W9-ALU-342

Illinois, Indiana & Ohio

Published by:
AAA Publishing
1000 AAA Drive
Heathrow, FL 32746-5063
Copyright AAA 2002

Send Written Comments to:
AAA Member Comments
1000 AAA Drive, Box 61
Heathrow, FL 32746-5063

**Advertising Rate and Circulation
Information**
Call: (407) 444-8280

Printed in the USA by Quebecor
World, Buffalo, NY

 Printed on recyclable paper.
Please recycle whenever possible.

Stock #4612

Illinois, Indiana & Ohio

TourBook Navigator

Follow our simple guide to make the most of this member benefit ... 11-27

■ *Ohio*

Featured Information

After eight hours in the car, you might think it's a mirage.

After a day of traveling, few sights are more welcome than a Hampton™ hotel. Because if you have a AAA membership card, you're entitled to savings at all Hampton locations nationwide. You'll also enjoy a free breakfast bar and our 100% Satisfaction Guarantee, and you can earn Hilton HHonors® hotel points and airline miles throughout your stay. So come join us. When you're on the road, there's no better place to stay.

We're with you all the way.™

A Member of the Hilton Family of Hotels.
Call 1-800-456-7793 for reservations.

Carry the card. Pocket the savings.

 Show Your Card & Save® at any participating hotel in the Hilton family. As a AAA member, you can count on the lowest available room rate at nearly 700 AAA approved locations in the U.S. Choose from conveniently situated properties ranging from luxury resorts to value-priced accommodations with all the amenities. To take advantage of an exceptional rate, just make advance reservations with a call to our dedicated AAA number at 1-877-655-5694 or your local AAA travel office.

Members of the Hilton Family of Hotels

hilton.com   doubletree.com   embassysuites.com   hiltongardeninn.com   homewood-suites.com

 Each of these Hilton family members is part of Hilton HHonors®, the only hotel rewards program to offer both hotel points and airline miles for the same stay. To join, visit hiltonhhonors.com.

100 years
OF SERVICE

In 1902 nine independent auto clubs formed the American Automobile Association to serve the interests of motorists. AAA's journey through the 20th century is marked with milestones of distinguished service to members and the public.

getting started

During the early years AAA promoted the automobile and a national highway system while gathering essential travel information.

- 1903 – Joined the Good Roads Movement and began an ongoing highway improvement campaign that led to the passage of the Federal Aid Road Act of 1916 and the 1956 Federal Aid Highway Act.

- 1905 – Published first map.

- 1915 – Automobile Club of Missouri rolled out the first AAA emergency road service (ERS) team.

On the road circa 1900

- 1917 – Published first travel guide, a hotel and garage directory.

- 1920 – Chicago Motor Club pioneered AAA's School Safety Patrol program.

- 1926 – Released first version of TourBook® guide and introduced Official Appointment program.

milestones

The 1930s and 1940s produced several AAA firsts: formal driver training, safety initiatives, a membership milestone and a customized routing system.

TripTik® shows the way

- 1936 – Partnered with Pennsylvania State College to gain nationwide acceptance of first driver education class.

- 1937 – Introduced the TripTik® routing system.

- 1940 – Membership reached 1 million.

- 1945 – Held first National School Traffic Safety Poster Contest.

School poster program

AAA Centennial Celebration
1902 10s 20s 30s 40s 50s

50th anniversary postage stamp

exciting times

At mid-century AAA celebrated its Golden Jubilee, reaffirming its commitment to motorists.

- 1952 – U.S. Postal Service issued a postage stamp commemorating AAA's 50th anniversary.

- 1963 – Created accommodations rating structure that became the Diamond Rating system in 1977.

- 1969 – Founded AAA Life Insurance Co.

In the '70s and '80s AAA offered more travel solutions for members, especially regarding roadside assistance and financial options.

- 1970 – Canadian Automobile Association signed affiliation agreement with AAA.

- 1975 – Established Approved Auto Repair program, a network of facilities that meets AAA's high standards.

- 1976 – Published a mobility guide for drivers with disabilities.

- 1979 – Offered Visa credit card, a first-time member benefit.

- 1981 – Introduced SUPERNUMBER®, a toll-free emergency assistance helpline.

- 1985 – AAA North American Road Atlas made *The New York Times* paperback best seller list.

Emergency road service call 1938

today and tomorrow...

AAA concluded its first century of service some 44 million members strong, sporting a contemporary version of the familiar oval and an array of products and services befitting the largest leisure travel organization in North America.

- 1993 – Instituted Show Your Card & Save® partner discount program on a national scale.
- 1997 – Welcomed 40-millionth member, unveiled a new logo and introduced aaa.com on the Internet.

- 1997 – Formed a strategic alliance with Disney to offer exclusive benefits to AAA members.

- 2000 – Made TripTik® routing system available to members via aaa.com.

AAA 100 years OF SERVICE

60s 70s 80s 90s 2002

Every Knight. Just Right.

Trust

the AAA TourBook® guide for objective travel information. Follow the pages of the TourBook Navigator to thoroughly understand this unique member benefit.

Making Your Way Through the AAA Listings

Attractions, lodgings and restaurants are listed on the basis of merit alone after careful evaluation, approval and rating by one of our full-time Tourism Editors or, in rare cases, a designated representative. Annual lodging evaluations are unannounced and conducted on site by random room sample.

Those lodgings and restaurants listed with an fyi icon have not gone through the same evaluation process as other rated properties. Individual listings will denote the reason why this icon appears. Bulleted recreational activity listings are not inspected but are included for member information.

An establishment's decision to advertise in the TourBook guide has no bearing on its inspection, evaluation or rating. Advertising for services or products does not imply AAA endorsement.

How the TourBook is

Organized

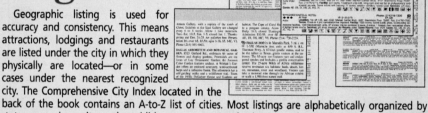

Geographic listing is used for accuracy and consistency. This means attractions, lodgings and restaurants are listed under the city in which they physically are located—or in some cases under the nearest recognized city. The Comprehensive City Index located in the back of the book contains an A-to-Z list of cities. Most listings are alphabetically organized by state or province, city, and establishment name. A color is assigned to each state or province so that you can match the color bars at the top of the page to switch from ❶ Points of Interest to ❷ Lodgings and Restaurants.

Destination Cities and Destination Areas

The TourBook guide also groups information by destination city and destination area. If a city is grouped in a destination vicinity section, the city name will appear at its alphabetical location in the book, and a handy cross reference will give the exact page on which listings for that city begin. Maps are placed at the beginning of these sections to orient you to the destinations.

❸ Destination cities, established based on government models and local expertise, are comprised of metropolitan areas plus nearby vicinity cities.

Destination areas are regions with broad tourist appeal. Several cities will comprise the area.

All information in this TourBook guide was reviewed for accuracy before publication. However, since changes inevitably occur between annual editions, we suggest you contact establishments directly to confirm prices and schedules.

Points of Interest Section

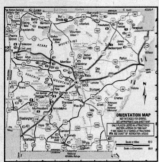

Orientation maps
near the start of each Attractions section show only those places we call points of interest. Coordinates included with the city listings depict the locations of those cities on the map. A GEM symbol (✿) accents towns with "must see" points of interest which offer a *Great Experience for Members*. And the black ovals with white numerals (**22** for example) locate items listed in the nearby Recreation Areas chart.

Destination area maps
illustrate key travel areas defined by local travel experts. Communities shown have listings for AAA approved attractions.

National park maps
represent the area in and around the park. Some campground sites and lodges spotted on the maps do not meet AAA/CAA criteria, but are shown for members who nevertheless wish to stay close to the park area.

Walking or self-guiding tour maps
correspond to specific routes described in TourBook guide text.

City maps
show areas where numerous points of interest are concentrated and indicate their location in relation to major roads, parks, airports and other landmarks.

Lodgings & Restaurants Section

Destination area maps
illustrate key travel areas defined by
local travel experts. Communities
shown have listings for AAA-RATED®
lodgings and/or restaurants.

Spotting maps
show the location of lodgings and
restaurants. Lodgings are spotted with
a black background (**22** for example);
restaurants are spotted with a white
background (**23** for example). Spotting map indexes have
been placed immediately after each map to provide the user
with a convenient method to identify what an area has to
offer at a glance. The index references the map page number
where the property is spotted, indicates if a property is an
Official Appointment and contains an advertising reference
if applicable. It also lists the property's diamond rating, high
season rate range and listing page number.

Downtown/city spotting maps
are provided when spotted facilities are very concentrated.
GEM points of interest also appear on these maps.

Vicinity spotting maps
spot those properties that are outside the downtown or city area. Major
roads, landmarks, airports and GEM points of interest are shown on vicinity
spotting maps as well. The names of suburban communities that have
AAA-RATED® accommodations are
shown in magenta type.

Featured Information Section

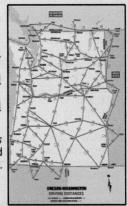

Driving distance maps
are intended to be used only for trip-distance and
driving-time planning.

Sample Attraction Listing

RED OAK is off I-95 exit 4A, then 2 mi. e. to 610 Magnolia St. The restored 1812 house has eight 60-foot columns and is furnished in period. Allow 1 hour minimum. Daily 9-5, Apr. 1-Labor Day; Thurs.-Sun. 9-5, mid-Feb. through Mar. 31 and day after Labor Day-Nov.30; by appointment rest of year. Closed holidays. Admission $4; over 65 and ages 6-12, $3; ages 2-5, $2; family rate $10. MC, VI ($10). Phone (601) 222-2222 or (800) 222-3333.

1

3 rest of year.
2 0. MC VI (
4 off I-95 exit

5

gn Mar. 31 and day after Labor Day-Nov. 30;
Admission $4; over 65 and ages 6-12, $3; a
(601) 222-2222   (800) 222-3333

1 This attraction is of exceptional interest and quality and therefore has been designated a AAA GEM—offering a *Great Experience for Members.*

2 Participating attractions offer AAA/CAA cardholders or holders of a AAA MasterCard or AAA Visa Card and up to six family members at least 10% off the attraction's standard admission for the validity period of the TourBook guide; members should inquire in advance concerning the validity of the discount for special rates. Present your card at the admissions desk. A list of participating points of interest appears in the Indexes section of the book. The SAVE discount may not be used in conjunction with other discounts. Attractions that already provide a reduced senior rate may not honor the SAVE discount for this age group. Discounts may not apply during special events or particular days or seasons.

3 AX = American Express   JC = Japan Credit Bureau
CB = Carte Blanche   MC = MasterCard
DC = Diners Club   VI = VISA
DS = Discover

Minimum amounts that may be charged appear in parentheses when applicable.

4 Unless otherwise specified, directions are given from the center of town, using the following highway designations: I (interstate highway), US (federal highway), Hwy. (Canadian highway), SR (state route), CR (county road), FM (farm to market road), FR (forest road), MM (mile marker).

5 Admission prices are quoted without sales tax. Children under the lowest age specified are admitted free when accompanied by an adult. Days, months and age groups written with a hyphen are inclusive. Prices pertaining to points of interest in the United States are quoted in U.S. dollars; prices for Canadian province and territory points of interest are quoted in Canadian dollars.

Bulleted Listings: Casino gambling establishments are visited by AAA personnel to ensure safety; casinos within hotels are presented for member information regardless of whether the lodging is AAA approved. Recreational activities of a participatory nature (requiring physical exertion or special skills) are not inspected. Wineries are inspected by AAA Tourism Editors to ensure they meet listing requirements and offer tours. All are presented in a bulleted format for informational purposes.

Attraction Partners

These Show Your Card & Save® partners provide the listed member benefits. Admission tickets that offer greater discounts may be available for purchase at the local AAA/CAA club. A maximum of six tickets is available at the discount price.

SeaWorld/Busch Gardens

[SAVE] Save at SeaWorld, Busch Gardens, Sesame Place, Water Country USA and Adventure Island

[SAVE] Save 10% on general admission

Six Flags Adventure Parks

[SAVE] Save $4 per adult on general admission at the gate

[SAVE] Save $12 per adult on general admission at the gate each Wednesday

[SAVE] Save 10% on selected souvenirs and dining (check at main gate for details)

Universal Orlando

Save $4 on a 2-day/2-park pass or $5 on a 3-day/2-park pass at Universal Orlando's theme parks (savings apply to tickets purchased at the gate)

Save 10% on select dining and souvenirs at both Universal Orlando theme parks and at all Universal CityWalk Orlando restaurants (except Emeril's)

Universal Studios Hollywood

Save $3 on a 1-day Universal Hollywood pass (savings applies to tickets purchased at the gate)

Save 10% on selected dining and souvenirs at Universal Studios Hollywood and Universal CityWalk

Restaurant Partners

Landry's Seafood House, The Crab House, Joe's Crab Shack

Save 10% on food and non-alcoholic beverages at Landry's Seafood House, The Crab House, Joe's Crab Shack and 10% on merchandise at Joe's Crab Shack.

Hard Rock Cafe

Save 10% on food, beverage, and merchandise at all U.S., Canada, and select International locations.

Visit aaa.com to discover all the great Show Your Card & Save® restaurants in your area.

Sample Lodging Listing

WHERE TO STAY

VISTA SUITES
Phone: (407)555-5522   **301**
XP: $10   F17

12/24-9/1 [CP]	1P: $139-$169	2P: $139-$169
12/1-12/23 & 9/2-11/30 [ECP]	1P: $129-$149	2P: $129-$149

Location: I-4, exit 26A, 1.8 mi e; at jct SR 535 and 536. 14450 International Dr 32803 (PO Box 22830). Fax 407/555-4411. **Facility:** A well-maintained, mature property offering a variety of room styles. 652 units. 646 one-bedroom standard units. 6 one-bedroom suites, some with efficiencies. 7 stories, interior corridors. *Bath:* combo or shower only. **Parking:** valet or street. **Terms:** 3 day cancellation notice-fee imposed. **Amenities:** voice mail, safes (fee), irons, hair dryers. *Some:* DVD players. *Fee:* Web TV, high-speed Internet. **Dining:** coffee shop, 6:30 am-9:30 pm, $4-$8, cocktails. **Pool(s):** outdoor, 2 heated indoor, wading pool, 2 outdoor saltwater. **Leisure Activities:** whirlpool, 2 lighted tennis courts, exercise room. **Guest Services:** gift shop, coin laundry. *Fee:* area transportation-major attractions. **Business Services:** meeting rooms, PC. *Fee:* fax. **Cards:** AX, CB, DC, JC, MC, VI. **Special Amenities:** free newspaper. *(See color ad p 12)*

SOME UNITS

1 **[AAA logo] [SAVE]** **[diamonds]** **Suite Hotel**

2

3 [BP]

4 F17

5 301

6 street. **Terms:** 3 day cancellation dryers. *Some:* DVD players. *Fee:* outdoor, 2 heated indoor, wading po

12/24-9/1 [CP]	1P: $139-$169	2P: $139-$169	XP: $10
12/1-12/23 & 9/2-11/30 [ECP]	1P: $129-$149	2P: $129-$149	

1 **[AAA]** or **[CAA]** indicates our Official Appointment (OA) lodgings. The OA program permits properties to display and advertise the **[AAA]** or **[CAA]** emblem. We highlight these properties with red diamonds and classification. Some OA listings include special amenities such as free continental breakfast; early check-in/late check-out; free room upgrade or preferred room, such as ocean view or poolside (subject to availability); free local phone calls; and free daily newspaper. This does not imply that only these properties offer these amenities. The **[AAA]** or **[CAA]** sign helps traveling members find accommodations that want member business.

[diamonds] or **[diamonds]** The number of diamonds—not the color—informs you of the overall level of quality in a lodging's amenities and service. More diamond details appear on page 18.

Suite Hotel or Suite Hotel: Diamond ratings are applied in the context of lodging type, or classification. See pages 24-25 for details about our Lodging Classifications.

Member Values

[SAVE] Official Appointment properties guarantee members a minimum 10% discount off the standard room rates published in TourBook guides or the lowest public rate available at the time of booking for the dates of stay, for standard rooms.

[SAVE] AAA's Show Your Card & Save® chain partners provide AAA's best rates and a satisfaction guarantee to our members: Select from Best Western, Choice Hotels, Hyatt Hotels, Days Inn, most Hilton brands, La Quinta Inn and most Marriott brands. Individual properties appearing in the TourBook guides have been evaluated and approved by AAA. Reservations can be made by calling the AAA member toll-free reservation line 866-AAA-SAVE or refer to page 22 for details and a complete listing of participating lodging chains.

[SD] Establishments offer a minimum senior discount of 10% off the listed rates. This discount is available to members 60 or older.

[ASK] Many TourBook guide properties offer discounts to members even though the lodgings do not participate in a formal discount program. The **[ASK]** is another reminder to inquire about available discounts when making your reservations or at check-in.

> **Discounts normally offered at some lodgings may not apply during special events or holiday periods. Special rates and discounts may not apply to all room types.**

To obtain published rates or discounts, you must identify yourself as a AAA or CAA member, request AAA rates when making reservations and have written confirmation sent to you. The SAVE or senior discount may not be used in conjunction with other discounts. At registration, show your membership card and verify the room rate.

The rates listed for approved properties are provided to AAA by each lodging and represent the regular (rack) rate for a standard room. Printed rates, based on rack rates and last room availability, are rounded to the nearest dollar. Rates do not include taxes and discounts. U.S. rates are in U.S. dollars; rates for Canadian lodgings are in Canadian dollars.

2 Rate Lines

Shown from left to right: dates the rates are effective; meal plan provided with rates (see Meal Plan Indicators-if no plan noted, rate includes room only); rates for 1 person or 2 persons; extra person charge (XP); and any applicable family plan indicator.

Rates Guaranteed

AAA/CAA members are guaranteed that they will not be charged more than the maximum regular rate printed in each rate range for a standard room. Rates may vary within the range depending on season and room type. Listed rates are based on last standard room availability. Rates for properties operating as concessionaires for the National Park Service are not guaranteed due to governing regulations.

Exceptions

Lodgings may temporarily increase room rates, not recognize discounts or modify pricing policies during special events. Examples of special events range from Mardi Gras and Kentucky Derby (including pre-Derby events) to college football games, holidays, holiday periods and state fairs. Although some special events are listed in AAA/CAA TourBook guides, it is always wise to check, in advance, with AAA travel professionals for specific dates.

Discounts

Member discounts will apply to rates quoted, within the rate range, applicable at the time of booking. Special rates used in advertising, and special short-term, promotional rates lower than the lowest listed rate in the range, are not subject to additional member discounts.

3 Meal Plan Indicators

The following types of meal plans may be available in the listed room rate:

AP = American Plan of three meals daily
BP = Breakfast Plan of full hot breakfast
CP = Continental Plan of pastry, juice and another beverage
ECP = Expanded Continental Plan, which offers a wider variety of breakfast items
EP = European Plan, where rate includes only room
MAP = Modified American Plan of two meals daily
See individual listing "Terms" section for additional meal plans that may be offered.

> Check-in times are shown in the listing only if they are after 3 p.m.; check-out times are shown only if they are before 10 a.m.
>
> Parking is on the premises and free unless otherwise noted.

4 Family Plan Indicators

F = Children stay free
D = Discounts for children
F17 = Children 17 and under stay free (age displayed will reflect property's policy)
D17 = Discount for children 17 and under

5 Lodging Locators

Numerals are used to locate, or "spot," lodgings on maps we provide for larger cities.

6 Unit Types

Unit types, amenities and room features preceded by the word "Some" indicate the item is available on a limited basis, potentially within only one unit.

The lodging listings with [fyi] in place of diamonds are included as an "information only" service for members. The icon indicates that a property has not been rated for one or more of the following reasons: too new to rate; under construction; under major renovation; not evaluated; or may not meet all AAA requirements. Listing prose will give insight as to why the [fyi] rating was assigned.

The Lodging Diamond Ratings

AAA Tourism Editors evaluate and rate each lodging based on the overall quality, the range of facilities and the level of services offered by a property. The size, age and overall appeal of an establishment are considered as well as regional decorating and architectural differences.

While guest services are an important part of all diamond ratings, they are particularly critical at the four and five diamond levels. A property must provide a high level of service, on a consistent basis, to obtain and support the four and five diamond rating.

These establishments reflect the characteristics of the ultimate in luxury and sophistication. Accommodations are first-class. The physical attributes are extraordinary in every manner. The fundamental hallmarks at this level are to meticulously serve and exceed all guest expectations while maintaining an impeccable standard of excellence. Many personalized services and amenities enhance an unmatched level of comfort.

These establishments are upscale in all areas. Accommodations are progressively more refined and stylish. The physical attributes reflect an obvious enhanced level of quality throughout. The fundamental hallmarks at this level include an extensive array of amenities combined with a high degree of hospitality, service and attention to detail.

These establishments appeal to the traveler with comprehensive needs. Properties are multifaceted with a distinguished style, including marked upgrades in the quality of physical attributes, amenities and level of comfort provided.

These establishments appeal to the traveler seeking more than the basic accommodations. There are modest enhancements to the overall physical attributes, design elements and amenities of the facility typically at a modest price.

These establishments typically appeal to the budget minded traveler. They provide essential, no-frills accommodations. They meet the basic requirements pertaining to comfort, cleanliness and hospitality.

Guest Safety

Room Security

In order to be approved for listing in AAA/CAA TourBook guides for the United States and Canada, all lodgings must comply with AAA's guest room security requirements.

In response to AAA/CAA members' concern about their safety at properties, AAA-RATED® accommodations must have dead-bolt locks on all guest room entry doors and connecting room doors.

If the area outside the guest room door is not visible from inside the room through a window or door panel, viewports must be installed on all guest room entry doors. Bed and breakfast properties and country inns are not required to have viewports. Ground floor and easily accessible sliding doors must be equipped with some other type of secondary security locks.

Tourism Editors view a percentage of rooms at each property since it is not feasible to evaluate every room in every lodging establishment. Therefore, AAA cannot guarantee that there are working locks on all doors and windows in all guest rooms.

Fire Safety

Because of the highly specialized skills needed to conduct professional fire safety inspections, AAA/CAA Tourism Editors cannot assess fire safety.

All U.S. and Canadian lodging properties must be equipped with an operational, single-station smoke detector, and all public areas must have operational smoke detectors or an automatic sprinkler system. A AAA/CAA Tourism Editor has evaluated a sampling of the rooms to verify this equipment is in place.

For additional fire safety information read the page posted on the back of your guest room door, or write:

National Fire Protection Association
1 Batterymarch Park / P.O. Box 9101 / Quincy, MA 02269-9101

Golden Passports – National Parks Pass

Citizens or permanent residents of the United States who are 62 and older can obtain Golden Age Passports for a one-time $10 fee.

Golden Access Passports are free to citizens or permanent residents of the United States (regardless of age) who are medically blind or permanently disabled.

Both cover entrance fees for the holder and accompanying private party to all national parks, historic sites, monuments, battlefields, recreation areas and wildlife refuges within the U.S. national park system, plus half off camping and other fees. Apply in person at most federally operated areas.

The Golden Eagle Passport is being replaced by the National Parks Pass. Although Golden Eagle Passports are no longer being sold, existing passports are still being accepted for the duration of their validity period.

The National Parks Pass, valid for 1 year from the date of purchase, allows unlimited admissions to all U.S. national parks. The $50 pass covers all occupants of a vehicle at parks where the entrance fee is per vehicle. At parks with individual entry fees, the pass covers the pass holder, spouse, parents and children.

As a result of a partnership with the National Park Service, AAA members may purchase the pass for $48, either through AAA's Internet site (www.aaa.com) or by phoning or visiting a participating AAA office or by phoning the National Park Foundation at (888) 467-2757. Non- members may purchase the pass through AAA for the full $50 price.

The passes are personalized at a distribution center and are mailed directly to the purchaser.

For an upgrade fee of $15, a Golden Eagle hologram sticker can be added to a National Parks Pass. The hologram covers entrance fees not just at national parks, but at any federal recreation area that has an admission fee. Valid for the duration of the National Parks Pass to which it is affixed, the Golden Eagle hologram is available at National Park Service, Fish and Wildlife Service and Bureau of Land Management fee stations.

Access for Mature Travelers and Travelers with Disabilities

Qualified properties listed in this guide are shown with symbols indicating they meet the needs of the hearing-impaired or offer some accessible features for mature travelers or travelers with disabilities.

Hearing Impaired

Indicates a property has the following equipment available for hearing-impaired travelers: TDD at front desk or switchboard; visual notification of fire alarm, incoming telephone calls, door knock or bell; closed caption decoder; text telephone or TDD for guest room use; telephone amplification device, with shelf or electric outlet next to guest room telephone.

Accessible Features

Indicates a property has some accessible features meeting the needs of mature travelers and travelers with disabilities. Lodging establishments will provide at least one guest room meeting the designated criteria as well as accessible restrooms and parking facilities. Restaurants provide accessible parking, dining rooms and restrooms.

AAA/CAA strongly urges members to call the property directly to fully understand the property's exact accessibility features. Some properties do not fully comply with AAA/CAA's exacting accessibility standards but may offer some design standards that meet the needs of some guests with disabilities.

AAA/CAA does not evaluate recreational facilities, banquet rooms, or convention or meeting facilities for accessibility.

Service Animals

No fees or deposits, even those normally charged for pets, may be charged for service animals. Service animals fulfill a critical need for their owners—they are *not* pets.

The Americans With Disabilities Act (ADA) prohibits businesses that serve the public from discriminating against persons with disabilities. Some businesses have mistakenly denied access to persons who use service animals. ADA, a federal mandate, has priority over all state and local laws, as well as a business owner's standard of business, which might bar animals from the premises. Businesses must permit entry to guests and their service animals, as well as allow service animals to accompany guests to all public areas of a property. A property is permitted to ask whether the animal is a service animal or a pet, and whether the guest has a disability. The property may not, however, ask questions about the nature of the disability, the service provided by the animal or require proof of a disability or certification that the animal is a service animal.

Additional Resources

Recognizing the need for more information, AAA/CAA also publishes a series of publications targeted to mature travelers and travelers with disabilities.

AAA Accessibility Criteria for Barrier-Free Travel (stock # 5024) is a free brochure that outlines the specific AAA criteria and accessibility categories used to evaluate properties on barrier-free attributes. (This brochure is available at your local AAA/CAA office).

AAA Barrier-Free Travel is a series of destination travel guides that provides detailed information on accessible features at AAA-RATED® lodgings, restaurants and points of interest. Also featured are accessible transportation and medical supply and equipment resources. (These books may be purchased at many AAA/CAA offices, through aaa.com, by calling 1-888-AAA-BOOK or at better bookstores).

What The Icons Mean

Member Values
(see p. 16)

AAA or **AA** Official Appointment

SAVE Offers minimum 10% discount or lowest public rate *(see p. 16)*

SAVE Show Your Card & Save partners

ASK May offer discount

S/D Offers senior discount

fyi Informational listing only

Member Services

➕ Airport transportation

🐾 Pets allowed

🍴 Restaurant on premises

🍴➕ Restaurant off premises (walking distance)

24🍴 24-hour room service

🍸 Cocktail lounge

👶 Child care

Accessibility Features
(see p. 20)

♿ Accessible features

♿ Roll-in showers

🦻 Hearing impaired

Leisure Activities

🏊 Pool

💪 Health club on premises

💪 Health club off premises

🎿 Recreational activities

In-Room Amenities

🚭 Non-smoking rooms

❄ No air conditioning

📺 No TV

VCR VCR

🎥 Movies

DATA PORT Data port/modem line

☎ No telephones

🧊 Refrigerator

🔲 Microwave

☕ Coffee maker

📻 Clock Radio

Availability

If an in-room amenity is available only on a limited basis (in one or more rooms), the term "SOME UNITS" will appear above those icons.

SOME UNITS

♿ 🦻 VCR 🎥 ☕ / 🚭 **DATA PORT** 🧊 /

Additional Fees

Fees may be charged for some of the services represented by the icons listed here. The word "FEE" will appear below each icon when an extra charge applies.

SOME UNITS

♿ 🦻 VCR 🎥 ☕ / 🚭 **DATA PORT** 🧊 /
      FEE FEE   FEE

Preferred Lodging Partners

Show Your Card & Save

AAA. Every Day.

Phone the member-only toll-free number below or your AAA/CAA club to get these member benefits.

Select the chain you want and have your membership card on hand when calling.

AAA's BEST RATES ON OVER 1,000,000 ROOMS - When calling the AAA-SAVE number below and selecting one of the partners listed you will automatically receive the lowest rate available for your dates of stay, except at Choice Hotels International where you will receive a 10-20% discount all the time. Your valid membership card must be presented at check-in.

SATISFACTION GUARANTEE - If you are not satisfied with any part of your stay, you must provide the property the opportunity to correct the situation during your stay. If the matter cannot be resolved, you will be entitled to recompense for a portion of, or your entire, stay. Satisfaction guarantee varies by chain.

Exclusive, Toll-Free Member Reservation Line
866-AAA-SAVE
(866-222-7283)

Making Reservations

Give Proper Identification

When making reservations, you must identify yourself as a AAA or CAA member. Give all pertinent information about your planned stay. Request written confirmation to guarantee: type of room, rate, dates of stay, and cancellation and refund policies. At registration, show your membership card. Note: Age restrictions may apply.

Confirm Deposit, Refund and Cancellation Policies

Most establishments give full deposit refunds if they have been notified at least 48 hours before the normal check-in time. Listing prose will note if more than 48 hours notice is required for cancellation. However, when making reservations, confirm the property's deposit, cancellation and refund policies. Some properties may charge a cancellation or handling fee.

When this applies, "cancellation fee imposed" will appear in the listing. If you cancel too late, you have little recourse if a refund is denied.

When an establishment requires a full or partial payment in advance, and your trip is cut short, a refund may not be given.

When canceling reservations, phone the lodging immediately. Make a note of the date and time you called, the cancellation number if there is one, and the name of the person who handled the cancellation. If your AAA/CAA club made your reservation, allow them to make the cancellation for you as well so you will have proof of cancellation.

Review Charges for Appropriate Rates

When you are charged more than the maximum rate listed in the TourBook guide for a standard room, question the additional charge. If management refuses to adhere to the published rate, pay for the room and submit your receipt and membership number to AAA/CAA within 30 days. Include all pertinent information: dates of stay, rate paid, itemized paid receipts, number of persons in your party, the room number you occupied, and list any extra room equipment used. A refund of the amount paid in excess of the stated maximum will be made if our investigation indicates that unjustified charging has occurred.

Get the Room You Reserved

When you find your room is not as specified, and you have written confirmation of reservations for a certain type of accommodation, you should be given the option of choosing a different room or finding one elsewhere. Should you choose to go elsewhere and a refund is refused or resisted, submit the matter to AAA/CAA within 30 days along with complete documentation, including your reasons for refusing the room and copies of your written confirmation and any receipts or canceled checks associated with this problem.

How to Get the Best Room Rates

You'll find the best room rate if you book your reservation in advance with the help of a travel professional or agent at your local AAA/CAA office.

If you're not yet ready to make firm vacation plans or if you prefer a more spontaneous trip, take advantage of the partnerships that preferred hotel chains have arranged with AAA. Phone the toll-free number on the previous page that have been set up exclusively for members for the purpose of reserving with these Show Your Card & Save® chain partners.

Even if you were unable to make a reservation, be sure to show your membership card at the desk and ask if you're being offered the lowest rate available for that time. Many lodgings offer reduced rates to members.

Lodging Classifications

AAA Tourism Editors evaluate lodgings based on classification, since all lodging types by definition do not provide the same level of service and facilities. Thus, hotels are rated in comparison to other hotels, resorts to other resorts—and so on. A lodging's classification appears beneath its diamond rating in the listing.

Hotel — *full service*
Usually high-rise establishments, offering a wide range of services and on-premise food/beverage outlets, shops, conference facilities and recreational activities.

Motel — *limited service*
Low-rise or multi-story establishment offering limited public and recreational facilities.

Country Inn — *moderate service*
Similar in definition to a bed and breakfast, but usually larger in size, with a dining facility that serves at least breakfast and dinner.

Resort — *full service*
Offers a variety of food/beverage outlets and an extensive range of recreational and entertainment programs—geared to vacation travelers.

Bed & Breakfast — *limited service*
Usually smaller, owner-operated establishments emphasizing an "at home" feeling. A continental or full, hot breakfast is served and included in the room rate.

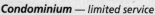

Condominium — *limited service*
Apartment-style units or homes primarily owned by individuals and available for rent. A variety of room styles and decor treatments, as well as limited housekeeping service, is typical.

Motor Inn — *moderate service*
Single or multi-story establishment offering on-premise food/beverage service, meeting and banquet facilities and some recreational facilities.

Complex — *service varies*
A combination of two or more types of lodging classifications.

Lodge — *moderate service*
Typically two or more stories with all facilities in one building. Rustic decor is common. Usually has food/beverage service.

Apartment — *limited service*
Primarily offers temporary guest accommodations with one or more bedrooms, a living room, a full kitchen and an eating area. Studio apartments may combine the sleeping and living areas into one room.

Cottage — *limited service*
Primarily individual housing units that may offer one or more separate sleeping areas, a living room and cooking facilities.

Ranch — *moderate service*
Often offers rustic decor treatments and food/beverage facilities. Entertainment and recreational activities are geared to a Western theme.

Lodging Subclassifications

The following are subclassifications that may appear along with the classifications listed above to provide a more specific description of the lodging.

Suite
One or more bedrooms and a living room/sitting area, closed off by a full wall. Note: May not have a partition bedroom door.

Extended Stay
Properties catering to longer-term guest stays. Will have kitchens or efficiencies and may have a separate living room area, evening office closure and limited housekeeping services.

Historic
Properties must meet one of the following criteria:
- Be listed on the National Register of Historic Places
- Be designated a National Historic Landmark
- Be located in a National Register Historic District

Classic
Renowned and landmark properties, older than 50 years, known for their unique style and ambience.

Sample Restaurant Listing

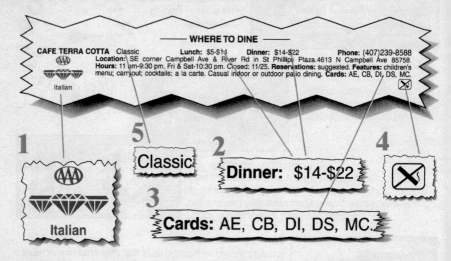

───── **WHERE TO DINE** ─────

CAFE TERRA COTTA Classic   **Lunch:** $5-$14   **Dinner:** $14-$22   **Phone:** (407)239-8588
Location: SE corner Campbell Ave & River Rd in St Phillips Plaza.4613 N Campbell Ave 85758.
Hours: 11 am-9:30 pm. Fri & Sat-10:30 pm. Closed: 11/25. **Reservations:** suggested. **Features:** children's menu; carryout; cocktails; a la carte. Casual indoor or outdoor patio dining. **Cards:** AE, CB, DI, DS, MC.

Italian

1   **5** Classic   **2** Dinner: $14-$22   **4**

Italian

3 Cards: AE, CB, DI, DS, MC.

1   (AAA) or (CAA) indicates our Official Appointment (OA) restaurants. The OA program permits properties to display and advertise the (AAA) or (CAA) emblem. We highlight these properties with red diamonds and cuisine type. The (AAA) or (CAA) sign helps traveling members find restaurants that want member business.

▼▼▼ or ▼▼▼▼ The number of diamonds—not the color—informs you of the overall level of quality for food and presentation, service and ambience.

A cuisine type is assigned for each restaurant listing. AAA currently recognizes more than 90 different cuisine types.

2   Prices represent the minimum and maximum entree cost per person. Exceptions may include one-of-a-kind or special market priced items.

3   AX = American Express
CB = Carte Blanche   DS = Discover   MC = MasterCard
DC = Diners Club   JC = Japan Credit Bureau   VI = VISA

4   This icon indicates that the restaurant has a designated non-smoking section or is entirely smoke-free.

5   If applicable, restaurants may be further defined as:

Classic—renowned and landmark properties, older than 25 years, known for unique style and ambience.

Historic—properties must meet one of the following criteria:
- Be listed on the National Register of Historic Places
- Be designated a National Historic Landmark
- Be located in a National Register Historic District

The restaurants with **fyi** in place of diamonds are included as an "information only" service for members. This designation indicates that the restaurant has not been evaluated.

The Restaurant Diamond Ratings

AAA Tourism Editors are responsible for determining a restaurant's diamond rating based on established criteria.

These criteria were established with input from AAA trained professionals, members and restaurant industry experts. They are purposely broad to capture what is typically seen throughout the restaurant industry at each diamond rating level.

Often renowned, these establishments impart a world-class and opulent, adult-oriented experience. This is "haute cuisine" at its best. Menus are often cutting edge, with an obvious dedication to use of only the finest ingredients available. Even the classic dishes become extraordinary under the masterful direction of highly acclaimed chefs. Presentations are spectacular, reflecting impeccable artistry and awareness. An expert, formalized staff continuously anticipates and exceeds guest expectations. Staff members' unfailing attention to detail appears effortless, well-rehearsed and unobtrusive. Undoubtedly, these restaurants appeal to those in search of the ultimate dining experience.

Examples include renowned dining rooms associated with luxury lodgings, or exclusive independent restaurants often found in metropolitan areas.

These establishments impart a luxurious and socially refined experience. This is consistent fine dining. Menus typically reflect a high degree of creativity and complexity, featuring elaborate presentations of market-driven or traditional dishes. A cultured, professional and highly proficient staff consistently demonstrates a profound desire to meet or exceed guest expectations. Restaurants of this caliber are geared to individuals with an appetite for an elite, fine-dining experience.

Examples include dining rooms associated with luxury lodgings, or exclusive independent restaurants often found in metropolitan areas.

These establishments impart an increasingly refined and upscale, adult-oriented experience. This is the entry level into fine dining. Creative and complex menus offer a blend of traditional and trendy foods. The service level is typically semi-formal with knowledgeable and proficient staff. Routinely these restaurants appeal to the diner in search of an experience rather than just a meal.

Examples include high-caliber, chic, boutique and conventional restaurants.

These establishments provide for dining needs that are increasingly complex, but still reasonably priced. They typically exhibit noticeable efforts in rising above the ordinary in many aspects of food, service and decor. Service is typically functional yet ambitious, periodically combining informal style with limited self-service elements. Often well-suited to traditional, special occasion and family dining.

Examples include a varied range of specific concept (theme) and multi-purpose establishments.

These establishments appeal to a diner seeking good, wholesome, no-nonsense eating at an affordable price. They typically provide simple, familiar and unadorned foods served in a sensible, casual or self-service style. Often quick service and family oriented.

Examples include coffee shops, diners, cafeterias, short order and modest full service eateries.

Only AAA offers an integrated travel information system that is tailored to your individual needs.

Our highly trained counselors can assist you with all facets of planning your trip, from designing the route to making reservations. In addition, only AAA travel counselors can provide our exclusive collection of travel materials selected especially for you.

TourBook® guides are comprehensive travel guides listing AAA Approved attractions, lodgings and restaurants. In addition to the coveted Diamond Ratings, you'll find descriptions of towns and cities and information on discounts available only to AAA members. TourBooks are updated annually and cover every state and province in the United States and Canada.

TripTik® routings trace your route mile-by-mile and are clearly marked with the vital information you need while on the road, such as highway exits and rest stops. These handy maps are custom-configured by your AAA travel counselor and can highlight the quickest, shortest or most scenic routes, as well as highway construction projects along the way.

Sheet maps are updated annually and cover every state and province, plus regional areas throughout North America. An extensive network of road reporters and club staff works with AAA cartographers to ensure that AAA maps are the most detailed and accurate maps available.

CampBook® guides list AAA Approved camping and RV facilities, both public and private, throughout the United States and Canada.

So the next time you're planning a trip, remember to visit your local AAA travel counselor or access AAA's renowned travel services on the internet - just type in www.aaa.com.

Travel With Someone You Trust®

Look For Savings

When you pick up a AAA TourBook® guide, look for establishments that display a bright red AAA logo, $\boxed{\text{SAVE}}$ icon, and Diamond rating in their listing. These Official Appointment establishments place a high value on the patronage they receive from AAA members. And, by offering members great room rates*, they are willing to go the extra mile to get your business.

So, when you turn to the AAA TourBook guide to make your travel plans, look for the establishments that will give you the special treatment you deserve.

See TourBook Navigator section, page 16, for complete details

The One That Does It All

*F*or years, people have turned to AAA for their emergency road service needs. But AAA is more than just towing. Access to AAA's travel services can give you the world. Its financial services can help you pay for it. And AAA insurance can give you the peace of mind to enjoy the ride. Plus, AAA gives you exclusive Show Your Card & Save® offers, bail bond benefits, and much more.

Discover the ways AAA can simplify your life. Call or stop by your nearest AAA office __today__ to find out about the specific products and services they offer.

Illinois

Rambling Riverboats

Step back to Mark Twain's day when paddlewheelers cruised along the muddy Mississippi

Architectural Delight

From art deco sky-scrapers to Prairie-style buildings, Chicago is known for its structural landmarks

Land of Lincoln

Historic sites trace the legendary footsteps of our 16th president

Amish Country

Split-rail fences and horse-drawn buggies welcome visitors to the plain and simple way of life

Kicks on Route 66

America's original two-lane road meanders past quaint towns and rolling farmland

old things that never grow old

W hat do Al Capone, Ernest Hemingway, Ronald Reagan and a John Deere tractor have in common?

Before you dream up a peculiar image of a gangster, an author and a president riding a giant green tractor, think Illinois instead.

The infamous Al Capone made Chicago his stomping ground; Hemingway called Oak Park his hometown; Reagan was born in Tampico and grew up in Dixon; and Moline is the home of Deere & Company.

The grasslands of Illinois served as a strong foundation for many people: Joseph Smith and his Mormon followers, who established Nauvoo; American poets Carl Sandburg and Edgar Lee Masters; George "Bugs" Moran who,

with help from his friends, expressed his displeasure with Prohibition; and the man for whom Illinois proudly displays "Land of Lincoln" on its license plates.

Lakes and streams are well-known residents as well. A seat atop the first Ferris wheel, unveiled at the 1893 Chicago World's Fair, provides a stunning view of the waters of Lake Michigan. And on most days, you can see lazy paddlewheelers, much like those Huck Finn encountered, rolling down the Mississippi River.

Let Illinois satisfy your appetite for travel. Like a slice of its Chicago deep-dish pizza, it's loaded with toppings and will leave you begging for more.

I was born on the prairie and the milk of its wheat, the red of its clover . . . gave me a song and a slogan.

Pulitzer Prize-winning poet Carl Sandburg sang the praises of the Illinois grasslands in his 1918 poem "Prairie." Sandburg was inspired by the state's countryside—where long grass sways in the wind, corn stands tall in neat rows and haystacks turn golden under the gleam of the sunset. And in the distance, the fields join sky in a clean seam.

Sons of the Prairie

Sandburg never *really* left Illinois: Behind the small cottage in his hometown of Galesburg (now the Carl Sandburg National Historic Site) sits Remembrance Rock, under which his ashes are scattered, per his request.

O prairie mother, I am one of your boys. I have loved the prairie as a man with a heart shot full of pain over love.

While Sandburg immortalized the plains in his melodious poetry, he also paid homage in volumes of biographies to the man whose jutting profile appears on the U.S. penny.

Strewn across Illinois are stops on the Lincoln Heritage Trail, which traces Abraham Lincoln's illustrious political career. Picture a postmaster in Petersburg; an aspiring law student in New Salem; a practicing lawyer in Mt. Pulaski and Lincoln; a member of the House of Representatives in Vandalia; and a father, legislator and president-elect in Springfield.

At the Lincoln Depot in Springfield, with its gender-specific waiting rooms, our 16th president eloquently bid a teary-eyed adieu to townsfolk before boarding a train for a journey that took him from his modest prairie home to the White House.

I know in the night I rest easy in the prairie arms, on the prairie heart.

Frank Lloyd Wright made a home of the prairie—literally. Mimicking the landscape he so adored, his unprecedented designs became known as the Prairie style of architecture.

Claiming that "the horizontal brings us serenity and peace," Wright contrived buildings that were in harmony with their surroundings. Oak Park, near Chicago, contains the country's largest concentration of Prairie-style homes—nearly 120, including 25 designed by Wright.

Among them is the Frank Lloyd Wright Home and Studio. Trademark diamond-patterned lead glass windows cast a glow

---

Illinois Historical Timeline

French missionaries Father Jacques Marquette and Louis Joliet found the Illinois country, opening it up for fur trading and other missionaries.
1673

Favorite son Abraham Lincoln becomes president of the United States.
1860

The Great Chicago Fire starts in the O'Leary's cowbarn, destroying one-third of the city and killing 300 people.
1871

1818
Illinois becomes the 21st state with Kaskaskia as the capital; Springfield becomes the capital in 1837.

1886
The Haymarket Affair in Chicago, which begins as a peaceful protest, turns deadly when a bomb explodes; the protest signifies labor unrest and marks the beginning of organized crime, bootleg liquor and newspaper wars.

upon furniture that Wright designed, and connecting rooms create flowing, open space throughout the home.

Within the town's historic district is the Frederick C. Robie House, with its long, low design and overhanging roofs. Earth-hugging and made from natural materials, it exemplifies Wright's fascination with the prairie.

In Arcola and Arthur, the land is a way of life for the Amish. Fields of straight-lined crops stretch off to the horizon. And quilts are made by sewing each tiny stitch by hand, much like the first Raggedy Ann and Andy dolls fashioned here in 1918.

Here the water went down, the icebergs slid with gravel, the gaps and the valleys hissed . . .

But Illinois isn't all grasslands. The Mississippi River rushes alongside the plains, forming the western border. Monks Mound, a huge man-made pile of earth, is one remnant of a prehistoric river-based civilization at Cahokia Mounds State Historic Site in Collinsville.

There's a seasonal show at Starved Rock State Park in La Salle: In spring, water cascades from the park's many canyons, forming a spectacular sight. Brisk winter air chills the falls to form crystal icefalls.

Not Your Average Metropolis

Here I saw a city rise and say to the peoples round world: Listen, I am strong, I know what I want.

Like a phoenix that rose from the ashes, Chicago not only survived the Great Fire of 1871, it came back with feathers flying. Home of the nation's first skyscraper and later such giants as the John Hancock Center, the "Windy City" makes its presence known with top-notch art collections, ritzy shops and action-packed commerce at the Chicago Board of Trade.

Another truly "super" city, Metropolis, lies at the southern tip of Illinois. Legendary home of Superman, the town is filled with monuments dedicated to the the man of steel.

And I know what the rainbow writes across the east or west in half-circle: A love-letter pledge to come again.

The Illinois prairie is wide and welcoming. Leave if you must, but return you will.

The World's Columbian Exposition, celebrating the 400th anniversary of the discovery of America by Columbus, takes place at Jackson Park in Chicago.
1893

The 1,454-foot Sears Tower is constructed, becoming the world's tallest building; today it remains North America's tallest building.
1973

The Democratic National Convention is held at Chicago's United Center.
1996

1942
Enrico Fermi and other scientists conduct the first controlled nuclear chain reaction in a lab at the University of Chicago.

1975
Richard J. Daley is reelected to an unprecedented sixth 4-year term as Chicago's mayor.

1997
The Chicago Bulls beat the Utah Jazz to claim their fifth National Basketball Association championship of the 1990s.

Recreation

Outdoor fun in the Prairie State is as simple as choosing a season. In summer, the sun shines warmly over lakes, rivers and trails. In winter, snowflakes cover the ground and make for chilly adventures. Either way, you're sure to find diversion in Illinois.

One of the best ways to get some fresh air as well as take in some splendid scenery is to hop on a bicycle. Illinois has wonderful, rolling hills that make **bicycling** a breeze. Chicago's Lake Shore Drive, which extends for 20 miles along the shore of Lake Michigan, has paths for bicycling or **inline skating.**

The Illinois Prairie Path is a 55-mile trail that begins in Elmhurst, just outside of Chicago. The trail stretches to Wheaton, where it then splits into four spurs leading to Elgin, Batavia, Aurora and Geneva. **Equestrians, joggers** and bicyclists all take advantage of the IPP's gravel paths.

In addition, a 27-mile greenway makes up the Rock Island Trail, which traverses Peoria and Stark counties. Near McHenry, scenic paths draped with trees wind through Moraine Hills State Park.

Trails in many state parks in Illinois convert to **cross-country skiing** and **snowmobiling** paths in winter. A minimum of 4 inches of snow must cover the trails before they are available for use, and snowmobilers should register with park officials before taking to the hills. **Tobogganing** runs at county forest preserve districts in River Forest and Lombard also create a flurry of winter thrills.

Snowflakes in northern Illinois make ideal conditions for **downhill skiing, ice skating** and **snowboarding.** Snake your way down the slopes in the Chain O'Lakes region (near Antioch); in the northwestern corner of the state; or head to Chestnut and Wilmot mountains near Galena. Four Lakes in Lisle and Ski Snowstar in Andalusia also welcome skiers.

Rivers of Opportunity

Illinois is bordered on almost all sides by water: The Illinois, Kaskaskia, Rock and Sangamon rivers feed into the great Mississippi; the Vermillion and Wabash rivers flow into the Ohio River along the southeastern border; and Lake Michigan splashes the northeast corner. It's no wonder that **water sports** are so popular.

Fishing, especially for bass, is excellent in numerous rivers, streams, lakes and ponds.

A license is required. Contact the Department of Natural Resources; phone (217) 782-7454.

Cool breezes on Lake Michigan make for smooth **sailing.** Lake Carlyle also is popular for **boating** and **swimming.** Near Mount Vernon, 19,000-acre Rend Lake is a great place for swimming, boating, **camping** and **picnicking.**

Hunting for deer is excellent in the western part of the state. Fine waterfowl hunting is the result of Illinois' location on the Mississippi flyway; the Chain O'Lakes resort area in the northeast and the Illinois Valley near Havana are notable locations. In winter, one of the largest concentrations of geese in the country gathers at Horseshoe Lake and Union County Wildlife Refuge near Cairo. Annual managed hunts are popular; permits are required.

The Shawnee National Forest, covering most of the southern tip of the state, offers tons of outdoor activities, and **camping** tops the list. In a setting of wooded hills and striking rock formations, campers can pitch a tent and sleep under the stars. The forest, in the foothills of the Ozark Mountains, contains several state parks.

All kinds of fun can be found within the state's extensive system of parks, conservation areas and memorials. You'll find restored American Indian mounds, old forts and pioneer homes to explore.

"Da Bulls" and "Da Bears"

In Chicago, sports fans speak a different language. Wild-eyed and face-painted, they pack Soldier Field to cheer on the Bears. Count the pennants at the United Center and you'll become an instant cheerleader for the city's beloved Bulls. And the Cubs and White Sox hit the diamonds at famous Wrigley Field and Comiskey Park, respectively.

Recreational Activities

Throughout the TourBook, you may notice a Recreational Activities heading with bulleted listings of recreation-oriented establishments listed underneath. Since normal AAA inspection criteria cannot be applied, these establishments are presented for information only. Age, height and weight restrictions may apply. Reservations are often recommended and sometimes required. Visitors should phone or write the attraction for additional information, and the address and phone number are provided for this purpose.

Fast Facts

POPULATION: 11,895,800.

AREA: 56,400 square miles; ranks 24th.

CAPITAL: Springfield.

HIGHEST POINT: 1,235 ft., Charles Mound.

LOWEST POINT: 279 ft., Mississippi River.

TIME ZONE: Central. DST.

MINIMUM AGE FOR DRIVERS: 18; 16 with completion of approved driver education course.

MINIMUM AGE FOR GAMBLING: 21.

SEAT BELT/CHILD RESTRAINT LAWS: Seat belts required for driver, front-seat passengers and all passengers in vehicles driven by a driver under 18. Child restraints required for under 4; ages 4 and 5 must be in a child restraint or seat belt.

HELMETS FOR MOTORCYCLISTS: Not required.

RADAR DETECTORS: Permitted.

FIREARMS LAWS: Vary by state and/or county. Contact the Illinois State Police, 3780 Lakeshore Dr., Springfield, IL 62708; phone (217) 786-6677.

HOLIDAYS: Jan. 1; Martin Luther King Jr. Day, Jan. (3rd Mon.); Lincoln's Birthday, Feb. 12; Washington's Birthday, Feb. (3rd Mon.); Memorial Day, May (last Mon.); July 4; Labor Day, Sept. (1st Mon.); Columbus Day, Oct. (2nd Mon.); Veterans Day, Nov. 11; Thanksgiving; Dec. 25.

TAXES: Illinois' statewide sales tax is 6.25 percent, with local options for additional increments. Cities and counties may impose a sales and/or lodgings tax of up to 5 percent.

STATE INFORMATION CENTERS: Welcome centers, which supply travel literature and other information, are off I-24 westbound near Metropolis; off I-57 northbound near Anna; off I-57 northbound and southbound near Monee; off I-70 eastbound near Highland; off I-70 westbound near Marshall; off I-74 westbound near Oakwood; off I-80 eastbound near Rapids City; off I-57 northbound and southbound near Whittington; off I-80 eastbound near South Holland; off I-64 eastbound near New Baden; and near I-90 southbound near South Beloit. All welcome centers are open daily 8:30-5.

FURTHER INFORMATION FOR VISITORS:
Illinois Bureau of Tourism
620 E. Adams
Springfield, IL 62701
(800) 226-6632
TDD (800) 406-6418

FISHING AND HUNTING REGULATIONS:
Illinois Department of Natural Resources
Division of Fisheries
524 S. Second St.
Springfield, IL 62706
(217) 782-7454

NATIONAL FOREST INFORMATION:
U.S. Forest Service, Eastern Region
310 W. Wisconsin Ave., Suite 500
Milwaukee, WI 53203
(877) 444-6777 (reservations)

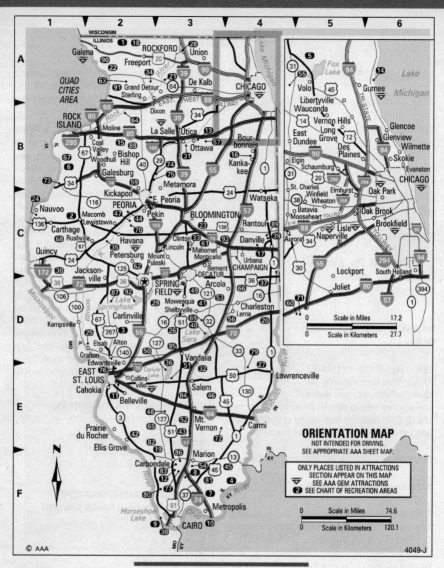

ORIENTATION MAP
NOT INTENDED FOR DRIVING.
SEE APPROPRIATE AAA SHEET MAP.

ONLY PLACES LISTED IN ATTRACTIONS
SECTION APPEAR ON THIS MAP
▽ SEE AAA GEM ATTRACTIONS
❷ SEE CHART OF RECREATION AREAS

© AAA

4049-J

Get on the Right Track

*T*he ***AAA New Car & Truck Buying Guide*** presents unbiased reviews on more than 180 new domestic and imported vehicles. You will find easy-to-read comparison data, ratings of key vehicle features, strong and weak points, specifications, pricing information, and more. Make sure your next vehicle is the right vehicle for you.
Purchase at participating AAA club offices or web sites (aaa.com) or by calling 1-877-AAA-BOOK.

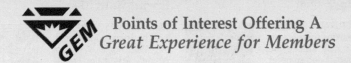

Points of Interest Offering A
Great Experience for Members

Brookfield (C-6)

BROOKFIELD ZOO— This 216-acre zoo houses animals in their natural habitats. See p. 75.

Chicago (C-6)

ADLER PLANETAR-IUM & ASTRONOMY MUSEUM— Highlights include a museum displaying space age hardware, a collection of timepieces, the history of space travel exhibit and a multimedia sky show. See p. 56.

ART INSTITUTE OF CHICAGO— One of the world's best collections of impressionist and post-impressionist paintings can be found here. See p. 58.

THE FIELD MUSEUM— This 1894 institution is one of the world's foremost museums of natural science with some 19 million specimens. See p. 59.

JOHN G. SHEDD AQUAR-IUM— Home to some 8,000 freshwater and saltwater animals, this aquarium also contains one of the world's largest indoor marine pavilions that is home to whales, dolphins, sea otters, harbor seals and a colony of penguins. See p. 61.

LINCOLN PARK— Home to Augustus Saint-Gaudens' Standing Statue of Lincoln, the city's largest park also features several beaches, a conservatory, a bird sanctuary and Lincoln Park Zoo. See p. 61.

MUSEUM OF BROADCAST COM-MUNICATIONS— Vintage televisions and radios in addition to a collection of historic television and radio programs are featured. See p. 59.

MUSEUM OF SCIENCE AND INDUSTRY— Housed in a reconstruction of the Palace of Fine Arts from the 1893 Columbian Exhibition, this museum contains interactive exhibits of applied sciences, engineering and industry. See p. 62.

MUSEUM OF SCIENCE AND INDUSTRY
CHICAGO

Collinsville (E-2)

CAHOKIA MOUNDS STATE HISTORIC SITE— This 2,200-acre site contains 65 preserved American Indian mounds that represent the Mississippian culture that flourished in the area in A.D. 900-1500. See p. 85.

Galena (A-1)

ULYSSES S. GRANT HOME STATE HISTORIC SITE— Many of Grant's possessions can be found in this home presented to him upon his return from the Civil War. See p. 89.

Gurnee (A-6)

SIX FLAGS GREAT AMERICA— This 300-acre theme park features nine roller coasters and four water rides. See p. 78.

La Salle (B-3)

STARVED ROCK STATE PARK— Hiking trails wind throughout the 18 canyons within this 2,630-acre wooded bluff where Fort St. Louis was built in 1682 by French explorer Robert de La Salle. See p. 92.

Lisle (C-5)

MORTON ARBORETUM— More than 4,800 species and varieties of plants are featured on this 1,700-acre site. See p. 79.

Naperville

NAPER SETTLEMENT— Revisit 1831 at this living-history village staffed by costumed "residents." See p. 80.

Oak Park (B-6)

ARCHITECTURAL TOURS—
Various walking tours are offered and may include the
historic district and some of
the buildings designed by
Oak Park resident Frank
Lloyd Wright. See p. 81.

Petersburg (C-2)

LINCOLN'S NEW SALEM HIS-
TORIC SITE—This 600-acre
replica of New Salem con-
tains buildings reconstructed
as they looked in the 1830s
when Abraham Lincoln lived
here as a young merchant.
See p. 97.

Springfield (D-3)

DANA-THOMAS HOUSE—
Built by Frank Lloyd Wright,
this 1902 home is one of
Wright's first major Prairie-
style houses and most elaborate. It contains more than
250 examples of art glass
doors, panels, windows and
lamps. See p. 102.

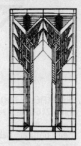

LINCOLN HOME NATIONAL
HISTORIC SITE—Built in
1839, this home is the only
one Abraham Lincoln ever owned. See p. 104.

LINCOLN'S TOMB STATE HISTORIC SITE—This
monument contains the tomb of Abraham Lincoln, his wife and three of their four children. See
p. 104.

RECREATION AREAS

	MAP LOCATION	CAMPING	PICNICKING	HIKING TRAILS	BOATING	BOAT RAMP	BOAT RENTAL	FISHING	SWIMMING	PETS ON LEASH	BICYCLE TRAILS	WINTER SPORTS	VISITOR CENTER	LODGE/CABINS	FOOD SERVICE
NATIONAL FOREST *(See place listing)*															
Shawnee 273,800 acres. Southern Illinois.		•	•	•	•	•	•	•	•	•					
ARMY CORPS OF ENGINEERS															
Blanding Landing (A-2) 18 acres 8 mi. n.w. of Hanover.	90	•	•		•	•		•		•					
Carlyle Lake (D-3) 37,508 acres on the n.e. edge of Carlyle. Historic. Hunting, water skiing; nature trail.	36	•	•	•	•	•	•	•	•	•			•	•	
Lake Shelbyville (D-3) 34,408 acres 1 mi. e. of Shelbyville. Golf, hunting, water skiing; nature trail. *(See Shelbyville p. 102)*	41	•	•	•	•	•	•	•	•	•			•	•	•
Rend Lake (E-3) 39,819 acres 1 mi. n. of Benton. Golf (18 holes), hunting, water skiing; horse rental.	43	•	•	•	•	•	•	•	•	•			•	•	•
Thomson Causeway (A-2) 64 acres 1 mi. w. of Thomson.	91	•	•	•	•	•		•		•	•				
STATE															
Anderson Lake (C-2) 2,135 acres 12 mi. s.w. of Havana off SR 100.	35	•	•		•	•		•		•		•			
Apple River Canyon (A-2) 298 acres 9 mi. n.w. of Stockton on CR 10. Scenic.	1	•	•	•				•		•					•
Argyle Lake (C-1) 1,700 acres 8 mi. s.w. of Macomb on US 136, then 1.5 mi. n. Cross-country skiing, snowmobiling, tobogganing.	2	•	•	•	•	•	•	•		•		•	•		•
Beaver Dam (D-2) 744 acres 7 mi. s.w. of Carlinville off CR 735.	3	•	•	•	•	•	•	•		•			•		
Big River (B-1) 3,027 acres 6 mi. n. of Oquawka on Oquawka-Keithsburg blacktop. Cross-country skiing, snowmobiling.	67	•	•	•				•		•		•	•		
Cave-in-Rock (F-4) 200 acres at Cave-in-Rock off SR 1.	4	•	•	•				•		•				•	•
Chain O'Lakes (A-5) 6,063 acres 3 mi. e. of Spring Grove off US 12. Cross-country skiing, snowmobiling, water skiing; horse rental.	5	•	•	•	•	•	•	•		•	•	•	•		•
Channahon (D-4) 20 acres at 2 W. Story St. in Channahon.	60	•	•		•			•		•					
Clinton Lake (C-3) 9,907 acres 5 mi. e. of Clinton on SR 54. Snowmobiling.	61	•	•	•	•	•		•		•		•			•
Delabar (B-1) 89 acres 2 mi. n. of Oquawka along the Mississippi River.	6	•	•		•	•		•		•					
Des Plaines (D-5) 5,012 acres 10 mi. s. of Joliet on I-55.	71	•	•	•				•		•					•

RECREATION AREAS

	MAP LOCATION	CAMPING	PICNICKING	HIKING TRAILS	BOATING	BOAT RAMP	BOAT RENTAL	FISHING	SWIMMING	PETS ON LEASH	BICYCLE TRAILS	WINTER SPORTS	VISITOR CENTER	LODGE/CABINS	FOOD SERVICE
Dixon Springs (F-3) 787 acres at Dixon Springs near jct. of SRs 145 and 146.	7	•	•	•				•	•						•
Eagle Creek (D-3) 1,463 acres 3 mi. s.e. of Findlay via SR 128. Cross-country skiing, golf, water skiing.	49	•	•	•	•			•				•		•	•
Eldon Hazlet (D-2) 3,500 acres 4 mi. n. of Carlyle on SR 127, then 2 mi. e.	50	•	•	•	•	•		•						•	•
Ferne Clyffe (F-3) 2,430 acres 1.5 mi. s. of Goreville off SR 37.	8	•	•	•				•	•						
Fort Defiance (F-2) 38 acres s. edge of Cairo. Historic.	9		•		•	•		•							
Fort Massac (F-3) 1,470 acres w. of Metropolis off I-24 via US 45. Historic. *(See Metropolis p. 94)*	10	•	•	•				•	•				•		
Fox Ridge (D-4) 1,838 acres 10 mi. s. of Charleston on SR 130.	56	•	•	•				•							
Frank Holten (E-2) 1,180 acres s. edge of East St. Louis on SR 111.	11		•		•	•		•	•						
Gebhard Woods (B-3) 30 acres on the w. edge of Morris. Historic.	57	•	•	•				•		•	•	•			
Giant City (F-3) 3,694 acres 12 mi. s. of Carbondale on US 51. Scenic. Horse rental. *(See Carbondale p. 46)*	12	•	•	•				•	•					•	•
Hamilton County (Dolan Lake) (E-3) 1,683 acres 8 mi. e. of McLeansboro off SR 14.	72	•	•	•	•	•	•	•				•			
Henderson County (B-1) 87 acres 20 mi. s.w. of Monmouth via US 34.	73	•	•		•	•	•	•	•			•			
Hennepin Canal Parkway (B-2) 5,773 acres off SR 34.	88	•	•	•	•	•		•		•	•	•	•		
Hidden Springs (D-3) 1,121 acres 7 mi. s.w. of Strasburg via CR 7.	69	•	•	•				•							
Horseshoe Lake (Alexander County) (F-3) 9,550 acres 13 mi. n.w. of Cairo off SR 3. *(See Cairo p. 46)*	38	•	•		•	•		•							
Horseshoe Lake (E-2) 2,854 acres s.e. of Granite City via SRs 162 and 111.	76	•		•	•			•							
Illini (B-3) 510 acres 1 mi. s. of Marseilles on the Illinois River. Tobogganing.	13	•	•	•				•	•			•			
Illinois Beach (A-6) 4,160 acres 4 mi. n. of Waukegan on SR 131. Cross-country skiing.	14	•	•	•				•	•	•	•	•	•	•	•
Johnson Sauk Trail (B-2) 1,361 acres 6 mi. n. of Kewanee off SR 78. Cross-country skiing, snowmobiling.	15	•	•	•	•	•		•				•			
Jubilee College (B-2) 3,500 acres .8 mi. w. on US 150, 2 mi. n. on Princeville Jubilee Rd., then w. on Jubilee College Rd. *(See Kickapoo p. 91)*	59	•	•	•				•				•	•		
Kankakee River (B-4) 3,932 acres 8 mi. n.w. of Kankakee on SR 102. Cross-country skiing, snowmobiling; horse rental.	16	•	•	•	•	•		•				•			
Kickapoo (C-4) 2,843 acres 7 mi. w. of Danville off I-74. Horse rental.	17	•	•	•	•	•		•	•						
Lake Le-Aqua-Na (A-2) 715 acres 4 mi. n. of Lena off SR 73. Cross-country skiing.	18	•	•	•	•	•	•	•	•	•		•			•
Lake Murphysboro (E-3) 1,024 acres 4 mi. w. of Murphysboro off SR 149.	19	•	•	•	•	•	•	•							
Lincoln's New Salem (C-2) 600 acres 2 mi. s. of Petersburg on SR 97. Historic. *(See Petersburg p. 97)*	62	•	•					•					•		•
Lincoln Trail (D-4) 1,022 acres 3 mi. s. of Marshall off SR 1. Historic.	20	•	•	•		•	•	•	•						
Lowden (A-3) 207 acres 2 mi. n. of Oregon off SR 64.	21	•	•	•	•	•		•							
Marshall (B-3) 5,658 acres 4 mi. s. of Lacon on SR 26. Cross-country skiing.	74	•	•	•	•	•		•				•			
Middle Fork (C-4) 2,778 acres 8 mi. n. of Oakwood on US 74.	89	•	•					•				•			
Mississippi Palisades (A-2) 2,500 acres 4 mi. n. of Savanna on SR 84. Scenic. Cross-country skiing, snowmobiling, tobogganing.	22	•	•	•	•	•	•	•				•	•		•

RECREATION AREAS

	MAP LOCATION	CAMPING	PICNICKING	HIKING TRAILS	BOATING	BOAT RAMP	BOAT RENTAL	FISHING	SWIMMING	PETS ON LEASH	BICYCLE TRAILS	WINTER SPORTS	VISITOR CENTER	LODGE/CABINS	FOOD SERVICE
Moraine Hills (A-5) 1,763 acres at 915 S. River Rd. in McHenry. Cross-country skiing.	55		•	•	•		•	•		•	•	•	•		•
Moraine View (C-3) 1,687 acres 7.5 mi. n.e. of LeRoy off CR 36. Cross-country skiing, snowmobiling; horse rental.	23	•	•	•	•	•	•	•	•	•			•		•
Morrison-Rockwood (A-2) 1,152 acres 2.5 mi. n. of Morrison on SR 78. Cross-country skiing; horse rental.	63	•	•	•	•	•	•	•		•		•	•		•
Nauvoo (C-1) 148 acres s. edge of Nauvoo off SR 96. Historic. *(See Nauvoo p. 96)*	24	•	•	•	•	•		•		•			•		•
Pere Marquette (D-2) 7,901 acres 5 mi. w. of Grafton on SR 100. Horse rental.	25	•	•	•	•			•		•	•		•	•	•
Prophetstown (B-2) 52 acres in Prophetstown.	64	•	•	•				•		•					
Pyramid (E-2) 7,041 acres 4 mi. s. of Pinckneyville on SR 13/127.	65	•	•	•	•	•		•		•	•				
Ramsey Lake (D-3) 1,880 acres 2 mi. n.w. of Ramsey off US 51. Snowmobiling, tobogganing; horse rental.	26	•	•	•	•	•	•	•		•		•			•
Randolph County (E-2) 1,031 acres 4 mi. n. of Chester off CR 1.	42	•	•	•	•	•		•		•					•
Red Hills (E-4) 948 acres 9 mi. w. of Lawrenceville on US 50. Horse rental.	27	•	•	•	•	•	•	•		•		•			•
Rice Lake (C-2) 5,660 acres 3.5 mi. s. of Banner off US 24.	44	•	•					•							
Rock Cut (A-3) 3,092 acres 5 mi. n.e. of Rockford on SR 51. Cross-country skiing, snowmobiling.	28	•	•	•	•	•	•	•	•	•		•			•
Saline County (F-4) 1,248 acres 6 mi. s.w. of Equality. Horse rental.	45	•	•	•	•	•		•		•					•
Sam Dale Lake (E-3) 1,301 acres 3 mi. w. of Johnsonville off CR 12.	46	•	•	•	•	•	•	•	•	•					•
Sand Ridge (C-2) 7,112 acres 10 mi. n.e. of Havana on Manito blacktop. Cross-country skiing, snowmobiling.	70	•	•	•						•		•			
Sangchris Lake (D-2) 3,576 acres 2 mi. w. of Kincaid on SR 104. Snowmobiling; horse rental.	29	•	•	•	•	•	•	•		•					•
Siloam Springs (C-1) 3,323 acres 11 mi. e. of Liberty off SR 104. Cross-country skiing, tobogganing; horse rental.	30	•	•	•	•	•	•	•		•		•			•
South Shore (E-3) 800 acres 3 mi. e. of Carlyle on US 50.	51	•	•	•	•			•		•					•
Spring Lake (C-2) 2,032 acres 1 mi. s. of Pekin on SR 29, 9 mi. s.w. on Manito blacktop, then 3 mi. w. on Spring Lake blacktop. Cross-country skiing, tobogganing.	47	•	•	•	•	•	•	•		•		•			•
Starved Rock (B-3) 2,630 acres 1 mi. s. of Utica, 4 mi. s. off I-80 on SR 178. Historic. Cross-country skiing, tobogganing; horse rental. *(See La Salle p. 92)*	31	•	•	•	•	•	•	•		•		•	•	•	•
Stephen A. Forbes (E-3) 3,100 acres 15 mi. n.e. of Salem on SR 37. Horse rental.	32	•	•	•	•	•	•	•	•	•			•		•
Walnut Point (D-4) 631 acres 5 mi. n. of Oakland on CR 669.	66	•	•	•	•	•	•	•		•		•			
Washington County (E-2) 1,417 acres 5 mi. s. of Nashville off SR 127.	48	•	•	•	•	•		•		•					•
Wayne Fitzgerrell (E-3) 3,302 acres 6 mi. n. of Benton on I-57, 1.5 mi. w. on SR 154, then .5 mi. n. Horse rental.	52	•	•	•	•	•	•	•		•			•	•	•
Weinburg-King (C-1) 772 acres 4 mi. e. of Augusta on SR 101. Snowmobiling; horse rental.	68	•	•	•				•		•			•		
Weldon Springs (C-3) 442 acres 3 mi. s.e. of Clinton off SR 10. Cross-country skiing; interpretive trails.	33	•	•	•				•		•		•			•
White Pines Forest (A-2) 385 acres 7 mi. w. of Oregon. Cross-country skiing, tobogganing.	34	•	•	•				•		•		•		•	•
Wolf Creek (D-3) 1,966 acres 8 mi. n.w. of Windsor via CR 1650. Snowmobiling; horse rental.	53	•	•	•	•	•	•	•	•	•		•			•
Woodford (B-2) 2,900 acres n. of Spring Bay on SR 26.	75	•	•	•	•			•		•					•

RECREATION AREAS

	MAP LOCATION	CAMPING	PICNICKING	HIKING TRAILS	BOATING	BOAT RAMP	BOAT RENTAL	FISHING	SWIMMING	PETS ON LEASH	BICYCLE TRAILS	WINTER SPORTS	VISITOR CENTER	LODGE/CABINS	FOOD SERVICE
OTHER															
Crab Orchard Lake (F-3) 6,965 acres 4 mi. e. of Carbondale via SR 13. Water skiing.	86	●	●	●	●	●	●	●	●	●			●		
Devils Kitchen Lake (F-3) 810 acres 8 mi. s.w. of Carbondale.	77	●	●	●	●	●	●	●	●	●					
East Fork Lake (D-4) 934 acres 1 mi. n. of Olney.	79	●	●		●	●		●		●					
Forest Glen Preserve (C-4) 1,800 acres 26 mi. s.e. of Danville.	37	●	●	●				●	●	●				●	
Grassy and Lyerle Lake (F-2) 310 acres 3 mi. s.e. of Ware.	80	●			●		●	●		●					
Kennekuk County Park (C-4) 2,500 acres 8 mi. n.w. of Danville.	39		●	●	●	●		●		●	●		●	●	
Lake Glendale (F-3) 79 acres 3 mi. n. of Dixon Springs via SR 145.	81	●	●		●	●	●	●	●	●					
Lake Jacksonville (D-2) 1,477 acres 3 mi. s. of Jacksonville off US 67.	87	●	●		●	●	●	●		●	●			●	●
Lake Kinkaid (E-2) 2,750 acres 8 mi. w. of Murphysboro via SRs 149 and 151.	82	●	●		●	●	●	●		●					
Lake of Egypt (F-3) 2,300 acres 8 mi. s. of Marion via I-57 and SR 37. Golf, water skiing.	54	●	●		●	●	●	●	●	●					
Lake of the Woods (C-3) 900 acres .5 mi. n. of Mahomet on SR 47. Golf; botanical gardens, museum.	93		●	●				●		●					
Lake Sara (D-3) 586 acres 5 mi. n.w. of Effingham on SR 32.	40	●	●		●	●	●	●	●	●			●		●
Lake Springfield (D-2) 4,235 acres s.e. off Lake Shore Dr. in Springfield. Golf; children's zoo, theater. *(See Springfield p. 103)*	92		●	●	●	●	●	●	●	●			●		
Little Grassy Lake (F-3) 1,000 acres near Makanda, 5 mi. s. of Crab Orchard Lake off CR 26.	83	●	●		●	●	●	●	●	●					
Raccoon Lake (E-3) 970 acres .2 mi. n. and 1 mi. e. of Centralia.	84	●	●		●	●	●	●		●					
Vandalia Lake (D-3) 660 acres n.w. of Vandalia via SR 185.	85	●	●		●	●	●	●		●					

Illinois Temperature Averages
Maximum / Minimum
From the records of the National Weather Service

	JAN	FEB	MAR	APR	MAY	JUNE	JULY	AUG	SEPT	OCT	NOV	DEC
Cairo	45/30	49/33	57/39	69/50	79/59	88/68	90/72	89/71	82/63	72/52	56/40	46/33
Chicago	33/19	35/20	44/29	59/40	71/50	81/60	86/66	84/65	77/56	65/46	48/32	36/22
Moline	32/15	35/18	45/27	61/39	72/50	82/61	87/64	85/62	77/54	66/42	48/30	35/19
Peoria	34/18	37/20	47/28	61/40	72/51	82/61	87/65	85/64	78/55	67/44	49/31	32/21
Rockford	30/14	33/16	43/25	59/37	71/48	81/58	86/62	84/61	76/52	64/41	46/28	34/18
Springfield	36/21	40/23	49/30	63/42	74/52	83/63	88/66	86/65	79/56	68/45	51/32	39/24

Points of Interest

ALTON (D-2) pop. 32,900, elev. 450'

Just north of the confluence of the Mississippi and Missouri rivers, Alton was founded 1814-17. Col. Rufus Easton obtained the land and named the town for his son. The Eagle Packet line of boats, once built in Alton, contributed to the local river traffic on the Mississippi. This portion of the Mississippi is tamed by the Melvin Price Locks and Dam, the last of a series of navigational and flood control dams that make up the Illinois Waterway. Riverfront Park offers a vantage point for viewing the Mississippi.

The issue of slavery found volatile expression in Alton when abolitionist editor Elijah Lovejoy was killed by a proslavery mob in 1837. The Alton Cemetery on Monument Avenue contains Lovejoy's tomb and a monument in his honor. In 1858 the last Lincoln-Douglas debate took place in town. The city's history and river heritage are among the themes addressed at Alton Museum of History and Art, 2809 College Ave.; phone (618) 462-2763.

Perhaps Alton's most renowned native son was Robert Pershing Wadlow; at 8 feet, 11.5 inches he remains the world's tallest person. A life-size statue of Wadlow can be seen on the campus of Southern Illinois University Dental School. Near the intersection of Broadway and William are the remnants of Alton Prison, where more than 1,300 Confederate soldiers died of various diseases. A portion of the cellblock wall remains.

Alton's Victorian, Federal and Greek Revival 19th-century houses draw attention. In autumn the surrounding bluffs blaze with color. The Great River Road, which runs north along the Mississippi River, has a bicycle path that affords views of the river and bluffs.

Alton Visitors Center: 200 Piasa St., Alton, IL 62002; phone (618) 465-6676 or (800) 258-6645.

Shopping areas: The antique district, in a 3-block area between George and State streets, contains more than 40 shops housed in buildings dating from the 1800s.

CASINOS

- *Alton Belle* **Riverboat Casino**, on the riverfront at 219 Piasa St. Sun.-Thurs. 8 a.m.-4 a.m., Fri.-Sat. 8 a.m.-6 a.m. Phone (800) 336-7568.

ARCOLA (D-3) pop. 2,700, elev. 678'

Platted in 1855, Arcola is in the northern corner of what was once known as the Broomcorn Belt. Broomcorn, used in broommaking, has a finer leaf and bushier tassel than grain corn. Homemade quilts and crafts can be found at a large Amish community west of town near Arthur.

Arcola Chamber of Commerce: P.O. Box 274, Arcola, IL 61910; phone (217) 268-4530.

SAVE **THE ILLINOIS AMISH INTERPRETIVE CENTER,** I-57 exit 203, 6 blks. w. on Springfield Rd. (SR 133) then 1.5 blks. n. to 111 S. Locust St., is dedicated to presenting the Amish way of life. A 15-minute videotape introduces visitors to the life of the Old Order Amish. Displays feature Amish crafts, traditional clothing, horse-drawn buggies and buildings.

Allow 1 hour minimum. Mon.-Sat. 10-5:30, Apr.-Nov.; Wed.-Sat. 10-4:30, rest of year. Closed major holidays. Admission $2.50; senior citizens $2.25; ages 6-11, $2. MC, VI. Phone (217) 268-3599 or (888) 452-6474.

ROCKOME GARDENS, 5 mi. w. off I-57 exit 203 following signs, has an array of rockwork, flower gardens and rides. Specialty shops such as a haunted cave, a craft shop and an Amish house also are on the grounds. The Christmas in the Country Craft Show is held Nov. 1-Dec.23. Gardens daily 9-5:30, late May through mid-Aug.; Sun.-Sun. 9-5:30, late Aug.-early Oct. and May 1 through mid-May; Sat.-Sun. 9-5:30, mid-Apr. through Apr. 30. Stores open 1 hour later than gardens and close 30 minutes earlier except on weekends. Free. A fee is charged for some rides. Admission may be charged for some special events. DS, MC, VI. Phone (217) 268-4106.

AURORA—*see Chicago p. 75.*

BATAVIA—*see Chicago p. 75.*

BELLEVILLE (E-2) pop. 42,800, elev. 500'

Founded in 1814, Belleville was named by its early French settlers. The discovery of coal in 1828 attracted many German miners. The town retains much of the Teutonic influence in language, song, festivals and architecture. Manufacturers produce a variety of goods, and area coal mines yield more than 3 million tons a year. Scott Air Force Base is nearby.

Belleville Tourism Bureau: 216 E. A St., Belleville, IL 62220; phone (800) 677-9255.

NATIONAL SHRINE OF OUR LADY OF THE SNOWS is w. on SR 15, just e. of I-255. A 200-acre religious center under direction of the Missionary Oblates of Mary Immaculate, the shrine includes a 2,400-seat amphitheater, a replica of the Lourdes Grotto, prayer gardens and chapels. Food is available. Daily 8-8. Donations. Phone (618) 397-6700.

SAVE **ST. CLAIR HISTORICAL SOCIETY,** 701 E. Washington St., is an 1866 Victorian adaptation of a Greek Revival home. Furnished in period, the home features changing displays of vintage clothing, toys, quilts and other articles. Tour guides explain the use of everyday items and provide information about the era. A historical research library is available. Mon.-Fri. 10-2; closed major holidays. Admission $2; ages 6-12, $1. Phone (618) 234-0600.

BEMENT (C-3) pop. 1,700, elev. 690′

BRYANT COTTAGE STATE HISTORIC SITE, jct. of SR 105 and Wilson St. at 146 E. Wilson St., is a four-room, period-furnished cottage built in 1856. Abraham Lincoln and Stephen Douglas allegedly met at the cottage in July 1858 to plan their well-known debates. Guided tours highlight local history. Allow 30 minutes minimum. Daily 9-5, Mar.-Oct.; 9-4, rest of year. Closed Jan. 1, Thanksgiving and Dec. 25. Donations. Phone (217) 678-8184.

BISHOP HILL (B-2) pop. 100, elev. 779′

Bishop Hill was settled in 1846 by a group of Swedish religious dissidents who believed that simplicity was the way to salvation. Their leader, Erik Jansson, named the colony for Biskopskulla, his birthplace in Sweden. The community was united by necessity and religious belief, but dissension arose within the following and the ideals were abandoned in 1861. The town, inhabited by descendants of the collective's original immigrants, is a good source for Swedish collectibles and crafts.

Bishop Hill Heritage Association: P.O. Box 92, Bishop Hill, IL 61419; phone (309) 927-3899.

BISHOP HILL STATE HISTORIC SITE, 2 mi. n. of US 34 on a 5-acre tract, commemorates the Swedish communal settlement with five museums. Skills and crafts of colony life are demonstrated, and 16 of the buildings have been restored.

Bishop Hill Museum contains an outstanding collection of early American primitive paintings by Olof Krans, now recognized as one of America's foremost folk artists. The Heritage Museum, in the Steeple Building, has exhibits depicting the story of the Swedish colonists; Bishop Hill Colony artifacts and crafts are featured. Cultural events are held. Allow 4 hours minimum. Daily 9-5; closed Jan. 1, Thanksgiving and Dec. 25. Donations. Phone (309) 927-3345.

HENRY COUNTY HISTORICAL MUSEUM, Knox and Park sts., has furnished period rooms and agricultural equipment. Daily 10-4, Apr.-Oct. Admission $1, under 16 free. Phone (309) 927-3528.

BLOOMINGTON (C-3) pop. 51,900, elev. 799′

Named in 1822 for its profusion of flowers and location just north of the town of Blooming Grove, Bloomington shares Franklin Avenue with the bordering city of Normal. This common avenue also was the only street in the nation with a university at each end: Illinois State University and Illinois Wesleyan University.

Majors Hall in Bloomington was the site of Abraham Lincoln's 1856 "Lost Speech" about the abolition of slavery, so named because reporters became so engrossed in the speech that none took notes. Although newspapers were unable to report the exact speech, most historians agree that this popular theme helped carry Lincoln to the presidency.

Bloomington-Normal Area Convention & Visitors Bureau: 210 S. East St., P.O. Box 1586, Bloomington, IL 61702-1586; phone (309) 829-1641 or (800) 433-8226.

DAVID DAVIS MANSION is at 1000 E. Monroe Dr. Built in 1872 for U.S. Supreme Court Judge David Davis and his wife Sarah, the home is considered a fine example of mid-Victorian residential architecture. Such features as indoor plumbing, a central heating system and a cast-iron cooking stove were considered luxuries. Original furnishings and other period pieces are enhanced by handsome woodwork, stencils and hand-painted ceilings.

Allow 1 hour, 30 minutes minimum. Thurs.-Mon. 9-4; closed Jan. 1, Martin Luther King Jr. Day, Presidents Day, Election Day, Veterans Day, Thanksgiving and Dec. 25. Donations. Phone (309) 828-1084.

McLEAN COUNTY MUSEUM OF HISTORY, 200 N. Main St., is in the former county courthouse, built in 1903. Four galleries depict the history of the county and life on the prairie through exhibits about its people, work, politics and farming. A courtroom, in use 1903-74, retains its judge's bench and jury box, and a library contains historical and genealogical information.

Allow 1 hour minimum. Mon.-Sat. 10-5 (also Tues. 5-9), Sun. 1-5, Sept.-May; Mon.-Sat. 10-5 (also Tues. 5-9), rest of year. Closed holidays. Admission $2; ages 3-12, $1; free to all Tues. Phone (309) 827-0428.

PRAIRIE AVIATION MUSEUM is on US 9, 2 mi. e. of jct. I-55 (Veterans Pkwy.) near the entrance of Central Illinois Regional Airport. Highlights include jets, helicopters and aircraft engine cutaways. A videotape presentation is of limited interest. Allow 30 minutes minimum. Thurs.-Sat. 11-4 (also Tues. 5-8 p.m., Apr.-Nov.), Sun. noon-4. Admission $1; over 65 and under 9, 50c. MC, VI. Phone (309) 663-7632.

BOURBONNAIS (B-4) pop. 13,900

Bourbonnais, just north of Kankakee, was one of the first settlements along the Kankakee River. The town has enjoyed a French flavor since the establishment of a French trading post in 1832 led to an influx of French Canadians. The home of George LeTourneau, the first mayor of Bourbonnais, has been restored and is now the headquarters for the Bourbonnais Grove Historical Society. Strickler Planetarium, at Olivet Nazarene University, has seasonal programs, many of which are written by campus astronomy students.

Bradley-Bourbonnais Chamber of Commerce: 1690 Newtowne Dr., Bourbonnais, IL 60914; phone (815) 932-2222.

EXPLORATION STATION, 459 N. Kennedy Dr., has interactive displays including a mock airplane cockpit, fire truck, ambulance, veterinary office, farm and castle. Mon.-Thurs. 10-6, Fri. noon-8, Sat. 10-5, Sun. 1-5, early June-Aug. 31; Mon.-Thurs. 10-5, Fri. noon-8, Sat. 10-5, Sun. 1-5, rest of year. Admission $4. Admission may vary; phone ahead. Phone (815) 933-9905.

BROOKFIELD—*see Chicago p. 75.*

CAHOKIA (E-2) pop. 17,600, elev. 401'

Cahokia was founded in 1699 by three missionaries from Québec. Its location along three rivers made it a center of commerce for the region by the mid-1700s. At the end of the French and Indian War in 1763, when the area was ceded to Great Britain, many citizens, uneasy about the possibility of a British occupation, moved across the Mississippi River and were instrumental in helping found St. Louis.

With the onset of the American Revolution, George Rogers Clark and his troops from Virginia occupied Cahokia, recruited a militia and organized a campaign against British forces at Vincennes, Ind. The Jarrot Mansion, completed in 1810, is probably the oldest brick building in the mid-Mississippi River Valley. Now a state historic site, it is open Tuesday through Saturday by appointment; phone (618) 332-1782.

Cahokia Area Chamber of Commerce: 905 Falling Springs Rd., Cahokia, IL 62206; phone (618) 332-1900.

CAHOKIA COURTHOUSE STATE HISTORIC SITE, off I-55/70, just w. of jct. SRs 3 and 157, was built in 1737 as a French residence and was used as a courthouse until 1814. The first U.S. court sessions and elections in the state were held in this building. The visitor center has interactive exhibits that trace the French influence in 18th-century Illinois. Courthouse and visitor center Tues.-Sat. 9-5; closed Jan. 1, Thanksgiving and Dec. 25. Donations. Phone (618) 332-1782.

 **CAHOKIA MOUNDS STATE HISTORIC SITE**—*see Collinsville p. 85.*

CHURCH OF THE HOLY FAMILY, 4 mi. s. of I-55/70 at jct. SRs 3 and 157, is the oldest church in Illinois. The 1699 stone and wood building has been in continuous use under French, British and American rule. Allow 30 minutes minimum. Daily 10-3, June-Aug.; by appointment rest of year. Donations. Phone (618) 337-4548.

CAIRO (F-3) pop. 4,800, elev. 326'

Illinois, Kentucky and Missouri are separated by Cairo by the confluence of the Ohio and Mississippi rivers. Built on a peninsula and protected by a huge levee, the settlement was named Cairo for its supposed resemblance to the Egyptian city.

During the Civil War Cairo was the site of a Union Army training and supply encampment. From this base Ulysses S. Grant waged his decisive campaigns against forts Henry and Donelson.

The Cairo Public Library, 1609 Washington Ave., houses various displays including a rare Tiffany grandfather clock and artwork, including a painting by Raphael; phone (618) 734-1840.

Cairo Chamber of Commerce: 220 Eighth St., Cairo, IL 62914; phone (618) 734-2737.

HORSESHOE LAKE STATE CONSERVATION AREA, 13 mi. n.w. off SR 3, contains public hunting grounds. During the winter 150,000 to 200,000 Canada geese migrate to this refuge. For hunting regulations contact the Horseshoe Lake Chamber of Commerce, R.R. 3, Olive Branch, IL 62969. Conservation area open daily 5 a.m.-10 p.m. Free. Phone (618) 776-5689. *See Recreation Chart.*

MAGNOLIA MANOR is at 27th and Washington Ave. The house was built in 1869 by merchant Charles A. Galigher, who supplied flour to the Union armies. Furnished with Victorian antiques and much of the original furniture, the house also contains local historical items. A winding staircase, marble fireplaces and chandeliers grace the interior. Allow 1 hour minimum. Guided tours Mon.-Sat. 9-5, Sun. 1-5; closed Jan. 1 and Dec. 24-25. Admission $5; ages 6-12, $2. Phone (618) 734-0201.

U.S. CUSTOM HOUSE MUSEUM is at 14th St. and Washington Ave. The Romanesque limestone building includes an 1865 fire pumper, American Indian artifacts and a desk used by Ulysses S. Grant. A display of an early 1900s post office also is presented. Photographs detail the history of this river town. Allow 30 minutes minimum. Mon.-Fri. 10-noon and 1-3. Free. Phone (618) 734-1019.

CARBONDALE (F-2) pop. 27,000, elev. 414'

South of Carbondale lie the popular recreational lands of Shawnee National Forest *(see place listing p. 102).* The Stage Co., 101 N. Washington, features plays as well as children's and dinner theater productions; phone (618) 549-5466.

Carbondale Convention & Tourism Bureau: 111 S. Illinois Ave., Carbondale, IL 62901; phone (618) 529-4451 or (800) 526-1500.

GIANT CITY STATE PARK, 12 mi. s. on US 51, is a 3,694-acre tract in the rugged, hilly section often called the Illinois Ozarks. The park was named for the large cubical blocks of stone that rise from its canyons. Of particular interest is the Old Stone Fort near the park's northern end. Daily 6 a.m.-10 p.m. Free. Phone (618) 457-4836. *See Recreation Chart.*

CARLINVILLE (D-2) pop. 5,400

MACOUPIN COUNTY COURTHOUSE, 201 E. Main St., cost more than $1 million when completed in 1870. Its lavish interiors include carved moldings and stained-glass windows. Self-guiding tour cassette tapes are available. Allow 1 hour minimum. Mon.-Fri. 8:30-4:30. Last tour begins 1 hour before closing. Free. Phone (217) 854-3211.

CARMI (E-4) pop. 5,600, elev. 400'

Outlined by the Little Wabash River, Carmi marks the transition between the open prairie and the hilly country of southern Illinois. The center of an oil-producing area shared by three states, Carmi also relies on farming and stock raising.

The Lincoln Heritage Trail enters the state just northeast of town. Also historically significant is the Robinson-Stewart House, the former residence of John M. Robinson, who served in the U.S. Senate 1835-43; phone (618) 382-7606.

Carmi Chamber of Commerce: 225 E. Main St., Carmi, IL 62821; phone (618) 382-7606.

CARTHAGE (C-1) pop. 2,700, elev. 678'

Located in the geographical center of Hancock County, Carthage was founded in the early 1830s and incorporated as a city in 1883.

Carthage College was founded in 1870 as a 4-year liberal arts college and the first Lutheran College in the Midwest. The college continued until 1964 when it moved to Kenosha, Wis.

THE HISTORIC CARTHAGE JAIL AND VISITOR CENTER, 307 Walnut St., was the scene of the deaths of Joseph Smith, founder of the Mormon Church, and his brother Hyrum. Jailed on charges of treason, they were killed by a mob in June 1844. Fifty-minute tours of the jail include an 18-minute videotape presentation about Joseph Smith's life.

Allow 1 hour minimum. Mon.-Sat. 9-6, Sun. 10:30-6, Memorial Day-Labor Day; Mon.-Sat. 9-5, Sun. noon-5, rest of year. Last tour begins 45 minutes before closing. Free. Phone (217) 357-2989.

CHAMPAIGN (C-4) pop. 63,500, elev. 738'

The towns of Champaign and Urbana *(see place listing p. 105)* are twin cities separated by a single street. Champaign was established in 1852, 30 years after Urbana, when the railroad laid tracks 2 miles outside of town. Some residents who chose to move near the depot later fought annexation by Urbana and won the incorporation of Champaign, which soon developed as a commercial center for prairie crops. A portion of the University of Illinois is within Champaign's borders.

The Starlight Dinner Theatre, 1501 S. Neil St., presents a mixture of old and new musical comedies and shows; phone (217) 359-4503.

Champaign County Convention & Visitors Bureau: 1817 S. Neil St., Suite 201, Champaign, IL 61820; phone (217) 351-4133.

UNIVERSITY OF ILLINOIS—see *Urbana p. 105.*

CHARLESTON (D-4) pop. 20,400, elev. 681'

The scene of the fourth Lincoln-Douglas debate, Charleston is rich in association with Abraham Lincoln. It also is the site of Eastern Illinois University, Lake Charleston, Fox Ridge State Park *(see Recreation Chart)* and Lincoln Log Cabin.

Charleston Area Chamber of Commerce: 501 Jackson Ave., P.O. Box 77, Charleston, IL 61920; phone (217) 345-7041.

Chicago

Population: 2,783,700 **Elevation:** 665 ft.

Popular Spots:

Art Institute of Chicago ....(see p. 58)
The Field Museum ....(see p. 59)
Museum of Science and Industry..(see p. 62)

Bright orange flames shot out of the O'Leary barn, licking the night sky in a fiery foreboding of the coming destruction. Dennis Sullivan ran inside and managed to save a calf before the heat and smoke drove him out, but beyond that all he or anyone else could do was stand by and watch as the wooden structure was consumed quickly.

Such a blaze would normally have been harmless to all but the O'Learys and possibly their neighbors, but Oct. 8, 1871, was no ordinary night. Sparks from the burning barn rode a stiff breeze onto nearby homes and buildings that, dry as kindling after a rainless summer, were ripe for ignition. Thus began the nightmare known as the Great Chicago Fire of 1871. By the time it was stopped—around 11 the following night—the disaster had claimed nearly 2,000 acres, more than 17,000 buildings and more than 250 lives.

But it would take more than a holocaust to destroy Chicago. The Gem of the Lakes rose from its ashy ruins to become the Hub of the Nation, the surprisingly swift recovery overshadowing the fire as the city's defining moment. Chicagoans responded with the same strength of character they used to build their city in the first place.

Chicago's origin may be its least glorious period. Long inhabited by various Native American tribes, the area supported a network of trade and travel routes snaking deep into the nation's interior. As European adventurers began to explore this region, they found the She-caw-gu portage a convenient shortcut between the Great Lakes and the Mississippi River.

Jean Baptiste Point DuSable, an enterprising trader of African and French descent, arrived in 1779 and established a substantial homestead. Within a few years the U.S. government decided to make the most of its newly acquired Northwest Territory, including the site of what is now Chicago, so Capt. John Whistler (grandfather of "Whistler's

Mother" painter James Abbott McNeill Whistler) was dispatched to found a military outpost.

Fort Dearborn was completed toward the end of 1804. The fledgling fort soon attracted a small corps of settlers determined to make a new life on the lonesome prairie. And though skirmishes between settlers and Indians ensued, the influx of new pioneers continued and Illinois became a state in 1818, hastening the end of the Indian wars.

Chicago was incorporated in 1837. Despite its rough edges, the bustling burg was the jumping-off spot for many a westbound pioneer. The city's proximity to fertile farmland, the Chicago Road and other highways, the Mississippi River and the Great Lakes made it a natural shipping center for the Midwest, a position bolstered by the opening of both the Illinois and Michigan Canal and the Galena and Chicago Union Railroad in 1848.

In 1860 the Republican party chose Chicago as the site of its national convention. This was an honor for such a young city, given the importance of that election. Relations between North and South were strained horribly, and an abolitionist administration led by Illinois lawyer Abraham Lincoln was certain to spur the slave states to secede. They did, igniting the Civil War shortly after Lincoln assumed the splintering nation's highest office.

Getting There — *starting on p. 54*

Getting Around — *starting on p. 55*

What To See — *starting on p. 56*

What To Do — *starting on p. 64*

Where To Stay — *starting on p. 295*

Where To Dine — *starting on p. 309*

The war's end brought both sorrow and joy. While citizens mourned the assassinated Lincoln, their grief was mitigated by the preservation of the Union and an economic boom. The establishment of stockyards and manufacturing concerns begat a wealth of jobs, inviting massive immigration. The city filled with opportunities and people—and row upon row of highly flammable wooden buildings.

So when the rains failed to come in the summer of 1871, Chicago—Gem of the Prairie, Jewel of the Lakes—went up in smoke. As the flames of the Great Chicago Fire died down, stunned citizens surveyed the wreckage with heartbroken disbelief but an undaunted spirit. They proclaimed that Chicago would rise again, and then they made it happen.

A bold new breed of architects looked upward for inspiration, designing the first lofty structures to be called skyscrapers. Most of the fire victims stayed, rebuilding old neighborhoods or forming new ones. They soon were joined by large numbers of immigrants, and Chicago grew from a prairie town to a major American city practically overnight.

The process sometimes was painful. Economic ups and downs were aggravated by the labor movement, as newly formed unions led strikes and rallies to demand better working conditions. The 1886 Haymarket Riot was a peaceful protest that turned deadly when a bomb blast rocked the police force monitoring the meeting; the ensuing gunfire left eight dead and dozens injured.

In 1893 Chicago won the honor of hosting the prestigious World's Columbian Exposition, topping such rivals as New York, St. Louis and Washington, D.C. The massive fair was a huge success, cementing Chicago's importance nationally.

As the 20th century began, Chicago had all the elements necessary for continued prosperity. This optimism, however, was tempered by some negative publicity. "The Jungle," Upton Sinclair's scathing 1906 exposé of the stockyards and meat-processing industry, focused unwelcome attention on the city's lifeblood and main employers.

The 1920s were even more chaotic. Gangland wars rocked the city during Prohibition as crime bosses vied for control of illegal—but highly profitable—bootlegging operations. The violence reached a horrifying climax in 1929 with the St. Valentine's Day massacre—allegedly mob boss Al Capone's revenge against his main rival, George "Bugs" Moran. Prohibition's end in 1933 subdued most of the overt gang activity, and another victory for law and order was won a year later, when police shot and killed bank robber John Dillinger, Public Enemy No. 1, outside the Biograph Theater.

The production boom that accompanied America's entry into World War II put people to work and local businesses in the black. More than any other city, Chicago may have hastened the war's end. In December 1942 a group of University of Chicago physicists led by Enrico Fermi created a nuclear chain reaction, the breakthrough that led to the development of the atomic bombs that forced Japan's surrender in 1945.

In 1955 a political dynasty began that would come to define the "toddlin' town," as Richard J. Daley assumed the first of his record six terms as mayor.

The 1960s rang in an era of change. Civil rights activists protested Chicago's entrenched policy of segregation, charges of corruption rattled the police force and Dr. Martin Luther King Jr.'s 1968 assassination sparked riots on the West Side. The end of the decade marked the setting of Daley's star, helped by rioting during the 1968 Democratic National Convention and a police raid that ended in the shooting deaths of two members of the militant civil rights group, the Black Panthers.

Machine politics held firm even after "hizzoner's" death in 1976, but by 1983 voters were ready for a change and elected their first African-American mayor, Harold Washington. Two years after his 1987 death, the populace returned to familiar ground and chose Daley's son, Richard M., as its leader.

The city's economy continues to thrive, bolstered by the financial powerhouse formed by the Chicago Board Options Exchange, Chicago Board of Trade, Chicago Mercantile Exchange and Chicago Stock Exchange. Heavyweights such as Amoco, Motorola, Sara Lee and Sears, Roebuck and Co. maintain a strong presence, joined by companies ranging from heavy manufacturing to health care to technology.

Chicago's architectural tradition, born in the rebuilding boom following the Great Fire, remains strong. Landmarks exist throughout the city, though perhaps the most notable is the Wrigley Building on Michigan Avenue at the Chicago River. Others include Mies van der Rohe's Federal Center Plaza; the soaring Gothic design of the 36-story Tribune Tower; the First National Bank Building, the tallest bank in the world; the scalloped cylindrical towers of Marina City; the 110-story Sears Tower, the tallest building in the United States; the John Hancock Center; and the Old Water Tower, one of only two public buildings to survive the fire.

In addition to its architecture Chicago is known for its sculpture. Imposing pieces by such greats as Alexander Calder, Marc Chagall, Claes Oldenburg and Pablo Picasso distinguish pedestrian plazas.

And topping off Chicago's stature as a capital of American culture, the city's most far-reaching contribution to popular culture lies under a pair of golden arches. Entrepreneur Ray Kroc opened his first McDonald's franchise in 1955, revolutionizing the fast-food industry.

In short, Chicago is a fascinating city, strengthened by its turbulent history and the indomitable spirit of its people. It is the epitome of an appropriately bold nickname: the City That Works.

JOHN G. SHEDD AQUARIUM

The Informed Traveler

Whom To Call

Emergency: 911

Police (non-emergency): 311

Time: (312) 976-1616

Temperature: (312) 976-1212

Hospitals: Holy Cross Hospital, (773) 471-8000; Northwestern Memorial, (312) 908-2000; Rush-Presbyterian-St. Luke's, (312) 942-5000; St. Anthony Hospital, (773) 521-1710; University of Chicago Hospital, (773) 702-1000.

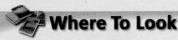 Where To Look

Newspapers

The two major dailies are the *Tribune* and the *Sun-Times,* both morning papers. These are supplemented by smaller journals and foreign-language papers.

The Reader, a free weekly newspaper, and *Chicago,* a monthly magazine, are helpful for visitors. *Key—This Week in Chicago* and *Where* are available at most major hotels in the metropolitan area and provide entertainment and event information.

Radio

Radio station WBBM (780 AM) is an all-news/weather station; WBEZ (91.5 FM) is a member of National Public Radio.

Visitor Information

The Chicago Office of Tourism, in the Chicago Cultural Center, 78 E. Washington St., Chicago, IL 60602, is open Mon.-Fri. 10-6, Sat. 10-5, Sun. 11-5; phone (312) 744-2400. Another visitor center is at Chicago Water Works, 163 E. Pearson St. at Michigan Avenue; the center is open daily 7:30-7. City and state maps and brochures are available. Cul-

tural events calendars are distributed at the information booth in the east lobby of the Richard J. Daley Center, Dearborn and Randolph streets.

What To Pack

Chicago weather is rarely boring. Summer is muggy, spring is damp and cool, and winter is downright challenging.

Temperatures peak in the 90s in July and August, the heat exacerbated by humidity. Lake Michigan breezes bring a hint of relief. In winter the breezes become chilling winds that combine with frigid temperatures to produce wind-chill factors that can drop to 20 below zero. Precipitation levels are highest April through September, but winter snow is a given. December and January are snowiest,

but flakes may pile up into March. *For additional information see temperature chart p. 43.*

A light casual look is appropriate in summer; add layers during the spring and fall. A heavy coat and winter boots are a must from October through March; a light jacket is advisable even in summer. An evening at a world-class restaurant or cultural institution is an occasion for finer fashion.

Sales Tax: Illinois sales tax is 6.25 percent; cities and counties impose additional increments. The Chicago area has a lodging tax of 14.9 percent.

Destination Chicago

John G. Shedd Aquarium, Chicago. Explore aquatic environments, including those of whales, dolphins, otters, seals and penguins at this Chicago landmark. (See listing page 61)

K nown by various nicknames-Gem of the Prairie, Jewel of the Lakes, Windy City-Chicago has come a long way since being destroyed in an 1871 fire set by the O'Learys' cow.

T he cultural center of the Midwest, the city's museums, galleries and architectural treasures are known worldwide.

Art Institute of Chicago. Two lions mark the entrance to the museum's extensive collections of ancient and contemporary art. (See listing page 58)

P laces included in this AAA Destination City:

Adler Planetarium & Astronomy Museum, Chicago.
Check out the StarRider Theater's virtual reality space journey as well as the museum and Sky Show Theater. (See listing page 56)

Navy Pier, Chicago.
Jutting into Lake Michigan, this entertainment mecca has shops, a Ferris wheel, carousel, IMAX and Shakespeare theaters, a conservatory and a children's museum. (See listing page 62)

See Downtown map page 57

Unity Temple, Oak Park.
Frank Lloyd Wright designed the temple in 1905 for a Unitarian Universalist congregation; said to be his greatest accomplishment, the structure is still in use. (See listing page 81)

Getting There

By Car

The primary route into Chicago from Milwaukee and other lakeside cities to the north is I-94. In the northern suburbs it divides; the eastern segment (Edens Expressway), still marked I-94, joins the John F. Kennedy Expressway, which enters downtown Chicago. The western leg, called the Tri-State Tollway, is numbered I-294; it forms a circumferential expressway around the city's west edge and ends at I-80.

From Madison and Rockford, I-90 (North-West Tollway) is the main highway. In the northwestern suburbs it intersects I-290, which curves southeast and continues into Chicago as the Eisenhower Expressway. Near O'Hare International Airport, the North-West Tollway intersects I-294, where it becomes the John F. Kennedy Expressway (I-90) as it heads into the city.

From the west direct access to Chicago from the Aurora area is via the East-West Tollway (I-88). Once inside the I-294 belt it becomes the Eisenhower Expressway (I-290). I-55 comes from Bloomington and other points in central Illinois; in the Chicago area, it is called the Adlai Stevenson Expressway. A major transcontinental route, I-80 passes to the south of Chicago and provides several connections into the city via I-55, I-57, I-90 and I-94.

The major routes from the south are I-94 (Bishop Ford Freeway), I-57 and I-90 (Chicago Skyway—toll). All three connect with the Dan Ryan Expressway (I-90/94), which leads into the city center. On the Indiana outskirts of Chicago, I-90 and I-80 form the Northern Indiana Toll Road, which is the main route to the city from the eastern seaboard; I-94 provides access to the city from Michigan.

Chicago's Loop, once defined as an area downtown encircled by the "L" elevated rapid transit line, now lends its name to the entire downtown area.

Air Travel

O'Hare International Airport, 18 miles northwest of the city proper, is considered the world's busiest, averaging some 180,000 passengers and 2,500 flights a day. The three domestic terminals service most major carriers and offer plenty of amenities for travelers as well. The international terminal is host to 30 airlines from around the world and is linked to the main building via the Airport Transit System (ATS). Allow yourself plenty of time to negotiate the airport.

The only highway exit is via I-190, which connects with I-90 directly east of the airport. I-90, a southeasterly route into the city proper, intersects

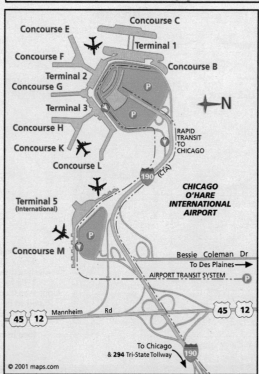

I-294 a short distance east of the I-190/90 junction. I-294 leads north to Wisconsin and south to Indiana. Allow plenty of time for traffic, which is always a factor in getting around greater Chicago.

The Chicago Transit Authority provides 24-hour service between O'Hare and downtown on the Blue Line, a 45-minute ride via rapid rail. Departures occur every 15 minutes from the lower pedestrian tunnel level of Terminal 3. The fare is $1.50. The transit authority also provides rapid rail service between O'Hare and Midway airports; phone (312) 836-7000 for details.

Midway Airport, though smaller than O'Hare, is closer to the Loop; it is only 10 miles southwest of the downtown core. It serves a much shorter roster of airlines—between 15 and 20—most of which are commuter services.

Exit Midway via Airport Drive, which intersects SR 50 (Cicero Avenue) along the airport's eastern edge. The most direct route downtown is on SR 50 north to I-55, then northeast to I-90/94 and east on Congress Parkway.

Rapid transit service on the Orange Line elevated train takes travelers from Midway to the heart of the city in less than 30 minutes. Visitors can board the train about every 15 minutes at the terminal just east of the airport building. The fare is $1.50.

Continental Air Transport Co., (312) 454-7800, provides buses between O'Hare, many downtown hotels, Union Station and Midway. One-way fare from O'Hare to the Loop is $17.50; round-trip $31. One-way from Midway to downtown is $12.50; round-trip $23.

Tri-State Coach Lines Inc., (773) 374-7200, operates between O'Hare and Midway every hour from 6:15 a.m. to 7:15 p.m.

Depending on traffic, a cab ride between either airport and downtown will run $28-$30.

Chicago is served by major car rental agencies. Arrangements should be made before you leave on your trip; your local AAA club can provide this assistance or additional information. Hertz, (312) 372-7600 or (800) 654-3080, offers discounts to AAA members. For listings of other agencies check the telephone directory.

Rail Service

Chicago Union Station, 210 S. Canal St., is the city's main train depot and Amtrak's local hub. Trains run to both coasts and well into the South, with stops at most major cities along the routes. For additional information phone (312) 558-1075 or (800) 872-7245.

Commuter rail service into Chicago from surrounding suburban communities is provided by METRA (Metropolitan Rail). Nearly a dozen lines run through the four downtown stations: Chicago Union Station, LaSalle Street Station at 414 S. LaSalle St., Randolph Street Station at Randolph and Michigan Avenue, and Union Pacific Station at Madison and Canal streets. For further details phone 836-7000 from any of the local area codes (312, 630, 708, 773, 815, 847).

Buses

Greyhound Lines Inc., (312) 408-5970, has its station at 630 W. Harrison St.

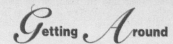

Getting Around

Street System

In driving around Chicago, as well as in approaching it, you should know where you are going and exactly how to get there. Plan your route in advance, particularly in regard to expressway interchanges, and be sure to keep a good street map handy.

Most Chicago streets follow an orderly grid running north-south and east-west. The few exceptions to this rule are outside the Loop—as downtown generally is known—and include N. Clark Street, N. Lincoln Avenue, Clybourn Avenue, I-90/94, N. Milwaukee Avenue, W. Ogden Avenue, S. Blue Island Avenue, S. Archer Avenue and Lake Shore Drive.

State Street is the east-west bisector; Madison Street divides north from south. The intersection of State and Madison streets in the Loop is ground zero for the street numbering system; all addresses begin at this intersection. The uniform numbering system from this point is an added help in finding an address. Downtown street numbers increase by

100 every two blocks leading away from this central intersection; outside the Loop they increase by 100 every block. For example, 800 W. Madison St. would be 16 blocks west of State Street.

In the northern section of the city all streets are designated by name. In the south, beginning at 8th, all east-west streets are numbered consecutively, and only north-south streets are named.

Unless otherwise posted, the speed limit on most streets is 25 to 30 mph. U-turns are allowed only where indicated by a sign. Many downtown streets are one-way. Rush hours, from 6:30 to 9:30 a.m. and 4 to 6:30 p.m., should be avoided.

Parking

Forget about street parking; it is illegal in the Loop area. As for metered street parking, there is little open to the heavy volume of determined drivers, and fines for parking violations are steep. Instead, take advantage of the city's numerous lots and garages.

City-owned lots are beneath Grant Park on N. Michigan and S. Michigan avenues and on E. Monroe Street; southeast of Adler Planetarium & Astronomy Museum on Solidarity Drive; south of John G. Shedd Aquarium on Lake Shore Drive; and at Burnham Park Harbor at the junction of 16th Street (Waldron Drive) and Lake Shore Drive. Full-day rates average $5-$10.

There are many public garages, both downtown and on the outskirts. Rates range from $5-$8 for 1 hour to $10-$18 for 8 hours. Four lots are available in Grant Park; for information phone (312) 747-2186. There also are many private garages; rates there average $7 to $9 a day but can be as high as $10 to $15.

Taxis

Expect to pay for the privilege of taking a taxi. Cabs are metered, with a basic charge of $1.60 plus $1.40 for each mile. Further charges for waiting time and extra passengers (50¢ per person ages 13 to 64) can add up. The largest cab company is Yellow, (312) 829-4222; others are listed in the telephone directory.

Public Transportation

Chicago has one of the nation's most convenient and accessible public transportation systems, serving the entire metro area. METRA commuter trains, augmented by the Chicago Transit Authority's (CTA) extensive network of buses and subway/elevated ("L") trains, connect suburbanites to the heart of the city. Stations are throughout the city; each has a color-coded map showing the system's myriad routes.

Rapid rail trains provide service around the city proper, north to Evanston, south to 95th Street and west to both airports. Routes are designated by colors and offer varying schedules. The Red and Blue lines (subway) operate daily 24 hours. The Orange, Brown, Purple, Green and Yellow lines ("L") all have different schedules, most beginning in the early morning hours and ending after midnight; all lines do not operate on weekends. The trains operate every 3 to 12 minutes during weekday rush hours, every 6 to 20 minutes at other times. Schedules are posted in each station.

Buses also provide transportation from numerous stops found throughout the city. The route number, name and destination of each vehicle are clearly displayed on the windshield sign, and many shelters offer graphical maps highlighting the routes. Service is offered daily, with most schedules beginning in the early morning and ending around midnight; some buses run on a more limited schedule.

The fare for all CTA vehicles is $1.50; exact change is required on buses and at the turnstiles. (Dollar bills are accepted.) Transfer cards cost 30¢ and permit an additional two rides, provided they occur within 2 hours and are not on the rider's original route. Reduced rates are available for senior citizens, the physically impaired and ages 7-11. CTA also offers a 1-, 2-, 3- or 5-day visitor pass.

For additional information phone CTA at 836-7000 from any of the local area codes (312, 630, 708, 773, 815, 847). The handy "Downtown Transit Sightseeing Guide" illustrating the CTA system is available at major downtown hotels, visitor centers and both airports.

Note: As in any major city, it pays to be cautious when using public transportation. Know where you are going and which trains to take before boarding, and avoid after-dark travel.

*W*hat *T*o *S*ee

ADLER PLANETARIUM & ASTRONOMY MUSEUM is just e. of Lake Shore Dr. (US 41) at 1300 S. Lake Shore Dr. The renovated 1930s planetarium building has a collection of sundials, early scientific instruments, rare books, photographs, early maps, charts and star atlases as well as an introductory gallery where the role of light, gravity, motion and energy is explained through interactive exhibits that display an image of the sun. The Sky Show Theater presents the night sky, with views of stars, planets and constellations as well as astronomy shows.

The Sky Pavilion includes four galleries and the StarRider Theater, a virtual reality space journey. A solar telescope displays an image of the sun. Food is available.

Allow 2 hours minimum. Open daily 9:30-4:30. Closed Thanksgiving and Dec. 25. Shows in the StarRider and Sky Show theaters are presented daily; phone for show selection and times. Admission (includes one Sky Show) $10; over 64 and ages 4-17, $9. Additional Sky Shows $5 each. Other combination tickets are available. Phone (312) 922-7827. *See ad p. 59.*

© AAA

DOWNTOWN
CHICAGO

Scale in Miles   0   0.5
Scale in Kilometers   0   0.8

RAPID TRANSIT
STATION

To Lincoln Park
Oak St. Beach

The Hancock
Observatory/
John Hancock
Center

Newberry Library

Washington Square Park

Untouchable Tours

Terra Museum of American Art

Mus. of Contemp. Art

Northwestern University Chicago Campus

Navy Pier Park

Navy Pier

Merchandise Mart

Tribune Tower

Wrigley Bldg.

Chicago Children's Museum

Wendella Sightseeing Boats

Mercury Cruise Lines

Coast Guard Station

James R. Thompson Ctr., Illinois Art Gallery

Illinois Center

City Hall & Co. Bldg.

Daley Civic Ctr.

Chicago Cultural Ctr. & Museum of Broadcast Comm.

Parking Area

Chicago & N.W. Station

Chicago Mercantile Exch.

Art Institute

Chicago Lake

Band Shell

Sears Tower Skydeck

Orchestra Hall Harold

Union Station

Chicago Washington Board Library of Trade Center

Chicago Architecture Foundation Shop & Tour Ctr.

Grant

Jane Addams Hull-House Museum

Greyhound Bus Term.

Spertus Museum

Buckingham Memorial Fountain

Harbor

University of Illinois at Chicago

Chicago Police Hdqrs.

Park

Shoreline Sightseeing Co. Harbor Tours

John G. Shedd Aquarium

The Field Museum

SOLIDARITY DR.

Adler Planetarium & Astronomy Museum

Soldier Field

Merrill C. Meigs Field

NORTHERLY

ISLAND

Chicago Trolley Co.

Glessner House Museum

Nat'l. Vietnam Veterans Art Mus.

Chinatown

McCormick Place

Burnham Park

Lake Michigan

Burnham Park

To Mus. of Science & Industry

2185-J

ART INSTITUTE OF CHICAGO, 111 S. Michigan Ave. at Adams St. in Grant Park, houses well-known paintings ranging from the 13th century to the present. The impressionist and post-impressionist collection is among the best in the world. Chinese, Japanese and Korean art are featured in other galleries. Also on display are prints and drawings, decorative arts, photographs, textiles, architectural fragments and drawings and art from Africa, Oceania and the Americas.

Outstanding collections include the George F. Harding Collection of arms and armor; the Mrs. James Ward Thorne Collection of miniature rooms, handmade to the smallest detail; and the works in the Modern and Contemporary galleries. Gallery walks, lectures and tours are available.

Allow 4 hours minimum. Mon.-Fri. and holidays 10:30-4:30 (also Tues. 4:30-8), Sat.-Sun. 10-5; closed Thanksgiving and Dec. 25. Admission $10; senior citizens, students with ID and ages 6-14, $6; free to all Tues. Phone (312) 443-3600. *See ad p. 59.*

Kraft Education Center includes galleries for changing exhibitions; a family room with an interactive computer program, reading nooks and a storytelling area; studios for student and family workshops; a teacher resource center; and an auditorium. Phone (312) 443-3836.

BAHA'I HOUSE OF WORSHIP—
see Wilmette p. 84.

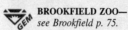
BALZEKAS MUSEUM OF LITHUANIAN CULTURE, 6500 S. Pulaski Rd., displays folk art, ambers, stamps, textiles, coins and other items spanning 1,000 years of Lithuanian history. It also houses the Children's Museum of Immigrant History, which features exhibits, demonstrations and performances that highlight tradition and culture brought to the United States. A library, an art gallery and a genealogy department also are included. Lectures and craft workshops are scheduled throughout the year.

Allow 1 hour minimum. Daily 10-4; closed Jan. 1, Easter, Thanksgiving and Dec. 25. Admission $4; over 65 and ages 12-18, $3; under 12, $1. Phone (773) 582-6500.

BROOKFIELD ZOO—
see Brookfield p. 75.

BURNHAM PARK is reached by Columbus Dr. and Lake Shore Dr. and connects Grant and Jackson parks. The Century of Progress World's Fair was held in the park 1932-33. Soldier Field, home of the Chicago Bears football team, is a memorial to Chicagoans who died serving their country. Recreation areas are available.

CANTIGNY—*see Wheaton p. 83.*

CHICAGO ARCHITECTURE FOUNDATION SHOP AND TOUR CENTER, at 224 S. Michigan Ave. in the Santa Fe Bldg., features exhibits and lectures detailing Chicago's contributions to architecture. It is the starting point for many architectural tours *(see What To Do, Sightseeing).* Mon.-Sat. 9-7, Sun. 9:30-6; closed holidays. Walking tour fare $3-$10. Boat tours $21. Bus tours $15-$25. AX, DS, MC, VI. Phone (312) 922-3432 for tour information.

CHICAGO BOARD OF TRADE, 141 W. Jackson Blvd. at La Salle St., is said to be the world's oldest and largest futures and options exchanges. It lists contracts based on such commodities as wheat, corn, oats, soybeans, precious metals and Treasury bonds and notes, as well as options on futures.

A viewing area of the visitor center on the fifth floor looks onto the agricultural futures trading rooms. The financial trading room, said to be the world's largest, is visible from an overhead observation area. Multi-lingual presentations lasting 45 minutes are offered. Mon.-Fri. 8-2; closed holidays. The first presentation begins at 9:15. Free. Phone (312) 435-3590 or 435-3625.

CHICAGO BOTANIC GARDEN—
see Glencoe p. 78.

CHICAGO CULTURAL CENTER, 78 E. Washington St., was built in 1897. The renovated building is noted for its Italian marble, mosaics and Tiffany domes. The center offers public programs and exhibits. Mon.-Wed. 10-7, Thurs. 10-9, Fri. 10-6, Sat. 10-5, Sun. 11-5; closed holidays. Free. Phone (312) 744-6630.

Museum of Broadcast Communications, jct. Michigan Ave. and Washington St. in the Chicago Cultural Center, contains a vast library of historic television and radio programs and commercials as well as a radio hall of fame. The MBC Television Center offers visitors the opportunity to anchor a newscast and purchase a videotape of the show. Vintage televisions and radios are on display, as are the ventriloquist dummies from Edgar Bergen's "The Charlie McCarthy Show." Allow 2 hours minimum. Mon.-Sat. 10-4:30, Sun. noon-5; closed holidays. Free. Phone (312) 629-6000.

CHICAGO HISTORICAL SOCIETY, at the s. end of Lincoln Park at Clark St. and North Ave., houses the oldest museum and library in the city. An original copy of the Declaration of Independence and Lincoln's death bed can be seen. There also are galleries devoted to Chicago history. Docents perform pioneer craft demonstrations including spinning, weaving, candle dipping and printing. Hands-on exhibits are featured. The Lincoln collection is noteworthy. Guided tours are available by reservation. Food is available.

Allow 2 hours minimum. Mon.-Sat. 9:30-4:30, Sun. noon-5; closed Jan. 1, Thanksgiving and Dec. 25. Admission $5; over 64 and students ages 13-22 with ID $3; ages 6-12, $1; free to all Mon. Phone (312) 642-4600.

CHICAGO MERCANTILE EXCHANGE, 30 S. Wacker Dr., is one of the world's largest financial exchanges, trading futures and options in currencies, interest rates, stock indexes and agricultural commodities. Interactive educational displays are featured. Visitors can watch "open outcry" and electronic trading of futures and options from the fourth-floor and the eighth-floor visitor galleries. Allow 30 minutes minimum. Fourth-floor gallery Mon.-Fri. 8:30-3:15. Eighth-floor Mon.-Fri. 7:15-2. Closed holidays. Free. Phone (312) 930-8249.

DALEY CIVIC CENTER, 50 W. Washington St., is the 31-story home of many municipal courts and offices. Of special interest is the plaza's 50-foot-high Cor-Ten sculpture by Pablo Picasso. The city offers free cultural programming weekdays at noon. For program listings phone (312) 744-6630.

DOUGLAS TOMB STATE HISTORIC SITE, 636 E. 35th St., is 96 feet high and surmounted by a bronze figure of Stephen A. Douglas by sculptor Leonard Volk. Douglas is buried in the tomb at the base of the monument. Daily 9-5; closed Jan. 1, Thanksgiving and Dec. 25. Free. Phone (312) 225-2620.

ELKS NATIONAL MEMORIAL AND HEADQUARTERS, 2750 N. Lakeview Ave. at Diversey Pkwy. in Lincoln Park, is a veterans memorial of classic design dedicated to all those who served in World War I and succeeding wars. The rotunda and reception room are elaborately decorated with marble, murals, sculpture and wood paneling. Daily 10-5,

mid-Apr. to mid-Nov.; Mon.-Fri. 10-5, rest of year. Free. Phone (773) 755-4700.

THE FIELD MUSEUM, across from Grant Park on Roosevelt Rd. at Lake Shore Dr., ranks among the world's foremost museums of natural sciences. Established in 1894, the Beaux Arts-style building houses more than 9 acres of exhibits consisting of world-renowned collections of some 20 million artifacts and specimens. The museum serves as an international center for public learning and scientific study of the world's diverse environments and cultures.

Exhibits include Sue: The Largest and Most Complete T. Rex; Life Over Time; Africa; Inside Ancient Egypt; Gems; The Webber Resource Center for Native American Cultures; and Traveling the Pacific.

Allow 4 hours minimum. Daily 9-5; closed Jan. 1 and Dec. 25. Admission $8; over 65, students with ID and ages 3-11, $4; military with ID free; free to all Wed. Parking $7 in Soldier Field lot (fee may vary depending on scheduled events). AX, MC, VI. Phone (312) 922-9410. *See ad.*

GARFIELD PARK CONSERVATORY is at the n.w. corner of Central Park Blvd. at Lake St. Built in 1907 by landscape architect Jens Jensen, the conservatory is considered the world's largest under one roof. More than 5,000 species and varieties of the world's flora as well as eight exhibit halls are

featured. Horticultural Hall and The Show House are the settings for five major annual flower shows: the Azalea/Camellia, Chrysanthemum, Spring, Summer and Celebration of Lights exhibitions. A demonstration urban garden features hardy plants in inner-city settings.

The Sensory Garden is next to the conservatory. Parking is available on Lake Street. Conservatory daily 9-5. Sensory Garden daily 9-5, May-Oct. Free. Phone (312) 746-5100.

[SAVE] **GLESSNER HOUSE MUSEUM**, 1800 S. Prairie Ave., is a 19th-century mansion built for John and Frances Glessner in 1887 by renowned architect Henry Hobson Richardson. Richardson's nontraditional approach to Victorian design helped reform domestic architecture. Features include William Morris wallpaper and fabric as well as decorative arts and crafts by notable designers. Guided tours on the hour Wed.-Sun. 1-3; closed holidays. Admission $7; over 65, college students with ID and ages 7-18, $6; free to all Wed. MC, VI. Phone (312) 326-1480.

GRANT PARK, on the lakefront between Randolph St. and Roosevelt Rd., is bordered on the w. by Columbus Dr. and on the e. by Lake Shore Dr. The park contains Augustus Saint-Gaudens' Seated Statue of Lincoln, the Gen. John A. Logan statue, a yacht basin, a rose garden and formal gardens. Free

evening concerts are presented at the bandshell June through August.

Buckingham Memorial Fountain is at the foot of Congress St. Made of red Georgia marble and surrounded by formal gardens, it is 280 feet at its greatest diameter; the central column of water rises to 135 feet. Fountain operates daily 10 a.m.-11 p.m., May 1-Oct. 1 (weather permitting). Color displays are presented at 15-minute intervals daily 9-11 p.m., May-Sept.

GRAUE MILL—*see Oak Brook p. 80.*

[SAVE] **THE HANCOCK OBSERVATORY/JOHN HANCOCK CENTER**, at 875 N. Michigan Ave. between Delaware Pl. and E. Chestnut St., is a 100-story complex. The center stands 1,127 feet high and contains offices, apartments, shops and parking facilities. The X-frames on the tower are the center's distinguishing features. An observatory is on the 94th floor. Allow 30 minutes minimum. Observatory open daily 9 a.m.-midnight. Admission $9; over 62, $7; ages 5-12, $6; military with ID free. DS, MC, VI. Phone (312) 751-3681, 751-3680 or (888) 875-8439. *See color ad & ad p. 59.*

HAROLD WASHINGTON LIBRARY CENTER (CHICAGO PUBLIC LIBRARY), 400 S. State St., houses more than 2 million books and periodicals. Among the library's many special features are the Civil War and American History research collections; Chicago Theater collection; Chicago Blues Music Archives, one of the Midwest's largest publicly accessible sound recording collections; a 385-seat auditorium/theater; a children's library; and a winter garden.

Allow 1 hour minimum. Mon., Wed. and Fri.-Sat. 9-5 (also Mon. 5-7), Tues. and Thurs. 11-7, Sun. 1-5. Tours Mon.-Fri. at 2. Closed holidays. Free. Phone (312) 747-4300.

ILLINOIS ART GALLERY, on the second floor of the James R. Thompson Center at 100 W. Randolph St., displays artwork by Illinois artists. Exhibits include sculpture, paintings and photography. Special exhibits rotate throughout the year. Guided tours are available. Allow 30 minutes minimum. Mon.-Fri. 9-5; closed major holidays. Free. Phone (312) 814-5322.

JACKSON PARK, adjoining Burnham Park on the s., is reached by Lake Shore Dr. The third largest of Chicago's parks, it has three beaches, an 18-hole golf course, playgrounds, tennis courts, bicycle and bridle paths and yacht moorings. The park was the scene of the Columbian Exposition of 1893.

The Midway Plaisance, a mile-long double boulevard, connects Jackson Park with Washington Park; the center portion was the midway of the 1893 Columbian Exposition. Skating is available in winter. At the west entrance is Lorado Taft's "Fountain of Time."

JOHN G. SHEDD AQUARIUM, on the Museum Campus of Grant Park at 1200 S. Lake Shore Dr. (US 41), exhibits more than 8,000 aquatic animals in naturalistic settings. The Oceanarium is said to be the largest indoor mammal marine pavilion in the world and contains beluga whales, Pacific white-sided dolphins, Alaska sea otters, harbor seals and a colony of penguins. Visitors can watch divers hand-feed fish in a 90,000-gallon Caribbean reef, wander through the Amazon rain forest in the Amazon Rising exhibit or explore the underwater world of seahorses in Seahorse Symphony.

Allow 2 hours minimum. Aquarium/Oceanarium open daily 9-6, Memorial Day-Labor Day; Mon.-Fri. 9-5, Sat-Sun. 9-6, rest of year. Closed Jan. 1 and Dec. 25. Admission for Aquarium and Oceanarium $15; over 64 and ages 3-11, $11. Aquarium only $8; over 64 and ages 3-11, $6. Aquarium, Caribbean Reef and Amazon Rising free to all Mon.-Tues., Sept.-Feb. Admission to Oceanarium and Seahorse Symphony Mon.-Tues., Sept.-Feb. $7; over 64 and ages 3-11, $5. Tickets should be purchased in advance through Ticketmaster (service charge $2 per ticket and 75c per order). AX, DS, MC, VI. Phone (312) 939-2438, or (312) 559-0200 for Ticketmaster. *See ad p. 59.*

LINCOLN PARK lies along Lake Shore Dr. from North Ave. to Hollywood Ave.

The largest park in the city, it contains Augustus Saint-Gaudens' Standing Statue of Lincoln, the Governor Oglesby State Monument, a monument to Alexander Hamilton by John Angel, a statue of Ulysses S. Grant and many others. In addition to several beaches, a bird sanctuary and playgrounds, there are facilities for golf, tennis, horseback riding and boating.

Lincoln Park Conservatory, 2391 N. Stockton Dr. in Lincoln Park, covers 4 acres and has four display houses. The showhouse presents a spring show early February through early May, a summer tropical show early June through early September, a chrysanthemum show mid-October through late November and a winter show early December through early January. Flower gardens can be viewed all summer. Allow 30 minutes minimum. Daily 9-5. Free. Phone (312) 742-7736.

Lincoln Park Zoo, Cannon Dr. at Fullerton Pkwy., houses more than 1,000 mammals, birds and reptiles from almost every part of the world; some are endangered species. Major exhibits house antelopes, zebras, penguins, birds, lions and primates. Other features include the children's zoo, the sea lion pool and a 5-acre replica of a working Illinois farm. **Note:** The large mammal area is closed until spring 2003.

Zoo tours, classes and educational programs are available; inquire at the information office. Food is available. Allow 3 hours minimum. Grounds daily 9-5. Animal habitats daily 10-4:30. Free. Parking $8. Phone (312) 742-2000.

LIZZADRO MUSEUM OF LAPIDARY ART— *see Elmhurst p. 77.*

MARTIN D'ARCY MUSEUM OF ART is at 6525 N. Sheridan Rd. in Cudahy Library on Loyola Univer-

sity's Lake Shore campus. The museum exhibits medieval, Renaissance and baroque art. Free lectures are offered. Open Tues.-Sat. noon-4, Sept.-May; Wed. and Fri. noon-4, in summer. Free. Phone (773) 508-2679.

MERCHANDISE MART is on the n. bank of the Chicago River between Wells and Orleans sts. Covering two square blocks, it is one of the world's largest commercial buildings. About 7.5 miles of corridors link hundreds of wholesale showrooms that display millions of dollars' worth of home furnishings. Shops on the first and second floors are open to the public.

Public tours are available by appointment Mon.-Fri., except during major trade shows; phone ahead. Admission $10, over 64 and full-time students with ID $9. Under 16 are not permitted. Phone (312) 527-4141.

MUSEUM OF CONTEMPORARY ART, 220 E. Chicago Ave., displays contemporary paintings, photography, sculpture and other visual art forms created since 1945. Among the artists represented in the museum's collections are Alexander Calder, Chuck Close, Jasper Johns, René Magritte, Robert Rauschenberg and Andy Warhol. Lectures and performances are scheduled frequently. Special exhibits also are presented. Food is available.

Tues.-Sun. 10-5 (also Tues. 5-8); closed Jan. 1, Thanksgiving and Dec. 25. Admission $10, over 65 and students with ID $6, under 12 free; free to all Tues. AX, DC, DS, MC, VI. Phone (312) 280-2660 or (888) 622-2442.

MUSEUM OF HOLOGRAPHY/CHICAGO, 1134 W. Washington Blvd., displays holograms—3-D images produced by laser light—in a gallery setting. Allow 30 minutes minimum. Wed.-Sun. 12:30-4:30; closed holidays. Admission $4, children $2.50, under 6 free. Phone (312) 226-1007.

MUSEUM OF SCIENCE AND INDUSTRY is in Jackson Park at 57th St. and S. Lake Shore Dr. The museum is a reconstruction of the Palace of Fine Arts from the 1893 Columbian Exposition. It contains exhibits of applied sciences, engineering and industry in 75 major exhibition halls spanning 15 acres. The museum is designed for visitor participation; there are buttons to push, cranks to turn, levers to lift and computers to operate.

Featured exhibits include the Take Flight aviation exhibit; Imagine, a virtual reality exhibit; a working replica of a coal mine, complete with mining equipment and an underground train; a German U-505 submarine captured during World War II; an incubator that hatches baby chicks; the Fairy Castle; a 16-foot walk-through human heart; a large model train; and Navy: Technology at Sea, which features two F-14 Tomcat flight simulators.

Allow 3 hours minimum. Daily 9:30-5:30, Memorial Day-Labor Day; Mon.-Fri. 9:30-4, Sat.-Sun. and holidays 9:30-5:30, rest of year. Closed Dec. 25. Admission $9; over 64, $7; ages 3-11, $4; free to all Thurs. Combination ticket for museum and theater $15; over 64, $12.50; ages 3-11, $10. AX, MC, VI. Phone (773) 684-1414. *See ad p. 59.*

Henry Crown Space Center and OMNIMAX Theater has exhibits about astronauts and space travel, including a simulated space station. Among the items on display are the Apollo 8 spacecraft that orbited the moon and the Aurora 7 Mercury spacecraft. The theater shows 70-millimeter films on a 76-foot-diameter aluminum-paneled screen that is 5 stories high. More than 70 speakers behind the screen enable sound to emanate from the section of the screen on which film action occurs.

Daily 9:30-5:30, Memorial Day-Labor Day; 9:30-4, rest of year. Admission $9; over 64, $7;

ages 3-11, $4. Combination ticket for museum and theater $15; over 64, $12.50; ages 3-11, $10. AX, MC, VI.

SAVE **NATIONAL VIETNAM VETERANS ART MUSEUM,** 1801 S. Indiana Ave., houses more than 700 works of art by 134 artists, all of whom were soldiers in the Vietnam War. The artists, from the United States, Australia, Cambodia and Thailand as well as North and South Vietnam, have created works illustrating their own experiences during that war. Food is available.

Allow 2 hours minimum. Tues.-Fri. 11-6, Sat. 10-5, Sun. noon-5; closed major holidays. Admission $5; over 65 and under 19, $4. MC, VI. Phone (312) 326-0270.

NAVY PIER, on the lakefront at 600 E. Grand Ave., originally served as an amusement park upon its opening in 1916. Today the restored pier is home to retail shops, a Ferris wheel, a carousel, a 1-acre indoor botanical garden, an IMAX Theater, the Chicago Children's Museum *(see attraction listing),* the Chicago Shakespeare Theater, the Smith Museum of Stained Glass Windows and other family attractions. Various cruise ships depart from the pier's dock for sightseeing tours. Food is available.

Allow 2 hours minimum. Daily 10-10 (also Fri.-Sat. 10 p.m.-midnight), Memorial Day-Labor Day; Mon.-Sat. 10-8 (also Fri.-Sat. 8 p.m.-11 p.m.), Sun. 10-7, rest of year. Free. Phone (312) 595-7437.

Chicago Children's Museum, 700 E. Grand Ave. on the Navy Pier, features such displays as Dinosaur Expedition, Inventing Process of Discovery, Waterways, a city hospital and the Tree House Trails for preschoolers. Other exhibits include the Climbing Schooner, a three-story replica of an 1850s sailing vessel; the Playmaze, a miniature city; an art studio; an electronic news bureau; and Under Construction, a hands-on exhibit where children construct buildings.

Allow 2 hours minimum. Daily 10-5 (also Thurs. 5-8), Memorial Day-Labor Day; Tues.-Sat. 10-5 (also Thurs. 5-8), rest of year. Closed Thanksgiving and Dec. 25. Admission $6.50, senior citizens $5.50, under 1 free; free to all Thurs. 5-8. AX, DS, MC, VI. Phone (312) 527-1000.

THE NEWBERRY LIBRARY, 60 W. Walton St., is a research library that focuses on the humanities. A gallery features changing exhibits. Lectures, seminars and special events are offered throughout the year. Allow 1 hour minimum. Library services Tues.-Thurs. 10-6, Fri.-Sat. 9-5. Gallery Mon.-Sat. 8:15-5:30 (also Tues.-Thurs. 5:30-7:30). Free. Phone (312) 943-9090.

NORTHWESTERN UNIVERSITY—
see Evanston p. 78.

SAVE **PEGGY NOTEBAERT NATURE MUSEUM,** in Lincoln Park at jct. Cannon and Fullerton drs., is an interactive museum featuring walkthrough nature dioramas, a city-science exhibit, a water lab and a butterfly haven. The Animal House is a play space for children. Food is available. Mon.-Fri., 9-4:30, Sat.-Sun., 10-5; closed Jan. 1, Thanksgiving and Dec. 25. Admission $6; over 60, $4; students with ID and ages 3-17, $3. AX, DS, MC, VI. Phone (773) 549-0606.

POLISH MUSEUM OF AMERICA, 984 N. Milwaukee Ave., documents the many Polish contributions to this country. The museum contains manuscripts of Thaddeus Kosciuszko and Casimir Pulaski, patriots in the war for America's independence; extensive displays concerning Ignace Jan Paderewski, a noted pianist and statesman; memorabilia of other noted Polish-Americans; coins, stamps and medals of Poland; Polish folk and fine art; and a library with archives.

Museum daily 11-4; closed Jan. 1, Easter, Thanksgiving and Dec. 25. Library Mon.-Tues. and Fri.-Sat. 10-4, Wed. 1-7. Admission $3, senior citizens and students with ID $2, children $1. Phone (773) 384-3352.

SEARS TOWER SKYDECK, 233 S. Wacker Dr., entrance on Jackson Blvd., in the United States' tallest building—110 stories—allows views of the city from 1,353 feet above the street. InfoVision kiosks present information in six languages. Knee-High Chicago is a 4-foot-high exhibit designed for children.

Daily 9 a.m.-11 p.m. Phone ahead to confirm schedule. Admission $9.50; senior citizens $7.75; ages 5-12, $6.75. A family rate is available. AX, DS, MC, VI. Phone (312) 875-9696. *See ad p. 59.*

SAVE **SPERTUS MUSEUM,** at 618 S. Michigan Ave. on the first two floors of the Spertus Institute of Jewish Studies, contains one of the largest collections of Jewish art and artifacts in the Midwest. The Holocaust Memorial includes objects and photographs, and the Artifact Center is an archeological hands-on exhibit for children. Special exhibitions explore contemporary and historical issues relating to the Jewish religion and culture.

Museum open Sun.-Thurs. 10-5 (also Thurs. 5-7, Mar.-Nov.), Fri. 10-3. Artifact Center open Sun.-Thurs. 1-4:30. Closed federal and Jewish holidays. Admission $5; over 60 and ages 3-16, $3; family rate $10; free to all Fri. MC, VI. Phone (312) 322-1747.

TERRA MUSEUM OF AMERICAN ART, 666 N. Michigan Ave., displays works by American artists spanning 3 centuries. Changing special exhibits feature noteworthy Chicago artists' works as well as the paintings of such masters as Winslow Homer, Maurice Prendergast and Jamie Wyeth. Tours are available. Allow 1 hour minimum. Tues.-Sat. 10-6

(also Tues. 6-8 p.m.), Sun. noon-5. Admission $7, senior citizens $3.50, students with ID and under 12 free; free Tues. and first Sun. of the month. AX, MC, VI. Phone (312) 664-3939.

UNIVERSITY OF CHICAGO, flanks the Midway between Stony Island and Cottage Grove aves. and extends n. to 55th St. and s. to 61st St. The university's modern buildings complement the older Gothic structures employing the traditional English quad design. Enrico Fermi and James Franck institutes, known as the Research Institutes, are at 5640 S. Ellis Ave. Henry Moore's sculpture "Nuclear Energy" commemorates the Manhattan Project's first controlled nuclear chain reaction that took place in 1942 in a squash-court laboratory.

Campus tours depart from Ida Noyes Hall, 1212 E. 59th St. For information write the Office of Special Events, 5710 Woodlawn Ave., Chicago, IL 60637. Allow 2 hours minimum. Campus tours depart Sat. at 10. Tours free. Phone (773) 702-9636.

David and Alfred Smart Museum of Art, 5550 S. Greenwood Ave., displays a collection of Chinese, ancient, modern and contemporary art as well as changing exhibitions. Tours are available. Allow 30 minutes minimum. Tues.-Fri. 10-4 (also Thurs. 4-9), Sat.-Sun. noon-6; closed holidays. Hours may vary; phone ahead. Free. Phone (773) 702-0200.

Frederick C. Robie House, 5757 S. Woodlawn Ave., is one of Frank Lloyd Wright's masterpieces of organic architecture and one of the best examples of his Prairie style of architecture. **Note:** The house is in the midst of a major renovation that will restore it to its 1910 appearance; the house will remain open during this 10-year period. Allow 1 hour minimum. Guided tours Mon.-Fri. at 11, 1 and 3, Sat.-Sun. on the half hour 11-3:30; closed Jan. 1, Thanksgiving and Dec. 25. Admission $9; over 65 and ages 7-18, $7. AX, DS, MC, VI. Phone (708) 848-1976 or (773) 834-1847

Oriental Institute, 1155 E. 58th St., contains a museum devoted to the archeology and art of the ancient Near East. The institute houses a large collection of antiquities, mainly from excavations in Egypt, Sudan, Turkey, Iraq, Iran, Syria and Israel. Artifacts on display include Egyptian mummies, a 40-ton Assyrian winged bull-man, a colossal statue of King Tutankhamen and a fragment of the Dead Sea Scrolls. Tues.-Sat. 10-4 (also Wed. 4-8:30), Sun. noon-4; closed Thanksgiving and Dec. 25. Films are shown Sun. at 2. Free. Phone (773) 702-9514.

Rockefeller Memorial Chapel, 5850 S. Woodlawn Ave., is a Gothic structure designed by Bertram Goodhue. The chapel houses a 72-bell carillon in its tower, the highest point on the university campus. Mon.-Fri. 8-4, Sat.-Sun. 9-4. Free. Phone (773) 702-9202 or 702-2100.

UNIVERSITY OF ILLINOIS AT CHICAGO, Halsted and Harrison sts., was formed in 1982 by the merger of the Medical Center and the Chicago

Circle campuses of the University of Illinois. This architecturally unusual campus accommodates approximately 25,000 students. Campus features include the Jane Addams' Hull-House Museum and the Pavilion, used for UIC athletic events and professional entertainment events. Campus tours leave from the Student Services Building at 1200 W. Harrison. Tours depart Mon.-Fri. at 2. Free. Phone (312) 996-5000.

Jane Addams' Hull-House Museum, 800 S. Halsted St., is inside the restored house used by Jane Addams, humanitarian, pioneer settlement worker and the first American woman to win the Nobel Peace Prize. The mansion contains original furnishings, paintings, memorabilia and photographs. A slide program is available. Changing exhibits also are presented. Mon.-Fri. 10-4, Sun. noon-5; closed holidays. Free. Phone (312) 413-5353.

𝒲hat 𝒯o 𝒟o

Sightseeing

Boat Tours

Boat trips travel along the Chicago River, through the locks into Chicago Harbor and Lake Michigan.

MERCURY CRUISE LINES, s. end of the river on the s.w. corner of Michigan Avenue Bridge at Wacker Dr., offers narrated cruises daily May-Oct. Ninety-minute cruises depart at 10, 11:30, 1:15, 2:30, 3:15, 4:30 and 7. A 2-hour cruise departs at 7:30 p.m. Ninety-minute cruise $14; under 12, $7. Two-hour cruise $16; under 12, $8. Tickets on sale 1 hour before departure. Phone (312) 332-1353.

SHORELINE SIGHTSEEING CO. HARBOR TOURS, in Grant Park next door to the John G. Shedd Aquarium at 1200 S. Lake Shore Dr., offers 30-minute narrated cruises of the Chicago skyline.

Guides give a historical rundown of Chicago's background and point out the city's main buildings.

Daily 11:15-6:15 (also 7:15-11:15 p.m. weather permitting), Apr. 1-Oct. 15. Tours from Buckingham Fountain in Grant Park depart daily every 30 minutes 7:15-11:15 p.m. Tours from the Navy Pier depart every hour Mon.-Fri. 10 a.m.-11 p.m., Sat.-Sun. 10 p.m.-midnight (weather permitting). Fare $9; senior citizens $8; under 11, $4. Phone (312) 222-9328.

WENDELLA SIGHTSEEING BOATS, at the n.w. corner of the Michigan Avenue Bridge, offers narrated 1-hour cruises daily at 5:45 and occasionally at 9:15 p.m., 90-minute cruises at 10, 11:30, 1:15, 2, 3, 4:30, 6, 7 and 8:30, mid-Apr. to late Oct. A 2-hour cruise is available daily, Memorial Day-Labor Day. Schedule may vary; phone ahead. Fare for 1-hour cruise $12; senior citizens $10; under 11, $6. Ninety-minute cruise $14; senior citizens $12; under 11, $7. Two-hour cruise $16; senior citizens $14; under 11, $8. Purchase tickets 1 hour before departure. Phone (312) 337-1446.

Bus Tours

One of the best ways to get oriented and view a multitude of sights in a short time is to take a bus tour. American Sightseeing Tours, (312) 251-3100, in the Palmer House at 17 E. Monroe St.; and Gray Line, (312) 251-3107 at 17 E. Monroe St., offer city orientation tours, including land and lake tours and dinner packages.

[SAVE] **UNTOUCHABLE TOURS** departs from 610 N. Clark St. Chicago's Original Gangster Tour features tommy gun-toting gangsters who take passengers on a 2-hour bus tour of Chicago's Prohibition-era landmarks. Guides, dressed in 1920s fedoras and spats, entertain passengers while offering a running dialogue of information about Al "Scarface" Capone, "Machine Gun" Jack McGurn, George "Bugs" Moran and others.

Tours depart Mon.-Wed. at 10, Thurs.-Sat. at 10 and 1 (also Fri. at 7:30 p.m. and Sat. at 5), Sun. at 11 and 2; closed major holidays. Fee $22; under 15, $16. Reservations are required. MC, VI. Phone (773) 881-1195.

Industrial Tours

Several of Chicago's manufacturers offer tours of their facilities; check with the Chicago Office of Tourism (see The Informed Traveler box).

NEWSPAPER TOURS are offered at the *Chicago Tribune* production plant, Freedom Center, 777 W. Chicago Ave. Allow 1 hour minimum. Tours given Tues.-Fri. at 9:30, 10:30, 11:30 and 1:30. Free. Children are permitted only with a guardian. Reservations are required. Phone (312) 222-2116.

Trolley Tours

CHICAGO TROLLEY CO. boards at 13 stops throughout downtown. This San Francisco-style trolley takes passengers on a 1.5-hour narrated tour of the city. On its winding, 11-mile route it stops at such places of interest as the Art Institute of Chicago, The Field Museum and the Navy Pier. Riders with a full-day pass can disembark and reboard at any of the stops.

Allow one hour, 30 minutes minimum. Daily 9-5, Memorial Day-Labor Day; 9:30-4, rest of year. Closed Jan. 1 and Dec. 24-25. All-day fare $18; over 64, $15; ages 3-11, $8. One loop $15. Two-day pass $20 Sun.-Thurs. AX, CB, DS, MC, VI. Phone (773) 254-6400.

Walking tours

Walking tours are available of the Pullman Historic District, a 19th-century industrial town. The model community was built in 1881 to house employees of George M. Pullman's Palace Car Co. Ninety-minute tours depart the Historic Pullman Foundation Visitor Center, 11141 S. Cottage Grove Ave., on the first Sunday of the month at 12:30 and 1:30, May-Oct. The fee is $4, senior citizens $3.50 and students with ID $2.50; phone (773) 785-8181. Open house tours in the Pullman Historic District take place the second weekend in October.

The Chicago Architecture Foundation, 224 S. Michigan Ave., offers more than 60 architecture tours of Chicago and the surrounding area via foot, bus, boat and bicycle. Two-hour walking tours devoted to either the early or modern architecture of the Loop depart daily. Two-hour walking tour fee $10 for one, $15 for both. The Architecture River Cruise runs daily May 1-Nov. 1. Fare $21. The Chicago Architecture Highlights by Bus is offered Sat. at 9:30 a.m. Fare $25. Phone (312) 922-3432 or 922-8687.

Not all of Chicago's art is confined to museums. The Richard J. Daley Plaza, Washington and Dearborn streets, offers the controversial sculpture known as "The Chicago Picasso." Farther south on Dearborn, at the First National Bank Plaza at Monroe Street, is "The Four Seasons," an acclaimed mosaic by Marc Chagall. The bright red "Flamingo" that dominates Chicago Federal Center Plaza, Adams and Dearborn streets, is by Alexander Calder. A wind-activated mobile is atop the Sporting Club at the corner of Stetson and Lake.

Spectator Sports

Chicago is one of the nation's great sports cities. From the early days of the Bears' gridiron glory to the 1990s reign of Air Jordan, locals turn out in droves year-round to cheer the home teams on to glory.

Those who would rather watch than work at their sports will find a full calendar of both amateur and professional contests. Do not forget the college and university teams; they can provide as much excitement as the professionals. A review of the sports and events pages in the daily newspapers will tell you who and what is scheduled where.

Baseball

The national pastime is alive and well in the Windy City, with teams from both professional leagues bringing the boys of summer to local stadiums. The **Chicago Cubs** have been an area fixture since baseball's origin in 1876; never-say-die fans still pack the stands of **Wrigley Field**, N. Clark and W. Addison streets, (773) 404-2827. And the **Chicago White Sox** play in the new **Comiskey Park**, which stands at 333 W. 35th St., directly across the street from a parking lot that once held the original ballpark; phone (312) 674-1000.

Basketball

The **Chicago Bulls**, the first team ever to win 70 games in a season, delight the hometown crowd during games at the state-of-the-art **United Center**, 1901 W. Madison; phone (312) 455-4000.

College hoops fans have plenty of teams to cheer. The **Chicago State University Cougars** play at **Jacoby Dickens Athletic Center**, (773) 995-2217; the **DePaul Blue Demons** take the court at **Allstate Arena**, 6920 N. Mannheim Rd. in Rosemont, (847) 635-6601; the **Loyola Ramblers** can be seen at the **Loyola University Alumni Gym**, (773) 508-2560; the home games of the **Northeastern Illinois University Golden Eagles** are at their **Physical Education Complex** at 5500 N. St. Louis Ave., (773) 583-4050; the **Northwestern Wildcats** defend their court at 1501 Central St. in Evanston, (847) 491-2287; and the **University of Illinois at Chicago Flames** meet their opponents at the **UIC Pavilion**, 1150 W. Harrison St., (312) 413-5740.

Football

The **Chicago Bears** boast a long and gloried history dating to 1921, the year the team moved to the Windy City. Fans clad in orange and blue still fill the bleachers of **Soldier Field** in support of the home team, even in the bitter cold of winter. The stadium is at 425 E. McFetridge Dr.; phone (312) 747-1285 for ticket information.

Oddly enough, the ultimate football town claims only one representative in NCAA Division I football: The Northwestern Wildcats take to the gridiron at **Ryan Field**, (847) 491-2287.

Hockey

Body checks and flying pucks are cheered with equal enthusiasm during the **Chicago Blackhawks'** icy matchups at United Center, (312) 455-4000, and during the **Chicago Wolves'** games at Allstate Arena, (847) 724-4625.

Horse Racing

The Thoroughbreds run at **Arlington International Racecourse**, 25 miles northwest of Chicago in Arlington Heights on Euclid Avenue. Races are held mid-June through October; post times vary. General admission is $4.75. For information phone (847) 255-4300.

Cicero's **Hawthorne Race Course**, 3501 S. Laramie Ave., offers Thoroughbred contests May 1-June 10 and Oct. 31-Dec. 31. The Thoroughbreds at neighboring **Sportsman's Park**, 3301 S. Laramie Ave., compete Friday through Tuesday from March through April. For information on post times phone (708) 780-3700 and (773) 242-1121, respectively.

Trotters and pacers command the course at **Maywood Park**, North and 5th avenues in Maywood, 8600 W. North Ave. Races are held year-round; post times vary. For information phone (708) 343-4800. Some 35 miles south of Chicago, **Balmoral Park**, 26435 S. Dixie Hwy. at Elm Court Lane and SR 1 in Crete, offers year-round racing; dates vary. For details phone (708) 672-1414.

Note: Policies on admitting children to parimutuel facilities vary. Phone in advance for specific information.

Recreation

Chicagoans also get in on the action themselves. And why not? Whether basking in the sun along **Lake Michigan**'s shore or enjoying wintry excursions in the surrounding heartland, you'll find the city's many recreational facilities offer a scenic playground in any season.

Information about the large variety of recreational facilities available in the Greater Chicago area can be obtained from the Chicago Park District, 425 E. McFetridge Dr., which distributes a free brochure describing all its offerings; phone (312) 747-2200.

In addition the Forest Preserve District of Cook County, 536 N. Harlem Ave. in River Forest, and the Cook County Building at 118 N. Clark have free brochures, maps and information detailing recreational opportunities. For more specific information regarding activities on the Forest Preserve District's 67,000 acres, phone (773) 261-8400, (708) 366-9420 in the suburbs, (800) 870-3666, or TDD (708) 771-1190.

Bicycling

Cyclists will appreciate the 20-mile path paralleling Lake Michigan from **Lincoln Park** south to **Jackson Park**, but should keep a watchful eye for joggers, power walkers and in-line skaters. The most convenient and scenic areas are concentrated among the museums, statuary and landscaped walkways of Lincoln and Grant parks.

Paths for bicycling also have been designated along some 20 miles of lakefront on the east bank of the **North Shore Channel**, the south end of which starts at W. Argyle Street. These paths are not continuous, and bicyclists must walk their bikes across intervening thoroughfares to the next trail. The path resumes on the west bank of the channel and continues north into the suburb of Skokie.

The Forest Preserve District maintains more than 109 miles of bicycle trails winding through Cook County's bucolic countryside. Bicyclists can ride continuously on the **North Branch Class 1 Bicycle Trail** from Caldwell and Devon to Lake County, about 20 miles north. The trail winds along the North Branch of the Chicago River, Skokie Lagoons and through the Chicago Botanic Garden. In addition there are eight designated bicycle trails at each end of the county as well as more than 200 miles of trails for hiking and horseback riding.

Equipment rentals are available from **Turin Bike Shop** in the River East Plaza, (847) 864-7660; **Village Cycle** at 1337 N. Wells St., (312) 335-8735; or at any of **Bike Chicago**'s three lakefront locations: Navy Pier, North Avenue Beach and the 63rd Street Beach. Bike Chicago also offers tours of the city and free trail maps; phone (312) 755-0488 or (800) 915-2453.

Cycling information and a "Chicago Bicycle Map" are available from the Bureau of Traffic, (312) 744-8093, and the Chicagoland Bicycle Federation, (312) 427-3325. The Department of Transportation Bicycle Hotline, (312) 742-2453, also has a bicycling map of Chicago and information about various bicycle tours.

Fishing

Local waterways teem with varying combinations of smelt, bass, perch, trout, walleye, pike, salmon and catfish. Harbors, piers and jetties nicking the Lake Michigan shoreline are popular, as are the Chicago Park District's two dozen ponds and lagoons. For information about fishing and other area recreation phone the Illinois Department of Natural Resources at (312) 814-2070.

Fishing piers on Lake Michigan are at 6900 N. Farwell Ave., 4400 N. Montrose Ave., 2300 S. McCormick Pl., 1600 N. North Ave., 3100 S. 31st St.,

5900 S. 59th St. and 6300 S. 63rd St. Other lake fishing is permitted except where it would interfere with designated public use areas.

Surrounding locales also provide plenty of good angling. The Forest Preserve District manages three dozen sites ranging from lakes to sloughs. The organization also produces a fishing guide complete with maps of the primary lakes.

Charter boat excursions are available for going after coho and chinook salmon in Lake Michigan; for information phone Chicago Sportfishing Charter at (312) 922-1100. The group also serves as the source of information about fishing regulations. Anglers must comply with state laws, and ages 16-65 must have a valid license. Residents need a season license; nonresidents must purchase a 1-day pass for each day they plan to fish. The license is $13, 1-day passes cost $5.50 and a salmon or trout stamp is an additional $6.50.

Golf

Chicago's harsh winters leave golfers yearning for spring. Family Golf Center, 221 N. Columbus Dr., is one of the area's most interesting. The downtown course—an unusual feature in such a large city—offers nine holes as well as the lovely backdrop of Lake Michigan; phone (312) 616-1234.

Golf enthusiasts can choose from the one 18-hole and five nine-hole courses of the Chicago Park District or from the eight 18-hole and two nine-hole courses operated by the Forest Preserve District of Cook County. Hours of operation and seasons vary. Generally, golf is possible from late March until November, depending upon weather and course conditions. The Forest Preserve District has four courses that are open throughout winter.

All of the following courses offer at least 18 holes and are open to the public. The Chicago Park District's 18-hole course is Jackson Park, 2 blocks east of Stony Island Avenue on 63rd Street, (312) 245-0909. Among the 18-hole courses operated by the Forest Preserve District are Burnham Woods, 142nd Street and 14201 Burnham Ave. in Burnham, (708) 862-9043; "Chick" Evans, Golf Road west of Harms Road in Morton Grove, (847) 965-5353; George W. Dunne, 163rd Street and 16310 S. Central Ave. in Oak Forest, (708) 429-6886; Joe Louis (The Champ), 131st Street and 13100 Halsted St. in Riverdale, (708) 849-1731; and River Oaks, 159th Street and 1 Park Ave. in Calumet City, (708) 868-4090.

Reduced fees are offered by the Forest Preserve District after 3 p.m. Special discounts are available for activity card holders, residents over 64 and ages 9-17. Activity cards cost $20 for Cook County residents and $50 for non-residents. Clubs and pull carts can be rented at the concession shops. For in-

formation about fees and tee times phone (773) 625-9676. An automated 24-hour tee-time registration system can be used up to 7 days in advance; phone (708) 366-9466 or (800) 870-3666.

Hiking

Nature lovers can enjoy the more than 200 miles of scenic trails winding through the Forest Preserve District's prairie wilderness.

Horseback Riding

The Forest Preserve District also maintains bridle paths winding through the Cook County landscape. Phone the district directly at (773) 261-8400 or (708) 366-9420 for information about licenses and trail maps.

In-line Skating

In-line skaters and bicyclists share the 20 miles of paths along Chicago's lakefront, both on the east and west banks of the North Shore Channel. *See Bicycling section.*

Jogging and Walking

Although the city is blessed with a multitude of parks and neighborhoods, your best bet for a stroll or run is along the lakefront trail. It's best to stick to Lincoln and Grant parks. The campus of Northwestern University, north of the city in Evanston, provides a scenic setting for walkers and joggers.

Tennis

As evidenced by the Chicago Park District's 700-plus courts, tennis is a favorite sport of Chicagoans. The season begins around the middle of April, when players throng municipal facilities daily. Public courts operate on a first-come, first-served basis. For details phone the district at (312) 747-2484.

Richard J. Daley Bicentennial Plaza, in the Loop at 337 E. Randolph St., also is open to the public and features a dozen lighted courts; phone (312) 742-7650. Courts must be reserved; the fee is $5 per hour.

Water Sports

With nearly 30 miles of shoreline fronting Lake Michigan and easy access to the **Des Plaines, Calumet and Chicago rivers,** Chicago is a water enthusiast's paradise. The Great Lake is a favorite spot for boating, sailing, swimming, water skiing, windsurfing and even scuba diving. Contact the Chicago Park District, (312) 747-2200, for details about water recreation opportunities and local boating policies.

Lakefront launching ramps for motorboats 20 feet and shorter are at **Burnham Harbor, Calumet Harbor, Diversey Harbor, Jackson Park Inner Harbor** and **Wilson Harbor.** Those wishing to use these ramps must register their boats and obtain a permit from the Chicago Park District; phone (312) 747-0737. The ramp attendant charge is $15; a seasonal pass is $110.

Motorboats also are permitted on the Calumet, Chicago and Des Plaines rivers. The **Little Calumet River** boat dock is on the east side of Ashland Avenue, north of Jackson Avenue; the Plank Road Meadow launching ramp is north of Ogden Avenue, east of First Avenue. Other lakes and waterways do not permit motorboats; check with the Forest Preserve District of Cook County; phone (773) 261-8400.

Canoes, rowboats and sailboats may be used on the following Forest Preserve District waterways (electric motors only): **Big Bend Lake, Busse Lake, E.J. Beck Lake, Maple Lake, Powderhorn Lake, Saganashkee Slough, Skokie Lagoons, Tampier Lake** and **Turtlehead Lake.** Contact district headquarters for restrictions and ramp locations.

Craft rentals are available through the **Chicago Sailing Club** in Lincoln Park's Belmont Harbor, (773) 871-7245, which also offers lessons to landlubbers; reservations are a good idea. Try **Chicagoland Canoe Base,** 4019 N. Narragansett Ave., for rentals and information about trails; phone (773) 777-1489.

Most major hotels have swimming pools, and the park district fills any gaps with more than 100 municipal pools, 40 of which are indoors. For locations and hours of operation phone (312) 747-0832. Popular beaches are those along the Lake Michigan shore from 9600 South to 7600 North. They are open daily 9 a.m.-9:30 p.m., mid-June through Labor Day. If you find yourself outside the city proper, take advantage of the Forest Preserve District's outdoor swimming areas: **Cermak Pool,** 7600 W. Ogden Ave. in Lyons, and **Green Lake,** at Torrence Avenue and 159th Street in Calumet City.

Winter Sports

Chicago's recreation scene thrives even in the dead of winter. The season generally runs from December through March, but can be longer at either end.

Ice skating is available at more than 200 locations during the winter. The largest and perhaps the most renowned is the **Midway Plaisance,** a mile-long depression that is flooded for skating in winter between the double boulevard of the same name. **Skate on State,** occupying a full block on the north side of Washington Street between State and Dearborn streets, features an ice rink open from late November to late February; admission is free and skate rentals are available.

Another favorite spot is the pond in Lincoln Park at N. Diversey and Sheridan Road. Ice skating in winter and roller skating the rest of the year are popular at the Richard J. Daley Bicentennial Plaza, 337 E. Randolph St. in Grant Park.

The hardy can indulge in skating and ice fishing at designated Forest Preserve District sites; the ice thickness is checked twice weekly. Skating is permitted at **Barrington Road Pond, Buffalo Woods, Busse Woods (North Pool), Cermak Quarry, Crawdad Slough, Deer Grove, Hidden Pond East** and **Schiller Woods.** Ice fishing is allowed at **Axehead Lake,** Beck Lake, **Belleau Lake, Bode Lakes,** Busse Lake (Main and South pools only), **Flatfoot Lake,** Maple Lake, **Papoose Lake,** Powderhorn Lake, Saganashkee Slough, **Sag Quarry West & East,** Tampier Lake, Turtlehead Lake and **Wampum Lake;** phone (708) 771-1330 for information about other sites.

Snow skiing, while not available within the city limits, can be enjoyed in the surrounding counties. Downhill skiing is offered at the **Four Lakes Ski Area** in Lisle and the **James Park Winter Sports Complex** in Evanston. For additional information contact the Chicago Metropolitan Ski Council, (312) 346-1268.

Cross-country skiers will find nearly 50 trails maintained by the Chicago Park District within the city limits. The Forest Preserve District also offers several miles of open trails throughout its property. Maps are available upon request for seven designated trails: **Arie Crown, Bemis Woods, Beverly Lake, Camp Sagawau,** Deer Grove, Maple Lake Area and **Swallow Cliff Area.** Ski rentals are available at Camp Sagawau, for use in that area only; phone (630) 257-2045.

The Forest Preserve District maintains several snowmobiling areas and toboggan runs. Snowmobiles are permitted at **Miller Meadow, Morrill Meadow, Ned Brown Meadow, North Creek Meadow** and Turtlehead Lake. Snowmobiles must be registered with both the district and the state. Toboggan slides are at Bemis Woods, **Dan Ryan Woods, Deer Grove (No. 5), Jensen Slides, River Forest** and Swallow Cliff; rentals are available at all slides. The James Park Winter Sports Complex in Evanston also has runs for tobogganing.

Most Forest Preserve District winter activities are available daily 8-dusk; toboggan slides and snowmobile areas are open 10-10. For information phone (773) 261-8400, (708) 366-9420, or TDD (708) 771-1190.

Shopping

Any shop 'til you drop aficionado is familiar with the **Magnificent Mile** and Marshall Field's, two Chicago landmarks. But savvy shoppers also know that virtually every type of store can be found in the Windy City and its environs.

Antiques

Antiquers will find the Near North neighborhoods, particularly in **River North, Lincoln Park, Lake View** and along the Magnificent Mile, the richest hunting grounds. **Halsted and Belmont streets** yield a wealth of gracefully aged treasures.

Noteworthy complexes include the mammoth **International Art and Antique Centre**, 2300 W. Diversey Pkwy.; and the **Chicago Riverfront Antique Mart**, 2929 N. Western Ave. **Antiques on the Avenue**, 104 S. Michigan Ave., offers wares dating to the mid-19th century. Art deco items are popular at **Armitage Antique Gallery**, 1529 W. Armitage Ave., and **Wrigleyville Antique Mall**, 3336 N. Clark St. Ethnic objects and more than 40 dealers make **Chicago Antique Mall**, 3045 N. Lincoln Ave., a good spot for browsing.

Malls

Local chains Carson Pirie Scott and Marshall Field's are particularly common in Chicago malls. Two stand-outs are Schaumburg's **Woodfield Mall** on Golf Road at SR 53, and **Old Orchard Shopping Center**, at Skokie Boulevard and Old Orchard Road in Skokie. The area's largest shopping center, Woodfield features anchor retailers JCPenney, Lord & Taylor, Marshall Field's, Nordstrom and Sears. Old Orchard offers an outdoor setting and 80 stores, including Lord & Taylor, Marshall Field's and Saks Fifth Avenue.

The vertical mall is a Chicago trademark, particularly on the Magnificent Mile. **Chicago Place**, 700 N. Michigan Ave., pays homage to another local tradition, evoking Chicago School architectural styles from its rounded exterior corners to its glass-topped winter garden on the eighth floor. A seven-story Saks Fifth Avenue is the center's fashionable anchor. The mall also offers more than 50 specialty shops and restaurants. Across the street shoppers encounter the omnipresent "swoosh" symbol in **NikeTown**.

Venerable retailers Lord & Taylor and Marshall Field's are the main attraction at **Water Tower Place**, 835 N. Michigan Ave. Dispersed between the two are more than 100 specialty stores and boutiques on eight floors. It also houses restaurants and seven cinemas. The last of the Mile's vertical malls, though certainly not the least, is **900 North Michigan Avenue**, featuring Bloomingdale's, Gucci and Henri Bendel.

Lincoln Park doesn't have a magnificent mile, but it does have a vertical mall, **Century Shopping Center**, in the shell of an old movie palace at 2828 Clark St. in the Lakeview neighborhood. Typical mall fare fills the seven-story structure that once was a vaudeville-era movie palace.

Other suburban malls include **Hawthorn Center**, SR 60 and Milwaukee Avenue in Vernon Hills; **Northbrook Court**, Lake-Cook Road in Northbrook;

Orland Square, 151st Street and US 45 in Orland Park; **Randhurst Shopping Plaza**, Rand Road off US 12 and SR 83 in Mount Prospect; **River Oaks Shopping Center**, 159th Street and Torrence in Calumet City; and **Stratford Square**, Army Trail Road and Gary Avenue in Bloomingdale.

Outlets

Chicago offers plenty of off-price retailers as alternatives to the Magnificent Mile and other ritzy districts. **Nordstrom Rack** is in Woodfield Village Green Center in Schaumburg, across from Woodfield Mall, and **Lord & Taylor Clearance Center** is at 445 E. Palatine Rd. in Arlington Heights.

Deeply discounted finds are offered at **Filene's Basement**, with downtown stores at 1 N. State St. and 830 N. Michigan Ave. Catalog giant **Lands' End** has outlets at 2121 N. Clybourn Ave. in Chicago, behind Yorktown Plaza in Lombard, 7205 W. Dempster St. in Niles and 1522 E. Golf Rd. in Schaumburg. Great deals on home furnishings delight bargain hunters at **Crate & Barrel Outlet Store**, 800 W. North Ave. **Syms**, 280 W. North Ave. in Addison, is awash in top-flight clothing goods selling for bottom dollar.

The 2-mile outlet paradise of **Gurnee Mills**, at I-94 and SR 132 in Gurnee, features Ann Taylor, Bally, Geoffrey Beene, Saks, Spiegel and Syms among its 230 stores. Also is in the complex is **Bass Pro Shops Outdoor World**, featuring an indoor waterfall and 30,000-gallon aquarium, wildlife exhibits and sporting demonstrations.

Specialty Districts

No shopping trip in Chicago is complete without at least a peek at the fine stores and galleries on N.

Michigan Avenue, called the "Magnificent Mile." This stretch of real estate above the Chicago River is a mercantile mecca of vertical malls and an outstanding selection of world-class shops and restaurants. Scattered between dozens of galleries are Bloomingdale's, Crate & Barrel, Lord and Taylor, Marshall Field's, Neiman Marcus, NikeTown, Tiffany and Co., and others.

If Neiman Marcus doesn't satisfy your craving for ritzy goods and sky-high prices, pop into Burberry's or Escada. Four levels filled with home furnishings entice shoppers at Crate & Barrel, and the electronic toys at Sony keep everyone plugged in. The inner child reigns at F.A.O. Schwarz; a toy-filled playground offers youthful diversions.

The seven blocks of State Street that lie within the Loop contain such a concentration of designer boutiques and independent merchants that one could spend a week shopping in this area alone. Two of the largest stores are Carson Pirie Scott, 1 S. State St., and the seven-story Marshall Field's at 111 N. State St. Carson Pirie Scott offers a shop devoted exclusively to Chicago Bulls memorabilia. Filene's Basement, T.J. Maxx and a host of specialty shops also entice shoppers to the area.

Equally glamorous is the trend-setting strip of Oak Street between Michigan Avenue and Rush Street. Standing at the entry to this ultra-chic thoroughfare is One Magnificent Mile, a three-building complex housing condominiums, restaurants and shops boasting the likes of Chanel and Ralph Lauren.

In town, you'll find the aptly named Atrium Mall in the James R. Thompson Center, 100 W. Randolph St., with about three dozen boutiques centered around a skylit atrium. Hyde Park's Harper Court is a collection of boutiques, galleries and eateries at Harper Avenue and 52nd Street. Though the showrooms of the massive Merchandise Mart, 300 N. Wells St., are closed to the public, the complex's Shops at the Mart provides two floors of retail operations.

Art galleries and boutiques line the streets of the Near North neighborhoods of River North, Lincoln Park and Old Town as well as New Town's Halsted Street. Those looking for something different will probably find it in the bazaars of Old Town, where everything from African zebra-skin rugs to pre-Columbian art is sold. New Town, from 2800 to 3400 North on Broadway, offers quaint pubs, boutiques and restaurants.

Imported goods from every corner of the earth fill stores in Andersonville, Chinatown, Devon Avenue, Lincoln Square, Little Saigon and Pilsen. On Lake Michigan east of downtown lies Navy Pier, which offers stores, restaurants, a promenade and a stunning lake view as well as family-oriented attractions (see attraction listing p. 62). Whimsicality is a characteristic of the shops at River East Plaza.

Performing Arts

Chicago's world-class cultural amenities set trends as well as standards. The arts are showcased in numerous venues and often are the focus of are events.

Ballets, concerts and legitimate theater productions with big-name entertainers are presented a Chicago's largest indoor theater, the Arié Crow Theatre, (312) 791-6190, in McCormick Place a 23rd Street and the lakefront. McCormick Place i reputed to be the largest exhibition and trade show facility in the Northern Hemisphere, featuring ma jor shows throughout the year. Performances als are held at Auditorium Theatre, (312) 922-4046 50 E. Congress Pkwy.; Chicago Theatre, (312 443-1130, on State and Lake streets; and Rosemon Theatre, (847) 671-5100, at 5400 N. River Rd. i Rosemont.

Other cultural centers that offer lectures an present dance and classical concerts include th Chicago Cultural Center, 78 E. Washington St (see attraction listing p. 58), and the Noyes Cul tural Arts Center, (847) 491-0266, 927 Noyes St. in nearby Evanston. Consult the newspapers fo complete information.

Dance

Small dance ensembles bring fluid expressior and graceful moves to every corner of the city. The Chicago Music Alliance and Dance Coalition (312) 987-9296, provides the Performance Hotline (312) 987-1123, and the Chicago Music Alliance Performance Guide.

Specializing in classical dance, Ballet Chicago (312) 251-8838, has a fondness for Balanchine pieces. American styles are the forte of the Hubbard Street Dance Chicago troupe, (312 850-9744, whose eclectic—and electric—performances honor such greats as Bob Fosse and Twyla Tharp. The Joffrey Ballet of Chicago, (312 739-0120, melds classic tradition and contemporary ideas into a unique vision of American dance.

Professional modern dance concerts are featured at the Dance Center of Columbia College, (312 344-8300, 1306 S. Michigan Ave., which sponsors a varied schedule anchored by the resident Mordine & Company Dance Theatre.

Film

Chicago was the original Tinseltown. Film pioneers of the early 1900s produced short "moving pictures" through such ventures as Essanay Studios, employer of the young Charlie Chaplin.

But the city's cinematic legacy is perhaps best honored in such independent theaters as Facets Multimedia, 1517 W. Fullerton Ave., and Chicago Filmmakers, 5243 N. Clark St.; phone (773) 281-4114 and 293-1447, respectively. Both screen experimental and obscure works by international artists. Two larger houses are Lowe's Cineplex Theater Fine Arts at 418 S. Michigan Ave., (312) 939-3700, and Music Box Theater at 3733 N. Southport Ave., (773) 871-6604, which offer acclaimed art films and documentaries. Three Penny Cinema, 2424 N. Lincoln Ave., operates in the same vein, albeit on a smaller scale; phone (773) 935-5744.

The **Gene Siskel Film Center at the School of the Art Institute**, (312) 443-3733, augments its dynamic schedule of independent efforts, revivals and retrospectives with lectures and classes.

Music

Chicago's music is almost unlimited in scope. Since its founding in 1891, the world-class **Chicago Symphony Orchestra** has established a tradition of excellence that has come to define symphonic music. Its devoted following virtually guarantees sold-out performances at stately **Orchestra Hall**, 220 S. Michigan Ave. The regular season features a blend of classical and contemporary pieces, in addition to CSO Presents, a diverse concert series. For schedule and ticket information phone (312) 294-3000. Future stars can be heard in the **Civic Orchestra of Chicago**, the symphony's ensemble of musicians in training.

The **Ravinia Music Festival** in Highland Park, a northern suburb, features a 12-week program, composed of a variety of concerts, dance and popular events presented daily. Internationally known artists and conductors take part. The Chicago Symphony Orchestra is featured for 8 weeks. For prices and information phone (847) 266-5100.

Performing Arts Chicago, (312) 225-5226, sponsors respected touring groups. The organization has its own resident ensemble, the Vermeer Quartet, (312) 663-1628. Most performances are given at **DePaul Concert Hall**, 800 W. Belden Ave. on the DePaul University campus.

Chicago Chamber Orchestra, (312) 922-5570, and **Chicago Ensemble**, (773) 334-4358, strike an eclectic note with classical and contemporary concerts at Chicago Cultural Center and **The Three Arts Club**, 1300 N. Dearborn Pkwy. Twentieth-century music is the province of **Concertante di Chicago**, performing at DePaul Concert Hall. The **Contemporary Chamber Players** perform at the University of Chicago, (773) 702-8068.

The **Grant Park Symphony Orchestra** entertains thousands of picnickers with free concerts at the **Petrillo Band Shell** in Grant Park on Wednesdays and Friday through Sunday, late June through August; phone (312) 742-7638.

One of Orchestra Hall's most revered traditions is the Christmastime performance of Handel's Messiah by the **Apollo Chorus of Chicago**, the city's oldest choir. The group also gives spring concerts at other venues; for information phone (630) 960-2251. Formed under the auspices of the Chicago Symphony Orchestra in 1957, the **Chicago Symphony Chorus**, (312) 294-3430, since has come into its own; it performs classical and modern pieces by itself and with the symphony at Orchestra Hall.

Music of the Baroque, (312) 551-1414, and the **Oriana Singers**, (773) 262-4558, focus primarily on 17th-century music but have branched out into other periods from time to time. The **William Ferris Chorale**, (773) 325-2000, specializes in modern composers. All perform throughout the year at various sites.

Opera

The city's premier company, **Lyric Opera of Chicago** performs classical and contemporary works at **Civic Opera House**, (312) 332-2244, 20 N. Wacker Dr.

Several smaller companies offer light fare in more intimate venues. English-language compositions are the fare of the contemporary **Chicago Opera Theatre**, which performs at DePaul University's **Merle Rushkin Theatre** at 60 E. Balbo St., and the occasionally offbeat **Chamber Opera Chicago**, which performs at **Ivanhoe Theater**; phone (312) 704-8420 or (713) 975-7171, respectively. Operettas and musicals dominate the repertoire of the **Light Opera Works**, (847) 869-6300, operating out of **Cahn Auditorium** on the Northwestern University campus.

Theater

Most of the houses that have become the main strongholds of legitimate theater are downtown. The grand dame of Chicago theater is the **Goodman Theater**, (312) 443-3800, 170 N. Dearborn St., whose reputation for excellence hasn't precluded innovation. Both Broadway shows and experimental productions are offered at the **Shubert**, (312) 902-1500, 22 W. Monroe St, and productions also can be seen at the Chicago Theatre.

The Auditorium Theatre, 50 E. Congress Pkwy., was designed by Louis Sullivan and Dankmar Adler in the 1880s and continues to serve as an active theater; phone (312) 922-2110 for general information or (312) 431-2354 for tours.

Cultural diversity is a common thread in **Court Theater** efforts at the University of Chicago, 5535

S. Ellis Ave., although the company also mines the classics on occasion; phone (773) 753-4472.

The **Chicago Shakespeare Theater** presents plays by the bard year-round at Navy Pier; phone (312) 595-5600. Shakespeare also takes center stage at **Ruth Page Theatre** with the Shakespeare Repertory, (312) 642-2273, which is dedicated solely to the Bard's works.

Summer has attractions of its own. The Chicago Park District offers a summer theater, "**Theater on the Lake**," at Fullerton Avenue and Lake Shore Drive; phone (312) 742-7994. Shows are held at 8 p.m. Wednesday through Sunday, June through August; admission is $10.

The **Tweeter**

Center, a 30,000-seat outdoor amphitheater at Ridgeland Avenue and Flossmoor Road in Tinley Park, offers concerts by top-name performers; phone (708) 614-1616.

Chicago also has many notable off-Loop theaters as well as several suburban playhouses that have been converted from abandoned warehouses, old ballrooms and garages. Since the flood of talent that swept through the city's North Side in the mid-1970s, the off-Loop theater circuit has become a launching pad for several Broadway shows.

Prominent off-Loop theaters include **Apollo Theater Center**, (773) 935-6100, 2540 N. Lincoln Ave.; **Briar Street Theatre**, (773) 348-4000, 3133

N. Halsted St.; Ivanhoe Theater, (773) 975-7171 750 W. Wellington Ave.; **Royal George Theatre Center**, (312) 988-9000, 1641 N. Halsted St.; **Steppenwolf Theatre**, (312) 335-1650, 1650 N. Halsted St.; and **Victory Gardens Theatre**, (773) 871-3000, 2257 N. Lincoln Ave.

Steppenwolf Theatre is noted for daring performances by such actors as John Mahoney, John Malkovich, Laurie Metcalf and Gary Sinise. The company conquered Broadway in 1990 with its Tony award-winning rendition of "The Grapes of Wrath."

Among the best known suburban theaters are the **Drury Lane Theatre**, (630) 530-8300, 100 Drury Ln. in Oakbrook Terrace; **Drury Lane South**, (708) 422-0404, 2500 W. 95th St. in Evergreen Park; and **Marriott's Theater**, (847) 634-0200, 10 Marriott Dr. in Lincolnshire. In addition, several colleges offer a variety of productions.

New plays are the forte of the **Organic Theatre Company**, (847) 475-2800, 1420 Maple Ave. in Evanston, a 1960s group whose radical attitude has mellowed with time. **Next Theatre Company**, (847) 475-1875, tackles social issues in an avant-garde style. The Next performs at 927 Noyes Ave. in Evanston.

The city's rich literary history is reflected in the philosophies of both **Northlight Theatre**, (847) 679-9501, and Victory Gardens Theater, which showcase new plays by emerging writers. Northlight productions are staged in venues around town.

For interactive theater, try the **Neo-Futurarium**, 5153 N. Ashland Ave., where offerings veer sharply off the beaten path; phone (773) 275-5255. The audience also is central to the antics of "Shear Madness" at the Blackstone Hotel's **Mayfair Theatre**, 636 S. Michigan Ave., and "Tony n' Tina's Wedding," 230 W. North Ave.; phone (312) 786-9120 or 664-1456, respectively. "Shear Madness" is a comedy whodunit that has reputedly become the longest-running, non-musical play in theater history.

Half-price tickets can be purchased with cash only on the day of performance, or on Saturday for Sunday performances, at the Hot Tixx Booths at 108 N. State St. or 811 N. Michigan Ave. Both booths are open Mon.-Sat. 10-6, Sun. noon-5. The Chicago Cultural Center also provides a recorded listing of art happenings in the city; phone (312) 346-3278.

Special Events

Throughout the year Chicago's calendar is full of special events, ranging from huge exhibitions of automobiles, vacation equipment and antiques to shopping center art fairs. The flower and garden shows change with the seasons; check the events sections of the newspapers.

One of the main horticultural events on Chicago's calendar is the **Chicago Flower & Garden Show**, bursting with exhibits of earthy pursuits. The show takes place at Navy Pier in mid-March.

Chicago so loves a parade that more than 200 parade permits are issued annually. There are parades to celebrate **Chinese New Year**, held late January or early February; **St. Patrick's Day**; **Polish Constitution Day**, in early May; **Bud Billiken Day**, a variable Saturday in August; **Mexican Independence Day** in September; **Columbus Day**; and the Saturday after Thanksgiving to welcome Santa.

The various ethnic communities throughout the city have some extraordinary celebrations. The Chinese celebrate the New Year in Chinatown, and the Scottish Americans perform the traditional **Highland Games** in mid-June. There are the **Irish Festival** in late May, the **Festival Polonaise** in mid-July, **Viva Mexico** and **Festa Italiana** in late July, the **Pan American Festival** in August, the German-American celebration of **Oktoberfest** in mid-September and the **Celtic Fest Chicago** in late September.

Summer brings several events, including the **Chicago Blues Festival** in early June, a 4-day jam where top musicians get down in Delta style at the **Petrillo Band Shell** in Grant Park. Chicagoans throng Lake Michigan's moonlit shore to enjoy the symphonic delights of the **Grant Park Music Festival**, also held in the shell mid-June to August. That "great street" gets its due at the **Celebrate on State Street Festival** in mid-June. The event is held, logically enough, on State Street between Wacker Drive and Van Buren Street. Chicago's culinary wizards demonstrate their prowess for the hungry multitudes at the **Taste of Chicago** food festival in late June in Grant Park.

Other events worth considering are the **Chicago International Art Exposition** in mid-May; the **Gospel Festival** and the **Chicago International Boat Show** in June; the **Air and Water Show**, **Jazz Fest** and **Venetian Night** in July; the **Chicago International New Art Forms Exposition** in September; and the **Chicago International Antiques Show** and **Chicago International Film Festival** in October.

Participating in the mid-October **Chicago Marathon** is a thorough, if strenuous, way to see the city, although just watching the 26.2-mile race can be exhausting. The contest begins and ends at Columbus and Balbo drives in Grant Park, running through various neighborhoods along the way.

The Chicago Office of Tourism, (312) 744-2400, can provide additional information about city events as can the Mayor's Office of Special Events, (312) 744-3370.

Nightlife

Chicago nightlife used to be summed up in two words: Rush Street. But as yuppies revitalized downtown neighborhoods, they also injected new life into the club scene. Hotspots now crop up all across the Near North, Loop and South Loop, with styles ranging from hip-hop to alternative to world music.

Sample this diversity at **Wild Hare**, 3530 N. Clark St., (773) 327-4273, featuring international bands and a reggae beat; **Tropicana Chicago**, 2047 N. Milwaukee Ave., (773) 489-9600, a swanky supper club where the salsa rhythms are as hot as the food; **Equator Club**, 4715 N. Broadway, (773) 728-2411, always packed with fans of African and Afro-Caribbean bands; and **Abbey Pub**, 3420 W. Grace St., (773) 478-4408, a popular hangout offering Irish acts along with rock and folk groups.

For club listings and band appearances check *The Reader,* the "Weekend Plus" section of the *Chicago Sun-Times* and the "Friday" section of the *Chicago Tribune.*

Blues

When it comes to the blues, few cities rival Chicago. **B.L.U.E.S.**, 2519 N. Halsted St., didn't get its name by chance—this bustling club is the real thing; phone (773) 528-1012. Wall-to-wall crowds also are a common sight at **Kingston Mines**, 2548 N. Halsted St., (773) 477-4646.

One of the city's coolest nightspots is **Blue Chicago**, where local hopefuls belt out the blues while an appreciative audience dances the evening away. The club has two locations, at 736 and 536 N. Clark St.; phone (312) 642-6261 and 661-0100. **House of Blues**, 329 N. Dearborn St., (312) 923-2000, serves up the blues with side dishes of Southern folk art and down-home cooking.

Buddy Guy's Legends at 754 S. Wabash Ave., (312) 427-0333, books stars to play the roomy hall owned by the guitar great. Guy himself has been known to show up for a set or two.

CityPass

CityPass offers savings to those who plan visits to many Chicago attractions. The pass covers the price of admission to six sites—Adler Planetarium & Astronomy Museum, Art Institute of Chicago, The Field Museum, The Hancock Observatory/John Hancock Center, John G. Shedd Aquarium, and Museum of Science and Industry.

A pass, valid for 9 days once the first attraction is visited, is $39; ages 3-11, $28. CityPass is available from visitor information centers, participating attractions and most major hotels.

Casinos

Gambling is not yet legal in Chicago city limits, bu you'll find a wealth of games to enjoy on the riverboa casinos in the outlying communities of Elgin, Aurora an Joliet.

Elgin's **Grand Victoria** Casino, (847) 888-1000, offe 80,000 square feet—most of them dedicated to gaming— and a Las Vegas feel. Aurora's **Hollywood Casino R verboats** splits games between two vessels *(City o Lights I* and *City of Lights II)*, as does **Empress** Casin Joliet *(Empress I* and *Empress II)* in Joliet; phone (80C 888-7777 and (815) 744-9400, respectively. Another Jc liet enterprise, **Harrah's Joliet Casino,** (800) 427-7247 features the *Southern Star* and *Northern Star* riverboa in addition to an entertainment complex at Harrah' Landing.

Comedy Clubs

Second City, Chicago's well-known improvisatio troupe that gave the world the inspired comedy of Da Aykroyd, Jim Belushi, John Candy, Bill Murray, Gild Radner and Martin Short, to name a few, still reduces au diences to tears—of laughter, that is—with its trademar blend of satire and comedy. The side-splitting continue at the offshoot **Second City, E.T.C.** The clubs are a 1616 and 1608 N. Wells St.; phone (312) 337-3992 an 642-8189.

Improvisation also is the force behind other clubs **ComedySportz,** (773) 549-8080, pits two teams of per formers in a hilarious competition spurred by audienc suggestions. Contests are staged at **TurnAround The atre,** 3209 N. Halsted St. Enjoy the antics of **Improv Olympic,** which stages "tag-team" improvisation at 354 N. Clark St.; phone (773) 880-0199.

Standard stand-up provides comic relief at **Zanie Comedy Nite Club,** 1548 N. Wells St.; phone (312 337-4027. The South Loop's **All Jokes Aside,** 1000 S Wabash Ave., promotes African-American comedians phone (773) 922-0577.

Dance Clubs

Variety is the spice at **Excalibur,** 632 N. Dearbori Pkwy., with four clubs offering a cabaret, a game room and progressive and top-40 music; phone (312 266-1944. Chicago clubbers generally dress to impress and fashion savvy is required at **Baja Beach Club,** (312 915-5986, a high-energy joint at 219 W. Erie St.

Jazz

Chicagoans tend to think *their* city is the true capita of American jazz. An abundance of jazz clubs in town lends ample evidence to support this view.

Step into **Green Mill** at 4802 N. Broadway, (773 878-5552, to get a taste of 1930s Chicago. The forme Capone hangout showcases fresh talent and the "Uptowr Poetry Slam" contest. Newcomers also catch the spot- light at the eclectic **Bop Shop,** 1443 W. Jarvis Ave.

Joe's Be-Bop Cafe & Jazz Emporium at Navy Pie features live music; phone (312) 595-5299. And stars crop up at **Andy's,** 11 E. Hubbard St., an old standby fo all kinds of jazz; phone (312) 642-6805.

ock

Alternative bands rock the Generation Xers ronging **Metro,** 3730 N. Clark St., which nurtures oth national and local talent. You'll find more of e same downstairs on the **Smart Bar** dance floor,

though the style tends more toward industrial/ thrash. Phone (773) 549-0203 for information about both clubs. To check out the newest trends in alternative rock, try the **Double Door** at 1572 N. Milwaukee Ave., (773) 489-3160.

The Chicago Vicinity

URORA (C-4) pop. 99,600, elev. 662′

Aurora was the site of a large Potawatomi Indian ettlement when Joseph McCarty of Elmira, N.Y., rived in 1834. He introduced industry by building dam on the Fox River to power a mill. Larger industry followed the completion of the first area railad in 1848.

Paramount Arts Centre on Galena Boulevard is a estored 1931 movie palace that presents musicals, aternational performances, comedy and holiday vents. Tours of the theater are available by appointment; phone (630) 896-6666.

Aurora Area Convention and Visitors Bureau: 4 W. Downer Pl., Aurora, IL 60506; phone (630) 97-5581 or (800) 477-4369.

hopping areas: Fox Valley Shopping Center, at R 59 and New York Street, features Carson Pirie cott, JCPenney, Marshall Field's and Sears among s shopping venues.

BLACKBERRY FARM AND PIONEER VILLAGE is w. on I-88 tollway to Orchard Rd. xit, s. to Galena Blvd., then 1.5 mi. w. following igns to 100 S. Barnes Rd. This re-creation of an Illnois farm village contains a commons, a smithy, a arriage museum, a one-room schoolhouse and a ioneer cabin. A museum representing the streets of ld Aurora features demonstrators dressed in eriod. The Discovery Barn contains farm animals.

Splash Country is a farm-themed water park feauring tube slides, pools and a simulated lazy river. ood is available.

Farm and village daily 10-4:30, last weekend in Apr.-Labor Day; Fri.-Sun. 10-4:30, day after Labor Day to mid-Oct. Water park Sun.-Fri. noon-7 (also Mon. and Wed. 7-8 p.m.), Sat. 10-6. Farm and village admission $7.50; senior citizens and ages 2-12, 6.50. Water park admission Mon.-Fri. $10. Admission Sat.-Sun. $11. MC, VI. Phone (630) 892-1550 or farm and village or 906-7981 for water park.

CITECH, .5 mi. w. of jct. SR 25 at 18 W. Benton t., offers more than 200 hands-on science exhibits xploring astronomy, heat, light and magnets. Alow 2 hours minimum. Tues.-Fri. and Sun. noon-5 also Thurs. 5-8), Sat. 10-5; closed Jan. 1, Easter, Thanksgiving and Dec. 25. Hours may vary; phone head. Admission $5; over 64, $4; under 2 free; amily rate (up to six immediate family members) 15. MC, VI. Phone (630) 859-3434.

CASINOS

• **Hollywood Casino**, 1 New York St. Bridge. *City of Lights I* daily 8:30 a.m.-6:30 a.m. *City of Lights II* daily 10:30 a.m.-12:30 a.m. (also Fri.-Sat. 12:30 a.m.-2:30 a.m. Phone (630) 801-1234 or (800) 888-7777.

BATAVIA (C-5) pop. 17,100, elev. 719′

Founded in 1833 by Christopher Columbus Payne, Batavia was incorporated as a village in 1856, then as a city in 1891. The nickname "Windmill City" was applied to Batavia after the Civil War, when three windmill manufacturers in Batavia shipped their whirling product worldwide.

Fox River, which flows through downtown, was the centerpiece of town and today it is the site for abundant recreational activities. The Batavia Riverwalk Project includes an activity center, park benches, an entry court and other amenities.

Batavia Chamber of Commerce: 100 N. Island Ave., Batavia, IL 60510; phone (630) 879-7134.

FERMI NATIONAL ACCELERATOR LABORATORY (FERMILAB) is off Farnsworth N. exit of I-88 tollway; follow Farnsworth to Kirk Rd., then 2 mi. n. to Pine St. entrance. Fermilab boasts the world's highest energy particle accelerator, a circular tunnel 4 miles in circumference that lets physicists explore the nucleus of an atom. The 15th-floor observation area has an audiovisual program, a super-conducting magnet and models of the accelerator tunnel and the laboratory site.

Pamphlets outline a self-guiding tour of the complex. The grounds contain a prairie trail and bicycle paths. Food is available. Allow 2 hours minimum. Daily 8:30-5. Free. Phone (630) 840-3351.

BROOKFIELD (C-6) pop. 18,900, elev. 620′

Until 1905 Brookfield was called Grossdale after Samuel Gross, who laid out this residential suburb of Chicago in 1893. Since then Brookfield has developed into three communities—Brookfield, Hollywood and Congress Park.

Brookfield Chamber of Commerce: 3724 Grand Blvd., Brookfield, IL 60513; phone (708) 485-1434.

BROOKFIELD ZOO, First Ave. and 31st St., is accessible by the First Ave. exit of the Eisenhower or Stevenson expwys. (I-290 or I-55) and the Ogden Ave. exit of the Tri-State Tollway (I-294). The 216-acre zoo contains an exceptional collection of mammals, birds and reptiles in cageless enclosures that simulate their natural habitats.

The Living Coast: A World of Surprising Connections is a re-creation of the western coasts of Chile and Peru. An underwater journey takes visitors from the ocean to the shore. Along the way they can see moon jellies, green sea turtles, small sharks, Humboldt penguins, vampire bats, Inca terns and chinchillas; graphics and displays explore the connections between animals, plants and their physical environment.

The Swamp: Wonders of our Wetlands features two American ecosystems—a southern cypress swamp and an Illinois river. Cypress and tupelo trees in the swamp area are inhabited by egrets, water snakes, siren salamanders and insect-eating mammals. A river system typical of Illinois has screech owls as well as underwater views of fish, an alligator snapping turtle and river otters.

Salt Creek Wilderness has a lake, a nature trail, a boardwalk and a representation of a northeastern Illinois wetland. Trumpeter swans, turtles, toads, dragonflies and raccoons can be seen.

Habitat Africa! The Savannah is a 5-acre savannah that includes a rocky outcropping and a water hole shared by giraffes, zebras, endangered African wild dogs and exotic birds and reptiles, while Habitat Africa! The Forest presents red river hogs, African lungfish, dwarf crocodiles and emperor scorpions.

The Children's Zoo features the Animals in Action program, in which demonstrations relating to such topics as horsemanship and animal training are given Memorial Day through Labor Day. Be a Bird allows guests to test their ability to fly (courtesy of a flying strength machine), and Australian House has a Walkabout exhibit with wombats and tree kangaroos. Food is available.

A Motor Safari tram provides guided tours of the zoo early spring through late fall. The Snowball Express shuttle bus runs between the exhibit buildings late fall through early spring. Zoo open daily 9:30-6, Memorial Day-Labor Day; 10-5, rest of year. All indoor animal exhibits close 30 minutes before the zoo. Admission $7; over 65 and ages 3-11, $3.50. Admission Tues. and Thurs., Oct.-Mar. free. Children's Zoo $1; over 65 and ages 3-11, 50c. Motor Safari $2.50; over 65 and ages 3-11, $1.50. Parking $6.75. Prices may vary; phone ahead. Phone (708) 485-0263. *See ad p. 58.*

The Fragile Kingdom reveals how animals in Africa and Asia depend on their environments and one another to survive. Three exhibit areas are unified by a global theme—the ecology of survival and the role humans play in the destruction and preservation of these worlds. The Fragile Desert reveals the diversity of life in the harsh African desert, while The Fragile Rain Forest examines the conglomeration of life in the warm, moist forests of Southeast Asia. The Fragile Hunters is a rocky, outdoor exhibit for African lions, tigers, snow leopards and Amur leopards.

Seven Seas Panorama has a 2,000-seat indoor dolphinarium where dolphins perform daily. Schedules are posted throughout the park. Near the building a rocky Pacific Northwest seascape with seals and sea lions. Admission to dolphin show $2.50; over 65 and ages 3-11, $2.

Tropic World: A Primate's Journey represents three rain forest regions: Africa, Asia and South America. A pathway overlooking pools and waterfalls allows visitors to view the animals coexisting amid 50-foot trees. Approximately 100 primates, other mammals and 30 birds can be seen. Rain storms occur in each exhibit area, though the animals are the only ones who get wet. Quest to Save the Earth is an interactive adventure game encouraging environmentally friendly behaviors.

DES PLAINES (B-5) pop. 53,200, elev. 641'

Spelled several ways since its founding—Plein, Plein, De Plein—Des Plaines originally was named Rand after an early settler, Socrates Rand. Most early citizens were German farmers who developed the town into a flourishing agrarian settlement.

In the 1920s truck farming became an important industry, with the town supplying most of the world's commercial flowers, particularly roses and carnations. The industry died after farmers realized it was wiser to grow flowers in more temperate southern climates.

In 1955 Ray Kroc built the first of many McDonald's in Des Plaines. As business boomed so did the number of McDonald's in town—the 1,000th franchise is on Oakton Street, and the 20,000th was built in Des Plaines in 1972.

Des Plaines Chamber of Commerce: 1401 Oakton St., Des Plaines, IL 60018; phone (847) 824-4200.

DES PLAINES HISTORICAL MUSEUM, 789 Pearson St., displays furniture, artifacts and clothing from the beginning of the 20th century in a restored Queen Anne-style house. Temporary and permanent exhibits chronicle local history. Allow 1 hour minimum. Mon.-Fri. 9-4, Sun. 1-4, Feb.-Dec.; closed Thanksgiving and Dec. 25. Donations. Phone (847) 391-5399.

McDONALD'S MUSEUM, 400 N. Lee St., is a red and white tiled re-creation of the first Ray Kroc's McDonald's restaurant at its original 1955 site. The museum includes original equipment, a menu board, photographs, documents and a brief videotape presentation. Four 1955 automobiles are parked outside. Allow 30 minutes minimum. Thurs.-Sat. 10:30-2:30, Memorial Day-Labor Day. Hours may vary; phone ahead. Free. Phone (847) 297-5022.

EAST DUNDEE (B-5)

THE HAEGER POTTERIES is 2 blks. s. of SR 72 at jct. Maiden Ln. and Van Buren St. Ceramic artware s made at the facility. Highlights include a museum, historical and manufacturing video presentations and one of the world's largest vases. Mon. and Thurs.-Fri. 10-6, Sat.-Sun. 11-5; closed Jan. 1, Easter, Thanksgiving and Dec. 25. Free. Phone (847) 426-3441.

SANTA'S VILLAGE THEME PARK, 2 mi. n. of I-90 exit 25 to jct. SRs 25 and 72, is a 55-acre amusement park that includes Santa's Village, Old McDonald's Farm, Coney Island, more than 40 rides, a petting zoo, arcades, live shows and picnic facilities. Racing Rapids water park and an ice-skating rink are on the grounds.

Allow 5 hours minimum. Santa's Village Mon.-Fri. 10-6, early June-late Aug. Park open Sat.-Sun. at 11, mid-May to early Oct.; closing hours vary. Racing Rapids open daily at 11 (closing hours vary), mid-June to mid-Aug.; open Sat.-Sun. at 11, mid-Aug. to early Sept. (closing hours vary). Hours may vary; phone ahead. Santa's Village admission $19.95; under 2 free. Racing Rapids $13.95; under 2 free. Both parks $27.95; under 2 free. AX, DS, MC, VI. Phone (847) 426-5525.

ELGIN (B-5) pop. 77,000, elev. 752'

Once noted for its contributions to the watchmaking industry, Elgin is rich in history and ethnic diversity. Here Gail Borden invented the process of condensing milk, a method in which the milk takes up less volume and can be packed in airtight cans making shipping easier.

Elgin Area Convention and Visitors Bureau: 77 Riverside Dr., Elgin, IL 60120; phone (847) 695-7540 or (800) 217-5362.

ELGIN AREA HISTORICAL MUSEUM, 1 mi. s. on SR 25, then .5 mi. w. to 360 Park St., is housed in an 1856 neoclassical building that once was home to Elgin Academy, one of the oldest preparatory schools in the Midwest. Various displays feature the history of the Elgin National Watch Co., Elgin Road Race memorabilia and an American Indian exhibit plus other local history items. Allow 2 hours minimum. Wed.-Sat. noon-4, Mar.-Dec. Admission $2, over 60 and students with ID $1, under 6 free. Phone (847) 742-4248.

CASINOS

• **Grand Victoria Casino**, 250 S. Grove Ave. Boarding daily 8:30 a.m.-6:30 a.m. Phone (847) 888-1000 or 468-7000.

ELMHURST (B-5) pop. 42,000, elev. 681'

White settlers first began to organize Elmhurst in the 1830s, when European immigrants claimed land along Salt Creek. Later, in 1842, Ohio native Gerry Bates established a formal community when he claimed a "treeless" area that today sits in the center of Elmhurst. At first the town was little more than a stagecoach stop, but in 1845 the town called Cottage Hill had begun to grow. In 1870 Cottage Hill changed its name to Elmhurst in recognition of the many elm trees dotting the city streets.

After World War II Elmhurst almost tripled in population, and growth continues. Elmhurst Historical Museum, 120 E. Park Ave., chronicles the people and customs that give the town its rich history; phone (630) 833-1457.

ELMHURST ART MUSEUM, off St. Charles Rd. .6 mi. n. to 150 Cottage Hill Ave., exhibits contemporary paintings, sculpture, prints and ceramics by American artists from the 19th century to the present. A glass gallery has collections tracing the history of glassmaking in America. Traveling exhibits also are featured. The 15,200-square-foot museum includes McCormick House—a 1952 row house prototype created by famed designer Mies van der Rohe. Guided tours are available.

Allow 1 hour minimum. Tues., Thurs. and Sat. 10-4, Wed., Fri. and Sun. 1-4; closed Jan. 1, Easter and Dec. 25. Admission $3, students with ID $2, under 12 free; free to all Tues. MC, VI. Phone (630) 834-0202.

[SAVE] **LIZZADRO MUSEUM OF LAPIDARY ART**, 220 Cottage Hill, is 2 blks. w. of York Rd., then 2 blks. n. of St. Charles Rd. in Wilder Park. The museum houses a large collection of jade and hardstone carvings as well as displays of gemstones and minerals. Allow 1 hour minimum. Tues.-Sat. 10-5, Sun. 1-5; closed holidays. Admission $3; over 60, $2; students with ID and ages 13-18, $1; free to all Fri. MC, VI. Phone (630) 833-1616.

EVANSTON (B-6) pop. 73,200, elev. 600'

In 1674 Father Jacques Marquette and his followers landed in the natural harbor of Evanston, originally named Grosse Point. This important lake port was later renamed Evanston for John Evans, one of the founders of Northwestern University.

Adjoining the northern limits of Chicago, Evanston has been likened to a New England village because of its nautical and academic atmosphere. It is the home of five institutions of higher learning and the headquarters of Rotary International and the Woman's Christian Temperance Union.

Frances E. Willard Home, 1730 Chicago Ave., offers tours by appointment. The National Woman's Christian Temperance Union, organized by Willard, is at the rear of the 1865 home; phone (847) 864-6170, or 864-1397 for tours.

Evanston Chamber of Commerce: 1560 Sherman Ave., Suite 860, Evanston, IL 60201; phone (847) 328-1500.

CHARLES GATES DAWES HOUSE, 225 Greenwood St., is in a historic district of restored Victorian homes and stately mansions. Active in international and domestic affairs, Nobel laureate Gen. Charles Gates Dawes served as vice president under Calvin Coolidge. Memorabilia and artifacts pertaining to his World War I service and public life are displayed. The restored 1894 home is furnished with original family pieces. Rotating exhibits and events also are featured.

Tours Thurs.-Sun. 1-5; closed holidays. Last tour begins 45 minutes before closing. Admission $5; over 60, students with ID and ages 6-18, $3. Phone (847) 475-3410.

NORTHWESTERN UNIVERSITY, at the corner of Sheridan Rd. and Chicago Ave., is one of the nation's leading private universities. Founded in 1851, it has a campus in Evanston and one in Chicago; the latter includes the medical, dental and law schools. Noted buildings include University Library, which has rare books and art exhibits; Dearborn Observatory, which offers public viewing by appointment; and Pick-Staiger Concert Hall. Campus tours are conducted Mon.-Fri. at 2 during the school year. Phone (847) 491-7271.

GLENCOE (B-6) pop. 8,500, elev. 673′

SAVE **CHICAGO BOTANIC GARDEN**, .5 mi. e. of Edens Expwy. on Lake Cook Rd. (County Line Rd.), is a 385-acre living museum featuring 23 gardens including a rose garden, a waterfall garden, an English walled garden, a three-island Japanese garden, a fruit and vegetable garden and native Illinois prairies. The education center houses three greenhouses and offers classes, lectures and exhibits. A narrated tram tour of the garden is available.

Garden open daily 8-dusk; closed Dec. 25. Garden free. Narrated tram tours $4; senior citizens, $3; ages 3-15, $2. Parking $7.75. Phone (847) 835-5440.

GLENVIEW (B-6) pop. 37,100, elev. 634′

THE GROVE, 1421 Milwaukee Ave., offers 124 acres of pioneer history. Visitors can tour the grounds of the Kennicotts, a pioneer family that settled on the site in 1836; the restored Kennicott House is furnished in period. Other highlights include an interpretive center, school house, an American Indian village, a log cabin and nature trails. Allow 1 hour, 30 minutes minimum. Mon.-Fri. 8-4:30, Sat.-Sun. 9-5. Hours may vary; phone ahead closed Jan. 1 and Dec. 25. Free. Phone (847) 299-6096.

GURNEE (A-6) pop. 13,700, elev. 676′

First settled in the 1830s, Gurnee went through its formative years as Wentworth, O'Plain and Gurnee Station before its current name was chosen. Once bolstered by commerce, Gurnee now relies on industrial parks, medical facilities and shopping for its economic stability.

Lake County, Illinois Convention and Visitors Bureau: 5455 Grand Ave., Suite 302, Gurnee, IL 60031; phone (847) 662-2700 or (800) 525-3669.

Shopping areas: The Gurnee Mills Mall, across from Six Flags Great America at 6170 W. Grand Ave., stretches nearly 2 miles. Included with more than 200 stores are Bass Pro Shops Outdoor World as well as Levi's, Saks Fifth Avenue and Spiegel phone (847) 263-7500.

GEM SIX FLAGS GREAT AMERICA, 1 mi. e. of I-94 on Grand Ave. (SR 132), is a family SAVE theme park with rides, shows and attractions. This 300-acre park features 12 roller coasters, four water rides, restaurants, shops, theaters and original show productions. Highlights include Batman the Ride, Iron Wolf, Raging Bull, V2, Déjà Vu, Viper and the Southwest Territory, which contains the Giant Drop. Camp Cartoon Network and Looney Tunes National Park contain 4 acres of rides and attractions for children under 55 inches tall.

Park open daily at 10, late May-late Aug.; Sat.-Sun., early May-late May and first 2 weekends in Sept.; Fri.-Sun., in Oct. Closing times vary; phone ahead. Admission $40.99; under 55 inches tall $30.99; over 59, $20.49; under age 4 free. Parking $10. AAA members save 10 percent on select in-park dining and merchandise. Check at the park's Guest Relations window for details. AX, DS, MC, VI. Phone (847) 249-4636.

JOLIET (D-5) pop. 76,800, elev. 538′

Originally named for Shakespeare's Juliet, the town became Joliet after it mistakenly was assumed to be named in honor of early French-Canadian explorer Louis Joliet, who visited the site in 1673.

Joliet's development directly benefited from the 1848 construction of the Illinois and Michigan Canal, which provided navigation between Lake Michigan and the Illinois River at La Salle. In 1900 the canal was replaced by the Chicago Sanitary and Ship Canal, which, along with the Des Plaines River, has established Joliet as one of the state's leading industrial and shipping centers.

The 1926 vaudeville Rialto Square Theatre presents entertainment and classic movies. Tours are available; phone (815) 726-6600.

Heritage Corridor Visitors Bureau: 81 N. Chicago St., Joliet, IL 60432; phone (815) 727-2323 or (800) 926-2262.

CASINOS

• *Empress* Casino Joliet, I-55 exit 248, then 3 mi. e. to Empress Dr. *Empress I* open Sun.-Thurs. 8:30 a.m.-1 a.m., Fri.-Sat. 8:30 a.m.-6:30 a.m. *Empress II* open daily 8:30 a.m.-6:30 a.m. Phone (815) 744-9400 or (888) 436-7737.

• *Harrah's Joliet Casino*, 151 N. Joliet St. *Southern Star* and *Northern Star* daily 8:30 a.m.-6:30 a.m. Phone (800) 427-7247.

LIBERTYVILLE (B-5) pop. 19,200, elev. 692′

Originally called Independence Grove, Libertyville assumed its present name when a post office was established in 1827. American Indians camped near the settlement while enjoying the mineral springs that dot the area. Wealthy Chicagoans later developed summer estates in the wooded hills and along the shores of the four lakes near the city limits.

The former summer home of the architect for whom it is named, David Adler Cultural Center presents art exhibits, folk music and craft shows; phone (847) 367-0707.

Independence Grove Forest Preserve covers 1,100 acres and surrounds a lake reclaimed from a gravel quarry. This outdoor recreation area features 5.5 miles of trails designed for bicycling, hiking and in-line skating. The marina offers boat rentals, fishing and swimming. A picnic pavilion and a visitors center also are available.

Green Oaks/Libertyville/Mundelein/Vernon Hills Chamber of Commerce: 1123 S. Milwaukee Ave., Libertyville, IL 60048; phone (847) 680-0750.

THE LAMBS FARM, I-94 n. to SR 176, is a nonprofit center providing residential, vocational and social support for developmentally disabled adults. Among the complex's vocational training sites are a bakery, pet shop, country store and restaurant. Outdoor activities include a children's farmyard, a petting zoo, miniature golf facilities, fire truck rides, train rides, a carousel and pony rides. Food is available.

Daily 9-6; closed holidays. Carousel, farmyard, fire truck, miniature golf and train $2 each. Phone (847) 362-4636; or 362-0048, ext. 5, for events information.

MARYTOWN/ST. MAXIMILIAN KOLBE SHRINE, 4 mi. w. of I-94 and SR 176 (Rockland Rd.) exit, honors the life of Conventual Franciscan priest and Polish saint Maximilian Kolbe. Four mosaics depict his charitable life and sacrifice in a German concentration camp during World War II. A Eucharistic adoration chapel contains stained glass patterned after the St. Paul Outside-the-Walls church in Rome. Allow 1 hour minimum. Chapel daily 24 hours. Donations. Phone (847) 367-7800.

LISLE (C-5) pop. 19,500, elev. 686'

Known as "Arboretum Village" because of the town's 1,700-acre Morton Arboretum, Lisle was incorporated in 1852. Lisle Station Park preserves much of Lisle Depot, an important shipping and passenger facility that served the town. The park includes a museum, a historic house and an old tavern; phone (630) 968-2747.

Lisle Convention and Visitors Bureau: 4746 Main St., Lisle, IL 60532; phone (800) 733-9811.

JURICA NATURE MUSEUM is on the second floor of the William Scholl Science Center at Benedictine University, 5700 College Rd. The museum contains a collection of northern Illinois, African and Pacific Ocean dioramas featuring birds, mammals, reptiles,

fish, insects and plants, including many extinct and endangered species. A 38-foot-long rorqual whale skeleton hanging from the ceiling dominates the room. Allow 1 hour, 30 minutes minimum. Mon.-Fri. 1-5, Sun. 2-4, Sept.-May; closed holidays. Donations. Phone (630) 829-6545.

MORTON ARBORETUM is on 1,700 acres about .25 mi. n. of I-88 exit SR 53N. More than 3,300 species and varieties of trees, shrubs and other plants are displayed in woodlands, wetlands, gardens and a restored native prairie. Crab apples and lilacs blossom in May. The fall foliage color display is outstanding during October. Trees and shrubs are labeled for identification along the 25 miles of trails; further information is available in the visitor center.

Open-air tram tours are available. Grounds open daily 7-7, Apr.-Oct.; 7-5, rest of year. Center open daily 9-5. Library open Tues.-Fri. 9-5, Sat. 10-4. Center and library closed Jan. 1, Thanksgiving and Dec. 25 and 31. Free. Parking $7 per private vehicle ($3 on Wed.). Pets are not permitted. Phone (630) 719-2465.

LOCKPORT (C-5) pop. 9,400, elev. 570'

Founded in 1836 when construction began on the Illinois and Michigan Canal, Lockport remains one of the best preserved canal towns in the country. A number of old locks as well as a modern lock on the Illinois Waterway can be seen.

The 1838 Gaylord Building initially was used as a materials depot during the construction of the Illinois and Michigan Canal, which linked Lake Michigan with the Mississippi River and created a trade corridor from New York to the Gulf of Mexico. An Italianate addition to the depot, built in 1859, served as a general store. A visitor center and a state museum gallery are inside. The building and canal area are part of I & M Canal National Heritage Corridor, which follows the canal route from Chicago to Peru.

Pioneer Settlement includes an early 19th-century log cabin, a village jail, a smithy, a tinsmith shop and other early buildings. Lockport Prairie Nature Preserve protects a remnant of the extensive prairies that once blanketed the Midwest.

Lockport Chamber of Commerce: 132 E. Ninth St., Lockport, IL 60441; phone (847) 634-0888.

Self-guiding tours: A walking tour through the Pioneer Settlement leads visitors past 19th-century homes, businesses and churches. Information is available from the Will County Historical Society, 803 S. State St., Lockport, IL 60441; phone (815) 838-5080.

ILLINOIS & MICHIGAN CANAL MUSEUM, 1 blk. n. of SR 7 at 803 S. State St. (SR 171), is in the original 1837 home of the canal commissioners. Displays recall 19th-century life along the canal. The Old Stone Annex Exhibit Building in the rear of the museum features displays of early banking, tools, a carriage and one of the two known scale models of Lincoln's Tomb. Daily 1-4:30, Jan. 3 to mid-Dec.; closed holidays and Thanksgiving week. Free. Phone (815) 838-5080.

LONG GROVE (B-5) pop. 4,700, elev. 733'

Originally called *Mutterscholz* by the German settlers who founded the area in the early 1800s, Long Grove began as a small farming community. By the 1930s the sleepy village fell into decline, and in the 1940s several women opened a successful antique resale shop. Other shops soon followed, thus turning the agricultural-based community into an antique haven. Today a Historic Landmark Ordinance guarantees the preservation of all the historic sites in the area—any new facades must conform to the architecture of the early 1800s.

Long Grove Visitor's Center: 307 Old McHenry Rd., Long Grove, IL 60047; phone (847) 634-0888.

Shopping areas: Historic Long Grove, at the junction of SRs 53 and 83, features some 90 shops housed in historic buildings.

MOOSEHEART (C-5) elev. 721'

Known as the Child City, Mooseheart gives educational, citizenship and moral training to children in need. The community includes a dairy farm, Baby Village, residence halls, schools, vocational centers, a museum, a church, a health center and a lake. Guided tours are available; phone (630) 859-2000.

NAPERVILLE (C-5) pop. 85,400, elev. 717'

Founded in 1831, Naperville has many restored Victorian homes downtown. The Riverwalk, a brick walkway with fountains and covered bridges, begins at the foot of Chicago Avenue and Main Street, and follows the DuPage River for several miles.

Naperville Convention & Visitors Bureau: 212 S. Webster St., Suite 104, Naperville, IL 60540-5347; phone (877) 236-2737.

[SAVE] **DuPAGE CHILDREN'S MUSEUM,** .5 mi. s. of Ogden Ave. (US 34) at 301 N. Washington St., offers children the opportunity to build a dam, fly a kite in a wind tunnel, explore the properties of sound and light and use hammers, saws and drills to construct inventions. Art, math and science related exhibits also are featured. Allow 2 hours minimum. Tues.-Sat. 9-5 (also Thurs. 5-8), Sun. noon-5; closed holidays. Admission $6.50; over 59, $5.50; under 1 free. DS, MC, VI. Phone (630) 637-8000.

[GEM] [SAVE] **NAPER SETTLEMENT** is 2 blks. w. of Washington St. at jct. Aurora Ave. and Webster St. Visitors can relive the pioneer and Victorian eras in this re-created 1831-1900 living-history village. Set on parklike grounds are a blacksmith shop, chapel, print shop, schoolhouse, log fort, meeting house and other buildings staffed by costumed interpreters. The 1883 Martin Mitchell Mansion, a grand Victorian

home, is original to the grounds. Activities include crafts, games and old-fashioned chores. Special events are held throughout the year.

Allow 3 hours minimum. Tues.-Sat. 10-4, Sun. 1-4, Apr.-Oct.; Tues.-Fri. 10-4, rest of year. Holiday hours vary; phone ahead. Admission Apr.-Oct. $6.50; over 55, $5.50; ages 4-17, $4. Admission rest of year $4.25; over 55, $3.75; ages 4-17, $3. MC, VI. Phone (630) 420-6010.

OAK BROOK (C-6) pop. 9,200, elev. 660'

West of Chicago, the suburb of Oak Brook has become an important center for international business and finance; more than 60 Fortune 500 companies are represented.

Oak Brook Area Association of Commerce and Industry: 1 Tower Ln., Suite LL20, Oakbrook Terrace, IL 60181; phone (630) 572-0616.

Shopping areas: Oakbrook Center, SR 83 and Cermak Road, lists Lord & Taylor, Marshall Field's, Neiman Marcus, Nordstrom, Saks Fifth Avenue and Sears among its stores.

CZECHOSLOVAK HERITAGE MUSEUM, LIBRARY & ARCHIVES is off I-294 Cermak Rd. exit, then just w. to 122 W. 22nd St. Dedicated to traditions and culture of Czech, Slovak and Moravian people, the museum displays dolls, puppets, crystal, ceramics, needlework, sculpture and art typical of the Czech Republic and Slovakia. Guided tours are available. Allow 1 hour minimum. Mon.-Fri. and the second Sat. of the month 10-4; closed holidays. Donations. Phone (630) 472-9909.

GRAUE MILL, on York and Spring rds. between 31st St. and Ogden Ave. (US 34), is a waterwheel gristmill dating from 1852. The milling process is demonstrated and explained. The basement is one of the few authenticated stations of the underground railroad system. A museum on the two upper floors contains items from the middle and late 1800s. Demonstrations of weaving and spinning are provided. Tues.-Sun. 10-4:30, mid-Apr. to mid-Nov. Admission $3.75; over 59, $3; ages 3-16, $1.50. Phone (630) 655-2090.

OAK PARK (B-6) pop. 53,600, elev. 630'

A suburb 9 miles west of Chicago, Oak Park reputedly is one of the world's largest communities that is governed as a village. It has been the home of several noted figures, including Ernest Hemingway, born in Oak Park in 1899, and Edgar Rice Burroughs.

Frank Lloyd Wright lived and worked in Oak Park 1889-1909, developing his distinctive Prairie style of architecture. There are 25 Wright-designed structures in Oak Park. The Frank Lloyd Wright Prairie School of Architecture National Historic District features a walking tour highlighting 13 of Wright's creations.

Oak Park Visitors Center: 158 N. Forest Ave., Oak Park, IL 60301; phone (708) 848-1500 or (888) 625-7275.

Self-guiding tours: Oak Park's diverse architecture can be explored courtesy of walking tour tapes available from the visitors center. The route, which takes approximately 1.5 to 2 hours to complete, traces the city's architectural evolution from the early Victorian period through the Prairie school to the Art Deco style. Tapes can be rented daily 10-3:30 for a fee of $6, senior citizens and children $4.

ARCHITECTURAL TOURS through local structures emphasize but are not limited to the historic district. Guided walking tours, which average 45 minutes, allow participants to view the exteriors of 13 Frank Lloyd Wright-designed buildings. Tours depart from the Frank Lloyd Wright Home and Studio at 951 Chicago Ave. Self-guiding tour audiotapes are available daily 10-3:30. Guided tours depart Sat.-Sun. at 10:30 and on the hour 11-4, Mar.-Oct.; at noon, 1 and 2, rest of year. Guided tour $8; over 64 and ages 7-18, $6. A combination rate is available with the Frank Lloyd Wright Home and Studio tour. AX, DS, MC, VI. Phone (708) 848-1976.

Frank Lloyd Wright Home and Studio, 951 Chicago Ave., offers tours of the famous architect's residence and workplace. The Wright Plus Housewalk—featuring interior tours of 10 architecturally significant buildings, some designed by Wright—is held the third Saturday in May and costs $100; phone after Mar. 1 for reservations. Home and studio tours are given Mon.-Fri. at 11, 1 and 3, Sat.-Sun. 11-3:30. Admission $8; over 65 and ages 7-18, $6. AX, DS, MC, VI. Phone (708) 848-1976.

SAVE Historic Pleasant Home, at 217 S. Home Ave., received its name due to its location at the corner of Pleasant Street and Home Avenue. George Maher designed the 30-room grand Prairie-style residence in 1897 with the use of simple geometric shapes. Guided tours are offered Thurs.-Sun. at 12:30, 1:30 and 2:30, Mar.-Nov.; at 12:30 and 1:30, rest of year. Admission $5; students with ID and ages 5-18, $3. Phone (708) 383-2654.

Unity Temple is at 875 Lake St. Designed by Frank Lloyd Wright in 1905 for a Universalist congregation, the building is an example of Wright's use of poured concrete. The congregation, now Unitarian Universalist, still occupies the building. Tours are provided by Unity Temple Restoration Foundation. Self-guiding tours Mon.-Fri. 10:30-4:30, Mar.-Nov.; 1-4, rest of year. Guided tours are given Sat.-Sun. at 1, 2 and 3. Guided tours $6; over 65 and students under 23, $4. AX, MC, VI. Phone (708) 383-8873.

ERNEST HEMINGWAY MUSEUM, 200 N. Oak Park Ave., includes samples of the author's writing. "Hemingway: The Oak Park Years" focuses on Hemingway's family life, love of nature, education and World War I and II experiences. Visitors can view an exhibit that features first-edition book jackets, photographs, a diary, artifacts and letters. A 6-minute videotape highlights the author's high school years. Other exhibits include his works on film and his writings during World War II.

Allow 1 hour minimum. Thurs.-Fri. and Sun. 1-5, Sat. 10-5; closed holidays. Admission (including Hemingway's Birthplace) $6, senior citizens and students with ID $4.50. AX, MC, VI. Phone (708) 848-2222.

HEMINGWAY'S BIRTHPLACE, 339 N. Oak Park Ave., is the 1890s home of Ernest Hemingway's maternal grandparents. Tours include the room in which Hemingway was born. Photographs of the family are displayed. Thurs.-Fri. and Sun. 1-5, Sat. 10-5; closed holidays. Admission (including Ernest Hemingway Museum) $6, senior citizens and students with ID $4.50. AX, MC, VI. Phone (708) 848-2222.

OAK PARK CONSERVATORY 615 Garfield St., features three thematic greenhouses filled with botanical specimens. The Desert House blazes with delicate cactus blooms in season; exotic plants from Hawaii, South America and China surround a lagoon with a waterfall in the Tropic House; and in the Fern House, seasonal flowering plants are displayed among the many species of ferns. Herbs, perennials and rare native flowers thrive in the

outdoor garden. Live parrots are on display throughout the buildings. Tues.-Sun. 10-4, Mon. 2-4. Donations. Phone (708) 386-4700.

ST. CHARLES (B-5) pop. 22,500, elev. 689′

An hour west of Chicago, St. Charles contains many historic buildings that have been restored to house shops, restaurants and other establishments. Visitors can explore more than a dozen antique stores housing more than 100 dealers. On the first Sunday (and preceding Saturday afternoon) of each month, the city holds one of the largest antique flea markets in the country.

St. Charles Convention and Visitors Bureau: 311 N. Second St., St. Charles, IL 60174; phone (630) 377-6161 or (800) 777-4373.

PADDLEWHEEL RIVERBOAT EXCURSIONS depart from Pottawatomie Park and cruise the scenic Fox River. Bordered by woods, the river has changed little since the Pottawatomie Indians inhabited its banks. The 4-mile cruise takes 60 minutes on weekdays and 45 minutes on weekends. Cruises depart Mon.-Fri. at 3:30, Sat. at 2, 3 and 4, Sun. at 2, 3, 4 and 5, June-Aug.; Sat.-Sun. at 2, 3 and 4 in May and Sept. 1 to mid-Oct. Fare $5; ages 2-15, $3.50. Phone (630) 584-2334.

SCHAUMBURG (B-5) pop. 68,600, elev. 799′

MEDIEVAL TIMES DINNER AND TOURNAMENT, 2001 N. Roselle Rd., presents a dinner show inside a replica of a medieval-style castle. Visitors enjoy a four-course feast served by wenches and serfs while knights on horseback compete in tournament games, jousting matches and sword fights. Contenders perform various feats on horseback, cheered on by guests in color-coded crowns that correspond to a particular knight.

Allow 2 hours minimum. Wed.-Thurs. at 7:30, Fri.-Sat. at 8, Sun. at 4. Hours may vary; phone ahead. Admission $37.95-$40.35; ages 1-12, $28.95. Reservations are required. AX, DS, MC, VI. Phone (847) 843-3900 or (800) 544-2001.

SPRING VALLEY NATURE SANCTUARY, .5 mi. w. of Meacham Rd. at 1111 E. Schaumburg Rd., is a 135-acre nature preserve that provides habitats for a variety of plants, birds and other wildlife. The Vera Meineke Nature Observation Building is a visitor center that offers a natural history library, interactive and seasonal exhibits, and a Backyard for Wildlife display. An 1880s living-history farm also is on the grounds. There are 3.5 miles of pedestrian nature trails throughout the preserve. Picnicking, bicycling and pets are not permitted.

Allow 1 hour minimum. Grounds open daily 8-8, Apr.-Oct.; 8-5, rest of year. Center open daily 9-5. Closed Jan. 1., Thanksgiving and Dec. 25. Free. Phone (847) 985-2100.

SKOKIE (B-6) pop. 59,400

SKOKIE NORTHSHORE SCULPTURE PARK, off I-94 at Dempster Ave., 2.8 mi. e. to McCormick Blvd., then just s., presents more than 70 sculptures on 2 landscaped acres along the Chicago River's north channel. Benches line a walking and bicycling trail. Self-guiding tour brochures are available. Allow 2 hours minimum. The park is open daily 24 hours. Free. Phone (847) 679-4265.

SOUTH HOLLAND (C-6)
pop. 22,100, elev. 600′

South Holland was founded by Dutch farmers in the 1840s; a few farmhouses of the era remain. The village's population increased dramatically following World War II, but this Chicago suburb has retained its small-town charm.

Chicago Southland Convention & Visitors Bureau: 2304 173rd St. Lansing, IL 60438; phone (888) 895-8233.

MIDWEST CARVERS MUSEUM, s. of US 6 at 16236 Vincennes Ave. (Thorton Blue Island Rd.), is in a restored farmhouse surrounded by other restored buildings. Hundreds of items, hand carved by local and national woodcarvers, represent examples of various woodcarving techniques. Mon.-Sat. 10-4; closed Jan. 1 and Dec. 25. Donations. Phone (708) 331-6011.

UNION (A-3) pop. 500, elev. 836′

DONLEY'S WILD WEST TOWN MUSEUM is 4.5 mi. n.w. of I-90 exit Marengo/US 20. This modern museum complex has antique phonographs and music boxes, telegraph equipment and collections pertaining to Thomas Edison as well as cowboy collectibles. The "Streets of Yesterday" includes a lamp shop, a doctor's office and a gun shop; a theater offers old-time movies. Visitors can pan for pyrite, turquoise and silver.

Pony rides and train rides are available. Wild West gunfights occur three times daily. Open daily 10-6, Memorial Day-Labor Day; Sat.-Sun. 10-6, Apr. 1-day before Memorial Day and day after Labor Day-Oct. 31. Admission $12.50, under 3 free. DS, MC, VI. Phone (815) 923-9000.

[SAVE] **ILLINOIS RAILWAY MUSEUM,** 1 mi. e. via Jefferson St., displays steam engines, streetcars, interurban electric cars, steam railroad cars and an 1851 railroad station. Admission includes unlimited rides on a diesel-powered train.

Mon.-Fri. 10-4, Sat.-Sun. 10:30-5, Memorial Day-Labor Day; Sat.-Sun. 10:30-5, May 1-day before Memorial Day and day after Labor Day-Oct. 31; Sun. 10:30-5, in Apr. Diesel trains run Sat.-Sun., May-Sept. Admission Mon.-Fri. $6; over 61 and ages 5-11, $4; family rate $20. Admission Sat.-Sun. $8; over 61 and ages 5-11, $6; family rate $30. Admission when train runs $9; over 61 and ages 5-11, $7; family rate $35. Rates may be higher for special events. DS, MC, VI. Phone (815) 923-4000 or (800) 244-7245.

VERNON HILLS (B-5) pop. 15,300, elev. 683'

SAVE **THE CUNEO MUSEUM AND GARDENS** is at 1350 N. Milwaukee Ave. Printing magnate John Cuneo purchased the 32-room, pink stucco Venetian-style mansion in 1937. Highlights include a chapel with stained-glass windows, a porcelain gallery, a 40-foot-high great hall with arcaded balconies, frescoed ceilings, a gilt grand piano and 17th-century tapestries. Seventy-five acres of landscaped grounds include a deer park, a conservatory, lakes and antique statuary.

Allow 2 hours minimum. Tues.-Sun. 10-5, Feb.-Dec.; closed Thanksgiving and Dec. 24-25. Tours are offered; phone ahead. Admission $10; over 55, $9; under 12, $5. Grounds only $5 per private vehicle. MC, VI. Phone (847) 362-3042.

VOLO (A-5) pop. 200, elev. 790'

The state's only open-water quaking bog is preserved in the Volo Bog State Natural Area. A receding glacier left an unusual formation now filled with quaking sphagnum moss and a wide variety of plant and animal life. Ferns, marsh marigolds, leatherleaf and blue flag iris are in abundance, along with many songbirds and waterfowls. Free weekend tours are available; phone (815) 344-1294.

VOLO ANTIQUE MALLS AND AUTO MUSEUM, 1 blk. n. of SR 12 and SR 120 on Volo Village Rd., is a complex that contains more than 250 vintage automobiles and antique malls with approximately 150 dealers. Daily 10-5; closed Easter, Thanksgiving and Dec. 25 Admission $5.95; over 65, $3.95; ages 6-12, $2.75. Phone (815) 385-3644.

WAUCONDA (B-5) pop. 6,300, elev. 803'

LAKE COUNTY MUSEUM is in Lakewood Forest Preserve at 27277 Forest Preserve Dr. American Indian artifacts, Victorian-era clothing and military memorabilia along with more than 15,000 historical maps and documents tell the story of Lake County. The museum also houses the Curt Teich Postcard Archives, a collection of more than 370,000 images once used by the Chicago-based postcard publisher. Mon.-Sat. 11-4:30, Sun. 1-4:30. Admission $5.50; ages 4-18, $2.75, under 18 free on Tues. MC, VI. Phone (847) 526-7878.

WHEATON (C-5) pop. 51,500, elev. 746'

Founded by brothers Jesse and Warren Wheaton, Wheaton is the home of Wheaton College, established in 1860. The college, railroad right-of-way and courthouse were given to the town by the founding fathers. About 24 religious publishers and organizations are headquartered in Wheaton. Such celebrated citizens as Billy Graham, Elbert Gary, Col. R.R. McCormick and Red Grange are the subjects of exhibits, mural displays and films at the DuPage Heritage Gallery/Red Grange Archives, 421 N. County Farm Rd.; phone (630) 682-7000.

Wheaton Chamber of Commerce: 108 E. Wesley St., Wheaton, IL 60187; phone (630) 668-6464.

BILLY GRAHAM CENTER, on the Wheaton College campus at 500 E. College Ave., has a museum, a library and archives devoted to Christian evangelism. The museum exhibits a visual history of the growth of evangelism in the United States from Colonial times to the present. Also featured are temporary exhibits about religious history and Christian art. Allow 1 hour, 30 minutes minimum. Mon.-Sat. 9:30-5:30, Sun. 1-5. Donations. Phone (630) 752-5909.

CANTIGNY is 3 mi. n. of I-88, then 1.5 blks. s. on Winfield Rd. The 500-acre grounds were formerly the property of Col. Robert R. McCormick, editor and publisher of the *Chicago Tribune* and a member of the First Infantry Division. The property includes 10 acres of formal gardens, wooded walks and picnic facilities. Outdoor concerts are held on the grounds at the gazebo Sundays at 3, Memorial Day through Labor Day.

Allow 2 hours minimum. Grounds open Tues.-Sun. 9-dusk. Museums open Tues.-Sun. 10-5, Memorial Day-Labor Day; Tues.-Sun. 10-4, Mar. 1-day before Memorial Day and day after Labor Day-Dec. 30; Fri.-Sun. 10-4 in Feb. Closed Thanksgiving and Dec. 25. Free. Parking $5. Phone (630) 668-5161.

First Division Museum, 1 S. 151 Winfield Rd., honors the U.S. Army's First Infantry Division, with units dating from 1776 as well as the men and women who have served in World War I, World War II, Vietnam and Desert Storm. Designed to allow visitors to experience what it was like to walk through war-torn France or land on Omaha Beach on D-Day, the museum also contains archives and an outdoor tank park. Phone (630) 668-5185.

Robert R. McCormick Museum, 1 S. 151 Winfield Rd., is the restored Georgian residence of Colonel McCormick and his grandfather, Joseph Medill. The museum contains antique furnishings, carpets and paintings; sword and miniature cannon collections; and an Art Deco bar and theater. A slide show is included in the tour. Phone (630) 668-5161.

COSLEY ZOO, 1356 Gary Ave. at Jewell Rd., is a small zoo with domestic and wild animals. Allow 1 hour minimum. Daily 9-9, day after Thanksgiving-Dec. 23; Mon.-Thurs. 9-4, Fri.-Sun. 10-6, Apr.-Oct.; daily 9-4, rest of year. Donations. Phone (630) 665-5534.

DUPAGE COUNTY HISTORICAL MUSEUM is at 102 E. Wesley St. The 1891 Richardsonian Romanesque building contains exhibits highlighting more than 150 years of county history. Displays include changing costume exhibits, period settings and a model railroad. Hands-on activities are available. Allow 30 minutes minimum. Museum open Mon., Wed. and Fri.-Sat. 10-4, Sun. 1-4; closed major holidays. Railroad operates 1:30-3:30, third and fifth Sat. of every month. Free. Phone (630) 682-7343.

WILMETTE (B-6) pop. 26,700, elev. 614'

The site of Wilmette, on Lake Michigan, originally belonged to an American Indian woman named Archange, who received a land grant under the Treaty of Prairie du Chien in 1829. She named the property for her French-Canadian husband, Antoine Ouilmette.

As the community developed, a small portion became known as "No Man's Land," as it was at this site that fireworks, illegal in other localities, were sold; the area was annexed into Wilmette in 1942. Wilmette attained further notoriety in 1860, when a lumber schooner struck the *Lady Elgin* and 293 people died. Dramatic changes took place 1908-10 when the Chicago Sanitary District experimented with a new waterway system. The landfills created by this work were later transformed into Gilson Park. The city is an exclusive residential area with many old homes on large acreages.

Wilmette Chamber of Commerce: 1150 Wilmette Ave., Wilmette, IL 60091; phone (847) 251-3800.

BAHA'I HOUSE OF WORSHIP, 100 Linden Ave. at Sheridan Rd., was built by the followers of Baha'u'llah, founder of the Baha'i faith. Symbolizing its basic principles of the oneness of God, religion and mankind, the temple is a nine-sided structure surmounted by a dome and surrounded by a formal garden. Daily 10-10, Apr.-Sept.; 10-5, rest of year. Tours are available daily 10-5 by request. Devotions are held Mon.-Sat. at 12:15, Sun. at 1:15 and are often followed by informative meetings in the visitor center. Free. Phone (847) 853-2300.

KOHL CHILDREN'S MUSEUM is at 165 Green Bay Rd.; take I-94 Lake Ave. exit 3 mi. e. to Green Bay Rd., then 5 blks. s. Based on the concept that children learn by doing, the museum is structured to allow a hands-on understanding of the world of science, basic life skills, the arts and world cultures. Exhibits include Music Makers, which allows children to create and play music; a child-size grocery store; People, a celebration of diversity; and All Aboard, a journey through Chicago.

Allow 2 hours minimum. Mon.-Sat. 9:30-5, Sun. noon-5, Memorial Day-Labor Day; Tues.-Sat. 9:30-5, Sun. noon-5, Mon. 9:30-noon, rest of year. Closed major holidays. Admission $6, senior citizens $5, under 1 free. AX, DS, MC, VI. Phone (847) 256-6056, or 251-7781 for activities.

WINFIELD (C-5) pop. 7,100, elev. 750'

KLINE CREEK FARM, on SR 43 (County Farm Rd.), .5 mi. s. of SR 64 (North Ave.), is a living-history farm depicting farm life during the late 19th century. Visitors can walk through the smokehouse, an apiary, a kitchen garden, a pumphouse and a chicken coop with costumed guides. Demonstrations and tours are available. Thurs.-Mon. 9-5. Free. Phone (630) 876-5900.

This ends listings for the Chicago Vicinity.
The following page resumes the alphabetical listings of cities in Illinois.

CLINTON (C-3) pop. 7,400, elev. 737'

A life-size statue of Abraham Lincoln created by Belgian artist Van den Bergen marks the site on Clinton's city square where Lincoln delivered his renowned aphorism "You can fool all the people part of the time and part of the people all the time, but you cannot fool all the people all the time." While campaigning against Stephen Douglas for a seat in the U.S. Senate in 1858, Lincoln gave his quotable speech in response to an accusation by Douglas.

Clinton Lake, with more than 130 miles of shoreline, is stocked with a wide variety of game fish and is an important stopover point for migrating waterfowls. Weldon Springs contains a 28-acre lake and a winter sled run. *See Recreation Chart.*

Clinton Chamber of Commerce: 100 S. Center St., Suite 100, Clinton, IL 61727; phone (217) 935-3364.

C. H. MOORE HOMESTEAD, 1 blk. e. of US 51 at 219 E. Woodlawn, was built in 1863 for John Bishop, a prosperous grain and lumber dealer. The house incorporates both Italianate and Second Empire styles of domestic architecture. Furnishings are early Victorian with a French influence. Exhibits include a doll collection, World War I weapons, American Indian artifacts and articles devoted to the history of DeWitt County.

A farm, carriage barn, covered bridge and general store are on the grounds. Tues.-Sat. 10-5, Sun. 1-5, first weekend in Apr.-Dec. 31; closed Easter, Thanksgiving and Dec. 25. Admission $2; ages 12-18, $1. Phone (217) 935-6066.

COAL VALLEY (B-2) pop. 3,800, elev. 700'

NIABI ZOO, 13010 Niabi Zoo Rd., lists an elephant, lions, tigers, bears and zebras among its inhabitants. Primate, bird and reptile exhibits also are available. Daily 9:30-5, mid-Apr. through Labor Day; otherwise varies. Admission $4.25; over 62, $3.25; ages 3-11, $3; free to all Tues. Zoo train $1.50. Phone (309) 799-5107.

COLLINSVILLE (E-2) pop. 22,400

Horseradishes, log cabins and coal all are a part of Collinsville's heritage that began when the town's first inhabitant built a log cabin overlooking the Mississippi basin in 1810. The city's name changed from Downing Station to Collinsville in 1825, and soon it became a bustling coal town.

Collinsville Convention and Visitors Bureau: 1 Gateway Dr., Collinsville, IL 62234; phone (618) 345-4999 or (800) 289-2388.

CAHOKIA MOUNDS STATE HISTORIC SITE, off I-255 exit 24 (Collinsville Rd.), then w. 1.5 mi., is a 2,200-acre site of 65 preserved American Indian tribal mounds. Monks Mound, the site's centerpiece, covers more than 14 acres at its base and is 100 feet tall. Evidence of a once-flourishing Mississippian civilization—the center of an enormous trade empire distinguished by social and political activity—spans the years A.D. 900-1500. At its peak Cahokia had about 20,000 residents.

Guided tours are available. Picnicking is permitted. Historic site and interpretive center open daily 9-5; closed Jan. 1, Martin Luther King Jr. Day, Presidents Day, Veterans Day, Thanksgiving and Dec. 25. Admission $2, children $1. Phone (618) 346-5160.

DANVILLE (C-4) pop. 33,800, elev. 602'

Formerly the site of a Painkeshaw Indian village where several trails converged, Danville was discovered by French explorers in search of salt, a precious commodity. The British, by right of conquest, were the next to colonize the area. Following the American capture of the British fort at Vincennes, Ind., by George Rogers Clark, the region temporarily became part of the Commonwealth of Virginia.

Named for first settler Dan Beckwith, the town was platted in 1827; it was incorporated as a city in 1869. Once a major center for the production of coal and clay, Danville now supports a diversity of industry. A landmark of note is Danville Soldiers Monument, a work by Lorado Taft at Main and Gilbert streets.

Danville Area Convention and Visitors Bureau: 100 W. Main St., Suite 146, P.O. Box 992, Danville, IL 61834-0992; phone (217) 442-2096 or (800) 383-4386.

[SAVE] **VERMILION COUNTY MUSEUM,** 4 mi. n. off I-74 exit SR 1 to 116 N. Gilbert, was built in 1855 and is furnished in the Victorian style. Of note is a balcony from which Abraham Lincoln spoke while he was running for the U.S. Senate. The bedroom in which Lincoln stayed is preserved. Alternating exhibits about natural history, quilts, photography and industry are presented; an herb garden also is on the grounds. The visitor center is a replica of the first courthouse in which Lincoln practiced law. Tues.-Sat. 10-5, Sun. 1-5; closed holidays. Admission $2; ages 6-14, 50c. Phone (217) 442-2922 or (800) 383-4386.

DECATUR (C-3) pop. 83,900, elev. 679'

Decatur, named for American naval hero Commodore Stephen Decatur, became the seat of Macon County in 1829. The city is known for its historic landmarks, mainly concentrated within an 80-acre tract of land. The historic district is said to contain buildings of every architectural style from the Civil War to the Depression eras. Houses of significance include Millikin Homestead, an 1875 mansion on N. Pine Street; the 1874 Oglesby Mansion on W. William; and the Prairie Style homes on Millikin Place, designed by Frank Lloyd Wright.

In 1830 Abraham Lincoln and his family arrived northeast of Decatur and built a log cabin along the

The Lincoln Highway

The horseless carriage rolled onto the American landscape in the 1890s. By 1910 there were more than 450,000 registered automobiles, yet the country still lacked a public road system.

Organized movements for better roads brought issues to the attention of the federal government, which had not participated in major road construction since it funded the National Road project in 1806.

But one particular initiative captured the public's support with a unique idea. In 1913 Carl Fisher—the man who built the Indianapolis Motor Speedway in 1909—and automobile industry leaders chartered the Lincoln Highway Association for the purpose of defining a direct coast-to-coast automobile route.

The LHA's first official act was to delineate a 3,389-mile, 12-state continuous route from New York to California—one that would be passable before the opening of the 1915 Panama-Pacific International Exposition in San Francisco. Although not perfect, the throughway was ready as promised, and a motion picture of America's transcontinental highway was shown at the exposition. Over time, the association improved surfaces by using better materials, shortened the driving distance with realignments and published guidebooks about the Lincoln Highway. Automobile touring had never been so good.

Through example, the LHA educated the public as well as state and federal governments about the value of good roads for almost 15 years. The 1919 moving of a military convoy over the "Lincolnway" foretold the utility of an integrated highway system for national defense and interstate commerce.

With the 1921 Federal Highway Act came the funds for states to construct and maintain connecting arteries. Four years later the United States adopted a highway numbering system, and most of the Lincoln route became US 30, 40 and 50. The Sangamon River. Working as a farmer and rail-splitter, 21-year-old Lincoln made his first political speech in what is now Lincoln Square. Discouraged after a severe winter, the family abandoned its homestead after only 1 year. Lincoln later moved to Decatur and worked as a circuit-riding attorney-at-law.

Statues of Lincoln as a young man stand on the campus of Millikin University, 1184 N. Main St., and in front of the county courthouse at 253 E. Wood St., where the first post of the Grand Army of the Republic was established in 1866. A bronze replica of Macon County's first courthouse, where Lincoln practiced law, is in Lincoln Square. The original log courthouse was relocated to Macon County Historical Society Museum Complex (see attraction listing).

Lake Decatur, off US 36, is 14 miles long and covers more than 2,800 acres. The lake offers boating, fishing and picnicking.

Decatur Area Convention and Visitors Bureau: 202 E. North St., Decatur, IL 62523; phone (217) 423-7000 or (800) 331-4479.

Self-guiding tours: Information about walking tours of the historic district is available at the convention and visitors bureau.

BIRKS MUSEUM is at 1184 W. Main St. on the Millikin University campus. The museum contains more than a thousand pieces of porcelain, fine china, glassware and crystal, including rare pieces from the 15th and 16th centuries. Special exhibits are held throughout the year. Daily 1-4, Aug.-May; by appointment rest of year. Free. Phone (217) 424-6337.

CHILDREN'S MUSEUM OF ILLINOIS, .5 mi. s. of US 36 at 55 S. Country Club Rd. in Scovill Park, features interactive displays including a virtual reality exhibit, a bubble-making area and a 22-foot vertical maze. Toddletown is designed to interest preschoolers. Tues.-Fri. 9:30-4:30 (also Mon. 9:30-4:30, Memorial Day-Labor Day), Sat. 10-5, Sun. 1-5; closed holidays. Admission $3.50; over 50 and ages 3-16, $3. MC, VI. Phone (217) 423-5437.

MACON COUNTY HISTORICAL SOCIETY MUSEUM COMPLEX, 5580 North Fork Rd., is a 3-acre complex that preserves the heritage of the area with changing and permanent exhibits of artifacts dating back to 1829—the Macon County settlement era. The complex includes galleries, a film about Lincoln in Macon county and a historic prairie village. Allow 1 hour minimum. Tues.-Sun. 1-4; closed holidays. Admission $2; ages 12-18, $1. Phone (217) 422-4919.

ROCK SPRINGS CENTER FOR ENVIRONMENTAL DISCOVERY, 3 mi. s.w. on SR 48 to Rock Springs Rd., then 1 mi. w. to Brozio Ln., provides educational and recreational activities and preserves plants and animals native to Macon County. Hiking trails span 6.5 miles. Trails are open December through March for cross-country skiing (weather permitting). The Rock Springs trail is 2.2 mi. and is open to bicyclists, joggers, hikers and the physically impaired. Living history programs are held in the 19th-century restored Homestead Prairie

Farm. Interpretive hikes, cultural programs and events are held on weekends and by appointment.

Allow 30 minutes minimum. Visitor center open Mon.-Sat. 9-4:30, Sun. 1-4:30; closed Jan. 1, Easter, Thanksgiving and Dec. 25. Trails open daily 8-dusk. Free. Phone (217) 423-4913 or 423-7708.

SCOVILL ZOO, 71 S. Country Club Rd., is home to 500 animals from six continents. The zoo contains an Oriental garden, a petting zoo, a picnic area, a train and a playground. Daily 10-8, Memorial Day-Labor Day; Mon.-Fri. 10-4, Sat.-Sun. 10-6:30, mid-Apr. through day before Memorial Day and day after Labor Day to mid-Oct. Admission $2.75; over 62, $1.50; ages 2-12, $1. Train ride $1; ages 2-12, 75c. MC, VI. Phone (217) 421-7435.

DEKALB (A-3) pop. 34,900, elev. 886′

Named for Baron Johann De Kalb, who served in the Revolution, DeKalb became synonymous with the first barbed wire manufacturing company and was nicknamed "Barb City." The city boasts one of the few remaining Egyptian-style movie palaces, restored to its early 20th-century appearance.

DeKalb Chamber of Commerce: 164 E. Lincoln Hwy., DeKalb, IL 60115; phone (815) 756-6306.

ELLWOOD HOUSE MUSEUM, 509 N. First St. at Augusta Ave., was built by Isaac Ellwood, the principal manufacturer of barbed wire. Guided tours of the 1879 Victorian mansion include all four floors, highlighted by an English-style living room and a three-story rotunda. Featured on the grounds are gardens; a visitor center with three exhibit galleries; and the "Little House," a Victorian-era playhouse.

Allow 1 hour, 30 minutes minimum. Guided tours Tues.-Fri. at 1 and 3, Sat.-Sun. at 1, 2 and 3, Mar. 1-early Dec.; closed holidays. Admission $5; ages 6-14, $1. Phone (815) 756-4609.

DES PLAINES—*see Chicago p. 76.*

DIXON (B-3) pop. 15,100, elev. 718′

Originally the site of a tavern and trading post served by a ferry on the Rock River, Dixon was associated with two U.S. presidents. Abraham Lincoln met with Jefferson Davis and Zachary Taylor here in 1832 during the Black Hawk War. Ronald Reagan, born in nearby Tampico, grew up in Dixon, the northernmost city on The Regan Trail. The trail includes eleven communities that played important roles in Regan's life in Illinois. A scenic portion of SR 2 follows the Rock River 41 miles from Dixon northeast to Rockford, intersecting SRs 64 and 72 along the way.

Dixon Area Chamber of Commerce: 101 W. Second St., Suite 210, Dixon, IL 61021; phone (815) 284-3361.

LINCOLN MONUMENT STATE MEMORIAL, on Lincoln Statue Dr. between Galena and Hennepin aves., marks the site of the Dixon Blockhouse. Jefferson Davis, Zachary Taylor and Abraham Lincoln met on the site

The Lincoln Highway
(*continued*)

association disbanded in 1928, but not before it engaged Boy Scout troops across the country to place some 3,000 concrete Lincoln Highway markers along the route in all 12 states: New York, New Jersey, Pennsylvania, Ohio, Indiana, Illinois, Iowa, Nebraska, Wyoming, Utah, Nevada and California. Many of these markers still exist.

Illinois boasted some of the finest roads of any Lincoln Highway state. The old route still can be traced following US 30 from Dyer, Ind., through Chicago Heights and around **Chicago** proper to **Joliet,** then **Aurora.** North of Aurora, SR 31 runs to Geneva and connects with SR 38. Westbound SR 38 passes through **DeKalb,** where the first "seedling mile"—a sample length of paved roadway—was laid by the association in 1914, then through Franklin Grove, home of the new Lincoln Highway Association. Original Lincoln Highway markers can be found in this area. Near **Sterling** US 30 marks the final link to Iowa, just across the Mississippi River from Fulton.

Look for these Illinois Lincoln Highway landmark towns in this TourBook guide.

For more information about the old Lincoln Highway, contact the new Lincoln Highway Association, P.O. Box 308, Franklin Grove, IL 61031; phone (815) 456-3030.

during the Black Hawk War in 1832. Overlooking the Rock River, this small park has a statue of Lincoln as a volunteer in the Black Hawk War.

RONALD REAGAN'S BOYHOOD HOME, off Galena Ave. at 816 S. Hennepin Ave., was the residence of Ronald Wilson Reagan and his family 1920-23. The house has been restored and furnished to appear as it did during that period. Guided tours are offered. Allow 30 minutes minimum. Mon.-Sat. 10-4, Sun. 1-4, Apr.-Nov.; Sat. 10-4, Sun. 1-4, Feb.-Mar. Closed Easter and Thanksgiving. Free. Phone (815) 288-3404.

EAST DUNDEE—*see Chicago p. 76.*

EAST PEORIA (C-3) pop. 21,400, elev. 480'

CASINOS

• *Par-a-dice* **Hotel and Casino,** 21 Blackjack Blvd. on the riverfront. Daily 8:30 a.m.-4:30 a.m. Phone (309) 698-7711, or (800) 727-2342 from Illinois and surrounding areas.

EAST ST. LOUIS (E-2)
pop. 40,900, elev. 418'

On the Mississippi River opposite St. Louis, East St. Louis was colonized by the French, who built a mission a few miles south at the village of Cahokia in 1699. Capt. James Piggott helped promote permanent settlement of the region when he established a ferry in 1795. Lots in Illinoistown, a village near the ferry, were auctioned off.

River traffic and trade, westward expansion and the development of the area's natural resource, coal, hastened expansion of the site. The coal was pulled by horses over wooden rails along the riverbanks; some note that this means of transporting the mineral constituted claim to the first railroad in the state. The area is now a railroad center.

The Gateway Geyser, Front Street and Trendley Avenue, is one of the world's highest fountains, reaching 627 feet and covering 6.4 acres. Holding 5 million gallons of water, the fountain is centered directly across from the Gateway Arch.

Fairmount Park Race Track, in Fairmount City at Collinsville Road and I-255, offers Thoroughbred racing; phone (314) 436-1516 for schedule.

Note: Policies concerning admittance of children to pari-mutuel betting facilities vary. Phone for information.

Greater East St. Louis Chamber of Commerce: 327 Missouri Ave., Room 602, East St. Louis, IL 62201; phone (618) 271-2855.

CASINOS

• **Casino Queen and Crown Hotel,** directly across from the Gateway Arch at 200 S. Front St. Daily 9 a.m.-6:30 a.m. Phone (618) 874-5000 or (800) 777-0777.

EDWARDSVILLE (D-2)
pop. 14,600, elev. 433'

Edwardsville has two historic areas that provide a glimpse of its past: the St. Louis Street Historic District and the LeClaire Historic District. Southern Illinois University at Edwardsville encompasses a picturesque 2,600-acre campus.

Edwardsville-Glen Carbon Chamber of Commerce: 115 S. Main St., P.O. Box 568, Edwardsville, IL 62025; phone (618) 656-7600.

MADISON COUNTY HISTORICAL MUSEUM AND ARCHIVAL LIBRARY, 715 N. Main St., is housed in a restored Federal-style residence built in 1836. The museum contains period furnishings, American Indian and pioneer artifacts, antique displays and a variety of changing seasonal exhibits that include quilts, needlework and historic costumes. A history and genealogy reference library is next to the museum. Allow 1 hour minimum. Wed.-Fri. 9-4, Sun. 1-4; closed holidays. Donations. Phone (618) 656-7562.

ELGIN—*see Chicago p. 77.*

ELLIS GROVE (E-2) pop. 400, elev. 592'

FORT KASKASKIA STATE HISTORIC SITE, 10 mi. n. off SR 3, occupies 275 acres on the Mississippi River. The fort, built during the French and Indian War, was destroyed by the townspeople to prevent it from falling into British hands. Garrison Hill Cemetery also is on the grounds. Camping is available. Allow 30 minutes minimum. Daily dawn-dusk. Donations. Phone (618) 859-3741.

Pierre Menard State Historic Site is at the foot of the hill where Fort Kaskaskia stood. Pierre Menard was the presiding officer of the territorial legislature and became the first lieutenant governor of Illinois in 1818. Built in 1802, his French Colonial-style home contains some of the original furnishings. The house also has a small museum and offers a slide show about local history. Behind the home is an original smokehouse and herb garden.

Daily 9-5, Mar.-Oct.; 9-4, rest of year. Closed Jan. 1, Veterans Day, Election Day, Thanksgiving and Dec. 25. Donations. Phone (618) 859-3031.

ELMHURST—*see Chicago p. 77.*

ELSAH (D-2) pop. 900, elev. 450'

An important steamboat stop on the Mississippi in the 19th century, Elsah has managed to retain the characteristics of a bygone era. The picturesque community, nestled in the river bluffs, has quaint stone cottages and winding, flower-lined streets. Elsah lies along the Great River Road, a popular daytrip route northwest of St. Louis known for scenic countryside set against the backdrop of the Mississippi and Illinois rivers.

EVANSTON—*see Chicago p. 77.*

FREEPORT (A-2) pop. 25,800, elev. 760'

A boulder and life-size statue in Freeport mark the site of the second Lincoln-Douglas debate of

1858. According to historians Stephen A. Douglas' renowned "Freeport Doctrine" speech helped to make Abraham Lincoln president and hastened the outbreak of the Civil War. Krape Park, about 100 acres on S. Park Boulevard and Empire Street, contains a creek, carousel, playground and picnic facilities.

Stephenson County Convention and Visitors Bureau: 2047 AYP Rd., Freeport, IL 61032; phone (815) 233-1357 or (800) 369-2955.

SAVE **FREEPORT ARTS CENTER,** 121 N. Harlem Ave., features six permanent galleries containing varied types of works—European, antiquities, Asian, Native American, contemporary and oceanic. The museum also houses rotating exhibits. Guided tours are available. Allow 1 hour minimum. Tues.-Sun. 10-5 (also Tues. 5-6); closed major holidays. Admission $3, over 60 and students with ID $2. Phone (815) 235-9755.

STEPHENSON COUNTY HISTORICAL SOCIETY MUSEUM, 1440 S. Carroll Ave., is in the Oscar Taylor Home, a two-story 1857 stone house surrounded by trees brought west by covered wagon. Noted as a stop on the underground railroad, the museum features 19th-century furnishings. On the grounds are a log cabin, an old schoolhouse, a farm museum and an arboretum containing 60 types of trees.

Museum Wed.-Sun. noon-4, May-Oct.; Fri.-Sun. noon-4, rest of year. Arboretum daily 9-dusk. Museum $3; ages 6-12, $1. Arboretum free. Phone (815) 232-8419.

GALENA (A-1) pop. 3,600, elev. 602′

Galena was once the largest Mississippi River port north of St. Louis and the center of trade for the upper Mississippi lead mine region. During the mid-19th century 80 percent of all lead mining in the world was done in this area. After the Civil War the town's prominence faded, but it remained a focal point of local trade until the early 20th century.

Galena is noteworthy for some of the finest period architecture in the Midwest. Galena's restored 19th-century homes include examples of Greek Revival, Italianate, Queen Anne, Second Empire and Federal architecture. Home tours are offered during the second full weekend in June and the last full weekend in September. Tour operators also offer guided tours throughout the year.

Galena/Jo Daviess County Convention and Visitors Bureau: 720 Park Ave., Galena, IL 61036; phone (815) 777-3557 or (800) 747-9377.

Self-guiding tours: Maps outlining a walking tour of historic Main and Bench streets are available at the visitor information centers at 101 Bouthillier and 121 N. Commerce sts.

SAVE **BELVEDERE MANSION,** 1008 Park Ave., was built in 1857 by J. Russell Jones, a steamboat owner and ambassador to Belgium. The 22-room Italianate mansion contains decorative arts,

items from Liberace's estate, draperies from "Gone With the Wind" and period furnishings. Daily 11-4 (also Sat. 4-5), Memorial Day-Oct. 31. Admission $10, ages 6-15, $3. Combination ticket with Dowling House $15; ages 6-15, $7. Phone (815) 777-0747.

SAVE **DOWLING HOUSE,** Main and Diagonal sts., was built in 1826 and is reputedly the oldest house in Galena. Restored, it contains artifacts and household utensils. Daily 10-5 (also Sat. 5-6), May-Oct.; Fri.-Sun. 10-4, Nov.-Dec. and in Apr. Admission $7; ages 6-15, $3.50. Combination ticket with Belvedere Mansion $15; ages 6-15, $7. Phone (815) 777-1250.

GALENA/JO DAVIESS COUNTY HISTORY MUSEUM, at 211 S. Bench St., highlights Galena's history. Exhibits about mining, steamboating and Gen. Ulysses S. Grant and the Civil War are featured along with period clothing and other artifacts. Featured in the 19th-century mansion is Thomas Nast's painting "Peace in Union," depicting Gen. Robert E. Lee's surrender to Grant. A brief video is shown hourly. Daily 9-4:30; closed Jan. 1, Easter, Thanksgiving and Dec. 24-25 and 31. Admission $4; ages 10-18, $3; under 10 free with adult. Phone (815) 777-9129.

OLD MARKET HOUSE STATE HISTORIC SITE, Market Sq., was built in 1845 and is one of the oldest remaining market houses in the Midwest. Until 1936 it also served as a city hall and public meeting place. The restored building contains numerous exhibits. Thurs.-Mon. 9-5; closed holidays. Hours may vary; phone ahead. Admission $2; under 19, $1. Phone (815) 777-2570 or 777-3310.

GEM **ULYSSES S. GRANT HOME STATE HISTORIC SITE,** 500 Bouthillier St., was presented by the citizens of Galena to General Grant on his return from the Civil War in 1865. He lived in the home until 1867 when he became secretary of war, and again 1879-81. The 1860 house contains many of Grant's possessions and original furnishings. Daily 9-4:45; closed Jan. 1, Martin Luther King Jr. Day, Presidents Day, Election Day, Veterans Day, Thanksgiving and Dec. 25. Admission $3; under 18, $1. Phone (815) 777-0248 or 777-3310.

VINEGAR HILL LEAD MINE, 6 mi. n. on SR 84 at 8885 N. Three Pines Rd., was founded by John Furlong, an Irish soldier captured and pressed into military service by the British. Sent to Canada, he deserted and came to the east bank of the Mississippi River to mine lead. Guided 30-minute tours are offered, and a museum contains artifacts from the area's early mining days. Daily 9-5, June-Aug.; Sat.-Sun. 9-5 in May and Sept.-Oct. Admission $5, students with ID $2.50, under 5 free. Phone (815) 777-0855.

GALESBURG (B-2) pop. 33,500, elev. 781′

Presbyterian minister George Washington Gale, for whom Galesburg was named, led a group of

Eastern pioneers to this site in 1836 to establish a college-centered community. The institution became Knox College.

Both the city and college were important to the underground railroad. The town was a station; the college was the site of one of the Lincoln-Douglas debates about slavery. On South Street, Knox College's Old Main was built in 1857 and is the only existing building of the 1858 Lincoln-Douglas debate sites. Two bronze plaques with the likenesses of Lincoln and Douglas can be found on the east wall.

Lake Storey Recreational Area offers 600 acres for outdoor activities including fishing, swimming, golf, paddleboating, bicycling and picnicking.

Galesburg Area Convention and Visitors Bureau: 2163 E. Main St., P.O. Box 60, Galesburg, IL 61402-0060; phone (309) 343-2485.

Shopping areas: The three-story Historic Galesburg Antique Mall, on the corner of Main and Seminary streets, houses antiques and collectibles. The downtown Seminary Street Historical Commercial District encompasses two blocks with specialty shops and restaurants in restored buildings.

CARL SANDBURG STATE HISTORIC SITE, at 331 E. Third St., is a three-room cottage that was the birthplace of Carl Sandburg. The neighboring visitor center contains a museum devoted to the life and works of the Pulitzer Prize-winning poet and Lincoln biographer. Behind the cottage is Remembrance Rock, Sandburg's gravesite and memorial garden. A 15-minute videotape presentation is presented. Allow 30 minutes minimum. Daily 9-5; closed Jan. 1, Thanksgiving and Dec. 25. Donations. Phone (309) 342-2361.

CENTRAL CONGREGATIONAL CHURCH, 60 Public Sq., is near the northern boundary of Knox College. The architecturally striking Romanesque church, built 1897-98, is made of red sandstone transported from Marquette, Mich., and is embellished with an extensive amount of stained glass. Mon.-Fri. 8:30-noon and 1-4:30; closed holidays. Tour fee $2. Phone (309) 343-5145.

GALESBURG RAILROAD MUSEUM, at 423 Mulberry St., exhibits railroad memorabilia in a restored 1921 Pullman parlor car. Displays focus primarily on Chicago, Burlington and Quincy Railroad, forerunner of Burlington Northern Santa Fe Railroad that still runs through town.

A 1930 caboose and locomotive, a 1920 baggage mail express car and two 1954 equipment cars are on the grounds. Section men's hand tools as well as gang and inspector's motor cars are displayed. Allow 30 minutes minimum. Tues.-Sun. 10-4, Memorial Day-Labor Day; by appointment, rest of year. Admission $2, children 50c. Phone (309) 342-9400.

[SAVE] **ORPHEUM THEATRE,** 57 S. Kellogg St., was built in 1916 as a vaudeville house and hosted such notables as Jack Benny, George Burns,

Harry Houdini and the Marx Brothers. The theater has been restored to its original eclectic style, with an elaborate Italian Renaissance plaster frieze in the mezzanine hall and French baroque medallions decorating the main hall; the exterior is French Second Empire.

A broad selection of performing arts is presented throughout the year. Tours are offered Mon.-Fri. 10-5, Sat. by appointment. Performance admission $6-$20. Tour fee $1. Reservations are recommended for shows and tours. MC, VI. Phone (309) 342-2299.

GLENCOE—*see Chicago p. 78.*

GLENVIEW—*see Chicago p. 78.*

GRAFTON (D-1) pop. 900, elev. 446′

Grafton sits along a scenic section of Great River Road (SR 100) near the confluence of the Mississippi and Illinois rivers. This river town offers antique shops and apple orchards. Autumn is a popular time to visit, when the harvest and fall foliage seasons coincide. The Brussels Ferry, just west of town, provides free passage across the Illinois River into Calhoun County.

Recreational opportunities are available at Pere Marquette State Park, 5 miles west on SR 100 (*see Recreation Chart*).

Alton Visitors Center: 200 Piasa St., Alton, IL 62002; phone (618) 465-6676 or (800) 258-6645.

RAGING RIVERS WATER PARK, off SR 100 at 100 Palisades Pkwy., has sun decks, two large body flumes, a whirlpool ride and a lazy river. A children's play area also is featured. Food is available. Allow 5 hours minimum. Daily 10:30-8, mid-June to mid-Aug.; 10:30-7, Memorial Day weekend, early June to mid-June, mid-Aug. to late Aug. and Labor Day weekend. Hours may vary; phone ahead. Admission $15.95; over 60 and ages 3-8, $12.95. Parking $4. DS, MC, VI. Phone (618) 786-2345 or (800) 548-7573.

GRAND DETOUR (A-2)

Originally known to pioneers as Great Bend, Grand Detour is in a horseshoe bend on the Rock River. Having laid out the village in 1834, Maj. Leonard Andrus of Vermont began construction of a dam to facilitate the operation of saw and flour mills. In 1837 John Deere, also of Vermont, settled in the village and developed the steel plow for which he became known.

Andrus and Deere formed a partnership in 1843 and began the state's first plow factory, one of the oldest major manufacturers in the state and one of the largest producers of farm implements in the world.

A scenic stretch of SR 2 parallels Rock River, passing through Grand Detour along its route from Rockford 41 miles southwest to Dixon.

JOHN DEERE HISTORIC SITE, just off SR 2, is where in 1837 John Deere developed the first steel plow that scoured itself clean. The historic complex includes Deere's restored homestead with furnishings from the 1830s, a visitor center, an archeological exhibition building on the excavated site of Deere's original smithy and a reconstructed blacksmith shop set up as a working forge. Allow 1 hour minimum. Daily 9-5, Apr.-Oct. Admission $3, under 11 free. Phone (815) 652-4551.

GURNEE—*see Chicago p. 78.*

HAVANA (C-2) pop. 3,600, elev. 477′

Since its early years as a steamboat and fishing town at the confluence of the Spoon and Illinois rivers, Havana has gracefully aged into a placid river port engaged in the grain trade. For 26 years Abraham Lincoln visited the town in his various roles of surveyor, returning soldier, lawyer and senatorial candidate. Both Lincoln and Stephen Douglas spoke in Havana's Rockwell Park during their 1858 senatorial campaign; the speeches, however, were on different days and before their famous series of debates.

Havana Area Chamber of Commerce: P.O. Box 116, Havana, IL 62644; phone (309) 543-3528.

CHAUTAUQUA NATIONAL WILDLIFE REFUGE covers 4,488 acres of Illinois River bottom land, including Lake Chautauqua. About 350,000 waterfowls have been seen at one time during fall migrations. Shorebird concentrations occur in August and September. Bald eagles can be seen in fall and winter. Such small mammals as raccoons, foxes and beavers are common within the refuge. A .5-mile interpretive nature trail and an observation overlook afford views of the area.

Fishing is permitted, except during the waterfowl migration season, mid-October to mid-January, when certain areas are closed. Waterfowl hunting is permitted in designated areas in season. Nut, berry and mushroom picking is allowed in areas open to wildlife observation. Allow 1 hour minimum. Daily dawn-dusk. Free. Phone (309) 535-2290.

JACKSONVILLE (C-2) pop. 19,300, elev. 602′

Shortly after its founding in 1825, Jacksonville became the home of Illinois College, the alma mater of William Jennings Bryan. Other prominent town figures were Stephen A. Douglas, who practiced law in town, and Abraham Lincoln, a frequent speaker in Jacksonville during the 1850s. The city also was an important station of the underground railroad.

Jacksonville is home to the Eli Bridge Co., said to be the oldest portable Ferris wheel manufacturer in the country. One of the company's original Ferris wheels is on display in Jacksonville Community Park.

Jacksonville Area Visitors and Conventions Bureau: 155 W. Morton Ave., Jacksonville, IL 62650; phone (217) 243-5678 or (800) 593-5678.

Self-guiding tours: Information and maps describing several walking tours of the historic district are available at the visitors and conventions bureau.

JOLIET—*see Chicago p. 78.*

KAMPSVILLE (D-1) pop. 400, elev. 430′

CENTER FOR AMERICAN ARCHEOLOGY (CAA), is on SR 100 at jct. Marquette and Broadway sts. The center is a repository for a region frequently referred to as the "Nile of North America." The valley surrounding the confluence of the Mississippi and Illinois rivers has been continuously inhabited for nearly 10,000 years by various civilizations and through changing natural environments. The CAA visitor center contains exhibits explaining archeological research methods as well as displays of artifacts. Mon.-Sat. 10-5, Sun. noon-5, mid-Apr. to mid-Nov. Donations. Phone (618) 653-4316.

KANKAKEE (B-4) pop. 27,500, elev. 632′

Kankakee, on the Kankakee River, served as a gateway for the first white settlers in the region, leaving behind a French heritage. Kankakee County Historical Society Museum documents local history, exhibiting a one-room schoolhouse and the childhood home of Gov. Len Small. Two of Frank Lloyd Wright's first Prairie-style houses can be seen in the area. Kankakee River State Park provides outdoor recreational opportunities *(see Recreation Chart).*

Between Kankakee and Wilmington, SR 113N and SR 102 are scenic drives that pass Rock Creek Falls and Rock Creek Canyon.

Kankakee County Convention and Visitors Bureau: 1270 Larry Power Rd., Bourbonnais, IL 60914; phone (815) 935-7390 or (800) 747-4837.

KICKAPOO (C-2)

JUBILEE COLLEGE STATE HISTORIC SITE is .8 mi. w. on US 150, 2 mi. n. on Princeville Jubilee Rd., then w. to 11817 Jubilee College Rd. The site occupies the grounds of the old Jubilee College, one of the first educational institutions in Illinois. It was founded in 1839 by Bishop Philander Chase, a Western missionary and educator for the Episcopal Church. The restored chapel/dormitory is constructed of native limestone. Bishop Chase is buried in the churchyard.

Allow 1 hour minimum. Daily 9-5, Apr.-Nov.; 9-4:30, rest of year. Closed Jan. 1, Thanksgiving and Dec. 25. Donations. Phone (309) 243-9489.

LA SALLE (B-3) pop. 9,700, elev. 465′

Named for the French explorer who came down the Illinois River to this region in 1679, La Salle was founded when plans for the Illinois and Michigan Canal were implemented in 1827. Before the completion of the Illinois Waterway, this canal, along with the mule-drawn barges that plied it, served as the first link between Lake Michigan and the Mississippi waterway systems.

Illinois Valley Area Chamber of Commerce and Economic Development: 300 Bucklin St., P.O. Box 446, La Salle, IL 61301; phone (815) 223-0227.

MATTHIESSEN STATE PARK, 1,938 acres 5 mi. s. off I-80 on SR 178, has 5 miles of hiking trails, canyon trails, waterfalls, cliffs and a reproduction of an old fort. Daily 5:30 a.m.-10 p.m. (weather permitting). Free. Phone (815) 667-4868.

STARVED ROCK STATE PARK, 2,630 acres of wooded bluffland, is 4 mi. s. off I-80 on SR 178. The rocky eminence that gives the park its name rises to a height of 125 feet. La Salle built Fort St. Louis at this site in 1682; the fort was closed in 1702 after the murder of Robert Cavelier de La Salle. In 1769 a band of Illinois American Indians took refuge on the summit of the rock, where, surrounded by their foes, they died from lack of food and water.

The park has 18 canyons that were formed by meltwaters from glaciers some 15,000 years ago. In early spring and after heavy rainfalls, waterfalls form at the head of each canyon. The spring-fed falls at St. Louis Canyon usually flow all summer. More than 15 miles of hiking trails lead to the canyons and traverse the park; hiking in unmarked areas is not permitted. Daily 5:30 a.m.-10 p.m. Free. Phone (815) 667-4906. *See Recreation Chart.*

LAWRENCEVILLE (E-4)
pop. 4,900, elev. 411′

Lawrenceville was named for Capt. James Lawrence, the commander of the *Chesapeake* during the War of 1812. His dying command was "Don't give up the ship."

Lawrence County Chamber of Commerce: 619 12th St., Lawrenceville, IL 62439; phone (618) 943-3516.

LINCOLN TRAIL STATE MEMORIAL is 9 mi. e. at the w. entrance to the Lincoln Memorial Bridge, which crosses the Wabash River. The bronze figure of Abraham Lincoln at the head of a covered wagon stands on the spot where the Lincoln family entered Illinois in 1830.

LERNA (D-4) pop. 300, elev. 754′

LINCOLN LOG CABIN STATE HISTORIC SITE, 10 mi. e. off I-57 from Charleston exit, then 8 mi. s. on Fourth St., is the site where Abraham Lincoln's father and stepmother lived from 1840 until their deaths. The site contains a visitor center and park office; an 86-acre homestead, including a replica of the Lincoln log cabin; outbuildings; root cellars; a mid-19th-century barn; and the Stephen Sargent farm. Interpretive living-history programs, offered in summer, provide a glimpse into the attitudes of the era.

Allow 1 hour minimum. Site open daily 8-dusk. Interpretive programs daily 9-5, Memorial Day-Labor Day; Sat.-Sun. 9-5 in May and Sept. Hours may vary; phone ahead. Closed Jan. 1, Thanksgiving and Dec. 25. Donations. Phone (217) 345-1845.

LEWISTOWN (C-2) pop. 2,600, elev. 600′

Lewistown was founded in 1821 by Ossian Ross, who named the town after his son. In 1823 Lewistown became the county seat for newly created Fulton County. Since then the town has had several noted visitors and citizens. Stephen A. Douglas served as circuit court judge in the Fulton County Courthouse, where on Aug. 17, 1858, Abraham Lincoln delivered his "Return to the Fountain" speech. Prolific author Edgar Lee Masters lived in Lewistown and modeled much of his most famous work, "Spoon River Anthology," about people and places in the town.

Lewistown Chamber of Commerce: 119 S. Adams St., Lewistown, IL 61542; phone (309) 547-4300.

DICKSON MOUNDS STATE MUSEUM is 2 mi. s.e. off SRs 78 and 97. The museum presents the history of the American Indians who lived in the Illinois River Valley through interactive exhibits, artifacts, multimedia presentations and special programs and events. There also is a children's room with hands-on exhibits. Picnicking is permitted. Food is available. Allow 2 hours minimum. Daily 8:30-5; closed Jan. 1, Easter, Thanksgiving and Dec. 25. Free. Phone (309) 547-3721.

LIBERTYVILLE—*see Chicago p. 78.*

LINCOLN (C-3) pop. 15,400, elev. 589′

Lincoln has the distinction of being the only town that was named for Abraham Lincoln before he became famous. Developers of the site used the young lawyer's services to prepare the necessary documents to sell lots. Upon being informed that the settlement would be named for him, Lincoln christened the new townsite with the juice of a watermelon. A historical marker near the Lincoln train station at Broadway and Chicago streets commemorates the christening site.

Abraham Lincoln Tourism Bureau of Logan County: 303 S. Kickapoo St., Lincoln, IL 62656; phone (217) 732-8687.

HERITAGE IN FLIGHT MUSEUM, at the Logan County Airport, displays planes, parachutes, helmets, uniforms and other aviation items from World War I to the present in a building that once held German prisoners of war. Visitors also can charter flights in old war planes and newer single-engine planes such as the Cessna 152. Allow 1 hour minimum. Daily 8-5; closed holidays. Donations. Phone (217) 732-3333.

LINCOLN COLLEGE MUSEUM consists of two rooms in the McKinstry Memorial Library of Lincoln College at 300 Keokuk. Items and documents related to Abraham Lincoln and other presidents are displayed. Mon.-Fri. 9-noon, Sat.-Sun. noon-4, Feb. 1-Dec. 15; closed holidays. Free. Phone (217) 732-3155 or 735-5050, ext. 295.

LISLE—*see Chicago p. 79.*

LOCKPORT—*see Chicago p. 79.*

LONG GROVE—*see Chicago p. 80.*

MACOMB (C-2) pop. 20,000, elev. 709'

Settled by veterans of the War of 1812 and land speculators from the East, Macomb was named in honor of the commanding general of the U.S. Army 1828-41, Alexander Macomb, who fought the British at Lake Champlain.

Western Illinois University is on the northwest side of the city. Recreational opportunities are available at Argyle Lake *(see Recreation Chart).*

Macomb Area Chamber of Commerce: 804 W. Jackson, P.O. Box 274, Macomb, IL 61455; phone (309) 837-4855.

MAHOMET (C-3) pop. 3,100, elev. 711'

EARLY AMERICAN MUSEUM AND BOTANICAL GARDENS is in Lake of the Woods Park, .5 mi. n. on SR 47. The museum's collection includes thousands of artifacts reflecting early 20th-century home and farm life in east-central Illinois with two floors of interpretive exhibits, vignettes and period furnishings. The Discovery Room provides hands-on opportunities for children. Exhibits appear throughout the year. Visitors may tour the adjoining botanical gardens, which contain annual, perennial and native plants and an herb garden.

Allow 2 hours minimum. Daily 10-5, Memorial Day-Labor Day; Sat.-Sun. 10-5, Apr. 1-day before Memorial Day and day after Labor Day-Dec. 31. Free. Phone (217) 586-2612.

MARION (F-3) pop. 14,500, elev. 433'

Standing in Marion's public square, Union general John Logan delivered a speech that was instrumental in winning southern Illinois to the Union cause during the Civil War. The city is a commercial and retail trade center for the region.

Williamson County Tourism Bureau: 8588 SR 148 S., P.O. Box 1088, Marion, IL 62959; phone (618) 997-3690 or (800) 433-7399.

CRAB ORCHARD NATIONAL WILDLIFE REFUGE, 2 mi. s. of jct. SRs 13 and 148, covers 43,000 acres. Natural areas are interspersed with recreational facilities, cornfields and active businesses housed in former World War II munitions buildings. Native wildlife species include deer, coyotes, beavers, woodchucks and thousands of wintering waterfowls. A 4,000-acre wilderness area is open to foot traffic only.

Irregularly shaped Crab Orchard Lake is one of the state's largest man-made bodies of water. Refuge and visitor center open daily 8-5. A 5-day pass costs $5 per private vehicle, annual pass $15. Phone (618) 997-3344. *See Recreation Chart.*

METAMORA (B-3) pop. 2,500, elev. 814'

METAMORA COURTHOUSE STATE HISTORIC SITE, off SR 116 at 113 E. Partridge St., was built in 1845 of bricks fired in Metamora and timbers cut nearby. Abraham Lincoln, traveling the Eighth Judicial Circuit, practiced law in the courthouse 1845-56. The courtroom has original furnishings and the museum displays period items. Tues.-Sat. 9-noon and 1-5; closed holidays. Donations. Phone (309) 367-4470.

METROPOLIS (F-4) pop. 6,700, elev. 339'

Legendary home of Superman, Metropolis has a telephone booth used by the hero and a statue honoring him. The *Daily Planet* office issues copies of the fictional newspaper.

Metropolis Area Chamber of Commerce, Tourism and Economic Development: 604 Market St., P.O. Box 188, Metropolis, IL 62960; phone (618) 524-2714 or (800) 949-5740.

FORT MASSAC STATE PARK, 1,470 acres w. off I-24 via US 45, is the site of 1757 Fort Massac. In 1778 Gen. George Rogers Clark and his Kentucky Long Knives rested at the fort on the way to capture Kaskaskia. A reconstructed fort and statue of Clark mark the site. The third weekend in October the fort celebrates its heritage with an 18th-century-style encampment with musket demonstrations and exhibitions of period arts and crafts. Park daily 7 a.m.-10 p.m. Museum daily 10-5:30. Free. Phone (618) 524-9321. *See Recreation Chart.*

SUPER MUSEUM, off SR 24 exit 37 to 517 Market St., contains items and memorabilia from the original "Superman" comic through the TV show featuring the superhero. Visitors are greeted out front by a 15-foot bronze Superman statue. Exhibits include outfits worn by Christopher Reeve, original drawings from the "Superman" creators and many of the props used in the Superman movies. Daily 9-5. Admission $3; over 65, $1; under 6 free. Phone (618) 524-5518.

CASINOS

- **Players Casino** is at 203 Ferry St. on Players Landing. Daily 9 a.m.-7 a.m. Phone (618) 524-2628 or (800) 929-5905.

MOLINE—*see Quad Cities p. 97.*

MONTICELLO (C-3) pop. 4,500, elev. 661'

Up until the early 19th century Monticello was a hunting ground for the Kickapoo and Pottawatomie tribes of the Algonquin Indians. The availability of buffaloes attracted the first white settlers, notably James A. Piatt Sr. who arrived in 1829. The area was called Piatt's Point until Maj. James McReynolds named it Monticello in honor of Thomas Jefferson.

In the 1850s Monticello was connected by two railroads and became an important transportation stop. Abraham Lincoln rode the rails to Monticello in 1856 and 1858 to campaign. Today's highways connect Monticello with Springfield, Decatur and Champaign; it is not unusual for a family to have one spouse commuting to Champaign while the other works in Decatur.

Monticello Chamber of Commerce: P.O. Box 313, Monticello, IL 61856; phone (217) 762-7921 or (800) 952-3396.

MONTICELLO RAILWAY MUSEUM, 2 mi. e. of I-72 exit 166 (Market St.), following Iron Horse Pl. to the frontage road, is a restored Illinois Central train depot with several railcars on exhibit. Round-trip train rides lasting a little over an hour include a stop at the historic Wabash Depot in Monticello. Picnicking is permitted. Food is available.

Grounds open Sat.-Sun. and holidays 10-6, May-Oct. Train departs from the museum Sat. at 11, 12:30, 2 and 3:30, Sun. at 12:30, 2 and 3:30. Train departs from the Wabash Depot Sat. at 11:30, 1 and 2:30, Sun. at 1 and 2:30. Museum free. Train ride $6; over 62 and ages 4-12, $4. Phone (217) 762-9011 or (800) 952-3396 Mon.-Fri.

ROBERT ALLERTON PARK, 2 mi. s. off I-72 exit 166 to SR 105, .2 mi. w. to Allerton Rd., then 3.5 mi. s. to entrance, is a 1,500-acre conservation area devoted to education and research. The park contains a University of Illinois conference center surrounded by Oriental and European sculpture and formal landscape gardens, hiking and walking trails, cross-country skiing trails, native forests and a visitor center. Many plant, animal and bird species are present.

For safety reasons, visitors are cautioned to stay on the trails. Allow 1 hour minimum. Daily 8-dusk. Visitor center open daily 8-5; closed Dec. 25. Free. Phone (217) 244-1035.

MOOSEHEART—*see Chicago p. 80.*

MOUNT PULASKI (C-3) pop. 1,600

MOUNT PULASKI COURTHOUSE STATE HISTORIC SITE is on Cook St. in the center of town. Abraham Lincoln once argued cases in this 1848 courthouse, which has also served as a school, jail, library and post office. Special events are held throughout the year. Guided tours are available. Allow 1 hour minimum. Tues.-Sat. noon-5, Mar.-Oct.; noon-4, rest of year. Closed holidays. Free. Phone (217) 732-8930.

MOUNT VERNON (E-3)
pop. 17,000, elev. 472'

In 1859 Abraham Lincoln successfully argued an important tax case in the Mount Vernon Appellate courthouse. In 1888 Clara Barton used the same building as a hospital following a large tornado. The city serves as a gateway to the expansive Rend Lake wildlife and recreation area *(see Recreation Chart)*.

Several landmarks are preserved in the Jefferson County Historical Society Historical Village, including The Mount Olive Log Church and a rail car made in Mount Vernon. The village is open by appointment; phone (618) 246-0033.

Mount Vernon Convention & Visitors Bureau: 200 Potomac Blvd., P.O. Box 2580, Mount Vernon, IL 62864; phone (618) 242-3151 or (800) 252-5464.

MITCHELL ART MUSEUM is 2 mi. e. on SR 15 off I-57, then n. on 27th St. to Richview Rd. following signs. The museum includes the works of such 19th- and 20th-century American artists as George Bellows, Mary Cassatt, Thomas Eakins and Childe Hassam. Changing exhibits display such contemporary art as ceramics, metalwork, painting, photography and sculpture.

Nature trails with interpretive braille markers and outdoor sculptures are on the 80-acre estate. Allow 1 hour minimum. Tues.-Sat. 10-5, Sun. 1-5; closed holidays. Free. Phone (618) 242-1236.

MOWEAQUA (D-3) pop. 1,800, elev. 637'

MOWEAQUA COAL MINE MUSEUM, 129 S. Main St., is a memorial to 54 coal miners killed in a 1932 mining disaster; the number killed amounted to 25 percent of the town's male population. The museum includes photographs, memorabilia, coal mining tools and implements and newspaper accounts of the accident. Allow 30 minutes minimum. Daily 1-4, Apr.-Oct.; otherwise by appointment. Free. Reservations are recommended. Phone (217) 768-3019.

NAPERVILLE—*see Chicago p. 80.*

NAUVOO (C-1) pop. 1,100, elev. 600'

Having fled persecution elsewhere, Joseph Smith and his religious followers established the headquarters of The Church of Jesus Christ of Latter-day Saints in Nauvoo in 1839. Both church and settlement flourished. By 1841 a university was projected, and the foundations for a great temple were laid. The temple, still unfinished when most of the Mormons left the state in 1846, was burned by vandals in 1848.

In 1849 the area was occupied by French Icarians, a socialist sect that lived by the creed "from each according to his ability and to each according to his need." Inner discord undermined the society and it was dissolved in 1858.

Monument to Women Statuary Gardens, next to Nauvoo Visitors Center, is a sculpture garden dedicated to women of the past, present and future. Each statue identifies a significant dimension in a woman's life.

Nauvoo Chamber of Commerce: 1295 Mulholland St., P.O. Box 41, Nauvoo, IL 62354; phone (217) 453-6648.

Self-guiding tours: Maps describing walking tours of the historic district are available from the Tourist Center, Page Street and SR 96; phone (217) 453-6648. Two-hour tape tours are available for $6.

JOSEPH SMITH HISTORIC CENTER, 1 blk. w. of SR 96 to 149 Water St. along the Mississippi River, is maintained by the Reorganized Church of Jesus Christ of Latter Day Saints. Guided tours are available Mon.-Sat. 9-5, Sun. 1-5; closed Thanksgiving weekend and Dec. 23-Jan. 31. Free. Phone (217) 453-2246.

The Homestead, on Water St., is an 1803 log building that was the first Nauvoo home of the Smith family. Original and antique furnishings are within. The graves of Joseph, Emma and Hyrum Smith are nearby. Demonstrations of 19th-century life are given at the kitchen in the summer.

Mansion House, Main and Water sts., was the permanent home of the prophet. The 1842 home has been restored as it was during the Smith family's residency 1842-69.

Red Brick Store, built in 1842, is the reconstructed general merchandise store operated by Joseph Smith. It was, for practical purposes, the church headquarters building of its day. Goods on display are typical of those that were sold 1842-46.

LDS VISITOR CENTER, Main and Young sts., provides an introduction to the 24 restored homes and shops in Nauvoo's historic district and also offers movies, musical productions, guide service and background information about the Mormon settlement 1839-46. Center open daily 8 a.m.-9 p.m., Memorial Day-Labor Day; 9-5, rest of year. Free. Phone (217) 453-2237 or (888) 453-6434.

Brigham Young Home, on Kimball St. 1 blk. w. of Main St., is the restored home of the second president of The Church of Jesus Christ of Latter-day Saints. The house contains the office where colonizer Brigham Young held meetings concerning westward expansion. Allow 30 minutes minimum. Daily 9-6, Memorial Day-Labor Day; 9-5, rest of year. Free.

Heber C. Kimball Home, Munson and Partridge sts., is the restored house of a prime counselor to Brigham Young. Allow 30 minutes minimum. Daily 9-6, Memorial Day-Labor Day; 9-5, rest of year. Free.

Jonathan Browning Home and Gunshop, on Main St., is a reconstruction of gunsmith Jonathan Browning's home and workshop. He invented several kinds of repeating firearms. The house contains a gun and rifle collection. Allow 30 minutes minimum. Daily 9-6, Memorial Day-Labor Day; 9-5, rest of year. Free.

Seventies Hall, on Parley St., was a training center for laymen wanting to improve their missionary skills under the direction of Brigham Young. The main floor was used for classes, lectures and worship; the second floor housed a library for the community. The 1844 building has been restored to its original design. Daily 9-6, Memorial Day-Labor Day; 9-5, rest of year. Free.

Wilford Woodruff House, on the corner of SR 96 and Hotchkiss St., was the home of the fourth president of The Church of Jesus Christ of Latter-day Saints. The 1843 house is a Midwest Federal-style building with arch bricks above the windows. Guided tours offered daily 9-6, Memorial Day-Labor Day; 9-5, rest of year. Free.

NAUVOO STATE PARK, off SR 96, features 148 acres. A 13-acre lake offers opportunities for fishing and boating. A house built by the Mormons in the 1840s, and later owned by the Rheinberger family, is now a museum and contains a room for each period in the city's history: American Indian, Mormon, Icarian and pioneer.

Contact the chamber of commerce, (217) 453-6648, for more information about the museum. Camping and picnicking are available on a first-come, first-served basis. Daily 1-5, May 1-Oct. 15; by appointment in Apr. Free. Phone (217) 453-2512. *See Recreation Chart.*

OAK BROOK—*see Chicago p. 80.*

OAK PARK—*see Chicago p. 80.*

OTTAWA (B-3) pop. 17,500

Nicknamed The Town of Two Rivers for its proximity to the Illinois and Fox rivers, Ottawa boasts two town squares dating from the 1800s, historic architecture and ample recreational opportunities.

The town's Washington Square is where Abraham Lincoln and Stephen A. Douglas held a senatorial debate on Aug. 21, 1858. Surrounded by examples of Greek Revival, Italianate and English High Gothic architecture, the square continues to be used for entertainment and recreational gatherings. The Main Street district offers antiques and specialty stores.

Ottawa Visitors Center: 100 W. Lafayette St., Ottawa, IL 61350; phone (815) 434-2737 or (888) 688-2924.

OTTAWA SCOUTING MUSEUM is s. on SR 23, then just w. on Washington St. to jct. Canal St. Dedicated to the history of scouting in America, the museum displays uniforms, badges, canteens, compasses, a mock campsite and historic photographs. Allow 30 minutes minimum. Thurs.-Mon. 10-4; closed holidays. Admission $3; ages 5-10, $2. Phone (815) 431-9353.

PEKIN (C-2) pop. 32,300, elev. 482'

In Pekin the young lawyer Abraham Lincoln won the case of "Black Nance," involving an escaped slave who had fled into the free state of Illinois.

Pekin also is the birthplace and gravesite of Sen. Everett McKinley Dirksen. Dirksen Congressional Center, Broadway and 4th Street, contains an exhibition hall with changing displays, photographs and other Dirksen memorabilia.

Pekin Chamber of Commerce: 402 Court St., P.O. Box 636, Pekin, IL 61555; phone (309) 346-2106.

PEORIA (C-2) pop. 113,500, elev. 474'

Louis Joliet and Jacques Marquette were the first Europeans to visit the region around Peoria in 1673. Named after one of the five Illinois American Indian tribes, Peoria is reputedly the oldest settlement in the state. Successively colonized under four flags, the early community developed from two French military establishments and three other French settlements on or near Peoria Lake.

The same natural resources that lured a continuous stream of settlers to the area contributed greatly to Peoria's later industrial and agricultural development. Flowing from its source for more than 14,000 years, Peoria Mineral Springs enticed several entrepreneurs to establish a successful brewery industry. One of the country's oldest commercial bottling companies continues to market Peoria mineral water.

This Corn Belt city now is an important manufacturing, railroad and shipping center, and is the headquarters of construction and mining equipment manufacturer Caterpillar Inc. Bradley University, a private institution composed of six colleges, provides an academic environment.

Tower Park, 1222 E. Kingman in Peoria Heights, includes a water tower that visitors can ascend in a glass-enclosed elevator to view the Illinois River and downtown Peoria. Forest Park Nature Center, also off Prospect Road in Peoria Heights, has 7 miles of marked trails as well as exhibits about local vegetation and animal life. Courthouse Plaza, at Main and Adams, offers free performances May through September.

Peoria Area Convention and Visitors Bureau: 456 Fulton, Suite 300, Peoria, IL 61602; phone (309) 676-0303 or (800) 747-0302.

GLEN OAK PARK, covering 100 acres, is at McClure and Prospect aves. in northeastern Peoria. The park has a zoo, conservatory, gardens, picnic areas, tennis courts and a wooden playground built by children and volunteers. Outdoor entertainment is offered at Glen Oak Amphitheater during the summer. Phone (309) 688-3667.

LAKEVIEW MUSEUM OF ARTS AND SCIENCES, 1125 W. Lake Ave., contains a children's discovery center, a planetarium, Illinois folk art and changing exhibits. Tues.-Sat. 10-5 (also Wed. 5-8), Sun. noon-5; closed major holidays. Admission for museum and planetarium $6; over 60 and ages 4-17, $4. Admission for one attraction $5; over 60 and ages 4-17, $3. DS, MC, VI. Phone (309) 686-7000.

Lakeview Planetarium presents sky shows. Show times vary. Admission for museum and planetarium $6; over 60 and ages 4-17, $4. Admission for one attraction $5; over 60 and ages 4-17, $3. DS, MC, VI. Phone (309) 686-6682.

SAVE **WHEELS O' TIME MUSEUM,** 9 mi. n. at 11923 N. Knoxville Ave. (SR 40), features interactive displays of airplanes, clocks, dolls, gasoline and steam engines, musical instruments, toys, tractors, vintage automobiles and real and model trains. Highlights include a reproduction of the Red Baron's fighter plane, an authentic firehouse and an 1855 fire engine. Wed.-Sun. noon-5, May-Oct. Admission $4.50; under 12, $2. Phone (309) 243-9020.

WILDLIFE PRAIRIE PARK, 10 mi. w. on I-74, then 4 mi. s. off exit 82 following signs, is dedicated to the preservation of Illinois animal and prairie life. On the grounds are bison, elk, wolves, cougars, bears, waterfowls, an American bald eagle and other animals native to Illinois. A 15-minute slide show precedes self-guiding nature walks. The park also has a country store, a museum, a one-room schoolhouse, a narrow-gauge railroad, a pioneer farmstead and a visitor center. Events are held throughout the year. Food is available.

Allow 1 hour minimum. Daily 9-6:30, May-Sept.; 9-4:30, mid-Mar. through Apr. 30 and Oct. 1 to mid-Dec. Admission $5; ages 4-12, $3. AX, DS, MC, VI. Phone (309) 676-0998.

PETERSBURG (C-2) pop. 2,300, elev. 552'

Petersburg was laid out next to the Sangamon River by a surveyor hired by George Warburton and Peter Lukins in 1833. John Taylor and Hezekiah King bought the town and hired Abraham Lincoln to resurvey the site in 1836. Many New Salem residents moved to Petersburg after it was made the seat of Menard County in 1839.

The grave of Ann Rutledge, an early acquaintance of Abraham Lincoln, is in Oakland Cemetery at the edge of town. Nearby is the grave of Edgar Lee Masters, author of "Spoon River Anthology." His home at Eighth and Jackson streets is open for tours. Artifacts, documents and mementos of Menard County's past are on display at Menard County Historical Museum, Seventh and Jackson streets.

Petersburg Chamber of Commerce: 125 S. Seventh St., P.O. Box 452, Petersburg, IL 62675; phone (217) 632-7363.

GEM **LINCOLN'S NEW SALEM HISTORIC SITE,** 2 mi. s. on SR 97, covers 600 acres. It is a reconstruction of the old town of New Salem, where Abraham Lincoln lived 1831-37. The only original building standing is the Onstot Cooper Shop, where Lincoln studied at night. A carding mill, a gristmill, the Rutledge Tavern, shops, a school, a sawmill and timber houses have been reconstructed to look as they did in the 1830s.

The visitor center offers exhibits and an orientation film about Lincoln's life in New Salem. An outdoor theater is open June through August. Picnicking and camping facilities are available. Allow 2 hours minimum. Buildings and museum open daily 9-5, Apr.-Oct.; 8-4, rest of year. Closed major holidays. Donations. Theater $7; under 13, $3. Phone (217) 632-4000 or 632-5440 for theater information. *See Recreation Chart.*

PRAIRIE DU ROCHER (E-2)
pop. 500, elev. 396'

Settlement of the region around Prairie du Rocher began in 1722 as a speculative land venture. Prairie du Rocher is thought to be the oldest town in Illinois. John Law obtained a charter that awarded him jurisdiction over the Louisiana Purchase; he promoted the area and pledged large profits to the French who speculated on the land. Within 2 years the venture failed, leaving the French financial system in ruin. The colonists sent to the area, however, remained.

FORT DE CHARTRES STATE HISTORIC SITE is off SR 3, 11 mi. w. on SR 155. Once the seat of the French government in the Illinois country, the fort was the last French possession to be surrendered to the British, who held it 1765-72. The present structure is a restoration of stone buildings erected during the 1750s and 1760s. The site includes the Peithman Museum, which features artifacts from the 18th-century French colony, picnic facilities and an interpretive center. Allow 1 hour minimum. Daily 9-5; closed Jan. 1, Martin Luther King Jr. Day, Thanksgiving and Dec. 25. Donations. Phone (618) 284-7230.

QUAD CITIES (A-1)

The unique community known collectively as the Quad Cities unites the states of Illinois and Iowa. **Bettendorf** and **Davenport, Iowa,** and **Moline** and **Rock Island, Ill.,** combine to create a commercial and manufacturing complex on the Mississippi River.

The quiet rural village of Gilbert was never the same after the arrival of Bettendorf Axle and Wagon Co. in 1903. Soon to be the largest railroad car shop west of the Mississippi, the company became the most important influence in the development of Gilbert, later renamed Bettendorf.

Cradled in a loop of the Mississippi River, Davenport developed around the river's Rock Island. River traffic flowing to either side of the island made it a natural place for early trade with American Indians. The island was garrisoned in 1816 with the establishment of Fort Armstrong, and it was at the fort in 1832 that the Sauk and Fox Indians signed the Black Hawk Treaty to open land west of the Mississippi to settlement. Col. George Davenport, who had established a fur trading post on the island, later bought a parcel. Davenport, named after the colonel, was founded in 1836.

Davenport's regional heritage is preserved at such places as the Village of East Davenport, which reflects the late 19th century in its brick-paved streets and small shops, and Scott County Park *(see the AAA North Central CampBook)*, north on US 61. The floral beds and rose gardens of Vander Veer Park and Conservatory are spectacular in summer.

The name Moline comes from the French word *moulin*, meaning "mill." Plotted by a mill company in June 1843, the town was incorporated 5 years later. Early settlers to Moline were of Swedish and German descent. Olde Town, 7th Street and 18th Avenue, reflects the heritage of the city's Belgian community. Home of the John Deere organization, Moline is known as the "Farm Implement Capital of America."

Playcrafters Barn Theatre offers productions in a renovated dairy barn; phone (309) 762-0330 8:30-noon for information or tickets. The MARK, 1201 River Dr., stages sports events, shows and other events; phone (309) 764-2000.

Rock Island's history was highlighted by American Indian settlement, the steamboat era and the Civil War. The onset of the Black Hawk War, which exterminated the Sauk and Fox Indians, was precipitated by the destruction of the tribes' ancient burial grounds to make way for the pioneers' cornfields. During the days of the steamboat about 2,000 vessels docked annually.

The Dred Scott Decision, handed down from the Supreme Court in response to a suit filed by the black servant of a Rock Island resident, pushed the country toward Civil War by stating that slaves were property and therefore not entitled to the rights of U.S. citizens. Rock Island Arsenal *(see attraction listing)* accommodated one of the most important Northern military prisons of the Civil War.

The Channel Cat Water Taxi is an open-air pontoon boat that explores the river and stops hourly at landings on both sides of the river. Bicycles are allowed on board so bicyclists can enjoy the many trails running along the Mississippi. Narrated trolley tours of the historic cities also are available.

American bald eagles winter in the Rock Island area. Prime viewing time is in January and February.

For information about local licensed operators of Mississippi riverboat gambling establishments contact the local AAA office; phone (319) 386-8159.

Quad Cities Convention & Visitors Bureau: 2021 River Dr., Moline, IL 61265; phone (309) 788-7800 or (800) 747-7800.

Shopping areas: Northpark Mall at US 6 and SR 130 in Davenport counts JCPenney and Younkers among its more than 150 stores. Southpark Mall, John Deere Road W. in Moline, features some 150 stores with JCPenney and Sears as the anchors. The Village of East Davenport on River Drive offers shops and eateries set in a historical village setting.

BLACK HAWK STATE HISTORIC SITE, 207 acres on SR 5 in Rock Island, was named for the warrior who led the Indians in the Black Hawk War. John Hauberg Indian Museum on Watch Tower Hill displays American Indian relics, including a wickiup, or hut. The park has facilities for picnicking, fishing and hiking. Museum open daily 9-noon and 1-5, Apr.-Oct.; 9-noon and 1-4, rest of year. Closed Jan. 1, Martin Luther King Jr. Day, President's Day, Veterans Day, Thanksgiving and Dec. 25. Donations. Phone (309) 788-9536 or 788-0177.

CELEBRATION RIVER CRUISES, 2501 River Dr. in Moline, offers non-gaming sightseeing cruises on the Mississippi River. All-day, lunch, dinner and show cruises also are available. The 1.5-hour sightseeing cruise departs Thurs.-Sun. at 2:30. Sightseeing cruise $9.50; ages 3-12, $6.50. AX, DS, MC, VI. Phone (309) 764-1952 or (800) 297-0034.

DAVENPORT MUSEUM OF ART, 1737 W. 12th St. in Davenport, Iowa, offers changing monthly exhibits from its collections of American, European, Mexican colonial and Haitian works of art. The permanent exhibit, Children's Orientation Gallery, allows children to learn about art at their own level. Tues.-Sat. 10-4:30 (also Thurs. 4:30-8), Sun. 1-4:30; closed holidays. Free. Admission is charged for special exhibits. Phone (319) 326-7804.

DEERE & COMPANY ADMINISTRATIVE CENTER about 7 mi. s. on John Deere Rd. in Moline, was designed by Eero Saarinen. Past and present Deere products and a collage depicting American agriculture 1837-1918 are exhibited on the display floor. Display floor open daily 9-5:30. Video presentations at 10:30 and 1:30. Free. Phone (877) 201-3924 or (800) 765-9588.

THE FAMILY MUSEUM OF ARTS & SCIENCE, 2900 Learning Campus Dr. in Bettendorf, Iowa, is designed with interactive exhibits for children and families. Visitors can investigate the science of music, explore the human heart and learn about healthy lifestyles, watch themselves on a giant interactive video screen, or learn about the industry of agriculture, "drive" a combine and help "harvest" a crop. Traveling national exhibits supplement permanent displays.

Allow 1 hour minimum. Tues.-Thurs. 9-7, Fri.-Sat. 9-5, Sun. noon-5; closed major holidays. Admission $4; over 59, $2; under 2 free. MC, VI. Phone (319) 344-4106.

JOHN DEERE PAVILION, off I-74 at 1400 River Dr. in downtown Moline, is housed in a glass-enclosed building. The pavilion showcases vintage and modern-day John Deere equipment. Interactive displays allow visitors to sit in the cab of a harvester, trace the progression of a family farm to the future of agri-business or take a virtual tour through the Harvester Works, the company's local combine factory. "The Bounty" is a film depicting a farm family's lifestyle as they meet the challenges of the changing season.

Allow 1 hour minimum. Mon.-Fri. 9-5 (also Mon.-Fri. 5-6 p.m., Apr.-Dec.), Sat. 10-5, Sun. noon-4; closed Jan. 1, Easter, Thanksgiving and Dec. 25. Free. Phone (309) 765-1000.

MISSISSIPPI RIVER VISITOR CENTER, Rodman Ave. on Island in Rock Island, overlooks Lock and Dam 15 on the Mississippi River. Visitors can watch as towboats and recreational boats pass through the locks. Park rangers are available to explain how water transportation works on the upper Mississippi. Various exhibits describe river navigation, and a videotape presentation provides a history of Lock and Dam 15. Allow 1 hour minimum. Daily 9-9, mid-May through Labor Day; 9-5, rest of year. Free. Phone (309) 794-5338.

SAVE **PUTNAM MUSEUM OF HISTORY AND NATURAL SCIENCE,** 1717 W. 12th St. in Davenport, Iowa, contains exhibits about the history of the region and the archeology of the Far East, Egypt and the Americas as well as wildlife, mineral and art collections. The River Boat Gallery displays paintings of early river transportation and miniature ship reproductions. The V.O. Figge Natural Science Wing displays historical artifacts and natural science specimens.

An IMAX Theatre was scheduled to open in March 2002; the discount does not apply to the theater. Allow 1 hour, 30 minutes minimum. Tues.-Fri. 9-5, Sat. 10-5, Sun. noon-5; closed major holidays. Admission $4; over 59, $3; ages 5-17, $2. DS, MC, VI. Phone (319) 324-1933.

QUAD CITY BOTANICAL CENTER is at 2525 4th Ave. in Rock Island. The focal point of the center is a 70-foot-tall conservatory with more than 100 tropical plants and trees, a 14-foot waterfall and reflecting pools stocked with Japanese koi and water plants. Outdoor gardens have plantings that change with the season. Allow 1 hour, 30 minutes minimum. Mon.-Sat. 10-5, Sun. 1-5; closed Jan. 1, Thanksgiving and Dec. 24-25. Admission $3.50; over 60, $3; ages 6-12, $1. MC, VI. Phone (309) 794-0991.

ROCK ISLAND ARSENAL is on Arsenal Island in the Mississippi River in Rock Island. The government's largest manufacturing arsenal, it was founded in 1862. Highlights include the Fort Armstrong Blockhouse, reconstructed near the site of the original 1816 fort; the Corps of Engineers Clock Tower Building; and the Confederate cemetery. A national cemetery at the east entrance is open daily 8-6. Free self-guiding tour booklets are available at the Rock Island Arsenal Museum.

The Col. Davenport House, on the n. shore of Arsenal Island, was built in 1833 by Col. George Davenport, the first settler in the area and the town's namesake. The house is the oldest in the Quad Cities. Thurs.-Sun. noon-4, early May-Oct. 31; by appointment rest of year. Admission $3; over 60 and ages 6-17, $2; students with ID $1; family rate $7. Phone (309) 786-7336.

Rock Island Arsenal Museum, Bldg. 60, North Ave., was established in 1905 and houses an extensive collection of military and civilian firearms with more than a thousand weapons on display. Exhibits interpret the history of Arsenal Island. Allow 1 hour minimum. Daily 10-4; closed Jan. 1, Thanksgiving and Dec. 24-25. Free. Phone (309) 782-5021.

CASINOS

- **Isle of Capri**, at the I-74 Bridge at State Street Landing in Bettendorf, Iowa. Daily 24 hours. Phone (319) 359-7280 or (800) 724-5825.

- **Jumer's Casino Rock Island**, 18th St. and the Mississippi riverfront in Rock Island. Daily 8 a.m.-1 a.m. (also Fri.-Sat. 1 a.m.-3 a.m.). Phone (800) 477-7747.

- **Rhythm City Casino** is at River Dr. and Brady St. in Davenport, Iowa. Casino open dockside daily 24 hours. Two-hour cruises depart Mon.-Fri. at 7:30 a.m., May-Oct. Phone (563) 328-8000 or (800) 262-8711.

QUINCY (C-1) pop. 39,700, elev. 488'

On the Mississippi River, Quincy is noted for its architecture; many 19th-century river estates exist. Of interest are Huffman House, Lorenzo Bull House, Newcomb House, Temple B'nai Shalom, Villa Katharine and Warfield House. Governor John Wood Mansion, 425 S. 12th St., is the headquarters of the Historical Society of Quincy and Adams County.

Quincy Convention & Visitors Bureau: 300 Civic Center Plaza, Suite 237, Quincy, IL 62301; phone (217) 223-1000 or (800) 978-4748.

ALL WARS MUSEUM, 1707 N. 12th St., is on the grounds of the Illinois Veterans Home—one of the nation's oldest and largest veterans homes. Exhibits span military involvement from the American Revolution to Desert Storm. Displays include vehicles, weapons, uniforms, medals, flags and a full-scale replica of a Revolutionary War cannon. Mon.-Sat. 9-noon and 1-4, Sun. 1-4. Free. Phone (217) 222-8641.

[SAVE] **THE GARDNER MUSEUM OF ARCHITECTURE AND DESIGN**, 332 Maine St., is in Quincy's Old Public Library and recounts the town's history through pictures, artifacts and changing architectural displays. The permanent collection entitled Aspirations in Glass displays stained glass from local churches and buildings. Children can practice their building and design skills in the Archiroom.

Allow 1 hour minimum. Tues.-Sun. 1-5, Mar. 2-Dec. 23; by appointment rest of year. Closed major holidays. Admission $2; over 59, $1; students 50c; under 5 free. Phone (217) 224-6873.

THE QUINCY MUSEUM is 3 blks. s. of SR 104 (Broadway) on the corner of 16th and Maine. Part of the 1891 Newcomb-Stillwell mansion, the first floor of the museum has been restored with late 19th-century furnishings. The parlor holds one of the few Square Baby Grand Pianos still in working condition. There are changing exhibits on the sec-

ond and third floors. The Discovery Area, with exhibits about dinosaurs, Mississippi River wildlife and American Indian lifestyles and cultures, has hands-on activities for children.

Allow 2 hours minimum. Tues.-Sun. 1-5; closed holidays. Admission $2, students $1, under 6 free. Phone (217) 224-7669.

RANTOUL (C-4) pop. 17,200

[SAVE] **OCTAVE CHANUTE AEROSPACE MUSEUM** is off I-57 exit 250, 1.4 mi. e. on Champaign Ave., .9 mi. s. on Century Blvd., then .2 mi. e. to 1011 Pacesetter Dr. Home of the Illinois Military Aviation Hall of Fame, the museum includes photographs, historic uniforms, interactive displays and 34 aircraft. Visitors can sit in the cockpit of a B-52 plane. Also featured are photographs and memorabilia that outline the history of the community of Rantoul. Guided tours are available.

Allow 1 hour minimum. Mon.-Sat. 10-5, Sun. noon-5; closed Jan. 1, Thanksgiving and Dec. 25. Admission $5; over 62, $4; grades K-12, $3. MC, VI. Phone (217) 893-1613 or (877) 726-8685.

ROCKFORD (A-3) pop. 139,400, elev. 716'

Bisected by the Rock River, Rockford is named for the shallow ford used by the Galena-Chicago Stagecoach Line before the area was settled. The city's founders were African-American slave Lewis Lemon, his master Germanicus Kent and Thatcher Blake, who built a sawmill near the ford in 1834. New Englanders of Scottish descent then settled the area, followed by Swedes, Italians, African Americans, Germans, Irish and Eastern Europeans. The ethnic heritage of the groups that have made the city their home survives in musical organizations and theater groups.

The city's streets were designed to accommodate the winding river without regard to uniformity. Parks, encompassing 6,000 acres, appear at oddly placed intervals; streets that begin as a boulevard narrow and stop at a wall or building. Its citizens nicknamed Rockford "The Forest City," because of the many trees. Today three public gardens and annual tours of the area's private gardens have transformed Rockford into a "City of Gardens."

Stock car racing takes place at Rockford Speedway. Local recreation includes boat and trolley rides and outdoor concerts offered in the summer by Rockford Park District. A scenic portion of SR 2 parallels the Rock River and intersects SRs 72 and 64 along its span from Rockford 41 miles southwest to Dixon.

Rockford Area Convention and Visitors Bureau: 211 N. Main St., Rockford, IL 61101-1010; phone (815) 963-8111 or (800) 521-0849.

ANDERSON JAPANESE GARDENS, 2.2 mi. n. on SR 251, then e. to 340 Spring Creek Rd., is home to 5 acres of formal Japanese gardens. Based on the style of gardens popular in Japan during the Kamakura Period A.D. 1185-1333, the area includes an authentic Sukiya-style guest house, a tea house, stone sculptures, viewing house and decorative bridges as well as a waterfall constructed of 700 tons of boulders. Staff are available to answer questions.

Allow 1 hour minimum. Mon.-Fri. 10-5 Sat. 10-4, Sun. noon-4, June-Aug.; Mon.-Fri. 10-5, Sun. noon-4 in May and Sept.-Oct. Admission $5; over 62, $4; ages 5-18, $2. AX, DS, MC, VI. Phone (815) 229-9390.

BURPEE MUSEUM OF NATURAL HISTORY, at 737 N. Main St., is housed in two Victorian-era mansions linked by a contemporary three-story gallery complex. Exhibits include collections relating to American Indians, animals, plants, minerals, fossils, a coal forest with thunderstorms, rocks and mounted birds and mammals as well as a full-size cast of an adult tyrannosaurus rex skeleton. The lifestyles and cultures of various American Indian tribes are examined through dioramas, artifacts and two full-size dwellings.

Mon.-Sat. 10-5, Sun. noon-5, mid-June through Aug. 31; Tues.-Sat. 10-5, Sun. noon-5, rest of year. Closed Jan. 1, Easter, Thanksgiving and Dec. 25. Admission $4; ages 3-17, $3. MC, VI. Phone (815) 965-3433.

DISCOVERY CENTER MUSEUM, 711 N. Main St. in Riverfront Museum Park, is designed for families to explore, experience and experiment with the many facets of science and art. More than 200 hands-on exhibits illustrate scientific and perceptual principles. Also featured are a planetarium show, an outdoor science park, a robotics lab and a children's TV studio. Tot's Spot is an activity area for preschoolers. Mon.-Sat. 10-5, Sun. noon-5, Memorial Day-Labor Day; Tues.-Sat. (also Mon. school holidays) 10-5, Sun. noon-5, rest of year. Admission $4; ages 2-18, $3. Phone (815) 963-6769.

KLEHM ARBORETUM AND BOTANIC GARDEN, 2701 Clifton Ave., features 150 acres of trees and plants. Featured are a children's garden, demonstration gardens, a botanical education center and changing exhibits. Allow 1 hour minimum. Daily 9-8, Memorial Day-Labor Day; 9-4, rest of year. Closed Jan. 1, Thanksgiving and Dec. 25. Admission $2, under 16 free; free to all Mon. AX, MC, VI. Phone (815) 965-8146 or (888) 419-0782.

MAGIC WATERS WATERPARK, off I-90 SR 20 exit, then 1.5 mi. s. on Bell School Rd., is a 43-acre water park featuring a wave pool, water slides, tube slides, a lazy river ride, a water roller coaster, a treehouse, beach volleyball and a Little Lagoon for kids. Allow 3 hours minimum. Daily 10-6, Memorial Day weekend-Labor Day. Admission $16.50; over 62 and under 48 inches tall $13.50; under 3, $1.50. Admission after 3pm. $9.50. DS, MC, VI. Phone (815) 332-3260 or (800) 373-1679.

SAVE **MIDWAY VILLAGE AND MUSEUM CENTER** is off US 20 Bus. Rte. exit of I-90, w. to Perryville Rd., n. to Guilford Rd., then w. to 6799

Guilford. This late 19th-century village set on 137 acres features some 24 historic buildings. The museum features exhibits about history, aviation and industry. Some of the village's events are Civil War Days and a World War II re-enactment; phone for schedule information.

Mon.-Fri. 10-5, Sat.-Sun. noon-5, Memorial Day-Labor Day; Thurs.-Sun. noon-4, Apr. 1-day before Memorial Day and day after Labor Day-Oct. 31. Admission $5; ages 3-15, $3; by donation on Thurs. Admission prices may vary for special events; phone ahead. DS, MC, VI. Phone (815) 397-9112.

ROCKFORD ART MUSEUM, 711 N. Main St. in Riverfront Museum Park, offers multimedia and changing exhibits and houses a permanent collection of 19th- and 20th-century art. Tues.-Fri. 11-5, Sat. 10-5, Sun. noon-5. Free. Phone (815) 968-2787.

SINNISSIPPI GARDENS, GREENHOUSE AND LAGOON, 1300 N. 2nd St., contains an aviary, a floral clock, formal gardens, a greenhouse, a lagoon and a recreation path. Daily 9-4; closed Thanksgiving and Dec. 25. Free. Phone (815) 987-8858.

TINKER SWISS COTTAGE MUSEUM, 411 Kent St., is an 1865 mansion with Victorian furnishings built by Robert Tinker. The cottage is adorned with more than 5,000 objects Tinker collected on his world travels. Tours are given Tues.-Sun. at 1, 2 and 3. Admission $4; over 65, $3.50; ages 5-17, $1. Phone (815) 964-2424.

ROCK ISLAND—*see Quad Cities p. 97.*

RUSHVILLE (C-1) pop. 3,200, elev. 676'

SCHUYLER COUNTY JAIL MUSEUM AND GENEALOGICAL CENTER is at 200 S. Congress St., at the corner of Congress and Madison sts. The restored 1857-58 jail, now a museum, contains historical displays of soldiers' uniforms, period clothing, American Indian relics, medical implements and household utensils. Museum and genealogical center open daily 1-5, Apr.-Oct.; Sat.-Sun. 1-5 in Nov. and Jan.-Mar. Closed major holidays. Donations. Phone (217) 322-6975.

ST. CHARLES—*see Chicago p. 82.*

SALEM (E-3) pop. 7,500, elev. 534'

William Jennings Bryan, known as The Great Commoner, was born in Salem. The Gutzon Borglum statue of Bryan that once stood in Washington, D.C., now stands in Salem's Bryan Memorial Park. Guided tours of Bryan's home at 408 Broadway are available; phone (618) 548-7791.

Bryan was the prosecuting attorney against John Thomas Scopes, principal in the so-called Scopes Monkey Trial. Scopes, who grew up in Salem and attended the University of Illinois, was accused of teaching Charles Darwin's theory of evolution; he was arrested, tried and fined for the incident.

Salem Chamber of Commerce: 615 W. Main, Salem, IL 62881; phone (618) 548-3010.

SCHAUMBURG—see *Chicago p. 82.*

SHAWNEE NATIONAL FOREST

Elevations in the forest range from 340 ft. at Olive Branch in Alexander County to 1,064 ft. at Williams Hill in Pope County. Refer to AAA maps for additional elevation information.

In the Shawnee Hills of southern Illinois, 273,800-acre Shawnee National Forest extends from the Mississippi River eastward to the Ohio. In sharp contrast to the level croplands of central Illinois, this region is characterized by hills and valleys, timber-producing land, scenic vistas and such wildlife as deer, foxes, waterfowls, turkeys and quails. A network of public roads and trails interlaces the forest, providing access to campgrounds, wildlife areas and unusual rock formations.

Hiking trails include the Rim Rock Forest Trail, a .7-mile circuit that winds past some of the state's most striking geological features; the .5-mile Garden of the Gods Trail, which explores 200 million-year-old rock formations; and the Bell Smith Springs Trail, which features caves and a natural bridge.

A short trail also begins at an iron furnace 4 miles north of Rosiclare; the 52-foot furnace was built in 1837, used during the Civil War and reconstructed in 1967. A nearby shelter house has explanatory graphics. For information contact the Forest Supervisor, 901 S. Commercial St., Harrisburg, IL 62946; phone (618) 253-7114 or (800) 699-6637. *See Recreation Chart and the AAA Great Lakes CampBook.*

SHELBYVILLE (D-3) pop. 4,900, elev. 650′

Lake Shelbyville's 172 miles of shoreline are a magnet for those looking to relax and enjoy the out of doors. Just northeast of Shelbyville, the lake is bordered by two state parks, Eagle Creek and Wolf Creek, and Hidden Springs State Forest. Among the recreational activities available are fishing, swimming, water skiing, camping, picnicking, boating, hiking and hunting. *See Recreation Chart.*

Greater Shelbyville Area Chamber of Commerce: 124 N. Morgan St., Shelbyville, IL 62565; phone (217) 774-2221.

HORACE M. TALLMAN HOUSE, 816 W. Main St., was the home of the inventor of the first successful pickup hay baler, which revolutionized agricultural work. The restored 1905 home contains original furnishings and restored brass hardware. Daily 6 a.m.-10 p.m. Free. Phone (217) 774-3991.

LAKE SHELBYVILLE VISITOR CENTER, 1 mi. e. on SR 16, overlooks Lake Shelbyville and houses aquariums, reptiles, wildlife displays and some

hands-on exhibits. Center open daily 9-4, Memorial Day-Labor Day; Sat.-Sun. 10-4, early May-day before Memorial Day and day after Labor Day-late Oct. Tours of the dam are offered Sat. at 3, Sun. at 11, Memorial Day-Labor Day. Free. Phone (217) 774-3951.

SHELBY COUNTY COURTHOUSE is at E. Main and Washington sts. The 1879 Victorian-Gothic courthouse, across the street from the site where the Lincoln-Thorton debate occurred, contains paintings of the debate and historically significant people. A restored courtroom downstairs contains oak furnishings similar to those used in the 1800s. Allow 30 minutes minimum. Mon.-Fri. 8-4; closed holidays. Free. Phone the office of tourism at (217) 774-2244 or (800) 874-3529.

SKOKIE—see *Chicago p. 82.*

SOUTH HOLLAND—see *Chicago p. 82.*

SPRINGFIELD (D-3) pop. 105,400, elev. 610′

Springfield did not exist when statehood was granted to Illinois in 1818, but in 1837 it was chosen as the state capital, and the state legislature moved to Springfield in 1839. It is now an important government center.

The city is rich in memories of Abraham Lincoln, who lived here for 24 years; he practiced law, married and is buried in Springfield. The 4-block Lincoln Home National Historic Site is closed to automobile traffic, forming a pedestrian court surrounding the neighborhood in which the Lincoln home is situated.

This historic area has gaslights and wooden sidewalks. At Bank One, East Old State Capitol Plaza, visitors can view an original ledger of Lincoln's account with Springfield Marine & Fire Insurance Co. Also, the Old State Capitol is the site of Lincoln's "House Divided" speech.

Reminders of Lincoln are but one facet of Springfield's historical significance. Springfield also was the birthplace of poet Vachel Lindsay. And its Governor's Mansion, Fifth and Jackson streets, is the oldest continuously occupied governor's mansion in the nation and a center of Springfield's social life since 1855.

Springfield Convention and Visitors Bureau: 109 N. Seventh St., Springfield, IL 62701; phone (217) 789-2360 or (800) 545-7300.

Shopping areas: Simon White Oaks Mall, 2501 W. Wabash Ave., has Famous Barr, Montgomery Ward, P.A. Bergners and Sears as its anchors. Springfield's downtown historic district offers a variety of specialty shops as well as restaurants.

DANA-THOMAS HOUSE, 301 E. Lawrence Ave., was designed by Frank Lloyd Wright for socialite Susan Lawrence Dana of Springfield. Built 1902-04, the home is one of Wright's first major Prairie-style houses and one of the most elaborate in terms of size, detailing, art glass and furnishings. Particularly noteworthy are more than 100 pieces of original Wright-designed furniture and more than 250 examples of art glass doors, windows, panels and lamps.

Tours include a 10-minute slide presentation. Allow 1 hour minimum. Tours offered Wed.-Sun. 9-4; closed Jan. 1, Thanksgiving and Dec. 25. Admission $3; under 17, $1. Phone (217) 782-6776.

FIRST PRESBYTERIAN CHURCH, 321 S. 7th St. at Capitol Ave., contains the pew used by the Lincoln family 1852-61. Seven windows designed by Tiffany are in the church. Allow 30 minutes minimum. Tours are available Mon.-Fri. 10-4, June-Sept. Free. Phone (217) 528-4311.

HENSON-ROBINSON ZOO, 1100 East Lake Dr., has more than 300 animals from six continents on 14 garden-style acres. Exhibits include rare and endangered species, birds, penguins, reptiles, monkeys and otters. The zoo also houses three species of en-

dangered lemurs from Madagascar. The lemur exhibit is one of only three collections in the country. Allow 1 hour minimum. Mon.-Fri. 10-5 (also Wed. 5-8, June-Aug.), Sat.-Sun. 10-6, Mar. 15-Oct. 18. Admission $2.50; over 62, $1.25; ages 3-12, $1. Phone (217) 753-6217.

ILLINOIS STATE MUSEUM, on the s.w. corner of the Capitol Complex at Spring and Edwards sts., has three floors of exhibits about art, anthropology and natural history. Fine and decorative arts displays emphasize 3 centuries of Illinois living. Habitat groups and dioramas show animals native to Illinois. The Peoples of the Past exhibit illustrates American Indian history. Audiophones explain exhibits. Allow 1 hour minimum. Mon.-Sat. 8:30-5, Sun. noon-5; closed Jan. 1, Easter, Thanksgiving and Dec. 25. Free. Phone (217) 782-7386.

LAKE SPRINGFIELD, s.e. off Lake Shore Dr., is a 4,235-acre man-made lake with 57 miles of shoreline. A surfaced drive encircles the lake. Some 70 landscaped acres constitute the Lincoln Memorial

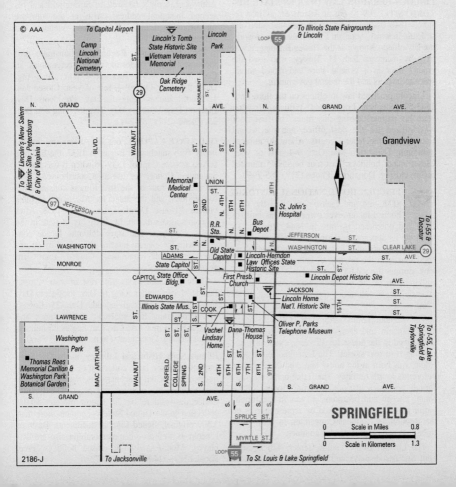

SPRINGFIELD

Garden and Nature Center, 2301 E. Lake Dr., which has 5 miles of rustic trails and an exhibit room. The recreational area, which offers boating, fishing, swimming, a children's zoo and a golf course, is at the east end of Vachel Lindsay Memorial Bridge.

Garden open daily dawn-dusk. Nature center open Tues.-Sat. 10-4, Sun. 1-4. Recreational schedules vary. Phone (217) 529-1111 for the nature center, 786-4075 for boating or fishing information or 786-4000 for golf information.

LINCOLN DEPOT HISTORIC SITE, at 10th and Monroe sts., originally was the Great Western Railroad Depot where Lincoln made his farewell address before leaving to assume the presidency. This concise and emotional speech has been compared with the Gettysburg Address for its eloquence. A video presentation re-creates Lincoln's journey to his inauguration. Allow 30 minutes minimum. Daily 10-4, Apr.-Aug. Free. Phone (217) 544-8695 or 788-1356.

LINCOLN-HERNDON LAW OFFICES STATE HISTORIC SITE, 209 S. 6th at Adams St., is in a restored 1840 building, said to be the only surviving structure in which Abraham Lincoln maintained working law offices. Known as the Tinsley Building, it was built by merchant Seth M. Tinsley, who used the ground floor as a general store and rented vacant space to lawyers and the federal government.

Lincoln practiced law in offices on the third floor 1843-52; Stephen Logan and William Herndon were his partners during this time. The first floor was utilized for the post office, and the second floor housed the federal courts. Allow 30 minutes minimum. Daily 9-5, Mar.-Oct.; 9-4, rest of year. Closed major holidays. Last tour begins 45 minutes before closing. Donations. Phone (217) 785-7960.

LINCOLN HOME NATIONAL HISTORIC SITE, 8th and Jackson sts., was the only home Lincoln ever owned; it was built in 1839 and purchased by him in 1844. Restored to resemble its appearance during the 1860s, the home is the centerpiece of a four-block historic neighborhood that is in the process of being returned to its look during the mid-19th century. A self-guiding walking tour of the neighborhood has signs posted at each house describing the home's residents in 1860.

The Lincoln family—Abraham, his wife Mary Todd Lincoln and their sons Robert, Willie and Tad—lived in the house for 17 years, eventually expanding it to two stories. The Lincolns' fourth son, Eddie, was born in the house and died there shortly before his fourth birthday. The frame home includes formal and back parlors, a dining room, sitting room, kitchen and bedrooms. It was in the formal parlor that Lincoln was asked by representatives of the Republican National Convention in May 1860 to be that party's presidential nominee.

The Lincoln Home Visitor Center, 426 S. Seventh St., has displays and sculptures and presents two orientation films on a continuous basis. The Dean House, across 8th Street, has an exhibit examining Lincoln's family life during his Springfield years; self-guiding tours are available.

Tours are conducted by park rangers; tickets can be acquired on a first-come, first-served basis on the day of the tour at the visitor center. Site daily 8-6, Apr.-Sept.; 8:30-5, rest of year. Closed Jan. 1, Thanksgiving and Dec. 25. Last tour begins 30 minutes before closing. Site and tour free. A fee is charged for parking. Phone (217) 492-4241.

 LINCOLN'S NEW SALEM HISTORIC SITE—see Petersburg p. 97.

LINCOLN'S TOMB STATE HISTORIC SITE, about 2 mi. n. of the Capitol in Oak Ridge Cemetery, is an impressive monument containing Lincoln's tomb and the crypts in which Mrs. Lincoln and three of their four children are buried. Statuettes depict Lincoln during his career. Bronze tablets bear the text of the Gettysburg Address, Lincoln's farewell to Springfield and his second inaugural address. Also at the site are memorials to Illinois' Korean and Vietnam war veterans.

The 114th Infantry Regiment demonstrates drill movements and performs retreat ceremonies in Civil War uniforms Tues. at 7 p.m., June-Aug. Daily 9-5, Mar.-Oct.; 9-4, rest of year. Closed Jan. 1, Martin Luther King Jr. Day, Presidents Day, Election Day, Veterans Day, Thanksgiving and Dec. 25. Phone (217) 782-2717.

OLD STATE CAPITOL, 6th and Adams sts., was Illinois' fifth statehouse. Begun in 1837, the building served as state Capitol 1839-76 when it was sold to Sangamon County for use as a courthouse. It was the scene of four of the five Illinois constitutional conventions, and the stage for Abraham Lincoln's famous "House Divided" speech in 1858. After Lincoln's assassination, his body lay in state in the House chambers. The stark dolomite facade contrasts with the elegant interior dominated by an impressive double staircase. Guided tours are available.

Daily 9-5, Mar.-Oct.; 9-4, rest of year. Closed Jan. 1, Martin Luther King Jr. Day, Presidents Day, Veterans Day, Thanksgiving and Dec. 25. Living-history programs take place Fri.-Sat. 10-noon and 1-4, June 1 to mid-Apr. Last tour begins 45 minutes before closing. Donations. Phone (217) 785-7960.

Illinois State Historical Library, in the Old State Capitol, houses a large collection of books about Illinois history, Civil War materials, manuscripts, Illinois newspapers, pictures and maps. The Lincoln Collection—said to be the largest pre-presidential collection in the United States—contains more than 1,500 original, signed Lincoln documents. Busts of Lincoln as well as other memorabilia also are displayed. Mon.-Fri. 8:30-5; closed holidays. Free. Phone (217) 524-6358 or 524-7216.

OLIVER P. PARKS TELEPHONE MUSEUM, 529 S. 7th St., contains a comprehensive collection of antique telephones and related memorabilia. Mon.-Fri. 9-4:30; closed holidays. Free. Phone the visitors bureau at (217) 789-5303 for information.

STATE CAPITOL is the central building of the State Capitol Group, extending more than 3 blks. along tree-shaded 2nd St. It was built 1868-88 and, at 405 feet high at the top of the flag pole, is one of the tallest buildings in central Illinois. The murals and relief work inside the dome are noteworthy. On the grounds are statues of Abraham Lincoln and Stephen A. Douglas. First floor open Mon.-Fri. 8-4, Sat.-Sun. 9-3; upstairs Mon.-Fri. 8-4. Closed Jan. 1, Easter, Thanksgiving, the day after Thanksgiving and Dec. 24-25. Tours are given daily 9-3. Free. Phone (217) 782-2099.

THOMAS REES MEMORIAL CARILLON, in Washington Park, is a 12-story tower with three observation decks that permit close inspection of the 67 imported bells. There is a videotape and guided explanation about the playing of the bells. Allow 30 minutes minimum. Carillon tours Tues.-Sun. noon-dusk, June-Aug.; Sat.-Sun. noon-dusk, Apr.-May and Sept.-Oct. (weather permitting). Concerts Wed. at 7 p.m., Sun. at 3 and 7 p.m., June-Aug.; Sun. at noon and 3, rest of year. Tours $2, children $1.50. Concerts free. Phone (217) 753-6219 for tour information.

Washington Park Botanical Garden, next to the Thomas Rees Memorial Carillon at 1740 W. Fayette St., is considered one of the finest horticultural attractions in central Illinois. It consists of a domed conservatory, a formal rose garden, a rockery and various floral display areas encompassing 20 acres. Six indoor flower shows are held annually. Mon.-Fri. noon-4, Sat.-Sun. noon-5; closed Dec. 24-25. Free. Phone (217) 753-6228.

STERLING (A-2) pop. 15,100, elev. 645′

An industrial city on the north bank of the Rock River, Sterling is noted as a national producer of builders' hardware. In 1839 the towns of Chatham and Harrisburgh combined as Sterling to capture the Whiteside County seat, which it held only briefly before losing the honor to Morrison.

Sterling Area Chamber of Commerce: 211 Locust St., Sterling, IL 61081; phone (815) 625-2400.

SAVE **DILLON HOME MUSEUM,** .5 mi. e. on SR 2 at 1005 E. Third St., dates from 1857. This former residence contains original furnishings and accessories of P.W. Dillon, son of the original owner of the Northwestern Steel & Wire Co. Local history exhibits are displayed in the museum carriage house. A vintage steam locomotive tender and caboose highlight the grounds. Allow 30 minutes minimum. Tues., Thurs. and Sat. 10-noon and 1-4, Sun. 1-5; closed major holidays. Admission $2; over 55, $1; under 12 free; family rate $4. Phone (815) 622-6202.

UNION—*see Chicago p. 82.*

URBANA (C-4) pop. 36,300, elev. 725′

The twin cities of Urbana and Champaign *(see place listing p. 47)* are separated by a single street. They also share the campus of the University of Illinois, though the majority of the university is within Urbana's property limits.

In 1822 William Tompkins built a cabin on land that would eventually become the city of Urbana. The town became the county seat of Champaign County in 1833, with the university opening its doors to students in 1868.

Plays and musicals are presented at The Station Theater, which features the Celebration Company, a local resident theater group. The theater is at 223 N. Broadway Ave.; phone (217) 384-4000.

Champaign County Convention & Visitors Bureau: 1817 S. Neil St., Suite 201, P.O. Box 1607, Champaign, IL 61820; phone (217) 351-4133.

UNIVERSITY OF ILLINOIS, I-74 Lincoln Ave. exit, was chartered in 1867 as the Illinois Industrial University. The center of campus activity is the Illini Union building, 1401 W. Green St. Prominent points of interest consist of Allerton Park, which includes a 1,500-acre woodland park near Monticello with lavish gardens, greenhouses and sculpture from around the world; Assembly Hall, an ultra-modern bowl-shaped building with a large edge-supported dome; and Memorial Stadium, which seats 75,000 people.

The University Library is said to be the third largest academic library in the nation. Morrow Plots is considered the nation's oldest agronomic experiment field; signposts describe experiments performed since 1876. For tour information contact the visitor center in Levis Faculty Center, 919 W. Illinois St., Urbana, IL 61801; phone (217) 333-0824. For general information phone (217) 333-1000.

John Philip Sousa Library & Museum, on the second floor of the Harding Band Building at 1103 S. 6th St., houses an extensive collection of Sousa's musical memorabilia including instruments, handwritten manuscripts and period band uniforms. Allow 1 hour minimum. Mon.-Fri. 8:30-noon and 1-5. Free. Phone (217) 244-9309.

Krannert Art Museum and Kinkead Pavilion, 500 E. Peabody Dr., houses an extensive collection of art from 4,000 B.C. to the present. More than 1,000 works include the old masters, Oriental paintings, photography, sculpture, ceramics and glassware. Allow 1 hour minimum. Tues.-Sat. 10-5 (also Wed. 5-8), Sun. 2-5. Free. Phone (217) 333-1860.

The Krannert Center for the Performing Arts, 500 S. Goodwin, is a $21 million complex of five theaters designed by Lincoln Center for the Performing Arts architect Max Abramovitz. A concert hall, theaters, an amphitheater, terraces and rehearsal spaces are connected by a marble and teak lobby. Allow 1 hour minimum. Tours daily at 3. Free. Phone (217) 333-6280 or (800) 527-2849.

UTICA (B-3) pop. 1,600, elev. 482′

ILLINOIS WATERWAY VISITOR CENTER, off SR 178 at 905 N. 27th Rd. (Dee Bennett Rd.), affords a view of the locking-through process at Starved Rock Lock and Dam. Towboats push heavy loads of grain, coal, petroleum and other products through the lock, one of eight along the 327-mile Illinois Waterway, which forms a navigable link between the Great Lakes and the Mississippi River.

The visitor center has displays devoted to the heritage of the region, a towboat pilot house and a slide presentation. Allow 1 hour minimum. Daily 9-8, Memorial Day-Labor Day; 8-5, rest of year. Free. Phone (815) 667-4054.

VANDALIA (D-3) pop. 6,100, elev. 512′

The wilderness site that developed into Vandalia was chosen by the state legislature as a second capital in 1819 in an effort to raise money. Lots were sold in this area of the Kaskaskia River Valley, and a town was created. Abraham Lincoln received his license to practice law and gained his first experience as legislator 1834-39. The community enjoyed its status as the state's political center for 20 years until a group of legislators under the leadership of Lincoln succeeded in moving the capital to Springfield.

The Little Brick House, 621 Saint Clair, is a simple 19th-century Italianate residence decorated with furnishings of the capital period, 1820-39. Displays feature memorabilia associated with important political and artistic figures from Illinois' early history, including Illinois writer James Hall, artist James Berry and Abraham Lincoln.

Vandalia Chamber of Commerce and Tourist Information Center: 1408 N. Fifth St., P. O. Box 238, Vandalia, IL 62471; phone (618) 283-2728.

OLD STATE CAPITOL, 315 W. Gallatin, was the last of three Vandalia buildings to serve as the state Capitol before the government was moved to Springfield. Abraham Lincoln served in the legislature. Used as a county courthouse until 1933, the 1836 building has been restored and furnished in period. Daily 8:30-5, Mar.-Oct.; 8-4, rest of year. Closed Jan. 1, Martin Luther King Jr. Day, Veterans Day, Thanksgiving and Dec. 25. Donations. Phone (618) 283-1161.

VERNON HILLS—see Chicago p. 83.

VOLO—see Chicago p. 83.

WATSEKA (C-4) pop. 5,400, elev. 634′

OLD COURTHOUSE MUSEUM, 103 W. Cherry St., displays local historical items in such re-created period settings as a Victorian parlor, a general store and the old county jail. A natural history area exhibits mounted animals native to the area. Allow 1 hour minimum. Mon.-Fri. 10:30-4:30 (also Sat.-Sun. 1-4, Apr.-Dec.); closed Jan. 1, Easter, Memorial Day, Labor Day, Thanksgiving and Dec. 25. Donations. Phone (815) 432-2215.

WAUCONDA—see Chicago p. 83.

WHEATON—see Chicago p. 83.

WILMETTE—see Chicago p. 84.

WINFIELD—see Chicago p. 84.

WOODHULL (B-2) pop. 800, elev. 824′

SAVE **MAX NORDEEN'S WHEELS MUSEUM,** 2 mi. n. via N. Division St., is on a 100-acre farm. The museum displays several rare and unique automobiles and a potpourri of more than 2,900 collectables. Exhibits include toys, clocks, radios, Civil War artifacts, American Indian relics and car emblems. Of particular interest are a Studebaker race car and John Deere's death notice. Tues.-Sun. 9-4, June-Aug.; Sat.-Sun. 9-4 in May and Sept.-Oct. Admission $3; ages 10-15, $1. Phone (309) 334-2589.

Indiana

Who's a Hoosier?

Poet James Whitcomb Riley, actor James Dean and comedian David Letterman

A Diverse Ecosystem

Shifting sands alter the landscape at Indiana Dunes National Lakeshore

Higher Learning and Boola Boola

South Bend boasts the University of Notre Dame and a football hall of fame

Wheels in Motion

Automobiles reach astounding speeds at the Indianapolis Motor Speedway

Hail to the Chiefs

Homes of three U.S. presidents welcome visitors

appealing at
any speed

REEVES & CO. ◇◇◇ COLUMBUS IND.

peed. It's what draws legions of racing fans to the center of Indiana every year. It's what the celebrated Indy 500 is all about.

But many of the state's most special treasures can be appreciated only if you ease up on the gas and downshift into a lower gear.

Browse through flea markets in the Amish country, where you'll discover masterfully crafted furniture as well as such whimsical delights as birdhouses and rocking horses.

Meander among fascinating flowstone and limestone formations in the caverns tunneling through the southern part of the state.

Sneak a smooch with your sweetheart before you emerge from the shadows of one of Parke County's romantic covered bridges.

Watch as swirling winds blow across the pristine Indiana Dunes to create a landscape that's in a continual state of transition.

The "crossroads of America" is made up of dusty country lanes and busy interstates, scenic drives and seemingly endless stretches of rural highway.

You can take it fast or take it slow, the latter coming more highly recommended. Regardless of the pace, Indiana welcomes you.

Hundreds of thousands of people converge on the center of Indiana each Memorial Day to watch a few dozen race cars whiz around a 2.5-mile oval track.

Perhaps they're enthralled by the strategic movements the racers employ, or maybe they're hoping to witness a spectacular 220-mph crash that results in screeching tires, plumes of smoke and bits of flying debris.

But there's a lot more to Indiana than the Indy 500.

Take Indianapolis, for instance. Tour the homes of President Benjamin Harrison and poet James Whitcomb Riley, or visit Crown Hill Cemetery to see the graves of outlaw John Dillinger, two-time Pulitzer Prize-winning novelist Booth Tarkington and vice presidents Charles Fairbanks, Thomas Hendricks and Thomas Marshall.

View the works of such famed artists as Georgia O'Keeffe, Frederic Remington, Charles Russell and J.M.W. Turner at the city's top-notch museums.

Cheer on the Indiana Pacers basketball team and thrill to hockey action by the Indianapolis Ice at Conseco Fieldhouse.

Venture outside the capital on one of the many highways that extend from the city limits like legs from the body of a spider, and you'll discover that the Hoosier State is simply loaded with possibilities.

A Treat for the Senses

You can satisfy all of your senses in northern Indiana. See how the Amish live in the quiet towns of Nappanee and Shipshewana. Listen to the "singing sands" of Indiana Dunes as the combination of quartz crystals, moisture, pressure and friction from your feet creates a rare musical ringing sound.

Test your pucker power at a pickle plant in St. Joe. Let the fragrance garden in South Bend's Leeper Park tickle your nose. Reach out to the touch-screens in Fort Wayne's Lincoln Museum to learn more about the country's 16th president.

Or head for one of the casino boats that leave from the shores of Lake Michigan. The melange of bright lights, food spreads and wall-to-wall *ka-chings!* strives for all-out sensory assault.

In contrast, the central part of the state is rich in history and heritage.

American Indians squared off with Gen. William Henry Harrison at Tippecanoe Battlefield, near Battle Ground.

French explorer Robert Cavelier reaches the area now known as Indiana by way of the St. Joseph River.
1679

Congress creates the Indiana Territory and appoints Gen. William Henry Harrison as governor.
1800

Indiana becomes a state, the 19th to be admitted to the Union.
1816

1787
Indiana becomes part of the Northwest Territory, which was ceded by the British in the Treaty of Paris 4 years earlier.

Indiana Historical Timeline

1824
Indianapolis succeeds Corydon as the state capital.

Thousands of escaping slaves passed through Fountain City, a Quaker community that served as a station of the Underground Railroad. Visitors can tour a Federal-style house that was a safe haven for many refugees.

Tours in Columbus focus on architectural diversity. A pool of talented designers—Alexander Girard, Robert Trent Jones, I.M. Pei, Eero and Eliel Saarinen and Harry Weese—have left their artful marks.

Innovators and Icons

In Elwood Haynes Museum in Kokomo, view the inventor's best creations: an early automobile and such alloys as stainless steel and cobalt-chromium, once used in dental and surgical instruments. Exhibits in the Dana birthplace of World War II correspondent Ernie Pyle detail his life and work.

The brief career of silver screen actor James Dean is outlined at his birthplace in Marion and in a gallery in Fairmount, the city in which he grew up and is buried.

In southern Indiana, you can leave human accomplishments behind and get down to communing with nature. Gaze into the trees along the shores of Bloomington's Lake Monroe to catch a glimpse of a nesting bald eagle. Watch a large herd of bison roaming on a farm in Elizabeth.

Pick up a walking stick and meander through the scenic back country hills of 195,000-acre Hoosier National Forest.

Settle into an electric boat and travel through Bluespring Caverns in Bedford. Pedestrian spelunkers have options, too. Daniel Boone and his brother Squire explored caverns in Corydon. Massive deposits of white flowstone characterize a cave in Marengo. Perhaps most impressive are the peculiar formations—such as an underground mountain and huge helictites—that mark the myriad rooms and passages in the caves of Wyandotte.

The many species of coral and prehistoric ocean life in the fossil bed at Falls of the Ohio State Park in Clarksville trace back to the Devonian Period, when land forms started to evolve from marine life.

Indianapolis Motor Speedway rightly grabs the spotlight for a day each year. But the "crossroads of America" is a whole lot more.

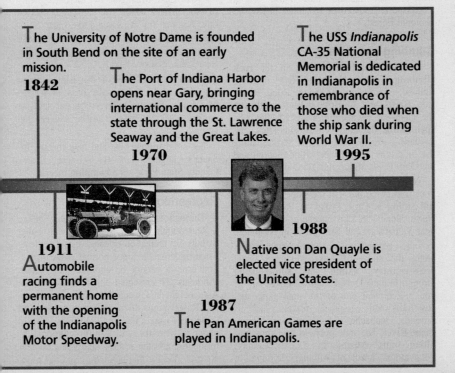

The University of Notre Dame is founded in South Bend on the site of an early mission.
1842

The Port of Indiana Harbor opens near Gary, bringing international commerce to the state through the St. Lawrence Seaway and the Great Lakes.
1970

The USS *Indianapolis* CA-35 National Memorial is dedicated in Indianapolis in remembrance of those who died when the ship sank during World War II.
1995

1911
Automobile racing finds a permanent home with the opening of the Indianapolis Motor Speedway.

1988
Native son Dan Quayle is elected vice president of the United States.

1987
The Pan American Games are played in Indianapolis.

Recreation

Although mountain treks are hard to come by in a state with no notable peaks, the 58-mile Knobstone Trail is rugged by average **hiking** standards. The trail—which stretches from Jackson-Washington State Forest, near Plattsburg, to Deam Lake State Recreation Area, west of Borden—passes through beautiful back country.

Invigorating short hikes also tempt hikers. Enjoy panoramic views of Celina and Indian lakes from the 12-mile Two Lakes Loop trail in Hoosier National Forest. Unusual limestone formations and scenic waterfalls at McCormick's Creek State Park, east of Spencer, make the thick woods worth exploring.

You'll find happy trails while **horseback riding** at Youngs Creek, south of Paoli, and German Ridge, 15 miles east of Tell City.

Comprising 800 miles of road and covering 11 routes throughout the state, the Hoosier Bikeway System is richly scenic. Guidebooks detailing each **bicycling** route are available; phone (317) 232-4180.

For more challenging **mountain biking** excursions, visit Wapehani Mountain Bike Park, near Bloomington; Bluhm County Park, west of Westville; and France Park, west of Logansport. Trails cover 157 miles in Hoosier National Forest.

Climbing and Caving

Head to Shoals if you're up for **rock climbing.** Follow the White River north to find such formations as House Rock, Riverside Bluffs and McBride's Bluff. Although the caves at Wyandotte make for the best **spelunking,** the many caves, sinkholes, disappearing streams and mineral springs along the limestone belt between Bloomington and the Ohio River all are intriguing diversions.

When the chills set *in*, don't let them keep you from going *out*. Hit the slopes for **downhill skiing** at Paoli Peaks, in Paoli; Perfect North Slopes, in Lawrenceburg; Pines Peak, near Valparaiso; and Ski World, in Nashville.

Take advantage of breathtaking sights along the shore of Lake Michigan while **cross-country skiing** or **snowshoeing** through Indiana Dunes National Lakeshore. If you prefer, visit one of the state parks that has trails and equipment rentals, such as Mounds, Ouabache, Potato Creek and Tippecanoe River. The state operates five **snowmobiling** trails: Miami, in Elkhart County; Potawatomi, north of Angola; Heritage, in southeast Allen County; Buffalo Run, west of South Bend; and Salamonie, along the south side of Salamonie Reservoir in Huntington and Wabash counties.

A quarter-mile track at Pokagon State Park, near Angola, lets you try **tobogganing** at speeds up to 40 mph.

Row, Row, Row Your Boat

Once the snow melts off and the lakes and rivers thaw, try your hand at water recreation. Go **canoeing** through 11 connecting lakes at Chain O' Lakes State Park, south of Albion; rentals are available from park concessionaires. Climb in your craft and go **kayaking** down Sugar Creek, which bisects Shades State Park.

After a heavy rain, put in at Big Pine Creek, near Rainsville, and paddle south to Attica. On the rare occasion that the water's high enough, you might catch a wild ride amid mild to exciting rapids. Arguably Indiana's swiftest river, the Whitewater—between Cambridge City and the Ohio state line—also is lively when conditions are right.

Boating and **sailing** opportunities abound on giant Lake Michigan, but there are plenty of other places where you can putter away a day. Set out for Wawasee Lake, near Syracuse; the Blue River, east of Marengo; Lake Monroe Reservoir, near Bloomington; or Patoka Lake, east of Jasper.

Catch a great view of the state's largest waterfall while **fishing** for bass in Cagles Mill Lake. The Ohio River is a hot spot for anglers seeking bass, catfish, sauger and crappie.

Set amid rolling hills and lush forests, Indiana's largest park—15,547-acre Brown County State Park—is a **camping** mecca.

Recreational Activities

Throughout the TourBook, you may notice a Recreational Activities heading with bullet listings of recreation-oriented establishments listed underneath. Since normal AAA inspection criteria cannot be applied, these establishments are presented only for information. Age, height and weight restrictions may apply. Reservations often are recommended and sometimes are required. Visitors should phone or write the attraction for additional information, and the address and phone number are provided for this purpose.

Fast Facts

POPULATION: 5,864,100.

AREA: 36,291 square miles; ranks 38th.

CAPITAL: Indianapolis.

HIGHEST POINT: 1,257 ft., near Bethel.

LOWEST POINT: 320 ft., Ohio River.

TIME ZONES: Eastern/Central. No DST except in counties near Louisville and Cincinnati (EDT) and near Chicago and Evansville (CDT).

MINIMUM AGE FOR DRIVERS: 16.

MINIMUM AGE FOR GAMBLING: 21.

SEAT BELT/CHILD RESTRAINT LAWS: Seat belts are required for driver and front-seat passengers; child restraints are mandatory for under 4.

HELMETS FOR MOTORCYCLISTS: Required for under 18.

RADAR DETECTORS: Permitted.

FIREARMS LAWS: Vary by state or county. Contact Indiana State Police, Attn: Firearms, Indiana Government Center N., 100 N. Senate, Indianapolis, IN 46204; phone (317) 232-8248.

HOLIDAYS: Jan. 1; Martin Luther King Jr. Day, Jan. (3rd Mon.); Lincoln's Birthday, Feb. 12; Washington's Birthday, Feb. (3rd Mon.); Good Friday; Primary Election Day, early May; Memorial Day, May (last Mon.); July 4; Labor Day, Sept. (1st Mon.); Columbus Day, Oct. (2nd Mon.); Election Day, Nov.; Veterans Day, Nov. 11; Thanksgiving; Dec. 25.

TAXES: Indiana's statewide sales tax is 5 percent. Local options are available for a 1 percent Food & Beverage Tax. Counties also may levy local lodgings taxes; rates range from 1 to 5 percent.

STATE INFORMATION CENTERS are on I-65N near the Kentucky state line; I-69S near the Michigan state line; I-70E near the Illinois state line; I-70W near the Ohio state line; I-74E near the Illinois state line; I-74W near the Ohio state line; and I-64W near the Illinois state line.

FURTHER INFORMATION FOR VISITORS:
Tourism Development Division
One N. Capitol, Suite 700
Indianapolis, IN 46204-2288
(800) 289-6646

FISHING AND HUNTING REGULATIONS:
Indiana Department of Natural Resources
402 W. Washington St., Rm. W160
Indianapolis, IN 46204
(317) 232-4200

NATIONAL FOREST INFORMATION:
Hoosier National Forest
811 Constitution Ave.
Bedford, IN 47421
(812) 275-5987
(877) 444-6777 (reservations)

Indiana Temperature Averages
Maximum / Minimum
From the records of the National Weather Service

	JAN	FEB	MAR	APR	MAY	JUNE	JULY	AUG	SEPT	OCT	NOV	DEC
Evansville	43 / 26	46 / 27	54 / 34	67 / 45	76 / 54	86 / 64	89 / 67	88 / 66	82 / 57	71 / 46	55 / 34	45 / 28
Fort Wayne	34 / 19	36 / 19	45 / 27	59 / 38	71 / 48	82 / 59	86 / 62	84 / 61	77 / 53	65 / 42	48 / 31	37 / 21
Indianapolis	37 / 21	39 / 23	48 / 30	61 / 40	72 / 51	82 / 60	86 / 64	85 / 63	78 / 55	67 / 44	50 / 32	39 / 23
South Bend	33 / 18	35 / 19	43 / 26	58 / 37	70 / 48	80 / 58	85 / 63	83 / 61	74 / 53	64 / 43	47 / 31	36 / 22

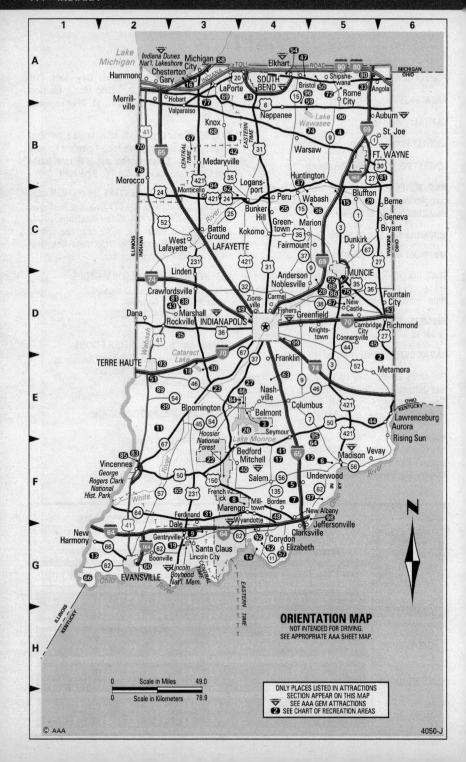

ORIENTATION MAP
NOT INTENDED FOR DRIVING.
SEE APPROPRIATE AAA SHEET MAP.

Scale in Miles 49.0
Scale in Kilometers 78.9

ONLY PLACES LISTED IN ATTRACTIONS
SECTION APPEAR ON THIS MAP.
SEE AAA GEM ATTRACTIONS
SEE CHART OF RECREATION AREAS

© AAA

4050-J

Points of Interest Offering A
Great Experience for Members

Auburn (A-6)

AUBURN CORD DUESEN-BERG MUSEUM—Indiana-made luxury motorcars are the pride of this collection of vintage vehicles. See p. 121.

Elkhart (A-4)

RUTHMERE MUSEUM—Beaux-arts architecture and opulent decor characterize this early 20th-century mansion built for A.R. Beardsley, a co-founder of Miles Laboratories Inc. See p. 127.

Fishers (D-4)

CONNER PRAIRIE—A settler's homestead and a pioneer village offer a 19th-century Indiana living-history experience. See p. 148.

Fort Wayne (B-6)

LINCOLN MUSEUM—Mementos spanning the 16th president's lifetime and reminiscent of his law career and presidency are displayed. See p. 131.

THE LINCOLN MUSEUM
The Life and Legacy of Abraham Lincoln

Indiana Dunes National Lakeshore (A-2)

INDIANA DUNES NATIONAL LAKESHORE—Miles of scenic trails traverse this diverse 15,000-acre landscape along the southern shore of Lake Michigan. See p. 134.

Indianapolis (D-4)

THE CHILDREN'S MUSEUM OF INDIANAPOLIS AND CINEDOME THEATER—Two theaters, a planetarium and five stories of exhibits invite young minds to explore. See p. 141.

EITELJORG MUSEUM OF AMERICAN INDIANS AND WESTERN ART—Original works by Georgia O'Keeffe, Frederic Remington and Charles Russell share the spotlight with American Indian objects of art and utility. See p. 143.

HOME OF JAMES WHITCOMB RILEY—The poet of the Hoosier dialect made this Victorian residence his home for 23 years. See p. 141.

INDIANAPOLIS MOTOR SPEEDWAY—See racing action past and present at the speedway's infield museum and the surrounding 2.5-mile oval racecourse. See p. 142.

INDIANAPOLIS MUSEUM OF ART—Four pavilions on 150 acres house paintings, sculpture, drawings and textiles from around the world, some dating to the Renaissance. See p. 142.

PRESIDENT BENJAMIN HARRISON HOME—Original furnishings, political mementos and family clothing serve as reminders that the nation's 23rd president occupied this Italianate mansion for many years. See p. 143.

Lincoln Boyhood National Memorial (G-3)

LINCOLN BOYHOOD NATIONAL MEMORIAL—Abraham Lincoln's formative years were spent on a rural family farm that has been recreated for visiting. See p. 151.

Madison (F-5)

LANIER MANSION STATE HISTORIC SITE—A banker who loaned the state $1 million during the Civil War built this Greek Revival home in 1844. See p. 152.

Mitchell (F-4)

SPRING MILL STATE PARK—Amid 100 acres of virgin woodland stands a restored 1815 frontier trading post complete with a gristmill, a sawmill, an apothecary and shops. See p. 155.

South Bend (A-4)

COLLEGE FOOTBALL HALL OF FAME—Every aspect of campus gridiron competition is featured here, from players to fans, cheerleaders to bands. See p. 161.

COPSHAHOLM, THE OLIVER MANSION—This turn-of-the-20th-century residence of a Scottish industrialist is appointed with luxuries from the era. See p. 161.

NORTHERN INDIANA CENTER FOR HISTORY—St. Joseph Valley history, from prehistoric times to the present, is the focus of this museum. See p. 161.

Wyandotte (G-4)

WYANDOTTE CAVES—A network of passages, an underground mountain and some of the largest helictites in the world are the natural marvels that await cave explorers. See p. 166.

RECREATION AREAS	MAP LOCATION	CAMPING	PICNICKING	HIKING TRAILS	BOATING	BOAT RAMP	BOAT RENTAL	FISHING	SWIMMING	PETS ON LEASH	BICYCLE TRAILS	WINTER SPORTS	VISITOR CENTER	LODGE/CABINS	FOOD SERVICE
NATIONAL FOREST (See place listing p. 134)															
Hoosier 197,000 acres. Southern Indiana.		●	●	●	●	●		●	●	●	●				
NATIONAL LAKESHORE (See place listing p. 134)															
Indiana Dunes (A-2) 15,000 acres on the southern shore of Lake Michigan.		●	●	●	●			●	●	●	●				
STATE															
Atterbury (E-4) 5,508 acres 2 mi. n.w. of Edinburgh off US 31. Boats with electric motors only. Hunting.	63	●		●	●			●		●					
Bass Lake Beach (B-3) 21 acres 12 mi. n. of Winamac on US 35. Water skiing; bathhouse, playground.	1	●	●		●				●						
Brookville Lake (E-6) 16,445 acres 3 mi. w. of Roseburg off SR 101. Interpretive program. Hunting, water skiing; horseshoe pits, playground, shooting range, volleyball courts.	2	●	●	●	●	●	●	●	●						●
Brown County (E-4) 15,696 acres 2 mi. s.e. of Nashville on SR 135. Nature program. Horse rental, horse trails, playground, pool. (See Bloomington p. 122)	3	●	●	●				●	●			●	●	●	●
Cagles Mill Lake (Lieber SRA) (E-3) 8,075 acres 10 mi. w. of Cloverdale on SR 42. Interpretive program. Hunting, water skiing; activity center, basketball court, fitness trail, horseshoe pits, playground. Hunting facilities include paved trails and deer blinds for the physically impaired.	18	●	●	●	●	●		●	●						
Cecil M. Harden Lake (Raccoon SRA) (D-3) 4,065 acres 9 mi. e. of Rockville on US 36. Interpretive program. Hunting, water skiing; basketball and volleyball courts, horseshoe pits, playground.	35	●	●	●	●	●		●	●						
Chain O' Lakes (B-5) 2,718 acres 6 mi. s. of Albion on SR 9. Nature program. Boats with electric motors only. Cross-country skiing.	4	●	●	●	●			●				●		●	
Charlestown (F-5) 2,300 acres 8 mi. e of Charlestown on SR 62.	97	●	●	●				●							
Clark (F-4) 23,979 acres 1 mi. n. of Henryville off US 31. Boats with electric motors only. Hunting; playground.	5	●	●	●	●			●							
Clifty Falls (F-5) 1,360 acres 1 mi. w. of Madison on SR 56. Nature program. Tennis; pool, waterslide.	6	●	●	●					●				●	●	●
Crosley (F-5) 4,084 acres 1 mi. s. of Vernon off SR 7. Boats with electric motors only. Hunting.	64	●		●	●	●		●							

RECREATION AREAS

Recreation Area	Map Location	Camping	Picnicking	Hiking Trails	Boating	Boat Ramp	Boat Rental	Fishing	Swimming	Pets on Leash	Bicycle Trails	Winter Sports	Visitor Center	Lodge/Cabins	Food Service
Deam Lake (F-4) 1,300 acres 5 mi. w. of Borden on SR 60. Boats with electric motors only. Hunting; bathhouse, playground.	7	•	•	•	•	•	•	•	•				•		
Falls of the Ohio (G-5) 65 acres 2 mi. w. of Clarksville on W. Riverside Dr. Fossil beds. *(See Clarksville p. 124)*	98	•	•	•	•			•							
Ferdinand (G-3) 7,657 acres 6 mi. e. of Ferdinand on SR 264. Boats with electric motors only. Hunting; playground. Primitive camping only.	9	•	•	•	•	•	•	•	•	•					
Fort Harrison (D-4) 1,700 acres off 56th St. in Indianapolis. Golf, horse trails. Historic military.	99	•	•					•						•	•
Glendale (F-3) 8,060 acres 7.5 mi. s. of Montgomery via Sportsman Rd. Hunting.	65	•	•		•	•	•	•		•					
Greene-Sullivan (E-2) 6,764 acres 7 mi. s. of Dugger on SR 159. Boats with electric motors only. Hunting; equestrian's campground, playground.	11	•	•	•	•	•	•	•							
Hardy Lake (F-5) 2,062 acres 8 mi. n.e. of Austin off SR 256. Interpretive program. Hunting, water skiing; basketball and volleyball courts, horseshoe pits, playground.	12	•	•	•	•	•	•	•	•						
Harmonie (G-1) 3,465 acres 4 mi. s. of New Harmony on SR 69. Nature program. Boat launch ramp into Wabash River, horse trails, playground, pool, waterslide.	13	•	•	•	•	•		•	•	•	•		•	•	
Harrison-Crawford (G-4) 25,619 acres 10 mi. s.w. of Corydon on SR 462. Nature program. Hunting; horse trails, playground, pool. *(See Corydon p. 125)*	14	•	•	•	•	•	•	•	•				•		
Wyandotte Woods (G-4) 2,000 acres within Harrison-Crawford State Forest, 10 mi. s.w. of Corydon on SR 462. Nature and cultural art program. Hunting, ice fishing; boat launch into Ohio River, equestrian's campground, horse trails, pool. *(See Corydon p. 125)*	92	•	•	•				•	•	•			•		
Hovey Lake (G-1) 7,000 acres 10 mi. s. of Mount Vernon on SR 69. Hunting.	66	•	•		•	•	•	•		•			•		
Huntington Lake (C-5) 8,295 acres 4 mi. s.e. of Huntington on US 224. Interpretive and cultural art programs. Archery, hunting, ice fishing, water skiing; fitness trail, model airport, playground. *(See Huntington p. 134)*	15	•	•					•	•	•					
Indiana Dunes (A-3) 2,182 acres along Lake Michigan, 3 mi. n. of Chesterton on SR 25E. Nature program. Cross-country skiing; playground. *(See Chesterton p. 124)*	16	•	•					•	•			•	•		
Jackson-Washington (F-4) 15,330 acres 3 mi. s.e. of Brownstown on SR 39. Boats with electric motors only. Hunting, ice fishing; horse trails, playground.	17	•	•	•	•	•		•		•					
Jasper-Pulaski (B-3) 8,022 acres 6 mi. n. of Medaryville on SR 143, just w. of US 421. Boats with electric motors only. Hunting, ice fishing; playground. *(See Medaryville p. 154)*	67	•	•					•		•					
Kankakee (B-3) 4,100 acres along the Kankakee River near Knox, 1 mi. n. on US 35, then 5 mi. w. on SR 8. Hunting, ice fishing. *(See Knox p. 150)*	68		•		•	•		•		•					
Kingsbury (A-3) 6,060 acres 8 mi. s. of LaPorte on US 35. Boats with electric motors only. Hunting, ice fishing. *(See LaPorte p. 151)*	69	•	•					•		•					
Lake Monroe (E-4) 23,952 acres 6 mi. s.e. of Bloomington on SR 446. Interpretive and cultural art program. Hunting, water skiing; playground, seasonal food service. *(See Bloomington p. 122)*	26	•	•	•	•	•	•	•	•	•			•		•
La Salle (B-2) 3,640 acres 3 mi. n. of Lake Village on US 41. Hunting.	70				•	•		•		•					
Lincoln (G-3) 1,747 acres .5 mi. s. of Dale on SR 162. Nature and cultural art programs. Boats with electric motors only. Canoeing; amphitheater, playground, seasonal food service. *(See Lincoln City p. 152)*	19	•	•	•	•	•	•	•	•	•			•	•	
Martin (F-3) 7,085 acres 4 mi. n.e. of Shoals on US 50. Boats with electric motors only. Hunting; playground.	22	•	•	•				•	•				•		

RECREATION AREAS

	MAP LOCATION	CAMPING	PICNICKING	HIKING TRAILS	BOATING	BOAT RAMP	BOAT RENTAL	FISHING	SWIMMING	PETS ON LEASH	BICYCLE TRAILS	WINTER SPORTS	VISITOR CENTER	LODGE/CABINS	FOOD SERVICE
McCormick's Creek (E-3) 1,852 acres 3 mi. e. of Spencer on SR 46. Nature and cultural arts programs. Tennis; amphitheater, horse rental, playground, pool.	23	•	•	•					•				•	•	•
Minnehaha (E-2) 12,500 acres 2 mi. s. of Sullivan on SR 54. Boats with electric motors only. Hunting.	89		•	•	•	•		•		•					
Mississinewa Lake (C-4) 14,386 acres 8 mi. s.e. of Peru off SR 124. Interpretive and cultural arts programs. Hunting, water skiing; frisbee golf course, playground.	25	•	•	•	•	•	•	•	•	•					
Morgan-Monroe (E-4) 23,443 acres 12 mi. s. of Martinsville off SR 37. Interpretive program. Boats with electric motors only. Hunting; playground, volleyball courts.	27	•	•	•	•	•		•		•					
Mounds (D-5) 288 acres 3 mi. e. of Anderson on SR 32. Nature and cultural arts programs. Canoe rental, cross-country ski equipment rental, horse trails, playground, pool. *(See Anderson p. 147)*	28	•	•	•				•	•				•	•	
Ouabache (C-5) 1,104 acres 4 mi. e. of Bluffton on SR 216. Nature and cultural arts programs. Boats with electric motors only. Cross-country skiing, tennis; basketball courts, firetower, horse trails, playground, pool, waterslide. *(See Bluffton p. 123)*	29	•	•	•	•	•	•	•	•	•			•		
Owen-Putman (E-3) 6,236 acres 5 mi. n. of Spencer on US 231. Hunting; horse trails.	30	•	•	•				•		•					
Patoka Reservoir (G-3) 26,000 acres 16 mi. e. of Jasper on SR 164. Interpretive and cultural arts programs. Archery, frisbee golf course, hunting, water skiing; fitness trail, playground.	31	•	•	•	•	•	•	•	•	•	•		•		
Pigeon River (A-5) 11,500 acres 1 mi. s. of Howe off SR 9. Boats with electric motors only. Hunting.	72	•	•	•		•		•		•					
Pokagon (A-6) 1,203 acres 5 mi. n. of Angola on SR 727. Nature program. Cross-country skiing, ice skating, tennis, water skiing; horse rental, playground, refrigerated .2-mile toboggan run, warming shelter. *(See Angola p. 121)*	33	•	•	•	•	•	•	•	•			•	•	•	•
Potato Creek (A-4) 3,840 acres 2 mi. e. of North Liberty on SR 4. Nature program. Boats with electric motors only. Bicycle rental, cross-country ski equipment rental, equestrian's campground, horse trails, playground. *(See South Bend p. 160)*	34	•	•	•	•	•	•	•	•	•	•	•			
Salamonie Lake (C-5) 11,506 acres 9 mi. s. of Andrews on SR 105. Nature center. Interpretive program. Cross-country skiing, hunting, snowmobiling, water skiing; equestrian's campground, horse trail, playground, volleyball courts.	36	•	•	•	•	•	•	•	•	•		•			
Salamonie River (B-4) 621 acres 2 mi. s. of Lagro on SR 524. Boats with electric motors only. Cross-country skiing, hunting; equestrian's campground, horse trails, playground.	37	•	•	•	•	•		•		•					
Shades (D-3) 3,084 acres 17 mi. w. of Crawfordsville on SR 234. Nature program. Playground.	38	•	•	•				•		•					
Shakamak (E-2) 1,766 acres 4 mi. w. of Jasonville on SR 48. Nature program. Boats with electric motors only. Tennis; horse rental, playground.	39	•	•	•	•			•	•				•	•	
Spring Mill (F-4) 1,319 acres 3.2 mi. e. of Mitchell on SR 60 from SR 37. Historic. Nature program. Boats with electric motors only. Cave exploration, tennis; horse rental, playground, pool, Spring Mill Theatre. *(See Mitchell p. 155)*	40	•	•	•	•			•	•				•	•	•
Starve Hollow Beach (F-4) 300 acres 2 mi. s. of Vallonia off SR 135. Interpretive program. Boats with electric motors only. Basketball and volleyball courts, playground, softball fields.	41	•	•	•	•	•		•	•	•			•		
Summit Lake (D-5) 2,683 acres 10 mi. s. of Muncie off SR 3. Nature and cultural arts programs. Cross-country skiing; bathhouse, bicycle rental.	86	•	•	•	•	•		•		•		•			
Tippecanoe River (B-3) 2,761 acres 6 mi. n. of Winamac on US 35. Nature program. Boats with electric motors only. Cross-country ski equipment rental, equestrian's campground, playground, tent rental.	42	•	•	•	•	•		•		•		•			
Tri County (B-5) 3,486 acres 6 mi. s. of Syracuse on SR 13. Boats with electric motors only. Hunting.	74		•	•	•		•		•						

RECREATION AREAS

	MAP LOCATION	CAMPING	PICNICKING	HIKING TRAILS	BOATING	BOAT RAMP	BOAT RENTAL	FISHING	SWIMMING	PETS ON LEASH	BICYCLE TRAILS	WINTER SPORTS	VISITOR CENTER	LODGE/CABINS	FOOD SERVICE
Turkey Run (D-3) 2,382 acres 5 mi. n. of Marshall on SR 47 via SR 236 and US 41. Scenic. Nature center with planetarium, wildlife window and live animal displays. Tennis; horse rental, museum, playground. *(See Marshall p. 153)*	43	•	•	•	•			•	•				•	•	•
Versailles (E-5) 5,909 acres 1 mi. e. of Versailles on US 50. Nature program. Boats with electric motors only. Horse rental, playground, pool, waterslide.	44	•	•	•	•	•	•	•	•						
Whitewater (D-5) 1,710 acres 3 mi. s. of Liberty off SR 101. Nature program. Boats with electric motors only. Bicycle rental, equestrian's campground, horse rental, horse trails, playground.	45	•	•	•	•	•	•	•	•				•	•	
Willow Slough (B-2) 9,938 acres 2 mi. w. of US 41. Boats with electric motors only. Hunting, ice fishing. *(See Morocco p. 155)*	76	•	•		•	•	•	•		•					
Yellowwood (E-4) 22,508 acres 5 mi. w. of Nashville off SR 46. Boats with electric motors only. Hunting; playground.	46	•	•	•	•			•		•			•		
OTHER															
Bixler Lake Park (A-5) 500 acres on Park Ave. in Kendallville. No motor boats permitted. Ice skating, tennis; jogging track, paddleboats, playground.	90	•	•	•	•			•	•	•	•				
Bonneyville Mill Park (A-4) 223 acres on the Little Elkhart River, 2.5 mi. e. of Bristol on SR 120, then .5 mi. s. on CR 131. Cross-country skiing, tobogganing. *(See Bristol p. 123)*	47		•	•				•		•		•	•		
Buffalo Trace Park (G-4) 147 acres .5 mi. e. of Palmyra on SR 150. Playground.	48	•	•	•	•	•	•	•	•	•					•
Clem's Lake (B-6) 57 acres 2.5 mi. n.e. of Decatur on CR 200E.	91	•	•		•			•	•	•					
Crooked Lake (A-5) 802 acres 2 mi. w. of Angola on US 20, then 3 mi. n. on I-69. Playground.	80	•	•		•	•	•	•	•						
Dobbs (E-2) 105 acres at SR 46 and Poplar St. in Terre Haute. Cross-country skiing, ice skating. *(See Terre Haute p. 162)*	93		•	•				•				•	•		
Eagle Creek (D-4) 3,800 acres 10 mi. n.w. of Indianapolis via 56th and 71st streets from I-65 or I-465. Historic. Nature program. Cross-country skiing, golf. *(See Indianapolis p. 141)*	49		•	•	•	•	•	•	•	•		•	•		
Eby Pines (A-5) 40 acres 3 mi. e. of Bristol on SR 120.	50	•	•	•				•	•	•					
Fowler Park (E-2) 163 acres 7 mi. s. of Terre Haute on US 41. Playground.	51	•	•	•				•	•	•					
France Park (B-3) 500 acres 4 mi. w. of Logansport via US 24. Cross-country skiing, ice fishing, ice skating, miniature golf, scuba diving, snowmobiling; waterslide. *(See Logansport p. 152)*	62	•	•	•	•			•	•	•		•			•
Hayswood Nature Reserve (G-4) 160 acres just s. of Corydon via SR 135.	52		•	•				•	•	•					
Henry County Memorial (D-5) 390 acres .5 mi. n. of New Castle off SR 3 on CR 100N. Golf (18 holes), ice skating, sledding; paddleboats, playgrounds.	87		•									•	•		•	•
Indiana Beach (B-3) 40 acres .5 mi. w. on US 24, then 3.2 mi. n. on W. Shafer Dr. Miniature golf; bathhouse, boardwalk, toboggan slide, water park. *(See Monticello p. 155)*	94	•	•		•			•	•					•	•
Kimmell Park (F-2) 16 acres on the Wabash River, 1.5 mi. n.w. of Vincennes on Oliphant Dr.	83	•	•		•	•		•							
Lake Lemon (E-3) 1,730 acres 10 mi. e. of Bloomington on SR 45 to Tunnel Rd. Canoe rental, nature trail.	84		•		•	•	•	•		•					
Marengo Cave National Landmark (F-4) 120 acres 9 mi. n. of I-64 via SRs 64 and 66. Canoeing, horse rental. *(See Marengo p. 153)*	8		•	•			•	•					•		•
Middlefork Reservoir (D-6) 175 acres 2 mi. n. of Richmond on US 27.	53		•	•	•	•	•	•		•	•				
Muscatatuck County Park (E-5) 200 acres at 325 N SR 7&3 in North Vernon. Ruins and historic buildings.	95	•	•	•											
Ouabache Trails (F-2) 254 acres 2 mi. n. of Vincennes off US 50 on Fort Knox Rd. Basketball courts, nature trails, playground, shelters.	85	•	•					•		•			•		

RECREATION AREAS

RECREATION AREAS	MAP LOCATION	CAMPING	PICNICKING	HIKING TRAILS	BOATING	BOAT RAMP	BOAT RENTAL	FISHING	SWIMMING	PETS ON LEASH	BICYCLE TRAILS	WINTER SPORTS	VISITOR CENTER	LODGE/CABINS	FOOD SERVICE
Oxbow (A-4) 223 acres 2.5 mi. s. of Elkhart on CR 45. Frisbee golf course.	54		•	•	•	•		•		•		•			
Prairie Creek Lake (D-5) 2,500 acres 5 mi. s.e. of Muncie off US 35.	55	•	•	•	•	•	•	•	•	•	•	•	•		
River Preserve County Park (A-5) 1,055 acres 1 mi. e. of SR 15 at the jct. of CRs 29 and 142 in Benton. Canoeing.	96	•	•	•				•		•		•			
Soldiers Memorial Park (A-3) 556 acres around Stone Lake on Grangemouth Rd., 1 mi. n.w. of LaPorte. *(See LaPorte p. 151)*	77		•	•	•	•		•		•			•		•
South Harrison (G-4) 220 acres 4 mi. s.w. of Elizabeth on SR 11. Miniature golf; playground.	57		•	•						•	•				•
Washington Park (A-3) 90 acres on the lakeshore at the end of Franklin Street in Michigan City. Tennis. Zoo. *(See Michigan City p. 154)*	58		•	•	•	•		•		•	•				•
Waveland Lake (D-3) 608 acres 13 mi. s. of Crawfordsville via SR 47 in Waveland. Tennis.	81	•	•		•	•		•	•						
Wawasee Lake (A-5) 3,000 acres at Wawasee on SR 13.	59		•	•	•	•	•	•	•	•			•		
Wesselman Park (G-2) 400 acres at 551 N. Boeke Rd. in Evansville. Golf (18-hole par 3), tennis; fitness trail; playground. Nature preserve adjacent. *(See Evansville p. 128)*	60		•	•						•	•		•		
Westwood (D-5) 735 acres 3 mi. w. of New Castle off SR 38. Boats with electric motors only. Ice fishing; horse trails, playground.	88	•	•	•	•	•		•		•		•		•	

AAA Spiral Guides

18 titles now available including:
- *Australia • Ireland • London*
- *New York • Orlando & Florida • Paris*

*I*ntroducing the AAA Spiral Guides, a series of one-of-a-kind travel companions, brought to you by AAA, the world's largest publisher of travel information.

The AAA Spiral Guides feature:

- Revolutionary design – exclusive lay-flat spiral binding

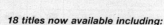

- Spectacular graphics – awesome photos and drawings

- Engaging text – entertaining, insightful descriptions

- Special member discount

Bound To Get You More For Your Vacation Dollars!

Points of Interest

ANDERSON—*see Indianapolis p. 147.*

ANGOLA (A-6) pop. 5,800, elev. 1,056′

Once a hunting ground for the Potawatomi and Miami Indians, Angola was settled in the mid-1800s by pioneers from the Northeast who named the town after a city in New York. Angola grew as its public square became a trading place for American Indians and farmers. Evidence of the Indians' presence can be found in many area fields, which yield an abundance of flint spearpoints and arrowheads.

Angola is a vacation center in Indiana's lake resort region, where more than 101 lakes provide recreational opportunities. Pokagon State Park *(see Recreation Chart)* is 5 miles north on SR 727.

Of interest is the Steuben County Courthouse on Public Square. Built in 1868, the courthouse is a replica of Boston's Faneuil Hall. Also on the square is the Soldiers' Monument, honoring county soldiers who served in the Civil War. Tri-State University is southwest.

Steuben County Tourism Bureau: 207 S. Wayne, Angola, IN 46703; phone (800) 581-0908.

AUBURN (A-6) pop. 9,400, elev. 862′

A light industrial center in a rich farming region, Auburn is one of the oldest towns in DeKalb County. One of the nation's earliest car manufacturers, the W.H. McIntyre Co., operated in Auburn 1908-15. From 1900 to 1937 the city was the site of the Auburn Automobile Co., maker of luxury cars, including the popular Auburn Boattail Speedster and the noted front-wheel-drive Cord.

DeKalb County Visitors Bureau: 204 N. Jackson St., Auburn, IN 46706; phone (219) 927-1499 or (877) 833-3282.

AUBURN CORD DUESENBERG MUSEUM, 1 mi. s.e. of I-69 via SR 8 following signs, at 1600 S. Wayne St., is in the 1930 Art Deco factory showroom built for the Auburn Automobile Co., manufacturer of the legendary Auburn, Cord and Duesenberg luxury motorcars. The museum features more than 100 antique and classic automobiles from the 19th century to the present. The focus is on the innovative and boldly styled Auburns, Cords and Duesenbergs produced in Indiana during the 1920s and 1930s.

Highlights also include automobiles produced by Packard, Cadillac and Rolls-Royce as well as rare cars built in Indiana. Allow 1 hour, 30 minutes minimum. Daily 9-5; closed Jan. 1, Thanksgiving and Dec. 25. Admission $7; ages 6-18, $4.50; family rate $20. Phone (260) 925-1444.

NATIONAL AUTOMOTIVE AND TRUCK MUSEUM, 1000 Gordon M. Buehrig Pl., displays vintage cars and trucks in a former automobile manufacturing facility. Also exhibited are displays of toy vehicles and other memorabilia. Daily 9-5. Admission $5; ages 5-12, $2. AX, MC, VI. Phone (260) 925-9100.

AURORA—*see Cincinnati in Ohio p. 204.*

BATTLE GROUND (C-3) pop. 800

TIPPECANOE BATTLEFIELD is off SR 43, 1.2 mi. s. of I-65. A monument marks the site of the 1811 battle in which Gen. William Henry Harrison, governor of the Indiana Territory in the early 1800s and ninth president of the United States, defeated the American Indians led by Prophet, the brother of Tecumseh. The battle is explained through a series of exhibits and audiovisual presentations at the interpretive center museum.

The 90-acre park includes picnic areas and scenic trails. Park daily dawn-dusk. Museum Mon.-Sat. 10-5, Sun. noon-5, June-Nov.; Tues.-Sun. noon-5, rest of year. Closed Jan. 1, Thanksgiving and Dec. 25. Park free. Museum $3; over 59, students with ID and ages 4-12, $2. Phone (765) 567-2147.

BEDFORD (F-4) pop. 13,800, elev. 694'

Several of the nation's buildings—the Empire State Building, the Chicago Museum of Fine Arts, the Mellon Institute in Pittsburgh and buildings of the Federal Triangle and the Washington Cathedral in Washington, D.C.—are partly constructed of limestone from the Bedford area.

Bedford Area Chamber of Commerce: 1116 16th St., Bedford, IN 47421-0068; phone (812) 275-4493.

SAVE **BLUESPRING CAVERNS** is 2 mi. s.w. on US 50 from jct. with SR 37, then .5 mi. w. on CR 450S. Lighted electric boats travel the underground passage of a large river on 1-hour guided tours. Blind cave fish and crayfish can be seen. A light jacket is recommended, as the cavern temperature is 52 F year-round. Daily 9-5, Memorial Day-Oct. 31; Sat.-Sun. 9-5, Apr. 1-day before Memorial Day. Admission $10; ages 3-15, $5. DS, MC, VI. Phone (812) 279-9471.

BELMONT (E-4)

T.C. STEELE STATE HISTORIC SITE, on 211 acres on T.C. Steele Rd. 1.5 mi. s. off SR 46, includes the home and studio of Theodore Clement Steele, Indiana landscape artist and founder of the Brown County Art Colony. More than 60 of his paintings are displayed. Also featured are five nature trails and gardens. Picnicking is permitted. Leashed pets are permitted. Allow 30 minutes minimum. Tues.-Sat. 9-5, Sun. 1-5, mid-Mar. to mid-Dec.; closed Easter and Thanksgiving. Donations. Phone (812) 988-2785.

BERNE (C-6) pop. 3,600, elev. 863'

Swiss architecture found throughout Berne reflects the influence of the Swiss Mennonites who settled in the region in 1852. More than 3,600 Amish operate farms in the area. Their horses and buggies can be seen at hitching posts in town on shopping days.

The Swiss Heritage Village and Museum, on 22-acres, has 15 buildings that depict the lives of Berne's early Swiss settlers; included is the oldest Mennonite church in Indiana.

Another point of interest is the Berne Furniture Co. at Berne and Behring streets; the manufacturer of upholstered furniture offers tours by appointment.

Berne Chamber of Commerce: 175 W. Main St., P.O. Box 85, Berne, IN 46711; phone (260) 589-8080.

BLOOMINGTON (E-3) pop. 60,600, elev. 748'

Indiana University, one of the oldest major state universities west of the Allegheny Mountains, began operation in Bloomington in 1820. Of particular interest on the beautiful 1,850-acre campus are the Thomas Hart Benton murals in the University Theatre, Woodburn Hall and the auditorium.

Some 30 working quarries in the area produce quality limestone; examples of this natural feature can be seen in local architecture. Within an hour's drive of the city are several state parks, including Brown County State Park near Lake Monroe *(see attraction listing)*. Lake Lemon, surrounded by a landscape of ridge and ravine that is typical of southern Indiana, is just east. *See Recreation Chart.*

Bloomington/Monroe County Convention and Visitors Bureau: 2855 N. Walnut St., Bloomington, IN 47404; phone (812) 334-8900 or (800) 800-0037.

Shopping areas: A major shopping center in the Bloomington area is College Mall, at the junction of the SR 46 bypass and E. Third Street, which features Lazarus, L.S. Ayres and Sears. The renovated historic district contains art galleries and specialty shops, including an antiques mall. An eclectic group of shops and restaurants line Kirkwood Avenue at the west edge of the Indiana University campus.

INDIANA UNIVERSITY ART MUSEUM, on the Fine Arts Plaza of the Indiana University campus at E. Seventh St., was designed by architect I.M. Pei. The museum contains more than 35,000 works in permanent and changing exhibits. Included are works by Henri Matisse, Claude Monet, Pablo Picasso, Auguste Rodin and Andy Warhol; an ancient and Asian art gallery with sculpture, jewelry, woodcarvings and other works; and the African, Oceanic and Art of the Americas collections. Tues.-Sat. 10-5, Sun. noon-5; closed major holidays. Donations. Phone (812) 855-5445 or 855-4826.

JORDAN HALL GREENHOUSE, 1001 E. 3rd St., is a botany research facility. Displays include exotic, tropical and desert plants from around the world. Allow 1 hour minimum. Mon.-Fri. 8-4, Sat.-Sun 9-3; closed major holidays. Free. Phone (812) 855-7717.

LAKE MONROE, 6 mi. s.e. via SR 446, is the largest lake in Indiana and is surrounded by the Hoosier National Forest *(see place listing p. 134)*. The lake is home to a wildlife refuge and provides a nesting area for bald eagles. Lake Monroe Reservoir offers water sports and other recreational opportunities. Daily 24 hours. Admission $5 per private vehicle. Phone (812) 837-9546. *See Recreation Chart and the AAA Great Lakes CampBook.*

LILLY LIBRARY, on the Indiana University campus at Seventh St. s. of Showalter Fountain, contains rare books and manuscripts, including a copy of the 1454 Gutenberg New Testament; a copy of the first complete Bible in English, dating from about 1535; and an extensive collection of works about Abraham Lincoln. Reading and exhibit rooms Mon.-Fri. 9-6, Sat. 9-1. Free. Phone (812) 855-2452.

MATHERS MUSEUM OF WORLD CULTURE, at 416 N. Indiana Ave. on the n.w. side of the Indiana

University campus, contains changing exhibits about anthropology, history and folklore from countries around the world. Allow 1 hour minimum. Tues.-Fri. 9-4:30, Sat.-Sun. 1-4:30; closed major holidays and during semester breaks. Donations. Phone (812) 855-6873.

Glenn A. Black Laboratory of Archaeology is at 423 N. Fess St. Weekend access is through the lobby of the Mathers Museum of World Culture. Artifacts revealing Indiana's history, from its first inhabitants to more recent American Indian cultures, are displayed. Tues.-Fri. 9-4:30, Sat.-Sun. 1-4:30, Sept.-May; closed major holidays. Free. Phone (812) 855-9544.

MONROE COUNTY HISTORICAL SOCIETY MUSEUM, 202 E. Sixth St., provides exhibits about early settlers, the local limestone industry and the natural history of Monroe County. Displays include farm and household implements and a log cabin. The museum is in the old library, an early 20th-century Classical limestone structure. Allow 30 minutes minimum. Tues.-Sat. 10-4, Sun. 1-4; closed holidays. Free. Phone (812) 332-2517.

WONDERLAB is at 116 W. 6th St. This museum of science, health and technology offers hands-on learning experiences. Activities include making a robot, digging for fossils, building a giant arch and experimenting with light, sound waves and gravity. Allow 1 hour minimum. Tues. and Thurs. 2-5, Sat. 10-5; closed Jan. 1, Thanksgiving and Dec. 25. Admission $2.75, under 3 free. MC, VI. Phone (812) 337-1337.

WINERIES

- **Oliver Winery**, 7 mi. n. to 8024 N. SR 37. Tasting room Mon.-Sat. 10-6, Sun. noon-6. Tours are given Fri.-Sat. noon-4:30, Sun. 1-4:30. Closed Jan. 1, election days, Thanksgiving and Dec. 25. Phone (812) 876-5800, or (800) 258-2783 in Ind.

BLUFFTON (B-5) pop. 9,000, elev. 828′

Established on the south bluffs of the Wabash River in the 1830s, Bluffton was later nicknamed the Parlor City for its wide, tree-lined paved streets. Information about area history can be found at the Wells County Historical Museum, a restored 1882 Victorian mansion at 420 W. Market St.; phone (260) 824-9956.

The River Greenway Trail, a scenic riverside walking and bicycling path, links Bluffton with Ouabache State Park *(see Recreation Chart and the AAA Great Lakes CampBook)*, 4 miles east on SR 216. Park activities include fishing, camping and swimming.

DEAM OAK, 4 mi. n.w. at jct. SR 116 and CR 250N, is a rare hybrid tree, a natural cross between the white and chinquapin oak. Marking the center of a small tract of state-owned land, it is a memorial to C.C. Deam, research forester, noted botanist and author. The tree is the first known of its kind,

and its acorns have been distributed to many gardens in the United States.

Wells County Chamber of Commerce: 202 S. Main St., Bluffton, IN 46714; phone (260) 824-0510.

BOONVILLE (G-2) pop. 6,700, elev. 395′

WARRICK COUNTY MUSEUM, 217 S. First St. at the corner of Walnut St., is housed in the 1901 Ella Williams School building. Six galleries display county history and local memorabilia. Smithsonian and Indiana Historical Society traveling exhibits are featured throughout the year. Guided tours are available. Allow 2 hours minimum. Mon.-Thurs. 11-2, Sun. 1-4; closed major holidays. Free. Phone (812) 897-3100.

BORDEN (NEW PROVIDENCE) (F-4)
elev. 560′

HUBER ORCHARD & WINERY is off I-64 exit 119, 4 mi. w. on SR 150 to Navilleton Rd., then 6 mi. n. to 19816 Huber Rd., following signs. This working farm has been maintained by the Huber family since 1843. Highlights include a wine cellar, ice-cream factory, farmer's market, playground and petting zoo. Food is available.

Allow 1 hour minimum. Farm and winery open daily 10-6, May-Dec. Winery also open Tues.-Sun. 10-5, Jan.-Apr. Petting zoo open Apr. 1-Dec. 24. Farmer's market open May-Dec. Closed Jan. 1, Easter, Thanksgiving and Dec. 25. Free. Petting zoo $3. Phone (812) 923-9463 or (800) 345-9463.

BRISTOL (A-4) pop. 1,100, elev. 771′

BONNEYVILLE MILL PARK is 2.5 mi. e. on SR 120, then .5 mi. s. on CR 131, on the Little Elkhart River. The 223-acre park contains one of the area's first water-powered gristmills with a turbine wheel. In operation since it was built in 1837, the mill still grinds corn, wheat, buckwheat and rye. Allow 1 hour minimum. Park open daily 8-dusk. Mill open daily 10-5, May-Oct. Milling takes place Sat.-Sun. and holidays at 11, 1, 2, 3 and 4, May-Oct. Free. Phone (574) 535-6458. *See Recreation Chart.*

ELKHART COUNTY HISTORICAL MUSEUM, 304 W. Vistula St. (SR 120), traces area history. Exhibits arranged in vignettes include a replica of an emporium, with yesteryear's shops and products; pioneer craftsmanship displayed in a barn setting; and a one-room schoolhouse recalling the origin of the 1903 museum building. Rooms furnished in period reveal the domestic side of late 19th- and mid-20th-century life. Allow 1 hour minimum. Wed.-Fri. 10-4, Sun. 1-5, Feb. 1-Dec. 1. Free. Phone (574) 848-4322.

BRYANT (C-6) pop. 300, elev. 875′

SAVE **BEARCREEK FARMS,** 8339 N. 400 E., is an entertainment resort complex with a children's amusement park, a musical theater, country shops and a museum featuring antique cars and tractors. Food is available. Amusement park Tues.-Sat. 11-7, Sun. 11-4, May-Sept. Museum Tues.-Sun. 11-5, early Mar.- late Dec. Show times vary. All-day ride pass $8, individual rides $1. Museum admission by donation. Shows $8-$25. DS, MC, VI. Phone (800) 288-7630.

BUNKER HILL (C-4) pop. 1,000, elev. 798'

GRISSOM AIR MUSEUM is off US 31, 2 mi. s. of US 24W at 6500 Hoosier Blvd. next to Grissom Air Reserve Base. Displays include aviation armaments, flight trainers, uniforms, models, survival gear, engines, war prizes and other military items. A theater shows aviation videotapes. The big show is outside, however, with a collection of 20 historic aircraft such as a B-17 Flying Fortress, a rare B-58 nuclear bomber and the A-10 Warthog. Visitors can sit in the cockpit of an F-4 jet.

Allow 1 hour, 30 minutes minimum. Grounds daily 7-dusk. Museum Tues.-Sat. 10-4, Feb.-Dec.; closed major holidays. Donations. Phone (765) 688-2654.

CAMBRIDGE CITY (D-5)
pop. 2,100, elev. 941'

Unlike other towns developed along the National Road, Cambridge City had the added advantage of straddling the Whitewater Canal. The canal failed to live up to its promise, but the National Road brought a steady stream of westbound wagons through Cambridge City, founded virtually overnight in 1836.

Cambridge City Area Chamber of Commerce: P.O. Box 206, Cambridge City, IN 47327; phone (765) 478-4689.

HUDDLESTON FARMHOUSE INN MUSEUM, 1 mi. w. of SR 1 on US 40, comprises a restored farmhouse, barn, smokehouse and springhouse. The three-story Federal-style farmhouse, constructed by a farming family 1839-41, accommodated many travelers along the National Road. It has been refurnished in period. Allow 30 minutes minimum. Tues.-Sat. 10-4, Sun. 1-4, May-Aug.; Tues.-Sat. 10-4, Feb.-Apr. and Sept.-Dec. Closed major holidays. Admission $3, students with ID $2, under 5 free. Phone (765) 478-3172.

CARMEL—see Indianapolis p. 148.

CHESTERTON (A-3) pop. 9,100, elev. 640'

INDIANA DUNES STATE PARK, 1600 N. SR 25E, is a spacious park that offers swimming, hiking trails, camping and a nature center. Daily 7 a.m.-11 p.m., Apr.-Sept.; 8 a.m.-10 p.m., rest of year. Admission $5. Phone (219) 926-1952. *See Recreation Chart.*

CLARKSVILLE (G-5) pop. 19,800

The Falls of the Ohio State Park and National Wildlife Conservation Area, 950 acres bordering Louisville, contains a coral reef of great geological importance. One of the world's few exposed formations from the Devonian Era, a time when terrestrial forms were beginning to evolve from marine life, the fossil bed contains more than 500 species of coral and prehistoric ocean life that are nearly 400 million years old. An interpretive center shows a film every 30 minutes about the history of the falls. A wildlife observation room also is featured.

The fossil bed area can best be viewed from the Indiana shore, where parking is available along Riverside Drive near the upper gates of McAlpine Dam. Accessibility to the beds is best from August through October, when the Ohio River is at its lowest level. However, due to the erratic level of the river, it is not always possible to view the beds. For information phone the park at (812) 280-9970. *See Recreation Chart.*

Clark-Floyd County Convention & Tourism Bureau: 315 Southern Indiana Ave., Jeffersonville, IN 47130-3218; phone (812) 282-6654 or (800) 552-3842.

RIVER FAIR FAMILY FUN PARK is off I-65 exit 4 on SR 131 on the second floor of the River Falls Mall. This indoor amusement park offers such rides as bumper cars, a carousel and a miniature train as well as a miniature golf course and a video arcade.

Park open Mon.-Sat. 10-9, Sun. noon-6. Hours may vary on holidays; phone for schedule. Rides open Sun.-Fri. at noon, Sat. at 10. Closed Easter, Thanksgiving and Dec. 25. Unlimited ride and golf pass $10, unlimited ride pass $6.50, unlimited golf pass $4 (or $2.95 per game), Megazone pass $4, 30-ticket ride book $8.95, 10-ticket ride book $3.95. DS, MC, VI. Phone (812) 284-3247.

COLUMBUS (E-4) pop. 31,800, elev. 631'

Advanced architectural design is a Columbus hallmark. Schools, banks, churches, a library, storefronts and golf courses—landmarks designed by such luminaries as Alexander Girard, Robert Trent Jones, I.M. Pei, Eero and Eliel Saarinen and Harry Weese—all contribute to the city's appearance.

In the 1950s a philanthropic foundation created a program that covered the architectural fees for the construction of public buildings. The program attracted distinguished architects and resulted in the construction of more than 60 architecturally renowned public and private buildings.

Columbus Area Visitor Center: 506 Fifth St., Columbus, IN 47201; phone (812) 378-2622 or (800) 468-6564.

Self-guiding tours: The visitor center offers driving and walking tour maps.

SAVE **COLUMBUS ARCHITECTURE TOURS** depart from the visitor center at 506 Fifth St. The 1- and 2-hour guided bus tours allow visitors to experience the rich architectural diversity of Columbus. The 1-hour tour concentrates on city highlights; the 2-hour tour continues to the town's outskirts.

Allow 2 hours, 30 minutes minimum. Tours depart Mon.-Fri. at 10, Sat. at 10 and 2, Sun. at 11, Mar.-Nov.; Mon.-Fri. at 10, Sat. at 10 and 2, rest of year. Visitor center open Mon.-Sat. 9-5, Sun. 10-4, Mar.-Nov.; Mon.-Sat. 9-5, rest of year. Closed major holidays. Visitor center free. One-hour tour $7; over 64, $6.50; students with ID $3; ages 6-12, $1.50. Two-hour tour $9.50; over 64, $9; students with ID $5; ages 6-12, $3. Reservations are required. MC, VI. Phone (812) 378-2622 or (800) 468-6564.

FIRST CHRISTIAN CHURCH, is at 531 Fifth St. at Lafayette Ave. A fine example of functional architecture, the church was designed by Eliel Saarinen. The 166-foot tower can be seen for miles. Mon.-Fri. 8:30-4:30; closed holidays and during church services. Free. Phone (812) 379-4491.

INDIANAPOLIS MUSEUM OF ART-COLUMBUS GALLERY, at 390 The Commons, is a satellite gallery displaying changing artwork by regional and nationally known artists. Tues.-Sat. 10-5, Sun. noon-4; closed holidays. Donations. Phone (812) 376-2597.

IRWIN GARDENS, Fifth St. and Lafayette Ave., consists of formal sunken gardens on the estate of the Irwin, Sweeney and Miller families. Sat.-Sun. 8-4, Apr. 15-Oct. 15 (weather permitting). Free.

NORTH CHRISTIAN CHURCH, 850 Tipton Ln., is a simple hexagonal structure tapering to a spire and topped by a gold leaf cross. The church was designed by Eero Saarinen, with interior furnishings by Alexander Girard. Mon.-Fri. 9-4:45, Sat. 9-noon; closed holidays and during church services. Free. Phone (812) 372-1531.

CONNERSVILLE (D-5)
pop. 15,600, elev. 828′

MARY GRAY BIRD SANCTUARY is 3.5 mi. s. on SR 121, then 3.5 mi. w. on CR 350S, following signs. The almost 700-acre nature preserve, owned by the Indiana Audubon Society, is laced with more than 6 miles of marked trails. Picnicking is permitted. Daily dawn-dusk. Donations. Phone (765) 825-9788.

WHITEWATER VALLEY RAILROAD, Fifth St. and Grand Ave., operates a 1950s diesel engine with a 1930s coach car along the towpath of the Whitewater Canal. A 2-hour layover in Metamora *(see place listing p. 204)* allows shopping and sightseeing. In addition to its regular schedule, the train makes special trips throughout the year. Dinner trips also are available.

Train departs Wed.-Fri. at 10, Sat.-Sun. and holidays at noon, in May; Sat.-Sun. and holidays at noon, June-Sept.; Thurs.-Fri. at 10, Sat.-Sun. at noon, in Oct. All trips return to Connersville by 5 p.m. Passengers are requested to arrive at the station 45 minutes before departure. Fare $14; ages 2-12, $7. Reservations are required for dinner trips. DS, MC, VI. Phone (765) 825-2054.

CORYDON (G-4) pop. 2,700

Through the influence of Indiana congressman Jonathon Jennings, the territorial capital of Indiana was moved from Vincennes to Corydon in 1813, and the state constitution was drawn up. The town served as the state capital 1816-25.

The Battle of Corydon, Indiana's only official Civil War conflict, took place a mile south when the home guard met the main force of Gen. John H. Morgan's Confederate Raiders on July 9, 1863. The home guard troops surrendered and were held captive during the famous raiders' brief stay.

Southwest, Harrison-Crawford State Forest *(see Recreation Chart)* covers more than 25,000 acres of hills overlooking the Ohio River. One of the largest state properties, the forest includes Wyandotte Woods State Recreation Area *(see Recreation Chart and the AAA Great Lakes CampBook)*, offering a full spectrum of recreational facilities; the Blue River, popular with canoeists; and Wyandotte Caves *(see Wyandotte p. 166).*

Harrison County Convention & Visitors Bureau: 310 N. Elm St., Corydon, IN 47112; phone (812) 738-2138 or (888) 738-2137. *See color ad.*

Self-guiding tours: Walking-tour maps pinpointing historic sites are available from the visitors bureau.

Shopping areas: Old Capital Square has a number of shops selling local art, solid-wood furniture, antiques, glassware and other specialties.

CORYDON CAPITOL STATE HISTORIC SITE, Old Capitol Sq. at Walnut St., preserves three sites that played roles in the political development of the state. The Old Capitol Building at Old Capitol Square on North Capitol Avenue served as the seat of government 1816-25. Built of native blue limestone and hand-hewn timbers, the square two-story structure is restored and furnished in period.

Governor Hendricks' Headquarters, the former home and headquarters of Indiana's second elected governor, is across the street from Old Capitol Square at 202 E. Walnut St. The house is furnished with period antiques. The Constitution Elm marks the site where Indiana delegates drafted the state's first constitution.

Allow 30 minutes minimum. Tues.-Sat. 9-5, Sun. 1-5, mid-Mar. to mid-Dec.; closed Easter and Thanksgiving. Donations. Phone (812) 738-4890.

SAVE **CORYDON SCENIC RAILROAD,** Walnut and Water sts., provides narrated, 90-minute sightseeing tours through the rolling hills of southern Indiana. The tour is especially scenic in the fall. Trips depart Wed.-Fri. at 1, Sat.-Sun. at 1 and 3, mid-June to mid-Aug.; Fri. at 1, Sat.-Sun. at 1 and 3, early June and Sept.-Oct.; Sat.-Sun. at 1 and 3, Memorial Day weekend and first Sat.-Sun. in Nov.

Fare $9; over 54, $8; ages 4-12, $5. MC, VI. Phone (812) 738-8000.

SAVE **SQUIRE BOONE CAVERNS AND VILLAGE** is 13 mi. s. of I-64 on SR 135, then 3 mi. e. on Squire Boone Caverns Rd. Discovered in 1790 by Daniel Boone and his brother Squire, the caverns feature twisted helictite formations and rare rimstone dams. A 67-step spiral staircase must be climbed on the 1-hour tour of the caverns.

Squire Boone's grave can be reached via a 2-mile trail. The village features crafts demonstrations, a large collection of American Indian artifacts, a farm animal petting zoo and a restored water-powered gristmill where cornmeal is ground. Food is available.

Allow 2 hours minimum. Village daily 10-5, Memorial Day weekend to mid-Aug.; Sat.-Sun. 10-6, mid-Aug. through Labor Day. Cavern tours daily every 30 minutes 9-5, Memorial Day weekend-Labor Day; daily every 2 hours 10-4, day after Labor Day-Dec. 31 and March 1-day before Memorial Day weekend; Sat.-Sun. every 2 hours 10-4, rest of year. Closed Jan. 1, Thanksgiving and Dec. 24-25. Admission $11; over 60, $10; ages 6-11, $6.50. Parking $3. Phone (812) 732-4381. *See ad.*

CRAWFORDSVILLE (D-3) pop. 13,600

Founded in 1882, Wabash was one of the earliest colleges west of the Alleghenies and is one of the few all-male colleges left in the country. Three noted men of letters who called the town home in the mid- and late 1800s were Gen. Lew Wallace, attorney and writer Maurice Thompson and novelist and diplomat Meredith Nicholson.

Crawfordsville-Montgomery County Visitors Center: 218 E. Pike St., Crawfordsville, IN 47933; phone (765) 362-5200 or (800) 866-3973

SAVE **THE BEN HUR MUSEUM,** 200 Wallace Ave. at E. Pike St., was built at Gen. Lew Wallace's home after his 1885 return from Turkey, where he served as U.S. Minister. Wallace wrote the majority of the novel "Ben Hur" on the study grounds; the book was completed in New Mexico. Displays of memorabilia chronicle Wallace's roles as lawyer, state senator, Civil War general, scholar and writer. Wed.-Sat. 10-4:30, Tues. and Sun. 1-4:30, June-Aug.; Tues.-Sun. 1-4:30, Apr.-May and Sept.-Oct.; Sat.-Sun. 1-4:30 in Mar. and Nov. Admission $3, students with ID $1. Phone (765) 362-5769.

THE OLD JAIL MUSEUM, 225 N. Washington St., is a restored 1882 county jail with a circular set of cellblocks that can be rotated by the turn of a crank. This arrangement enabled the sheriff to check on each of his prisoners without moving from his desk. The sheriff's living quarters contain prehistoric, American Indian and pioneer artifacts as well as period costumes, tools, toys and works by local artists. Guided tours are available.

Wed.-Sat. 10-4:30, Tues. and Sun. 1-4:30, June-Aug.; Wed.-Sun. 1-4:30, Apr.-May and Sept.-Oct.

Donations. Reservations are required for guided tours. Phone (765) 362-5222.

DALE (G-3) pop. 1,600, elev. 470'

SAVE **DR. TED'S MUSICAL MARVELS**, off I-64 exit 57, then .5 mi. n. on SR 231, houses a collection of self-playing antique musical instruments from around the world. Included are gramophones, player pianos, street organs, nickelodeons, orchestrions, music boxes, a Wurlitzer carousel organ and a giant dance organ. Guided tours are available.

Allow 1 hour minimum. Mon.-Sat. 10-6, Sun. 1-6, Memorial Day-Labor Day; Sat. 10-6, Sun. 1-6, May 1-day before Memorial Day and day after Labor Day-Sept. 30. Admission $6; over 49, $5; ages 6-12, $2. MC, VI. Phone (812) 937-4250.

DANA (D-2) pop. 700, elev. 642'

ERNIE PYLE STATE HISTORIC SITE, .5 mi. n. of US 36 on SR 71, highlights the life and career of the Pulitzer Prize-winning journalist who gained national acclaim for his work as a newspaper correspondent during World War II. The restored farmhouse where Pyle was born in 1900 is decorated with photographs and Victorian furniture and antiques. Two World War II Quonset huts serve as the visitor center, which contains multimedia exhibits and life-size scenes interpreting Pyle's wartime experiences. Pyle memorabilia also is displayed.

Allow 30 minutes minimum. Wed.-Sat. 9-5, Sun. 1-5, mid-Mar. to mid-Dec.; closed Easter and Thanksgiving. Donations. Phone (765) 665-3633.

DUNKIRK (C-5) pop. 2,700, elev. 946'

SAVE **THE GLASS MUSEUM**, 309 S. Franklin St., displays 5,000 pieces of glass from 110 factories, bottles from 50 factories, leaded lamps, 25 leaded windows and glass canes. The collection of Depression glass is particularly comprehensive. Glass manufacturers from central Indiana and elsewhere are represented by stemware, plates, bowls, candlesticks and vases. Guided tours are available. Allow 30 minutes minimum. Tues.-Sat. 10-4, May-Oct. Admission $2, under 12 free when accompanied by a parent. Phone (765) 768-6872.

ELIZABETH (G-4) pop. 200

CASINOS

- **Caesars Riverboat Casino**, 11999 Avenue of the Emperors. Cruise boards every 2 hours Sun.-Thurs. 9 a.m.-1 a.m., Fri.-Sat. 9 a.m.-3 a.m. Phone (812) 969-6400 or (888) 766-2648.

ELKHART (A-4) pop. 43,600, elev. 754'

Elkhart grew from the crossroads of several American Indian trails to a bustling junction of major railways in the mid-1800s. Small industries lured by the combined water power of the St. Joseph and Elkhart rivers began relocating to Elkhart in the late 1800s.

The town, now a prominent center of diversified manufacturing, produces more than 50 percent of the nation's band instruments. Other products include pharmaceuticals, plastics machinery, mechanical rubber, firefighting equipment and recreational vehicles.

Amish Country/Elkhart County Visitors Center: 219 Caravan Dr., Elkhart, IN 46514; phone (574) 262-8161 or (800) 251-2676.

Self-guiding tours: Materials for audio driving tours and bicycling and hiking routes are available at the visitors center.

SAVE **MIDWEST MUSEUM OF AMERICAN ART**, 429 S. Main St., presents a permanent collection of American paintings, prints, drawings, watercolors, sculpture and photographs spanning 150 years. Particularly noteworthy are works by Alexander Calder, Grandma Moses and Norman Rockwell. The gallery, in a restored bank building, also sponsors changing multimedia art exhibits. Audiotape tours are available.

Allow 1 hour minimum. Tues.-Fri. 11-5, Sat.-Sun. 1-4; closed holidays. Admission $3; over 62, $2; students with ID $1; free to all Sun. Phone (574) 293-6660.

NATIONAL NEW YORK CENTRAL RAILROAD MUSEUM, 721 S. Main St., houses two 1915 rail coaches, a loading dock built in the 1880s, a stationmaster's office, a scale model of a New York Central Mohawk steam locomotive and more than 10,000 photographs and papers. Several locomotives and rail cars are displayed on the grounds. In addition, a viewing room shows railroad films. Allow 1 hour minimum. Tues.-Fri. 10-2, Sat. 10-4, Sun. noon-4; closed holidays. Admission $2; over 62 and ages 6-12, $1. Phone (574) 294-3001.

OLD WAKARUSA RAILROAD is 10 mi. s. on SR 19. Open-sided sightseeing cars, steam powered by a one-third scale replica of an 1862 locomotive, are used for a 1.5-mile ride over a completely hand-laid railway. The tracks wind over low hills, curve around a small lake, overlook farmland, intersect with a street, pass through a 100-foot tunnel and cross over and under handmade trestles. Allow 30 minutes minimum. Trains depart every 30 minutes Mon.-Sat. 11-dusk, Apr.-Dec. Fare $4, under 4 free. Phone (574) 862-2714.

GEM **RUTHMERE MUSEUM**, .5 mi. n.e. on SR 19 at 302 E. Beardsley Ave., is a magnificent Beaux-arts mansion erected in 1908 for A.R. Beardsley, one of the founders of Miles Laboratories Inc. Restored velvet and silk wall coverings and elaborately painted ceilings distinguish the interior; the exterior is highlighted by a wraparound marble veranda. The mansion, furnished in the luxurious style of the period, includes some original furnishings.

In addition, the house contains three Tiffany lamps, fine art, sculpture and changing exhibits. A 1915 Choralcelo piano-organ, which can be played manually or with player rolls, is heard as a piano in some rooms and as an organ in others, thanks to banks of organ pipes. An audiotape tour is available.

A guided house tour includes the garage, inside which are two classic cars in working order. Stair climbing is required. Allow 1 hour minimum. Tours are given Tues.-Sat. at 10, 11, 1, 2 and 3 (also Sun. at 2 and 3, July-Aug.), first Tues. in Apr.-Dec.-31; closed Thanksgiving. Admission $6; over 61, $5; students with ID $3; under 5 free. Phone (574) 264-0330 or (888) 287-7696..

RV/MH HALL OF FAME MUSEUM AND LIBRARY, 801 Benham Ave., depicts the history of recreational vehicles and manufactured homes through photographs, displays and examples from as early as the 1920s. A library provides books and artifacts. Allow 1 hour minimum. Mon.-Fri. 9-5. Admission $3, family rate $10. Phone (574) 293-2344 or (800) 378-8694.

S. RAY MILLER AUTO MUSEUM, 2130 Middlebury St., contains 40 restored cars, many of which are the last of their kind. Included in the collection is a 1930 Duesenberg "J" Murphy Convertible once owned by Jake "The Barber" Factor, Al Capone's lawyer. Also on display are a 1932 Nash Advanced Series Victoria, a 1900 locomobile steam car, a 1954 Corvette, a 1978 Avanti and a 1903 Ford Runabout. The museum also contains a collection of vintage clothing and memorabilia from the eras dominated by the types of automobiles found in the museum. An audiotape tour is available.

Allow 1 hour minimum. Mon.-Fri. 10-4 (also last complete weekend of the month noon-4). Phone for holiday hours. Admission $6; over 62 and ages 7-18, $5. Phone (574) 522-0539.

EVANSVILLE (G-2) pop. 126,300, elev. 397′

A busy river port during the steamboat era, Evansville has retained much of its historic appearance. Visitors will find houses representing nearly every major architectural style of the late 19th and early 20th centuries.

At Fourth and Vine streets is the restored Beauxarts Old Vanderburgh County Courthouse, which houses offices and the Vanderburgh County History Museum and Art Gallery. The courthouse interior is noted for its marble floors, wainscots, oak woodwork, brass handrails and hardware.

Other period structures are the 1885 Italianate Gothic Willard Library at 21 First Ave., the Old Post Office at 100 N.W. Second St. and the Soldiers and Sailors Memorial Coliseum, 300 Court St. A number of other historic structures line the serpentine Downtown Walkway, a traffic-free redevelopment of the old Main Street shopping district. A motorized trolley traverses the walkway and the downtown area.

Wesselman Park *(see Recreation Chart),* 551 N. Boeke Rd., offers diverse recreational facilities including softball fields, sand volleyball courts, hand-

ball and tennis courts, batting cages and a fitness trail. Marked trails score the 200-acre park and adjacent 200-acre Wesselman Woods Nature Preserve, an area of virgin hardwood forest.

Evansville Convention and Visitors Bureau: 401 S.E. Riverside Dr., Evansville, IN 47713; phone (812) 421-2200 or (800) 433-3025.

Shopping areas: A major shopping area in Evansville is Eastland Mall, 3 miles east of US 41 at 800 N. Green River Rd. The mall contains 140 stores, including DeJongs, Famous-Barr, JCPenney and Lazarus. Washington Square Mall, east of town at Washington Avenue and Green River Road, has Sears and Elder-Beerman as well as a number of specialty shops.

ANGEL MOUNDS STATE HISTORIC SITE, off I-164 Covert Ave. exit at 8215 Pollack Ave., following signs, is a 103-acre archeological site that was once the location of a prehistoric Moundbuilders' village. These Indians, part of the ancient Mississippian culture, occupied the land along the banks of the Ohio River A.D. 1100-1450. A reconstructed community includes family dwellings and ceremonial structures. An interpretive center shows a videotape, and a nature preserve offers birdwalks and trails. Picnic areas are available.

Allow 1 hour minimum. Tues.-Sat. 9-5, Sun. 1-5, mid-March to mid-Dec.; closed Easter and Thanksgiving. Donations. Phone (812) 853-3956.

EVANSVILLE MUSEUM OF ARTS AND SCIENCE, 411 S.E. Riverside Dr. in Sunset Park, contains works of art and artifacts covering the disciplines of art, history and science. Artistic efforts range from 2nd-century Roman sculpture to contemporary American paintings.

Family Place and the Koch Science Center offer hands-on looks at science and technology, while the Koch Planetarium allows visitors to experience the Midwestern night sky. Rivertown USA is a reproduction of a 19th-century Midwestern village. The museum also sponsors more than 30 changing exhibitions and cultural events each year.

The Evansville Museum of Transportation Center (EMTRAC) features exhibits about modes of travel from the mid-19th century to the early 20th century. Included are five historic vehicles constructed or utilized in Evansville; a presentation on local river, rail and aviation history; four vintage rail cars; and a model railroad diorama.

Allow 1 hour minimum. Tues.-Sat. 10-5, Sun. noon-5. Planetarium shows Tues. and Thurs. at 1, Sat.-Sun. at 1 and 3. Closed Jan. 1, July 4, Thanksgiving and Dec. 24-25. Museum admission by donations. Planetarium show $2.50, children $1.50. EMTRAC $2, under 12 free. Phone (812) 425-2406, or TDD (812) 421-7506.

MESKER PARK ZOO AND BOTANIC GARDEN, 2421 Bement Ave. off St. Joseph Ave., occupies 70 acres and features more than 700 animals that roam freely in natural habitats surrounded by exotic plants, wildflowers and trees. In addition, the Discovery Center focuses on the world's vanishing rain forests and animals. A butterfly house, a children's zoo, paddle boats and a train also are available. Allow 2 hours minimum. Zoo daily 9-4. Butterfly house daily 10-4, May-Oct. Admission $4.75; ages 3-12, $3.75. Phone (812) 435-6143.

[SAVE] **REITZ HOME MUSEUM** is at 224 S.E. First St. Guided tours are offered of the restored 1871 French Second Empire mansion of John Augustus Reitz, who was once known as the Lumber Baron. His son, Francis Joseph Reitz, redecorated the mansion in the 1890s.

The house contains period furnishings, many of them original. Ornate hand-painted ceilings, intricate plasterwork, gilded chandeliers, decorative mantels, stained-glass windows and parquet flooring are evident throughout. Tours begin in the carriage house visitor center. Tues.-Sat. 11-3:30, Sun. 1-3:30. Admission $5; students with ID $2.50; under 12, $1.50. Phone (812) 426-1871.

CASINOS

- **Casino Aztar Evansville**, 421 N.W. Riverside Dr. Daily 9 a.m.-3 a.m. Phone (812) 433-4000 or (800) 342-5386.

FAIRMOUNT (C-4) pop. 3,100, elev. 880′

FAIRMOUNT HISTORICAL MUSEUM, 203 E. Washington St., contains exhibits about the history of Grant County and the lives of actor James Dean, born in nearby Marion; CBS reporter Phil Jones; and cartoonist Jim Davis, creator of "Garfield." Allow 1 hour minimum. Mon.-Sat. 10-5, Sun. noon-5, Mar.-Nov.; by appointment rest of year. Donations. Phone (765) 948-4555.

[SAVE] **THE JAMES DEAN MEMORIAL GALLERY**, 425 N. Main St., houses a large collection of James Dean memorabilia, including clothes, photographs, yearbooks, screenplays and posters. A 45-minute videotape presentation in the theater includes screen clips, tests and television appearances made by the actor. Guided tours are available. Daily 9-6. Closed Jan. 1, Thanksgiving and Dec. 25. Admission $3.75, under 11 free. AX, DS, MC, VI. Phone (765) 948-3326.

FERDINAND (G-3) pop. 2,300, elev. 504′

MONASTERY IMMACULATE CONCEPTION, off I-64 exit 63 (SR 162) to 802 E. 10th St., is one of the largest communities of Benedictine women in the United States. The 190-acre complex features a majestic domed church, outdoor Stations of the Cross, rosary steps, a labyrinth and a Lourdes grotto. In addition, there are the Kordes Enrichment Center, a retreat and conference facility, and Marian Heights Academy, a boarding and day college-prep school for girls.

An information office presents historical displays and a videotape about the sisters' way of life. Guided tours of the complex are given Tues.-Fri. at

10, 11, 1, 2 and 3, Sat.-Sun. at 1, 2 and 3, other times by appointment. Information center open daily 8:30-4:30. Donations. Phone (812) 367-1411.

FISHERS—*see Indianapolis p. 148.*

FORT WAYNE (B-6) pop. 173,000, elev. 839′

This region at the confluence of three rivers was originally inhabited by the Miami Indians. The area was later named for the renowned Revolutionary War figure Gen. "Mad" Anthony Wayne after he made peace with the Indians.

The city became an important center of trade, due largely to the Wabash-Erie Canal, the longest canal in the country. Today Fort Wayne is known as The City of Attractions, with 11 museums and historic sites within walking distance in the downtown area. Historically noteworthy is the 1928 Embassy Theatre, 125 W. Jefferson Blvd., distinguished by a rare Grand Page organ.

Lakeside Rose Garden in northeast Fort Wayne is recognized as one of the nation's largest rose gardens, with displays of 2,500 labeled plants.

John Chapman, better known as Johnny Appleseed, is buried in Johnny Appleseed Park, just south of the War Memorial Coliseum on Parnell Avenue.

Fort Wayne-Allen County Convention and Visitor Bureau: 1021 S. Calhoun, Fort Wayne, IN 46802; phone (800) 767-7752.

Shopping areas: Glenbrook Square, Coliseum Boulevard and Coldwater Road, has 186 stores, including JCPenney, L.S. Ayres, Marshall Field's and Sears. The Jefferson Pointe complex at Illinois Road (SR 14) and W. Jefferson Boulevard counts Ann Taylor, Old Navy, Talbots and Von Maur among its 60 stores.

ALLEN COUNTY COURTHOUSE, 715 S. Calhoun St., was dedicated in 1902; its cornerstone was laid in 1897. The building's exterior is blue limestone, and inside are walls and columns of scagliola (faux marble), intricate stained-glass windows and murals. Booklets are available for self-guiding walking tours. Mon.-Fri. 8-4:30. Free. Phone (260) 449-4246.

ALLEN COUNTY—FORT WAYNE HISTORICAL MUSEUM is at Berry and Barr sts.; entry is at the rear of the building. The museum, in an 1893 Richardsonian city hall, relates the history of the area from the glacial age to the present. Included are exhibits about the Wabash-Erie Canal and the railroad's importance to the city. Tues.-Fri. 9-5, Sat.-Sun. noon-5, Feb.-Dec.; closed holidays. Admission $3, senior citizens and students with ID $2. Phone (260) 426-2882.

ALLEN COUNTY PUBLIC LIBRARY, 900 Webster St., features rare books and documents. A large genealogical department includes thousands of family genealogies, plus state, county and town histories.

The Lincoln Highway

The horseless carriage rolled onto the American landscape in the 1890s. By 1910 there were more than 450,000 registered automobiles, yet the country still lacked a public road system.

Organized movements for better roads brought issues to the attention of the federal government, which had not participated in major road construction since it funded the National Road project in 1806.

But one particular initiative captured the public's support with a unique idea. In 1913 Carl Fisher—the man who built the Indianapolis Motor Speedway in 1909—and automobile industry leaders chartered the Lincoln Highway Association for the purpose of defining a direct coast-to-coast automobile route.

The LHA's first official act was to delineate a 3,389-mile, 12-state continuous route from New York to California—one that would be passable before the opening of the 1915 Panama-Pacific International Exposition in San Francisco. Although not perfect, the throughway was ready as promised, and a motion picture of America's transcontinental highway was shown at the exposition. Over time, the association improved surfaces by using better materials, shortened the driving distance with realignments and published guidebooks about the Lincoln Highway. Automobile touring had never been so good.

Through example, the LHA educated the public as well as state and federal governments about the value of good roads for almost 15 years. The 1919 moving of a military convoy over the "Lincolnway" foretold the utility of an integrated highway system for national defense and interstate commerce.

With the 1921 Federal Highway Act came the funds for states to construct and maintain connecting arteries. Four years later the United States adopted a highway numbering system, and most of the Lincoln route became US 30, 40 and 50. The

Mon.-Thurs. 9-9, Fri.-Sat. 9-6, Sun. 1-6, Labor Day-Memorial Day; Mon.-Thurs. 9-9, Fri.-Sat. 9-6, rest of year. Closed major holidays. Free. Phone (260) 421-1200.

ALLEN COUNTY WAR MEMORIAL COLISEUM, 4000 Parnell Ave., is a memorial to members of the armed forces who died in World Wars I and II and the Korean War. The coliseum seats 10,000. A sports stadium on the grounds features baseball, basketball and hockey games. Phone (260) 482-9502.

CONCORDIA THEOLOGICAL SEMINARY, .2 mi. n. of St. Joseph Center Rd. at 6600 N. Clinton St., is a school of the Lutheran Church-Missouri Synod. The campus, designed by internationally acclaimed architect Eero Saarinen, was patterned after a North European village. Guided tours are available. Campus buildings open Mon.-Fri. 7:30-4:30. Free. Phone (260) 452-2100 or (800) 481-2155.

[SAVE] **FOELLINGER-FREIMANN BOTANICAL CONSERVATORY,** 1 blk. w. of US 27/33S at 1100 S. Calhoun St., consists of three gardens under glass in the heart of Fort Wayne. The Floral Showcase displays six distinct and colorful seasonal gardens each year. Exotic plants surround a waterfall in the Tropical House. The Desert House, with its cactuses, offers a quiet retreat. Also of interest is an interactive exhibit gallery. Mon.-Sat. 10-5, Sun. noon-4; closed Dec. 25. Admission $3; ages 4-14, $2. Phone (260) 427-6440.

FORT WAYNE CHILDREN'S ZOO, 3411 Sherman Blvd. in Franke Park, houses more than 1,200 animals and birds from around the world on 42 landscaped acres. Animals from the East African plains roam freely on the 22-acre African veldt, which can be toured on an elevated boardwalk or in protected electric cars. The Indonesian Rain Forest includes Orangutan Valley and Tiger Forest. The petting zoo features more than 100 animals. An endangered species carousel as well as pony and miniature train rides are available.

The Adventure Canoe Ride or a stroll down the walkways through the 5-acre Australian Adventure reveals the Great Barrier Reef aquarium, walk-through aviary and down-under wildlife, including Tasmanian devils, kangaroos and spiny anteaters. Daily 9-5, late Apr.-Oct. 11. Admission $6.50; over 60 and ages 2-14, $4. Pony rides $2. All other rides $1. Phone (260) 427-6800.

[SAVE] **FORT WAYNE MUSEUM OF ART,** 311 E. Main St., displays a permanent art collection featuring more than 1,300 pieces from the 19th century to the present. Changing exhibits show contemporary artwork. Tues.-Sat. 10-5, Sun. noon-5. Admission $3, students with ID $2, family rate $8. Free to all first Sun. of month and Wed. Phone (260) 422-6467.

THE GREATER FORT WAYNE AVIATION MUSEUM, in the Lt. Paul Barr Terminal at Fort Wayne International Airport, showcases area aviation history with memorabilia relating to military and commercial flight. Daily 7-7. Free. Phone (260) 478-7146.

JACK D. DIEHM MUSEUM OF NATURAL HISTORY, 600 Franke Park Dr., displays mounted animals, birds and fish in dioramas depicting their natural habitats.

Other exhibits include minerals, gems and Far East artifacts. Written and audiotape descriptions of the exhibits
are provided. Allow 30 minutes minimum. Wed.-Sun.
noon-5, late Apr. to mid-Oct. Admission $2; ages 2-12,
$1. Phone (260) 427-6708.

LINCOLN MUSEUM, 200 E. Berry St. at Clinton St., displays a comprehensive collection of
personal possessions of Abraham Lincoln and
his family. Among the memorabilia are original
photographs and paintings, including the last portrait of
the 16th president done during his lifetime as well as the
inkwell he used when he signed the Emancipation Proc-
lamation.

Exhibits and audiovisual presentations focus on Lincoln's life, from his boyhood years to his law career and
presidency. Touchscreen computer exhibits allow visitors
to redecorate the White House as Mary Todd Lincoln
did, fight a Civil War battle and read Lincoln's mail. A library and an archives also are available.

Allow 2 hours minimum. Tues.-Sat. 10-5, Sun. 1-5;
closed Jan. 1, Easter, Thanksgiving and Dec. 25. Library
and archives available Tues.-Fri. by appointment. Admission $2.99; over 60 and ages 5-12, $1.99. AX, CB, DS,
MC, VI. Phone (260) 455-3864.

SCIENCE CENTRAL is off I-69 exit 111, then 2 mi. s.
on US 33/27 to 1950 N. Clinton St. At this former electrical plant refurbished as an interactive, hands-on science center for all ages, visitors can bend rainbows,
create earthquakes, dance on giant piano keys, experience weightlessness and ride a bicycle on a rail 20 feet
in the air. Changing exhibits also are featured. Picnicking
is permitted in the adjacent park. Food is available.

Allow 2 hours, 30 minutes minimum. Tues.-Sat. 10-5,
Sun. and Labor Day noon-5; closed Jan. 1, Thanksgiving
and Dec. 25. Admission $5.50; over 65, $5; ages 3-12,
$4.50. DS, MC, VI. Phone (260) 424-2400.

UNIVERSITY OF ST. FRANCIS LIBRARY, on the university campus at 2701 Spring St., is housed in the 33-
room castlelike Bass Mansion. Self-guiding tours take
visitors through many of the grand and beautifully restored rooms. Allow 1 hour minimum. Mon.-Thurs. 8
a.m.-9 p.m., Fri. 8-4:30, Sat. 11-5, Sun. 1-9, during the
academic year; hours vary during summer sessions.
Closed major and university holidays. Donations. Phone
(260) 434-3100 or (800) 729-4732.

FOUNTAIN CITY (D-6) pop. 800

Fountain City, largely settled by Quakers, served as an
important station of the Underground Railroad, the route
covertly followed by thousands of fugitive slaves seeking
freedom in Canada. At one time almost the entire community of 30 families was involved in Underground Railroad activities. They essentially were directed by Levi
and Catharine Coffin, North Carolina Quakers after
whom the characters Simeon and Rachel Halliday of
"Uncle Tom's Cabin" were patterned.

THE LEVI COFFIN HOUSE STATE HISTORIC SITE, 6
mi. n. of I-70 exit 151 on US 27, is a Federal-style house
that was known as the Grand Central Station of the Underground Railroad. During their 20 years in residence

The Lincoln Highway
(continued)

association disbanded in 1928, but
not before it engaged Boy Scout
troops across the country to place
some 3,000 concrete Lincoln Highway
markers along the route in all 12
states: New York, New Jersey, Pennsylvania, Ohio, Indiana, Illinois, Iowa,
Nebraska, Wyoming, Utah, Nevada
and California. Many of these markers still exist.

In **Fort Wayne,** the first major city
reached by Lincolnway motorists entering Indiana from the east, a restored bridge built over the St.
Mary's River around 1915 preserves
original mileage plaques like those so
often seen by early travelers. The 76-
mile corridor to **South Bend,** which
passes through Ligonier and **Elkhart,**
corresponds to today's US 33. West of
South Bend, the towns of **LaPorte,**
Valparaiso and **Merrillville** welcomed
Illinois-bound travelers.

Between Schererville and Dyer motorists were treated to a glimpse of
the future with the 1923 completion
of the Lincoln Highway's "Ideal Section"—a 1.3-mile lighted, four-lane
concrete model highway with wide
shoulders and landscaping. **Look for
these Indiana Lincoln Highway landmark towns in this TourBook guide.**

For more information about the
old Lincoln Highway, contact the new
Lincoln Highway Association, P.O.
Box 308, Franklin Grove, IL 61031;
phone (815) 456-3030.

Levi and Catharine Coffin opened their home to more than 2,000 fleeing slaves, none of whom was ever captured en route to Canada. The 1839 house contains furnishings typical of the area in the early 19th century.

Allow 1 hour minimum. Guided tours are given Tues.-Sat. 1-4, June-Aug.; Sat. 1-4, Sept.-Oct. Closed July 4. Fee $2; ages 6-18, $1. Phone (765) 847-2432.

FRANKLIN—*see Indianapolis p. 148.*

FRENCH LICK (F-3) pop. 2,100, elev. 484'

Founded in 1811, French Lick was named for a nearby salt lick and a French trading post established in the early 1700s. The town evolved into a resort and health center in the mid-1800s after a local doctor realized the commercial value of the area's three artesian springs. Water from Pluto Spring is available to the public; bring your own container.

French Lick-West Baden Chamber of Commerce: 1 Monon St., P.O. Box 347, French Lick, IN 47432; phone (812) 936-2405.

SAVE **INDIANA RAILWAY MUSEUM,** 1 Monon St., displays railroad memorabilia and old railroad cars and engines. A 20-mile round trip on a 1920s train is offered. Allow 2 hours minimum. Museum open daily 10-4; closed Jan. 1, Thanksgiving and Dec. 25. Train rides Sat.-Sun. at 10, 1 and 4, Apr.- Oct. (also Tues. at 1, June-Oct.); Sat.-Sun. at 1 in Nov. Museum free. Train ride $8; ages 3-11, $4. Phone (812) 936-2405 or (800) 748-7246.

GARY (A-3) pop. 116,600, elev. 599'

Gary is in the Calumet district, formerly one of the country's greatest steel producing areas. Midway between the vast iron ore beds of Minnesota and the great coal region to the south, Gary was chosen in 1906 as the site of the main plant of the U.S. Steel Corp. Gary also lies at the western end of scenic US 12, which follows the Lake Michigan shoreline through Indiana Dunes National Lakeshore *(see place listing p. 134)* before crossing into Michigan northeast of Michigan City.

Gary Chamber of Commerce: 504 Broadway #328, Gary, IN 46402; phone (219) 885-7407.

CASINOS

- **Majestic Star**, 1 Buffington Harbor Dr. Cruise boards every 2 hours daily 8 a.m.-2 a.m. Phone (219) 977-7777 or (888) 225-8259.

- **Trump Casino**, 1 Buffington Harbor Dr. Cruise boards every 2 hours daily 9 a.m.-3 a.m. Phone (888) 218-7867.

GENEVA (C-6) pop. 1,400, elev. 840'

Geneva lies in the Limberlost country made known in the first quarter of the 20th century by

the writings of Gene Stratton Porter, author of "Freckles" and "Girl of the Limberlost." Many of her stories and characters were based on the lives of local people. A large Amish community is nearby.

LIMBERLOST STATE HISTORIC SITE, 200 E. Sixth St., contains the original two-story Limberlost cabin, home of author, photographer and naturalist Gene Stratton Porter for 18 years. She designed the 14-room house constructed of white cedar logs and redwood shingles to blend with the environment of Limberlost Swamp, the inspiration for her work. Some of her furnishings, personal belongings and photographic works are displayed. Guided tours are available.

The Porters moved to Rome City (*see place listing p. 159*) after the swamp was drained in 1913. A preserve with nature trails and a bird sanctuary were created through the restoration of some of Limberlost's wetlands; brochures and maps for self-guiding walks are available.

Allow 30 minutes minimum. Wed.-Sat. 9-5, Sun. 1-5, mid-Mar. to mid-Dec.; closed Easter and Thanksgiving. Last tour begins 30 minutes before closing. Donations. Phone (260) 368-7428.

GENTRYVILLE (G-3) pop. 300, elev. 405′

COLONEL WILLIAM JONES STATE HISTORIC SITE, .5 mi. w. of US 231 on Boone St., contains period furnishings. The restored house was built 1834-44 by Col. William Jones, a merchant, lieutenant colonel in the Union Army and lifelong friend of Abraham Lincoln. Surrounded by 100 acres of forest, the site includes an herb garden, a 1-mile hiking trail and a reconstructed log barn. Guided tours are available. Allow 1 hour, 30 minutes minimum. Wed.-Sat. 9-5, Sun. 1-5, mid-March to mid-Dec.; closed Easter and Thanksgiving. Donations. Phone (812) 937-2802.

GEORGE ROGERS CLARK NATIONAL HISTORICAL PARK—*see Vincennes p. 164.*

GREENFIELD—*see Indianapolis p. 148.*

GREENTOWN (C-4) pop. 2,200, elev. 844′

GREENTOWN GLASS MUSEUM, 112 N. Meridian, houses glassware produced at the turn of the 20th century by the Indiana Tumbler and Goblet Co., including a large collection of chocolate glass and golden agate glass. Rare colors popular among collectors, these distinctive hues were products of secret formulas. Opaque whites and Nile greens, also fairly scarce today, are represented as well. Guided tours are available.

Allow 1 hour minimum. Tues.-Fri. 10-noon and 1-4, Sat.-Sun. 1-4, mid-May through Oct. 31; Sat.-Sun. 1-4, Mar. 1 and Nov.-Jan. Donations. Phone (765) 628-6206.

HAGERSTOWN (D-5) elev. 1,015′

WILBUR WRIGHT BIRTHPLACE AND MUSEUM is 5.8 mi. w. on SR 38, 2.1 mi. n. on Wilbur Wright Rd., .4 mi. e. on CR 100N, then .5 mi. n. to 1525

N. CR 750E. The restored farmhouse where inventor Wilbur Wright was born in 1867 features period furnishings, family memorabilia and a life-size replica of Wright's flying machine. Allow 1 hour minimum. Mon.-Sat. 10-5, Sun. 1-5, Apr.-Oct.; by appointment rest of year. Admission $2.50, students with ID $1.50. Phone (765) 332-2495.

HAMMOND (A-2) pop. 84,200, elev. 590′

The oldest city in the Calumet region, Hammond dates back to 1851 when Ernest Hohman, a German immigrant, built a log cabin on the north bank of the Grand Calumet. The area's first industrial enterprise was a meat packing company begun by George H. Hammond some 17 years later just across the river. Over the years the original name of Hohmanville was abandoned, and the town came to be called Hammond.

Lake County Convention and Visitors Bureau: 7770 Corinne Dr., Hammond, IN 46323; phone (219) 989-7770. *See ad.*

GIBSON WOODS NATURE PRESERVE is off I-80/94 Kennedy Ave. exit, n. to 169th Ave., then e. to 6201 Parrish Ave. The 130-acre preserve features a nature center with reptiles, amphibians and mounted wildlife. Of note is a display about the inland dune and swale complex. Nature trails are available. Allow 2 hours minimum. Preserve daily 9-5. Nature center daily 11-4. Free. Phone (219) 844-3188.

CASINOS

- **Jack Binion's Horseshoe**, 777 Casino Center Dr. at the Hammond Marina. Daily 8 a.m.-2 a.m. Phone (866) 711-7463.

HOBART (A-3) pop. 21,800, elev. 623'

WOOD'S HISTORIC GRIST MILL is .2 mi. n. from US 30 on Randolph St., then 1 mi. e. on Old Lincoln Hwy. to Deep River County Park. Considered one of the finest mills in the county in the late 1800s, Wood's Mill could grind 12 bushels of grain per hour. Today visitors can watch demonstrations of the powerful stone wheel as it grinds corn into meal. The park offers picnicking and hiking. Park daily 7 a.m.-dusk. Mill daily 10-5, May-Oct. Park and mill free. Phone (219) 947-1958.

HOOSIER NATIONAL FOREST

Elevations in the forest range from 400 ft. in Cannelton around the Ohio River to 930 ft. at Browning Hill.

Covering 197,000 acres in south-central Indiana, Hoosier National Forest offers many miles of scenic driving over back country hills; the roads are particularly beautiful in the autumn and spring. Principal recreation areas are Hardin Ridge on Lake Monroe and Celina, Indian and Tipsaw lakes. The forest has more than 239 miles of hiking, mountain biking and horse trails. Facilities for horse camping are available. Hunting for a variety of wildlife is permitted in season.

There are several remote areas for backpacking and nature study. Pioneer Mothers' Memorial Forest, a tract of virgin timber 1 mile south of Paoli, is used in ecological studies and is renowned for its large trees. Nearby towns listed separately are Bedford, Bloomington and Evansville. Open daily 24 hours (weather permitting). For more information contact the Forest Supervisor, 811 Constitution Ave., Bedford, IN 47421; phone (812) 275-5987. *See Recreation Chart and the AAA Great Lakes CampBook.*

HUNTINGTON (B-5) pop. 16,400, elev. 742'

Much of the early history of Huntington centers on the forks of the Wabash River, where many American Indian treaties were signed. Today the Forks of the Wabash Historic Park preserves the history of life in Huntington during the mid-1800s. Francis LaFontaine, chief of the Miami Indians, is buried in Mount Calvary Cemetery. His house, built in 1833, is in the historic park.

Among the houses in Huntington's historic district is the Taylor-Zent House, one of the state's finest examples of Romanesque Revival architecture. On Polk Street is a dwelling of more recent vintage, the boyhood home of former Vice President Dan Quayle. Memorial Park, on the western edge of the city, contains Romanesque gardens.

Recreational activities at Huntington Lake State Park (*see Recreation Chart and the AAA Great*

Lakes CampBook), southeast on US 224, include swimming, boating, camping, hiking, fishing, hunting, picnicking and interpretive programs.

Huntington County Visitor and Convention Bureau: 407 N. Jefferson St., Huntington, IN 46750; phone (800) 848-4282.

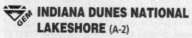

INDIANA DUNES NATIONAL LAKESHORE (A-2)

Covering 15,000 acres on the southern shore of Lake Michigan, Indiana Dunes National Lakeshore is traversed by a scenic stretch of US 12.

The area emerged from the most recent ice age with a natural landscape that accommodates an unusual ecosystem of dunes, plants and animals. The surface is constantly altered as a result of sand dropped by the continuous northwest winds. Back-dunes thousands of years old have been stabilized by soil and vegetation, while dunes closer to the shore shift with the winds and soil deposits. The largest dune, 123-foot high Mount Baldy, moves 4 to 5 feet south from the lake each year. Marshes, swamps, bogs and ponds also are part of the lakeshore.

This environment supports southern dogwood, arctic bearberry, plains flowers, cactus and other species. Equally diverse types of birds are drawn to the lakeshore. North and south migration routes nearby attract birds more common to other parts of the continent.

Hikers will find many trails around the lakeshore, including one that was used by American Indians for centuries—the Old Sauk Trail. Near the homestead of French fur trader Joseph Bailly and the 19th-century Chellberg Farm is the 2-mile Bailly-Chellberg Trail. The farm grounds are open daily, and self-guided tours of the homestead are available Sun. 1-4, Memorial Day-Oct. 31. The .5-mile Calumet Dune Trail originates at the visitor center. Stay on designated routes, as the dunes can easily be destroyed by too many independent trails.

The visitor center at Kemil Road and US 12 explains the development of the lakeshore's plant and animal life through literature, exhibits and an audiovisual program. Maps and activity schedules are available. The center is open daily 8-6, Memorial Day weekend-Labor Day; 8-5, rest of year. Closed Jan. 1, Thanksgiving and Dec. 25.

Other lakeshore activities include swimming (West Beach has lifeguards during the summer), camping, fishing and cross-country skiing on the Ly-co-ki-we Trail near US 20 and Kemil Road. A fishing license is required; hunting and open fires are prohibited. Swimming is unsafe when north winds cause rip currents in the lake.

For more information and a schedule of ranger-guided activities, contact the Superintendent, Indiana Dunes National Lakeshore, 1100 N. Mineral Springs Rd., Porter, IN 46304; phone (219) 926-7561, ext. 225. *See Recreation Chart.*

Special People Get Special Treatment

Want to be sure you'll be treated right on your next travel adventure?

*L*ook for establishments that advertise in the AAA TourBook® guides. These are the businesses that cater to AAA members. They value the business they receive from AAA members, and are willing to go the extra mile to get it. And in turn, they pass value on to you.

Indianapolis

Capital and largest city in the state, Indianapolis pulses with the activity forged by its high-tech industries, governmental and educational sectors and sports and cultural institutions. Progress has been the catalyst behind its growth from a wilderness camp in 1820 to a Midwestern giant today.

Indianapolis owes its start to location. In 1820 state legislators in Corydon asked 10 commissioners to find a new site for the capital. The commissioners headed for the center of the state and decided on Fall Creek, then a swampy little settlement on the shallow White River. Alexander Ralston, assistant to Pierre L'Enfant in the designing of Washington, D.C., mapped the new town, and settlers began to arrive.

In 1825 the state government brought in many jobs and people, and the National Road (US 40) stimulated more growth when it came through in 1834. However, not until the Central Canal was built on the White River in 1836 did industry come to town. The canal provided the transportation link and water power needed to run factories, paper mills and sawmills. But the soft, muddy shores of the White River were too fluid to maintain the canal, and without a water supply, the mills and factories left.

With the arrival of the railroad in 1847 manufacturing concerns that did not have to rely on inexpensive water power or transportation also began to arrive. By the turn of the 20th century Indianapolis had become a sophisticated city with sidewalks, streetlights, streetcars, and musical and literary organizations.

A major new industry emerged as entrepreneurs set up factories to produce automobiles. In 1911 the first Indianapolis 500 was held, setting a Memorial Day tradition that has become the largest single-day sporting event in the world. Although it kept its race, Indianapolis eventually lost the automobile industry to areas that could provide steel and coal more economically—by water.

Since the World Wars Indianapolis' industrial progress has been in technology. Eli Lilly and Co., a pharmaceutical giant, more than 100 computer software companies, and several enterprises that specialize in automation equipment and robotics are based in Indianapolis. But with all of its technology, Indianapolis is still a Midwestern city, and as such it serves as one of the country's leading grain markets and a major livestock and meat processing center.

As notable as high-tech industries are the many academic institutions, the largest of which is Indiana University-Purdue University at Indianapolis. The Indiana University Medical School is one of the largest in the nation, and Purdue is noted for its research in the areas of computers and automation. Butler University, Marian

College and the University of Indianapolis, all private colleges, also are part of the city's educational environment. Martin University was founded by Fr. Boniface Hardin in 1977. The institution was created to serve minorities and low-income groups.

The effects of explosive industrial growth have not always been positive. Indianapolis was proclaimed one of America's dirtiest cities in the 1960s. A major cleanup and revitalization project resulted, and by the late 1970s Indianapolis was considered one of the nation's cleanest urban centers. Of the country's 50 largest cities, it has one of the lowest crime rates. Urban blight has been counteracted by an unusual Unigov structure of government, a consolidation of city and county agencies that work cooperatively to perpetuate the city's renaissance.

A resurgence in the arts has accompanied this revitalization project. Home of a nationally acclaimed children's museum and an equally noted museum of art, Indianapolis also claims a respected symphony orchestra, ballet and opera companies as well as several theater groups. The headquarters of such organizations as the American Legion and Kiwanis International further define the metropolitan atmosphere.

The city also has grown into a major sports center. Both professional and amateur teams are supported, and Indianapolis is home to the national governing bodies of seven sports. World-class facilities, combined with a tremendous volunteer commitment, have helped bring success to both national and international sporting events. Indianapolis is still best known, however, as the home of the Indianapolis 500, the jewel in the automobile racing crown. On that one day in May the city becomes as central to the nation as it has always been to the state.

Approaches

By Car

Both I-70, a major east-west superhighway spanning two-thirds of the country, and I-65, the Lake Michigan-Gulf of Mexico link, pass directly through downtown, enabling travelers to reach the city's center from the suburbs in 15 to 20 minutes.

I-74, connecting several important highways, angles toward Indianapolis from Cincinnati to the southeast and from the Quad Cities area to the northwest; it merges with part of the Indianapolis bypass route, I-465. I-69 brings in traffic from central and southern Michigan.

Approaches serving local traffic include east-west routes US 40 (which closely parallels I-70), US 36 and US 52, and north-south highways US 31, US 421 and SRs 37 and 67. The beltway, I-465, encircles the city and provides direct access to all main approaches and to all parts of Indianapolis.

(continued on p. 141)

The Informed Traveler

City Population: 731,300

Elevation: 708 ft.

WHOM TO CALL

Emergency: 911

Police (nonemergency): (317) 327-3811

Time and Temperature: (317) 635-5959

Hospitals: St. Vincent Hospital, (317) 338-2345; Wishard Health Services, (317) 639-6671.

WHERE TO LOOK

Newspapers

The city's major daily newspaper is the *Indianapolis Star.*

Radio

Indianapolis radio station WIBC (1070 AM) is an all-news/weather station; WFYI (90.1 FM) is a member of National Public Radio. For a complete list of radio programs consult the daily newspaper.

Visitor Information

The Indianapolis City Center in Pan Am Plaza provides visitor information and current events listings. Contact 201 S. Capitol Ave., Indianapolis, IN 46225; phone (317) 237-5200. The center is open Mon.-Fri. 10-5, Sun. noon-5.

This is Indianapolis contains extensive information about the city and is available at hotels and visitor centers or by phoning (800) 323-4639. Also providing current events information is *Indianapolis Monthly* magazine, available at newsstands.

TRANSPORTATION

Air Travel

The city is served by Indianapolis International Airport, just outside I-465 on the southwest edge; the drive to downtown is via I-70 and takes about 12 minutes.

Carey Indiana, (317) 241-6700, offers transportation to and from downtown; the fare is $10 per passenger. Many hotels also provide limousine service between downtown and the airport. For airport information phone (317) 487-9594.

Rental Cars

Hertz, (317) 243-9321 or (800) 654-3080, offers discounts to AAA members. For other agencies consult a telephone directory.

Rail Service

Passenger train service is available through Amtrak, which departs from Union Station, 350 S. Illinois St. For details phone (800) 872-7245.

Buses

Greyhound Lines Inc. bus connections can be made at 127 N. Capitol Ave; phone (800) 231-2222.

Taxis

Major cab companies include Airline Taxi, (317) 631-7521; and Yellow Cab, (317) 487-7777. Fares range from $2.69 to $3.60 for the first mile, and $1.70 to $2 for each additional mile. Consult a telephone directory for other companies.

Public Transport

IndyGo operates 34 city bus routes serving downtown and most of Marion County. The fare is $1; transfers are free.

Schedule and trip planning information is available; phone (317) 635-3344 Mon.-Fri. 7-7, Sat. 9-4.

Destination Indianapolis

*I*ndiana's capital is perhaps best known for its renowned Indianapolis 500, but racing isn't all this historic city has to offer.

*A*fter touring the track, you can visit memorials and walk through several of the city's beautiful old buildings. And you may just learn a thing or two the fun way at a children's museum that's reputedly the largest in the world.

White River State Park, Indianapolis.
Take in a zoo and an art museum, or wind down with a relaxing stroll or paddleboat ride. (See listing page 143)

Scottish Rite Cathedral, Indianapolis.
A very beautiful building, the cathedral features tours and a 7,000-pipe organ. (See listing page 143)

The Children's Museum of Indianapolis and CineDome Theater.
This gigantic museum proves learning can be tons of fun. Inside are nature, history and cultural exhibits and a planetarium; and don't miss the life-size Tyrannosaurus rex. (See listing page 141)

See Downtown map page 140

Indianapolis Motor Speedway.
Take a bus tour through the home of the famous Indy 500 and visit its hall of fame. (See listing page 142)

*P*laces included in this AAA Destination City:

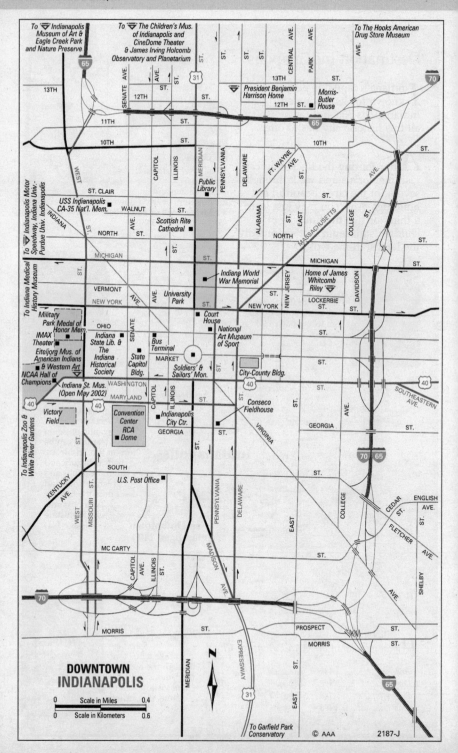

To Indianapolis Museum of Art & Eagle Creek Park and Nature Preserve

To The Children's Mus. of Indianapolis and CineDome Theater & James Irving Holcomb Observatory and Planetarium

To The Hooks American Drug Store Museum

President Benjamin Harrison Home

Morris-Butler House

13TH

12TH

11TH

10TH

SENATE AVE.

CAPITOL

ILLINOIS

MERIDIAN

PENNSYLVANIA

DELAWARE

FT. WAYNE   AVE.

CENTRAL   AVE.

PARK   AVE.

MASSACHUSETTS

COLLEGE   AVE.

Public Library

ST. CLAIR

WALNUT

NORTH

MICHIGAN

To Indianapolis Motor Speedway, Indiana Univ.- Purdue Univ. Indianapolis

USS Indianapolis CA-35 Nat'l. Mem.

Scottish Rite Cathedral

INDIANA

WEST

ALABAMA

EAST

Indiana World War Memorial

Home of James Whitcomb Riley

LOCKERBIE ST.

DAVIDSON

To Indiana Medical History Museum

VERMONT

NEW YORK

University Park

Court House

National Art Museum of Sport

NEW JERSEY

NEW YORK

Military Park Medal of Honor Mem.

IMAX Theater

Eiteljorg Mus. of American Indians & Western Art

NCAA Hall of Champions

Indiana St. Mus. (Open May 2002)

OHIO

Indiana State Lib. & The Indiana Historical Society

SENATE

Bus Terminal

State Capitol Bldg.

MARKET

Soldiers' & Sailors' Mon.

City-County Bldg.

WASHINGTON

MARYLAND

CAPITOL

ILLINOIS

To Indianapolis Zoo & White River Gardens

Victory Field

Convention Center RCA Dome

Indianapolis City Ctr.

GEORGIA

Conseco Fieldhouse

VIRGINIA

GEORGIA

SOUTHEASTERN AVE.

SOUTH

U.S. Post Office

KENTUCKY   AVE.

WEST   ST.

MISSOURI   ST.

CAPITOL   AVE.

ILLINOIS   ST.

PENNSYLVANIA   ST.

DELAWARE   ST.

EAST   ST.

COLLEGE   AVE.

CEDAR   ST.

ENGLISH AVE.

FLETCHER   AVE.

MC CARTY

SHELBY   AVE.

MORRIS

MADISON   AVE.

PROSPECT

MORRIS

EXPRESSWAY

MERIDIAN   ST.

EAST   ST.

To Garfield Park Conservatory

To Indianapolis Zoo & White River Gardens

DOWNTOWN INDIANAPOLIS

| 0 | Scale in Miles | 0.4 |
| 0 | Scale in Kilometers | 0.6 |

© AAA

2187-J

Getting Around

Street System

The Indianapolis street system is a grid with four broad avenues branching at angles from a central circle. Meridian Street runs in a north-south direction and divides the city into east and west. Washington Street runs in an east-west direction and divides the city into north and south. Street addresses emanate from the junction of Washington and Meridian, beginning at 0/0. Numbered streets are generally found north of Washington Street, with the numbers corresponding to the distance in blocks from Washington Street.

Most north-south routes are named avenues, roads or boulevards. The four angled avenues—Virginia, Massachusetts, Indiana and Kentucky—can be disconcerting to first-time visitors, who might find the I-70/I-65 inner beltway more convenient. The city has several one-way streets, and during rush hour many left turns are prohibited. Consult a good city map and plan to avoid rush hours, 6-9 a.m. and 3-6 p.m. Speed limits generally range from 25 to 45 mph.

Parking

On-street metered parking is often difficult to find. Rates begin at 25c for 20 minutes. There are many parking lots and garages in the city, and most hotels provide parking for their guests. Lots and garages cost from $1.50 to $7 per day. The Pan American Plaza next to the RCA Dome and Union Station provides convenient parking; the fee is $5 per day.

What To See

 THE CHILDREN'S MUSEUM OF INDIANAPOLIS AND CINEDOME THEATER, on the n. side of 30th St. between Meridian and Illinois sts., offers exhibits about history, foreign cultures, physical and natural science, trains and the arts. Featured are a life-size Tyrannosaurus rex model, a water clock, a log cabin and a late 19th-century carousel. The five-story museum also houses a children's theater, a planetarium and CineDome, a large-format theater.

Allow 2 hours minimum. Daily 10-5 (also first Thurs. of the month 5-8), Mar. 1-Labor Day; Tues.-Sun. 10-5 (also first Thurs. of the month 5-8), rest of year. CineDome and planetarium hours may vary; phone ahead. Closed Easter, Thanksgiving and Dec. 25. Museum admission $8; over 59, $7; ages 2-17, $3.50. CineDome $6.50; ages 2-17, $4.50. Combination ticket $12.50; over 59, $11.50; ages 2-17, $7. Carousel 50c. Museum free to all Thurs. 5-8, Martin Luther King Jr. Day, Presidents Day and Dec. 24. MC, VI. Phone (317) 334-3322.

EAGLE CREEK PARK AND NATURE PRESERVE, 7840 W. 56th St., is a city park with a 1,300-acre reservoir and 3,900 acres of land. White-tailed deer, many species of birds and small field and woods animals inhabit the park, which also has a nature center and a golf course, plus a pistol and archery range. Hiking trails, a canine companion zone, bicycling, fishing, swimming, a marina and boat rentals are available. The park's rowing course is sanctioned for international competition.

Daily dawn-dusk. Admission $3 per private vehicle Sat.-Sun. and holidays; $2 per private vehicle (up to six people) Mon.-Fri. . There is a 25c fee for each additional passenger. Bicyclists and hikers 50c. Phone (317) 327-7110. *See Recreation Chart.*

 EITELJORG MUSEUM OF AMERICAN INDIANS AND WESTERN ART— *see White River State Park p. 143.*

GARFIELD PARK CONSERVATORY, 2505 Conservatory Dr. in Garfield Park, houses a large collection of tropical plants. Various floral displays are exhibited throughout the year. The neoclassical, formal European-style sunken garden set outside the conservatory dates from 1916. Guided tours are available. Daily 10-6. Free. Guided tours $1. Phone (317) 327-7184.

HOME OF JAMES WHITCOMB RILEY, just n. of E. New York St. at 528 Lockerbie St., was built in 1872. Preserved as it was during the poet's residence 1893-1916, the house is an excellent example of Victorian architecture. Many of Riley's personal possessions—including his pen—are on display. Allow 30 minutes minimum. Tues.-Sat. 10-3:30, Sun. noon-3:30; closed major holidays and first 3 weeks in Jan. Admission $3; over 64, $2; ages 7-17, 50c. Phone (317) 631-5885.

THE HOOKS AMERICAN DRUG STORE MUSEUM, 1180 E. 38th St. on the Indiana State Fairgrounds, displays an array of drugstore and pharmacy artifacts amid ornate furnishings. A vintage soda fountain is in operation. Allow 30 minutes minimum. Daily 9-9 during the state fair in Aug.; by appointment rest of year. Free with fair admission. Phone (317) 951-2222.

THE INDIANA HISTORICAL SOCIETY is at 450 W. Ohio St. The society was founded in 1830 to promote and preserve the Hoosier State's heritage. Inside are interactive exhibits, educational programs and a music room highlighting Indiana musicians. It also has a research library that contains rare books, manuscripts, maps and pictures relating to the history of Indiana and the Old Northwest. Tues.-Sat. 10-5, Sun. noon-5. The library is closed on Sundays. Closed major holidays. Donations. Phone (317) 232-1882 or (800) 447-1830.

SAVE INDIANA MEDICAL HISTORY MUSEUM, n. on Warman Ave. from Washington St., then w. to 3045 W. Vermont St., provides guided tours of the 1896 Old Pathology Building, which was once used to study mental and nervous disorders. Features include more than 15,000 medical artifacts, surgical and dental equipment, laboratories and an amphitheater formerly used as a medical classroom. Allow 1 hour minimum. Thurs.-Sat. 10-4; closed Jan. 1, July 4, Thanksgiving and Dec. 25. Admission $5; ages 6-18, $1. Phone (317) 635-7329.

INDIANAPOLIS MOTOR SPEEDWAY, 4790 W. 16th St., was built in 1909 as a proving ground and racetrack for automobiles. The facility's Indianapolis 500 race has resulted in such automotive improvements as the rearview mirror, balloon tires and ethyl gasoline. The speedway, also the site of NASCAR's Brickyard 400 and the Formula One U.S. Grand Prix, covers more than 433 acres, with an 18-hole PGA course inside and around the track.

Also inside the 2.5-mile oval is the Hall of Fame Museum, which displays many of the races' winning cars, car and driver memorabilia, antique automobiles and equipment. Bus tours of the track are available when it is not in use (weather permitting). A film about the track's history and highlights is shown every half-hour in the Tony Hulman Theatre.

Allow 1 hour minimum. Daily 9-5; closed Dec. 25. Last tour begins 30 minutes before closing. Museum $3; ages 6-15, $1. Bus tour $3; ages 6-15, $1. Phone (317) 484-6747.

INDIANAPOLIS MUSEUM OF ART, 1200 W. 38th St., is set among 152 acres of grounds and gardens incorporating Oldfields, the former J.K. Lilly Jr. estate. Permanent and changing exhibitions range from ancient artifacts to contemporary masterpieces and feature paintings, sculpture, decorative arts, textiles, costumes, photographs, prints and drawings.

Highlights include more than 2,000 objects of African art, the Clowes Collection of old master works, a comprehensive collection of works by English artist J.M.W. Turner, the Holliday collection of neo-impressionist paintings by Georges Suerat and his followers, and paintings and prints by Paul Gaugin and followers of the School of Pont-Aven. Japanese artwork from the Edo period, Chinese ceramics, West Asian rugs, contemporary studio glass and works by Indiana artists also are displayed.

The centerpiece of Oldfields is Lilly House, which dates from the early 20th century. Built in the style of an 18th-century French country mansion, it serves as a display pavilion. **Note:** The house is closed for renovations until summer 2002.

Tues.-Sat. 10-5 (also Thurs. 5-8:30), Sun. noon-5; closed Jan. 1, Thanksgiving and Dec. 25. Free. Admission to special exhibits is by donation. Phone (317) 923-1331.

INDIANA STATE LIBRARY, opposite the Capitol at 140 N. Senate Ave., has more than 34,000 volumes about Indiana. Tours are available by appointment. Library Mon.-Fri. 8-4:30. Genealogy department Mon.-Fri. 8-4:30 (also Tues. and Thurs. 4:30-8), Sat. 8:30-4. Closed state holidays. Free. Phone (317) 232-0023, or 232-3689 for the genealogy department.

INDIANA STATE MUSEUM, 202 N. Alabama St., is in the old City Hall building. A museum of Indiana's history and culture, its main feature is a four-story Foucault pendulum suspended from a stained-glass skylight in the rotunda. Displays include scenes of early Indiana and the animals that inhabited the area.

Of note are the Streets of Indiana, with a living-history variety store, and On the Air: Indiana Radio 1920-1950, which chronicles Indiana's broadcast history. Freetown Village represents an actual community that existed on the west side of town along the White River. Also on the grounds is the Indiana Museum of Sports, which highlights Indiana sports history. Traveling exhibits focus on social and cultural history, art and science.

Allow 1 hour minimum. Mon.-Sat. 9-4:45, Sun. noon-4:45; closed Jan. 1, Easter, Thanksgiving and Dec. 24-25. **Note:** The museum is scheduled to move to White River State Park spring 2002. Phone ahead to verify hours. Free. Phone (317) 232-1637.

INDIANA UNIVERSITY-PURDUE UNIVERSITY INDIANAPOLIS occupies a 285-acre campus on the east bank of the White River. Indiana University Medical Center is one of the country's great research centers. Other facilities include the Indianapolis Tennis Center, site of several national and international tennis competitions; the Natatorium, where U.S. Olympic swimming and diving trials and other national and international events are held; and the Track and Field Stadium, site of world-class meets.

Campus tours are available. For tour information phone the Director of Orientation, (317) 274-4240; for general information phone (317) 274-5555.

INDIANA WORLD WAR MEMORIAL occupies a plaza of five city blocks between Meridian, Pennsylvania, St. Clair and New York sts. The four-story limestone building in the northeast corner houses the national headquarters of the American Legion. A cenotaph honoring Indiana's war dead is in the north square, and a 100-foot obelisk rises from the center square. Wed.-Sun 9-6; closed Jan. 1 and Dec. 25. Free. Phone (317) 232-7615.

Memorial Building, the main edifice in the plaza, has an auditorium and meeting rooms. On the south side of the shrine a flight of steps leads past the statue "Pro Patria," one of the largest bronze castings ever made, and to the entrance of the Memorial Shrine Room honoring the American flag.

The Military Museum in the lower concourse pays tribute to the contributions of Hoosiers in the armed forces. Exhibits include a World War I French 75mm cannon, a Navy Terrier missile, combat maps and pictures. Wed.-Sun 9-6; closed Jan. 1, Dec. 25 and during events. Free.

JAMES IRVING HOLCOMB OBSERVATORY AND PLANETARIUM, W. 46th and Sunset sts. at Butler University, has the state's largest telescope. Tours are available on selected Fridays and Saturdays during the school year; phone for dates and times.

Planetarium shows are given Fri.-Sat. at 8. Admission $2.50, senior citizens, students with ID and children $1, family rate $6. Phone (317) 940-9333.

SAVE **MORRIS-BUTLER HOUSE**, 1204 N. Park Ave., is a restored 16-room Second Empire house completed in 1865. The interior is a museum that represents a local upper class Victorian family lifestyle, with period furniture, rich floral carpets and draperies, elegant chandeliers and intricate mantelpieces and other woodwork.

Allow 30 minutes minimum. Guided tours are given every 30 minutes Tues.-Sat. 10-4, Sun. 1-4, June-Aug.; Thurs.-Sat. 10-4 and first Sun. of the month 1-4, rest of year. Closed holidays. Last tour begins 30 minutes before closing. Admission $5; over 65, $4; ages 6-16, $3. Phone (317) 636-5409.

NATIONAL ART MUSEUM OF SPORT is in the University Place Conference Center and Hotel, 850 W. Michigan St., on the campus of Indiana University-Purdue University Indianapolis. The collection of fine art focusing on sports consists of drawings, paintings, sculptures and prints. Allow 1 hour minimum. Mon.-Fri. 8-5; closed major holidays. Sat.-Sun. hours vary; phone ahead. Free. Phone (317) 274-3876.

GEM **PRESIDENT BENJAMIN HARRISON HOME**, 1 mi. n. of Washington St. (US 40) at 1230 N. Delaware St., was completed in 1875. Harrison occupied the 16-room Italianate Victorian mansion, except during his term as 23rd president of the United States, until his death in 1901. The restored house contains original furnishings, political mementos and a collection of gowns belonging to both Mrs. Harrison and her daughter. T.C. Steele's portrait of President Harrison hangs in the rear parlor. A reconstructed carriage house contains a carriage room, stable and replica of Harrison's law office.

Allow 1 hour minimum. Guided tours are given every half-hour Mon.-Sat. 10-3:30, Sun. 12:30-3:30, late Jan.-Dec. 31; closed Easter, Memorial Day weekend, Labor Day, Thanksgiving and Dec. 24-25. Admission $5.50; over 64, $4.50; students with ID $2.50. Phone (317) 631-1888.

SCOTTISH RITE CATHEDRAL, 650 N. Meridian St., is a Gothic structure containing a 54 bell-carillon. Considered one of the most beautiful buildings in the country after its completion in 1929, the cathedral houses a 7,000-pipe organ. Food is available. Allow 30 minutes minimum. Guided tours are given Mon.-Fri. 10-3; closed holidays. Free. Phone (317) 262-3100.

SOLDIERS' & SAILORS' MONUMENT, in the center of Monument Circle, is 284 feet high and surmounted by a 30-foot statue of Miss Victory. Constructed of Indiana limestone and featuring exterior historical and mythological sculptures, the monument was originally dedicated in 1902 and underwent major restoration in the late 1980s. A glass-enclosed observation deck surrounding the base of the pinnacle statue can be reached by elevator or stairs. Wed.-Sun. 9-6; closed major holidays. Free. Phone (317) 232-7615.

Col. Eli Lilly Civil War Museum is in the Soldiers' & Sailors' Monument. Exhibits chronicle the Civil War experiences of Indiana residents, with topics ranging from the homefront to camp life, battlefields to imprisonment. Allow 1 hour minimum. Wed.-Sun. 9-6; closed major holidays. Free. Phone (317) 232-7615.

STATE CAPITOL BUILDING is on 9 acres bounded by Capitol Ave., Washington St., Senate Ave. and Ohio St. Completed in 1888, the Renaissance Revival limestone structure incorporates classical neo-Greco architectural details in its interior, which features various marbles and granite. The stained-glass window in the rotunda is the original. Unlike many old capitols, it is functional and houses all three branches of government.

Visitors may take a self-guiding tour; brochures are available at the information desk or tour office. Guided tours are available. Allow 30 minutes minimum. Mon.-Fri. 9-3. Free. Phone (317) 233-5293.

WHITE RIVER GARDENS is off I-65 exit 114, then 1 mi. w. to 1200 W. Washington St. More than 3 acres of botanical gardens contain plantings, sculpture, water features, flowered pathways, meandering trails and a conservatory. A resource center offers gardening tips, horticultural information and ideas for landscape design. Allow 1 hour, 30 minutes minimum. Daily 9-5; closed Jan. 1, Thanksgiving and Dec. 25. Admission $6.50; over 62, $5.50; ages 3-12, $4.50. Parking $3. DS, MC, VI. Phone (317) 630-2001.

WHITE RIVER STATE PARK, on W. Washington St., features sports, entertainment and cultural venues on 250 acres in the heart of the city. Included are Victory Field, home of Indianapolis' professional baseball team; a riverside promenade made of Indiana limestone; and a pedestrian path along a canal built in the mid-1800s. Paddle boats can be rented. The visitor center is in a restored 1870 pumphouse at 801 W. Washington St. Visitor center open Mon.-Fri. 8:30-7, Sat. 10-7, Sun. noon-7. Apr.-Oct.; Mon.-Fri. 8:30-5. Sat. 10-5, Sun. noon-5, rest of year. Free. Phone (317) 233-2434 or (800) 665-9056.

GEM **Eiteljorg Museum of American Indians and Western Art**, 500 W. Washington St., houses two major permanent collections and provides gallery space for traveling exhibitions of artistic representations of the American West. The adobe building was designed especially as a showcase for paintings depicting the West and for American Indian artifacts collected by Harrison Eiteljorg, Indianapolis businessman and philanthropist.

The Western Collection displays paintings, drawings, graphics and sculpture from the early 19th century to the present and includes works by Georgia O'Keeffe, Frederic Remington, Charles Russell and members of the original Taos, N.M., art colony. The Native American Collection exhibits such objects as woodcarvings, basketry, pottery and clothing from American Indian cultural regions all over North America. Plantings, a fountain and three commissioned sculptures enhance the building, itself considered a work of art.

Allow 2 hours minimum. Tues.-Sat. 10-5, Sun. noon-5 (also Mon. 10-5, Memorial Day-Labor Day); closed Jan. 1, Thanksgiving, evening of Dec. 24, and Dec. 25. Guided tours are given at 1. Admission $6; over 65, $5; full-time students with ID and ages 5-17, $3. MC, VI. Phone (317) 636-9378.

IMAX Theater, 650 W. Washington St., shows IMAX and 3-D films on a six-story, 80-foot-wide screen. The auditorium seats more than 400 viewers. Underground parking is available. Allow 2 hours minimum. Mon.-Wed. 10-4, Thurs.-Sun. 10-8. Admission $7.50-$10; over 60, $7-$9; ages 3-12, $4.50-$7.50. Parking $2. Phone (317) 233-4629.

SAVE **The Indianapolis Zoo** is at 1200 W. Washington St. The 64-acre cageless zoo exhibits animals in such simulated habitats as deserts, plains, forests and the ocean. The zoo contains one of the world's largest enclosed dolphin pavilions; an aquarium; Living Deserts of the World, where desert animals and plants coexist as they would in nature; and the Encounters Arena, where domestic animal shows are presented.

Visitors can ride a train, a family roller coaster and ponies April through October. Food is available. Daily 9-5. Hours may vary; phone ahead. Closed Jan. 1, June 8 and Dec. 24-25 and 31. Admission $9.75; over 62, $7; ages 3-12, $6. Roller coaster $2. Train fare and pony rides $1.50. Parking $3. DS, MC, VI. Phone (317) 630-2001.

Medal of Honor Memorial is on the n. bank of Central Canal in White River State Park. Twenty-seven curved glass walls are etched with the names of recipients of the nation's highest award for military valor. At dusk the walls are illuminated one at a time while a recording tells honorees' stories. Allow 30 minutes minimum. Daily dawn-dusk. Free. Phone (317) 233-2434.

NCAA Hall of Champions is at 700 W. Washington St. in White River State Park. The National Collegiate Athletic Association's museum highlights outstanding college athletes, coaches and teams through multimedia exhibits. Guided tours are available. Allow 1 hour, 30 minutes minimum. Mon.-Sat. 10-5, Sun. noon-5; closed Jan. 1, Thanksgiving and Dec. 25. Admission $7; over 55, $6; ages 6-22, $4. Parking $2-$8. AX, DS, MC, VI. Phone (317) 917-6222 or (800) 735-6222.

What To Do

Sightseeing

Bus or Carriage Tours

SAVE Gray Line bus tours of the city depart from the Omni Severin Hotel at Illinois and Jackson streets Wednesday at 1 p.m. The 3-hour tour is offered April through October; phone (317) 573-0403 or (800) 447-4526 on Mondays for reservations.

A popular way to see the area at night is on a horse-drawn carriage ride offered by one of three carriage companies. Most are offered 7 p.m.-midnight and are stationed along Washington Street at Meridian Street or at the Hyatt Regency at 1 S. Capitol Ave.

Walking Tours

An especially interesting area for a walking tour is Lockerbie Square, a six-block district bounded by New York, College, Michigan and East streets. Featured are restored 19th-century private houses, cobblestone streets, antique gas streetlights and the Victorian home of James Whitcomb Riley. Another interesting area for a stroll is Broad Ripple, a neighborhood north of the downtown area. Similar to New York City's Greenwich Village, the area contains boutiques, art galleries, sidewalk cafes, antique shops and ethnic restaurants.

Also of interest is the Madame Walker Theatre Center at 617 Indiana Ave., a restoration of the former headquarters of the cosmetic business of Madame C.J. Walker, one of the country's first female millionaires. Thirty-minute tours are available by appointment; phone (317) 236-2099.

A relatively new addition is the Canal Walk, a portion of the historic Central Canal that has been

renovated into a pathway popular with walkers, joggers and downtown workers. The junction of Ohio and West streets is a good starting point. At Walnut Street and Senate Avenue is the USS Indianapolis CA-35 National Memorial, a granite memorial to the shipmates who died when the USS *Indianapolis* sank in World War II.

An observation tower atop the City-County Building offers a 360-degree view from more than 300 feet above street level and includes exhibits and a telescope; phone (317) 327-4345. Commemorating Civil War and Spanish-American War veterans, the Soldiers' & Sailors' Monument at Monument Circle also provides a panorama of downtown.

Another good vantage point is Crown Hill Cemetery at 3402 Boulevard Pl., where such notables as James Whitcomb Riley, John Dillinger, President Benjamin Harrison and three vice presidents are buried.

Sports and Recreation

Indianapolis' 113 city parks provide sports-minded visitors and residents with almost every recreational activity imaginable. Eagle Creek Park, 10 miles northwest via 56th and 71st streets, is well equipped for such activities as **bicycling, boating, cross-country skiing, fishing, golfing** (27 holes), **hiking, ice skating, jogging, picnicking** and **swimming** (beach).

Centrally located White River State Park is a diverse urban oasis suitable for hiking, bicycling and **roller skating**. In addition to museums and the zoo, the park features a sports fitness center, outdoor entertainment venues and picnic areas.

Ice skating facilities are at Carmel Ice Skadium, 1040 3rd Ave., Carmel; Pepsi Coliseum Ice Rink at the State Fairgrounds, 1202 E. 38th St.; Eagle Creek Park, 9026 W. 56th St.; Ellenberger Ice Rink, 5301 E. St. Clair; Pan Am Plaza, 201 S. Capitol Ave.; and Perry Ice Rink, 415 E. Stop 11 Rd. Eagle Creek Park and Sahm Park, 6801 E. 91st St., offer cross-country skiing.

Boating and **sailing** are available at Geist and Morse reservoirs, both north of the city, and at Eagle Creek Reservoir in Eagle Creek Park; boats can be rented at Eagle Creek. Phone (317) 327-7110 or (317) 327-7130.

Golfing is available at 12 public courses. Some of the most popular are Eagle Creek, 9026 W. 56th St. (nine and 18 holes); Pleasant Run, 601 N. Arlington (18 holes); Riverside Park, 3501 Cold Spring Rd. (18 holes); Sahm Park, 6800 E. 91st St. (18 holes); and South Grove, 1800 W. 18th St. (18 holes).

Fans of swimming, **running** and bicycling enjoy specially designed facilities in Indianapolis. The Natatorium, 901 W. New York St., is one of the most advanced swimming and diving pools in the country; phone (317) 274-3518.

Across the street is Indiana University's Michael A. Carroll Track and Field Stadium, available 5:30 a.m.-8 p.m. for running, except during official meets. The stadium also contains fitness trails. The Major Taylor Velodrome at 3649 Cold Spring Rd. has a concrete surface banked at 28 degrees. It is open to bicyclists daily from May to November, unless it is being used for competitions; a limited quantity of rental bicycles and helmets is available. Phone (317) 327-8356. Eagle Creek Park has 1,000 acres with bicycle routes.

In addition to the many public **tennis** courts, the Indianapolis Tennis Center, 150 University Blvd., has 14 outdoor hard-surface courts, four outdoor clay-surface courts and six indoor hard-surface courts. Phone (317) 278-2100 to reserve a court. The Indianapolis Tennis Center is the site of the RCA men's professional tournament held each August.

Automobile racing is another popular pastime. The Indianapolis 500 race, held during Memorial Day weekend, is considered the biggest 1-day sporting event in the world, drawing more than 400,000 fans to the speedway each year. Also at the Indianapolis Motor Speedway is NASCAR's Brickyard 400, held in early August, and the Formula One U.S. Grand Prix in September. Rounding out the summer are the National Hot Rod Association Championship Drag Races on Labor Day at Indianapolis Raceway Park; phone (317) 291-4090.

The city also is home to the National **Football** League's Indianapolis Colts, who play in the 60,500-seat RCA Dome; phone (317) 262-3389 or 239-5151. The 18,500-seat Conseco Fieldhouse is the showcase for the National **Basketball** Association's Indiana Pacers and the Women's National Basketball Association's Indiana Fever; phone (317) 917-2500 or 239-5151. The International **Hockey** League's Indianapolis Ice also play at the fieldhouse and at the Pepsi Coliseum; phone (317) 925-4423 or 239-5151. The Indianapolis Indians, an affiliate of the Milwaukee Brewers, play **baseball** at Victory Field in White River State Park; phone (317) 269-3545 or 239-5151. The Western Conference of the United **Soccer** League is represented by the Indiana Blast, who play at Kuntz Stadium; phone (317) 585-9203. The Blaze, Indiana's only women's soccer team, also kick it up at Kuntz Stadium.

Shopping

Shoppers will find a wide range of places where they can spend their money—from international food stands to specialty stores and boutiques to traditional department stores.

City Market, 222 E. Market St., offers exotic foods and imported items. The 1886 market has been restored as part of a revitalization project and is noted for its fresh produce, ethnic food, flowers, meats, pastries, cheeses, fruits, coffees and teas. The market is open Mon.-Sat. 6-6.

Specialty shops can be found at Merchants Plaza, 2 W. Washington St. Local wines can be sampled and purchased at Chateau Thomas Winery, 6291

Cambridge Way, and at Easley's Winery, 205 N. College Ave.

Indianapolis has a number of shopping malls. Castleton Square Mall, 6020 E. 82nd St., features JCPenney, Lazarus, L.S. Ayres and Sears among its 120 stores. Circle Centre Mall, 49 W. Maryland St., counts Nordstrom, Parisian and FAO Schwarz among its more than 100 shops. The mall also includes the Indianapolis Artsgarden, a glass-domed structure that shows local art. At 7150 E. Washington St., the Eastgate Consumer Mall contains 63 shops, including the Burlington Coat Factory and Dunham's Sporting Goods.

Glendale Center, 6101 N. Keystone Ave., has 105 shops, including Old Navy and L.S. Ayres. At 3919 N. Lafayette Rd., Lafayette Square contains 90 stores, including JCPenney. Additional stores include Lazarus, L.S. Ayres and Sears, which also can be found among the 100 shops at Washington Square, 10202 E. Washington St.

The Broad Ripple area, about 15 minutes from downtown, offers the chic, the unusual, the extraordinary and the unexpected. Many of the stores are small boutiques in old restored houses. Another interesting shopping area is the Fashion Mall at Keystone at the Crossing, offering luxury items ranging from fine crystal to handmade Italian sportswear; the 95-store complex features Brooks Brothers, Crabtree and Evelyn, Jacobson's, Laura Ashley and Parisian.

Farther out are several plazas and malls. In Zionsville *(see place listing p. 149)*, shoppers can browse through fashionable specialty shops in a restored 19th-century village. At 1251 US 31N in Greenwood, the Greenwood Park Mall contains 135 stores, including JCPenney, Lazarus, L.S. Ayres, Sears and Service Merchandise.

Theater and Concerts

The arts are a priority in Indianapolis, as the city is undergoing a sustained cultural renaissance. The Indianapolis Symphony Orchestra is directed by Raymond Leppard, said to be one of the top conductors in the world, and performs in the renovated Hilbert Circle Theatre at 45 Monument Cir. The regular season runs from September through May and includes classical, pop and family series as well as morning coffee and Yuletide concerts.

In the summer the symphony presents its free Concert in the Park programs. Summer also brings the Symphony on the Prairie series to Conner Prairie in nearby Fishers *(see attraction listing p. 148)*, where music is combined with picnics and sunsets. For ticket and performance information phone (317) 776-6004.

Local chamber groups play on a regular basis at Butler University, the Indianapolis Museum of Art and the University of Indianapolis. National and international chamber group performances include the Festival Music Society's July series at the Indianapolis Museum of Art; the Ensemble Music Society's concerts at the Children's Museum, October

through May; and the Ronen Chamber Ensemble's season at the Hilbert Circle Theatre, November through May.

The American Pianists Association presents nationally known pianists at Christ Church Cathedral on Monument Circle throughout the year.

The Indianapolis Artsgarden, run by the Arts Council of Indianapolis, has a monthly jazz series, various other performing arts presentations and a celebration of song at Christmas. The Artsgarden, in Circle Center Mall on W. Maryland Street, also has family shows, art exhibits and a Black History Month celebration; phone (317) 631-3301.

Concerts regularly take place at Clowes Hall on the Butler University campus; at Verizon Wireless Music Center in Noblesville; at the Indiana State Fairgrounds; and at Conseco Fieldhouse, 125 S. Pennsylvania St. Local jazz groups perform frequently at the Madame Walker Urban Life Center, 617 Indiana Ave.

Opera buffs can enjoy presentations of the Indianapolis Opera at Clowes Hall, 4600 Sunset Ave. For information phone (317) 283-3470.

The Indiana Repertory Theatre, housed in a renovated movie palace downtown at 140 W. Washington St., is the city's Equity company. The company's Mainstage offers a full schedule of plays running from October through May. For information phone (317) 635-5252.

The MacAllister Center for the Performing Arts, in Garfield Park, presents theatrical performances and concerts throughout the summer.

Professional dance is represented by Dance Kaleidoscope and the Indianapolis Ballet Theatre, both of which present a regular concert series. Dance Kaleidoscope, based at the Indiana Repertory Theatre's Upperstage, offers contemporary dance by nationally known choreographers; the Indianapolis Ballet Theatre presents several major ballets September through May at Butler University's Clowes Hall.

The Beef and Boards Dinner Theatre, 9301 Michigan Rd., presents well-known entertainers in concert and in Broadway musicals all year; phone (317) 872-9664

For more details about current shows and concerts, contact the Indianapolis City Center in Pan Am Plaza or phone the city's tourism hotline, (800) 468-4639, for 24-hour information about events.

Special Events

The biggest event in Indianapolis, as well as in automobile racing, is the Indianapolis 500, held Memorial Day weekend. Preceding the grand race is the Indianapolis 500 Festival, a monthlong celebration that includes a festival queen contest and coronation ceremony, a minimarathon, art exhibits and a parade with floats. The Brickyard 400, in early August, is another favorite racing event. The U.S. National Hot Rod Association Drag Racing Championship is held at Indianapolis Raceway Park in early September.

Throughout the spring, summer and fall Indianapolis' ethnic communities hold a wide variety of festivals, including those celebrating Italian, German, Greek and Spanish heritages.

Spring is ushered in by the Indiana Flower and Patio Show the second full week in March. June brings the Midsummer Festival to welcome the summer solstice. The event takes place on Monument Circle, where more than 50 restaurants serve their specialties as live bands provide entertainment. Indiana Black Expo Summer Celebration, held around the Fourth of July, is a weeklong event highlighting African-American achievements, commerce, artists and culture. Circlefest, held in July, provides a wide range of activities and entertainment.

A perennial August favorite is the Indiana State Fair, featuring amusement park fun, national entertainment, horse shows and harness racing. Also in August is the RCA Tennis Championship, held at the Indianapolis Tennis Center. Benjamin Harrison's Birthday Celebration in mid-August honors the 23rd president of the United States.

The Penrod Arts Fair, held at the Indianapolis Museum of Art on the first Saturday after Labor Day, is a festival of arts and crafts. Highlighting the day is the live entertainment—including opera, theater, ballet and mime—provided by Indianapolis' performing artists. Circle City Classic, one of the largest bowl games between historically African-American colleges, has grown from a football game played at RCA Dome to a festival with more than 20 events and a parade.

The first full weekend in October brings the Blue River Valley Pioneer Craft Fair at the Shelby County Fairgrounds. The fair features demonstrations of pioneer crafts of the 1830s and '40s. Rounding out the month, the International Festival celebrates the heritages of cultures from around the world at Butler University from mid- to late October; highlights include art, dancing and food.

Setting the scene for the Christmas season is the Christmas Gift and Hobby Show the first week in November. Throughout December thousands of tiny lights turn the Indiana Soldiers' & Sailors' Monument into the world's tallest Christmas tree. Christmas at the Zoo includes 150,000 twinkling lights and more than 30 other displays. Details about when and where events are scheduled are available at the Indianapolis City Center in Pan Am Plaza.

The Indianapolis Vicinity

ANDERSON (D-4) pop. 59,500, elev. 875'

Anderson is the summer home of the National Football League's Indianapolis Colts, who practice on the Anderson University campus from late July through August. The university's Warner Auditorium has one of the largest circular domes ever to be lifted during construction. The city also is the international headquarters for the Church of God and the site of its annual convention.

Historic West Eighth Street is an 11-block neighborhood with Victorian houses built 1870-1920; more than 100 Newport-style gaslights adorn the streets.

Several hiking, bicycling and canoeing trails are found along the White River; most of these travel through Mounds State Park (see Recreation Chart), which has ancient earthworks built by the Adena and Hopewell Indians.

Hoosier Park at Anderson offers Standardbred and Thoroughbred racing from early spring to late fall; phone (765) 642-7223.

Note: Policies concerning admittance of children to pari-mutuel betting facilities vary. Phone for information.

Anderson/Madison County Visitors & Convention Bureau: 6335 S. Scatterfield Rd., Anderson, IN 46013; phone (765) 643-5633 or (800) 633-6569.

Shopping areas: Mounds Mall, at the junction of Scatterfield Road and SR 32, contains Sears and 35 specialty stores. Applewood Centre, at Scatterfield Road and I-69, contains a number of shops and restaurants. The Anderson Antique Mall is at 14th and Main Street, and Pendleton Antique Mall is 3 miles southeast off I-69 in Pendleton.

ANDERSON FINE ARTS CENTER, 32 W. 10th St., in the 1905 Carnegie Building, presents changing art exhibits that show the works of local, regional and national artists. Guided tours are available. Allow 1 hour minimum. Tues.-Sat. 10-5, Sun. 2-5; closed holidays. Admission $2; over 59, $1.50; students with ID $1; under 4 free; family rate $5; free to all Tues. and first Sun. of the month. Phone (765) 649-1248 or (800) 213-7656.

[SAVE] **GRUENEWALD HISTORIC HOUSE,** 626 Main St., is a three-story French Second Empire house dating from 1860. Living-history guided tours, available by appointment, present the house as it was when Martin Gruenewald, a successful local businessman, completed it. Its 12 rooms are decorated with late 18th- and 19th-century furnishings and household items.

Allow 1 hour minimum. Tues.-Fri. 10-3, Apr. 1-Dec. 15; by appointment rest of year. Closed major holidays. Admission $4, ages 5-16 and students with ID $2. Phone (765) 648-6875.

THE PARAMOUNT THEATRE, 1124 Meridian Plaza, was designed by architect John Eberson and includes a grand ballroom. The theater features a starlit night sky projected onto a dome ceiling. The interior is reminiscent of an ancient Spanish villa, with interesting architectural features and an unusual pipe organ. Brochures are available for self-guiding tours. Mon.-Fri. 9-5; closed holidays. Donations. Phone (765) 642-1234 or (800) 523-4658.

CARMEL (D-4) pop. 25,400, elev. 829'

Carmel, founded in the early 19th century, was initially called Bethlehem; when the town was incorporated, its name was changed to Carmel. Resident, Leslie Haines manufactured and installed in Carmel what is believed to be the first automatic traffic signal in the country.

Hamilton County Convention and Visitors Bureau: 11601 Municipal Dr., Fishers, IN 46038; phone (317) 598-4444 or (800) 776-8687.

[SAVE] **MUSEUM OF MINIATURE HOUSES,** 111 E. Main St., displays antique and contemporary doll houses, room boxes and vignettes furnished in period. Special collections also are displayed. Allow 1 hour minimum. Wed.-Sat. 11-4, Sun. 1-4; closed holidays. Donations. Phone (317) 575-9466.

FISHERS (D-4) pop. 7,500, elev. 816'

William Conner, an early pioneer, arrived in the area during the winter of 1800-01. His two-story brick home serves as one of the focal points of nearby Conner Prairie.

Originally known as Fishers Switch, then Fishers Station, Fishers officially came into being in 1872. Its ties to a railroad heritage are obvious. The railroad drew residents and businesses to the area, and the growth began that has led to Fishers' status as a residential and commercial center.

Hamilton County Convention and Visitors Bureau: 11601 Municipal Dr., Fishers, IN 46038; phone (317) 598-4444 or (800) 776-8687.

[GEM] [SAVE] **CONNER PRAIRIE** is 6 mi. n. on Allisonville Rd. This living-history museum depicts the lifestyles, values and experiences of Indiana settlers through five interpretive areas along the White River. The Conner Estate includes a barn, spring house, garden and the restored 1823 Federal-style home of fur trader, entrepreneur and legislator William Conner. Dyeing, spinning and weaving techniques are demonstrated at a loom house.

Prairietown, a re-creation of a typical 1836 Midwestern village, comprises a restored schoolhouse and general store as well as blacksmith, carpentry and pottery shops. Costumed interpreters portray fictional residents in re-enactments of elections, weddings and funerals. Liberty Corner, reminiscent of an 1886 rural crossroad community, features a Victorian-era farmhouse, a Quaker meeting house and a covered bridge. Delaware Indian history is explained at the Lenape Indian Camp, with five Delaware wigwams and a log trading post. In the PastPort Discovery Area visitors can try 19th-century crafts, skills and games.

The Museum Center serves as a starting point for visits to the outdoor areas; it contains exhibits and presents an orientation film. Thirty-minute guided tours of the Conner home begin at the Conner barn. Food is available.

Allow 3 hours minimum. Museum Center open Tues.-Sat. 9:30-5, Sun. 11-5. Historic areas open Tues.-Sat. 9:30-5, Sun. 11-5, Apr.-Nov. Closed Jan. 1, Easter, Thanksgiving and Dec. 24-25 and 31. Guided tours of the Conner home are given every 20 minutes. Historic areas admission $10; over 64, $9; ages 5-12, $6. Conner home tour included with admission; reservations should be made when tickets are purchased. DS, MC, VI. Phone (317) 776-6006 or (800) 966-1836.

RITCHEY WOODS NATURE PRESERVE, 10410 Hague Rd., includes forest and wetlands as well as nature trails for viewing wildlife and plants. Guided nature hikes are available Saturday and Sunday at 1 for a fee. Allow 1 hour minimum. Daily 10-5, June-Aug.; Sat.-Sun. 10-5, Apr.-May and Sept.-Oct. Admission $2. Phone (317) 334-3826.

FRANKLIN (E-4) pop. 12,900, elev. 731'

JOHNSON COUNTY MUSEUM OF HISTORY, 1.5 blks. n. of Jefferson St. at 135 N. Main St., in a former Masonic Temple, houses a collection of items relating to the history of Johnson County. Exhibits include 19th-century furnishings and fashions, a log cabin, dolls and Civil War memorabilia. A 1940s-style room depicts the history of Camp Atterbury, a training camp established during World War II. A genealogical research room is available.

Allow 1 hour minimum. Mon.-Fri. 9-4, second Sat. of the month 10-3; closed county holidays. Donations. Phone (317) 736-4655.

GREENFIELD (D-5) pop. 11,700, elev. 993'

[SAVE] **JAMES WHITCOMB RILEY BIRTHPLACE AND MUSEUM,** 250 W. Main St., is in the renovated Riley home, where Indiana's poet laureate was born in 1849 and spent a lively childhood. His most celebrated poems drew on these experiences and later inspired the Raggedy Ann and Andy dolls and the "Little Orphan Annie" comic strip. The Annie character was based on Little Orphaned Annie, a worker at the Riley home; her room is part of the guided tour. The house next door chronicles the poet's life with displays of his works, period antiques and photographs. The gardens contain flowers and herbs of the period.

Allow 1 hour minimum. Tues.-Sat. 10-4, Sun. 1-4, mid-April to mid-Nov.; closed major holidays. Admission $3; ages 6-17, $1. Phone (317) 462-8539.

NOBLESVILLE (D-4) pop. 17,700, elev. 801'

Noblesville was founded in 1823 by William Conner, who ran a trading post in the region 1802-23. With the arrival of the railroad and the industrial age in the mid-1800s, Noblesville developed into a light manufacturing center in a prosperous farming region. A historic Victorian Square is centered around the renovated 1878 courthouse. Forest Park is a half-mile northwest on SR 19.

Hamilton County Convention and Visitors Bureau: 11601 Municipal Drive, Fishers, IN 46038; phone (317) 598-4444 or (800) 776-8687.

ZIONSVILLE (D-4) pop. 5,300, elev. 885'

A northern suburb of Indianapolis, Zionsville materialized in 1852 as a community along the Cincinnati, Indianapolis and Lafayette Railroad. With the establishment of the Zion Park Assembly on the banks of Lake Como in the late 19th century, Zionsville developed into a cultural center frequented by such intellectuals as Democratic and Populist leader William Jennings Bryan, best known for his assistance in prosecuting the Scopes trial, and Albert J. Beveridge, a U.S. senator and historian.

En route to Washington, D.C., for his presidential inauguration in 1861, Abraham Lincoln addressed Zionsville's citizens from the platform of his train; the site of the former railroad station where this event took place is marked by a stone monument in Lincoln Park.

Zionsville has preserved a Victorian village atmosphere, most evident in the many examples of period architecture. Six blocks of brick Main Street are lined with trees, flowering planters, candlelit windows, historical markers and specialty shops. Docents give guided walking tours; contact the chamber of commerce for reservations.

Greater Zionsville Chamber of Commerce: 135 S. Elm St., P.O. Box 148, Zionsville, IN 46077; phone (317) 873-3836.

Self-guiding tours: A brochure identifying period structures is available at the chamber of commerce.

P.H. SULLIVAN MUSEUM AND GENEALOGY LIBRARY, 1 blk. w. of jct. SR 334 at 225 W. Hawthorne St., presents permanent and changing displays about the history of Boone County and Indiana. Exhibits include period furniture, quilts, photographs and paintings. A genealogical library is available. Allow 1 hour minimum. Tues.-Sat. 10-4 (also Thurs. 4-8), mid-Jan. to mid-Dec.; closed major holidays. Donations. Phone (317) 873-4900.

This ends listings for the Indianapolis Vicinity.
The following page resumes the alphabetical listings
of cities in Indiana.

JEFFERSONVILLE (G-5)
pop. 22,000, elev. 844'

In 1834 James Howard launched his first steamboat, the *Hyperion,* at Jeffersonville. For nearly a century the Howard family turned out some of the finest ships on American rivers, and shipbuilding remains a major component in Jeffersonville's economy. The town promotes its river heritage through preservation of the historic commercial architecture along the scenic Ohio River.

Southern Indiana Chamber of Commerce: 4100 Charlestown Rd., New Albany, IN 47150; phone (812) 945-0266.

[SAVE] **HOWARD STEAMBOAT MUSEUM,** 1101 E. Market St., depicts riverboat history through craft models and tools used to build boats in the Howard Shipyards 1834-1941. Housed in an 1890 Victorian mansion built by Edmonds J. Howard, the museum contains original family furnishings. Guided tours are given Tues.-Sat. 10-4, Sun. 1-4; closed major holidays. Admission $4; over 65, $3; students over age 6 and college students with ID $2. Phone (812) 283-3728.

KNIGHTSTOWN (D-5) pop. 2,000, elev. 938'

CARTHAGE, KNIGHTSTOWN & SHIRLEY RAILROAD departs from the CKS Depot at 112 W. Carey St., 2 blks. e. of SR 109. This round-trip tour covers 10 miles through scenic countryside and over the Big Blue River. Passengers sit in enclosed or open-air train cars and listen to the engineer spin anecdotes about the journey and the old line that used to run on the same tracks.

Allow 1 hour minimum. Train departs Sat.-Sun. and holidays at 11, 1 and 3, Fri. at 11, May-Oct. Fare $7; ages 3-11, $5. DS, MC, VI. Phone (765) 345-5561, or (800) 345-2704 in Ind.

KNOX (B-3) pop. 3,700, elev. 713'

KANKAKEE STATE FISH AND WILDLIFE AREA is 1 mi. n. on US 35, then 5 mi. w. on SR 8. The area lies along both sides of the Kankakee River and contains 4,100 acres in what was once Indiana's finest hunting and fishing district. Other popular activities include birdwatching, picnicking, canoeing, boating, and berry and mushroom picking. Daily 24 hours. Free. Phone (574) 896-3522. *See Recreation Chart.*

KOKOMO (C-4) pop. 45,000, elev. 806'

Kokomo experienced growth with the discovery of natural gas in 1886. Among those drawn by the area's natural resources was Elwood Haynes, a specialist in metallurgy and machinery who is said to have created America's first automobile as well as stainless steel and several other alloys. Haynes opened Indiana's first automobile plant in Kokomo in 1898.

Kokomo industrialists were the first to produce the pneumatic rubber tire, the carburetor and a push-button car radio. The Automotive Heritage Museum, 1500 N. Reed Rd., highlights the area's automotive history with a collection of antique vehicles, including Haynes' second car; phone (765) 454-9999.

The Kokomo Opalescent Glass Co. has been in operation since 1888 and offers tours of the factory Wednesday and Friday mornings; phone (765) 457-1829.

Old Ben, a 4,700-pound steer preserved by taxidermy, is displayed in Kokomo's Highland Park near another novelty, a huge sycamore tree stump measuring about 51 feet in circumference at its base.

Kokomo/Howard County Visitors Bureau: 1504 N. Reed Rd., Kokomo, IN 46901; phone (765) 457-6802 or (800) 837-0971.

ELWOOD HAYNES MUSEUM, 1915 S. Webster St., contains articles relating to the inventor's life, including 1905, 1923 and 1924 Haynes automobiles. The second floor contains industrial displays. A monument east of the city marks the place where Haynes' original car, one of the first American automobiles, made its initial road test on July 4, 1894. Guided tours and a film presentation are available. Allow 30 minutes minimum. Tues.-Sat. 1-4, Sun. 1-5; closed holidays. Free. Phone (765) 456-7500.

[SAVE] **HOWARD COUNTY MUSEUM,** 1200 W. Sycamore St., is housed in the 1891 Seiberling Mansion, an elegantly restored example of late Victorian architecture. The mansion's features include hand-carved interior woodwork, brass hardware and priceless Art Nouveau stained-glass windows. Some rooms are furnished in period; others reflect past lifestyles in Indiana. Medical, Civil War and sports exhibits also are featured.

Allow 1 hour minimum. Tues.-Sun. 1-4, Feb.-Dec.; phone for holiday schedule. Admission $2, under 12 free. Phone (765) 452-4314.

LAFAYETTE (C-3) pop. 43,800, elev. 578'

Founded in 1825 and named for the French general Marquis de Lafayette, Lafayette grew as a shipping and trade center on the busy Wabash River. The city, surrounded by farmland, is a center for food processing and is a manufacturing site for pharmaceuticals, automobiles, electrical equipment and other diversified products. The site of Fort Ouiatenon, the first military post in Indiana, is on South River Road. Purdue University is across the Wabash River in West Lafayette *(see place listing p. 166).*

Perrin Avenue and the historic districts contain many examples of 19th- and 20th-century architecture. The Tippecanoe County Courthouse and the Fowler House Historical Museum are notable architectural highlights.

Columbian Park, Lafayette's largest, contains a zoo and an amusement park. A variety of concerts is presented in the gazebo from June through August. Another noteworthy attraction is the Wabash

Heritage Trail, which begins at the Lafayette municipal golf course and follows Burnett's Creek and the Wabash River north to Tippecanoe Battlefield.

Greater Lafayette Chamber of Commerce: 337 Columbia St., P.O. Box 348, Lafayette, IN 47902; phone (765) 742-4041.

ART MUSEUM OF GREATER LAFAYETTE, 102 S. Tenth St., displays collections of paintings by both Indiana and other American artists, American art pottery, contemporary art and Latin American paintings. Temporary exhibits feature historical themes in art, regional cultures and local artists. Tues.-Sun. 11-4; closed major holidays. Donations. Phone (765) 742-1128.

TIPPECANOE COUNTY HISTORICAL ASSOCIATION MUSEUM, 909 South St., is in the Fowler House, a Victorian mansion built 1851-52. Highlights include original design features of the house and county history exhibits. The Allameda McCollough Resource Library, across from the museum in the Wetherill Historical Resource Center at 1001 South St., contains historical and genealogical material.

Museum open Tues.-Sun. 1-5. Resource center Tues.-Wed. 1-7, Thurs.-Fri. 1-5, third Sat. of the month 10-2. Closed holidays. Museum $3; ages 4-12, $1.50. Resource center free. Phone (765) 476-8411.

LaPORTE (A-3) pop. 21,500, elev. 812'

Founded in 1830, LaPorte, French for "the door," was so named because of its strategic location near several lakes at the northern edge of Indiana's central forests, where the land opens onto rolling prairie. LaPorte is a center of diversified industries. Products manufactured include rubber items, industrial blowers and radiators.

Fox Memorial Park features picnic areas and playgrounds as well as an outdoor amphitheater. Fishing, hiking, cross-country skiing and a nature center are offered at Luhr County Park. Recreational pursuits available at Soldiers Memorial Park (see Recreation Chart) include a beach and hiking trails around Stone and Pine lakes.

The LaPorte Little Theater, one of the oldest theater groups in the country, stages productions from October through May. The LaPorte Symphony Orchestra performs between November and May.

LaPorte County Convention & Visitors Bureau: 1503 S. Meer Rd., Michigan City, IN 46360-9115; phone (219) 872-5055 or (800) 634-2650.

Self-guiding tours: The visitor center has brochures titled "A Stroll Along the Avenues." The tour takes visitors past many fine houses built in the late 1800s and early 1900s; phone (219) 872-5055 or (800) 634-2650. The brochure "Lighthouses, Lakes and Lanes," a driving tour of northern Indiana harbor country, also is available at the convention and visitors bureau.

DOOR PRAIRIE AUTO MUSEUM, 1 mi. s. on US 35 at 2405 Indiana Ave., displays three floors of antique and classic automobiles and vintage toys representing 100 years of automotive history. Also featured is a block on old Main Street in LaPorte, re-created to show business storefronts from three eras. The Indiana room has a collection of Indiana license plates, Rumely model tractors and antique photos.

Allow 1 hour minimum. Tues.-Sat. 10-4:30, Sun. noon-4:30, Apr.-Dec.; closed major holidays. Admission $5; over 60, $4; ages 10-18, $3. MC, VI. Phone (574) 326-1337.

KINGSBURY STATE FISH AND WILDLIFE AREA, 8 mi. s. on US 35, consists of 6,060 acres where wildlife can be viewed in a natural setting. Fishing and hunting (in season) are permitted; a primitive campground and shooting range also are available. Park daily 24 hours. Office daily 8-3:30. Free. Phone (574) 393-3612. See Recreation Chart and the AAA Great Lakes CampBook.

LaPORTE COUNTY HISTORICAL SOCIETY MUSEUM, in the county complex building at Michigan Ave. and State St. behind the courthouse, has history exhibits, including antique toys, portraits and manuscripts. Of particular note is the Jones collection of firearms, said to be one of the best in the nation. Tues.-Sat. 10-4:30. Admission $4; under 18, $2; family rate (2 adults and 2 children) $10. Phone (574) 326-6808, ext. 276.

LAWRENCEBURG—

see Cincinnati in Ohio p. 204.

LINCOLN BOYHOOD NATIONAL MEMORIAL (G-3)

On SR 162 just south of Dale, the 200-acre Lincoln Boyhood National Memorial preserves the farm where Abraham Lincoln lived 1816-30. The memorial park includes the reconstructed farm site, a visitor center and the burial site of Lincoln's mother, Nancy Hanks Lincoln, who died when Lincoln was 9 years old.

Allow 1 hour, 30 minutes minimum. Grounds daily 8-5; closed Jan. 1, Thanksgiving and Dec. 25. Admission (including Living Historical Farm and Memorial Visitor Center) $2, under 17 free, family rate $4. Phone (812) 937-4541.

LIVING HISTORICAL FARM, s.w. corner of the original Thomas Lincoln farm, re-creates the rural environment that influenced Lincoln from the age of 7 to 21. Reconstructed log buildings, restored fields and a garden area are reminiscent of the 1820s. Daily 8-5, May-Sept. Admission (including grounds and Memorial Visitor Center) $2, under 17 free, family rate $4.

MEMORIAL VISITOR CENTER is an architecturally unusual structure built of native stone and wood. Included in the building are halls honoring Abraham and Nancy Hanks Lincoln; exterior sculptured panels depict important periods in Lincoln's life. Also featured are a 24-minute film and a museum based on Lincoln's 14 years in the state. Interpretive material is available.

Daily 8-5; closed Jan. 1, Thanksgiving and Dec. 25. Admission (including grounds and Living Historical Farm) $2, under 17 free, family rate $4. Phone (812) 937-4541.

LINCOLN CITY (G-3)

Lincoln Amphitheatre, in Lincoln State Park *(see Recreation Chart and the AAA Great Lakes CampBook)*, stages two outdoor musicals on summer evenings. "Young Abe Lincoln" tells the story of Lincoln's boyhood years in southern Indiana. The amphitheater offers covered seating. For information and reservations phone (800) 264-4223.

LINDEN (C-3) pop. 700, elev. 789'

LINDEN JUNCTION DEPOT RAILROAD MUSEUM, 1 mi. n. on US 231, houses railroad memorabilia, scale models, railroad devices and a caboose that visitors can tour. Allow 30 minutes minimum. Fri.-Sun. 1-5, May-Sept.; by appointment rest of year. Closed holidays. Admission $2; ages 13-18, $1; ages 6-12, 50c. Phone (765) 339-7245 or (800) 866-3973.

LOGANSPORT (B-4) pop. 16,800, elev. 599'

Unlike his uncles Tecumseh and Prophet, the Shawnee chief Spemicalawwah, who also was known as Capt. James John Logan, fought for the United States in Indiana, western Ohio and southeastern Michigan during the War of 1812. He was killed in November 1812 in a clash with the British along the Maumee River. Logansport was named in his honor by Col. John B. Duret, who won the right to name the town at a marksmanship competition.

Logansport, on the Wabash and Eel rivers, offers such recreational opportunities as scuba diving and fishing. Just west on US 24 is France Park *(see Recreation Chart and the AAA Great Lakes CampBook)*, featuring a waterfall and an 1839 cabin as well as winter and summer recreation facilities. Riverside Park, 11th and High streets, has a model train as well as an antique carousel with animals hand-carved by Gustav Dentzel; activities include miniature golf and picnicking.

Logansport/Cass County Chamber of Commerce: 300 E. Broadway #103, Logansport, IN 46947-3139; phone (574) 753-6388.

MUSEUM OF THE CASS COUNTY HISTORICAL SOCIETY, 1004 E. Market St., consists of the 1853 Jerolaman-Long Home, a cabin, a carriage barn and a schoolroom furnished in period. Seventeen rooms contain displays depicting life in the 1800s. Also on display is a restored 1920 ReVere Touring Car, manufactured in Logansport by the ReVere Motor Co. 1917-1926. Tues.-Sat. 1-5, also first Mon. of the month 1-7; closed holidays. Free. Phone (574) 753-3866.

MADISON (F-5) pop. 12,000, elev. 455'

Founded in 1809 along the Ohio River, Madison was a supply town for westbound settlers and enjoyed growth in the steamboat area through its boat-building industry and livestock exports. The city's prominence as a port declined with the construction of the first railroad west of the Alleghenies, connecting Madison with Indianapolis.

Madison's shaded streets are bordered by 19th-century Federal, Classical Revival and Italianate buildings. Georgian structures distinguish the 550-acre hilltop campus of Hanover College, overlooking the Ohio River. A year-round showpiece of pioneer gardening that dates from 1820 is on Poplar Street between First and Second streets.

Local farmers sell their produce in the courthouse square on Tuesday, Thursday and Saturday mornings in the summer.

Madison Area Convention & Visitors Bureau: 301 E. Main St., Madison, IN 47250; phone (812) 265-2956 or (800) 559-2956.

DR. WILLIAM D. HUTCHINGS OFFICE AND HOSPITAL, 120 W. Third St., is the two-story, four-room Greek Revival building where Dr. William D. Hutchings practiced medicine from 1882 until his death in 1903. The building served as the first and only hospital in the Ohio River Valley between Louisville and Cincinnati until 1889. Soon after Hutchings' death his office and hospital were closed and left untouched until 1967.

The restoration is notable for its completeness. Virtually all the contents belonged to Dr. Hutchings, and no item dates from after 1903. The waiting room, surgery, and upstairs rooms for convalescing patients contain original furnishings, medical instruments and books. Such items as a pair of galvanic energy boxes for electrotherapy treatments and a book about acupuncture testify to Dr. Hutchings' progressive practice.

Allow 30 minutes minimum. Mon.-Sat. and holidays 10-4:30, Sun. 1:15-4:30, mid-Apr. through Oct. 31. Admission $3, under 18 free. Phone (812) 265-2967.

LANIER MANSION STATE HISTORIC SITE, Elm and W. First sts., overlooks the Ohio River and Kentucky hills. Designed by architect Francis Costigan and completed in 1844, the mansion was the home of James F.D. Lanier, a banker who financed the state during a difficult period of the Civil War with a loan of more than $1 million. Within are some pieces of original furniture as well as a three-story spiral staircase. Formal gardens feature plantings and landscaping styles typical of the late 19th century.

Allow 30 minutes minimum. Tours are given every half-hour Tues.-Sat. 9-5, Sun. 1-5, mid-Mar. to mid-Dec.; Sat. 9-5, Sun. 1-5, Tues.-Fri.; by appointment, rest of year. Last tour departs 30 minutes before closing. Closed Jan. 1, Easter, Thanksgiving and Dec. 24-25. Donations. Phone (812) 265-3526.

SAVE **LANIER-SCHOFIELD HOUSE** is at 217 W. Second St. The restored Federal-style house was the first meeting place for Indiana Freemasons. Built about 1815 and furnished in period, the structure boasts fine flooring, walls, brickwork and handmade glass windows. Allow 30 minutes minimum. Mon., Thurs.-Sat. and holidays 10-4:30, Sun. 1-4:30, Apr.-Oct. Admission $3. Phone (812) 265-4759.

MADISON RAILROAD STATION AND JEFFERSON COUNTY HISTORICAL SOCIETY MUSEUM is at 615 W. First St.. The restored 1895 octagonal wooden railroad depot has a two-story waiting room with stained glass windows and features a collection of railroad posters and relics. The museum displays American Indian artifacts and exhibits relating to the history of southeastern Indiana. An antique caboose is on the grounds. Allow 30 minutes minimum. Mon.-Sat. 10-4:30, Sun. 1-4, late Apr.-Oct. 31.; Mon.-Fri. 10-4:30, rest of year. Admission $3, under 16 free. Phone (812) 265-2335.

SULLIVAN HOUSE, n.w. corner of Second and Poplar sts., was the town's earliest mansion and the home of Judge Jeremiah Sullivan, an early 19th-century justice of the Indiana Supreme Court. Sullivan was credited with naming Indianapolis. His home, restored and furnished with many original pieces, is an example of Federal-style architecture. Allow 30 minutes minimum. Mon.-Sat. 10-4:30, Sun. 1:15-4:30, mid-Apr. through Oct. 31. Admission $3, under 18 free. Phone (812) 265-2967.

MARENGO (F-3) pop. 800, elev. 469′

Marengo is 4 miles west of the Blue River, part of Indiana's natural and scenic river system. The spring-fed river flows through the hills of Indiana cave country and is popular with canoeists.

SAVE **MARENGO CAVE NATIONAL LANDMARK** is 9 mi. n. of I-64 via SRs 66 and 64. Two guided tours examine the stalagmites and white flowstone formations found in the illuminated limestone cavern. The huge corridors, soda-straw formations, delicate helictites and totem pole stalagmites of Dripstone Trail contrast with the massive flowstone deposits throughout the Crystal Palace.

The lower levels of the cavern contain underground rivers, blind fish and great mountain rooms. A jacket is recommended, as the temperature inside the cave is a constant 52 F. Park facilities are available for horseback riding, picnicking, canoeing, gemstone mining and hiking. Also available are a 300-foot zip line and "The Crawl," a cave-exploring simulator. Food is available.

Park open daily 9-6, Memorial Day weekend-Labor Day; 9-5, rest of year. Closed Thanksgiving and Dec. 25. Cave tours are given every 30 minutes. Park free. Crystal Palace 40-minute tour (.33 mile) $11; ages 4-12, $5.50. Dripstone Trail 70-minute tour (1 mile) $12; ages 4-12, $6. Combination ticket $16; ages 4-12, $8. DS, MC, VI. Phone (812) 365-2705. *See Recreation Chart.*

MARION (C-4) pop. 32,600, elev. 810′

Marion, in the heart of a rich corn, hog and soybean agricultural area, is the home of Indiana Wesleyan University, which evolved from the Indiana Normal School and Business Institute founded in 1889. The Roman Gothic administration building dates from the original school.

The birthplace of movie idol James Dean is at Fourth and McClure sts. The Miami Indian Historical Site, on CRs 600N and 380W, marks the site of the 1812 Battle of Mississinewa, the last conflict between Indiana's settlers and the Miami Indians. Hiking trails traverse the former Miami reservation and village. The Mississinewa Riverwalk is a walking and jogging path that follows the Mississinewa River to Matter Park.

Marion/Grant County Convention and Visitors Bureau: 217 S. Adams St., Marion, IN 46952; phone (765) 668-5435 or (800) 662-9474.

MARSHALL (D-3) pop. 400 elev. 700′

TURKEY RUN STATE PARK, 5 mi. n. on SR 47 via SR 236 and US 41, is noted for its deep canyons and scenic gorges. Still standing is the home of Salmon Lusk, who arrived in 1821 and was the

---

original owner of the area. The park's nature center has a Spitz-Nova star projection system and a wildlife observation room. Daily 7 a.m.-11 p.m. Admission $5 per private vehicle, or $1 per person for bus riders or pedestrians. Phone (765) 597-2635. *See Recreation Chart and the AAA Great Lakes CampBook.*

MEDARYVILLE (B-3) pop. 700, elev. 687′

JASPER-PULASKI FISH AND WILDLIFE AREA is on SR 143 just w. of US 421. A marsh and pond provide refuge for thousands of waterfowls; in spring and fall sandhill cranes can be seen. Picnicking, camping, fishing, berry picking, hiking and hunting are permitted. Office open Mon.-Fri. 8-3:30. Check station open during hunting season; phone for hours. Free. Phone (219) 843-4841. *See Recreation Chart and the AAA Great Lakes CampBook.*

MERRILLVILLE (A-2) pop. 27,300, elev. 645′

Merrillville is in Indiana's far northwest corner. As a stopping point for wagon trains heading west, 16 trails radiated in all directions—much like the transportation system that exists now. Of regional importance is the John Wood Mill, part of Old Mill Park, about 8 miles east of SR 53 on CR 330. The first industry in Lake County, the mill has been refurbished and once again grinds corn, wheat and rye.

Noteworthy for its unusual decor is the Sts. Constantine and Helen Greek Orthodox Cathedral, the only one of this denomination in the state. Dominating 37 acres at 8000 Madison St., the cathedral features a rotunda 100 feet in diameter, 25 large stained-glass windows and Byzantine mosaic work.

The dramatic arts also are represented in Merrillville. The Star Plaza Theatre, part of the Radisson Hotel at Star Plaza resort, I-65 and US 30, presents top-name performers.

Lake County Convention and Visitors Bureau: 7770 Corinne Dr., Hammond, IN 46323; phone (219) 989-7770.

DEEP RIVER WATERPARK is 4 mi. e. on US 30. Water rides for all ages include a wave pool, a slow river ride, and body, speed and tube slides. A children's play area and a volleyball beach also are offered. Food is available. Allow 4 hours minimum. Daily 10-6, Memorial Day to mid-Aug.; Sat.-Sun. 10-6, mid-Aug. through Labor Day. Admission $12.25; under 46 inches tall, $5.50. Admission after 2 p.m. $10.50; under 46 inches tall, $5.50. Phone (219) 945-7850.

METAMORA—*see Cincinnati in Ohio p. 204.*

MICHIGAN CITY (A-3) pop. 33,800

Michigan City was founded in 1675 by French explorer Father Jacques Marquette. Now a popular summer resort, the city is part of the sand dune country at the southern end of Lake Michigan (see

Indiana Dunes National Lakeshore p. 134). The city lies at the eastern end of scenic US 12, which follows the Lake Michigan shoreline before crossing into Illinois.

Michigan City is widely known as the Coho Capital of the Midwest. The waters abound with coho and chinook salmon as well as brown, lake and steelhead trout. Charter fishing boats are available.

Summer theater and art are popular in Michigan City. The Main Street Theater, 807 Franklin St., stages productions by a resident company. The Dunes Summer Theater, east of town, presents plays in the summer.

The John G. Blank Center for the Arts, 312 E. Eighth St., has exhibits ranging from the pre-Columbian period to the present.

LaPorte County Convention and Visitors Bureau: 1503 S. Meer Rd., Michigan City, IN 46360-9115; phone (219) 872-5055 or (800) 634-2650.

Self-guiding tours: "Lighthouses, Lakes and Lanes," a brochure for a driving tour of northern Indiana harbor country, is available at the convention and visitors bureau.

Shopping areas: Lighthouse Place Outlet Mall, at Sixth and Wabash streets, is an upscale center with more than 120 shops, including Esprit, Fila, Gap and Tommy Hilfiger.

[SAVE] **BARKER MANSION,** 1 blk. n.w. at 631 Washington St., is the former estate of John H. Barker, the founder of the Haskell & Barker Railroad Car Co. The 38-room mansion, built in 1857 and modeled after English Victorian manors, features hand-carved marble fireplaces; mahogany, walnut and teak woodwork; baroque ceilings; a third-story ballroom; and a sunken garden. The house contains many original furnishings and works of art.

Guided tours are given Mon.-Fri. at 10, 11:30 and 1, Sat.-Sun. at noon and 2, June-Oct.; Mon.-Fri. at 10, 11:30 and 1, rest of year. Holiday tours are given Sat.-Sun. early Dec. to mid-Jan.; phone ahead for schedule. Closed holidays. Fee $4; ages 4-18, $2. Phone (219) 873-1520.

[SAVE] **GREAT LAKES MUSEUM OF MILITARY HISTORY,** 360 Dunes Plaza, exhibits military memorabilia from the Revolutionary War to the present. Among the displays are uniforms, edged weapons, flags, maps, a large collection of firearms and a World War II Japanese Declaration of War captured by the U.S. Army. The reference library contains books and videotapes. Guided tours are available.

Allow 1 hour minimum. Tues.-Fri. 9-4, Sat. 10-4 (also Sun. noon-4, Memorial Day-Labor Day); closed Jan. 1, Easter, Thanksgiving and Dec. 24-25 and 31. Admission $2; over 60 and ages 8-18, $1. MC, VI. Phone (219) 872-2702 or (800) 726-5912.

WASHINGTON PARK, on the lakeshore at the end of Franklin St., features a beach, marina, lighthouse museum, Coast Guard station, observation tower and the Washington Park Zoo. Band concerts are held on Thursday evenings mid-June to mid-August in the amphitheater. The Old Lighthouse Museum on the waterfront contains maritime artifacts and exhibits about local history.

Park daily 6 a.m.-11 p.m. Zoo daily 10:30-5, Memorial Day-Labor Day; 10:30-4, Apr. 1-day before Memorial Day and day after Labor Day-Oct. 31. Lighthouse museum Tues.-Sun. 1-4. Park admission $2 per private vehicle Mon.-Fri., $4 per private vehicle Sat.-Sun. and holidays, Apr.-Sept.; free rest of year. Admission is charged during special events. An additional fee may be charged for vehicles with trailers. Zoo admission $3; over 62, $2; ages 3-11, $1.75. Lighthouse museum admission $2; ages 5-12, 50c. Phone (219) 873-1506 for the park, (219) 873-1510 for the zoo, (219) 872-6133 for the lighthouse museum and (219) 872-1712 for the marina. *See Recreation Chart.*

CASINOS

- **Blue Chip Casino**, 2 Easy St. Cruise boards every 2 hours Sun.-Thurs. 9 a.m.-1 a.m.; Fri.-Sat. 9 a.m.-3 a.m. Phone (219) 879-7711 or (888) 879-7711.

MILLTOWN (F-4) pop. 900, elev. 552′

RECREATIONAL ACTIVITIES
Canoeing

- SAVE **Cave Country Canoes**, 112 Main St. Write P.O. Box 217, Marengo, IN 47140. Daily Apr.-Oct. Phone (812) 365-2705.

MITCHELL (F-4) pop. 4,700, elev. 676′

The Mitchell area was settled in 1813 when Canadian Samuel Jackson opened a gristmill on land given him by the U.S. government as a reward for his services in the War of 1812. A village soon grew up around the mill, and a lucrative trade of shipping grain, meat and whiskey to New Orleans began. With the coming of two railroads in the mid-1800s, the town's position as a trade and shipping center was solidified.

Greater Mitchell Chamber of Commerce: 602 W. Main, P.O. Box 216, Mitchell, IN 47446; phone (812) 849-4441 or (800) 580-1985.

SPRING MILL STATE PARK is 3.2 mi. e. on SR 60 from SR 37. In the park is the restoration of Spring Mill Village, a frontier trading post founded about 1815. Included are a functioning water-powered gristmill, the remains of a limekiln and a reconstructed sawmill, hat shop, post office, stillhouse, boot shop and apothecary. The Virgil I. Grissom Memorial Visitor Center features a space capsule and an audiovisual presentation about space exploration.

The park contains an artificial lake and approximately 100 acres of virgin woodland with some large specimens of white oak and tulip poplar; there

also are many unusual caverns and underground streams with rare species of blind fish. Boat trips are available in season. Donaldson Cave can be explored partially, but only with a park guide.

Park open daily 7 a.m.-11 p.m. Visitor center daily 8:30-4. Park admission $5 per private vehicle or $1 per person for bus riders or pedestrians. Phone (812) 849-4129. *See Recreation Chart and the AAA Great Lakes CampBook.*

MONTICELLO (B-3) pop. 5,200

Monticello's man-made twin lakes, Freeman and Shafer, are the site of many fishing tournaments throughout the summer. The lakes' black and hybrid bass are noted for their record sizes.

INDIANA BEACH, .5 mi. w. on US 24, then 3.2 mi. n. on W. Shafer Dr., is an amusement park and campground on Lake Shafer. A boardwalk with rides, games, miniature golf courses and shops fronts a pier-enclosed public beach. Other features include a roller coaster, a water park, boat launching ramps, a speed slide, a bathhouse, boat rentals and campsites. Food is available.

Daily 11-11, mid-May through day before Labor Day; Sat.-Sun. 11-6, early to mid-May and Labor Day. Water-ski shows daily at 1:30, 3:30, 5:30 and 7:45, mid-June to mid-Aug.. Park admission $2, under 4 free. Beach $2. Individual ride tickets $1-$4; 10-ticket book $15. Ride pass, good toward unlimited rides over a 7-hour period (11-6 or 4-11), $15; under 48 inches tall $10. Water park admission $13 in addition to park admission. Combination ride and water park pass $24; 44-48 inches tall $19. AX, DC, DS, MC, VI. Phone (574) 583-4141. *See Recreation Chart and the AAA Great Lakes CampBook.*

The Shafer Queen, departing from the boardwalk dock, is a double-decker paddle-wheel steamer that makes half-hour trips around the southern end of Shafer Lake and 1.2-hour cruises around the northern end. The 1.2-hour cruise departs daily at 12:15 and 6, mid-May through Labor Day. Half-hour cruise departs daily at 11:15, every 30 minutes 1:30-5:15, and at 8, mid-May through Labor Day; Sat.-Sun. at 11:15 and every 30 minutes 1:30-6, first weekend in May to mid-May.

Fare for 1.2-hour cruise $5; under 12, $3. Fare for half-hour cruise $4; under 12, $2. AX, DS, MC, VI. Phone (574) 583-4141.

MOROCCO (B-2) pop. 1,000, elev. 678′

WILLOW SLOUGH STATE FISH AND WILDLIFE AREA is 2 mi. w. of US 41. This wildlife management area encompasses a 1,300-acre lake and offers camping, fishing and hunting for ducks, small game and deer. Boat rentals are available. Daily dawn-dusk. Free. Boat rental fee $10.50 per day. Phone (219) 285-2704. *See Recreation Chart and the AAA Great Lakes CampBook.*

MUNCIE (C-5) pop. 71,000, elev. 945′

Muncie grew into an agricultural trading center on lands originally occupied by the Munsee tribe of the Delaware Indians. Cyrus E. Dallin's life-size image of an Indian on his pony, "The Appeal to the Great Spirit," marks a former Munsee campsite at Walnut Street and Granville Avenue.

With the arrival of the railroads and the discovery of natural gas during the second half of the 19th century, Muncie became industrialized. Ball Corp., makers of the well-known canning jars, was among the many industries established. Though the jars are no longer produced in Muncie, collections of glass canning jars are displayed at Minnetrista Cultural Center (see attraction listing) and Robinson Jars, 1201 W. Cowing St.

Ball State University was founded in 1918 largely through substantial contributions from the five Ball brothers, who also were involved in many other local philanthropic ventures. The university, at Riverside and University avenues, has The Museum of Art (see attraction listing); a planetarium and an observatory; Emens Auditorium, an acoustically perfect concert hall; and Christy Woods, a 17-acre area with greenhouses, trails and labeled trees.

During the 1930s Muncie became the focus of a sociological study about a typical small city. The researchers, Robert and Helen Lynd, wrote "Middletown" and "Middletown in Transition."

The Muncie Motor Speedway/Muncie Dragway is the site of national dragstrip competitions, including the World Title Drag Series.

Muncie Visitors Bureau: 425 N. High St., Muncie, IN 47305; phone (765) 284-2700 or (800) 568-6862.

BALL STATE UNIVERSITY MUSEUM OF ART, in the Fine Arts Building on the Ball State University campus at the jct. of Riverside Ave. and Warwick Rd., houses Italian Renaissance and 19th-century American art, decorative arts and contemporary drawings and prints. Allow 30 minutes minimum. Mon.-Fri. 9-4:30, Sat.-Sun. 1:30-4:30; closed major holidays. Donations. Phone (765) 285-5242.

[SAVE] **ME'S ZOO** is 7 mi. e. on SR 32, 5 mi. s. on CR 700E, then 2.5 mi. e on CR 500S. The zoo contains more than 300 animals, including a white tiger, and features a children's petting area and a parrot arena. Picnic and playground facilities are available. Allow 1 hour, 30 minutes minimum. Tues.-Thurs. and Sat. 10-6, Sun. noon-6, May-Sept. Admission $5.50; over 64, $5; under 13, $4.50; 50¢ less on Wed. Phone (765) 468-8559.

MINNETRISTA CULTURAL CENTER AND OAK-HURST GARDENS, 1200 N. Minnetrista Pkwy., is a museum with four galleries for the display of local, national and international changing exhibits about history, art and science. Free outdoor concerts and festivals are held in the performance pavilion on the center's 35 landscaped acres.

Allow 1 hour minimum. Mon.-Fri. 8-5:30, Sat. 9-8, Sun. 11-5:30; closed Jan. 1, Easter and Dec. 25. Admission $5, over 65 and students with ID $3, family rate $15. MC, VI. Phone (765) 282-4848 or (800) 428-5887.

MUNCIE CHILDREN'S MUSEUM, 515 S. High St., is a hands-on center for children. The museum's featured permanent exhibit is based on "Garfield," the lasagna-loving character created by local cartoonist Jim Davis. Other exhibits allow children to pretend to be truck drivers, geologists, ants, farmers, paleontologists, grocers, engineers or birds. An outdoor learning area also provides insights.

Allow 2 hours minimum. Tues.-Sat. 10-5, Sun. 1-5; closed major holidays. Admission $5, under age 1 free. MC, VI. Phone (765) 286-1660.

NATIONAL MODEL AVIATION MUSEUM, 5151 E. Memorial Dr., displays all levels of model airplanes—from simple balsa construction to elaborate radio-controlled planes. Aeromodeling history is portrayed through examples of flying models, engines, radio equipment, accessories and model kits. A reference library also is available. Picnicking is permitted. Allow 1 hour minimum. Mon.-Fri. 8-4:30, Sat.-Sun. 10-4, day after Easter-Thanksgiving; Mon.-Fri. 8-4:30, Sat. 10-4, rest of year. Admission $2; ages 6-17, $1. Phone (765) 289-4236.

NAPPANEE (A-4) pop. 5,500

Spawned by the Baltimore and Ohio Railroad in 1874, Nappanee is in an agricultural region known for its mint and onion crops. Many of the area's farmers are Amish.

Nappanee Area Chamber of Commerce: 451 N. Main, Suite 100, Nappanee, IN 46550; phone (574) 773-7812.

Shopping areas: Borkholder Dutch Village, on CR 101 north of US 6, has an auction barn, a flea market, arts and crafts boutiques and antiques shops.

[SAVE] **AMISH ACRES,** 1 mi. w. on US 6 at 1600 W. Market St., is an 80-acre, 19th-century Amish farm with 18 restored buildings, some of which are used for crafts demonstrations. Guides conduct a 1-hour tour of five buildings, including a 12-room farmhouse and a barn. A 15-minute film introduces the Amish lifestyle; Broadway musicals are presented in matinee and evening shows. Horse-drawn buggy rides are available. Food is available.

Farm daily 10-5, Mar.-Dec.; closed Dec. 24-25. Phone ahead for musical theater schedule. Guided tour and film $6.95; ages 4-11, $2.95. Twenty-minute horse-drawn buggy ride $3.95; ages 4-11, $1.95. Musical productions $20-$30; ages 4-17, $6. Combination package (includes tour, film, family-style dinner and buggy ride) $23.95; ages 4-11, $9.95. DC, DS, MC, VI. Phone (574) 773-4188 or (800) 800-4942.

NASHVILLE (E-4) pop. 900, elev. 800'

The foothills of the Cumberlands first lured lumber industries in the early 1800s. By 1870 word of the area's beauty had spread, and Nashville became an artists' colony. Noted resident painters included Marie Goth, Adolph Shulz and T.C. Steele.

Nashville's artistic evolution also has encouraged participation in the performing arts. Operated by Indiana University, the Brown County Playhouse has been active since 1948. Little Nashville Opry, south on SR 46, is the site of country music shows. The Countrytime Jamboree, 1 mile east on SR 46, features country and gospel music on Friday and Saturday nights.

In July and September through October the small outdoor Melchior Marionette Theatre on S. Van Buren Street presents cabaret puppet shows, using marionettes up to 3 feet tall.

Many of Nashville's attractions are easily reached by taking the Nashville Express Trains, which offer 2.5-mile narrated tours spring through fall. One point of interest is the Brown County Art Barn at Gould and Van Buren streets. Skiing is available west of town.

Brown County Convention and Visitors Bureau: 10 N. Van Buren, P.O. Box 840, Nashville, IN 47448; phone (812) 988-7303 or (800) 753-3255.

BROWN COUNTY ART GALLERY & MUSEUM, 2 blks. e. of the courthouse at the corner of Artist Dr. and Main St., is one of the oldest art associations in the Midwest. Early Indiana/Brown County works are exhibited in the permanent museum room. Changing exhibits also are offered. There also is a memorial to Glen Cooper Henshaw, an area artist active from the turn of the 20th century through the 1940s.

Allow 30 minutes minimum. Mon.-Sat. 10-5, Sun. noon-5; closed Jan. 1, Thanksgiving and Dec. 25. Free. Phone (812) 988-4609.

BROWN COUNTY ART GUILD INC., 1 blk. s. of jct. Van Buren (SR 135) and Main sts., presents the work of local and regional artists in the historic Minor House. Monthly one-person shows supplement a permanent collection of paintings by early Indiana artists as well as pioneer members of the guild. Mon.-Sat. 10-5, Sun. 11-5, Mar.-Dec.; Mon.-Fri. by appointment, Sat. 10-5, Sun. 11-5, rest of year. Closed Easter, Thanksgiving and Dec. 25. Free. Phone (812) 988-6185.

NEW ALBANY (G-5) pop. 36,300, elev. 442'

New Albany is across the Ohio River from Louisville, Ky. Local shipbuilders of the 19th century produced speed record-setting steamships, including the *Robert E. Lee* and the *City of Louisville*.

Southern Indiana Chamber of Commerce: 4100 Charleston Rd., New Albany, IN 47150; phone (812) 945-0266.

CULBERTSON MANSION STATE HISTORIC SITE, 9 blks. e. at 914 E. Main St., is the French Second Empire mansion of 19th-century entrepreneur and philanthropist William S. Culbertson. Furnished in period, the 1869 house has such Victorian effects as hand-painted ceilings, Italian marble fire-

places and elaborate woodwork, including a three-story mahogany and rosewood staircase.

Allow 1 hour minimum. Tues.-Sat. 9-5, Sun. 1-5, mid-Mar. to mid-Dec.; closed Easter and Thanksgiving. Donations. Phone (812) 944-9600.

NEW CASTLE (D-5) pop. 17,800, elev. 997'

SAVE **INDIANA BASKETBALL HALL OF FAME MUSEUM,** 1 blk. e. of SR 3 at 408 Trojan Ln., showcases the history of Indiana basketball. Displays include memorabilia from every state championship team and such all-star players such as Larry Bird and Oscar Robertson. A tribute to Hoosier hysteria, an inspirational videotape about coach John Wooden and hands-on exhibits are additional highlights.

Allow 1 hour, 30 minutes minimum. Tues.-Sat. 10-5, Sun. 1-5; closed Jan. 1, Easter, Thanksgiving and Dec. 25. Admission $4; over 64, $3; ages 5-12, $2. Phone (765) 529-1891.

NEW HARMONY (G-1) pop. 800

The Harmonie Society, a German religious communal group, moved to Indiana in 1814, purchased 30,000 acres of forest land and built a planned town in the Indiana wilderness within a year of their arrival. They perfected a cosmopolitan and efficient community 1814-24.

By 1824 more than 150 structures were built and the town marketed 20 different products as far away as Pittsburgh and New Orleans. Per-capita income and cultural amenities in the town rivaled those of eastern cities.

The following year Welsh philanthropist Robert Owen and geologist and philanthropist William Maclure bought the settlement from founder George Rapp and tried to organize a model community where educational and social equality would prosper.

Naturalists, educators, geologists and feminists all came to New Harmony, and their pioneering contributions to education, geology, trade schools and women's suffrage had national importance.

The New Harmony Theatre, at 419 Tavern St., offers summer productions mid-June to mid-August; phone (812) 682-3115.

Shopping areas: The historic downtown area offers a number of stores selling crafts, antiques, home and garden accessories and fine art.

ATHENEUM is 4 blks. n.w. of jct. SRs 66 and 69 at North and Arthur sts. This striking contemporary structure designed by architect Richard Meier stands as a monument to the cultural, artistic and scientific explorations fostered by the two communal societies. The Atheneum serves as a visitor center and features a film about the history of New Harmony. Also displayed are models of the town as it looked in 1824 and of the second Harmonist Church.

A biographical exhibit about the Owenite community focuses on the 19th-century intellectuals and scientists who lived in the town. The Atheneum also is the point of departure for historic tours of the town (see attraction listing). Picnicking is permitted. Allow 30 minutes minimum. Daily 9:30-5, Mar.-Dec. Visitor center free. Film $3 (includes Atheneum exhibit). MC, VI. Phone (812) 682-4474 or (800) 231-2168.

SAVE **HISTORIC NEW HARMONY WALKING TOURS**, departing from the Atheneum at North and Arthur sts., cover an area of approximately 1 square mile and include restored buildings from the Harmonist and Owen-Maclure periods. The guided walking tours last from 1 to 3 hours. All tours include a 7-minute historical overview on film shown at the Atheneum. Tours are given daily 10-4, Mar.-Dec. Fee $10; over 55, $9; ages 7-17, $5; family rate $25. MC, VI. Phone (812) 682-4474.

NEW HARMONY GALLERY OF CONTEMPORARY ART, 506 Main St., displays changing contemporary works by Midwestern artists, including paintings, sculpture, prints and pottery. Allow 1 hour minimum. Tues.-Sat. 9-5, Sun. noon-4. Free. Phone (812) 682-3156.

ROOFLESS CHURCH, at North and Main sts., is a nonsectarian open-air church designed by architect Philip Johnson. Outstanding features include a cedar shake dome covering the bronze sculpture "Descent of the Holy Spirit," by Jacques Lipchitz. Allow 30 minutes minimum. Daily 24 hours. Free. Phone (812) 682-4431.

WORKINGMEN'S INSTITUTE, 407 W. Tavern St., houses a museum that contains artifacts from the two Utopian communities established in New Harmony. It also has a variety of natural history exhibits, an art gallery and a public library with archives. Allow 1 hour minimum. Museum Tues.-Sat. 10--4. Admission $1; ages 6-12, 50c. Phone (812) 682-4806.

NOBLESVILLE—see Indianapolis p. 148.

PERU (C-4) pop. 12,800, elev. 643'

An industrial community and the former site of a Miami Indian village, Peru is best known as the former home base of the various traveling circuses that crisscrossed the country. Troupes, including the well-known Hagenback-Wallace circus, wintered in the area as early as the 1800s, and for many years the city's economy focused on the circus. Songwriter Cole Porter, born in Peru in 1891, is buried in Mount Hope Cemetery.

Peru/Miami County Chamber of Commerce: 13 E. Main St., Peru, IN 46970; phone (765) 472-1923.

CIRCUS CITY FESTIVAL MUSEUM, 154 N. Broadway, contains circus posters, newspaper clippings, costumes of celebrated performers and other circus memorabilia. Allow 1 hour minimum. Mon.-Fri. 9-1 and 2-4; closed holidays. Donations. Phone (765) 472-3918.

MIAMI COUNTY MUSEUM, 51 N. Broadway, contains more than 75,000 items of historical significance. Twenty-five buildings built 1900-1925 include a Victorian house, a church, a one-room schoolhouse and a garage. Displays include pioneer and Miami Indian artifacts, many circus relics and Cole Porter memorabilia, featuring his 1955 Fleetwood Cadillac. Allow 1 hour minimum. Tues.-Sat. 9-5; closed Jan. 1, July 4, Thanksgiving and Dec. 25. Free. Phone (765) 473-9183.

RICHMOND (D-6) pop. 38,700, elev. 979'

Quakers from North Carolina and German immigrants established Richmond on the Whitewater River in 1806. The city has become one of Indiana's leading industrial communities as well as the trade and distribution center for agriculturally rich Wayne County.

In Glen Miller Park the Hill Memorial Rose Garden cultivates more than 73 varieties of roses, and the All-American Rose Garden propagates 2,000 rose bushes, annuals and perennials.

At the entrance to Glen Miller Park is the Madonna of the Trail, a monument to pioneer women. It is one of the many historic structures along the Old National Road (US 40), the 1800s avenue of trade, culture and migration that extended westward from Cumberland, Md., to St. Louis.

Whitewater River Gorge, a deep channel formed by retreating Wisconsin glaciers during the most recent ice age, is bordered by a 3.5-mile trail that passes several natural and historical attractions. The trail extends from Test Road to Thistlethwaite Falls.

From October to April the Whitewater Opera Company presents several performances at the Civic Hall. Also offering productions in season are the Richmond Civic Theatre and the Richmond Symphony Orchestra.

The Old Richmond Historic District, covering some 250 acres and encompassing more than 213 historical structures, is in an area bounded by the Chesapeake and Ohio Railroad and South A, North 10th and South E streets. The district contains Federal, Greek Revival, Victorian and early 20th-century houses and churches. The Starr Historic District has many structures dating to the early 1800s.

Richmond/Wayne County Convention and Tourism Bureau: 5701 National Rd. E., Richmond, IN 47374; phone (765) 935-8687 or (800) 828-8414.

Self-guiding tours: Maps and information for tours of the districts and surrounding area are available from the convention and tourism bureau.

HAYES REGIONAL ARBORETUM, 2 mi. w. on US 40 from I-70 exit 156, then .5 mi. n. on Elks Rd., is an education center as well as a 358-acre nature

So Many Reasons To Travel.
So Many Marriotts.

Whatever your reasons for traveling, there's a Marriott that has exactly what you're looking for. And as a AAA member, you can show your card and save at participating Marriott locations. You'll receive special rates and packages throughout the year, and earn Marriott Rewards® points or miles with every stay.

Rejuvenate at a full service hotel where great dining, caring service and well-appointed guest rooms and suites ensure a memorable stay.

Experience a full service hotel with a style inspired by local surroundings, history and culture; where function and delight are inseparable.

Designed with your needs in mind, you'll get just the right space, service and amenities so you can be rested and refreshed for the day ahead.

Always a clean, comfortable room and smart, friendly service. Plus, a free continental breakfast to start your day.

Combines all the comforts of home with an array of services and amenities to ensure an exceptional stay. It's the perfect place to bring the family together.

The space your family needs at an unexpected value. All-suite comfort so you can stretch out and relax. Complimentary Suite Season Breakfast℠ buffet, makes it the smart choice.

Spend time with your family in a comfortable, home-like, neighborhood setting. There are three different suite designs to suit your needs. You can even bring the family pet.

For reservations or more information, call your travel agent or toll-free 1-866-211-4607 or visit marriott.com.
Your Marriott Awaits.

preserve for flora and fauna native to the Whitewater Valley. Highlights include a bird sanctuary, a butterfly house, a museum, a nature center, three scenic hiking trails, a 4-mile driving tour route and a variety of family weekend programs. Tues.-Sat. 9-5 (also Sun. 1-5, Easter-Dec. 24); closed holidays. Donations. Fee for automobile tour. Phone (765) 962-3745.

INDIANA FOOTBALL HALL OF FAME, 815 North A St., displays pictures, statistics and memorabilia pertaining to Indiana football players and high school, college and professional football teams. Mon.-Fri. 10-4, Sat.-Sun. by appointment, May-Sept.; Mon.-Fri. 10-2, Sat.-Sun. by appointment, rest of year. Closed holidays. Donations. Phone (765) 966-2235.

RICHMOND ART MUSEUM, McGuire Hall in the north wing of Richmond High School at 350 Hub Etchison Pkwy., offers a large permanent collection of works by local and nationally known artists. Changing exhibits also are presented. Tues.-Fri. 10-4, Sat.-Sun. 1-4; closed holidays. Donations. Phone (765) 966-0256.

[SAVE] **WAYNE COUNTY HISTORICAL MUSEUM,** 1150 North A St., occupies the 1865 former Quaker meetinghouse of the Whitewater Society of Friends. Glass, china, tools and clothing of the area's early settlers are displayed. Other items include an Egyptian mummy, a Japanese samurai warrior's uniform, a 1929 Davis airplane, and carriages, vintage cars and steam engines made in Richmond. Among the highlights are a pioneer general store, an 1823 log cabin and a loom house as well as cobbler, blacksmith and apothecary shops.

Allow 1 hour, 30 minutes minimum. Tues.-Fri. 9-4, Sat.-Sun. 1-4, mid-Feb. to mid-Dec.; closed major holidays. Admission $4; over 60, $3.50; ages 6-18, $1. Phone (765) 962-5756.

RISING SUN—see Cincinnati in Ohio p. 204.

ROCKVILLE (D-3) pop. 2,700, elev. 678'

Rockville is centrally located in Parke County, the state's covered bridge capital. Tour maps of scenic back roads and 32 historic covered bridges are available from the visitor center.

Parke County Convention & Visitors Bureau: 401 E. Ohio, P.O. Box 165, Rockville, IN 47872; phone (765) 569-5226.

[SAVE] **BILLIE CREEK VILLAGE,** 1 mi. e. on US 36, is a re-created early 20th-century village with three covered bridges, a farmstead, a living-history museum and a historic inn. There are 38 authentic buildings, moved from various sites in Parke County, that feature 25 historical exhibits. Free horse-drawn wagon rides depart from the village farmhouse. Pet kennels are available nearby.

Exhibiting artisans are in residence on selected weekends and holidays. A Maple Syrup Camp operates from the last weekend in February to the first weekend in March. Allow 2 hours minimum. For

additional information write R.R. 2, Box 27, Rockville, IN 47872.

Daily 9-4. Admission $3.50; over 60, $3; under 4 free. A $5 fee is charged for some events. AX, DS, MC, VI. Phone (765) 569-3430.

ROME CITY (A-5) pop. 1,200, elev. 928'

Rome City began as an encampment of Irish laborers working on a dam across the Elkhart River in 1837. After complaining about the shabby living conditions, they were told, "do as the Romans do." Thus they named their collection of shacks Rome. Later citizens added City to the name to distinguish their town from another in Indiana with the same name.

GENE STRATTON PORTER STATE HISTORIC SITE, 1 mi. s. on SR 9, preserves the cabin that was the novelist's home for several years. Surrounded by woods, wildflowers and wildlife, the two-story log cabin on 123 acres of Sylvan Lake shoreline was the perfect setting for Porter's writing, photography and nature studies in the first quarter of the 20th century.

The furniture and interior design of the house reflect the author's taste and lifestyle during her occupancy. The cabin also houses memorabilia and a personal library. Formal gardens are featured. Pontoon boat rides are offered May through September. Picnic facilities and a visitor center are available.

Allow 1 hour minimum. Visitor center Tues.-Sat. 9-5, Sun. 1-5, Apr. 1 to mid-Dec. Closed Easter and Thanksgiving. Guided cabin tours are given on the hour. Last tour begins 1 hour before closing. Donations. Boat fare $5. Reservations are recommended for boat rides. Phone (260) 854-3790.

ST. JOE (B-6) pop. 500

RALPH SECHLER & SON PICKLES, 1.5 mi. n.e. on SR 1, offers guided plant tours demonstrating the processing, bottling and labeling of more than 50 varieties of pickle products. Allow 30 minutes minimum. Tours are given Mon.-Fri. 9-11 and 12:30-2, Apr.-Oct.; closed holidays. Free. Phone (260) 337-5461 or (800) 332-5461.

SALEM (F-4) pop. 5,600, elev. 723'

Founded in 1814, Salem was the birthplace in 1838 of John Milton Hay, a noted author, statesman and diplomat.

Washington County Chamber of Commerce: 210 N. Main St., Salem, IN 47167; phone (812) 883-4303.

JOHN HAY CENTER, 307 E. Market St., houses a reconstructed pioneer village that includes a blacksmith shop, a carriage house, a jail, a general store, a school, a church, a log cabin, a smokehouse, a barn and a loom house. The center also contains the John Hay Home and the Stevens Memorial Museum.

The statesman's birthplace has been restored and furnished in 1840s style. The museum houses a large genealogical library, historical artifacts and replicas of 19th-century professional offices and a train depot. Tours of the village and the museum are available. Allow 1 hour minimum. Library Tues.-Sat. 9-5. Museum Tues.-Sat. 1-5. Guided tours of the village are given Tues.-Sat. 1-5. Closed holidays. Museum admission (includes library) $2, under 13 free. Village tour $2, under 13 free. Phone (812) 883-6495.

SANTA CLAUS (G-3) pop. 900

SAVE **HOLIDAY WORLD THEME PARK AND SPLASHIN' SAFARI WATER PARK**, 7 mi. s. of I-64 at jct. SRs 162 and 245, features areas thematic to Christmas, the Fourth of July and Halloween. In the complex are more than 60 rides, games and shows, including a white-water raft ride, a log-flume ride and two roller coasters; live musical entertainment; a high-dive show; games; a Lincoln era exhibit; a wax museum; a doll museum; antique toy displays; and visits with Santa Claus. Splashin' Safari is a water park featuring many waterslides, an action river, a wave pool, and three children's pools. Food is available. Kennel facilities are available.

Theme park open daily at 10 a.m., mid-May to late Aug. and on Labor Day; Sat.-Sun. at 10, early to mid-May and late Aug.- early Oct. Water park open daily at 11 a.m., late May-late Aug.; Sat.-Sun at 11, late Aug.-early Sept. Closing times vary. Schedule may vary; phone ahead. Admission (includes both parks) $26.95, over age 60 and under 54 inches tall $20.95, under age 2 free. DS, MC, VI. Phone (812) 937-4401 or (800) 467-2682.

SEYMOUR (E-4) pop. 15,600

MUSCATATUCK NATIONAL WILDLIFE REFUGE, 3 mi. e. of jct. I-65 and US 50, is a 7,700-acre tract featuring a hardwood forest and wetland habitats that are home to a variety of birds and wildlife. With a network of 9 miles of roads and 11 miles of hiking trails, the refuge offers opportunities for wildlife observation, photography, fishing, hunting, hiking and mushroom and berry picking. The visitor center features exhibits about the refuge and its inhabitants. A self-guiding automobile tour route and interpretive trail also are available. Allow 1 hour minimum. Daily dawn-dusk. Free. Phone (812) 522-4352.

SOUTHERN INDIANA CENTER FOR THE ARTS is 3 mi. n. on SR 11 to 2001 N. Ewing St. Works by regional artists and a collection of paintings by John Mellencamp are displayed in an 1851 Greek Revival building. Allow 30 minutes minimum. Tues.-Sat. noon-5; closed Jan. 1, Thanksgiving and Dec. 25. Free. Phone (812) 522-2278.

SHIPSHEWANA (A-5) elev. 904'

Shipshewana is home to one of the largest Amish communities in the world. The Shipshewana Auction and Flea Market, said to be the largest outdoor flea market in the Midwest, is open Tuesday and Wednesday, May through October.

LaGrange County Convention and Visitors Bureau: 440½ S. Van Buren St., Shipshewana, IN 46565; phone (260) 768-4008 or (800) 254-8090.

MENNO-HOF MENNONITE-AMISH VISITORS CENTER, on SR 5, is in a house and a barn built by Mennonite and Amish groups in a 6-day barn-raising. A guided 1-hour tour provides an introduction to these distinctive religious communities. Audiovisual presentations, historical exhibits and a playground with handmade toys also are featured. Videotape cameras are not permitted.

Allow 1 hour minimum. Mon.-Sat. 10-5 (also Tues. 5-7, June-Aug.), Apr.-Dec.; Tues.-Fri. noon-4, Sat. 10-5, rest of year. Closed Jan. 1, Thanksgiving and Dec. 25. Last tour begins 30 minutes before closing. Hours may vary in Jan.; phone ahead. Donations. Phone (260) 768-4117.

SOUTH BEND (A-4) pop. 105,500, elev. 719'

In 1842 Edward Sorin, a priest of the Congregation of the Holy Cross, arrived at the present site of the University of Notre Dame in South Bend to head a mission for the Potawatomi Indians and start a school for both secular students and those studying for the Holy Cross Order. The university that he founded, characterized by its distinctive golden dome *(see attraction listing)*, is one of the state's most visited sites.

South Bend resident James Oliver took his place in agricultural history in 1864 when he discovered a chilling process that allowed steel to replace iron in the curved moldboard of plows. In addition to being harder, the treated steel resisted the tendency of moist earth to build up on and clog plow blades. Factories producing goods ranging from automobile parts to guided missiles represent the importance of manufacturing to the economy of South Bend.

Tippecanoe Place, now a gourmet restaurant, was the home of the Studebakers, who founded an automobile dynasty. Balancing South Bend's industrial image are its fine city parks. Leeper Park is noted for its fragrance garden; Pinhook provides a lagoon; and Rum Village has a nature center and hiking and nature trails.

The East Race Waterway is one of the first man-made white-water raceways in the world. Capable of matching the Colorado River in power, it offers kayaking and rafting during the summer. A bordering fitness trail is part of a 5-mile system of inter-locking parks that stretches throughout the downtown core along the St. Joseph River. National and international competitions take place on the raceway.

The 5,000-seat Stanley Coveleski Regional Baseball Stadium is home to minor league baseball, other sporting events and concerts. St. Patrick's Park and Bendix Woods offer cross-country skiing.

Ferrettie/Baugo Creek County Park and St. Patrick's provide inner tubing and canoeing opportunities. Nearby Potato Creek State Park *(see Recreation Chart)* has a full spectrum of recreational facilities.

Convention & Visitors Bureau of South Bend/ Mishawaka: 401 E. Colfax Ave., P.O. Box 1677, South Bend, IN 46634; phone (574) 234-0051, ext. 345 or (800) 828-7881.

COLLEGE FOOTBALL HALL OF FAME, 111 S. St. Joseph, is a 58,000-square-foot museum of historic artifacts, mementos, photographs and interactive exhibits. In addition, it is a caretaker of college football history and features archives and a library.

Various galleries focus on different aspects of the game. The Locker Room provides a look at the way coaches train and inspire players. Visitors can test their football skills through a series of challenges and activities in the Training Center. The Pigskin Pageantry area is an interactive salute to fans, cheerleaders, marching bands and mascots. Other galleries highlight the media, equipment, bowl games and national championships.

In the Hall of Honor, more than 700 coaches and players are recognized; touch-screen monitors can be used to access information about them and to see them in action. The Stadium Theater, with its 360-degree screen, catches the action of a college football game. Food is available. Allow 2 hours minimum. Daily 10-7, June-Dec.; 10-5, rest of year. Closed major holidays. Admission $10; over 61, $7; ages 6-14, $4. Phone (574) 235-9999. *See color ad.*

COPSHAHOLM, THE OLIVER MANSION, 808 W. Washington St., was built in 1895 by Joseph Doty Oliver, president of the Oliver Chilled Plow Works, and named for the Scottish village in which his father was born. The 38-room stone mansion contains leaded glass windows, parquet floors, nine bathrooms and 14 fireplaces. Original furnishings include porcelains, glass, silver, prints and bronzes. The 2.5 acres of gardens show a formal Italianate garden, a rose garden, a tea house, a pergola, a fountain and a carriage house.

Also on the grounds is *Dom Robotnika,* the Worker's Home Museum. This furnished two-story, front-gable house built around 1870 represents the working-class heritage of the community.

Allow 1 hour, 30 minutes minimum. Guided tours are given hourly Tues.-Sat. 10:30-5, Sun. noon-5; closed major holidays. Last tour departs at 3:30. House tour $6, over 60, $5; students with ID $3. Combination admission for Copshaholm and Northern Indiana Center for History $8; over 60, $6.50; students with ID $4. AX, DS, MC, VI. Phone (574) 235-9664.

NORTHERN INDIANA CENTER FOR HISTORY, 808 W. Washington St., uses audiotapes, artifacts and photographs to re-create the history of the St. Joseph Valley. The core of the museum, Voyages Gallery, houses nine

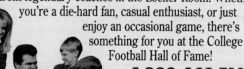

exhibitions that present different aspects of the area's development, including the prehistoric era and the advent of European settlement.

The history of the University of Notre Dame is chronicled in the Raclin Gallery. Kidsfirst Children's Museum offers a playful setting, including a canoe that children can climb in and out of and hands-on objects representing area history.

Allow 1 hour minimum. Tues.-Sat. 10-5, Sun. noon-5; closed holidays. Last house tour departs 1 hour, 30 minutes before closing. Center for History admission (including children's museum) $5; over 60, $4; ages 6-17 and students with ID $3. Combination admission for Center for History and Copshaholm $8; over 60, $6.50; students with ID $4; under 6 free. AX, DS, MC, VI. Phone (574) 235-9664.

POTAWATOMI ZOO, 1.5 mi. e. on Jefferson Blvd., then .2 mi. s. on Greenlawn Ave., is in 64-acre Potawatomi Park. Featured are a learning center, animals from five continents and a petting zoo. Allow 1 hour minimum. Daily 10-5, Apr.-Dec.; closed Thanksgiving and Dec. 25. Admission $4; over 62 and ages 3-14, $2.50. Phone (574) 235-9800.

SAVE **STUDEBAKER NATIONAL MUSEUM,** 525 S. Main St., displays horse-drawn and motorized Studebaker vehicles manufactured in South Bend. Some of the motor vehicles set speed and endurance records in the 1920s. In addition, the museum details the economic development of the area.

Highlights include carriages belonging to Presidents Grant and McKinley, the carriage in which President Lincoln rode to Ford's Theater, World War I horse-drawn wagons, an amphibious World War II Weasel and an electric 1909 backward/forward car that transported senators between their office building and the U.S. Capitol.

Allow 30 minutes minimum. Mon.-Sat. 9-5, Sun. noon-5. Admission $5.50; over 60 and students with ID $4.50; ages 2-12, $3. Phone (574) 235-9714.

UNIVERSITY OF NOTRE DAME, off I-80/90 exit 77, s. on SR 933 to Angela Blvd., then e. to Notre Dame Ave. following signs to the 1,250-acre main campus, was founded in 1842 on the site of an early mission.

Student-guided historical campus tours depart from the Eck Notre Dame Visitor's Center on Notre Dame Avenue. Free. Phone (574) 631-5726.

Basilica of the Sacred Heart, on the campus grounds, was built in the late 1800s. The ornate structure is adorned with gold and brass. Rich, detailed murals by the 19th-century artist Luigi Gregori cover the walls and ceiling. Built in the shape of a Latin cross, the basilica includes a chancel and apsidal chapels that contain relics and works or art. Tours are available by appointment. Free. Phone (574) 631-5726.

Grotto of Our Lady of Lourdes, w. of the Main Building, is a beautiful reproduction of the Grotto of Lourdes in France. Daily 24 hours.

Log Chapel, at the edge of St. Mary's Lake, is a replica of the chapel built in 1830 by Father Stephen Badin, the first Roman Catholic priest ordained in the United States. Open for Notre Dame events only.

Main Building (Golden Dome), center of campus, has a magnificent golden dome surmounted by a statue of the Virgin Mary. The murals depicting the life of Christopher Columbus are the work of Luigi Gregori, a Vatican artist who spent 17 years at Notre Dame. A $58 million renovation has restored the five-story Victorian building's woodwork, lighting fixtures and walls.

Snite Museum of Art, n. of the football stadium, houses rare religious artworks as well as masterpieces by European and American artists. Allow 30 minutes minimum. Tues.-Wed. 10-4, Thurs.-Sat. 10-5, Sun. 1-5; closed major holidays. Free. Phone (574) 631-7960.

Theodore M. Hesburgh Library, at the center of the east campus quadrangle, has an 11-story granite mosaic mural on an outer wall. The library holds more than 2 million volumes and can accommodate more than half the student body. Mon.-Fri. 7:30 a.m.-2 a.m., Sat. 8 a.m.-2 a.m., Sun. 10 a.m.-2 a.m., fall and spring sessions; otherwise varies. Phone (574) 631-6258.

TERRE HAUTE (E-2) pop. 55,400, elev. 485′

Named "high land" by the French, Terre Haute is an industrial center in the fertile lower Wabash Valley. Eugene V. Debs founded one of the first labor unions in the nation in Terre Haute, the American Railway Union.

Area parks offer many opportunities for recreational pursuits. Hiking, nature and cross-country ski trails, a well-stocked fishing lake and a nature center are on the 105 acres of Dobbs Park at SR 46 and Poplar Street (see Recreation Chart). Fairbanks Park contains the birthplace of Paul Dresser, who wrote Indiana's state song, "On the Banks of the Wabash."

Next to the business district is the Farrington's Grove Historical District, an 80-square-block area of more than 800 historic buildings.

Notable attractions on the campus of Indiana State University, include an anthropology museum and an astronomical observatory.

Saint Mary-of-the-Woods College, the oldest Catholic women's college in the United States, occupies 67 wooded acres northwest of Terre Haute on SR 150. Architectural guided tours of its buildings, which date from 1860, are available; art collections, dioramas and a gallery are among the noteworthy features on campus.

Terre Haute Convention and Visitors Bureau: 643 Wabash Ave., Terre Haute, IN 47807; phone (812) 234-5555 or (800) 366-3043.

Self-guiding tours: Maps for tours of the historic district, the arts corridor and the riverfront are available at the visitors bureau.

CHILDREN'S SCIENCE AND TECHNOLOGY MUSEUM OF TERRE HAUTE, off I-70 exit 7 at 523 Wabash Ave., contains hands-on exhibits, fossils, a studio and changing exhibits. Allow 1 hour minimum. Tues.-Sat. 9-4; closed major holidays. Admission $2.50; over 65 and ages 2-12, $2. Phone (812) 235-5548.

EUGENE V. DEBS HOME, 451 N. Eighth St., is a memorial to the labor and Socialist Party leader. Of interest are the murals by John Joseph Laska and plaques honoring historic labor leaders. Allow 30 minutes minimum. Wed.-Sun. 1-4:30; other times by appointment. Closed holidays. Free. Phone (812) 232-2163.

THE ROSE-HULMAN INSTITUTE OF TECHNOLOGY GALLERY, 5500 Wabash Ave. in the Hulman Union Building, displays 115 works by such noted 19th-century artists as Paul Sandby, father of the British watercolor movement, and caricaturist John Nixon.

Other featured works include 94 paintings from the state's Tri Kappa collection housed in the John A. Logan Library, more than 50 watercolors by Hoosier artist D. Omer Seamon in Hadley and Olin halls, and a variety of changing exhibits throughout the institute's campus. Mon.-Fri. 8-5; closed holidays. Free. Phone (812) 877-1511.

SWOPE ART MUSEUM, 25 S. Seventh St., exhibits 19th- and 20th-century works by American artists, including Edward Hopper, Andy Warhol, Robert Motherwell, Janet Scudder, Thomas Hart Benton and Grant Wood. The collection is housed in a 1901 Italian Renaissance-style building with an art deco interior. Also featured are films, lectures, concerts and special exhibits. Allow 1 hour minimum. Tues.-Fri. 10-5 (also Thurs. 5-8), Sat.-Sun. noon-5; closed holidays. Free. Phone (812) 238-1676.

UNIVERSITY ART GALLERY, 300 N. Seventh St. in the Indiana State University Center for Performing and Fine Arts, displays changing exhibitions by well-known national artists and ISU faculty and students. Allow 30 minutes minimum. Mon.-Wed. and Fri. 11-4, Thurs. 4-8; closed holidays. Free. Phone (812) 237-3720.

VIGO COUNTY HISTORICAL MUSEUM, 1411 S. Sixth St., is in an 1868 Victorian house. Wabash Valley history is depicted through antiques and local memorabilia; changing exhibits also are presented. Coca-Cola memorabilia and re-creations of a general store and post office, turn-of-the-20th-century pharmacy, late 19th-century schoolroom, dressmaker's shop, Victorian rooms and toy shop are among the displays. Allow 1 hour minimum. Tues.-Sun. 1-4, Feb.-Dec.; closed major holidays. Free. Phone (812) 235-9717.

UNDERWOOD (F-5)

PIGEON ROOST STATE HISTORIC SITE, 1 mi. n. on US 31, features a 44-foot obelisk marking the

burial site of settlers killed when the village of Pigeon Roost was burned by American Indians in 1812. Daily dawn-dusk. Free. Phone (812) 265-3526.

VALPARAISO (A-3) pop. 24,400, elev. 784'

Valparaiso—Spanish for "Vale of Paradise"—is the center of an agricultural area that produces corn, popcorn, wheat, oats and soybeans as well as livestock and dairy products.

The 310-acre campus of Valparaiso University is entered from the east end of Union Street or from just north of the junction of US 30 and SR 130. The Brauer Museum of Art, next to the university's Moellering Library, contains more than 2,500 works of American art dating from the 19th century.

Greater Valparaiso Chamber of Commerce: 150 W. Lincolnway, P.O. Box 330, Valparaiso, IN 46384-0330; phone (219) 462-1105.

Self-guiding tours: Brochures outlining walking tours of the historic sites are available at the Valparaiso Public Library, 103 Jefferson St.; phone (219) 462-0524.

CHAPEL OF THE RESURRECTION (Lutheran), at jct. SR 130 and US 30 on the Valparaiso University campus, is noted for its interesting architecture and stained-glass windows. A free-standing 140-foot campanile houses bells that chime several times per hour. The chapel seats 2,400. Guided tours are available. Daily 8 a.m.-10:30 p.m., Sept. 1-May 15; Mon.-Fri. 8-4:45, rest of year. Free. Reservations are required for guided tours. Phone (219) 464-5112.

VEVAY—*see Cincinnati in Ohio p. 204.*

VINCENNES (F-2) pop. 19,900, elev. 429'

Vincennes was established in 1732 by François Marie Bissot, who was commissioned in the early 18th century to construct a series of forts to combat British expansion in the Northwest Territory. In 1763 the post was turned over to the British, although many French settlers stayed in the area.

During the American Revolution 25-year-old George Rogers Clark attempted to seize all the land northwest of the Ohio River for Virginia and successfully defeated the British garrison in 1779. Virginia, however, failed to prevent the lawlessness and violence that beset the territory, and in 1784 the state ceded the land to the United States as a public domain.

Vincennes/Knox County Convention and Visitors Bureau: P.O. Box 602, Vincennes, IN 47591; phone (812) 886-0400 or (800) 886-6443.

GEORGE ROGERS CLARK NATIONAL HISTORICAL PARK, off US 50 and US 41, contains a granite and marble memorial building commemorating the George Rogers Clark campaign during the American Revolution. At this site in 1779 Clark and his small force of frontiersmen captured Fort Sackville from the British. A visitor center presents exhibits and shows a 23-minute film about the campaign.

Allow 1 hour minimum. Park open daily 9-5; closed Jan. 1, Thanksgiving and Dec. 25. Admission $2; under 17 free. Phone (812) 882-1776, ext. 110.

HARRISON MANSION (Grouseland), 3 W. Scott St., was built 1803-04 by William Henry Harrison, later the ninth president of the United States. The mansion was his home while he served as the first governor of the Indiana Territory. Some original furniture is displayed. A genealogical library is available. Allow 30 minutes minimum. Mon.-Sat. 9-5, Sun. 11-5, Mar.-Dec.; daily 11-4, rest of year. Closed Jan. 1, Thanksgiving and Dec. 25. Admission $5; ages 12-18, $3; ages 6-11, $2. Phone (812) 882-2096.

THE OLD CATHEDRAL (St. Francis Xavier Church), 205 Church St., was built in 1826 on the site of the first log church. In the spire is the bell, since recast, that hung in the original tower. Daily 7-4; closed during services. Donations. Phone (812) 882-5638.

OLD CATHEDRAL LIBRARY AND MUSEUM, 205 Church St. behind The Old Cathedral *(see attraction listing),* was founded in 1794 and is the oldest library in Indiana. It contains 10,000 volumes dating from the 12th to 18th centuries. Mon.-Fri. 1-4, Memorial Day-Labor Day. Admission 50c; under 12, 25c. Phone (812) 882-5638.

VINCENNES STATE HISTORIC SITES, at First and Harrison sts., includes buildings that played an important role in the development of the Indiana Territory. Phone (812) 882-7422.

Fort Knox II is 3 mi. n. on the Wabash River. Interpretive markers tell the history of the fort, which served as a military outpost 1803-13. Only the outline of the fort is visible. Picnicking and self-guiding tours permitted daily 9-5. Free.

Indiana Territory Capitol, also known as the Red House, served as the territory's first capitol. The two-story frame structure, held together by wooden pegs, was built about 1805. It housed a series of businesses before it became the home of the General Assembly 1811-13. Tues.-Sat. 9-5, Sun. 1-5, mid-Mar. to mid-Dec. Donations.

Maurice Thompson Birthplace was the birthplace of Maurice Thompson, author of "Alice of Old Vincennes," a 1900 novel set during the Revolutionary War. The small white house features frame construction and a cast-iron stove. Tues.-Sat. 9-5, Sun. 1-5, mid-Mar. to mid-Dec. Donations.

The Print Shop of Elihu Stout, next to the territorial capitol, is a replica of Stout's first print shop. Stout was brought to Vincennes by Territorial Governor William Henry Harrison to print the laws enacted by the legislature. His newspaper, called the *Indiana Gazette* when it was established in 1804, and his printing press were the first in the Indiana Territory. The wooden printing press displayed is an original Adam Ramage Printing Press, the same type used by Stout. Tues.-Sat. 9-5, Sun. 1-5, mid-Mar. to mid-Dec. Donations.

WABASH (C-5) pop. 12,100, elev. 727'

Light radiating from the courthouse dome on March 31, 1880, reputedly made Wabash the first city in the world to be illuminated by electricity. One of the first electric lights is displayed in the courthouse lobby. Several other period buildings (including residences) in Wabash's historic district reflect the city's development, first as a port on the Wabash and Erie Canal and later as a manufacturing center on the edge of the Indiana gas belt.

The Honeywell Center, at 275 W. Market St., was built in the 1940s by Wabash native Mark C. Honeywell, co-founder of Honeywell Inc. The center contains a theater, an art gallery and a sculpture plaza. For information phone (260) 563-1102.

Paradise Spring Historical Park preserves the site of an 1826 peace treaty between the U.S. government and the Potawatomi and Miami Indians. The park features cabins built to represent a mid-19th-century military post. Overlooking the Wabash River is Riverwalk Trail, a popular half-mile loop for walking, skating, bicycling, jogging.

Wabash County Convention and Visitors Bureau: 111 S. Wabash St., P.O. Box 746, Wabash, IN 46992; phone (260) 563-7171 or (800) 563-1169.

WABASH COUNTY HISTORICAL MUSEUM, 89 W. Hill St., in the 1899 Memorial Hall building, was constructed as a memorial to Civil War veterans. The museum contains natural history exhibits and American Indian artifacts, pioneer clothing and furniture, Civil War records and a display featuring Wabash-born country singer Crystal Gayle. Allow 1 hour minimum. Tues.-Sat. 9-1; closed major holidays. Donations. Phone (260) 563-0661.

WARSAW (B-4) pop. 11,000, elev. 824'

Warsaw was incorporated in 1854, nearly 20 years after the surrounding area was organized as a county and named for Polish nobleman Thaddeus Kosciuszko, who served with George Washington in the Revolutionary War. It is believed that the town was named for Kosciuszko's birthplace.

Kosciuszko County Convention and Visitors Bureau: 111 Capital Dr., Warsaw, IN 46582; phone (574) 269-6090 or (800) 800-6090.

KOSCIUSKO COUNTY OLD JAIL MUSEUM AND LIBRARY, corner of Indiana and Main sts., is an 1871 complex composed of bull pens, a catwalk, two floors of cells and the eight-room sheriff's residence. Throughout the facility are displays of medical equipment, military artifacts, antique tools and school nostalgia. Of particular interest is a jail cell that has been preserved in its starkness. A display

about gangster John Dillinger, who robbed the city police in 1934, also is included.

The library contains genealogical records. Allow 30 minutes minimum. Thurs.-Sat. 10-4, Sun. 1-4; closed holidays. Donations. Phone (574) 269-1078.

WEST LAFAYETTE (C-3) pop. 25,900

PURDUE UNIVERSITY is bounded by Northwestern Ave., State St. and Airport Rd. Founded in 1869 as a land-grant college, it is one of the nation's leading universities. Noteworthy are the Memorial Union, containing an art gallery, and the Stewart Center, comprising an experimental theater, art gallery, playhouse and audiovisual center as well as a hotel and restaurants.

Guided tours of Purdue's central campus are available. Self-guiding walking-tour maps also are available. Visitor information center open Mon.-Fri. 8-5, Sat. 8-4 (closed Sat. at noon during home football games). Guided tours of the campus are given Mon.-Fri. at 10 and 2, Sat. at 10. Reservations are required for guided tours. Phone (765) 494-4636.

WYANDOTTE (G-4)

WYANDOTTE CAVES are at 7315 S. Wyandotte Cave Rd. Wear good walking shoes and bring a jacket; the caves are always chilly. Phone (812) 738-2782.

Big Wyandotte Cave, used by prehistoric peoples for shelter and as a source of material to fashion tools, has extensive rooms and passages with many unusual formations, including an underground mountain and rare helictites that are said to be the largest of their type in the world. A variety of guided tours over lighted trails is offered year-round. The tours require climbing many long stairways.

Allow 2 hours minimum. Tours are given daily on the hour 9-4, Memorial Day weekend-Labor Day; Tues.-Sun. at 9, 11, 1 and 3, rest of year. Closed Jan. 1, Martin Luther King Jr. Day, Good Friday, Easter, election days, Nov. 11, Thanksgiving, day after Thanksgiving and Dec. 25. Fee $7; ages 4-12, $4.

Little Wyandotte Cave, discovered in 1851, has a variety of cave formations highlighted by indirect electrical lighting. A visitor center has displays relating to the cave. Thirty-minute guided tours are given daily every hour 10-5, Memorial Day weekend-Labor Day; Tues.-Sun. every two hours 10-4, rest of year. Visitor center daily 9-5, Memorial Day weekend-Labor Day; Tues.-Sun. 9-5, rest of year. Closed Jan. 1, Good Friday, Easter, election days, Nov. 11, Thanksgiving and Dec. 25. Fee $5; ages 4-12, $3. Visitor center free. For information about swimming and camping phone (812) 738-2782.

ZIONSVILLE—see Indianapolis p. 149.

Ohio

America's Roller Coast

The wild rides of Ohio's amusement parks will take your breath away

The Three C's

Century-old landmarks and cutting-edge attractions await in Cincinnati, Cleveland and Columbus

Beautiful Ohio

Go off the beaten path and discover Ohio's scenic state parks

Famous Faces

Whether you're a football fan or a rock 'n' roller, learn more about your heros at Ohio's halls of fame

Simple Pleasures

Take a buggy ride over the gently rolling hills of Ohio's Amish Country

all things are possible

The word Ohio means "great" in the Iroquois language, and what better way to describe a state that has produced eight U.S. presidents, two pioneering astronauts, many respected authors and more than a few inventors. You might wonder what has made the Buckeye State such a prolific source of important leaders, innovators and artists. It may be the optimism tempered with a belief in hard work that has characterized Ohioans since Revolutionary War veterans first settled the area. The state motto, "With God, all things are possible," reflects this positive outlook.

Visitors to Ohio have ample reason to be optimistic as well, for when it comes to attractions and pleasant pastimes—nearly anything is possible. Interested

in Ohio's favorite sons? Tour the Neil Armstrong Air and Space Museum, the Hayes Presidential Center or the President Harding Home and Museum.

Need to get away from it all? Try Wayne National Forest, Cuyahoga Valley National Recreation Area or Hocking Hills State Park. Crave amusement park thrills? There's Paramount's Kings Island and Cedar Point.

What about zoos, art museums, halls of fame and science centers? Ohio has these, too.

And the list goes on. So if you ever forget what the word Ohio means in Iroquois, just visit and you'll remember: Ohio means great!

Like a coin, there are two sides to Ohio. On one side you'll see the heavily industrialized and urbanized cities typified by Cleveland, Toledo and Cincinnati. Travelers looking for big city diversions—top-notch art museums, child-friendly science centers and world-class zoos—will find them here.

Turn the coin over and you'll discover the small towns and family farms of Middle America. Here remnants of a simpler time are preserved among carefully restored historic villages and Amish-populated rural counties. Craft demonstrations, barn raisings and horse-drawn buggies distinguish this side of Ohio.

Which is the real Ohio? The answer is both. Urban and rural, modern and quaint, the state turns two faces to the world.

Destined for Success

"Our position in the nation," one 19th-century historian wrote of his adopted state, "is peculiarly felicitous as to soil, climate and productions, and it will be our own fault if we are not the happiest people in the Union." To many early settlers, success among the fertile lands of Ohio seemed guaranteed.

As immigrants poured westward along the Ohio River, a shimmering liquid highway into the continent's heart, towns along the river boomed. The initial wave of settlement occurred after the Revolutionary War. Within 2 decades Ohio had become a state—the first to be carved from the Northwest Territory.

Cincinnati became the first industrial city in what was then the American West thanks to its location on the Ohio River, and by the late 19th century it was Cleveland's turn to boom. Proximity to coal fields in West Virginia and Pennsylvania and iron mines in Minnesota turned this Great Lakes port into one of America's leading manufacturing centers.

Though recent decades have not been kind to the heavy industry many Ohioans depend upon, the state's corner of the "rust belt" has rebounded. Nothing illustrates this renewal more vividly than numerous attractions that lure thousands of tourists each year.

On a quest for culture? Serious about science? Many of the Buckeye state's top draws are museums. The Cleveland Museum of Art features a large, widely respected collection of art ranging from ancient Egyptian statues to Impressionist masterpieces. Boasting "Lucy," one of the oldest known fossils of our early ancestors, and myriad other science

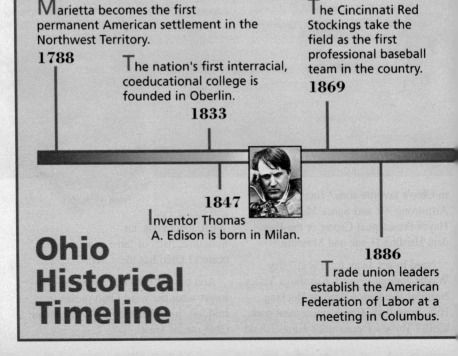

Marietta becomes the first permanent American settlement in the Northwest Territory.
1788

The nation's first interracial, coeducational college is founded in Oberlin.
1833

1847
Inventor Thomas A. Edison is born in Milan.

The Cincinnati Red Stockings take the field as the first professional baseball team in the country.
1869

1886
Trade union leaders establish the American Federation of Labor at a meeting in Columbus.

Ohio Historical Timeline

exhibits, the Cleveland Museum of Natural History is large enough to display looming dinosaur skeletons.

Standing on Cleveland's reinvigorated lakeshore is an eye-popping, glass-and-concrete monument to the music that has defined generations: the Rock and Roll Hall of Fame and Museum. Interactive exhibits recount this musical genre's history.

At the opposite corner of the state is Cincinnati's standout museum complex centered around its beautiful Art Deco train station. The Museum of Natural History and Science, the Cincinnati History Museum and The Children's Museum are housed here.

Intrepid explorers and wildlife lovers who don't have time for a safari in Africa or a cruise on the Amazon will want to spend the day at one of Ohio's famous zoos. Foremost among these is Cincinnati's Zoo and Botanical Garden, home to Bengal tigers and lowland gorillas. Gorillas also thrive at Toledo's Zoological Gardens along with hippopotamuses and koalas. And you won't need scuba gear to get close to dolphins and other deep-sea denizens at Six Flags Worlds of Adventure near Cleveland, but sit too near the killer whale show and you might get wet.

A Simpler Life

On the other side of the Ohio coin are many rustic locales that harken back to a past when life was simpler. You can give nostalgia free reign at Historic Roscoe Village in Coshocton, a restored canal town where costumed interpreters demonstrate craft skills. Similar sites offering living-history tours include Ohio Village at the Ohio Historical Center in Columbus; Hale Farm and Village near Bath; and Sauder Farm and Craft Village in Archbold.

Though these restored villages carefully recreate the past, they are still recreations. If it's the real thing you're after, visit Ohio's Amish country. For generations the Amish and Mennonites of eastern Ohio have shunned modern conveniences by continuing a farming tradition that enchants modern observers with its simplicity. Berlin is the best place to be introduced to Amish life. Buggy tours of the area are available, as well as handcrafted souvenirs.

One state, two faces. If you can't choose between Ohio's urban attractions and its pastoral countryside, flip a coin. Either way you win.

The National Football League is founded in Canton.
1920

Neil Armstrong of Wapakoneta becomes the first person to walk on the moon.
1969

U.S. Sen. John Glenn returns to space aboard the shuttle *Discovery*, becoming the world's oldest astronaut.
1998

1962
John Glenn of New Concord becomes the first American astronaut to orbit Earth.

1970
Four students are killed by National Guardsmen during anti-war demonstrations at Kent State University.

1967
Carl Stokes is elected mayor of Cleveland, the first African-American mayor of a major U.S. city.

Recreation

The presence of Lake Erie on its northern border is a favorite fringe benefit for Ohioans. The lake's warm temperatures, its shallow reefs, shoals and rocky shorelines produce greater numbers and varieties of fish than any other of the Great Lakes. Resorts have popped up along its sandy beaches, offering **parasailing**, **jet skiing** and **power boating**. Charter boats offer **fishing** trips and **diving** excursions to shipwreck sites. When temperatures drop and the waters of Lake Erie freeze, ice shanty camps appear off the west shore of Put-In-Bay between Rattlesnake and Middle Bass Island.

Canoeing is one of the few water activities not recommended for Lake Erie. However, the northern third of the scenic Sandusky River, which empties into the lake, is perfect for paddling. Formed by receding glaciers, the river passes limestone outcroppings.

State Treasures

Mohican State Park near Mansfield encompasses both the meandering Clear Fork River and the dramatic Clear Fork Gorge. More than 100,000 brown trout have been released in the Clear Fork, creating a paradise for fishing.

The lower section of the river is completely contained within the state park and is the most accessible. A trail that follows the Clear Fork through its magnificent gorge (more than 1,000 feet wide and 300 feet deep) passes two waterfalls, offering both spectacular scenery and easy access for anglers.

Hocking State Forest and neighboring Hocking Hills State Park in southern Ohio are considered to be the most diverse recreational areas in the state. The forest's **climbing** and **rappelling** area consists of 99 acres of challenging cliffs and sheer rock faces. Climbs range from 20 to 120 feet.

For the less ambitious, Hocking Hills has a concrete trail that snakes past sandstone cliffs, time-carved gorges and a 90-foot waterfall to Ash Cave. This path is an alternative for those physically impaired or traveling with small children.

In the rugged foothills of the Appalachian Mountains in southeastern Ohio, Wayne National Forest is home to cedar, pine and hardwoods laden with such wildlife as songbirds, deer, wild turkeys—a perfect place for **hunting** or just **bird watching**. Of Ohio's 72 state parks, 57 offer campgrounds with a variety of facilities.

Out of the Woods

You don't have to head into rural wilderness for outdoor fun in Ohio. Cleveland's 19,000-acre, 100-mile chain of metropolitan parks, known as the "Emerald Necklace," is one of the largest park districts in the country. The 14 Reservations showcase **hiking**, **water sports**, **horseback riding** and **inline skating** during warm weather and **tobogganing**, **cross-country skiing** and **sledding** in winter.

Cleveland Lakefront State Park's Edgewater Unit, adjacent to downtown, offers a beach, a fishing pier and boat ramps. For a unique adventure, spend an afternoon **scuba diving** along the park's shoreline and explore a freshwater reef created by remnants of the demolished Cleveland Municipal Stadium.

Once you've seen the natural sights surrounding Cleveland, you can go **biking**, hiking or cross-country skiing along the Ohio and Erie Canal Towpath Trail. Running the 22-mile length of the Cuyahoga Valley National Park from Cleveland to Akron, it passes historic homes, locks, spillways, an aqueduct and other canal features.

If a **golf** cart seems more comfortable than a pair of hiking boots, you don't have to try hard to find a course. Right outside Cincinnati in Mason is the Golf Center at Kings Island, home of the Senior PGA Kroger Classic each autumn. The center offers two courses: the Bruin, an 18-hole, par 61 mid-length course ideal for families and the Championship Course, called "The Grizzly" in honor of designer Jack Nicklaus, the "Golden Bear."

Akron has its own claim to golf fame—the NEC Invitational World Series of Golf, one of the most prestigious tournaments of the PGA Tour. An annual international event, it features a field of the world's best golfers.

Recreational Activities

Throughout the TourBook, you may notice a Recreational Activities heading with bulleted listings of recreation-oriented establishments listed underneath. Since normal AAA inspection criteria cannot be applied, these establishments are presented for information only. Age, height and weight restrictions may apply. Reservations are often recommended and sometimes required. Visitors should phone or write the attraction for additional information, and the address and phone number are provided for this purpose.

Fast Facts

POPULATION: 11,186,300.

AREA: 41,422 square miles; ranks 35th.

CAPITAL: Columbus.

HIGHEST POINT: 1,550 ft., Campbell Hill, Bellefontaine.

LOWEST POINT: 433 ft., Ohio River.

TIME ZONES: Eastern. DST.

MINIMUM AGE FOR DRIVERS: 18, 16 with driver education.

SEAT BELT/CHILD RESTRAINT LAWS: Seat belts required for driver and front-seat passengers; child restraints required for under age 4 or under 40 lbs.

HELMETS FOR MOTORCYCLISTS: Required for persons under 18, or with less than 1 year driving experience.

RADAR DETECTORS: Permitted, except in commercial vehicles.

FIREARMS LAWS: Vary by state and/or county. Contact the Ohio Highway Patrol/State Police at 1970 W. Broad St., Columbus, OH 43218-2074; phone (614) 466-2660.

HOLIDAYS: Jan. 1; Martin Luther King Jr. Day, Jan. (3rd Mon.); Washington-Lincoln Day, Feb. (3rd Mon.); Memorial Day, May (last Mon.); July 4; Labor Day, Sept. (1st Mon.); Columbus Day, Oct. (2nd Mon.); Veterans Day, Nov. 11; Thanksgiving; Dec. 25.

TAXES: Ohio's statewide sales tax is 5 percent, with local options for additional increments up to 3 percent. Local options also allow lodgings taxes up to 7 percent.

STATE INFORMATION CENTERS: Highway welcome centers, which supply travel literature and other information, are off I-90 westbound near Conneaut; I-71 north- and southbound near Lebanon; I-80 westbound near Hubbard; I-70 westbound near St. Clairsville; I-77 northbound near Marietta; I-75 north- and southbound near Bowling Green; I-70 eastbound near Gettysburg; I-75 north- and southbound near Monroe; US 23 southbound between Wakefield and Lucasville; and in the Ohio Statehouse, Broad and High sts. in Columbus. Centers are open daily except Jan. 1, Thanksgiving and Dec. 25.

FURTHER INFORMATION FOR VISITORS:

Ohio Dept. of Development
Division of Travel and
Tourism
Box 1001
Columbus, OH 43216
(800) 282-5393

NATIONAL FOREST INFORMATION:

Forest Supervisor
Wayne National Forest
13700 US 33
Nelsonville, OH 45764
(740) 753-0101
(information)
(877) 444-6777
(reservations)
TDD (877) 833-6777

RECREATION INFORMATION:

Division of Parks and Recreation
Dept. of Natural Resources
1952 Belcher Dr., Bldg. C-3
Columbus, OH 43224-1386
(614) 265-6561 or 265-7000

FISHING AND HUNTING REGULATIONS:

Division of Wildlife
Dept. of Natural Resources
1840 Belcher Dr.
Columbus, OH 43224-1329
(614) 265-6300

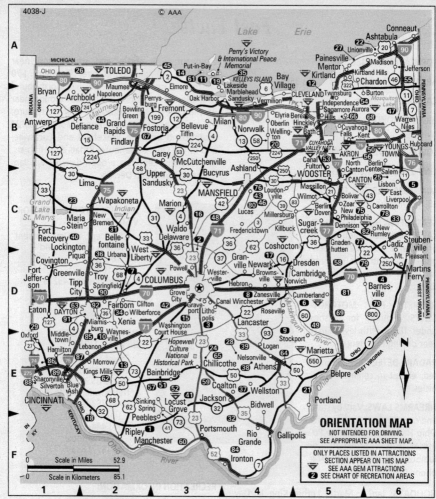

4038-J
© AAA

ORIENTATION MAP
NOT INTENDED FOR DRIVING.
SEE APPROPRIATE AAA SHEET MAP.

ONLY PLACES LISTED IN ATTRACTIONS
SECTION APPEAR ON THIS MAP.
▽ SEE AAA GEM ATTRACTIONS
② SEE CHART OF RECREATION AREAS

Scale in Miles   52.9
Scale in Kilometers   85.1

Points of Interest Offering A
Great Experience for Members

Akron (B-5)

NATIONAL INVENTORS HALL OF FAME—Interactive displays demonstrate some of history's greatest inventions, while a workshop allows you to express your own creativity. See p. 183.

STAN HYWET HALL AND GARDENS—One of the finest examples of Tudor Revival architecture in America, this majestic country house

situated on a beautiful garden landscape reflects a time of elegance and opulence. See p. 183.

Archbold (B-1)

HISTORIC SAUDER VILLAGE—Relive the taming of the Great Black Swamp of northwest Ohio in the mid-1800s with costumed interpreters and skilled craftspeople. See p. 184.

Aurora (B-5)

SIX FLAGS WORLDS OF AD-VENTURE—Three parks form this massive, self-titled "mega-park," complete with thrill rides, animal shows, marine exhibits and a water park. You might need a nap when you get home. See p. 185.

Bath (B-5)

HALE FARM AND VILLAGE—Artisans at this restored village re-enact small town life in the 1800s. See p. 186.

Canton (C-5)

PRO FOOTBALL HALL OF FAME—The defining moments of football history are combined with the thrills of today's game. See p. 190.

Cincinnati (E-1)

CINCINNATI ART MUSEUM—From mummies to Monet, this museum's collections span 5,000 years. See p. 195.

CINCINNATI
ART
MUSEUM
Great Art In Eden Park

CINCINNATI HISTORY MUSEUM—The riverboat era and World War II are depicted as poignant times in the city's history. See p. 199.

CINCINNATI ZOO AND BOTANICAL GARDEN—Lush plants represent the natural habitats of many zoo inhabitants. See p. 195.

THE MUSEUM CENTER AT UNION TERMINAL—This renovated, Art Deco-style train station houses an IMAX theater as well as the city's history, science and children's museums. See p. 199.

MUSEUM OF NATURAL HISTORY AND SCIENCE—The waterfalls and winged mammals of the re-created cave will drive you batty. See p. 199.

Cleveland (B-5)

CLEVELAND MUSEUM OF ART—Japanese and Egyptian collections are highlights in this elegant Beaux Arts-style building. See p. 213.

CLEVELAND MUSEUM OF NATURAL HISTORY—Geology, astronomy and archeology are just a few of the sciences explored in this ever-evolving museum. See p. 213.

GREAT LAKES SCIENCE CENTER—The indoor tornado will blow your mind. See p. 214.

GREAT LAKES
Science Center

THE HEALTH MUSEUM OF CLEVELAND—Have a chat with "Juno the Transparent Talking Woman," just one of this museum's 150 exhibits. See p. 214.

THE RAINFOREST—This tropical paradise features a spectacular two-story atrium with a 25-foot waterfall and a simulated thunderstorm every 15 minutes. See p. 213.

ROCK AND ROLL HALL OF FAME AND MUSEUM—Dedicated to the energy and evolution of rock 'n' roll, the museum highlights the greats who started it all. See p. 214.

WESTERN RESERVE HISTORICAL SOCIETY—Features include a 1911 mansion, a top-ranked costume collection, antique automobiles and aircraft, and archives of urban, ethnic and labor histories. See p. 215.

Columbus (D-3)

COLUMBUS ZOO—Visit with kangaroos or investigate a coral reef in the heart of Ohio. See p. 223.

COSI COLUMBUS—This center of science and industry offers interactive exhibits about the world around us. See p. 223.

FRANKLIN PARK CONSERVA-TORY AND BOTANICAL GAR-DEN—The climates of a Himalayan mountain, a rain forest, a desert and a Pacific island are re-created in a fantastic glass structure. See p. 223.

OHIO HISTORICAL CENTER—Follow Ohio's history from the ice age to the present with the help of modern technology. See p. 223.

OHIO VILLAGE—Revisit the past as you stroll through the shops and residences of this 1860s village. See p. 223.

Coshocton (C-4)

HISTORIC ROSCOE VILLAGE—Discover historic America in this restored 1830s canal town. See p. 232.

Cumberland (D-5)

THE WILDS—Reputed to be North America's largest wildlife research and conservation facility, this refuge is home to such exotic species as the southern white rhino and the scimitar-horned oryx. See p. 232.

Cuyahoga Valley National Park (B-5)

CUYAHOGA VALLEY NATIONAL PARK—Walk, bike or cross-country ski alongside the 22-mile Ohio & Erie Canal Towpath Trail, a popular feature of this historic area. See p. 232.

Dayton (D-1)

DAYTON ART INSTI-TUTE—Best known for its collections of European and American paintings, this museum has expanded its galleries to include regional, modernistic and photographic art. See p. 234.

UNITED STATES AIR FORCE MUSEUM—Follow aviation history from the days of the Wright Brothers to the age of the space shuttle. See p. 236.

Dover (C-5)

WARTHER CARV-INGS—Ernest "Mooney" Warther's fascination with trains can be seen in his working carvings of 64 steam locomotives and his collection of railroad memorabilia. See p. 237.

East Liverpool (C-6)

MUSEUM OF CERAMICS—The local history of the ceramics industry is highlighted with examples ranging from primitive pottery to collector's items. See p. 237.

Fremont (B-3)

HAYES PRESIDENTIAL CEN-TER—Tour the restored mansion of the 19th president and the nation's first presidential library at this 25-acre estate. See p. 239.

Kings Mills (E-2)

THE BEACH WATERPARK—The first water-coaster in the Midwest as well as 35 acres of sand and sun provide hours of splashing, floating fun. See p. 202.

PARAMOUNT'S KINGS ISLAND—Wild rides and cool waterslides provide a full day of entertainment. See p. 202.

Kirtland (A-5)

LAKE FARMPARK—Hop aboard a horse-drawn wagon for a tour of orchards, vineyards, gardens and a barnyard full of your favorite farm friends. See p. 244.

Locust Grove (E-3)

SERPENT MOUND—Overlooking the Brush Creek Valley, this is considered to be the largest and finest serpent effigy in the United States. See p. 245.

Mansfield (C-4)

KINGWOOD CENTER—Tiptoe through the tulips—and other perennials—as you enjoy the scenic beauty of this 47-acre center. See p. 246.

THE LIVING BIBLE MUSEUM—Life-size dioramas of the Old and New Testaments are accompanied by striking narratives and special effects. See p. 246.

Marietta (E-5)

CAMPUS MARTIUS MUSEUM—This facility is Ohio's only museum devoted to the history of settlement and migration in the state. See p. 247.

Marion (C-3)

THE PRESIDENT HARDING HOME AND MUSEUM—Harding's famous "front porch" campaign was conducted from this restored Victorian house. See p. 248.

New Philadelphia (C-5)

SCHOENBRUNN VILLAGE STATE MEMORIAL—This restored 1772 Moravian mission built for the Delaware Indians was the first attempt to settle Ohio. See p. 251.

Newport, Ky

NEWPORT AQUARIUM—The inhabitants and visitors get along swimmingly at this aquarium. See p. 206.

Norwich (D-5)

NATIONAL ROAD-ZANE GREY MUSEUM—This museum pays homage to the country's first highway and the father of the Western novel. See p. 252.

Perry's Victory and International Peace Memorial (A-4)

PERRY'S VICTORY AND INTERNATIONAL PEACE MEMORIAL—Rising 352 feet above Lake Erie, this imposing tower honors Admiral Perry's victory during the War of 1812. See p. 253.

Sandusky (B-4)

CEDAR POINT—This 364-acre amusement park/resort is home to 60 rides, including an amazing 13 roller coasters. See p. 256.

Toledo (A-2)

COSI TOLEDO—This center of science and industry offers interactive exhibits about the world around us. See p. 259.

TOLEDO MUSEUM OF ART—Don't let its Grecian exterior fool you—there are treasures from Eygpt, Africa, Asia and an exceptional U.S. glass collection exhibited inside. See p. 259.

TOLEDO ZOO—Check out an underwater view of a hippopotamus family or meet a distant cousin in the Primate Forest. See p. 259.

Wapakoneta (C-2)

NEIL ARMSTRONG AIR AND SPACE MUSEUM—Fly to the moon in the dome-shaped "astrotheater" and examine the history of space travel. See p. 261.

West Liberty (C-2)

OHIO CAVERNS—Sparkling white formations contrast with these caverns' colorful interiors. See p. 263.

Youngstown (B-6)

MILL CREEK METROPARKS—A beautiful formal garden, waterfalls and scenic vistas make this a perfect picnic spot. See p. 264.

Zanesville (D-5)

ZANESVILLE ART CENTER—In a community known for its glass and pottery, this center emphasizes the work of local artists. See p. 265.

Zoar (C-5)

ZOAR VILLAGE—This former German communal settlement dates from the early 19th century. See p. 265.

RECREATION AREAS

	MAP LOCATION	CAMPING	PICNICKING	HIKING TRAILS	BOATING	BOAT RAMP	BOAT RENTAL	FISHING	SWIMMING	PETS ON LEASH	BICYCLE TRAILS	WINTER SPORTS	VISITOR CENTER	LODGE/CABINS	FOOD SERVICE
NATIONAL FOREST *(See place listing)*															
Wayne 230,000 acres. Southeastern Ohio. Horse rental.		●	●	●	●	●		●	●						
NATIONAL PARK *(See place listing)*															
Cuyahoga Valley (B-5) Northeastern Ohio.			●	●				●			●	●	●		
STATE															
Adams Lake (F-2) 95 acres 1 mi. n.e. of West Union on SR 41.	①		●	●	●	●	●	●	●		●				
Alum Creek (C-3) 8,600 acres 7 mi. s.e. of Delaware off SRs 36 and 37, 1 mi. w. of jct. I-71. Hunting.	②	●	●	●	●	●	●	●	●	●			●		●
A.W. Marion (D-3) 454 acres 5 mi. e. of Circleville off US 22. Hunting.	③	●	●	●	●	●		●		●			●		
Barkcamp (D-6) 1,349 acres 1 mi. e. of Belmont off SR 149. Nature programs. Hunting; bridle trails.	④	●	●	●	●	●		●	●	●			●		
Beaver Creek (C-6) 3,038 acres 8 mi. n. of East Liverpool off SR 7. Hunting.	⑤	●	●	●				●		●			●		
Blue Rock (D-5) 350 acres 12 mi. s.e. of Zanesville off SR 60 on CR 45.	⑥	●	●	●	●	●		●	●	●			●		
Buck Creek (D-2) 4,030 acres 4 mi. e. of Springfield on SR 4. Hunting.	⑦	●	●	●	●	●	●	●	●	●			●	●	●
Buckeye Lake (D-4) 3,557 acres 9 mi. s. of Newark off SR 13. Hunting. *(See Newark p. 230)*	⑧		●		●	●		●	●	●					
Burr Oak (D-4) 3,256 acres 6 mi. n.e. of Glouster off SR 13. Nature programs. Hunting; bridle trails.	⑨	●	●	●	●	●	●	●	●	●			●		
Caesar Creek (E-2) 10,771 acres on SR 73 6 mi. w. of jct. I-71. Hunting; bridle trails. *(See Waynesville p. 204)*	⑩	●	●	●	●	●		●	●	●			●		
Catawba Island (A-3) 18 acres in Catawba off SR 53.	⑪		●		●	●		●					●		
Cleveland Lakefront (A-5) 517 acres off I-90 in downtown Cleveland.	⑫		●					●	●		●	●			●
Cowan Lake (E-2) 1,775 acres 5 mi. s. of Wilmington off US 68. Nature programs. Hunting; bike rental.	⑬	●	●	●	●	●	●	●	●	●	●		●	●	●
Crane Creek (A-3) 79 acres n.w. of Locust Point off SR 2. Hunting.	⑭		●	●	●			●	●				●		
Deer Creek (D-3) 4,897 acres 7 mi. s. of Mount Sterling on SR 207. Nature programs. Hunting; bike rental, bridle trails.	⑮	●	●	●	●	●	●	●	●	●	●		●	●	●
Delaware (C-3) 3,145 acres 6 mi. n. of Delaware on US 23. Hunting.	⑯	●	●	●	●	●		●	●	●			●		
Dillon (D-4) 7,690 acres 5 mi. n.w. of Zanesville off SR 146. Hunting.	⑰	●	●	●	●	●	●	●	●	●			●	●	●
East Fork (F-2) 10,580 acres 4 mi. s.e. of Amelia off SR 125. Hunting; bridle trails.	⑱	●	●	●	●	●		●	●	●			●		
East Harbor (A-3) 1,152 acres 8 mi. e. of Port Clinton off SR 269. Nature programs. Hunting.	⑲	●	●	●	●	●		●	●	●			●		●
Findley (B-4) 931 acres 3 mi. s. of Wellington on SR 58. Nature programs. Hunting; bike rental.	⑳	●	●	●	●	●	●	●	●	●			●		●
Forked Run (E-5) 817 acres 3 mi. s.w. of Reedsville off SR 124. Hunting.	㉑	●	●	●	●	●		●	●	●			●		
Geneva (A-5) 698 acres on the shore of Lake Erie at Geneva-on-the-Lake. Hunting; marina.	㉒	●	●	●	●	●		●	●	●			●	●	
Grand Lake St. Marys (C-1) 14,000 acres 2 mi. w. of St. Marys on SR 703. Nature programs. Hunting.	㉓	●	●		●	●	●	●		●			●		

RECREATION AREAS

RECREATION AREAS	MAP LOCATION	CAMPING	PICNICKING	HIKING TRAILS	BOATING	BOAT RAMP	BOAT RENTAL	FISHING	SWIMMING	PETS ON LEASH	BICYCLE TRAILS	WINTER SPORTS	VISITOR CENTER	LODGE/CABINS	FOOD SERVICE
Great Seal (E-3) 1,864 acres 3 mi. n.e. of Chillicothe on Marietta Pike. Cross-country skiing, hunting; bridle trails.	24	•	•	•								•			
Guilford Lake (C-6) 488 acres 6 mi. n.w. of Lisbon off SR 172.	25	•	•	•	•	•	•	•	•						
Harrison Lake (A-1) 247 acres 4 mi. s. of Fayette off SR 66.	26	•	•	•	•	•	•		•	•	•				
Headlands Beach (A-5) 125 acres 2 mi. n.w. of Painesville at SR 44 terminus.	27		•	•	•	•		•	•						•
Hocking Hills (E-4) 2,348 acres. Nature programs. *(See Logan p. 245)*	28	•	•	•	•				•	•			•	•	•
Hueston Woods (D-1) 3,596 acres 5 mi. n. of Oxford off SR 732. Nature programs. Hunting; bike rental, bridle trails.	29	•	•	•	•	•	•	•	•	•	•		•	•	•
Independence Dam (B-1) 606 acres 4 mi. e. of Defiance on SR 424.	30	•	•	•	•	•	•	•		•	•				
Indian Lake (C-2) 6,452 acres 2 mi. n. of Lakeview on SR 235. Nature programs. Hunting.	31	•	•	•	•	•	•	•	•	•	•	•			
Jackson Lake (F-4) 334 acres 2 mi. w. of Oak Hill on SR 279.	32	•	•	•		•	•	•	•	•					
Jefferson Lake (C-6) 961 acres 16 mi. n.w. of Steubenville off SR 43. Hunting; bridle trails.	33	•	•	•		•	•	•	•	•					
John Bryan (D-2) 750 acres 2 mi. e. of Yellow Springs on SR 370.	34	•	•	•	•				•	•					
Kelleys Island (A-4) 661 acres. Scenic. Hunting. *(See Kelleys Island p. 243)*	35	•	•	•	•	•		•	•	•			•		
Kiser Lake (D-2) 870 acres 17 mi. n.w. of Urbana on SR 235.	36	•	•	•	•			•	•			•			•
Lake Alma (E-4) 350 acres 3 mi. n.e. of Wellston on SR 349. Hunting.	37	•	•	•	•			•	•	•					
Lake Hope (E-4) 3,223 acres 12 mi. n.e. of McArthur on SR 278. Nature programs.	38	•	•	•	•	•	•	•	•					•	•
Lake Logan (E-4) 719 acres 4 mi. w. of Logan off SR 664. Hunting.	39	•	•	•	•	•	•	•	•			•			•
Lake Loramie (C-1) 2,080 acres 3 mi. s.e. of Minster off SR 66. Hunting.	40	•	•	•	•	•	•	•	•						
Lake Milton (B-6) 2,685 acres 1 mi. s. of I-76 off SR 534. Hunting.	50		•	•	•	•	•	•	•	•					
Lake White (E-3) 444 acres 4 mi. s.w. of Waverly on SR 104.	41	•	•			•	•		•						
Little Miami (E-2) 707 acres n. of Corwin. Bridle trails.	85		•	•						•	•	•	•	•	•
Madison Lake (D-3) 186 acres 3 mi. e. of London off SR 665. Hunting.	42		•			•	•		•	•					
Malabar Farm (C-4) 917 acres. Nature programs. Hunting; bridle trails. *(See Lucas p. 245)*	43	•	•	•					•			•			•
Mary Jane Thurston (B-2) 555 acres 2 mi. w. of Grand Rapids on SR 65. Hunting; bridle trails.	44	•	•	•	•	•	•	•				•			
Maumee Bay (A-3) 1,350 acres 8 mi. e. of Toledo, then 3 mi. n. off SR 2. Hunting.	45	•	•	•	•		•	•	•		•		•	•	•
Mohican (C-4) 1,294 acres. Nature programs. Scenic. Bicycle and canoe rental, bridle trails. *(See Loudonville p. 245)*	46	•	•	•					•	•			•	•	•
Mosquito Lake (B-6) 11,811 acres 10 mi. n. of Warren off SR 305. Hunting; bridle trails.	47	•	•	•	•	•	•	•	•	•			•		
Mount Gilead (C-3) 172 acres 1 mi. e. of Mount Gilead on SR 95.	48	•	•	•	•	•	•	•				•			

RECREATION AREAS

	MAP LOCATION	CAMPING	PICNICKING	HIKING TRAILS	BOATING	BOAT RAMP	BOAT RENTAL	FISHING	SWIMMING	PETS ON LEASH	BICYCLE TRAILS	WINTER SPORTS	VISITOR CENTER	LODGE/CABINS	FOOD SERVICE
Muskingum River (D-5) 120 acres along 80 miles of the Muskingum River extending from Devola to Ellis Locks.	49	•	•	•	•	•		•		•					
Paint Creek (E-3) 10,200 acres 17 mi. e. of Hillsboro on US 50. Nature programs. Pioneer farm. Hunting; bridle trails.	51	•	•	•	•	•	•	•	•	•	•				•
Pike Lake (E-3) 613 acres 6 mi. s.e. of Bainbridge. Nature programs.	52	•	•	•		•	•	•		•				•	•
Portage Lakes (B-5) 3,520 acres in Akron on SR 93. Hunting.	53	•	•	•	•	•		•	•	•			•		
Punderson (B-5) 996 acres 2 mi. e. of Newbury off SR 87. Nature programs. Hunting; tennis.	54	•	•	•	•	•		•	•	•			•	•	•
Pymatuning (A-6) 17,500 acres 6 mi. s.e. of Andover off US 85. Nature programs. Hunting.	55	•	•	•	•	•	•	•	•				•	•	•
Quail Hollow (B-6) 700 acres 2 mi. n. of Hartville on Congress Lake Rd. Nature programs. Bridle trails.	56		•	•								•	•		
Rocky Fork (E-3) 3,464 acres 3 mi. e. of Hillsboro off SR 124. Hunting.	57	•	•	•	•	•	•	•	•	•			•		
Salt Fork (D-5) 20,181 acres 7 mi. n.e. of Cambridge on US 22. Nature programs. Hunting; bicycle rental, bridle trails.	58	•	•	•	•	•	•	•	•	•			•	•	•
Scioto Trail (E-3) 248 acres 10 mi. s. of Chillicothe off US 23. Hunting.	59	•	•	•	•		•		•		•		•		
Shawnee (F-3) 1,168 acres 8 mi. w. of Portsmouth on SR 125. Nature programs. Hunting.	60	•	•	•	•		•		•		•		•	•	•
South Bass Island (A-3) 35 acres on South Bass Island by summer ferry.	61	•	•		•	•		•			•				
Stonelick (E-2) 1,258 acres 1 mi. s. of Edenton off SR 727. Hunting.	62	•	•	•	•	•	•	•	•	•	•		•		
Strouds Run (E-4) 2,606 acres 8 mi. n.e. of Athens off US 50A on CR 20. Hunting; bridle trails.	64	•	•	•	•	•		•	•	•			•		
Sycamore (D-1) 2,373 acres 1 mi. w. of Trotwood on SR 49. Hunting, snowmobiling; bridle trails.	63		•	•				•		•		•			
Tar Hollow (E-3) 634 acres 10 mi. s. of Adelphi off SR 540. Hunting.	65	•	•	•	•		•	•		•			•		
Tinker's Creek (B-5) 369 acres 2 mi. w. of SR 43 on Aurora-Hudson Road near Portage.	66		•	•				•	•				•		
Van Buren (B-2) 296 acres 1 mi. e. of Van Buren on SR 613. Hunting; bridle trails.	67	•	•	•	•		•		•	•	•				
West Branch (B-5) 8,002 acres 5 mi. e. of Ravenna off SR 5. Nature programs. Hunting; bridle trails.	68	•	•	•	•	•	•	•	•	•			•		•
Wolf Run (D-5) 1,363 acres 1 mi. e. of Belle Valley off I-77. Hunting.	69	•	•	•	•	•		•	•	•			•		
MUSKINGUM WATERSHED CONSERVANCY DISTRICT															
Atwood Lake (C-5) 4,536 acres 2 mi. s.e. of New Cumberland off SR 212. Nature programs. Hunting; playground.	75	•	•	•	•	•	•	•	•	•			•	•	•
Charles Mill Lake (C-4) 3,347 acres 9 mi. e. of Mansfield on SR 430. Nature programs. Hunting.	76	•	•	•	•	•	•	•	•		•		•		•
Clendening Lake (C-5) 6,550 acres 3 mi. n. of Freeport off SR 800. Hunting.	77	•	•		•	•	•	•						•	•
Leesville Lake (C-6) 3,625 acres 4 mi. s. of Sherrodsville off SR 212. Hunting.	78	•	•	•	•	•	•		•					•	•
Piedmont Lake (D-6) 6,642 acres 2 mi. s.e. of Smyrna off SR 800. Hunting.	79	•	•		•	•	•	•		•				•	•

RECREATION AREAS

Recreation Area	MAP LOCATION	CAMPING	PICNICKING	HIKING TRAILS	BOATING	BOAT RAMP	BOAT RENTAL	FISHING	SWIMMING	PETS ON LEASH	BICYCLE TRAILS	WINTER SPORTS	VISITOR CENTER	LODGE/CABINS	FOOD SERVICE
Pleasant Hill Lake (C-4) 2,195 acres 3 mi. s.w. of Perrysville on SR 95. Nature programs. Hunting.	80	•	•	•	•	•	•	•	•	•			•	•	•
Senecaville Lake (D-5) 7,613 acres 3 mi. s.e. of Senecaville on SR 547. Nature programs. Hunting.	81	•	•	•	•	•	•	•	•	•			•	•	•
Tappan Lake (C-6) 7,597 acres 12 mi. n.w. of Cadiz off US 250. Nature programs. Hunting.	82	•	•	•	•	•	•	•	•	•			•	•	•
OTHER															
Carriage Hill Metro Park Farm (D-2) 868 acres n.e. of Dayton at jct. I-70 and SR 201. *(See Dayton p. 234)*	90	•	•	•						•	•	•			
Lake Vesuvius (F-4) 200 acres 6 mi. n. of Ironton off SR 93. Nature programs.	84	•	•	•	•	•	•	•	•	•			•		
Miami Whitewater Forest (E-1) n.w. of Cincinnati off I-74. Golf; playground.	86	•	•	•				•	•				•		
Piatt (D-6) 119 acres 4 mi. e. of Woodsfield on SR 78. Bridle trails.	70	•	•	•											
Possum Creek Reserve (D-1) 518 acres w. of Dayton at jct. Gettysburg Avenue and SR 4.	91	•	•	•					•				•		
Sharon Woods (E-1) n.e. of Cincinnati off Reading Road. Golf; bicycle rental, playground.	87		•	•								•	•		•
Shawnee Lookout (E-1) w. of Cincinnati via US 50. Golf; playground.	88		•	•		•		•							
Sugarcreek Reserve (D-1) 596 acres s.e. of Dayton on Wilmington Pike. Horse rental.	92		•	•									•		
Winton Woods (E-1) n. of Cincinnati off Winton Road. Golf; bicycle rental, horse rental, playground.	89	•	•	•	•			•	•				•	•	

Ohio Temperature Averages
Maximum / Minimum
From the records of the National Weather Service

	JAN	FEB	MAR	APR	MAY	JUNE	JULY	AUG	SEPT	OCT	NOV	DEC
Cincinnati	41 / 26	43 / 27	52 / 33	64 / 44	75 / 54	84 / 63	88 / 66	86 / 65	80 / 58	69 / 47	53 / 36	43 / 28
Cleveland	35 / 20	36 / 21	44 / 30	58 / 36	69 / 46	78 / 52	82 / 60	80 / 59	74 / 51	63 / 41	48 / 31	37 / 22
Columbus	39 / 23	41 / 24	49 / 30	62 / 40	74 / 50	83 / 60	87 / 63	85 / 61	79 / 54	67 / 44	52 / 33	41 / 24
Dayton	37 / 22	39 / 23	48 / 30	61 / 41	72 / 51	81 / 62	85 / 65	84 / 64	77 / 56	66 / 45	50 / 34	38 / 24
Toledo	34 / 18	36 / 19	45 / 26	58 / 35	70 / 46	80 / 56	81 / 60	83 / 59	76 / 51	64 / 40	47 / 30	36 / 21
Youngstown	35 / 21	36 / 21	45 / 28	59 / 37	70 / 47	79 / 56	83 / 59	81 / 59	74 / 52	62 / 42	48 / 33	37 / 24

Points of Interest

AKRON (B-5) pop. 223,000, elev. 873′

The center of global rubber empires, Akron once led the world in the manufacturing of rubber products. Although local production is now minimal, Akron is still the corporate home of such companies as Genic, Goodyear and Uniroyal-Goodrich. Akron also is a merchandising center—a vital distribution gateway between the industrial East and Midwest.

From the standpoint of scientific research, Akron is perhaps the nation's fastest growing city. The Firestone and Goodyear laboratories specialize in research involving rubber and plastics. The original space suits worn by U.S. astronauts were made and fitted at B.F. Goodrich. The University of Akron's Institute of Polymer Science has gained renown for its work in combining molecules through chemical reactions.

The Akron area offers a variety of cultural and sporting activities, including events at E.J. Thomas Center for the Performing Arts. Akron Civic Theatre, with its opulent design and ceiling replete with blinking stars and floating clouds, is one of the few remaining "atmospheric" theaters. Guided tours are offered; phone (330) 535-3175. Carousel Dinner Theatre, 1275 E. Waterloo Rd., presents touring productions of Broadway shows, and visitors have a choice of purchasing dinner-and-show or show-only tickets; phone (330) 724-9855. Akron's Blossom Music Center is the summer home of the renowned Cleveland Orchestra from June to mid-September; phone (330) 920-8040.

April through September, the Akron Aeros AA minor league baseball team plays at state-of-the-art Canal Park, on the corner of S. Main and W. Exchange Streets.

August brings two of the city's most popular sporting events, the All-American Soap Box Derby in mid-month and the NEC Invitational World Series of Golf at the end of the month.

Goodwill Industries of Akron, 570 E. Waterloo Rd., offers tours of its rehabilitation training facility; phone (330) 724-6995.

Akron/Summit Convention and Visitors Bureau: 77 E. Mill St., Akron, OH 44308; phone (330) 374-7560 or (800) 245-4254.

Shopping areas: Chapel Hill Mall, at Howe and Brittain roads, and Rolling Acres Mall, 2 miles

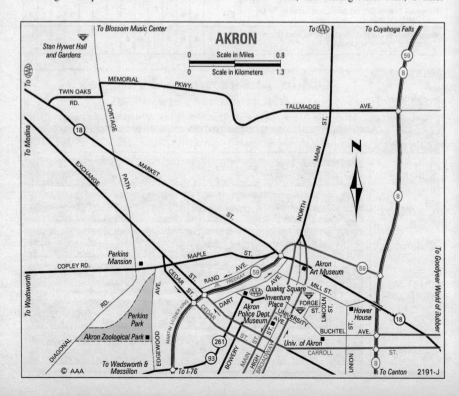

west of I-77 exit 130 at 2400 Romig Rd., both feature Kaufmann's, JCPenney and Sears; Summit Mall, 1.5 miles east of I-77 exit 137 on SR 18, houses Kaufmann's and Dillard's. Quaker Square *(see attraction listing),* I-77 exit 22A (Broadway) to 120 E. Mill St., has many unusual boutiques and shops. A Colonial charm is reflected in the shops of Liberty Commons, 1236 Weathervane Ln.

AKRON ART MUSEUM is at 70 E. Market St. in the Old Akron Post Office, a restored late 19th-century Italian Renaissance structure. Three floors of galleries present changing exhibits from American and international collections. The museum's permanent collection presents a distinctive look at regional, national and international art from 1850 to the present, with a special focus on contemporary paintings and photography. Allow 1 hour minimum. Daily 11-5; closed major holidays. Free. Phone (330) 376-9185.

AKRON POLICE DEPARTMENT MUSEUM, 217 S. High St., features confiscated weapons, gambling and narcotics paraphernalia, counterfeit money and other police-related items. Police uniforms and more than 200 photographs also are displayed. Allow 30 minutes minimum. Mon.-Fri. 10-2; closed holidays. Free. Phone (330) 375-2390.

[SAVE] **AKRON ZOOLOGICAL PARK,** 500 Edgewood Ave., covers 25 acres in Perkins Woods. Among the zoo's 400 animals are endangered Chinese alligators, rare red pandas and bald eagles. The interactive Tiger Valley exhibit includes Sumatran tigers, sun bears and flamingos as well as a train, a tree house and a conservation camp. Children may feed the animals at the Ohio Farmyard Encounter or take a train or pony ride.

Allow 3 hours minimum. Mon.-Sat. 10-5, Sun. and holidays 10-6, May 1 to mid-Oct.; daily 1-4, rest of year. Closed major holidays. Admission $7.50; over 64, $6; ages 2-14, $5. Parking $1.50. DS, MC, VI. Phone (330) 375-2550 or 375-2525.

GOODYEAR WORLD OF RUBBER, 1201 E. Market St., is a museum depicting the history of rubber. Exhibits include a replica of a rubber plantation, displays of tires, memorabilia of Charles Goodyear and a reproduction of his workshop. A videotape describing the tire production process and a self-guiding tour are available. Allow 1 hour minimum. Mon.-Fri. 8-4:30; closed holidays. Free. Phone (330) 796-7117.

HOWER HOUSE is on the edge of the University of Akron campus, .1 mi. s. on Fir Hill from E. Market St. This 28-room Victorian mansion (owned by the university), designed in the Second Empire Italianate style, was built in 1871 by John Henry Hower, one of Akron's leading industrialists. The house contains octagonal rooms with oak parquet floors, black walnut woodwork and is filled with Hower family furnishings and treasures collected from around the world. Allow 1 hour minimum. Wed.-Sat. noon-3:30, Sun. 1-4, Feb.-Dec.; closed

major holidays. Admission $5; over 64, $4; students with ID and ages 6-18, $2. Phone (330) 972-6909.

 NATIONAL INVENTORS HALL OF FAME, 221 S. Broadway, has hands-on exhibits that allow visitors to play a harp with light [SAVE] beams, take gadgets apart, experiment with science and create their own inventions. Allow 2 hours minimum. Tues.-Sat. 9-5, Sun. noon-5; closed Jan. 1, Easter, Thanksgiving and Dec. 25. Admission $7.50; over 54 and ages 3-17, $6; family rate $25. AX, DS, MC, VI. Phone (330) 762-4463 or (800) 968-4332.

[SAVE] **PERKINS MANSION,** Copley Rd. and S. Portage Path, was built in 1837 by Col. Simon Perkins, son of Akron's founder, Gen. Simon Perkins. This Greek Revival mansion is furnished in period. Across the street is the house where abolitionist John Brown lived for 2 years. Allow 1 hour, 30 minutes minimum. Both houses are open Wed.-Sun. 1-4, Mar.-Dec.; closed holidays. Admission $5; over 59 and ages 5-12, $4. MC, VI. Phone (330) 535-1120.

QUAKER SQUARE is at 135 S. Broadway. The square encompasses the renovated factory buildings of the original Quaker Oats Co. The structures, where oatmeal and other products were produced from the late 1800s until 1970, include restaurants, specialty shops, boutiques and a hotel with rooms built into the original grain silos. Inside the hotel are hand-sculpted wall murals, relics and historical displays.

A restaurant is built in and around original 1938 Broadway Limited train cars. The diner houses a collection of railroad memorabilia; displays are free and open to the public. Allow 2 hours minimum. Mon.-Sat. 10-9, Sun. noon-6; closed Jan. 1, Easter, Thanksgiving and Dec. 25. Free. Phone (330) 253-5970.

 STAN HYWET HALL AND GARDENS, 714 N. Portage Path, was built 1911-15 by Frank A. Seiberling, co-founder of Goodyear and Seiberling Rubber companies. [SAVE] Considered one of the finest examples of Tudor Revival architecture in the United States, the 65-room manor house contains art treasures from around the world.

Features include an impressive music room, a three-story great hall and a west porch fountain portraying the Well of St. Keyne. Modern fixtures such as radiators, telephones and closets are concealed behind decorative grillwork and carved panels so as not to disturb the elegance of the decor.

Guided tours are offered. An audio tour describes acres of artfully landscaped grounds, which include a fully-restored English garden, a lagoon and scenic vistas. Food is available.

Allow 1 hour minimum. Tours daily 10-4:30, Apr.-Dec.; Tues.-Sat. 10-4, Sun. 1-4, Feb.-Mar. Closed major holidays. Admission $8; ages 6-12, $4; under 6 free with adult. MC, VI. Phone (330) 836-5533 or (888) 836-5533.

ANTWERP (B-1) pop. 1,700

Antwerp is in the middle of a region once known as the Black Swamp. This thickly forested area, almost completely submerged, was avoided by all westbound settlers until draining encouraged the development of small industries, such as bucket and oar factories.

In the 1840s canals built along the Maumee River provided a means of transportation through the area. Interest in the fertile swampland grew, and a vast reclamation project transformed the once forbidding region into farmland. Antwerp soon developed into the farming community it now is.

EHRHART MUSEUM, in the city hall at 118 N. Main St., is filled with hundreds of mounted birds and animals caught and preserved by Otto Ehrhart, a local naturalist. A historical collection that includes American Indian artifacts also is displayed. Allow 30 minutes minimum. Mon.-Thurs. 11:30-5; by appointment rest of week. Free. Phone (419) 258-2665.

ARCHBOLD (B-1) pop. 3,400

Archbold is home to the world's premier ready-to-assemble furniture manufacturer and the country's eighth largest furniture manufacturer, Sauder Woodworking. No matter the season outside, it is always the yuletide in The Candy Cane Christmas Shoppe, where 30 themed trees lift spirits and promote nostalgia.

Archbold Chamber of Commerce: 300 N. Defiance St., Archbold, OH 43502; phone (419) 445-2222.

HISTORIC SAUDER VILLAGE is 1.7 mi. n.e. on SR 2. Craftsmen, including a potter, blacksmith, gunsmith, woodworker, spinner, weaver, cooper, broom maker, glassblower and tinsmith, and a costumed staff work in a community setting of restored buildings. A turn-of-the-20th-century homestead, complete with a barn and animals, is on the grounds. The village museum displays antique tools and equipment left by the region's settlers.

Allow 4 hours minimum. Mon.-Sat. 10-5, Sun. 1-5, late Apr. to mid-Oct. Admission $9.50; ages 6-16, $4.75. Carriage, train or wagon ride $1.50. MC, VI. Phone (800) 590-9755. *See color ad.*

ASHLAND (B-4) pop. 20,100, elev. 1,076'

Founded in 1815 and situated in the rolling hills of mainly agricultural Ashland County, Ashland maintains a prosperous economy thanks to light industry and its location off I-71 approximately halfway between Cleveland and Columbus. The city is home to the 1,800-student Ashland University, the John M. Ashbrook Center for Public Affairs and Ashland Theological Seminary. At 414 Center St. is the Ashland County Historical Society Museum with its fine, wide-ranging collections and replicas of late-19th-century/early-20th-century establishments housed in an 1859 house, carriage house and a barn. The museum is open Wednesday, Friday and Sunday from 1 to 4; phone (419) 289-3111.

During the summer months, a variety of free concerts are performed at the Guy C. Myers Band Shell. The city also serves as a base for visitors to Charles Mill Lake and Pleasant Hill Lake recreational areas *(see Recreation Chart and Mansfield and Perrysville in the AAA Great Lakes CampBook),* Mohican State Park *(see Loudonville p. 245)* and Malabar Farm State Park *(see Lucas p. 245).*

Ashland Area Chamber of Commerce: 10 W. 2nd St., Suite 210, Ashland, OH 44805; phone (419) 281-4584.

ASHTABULA (A-6) pop. 21,600, elev. 647'

Moses Cleaveland's 1796 discovery of a harbor in northeast Ohio on Lake Erie led to the settlement of Ashtabula, a major coal and iron port. In addition to its role as a manufacturing center, the city also is a waterfront resort and home to a 1,250-student regional campus of Kent State University. The city's name reputedly was derived from an American Indian phrase meaning "river of many fish."

Walnut Beach, on Lake Erie at Walnut Boulevard and Lake Avenue, is a municipal park with a white

sand beach, tennis courts, a playground and picnic facilities; food is available. Lake Shore Park, northeast of Walnut Beach on SR 531, has a boat ramp and concessions. The parks close at dusk.

Nearby Countryside offers opportunities for scenic drives visiting 16 covered bridges and 11 wineries.

Ashtabula County Convention and Visitors Bureau: 1850 Austinburg Rd., Austinburg, OH 44010; phone (440) 275-3202 or (800) 337-6746.

Self-guiding tours: Brochures outlining a walking tour past about 25 historic buildings at Ashtabula Harbor are available by contacting the visitors bureau or Silhouette Gift Shop, 1038 Bridge St. Maps for covered bridge driving tours also are available.

Shopping areas: Historic Ashtabula Harbor District Village, 5 miles north of I-90 on SR 11, then west 1 mile on SR 531, features specialty shops, museums and restaurants. Nearby at SR 11 and SR 20 is the Astabula Mall.

GREAT LAKES MARINE & U.S. COAST GUARD MEMORIAL MUSEUM is at Ashtabula Harbor; exit 229 off I-90, 4 mi. n. on SR 11, w. on SR 531, 2 blks. n. on Franklin St., then e. on Walnut Blvd. This museum, housed in an 1898 lighthouse keeper's quarters, displays marine artifacts, paintings, photographs, equipment and models of ships. A restored pilot house and a scale model of an ore-unloading machine also are featured. A narrative account of the sinking of the iron-ore freighter *Daniel J. Morrell* is given by a survivor.

A picnic area is available. Allow 1 hour minimum. Thurs.-Mon. and holidays 11-6, mid-Apr. through Labor Day; Fri.-Sun. noon-5, day after Labor Day-Oct. 31. Admission $3; under 12, $1. Phone (440) 964-6847.

HUBBARD HOUSE UNDERGROUND RAILROAD MUSEUM is at the corner of Walnut Blvd. and Hibbard Hill Dr. on Lake Erie. The 1840s brick house was an important stop on the Underground Railroad, the network of abolitionist-run safe houses that helped slaves to escape to freedom before the Civil War. Fugitive slaves would wait in the barn until a ship arrived to take them to Canada. The house contains exhibits relating to the Underground Railroad, the Civil War and local history and is furnished in period.

Allow 30 minutes minimum. Fri.-Sun. noon-6, Memorial Day weekend-Labor Day; Fri.-Sun. 1-5, day after Labor Day-Sept. 30. Admission $5; ages 6-16, $3. Phone (440) 964-8168.

ATHENS (E-4) pop. 21,300, elev. 650'

Athens is best known as the home of Ohio University, home to 19,000 students. Guided tours of the university campus can be arranged by phoning the admissions office at (740) 593-4100.

THE DAIRY BARN CULTURAL ARTS CENTER is off the US 33/50 bypass; take SR 682N/Ohio University exit, go 2 blks. s. on Richland Ave., then .2 mi. and turn w. to 8000 Dairy Ln., following signs. The Dairy Barn is the site of international, national and regional arts and crafts exhibitions and festivals. The center also holds special events throughout the year, such as Quilt National, a quilt show that attracts entries from around the world. For a schedule of events send a self-addressed stamped envelope to P.O. Box 747, Athens, OH 45701.

Allow 1 hour minimum. Tues.-Sun. 11-5 (also Thurs. 5-8); closed between shows. Admission $3, over 64 and students with ID $2.50, under 12 free; free to all Thurs. 5-8. Special events admission $5, over 64 and students with ID $3.50, under 12 free. AX, MC, VI ($10). Phone (740) 592-4981 for schedule and events information.

AURORA (B-5) pop. 9,200

Founded in 1799, Aurora was originally settled by Revolutionary War veterans during the land grant period resulting from the Northwest Territory Ordinance of 1787. The town was once considered the cheese-making capital of the United States. Boasting a diverse economy and a growing cultural community, Aurora maintains its Western Reserve style, heritage and history.

Aurora Chamber of Commerce: 173 S. Chillicothe Rd., Aurora, OH 44202; phone (330) 562-3373 or (800) 648-6342.

Shopping areas: Aurora Premium Outlets, on SR 43, is comprised of 70 outlet stores and specialty and antique shops in a village setting.

SIX FLAGS WORLDS OF ADVENTURE is 3 mi. w. on SR 43 to 1060 N. Aurora Rd. Three entities—a thrill park, a marine life park and a water park—comprise this 240-acre entertainment complex, which surrounds Geauga Lake. A ferry and a boardwalk provide transportation between the three worlds.

More than 100 rides and attractions are featured, including 10 roller coasters. Daredevils will not want to miss the U-shaped Superman Ultimate Escape, the X-Flight flying coaster or the floorless Batman Knight Flight, which sends riders 161 feet in the air at speeds approaching 65 mph.

Dolphins, otters and walruses—as well as dogs and cats—are stars of their own shows. Marine exhibits showcase penguins, sharks and hundreds of exotic fish. A 25,000-square-foot wave pool and a lazy river are highlights at Hurricane Harbor. Turtle Beach caters to toddlers, while visitors can meet Bugs Bunny and other characters at Looney Tunes Boomtown. Food is available.

Park open daily, Memorial Day-Labor Day; some Sat.-Sun., May 1-day before Memorial Day and day after Labor Day-Oct. 31. Hours vary; phone ahead to confirm schedule. Admission $39.99, over 60 and under 48 inches tall $19.99, under age 2 free. Parking $9. AAA members save 10 percent on select in-park dining and merchandise. Check at the park's Guest Relations window for details. AX, MC, VI. Phone (330) 562-8303.

BAINBRIDGE (E-3) pop. 1,000

Once the land of the Shawnee, Bainbridge was founded in 1805 by surveyor Nathaniel Massie, a wealthy landowner from Chillicothe. This rural trade center became known as the "cradle of American dentistry" after the profession's first school was established in 1827.

Two scenic routes to Bainbridge are US 50 from the east and SR 41 from the south.

PAINT VALLEY SKYLINE DRIVES radiate from Bainbridge. Four loop routes varying from 19 to 50 miles in length traverse the valley and lead to the summits of some of Ohio's most spectacular hills. Allow 4 hours minimum. Phone (740) 634-2085.

SEIP MOUND STATE MEMORIAL, 10 acres 3 mi. e. on US 50, contains the great central mound (240 ft. long, 160 ft. wide and 30 ft. high) of a group of geometric earthworks built by the Hopewell Indians for burials. This complex originally comprised several mounds and engulfed more than 100 acres. A pavilion has related displays. Picnic facilities are available. Daily dawn-dusk. Free. Phone (800) 686-1535 Mon.-Fri.

SAVE **SEVEN CAVES** is 4 mi. w. on US 50, then 1 mi. s. on Cave Rd., following signs. Three nature trails lead to the caves, which have cement walks, handrails and push-button lighting emphasizing specific formations; the tours are self-guiding. Cliffs, canyons, waterfalls and more than 300 species of plants and trees are found throughout the park.

Note: Stone trails may be uneven, narrow or steep. Visitors should be physically capable of climbing stairs; walking shoes are recommended. Picnicking is permitted. Food is available. Allow 1 hour, 30 minutes minimum. Daily 9-7. Admission $10; ages 4-14, $5. MC, VI. Phone (937) 365-1283.

BARNESVILLE (D-6) pop. 4,300, elev. 1,276'

Barnesville was so named because it was settled by the family that had established Barnesville, Md. During the late 18th and early 19th centuries the town was the home of many affluent leaders in the area's tobacco, strawberry and glass industries. The scenic portions of two highways, SR 147 and SR 800, meet in Barnesville.

Barnesville Visitor Information Center: 300 E. Church St., Barnesville, OH, 43713; phone (740) 425-4300.

BARBARA BARBE DOLL MUSEUM 211 N. Chestnut St., displays more than 3,000 dolls from noted doll collector and designer Barbara Barbe. The collection includes early bisque dolls, wax dolls, tin heads, hard plastics and vinyls as well as more recent models by Ideal and Sun Rubber. Allow 1 hour minimum. Wed.-Sun. 1-4, May-Sept. Admission $2; ages 6-12, $1. Phone (740) 425-4300 or 425-2301.

BELMONT COUNTY VICTORIAN MANSION MUSEUM, 532 N. Chestnut St., is a brick Romanesque-style house featuring 26 rooms elegantly appointed and furnished in the 1890s style. Allow 1 hour minimum. Guided 45-minute tours are conducted as needed Thurs.-Sun. 1-4:30, May-Sept.; by appointment in Dec. Last tour begins at closing. Fee $4; ages 6-18, $1. Phone (740) 425-2926.

BATH (B-5) pop. 2,200

▼GEM **HALE FARM AND VILLAGE** is 5 mi. s.e. of I-77 Richfield exit 143, following signs to 2686 Oak Hill Rd. This working farm and restored village simulates the sights, sounds and smells of a bustling Western Reserve township of 1848. Artisans demonstrate blacksmithing, candle making, glass blowing, weaving and other activities of the mid-1800s. Visitors can see cattle, horses, sheep, pigs and chickens. Maple sugaring is demonstrated during select weekends in winter.

Allow 3 hours minimum. Mon.-Sat. 10-5, Sun. noon-5, Memorial Day-Oct. 31; phone for hours in Dec. Admission $12; over 59, $10; ages 3-12, $7. AX, DS, MC, VI. Phone (330) 666-3711, or (800) 589-9703.

BAY VILLAGE—see Cleveland p. 219.

BELLEFONTAINE (C-2)
pop. 12,100, elev. 1,216'

When Marmaduke Swearingen was captured by Shawnees during the 18th century, he was wearing a blue hunting shirt; thus, his captors called him Blue Jacket. After the tribe moved from Pennsylvania and he married the chief's daughter, the site was named in his honor. As chief of the tribe, Blue Jacket played an active part in treaty negotiations with American pioneers.

Natural springs gave the town its current name, derived from the French for "beautiful fountain." Bellefontaine is a trading center for a rich agricultural region. Nearby 1,550-foot Sample Hill is the highest point in Ohio.

Logan County Convention and Tourist Bureau: 100 S. Main St., Bellefontaine, OH 43311-2083; phone (937) 599-5121.

THE LOGAN COUNTY HISTORICAL MUSEUM, 521 E. Columbus Ave., is housed in a spacious 1906 mansion built by a local lumber baron. Exhibits describe local history and include American Indian artifacts, railroad memorabilia, toys, clothes, household objects and items manufactured in Logan County. A 19th-century schoolroom is re-created in one room of the museum while another room contains military memorabilia from area veterans.

Allow 1 hour minimum. Wed. and Fri.-Sun. 1-4, May-Oct.; Fri.-Sat. 1-4, rest of year. Closed major holidays. Donations. Phone (937) 593-7557.

ZANE SHAWNEE CAVERNS, 6 mi. e. on SR 540, offers 1-hour tours. Cave pearls are among the caverns' formations. A museum at the entrance displays

American Indian artifacts, including weapons and a scale model of an early Shawnee village. Tours are given as needed daily 9-5. Admission to caverns $7; ages 2-12, $4. Museum $6; ages 2-12, $4. DS, MC, VI. Phone (937) 592-9592.

BELLEVUE (B-3) pop. 8,100, elev. 743′

An important railroad center in its early development, this area continues to flourish as an agricultural region noted for its cherries, grains, soy beans and livestock.

Bellevue Area Tourism and Visitors Bureau: Box 63, Bellevue, OH 44811; phone (419) 483-5359 or (800) 562-6978.

[SAVE] **HISTORIC LYME VILLAGE** is 3 mi. e. on US 20, then 1.5 mi. n. to 5001 SR 4 This complex and visitors center contains 21 restored 19th-century buildings, including houses, barns, shops, a mansion, schoolhouse, general store, a log church, post office and several museums. The Groton Postmark Research Center contains the National Museum of the Postmark Collectors Club. The village is open only by guided tour. Tours start when visitors arrive and may be joined in progress; visitors seldom wait more than 20 minutes to begin a tour.

Allow 2 hours, 30 minutes minimum. Guided 2.5-hour tours of the village begin as needed Tues.-Sun. 1-5, June-Aug.; Sun. 1-5 in May and Sept.; by appointment rest of year. Last complete tour begins 2.5 hours before closing; an abbreviated tour begins 1 hour before closing. Fee $7; over 64, $6; ages 6-12, $3. Phone (419) 483-4949 or 483-6052.

MAD RIVER AND NKP RAILROAD SOCIETY MUSEUM, 2 blks. s. of US 20 at 253 Southwest St., houses railroad memorabilia. Many restored railroad cars, including a Wabash F-7 diesel, are displayed on the grounds. Daily 1-5, Memorial Day-Labor Day; Sat.-Sun. 1-5, May 1-day before Memorial Day and day after Labor Day-Oct. 31. Admission $3; ages 3-12, $1. Phone (419) 483-2222.

[SAVE] **SENECA CAVERNS** is 3.5 mi. s. off SR 269, then 2 mi. w. on Rte. 178. This limestone cavern has seven levels open to the public. Unique varieties of fossilized fish, shells and coral can be seen, along with inscriptions dating back to 1872. Some bending and stooping is required to negotiate the sometimes narrow passages. Picnicking is permitted. Allow 1 hour minimum. One-hour tours depart every 20 minutes daily 9-7, Memorial Day-Labor Day; Sat.-Sun. 10-5, May 1-day before Memorial Day and day after Labor Day to mid-Oct. Fee $9.50; over 62, $7.50; ages 5-12, $5. Phone (419) 483-6711.

SORROWFUL MOTHER SHRINE is 5.5 mi. s. of US 20/18 on SR 269. The shrine includes 120 acres of lawns, flower gardens and woods. A mile-long trail leads to grottoes and an outdoor Way of the Cross. Food is available May-Oct. Daily 9-5; mass and daily devotions at 11 and 4:30. Free. Phone (419) 483-3435.

BELPRE (E-5) pop. 6,800, elev. 622′

LEE MIDDLETON ORIGINAL DOLLS INC. is 1 mi. w. on SR 618 at 1301 Washington Blvd. This factory offers 30-minute tours of its facilities during which visitors can witness the various stages of doll production. A life-size dollhouse with gingerbread facade covers 50,000 square feet. Allow 30 minutes minimum. Tours Mon.-Fri. at 9, 10:15, 11, 12:30, 1:15 and 2:15, Feb.-Dec. Outlet open Mon.-Fri. 9-6, Sat. 9-5, Sun. noon-4, May-Dec.; Mon.-Fri. noon-5, Sat. 9-5 in Jan.; Mon.-Sat. 9-5, rest of year. Phone for holiday schedules. Tours free. Phone (740) 423-1481 or (800) 233-7479.

BEREA—*see Cleveland p. 219.*

BERLIN (C-5) pop. 3,100, elev. 954′

Berlin, in the heart of Amish country, offers visitors a chance to view a lifestyle different from their own. The Amish have maintained their simplified way of life, rejecting many modern conveniences. Visitors are captivated by the charming country roads on which Amish families travel in horse-drawn buggies. Crafts, antiques and homemade foods can be bought from the Amish at roadside stands or in area shops.

The Wendell August Forge, 4 miles north of Berlin on SR 62, features forged aluminum, bronze, pewter and sterling silver items. Visitors can watch the craftsmen at work, take a self-guiding tour or visit a museum area Monday through Saturday. Phone (330) 893-3713.

"BEHALT" is .5 mi. e. on SR 39, then 1.2 mi. n. on CR 77. This 265-foot cyclorama illustrates the heritage of the Amish and Mennonite people. Allow 1 hour minimum. Mon.-Thurs. 9-5, Fri.-Sat. 9-8, June-Oct.; Mon.-Sat. 9-5, rest of year. Closed Jan. 1, Thanksgiving, and Dec. 25. Admission $5.50; ages 6-12, $2.50. Phone (330) 893-3192.

THE ROLLING RIDGE RANCH, 1 mi. n. on SR 62 then 1.5 mi. to 3961 CR 168, offers a 1.5-mile self-guiding drive or a wagon ride through 80 acres of woods and pasturelands. The 350 domestic and exotic animals from around the world include camels, Watusi cattle and zebras. Mon.-Sat. 9-dusk, first Mon. in Apr.-Oct. 31. Last wagon leaves at 5. Allow 1 hour minimum. Drive-through fee $7.50; over 65 and ages 3-12, $4.50. Wagon ride fee $12.50; over 65 and ages 3-12, $7.50. Phone (330) 893-3777.

[SAVE] **SCHROCK'S AMISH FARM,** 1 mi. e. on SR 39, includes a guided tour of an Amish farm and a videotape presentation about Amish life in the surrounding area. Baked goods are prepared at the farm daily. Buggy rides are available, and picnicking is permitted. Mon.-Fri. 10-5, Sat. 10-6, Apr.-Oct. Admission $4; ages 3-12, $3. Admission including buggy ride, $7.50; ages 3-12, $5.50. Phone (330) 893-2951.

BERLIN CENTER (B-6) elev. 1,075′

SAVE **NOAH'S LOST ARK ANIMAL SANCTUARY,** 2 mi. w. on US 224 then s. 2 mi. to 8424 Bedell Rd., allows visitors to get an up-close view of rehabilitated, formerly mistreated exotic animals such as tigers, lions, bears and wolves. Children may pet and feed some of the animals. Picnicking is permitted. Allow 30 minutes minimum. Sun. and Tues.-Fri. 10-5, Sat. 10-6, May-Oct. Schedule may vary; phone ahead. Admission $5.50; ages 2-17, $4.50. A fee is charged for animal food. Phone (330) 584-7835.

BIDWELL (F-4) pop. 400, elev. 685′

JEWEL EVANS GRIST MILL is at jct. US 35 and SR 850. Built by Amish workers, the mill uses rare French buhrstone millstones to grind cornmeal and wheat flour. A viewing room allows visitors to watch the milling operation. Mon.-Fri., 7:30-4; closed holidays. Free. Phone (740) 245-5654.

BLUE ASH—see Cincinnati p. 202.

BOLIVAR (C-5) pop. 900

SAVE **FORT LAURENS STATE MEMORIAL AND MUSEUM** is .5 mi. w. of jct. I-77 and SR 212. This 81-acre park was the site of the only U.S. military fort in Ohio during the American Revolution. A museum includes Revolutionary War displays and an audiovisual presentation.

Park open daily 9:30-dusk, Apr.-Oct. Museum open Wed.-Sat. 9:30-5, Sun. and holidays noon-5, Memorial Day weekend-Labor Day; Sat. 9:30-5, Sun. noon-5, day after Labor Day-Oct. 31. Park admission free except during special events. Museum admission $3; over 64, $1.60; ages 6-12, $1.25. AX, DS, MC, VI. Phone (330) 874-2059 or (800) 283-8914.

BROWNSVILLE—see Columbus p. 229.

BOWLING GREEN (B-2)
pop. 28,200, elev. 696′

SAVE **THE WOOD COUNTY HISTORICAL MUSEUM** is off I-75 exit 179; take US 6 e. .5 mi. to County Home Rd., then s. following signs. Formerly the Wood County Infirmary, the museum is on the site of what was once a "poor farm," a place that functioned as a commune where each resident was expected to contribute according to his or her ability. The main building, a 60-room Victorian structure completed in 1868, contains exhibits about northwest Ohio history. The grounds include hiking trails, a large ice house, horse barn, hog barn, slaughter house, granary, pauper's cemetery, herb garden and a hospital for the violently insane which was known as the Lunatic House.

Outdoor exhibits include a large collection of antique agricultural equipment and a fully operational oil derrick. Drilling equipment on the site relate the oil-rich history of this area once known as the Black Swamp. Allow 1 hour minimum. Tues.-Fri.

9:30-4:30, Sat.-Sun. 1-4, Apr.-Oct.; Mon.-Fri. 9:30-4:30, rest of year. Guided tours are given Sat.-Sun. 1-4, Apr.-Oct. and the first weekend in Dec. Admission $2. Phone (419) 352-0967.

BRYAN (B-1) pop. 8,300, elev. 764′

More than 150 years old, the town of Bryan was named for Ohio Secretary of State John A. Bryan. A prominent landmark in the town square is the Romanesque Revival-style Williams County Courthouse. The courthouse was built in 1888, using stones weighing as much as 6 tons each. Stone cutters were brought from Scotland to create the building's exterior carvings.

BUCYRUS (C-3) pop. 13,500, elev. 1,004′

Settled by Pennsylvanians in the early 1820s, Bucyrus (bu-SIGH-rus) was named for its beauty, "bu-" and for Cyrus, founder of the Persian Empire.

D. PICKING & CO., 119 S. Walnut St., makes its copper products primarily by hand. Guided 30-minute shop tours begin every half-hour Mon.-Fri. 10-11 and 12:30-2; closed holidays. Free. Phone (419) 562-6891.

BURTON (B-6) pop. 1,300, elev. 1,310′

SAVE **CENTURY VILLAGE MUSEUM AND CROSSROADS COUNTRY STORE,** jct. SRs 87 and 168/700, is a completely restored Western Reserve community with five fully-furnished houses, an 1846 church, a marshall's office, a one-room schoolhouse, a seamstress' shop, a blacksmith's shop and a crossroads store. The buildings are accessible by guided tour. The historical and genealogical library contains the Thoburn Toy Soldier Collection of lead miniatures that depicts the soldier's life throughout 3,000 years of military history.

Tues.-Fri. 10-4, Sat.-Sun. 1-4, May 1-Nov. 15. Guided 90-minute tours are given Tues.-Fri. at 10:30, 1 and 3, Sat.-Sun. at 1 and 3. Fee $5; senior citizens $4; ages 6-12, $3. Phone (440) 834-1492.

CADIZ (C-6) pop. 3,400, elev. 1,280′

CLARK GABLE BIRTHPLACE is s. of downtown at jct. Charleston St./SR 250, following signs. This is a reproduction of the house in which Clark Gable was born. A museum houses some of the actor's personal belongings, including his 1954 Cadillac, as well as antiques. Tues.-Sun. 10-4, May-Sept.; Tues.-Fri. 10-4, rest of year. Closed holidays. Admission $4.50; over 60, $4; ages 5-16, $3. Phone (740) 942-4989.

CAMBRIDGE (D-5) pop. 11,700, elev. 800′

Cambridge was the boyhood home of actor William Boyd, who became famous for his film and television role as Hopalong Cassidy. The Hopalong Cassidy Museum is at 127 S. 10th St.; phone (740) 432-3364.

The Guernsey County Historical Society Museum, 218 N. 8th St., is a restored early 19th-century house containing Cambridge memorabilia from the town's beginning through the present; phone (740) 439-5884.

Nearby parks, including Salt Fork, Senecaville Lake and Wolf Run offer recreational activities throughout the year. *See Recreation Chart and the AAA Great Lakes CampBook.*

Cambridge Visitors and Convention Bureau: 2146 Southgate Pkwy., P.O. Box 427, Cambridge, OH 43725; phone (740) 432-2022 or (800) 933-5480. *See color ad.*

BOYD'S CRYSTAL ART GLASS CO., 1203 Morton Ave., offers guided tours through the factory, where antique glass reproductions are made. Allow 30 minutes minimum. Guided 20-minute tours are given as needed Mon.-Fri. 8-3:30; closed major holidays. Last tour begins 20 minutes before closing. Free. Phone (740) 439-2077.

THE CAMBRIDGE GLASS MUSEUM, 1.5 mi. n. on SR 209 from jct. I-70 exit 178, then 500 ft. w., following signs to 812 Jefferson Ave., reputedly has the largest private collection of Cambridge glass in the country. More than 5,000 pieces are displayed. Allow 30 minutes minimum. Mon.-Sat. 1-4, June-Oct. Admission $2; over 59, $1; under 12 free. Phone (740) 432-3045.

DEGENHART PAPERWEIGHT AND GLASS MUSEUM, jct. SR 22 and I-77, contains the personal collection of Elizabeth Degenhart, owner of the Crystal Art Glass Co. until her death in 1978. Exhibits include Midwestern pattern glass, cruets and Degenhart glass and paperweights. A videotape presentation is shown.

Allow 1 hour minimum. Mon.-Sat. 9-5, Sun. 1-5, Apr.-Dec.; Mon.-Fri. 10-5, rest of year. Closed Jan. 1, Thanksgiving and Dec. 24-26 and 31. Admission $1.50; over 55, $1; under 18 free. Phone (740) 432-2626.

SAVE **"LIVING WORD" OUTDOOR DRAMA,** 3 mi. n.w. on SR 209, portrays the life of Jesus. Performances are staged in a natural outdoor amphitheater. Free guided tours of the sets and stage are conducted 45 minutes prior to each performance. Allow 2 hours, 30 minutes minimum. Thurs.-Sat. at 8, mid-June through August 31; Sat. at 7 in Sept. Tickets $12; over 59, $10; ages 4-12, $6. Inquire about refund and weather policies. Reservations are recommended. MC, VI. Phone (740) 439-2761.

MOSSER GLASS INC., .5 mi. w. of I-77 on US 22, offers 1-hour guided tours of its glassmaking operations. Tours are available Mon.-Fri. at 8:15, 9:15, 10:15, 11:45, 1, 2 and 3; closed first 2 weeks in July. Free. Phone (740) 439-1827.

CANAL FULTON (B-5) pop. 4200, elev. 947'

HELENA III CANAL BOAT departs from 103 Tuscarawas St. W. This horse-drawn canalboat offers guided tours with a narrative history of the canal and the area. A museum features a collection of canal memorabilia and local history displays; a videotape is shown. Museum Tues.-Sun. 1-4, cruises at 1, 2 and 3, June-Aug.; museum Sat.-Sun. 1-4, cruises at 1, 2 and 3 in May and Sept. (weather permitting) One-hour cruise (includes museum admission) $6.50; over 59, $5.50; ages 3-12, $4.50. Phone (330) 854-3808 or (800) 435-3623.

CANAL WINCHESTER—
see Columbus p. 229.

CANTON (C-5) pop. 84,200, elev. 1,052'

Canton derived its name from the wealthy estate near Baltimore, where Bezaleel Wells lived before settling in Ohio around 1805. Although Canton grew into a major industrial center, the city maintains an informal neatness dating from the 19th century, when immigrant Swiss and German watchmakers influenced city planning.

Canton was the home of President William McKinley. He attended the Church of the Savior United Methodist at Cleveland Avenue and W. Tuscarawas Street. Four memorial windows presented by Mrs. McKinley adorn the structure.

In 1918, after delivering a speech in Canton, one-time Socialist presidential candidate Eugene V.

Debs was arrested for violating the Espionage Act of 1917.

Canton/Stark County Convention and Visitors Bureau: 229 Wells Ave. N.W., Canton, OH 44703-2642; phone (330) 454-1439 or (800) 533-4302.

Shopping areas: A major shopping complex is Canton Centre, Whipple and W. Tuscarawas streets, featuring JCPenney and Kaufmann's.

SAVE **CANTON CLASSIC CAR MUSEUM,** off I-77 Tuscarawas St. exit, then .5 mile e. to 555 Market Ave. S.W., has more than 45 antique, classic and special interest cars. Housed in the 1915 showroom of a Ford-Lincoln dealership, the automobiles are displayed in an atmosphere of period memorabilia, including fashions, advertisements, a jukebox and a photograph collection of automobile pioneers.

Allow 1 hour minimum. Daily 10-5; closed major holidays. Admission $6; over 64, $5; students with ID $4; under 5 free. MC, VI. Phone (330) 455-3603.

THE CULTURAL CENTER FOR THE ARTS, 1001 Market Ave. N., presents performances by the Canton Ballet, Canton Symphony, Civic Opera and Players Guild. The center also houses the Art Museum, which presents multimedia exhibitions with an emphasis on Ohio artists. Allow 1 hour minimum. Mon.-Fri. 9-5. Art Institute $2.50; students with ID, $1.50; over 59 and under 12, $1.25; free to all Tues. Phone (330) 452-4096.

GREATER CANTON AMATEUR SPORTS HALL OF FAME, 1414 Market Ave. N., is within a renovated house built in 1908. The hall of fame contains exhibits that recognize the accomplishments of local amateur athletes, some of whom have achieved international prominence. Allow 1 hour minimum. Tues.-Sun. noon-4. Free. Phone (330) 453-1552.

HARRY LONDON CHOCOLATE FACTORY—
see North Canton p. 251.

McKINLEY MUSEUM, 800 McKinley Monument Dr. N.W., off I-77 exit 106, features scientific, industrial and historic displays. The Street of Shops re-creates a late-19th- to early 20th-century Ohio town and includes a pioneer house, general store, print shop and other shops. McKinley Hall features items related to President William McKinley.

Discover World offerings include science displays and hands-on exhibits, a robotic dinosaur and live ponds. The Hoover-Price Planetarium presents nine different sky productions that correspond to changing seasons.

Allow 2 hours minimum. Museum open Mon.-Sat. 9-6, Sun. noon-6, day after Memorial Day-day before Labor Day; Mon.-Sat. 9-5, Sun. noon-5, rest of year. Closed holidays. Planetarium shows daily Memorial Day-day before Labor Day; Sat.-Sun., rest of year. Admission $6; over 59, $5; ages 3-18,

$4; family rate $18. MC, DS, VI. Phone (330) 455-7043.

McKINLEY NATIONAL MEMORIAL, 800 McKinley Monument Dr. N.W., off I-77 exit 106, is a 26-acre national landmark dedicated to the 25th president, William McKinley, who is entombed there along with his wife Ida Saxton McKinley and their two daughters. The patio of the monument provides a fine view of downtown Canton. Allow 30 minutes minimum. Mon.-Sat. 9-6, Sun. noon-6, Memorial Day-Labor Day; Mon.-Sat. 9-5, Sun. noon-5, rest of year. Free. Phone (330) 455-7043.

GEM SAVE **PRO FOOTBALL HALL OF FAME** is at 2121 George Halas Dr. N.W., next to Fawcett Stadium (exit 107A, jct. I-77 and US 62). The hall presents films and memorabilia of professional football history; teams and individual stars are highlighted. The Game Day Stadium Theatre rotates 180 degrees to offer its audience two separate videotape presentations. Access to the hall's research library is available by appointment. Induction ceremonies, parades, an exhibition football game and other events are held in August during the Pro Football Hall of Fame Festival.

Allow 2 hours minimum. Daily 9-8, Memorial Day weekend-Labor Day; 9-5, rest of year. Closed Dec. 25. Admission $12; over 62, $8; ages 6-14, $6; family rate $30 (parents and dependent children). VI. Phone (330) 456-8207.

CAREY (B-3) pop. 3,700, elev. 823′

BASILICA AND NATIONAL SHRINE OF OUR LADY OF CONSOLATION, 315 Clay St., is served by the Conventual Franciscans. The statue of the Virgin Mary was brought to Carey in 1875 from Luxembourg. Shrine devotions are held Sunday at 2:30. Three blocks west of the basilica, the 23-acre park contains a memorial altar and the Stations of the Cross. Daily 24 hours. Phone (419) 396-7107 or 396-3355.

CARROLLTON (C-6) pop. 3,000, elev. 1,138′

Carroll County Convention & Visitors Bureau: 203 2nd St. N.W., P.O. Box 505, Carrollton, OH 44615; phone (330) 627-0103 or (877) 727-0103.

ELDERBERRY LINE is 1 blk. n. of downtown at 203 Second St. N.W. Train trips from Carrollton to nearby Minerva are offered; round-trips are three hours long, including a one-hour stopover in Minerva. Trips depart Sat. at 11, Sun. at 1, mid-June through October 31. Fare $12; ages 1-12, $9. MC, VI. Phone (330) 627-2282.

McCOOK HOUSE AND CIVIL WAR MUSEUM, on the square, is the restored home of the "Fighting McCooks," 16 family members who were Union soldiers. Civil War materials are displayed. Fri.-Sun. 10-5, Sun. 1-5, Memorial Day weekend-Labor Day; Sat. 10-5, Sun. 1-5, day after Labor Day to mid-Oct. Admission $3; over 54, $2.50; ages 6-12, $1. Phone (330) 627-3345 or (800) 600-7172.

CHARDON (A-6) pop. 4,400, elev. 1,230'

SAVE **PIONEER WATERLAND & DRY FUN PARK,** 10661 Kile Rd., is a 75-acre park featuring wet and dry activities for all ages. Facilities include giant waterslides, a lazy innertube ride, paddleboats, miniature golf, a 3-acre cement pool and a play area for young children. A grand prix go-cart race track, bumper cars and golf and batting cages are available on a pay-as-you-play basis. Picnic facilities with grills are available.

Daily 10-8, early June-last weekend in Aug. and Labor Day weekend. Hours may vary; phone ahead. Admission $14.95, children under 40 inches tall free. DS, MC, VI. Phone (440) 951-7507 or 285-0909.

CHILLICOTHE (E-3) pop. 21,900, elev. 632'

Founded in 1796, Chillicothe served as capital of the Northwest Territory and was governed by Gen. Arthur St. Clair 1800-1802. The city was host to the state's first constitutional convention in 1802, and Chillicothe was Ohio's first capital. Now an industrial center, the city has many early 19th-century Greek Revival mansions.

Chillicothe is at the junction of two scenic highways. A picturesque portion of SR 159 runs 34 miles southwest from Lancaster, while an impressive portion of US 50 runs 19 miles northeast from Bainbridge.

Ross-Chillicothe Convention and Visitors Bureau: 25 E. Main St., P.O. Box 353, Chillicothe, OH 45601; phone (740) 702-7677 or (800) 413-4118.

CHILLICOTHE GAZETTE, 50 W. Main St., was first published in 1800 and is the oldest continuously published newspaper west of the Alleghenies. Two wall-mounted cases display written matter from Babylonian times, wooden printing blocks from Asia and a page from the Gutenberg Bible. Mon.-Fri. 8-5; closed major holidays. Free. Phone (740) 773-2111.

HOPEWELL CULTURE NATIONAL HISTORICAL PARK—*see place listing p. 242.*

JAMES M. THOMAS MUSEUM, in the phone company building at 68 E. Main St., exhibits equipment and displays chronicling the history and development of the telephone. Allow 30 minutes minimum. Mon.-Fri. 8:30-5; closed holidays. Free. Phone (740) 772-8200 or (800) 500-3134.

ROSS COUNTY HISTORICAL SOCIETY MUSEUM, 45 W. 5th St., includes McKell Library, 39 W. 5th St., the adjacent Knoles Log House and Franklin House, 80 S. Paint St. Displays include pioneer articles, a prehistoric culture exhibit, Ohio's Constitution Table, a Civil War room, an early Ohio settlement room and a World War I room. The museum also contains a Conestoga wagon and historic toys and dolls.

The Franklin House has a large collection of textiles from the 19th and 20th centuries, furniture and decorative arts. The Knoles Log House is a restored early 19th-century pioneer house. Guided 1-hour tours of the museum and the log house are available. Tues.-Sun. 1-5, Apr.-Aug.; Sat.-Sun. 1-5, Sept.-Dec.; by appointment, rest of year. Closed holidays. Last tour departs 1 hour before closing. Library Tues.-Wed. and Fri.-Sat. 1-5. Admission $4; over 64 and ages 13-21, $2. Fee for library use $2. Phone (740) 772-1936.

"TECUMSEH!"—HISTORICAL OUTDOOR DRAMA, 6.5 mi. n.e. on Delano Rd. off SR 159 at Sugarloaf Mountain Amphitheatre, traces the life of Tecumseh and his struggle to preserve a home for the Shawnee Nation on America's frontier. Inquire about refund and weather policies. For information write "Tecumseh!", Box 73, Chillicothe, OH 45601.

Allow 3 hours minimum. Performances Mon.-Sat. at 8, June 7-Aug. 31. The box office is open Mon.-Sat. 9-9, Mar. 1-Sept. 1. Tickets Mon.-Thurs. $14; under 11, $7. Tickets Fri.-Sat. $16; under 11, $8. Advanced payment is required for all performances. All tickets are held at the box office. Reservations are recommended. All seats are reserved. AX, DS, MC, VI. Phone (866) 775-0700 Mar.-Aug.

Cincinnati

Winston Churchill called Cincinnati "the most beautiful of America's inland cities." Cincinnati's location has much to do with its aesthetic appeal and stable business community. On the north shore of the Ohio River, the downtown section is in a basin surrounded by hills. The city also is near the Ohio River's midpoint and on the Mason-Dixon line, both major factors in its economic development.

Cincinnati was first platted in 1788 by three land speculators. In 1789 Fort Washington was built to protect the settlers from the American Indians, but it was not until the defeat of the Ohio Indians at Fallen Timbers in 1794 that the area became open for further settlement. Cincinnati's accessibility increased in 1811 with the arrival of the *New Orleans,* the first steamboat to reach its shores.

The construction of the Miami and Erie canals in the late 1820s provided farmers with transportation to the city where they could market their produce. Businessmen created new industries to process such raw products as corn, hogs and wheat into the marketable forms of whiskey, pork and flour. Plagued by religious and political conflicts, many Germans immigrated in the 1830s, followed in the 1840s by Irish driven from their country by the potato famine.

By 1850 Cincinnati was the world's largest pork-packing center, a status that brought the nickname Porkopolis. The South became the city's major market. This caused residents' loyalties to be divided with the approach of the Civil War, but the city eventually supported the Union forces.

Following the war, Cincinnati experienced another burst of prosperity as the resumption of trade between North and South created heavy river commerce. In the 1870s Cincinnati businessmen arranged for the building of a railroad to reach their southern markets. The city's industry stabilized but did not grow during the next several decades.

Compared with most cities, Cincinnati was not hampered by the Depression, sheltered again by its river location. Modern Cincinnati businesses have given downtown a facelift. The award-winning Fountain Square is the hub of downtown. Centered on the historic 1871 Tyler Davidson Fountain, which tops a large underground garage, the square is surrounded by modern office buildings and hotels.

With its central location and revitalized downtown atmosphere, the city attracts many companies, including a large number of corporate headquarters. The river community also is considered a convention center.

Near Fountain Square are the Dr. Albert B. Sabin Cincinnati Convention Center and Tower Place at the Carew

Tower. Cinergy Field, linked to downtown by a pedestrian bridge, is home to baseball's Reds, while the Bengals revel in the state-of-the-art, 21st-century Paul Brown Stadium. The Firstar Center features hockey, basketball, circuses, ice shows and concerts.

Yeatman's Cove Park is adorned with fountains, a serpentine wall, concert podium and sculpture garden. Bicentennial Commons at Sawyer Point offers a wide variety of activities with sports facilities, gardens, scenic overlooks and public performance arenas. Each spring 186-acre Eden Park—home to the Cincinnati Art Museum, Cincinnati Art Academy, Murray Seasongood Pavilion, Playhouse in the Park and the Irwin M. Krohn Conservatory—explodes into color with flowering trees and 50,000 daffodils. The riverfront's historical focal point is Public Landing, where riverboats are welcomed and where the Showboat *Majestic* entertains audiences.

Cincinnati is the home of the 33,600-student University of Cincinnati, founded in 1819; phone (513) 556-6000. Xavier University, founded in 1831, offers free guided tours of its 6,400-student campus upon request; phone (513) 745-3301.

Approaches

By Car

Cincinnati straddles I-75, one of the nation's major north-south routes, shuttling traffic from the Canadian border to the north and Florida's Gulf Coast to the south. A shorter artery, I-71, angles through the city, providing a fast route from Louisville, central Ohio and Lake Erie cities.

Both routes join in the Kentucky suburbs to cross the river via the Brent Spence Bridge. From the north they follow separate alignments to the river but are connected across Ohio suburban areas by the Norwood Lateral Expressway (SR 562) and the Ronald Reagan Cross County Highway (SR 126).

I-71 and I-75 provide good access from I-70, a major transcontinental route that bisects Ohio some 55 miles north of the city, and each interchanges with primary city streets.

US 50 and scenic US 52 funnel east-west travelers to the city from the Indiana and Ohio countrysides; these older roads accommodate mostly local traffic. US 52 offers a scenic trip along the Ohio River east of Cincinnati.

I-74 is the principal link from the west, collecting traffic from some of the nation's busiest thoroughfares, I-80 and I-70, as well as highways from the Chicago area. SR 32 (Appalachian Highway) is a good route from rural areas east of the city.

I-275 (Circle Freeway) swings in a full orbit through the Ohio, Kentucky and Indiana environs. It provides a complete bypass of the city proper and interchanges with all major intersecting routes for easy access to downtown. I-471 offers an additional spur from the Kentucky portion

(continued on p. 195)

The Informed Traveler

City Population: 364,000

Elevation: 820 ft.

Sales Tax: The Cincinnati area has a 6 percent sales tax, a 12 percent lodging tax and a 9 percent rental car tax with an additional 9 percent recoupment tax. The northern Kentucky lodging tax is 9.18 percent.

WHOM TO CALL

Emergency: 911

Police (non-emergency): (513) 765-1212

Fire: (513) 241-2525

Time and Temperature: (513) 721-1700

Hospitals: Christ Hospital, (513) 585-2000; Good Samaritan, (513) 872-1400; University Hospital, (513) 584-1000.

WHERE TO LOOK

Newspapers

The two major newspapers are the *Cincinnati Enquirer* (morning) and the *Cincinnati Post* (afternoon). The *Cincinnati Enquirer* publishes a Sunday edition.

Downtowner, a free weekly, details the city's events, attractions and nightlife. It is distributed at hotels, restaurants and shops.

Radio

Cincinnati radio station WLW (700 AM) is a news/talk/weather station; WGUC (90.9 FM) and WUXU (91.7) are members of National Public Radio.

Visitor Information

The Cincinnati Convention and Visitors Bureau, 300 W. 6th St., Cincinnati, OH 45202, distributes a wide array of visitor information, including maps and a helpful visitors' guide. The bureau's office is open Mon.-Fri. 9-5; phone (513) 621-2142 or (800) 246-2987. The bureau also operates a visitors center at Fountain Square Mon.-Sat. 10-6, Sun. noon-5.

TRANSPORTATION

Air Travel

Most major passenger airlines serve the Greater Cincinnati International Airport. Long-term airport parking costs $5 per day, with free shuttle service to the terminals. The Airport Taxi Association offers cabs with fixed fares to and from downtown. The fare is approximately $24 (one to five passengers). Many hotels provide courtesy car service.

Rental Cars

Hertz offers discounts to AAA members; phone (859) 767-3535 or (800) 654-3080.

Rail Service

The Amtrak station, (800) 872-7245, is at 1301 Western Ave. inside historic Union Terminal.

Buses

Greyhound Lines Inc., (800) 231-2222, 1005 Gilbert Ave., is the major company serving the city.

Taxis

Taxis are metered and charge $2.60 for a pickup and $1.60 per mile. There is a minimum charge of $3 and no charge for additional passengers. Taxis can be hailed at downtown hotels or ordered by phone. The largest company is Cincinnati Yellow; phone (513) 241-2100.

Public Transport

Metro operates buses throughout the metropolitan area. The weekday base fare is 65c, 80c during rush hours (6-9 a.m. and 3-6 p.m.) and 50c on weekends. Exact change is required, and zone and transfer charges are additional. Signs at many bus stops list the numbers of the routes that stop there. For route and schedule information phone (513) 621-4455, Mon.-Fri. 6:30 a.m.-6 p.m., 8-4, Sat. Information also is available at MetroCenter Sales, 120 E. Fourth St., Mon.-Fri. 6:30-6; phone (513) 632-7699.

of this circumferential highway into downtown via the Daniel Carter Beard Bridge.

Getting Around

Street System

With the aid of a good city map, driving in Cincinnati is relatively easy. The downtown area is laid out in a grid pattern with streets running either north-south or east-west. The numbered streets run east-west beginning with 2nd Street near the Ohio River; named north-south streets intersect them. East-west address numbers start at Vine Street.

Unless otherwise posted, the speed limit on most streets is 25 or 30 mph. Rush-hour traffic, 7-9 a.m. and 3-6 p.m., should be avoided. Right turns on red are permitted unless otherwise posted. For updated traffic and road construction information, phone the Cincinnati Traffic Hotline at (513) 333-3333.

Parking

Metered parking is found on many downtown streets; be sure to check signs and meters for restricted times and limits. There are several commercial garages and lots, and most hotels provide parking for guests. Municipal garage rates are $1 for the first 2 hours, $2 for each additional hour up to $15 per day.

What To See

ABRAHAM LINCOLN STATUE, in Lytle Park at 4th and Pike sts., is the work of noted sculptor George Grey Barnard.

CAREW TOWER OBSERVATORY, at 5th and Vine sts., is perched 49 stories above ground atop Cincinnati's tallest building and provides excellent views of downtown as well as the surrounding metropolitan area. Mon.-Thurs. 9:30-5:15, Fri.-Sat. 9:30-8:45, Sun. 11-4:45. Admission $2; under 12, $1. Phone (513) 579-9735.

CINCINNATI ART MUSEUM is off I-71 exit 2, following signs to Eden Park. The museum's more than 88 galleries review the visual arts of most major civilizations over the past 6,000 years through sculpture, paintings, prints, musical instruments, costumes, photographs, decorative arts and period rooms. Masterpieces from such artists as Claude Monet, Pablo Picasso and Vincent van Gogh are on display as well as artifacts from Ancient Egypt, Rome and Greece. Asian, African and American Indian works of art also are included. Food is available.

Tues.-Sat. 11-5 (also Wed. 5-9), Sun. noon-6; closed Thanksgiving and Dec. 25. Admission $5; over 54 and students with ID $4; under 18 free. AX, MC, VI. Phone (513) 639-2995.

CINCINNATI FIRE MUSEUM, 315 W. Court St., chronicles firefighting history. The museum contains hands-on exhibits, restored antique firefighting equipment, photographs and memorabilia. Tues.-Fri. 10-4, Sat.-Sun. noon-4; closed holidays. Admission $5; over 54 and ages 2-12, $3. MC, VI. Phone (513) 621-5553.

CINCINNATI NATURE CENTER, n. on I-275 to exit 63B, then 1 mi. e. on SR 32, n. on Glen Este-Withamsville Rd., e. on Batavia Pike and 3.5 mi. n.e. to 4949 Tealtown Rd., contains 790 acres with numerous nature trails covering more than 14 miles. The Nature Center building houses a library, displays and a bird-viewing area. Allow 2 hours minimum. Park open daily dawn-dusk. Nature Center open Mon.-Sat. 9-5, Sun. 1-5; closed holidays. Admission Mon.-Fri. $3; ages 3-12, $1. Admission Sat.-Sun. $5; ages 3-12, $1. Phone (513) 831-1711.

CINCINNATI ZOO AND BOTANICAL GARDEN is reached via I-75 exit 6, following signs to the Auto Gate. In a garden setting, the zoo houses some of the world's rarest animals, including Sumatran rhinoceroses, white Bengal tigers and lowland gorillas. Manatee Springs house two manatees, alligators and crocodiles; orangutans reside in the Jungle Trail; Vanishing Giants is home to elephants, giraffes and okapi; and the highlight of Lords of the Arctic is an underwater view of four young polar bears. Animal shows are offered in the summer, as are tram and train rides. More than 3,000 varieties of plants grace the grounds.

Allow 3 hours minimum. Daily 8-6, Memorial Day weekend-Labor Day; 9-5 (also Sun.-Thurs. 5-9, Fri.- Sat. 5-9:30, late Nov.-early Jan. during the Festival of Lights), rest of year. Admission $11.50; over 62, $9; ages 2-12, $6. Children's zoo $1. Parking $6.50. Phone (513) 281-4700 or (800) 944-4776.

CONEY ISLAND, off I-275 at 6201 Kellogg Ave., offers a range of recreational activities. Visitors can swim in the Sunlite Pool which, at 200 feet wide and more than 400 feet long, is said to be the world's largest recirculating pool. The park also has a 500-foot-long waterslide and a 180-foot-long water coaster. Pedal boats, bumper boats, a miniature golf course and rides designed for children are offered, along with a garden and areas for picnicking and volleyball.

Allow 2 hours minimum. Pool open daily 10-8, rides noon-9, Memorial Day weekend-Labor Day. Pool and rides $16.95; ages 4-11, $14.95; over 54, $12.95. Pool only $11.95; ages 4-11, $8.95; over 54, $7.95. Parking $4. MC, VI. Phone (513) 232-8230.

CONTEMPORARY ARTS CENTER, 115 E. 5th St., presents changing exhibits of paintings, sculpture and photography. Mon.-Sat. 10-6, Sun. noon-5; closed holidays. Admission $3.50, over 61 and students with ID $2, under 12 free; free to all Mon. Phone (513) 345-8400.

HARRIET BEECHER STOWE HOUSE, 2950 Gilbert Ave., was the Cincinnati home of the author of "Uncle Tom's Cabin," the novel that brought the

Destination Cincinnati

Cincinnati Museum Center at Union Terminal.
Take a journey of the imaginary kind by watching an OMNIMAX movie or exploring the museums. (See listing page 199)

*F*or the Queen City the Three Rs have always been paramount: River, Railroad and Recreation.

*S*hipping on the Ohio River, the Miami and Erie canals and the great railroads of the late 19th and early 20th centuries made Cincinnati an industrial giant which spent its wealth on such recreational amenities as a great symphony orchestra, zoo and several museums.

The Beast at Paramount's Kings Island, Kings Mills. For more than 20 years The Beast has been churning stomachs and providing the wind-swept look to brave souls. (See listing page 202)

*P*laces included in this AAA Destination City:

Tiger cub, Cincinnati Zoo and Botanical Garden. This tiger may aspire to join his distant cousins when the Bengals take to the field at Paul Brown Stadium in autumn. (See listing page 195)

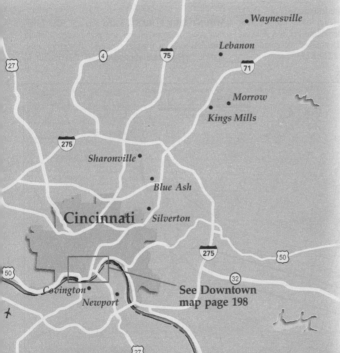

Waynesville

Lebanon

Morrow

Kings Mills

Sharonville

Blue Ash

Cincinnati Silverton

Covington

Newport

See Downtown
map page 198

Ripley

Union

Cincinnati Art Museum. Centuries are bridged when viewing this family scene. (See listing page 195)

Irwin M. Krohn Conservatory, Cincinnati. During the annual Butterfly Show, butterflies swoop and flutter among the lush tropical plants. (See listing page 198)

evils of slavery to the attention of the world. Exhibits describe the Beecher family, the abolitionist movement and the history of African-Americans. Allow 30 minutes minimum. Tues.-Thurs. 10-4; closed major holidays. Donations. Phone (513) 632-5120.

HEBREW UNION COLLEGE—JEWISH INSTITUTE OF RELIGION is at 3101 Clifton Ave. The Skirball Museum Cincinnati Branch, in Mayerson Hall, houses displays exploring the cultural heritage of Jewish people, focusing on immigration, American Judaism, archeology, the Torah, Jewish life cycles and festivals and the Holocaust.

The American Jewish Archives is a research facility for American Jewish history. The Klau Library Rare Book Room contains collections of incunabula, periodicals and ancient manuscripts. Guided tours of the 150-student campus are available by appointment. Museum open Mon.-Thurs. 11-4, Sun. 2-5. Library open Mon.-Fri. 8-5. Closed major holidays. Free. Donations accepted for guided tours. Phone (513) 221-1875.

HERITAGE VILLAGE MUSEUM— *see Sharonville in Cincinnati vicinity p. 203.*

HILLEL JEWISH STUDENT CENTER, across from the University of Cincinnati campus at 2615 Clifton Ave., contains a collection of antique architectural Judaica from synagogues throughout the Midwest. The complex also displays commissioned Jewish ritual objects and changing art exhibits. A small library is available. Mon.-Thurs. 9-5, Fri. 9-3; closed holidays. Free. Phone (513) 221-6728.

IRWIN M. KROHN CONSERVATORY, in Eden Park, has permanent and six seasonal displays of flowers and plants. Permanent plantings include desert, orchid and tropical rain forest flora. Guided tours are offered by reservation. Daily 10-5; extended hours in mid-Dec. Donations. Phone (513) 421-4086.

MOUNT AIRY FOREST, 1,466 acres at 5083 Colerain Ave., features hiking and picnic areas. Mount Airy Arboretum displays lilacs, flowering crab apples, azaleas and rhododendrons that bloom in

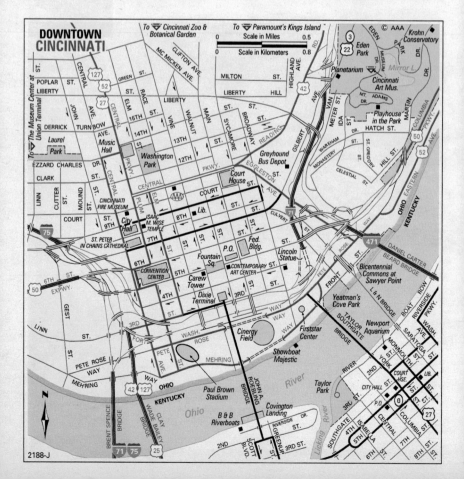

spring. Dwarf evergreens decorate the grounds. Guided tours are given by appointment. Daily 6 a.m.-10 p.m. Free. Phone (513) 352-4080.

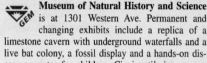 **THE MUSEUM CENTER AT UNION TERMINAL** is off I-75N to Ezzard Charles Dr. The center is home to Cinergy Children's Museum, the Museum of Natural History & Science, the Cincinnati Historical Society Library and an OMNIMAX theater. The restored Art Deco-style train station was a major departure point for troops during World War II and is a National Historic Landmark. The building features several large mosaic tile murals created in the 1930s. Food is available.

Allow 2 hours minimum. Museums open Mon.-Sat. 10-5, Sun. 11-6 (closes at 3 Dec. 24); closed Thanksgiving and Dec. 25. Admission for each museum $6.75; over 59, $5.75; ages 3-12, $4.75. Admission to all museums for ages 1-2, $3.75. Combination ticket to the museums and the OMNIMAX is available. AX, DS, MC, VI. Phone (513) 287-7000 or (800) 733-2077, or TTY (800) 750-0750.

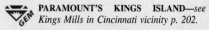 **Cincinnati History Museum** is at 1301 Western Ave. Various exhibits relate the history of Cincinnati, including a re-creation of the 1850s Public Landing, a World War II exhibit, vintage automobiles, a 1920s streetcar and various changing displays. A research library contains books, manuscripts, photographs and graphics pertaining to the histories of Cincinnati, Hamilton County and southwestern Ohio.

Cinergy Children's Museum is at 1301 Western Ave. The museum's nine hands-on exhibit areas are designed for infants to 10-year-old children. "Waterworks," which simulates a river, contains a bridge, boats, dam, locks and a waterfall. An aquarium houses fish and turtles; a wooded area includes a cave, stuffed animals, tunnels and fossils; and an energy exhibit allows kids to see how pulleys, treadmills and pneumatic tubes work. Also included is an indoor play area for infants and toddlers.

Museum of Natural History and Science is at 1301 Western Ave. Permanent and changing exhibits include a replica of a limestone cavern with underground waterfalls and a live bat colony, a fossil display and a hands-on discovery center for children. Cincinnati's ice age re-creates a prehistoric glacial environment.

The Robert D. Linder Family OMNIMAX Theater is at 1301 Western Ave. The theater presents various shows on the hour Mon.-Fri. 11-4 and 7-8 (also Fri. 8-9 p.m.), Sat.-Sun. and holidays 11-5 (also Sat. 7-9 p.m.), June-Aug.; Mon. at 1, 2 and 3, Tues.-Thurs. at 1, 2, 3, 7 and 8, Fri. at 1, 2, 3, 7, 8 and 9, Sat. 11-9, Sun. 11-6, rest of year. Phone for titles and to verify show times. Admission $6.50; over 59, $5.50; ages 3-12, $4.50. AX, DS, MC, VI. Phone (513) 287-7000.

PARAMOUNT'S KINGS ISLAND—*see Kings Mills in Cincinnati vicinity p. 202.*

ST. PETER IN CHAINS CATHEDRAL, 8th and Plum sts., was dedicated in 1845 and renovated in 1957. An outstanding example of Greek Revival architecture, this Roman Catholic cathedral contains a 25-foot gold leaf reredos in the Blessed Sacrament Chapel. Mon.-Fri. 6:30-6, Sat. 10-6, Sun. 8-noon and 5-7. Guided tours are conducted at noon the second Sun. of each month. Phone (513) 421-5354.

SURF CINCINNATI WATERPARK, 11460 Sebring Dr., offers a half-acre wave pool, an inner tube ride, body flumes, speed slides, a small pool and beach for children and a sun deck. Food and picnic areas are available. Daily 11-7, Memorial Day weekend-Labor Day. Phone ahead to verify schedule. Admission $15; ages 6-12, $7.50. Admission after 4, $5. AX, DS, MC, VI. Phone (513) 742-0620.

WILLIAM HOWARD TAFT NATIONAL HISTORIC SITE, 2038 Auburn Ave., is the birthplace and boyhood home of the 27th president and 10th chief justice of the United States. The Greek Revival brick house has four rooms furnished to reflect the Taft's family life 1857-77. Other rooms have exhibits depicting the Taft family and President Taft's devotion

to his public career. Tours begin in the Taft Education center next door. Daily 8-4; closed Jan. 1, Thanksgiving and Dec. 25. Free. Phone (513) 684-3262.

What To Do

Sightseeing

Boat Tours

A river view of Cincinnati is possible aboard BB Riverboats *(see attraction listing p. 205)* in nearby Covington, Ky.

Carriage Tours

A guided tour is a good way to become familiar with the city. For those who would like to navigate the downtown area in 18th- and 19th-century style, horse-drawn carriage tours leave from Fountain Square.

Sports and Recreation

Cincinnati's city parks, Hamilton County's 16 parks and several state parks are easily accessible to Cincinnati visitors. Among these choices, the sports-minded can find facilities for almost any activity. Many of the parks have tennis courts, **camping** sites and lakes for **boating**, **fishing** and **swimming.**

Hiking trails are plentiful, especially at Mount Airy Forest. Eden Park, 186 acres off Gilbert Avenue between Elsinore and Morris, offers picnic facilities, lakes for **ice skating** and an exercise course. An enjoyable activity is a stroll along the riverfront at Bicentennial Commons at Sawyer Point or Yeatman's Cove Park. For information about city park facilities phone (513) 352-4080.

There are many **golf** courses in the area, including seven city-owned and seven county-owned

courses. The most well-known course is The Golf Center at Kings Island, (513) 398-7700, at Paramount's Kings Island near Kings Mills.

For those more interested in spectator sports, the city has much to offer. When in Cincinnati, if your favorite **baseball** team is not the Reds, it is best to keep that fact under your hat. World Series winners in 1975, 1976 and 1990, the Big Red Machine has a large following. The Reds play at Cinergy Field. For ticket and schedule information phone (513) 421-4510.

When all eyes turn from the diamond to the gridiron, **football's** Cincinnati Bengals become the city's stars. The team plays at the Paul Brown Stadium which opened in 2000. They gained a lofty status when they captured the 1981 and 1988 American Football Conference championships. For ticket and schedule information phone (513) 621-3550.

Tennis fans won't want to miss the Tennis Masters Series Cincinnati, Aug. 1-11, 2002, in nearby Mason; phone (513) 651-0303. And Cincinnati has two professional **soccer** teams, the A-league Riverhawks and the W-league Ladyhawks. Both teams play at Galbreath Field, near Kings Island, May through September. For ticket information phone (513) 853-7070.

Sports fans can head indoors October through March to root for the American **Hockey** League's Cincinnati Mighty Ducks. The team plays at Cincinnati Gardens; phone (513) 351-3999 for ticket information. Representing the East Coast Hockey League, the Cincinnati Cyclones play at the Firstar Center, 100 Broadway next to Cinergy Field; phone (513) 421-7825.

Perhaps because of Cincinnati's proximity to Kentucky, **horse racing** events are popular. River Downs

Racetrack, (513) 232-8000, at 6301 Kellogg Ave., offers Thoroughbred racing late April through Labor Day. The Kentucky Speedway, in nearby Sparta, Ky., hosts **automobile racing** mid-May to mid-August; phone (888) 652-7223 for ticket information.

Note: Policies vary concerning admittance of children to pari-mutuel betting facilities. Phone for information.

Shopping

Whether you are looking for designer fashions or clothing from grandmother's attic, it can be found in Cincinnati's array of department stores, boutiques and specialty shops. Downtown's major department stores are Lazarus, 5th and Race streets, and Saks Fifth Avenue, 101 W. 5th St. The Carew Tower Arcade and Tower Place offer more than 70 shops and eateries.

Trend setters must visit Mount Adams, a San Francisco-style hillside shopping and dining area. Novelty shops and fashion boutiques are scattered among restaurants, nightspots and parks. Collegiate-style attire is found in Clifton, where many shops cater to University of Cincinnati students.

Consumer frenzy also can be satisfied at the shopping malls and centers, including Eastgate Mall, I-275 exit 63; Florence Mall, in Florence, Ky.; Forest Fair Mall, I-275 exit 39; Kenwood Towne Centre, Kenwood and Montgomery roads; Northgate Mall, I-275 exit 33; and Tri-County Mall, I-275 exit 42.

Bargain hunters willing to spend time traveling will particularly enjoy shopping at Dry Ridge Outlet Center 35 miles south in Dry Ridge, Ky., and the VF Factory Outlet, 55 miles southwest in Carrollton, Ky. Die-hard discount shoppers can travel 60 miles northeast to Ohio Factory Shops and the Jeffersonville Outlet Center, both in Jeffersonville.

Bass Pro Shops Outdoor World, 300 Forest Fair Dr., features an aquarium, waterfall, wildlife exhibits and sporting demonstrations; phone (513) 826-5200.

Theater and Concerts

The city's arts and entertainment centerpiece is the Arnoff Center for the Performing Arts, 650 Walnut St. between 6th and 7th streets; (513) 721-3344. The center's three theaters present more than 10,000 exhibits and performances throughout the year, including Broadway shows and children's theater. In addition, the center is the main performance hall for the Cincinnati Ballet; phone (513) 621-5219 for information.

Other professional theaters include Playhouse in the Park, (513) 421-3888, with its two theaters, the Robert S. Marx and the Shelterhouse, on Mount Adams Circle in Eden Park. These stages present modern American and European plays September through June.

The Showboat *Majestic*, (513) 241-6550, draws theatergoers to the riverfront April to mid-October. Docked at the Public Landing behind The Firstar Center, it is one of the last original floating theaters still in operation. Dramas, comedies, old-fashioned melodramas and musical productions are performed on the old showboat Wednesday through Saturday evenings and Sunday afternoons and evenings.

The Ensemble Theatre of Cincinnati, (513) 421-3555, downtown at 1127 Vine St., presents live theatrical shows season from September through June. Performances of new plays and well-known modern works are given Wednesday through Saturday evenings and Sunday afternoons.

The SAVE Cincinnati Shakespeare Festival Theatre Company performs seven plays from September through June; phone (513) 381-2273 for additional information.

Music Hall, 1241 Elm St., was built by philanthropic leaders in 1878 and is fondly referred to as the Grand Dame of the Queen City. The interior of the red brick edifice is adorned with crystal chandeliers and woodwork. The hall is a fitting home to the Cincinnati Pops Orchestra and the Cincinnati Symphony; phone (513) 381-3300. The Cincinnati Opera also performs in Music Hall; its mid-June to mid-July season includes grand operas, operettas and musicals. Phone (513) 241-2742 for more information.

The University of Cincinnati's College Conservatory of Music at Clifton and Calhoun streets makes impressive contributions to the area's music scene. A prominent music school, the 1,400-student college offers a variety of performing arts entertainment, ranging from opera and musical theater to dance and drama. There are more than 800 performances a year and many of them are free; phone (513) 556-4183 for schedule and ticket information.

Concerts by popular entertainers and groups are often held at the Riverbend Music Center, (513) 232-6220, the summer home of the Cincinnati Symphony and the Cincinnati Pops Orchestra. The Cincinnati Gardens, (513) 631-8287, and The Firstar Center, (513) 421-4111, also host many entertainment and sporting events.

Special Events

Cincinnatians are proud of their city and don't hesitate to celebrate their heritage. The Appalachian Folk Festival held at Coney Island in May begins the array of events. This festival is said to be the largest craft show in the nation.

During two weekends in May, the city's renowned music community celebrates May Festival, the oldest continuing festival of choral and orchestral music in the United States. The tradition began in 1873; performances consist of a 200-voice chorus accompanied by the Cincinnati Symphony and joined by top-name guest conductors and opera singers.

Restaurateurs show off their talents on Memorial Day weekend during the Taste of Cincinnati, a sidewalk smorgasbord along Central Parkway.

Cincinnati heralds the summer season with its Summerfair in mid-June. More than 200 artists gather at Coney Island and display their works, while musicians perform classical, pop, country and jazz pieces.

The summer draws to a close in September with Cincinnati's largest celebration, Riverfest. In honor of their river heritage, more than 500,000 people gather along the riverfront to watch water skiing, sky diving and air shows, and enjoy riverboat cruises. The festival climaxes with a spectacular fireworks display accompanied by a soundtrack broadcast by a radio station.

Another major end-of-summer event is the Harvest Home Fair, held the weekend following Labor Day in nearby Cheviot. A parade marks the traditional kickoff

for what is dubbed "the biggest little fair in Ohio." Fairgoers can view horse, artwork and flower shows, attend a 4-H auction, play jumbo poker or visit a petting zoo, among other diversions. Food, drink and stage entertainment are available.

With more than half the city's population of German ancestry, it is little wonder Oktoberfest Zinzinnati is celebrated with almost as much vigor as its counterpart in Munich, Germany. During a mid-September weekend, six blocks of downtown around Fountain Square are transformed into a German *biergarten*, complete with music, dancing, singing and, of course, lots of sauerkraut and beer.

The Cincinnati Vicinity

BLUE ASH (E-1) pop. 11,900, elev. 846'

BLUE ASH BICENTENNIAL VETERANS MEMORIAL is downtown at Hunt and Cooper rds. Created for the town's 1991 bicentennial celebration, the memorial consists of 11 life-size statues of members of the armed forces representing America's major wars from the American Revolution to the Persian Gulf War. Behind each statue flies a U.S. flag from the corresponding era. Daily 24 hours. Free. Phone (513) 745-8510.

KINGS MILLS (E-2)

THE BEACH WATERPARK, off I-71 exit 25 at 2590 Waterpark Dr., is a 35-acre park with more than 30 waterslides and rides, inner tube rides, children's water areas, a wave pool, a leisure pool, sand volleyball courts and live entertainment. Food is available. Open daily at 10, Memorial Day weekend-Labor Day; closing times vary. All-day pass $23.95, over 59 and under 48 inches tall $7.95. AX, DS, MC, VI. Phone (513) 398-7946 or (800) 886-7946.

PARAMOUNT'S KINGS ISLAND is on Kings Island Dr., .5 mi. s.w. via I-71 exit 25A. This family entertainment park offers more than 80 rides and attractions, including 13 roller coasters. Thrills are provided by the Son of Beast wooden, looping roller coaster; the 26-story, free-fall gyro ride Drop Zone; the face-to-face inverted Face/Off; and The Beast, reputed to be the world's longest wooden roller coaster.

Nickelodeon Central features one of the first inverted roller coasters for children, while favorite cartoon characters populate Hanna-Barbera Land. WaterWorks, the park's 30-acre water playground, offers 22 waterslides, a heated wave pool and a surfing pool. An array of live shows rounds out the fun.

Allow a full day. Park opens daily at 9, rides begin operation at 10, May 24-Aug. 25, Aug. 31-Sept. 2; Sat.-Sun., Apr. 6-May 19 and Sept. 28-Nov. 3. Closing times vary. WaterWorks open daily at 11, May 25-Aug. 25 (weather permitting). Both parks closed June 2. Admission (includes WaterWorks) $41.99; over 59,

ages 3-6 or under 48 inches tall $20.99. Parking $8. DS, MC, VI. To confirm hours and prices phone (513) 754-5700 or (800) 288-0808.

LEBANON (E-2) pop. 10,500, elev. 696'

Old houses and buildings, including the 1803 Golden Lamb Inn *(see attraction listing),* give Lebanon a Colonial atmosphere that is unusual in the Midwest. Many of the city's historic structures are within an area bounded by Orchard Avenue and West, Silver, Pleasant and High streets; most are private residences and are closed to the public.

The Lebanon Raceway, 665 N. Broadway, presents harness racing from October through May. For information phone (513) 932-4936.

Note: Policies vary concerning admittance of children to pari-mutuel betting facilities. Phone for information.

Warren County Convention & Visitors Bureau: 1073 Oregonia Rd., Suite A, P.O. Box 239, Lebanon, OH 45036; phone (513) 925-1138 or (800) 791-4386.

Self-guiding tours: A map detailing a tour of the historic area is available at Warren County Historical Society Museum *(see attraction listing).*

Shopping areas: Downtown Lebanon offers more than 50 antiques and specialty shops.

(SAVE) **FORT ANCIENT** is 7 mi. s.e. off Middleboro Rd. on SR 350. A prehistoric earthwork built on a plateau by the Hopewell Indians, Fort Ancient encompasses about 100 acres containing circular mounds used as a calendar, and the remains of village sites. Fort Ancient Museum illustrates the religion, customs and cultures of the prehistoric period. Picnic facilities and hiking trails are available.

Daily 10-5, Memorial Day weekend-Labor Day; Wed.-Sun. 10-5, Mar. 1-day before Memorial Day weekend and day after Labor Day-Nov. 30. Admission $5; ages 6-12, $1.25. AX, DS, MC, VI. Phone (513) 932-4421.

GLENDOWER STATE MEMORIAL, 3 blks. s.w. of jct. US 42 and SR 123 on US 42, is a restored 1840 Greek Revival mansion reflecting 19th-century Ohio home life. The structure is furnished in period. Wed.-Sat. noon-4, Sun. 1-4, first Wed. in June -Labor Day; Sat. noon-4, Sun. 1-4, day after Labor Day-Oct. 31 Admission $3, students with ID $1. Phone (513) 932-1817.

THE GOLDEN LAMB INN is on US 42 at SRs 63 and 123 (27 S. Broadway). Built in 1803, the inn houses an extensive collection of Shaker furniture and other items, including toys from the late 1890s. Food is available. Allow 30 minutes minimum. Daily 10:30-9. Free. Phone (513) 932-5065.

WARREN COUNTY HISTORICAL SOCIETY MUSEUM, on US 42 just s. of SR 63 at 105 S. Broadway, displays artifacts dating from prehistoric times to the present. Highlights include paleontology and archeology collections, a village green exhibit and a Shaker gallery. A local history and genealogy library also is on the premises. Maps detailing driving and walking tours of Lebanon are available. Allow 1 hour minimum. Tues.-Sat. 9-4, Sun. noon-4; closed holidays. Admission $3; grades K-12, $1. AX, MC, VI ($10). Phone (513) 932-1817.

MORROW (E-2) pop. 1,200, elev. 640′

RECREATIONAL ACTIVITIES

Horseback Riding

• [SAVE] **The Dude Ranch,** on the Ripple Creek Farm at 3205 Waynesville Rd. Write 4010 Executive Park Dr., Suite 100, Cincinnati, OH 45241. Rides and cattle drives daily. Phone (513) 956-8099.

WINERIES

• **Valley Vineyards,** 2.5 mi. s.w. at 2276 E. US 22/SR 3. Mon.-Thurs. 11-8, Fri.-Sat. 11-11, Sun. 1-6; closed Jan. 1, Thanksgiving and Dec. 25. Phone (513) 899-2485.

RIPLEY (F-2) pop. 1,800, elev. 447′

RANKIN HOUSE STATE MEMORIAL, n. off US 52 on Rankin Hill, is the restored home of Rev.

John Rankin, an early Ohio abolitionist. A station on the Underground Railroad, the house is reputedly the one in which Eliza, a character in "Uncle Tom's Cabin," found refuge after crossing the ice on the Ohio River. Wed.-Sat. 10-5, Sun. noon-5, Memorial Day weekend-Labor Day; Sat. 10-5, Sun. noon-5, day after Labor Day-Oct. 31. Admission $2; ages 6-12, 75c. Phone (937) 392-1627.

SHARONVILLE (E-1) pop. 13,200

[SAVE] **HERITAGE VILLAGE MUSEUM,** 1 mi. s. of I-275 exit 46 on US 42, is in Sharon Woods Park. The village consists of restored 19th-century buildings brought from other sections of southwest Ohio.

A medical office exhibits Civil War medical and pharmaceutical equipment. The 1804 Kemper Log House contains period furnishings. Greek Revival, rural Federal and Carpenter Gothic architecture are represented. Outbuildings include an early 1800s barn with agricultural tools, a corncrib, an icehouse and a smokehouse. Allow 2 hours minimum. Wed.-Sat. noon-4, Sun. 1-5, May-Oct.; Sat. noon-4, Sun. 1-5, in Apr. and Nov.; phone for Dec. schedule. Admission $5; over 59, $4; ages 5-11, $3. MC, VI ($20). Phone (513) 563-9484.

SILVERTON (E-1) pop. 5,000, elev. 840′

WINERIES

• **Meier's Wine Cellars** is off I-71 exit 12, then s. on Montgomery Rd. and 1 mi. w. to 6955 Plainfield Rd. Mon.-Sat. 9-5. Guided tours begin 10 minutes before the hour Mon.-Sat. 10-3, June-Oct. Closed Jan. 1, Thanksgiving and Dec. 25. Phone (513) 891-2900 or (800) 346-2941.

WAYNESVILLE (E-2) pop. 1,900, elev. 940′

Waynesville, renowned throughout the state for its antiques, has more than 30 antiques shops and nearly as many specialty shops housed in historic buildings along brick sidewalks sporting flower boxes and copper street lamps.

Waynesville Area Chamber of Commerce: 10 B Main St., P.O. Box 281, Waynesville, OH 45068; phone (513) 897-8855.

CAESAR CREEK STATE PARK, Clarksville Rd. off SR 73, 6 mi. w. of jct. I-71, with a 2,800-acre lake offers a variety of recreational opportunities and also serves as a nature preserve and wildlife area, where licensed hunting is permitted in season. The Caesar Creek Lake Visitor Center provides information about the role of the Army Corps of Engineers in water resource management and flood control. Trilobite fossils and American Indian artifacts also are displayed.

Allow 1 hour minimum. Park and village open daily dawn-dusk. Visitor center open Mon.-Fri. and holidays 8-4, Sat.-Sun. 8-5, Apr.-Oct. Free. Phone (513) 897-3055. *See Recreation Chart and the AAA Great Lakes CampBook.*

Pioneer Village is at 3999 Pioneer Village Rd. This re-created 19th-century town consists of rebuilt and restored structures, including a Quaker meetinghouse and the 1807 Levi Lukens house, the only building original to the site. Other buildings include a toll house, broom shop, weaver's shop and maple syrup shed. Allow 1 hour minimum. Buildings open by appointment Sat.-Sun. 9-8.

Nearby Indiana

AURORA pop. 3,800, elev. 459′

A hilly town on the Ohio River, Aurora has been home to such notables as Judge Jesse Holman, one of Indiana's first supreme court justices, and Edwin C. Hill and Elmer Davis, popular writers and radio commentators of the early 1900s. Not long after the town was founded in 1819, Judge Holman chose Aurora as its name, in honor of the goddess of dawn.

SAVE **HILLFOREST**, 213 Fifth St., was the residence of Thomas Gaff, an Ohio Valley industrialist. Built in 1855, the 10-acre estate reflects the grand lifestyle of the state's wealthy citizens during the mid- to late 1800s. The Italian Renaissance mansion's "steamboat" verandas and wrought-iron balconies offer excellent views of the Ohio River. Allow 1 hour minimum. Tues.-Sun. 1-5 (also Mon. 1-5, Memorial Day-Labor Day) Cincinnati time, Apr. 1-Dec. 30. Admission $5; ages 7-18, $2.50. MC, VI ($10). Phone (812) 926-0087.

LAWRENCEBURG pop. 4,400, elev. 486′

Lawrenceburg, founded on a bend in the Ohio River in 1803 by Capt. Samuel Vance, grew quickly after the advent of steamboat shipping. During this era the city's Gamblers' Row was notorious from Pittsburgh to New Orleans. In 1819 Lawrenceburg became the site of the state's first "skyscraper"— The Jessie Hunt House, a three-story brick building at Walnut and High streets. Due to its location, Lawrenceburg offers many scenic views of the river as well as numerous year-round recreational activities.

Dearborn County Convention and Tourism Bureau: 555 E. Eads Pkwy., P.O. Box 4086, Lawrenceburg, IN 47025; phone (812) 537-0814 or (800) 322-8198.

Self-guiding tours: A brochure detailing a walking tour of downtown is available for 25c from Dearborn County Historical Society in the 1818 home of Capt. Samuel Vance at 508 W. High St.; phone (812) 537-4075.

CASINOS

• *Argosy VI* departs from 777 Argosy Pkwy. Cruises depart every 2 hours Sun.-Thurs. 9 a.m.-1 a.m., Fri.-Sat. and holidays 9 a.m.-3 a.m. Phone (888) 274-6797.

METAMORA pop. 900

Old Metamora, next to the Whitewater Canal State Historic Site *(see attraction listing)*, in Metamora is a capsule version of a 19th-century canal town, complete with one of the few operating aqueducts in the nation. The many restored period buildings contain an array of interesting restaurants as well as crafts, art and specialty shops. Flags posted on buildings in Old Metamora indicate when an establishment is open for business. The complex is open mid-April to mid-December; phone (765) 647-2109.

WHITEWATER CANAL STATE HISTORIC SITE, on US 52 just s. of town, is a restored 14-mile section of the old waterway built 1836-47. A replica of an 1840s flat-bottom boat, pulled by a team of horses, takes visitors on canal rides; historical narration is provided. Visitors can purchase cornmeal and corn grits at the restored, operating 1845 gristmill. Concerts and performances are staged periodically in a 19th-century-style gazebo bandstand. Picnic facilities are near the gristmill.

Allow 1 hour minimum. Gristmill open Tues.-Sun. 9-5, mid-Mar. to mid-Dec. Closed major holidays, except Memorial Day, July 4 and Labor Day. Canalboat operates on the hour Tues.-Fri. noon-4, Sat.-Sun. noon-4, May-Oct. (weather permitting). Site and gristmill free. Canalboat fare $1, under 3 free. Phone (765) 647-6512.

RISING SUN pop. 2,300, elev. 420′

CASINOS

• **Grand Victoria**, 600 Grand Victoria Dr. Gambling cruises depart every 2 hours Sun.-Thurs. 9:30 a.m.-1:30 a.m., Fri.-Sat. 9:30 a.m.-5:30 a.m. Phone (800) 472-6311.

VEVAY elev. 525′

The area around Vevay was settled in the late 18th and early 19th centuries by French and Swiss immigrants. Many historic houses of Greek Revival, Federal, Italianate and Gothic architecture remain. Vevay was the 1837 birthplace of Edward

Eggleston, editor and author of such works as "The Hoosier Schoolmaster" and "The Hoosier Schoolboy."

Switzerland County Welcome Center: 105 W. Pike St., P.O. Box 149, Vevay, IN 47043; phone (812) 427-3237 or (800) 435-5688.

SWITZERLAND COUNTY HISTORICAL SOCIETY MUSEUM, at Main and Market sts., 2 blks. e. of SR 56 on SR 156, is in the former Vevay Presbyterian Church, built in 1860. Exhibits include items pertaining to local history, steamboat models and Indiana's first piano. Guided tours are available. Allow 30 minutes minimum. Daily noon-4, Apr.-Oct.; by appointment rest of year. Admission $1, under 14 free with parent. Phone (812) 427-3560.

CASINOS

• **Belterra,** 7777 Belterra Dr. Sun.-Thurs. 9:30-3:30, Fri.-Sat. 9:30-5. Phone (812) 427-7777 or (888) 235-8377.

Nearby Kentucky

CARROLLTON pop. 3,700, elev. 404'

Carrollton, on a bend where the Ohio and Kentucky rivers meet, was established in 1794 as Port William. It was renamed in 1838 for Charles Carroll, a native of Maryland and a signer of the Declaration of Independence. The city is one of the largest burley tobacco markets in the world.

Carrollton/Carroll County Tourism and Convention Commission: P.O. Box 293, Carrollton, KY 41008; phone (502) 732-7036 or (800) 325-4290.

GENERAL BUTLER STATE RESORT PARK, 2 mi. s.e. on SR 227, is a multi-use, year-round recreation area. Facilities include a boat dock, rentals of paddleboats, rowboats and canoes, basketball courts, a nine-hole golf course, a miniature golf course and tennis courts. The furnished home of Kentucky's Butler family, which included Gens. William Orlando and Thomas Butler, also is on the park grounds.

Park open daily dawn-11 p.m.; closed Dec. 21-25. Tours of the Butler House are given on the hour 10-11 and 1-3, Feb. 1 to mid-Dec. Park free. House $3; ages 6-12, $1. AX, DS, MC, VI. Phone (502) 732-4384. *See Recreation Chart in Kentucky/Tennessee TourBook and the AAA Southeastern CampBook.*

COVINGTON pop. 43,300, elev. 515'

Three bridges spanning the Ohio River connect Covington to Cincinnati. During the Civil War Covington's ties with its northern neighbor greatly divided the people's loyalty. The connection has spurred industrial ventures and trade between the two states and has made Covington a part of the Cincinnati metropolitan area.

The five- to six-block area making up Main-Strasse Village is a restored 19th-century German neighborhood. Shops and restaurants are housed in renovated buildings. Of interest in the village is the Goose Girl Fountain, a life-size bronze sculpture of a German maiden carrying two geese to the market. Greek-born sculptor Eleftherios Karkadoulias destroyed the mold from which the fountain was cast, making the sculpture a unique piece.

Turfway Park, about 10 miles southwest off I-75 exit 182 at 7500 Turfway Rd., is the scene of Thoroughbred racing in the fall; phone (859) 371-0200 or (800) 733-0200 for exact dates.

Note: Policies concerning admittance of children to pari-mutuel betting facilities vary. Phone for information.

Northern Kentucky Convention and Visitor Center: 605 Philadelphia St., Covington, KY 41011; phone (859) 655-4159 or (800) 354-9718.

BB RIVERBOATS, departing from the foot of Madison Ave., offers 1-hour narrated sightseeing cruises on the Ohio River. Lunch and dinner cruises also are available. Cruises depart several times daily, May-Oct. Fare $12.50; over 59, $11.50; ages 4-12, $6.25. Reservations are recommended. AX, DS, MC, VI. Phone (859) 261-8500 or (800) 261-8586.

CARROLL CHIMES BELL TOWER, 6th and Philadelphia sts. in MainStrasse Village (Goebel Park), is a 43-bell carillon in a German Gothic clock tower. On the hour the bells chime and mechanical figures move onto a balcony and act out the story of the Pied Piper of Hamelin. The tower is illuminated after dark April through December. An adjacent visitor center offers an audiovisual presentation on the half-hour showcasing northern Kentucky and Cincinnati attractions.

Allow 30 minutes minimum. Visitor center daily 9-5; closed Jan. 1, Thanksgiving and Dec. 25. Free. Phone (859) 655-4159.

CATHEDRAL BASILICA OF THE ASSUMPTION, 1140 Madison Ave. at 12th St., is modeled after Notre Dame in Paris. This basilica has 82 stained-glass windows, including what is reputedly the largest stained-glass church window in the world. Four large murals on canvas painted by Covington native Frank Duveneck also are on display. Guided tours are available by appointment. Allow 1 hour minimum. Mon.-Fri. 10:30-3:30. Donations. Guided tour $2 per person. Phone (859) 431-2060.

MOTHER OF GOD CHURCH is at 119 W. Sixth St. This Italian Renaissance-style church is enhanced by stained-glass windows imported from Germany in 1890 and five murals created by parishioner Johann Schmitt, some of whose works are in the Vatican. Use the entrance between the church and the rectory. Allow 30 minutes minimum. Mon.-Sat. 9-4:30; closed holidays. Free. Phone (859) 291-2288.

NEWPORT pop. 18,900, elev. 508′

NEWPORT AQUARIUM is off I-471 exit 5 (SR 8), then w. following signs to Newport on the Levy. The aquarium displays 11,000 creatures in 60 exhibits, with examples of aquatic life from every continent and ocean. Among the aquarium's 16 themed areas are Rivers of the World; Shore Gallery, with a touch pool populated by starfish, crabs and urchins; The Bizarre and the Beautiful; The Dangerous and Deadly, inhabited by piranhas, poison frogs and pufferfish; and The Riverbank, featuring fish and foliage native to the Ohio River region.

'Gator Bayou, a swampland where alligators can be seen snapping beneath a footbridge; Surrounded by Sharks, with an up-close view of 25 of the sharp-toothed creatures; Kingdom of Penguins; and Jelly Fish Gallery are other major exhibits.

Visitors follow a one-way path past numerous exhibits of ocean fauna such as graceful jellyfish, splendidly attired penguins, and sharks the design of whose tank allows them to swim over and around the visitor. Acrylic flooring and tunnels, murals and a theater disguised as a pirate's ship help set the tone. Food is available. Allow 2 hour minimum. Daily 10-6. Admission $15.95; over 64, $13.95; ages 3-12, $9.95. Parking $3. AX, DS, MC, VI. Phone (859) 261-7444 or (800) 406-3474. *See color ad p. 570.*

UNION pop. 1,000, elev. 515′

BIG BONE LICK STATE PARK, off SR 338 at 3380 Beaver Rd., is the site of prehistoric animal remains. The creatures came to lick the salt produced by the springs; some became mired in the mud and died. A museum displays some of the items discovered during archeological digs. A herd of bison can be seen from the park's discovery trail.

Park open daily dawn-dusk. Museum hours vary; phone ahead. Park free. Museum $1; under 13, 50c. Phone (859) 384-3522 for the park or 384-3906 for the museum. *See Recreation Chart in Kentucky/Tennessee TourBook and the AAA Southeastern CampBook.*

This ends listings for the Cincinnati Vicinity.
The following page resumes the alphabetical listings
of cities in Ohio.

For nearly 100 years members have counted on AAA for their emergency road service needs, maps, TripTiks and travel information & services.

*B*ut did you know...

you can also trust AAA to provide you with insurance protection. Most[1] AAA clubs provide a variety of insurance products for all phases of your life, at competitive rates from leading companies in their markets. Policies most often available include coverage for your:

- Automobile
- Home
- Life
- Boat
- RV
- Trip Cancellation
- Travel Delay/Lost Baggage

Call your local AAA office today and ask for one of our knowledgeable insurance representatives to help you with your insurance needs.

[1]Due to state regulations and local restrictions, insurance is not available through all AAA clubs.

Travel With Someone You Trust®

Cleveland

Cleveland began in 1796 when surveyor Moses Cleaveland picked his townsite on Lake Erie. Only three of his malaria-ridden group agreed to remain. The town grew slowly until the late 1820s, when New York finished its Erie Canal and Ohio decided to build a canal of its own.

By 1832 the Ohio and Erie Canal was completed, and Cleveland, the northern terminus, had already doubled its population. Over the next 10 years the town grew by almost 500 percent. The city also acquired a trimmer name for its bright new future. Because the editor of a newspaper called *The Cleveland Gazette and Commercial Register* had to drop a letter from his masthead for it to fit across the page, he chose the first "a" in Cleaveland to be expendable.

During the 1800s, Cleveland was an important stop on the Underground Railroad. The city's port provided a route to freedom across the Canadian border for slaves fleeing the South.

With the canal came Cleveland's first wave of immigrants, the backbone of its labor force. The city grew quickly from a bustling port to a shipping and industrial giant. The Civil War briefly halted the city's progress, but the subsequent demand for iron spurred new growth. Fortunes were made in shipping coal, limestone and iron ore, in manufacturing steel and iron, and in communications, railroads and oil. Between 1910-20 Cleveland was the country's second largest center for automobile production.

Behind this growth were the great industrialists: Jephtha Wade I, whose telegraph company evolved into the Western Union system; Charles Brush, who invented the carbon arc lamp that lighted the city's streets; Sam Mather, a steel and shipping magnate; Mark Hanna, a steel and shipping baron and political boss; and John D. Rockefeller, the world's first billionaire, who made his fortune in the Standard Oil Co.

By the late 19th century Cleveland had matured. Public transportation was made cheap and easy, and projects were initiated to build the Cleveland Union Terminal, a 52-story skyscraper that contained the Union Railroad Station. Now a three-level mall called The Avenue fills the former railroad station concourse beneath what has become known as the Terminal Tower. The Society Center on Cleveland's Public Square, opened in 1992, stands at 948 feet, making this 56-story structure the tallest in Cleveland and among the 25 tallest buildings in the world.

Since 1950, the population of Cleveland proper has declined by nearly one third as increasing numbers of residents have moved to the suburbs. In recent years,

however, Cleveland has attracted new enterprises and created new jobs. As the nation's 12th largest consumer market, Cleveland is headquarters for more than 20 major industrial corporations and many smaller companies.

Despite its industrial bent, Cleveland has not overlooked the finer things in life. The almost 19,000 acres of the metropolitan parks districts and the surrounding rivers, streams and lakes, including Lake Erie and the Cleveland lakefront, offer ample opportunities for recreation. Professional theater is showcased at the Cleveland Play House, founded in 1915, it is one of the nation's longest-running resident theater companies, and at the restored Playhouse Square, a five-theater complex on Euclid Avenue.

The city also is home of the Cleveland Orchestra; several art, science and health museums, including the Cleveland Museum of Art, the Great Lakes Science Center, the Rock and Roll Hall of Fame and Museum and the Western Reserve Historical Society; the Cleveland Clinic, which administers some of the world's most advanced medical treatments; and Case Western Reserve and Cleveland State universities.

Entertainment alternatives are numerous and continue to expand. The Flats, a riverfront area once known for its heavy industry, now comprises the city's primary entertainment district along both banks of the Cuyahoga River. Converted warehouses line the docks with restaurants and nightclubs. The Historic Warehouse District, just east of The Flats, provides a backdrop of 19th-century architecture and traditions for shopping, dining and entertainment. Jacob's Field Stadium and Gund Arena, the all-purpose sports and entertainment complex, as well as a state-of-the-art stadium for the resurrected Cleveland Browns have re-energized Cleveland's sports fans and stimulated economic development in the downtown area.

All these facets combine to make Cleveland a livable place with much to offer and much to be proud of.

Approaches

By Car

Cleveland sits in the middle of a "Y" formed by two of the nation's major transcontinental routes: I-90 and I-80. I-90 passes through the heart of the city, bringing traffic along the lakeshore from the east; I-80 channels motorists from the interior through the southern suburbs. From the west, these routes combine over the Ohio Turnpike, with the "Y" beginning at neighboring Elyria.

Both highway systems interchange with important intersecting routes for easy access to the suburbs, and I-90 links conveniently to important city streets. Other supplemental east-west roads are SR 2, US 6 and US 20. These routes primarily serve local traffic, but also follow some of the major city arteries.

(continued on p. 212)

The Informed Traveler

City Population: 505,600

Elevation: 865 ft.

Sales Tax: The Cleveland area levies a 7 percent sales tax. The lodging tax rate within the city of Cleveland is 14.5 percent. Cars rented at Cleveland Hopkins Airport are subject to a 7 percent sales tax and 11.10 percent concession fee as well as a one-time charge of $11.30.

WHOM TO CALL

Emergency: 911

Police (non-emergency): (216) 623-5000

Fire: 911

Time and Temperature: (216) 931-1212

Hospitals: Cleveland Clinic, (216) 444-2200; Huron Hospital, (216) 761-3300; St. Vincent Charity, (216) 861-6200; University Hospitals of Cleveland, (216) 844-1000.

WHERE TO LOOK

Newspapers

The Cleveland Plain Dealer is published in the morning. The suburbs receive the daily *Sun.*

Radio

Cleveland radio station WTAM (1100 AM) is an all-news/weather station; WCPN (90.3 FM) is a member of National Public Radio.

Visitor Information

Brochures, maps and information are available from the Greater Cleveland Convention and Visitors Bureau in Suite 3100 of the Terminal Tower, 50 Public Sq., Cleveland, OH 44113; phone (216) 621-5555 or (800) 321-1004.

TRANSPORTATION

Air Travel

Cleveland Hopkins International Airport is 12 miles southwest of downtown via I-71; airport information is available at 1620 AM on the radio. Hopkins Limousine, (216) 267-8282, provides transportation Sun.-Fri. 6 a.m.-11 p.m., Sat. and holidays 6 a.m.-8 p.m.; fares average $37 and reservations are required. Taxi fare to downtown is approximately $25. Selected Greater Cleveland Regional Transit Authority (RTA) rapid transit trains provide service to downtown from 4:30 a.m. to 12:30 a.m.

Rental Cars

Hertz, at the airport, (216) 267-8900 or (800) 654-3080, and at 3663 Park East, Beachwood, (216) 831-3836 or (800) 654-3080, offers discounts to AAA members. For listings of other agencies check the telephone directory.

Rail Service

The Amtrak station is at Ninth Street and Cleveland Memorial Shoreway; phone (800) 872-7245.

Buses

Greyhound Lines Inc., (800) 231-2222, is at 1465 Chester Ave.

Taxis

Cabs are available at the taxi stands in Public Square or can be ordered by phone. Average rates are $1.80 for the first one-sixth mile and 40c for each additional quarter-mile; the average fee for waiting is $15 an hour. Companies include Ace Cab, (216) 361-4700; Americab, (216) 429-1111; and Yellow, (216) 623-1500.

Public Transport

The transit authority offers bus or rapid transit train service. Rail service runs from the airport to Tower City Center on Public Square through the Louis Stokes Transit Center/Windermere in East Cleveland, as well as from Tower City Center to points in Shaker Heights along Van Aken and Shaker boulevards. Connecting bus routes serve almost every downtown spot and surrounding suburbs. Train and express bus fare is $1.50, local bus service is $1.25 and loop and community circulator bus service is 50c; transfers are free. Phone the RTA answer line at (216) 621-9500 for schedule information.

Destination Cleveland

*I*f you're ready to kick up your heels and rock 'n' roll, Cleveland is the place to do it.

*P*ut on your blue suede shoes and boogie on down to the Rock and Roll Hall of Fame. Slip into your high-heel sneakers and Bach on down to Severance Hall for the Cleveland Orchestra. Don your cleats and broken field run to Cleveland Browns Stadium or slide into Jacob's Field. Rock on!

Cleveland Museum of Art. A Romanesque fountain greets visitors at the south end of this renowned museum. (See listing page 213)

Cleveland Museum of Natural History. Wide-eyed children gape at dinosaur skeletons in the Kirtland Hall of Prehistoric Life. (See listing page 213)

Bay Village

Cleveland

See Vicinity map page 212

See Insert on page 212

Berea

Independence

The RainForest at Cleveland Metroparks Zoo. Visitors approach the 2-acre enclosure. (See listing page 213)

*P*laces included in this AAA Destination City:

Downtown Cleveland is the northern terminus of I-71 and I-77, which bring traffic from the southwest and the south respectively. I-490, south of the city, provides a connector for I-71 and I-77. SR 176 also channels traffic from the south connecting to I-490 and I-90. Approaching the city, each interchanges frequently with other routes, including I-80, before joining I-90 near the city's center.

Other routes from the south include SR 8, SR 21 and US 42, which are used chiefly by local traffic. Upon entering Cleveland, these roads constitute some of the principal thoroughfares.

I-271, forming an irregular arc between I-71 and I-90, provides a bypass around Cleveland's east side. I-80 (the Ohio Turnpike), I-480 and I-271 that bypass the city to the east and south, provide connections for I-90 corridor traffic.

Getting Around

Street System

Cleveland's streets are in a grid pattern that centers on Public Square, from which all major avenues radiate. Euclid Avenue is the major business thoroughfare, running from the square through downtown to the eastern suburbs. Ontario Avenue,

running north-south through Public Square, divides the city into east and west. North-south routes are numbered streets, while the majority of east-west thoroughfares are named avenues, roads or boulevards. Right turns on red are permitted unless otherwise posted.

Parking

On-street metered parking is available but finding a spot is often difficult. Meters operate from a minimum of 30 minutes to a maximum of 4 hours from 7 a.m. or 9:30 a.m. to 6 p.m. Parking is available in the municipal parking lot on the Memorial Shoreway (I-90) just east of the 9th Street exit; this affords easy access to the Waterfront Rapid Transit Train serving Tower City, The Flats and other Cleveland attractions. Parking lot and garage charges can vary from $2 to $9 daily. Park and ride lots are at some RTA stations.

What To See

THE CHILDREN'S MUSEUM OF CLEVELAND, 10730 Euclid Ave. in University Circle, is a hands-on and creative learning environment where children and families discover the world through

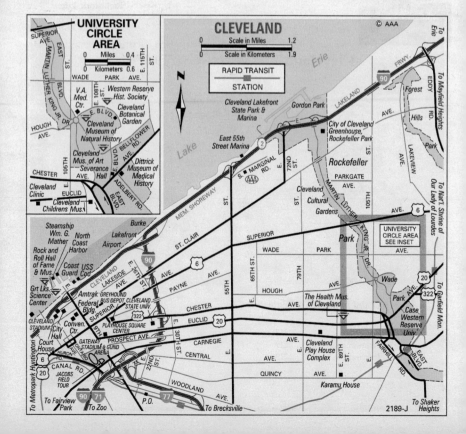

2189-J

play. Daily programs and special activities are offered year-round.

Allow 1 hour minimum. Daily 10-5 (also second Wed. of the month 5-8); closed Jan. 1 and Dec. 25. Admission $5; over 64 and ages 18 months-15 years, $4.50. Admission second Wed. of the month 5-8, $1. DS, MC, VI. Phone (216) 791-5437.

CITY OF CLEVELAND GREENHOUSE AND BOTANICAL GARDEN, ROCKEFELLER PARK, 750 E. 88th St., has 4 acres of outdoor gardens and indoor showhouses. The Talking Garden has taped descriptions of plants, which visitors are encouraged to touch and smell. Japanese and peace gardens also are on the grounds. The showhouses include a water garden, tropical plants, fruits and seasonal flowers. Special seasonal displays are presented. Allow 1 hour minimum. Daily 10-4. Free. Phone (216) 664-3103.

CLEVELAND BOTANICAL GARDEN, 11030 East Blvd., includes 10 acres of landscaped grounds with 12 distinct gardens which include Japanese, herb, rose and children's gardens. The garden also features a horticultural library, a visitor center, plant exhibits, gardening lectures and public programs. Grounds open Mon.-Sat. 9-5, Sun. noon-5, Apr.-Oct. Closed holidays. **Note:** the visitor center is undergoing expansion and is closed until fall 2003. Free. Phone (216) 721-1600.

CLEVELAND METROPARKS includes 14 reservations, Cleveland Metroparks Zoo and more than 100 miles of connecting parkways. Containing more than 19,000 acres, the park district features picnic grounds; two riding stables; bridle trails; golf courses; boating, swimming and fishing areas; wildlife management areas and waterfowl sanctuaries; and seven outdoor education centers. All-purpose trails are designed for walking, running, skating and bicycling. The park district also offers winter recreation facilities and activities such as tobogganing, sledding, ice skating and cross-country skiing. Phone (216) 351-6300, or TDD (216) 351-0808.

CLEVELAND METROPARKS ZOO, off Wildlife Way, is the 165-acre home to thousands of mammals, birds, reptiles, amphibians and fish living in naturalistic habitats. Ostriches, zebras and giraffes roam through the African Plains Savanna, while kangaroos, wallabies and koalas live in the Australian Adventure.

Wolf Wilderness immerses visitors in a northern temperate forest, home to a pack of gray wolves, beavers and a variety of birds, reptiles and amphibians. Nearby are exhibits featuring bears, Bactrian camels and Thorold's deer as well as a seal and sea lion pool.

An aquatics exhibit, which displays the underwater world of sharks, lungfish and piranhas, is housed in the same building as many of the zoo's primates and big cats. Also of interest are the Birds of Prey, the Public Greenhouse and the outdoor gorilla exhibits. Picnicking is permitted. Food is available.

Zoo grounds open Mon.-Fri. 10-5, Sat.-Sun. and holidays 10-7, Memorial Day weekend-Labor Day; daily 10-5, rest of year. Closed Jan. 1 and Dec. 25. Last admission 1 hour before closing. Admission to Zoo and The RainForest $8; ages 2-11, $4. Parking is free. MC, VI. Phone (216) 661-6500, or TDD (216) 661-1090.

The RainForest features 600 animals and 10,000 varieties of plants, trees and shrubs from around the jungles of Africa, Asia and the Americas. The elaborate 2-acre, bi-level recreation of a tropical habitat includes a 25-foot waterfall and a simulated thunderstorm every 15 minutes. Allow 1 hour minimum. Mon.-Fri. 10-5, Sat.-Sun. 10-7, Memorial Day weekend-Labor Day; daily 10-5 rest of year. Closed Jan. 1 and Dec. 25. Last admission 1 hour before closing.

CLEVELAND MUSEUM OF ART, 11150 East Blvd., overlooks the Fine Arts Gardens, with its seasonal flower displays. A permanent collection of more than 40,000 works of art is displayed in 70 galleries. Works are displayed chronologically from the ancient Mediterranean period to present. Especially noteworthy are collections of Medieval European, Asian and pre-Columbian art. Paintings include those of Caravaggio, Francisco Goya, El Greco, Frans Hals, Michelangelo, Claude Monet, Pablo Picasso, Rembrandt, Pierre Auguste Renoir, J.M.W. Turner and Vincent van Gogh.

The museum includes an auditorium, lecture and recital halls, and classrooms where film and music series are offered. Food is available. Tues.-Sun. 10-5 (also Wed. and Fri. 5-9); closed Jan. 1, July 4, Thanksgiving and Dec. 25. Free. Admission may be charged for special exhibitions and programs. Phone (216) 421-7350 or (888) 262-0033.

CLEVELAND MUSEUM OF NATURAL HISTORY is at 1 Wade Oval Dr. in University Circle. A planetarium features more than 5,000 stars, nebulae, galaxies and planets. "Planet e" integrates the sciences of geology and astronomy through high-tech, interactive displays. The Gallery of Gems and Jewels showcases more than 1,500 dazzling objects. A wildlife center and garden displays flora and fauna indigenous to Ohio. Exhibits in other galleries deal with dinosaurs and other ancient creatures such as armored fish, artifacts from nine cultures and "Lucy," one of the oldest known human ancestors. An observatory, live animal shows and an outdoor courtyard also are offered.

Museum open Mon.-Sat. 10-5, Sun. noon-5. Observatory open Wed. 8:30 p.m.-10 p.m., Sept.-May. Admission $6.50; over 59, college students with ID and ages 7-18, $4.50; ages 3-6, $3.50. Planetarium show $3 extra. MC, VI. Phone (216) 231-4600 or (800) 317-9155.

DITTRICK MUSEUM OF MEDICAL HISTORY, 11000 Euclid Ave. on the third floor of the Allen Memorial Medical Library, deals with the history of medicine in the Western Reserve. Exhibits include two doctors' offices and an 1880s pharmacy. Mon.-Fri. 10-5; closed holidays and day after Thanksgiving. Free. Phone (216) 368-3648.

GARFIELD MONUMENT, 12316 Euclid Ave., is in Lake View Cemetery at the tomb of President James A. Garfield. The 285-acre cemetery also contains the graves of Myron T. Herrick, ambassador to France; Mark Hanna, U.S. senator; John Hay, secretary of state under President William McKinley; and industrialist John D. Rockefeller.

The cemetery maintains more than 100 varieties of trees, shrubs and flowers. Guided tours are available. Daily 9-4, Apr. 1-late Nov. Phone (216) 421-2665.

GREAT LAKES SCIENCE CENTER is at E. 9th St. and SR 2, 3 blks. n. of Public Sq. to 601 Erieside Ave. Through extensive use of more than 340 interactive exhibits, daily demonstrations and educational programming, the center stimulates interest and understanding of science, the environment and technology. Highlights include major traveling exhibits, an indoor tornado, a bridge of fire, Polymer FunHouse and a large hands-on exhibit area about the Great Lakes Region. The center also incorporates a six-story domed OMNIMAX theater.

Allow 2 hours minimum. Daily 9:30-5:30; closed Thanksgiving and Dec. 25. Admission to either the exhibits or the film $7.95; ages 3-17, $5.95. Com-bination exhibit and film admission $10.95; ages 3-17, $7.95. AX, DS, MC, VI. Phone (216) 694-2000.

THE HEALTH MUSEUM OF CLEVELAND, 8911 Euclid Ave., dramatizes the workings of the human body and promotes healthy lifestyle choices. The more than 150 permanent exhibits include Juno, the Transparent Talking Woman; The Giant Tooth; Come To Your Senses; the Body Stops; and the theaters of Hearing, Sight and Social Concerns. These are supplemented by timely temporary traveling exhibitions and special weekend programs suitable for all ages.

Mon.-Fri. 9-5, Sat. 10-5, Sun. noon-5; closed holidays. Admission $5; over 64 and ages 4-17, $3.50. MC, VI ($10). Phone (216) 231-5010.

JACOBS FIELD TOUR, 2401 Ontario St., makes stops at the press box, the indoor batting cages and the dugout. Guided 1-hour tours depart every half-hour Mon.-Sat. 10-2, June-Aug.; Mon.-Fri. at 1 and 2, on the hour Sat. 10-2 in May and Sept. No tours are given when day games are scheduled, during special events and on holidays. Fee $6.50; over 59 and ages 3-14, $4.50. AX, CB, DC, DS, JC, MC, VI. Phone (216) 420-4200.

NASA GLENN RESEARCH CENTER VISITOR CENTER, next to Cleveland Hopkins International Airport on SR 17 (Brookpark Rd.), offers 8,000 square feet of exhibit space devoted to a variety of visual, auditory and interactive displays about such topics as aeronautics, space exploration, the solar system, satellites and other NASA programs. Weekend programs change quarterly. Special programs throughout the year coincide with national events.

Mon.-Fri. 9-4, Sat. and holidays 10-3, Sun. 1-5; closed Jan. 1, Easter, Thanksgiving and Dec. 24-25 and 31. Guided tours are offered Wed. at 2 and the third Sat. of the month at 11 for visitors at least 13 years old. Free. Non-residents must present a visa or passport. Reservations are required for tours. Phone (216) 433-2000, or TDD (216) 433-9834.

NATIONAL SHRINE OF OUR LADY OF LOURDES is 10 mi. e. via US 20 (Euclid Ave.) and US 6 (Chardon Rd.) at 21281 Chardon Rd. The grotto in the hillside resembles the original in France. A chapel and the Way of the Cross, with its hillside woods and shrines, also are on the grounds. Daily dawn-dusk. Phone (216) 481-8232 for Mass and pilgrimage schedules.

ROCK AND ROLL HALL OF FAME AND MUSEUM is at E. 9th St. and Erieside Ave. at 1 Key Plaza. The giant, 150,000-square-foot space is dedicated to the living legacy of music from Delta blues to rock 'n' roll and to the continuing evolution of music today. Visitors can listen to the songs that shaped rock 'n' roll, a sample of the most popular and influential recordings in the history of the genre. A retrospective of music videos from MTV's beginnings to the present as well as several films are shown daily.

A large collection of images, artifacts and instruments from current performers, Hall of Famers and other legends is imaginatively presented. Food is available.

Allow 3 hours minimum. Daily 10-5:30 (also Wed. and Sat. 5:30-9), Memorial Day-Labor Day; daily 10-5:30 (also Wed. 5:30-9), rest of year. Closed Thanksgiving and Dec. 25. Admission $15; over 55 and ages 9-11, $11.50. Parking garages are available nearby for a fee. AX, DS, MC, VI. Phone (216) 781-7625 or (888) 764-7625. *See color ad.*

[SAVE] **STEAMSHIP** *WILLIAM G. MATHER* **MUSEUM**, 1001 E. 9th St. Pier, is a restored 1925 Great Lakes freighter that has been preserved as a floating museum ship. Visitors can explore the historic cargo holds, four-story engine room, elegant dining rooms, galley and the brass and oak pilothouse of this 618-foot steamer. Exhibits and introductory videotapes portray the evolution of the shipping industry. Guided tours are available. **Note:** Visitors are encouraged to wear flat, rubber-soled shoes. Accessibility for the physically impaired is very limited.

Allow 1 hour minimum. Mon.-Sat. 10-5, Sun. noon-5, June-Aug.; Fri.-Sat. 10-5, Sun. noon-5 in May and Sept.-Oct.; by reservation only, Labor Day weekend. Admission $5; over 59, $4; ages 5-18, $3. Nearby parking $5 and up. MC, VI. Phone (216) 574-6262.

USS *COD*, 1089 N. Marginal Rd., is a World War II fleet submarine which must be boarded through vertical ladders and narrow hatchways. Self-guiding tours of this fully-intact vessel include the control room, the torpedo room, the engine rooms, crew berths and compartments. Allow 30 minutes minimum. Daily 10-5, May-Sept. Last tour departs 30 minutes before closing. Admission $5; senior citizens $4; grades 1-12, $3. Phone (216) 566-8770.

[GEM] [SAVE] **WESTERN RESERVE HISTORICAL SOCIETY**, 10825 East Blvd., University Circle, is housed in two early 20th-century mansions built in the Italian Renaissance style. The society offers changing exhibitions, including an auto-aviation collection, as well as a historical museum and a library. Mon.-Sat. 10-5, Sun. noon-5. Library Tues.-Sat. 9-5 (also Wed. 5-9), Sun. noon-5. Closed holidays. Admission $7.50; over 59, $6.50; students $5. Phone (216) 721-5722.

Crawford Auto-Aviation Museum houses nearly 200 antique, vintage and classic vehicles that highlight the technological and stylistic development of the automobile. Displays tracing the evolution of the automobile 1895-1981 accent Cleveland's importance as an early car-manufacturing center. Models ranging from an 1895 Panhard et Levassor to a 1981 Aston Martin Lagonda are exhibited.

On the lower level is a late 1890s cobblestone street that portrays the horseless carriage era with a blacksmith shop, music store, general store, barbershop, pharmacy, saloon and tobacco shop. Allow 1 hour, 30 minutes minimum.

The History Museum has exhibits about the history of Northeast Ohio. Displays in the Chisholm Halle Costume Wing include clothing from the late 1700s to the present. Other areas chronicle the settlement of the region. Many interesting architectural details can be seen both inside and outside the museum's buildings, and the grounds include formal gardens.

Guided tours of the Hay-McKinney Mansion describe the early-1900s lifestyles of the family that occupied this house and of their servants. Rotating special exhibitions focus on everything from costumes to crime solving. Free guided tours of the mansion are offered daily noon-5.

Rock and Roll Hall of Fame and Museum
One Key Plaza, Cleveland, OH 44114 • www.rockhall.com

Nothing captures the essence of human spirit like music. And no place captures the music like that of the Rock and Roll Hall of Fame and Museum in Cleveland, Ohio. The Museum contains over 50 exhibits, dynamic cinema presentations, rare collectibles, plus the world's largest single collection of rock and roll artifacts. Regular Hours: Open daily 10:00 a.m.–5:30 p.m., Wednesday until 9:00 p.m. Memorial Day - Labor Day, open daily 10:00 a.m.–5:30 p.m., Wednesday and Saturday until 9:00 p.m. For up to date information on upcoming events, visit www.rockhall.com. For travel information, hotel packages and discounts, call 888.764.ROCK.

The Research Library has books and manuscripts related to African-American, Jewish, Ohio Labor, urban and general American history, with emphasis on the Civil War and 19th-century publications. Family history research material is featured.

What To Do

Sightseeing

A good way to see the city is from the observation deck on the 42nd floor of the Terminal Tower. This 52-story edifice over a three-level railroad passenger station was built 1927-30 and is considered the showpiece of Cleveland's lakefront. The observation deck is open Sat.-Sun. 11-4:30, May-Sept.; Sat.-Sun. 11-3:30, rest of year. Admission is $2; ages 6-16, $1. Tickets may be purchased at the Tower City Center Visitor Information Center in Public Square; phone (216) 621-7981.

Boat Tours

GOODTIME CRUISE LINES, 825 E. Ninth St. Pier at the North Coast Harbor, offers excursions on the Cuyahoga River and in the harbor aboard the 1,000-passenger *Goodtime III*. Additional cruises also are offered. Combination 2-hour lake and river cruises are offered Mon.-Sat. at noon and 3, Sun. at noon, 3 and 6, June 15-Labor Day; Fri.-Sun. at noon and 3, day after Labor Day-Sept. 30. Fare $15; over 60, $14; ages 2-11, $9. Phone (216) 861-5110.

NAUTICA QUEEN, in the Nautica Entertainment Complex on the w. bank of the Flats at 1153 Main Ave., provides 2-hour narrated lunch cruises with live music and 3-hour dinner cruises on the Cuyahoga River and Lake Erie. Cruises are available Easter-Dec. 31. Lunch trips depart Mon.-Fri. at noon, Sat.-Sun. at 11. Dinner cruises depart Mon.-Thurs. at 7, Fri.-Sat. at 7:30, Sun. at 4. Boarding begins 1 hour before departure. Fare $22.95-$44.95. Reservations are recommended. AX, DI, DS, MC, VI. Phone (216) 696-8888 or (800) 837-0604.

Trolley and Train Tours

There are other ways to see the sights in Cleveland. Trolley Tours of Cleveland provides narrated trolley tours of the city. Reservations are required; phone (216) 771-4484.

The Cuyahoga Valley Scenic Railroad offers historic train rides through Cuyahoga Valley National Park *(see attraction listing p. 219)*. Trips range from 90-minute scenic tours of the valley to a 52-mile round trip to various Akron destinations *(see place listing p. 182)*.

Walking Tours

Self-guiding walking or driving tours are good ways to experience the restoration of Ohio City on Cleveland's west side. A separate municipality that was later annexed, Ohio City is a neighborhood of old Victorian houses, many of which now house boutiques, restaurants and antique shops. Saturdays May through August the district hosts an urban flea market. Many of the neighborhood's restored homes open their doors to the public during the annual "Weekend in Ohio City " celebration held the third weekend in May. Brochures of the area are provided by the Ohio City Near West Development Corp., 2525 Market Ave., Suite A, Cleveland, OH 44113; phone (216) 781-3222.

Sports and Recreation

The more than 19,000 acres of Cleveland Metroparks constitute one of the largest concentrations of parkland per capita in the nation. The natural woodland parks encircle the city, offering facilities for hiking, biking, picnicking, horseback riding, golfing, swimming, boating, other water sports and many winter sports. Phone (216) 351-6300.

Various recreational opportunities also are found at the Cuyahoga Valley National Park, just southeast of the city *(see place listing p. 232 and Recreation Chart)*.

Golf enthusiasts can try their skill at any one of the dozens of public courses, including Cleveland Metroparks' Big Met, 4811 Valley Pkwy., (440) 331-1070; Manakiki, 35501 Eddy Rd., (440) 942-2500; and Shawnee Hills, 18753 Egbert Rd., (440) 232-7184. Other courses are listed in the telephone directory.

More than 80 miles of bridle trails are provided by Cleveland Metroparks. Stables offering **horseback riding** lessons and boarding only are at Rocky River Stables, (216) 267-2525, and Brecksville Stables, (440) 526-6767. **Hiking, biking** and **jogging** paths also are available. **Swimming** can be enjoyed at the sandy Lake Erie beaches, such as the ones found in Cleveland Metropark Huntington Reservation in Bay Village *(see place listing p. 219)*, Cleveland Lakefront State Park and Mentor Headlands Beach State Park.

Fishing and **boating** also are popular pastimes on Lake Erie. Public boat rentals and ramps are at Cleveland Metroparks Rocky River and Hinckley, and fishing piers are at Huntington. Trident Marine Corp. offers custom-designed group cruise service; phone (216) 771-2628. Wildwood Marina offers public and private fishing excursions; phone (216) 481-5771.

Downhill skiing is popular at several nearby sites, including Alpine Valley, (440) 285-2211, and Boston Mills/Brandywine, (330) 467-2242 or (800) 875-4241. Several Cleveland Metroparks offer **cross-country skiing**.

Because Cleveland is home to several professional sports teams, spectator sports enthusiasts can choose from a variety of activities. At Jacobs Field on Carnegie Avenue between Ontario Avenue and E. 9th Street, the Indians play **baseball** in the spring and summer and guided tours are offered Monday through Saturday, May through September, excluding day games, special events and holidays *(see attraction listing p. 214)*; phone (216) 420-4200. During the summer, the Rockers play women's **basketball** at the Gund Arena. The arena also is where the NBA's Cavaliers play in winter; for tickets phone (216) 420-2200. The Cleveland Crunch play **soccer** in fall and spring at Cleveland State University's Convocation Centre; phone (216) 687-5555.

Cleveland Browns **football** fans do the wave in their 1999 Cleveland Browns Stadium at 1085 W. 3rd St. near the North Coast Harbor; phone (440) 891-5050 or (888) 891-1999.

Thoroughbred racing is held throughout the year at the Thistledown Racing Club, 21501 Emery Rd., (216) 662-8600. **Harness races** are featured year-round at Northfield Park, 15 miles south on Northfield Road; reservations are suggested. Phone (330) 467-4101.

Note: Policies vary concerning admittance of children to pari-mutuel betting facilities. Phone for information.

Shopping

Cleveland is a shopper's delight: It is one of the largest consumer markets in the country, with numerous retail establishments in the downtown area alone.

The Avenue, within the Tower City Center at 50 Public Sq., is a shopping, dining and entertainment complex surrounding a modernized commuter rail station. Skylights, light and water shows, marble staircases, historic brass storefronts and a glass dome accent the three levels of retail stores and eateries. The Galleria at Erieview, 1301 E. 9th and St. Clair streets, offers a distinctive collection of shops and eating places.

In the surrounding suburbs are major shopping centers and malls, offering such department stores as JCPenney, Northrop's, Saks Fifth Avenue and Sears as well as many smaller shops. Among the more popular malls are Beachwood Place, 26300 Cedar Rd. at Richmond Road in Beachwood; Great Northern Mall, 4954 Great Northern Blvd. at I-480 in North Olmsted; Parmatown Mall, 7899 W. Ridgewood Dr. in Parma; Randall Park Mall, Northfield and Emery roads in North Randall; Great Lakes Mall, 7850 Mentor Ave. in Mentor;

SouthPark Center, 500 SouthPark in Strongsville; and Westgate Mall, 3211 Westgate Mall in Fairview Park.

Shopping areas with a special flavor or theme also are abundant in Cleveland. At Coventry Road in Cleveland Heights between Mayfield and Euclid Heights roads., colorful shops and boutiques offer offbeat clothing, artworks and crafts. Antique Row, Lorain Avenue from W. 25th to W. 117th streets, and Detroit Avenue from Westwood Avenue to W. Clifton Boulevard, are popular with antiques hunters. And those seeking the novel may want to check out the offerings in The Cop Shop, the police department museum's gift shop at 1300 Ontario St.

The Arcade, 401 Euclid Ave., is considered to have been the first indoor mall in the country. This historical 19th-century landmark has been renovated to include a hotel, but continues to offer a variety of shops and boutiques. Shaker Square, at the junction of Van Aken Boulevard, Shaker Boulevard and E. 130th Street, offers shops and entertainment.

Beachcliff Market Square, 19300 Detroit Rd., is a converted landmark 1930 movie house with a central atrium and dozens of specialty shops. Old River Shopping Area, on Old Detroit and Wooster roads in Rocky River, is home to shops that specialize in gifts, antique clocks, sailboat sails, gourmet food, wines and specialty clothing.

For those who get hungry after all that shopping, the West Side Market at W. 25th Street and Lorain Avenue sells fresh fruit, vegetables, meats, fish, poultry, cheese and ethnic foods Mon. and Wed. 7-4 and Fri.-Sat. 7 a.m.-6 p.m. For those traveling east of the city, the Eastside Market at E. 105th and St. Clair, is another indoor/outdoor bazaar offering culinary delights Tues.-Fri. 9-6, Sat. 8-6.

Theater and Concerts

The Cleveland Orchestra, one of the world's finest, performs mid-September through May at the restored Severance Hall in the University Circle area and at the open-air Blossom Music Center in Cuyahoga National Park from July 4 through Labor Day. The center is the site of opera, classical, pop, jazz, rock and folk music events at other times, such as

holiday orchestra and chorus events. Phone (800) 686-1141 for Cleveland Orchestra ticket information. While food is available at both facilities, the patrons of Blossom Music Center can opt to bring a picnic.

The Cleveland Chamber Music Society performs at the Fairmont Temple Auditorium and occasionally other locations on selected Tuesdays, October through May. The renowned Cleveland Chamber Symphony, in the Music and Communications Building of Cleveland State University, gives concerts of contemporary music; phone (216) 687-9243 for scheduled programs.

Musical events are presented regularly at various sites across the city, including the Cleveland Museum of Art, The Cleveland Music School Settlement, Gund Arena and the civic auditorium at Lakewood High School. The students and faculty as well as visiting artists of the Cleveland Institute of Music, 11021 East Blvd. in University Circle, perform chamber, orchestra and opera music throughout the year; phone (216) 791-5000 for schedule information. Summer months at the institute are enlivened by Lyric Opera Cleveland; phone (216) 231-2910.

Playhouse Square Center (see color ad), on Euclid Avenue between E. 14th and E. 17th streets, is comprised of the recently acquired Hanna Theatre and five restored, landmark theaters: the Ohio, the State, the Palace, Allen and Kennedy's. The center is home to the ballet companies Ohio Ballet (see color ad) and DanceCleveland (see color ad), the Cleveland Opera (see color ad) and the CCC Jazz Festival; for ticket information phone (216) 241-6000, or (800) 766-6048 outside the Cleveland area. The Great Lakes Theater Festival (see color ad) mounts five productions yearly in the center's Ohio Theatre; phone (216) 241-5490 for festival information.

The Cleveland Play House, established in 1915, is a four-theater complex at 8500 Euclid Ave. It is reputedly one of the longest-running regional theaters in the country. A Romanesque addition, designed by internationally acclaimed architect, Phillip Johnson, was built in 1983. Productions range from the classics to new plays and from comedies to musicals; phone (216) 795-7000.

Other city theaters include the Karamu House, (216) 795-7070, at 2355 E. 89th St., a multiracial, multicultural center for the arts; and the Beck Center for the Arts, (216) 521-2540, at 17801 Detroit Ave.

Special Events

Every season offers a wealth of events in Cleveland. Cleveland plays host to the Mid-American Sail and Power Boat Show at the International Exposition Center near Cleveland Hopkins Airport in January and the National Home and Flower Show and the Greater Cleveland International Auto Show in February.

March brings the American and Canadian Sport Travel and Outdoor Show to the International Exposition Center, and one of Cleveland's most popular traditions, the St. Patrick's Day parade, is held March 17. Each year the Sunday following March 15 is declared Buzzard Sunday in nearby Hinckley (see place listing p. 242); residents and visitors celebrate the return of buzzards to the town.

April is the month for the Geauga County Maple Festival in nearby Chardon featuring crafts, parades, carnival rides, contests and the Sap Run marathon. Also in April are the Earthfest at Cleveland Metroparks Zoo, which celebrates the world's natural resources; and the Tri-C Jazz Fest, a musical event that takes place at various downtown locations. In May the Great American Rib Cook-Off includes entertainment. The Revco-Cleveland Marathon and 10K Race in May includes participants from all over the world.

The Annual Grand Prix of Cleveland, featuring some of the top Indy car drivers, is held at Burke Lakefront Airport in June. Also in June is the Boston Mills Art Festival in nearby Cuyahoga Valley National Park (see place listing p. 232 and Recreation Chart).

Early July is marked by the Festival of Freedom, which offers a fireworks display, and the Tower City Star-Spangled Celebration, which features performances by the Cleveland Orchestra. Also in July

is the KidFest and Interactive Environment for children and parents held at the Nautica Entertainment Complex.

The first full weekend in August brings the Twins Days Festival at Chamberlin Park in nearby Twinsburg *(see place listing p. 260)*, a 2-day affair attended by more than 3,000 sets of twins each year. In mid-August the Feast of the Assumption Italian Festival is held in the Little Italy section of Cleveland (also known as Murray Hill). Also in August is the Cuyahoga County Fair, one of the largest fairs in the state, at the fairgrounds in nearby Berea. The Cleveland National Air Show takes place Labor Day weekend at Burke Lakefront Airport.

The Christmas season is welcomed by the Holiday Lighting Program, held the day after Thanksgiving on Public Square.

The Cleveland Vicinity

BAY VILLAGE (A-4) pop. 17,000

LAKE ERIE NATURE & SCIENCE CENTER is off US 6 and near I-90/SR 2 exit 156 at 28728 Wolf Rd., within the 103 wooded acres of the Cleveland Metroparks' Huntington Reservation. The center includes live animals native to the area, educational programs and exhibits. Visitors are invited to explore the local forests and beaches, examine fossils, rocks and minerals, and learn about environmental issues. The Schuele Planetarium offers public programs; phone for schedule and reservations.

Allow 1 hour minimum. Daily 10-5; closed Jan. 1, Easter, Thanksgiving and Dec. 25. Admission free. A nominal fee is charged for most programs. Phone (440) 871-2900.

BEREA (B-5) pop. 19,100, elev. 788′

At one time four-fifths of the grindstones in the United States were made of sandstone quarried at Berea. Now cultural pursuits are the highlight. On the 4,500-student Baldwin-Wallace College campus are replicas of Independence Hall and the Liberty Bell. Riemenschneider Bach Institute, in the school's Merner-Pfeiffer Hall, has works by and about Johann Sebastian Bach as well as original work and first editions by other major composers. Throughout the academic year a wide array of speakers, and art and music events is open to the public, usually without charge.

INDEPENDENCE (B-5) pop. 6,500, elev. 855′

CUYAHOGA VALLEY SCENIC RAILROAD, I-77 exit 155 (Rockside Rd.), 1.2 mi. e. on Rockside Rd., 1 blk. n. on Canal Rd., then w. on Old Rockside Rd., following signs, runs through the Cuyahoga Valley National Park. Aboard coaches built 1939-41, passengers can take sightseeing tours or trips to regional attractions. Trips are offered daily in Oct.; Wed.-Sun., June-Aug.; Sat.-Sun., Feb.-May, in Sept. and Nov.-Dec. Departure times vary; phone ahead. Fare $11-$21; over 59, $10-$19; ages 3-12, $7-$16; under 3 free when on an adult's lap. Reservations are recommended. MC, VI. Phone (330) 657-2000 or (800) 468-4070.

The previous listings were for the Cleveland Vicinity. This page resumes the alphabetical listings of cities in Ohio.

CLIFTON (D-2) pop. 200, elev. 1,010′

CLIFTON MILL is off I-70 exit 54, 7 mi. s. on SR 72, then just w. to 75 Water St. In 1802 the water-powered flour mill was built on the banks of the Little Miami River in what is now Clifton; it operated commercially until 1948. Tours of the 20-foot-tall water wheel and 7-foot-tall mill are offered, and a country store displays antiques and collectibles. From the day after Thanksgiving through Jan. 3 the mill is decorated with 2.5 million holiday lights. Mon.-Fri. 9-5, Sat.-Sun. 8-5; closed holidays. Free. Phone (937) 767-5501.

COALTON (E-4) pop. 600, elev. 709′

LEO PETROGLYPH STATE MEMORIAL is e. on CR 28 to Township Rd. 224, then 4 mi. n.w. The 12-acre area contains several figures cut into a flat sandstone surface by prehistoric Indians. Hiking trails and a covered area with picnic tables are available. Daily dawn-dusk. Free. Phone (614) 297-2630 or (800) 686-1535 Mon.-Fri.

Columbus

Author James Thurber said of his birthplace, "Columbus is a town in which almost anything is likely to happen and in which almost everything has." He would not be surprised to find the city on the cutting edge of scientific and technological progress. Columbus is not just the capital of the state of Ohio; it also is a capital of state of the art.

Columbus is a city that almost was not. When Ohio gained statehood in 1803, it had yet to designate a permanent capital. Political maneuvering almost landed the state government in such thriving communities as Zanesville and Chillicothe.

However, in 1812 the residents of Franklinton, a county seat in the heart of Ohio along the Scioto River, tempted the state with 1,200 acres of land and a commitment to spend $50,000 to construct a capitol building and a penitentiary if that site were named capital. Within a matter of days the general assembly accepted the offer, and Columbus was born on the opposite bank of the river.

During the next 20 years Columbus began to overshadow its maternal city. By 1824 the county seat had shifted to Columbus, and as Franklinton residents relocated to the capital, Columbus merged with—if not engulfed—its predecessor.

The Civil War era saw the State Capitol building completed. It also initiated a wave of unprecedented growth: The population soared fivefold, and manufacturing soon competed with government as the city's main concern.

The opening in 1873 of Ohio Agriculture and Mechanical College, later renamed Ohio State University, spawned a new outlook for the city. Education was thrust to the forefront, and the intellectual atmosphere helped contribute to the forerunner of the computer, the development of the xerography process and numerous advancements in the medical treatment of the physically impaired. Current enrollment is 48,500.

This city continues to lead the way to the future. State of the art is synonymous with Columbus, which ranks with Washington, D.C., as a center for scientific and technological information; more than 150 high-tech companies are in Columbus.

These businesses made Columbus one of the first areas offering citywide cable television and introduced such technology as the 24-hour banking machine, interactive cable television and the electronic newspaper. The city also is a center for retail banking, insurance and real estate, and it has emerged as a leading convention city.

Columbus' residents make up a demographically representative slice of America, making its main distinction the fact that it is not too distinctive. Columbus offers a perfect cross section of consumers for the testing of new

products. Because so many fast-food chains develop their menus in Columbus, the city is often referred to as "Test Market, U.S.A."

Ordinary and extraordinary, the city has never looked back since shedding the industrial tradition of the Northeast. By relying on the mind instead of muscle, Columbus looks smarter all the time.

Approaches

By Car

The intersection of two interstate highways and a number of lesser routes makes Columbus accessible from all directions. The primary east-west highway is I-70, which spans about two-thirds of the nation and connects such cities as Baltimore, Wheeling, W.Va., and Indianapolis; I-70 passes through downtown Columbus, with convenient interchanges at major streets.

Closely paralleling the freeway is old US 40, which serves local traffic and provides a link to other downtown avenues. US 62 approaches Columbus from the northeast and southwest to bring the city a steady flow of in-state traffic, as does SR 16, combining with US 40 coming in from the northeastern suburbs.

Mainly an intrastate interstate, I-71 links Cleveland to the north and Cincinnati to the south, passing through Columbus and continuing southward to Louisville.

Running north-south through the city is US 23, which collects traffic from northern Ohio and Michigan as well as from southern Ohio, Kentucky and West Virginia. US 33, leading directly downtown, connects towns northwest and southeast of Columbus.

I-270 is a circumferential freeway that swings in a wide path around Columbus and, with interchanges with all major highways, provides a bypass of the city. When complete, I-670 will combine with I-70 and I-71 to form a tight rectangle around downtown Columbus, offering the usual convenient interchanges.

Getting Around

Street System

Despite Columbus' growth to big-city status, driving in and around the city is not as hectic as in many metropolitan areas. Driving from one end of downtown to the opposite end averages 25 minutes, and few suburban commutes take more than 45 minutes at non-peak traffic hours. Right turns on red are permitted unless otherwise posted.

Streets are organized on a grid system, with addresses beginning at 1 at the corner of Broad and High streets in the center of downtown and increasing as routes go out of the city. Numbered streets, running north-south, are divided by Broad Street; numbered avenues, running east-west, are divided by High Street.

(continued on p. 223)

The Informed Traveler

City Population: 632,900

Elevation: 777 ft.

Sales Tax: Columbus has a sales tax of 5.75 percent and a lodging tax of 15.75 percent. There is a 10 percent concession fee on rental cars picked up at Port Columbus International Airport.

WHOM TO CALL

Emergency: 911

Police (non-emergency): (614) 645-4545

Fire: (614) 221-2345

Time and Temperature: (614) 281-8211

Hospitals: Grant/Riverside Methodist Hospital (Downtown), (614) 566-9000; Grant/Riverside Methodist Hospital (Northwest), (614) 566-5000; Mount Carmel Health, (614) 234-5000; Ohio State University, (614) 257-3000.

WHERE TO LOOK

Newspapers
Columbus' major daily, published mornings, is the *Columbus Dispatch*.

Radio and TV
Columbus radio station WTVN (610 AM) is an all-news/weather station; WCBE (90.5 FM) is a member of National Public Radio.

Visitor Information
The Greater Columbus Convention and Visitors Bureau distributes information through its visitor information center on the second level of the City Center Mall at S. Third and Rich streets. The center is open Mon.-Sat. 10-9 and Sun. noon-6; the center is closed Thanksgiving and Dec. 25. Phone (614) 221-6623 or (800) 345-4386. The bureau's headquarters is at 90 N. High St., Columbus, OH 43215. This location is open Mon.-Fri. 9-5:30.

TRANSPORTATION

Air Travel
Port Columbus International Airport, 7 miles east of downtown inside the beltway off Stelzer Road, is served by major carriers. A free shuttle bus runs to the terminal from remote parking areas. Taxi service is offered to downtown, with average fares between $13 and $15.

Rental Cars
Hertz offers discounts to AAA members; phone (614) 239-1084 or (800) 654-3080. For listings of other agencies check the telephone directory.

Buses
Greyhound Lines Inc., (614) 221-2389 or (800) 231-2222, 111 E. Town St. between S. 3rd and S. 4th streets, serves Columbus.

Taxis
Major cab companies include Northway Cab, (614) 299-1191, and Yellow Cab, (614) 444-4444. Fixed fares are $2 base rate, $3.20 for the first mile, $1.35 for each additional mile and $1.50 for each mile outside Franklin County.

Public Transport
Central Ohio Transit Authority (COTA) provides bus transportation throughout the city and suburbs Mon.-Fri. 6 a.m.-8 p.m., Sat.-Sun. 8-6. The basic fare is $1.10, express fare $1.50 and transfers 10c. Passengers must have exact change. For details about routes and timetables, contact the COTA Information Center, 177 N. High St.; phone (614) 228-1776.

Parking

Parking lots and garages are plentiful downtown, with rates ranging from $4 to $7 Monday through Friday and generally decreasing to $1 on the weekends. On-street metered parking, costing approximately $1 per hour, can be found along most downtown streets; parking is restricted to 2 hours or less at most meters. Park and Ride lots are at many suburban shopping centers.

What To See

COLUMBUS MUSEUM OF ART, 480 E. Broad St., includes the Ferdinand Howald Collection of early Modernist paintings, the Frederick Schumacher Collection of Old Masters and modern American paintings, and the Sirak Collection of Impressionist, post-Impressionist and Expressionist works. The museum also has a sculpture garden and a continuing program of traveling exhibitions. Guided tours are available. Food is available.

Allow 1 hour minimum. Tues.-Sun. 10-5:30 (also Thurs. 5:30-8:30); closed major holidays. Admission $6; over 54, students with ID and ages 6-12, $4; free to all Thurs. 5:30-8:30. Parking $2. DS, MC, VI. Phone (614) 221-4848 or 221-6801.

COLUMBUS ZOO is off I-270, Sawmill Rd. exit, following signs. This zoo has almost 100 acres of gardens and natural habitats and includes the first gorilla born in captivity, a koala, a North American animal exhibit, a coral reef exhibit, a 250,000-gallon home for manatees and one of the largest collections of reptiles in the United States. Daily 9-6, Memorial Day weekend-Labor Day; 9-5, rest of year. Admission $8; over 59, $7; ages 2-11, $4. Parking $3. DS, MC, VI. Phone (614) 645-3500 or (800) 666-5397.

COSI COLUMBUS is off I-70W to exit 100B, or I-70E to exit 97, following signs to 333 W. Broad St. Three floors at the science learning center house more than 1,000 interactive exhibits. Eight major learning worlds, three theaters, attractions and an outdoor science park are included. Highlights include an ocean playground, 3-D theater, and exhibits about technology, adventure, history, gadgets and the human body. Courtesy strollers, wheelchairs and food are available.

Allow 2 hours minimum. Daily 10-5. Theaters Fri.-Sat. 10-9, Sun. noon-9. Closed Jan. 1, Easter, July 4, Thanksgiving and Dec. 24-25. Admission $12; over 59, $10; ages 2-12, $7. AX, CB, DI, DS, MC, VI. Phone (614) 228-2674, (877) 257-2674, or TDD (614) 228-6400.

FRANKLIN PARK CONSERVATORY AND BOTANICAL GARDEN is in Franklin Park at 1777 E. Broad St. This 12,500-square-foot glass structure, built in 1895, was designed in the style of London's Crystal Palace. Self-guiding tours travel through simulated habitats of the world including a tropical rain forest, the Himalayan Mountains, an arid desert and a Pacific Island water garden.

Other exhibits include a bonsai collection, an orchid collection and seasonal displays. The 28-acres of botanical gardens include a Japanese garden, an education garden, the Grand Mall Way, sculptures. Food and courtesy wheelchairs are available.

Allow 1 hour minimum. Tues.-Sun. 10-5 (also Wed. 5-8); closed Jan. 1, Thanksgiving and Dec. 25. Admission $5; over 61 and students with ID $3.50; ages 2-12, $2. Phone (614) 645-8733 or (800) 214-7275.

GERMAN VILLAGE, 1 mi. s., is reached via I-70 exit 100B. Originally established in the 1800s by German-speaking settlers, the restored district is now 233 acres of houses, shops and restaurants. Allow 1 hour, 30 minutes minimum. Hours for the various village enterprises vary. Phone (614) 221-8888.

OHIO HISTORICAL CENTER, jct. I-71 and 17th Ave., houses the Ohio Historical Society's administrative offices, a historical research library and the state archives. Exhibits include archeological, historical and natural history material. Food is available.

Allow 1 hour, 30 minutes minimum. Self-guiding tours Mon.-Sat. 9-5, Sun. and holidays 10-5; closed Jan. 1, Thanksgiving and Dec. 25. Library open Tues.-Sat. 9-5. Admission (includes historical center and Ohio Village) $5; over 61, $4; ages 6-12, $1.25; half-price to all Mon.-Tues. Phone (614) 297-2300 or (800) 653-6446.

Ohio Village, 1982 Velma Ave., is a reconstruction of a 19th-century rural Ohio community. Buildings include a town hall, hotel, schoolhouse, church, physician's residence, print shop and craft shops, all attended by costumed workers. Food is available. Wed.-Sat. 9-5, Sun. 10-5; hours vary in Dec. Closed Jan. 1, Thanksgiving and Dec. 24-25 and 31.

OHIO STATEHOUSE, Broad and High sts., is considered to be one of the best examples of Greek Revival architecture in the United States. The 1861 building contains historical documents, portraits and other works commemorating Ohio's noted governors and U.S. presidents. A painting of the Great Seal of Ohio is in the center of the rotunda dome. An Ohio travel information center is located in the building.

Self-guided tours daily 7-7. Guided 45- to 60-minute tours depart Mon.-Fri. at 10, 11:30, 1 and 3, Sat.-Sun. at 11:15, 12:30, 2 and 3. Closed holidays. Free. Phone (614) 752-6350.

OHIO STATE UNIVERSITY, N. High St. between 11th and Lane aves., was opened in 1873. On the campus is the Hopkins Hall Gallery, featuring changing art exhibits. Ohio Stadium, with seating for more than 95,000, was the first double-deck, horseshoe-shaped stadium built in the country.

Destination Columbus

Franklin Park Conservatory, Columbus.
Modern sculptures reflect the
curvilinearity of this 1895 copy
of London's Crystal Palace.
(See listing page 223)

*C*olumbus is a vibrant,
fast-growing city where
industry ranges from traditional
beer brewing to information
technology, and the architecture
ranges from late 19th-century
granite and gargoyles to
contemporary steel and glass.

*I*ts demographics are
representative of those
of the nation, and that means
you can expect to feel at home
in Columbus!

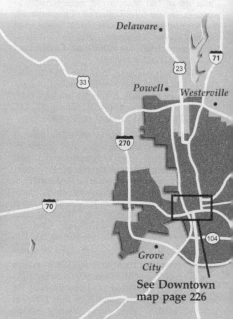

Ohio Statehouse, Columbus.
The uncluttered Doric lines of this Greek
Revival building make it unusual among
its peers. (See listing page 223)

See Downtown
map page 226

*P*laces included in this AAA Destination City:

COSI Columbus.
This unusual
structure contains
a hands-on science
learning center
which bills itself as
"The Fascination
Destination." (See
listing page 223)

Columbus

German Village, Columbus.
Visitors enjoy strolling
through this district of late
19th-century houses, shops
and restaurants. (See
listing page 223)

Self-guiding tours of the Chadwick Arboretum, Fyffe Road and Lane Avenue, are available. Two-hour guided tours of the campus leave the Student Visitor Center, Room 132, Enarson Hall, 154 W. 12th Ave., Mon.-Fri. at 10 and 2; no tours on university holidays. Student Center open Mon.-Fri. 8-5; closed university holidays. The gallery is open Mon.-Fri. 8:30-5:30 (also Tues. and Thurs. 5:30-7:30), Sat. 10-2. Reservations are required for the campus tour at least 2 weeks in advance. Phone (614) 292-3980 for tour reservations.

Wexner Center for the Arts, N. High St. at 15th Ave., is devoted to contemporary visual, performing and media arts. Changing exhibits are featured. Special performances and films are offered for a fee. Allow 1 hour minimum. Tues.-Sun. 10-6 (also Thurs. 6-9 p.m.); phone for holiday schedule. Admission $3, over 54 and students with ID $2, under 12 free; free to all Thurs. 5-9. Phone (614) 292-3535.

THE *SANTA MARIA*, at Battelle Park on Broad St. and Marconi Blvd., is a full-scale replica of the 15th-century cargo vessel that served as Christopher Columbus' flagship during his historic journey to America. A 45-minute guided tour of the ship led by costumed docents highlights the challenges and hardships faced by Columbus and his crew; tours begin as needed.

Allow 1 hour minimum. Wed.-Fri. 10-5, Sat.-Sun. 11:30-6, Memorial Day weekend-Labor Day; Wed.-Fri. 10-3, Sat.-Sun. noon-5, first Sat. in Apr.-day before Memorial Day weekend and day after Labor Day-last Sun. in Oct. Last tour begins 30 minutes before closing. Admission $3; over 59, $2.50; ages 5-17, $1.50. Phone (614) 645-8760.

THE THURBER HOUSE, 77 Jefferson Ave., is a restored 19th-century house containing memorabilia and drawings of author, humorist, cartoonist and playwright James Thurber. Special readings and programs are offered. Allow 30 minutes minimum. Daily noon-4; closed holidays. Guided tours are available Sun. Admission free. Guided tour $2, over 64 and students with ID $1.50, under 6 free. Phone (614) 464-1032.

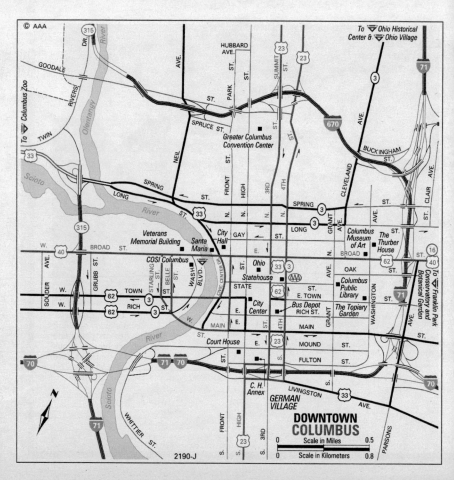

DOWNTOWN COLUMBUS

THE TOPIARY GARDEN, 480 E. Town St. at Washington Ave. in Old Deaf School Park, is a landscape rendition of Georges Seurat's post-impressionist landscape painting "A Sunday After-noon on the Island of La Grande Jatte." Sculptor James T. Mason designed, created and installed the metal frames and topiaries which represent 54 people, eight boats, three dogs, a monkey and a cat; the largest figure is 12 feet high. A pond represents the river Seine. A visitor center is at the Town Street park entrance. Allow 30 minutes minimum. Daily dawn-dusk. Free. Phone (614) 645-0197 11-4 for guided tour information.

What To Do

Sightseeing

An excellent vantage point from which to view the city is the 40th-floor observation deck of the Rhodes State Office Tower. The building, Colum-bus' tallest structure, also can be toured. Specific points of interest on the free tour include the obser-vation deck and the Ohio Supreme Court Lobby. The Supreme Court is in session September through May and is open to the public. Phone (614) 466-7361 for more information.

Carriage Tours

Half-hour horse-drawn carriage rides of the Vic-torian Village and the riverfront are available Friday and Saturday evenings for $30 per couple; phone (614) 444-0608 for reservations.

Sports and Recreation

Columbus does not lack sports enthusiasts. Ohio State University **football** commands the attention of the city on autumn Saturdays; tailgate parties, Buckeye banners and 95,000 fervent fans color horseshoe-shaped Ohio Stadium scarlet and gray with excitement. Ohio State also fields competitive **basketball** and **ice hockey** teams. For information contact the OSU ticket office, in the Jerome Schot-tenstein Center at 555 Donald A. Borror Dr.; phone (614) 292-2624 or (800) 462-8257.

The Columbus Blue Jackets, (614) 431-3600, plays major league **hockey** at the Nationwide Arena at 200 W. Nationwide Blvd. The Columbus Crew, (614) 447-2739, plays major league **soccer** at the Crew Stadium at the Ohio State Expo Center.

Baseball is also a popular spectator sport in Co-lumbus. The Columbus Clippers, the New York Yan-kees' AAA minor league affiliate, has established a winning tradition since joining the International League in 1977. Cooper Stadium, (614) 462-5250, at 1155 W. Mound St., is the site of more than 70 home games April through September.

Horse racing fans have a variety of tracks and styles from which to choose. Quarter horse and Thoroughbred racing can be found September through May at Beulah Park, (614) 871-9600, 3664 Grant Ave. in Grove City. Harness racing is held May to mid-September at Scioto Downs, (614)

491-2515, 6000 S. High St. The biggest pacing event of the year, the Little Brown Jug, is held the third Thursday in September at the Delaware County Fairgrounds.

Note: Policies vary concerning admittance of children to pari-mutuel betting facilities. Phone for information.

For racing fans who demand more horsepower, **stock car racing** is held Saturday nights at 7 p.m. during the summer at the Columbus Motor Speed-way, (614) 491-1047, at 1845 Williams Rd. **Drag racing** excitement revs engines May through Octo-ber at National Trail Raceway, 2650 National Rd. S.W. in nearby Hebron; phone (614) 928-5706.

Columbus offers an abundance of public **golf** courses, including Blacklick Woods, (614) 861-3193, 7309 E. Livingston Ave.; Minerva Lake, (614) 882-9988, 2955 Minerva Lake Rd.; Raymond Memorial, (614) 645-3276, 3860 Trabue Rd.; and Thorn Apple, (614) 878-7703, 1051 Alton at Darby Creek Rd. Other public courses are listed in the telephone directory.

Columbus also is the home of the Memorial Tournament, a professional golf event. The 4-day competition is held at the end of May at Muirfield Village, a course in Dublin designed by Columbus native Jack Nicklaus; phone (614) 889-6700.

Tennis courts are abundant in Columbus, with more than 140 run by the city and numerous others at local colleges and high schools. Phone the con-vention and visitors bureau at (614) 221-6623 for details.

Despite its moderate climate, Columbus is within about an hour's drive of several popular **skiing** ar-eas. Clear Fork, (800) 237-5673, 55 miles northeast in Butler, offers an excellent beginner's slope and other more demanding runs. Snow Trails, (419) 774-9818, is 60 miles northeast near Mansfield and is considered to be Ohio's first ski area.

Mad River Mountain, (937) 599-1015, or (800) 231-7669 outside Ohio, about 40 miles northwest near Bellefontaine, is a large resort with night skiing.

For **bicyclists** and **joggers**, Columbus operates an extensive park system with miles of trails. One of the most scenic routes takes bicyclists 8 miles along the Olentangy River. Columbus plays host to the Columbus Marathon in October and other long-distance running events throughout the year.

Shopping

Columbus, the home of the original regional shopping center, is a natural for discovering bar-gains and hard-to-find items. While the bulk of shopping is done at five suburban malls—Eastland, off I-70 and Hamilton Rd.; Easton Market, off I-270 and Easton Way; The Mall at Tuttle Crossing, off I-270 and Tuttle Crossing Road; Northland, 3 miles east of I-71 on Morse Road; and Westland at W. Broad Street and I-270—specialty shops are sprinkled throughout the area.

The chief landmark of the downtown shopping district is the City Center Mall at 111 S. 3rd St. Anchored by both Jacobsons and Marshall Field's, the mall is connected by a bridge over High Street to the eight-floor Lazarus department store—the flagship of Ohio's noted chain. The Ohio Center Mall, 400 N. High St., contains about 25 stores and is one facet of the hotel-convention center complex. A Show of Hands in the City Center Mall specializes in contemporary Ohio crafts and focuses on one-of-a-kind pieces.

College Traditions, 286 W. Lane Ave., and Conrads College Gifts, 316 W. Lane Ave., carry Ohio State University memorabilia for avid Buckeye boosters. German Village, a restored 19th-century German community on 3rd Street south of I-70/I-71, has antiques, books and baked goods.

In the quaint suburb of Grandview Heights, The Marketplace at Grandview Avenue, located between 3rd and 5th avenues, offers a variety of interesting restaurants, cafes, shops and galleries. The Lane Avenue Shopping Center, 1585 W. Lane Ave., features more than 90 specialty shops, many of which are unique to Columbus.

Brice Outlet Mall, I-70 and Brice Road, offers around 20 discount outlets for stores such as Ben Franklin and Sears. Also off the I-70 Brice Road exit, at 2361 Park Crescent, is JCPenney's Catalog Outlet Store, which posts reductions on merchandise no longer sold in its catalog. Schottenstein Department Store, with locations at 3251 Westerville Rd., 1887 Parsons Ave., 3400 North Blvd., and 6055 E. Main St., features clothing bargains.

Theaters and Concerts

With "Sold Out" stamped on many dates of the performing arts calendar, it is evident that a cultural explosion has hit Columbus. When it comes to entertainment, residents like it big and brassy.

Jazz is prevalent in Columbus, with the Jazz Arts Group's Columbus Jazz Orchestra playing the familiar Big Band sounds of Count Basie, Louis Armstrong and Woody Herman; phone (614) 294-5200. The 17-musician band plays a subscription series at Battelle Auditorium on the OSU campus, (614) 424-7700, and the Palace Theatre, 34 W. Broad St.; phone (614) 469-9850. Aspiring musicians compose the Ohio State University Jazz Ensemble, which performs on campus.

The Columbus Symphony Orchestra plays a regular 9-month concert season in the opulent Ohio Theatre, directly across from the Ohio Statehouse (see attraction listing p. 223). The venue is decorated with plaster ceilings, brocaded paneling, gold leaf trim and a chandelier in the grand foyer; phone (614) 228-9600. The symphony also presents pops and chamber music concerts as well as youth concerts. Another ensemble, the Pro Musica Chamber Orchestra, offers concert series at the Southern Theatre at the corner of High and Main streets; phone (614) 464-0066.

Opera-Columbus performs several major opera productions throughout the year; phone (614) 461-0022. Ballet Met, (614) 229-4848, produces classical and contemporary works. Zivili performs the dance and music of the former Yugoslavia; phone (614) 855-7805.

The Columbus Association for the Performing Arts, (614) 469-1045, brings to the area productions including well-known musical performers and plays. Professional theater and Broadway shows visit area stages on a regular basis. However, the bulk of theater presentations are produced by community groups. Gallery Players at the Jewish Center offers productions, including musicals; phone (614) 231-2731, ext. 260. Grove City's Little Theatre Off Broadway performs cabaret-style theater; phone (614) 875-3919.

Special Events

Highlighted by a celebration honoring the city's namesake, Columbus' calendar is filled with an array of events. Ohio State University is the site of the OSU Jazz Festival in April, with college and high school bands. Origami, kite-making and exotic foods are on tap at the Asian Festival, held mid-May in Franklin Park.

In June the Columbus Arts Festival features music, dance and theater performances, arts, crafts and food. Also during June a guided walking tour of the renovated homes of German Village is offered in the Haus und Garten Tour. The city celebrates our nation's independence with Red, White and Boom in July.

In August, Columbus is the home of the Ohio State Fair, probably the biggest shindig in the state and one of the largest fairs in the nation. Held at the Ohio Expo Center off I-71 between 11th and 17th avenues, the fair has livestock displays, exhibits, entertainment and food.

The birth of the commercially sold tomato is hailed in September by the residents of Reynoldsburg. Later that month private residences in Victorian Village are opened during its Festival and Tour.

Polka bands, bratwurst, beer and thousands of people combine in September to give Columbus one of its grandest celebrations: German Village Oktoberfest. In October, the convening of the All-American Quarter Horse Congress brings one of the world's largest quarter horse shows to the city. Columbus Day activities involve a 3-day weekend and include a parade.

The Columbus International Festival in November mixes ethnic foods, cultures and souvenirs while musicians and dancers of many different nationalities continuously perform on several stages; for more information phone (614) 228-4010. Wildlight Wonderland, held Thanksgiving through New Year's, includes musical performances, animal exhibits at the Columbus Zoo and a display of holiday lights. The year ends with First Night Columbus, a communitywide event featuring dancing, music and fun in downtown.

The Columbus Vicinity

BROWNSVILLE (D-4)

SAVE **FLINT RIDGE STATE MEMORIAL AND MUSEUM**, 3 mi. n. of US 40 on SR 668, encompasses 525 acres. Trails through woods overlook pit areas where American Indians once quarried flint. The museum contains a flint pit and traces the mineral from its raw state to its many uses by tribes. A paved nature trail also is on the grounds.

Park trails and picnic areas open daily dawn-dusk, Apr.-Oct. Museum open Wed.-Sat. 9:30-5, Sun. and holidays noon-5, Memorial Day weekend-Labor Day; Sat. 9:30-5, Sun. noon-5, day after Labor Day-Oct. 31. Museum admission $3; over 59, $2.70; ages 6-12, $1.25. Park admission free except during special events. Phone (740) 787-2476.

CANAL WINCHESTER (D-4) pop. 2,900

SAVE **MID-OHIO HISTORICAL MUSEUM**, SR 33 and Gender Rd., houses a collection of antique dolls and accessories. Featured are rare 18th-century Queen Anne dolls; French and German bisque dolls; and porcelain, papier-mâché and contemporary dolls. Also featured is a handmade miniature circus and midway. Allow 1 hour minimum. Wed.-Sat. 11-5, Apr. 1-Dec. 15; closed holidays. Admission $3, under 6 free. MC, VI. Phone (614) 837-5573.

DELAWARE (D-4) pop. 20,000

OLENTANGY INDIAN CAVERNS are 6 mi. n. of jct. US 23 and I-270, then 2 mi. w. to 1779 Home Rd., following signs. Used by the Wyandot Indians for shelter, the caverns are a series of natural passageways and rooms 55 to 105 feet below ground. The Cave-House Museum features American Indian artifacts and archeological displays. Gem mining is available. Guided tours are available. Allow 1 hour minimum. Daily 9:30-5, Apr.-Oct. Admission $8; over 59, $7.20; ages 7-17, $5. MC, VI. Phone (740) 548-7917.

GRANVILLE (D-4) pop. 4,400

ROBBINS HUNTER MUSEUM, 221 E. Broadway, is in the 1842 Avery-Downer House, a classic example of the temple form of Greek Revival architecture. Eleven furnished rooms contain 18th- and 19th-century American, European and Asian antiques, including furniture, paintings, sculpture, Oriental carpets, musical instruments, clocks, silver, china and Cornelius chandeliers. Wed.-Sun. 1-4, May-Oct.; otherwise by appointment. Admission $2. Phone (740) 587-0430.

GROVE CITY (D-3) pop. 19,700, elev. 851'

THE GARDENS AT GANTZ FARM, 2255 Home Rd. W., offers visitors a self-guiding tour of a series of carefully cultivated herb beds. Many of the plants have been used for centuries to create fragrances, flavors, dyes and medicines. Allow 30 minutes minimum. Daily dawn-11 p.m. Free. Phone (614) 871-6323.

GROVEPORT (D-3) pop. 2,900, elev. 745'

MOTTS MILITARY MUSEUM is at 5075 S. Hamilton Rd. The museum represents military history from pre-Revolutionary War times through the Persian Gulf War. Uniforms, weapons, vehicles and a wealth of memorabilia are on display. Tues.-Sat. 9-5, Sun. 1-5; closed major holidays. Admission $5; over 62, $4; ages 5-18, $3. DS, MC, VI. Phone (614) 836-1500.

HEBRON (D-4) pop. 2,100, elev. 889'

BUCKEYE CENTRAL SCENIC RAILROAD, 2 mi. e. of SR 79 on US 40, offers 12-mile train rides along the old Shawnee Branch of the Baltimore and Ohio Railroad. The train includes four 1930 vintage enclosed cars. Departures Sat.-Sun. at 1 and 3, Memorial Day weekend-Oct. 31. Fare $7; ages 2-11, $5. Special Haunted Halloween trips run Fri.-Sat. at 7 during the last week of Oct. Santa Specials depart at 1 and 3 during the first two weekends in Dec. Phone (740) 928-3827.

LANCASTER (D-4) pop. 34,500, elev. 898'

Settled in 1800 and designated as the county seat by 1806, Lancaster grew even faster after 1836, when the Lancaster Lateral Canal was connected with the Ohio and Erie Canal. With the coming of the railroads in the 1850s and the discovery of natural gas in 1887, the town became one of Ohio's manufacturing and distribution centers, a status it retains.

Preserving the city's heritage are the early 19th-century houses on Square 13, which is bounded by N. High, Broad, Main and Wheeling streets.

THE GEORGIAN, 105 E. Wheeling and Broad sts., is an 1832 Federal-style house. The house displays period furnishings, including an early glass collection. Allow 1 hour minimum. Guided 45-minute tours leave as needed Tues.-Sun. 1-4, Apr. 1-early Dec.; closed holidays. Last tour begins 45 minutes before closing. Admission $2.50; ages 6-18, $1. Combination ticket, including The Sherman House, $4; ages 6-18, $1.50. Phone (740) 654-9923.

MOUNT PLEASANT, in Rising Park, is a sandstone rock 250 feet high with 2 acres of flat top area. Used by the American Indians and settlers as an observation point and a fortress, the rock commands an excellent view of the surrounding country. Its south side projections resemble the profile of an American Indian.

THE SHERMAN HOUSE, 137 E. Main St., was the birthplace and early home of brothers William T. Sherman, Civil War general, and Sen. John Sherman, author of the Sherman Anti-Trust Act. Civil

War mementos and other antiques are displayed. Allow 1 hour minimum. Guided 1-hour tours leave as needed Tues.-Sun. 1-4, Apr. 1-early Dec. Last tour departs 1 hour before closing. Admission $2.50; ages 6-18, $1. Combination ticket, including The Georgian, $4; ages 6-18, $1.50. Phone (740) 687-5891.

[SAVE] **WAHKEENA NATURE PRESERVE**, 6 mi. s. on US 33, then w. on CR 86, following signs, contains trees, wildflowers, rhododendrons, mountain laurels, ferns and eight varieties of native orchids. Some 70 species of birds and 15 species of mammals inhabit the area; among the most common are pileated woodpeckers and white-tailed deer. A museum and nature trails are on the grounds.

Allow 1 hour minimum. Wed.-Sun. 8-4:30, Apr.-Oct.; by appointment rest of year. Admission $2 per private vehicle. Phone (740) 746-8695 or (800) 297-1883.

LITHOPOLIS (D-3) pop. 600, elev. 902'

SLATE RUN LIVING HISTORICAL FARM, 4.5 mi. s. at 1375 SR 674, is an 1880s working farm that includes restored buildings and employs the methods of the late 19th century. The self-guiding tour allows visitors to see farm routines that change with the seasons. Work may include planting or harvesting; cider-, soap- or toy-making; and such daily chores as sewing, cooking and milking.

Allow 1 hour, 30 minutes minimum. Tues.-Thurs. 9-4, Fri.-Sat. 9-6, Sun. 11-6, June-Aug.; Tues.-Sun. 11-4, Apr.-May and Sept.-Dec. Closed Thanksgiving and Dec. 25. Free. Phone (614) 833-1880.

WAGNALLS MEMORIAL is at 150 E. Columbus St. The memorial is dedicated to Adam Willis Wagnalls, one of the founders of Funk and Wagnalls publishing house in 1877. The memorial contains original letters from writer O. Henry to Mabel Wagnalls, paintings by John Ward Dunsmore and paintings once used on covers of literary digests. There also are original paintings by Norman Rockwell. Guided tours are available by appointment.

Mon.-Thurs. 9-9, Fri.-Sat. 9-5 (also Sun. 1-5, Sept.-May); closed holidays. Travelogues are offered Sun. at 2:30, Jan.-May and Sept.-Nov. Free. Fee charged for travelogues. Phone (614) 837-4765.

NEWARK (D-4) pop. 44,400, elev. 822'

The site of several large prehistoric American Indian mounds, Newark was founded in 1802 by a New Jersey man who named the new plot after his hometown. Like its namesake, Newark became a busy center of trade and industry, especially after the completion of the Ohio and Erie Canal in 1832 and the arrival of railroads in the 1850s.

A monument commemorating the canal's groundbreaking ceremony, presided over by New York governor DeWitt Clinton on July 4, 1825, is 3 miles south on SR 79. Also of interest is Cranberry Island on nearby Buckeye Lake *(see Recreation Chart)*. The island is a sphagnum bog that was formed at the end of the ice age; it contains various species of plants, including alder bush, sundew and poison sumac.

Don't miss driving by the Longaberger National Headquarters at 1500 East Main St., a seven-story replica of a Longaberger market basket. The lobby area is open for viewing 8-5, Monday through Saturday, and noon-5 Sunday. The structure is approximately 18 miles west of The Longaberger Basket Company manufacturing campus *(see attraction listing p. 237)* is about 18 miles east in Dresden.

Licking County Convention and Visitors Bureau: 50 W. Locust St., Newark, OH 43058; phone (740) 345-8224 or (800) 589-8224.

DAWES ARBORETUM, 5 mi. s. on SR 13, is a 1,149-acre area with both virgin forest and formally planted sections. Daweswood House, the former home of arboretum founders Beman and Bertie Dawes, is on the grounds. Tour areas are accessible by road. Allow 1 hour minimum. Arboretum open daily dawn-dusk. Visitor center open Mon.-Sat. 8-5, Sun. 1-5. Closed Jan. 1, Thanksgiving and Dec. 25. Free. Phone (740) 323-2355 or (800) 443-2937.

THE INSTITUTE OF INDUSTRIAL TECHNOLOGY is downtown at First and Scheidler sts. Housed in an 1881 steam engine factory, the museum contains interactive history and science exhibits relating to Licking County and central Ohio. Glass-blowing demonstrations are offered. Allow 2 hours minimum. Tues.-Fri. 9-4, Sat.-Sun. noon-4; closed holidays. Admission $4; over 54, $3; ages 4-16, $1. Phone (740) 349-9277.

LICKING COUNTY HISTORICAL SOCIETY, at N. 6th and W. Main sts., includes three restored structures. The 1835 Greek Revival Buckingham House is open for private functions only. The 1815 Sherwood-Davidson House is an example of Federal architecture and displays period furnishings. The historic Webb House, 303 Granville St., focuses on the early 20th century.

Allow 30 minutes minimum for each house. Sherwood-Davidson House open Tues.-Sun. 1-4, Apr.-Dec. Webb House open Thurs.-Fri. and Sun. 1-4, Apr.-Nov. Donations. Phone (740) 345-6525.

NATIONAL HEISEY GLASS MUSEUM, 6th and Church sts., features a collection of 5,000 pieces of glassware made at A.H. Heisey & Co. 1896-1957. Allow 30 minutes minimum. Tues.-Sat. 10-4, Sun. 1-4; closed major holidays. Admission $2, under 18 free with an adult admission. MC, VI. Phone (740) 345-2932.

NEWARK EARTHWORKS is 1 mi. s.w. of SR 16 on SR 79. The 66-acre memorial preserves one portion of the Newark Earthworks, a system of prehistoric Indian mounds. It contains a circular earthwork 1,200 feet in diameter with grass-covered earthen walls ranging from 8 to 14 feet in height. In the center are four lower connected mounds. Another portion of the earthworks, Octagon State Memorial, is nearby. Daily 8-7, Apr.-Oct. Free.

[SAVE] **Ohio Indian Art Museum,** on the Newark Earthworks Memorial grounds, is devoted to prehistoric American Indian art. Objects in various media represent the prehistoric cultures of Ohio. Museum staff provide directions to nearby Octagon and Wright Earthworks State Memorial. Wed.-Sat. 9:30-5, Sun. and holidays noon-5, Memorial Day weekend-Labor Day; Sat. 9:30-5, Sun. noon-5, day after Labor Day-Oct. 31. Admission $3; over 64, $2.70; ages 6-12, $1.25. Phone (740) 344-1920, or (800) 600-7174.

PICKERINGTON (D-3) pop. 5,700, elev. 842′

The town was established shortly after 1811 when Abraham and Ann Pickering built a home and trading post. In 1815 it was finally given a name, Jacksonville, commemorating Andrew Jackson's defeat of British forces in the battle of New Orleans during the War of 1812; citizens changed the name to Pickerington in 1827. The 413 acres of Pickerington Ponds Wetlands Wildlife Refuge feature observation areas with waterfowl, shorebirds and raptors.

Pickerington Area Chamber of Commerce: 13 W. Columbus St., P.O. Box 58, Pickerington, OH 43147; phone: (614) 837-1958.

[SAVE] **MOTORCYCLE HALL OF FAME MUSEUM** is off I-70 exit 112, s. on SR 256, e. on SR 204, following signs to 13515 Yarmouth Dr. Rotating exhibits in four galleries feature motorcycles—from antiques to present-day machines—and displays relating to the sport. The hall of fame contains motorcycles once ridden by inductees. Allow 1 hour minimum. Daily 9-5, noon-4 on Memorial Day, July 4 and Labor Day; closed Jan. 1, Easter, Thanksgiving and Dec. 25. Admission $4; over 62, $3; under 17 free. AE, CB, DI, DS, MC, VI. Phone (614) 856-2222.

POWELL (D-3) pop. 2,200, elev. 922′

[SAVE] **WYANDOT LAKE ADVENTURE PARK,** off I-270 Sawmill Rd. exit next to the Columbus Zoo at 10101 Riverside Dr., is a combination water/amusement park featuring antique carnival rides, a carousel, a roller coaster and a magic show, as well as flumes, a wave pool, water playgrounds and a lazy river. Food is available.

Allow 1 hour, 30 minutes minimum. Park opens daily at 10, late May-late Aug. and Labor Day weekend; Sat.-Sun. the weekend before Memorial Day weekend; Thurs.-Sun. in Oct. Closing times vary; phone ahead. Admission $24.99; under 42 inches tall $17.99; over age 60, $9.99; under age 2 free. Admission after 4 p.m. $13.50. Parking $3. AX, DS, MC, VI. Phone (614) 889-9283 or (800) 328-9283.

WESTERVILLE (D-3) pop. 30,300, elev. 874′

Westerville was established in 1806 by New England settlers. The town became known as the "dry capital of the world" when the Anti-Saloon League settled here in 1918. The Hanby House at 160 W. Main St. is the restored and furnished pre-Civil War home of Benjamin Hanby, author and composer of "Darling Nelly Gray" and "Up on the House Top"; phone (614) 891-6282 or (800) 600-6843. The Westerville Public Library houses the desk where the 18th Amendment to the U.S. Constitution was penned.

Westerville Visitors and Convention Bureau: 28 S. State St., Westerville, OH 43081; phone (614) 794-0401 or (800) 824-8461.

INNISWOOD METRO GARDENS, I-270 exit 27 and .2 mi. n. to Schrock Rd., then 3 mi. e. to 940 S. Hempstead Rd., features plant exhibits, including a large herb garden; landscaped grounds; paved walking paths and a boardwalk that passes through a hardwood forest. Allow 1 hour, 30 minutes minimum. Daily 7-dusk. Free. Phone (614) 895-6216.

THE ROSS C. PURDY MUSEUM OF CERAMICS is off I-270 exit 27; take Cleveland Rd. .5 mi. n. to Schrock Ave., then .5 mi. e. to 735 Ceramic Pl. The museum houses exhibits of traditional and high-tech ceramics produced during the last 150 years. Items include pottery, glass, brick, tile, dinnerware, shuttle tiles, military armor, sporting goods, a working automotive engine and elaborate works of art. Allow 30 minutes minimum. Mon.-Fri. 8-5; closed major holidays. Free. Phone (614) 890-4700.

This ends listings for the Columbus Vicinity.
The following page resumes the alphabetical listings
of cities in Ohio.

CONNEAUT (A-6) pop. 13,200, elev. 650'

The first survey party of the Western Reserve Region reached Conneaut Harbor on July 4, 1796. Later, as settlers arrived, the town adopted the name the Seneca Indians had given to the nearby river, Conneaut, meaning "river of many fishes." On Lake Erie, the development of industry along the harbor made the town a busy port, with shipments running into millions of tons annually.

Today Conneaut's economy also encompasses tourism, with an increasing number of tourists and sportsmen visiting this waterfront community where amenities include marinas, summer cottages, golf courses and a developing wine producing industry. Three local covered bridges are part of nearby Ashtbula's October county covered bridge festival.

Conneaut Area Chamber of Commerce/Board of Tourism: P.O. Box 722, Conneaut, OH 44030; phone (440) 593-2402.

CONNEAUT HISTORICAL RAILROAD MUSEUM, Depot St. at Mill St., is in the old New York Central Station. The museum houses such relics from the railroad steam era as an old steam engine and railroad cars. Allow 30 minutes minimum. Daily noon-5, Memorial Day weekend-Labor Day. Donations. Phone (440) 599-7878.

COSHOCTON (C-4) pop. 12,200, elev. 790'

Coshocton, once the capital for the Delaware Indians, is now a specialty advertising and manufacturing center. Of interest is the Experiment Station, 11 miles northeast on SR 621, one of six in the country where soil and water conservation research on agricultural basins is conducted.

Coshocton County Convention and Visitors Bureau: P.O. Box 905, Coshocton, OH 43812; phone (800) 338-4724.

HISTORIC ROSCOE VILLAGE, on SRs 16 and 83 at jct. US 36, is a restored 1830s Ohio & Erie Canal town, with houses, shops, restaurants and a 50-room inn. The Living History Tour includes crafts demonstrations and displays of canal relics illustrating aspects of daily life on the canal. Many annual festivals and special events are held. Food is available. Tours are given daily 10-3, Mar.-Dec. Shops open daily 10-5. Closed Jan. 1, Thanksgiving and Dec. 25. Living History Tour $9.95; ages 5-12, $4.95. AX, DS, MC, VI. Phone (740) 622-9310 or (800) 877-1830.

Johnson-Humrickhouse Museum, 300 N. Whitewoman St., contains American Indian, European, Oriental and Newark Holy Stones, as well as early American and Ohio displays. Basketry, pottery, lacquerware, cloisonne, carvings, porcelain, pewter and glass are included in the exhibitions. Daily noon-5, May-Oct.; Tues.-Sun. 1-4:30, rest of year. Closed Jan. 1, Thanksgiving and Dec. 24-25. Donations. Phone (740) 622-8710.

Monticello III, .5 mi. n. of the village on SR 83, offers 45-minute horse-drawn canal boat rides on the hour daily 1-5, Memorial Day weekend-Labor Day; Sat.-Sun. 1-5, day after Labor Day-early Oct. Fare $6; over 59, $5; ages 5-12, $3. AX, DS, MC, VI. Phone (740) 622-7528.

COVINGTON (D-1) pop. 2,600, elev. 930'

STILLWATER PRAIRIE RESERVE, 2 mi. w. of SR 48 on SR 185, encompasses 254 acres. The reserve includes woodlands, rolling hills, meadows, wildlife, fishing ponds, boardwalks and 2 miles of nature trails. Daily 8-dusk. Free. Phone (937) 667-1086 or 335-9547.

CUMBERLAND (D-5) pop. 300, elev. 857'

THE WILDS is 4.5 mi. w. on SR 146, 4 mi. s. on Zion Ridge Rd., 1 mi. s. on SR 284, then 1 mi. w. to 14000 International Rd. Situated on 10,000 acres of reclaimed mining land, this wildlife preserve and research facility provides an open-range habitat for threatened and endangered species from Africa, Asia and North America. Visitors take a guided 1-hour bus tour and view such species as the southern white rhino, Prezewalski's wild horses, scimitar-horned oryx and North American bison. Visitors also can learn about the preserve's research and conservation programs at the visitor center and in the educational center which has interactive exhibits. A wetlands walking trail is on the grounds. Food is available.

Allow 2 hours minimum. Tours on the hour daily 9-5, May-Oct. Last tour begins 1 hour before closing. Admission $10; over 59, $9; ages 4-12, $7. Parking $2. Phone (740) 638-5030.

CUYAHOGA FALLS (B-5)
pop. 49,000, elev. 870'

BLOSSOM MUSIC CENTER, 1145 W. Steels Corner Rd., is the summer home of the Cleveland Orchestra. The pavilion, in an 800-acre woodland, has perfect acoustics and unobstructed views. It seats more than 5,000 people under cover and an additional 13,500 on the lawns. Performers range from symphony orchestras to rock groups; concerts take place May-Sept. Phone (330) 920-8040.

CUYAHOGA VALLEY NATIONAL PARK (B-5)

The Cuyahoga Valley National Park is 33,000 acres of valley along a 22-mile section of the Cuyahoga River between Cleveland and Akron. The area is characterized by a river flood plain, streams and creeks, forested valleys and upland plateaus. It offers picnicking, hiking, bicycle trails, bridle trails, winter sports and ranger-guided programs. Special events are held throughout the year.

The recently reconstructed Ohio & Erie Canal Towpath Trail runs the length of the recreation area and parallels remnants of the Ohio & Erie Canal and the twisting Cuyahoga River. Many historical structures, canal locks and wayside exhibits highlighting the history of the Cuyahoga Valley can be seen along the trail.

The national park has four visitor centers: The Canal Visitor Center, on Canal Road in the northwestern tip of the area; Boston Store, on Boston Mills Road in Boston; Happy Days Visitor Center, 300 W. Streetsboro Rd. (SR 303) in Boston Heights; and Hunt Farm Visitor Information Center, on Bolanz Road in Everett. The park is open daily dawn-dusk. The Canal Visitor Center is open daily 8-5; closed major holidays. Hours vary at the other visitor centers, especially in winter; phone ahead.

For further information contact the Cuyahoga Valley National Park, 15610 Vaughn Rd., Brecksville, OH 44141; phone (216) 524-1497. *See Recreation Chart.*

DAYTON (D-1) pop. 182,000, elev. 740′

Dayton is at the confluence of four shallow streams that drain the upper portion of the rich Miami Valley. The site was first surveyed in November 1795, and the following spring three small groups of settlers named the new settlement in honor of Gen. Jonathan Dayton. Today Dayton is home to more than 830 high-technology companies.

Many original buildings still stand in one of the city's first communities, now known as the Oregon Historic District. This 12-block area is bounded by 5th Street, Wayne Avenue, US 35 and Patterson Boulevard. Christmas tours of the district take place the first Tuesday and Wednesday evenings of December; spring garden tours are available in late May and June. Both require reservations; write to the Oregon Historic District, P.O. Box 383, Dayton, OH 45401.

Dayton was the home of the Wright brothers. Wilbur and Orville's original laboratory has been moved to Greenfield Village in Dearborn, Mich. Orville Wright's house is at Harmon and Park avenues in Oakwood. Both brothers are buried at Woodland Cemetery and Arboretum, 118 Woodland Ave.

Courthouse Square, at 3rd and Main streets, is the center of downtown and the site of many events such as concerts and impromptu entertainment.

At 130 Riverside Dr. is the Ohio Korean War Memorial and Veterans Walkway. Vandalia, north of Dayton on I-75, is the site of the Trap Shooting Hall of Fame. The complex houses displays relating to the sport; in August it plays host to marksmen competing for the Grand American Tournament title.

The greater Dayton area is home to the University of Dayton. A variety of nature programs and activities is available in the area. Recreational opportunities in the area include bicycling and hiking on the River Bikeway, which follows the Great Miami and Stillwater rivers for 24 miles. For information about area parks contact Five Rivers Metroparks, 1375 E. Siebenthaler Ave., Dayton, OH 45414; phone (937) 275-7275.

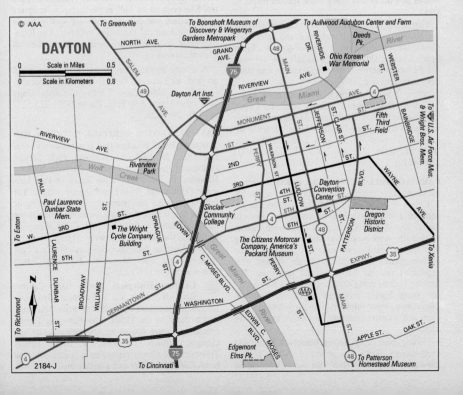

Dayton and Montgomery County Convention and Visitors Bureau: 5th and Main sts. in the Dayton Convention Center, 1 Chamber Plaza, Suite A, Dayton, OH 45402-2400; phone (937) 226-8211, (800) 221-8234 in Ohio, or (800) 221-8235 out of Ohio.

SAVE **AULLWOOD AUDUBON CENTER AND FARM,** 1000 Aullwood Rd., is 10 mi. n. near I-70 at Englewood Dam (US 40). This 350-acre wildlife sanctuary includes 6 miles of hiking trails winding through prairie, woods, marsh ponds, farmland and meadows. The Marie S. Aull Education Center contains hands-on exhibits about southwest Ohio's flora and fauna. Aullwood's Farm is home to pigs, goats and other livestock; an education building features exhibits about farming. Allow 2 hours minimum. Mon.-Sat. 9-5, Sun. 1-5; closed major holidays. Admission $4; ages 2-18, $2. MC, VI. Phone (937) 890-7360.

BOONSHOFT MUSEUM OF DISCOVERY is w. off I-75. Take exit 57B to Siebenthaler Ave. and follow signs to 2600 DeWeese Pkwy. This museum offers interactive exhibits for the entire family. Science Central features a science lab, science theater, a physics lab and a three-story climbing tower. EcoTrek takes visitors through reproductions of desert, ice-age, tropical, woodland and coastal environments, while the Mead Treehouse takes visitors on a forest adventure. In the Exley Wild Ohio zoo, visitors get up close and personal with otters, snakes and ducks and many other species native to Ohio.

That Kid's Playce features activities specifically for children under 6. Planetarium and laser light shows are presented in a state-of-the-art Philips Space Theater. Other features include a 3,000-year-old Egyptian mummy, traveling exhibits and daily demonstrations and activities.

Allow 2 hours minimum. Museum open Mon.-Sat. 9-5, Sun. noon-5; closed Jan. 1, Easter, Thanksgiving, Dec. 24-25 and 31. Space Theater schedule varies; phone for show times. Museum admission $7; over 59, $5; ages 2-12, $4.50. Laser show $6; under 12, $4. MC, VI. Phone (937) 275-7431.

CARRIAGE HILL METRO PARK FARM is reached by taking I-70 exit 38 and going 1 mi. n. on SR 201, then .5 mi. e. on E. Shull Rd. Visitors can experience a working farm as it would have been in the 1880s. A summer kitchen and wash house, blacksmith shop, woodshop and barns are among the reconstructed and restored buildings. The kitchen garden and truck patch are planted with vegetables that are harvested and preserved. The farming is done using draft horses and 19th-century equipment. Special programs are offered Sundays. The visitor center offers exhibits, a videotape program and a center featuring interactive exhibits for children.

Fishing, picnicking, hiking, horseback riding and cross-country skiing are permitted. Allow 1 hour minimum. Mon.-Fri. 10-5, Sat.-Sun. 1-5; closed

Jan. 1 and Dec. 25. Donations. Phone (937) 879-0461. *See Recreation Chart.*

THE CITIZENS MOTORCAR COMPANY, AMERICA'S PACKARD MUSEUM, 420 S. Ludlow St., is housed in an authentic, restored dealership building. About 20-30 Packard models dating 1909-56 are displayed in an Art Deco showroom and a working service department. Visitors may actually climb in and take the wheel of some cars. Allow 1 hour minimum. Mon.-Fri. noon-5, Sat.-Sun. 1-5. Admission $5; under 13, $4. MC, VI. Phone (937) 226-1917 or 226-1710.

COX ARBORETUM AND GARDENS METROPARK, 6733 Springboro Pike, is off I-75 exit 44 and e. onto Miamisburg-Centerville Rd. (SR 725), then 1 mi. n. on Springboro Pike (SR 741). This 186-acre preserve provides 3 miles of nature trails, a shrub garden, water garden, children's boxwood maze, conifer collection, edible landscape garden, plant collections and a butterfly house. The Butterfly House is open seasonally; phone for the schedule.

Allow 1 hour minimum. Grounds open daily 8-dusk. Visitor center open Mon.-Fri. 8-4:30, Sat.-Sun. 1-4. Closed Jan. 1 and Dec. 25. Donations. Phone (937) 434-9005.

GEM **DAYTON ART INSTITUTE,** Forest and Riverview aves. at 456 Belmonte Park N., is in a 1930 Italian Renaissance building. An extensive collection of African, American, Asian and European art as well as photography, sculpture and furniture and decorative art are spotlighted in cultural and special exhibition galleries. The Experiencenter, a participatory family center, presents thematic shows.

A library contains books and periodicals about art and architecture. Guided tours are available. Food is available. Allow 2 hours minimum. Daily 10-5 (also Thurs. 5-9) Free. Phone (937) 223-5277 or (800) 296-4426.

DAYTON AVIATION HERITAGE NATIONAL HISTORICAL PARK contains four geographically separate sites. In 1992 the National Park Service established the Dayton Aviation Heritage National Historical Park to preserve the legacy of Paul Laurence Dunbar and Wilbur and Orville Wright. The four units of the park currently open to the public include the Wright Brothers Aviation Center at the Carillon Historical Park, Wright Cycle Company Building, the Huffman Prairie Flying Field at Wright-Patterson Air Force Base and the Paul Laurence Dunbar State Memorial. Admission varies with site. Phone (937) 225-7705.

SAVE **Carillon Historical Park,** 1000 Carillon Blvd., is 2 mi. s. off S. Patterson Blvd. Four handsome contemporary buildings grace this park, which dates to the 1950s. The Kettering Family Education Center houses an orientation center and changing exhibits. The James F. Dickie Family Transportation Center represents a roundhouse and holds five rail exhibits and a trolley bus.

The John W. Berry, Sr., Wright Brothers Aviation Center is a complex of four buildings. One of them, Wright Hall, houses the original 1905 Wright Flyer III airplane. Other exhibits include antique automobiles and bicycles, a canal lock, a working 1930s print shop, a 1796 log house and a circa 1815 stone house. Food is available.

Allow 2 hours minimum. Tues.-Sat. 9:30-5, Sun. and holidays noon-5, Apr.-Oct. Carillon concerts are held Sun. at 3, Apr.-Aug. (also Sat. at 3, June-Aug.). Admission $5; over 59, $4; ages 3-17, $3. Phone (937) 293-2841.

Huffman Prairie Flying Field, on Wright-Patterson Air Force Base, Area A, was used by the Wright brothers for test flying and perfecting their airplanes as well as their piloting skills. Tests were conducted in secret 1904-05 and in 1910 the brothers established a school of flight on the site. A re-creation of the 1905 hangar and the catapult launch device are on the site. Allow 30 minutes minimum. Daily 8-6. Free. Phone (937) 257-5535, ext. 254.

Paul Laurence Dunbar State Memorial, 219 N. Paul Laurence Dunbar St., is the restored former home of poet, novelist and civil rights advocate Paul Laurence Dunbar. The house contains many of his personal belongings dating from the late 19th and early 20th centuries.

Allow 1 hour minimum. Mon.-Fri. 9:30-4:30, Nov. 1-day before Memorial Day; Wed.-Sat. 9:30-

4:30, Sun. noon-4:30, Memorial Day-Labor Day; Sat. 9:30-4:30, Sun. 12:30-4:30, rest of year. Closed major holidays. Admission $3; over 59, $2.40; ages 6-12, $1.25. Phone (937) 224-7061.

The Wright Cycle Company Building is at 22 S. Williams St. This restored building was the site of the Wright brothers' bicycle and printing businesses 1895-97. A re-created shop exhibit contains period artifacts, bicycles and machinery. Their active interest in flight began while working in this building. Allow 30 minutes minimum. Mon.-Sat. 8:30-4:30, Sun. 11-4:30, Memorial Day-Labor Day; Wed.-Sat. 8:30-4:30, Sun. 11:30-4:30, rest of year. Closed Jan. 1, Thanksgiving and Dec. 25. Free. Phone (937) 225-7705.

PATTERSON HOMESTEAD MUSEUM, 1815 Brown St., was built in the 1820s by Col. Robert Patterson, Revolutionary War hero and founder of Lexington, Ky. Remodeled by Col. Patterson's son Jefferson in 1850, the house contains portraits and family memorabilia along with 18th- and early 19th-century furnishings. Several heirloom flower gardens provide seasonal foliage around the property. Allow 1 hour minimum. Wed.-Sat. 1-4, May-Oct.; closed holidays. Admission $2. Phone (937) 222-9724.

SAVE **SUNWATCH INDIAN VILLAGE** is s. on I-75 to exit 51 and 1 mi. w. on Edwin C. Moses Blvd., then 1 mi. s. on W. River Rd. to 2301 W.

River Rd. More than 800 years ago a group of early American Indian farmers, known as the Fort Ancient Indians, developed a complex system of charting time based on observations of the sun's position. Sunwatch is a reconstruction at the site of one of their villages. Visitors can explore the rebuilt houses, gardens and learn about the way of life of the Fort Ancient Indians.

Special demonstrations and children's programs are offered on the first Saturday of the month; phone ahead for event schedules. Allow 2 hours minimum. Tues.-Sat. 9-5, Sun. and holidays noon-5; closed Jan. 1, Easter, Thanksgiving and Dec. 24-25 and 31. Admission $5; over 54 and ages 6-17, $3. MC, VI. Phone (937) 268-8199.

UNITED STATES AIR FORCE MUSEUM, is off I-675 exit 15, 4.7 mi. n.e. on Springfield Pike. One of the oldest and largest military aviation museums in the world, this museum features more than 300 aircraft and missiles in six main galleries. Displays include the advanced missiles and bombs used during the Persian Gulf War and early spacesuits.

The aircraft of Presidents Franklin D. Roosevelt, Harry S. Truman, Dwight D. Eisenhower, John F. Kennedy and Lyndon B. Johnson are housed in the museum's Presidential Aircraft Hangar, about 1 mile from the main building. Also exhibited is the only remaining XB-70, as well as a YF-22, an F-117, an F-111, a B-1, an SR-71 and aircraft from World War I, World War II and foreign nations. The IMAX theater presents 40-minute space and aviation films every hour. Food is available.

Allow 4 hours minimum. Daily 9-5; closed Jan. 1, Thanksgiving and Dec. 25. Museum free. IMAX $6; over 59, $5.50; students with ID $4.50; ages 3-7, $3. MC, VI. Phone (937) 255-3286, or 253-4629 for the IMAX theater.

WEGERZYN GARDENS METROPARK is 1.5 mi. off I-75 exit 57B; take Siebenthaler Ave. w., following signs to 1301 E. Siebenthaler Ave. These formal gardens feature Victorian, English and Federal theme gardens as well as rose, shade and children's gardens. Planted limestone walls and perennial borders flank the Garden Green. Also featured are the scenic Stillwater River, the Marie Aull Nature Trail and a mature swamp forest through which a 350-foot boardwalk meanders. Programs about horticulture are presented. Gardens open daily 8 a.m.-dusk; closed Jan. 1 and Dec. 25. Center open Mon.-Fri. 8-5; closed major holidays. Free. Phone (937) 277-6545.

WRIGHT BROTHERS MEMORIAL is 5 mi. n. on SR 4 to SR 444, then e. on Kauffman Rd. The memorial was erected in 1940 to honor Wilbur and Orville Wright. The brothers made the first powered flight Dec. 17, 1903, at Kitty Hawk, N.C. The site overlooks Huffman Prairie Flying Field on Wright-Patterson Air Force Base, where the Wrights ran a flight school 1910-16. Daily 8-8. Free. Phone (937) 257-5535, ext. 254.

DEFIANCE (B-2) pop. 16,800, elev. 710′

Gen. Anthony Wayne chose a location in the Maumee Valley for Fort Defiance, which he built in 1794. The site of the fort is marked by plaques and stones in the Defiance city park. Old earthworks are visible. Other marked historic sites in Defiance include Fort Winchester, built in 1812 by Gen. William Henry Harrison; the 1650 French Mission in Kingsbury Park; the 1811-28 Johnny Appleseed Nursery; and the birthplace of Ottawa Indian Chief Pontiac.

Defiance Area Chamber of Commerce: P.O. Box 130, Defiance, OH 43512; phone (419) 782-7946.

DELAWARE—see Columbus p. 229.

DENNISON (C-5) pop. 3,300, elev. 908′

(SAVE) **DENNISON RAILROAD DEPOT MUSEUM,** 400 Center St., is housed in an 1873 railroad depot that came to be called the Servicemen's Canteen in 1942. Better known as "Dreamsville," this depot was a popular stop for servicemen during World War II. Volunteers and the Salvation Army offered free food and comfort to more than 1.5 million transient soldiers. Seven rooms of displays include railroad memorabilia, uniforms, photographs

and World War II relics. A 1950s caboose and loco-motive are on the grounds. Food is available.

Allow 1 hour minimum. Tues.-Sat. 10-5, Sun. 11-3; closed major holidays. Admission $3; over 59, $2.50; ages 7-17, $1.75. MC, VI. Phone (740) 922-6776.

DOVER (C-5) pop. 11,300, elev. 875′

J.E. REEVES VICTORIAN HOME AND CAR-RIAGE HOUSE MUSEUM is at 325 E. Iron Ave. (SR 800). The Victorian mansion contains period furnishings. The adjoining museum displays antique vehicles and other historical items. Allow 1 hour minimum. Tues.-Sun. noon-4, June-Oct.; daily noon-8, Dec. 1-20; by appointment rest of year. Admission $5; over 64, $4; ages 6-17, $2. Phone (330) 343-7040 or (800) 815-2794.

WARTHER CARVINGS, 331 Karl Ave., is .5 mi. e. of I-77 exit 83. This museum displays items fashioned by "world master carver" Ernest "Mooney" Warther. Using only a knife, files and ingenuity, Warther became known for carving models of steam locomotives. One carving is a scaled-down replica of the steel mill where he worked for 24 years.

A highlight is the Tree of Pliers—more than 500 interconnecting pairs of working pliers carved out of a solid piece of walnut. Also displayed are Warther's 1912 workshop, carvings depicting Abraham Lincoln's life and death, an arrowhead collection and his wife Frieda's collection of 73,000 buttons. A caboose, railroad memorabilia and a Swiss-style garden are on the grounds. Visitors also can view Warther knives being made.

Allow 1 hour, 30 minutes minimum. Daily 9-5, Mar.-Nov.; 10-4 rest of year. Closed Jan. 1, Easter, Thanksgiving and Dec. 25. Last tour begins 1 hour before closing. Guided 1-hour tour $8.50; ages 6-17, $4. MC, VI. Phone (330) 343-7513. *See color ad.*

DRESDEN (D-4) pop. 1,600

Founded in 1817, Dresden is now the home of reportedly the world's largest basket. Measuring 48 feet long, 11 feet wide and 23 feet high, the basket is made of 10 hardwood maples and took 2,000

hours to complete. Don't miss driving by the Long-aberger National Headquarters in Newark *(see place listing p. 230)*, about 18 miles west of Dresden; the building is a seven-story replica of a Long-aberger market basket.

LONGABERGER BASKET COMPANY, 2.9 mi. w. of jct. SRs 60 and 16, offers self-guided tours where visitors witness the art of basket making. Weaving demonstrations are given in the gallery. The best time to visit is Mon.-Fri. before 1; production generally is not scheduled on the weekends. Allow 1 hour minimum. The entire production process may be viewed Mon.-Fri. 8-1. Tours of the facility are available Mon.-Sat. 8-5 (Labor Day 11-4), Sun. noon-5; closed Jan. 1-2, Easter, Thanksgiving, Dec. 24-25 and 31. Free. Phone (740) 322-5588.

EAST LIVERPOOL (C-6)
pop. 13,700, elev. 686′

Founded in 1798 on the banks of the Ohio River, East Liverpool was once a leading producer of pottery. Surrounded by an area rich in natural clays and coal, the city manufactured about half the nation's pottery until the industry declined in the early 1930s. The city's downtown sits along the route of the Old Lincoln Highway and is near the first survey line for the Northwest Territory.

HALL CHINA CO., e. edge of town on SR 39, offers self-guiding tours explaining the making of chinaware from raw clay to the finished product. Mon.-Fri. 9:15-2. Free. Children must be with an adult. Phone (330) 385-2900.

MUSEUM OF CERAMICS, 400 E. Fifth St., traces the rise and decline of the ceramics industry in East Liverpool and covers the industry's effects on the town and its people. Displayed are life-size dioramas of a jigger shop, kiln and decorating shop; photographs, charts and maps tracing local history; and a collection of ceramics ranging from primitive yellow ware to highly refined Lotus Ware. A videotape presentation is shown, and guide service is available upon request.

Allow 1 hour minimum. Wed.-Sat. 9:30-5, Sun. and holidays noon-5, Mar.-Nov.; by appointment rest of year. Closed major holidays. Admission $5; over 64, $4.50; ages 6-12, $1.25. DS, MC, VI. Phone (330) 386-6001.

EATON (D-1) pop. 7,400

Eaton-Preble County Chamber of Commerce: 110 W. Main St., P.O. Box 303, Eaton, OH 45320; phone (937) 456-4949.

FORT ST. CLAIR PARK, 1 mi. w. off SR 122, encompasses 89 acres. Fort St. Clair, built in 1792, was the scene of a battle that year between Maj. John Adair's Kentucky soldiers and the Miami Indians under Chief Little Turtle. Picnic facilities are available. Daily 8-8, Apr.-Oct.; 6 p.m.-10 p.m. in Dec. Free. Phone (937) 456-4125.

ELMORE (B-3) pop. 1,300, elev. 616′

SAVE **SCHEDEL FOUNDATION ARBORETUM AND GARDENS,** n. of Ohio Turnpike exit 81 on SR 51, was established by German immigrants in the early 1930s. The 17-acre arboretum and numerous gardens include a bonsai exhibit, rose and iris gardens, a perennial garden and a Japanese garden with pagodas and waterfalls; more than 20,000 annuals are planted yearly. A Victorian mansion on the grounds houses antiques, Persian rugs and a jade collection. Guided tours of the house and/or gardens are available by reservation and for an additional fee. Allow 30 minutes minimum. Mon.-Sat. 10-4, Sun. noon-4, May-Oct.; closed holidays. Admission $5. Phone (419) 862-3182.

ELYRIA (B-4) pop. 56,700, elev. 733′

HICKORIES MUSEUM is 6 blks. n. of town square at 509 Washington Ave. Guides offer tours of the mansion, which was state-of-the-art when completed in 1896. Numerous architectural details employ various styles. A library offers genealogical information. Tues.-Sat. 11-2:30. Admission $3.50; ages 6-12, $1. Phone (440) 322-3341.

FAIRBORN (D-2) pop. 31,300

Wright-Patterson Air Force Base, contiguous to Fairborn, is headquarters of the Air Force Logistics Command, the procurement, maintenance, transportation and supply agency for the U.S. Air Force. It also is the home of the Aeronautical Systems Division, which manages the development and acquisition of aeronautical systems for the Air Force, and the Air Force Institute of Technology, the service's graduate school for engineers. Fairborn is also the home of 16,000-student Wright State University.

For an old-time shopping experience try Foy's Variety, Halloween Store at 18-20 E. Main St. The variety store has been open since the 1920s and maintains its original ambience. The Halloween store and the costume store at 10 W. Main st. are more recent, and from late September through All Hallows' Eve are joined by other temporary estab-

lishments such as the Haunted Museum and the Glow in the Dark Shop to form the Halloween Mini Mall; look for appropriate decorations on some of the stores downtown. Phone (800) 642-9686.

Fairborn Ohio Area Chamber of Commerce: 12 N Central Ave. Fairborn, OH 45324; phone (937) 878-3191.

 **UNITED STATES AIR FORCE MUSEUM**—*see Dayton p. 236.*

FINDLAY (B-2) pop. 35,700

Findlay was the home of the *Findlay Jeffersonian,* which published the fictitious Civil War letters of "Petroleum Vesuvius Nasby," a stupid Copperhead whose arguments made the Confederacy appear ridiculous. The town also was an active stop on the Underground Railroad. Diverse industries now support the city.

Hancock Historical Museum, 422 W. Sandusky St., presents glass displays and historical items. A research library is available. Phone (419) 423-4433.

The University of Findlay's Center for Equine and Pre-Veterinary Studies, 11613 CR 40, where students and instructors ride and train horses, features guided tours by appointment and summer horse shows; phone (419) 424-4656.

Findlay-Hancock County Chamber of Commerce: 123 E. Main Cross St., Findlay, OH 45840; phone (419) 422-3313.

Shopping areas: Jeffrey's Antique Gallery, I-75 exit 161, features more than 250 antiques dealers.

GHOST TOWN MUSEUM PARK, 6 mi. s. on US 68, then 1.5 mi. w. on CR 40, is a re-creation of a town of the 1880s. Among the 28 buildings are a barbershop, print shop and general store. Allow 1 hour minimum. Tues.-Sun. 7:30-5, Memorial Day-Labor Day. Admission $4; over 55, $3.50; under 12, $3. Phone (419) 326-5874 to verify schedule.

HANCOCK COUNTY COURTHOUSE, jct. Main Cross and Main sts. to 300 S. Main St., still houses the governmental operations of Findlay. The 1886 courthouse is noted for its stained glass, original furnishings in the courtroom and a painting of Lady Justice. Allow 30 minutes minimum. Mon.-Fri. 8:30-4:30; closed holidays. Free. Phone (419) 424-7037.

THE MAZZA COLLECTION GALLERIA, in the Virginia B. Gardner Fine Arts Pavilion on the University of Findlay campus at 1000 N. Main St., houses original artwork by renowned illustrators of children's books. The galleria claims to be the world's first and largest gallery specializing in such art, and the collection contains more than 1,800 pieces, including Marcia Brown's illustrations from "Cinderella" and several drawings by Randolph J. Caldecott, for whom the Caldecott Medal is named. Wed.-Fri. noon-5, Sun. 1-4; closed holidays. Donations. Phone (419) 424-4560.

No matter where you go, you'll find a 10% discount.

CHOICE HOTELS
INTERNATIONAL ®

1.800.228.1AAA
choicehotels.com

The Power of Being There. Go SM

FORT JEFFERSON (D-1) elev. 1,035'

FORT JEFFERSON STATE MEMORIAL, 6 acres off SR 121, marks the site of the fort built in 1791 by Gen. Arthur St. Clair's army. Picnicking is permitted. Daily dawn-dusk. Free. Phone (614) 297-2300.

FORT RECOVERY (C-1)
pop. 1,300, elev. 923'

[SAVE] **FORT RECOVERY STATE MEMORIAL,** on SR 49 at SR 119, is where Gen. Arthur St. Clair was defeated by Miami Indians in 1791. The 9-acre site contains two blockhouses with a connecting stockade wall. The Fort Recovery Museum depicts the Indian Wars of the 1790s, and an adjacent museum displays local artifacts. Dedicated to those who fought in the disputes of 1791-94, a monument stands at SR 49 and W. Butler Street. A pioneer cemetery is 2 blocks south on Gwendolyn Street.

Allow 1 hour minimum. Museum open daily noon-5, June-Aug.; Sat.-Sun. noon-5 in May and Labor Day-third weekend in Sept. Admission $3; ages 6-12, $1. Phone (419) 375-4649.

FOSTORIA (B-3) pop. 15,000, elev. 780'

Fostoria was created when the two small villages of Risdon and Rome were unified in 1854. The new town was named in honor of C.W. Foster, a prominent pioneer whose son Charles later became governor of Ohio and secretary of the U.S. Treasury.

During the late 19th and early 20th centuries, Fostoria was the home of several glass manufacturing plants. Although their furnaces are now cold, the local glass companies and the craftsmanship for which they were known are remembered at Glass Heritage Gallery at 109 N. Main St.; phone (419) 435-5077.

FREDERICKTOWN (C-4)
pop. 2,400, elev. 1,130'

RECREATIONAL ACTIVITIES
Horseback Riding

• **Heartland Resort Riding Stable,** 2994 Township Rd. 190, Fredericktown, OH 43019. Daily 9-4 and by appointment. Phone (419) 768-9100 or 768-9300.

FREMONT (B-3) pop. 17,600, elev. 613'

Fremont is on the site of 1813 Fort Stephenson, where 21-year-old Maj. George Croghan and 150 American soldiers repelled an attack by 400 British soldiers and 300 American Indians.

Rodger Young Park, on the Sandusky River, is dedicated to the World War II hero and to all the Sandusky County servicemen and women.

Fremont/Sandusky County Convention and Visitors Bureau: 1510 E. State St., Fremont, OH 43420; phone (419) 332-4470 or (800) 255-8070.

 HAYES PRESIDENTIAL CENTER, Hayes and Buckland aves., occupies a 25-acre site known as Spiegel Grove. The center encompasses the Victorian mansion and [SAVE] wooded estate of President and Mrs. Rutherford B. Hayes. Also on the grounds is the first official presidential museum, which contains family mementos, a library and the public and private papers and books of the president and his family. The iron gates at the six entrances to the area were at the White House during the Hayes administration.

Museum and mansion open Mon.-Sat. 9-5, Sun. and holidays noon-5. Library open Mon.-Sat. 9-5. Closed Jan. 1, Thanksgiving and Dec. 25. Museum or mansion $5; over 59, $4; ages 6-12, $1.25. Combination admission to both museum and mansion $8.50; over 59, $7.50; ages 6-12, $2.50. Library free. MC, VI. Phone (419) 332-2081 or (800) 998-7737.

MEMORIAL MONUMENT, 423 Croghan St. in Birchard Library Park, is dedicated to the soldiers and sailors of Sandusky County who fought in U.S. wars. The monument marks the site of Maj. George Croghan's grave. The single cannon used by the Americans in their 1813 victory at Fort Stephenson is on the grounds. Daily dawn-dusk. Free.

GALLIPOLIS (F-4) pop. 4,800, elev. 561'

The second permanent settlement in the state, Gallipolis (galli-po-LEECE), meaning "the city of Gauls," was founded in 1790 by French Royalists who were fleeing the French Revolution.

Le Place, a community park overlooking the Ohio River, is the site of the original settlement of the "French 500." The town's heritage is evident in the old houses surrounding the park.

Fortification Hill, in Mound Hill Cemetery, offers a view of Gallipolis and the Ohio River Valley to the hills of West Virginia. French Art Colony, 530 1st Ave., is a multicultural arts center housed in an 1855 Greek Revival house; phone (740) 446-3834.

Gallia County Convention and Visitors Bureau: 61 Court St., Gallipolis, OH 45631; phone (800) 765-6482.

OUR HOUSE MUSEUM, 432 1st Ave., is 1 blk. s. of the courthouse off SR 7. Built in 1819, this restored river inn is furnished in period and contains a museum of early Americana. Wed.-Sat. 10-4, Sun. 1-4, Memorial Day-Labor Day; Sat. 10-4, Sun. 1-4, May 1-day before Memorial Day and day after Labor Day-Oct. 31. Admission $4; senior citizens $3; under 12, $1. Phone (740) 446-0586.

GNADENHUTTEN (C-5) pop. 1,200

GNADENHUTTEN MONUMENT (ja-NA-den-hutten), 1 mi. s., following historical tour signs, is a 9-acre memorial that includes a log church and cooper's cabin reconstructed on the site of the original village. In 1782 more than 90 Christian

The Lincoln Highway

The horseless carriage rolled onto the American landscape in the 1890s. By 1910 there were more than 450,000 registered automobiles, yet the country still lacked a public road system.

Organized movements for better roads brought issues to the attention of the federal government, which had not participated in major road construction since it funded the National Road project in 1806.

But one particular initiative captured the public's support with a unique idea. In 1913 Carl Fisher—the man who built the Indianapolis Motor Speedway in 1909—and automobile industry leaders chartered the Lincoln Highway Association for the purpose of defining a direct coast-to-coast automobile route.

The LHA's first official act was to delineate a 3,389-mile, 12-state continuous route from New York to California—one that would be passable before the opening of the 1915 Panama-Pacific International Exposition in San Francisco. Although not perfect, the throughway was ready as promised, and a motion picture of America's transcontinental highway was shown at the exposition. Over time, the association improved surfaces by using better materials, shortened the driving distance with realignments and published guidebooks about the Lincoln Highway. Automobile touring had never been so good.

Through example, the LHA educated the public as well as state and federal governments about the value of good roads for almost 15 years. The 1919 moving of a military convoy over the "Lincolnway" foretold the utility of an integrated highway system for national defense and interstate commerce.

With the 1921 Federal Highway Act came the funds for states to construct and maintain connecting arteries. Four years later the United States adopted a highway numbering

American Indians were massacred at this Moravian mission by soldiers. A museum containing area relics and American Indian artifacts also is on the grounds.

Mon.-Sat. 10-5, Sun. noon-5, June 1-Labor Day; Sat. 10-5, Sun. noon-5, day after Labor Day-Oct. 31; by appointment rest of year. Donations. Phone (740) 254-4143 or 254-4756.

GRAND RAPIDS (B-2) pop. 1,000, elev. 654′

ISAAC LUDWIG MILL, .2 mi. e. on SR 65, then n. on SR 578, is a restored 19th-century mill on the banks of the Maumee River. Visitors can see demonstrations of frontier crafts and a flour mill, saw mill and electric generator powered by water from the Old Miami and Erie Canal. Living-history characters are stationed throughout the mill to answer visitors' questions. Narrated, 45-minute mule-drawn canalboat rides are available.

Allow 1 hour minimum. Mill open Wed.-Sun. 10-5, May-Oct. Canal rides are offered on the hour Wed.-Fri. 10-4, Sat.-Sun. 11-5, May-Oct. Mill free. Canal ride $4; over 59, $3; ages 3-12, $2. DS, MC, VI. Phone (419) 535-3050 or 535-3058.

TOLEDO, LAKE ERIE AND WESTERN RAILWAY *BLUEBIRD* PASSENGER TRAIN, departing from Third and Mill sts., uses restored engines and coaches as its rolling stock and displays other equipment. Trains depart from both Waterville and Grand Rapids for a 20-mile, 1.5-hour round trip. The trip includes a spectacular view from a 900-foot-long bridge over the Maumee River.

The train leaves Wed.-Thurs. at 10:30, noon and 1:30, Sat.-Sun. and holidays at 1, 2:30 and 4, June-Aug.; otherwise varies. Fare $8; over 64, $7; ages 3-12, $4.50. Phone (419) 878-2177.

GRANVILLE—see Columbus p. 229.

GREENVILLE (D-1) pop. 12,900, elev. 1,030′

Greenville was the site of Fort Greenville, built in 1793 by Gen. Anthony Wayne and named for Gen. Nathanael Greene. After his victory at Fallen Timbers, Wayne signed a treaty at the fort with several tribes, which opened up the Northwest Territory for settlement. The fort was later burned and abandoned, but the site is marked by the Fort Greenville Treaty Memorial in front of the City Building. The Greenville Treaty scene is etched on a stone at the corner of Elm and West Main.

Darke County Visitors Bureau: 202 E. Main St., Greenville, OH 45331; phone (937) 548-5158 or (800) 504-2995.

BEAR'S MILL, 5 mi. e. on US 36, then .2 mi. s. on Arcanum-Bear's Mill Rd., is a water-powered flour mill built in 1849; President James Monroe granted the land and water rights to Maj. George Adams in 1824. Said to be one of the last operating mills in the state, the mill grinds cornmeal and flours using water power from Greenville Creek. A self-guiding tour of the four-story structure is available. Allow 1 hour minimum. Thurs.-Sun. 11-5, June-Nov.; daily 11-5 in Dec.; Sat.-Sun. 11-5, Jan.-Mar.; Fri.-Sun. 11-5, rest of year. Donations. Phone (937) 548-5112.

GARST MUSEUM, 205 N. Broadway (SR 118N), with the main entrance on Wilson Dr., was built in 1852 as an inn for railroad passengers. Displays include relics of the Indian Wars, pioneer artifacts and Annie Oakley's prizes and mementos. Lowell Thomas, a pioneer of broadcast journalism, was born in nearby Woodington; his early home has been moved to the museum grounds.

A painting by Howard Chandler Christy depicts the signing of the 1795 Treaty of Greenville. A research library also is on the grounds. Allow 2 hours minimum. Tues.-Sat. 11-5, Sun. 1-5, Feb.-Dec. Admission $3; over 59, $2; ages 6-18, $1. Phone (937) 548-5250.

GROVE CITY—see Columbus p. 229.

GROVEPORT—see Columbus p. 229.

HAMILTON (E-1) pop. 61,400, elev. 593'

Founded as Fort Hamilton in 1791, Hamilton became a prosperous industrial community due to immigrant labor and canals. In the late 1820s a wharf basin was dug, linking the town to the Miami and Erie Canal. At the same time an influx of German and Irish immigrants provided the labor for new enterprises.

Heavy industry expanded when Hamilton Hydraulic was completed in 1852. In addition to industry, the Hamilton region enjoys the agricultural yields of the fertile Great Miami River Valley. Hamilton's historic houses and commercial buildings, which show a variety of architectural styles, are concentrated in three districts: Rossville, Dayton Lane and German Village.

On Monument Street, the Soldiers, Sailors and Pioneers Monument is topped by a 17-foot brass figure of a Civil War private. The monument contains a library with the names of all Ohioans who served in the Civil War and World War I.

Hamilton Convention and Visitors Bureau: 1 Riverfront Plaza, Hamilton, OH 45011; phone (513) 844-8080 or (800) 311-5353.

Self-guiding tours: Brochures describing walking tours of all three historic districts are available from the convention and visitors bureau.

BUTLER COUNTY HISTORICAL MUSEUM, 327 N. 2nd St. in the Benninghofen House, contains Victorian furnishings. Displays include antique clocks, dolls, American Indian artifacts and antique farming and kitchen items. Allow 1 hour minimum. Tues.-Sun. 1-4; closed holidays. Free. Phone (513) 896-9930.

FITTON CENTER FOR CREATIVE ARTS, at 101 S. Monument Ave., is a three-story center promoting local and regional artists. Two galleries on the second floor feature rotating exhibits of paintings and sculpture, while the Vista Room offers a fine view of the Miami River. Allow 30 minutes minimum. Mon.-Thurs. 9-8, Fri. 9-6, Sat. 9-noon; closed holidays. Free. Phone (513) 863-8873.

LANE-HOOVEN HOUSE, 319 N. 3rd St., is a restored octagonal 1863 Gothic Revival-style brick house. The house has an unusual spiral staircase that winds to the

The Lincoln Highway
(continued)

system, and most of the Lincoln route became US 30, 40 and 50. The association disbanded in 1928, but not before it engaged Boy Scout troops across the country to place some 3,000 concrete Lincoln Highway markers along the route in all 12 states: New York, New Jersey, Pennsylvania, Ohio, Indiana, Illinois, Iowa, Nebraska, Wyoming, Utah, Nevada and California. Many of these markers still exist.

Carl Fisher envisioned that the Lincoln Highway would represent the most direct route across the country. While terrain in some states made this nearly impossible, the Ohio Lincolnway took a fairly straight course across the state. Minor realignments over the years diverted the original route slightly to the north in one area, or to the south in another, resulting in a line that can be followed today using US 30. Principal cities along the route included **East Liverpool,** just across the Ohio River from Pennsylvania, and **Canton, Wooster, Ashland** and **Mansfield. Lima,** on the early highway, was bypassed as a result of a later adjustment through **Cairo.** Through Van Wert, travelers approached Indiana. **Look for these Ohio Lincoln Highway landmark towns in this TourBook guide.**

For more information about the old Lincoln Highway, contact the new Lincoln Highway Association, P.O. Box 308, Franklin Grove, IL 61031; phone (815)456-3030.

third-floor turret. The main floor boasts detailed butternut and ash woodwork and a stained-glass entrance. The house is partially furnished in period. Allow 1 hour minimum. Mon.-Fri. 9-4. Donations. Phone (513) 863-1389.

[SAVE] **PYRAMID HILL SCULPTURE PARK & MU-SEUM**, 1 mi. s. on SR 128/Hamilton-Cleves Rd., is a 265-acre wooded park featuring natural galleries showcasing large-scale contemporary 3-dimensional works of art. One-way roads wind past an arboretum, gardens, an amphitheater, the ruins of a 19th-century stone house and seven lakes. Allow 30 minutes minimum. Pets, motorcycles and bicycles are not permitted. Tues.-Sun. 10-6, Apr.-Oct.; Sat.-Sun. 10-4 (weather permitting), rest of year. Schedule may vary; phone ahead. Admission Tues.-Fri. $3; Sat.-Sun. $4; ages 5-12, $1.50. Phone (513) 868-8336.

HEBRON—*see Columbus p. 229.*

HINCKLEY (B-5) pop. 5,400

Hinckley has the dubious honor of being the place where buzzards return every March 15 after wintering in the Smoky Mountains. Rivaling the legendary swallows that return to Capistrano, more than 75 buzzards descend upon Hinckley Reservation and Whipp's Ledges on the same day each year.

Two local legends speculate about the buzzards' initial attraction to Hinckley. One story claims that the scavengers were drawn to the town in 1808 by the body of a Wyandot woman who was hanged for witchcraft. Another tale suggests that they arrived in 1819 after The Great Hunt, during which hundreds of predators were killed to curb livestock losses.

The curious event first was documented by a park patrolman who logged their arrival for 23 years. In February 1957, a *Cleveland Press* reporter recounted the story, and the following March 15 Hinckley was descended upon by more than just buzzards: Thousands of spectators came to see these turkey vultures arrive at their nesting grounds. To prepare for future deluges, the town proclaimed the Sunday following March 15 as Buzzard Sunday. Hinckley welcomes its visitors with a pancake breakfast in area schools, and naturalists and park rangers supervise a "birdwalk."

HOPEWELL CULTURE NATIONAL HISTORICAL PARK (E-3)

About 3 miles north of Chillicothe on SR 104, this 120-acre tract with a 13-acre earth wall enclosure preserves 23 prehistoric burial mounds that lie within a low embankment. The Hopewell Indians, who inhabited the area from about 200 B.C. to A.D. 500, were noted for their artistry and their practice of erecting earth mounds over their dead. These artisans fashioned ornaments from materials foreign to Ohio.

A visitor center contains exhibits and public facilities, including an auditorium with a 17-minute orientation film and recorded description about the history of the site. Marked trails and trailside exhibits also can be found. Pets must remain on a leash.

Allow 1 hour minimum. Visitor center open daily 8:30-5; closed Jan. 1, Thanksgiving and Dec. 25. Monument open daily dawn-dusk. Admission $3, under 17 free; free to all Dec.-Feb. Maximum charge per private vehicle is $5. Phone (740) 774-1125.

HUBBARD (B-6) pop. 8,000, elev. 970′

WORLD WAR II VEHICLE MUSEUM, 1.5 mi. w. to 5959 W. Liberty St., contains a very large collection of military vehicles and tanks in good to excellent condition, all housed in a building large enough to allow visitors to walk around them for good views. Also displayed are weapons, uniforms and other military artifacts from various countries. Guided 1-hour tours are available. Mon.-Fri. 9-noon and 1-5; closed holidays. Admission $5; under 11, $3. Phone (330) 534-8125.

INDEPENDENCE—*see Cleveland p. 219.*

IRONTON (F-4) pop. 12,800, elev. 540′

LAWRENCE COUNTY MUSEUM, 506 S. 6th St., features permanent and rotating exhibits about the iron industry as well as vintage clothing and furniture. It is housed in a restored 1870 Victorian house that once served as a way station on the Underground Railroad. Rev. John Rankin, a prominent abolitionist, lived in the house until his death in 1886. Allow 1 hour minimum. Fri.-Sun. 1-5, Apr. 9-Dec. 16 Donations. Phone (740) 532-1222.

JACKSON (E-3) pop. 6,100

Jackson was settled by accident in the early 1800s when a group of Welsh immigrants traveling down the Ohio River was stranded in Gallipolis after its boats were stolen. Making the best of the situation, the six families decided to stay.

Copies of a pamphlet describing Welsh communities in America brought more Welsh settlers to the area. Many of the men took jobs working on the Gallipolis/Chillicothe road and at the many coal mines and iron furnaces in Jackson County.

The region's once-great iron industry has since diversified into aluminum, wood and plastic products, and food processing.

Jackson Chamber of Commerce: 200 Broadway, Jackson, OH 45640; phone (740) 286-2722.

Shopping areas: Art & Craft Mall, off SR 32 at 110 Twin Oak Dr., offers handcrafted items including collectible dolls, ceramics, jewelry and toys.

NOAH'S ARK ANIMAL FARM, 5 mi. e. on SR 32, contains more than 100 animals and birds on 35 acres. The farm's inhabitants include bears and llamas. Facilities include a miniature golf course, a .75-mile ride on a scale model train, picnic areas, a campground and a 4-acre pay fishing lake. Allow 2 hours minimum. Mon.-Sat. 10-5, Sun. noon-6, Apr.-Oct. Admission $5.50; ages 3-12, $4. Train ride $1. AX, DS, MC, VI. Phone (740) 384-3060 or (800) 282-2167.

JEFFERSON (A-6) pop. 3,300, elev. 967'

Founded in 1813, Jefferson was part of the area of Ohio known as the Western Reserve, a colony of Connecticut. The community experienced a burst of prosperity in the 1870s during the era of the railroad steam engine. Today Jefferson is the county seat for Ashtabula County, where the mainstays of the economy are transportation equipment, fabricated metals, chemicals and Fiberglas boats. The primary component of the agricultural sector is dairy products.

Ashtabula County Convention and Visitors Bureau: 1850 Austinburg Rd., Austinburg, OH 44010; phone (440) 275-3202 or (800) 337-6746.

THE VICTORIAN PERAMBULATOR MUSEUM OF JEFFERSON, 26 E. Cedar St., displays close to 200 early wicker children's and doll's carriages, as well as children's pre-1900 toys, books and games. To celebrate the holidays, the museum hosts the Victorian Extravaganza the first Saturday in November through the first Saturday in January. Wed. and Sat. 11-5, June-Dec.; by appointment rest of year. Closed Dec. 25. Admission $3; under12, $2.50. Phone (440) 576-9588.

KELLEYS ISLAND (A-4) pop. 200, elev. 614'

Once the site of an active limestone quarry, Kelleys Island in Lake Erie is a summer resort and the center of a grape-growing region. The island was inhabited by Erie Indians more than 300 years ago, as evidenced by pictographs at Inscription Rock State Memorial.

The island is reached by ferry trips from Marblehead and Port Clinton, or by plane from Port Clinton and Sandusky. Jet Express Ferry, (800) 245-1538, provides service May through October. Neuman's Kelleys Island Ferry, (419) 798-5800 or (800) 876-1907, makes trips April through November.

KELLEYS ISLAND STATE PARK is on the southern tip of the island. Within the 800-acre park are the Glacial Grooves, where fossilized marine life is embedded in limestone bedrock. These grooves are considered among the finest glacial carvings in America.

Note: There are limited facilities at the park, which is not staffed November through March.

The park is accessible by ferry Apr.-Nov. Park admission free. Fare for ferry varies. Phone (419) 746-2546. *See Recreation Chart and the AAA Great Lakes CampBook.*

KENT (B-5) pop. 28,800

Established in 1910 as Kent Normal School, a teacher-training facility, Kent State University has earned many national and international distinctions, including recognition by the Carnegie Foundation for an optimal blending of teaching and research. Of interest on this 32,000-student campus are the planetarium, art galleries, gardens, the Liquid Crystal Institute and the Kent State University Museum *(see attraction listing).*

The May 4th Memorial commemorates the events of May 4, 1970, when four students were killed and nine wounded by the Ohio National Guard troops during a protest against the Vietnam War. The memorial sits on a sloped, wooded area at the northern corner of Taylor Hall overlooking the University Commons.

[SAVE] **KENT STATE UNIVERSITY MUSEUM** is in Rockwell Hall at the corner of E. Main and S. Lincoln sts. Focusing on fashion and decorative arts, the museum houses one of the nation's largest and finest collections of 18th- through 21st-century costumes as well as creations by some of today's most celebrated fashion designers. Also featured are Ohio art pottery, collectible glass, ivory, and international textiles. Nine galleries feature changing exhibitions. Guided tours are available by reservation.

Allow 1 hour minimum. Wed.-Sat. 10-4:45 (also Thurs. 4:45-8:45), Sun. noon-4:45; closed holidays. Admission $5; over 54, $4; ages 7-18, $3. Phone (330) 672-3450.

KINGS MILLS—*see Cincinnati p. 202.*

KIRTLAND (A-5) pop. 5,900

The first permanent settler came to this area in 1811 and the township was formed in 1822. In 1830 the largest settlement began when the Mormon leader Joseph Smith and many of his followers arrived; nearly 3,000 people lived in Kirtland by the time the Mormons moved westward in 1838.

Today this small town is known for its amenities, both man-made and natural. Lakeland Community College occupies 400 rolling, wooded acres. Old South Church, whose belfry was used by surveyors as a fixed point, was built in 1859 to replace the original 1819 Western Reserve pioneer church.

Chapin Forest's 362 acres offer an opportunity to picnic or hike. Penitentiary Glen allows visitors to observe wildlife, including animals in its wildlife rehabilitation center; phone (440) 256-1404.

THE HOLDEN ARBORETUM is 4 mi. e. of SR 306 on Kirtland-Chardon Rd., then 1.5 mi. n. on Sperry Rd. Walking trails weave through this 3,400-acre natural woodland museum containing horticultural display gardens, woods, fields, lakes and ravines. Plants include rhododendrons, crab apples, maples, conifers, nut trees, wildflowers, lilacs and viburnums.

A visitor center, reference library and picnic area are on the grounds. Guided tours are available by reservation. Arboretum open Tues.-Sun. 10-5. Admission $4; over 60, $3; ages 6-15, $2. MC, VI. Phone (440) 946-4400.

KIRTLAND TEMPLE is at 9020 Chillicothe Rd. Owned and maintained by the Reorganized Community of Christ, the building was completed in 1836. This temple is a tribute to the early Latter Day Saints who, under the leadership of Joseph Smith Jr., built this house of worship. Guided 30- to 40-minute tours of this National Historic Landmark, which has unusual architecture and window design, begin in the visitor center with an DVD presentation. Allow 1 hour minimum. Mon.-Sat. 9-5, Sun. 1-5. Last tour begins at closing. Free. Phone (440) 256-3318.

LAKE FARMPARK is located 5 mi. s. of I-90 on SR 306 to SR 6, then 1.2 mi. e. at 8800 Chardon Rd. More than 60 breeds of farm animals, some of which are rare and endangered, are exhibited on this 235-acre park. The visitor center houses interactive exhibits and a theater as well as the Dairy Parlor, where visitors can meet and milk various breeds of dairy cows. Antique and modern farm machinery also is displayed. Both indoor and outdoor demonstrations are scheduled daily, and horse-drawn or tractor-drawn wagon rides are included.

The Barnyard area features alpacas, cattle, llamas, poultry, sheep, swine, and animal care. Newborn farm animals, horses and tractor demonstrations are featured in the arena. The Plant Science Center showcases The Great Tomato Works exhibit, a complex of traditional and hydroponic greenhouses, established orchards, vineyards, themed gardens and field crops. Picnicking is permitted. Food is available.

Allow 1 hour minimum. Tues.-Sun. 9-5 (also Mon. 9-5, Apr.-Dec.); closed Jan. 1 and Dec. 25. Admission $6; over 60, $5; ages 2-11, $4. DS, MC, VI. Phone (440) 256-2122.

NEWELL K. WHITNEY STORE AND MUSEUM is at jct. SR 306 and Chillicothe Rd. The buildings interpret the history of Kirtland and the Mormon Church in America. Joseph Smith Jr., leader and first president of the Mormon Church, developed and taught church doctrine in the store's apartment. Plans are underway for the renovation of a historic village that includes other restored structures. Guided tours are available. Allow 1 hour minimum. Daily 9-dusk; closed Thanksgiving and Dec. 25. Free. Phone (440) 256-9805.

KIRTLAND HILLS (A-5) pop. 600, elev. 700′

LAKE COUNTY HISTORY CENTER is at 8610 Mentor Rd. The center is housed in the 1926 summer home of Arthur Baldwin and his wife, Reba Williams, heiress to the Sherwin-Williams Paint fortune. The home/museum contains 19th-century music boxes and an Underground Railroad hideaway. A working steam engine also is on display.

A self-guiding walking trail of the 15-acre grounds includes an early 19th-century log house and replicas of a one-room school house and an American Indian site circa 1400. Picnicking is permitted. Allow 1 hour minimum. Tues.-Fri. 10-4,

Sat.-Sun. 1-4, May-Oct. Donations. Phone (440) 255-8979.

LAKESIDE (A-4)

Founded on Marblehead Peninsula in 1873, Lakeside is a resort with some of the largest summer conference facilities in the Midwest. One of the few remaining chautauquas in the country, it serves as a center for culture, religion, education, recreation and the arts.

Lakeside is open June through August, and nationally known performers are featured throughout the season. The scenic portion of SR 53/163 runs to the resort.

LANCASTER—see Columbus p. 229.

LEBANON—see Cincinnati p. 202.

LIMA (C-2) pop. 45,500, elev. 860′

Lima (LYE-ma) was the remaining name among suggestions pulled from a hat in 1831, after residents argued about the name for this new county seat. During the late 19th century the town prospered from the region's oil, but residents also had the foresight to diversify industry, ensuring survival after a short-lived boom. Now Lima's industries range from building automobile engines to making neon signs.

Lima gained national attention in 1933 when members of John Dillinger's gang murdered the town sheriff. The shooting precipitated a nationwide manhunt that led to the gangster's death in Chicago.

Lincoln Park, on E. Elm Street, offers picnic facilities and a display of the last steam locomotive built in Lima, along with other trains and an 1895 country railroad station.

Lima/Allen County Convention & Visitors Bureau: 147 N. Main St., Lima, OH 45801; phone (419) 222-6075 or (888) 222-6075.

Shopping areas: Lima Mall (Lima Center), I-75 exit 125 onto SR 309W to 2400 Elida Rd., features Elder-Beerman, JCPenney, Lazarus and Sears.

ALLEN COUNTY MUSEUM, 620 W. Market St., houses antiques, historical exhibits and a library. Displays include American Indian and pioneer artifacts, steam and electric railroad items, musical instruments, antique automobiles and bicycles, a country store, doctor's office and barber shop. A 10- by 15-foot model of Mount Vernon is decorated in period. A Shay-geared locomotive and a log house with exhibits depict pioneer life. A children's hands-on museum and garden are on the grounds.

Allow 1 hour minimum. Museum open Tues.-Sat. 10-5, Sun. 1-5, June-Aug.; Tues.-Sun. 1-5, rest of year. Children's museum open Tues.-Sat. 1-5, June-Aug. Closed holidays. Free. Phone (419) 222-9426.

THE MACDONELL HOUSE, 632 W. Market St., is a lavishly decorated Victorian house with period furnishings. A trophy room contains big game and smaller animals and birds. Allow 30 minutes minimum. Tues.-Sat. 10-5, Sun. 1-5, June-Aug.; Tues.-Sun. 1-5, rest of year. Closed holidays. Donations. Phone (419) 222-9426.

LISBON (C-6) pop. 3,000, elev. 955'

One of the oldest communities in the state, Lisbon is home to the Old Stone Tavern, 100 E. Washington St. Built in 1805, the house is furnished with antiques. A monument 5 miles south of town on SR 518 marks the northernmost Civil War penetration of Confederate raider, Gen. John Morgan and commemorates his surrender to Union forces on July 26, 1863, in one of Ohio's few Civil War skirmishes.

LITHOPOLIS—see Columbus p. 230.

LOCKINGTON (D-1) pop. 200, elev. 949'

LOCKINGTON LOCKS STATE MEMORIAL is off I-75 exit 83, 1.5 mi. w. on SR 25A, then 2.5 mi. n. on SR 66 to Hardin Rd. at Fessler-Buxton Rd. This memorial provides a view of an aqueduct and portions of the six original locks that lowered boats 67 feet in the Miami and Erie Canal. Daily dawn-dusk. Free. Phone (937) 773-2522.

LOCUST GROVE (E-3)

SERPENT MOUND, 4 mi. n.w. on SR 73, is one of the finest remaining prehistoric American Indian effigy mounds. On the crest of a ridge paralleling Brush Creek, the serpent-shaped mound is nearly a quarter-mile long and is 5 feet high at some places. Excavations have shown that the serpent form was traced on the ground with stones and lumps of clay, then basketfuls of earth were piled over the pattern. A museum features exhibits about the mound and the geology of Brush Creek Valley. Picnic facilities are available.

Park open daily 9:30-8, Memorial Day weekend-Labor Day; 10-5, rest of year. Museum open daily 9:30-5, Memorial Day weekend-Labor Day; 10-5, Apr. 1-day before Memorial Day and day after Labor Day-Oct. 31. Admission $5 per private vehicle; $8 per vans; over 64, $4 per private vehicle. AX, DS, MC, VI. Phone (937) 587-2796.

LOGAN (E-4) pop. 6,700

HOCKING HILLS STATE PARK, in Hocking State Forest, is 10 mi. s.w. of US 33 on SR 664. This 2,348-acre area has a wide variety of regional trees and plants. About 110 kinds of birds are known to nest in the park—50 species spend the winter, others are migratory. The forest shelters most species of wildlife native to the Midwest. Picnicking and hiking are popular activities. Allow 2 hours minimum. Daily dawn-dusk. Free. Phone (740) 385-6841. See Recreation Chart and the AAA Great Lakes CampBook.

Ash Cave is 15 mi. s. of Logan and 5 mi. e. of South Bloomingville on SR 56. This 80-acre cave is a semicircular recess in a great rock, 700 feet long and 90 feet high. A stream falls from the rock into a pool. Daily dawn-dusk. Free.

Cantwell Cliffs, 12 mi. w. of Logan and 5 mi. s.w. of Rockbridge on SR 374, is 386 acres consisting of impressive cliffs and a deeply cut, rugged glen. Daily dawn-dusk. Free.

Cedar Falls, 13 mi. s. of Logan and 2 mi. n. of Ash Cave on SR 374, includes 50 acres. A path leads from Old Man's Cave up the gorge of Clear Creek. Cedar Falls is found at the head of the gorge; just below it is a saltpeter cave. A 3-mile trail connects with Old Man's Cave. Daily dawn-dusk. Free.

Conkles Hollow is on SR 374, 14 mi. s.w. of Logan and 4 mi. n. of South Bloomingville. This rugged 87-acre area contains a deep gorge that ends in a small recessed cave and waterfalls. Daily dawn-dusk. Free.

Old Man's Cave, 12 mi. s.w. of Logan on SR 664, is 417 acres containing 2 miles of a heavily wooded, winding ravine, picturesque waterfalls, two recessed caves and interesting rock formations. Daily dawn-dusk. Free.

Rock House, 165 acres, is 12 mi. w. of Logan on SR 374. An unusual rock dwelling is built into the face of a perpendicular cliff. Daily dawn-dusk. Free.

HOCKING VALLEY SCENIC RAILWAY— see Nelsonville p. 250.

LOUDONVILLE (C-5) pop. 2,900

Loudonville was the birthplace of Charles F. Kettering, an engineer whose invention of the electric starter was an important milestone in the development of the modern automobile. Because of the many picturesque streams and rivers in the area, Loudonville is called the "Canoe Capital of Ohio."

Mohican Tourist Association: 425 E. Haskell St., P.O. Box 24, Loudonville, OH 44842; phone (419) 994-5225 or (800) 722-7588.

MOHICAN STATE PARK is in Mohican State Forest, just s. off SR 3. At the upper edge of the forest is the 113-foot Pleasant Hill Dam, the highest dam in the Muskingum Conservancy District. Within the park, the Mohican River (popular for canoeing) forms the striking Clearfork Gorge, which is 1,000 feet wide at the top and 200 to 300 feet deep. A hemlock forest also fills the park. Park daily 8 a.m.-9 p.m. Office daily 8-5. Free. Phone (419) 994-4290. See Recreation Chart and the AAA Great Lakes CampBook.

LUCAS (C-4) pop. 700

MALABAR FARM STATE PARK, take SR 39 e., then s. on SR 603, then w. on Pleasant Valley Rd. to 4050 Bromfield Rd. This conservation, demonstration and educational farm was home to Louis

Bromfield, early 20-century author, farmer and conservationist; it is the only working farm in the Ohio state park system.

Allow 1 hour minimum. Park open daily dawn-dusk. Tractor-drawn 45-minute wagon tours are given Thurs.-Mon. on the hour noon-3, Memorial Day-Labor Day; Sat.-Sun. on the hour noon-3, May 1-day before Memorial Day and day after Labor Day-Oct. 31; by appointment Jan.-Mar. Closed non-summer holidays. Wagon tours $1, under 6 free. Phone (419) 892-2784. *See Recreation Chart and the AAA Great Lakes CampBook.*

The Big House Bromfield's 32-room country manor contains a variety of antiques, art items and rare books. Guided 45-minute tours are given daily at 10-5, Memorial Day-Labor Day; Tues.-Sun. 10-5, May 1-day before Memorial Day and day after Labor Day-Oct. 31; Tues.-Sun. 11-5, Nov.-Dec.; otherwise varies. Closed non-summer holidays. Admission $3; ages 6-18, $1. AX, DS, MC, VI. Phone (419) 892-2784.

MADISON (A-6) pop. 2,500, elev. 714′

WINERIES

- **Chalet Debonne Vineyards**, 7743 Doty Rd. Tues. noon-6, Thurs. and Sat. noon-8, Wed. and Fri. noon-midnight, Feb.-Dec.; Tues.-Sat. noon-5, rest of year. Phone (440) 466-3485.

MANCHESTER (F-3) pop. 2,200

WINERIES

- **Moyer Vineyards**, 3859 US 52. Mon.-Thurs. 11:30-9, Fri.-Sat. 11:30-10; closed Jan. 1, Thanksgiving and Dec. 25. Phone (937) 549-2957.

MANSFIELD (C-4) pop. 50,600, elev. 1,152′

Mansfield was laid out in 1808 under the direction of Surveyor General of the United States Jared Mansfield. As the surrounding lands were cleared and cultivated in the 1820s, Mansfield became a center of trade and commerce. In the late 1840s and 1850s the arrivals of the railroads and telegraph drew the first industries, such as the Ohio Brass Co. and Aultman and Taylor, makers of threshing machines.

Mansfield is rich in well-known native sons, including John Sherman, brother of Gen. William T. Sherman and author of the Sherman Anti-Trust Act; and Pulitzer Prize-winning author Louis Bromfield. Mansfield also has fostered artists. Displays of their works, including acrylic paintings, watercolors, photographs, quiltings and weavings, can be seen at the Mansfield Art Center, 700 Marion Ave; phone (419) 756-1700.

Mansfield-Richland Area Chamber of Commerce: 55 N. Mulberry St., Mansfield, OH 44902; phone (419) 522-3211.

Shopping areas: Richland Mall, 1 mile south of US 30 at W. Fourth Street and Lexington-Springmill Road, features JCPenney, Kaufmann's, Lazarus and Sears.

KINGWOOD CENTER is 1.5 mi. w.; from I-71 exit at US 30, go w. to Trimble Rd., then s. to entrance at 900 Park Ave. W. The public garden covers 47 acres and contains landscaped gardens, trails that meander through woodland settings and two ponds that harbor waterfowl. Greenhouses filled with flowers and other plants are highlights.

The gardens have one of the largest displays of tulips and daffodils in the country. Also outstanding are other perennials—irises, peonies, day lilies, roses—and terrace and historic gardens. Allow 1 hour minimum. Center open daily 8 a.m.-30 minutes before dusk, Apr.-Oct.; 8-5, rest of year. Greenhouse open daily 8 a.m.-1 hour before dusk, Apr.-Oct.; 8-4:30, rest of year. Free. Phone (419) 522-0211.

Kingwood Hall is a French Provincial-style mansion containing a horticultural reference library. Allow 30 minutes minimum. Tues.-Sat. 9-5, Sun. 1-5, Apr.-Oct.; Tues.-Sat. 9-5, rest of year. Closed holidays. Free. Phone (419) 522-0211.

THE LIVING BIBLE MUSEUM, .5 mi. n. of US 30 via SR 545 at 500 Tingley Ave., features three museums. The Museum of Christian Martyrs and Life of Christ present life-size dioramas with an accompanying non-denominational audiovisual presentation about the life of Jesus. Miracles of the Old Testament presents 19 additional dioramas giving an in-depth glimpse into the Old Testament. Also displayed are a collection of rare Bibles, American votive folk art, wood carvings and animated scenes. A gallery and a theater also are included.

Allow 1 hour minimum. Guided tours of each museum are offered. Mon.-Fri. 10-5, Sat. 10-7, Sun. 2-7. Admission to Life of Christ or Miracles of the Old Testament $4.50; over 54, $4.25; ages 6-18, $3.50. Admission to Christian Martyrs $3.75; over 54, $3.50; ages 6-18, $2.75. Admission to all three $11.75; over 54, $11; ages 6-18, $8.75. Phone (419) 524-0139.

RICHLAND CARROUSEL PARK is at 75 N. Main St. The downtown historic district houses a hand-carved carousel that features 52 animals, including 30 horses and 22 menagerie figures; a Stinson Band Organ provides music. Food is available. Daily 11-5 (also Wed. 5-8). Rides 80c. Phone (419) 522-4223.

MARBLEHEAD (B-4) pop. 700, elev. 579′

A summer resort and popular fishing center, Marblehead is on the tip of Marblehead Peninsula, which forms the northern shore of Sandusky Bay. The town is the site of a lighthouse built in 1821 which is one of the oldest lighthouses in continuous operation on the Great Lakes. Many sections of the 20-mile drive around the peninsula afford fine views. The western part of the peninsula is noted for peach and apple orchards.

Peninsula Chamber of Commerce: P.O. Box 268, Marblehead, OH 43440; phone (419) 798-9777.

MARIA STEIN (C-1)

SHRINE OF THE HOLY RELICS, .5 mi. n. of SR 119 on St. Johns Rd., is part of what was originally the Motherhouse of the Sisters of the Precious Blood. The shrine's buildings were constructed 1846-1900. A small museum contains mid-19th-century artifacts of the order and of the Low German Catholic farmers who settled in Mercer County. The museum is said to contain the second largest collection of relics in the country.

Allow 1 hour, 30 minutes minimum. Museum open Tues.-Sun. noon-4, May-Oct. Shrine open Tues.-Sun. 9:30-4:30. Both museum and shrine closed holidays. Donations. Phone (419) 925-4532.

MARIETTA (E-5) pop. 15,000, elev. 618'

Forty-eight pioneers led by Rufus Putnam arrived in Marietta during April 1788. They platted the future community, built a land office, erected a fort and chose the name Marietta in honor of Queen Marie Antoinette, in recognition of the aid rendered to the Colonies by France during the American Revolution.

Marietta, at the confluence of the Muskingum and Ohio rivers, honors its water transportation history with the 1926 stern-wheeler showboat *Becky Thatcher* Theatre, permanently moored at 237 Front St. Phone (740) 373-6033.

In Muskingum Park is the Memorial to the Start Westward, created by Mount Rushmore sculptor Gutzon Borglum.

Marietta/Washington County Convention and Visitors Bureau: 316 Third St., Marietta, OH 45750; phone (740) 373-5178 or (800) 288-2577. *See color ad.*

Self-guiding tours: A map and brochure detailing a tour of scenic and historic points is available from the tourist and convention bureau.

CAMPUS MARTIUS MUSEUM is at 2nd and Washington sts. Exhibits re-create the founding and early development of Marietta as the first organized American settlement in the Northwest Territory as well as its progress in later years. Campus Martius is Latin for "Field of Mars," the military camp where the legions of ancient Rome trained.

The museum encloses the Putnam House, the only surviving dwelling of the original settlement, and contains exhibits relating to the establishment of the surrounding area.

Allow 1 hour minimum. Mon.-Sat. 9:30-5, Sun. and holidays noon-5, May-Sept.; Wed.-Sat. 9:30-5, Sun. noon-5, Mar.-Apr. and Oct.-Nov. Closed Nov. 11 and Thanksgiving. Campus admission $5; ages 6-12, $1.25. AX, DS, MC, VI. Phone (740) 373-3750 or (800) 860-0145.

Ohio River Museum and the *W.P. Snyder Jr.* are at Washington and Front sts. The museum displays steamboat-era items, including scale models of late 19th-century riverboats, pictures, whistles and a full-size calliope. The theater presents the 30-minute videotape "Fire on the Water." The *W.P. Snyder Jr.,* moored alongside the museum, is the last steam-powered, stern-wheeled towboat of its type in America.

Museum open Mon.-Sat. 9:30-5, Sun. and holidays noon-5, May-Sept.; Wed.-Sat. 9:30-5, Sun. noon-5, Mar.-Apr. and Oct.-Nov. Closed Nov. 11 and Thanksgiving. *W.P. Snyder Jr.* open Mon.-Sat. 9:30-5, Sun. noon-5, mid-Apr. through last weekend in Oct., except during high water; phone to verify its schedule. Admission $5; ages 6-12, $1.25. AX, DS, MC, VI. Phone (740) 373-3750 or (800) 860-0145.

THE CASTLE is in the heart of the historic district at 418 Fourth St. between Wooster and Scammel sts. This 1855 mansion is an outstanding example of Gothic Revival architecture. Special events, exhibitions and concerts are scheduled throughout the year. Guided 45- to 60-minute tours Mon.-Fri. 10-4, Sat.-Sun. 1-4, June-Aug.; Mon. and Thurs.-Fri. 10-4, Sat.-Sun. 1-4, Apr.-May and Sept.-Dec. Closed Easter, Thanksgiving and

Dec. 25. Last tour begins 30 minutes before closing. Fee $4; over 59, $3.50; children and students $2.50; under 5 free. MC, VI. Phone (740) 373-4180.

HARMAR VILLAGE can be reached by automobile by taking the Putnam Bridge or on foot by taking the Harmar Bridge. This village, which started as a fort in 1785, contains specialty shops, eateries and four museums. Marietta Soda Museum takes a look at these beverages since their inception. Harmar Station displays one of the largest collections of authentic electric toy trains in the country. The Children's Toy and Doll Museum and the 1847 Henry Fearing House, furnished in period, are included.

Village open daily. Museum schedules vary. Admission to village is free; fees are charged for the museums. Phone (740) 373-3395 or the Marietta/Washington County Convention & Visitors Bureau at (800) 288-2577.

MOUND CEMETERY, on 5th St., contains the 30-foot-high *conus*. The burial place of a chief, this is an example of the Mound Builders' art. Also within the cemetery are graves of settlers and Revolutionary War soldiers. Daily dawn-dusk. Free.

TROLLEY TOURS OF MARIETTA depart from the Levee House Cafe, Second and Ohio sts. at 127 Ohio St. Narrated tours detail points of interest in historic downtown Marietta.

Allow 1 hour minimum. Trolleys depart Tues.-Sun. at 12:30 and 2:30 (also Thurs.-Sat. at 10:30), July-Aug.; Wed.-Sun. at 12:30 and 2:30 (also Sat. at 10:30), June 15-30; Thurs.-Sun. at 12:30 and 2:30 (also Sat. at 10:30), June 1-14; Thurs.-Sat. at 10:30, 12:30 and 2:30 in Sept.; Fri.-Sat. at 10:30, 12:30 and 2:30, Sun. at 12:30 and 2:30, in Oct.; Sat.-Sun. at 12:30 and 2:30, Apr.-May. Fare $7.50; over 54, $7; ages 5-12, $5. DS, MC, VI. Phone (740) 374-2233.

[SAVE] **THE *VALLEY GEM***, at Washington and Front sts., is a replica of a stern-wheeler. Cruises along the Muskingum and Ohio rivers depart hourly Tues.-Sun. 1-4, mid-June to mid-Aug.; Sat. 1-4, Sun. and holidays 1-4, May 1 to mid-June and mid-Aug. through Sept. 30. Fall foliage tours are given Sat.-Sun. at 10 and 2 in Oct. Two-hour dinner cruise is available Sat. at 5:30, mid-June through Oct. 31. One-hour cruise $5.50; ages 2-10, $3. Fall foliage tour $15; ages 2-10, $6. Reservations are required for the fall foliage tour and dinner cruise. MC, VI. Phone (740) 373-7862.

MARION (C-3) pop. 34,100, elev. 923'

In 1821 the combination of a steady diet of salt pork and a lack of water caused Jacob Foos to dig into a few feet of moist dirt. Discovering an abundant spring, he named the site Jacob's Well, and the area grew to become the county seat. The town was renamed in honor of Revolutionary War general Francis Marion, the "Swamp Fox."

Marion's economy, once based upon the manufacture of the steam shovel and road roller, now depends on such agricultural goods as popping corn and dairy products.

Marion Area Convention and Visitors Bureau: 1952 Marion-Mt. Gilead Rd., Suite 120, Marion, OH 43302; phone (740) 389-9770 or (800) 371-6688.

HARDING MEMORIAL, Delaware Ave. at Vernon Heights Blvd., is a circular, pillared monument of white Georgian marble. The memorial contains the tombs of President and Mrs. Warren G. Harding. Daily dawn-dusk. Free.

MARION COUNTY MUSEUM OF HISTORY, 1 blk. e. of Main St. at 169 E. Church St., chronicles the area's history. Of note is the Harding Presidential Room, with exhibits about former U.S. President Warren Harding, a native of Marion. Guided tours are available. Allow 30 minutes minimum. Wed.-Sun. 1-4, May-Oct.; Sat.-Sun. 1-4, rest of year. Closed Easter and Dec. 25. Free. Phone (740) 387-4255.

Wyandot Popcorn Museum, 169 E. Church St. in the Marion County Museum of History, showcases 50 popcorn popping machines, peanut roasters, concession trucks and vending wagons. Guided tours are available. Allow 30 minutes minimum. Wed.-Sun. 1-4, May-Oct.; Sat.-Sun. 1-4, rest of year. Closed Easter and Dec. 25. Free. Phone (740) 387-4255.

[GEM] **THE PRESIDENT HARDING HOME AND MUSEUM**, 380 Mount Vernon Ave., is 4 mi. w. of SR 23 on SR 95. It was from this house that Warren G. Harding conducted his "Front Porch Campaign" in the 1920 presidential election. From wallpaper to gaslight fixtures and original furnishings, the house is authentically restored. In the back of the house, the former campaign press building, purchased for about $1,000 through the Sears Roebuck catalogue in 1920, contains a museum chronicling the Harding life and campaign and the construction of the Harding Memorial.

Allow 1 hour minimum. Guided 45-minute tours depart at quarter past the hour Mon.-Sat. 9:30-4, Sun. noon-5, Memorial Day weekend-Labor Day; Sat. 9:30-5, Sun. noon-5, day after Labor Day-Oct. 31; by appointment Apr. 1-day before Memorial Day weekend. Last tour departs 45 minutes before closing. Admission $3; over 64, $2; ages 6-12, $1.25. AX, DS, MC, VI. Phone (740) 387-9630.

VETERANS MEMORIAL PARK, at jct. Delaware Ave. and Vernon Heights Blvd. across from the Harding Memorial, is a park dedicated to those involved in every conflict the United States has fought. Monuments throughout the 7.5-acre park honor veterans from the American Revolution through the Persian Gulf War. Daily dawn-dusk. Free. Phone (740) 383-5027.

MARTINS FERRY (D-6)
pop. 8,000, elev. 660'

The Betty Zane Memorial at the entrance of Walnut Grove Cemetery honors the Revolutionary War heroine for her bravery during the siege of Fort Henry in 1782. Pulitzer Prize winner James Wright and Pro Football Hall of Fame member Lou Groza were born in Martins Ferry.

SAVE **SEDGWICK HOUSE MUSEUM** is w. of SR 7 at 627 Hanover St. The collection includes historical materials relevant to the area. Allow 1 hour minimum. Wed.-Sun. noon-4, May-Sept.; by appointment rest of year. Closed holidays. Admission $2. Phone (740) 633-5046.

MASSILLON (C-5) pop. 31,000, elev. 975′

Named for Bishop Jean-Baptiste Massillon, a clergyman and writer at the French court of Louis XIV, Massillon came into being in the 19th century when five villages joined together. The city prospered during the Ohio & Erie Canal era, thrived as a site of steam engine manufacturing in the latter half of the 1800s and continued to grow as a center of steel production through the first half of the 1900s.

Massillon's heritage is most visible in the 19th-century architecture of its downtown area and brick-paved Fourth Street historic district between Lincoln Way and Cherry Road. One of the most notable buildings in this area is the three-story Five Oaks house at 210 Fourth St. This Romanesque-Gothic structure was designed in the early 1890s by noted architect Charles Schweinfurth, designer of many of of the mansions on Cleveland's Millionaires' Row. St. Mary Church, an impressive Gothic-style stone church at Cherry Street and First Street N.E., was begun in 1876 and dedicated in 1892.

One of Massillon's historic houses, Spring Hill, off Wales Rd. N.E. at 1401 Spring Hill Ln., was built about 1821 and was a stop on the Underground Railroad. The grounds of the restored house have herb and flower gardens, a smokehouse, springhouse and other outbuildings; phone (330) 833-6749 for tour information.

Massilon Chamber of Commerce: 137 Lincoln Way E., Massilon, OH 44646; phone (330) 833-3146.

MASSILLON MUSEUM is at 121 Lincoln Way E. in the former Stark Dry Goods building. This museum has historical and art exhibits including a room containing circus memorabilia. Allow 30 minutes minimum. Tues.-Sat. 9:30-5, Sun. 2-5; closed holidays. Free. Phone (330) 833-4061.

NATIONAL SHRINE OF ST. DYMPHNA, is 3.5 mi. s. on SR 21 to Erie St. S. exit, then e. to Old SR 21 to the main entrance at 3000 Erie St. S. This shrine is on the grounds of the Heartland Behavioral Healthcare Center and is a memorial to the patroness of those afflicted with mental and nervous disorders. The chapel and outdoor shrine are open Mon.-Fri. 8-4:30. Free. Phone (330) 833-8478.

OHIO SOCIETY OF MILITARY HISTORY, 2 blks. e. on Lincoln Way E., features a collection of congressional medals, photographs, clothing and other items dating from the Civil War through Operation Desert Storm. Allow 30 minutes minimum. Tues.-Fri. 10-5, Sat. 10-3; closed major holidays. Donations. Phone (330) 832-5553.

MAUMEE (B-2) pop. 15,600, elev. 638′

During the late 18th century much of Ohio's American Indian population was concentrated along the Maumee River, a vital link to the British army post in Detroit. Repeated American Indian raids delayed settlement of the area until 1794, when American forces led by Gen. Anthony Wayne won the decisive Battle of Fallen Timbers.

The War of 1812 permanently secured the area for the United States, and Maumee was founded in 1817 by William Oliver, a former scout and officer at nearby Fort Meigs. The blockhouse and stockade of Fort Meigs can be seen from the old canal towpath. By the mid-1800s the Miami and Erie Canal had made Maumee a center of trade and commerce. The locks that connected the Maumee River and the canal can be seen in Sidecut Metropark.

SAVE **WOLCOTT HOUSE MUSEUM COMPLEX,** 1031 River Rd., centers on the original Federal-style house of James and Mary Wolcott. This 1836 house has displays of period antiques and American Indian artifacts. Other buildings include a log cabin, an 1840s saltbox farmhouse, a 19th-century church and the Toledo and Grand Rapids Railroad depot. Allow 1 hour minimum. Wed.-Sun. 1-4, Apr.-Dec.; closed holidays. Admission $3.50; ages 6-18, $1.50. MC, VI. Phone (419) 893-9602.

McCUTCHENVILLE (B-3)

McCUTCHEN OVERLAND INN, on SR 53, was built as a stagecoach stop in 1829. The restored inn has an old spring well, fireplaces and period furnishings. Allow 1 hour minimum. Thurs.-Sun. 1-4:30, June-Oct. Admission $1; ages 6-18, 50c. Phone (419) 981-2052.

MENTOR (A-5) pop. 47,400, elev. 651′

SAVE **JAMES A. GARFIELD NATIONAL HISTORIC SITE** is 2 mi. e. on US 20. The home of the 20th president features the first presidential memorial library as well as original furnishings and Garfield memorabilia. A visitor center featuring permanent exhibits describing Garfield's life is housed in an 1893 carriage house on the grounds. Guided tours are available. Mon.-Sat. 10-5, Sun. noon-5. Admission to main house $6; over 56, $5; ages 6-12, $4. Visitor center free. AX, DS, MC, VI. Phone (440) 255-8722.

MIAMISBURG (D-2) pop. 17,800, elev. 704′

MIAMISBURG MOUND STATE MEMORIAL is 1 mi. s.e. on I-75 (exit 44) and SR 725. The prehistoric remains that form the largest conical mound in Ohio are on the grounds. The mound is 68 feet high and covers 1.5 acres. Picnic facilities are available. Daily dawn-dusk. Free. Phone (614) 297-2300 or (800) 686-1535.

WRIGHT "B" FLYER, 10550 Springboro Pike at the Dayton Wright Brothers Airport, is a replica of the 1911 Wright "B" Flyer, the first mass produced airplane in the world. The plane, which periodically is flown, is housed in a hangar built to resemble the original Wright Co. Hangar. Tues., Thurs. and Sat. 9-2:30; closed holidays. Free. Phone (937) 885-2327.

MILAN (B-4) pop. 1,500, elev. 602′

Founded in the early 1800s on a bluff overlooking the Huron River, Milan overcame its landlocked handicap by building a canal to the river, which flows into Lake Erie. By the early 1840s, with the canal newly completed, Milan was booming as one of the largest wheat-shipping centers in the country.

The prosperity lasted until the town refused right-of-way to the Lake Shore and Michigan Southern Railroad. The railroad went through Norwalk instead, and Milan's commerce abruptly declined. To add to the city's problems, deforestation caused the river to diminish and become unnavigable. By the 1870s the canal was abandoned, and Milan entered an era of light industry and farming.

EDISON BIRTHPLACE MUSEUM, 9 Edison Dr., is the house where inventor Thomas A. Edison spent his first 7 years. Guided 45- to 60-minute tours of the well-preserved house are available. Allow 1 hour minimum. Tours on the half-hour Tues.-Sat. 10-5, Sun. 1-5, June-Aug.; Tues.-Sun. 1-5, Apr.-May and Sept.-Oct.; by appointment Nov.-Dec. and Feb.-Mar. Closed Easter. Last tour begins 30 minutes before closing. Admission $5; over 59, $4; ages 6-12, $2. AX, MC, VI. Phone (419) 499-2135.

MILAN HISTORICAL MUSEUM, 10 Edison Dr., contains collections of dolls, artworks, pressed glass, china and other historical items in an 1846 house. A complex of other buildings includes a general store, blacksmith shop and the 1843 Robert Sayles House. Allow 1 hour minimum. Tues.-Sat. 10-5, Sun. 1-5, June-Aug.; Tues.-Sun. 1-5, Apr.-May and Sept.-Oct.; by appointment, Feb.-Mar. and Nov.-Dec. Closed Labor Day weekend. Admission $5; senior citizens $4; ages 6-12, $3. Phone (419) 499-2968.

Edna Roe Newton Memorial Building, 12 Edison Dr. next door to the Milan Historical Museum, houses items Edna and Bert Newton collected as they traveled throughout the world. Antiques, artwork and needlework are displayed. Tues.-Sat. 1-5, May-Oct. Free. Phone (419) 499-2968.

MILLERSBURG (C-4) pop. 3,100

[SAVE] **VICTORIAN HOUSE,** 4 blks. n. from Courtyard Square on SR 83 to 484 Wooster Rd., is a 28-room Queen Anne-style house built in 1902. Highlights include parquet floors, elegant window treatments, hand-painted ceilings, a third-floor ballroom, a 1920s steam bath and a summer kitchen. Allow 1 hour minimum. Self-guiding tours Tues.-Sun. 1:30-4, May-Oct. Phone for additional sea-

sonal hours and special events. Admission $5; ages 12-18, $3. Phone (330) 674-0022 or (888) 201-0022.

MORROW—see Cincinnati p. 203.

MOUNT PLEASANT (D-6) pop. 500

Many of Mount Pleasant's original buildings are still standing. The Quaker Meeting House State Memorial, just west off Union Street on SR 150, was built in 1814 and is reputedly the first yearly meetinghouse west of the Alleghenies.

The building seats 2,000 and is open by appointment; phone (740) 769-2893 or (800) 752-2631. A Christmas Tour is given the first weekend in December, and a garden tour is available in early August. A log cabin, a mansion, a tin shop, a general store and a historical center also can be toured April through December.

NAPOLEON (B-2) pop. 8,900, elev. 677′

HENRY COUNTY COURTHOUSE is at 660 N. Perry St. Constructed of brick and stone, this 1882 courthouse is graced by a 160-foot tower and topped by a 15-foot figure of the goddess of justice. Recently restored, the building houses exhibits pertaining to its construction and the county's history. Guided tours are available by appointment. Mon.-Fri. 8:30-4:30. Free. Phone (419) 592-1786.

NELSONVILLE (E-4) pop. 4,600, elev. 681′

HOCKING VALLEY SCENIC RAILWAY depot is at US 33 and Hocking Pkwy. A 1952 GP7 diesel locomotive offers a 14-mile round trip from Nelsonville to Haydenville and a 22-mile round trip to East Logan. Both rides include a 30-minute stopover in Robbins Crossing, where a visitors center recreates a small 1860s settlers village. For more information write P.O. Box 427, Nelsonville, OH 45764.

Allow 2 hours minimum. Departures Sat.-Sun. at noon to Haydenville and at 2:30 to East Logan, Memorial Day weekend to early Nov.; Santa Trains, to East Logan only, depart at 11 and 2:30 the last weekend in Nov. and the first three weekends in Dec.

Fare $11 to East Logan and $8 to Haydenville; ages 3-12, $7 to East Logan and $5 to Haydenville. Santa train $11; ages 3-12, $7.50 Reservations are recommended for fall foliage and Santa trains. MC, VI. Phone (800) 967-7834 Mon.-Fri., or (740) 753-9531 Sat.-Sun. 10-5.

NEWARK—see Columbus p. 230.

NEW BREMEN (C-2) pop. 2,600, elev. 941′

BICYCLE MUSEUM OF AMERICA is downtown at the corner of SRs 66 and 274. Featuring a broad selection of memorabilia, the museum houses antique bicycles from the 1800s, balloon tire models of the 1940s and banana-seat, high-rise handle bar bicycles of the 1960s. Allow 1 hour minimum. Mon.-Fri. 11-7, Sat. 11-2, Memorial Day-Labor Day;

Mon.-Fri. 11-5, Sat. 11-2, rest of year. Closed major holidays. Admission $3; over 60, $2; students under 18, $1; family rate $7. Phone (419) 629-9249.

NEW PHILADELPHIA (C-5)
pop. 15,700, elev. 878'

New Philadelphia was founded in the early 1800s by Moravian missionaries and Swiss-German immigrants who were undaunted by the hard times faced by their brethren in previous unsuccessful settlements. Surviving American Indian raids and the War of 1812, the village soon saw economic growth and prosperity.

A light industrial center, New Philadelphia also is a popular vacation spot. Recreational opportunities are abundant on the 16,000 acres of lakes in the Muskingum Conservancy District (see Recreation Chart and the AAA Great Lakes CampBook).

Tuscarawas County Convention and Visitors Bureau: 125 McDonald Dr. S.W., New Philadelphia, OH 44663; phone (330) 339-5453 or (800) 527-3387.

Shopping areas: Riverfront Antique Mall, 1203 Front St. S.W., has more than 400 dealers who specialize in everything from furniture to jewelry.

SCHOENBRUNN VILLAGE STATE MEMORIAL is on SR 259, 1 mi. s.e. of town and 4 mi. e. of I-77 exit 81. Founded by David Zeisberger in 1772 as a Moravian mission to the Delaware Indians, Schoenbrunn was the first settlement in Ohio. The town grew to include more than 60 log buildings. Its 300 settlers drew up Ohio's first civil code and built the first church and schoolhouse. British and American Indian hostilities caused the abandonment of Schoenbrunn in 1777; the village was later destroyed.

The village has 17 reconstructed log buildings, an original mission cemetery and 2.5 acres of planted fields. Picnic facilities are available. Mon.-Sat. 9:30-5, Sun. noon-5, Memorial Day weekend-Labor Day; Sat. 9:30-5, Sun. noon-5, day after Labor Day-Oct. 31. Admission $5; over 59, $4.50; ages 6-12, $1.25. AX, DS, MC, VI. Phone (330) 339-3636 or (800) 752-2711.

"TRUMPET IN THE LAND" is performed in the Schoenbrunn Amphitheatre, I-77 exit 81. This outdoor historical drama recounts the efforts of Moravian missionary David Zeisberger as he brought Christianity to the Delaware Indians during the late 1700s. "The White Savage," the story of border renegade Simon Gurty, also is performed. Ask about refund and weather policies. Performances Mon.-Sat. and holidays at 8:30 p.m., mid-June to late Aug. Admission $15; over 59, $13; under 12, $7. Reservations are recommended. MC, VI. Phone (330) 339-1132 to verify schedule and prices.

NEW RUMLEY (C-6)

CUSTER MONUMENT, on SR 646, is a bronze statue of George A. Custer that marks his 1839 birthplace. A cavalry officer in the Civil War and Indian Wars, Custer was killed in 1876. Exhibits depict the soldier's life. Picnic facilities are available. Daily dawn-dusk. Free. Phone (740) 946-3781.

NILES (B-6) pop. 21,100, elev. 882'

Founded in 1806 by James Heaton, the settlement was originally named Nilestown. Heaton is credited with manufacturing the first bar iron in Ohio in 1809; by 1880 Niles had become one of the leading iron manufacturers in the state due to local industrialists.

The town is the birthplace of William McKinley, the nation's 25th president.

Shopping areas: On SR 422, the Eastwood Mall Shopping and Entertainment Complex features more than 180 stores.

NATIONAL MCKINLEY BIRTHPLACE MEMORIAL, 40 N. Main St., is an imposing Classical Greek structure constructed of Georgian marble 1915-17. William McKinley was born in Niles Jan. 29, 1843, and served as the 25th president of the United States from 1897 until his assassination in 1901. A museum with ornate ceiling scrollwork, walnut woodwork and marble columns contains McKinley memorabilia, Civil War and Spanish-American War artifacts and bronze busts. An auditorium and public library also are featured.

Allow 30 minutes minimum. Mon.-Thurs. 9-8, Fri.-Sat. 9-5:30, Sun. 1-5, Sept.-May; Mon.-Thurs. 9-8, Fri.-Sat. 9-5:30, rest of year. All facilities free. Phone (330) 652-1704.

NORTH CANTON (C-5) pop. 14,700

SAVE **HARRY LONDON CHOCOLATE FACTORY,** just n. of I-77 exit 113 to 5353 Lauby Rd., produces more than 500 varieties of chocolate and gourmet candies. Tour guides take visitors on a 45-minute trip through the Chocolate Hall of Fame, provide insight into the candy-making process and offer samples of the products. Allow 1 hour minimum. Tours are given on the half-hour Mon.-Sat. 9-4, Sun. noon-3:30; closed major holidays. Fee $2; ages 3-18, $1. Reservations are required. MC, VI. Phone (330) 494-0833 or (800) 321-0444.

HOOVER HISTORICAL CENTER is in Hoover Park at 1875 Easton St. N.W. The Victorian house is the boyhood home of William H. "Boss" Hoover, founder of the Hoover Co. "Sweeping Changes" traces the history of the Hoover family and of cleaning devices, especially Hoover products; items include vintage advertisements, military items produced during World War II, and past and current products. Herb gardens are on the grounds. Allow 30 minutes minimum. Guided tours are available Tues.-Sun. at 1, 2, 3 and 4; closed major holidays. Free. Phone (330) 499-0287.

NORWALK (B-4) pop. 14,700, elev. 713'

During the Western Reserve era, settlers came to the Norwalk area from parts of New England ravaged by British raids. Because the land was deeded as compensation for Revolutionary War fire destruction, it was called the "Firelands." The West Main Historic District showcases some of the Classic Revival houses built by the original settlers. Today the area offers an abundance of leisure activities, including golf courses, historic attractions, a revitalized uptown district and access to recreation on Lake Erie.

Norwalk Raceway Park on SR 18 hosts more than 90 drag racing events April through October, including the International Hod Rod Association's World Nationals. Phone (419) 668-5555 for event and ticket information.

FIRELANDS MUSEUM, behind the public library at 4 Case Ave., is in an 1836 Federal-style house. Among the displays are period rooms, firearms, dishes, glassware, costumes, toys, pioneer articles and American Indian relics. Archives are available for genealogy and history research. Allow 1 hour minimum. Tues.-Sun. noon-5, June-Aug.; Sat.-Sun. noon-4, Apr.-May and Sept.-Oct.; by appointment rest of year. Admission $3; over 59, $2.50; ages 13-18, $2. Phone (419) 668-6038.

NORWICH (D-5) pop. 100

NATIONAL ROAD-ZANE GREY MUSEUM, off I-70 exit 164, traces the development of the country's first "highway," the National Road from Cumberland, Md., to Vandalia, Ill. A series of exhibits, including a 136-foot miniature diorama, depicts the history of both the road and vehicle technology. The museum features an original Conestoga wagon and harnesses, as well as commercial art pottery and decorative tile produced by local potteries. Objects belonging to Western novelist Zane Grey and copies of his manuscripts also are displayed.

Allow 1 hour minimum. Mon.-Sat. 9:30-5, Sun. noon-5, May-Sept.; Wed.-Sat. 9:30-5, Sun. noon-5, Mar.-Apr. and Oct.-Nov. Closed Thanksgiving. Admission $5; over 59, $4.50; ages 6-12, $1.25. AX, DS, MC, VI. Phone (740) 872-3143 or (800) 752-2602.

OAK HARBOR (B-3) pop. 2,600, elev. 590'

MAGEE MARSH WILDLIFE AREA, 2 mi. w. of SR 19 on SR 2, is a 2,000-acre marsh where large flocks of migrating waterfowls can be seen March through April and October through November. The Sportsmen Migratory Bird Center offers displays about wildlife lore, antique decoys and wildlife as well as an observation deck and boardwalk. Visitors should bring binoculars.

Mon.-Fri. 8-5, Sat.-Sun. 11-5, Mar.-Nov.; Mon.-Fri. 8-5, rest of year. Closed holidays. Free. Phone (419) 898-0960.

OBERLIN (B-4) pop. 8,200, elev. 855'

Co-founded with Oberlin College, the town of Oberlin was established as a colony pledged to "plainest living and highest thinking." The town

and college were a hotbed of abolitionist sentiment, and a major stop on the Underground Railroad; it has been called "The town that started the Civil War." The electrolytic process of producing aluminum was discovered in the town in 1886 by Charles M. Hall, an Oberlin graduate; he later co-founded the Aluminum Company of America, Alcoa.

Oberlin Area Chamber of Commerce: 13 S. Main St., Oberlin, Ohio 44074-1613; phone (440) 774-6262.

OBERLIN COLLEGE, a leading college of liberal arts and sciences, was founded in 1833. Two years later, Oberlin established a formal open-admissions policy which ignored race and gender. It is said that in 1900 nearly one-third of the nation's African American college graduates of predominantly white institutions were graduates of Oberlin.

Oberlin's renowned Conservatory of Music, reputed to be the oldest continuing conservatory in the country, presents ticketed and free concerts throughout the year. Free tours of the campus are available. Guided tours may be arranged Mon.-Sat. at the admissions office in the Carnegie Building on N. Professor Street. Free. Phone (440) 775-8411 or (800) 622-6243.

Allen Memorial Art Museum, 87 N. Main St., has a collection that covers the entire history of art and is particularly strong in the areas of 17th-century Dutch and Flemish paintings, European art of the late 19th and early 20th centuries, contemporary American art and Japanese prints. A wing of the building was designed by Robert Venturi. The museum includes the Usonian-style Weltzheimer/Johnson House, a 1949 house designed by Frank Lloyd Wright.

Museum open Tues.-Sat. 10-5, Sun. 1-5; closed major holidays. Tours of the Weltzheimer/Johnson House are offered the first and the third Sun. of the month 1-5. Museum free; Wright house tours $5. Maps to the house are available at the museum store. Phone (440) 775-8665.

OBERLIN HERITAGE CENTER, s. of SR 511 on SR 58 then w. on Vine St. to 73½ S. Professor St., offers guided 75-minute tours of the 1866 James Monroe House, the 1836 Little Red Schoolhouse and the 1884 Jewett House, which includes an exhibit about the development of aluminum. Guides tell about Oberlin's role as an early stop on the Underground Railroad.

Allow 1 hour, 30 minutes minimum. Tours are given Tues., Thurs. and Sat. at 10:30 and 1:30. Admission $4, under 19 free with an adult. Phone (440) 774-1700.

OXFORD (E-1) pop. 18,900, elev. 918'

A college town with many beautiful and architecturally significant older houses and buildings, Oxford derives much of its charm from the attractive campus of 16,000-student Miami University, founded in 1809. Points of interest include outdoor sculpture, formal gardens, Kumler Chapel and University Art Museum. Guided tours of the campus are available; phone (513) 529-1809.

William Holmes McGuffey established his first reading audience while a professor at Miami in the 1830s. His home is now McGuffey Museum on campus. Paul Brown, Weeb Ewbank, Ara Parseghian and other gridiron notables are a part of Miami's football history.

Other attractions of the town include: self guided walking tours of the historic uptown area; red brick streets; unusual shops and restaurants; the 1870 Black Covered Bridge; Pioneer Farm & House Museum; golf courses and other recreational facilities. Oxford's historic houses include the 1838 Lewis Place, traditional home of the Miami University presidents; the 1837 Simpson House, a guesthouse; the "Coffee Mill House"; and the home of Lorenzo Lorrain Langstroth, inventor of the revolutionary movable comb beehive.

Hueston Woods State Park, 5 miles north on SR 732, offers a variety of recreational opportunities including hiking, biking, sailing, as well as a nature center. *See Recreation Chart.*

Oxford Visitors & Convention Bureau: 30 W. Park Place, Oxford, OH 45056; phone (513) 523-8687.

MIAMI UNIVERSITY ART MUSEUM, Patterson Ave., has five galleries of changing exhibits ranging from national loan shows to the museum's permanent collection of contemporary, historical, decorative and ethnographical art. Allow 1 hour minimum. Tues. Fri. 10-5, Sat.-Sun. noon-5; closed major holidays. Free. Phone (513) 529-2232.

PAINESVILLE (A-5) pop. 15,700, elev. 702'

Painesville, near the mouth of the Grand River, has had a major nursery business since the 1850s and now has a strong chemical industry. The town is also home of Lake Erie College, a 750-student co-educational liberal arts institution. Western Reserve architect Jonathan Goldsmith designed and built the city hall in 1840; Also on the town square are many other historic buildings.

INDIAN MUSEUM OF LAKE COUNTY, in the Kilcawley Center at the w. end of Lake Erie College off Mentor Ave., traces the history of early native inhabitants of the Ohio area from 10,000 B.C. to 1650 AD. Artifacts from cultures throughout North America, including Inuits (Eskimos), from 1800 to the present also are displayed. There are hands-on activities for all ages. Allow 30 minutes minimum. Mon.-Fri. 9-4, Sat.-Sun. 1-4, Sept.-Apr.; Mon.-Fri. 10-4, Sat.-Sun. 1-4, rest of year. Closed major holiday weekends and college winter and spring breaks. Admission $2, senior citizens $1.50, grades K-12, $1. Prices may be slightly higher during special events. Phone (440) 352-1911.

PEEBLES (F-2) pop. 1,800

EDWIN H. DAVIS STATE MEMORIAL is at the jct. of Township Roads 126 and 129; take SR 41 s. to SR 32, head e. on SR 32 for about 3 mi., n. on Steam Furnace Rd., then .25 mi. to Township Rd. 129 (Davis Memorial Rd.). This 88-acre nature preserve contains redbud, arrowwood, witch hazel, linden, black walnut, tulip and red cedar trees. Nature trails are on the grounds. Daily dawn-dusk. Free. Phone (614) 297-2630 or (800) 686-1535 Mon.-Fri.

PERRYSBURG (B-3) pop. 12,600, elev. 628'

FORT MEIGS, on SR 65, 1 mi. s.w. of jct. SR 25, is a reconstruction of a fortification built in 1813. The fort played a critical role in safeguarding the Western frontier against British forces in the War of 1812. On 10 acres of land, Fort Meigs contains seven blockhouses with items that illustrate events of the war. Wed.-Sat. 9:30-5, Sun. and holidays noon-5, Memorial Day weekend-Labor Day; Sat. 9:30-5, Sun. noon-5, day after Labor Day-Oct. 31. Admission $5; over 59, $4.25; ages 6-12, $1.25. AX, DS, MC, VI. Phone (419) 874-4121 or (800) 283-8916.

⚡GEM PERRY'S VICTORY AND INTERNATIONAL PEACE MEMORIAL (A-4)

Perry's Victory and International Peace Memorial is reached during summer by automobile and passenger ferry from Catawba and Port Clinton and by plane from Port Clinton and Sandusky. The memorial, at Put-in-Bay on South Bass Island *(see place listing p. 254)* in Lake Erie, commemorates the Battle of Lake Erie and the ensuing years of peace.

During the War of 1812 Commodore Oliver Hazard Perry commanded the American fleet, consisting of the *Lawrence*, the *Niagara* and seven smaller vessels assembled on the British-controlled lake. On Sept. 10, 1813, he met and defeated the British fleet, and forced Robert Heriot Barclay's flagship and five other vessels to surrender. Perry then sent his famous message to Gen. William Henry Harrison, "We have met the enemy and they are ours." This victory made possible both the recapture of Detroit and Gen. Harrison's invasion of Canada.

The memorial is 352 feet high and 45 feet in diameter at its base. Built of pink granite from Milford, Mass., the memorial has an observation deck at 317 feet. Allow 30 minutes minimum. Daily 10-7, mid-June through Labor Day; 10-5, mid-Apr. to mid-June and day after Labor Day-late Oct.; by appointment rest of year. Elevator fee $3, under 17 free with adult. Phone (419) 285-2184.

PICKERINGTON—*see Columbus p. 231.*

PIQUA (D-1) pop. 20,600, elev. 884'

A major village of the Miami Indians was 1 mile north of the present city. An English trading post, Fort Pickawillany, was established there in 1748 and destroyed in 1752 by the French and their American Indian allies. In 1780 the Shawnees took possession of this territory. The town's name, derived from a Shawnee creation myth, means "a man formed out of the ashes."

The Piqua Historical Museum relates the history of the Upper Miami Valley; phone (937) 773-6752. Just north off I-75 are the ruins of Lockington Locks, a series of six locks on the old Miami and Erie Canal, which was extended to reach Piqua in 1837 and served the area until 1913. The locks were capable of raising or lowering boats 67 feet within a distance of half a mile.

Miami County Visitors and Convention Bureau: 405 S.W. Public Square, Suite 272, Troy, OH 45373; phone (937) 339-1044 or (800) 348-8993.

Self-guiding tours: A map and brochure detailing a tour of the historic district is available from the Piqua Historical Society, 124 W. Greene St.; phone (937) 773-6753.

Shopping areas: Miami Valley Centre Mall, at the junction of I-75 and SR 36, features Ames, Elder-Beerman, JCPenney and Sears.

GARBY'S BIG WOODS RESERVE AND SANCTUARY, I-75 exit 82, then 3 mi. e. on SR 36 and 1 mi. s. on Casstown-Sidney Rd., contains 272 acres of woodland. The area features a 3,800-foot boardwalk. Picnic facilities, on the reserve side, and nature trails are available. Daily 8-dusk. Free. Phone (937) 667-1086 or 335-9547.

SAVE **PIQUA HISTORICAL AREA STATE MEMORIAL** is off I-75 exit 83, 1 mi. w. on CR 25A, 2.5 mi. n. on SR 66, then .2 mi. e. on Hardin Rd. This 174-acre farmstead was the home of John Johnston and his family. Johnston was a federal Indian agent in Ohio, an Ohio Canal commissioner, an early Miami County settler and an innovative farmer. The farm includes his 1815 two-story brick house, summer kitchen, two-story springhouse, stone cider house and an 1808 barn, reputed to be the oldest double-pen log barn in Ohio. Guided tours by costumed interpreters and demonstrations of pioneer craftmaking are offered.

The museum features displays about the Eastern Woodland Indians who inhabited the area; Pickawillany, the first English trading post in Ohio; and the story of the canal era in Ohio. A mule-drawn canalboat ride takes visitors and costumed interpreters through the restored section of the Miami-Erie Canal. Picnicking is permitted.

Allow 2 hours minimum. Wed.-Sat. 9:30-5, Sun. noon-5, Memorial Day weekend-Labor Day; Sat. 9:30-5, Sun. noon-5, day after Labor Day-Oct. 31. Admission (includes canal boat ride) $5; over 59, $4.50; ages 6-12, $1.25. Phone (937) 773-2522 or (800) 752-2619.

PORTLAND (E-5) elev. 666'

BUFFINGTON ISLAND STATE MONUMENT, 4 acres on SR 124 and the Ohio River, marks the site of one of the few Civil War battles fought in Ohio. Picnic facilities are available. Daily dawn-dusk. Free. Phone (614) 297-2630 or (800) 686-1535 Mon.-Fri.

PORTSMOUTH (F-3) pop. 22,700, elev. 532'

At the confluence of the Ohio and Scioto rivers, Portsmouth is a manufacturing center where steel and clay products have been made for more than 100 years. Many of the city's 19th-century buildings are restored, including structures in the Boneyfiddle District. Portsmouth was the boyhood home of movie cowboy Roy Rogers and baseball great Branch Rickey, both of whom are depicted in the Portsmouth Floodwall Murals.

When completed, the 35-40 murals by Robert Dafford will depict more than 300 years of history of Portsmouth and the surrounding area. The murals may be viewed free of charge along the .3-mile floodwall on Front Street.

About 10 miles up the Ohio River from Portsmouth is the Greenup Locks and Dam complex; the best access is from the Kentucky side of the river. Observation buildings are open daily dawn-dusk. The Shawnee State Park *(see Recreation Chart and the AAA Great Lakes CampBook)* lies west; phone (740) 858-6621.

Portsmouth Area Convention and Visitors Bureau: 324 Chillicothe St., P.O. Box 509, Portsmouth, OH 45662; phone (740) 353-1116.

SOUTHERN OHIO MUSEUM AND CULTURAL CENTER, 825 Gallia St., presents changing exhibits relating to art, history and local interests. Music and theater events, films, lectures and classes are offered. Allow 1 hour minimum. Tues.-Fri. 10-5, Sat.-Sun. 1-5; closed holidays. Admission $2, students with ID $1; free to all Fri. Phone (740) 354-5629.

POWELL—*see Columbus p. 231.*

PUT-IN-BAY (A-3) pop. 100

Put-in-Bay, on South Bass Island, is known for its wineries and caves. Perry's Victory and International Peace Memorial *(see place listing p. 253)* is just outside the village.

The island can be reached by ferry from Port Clinton. Jet Express Ferry, (800) 245-1538, provides service May through October. Miller Ferries, (419) 285-2421 or (800) 500-2421, makes trips late March through September.

Put-in-Bay Chamber of Commerce: 250 Delaware Ave., P.O. Box 250, Put-in-Bay, OH 43456; phone (419) 285-2832.

LAKE ERIE ISLANDS HISTORICAL SOCIETY MUSEUM, s. of De Rivera Park at 441 Catawba Ave., displays more than 75 model ships showing 100 years of changes, paintings, records recounting the 1813 Battle of Lake Erie, the original lens from the 1897 South Bass Island Lighthouse, historic postcards and photographs, local wildlife exhibits, a sleigh and an old wine press. A display details more than 125 years winemaking on the island. A restored carriage barn and bottling works are on the grounds. Allow 30 minutes minimum. Daily 10-6, mid-June through Labor Day; Fri.-Sun. 11-5, day after Labor Day-Oct. 31 and May 1-early June. Donations. Phone (419) 285-2804.

PERRY'S CAVE & GEMSTONE MINING is .5 mi. s. of downtown at 979 Catawba Ave. The attraction offers 20-minute guided tours of a limestone cavern, which includes an underground lake. Since the cave is a constant 50 degrees F, warm clothing is recommended. The stairs leading into the cave are steep and narrow; wear good walking shoes. Daily 10:30-6, May 15-Sept. 15; Sat.-Sun. 10:30-5, Sept. 16-Oct. 15. Allow 30 minutes minimum. Admission $5.50; ages 5-11, $2.50. Phone (419) 285-2405.

PUT-IN-BAY TOUR TRAIN, boarding at the depot, conducts a 1-hour narrated guided tour of South Bass Island. The tours, which depart every 30 minutes, allow passengers to depart at three different areas and reboard without cost. Daily 10-5, Memorial Day-Labor Day; Sat.-Sun. 10-5, May 1-day before Memorial Day and day after Labor Day-Sept. 30 (weather permitting). Fare $8; ages 6-11, $1.50. Phone (419) 285-4855.

SAVE **STONEHENGE ESTATE** is .4 mi. n. of the ferry docks at 808 Langram Rd. Comprised of four buildings on 7 acres, the former working winery dates to the 1800s and has been meticulously restored. An audio tape tour relays the history of the estate, which includes a stone farmhouse and wine press cottage, both listed on the National Register of Historic Places. Antiques and photographs are on display. Allow 30 minutes minimum. Daily 11-5, late May through Sept. 30. Admission $5; ages 6-15, $2. Phone (419) 285-6134.

WINERIES

- **Heineman Winery**, 978 Catawba Ave. Mon.-Sat. and holidays 10:30-5, Sun. noon-5, May-Sept. Phone (419) 285-2811.

RIO GRANDE (F-4) pop. 1,000, elev. 682'

BOB EVANS FARMS, 2 mi. e. on SR 588, is a 1,000-acre working farm offering weekend horseback riding and canoe trips, a restored log cabin village, a craft barn, hayrides, camping, a baby animal barnyard, weekend events and festivals. Daily 9-5, Memorial Day weekend-Labor Day. Free. Reservations are required for overnight activities. Phone (740) 245-5305 or (800) 994-3276.

RIPLEY—*see Cincinnati p. 203.*

ROSEVILLE (D-4) pop. 1,800

Roseville and neighboring Crooksville have been pottery centers since the 19th century.

OHIO CERAMIC CENTER, 1 mi. s. on SR 93, consists of five themed buildings housing an artist

Traveling With Tabby

Man's best friend likes to travel, too. With *Traveling With Your Pet – The AAA PetBook*® you get listings of more than 10,000 pet-friendly AAA lodgings throughout North America. This guide provides valuable information such as traveling by car, taking your pet on an airplane, and animal clinic listings. Lodging listings feature pet-specific information, including fees and deposits, pet policies and more.

So before you pack for your pet, drop by your local AAA office* and purchase *Traveling With Your Pet–The AAA PetBook*. Then you and your furry friend will be ready to roam.

* Available at participating AAA club offices or web sites (aaa.com) or by calling 1-877-AAA-BOOK.

studio, a production area and art pottery and utilitarian ware exhibitions. Also displayed are items on loan from private collectors. Mon.-Sat. 9-5, Sun. noon-5, mid-May through Oct. 15; closed holidays. Admission $2, under 13 free. Phone (740) 697-7021 or (800) 752-2604.

SAGAMORE HILLS (B-5)

DOVER LAKE WATERPARK is off the Ohio Tpke. at exit 173N, .7 mi. on SR 21 to Snowville Rd., then e. 3.4 mi. to 1150 W. Highland Rd. Waterslides, tube rides, a wave pool, a children's area, a lake with a beach, amusement park rides for children, miniature golf and a petting zoo with alpacas are offered. Food is available. Park open daily 10-8, rides open 11-7, June 9-Aug. 20 and Aug. 26-27. Phone for Oct. Halloween schedule. Admission Sat.-Sun. $12.95, Mon.-Fri. $9.95, children under 40 inches tall free. Parking $3. DS, MC, VI. Phone (330) 467-7946.

SALEM (C-6) pop. 12,200

Salem is a Quaker town founded in 1806 by Zadok Street and John Strawn. Before the Civil War the town was a station on the Underground Railroad and headquarters for the Western Anti-Slavery Society. One of John Brown's raiders, Edwin Coppock, is honored with a 12-foot sandstone monument in Hope Cemetery on N. Lincoln Street.

SANDUSKY (B-4) pop. 29,800, elev. 597'

Although Sandusky was explored by Robert La-Salle in 1679 and visited by English trader George Croghan in 1760, it was not until 1816 that the town was settled. Its location on Sandusky Bay, a natural harbor on Lake Erie formed by the Cedar Point and Marblehead peninsulas, quickly made it a major center of shipping and industry. It is one of the largest coal-shipping ports on the Great Lakes.

Sandusky still has time for relaxation; its lakeside resorts, wineries, abundant fishing opportunities and access to Lake Erie's islands make it a popular summer vacation spot.

Sandusky/Erie County Visitors and Convention Bureau: 4424 Milan Rd., Sandusky, OH 44870; phone (419) 625-2984 or (800) 255-3743.

Shopping areas: Off the Ohio Turnpike exit 118 on US 250 is Sandusky Mall, whose stores include Elder-Beerman, JCPenney, Kaufmann's and Sears.

CEDAR POINT, off US 6, 10 mi. n. of Ohio Tpke. exit 118, is a 364-acre amusement/theme park and resort. Opened in 1870, Cedar Point offers more than 68 rides, including 15 roller coasters, thought to be the largest collection on Earth. Millennium Force is a 310-foot-tall world record-breaking roller coaster that gives riders a 93-miles-per-hour thrill. Other scream machines include the stand-up Mantis; the six-inversion Raptor; the wooden Mean Streak; the 215-foot-tall Wicked Twister; and the Magnum XL-200, the first roller coaster to break the 200-foot barrier. Three water rides offer refreshing thrills, while the 300-foot-tall Power Tower plunges riders to earth or rockets them into the sky.

The park also features Camp Snoopy, a PEANUTS family area; two more children's areas; an IMAX theater; 10 musical shows in three theatres and along the midways; pioneer crafts; a sandy Lake Erie beach; marina; and picnic facilities. Two miniature golf courses, a 152-foot-tall Skycoaster and Triple Challenge Racepark are next door at Challenge Park, which has separate fees. Food is available.

Park opens daily at 10, May 12 through Labor Day; Sat.-Sun., day after Labor Day-Oct. 27. Closing hours vary. Admission for over 48 inches tall in shoes $42; over age 59, $25; over 4 and under 48 inches tall in shoes $20; under 4 free. Multi-day and combination tickets with Soak City are available. Challenge Park activities have separate fees. Combined causeway toll and parking $6; phone to verify. AX, DS, MC, VI. Phone (419) 627-2350.

FOLLETT HOUSE MUSEUM, 2 blks. s. of US 6 at 404 Wayne St., is an 1834 Greek Revival stone mansion built by prominent businessman Oran Follett, who fought against slavery and helped establish the Republican Party. Items displayed reflect Erie County history from its earliest times to the present, including a collection of Civil War items from the Confederate officers' prison on Johnson's Island. Guided tours are available by appointment.

Allow 1 hour minimum. Tues.-Sat. noon-4, June-Aug.; Sat.-Sun. noon-4, Apr.-May and Sept.-Dec; by appointment rest of year. Closed Dec. 25. Free. Phone (419) 627-9608 or the Sandusky Library at 625-3834 to schedule a guided tour.

GRIFFING FLYING SERVICE, 1 mi. e. of Cedar Point entrance at 3115 Cleveland Rd., offers 15-minute (2 person minimum) and 30-minute airborne sightseeing tours over the islands of Lake Erie. Air transportation to the islands and other destinations also is available. Daily 8-dusk; closed Dec. 25. Fifteen-minute tour $43 per person ($34 per person for two or more); 30-minute tour $125 for one to three persons, $175 for four to five persons. AX, DS, MC, VI. Phone (419) 626-5161.

LAKESIDE—see place listing p. 244.

SAVE **MERRY-GO-ROUND MUSEUM**, at W. Washington and Jackson sts., features a working merry-go-round, exhibits, photographs and carving demonstrations, as well as animals and chariots from carousels. Allow 1 hour minimum. Mon.-Sat. 10-5, Sun. noon-5, Memorial Day-Labor Day; Wed.-Sat. 11-5, Sun. noon-5, Mar. 1-day before Memorial Day and day after Labor Day-Dec. 31; Sat. 11-5, Sun. noon-5, rest of year. Last tour departs 1 hour, 15 minutes before closing. Admission $4; over 59, $3; ages 4-14, $2. MC, VI. Phone (419) 626-6111.

SOAK CITY is at the n.e. corner of Cedar Point amusement park off US 6, 10 mi. n. of Ohio Tpke. exit 118. This 18.5-acre water park's splashing fun includes Breakers Bay, a half-million gallon wave pool; Adventure Cove family activity pool; Eerie Falls' three twisting enclosed slides; Zoom Flume's raft plunge; 10 more tube and body slides; Renegade River, a whitewater inner tube river; Main Stream, a relaxing tube river; and a special 21-and-over area with a pool, hot tub and refreshments. Children and their parents have two water playgrounds and mini inner tube river.

Opens daily at 10, May 25-Labor Day; closing times vary. Admission for over 48 inches tall in bare feet $23; over 59, $13; over 4 and under 48 inches tall in bare feet $10; under 4 free. Reduced admission (after 4 p.m. when park closes at 7 p.m., after 5 p.m. other days), $15; Multi-day and combination tickets with Cedar Point are available. Combined causeway toll and parking $6. AX, DS, MC, VI. Phone (419) 627-2350.

SAVE **SPORTS CITY,** 5205 Milan Rd. (US 250) .25 mi. n. of SR 2, has two 18-hole miniature golf courses, go-cart tracks, bumper boats and batting cages. Open daily, Memorial Day-Labor Day. Hours vary; phone ahead. Rates vary with facilities and ages. DS, MC, VI. Phone (419) 627-1701 or (800) 733-3353.

WINERIES

• **Firelands Winery,** 917 Bardshar Rd., US 6 off SR 2. Mon.-Sat. 9-5, Sun. 1-5, June-Sept.; Mon.-Fri. 9-5, Sat. 10-4, Oct.-Dec. Phone (419) 625-5474 or (800) 548-9463.

SHARONVILLE—*see Cincinnati p. 203.*

SILVERTON—*see Cincinnati p. 203.*

SINKING SPRING (E-2) pop. 200

FORT HILL STATE MEMORIAL, 1,186 acres 3 mi. n. off SR 41, is the site of Fort Hill, a prehistoric earthwork believed to have been built by the Hopewell Indians. Enclosing 48 acres, the walls are about 8,500 feet long, 10 to 20 feet high and 30 to 40 feet thick at the base. A deep gorge cut by the Baker's Fork of Brush Creek borders the area on the north and west.

A museum offers displays about American Indians and the natural history of the site. Picnic facilities and 12 miles of hiking trails are on the grounds. Site daily dawn-dusk. Museum Wed.-Sat. 9:30-5, Sun. noon-5. Site free. Museum $3; ages 6-12, $1.25. Phone (937) 588-3221 or (800) 283-8905.

SPRINGFIELD (D-2) pop. 70,500, elev. 984′

Springfield was settled about 1800 by a group of Kentuckians, including the frontiersman and American Indian scout Simon Kenton. Kenton's wife named the town for the numerous springs found there. In 1802 a water-powered flour mill was built nearby on a gorge in what is now Clifton *(see place listing p. 219);* visitors can take a self-guiding tour of the mill and explore a country store.

After the road came through in 1838 it became known as the "town at the end of the National Pike." Now US 40, the pike connected Springfield with industrial cities as far east as Cumberland, Md., and opened new markets for the city's harvests. Agricultural machinery firms set up shops, and slowly Springfield's complexion changed from rural to industrial. Its industries have diversified, producing turbines, engines and piano plates. Wittenberg University and its 2,100 students add a college-town flavor to this bustling city.

Springfield Area Convention and Visitors Bureau: 333 N. Limestone, Suite 201, Springfield OH 45503; phone (937) 325-7621.

SPRINGFIELD MUSEUM OF ART, 107 Cliff Park Rd., houses temporary exhibits and a permanent collection of 19th- and 20th-century American art. Classes and an art library also are featured. Guided tours are available. Allow 1 hour minimum. Tues.-Fri. 9-5 (also Wed. 5-9), Sat. 9-3, Sun. 2-4; closed Jan. 1, Thanksgiving and Dec. 24-25 and 31. Free. Phone (937) 325-4673.

WEAVER CHAPEL, part of Wittenberg University, is off Woodlawn Ave. This chapel is known for its leaded stained-glass windows. Allow 30 minutes minimum. Daily 8-5. Free. Phone (937) 327-7411.

STEUBENVILLE (C-6) pop. 22,100, elev. 719′

Steubenville, across the Ohio River from West Virginia, is one of the oldest communities in Ohio. The city's location and the nearby supply of coal and clay have helped it become an industrial center.

As part of Steubenville's City of Murals, 21 downtown buildings are decorated with large murals depicting historical scenes. New murals in this project are in progress each year from May through October.

Another local attraction is Creegan Co., 510 Washington St., one of the nation's largest manufacturers of animated and costume characters. Free guided tours of the manufacturing operations are available by appointment; phone (740) 283-3708.

Jefferson County Chamber of Commerce: 630 Market St., Steubenville, OH 43952; phone (740) 282-6226.

Shopping areas: Fort Steuben Mall, half a mile south of US 22 on John Scott Memorial Highway at 100 Mall Dr., has more than 60 stores, including JCPenney and Sears.

WELSH JAGUAR CLASSIC CAR MUSEUM, 501 Washington St., features 20 classic automobiles including Jaguars and muscle cars of the 1960s. Several car-related murals also can be seen. Allow 30 minutes minimum. Wed.-Sun. noon-5; closed major holidays. Admission $1. Phone (740) 282-8649 or (800) 875-5247.

STOCKPORT (E-4) pop. 500, elev. 661'

BIG BOTTOM STATE MONUMENT, 1 mi. s.e. on SR 266, marks the site of a massacre of settlers by American Indians on Jan. 2, 1791. A marble obelisk commemorates the 3-acre site on the Muskingum River. Picnic facilities are available. Daily dawn-dusk. Free. Phone (614) 297-2630 or (800) 686-1535.

SUGARCREEK (C-5) pop. 2,100, elev. 990'

In a predominately Amish dairying and farming region, Sugarcreek is known as the "Little Switzerland of Ohio" because of its Swiss settlers and architecture. The town has numerous Swiss cheese factories.

Sugarcreek Tourist Information: 106 W. Main St., P.O. Box 158, Sugarcreek, OH 44681; phone (330) 852-4113.

Shopping areas: There are several Amish and Swiss heritage shops in the Sugarcreek area. Dutch Valley, 1343 Old SR 39, contains stores featuring antiques, furniture, gifts and Amish baked goods.

ALPINE HILLS MUSEUM, on the public square, depicts the history of the community and its Swiss and Amish heritage. Three floors of exhibits include a Swiss cheese factory from the early 1800s, an Amish kitchen from the 1890s, a restored 19th-century woodworking shop and the Sugarcreek Firehouse from 1895, with its original equipment. A 10-minute videotape is presented in the tourist information center at the front of the museum.

Allow 1 hour minimum. Mon.-Sat. 10-4:30, Apr.-Nov. Donations. Phone (330) 852-4113, 852-2223 or (800) 609-7592.

SAVE **DAVID WARTHER CARVINGS** is 1 mi. e. at 1387 Old SR 39 in the Dutch Valley complex. Warther's intricate solid ivory carvings depict the history of ships. The *Santa Maria* and the *Mayflower* are among the miniature scale models displayed. Allow 30 minutes minimum. Guided 45-minute tours are given as needed Mon.-Sat. 9-5; closed Thanksgiving and Dec. 25. Last tour begins at closing. Admission $4, under 18 free. Phone (330) 852-3455.

TIFFIN (B-3) pop. 18,600, elev. 760'

The meticulously restored 1928 Ritz Theatre is the venue for live performances and motion pictures on many weekends. During the week, guided tours reveal design delights such as garden murals, intricate stencil- and plasterwork, and a 1,200-pound crystal chandelier; advance reservations are required for the tour. Phone the box office at (419) 448-8544 for tour reservations and show schedules.

Tiffin Area Chamber of Commerce: 62 S. Washington St., Tiffin, Ohio 44883; phone (419) 447-4141.

TIFFIN GLASS MUSEUM, 25 S. Washington St., houses a display of original Tiffin glassware produced at the Tiffin Glass Factory 1889-1984. A guided tour is offered. Allow 30 minutes minimum. Tues.-Sat. 1-5; closed holidays. Free. Phone (419) 448-0200.

TIPP CITY (D-1) pop. 6,000 elev. 830'

Tipp City was named for presidential candidate William Henry Harrison's campaign slogan, "Tippecanoe and Tyler too." The 19th-century downtown of this town along the Miami-Erie Canal draws antiques shoppers and those looking for crafts objects. The restored 1839 Roller Mill at 225 E. Main St. now houses specialty shops and a theater which offers melodramas on Saturday; phone (937) 667-3696.

Miami County Visitors and Convention Bureau: 405 S.W. Public Square, Suite 272, Troy, OH 45373; phone (937) 339-1044 or (800) 348-8993.

CHARLESTON FALLS PRESERVE, I-75 exit 68, SR 571 e., then s. on SR 202 and 1 mi. w. on Ross Rd., is a 169-acre preserve consisting of a 37-foot waterfall, a limestone cave, 2.5 miles of hiking trails, a small pond, a planted prairie site and an observation tower; there are easy-access boardwalks. Picnicking is permitted; alcoholic beverages and fires are not permitted. Daily dawn-dusk. Free. Phone (937) 667-1086.

TOLEDO (A-2) pop. 332,900, elev. 572'

A great industrial center, Toledo is one of the world's busiest freshwater ports, ranking third on the Great Lakes. The city's importance as a port stems from its location at the mouth of the Maumee River, the largest river flowing into the lakes. Its natural harbor has 35 miles of frontage. Pipelines for crude oil and gas terminate in Toledo, a major refining center as well as a large producer of glass.

Toledo occupies the site of old Fort Industry, which was built in 1794 and stood near the present Summit and Monroe streets. Fallen Timbers Monument, off SR 24 on Jerome Road, commemorates Gen. Anthony Wayne's 1794 defeat of the American Indians, ending the bloody conflicts between the colonists and American Indians.

As a result of his victory the American Indians relinquished their rights to the Firelands (*see Norwalk p. 251*), which comprised most of the American Indian lands remaining in the vicinity. A consequence of the Toledo War of 1835, a vociferous boundary dispute with Michigan, gave Toledo to Ohio and granted Michigan its northern peninsula in compensation.

The Erie and Kalamazoo Railroad, completed in 1836, was the first American railroad built west of the Alleghenies. Toledo is now one of the nation's largest rail centers.

Toledo provides opportunities for outdoor recreation at its numerous public Metroparks. Promenade Park, a peaceful, landscaped setting along the

Maumee River, is a favorite spot for viewing freighters and towboats. Sidecut Park offers picnicking by canal locks along the Maumee River. Horse racing enthusiasts can find satisfaction at nearby Raceway Park; phone (419) 476-7751.

Note: Policies vary concerning admittance of children to pari-mutuel betting facilities. Phone for information.

Notable among institutions of higher learning in the city is the 21,500-student University of Toledo, established in 1872. Guided tours of the campus, at 2801 W. Bancroft St., are available by appointment; phone (419) 530-8888 or (800) 586-5336. The university's Ritter Planetarium offers weekend shows throughout the year; phone (419) 530-2650 or 530-4037.

Toledo Convention and Visitors Bureau: 401 Jefferson Ave., Toledo, OH 43604; phone (419) 321-6404 or (800) 243-4667.

Self-guiding tours: Brochures and maps of a walking or driving tour of Old West End are available from the convention and visitors bureau. Discover Downtown Toledo highlights the history and architecture of Toledo through a downtown walking tour. For information phone the Urban Affairs Center at the University of Toledo, (419) 530-3591.

Shopping areas: Woodville Mall, 3725 Williston Rd., features Elder-Beerman. Franklin Park, 5001 Monroe St., contains Dillard's, Marshall Field's and Jacobson's, while Southwyck Mall, 2040 S. Reynolds Rd., has Dillard's.

COSI TOLEDO, 1 Discovery Way, at jct. Summit and Adams sts. on the riverfront (parking is at Adams and Superior sts.), is a hands-on science learning center where visitors can ride a high wire cycle above the atrium, design a roller coaster and apply aerodynamics to create the perfect baseball pitch. In addition to hundreds of hands-on exhibits, dramatic demonstrations are presented. Food is available. Mon.-Sat. 10-5, Sun. noon-5; closed Jan. 1, Easter, Thanksgiving and Dec. 24-25. Admission $8; over 64 and ages 3-18, $6.50. MC, VI. Phone (419) 244-2674.

FORT MEIGS—*see Perrysburg p. 253.*

TOLEDO BOTANICAL GARDENS, 5403 Elmer Dr., encompasses 57 acres and includes roses and herbs, wildflowers, azaleas, rhododendrons, a shade and hosta garden, a vegetable garden and a fragrance section. Also on the grounds is a re-created pioneer homestead and artists' guilds. Allow 1 hour minimum. Daily 8 a.m.-9 p.m., Apr.-Oct.; 8-6, rest of year. Free. Phone (419) 936-2986.

TOLEDO MUSEUM OF ART, at 2445 Monroe St., is 1 blk. e. of I-75. This Grecian-style marble structure contains works tracing the history of art from ancient Egypt to the present. Among its more than 700 paintings are works by such European artists as El Greco,

Rembrandt, Peter Paul Rubens and Vincent Van Gogh, as well as works by American artists.

Also featured are books, manuscripts, prints, sculptures, medieval ivories, glass items, decorative arts objects and tapestries. A glass collection chronicles the history of glass over the course of 3,500 years. Allow 2 hours minimum. Tues.-Sat. 10-4 (also Fri. 4-10), Sun. 11-5; closed holidays. Free. Phone (419) 255-8000.

TOLEDO ZOO is 3 mi. s.w. on SR 25. Among the zoo's 62 acres are more than 700 species of mammals, birds and reptiles. An African Savanna area features animals in their natural habitat. The Hippoaquarium features an underwater view of a hippopotamus family. Kingdom of the Apes is a 17,000-sq.-ft. gorilla meadow with an interpretive center offering hands-on exhibits. Large freshwater and saltwater aquariums, a conservatory and botanical gardens also are included.

Daily 10-5, Apr.-Sept.; 10-4, rest of year. Closed Jan. 1, Thanksgiving and Dec. 25. Admission $7.50; over 60 and ages 2-11, $4.50. Parking $3. DS, MC, VI. Phone (419) 385-5721.

Children's Zoo includes a petting zoo and hands-on exhibits.

Museum of Natural Science contains "Diversity of Life," a hands-on activity center.

WILDWOOD MANOR HOUSE, 5 mi. n.w. at 5100 W. Central Ave. in Wildwood Preserve Metropark, reflects the 18th-century Georgian architectural style. The former home of Champion Spark Plug Co. founder Robert A. Strannahan Sr., the 1930s manor includes 16 fireplaces and more than 50 rooms. Wildwood is furnished in period. Guided 45-minute tours are available as needed.

Allow 1 hour minimum. Guided tours Wed.-Sun. and holidays noon-5; closed Jan. 1, Thanksgiving, Nov. 29-Dec. 4 and Dec. 25. Last tour begins 1 hour before closing. Free. Admission may be charged for special events. Phone (419) 535-3050.

WILLIS B. BOYER, docked at International Park across from Portside, was launched in 1911 and retired in 1980. The *Willis B. Boyer* has been refurbished to depict how the biggest, most modern ship on the Great Lakes looked in its day. The museum depicts freighter history on the lakes. Allow 1 hour, 30 minutes minimum. Mon.-Sat. 10-5, Sun. noon-5, May-Sept.; Wed.-Sun. 10-5, rest of year. Last tour departs 1 hour before closing. Admission $6; students with ID and ages 5-18, $4. Phone (419) 936-3070.

WOLCOTT HOUSE MUSEUM COMPLEX— *see Maumee p. 249.*

TROY (D-2) pop. 19,500, elev. 836'

The Eldean Bridge, 2 miles north of Troy, is a long-type truss bridge. Built in 1860, the 223-foot bridge crosses the Great Miami River. Also noteworthy is Troy's public square at Main Street and

SR 55. The restored Miami County Courthouse, with its frescoes and five domes, is particularly impressive.

Miami County Visitors and Convention Bureau: 405 S.W. Public Square, Suite 272, Troy, OH 45373; phone (937) 339-1044 or (800) 348-8993.

BRUKNER NATURE CENTER is 3 mi. s.w. on SR 55, off I-75 exit 73, then 3 mi. w. to 5995 Horseshoe Bend Rd., following signs. This 165-acre nature preserve, dedicated to environmental education and wildlife rehabilitation, offers 6 miles of hiking trails through a diversity of habitats, including pine forest, fen and prairie. The interpretive center features a tree-top-level bird-viewing room and interpretative displays. The restored 1804 Iddings log house is open for viewing. Rehabilitated but permanently impaired animals, including a bobcat and a bald eagle, can be seen.

Frequently scheduled events include live wildlife programs, night walks and stargazing. Pets and picnicking are not permitted. Allow 4 hours minimum. Center open Mon.-Sat. 9-5, Sun. 12:30-5; trails open daily dawn-dusk. Buildings closed major holidays. Admission Mon.-Sat. free. Sun. $1; under 12, 25c; family rate $2. Phone (937) 698-6493 for program information.

TROY-HAYNER CULTURAL CENTER, 301 W. Main St., is in the former home of Mary Jane Harter Coleman Hayner, a prominent local citizen who filled her house with objects she collected during her many travels. Built in 1914, the house has been restored and is used for exhibits, seminars, classes and community programs. Allow 1 hour minimum. Tues.-Sat. 9-5 (also Tues.-Thurs. 7-9 p.m.), Sun. 1-5; closed major holidays. Free. Phone (937) 339-0457.

TWINSBURG (B-5) pop. 9,600, elev. 1,004′

Settled in 1817, Twinsburg was originally called Millsville; however, in 1819 the town was renamed for two merchants from Connecticut, Moses and Aaron Wilcox, who were instrumental in the expansion of this community. Settling in Twinsburg in 1823, these identical twins married sisters, were life-long business partners, died within hours of one another and are buried together.

Today Twinsburg, one of the fastest growing communities in the state, is the site of the area's largest festival. Twinsburg residents and nearly 100,000 visitors see double the first weekend in August during the Twins Days Festival. Highlights of this gathering of twins, triplets and quadruplets from around the world include a parade, arts and crafts show, fireworks display, talent show and a golf tournament. Phone (330) 425-3652.

Twinsburg Visitors Center: 9044 Church St., Twinsburg, OH 44087; phone (330) 963-6311 or (877) 542-1435.

UNIONVILLE (A-5) elev. 705′

SHANDY HALL, 1 mi. e. on SR 84, was built in 1815 and is believed to be the oldest house in the

Western Reserve. The hall contains the original furnishings and collections of the Robert Harper family. Outstanding among the 17 rooms is the banquet room. The house also includes the original cellar kitchen and a formal parlor with American Empire furniture. Tues.-Sat. 10-5, Sun. 1-5, May-Oct. Admission $3; over 59 and ages 6-12, $2. Phone (440) 466-3680.

UPPER SANDUSKY (C-3)
pop. 5,900, elev. 850′

Established in 1843, Upper Sandusky overlooks the Sandusky River, whose name comes from an American Indian word meaning "water within pools." This site was headquarters for the Wyandot Indians, who controlled the area that is now Ohio.

Swartz Bridge, southeast of town on CR 130, and Parker Bridge, northeast of town on CR 40, are covered bridges found within the area.

Wyandot County Visitors Bureau: P.O. Box 357, Upper Sandusky, OH 43351; phone (419) 294-3556 or (877) 992-6368.

INDIAN MILL STATE MEMORIAL is 2.5 mi. n.e. on SR 67, then 1 mi. e. on TR 47. The museum, housed in a converted gristmill built in 1861, depicts the history of milling. Fri.-Sat. 9:30-5, Sun. 1-6, June-Oct. Admission $1; ages 6-12, 50c. Phone (419) 294-4022 or (800) 600-7147.

WYANDOT COUNTY HISTORICAL SOCIETY, 130 S. 7th St., is in an 1853 Normandy-style mansion. Displays include American Indian and pioneer artifacts, antique toys and clothing. A restored one-room schoolhouse furnished with items reminiscent of the 19th century is on the grounds. Allow 1 hour minimum. Thurs.-Sun. 1-4:30, May-Oct. Admission $1, students with ID 50c. Phone (419) 294-3857.

URBANA (D-2) pop. 11,400

Urbana-Champaign County Chamber of Commerce: 113 Miami St., Urbana, OH 43078; phone (937) 653-5764.

SAVE **CEDAR BOG NATURE PRESERVE,** 4 mi. s. on US 68, then 1 mi. w. on Woodburn Rd., offers such uncommon flora and fauna as tundra swamp birch, prairie dock, swamp rattlesnake, spotted turtle and more than 100 species of birds. Much of the plant life in the preserve dates to the last ice age. Wed.-Sun. 9-4:30, Apr.-Sept.; by appointment rest of year. Admission $3; ages 6-11, $1.25. Phone (937) 484-3744 or (800) 860-0147.

VERMILION (B-4) pop. 11,100, elev. 604′

The banks of the Vermilion River were first settled by the Ottawa Indians, who found that the clay soil made a bright and durable red paint. In 1808 pioneers moved in and established homesteads, and soon a thriving harbor town was born.

The Farmer's Exchange Park, Liberty Avenue and Main Street, provides scenic views of the river. Main Street Beach, at the Great Lakes Historical

Museum, overlooks Lake Erie. A section of Vermilion's old downtown area, Harbour Town, encompasses restored houses, the Town Hall, the 1883 Opera House, the Old School House and shops.

Sandusky/Erie County Visitors and Convention Bureau: 4424 Milan Rd., Sandusky, OH 44870; phone (419) 625-2984 or (800) 255-3743.

Self-guiding tours: Information about tours of Harbour Town is available from Friends of Harbour Town 1837, Old Jib's Corner, 5741 Liberty Ave., Vermilion, OH 44089; phone (440) 967-4262.

INLAND SEAS MARITIME MUSEUM, 480 Main St., exhibits models of sailing ships, yachts and lake freighters and displays paintings, photographs, a steam tug engine, a pilothouse and items depicting navigation on the Great Lakes. A 62-foot, full-size replica of the 1877 Vermilion lighthouse stands adjacent to the museum. Allow 30 minutes minimum. Daily 10-5; closed Jan. 1, Easter, Thanksgiving and Dec. 25. Admission $5; over 64, $4; ages 6-15, $3; family rate $10. AX, DS, MC, VI. Phone (440) 967-3467 or (800) 893-1485.

WALDO (C-3) pop. 340

WINERIES

- **Shamrock Vineyards,** 111 CR 25 (Rengert Rd.). Mon.-Sat. 1-6, Apr.-Oct.; 1-5, rest of year. Closed major holidays. Phone (740) 726-2883.

WAPAKONETA (C-2) pop. 9,200, elev. 898′

Neil Armstrong, who on July 20, 1969, became the first person to walk on the moon, was born in Wapakoneta in 1930.

FORT AMANDA STATE MEMORIAL, 9 mi. n.w. on SR 198, is the site of Fort Amanda, built during the War of 1812. Picnic facilities are available. Daily dawn-dusk, Apr.-Oct. Free. Phone (419) 221-1232.

NEIL ARMSTRONG AIR AND SPACE MUSEUM, I-75 business loop at exit 111, follows the history of flight from balloon travel to space exploration. On view are model airplanes, the Gemini 8 capsule in which Armstrong completed the first spacecraft docking in orbit, a Jupiter rocket engine and several motion picture presentations.

A dome-shaped "astrotheater" creates the impression of a trip to the moon. The infinity cube, an 18-foot square lined with mirrors, offers the illusion of being projected into space. Allow 2 hours minimum. Mon.-Sat. 9:30-5, Sun. noon-5; closed Jan. 1, Thanksgiving and Dec. 25. Admission $5; over 59, $4.50; ages 6-12, $1.25. AX, DS, MC, VI. Phone (419) 738-8811 or (800) 860-0142.

WARREN (B-6) pop. 50,800, elev. 894′

Settled in 1799, Warren was named after the territorial surveyor Moses Warren. An early iron and

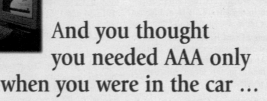

coal producer, the city served as the first capital of the historic Connecticut Western Reserve.

Local industrialists William Doud and James Ward Packard established the Packard Electric Co. in 1890. The first Packard automobile was built in Warren. The success of the Packard brought prosperity to the town, as evidenced by the unusual architectural styles of the grand homes along "Millionaires Row" on Mahoning Avenue. Warren was the first U.S. city to light its streets with incandescent bulbs. The W.D. Packard Music Hall, built in 1955, is used for concerts, lectures and other programs. Camping, fishing, boating and swimming are possible at nearby Mosquito Lake State Park (see Recreation Chart).

The world's top women golfers visit each summer for the Giant Eagle LPGA Classic.

Trumbull County Convention & Visitors Bureau: 650 Youngstown-Warren Rd., Niles, OH 44446; phone (330) 544-3468 or (800) 672-9555.

SAVE **NATIONAL PACKARD MUSEUM** is 2 mi. n. to 1899 Mahoning Ave. Displays detail the history of the Packard Electric Company, located in Warren, and little-known facts about it and its innovative technology. A collection of Packard automobiles built at the Warren Packard Motor Car Company and 8-and 12-cylinder models built in Detroit, Mich., also are on display. Tues.-Sat. noon-5, Sun. 1-5; closed Jan. 1, July 4, Thanksgiving and Dec. 25. Admission $5; ages 7-12 and over 64, $3. Allow 1 hour minimum. Phone (330) 394-1899.

WASHINGTON COURT HOUSE (D-3)
pop. 12,600, elev. 973'

Originally named Washington, the affix "Court House" was added in the late 1820s to distinguish the town from four other Washingtons in Ohio.

The Fayette County Court House contains murals by Archibald M. Willard, who created the painting "Spirit of '76." Many fine saddle horses, pacers and trotters are raised in the area, with several farms open to the public.

Fayette County Chamber of Commerce: 101 E. East St., Washington Court House, OH 43160; phone (740) 335-0761.

WAYNE NATIONAL FOREST

Elevations in the forest range from 630 ft. on the Ohio River near Newport to 1,320 ft. on the Narrows River near Sardis. Refer to AAA maps for additional information.

In the southeastern portion of the state, Wayne National Forest was named in honor of Revolutionary War hero Gen. Anthony Wayne. The forest encompasses several divisions totaling 230,000 acres. More than 360 miles of hiking, horse and vehicle trails wind through the forest. Redbuds and dog-

woods bloom in spring, and the fall foliage is stunning. There are several covered bridges in the area.

Flowing through the forest's Marietta unit, the Little Muskingum River offers canoeing and fishing. Vesuvius Furnace, north of Ironton off SR 93, is a 19th-century relic of Ohio's iron industry. Primitive camping is available; a fee is charged for developed campsites. The Athens and Ironton units have developed campgrounds; a small fee is charged. Hunting is permitted in season.

The forest is free and open all year. For maps and information contact the Ironton District, (740) 534-6500, at 6518 State Route 93, Pedro, OH 45659; the Athens District, (740) 753-0101, at 13700 US 33, Nelsonville, OH 45764; or the Marietta District, (740) 373-9055, Rte. 1, Box 132, Marietta, OH 45750. See Recreation Chart and the AAA Great Lakes CampBook.

WAYNESVILLE—see Cincinnati p. 203.

WELLINGTON (B-4) pop. 4,100, elev. 855'

Established in 1818, Wellington did not achieve its potential until 1850 when the railroad arrived. A station on the Underground Railroad, the town was the site of the Oberlin/Wellington Slave Rescue of 1857. By 1880 the town was known as the "Cheese Capital of the United States," with more than 40 cheese factories in the area. Wellington was the 1855-75 home of Archibald M. Willard, painter of the classic "Spirit of '76." A copy of the artwork, along with many Willard originals, hangs in the town library on Main Street and in the Spirit of '76 Museum, which is open Saturday and Sunday at 201 N. Main Street; phone (440) 647-4367. Other notables natives include Myron T. Herrick, Governor of Ohio 1904-06 and Ambassador to France, 1912-14 and 1921-29.

WELLSTON (E-4) pop. 6,000

Founded in 1873 by Harvey Wells, Wellston is a hunter's paradise. Its abundance of game attracts hunters, especially deer hunters. Lake Alma offers fishing, swimming, boating, camping and picnicking on its 90 acres. See Recreation Chart and the AAA Great Lakes CampBook.

BUCKEYE FURNACE is 2 mi. s. on SR 327, 3.5 mi. e. on SR 124, then 2 mi. s. on CR 58 and s. on Buckeye Park Rd. following signs. Built in 1851 and closed in 1894, the furnace is one of the last 19th-century charcoal-fired iron ore furnaces in existence. Five buildings within the furnace complex include the charging house, casting shed, charcoal shed, engine house and a company store that contains a visitor center and museum. Nature trails are on the grounds.

Grounds daily dawn-dusk. Buildings are open by appointment. Admission $3; ages 6-12, $1.25. Phone (740) 384-3537 or (800) 860-0144.

WESTERVILLE—see Columbus p. 231.

WEST LIBERTY (C-2) pop. 1,600, elev. 1,009'

 OHIO CAVERNS, 4 mi. s.e. on SR 245, contrasts vividly colored walls with pure white stalactites and stalagmites. Discovered in 1897, the caves maintain a constant temperature of 54 degrees F. Electrically lighted passageways wind through the caverns. Picnic facilities are available.

Allow 1 hour minimum. Guided 45-minute tours are given as needed daily 9-5, Apr.-Oct.; 9-4, rest of year. Closed Thanksgiving and Dec. 25. Last tour departs 30 minutes before closing. Admission $9.50; ages 5-12, $5. DS, MC, VI. Phone (937) 465-4017.

SAVE **THE PIATT CASTLES** are 1 and 2 mi. e. on SR 245. Mac-A-Cheek Castle is a limestone structure completed in 1871. A guided tour of many of the castle's rooms acquaints visitors with the lives of several generations of former occupants. Mac-O-Chee Castle was begun in the 1860s as a modest Gothic retreat and was completed in 1881 with a Flemish-inspired limestone facade. This building contains American, European and Asian furnishings and objects. Both buildings are shown only by 45-minute, as-needed, guided tours.

Allow 1 hour minimum. Both castles open daily 11-5, Memorial Day weekend-Labor Day; daily noon-4 Apr. 1-Sat. before Memorial Day, day after Labor Day-Oct. 31, and day after Thanksgiving-Dec. 31; Sat.-Sun. noon-4 in Mar.; otherwise varies. Last tour begins at closing. Closed Jan. 1, Easter and Dec. 24-25. Admission per castle $8; over 59, $7; students ages 13-21 with ID $6; ages 5-12, $5. Combination ticket for both castles $15; over 59, $13; students ages 13-21 with ID $11; ages 5-12, $9. Phone (937) 465-2821.

WILBERFORCE (D-2) pop. 2,700

In 1856 the Methodist Episcopal Church purchased a tract of land in southwest Ohio for the purpose of opening a college, then known as Ohio African University, for escaped and freed slaves. This college, the first African-American university in the country, is now Wilberforce University, named after the 18th-century British abolitionist William Wilberforce. Student enrollment is 750.

THE NATIONAL AFRO-AMERICAN MUSEUM AND CULTURAL CENTER, is at 1350 Brush Row Rd., off US 42. The museum serves as a repository for the preservation, study and interpretation of African-American history and culture. A permanent exhibit, "From Victory to Freedom: Afro-American Life in the Fifties," chronicles African-American lives from World War II to the passage of the Voting Rights Act in 1965.

Also presented are changing exhibits as well as an expanding collection of artifacts, manuscripts and other library materials. Guided tours are available with 2-weeks advance notice. Allow 1 hour, 30 minutes minimum. Tues.-Sat. 9-5, Sun. 1-5; closed major holidays, except Martin Luther King Jr. Day. Admission $4, senior citizens, $3.60, kindergarten-

college students with ID $1.50. AX, DS, MC, VI. Phone (937) 376-4944 or (800) 752-2603.

WILMOT (C-5) pop. 300

ALPINE-ALPA is 2.5 mi. s.w. on US 62. Visitors can view what is believed to be the world's largest cuckoo clock, standing more than 23 feet tall. The clock features hand-carved wooden band members and dancers that perform every half-hour. This Swiss village market also features a life-size mural and one of the largest collections of cuckoo clocks in the country. Food is available. Allow 30 minutes minimum. Cuckoo clock daily 9-8, May-Nov. Village open daily 9-8. Village free. Clock 25c. Phone (330) 359-5454.

THE WILDERNESS CENTER, 1 mi. w. on US 250, consists of 573 acres of forests, prairies and marshes with winding trails. The Interpretive Building features nature exhibits and an observation room. Picnic facilities are available; no camping or fires are permitted. Pets and bicycles are not allowed on trails. Allow 1 hour minimum. Trails open daily dawn-dusk. Interpretive Building open Tues.-Sat. 9-5, Sun. 1-5. Holiday hours vary. Donations. Phone (330) 359-5235.

WOOSTER (C-4) pop. 22,200, elev. 912'

During the War of 1812, an Army headquarters and a land office were established in Wooster. These drew permanent settlers, including the young German immigrant August Imgard, whom local historians claim introduced Christmas trees to America in 1847.

Wayne County Convention and Visitors Bureau: 428 West Liberty St., Wooster, OH 44691; phone (330) 264-1800 or (800) 362-6474.

OHIO AGRICULTURAL RESEARCH AND DEVELOPMENT CENTER of Ohio State University is 1 mi. s. on SR 83 at 1680 Madison Ave. This 2,100-acre research center includes the Secrest Arboretum and the Garden of Roses of Legend and Romance. Allow 1 hour, 30 minutes minimum. Visitor center open Mon.-Fri. 8-5. Grounds open daily dawn-dusk. Free. Phone (330) 263-3700.

XENIA (D-2) pop. 24,700, elev. 910'

Xenia (ZEEN-yuh), once the site of the Shawnee Nation's largest settlement, was the birthplace of Tecumseh. In the 1790s and early 1800s, Tecumseh tried to create a pan-Indian alliance to protect tribal lands and culture from the encroaching frontiersmen. Tecumseh joined forces with the British during the War of 1812. Tecumseh's cause died with him in 1813 at the Battle of the Thames in Ontario.

Greene County Convention and Visitors Bureau: 1221 Meadowbridge Dr., Suite A, Beavercreek, OH 45434; phone (937) 429-9100 or (800) 733-9109.

SAVE **"BLUE JACKET"** is performed in a 1,500-seat amphitheater in Caesar's Ford Park, 2-3 mi. e. on US 35; then 4.5 mi. s. on Jasper Rd. to Stringtown Rd. and follow signs. The 2.5-hour outdoor drama recounts the struggle for freedom among Ohio's Shawnee Indians, frontiersmen and escaping slaves during the late 18th century. Performances feature a large professional cast, 17 horses and period weapons, including three historically accurate cannons.

Frontier-style dinners and backstage tours are available. Performances Tues.-Sun. at 8 p.m., early June-Labor Day. Play admission Tues.-Sat. $9-$15; over 60, $8-$13; under 13, $6. Admission on Sun. $8; under 13, $6. No refunds are given; exchanges are made with 24-hour notice; rain checks are issued for canceled performances. Reservations are recommended. MC, VI. Phone (937) 376-4318 or (877) 465-2583.

GREENE COUNTY HISTORICAL SOCIETY, 74 W. Church St., is in the Brantley Carriage House Museum, which contains exhibits chronicling 19th-century living, antiques, an HO model railway diorama showing Xenia 1920-50 and documents of Greene County. A restored Victorian townhouse and the 1799 James Galloway Log House also are on the grounds. The log house has withstood both a dismantling and rebuilding in 1936 and 1974.

Allow 1 hour minimum. Tues.-Fri. 1:30-3:30, Sat.-Sun. 1:30-4, June-Sept.; Tues.-Fri. 1:30-3:30, rest of year. Closed holidays. Guided tours are available at 1:30. Donations. Phone (937) 372-4606.

YOUNGSTOWN (B-6) pop. 95,700

Youngstown was named after John Young, a surveyor who purchased 15,600 acres of land in 1797. The town's development was slow until 1803, when iron ore was discovered and the first blast furnace was established in the area. The opening of the Pennsylvania and Ohio Canal increased both the population and industrialization of the area during the 1820s. In 1862 the first coal mine was opened, and the first steel plant, the Union Iron and Steel Co., was built in 1892. Most early settlers came from Pennsylvania, New York and New England; however, the growing industrial economy soon attracted European emigrants.

Youngstown now has a strong and diversified industrial base and a rich cultural background, due in part to the 12,500-student Youngstown State University, which was established in 1908.

Youngstown/Mahoning County Convention and Visitors Bureau: 100 Federal Plaza E., Suite 101, Youngstown, OH 44503; phone (330) 747-8200 or (800) 447-8201.

Shopping areas: Southern Park Mall, US 224 and SR 7, features Dillard's, JCPenney, Kaufmann's and Sears.

THE ARMS FAMILY MUSEUM OF LOCAL HISTORY, is 1 mi. n. of Federal Plaza St., s. of US 422. Greystone, the former home of Wilford and Olive Arms, represents the arts-and-crafts style of the early 20th century. The first floor has period rooms; the second floor has exhibits about the history of the Mahoning Valley. On the grounds is a carriage house of the same era containing an archival library. Allow 1 hour minimum. Museum open Tues.-Fri. 1-4, Sat.-Sun. 1:30-5. Library open Tues.-Fri. 9-4, Sat. 1-5. Admission $3; over 59 and college students with ID $2; under 18, $1. Phone (330) 743-2589.

THE BUTLER INSTITUTE OF AMERICAN ART is at 524 Wick Ave. Founded in 1919 by Youngstown industrialist Joseph G. Butler Jr., this museum was one of the first in the country built specifically to house American artworks. The permanent collection surveys American art from the Colonial period to the present. Highlights include major works by Mary Cassatt, John Copley, Thomas Eakins, Adolph Gottlieb, Winslow Homer, Frederic Remington, Charles Sheeler, Charles Vonnoh, Andy Warhol and Benjamin West.

There also are monthly exhibits. Allow 1 hour minimum. Tues.-Sat. 11-4 (also Wed. 4-8 p.m.), Sun. noon-4; closed holidays. Free. Phone (330) 743-1107.

GEM **MILL CREEK METROPARKS,** s. of Mahoning Ave. off Glenwood Ave., is a 3,600-acre park containing a 6-mile-long gorge, foot trails, drives, three lakes and Lanterman Falls. Golf, tennis, fishing and picnic facilities are available. Daily dawn-dusk. Free. Phone (330) 702-3000.

Fellows Riverside Gardens is off Mattoning Ave. on McKinley Ave. at the north end of the Mill Creek Metroparks. The 11-acre garden encompasses a formal rose garden, perennials, shrubs, trees and seasonal displays of 25,000 tulips in the spring and flowering annuals in the summer. Two overlooks provide views of the park and the city. The architecturally interesting visitors center provides maps and other visitor information. Allow 1 hour minimum. Grounds open daily 10-dusk. Visitors center open Tues.-Sun.10-5. Free. Phone (330) 740-7116.

Ford Nature Center is at 840 Old Furnace Rd. This former residence built of stone now houses a naturalist staff and a variety of displays. Three rooms display live reptiles and hands-on exhibits. Nature programs and weekly nature hikes are offered. Daily 9-5; closed Jan. 1, Thanksgiving and Dec. 25. Free. Phone (330) 740-7107.

Lanterman's Mill, 980 Canfield Rd., is a restored 19th-century water-powered gristmill. The 1845 mill has been completely renovated and is still in operation. Allow 30 minutes minimum. Tues.-Fri. 10-5, Sat.-Sun. 11-6, May-Oct. Admission $1; over 59 and ages 6-18, 50c. Phone (330) 740-7115.

SAVE **YOUNGSTOWN HISTORICAL CENTER OF INDUSTRY AND LABOR,** 151 W. Wood St., chronicles the impact of the iron and steel industry upon Mahoning Valley communities. The museum's permanent exhibit explores labor, immigration and urban history, using videotapes, photographs, reconstructed scenes and historic objects. Items displayed range from workers' tools and clothing to "last heats," the final batches of steel produced at a mill before it closes. Life-size scenes interpret the lives of steelworkers.

Allow 1 hour minimum. Center open Wed.-Sat. 9-5, Sun. noon-5. Archives and library open Tues.-Sat. 9-5. Closed Jan. 1, Thanksgiving and Dec. 25. Admission to center $5; senior citizens $4.50; ages 6-12, $1.25. Archives and library free. DS, MC, VI. Phone (330) 743-5934.

ZANESVILLE (D-5) pop. 26,800, elev. 699′

Settled in 1799, Zanesville was once considered the pottery capital of the United States; its surrounding areas still support a number of pottery factories. Architect Cass Gilbert and novelists Zane Grey and Charles D. Stewart were born in Zanesville.

The Y-Bridge carries US 40 over the junction of the Muskingum and Licking rivers. The design is uncommon in the United States.

Zanesville is at the junction of two scenic highways. US 22 runs southwest to Lancaster, and a scenic portion of I-70 runs east to Bridgeport, then through West Virginia and into Pennsylvania.

Zanesville-Muskingum County Convention and Visitors Bureau: 205 N. Fifth St., Zanesville, OH 43701; phone (740) 455-8282 or (800) 743-2303.

Shopping areas: Colony Square, 3575 N. Maple Ave., features Elder-Beerman, JCPenney, Lazarus and Sears. Freight Shops, at Third and Market streets, offers shops in the restored 1917 New York Central Railroad Depot.

THE LORENA **STERNWHEELER** is moored at Zane's Landing Park. This riverboat offers 1-hour cruises on the Muskingum River. Dinner cruises also are available. Sightseeing cruises depart daily at 1, 2:30 and 4, June-Aug.; Sat.-Sun. at 1, 2:30 and 4, Sept.-Oct. (weather permitting). Fare $5; senior citizens $4.50; ages 2-12, $3. Phone (740) 455-8883 or (800) 246-6303.

NATIONAL ROAD-ZANE GREY MUSEUM— *see Norwich p. 252.*

 **ZANESVILLE ART CENTER,** 3.2 mi. n. via Maple Ave. at 620 Military Rd., displays Ohio art, pottery and glass, as well as a diverse collection of traditional and contemporary art from America, Asia and Europe. Displayed are paintings, drawings, sculpture, prints and ceramics. Highlighted is a 300-year-old London panel room with paintings by Old Masters, drawings and decorative arts pieces. Traveling exhibitions are presented. An art library is on the premises. Allow 1 hour minimum. Tues.-Wed. and Fri. 10-5 (also Thurs. 5-8:30), Sat.-Sun. 1-5; closed holidays. Free. Phone (740) 452-0741.

ZOAR (C-5) pop. 200, elev. 883′

 **ZOAR VILLAGE,** on SR 212, 3 mi. s.e. of I-77 exit 93 to 198 Main St., is in the center of what was once the Zoar Community. The village was founded in 1817 by German immigrants who acquired several thousand acres along the Tuscarawas River. Their practically self-sustaining community prospered until it was dissolved in 1898, when the industries of the village failed to keep pace with those of the rest of the country.

Restored buildings include Number One House, the home of leader Joseph Bimeler; a bakery; tin shop; wagon shed; general store; kitchen; dairy; blacksmith shop; and garden house. The Bimeler Museum contains historic items of the period. The community garden is geometrically patterned to symbolize the New Jerusalem.

Wed.-Sat. 9:30-5, Sun. and holidays noon-5, Memorial Day-Labor Day; Sat. 9:30-5, Sun. and holidays noon-5, Apr. 1-day before Memorial Day and day after Labor Day-Oct. 31. Admission $5; over 64, $4.50; ages 6-12, $1.25. AX, DS, MC, VI. Phone (330) 874-3011 or (800) 262-6195.

Illinois

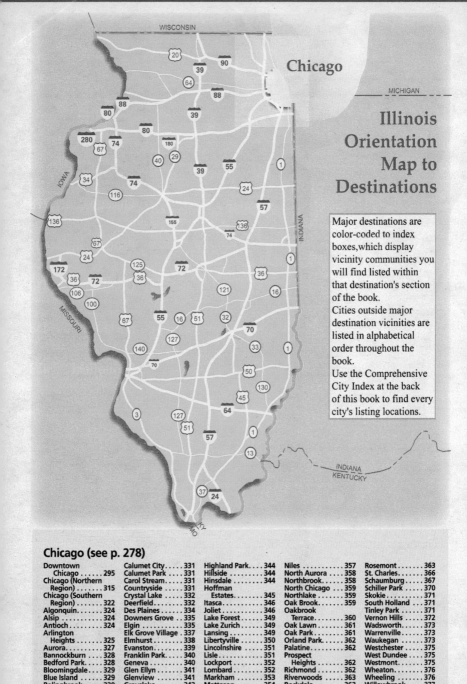

Chicago

Illinois
Orientation
Map to
Destinations

Major destinations are
color-coded to index
boxes, which display
vicinity communities you
will find listed within
that destination's section
of the book.
Cities outside major
destination vicinities are
listed in alphabetical
order throughout the
book.
Use the Comprehensive
City Index at the back
of this book to find every
city's listing locations.

ALGONQUIN —*See Chicago p. 324.*

ALSIP —*See Chicago p. 324.*

ALTON pop. 32,900

———— **WHERE TO STAY** ————

COMFORT INN

Motel

Phone: (618)465-9999
All Year [ECP]   1P: $69-$81   2P: $74-$86   XP: $5   F18
Location: Jct SR 140, off SR 3. 11 Crossroads Ct 62002. Fax: 618/465-0055. **Facility:** 62 one-bedroom standard units, some with whirlpools. 3 stories, interior corridors. *Bath:* combo or shower only. **Parking:** on-site. **Terms:** package plans, pets (with prior approval). **Amenities:** extended cable TV, safes (fee). *Some:* irons, hair dryers. **Pool(s):** heated indoor. **Leisure Activities:** limited exercise equipment. **Business Services:** business center, PC, fax. **Cards:** AX, CB, DC, DS, MC, VI. **Special Amenities:** free continental breakfast and free local telephone calls.

SOME UNITS

SUPER 8 MOTEL
Motel
JC, MC, VI.

Phone: (618)465-8885
All Year [ECP]   1P: $48-$66   2P: $54-$72   XP: $6   F12
Location: SR 111, 1.8 mi e of jct SR 67. 1800 Homer Adams Pkwy 62002. Fax: 618/465-8964. **Facility:** 63 one-bedroom standard units. 3-4 stories (no elevator), interior corridors. *Bath:* combo or shower only. **Parking:** on-site. **Amenities:** extended cable TV, safes (fee). **Business Services:** fax (fee). **Cards:** AX, CB, DC, DS, JC, MC, VI.

SOME UNITS

———— **WHERE TO DINE** ————

CASTELLI'S MOONLIGHT RESTAURANT   Lunch: $5-$7   Dinner: $5-$19   Phone: 618/462-4620
Italian
Location: Jct SR 3/140/111, 0.4 mi e, then 1.2 mi n. 3400 Fosterburg Rd 62002. **Hours:** 11:15 am-10 pm, Fri-11 pm, Sat 4 pm-11 pm. Closed major holidays. **Features:** casual dress; children's menu; carryout; cocktails & lounge; buffet. Since 1937, patrons have enjoyed the casual atmosphere and homemade specialties here. The Roman house salad with creamy Italian dressing and the "Talk-n-Chic" fried chicken are notable hits in this cozy and friendly eatery convenient for travelers. **Parking:** on-site. **Cards:** AX, DS, MC, VI.

TONY'S RESTAURANT & 3RD ST CAFE   Dinner: $9-$22   Phone: 618/462-8384
Steak House
Location: US 67, just n of jct SR 100. 312 Piasa St 62002. **Hours:** 4:30 pm-10 pm, Fri & Sat-11 pm. **Reservations:** suggested. **Features:** casual dress; children's menu; carryout; cocktails & lounge. Located at the foot of Piasa Street, close to the banks of the Mississippi River, Tony's of Alton occupies a building which once housed a popular department store. Now, this building is home to a restaurant with several dining rooms, each with different levels of sophistication and elegance. At Tony's, you will be able to select from pasta, pizza, steak and seafood and a wide variety of cheesecake desserts. **Parking:** on-site and valet. **Cards:** AX, CB, DC, DS, JC, MC, VI.

ANTIOCH —*See Chicago p. 324.*

ARCOLA pop. 2,700

——— WHERE TO STAY ———

COMFORT INN
[SAVE]
Motel

5/1-10/31	1P: $45-$95	2P: $49-$99	XP: $7 F12
4/1-4/30	1P: $45-$85	2P: $49-$89	XP: $7 F12
11/1-12/31	1P: $45-$75	2P: $49-$79	XP: $7 F12
1/1-3/31	1P: $39-$69	2P: $49-$79	XP: $7 F12

Phone: (217)268-4000

Location: I-57, exit 203, just w. 610 E Springfield Rd 61910. Fax: 217/268-4001. **Facility:** 41 one-bedroom standard units, some with whirlpools. 2 stories, interior corridors. **Parking:** on-site, winter plug-ins. **Amenities:** extended cable TV. *Some:* irons, hair dryers. **Pool(s):** outdoor. **Business Services:** fax (fee). **Cards:** AX, CB, DC, DS, MC, VI.

SOME UNITS

THE FLOWER PATCH BED & BREAKFAST
Historic Bed & Breakfast

| All Year [BP] | 1P: $60-$87 | 2P: $60-$87 | XP: $15 |

Phone: 217-268-4876

Location: I-57, exit 203, 0.8 mi w on E Springfield Rd to Locust St, 0.3 mi n to Jefferson St, then just e. 225 E Jefferson St 61910. Fax: 217/268-4900. **Facility:** Smoke free premises. 5 one-bedroom standard units. 2 stories, interior corridors. *Bath:* some shared or private, shower only. **Parking:** on-site. **Terms:** check-in 4:30 pm, age restrictions may apply, 7 day cancellation notice-fee imposed. **Amenities:** *Some:* hair dryers. **Guest Services:** gift shop, afternoon tea. **Cards:** DS, MC, VI.

SOME UNITS

ARLINGTON HEIGHTS —See Chicago p. 325.

ARTHUR pop. 2,100

——— WHERE TO DINE ———

YODER'S KITCHEN
Regional American

| **Lunch:** $5-$10 | **Dinner:** $8-$12 | **Phone:** 217-543-2714 |

Location: Just e on SR 133. 1195 E Columbia 61911. **Hours:** 6 am-8 pm. Closed major holidays; also Sun. **Reservations:** accepted. **Features:** casual dress; carryout; salad bar; buffet. In the heart of Central Illinois' Old Order Amish country, you'll find Yoder's Kitchen. Yoder's is known for simple country cooking done well. Their ham, chicken, chops and sausages are very popular. You may order them from the menu or select from the buffet. But please save room for pie. If you wonder why this restaurant is so busy, the pie is why. Smoke free premises. **Parking:** on-site. **Cards:** DS, MC, VI.

AURORA —See Chicago p. 327.

BANNOCKBURN —See Chicago p. 328.

BEARDSTOWN pop. 5,300

——— WHERE TO STAY ———

SUPER 8 MOTEL
Motel

| All Year | 1P: $35-$45 | 2P: $45-$52 | XP: $7 F12 |

Phone: 217/323-5858

Location: US 67, just w from SR 125. 1903 Grand Ave 62618 (RR 2, Box 101A). Fax: 217/323-5858. **Facility:** 40 one-bedroom standard units, some with whirlpools. 2 stories, interior corridors. **Parking:** on-site. **Terms:** pets ($25 deposit). **Amenities:** extended cable TV. **Pool(s):** outdoor. **Business Services:** meeting rooms. **Cards:** AX, CB, DC, DS, MC, VI.

SOME UNITS
FEE FEE

BEDFORD PARK —See Chicago p. 328.

BELLEVILLE pop. 42,800

——— WHERE TO STAY ———

THE SHRINE MOTEL
[AAA] [SAVE]
Motel

| All Year | 1P: $60 | 2P: $60 | XP: $7 F16 |

Phone: 618/397-1162

Location: I-255, exit 17A, 1 mi e on SR 15. 451 S De Mazenod Dr 62223. Fax: 618/394-6524. **Facility:** 78 one-bedroom standard units. 2 stories, interior corridors. *Bath:* combo or shower only. **Parking:** on-site. **Leisure Activities:** hiking trails, playground. **Business Services:** fax (fee). **Cards:** AX, CB, DC, DS, MC, VI. **Special Amenities:** free continental breakfast and free local telephone calls.

SOME UNITS

SUPER 8 MOTEL
Motel

| All Year | 1P: $43 | 2P: $50 | XP: $5 F12 |

Phone: 618/234-9670

Location: 0.4 mi e from SR 159. 600 E Main St 62220. Fax: 618/234-0177. **Facility:** 42 one-bedroom standard units, some with whirlpools. 2 stories, exterior corridors. **Parking:** on-site, winter plug-ins. **Terms:** [CP] meal plan available, pets ($5 extra charge). **Amenities:** extended cable TV. **Guest Services:** coin laundry. **Business Services:** fax (fee). **Cards:** AX, DC, DS, MC, VI.

SOME UNITS

SWANS COURT BED & BREAKFAST
Phone: (618)233-0779

[AAA] [SAVE]
▼▼▼
Historic Bed & Breakfast

All Year [BP]   1P: $45-$90   2P: $65-$90   XP: $20
Location: Jct SR 15 and 159, 3.6 mi n to D St, just e to Court St, then just n. 421 Court St 62220. Fax: 618/277-3150. **Facility:** Second Empire architecture defines this restored 1883 B&B, which is in a residential area; furnishings include period pieces. Smoke free premises. 4 one-bedroom standard units. 2 stories, interior corridors. *Bath:* some shared or private, combo or shower only. **Parking:** on-site. **Terms:** age restrictions may apply. **Amenities:** extended cable TV. **Guest Services:** complimentary laundry. **Cards:** AX, DS, MC, VI. **Special Amenities:** early check-in/late check-out and free local telephone calls.

SOME UNITS
[S/D] [X] [🖨] / [TV] [VCR] /

VICTORY INN
Phone: (618)277-1538

▼▼▼
Historic Bed & Breakfast

All Year [ECP]   1P: $60-$115   2P: $60-$115   XP: $10   F3
Location: Jct SR 15 and 159, just n to SR 13, just e to Jackson St, then 0.4 mi n. 712 S Jackson St 62220. Fax: 618/277-1576. **Facility:** Victorian architecture is a feature of this inn, which is in a residential area. Smoke free premises. 4 one-bedroom standard units. 2 stories, interior corridors. *Bath:* some shared or private. **Parking:** on-site. **Terms:** check-in 4 pm, age restrictions may apply, 7 day cancellation notice, no pets allowed (dogs & cats on premises). **Business Services:** fax. **Cards:** AX, MC, VI.

SOME UNITS
[ASK] [S/D] [X] / [TV] [VCR] /

----------------- **WHERE TO DINE** -----------------

THE PIE PANTRY
Lunch: $5-$12   **Dinner:** $5-$12   **Phone:** 618/277-4140   (135)

◆
American

Location: I-64, exit 12, 6 mi s on SR 159, then just e. 310 E Main St 62220. **Hours:** 7 am-8 pm, Fri & Sat-9 pm, Sun 7 am-2 pm. Closed major holidays. **Reservations:** suggested; for lunch. **Features:** casual dress; children's menu; carryout; a la carte. The courtyard of this 100-year-old carriage house with a cobblestone floor, antique furniture, large skylights and high beamed ceiling is striking. The pie is the definite show stopper though and is an excellent ending to any meal you choose here. **Parking:** street. **Cards:** AX, DC, DS, MC, VI.

[X]

THE SHRINE RESTAURANT
Lunch: $6-$10   **Dinner:** $10-$14   **Phone:** 618/397-6700   (134)

[AAA]
◆◆◆
American

Location: I-255, exit 17A, 1 mi e on SR 15; in the Shrine of Our Lady of the Snows Complex. 442 S De Mazenod Dr 62223. **Hours:** 11 am-8 pm, Fri & Sat-9 pm, Sun 8 am-8 pm. Closed: 12/25. **Features:** casual dress; Sunday brunch; children's menu; carryout; cocktails; buffet. Homemade soup and a varied salad bar that includes a pasta station are favorites at the casual family restaurant, which is known for its comfort foods. The setting, on the grounds of the national shrine for which it is named, is beautiful and serene. **Parking:** on-site. **Cards:** AX, DS, MC, VI.

[X]

VIVIANO'S ITALIAN RESTAURANT
Lunch: $6   **Dinner:** $7-$16   **Phone:** 618/235-1558   (136)

◆◆
Italian

Location: Jct SR 161 and Lebanon Ave; in Wade Square Shopping Center. 6 Wade Square 62221. **Hours:** 11 am-10 pm, Fri & Sat-11 pm, Sun & Mon-9 pm. Closed major holidays. **Reservations:** suggested. **Features:** casual dress; Sunday brunch; children's menu; carryout; salad bar; cocktails & lounge; buffet. In a small strip mall, the neighborhood Italian restaurant has been offering casual service and hearty southern Italian pasta, chicken, pizza and veal dishes since 1975. Bread is homemade, as is the delicious cannoli. **Parking:** on-site. **Cards:** AX, CB, DC, DS, MC, VI.

[X] [🍸]

BLOOMINGDALE —*See Chicago p. 329.*

BLOOMINGTON pop. 51,900

----------------- **WHERE TO STAY** -----------------

COUNTRY INN & SUITES BY CARLSON-BLOOMINGTON/NORMAL-WEST
Phone: (309)828-7177

▼▼▼
Motel

1/1-3/31 [ECP]   1P: $78-$116   2P: $84-$116   XP: $6   F19
4/1-12/31 [ECP]   1P: $76-$116   2P: $82-$116   XP: $6   F19
Location: I-55/74, exit 160B (SR 9), 0.3 mi w to Wylie Dr, just n, then just e. 923 Maple Hill Rd 61704. Fax: 309/828-4601. **Facility:** 63 units. 53 one-bedroom standard units, some with whirlpools. 10 one-bedroom suites ($91-$116). 3 stories, interior corridors. *Bath:* combo or shower only. **Parking:** on-site, winter plug-ins. **Terms:** small pets only (in smoking units). **Amenities:** extended cable TV, high-speed Internet (fee), hair dryers. *Some:* irons. **Pool(s):** small heated indoor. **Leisure Activities:** whirlpool, exercise room. **Guest Services:** valet and coin laundry. **Cards:** AX, DC, DS, MC, VI. *(See color ad p 322)*

SOME UNITS
[ASK] [S/D] [🐾] [🍴] [&M] [🏊] [⛱] [📷] [DATA PORT] [💻] [🖨] / [X] [📶] [🍽] /
FEE

DAYS INN
Phone: 309/829-6292

[SAVE]
▼▼
Motel

All Year [CP]   1P: $59-$74   2P: $64-$79   XP: $5   F17
Location: I-55/74, exit 160A (SR 9), 0.5 mi e. 1707 W Market St 61701. Fax: 309/829-6292. **Facility:** 58 one-bedroom standard units. 3 stories, interior corridors. **Parking:** on-site, winter plug-ins. **Terms:** package plans, small pets only (in smoking units). **Amenities:** extended cable TV, hair dryers. *Some:* irons. **Pool(s):** small heated indoor. **Leisure Activities:** whirlpool. **Guest Services:** valet laundry. **Cards:** AX, CB, DC, DS, MC, VI.

SOME UNITS
[S/D] [🐾] [&M] [🏊] [⛱] [📷] [🖨] / [X] [DATA PORT] [🍽] [🍽] /
FEE

GUESTHOUSE INTERNATIONAL INN
Phone: (309)663-1361

▼▼
Motel

All Year [ECP]   1P: $65   2P: $65   XP: $5   F17
Location: SR 9, just e of I-55 business route (Veterans Pkwy). 1803 E Empire St 61704. Fax: 309/662-6113. **Facility:** 99 one-bedroom standard units, some with whirlpools. 2 stories, interior corridors. **Parking:** on-site. **Terms:** pets ($6 extra charge). **Amenities:** irons. **Guest Services:** valet and coin laundry. **Business Services:** meeting rooms. **Cards:** AX, CB, DC, DS, MC, VI.

SOME UNITS
[ASK] [S/D] [✈] [🐾] [🖊] [⛱] [DATA PORT] [🖨] [💻] [🍽] / [X] [VCR] [🍽] /
FEE

HAMPTON INN-VETERANS PARKWAY

Phone: (309)662-2800

SAVE

Motel

11/1-3/31 [ECP]	1P: $75-$79	2P: $75-$79
7/1-10/31 [ECP]	1P: $75-$77	2P: $75-$77
4/1-6/30 [ECP]	1P: $73-$75	2P: $73-$75

Location: I-55, exit 67, follow I-55 business route (Veterans Pkwy) 2.8 mi s to jct SR 9, just e, then just n via service road; exit 157B (Veterans Pkwy) northbound, 4 mi n to SR 9. 604 1/2 IAA Dr 61701. Fax: 309/662-2811. **Facility:** 108 one-bedroom standard units. 3 stories, interior corridors. **Parking:** on-site. **Terms:** 14 day cancellation notice-fee imposed, package plans. **Amenities:** high-speed Internet (fee), voice mail, irons, hair dryers. **Pool(s):** heated outdoor. **Guest Services:** valet laundry. **Business Services:** meeting rooms. **Cards:** AX, CB, DC, DS, MC, VI.

SOME UNITS

HAWTHORN SUITES LTD

Phone: (309)829-8111

Motel

| All Year [BP] | 1P: $88-$125 | 2P: $98-$129 | XP: $7 | F5 |

Location: I-55/74, exit 160 (W Market St), just e to Brock Dr, then 0.4 mi sw. 1 Lyon Ct 61701. Fax: 309/829-1811. **Facility:** 75 one-bedroom standard units. 3 stories, interior corridors. **Parking:** on-site. **Amenities:** high-speed Internet, voice mail, irons, hair dryers. **Pool(s):** heated indoor. **Leisure Activities:** exercise room. **Guest Services:** complimentary evening beverages: Mon-Thurs. **Business Services:** meeting rooms, business center, PC, fax (fee). **Cards:** AX, CB, DC, DS, MC, VI.

SOME UNITS

JUMER'S CHATEAU

Phone: (309)662-2020

AAA SAVE

Motor Inn

| 8/1-3/31 | 1P: $109 | 2P: $119 | | |
| 4/1-7/31 | 1P: $105 | 2P: $115 | XP: $10 | F18 |

Location: I-55 business route (Veterans Pkwy), 1.3 mi n of jct SR 9, 1 mi s of jct I-55. 1601 Jumer Dr 61704. Fax: 309/662-6522. **Facility:** 180 one-bedroom standard units. 5 stories, interior corridors. **Parking:** on-site and valet, winter plug-ins. **Terms:** [MAP] meal plan available, package plans, pets ($25 deposit). **Amenities:** video games, dual phone lines, voice mail, irons, hair dryers. **Dining:** Le Radis Rouge, see separate listing, entertainment. **Pool(s):** heated indoor. **Leisure Activities:** saunas, whirlpool, exercise room. **Guest Services:** gift shop, massage (fee), valet laundry, area transportation. **Business Services:** conference facilities, fax. **Cards:** AX, CB, DC, DS, JC, MC, VI. **Special Amenities:** free local telephone calls and free newspaper.

SOME UNITS

MICROTEL INN & SUITES

Phone: (309)828-0900

Motel

| All Year [ECP] | 1P: $60-$107 | 2P: $66-$107 | XP: $6 | F16 |

Location: I-55/74, exit 160B (SR 9), 0.4 mi w to Wylie Rd, just n, then just e. 919 Maple Hill Rd 61704. Fax: 309/828-0131. **Facility:** 64 one-bedroom standard units, some with whirlpools. 3 stories, interior corridors. *Bath:* combo or shower only. **Parking:** on-site. **Terms:** [ECP] meal plan available, pets (in smoking units). **Amenities:** voice mail. *Some:* irons, hair dryers. **Pool(s):** small heated indoor. **Leisure Activities:** exercise room. **Guest Services:** valet and coin laundry. **Cards:** AX, DC, DS, JC, MC, VI.

SOME UNITS

RADISSON HOTEL & CONFERENCE CENTER-BLOOMINGTON

Phone: (309)664-6446

Motor Inn

| All Year [BP] | 1P: $99-$122 | 2P: $109-$132 | XP: $10 | F18 |

Location: I-55 business route (Veterans Pkwy), just n of US 150. 10 Brickyard Dr 61701. Fax: 309/664-6135. **Facility:** 197 units. 187 one-bedroom standard units, some with whirlpools. 10 one-bedroom suites ($182-$258), some with whirlpools. 5 stories, interior corridors. *Bath:* combo or shower only. **Parking:** on-site, winter plug-ins. **Terms:** package plans, pets ($40 deposit). **Amenities:** extended cable TV, dual phone lines, voice mail, irons, hair dryers. **Pool(s):** heated indoor. **Leisure Activities:** whirlpool, exercise room. **Guest Services:** complimentary evening beverages, valet and coin laundry. **Business Services:** conference facilities. **Cards:** AX, CB, DC, DS, JC, MC, VI.

SOME UNITS

WINGATE INN

Phone: (309)820-9990

Motel

| All Year | 1P: $79 | 2P: $89 | XP: $10 | F18 |

Location: I-55/74, exit 160B (SR 9), just w, then just n. 1031 Wylie Dr 61704. Fax: 309/820-0895. **Facility:** 80 one-bedroom standard units, some with whirlpools. 3 stories, interior corridors. *Bath:* combo or shower only. **Parking:** on-site. **Amenities:** dual phone lines, voice mail, safes, irons, hair dryers. *Fee:* video games, Web TV, high-speed Internet. **Pool(s):** small heated indoor. **Leisure Activities:** whirlpool, exercise room. **Guest Services:** valet and coin laundry. **Business Services:** meeting rooms, business center, PC, fax. **Cards:** AX, CB, DC, DS, JC, MC, VI.

SOME UNITS

—————— WHERE TO DINE ——————

CENTRAL STATION CAFE

Lunch: $6-$9   **Dinner: $9-$20**   **Phone: 309/828-2323**

American

Location: At Front and East sts. 220 E Front St 61701. **Hours:** 11 am-3 & 5-10 pm, Fri & Sat-midnight. Closed major holidays; also Sun & Mon 5/30-9/2. **Reservations:** suggested; weekends. **Features:** casual dress; children's menu; carryout; cocktails & lounge. This former fire station built in 1902 serves house specials of fresh seafood and garlic-crusted prime rib to a mostly family and business crowd. The surroundings are reminiscent of the past with brick and dark wood accents and afford a cozy ambience. **Parking:** street. **Cards:** AX, DC, MC, VI.

LE RADIS ROUGE

(AAA)

▽▽▽▽

American

Lunch: $5-$8   **Dinner:** $12-$20   **Phone:** 309/662-2525

Location: I-55 business route (Veterans Pkwy), 1.3 mi n of jct SR 9, 1 mi s of jct I-55; in Jumer's Chateau. 1601 Jumer Dr 61704. **Hours:** 6:30-11 am, 11:30-4 & 4:30-10 pm, Sat-11 pm, Sun 7 am-2 & 2:30-10 pm. **Reservations:** suggested. **Features:** casual dress; Sunday brunch; children's menu; early bird specials; cocktails & lounge; entertainment. With a name like "Le Radis Rouge" and a location in Jumer's Chateau, you might expect French cuisine. This restaurant, however, serves from a varied menu with dishes that reflect a number of cultures and national influences. You might want to consider the Mediterranean Shrimp appetizer as a spicy way to start. The Coq Au Vin makes a delightful entree. And everything comes with legendary cinnamon rolls. **Parking:** on-site and valet. **Cards:** AX, CB, DC, DS, JC, MC, VI.

⊠

BLUE ISLAND —See Chicago p. 329.

BOLINGBROOK —See Chicago p. 330.

BOURBONNAIS pop. 29,100

------- **WHERE TO STAY** -------

FAIRFIELD INN BY MARRIOTT

(AAA) [SAVE]

▽▽▽ ▽▽

Motel

All Year [ECP]   1P: $69-$99   2P: $69-$99   XP: $5   F18

Location: I-57, exit 315 (SR 50). 1550 SR 50 60914. Fax: 815/935-1334. **Facility:** 57 one-bedroom standard units. 3 stories, interior corridors. *Bath:* combo or shower only. **Parking:** on-site. **Amenities:** extended cable TV, irons. **Pool(s):** small heated indoor. **Leisure Activities:** whirlpool. **Guest Services:** valet laundry. **Cards:** AX, DC, DS, MC, VI. **Special Amenities:** free continental breakfast and free local telephone calls. *(See color ad card insert)*

SOME UNITS

[S◑] [↑] [🐾] [♿] [◎] [🏊] [👶] [🐕] [DATA PORT] [📠] / [⊠] [🔒] [🍽] [📺] /
FEE

HOLIDAY INN EXPRESS HOTEL & SUITES

▽▽▽▽

Motel

All Year [ECP]   1P: $83-$125   2P: $83-$125   XP: $5   F12

Location: I-57, exit 315 (SR 50). 62 Ken Hayes Dr 60914. Fax: 815/932-4439. **Facility:** 101 one-bedroom standard units. 3 stories, interior corridors. *Bath:* combo or shower only. **Parking:** on-site. **Terms:** package plans, pets ($50 deposit, small dogs only). **Amenities:** dual phone lines, voice mail, irons, hair dryers. **Pool(s):** small heated indoor. **Leisure Activities:** exercise room. **Guest Services:** valet and coin laundry. **Business Services:** meeting rooms. **Cards:** AX, CB, DC, DS, MC, VI.

SOME UNITS

[ASK] [S◑] [🐕] [↑] [♿M] [🏊] [👶] [DATA PORT] [📺] [📠] / [⊠] [🔒] [🍽] /
FEE FEE

LEES INN & SUITES

▽▽▽▽

Motel

All Year [BP]   1P: $79-$199   2P: $89-$209   XP: $10   F18

Location: I-57, exit 315 (SR 50). 1500 N SR 50 60914. Fax: 815/935-5858. **Facility:** 114 units. 106 one-bedroom standard units, some with whirlpools. 8 one-bedroom suites ($129-$199). 3 stories, interior corridors. **Parking:** on-site. **Terms:** 7 day cancellation notice, [ECP] meal plan available, package plans, small pets only. **Amenities:** extended cable TV, irons, hair dryers. **Pool(s):** heated indoor. **Leisure Activities:** whirlpool. **Guest Services:** complimentary evening beverages: Mon-Thurs, valet and coin laundry. **Business Services:** meeting rooms. **Cards:** AX, DC, DS, MC, VI.

SOME UNITS

[ASK] [S◑] [🐕] [↑] [◎] [🏊] [👶] [DATA PORT] [📺] [📠] / [⊠] [🔒] [🍽] /
FEE FEE

SUPER 8 MOTEL

▽▽▽▽

Motel

All Year   1P: $51-$56   2P: $61-$66   XP: $6

Location: I-57, exit 315 (SR 50), just s. 1390 Lock Dr 60914. Fax: 815/939-7888. **Facility:** 41 one-bedroom standard units. 2 stories, interior corridors. **Parking:** on-site. **Terms:** 7 day cancellation notice. **Amenities:** extended cable TV, hair dryers. **Pool(s):** small heated indoor. **Guest Services:** coin laundry. **Cards:** AX, CB, DC, DS, JC, MC, VI.

SOME UNITS

[↑] [🏊] [👶] [DATA PORT] [🔒] [🍽] [📠] / [⊠] [VCR] /
FEE

BRIDGEVIEW —See Chicago p. 330.

BUFFALO GROVE —See Chicago p. 330.

BURR RIDGE —See Chicago p. 331.

CALUMET CITY —See Chicago p. 331.

CALUMET PARK —See Chicago p. 331.

CARBON CLIFF pop. 1,500

------- **WHERE TO STAY** -------

SUPER 8 MOTEL-EAST MOLINE

▽▽▽▽

Motel

All Year   1P: $50-$70   2P: $56-$80   XP: $6   F12

Location: I-80, exit 4A (John Deere Rd), 5 mi w on SR 5. 2201 John Deere Rd 61244. Fax: 309/796-1999. **Facility:** 63 one-bedroom standard units. 2 stories, interior corridors. **Parking:** on-site, winter plug-ins. **Terms:** 7 day cancellation notice, small pets only ($150 deposit). **Amenities:** extended cable TV. **Leisure Activities:** exercise room. **Guest Services:** coin laundry. **Business Services:** meeting rooms. **Cards:** AX, DC, DS, MC, VI.

SOME UNITS

[ASK] [S◑] [🐕] [↑] [👶] [DATA PORT] / [⊠] [🔒] [🍽] /
FEE   FEE FEE

------ **WHERE TO DINE** ------

DEERFIELD FAMILY RESTAURANT   **Lunch:** $5-$12   **Dinner:** $5-$18   **Phone:** 309/792-3900
American
Location: I-80, exit 4A (John Deere Rd), 5 mi w on SR 5. 2215 John Deere Rd 61239. **Hours:** 7 am-10 pm. **Features:** casual dress; children's menu; carryout. Enjoy a family atmosphere with no frills, just home cooking that offers breakfast, lunch and dinner. Friendliness is served in abundance. Smoke free premises. **Parking:** on-site. **Cards:** AX, DS, MC, VI.

CARBONDALE pop. 27,000

------ **WHERE TO STAY** ------

BEST INNS   **Phone:** (618)529-4801
Motel
All Year [ECP]   1P: $42-$63   2P: $49-$70   XP: $7   F17
Location: I-57, exit 54B, 13 mi w on SR 13; next to University Mall. 1345 E Main St 62901. **Fax:** 618/529-7212. **Facility:** 86 one-bedroom standard units. 2 stories, exterior corridors. **Parking:** on-site, winter plug-ins. **Terms:** package plans, small pets only. **Amenities:** extended cable TV. **Pool(s):** small outdoor. **Business Services:** fax (fee). **Cards:** AX, CB, DC, DS, MC, VI. **Special Amenities: free continental breakfast and free local telephone calls.**
SOME UNITS

COMFORT INN   **Phone:** (618)549-4244
Motel
5/1-5/31   1P: $59-$79   2P: $69-$99   XP: $6   F12
4/1-4/30 & 6/1-11/30   1P: $49-$79   2P: $59-$89   XP: $6   F12
12/1-3/31   1P: $49-$59   2P: $59-$89   XP: $6   F12
Location: I-57, exit 54B, 13.5 mi e on SR 13; next to University Mall. 1415 E Main St 62901. **Fax:** 618/549-3008. **Facility:** 64 one-bedroom standard units, some with whirlpools. 2 stories, interior corridors. *Bath:* combo or shower only. **Parking:** on-site, winter plug-ins. **Terms:** [CP] meal plan available. **Amenities:** hair dryers. *Some:* irons. **Pool(s):** heated indoor. **Guest Services:** coin laundry. **Business Services:** fax (fee). **Cards:** AX, CB, DC, DS, JC, MC, VI.
SOME UNITS
FEE

DAYS INN CARBONDALE   **Phone:** (618)457-3347
Motel
All Year   1P: $40-$120   2P: $40-$120   XP: $10   F12
Location: 1 mi e on SR 13. 801 E Main St 62901. **Fax:** 618/549-2897. **Facility:** 70 one-bedroom standard units, some with whirlpools. 2 stories, exterior corridors. **Parking:** on-site. **Amenities:** extended cable TV, hair dryers. **Pool(s):** heated indoor. **Business Services:** fax (fee). **Cards:** AX, DC, DS, MC, VI.
SOME UNITS

HAMPTON INN   **Phone:** 618/549-6900
Motel
All Year [ECP]   1P: $69-$99   2P: $75-$125
Location: I-57, exit 54B, 12 mi e on SR 13. 2715 Reed Station Pkwy 62901. **Fax:** 618/549-8448. **Facility:** 80 one-bedroom standard units, some with whirlpools. 3 stories, interior corridors. *Bath:* combo or shower only. **Parking:** on-site. **Terms:** 5 day cancellation notice. **Amenities:** voice mail, irons, hair dryers. **Pool(s):** heated indoor. **Guest Services:** valet laundry. **Business Services:** meeting rooms, business center, fax (fee). **Cards:** AX, CB, DC, DS, JC, MC, VI.
SOME UNITS
FEE FEE

HOLIDAY INN CARBONDALE   **Phone:** 618/529-1100
Motor Inn
All Year   1P: $63   2P: $63   XP: $7   F18
Location: 1 mi e on SR 13. 800 E Main St 62901. **Fax:** 618/457-0292. **Facility:** 95 one-bedroom standard units. 2 stories, interior corridors. **Parking:** on-site. **Terms:** package plans, pets ($40 deposit). **Amenities:** extended cable TV, video games, irons, hair dryers. **Pool(s):** heated indoor. **Leisure Activities:** whirlpool. *Fee:* game room. **Guest Services:** valet laundry. **Business Services:** conference facilities, fax (fee). **Cards:** AX, CB, DC, DS, JC, MC, VI.
SOME UNITS
FEE   FEE FEE

SUPER 8 MOTEL   **Phone:** (618)457-8822
Motel
All Year [ECP]   1P: $48-$68   2P: $54-$70   XP: $6   F12
Location: 1 mi e on SR 13. 1180 E Main St 62901. **Fax:** 618/457-4186. **Facility:** 63 one-bedroom standard units. 3 stories (no elevator), interior corridors. **Parking:** on-site, winter plug-ins. **Amenities:** extended cable TV, safes. **Business Services:** fax (fee). **Cards:** AX, CB, DC, DS, MC, VI.
SOME UNITS
FEE   FEE

------ **WHERE TO DINE** ------

HUNAN   **Lunch:** $4-$6   **Dinner:** $7-$12   **Phone:** 618/529-1108
Regional Chinese
Location: 1 mi e on SR 13. 710 E Main St 62901. **Hours:** 11 am-9:30 pm, Fri-10 pm, Sat 11:30 am-10 pm, Sun 11:30 am-9:30 pm. Closed major holidays. **Features:** casual dress; carryout; cocktails; a la carte. Hunan, Cantonese, Szechuan, Shanghai, Peking and Mandarin specialties abound at this eatery amid an upscale atmosphere. But the menu is the real treat and promises something for every taste preference. A delicious rice pudding is presented with flair. **Parking:** on-site. **Cards:** AX, DS, MC, VI.

CARLINVILLE pop. 5,400

——— WHERE TO STAY ———

BEST VALUE INN-CARLIN VILLA

▼▼▼ ◆◆
Motel

All Year [CP]   1P: $39-$55   2P: $47-$64   **Phone:** (217)854-3201
                                                                   XP: $5   F18
Location: 0.5 mi s from jct SR 108 and 4. 18891 Rt 4 62626. Fax: 217/854-8414. **Facility:** 35 one-bedroom standard units. 1 story, interior/exterior corridors. **Parking:** on-site, winter plug-ins. **Terms:** small pets only ($5 extra charge). **Amenities:** extended cable TV, video tape library (fee), voice mail. **Pool(s):** heated indoor. **Leisure Activities:** whirlpool. **Business Services:** meeting rooms. **Cards:** AX, CB, DC, DS, MC, VI.

SOME UNITS

🛏 🍴 🛟 🎣 / ✕ VCR 🔌 📠 🖥 /
FEE

HOLIDAY INN-CARLINVILLE

▼▼▼▼
Motor Inn

All Year   1P: $62-$72   2P: $67-$77   **Phone:** (217)324-2100
                                                                   XP: $5   F19
Location: I-55, exit 60 (SR 108), just w. 19067 W Frontage Rd 62626 (PO Box 377). Fax: 217/324-2100. **Facility:** 101 one-bedroom standard units. 2 stories, interior corridors. **Parking:** on-site. **Terms:** pets ($10 extra charge). **Amenities:** video tape library (fee), irons, hair dryers. **Pool(s):** heated indoor. **Leisure Activities:** whirlpool, fishing, playground. *Fee:* game room. **Guest Services:** coin laundry. **Business Services:** conference facilities. **Cards:** AX, CB, DC, DS, JC, MC, VI.

SOME UNITS

(ASK) S🔌 🛏 🍴 🍸 🔥M 🛟 ✕ DATA PORT 🖥 📠 / ✕ VCR 🔌 /
                                                          FEE FEE

——— WHERE TO DINE ———

ANGUS BAILEY'S

▼▼▼ ◆◆
American

Lunch: $5-$8   **Dinner:** $7-$16   **Phone:** 217/854-5250
Location: Downtown; northwest corner of the square. 510 North Side Square 62626. **Hours:** 11 am-2 & 5-9 pm, Fri & Sat-10 pm, Sun 5 pm-9 pm. Closed major holidays. **Reservations:** suggested. **Features:** casual dress; children's menu; carryout; cocktails & lounge; a la carte. A short walk from the historic Macoupin County Courthouse, the restaurant sits on the northwest corner of the town square. Lunch is mostly soup, salad and sandwiches although an extensive list of appetizers is offered. Visit during the dinner hour for a more sophisticated menu with more complex entrees. **Parking:** street. **Cards:** MC, VI.

✕

CARLYLE pop. 3,500

——— WHERE TO STAY ———

MARINER'S VILLAGE/MICROTEL INN & SUITES

▼▼ ◆◆
Complex

All Year [CP]   1P: $47-$65   2P: $47-$65   **Phone:** (618)594-7666
                                                                   XP: $5   F16
Location: Just n from jct US 50 and SR 127 to William Rd, then just e. 1 Resort Dr 62231 (PO Box 206). Fax: 618/594-7676. **Facility:** 70 units. 65 one-bedroom standard units. 5 two-bedroom vacation rentals ($100-$150). 1-3 stories, interior/exterior corridors. *Bath:* combo or shower only. **Parking:** on-site. **Amenities:** voice mail. **Pool(s):** heated outdoor. **Business Services:** meeting rooms. **Cards:** AX, CB, DC, DS, JC, MC, VI.

SOME UNITS

(ASK) S🔌 🍴 🍸 🔥 🌀 🛟 DATA PORT 📠 / ✕ 🔌 🖥 /

CAROL STREAM —See Chicago p. 331.

CASEY pop. 2,900

——— WHERE TO STAY ———

COMFORT INN

(AAA) SAVE
▼▼▼▼
Motel

All Year   1P: $51-$61   2P: $55-$65   **Phone:** (217)932-2212
Location: I-70, exit 129, 0.3 mi se. (PO Box 248, 62420). Fax: 217/932-2232. **Facility:** 52 one-bedroom standard units, some with whirlpools. 2 stories, interior corridors. **Parking:** on-site, winter plug-ins. **Terms:** 7 day cancellation notice, pets ($5 extra charge). **Amenities:** extended cable TV. *Some:* irons, hair dryers. **Pool(s):** outdoor. **Leisure Activities:** exercise room. **Guest Services:** coin laundry. **Business Services:** meeting rooms, fax (fee). **Cards:** AX, CB, DC, DS, JC, MC, VI. **Special Amenities:** free continental breakfast and free newspaper.

SOME UNITS

S🔌 🛏 🛟 DATA PORT 📠 / ✕ VCR 🔌 🖥 🖥 /
                                     FEE

——— WHERE TO DINE ———

RICHARDS FARM RESTAURANT

▼▼ ◆◆
American

Lunch: $6-$19   **Dinner:** $7-$19   **Phone:** 217/932-5300
Location: I-70, exit 129, 1 mi s on SR 49, 0.5 mi e on US 40, just n at marker 170 E Rd. 607 NE 13th St 62420. **Hours:** 11 am-8:30 pm, Fri & Sat-9:30 pm. Closed: 12/25. **Reservations:** suggested; weekends. **Features:** casual dress; Sunday brunch; children's menu; carryout; salad bar; cocktails; buffet. In a 1930s style hip-roof barn, the relaxed restaurant serves country cooking, such as the specialty one-pound pork chops and other pork, chicken and beef entrees. Paintings, farm tools and quilts add to the ambience. **Parking:** on-site. **Cards:** AX, DC, DS, MC, VI.

✕

CASEYVILLE pop. 4,400

—— WHERE TO STAY ——

BEST INNS
AAA [SAVE]
◇◇◇ ◇◇
Motel

All Year — 1P: $45-$65 — 2P: $55-$85 — XP: $9 — F17
Location: I-64, exit 9 (SR 157), just s. 2423 Old Country Inn Dr 62232. Fax: 618/397-3300. **Facility:** 84 one-bedroom standard units, some with whirlpools. 2 stories, interior corridors. *Bath:* combo or shower only. **Parking:** on-site. **Terms:** 7 day cancellation notice, pets ($25 deposit, $75 extra charge). **Pool(s):** outdoor. **Guest Services:** coin laundry. **Cards:** AX, CB, DC, DS, MC, VI. **Special Amenities: free continental breakfast and free local telephone calls.**

Phone: (618)397-3300

SOME UNITS
[icons]

CENTRALIA pop. 14,300

—— WHERE TO STAY ——

BELL TOWER INN
◇◇◇
Motel

All Year — 1P: $44 — 2P: $49 — XP: $5 — F18
Location: Jct US 51 S and SR 161. 200 E Noleman St 62801. Fax: 618/533-1461. **Facility:** 57 one-bedroom standard units. 4 stories, interior corridors. **Parking:** on-site. **Terms:** [CP] meal plan available, small pets only. **Amenities:** extended cable TV. **Pool(s):** heated indoor. **Leisure Activities:** playground. **Guest Services:** valet laundry. **Business Services:** meeting rooms, fax (fee). **Cards:** AX, CB, DC, DS, MC, VI.

Phone: (618)533-1300

SOME UNITS
[ASK] [icons] FEE FEE

CHAMPAIGN pop. 63,500—See also URBANA.

—— WHERE TO STAY ——

BAYMONT INN & SUITES
AAA [SAVE]
◇◇◇ ◇◇
Motel

All Year [ECP] — 1P: $65-$80 — 2P: $65-$80
Location: I-74, exit 182 (Neil St), just nw. 302 W Anthony Dr 61821. Fax: 217/356-9253. **Facility:** 96 one-bedroom standard units, some with whirlpools. 3 stories, interior corridors. **Parking:** on-site. **Terms:** cancellation fee imposed, pets (in smoking units). **Amenities:** extended cable TV, video games, voice mail, safes, irons, hair dryers. **Leisure Activities:** exercise room. **Guest Services:** coin laundry. **Business Services:** meeting rooms, fax (fee). **Cards:** AX, CB, DC, DS, MC, VI. **Special Amenities: free continental breakfast and free newspaper.**

Phone: (217)356-8900

SOME UNITS
[icons] FEE

COMFORT INN
[SAVE]
◇◇◇ ◇◇
Motel

All Year — 1P: $49-$99 — 2P: $54-$99 — XP: $5 — F18
Location: I-74, exit 182B (Neil St), just n to Marketview Dr, then just w. 305 Marketview Dr 61821. Fax: 217/352-4055. **Facility:** 66 one-bedroom standard units. 2 stories, interior corridors. **Parking:** on-site. **Terms:** 7 day cancellation notice, small pets only. **Amenities:** extended cable TV. *Some:* irons, hair dryers. **Pool(s):** heated indoor. **Leisure Activities:** whirlpool. **Guest Services:** valet laundry. **Business Services:** meeting rooms, fax (fee). **Cards:** AX, CB, DC, DS, MC, VI.

Phone: (217)352-4055

SOME UNITS
[icons] FEE

COURTYARD BY MARRIOTT
AAA [SAVE]
◇◇◇ ◇◇
Motel

All Year — 1P: $85-$125 — 2P: $90-$130 — XP: $5 — F18
Location: I-74, exit 182 (Neil St), just nw via service road. 1811 Moreland Blvd 61820. Fax: 217/355-0411. **Facility:** 78 one-bedroom standard units. 3 stories, interior corridors. *Bath:* combo or shower only. **Parking:** on-site. **Terms:** 7 day cancellation notice. **Amenities:** extended cable TV, voice mail, irons, hair dryers. **Dining:** coffee shop, 6-9:30 am, Sat & Sun 7-11 am. **Pool(s):** heated indoor. **Leisure Activities:** whirlpool, exercise room. **Guest Services:** valet and coin laundry. **Business Services:** meeting rooms, fax (fee). **Cards:** AX, DC, DS, MC, VI. *(See color ad card insert)*

Phone: (217)355-0411

SOME UNITS
[icons] FEE FEE

DAYS INN
[SAVE]
◇◇◇ ◇◇
Motel

All Year [CP] — 1P: $50-$75 — 2P: $59-$89 — XP: $5 — F12
Location: I-74, exit 181 (Prospect Blvd), just s, then 0.5 mi w. 1019 Bloomington Rd 61821. Fax: 217/356-6950. **Facility:** 42 one-bedroom standard units. 2 stories, interior corridors. **Parking:** on-site, winter plug-ins. **Leisure Activities:** sauna, whirlpool. **Guest Services:** coin laundry. **Business Services:** meeting rooms, fax (fee). **Cards:** AX, CB, DC, DS, JC, MC, VI.

Phone: (217)356-6873

SOME UNITS
[icons] FEE

DRURY INN & SUITES-CHAMPAIGN
◇◇◇ ◇◇

All Year [ECP] — 1P: $73-$105 — 2P: $73-$105 — XP: $10 — F18
Location: I-74, exit 181 (Prospect Blvd). 905 W Anthony Dr 61821. Fax: 217/398-0030. **Facility:** 133 units. 122 one-bedroom standard units. 11 one-bedroom suites ($98-$118). 1-5 stories, interior corridors. *Bath:* combo or shower only. **Parking:** on-site. **Terms:** small pets only. **Amenities:** extended cable TV, voice mail, irons, hair dryers. **Pool(s):** heated indoor/outdoor. **Leisure Activities:** whirlpool, exercise room. **Guest Services:** complimentary evening beverages: Mon-Thurs, valet and coin laundry. **Business Services:** meeting rooms. **Cards:** AX, CB, DC, DS, MC, VI. *(See color ad p 5)*

Phone: (217)398-0030

SOME UNITS
[icons]

FAIRFIELD INN BY MARRIOTT

(AAA) [SAVE]

◆◆◆ Motel

All Year	1P: $59-$99	2P: $65-$99	XP: $6

Phone: (217)355-0604
XP: $6 F18

Location: I-74, exit 182 (Neil St), just nw via service road. 1807 Moreland Blvd 61821. Fax: 217/355-0604. **Facility:** 62 one-bedroom standard units. 3 stories, interior corridors. *Bath:* combo or shower only. **Parking:** on-site. **Terms:** 7 day cancellation notice. **Amenities:** extended cable TV, irons. **Pool(s):** heated indoor. **Leisure Activities:** whirlpool. **Guest Services:** valet laundry. **Business Services:** fax (fee). **Cards:** AX, DC, DS, MC, VI. **Special Amenities:** free continental breakfast and free local telephone calls.

(See color ad card insert)

SOME UNITS

LA QUINTA INN

(AAA) [SAVE]

◆◆◆ Motel

All Year	1P: $55-$77	2P: $62-$84	XP: $7

Phone: (217)356-4000
XP: $7 F18

Location: I-74, exit 182B (Neil St), just n. 1900 Center Dr 61820. Fax: 217/352-7783. **Facility:** 122 units. 120 one-bedroom standard units. 2 one-bedroom suites ($85-$124). 2 stories, interior corridors. **Parking:** on-site, winter plug-ins. **Amenities:** video games, voice mail, irons, hair dryers. **Pool(s):** heated outdoor. **Guest Services:** valet and coin laundry. **Business Services:** fax (fee). **Cards:** AX, CB, DC, DS, MC, VI. **Special Amenities:** free continental breakfast and free local telephone calls.

SOME UNITS

RED ROOF INN #170

(AAA) [SAVE]

◆◆ Motel

6/3-9/2	1P: $37-$62	2P: $42-$67	XP: $5
4/1-6/2 & 9/3-3/31	1P: $35-$56	2P: $40-$61	XP: $5

Phone: (217)352-0101
XP: $5 F18
XP: $5 F18

Location: I-74, exit 182B (Neil St), just n, then just w. 212 W Anthony Dr 61820. Fax: 217/352-1891. **Facility:** 112 one-bedroom standard units. 2 stories, exterior corridors. **Parking:** on-site. **Terms:** small pets only. **Amenities:** video games, voice mail. **Cards:** AX, CB, DC, DS, MC, VI. **Special Amenities:** free local telephone calls and free newspaper.

SOME UNITS

——— WHERE TO DINE ———

FORTUNE HOUSE

◆◆ Chinese

Lunch: $6   Dinner: $10   Phone: 217-398-5886

Location: I-74, exit 182B (Neil St N), just n. 1903 Convenience Pl 61820. **Hours:** 11 am-10 pm, Fri & Sat-11 pm. **Reservations:** accepted. **Features:** casual dress; carryout; beer & wine only; buffet, a la carte. An extensive buffet awaits with a wealth of choices that successfully blend traditional and unusual offerings. Crispy duck, crab legs, soup, noodles, salad and dessert are all well prepared and plentiful. The service is prompt, efficient and attentive. **Parking:** on-site. **Cards:** AX, MC, VI.

MANZELLA'S ITALIAN PATIO RESTAURANT

◆◆ Italian

Lunch: $4-$8   Dinner: $9-$13   Phone: 217-352-7624

Location: I-74, exit 182B (Lincoln Ave), 1 mi s to University Ave, just w, 0.5 mi e to First St, then just s. 115 S First St 61820. **Hours:** 11 am-1:30 & 5-9:30 pm, Fri-10 pm, Sat 5 pm-10 pm, Sun 5 pm-9 pm. Closed major holidays. **Features:** casual dress; carryout; cocktails; a la carte. Empty Chianti bottles hang from the ceiling cove of the casual restaurant, which serves traditional dishes with some American preparations of steak, chops and seafood. The toasted ravioli appetizer, served with marinara sauce, is exceptionally tasty. **Parking:** on-site. **Cards:** AX, CB, DC, MC, VI.

MINNECI'S

◆◆ Italian

Lunch: $4-$8   Dinner: $8-$19   Phone: 217-352-4425

Location: Corner of First and Springfield sts. 401 S First St 61820. **Hours:** 11:30 am-1:30 & 5-9:30 pm, Sat from 5 pm. Closed major holidays; also Sun. **Features:** casual dress; children's menu; carryout; cocktails; a la carte. Since 1978, this family-owned and operated restaurant has featured traditional Italian and American cuisine prepared with healthful ingredients including extra virgin olive oil, crisp vegetables and fresh meat. Sauces are made from scratch according to traditional family recipes. **Parking:** on-site. **Cards:** AX, CB, DC, DS, MC, VI.

CHARLESTON pop. 20,400

——— WHERE TO STAY ———

DAYS INN CHARLESTON

[SAVE]

◆◆ Motel

4/1-10/31 & 2/11-3/31	1P: $49-$69	2P: $55-$69	XP: $8
11/1-2/10	1P: $46-$64	2P: $54-$65	XP: $8

Phone: 217-345-7689
XP: $8 F12
XP: $8 F12

Location: SR 130, 1.8 mi w on SR 16 (Lincoln Hwy). 810 W Lincoln Hwy 61920. Fax: 217/345-7697. **Facility:** 52 one-bedroom standard units. 2 stories, interior/exterior corridors. **Parking:** on-site, winter plug-ins. **Terms:** 21 day cancellation notice-fee imposed. **Amenities:** extended cable TV, hair dryers. **Cards:** AX, CB, DC, DS, JC, MC, VI.

SOME UNITS
FEE FEE FEE

CHESTER pop. 8,200

——— WHERE TO STAY ———

BEST WESTERN REIDS' INN

◆◆◆ Motel

All Year	1P: $49-$59	2P: $54-$64	XP: $5

Phone: (618)826-3034
XP: $5 F12

Location: SR 150 E, 1 mi e of SR 3. 2150 State St 62233. Fax: 618/826-3034. **Facility:** 46 one-bedroom standard units. 2 stories, interior corridors. **Parking:** on-site. **Terms:** cancellation fee imposed. **Amenities:** extended cable TV. **Pool(s):** outdoor. **Leisure Activities:** whirlpool, exercise room. **Guest Services:** coin laundry. **Business Services:** fax (fee). **Cards:** AX, CB, DC, DS, MC, VI.

SOME UNITS
FEE FEE FEE

Destination Chicago
pop. 2,783,700

Soldier Field, Chicago.
Fans fill the stands for
gridiron action at Soldier
Field, home of "da Bears."
(See mention page 66)

*C*hicago imposes on you—
demanding to be noticed
and explored.

*I*ts architectural heritage is evident
in downtown skyscrapers and the
legacy of buildings designed by
master architect Frank Lloyd Wright.
Professional sports enthusiasts have
their choice of teams to root for.
Downtown streets are lined with
legends of the retail world. And
recreational opportunities abound at
lakefront parks and piers.

*Lincoln Park,
Chicago.*
In addition to
impressive
statuary, a
conservatory and
a zoo, the park
has multiple
recreational
facilities. (See
listing page 61)

*P*laces included in this AAA Destination City:

Antioch

Richmond

Harvard

12

14

Woodstock

Crystal
Lake

Lake
Zurich

Algonquin

47

Rolling
Meadows

90

West
Dundee

Elgin

Hoffman
Estates

31

Schaumburg

Bloomingdale

St. Charles

Carol
Stream

64

Geneva

Glen Ellyn
Wheaton

North
Aurora

88

Warrenville

Aurora

Naperville Lisle

Bolingbrook

Romeoville

55

Rockdale

80

55

State Street, Chicago. Boutiques and specialty shops join such retail giants as Marshall Field's along this shopping promenade. (See mention page 70)

94
•Wadsworth

Gurnee   •Waukegan
•Grayslake   •North Chicago
•Libertyville
•Mundelein
          Bannockburn
•Vernon   •Lake Forest
Hills
    Lincolnshire
Buffalo•Riverwoods •Highland Park
Grove
•Wheeling•   •Deerfield
Palatine   •Northbrook
•Arlington Heights •Glenview
     •Prospect Heights
•Mount Prospect   •Wilmette
Elk Grove •Des Plaines   •Evanston
Village   •Skokie
•Itasca
     •Niles
Wood   •Rosemont
Dale   Schiller Park
North Lake •Franklin Park
•Elmhurst
•Oakbrook   •Oak Park
Terrace •Hillside
Lombard
  •Westchester

Chicago

90
94

290

55

•Hinsdale
Oak   •Burr •Bedford Park
Brook Ridge •Westmont
•Downers Grove •Countryside
Willowbrook   •Bridgeview

90

294   •Oak Lawn   **394**

Alsip •Calumet Park
Blue Island •Harvey
Orland   •Calumet
Park Tinley •Markham City
•Lockport Park •South
45   Holland
57
80   **94** **80**

•Joliet   Lansing
30
    •Matteson

52
57
45

ILLINOIS
INDIANA

See Downtown
map page 280

See Northern
Region map
page 284

See Southern
Region map
page 292

N. Michigan Avenue, Chicago. Fine stores and galleries line this section of Michigan Avenue, known as the "Magnificent Mile." (See mention page 69)

Chicago skyline. In a city where art and architecture are revered, the skyline itself is a masterpiece.

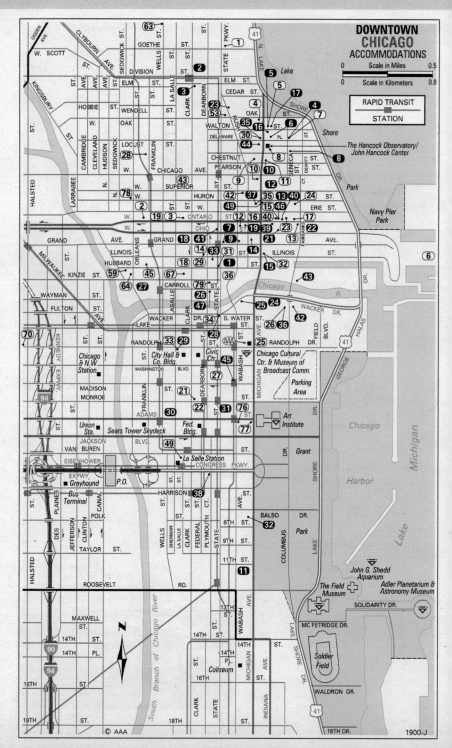

DOWNTOWN
CHICAGO
ACCOMMODATIONS

Scale in Miles
0 .... 0.5

Scale in Kilometers
0 .... 0.8

RAPID TRANSIT

STATION

The Hancock Observatory/
John Hancock Center

Navy Pier
Park

Park

The Field
Museum

John G. Shedd
Aquarium

Adler Planetarium &
Astronomy Museum

SOLIDARITY DR.

MC FETRIDGE DR.

Soldier
Field

WALDRON DR.

Chicago

Michigan

Harbor

Lake
Michigan

Chicago Cultural
Ctr. & Museum of
Broadcast Comm.

Parking
Area

Art
Institute

Chicago & N.W.
Station

Union
Sta.

Sears Tower Skydeck

Fed.
Bldg.

La Salle Station

Greyhound
Bus
Terminal

P.O.

City Hall &
Co. Bldg.

Civic
Ctr.

Coliseum

© AAA

1900-J

Downtown Chicago

This index helps you "spot" where approved accommodations and restaurants are located on the corresponding detailed maps. Lodging rate ranges are for comparison only and show the property's high season; rates are per night, unless only weekly (W) or monthly (M) rates are available. Restaurant rate range is for dinner, unless only lunch (L) is served. Turn to the listing page for more detailed rate information and consult display ads for special promotions.

Spotter/Map Page Number	OA	DOWNTOWN CHICAGO - Lodgings	Diamond Rating	Rate Range High Season	Listing Page
1 / p. 280	AAA	**Courtyard by Marriott Chicago Downtown -** see ad p 299 & color ad card insert	◆◆◆	$189-$320 SAVE	298
2 / p. 280	AAA	**Claridge Hotel**	◆◆	$149-$189 SAVE	298
3 / p. 280		Gold Coast Guest House Bed & Breakfast	◆◆◆	$119-$189	301
4 / p. 280	AAA	**Doubletree Guest Suites Chicago**	◆◆◆	$169-$399 SAVE	299
5 / p. 280	AAA	**The Drake Hotel, Chicago**	◆◆◆◆	$295-$395 SAVE	299
6 / p. 280	AAA	**The Westin Michigan Avenue Chicago -** see color ad p 307	◆◆◆	$219-$424 SAVE	307
7 / p. 280		Hilton Garden Inn Chicago Downtown North - see color ad p 301	◆◆◆	$129-$309	301
8 / p. 280	AAA	**The Seneca Hotel & Suites -** see color ad p 305	◆◆◆	$129-$199 SAVE	305
9 / p. 280	AAA	Homewood Suites by Hilton - see ad p 302	◆◆◆	$129-$329	302
10 / p. 280	AAA	**The Ritz-Carlton, Chicago (A Four Seasons Hotel)**	◆◆◆◆◆	$385-$585	305
11 / p. 280	AAA	**Best Western Grant Park Hotel**	◆◆	$139-$199 SAVE	295
12 / p. 280		Summerfield Suites by Wyndham	◆◆◆	$309-$419	306
13 / p. 280	AAA	**Radisson Hotel & Suites Chicago -** see ad p 304	◆◆◆	$279-$389 SAVE	304
14 / p. 280	AAA	**Chicago Marriott Downtown -** see color ad card insert	◆◆◆	$199-$249 SAVE	298
15 / p. 280		Hotel Inter-Continental Chicago	◆◆◆◆	$269-$289	302
16 / p. 280	AAA	**Millennium Knickerbocker Hotel**	◆◆◆	$250-$270 SAVE	303
17 / p. 280	AAA	**Residence Inn by Marriott Chicago Downtown -** see color ad card insert	◆◆◆	$219 SAVE	304
18 / p. 280	AAA	**Best Western River North Hotel -** see ad p 297	◆◆◆	$139-$159 SAVE	297
19 / p. 280	AAA	Chicago's Lenox Suites Hotel - see color ad p 297	◆◆	$99-$199 SAVE	298
21 / p. 280	AAA	**Best Western Inn of Chicago**	◆◆◆	$129-$209 SAVE	295
22 / p. 280	AAA	**Holiday Inn-Chicago City Centre**	◆◆◆	$127-$300 SAVE	301
23 / p. 280	AAA	The Sutton Place Hotel - see color ad p 306	◆◆◆	$209 SAVE	306
24 / p. 280	AAA	**Hyatt Regency Chicago -** see color ad p 295	◆◆◆	$155-$295 SAVE	303
25 / p. 280		Clarion Executive Plaza Hotel	◆◆◆	$129-$199	298
26 / p. 280	AAA	**Westin Chicago River North -** see ad p 307	◆◆◆	$169-$399 SAVE	307
27 / p. 280		Holiday Inn Chicago Mart Plaza	◆◆◆	$285-$305	302
28 / p. 280	AAA	**Renaissance Chicago Hotel -** see color ad card insert	◆◆◆◆	$279-$319 SAVE	304
29 / p. 280		Hotel Allegro Chicago	◆◆◆	$279	302
30 / p. 280		W Chicago City Center	◆◆◆	$219-$279	307
31 / p. 280	AAA	**The Palmer House Hilton**	◆◆◆	$159-$354 SAVE	303
32 / p. 280	AAA	**Hilton Chicago**	◆◆◆	$159-$354 SAVE	301
33 / p. 280		Hampton Inn & Suites-Chicago Downtown	◆◆◆	$119-$299	301

Spotter/Map Page Number	OA	DOWNTOWN CHICAGO - Lodgings (continued)	Diamond Rating	Rate Range High Season	Listing Page
35 / p. 280	AAA	Four Seasons Hotel Chicago	◆◆◆◆◆	$375-$575	300
36 / p. 280		The Fairmont Chicago	◆◆◆◆	$189-$414	300
37 / p. 280		Omni Chicago Hotel	◆◆◆◆	$309-$329	303
38 / p. 280	AAA	Hyatt on Printers Row - see color ad p 295	◆◆◆	$149-$240 [SAVE]	303
39 / p. 280	AAA	Red Roof Inn	◆	$86-$146 [SAVE]	304
40 / p. 280	AAA	Fairfield Inn & Suites Chicago/Downtown - see color ad card insert	◆◆	$199-$219 [SAVE]	300
41 / p. 280		Embassy Suites Hotel Chicago-Downtown	◆◆◆	$189-$419	299
42 / p. 280	AAA	Swissotel Chicago	◆◆◆◆	$299-$349 [SAVE]	306
43 / p. 280	AAA	Sheraton Chicago Hotel & Towers - see ad p 306	◆◆◆	$169-$399 [SAVE]	305
44 / p. 280	AAA	Whitehall Hotel	◆◆◆◆	$189-$359 [SAVE]	308
45 / p. 280		Crowne Plaza Chicago-The Silversmith	◆◆◆	$189-$259	298
46 / p. 280	AAA	Wyndham Chicago	◆◆◆	$199-$279 [SAVE]	308
47 / p. 280		House of Blues Hotel A Loews Hotel	◆◆◆	$189-$309	303
49 / p. 280		The Allerton Crowne Plaza	◆◆◆	$189-$249	295
		DOWNTOWN CHICAGO - Restaurants			
1 / p. 280		The Pump Room	◆◆◆	$21-$35	312
2 / p. 280		Lino's Ristorante	◆◆	$9-$25	312
3 / p. 280		Chicago Chop House	◆◆	$16-$30	310
4 / p. 280		Spiaggia	◆◆◆	$29-$40	313
5 / p. 280		Cape Cod Room	◆◆◆	$35-$60	309
6 / p. 280		Riva	◆◆◆	$13-$30	312
7 / p. 280		Park Avenue Cafe	◆◆◆	$20-$33	312
8 / p. 280	AAA	The Signature Room at the 95th	◆◆◆	$20-$34	313
9 / p. 280		Bistro 110	◆◆◆	$12-$28	309
10 / p. 280		RL	◆◆◆	$17-$35	313
11 / p. 280		The Dining Room	◆◆◆◆	$29-$37	310
12 / p. 280		Su Casa	◆	$9-$14	314
13 / p. 280		The Indian Garden	◆◆	$9-$20	311
14 / p. 280		Spago	◆◆◆	$12-$34	313
15 / p. 280		Caliterra Cal-Ital Bar & Grille	◆◆◆	$13-$35	309
16 / p. 280		Lawry's-The Prime Rib	◆◆◆	$25-$39	311
17 / p. 280		Ron of Japan	◆◆	$16-$50	313
18 / p. 280		Frontera Grill/Topolobampo	◆◆◆	$10-$21	310
19 / p. 280		Ed Debevic's	◆	$4-$9	310
21 / p. 280	AAA	Nick's Fishmarket & Grill	◆◆◆◆	$20-$48	312
22 / p. 280	AAA	The Italian Village	◆◆	$11-$22	311
23 / p. 280		Les Nomades	◆◆◆◆	$72	311
24 / p. 280		Tru	◆◆◆◆◆	$75-$125	314
25 / p. 280		Chicago-A Bar & Grill	◆◆	$12-$26	309

Spotter/Map Page Number	OA	**DOWNTOWN CHICAGO - Restaurants (continued)**	Diamond Rating	Rate Range High Season	Listing Page
26 / p. 280		Entre Nous	▼▼▼	$19-$36	310
27 / p. 280		Trattoria No 10	▼▼▼	$12-$26	314
28 / p. 280		mk	▼▼▼	$15-$36	312
29 / p. 280		Ben Pao	▼▼	$9-$18	309
30 / p. 280		Seasons Restaurant	▼▼▼▼	$32-$42	313
31 / p. 280		Vong	▼▼▼▼	$18-$32	314
32 / p. 280		Zest	▼▼▼	$14-$22	314
33 / p. 280		312 Chicago	▼▼▼	$11-$26	309
34 / p. 280		Cuisines	▼▼▼	$12-$28	310
35 / p. 280		Cielo	▼▼▼	$12-$29	310
36 / p. 280		Shaw's Crab House	▼▼	$11-$40	313
40 / p. 280		Bice Ristorante	▼▼▼	$11-$24	309
42 / p. 280		Blackhawk Lodge	▼▼▼	$16-$30	309
43 / p. 280		Cafe Iberico	▼▼	$6-$13	309
45 / p. 280		Coco Pazzo Restaurant	▼▼▼	$14-$29	310
49 / p. 280	AAA	**Everest**	▼▼▼▼▼	$33-$44	310
53 / p. 280	AAA	**Gibsons Bar & Steakhouse**	▼▼▼	$19-$41	311
59 / p. 280		Hubbard Street Grill	▼▼	$10-$24	311
63 / p. 280		Kamehachi	▼▼	$9-$25	311
64 / p. 280		Klay Oven	▼▼	$15-$25	311
67 / p. 280		Mambo Grill	▼	$9-$22	312
70 / p. 280		Marche	▼▼▼	$14-$34	312
76 / p. 280		Rhapsody	▼▼▼	$14-$25	312
77 / p. 280		Russian Tea Time	▼▼▼	$15-$26	313
78 / p. 280		Scoozi!	▼▼	$8-$30	313
79 / p. 280		Harry Caray's Restaurant	▼▼	$11-$33	311

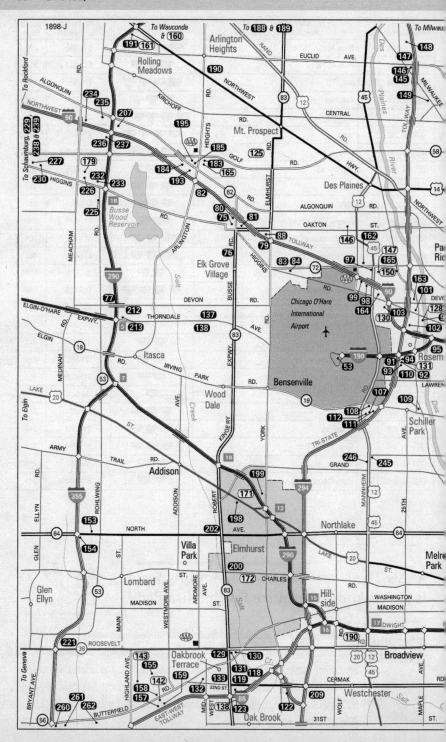

CHICAGO
NORTHERN REGION
ACCOMMODATIONS

✈ Airport Accommodations

Spotter/Map Page Number	OA	CHICAGO O'HARE INTERNATIONAL	Diamond Rating	Rate Range High Season	Listing Page
53 / p. 284	AAA	Hilton Chicago O'Hare Airport, at O'Hare Airport	◆◆◆	$159-$314 (SAVE)	318
165 / p. 284	AAA	Comfort Inn-O'Hare, 2.5 mi ne of airport	◆◆◆	$109-$160 (SAVE)	334
163 / p. 284	AAA	Courtyard by Marriott O'Hare, 3.5 mi ne of airport	◆◆◆	$82-$194 (SAVE)	334
162 / p. 284		Doubletree Club Hotel Chicago O'Hare, 3 mi n of airport	◆◆◆	Failed to provide	334
164 / p. 284	AAA	Travelodge Chicago O'Hare/Rosemont, 2 mi n of airport	◆◆	$84-$159 (SAVE)	334
99 / p. 284	AAA	Best Western At O'Hare, 2 mi n of airport	◆◆◆	$109-$139 (SAVE)	363
91 / p. 284	AAA	Embassy Suites Hotel O'Hare Rosemont, 2 mi e of airport	◆◆◆	$119-$265 (SAVE)	364
93 / p. 284	AAA	Holiday Inn O'Hare International, 2 mi e of airport	◆◆◆	$139-$199 (SAVE)	364
95 / p. 284	AAA	Hyatt Regency O'Hare, 2 mi e of airport	◆◆◆	$119-$224 (SAVE)	364
96 / p. 284	AAA	Marriott Suites Chicago O'Hare, 2 mi ne of airport	◆◆◆	$139-$289 (SAVE)	365
98 / p. 284	AAA	Ramada Plaza Hotel-O'Hare, 2 mi n of airport	[fyi]	$99-$155 (SAVE)	365
103 / p. 284		Sheraton Gateway Suites O'Hare, 1.5 mi n of airport	◆◆◆	$85-$194	365
94 / p. 284	AAA	Sofitel Chicago O'Hare, 2 mi e of airport	◆◆◆	$199 (SAVE)	365
102 / p. 284	AAA	The Westin O'Hare, 3 mi ne of airport	◆◆◆	$99-$179 (SAVE)	365
112 / p. 284	AAA	Days Inn-O'Hare International, 2 mi s of airport	◆◆	$79-$169 (SAVE)	370
108 / p. 284		Four Points by Sheraton Chicago O'Hare Airport, 2 mi s of airport	◆◆◆	$129-$139	370
111 / p. 284		Hampton Inn O'Hare Airport, 2 mi s of airport	◆◆◆	$119	370
107 / p. 284	AAA	Howard Johnson Express Inn, 0.8 mi s	◆◆	$99-$109 (SAVE)	370
110 / p. 284	AAA	Residence Inn by Marriott O'Hare-Schiller Park, 1.5 mi e of airport	◆◆◆	$99-$179 (SAVE)	371

Chicago Northern Region

This index helps you "spot" where approved accommodations and restaurants are located on the corresponding detailed maps. Lodging rate ranges are for comparison only and show the property's high season; rates are per night, unless only weekly (W) or monthly (M) rates are available. Restaurant rate range is for dinner, unless only lunch (L) is served. Turn to the listing page for more detailed rate information and consult display ads for special promotions.

Spotter/Map Page Number	OA	CHICAGO (NORTHERN REGION) - Lodgings	Diamond Rating	Rate Range High Season	Listing Page
52 / p. 284	AAA	AmeriSuites Chicago/O'Hare - see color ad p 296	◆◆◆	$129 (SAVE)	315
53 / p. 284	AAA	Hilton Chicago O'Hare Airport	◆◆◆	$159-$314 (SAVE)	318
54 / p. 284	AAA	Heart O' Chicago Motel	◆	$75-$95 (SAVE)	318
55 / p. 284	AAA	Best Western Hawthorne Terrace - see color ad p 316	◆◆◆	$149-$199 (SAVE)	316
56 / p. 284	AAA	Majestic Hotel - see color ad p 317	◆◆◆	$139-$199 (SAVE)	319
57 / p. 284	AAA	City Suites Hotel - see color ad p 317	◆◆◆	$139-$199 (SAVE)	316
58 / p. 284		Comfort Inn	◆◆	Failed to provide	316
59 / p. 284	AAA	Days Inn-Lincoln Park North - see color ad p 318	◆◆	$106-$141 (SAVE)	318
60 / p. 284		Holiday Inn O'Hare Kennedy	◆◆◆	$179	319
61 / p. 284		Days Inn Gold Coast	◆◆	$119-$159	316

Spotter/Map Page Number	OA	CHICAGO (NORTHERN REGION) - Lodgings (continued)	Diamond Rating	Rate Range High Season	Listing Page
62 / p. 284	AAA	The Willows - see color ad p 317	▽▽▽	$139-$199 SAVE	319
63 / p. 284	AAA	Hyatt Regency McCormick Place Chicago - see color ad p 295	▽▽▽▽	$175-$255 SAVE	319
64 / p. 284	AAA	Hyatt at University Village	▽▽▽	$135-$224 SAVE	319
		CHICAGO (NORTHERN REGION) - Restaurants			
85 / p. 284		Monastero's Ristorante	▽▽	$9-$19	320
88 / p. 284	AAA	Ambria	▽▽▽▽▽	$29-$34	319
89 / p. 284		Rudi Fazuli's West Side Italian	▽▽	$10-$19	321
90 / p. 284	AAA	Yoshi's Cafe	▽▽▽	$13-$25	321
91 / p. 284		Arun's	▽▽▽▽	$75	319
92 / p. 284		PS Bangkok	▽▽	$6-$11	321
94 / p. 284		Basta Pasta Restaurant	▽▽	$9-$26	320
96 / p. 284		Cafe Absinthe	▽▽▽	$15-$26	320
97 / p. 284		Topo Gigio Ristorante	▽▽	$12-$23	321
99 / p. 284		Cafe Ba-Ba-Reeba!	▽▽▽	$15-$25	320
100 / p. 284		Charlie Trotter's	▽▽▽▽▽	$100-$125	320
102 / p. 284		Erwin-An American Cafe	▽▽▽	$13-$26	320
107 / p. 284		La Bocca della Verita	▽▽	$11-$24	320
108 / p. 284		Le Bouchon	▽▽▽	$12-$17	320
111 / p. 284		Lutz's Continental Cafe & Pastry Shop	▽	$12-$18	320
116 / p. 284		one sixtyblue	▽▽▽	$19-$30	320
118 / p. 284		Wishbone	▽	$7-$14	321
119 / p. 284		Stefani's	▽▽	$10-$24	321
120 / p. 284		Tuscany	▽▽	$9-$24	321
		ELK GROVE VILLAGE - Lodgings			
75 / p. 284	AAA	Best Western Midway Hotel	▽▽	$94-$140 SAVE	337
76 / p. 284		Holiday Inn of Elk Grove	▽▽▽	$79-$119	338
77 / p. 284	AAA	Exel Inn of Elk Grove Village - see color ad p 318	▽▽	$50-$74 SAVE	337
79 / p. 284	AAA	Comfort Inn International	▽▽▽	$72-$189 SAVE	337
80 / p. 284	AAA	Hampton Inn Elk Grove Village	▽▽	$87-$97 SAVE	337
81 / p. 284		La Quinta Inn O'Hare Airport - see color ad p 325	▽▽▽	$80-$149	338
82 / p. 284		Sheraton Suites Elk Grove/O'Hare	▽▽▽	$99-$249	338
83 / p. 284	AAA	Exel Inn of O'Hare - see color ad p 318	▽▽	$67-$91 SAVE	337
84 / p. 284	AAA	Super 8 Motel O'Hare	▽▽	$55-$78 SAVE	338
		MOUNT PROSPECT - Lodgings			
88 / p. 284	AAA	Country Inn & Suites By Carlson Chicago/O'Hare - see color ad p 322	▽▽▽	$99-$109 SAVE	354
		MOUNT PROSPECT - Restaurant			
125 / p. 284		Retro Bistro	▽▽▽	$11-$22	354
		ROSEMONT - Lodgings			
91 / p. 284	AAA	Embassy Suites Hotel O'Hare Rosemont	▽▽▽	$119-$265 SAVE	364

Spotter/Map Page Number	OA	**ROSEMONT** - Lodgings (continued)	Diamond Rating	Rate Range High Season	Listing Page
92 / p. 284		Doubletree Hotel Chicago O'Hare Airport-Rosemont	◇◇◇	$189	364
93 / p. 284	AAA	Holiday Inn O'Hare International - see color ad p 364	◇◇◇	$139-$199 SAVE	364
94 / p. 284	AAA	Sofitel Chicago O'Hare	◇◇◇	$199 SAVE	365
95 / p. 284	AAA	Hyatt Regency O'Hare - see color ad p 295	◇◇◇	$119-$224 SAVE	364
96 / p. 284	AAA	Marriott Suites Chicago O'Hare - see color ad card insert	◇◇◇	$139-$289 SAVE	365
97 / p. 284	AAA	Residence Inn by Marriott O'Hare-Rosemont - see color ad card insert	◇◇◇	$139-$189 SAVE	365
98 / p. 284	AAA	Ramada Plaza Hotel-O'Hare	fyi	$99-$155 SAVE	365
99 / p. 284	AAA	Best Western At O'Hare	◇◇◇	$109-$139 SAVE	363
101 / p. 284	AAA	Hyatt Rosemont - see color ad p 295	◇◇◇	$199 SAVE	364
102 / p. 284	AAA	The Westin O'Hare	◇◇◇	$99-$179 SAVE	365
103 / p. 284		Sheraton Gateway Suites O'Hare	◇◇◇	$85-$194	365
		ROSEMONT - Restaurants			
128 / p. 284		Carlucci	◇◇◇	$15-$30	366
130 / p. 284		Nick's Fishmarket	◇◇◇◇	$20-$48	366
131 / p. 284	AAA	Gibson's Steakhouse	◇◇◇	$13-$60	366
		SCHILLER PARK - Lodgings			
107 / p. 284	AAA	Howard Johnson Express Inn	◇◇	$99-$109 SAVE	370
108 / p. 284		Four Points by Sheraton Chicago O'Hare Airport	◇◇◇	$129-$139	370
109 / p. 284		Comfort Suites & Conference Center	◇◇◇	$79-$139	370
110 / p. 284	AAA	Residence Inn by Marriott O'Hare-Schiller Park - see color ad card insert	◇◇◇	$99-$179 SAVE	371
111 / p. 284		Hampton Inn O'Hare Airport	◇◇◇	$119	370
112 / p. 284	AAA	Days Inn-O'Hare International - see color ad p 370	◇◇◇	$79-$169 SAVE	370
		OAK BROOK - Lodgings			
118 / p. 284	AAA	Hyatt Regency Oak Brook	◇◇◇	$79-$200 SAVE	359
119 / p. 284	AAA	Renaissance Oak Brook Hotel - see color ad card insert	◇◇◇	$159-$194 SAVE	360
122 / p. 284	AAA	Wyndham Drake-Oak Brook	◇◇◇◇	$99-$179 SAVE	360
123 / p. 284	AAA	Marriott Oak Brook Hotel - see color ad card insert	◇◇◇	$159-$209 SAVE	360
		OAK BROOK - Restaurant			
138 / p. 284		Tuscany	◇◇◇	$8-$26	360
		OAKBROOK TERRACE - Lodgings			
129 / p. 284		Comfort Suites-Oakbrook Terrace	◇◇◇	$109-$129	360
130 / p. 284		Hilton Suites Oakbrook Terrace	◇◇◇	$109	361
131 / p. 284		Hilton Garden Inn	◇◇◇	$79	361
132 / p. 284		La Quinta Inn-Oakbrook Terrace - see color ad p 325	◇◇◇	$79-$129	361
133 / p. 284		Four Points Barcelo Hotel Oakbrook	◇◇◇	$69-$199	360
		WOOD DALE - Lodgings			
137 / p. 284	AAA	Wyndham Garden Hotel-Wood Dale	◇◇◇	$79-$145 SAVE	378
138 / p. 284	AAA	Courtyard by Marriott Wood Dale - see ad p 299 & color ad card insert	◇◇◇	$49-$149 SAVE	377

Spotter/Map Page Number	OA	GLENVIEW - Lodgings	Diamond Rating	Rate Range High Season	Listing Page
145 / p. 284		Motel 6 - 1040	◆	$51-$67	342
146 / p. 284	AAA	Baymont Inn & Suites Chicago-Glenview - see color ad opposite title page	◆◆	$74-$84 SAVE	341
147 / p. 284	AAA	Courtyard by Marriott-Glenview - see ad p 299 & color ad card insert	◆◆◆	$129-$139 SAVE	342
148 / p. 284	AAA	Fairfield Inn Chicago/Glenview - see color ad card insert	◆◆	$84 SAVE	342
149 / p. 284	AAA	Doubletree Guest Suites O'Hare North-Glenview - see ad p 317	◆◆◆	$99-$159 SAVE	342
		LOMBARD - Lodgings			
153 / p. 284		Comfort Suites Lombard/Oak Brook	◆◆◆	$99-$129	353
154 / p. 284		Quality Inn & Suites	◆◆◆	$81	353
155 / p. 284		Hampton Inn-Lombard	◆◆◆	$69-$119	353
157 / p. 284		Embassy Suites Hotel-Lombard/Oak Brook	◆◆◆	$99-$229	353
158 / p. 284	AAA	AmeriSuites Chicago/Lombard - see color ad p 296	◆◆◆	$69-$159 SAVE	352
159 / p. 284		Homestead Studio Suites Hotel	◆◆◆	$84-$99	353
		LOMBARD - Restaurants			
142 / p. 284		Magnum's Prime Steak House	◆◆◆	$14-$35	353
143 / p. 284		Bistro Banlieue	◆◆◆	$10-$25	353
		DES PLAINES - Lodgings			
162 / p. 284		Doubletree Club Hotel Chicago O'Hare	◆◆◆	Failed to provide	334
163 / p. 284	AAA	Courtyard by Marriott O'Hare - see ad p 299 & color ad card insert	◆◆◆	$82-$194 SAVE	334
164 / p. 284	AAA	Travelodge Chicago O'Hare/Rosemont	◆◆	$84-$159 SAVE	334
165 / p. 284	AAA	Comfort Inn-O'Hare	◆◆◆	$109-$160 SAVE	334
		DES PLAINES - Restaurants			
146 / p. 284		Grazie	◆◆	$10-$18	334
147 / p. 284		Cafe La Cave	◆◆◆	$21-$45	334
150 / p. 284		Tiffany's	◆	$10-$20	334
		SKOKIE - Lodgings			
170 / p. 284		Holiday Inn Northshore	◆◆◆	$149-$189	371
171 / p. 284	AAA	Howard Johnson Hotel-Skokie	◆◆	$105-$164 SAVE	371
		EVANSTON - Lodgings			
174 / p. 284	AAA	Hilton Garden Inn-Evanston - see ad p 339	◆◆◆	$109-$219 SAVE	339
175 / p. 284		Omni Orrington Hotel	◆◆◆	$179-$189	340
176 / p. 284		The Evanston Holiday Inn & Conference Center	◆◆◆	$129-$199	339
		EVANSTON - Restaurants			
156 / p. 284		Trio	◆◆◆◆	$65-$85	340
157 / p. 284		Va Pensiero	◆◆◆	$16-$29	340
		ARLINGTON HEIGHTS - Lodgings			
183 / p. 284	AAA	AmeriSuites (Chicago/Arlington Heights) - see color ad p 296	◆◆◆	$99-$109 SAVE	325
184 / p. 284		Motel 6 - 1048	◆	$51-$67	326
185 / p. 284	AAA	Holiday Inn Express - see color ad p 325	◆◆◆	$79-$139 SAVE	326
188 / p. 284		La Quinta Inn-Arlington Heights - see color ad p 325	◆◆◆	$80-$129	326

Spotter/Map Page Number	OA	ARLINGTON HEIGHTS - Lodgings (continued)	Diamond Rating	Rate Range High Season	Listing Page
189 / p. 284	AAA	Courtyard by Marriott-North - see ad p 299 & color ad card insert	◆◆◆	$59-$109 SAVE	326
190 / p. 284	AAA	Best Western Arlington Inn	◆◆	$65-$91 SAVE	325
191 / p. 284		Sheraton Chicago Northwest	◆◆◆	$239	327
193 / p. 284	AAA	Radisson Hotel Arlington Heights - see color ad p 326	◆◆◆	$45-$209 SAVE	327
195 / p. 284	AAA	Red Roof Inn #7102	◆◆	$55-$81 SAVE	327
		ARLINGTON HEIGHTS - Restaurants			
160 / p. 284		Le Titi de Paris	◆◆◆◆	$21-$28	327
161 / p. 284		Delaney & Murphy, A Steak House	◆◆◆	$18-$35	327
165 / p. 284		Wellington of Arlington	◆◆	$13-$19	327
		ELMHURST - Lodgings			
198 / p. 284	AAA	AmeriSuites (Chicago/Elmhurst-O'Hare Area) - see color ad p 296	◆◆◆	$79-$109 SAVE	338
199 / p. 284	AAA	Holiday Inn Chicago-Elmhurst	◆◆◆	$119-$129 SAVE	338
200 / p. 284	AAA	Holiday Inn Express Oak Brook/Elmhurst	◆◆◆	$79-$109 SAVE	339
202 / p. 284	AAA	Courtyard by Marriott-Elmhurst - see color ad card insert	◆◆◆	$119 SAVE	338
		ELMHURST - Restaurants			
171 / p. 284		Our Kitchen	◆	$4-$9(L)	339
172 / p. 284		Dave and Jack's Silverado Grill	◆	$9-$18	339
		ROLLING MEADOWS - Lodgings			
207 / p. 284	AAA	Holiday Inn Rolling Meadows/Schaumburg Area	◆◆◆	$99-$119 SAVE	363
		WESTCHESTER - Lodgings			
209 / p. 284		Hampton Inn-Westchester/Oak Brook	◆◆◆	$79-$129	375
		ITASCA - Lodgings			
212 / p. 284	AAA	AmeriSuites Chicago/Itasca - see color ad p 296	◆◆◆	$111 SAVE	346
213 / p. 284	AAA	Wyndham Northwest Chicago	◆◆◆	$99-$189 SAVE	346
		GLEN ELLYN - Lodgings			
221 / p. 284		Holiday Inn	◆◆◆	$89-$109	341
		SCHAUMBURG - Lodgings			
225 / p. 284	AAA	Chicago Marriott Schaumburg - see color ad card insert	◆◆◆	$69-$209 SAVE	367
226 / p. 284	AAA	Hampton Inn Schaumburg	◆◆◆	$99-$119 SAVE	368
227 / p. 284		Homewood Suites Schaumburg	◆◆◆	$159-$189	368
229 / p. 284		Holiday Inn Schaumburg/Hoffman Estates	◆◆◆	$99-$139	368
230 / p. 284	AAA	Summerfield Suites by Wyndham-Chicago/Schaumburg	◆◆◆	$99-$165 SAVE	369
232 / p. 284		Drury Inn-Schaumburg - see color ad p 5	◆◆◆	$70-$125	368
233 / p. 284		La Quinta Inn Schaumburg - see color ad p 325	◆◆◆	$79-$139	369
234 / p. 284	AAA	Embassy Suites Hotel Schaumburg-Woodfield - see color ad p 368	◆◆◆	$99-$209 SAVE	368
235 / p. 284	AAA	Radisson Hotel Schaumburg - see color ad p 326	◆◆◆	$95-$209 SAVE	369
236 / p. 284	AAA	Hyatt Regency Woodfield	◆◆◆	$99-$220 SAVE	369
237 / p. 284	AAA	AmeriSuites (Chicago/Schaumburg) - see color ad p 296	◆◆◆	$112 SAVE	367

Spotter/Map Page Number	OA	**SCHAUMBURG** - Lodgings (continued)	Diamond Rating	Rate Range High Season	Listing Page
238 / p. 284		Country Inn & Suites - see color ad p 322	▼▼▼	$99-$179	367
239 / p. 284		Homestead Studio Suites-Chicago/Schaumburg	▼▼▼	$79-$94	368
		SCHAUMBURG - Restaurant			
179 / p. 284		California Cafe	▼▼▼	$11-$20	369
		FRANKLIN PARK - Lodgings			
245 / p. 284		Comfort Inn	▼▼	$99-$119	340
246 / p. 284		Super 8 O'Hare South	▼▼	$54-$114	340
		DOWNERS GROVE - Lodgings			
260 / p. 284	AAA	**Comfort Inn**	▼▼	$79-$89 [SAVE]	335
261 / p. 284	AAA	**Holiday Inn Express - see color ad p 322**	▼▼▼	$104-$139 [SAVE]	335
262 / p. 284	AAA	**Red Roof Inn**	▼▼	$55-$74 [SAVE]	335
		HILLSIDE - Restaurant			
190 / p. 284		Emilio's Tapas Bar Restaurant	▼▼▼	$7-$18	344
		OAK PARK - Restaurants			
199 / p. 284		Cafe Winberie	▼▼	$10-$18	361
200 / p. 284		Philander's Oak Park	▼▼▼	$14-$26	361
		WILMETTE - Restaurants			
205 / p. 284	AAA	**Old Quilmette Depot Restaurant**	▼▼	$10-$24	377
206 / p. 284		Akai Hana	▼▼	$12-$19	377

Look for our Partners in Savings!

When selecting a AAA Approved lodging, look for properties that participate in our various partnership programs. In addition to actively soliciting AAA business, many of them also offer discounts to AAA members.

• Properties that advertise in the TourBook® guide want to provide members with a more complete picture of their property. Please refer to their ads for more details on what these properties have to offer.

• A red [SAVE] icon in their TourBook guide listing indicates an **Official Appointment** property that offers a minimum 10% discount off published TourBook standard room rates or the lowest public room rate, at the time of booking, for the dates of stay.

• A black [SAVE] icon indicates a chain hotel that participates in the **Show Your Card & Save®** program. These properties offer a satisfaction guarantee and AAA's best rates for your dates of stay. Please refer to page 22 in the TourBook Navigator section for complete details and a list of participating hotel chains or call **866-AAA-SAVE** to make a reservation.

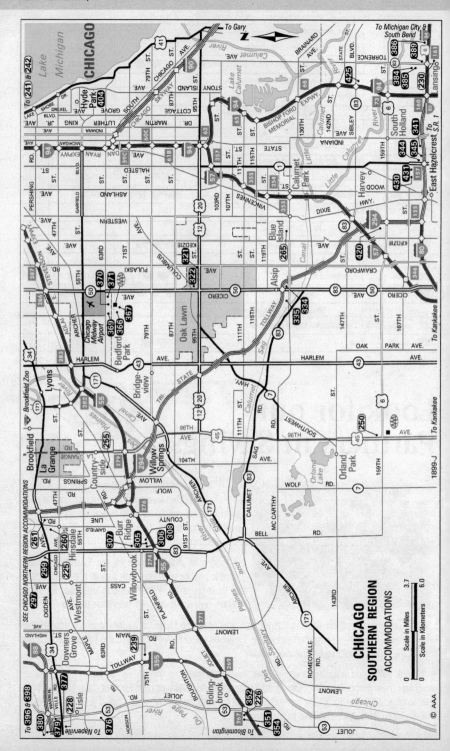

CHICAGO
SOUTHERN REGION
ACCOMMODATIONS

© AAA

1899-J

✈ Airport Accommodations

Spotter/Map Page Number	OA	CHICAGO MIDWAY	Diamond Rating	Rate Range High Season	Listing Page
366 / p. 292	◇◇◇	Courtyard by Marriott-Chicago/Midway Airport, 0.8 mi s of airport	▽▽▽	$149-$179 SAVE	328
367 / p. 292	◇◇◇	Fairfield Inn by Marriott, 0.8 mi s of airport	▽▽▽	$109-$159 SAVE	329
370 / p. 292		Hampton Inn Midway Airport, 0.8 mi s of airport	▽▽▽	$89-$179	329
371 / p. 292		Holiday Inn Express Hotel & Suites Chicago/Midway, 0.8 mi s of airport	▽▽▽	$149-$199	329
369 / p. 292		Sleep Inn-Midway Airport, 0.8 mi s of airport	▽▽	$89-$159	329

Chicago Southern Region

This index helps you "spot" where approved accommodations and restaurants are located on the corresponding detailed maps. Lodging rate ranges are for comparison only and show the property's high season; rates are per night, unless only weekly (W) or monthly (M) rates are available. Restaurant rate range is for dinner, unless only lunch (L) is served. Turn to the listing page for more detailed rate information and consult display ads for special promotions.

Spotter/Map Page Number	OA	WESTMONT - Lodgings	Diamond Rating	Rate Range High Season	Listing Page
297 / p. 292		Homestead Studio Suites-Chicago/Westmont/Oak Brook	▽▽▽	$79-$119	375
299 / p. 292		ClubHouse Inn & Suites - see ad p 375	▽▽▽	$81-$109	375
		WESTMONT - Restaurant			
225 / p. 292		Cucina Roma	▽▽▽	$12-$21	375
		WILLOWBROOK - Lodgings			
305 / p. 292	◇◇◇	Fairfield Inn Willowbrook - see color ad card insert	▽▽	$59-$79 SAVE	377
306 / p. 292		Holiday Inn-Willowbrook	▽▽▽	$119-$139	377
307 / p. 292	◇◇◇	Red Roof Inn	▽▽	$59-$87 SAVE	377
308 / p. 292	◇◇◇	Baymont Inn & Suites Chicago-Willowbrook - see color ad opposite title page	▽▽▽	$69-$89 SAVE	377
		OAK LAWN - Lodgings			
321 / p. 292	◇◇◇	Holiday Inn-Oak Lawn (Chicago Southwest)	▽▽	$104 SAVE	361
322 / p. 292		Hilton Oak Lawn	▽▽▽	$150-$194	361
		ALSIP - Lodgings			
334 / p. 292	◇◇◇	Baymont Inn-Chicago Midway South	▽▽	$70-$95 SAVE	324
335 / p. 292	◇◇◇	Radisson Hotel-Alsip	▽▽▽	$109-$169 SAVE	324
		SOUTH HOLLAND - Lodgings			
341 / p. 292	◇◇◇	Hilton Garden Inn South Holland	▽▽▽	$95-$135	371
344 / p. 292		Motel 6	▽▽	$34-$55	371
345 / p. 292		Hampton Inn	▽▽▽	$79-$85	371
		BOLINGBROOK - Lodgings			
351 / p. 292	◇◇◇	Holiday Inn Hotel & Suites	▽▽▽	$129 SAVE	330
352 / p. 292	◇◇◇	Ramada Limited	▽▽▽	$80-$85 SAVE	330
354 / p. 292		Comfort Inn	▽▽▽	$79-$85	330
		BOLINGBROOK - Restaurant			
226 / p. 292		Bourbon Street Cafe	▽▽	$8-$20	330
		BEDFORD PARK - Lodgings			
366 / p. 292	◇◇◇	Courtyard by Marriott-Chicago/Midway Airport - see color ad card insert	▽▽▽	$149-$179 SAVE	328
367 / p. 292	◇◇◇	Fairfield Inn by Marriott - see color ad card insert	▽▽▽	$109-$159 SAVE	329
369 / p. 292		Sleep Inn-Midway Airport	▽▽	$89-$159	329
370 / p. 292		Hampton Inn Midway Airport	▽▽▽	$89-$179	329

Spotter/Map Page Number	OA	BEDFORD PARK - Lodgings (continued)	Diamond Rating	Rate Range High Season	Listing Page
371 / p. 292		Holiday Inn Express Hotel & Suites Chicago/Midway Airport	◆◆◆	$149-$199	329
		LISLE - Lodgings			
376 / p. 292	AAA	Hickory Ridge Marriott Conference Hotel - see color ad card insert	◆◆◆	$79-$159 SAVE	351
377 / p. 292	AAA	Hyatt Lisle	◆◆◆	$89-$180 SAVE	352
379 / p. 292	AAA	Hilton Lisle/Naperville	◆◆◆	$95-$175 SAVE	352
380 / p. 292	AAA	Wyndham Lisle/Naperville	◆◆◆	$79-$165 SAVE	352
		LISLE - Restaurant			
228 / p. 292		Chinn's 34th Street Fishery	◆◆	$9-$27	352
		LANSING - Lodgings			
384 / p. 292		Sleep Inn	◆◆	Failed to provide	350
385 / p. 292		Comfort Suites	◆◆◆	Failed to provide	349
386 / p. 292	AAA	Fairfield Inn by Marriott-Lansing - see color ad card insert	◆◆	$73 SAVE	349
389 / p. 292	AAA	Red Roof Inn	◆◆	$51-$79 SAVE	349
		LANSING - Restaurant			
230 / p. 292		Cafe Borgia	◆◆	$10-$25	350
		DOWNERS GROVE - Lodgings			
396 / p. 292	AAA	Marriott Suites Downers Grove - see color ad card insert	◆◆◆	$159-$209 SAVE	335
398 / p. 292		Doubletree Guest Suites	◆◆◆	$69-$169	335
		CHICAGO (SOUTHERN REGION) - Lodgings			
404 / p. 292		Wooded Isle Suites	◆◆	$164-$198	322
		CHICAGO (SOUTHERN REGION) - Restaurants			
239 / p. 292		Sher-A Punjab	◆◆	$9	323
241 / p. 292		Emperor's Choice	◆◆	$8-$24	323
242 / p. 292		Evergreen Restaurant	◆◆	$8-$17	323
		MARKHAM - Lodgings			
420 / p. 292		Holiday Inn Express	◆◆	$65-$95	353
		CALUMET CITY - Lodgings			
425 / p. 292		Baymont Inn & Suites Chicago-Calumet City	◆◆	$79-$89	331
		HARVEY - Lodgings			
430 / p. 292		Comfort Suites	◆◆◆	$79-$109	344
431 / p. 292		Sleep Inn	◆◆	$59-$89	344
		ORLAND PARK - Restaurant			
250 / p. 292		The Charley Horse	◆	$6-$14	362
		COUNTRYSIDE - Restaurant			
255 / p. 292		Flame of Countryside	◆◆	$15-$25	331
		HINSDALE - Restaurants			
260 / p. 292		Salbute	◆◆	$12-$25	344
261 / p. 292		Egg Harbour Cafe I	◆	$5-$9(L)	344
		BLUE ISLAND - Restaurant			
265 / p. 292		Babe's Farm House Inn Restaurant	◆	$8-$16	329

DOWNTOWN CHICAGO   (See map p. 280; index p. 281)

———— WHERE TO STAY ————

THE ALLERTON CROWNE PLAZA

Phone: (312)440-1500   **49**

4/1-6/30 & 9/5-12/31	1P: $189-$249	2P: $189-$249	XP: $25
7/1-9/4	1P: $179-$219	2P: $179-$219	XP: $25
1/1-3/31	1P: $139-$179	2P: $139-$179	XP: $25

Hotel   **Location:** Jct Huron St and N Michigan Ave. 701 N Michigan Ave 60611. Fax: 312/440-1819. **Facility:** 443 units. 395 one-bedroom standard units. 48 one-bedroom suites ($375-$875). 25 stories, interior corridors. *Bath:* combo or shower only. **Parking:** valet only (fee). **Terms:** [AP], [BP], [CP] & [ECP] meal plans available, package plans. **Amenities:** dual phone lines, voice mail, safes, honor bars, irons, hair dryers. **Leisure Activities:** sauna, exercise room. **Guest Services:** gift shop, massage (fee), valet and coin laundry. **Business Services:** conference facilities, business center, PC (fee), fax. **Cards:** AX, CB, DC, DS, JC, MC, VI.

SOME UNITS

(ASK) (SD) (¶¶) (24¶) (Y) (&) (✍) (☂) (DATA PORT) (▯) (▤) / (⊠) /
FEE

BEST WESTERN GRANT PARK HOTEL

Phone: (312)922-2900   **11**

4/1-9/30	1P: $139-$189	2P: $149-$199	XP: $10	F17
10/1-3/31	1P: $109-$159	2P: $119-$159	XP: $10	F17

Hotel   **Location:** Jct Congress Pkwy and S Michigan Ave. 0.3 mi s at 11th St. 1100 S Michigan Ave 60605. Fax: 312/922-8812. **Facility:** 172 one-bedroom standard units. 9 stories, interior corridors. *Bath:* combo or shower only. **Parking:** valet only (fee). **Terms:** cancellation fee imposed, package plans. **Amenities:** extended cable TV, voice mail. **Dining:** restaurant, 7 am-10 pm, $10-$19, cocktails. **Pool(s):** heated outdoor. **Leisure Activities:** exercise room. **Guest Services:** valet laundry. **Cards:** AX, CB, DC, DS, JC, MC, VI. **Special Amenities: free newspaper and preferred room (subject to availability with advanced reservations).**

SOME UNITS

(SD) (¶¶) (Y) (&) (✍) (☂) (DATA PORT) (▤) / (⊠) (▯) (▯) /
FEE

BEST WESTERN INN OF CHICAGO

Phone: (312)787-3100   **21**

7/1-10/31	1P: $129-$209	2P: $129-$209
4/1-6/30	1P: $119-$209	2P: $119-$209
11/1-3/31	1P: $99-$209	2P: $99-$209

Hotel   **Location:** Just e of N Michigan Ave. 162 E Ohio St at Michigan Ave 60611. Fax: 312/573-3136. **Facility:** 357 units. 343 one-bedroom standard units. 14 one-bedroom suites ($240-$390). 22 stories, interior corridors. *Bath:* combo or shower only. **Parking:** *Fee:* off-site and valet. **Terms:** cancellation fee imposed, package plans. **Amenities:** extended cable TV, voice mail, irons. *Some:* hair dryers. **Dining:** restaurant, 6 am-10 pm, Fri & Sat-11 pm, $8-$15, cocktails. **Leisure Activities:** exercise room. **Guest Services:** gift shop. **Business Services:** meeting rooms. **Cards:** AX, CB, DC, JC, MC, VI. **Special Amenities: early check-in/late check-out.**

SOME UNITS

(SD) (¶¶) (Y) (☂) (☂) (DATA PORT) (▯) (▤) / (⊠) (▯) /
FEE

(See map p. 280)

BEST WESTERN RIVER NORTH HOTEL   Phone: (312)467-0800

	5/1-11/15	1P: $139-$149	2P: $149-$159	XP: $10	F16
	11/16-3/31	1P: $109-$119	2P: $119-$129	XP: $10	F16
Motor Inn	4/1-4/30	1P: $99-$119	2P: $109-$129	XP: $10	F16

Location: Corner of Ohio and LaSalle sts. 125 W Ohio St 60610. Fax: 312/467-1665. **Facility:** 150 units. 147 one-bedroom standard units. 3 one-bedroom suites ($255-$325). 6 stories, interior corridors. **Parking:** on-site and valet. **Amenities:** extended cable TV, video games (fee), voice mail, safes, irons, hair dryers. *Some:* dual phone lines. **Dining:** restaurant, 6:30 am-midnight, $10-$22, cocktails. **Pool(s):** heated indoor. **Leisure Activities:** sun deck, exercise room. **Guest Services:** valet laundry. **Business Services:** meeting rooms. **Cards:** AX, CB, DC, DS, JC, MC, VI. **Special Amenities:** early check-in/late check-out and free room upgrade (subject to availability with advanced reservations). *(See ad below)*

SOME UNITS

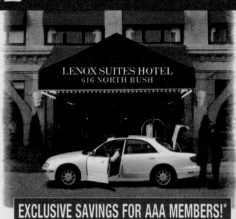

(See map p. 280)

CHICAGO'S LENOX SUITES HOTEL
Phone: (312)337-1000   ⑲
All Year [CP]   1P: $99-$199   2P: $99-$199   XP: $15   F16
Location: Jct Rush and Ontario sts, just w of N Michigan Ave. 616 N Rush St 60611. Fax: 312/337-7217. **Facility:** 324 units. 204 one-bedroom standard units. 120 one-bedroom suites. 17 stories, interior corridors. **Parking:** valet only (fee). **Terms:** package plans. **Amenities:** extended cable TV, voice mail, honor bars, irons, hair dryers. *Some:* dual phone lines. **Dining:** 2 restaurants, 6 am-midnight, $8-$26, cocktails. **Leisure Activities:** exercise room. **Guest Services:** gift shop, valet and coin laundry. **Business Services:** meeting rooms, business center. *Fee:* PC, fax. **Cards:** AX, CB, DC, DS, JC, MC, VI. *(See color ad p 297)*
Hotel

SOME UNITS

CHICAGO MARRIOTT DOWNTOWN
Phone: (312)836-0100   ⑭
5/4-11/23   1P: $199-$249
4/1-5/3   1P: $189-$229
11/24-3/31   1P: $169-$189
Location: Jct Rush and Ohio sts. 540 N Michigan Ave 60611. Fax: 312/836-6139. **Facility:** 1192 units. 1168 one-bedroom standard units. 24 one-bedroom suites ($209-$269). 46 stories, interior corridors. *Bath:* combo or shower only. **Parking:** valet only (fee). **Terms:** check-in 4 pm, package plans. **Amenities:** voice mail, safes, irons, hair dryers. *Some:* CD players. **Dining:** dining room, restaurant, coffee shop, 6 am-10 pm, $10-$30, cocktails, entertainment. **Pool(s):** small heated outdoor. **Leisure Activities:** saunas, whirlpool, steamrooms, exercise room, basketball. *Fee:* game room, beauty salon, custom clothing store. **Guest Services:** gift shop, massage (fee), valet laundry. **Business Services:** conference facilities, business center, fax. *Fee:* administrative services, PC. **Cards:** AX, CB, DC, DS, JC, MC, VI.
(See color ad card insert)
Hotel

SOME UNITS

CLARIDGE HOTEL
Phone: (312)787-4980   ②
4/1-12/31   1P: $149-$189   2P: $149-$189   XP: $20   F18
1/1-3/31   1P: $129-$169   2P: $129-$169   XP: $20   F18
Location: Just s of Goethe St. 1244 N Dearborn St 60610. Fax: 312/266-0978. **Facility:** 161 units. 159 one-bedroom standard units. 2 one-bedroom suites with whirlpools. 13 stories, interior corridors. **Parking:** *Fee:* off-site and valet. **Terms:** [CP] meal plan available, package plans - seasonal, small pets only. **Amenities:** video games (fee), voice mail, honor bars, irons, hair dryers. **Dining:** dining room, 6:30 am-2 & 5-10 pm, Fri & Sat-10:30 pm, $14-$23, cocktails. **Guest Services:** valet laundry. **Business Services:** meeting rooms. **Cards:** AX, CB, DC, DS, JC, MC, VI. **Special Amenities:** free continental breakfast and free newspaper.
Hotel

SOME UNITS

CLARION EXECUTIVE PLAZA HOTEL
Phone: (312)346-7100   ㉕
4/1-12/4   1P: $129-$189   2P: $139-$199   XP: $20   F18
12/5-3/31   1P: $109-$169   2P: $119-$179   XP: $20   F18
Location: Between Michigan and Wabash aves. 71 E Wacker Dr 60601. Fax: 312/346-1721. **Facility:** 421 units. 361 one-bedroom standard units. 60 one-bedroom suites. 39 stories, interior corridors. *Bath:* combo or shower only. **Parking:** *Fee:* off-site and valet. **Terms:** 3 day cancellation notice-fee imposed, package plans. **Amenities:** video games (fee), voice mail, irons, hair dryers. *Some:* dual phone lines, safes. **Leisure Activities:** exercise room. **Guest Services:** gift shop, valet laundry. **Business Services:** meeting rooms, business center. *Fee:* PC, fax. **Cards:** AX, CB, DC, DS, MC, VI.
Hotel

SOME UNITS

COURTYARD BY MARRIOTT CHICAGO DOWNTOWN
Phone: 312-329-2500   ①
6/1-11/30   1P: $189-$300   2P: $209-$320   XP: $10   F12
12/1-3/31   1P: $179-$300   2P: $199-$320   XP: $10   F12
4/1-5/31   1P: $159-$300   2P: $179-$320   XP: $10   F12
Location: State and Hubbard sts. 30 E Hubbard St 60611. Fax: 312/329-9452. **Facility:** 337 units. 303 one-bedroom standard units. 34 one-bedroom suites ($250-$400). 15 stories, interior corridors. *Bath:* combo or shower only. **Parking:** *Fee:* on-site and valet. **Amenities:** high-speed Internet, dual phone lines, voice mail, irons, hair dryers. **Dining:** restaurant, 6:30 am-11 pm, Sat & Sun from 7 am, $12-$17, cocktails. **Pool(s):** heated indoor. **Leisure Activities:** whirlpool, exercise room, sun deck. **Guest Services:** gift shop, coin laundry. **Business Services:** conference facilities, PC, fax. **Cards:** AX, CB, DC, DS, JC, MC, VI. *(See ad p 299 & color ad card insert)*
Hotel

SOME UNITS

CROWNE PLAZA CHICAGO-THE SILVERSMITH
Phone: (312)372-7696   ㊺
4/1-11/30   1P: $189-$259   2P: $189-$259   XP: $20   F18
12/1-3/31   1P: $169-$259   2P: $169-$259   XP: $20   F18
Location: Just n of jct Wabash Ave and Madison St. 10 S Wabash Ave 60603. Fax: 312/372-7320. **Facility:** 143 units. 80 one-bedroom standard units. 63 one-bedroom suites ($199-$350), some with whirlpools. 10 stories, interior corridors. *Bath:* combo or shower only. **Parking:** valet only (fee). **Terms:** cancellation fee imposed, package plans. **Amenities:** extended cable TV, video games (fee), CD players, dual phone lines, voice mail, safes, irons, hair dryers. **Leisure Activities:** exercise room. **Guest Services:** valet laundry. **Business Services:** meeting rooms, business center, PC (fee). **Cards:** AX, CB, DC, DS, JC, MC, VI.
Historic Hotel

SOME UNITS

(See map p. 280)

DOUBLETREE GUEST SUITES CHICAGO

Phone: (312)664-1100   **4**

AAA SAVE

4/1-6/30 & 9/1-12/14   1P: $169-$399   XP: $25   F12
7/1-8/31 & 12/15-3/31   1P: $129-$399   XP: $25   F12

◆◆◆◆ Suite Hotel

Location: Just e of Michigan Ave. 198 E Delaware Pl 60611. Fax: 312/664-8627. **Facility:** 345 units. 25 one-bedroom standard units. 320 one-bedroom suites, some with whirlpools. 30 stories, interior corridors. **Parking:** valet only (fee). **Terms:** cancellation fee imposed, package plans. **Amenities:** high-speed Internet (fee), dual phone lines, voice mail, honor bars, irons, hair dryers. *Some:* CD players. **Dining:** restaurant, coffee shop, 7 am-2 am, $10-$19, cocktails, also, Park Avenue Cafe, see separate listing. **Pool(s):** heated indoor. **Leisure Activities:** sauna, whirlpool, exercise room. *Fee:* spa services. **Guest Services:** massage (fee), valet laundry. **Business Services:** conference facilities, business center. *Fee:* PC, fax. **Cards:** AX, CB, DC, DS, JC, MC, VI.

SOME UNITS

(icons) FEE

THE DRAKE HOTEL, CHICAGO

Phone: (312)787-2200   **5**

AAA SAVE

4/1-6/30 & 9/3-12/8   1P: $295-$365   2P: $325-$395   XP: $30   F18
7/1-9/2   1P: $270-$305   2P: $300-$335   XP: $30   F18
12/9-3/31   1P: $235-$305   2P: $265-$335   XP: $30   F18

◆◆◆◆ ◆◆◆◆ Historic Hotel

Location: N Michigan Ave at Lake Shore Dr and Walton Pl. 140 E Walton Pl 60611-1545. Fax: 312/787-1431. **Facility:** Old-World elegance is embodied in this Chicago-landmark hotel. 537 units. 514 one-bedroom standard units. 23 one-bedroom suites ($435-$2500). 10 stories, interior corridors. *Bath:* combo or shower only. **Parking:** valet only (fee). **Terms:** package plans, small pets only. **Amenities:** voice mail, safes, honor bars, irons, hair dryers. *Some:* CD players. **Dining:** 2 restaurants, 7 am-1 am, $15-$30, cocktails, also, Cape Cod Room, see separate listing, entertainment. **Leisure Activities:** exercise room. **Guest Services:** gift shop, afternoon tea, valet laundry. **Business Services:** conference facilities, business center. *Fee:* PC, fax. **Cards:** AX, CB, DC, DS, JC, MC, VI. **Special Amenities:** early check-in/late check-out and free newspaper. Affiliated with A Hilton Hotel.

SOME UNITS

(icons) FEE   FEE

EMBASSY SUITES HOTEL CHICAGO-DOWNTOWN

Phone: (312)943-3800   **41**

SAVE

All Year [BP]   1P: $189-$399   2P: $209-$419   XP: $20   F17

◆◆◆◆ Suite Hotel

Location: Corner of Ohio and State sts. 600 N State St 60610. Fax: 312/943-5979. **Facility:** 358 one-bedroom suites. 11 stories, interior corridors. **Parking:** valet only (fee). **Terms:** check-in 5 pm, cancellation fee imposed. **Amenities:** dual phone lines, voice mail, honor bars, irons, hair dryers. *Fee:* video games, Web TV, high-speed Internet. *Some:* fax. **Pool(s):** heated indoor. **Leisure Activities:** sauna, whirlpool, exercise room. **Guest Services:** gift shop, complimentary evening beverages, valet and coin laundry. **Business Services:** meeting rooms. **Cards:** AX, CB, DC, DS, JC, MC, VI.

SOME UNITS

(icons) FEE

(See map p. 280)

FAIRFIELD INN & SUITES CHICAGO/DOWNTOWN

Phone: (312)787-3777 **40**

1/1-3/31 [ECP]	1P: $199-$209	2P: $209-$219	XP: $10	F17
4/1-11/13 [ECP]	1P: $189-$209	2P: $199-$219	XP: $10	F17
11/14-12/31 [ECP]	1P: $179-$189	2P: $189-$199	XP: $10	F17

Hotel

Location: Jct N Michigan Ave and Ontario St, 1 blk e. 216 E Ontario St 60611. Fax: 312/787-8714. **Facility:** 185 units. 159 one-bedroom standard units. 26 one-bedroom suites. 15 stories, interior corridors. *Bath:* combo or shower only. **Parking:** valet only (fee). **Amenities:** dual phone lines, voice mail, irons, hair dryers. *Some:* CD players. **Leisure Activities:** exercise room. **Guest Services:** valet laundry. **Business Services:** meeting rooms. **Cards:** AX, DC, DS, MC, VI. **Special Amenities:** free continental breakfast and free local telephone calls. *(See color ad card insert)*

SOME UNITS / FEE FEE

THE FAIRMONT CHICAGO

Phone: (312)565-8000 **36**

All Year   1P: $189-$389   2P: $214-$414   XP: $25   F18

Hotel

Location: Jct Michigan Ave and Wacker Dr, just e. 200 N Columbus Dr 60601. Fax: 312/856-9020. **Facility:** From its lake views to its piano-furnished, circular lobby, this downtown hotel has a posh, sophisticated ambience. 692 units. 630 one-bedroom standard units. 58 one- and 4 two-bedroom suites ($289-$489), some with whirlpools. 42 stories, interior corridors. **Parking:** valet only (fee). **Terms:** package plans, small pets only. **Amenities:** extended cable TV, high-speed Internet (fee), dual phone lines, voice mail, fax, honor bars, irons, hair dryers. **Dining:** Entre Nous, see separate listing. **Guest Services:** gift shop, massage (fee), afternoon tea, valet laundry. **Business Services:** conference facilities, business center. *Fee:* administrative services, PC, fax. **Cards:** AX, CB, DC, DS, JC, MC, VI.

SOME UNITS / FEE FEE FEE

FOUR SEASONS HOTEL CHICAGO

Phone: (312)280-8800 **35**

All Year   1P: $375-$535   2P: $415-$575   XP: $40   F17

Hotel

Location: Jct Michigan Ave. 120 E Delaware Pl 60611. Fax: 312/280-7585. **Facility:** Each luxuriously appointed room at this upscale hotel has an outstanding view. 343 units. 161 one-bedroom standard units. 148 one- and 34 two-bedroom suites ($700-$3500), some with kitchens. 46 stories, interior corridors. *Bath:* combo or shower only. **Parking:** *Fee:* on-site and valet. **Terms:** cancellation fee imposed, package plans, small pets only. **Amenities:** extended cable TV, video tape library, video games, CD players, Web TV, dual phone lines, voice mail, fax, safes, honor bars, irons, hair dryers. **Dining:** dining room, restaurant, 24 hours, $14-$27, cocktails, also, Seasons Restaurant, see separate listing. **Pool(s):** heated indoor. **Leisure Activities:** saunas, whirlpool. *Fee:* full spa services. **Guest Services:** gift shop, massage (fee), afternoon tea, valet laundry. **Business Services:** conference facilities, business center, PC, fax. **Special Amenities:** free newspaper.

SOME UNITS / FEE FEE

(See map p. 280)

GOLD COAST GUEST HOUSE BED & BREAKFAST

Phone: (312)337-0361   **3**

Bed & Breakfast

All Year [BP]   1P: $119-$189   2P: $119-$189

Location: Just w of Dearborn St. 113 W Elm St 60610. Fax: 312/337-0362. **Facility:** A spiral staircase leads to most guest rooms at this three-story townhouse B&B, which features a loft dining area. Smoke free premises. 4 one-bedroom standard units. 3 stories (no elevator), interior corridors. *Bath:* combo or shower only. **Parking:** off-site (fee). **Terms:** age restrictions may apply, 14 day cancellation notice. **Amenities:** video tape library, CD players, irons, hair dryers. **Guest Services:** complimentary evening beverages, complimentary laundry. **Cards:** AX, DS, MC, VI.

HAMPTON INN & SUITES-CHICAGO DOWNTOWN

Phone: (312)832-0330   **33**

[SAVE]

Hotel

1/1-3/31 [ECP]   1P: $119-$299   2P: $119-$299   XP: $10   F18
4/1-12/31 [ECP]   1P: $109-$269   2P: $119-$279   XP: $10   F18

Location: Jct of Dearborn and W Illinois sts, just w of State St. 33 W Illinois St 60610. Fax: 312/832-0333. **Facility:** 230 units. 170 one-bedroom standard units. 60 one-bedroom suites ($209-$399). 12 stories, interior corridors. *Bath:* combo or shower only. **Parking:** valet only (fee). **Terms:** package plans. **Amenities:** video games (fee), dual phone lines, voice mail, safes, irons, hair dryers. **Pool(s):** heated indoor. **Leisure Activities:** sauna, whirlpool, business center. **Business Services:** meeting rooms, business center. *Fee:* PC, fax. **Cards:** AX, CB, DC, DS, JC, MC, VI.

SOME UNITS

HILTON CHICAGO

Phone: (312)922-4400   **32**

[AAA] [SAVE]

Classic Hotel

4/1-12/8   1P: $159-$329   2P: $184-$354   XP: $25   F18
12/9-3/31   1P: $129-$249   2P: $154-$274   XP: $25   F18

Location: I-290 (Congress Pkwy), just s; overlooking Lake Michigan and Grant Park. 720 S Michigan Ave 60605. Fax: 312/922-5240. **Facility:** Historic. 1544 units. 1531 one-bedroom standard units. 13 one-bedroom suites ($479-$5000), some with whirlpools. 27 stories, interior corridors. *Bath:* some combo or shower only. **Parking:** Fee: on-site and valet. **Terms:** cancellation fee imposed, package plans. **Amenities:** Web TV (fee), dual phone lines, voice mail, honor bars, irons, hair dryers. *Some:* high-speed Internet (fee). **Dining:** 2 dining rooms, restaurant, 5:30 am-1:30 am, $10-$36, cocktails, entertainment. **Pool(s):** heated indoor. **Leisure Activities:** saunas, whirlpools, sun deck, jogging. *Fee:* tanning beds. **Guest Services:** gift shop, massage (fee), valet laundry, area transportation. **Business Services:** conference facilities, business center. *Fee:* PC, fax. **Cards:** AX, CB, DC, DS, JC, MC, VI.

SOME UNITS

HILTON GARDEN INN CHICAGO DOWNTOWN NORTH

Phone: (312)595-0000   **7**

[SAVE]

Hotel

All Year   1P: $129-$309   2P: $129-$309   XP: $20   F18

Location: Jct Grand Ave and State St. 10 E Grand Ave 60611. Fax: 312/595-0955. **Facility:** 357 units. 351 one-bedroom standard units. 6 one-bedroom suites ($250-$450). 23 stories, interior corridors. *Bath:* combo or shower only. **Parking:** Fee: on-site and valet. **Terms:** package plans. **Amenities:** dual phone lines, voice mail, irons, hair dryers. *Fee:* video games, high-speed Internet. **Pool(s):** small heated indoor. **Leisure Activities:** whirlpool, exercise room. **Guest Services:** valet laundry. **Business Services:** meeting rooms, business center, PC, fax. **Cards:** AX, CB, DC, DS, JC, MC, VI. *(See color ad below)*

SOME UNITS

HOLIDAY INN-CHICAGO CITY CENTRE

Phone: (312)787-6100   **22**

[AAA] [SAVE]

Hotel

All Year   1P: $127-$280   2P: $145-$300   XP: $20   F18

Location: Just e of Michigan Ave. 300 E Ohio St 60611. Fax: 312/787-6238. **Facility:** 500 units. 496 one-bedroom standard units. 4 one-bedroom suites ($600-$900). 26 stories, interior corridors. *Bath:* combo or shower only. **Parking:** on-site (fee). **Terms:** package plans. **Amenities:** video games (fee), dual phone lines, irons, hair dryers. **Dining:** restaurant, 6:30 am-11 pm, $9-$22, cocktails. **Leisure Activities:** sauna, whirlpool. *Fee:* racquetball courts. **Guest Services:** gift shop, massage (fee), valet and coin laundry. **Business Services:** conference facilities, business center. **Cards:** AX, CB, DC, DS, JC, MC, VI.

SOME UNITS

(See map p. 280)

HOLIDAY INN CHICAGO MART PLAZA
Phone: (312)836-5000   27

	4/1-11/1	1P: $285-$305	2P: $285-$305	XP: $25	F19
	11/2-1/31	1P: $265-$285	2P: $265-$285	XP: $25	F19
Hotel	2/1-3/31	1P: $245-$265	2P: $245-$265	XP: $25	F19

Location: Atop the Apparel Center, at the Merchandise Mart, 14th-23rd floors. 350 N Orleans 60654. Fax: 312/222-9508. **Facility:** 521 units. 508 one-bedroom standard units. 13 one-bedroom suites. 23 stories, interior corridors. *Bath:* combo or shower only. **Parking:** on-site (fee). **Terms:** package plans, small pets only. **Amenities:** dual phone lines, voice mail, irons, hair dryers. **Pool(s):** heated indoor. **Leisure Activities:** sauna, exercise room. **Guest Services:** massage (fee), valet and coin laundry. **Business Services:** conference facilities, business center. *Fee:* PC, fax. **Cards:** AX, CB, DC, DS, JC, MC, VI.

SOME UNITS
(ASK) (S/D) (✈) (🐾) (🍴) (Y) (🎬) (🌀) (🏊) (🐕) (DATA PORT) (📟) (🖨) / (✕) (/)
FEE   FEE

HOMEWOOD SUITES BY HILTON
Phone: (312)644-2222   9

(SAVE)   All Year [ECP]   1P: $129-$329   2P: $129-$329   XP: $10   F18

Location: Jct Grand and Wabash aves, just w of Michigan Ave. 40 E Grand Ave 60611. Fax: 312/644-7777. **Facility:** 233 one-bedroom suites with kitchens. 19 stories, interior corridors. *Bath:* combo or shower only. **Parking:** valet only (fee). **Terms:** check-in 4 pm, package plans. **Amenities:** extended cable TV, dual phone lines, voice mail, irons, hair dryers. **Pool(s):** small heated indoor. **Leisure Activities:** exercise room. **Guest Services:** gift shop, complimentary evening beverages: Mon-Thurs, valet and coin laundry. **Business Services:** meeting rooms, business center, PC, fax. **Cards:** AX, CB, DC, DS, JC, MC, VI. *(See ad below)*

Suite Hotel

SOME UNITS
(S/D) (🍴) (&M) (🎬) (🌀) (🏊) (📹) (DATA PORT) (🔲) (📟) (💻) (🖨) / (✕) /
FEE

HOTEL ALLEGRO CHICAGO
Phone: (312)236-0123   29

All Year   1P: $279   2P: $279   XP: $20   F18

Hotel   **Location:** Jct Randolph and LaSalle sts. 171 W Randolph St 60601. Fax: 312/236-0917. **Facility:** 483 units. 452 one-bedroom standard units. 31 one-bedroom suites with whirlpools. 19 stories, interior corridors. *Bath:* combo or shower only. **Parking:** *Fee:* off-site and valet. **Terms:** package plans, small pets only. **Amenities:** CD players, dual phone lines, voice mail, fax, honor bars, irons, hair dryers. video games, high-speed Internet. **Dining:** 312 Chicago, see separate listing. **Leisure Activities:** exercise room. **Guest Services:** gift shop, complimentary evening beverages, valet laundry. **Business Services:** conference facilities. **Cards:** AX, CB, DC, DS, JC, MC, VI.

SOME UNITS
(ASK) (S/D) (🐕) (🍴) (Y) (📹) (DATA PORT) (📟) (🖨) / (✕) (VCR) (🔲) /
FEE   FEE FEE

HOTEL INTER-CONTINENTAL CHICAGO
Phone: (312)944-4100   15

	9/4-12/31	1P: $269	2P: $289	XP: $20
	4/1-6/30	1P: $259	2P: $279	XP: $20
Hotel	7/1-9/3	1P: $239	2P: $259	XP: $20
	1/1-3/31	1P: $189	2P: $209	XP: $20

Location: Just n of Chicago River. 505 N Michigan Ave 60611. Fax: 312/944-3050. **Facility:** This expansive hotel, set on Michigan Avenue, features interior design with Egyptian, Roman, Grecian and Oriental influences. 814 units. 762 one-bedroom standard units. 52 one-bedroom suites. 42 stories, interior corridors. *Bath:* combo or shower only. **Parking:** valet only (fee). **Terms:** 3 day cancellation notice-fee imposed, package plans. **Amenities:** video games (fee), dual phone lines, voice mail, safes, honor bars, irons, hair dryers. *Some:* fax. **Dining:** Zest, see separate listing. **Pool(s):** heated indoor. **Leisure Activities:** saunas. **Guest Services:** gift shop, massage (fee), afternoon tea, valet laundry. **Business Services:** conference facilities, business center. *Fee:* PC, fax. **Cards:** AX, CB, DC, DS, JC, MC, VI.

SOME UNITS
(ASK) (🍴) (24↑) (Y) (🎬) (🌀) (🏊) (🐕) (📹) (DATA PORT) (📟) (🖨) / (✕) (VCR) /
FEE FEE   FEE

(See map p. 280)

HOUSE OF BLUES HOTEL A LOEWS HOTEL
Phone: (312)245-0333 47

Hotel

9/3-12/14	1P: $189-$309	2P: $189-$309	XP: $20	F18
4/1-6/30	1P: $169-$279	2P: $169-$279	XP: $20	F18
7/1-9/2	1P: $169-$249	2P: $169-$249	XP: $20	F18
12/15-3/31	1P: $129-$209	2P: $129-$209	XP: $20	F18

Location: On Chicago River; between Dearborn and State sts. 333 N Dearborn St 60610. Fax: 312/923-2444. **Facility:** 367 units. 353 one-bedroom standard units. 14 one-bedroom suites ($350-$1500). 13 stories, interior corridors. *Bath:* combo or shower only. **Parking:** valet only (fee). **Terms:** cancellation fee imposed, package plans. **Amenities:** CD players, dual phone lines, voice mail, fax, irons, hair dryers. *Fee:* video games, Web TV. *Some:* high-speed Internet (fee), honor bars. **Guest Services:** gift shop, massage (fee), valet laundry. **Business Services:** meeting rooms, business center. *Fee:* PC, fax. **Cards:** AX, CB, DC, DS, JC, MC, VI.

HYATT ON PRINTERS ROW
AAA SAVE
Phone: (312)986-1234 38

Hotel

All Year	1P: $149-$215	2P: $174-$240	XP: $25	F18

Location: Jct Congress Pkwy and Dearborn St. 500 S Dearborn St 60605. Fax: 312/939-2468. **Facility:** 161 units. 158 one-bedroom standard units. 3 one-bedroom suites. 12 stories, interior corridors. *Bath:* combo or shower only. **Parking:** *Fee:* off-site and valet. **Terms:** cancellation fee imposed, package plans. **Amenities:** voice mail, honor bars, irons, hair dryers. *Some:* CD players, fax. **Dining:** restaurant, 6 am-10 pm, $23-$28, cocktails. **Leisure Activities:** exercise room. **Guest Services:** valet laundry. **Business Services:** meeting rooms. **Cards:** AX, CB, DC, DS, JC, MC, VI. *(See color ad p 295)*

HYATT REGENCY CHICAGO
AAA SAVE
Phone: (312)565-1234 24

Hotel

All Year	1P: $155-$270	2P: $180-$295	XP: $25	F18

Location: Just e of jct Wacker Dr and N Michigan Ave. 151 E Wacker Dr 60601. Fax: 312/565-2966. **Facility:** 2019 units. 1874 one-bedroom standard units. 145 one-bedroom suites, some with whirlpools. 36 stories, interior corridors. *Bath:* combo or shower only. **Parking:** valet only (fee). **Terms:** cancellation fee imposed, package plans. **Amenities:** extended cable TV, voice mail, safes, honor bars, irons, hair dryers. *Some:* CD players, dual phone lines, fax. **Dining:** dining room, 2 restaurants, 2 coffee shops, deli, 6 am-midnight, $10-$30, cocktails. **Leisure Activities:** exercise room. **Guest Services:** gift shop, valet laundry. **Business Services:** conference facilities, business center. *Fee:* administrative services, PC, fax. **Cards:** AX, CB, DC, DS, JC, MC, VI. *(See color ad p 295)*

MILLENNIUM KNICKERBOCKER HOTEL
AAA SAVE
Phone: (312)751-8100 16

Classic Hotel

9/3-12/7	1P: $250-$270	XP: $20	F17
4/1-6/29	1P: $225-$245	XP: $20	F17
6/30-9/2	1P: $196-$216	XP: $20	F17
12/8-3/31	1P: $172-$192	XP: $20	F17

Location: Just e of N Michigan Ave. 163 E Walton Pl 60611. Fax: 312/751-9205. **Facility:** The Millennium Knickerbocker occupies a restored historic building. 305 units. 295 one-bedroom standard units. 10 one-bedroom suites ($245-$295). 12 stories, interior corridors. **Parking:** valet only (fee). **Terms:** cancellation fee imposed, package plans. **Amenities:** CD players, voice mail, honor bars, irons, hair dryers. **Dining:** dining room, 6:30 am-2 & 5-10 pm, $18-$27, cocktails. **Leisure Activities:** exercise room. **Guest Services:** gift shop, valet laundry. **Business Services:** conference facilities, business center, PC. **Cards:** AX, CB, DC, DS, JC, MC, VI.

OMNI CHICAGO HOTEL
Phone: (312)944-6664 37

Suite Hotel

9/3-12/31	1P: $309-$329	2P: $309-$329	XP: $20	F18
4/1-6/29	1P: $299-$319	2P: $299-$319	XP: $20	F18
6/30-9/2	1P: $289-$309	2P: $289-$309	XP: $20	F18
1/1-3/31	1P: $269-$289	2P: $269-$289	XP: $20	F18

Location: N Michigan Ave at Huron St. 676 N Michigan Ave 60611. Fax: 312/266-3015. **Facility:** Located in the heart of Chicago. 347 one-bedroom suites ($319-$2500). 25 stories, interior corridors. **Parking:** valet only (fee). **Terms:** cancellation fee imposed, package plans. **Amenities:** extended cable TV, CD players, dual phone lines, voice mail, fax, safes, honor bars, irons, hair dryers. *Fee:* video games, Web TV. **Dining:** Cielo, see separate listing. **Pool(s):** heated indoor. **Leisure Activities:** saunas, whirlpool, exercise room. **Guest Services:** valet laundry. **Business Services:** meeting rooms, business center. *Fee:* PC, fax. **Cards:** AX, CB, DC, DS, MC, VI.

THE PALMER HOUSE HILTON
AAA SAVE
Phone: (312)726-7500 31

Historic Hotel

4/1-12/8	1P: $159-$329	2P: $184-$354	XP: $25	F18
12/9-3/31	1P: $129-$249	2P: $154-$274	XP: $25	F18

Location: Between State St and Wabash Ave. 17 E Monroe St 60603. Fax: 312/917-1707. **Facility:** An ornately decorated public space defines this hotel, which has guest rooms of varying sizes. 1639 units. 1583 one-bedroom standard units. 55 one- and 1 two-bedroom suites ($479-$1500), some with whirlpools. 23 stories, interior corridors. *Bath:* combo or shower only. **Parking:** *Fee:* on-site and valet. **Terms:** cancellation fee imposed, package plans, pets ($250 deposit). **Amenities:** dual phone lines, voice mail, honor bars, irons, hair dryers. *Fee:* video games, Web TV. *Some:* high-speed Internet (fee). **Dining:** dining room, 2 restaurants, coffee shop, 6 am-11:30 pm; Sunday brunch, $13-$29, cocktails. **Pool(s):** heated indoor. **Leisure Activities:** whirlpool, barber shop, beauty salon. *Fee:* golf simulator. **Guest Services:** gift shop, massage (fee), valet laundry. **Business Services:** conference facilities, business center. *Fee:* PC, fax. **Cards:** AX, CB, DC, DS, JC, MC, VI.

(See map p. 280)

RADISSON HOTEL & SUITES CHICAGO

Phone: (312)787-2900 **13**

(AAA) (SAVE)

WWW Hotel

All Year   1P: $279-$369   2P: $299-$389   XP: $20   F17
Location: Just e of N Michigan Ave. 160 E Huron St 60611. Fax: 312/787-5158. **Facility:** 350 units. 251 one-bedroom standard units. 99 one-bedroom suites. 40 stories, interior corridors. **Bath:** combo or shower only. **Parking:** valet only (fee). **Terms:** package plans, small pets only ($75 deposit). **Amenities:** extended cable TV, video games (fee), voice mail, honor bars, irons, hair dryers. *Some:* dual phone lines. **Dining:** restaurant, 6 am-11 pm, $14-$24, cocktails. **Pool(s):** heated outdoor. **Leisure Activities:** sun deck, exercise room. **Guest Services:** valet laundry. **Business Services:** meeting rooms, business center. *Fee:* PC, fax. **Cards:** AX, CB, DC, DS, MC, VI. **Special Amenities:** free newspaper. *(See ad below)*

SOME UNITS

FEE

RED ROOF INN

Phone: 312/787-3580 **39**

(AAA) (SAVE)

WW Hotel

All Year   1P: $86-$140   2P: $92-$146   XP: $3   F17
Location: Just e of Michigan Ave. 162 E Ontario St 60611. Fax: 312/787-1299. **Facility:** 195 units. 182 one-bedroom standard units. 13 one-bedroom suites. 15 stories, interior corridors. **Bath:** combo or shower only. **Parking:** valet only (fee). **Terms:** package plans, small pets only (must be attended). **Amenities:** video games (fee), voice mail. **Dining:** restaurant, 11:30 am-11 pm, Sun-9 pm, $11-$17, cocktails. **Cards:** AX, DC, DS, MC, VI. **Special Amenities:** free local telephone calls and free newspaper.

SOME UNITS

FEE

RENAISSANCE CHICAGO HOTEL

Phone: (312)372-7200 **28**

(AAA) (SAVE)

WWW WW Hotel

5/4-11/23   1P: $279-$299   2P: $299-$319   XP: $20   F18
4/1-5/3 & 11/24-3/31   1P: $229-$249   2P: $249-$269   XP: $20   F18
Location: Jct State St and Wacker Dr. 1 W Wacker Dr 60601. Fax: 312/372-0093. **Facility:** Luxury touches are featured in the lobby and meeting areas of this refined hotel; guest rooms offer business-friendly conveniences. 553 units. 513 one-bedroom standard units. 40 one-bedroom suites, some with whirlpools. 27 stories, interior corridors. **Bath:** combo or shower only. **Parking:** *Fee:* off-site and valet. **Terms:** package plans, small pets only ($45 extra charge). **Amenities:** extended cable TV, voice mail, honor bars, irons, hair dryers. *Fee:* video games, high-speed Internet. *Some:* fax. **Dining:** restaurant, 11:30 am-10 pm, $10-$25, cocktails, also, Cuisines, see separate listing, entertainment. **Pool(s):** heated indoor. **Leisure Activities:** sauna, whirlpool, exercise room. **Guest Services:** gift shop, massage (fee), afternoon tea, valet laundry. **Business Services:** conference facilities, business center. *Fee:* PC, fax. **Cards:** AX, CB, DC, DS, JC, MC, VI. *(See color ad card insert)*

SOME UNITS

FEE

RESIDENCE INN BY MARRIOTT CHICAGO DOWNTOWN

Phone: (312)943-9800 **17**

(AAA) (SAVE)

WWW Apartment

5/4-11/24 [BP]   1P: $219
4/1-5/3 [BP]   1P: $195
11/25-3/31 [BP]   1P: $155
Location: Just e of Michigan Ave at jct Walton and Mies van der Rohe. 201 E Walton St 60611. Fax: 312/943-8579. **Facility:** 221 units. 110 one-bedroom standard units with efficiencies. 80 one- and 31 two-bedroom suites with kitchens. 19 stories, interior corridors. **Bath:** combo or shower only. **Parking:** valet only (fee). **Terms:** cancellation fee imposed, pets ($15 fee). **Amenities:** extended cable TV, high-speed Internet (fee), dual phone lines, voice mail, irons, hair dryers. **Leisure Activities:** exercise room. **Guest Services:** complimentary evening beverages: Mon-Thurs, valet and coin laundry. **Cards:** AX, CB, DC, DS, JC, MC, VI. *(See color ad card insert)*

SOME UNITS

FEE

(See map p. 280)

THE RITZ-CARLTON, CHICAGO (A FOUR SEASONS HOTEL)

Phone: (312)266-1000 🔟

ⒶⒶⒶ ◆◆◆◆◆ Hotel

All Year 1P: $385-$545 2P: $425-$585 XP: $40 F17
Location: Jct N Michigan Ave and E Pearson St; in Water Tower Place. 160 E Pearson St 60611. Fax: 312/621-6906. **Facility:** Understated, traditional elegance characterizes this Windy City property. 435 units. 344 one-bedroom standard units. 64 one- and 27 two-bedroom suites ($775-$3500), some with kitchens. 32 stories, interior corridors. *Bath:* combo or shower only. **Parking:** off-site and valet (fee). **Terms:** cancellation fee imposed, package plans, small pets only. **Amenities:** extended cable TV, video games, CD players, Web TV, high-speed Internet, dual phone lines, voice mail, safes, honor bars, irons, hair dryers. *Some:* fax. **Dining:** dining room, restaurant, 6:30 am-midnight, $29-$37, cocktails, also, The Dining Room, see separate listing, entertainment. **Pool(s):** heated indoor. **Leisure Activities:** steamroom. *Fee:* sauna, whirlpool, aerobic instruction. **Guest Services:** gift shop, massage (fee), afternoon tea, valet laundry. **Business Services:** conference facilities, business center, administrative services, PC, fax (fee). **Cards:** AX, CB, DC, DS, JC, MC, VI. **Special Amenities:** free newspaper.

SOME UNITS

🛏️ 🍴 24️⃣ 🍸 🏋️M ✋ 🌀 🏊 ⊞ ⊠ 🔼 [DATA PORT] 📠 / ⊠ [VCR] 🔲 📼 📱 /
FEE FEE

THE SENECA HOTEL & SUITES

Phone: (312)787-8900 🔢

ⒶⒶⒶ SAVE ◆◆◆ Hotel

All Year [CP] 1P: $129-$199 2P: $129-$199 XP: $20 F18
Location: Just e of Michigan Ave. 200 E Chestnut St 60611. Fax: 312/988-4438. **Facility:** 130 units. 52 one-bedroom standard units. 78 one-bedroom suites ($149-$279). 17 stories, interior corridors. **Parking:** *Fee:* off-site and valet. **Terms:** cancellation fee imposed. **Amenities:** extended cable TV. **Dining:** 2 restaurants, deli, 7:30 am-11:30 pm, $8-$35, cocktails. **Leisure Activities:** sun deck, exercise room. **Guest Services:** valet and coin laundry. **Business Services:** meeting rooms, business center, fax (fee). **Cards:** AX, CB, DC, DS, JC, MC, VI. **Special Amenities:** free newspaper and free room upgrade (subject to availability with advanced reservations).** *(See color ad below)*

SOME UNITS

[S/D] 🍴 🍸 [DATA PORT] 🔲 📱 📠 / ⊠ /

SHERATON CHICAGO HOTEL & TOWERS

Phone: (312)464-1000 🔢

ⒶⒶⒶ SAVE ◆◆◆ Hotel

All Year 1P: $169-$399 2P: $169-$399 XP: $30 F17
Location: Columbus Dr at Chicago River, just e of Michigan Ave. 301 E North Water St 60611. Fax: 312/464-9140. **Facility:** 1209 units. 1176 one-bedroom standard units. 33 one-bedroom suites ($500-$3500). 34 stories, interior corridors. *Bath:* combo or shower only. **Parking:** valet only (fee). **Terms:** cancellation fee imposed, package plans, small pets only ($100 deposit). **Amenities:** video games (fee), voice mail, safes, honor bars, irons, hair dryers. *Some:* fax. **Dining:** dining room, 2 restaurants, coffee shop, 6 am-11 pm, $9-$45, cocktails. **Pool(s):** heated indoor. **Leisure Activities:** saunas, sun deck. **Guest Services:** gift shop, massage (fee), valet laundry. **Business Services:** conference facilities, business center. *Fee:* PC, fax. **Cards:** AX, CB, DC, DS, JC, MC, VI. **Special Amenities:** free newspaper. *(See ad p 306)*

SOME UNITS

[S/D] 🛏️ 🍴 24️⃣ 🍸 ✋ 🌀 🏊 ⊞ 🔼 [DATA PORT] 📱 📠 / ⊠ [VCR] /
FEE FEE FEE

(See map p. 280)

SUMMERFIELD SUITES BY WYNDHAM

Phone: (312)787-6000 🔟2️⃣

9/3-12/14	1P: $309-$419	2P: $309-$419	XP: $30 F12
4/1-9/2	1P: $279-$389	2P: $279-$389	XP: $30 F12
1/1-3/31	1P: $249-$359	2P: $249-$359	XP: $30 F12
12/15-12/31	1P: $229-$329	2P: $229-$329	XP: $30 F12

Hotel

Location: Just e of Michigan Ave. 166 E Superior 60611. Fax: 312/787-4331. **Facility:** 120 units. 60 one-bedroom standard units. 60 one-bedroom suites ($329-$419) with kitchens. 29 stories, interior corridors. **Parking:** Fee: off-site and valet. **Terms:** check-in 4 pm, 2 night minimum stay - weekends, cancellation fee imposed. **Amenities:** extended cable TV, voice mail, irons, hair dryers. **Pool(s):** outdoor. **Leisure Activities:** exercise room. **Guest Services:** gift shop, valet and coin laundry. **Business Services:** meeting rooms. **Cards:** AX, CB, DC, DS, JC, MC, VI.

SOME UNITS

THE SUTTON PLACE HOTEL

Phone: (312)266-2100 2️⃣3️⃣

4/1-6/30	1P: $209	2P: $209	XP: $25 F18
7/1-11/30	1P: $189	2P: $189	XP: $25 F18
12/1-3/31	1P: $169	2P: $169	XP: $25 F18

Hotel

Location: Jct of Rush St. 21 E Bellevue Pl 60611. Fax: 312/266-2103. **Facility:** Appointments such as CD players, bathrobes and mahogany "Art Deco" furniture distinguish this downtown hotel. 246 units. 240 one-bedroom standard units. 6 one-bedroom suites. **Parking:** valet only (fee). **Terms:** cancellation fee imposed, package plans, small pets only ($250 deposit). **Amenities:** CD players, dual phone lines, voice mail, honor bars, irons, hair dryers. Fee: video games, high-speed Internet. Some: safes. **Dining:** restaurant, 6 am-11 pm, $12-$27, cocktails. **Leisure Activities:** exercise room. **Guest Services:** valet laundry, area transportation-Loop area. **Business Services:** meeting rooms, business center. Fee: PC, fax. **Cards:** AX, CB, DC, DS, JC, MC, VI. **Special Amenities:** free local telephone calls and free newspaper. (See color ad below)

SOME UNITS

FEE   FEE

SWISSOTEL CHICAGO

Phone: (312)565-0565 4️⃣2️⃣

4/1-6/15 & 9/4-11/30	1P: $299-$349	2P: $299-$349	XP: $20 F12
6/16-9/3 & 12/1-3/31	1P: $239-$279	2P: $239-$279	XP: $20 F12

Hotel

Location: Just e of Michigan Ave. 323 E Wacker Dr 60601. Fax: 312/565-0540. **Facility:** Marble-accented bathrooms and large, contemporary-style guest rooms with downtown and lake views enhance this conference hotel. 632 units. 597 one-bedroom standard units. 35 one-bedroom suites, some with whirlpools. 43 stories, interior corridors. Bath: combo or shower only. **Parking:** valet only (fee). **Terms:** cancellation fee imposed, package plans. **Amenities:** dual phone lines, voice mail, honor bars, irons, hair dryers. Some: CD players, high-speed Internet (fee), fax. **Dining:** restaurant, coffee shop, 6 am-11 pm, $9-$32, cocktails. **Pool(s):** heated indoor. **Leisure Activities:** sauna, whirlpool. **Guest Services:** gift shop, massage (fee), valet laundry. **Business Services:** conference facilities, business center. Fee: administrative services, PC, fax. **Cards:** AX, CB, DC, DS, JC, MC, VI. **Special Amenities:** free newspaper and free room upgrade (subject to availability with advanced reservations).

SOME UNITS

FEE FEE   FEE

(See map p. 280)

W CHICAGO CITY CENTER

▽▽▽▽ Classic Hotel

			Phone: (312)332-1200	**30**
	4/16-12/31	1P: $219-$279	XP: $25	F18
	1/1-3/31	1P: $169-$209	XP: $25	F18
	4/1-4/15	1P: $149-$179	XP: $25	F18

Location: Between LaSalle and Wells sts. 172 W Adams St 60603-3604. Fax: 312/332-5909. **Facility:** Historic. 390 units. 388 one-bedroom standard units. 2 one-bedroom suites. 22 stories, interior corridors. *Bath:* combo or shower only. **Parking:** valet only (fee). **Terms:** 7 day cancellation notice-fee imposed, small pets only. **Amenities:** extended cable TV, video tape library, CD players, Web TV (fee), dual phone lines, voice mail, safes, honor bars, irons, hair dryers. *Some:* fax. **Leisure Activities:** exercise room. **Guest Services:** gift shop, valet laundry. **Business Services:** conference facilities. **Cards:** AX, CB, DC, DS, JC, MC, VI.

SOME UNITS
(ASK) 🛏 🍴 📺 🛗 📞 VCR 🐾 DATA PORT 💻 🖨 / ⊠ 🧴 /
FEE

WESTIN CHICAGO RIVER NORTH

AAA SAVE ▽▽▽▽ Hotel

				Phone: (312)744-1900	**26**
	All Year	1P: $169-$399	2P: $169-$399	XP: $30	F17

Location: Just n of Chicago River; between Dearborn St and Clark. 320 N Dearborn St 60610. Fax: 312/527-2650. **Facility:** 424 units. 407 one-bedroom standard units. 17 one-bedroom suites ($650-$2900), some with whirlpools. 20 stories, interior corridors. **Parking:** valet only (fee). **Terms:** cancellation fee imposed, package plans, small pets only ($75 deposit). **Amenities:** video games (fee), dual phone lines, voice mail, honor bars, irons, hair dryers. *Some:* CD players. **Dining:** dining room, 6 am-11 pm, $16-$26, cocktails, entertainment. **Leisure Activities:** saunas. **Guest Services:** gift shop, massage (fee), valet laundry. **Business Services:** conference facilities, business center. *Fee:* PC, fax. **Cards:** AX, CB, DC, DS, JC, MC, VI. **Special Amenities:** free newspaper. *(See ad below)*

SOME UNITS
🅢🅓 🛏 🍴 24⏰ 📺 📞 ♨ 🐾 DATA PORT 💻 🖨 / ⊠ /
FEE FEE

THE WESTIN MICHIGAN AVENUE CHICAGO

AAA SAVE ▽▽▽▽ Hotel

				Phone: (312)943-7200	**6**
	9/4-12/31	1P: $219-$399	2P: $244-$424	XP: $25	F16
	4/1-6/30	1P: $219-$369	2P: $244-$394	XP: $25	F16
	7/1-9/3	1P: $179-$339	2P: $204-$364	XP: $25	F16
	1/1-3/31	1P: $179-$319	2P: $204-$344	XP: $25	F16

Location: Across from John Hancock Center. 909 N Michigan Ave 60611. Fax: 312/397-5580. **Facility:** 751 units. 723 one-bedroom standard units. 28 one-bedroom suites. 16-27 stories, interior corridors. *Bath:* some combo or shower only. **Parking:** valet only (fee). **Terms:** cancellation fee imposed, package plans, small pets only. **Amenities:** video games (fee), dual phone lines, voice mail, safes, honor bars, irons, hair dryers. *Some:* fax. **Dining:** dining room, coffee shop, 6:30 am-10 pm, $18-$30, cocktails. **Leisure Activities:** saunas, exercise room. **Guest Services:** gift shop, massage (fee), valet laundry. **Business Services:** conference facilities, business center, PC, fax. **Cards:** AX, CB, DC, DS, JC, MC, VI. **Special Amenities:** free newspaper and free room upgrade (subject to availability with advanced reservations). *(See color ad below)*

SOME UNITS
🛏 🍴 24⏰ 📺 🛗M 📞 🐾 ♨ DATA PORT 💻 🖨 / ⊠ VCR /
FEE

(See map p. 280)

WHITEHALL HOTEL   **Phone: (312)944-6300**   44

AAA SAVE

4/1-10/31	1P: $189-$339	2P: $209-$359	XP: $15 F18
11/1-3/31	1P: $159-$339	2P: $179-$359	XP: $15 F18

Location: Just w of Michigan Ave. 105 E Delaware Pl 60611. Fax: 312/944-8552. **Facility:** This historic property is in a prime location; a bistro is on site. 221 units. 213 one-bedroom standard units. 8 one-bedroom suites ($575-$1200). 21 stories, interior corridors. **Parking:** valet only (fee). **Terms:** cancellation fee imposed, package plans, small pets only ($100 deposit). **Amenities:** dual phone lines, voice mail, safes, honor bars, irons, hair dryers. *Fee:* video games, Web TV. *Some:* CD players, fax. **Dining:** dining room, 7 am-1 am, $12-$29, cocktails. **Leisure Activities:** exercise room. **Guest Services:** valet laundry, area transportation-within 2 mi. **Business Services:** meeting rooms, fax. **Cards:** AX, DC, DS, JC, MC, VI. **Special Amenities:** free newspaper.

Hotel

SOME UNITS

[icons] FEE   FEE   / VCR /

WYNDHAM CHICAGO   **Phone: (312)573-0300**   46

AAA SAVE

4/1-6/30	1P: $199-$259	2P: $219-$279	XP: $20 F18
9/3-3/31	1P: $189-$259	2P: $209-$279	XP: $20 F18
7/1-9/2	1P: $189-$199	2P: $209-$219	XP: $20 F18

Location: Just e of Michigan Ave at jct Erie and St Claire sts. 633 N St Claire St 60611. Fax: 312/274-0164. **Facility:** Desks, ergonomic chairs and bathrobes are among the amenities offered at this luxurious full-service hotel. 417 units. 368 one-bedroom standard units. 49 one-bedroom suites ($189-$329). 28 stories, interior corridors. **Bath:** combo or shower only. **Parking:** valet only (fee). **Terms:** cancellation fee imposed, package plans. **Amenities:** CD players, dual phone lines, voice mail, honor bars, irons, hair dryers. *Fee:* video games, Web TV, high-speed Internet. **Dining:** Caliterra Cal-Ital Bar & Grille, see separate listing, entertainment. **Pool(s):** small heated indoor. **Leisure Activities:** sauna, whirlpool, steamroom, exercise room. **Guest Services:** gift shop, massage (fee), valet laundry. **Business Services:** conference facilities, business center. *Fee:* PC, fax. **Cards:** AX, CB, DC, DS, JC, MC, VI.

Hotel

SOME UNITS

[icons] FEE   /   FEE

---

*The following lodgings were either not evaluated or did not
meet AAA rating requirements but are listed for your information only.*

COMFORT INN & SUITES DOWNTOWN   **Phone: 312/494-1515**

fyi

All Year [ECP]	1P: $139-$249	2P: $149-$259	XP: $10 F18

Too new to rate, opening scheduled for March 2002. **Location:** I-90/94, exit 50B, 1.5 mi e. 15 E Ohio St 60611 (1017 W Belmont Ave, CHICAGO, 60657). **Amenities:** radios, coffeemakers, microwaves, refrigerators. **Terms:** cancellation fee imposed. **Cards:** AX, CB, DC, DS, MC, VI. *(See color ad below)*

Motor Inn

(See map p. 280)

EMBASSY SUITES HOTEL CHICAGO DOWNTOWN LAKEFRONT   Phone: 312/836-5900
(fyi)   All Year   1P: $139-$399   2P: $159-$419   XP: $20   F18
        Too new to rate. **Location:** I-90/94, exit Ohio St, just e. 511 N Columbus Dr 60611. **Fax:** 312/836-5901.
Motel   **Amenities:** radios, coffeemakers, microwaves, refrigerators, pool. **Terms:** cancellation fee imposed.
        (See color ad p 308)

──────── **WHERE TO DINE** ────────

312 CHICAGO   **Lunch:** $11-$22   **Dinner:** $11-$26   **Phone:** 312/696-2420   33
▼▼▼   **Location:** Jct Randolph and LaSalle sts; in Hotel Allegro Chicago. 136 N LaSalle St 60602. **Hours:** 7-10 am, 11-3 &
          5-10 pm, Fri & Sat-11 pm. Closed major holidays. **Reservations:** suggested. **Features:** dressy casual;
American Sunday brunch; health conscious menu items; cocktails; a la carte. Near many major theaters in the heart
          of the city, the popular, casual restaurant builds its menu around Italian-inspired American cuisine prepared
with fresh ingredients. A prix-fixe theater menu is available for guests needing to get to the theater on time. **Parking:** valet only
(fee). **Cards:** AX, CB, DC, DS, MC, VI.

BEN PAO   **Lunch:** $10-$15   **Dinner:** $9-$18   **Phone:** 312/222-1888   29
▼▼▼   **Location:** Jct Illinois and Dearborn sts. 52 W Illinois St 60610. **Hours:** 11:30 am-10 pm, Fri-11 pm, Sat & Sun 5
          pm-10 pm. Closed major holidays. **Reservations:** accepted. **Features:** dressy casual; cocktails & lounge;
Chinese   a la carte. A stylish, contemporary decor and fun, bustling atmosphere breathe life into the upscale
          restaurant. Enjoy the moist texture of the shrimp dumplings. Spicy peppers add punch to the kung pao
chicken. Save room for one of the delicious desserts. **Parking:** valet only (fee). **Cards:** AX, CB, DC, DS, JC, MC, VI.

BICE RISTORANTE   **Lunch:** $8-$20   **Dinner:** $11-$24   **Phone:** 312/664-1474   40
▼▼▼   **Location:** Just e of Michigan Ave. 158 E Ontario St 60611. **Hours:** 11:30 am-10:30 pm, Fri & Sat-11:30 pm.
          Closed: 1/1, 12/25. **Reservations:** accepted. **Features:** casual dress; cocktails & lounge; a la carte. The
Italian   setting is sleek with contemporary dining rooms and a wait staff to match. Fine Northern Italian cuisine, the
          likes of rigatoni with meat sauce, is presented with flair. Patio dining is available in summer; valet parking
is offered at dinner. **Parking:** on-site. **Cards:** AX, DC, DS, MC, VI.

BISTRO 110   **Lunch:** $9-$20   **Dinner:** $12-$28   **Phone:** 312/266-3110   9
▼▼▼   **Location:** Jct Pearson St and Michigan Ave; across from Water Tower Square. 110 E Pearson St 60611.
          Hours: 11:30 am-11 pm, Fri & Sat-midnight, Sun-10 pm. Closed major holidays. **Reservations:** suggested.
French   **Features:** casual dress; Sunday brunch; children's menu; carryout; cocktails; a la carte. This fast-paced
          bistro features a wood-burning oven and an array of delectable grilled and roasted entrees. Enjoy both the
taste and the colorful presentation of roasted chicken with a melange of similarly prepared vegetables. Valet parking is offered
after 5 pm. **Parking:** on-site. **Cards:** AX, CB, DC, DS, MC, VI.

BLACKHAWK LODGE   **Lunch:** $12-$19   **Dinner:** $16-$30   **Phone:** 312/280-4080   42
▼▼▼   **Location:** Superior at Wabash. 41 E Superior 60611. **Hours:** 11:30 am-2 & 5-10 pm, Fri-11 pm, Sat 5 pm-11
          pm, Sun 10 am-3 & 5-10 pm. Closed major holidays. **Reservations:** suggested. **Features:** dressy casual;
American Sunday brunch; children's menu; carryout; cocktails & lounge; a la carte. Imaginative American cuisine is
          evident at each seating and served in a rustically casual dining room. The moist brick oven baked Atlantic
Salmon is colorfully presented and delicious. Service is welcoming and capable. **Parking:** on-site and valet (fee). **Cards:** AX,
DC, DS, MC, VI.

CAFE IBERICO   **Lunch:** $6-$13   **Dinner:** $6-$13   **Phone:** 312/573-1510   43
▼▼   **Location:** Between Chicago and Superior. 739 N LaSalle St 60610. **Hours:** 11 am-11 pm, Fri-1:30 am, Sat
          noon-1:30 am, Sun noon-11 pm. Closed major holidays. **Reservations:** accepted. **Features:** casual dress;
Spanish   carryout; cocktails & lounge; a la carte. Bright colors boost the energy level in this lively, festive restaurant.
          The casual eatery features an extensive menu of Spanish tapas and an impressive selection of
international beers. Caramel flan served with fresh mixed berries is exceptional. **Parking:** street. **Cards:** AX, DC, DS, MC, VI.

CALITERRA CAL-ITAL BAR & GRILLE   **Lunch:** $11-$24   **Dinner:** $13-$35   **Phone:** 312/274-4444   15
▼▼▼   **Location:** Just e of Michigan Ave at jct Erie and St Claire sts; in Wyndham Chicago. 633 N St Claire St 60611.
          Hours: 6:30 am-11 pm. **Reservations:** suggested. **Features:** dressy casual; children's menu; cocktails &
California lounge; entertainment; a la carte, also prix fixe. The creative chef masterfully fuses Italian and Northern
          Californian influences in the open kitchen of the moderately upscale dining room. Such dishes as the
signature porcini-crusted halibut are flavorful and eye catching. The wine list is extensive. **Parking:** valet only (fee).
Cards: AX, CB, DC, DS, JC, MC, VI.

CAPE COD ROOM   **Lunch:** $15-$35   **Dinner:** $35-$60   **Phone:** 312/440-8486   5
▼▼▼   **Location:** N Michigan Ave at Lake Shore Dr and Walton Pl; in The Drake Hotel, Chicago. 140 E Walton Pl 60611.
          Hours: 11:30 am-2:30 & 4:30-11 pm, Sat & Sun 11:30 am-11 pm. Closed: 12/25.
Seafood   **Reservations:** suggested. **Features:** dressy casual; cocktails. A cozy, intimate atmosphere envelops the
          relaxed restaurant, which benefits from such decor touches as wooden beams, hanging copper pots and
red-checked tablecloths. Zesty Maryland crab cakes, bookbinder soup and fresh Dover sole are favorite dishes. **Parking:**
on-site and valet (fee). **Cards:** AX, CB, DC, DS, JC, MC, VI.

CHICAGO-A BAR & GRILL   **Lunch:** $8-$15   **Dinner:** $12-$26   **Phone:** 312/856-1844   25
▼▼   **Location:** E Randolph at Michigan Ave; in Prudential Plaza. 120 E Randolph St 60601. **Hours:** 11 am-9 pm, Fri-10
          pm. Closed major holidays; also Sat & Sun. **Reservations:** accepted. **Features:** dressy casual; children's
American menu; carryout; cocktails & lounge. On the menu are lots of choices of chicken, seafood, beef, salads,
          soups and sandwiches. The plentiful lobster and rock shrimp salad certainly doesn't skimp on seafood. The
Tollhouse tart—vanilla ice cream, chocolate sauce and chopped pecans—is a real sweet-tooth pleaser. **Parking:** on-site.
Cards: AX, DC, DS, MC, VI.

(See map p. 280)

CHICAGO CHOP HOUSE   Historical   **Lunch:** $10-$17   **Dinner:** $16-$30   **Phone:** 312/787-7100   ③
Steak House   **Location:** Between Clark and Dearborn sts. 60 W Ontario St 60610. **Hours:** 11:30 am-11 pm, Fri-11:30 pm, Sat 4 pm-11:30 pm, Sun 4 pm-11 pm. Closed major holidays. **Reservations:** suggested. **Features:** dressy casual; cocktails & lounge. Patrons dine on aged prime steak, lamb, veal, chicken and seafood while surrounded by oak-paneled walls sporting Chicago photographs taken 1830-1930. The New York strip steak is remarkable, as is the excellent wine selection. **Parking:** Fee: on-site and valet. **Cards:** AX, CB, DC, DS, JC, MC, VI.
✕

CIELO   **Lunch:** $8-$18   **Dinner:** $12-$29   **Phone:** 312/944-7676   ㉟
Regional American   **Location:** N Michigan Ave at Huron St; in Omni Chicago Hotel. 676 N Michigan Ave 60611. **Hours:** 6:30 am-10 pm, Fri & Sat-11 pm. **Reservations:** suggested. **Features:** dressy casual; Sunday brunch; children's menu; cocktails & lounge. Entree selections run the gamut, but all are faithful to Cielo's signature Italian cuisine accented by Mediterranean influences. Pizza and grilled entrees are cooked on a wood-burning stove. A variety of healthy, light entrees also is served. **Parking:** on-site and valet (fee). **Cards:** AX, CB, DC, DS, JC, MC, VI.
♿M ✕

COCO PAZZO RESTAURANT   **Lunch:** $10-$16   **Dinner:** $14-$29   **Phone:** 312/836-0900   ㊺
Italian   **Location:** Hubbard St at Franklin St. 300 W Hubbard St 60610. **Hours:** 11:30 am-2:30 & 5:30-10:30 pm, Fri & Sat-11:30 pm, Sun 5 pm-10 pm. Closed major holidays. **Reservations:** suggested. **Features:** dressy casual; cocktails; a la carte. The cozy, inviting loft boasts contemporary styling, crisp white linen tabletops, open kitchen and a festive energetic ambience. The menu features inventive preparations of classic Tuscan Italian cuisine. The signature preparation is the Leg of Lamb that is finished in their wood burning oven and attractively presented. The flourless chocolate cake is served warm and is outstanding in flavor, a decadent diet-breaker. **Parking:** valet only (fee). **Cards:** AX, CB, DC, MC, VI.
✕

CUISINES   **Lunch:** $11-$18   **Dinner:** $12-$28   **Phone:** 312/795-3330   ㉞
Mediterranean   **Location:** Jct State St and Wacker Dr; in Renaissance Chicago Hotel. 1 W Wacker Dr 60601. **Hours:** 11:30 am-2 & 5:30-9 pm, Sat from 5:30 pm. Closed major holidays; also Sun. **Reservations:** suggested. **Features:** dressy casual; cocktails & lounge; a la carte. Lending to the luxurious atmosphere are fresh flowers, lovely fabric seat coverings, elegant table settings and oak wine cabinets on opposite sides of the dining room. Fine grilled specialties include swordfish, tuna, salmon, shrimp, filet mignon, lamb chops and veal medallions. **Parking:** on-site and valet (fee). **Cards:** AX, CB, DC, DS, MC, VI.
♿M ✕

THE DINING ROOM   **Dinner:** $29-$37   **Phone:** 312/573-5223   ⑪
French   **Location:** Jct N Michigan Ave and E Pearson St; in Water Tower Place; in The Ritz-Carlton, Chicago (A Four Seasons Hotel). 160 E Pearson 60611. **Hours:** 6 pm-11 pm, Sun-10 pm. **Reservations:** suggested. **Features:** semi-formal attire; Sunday brunch; cocktails & lounge; a la carte. Striking creations of modern French cuisine include such dishes as roasted salmon with truffle potato terrine and Maine lobster with golden potato ravioli. Mahogany-paneled walls and cut-glass chandeliers adorn the dining room. **Parking:** off-site and valet (fee). **Cards:** AX, CB, DC, DS, JC, MC, VI.
♿M ✕

ED DEBEVIC'S   **Lunch:** $4-$9   **Dinner:** $4-$9   **Phone:** 312/664-1707   ⑲
American   **Location:** Jct N Wells and W Ontario sts. 640 N Wells St 60610. **Hours:** 11 am-11 pm, Fri & Sat-1 am, Sun-10 pm. Closed: 11/28, 12/25. **Features:** casual dress; carryout; cocktails; a la carte. A modern version of a 1950s diner, the whimsical, friendly restaurant is ultra-casual and tilts toward the downright wacky. Costumed servers are amusing for the often incompetent and rude, but always good-spirited, service they intentionally provide. **Parking:** street and valet (fee). **Cards:** AX, DC, DS, MC, VI.
✕

ENTRE NOUS   **Dinner:** $19-$36   **Phone:** 312/565-7997   ㉖
American   **Location:** Jct Michigan Ave and E Pearson St, just e; in The Fairmont Chicago. 200 N Columbus 60601. **Hours:** 5:30 pm-10:30 pm. Closed: 7/4; also Sun & Mon. **Reservations:** suggested. **Features:** dressy casual; cocktails & lounge; a la carte. A sophisticated atmosphere prevails in the stately and elegant dining room, which is made comfortable by the gracious manner exhibited by the experienced service staff. Expertly prepared food can be described as contemporary American with a distinct Asian influence. Smoke free premises. **Parking:** valet only (fee). **Cards:** AX, CB, DC, DS, JC, MC, VI.
✕

EVEREST   **Dinner:** $33-$44   **Phone:** 312/663-8920   ㊾
French   **Location:** Jct Congress Pkwy and LaSalle St; on 40th Floor at One Financial Place. 440 S LaSalle St 60605. **Hours:** seatings from 5:30 pm-9 pm, Fri & Sat-10 pm. Closed major holidays; also Sun & Mon. **Reservations:** required. **Features:** semi-formal attire; cocktails; a la carte, also prix fixe. Alsatian influences flavor the exhilarating French cuisine of chef Jean Joho. Diners can select from a la carte, pre-theater and six-course degustation menus. Mirrored walls, leopard-print carpet, luxurious table settings and a dramatic view of the city lights 40 floors below make this a perfect spot for a special-occasion meal. **Parking:** on-site. **Cards:** AX, CB, DC, JC, MC, VI.
✕

FRONTERA GRILL/TOPOLOBAMPO   **Lunch:** $7-$14   **Dinner:** $10-$21   **Phone:** 312/661-1434   ⑱
Regional Mexican   **Location:** Between Hubbard and Illinios sts. 445 N Clark St 60610. **Hours:** 11:30 am-2:30 & 5:30-10 pm, Fri-11 pm, Sat 10:30 am-2:30 & 5-11 pm. Closed major holidays; also Sun & Mon. **Reservations:** accepted. **Features:** casual dress; children's menu; cocktails & lounge; a la carte. Brilliantly prepared and artfully presented meals are served in Frontera's casual, festive atmosphere. The flavorful pork tenderloin atop a bed of sweet potatoes and accompanied by fried bananas is most memorable. Outdoor dining is available. **Parking:** valet only (fee). **Cards:** AX, CB, DC, DS, MC, VI.
✕

(See map p. 280)

GIBSONS BAR & STEAKHOUSE   Dinner: $19-$41   Phone: 312/266-8999   53
Steak House
Location: Corner of Bellevue Pl and Rush St. 1028 N Rush St 60611. **Hours:** 5 pm-midnight. **Reservations:** suggested. **Features:** dressy casual; carryout; cocktails & lounge; entertainment; a la carte. The atmosphere is bustling amid an old-fashioned steakhouse ambience. Huge portions of tender prime aged beef are the hands-down attraction for locals and visitors alike. Lamb, pork, veal and a few seafood entrees are also served by an experienced staff. **Parking:** street and valet (fee). **Cards:** AX, DC, DS, MC, VI.

HARRY CARAY'S RESTAURANT   Lunch: $9-$20   Dinner: $11-$33   Phone: 312/828-0966   79
Steak House
Location: Jct Dearborn and Kinzie, just w of State St. 33 W Kinzie 60610. **Hours:** 11:30 am-3 & 5-10:30 pm, Fri & Sat-11 pm, Sun 4 pm-10 pm. Closed major holidays. **Reservations:** accepted. **Features:** casual dress; children's menu; cocktails & lounge; a la carte. As you might expect from a restaurant bearing the name of the beloved Cubs announcer, the popular steakhouse has a decidedly sports-oriented theme. Expect large portions of Italian-American food including plenty of prime-aged beef, pasta and seafood. **Parking:** valet only (fee). **Cards:** AX, DC, DS, MC, VI.

HUBBARD STREET GRILL   Lunch: $10-$14   Dinner: $10-$24   Phone: 312/222-0770   59
American
Location: Just w of Orleans St. 351 W Hubbard St 60610. **Hours:** 11:30 am-9 pm, Fri-10 pm, Sat 5 pm-10 pm. Closed major holidays; also Sun. **Reservations:** suggested. **Features:** casual dress; carryout; cocktails & lounge; a la carte. Ample portions of such hearty fare as filet mignon, herb roasted chicken, barbecue ribs and grilled shrimp with pasta are the draw at the laid-back restaurant. The black bean soup is thick and flavorful. Servers are prompt and knowledgeable. **Parking:** street and valet (fee). **Cards:** AX, DC, DS, MC, VI.

THE INDIAN GARDEN   Lunch: $8   Dinner: $9-$20   Phone: 312/280-4910   13
Northern Indian
Location: Just e of Michigan Ave. 247 E Ontario St, 2nd Floor 60611. **Hours:** 11 am-2:30 & 5-10 pm, Fri-10:30 pm, Sat & Sun noon-2:45 & 5-10 pm. Closed: 1/1. **Reservations:** accepted. **Features:** casual dress; carryout; cocktails; a la carte. Thoughtfully prepared dishes of northern Indian cuisine are piquant and delicious. Sizzling plates of tandoori chicken and mouthwatering white flour bread are among items on the well-labeled lunch buffet. Steep stairs lead into the restaurant. **Parking:** street and valet (fee). **Cards:** AX, DS, MC, VI.

THE ITALIAN VILLAGE   Lunch: $8-$17   Dinner: $11-$22   Phone: 312/332-7005   22
Italian
Location: Between Dearborn and Clark sts. 71 W Monroe 60603. **Hours:** 11:30 am-2 am, Sun noon-midnight. Closed: 11/28, 12/25. **Reservations:** suggested. **Features:** dressy casual; carryout; cocktails & lounge; a la carte. Traditional and contemporary Italian cuisine is served in three dining rooms by an attentive and knowledgeable wait staff. Large portions of well prepared food are featured at this locally popular dining spot. Pollo a la Vesuvio is the house specialty. **Parking:** street and valet (fee). **Cards:** AX, CB, DC, DS, MC, VI.

KAMEHACHI   Lunch: $7-$18   Dinner: $9-$25   Phone: 312/664-3663   63
Japanese
Location: I-94, exit North Ave, 3 mi e to Wells St, then 3 blks s. 1400 N Wells St 60610. **Hours:** 11:30 am-2 & 5-12:30 am, Fri & Sat-1:30 am, Sun 4:30 pm-11:30 pm. Closed major holidays. **Reservations:** accepted. **Features:** casual dress; carryout; cocktails; a la carte. Sushi and sashimi are among traditional offerings at the small, comfortable restaurant. Wander through the delightful garden in the back or enjoy the Western style tatami room or private dining room. The competent service staff is cordial and efficient. **Parking:** street and valet (fee). **Cards:** AX, CB, DC, DS, MC, VI.

KLAY OVEN   Lunch: $9-$15   Dinner: $15-$25   Phone: 312/527-3999   64
Ethnic
Location: Orleans at Hubbard St. 414 N Orleans St 60610. **Hours:** 11:30 am-2:30 & 5:30-10 pm, Fri & Sat noon-3 & 5:30-10 pm. Closed major holidays. **Reservations:** suggested. **Features:** casual dress; cocktails & lounge; a la carte. Northern Indian cuisine prevails, with clay-oven dishes such as rack of lamb and tiger prawns taking center stage. A recent meal consisted of tender chicken kabob with sweet and sour sauce and vegetarian rice with potatoes and peppers throughout. **Parking:** street. **Cards:** AX, DC, MC, VI.

LAWRY'S-THE PRIME RIB   Lunch: $6-$14   Dinner: $25-$39   Phone: 312/787-5000   16
American
Location: Between N Michigan Ave and Rush St. 100 E Ontario St 60611. **Hours:** 11:30 am-2 & 5-10:30 pm, Fri-11 pm, Sat from 5 pm, Sun 3 pm-10 pm. Closed: 12/25. **Reservations:** suggested. **Features:** dressy casual; children's menu; cocktails & lounge. A distinguished eatery known for it's single dinner entree of roasted prime rib that is carved and prepared tableside according to each guest's desire. Lawry's has expanded its menu to now offer lobster and fresh fish. The atmosphere is reminiscent of an elegant English manor featuring cherry wood walls, chandeliers, high back brown leather chairs and brass framed paintings that are individually lighted. Lunch is self-service and valet parking is available at dinner only. **Parking:** on-site and valet (fee). **Cards:** AX, CB, DC, DS, JC, MC, VI.

LES NOMADES   Dinner: $72   Phone: 312/649-9010   23
French
Location: Just e of N Michigan Ave. 222 E Ontario St 60611. **Hours:** 5 pm-10 pm. Closed major holidays; also Sun & Mon. **Reservations:** suggested. **Features:** semi-formal attire; cocktails & lounge; prix fixe, a la carte. The restaurant nurtures a quiet, refined, intimate atmosphere. After passing through a narrow gate and up a few steps through the narrow entry door, diners reach a cozy, elegant salon with crisp white linen tablecloths and a shimmering flower petal chandelier. The seasoned chef's contemporary French food reflects a distinct Asian influence. Servers exhibit a quiet professionalism in their manner with guests. Smoke free premises. **Parking:** street and valet (fee). **Cards:** AX, DC, MC, VI.

(See map p. 280)

LINO'S RISTORANTE
◆◆◆
Italian

Lunch: $9-$25　　**Dinner:** $9-$25　　**Phone:** 312/266-0616　　②
Location: Just w of Wells St. 222 W Ontario St 60610. **Hours:** 11 am-11 pm. Closed major holidays; also Sun. **Reservations:** accepted. **Features:** casual dress; cocktails; a la carte. The casual, festive dining room is an inviting place in which to enjoy classic Northern Italy dishes, some of which are prepared tableside. Colorful garnishes give the offerings great eye appeal. Save room for one of the scrumptious homemade desserts. **Parking:** valet only (fee). **Cards:** AX, CB, DC, DS, MC, VI.　　✕

MAMBO GRILL
◆
Latino

Lunch: $7-$14　　**Dinner:** $9-$22　　**Phone:** 312/467-9797　　67
Location: Between Hubbard and Kinzie sts. 412 N Clark St 60610. **Hours:** 11 am-10 pm, Fri & Sat-11 pm. Closed major holidays; also Sun. **Reservations:** accepted. **Features:** casual dress; carryout; cocktails; a la carte. Well-prepared cuisine represents a creative fusion of Mexican, South American, Puerto Rican and Cuban influences. Fresh ingredients, flavorful seasonings and colorful garnishes enhance the excellent arroz con pollo. Serving sizes are substantial. **Parking:** street. **Cards:** AX, MC, VI.　　✕

MARCHE
◆◆◆
French

Lunch: $12-$19　　**Dinner:** $14-$34　　**Phone:** 312/226-8399　　70
Location: Just w of Halsted st. 833 W Randolph St 60607. **Hours:** 11:30 am-2 & 5:30-10 pm, Thurs-11 pm, Fri & Sat-midnight. Closed major holidays. **Reservations:** suggested. **Features:** dressy casual; carryout; cocktails; a la carte. A bright, whimsical circus theme awaits diners at the locally popular restaurant. Lovely plate presentations are outdone only by the skilled kitchen staff's excellent food preparation. Among well-prepared seafood dishes are grilled striped sea bass and pan-fried skate. Steak and pasta dishes round out the menu. **Parking:** street and valet (fee). **Cards:** AX, CB, DC, MC, VI.　　✕

MK
◆◆◆
American

Lunch: $11-$17　　**Dinner:** $15-$36　　**Phone:** 312/482-9179　　28
Location: Just n of W Chicago Ave. 868 N Franklin St 60610. **Hours:** 11:30 am-2 & 5:30-10 pm. Closed major holidays. **Reservations:** accepted. **Features:** dressy casual; cocktails & lounge; a la carte, also prix fixe. A trendy dining spot featuring well conceived Contemporary American cuisine. MK presents a casual atmosphere with a fashionable and airy two-level dining room that includes linen covered tables, fine crystal stemware, white walls and track lighting. The varied menu changes regularly and the food is fresh, remarkably innovative and delightful. The wait staff is casually clad but offer astute as well as welcoming service. **Parking:** street and valet (fee). **Cards:** AX, CB, DC, MC, VI.　　✕

NICK'S FISHMARKET & GRILL
◈◈◈
◆◆◆◆
Seafood

Lunch: $12-$28　　**Dinner:** $20-$48　　**Phone:** 312/621-0200　　21
Location: Jct Monroe and Clark. 51 S Clark St 60603. **Hours:** 11:30 am-2 & 5:30-10:30 pm, Fri & Sat-11 pm. Closed major holidays; also Sun. **Reservations:** suggested. **Features:** dressy casual; cocktails & lounge; a la carte. Overlooking an attractive plaza fountain, the contemporary, upscale dining room features colorful, drop-down lighting, blue-wave partitions and linen tablecloths. High-quality seafood preparations include fresh items that are flown in daily. Many Hawaiian fish are offered along with plenty of American favorites. Service is exemplary. Smoke free premises. **Parking:** valet only (fee). **Cards:** AX, CB, DC, DS, MC, VI.　　✕

PARK AVENUE CAFE
◆◆◆◆
American

Dinner: $20-$33　　**Phone:** 312/944-4414　　⑦
Location: Just e of Michigan Ave; in Doubletree Guest Suites Chicago. 199 E Walton 60611. **Hours:** 5 pm-11:30 pm, Sun 10:30 am-2:20 & 5-10 pm. Closed: 1/1; also Super Bowl Sun. **Reservations:** suggested. **Features:** dressy casual; Sunday brunch; children's menu; cocktails & lounge; a la carte, also prix fixe. Imaginatively conceived and artistically presented dishes are served in a relaxed atmosphere. Allow the chef to delight you with his creative degustation menu, or go it on your own with the red snapper with paella. The wine list is heavily American. Hardwood floors and dim lighting along with urban Chicago views all add to the ambience and experience. **Parking:** valet only (fee). **Cards:** AX, CB, DC, DS, MC, VI.　　✕

THE PUMP ROOM
◆◆◆◆
American

Lunch: $11-$16　　**Dinner:** $21-$35　　**Phone:** 312/266-0360　　①
Location: Corner of Goethe and State Pkwy; in Omni Ambassador East. 1301 N State & Goethe St 60610. **Hours:** 6:30-10:30 am, 11:30-2:30 & 6-10 pm, Fri & Sat-11 pm, Sun 11 am-2:30 & 5:30-10 pm. **Reservations:** suggested. **Features:** dressy casual; Sunday brunch; cocktails & lounge; entertainment; a la carte, also prix fixe. The Pump Room occupies space in an elegant hotel and is just a short walk from the city's bustling theatre and business district. The cuisine is French-inspired American, well-prepared and attractively presented. The luxurious dining room features brilliant chandeliers, high ceilings, large columns and lovely floral arrangements. The walls leading into the restaurant read like a "who's who" of Hollywood movie stars, moguls and celebrities. **Parking:** valet only (fee). **Cards:** AX, CB, DC, DS, MC, VI.　　✕

RHAPSODY
◆◆◆
American

Lunch: $10-$18　　**Dinner:** $14-$25　　**Phone:** 312/786-9911　　76
Location: Just w of Michigan Ave at jct Adams St and Wabash Ave. 65 E Adams at Symphony Center 60603. **Hours:** 11:30 am-2 & 5-9 pm, Thurs-Sat to 10:30 pm. **Reservations:** suggested. **Features:** dressy casual; health conscious menu items; cocktails & lounge; a la carte. Rhapsody features an upscale festive setting overlooking a lovely garden. Guests can also enjoy the downtown views. The menu predominantly features fresh seafood and fine meats. The staff is well-trained and dressed sharply. Smoke free premises. **Parking:** valet only (fee). **Cards:** AX, DC, DS, MC, VI.　　✕

RIVA
◆◆◆
Steak & Seafood

Lunch: $7-$15　　**Dinner:** $13-$30　　**Phone:** 312/644-7482　　⑥
Location: At Navy Pier. 700 E Grand Ave 60611. **Hours:** 11:30 am-3 & 5-11 pm, Fri & Sat-midnight. **Reservations:** suggested; for dinner. **Features:** dressy casual; cocktails & lounge; a la carte. Overlooking Lake Michigan, the restaurant has a split personality: comfy and casual downstairs, upscale and semiformal upstairs. Well-prepared steak, seafood and pasta entrees mingle with raw bar offerings. The white chocolate cheesecake is a must. **Parking:** Fee: on-site and valet. **Cards:** AX, CB, DC, DS, MC, VI.　　✕

(See map p. 280)

RL
~~~ ~~~
American
DC, DS, MC, VI.

Lunch: $13-$21   Dinner: $17-$35   Phone: 312/475-1100   ⑩
Location: Just e of N Michigan Ave. 115 E Chicago Ave 60611. **Hours:** 11:30 am-10 pm, Fri & Sat-11 pm, Sun noon-5 pm. **Reservations:** suggested. **Features:** dressy casual; cocktails & lounge. On the Magnificent Mile, this upscale eatery features well-prepared Italian cuisine. The presentations are clever, and service is capable. Beautiful artwork and dark wood molding completes the setting. **Parking:** on-site. **Cards:** AX, CB,
☒

RON OF JAPAN
~~~ ~~~
Japanese
MC, VI.

Dinner: $16-$50   Phone: 312/644-6500   ⑰
Location: Between Fairbanks and St Claire sts, e of Michigan Ave. 230 E Ontario St 60611. **Hours:** 5 pm-9:30 pm, Fri & Sat-10 pm, Sun 4:30 pm-9:30 pm. Closed: 1/1, 11/28; also 4/4. **Reservations:** suggested. **Features:** casual dress; children's menu; cocktails. You'll enjoy the personalized service you'll receive from the chef at this popular Japanese eatery where all meals are prepared tableside. Seating around the grill is for eight so you'll have a chance to socialize with others in this festive atmosphere. **Parking:** street. **Cards:** AX, DC, DS, JC,
☒

RUSSIAN TEA TIME
~~~ ~~~
Ethnic

Lunch: $7-$15   Dinner: $15-$26   Phone: 312/360-0000   ⑰⑰
Location: Adams St at Michigan Ave. 77 E Adams St 60603. **Hours:** 11 am-11 pm, Sun & Mon-9 pm, Fri & Sat-midnight. Closed major holidays. **Reservations:** suggested; for dinner. **Features:** casual dress; carryout; cocktails; a la carte. The Russian and Soviet regional cuisine offered includes sturgeon, caviar, wild game, poultry and vegetarian courses. The fine appointments, Russian background music and friendly, knowledgeable staff make this an elegant and enjoyable dining experience. Smoke free premises. **Parking:** on-site. **Cards:** AX, CB, DC, DS, JC, MC, VI.
☒

SCOOZI!
~~~
Italian

Lunch: $7-$20   Dinner: $8-$30   Phone: 312/943-5900   ⑰⑧
Location: Just w of Orleans St. 410 W Huron St 60610. **Hours:** 11:30 am-2 & 5:30-9:30 pm, Fri & Sat 5 pm-10:30 pm, Sun 4 pm-9 pm. Closed: 11/28, 12/25. **Reservations:** suggested. **Features:** dressy casual; children's menu; carryout; cocktails & lounge; a la carte. Bruschetta, wood-roasted prosciutto and mozzarella are good starters to gourmet pizza, which sports a delicious crust and plenty of fresh toppings. The bustling trattoria also offers a wide range of pasta entrees and salads, all served by a friendly staff. **Parking:** street and valet (fee). **Cards:** AX, CB, DC, DS, MC, VI.
☒

SEASONS RESTAURANT
~~~ ~~~
American

Lunch: $13-$26   Dinner: $32-$42   Phone: 312/649-2349   ㉚
Location: Jct Michigan Ave; in Four Seasons Hotel Chicago. 120 E Delaware Pl 60611. **Hours:** 6:30-10:30 am, 11:30-2 & 6-10 pm. **Reservations:** suggested. **Features:** semi-formal attire; Sunday brunch; children's menu; cocktails & lounge; a la carte, also prix fixe. Full-length drapes, crown molding, chandeliers and sconces set a decidedly elegant mood in the traditional dining room. Striking presentation characterizes such confident, imaginative cuisine as Colorado rack of lamb with an array of colorful sauces. **Parking:** on-site and valet (fee). **Cards:** AX, CB, DC, DS, JC, MC, VI.
🄼 ☒

SHAW'S CRAB HOUSE
~~~ ~~~
Seafood

Lunch: $11-$40   Dinner: $11-$40   Phone: 312/527-2722   ㊱
Location: Between State St and Wabash Ave. 21 E Hubbard St 60611. **Hours:** 11:30 am-2 pm, & 5:30-10 pm, Fri-11 pm, Sat 5 pm-11 pm, Sun 5 pm-10 pm. Closed: 11/28, 12/25. **Reservations:** suggested. **Features:** dressy casual; carryout; cocktails & lounge; a la carte. Large fish displays and pictures of fish hang on the walls of the relaxed restaurant, an area favorite for seasonal seafood. The grilled Alaskan halibut is served with asparagus. The casual but capable servers are well-versed in menu preparations. **Parking:** valet only (fee). **Cards:** AX, CB, DC, DS, MC, VI.
☒

THE SIGNATURE ROOM AT THE 95TH   Lunch: $9-$16   Dinner: $20-$34   Phone: 312/787-9596   ⑧
🔺
~~~ ~~~
American

Location: In John Hancock Center; Chestnut St entrance. 875 N Michigan Ave 60611. **Hours:** 11 am-2:30 & 5-10 pm, Fri & Sat-11 pm, Sun 10 am-2 & 5-10 pm. Closed: 1/1, 12/25. **Reservations:** suggested. **Features:** dressy casual; Sunday brunch; cocktails & lounge; a la carte, buffet. On the 95th floor of the John Hancock building, the busy, moderately upscale restaurant offers unmatched views of the city and Lake Michigan. The great view is not all you will get at this fine restaurant. An excellent buffet is popular at lunch and a more varied and creative menu for dinner featuring fresh seafood, duck, lamb, fine steaks and pork chops. **Parking:** on-site (fee). **Cards:** AX, DC, DS, MC, VI.
☒

SPAGO
~~~ ~~~
American
MC, VI.

Lunch: $10-$17   Dinner: $12-$34   Phone: 312/527-3700   ⑭
Location: Jct Grand Ave and Dearborn St. 520 N Dearborn St 60610. **Hours:** 11:30 am-2 & 5:30-9 pm, Sat from 5 pm. Closed major holidays; also Sun. **Reservations:** suggested. **Features:** dressy casual; cocktails & lounge; a la carte, also prix fixe. Distinct Asian influences kiss the restaurant's contemporary American dishes. Recessed and track lighting adds a touch of sophistication to the trendy, moderately upscale dining room. The in-house desserts are as attractive as they are delicious. **Parking:** street and valet (fee). **Cards:** AX, CB, DC, DS,
☒

SPIAGGIA
~~~ ~~~
Italian

Lunch: $19-$26   Dinner: $29-$40   Phone: 312/280-2750   ④
Location: Corner of Oak St and Michigan Ave; in One Magnificent Mile Bldg. 2nd Floor. 980 N Michigan Ave 60611. **Hours:** 11:30 am-2 & 5:30-9:30 pm, Fri 5:30 pm-10:30 pm, Sat-10:30 pm, Sun 5:30 pm-9 pm. Closed major holidays. **Reservations:** suggested. **Features:** semi-formal attire; cocktails & lounge; a la carte. Overlooking Lake Michigan, the posh, upscale dining room has seating on two levels. Authentic and creative regional Italian cuisine includes such dishes as wood-roasted monkfish and seared filet of beef tenderloin. The coffees are wonderful. A three course prix fixe menu available at lunch. **Parking:** on-site (fee). **Cards:** AX, CB, DC, DS, MC, VI.
☒

(See map p. 280)

SU CASA
Mexican

Lunch: $6-$11   Dinner: $9-$14   Phone: 312/943-4041   ⑫
Location: Just w of N Michigan Ave. 49 E Ontario St 60611. **Hours:** 11:30 am-11 pm, Fri & Sat-midnight. Closed: 11/28, 12/25. **Reservations:** suggested. **Features:** casual dress; carryout; cocktails & lounge; a la carte. All of the home-style Mexican menu choices are nicely prepared at this bustling eatery where the service is friendly and prompt. A recent visit found the chicken taco special with refried beans, melted cheese and tomato garnish delightful. **Parking:** on-site. **Cards:** AX, DC, DS, MC, VI.   ✕

TRATTORIA NO 10
Italian

Lunch: $12-$26   Dinner: $12-$26   Phone: 312/984-1718   ㉗
Location: Just n of Madison Ave. 10 N Dearborn St 60602. **Hours:** 11:30 am-2 & 5:30-9 pm, Fri & Sat 5:30 pm-10 pm. Closed major holidays; also Sun. **Reservations:** suggested. **Features:** dressy casual; cocktails & lounge; a la carte. An impressively cheerful and skilled staff serves contemporary Italian dishes amid the distinctive illusion of a Tuscan atmosphere. Sausage ravioli boasts a "to-die-for" sauce with wonderful seasonings. Caesar salad is delicious. **Parking:** on-site and valet (fee). **Cards:** AX, CB, DC, DS, MC, VI.   ✕

TRU
French

Dinner: $75-$125   Phone: 312/202-0001   ㉔
Location: Jct Huron and N St Claire St, just e of Michigan Ave. 676 N St Claire St 60611. **Hours:** 5:30 pm-10 pm, Fri & Sat 5 pm-11 pm. Closed major holidays; also Sun. **Reservations:** required. **Features:** semi-formal attire; cocktails & lounge; prix fixe. The dining room resembles an art gallery, with stark, white walls, high ceilings, white-draped floor-to-ceiling windows and crisp, white-linen tabletops. Spot lighting directed at each table showcases the real masterpieces: stunning food presentations accentuated by unusually shaped pieces of fine china. Remarkably well-conceived progressive French cuisine is featured on four prix-fixe menus. The wait staff is outstanding. Smoke free premises. **Parking:** street and valet (fee). **Cards:** AX, CB, DC, DS, JC, MC, VI.   ✕

VONG
Thai

Lunch: $18-$32   Dinner: $18-$32   Phone: 312/644-8664   ㉛
Location: Jct State and Hubbard sts. 6 W Hubbard St 60610. **Hours:** 11:30 am-2 & 5:30-9:30 pm, Sat 5 pm-11 pm, Sun 5 pm-9 pm. Closed major holidays. **Reservations:** suggested. **Features:** dressy casual; health conscious menu items; cocktails & lounge; a la carte, also prix fixe. Vong features a modish and sophisticated atmosphere with high ceilings, soft track lighting, floor to ceiling gold drapes and polished black granite tables. The cuisine is highly imaginative and described as Thai inspired French with the Thai influence dominant. The Black plate is perfect for those dining with others and allows you to sample five different appetizers from a single plate. The Muscovy duck breast roasted rare and served in a tamarind-sesame sauce is outstanding. **Parking:** street and valet (fee). **Cards:** AX, CB, DC, DS, MC, VI.   ✕

ZEST
Pacific Rim

Lunch: $9-$16   Dinner: $14-$22   Phone: 312/321-8766   ㉜
Location: Just n of Chicago River; in Hotel Inter-Continental Chicago. 525 N Michigan Ave 60618. **Hours:** 6 am-11 pm. **Reservations:** accepted. **Features:** casual dress; children's menu; cocktails; a la carte. The stylish, moderately upscale dining room is characterized by polished light wood floors and crisp white-linen-covered tabletops accentuated by deep blue water glasses. The menu centers on well-prepared globally influenced cuisine. The excellent trio of micro greens includes three Parmesan cups filled with greens-one cup contains tandoori duck, another, quail egg, and the third, confit of duck-and dressed with an Indonesian vinaigrette. **Parking:** on-site and valet (fee). **Cards:** AX, CB, DC, DS, JC, MC, VI.   ✕

The following restaurants have not been evaluated by AAA but are listed for your information only.

BACINO'S   [fyi]   Phone: 312/263-0070
Not evaluated. **Location:** Between Michigan and Wabash aves. 75 E Wacker Dr. On the restaurant's menu are well-prepared thin and stuffed-crust gourmet pizza.

BIN 36   [fyi]   Phone: 312/245-0333
Not evaluated. **Location:** On Chicago River; between Dearborn and State sts; in House of Blues Hotel A Loews Hotel. 333 N Dearborn St 60610. An extensive wine list complements the distinctive menu selections.

CITE   [fyi]   Phone: 312/644-4050
Not evaluated. **Location:** 505 N Lake Shore Dr. Affording Chicago skyline views, the restaurant serves such fare as steak and Maine lobster.

EMILIO'S TAPAS SOL Y NIEVE   [fyi]   Phone: 312/467-7177
Not evaluated. **Location:** 215 E Ohio St. Tapas and Spanish cuisine are served in the festive dining room.

GRACE   [fyi]   Phone: 312/928-9200
Not evaluated. **Location:** Between Jefferson and Des Plaines aves. 623 W Randolph St 60661. Well-prepared game courses include fresh rabbit, venison, wild boar and lamb.

HATSUHANA   [fyi]   Phone: 312/280-8808
Not evaluated. **Location:** 160 E Ontario St 60611. This casual restaurant features Japanese cuisine with sushi and sashimi.

HUDSON CLUB RESTAURANT & BAR   [fyi]   Phone: 312/467-1947
Not evaluated. **Location:** Between Grand and Illinois. 504 N Wells St. American cuisine and many wines by the glass are featured at this sophisticated club.

HUGO'S FROG BAR & FISH HOUSE   [fyi]   Phone: 312/640-0999
Not evaluated. **Location:** 1024 N Rush St 60611. Popular, nautical-themed restaurant featuring fresh fish.

ISAAC HAYES RIBS N' BLUES   [fyi]   Phone: 312/266-2400
Not evaluated. **Location:** 739 N Clark St 60610. Nightly jump-style blues music plays in the background in the dining room.

(See map p. 280)

KIKI'S BISTRO

(fyi)   Not evaluated. **Location:** At jct N Franklin and Locust sts. 900 N Franklin St 60610. Well-prepared offerings of French cuisine await diners at the casual restaurant.

Phone: 312/335-5454

KINZIE STREET CHOPHOUSE

(fyi)   Not evaluated. **Location:** At corner of Wells and Kinzie sts. 400 N Wells St. Adorned with paintings by Chicago artists, the chop house offers steaks, chops, seafood and pasta.

Phone: 312/822-0191

MAGNUM'S PRIME STEAKHOUSE

(fyi)   Not evaluated. **Location:** 225 W Ontario St 60610. The upscale steakhouse serves prime-aged steaks and crab, fish and lobster dishes.

Phone: 312/337-8080

MIKE DITKA'S RESTAURANT

(fyi)   Not evaluated. **Location:** In the Tremont Hotel. 100 E Chestnut St 60011. The sports-themed restaurant features American bistro fare.

Phone: 312/587-8989

MOLIVE-AN AMERICAN BISTRO

(fyi)   Not evaluated. **Location:** In Whitehall Hotel. 107 E Delaware Pl 60611. The swanky new eatery features Asian-influenced California cuisine rooted in classic Mediterranean cooking.

Phone: 312/573-6300

NACIONAL 27

(fyi)   Not evaluated. **Location:** Huron at Orleans. 325 W Huron St 60613. Cuisine from 27 South and Central American countries makes up the menu.

Phone: 312/664-2727

PALETTE'S RESTAURANT

(fyi)   Not evaluated. **Location:** Just n of Oak St; in Newberry Plaza Office/Condo Bldg. 1030 N State St 60610. The restaurant offers a funky atmosphere and contemporary American cuisine.

Phone: 312/440-5200

PAPAGUS GREEK TAVERNA

(fyi)   Not evaluated. **Location:** Corner of Ohio and State sts; in Embassy Suites Hotel Chicago-Downtown. 620 N State St 60610. Oven-roasted Greek chicken is the signature dish at the casual eatery.

Phone: 312/642-8450

QP

(fyi)   Not evaluated. **Location:** In Seneca Hotel. 200 E Chestnut St 60611. The stylish eatery presents a large menu of both Greek and American cuisine.

Phone: 312/751-2100

SAVARIN

(fyi)   Not evaluated. **Location:** 713 N Wells St. The refined restaurant presents daily tasting menus of distinguished French cuisine.

Phone: 312/255-9520

TAVERN ON RUSH

(fyi)   Not evaluated. **Location:** 1031 N Rush St. Steak, seafood, pasta and poultry are offered at the upscale steakhouse.

Phone: 312/664-9600

THYME

(fyi)   Not evaluated. **Location:** 464 N Halsted St. Innovative American cuisine and a modern decor are offered here.

Phone: 312/226-4300

TSUNAMI

(fyi)   Not evaluated. **Location:** 1160 N Dearborn. The upscale dining spot builds its menu on contemporary and eclectic Japanese cuisine.

Phone: 312/642-9911

TYPHOON

(fyi)   Not evaluated. **Location:** On level 6 at 900 N Michigan Shops. 900 N Michigan Ave 60611. Sushi and traditional Asian cuisine is served in an eclectic dining room.

Phone: 312/642-5030

CHICAGO (NORTHERN REGION)   (See map p. 284; index p. 286)

──────── WHERE TO STAY ────────

AMERISUITES CHICAGO/O'HARE

Phone: (773)867-0000   **52**

(AAA) (SAVE)   All Year   1P: $129   2P: $129   XP: $10   F18
Hotel   **Location:** I-90, exit 79B (Cumberland Ave N), just n to Higgins Rd, then just e. 8101 W Higgins Rd 60631-2916.
Fax: 773/867-0001. **Facility:** 245 one-bedroom standard units. 7-10 stories, interior corridors. *Bath:* combo or shower only. **Parking:** on-site. **Terms:** [ECP] meal plan available. **Amenities:** dual phone lines, voice mail, irons, hair dryers. *Fee:* video games, Web TV. **Pool(s):** heated indoor. **Leisure Activities:** exercise room. *Fee:* full service beauty salon. **Guest Services:** gift shop, valet and coin laundry, area transportation-within 5 mi. **Business Services:** meeting rooms, business center. *Fee:* PC, fax. **Cards:** AX, CB, DC, DS, JC, MC, VI.
Special Amenities: free continental breakfast and free newspaper. *(See color ad p 296)*   SOME UNITS

(See map p. 284)

BEST WESTERN HAWTHORNE TERRACE   Phone: (773)244-3434   55

    AAA SAVE   3/1-3/31   1P: $149-$189   2P: $159-$199   XP: $10   F12
             4/1-2/28   1P: $139-$179   2P: $149-$189   XP: $10   F12

▼▼▼▼   **Location:** Between Belmont and Addison. 3434 N Broadway 60657. Fax: 773/244-3435. **Facility:** 59 one-bedroom
Historic Motel   standard units, some with whirlpools. 4 stories, interior corridors. *Bath:* combo or shower only. **Parking:** on-site (fee). **Terms:** cancellation fee imposed, [ECP] meal plan available. **Amenities:** dual phone lines, voice mail, irons. **Leisure Activities:** sauna, whirlpool, exercise room. **Guest Services:** valet and coin laundry.
Cards: AX, CB, DC, DS, MC, VI. **Special Amenities:** free continental breakfast and free newspaper. *(See color ad below)*

SOME UNITS
⬛🛏️📺🐕🎬📠/⬛📠/

CITY SUITES HOTEL   Phone: (773)404-3400   57

    AAA SAVE   All Year   1P: $139-$189   2P: $149-$199   XP: $10   F12
▼▼▼▼   **Location:** Just w of Clark St. 933 W Belmont Ave 60657. Fax: 773/404-3405. **Facility:** 45 units. 33 one-bedroom stan-
Historic Motel   dard units. 12 one-bedroom suites. 4 stories, interior corridors. **Parking:** off-site (fee). **Terms:** 3 day cancellation notice-fee imposed, package plans. **Amenities:** extended cable TV, dual phone lines, voice mail, hair dryers. **Guest Services:** valet laundry. **Cards:** AX, CB, DC, DS, MC, VI. **Special Amenities:** free continental breakfast and free newspaper. *(See color ad p 317)*

SOME UNITS
⬛🛏️📡🎬📠⬛📠/⬛/

COMFORT INN   Phone: 773/348-2810   58

▼▼   Property failed to provide current rates
Historic Motel   **Location:** Just e of jct Clark and Broadway sts. 601 W Diversey Pkwy 60614. Fax: 773/348-1912. **Facility:** 74 units. 71 one-bedroom standard units. 3 one-bedroom suites with whirlpools. 4 stories, interior corridors. **Parking:** on-site (fee). **Amenities:** extended cable TV, voice mail. *Some:* irons, hair dryers. **Business Services:**
meeting rooms. **Cards:** AX, CB, DC, DS, JC, MC, VI.

SOME UNITS
🛏️📡🎬📠⬛/⬛📠/

DAYS INN GOLD COAST   Phone: (312)664-3040   61

    SAVE   4/1-12/4 [CP]   1P: $119-$159   2P: $119-$159   XP: $10   F16
             12/5-3/31 [CP]   1P: $89-$129   2P: $89-$129   XP: $10   F16
▼▼▼   **Location:** Just n of North Ave (SR 64); adjacent to Lincoln Park Zoo. 1816 N Clark St 60614. Fax: 312/664-0568.
Hotel   **Facility:** 236 units. 235 one-bedroom standard units. 1 one-bedroom suite with whirlpool. 13 stories, interior corridors. *Bath:* combo or shower only. **Parking:** off-site (fee). **Terms:** check-in 4 pm, cancellation fee imposed. **Amenities:** extended cable TV, voice mail, irons, hair dryers. **Business Services:** meeting rooms.
Cards: AX, DC, DS, MC, VI.

SOME UNITS
⬛🛏️🍸🎬📠⬛/⬛📠/

(See map p. 284)

DAYS INN-LINCOLN PARK NORTH   Phone: (773)525-7010 [59]

  (AAA) [SAVE]   6/1-11/30 [ECP]   1P: $106-$131   2P: $116-$141   XP: $10   F17

  ▼▼ ▼▼   4/1-5/31 & 12/1-3/31 [ECP]   1P: $101-$126   2P: $111-$136   XP: $10   F17

Location: Just w of jct Clark and Broadway sts, just e of Halsted. 644 W Diversey Pkwy 60614. Fax: 773/525-6998.

Historic Motel   **Facility:** 133 units. 129 one-bedroom standard units. 4 one-bedroom suites ($215-$230). 4 stories, interior corridors. *Bath:* combo or shower only. **Parking:** *Fee:* on-site and valet. **Terms:** cancellation fee imposed. **Amenities:** extended cable TV, voice mail, safes (fee), hair dryers. *Some:* irons. **Guest Services:** valet and coin laundry. **Business Services:** meeting rooms. **Cards:** AX, CB, DC, DS, JC, MC, VI. **Special Amenities:** free continental breakfast and free newspaper. *(See color ad below)*

SOME UNITS

[S D] [♿] [➕] [📺] [🖥] / [✕] [DATA PORT] [🔌] [🛏] [💻] /

HEART O' CHICAGO MOTEL   Phone: (773)271-9181 [54]

  (AAA) [SAVE]   All Year [CP]   1P: $75-$85   2P: $85-$95   D12

  ▼   **Location:** Corner of N Ridge Ave and Peterson, just w of Clark Ave. 5990 N Ridge Ave 60660. Fax: 773/271-6804.

Motel   **Facility:** 45 one-bedroom standard units. 2 stories, exterior corridors. **Parking:** on-site. **Cards:** AX, DC, DS, MC, VI. **Special Amenities:** free continental breakfast.

SOME UNITS

[📶] [📺] / [🖥] /

HILTON CHICAGO O'HARE AIRPORT   Phone: (773)686-8000 [53]

  (AAA) [SAVE]   All Year   1P: $159-$299   2P: $174-$314   XP: $15   F18

  ▼▼ ▼▼▼   **Location:** Opposite and connected to terminal buildings at O'Hare International Airport, accessed via I-190. (PO Box 66414 O'Hare Intl Airport, CHICAGO, 60666). Fax: 773/601-2873. **Facility:** 858 units. 846 one-bedroom standard units. 12 one-bedroom suites ($1500-$3500). 10 stories, interior corridors. **Parking:** valet only (fee).

Hotel   **Terms:** cancellation fee imposed, package plans. **Amenities:** dual phone lines, voice mail, honor bars, irons, hair dryers. *Fee:* video games, Web TV. *Some:* CD players, high-speed Internet (fee). **Dining:** 2 restaurants, 6 am-2 am, $8-$29, cocktails, entertainment. **Pool(s):** heated indoor. **Leisure Activities:** sauna, whirlpool, steamroom. *Fee:* pool, tanning bed. **Guest Services:** gift shop, massage (fee), valet laundry. **Business Services:** conference facilities, business center. *Fee:* PC, fax. **Cards:** AX, CB, DC, DS, JC, MC, VI.

SOME UNITS

[✈] [🐕] [🍴] [24] [Y] [🌀] [🏊] [♨] [✕] [📺] [DATA PORT] [💻] [🖥] / [✕] /
                FEE   FEE

(See map p. 284)

HOLIDAY INN O'HARE KENNEDY   Phone: (773)693-2323   60

Motor Inn

All Year   1P: $179   2P: $179   XP: $10   F18
Location: I-90, exit Cumberland Ave N, just n to Higgins (SR 72), then just e. 8201 W Higgins 60631. Fax: 773/693-3771. **Facility:** 122 one-bedroom standard units. 2 stories, interior corridors. *Bath:* combo or shower only. **Parking:** on-site. **Terms:** package plans. **Amenities:** dual phone lines, voice mail, safes, irons, hair dryers. *Fee:* video games, high-speed Internet. **Pool(s):** heated outdoor. **Leisure Activities:** exercise room. **Guest Services:** valet laundry. **Business Services:** meeting rooms. **Cards:** AX, CB, DC, DS, JC, MC, VI.

HYATT AT UNIVERSITY VILLAGE   Phone: (312)491-1234   64

Hotel

All Year   1P: $135-$199   2P: $160-$224   XP: $25   F18
Location: I-290, exit Ashland Ave, just s. 625 S Ashland Ave 60607. Fax: 312/529-6095. **Facility:** Designated smoking area. 114 units. 111 one-bedroom standard units. 3 one-bedroom suites. 4 stories, interior corridors. *Bath:* combo or shower only. **Parking:** valet only (fee). **Terms:** cancellation fee imposed, package plans. **Dining:** dining room, 6 am-10 pm, $9-$26, cocktails. **Leisure Activities:** exercise room. *Fee:* access to University of Illinois Chicago athletic complex. **Guest Services:** valet laundry, area transportation-within 1 mi. **Business Services:** meeting rooms, administrative services (fee). **Cards:** AX, CB, DC, DS, JC, MC, VI.

HYATT REGENCY MCCORMICK PLACE CHICAGO   Phone: (312)567-1234   63

Hotel

All Year   1P: $175-$230   2P: $200-$255   XP: $25   F18
Location: I-55, exit Martin Luther King Dr, just n at jct Cermak Rd. 2233 S Martin Luther King Dr 60616. Fax: 312/528-4000. **Facility:** An upscale convention hotel, this Hyatt offers oversize public areas tastefully appointed with modern architecture and decor. 800 units. 752 one-bedroom standard units. 48 one-bedroom suites, some with whirlpools. 33 stories, interior corridors. *Bath:* combo or shower only. **Parking:** *Fee:* on-site and valet. **Terms:** cancellation fee imposed, package plans. **Amenities:** high-speed Internet (fee), dual phone lines, voice mail, irons, hair dryers. *Some:* fax. **Dining:** restaurant, coffee shop, 6 am-3 & 5:30-11 pm, $12-$28, cocktails. **Pool(s):** outdoor lap. **Leisure Activities:** saunas, sun deck, exercise room. **Guest Services:** gift shop, valet and coin laundry, area transportation-within 6 mi. **Business Services:** conference facilities, business center. *Fee:* PC, fax. **Cards:** AX, CB, DC, DS, JC, MC, VI. *(See color ad p 295)*

MAJESTIC HOTEL   Phone: (773)404-3499   56

Historic Motel

All Year   1P: $139-$189   2P: $149-$199   XP: $10   F12
Location: Just s of Addison, then just w of Lake Shore Dr. 528 W Brompton Pl 60657. Fax: 773/404-3495. **Facility:** 52 units. 28 one-bedroom standard units. 24 one-bedroom suites. 1-4 stories, interior corridors. **Parking:** off-site (fee). **Terms:** 3 day cancellation notice-fee imposed, package plans. **Amenities:** extended cable TV, dual phone lines, voice mail, hair dryers. *Some:* irons. **Guest Services:** valet laundry. **Cards:** AX, CB, DC, DS, MC, VI. **Special Amenities:** free continental breakfast and free newspaper.
(See color ad p 317)

THE WILLOWS   Phone: (773)528-8400   62

Historic Motel

All Year   1P: $139-$189   2P: $149-$199   XP: $10   F12
Location: Just e of Broadway, just n of Diversey Pkwy. 555 W Surf St 60657 (528 W Brompton Pl, CHICAGO). Fax: 773/528-8483. **Facility:** 55 units. 51 one-bedroom standard units. 4 one-bedroom suites. 4 stories, interior corridors. *Bath:* combo or shower only. **Parking:** on-site (fee). **Terms:** 3 day cancellation notice-fee imposed, package plans. **Amenities:** extended cable TV, dual phone lines, voice mail, hair dryers. **Guest Services:** valet laundry. **Cards:** AX, CB, DC, DS, MC, VI. **Special Amenities:** free continental breakfast and free newspaper. *(See color ad p 317)*

──────── **WHERE TO DINE** ────────

AMBRIA   Dinner: $29-$34   Phone: 773/472-5959   88

French

Location: Just s of jct Fullerton Ave; in The Belden-Stratford. 2300 N Lincoln Park W 60614. **Hours:** 6 pm-9:30 pm, Fri-10:30 pm, Sat 5 pm-10:30 pm. Closed major holidays; also Sun. **Reservations:** suggested. **Features:** semi-formal attire; cocktails & lounge; a la carte, also prix fixe. The warm, wood-paneled dining room, beautiful floral arrangements and exquisite table settings create a classical backdrop for the chef's imaginative and contemporary French selections. Among degustation choices are five- and eight-course menus and a five-course vegetarian menu. A la carte selections also can be ordered. Desserts, including tempting soufflés, are sinful. Gentlemen are asked to wear jackets. Smoke free premises. **Parking:** valet only (fee). **Cards:** AX, CB, DC, DS, MC, VI.

ARUN'S   Dinner: $75   Phone: 773/539-1909   91

Thai

Location: Just n of jct Irving Park Rd. 4156 N Kedzie 60618. **Hours:** 5 pm-9 pm, Sat-10 pm. Closed major holidays; also Mon. **Reservations:** required. **Features:** dressy casual; cocktails; prix fixe. The renowned chef's creative vision shines in impeccably prepared and artfully displayed examples of Thai cuisine. The 12-course tasting menu presents innovative preparations of six appetizers, four entrees and two desserts. Entrees come all at once in Thai family-style. Each course's varied flavors and textures are sure to dazzle taste buds. Service is highly skilled and gracious. Smoke free premises. **Parking:** street and valet (fee). **Cards:** AX, CB, DC, DS, MC, VI.

(See map p. 284)

BASTA PASTA RESTAURANT   Lunch: $7-$11   Dinner: $9-$26   Phone: 773/763-0667   94
Italian
Location: Just s on Oshkosh from jct Northwest Hwy; near Park Ridge. 6733 N Olmstead 60631. **Hours:** 11:30 am-2 & 4:30-10 pm, Fri & Sat-11 pm, Sun 4 pm-9 pm. **Closed:** 11/28, 12/25; also Mon. **Features:** casual dress; carryout; cocktails & lounge. As the name states, large portions of very well-prepared Italian cuisine, with an emphasis on pasta, are served in a friendly, energetic atmosphere. Try the excellent spicy linguine with grilled chicken and peppers. The staff is knowledgeable and prompt. **Parking:** on-site and valet. **Cards:** AX, DC, MC, VI.

CAFE ABSINTHE   Dinner: $15-$26   Phone: 773/278-4488   96
Nouvelle French
Location: Corner of North and Damen aves. 1954 W North Ave 60622. **Hours:** 5:30 pm-10 pm, Fri & Sat-11 pm, Sun-9 pm. Closed major holidays. **Reservations:** suggested. **Features:** casual dress; cocktails; a la carte. The cozy, romantically lit dining room features excellently prepared and upscale French bistro cuisine. Among selections diner might find on the often-changing menu are preparations of ostrich, venison, baby octopus, skatewing, monkfish, quail, duck and lamb chops. **Parking:** on-site and valet. **Cards:** AX, MC, VI.

CAFE BA-BA-REEBA!   Lunch: $7-$10   Dinner: $15-$25   Phone: 773/935-5000   99
Spanish
Location: Just n of Armitage Ave. 2024 N Halsted St 60614. **Hours:** noon-10 pm, Fri & Sat-midnight. Closed: 11/28, 12/25. **Reservations:** suggested; weekends. **Features:** casual dress; children's menu; cocktails & lounge; a la carte. The menu emphasizes authentic Spanish cuisine and is served in friendly, spirited dining rooms. If dining alone or with friends, try the tapas (varied appetizers) when several types can be ordered and shared. The service is friendly and attentive. Outdoor patio dining in season. **Parking:** street and valet (fee). **Cards:** AX, CB, DC, DS, MC, VI.

CHARLIE TROTTER'S   Dinner: $100-$125   Phone: 773/248-6228   100
American
Location: Just w of jct Halsted St. 816 W Armitage Ave 60614. **Hours:** 6 pm-10 pm. Closed major holidays; also Sun, Mon & last week of March. **Reservations:** required. **Features:** semi-formal attire; cocktail lounge; wine only; prix fixe. Courses on the bold, dazzlingly presented degustation menu are prepared from the freshest natural products and emphasize pure flavors and taste. Understated dining rooms and superior service also add to a long-memorable dining experience. Smoke free premises. **Parking:** valet only (fee). **Cards:** AX, CB, DC, DS, MC, VI.

ERWIN-AN AMERICAN CAFE   Dinner: $13-$26   Phone: 773/528-7200   102
American
Location: Between Diversey Pkwy and Belmont St. 2925 N Halsted St 60657. **Hours:** 5:30 pm-10 pm, Fri & Sat-11 pm, Sun 10:30 am-2:15 & 5-9 pm. Closed major holidays; also Mon. **Reservations:** suggested. **Features:** casual dress; Sunday brunch; carryout; cocktails & lounge; a la carte. Seafood, organic poultry and a handful of steaks make up the seasonally changing menu. Freshly baked bread and such homemade desserts as passion fruit cheesecake set the casual cafe apart. The modern dining room has a charming bistro feel. **Parking:** street and valet (fee). **Cards:** AX, DC, DS, MC, VI.

LA BOCCA DELLA VERITA   Dinner: $11-$24   Phone: 773/784-6222   107
Italian
Location: Jct Wilson St and Lincoln Ave. 4618 N Lincoln Ave 60625. **Hours:** 5 pm-11 pm, Sun 4 pm-10 pm. Closed major holidays; also Mon. **Reservations:** suggested. **Features:** casual dress; carryout; cocktails; a la carte. The menu comprises a large selection of pasta, poultry and seafood. Simple preparations are nicely garnished and wonderfully seasoned. Frosted ceiling drop down lights, stucco walls and quality artwork are charming touches in the dining room. **Parking:** street. **Cards:** AX, DS, MC, VI.

LE BOUCHON   Dinner: $12-$17   Phone: 773/862-6600   108
French
Location: Corner of Damen and Armitage aves. 1958 N Damen Ave 60647. **Hours:** 5:30 pm-11 pm, Fri & Sat 5 pm-midnight. Closed major holidays; also Sun. **Reservations:** suggested. **Features:** casual dress; cocktails; a la carte. Guests will feel like they are in Paris while dining at this cozy neighborhood bistro. Everything from the lace tablecloth curtains to the etched-glass wall sconces reflects a French influence. Among examples of the excellently prepared food are variations of seafood, steak, chicken and lamb. The service staff is welcoming. **Parking:** street and valet (fee). **Cards:** AX, CB, DC, DS, MC, VI.

LUTZ'S CONTINENTAL CAFE & PASTRY SHOP   Lunch: $8-$16   Dinner: $12-$18   Phone: 773/478-7785   111
Continental
Location: Just w of Western Ave. 2458 W Montrose Ave 60618. **Hours:** 11 am-10 pm; call for hours 10/1-3/31, 4/1-4/30. Closed major holidays; also Mon. **Reservations:** accepted. **Features:** casual dress; carryout; cocktails; a la carte. The comfortable, European-feeling cafe is known for its pastries and such German specialties as Konigsberger klopse: boiled potatoes served separately from lamb and beef. A visit isn't complete without a stroll through the lovely garden out back. Smoke free premises. **Parking:** street. **Cards:** MC, VI.

MONASTERO'S RISTORANTE   Lunch: $7-$11   Dinner: $9-$19   Phone: 773/588-2515   85
Regional Italian
Location: E of Crawford (Pulaski). 3935 W Devon Ave 60659. **Hours:** 11 am-2 & 4-11 pm, Sat from 4 pm, Sun 4 pm-10 pm. Closed: 1/1, 11/28, 12/25; also Mon. **Reservations:** suggested. **Features:** casual dress; children's menu; carryout; cocktails & lounge. Skylights, hanging plants and bentwood chairs create a comfortable environment in the casual restaurant. Simply prepared classics, such as lasagna, and a few steak and American choices make up the casual restaurant's menu. Service is rapid and accurate. **Parking:** on-site. **Cards:** AX, DS, MC, VI.

ONE SIXTYBLUE   Dinner: $19-$30   Phone: 312/850-0303   116
American
Location: Corner of Randolph and Ogden. 160 N Loomis 60607. **Hours:** 5 pm-9:30 pm, Fri & Sat-10:30 pm. Closed major holidays. **Reservations:** suggested. **Features:** dressy casual; health conscious menu items; cocktails & lounge; a la carte. The upscale, trendy dining spot is known for contemporary American cuisine prepared in an open kitchen. Presentations are lovely, and the food outstanding. Complex, flavorful sauces complement preparations of seafood, lamb and beef. Chocolate souffle is memorable. **Parking:** street and valet (fee). **Cards:** AX, CB, DC, MC, VI.

(See map p. 284)

PS BANGKOK
Ethnic
Lunch: $6-$9   **Dinner:** $6-$11   **Phone:** 773/871-7777   [92]
Location: Between Buckingham and Roscoe. 3345 N Clark St 60657. **Hours:** 11:30 am-10 pm, Fri & Sat-11:30 pm. Closed: 11/28, 12/24, 12/25; also Mon. **Reservations:** accepted. **Features:** casual dress; Sunday brunch; carryout; beer & wine only; a la carte. Beautiful Asian art decorates the storefront of the comfortable restaurant. The enormous, but well-organized, menu includes piquant Thai dishes at moderate prices. The Sunday brunch lays out 100 tempting choices. Service is rapid but not hurried. **Parking:** street. **Cards:** AX, CB, DC, DS, MC, VI.

RUDI FAZULI'S WEST SIDE ITALIAN
Italian
Lunch: $7-$14   **Dinner:** $10-$19   **Phone:** 773/388-0100   [89]
Location: Jct Fullerton Ave and N Clark St, just n. 2442 N Clark St 60614. **Hours:** 11:30 am-10:30 pm, Fri & Sat-11:30 pm, Sun 10:30 am-9:30 pm. Closed major holidays; also Mon. **Reservations:** accepted. **Features:** casual dress; cocktails & lounge; a la carte. A raised platform sits outside the casual eatery, providing outdoor dining in nice weather. An extensive menu of well-prepared choices includes the wonderfully seasoned bruscetta and the heaping helping of pasta pasquale. The spumoni is a great dessert. **Parking:** street and valet (fee). **Cards:** AX, DC, DS, MC, VI.

STEFANI'S
Northern Italian
Lunch: $8-$14   **Dinner:** $10-$24   **Phone:** 773/348-0111   [119]
Location: I-90/94, exit Fullerton Ave, 1 mi e. 1418 W Fullerton Ave 60614. **Hours:** 11 am-10 pm, Fri-11 pm, Sat 5 pm-11 pm, Sun 4 pm-9 pm. Closed major holidays. **Reservations:** accepted. **Features:** dressy casual; carryout; cocktails; a la carte. Tasty pasta and pizza cooked in a wood-burning oven stand out on the restaurant's traditional menu. The pace here is rapid, and the servings are large. The light cappuccino mousse cake is a favorite dessert choice. Request outdoor seating during summer. **Parking:** street and valet (fee). **Cards:** AX, DC, DS, MC, VI.

TOPO GIGIO RISTORANTE
Italian
Lunch: $8-$13   **Dinner:** $12-$23   **Phone:** 312/266-9355   [97]
Location: Jct Wells St and North Ave (SR 64), just s. 1516 N Wells St 60614. **Hours:** 11 am-11 pm, Sun 4 pm-10 pm. Closed major holidays. **Reservations:** accepted. **Features:** casual dress; carryout; cocktails; a la carte. This long-established Italian restaurant caters to a strong local following. The wood floors, brick walls and wine bottles on high-mounted shelves set the stage for a casual, intimate ambience in which to enjoy traditional Italian cuisine. The food is simply presented and excellently prepared. **Parking:** street. **Cards:** AX, MC, VI.

TUSCANY
Italian
Lunch: $9-$18   **Dinner:** $9-$24   **Phone:** 312/829-1990   [120]
Location: W Taylor at S Morgan St, near UIC Campus. 1014 W Taylor 60607. **Hours:** 11 am-3:30 & 5-11 pm, Fri-midnight, Sat 5 pm-midnight, Sun 2 pm-9:30 pm. Closed major holidays. **Reservations:** suggested. **Features:** dressy casual; cocktails & lounge; a la carte. The bustling eatery boasts wonderful pizza topped with fresh tomato, whole basil, grilled eggplant and goat and mozzarella cheeses. Pasta dishes and chicken roasted in a wood-burning oven also are tempting. Service is casual and competent. **Parking:** street and valet (fee). **Cards:** AX, DC, MC, VI.

WISHBONE
American
Lunch: $6-$9   **Dinner:** $7-$14   **Phone:** 312/850-2663   [118]
Location: Corner of Morgan St and Washington Blvd. 1001 W Washington Blvd 60607. **Hours:** 7 am-3 & 5-10 pm, Sat 8 am-2:30 & 5-11 pm, Sun 8 am-2:30 & 5-9 pm. **Features:** casual dress; Sunday brunch; children's menu; carryout; cocktails & lounge. Whimsically decorated with farmyard paintings by the owner's mother, Wishbone prides itself on very well-prepared Southern cuisine served with style. Some vegetarian dishes also grace the extensive menu. Outdoor seating is available in summer. **Parking:** street. **Cards:** AX, CB, DC, DS, JC, MC, VI.

YOSHI'S CAFE
American
Dinner: $13-$25   **Phone:** 773/248-6160   [90]
Location: Just n of Belmont at corner of W Aldine Ave. 3257 N Halsted 60657. **Hours:** 5 pm-10:30 pm, Fri & Sat-11 pm, Sun 11 am-2:30 & 5-9:30 pm. Closed major holidays; also Mon. **Reservations:** suggested. **Features:** casual dress; Sunday brunch; children's menu; carryout; cocktails; a la carte. The attractive, upscale cafe has a charming bistro feel. Fresh ingredients and beautiful presentation marks such seasonally changing dishes as mixed seafood tempura, three-kind mushroom soup and grilled lamb chops. The mascarpone berry cake is exquisite. **Parking:** street and valet (fee). **Cards:** AX, CB, DC, JC, MC, VI.

─────── *The following restaurants have not been evaluated by AAA* ───────
but are listed for your information only.

FEAST   **Phone:** 773/772-7100
[fyi]   Not evaluated. **Location:** Jct North and N Damen aves. 1616 N Damen Ave. The restaurant's international cuisine reflects a distinctively Asian influence.

GREEN DOLPHIN STREET   **Phone:** 773/395-0066
[fyi]   Not evaluated. **Location:** 2200 N Ashland Ave. The 1940s style dining room has photographs of jazz musicians on the walls.

OFIE   **Phone:** 773/248-6490
[fyi]   Not evaluated. **Location:** Just s of Irving Park Rd. 3911 N Sheridan Rd 60613. The menu features cuisine from Nigeria, Ghana and Sierra Leone. Smoke free premises.

TROTTER'S TO GO   **Phone:** 773/868-6510
[fyi]   Not evaluated. **Location:** Between Southport and Racine aves. 1337 W Fullerton Ave 60614. The world-class chef prepares an extensive variety of soups, salads, sandwiches and entrees.

CHICAGO (SOUTHERN REGION)   (See map p. 292; index p. 294)

——— WHERE TO STAY ———

WOODED ISLE SUITES
◆◆ ◆◆ 5/19-6/15
         4/1-5/18 & 6/16-1/1
Historic Apartment 1/2-3/31

Phone: (773)288-5578 404
2P: $164-$198   XP: $15
2P: $148-$178   XP: $15
2P: $139-$169   XP: $15

Location: Lake Shore Dr, exit 57th Dr, follow to Stoney Island Ave, just s. 5750 S Stony Island Ave 60637. Fax: 773/288-8972. **Facility:** Smoke free premises. 13 units. 6 one-bedroom standard units. 7 one-bedroom suites ($139-$198). 3 stories (no elevator), interior corridors. **Parking:** street. **Terms:** 14 day cancellation notice-fee imposed. **Amenities:** extended cable TV, irons, hair dryers. **Guest Services:** coin laundry. **Cards:** AX, DS, MC, VI.

SOME UNITS

In Illinois:
Bloomington/Normal–West
Chicago–O'Hare N.W.
Crystal Lake

Decatur
Elgin
Freeport
Galena

Galesburg
Gurnee
Manteno
Matteson

(See map p. 292)

------ WHERE TO DINE ------

EMPEROR'S CHOICE   Lunch: $8-$24   Dinner: $8-$24   Phone: 312/225-8800   (241)

Chinese

Location: Between Cermak Rd and 23rd St; in Chinatown. 2238 S Wentworth Ave 60616. **Hours:** 11:30 am-1 am, Sun-midnight. **Reservations:** suggested. **Features:** casual dress; carryout; cocktails; a la carte, also prix fixe. Cantonese seafood dishes are the specialty at this handsome storefront eatery located in the heart of Chinatown. Mandarin, Hunan and Szechuan cuisines also are served in large portions and by an efficient service staff that caters to your every need. **Parking:** street. **Cards:** AX, DS, MC, VI.

EVERGREEN RESTAURANT   Lunch: $5-$7   Dinner: $8-$17   Phone: 312/225-8898   (242)

Chinese

Location: Jct Cermak Rd and Wentworth Ave, 3 blks s; in Chinatown. 2411 S Wentworth Ave 60616. **Hours:** 11:30 am-2 am. **Reservations:** accepted. **Features:** casual dress; health conscious menu; carryout; cocktails. In the heart of Chinatown, the popular restaurant serves excellently prepared, "Hong Kong-style" Cantonese and Szechuan cuisine. Elements of the traditional decor include attractive floral arrangements and large brass framed art. Family dinners are available. **Parking:** street. **Cards:** AX, DS, MC, VI.

SHER-A PUNJAB   Lunch: $7   Dinner: $9   Phone: 630/971-8111   (239)

Indian

Location: I-355, exit 63rd St, 0.5 mi e; in Meadowbrook Shopping Center. 2113 W 63rd St 60516. **Hours:** 11:30 am-4 pm, Fri & Sat-10:30 pm, Sun-10 pm. **Reservations:** accepted. **Features:** casual dress; carryout; beer & wine only; buffet, a la carte. Diners can experience a great introduction to Indian food on the lunch and dinner buffet lines. The relaxed atmosphere is helped along by the sounds of Indian sitar music. Sizzling plates of tandoori chicken are delivered to each table. Pita bread baked in a brick oven is wonderful. **Parking:** on-site. **Cards:** AX, MC, VI.

The Chicago Vicinity

ALGONQUIN pop. 11,700

——— WHERE TO DINE ———

PORT EDWARD
AAA
♦♦♦
Seafood
DS, MC, VI.

Lunch: $7-$13   **Dinner:** $15-$35   **Phone:** 847/658-5441
Location: On SR 62, just e of jct SR 31. 20 W Algonquin Rd 60102. **Hours:** 11:30 am-3 & 5-10 pm, Fri-11 pm, Sat 5 pm-11 pm, Sun 9:30 am-1 & 3-9 pm. Closed major holidays; also 12/24. **Reservations:** suggested; weekends. **Features:** casual dress; Sunday brunch; carryout; cocktails & lounge. Along the Fox River, the rustic, two-story restaurant is big on seafood, with extensive offerings of such dishes as live Maine lobster and Alaskan king crab. A fishing boat sits in a pond just inside the dining room and other nautical scenes make up the large all wood dining area. Enjoy the buffet on Fridays. **Parking:** on-site. **Cards:** AX, CB, DC,

⊠

ALSIP pop. 18,200   (See map p. 292; index p. 293)

——— WHERE TO STAY ———

BAYMONT INN-CHICAGO MIDWAY SOUTH   **Phone:** 708/597-3900   `334`
AAA SAVE
♦♦♦
Motel

All Year [ECP]   1P: $70-$95
Location: I-294, exit Cicero Ave S. 12801 S Cicero Ave 60803. Fax: 708/597-3979. **Facility:** 101 units. 100 one-bedroom standard units, some with whirlpools. 1 one-bedroom suite ($95-$130) with kitchen. 3 stories, interior corridors. *Bath:* combo or shower only. **Parking:** on-site. **Terms:** check-in 4 pm, package plans, small pets only. **Amenities:** voice mail, irons, hair dryers. *Some:* Web TV (fee). **Guest Services:** valet and coin laundry. **Business Services:** meeting rooms. **Cards:** AX, CB, DC, DS, MC, VI. **Special Amenities:** free continental breakfast and free newspaper.

SOME UNITS
🛏 ⎙M ⎙ ⌨ 📺 DATA PORT ⎚ 🖨 / ⊠ 🔒 🖼
FEE

RADISSON HOTEL-ALSIP   **Phone:** (708)371-7300   `335`
AAA SAVE
♦♦♦
Motor Inn

All Year   1P: $109-$159   2P: $119-$169   XP: $10   F17
Location: I-294, exit Cicero Ave S, just w. 5000 W 127th St at Cicero Ave 60803. Fax: 708/371-9949. **Facility:** 193 units. 188 one-bedroom standard units. 5 one-bedroom suites ($199). 5 stories, interior corridors. *Bath:* combo or shower only. **Parking:** on-site. **Terms:** 14 day cancellation notice, package plans, small pets only ($50 deposit). **Amenities:** dual phone lines, voice mail, irons, hair dryers. *Fee:* video games, high-speed Internet. **Dining:** restaurant, 6 am-2 & 5-10 pm, $12-$22, cocktails. **Pool(s):** heated indoor. **Leisure Activities:** sun deck, exercise room. **Guest Services:** valet and coin laundry, area transportation-within 3 mi. **Business Services:** conference facilities, fax. **Cards:** AX, CB, DC, DS, JC, MC, VI. **Special Amenities:** free newspaper and free room upgrade (subject to availability with advanced reservations).

SOME UNITS
S/D 🛏 🍴 Y ⎙M ⌨ 🛟 📺 DATA PORT ⎚ 🖨 / ⊠ 🔒
FEE

ANTIOCH pop. 6,100

——— WHERE TO STAY ———

BEST WESTERN REGENCY INN   **Phone:** (847)395-3606
AAA SAVE
♦♦♦
Motel

5/1-9/1 [CP]   1P: $93-$107   2P: $93-$107
4/1-4/30 & 9/2-12/31 [CP]   1P: $78-$93   2P: $78-$93
1/1-3/31 [CP]   1P: $72-$90   2P: $72-$90
Location: SR 173, 0.5 mi w of jct SR 83. 350 Rt 173 60002. Fax: 847/395-3606. **Facility:** 68 one-bedroom standard units. 3 stories, interior corridors. **Parking:** on-site. **Terms:** 3 day cancellation notice, package plans, small pets only ($25 deposit). **Amenities:** hair dryers. **Guest Services:** valet laundry. **Business Services:** meeting rooms. **Cards:** AX, CB, DC, DS, JC, MC, VI. **Special Amenities:** free continental breakfast and free newspaper.

SOME UNITS
S/D 🛏 🍴 Y 🛟 📺 DATA PORT 🖨 / ⊠ 🔒 /

Travel With Someone You Trust®

ARLINGTON HEIGHTS pop. 75,500   (See map p. 284; index p. 289)

———— **WHERE TO STAY** ————

AMERISUITES (CHICAGO/ARLINGTON HEIGHTS)
Phone: (847)956-1400   183
(AAA) (SAVE)   All Year   1P: $99-$109   XP: $10   F18
Location: I-90, exit Arlington Heights Rd, 0.6 mi n. 2111 S Arlington Heights Rd 60005. Fax: 847/956-0804.
Motel   **Facility:** 114 one-bedroom standard units. 6 stories, interior corridors. *Bath:* combo or shower only. **Parking:** on-site. **Terms:** package plans, pets ($50 fee). **Amenities:** high-speed Internet (fee), voice mail, irons, hair dryers. **Leisure Activities:** whirlpool, exercise room. **Guest Services:** complimentary evening beverages: Wed, valet laundry, area transportation-within 5 mi. **Business Services:** meeting rooms, business center.
Fee: PC, fax. **Cards:** AX, CB, DC, DS, JC, MC, VI. **Special Amenities:** free continental breakfast and free newspaper.
(See color ad p 296)

SOME UNITS

FEE

BEST WESTERN ARLINGTON INN
Phone: (847)255-2900   190
(AAA) (SAVE)   All Year [CP]   1P: $65-$88   2P: $70-$91   XP: $5   F12
Location: US 14, just e of Arlington Heights Rd. 948 E Northwest Hwy 60004. Fax: 847/394-1093. **Facility:** 81 one-
Motor Inn   bedroom standard units. 2 stories, interior/exterior corridors. **Parking:** on-site. **Terms:** package plans.
Amenities: hair dryers. **Dining:** restaurant, 7 am-2 & 5-9 pm, Fri & Sat-10 pm, Sun 3 pm-9 pm, $6-$12, cocktails. **Pool(s):** small heated indoor. **Leisure Activities:** whirlpool, exercise room. **Business Services:** meeting rooms. **Cards:** AX, CB, DC, DS, JC, MC, VI. **Special Amenities:** free continental breakfast and
free local telephone calls.

SOME UNITS

FEE

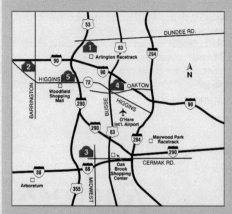

(See map p. 284)

COURTYARD BY MARRIOTT-NORTH
Phone: (847)394-9999 ⑱⑨

AAA SAVE
♦♦♦♦
Motor Inn

All Year   1P: $59-$99   2P: $69-$109
Location: SR 53, exit Dundee Rd, just e, then 0.8 mi n. 3700 N Wilke Rd 60004. Fax: 847/394-9532. **Facility:** 152 units. 140 one-bedroom standard units. 12 one-bedroom suites ($109-$119). 4 stories, interior corridors. *Bath:* combo or shower only. **Parking:** on-site. **Amenities:** high-speed Internet (fee), voice mail, irons, hair dryers. **Dining:** dining room, 6:30 am-10 & 5-10 pm, Sat & Sun 7 am-noon, $6-$12, cocktails. **Pool(s):** heated indoor. **Leisure Activities:** whirlpool, exercise room, patio deck. **Guest Services:** valet and coin laundry. **Business Services:** meeting rooms. **Cards:** AX, CB, DC, DS, MC, VI. *(See ad p 299 & color ad card insert)*

SOME UNITS
[icons] FEE

HOLIDAY INN EXPRESS
Phone: (847)593-9400 ⑱⑤

AAA SAVE
♦♦♦♦
Motel

All Year [ECP]   1P: $79-$139   2P: $79-$139
Location: I-90, exit Arlington Heights Rd, 0.6 mi n. 2120 S Arlington Heights Rd 60005. Fax: 847/593-3632. **Facility:** 125 units. 121 one-bedroom standard units. 4 one-bedroom suites ($99-$149). 3 stories, interior corridors. *Bath:* combo or shower only. **Parking:** on-site. **Terms:** 3 day cancellation notice-fee imposed, package plans. **Amenities:** voice mail, irons, hair dryers. **Guest Services:** valet laundry. **Business Services:** meeting rooms. **Cards:** AX, CB, DC, DS, JC, MC, VI. **Special Amenities:** free continental breakfast and free local telephone calls. *(See color ad p 325)*

SOME UNITS
[icons] FEE

LA QUINTA INN-ARLINGTON HEIGHTS
Phone: (847)253-8777 ⑱⑧

SAVE
♦♦♦
Motel

All Year   1P: $80-$119   2P: $90-$129   XP: F18
Location: SR 53, exit Dundee Rd, just e. 1415 W Dundee Rd 60004. Fax: 847/818-9167. **Facility:** 121 units. 119 one-bedroom standard units. 2 one-bedroom suites ($110-$169). 4 stories, interior corridors. **Parking:** on-site. **Terms:** small pets only. **Amenities:** video games, voice mail, irons, hair dryers. **Pool(s):** heated outdoor. **Leisure Activities:** exercise room. **Guest Services:** valet laundry. **Business Services:** meeting rooms. **Cards:** AX, CB, DC, DS, MC, VI. *(See color ad p 325)*

SOME UNITS
[icons] FEE

MOTEL 6 - 1048
Phone: 847/806-1230 ⑱④

♦♦
Motel

5/23-8/31	1P: $51-$61	2P: $57-$67	XP: $3 F17
9/1-3/31	1P: $46-$56	2P: $52-$62	XP: $3 F17
4/1-5/22	1P: $43-$53	2P: $49-$59	XP: $3 F17

Location: I-90, exit Arlington Heights Rd, just n, then 0.5 mi w. 441 W Algonquin Rd 60005. Fax: 847/364-7413. **Facility:** 144 one-bedroom standard units. 2 stories, interior corridors. **Parking:** on-site. **Terms:** small pets only (must be attended). **Guest Services:** coin laundry. **Cards:** AX, CB, DC, DS, MC, VI.

SOME UNITS
[icons]

(See map p. 284)

RADISSON HOTEL ARLINGTON HEIGHTS
Phone: (847)364-7600   [193]

(AAA) (SAVE)
◇◇◇◇
Motor Inn

All Year   1P: $45-$209   2P: $95-$209
Location: I-90, exit Arlington Heights Rd, just n. 75 W Algonquin Rd 60005. Fax: 847/364-7665. **Facility:** 247 units. 237 one-bedroom standard units. 10 one-bedroom suites ($129-$289), some with whirlpools. 6 stories, interior corridors. **Parking:** on-site. **Terms:** [BP] meal plan available, package plans. **Amenities:** video games (fee), dual phone lines, voice mail, irons, hair dryers. *Some:* high-speed Internet (fee). **Dining:** restaurant, 6:30 am-10 pm, Fri & Sat-11 pm, $10-$29, cocktails. **Pool(s):** heated indoor. **Leisure Activities:** sauna, whirlpool, exercise room. **Guest Services:** gift shop, valet laundry. **Business Services:** conference facilities. **Cards:** AX, CB, DC, DS, JC, MC, VI. **Special Amenities: free local telephone calls and free newspaper.** *(See color ad p 326)*

SOME UNITS

RED ROOF INN #7102
Phone: (847)228-6650   [195]

(AAA) (SAVE)
◇◇
Motel

5/26-10/26   1P: $55-$76   2P: $59-$81   XP: $5   F18
4/1-5/25 & 10/27-3/31   1P: $49-$64   2P: $54-$69   XP: $5   F18
Location: I-90, exit Arlington Heights Rd, 0.5 mi n, then just w. 22 W Algonquin Rd 60005. Fax: 847/228-6709. **Facility:** 136 one-bedroom standard units. 2 stories, exterior corridors. *Bath:* combo or shower only. **Parking:** on-site. **Terms:** small pets only. **Amenities:** video games (fee), voice mail. **Cards:** AX, CB, DC, DS, JC, MC, VI. **Special Amenities: free local telephone calls and free newspaper.**

SOME UNITS

SHERATON CHICAGO NORTHWEST
Phone: (847)394-2000   [191]

◇◇◇
Hotel

1/1-3/31   1P: $239   2P: $239   XP: $20   F18
4/1-12/31   1P: $229   2P: $229   XP: $20   F18
Location: Jct Euclid Ave E and SR 53; at Arlington Park Race Track. 3400 W Euclid Ave 60005. Fax: 847/394-2095. **Facility:** 429 units. 428 one-bedroom standard units. 1 one-bedroom suite ($279-$550) with whirlpool. 24 stories, interior corridors. *Bath:* combo or shower only. **Parking:** on-site. **Terms:** cancellation fee imposed, package plans. **Amenities:** video games (fee), dual phone lines, voice mail, irons, hair dryers. *Some:* fax. **Dining:** Delaney & Murphy, A Steak House, see separate listing. **Pool(s):** heated indoor. **Leisure Activities:** sauna, whirlpool, 2 lighted tennis courts, basketball, horseshoes, volleyball. **Guest Services:** gift shop, massage (fee), valet laundry. **Business Services:** conference facilities, business center. **Fee:** PC, fax. **Cards:** AX, CB, DC, DS, JC, MC, VI.

SOME UNITS

WHERE TO DINE

DELANEY & MURPHY, A STEAK HOUSE
Dinner: $18-$35   Phone: 847/394-3090   [161]

◇◇◇
Steak House

Location: Jct Euclid Ave E and SR 53; at Arlington Park Race Track; in Sheraton Chicago Northwest. 3400 W Euclid Ave 60005. **Hours:** 5:30 pm-9:30 pm. Closed major holidays. **Reservations:** suggested. **Features:** dressy casual; cocktails & lounge; a la carte. The finest cuts of prime steak are the feature of this upscale steakhouse that is located in a residential hotel next to the Arlington Park Racetrack. The pepperloin steak is marinated for days in special herbs and spices and is the signature dish. The food is superbly prepared and presented without a lot of flair. The white chocolate cheesecake is particularly rich and delicious. **Parking:** on-site. **Cards:** AX, CB, DC, DS, MC, VI.

LE TITI DE PARIS
Lunch: $12-$21   Dinner: $21-$28   Phone: 847/506-0222   [160]

◇◇◇◇
French

Location: SR 53, exit Dundee Rd, 0.5 mi e. 1015 W Dundee Rd 60004. **Hours:** 5:30 pm-9:30 pm, Thurs 11:30 am-2:30 & 5:30-9:30 pm, Fri 11:30 am-2:30 & 5:30-10 pm, Sat 5:30 pm-10 pm. Closed major holidays; also Sun & Mon. **Reservations:** suggested. **Features:** dressy casual; cocktails; a la carte, also prix fixe. Highly creative presentations of modern French cuisine distinguish this elegant restaurant. Recommend the tasting menu to really experience the range of superbly prepared seafood, fowl and filets coupled with an excellent array of fine desserts. Dining room complemented by a fine, welcoming service staff. An extensive selection of wines complements the dishes. Private dining rooms available. **Parking:** on-site. **Cards:** AX, CB, DC, DS, JC, MC, VI.

WELLINGTON OF ARLINGTON
Lunch: $8-$13   Dinner: $13-$19   Phone: 847/439-6610   [165]

◇◇ ◇◇
American

Location: I-90, exit Arlington Heights Rd, 0.6 mi w. 2121 S Arlington Heights Rd 60005. **Hours:** 11 am-3:30 & 5-11 pm, Sat 4:30 pm-midnight, Sun noon-10 pm. Closed: 12/25. **Reservations:** accepted. **Features:** dressy casual; cocktails & lounge; entertainment. Fresh beef Wellington is tender, well seasoned and definitely worth a try as are any of the extensive variety of entrees and sandwiches that make up the menu. A traditional decor and an attentive, smiling service staff makes the experience a pleasure. **Parking:** on-site. **Cards:** AX, CB, DC, MC, VI.

AURORA pop. 99,600

WHERE TO STAY

BEST WESTERN FOX VALLEY INN
Phone: (630)851-2000

◇◇ ◇◇
Motel

All Year   1P: $55-$70   2P: $60-$75   XP: $5   F12
Location: I-88, exit Farnsworth Ave, 0.3 mi n. 2450 N Farnsworth Ave 60504. Fax: 630/851-8885. **Facility:** 114 units. 111 one-bedroom standard units. 3 one-bedroom suites ($85-$95), some with kitchens. 2 stories, interior corridors. **Parking:** on-site, winter plug-ins. **Terms:** package plans. **Pool(s):** outdoor. **Leisure Activities:** exercise room. **Guest Services:** coin laundry. **Business Services:** meeting rooms. **Cards:** AX, CB, DC, DS, MC, VI.

SOME UNITS

COMFORT INN AURORA
SAVE
Motel
Phone: (630)820-3400

| 4/1-9/30 | 1P: $69-$119 | 2P: $69-$119 | XP: $10 | F18 |
| 10/1-3/31 | 1P: $59-$99 | 2P: $59-$99 | XP: $10 | F18 |

Location: I-88, exit SR 59, 3 mi s, 0.8 mi w on New York St. 4005 Gabrielle Ln 60504. Fax: 630/820-7081. **Facility:** 51 one-bedroom standard units. 2 stories, interior corridors. **Parking:** on-site. **Terms:** package plans. **Amenities:** extended cable TV, hair dryers. **Leisure Activities:** limited exercise equipment. **Guest Services:** valet laundry. **Business Services:** meeting rooms. **Cards:** AX, CB, DC, DS, JC, MC, VI.

SOME UNITS

COMFORT SUITES
SAVE
Motel
Phone: (630)896-2800

| 5/1-10/31 | 1P: $109-$189 | 2P: $119-$199 | XP: $10 | F17 |
| 4/1-4/30 & 11/1-3/31 | 1P: $89-$189 | 2P: $99-$199 | XP: $10 | F17 |

Location: I-88, exit SR 31, 2.5 mi s to Illinois St, just e to Broadway Ave, then 0.7 mi s. 111 N Broadway Ave 60505. Fax: 630/896-2887. **Facility:** 82 units. 78 one-bedroom standard units, some with whirlpools. 4 one-bedroom suites with whirlpools. 3 stories, interior corridors. *Bath:* combo or shower only. **Parking:** on-site. **Terms:** check-in 4 pm, 5 day cancellation notice, package plans. **Amenities:** video tape library (fee), dual phone lines, voice mail, irons, hair dryers. **Pool(s):** small heated outdoor. **Leisure Activities:** whirlpool, exercise room. **Guest Services:** complimentary evening beverages: Mon-Thurs, valet and coin laundry. **Business Services:** meeting rooms, business center, PC, fax. **Cards:** AX, CB, DC, DS, JC, MC, VI.

SOME UNITS

SUPER 8 MOTEL
Motel
Phone: (630)898-5419

| 4/1-10/31 [ECP] | 1P: $64-$69 | 2P: $64-$74 | XP: $5 | F13 |
| 11/1-3/31 [ECP] | 1P: $59-$64 | 2P: $59-$64 | XP: $5 | F13 |

Location: I-88, exit SR 59, 3.5 mi s to US 34, then 0.4 mi w. 4228 Longmeadow Dr 60504. Fax: 630/898-6087. **Facility:** 65 units. 62 one-bedroom standard units, some with whirlpools. 3 one-bedroom suites ($110-$199) with whirlpools. 3 stories, interior corridors. *Bath:* combo or shower only. **Parking:** on-site, winter plug-ins. **Terms:** package plans. **Amenities:** extended cable TV, high-speed Internet (fee). *Some:* irons, hair dryers. **Pool(s):** small heated indoor. **Leisure Activities:** whirlpool, limited exercise equipment. **Guest Services:** valet and coin laundry. **Business Services:** meeting rooms. **Cards:** AX, DC, DS, MC, VI.

SOME UNITS

The following lodging was either not evaluated or did not meet AAA rating requirements but is listed for your information only.

HAMPTON INN & SUITES
[fyi]
Motel
Phone: 630/907-2600

| All Year | 1P: $99-$200 | | XP: $10 | F18 |

Too new to rate. **Location:** I-88, exit Orchard Rd, just s. 2423 Bushwood Dr 60506. Fax: 630/907-2919. **Amenities:** radios, coffeemakers, pool. **Terms:** 7 day cancellation notice-fee imposed. **Cards:** AX, CB, DC, DS, JC, MC, VI.

--- **WHERE TO DINE** ---

LUIGI'S HOUSE
Italian
Lunch: $8-$12   Dinner: $10-$25   Phone: 630/375-6400

Location: I-88, exit SR 59, 2.5 mi s. 778 N Rt 59 60504. **Hours:** 11 am-10 pm, Fri & Sat-11 pm, Sun 11 am-9 pm. Closed major holidays. **Features:** casual dress; children's menu; carryout; cocktails & lounge; entertainment; a la carte. The distinctive, casual Italian eatery invites patrons to dine in a room of Luigi's home: his kitchen, library, living room or the pottery room, complete with ceiling-hung clay pots and twinkle lights. Excellently prepared food is served in generous portions. **Parking:** on-site. **Cards:** AX, DC, DS, MC, VI.

BANNOCKBURN pop. 1,400

--- **WHERE TO STAY** ---

WOODFIELD SUITES CHICAGO NORTH SHORE
AAA SAVE
Motel
Phone: 847/317-7300

| 4/1-10/1 | 1P: $99-$129 | 2P: $105-$139 | XP: $10 | F18 |
| 10/2-3/31 | 1P: $89-$119 | 2P: $99-$129 | XP: $10 | F18 |

Location: I-94, exit Half Day Rd (SR 22), just e to Lakeside Dr, then just s. 2000 Lakeside Dr 60015. Fax: 847/317-3350. **Facility:** 127 units. 121 one-bedroom standard units. 6 one-bedroom suites with whirlpools. 3 stories, interior corridors. *Bath:* some combo or shower only. **Parking:** on-site. **Terms:** 7 day cancellation notice-fee imposed, package plans, small pets only ($50 fee). **Amenities:** extended cable TV, video games (fee), dual phone lines, voice mail, irons, hair dryers. **Pool(s):** heated indoor. **Leisure Activities:** whirlpool, sun deck, exercise room, childrens play room, foosball. **Guest Services:** complimentary evening beverages, valet and coin laundry, area transportation-within 5 mi. **Business Services:** meeting rooms. **Cards:** AX, CB, DC, DS, MC, VI. **Special Amenities:** free local telephone calls and free newspaper.

SOME UNITS

BEDFORD PARK pop. 600 (See map p. 292; index p. 293)

--- **WHERE TO STAY** ---

COURTYARD BY MARRIOTT-CHICAGO/MIDWAY AIRPORT
AAA SAVE
Motel
Phone: (708)563-0200   366

| All Year | 1P: $149-$179 | | | |

Location: Jct Cicero Ave and 65th St. 6610 S Cicero Ave 60638. Fax: 708/728-2841. **Facility:** 174 one-bedroom standard units, some with whirlpools. 5 stories, interior corridors. *Bath:* combo or shower only. **Parking:** on-site. **Amenities:** video games (fee), voice mail, irons, hair dryers. **Dining:** coffee shop, 5:30-10:30 am, Sat & Sun 6 am-noon. **Pool(s):** heated indoor. **Leisure Activities:** whirlpool, exercise room. **Guest Services:** valet and coin laundry, airport transportation-Midway Airport, area transportation-local train. **Business Services:** meeting rooms, business center, PC, fax. **Cards:** AX, CB, DC, DS, JC, MC, VI. *(See color ad card insert)*

SOME UNITS

(See map p. 292)

FAIRFIELD INN BY MARRIOTT   Phone: (708)594-0090   367
(AAA) [SAVE]   4/1-11/23 & 2/28-3/31   1P: $109-$159
▽▽▽▽▽   11/24-2/27   1P: $89-$159
Motel   **Location:** Jct Cicero Ave and 65th St. 6630 S Cicero Ave 60638. Fax: 708/728-2842. **Facility:** 113 one-bedroom
standard units. 5 stories, interior corridors. *Bath:* combo or shower only. **Parking:** on-site. **Amenities:** video
games (fee), voice mail, irons, hair dryers. **Pool(s):** small heated indoor. **Leisure Activities:** whirlpool, exercise room. **Guest Services:** valet laundry, airport transportation-Midway Airport, area transportation-local
train station. **Business Services:** meeting rooms. **Cards:** AX, CB, DC, DS, JC, MC, VI. **Special Amenities: free continental
breakfast and free local telephone calls.** *(See color ad card insert)*

SOME UNITS

HAMPTON INN MIDWAY AIRPORT   Phone: (708)496-1900   370
[SAVE]   All Year   1P: $89-$179
▽▽▽▽▽   **Location:** Jct Cicero Ave and 65th St. 6540 S Cicero Ave 60638. Fax: 708/496-1997. **Facility:** 170 one-bedroom
Motel   standard units. 5 stories, interior corridors. **Parking:** on-site. **Terms:** package plans. **Amenities:** video
games (fee), dual phone lines, voice mail, irons, hair dryers. **Leisure Activities:** exercise room. **Guest Serv-
ices:** valet laundry. **Business Services:** meeting rooms. **Cards:** AX, CB, DC, DS, MC, VI.

SOME UNITS

HOLIDAY INN EXPRESS HOTEL & SUITES CHICAGO/MIDWAY AIRPORT   Phone: (708)458-0202   371
▽▽▽▽   All Year [CP]   1P: $149   2P: $199
Motel   **Location:** Jct Cicero Ave and 65th St. 6500 S Cicero Ave 60638. Fax: 708/458-0994. **Facility:** 104 units. 98 one-
bedroom standard units, some with whirlpools. 6 one-bedroom suites ($169-$250). 4 stories, interior corridors. *Bath:* combo or shower only. **Parking:** on-site. **Terms:** package plans. **Amenities:** video games (fee),
dual phone lines, voice mail, irons, hair dryers. **Leisure Activities:** exercise room. **Guest Services:** valet laundry. **Business
Services:** meeting rooms, business center, PC, fax. **Cards:** AX, CB, DC, DS, JC, MC, VI.

SOME UNITS

SLEEP INN-MIDWAY AIRPORT   Phone: (708)594-0001   369
[SAVE]   All Year   XP: $10   F17
▽▽▽▽   **Location:** Jct Cicero Ave and 65th St. 6650 S Cicero Ave 60638. Fax: 708/594-0058. **Facility:** 120 one-bedroom
Motel   standard units. 3 stories, interior corridors. *Bath:* combo or shower only. **Parking:** on-site. **Terms:** cancella-
tion fee imposed. **Amenities:** video games (fee), irons, hair dryers. **Leisure Activities:** whirlpool, limited
exercise equipment. **Guest Services:** valet laundry. **Business Services:** meeting rooms. **Cards:** AX, CB, DC,
DS, JC, MC, VI.

SOME UNITS

BLOOMINGDALE pop. 16,600

———— WHERE TO STAY ————

INDIAN LAKES GOLF RESORT AND CONFERENCE CENTER   Phone: (630)529-0200
▽▽▽▽▽   All Year   1P: $99-$169   2P: $99-$169
Resort   **Location:** I-355, exit US 20 (Lake St), 2.5 mi w, just s on Bloomingdale Rd, then 0.6 mi w. 250 W Schick Rd 60108.
Fax: 630/529-9271. **Facility:** Circular rooms are an unusual feature of this long-established resort, which is
surrounded by a golf course in a residential area. 314 one-bedroom standard units, some with whirlpools. 6
stories, interior corridors. *Bath:* combo or shower only. **Parking:** on-site. **Terms:** check-in 4 pm, package plans. **Amenities:** video
games (fee), voice mail, irons. **Pool(s):** heated outdoor, heated indoor. **Leisure Activities:** saunas, whirlpool. *Fee:* golf-36 holes,
miniature golf, 3 lighted tennis courts, game room. **Guest Services:** gift shop, massage (fee), valet laundry. **Business Services:**
conference facilities, business center. *Fee:* PC, fax. **Cards:** AX, CB, DC, DS, MC, VI.

SOME UNITS

———— WHERE TO DINE ————

SALVATORE'S RESTAURANT   Lunch: $7-$12   Dinner: $9-$18   Phone: 630/582-1201
▽▽▽ ▽▽▽   **Location:** US 20 (Lake St), just e of Bloomingdale Rd. 170 E Lake St 60108. **Hours:** 11:30 am-10 pm, Fri-11 pm,
Italian   Sat 4 pm-11 pm, Sun 3 pm-9 pm. Closed major holidays. **Reservations:** accepted. **Features:** casual
dress; carryout; cocktails; a la carte. In a quiet and mostly residential area, the casual eatery serves
classic cuisine from all over Italy including Sicily and the northern part of the country. The intimate dining
room features lovely framed artwork and tables covered in red cloths. The restaurant prides itself on the fresh pasta that is
prepared daily. Excellent ravioli can be enjoyed with meat or cheese filling and in a cream or tomato sauce. **Parking:** on-site.
Cards: AX, CB, DC, DS, MC, VI.

BLUE ISLAND pop. 21,200   (See map p. 292; index p. 294)

———— WHERE TO DINE ————

BABE'S FARM HOUSE INN RESTAURANT   Lunch: $5-$8   Dinner: $8-$16   Phone: 708/389-0394   265
▽▽▽   **Location:** I-57, exit 127th St (Burr Oak Ave), just w; between Western and Kedzie aves. 2824 W 127th St 60406.
American   **Hours:** 11 am-9 pm, Fri-10 pm, Sat 4 pm-10 pm. Closed: 1/1, 12/25; also Mon. **Reservations:** accepted.
Features: casual dress; children's menu; early bird specials; carryout; cocktails. You'll delight in the fine
country-style cooking presented in a beautifully restored farm house. Chicken and dumplings, roast loin of
pork and pot roast with mashed potatoes top the list of house specials. Stroll through the accompanying antique shop.
Parking: on-site. **Cards:** AX, MC, VI.

BOLINGBROOK pop. 40,800   (See map p. 292; index p. 293)

——— WHERE TO STAY ———

COMFORT INN
Phone: 630/226-0000 ⟨354⟩

Motel

All Year   1P: $79   2P: $85   XP: $10   F18
Location: I-55, exit 267, 0.5 mi sw. 225 W South Frontage Rd 60440. Fax: 630/226-1111. **Facility:** 101 units. 97 one-bedroom standard units, some with whirlpools. 4 one-bedroom suites ($119-$150), some with whirlpools. 3 stories, interior corridors. *Bath:* combo or shower only. **Parking:** on-site. **Terms:** 14 day cancellation notice, [CP] meal plan available, package plans. **Pool(s):** small heated indoor. **Leisure Activities:** whirlpool, limited exercise equipment. **Guest Services:** valet and coin laundry. **Cards:** AX, DC, DS, MC, VI.

SOME UNITS

HOLIDAY INN HOTEL & SUITES
Phone: (630)679-1600 ⟨351⟩

Motor Inn

All Year   1P: $129   2P: $129
Location: I-55, exit 267, just n, then 0.4 mi sw. 205 Remington Blvd 60440. Fax: 630/679-1616. **Facility:** 145 units. 118 one-bedroom standard units. 27 one-bedroom suites ($139-$179), some with whirlpools. 5 stories, interior corridors. *Bath:* combo or shower only. **Parking:** on-site. **Terms:** package plans, small pets only. **Amenities:** extended cable TV, dual phone lines, voice mail, irons, hair dryers. **Dining:** restaurant, 6 am-2 & 5-10 pm, $9-$17, cocktails. **Pool(s):** heated indoor. **Leisure Activities:** sauna, whirlpool, exercise room. **Guest Services:** gift shop, valet and coin laundry, area transportation-within 5 mi. **Business Services:** conference facilities, business center, fax (fee). **Cards:** AX, CB, DC, DS, JC, MC, VI. **Special Amenities:** early check-in/late check-out.

SOME UNITS

RAMADA LIMITED
Phone: (630)972-9797 ⟨352⟩

Motel

All Year [ECP]   1P: $80   2P: $85   XP: $5   F18
Location: I-55, exit 267, 0.4 mi s. 520 S Bolingbrook Dr 60440. Fax: 630/972-1991. **Facility:** 59 one-bedroom standard units, some with whirlpools. 3 stories, interior corridors. *Bath:* combo or shower only. **Parking:** on-site. **Terms:** 7 day cancellation notice. **Amenities:** extended cable TV, voice mail, safes (fee), irons, hair dryers. *Some:* high-speed Internet (fee). **Pool(s):** small heated indoor. **Leisure Activities:** whirlpool. **Guest Services:** valet and coin laundry. **Business Services:** meeting rooms. **Cards:** AX, CB, DC, DS, MC, VI. **Special Amenities: free continental breakfast and free newspaper.**

SOME UNITS

——— WHERE TO DINE ———

BOURBON STREET CAFE
Lunch: $8-$20   **Dinner:** $8-$20   **Phone:** 630/771-1111 ⟨226⟩

Seafood

Location: I-55, exit 267, just n to Remington Blvd, then 0.4 mi sw. 195 W Remington Blvd 60440. **Hours:** 11 am-10 pm, Fri & Sat-11 pm, Sun 10:30 am-9 pm. Closed major holidays. **Reservations:** accepted. **Features:** dressy casual; Sunday brunch; children's menu; carryout; cocktails & lounge. This popular restaurant features a casual, upbeat and fast paced dining experience. The menu has an enormous variety of fresh fish. Be sure to try the lobster bisque, which has a rich consistency and a Cajun twang. **Parking:** on-site. **Cards:** AX, CB, DC, DS, MC, VI.

BRIDGEVIEW pop. 14,400

——— WHERE TO STAY ———

EXEL INN OF BRIDGEVIEW
Phone: (708)430-1818

Motel

4/1-10/31 [CP]   1P: $58-$79   2P: $64-$85   XP: $6   F18
11/1-3/31 [CP]   1P: $58-$66   2P: $64-$72   XP: $6   F18
Location: I-294, exit 95th St, just s. 9625 S 76th Ave 60455. Fax: 708/430-1894. **Facility:** 113 one-bedroom standard units, some with efficiencies (no utensils) and/or whirlpools. 3 stories, interior corridors. **Parking:** on-site. **Terms:** small pets only ($100 deposit). **Amenities:** irons, hair dryers. **Leisure Activities:** exercise room. **Guest Services:** valet and coin laundry. **Cards:** AX, CB, DC, DS, MC, VI. **Special Amenities: early check-in/late check-out and free continental breakfast.** *(See color ad p 318)*

SOME UNITS

BUFFALO GROVE pop. 36,400

——— WHERE TO STAY ———

WYNDHAM GARDEN-BUFFALO GROVE
Phone: (847)215-8883

Motor Inn

All Year   1P: $75-$110   XP: $10   F18
Location: Jct US 53 and Lake Cook Rd, 2 mi e, just e of Arlington Heights Rd. 900 W Lake Cook Rd 60089. Fax: 847/215-9304. **Facility:** 155 one-bedroom standard units. 2 stories, interior corridors. **Parking:** on-site. **Terms:** check-in 4 pm, cancellation fee imposed, package plans. **Amenities:** high-speed Internet (fee), voice mail, irons, hair dryers. **Pool(s):** heated indoor. **Leisure Activities:** whirlpool, sun deck, 2 lighted tennis courts, exercise room. **Guest Services:** valet and coin laundry. **Business Services:** meeting rooms. **Cards:** AX, CB, DC, DS, JC, MC, VI.

SOME UNITS

——— WHERE TO DINE ———

CAFE WINBERIE
American

Lunch: $7-$13   **Dinner:** $7-$14   **Phone:** 847/520-7447
Location: Jct US 53 and Lake Cook Rd, 2 mi e; just e of Arlington Heights Rd. 800 W Lake Cook Rd 60089. **Hours:** 11:30 am-10 pm, Fri & Sat-11 pm, Sun 10 am-9 pm. Closed: 11/28, 12/25. **Reservations:** accepted; Sunday brunch. **Features:** casual dress; Sunday brunch; children's menu; carryout; cocktails & lounge; a la carte. The dining room's sleek, modern design adds to the casual ambience of the restaurant, where fine pasta, steak and chicken dishes are among menu choices. Food is attractively presented and skillfully prepared. Patio dining is popular when the weather is nice. **Parking:** on-site. **Cards:** AX, DC, DS, MC, VI.

BURR RIDGE pop. 7,700

——— WHERE TO STAY ———

AMERISUITES CHICAGO/BURR RIDGE
Motel

Phone: (630)323-7530
All Year   1P: $99-$125   2P: $99-$125
Location: I-55, exit 276B (County Line Rd), 0.3 mi n. 15 W 90 N Frontage Rd 60521. Fax: 630/323-7605. **Facility:** 128 one-bedroom standard units. 6 stories, interior corridors. *Bath:* combo or shower only. **Parking:** on-site. **Terms:** package plans, small pets only. **Amenities:** voice mail, irons, hair dryers. *Fee:* video games, high-speed Internet. *Some:* dual phone lines. **Pool(s):** heated indoor. **Leisure Activities:** exercise room. **Guest Services:** complimentary evening beverages: Wed, valet and coin laundry, area transportation-within 5 mi. **Business Services:** meeting rooms, business center, PC. **Cards:** AX, CB, DC, DS, JC, MC, VI. **Special Amenities:** free continental breakfast and free newspaper. *(See color ad p 296)*

SOME UNITS

CALUMET CITY pop. 37,800 (See map p. 292; index p. 294)

——— WHERE TO STAY ———

BAYMONT INN & SUITES CHICAGO-CALUMET CITY
Motel

Phone: 708/891-2900   [425]
All Year   1P: $79-$89
Location: I-94, exit 71B (Sibley Blvd E). 510 East End Ave 60409. Fax: 708/891-2900. **Facility:** 81 units. 79 one-bedroom standard units, some with whirlpools. 2 one-bedroom suites ($99-$175), some with whirlpools. 3 stories, interior corridors. *Bath:* combo or shower only. **Parking:** on-site. **Terms:** small pets only ($50 deposit). **Amenities:** video games (fee), dual phone lines, voice mail, irons, hair dryers. **Pool(s):** small heated indoor. **Leisure Activities:** whirlpool. **Guest Services:** coin laundry. **Business Services:** meeting rooms. **Cards:** AX, CB, DC, DS, MC, VI.

SOME UNITS

CALUMET PARK pop. 8,400

——— WHERE TO STAY ———

SUPER 8 MOTEL CHICAGO SOUTHWEST
Motel

Phone: (708)385-9100
All Year [ECP]   1P: $69-$99   2P: $69-$99   XP: $10   F17
Location: I-57, exit 353, just e. 12808 S Ashland Ave 60827. Fax: 708/388-4999. **Facility:** 94 one-bedroom standard units, some with whirlpools. 3 stories, interior corridors. *Bath:* combo or shower only. **Parking:** on-site. **Terms:** small pets only. **Amenities:** extended cable TV. **Guest Services:** coin laundry. **Business Services:** meeting rooms. **Cards:** AX, CB, DC, DS, JC, MC, VI.

SOME UNITS

CAROL STREAM pop. 31,800

——— WHERE TO STAY ———

HOLIDAY INN HOTEL & SUITES
Motor Inn

Phone: (630)665-3000
All Year   1P: $99-$119   2P: $99-$119
Location: Jct SR 64, just s. 150 S Gary Ave 60188. Fax: 630/665-9389. **Facility:** 198 units. 161 one-bedroom standard units, some with whirlpools. 37 one-bedroom suites ($119-$159), some with whirlpools. 4 stories, interior corridors. *Bath:* combo or shower only. **Parking:** on-site. **Terms:** package plans. **Amenities:** extended cable TV, dual phone lines, voice mail, irons, hair dryers. **Pool(s):** heated indoor. **Leisure Activities:** whirlpool, exercise room. *Fee:* game room. **Guest Services:** gift shop, valet and coin laundry. **Business Services:** conference facilities, business center, PC (fee), fax. **Cards:** AX, CB, DC, DS, JC, MC, VI.

SOME UNITS

COUNTRYSIDE pop. 5,700 (See map p. 292; index p. 294)

——— WHERE TO DINE ———

FLAME OF COUNTRYSIDE
Steak House

Lunch: $6-$12   **Dinner:** $15-$25   **Phone:** 708/352-3442   [255]
Location: Corner of Joliet Rd and Brainard, 0.5 mi w of jct US 45. 803 Joliet Rd 60525. **Hours:** 11 am-10 pm, Fri & Sat-11 pm, Sun noon-10 pm. Closed: 5/27, 7/4. **Reservations:** suggested. **Features:** dressy casual; cocktails & lounge; entertainment. Classic steak and seafood entrees and a tantalizing assortment of desserts prepared in house make up the restaurant's menu. Wood walls, a beamed ceiling and cloth-covered tables with excellent flatware set the stage for a fine meal. **Parking:** on-site. **Cards:** AX, DC, MC, VI.

CRYSTAL LAKE pop. 24,500

―――― WHERE TO STAY ――――

COUNTRY INN & SUITES BY CARLSON
Phone: (815)477-3500

(AAA) [SAVE]

Motel

5/15-9/15 [ECP]	1P: $94-$104	2P: $94-$104	XP: $5 F18
4/1-5/14 & 9/16-3/31 [ECP]	1P: $84-$94	2P: $84-$94	XP: $5 F18

Location: Jct SR 31 and 14, 0.4 mi w, then just s on Pingree St. 600 Tracy Tr 60014. Fax: 815/477-0189. **Facility:** 80 units. 58 one-bedroom standard units. 20 one- and 2 two-bedroom suites, some with kitchens and/or whirlpools. 3 stories, interior corridors. *Bath:* combo or shower only. **Parking:** on-site. **Terms:** 14 day cancellation notice. **Amenities:** voice mail, irons, hair dryers. *Some:* dual phone lines. **Pool(s):** small heated indoor. **Leisure Activities:** whirlpool, exercise room. **Guest Services:** valet and coin laundry. **Business Services:** meeting rooms. **Cards:** AX, CB, DC, DS, MC, VI. **Special Amenities: free continental breakfast and free newspaper.** *(See color ad p 322)*

SOME UNITS

HOLIDAY INN CRYSTAL LAKE
Phone: 815/477-7000

(AAA) [SAVE]

Motor Inn

All Year   1P: $129   2P: $129

Location: At Three Oaks Rd and SR 31, 0.3 mi s of jct US 14. 800 S SR 31 60014. Fax: 815/477-7027. **Facility:** 196 units. 192 one-bedroom standard units, some with whirlpools. 4 one-bedroom suites ($159-$189). 6 stories, interior corridors. *Bath:* combo or shower only. **Parking:** on-site. **Terms:** package plans. **Amenities:** video games (fee), dual phone lines, voice mail, irons, hair dryers. **Dining:** restaurant, 6 am-10 pm, Sat & Sun from 7 am, $8-$20, cocktails. **Pool(s):** heated indoor. **Leisure Activities:** sauna, whirlpool, sun deck, weight room. *Fee:* game room, aerobic classes. **Guest Services:** gift shop, valet and coin laundry, area transportation-within 10 mi. **Business Services:** conference facilities. **Cards:** AX, CB, DC, DS, MC, VI. *(See color ad below)*

SOME UNITS
FEE

SUPER 8 MOTEL
Phone: (815)455-2388

Motel

7/1-8/31	1P: $71-$76	2P: $76-$81	XP: $5 F12
5/1-6/30	1P: $61-$66	2P: $66-$71	XP: $5 F12
9/1-3/31	1P: $58-$63	2P: $63-$68	XP: $5 F12
4/1-4/30	1P: $56-$60	2P: $60-$65	XP: $5 F12

Location: On US 14, 1 mi w of jct SR 31. 577 Crystal Point Dr 60014. Fax: 815/455-2388. **Facility:** 59 one-bedroom standard units. 2 stories, interior corridors. **Parking:** on-site, winter plug-ins. **Terms:** [CP] meal plan available. **Amenities:** extended cable TV, safes. *Some:* hair dryers. **Guest Services:** valet and coin laundry. **Cards:** AX, CB, DC, DS, MC, VI.

SOME UNITS
FEE

DEERFIELD pop. 17,300

―――― WHERE TO STAY ――――

COURTYARD BY MARRIOTT
Phone: (847)940-8222

(AAA) [SAVE]

Motel

5/4-12/31	1P: $139	2P: $149
4/1-5/3 & 1/1-3/31	1P: $119	2P: $129

Location: I-94, exit Lake Cook Rd, 1.3 mi e; 2.5 mi w of jct SR 41. 800 W Lake Cook Rd 60015. Fax: 847/940-7741. **Facility:** 131 units. 118 one-bedroom standard units. 13 one-bedroom suites. 2 stories, interior corridors. *Bath:* combo or shower only. **Parking:** on-site. **Amenities:** high-speed Internet (fee), dual phone lines, voice mail, irons, hair dryers. **Dining:** coffee shop, 6:30-10 am, Sat & Sun 7-11 am. **Pool(s):** heated indoor. **Leisure Activities:** whirlpool, exercise room. **Guest Services:** valet and coin laundry, area transportation-within 3 mi. **Business Services:** meeting rooms. **Cards:** AX, CB, DC, DS, JC, MC, VI. *(See ad p 299 & color ad card insert)*

SOME UNITS
FEE

EMBASSY SUITES-CHICAGO NORTH SHORE

Phone: (847)945-4500

6/1-11/15 [BP]	1P: $89-$209	2P: $109-$229	XP: $20	F18
4/1-5/31 & 11/16-3/31 [BP]	1P: $79-$179	2P: $99-$199	XP: $20	F18

Suite Hotel

Location: I-94, exit Lake Cook Rd, just e. 1445 Lake Cook Rd 60015. **Fax:** 847/945-7795. **Facility:** 237 one-bedroom suites, some with whirlpools. 7 stories, interior corridors. **Parking:** on-site. **Terms:** check-in 4 pm, package plans. **Amenities:** voice mail, irons, hair dryers. **Dining:** restaurant, 11 am-10 pm, Fri & Sat-11 pm, $10-$25, cocktails. **Pool(s):** heated indoor. **Leisure Activities:** sauna, whirlpool, sun deck, exercise room. **Guest Services:** gift shop, complimentary evening beverages, valet and coin laundry, area transportation-within 5 mi. **Business Services:** conference facilities. **Cards:** AX, CB, DC, DS, JC, MC, VI. **Special Amenities:** free continental breakfast and free newspaper. *(See color ad below)*

SOME UNITS

HYATT DEERFIELD

Phone: (847)945-3400

All Year	1P: $95-$155	2P: $120-$180	XP: $25	F18

Hotel

Location: I-94, exit Lake Cook Rd, just ne. 1750 Lake Cook Rd 60015. **Fax:** 847/945-3563. **Facility:** 301 units. 300 one-bedroom standard units. 1 one-bedroom suite. 6 stories, interior corridors. *Bath:* combo or shower only. **Parking:** on-site. **Terms:** cancellation fee imposed, package plans. **Amenities:** extended cable TV, voice mail, irons, hair dryers. *Some:* dual phone lines, fax, safes. **Dining:** dining room, 6:30 am-10 pm, $10-$23, cocktails. **Pool(s):** heated indoor. **Leisure Activities:** sauna, whirlpool, exercise room. **Guest Services:** valet laundry, area transportation-within 5 mi. **Business Services:** conference facilities. **Cards:** AX, CB, DC, DS, JC, MC, VI.

SOME UNITS

MARRIOTT SUITES DEERFIELD

Phone: (847)405-9666

All Year	1P: $69-$179	2P: $69-$179

Suite Hotel

Location: I-94, exit Deerfield Rd northbound, just w; exit Lake Cook Rd southbound, 0.3 mi e to Saunders Rd, 0.5 mi n; in Parkway North Center. 2 Parkway Blvd N 60015. **Fax:** 847/405-0354. **Facility:** 248 one-bedroom suites. 7 stories, interior corridors. **Parking:** on-site. **Terms:** check-in 4 pm, package plans, pets ($50 fee). **Amenities:** voice mail, irons, hair dryers. *Fee:* video games, Web TV, high-speed Internet. *Some:* dual phone lines. **Dining:** dining room, 7 am-1 & 5-10:30 pm, $9-$23, cocktails. **Pool(s):** heated outdoor, heated indoor. **Leisure Activities:** saunas, whirlpool, exercise room. **Guest Services:** valet and coin laundry, area transportation-within 5 mi. **Business Services:** conference facilities, business center. *Fee:* PC, fax. **Cards:** AX, CB, DC, DS, JC, MC, VI. *(See color ad card insert)*

SOME UNITS

RESIDENCE INN BY MARRIOTT

Phone: (847)940-4644

5/16-8/15 [BP]	1P: $134-$161	2P: $134-$161
4/1-5/15 & 8/16-10/15 [BP]	1P: $116-$134	2P: $116-$134
10/16-3/31 [BP]	1P: $107-$116	2P: $107-$116

Apartment

Location: I-94, exit Lake Cook Rd, 1.8 mi e, 3 blks n on Corporate 500 Dr Access Rd. 530 Lake Cook Rd 60015. **Fax:** 847/940-7639. **Facility:** 128 units. 96 one-bedroom standard units with efficiencies. 24 one- and 8 two-bedroom suites with kitchens. 2 stories, exterior corridors. *Bath:* combo or shower only. **Parking:** on-site. **Terms:** pets ($15 extra charge). **Amenities:** extended cable TV, voice mail, irons, hair dryers. **Pool(s):** heated outdoor. **Leisure Activities:** whirlpool, exercise room, sports court. **Guest Services:** valet and coin laundry, area transportation-within 5 mi. **Business Services:** meeting rooms. **Cards:** AX, CB, DC, DS, JC, MC, VI. *(See color ad card insert)*

SOME UNITS

------ **WHERE TO DINE** ------

SHAW'S SEAFOOD GRILL

Lunch: $9-$15   **Dinner:** $10-$30   **Phone:** 847/948-1020

Seafood

Location: I-294/94, exit Lake Cook Rd, 1.5 mi e; 2.3 mi w of jct SR 41. 660 W Lake Cook Rd 60015. **Hours:** 11:30 am-2:30 & 5-9:30 pm, Fri & Sat-10:30 pm, Sun 4:30 pm-9 pm. **Closed:** 11/28, 12/25. **Reservations:** suggested. **Features:** casual dress; children's menu; early bird specials; carryout; cocktails; a la carte. Key West decor throughout the bustling restaurant gives it a breezy, tropical feel. Fresh seafood, such as the rich shrimp bisque and Wisconsin trout with red potatoes, is complemented by a selection of mostly domestic wines and many beers. **Parking:** on-site. **Cards:** AX, DC, DS, MC, VI.

DES PLAINES pop. 53,200 (See map p. 284; index p. 289)

———— WHERE TO STAY ————

COMFORT INN-O'HARE
Phone: (847)635-1300 (165)
All Year [ECP]   1P: $109-$160   2P: $109-$160   XP: $10   F18
Location: I-294, exit Touhy Ave W, corner of Touhy Ave and River Rd. 2175 E Touhy Ave 60018-3637.
Fax: 847/635-7572. **Facility:** 145 units. 142 one-bedroom standard units. 3 one-bedroom suites ($140-$160).
3 stories, interior corridors. **Parking:** on-site. **Amenities:** video games (fee), voice mail, irons, hair dryers.
Some: high-speed Internet. **Dining:** Tiffany's, see separate listing. **Leisure Activities:** whirlpool, exercise
room, patio. **Guest Services:** valet and coin laundry. **Business Services:** meeting rooms. **Cards:** AX, CB,
DC, DS, JC, MC, VI. **Special Amenities: free continental breakfast and free local telephone calls.**

Motel

SOME UNITS

COURTYARD BY MARRIOTT O'HARE
Phone: (847)824-7000 (163)
All Year   1P: $82-$194   2P: $87-$194
Location: I-294, exit Touhy Ave northbound, just sw, 0.3 mi s; exit Golf Rd southbound, 0.3 mi w to River Rd, 6 mi s.
2950 River Rd 60018. Fax: 847/824-4574. **Facility:** 180 units. 165 one-bedroom standard units. 15 one-
bedroom suites ($129-$209). 5 stories, interior corridors. **Bath:** combo or shower only. **Parking:** on-site.
Terms: package plans. **Amenities:** high-speed Internet (fee), voice mail, irons, hair dryers. **Dining:** restaurant, 6 am-2 & 5-10 pm, Sat & Sun 7 am-1 & 5-10 pm, $7-$17, (cocktails). **Pool(s):** heated indoor. **Leisure**
Activities: whirlpool, exercise room, patio & gazebo. **Guest Services:** gift shop, valet and coin laundry, area transportation-train
station & local restaurants. **Business Services:** meeting rooms. **Cards:** AX, CB, DC, DS, MC, VI.
(See ad p 299 & color ad card insert)

Motor Inn

SOME UNITS

DOUBLETREE CLUB HOTEL CHICAGO O'HARE
Phone: 847/296-8866 (162)
Property failed to provide current rates
Location: On US 12 and 45, Mannheim Rd at Touhy Ave. 1450 E Touhy Ave 60018. Fax: 847/296-8268. **Facility:** 246
one-bedroom standard units. 4 stories, interior corridors. **Bath:** combo or shower only. **Parking:** on-site.
Terms: package plans. **Amenities:** extended cable TV, video games (fee), dual phone lines, voice mail,
irons, hair dryers. **Pool(s):** heated outdoor. **Leisure Activities:** exercise room. **Guest Services:** gift shop, valet laundry. **Busi-**
ness Services: meeting rooms, business center, fax (fee). **Cards:** AX, CB, DC, DS, MC, VI.

Motor Inn

SOME UNITS

TRAVELODGE CHICAGO O'HARE/ROSEMONT
Phone: (847)296-5541 (164)
All Year   1P: $84-$129   2P: $99-$159   XP: $5   F
Location: US 12 and 45, just n of jct SR 72 (Mannheim Rd). 3003 Mannheim Rd 60018. Fax: 847/803-1984.
Facility: 94 one-bedroom standard units. 2 stories, interior/exterior corridors. **Bath:** combo or shower only.
Parking: on-site. **Terms:** package plans, small pets only. **Amenities:** hair dryers. **Pool(s):** outdoor. **Busi-**
ness Services: meeting rooms. **Cards:** AX, CB, DC, DS, JC, MC, VI. **Special Amenities: free local tele-**
phone calls and free newspaper.

Motel

SOME UNITS

———— WHERE TO DINE ————

CAFE LA CAVE
Lunch: $12-$25   Dinner: $21-$45   Phone: 847/827-7818 (147)
Location: Between Higgins Rd and Touhy Ave. 2777 Mannheim Rd 60018. **Hours:** 11:30 am-11 pm, Sat 5
pm-11:30 pm, Sun 5 pm-10 pm. Closed major holidays; also Mon for lunch. **Reservations:** suggested.
Features: semi-formal attire; cocktails & lounge; a la carte. Beyond the traditional dining area is a more
distinctive cave-like area, hence the name. The menu has some excellent selections including the
crabmeat appetizer with zesty sauce, the succulent veal chop, or the delicious Steak Diane. Service is dept by tuxedo-clad
servers. **Parking:** on-site and valet. **Cards:** AX, CB, DC, DS, MC, VI.

Continental

GRAZIE
Lunch: $7-$14   Dinner: $10-$18   Phone: 847/299-0011 (146)
Location: Just w of US 12/45 (Lee St), between Lee St and Wolf Rd. 1050 E Oakton 60018. **Hours:** 11 am-10 pm,
Fri & Sat-midnight, Sun 10:30 am-2:30 & 4-10 pm. Closed major holidays. **Reservations:** accepted.
Features: dressy casual; Sunday brunch; carryout; cocktails & lounge. A stylish and festive restaurant with
gold trim drapes, large colorful wall murals and wood floors sets the stage for a fine meal at Grazie. The
menu is equal parts traditional and contemporary, with such offerings as shrimp crostini and veal and portobello mushroom
ravioli. The in-house bakery whips up sinful desserts. **Parking:** on-site. **Cards:** AX, DC, MC, VI.

Italian

TIFFANY'S
Lunch: $7-$15   Dinner: $10-$20   Phone: 847/298-7733 (150)
Location: I-294, exit Touhy Ave W, corner of Touhy Ave and River Rd; in Comfort Inn-O'Hare. 2179 E Touhy Ave
60018. **Hours:** 5:30 am-1 am, Fri & Sat-2 am. **Features:** casual dress; children's menu; carryout; cocktails
& lounge. A locally popular breakfast and lunch spot with an extensive menu of sandwiches, salad, soup,
burgers and some Greek specialties. The portions are large and the dining room features a sleek,
contemporary look with lovely Tiffany drop down lights and polished cherry wood millwork. **Parking:** on-site. **Cards:** AX, DC,
MC, VI.

American

DOWNERS GROVE pop. 46,900 (See map p. 284 & p. 292; index p. 291 & p. 294)

———— WHERE TO STAY ————

COMFORT INN
AAA SAVE
◆◆◆◆
Motel

Phone: (630)515-1500 260
All Year [ECP]   1P: $79-$89   2P: $79-$89   XP: $5   F12
Location: I-355, exit Butterfield Rd (SR 56), just e. 3010 Finley Rd 60515. Fax: 630/515-1595. **Facility:** 121 units. 120 one-bedroom standard units. 1 one-bedroom suite. 3 stories, interior corridors. **Parking:** on-site. **Amenities:** irons, hair dryers. **Pool(s):** heated outdoor. **Leisure Activities:** whirlpool, exercise room. **Guest Services:** valet and coin laundry. **Business Services:** meeting rooms. **Cards:** AX, CB, DC, DS, JC, MC, VI. **Special Amenities: free continental breakfast and free local telephone calls.**

SOME UNITS

DOUBLETREE GUEST SUITES
SAVE
◆◆◆◆
Suite Hotel

Phone: (630)971-2000 398
4/1-11/14   1P: $69-$169   2P: $69-$169   XP: $10
1/1-3/31   1P: $69-$159   2P: $69-$159   XP: $10
11/15-12/31   1P: $69-$149   2P: $69-$149   XP: $10
Location: I-355, exit Butterfield Rd (SR 56), just w. 2111 Butterfield Rd 60515. Fax: 630/971-1021. **Facility:** 247 one-bedroom suites. 7 stories, interior corridors. **Parking:** on-site. **Terms:** cancellation fee imposed, package plans. **Amenities:** video games, dual phone lines, voice mail, irons, hair dryers. **Leisure Activities:** sauna, whirlpool, sun deck, pool privileges for adults. *Fee:* tennis court, racquetball courts. **Guest Services:** gift shop, valet and coin laundry. **Business Services:** conference facilities. **Cards:** AX, DC, DS, MC, VI.

SOME UNITS
FEE

HOLIDAY INN EXPRESS
AAA SAVE
◆◆◆
Motel

(See color ad p 322)

Phone: (630)810-9500 261
All Year   1P: $104-$139
Location: I-355, exit Butterfield Rd (SR 56), just e. 3031 Finley Rd 60515. Fax: 630/810-0059. **Facility:** 123 units. 115 one-bedroom standard units, some with whirlpools. 8 one-bedroom suites ($119). 3 stories, interior corridors. **Parking:** on-site. **Terms:** [ECP] meal plan available, package plans. **Amenities:** voice mail, irons, hair dryers. **Guest Services:** valet laundry. **Business Services:** meeting rooms. **Cards:** AX, CB, DC, DS, JC, MC, VI. **Special Amenities: free continental breakfast and free local telephone calls.**

SOME UNITS
FEE

MARRIOTT SUITES DOWNERS GROVE
AAA SAVE
◆◆◆◆
Suite Hotel

Phone: (630)852-1500 396
1/1-3/31   1P: $159-$199   2P: $169-$209
4/1-12/31   1P: $149-$189   2P: $159-$199
Location: I-355, exit Butterfield Rd (SR 56), just e, 0.3 mi s on Finley Rd. 1500 Opus Pl 60515. Fax: 630/852-6527. **Facility:** 254 one-bedroom suites. 7 stories, interior corridors. **Parking:** on-site. **Terms:** check-in 4 pm, package plans. **Amenities:** extended cable TV, dual phone lines, voice mail, irons, hair dryers. *Fee:* video games, high-speed Internet. **Dining:** restaurant, 6:30 am-11:30 pm, $12-$18, cocktails. **Pool(s):** heated indoor. **Leisure Activities:** saunas, whirlpool, exercise room. **Guest Services:** gift shop, valet and coin laundry, area transportation-within 5 mi. **Business Services:** meeting rooms, business center. *Fee:* PC, fax. **Cards:** AX, CB, DC, DS, JC, MC, VI. *(See color ad card insert)*

SOME UNITS
FEE

RED ROOF INN
AAA SAVE
◆◆ ◆
Motel

Phone: (630)963-4205 262
6/16-9/28   1P: $55-$69   2P: $61-$74   XP: $5   F18
9/29-3/31   1P: $41-$63   2P: $46-$68   XP: $5   F18
5/5-6/15   1P: $44-$59   2P: $49-$64   XP: $5   F18
4/1-5/4   1P: $39-$49   2P: $44-$54   XP: $5   F18
Location: I-355, exit Butterfield Rd (SR 56), on frontage road; I-88, exit Highland Ave N, just w. 1113 Butterfield Rd 60515. Fax: 630/963-4425. **Facility:** 135 one-bedroom standard units. 2 stories, exterior corridors. **Parking:** on-site. **Terms:** small pets only. **Amenities:** video games, voice mail. **Cards:** AX, CB, DC, DS, MC, VI. **Special Amenities: free local telephone calls and free newspaper.**

SOME UNITS
FEE

ELGIN pop. 77,000

———— WHERE TO STAY ————

BAYMONT INN
AAA SAVE
◆◆ ◆
Motel

Phone: (847)931-4800
11/1-3/31 [ECP]   1P: $65-$85
4/1-6/1 [ECP]   1P: $65-$75
6/2-10/31 [ECP]   1P: $60-$75
Location: I-90, exit SR 31 N, just n. 500 Toll Gate Rd 60123. Fax: 847/931-4894. **Facility:** 80 one-bedroom standard units. 3 stories, interior corridors. *Bath:* combo or shower only. **Parking:** on-site, winter plug-ins. **Amenities:** voice mail, irons, hair dryers. **Leisure Activities:** exercise room. **Guest Services:** valet and coin laundry. **Cards:** AX, CB, DC, DS, JC, MC, VI. **Special Amenities: free continental breakfast and free newspaper.**

SOME UNITS

COUNTRY INN & SUITES BY CARLSON IN ELGIN
Phone: (847)426-6400

[AAA] [SAVE]

Motel

| 4/1-9/30 | 1P: $89 | XP: $10 | F17 |
| 10/1-3/31 | 1P: $59 | XP: $10 | F17 |

Location: I-90, exit Randall Rd, just n to Point Blvd, then just e. 2270 Point Blvd 60123. Fax: 847/426-6410. **Facility:** 74 units. 59 one-bedroom standard units. 15 one-bedroom suites ($99-$149), some with whirlpools. 3 stories, interior corridors. *Bath:* combo or shower only. **Parking:** on-site. **Terms:** cancellation fee imposed. **Amenities:** extended cable TV, dual phone lines, voice mail, irons, hair dryers. **Pool(s):** heated indoor. **Leisure Activities:** whirlpool, limited exercise equipment. **Guest Services:** valet and coin laundry. **Business Services:** meeting rooms. **Cards:** AX, DC, DS, MC, VI. *(See color ad p 322)*

SOME UNITS

CROWNE PLAZA
Phone: (847)488-9000

[AAA] [SAVE]

Hotel

All Year   1P: $89   2P: $89

Location: I-90, exit SR 31 N, just n. 495 Airport Rd 60123. Fax: 847/488-9800. **Facility:** 243 units. 175 one-bedroom standard units. 68 one-bedroom suites, some with whirlpools. 8 stories, interior corridors. *Bath:* combo or shower only. **Parking:** on-site and valet. **Terms:** package plans. **Amenities:** voice mail, irons, hair dryers. *Fee:* video games, Web TV. *Some:* CD players. **Dining:** dining room, restaurant, 6 am-midnight, $8-$19, cocktails, entertainment. **Pool(s):** heated indoor. **Leisure Activities:** whirlpool, exercise room. **Guest Services:** gift shop, valet and coin laundry, area transportation-within 3 mi. **Business Services:** conference facilities, business center, PC, fax. **Cards:** AX, CB, DC, DS, JC, MC, VI. **Special Amenities:** free continental breakfast and free newspaper. *(See color ad below)*

SOME UNITS

FEE   FEE FEE

HAMPTON INN
Phone: 847/931-1940

Motel

Property failed to provide current rates

Location: I-90, exit SR 31 N, just n. 405 Airport Rd 60123. Fax: 847/931-5190. **Facility:** 108 one-bedroom standard units. 3 stories, interior corridors. *Bath:* combo or shower only. **Parking:** on-site. **Terms:** package plans. **Amenities:** extended cable TV, dual phone lines, voice mail, irons, hair dryers. **Pool(s):** small heated indoor. **Leisure Activities:** whirlpool, sun deck, exercise room. **Guest Services:** valet and coin laundry. **Business Services:** meeting rooms, business center, fax. **Cards:** AX, CB, DC, DS, MC, VI.

SOME UNITS

RAMADA INN ELGIN
Phone: 847/695-5000

Motor Inn

All Year   1P: $59-$71   2P: $62-$80

Location: I-90, exit SR 31 S, 0.5 mi e. 345 W River Rd 60123. Fax: 847/695-6556. **Facility:** 203 units. 198 one-bedroom standard units. 5 one-bedroom suites ($89), some with whirlpools. 2-5 stories, interior corridors. **Parking:** on-site. **Terms:** package plans, pets ($40 deposit, $10 extra charge). **Amenities:** voice mail. *Some:* irons, hair dryers. **Pool(s):** heated indoor. **Leisure Activities:** sauna, whirlpool, limited exercise equipment. **Guest Services:** valet and coin laundry. **Business Services:** conference facilities. **Cards:** AX, CB, DC, DS, JC, MC, VI.

SOME UNITS

SUPER 8 MOTEL
Phone: (847)697-8828

Motel

5/31-9/30 [CP]	1P: $70-$75	2P: $80-$85
10/1-12/31 [CP]	1P: $65-$72	2P: $75-$80
1/1-3/31 [CP]	1P: $63-$70	2P: $70-$80
4/1-5/30 [CP]	1P: $70	2P: $74

Location: I-90, exit SR 31 N, just n. 435 Airport Rd 60123. Fax: 847/697-6659. **Facility:** 63 one-bedroom standard units. 2 stories, interior corridors. **Parking:** on-site, winter plug-ins. **Terms:** 5 day cancellation notice. **Amenities:** irons, hair dryers. **Cards:** AX, CB, DC, DS, JC, MC, VI.

SOME UNITS

──── WHERE TO DINE ────

PRAIRIE ROCK BREWING COMPANY   **Lunch:** $8-$14   **Dinner:** $11-$26   **Phone:** 847/622-8888
♦♦♦ ♦♦♦   **Location:** Just n of Riverboat Casino. 127 S Grove 60120. **Hours:** 11:30 am-2:30 & 5-10 pm, Fri & Sat-11 pm,
American   Sun 4 pm-9 pm. **Reservations:** accepted. **Features:** casual dress; children's menu; carryout; cocktails &
   lounge; a la carte. While known primarily as a microbrewery with a variety of beers including both famous
   flavors and seasonal brews, this place also has made a name for itself with its fine food. Prime steak,
seafood and pasta are the emphasis, but the rich bowl of red chili is exceptional. A large, sleek-looking, two-tiered dining room
is accented with wood trim and walls, tabletops draped in white cloths, street lamp lighting and a sensational two-story stone
fireplace that serves as the room's centerpiece. **Parking:** on-site. **Cards:** AX, CB, DC, DS, MC, VI.   ⊠

──── *The following restaurant has not been evaluated by AAA* ────
but is listed for your information only.

AL'S CAFE & CREAMERY   **Phone:** 847/742-1180
[fyi]   Not evaluated. **Location:** 43 DuPage Ct 60120. Patrons of the casual downtown cafe can enjoy milkshakes with a
   wide variety of sandwiches.

ELK GROVE VILLAGE pop. 33,400   (See map p. 284; index p. 287)

──── WHERE TO STAY ────

BEST WESTERN MIDWAY HOTEL   **Phone:** (847)981-0010   **75**
AAA [SAVE]   9/1-3/31 [ECP]   1P: $94-$130   2P: $104-$140   XP: $10   F
   4/1-8/31 [ECP]   1P: $88-$124   2P: $98-$134   XP: $10   F
♦♦♦ ♦♦♦   **Location:** Jct Higgins and Busse rds with Oakton St. 1600 Oakton St 60007. **Fax:** 847/364-7365. **Facility:** 165 units.
Motor Inn   159 one-bedroom standard units. 6 one-bedroom suites ($99-$139). 3 stories, interior corridors. **Parking:**
   on-site. **Terms:** [BP] meal plan available, package plans. **Amenities:** extended cable TV, voice mail, irons,
   hair dryers. **Dining:** restaurant, 6:30-10:30 am, 11-1:30 & 5-10 pm, $9-$24, cocktails. **Pool(s):** heated indoor.
Leisure Activities: saunas, whirlpool, exercise room, indoor recreation area. **Guest Services:** valet laundry, area transportation-
within 5 mi. **Business Services:** conference facilities. **Cards:** AX, CB, DC, DS, MC, VI. **Special Amenities: free continental
breakfast and free newspaper.**
SOME UNITS
[icons] ⊠ 🛏

COMFORT INN INTERNATIONAL   **Phone:** (847)364-6200   **79**
AAA [SAVE]   4/1-9/30   1P: $72-$189   2P: $72-$189   XP: $10   F18
   10/1-3/31   1P: $59-$169   2P: $59-$169   XP: $10   F18
♦♦♦ ♦♦♦ ♦♦♦   **Location:** Just s of I-90, jct Elmhurst and Landmeier rds, just n of Higgins. 2550 Landmeier Rd 60007.
Motel   Fax: 847/364-0957. **Facility:** 102 one-bedroom standard units. 3 stories, interior corridors. **Parking:** on-site.
   Terms: cancellation fee imposed, package plans. **Amenities:** dual phone lines, voice mail, irons, hair dryers.
   Fee: video games, high-speed Internet, safes. **Leisure Activities:** exercise room. **Guest Services:** valet
laundry, airport transportation-O'Hare International Airport. **Business Services:** meeting rooms. **Cards:** AX, CB, DC, DS, JC,
MC, VI. **Special Amenities: free continental breakfast and free local telephone calls.**
SOME UNITS
[icons] FEE

EXEL INN OF ELK GROVE VILLAGE   **Phone:** (847)895-2085   **77**
AAA [SAVE]   All Year [CP]   1P: $50-$68   2P: $56-$74   XP: $6   F18
♦♦♦ ♦♦♦   **Location:** I-290, exit Thorndale Ave, 0.5 mi w to Rohlwing Rd, 0.3 mi n to Devon Ave, then 0.3 mi e. 1000 W Devon Ave
Motel   60007. Fax: 847/895-2471. **Facility:** 113 one-bedroom standard units, some with whirlpools. 3 stories, interior corridors. **Parking:** on-site. **Terms:** small pets only. **Amenities:** extended cable TV, irons. **Leisure Activities:** exercise room. **Guest Services:** coin laundry. **Cards:** AX, CB, DC, DS, MC, VI. **Special Amenities:
   early check-in/late check-out and free continental breakfast.** *(See color ad p 318)*
SOME UNITS
[icons] FEE   ⊠   FEE FEE

EXEL INN OF O'HARE   **Phone:** (847)803-9400   **83**
AAA [SAVE]   All Year [CP]   1P: $67-$85   2P: $73-$91   XP: $6   F18
♦♦♦ ♦♦♦   **Location:** Jct SR 83 and 72, 1.5 mi e on SR 72 (Higgins/Touhy Ave). 2881 Touhy Ave 60007. Fax: 847/803-9771.
Motel   **Facility:** 123 one-bedroom standard units, some with whirlpools. 3 stories, interior corridors. **Parking:** on-
   site. **Terms:** small pets only. **Amenities:** extended cable TV, irons, hair dryers. **Leisure Activities:** exercise
   room. **Guest Services:** valet and coin laundry. **Business Services:** business center, PC, fax. **Cards:** AX,
   CB, DC, DS, MC, VI. **Special Amenities: early check-in/late check-out and free continental breakfast.**
(See color ad p 318)
SOME UNITS
[icons] FEE   ⊠   FEE FEE

HAMPTON INN ELK GROVE VILLAGE   **Phone:** 847/593-8600   **80**
AAA [SAVE]   All Year   1P: $87   2P: $97   XP: $10   F18
♦♦♦ ♦♦♦   **Location:** Just n of jct Higgins Rd. 100 Busse Rd 60007. Fax: 847/593-8607. **Facility:** 125 one-bedroom standard
Motel   units. 4 stories, interior corridors. **Parking:** on-site. **Terms:** 5 day cancellation notice, [CP] meal plan available, package plans. **Amenities:** video games (fee), voice mail, irons, hair dryers. **Guest Services:** valet
   laundry. **Business Services:** meeting rooms. **Cards:** AX, CB, DC, DS, MC, VI. **Special Amenities: free
continental breakfast and free local telephone calls.**
SOME UNITS
[icons] FEE   ⊠

(See map p. 284)

HOLIDAY INN OF ELK GROVE

Phone: 847/437-6010   **76**

All Year [BP]   1P: $79-$119   2P: $79-$119   XP: $10   F18

Motor Inn

Location: SR 83 (Busse Rd), 0.3 mi s of jct Higgins Rd (SR 72). 1000 Busse Rd 60007. Fax: 847/806-9369. **Facility:** 159 units. 158 one-bedroom standard units. 1 one-bedroom suite ($125-$225) with whirlpool. 4 stories, interior corridors. *Bath:* combo or shower only. **Parking:** on-site. **Terms:** [CP] meal plan available, small pets only. **Amenities:** voice mail, irons, hair dryers. *Some:* honor bars. **Pool(s):** heated indoor. **Leisure Activities:** saunas, whirlpool, exercise room. **Guest Services:** valet and coin laundry. **Business Services:** conference facilities. **Cards:** AX, CB, DC, DS, JC, MC, VI.

SOME UNITS

ASK ⓢⓓ ✚ 🐾 🍴 🍽 🍸 🅿 🏊 🔀 📺 DATA PORT 💻 🖨 / ✗ /   FEE

LA QUINTA INN O'HARE AIRPORT

Phone: (847)439-6767   **81**

SAVE

All Year   1P: $80-$139   2P: $90-$149   XP: $10   F18

Motel

Location: Jct of Higgins and Busse rds with Oakton St. 1900 Oakton St 60007. Fax: 847/439-5464. **Facility:** 142 one-bedroom standard units. 4 stories, interior corridors. **Parking:** on-site. **Terms:** package plans, small pets only. **Amenities:** video games, voice mail. *Some:* irons, hair dryers. **Pool(s):** heated outdoor. **Guest Services:** valet laundry. **Cards:** AX, CB, DC, DS, MC, VI. *(See color ad p 325)*

SOME UNITS

✚ 🐾 🍽 🏊 🔀 📺 DATA PORT 💻 / ✗ 🛢 🖨 /   FEE

SHERATON SUITES ELK GROVE/O'HARE

Phone: (847)290-1600   **82**

All Year   1P: $99-$239   2P: $109-$249   XP: $10   F17

Suite Hotel

Location: I-90, exit Arlington Heights Blvd S; in Northwest Point Corp Park. 121 Northwest Point Blvd 60007. Fax: 847/290-1129. **Facility:** 253 one-bedroom suites. 7 stories, interior corridors. **Parking:** on-site. **Terms:** cancellation fee imposed, package plans. **Amenities:** video games (fee), voice mail, honor bars, irons, hair dryers. *Some:* dual phone lines, fax. **Pool(s):** heated outdoor, heated indoor. **Leisure Activities:** whirlpool, jogging, exercise room. **Guest Services:** valet and coin laundry. **Business Services:** meeting rooms. **Cards:** AX, CB, DC, DS, JC, MC, VI.

SOME UNITS

✚ 🍴 🍸 🦽 🅿 🏊 🔀 📺 DATA PORT 💻 🖨 / ✗ 🖨 /   FEE

SUPER 8 MOTEL O'HARE

Phone: (847)827-3133   **84**

AAA SAVE

All Year   1P: $55-$59   2P: $65-$78   XP: $7   D18

Motel

Location: Jct SR 83 and 72, 1.5 mi e on SR 72 (Higgins Ave). 2951 Touhy Ave 60007. Fax: 847/827-3246. **Facility:** 98 units. 95 one-bedroom standard units, some with whirlpools. 3 one-bedroom suites ($110-$125). 2 stories, interior corridors. *Bath:* combo or shower only. **Parking:** on-site. **Terms:** [CP] & [ECP] meal plans available, package plans. **Amenities:** extended cable TV, safes. *Some:* dual phone lines, hair dryers. **Pool(s):** small heated indoor. **Leisure Activities:** whirlpool, exercise room. **Guest Services:** valet and coin laundry. **Cards:** AX, CB, DC, DS, JC, MC, VI. **Special Amenities:** free continental breakfast and free local telephone calls.

SOME UNITS

ⓢⓓ ✚ 🦽 🅿 🏊 🔀 📺 DATA PORT 🖨 / ✗ 🛢 🖨 💻 /   FEE   FEE

ELMHURST   pop. 42,000   (See map p. 284; index p. 290)

——— **WHERE TO STAY** ———

AMERISUITES (CHICAGO/ELMHURST-O'HARE AREA)

Phone: (630)782-6300   **198**

AAA SAVE

All Year [ECP]   1P: $79-$109   2P: $79-$109   XP: $10   F17

Motel

Location: I-20, exit 12, just w on US 20 (Lake St). 410 W Lake St 60126. Fax: 630/782-6303. **Facility:** 128 one-bedroom standard units. 6 stories, interior corridors. *Bath:* combo or shower only. **Parking:** on-site. **Terms:** package plans, small pets only. **Amenities:** voice mail, irons, hair dryers. *Fee:* video games, high-speed Internet. *Some:* dual phone lines. **Pool(s):** heated indoor. **Leisure Activities:** sun deck, exercise room. **Guest Services:** complimentary evening beverages: Wed, valet and coin laundry, airport transportation-O'Hare International Airport, area transportation-within 5 mi. **Business Services:** meeting rooms, business center, PC, fax. **Cards:** AX, CB, DC, DS, JC, MC, VI. **Special Amenities:** free continental breakfast and free newspaper. *(See color ad p 296)*

SOME UNITS

ⓢⓓ ✚ 🐾 🍽 🦽 🅖 🅿 🏊 VCR 📺 DATA PORT 🛢 🖨 💻 🖨 / ✗ /   FEE

COURTYARD BY MARRIOTT-ELMHURST

Phone: (630)941-9444   **202**

AAA SAVE

All Year   1P: $119

Motel

Location: I-290, exit 10A (SR 83), 1 mi s on SR 83, at jct SR 64 (North Ave). 370 N Rt 83 60126. Fax: 630/941-3539. **Facility:** 140 units. 126 one-bedroom standard units. 14 one-bedroom suites with whirlpools. 7 stories, interior corridors. **Parking:** on-site. **Terms:** 30 day cancellation notice, [BP] meal plan available. **Amenities:** video games (fee), dual phone lines, voice mail, irons, hair dryers. **Dining:** coffee shop, 6-10 am, Sat & Sun 7-11 am. **Pool(s):** heated indoor. **Leisure Activities:** sauna, whirlpool, exercise room. **Guest Services:** valet and coin laundry. **Business Services:** meeting rooms. **Cards:** AX, CB, DC, DS, MC, VI. *(See color ad card insert)*

SOME UNITS

🍴 🍸 🅿 🏊 🔀 📺 DATA PORT 💻 / ✗ 🛢 🖨 /   FEE

HOLIDAY INN CHICAGO-ELMHURST

Phone: (630)279-1100   **199**

AAA SAVE

All Year   1P: $119   2P: $129   XP: $10   F18

Motor Inn

Location: I-290, exit 12, just n. 624 N York Rd 60126. Fax: 630/279-4038. **Facility:** 237 one-bedroom standard units, some with whirlpools. 4 stories, interior corridors. **Parking:** on-site. **Terms:** check-in 4 pm, [AP] meal plan available, package plans, pets ($25 fee). **Amenities:** voice mail, irons, hair dryers. **Dining:** restaurant, 6:30 am-2 & 5-10 pm, weekends from 7 am, $8-$21, cocktails. **Pool(s):** heated indoor. **Leisure Activities:** sauna, whirlpool, exercise room, sports court, basketball, volleyball, indoor recreation area. *Fee:* game room. **Guest Services:** valet and coin laundry, area transportation-within 3 mi. **Business Services:** meeting rooms, business center. *Fee:* PC, fax. **Cards:** AX, CB, DC, DS, JC, MC, VI. **Special Amenities:** early check-in/late check-out and free local telephone calls.

SOME UNITS

ⓢⓓ ✚ 🐾 🍴 🍸 🅿 🏊 🔀 📺 DATA PORT 💻 🖨 / ✗ 🛢 /   FEE

(See map p. 284)

HOLIDAY INN EXPRESS OAK BROOK/ELMHURST

AAA (SAVE) — Motel

All Year   1P: $79   2P: $109   **Phone:** (630)279-0700   200

XP: $10   F19

Location: At Riverside Dr, off SR 83, 2.4 mi s of SR 64. 933 Rt 83 S 60126. **Fax:** 630/279-0131. **Facility:** 102 units. 101 one-bedroom standard units. 1 one-bedroom suite ($149-$199). 2 stories, interior corridors. *Bath:* combo or shower only. **Parking:** on-site. **Terms:** cancellation fee imposed, [ECP] meal plan available. **Amenities:** extended cable TV, dual phone lines, voice mail, irons, hair dryers. **Pool(s):** heated outdoor. **Leisure Activities:** Fee: driving range. **Guest Services:** complimentary evening beverages: Mon-Thurs, valet laundry. **Business Services:** meeting rooms, business center, PC (fee). **Cards:** AX, CB, DC, DS, JC, MC, VI. **Special Amenities:** free continental breakfast and free local telephone calls.

SOME UNITS

───────── WHERE TO DINE ─────────

DAVE AND JACK'S SILVERADO GRILL

Steak House

Lunch: $8-$14   **Dinner:** $9-$18   **Phone:** 630/833-1602   172

Location: SR 83, 0.6 mi e on St Charles Rd, just s. 447 Spring Rd 60126. **Hours:** 11:30 am-10 pm, Fri-11 pm, Sat 5 pm-11 pm, Sun 5 pm-9:30 pm. Closed major holidays. **Reservations:** accepted. **Features:** casual dress; children's menu; carryout; cocktails & lounge. You'll enjoy the casual country western decor at Dave and Jack's Silverado along with the steak and rib house specialties. You can't go wrong when ordering the teriyaki steak cooked to order and seasoned just right. Fine selections of sandwiches and hamburgers also available and the service is prompt and friendly. **Parking:** on-site. **Cards:** AX, DC, DS, MC, VI.

OUR KITCHEN

American

Lunch: $4-$9   **Phone:** 630/279-3738   171

Location: I-290, exit 12, then 0.3 mi w on US 20. 363 W Lake St 60126. **Hours:** 7 am-3 pm, Sun-2 pm. Closed: 11/28, 12/25. **Features:** casual dress; carryout. This cozy, country-style restaurant specializes in pancake and omelet creations, but there are also quite a few other notable menu selections such as a variety of waffles, club sandwiches and thick burgers. Our Kitchen only serves breakfast and lunch. **Parking:** on-site.

Cards: AX, DC, DS, MC, VI.

EVANSTON pop. 73,200 (See map p. 284; index p. 289)

───────── WHERE TO STAY ─────────

THE EVANSTON HOLIDAY INN & CONFERENCE CENTER

Hotel

			Phone: (847)491-6400 176
4/1-11/15 & 3/1-3/31	1P: $129-$189	2P: $139-$199	XP: $10 F12
11/16-2/28	1P: $79-$129	2P: $99-$139	XP: $10 F12

Location: Just s of Evanston Towne Centre, at Sherman and Lake sts. 1501 Sherman Ave 60201. **Fax:** 847/328-3090. **Facility:** 159 one-bedroom standard units. 12 stories, interior corridors. *Bath:* combo or shower only. **Parking:** on-site. **Terms:** cancellation fee imposed, [BP] meal plan available, package plans. **Amenities:** dual phone lines, voice mail, irons, hair dryers. **Pool(s):** heated outdoor, wading. **Leisure Activities:** sauna, exercise room. **Guest Services:** valet and coin laundry. **Business Services:** conference facilities. **Cards:** AX, CB, DC, DS, JC, MC, VI.

SOME UNITS

HILTON GARDEN INN-EVANSTON

AAA (SAVE) — Motor Inn

All Year   1P: $109-$209   2P: $119-$219   **Phone:** (847)475-6400   174

XP: $10   F18

Location: US 41 (Skokie Blvd), 1.8 mi e to McDormick, 0.7 mi n to Golf/Emerson, 1.2 mi e to Maple Ave, then just s. 1818 Maple Ave 60201. **Fax:** 847/475-6460. **Facility:** 178 units. 172 one-bedroom standard units. 6 one-bedroom suites ($149-$299), some with whirlpools. 6 stories, interior corridors. *Bath:* combo or shower only. **Parking:** on-site (fee). **Terms:** 14 day cancellation notice, package plans. **Amenities:** dual phone lines, voice mail, irons, hair dryers. **Fee:** video games, Web TV. **Dining:** restaurant, 6 am-11 pm, $9-$19, cocktails. **Pool(s):** small heated indoor. **Leisure Activities:** exercise room. **Guest Services:** valet and coin laundry. **Business Services:** conference facilities, business center, PC, fax. **Cards:** AX, CB, DC, DS, JC, MC, VI. **Special Amenities:** free local telephone calls and free newspaper. *(See ad below)*

SOME UNITS

FEE

(See map p. 284)

OMNI ORRINGTON HOTEL
Phone: (847)866-8700 〔175〕

▼▼▼▼
Classic Hotel

All Year [BP]   1P: $179-$189   2P: $179-$189   XP: $10   F17
Location: Adjacent to Northwestern University. 1710 Orrington Ave 60201. Fax: 847/866-8724. **Facility:** Historic. 270 one-bedroom standard units. 8 one- and 2 two-bedroom suites, some with kitchens. 9 stories, interior corridors. *Bath:* combo or shower only. **Parking:** valet only (fee). **Terms:** package plans. **Amenities:** video games (fee), voice mail, irons, hair dryers. **Leisure Activities:** exercise room. **Guest Services:** gift shop, valet laundry. **Business Services:** conference facilities. **Cards:** AX, CB, DC, DS, JC, MC, VI.

SOME UNITS

—— WHERE TO DINE ——

TRIO
Lunch: $29   **Dinner: $65-$85**   **Phone: 847/733-8746** 〔156〕

▼▼▼ ▼▼
American

Location: From Dempster St, 0.3 mi n; in The Homestead; just s of jct Church St. 1625 Hinman Ave 60201. **Hours:** 6 pm-9:30 pm, Fri noon-1 & 6-10 pm, Sat 5 pm-10 pm, Sun 5 pm-9 pm. Closed major holidays; also Mon. **Reservations:** suggested. **Features:** semi-formal attire; cocktails & lounge; prix fixe. In the heart of historic Evanston, Trio is fine dining at it's very best. Here you will find wonderfully prepared fusion cuisine that combines French, Italian and Asian influences. Each plate is handsomely presented and imaginatively conceived with each ingredient coordinated perfectly to enhance the overall flavor of the dish. The menu is ala carte but you may also opt for the chef's five course tasting menu that features a variety of dishes that give you a great exposure to this unique cuisine. Smoke free premises. **Parking:** street and valet (fee). **Cards:** AX, DS, JC, MC, VI.

VA PENSIERO
Dinner: $16-$29   **Phone: 847/475-7779** 〔157〕

▼▼ ▼▼
Italian

Location: Just s of Davis, 0.3 mi n of Dempster; in Margarita European Inn. 1566 Oak Ave 60201. **Hours:** 5:30 pm-9 pm, Fri & Sat-10 pm, Sun-8 pm. Closed major holidays. **Reservations:** suggested. **Features:** dressy casual; cocktails; a la carte. Superb Italian cuisine is served in a classic European atmosphere their service is consistently attentive and knowledgeable. Any of the seafood appetizers or entrees make fine choices and are skillfully presented. The Australian rack of lamb is extraordinary. Smoke free premises. **Parking:** on-site and valet (fee). **Cards:** AX, CB, DC, DS, MC, VI.

FRANKLIN PARK pop. 18,500   (See map p. 284; index p. 291)

—— WHERE TO STAY ——

COMFORT INN
SAVE
Phone: (847)233-9292 〔245〕

▼▼▼ ▼
Motel

All Year   1P: $99-$119   2P: $99-$119   XP: $10   F16
Location: Jct US 12/45 (Mannheim Rd) and Grand Ave, just n. 3001 N Mannheim Rd 60131. Fax: 847/233-9255. **Facility:** 56 one-bedroom standard units, some with whirlpools. 4 stories, interior corridors. *Bath:* combo or shower only. **Parking:** on-site. **Terms:** pets ($50 deposit). **Amenities:** extended cable TV, safes (fee), irons, hair dryers. **Pool(s):** small heated indoor. **Leisure Activities:** limited exercise equipment. **Guest Services:** valet laundry. **Cards:** AX, CB, DC, DS, JC, MC, VI.

SOME UNITS

SUPER 8 O'HARE SOUTH
Phone: (847)288-0600 〔246〕

▼▼ ▼▼
Motel

All Year   1P: $59-$109   2P: $54-$114   XP: $7   F12
Location: Jct SR 64, 1.4 mi n. 3010 N Mannheim Rd 60131. Fax: 847/288-1251. **Facility:** 91 units. 89 one-bedroom standard units, some with whirlpools. 2 one-bedroom suites ($109-$209). 2-3 stories, interior corridors. *Bath:* combo or shower only. **Parking:** on-site. **Terms:** 3 day cancellation notice, package plans. **Amenities:** extended cable TV, safes (fee), irons, hair dryers. **Leisure Activities:** limited exercise equipment. **Business Services:** meeting rooms. **Cards:** AX, CB, DC, DS, MC, VI.

SOME UNITS

GENEVA pop. 12,600

—— WHERE TO STAY ——

THE HERRINGTON INN
AAA SAVE
Phone: (630)208-7433

▼▼▼ ▼
Country Inn

All Year   1P: $159-$385   2P: $159-$385   XP: $15   F18
Location: Banks of Fox River, just off SR 38, 0.5 mi w of jct SR 25. 15 S River Ln 60134. Fax: 630/208-8930. **Facility:** Each guest room has a fireplace at this intimate inn designed in a European style. 63 units. 55 one-bedroom standard units with whirlpools. 8 one-bedroom suites ($345-$425) with whirlpools. 3 stories, interior corridors. **Parking:** on-site. **Terms:** check-in 4 pm, package plans, small pets only ($40 fee, $210 deposit). **Amenities:** extended cable TV, CD players, dual phone lines, voice mail, honor bars, irons, hair dryers. *Some:* high-speed Internet (fee). **Dining:** Atwater's, see separate listing. **Guest Services:** afternoon tea, valet laundry, area transportation-within 5 mi. **Business Services:** meeting rooms. **Cards:** AX, CB, DC, DS, MC, VI. **Special Amenities:** free continental breakfast and free local telephone calls.

SOME UNITS

—— WHERE TO DINE ——
---

302 WEST
Dinner: $18-$28   **Phone: 630/232-9302**

▼▼▼
American

Location: Center; on SR 38, w of SR 31. 302 W State St 60134. **Hours:** 6 pm-9 pm, Fri & Sat-10 pm. Closed major holidays; also Sun & Mon. **Reservations:** suggested. **Features:** casual dress; cocktails & lounge. 302 West occupies what was formerly a large bank and features a stylish two-tier dining room. The dining room is casual-upscale with an enormously high ceiling, tall stately arched windows on two sides, light wood wanescoating, crisp linen tabletops and blue vases with fresh flowers. The creative and well-prepared cuisine is described as Modern American. The menu features a variety of fresh seafood, a venison chop, veal and beef tenderloin. **Parking:** street. **Cards:** AX, CB, DC, DS, MC, VI.

ATWATER'S
Continental

Lunch: $10-$16   Dinner: $18-$30   Phone: 630/208-7433
Location: Banks of Fox River, just off SR 38, 0.5 mi w of jct SR 25; in The Herrington Inn. 15 S River Ln 60134. **Hours:** 6:30-10 am, 11-2 & 5:30-9 pm, Fri & Sat-10 pm. **Reservations:** suggested. **Features:** dressy casual; Sunday brunch; cocktails; a la carte. Overlooking the Fox River, the romantic European-style inn has a cozy, intimate feel. Well-prepared dishes include succulent steaks and tasty seafood salad with smoked fish, tuna and lobster in lemon ginger vinaigrette and Thai green curry sauce. Smoke free premises. **Parking:** on-site. **Cards:** AX, DC, DS, MC, VI.

GRANADA TAPAS BAR & RESTAURANT
Spanish

Lunch: $7-$16   Dinner: $9-$18   Phone: 630/262-1000
Location: SR 31, just w on SR 38, then just s. 14 S Third 60134. **Hours:** 11:30 am-9:30 pm, Fri-11 pm, Sat noon-11 pm, Sun 3 pm-9 pm. Closed major holidays. **Reservations:** accepted. **Features:** casual dress; children's menu; carryout; cocktails & lounge; a la carte. An extensive menu of excellently prepared Spanish paellas, small casseroles and hot and cold tapas awaits diners. Vivid murals of a Spanish village and countryside decorate the energetic dining room. Varied desserts and coffees are also available. Smoke free premises. **Parking:** street. **Cards:** AX, DC, MC, VI.

MILL RACE INN
American

Country Inn   Lunch: $9-$16   Dinner: $11-$25   Phone: 630/232-2030
Location: Center; on SR 38 at jct SR 25, entrance off SR 25. 4 E State St 60134. **Hours:** 11:30 am-3 & 5-9 pm, Fri & Sat-10 pm, Sun 10 am-9 pm. Closed: 12/25. **Reservations:** suggested. **Features:** casual dress; Sunday brunch; children's menu; cocktails & lounge; entertainment. A cozy country feel settles over the rustic dining room, which features a large stone fireplace, vines twisted along the top of the windows and splendid Fox River views from every table. Offerings of classic American cuisine include preparations of prime rib, steak, chicken, lamb and fresh seafood. **Parking:** on-site and valet. **Cards:** AX, CB, DC, MC, VI.

GLEN ELLYN pop. 24,900   (See map p. 284; index p. 290)

─────── WHERE TO STAY ───────

HOLIDAY INN
Motor Inn

All Year   1P: $89-$109   2P: $89-$109   Phone: (630)629-6000   221
Location: I-355, exit Roosevelt Rd, 0.8 mi e on SR 38. 1250 Roosevelt Rd 60137. Fax: 630/629-0025. **Facility:** 119 one-bedroom standard units. 4 stories, interior corridors. **Bath:** combo or shower only. **Parking:** on-site. **Terms:** cancellation fee imposed, package plans, small pets only ($25 fee). **Amenities:** irons, hair dryers. **Pool(s):** heated outdoor. **Leisure Activities:** exercise room. **Guest Services:** complimentary evening beverages: Tues, valet and coin laundry. **Business Services:** conference facilities. **Cards:** AX, CB, DC, DS, JC, MC, VI.

SOME UNITS

GLENVIEW pop. 37,100   (See map p. 284; index p. 289)

─────── WHERE TO STAY ───────

BAYMONT INN & SUITES CHICAGO-GLENVIEW
Motel

All Year   1P: $74-$84   2P: $74-$84   Phone: (847)635-8300   146
Location: I-294, exit Willow Rd, 0.3 mi w to Sanders Rd, 1.3 mi s to Milwaukee Ave (SR 21), 0.5 mi se to Lake Ave. 1625 Milwaukee Ave 60025. Fax: 847/635-8166. **Facility:** 142 units. 138 one-bedroom standard units. 4 one-bedroom suites ($84-$124). 3 stories, interior corridors. **Parking:** on-site, winter plug-ins. **Terms:** small pets only. **Amenities:** video games (fee), voice mail, irons, hair dryers. **Leisure Activities:** exercise room. **Guest Services:** valet and coin laundry. **Business Services:** meeting rooms. **Cards:** AX, CB, DC, DS, MC, VI. **Special Amenities:** free continental breakfast and free newspaper. *(See color ad opposite title page)*

SOME UNITS

(See map p. 284)

COURTYARD BY MARRIOTT-GLENVIEW
Phone: (847)803-2500   **147**

ⒶⒶⒶ (SAVE)   All Year   1P: $129-$139   2P: $129-$139
▼▼▼   Location: I-294, exit Willow Rd, 0.3 mi w to Sanders Rd, 1.3 mi s to Milwaukee Ave (SR 21), 0.5 mi se to Lake Ave.
Motel   1801 Milwaukee Ave 60025. Fax: 847/803-2520. Facility: 149 units. 137 one-bedroom standard units. 12 one-
bedroom suites. 3 stories, interior corridors. Bath: combo or shower only. Parking: on-site. Terms: [BP] meal
plan available, package plans. Amenities: high-speed Internet (fee), voice mail, irons, hair dryers.
Dining: coffee shop, 6:30-10:30 am, Sat & Sun 7-11 am. Pool(s): heated indoor. Leisure Activities: whirlpool, exercise room. Guest Services: valet and coin laundry. Business Services: meeting rooms. Cards: AX, CB, DC, DS, JC,
MC, VI. (See ad p 299 & color ad card insert)

SOME UNITS

DOUBLETREE GUEST SUITES O'HARE NORTH-GLENVIEW
Phone: (847)803-9800   **149**

ⒶⒶⒶ (SAVE)   4/1-8/31   1P: $99-$159   2P: $99-$159   XP: $20   F18
▼▼▼   9/1-11/30   1P: $99-$139   2P: $99-$139   XP: $20   F18
        12/1-3/31   1P: $79-$129   2P: $79-$129   XP: $20   F18
Suite Hotel   Location: I-294, exit Willow Rd, 0.3 mi w to Sanders Rd, 1.3 mi s to Milwaukee Ave (SR 21), then 1 mi s. 1400 N Milwaukee Ave 60025. Fax: 847/803-0380. Facility: 252 one-bedroom suites. 7 stories, interior corridors.
Parking: on-site. Terms: package plans. Amenities: dual phone lines, voice mail, honor bars, irons, hair
dryers. Fee: video games, high-speed Internet. Some: DVD players (fee), fax. Dining: restaurant, 6:30 am-9:30 & 11-11 pm, Sat
& Sun 7:30-10:30 am, $9-$21, cocktails. Pool(s): heated indoor. Leisure Activities: sauna, whirlpool, sun deck, exercise room,
volleyball. Guest Services: gift shop, valet and coin laundry, area transportation-within 5 mi. Business Services: conference
facilities. Cards: AX, CB, DC, DS, JC, MC, VI. (See ad p 317)

SOME UNITS

FAIRFIELD INN CHICAGO/GLENVIEW
Phone: (847)299-1600   **148**

ⒶⒶⒶ (SAVE)   All Year [ECP]   1P: $84   2P: $84
▼▼▼   Location: I-294, exit Willow Rd, 0.3 mi w to Sanders Rd, 1.3 mi s to Milwaukee Ave (SR 21), 0.5 mi se. 4514 W Lake
Motel   Ave 60025. Fax: 847/803-9943. Facility: 138 one-bedroom standard units. 3 stories, interior corridors.
Parking: on-site. Terms: 3 day cancellation notice. Amenities: voice mail, irons, hair dryers. Pool(s): heated
outdoor. Guest Services: valet laundry. Cards: AX, DC, DS, MC, VI. Special Amenities: free continental
breakfast and free local telephone calls. (See color ad card insert)

SOME UNITS

MOTEL 6 - 1040
Phone: 847/390-7200   **145**

▼▼   5/23-10/19   1P: $51-$61   2P: $57-$67   XP: $3   F17
Motel   4/1-5/22 & 10/20-3/31   1P: $45-$55   2P: $51-$61   XP: $3   F17
Location: I-294, exit Willow Rd, 0.3 mi w to Sanders Rd, 1.3 mi s to Milwaukee Ave (SR 21), 0.5 mi se. 1535 Milwaukee
Ave 60025. Fax: 847/390-0845. Facility: 110 one-bedroom standard units. 2 stories, interior corridors. Bath:
combo or shower only. Parking: on-site. Terms: small pets only. Guest Services: coin laundry. Cards: AX, CB, DC, DS,
MC, VI.

SOME UNITS

GRAYSLAKE pop. 7,500

──────── WHERE TO DINE ────────

THE COUNTRY SQUIRE Historical
Lunch: $7-$17   Dinner: $13-$23   Phone: 847/223-0121

▼▼ ▼▼   Location: On SR 120, just w of jct US 45. 19133 W Hwy 120 60030. Hours: 11 am-10 pm, Sat-11 pm, Sun 10
Continental   am-9 pm. Closed: Mon. Reservations: suggested. Features: casual dress; Sunday brunch; children's
menu; cocktails & lounge. Shrimp DeJonghe prepared in garlic butter keeps excellent company with other
menu offerings, including preparations of steak, seafood, chicken and roast duck. Fourteen acres of
grounds accented by a fountain, gazebos and gardens surround the restored Georgian mansion. A pianist performs on
weekends. Parking: on-site. Cards: AX, DC, DS, MC, VI.

GURNEE pop. 13,700

──────── WHERE TO STAY ────────

BAYMONT INN & SUITES CHICAGO-GURNEE
Phone: (847)662-7600

ⒶⒶⒶ (SAVE)   All Year   1P: $89-$119   2P: $89-$119
▼▼▼▼   Location: I-94, exit Grand Ave (SR 132 E), just e via service road. 5688 N Ridge Rd 60031. Fax: 847/662-5300.
Motel   Facility: 102 units. 99 one-bedroom standard units. 3 one-bedroom suites ($99-$159). 4 stories, interior cor-
ridors. Bath: combo or shower only. Parking: on-site, winter plug-ins. Terms: small pets only.
Amenities: video games (fee), voice mail, irons, hair dryers. Pool(s): small heated indoor. Leisure Activi-
ties: whirlpool. Guest Services: valet and coin laundry. Cards: AX, CB, DC, DS, MC, VI.
Special Amenities: free continental breakfast and free newspaper. (See color ad opposite title page)

SOME UNITS

COMFORT INN
Phone: (847)855-8866

(SAVE)   5/26-9/1 [CP]   1P: $110-$120   2P: $110-$120   XP: $5   F17
▼▼▼▼   4/1-5/25 & 9/2-3/31 [CP]   1P: $69-$75   2P: $69-$75   XP: $5   F17
Motel   Location: I-94, exit Grand Ave (SR 132 W), just w. 6080 Gurnee Mills Blvd E 60031. Fax: 847/855-8866. Facility: 63
one-bedroom standard units. 3 stories, interior corridors. Bath: combo or shower only. Parking: on-site.
Terms: 14 day cancellation notice-fee imposed, package plans, small pets only (on ground floor).
Amenities: extended cable TV. Some: irons. Pool(s): small heated indoor. Leisure Activities: whirlpool.
Guest Services: valet laundry. Cards: AX, CB, DC, DS, MC, VI.

SOME UNITS

COMFORT SUITES

[SAVE]

Motel

5/22-9/19	1P: $99-$149	2P: $99-$149	XP: $10	F18
4/1-5/21 & 9/20-3/31	1P: $79-$139	2P: $79-$139	XP: $10	F18

Phone: (847)782-0890

Location: I-94, exit Grand Ave (SR 132 E), 0.5 mi e. 5430 Grand Ave 60031. Fax: 847/782-0809. **Facility:** 65 units. 64 one-bedroom standard units, some with whirlpools. 1 one-bedroom suite ($99-$139) with whirlpool. 3 stories, interior corridors. *Bath:* combo or shower only. **Parking:** on-site. **Terms:** package plans, small pets only ($30 deposit). **Amenities:** extended cable TV, voice mail, irons, hair dryers. **Pool(s):** small heated indoor. **Leisure Activities:** whirlpool, limited exercise equipment. **Guest Services:** valet and coin laundry. **Business Services:** meeting rooms. **Cards:** AX, CB, DC, DS, MC, VI.

SOME UNITS

COUNTRY INN & SUITES BY CARLSON

Motel

5/22-9/19	1P: $99-$149	2P: $99-$149	XP: $10	F18
4/1-5/21 & 9/20-3/31	1P: $79-$139	2P: $79-$139	XP: $10	F18

Phone: (847)625-9700

Location: I-94, exit Grand Ave (SR 132 E), 0.5 mi e. 5420 Grand Ave 60031. Fax: 847/625-4251. **Facility:** 68 units. 57 one-bedroom standard units. 11 one-bedroom suites ($99-$139). 3 stories, interior corridors. *Bath:* combo or shower only. **Parking:** on-site. **Terms:** package plans, small pets only ($30 deposit). **Amenities:** extended cable TV, voice mail, irons, hair dryers. **Pool(s):** small heated indoor. **Leisure Activities:** whirlpool. **Guest Services:** valet and coin laundry. **Business Services:** meeting rooms. **Cards:** AX, CB, DC, DS, JC, MC, VI. *(See color ad p 322)*

SOME UNITS

FAIRFIELD INN BY MARRIOTT

[AAA] [SAVE]

Motel

5/24-8/25 [CP]	1P: $100-$110	2P: $110-$140
4/1-5/23 & 8/26-3/31 [CP]	1P: $75-$90	2P: $80-$95

Phone: (847)855-8868

Location: I-94, exit Grand Ave (SR 132 W), just nw. 6090 Gurnee Mills Blvd E 60031. Fax: 847/855-8868. **Facility:** 62 one-bedroom standard units. 3 stories, interior corridors. **Parking:** on-site, winter plug-ins. **Terms:** 3 day cancellation notice. **Amenities:** extended cable TV, irons. **Pool(s):** small heated indoor. **Leisure Activities:** whirlpool. **Guest Services:** valet laundry. **Cards:** AX, DC, DS, MC, VI. **Special Amenities:** free continental breakfast and free local telephone calls. *(See color ad card insert)*

SOME UNITS

FEE

HAMPTON INN

[SAVE]

Motel

7/1-8/24 [ECP]	1P: $99-$109	2P: $99-$109
5/24-6/30 [ECP]	1P: $79-$89	2P: $79-$89
8/25-3/31 [ECP]	1P: $69-$79	2P: $69-$79
4/1-5/23 [ECP]	1P: $69	2P: $69

Phone: (847)662-1100

Location: I-94, exit Grand Ave (SR 132 E), 0.3 mi e. 5550 Grand Ave 60031. Fax: 847/662-2556. **Facility:** 134 one-bedroom standard units. 5 stories, interior corridors. **Parking:** on-site, winter plug-ins. **Amenities:** extended cable TV. **Pool(s):** heated outdoor. **Guest Services:** valet laundry. **Business Services:** meeting rooms. **Cards:** AX, CB, DC, DS, MC, VI.

SOME UNITS

FEE

HOLIDAY INN-GURNEE (WAUKEGAN)

Motor Inn

7/1-8/31	1P: $119-$129	2P: $119-$129
9/1-12/31	1P: $79-$99	2P: $79-$99
4/1-6/30 & 1/1-3/31	1P: $69-$79	2P: $69-$79

Phone: (847)336-6300

Location: I-94, exit Grand Ave (SR 132 W), 0.3 mi w. 6161 W Grand Ave 60031. Fax: 847/336-6303. **Facility:** 224 one-bedroom standard units. 4 stories, interior corridors. **Parking:** on-site. **Terms:** 3 day cancellation notice, [AP], [BP], [CP] & [ECP] meal plans available, package plans. **Amenities:** video games (fee), voice mail, irons, hair dryers. **Pool(s):** heated indoor. **Leisure Activities:** whirlpool, exercise room. *Fee:* game room. **Guest Services:** valet and coin laundry. **Business Services:** conference facilities, business center. *Fee:* PC, fax. **Cards:** AX, CB, DC, DS, JC, MC, VI.

SOME UNITS

FEE

─── WHERE TO DINE ───

MING'S OF CHINA

Chinese

Lunch: $5-$8   **Dinner:** $7-$14   **Phone:** 847/662-5597

Location: I-94, exit Grand Ave (SR 132 E), just e. 5572 Grand Ave 60031. **Hours:** 11:30 am-10:30 pm, Fri & Sat-11 pm, Sun-9:30 pm. Closed: 11/28. **Reservations:** accepted. **Features:** casual dress; health conscious menu items; carryout; cocktails; a la carte, buffet. Cherry wood columns, luxurious sconce lighting, plush tie-back drapes with tassels and ornate vases characterize the elegant, upscale dining room. Expertly prepared Mandarin and Szechwan cuisine factors heavily on the extensive menu. **Parking:** on-site. **Cards:** AX, CB, DC, DS, MC, VI.

HARVARD pop. 6,000

─── WHERE TO STAY ───

AMERIHOST INN-HARVARD

[AAA] [SAVE]

Motel

All Year	1P: $99-$109	2P: $109-$129	XP: $10	F16

Phone: (815)943-0700

Location: Jct US 14 and SR 23. 1701 S Division St 60033. Fax: 815/943-0707. **Facility:** 60 one-bedroom standard units, some with whirlpools. 2 stories, interior corridors. *Bath:* combo or shower only. **Parking:** on-site. **Terms:** 14 day cancellation notice, [CP] meal plan available, package plans, small pets only. **Amenities:** voice mail, safes, irons, hair dryers. **Pool(s):** heated indoor. **Leisure Activities:** sauna, whirlpool, exercise room. **Business Services:** meeting rooms. **Cards:** AX, CB, DC, DS, MC, VI. **Special Amenities:** free continental breakfast and free local telephone calls.

SOME UNITS

FEE

HARVEY pop. 29,800 (See map p. 292; index p. 294)

——— **WHERE TO STAY** ———

COMFORT SUITES   **Phone:** (708)331-7000   **430**

SAVE   4/1-9/30 [ECP]   1P: $79-$99   2P: $89-$109   XP: $10   F17
                  10/1-3/31 [ECP]   1P: $69-$89   2P: $79-$99   XP: $10   F17

Motel   **Location:** I-80/294, exit Halsted St N, just n. 16920 Halsted St 60421. **Fax:** 708/333-4746. **Facility:** 73 units. 72 one-bedroom standard units, some with whirlpools. 1 one-bedroom suite. 3 stories, interior corridors. *Bath:* combo or shower only. **Parking:** on-site. **Terms:** package plans. **Amenities:** hair dryers. **Pool(s):** heated indoor. **Leisure Activities:** exercise room. **Guest Services:** valet laundry. **Business Services:** meeting rooms. **Cards:** AX, CB, DC, DS, MC, VI.

SOME UNITS

SLEEP INN   **Phone:** (708)331-3400   **431**

SAVE   4/1-9/30 [CP]   1P: $59-$79   2P: $69-$89   XP: $10   F17
                  10/1-3/31 [CP]   1P: $49-$69   2P: $59-$79   XP: $10   F17

Motel   **Location:** I-80/294, exit Halsted St N, just n. 16940 Halsted St 60426. **Fax:** 708/331-5510. **Facility:** 74 one-bedroom standard units. 3 stories, interior corridors. *Bath:* combo or shower only. **Parking:** on-site. **Terms:** package plans. **Guest Services:** valet laundry. **Cards:** AX, CB, DC, DS, MC, VI.

SOME UNITS

HIGHLAND PARK pop. 30,600

——— **WHERE TO STAY** ———

COURTYARD BY MARRIOTT-HIGHLAND PARK   1P: $69-$159   2P: $69-$159   **Phone:** 847/831-3338

AAA **SAVE**   All Year [BP]   1P: $69-$159   2P: $69-$159
            Location: Jct of Lake Cook Rd, US 41 and Skokie Blvd. 1505 Lake Cook Rd 60035. **Fax:** 847/831-0782. **Facility:** 149 units. 137 one-bedroom standard units. 12 one-bedroom suites ($129-$169). 3 stories, interior corridors. **Parking:** on-site. **Terms:** 7 day cancellation notice, package plans. **Amenities:** high-speed Internet (fee), dual phone lines, voice mail, irons, hair dryers. **Dining:** coffee shop, 6:30-10:30 am, Sat & Sun 7 am-

Motel   noon. **Pool(s):** heated indoor. **Leisure Activities:** whirlpool, exercise room. **Guest Services:** valet and coin laundry, area transportation-within 5 mi. **Business Services:** meeting rooms. **Cards:** AX, DC, DS, MC, VI.
(See ad p 299 & color ad card insert)

SOME UNITS

FEE

——— **WHERE TO DINE** ———

CARLOS'   **Dinner:** $29-$39   **Phone:** 847/432-0770
            Location: Jct SR 22 and Green Bay Rd, just n on Green Bay Rd, just e on Highwood/Temple Ave. 429 Temple Ave

French   60035. **Hours:** seatings 5 pm-6:30 & 8-8:30 pm, Fri & Sat 5:30 pm-6:30 & 9-9:30 pm. Closed major holidays; also Tues. **Reservations:** required. **Features:** dressy casual; cocktails; a la carte, also prix fixe. Nestled in the historic section of the city, the cozy, upscale restaurant invites patrons to enjoy a wonderful dining experience. The masterful chef works wonders in the kitchen in preparing fine French cuisine. Fresh ingredients go into dishes that are both colorfully presented and piping hot. **Parking:** on-site and valet. **Cards:** AX, DC, DS, MC, VI.

HILLSIDE pop. 7,700 (See map p. 284; index p. 291)

——— **WHERE TO DINE** ———

EMILIO'S TAPAS BAR RESTAURANT   **Lunch:** $7-$18   **Dinner:** $7-$18   **Phone:** 708/547-7177   **190**
            Location: On SR 38, just w of US 12/20/45. 4100 W Roosevelt Rd 60162. **Hours:** 11:30 am-10 pm, Fri & Sat-11

Ethnic   pm, Sun noon-9 pm. Closed major holidays. **Reservations:** accepted. **Features:** casual dress; cocktails; a la carte. Delicious Spanish tapas (small dishes meant for sharing) are served in the gaily decorated dining rooms of this chef-owned restaurant. Try the grilled shrimp with garlic sauce, the flavorful pork tenderloin, or the very popular seafood filled paellas which takes 30 minsutes to prepare. Patio dining available in season. **Parking:** on-site. **Cards:** AX, DC, MC, VI.

HINSDALE pop. 16,000 (See map p. 292; index p. 294)

——— **WHERE TO DINE** ———

EGG HARBOUR CAFE I   **Lunch:** $5-$9   **Phone:** 630/920-1344   **261**
            Location: I-294, exit Ogden Ave (US 34), 0.5 mi w, just s on York Rd; in center of Gateway Square Shopping Center. 777 N York Rd 60521. **Hours:** 6:30 am-2 pm. Closed: 11/28, 12/25. **Features:** casual dress; children's menu;

American   carryout. Chickens, eggs and pictures of farm animals decorate the cozy country interior of the breakfast and lunch restaurant. Sandwiches, salad, a handful of appetizers and soups complement a generous selection of egg choices. Service is prompt. Smoke free premises. **Parking:** on-site. **Cards:** DS, MC, VI.

SALBUTE   **Dinner:** $12-$25   **Phone:** 630/920-8077   **260**
            Location: I-294, exit Ogden Ave (US 34), 0.4 mi w to York Rd, 0.4 mi s to Garfield Ave, 0.6 mi s to First St, then just

Mexican   e. 20 E First St 60521. **Hours:** 5 pm-9 pm, Fri & Sat-10 pm. Closed major holidays. **Reservations:** suggested. **Features:** casual dress; carryout; a la carte. The popular restaurant prides itself on using only fresh ingredients in such authentic, well-seasoned dishes as enchiladas with shrimp, green peppers, sour cream and black beans. Leave room for the delectable pecan pie, an absolute must try. Smoke free premises. **Parking:** street. **Cards:** AX, DC, DS, MC, VI.

HOFFMAN ESTATES pop. 46,600

──── WHERE TO STAY ────

AMERISUITES (CHICAGO/HOFFMAN ESTATES)
Phone: (847)839-1800

(AAA) (SAVE)

4/1-9/30 [ECP]	1P: $69-$149	2P: $79-$159	XP: $10	F18
10/1-3/31 [ECP]	1P: $59-$139	2P: $69-$149	XP: $10	F18

Motel

Location: I-90, exit Barrington Rd, 0.3 mi s. 2750 Greenspoint Pkwy 60195. Fax: 847/839-1860. **Facility:** 128 one-bedroom standard units. 6 stories, interior corridors. *Bath:* combo or shower only. **Parking:** on-site. **Terms:** package plans, small pets only. **Amenities:** high-speed Internet (fee), dual phone lines, voice mail, irons, hair dryers. **Pool(s):** heated indoor. **Leisure Activities:** exercise room. **Guest Services:** valet and coin laundry, area transportation-within 3 mi. **Business Services:** meeting rooms, business center. *Fee:* PC, fax. **Cards:** AX, CB, DC, DS, JC, MC, VI. **Special Amenities: free continental breakfast and free newspaper.** *(See color ad p 296)*

SOME UNITS

BAYMONT INN & SUITES CHICAGO-HOFFMAN ESTATES
Phone: (847)882-8848

(AAA) (SAVE)

All Year   1P: $69-$89   2P: $69-$89

Motel

Location: I-90, exit Barrington Rd, 0.3 mi s. 2075 Barrington Rd 60195. Fax: 847/882-9145. **Facility:** 99 units. 97 one-bedroom standard units. 2 one-bedroom suites ($99-$159). 3 stories, interior corridors. **Parking:** on-site. **Terms:** small pets only ($50 deposit, in smoking units). **Amenities:** extended cable TV, video games (fee), voice mail, irons, hair dryers. **Guest Services:** valet laundry. **Cards:** AX, CB, DC, DS, MC, VI. **Special Amenities: free continental breakfast and free newspaper.** *(See color ad opposite title page)*

SOME UNITS

HILTON GARDEN INN HOFFMAN ESTATES
Phone: (847)277-7889

(SAVE)

All Year   1P: $149   XP: $10   F18

Motel

Location: I-90, exit Barrington Rd, just n. 2425 Barrington Rd 60195. Fax: 847/277-7899. **Facility:** 184 one-bedroom standard units. 7 stories, interior corridors. *Bath:* combo or shower only. **Parking:** on-site. **Terms:** [BP], [CP] & [ECP] meal plans available, package plans. **Amenities:** dual phone lines, voice mail, irons, hair dryers. *Fee:* video games, Web TV. **Pool(s):** small heated indoor. **Leisure Activities:** whirlpool, exercise room. **Guest Services:** valet and coin laundry. **Business Services:** meeting rooms, business center, PC, fax. **Cards:** AX, CB, DC, DS, JC, MC, VI.

SOME UNITS

LA QUINTA INN
Phone: (847)882-3312

(SAVE)

All Year   1P: $70-$119   2P: $80-$129   XP: $10   F18

Motel

Location: I-90, exit Barrington Rd, 0.3 mi s. 2280 Barrington Rd 60195. Fax: 847/882-5960. **Facility:** 130 units. 122 one-bedroom standard units. 8 one-bedroom suites ($110-$159). 3 stories, interior corridors. *Bath:* combo or shower only. **Parking:** on-site. **Terms:** small pets only. **Amenities:** voice mail, irons, hair dryers. **Pool(s):** heated outdoor. **Leisure Activities:** exercise room. **Guest Services:** valet laundry. **Business Services:** meeting rooms. **Cards:** AX, CB, DC, DS, MC, VI. *(See color ad p 325)*

SOME UNITS

RED ROOF INN
Phone: (847)885-7877

(AAA) (SAVE)

6/2-9/28	1P: $55-$69	2P: $61-$75	XP: $6	F18
9/29-3/31	1P: $47-$61	2P: $53-$73	XP: $6	F18
4/1-6/1	1P: $45-$60	2P: $51-$67	XP: $6	F18

Motel

Location: I-90, exit Barrington Rd, 0.3 mi s. 2500 Hassell Rd 60195. Fax: 847/885-8616. **Facility:** 119 one-bedroom standard units. 3 stories, exterior corridors. **Parking:** on-site. **Terms:** small pets only. **Amenities:** video games (fee), voice mail. **Guest Services:** coin laundry. **Cards:** AX, CB, DC, DS, MC, VI. **Special Amenities: free local telephone calls and free newspaper.**

SOME UNITS

―――――― *The following lodging was either not evaluated or did not* ――――――
meet AAA rating requirements but is listed for your information only.

CHICAGO MARRIOTT NORTHWEST
Phone: 847/645-9500
[fyi]
Motel
Under construction, scheduled to open September 2002. **Location:** I-90, exit 59. 4800 Columbine Blvd 60192 (4243 Hunt Rd, CINCINNATI, OH, 45242). Fax: 847/645-9600. **Planned Amenities:** restaurant, radios, coffeemakers, pool. *(See color ad p 345)*

ITASCA pop. 6,900 (See map p. 284; index p. 290)

―――――― **WHERE TO STAY** ――――――

AMERISUITES CHICAGO/ITASCA
Phone: (630)875-1400　212
(AAA) [SAVE]
▼▼▼
Motel
All Year [ECP]　　1P: $111　　2P: $111　　XP: $10　　F18
Location: I-290, exit Thorndale Ave, 0.6 mi e on Thorndale Heights Rd, 0.5 mi n. 1150 Arlington Heights Rd 60143. Fax: 630/875-9756. **Facility:** 128 one-bedroom standard units. 6 stories, interior corridors. *Bath:* combo or shower only. **Parking:** on-site. **Terms:** package plans, small pets only. **Amenities:** high-speed Internet (fee), voice mail, irons, hair dryers. *Some:* dual phone lines. **Pool(s):** heated indoor. **Leisure Activities:** sun deck, exercise room. **Guest Services:** valet and coin laundry, area transportation-within 10 mi. **Business Services:** meeting rooms, business center. *Fee:* PC, fax. **Cards:** AX, CB, DC, DS, JC, MC, VI. **Special Amenities:** free continental breakfast and free newspaper. *(See color ad p 296)*
SOME UNITS
⬛🛏️⬛♿⬛🔲🐕‍🦺 VCR 🔲 DATA PORT 🔲🔲🔲🔲 / ✕
FEE

WYNDHAM NORTHWEST CHICAGO
Phone: (630)773-4000　213
(AAA) [SAVE]
▼▼▼
Hotel
4/1-6/30 & 9/8-3/31　1P: $99-$169　　2P: $99-$189　　XP: $20　　F18
7/1-9/7　　　　　　1P: $99-$159　　2P: $99-$179　　XP: $20　　F18
Location: I-290, exit Thorndale Ave, just e. 400 Park Blvd 60143. Fax: 630/773-4088. **Facility:** 408 units. 379 one-bedroom standard units. 29 one-bedroom suites. 12 stories, interior corridors. **Parking:** on-site and valet (fee). **Terms:** cancellation fee imposed, package plans. **Amenities:** dual phone lines, voice mail, irons, hair dryers. *Fee:* video games, Web TV, high-speed Internet. *Some:* CD players. **Dining:** restaurant, 6:30 am-2:30 & 5-10 pm, $8-$60, cocktails. **Pool(s):** heated indoor. **Leisure Activities:** saunas, whirlpools, jogging, basketball. *Fee:* lighted tennis court, racquetball courts, aerobic instruction. **Guest Services:** gift shop, massage (fee), valet laundry, area transportation-within 3 mi. **Business Services:** conference facilities, business center. *Fee:* PC, fax. **Cards:** AX, CB, DC, DS, JC, MC, VI.
SOME UNITS
🔲🍴🔲🔲🐕‍🦺➕✕🔲 DATA PORT 🔲🔲🔲 / ✕
FEE　　FEE

JOLIET pop. 76,800

―――――― **WHERE TO STAY** ――――――

BEST WESTERN JOLIET INN & SUITES
Phone: 815/730-7500
(AAA) [SAVE]
▼▼▼
Motel
4/1-9/30　　　1P: $64　　2P: $69　　XP: $5
10/1-3/31　　 1P: $54　　2P: $59　　XP: $5
Location: I-55, exit 253, just e via frontage road. 4380 Enterprise Dr 60431. Fax: 815/730-7400. **Facility:** 62 units. 50 one-bedroom standard units. 12 one-bedroom suites ($64-$129), some with whirlpools. 3 stories, interior corridors. *Bath:* combo or shower only. **Parking:** on-site. **Terms:** package plans. **Amenities:** extended cable TV, high-speed Internet, dual phone lines, voice mail, hair dryers. *Some:* irons. **Pool(s):** heated indoor. **Leisure Activities:** whirlpool, exercise equipment available. **Guest Services:** valet and coin laundry, area transportation (fee)-local attractns. **Cards:** AX, CB, DC, DS, MC, VI.
SOME UNITS
🔲🔲🔲🔲🐕‍🦺✕ DATA PORT 🔲 / ✕🔲🔲🔲 /
FEE　FEE　FEE

COMFORT INN-JOLIET SOUTH
Phone: (815)744-1770
[SAVE]
▼▼▼
Motel
6/1-9/1 [CP]　　　　1P: $80-$130　　2P: $85-$135　　XP: $5　　F17
4/1-5/31 & 9/2-3/31 [CP]　1P: $70-$75　　2P: $75-$80　　XP: $5　　F17
Location: I-80, exit 130B, 0.5 mi n. 135 S Larkin Ave 60436. Fax: 815/744-1770. **Facility:** 67 one-bedroom standard units. 2 stories, interior corridors. **Parking:** on-site. **Terms:** cancellation fee imposed, package plans, small pets only. **Amenities:** extended cable TV. *Some:* irons, hair dryers. **Pool(s):** small heated indoor. **Leisure Activities:** whirlpool. **Guest Services:** valet laundry. **Cards:** AX, CB, DC, DS, JC, MC, VI.
SOME UNITS
🔲🛏️🔲🔲🐕‍🦺✕ DATA PORT 🔲 / ✕🔲🔲🔲 /
FEE　　　　　FEE　FEE

COMFORT INN NORTH
Phone: (815)436-5141
[SAVE]
▼▼▼
Motel
All Year [CP]　1P: $65-$75　　2P: $65-$75
Location: I-55, exit 257, just e. 3235 Norman Ave 60435. Fax: 815/436-5141. **Facility:** 64 one-bedroom standard units. 3 stories, interior corridors. **Parking:** on-site, winter plug-ins. **Terms:** package plans, small pets only ($20 extra charge, in smoking units). **Amenities:** extended cable TV. *Some:* irons, hair dryers. **Pool(s):** small heated indoor. **Leisure Activities:** whirlpool. **Guest Services:** valet laundry. **Cards:** AX, CB, DC, DS, JC, MC, VI.
SOME UNITS
🔲🛏️🔲🔲🐕‍🦺✕🔲 / ✕🔲🔲🔲 /
FEE

EMPRESS CASINO HOTEL
Phone: (815)744-9400
▼▼▼
Motel
All Year [CP]　1P: $89-$119　　2P: $89-$119
Location: I-80, exit 127, 1.3 mi s follow signs; opposite Empress Casino. 2200 Empress Rd 60435. Fax: 815/741-4410. **Facility:** 102 units. 97 one-bedroom standard units, some with whirlpools. 5 one-bedroom suites. 3 stories, interior corridors. *Bath:* combo or shower only. **Parking:** on-site. **Terms:** cancellation fee imposed, package plans. **Amenities:** safes, irons, hair dryers. *Some:* CD players. **Pool(s):** heated indoor. **Leisure Activities:** whirlpool. **Business Services:** meeting rooms. **Cards:** AX, CB, DC, DS, JC, MC, VI. *(See color ad p 347)*
SOME UNITS
ASK 🔲🔲🐕‍🦺✕ DATA PORT 🔲🔲 / ✕🔲🔲🔲 /
FEE　FEE

FAIRFIELD INN BY MARRIOTT-NORTH

Phone: (815)436-6577

AAA SAVE
◊◊◊
Motel

	6/1-8/31 [CP]	1P: $70-$75	2P: $70-$75
	4/1-5/31 & 9/1-10/31 [CP]	1P: $60-$65	2P: $60-$65
	11/1-3/31 [CP]	1P: $55-$60	2P: $55-$60

Location: I-55, exit 257, just e. 3239 Norman Ave 60435. Fax: 815/436-6577. **Facility:** 63 one-bedroom standard units. 3 stories, interior corridors. **Parking:** on-site. **Terms:** package plans. **Amenities:** extended cable TV, irons. **Pool(s):** small heated indoor. **Leisure Activities:** whirlpool. **Guest Services:** valet laundry. **Cards:** AX, CB, DC, DS, JC, MC, VI. **Special Amenities:** free continental breakfast and free local telephone calls. *(See color ad card insert)*

SOME UNITS

FEE

FAIRFIELD INN BY MARRIOTT-RIVERBOAT CENTER

Phone: (815)741-3499

AAA SAVE
◊◊◊
Motel

| | 6/1-9/1 [CP] | 1P: $80-$130 | 2P: $85-$135 | XP: $5 | F17 |
| | 4/1-5/31 & 9/2-3/31 [CP] | 1P: $70-$75 | 2P: $75-$80 | XP: $5 | F17 |

Location: I-80, exit 127, just n. 1501 Riverboat Center Dr 60431. Fax: 815/741-3499. **Facility:** 64 one-bedroom standard units. 3 stories, interior corridors. *Bath:* combo or shower only. **Parking:** on-site. **Terms:** cancellation fee imposed, package plans. **Amenities:** irons. **Pool(s):** small heated indoor. **Leisure Activities:** whirlpool. **Guest Services:** valet laundry. **Business Services:** meeting rooms. **Cards:** AX, DC, DS, MC, VI. **Special Amenities:** free continental breakfast and free local telephone calls. *(See color ad card insert)*

SOME UNITS

FEE   FEE FEE

HAMPTON INN JOLIET (I-55)

Phone: (815)439-9500

SAVE
◊◊◊
Motel

	1/1-3/31	1P: $71-$75	2P: $75-$80
	4/1-5/31	1P: $71-$72	2P: $75-$76
	10/1-12/31	1P: $63-$71	2P: $67-$75
	6/1-9/30	1P: $71-$72	2P: $71-$72

Location: I-55, exit 257, 0.4 mi e on US 30 to Mall Loop Dr, then 0.4 mi s. 3555 Mall Loop Dr 60431. Fax: 815/439-9550. **Facility:** 106 one-bedroom standard units. 3 stories, interior corridors. *Bath:* combo or shower only. **Parking:** on-site. **Terms:** package plans. **Amenities:** extended cable TV, dual phone lines, voice mail, irons. *Some:* hair dryers. **Pool(s):** small heated indoor. **Leisure Activities:** whirlpool, exercise room. **Guest Services:** valet and coin laundry. **Business Services:** meeting rooms. **Cards:** AX, CB, DC, DS, MC, VI.

SOME UNITS

FEE FEE

HAMPTON INN-JOLIET I-80

Phone: (815)725-2424

SAVE
◊◊◊
Motel

	5/28-10/21 [ECP]	1P: $69-$99	2P: $79-$99
	1/1-3/31 [ECP]	1P: $71-$85	2P: $79-$95
	4/1-5/27 [ECP]	1P: $65-$79	2P: $75-$84
	10/22-12/31 [ECP]	1P: $65-$79	2P: $65-$79

Location: I-80, exit 127, just n. 1521 Riverboat Center Dr 60436. Fax: 815/725-3110. **Facility:** 89 one-bedroom standard units. 3 stories, interior corridors. *Bath:* combo or shower only. **Parking:** on-site. **Terms:** 7 day cancellation notice. **Amenities:** extended cable TV, voice mail, irons. **Pool(s):** small heated indoor. **Leisure Activities:** whirlpool. **Guest Services:** valet and coin laundry. **Business Services:** meeting rooms. **Cards:** AX, CB, DC, DS, JC, MC, VI.

SOME UNITS

HOLIDAY INN EXPRESS-JOLIET

Phone: (815)729-2000

◊◊◊◊
Motel

| | All Year | 1P: $69-$119 |

Location: I-80, exit 130B. 411 S Larkin Ave 60436. Fax: 815/729-4231. **Facility:** 200 one-bedroom standard units. 4 stories, interior corridors. *Bath:* combo or shower only. **Parking:** on-site. **Terms:** small pets only. **Amenities:** voice mail, irons, hair dryers. **Pool(s):** heated outdoor. **Leisure Activities:** exercise room. *Fee:* game room. **Guest Services:** valet and coin laundry. **Business Services:** meeting rooms. **Cards:** AX, CB, DC, DS, JC, MC, VI.

SOME UNITS

FEE   FEE

MOTEL 6 JOLIET I-55 - 1296

Phone: 815/439-1332

5/23-11/2	1P: $41-$51	2P: $47-$57	XP: $3	F17
11/3-3/31	1P: $39-$49	2P: $45-$55	XP: $3	F17
4/1-5/22	1P: $35-$45	2P: $41-$51	XP: $3	F17

Motel

Location: I-55, exit 257, 0.4 mi e on US 30, then 0.4 mi s. 3551 Mall Loop Dr 60431. Fax: 815/254-3075. **Facility:** 121 one-bedroom standard units. 3 stories, interior corridors. *Bath:* combo or shower only. **Parking:** on-site. **Terms:** small pets only. **Guest Services:** coin laundry. **Cards:** AX, CB, DC, DS, MC, VI.

SOME UNITS

MOTEL 6 JOLIET I-80 - 694

Phone: 815/729-2800

5/23-10/5	1P: $39-$49	2P: $45-$55	XP: $3	F17
10/6-3/31	1P: $34-$44	2P: $40-$50	XP: $3	F17
4/1-5/22	1P: $32-$42	2P: $38-$48	XP: $3	F17

Motel

Location: I-80, exit 130B, 0.3 mi n on SR 7. 1850 McDonough St 60436. Fax: 815/729-9528. **Facility:** 129 one-bedroom standard units. 2 stories, exterior corridors. *Bath:* combo or shower only. **Parking:** on-site. **Terms:** small pets only. **Guest Services:** coin laundry. **Cards:** AX, CB, DC, DS, MC, VI.

SOME UNITS

RAMADA LIMITED-NORTH

Phone: (815)439-4200

9/1-12/31	1P: $79
4/1-8/31	1P: $69
1/1-3/31	1P: $59

Motel

Location: I-55, exit 257, just e. 3231 Norman Ave 60431. Fax: 815/439-4211. **Facility:** 63 one-bedroom standard units, some with whirlpools. 3 stories, interior corridors. *Bath:* combo or shower only. **Parking:** on-site, winter plug-ins. **Terms:** [CP] meal plan available, package plans. **Amenities:** extended cable TV, voice mail, safes (fee), irons, hair dryers. **Pool(s):** small heated indoor. **Leisure Activities:** whirlpool, exercise room. **Guest Services:** valet and coin laundry. **Business Services:** meeting rooms. **Cards:** AX, CB, DC, DS, JC, MC, VI.

SOME UNITS

RAMADA LIMITED-SOUTH

Phone: 815/730-1111

4/1-10/15 [CP]	1P: $69-$79	2P: $69-$79	XP: $7
10/16-3/31 [CP]	1P: $59-$69	2P: $59-$69	XP: $7

Motel

Location: I-80, exit 127, just n. 1520 Commerce Ln 60431. Fax: 815/730-1111. **Facility:** 70 one-bedroom standard units, some with whirlpools. 3 stories, interior corridors. **Parking:** on-site. **Amenities:** voice mail, irons, hair dryers. **Pool(s):** heated indoor. **Leisure Activities:** whirlpool. **Guest Services:** valet and coin laundry. **Business Services:** meeting rooms. **Cards:** AX, CB, DC, DS, MC, VI. **Special Amenities:** free continental breakfast and free local telephone calls.

SOME UNITS

RED ROOF INN

Phone: (815)741-2304

5/19-8/31	1P: $45-$69	2P: $50-$74	XP: $5	F18
9/1-10/26	1P: $41-$64	2P: $45-$69	XP: $5	F18
4/1-5/18	1P: $39-$59	2P: $44-$64	XP: $5	F18
10/27-3/31	1P: $34-$55	2P: $39-$60	XP: $5	F18

Motel

Location: I-80, exit 130B, just off Larkin Ave. 1750 McDonough St 60436. Fax: 815/741-2330. **Facility:** 108 one-bedroom standard units. 2 stories, exterior corridors. **Parking:** on-site. **Terms:** small pets only (in smoking units). **Amenities:** extended cable TV, video games, voice mail. **Cards:** AX, CB, DC, DS, MC, VI. **Special Amenities:** free local telephone calls and free newspaper.

SOME UNITS

SUPER 8 MOTEL

Phone: (815)725-8855

All Year	1P: $59-$69	2P: $69-$79	XP: $10	F12

Motel

Location: I-80, exit 130B, just off Larkin Ave. 1730 McDonough St 60436. Fax: 815/725-2975. **Facility:** 64 one-bedroom standard units. 2 stories, interior corridors. **Parking:** on-site, winter plug-ins. **Amenities:** extended cable TV. **Business Services:** meeting rooms. **Cards:** AX, CB, DC, DS, MC, VI.

SOME UNITS

SUPER 8 MOTEL I-55 NORTH

Phone: (815)439-3838

All Year [CP]	1P: $55-$67	2P: $65-$87	XP: $6	F12

Motel

Location: I-55, exit 257, 0.4 mi e on US 30, just s. 3401 Mall Loop Dr 60431. Fax: 815/439-3940. **Facility:** 62 one-bedroom standard units, some with whirlpools. 3 stories, interior corridors. *Bath:* combo or shower only. **Parking:** on-site, winter plug-ins. **Terms:** small pets only. **Amenities:** extended cable TV. *Some:* hair dryers. **Pool(s):** small heated indoor. **Leisure Activities:** whirlpool. **Guest Services:** coin laundry. **Business Services:** meeting rooms. **Cards:** AX, CB, DC, DS, MC, VI.

SOME UNITS

WINGATE INN

Phone: (815)741-2100

All Year [ECP]	1P: $60-$79	2P: $60-$79	XP: $5	F18

Motel

Location: I-55, exit 253, just e via frontage road. 101 McDonald Ave 60431. Fax: 815/741-0406. **Facility:** 81 one-bedroom standard units, some with whirlpools. 3 stories, interior corridors. *Bath:* combo or shower only. **Parking:** on-site. **Terms:** package plans. **Amenities:** extended cable TV, video games, high-speed Internet, dual phone lines, voice mail, safes, irons. **Pool(s):** small heated indoor. **Leisure Activities:** whirlpool, exercise room. *Fee:* game room. **Guest Services:** complimentary laundry. **Business Services:** meeting rooms, business center. **Cards:** AX, CB, DC, DS, JC, MC, VI.

SOME UNITS

--------- WHERE TO DINE ---------

AL'S STEAK HOUSE
▼▼▼ ▼▼▼▼
Steak House

Lunch: $7-$12   **Dinner:** $10-$25   **Phone:** 815/725-2388
Location: I-55, exit 253A, 3 mi e on US 52; just w of jct SR 7. 1990 W Jefferson 60435. **Hours:** 11 am-11 pm, Fri & Sat-12:30 am, Sun 10 am-11 pm. Closed: 12/25. **Reservations:** accepted. **Features:** dressy casual; Sunday brunch; children's menu; salad bar; cocktails & lounge. Steak and prime rib are the primary choices at the enormous, locally popular eatery. The '60s- and '70s-style decor, with brick walls and raftered ceilings, reflects a supper-club atmosphere. The Sunday buffet and Friday seafood buffet draw a good crowd. **Parking:** on-site. **Cards:** AX, CB, DC, MC, VI.   ✕

LAKE FOREST pop. 17,800

--------- WHERE TO DINE ---------

EGG HARBOR CAFE
▼▼▼
American

Lunch: $5-$9   **Phone:** 847/295-3449
Location: Jct US 41 (Skokie Hwy) and Deerpath Rd, 1.3 mi e to Western Ave, then just s; in Lake Forest Plaza. 512 N Western Ave 60045. **Hours:** 6:30 am-2 pm. **Features:** casual dress; children's menu; carryout. The country decor and lively atmosphere complement the distinctive breakfast and lunch creations served here. Colorful fabric, ceramic, and wood carved chickens and roosters decorate the walls as you enjoy eggs Benedict, blueberry pancakes, a Malibu chicken sandwich or an item from the enormous menu. Smoke free premises. **Parking:** on-site. **Cards:** AX, DS, MC, VI.   ✕

SOUTH GATE CAFE
▼▼▼ ▼▼▼
American

Lunch: $8-$24   **Dinner:** $8-$24   **Phone:** 847/234-8800
Location: US 41, 1.1 mi e on Deer Path Rd, just n; in Market Square. 655 Forest Ave 60045. **Hours:** 11:30 am-9 pm, Fri & Sat-10 pm, Sun-8 pm. Closed major holidays. **Reservations:** accepted. **Features:** casual dress; carryout; cocktails & lounge. Imaginative daily specials stand out on the lengthy all day menu that spans a broad price range. Aromas from the on-premises bakery make your mouth water. The dining room is warm and inviting, with painted walls, attractive art and French windows. **Parking:** on-site. **Cards:** AX, CB, DC, DS, MC, VI.   ✕

LAKE ZURICH pop. 14,900

--------- WHERE TO DINE ---------

D & J BISTRO
▼▼▼ ▼▼▼
French

Lunch: $8-$15   **Dinner:** $13-$21   **Phone:** 847/438-8001
Location: On US 12, just s of jct SR 22 and US 12; next to 1st Bank Plaza Business Center. 466 S Rand Rd 60012. **Hours:** 11:30 am-2:30 & 5:30-9 pm, Fri-10 pm, Sat 5 pm-10 pm, Sun 5 pm-8:30 pm. Closed: 1/1, 11/28, 12/25; also Mon. **Reservations:** accepted. **Features:** casual dress; cocktails & lounge; a la carte, also prix fixe. The bistro menu boasts a variety of very well-prepared dishes that spotlight an attentive eye toward flavor but also creativity. Appetizers, salad, soup, paella, sandwiches, steak and seafood all make a wonderful showing in taste and presentation. **Parking:** on-site. **Cards:** AX, DC, MC, VI.   ✕

JULIO'S LATIN CAFE
▼▼▼
Latino

Lunch: $8-$14   **Dinner:** $13-$22   **Phone:** 847/438-3484
Location: On US 12, 0.5 mi nw of jct SR 22; in Lakeview Plaza. 99 S Rand Rd 60047. **Hours:** 11:30 am-2:30 & 5-9 pm, Sat from 5 pm, Sun 4:30 pm-8:30 pm. Closed major holidays; also Sun 11/1-4/30. **Reservations:** accepted. **Features:** casual dress; carryout; cocktails & lounge; a la carte. The artful Mexican menu showcases a variety of creations enhanced by the flavors of the Caribbean and Central and South America, including a signature dessert: a tortilla-wrapped banana, fried and dusted with cinnamon sugar and served with ice cream. **Parking:** on-site. **Cards:** AX, DC, DS, MC, VI.   ✕

LANSING pop. 28,100   (See map p. 292; index p. 294)

--------- WHERE TO STAY ---------

COMFORT SUITES
▼▼▼ ▼▼▼
Motel

Phone: 708/418-3337   [385]
Property failed to provide current rates
Location: I-80/94, exit 161 (Torrence Ave), just n, then just w, follow signs. 2235 W 173rd St 60438. **Fax:** 708/418-4340. **Facility:** 65 one-bedroom standard units, some with whirlpools. 3 stories, interior corridors. *Bath:* combo or shower only. **Parking:** on-site. **Amenities:** hair dryers. *Some:* irons. **Pool(s):** small heated indoor. **Leisure Activities:** exercise room. **Guest Services:** valet laundry. **Cards:** AX, CB, DC, DS, MC, VI.

SOME UNITS
♿ 🛏 📶 [DATA PORT] 🍴 🛗 🖥 🖨 / ✕ /

FAIRFIELD INN BY MARRIOTT-LANSING
[AAA] [SAVE]
▼▼▼ ▼▼▼
Motel
(See color ad card insert)

Phone: 708/474-6900   [386]

4/1-10/15 [ECP]	1P: $73	XP: $7	F18
10/16-3/31 [ECP]	1P: $65	XP: $7	F18

Location: I-80/94, exit 161 (Torrence Ave), just n. 17301 Oak Ave 60438. **Fax:** 708/474-6900. **Facility:** 135 one-bedroom standard units. 3 stories, interior/exterior corridors. **Parking:** on-site, winter plug-ins. **Terms:** cancellation fee imposed. **Amenities:** irons. **Pool(s):** heated outdoor. **Guest Services:** valet laundry. **Cards:** AX, DC, DS, MC, VI. **Special Amenities:** free continental breakfast and free local telephone calls.

SOME UNITS
🛗 📶 🛏 📠 🍴 [DATA PORT] 🖨 / ✕ 🍴 🖥 /
FEE

RED ROOF INN
[AAA] [SAVE]
▼▼▼ ▼▼▼
Motel

Phone: (708)895-9570   [389]

5/20-9/16	1P: $51-$74	2P: $56-$79	XP: $5	F18
4/1-5/19	1P: $39-$66	2P: $44-$71	XP: $5	F18
9/17-11/2	1P: $48-$59	2P: $53-$64	XP: $5	F18
11/3-3/31	1P: $39-$59	2P: $44-$64	XP: $5	F18

Location: I-80/94, exit 161 (Torrence Ave), just n. 2450 E 173rd St 60438. **Fax:** 708/895-7686. **Facility:** 108 one-bedroom standard units. 2 stories, exterior corridors. *Bath:* combo or shower only. **Parking:** on-site. **Terms:** small pets only. **Amenities:** video games. **Cards:** AX, CB, DC, DS, MC, VI. **Special Amenities:** free local telephone calls and free newspaper.

SOME UNITS
🛏 🛗 📶 📺 [DATA PORT] 🖨 / ✕ 🍴 🖥 /
FEE   FEE FEE

(See map p. 292)

SLEEP INN

Motel

Phone: 708/418-3770 **384**

Property failed to provide current rates

Location: I-80/94, exit 161 (Torrence Ave), just n, then just w, follow signs. 2255 W 173rd St 60438. Fax: 708/418-4330. **Facility:** 73 one-bedroom standard units. 4 stories, interior corridors. *Bath:* combo or shower only. **Parking:** on-site. **Guest Services:** valet laundry. **Cards:** AX, DC, DS, MC, VI.

SOME UNITS

─── **WHERE TO DINE** ───

CAFE BORGIA

Regional Italian

Lunch: $8-$17   **Dinner:** $10-$25   **Phone:** 708/474-5515 **230**

Location: I-80/94, exit 161 (Torrence Ave), 0.4 mi s. 17923 Torrence Ave 60438. **Hours:** 11 am-11 pm, Fri & Sat-midnight. Closed major holidays. **Features:** casual dress; carryout; beer & wine only; a la carte. Fine Italian food is served in a small but festive dining room featuring vivid murals of scenes from Italy. Pan-fried scallops in roasted garlic mayonnaise sauce are delightful, as is veal limone, which is sauteed in olive oil, garlic and white wine. **Parking:** on-site. **Cards:** AX, MC, VI.

LIBERTYVILLE pop. 19,200

─── **WHERE TO STAY** ───

BEST WESTERN HITCH INN POST

Motel

All Year [ECP]   1P: $69-$139   2P: $69-$139   XP: $8   F12

Location: Jct SR 137 and 21. 1765 N Milwaukee Ave 60048. Fax: 847/362-8725. **Facility:** 136 units. 126 one-bedroom standard units, some with whirlpools. 10 one-bedroom suites ($99-$149). 2 stories, interior corridors. *Bath:* combo or shower only. **Parking:** on-site, winter plug-ins. **Terms:** 7 day cancellation notice. **Amenities:** voice mail, irons, hair dryers. **Pool(s):** heated indoor. **Leisure Activities:** sauna, whirlpool, exercise room, indoor recreation area. **Guest Services:** gift shop, valet and coin laundry, area transportation-Great America & Naval Base. **Business Services:** meeting rooms. **Cards:** AX, CB, DC, DS, MC, VI. **Special Amenities:** free continental breakfast and free local telephone calls.

Phone: (847)362-8700

SOME UNITS

CANDLEWOOD SUITES CHICAGO-LIBERTYVILLE

Extended Stay Motel

Phone: 847/247-9900

Property failed to provide current rates

Location: I-94, exit SR 137 (Buckley Rd), 5.6 mi w to US 45, 1.4 mi s. 1100 N US 45 60048. Fax: 847/247-9971. **Facility:** 122 units. 98 one-bedroom standard units with efficiencies. 24 one-bedroom suites with kitchens. 3 stories, interior corridors. *Bath:* combo or shower only. **Parking:** on-site. **Terms:** small pets only ($150 fee). **Amenities:** extended cable TV, video tape library, CD players, dual phone lines, voice mail, irons, hair dryers. **Leisure Activities:** exercise room. **Guest Services:** complimentary laundry. **Business Services:** business center, fax. **Cards:** AX, CB, DC, DS, JC, MC, VI.

SOME UNITS

DAYS INN

Motel

All Year [ECP]   1P: $63-$79   2P: $68-$89   XP: $5   F16

Location: Jct SR 137 and 21. 1809 N Milwaukee Ave 60048. Fax: 847/816-9771. **Facility:** 90 one-bedroom standard units. 3 stories, interior corridors. **Parking:** on-site. **Terms:** small pets only. **Amenities:** extended cable TV. **Pool(s):** heated outdoor. **Business Services:** meeting rooms. **Cards:** AX, CB, DC, DS, MC, VI. **Special Amenities:** free continental breakfast and free newspaper.

Phone: (847)816-8006

SOME UNITS

LIBERTYVILLE TRAVELODGE & SUITES

Motel

All Year [ECP]   1P: $94-$139   2P: $99-$149   XP: $5   F16

Location: I-94, exit SR 137 (Buckley Rd), 2.3 mi w. 77 W Buckley Rd 60048. Fax: 847/549-7898. **Facility:** 73 units. 68 one-bedroom standard units. 5 one-bedroom suites ($139-$159), some with whirlpools. 3 stories, interior corridors. *Bath:* combo or shower only. **Parking:** on-site. **Terms:** 7 day cancellation notice. **Amenities:** extended cable TV, dual phone lines, voice mail, safes, irons, hair dryers. **Pool(s):** small heated indoor. **Leisure Activities:** limited exercise equipment. **Guest Services:** valet laundry. **Business Services:** meeting rooms. **Cards:** AX, CB, DC, DS, JC, MC, VI. **Special Amenities:** free continental breakfast. *(See color ad below)*

Phone: (847)549-7878

SOME UNITS

LINCOLNSHIRE pop. 4,900

──────── **WHERE TO STAY** ────────

HAMPTON INN & SUITES
Phone: (847)478-1400

SAVE

Motel

All Year [ECP]   1P: $99-$165   2P: $109-$185
Location: I-94, exit Half Day Rd northbound, 2.2 mi w to Milwaukee Ave, 1.3 mi s; exit Deerfield Rd southbound, 2 mi w to Milwaukee Ave (US 45/SR 21), 0.7 mi n. 1400 Milwaukee Ave 60069. Fax: 847/478-1451. **Facility:** 117 units. 84 one-bedroom standard units. 33 one-bedroom suites ($129-$159), some with whirlpools. 3 stories, interior corridors. *Bath:* combo or shower only. **Parking:** on-site. **Amenities:** video games (fee), dual phone lines, voice mail, irons, hair dryers. **Pool(s):** heated indoor. **Leisure Activities:** whirlpool, exercise room. **Guest Services:** complimentary evening beverages: Wed, valet and coin laundry. **Business Services:** meeting rooms. **Cards:** AX, CB, DC, DS, JC, MC, VI.

HAWTHORN SUITES HOTEL
Phone: (847)945-9300

Suite Motel

All Year [BP]   1P: $79-$160
Location: I-94, exit Half Day Rd, just w. 10 Westminister Way 60069. Fax: 847/945-0013. **Facility:** 125 units. 103 one- and 22 two-bedroom suites with kitchens. 3 stories, interior corridors. **Parking:** on-site. **Terms:** check-in 4 pm, 14 day cancellation notice-fee imposed, package plans. **Amenities:** extended cable TV, voice mail, irons, hair dryers. **Pool(s):** heated indoor. **Leisure Activities:** whirlpool, sun deck, courtyard area, exercise room. **Guest Services:** complimentary evening beverages: Mon-Thurs, valet and coin laundry. **Business Services:** meeting rooms. **Cards:** AX, CB, DC, DS, MC, VI.

MARRIOTT'S LINCOLNSHIRE RESORT
Phone: (847)634-0100

AAA **SAVE**

Resort

All Year   1P: $79-$189   2P: $89-$199
Location: I-94, exit Half Day Rd, 2 mi w to jct US 45, SR 21 and 22, just s. 10 Marriott Dr 60069. Fax: 847/634-1278. **Facility:** This sprawling resort, set in a quiet residential area, features a three-story lobby with an oversize fireplace, plush seating and high-end lighting. 390 units. 386 one-bedroom standard units. 4 one-bedroom suites ($325-$390). 3 stories, interior corridors. *Bath:* combo or shower only. **Parking:** on-site. **Terms:** check-in 4 pm, cancellation fee imposed, package plans, small pets only ($25 fee). **Amenities:** high-speed Internet (fee), voice mail, irons, hair dryers. **Dining:** 2 restaurants, coffee shop, 6:30 am-11 pm, $10-$27, cocktails. **Pool(s):** heated outdoor, heated indoor, wading. **Leisure Activities:** whirlpool, rental boats, rental paddleboats, golf practice facility, jogging, playground, horseshoes, volleyball, theater in-the-round. *Fee:* golf-18 holes, 5 indoor tennis courts, racquetball courts, game room. **Guest Services:** gift shop, massage (fee), valet and coin laundry, area transportation-within 5 mi. **Business Services:** conference facilities, business center, fax. *Fee:* administrative services, PC. **Cards:** AX, CB, DC, DS, JC, MC, VI. *(See color ad card insert)*

SPRINGHILL SUITES BY MARRIOTT
Phone: (847)793-7500

AAA **SAVE**

Motel

All Year [CP]   1P: $129   2P: $139
Location: I-294, exit Half Day Rd, 2 mi w to SR 21 (Milwaukee Ave), then just s. 300 Marriott Dr 60069. Fax: 847/793-0322. **Facility:** 161 one-bedroom standard units. 6 stories, interior corridors. *Bath:* combo or shower only. **Parking:** on-site. **Amenities:** extended cable TV, dual phone lines, voice mail, irons, hair dryers. **Pool(s):** small heated indoor. **Leisure Activities:** whirlpool, exercise room, patio, sundries shop. **Guest Services:** valet and coin laundry. **Cards:** AX, CB, DC, DS, JC, MC, VI. **Special Amenities:** free continental breakfast and free local telephone calls. *(See color ad card insert)*

──────── *The following lodging was either not evaluated or did not* ────────
meet AAA rating requirements but is listed for your information only.

COURTYARD BY MARRIOTT
Phone: 847/634-9555

[fyi]

Not evaluated. **Location:** I-94, exit Half Day Rd, 2 mi w, just s of jct US 45, SR 21 and 22. 505 N Milwaukee Ave 60069. Facilities, services, and decor characterize a mid-range property.

LISLE pop. 19,500 (See map p. 292; index p. 294)

──────── **WHERE TO STAY** ────────

HICKORY RIDGE MARRIOTT CONFERENCE HOTEL
Phone: (630)971-5000 [376]

AAA **SAVE**

Hotel

4/1-11/15   1P: $79-$149   2P: $79-$159
11/16-3/31   1P: $69-$129   2P: $69-$129
Location: I-88, exit SR 53, 2.5 mi s, then just w. 1195 Summerhill Dr 60532. Fax: 630/971-6989. **Facility:** 383 units. 342 one-bedroom standard units. 41 one-bedroom suites. 10 stories, interior corridors. *Bath:* combo or shower only. **Parking:** on-site. **Terms:** cancellation fee imposed, package plans. **Amenities:** dual phone lines, voice mail, irons, hair dryers. *Fee:* video games, high-speed Internet. **Dining:** dining room, restaurant, 6:30-9:30 am, 11:15-1:15 & 4-midnight, $7-$20, cocktails. **Pool(s):** heated indoor. **Leisure Activities:** saunas, 2 lighted tennis courts, racquetball court, nature trails, bicycles, basketball, volleyball, picnic grove. *Fee:* aerobics class. **Guest Services:** gift shop, valet and coin laundry, area transportation-within 10 mi. **Business Services:** conference facilities, business center. *Fee:* PC, fax. **Cards:** AX, CB, DC, DS, JC, MC, VI. *(See color ad card insert)*

(See map p. 292)

HILTON LISLE/NAPERVILLE
Phone: (630)505-0900 🔵379

AAA SAVE

| | 4/1-10/31 | 1P: $95-$155 | 2P: $95-$175 | XP: $20 | F18 |
| | 11/1-3/31 | 1P: $89-$155 | 2P: $89-$175 | XP: $20 | F18 |

Hotel

Web TV.

Location: I-88, exit Naperville Rd, just n, then 0.3 mi e on Warrenville Rd. 3003 Corporate West Dr 60532. Fax: 630/505-0479. **Facility:** 309 units. 307 one-bedroom standard units. 2 one-bedroom suites ($325-$425) with whirlpools. 8 stories, interior corridors. **Parking:** on-site. **Terms:** cancellation fee imposed, package plans. **Amenities:** extended cable TV, dual phone lines, voice mail, irons, hair dryers. *Fee:* video games, *Some:* high-speed Internet (fee). **Dining:** restaurant, 6:30-10:30 am, Sat & Sun from 7 am, $13-$29, cocktails. **Pool(s):** heated indoor. **Leisure Activities:** whirlpool, exercise room, sun deck. **Guest Services:** valet laundry, area transportation-within 3 mi. **Business Services:** conference facilities, business center. *Fee:* PC, fax. **Cards:** AX, CB, DC, DS, JC, MC, VI. **Special Amenities:** free newspaper and free room upgrade (subject to availability with advanced reservations).

SOME UNITS

HYATT LISLE
Phone: (630)852-1234 🔵377

AAA SAVE

| | All Year | 1P: $89-$155 | 2P: $114-$180 | XP: $25 | F18 |

Hotel

Location: I-88, exit SR 53 westbound, 0.3 mi s; exit Naperville Rd eastbound to Warrenville Rd, 2 mi e to jct SR 53. 1400 Corporetum Dr 60532. Fax: 630/852-1260. **Facility:** 312 units. 310 one-bedroom standard units. 2 one-bedroom suites. 13 stories, interior corridors. *Bath:* combo or shower only. **Parking:** on-site. **Terms:** cancellation fee imposed, package plans. **Amenities:** dual phone lines, voice mail, fax, irons, hair dryers. **Dining:** restaurant, 6 am-midnight, $10-$25, cocktails. **Pool(s):** heated indoor. **Leisure Activities:** sauna, whirlpool, sun deck, exercise room. **Guest Services:** valet laundry, area transportation-local businesses. **Business Services:** conference facilities. **Cards:** AX, CB, DC, DS, JC, MC, VI.

SOME UNITS

WYNDHAM LISLE/NAPERVILLE
Phone: (630)505-1000 🔵380

AAA SAVE

| | All Year | 1P: $79-$155 | 2P: $79-$165 | XP: $10 | F18 |

Hotel

Location: I-88, exit Naperville Rd, just n, then 0.3 mi e. 3000 Warrenville Rd 60532. Fax: 630/505-1165. **Facility:** 242 one-bedroom standard units, some with whirlpools. 8 stories, interior corridors. *Bath:* combo or shower only. **Parking:** on-site and valet (fee). **Terms:** cancellation fee imposed, package plans, small pets only ($25 fee). **Amenities:** extended cable TV, dual phone lines, voice mail, irons, hair dryers. *Fee:* video games, high-speed Internet. *Some:* CD players. **Dining:** dining room, restaurant, 6 am-11 pm, $8-$50, cocktails, nightclub. **Pool(s):** heated indoor. **Leisure Activities:** sauna, whirlpool. *Fee:* racquetball courts, aerobic classes, tanning beds. **Guest Services:** gift shop, massage (fee), valet laundry, area transportation-within 5 mi. **Business Services:** conference facilities. **Cards:** AX, CB, DC, DS, JC, MC, VI.

SOME UNITS

------ WHERE TO DINE ------

CHINN'S 34TH STREET FISHERY
Lunch: $6-$17   **Dinner:** $9-$27   **Phone:** 630/637-1777 🔵228

Seafood

Location: On US 34, 1.7 mi w of SR 53. 3011 W Ogden Ave 60532. **Hours:** 11 am-10 pm, Fri-11 pm, Sat 11:30 am-11 pm, Sun 3 pm-9 pm. **Closed:** 11/28, 12/25. **Reservations:** accepted. **Features:** casual dress; children's menu; early bird specials; carryout; cocktails & lounge; a la carte. Diners who appreciate fresh seafood served in a casual setting by a friendly, no-nonsense service staff have plenty to like here. Choose from a menu that features selections such as fresh catch, surf 'n' turf, pasta lovers or shellfish from the lobster and crab tank. There are also plenty of choices for those who aren't in a seafood mood, including prime steak, ribs and chicken. **Parking:** on-site. **Cards:** AX, CB, DC, DS, MC, VI.

LOCKPORT pop. 9,400

------ WHERE TO DINE ------

TALLGRASS
Dinner: $45-$65
Phone: 815/838-5566

French

Location: SR 171, just s of jct SR 7. 1006 S State 60441. **Hours:** 6 pm to close. Closed major holidays; also Mon & Tues. **Reservations:** required. **Features:** semi-formal attire; cocktails; prix fixe. Guests can unwind in the intimate, formal restaurant's beautifully renovated Victorian-style dining room to enjoy the chef-owner's superbly prepared cuisine. The menu outlines three-, four- and five-course meals that showcase abundant variety and creativity. Plate presentations are marvelous. Smoke free premises. **Parking:** street. **Cards:** MC, VI.

LOMBARD pop. 39,400   (See map p. 284; index p. 289)

------ WHERE TO STAY ------

AMERISUITES CHICAGO/LOMBARD
Phone: (630)932-6501 🔵158

AAA SAVE

| | 4/1-9/30 [ECP] | 1P: $69-$149 | 2P: $79-$159 | XP: $10 | F18 |
| | 10/1-3/31 [ECP] | 1P: $59-$139 | 2P: $69-$149 | XP: $10 | F18 |

Motel

Location: I-88, exit Highland Ave, just n to Butterfield Rd (SR 56), 0.9 mi e, just n. 2340 S Fountain Square Dr 60148. Fax: 630/932-6502. **Facility:** 151 one-bedroom standard units. 6 stories, interior corridors. *Bath:* combo or shower only. **Parking:** on-site. **Terms:** package plans, small pets only. **Amenities:** video games, high-speed Internet (fee), voice mail, irons, hair dryers. **Pool(s):** heated indoor. **Leisure Activities:** sun decks, exercise room. **Guest Services:** valet and coin laundry. **Business Services:** meeting rooms, business center. *Fee:* PC, fax. **Cards:** AX, CB, DC, DS, JC, MC, VI. **Special Amenities:** free continental breakfast and free newspaper. (See color ad p 296)

SOME UNITS

(See map p. 284)

COMFORT SUITES LOMBARD/OAK BROOK
SAVE
Motel

All Year [ECP] 1P: $99-$119 2P: $109-$129 **Phone:** (630)268-1300 **153**
XP: $10 F18
Location: I-355, exit North Ave (SR 64), 0.3 mi e. 530 W North Ave 60148. Fax: 630/268-1400. **Facility:** 66 one-bedroom standard units, some with whirlpools. 3 stories, interior corridors. *Bath:* combo or shower only. **Parking:** on-site. **Terms:** package plans. **Amenities:** extended cable TV, dual phone lines, voice mail, safes (fee), irons, hair dryers. *Some:* CD players. **Pool(s):** heated indoor. **Leisure Activities:** whirlpool, exercise room. **Guest Services:** valet and coin laundry. **Cards:** AX, CB, DC, DS, JC, MC, VI.

SOME UNITS

EMBASSY SUITES HOTEL-LOMBARD/OAK BROOK
SAVE
Suite Hotel

All Year 1P: $99-$229 2P: $99-$229 **Phone:** (630)969-7500 **157**
XP: $10 F
Location: I-88, exit Highland Ave (SR 56), 0.5 mi e. 707 E Butterfield Rd 60148. Fax: 630/969-9821. **Facility:** 262 one-bedroom suites, some with whirlpools. 10 stories, interior corridors. **Parking:** on-site. **Terms:** [BP] meal plan available, package plans. **Amenities:** video games, dual phone lines, voice mail, irons, hair dryers. **Leisure Activities:** sauna, whirlpool, exercise room. **Guest Services:** gift shop, complimentary evening beverages, valet and coin laundry. **Business Services:** meeting rooms.
Cards: AX, CB, DC, DS, JC, MC, VI.

SOME UNITS

HAMPTON INN-LOMBARD
SAVE
Motel

All Year [ECP] 1P: $69-$109 2P: $79-$119 **Phone:** (630)916-9000 **155**
XP: $10 F18
Location: I-88, exit Highland Ave, 0.8 mi n, just e. 222 E 22nd St 60148. Fax: 630/916-8016. **Facility:** 128 one-bedroom standard units. 4 stories, interior corridors. **Parking:** on-site. **Terms:** cancellation fee imposed, package plans. **Amenities:** video games, voice mail, irons, hair dryers. **Leisure Activities:** exercise room. **Guest Services:** valet laundry. **Business Services:** meeting rooms. **Cards:** AX, CB, DC, DS, JC, MC, VI.

SOME UNITS

HOMESTEAD STUDIO SUITES HOTEL
Extended Stay Motel

4/1-9/30 1P: $84-$99 **Phone:** (630)928-0202 **159**
XP: $5 F18
10/1-3/31 1P: $74-$94 XP: $5 F18
Location: I-88, exit Highland Ave, just n, 0.6 mi e on Butterfield Rd (SR 53), just s. 2701 Technology Dr 60148. Fax: 630/928-0505. **Facility:** 136 one-bedroom standard units with efficiencies. 3 stories, interior corridors. *Bath:* combo or shower only. **Parking:** on-site. **Terms:** small pets only ($75 fee). **Amenities:** dual phone lines, voice mail, irons. **Guest Services:** valet and coin laundry. **Cards:** AX, DC, DS, MC, VI.

SOME UNITS

QUALITY INN & SUITES
SAVE
Motel

All Year [ECP] 1P: $81 2P: $81 **Phone:** (630)629-1500 **154**
XP: $10 F18
Location: I-355, exit North Ave (SR 64), just e. 645 W North Ave 60148. Fax: 630/629-2957. **Facility:** 112 one-bedroom standard units, some with whirlpools. 3 stories, interior corridors. *Bath:* combo or shower only. **Parking:** on-site. **Terms:** 5 day cancellation notice-fee imposed. **Amenities:** extended cable TV, dual phone lines, voice mail, irons, hair dryers. **Leisure Activities:** whirlpool, exercise room. **Guest Services:** valet laundry. **Business Services:** meeting rooms. **Cards:** AX, CB, DC, DS, JC, MC, VI.

SOME UNITS

——— WHERE TO DINE ———

BISTRO BANLIEUE
French

Lunch: $9-$22 **Dinner:** $10-$25 **Phone:** 630/629-6560 **143**
Location: I-88, exit Highland Ave, 0.5 mi n; in Yorktown Convenience Center, behind Yorktown Mall. 44 Yorktown Convenience Center 60148. **Hours:** 11:30 am-9 pm, Fri-10 pm, Sat 5 pm-10 pm, Sun 4 pm-8 pm. Closed major holidays. **Reservations:** suggested. **Features:** dressy casual; cocktails & lounge; a la carte. The casual, moderately upscale bistro serves well-prepared French cuisine. On the menu are beef tenderloin, venison, lamb and duck, as well as the highly recommended roasted salmon with stone-ground mustard and honey glaze. Patio dining is available seasonally. **Parking:** on-site. **Cards:** AX, DC, DS, MC, VI.

MAGNUM'S PRIME STEAK HOUSE
Steak & Seafood

Lunch: $8-$17 **Dinner:** $14-$35 **Phone:** 630/573-1010 **142**
Location: I-88, exit Highland Ave, just n to Butterfield Rd (SR 56), 0.5 mi e. 777 E Butterfield Rd 60148. **Hours:** 11 am-11 pm, Fri & Sat 4 pm-midnight, Sun 4 pm-10 pm. **Reservations:** suggested. **Features:** casual dress; carryout; cocktails & lounge; a la carte. Stone fireplaces and a swanky, upscale decor lend warmth to the sophisticated dining room. Excellent prime cuts of steak and fresh seafood are superbly prepared and cleverly presented. The professional and engaging service staff is responsive to diners' every need. **Parking:** on-site. **Cards:** AX, CB, DC, DS, MC, VI.

MARKHAM pop. 13,100 (See map p. 292; index p. 294)

——— WHERE TO STAY ———

HOLIDAY INN EXPRESS
Motel

4/1-8/31 1P: $65-$95 **Phone:** (708)331-5000 **420**
9/1-3/31 1P: $60
Location: I-294, exit 159th St W; I-57, exit 348, 1 mi e. 2850 W 159th St 60426. Fax: 708/331-5502. **Facility:** 59 one-bedroom standard units, some with whirlpools. 2 stories, interior corridors. *Bath:* combo or shower only. **Parking:** on-site. **Terms:** 15 day cancellation notice, package plans. **Amenities:** irons, hair dryers. *Some:* dual phone lines. **Guest Services:** valet laundry. **Cards:** AX, CB, DC, DS, MC, VI.

SOME UNITS

MATTESON pop. 11,400

──────── **WHERE TO STAY** ────────

BAYMONT INN & SUITES CHICAGO-MATTESON
Phone: (708)503-0999

AAA (SAVE)
◆◆◆
Motel

All Year   1P: $69-$89   2P: $69-$89
Location: I-57, exit 340A, 0.3 mi e on US 30, 0.3 mi s on Cicero Ave to entrance. 5210 W Southwick Dr 60443. Fax: 708/503-0444. **Facility:** 111 one-bedroom standard units. 3 stories, interior corridors. **Parking:** on-site, winter plug-ins. **Terms:** 18 day cancellation notice, small pets only ($50 deposit). **Amenities:** video games, voice mail, irons, hair dryers. **Guest Services:** valet and coin laundry. **Cards:** AX, CB, DC, DS, MC, VI. **Special Amenities: free continental breakfast and free newspaper.** *(See color ad opposite title page)*

SOME UNITS
[icons] FEE

COUNTRY INN & SUITES BY CARLSON
Phone: (708)748-4740

◆◆◆
Motel

All Year   1P: $69-$149   2P: $69-$149
Location: I-57, exit 340A, 0.3 mi e, then 0.3 mi n. 950 Lake Superior Dr 60443. Fax: 708/748-4916. **Facility:** 84 units. 55 one-bedroom standard units, some with whirlpools. 29 one-bedroom suites ($79-$179). 3 stories, interior corridors. **Bath:** combo or shower only. **Parking:** on-site. **Terms:** package plans. **Amenities:** dual phone lines, voice mail, irons, hair dryers. **Pool(s):** small heated indoor. **Leisure Activities:** whirlpool, exercise room. **Guest Services:** valet and coin laundry. **Business Services:** meeting rooms. **Cards:** AX, CB, DC, DS, MC, VI. *(See color ad p 322)*

SOME UNITS
[icons] FEE FEE

HOLIDAY INN-MATTESON
Phone: 708/747-3500

◆◆◆
Hotel

All Year   1P: $112   2P: $112   XP: $10   F18
Location: I-57, exit 340A, just e. 500 Holiday Plaza Dr 60443. Fax: 708/747-8495. **Facility:** 204 units. 202 one-bedroom standard units, some with whirlpools. 2 one-bedroom suites with whirlpools. 5 stories, interior corridors. **Parking:** on-site. **Terms:** package plans. **Amenities:** dual phone lines, voice mail, irons, hair dryers. **Pool(s):** heated indoor. **Leisure Activities:** sauna, whirlpool, exercise room. *Fee:* game room. **Guest Services:** valet and coin laundry. **Business Services:** conference facilities, business center, PC, fax. **Cards:** AX, CB, DC, DS, JC, MC, VI.

SOME UNITS
[icons] FEE FEE

MOUNT PROSPECT pop. 53,200 (See map p. 284; index p. 287)

──────── **WHERE TO STAY** ────────

COUNTRY INN & SUITES BY CARLSON CHICAGO/O'HARE
Phone: (847)290-0909 **88**

AAA (SAVE)
◆◆◆
Motel

All Year [ECP]   1P: $99-$109   XP: $10   F17
Location: Jct I-90 and SR 83, 0.5 mi n. 2200 S Elmhurst Rd 60056. Fax: 847/290-1774. **Facility:** 94 units. 90 one-bedroom standard units, some with whirlpools. 4 one-bedroom suites ($129-$149). 3 stories, interior corridors. **Bath:** combo or shower only. **Parking:** on-site. **Terms:** package plans. **Amenities:** dual phone lines, voice mail, irons, hair dryers. **Pool(s):** small heated indoor. **Leisure Activities:** whirlpool, exercise room. **Guest Services:** valet and coin laundry. **Business Services:** meeting rooms. **Cards:** AX, CB, DC, DS, MC, VI. **Special Amenities: free continental breakfast and free newspaper.** *(See color ad p 322)*

SOME UNITS
[icons]

──────── **WHERE TO DINE** ────────

RETRO BISTRO
Lunch: $7-$13   **Dinner:** $11-$22   **Phone:** 847/439-2424 **125**

◆◆◆
French

Location: At northwest corner of jct Golf and Busse rds; in Mt Prospect Commons. 1746 W Golf Rd 60056. **Hours:** 11:30 am-2:30 & 5:30-9 pm, Sat 5 pm-10 pm. Closed major holidays; also Sun. **Reservations:** suggested; on weekends. **Features:** casual dress; cocktails & lounge; a la carte. A bustling and colorful atmosphere await diners at the popular French bistro. Fresh ingredients are blended to create thoughtful preparations of lamb shank, rabbit, venison, pork tenderloin, steak, Cornish hen and fresh seafood. Brilliantly presented desserts are made in house. **Parking:** on-site. **Cards:** AX, CB, DC, DS, MC, VI.

[icon]

MUNDELEIN pop. 21,200

──────── **WHERE TO STAY** ────────

CROWNE PLAZA CHICAGO-NORTHSHORE
Phone: (847)949-5100

◆◆◆
Motor Inn

All Year   1P: $159-$229   2P: $159-$229   XP: $20   F19
Location: Jct US 45 and SR 83. 510 SR 83 E 60060. Fax: 847/949-0117. **Facility:** 183 units. 177 one-bedroom standard units. 6 one-bedroom suites ($400-$600). 4 stories, interior corridors. **Parking:** on-site. **Terms:** package plans. **Amenities:** CD players, dual phone lines, voice mail, safes, irons, hair dryers. **Pool(s):** heated indoor. **Leisure Activities:** exercise room. **Guest Services:** valet and coin laundry. **Business Services:** conference facilities, business center, PC, fax. **Cards:** AX, CB, DC, DS, JC, MC, VI.

SOME UNITS
 FEE

RAMADA GRAND COURT INN

AAA SAVE
◊◊◊ ◊◊◊

Motel

All Year [ECP]　　　　　　1P: $79-$199　　　2P: $79-$199　　　XP: $10　　　F16

Phone: (847)566-5400

Location: Jct US 45 and SR 83 E. 517 SR 83 E 60060. **Fax:** 847/566-2760. **Facility:** 93 one-bedroom standard units, some with whirlpools. 2 stories, interior corridors. **Parking:** on-site, winter plug-ins. **Terms:** 3 day cancellation notice, package plans. **Amenities:** extended cable TV, dual phone lines, voice mail, irons, hair dryers. **Pool(s):** heated outdoor. **Leisure Activities:** whirlpool, steamroom, exercise room. **Guest Services:** valet and coin laundry, area transportation-local business. **Business Services:** meeting rooms, PC. **Cards:** AX, CB, DC, DS, JC, MC, VI. **Special Amenities:** free continental breakfast.

SOME UNITS
[icons] FEE ／ ⊠ VCR ／

SUPER 8 MOTEL

◊◊◊◊◊ ◊◊◊◊◊

Motel

5/31-9/30 [CP]　　　　　1P: $58　　　　　2P: $64　　　　　XP: $6　　　F17
4/1-5/30 & 10/1-3/31 [CP]　1P: $53　　　　　2P: $59　　　　　XP: $6　　　F17

Phone: (847)949-8842

Location: Jct of US 45/60 and SR 83. 1950 S Lake St 60060. **Fax:** 847/949-8848. **Facility:** 72 one-bedroom standard units. 3 stories, interior corridors. **Parking:** on-site, winter plug-ins. **Terms:** package plans. **Amenities:** extended cable TV, safes (fee). **Cards:** AX, DC, DS, MC, VI.

SOME UNITS
ASK [icons] FEE ／ ⊠ FEE FEE

——— WHERE TO DINE ———

DOVER STRAITS RESTAURANT　　　**Lunch:** $7-$15　　　**Dinner:** $14-$22　　　**Phone:** 847/949-1550

◊◊ ◊◊

Seafood

Location: On US 45, 0.5 mi s of jct SR 83. 890 E US 45 60060. **Hours:** 11 am-midnight, Sat 4 pm-2 am, Sun 2 pm-10 pm. **Closed:** 1/1, 11/28, 12/25; also Sat for lunch. **Reservations:** suggested; weekends. **Features:** dressy casual; children's menu; early bird specials; carryout; cocktails & lounge; entertainment. Rope door handles, shark and swordfish wall mounts and framed beach and boat scenes set a nautical tone in the casual dining room. The menu comprises many fresh seafood choices, such as lobster, whitefish, crab, shrimp, grouper, halibut and trout. **Parking:** on-site. **Cards:** AX, CB, DC, DS, MC, VI.

⊠M ⊠

NAPERVILLE pop. 85,400

——— WHERE TO STAY ———

BEST WESTERN NAPERVILLE INN

AAA SAVE
◊◊◊ ◊◊◊

Motel

4/1-10/31　　　　　　1P: $79-$129　　　2P: $89-$139　　　XP: $10　　　F12
11/1-3/31　　　　　　1P: $59-$109　　　2P: $69-$119　　　XP: $10　　　F12

Phone: (630)505-0200

Location: I-88, exit Naperville Rd, 0.4 mi s. 1617 N Naperville/Wheaton Rd 60563. **Fax:** 630/505-4291. **Facility:** 105 one-bedroom standard units, some with whirlpools. 3 stories, interior/exterior corridors. **Parking:** on-site. **Amenities:** extended cable TV, safes, irons, hair dryers. **Leisure Activities:** exercise room. **Guest Services:** valet and coin laundry. **Cards:** AX, CB, DC, DS, JC, MC, VI. **Special Amenities:** free continental breakfast and free local telephone calls. *(See color ad below)*

SOME UNITS
[icons] FEE ／ ⊠ [icons] ／

COUNTRY INN & SUITES BY CARLSON

◊◊◊ ◊◊◊

Motel

6/3-10/10 [ECP]　　　　1P: $90-$125　　　2P: $90-$125　　　XP: $7　　　F18
10/11-3/31 [ECP]　　　1P: $84-$114　　　2P: $84-$114　　　XP: $5　　　F18
4/1-6/2 [ECP]　　　　　1P: $80-$110　　　2P: $80-$110　　　XP: $5　　　F18

Phone: (630)548-0966

Location: I-88, exit SR 59, just s. 1847 W Diehl Rd 60563. **Fax:** 630/548-0966. **Facility:** 64 units. 54 one-bedroom standard units. 10 one-bedroom suites. 3 stories, interior corridors. **Bath:** combo or shower only. **Parking:** on-site. **Terms:** 14 day cancellation notice-fee imposed, package plans, small pets only ($5 fee, in smoking units). **Amenities:** extended cable TV, irons, hair dryers. **Pool(s):** heated indoor. **Leisure Activities:** whirlpool. **Guest Services:** valet laundry. **Cards:** AX, DC, DS, MC, VI. *(See color ad p 322)*

SOME UNITS
ASK [icons] FEE ／ ⊠ [icons] ／

COURTYARD BY MARRIOTT
Phone: 630/505-0550
🔵🔵 (SAVE) All Year   1P: $59-$124
▼▼▼
            Location: I-88, exit Naperville Rd, 0.3 mi s to Diehl Rd, then 0.5 mi w. 1155 E Diehl Rd 60563. Fax: 630/505-8337.
  Motel   **Facility:** 147 units. 131 one-bedroom standard units. 16 one-bedroom suites ($119-$149). 2-3 stories, interior corridors. *Bath:* combo or shower only. **Parking:** on-site. **Terms:** 7 day cancellation notice-fee imposed, [BP] meal plan available. **Amenities:** high-speed Internet, voice mail, irons, hair dryers. **Dining:** coffee shop, 6:30-10 am, Sat & Sun 7-11 am, $5-$7. **Pool(s):** heated indoor. **Leisure Activities:** whirlpool, exercise room.
Guest Services: valet and coin laundry. **Business Services:** meeting rooms. **Cards:** AX, DC, DS, MC, VI.
(See ad p 299 & color ad card insert)

SOME UNITS

EXEL INN OF NAPERVILLE
Phone: (630)357-0022
🔵🔵 (SAVE) 6/1-10/31 [CP]   1P: $50-$70   2P: $55-$75   XP: $6   F18
▼▼▼   4/1-5/31 & 11/1-3/31 [CP] 1P: $50-$62   2P: $55-$69   XP: $6   F18
  Motel   **Location:** I-88, exit Naperville Rd, 0.5 mi s. 1585 N Naperville Rd/Wheaton Rd 60563. Fax: 630/357-9817. **Facility:** 123 one-bedroom standard units, some with whirlpools. 3 stories, interior corridors. **Parking:** on-site. **Terms:** small pets only ($100 per week). **Amenities:** irons, hair dryers. **Leisure Activities:** exercise room. **Guest Services:** valet and coin laundry. **Cards:** AX, CB, DC, DS, MC, VI. **Special Amenities:** early check-in/late check-out and free continental breakfast. *(See color ad p 318)*

SOME UNITS

FAIRFIELD INN BY MARRIOTT
Phone: 630/577-1820
🔵🔵 (SAVE) All Year [ECP]   1P: $94
▼▼▼
            Location: I-88, exit Naperville Rd, 0.3 mi s to Diehl Rd, 0.5 mi w. 1820 Abriter Ct 60563. Fax: 630/577-0120.
  Motel   **Facility:** 105 one-bedroom standard units, some with whirlpools. 3 stories, interior corridors. *Bath:* combo or shower only. **Parking:** on-site. **Amenities:** voice mail, irons. **Leisure Activities:** whirlpool, exercise room. **Guest Services:** valet and coin laundry. **Business Services:** meeting rooms. **Cards:** AX, CB, DC, DS, MC, VI. **Special Amenities:** free continental breakfast and free local telephone calls.
(See color ad card insert)

SOME UNITS

HAMPTON INN
Phone: (630)505-1400
(SAVE) 7/1-9/30 [ECP]   1P: $79-$114   2P: $79-$114   XP: $10   F17
▼▼▼   4/1-6/30 & 10/1-3/31 [ECP] 1P: $69-$104   2P: $69-$104   XP: $10   F17
  Motel   **Location:** I-88, exit Naperville Rd, 0.3 mi s to Diehl Rd, then 0.5 mi w. 1087 E Diehl Rd 60563. Fax: 630/505-1416. **Facility:** 130 one-bedroom standard units. 4 stories, interior corridors. **Parking:** on-site, winter plug-ins. **Terms:** package plans. **Amenities:** video games (fee), voice mail, irons, hair dryers. **Pool(s):** heated outdoor. **Leisure Activities:** exercise room. **Guest Services:** valet laundry. **Business Services:** meeting rooms. **Cards:** AX, CB, DC, DS, JC, MC, VI. *(See ad below)*

SOME UNITS

HAWTHORN SUITES-NAPERVILLE
Phone: (630)548-0881
▼▼▼   All Year [BP]   1P: $109-$129
            Location: I-88, exit SR 59, just s to Diehl Rd, then just w. 1843 W Diehl Rd 60563. Fax: 630/548-0882. **Facility:** 72
Extended Stay units. 28 one-bedroom standard units, some with efficiencies. 37 one- and 7 two-bedroom suites with
  Motel   kitchens. 4 stories, interior corridors. *Bath:* combo or shower only. **Parking:** on-site. **Terms:** package plans, pets ($150 fee). **Amenities:** dual phone lines, voice mail, irons. **Pool(s):** heated indoor. **Leisure Activities:** whirlpool, exercise room, sports court. **Guest Services:** complimentary evening beverages: Mon-Thurs, valet and coin laundry. **Business Services:** meeting rooms. **Cards:** AX, CB, DC, DS, MC, VI.

SOME UNITS

HOLIDAY INN SELECT CHICAGO/NAPERVILLE
Phone: (630)505-4900
▼▼▼   All Year   1P: $111   2P: $111   XP: $10   F18
            Location: I-88, exit Naperville Rd, just s. 1801 N Naper Blvd 60563. Fax: 630/505-8239. **Facility:** 299 units. 292
Motor Inn   one-bedroom standard units. 7 one-bedroom suites ($134-$280), some with whirlpools. 7 stories, interior corridors. **Parking:** on-site. **Terms:** package plans. **Amenities:** extended cable TV, video games, voice mail, irons, hair dryers. **Pool(s):** heated indoor. **Leisure Activities:** sauna, sun deck, exercise room. **Guest Services:** gift shop, valet laundry. **Business Services:** conference facilities, business center. *Fee:* PC, fax. **Cards:** AX, CB, DC, DS, JC, MC, VI.

SOME UNITS

HOMESTEAD STUDIO SUITES-CHICAGO/NAPERVILLE

Phone: (630)577-0200

Extended Stay Motel

All Year   1P: $79-$84   2P: $84-$95   XP: $5   F18
Location: I-88, exit Naperville Rd, just s to Diehl Rd, 0.8 mi w, then just n. 1827 Centre Point Cir 60563. Fax: 630/577-0260. **Facility:** 137 one-bedroom standard units with efficiencies. 3 stories, interior corridors. *Bath:* combo or shower only. **Parking:** on-site. **Terms:** small pets only ($75 fee). **Amenities:** voice mail, irons. **Guest Services:** valet and coin laundry. **Cards:** AX, CB, DC, DS, MC, VI.

SOME UNITS

RED ROOF INN

Phone: (630)369-2500

Motel

6/3-9/28	1P: $61-$78	2P: $67-$84	XP: $6 F18
5/12-6/2	1P: $59-$77	2P: $65-$83	XP: $6 F18
9/29-3/31	1P: $49-$63	2P: $55-$69	XP: $6 F18
4/1-5/11	1P: $47-$63	2P: $53-$69	XP: $6 F18

Location: I-88, exit SR 59, just s. 1698 W Diehl Rd 60563. Fax: 630/369-9987. **Facility:** 119 one-bedroom standard units. 3 stories, exterior corridors. **Parking:** on-site. **Terms:** small pets only. **Amenities:** video games (fee), voice mail. **Cards:** AX, CB, DC, DS, MC, VI. **Special Amenities:** free local telephone calls and free newspaper.

SOME UNITS

SLEEP INN

Phone: (630)778-5900

Motel

4/1-9/30	1P: $69-$109	2P: $69-$109	XP: $10 F18
10/1-3/31	1P: $59-$79	2P: $59-$79	XP: $10 F18

Location: I-88, exit SR 59, just sw. 1831 W Diehl Rd 60563. Fax: 630/778-1441. **Facility:** 69 one-bedroom standard units, some with whirlpools. 3 stories, interior corridors. *Bath:* combo or shower only. **Parking:** on-site. **Amenities:** extended cable TV, dual phone lines, voice mail. *Some:* irons. **Guest Services:** valet laundry. **Cards:** AX, DC, DS, MC, VI.

SOME UNITS

WYNDHAM GARDEN HOTEL-NAPERVILLE

Phone: (630)505-3353

Motor Inn

All Year   1P: $89-$122   2P: $89-$132   XP: $10   F18
Location: I-88, exit Naperville Rd, 0.3 mi s to Diehl Rd, 0.7 mi w, then just n. 1837 Centre Point Cir 60563. Fax: 630/505-0176. **Facility:** 143 units. 140 one-bedroom standard units. 3 one-bedroom suites. 4 stories, interior corridors. **Parking:** on-site. **Terms:** cancellation fee imposed, package plans. **Amenities:** voice mail, irons, hair dryers. *Fee:* video games, high-speed Internet. **Dining:** restaurant, 6:30 am-2 & 5-10 pm, Sat & Sun 7 am-noon, $8-$20, cocktails. **Leisure Activities:** whirlpool, exercise room. **Guest Services:** valet and coin laundry. **Business Services:** meeting rooms. **Cards:** AX, CB, DC, DS, JC, MC, VI.

SOME UNITS

------- **WHERE TO DINE** -------

MESON SABIKA

Lunch: $10-$24   Dinner: $10-$24   Phone: 630/983-3000

Spanish

Location: 1 mi e of jct US 34 (Ogden Ave). 1025 Aurora Ave 60540. **Hours:** 11:30 am-10 pm, Fri-11 pm, Sat 5 pm-11 pm, Sun 11 am-2 & 4-9 pm. Closed major holidays. **Reservations:** accepted. **Features:** casual dress; Sunday brunch; children's menu; carryout; cocktails & lounge; a la carte. An enormous menu of well-prepared Spanish tapas is presented at the upscale dining room, set in a stately 1847 Colonial home. Sparkling vintage crystal chandeliers and decorative imported ceramic plates adorn the lovely, yet casual, dining room. Outdoor patio dining is available in season, and entertainment is featured on weekends. **Parking:** on-site. **Cards:** AX, DC, MC, VI.

RAFFI'S ON 5TH

Lunch: $9-$15   Dinner: $11-$25   Phone: 630/961-8203

Mediterranean

Location: Between Columbia and Washington sts; in 5th Ave Station. 200 E 5th Ave 60563. **Hours:** 11:30 am-2 & 6-9:30 pm, Sat from 6 pm. Closed major holidays; also Sun. **Reservations:** suggested. **Features:** dressy casual; cocktails; a la carte. Expertly prepared Mediterranean cuisine is served in a moderately upscale dining room with crisp white linen tablecloths and fine china. The restaurant shares its location—a converted antique brick train station that was also a huge furniture factory—with trendy shops and stores. Service is skilled though casual. Smoke free premises. **Parking:** on-site. **Cards:** AX, CB, DC, DS, MC, VI.

WASHINGTON SQUARE

Lunch: $8-$15   Dinner: $18-$30   Phone: 630/357-3462

American

Location: From US 34 (Ogden Ave) 0.8 mi s; in historic downtown. 218 S Washington St 60540. **Hours:** 11 am-11 pm. Closed: Sun. **Reservations:** suggested; weekends. **Features:** dressy casual; cocktails & lounge. In the heart of the charming historic downtown area, the restaurant nurtures an elegant, yet casual, atmosphere. Continental and American cuisine, including the house special Athenian-style lamb chops, is capably prepared. Guests may request seating in one of five dining rooms. **Parking:** street. **Cards:** AX, CB, DC, DS, MC, VI.

NILES pop. 28,300

------- **WHERE TO STAY** -------

DAYS INN-NILES/SKOKIE/CHICAGO

Phone: (847)647-7700

Motel

All Year [CP]   1P: $79   2P: $85   XP: $10   F18
Location: At jct W Touhy Ave and N Caldwell. 6450 W Touhy Ave 60714. Fax: 847/647-7716. **Facility:** 149 units. 139 one-bedroom standard units. 10 one-bedroom suites ($129) with whirlpools. 1-2 stories, exterior corridors. *Bath:* combo or shower only. **Parking:** on-site. **Terms:** 3 day cancellation notice, package plans. **Amenities:** safes (fee), hair dryers. **Guest Services:** valet laundry. **Business Services:** meeting rooms. **Cards:** AX, CB, DC, DS, JC, MC, VI. **Special Amenities:** free continental breakfast and free newspaper.

SOME UNITS

NORTH AURORA pop. 5,900

―――――― WHERE TO STAY ――――――

BAYMONT INNS & SUITES NORTH AURORA
Phone: (630)897-7695

Ⓐ SAVE   All Year   1P: $69-$90   2P: $76-$90   XP: $7   F18

Motel

Location: I-88, exit SR 31, just s. 308 S Lincoln Way 60542. Fax: 630/897-8130. **Facility:** 71 one-bedroom standard units, some with whirlpools. 3 stories, interior corridors. *Bath:* combo or shower only. **Parking:** on-site. **Terms:** 7 day cancellation notice-fee imposed, small pets only. **Amenities:** extended cable TV, dual phone lines, voice mail, irons, hair dryers. **Pool(s):** small heated outdoor. **Leisure Activities:** exercise room. **Guest Services:** valet laundry. **Business Services:** meeting rooms. **Cards:** AX, CB, DC, DS, MC, VI.
Special Amenities: free continental breakfast and free newspaper.

SOME UNITS

NORTHBROOK pop. 32,300

―――――― WHERE TO STAY ――――――

ADAM'S MARK HOTEL
Phone: (847)298-2525

Ⓐ SAVE   9/8-11/23   1P: $139-$219   2P: $154-$235
            4/1-9/7   1P: $129-$209   2P: $144-$224
            11/24-3/31   1P: $119-$199   2P: $134-$214

Motor Inn

Location: I-294, exit Willow Rd, 1 mi w to SR 21 and US 45 (Milwaukee Ave), 0.6 mi s. 2875 N Milwaukee Ave 60062-6191. Fax: 847/298-5592. **Facility:** 318 one-bedroom standard units. 4-7 stories, interior corridors. *Bath:* combo or shower only. **Parking:** on-site. **Terms:** [AP] meal plan available, package plans. **Amenities:** dual phone lines, voice mail, irons, hair dryers. *Fee:* video games, Web TV. **Dining:** restaurant, 6 am-10 pm, $12-$22, cocktails. **Pool(s):** heated outdoor. **Leisure Activities:** whirlpool, exercise room. **Guest Services:** gift shop, valet and coin laundry, area transportation-within 5 mi. **Business Services:** conference facilities, business center. *Fee:* PC, fax. **Cards:** AX, CB, DC, DS, JC, MC, VI. **Special Amenities: early check-in/late check-out and preferred room (subject to availability with advanced reservations).**

SOME UNITS

FEE   FEE

THE HILTON NORTHBROOK
Phone: 847/480-7500

Ⓐ SAVE   All Year   1P: $99-$124   2P: $119-$144   XP: $20   F18

Hotel

Location: On SR 21, s of jct US 45 and Willow Rd. 2855 N Milwaukee Ave 60062. Fax: 847/509-1043. **Facility:** 246 units. 245 one-bedroom standard units, some with whirlpools. 1 one-bedroom suite ($184-$260). 10 stories, interior corridors. **Parking:** on-site. **Terms:** cancellation fee imposed, package plans. **Amenities:** video games (fee), dual phone lines, voice mail, honor bars, irons, hair dryers. *Some:* high-speed Internet (fee). **Dining:** restaurant, coffee shop, 6 am-10 pm, Sat & Sun from 7 am, cocktails, also, Allgauer's On The Riverfront, see separate listing. **Pool(s):** heated indoor. **Leisure Activities:** sauna, whirlpool, hiking trails, jogging, exercise room. **Guest Services:** gift shop, valet laundry, area transportation-within 5 mi. **Business Services:** conference facilities, business center, administrative services. *Fee:* PC, fax. **Cards:** AX, CB, DC, DS, JC, MC, VI.

SOME UNITS

FEE   FEE

RED ROOF INN
Phone: (847)205-1755

Ⓐ SAVE   6/3-9/8   1P: $61-$74   2P: $66-$79   XP: $5   F18
            5/13-6/2   1P: $56-$72   2P: $61-$77   XP: $5   F18
            9/9-3/31   1P: $49-$72   2P: $54-$77   XP: $5   F18
            4/1-5/12   1P: $45-$62   2P: $50-$67   XP: $5   F18

Motel

Location: I-94, exit SR 43 (Waukegan Rd). 340 Waukegan Rd 60062. Fax: 847/205-1891. **Facility:** 118 one-bedroom standard units. 3 stories, exterior corridors. **Parking:** on-site. **Terms:** small pets only ($100 deposit). **Amenities:** video games (fee), voice mail. **Business Services:** meeting rooms. **Cards:** AX, CB, DC, DS, MC, VI. **Special Amenities: free local telephone calls and free newspaper.**

SOME UNITS

FEE

RENAISSANCE CHICAGO NORTH SHORE

[AAA] [SAVE]

Hotel

1/1-3/31	1P: $99-$169	2P: $99-$169	XP: $10	F12
4/1-12/31	1P: $99-$159	2P: $99-$159	XP: $10	F12

Phone: (847)498-6500

Location: I-94, exit Dundee Rd W northbound; exit Waukegan Rd southbound, 0.5 mi s to SR 68, 1.5 mi e. 933 Skokie Blvd 60062. Fax: 847/498-9558. **Facility:** 386 units. 383 one-bedroom standard units. 3 one-bedroom suites. 8-10 stories, interior corridors. *Bath:* combo or shower only. **Parking:** on-site. **Terms:** package plans. **Amenities:** video games (fee), voice mail, irons, hair dryers. *Some:* dual phone lines, fax. **Dining:** dining room, restaurant, 6 am-11 pm, Sun from 6:30 am, $8-$40, cocktails. **Pool(s):** heated indoor. **Leisure Activities:** exercise room, sun deck. **Guest Services:** gift shop, valet and coin laundry, area transportation-within 5 mi. **Business Services:** conference facilities. **Cards:** AX, CB, DC, DS, JC, MC, VI. *(See ad p 358 & color ad card insert)*

SOME UNITS

——— WHERE TO DINE ———

ALLGAUER'S ON THE RIVERFRONT

Continental

Lunch: $8-$15   **Dinner:** $15-$30   **Phone:** 847/664-7999

Location: On SR 21, s of jct US 45 and Willow Rd; in The Hilton Northbrook. 2855 N Milwaukee 60062. **Hours:** 6 am-10 pm, Sat & Sun from 7 am. **Reservations:** suggested. **Features:** casual dress; Sunday brunch; early bird specials; cocktails & lounge. Take a seat in the spacious dining room or outdoor area overlooking the river and sample any one of the specialties of the house, such as steak Diane and Dover sole. The service is knowledgeable and skilled in tableside preparations. **Parking:** on-site. **Cards:** AX, CB, DC, DS, JC, MC, VI.

RON OF JAPAN

Japanese

Dinner: $16-$30   **Phone:** 847/564-5900

Location: I-94, exit Dundee Rd W, just w, then just n. 633 Skokie Blvd 60062. **Hours:** 5 pm-9 pm, Sun from 4:30 pm. Closed: 1/1, 11/28. **Reservations:** suggested. **Features:** casual dress; children's menu; cocktails; a la carte. The festive atmosphere blends well with the popular Japanese tableside preparations served here. Fresh vegetables and a good variety of choice steak, chicken, seafood and prime rib are cooked just right. A children's menu is also available. **Parking:** on-site. **Cards:** AX, DC, DS, JC, MC, VI.

NORTH CHICAGO pop. 35,000

——— WHERE TO STAY ———

NORTH CHICAGO DAYS INN

[SAVE]

Motel

4/1-11/30	1P: $50-$75	2P: $60-$85	XP: $10	F17
12/1-3/31	1P: $45-$65	2P: $55-$75	XP: $10	F17

Phone: (847)887-9000

Location: Jct US 41 and SR 137, just s. 3000 Hwy 41 60064 (3000 N Skokie Hwy, LAKE BLUFF, 60044). Fax: 847/887-9601. **Facility:** 58 one-bedroom standard units. 2 stories, interior corridors. *Bath:* combo or shower only. **Parking:** on-site. **Amenities:** *Some:* hair dryers. **Cards:** AX, CB, DC, DS, MC, VI.

SOME UNITS

RED CARPET INN

[AAA] [SAVE]

Motel

All Year   1P: $59-$69   2P: $69-$79   XP: $5   F16

Phone: (847)689-9400

Location: Jct US 41 and SR 137. 3207 Buckley Rd 60064. Fax: 847/689-0025. **Facility:** 100 one-bedroom standard units. 2 stories, exterior corridors. **Parking:** on-site. **Terms:** [CP] meal plan available. **Amenities:** voice mail. *Some:* irons. **Leisure Activities:** whirlpool. **Guest Services:** coin laundry. **Cards:** AX, CB, DC, DS, MC, VI. **Special Amenities:** free continental breakfast and preferred room (subject to availability with advanced reservations).

SOME UNITS

NORTHLAKE pop. 12,500

——— WHERE TO STAY ———

ECONO LODGE O'HARE

[AAA] [SAVE]

Motor Inn

All Year   1P: $60-$70   2P: $65-$75   XP: $5   F12

Phone: (708)681-0220

Location: On US 45, 0.5 mi n of jct SR 64. 2080 N Mannheim Rd 60164. Fax: 708/681-9533. **Facility:** 95 one-bedroom standard units. 2 stories, interior corridors. **Parking:** on-site. **Dining:** restaurant, 6 am-10 pm, $6-$12. **Cards:** AX, CB, DC, DS, JC, MC, VI. **Special Amenities:** early check-in/late check-out.

SOME UNITS

OAK BROOK pop. 9,200   (See map p. 284; index p. 288)

——— WHERE TO STAY ———

HYATT REGENCY OAK BROOK

[AAA] [SAVE]

Hotel

All Year   1P: $79-$175   2P: $104-$200   XP: $25   F18

Phone: (630)573-1234   **[118]**

Location: Spring and Harger rds; n of 22nd St (Cermak Rd). 1909 Spring Rd 60523. Fax: 630/573-1133. **Facility:** 423 units. 410 one-bedroom standard units. 12 one- and 1 two-bedroom suites. 7 stories, interior corridors. *Bath:* combo or shower only. **Parking:** on-site. **Terms:** cancellation fee imposed, package plans. **Amenities:** voice mail, irons, hair dryers. *Fee:* video games, Web TV. **Dining:** dining room, restaurant, coffee shop, 6:30 am-10:30 pm, $10-$32, cocktails. **Pool(s):** heated indoor. **Leisure Activities:** whirlpool, sun deck. *Fee:* barber shop, shoe shine. **Guest Services:** gift shop, valet and coin laundry, area transportation-within 5 mi. **Business Services:** conference facilities, business center. *Fee:* PC, fax. **Cards:** AX, CB, DC, DS, JC, MC, VI.

SOME UNITS

(See map p. 284)

MARRIOTT OAK BROOK HOTEL
Phone: (630)573-8555 [123]

(AAA) (SAVE)

Hotel

| | 1/1-3/31 | 1P: $159-$199 | 2P: $169-$209 |
| | 4/1-12/31 | 1P: $149-$189 | 2P: $159-$199 |

Location: I-88, exit Cermak Rd westbound, exit Midwest Rd eastbound to Butterfield Rd/22nd St, then 2 mi e. 1401 W 22nd St 60523. **Fax:** 630/573-1026. **Facility:** 347 units. 336 one-bedroom standard units. 11 one-bedroom suites. 12 stories, interior corridors. *Bath:* combo or shower only. **Parking:** on-site. **Terms:** check-in 4 pm. **Amenities:** dual phone lines, voice mail, safes, irons, hair dryers. *Fee:* video games, high-speed Internet. **Dining:** dining room, restaurant, coffee shop, 6:30 am-11 pm, $9-$30, cocktails. **Leisure Activities:** whirlpool, exercise room. **Guest Services:** valet and coin laundry, area transportation-within 3 mi. **Business Services:** conference facilities, business center. *Fee:* PC, fax. **Cards:** AX, CB, DC, DS, JC, MC, VI. *(See color ad card insert)*

SOME UNITS

(icons) FEE

RENAISSANCE OAK BROOK HOTEL
Phone: (630)573-2800 [119]

(AAA) (SAVE)

Motor Inn

	7/1-12/31	1P: $159-$179	2P: $174-$194
	4/23-6/30	1P: $169	2P: $184
	4/1-4/22 & 1/1-3/31	1P: $149	2P: $164

Location: E of SR 83, n of 22nd St (Cermak Rd); in Oak Brook Shopping Center. 2100 Spring Rd 60523. **Fax:** 630/573-7134. **Facility:** 166 units. 164 one-bedroom standard units. 2 one-bedroom suites ($300). 10 stories, interior corridors. **Parking:** on-site and valet (fee). **Terms:** package plans. **Amenities:** video games (fee), voice mail, honor bars, irons, hair dryers. **Dining:** dining room, 6:30 am-2:30 & 5:30-10 pm, Fri & Sat-10:30 pm, Sun 7 am-2:30 pm, $12-$25, cocktails. **Pool(s):** heated outdoor, wading. **Leisure Activities:** sauna, exercise room. **Guest Services:** valet laundry, area transportation-within 5 mi. **Business Services:** conference facilities, PC. **Cards:** AX, DC, DS, JC, MC, VI. *(See color ad card insert)*

SOME UNITS

(icons) FEE

WYNDHAM DRAKE-OAK BROOK
Phone: (630)574-5700 [122]

(AAA) (SAVE)

Motor Inn

| | All Year | 1P: $99-$169 | 2P: $99-$179 | XP: $18 | F18 |

Location: York Rd and 22nd St (Cermak Rd). 2301 York Rd 60523. **Fax:** 630/574-0830. **Facility:** The hotel's rooms are of varied size but all feature a large desk and comfortable ergonomic chair. 160 units. 149 one-bedroom standard units. 11 one-bedroom suites. 2-4 stories, interior corridors. *Bath:* combo or shower only. **Parking:** on-site and valet. **Terms:** cancellation fee imposed, package plans. **Amenities:** extended cable TV, video games (fee), dual phone lines, irons, hair dryers. **Dining:** dining room, 6:30 am-11 pm, $15-$27, cocktails. **Pool(s):** heated outdoor, heated indoor. **Leisure Activities:** whirlpool, jogging. **Guest Services:** massage (fee), valet laundry, area transportation-within 7 mi. **Business Services:** conference facilities, business center. *Fee:* PC, fax. **Cards:** AX, CB, DC, DS, MC, VI.

SOME UNITS

(icons) FEE

------ WHERE TO DINE ------

TUSCANY

Italian

Lunch: $8-$26   **Dinner:** $8-$26   **Phone:** 630/990-1993 [138]

Location: At se jct of 22nd St and SR 83. 1415 W 22nd St 60521. **Hours:** 11:30 am-3:30 & 5-10 pm, Fri & Sat 5 pm-11 pm, Sun 4 pm-9 pm. Closed major holidays. **Reservations:** suggested. **Features:** dressy casual; carryout; cocktails & lounge; a la carte. The bustling eatery boasts a wonderful minestrone, chock full of carrots, celery, cabbage and light seasonings. Pasta dishes, sausage with peppers, and chicken roasted in a wood-burning oven also are tempting. Service is casual and competent. **Parking:** on-site and valet (fee). **Cards:** AX, DC, DS, JC, MC, VI.

(icon)

------ *The following restaurant has not been evaluated by AAA but is listed for your information only.* ------

CAFE AT THE DRAKE

[fyi]

Phone: 630/574-5700

Not evaluated. **Location:** York Rd and 22nd St (Cermak Rd); in Wyndham Drake-Oak Brook. 2301 York Rd 60523. Dishes include rack of lamb, beef tenderloin and the signature bookbinder soup.

OAKBROOK TERRACE pop. 1,900 (See map p. 284; index p. 288)

------ WHERE TO STAY ------

COMFORT SUITES-OAKBROOK TERRACE
Phone: (630)916-1000 [129]

(SAVE)

Suite Motel

| | All Year [BP] | 1P: $109-$129 | 2P: $119-$129 | XP: $10 | F18 |

Location: SR 38, just w of jct SR 83. 17 W 445 Roosevelt Rd 60181. **Fax:** 630/916-1068. **Facility:** 103 one-bedroom suites. 3 stories, interior corridors. **Parking:** on-site. **Amenities:** extended cable TV, voice mail, irons, hair dryers. **Pool(s):** heated indoor. **Leisure Activities:** sauna, exercise room. **Guest Services:** complimentary evening beverages: Mon-Thurs, valet and coin laundry. **Business Services:** meeting rooms. **Cards:** AX, CB, DC, DS, JC, MC, VI.

SOME UNITS

(icons)

FOUR POINTS BARCELO HOTEL OAKBROOK
Phone: (630)833-3600 [133]

(AAA)

Motor Inn

| | All Year | 1P: $69-$199 | 2P: $69-$199 | XP: $10 | F18 |

Location: I-88 E, exit Midwest Rd, just on Midwest Rd, 0.3 mi e; 0.5 mi w of jct SR 83. 17 W 350 22nd St 60181. **Fax:** 630/833-7037. **Facility:** 228 units. 223 one-bedroom standard units. 5 one-bedroom suites ($144-$300). 7 stories, interior corridors. **Parking:** on-site. **Terms:** cancellation fee imposed, package plans. **Amenities:** dual phone lines, voice mail, irons, hair dryers. **Pool(s):** heated indoor. **Leisure Activities:** whirlpool, sun deck, exercise room. **Guest Services:** valet laundry. **Business Services:** conference facilities, fax. **Cards:** AX, CB, DC, DS, JC, MC, VI.

SOME UNITS

FEE   FEE FEE

(See map p. 284)

HILTON GARDEN INN

Motel

Phone: 630/941-1177   [131]
All Year [BP]   1P: $79   2P: $79   XP: $20   F18
Location: Just se of jct SR 83 and 38. 1000 Drury Ln 60181. Fax: 630/941-1188. **Facility:** 128 one-bedroom standard units. 5 stories, interior corridors. *Bath:* combo or shower only. **Terms:** cancellation fee imposed. **Amenities:** dual phone lines, voice mail, irons, hair dryers. **Pool(s):** heated indoor. **Leisure Activities:** whirlpool, sun deck, exercise room. **Guest Services:** valet and coin laundry. **Business Services:** meeting rooms, business center, PC (fee), fax. **Cards:** AX, CB, DC, DS, JC, MC, VI.

SOME UNITS

HILTON SUITES OAKBROOK TERRACE

Suite Hotel

Phone: 630/941-0100   [130]
All Year [AP]   1P: $109   2P: $109   XP: $20   F18
Location: Just se of jct SR 83 and 38. 1000 Drury Ln 60181. Fax: 630/941-0299. **Facility:** 212 one-bedroom suites ($109). 10 stories, interior corridors. *Bath:* combo or shower only. **Parking:** on-site. **Terms:** cancellation fee imposed, package plans. **Amenities:** high-speed Internet (fee), dual phone lines, voice mail, irons, hair dryers. **Pool(s):** small heated indoor. **Leisure Activities:** sauna, whirlpool, exercise room. **Guest Services:** gift shop, complimentary evening beverages, valet laundry. **Business Services:** meeting rooms, business center, PC, fax. **Cards:** AX, CB, DC, DS, JC, MC, VI.

SOME UNITS

LA QUINTA INN-OAKBROOK TERRACE

Motel

Phone: (630)495-4600   [132]
All Year   1P: $79-$119   2P: $89-$129   XP: $10   F18
Location: I-88, exit Midwest Rd, 0.4 mi n, just n of 22nd St/Cermak Rd. 1 S 666 Midwest Rd 60181-4429. Fax: 630/495-2558. **Facility:** 151 units. 150 one-bedroom standard units. 1 one-bedroom suite ($109-$159). 3 stories, interior corridors. **Parking:** on-site. **Terms:** small pets only. **Amenities:** video games, voice mail, irons, hair dryers. **Pool(s):** heated outdoor. **Leisure Activities:** exercise room. **Guest Services:** valet laundry. **Business Services:** meeting rooms. **Cards:** AX, CB, DC, DS, MC, VI. *(See color ad p 325)*

SOME UNITS

OAK LAWN pop. 56,200   (See map p. 292; index p. 293)

──── **WHERE TO STAY** ────

HILTON OAK LAWN

Hotel

Phone: (708)425-7800   [322]
All Year   1P: $150-$184   2P: $160-$194   XP: $10   F18
Location: SR 50, just n of US 12 and 20. 9333 S Cicero Ave 60453. Fax: 708/425-8111. **Facility:** 180 units. 177 one-bedroom standard units. 3 one-bedroom suites ($329-$629), some with whirlpools. 12 stories, interior corridors. **Parking:** on-site. **Terms:** 21 day cancellation notice-fee imposed, package plans. **Amenities:** high-speed Internet (fee), voice mail, irons, hair dryers. *Some:* honor bars. **Pool(s):** heated indoor. **Leisure Activities:** sauna, whirlpool, exercise room. **Guest Services:** gift shop, valet laundry. **Business Services:** conference facilities, fax. **Cards:** AX, CB, DC, DS, JC, MC, VI.

SOME UNITS

HOLIDAY INN-OAK LAWN (CHICAGO SOUTHWEST)
Motor Inn

Phone: (708)425-7900   [321]
6/1-3/31   1P: $104   2P: $104
4/1-5/31   1P: $95   2P: $95
Location: US 12 and 20, 1 mi e of jct Cicero Ave. 4140 W 95th St 60453. Fax: 708/425-7918. **Facility:** 139 one-bedroom standard units, some with whirlpools. 5 stories, interior corridors. *Bath:* combo or shower only. **Parking:** on-site. **Terms:** 10 day cancellation notice, package plans. **Amenities:** video games (fee), irons, hair dryers. **Dining:** restaurant, 6:30 am-10:30 & 5-9 pm, Sat & Sun 7 am-noon & 5-8 pm, $8-$16, cocktails. **Pool(s):** heated outdoor. **Leisure Activities:** exercise room. **Guest Services:** valet laundry, airport transportation-Midway Airport. **Business Services:** conference facilities. **Cards:** AX, CB, DC, DS, JC, MC, VI.

SOME UNITS

OAK PARK pop. 53,600   (See map p. 284; index p. 291)

──── **WHERE TO DINE** ────

CAFE WINBERIE
American

Lunch: $7-$14   **Dinner:** $10-$18   **Phone:** 708/386-2600   [199]
Location: Corner of Oak Park Ave and Lake St. 151 N Oak Park Ave 60301. **Hours:** 11 am-10:30 pm, Fri & Sat-midnight, Sun 10 am-10 pm. **Closed:** 11/28, 12/25. **Reservations:** suggested; Sunday. **Features:** casual dress; Sunday brunch; children's menu; carryout; cocktails & lounge; a la carte. Coq au vin, wild mushroom risotto and the grilled swordfish sandwich are popular dishes at the casual eatery. The dining rooms have the feel of a European bistro, with lots of windows, plants, flowers and interesting artwork. The atmosphere is cheery. **Parking:** street. **Cards:** AX, DC, DS, MC, VI.

PHILANDER'S OAK PARK
Seafood

Dinner: $14-$26   **Phone:** 708/848-4250   [200]
Location: I-290, exit Harlem Ave, 0.8 mi n to Pleasant St, just e. 1120 Pleasant St 60302. **Hours:** 4 pm-10 pm, Fri & Sat-12:30 am. Closed major holidays; also Sun. **Reservations:** suggested. **Features:** dressy casual; cocktails; entertainment; a la carte. You'll delight in both the comfortably classic, turn-of-the-20th-century decor and any one of Philander's signature seafood dishes. A recent visit produced a delicious fresh flounder accompanied by scalloped potatoes. Live jazz is presented nightly. **Parking:** on-site and valet (fee). **Cards:** AX, DC, DS, MC, VI.

ORLAND PARK pop. 35,700   (See map p. 292; index p. 294)

——— WHERE TO DINE ———

THE CHARLEY HORSE   **Lunch:** $6-$10   **Dinner:** $6-$14   **Phone:** 708/460-1771   〔250〕

American

Location: US 6 and 45, 1 mi n on US 45; in Orland Square. 39 Orland Square Dr 60462. **Hours:** 11 am-10 pm, Fri & Sat-midnight, Sun 11:30 am-9 pm. Closed: 11/28, 12/25. **Reservations:** suggested; weekends. **Features:** casual dress; children's menu; carryout; cocktails & lounge; a la carte. Sports is the name of the game here, and the atmosphere and decor speak volumes on the subject. There are plenty of sandwich specialties and some Mexican entrees, but burgers are what hit home runs. Try the "Big Bagger" with barbecue dressing and fries. **Parking:** on-site. **Cards:** AX, DC, DS, MC, VI.

PALATINE pop. 38,900

——— WHERE TO STAY ———

DOUBLETREE CLUB CHICAGO WOODFIELD/SCHAUMBURG AREA   **Phone:** (847)359-6900

SAVE

Motor Inn

All Year   1P: $79-$139

Location: SR 53, exit Northwest Hwy (US 14), just w. 920 E Northwest Hwy (US 14) 60067. Fax: 847/359-6991. **Facility:** 196 one-bedroom standard units. 5 stories, interior corridors. *Bath:* combo or shower only. **Parking:** on-site, winter plug-ins. **Terms:** package plans. **Amenities:** extended cable TV, dual phone lines, voice mail, irons, hair dryers. *Fee:* video games, high-speed Internet. **Pool(s):** heated indoor. **Leisure Activities:** saunas, exercise room. **Guest Services:** valet and coin laundry. **Business Services:** conference facilities, business center. *Fee:* PC, fax. **Cards:** AX, CB, DC, DS, JC, MC, VI.

SOME UNITS

HOLIDAY INN EXPRESS PALATINE/ARLINGTON HEIGHTS   **Phone:** (847)934-4900

4/1-10/15 [CP]	1P: $65-$99	2P: $65-$99	XP: $10 F17
10/16-3/31 [CP]	1P: $62-$87	2P: $62-$87	XP: $10 F17

Motel

Location: SR 53, exit Dundee Rd (SR 68), just w. 1550 E Dundee Rd 60074. Fax: 847/934-6079. **Facility:** 183 units. 178 one-bedroom standard units, some with whirlpools. 5 one-bedroom suites ($129-$149). 6 stories, interior corridors. *Bath:* combo or shower only. **Parking:** on-site. **Terms:** package plans. **Amenities:** video games (fee), voice mail, irons, hair dryers. **Pool(s):** heated indoor. **Leisure Activities:** saunas, whirlpool, steamroom, jogging, basketball, volleyball. *Fee:* racquetball court. **Guest Services:** valet and coin laundry. **Business Services:** conference facilities. **Cards:** AX, CB, DC, DS, JC, MC, VI.

SOME UNITS

——— WHERE TO DINE ———

MIA CUCINA   **Lunch:** $7-$14   **Dinner:** $8-$18   **Phone:** 847/358-4900

Italian

Location: Jct Northwest Hwy (US 14) and Palatine Rd, 0.5 mi w on Palatine Rd to Brockway St, then just n. 56 W Wilson St 60067. **Hours:** 11:30 am-2 & 5-10:30 pm, Sat from 5 pm, Sun 5 pm-9 pm. Closed major holidays. **Reservations:** accepted. **Features:** casual dress; cocktails & lounge; a la carte. High-domed and wood-rafter ceilings wrapped with twinkle lights, white linen tabletops and colorful murals characterize the snazzy, festive eatery. Fresh pasta dishes with rich, well-prepared sauces are among examples of the delicious Italian cuisine. **Parking:** on-site. **Cards:** AX, DC, DS, MC, VI.

PROSPECT HEIGHTS pop. 15,200

——— WHERE TO STAY ———

EXEL INN OF PROSPECT HEIGHTS   **Phone:** (847)459-0545

AAA SAVE

Motel

4/1-9/30 [CP]	1P: $40-$65	2P: $46-$71	XP: $6 F18
10/1-3/31 [CP]	1P: $40-$52	2P: $46-$55	XP: $6 F18

Location: Jct SR 21 and US 45. 540 Milwaukee Ave 60070. Fax: 847/459-8639. **Facility:** 123 one-bedroom standard units, some with efficiencies (no utensils) and/or whirlpools. 3 stories, interior corridors. **Parking:** on-site. **Terms:** package plans, small pets only. **Amenities:** extended cable TV, irons, hair dryers. **Guest Services:** valet and coin laundry. **Cards:** AX, CB, DC, DS, MC, VI. **Special Amenities:** early check-in/late check-out and free continental breakfast. *(See color ad p 318)*

SOME UNITS

RICHMOND pop. 1,000

——— WHERE TO STAY ———

DAYS INN   **Phone:** (815)678-4711

SAVE

Motel

5/1-9/30	1P: $69-$99	2P: $75-$110	XP: $6 F13
4/1-4/30	1P: $69-$74	2P: $75-$86	XP: $6 F13
10/1-3/31	1P: $69	2P: $75	XP: $6 F13

Location: On SR 12, 0.5 mi n of jct SR 173. 11200 N Rt 12 60071. Fax: 815/678-4623. **Facility:** 60 one-bedroom standard units. 2 stories, interior corridors. **Parking:** on-site, winter plug-ins. **Amenities:** extended cable TV, video tape library, hair dryers. **Pool(s):** small outdoor. **Cards:** AX, CB, DC, DS, MC, VI.

SOME UNITS

RIVERWOODS pop. 2,900

——— WHERE TO STAY ———

COUNTRY INN & SUITES BY CARLSON **Phone:** (847)374-0260
All Year   1P: $119
▼▼▼ **Location:** I-94, exit Lake Cook Rd, 0.8 mi w. 2600 Lake Cook Rd 60015. Fax: 847/374-0535. **Facility:** 115 units. 64
Motel one-bedroom standard units, some with whirlpools. 51 one-bedroom suites ($129-$149). 3 stories, interior
corridors. *Bath:* combo or shower only. **Parking:** on-site. **Terms:** package plans. **Amenities:** extended cable
TV, dual phone lines, voice mail, irons, hair dryers. **Pool(s):** small heated indoor. **Leisure Activities:** whirlpool, exercise room.
Guest Services: valet and coin laundry. **Business Services:** meeting rooms, business center, PC. **Cards:** AX, DC, DS,
MC, VI. *(See color ad p 322)*

ROCKDALE pop. 1,700

——— WHERE TO DINE ———

SYL'S RESTAURANT **Lunch:** $7-$15 **Dinner:** $11-$25 **Phone:** 815/725-1977
▼▼ ▼▼ **Location:** I-80, exit 130A, 0.5 mi s on Larkin Ave, then 0.3 mi e. 829 Moen Ave 60436. **Hours:** 11:30 am-2 & 5-10
American pm, Sat-Mon from 5 pm. Closed: 11/28, 12/25. **Reservations:** suggested; Fri & Sat night.
Features: casual dress; children's menu; carryout; cocktails & lounge. Prime steak, ribs and fresh seafood
are menu mainstays at the cozy eatery, just a few miles from two casino venues. The service staff is
friendly and knowledgeable. Private dining rooms are available. **Parking:** on-site. **Cards:** AX, MC, VI.

ROLLING MEADOWS pop. 22,600 (See map p. 284; index p. 290)

——— WHERE TO STAY ———

HOLIDAY INN ROLLING MEADOWS/SCHAUMBURG AREA **Phone:** (847)259-5000
▲▲▲ SAVE 9/1-12/31   1P: $99-$119
4/1-8/31 & 1/1-3/31   1P: $89-$109
▼▼▼▼ **Location:** On SR 62, just e of SR 53, 0.3 mi ne of I-90. 3405 Algonquin Rd 60008. Fax: 847/259-0597. **Facility:** 422
Motor Inn units. 409 one-bedroom standard units. 13 one-bedroom suites ($150-$250). 2-9 stories, interior/exterior corridors. *Bath:* combo or shower only. **Parking:** on-site. **Terms:** package plans. **Amenities:** dual phone lines,
voice mail, irons, hair dryers. **Dining:** restaurant, 6:30 am-2 & 4-10 pm, $7-$22, cocktails. **Pool(s):** heated
outdoor, 2 heated indoor. **Leisure Activities:** sauna, whirlpools, exercise room, sports court, shuffleboard, domed recreation
area, kids play port. **Guest Services:** gift shop, complimentary evening beverages: Tues, valet and coin laundry, area
transportation-within 5 mi. **Business Services:** conference facilities. **Cards:** AX, CB, DC, DS, JC, MC, VI.

ROMEOVILLE pop. 14,000

——— WHERE TO STAY ———

COUNTRY INN & SUITES BY CARLSON **Phone:** (630)378-1052
All Year   1P: $89   2P: $159
▼▼▼ **Location:** I-55, exit 263, just n. 1265 Lakeview Dr 60446. Fax: 630/378-1053. **Facility:** Smoke free premises. 84
Motel units. 51 one-bedroom standard units. 33 one-bedroom suites ($105-$199), some with whirlpools. 3 stories,
interior corridors. *Bath:* combo or shower only. **Parking:** on-site. **Terms:** package plans. **Amenities:** high-
speed Internet (fee), voice mail, irons, hair dryers. **Pool(s):** small heated indoor. **Leisure Activities:** whirlpool, exercise room.
Guest Services: valet and coin laundry. **Business Services:** meeting rooms. **Cards:** AX, CB, DC, DS, JC, MC, VI.
(See color ad p 322)

SPRINGHILL SUITES **Phone:** (630)759-0529
▲▲▲ SAVE 5/1-8/31 [ECP]   1P: $124-$169   2P: $124-$169
9/1-11/30 [ECP]   1P: $119-$159   2P: $119-$159
▼▼▼▼ 4/1-4/30 [ECP]   1P: $114-$159   2P: $114-$159
Motel 12/1-3/31 [ECP]   1P: $109-$159   2P: $109-$159
Location: I-55, exit 267, just n. 125 Remington Blvd 60440. Fax: 630/759-0530. **Facility:** 82 one-bedroom stan-
dard units, some with whirlpools. 3 stories, interior corridors. *Bath:* combo or shower only. **Parking:** on-site.
Amenities: extended cable TV, dual phone lines, voice mail, irons, hair dryers. **Pool(s):** small heated indoor. **Leisure Activi-
ties:** whirlpool, exercise room. **Guest Services:** valet and coin laundry. **Business Services:** meeting rooms, business center,
PC. **Cards:** AX, CB, DC, DS, JC, MC, VI. **Special Amenities:** free continental breakfast and free local telephone calls.
(See color ad card insert)

ROSEMONT pop. 4,000 (See map p. 284; index p. 287)

——— WHERE TO STAY ———

BEST WESTERN AT O'HARE **Phone:** (847)296-4471
▲▲▲ SAVE 5/6-12/4   1P: $109-$139   2P: $109-$139   XP: $10   F12
12/5-3/31   1P: $99-$119   2P: $99-$119   XP: $10   F12
▼▼▼ 4/1-5/5   1P: $99-$109   2P: $99-$109   XP: $10   F12
Motor Inn **Location:** Jct US 12/45 and SR 72. 10300 W Higgins Rd 60018. Fax: 847/296-4958. **Facility:** 143 one-bedroom
standard units, some with whirlpools. 3 stories, interior corridors. **Parking:** on-site. **Amenities:** extended
cable TV, voice mail, irons. *Fee:* video games, Web TV. **Dining:** 2 restaurants, 24 hours, $9-$25, cocktails.
Leisure Activities: exercise room. **Guest Services:** valet and coin laundry, area transportation-within 1 mi. **Business Services:**
meeting rooms. **Cards:** AX, CB, DC, DS, JC, MC, VI. **Special Amenities:** free newspaper and free room upgrade (subject
to availability with advanced reservations).

(See map p. 284)

DOUBLETREE HOTEL CHICAGO O'HARE AIRPORT-ROSEMONT   **Phone:** (847)292-9100 92

	9/1-11/15	1P: $189	2P: $189	XP: $15	F18
SAVE	4/1-8/31	1P: $169	2P: $169	XP: $15	F18
	11/16-3/31	1P: $149	2P: $149	XP: $15	F18

Hotel   **Location:** I-190, exit 1B, just s. 5460 N River Rd 60018. Fax: 847/292-9295. **Facility:** 369 one-bedroom standard units. 9 stories, interior corridors. *Bath:* combo or shower only. **Parking:** off-site (fee). **Terms:** cancellation fee imposed, package plans, small pets only ($75 deposit). **Amenities:** dual phone lines, voice mail, honor bars, irons, hair dryers. *Fee:* video games, Web TV. **Dining:** Gibson's Steakhouse, see separate listing. **Pool(s):** heated indoor. **Leisure Activities:** whirlpool, exercise room. **Guest Services:** valet laundry. **Business Services:** conference facilities, business center. *Fee:* PC, fax. **Cards:** AX, CB, DC, DS, JC, MC, VI.

SOME UNITS

EMBASSY SUITES HOTEL O'HARE ROSEMONT   **Phone:** (847)678-4000 91

| | All Year [BP] | 1P: $119-$265 | 2P: $119-$265 | XP: $15 | F18 |

Suite Hotel   **Location:** I-190, exit 1B, just s. 5500 N River Rd 60018. Fax: 847/928-7659. **Facility:** 296 one-bedroom suites. 8 stories, interior corridors. *Bath:* combo or shower only. **Parking:** on-site. **Terms:** package plans. **Amenities:** video games, high-speed Internet (fee), voice mail, honor bars, irons, hair dryers. **Dining:** restaurant, 11 am-2 & 5-11 pm, $12-$25, cocktails. **Pool(s):** heated indoor. **Leisure Activities:** sauna, whirlpool, exercise room. **Guest Services:** gift shop, complimentary evening beverages, valet and coin laundry. **Business Services:** conference facilities, business center, PC (fee), fax. **Cards:** AX, CB, DC, DS, JC, MC, VI. **Special Amenities:** free continental breakfast and free newspaper.

SOME UNITS

HOLIDAY INN O'HARE INTERNATIONAL   **Phone:** (847)671-6350 93

| | 4/1-11/15 | 1P: $139-$199 | 2P: $139-$199 | XP: $10 | F12 |
| | 11/16-3/31 | 1P: $109-$179 | 2P: $109-$179 | XP: $10 | F12 |

Hotel   **Location:** I-190, exit 1B, just s. 5440 N River Rd 60018. Fax: 847/671-5406. **Facility:** 505 units. 502 one-bedroom standard units. 3 one-bedroom suites. 14 stories, interior corridors. *Bath:* combo or shower only. **Parking:** on-site (fee). **Terms:** 3 day cancellation notice-fee imposed, package plans. **Amenities:** high-speed Internet (fee), voice mail, irons, hair dryers. **Dining:** restaurant, coffee shop, 6 am-1:30 am, $12-$25, cocktails. **Leisure Activities:** sauna, whirlpool, exercise room. **Guest Services:** gift shop, valet and coin laundry. **Business Services:** conference facilities, business center. *Fee:* PC, fax. **Cards:** AX, CB, DC, DS, JC, MC, VI. **Special Amenities:** early check-in/late check-out and free room upgrade (subject to availability with advanced reservations). *(See color ad below)*

SOME UNITS

HYATT REGENCY O'HARE   **Phone:** (847)696-1234 95

| | All Year | 1P: $119-$199 | 2P: $144-$224 | XP: $25 | F18 |

Hotel   **Location:** I-190, exit 1B, just s. 9300 W Bryn Mawr Ave 60018. Fax: 847/698-0139. **Facility:** 1099 units. 1096 one-bedroom standard units, some with whirlpools. 3 one-bedroom suites. 10 stories, interior corridors. *Bath:* combo or shower only. **Parking:** *Fee:* on-site and valet. **Terms:** cancellation fee imposed, package plans. **Amenities:** extended cable TV, voice mail, fax, irons, hair dryers. **Dining:** 2 dining rooms, 2 restaurants, coffee shop, 6 am-midnight, Fri & Sat-1 am, $8-$30, cocktails. **Leisure Activities:** saunas. **Guest Services:** gift shop, massage (fee), valet laundry. **Business Services:** conference facilities, business center, PC, fax (fee). **Cards:** AX, CB, DC, DS, JC, MC, VI. *(See color ad p 295)*

SOME UNITS

HYATT ROSEMONT   **Phone:** (847)518-1234 101

| | All Year | 1P: $199 | | XP: $25 | F18 |

Hotel   **Location:** I-190, exit 1B, 0.4 mi n. 6350 N River Rd 60018. Fax: 847/518-0855. **Facility:** 206 units. 201 one-bedroom standard units. 5 one-bedroom suites ($350-$550). 8 stories, interior corridors. *Bath:* combo or shower only. **Parking:** on-site. **Terms:** check-in 4 pm, cancellation fee imposed. **Amenities:** extended cable TV, dual phone lines, voice mail, safes, irons, hair dryers. *Some:* fax. **Dining:** restaurant, 6 am-10 pm, $10-$28, cocktails. **Leisure Activities:** exercise room. **Guest Services:** valet laundry. **Business Services:** conference facilities. **Cards:** AX, CB, DC, DS, JC, MC, VI. *(See color ad p 295)*

SOME UNITS

(See map p. 284)

MARRIOTT SUITES CHICAGO O'HARE
Phone: (847)696-4400 96

AAA SAVE

Suite Hotel

All Year   1P: $139-$269   2P: $139-$289
Location: I-190, exit 1B, then n. 6155 N River Rd 60018. Fax: 847/696-2122. **Facility:** 256 one-bedroom suites. 11 stories, interior corridors. **Parking:** on-site. **Terms:** check-in 4 pm, cancellation fee imposed, package plans, small pets only ($50-$100 deposit). **Amenities:** high-speed Internet (fee), dual phone lines, voice mail, irons, hair dryers. **Dining:** restaurant, 6:30 am-11 pm, $9-$30, cocktails. **Pool(s):** heated indoor. **Leisure Activities:** saunas, whirlpool, exercise room, large patio. **Guest Services:** valet and coin laundry. **Business Services:** meeting rooms, business center, fax (fee). **Cards:** AX, CB, DC, DS, JC, MC, VI. *(See color ad card insert)*

SOME UNITS

RESIDENCE INN BY MARRIOTT O'HARE-ROSEMONT
Phone: 847/375-9000 97

AAA SAVE

Extended Stay
Apartment

All Year [MAP]   1P: $139-$189   2P: $139-$189
Location: At jct Touhy Ave and Mannheim Rd (US 12 and 45), 3 mi n of O'Hare Airport. 7101 Chestnut St 60018. Fax: 847/375-9010. **Facility:** 192 units. 100 one-bedroom standard units with efficiencies. 62 one- and 30 two-bedroom suites with kitchens. 3 stories, interior corridors. *Bath:* combo or shower only. **Parking:** on-site. **Terms:** pets ($100 fee, $10 extra charge). **Amenities:** dual phone lines, voice mail, irons, hair dryers. *Fee:* video games, high-speed Internet. **Pool(s):** heated outdoor. **Leisure Activities:** whirlpool, exercise room, sports court, patio, gazebo. **Guest Services:** complimentary evening beverages: Mon-Thurs, valet and coin laundry. **Business Services:** meeting rooms. **Cards:** AX, CB, DC, DS, JC, MC, VI. *(See color ad card insert)*

SOME UNITS

SHERATON GATEWAY SUITES O'HARE
Phone: (847)699-6300 103

Suite Hotel

All Year   1P: $85-$194   XP: $10
Location: On US 12 and 45, at jct SR 72. 6501 N Mannheim Rd 60018. Fax: 847/699-0617. **Facility:** 297 units. 295 one- and 2 two-bedroom suites, some with whirlpools. 11 stories, interior corridors. *Bath:* combo or shower only. **Parking:** on-site (fee). **Terms:** cancellation fee imposed, package plans. **Amenities:** video games (fee), dual phone lines, voice mail, honor bars, irons, hair dryers. *Some:* high-speed Internet (fee), fax. **Pool(s):** heated indoor. **Leisure Activities:** sauna, whirlpool. **Guest Services:** gift shop, valet laundry. **Business Services:** conference facilities, business center. *Fee:* PC, fax. **Cards:** AX, CB, DC, DS, JC, MC, VI.

SOME UNITS

SOFITEL CHICAGO O'HARE
Phone: (847)678-4488 94

AAA SAVE

Hotel

All Year   1P: $199   2P: $199   XP: $20   F12
Location: I-190, exit 1B, just s. 5550 N River Rd 60018. Fax: 847/678-4244. **Facility:** 300 units. 292 one-bedroom standard units. 8 one-bedroom suites. 10 stories, interior corridors. *Bath:* combo or shower only. **Parking:** *Fee:* on-site and valet. **Terms:** cancellation fee imposed, package plans, small pets only. **Amenities:** dual phone lines, voice mail, honor bars, irons, hair dryers. **Dining:** restaurant, coffee shop, 6:30 am-12:30 am, $12-$25, cocktails. **Pool(s):** heated indoor. **Leisure Activities:** sauna, sun deck, exercise room. **Guest Services:** gift shop, massage (fee), valet laundry. **Business Services:** conference facilities, business center. *Fee:* PC, fax. **Cards:** AX, CB, DC, DS, JC, MC, VI. **Special Amenities:** free local telephone calls and free newspaper.

SOME UNITS

THE WESTIN O'HARE
Phone: (847)698-6000 102

AAA SAVE

Hotel

4/7-3/31   1P: $99-$179   2P: $99-$179   XP: $25   F18
4/1-4/6   1P: $89-$159   2P: $89-$159   XP: $25   F18
Location: I-190, exit 1B, just n. 6100 N River Rd 60018. Fax: 847/698-4591. **Facility:** 525 units. 499 one-bedroom standard units. 26 one-bedroom suites ($325-$800), some with whirlpools. 12 stories, interior corridors. *Bath:* combo or shower only. **Parking:** *Fee:* on-site and valet. **Terms:** cancellation fee imposed, package plans. **Amenities:** dual phone lines, voice mail, honor bars, irons, hair dryers. *Some:* fax. **Dining:** restaurant, coffee shop, 6 am-10:30 pm, $18-$32, cocktails. **Pool(s):** heated indoor. **Leisure Activities:** saunas, whirlpool, sun deck, racquetball courts. **Guest Services:** gift shop, massage (fee), valet laundry, area transportation-CTA train. **Business Services:** conference facilities, business center. *Fee:* PC, fax. **Cards:** AX, CB, DC, DS, JC, MC, VI. **Special Amenities:** free newspaper.

SOME UNITS

The following lodging was either not evaluated or did not meet AAA rating requirements but is listed for your information only.

RAMADA PLAZA HOTEL-O'HARE
Phone: (847)827-5131 98

AAA SAVE

[fyi]

Hotel

9/1-3/31   1P: $99-$155
4/1-8/31   1P: $99-$152
Under major renovation, scheduled to be completed March 2002. Last rated: ▼▼ **Location:** US 12 and 45, n of SR 72. 6600 N Mannheim Rd 60018. Fax: 847/827-5659. **Facility:** 273 units. 242 one-bedroom standard units. 31 one-bedroom suites ($225-$1000). 9 stories, interior corridors. *Bath:* combo or shower only. **Parking:** on-site (fee). **Terms:** package plans. **Amenities:** video games (fee), voice mail. **Dining:** dining room, 2 restaurants, 6 am-2 & 5-11 pm, Sat & Sun from 6:30 am, $9-$26, cocktails. **Leisure Activities:** sauna, whirlpool, exercise room. **Guest Services:** gift shop, valet laundry. **Business Services:** conference facilities, business center. *Fee:* PC, fax. **Cards:** AX, CB, DC, DS, JC, MC, VI. **Special Amenities:** early check-in/late check-out and free newspaper.

SOME UNITS

(See map p. 284)

———— WHERE TO DINE ————

CARLUCCI
▼▼▼▼

Northern
Italian

Lunch: $9-$16   **Dinner:** $15-$30   **Phone:** 847/518-0990   128
Location: I-190, exit 1B, 0.3 mi n to jct Higgins Rd. 6111 N River Rd 60018. **Hours:** 11:30 am-2:30 & 5-10 pm, Fri-11 pm, Sat 5 pm-11 pm, Sun 4:30 pm-9 pm. Closed major holidays. **Reservations:** suggested. **Features:** casual dress; carryout; cocktails & lounge; a la carte. The atmosphere bustles in the casual Italian eatery's dining room, which features lovely light-wood floors, linen tablecloths and decorative sconce lighting. Fine food—mostly pasta, pizza and salads—lines an enormous menu. **Parking:** on-site and valet.
Cards: AX, DC, DS, MC, VI.

⊠

GIBSON'S STEAKHOUSE
ⓐⓐⓐ
▼▼▼▼

Steak House

Lunch: $10-$34   **Dinner:** $13-$60   **Phone:** 847/928-9900   131
Location: I-190, exit 1B, just s; in Doubletree Hotel Chicago O'Hare Airport-Rosemont. 5464 N River Rd 60018. **Hours:** 11 am-midnight, Fri-1 am, Sat & Sun 5 pm-1 am. **Reservations:** suggested. **Features:** dressy casual; cocktails & lounge; entertainment; a la carte. Prime cuts of aged beef are the specialty at the fine steakhouse. An upscale ambience punctuates the sleek, modern dining room. The enthusiastic, highly skilled wait staff provides excellent information about the steaks offered. **Parking:** valet only. **Cards:** AX, DS, MC, VI.

⊠

NICK'S FISHMARKET
▼▼▼▼▼

Seafood

Dinner: $20-$48   **Phone:** 847/298-8200   130
Location: Higgins at Mannheim Rd. 10275 W Higgins 60018. **Hours:** 5:30 pm-10 pm, Fri & Sat-10:30 pm, Sun-9 pm. Closed major holidays. **Reservations:** suggested. **Features:** dressy casual; cocktails & lounge; a la carte. The restaurant provides a fine-dining experience with excellently prepared seafood and a superb wait staff that provides welcoming service. Multiple dining rooms are united in an aquatic theme, as large tanks with colorful fish and coral provide an interesting focal point. Lobster bisque is delightful, as are the many Hawaiian seafood specialties. **Parking:** on-site and valet. **Cards:** AX, CB, DC, DS, MC, VI.

⊠

ST. CHARLES pop. 22,500

———— WHERE TO STAY ————

BEST WESTERN INN OF ST. CHARLES
ⓐⓐⓐ SAVE
▼▼▼▼

Motel

All Year [ECP]   1P: $79   2P: $89   **Phone:** (630)584-4550
Location: On SR 64, 0.5 mi e of SR 25. 1635 E Main St 60174. Fax: 630/584-5221. **Facility:** 54 units. 52 one-bedroom standard units. 2 one-bedroom suites, some with kitchens. 2 stories, interior/exterior corridors. *Bath:* combo or shower only. **Parking:** on-site. **Amenities:** extended cable TV, voice mail, irons, hair dryers. **Pool(s):** heated outdoor. **Leisure Activities:** exercise room. **Guest Services:** coin laundry, area transportation-within 5 mi. **Business Services:** meeting rooms. **Cards:** AX, CB, DC, DS, JC, MC, VI.
Special Amenities: free continental breakfast and free local telephone calls.

SOME UNITS
⟦Ⓢ⟧ ⟦ⓣ⟧ ⟦≋⟧ ⟦📷⟧ ⟦DATA PORT⟧ 🔊 💻 🖨 / ⊠ 📷

COUNTRY INN & SUITES BY CARLSON
▼▼▼▼

Motel

All Year [ECP]   1P: $69-$119   2P: $69-$119   **Phone:** (630)587-6564
Location: On SR 64, 3.1 mi w of SR 59. 155 S 38th Ave 60174. Fax: 630/587-6568. **Facility:** 84 units. 51 one-bedroom standard units. 33 one-bedroom suites ($79-$129), some with whirlpools. 3 stories, interior corridors. *Bath:* combo or shower only. **Parking:** on-site. **Terms:** package plans. **Amenities:** extended cable TV, high-speed Internet, voice mail, irons, hair dryers. **Pool(s):** small heated indoor. **Leisure Activities:** whirlpool, exercise room. **Guest Services:** valet and coin laundry. **Business Services:** meeting rooms. **Cards:** AX, CB, DC, DS, MC, VI.
(See color ad p 322)

SOME UNITS
ASK ⟦Ⓢ⟧ ⟦✈⟧ ⟦ⓣ⟧ ⟦Ⓜ⟧ ⟦✆⟧ ⟦⌒⟧ ⟦≋⟧ ⟦📷⟧ ⟦DATA PORT⟧ 💻 🖨 / ⊠ 🔊 📷 /

HILTON GARDEN INN ST. CHARLES
SAVE
▼▼▼▼

Motor Inn

All Year   1P: $109   2P: $109   XP: $10   F18   **Phone:** (630)584-0700
Location: On SR 64, 2.4 mi w of SR 59. 4070 E Main St 60174. Fax: 630/762-9152. **Facility:** 120 units. 118 one-bedroom standard units, some with whirlpools. 2 one-bedroom suites with whirlpools. 3 stories, interior corridors. *Bath:* combo or shower only. **Parking:** on-site. **Terms:** check-in 4 pm, package plans. **Amenities:** video games, high-speed Internet, dual phone lines, voice mail, irons, hair dryers. **Pool(s):** small heated indoor. **Leisure Activities:** whirlpool, exercise room. **Guest Services:** valet and coin laundry. **Business Services:** conference facilities, business center, PC, fax. **Cards:** AX, CB, DC, DS, JC, MC, VI.

SOME UNITS
⟦Ⓢ⟧ ⟦ⓣ⟧ ⟦Ⓜ⟧ ⟦✆⟧ ⟦⌒⟧ ⟦≋⟧ ⟦📷⟧ ⟦DATA PORT⟧ 🔊 🖨 💻 🖨 / ⊠ /
FEE

HOLIDAY INN EXPRESS
▼▼▼▼

Motel

All Year   1P: $91   2P: $91   **Phone:** (630)584-5300
Location: On SR 64, 0.5 mi e of SR 25. 1600 E Main St 60174. Fax: 630/584-5395. **Facility:** 122 one-bedroom standard units. 2 stories, interior corridors. *Bath:* combo or shower only. **Parking:** on-site. **Terms:** check-in 4 pm, cancellation fee imposed. **Amenities:** extended cable TV, irons, hair dryers. *Some:* dual phone lines. **Pool(s):** heated outdoor. **Leisure Activities:** exercise room. **Guest Services:** valet and coin laundry. **Business Services:** meeting rooms. **Cards:** AX, CB, DC, DS, JC, MC, VI.

SOME UNITS
ASK ⟦Ⓢ⟧ ⟦ⓣ⟧ ⟦≋⟧ ⟦📷⟧ ⟦DATA PORT⟧ 💻 🖨 / ⊠ 🔊 📷 /
FEE FEE

THE HOTEL BAKER
▼▼▼▼

Classic Hotel

All Year   1P: $99-$179   **Phone:** (630)584-2100
Location: Jct SR 25 and 64, 0.3 mi w. 100 W Main St 60174. Fax: 630/443-0795. **Facility:** Designated smoking area. 53 units. 43 one-bedroom standard units, some with whirlpools. 10 one-bedroom suites ($199-$499) with whirlpools, some with kitchens. 6 stories, interior corridors. *Bath:* combo or shower only. **Parking:** street and valet. **Terms:** check-in 4 pm, cancellation fee imposed, [CP] meal plan available, package plans. **Amenities:** extended cable TV, dual phone lines, voice mail, irons, hair dryers. *Some:* honor bars. **Leisure Activities:** exercise room. **Business Services:** meeting rooms, business center, fax (fee). **Cards:** AX, CB, DC, DS, MC, VI.

SOME UNITS
ASK ⟦Ⓢ⟧ ⟦ⓣ⟧ ⟦Ⓨ⟧ ⊠ ⟦VCR⟧ ⟦📷⟧ ⟦DATA PORT⟧ 🖨 / 🔊 📷 /
FEE FEE

ST. CHARLES COURTYARD BY MARRIOTT
Phone: (630)377-6370

(AAA) SAVE

Motel

All Year   1P: $79-$110
Location: Jct SR 59 and 64, 3.4 mi w on SR 64, just n on Kirk Rd, then just w on Foxfield. 700 Courtyard Dr 60174. Fax: 630/377-6709. **Facility:** 121 units. 119 one-bedroom standard units, some with whirlpools. 2 one-bedroom suites. 4 stories, interior corridors. *Bath:* combo or shower only. **Parking:** on-site. **Terms:** [BP] meal plan available. **Amenities:** dual phone lines, voice mail, irons, hair dryers. **Dining:** coffee shop, 6:30-10 am, Sat & Sun from 7 am. **Pool(s):** small heated indoor. **Leisure Activities:** whirlpool, exercise room. **Guest Services:** valet and coin laundry. **Business Services:** meeting rooms. **Cards:** AX, CB, DC, DS, MC, VI.
(See ad p 299 & color ad card insert)

SOME UNITS

SUPER 8 MOTEL-ST. CHARLES
Phone: (630)377-8388

Motel

4/1-8/31	1P: $70-$75	2P: $75-$80	XP: $7 F12
9/1-3/31	1P: $65-$75	2P: $75-$80	XP: $7 F12

Location: On SR 64, 1 mi e. 1520 E Main St 60174. Fax: 630/377-1340. **Facility:** 67 one-bedroom standard units. 3 stories, interior corridors. **Parking:** on-site, winter plug-ins. **Terms:** 14 day cancellation notice-fee imposed, [CP] meal plan available, small pets only ($50 deposit). **Amenities:** safes (fee). *Some:* hair dryers. **Cards:** AX, CB, DC, DS, MC, VI.

SOME UNITS

-------- **WHERE TO DINE** --------

LA ZAZA'S TRATTORIA
Lunch: $7-$18   **Dinner:** $8-$19   **Phone:** 630/443-9304

Italian

Location: Jct SR 64 and First St, just e of SR 31. 5 S First St 60174. **Hours:** 11:30 am-2 & 5-9 pm, Fri & Sat-10 pm, Sun 4 pm-8 pm. Closed major holidays. **Reservations:** accepted. **Features:** dressy casual; carryout; cocktails & lounge; a la carte. In the downtown area of a charming village along the Fox River, the triangular dining room has a lovely stone wall on one side and windows on the other. Wood floors, lovely drapes and linen-covered tables set the stage for the excellently prepared Italian food. Bruscetta with spinach is delightful. **Parking:** street. **Cards:** AX, DC, DS, MC, VI.

-------- *The following restaurant has not been evaluated by AAA* --------
but is listed for your information only.

THE TROPHY ROOM
Phone: 630/584-2121

[fyi]

Not evaluated. **Location:** 100 W Main St 60174. Overlooking the Fox River, the restaurant serves Mediterranean cuisine.

SCHAUMBURG pop. 68,600 (See map p. 284; index p. 290)

-------- **WHERE TO STAY** --------

AMERISUITES (CHICAGO/SCHAUMBURG)
Phone: (847)330-1060   [237]

(AAA) SAVE

Motel

All Year [ECP]   1P: $112   2P: $112   XP: $10   F18
Location: I-290, exit 1A (Woodfield/Golf Rd) northbound, just n to Golf Rd, just w to McConner Pkwy, just n; exit 1B (Woodfield/Golf Rd) southbound. 1851 McConnor Pkwy 60173. Fax: 847/330-1001. **Facility:** 128 units. 6 stories, interior corridors. *Bath:* combo or shower only. **Parking:** on-site. **Terms:** 30 day cancellation notice, package plans, small pets only. **Amenities:** video games, high-speed Internet, voice mail, irons, hair dryers. **Leisure Activities:** exercise room. **Guest Services:** valet and coin laundry, area transportation-within 5 mi. **Business Services:** meeting rooms, business center. *Fee:* PC, fax. **Cards:** AX, CB, DC, DS, JC, MC, VI. **Special Amenities:** free continental breakfast and free newspaper. *(See color ad p 296)*

SOME UNITS

CHICAGO MARRIOTT SCHAUMBURG
Phone: (847)240-0100   [225]

(AAA) SAVE

Hotel

All Year   1P: $69-$199   2P: $79-$209
Location: I-290, exit Higgins Rd W (SR 72), 0.5 mi s. 50 N Martingale Rd 60173. Fax: 847/240-2388. **Facility:** 398 units. 394 one-bedroom standard units. 4 one-bedroom suites ($250). 4-13 stories, interior corridors. *Bath:* combo or shower only. **Parking:** on-site. **Terms:** package plans, small pets only ($25 fee). **Amenities:** high-speed Internet (fee), dual phone lines, voice mail, irons, hair dryers. **Dining:** restaurant, 6:30 am-2 & 5-10 pm, Sat & Sun from 7 am, $7-$20, cocktails. **Leisure Activities:** saunas, whirlpool, exercise room. **Guest Services:** gift shop, valet and coin laundry, area transportation-mall & corporate ctrs. **Business Services:** conference facilities, business center. *Fee:* PC, fax. **Cards:** AX, CB, DC, DS, JC, MC, VI. *(See color ad card insert)*

SOME UNITS

COUNTRY INN & SUITES
Phone: (847)839-1010   [238]

Motel

All Year   1P: $99-$179   2P: $99-$179   XP: $10   F18
Location: I-90, exit Roselle Rd, 0.8 mi s. 1401 N Roselle Rd 60195. Fax: 847/839-1212. **Facility:** 73 one-bedroom standard units, some with whirlpools. 3 stories, interior corridors. *Bath:* combo or shower only. **Parking:** on-site. **Terms:** package plans. **Amenities:** DVD players, video games (fee), CD players, voice mail, irons, hair dryers. *Some:* fax. **Pool(s):** small heated indoor. **Leisure Activities:** whirlpool, exercise room. **Guest Services:** complimentary evening beverages: Mon-Thurs & Sat, valet and coin laundry. **Business Services:** business center, PC, fax. **Cards:** AX, CB, DC, DS, MC, VI. *(See color ad p 322)*

SOME UNITS

(See map p. 284)

DRURY INN-SCHAUMBURG
Phone: (847)517-7737 　232

Motel

All Year [ECP]　　　　　1P: $70-$125　　　2P: $70-$125　　　XP: $10　　　F18
Location: I-290, exit Higgins Rd W (SR 72), just w, then just n. 600 N Martingale Rd 60173. Fax: 847/517-7737. **Facility:** 124 one-bedroom standard units. 4 stories, interior corridors. **Parking:** on-site. **Terms:** small pets only. **Amenities:** voice mail, irons. **Pool(s):** heated indoor. **Leisure Activities:** whirlpool, exercise room. **Guest Services:** complimentary evening beverages: Mon-Thurs, valet and coin laundry. **Business Services:** meeting rooms. **Cards:** AX, CB, DC, DS, MC, VI. *(See color ad p 5)*

SOME UNITS

EMBASSY SUITES HOTEL SCHAUMBURG-WOODFIELD
Phone: (847)397-1313 　234

Suite Hotel

All Year [BP]　　　　　1P: $99-$209　　　　　　　　XP: $10　　　F18
Location: Jct of Meacham and Algonquin rds. 1939 N Meacham Rd 60173. Fax: 847/397-9007. **Facility:** 209 one-bedroom suites. 7 stories, interior corridors. *Bath:* combo or shower only. **Parking:** on-site. **Terms:** package plans. **Amenities:** extended cable TV, dual phone lines, voice mail, irons, hair dryers. *Fee:* video games, Web TV, high-speed Internet. **Dining:** restaurant, 11 am-2 & 5-10 pm, Sun-9 pm, $11-$25, cocktails. **Pool(s):** heated indoor. **Leisure Activities:** sauna, whirlpool, fitness equipment available. **Guest Services:** gift shop, complimentary evening beverages, valet and coin laundry, area transportation-within 3 mi. **Business Services:** conference facilities. **Cards:** AX, DC, DS, MC, VI. **Special Amenities:** free newspaper. *(See color ad below)*

FEE　　　　SOME UNITS

HAMPTON INN SCHAUMBURG
Phone: (847)619-1000 　226

Motel

All Year　　　　　　　1P: $99-$119　　　2P: $109-$119
Location: I-290, exit Higgins Rd (SR 72), 0.5 mi w. 1300 E Higgins Rd 60173. Fax: 847/619-1019. **Facility:** 128 one-bedroom standard units. 4 stories, interior corridors. **Parking:** on-site. **Amenities:** video games (fee), voice mail, irons, hair dryers. **Leisure Activities:** exercise room. **Guest Services:** valet laundry, area transportation-within 5 mi. **Business Services:** meeting rooms. **Cards:** AX, CB, DC, DS, JC, MC, VI. **Special Amenities:** free continental breakfast and free local telephone calls.

FEE　　　　SOME UNITS

HOLIDAY INN SCHAUMBURG/HOFFMAN ESTATES
Phone: (847)310-0500 　229

Motor Inn

4/1-11/30 [ECP]　　　1P: $99-$139　　　2P: $99-$139　　　XP: $10　　　F19
12/1-3/31 [ECP]　　　1P: $89-$129　　　2P: $89-$129　　　XP: $10　　　F19
Location: I-90, exit Roselle Rd, then 0.8 mi s. 1550 N Roselle Rd 60195. Fax: 847/310-0579. **Facility:** 143 one-bedroom standard units, some with whirlpools. 6 stories, interior corridors. *Bath:* combo or shower only. **Parking:** on-site. **Terms:** package plans. **Amenities:** video games (fee), dual phone lines, voice mail, safes, irons, hair dryers. **Pool(s):** outdoor. **Leisure Activities:** exercise room. **Guest Services:** valet laundry. **Business Services:** meeting rooms, business center. *Fee:* PC, fax. **Cards:** AX, CB, DC, DS, JC, MC, VI.

FEE　　　　SOME UNITS

HOMESTEAD STUDIO SUITES-CHICAGO/SCHAUMBURG
Phone: (847)882-6900 　239

Extended Stay Motel

All Year　　　　　　　1P: $79-$89　　　2P: $84-$94　　　XP: $5　　　F18
Location: I-90, exit Roselle Rd, 0.8 mi s, then just e. 51 E State Pkwy 60173. Fax: 847/882-6925. **Facility:** 136 one-bedroom standard units, some with efficiencies or kitchens. 3 stories, interior corridors. *Bath:* combo or shower only. **Parking:** on-site. **Terms:** pets ($75 fee). **Amenities:** voice mail, irons. **Guest Services:** valet and coin laundry. **Cards:** AX, CB, DC, DS, JC, MC, VI.

SOME UNITS

HOMEWOOD SUITES SCHAUMBURG
Phone: (847)605-0400 　227

Apartment

All Year [ECP]　　　　1P: $159-$179　　　2P: $169-$189
Location: I-290, exit Higgins Rd (SR 72), 0.5 mi w, 0.8 mi n on Meacham, then 0.8 mi w. 815 E American Ln 60173. Fax: 847/619-0990. **Facility:** 108 one-bedroom suites with kitchens. 2-3 stories, interior/exterior corridors. **Parking:** on-site. **Terms:** package plans, pets ($10 fee, $75 deposit). **Amenities:** video tape library (fee), dual phone lines, voice mail, irons, hair dryers. **Leisure Activities:** whirlpool, exercise room, basketball. **Guest Services:** gift shop, complimentary evening beverages: Mon-Thurs, valet and coin laundry. **Business Services:** meeting rooms, business center, PC, fax (fee). **Cards:** AX, CB, DC, DS, MC, VI.

SOME UNITS

(See map p. 284)

HYATT REGENCY WOODFIELD   Phone: (847)605-1234 236
  (AAA) (SAVE)   All Year   1P: $99-$195   2P: $124-$220   XP: $25   F18
  ▼▼▼▼▼ **Location:** I-90, exit Woodfield Rd southbound; exit SR 72 and 58 northbound, follow signs to Golf Rd, then 0.3 mi w.
  Hotel   1800 E Golf Rd 60173. Fax: 847/605-0328. **Facility:** 469 units. 464 one-bedroom standard units. 5 one-
                bedroom suites. 5 stories, interior corridors. **Bath:** combo or shower only. **Parking:** on-site and valet (fee).
                Terms: cancellation fee imposed, package plans. **Amenities:** high-speed Internet (fee), voice mail, irons,
                hair dryers. *Some:* CD players, dual phone lines, fax, safes. **Dining:** restaurant, 6:30 am-midnight, Sat & Sun
from 7 am, $9-$23, cocktails. **Pool(s):** heated outdoor, heated indoor. **Leisure Activities:** sauna, whirlpool, exercise room. *Fee:*
barber shop. **Guest Services:** gift shop, valet laundry, area transportation-shopping mall. **Business Services:** conference facilities, PC. **Cards:** AX, CB, DC, DS, JC, MC, VI.
                                                                                               SOME UNITS

LA QUINTA INN SCHAUMBURG   Phone: (847)517-8484 233
  (SAVE)   All Year   1P: $79-$129   2P: $89-$139   XP: $10   F18
  ▼▼▼▼ **Location:** I-290, exit Higgins Rd W (SR 72), just w. 1730 E Higgins Rd 60173-4702. Fax: 847/517-4477. **Facility:** 127
  Motel   one-bedroom standard units. 3 stories, interior corridors. **Parking:** on-site, winter plug-ins. **Terms:** small pets
                only. **Amenities:** video games (fee), voice mail. **Pool(s):** heated outdoor. **Guest Services:** valet and coin
                laundry. **Business Services:** meeting rooms. **Cards:** AX, CB, DC, DS, JC, MC, VI. *(See color ad p 325)*
                                                                                               SOME UNITS

RADISSON HOTEL SCHAUMBURG   Phone: (847)397-1500 235
  (AAA) (SAVE)   All Year   1P: $95-$209   2P: $95-$209   F18
  ▼▼▼▼ **Location:** SR 53, exit Algonquin Rd (SR 62), 0.5 mi w. 1725 E Algonquin Rd 60173. Fax: 847/397-0665. **Facility:** 200
  Motor Inn   units. 199 one-bedroom standard units, some with whirlpools. 1 one-bedroom suite ($129-$289) with whirl-
                pool. 4 stories, interior corridors. **Bath:** combo or shower only. **Parking:** on-site. **Terms:** [BP] meal plan avail-
                able, package plans. **Amenities:** video games (fee), dual phone lines, voice mail, irons, hair dryers.
                Dining: restaurant, 6:30 am-11 pm, $8-$18, cocktails. **Pool(s):** heated outdoor. **Leisure Activi-**
ties: whirlpool, exercise room. **Guest Services:** valet laundry, area transportation-within 5 mi. **Business Services:** conference
facilities, business center. *Fee:* PC, fax. **Cards:** AX, CB, DC, DS, JC, MC, VI. **Special Amenities:** free newspaper.
(See color ad p 326)
                                                                                               SOME UNITS

SUMMERFIELD SUITES BY WYNDHAM-CHICAGO/SCHAUMBURG   Phone: (847)619-6677 230
  (AAA) (SAVE)   All Year   1P: $99-$165   2P: $99-$165   XP: $20   F18
  ▼▼▼▼ **Location:** Jct SR 53, 1.5 w on SR 72 (Higgins Rd), then 0.3 mi n on Plum Grove Rd. 901 E Woodfield Office Ct 60173.
  Apartment   Fax: 847/619-9184. **Facility:** 112 units. 50 one- and 62 two-bedroom suites with kitchens. 2-3 stories,
                interior/exterior corridors. **Parking:** on-site. **Terms:** cancellation fee imposed, [BP] meal plan available,
                package plans, pets ($150 fee). **Amenities:** extended cable TV, voice mail, irons, hair dryers. *Fee:* video tape
                library, high-speed Internet. **Pool(s):** heated outdoor. **Leisure Activities:** whirlpool, exercise room, sports
court, barbecue area. **Guest Services:** complimentary evening beverages: Mon-Thurs, valet and coin laundry. **Business Serv-**
ices: meeting rooms. **Cards:** AX, DC, DS, JC, MC, VI.
                                                                                               SOME UNITS

---

*The following lodgings were either not evaluated or did not
meet AAA rating requirements but are listed for your information only.*

RESIDENCE INN BY MARRIOTT-SCHAUMBURG   Phone: 847/517-9200
  (fyi)   Property failed to provide current rates
  Motel   Too new to rate. **Location:** I-90, exit 1A (SR 53). 1610 McConnor Pkwy 60193. Fax: 847/517-9800. **Amenities:** 124
                units, pets, radios, coffeemakers, microwaves, refrigerators. **Cards:** AX, DS, MC, VI.
                (See color ad card insert)

SPRINGHILL SUITES BY MARRIOTT-SCHAUMBURG   Phone: 847/995-1500
  (fyi)   Property failed to provide current rates
  Motel   Too new to rate, opening scheduled for October 2001. **Location:** I-90, exit 1A (SR 53). 1550 McConnor Pkwy
                60193. Fax: 847/995-1900. **Amenities:** 132 units, coffeemakers, microwaves, refrigerators. **Cards:** AX, DS,
                MC, VI. *(See color ad card insert)*

--- **WHERE TO DINE** ---

CALIFORNIA CAFE   Lunch: $9-$14   Dinner: $11-$20   Phone: 847/330-1212 179
  ▼▼▼▼ **Location:** I-290, exit Higgins Rd (SR 72), 0.5 mi w to Mall Dr, 0.5 mi n to southwest corner of Woodfield Mall. 5
                Woodfield Mall Shopping Center 60173. **Hours:** 11:30 am-4 & 5-10 pm, Fri & Sat-10:30 pm, Sun 11 am-3:30 &
  California   4:30-8:30 pm. Closed: 11/28, 12/25; also 4/4. **Reservations:** accepted. **Features:** casual dress; Sunday
                brunch; children's menu; carryout; cocktails & lounge; a la carte. The moderately upscale, contemporary,
eclectic-style restaurant serves innovative multi-ethnic cuisine. Featured are fresh seafood, steak and pasta dishes, all
well-prepared and dynamically presented. A very fine wine list complements the menu. **Parking:** on-site and valet (fee).
Cards: AX, CB, DC, DS, MC, VI.

SCHILLER PARK pop. 11,200   (See map p. 284; index p. 288)

──────── WHERE TO STAY ────────

COMFORT SUITES & CONFERENCE CENTER   Phone: (847)233-9000   `109`
[SAVE]   All Year [ECP]   1P: $79-$139   2P: $79-$139   XP: $5   F12
         Location: Jct Irving Park Rd (SR 19) and Des Plaines/River Rd, just n. 4200 N River Rd 60176. Fax: 847/233-0842.
Motel   **Facility:** 160 one-bedroom suites ($129-$209), some with whirlpools. 9 stories, interior corridors. *Bath:* combo or shower only. **Parking:** on-site. **Amenities:** extended cable TV, video games (fee), dual phone lines, voice mail. *Some:* irons, hair dryers. **Leisure Activities:** exercise room. **Guest Services:** valet laundry. **Business Services:** conference facilities. **Cards:** AX, CB, DC, DS, JC, MC, VI.
                                                                                       SOME UNITS

DAYS INN-O'HARE INTERNATIONAL   Phone: (847)678-0670   `112`
[AAA] [SAVE]   4/1-10/31   1P: $79-$159   2P: $89-$169   XP: $10   F12
              11/1-3/31   1P: $59-$159   2P: $69-$169   XP: $10   F12
         Location: 2 mi s of O'Hare Airport on US 12 and 45. 3801 N Mannheim Rd 60176. Fax: 847/678-0690. **Facility:** 14 one-bedroom standard units, some with whirlpools. 2 stories, interior corridors. **Parking:** on-site.
Motor Inn   **Terms:** package plans. **Amenities:** extended cable TV. **Dining:** coffee shop, 11 am-3 am, $5-$12, cocktails. **Pool(s):** outdoor. **Leisure Activities:** exercise room. **Guest Services:** valet and coin laundry. **Business Services:** meeting rooms. **Cards:** AX, CB, DC, DS, JC, MC, VI. **Special Amenities:** free continental breakfast and free newspaper. *(See color ad below)*

FOUR POINTS BY SHERATON CHICAGO O'HARE AIRPORT   Phone: (847)671-6000   `108`
         All Year   1P: $129-$139   2P: $129-$139   XP: $10   F16
         Location: Jct US 12 and 45; Mannheim Rd and SR 19, exit I-190, 1.3 mi s on Mannheim. 10249 W Irving Park Rd 60176.
Hotel   Fax: 847/671-0371. **Facility:** 296 one-bedroom standard units. 7 stories, interior corridors. **Parking:** on-site. **Terms:** package plans. **Amenities:** dual phone lines, voice mail, irons, hair dryers. *Fee:* video games, Web TV, high-speed Internet. **Pool(s):** heated indoor. **Leisure Activities:** saunas, whirlpool, exercise room. **Guest Services:** gift shop, valet laundry. **Business Services:** conference facilities, business center. *Fee:* PC, fax. **Cards:** AX, CB, DC, DS, MC, VI.
                                                                                       SOME UNITS

HAMPTON INN O'HARE AIRPORT   Phone: (847)671-1700   `111`
[SAVE]   All Year [ECP]   1P: $119   2P: $119
         Location: US 12 and 45 (Mannheim Rd), 0.5 mi s of Irving Park Rd. 3939 N Mannheim Rd 60176. Fax: 847/671-5909.
Motel   **Facility:** 150 one-bedroom standard units. 5 stories, interior corridors. **Parking:** on-site. **Terms:** package plans. **Amenities:** video games (fee), dual phone lines, voice mail, honor bars, irons, hair dryers. **Pool(s):** heated outdoor. **Leisure Activities:** exercise room. **Guest Services:** valet laundry. **Business Services:** meeting rooms. **Cards:** AX, CB, DC, DS, JC, MC, VI.
                                                                                       SOME UNITS

HOWARD JOHNSON EXPRESS INN   Phone: (847)678-4470   `107`
[AAA] [SAVE]   6/1-3/31   1P: $99   2P: $109   XP: $10   F16
              4/1-5/31   1P: $89   2P: $94   XP: $10   F16
         Location: On US 45, just s of SR 19. 4101 N Manheim Rd 60176. Fax: 847/678-3837. **Facility:** 66 one-bedroom standard units, some with whirlpools. 2-3 stories, interior/exterior corridors. *Bath:* combo or shower only.
Motel   **Parking:** on-site. **Terms:** package plans. **Amenities:** extended cable TV, voice mail, irons, hair dryers. **Leisure Activities:** sauna, whirlpool, limited exercise equipment. **Guest Services:** coin laundry. **Cards:** AX, DC, DS, MC, VI.
                                                                                       SOME UNITS

(See map p. 284)

RESIDENCE INN BY MARRIOTT O'HARE-SCHILLER PARK

Phone: (847)725-2210   **110**

AAA **SAVE**
▽▽▽▽

Apartment

All Year [BP]   1P: $99-$169   2P: $109-$179
Location: 0.5 mi e of US 12 and 45. 9450 W Lawrence Ave 60176. Fax: 847/725-2211. **Facility:** 171 units. 49 one-, 117 two- and 5 three-bedroom suites with kitchens. 6 stories, interior corridors. **Parking:** on-site. **Terms:** [MAP] meal plan available, pets ($7 fee, $100 extra charge). **Amenities:** extended cable TV, voice mail, irons, hair dryers. *Some:* CD players. **Dining:** restaurant, 4 pm-11 pm, Sat 5 pm-midnight, Sun 3 pm-10 pm, $11-$22, wine/beer only. **Leisure Activities:** whirlpool, sports court. **Guest Services:** valet laundry. **Business Services:** meeting rooms, PC. **Cards:** AX, CB, DC, DS, JC, MC, VI. *(See color ad card insert)*

SOME UNITS

[S/D] [✈] [🐾] [¶¶] [♿] [VCR] [💆] [DATA PORT] [🛏] [📷] [📺] [🖨] / [✕] /
                                          FEE

SKOKIE pop. 59,400   (See map p. 284; index p. 289)

──────── WHERE TO STAY ────────

HOLIDAY INN NORTHSHORE

Phone: (847)679-8900   **170**

▽▽▽
Motor Inn

All Year   1P: $149-$189   2P: $149-$189
Location: I-94, exit 39A, 0.5 mi w. 5300 W Touhy Ave 60077. Fax: 847/679-7447. **Facility:** 244 one-bedroom standard units. 2-4 stories, interior/exterior corridors. *Bath:* combo or shower only. **Terms:** package plans, small pets only (in limited units). **Amenities:** voice mail, irons, hair dryers. **Pool(s):** heated indoor. **Leisure Activities:** sauna, whirlpool, exercise room. **Guest Services:** gift shop, valet and coin laundry. **Business Services:** conference facilities. **Cards:** AX, CB, DC, DS, MC, VI.

SOME UNITS

[A$K] [S/D] [🐾] [¶¶] [📷] [♿] [🧖] [🏊] [✕] [💆] [DATA PORT] [📺] [🖨] / [✕] [🛏] [📷] /
                                                    FEE

HOWARD JOHNSON HOTEL-SKOKIE

Phone: (847)679-4200   **171**

AAA **SAVE**
▽▽▽ ▽▽▽
Motor Inn

All Year [BP]   1P: $105-$149   2P: $137-$164   XP: $10   F18
Location: On US 41, just n of Gross Point Rd. 9333 Skokie Blvd 60077. Fax: 847/679-4218. **Facility:** 134 one-bedroom standard units. 2-5 stories, interior corridors. *Bath:* combo or shower only. **Parking:** on-site. **Terms:** package plans, small pets only. **Amenities:** extended cable TV, voice mail, irons, hair dryers. **Dining:** 2 restaurants, 11:30 am-11 pm, Sun from 4 pm, $8-$25, cocktails. **Pool(s):** heated indoor. **Leisure Activities:** saunas, whirlpool, exercise room. **Guest Services:** complimentary evening beverages: Mon, valet laundry, area transportation-within 3 mi. **Business Services:** meeting rooms. **Cards:** AX, CB, DC, DS, JC, MC, VI. **Special Amenities:** free continental breakfast and free newspaper.

SOME UNITS

[S/D] [🐾] [¶¶] [🍸] [♿] [🧖] [🏊] [✕] [📷] [DATA PORT] [📺] [🖨] / [✕] [🛏] [📷] /
                                                    FEE   FEE

SOUTH HOLLAND pop. 22,100   (See map p. 292; index p. 293)

──────── WHERE TO STAY ────────

HAMPTON INN

Phone: (708)331-3200   **345**

SAVE
▽▽▽
Motel

4/1-8/31 [CP]   1P: $79   2P: $85
9/1-3/31 [CP]   1P: $69   2P: $69
Location: I-80/294, exit Halsted St N. 17345 Halsted St 60473. Fax: 708/331-3210. **Facility:** 105 one-bedroom standard units, some with whirlpools. 4 stories, interior corridors. *Bath:* combo or shower only. **Parking:** on-site. **Amenities:** voice mail, irons, hair dryers. **Leisure Activities:** whirlpool, exercise room. **Guest Services:** valet and coin laundry. **Business Services:** meeting rooms. **Cards:** AX, CB, DC, DS, MC, VI.

SOME UNITS

[S/D] [¶¶] [♿] [📷] [🏊] [DATA PORT] [📺] [🖨] / [✕] [🛏] /
                                          FEE

HILTON GARDEN INN SOUTH HOLLAND

Phone: (708)225-1300   **341**

SAVE
▽▽▽ ▽▽▽
Motor Inn

All Year   1P: $95-$125   2P: $105-$135   XP: $10   F17
Location: I-80/294, exit Halsted St N. 610 Tollview Dr 60473. Fax: 708/225-1328. **Facility:** 80 units. 79 one-bedroom standard units. 1 one-bedroom suite. 3 stories, interior corridors. *Bath:* combo or shower only. **Parking:** on-site. **Terms:** package plans. **Amenities:** video games, voice mail, irons, hair dryers. **Pool(s):** heated indoor. **Leisure Activities:** whirlpool, exercise room. **Guest Services:** valet and coin laundry. **Business Services:** meeting rooms, business center, PC (fee), fax. **Cards:** AX, CB, DC, DS, JC, MC, VI.

SOME UNITS

[S/D] [¶¶] [♿] [📷] [🏊] [DATA PORT] [🛏] [📺] [🖨] / [✕] /
                                          FEE

MOTEL 6

Phone: 708/331-1621   **344**

▽▽ ▽▽
Motel

All Year   1P: $34-$49   2P: $40-$55   XP: $3   F17
Location: I-80/294, exit Halsted St N. 17301 S Halsted St 60473. Fax: 708/331-1645. **Facility:** 136 one-bedroom standard units. 2 stories, exterior corridors. **Parking:** on-site. **Amenities:** voice mail. **Cards:** AX, CB, DC, DS, MC, VI.

SOME UNITS

[S/D] [🐾] [¶¶] [💆] [DATA PORT] / [✕] /
                        FEE

TINLEY PARK pop. 37,100

──────── WHERE TO STAY ────────

BAYMONT INN & SUITES CHICAGO-TINLEY PARK

Phone: (708)633-1200

AAA **SAVE**
▽▽▽

Motel

All Year   1P: $74-$94   2P: $74-$94
Location: I-80, exit 148B, just n. 7255 W 183rd St 60477. Fax: 708/633-1444. **Facility:** 99 units. 95 one-bedroom standard units. 4 one-bedroom suites ($84-$134), some with kitchens. 4 stories, interior corridors. *Bath:* combo or shower only. **Parking:** on-site. **Terms:** small pets only ($50 deposit). **Amenities:** video games (fee), voice mail, irons, hair dryers. *Some:* dual phone lines. **Pool(s):** heated indoor. **Leisure Activities:** whirlpool, exercise room. **Guest Services:** valet and coin laundry. **Cards:** AX, CB, DC, DS, MC, VI. **Special Amenities:** free continental breakfast and free newspaper.

SOME UNITS

[S/D] [🐾] [♿M] [📷] [🏊] [💆] [DATA PORT] [📺] [🖨] / [✕] [🛏] [📷] /
                                          FEE   FEE FEE

COMFORT SUITES

SAVE

Motel

Phone: (708)342-1425

10/1-12/31	1P: $100-$189	2P: $100-$189	XP: $10 F15
5/31-9/30	1P: $120-$150	2P: $120-$150	XP: $10 F15
1/1-3/31	1P: $100-$130	2P: $100-$130	XP: $10 F15
4/1-5/30	1P: $89-$100	2P: $89-$100	XP: $10 F15

Location: I-80, exit 148, 0.5 mi n to 183rd St, just w to North Creek Business Center, just s. 18400 Spring Creek Dr 60477. Fax: 708/342-1710. **Facility:** 67 one-bedroom standard units, some with whirlpools. 3 stories, interior corridors. *Bath:* combo or shower only. **Parking:** on-site. **Terms:** [ECP] meal plan available. **Amenities:** voice mail, irons, hair dryers. **Pool(s):** small heated indoor. **Leisure Activities:** exercise room. **Guest Services:** valet laundry. **Business Services:** meeting rooms. **Cards:** AX, CB, DC, DS, MC, VI.

SOME UNITS

FAIRFIELD INN

AAA **SAVE**

Motel

Phone: (708)633-1050

4/1-9/29 [CP]	1P: $64-$95	2P: $70-$100	XP: $6 F17
9/30-12/1 [CP]	1P: $60-$75	2P: $66-$81	XP: $6 F17
12/2-3/31 [CP]	1P: $57-$67	2P: $63-$73	XP: $6 F17

Location: I-80, exit 148B, just nw. 18511 N Creek Dr 60477. Fax: 708/633-1050. **Facility:** 64 one-bedroom standard units. 3 stories, interior corridors. *Bath:* combo or shower only. **Parking:** on-site. **Amenities:** extended cable TV, irons. **Pool(s):** small heated indoor. **Leisure Activities:** whirlpool. **Guest Services:** valet laundry. **Cards:** AX, CB, DC, DS, MC, VI. **Special Amenities:** free continental breakfast and free local telephone calls.

(See color ad card insert)

SOME UNITS

FEE

HAMPTON INN-TINLEY PARK

SAVE

Motel

Phone: (708)633-0602

5/27-9/30 [CP]	1P: $69-$119	2P: $79-$119	XP: $6 F17
10/1-3/31 [CP]	1P: $58-$74	2P: $64-$79	XP: $6 F17
4/1-5/26 [CP]	1P: $59-$69	2P: $65-$74	XP: $6 F17

Location: I-80, exit 148B, just nw. 18501 N Creek Dr 60477. Fax: 708/633-1768. **Facility:** 64 one-bedroom standard units. 3 stories, interior corridors. *Bath:* combo or shower only. **Parking:** on-site. **Amenities:** extended cable TV, irons, hair dryers. **Pool(s):** small heated indoor. **Leisure Activities:** whirlpool. **Guest Services:** valet laundry. **Cards:** AX, CB, DC, DS, JC, MC, VI.

SOME UNITS

FEE   FEE FEE

HOLIDAY INN SELECT & CONVENTION CENTER

Hotel

Phone: 708/444-1100

All Year	1P: $108-$117	2P: $108-$117

Location: I-80, exit 148. 18501 S Harlem Ave 60477. Fax: 708/444-1104. **Facility:** 202 units. 192 one-bedroom standard units. 10 one-bedroom suites ($225-$295) with whirlpools. 6 stories, interior corridors. *Bath:* combo or shower only. **Parking:** on-site. **Terms:** check-in 4 pm, package plans. **Amenities:** extended cable TV, dual phone lines, voice mail, irons, hair dryers. *Fee:* video games, Web TV. *Some:* safes. **Leisure Activities:** sauna, whirlpool, exercise room. **Guest Services:** gift shop, valet and coin laundry. **Business Services:** conference facilities, business center, PC, fax. **Cards:** AX, CB, DC, DS, JC, MC, VI.

SOME UNITS

FEE

SLEEP INN

SAVE

Motel

Phone: (708)342-1700

10/1-12/31 [CP]	1P: $89-$110	2P: $89-$110	XP: $10 F15
5/30-9/30 [CP]	1P: $79-$89	2P: $79-$89	XP: $10 F15
1/1-3/31 [CP]	1P: $69-$79	2P: $69-$79	XP: $10 F15
4/1-5/29 [CP]	1P: $59-$69	2P: $59-$69	XP: $10 F15

Location: I-80, exit 148B, 0.5 mi n to North Creek Business Center, just s. 18420 Spring Creek Dr 60477. Fax: 708/342-1709. **Facility:** 73 one-bedroom standard units. 4 stories, interior corridors. *Bath:* combo or shower only. **Parking:** on-site. **Terms:** 7 day cancellation notice. **Amenities:** extended cable TV. **Guest Services:** valet laundry. **Cards:** AX, CB, DC, DS, JC, MC, VI.

SOME UNITS

WINGATE INN

AAA **SAVE**

Motel

Phone: 708/532-9300

5/1-11/15 [ECP]	1P: $70-$79	2P: $70-$79
4/1-4/30 & 2/16-3/31 [ECP]	1P: $61-$70	2P: $61-$70
11/16-2/15 [ECP]	1P: $58-$60	2P: $58-$60

Location: I-80, exit 148B, 0.5 mi n to 183rd St, just w to North Creek Business Center, just s. 18421 North Creek Dr 60477. Fax: 708/614-9222. **Facility:** 86 one-bedroom standard units. 4 stories, interior corridors. *Bath:* combo or shower only. **Parking:** on-site. **Amenities:** extended cable TV, video games, high-speed Internet, voice mail, safes, irons, hair dryers. **Pool(s):** small heated indoor. **Leisure Activities:** whirlpool, exercise room. **Guest Services:** valet laundry. **Business Services:** meeting rooms, business center, PC, fax. **Cards:** AX, CB, DC, DS, JC, MC, VI. **Special Amenities:** free continental breakfast and free local telephone calls.

SOME UNITS

FEE   FEE FEE

VERNON HILLS pop. 15,300

——— WHERE TO STAY ———

AMERISUITES (CHICAGO/VERNON HILLS)

AAA **SAVE**

Motel

Phone: (847)918-1400

All Year	1P: $99-$159

Location: SR 21, 0.3 mi s of jct SR 60. 450 N Milwaukee Ave 60061. Fax: 847/918-1474. **Facility:** 128 one-bedroom standard units. 6 stories, interior corridors. *Bath:* combo or shower only. **Parking:** on-site. **Terms:** cancellation fee imposed, [CP] meal plan available, package plans, small pets only (in smoking units). **Amenities:** high-speed Internet (fee), voice mail, irons, hair dryers. **Pool(s):** heated indoor. **Leisure Activities:** exercise room. **Guest Services:** complimentary evening beverages: Wed, valet and coin laundry, area transportation-corporate within 3 mi. **Business Services:** meeting rooms, business center. *Fee:* PC, fax. **Cards:** AX, CB, DC, DS, JC, MC, VI. **Special Amenities:** free continental breakfast and free newspaper. *(See color ad p 296)*

SOME UNITS

FEE

HOMESTEAD STUDIO SUITES-CHICAGO/VERNON HILLS

Phone: (847)955-1111

All Year   1P: $74-$99   2P: $79-$104   XP: $5   F18

Extended Stay Motel

Location: I-94, exit SR 60 (Town Line Rd), 2.1 mi w to Milwaukee Ave (SR 21), 1.9 mi s to Woodlands Pkwy, then just w. 675 Woodlands Pkwy 60061. Fax: 847/955-0446. **Facility:** 124 one-bedroom standard units with efficiencies. 3 stories, interior corridors. *Bath:* combo or shower only. **Parking:** on-site. **Terms:** small pets only ($75 fee). **Amenities:** video tape library, dual phone lines, voice mail, irons. **Guest Services:** valet and coin laundry.

Cards: AX, DC, DS, JC, MC, VI.

——— WHERE TO DINE ———

SILK MANDARIN

Lunch: $6-$10   **Dinner:** $8-$18   **Phone:** 847/680-1760

Chinese

Location: Just off SR 60, 1 mi w of jct SR 21 (Milwaukee Ave). 4 E Phillips Rd 60061. **Hours:** 11:30 am-10 pm, Fri & Sat-11 pm, Sun-9 pm. **Reservations:** accepted. **Features:** casual dress; Sunday brunch; carryout; cocktails & lounge; a la carte, buffet. Red and gold trim, along with artwork of colorfully masked Chinese faces, set the tone for a festive atmosphere. The new sushi bar adds variety to the already fine menu. Szechwan, Hunan and Mandarin dishes are well-prepared. **Parking:** on-site. **Cards:** AX, DC, MC, VI.

WADSWORTH pop. 1,800

——— WHERE TO STAY ———

HAWTHORN SUITES AT MIDLANE GOLF RESORT

Phone: (847)360-0550

All Year [BP]   1P: $99-$109   2P: $119-$129

Motor Inn

Location: SR 41, 2.5 mi e on Delaney Rd, then 0.5 mi n. 4555 W Yorkhouse Rd 60083. Fax: 847/625-8186. **Facility:** 86 units. 59 one-bedroom standard units. 21 one- and 6 two-bedroom suites ($119-$209) with kitchens. 3 stories, interior corridors. *Bath:* combo or shower only. **Parking:** on-site. **Amenities:** *Some:* video games, dual phone lines, voice mail, irons, hair dryers. **Pool(s):** heated indoor. **Leisure Activities:** 2 tennis courts, exercise room. **Fee:** golf-27 holes. **Guest Services:** complimentary evening beverages: Mon-Thurs, valet and coin laundry. **Business Services:** conference facilities. **Cards:** AX, CB, DC, DS, MC, VI.

WARRENVILLE pop. 11,300

——— WHERE TO STAY ———

AMERISUITES (CHICAGO/WARRENVILLE)

Phone: (630)393-0400

All Year [ECP]   1P: $79-$129   2P: $79-$129   XP: $10   F18

Motel

Location: I-88, exit Winfield Rd, just s. 4305 Weaver Pkwy 60555. Fax: 630/393-3103. **Facility:** 128 one-bedroom standard units. 6 stories, interior corridors. *Bath:* combo or shower only. **Parking:** on-site. **Terms:** package plans, small pets only ($50 fee). **Amenities:** voice mail, irons, hair dryers. **Fee:** video games, high-speed Internet. **Pool(s):** heated indoor. **Leisure Activities:** exercise room. **Guest Services:** valet and coin laundry, area transportation-within 10 mi. **Business Services:** meeting rooms, business center. **Fee:** PC, fax. **Cards:** AX, CB, DC, DS, MC, VI. **Special Amenities:** free continental breakfast and free newspaper. *(See color ad p 296)*

WAUKEGAN pop. 69,400

——— WHERE TO STAY ———

BEST INN

Phone: 847/336-9000

Property failed to provide current rates

Motel

Location: I-94, exit Grand Ave (SR 132 E), 3.5 mi e to SR 131, 0.7 mi s. 31 N Green Bay Rd 60085. Fax: 847/336-9000. **Facility:** 89 one-bedroom standard units. 2 stories, interior corridors. **Parking:** on-site. **Terms:** package plans, small pets only ($10 fee). **Amenities:** extended cable TV. **Pool(s):** heated outdoor. **Cards:** AX, CB, DC, DS, MC, VI.

CANDLEWOOD SUITES CHICAGO/WAUKEGAN

Phone: (847)578-5250

All Year   1P: $99-$119

Extended Stay Apartment

Location: I-94, exit Buckley Rd (SR 137), 0.5 mi e to SR 43 (Waukegan Rd), 1.9 mi n. 1151 S Waukegan Rd 60085. Fax: 847/578-5256. **Facility:** 122 units. 98 one-bedroom standard units with efficiencies. 24 one-bedroom suites ($129-$179) with efficiencies. 3 stories, interior corridors. *Bath:* combo or shower only. **Parking:** on-site. **Terms:** small pets only ($50 fee, $100 deposit). **Amenities:** extended cable TV, video tape library, CD players, dual phone lines, voice mail, irons, hair dryers. **Leisure Activities:** exercise room. **Guest Services:** complimentary laundry. **Cards:** AX, CB, DC, DS, JC, MC, VI.

COMFORT INN

Phone: (847)623-1400

4/1-12/31 [ECP]   1P: $99   2P: $99   XP: $6   D12
1/1-3/31 [ECP]   1P: $89   2P: $89   XP: $6   D12

Motel

Location: I-94, exit Belvidere Rd E (SR 120), 2.1 mi e. 3031 Belvidere Rd 60085. Fax: 847/623-0686. **Facility:** 64 one-bedroom standard units. 2 stories, interior corridors. **Parking:** on-site. **Terms:** cancellation fee imposed. **Amenities:** extended cable TV. **Cards:** AX, CB, DC, DS, JC, MC, VI. **Special Amenities:** free continental breakfast and free newspaper.

COURTYARD BY MARRIOTT

AAA **SAVE**   **Phone: 847/689-8000**

Motel

All Year   1P: $89-$129   2P: $89-$129

Location: I-94, exit Belvidere Rd (SR 120 E), 1.3 mi e, exit Lakehurst Rd, follow to north side of Lakehurst Mall. 800 Lakehurst Rd 60085. Fax: 847/689-0135. **Facility:** 149 units. 137 one-bedroom standard units. 12 one-bedroom suites ($129-$159). 3 stories, interior corridors. *Bath:* combo or shower only. **Parking:** on-site. **Terms:** cancellation fee imposed, package plans. **Amenities:** high-speed Internet (fee), voice mail, irons, hair dryers. **Dining:** coffee shop, 6:30-10:30 am, Sat & Sun 7-11 am. **Pool(s):** heated indoor. **Leisure Activities:** whirlpool, limited exercise equipment. **Guest Services:** valet and coin laundry. **Business Services:** meeting rooms. **Cards:** AX, CB, DC, DS, MC, VI. *(See ad p 299 & color ad card insert)*

SOME UNITS

DAYS INN-WAUKEGAN

AAA **SAVE**   **Phone: (847)249-7778**

Motel

6/2-10/27	1P: $67-$120	2P: $67-$120	XP: $6 F13
4/1-6/1	1P: $62-$114	2P: $62-$114	XP: $6 F13
10/28-12/31	1P: $65-$105	2P: $65-$105	XP: $6 F13
1/1-3/31	1P: $62-$100	2P: $62-$100	XP: $6 F13

Location: I-94, exit Grand Ave (SR 132), 4.5 mi e to Lewis Ave, 3.2 mi n. 3633 N Lewis Ave 60087. Fax: 847/249-4970. **Facility:** 73 one-bedroom standard units, some with efficiencies (no utensils) and/or whirlpools. 2 stories, interior corridors. **Parking:** on-site. **Terms:** cancellation fee imposed, package plans. **Amenities:** hair dryers. **Guest Services:** valet laundry. **Cards:** AX, DC, DS, JC, MC, VI. **Special Amenities: free continental breakfast and free newspaper.**

SOME UNITS

HOLIDAY INN EXPRESS CHICAGO, WAUKEGAN (GREAT LAKES)

   Phone: (847)662-3200

Motel

7/1-8/31 [ECP]	1P: $80-$100	2P: $80-$100	XP: $7 F18
6/1-6/30 [ECP]	1P: $80-$90	2P: $80-$90	XP: $7 F18
4/1-5/31 & 9/1-3/31 [ECP]	1P: $70-$80	2P: $70-$80	XP: $7 F18

Location: I-94, exit Belvidere Rd (SR 120 E), 2.3 mi e on Belvidere Rd (SR 120); at jct Belvidere and Green Bay rds. 619 S Green Bay Rd 60085. Fax: 847/662-7275. **Facility:** 87 one-bedroom standard units. 2 stories, interior corridors. *Bath:* combo or shower only. **Parking:** on-site. **Terms:** package plans. **Amenities:** extended cable TV, irons, hair dryers. **Guest Services:** valet laundry. **Cards:** AX, CB, DC, DS, JC, MC, VI.

SOME UNITS

FEE   FEE

RAMADA INN WAUKEGAN

   Phone: (847)244-2400

Motor Inn

6/1-8/31	1P: $90	2P: $105	XP: $5 F18
9/1-3/31	1P: $85	2P: $90	XP: $5 F18
4/1-5/31	1P: $82	2P: $87	XP: $5 F18

Location: On SR 131, 0.6 mi s of jct SR 132 (Grand Ave). 200 N Green Bay Rd 60085. Fax: 847/249-9716. **Facility:** 185 units. 182 one-bedroom standard units. 3 one-bedroom suites ($100-$160). 2 stories, interior corridors. **Parking:** on-site. **Terms:** package plans, pets ($75 fee, $5 extra charge). **Amenities:** voice mail, irons. **Pool(s):** heated indoor. **Leisure Activities:** sauna, whirlpool, exercise room. *Fee:* game room. **Guest Services:** gift shop, valet laundry. **Business Services:** conference facilities. **Cards:** AX, CB, DC, DS, MC, VI.

SOME UNITS

FEE

RESIDENCE INN BY MARRIOTT-WAUKEGAN

AAA **SAVE**   **Phone: (847)689-9240**

Extended Stay
Apartment

All Year   1P: $99-$169   2P: $99-$179   XP: $10   F12

Location: I-94, exit SR 137 (Buckley Rd), 0.5 mi e to SR 43 (Waukegan Rd), 1.5 mi n. 1440 S White Oak Dr 60085. Fax: 847/689-9260. **Facility:** 126 units. 55 one-bedroom standard units with efficiencies. 48 one- and 23 two-bedroom suites, some with kitchens. 1-3 stories, interior corridors. *Bath:* combo or shower only. **Parking:** on-site. **Terms:** package plans, pets ($75 fee, $5 extra charge). **Amenities:** video games (fee), dual phone lines, voice mail, irons, hair dryers. **Pool(s):** small heated outdoor. **Leisure Activities:** whirlpool, exercise room, sports court. **Guest Services:** complimentary evening beverages: Mon-Thurs, valet and coin laundry, area transportation-local corporate offices. **Business Services:** meeting rooms. **Cards:** AX, CB, DC, DS, MC, VI. *(See color ad card insert)*

SOME UNITS

FEE

------- **WHERE TO DINE** -------

MADISON AVENUE

American

Lunch: $7-$12   **Dinner:** $10-$21   **Phone:** 847/662-6090

Location: Just s of Grand Ave (SR 132). 34 N Sheridan Rd 60085. **Hours:** 11 am-10 pm, Fri-11 pm, Sat 4 pm-11 pm, Sun 4 pm-10 pm. **Closed:** 1/1, 11/28, 12/25. **Reservations:** accepted. **Features:** casual dress; cocktails & lounge. "Fresh ingredients" and "made in-house" are the buzz words at this restaurant overlooking Lake Michigan. Prime rib, homemade soup, steak, chicken and fresh seafood are served by a prompt and courteous wait staff. Live entertainment performs Friday and Saturday. **Parking:** on-site (fee). **Cards:** AX, DC, DS, MC, VI.

YAN'S HUNAN INN

Chinese

Lunch: $5-$7   **Dinner:** $7-$12   **Phone:** 847/473-1660

Location: I-94, exit Belvidere Rd (SR 120), 2 mi e, exit on Lakehurst Rd, follow to north side of Lakehurst Mall. 900 Lakehurst Rd 60085. **Hours:** 11 am-9:30 pm, Fri & Sat-10:30 pm. **Closed:** 11/28. **Reservations:** accepted. **Features:** casual dress; carryout; cocktails & lounge; a la carte, buffet. The restaurant sustains a bustling, bright atmosphere. The large, well-stocked lunch buffet lays out a variety of primarily Hunan preparations. The extensive dinner menu centers on house specialties of seafood, vegetables, pork, beef, lamb and poultry. **Parking:** on-site. **Cards:** AX, DC, DS, MC, VI.

WESTCHESTER pop. 17,300 (See map p. 284; index p. 290)

—— WHERE TO STAY ——

HAMPTON INN-WESTCHESTER/OAK BROOK
Phone: (708)409-1000 **209**
All Year [ECP] 1P: $79-$119 2P: $79-$129 XP: $10 F18

[SAVE]
Location: I-294, exit Cermak Rd southbound, 0.5 mi e; exit Ogden Ave W northbound, 0.5 mi w to York Rd, 2 mi n, then 1 mi e Cermak Rd. 2222 Enterprise Dr 60154. Fax: 708/409-1055. **Facility:** 112 one-bedroom standard units. 4 stories, interior corridors. **Parking:** on-site. **Terms:** 3 day cancellation notice, package plans.
Motel
Amenities: video games (fee), voice mail, irons, hair dryers. **Leisure Activities:** exercise room. **Guest Services:** valet laundry. **Business Services:** meeting rooms. **Cards:** AX, CB, DC, DS, JC, MC, VI.

SOME UNITS

WEST DUNDEE

—— WHERE TO STAY ——

TOWNEPLACE SUITES
Phone: 847/608-6320
All Year 1P: $58-$104

[AAA] [SAVE]
Location: I-90, exit SR 31, 0.4 mi n to Marriott Dr, just e. 2185 Marriott Dr 60118. Fax: 847/608-6319. **Facility:** 143 units. 103 one-bedroom standard units with efficiencies. 6 one- and 34 two-bedroom suites with kitchens. 3 stories, interior corridors. *Bath:* combo or shower only. **Parking:** on-site. **Terms:** pets ($100 extra charge).
Apartment
Amenities: extended cable TV, dual phone lines, voice mail, irons, hair dryers. **Pool(s):** small heated outdoor. **Leisure Activities:** exercise room. **Guest Services:** valet and coin laundry. **Cards:** AX, CB, DC, DS, MC, VI. **Special Amenities:** free local telephone calls. *(See color ad card insert)*

SOME UNITS

WESTMONT pop. 21,200 (See map p. 292; index p. 293)

—— WHERE TO STAY ——

CLUBHOUSE INN & SUITES
Phone: (630)920-2200 **299**
All Year [BP] 1P: $81-$99 2P: $81-$109 XP: $5 F17

Location: Just off US 34, 0.3 mi nw of jct SR 83. 630 Pasquinelli Dr 60559. Fax: 630/920-2766. **Facility:** 137 units.
Motel
118 one-bedroom standard units. 19 one-bedroom suites ($135), some with whirlpools. 2 stories, interior corridors. **Parking:** on-site. **Terms:** package plans. **Amenities:** extended cable TV, high-speed Internet (fee), irons, hair dryers. **Pool(s):** heated indoor. **Leisure Activities:** whirlpool. **Guest Services:** complimentary evening beverages, valet and coin laundry. **Business Services:** meeting rooms. **Cards:** AX, CB, DC, DS, MC, VI. *(See ad below)*

SOME UNITS
FEE FEE

HOMESTEAD STUDIO SUITES-CHICAGO/WESTMONT/OAK BROOK
Phone: (630)323-9292 **297**
4/1-10/31 1P: $79-$99 2P: $99-$119 XP: $10 F17
11/1-3/31 1P: $69-$89 2P: $89-$109 XP: $10 F17

Extended Stay
Location: SR 83, exit Ogden Ave (US 34), just w to Pasquinelli Dr, 0.5 mi n. 855 Pasquinelli Dr 60559. Motel Fax: 630/323-9536. **Facility:** 141 one-bedroom standard units, some with efficiencies or kitchens. 3 stories, interior corridors. *Bath:* combo or shower only. **Parking:** on-site. **Terms:** pets ($75 extra charge).
Amenities: *Some:* voice mail, irons. **Guest Services:** valet and coin laundry. **Cards:** AX, CB, DC, DS, JC, MC, VI.

SOME UNITS

—— WHERE TO DINE ——

CUCINA ROMA
Lunch: $7-$11 **Dinner:** $12-$21 **Phone:** 630/654-9600 **225**
Location: On US 34, just w of jct SR 83; in St. James Crossing. 800 E Ogden Ave & Rt 83 60559. **Hours:** 11 am-10 pm, Fri-11 pm, Sat 11:30 am-11 pm, Sun noon-9 pm. Closed major holidays. **Reservations:** accepted.
Italian
Features: casual dress; carryout; cocktails & lounge; a la carte. The well-prepared country Italian food is delicious. May we recommend lasagna and bruscetta (hard-crusted bread with seasoned tomato chunks)? Or how about the fresh pizza, pasta and house specialties? You'll be pleased no matter what you choose. **Parking:** on-site. **Cards:** AX, DC, DS, MC, VI.

WHEATON pop. 51,500

──────── WHERE TO STAY ────────

THE WHEATON INN
▼▼▼▼
Bed & Breakfast

Phone: (630)690-2600

All Year [BP]   1P: $145-$225   2P: $145-$225   XP: $35   F3
Location: On SR 38, 0.3 mi w of jct SR 23. 301 W Roosevelt Rd 60187. Fax: 630/690-2623. **Facility:** Large, traditional-style rooms, many with fireplaces and large bathrooms, make this inn comfortable. Smoke free premises. 16 one-bedroom standard units, some with whirlpools. 3 stories, interior corridors. **Parking:** on-site. **Terms:** check-in 4 pm, 7 day cancellation notice-fee imposed, package plans. **Amenities:** voice mail, hair dryers. **Guest Services:** complimentary evening beverages. **Business Services:** meeting rooms. **Cards:** AX, DC, DS, JC, MC, VI.

SOME UNITS

(ASK) (S☐) (Ⓣ) (✕) (DATA PORT) (🖨) / (VCR) /

WHEELING pop. 29,900

──────── WHERE TO STAY ────────

PALWAUKEE INN HOTEL AND CONFERENCE CENTER
(AAA) (SAVE)
▼▼▼▼
Motor Inn

Phone: (847)537-9100

All Year [BP]   1P: $85-$95   2P: $85-$95   XP: $10   F17
Location: I-294, exit Willow Rd, 0.6 mi w to Milwaukee Ave, 0.3 mi n. 1090 S Milwaukee 60090. Fax: 847/520-8420. **Facility:** 144 one-bedroom standard units. 2 stories, interior corridors. *Bath:* combo or shower only. **Parking:** on-site. **Terms:** package plans. **Amenities:** dual phone lines, voice mail, irons, hair dryers. **Dining:** restaurant, 6:30 am-10:30 pm, Fri & Sat-11:30 pm, $10-$25, cocktails. **Leisure Activities:** exercise room. *Fee:* 4 lane bowling alley. **Guest Services:** valet and coin laundry. **Business Services:** conference facilities.
Cards: AX, CB, DC, DS, MC, VI.

SOME UNITS

(S☐) (Ⓣ) (Ⓨ) (Ⓖ) (Ⓓ) (DATA PORT) (💻) (🖨) / (✕) /

──────── WHERE TO DINE ────────

BOB CHINN'S CRAB HOUSE
▼▼▼ ▼▼▼
Seafood

Lunch: $6-$25   **Dinner:** $11-$39   Phone: 847/520-3633
Location: US 45, 0.4 mi s of jct Dundee Rd (SR 68). 393 S Milwaukee Ave 60090. **Hours:** 11 am-2:30 & 4:30-10:30 pm, Fri-11:30 pm, Sat noon-11:30 pm, Sun noon-10 pm. Closed: 11/28, 12/25. **Reservations:** suggested. **Features:** casual dress; children's menu; carryout; salad bar; cocktails & lounge; a la carte. The busy atmosphere at Bob Chinn's is uncannily well orchestrated by the friendly, enthusiastic service staff. And the food follows suit: Fresh Kona crab and lobster are just two of the varied seafood items and appetizers you'll encounter here. Locally popular so a good idea to call ahead. **Parking:** on-site and valet. **Cards:** AX, CB, DC, DS, JC, MC, VI.

(✕)

LE FRANCAIS
(AAA)
▼▼▼ ▼▼▼
French

Lunch: $14-$20   **Dinner:** $22-$38   Phone: 847/541-7470
Location: On US 45, just s of jct SR 68 (Dundee Rd). 269 S Milwaukee Ave 60090. **Hours:** 11:30 am-2 & 6-9 pm, Fri & Sat seating at 6 pm-6:30 pm & 9 pm-10 pm. Closed major holidays; also Sun. **Reservations:** required. **Features:** semi-formal attire; early bird specials; cocktails; a la carte, also prix fixe. Polished, light-maple woodwork accents the dining room of the refined restaurant, where contemporary elegance abounds. Visible through a large window, the open kitchen enables patrons to watch masterful chefs prepare creative, eye-catching and expertly seasoned food presentations that are world class in every way. Service is formal and accomplished, yet unassuming. Smoke free premises. **Parking:** on-site and valet. **Cards:** AX, CB, DC, DS, MC, VI.

(✕)

WILLOWBROOK pop. 8,600 (See map p. 292; index p. 293)

------ WHERE TO STAY ------

BAYMONT INN & SUITES CHICAGO-WILLOWBROOK
Phone: (630)654-0077   **308**

AAA SAVE
◇◇◇◇
Motel

All Year   1P: $69-$89   2P: $69-$89
Location: I-55, exit 274, just n. 855 79th St 60521. Fax: 630/654-0181. **Facility:** 130 units. 127 one-bedroom standard units. 3 one-bedroom suites ($79-$124). 3 stories, interior corridors. **Parking:** on-site. **Amenities:** video games (fee), voice mail, irons, hair dryers. **Leisure Activities:** exercise room. **Guest Services:** valet and coin laundry. **Cards:** AX, CB, DC, DS, MC, VI. **Special Amenities:** free continental breakfast and free newspaper. *(See color ad opposite title page)*

SOME UNITS
[icons] FEE

FAIRFIELD INN WILLOWBROOK
Phone: (630)789-6300   **305**

AAA SAVE
◇◇◇
Motel

11/1-3/31 [ECP]   1P: $59-$72   2P: $66-$79
4/1-10/31 [ECP]   1P: $67-$74   2P: $70-$77
Location: I-55, exit 274, 0.3 mi n to Midway Dr, then e on frontage road. 820 W 79th St 60521. Fax: 630/789-6300. **Facility:** 129 one-bedroom standard units. 3 stories, interior/exterior corridors. **Parking:** on-site, winter plug-ins. **Terms:** 30 day cancellation notice. **Amenities:** voice mail, irons. **Pool(s):** heated outdoor. **Guest Services:** valet laundry. **Cards:** AX, DC, DS, MC, VI. **Special Amenities:** free continental breakfast and free local telephone calls. *(See color ad card insert)*

SOME UNITS
[icons] FEE

HOLIDAY INN-WILLOWBROOK
Phone: (630)325-6400   **306**

◇◇◇
Motor Inn

All Year   1P: $119-$139   2P: $119-$139   XP: $10   F18
Location: I-55, exit 274, 0.3 mi n. 7800 Robert Kingery Hwy 60521. Fax: 630/325-2362. **Facility:** 220 units. 219 one-bedroom standard units. 1 one-bedroom suite. 2-3 stories, interior corridors. **Parking:** on-site. **Terms:** package plans. **Amenities:** video tape library (fee), dual phone lines, voice mail, irons, hair dryers. **Pool(s):** heated outdoor. **Leisure Activities:** sauna, sun deck, exercise room. **Guest Services:** gift shop, valet and coin laundry. **Business Services:** conference facilities, PC. **Cards:** AX, CB, DC, DS, MC, VI.

SOME UNITS
[icons] FEE

RED ROOF INN
Phone: (630)323-8811   **307**

AAA SAVE
◇◇◇
Motel

5/20-10/26   1P: $59-$81   2P: $65-$87   XP: $6   F18
4/1-5/19 & 10/27-3/31   1P: $51-$71   2P: $57-$77   XP: $6   F18
Location: I-55, exit 274, 0.5 mi n on SR 83. 7535 Robert Kingery Hwy 60521. Fax: 630/323-2714. **Facility:** 109 one-bedroom standard units. 3 stories, exterior corridors. **Bath:** combo or shower only. **Parking:** on-site. **Terms:** small pets only. **Amenities:** video games (fee), voice mail. **Cards:** AX, CB, DC, DS, MC, VI. **Special Amenities:** free local telephone calls and free newspaper.

SOME UNITS
[icons] FEE   FEE FEE

WILMETTE pop. 26,700 (See map p. 284; index p. 291)

------ WHERE TO DINE ------

AKAI HANA
Lunch: $7-$15   Dinner: $12-$19   Phone: 847/251-0384   **206**

◇◇
Japanese

Location: On Lake Ave, just e of jct I-94; in Edens Bank shopping area. 3223 W Lake Ave 60091. **Hours:** 11:30 am-10 pm, Sun-9 pm. Closed major holidays. **Features:** casual dress; carryout; beer & wine only; a la carte. The backdrop is an unpretentious Japanese dining room where sushi, sashimi and tempura specialties are offered by servers both efficient and friendly. A large bowl of beef teriyaki with rice, peppers and various fresh vegetables is a very good choice. Smoke free premises. **Parking:** on-site. **Cards:** AX, DC, DS, JC, MC, VI.

[icon]

OLD OUILMETTE DEPOT RESTAURANT
Lunch: $7-$14   Dinner: $10-$24   Phone: 847/256-0771   **205**

AAA
◇◇◇
American

Location: Between Green Bay Rd and Lake Ave. 1139 Wilmette Ave 60091. **Hours:** 11 am-9:30 pm, Fri & Sat-10:30 pm, Sun-8:30 pm. Closed major holidays. **Reservations:** suggested. **Features:** casual dress; children's menu; carryout; cocktails; a la carte. The inviting train depot decor and good traditional American food at Old Ouilmette prove to be real treats for travelers. The barbecued ribs or seafood Florentine are notable and served either indoors or out. Some vegetarian dishes also are offered. **Parking:** on-site. **Cards:** DS, MC, VI.

[icon]

WOOD DALE pop. 12,400 (See map p. 284; index p. 288)

------ WHERE TO STAY ------

COURTYARD BY MARRIOTT WOOD DALE
Phone: (630)766-7775   **138**

AAA SAVE
◇◇◇
Motor Inn

All Year   1P: $49-$139   2P: $59-$149
Location: I-290, exit Thorndale Ave, 2 mi e, 0.3 mi s. 900 N Wood Dale Rd 60191. Fax: 630/766-7552. **Facility:** 149 units. 137 one-bedroom standard units. 12 one-bedroom suites. 2-3 stories, interior corridors. **Bath:** combo or shower only. **Parking:** on-site. **Amenities:** high-speed Internet, dual phone lines, voice mail, irons, hair dryers. **Dining:** dining room, 6:30 am-10:30 & 5-10 pm, Sat & Sun 7 am-11 & 5-10 pm; closed Fri & Sat evenings, $8-$14, cocktails. **Pool(s):** heated indoor. **Leisure Activities:** whirlpool, exercise room. **Guest Services:** valet and coin laundry, area transportation-within 5 mi. **Business Services:** meeting rooms. **Cards:** AX, CB, DC, DS, JC, MC, VI. *(See ad p 299 & color ad card insert)*

SOME UNITS
[icons] FEE

(See map p. 284)

WYNDHAM GARDEN HOTEL-WOOD DALE

Phone: (630)860-2900 [137]

(AAA) [SAVE]   All Year   1P: $79-$135   2P: $79-$145   XP: $10   F18

Motor Inn   **Location:** I-290, exit 5, 1.5 mi e on Thorndale Ave. 1200 N Mittel Blvd 60191. Fax: 630/860-2945. **Facility:** 162 one-bedroom standard units. 2-3 stories, interior corridors. *Bath:* combo or shower only. **Parking:** on-site. **Terms:** cancellation fee imposed, package plans. **Amenities:** voice mail, irons, hair dryers. *Fee:* Web TV, high-speed Internet. **Dining:** restaurant, 6:30 am-2 & 5-10 pm, Sat & Sun 7 am-noon, $10-$21, cocktails. **Pool(s):** heated indoor. **Leisure Activities:** sauna, whirlpool, jogging. **Guest Services:** valet laundry, area transportation-within 5 mi. **Business Services:** meeting rooms. **Cards:** AX, CB, DC, DS, JC, MC, VI.

SOME UNITS

WOODSTOCK pop. 14,400

—— **WHERE TO STAY** ——

DAYS INN

Phone: (815)338-0629

[SAVE]   All Year [CP]   1P: $60-$100   2P: $67-$107   XP: $7   F12

Motel   **Location:** On SR 47, 0.5 mi n of SR 14. 990 Lake Ave 60098. Fax: 815/338-0895. **Facility:** 45 one-bedroom standard units. 3 stories, interior corridors. **Parking:** on-site, winter plug-ins. **Terms:** package plans. **Amenities:** extended cable TV, video tape library (fee), safes, irons, hair dryers. **Pool(s):** heated indoor. **Leisure Activities:** sauna, whirlpool. **Guest Services:** gift shop. **Business Services:** meeting rooms. **Cards:** AX, CB, DC, DS, MC, VI.

SOME UNITS

HOLIDAY INN EXPRESS

Phone: (815)334-9600

All Year [ECP]   1P: $79   XP: $5   F19

Motel   **Location:** Jct SR 47 and US 14. 1785 S Eastwood Dr 60098. Fax: 815/334-9614. **Facility:** 51 units. 50 one-bedroom standard units, some with whirlpools. 1 one-bedroom suite ($105). 2 stories, interior corridors. *Bath:* combo or shower only. **Parking:** on-site. **Amenities:** irons, hair dryers. **Pool(s):** small heated indoor. **Leisure Activities:** whirlpool, exercise room. **Guest Services:** valet and coin laundry. **Business Services:** meeting rooms. **Cards:** AX, CB, DC, DS, JC, MC, VI.

SOME UNITS

This ends listings for the Chicago Vicinity.
The following page resumes the alphabetical listings of cities in Illinois.

CHILLICOTHE pop. 6,000

—— WHERE TO STAY ——

SUPER 8 MOTEL

Motel

Phone: (309)274-2568

| All Year [CP] | 1P: $45-$55 | 2P: $55-$65 | XP: $4 | F12 |

Location: 1.1 mi s on SR 29. 615 S Fourth St 61523. Fax: 309/274-2568. **Facility:** 36 one-bedroom standard units, some with whirlpools. 2 stories, interior corridors. **Parking:** on-site, winter plug-ins. **Terms:** small pets only ($10 fee, $50 deposit). **Amenities:** extended cable TV. **Cards:** AX, CB, DS, JC, MC, VI.

SOME UNITS

COLLINSVILLE pop. 22,400

—— WHERE TO STAY ——

DRURY INN COLLINSVILLE

Motel

Phone: (618)345-7700

| All Year [ECP] | 1P: $82-$108 | 2P: $82-$108 | XP: $10 | F18 |

Location: I-55/70, exit 11 (SR 157), just n. 602 N Bluff Rd 62234. Fax: 618/345-7700. **Facility:** 123 one-bedroom standard units. 4 stories, interior corridors. **Parking:** on-site, winter plug-ins. **Amenities:** extended cable TV, dual phone lines, voice mail, irons, hair dryers. **Pool(s):** small heated indoor. **Leisure Activities:** exercise room. **Guest Services:** complimentary evening beverages: Mon-Thurs, valet and coin laundry. **Business Services:** meeting rooms, fax (fee). **Cards:** AX, CB, DC, DS, MC, VI. *(See color ad p 5)*

SOME UNITS

FEE

FAIRFIELD INN BY MARRIOTT

Motel

Phone: 618/346-0607

6/1-10/31	1P: $66-$72		XP: $5	F18
4/1-5/31	1P: $56-$66		XP: $5	F18
11/1-12/31	1P: $53-$61		XP: $5	F18
1/1-3/31	1P: $52-$57		XP: $5	F18

Location: I-55/70, exit 11 (SR 157), just nw. 4 Gateway Dr 62234. Fax: 618/346-0607. **Facility:** 64 one-bedroom standard units. 3 stories, interior corridors. *Bath:* combo or shower only. **Parking:** on-site. **Amenities:** extended cable TV, irons. **Pool(s):** small heated indoor. **Leisure Activities:** whirlpool. **Guest Services:** valet laundry. **Business Services:** fax (fee). **Cards:** AX, DC, DS, MC, VI. **Special Amenities: free continental breakfast and free local telephone calls.**

SOME UNITS

HOLIDAY INN COLLINSVILLE/ST. LOUIS

Motor Inn

Phone: (618)345-2800

| 5/1-3/31 | 1P: $129-$139 | 2P: $141-$151 | XP: $12 | F18 |
| 4/1-4/30 | 1P: $109-$119 | 2P: $121-$131 | XP: $12 | F18 |

Location: I-55/70, exit 11 (SR 157), just nw. 1000 Eastport Plaza Dr 62234. Fax: 618/345-9804. **Facility:** 229 units. 228 one-bedroom standard units. 1 one-bedroom suite ($150-$200). 4-5 stories, interior corridors. **Parking:** on-site. **Terms:** [BP], [CP] & [ECP] meal plans available, package plans, pets ($50 deposit, dogs only). **Amenities:** video games, voice mail, safes (fee), irons, hair dryers. **Dining:** Porter's Steakhouse, see separate listing. **Pool(s):** heated indoor. **Leisure Activities:** whirlpool, sun deck, exercise room, basketball, horseshoes, volleyball. *Fee:* game room. **Guest Services:** valet and coin laundry. **Business Services:** conference facilities, fax. **Cards:** AX, CB, DC, DS, JC, MC, VI.

SOME UNITS

FEE

MOTEL 6 - 1133

Motel

Phone: 618/345-2100

5/23-11/9	1P: $39-$55	2P: $45-$61	XP: $3	F17
11/10-2/28	1P: $35-$45	2P: $41-$51	XP: $3	F17
3/1-5/22	1P: $33-$43	2P: $39-$49	XP: $3	F17

Location: I-55/70, exit 11 (SR 157), just s. 295A N Bluff Rd 62234. Fax: 618/345-9160. **Facility:** 86 one-bedroom standard units. 2 stories, interior corridors. *Bath:* combo or shower only. **Parking:** on-site. **Terms:** small pets only. **Amenities:** extended cable TV. **Cards:** AX, CB, DC, DS, MC, VI.

SOME UNITS

PEAR TREE INN BY DRURY

Motel

Phone: (618)345-9500

| 4/1-9/30 [CP] | 1P: $62-$79 | 2P: $62-$79 | XP: $10 | F18 |
| 10/1-3/31 [CP] | 1P: $40-$55 | 2P: $40-$55 | XP: $10 | F18 |

Location: I-55/70, exit 11 (SR 157), just s. 552 Ramada Blvd 62234. Fax: 618/345-9500. **Facility:** 105 one-bedroom standard units. 2 stories, exterior corridors. *Bath:* combo or shower only. **Parking:** on-site. **Amenities:** extended cable TV, voice mail. **Pool(s):** outdoor. **Guest Services:** valet laundry. **Cards:** AX, CB, DC, DS, MC, VI. *(See color ad p 5)*

SOME UNITS

FEE

RAMADA LIMITED

Motel

Phone: (618)345-2000

| All Year [ECP] | 1P: $72-$125 | 2P: $82-$125 | XP: $7 | F17 |

Location: I-55/70, exit 11 (SR 157), just nw. 12 Commerce Dr 62234. Fax: 618/345-2626. **Facility:** 56 one-bedroom standard units, some with whirlpools. 3 stories, interior corridors. *Bath:* combo or shower only. **Parking:** on-site. **Terms:** 7 day cancellation notice. **Amenities:** extended cable TV, voice mail. **Pool(s):** small heated indoor. **Guest Services:** valet laundry. **Business Services:** fax (fee). **Cards:** AX, CB, DC, DS, MC, VI. **Special Amenities: free continental breakfast and free local telephone calls.**

SOME UNITS

FEE   FEE

——— WHERE TO DINE ———

PORTER'S STEAKHOUSE
▼▼▼▼
American

Lunch: $8-$15   **Dinner:** $18-$35   **Phone:** 618/345-2400   [64]

Location: I-55/70, exit 11 (SR 157), just nw; in Holiday Inn Collinsville/St. Louis. 1000 E Port Plaza Dr 62234. **Hours:** 6:15 am-2 & 4:30-10:30 pm, Sat from 7 am, Sun 7 am-10 pm. **Reservations:** suggested. **Features:** dressy casual; Sunday brunch; children's menu; cocktails & lounge; a la carte. The warm glow of a fireplace, jade banker's lamps and lots of natural wood provide the classic setting in which to enjoy huge portions of good food. The restaurant is known for pepper loin served with sizzling mustard sauce and a monstrous six-layer cake. **Parking:** on-site. **Cards:** AX, CB, DC, DS, MC, VI.

ZEPPETELLA'S
▼
Italian

Lunch: $4-$15   **Dinner:** $6-$15   **Phone:** 618/344-8020   [63]

Location: I-70, exit 15A (SR 159), 1.5 mi s. 1813 Vandalia St 62234. **Hours:** 11:30 am-10 pm, Fri & Sat-11 pm, Sun-9:30 pm. Closed: 11/28, 12/25; also Mon. **Reservations:** suggested; weekends. **Features:** casual dress; children's menu; carryout; cocktails & lounge; a la carte. The locals love the family-style eats and casual atmosphere. Offering many house specials with an array of pasta, steak, seafood and chicken entrees. Plus homemade dressing, spaghetti sauce and cheesecake make up the menu. **Parking:** on-site. **Cards:** MC, VI.

COLUMBIA pop. 5,500

——— WHERE TO DINE ———

THE LANTERN RESTAURANT
▼
American

Lunch: $5-$12   **Dinner:** $5-$18   **Phone:** 618/281-7312

Location: Downtown; Main St at Walnut. 230 N Main St 62236. **Hours:** 11 am-9 pm, Fri & Sat-10 pm. Closed major holidays; also Mon. **Features:** casual dress; children's menu; carryout; cocktails. A popular, casual family dining spot. This casual tone is carried through to the service staff, who are quite informal. The fried cod is a good choice. **Parking:** on-site. **Cards:** AX, DS, MC, VI.

COUNTRYSIDE —See Chicago p. 331.

CRAINVILLE pop. 1,000

——— WHERE TO DINE ———

THE PIONEER'S CABIN
▼
Regional American

Lunch: $5-$7   **Dinner:** $5-$8   **Phone:** 618/985-8290

Location: I-57, exit 54B (SR 13), 5 mi w. 1325 Main St 62918. **Hours:** 6:30 am-9 pm, Sun 10:30 am-4 pm. Closed major holidays; also Mon. **Reservations:** accepted; weekdays. **Features:** casual dress; carryout; also prix fixe. Settle down at a table in the rustic pine log cabin, where you can drink from glass jars and enjoy down-home food like Grandma used to make when she had company. Fried chicken, family-style catfish and homemade desserts are favorite offerings. **Parking:** on-site. **Cards:** CB, DC, DS, MC, VI.

CRYSTAL LAKE —See Chicago p. 332.

DANVILLE pop. 33,800

——— WHERE TO STAY ———

BEST WESTERN REGENCY INN
AAA SAVE
▼▼▼
Motel

Phone: (217)446-2111

All Year   1P: $60-$80   2P: $70-$90   XP: $10   D10

Location: I-74, exit 220 (Lynch Dr), just n. 360 Eastgate Dr 61834. Fax: 217/446-2444. **Facility:** 42 one-bedroom standard units. 2 stories, interior/exterior corridors. **Parking:** on-site. **Terms:** 3 day cancellation notice-fee imposed, pets ($10 extra charge). **Amenities:** extended cable TV, irons, hair dryers. **Leisure Activities:** whirlpool. **Guest Services:** valet and coin laundry. **Cards:** AX, CB, DC, DS, MC, VI. **Special Amenities:** free continental breakfast and preferred room (subject to availability with advanced reservations).

SOME UNITS

BEST WESTERN RIVERSIDE
AAA SAVE
▼▼▼
Motel

Phone: (217)431-0020

All Year   1P: $65-$85   2P: $75-$95   XP: $10   D10

Location: I-74, exit 215, 0.8 mi n, on US 150 and SR 1. 57 S Gilbert St 61832. Fax: 217/431-8980. **Facility:** 42 units. 40 one-bedroom standard units, some with whirlpools. 2 one-bedroom suites ($125-$145). 2 stories, interior/exterior corridors. **Parking:** on-site. **Terms:** cancellation fee imposed, small pets only ($10 extra charge). **Amenities:** extended cable TV, irons, hair dryers. **Pool(s):** outdoor. **Guest Services:** valet and coin laundry. **Business Services:** fax (fee). **Cards:** AX, CB, DC, DS, MC, VI. **Special Amenities:** free continental breakfast and preferred room (subject to availability with advanced reservations).

SOME UNITS

COMFORT INN
SAVE
▼▼▼
Motel

Phone: (217)443-8004

All Year   1P: $49-$79   2P: $54-$84   XP: $5   F18

Location: I-74, exit 220 (Lynch Dr), just n. 383 Lynch Dr 61834. Fax: 217/443-8004. **Facility:** 56 one-bedroom standard units. 2 stories, interior corridors. **Parking:** on-site, winter plug-ins. **Terms:** 7 day cancellation notice. **Amenities:** Some: irons, hair dryers. **Pool(s):** small heated outdoor. **Leisure Activities:** whirlpool. **Guest Services:** valet laundry. **Business Services:** fax (fee). **Cards:** AX, CB, DC, DS, MC, VI.

SOME UNITS

DAYS INN DANVILLE   Phone: (217)443-6600

[SAVE]

4/1-10/31	1P: $76-$81	2P: $86-$91	XP: $10 F18
11/1-3/31	1P: $73-$78	2P: $83-$88	XP: $10 F18

Motor Inn

Location: I-74, exit 215, 1 mi n on US 136 W. 77 N Gilbert St 61832. Fax: 217/443-2345. **Facility:** 95 units. 94 one-bedroom standard units. 1 one-bedroom suite with whirlpool. 6 stories, interior corridors. *Bath:* combo or shower only. **Parking:** on-site. **Amenities:** extended cable TV, voice mail, hair dryers. *Some:* irons. **Pool(s):** outdoor. **Guest Services:** valet laundry. **Business Services:** conference facilities. **Cards:** AX, CB, DC, DS, JC, MC, VI.

SOME UNITS

FAIRFIELD INN BY MARRIOTT   Phone: (217)443-3388

[AAA] [SAVE]

4/1-10/31	1P: $65-$96	2P: $70-$96	XP: $5 F18
11/1-3/31	1P: $60-$86	2P: $65-$86	XP: $5 F18

Motel

Location: I-14, exit 220 (Lynch Dr), just n. 389 Lynch Dr 61834. Fax: 217/443-3388. **Facility:** 56 one-bedroom standard units. 3 stories, interior corridors. *Bath:* combo or shower only. **Parking:** on-site, winter plug-ins. **Amenities:** irons, hair dryers. **Pool(s):** small heated outdoor. **Leisure Activities:** whirlpool. **Guest Services:** valet laundry. **Cards:** AX, CB, DC, DS, MC, VI. **Special Amenities:** free continental breakfast and free local telephone calls. *(See color ad card insert)*

SOME UNITS

SLEEP INN & SUITES   Phone: (217)442-6600

[SAVE]

4/1-10/31 [ECP]	1P: $90-$159	2P: $90-$159	XP: $10 F18
11/1-3/31 [ECP]	1P: $70-$139	2P: $70-$139	XP: $10 F18

Motel

Location: I-74, exit 220 (Lynch Dr), just n, then just e. 361 Lynch Dr 61834. Fax: 217/442-1350. **Facility:** 76 one-bedroom standard units. 3 stories, interior corridors. *Bath:* combo or shower only. **Parking:** on-site. **Terms:** small pets only ($15 deposit, in carrier). **Amenities:** extended cable TV, dual phone lines, voice mail, hair dryers. *Some:* irons. **Pool(s):** heated indoor. **Leisure Activities:** whirlpool, exercise room. **Guest Services:** valet and coin laundry. **Business Services:** meeting rooms, business center, PC, fax (fee). **Cards:** AX, CB, DC, DS, JC, MC, VI.

SOME UNITS

SUPER 8-DANVILLE   Phone: (217)443-4499

All Year	1P: $53-$60	2P: $53-$60

Motel

Location: I-74, exit 220 (Lynch Dr), just n. 377 Lynch Dr 61834. Fax: 217/443-4499. **Facility:** 50 one-bedroom standard units. 2 stories, interior corridors. **Parking:** on-site. **Terms:** pets (in smoking units). **Guest Services:** valet laundry. **Business Services:** fax (fee). **Cards:** AX, DC, DS, MC, VI.

SOME UNITS

DECATUR pop. 83,900

———— **WHERE TO STAY** ————

BAYMONT INN-DECATUR   Phone: (217)875-5800

[AAA] [SAVE]

All Year	1P: $59-$69	2P: $59-$69

Motel

Location: I-72, exit 141B (US 51 N), then s on frontage road. 5100 Hickory Pt Frontage Rd 62526. Fax: 217/875-7537. **Facility:** 102 one-bedroom standard units. 2 stories, interior corridors. **Parking:** on-site, winter plug-ins. **Terms:** small pets only. **Amenities:** extended cable TV, video games, voice mail, irons, hair dryers. **Guest Services:** valet laundry. **Business Services:** meeting rooms. **Cards:** AX, CB, DC, DS, MC, VI. **Special Amenities:** free continental breakfast and free newspaper. *(See color ad opposite title page)*

SOME UNITS

COUNTRY INN & SUITES BY CARLSON   Phone: (217)872-2402

[AAA] [SAVE]

All Year [ECP]	1P: $75-$85	2P: $75-$85	XP: $8 F17

Motel

Location: I-72, exit 141B (US 51 N), then s on frontage road. 5150 Hickory Pt Frontage Rd 62526. Fax: 217/872-2403. **Facility:** 72 one-bedroom standard units, some with whirlpools. 3 stories, interior corridors. *Bath:* combo or shower only. **Parking:** on-site, winter plug-ins. **Amenities:** video games, voice mail, irons, hair dryers. **Pool(s):** indoor. **Leisure Activities:** whirlpool, exercise room. **Guest Services:** valet and coin laundry, area transportation. **Business Services:** meeting rooms. **Cards:** AX, CB, DC, DS, JC, MC, VI. **Special Amenities:** free continental breakfast and free newspaper. *(See color ad p 322)*

SOME UNITS

HAWTHORN SUITES LTD   Phone: (217)864-9311

All Year [BP]	1P: $84-$89	2P: $84-$89

Motel

Location: SR 121, 0.5 mi s from jct US 36. 2370 S Mount Zion Rd 62521. Fax: 217/864-9611. **Facility:** 60 units. 59 one-bedroom standard units, some with efficiencies. 1 one-bedroom suite. 3 stories, interior corridors. *Bath:* combo or shower only. **Parking:** on-site. **Terms:** 14 day cancellation notice-fee imposed. **Amenities:** extended cable TV, dual phone lines, voice mail, irons, hair dryers. **Leisure Activities:** limited exercise equipment. **Guest Services:** complimentary evening beverages: Wed, valet and coin laundry. **Business Services:** meeting rooms. **Cards:** AX, CB, DC, DS, MC, VI.

SOME UNITS

HOLIDAY INN SELECT CONFERENCE HOTEL

Phone: (217)422-8800

AAA [SAVE]
▼▼▼▼

Motor Inn

2/9-3/31	1P: $99	2P: $109	XP: $10	F18
4/1-10/31	1P: $79	2P: $89	XP: $10	F18
11/1-2/8	1P: $59	2P: $69	XP: $10	F18

Location: I-72, exit 133A (US 36), 1 mi e. 4191 W Hwy 36 62522. Fax: 217/422-9690. **Facility:** 370 one-bedroom standard units. 2-4 stories, interior corridors. *Bath:* combo or shower only. **Parking:** on-site, winter plug-ins. **Terms:** check-in 4 pm, cancellation fee imposed. **Amenities:** extended cable TV, high-speed Internet, voice mail, irons, hair dryers. **Dining:** dining room, restaurant, 6 am-10 pm, Fri & Sat-11 pm, $16-$25, cocktails, entertainment. **Pool(s):** heated indoor. **Leisure Activities:** sauna, whirlpools, fishing, tennis court, playground, exercise room, volleyball, domed recreation area, heliport, outdoor pavillion, ping pong, volleyball, tended nature area. *Fee:* game room, billiards. **Business Services:** gift shop, coin laundry, airport transportation-Decatur Municipal Airport, area transportation-within 5 mi. **Business Services:** conference facilities, business center, PC, fax (fee). **Cards:** AX, CB, DC, DS, JC, MC, VI. **Special Amenities:** free newspaper. *(See ad below)*

SOME UNITS

RAMADA LIMITED DECATUR

Phone: (217)876-8011

AAA [SAVE]
▼▼▼

Motor

All Year   1P: $62   2P: $62

Location: I-72, exit 141B (US 51 N), just n, then s on frontage road. 355 E Hickory Pt Rd 62526. Fax: 217/876-8951. **Facility:** 61 one-bedroom standard units, some with whirlpools. 3 stories, interior corridors. *Bath:* combo or shower only. **Parking:** on-site. **Terms:** [ECP] meal plan available, package plans. **Amenities:** voice mail, irons, hair dryers. **Pool(s):** small heated indoor. **Leisure Activities:** whirlpool, limited exercise equipment. **Guest Services:** valet laundry, area transportation. **Cards:** AX, CB, DC, DS, MC, VI. **Special Amenities:** free continental breakfast and free local telephone calls.

SOME UNITS

SLEEP INN OF DECATUR

Phone: (217)872-7700

AAA [SAVE]
▼▼▼

Motor

All Year   1P: $59-$79   XP: $5   F15

Location: I-72, exit 144 (SR 48), just s to Brush College Rd, then just e. 3920 E Hospitality Ln 62521. Fax: 217/872-7711. **Facility:** 69 one-bedroom standard units. 3 stories, interior corridors. *Bath:* combo or shower only. **Parking:** on-site. **Terms:** 14 day cancellation notice. **Amenities:** extended cable TV, voice mail, irons, hair dryers. **Pool(s):** heated indoor. **Leisure Activities:** whirlpool, exercise room. **Guest Services:** coin laundry. **Business Services:** meeting rooms, business center, PC, fax. **Cards:** AX, DC, DS, MC, VI. **Special Amenities:** free continental breakfast and free room upgrade (subject to availability with advanced reservations).

SOME UNITS

SUPER 8 MOTEL-DECATUR

Phone: (217)877-8888

▼
Motel

All Year [CP]   1P: $50   2P: $55

Location: I-72, exit 141A (US 51 S), 1.8 mi s. 3141 N Water St 62526. Fax: 217/887-8888. **Facility:** 58 one-bedroom standard units. 3 stories (no elevator), interior corridors. **Parking:** on-site. **Terms:** small pets only ($10 fee). **Amenities:** extended cable TV, safes (fee). **Guest Services:** coin laundry. **Business Services:** meeting rooms. **Cards:** AX, DC, DS, MC, VI.

SOME UNITS

DEERFIELD —See *Chicago p. 332.*

DEKALB pop. 34,900

─────── **WHERE TO STAY** ───────

BAYMONT INNS & SUITES DEKALB/SYCAMORE
Phone: (815)748-4800

(AAA) (SAVE)
All Year [ECP]　　　　1P: $89-$109　　　2P: $99-$129　　　XP: $10　　　F18
▼▼▼▼　**Location:** I-88, exit Annie Glidden Rd, 2 mi n to W Lincoln Hwy (SR 38), 0.4 mi w. 1314 W Lincoln Hwy 60115.
Motel　　Fax: 815/756-5047. **Facility:** 53 units. 50 one-bedroom standard units. 3 one-bedroom suites ($109-$159)
with whirlpools. 3 stories, interior corridors. *Bath:* combo or shower only. **Parking:** on-site. **Amenities:** extended cable TV, video games (fee), dual phone lines, voice mail, irons, hair dryers. **Pool(s):** small heated
indoor. **Leisure Activities:** exercise room. **Guest Services:** valet and coin laundry. **Business Services:**
meeting rooms. **Cards:** AX, CB, DC, DS, MC, VI. **Special Amenities:** free continental breakfast and free newspaper.

SOME UNITS

[icons] FEE

BEST WESTERN DEKALB INN & SUITES
Phone: (815)758-8661

(AAA) (SAVE)
All Year　　　　1P: $79-$89　　　2P: $79-$89　　　XP: $5　　　F18
▼▼▼▼　**Location:** I-88, exit Annie Glidden Rd, 2 mi n to W Lincoln Hwy (SR 38), then just w. 1212 W Lincoln Hwy 60115.
Motel　　Fax: 815/758-0001. **Facility:** 95 units. 76 one-bedroom standard units, some with whirlpools. 19 one-bedroom suites ($99-$140) with kitchens. 2 stories, interior/exterior corridors. *Bath:* combo or shower only.
Parking: on-site. **Terms:** [CP] meal plan available, package plans, small pets only ($10 fee, in limited units).
Amenities: video games, dual phone lines, voice mail, irons, hair dryers. **Pool(s):** heated outdoor. **Leisure
Activities:** sauna, exercise room. **Guest Services:** valet and coin laundry. **Business Services:** conference facilities, business
center, fax (fee). **Cards:** AX, CB, DC, DS, JC, MC, VI. **Special Amenities:** free continental breakfast and free local telephone
calls.

SOME UNITS

[icons] FEE

─────── **WHERE TO DINE** ───────

YEN CHING　　　　　　**Lunch:** $5-$13　　　**Dinner:** $7-$13　　　**Phone:** 815/758-2007
▼▼▼ ▼▼▼　**Location:** I-88, exit Annie Glidden Rd, 2 mi n to W Lincoln Hwy (SR 38), just e. 810 W Lincoln Hwy 60115. **Hours:** 11
Chinese　　am-9 pm, Fri & Sat-10 pm. Closed: 11/28, 12/25. **Reservations:** accepted. **Features:** casual dress;
carryout; cocktails & lounge; a la carte. Large stone lion statuettes are perched near the entry of this
well-established restaurant. An intimate atmosphere with a colorful oriental decor featuring attractive art, a
large black colored figurine of Buddha and a lattice-design wall await you at Yen Ching. The service is friendly and the menu
comprises an extensive selection of traditional Mandarin and Szechwan dishes. Many beers and wines are offered. **Parking:**
on-site. **Cards:** AX, DS, MC, VI.

[icon]

DES PLAINES —See *Chicago p. 334.*

DIXON pop. 15,100

─────── **WHERE TO STAY** ───────

BEST WESTERN BRANDYWINE LODGE
Phone: (815)284-1890

(AAA) (SAVE)
1/1-3/31　　　　1P: $63-$67　　　2P: $72-$76　　　XP: $7　　　F17
▼▼ ▼▼　4/1-12/31　　　　1P: $61-$65　　　2P: $70-$74　　　XP: $7　　　F17
Motor Inn　　**Location:** SR 2, 3.6 mi w of jct SR 26. 443 Illinois Rt 2 61021. Fax: 815/284-1174. **Facility:** 89 units. 85 one-bedroom standard units, some with whirlpools. 4 one-bedroom suites ($115-$180). 2 stories, interior corridors. **Parking:** on-site, winter plug-ins. **Terms:** pets ($25 deposit). **Amenities:** extended cable TV, irons, hair
dryers. **Dining:** dining room, coffee shop, 6:30 am-9 pm, Sun-2 pm, Mon from 11 am, $6-$15, cocktails.
Pool(s): heated outdoor. **Business Services:** meeting rooms. **Cards:** AX, CB, DC, DS, JC, MC, VI. **Special Amenities:** free
local telephone calls and free newspaper.

SOME UNITS

[icons] FEE FEE FEE

COMFORT INN
Phone: (815)284-0500

(AAA) (SAVE)
All Year [ECP]　　　　1P: $59-$70　　　2P: $64-$74　　　XP: $5　　　F18
▼▼▼▼　**Location:** I-88, exit SR 26, just n, then just e. 136 Plaza Dr 61021. Fax: 815/284-0509. **Facility:** 48 units. 45 one-bedroom standard units, some with whirlpools. 3 one-bedroom suites ($83-$104). 2 stories, interior corridors.
Motel　　*Bath:* combo or shower only. **Parking:** on-site. **Terms:** package plans, pets ($100 deposit). **Amenities:** extended cable TV, voice mail, hair dryers. *Some:* dual phone lines, irons. **Pool(s):** small heated indoor.
Leisure Activities: exercise room. **Guest Services:** coin laundry. **Business Services:** meeting rooms.
Cards: AX, CB, DC, DS, JC, MC, VI. **Special Amenities:** free continental breakfast and free local telephone calls.

SOME UNITS

[icons]

DOWNERS GROVE —See *Chicago p. 335.*

DU QUOIN pop. 6,700

─────── **WHERE TO STAY** ───────

FRANCIE'S INN ON LINE
Phone: (618)542-6686

▼▼▼ ▼▼▼
All Year [BP]　　　　1P: $60-$85　　　2P: $70-$95　　　XP: $10　　　F8
Location: 0.4 mi e of US 51 via Poplar St. 104 S Line St 62832. Fax: 618/542-4834. **Facility:** Designated smoking
Historic Bed　　area. 6 one-bedroom standard units. 3 stories, interior corridors. *Bath:* some shared or private. **Parking:** on-
& Breakfast　　site. **Terms:** 10 day cancellation notice-fee imposed. **Amenities:** extended cable TV. **Leisure Activities:** bicycles, horseshoes. **Guest Services:** valet laundry. **Business Services:** meeting rooms. **Cards:** AX, DC,
DS, MC, VI.

SOME UNITS

[icons] [VCR]

EAST CAPE GIRARDEAU pop. 500

———— WHERE TO DINE ————

JOEY'S RESTAURANT **Lunch:** $4-$6 **Dinner:** $4-$6 **Phone:** 618/661-1644
American
Location: SR 146, 0.7 mi e from Mississippi River. 107 Iriquois 62957. **Hours:** 7 am-8 pm, Sun-2 pm. Closed major holidays; also Mon. **Reservations:** accepted. **Features:** casual dress; children's menu. Family comfort food such as fried chicken, roast beef, sandwiches, spaghetti, catfish and homemade dessert is served in a casual and comfortable atmosphere. The service staff is friendly. Fried catfish specials are offered Friday and Saturday night. **Parking:** on-site. **Cards:** MC, VI.

EAST DUBUQUE pop. 1,900

———— WHERE TO DINE ————

TIMMERMAN'S SUPPER CLUB **Dinner:** $12-$25 **Phone:** 815/747-3316
American
Location: Just s off SR 20 E. 7777 Timmerman Dr 61025. **Hours:** 4:30 pm-9:30 pm, Fri & Sat-10 pm, Sun 10 am-2 & 4:30-9 pm. Closed: 12/24, 12/25. **Reservations:** suggested. **Features:** casual dress; Sunday brunch; cocktails & lounge; a la carte. On a bluff high above the Mississippi River, you can enjoy prime steak, fresh seafood, tasty pasta and creative poultry dishes while dining in casual elegance. You will find the servers to be as professional as they look in their black slacks, white formal dress shirt, maroon cummerbunds and bow ties. **Parking:** on-site. **Cards:** AX, DS, MC, VI.

EAST PEORIA pop. 21,400—*See also PEORIA.*

———— WHERE TO STAY ————

BAYMONT INN & SUITES-EAST PEORIA **Phone:** (309)694-4959
[AAA] [SAVE]
All Year 1P: $69 2P: $69 XP: $10 F18
[diamond][diamond][diamond]
Motel
Location: I-74, exit 95A (Main St), 0.4 mi w to Venture Dr, just s to E Light Ct, then just e. 300 Eastlight Ct 61611. Fax: 309/694-4727. **Facility:** 85 one-bedroom standard units, some with whirlpools. 4 stories, interior corridors. *Bath:* combo or shower only. **Parking:** on-site. **Terms:** [ECP] meal plan available. **Amenities:** extended cable TV, video games, voice mail, irons, hair dryers. **Pool(s):** indoor. **Leisure Activities:** sun deck, exercise room. **Guest Services:** valet and coin laundry. **Business Services:** meeting rooms. **Cards:** AX, CB, DC, DS, MC, VI. **Special Amenities:** free continental breakfast and free newspaper.

SOME UNITS

HAMPTON INN **Phone:** (309)694-0711
[SAVE]
All Year 1P: $72-$102 2P: $82-$112 XP: $10
[diamond][diamond][diamond]
Motel
Location: I-74, exit 95B, just e. 11 Winner's Way 61611. Fax: 309/694-0407. **Facility:** 154 one-bedroom standard units. 5 stories, interior corridors. **Parking:** on-site, winter plug-ins. **Terms:** [ECP] meal plan available. **Amenities:** extended cable TV, high-speed Internet, voice mail, irons, hair dryers. **Pool(s):** heated indoor. **Leisure Activities:** whirlpool, exercise room. **Guest Services:** valet laundry. **Business Services:** meeting rooms. **Cards:** AX, DC, DS, MC, VI.

SOME UNITS

MOTEL 6 **Phone:** 309/699-7281
[diamond]
Motel
Property failed to provide current rates
Location: I-74, exit 95A (Main St), 0.3 mi w. 104 W Camp St 61611. Fax: 309/694-7636. **Facility:** 78 one-bedroom standard units. 2 stories, interior corridors. *Bath:* shower only. **Parking:** on-site. **Amenities:** extended cable TV. **Pool(s):** outdoor. **Cards:** AX, DC, DS, MC, VI.

SOME UNITS

SUPER 8 MOTEL **Phone:** (309)698-8889
[diamond][diamond][diamond]
Motel
All Year [ECP] 1P: $47-$67 2P: $52-$72 XP: $6 F12
Location: I-74, exit 96, just e. 725 Taylor St 61611. Fax: 309/698-8885. **Facility:** 64 one-bedroom standard units. 3 stories, interior corridors. **Parking:** on-site, winter plug-ins. **Amenities:** extended cable TV. *Some:* hair dryers. **Cards:** AX, CB, DC, DS, MC, VI.

SOME UNITS

EFFINGHAM pop. 11,900

———— WHERE TO STAY ————

BEST WESTERN RAINTREE INN **Phone:** (217)342-4121
[AAA] [SAVE]
All Year 1P: $42-$55 2P: $48-$65 XP: $9 F18
[diamond][diamond]
Motel
Location: I-57/70, exit 159. 1811 W Fayette Ave 62401 (PO Box 663). Fax: 217/342-4121. **Facility:** 65 one-bedroom standard units. 2 stories, interior/exterior corridors. **Parking:** on-site, winter plug-ins. **Terms:** 10 day cancellation notice, pets (in smoking units). **Amenities:** extended cable TV, irons, hair dryers. **Pool(s):** outdoor. **Guest Services:** valet laundry. **Business Services:** fax (fee). **Cards:** AX, CB, DC, DS, MC, VI. **Special Amenities:** free continental breakfast and free newspaper.

SOME UNITS

COMFORT INN

Motel

Phone: (217)347-5050

All Year [ECP]   1P: $48-$75   2P: $48-$75   XP: $6   F18

Location: I-57/70, exit 160, just e, then just n. 1304 W Evergreen Dr 62401. Fax: 217/347-5084. **Facility:** 61 one-bedroom standard units, some with whirlpools. 2 stories, interior corridors. *Bath:* combo or shower only. **Parking:** on-site. **Terms:** 10 day cancellation notice, small pets only (in smoking units). **Amenities:** extended cable TV, safes (fee). *Some:* irons, hair dryers. **Pool(s):** heated indoor. **Leisure Activities:** sauna, whirlpool, exercise room. **Guest Services:** valet laundry. **Business Services:** meeting rooms, fax (fee). **Cards:** AX, CB, DC, DS, JC, MC, VI. **Special Amenities: free continental breakfast and free newspaper.** *(See ad below)*

SOME UNITS

COMFORT SUITES

Motel

Phone: (217)342-3151

All Year   1P: $55-$89   2P: $59-$89   XP: $6   F18

Location: I-57/70, exit 159, 0.4 mi e. 1310 W Fayette Ave 62401 (PO Box 1168). Fax: 217/342-3555. **Facility:** 65 one-bedroom standard units, some with whirlpools. 3 stories, interior corridors. *Bath:* combo or shower only. **Parking:** on-site. **Terms:** 10 day cancellation notice, pets (in smoking units). **Amenities:** extended cable TV, voice mail, safes, irons, hair dryers. **Leisure Activities:** sauna. **Guest Services:** valet and coin laundry. **Business Services:** meeting rooms, fax (fee). **Cards:** AX, CB, DC, DS, MC, VI. **Special Amenities: free continental breakfast and preferred room (subject to availability with advanced reservations).**

SOME UNITS

DAYS INN

Motel

Phone: (217)342-9271

4/1-10/15   1P: $49   2P: $69   XP: $5   F18
10/16-3/31   1P: $39   2P: $59   XP: $5   F18

Location: I-57/70, exit 159, just e. 1412 W Fayette Ave 62401 (PO Box 626). Fax: 217/342-5850. **Facility:** 115 one-bedroom standard units, some with whirlpools. **Parking:** on-site. **Terms:** pets (in smoking units). **Amenities:** extended cable TV. *Some:* irons, hair dryers. **Pool(s):** outdoor. **Business Services:** meeting rooms, fax (fee). **Cards:** AX, DC, DS, MC, VI. **Special Amenities: early check-in/late check-out and free continental breakfast.**

SOME UNITS

FEE FEE

HAMPTON INN

Motel

Phone: (217)342-4499

All Year   1P: $62-$79   2P: $66-$84

Location: I-57/70, exit 160, just s. 1509 Hampton Dr 62401 (PO Box 666). Fax: 217/347-2828. **Facility:** 62 one-bedroom standard units, some with whirlpools. 2 stories, interior corridors. *Bath:* combo or shower only. **Parking:** on-site, winter plug-ins. **Terms:** 10 day cancellation notice, small pets only (in smoking units). **Amenities:** extended cable TV, voice mail, irons, hair dryers. **Pool(s):** heated indoor. **Guest Services:** valet laundry. **Business Services:** meeting rooms, fax (fee). **Cards:** AX, CB, DC, DS, MC, VI.

SOME UNITS

FEE FEE

HOLIDAY INN EXPRESS

Motel

Phone: (217)540-1111

All Year   1P: $69-$139   2P: $69-$139   XP: $10   F18

Location: I-57/70, exit 160 (SR 32/33), just n. 1103 Ave of Mid-America 62401. Fax: 217/347-7341. **Facility:** 118 one-bedroom standard units, some with whirlpools. 4 stories, interior corridors. *Bath:* combo or shower only. **Parking:** on-site, winter plug-ins. **Terms:** small pets only. **Amenities:** extended cable TV, dual phone lines, voice mail, irons, hair dryers. **Pool(s):** small heated indoor. **Leisure Activities:** exercise room. **Guest Services:** valet and coin laundry. **Business Services:** meeting rooms, fax. **Cards:** AX, DC, DS, MC, VI.

SOME UNITS

KELLER INN

Motel

Phone: (217)342-2131

All Year [CP]   1P: $75-$149   2P: $75-$149   XP: $7   F18

Location: I-57/70, exit 160 (SR 32/33), just ne. 1201 N Keller Dr 62401 (PO Box 747). Fax: 217/347-8757. **Facility:** 162 units. 153 one-bedroom standard units, some with whirlpools. 9 one-bedroom suites, some with whirlpools. 2 stories, interior/exterior corridors. **Parking:** on-site, winter plug-ins. **Terms:** pets (in smoking units). **Amenities:** extended cable TV, voice mail, irons, hair dryers. **Pool(s):** heated outdoor, heated indoor. **Leisure Activities:** sauna, whirlpool, playground. *Fee:* miniature golf, game room. **Guest Services:** massage (fee), valet laundry. **Business Services:** conference facilities. **Cards:** AX, CB, DC, DS, MC, VI.

SOME UNITS

FEE FEE

PARADISE INN

Motel

All Year	1P: $29-$33	2P: $34-$39	XP: $5	F12

Phone: 217/342-2165

Location: I-57/70, exit 159, 1 mi e. 1000 W Fayette Ave 62401. Fax: 217/347-3373. **Facility:** 33 one-bedroom standard units. 1 story, exterior corridors. **Parking:** on-site. **Terms:** cancellation fee imposed, pets ($5 extra charge, with prior approval). **Amenities:** extended cable TV. **Cards:** AX, CB, DC, DS, JC, MC, VI. **Special Amenities:** free local telephone calls and preferred room (subject to availability with advanced reservations).

SOME UNITS

SUPER 8 MOTEL
Motel

All Year	1P: $48-$68	2P: $56-$76	XP: $6	F12

Phone: (217)342-6888

Location: I-57/70, exit 160 (SR 32/33), 0.5 mi n. 1400 Thelma Keller Ave 62401. Fax: 217/347-2863. **Facility:** 49 one-bedroom standard units. 2 stories, interior corridors. **Parking:** on-site. **Amenities:** extended cable TV, safes. **Cards:** AX, CB, DC, DS, MC, VI.

SOME UNITS

TRAVELODGE & SUITES

Motel

4/1-9/30	1P: $39-$49	2P: $49-$59	XP: $6	F18
10/1-3/31	1P: $35-$45	2P: $39-$49	XP: $6	F18

Phone: (217)347-7515

Location: I-57/70, exit 160, just n. 1205A N Keller Dr 62401. Fax: 217/347-3339. **Facility:** 39 one-bedroom standard units. 2 stories, interior corridors. **Parking:** on-site, winter plug-ins. **Amenities:** extended cable TV, dual phone lines, safes (fee), irons, hair dryers. **Leisure Activities:** pool privileges, playground, exercise room, basketball, volleyball. **Guest Services:** coin laundry. **Business Services:** fax (fee). **Cards:** AX, DC, DS, JC, MC, VI. **Special Amenities:** early check-in/late check-out and free continental breakfast.

SOME UNITS

——— WHERE TO DINE ———

NIEMERG'S STEAK HOUSE
American

Lunch: $4-$8   **Dinner:** $5-$13   **Phone:** 217/342-3921

Location: I-57/70, exit 159, just s. 1410 W Fayette Ave 62401. **Hours:** 6 am-2 am, Sun-midnight. Closed: 12/25. **Features:** casual dress; children's menu; early bird specials; carryout; salad bar; cocktails & lounge. All American staples—fried chicken, seafood, steak, syrupy sundaes and homemade pies—entice families to the friendly, comfortable restaurant. A cozy coffee shop, decorated with grapevines and flowers, sits adjacent to the main dining room. **Parking:** on-site. **Cards:** AX, DC, MC, VI.

REXROATS
American

Lunch: $6   **Dinner:** $8-$25   **Phone:** 217/347-5831

Location: Banker and Jefferson sts. 221 W Jefferson St 62401. **Hours:** 11 am-2 & 5-9 pm, Fri-10 pm, Sat 5 pm-10 pm. Closed major holidays; also Sun. **Reservations:** accepted. **Features:** casual dress; children's menu; carryout; salad bar; cocktails; a la carte. A classic small town restaurant in a downtown building serving Midwestern favorites with an emphasis on steak and seafood. The lunch buffet is locally popular with the business community and the dinner menu is a favorite for a special night out. **Parking:** street. **Cards:** AX, DC, DS, MC, VI.

TRAILWAYS RESTAURANT
American

Lunch: $6   **Dinner:** $5-$14   **Phone:** 217/342-2680

Location: I-57/70, exit 162 (US 45), just n. 2402 N 3rd St 62401. **Hours:** 6 am-9 pm, Fri & Sat-9:30 pm. Closed: 12/25. **Reservations:** accepted. **Features:** casual dress; children's menu; carryout; salad bar; a la carte. Casual, country dining is what you'll discover at Trailways. The menu features such palate-pleasers as fried chicken, steak, cod, catfish, pork chops and hickory-smoked barbecued ribs. The atmosphere is comfortable and contemporary with lots of pictures. The lunch buffet is a local favorite. **Parking:** on-site. **Cards:** AX, DS, MC, VI.

ELGIN —See Chicago p. 335.

ELK GROVE VILLAGE —See Chicago p. 337.

ELMHURST —See Chicago p. 338.

ELSAH pop. 900

——— WHERE TO DINE ———

ELSAH LANDING RESTAURANT Historical
American

Lunch: $6-$10   **Dinner:** $6-$10   **Phone:** 618/786-7687

Location: At south edge of town; in the Brainerd House Bed & Breakfast. 420 E Main St 62037. **Hours:** 11:30 am-7:30 pm. Closed major holidays; also Mon & 12/23-1/2. **Features:** carryout. The charming, comfortable restaurant is known for its four S's: soup, salad, sandwiches and sensational desserts. Everything is made on the premises, including an award winning, mouthwatering mountain berry pie. Smoke free premises. **Parking:** on-site. **Cards:** MC, VI.

EVANSTON —See Chicago p. 339.

FAIRFIELD pop. 5,400

——— WHERE TO STAY ———

GLASS DOOR INN BED & BREAKFAST   **Phone:** (618)847-4512
▼▼▼   All Year   1P: $52-$65   2P: $58-$72   XP: $8
Bed & Breakfast   **Location:** Jct US 45 and SR 15, 2.3 mi e on SR 15, 0.5 mi n on CR 2090 E. RR 3, Box 101 62837. **Facility:** This contemporary home in a rural setting offers flower gardens, fountains, individually decorated rooms and 70 acres of open fields. Smoke free premises. 4 one-bedroom standard units. 2 stories, interior corridors. *Bath:* combo or shower only. **Parking:** on-site. **Terms:** age restrictions may apply, cancellation fee imposed, [ECP] meal plan available. **Amenities:** hair dryers. **Leisure Activities:** whirlpool, paddleboats, fishing, hiking trails. **Business Services:** fax. **Cards:** DS, MC, VI.

SOME UNITS

$\boxed{S_D}$ $\boxed{\otimes}$ $\boxed{\times}$ $\boxed{\text{DATA PORT}}$ $\boxed{\text{🖨}}$ / $\boxed{VCR}$ /

FAIRVIEW HEIGHTS pop. 14,400

——— WHERE TO STAY ———

DRURY INN-FAIRVIEW HEIGHTS   **Phone:** (618)398-8530
▼▼▼ ▼▼▼   All Year [ECP]   1P: $78-$108   2P: $78-$108   XP: $10   F18
▼▼ ▼▼
Motel   **Location:** I-64, exit 12 (SR 159). 12 Ludwig Dr 62208. Fax: 618/398-8530. **Facility:** 102 one-bedroom standard units. 4 stories, interior corridors. **Parking:** on-site. **Amenities:** dual phone lines, voice mail, irons, hair dryers. **Pool(s):** outdoor. **Leisure Activities:** exercise room. **Guest Services:** complimentary evening beverages: Mon-Thurs, valet and coin laundry. **Business Services:** meeting rooms. **Cards:** AX, CB, DC, DS, MC, VI.
(See color ad p 5)

SOME UNITS

$\boxed{🛏}$ $\boxed{\text{¶⊹}}$ $\boxed{\text{🏊}}$ $\boxed{\text{📺}}$ $\boxed{\text{DATA PORT}}$ $\boxed{\text{🖥}}$ $\boxed{\text{🖨}}$ / $\boxed{\times}$ $\boxed{🚽}$ $\boxed{\text{🍴}}$ /

FAIRFIELD INN BY MARRIOTT   **Phone:** (618)398-7124
(AAA) [SAVE]   All Year   1P: $65-$85   2P: $70-$90   XP: $5   F18
▼▼▼ ▼▼▼
Motel   **Location:** I-64, exit 12 (SR 159), 1 mi nw. 140 Ludwig Dr 62208. Fax: 618/398-7124. **Facility:** 63 one-bedroom standard units. 3 stories, interior corridors. *Bath:* combo or shower only. **Parking:** on-site, interior plug-ins. **Amenities:** extended cable TV. **Pool(s):** small heated indoor. **Leisure Activities:** whirlpool. **Guest Services:** valet laundry. **Cards:** AX, DC, DS, MC, VI. **Special Amenities:** free continental breakfast and free local telephone calls.

SOME UNITS

$\boxed{S_D}$ $\boxed{\text{¶⊹}}$ $\boxed{\text{&M}}$ $\boxed{\text{📺}}$ $\boxed{\text{🏊}}$ $\boxed{\text{🏊}}$ $\boxed{\text{🖨}}$ / $\boxed{\times}$ $\boxed{🚽}$ $\boxed{\text{🍴}}$ /
                                        FEE

HAMPTON INN FAIRVIEW HEIGHTS   **Phone:** (618)397-9705
[SAVE]   5/1-8/31   1P: $69-$84   2P: $74-$89   XP: $5   F18
▼▼▼   4/1-4/30 & 9/1-3/31   1P: $65-$79   2P: $70-$84   XP: $5   F18
Motel   **Location:** I-64, exit 12 (SR 159), 1 mi nw. 150 Ludwig Dr 62208. Fax: 618/397-7829. **Facility:** 63 one-bedroom standard units. 3 stories, interior corridors. *Bath:* combo or shower only. **Parking:** on-site. **Amenities:** extended cable TV, voice mail, irons. **Pool(s):** small heated indoor. **Leisure Activities:** whirlpool. **Guest Services:** valet laundry. **Cards:** AX, DC, DS, MC, VI.

SOME UNITS

$\boxed{S_D}$ $\boxed{\text{&M}}$ $\boxed{\text{♿}}$ $\boxed{\text{📢}}$ $\boxed{\text{🏊}}$ $\boxed{\text{📺}}$ $\boxed{\text{DATA PORT}}$ $\boxed{\text{🖥}}$ $\boxed{\text{🖨}}$ / $\boxed{\times}$ $\boxed{🚽}$ $\boxed{\text{🍴}}$ /
                                        FEE

RAMADA INN FAIRVIEW HEIGHTS   **Phone:** (618)632-4747
(AAA) [SAVE]   5/24-9/21 [ECP]   1P: $79   2P: $89   XP: $9   F18
▼▼▼ ▼▼▼   4/26-5/23 [ECP]   1P: $67   2P: $77   XP: $9   F18
Motor Inn   9/22-3/31 [ECP]   1P: $62   2P: $72   XP: $9   F18
           4/1-4/25 [ECP]   1P: $59   2P: $69   XP: $9   F18
Location: I-64, exit 12 (SR 159), just n. 6900 N Illinois Ave 62208. Fax: 618/632-9428. **Facility:** 159 one-bedroom standard units, some with whirlpools. 5 stories, interior corridors. **Parking:** on-site, winter plug-ins. **Terms:** small pets only ($10 extra charge). **Amenities:** voice mail, irons. *Some:* hair dryers. **Dining:** restaurant, 11 am-2 am, $6-$15, nightclub, entertainment. **Leisure Activities:** exercise room. *Fee:* video games. **Guest Services:** valet and coin laundry. **Business Services:** conference facilities. **Cards:** AX, CB, DC, DS, JC, MC, VI. **Special Amenities:** free continental breakfast and free local telephone calls.

SOME UNITS

$\boxed{S_D}$ $\boxed{🛏}$ $\boxed{\text{🍴}}$ $\boxed{\text{📺}}$ $\boxed{\text{DATA PORT}}$ $\boxed{\text{🖥}}$ $\boxed{\text{🖨}}$ / $\boxed{\times}$ $\boxed{🚽}$ $\boxed{\text{🍴}}$ /
                                        FEE   FEE

SUPER 8 MOTEL   **Phone:** (618)398-8338
▼▼▼ ▼▼▼   All Year [ECP]   1P: $50-$71   2P: $56-$77   XP: $6   F12
▼▼
Motel   **Location:** I-64, exit 12 (SR 159). 45 Ludwig Dr 62208. Fax: 618/398-8158. **Facility:** 81 one-bedroom standard units. 3 stories, interior corridors. **Parking:** on-site. **Terms:** check-in 4 pm, pets (in carriers, with prior approval). **Amenities:** extended cable TV, safes. **Guest Services:** coin laundry. **Business Services:** meeting rooms. **Cards:** AX, CB, DC, DS, MC, VI.

SOME UNITS

$\boxed{ASK}$ $\boxed{S_D}$ $\boxed{🛏}$ $\boxed{\text{¶⊹}}$ $\boxed{\text{📺}}$ $\boxed{🚽}$ / $\boxed{\times}$ $\boxed{\text{DATA PORT}}$ $\boxed{🚽}$ $\boxed{\text{🍴}}$ /
                                        FEE   FEE   FEE

——— WHERE TO DINE ———

LOTAWATA CREEK SOUTHERN GRILL   **Lunch:** $10-$19   **Dinner:** $10-$19   **Phone:** 618/628-7373   (117)
▼▼▼   **Location:** I-64, exit 12 (SR 159), just n. 311 Salem Pl 62208. **Hours:** 11 am-10 pm, Fri & Sat-11 pm. Closed:
Regional American   11/28, 12/25. **Features:** casual dress; children's menu; cocktails & lounge; a la carte. Traditional Southern food served in a casual setting is what you'll find, along with lots of country-fried items and blackened Cajun fare. The quality is consistently high, especially among the hand-cut beef and homemade bread and dessert. **Parking:** on-site. **Cards:** AX, CB, DC, DS, MC, VI.

$\boxed{\times}$

FORSYTH pop. 1,300

——— WHERE TO STAY ———

COMFORT INN OF FORSYTH
Phone: (217)875-1166

SAVE

▼▼▼

Motel

4/1-10/31	1P: $52-$57	2P: $57-$62	XP: $5 F18
11/1-3/31	1P: $49-$55	2P: $54-$60	XP: $5 F18

Location: I-72, exit 141B (US 51), 0.5 mi n. 134 Barnett Ave 62535. **Fax:** 217/875-1166. **Facility:** 56 one-bedroom standard units. 2 stories, interior corridors. **Parking:** on-site, winter plug-ins. **Terms:** 7 day cancellation notice, small pets only ($10 deposit). **Amenities:** extended cable TV. *Some:* irons, hair dryers. **Pool(s):** heated indoor. **Leisure Activities:** whirlpool. **Guest Services:** valet laundry. **Cards:** AX, CB, DC, DS, JC, MC, VI.

SOME UNITS

FAIRFIELD INN BY MARRIOTT
Phone: (217)875-3337

(AAA) **SAVE**

▼▼▼

Motel

All Year ... 1P: $59-$75 ... 2P: $59-$75

Location: I-72, exit 141B (US 51), 0.5 mi n. 1417 Hickory Point Dr 62535. **Fax:** 217/875-3337. **Facility:** 62 one-bedroom standard units. 3 stories, interior corridors. **Parking:** on-site, winter plug-ins. **Amenities:** extended cable TV, irons. **Pool(s):** heated indoor. **Leisure Activities:** whirlpool. **Guest Services:** valet laundry. **Cards:** AX, DC, DS, MC, VI. **Special Amenities:** free continental breakfast and free local telephone calls. *(See color ad card insert)*

SOME UNITS

HAMPTON INN
Phone: (217)877-5577

SAVE

▼▼▼

Motel

All Year ... 1P: $59-$69 ... 2P: $64-$74 ... XP: $5 F18

Location: I-72, exit 141B (US 51), 0.5 mi n. 1429 Hickory Point Dr 62535. **Fax:** 217/877-9963. **Facility:** 61 one-bedroom standard units. 3 stories, interior corridors. **Parking:** on-site. **Terms:** 5 day cancellation notice. **Amenities:** extended cable TV, voice mail, irons. **Pool(s):** heated indoor. **Leisure Activities:** whirlpool. **Guest Services:** valet laundry. **Business Services:** meeting rooms. **Cards:** AX, CB, DC, DS, JC, MC, VI.

SOME UNITS

FRANKLIN PARK —See Chicago p. 340.

FREEPORT pop. 25,800

——— WHERE TO STAY ———

AMERIHOST INN & SUITES-FREEPORT
Phone: (815)599-8510

(AAA) **SAVE**

▼▼▼

Motel

All Year [ECP] ... 1P: $64-$175 ... 2P: $64-$175 ... XP: $6 F18

Location: Jct US 20 Bypass and SR 26, just s. 1060 Riverside Dr 61032. **Fax:** 815/599-8610. **Facility:** 64 one-bedroom standard units, some with whirlpools. 3 stories, interior corridors. *Bath:* combo or shower only. **Parking:** on-site. **Terms:** package plans. **Amenities:** extended cable TV, voice mail, safes (fee), irons, hair dryers. **Pool(s):** heated indoor. **Leisure Activities:** whirlpool, exercise room. **Guest Services:** valet laundry. **Business Services:** meeting rooms. **Cards:** AX, CB, DC, DS, JC, MC, VI. **Special Amenities:** free continental breakfast and free newspaper.

SOME UNITS

FEE ... FEE FEE

COUNTRY INN & SUITES BY CARLSON
Phone: (815)233-3300

▼▼▼

Motel

All Year [BP] ... 1P: $71-$76 ... 2P: $77-$82 ... XP: $6 F18

Location: Jct SR 26 and South Ave, just w. 1710 S Dirck Dr 61032. **Fax:** 815/233-3333. **Facility:** 66 one-bedroom standard units, some with whirlpools. 2 stories, interior corridors. *Bath:* combo or shower only. **Parking:** on-site. **Amenities:** extended cable TV, irons, hair dryers. *Some:* dual phone lines. **Pool(s):** small heated indoor. **Leisure Activities:** whirlpool, exercise room. **Guest Services:** valet and coin laundry. **Business Services:** meeting rooms. **Cards:** AX, DC, DS, MC, VI. *(See color ad p 322)*

SOME UNITS

FEE ... FEE FEE

——— WHERE TO DINE ———

COPPERFIELD INN FAMILY RESTAURANT
Lunch: $6-$11 ... Dinner: $6-$11 ... Phone: 815/235-2466

▼▼ ▼▼

American

Location: Jct Business Rt and Bypass US 20 W. 2051 AYP Rd 61032. **Hours:** 6 am-9 pm. Closed major holidays. **Reservations:** accepted. **Features:** casual dress; Sunday brunch; children's menu; carryout; a la carte, buffet. With its rural location on the northwest side of town and its traditional American comfort food menu, there is a certain down-home, country casual feel to Copperfield. They offer fried chicken and catfish, steak and shrimp as well as a breakfast menu which is served all day long. **Parking:** on-site. **Cards:** MC, VI.

IMPERIAL PALACE
Lunch: $4-$6 ... Dinner: $6-$12 ... Phone: 815/233-5944

▼▼ ▼▼

Traditional Chinese

Location: Just s of South St, 1.2 mi e of SR 26. 1735 Ihm Blvd 61032. **Hours:** 11 am-2:30 & 5-10 pm, Fri-11 pm, Sat 11 am-11 pm, Sun noon-9 pm. Closed major holidays. **Reservations:** accepted. **Features:** casual dress; children's menu; carryout; cocktails. The menu at Imperial Palace represents various Chinese influences such as Mandarin, Szechuan and Hunan as well as traditional American fare and a number of choices for children. You will find the dining room to be bright and colorful with cheerful red and gold tones throughout. **Parking:** on-site. **Cards:** DS, MC, VI.

GALENA pop. 3,600

──── WHERE TO STAY ────

BELLE AIRE MANSION

Phone: (815)777-0893

All Year [BP]	1P: $90-$180	2P: $95-$185	XP: $10	F12

Historic Bed & Breakfast

Location: 2.5 mi w on US 20. 11410 Rt 20 NW 61036. **Facility:** Fireplaces are featured in three guest rooms at this 1834 farmhouse, which has children in residence. Smoke free premises. 5 units. 4 one-bedroom standard units, some with whirlpools. 1 one-bedroom suite with whirlpool. 2 stories, interior corridors. *Bath:* combo or shower only. **Parking:** on-site. **Terms:** check-in 4 pm, 7 day cancellation notice, no pets allowed (small dog on premises). **Amenities:** video tape library. *Some:* CD players, hair dryers. **Cards:** DS, MC, VI.

SOME UNITS

BEST WESTERN QUIET HOUSE SUITES

Phone: (815)777-2577

All Year	1P: $91	2P: $211	XP: $10	F16

Motel

Location: On US 20, 1 mi e. 9915 US 20 W 61036. Fax: 815/777-0584. **Facility:** 42 units. 41 one-bedroom standard units, some with whirlpools. 1 one-bedroom suite. 3 stories (no elevator), interior/exterior corridors. **Parking:** on-site. **Terms:** package plans, pets [$15 extra charge, with prior approval, in designated units). **Amenities:** extended cable TV, irons, hair dryers. **Pool(s):** small heated indoor/outdoor. **Leisure Activities:** whirlpool, exercise room. **Cards:** AX, CB, DC, DS, JC, MC, VI. **Special Amenities:** free local telephone calls and free newspaper.

SOME UNITS

FEE

COUNTRY INN & SUITES

Phone: (815)777-2400

9/1-10/31 [ECP]	1P: $110-$150		XP: $10	F18
6/2-8/31 [ECP]	1P: $100-$130		XP: $10	F18
11/1-3/31 [ECP]	1P: $90-$100			
4/1-6/1 [ECP]	1P: $80-$100		XP: $10	F18

Motel

Location: On US 20, 2.5 mi w of downtown. 11334 Oldenburg Ln 61036. Fax: 815/777-2702. **Facility:** 75 units. 63 one-bedroom standard units, some with whirlpools. 12 one-bedroom suites ($195). 3 stories, interior corridors. *Bath:* combo or shower only. **Parking:** on-site. **Terms:** 7 day cancellation notice-fee imposed, package plans. **Amenities:** extended cable TV, voice mail, irons, hair dryers. **Pool(s):** heated indoor, wading. **Leisure Activities:** whirlpool, waterslide, exercise room. *Fee:* game room. **Guest Services:** valet and coin laundry. **Business Services:** meeting rooms. **Cards:** AX, DC, DS, MC, VI. *(See color ad p 322)*

SOME UNITS

FEE FEE

DESOTO HOUSE HOTEL

Phone: (815)777-0090

7/1-10/31	1P: $120-$135	2P: $145-$195	XP: $10	F18
5/1-6/30	1P: $109	2P: $135-$169	XP: $10	F18
4/1-4/30	1P: $99	2P: $99-$149	XP: $10	F18
11/1-3/31	1P: $99	2P: $119-$145	XP: $10	F18

Classic Hotel

Location: Just n of US 20. 230 S Main St 61036. Fax: 815/777-9529. **Facility:** Historic. 55 units. 53 one-bedroom standard units. 2 one-bedroom suites ($145-$195). 3-4 stories, interior corridors. **Parking:** on-site. **Terms:** 3 day cancellation notice-fee imposed, package plans. **Amenities:** extended cable TV. *Some:* hair dryers. **Dining:** dining room, restaurant, 7 am-9 pm, Fri & Sat-10 pm, $13-$27, cocktails. **Guest Services:** valet laundry. **Business Services:** meeting rooms. **Cards:** AX, CB, DC, DS, MC, VI. **Special Amenities:** early check-in/late check-out and free local telephone calls.

SOME UNITS

FEE

EAGLE RIDGE INN & RESORT

Phone: (815)777-2444

5/17-10/24	1P: $199-$279	2P: $199-$279	XP: $10	F17
4/1-5/16 & 10/25-12/31	1P: $149-$269	2P: $149-$269	XP: $10	F17
1/1-3/31	1P: $129-$259	2P: $129-$259	XP: $10	F17

Resort

Location: 6 mi e on US 20, 4.5 mi n. 444 Eagle Ridge Dr 61036 (PO Box 777). Fax: 815/777-4502. **Facility:** Championship golf facilities are the main draw at this resort, which has manicured grounds, attentive service and well-appointed guest rooms. 470 units. 127 one-bedroom standard units. 140 one-, 129 two- and 74 three-bedroom suites. 2-3 stories, interior/exterior corridors. **Parking:** on-site, winter plug-ins. **Terms:** check-in 4 pm, 15 day cancellation notice-fee imposed, package plans. **Amenities:** extended cable TV, irons, hair dryers. *Some:* video games (fee), CD players, voice mail. **Pool(s):** heated indoor. **Leisure Activities:** saunas, whirlpools, rental boats, rental canoes, rental paddleboats, boat dock, fishing, ice skating, children's program, nature program, recreation program in summer, hiking trails, jogging, playground, exercise room. *Fee:* water aerobics, golf-63 holes, 4 lighted tennis courts, cross country skiing, bicycles, horseback riding. **Guest Services:** gift shop, massage (fee), valet laundry. **Business Services:** conference facilities. *Fee:* PC, fax. **Cards:** AX, DC, DS, MC, VI.

SOME UNITS

PARK AVENUE GUEST HOUSE

Phone: 815/777-1075

All Year	1P: $95-$135	2P: $105-$145	XP: $15	

Historic Bed & Breakfast

Location: 0.5 mi n from US 20. 208 Park Ave 61036. Fax: 815/777-1097. **Facility:** A wraparound screened porch greets visitors at this 1893 Queen Anne home, which has a garden, a gazebo and three rooms with gas fireplaces. Smoke free premises. 4 units. 3 one-bedroom standard units. 1 one-bedroom suite. 3 stories, interior corridors. *Bath:* combo or shower only. **Parking:** street. **Terms:** check-in 4 pm, age restrictions may apply, 7 day cancellation notice-fee imposed, [BP] meal plan available, no pets allowed (cat on premises). **Amenities:** extended cable TV. **Cards:** DS, MC, VI.

SOME UNITS

QUEEN ANNE GUEST HOUSE

Phone: 815/777-3849

All Year	1P: $75-$85	2P: $95-$125	

Historic Bed & Breakfast

Location: 0.5 mi n of US 20. 200 Park Ave 61036. **Facility:** An elegant country decor distinguishes this service-oriented 1891 Queen Anne inn located near Grant Park. Smoke free premises. 4 one-bedroom standard units. 2 stories, interior corridors. **Parking:** street. **Terms:** check-in 4 pm, age restrictions may apply, 7 day cancellation notice-fee imposed, no pets allowed (cats on premises). **Cards:** DS, MC, VI.

--- **WHERE TO DINE** ---

BUBBA'S SEAFOOD, PASTA & SMOKEHOUSE
Dinner: $9-$19 **Phone:** 815/777-8030

American

Location: 0.5 mi n of US 20. 300 N Main St 61036. **Hours:** 5 pm-10 pm, Fri-Sun from 11 am. Closed: 12/25. **Reservations:** suggested. **Features:** casual dress; carryout; cocktails & lounge; a la carte. At the north end of the busy and historic Main Street shopping area, in a corner store-front location, Bubba's serves up classic hamburgers, quality steak and tasty pasta in a timeless malt shop atmosphere. On a good night, service can be friendly and attentive but at times it can be indifferent and detracting. Smoke free premises. **Parking:** street. **Cards:** AX, CB, DC, DS, MC, VI.

CAFE ITALIA/TWISTED TACO CAFE
Lunch: $6-$10 **Dinner: $8-$18** **Phone:** 815/777-0033

Italian

Location: US 20, 0.6 mi n. 301 N Main St 61036. **Hours:** 11 am-3 & 5-9 pm, Fri-Sun to 10 pm. Closed: 11/28; also Tues. **Reservations:** suggested. **Features:** dressy casual; Sunday brunch; children's menu; carryout; cocktails & lounge. Artful presentations & imaginative creations on standard meat, fish & chicken dishes make Rainwater an inviting dining destination. The chic, vineyard-themed ambiance also enhance the experience here. **Parking:** street. **Cards:** AX, CB, DC, DS, MC, VI.

VINNY VANUCCHI'S
Lunch: $5-$10 **Dinner: $9-$15** **Phone:** 815/777-8100

Traditional Italian

Location: Just n of US 20; set well back from street. 201 S Main St 61036. **Hours:** 11 am-10 pm. Closed: 11/28, 12/25. **Reservations:** suggested; required on Sat. **Features:** casual dress; carryout; cocktails. Perched on a quaint cobblestone pedestrian way just above Main Street, Vinny Vanucchi's will allow you to enjoy traditional Italian dishes in a Chicago-style restaurant located in the heart of this historic community. Classic food, good wine and friendly service combine to make for consistently pleasurable dining experiences. **Parking:** street. **Cards:** AX, DC, DS, MC, VI.

GALESBURG pop. 33,500

--- **WHERE TO STAY** ---

COMFORT INN
Phone: (309)344-5445

[SAVE]

Motel

All Year [ECP] 1P: $59-$94 2P: $64-$99 XP: $5 F18
Location: US 34, exit US 150 E. 907 W Carl Sandburg Dr 61401. Fax: 309/344-5445. **Facility:** 46 one-bedroom standard units. 2 stories, interior corridors. **Parking:** on-site, winter plug-ins. **Terms:** pets ($15 extra charge, in non-smoking units). **Amenities:** extended cable TV. *Some:* irons, hair dryers. **Guest Services:** valet laundry. **Cards:** AX, DC, DS, MC, VI.

SOME UNITS

COUNTRY INN & SUITES BY CARLSON
Phone: (309)344-4444

Motel

All Year 1P: $75-$110 2P: $75-$110 XP: $10 F17
Location: US 34, exit US 150 E, just s to Carl Sandburg Dr, then 0.5 mi w. 2284 Promenade Ct 61401. Fax: 309/344-4445. **Facility:** 61 one-bedroom standard units. 3 stories, interior corridors. *Bath:* combo or shower only. **Parking:** on-site. **Terms:** 7 day cancellation notice, [CP] meal plan available. **Amenities:** extended cable TV, voice mail, irons, hair dryers. **Pool(s):** heated indoor. **Leisure Activities:** whirlpool, exercise room. **Guest Services:** coin laundry. **Business Services:** meeting rooms. **Cards:** AX, CB, DC, DS, MC, VI. *(See color ad p 322)*

SOME UNITS

FAIRFIELD INN BY MARRIOTT
Phone: (309)344-1911

[AAA] [SAVE]

Motel

All Year [ECP] 1P: $64-$94 2P: $69-$99 XP: $5 F18
Location: US 34, exit US 150 E, just s. 901 W Carl Sandburg Dr 61401. Fax: 309/344-1911. **Facility:** 56 one-bedroom standard units. 3 stories, interior corridors. *Bath:* combo or shower only. **Parking:** on-site, winter plug-ins. **Amenities:** extended cable TV, irons. **Pool(s):** indoor. **Leisure Activities:** whirlpool. **Guest Services:** valet laundry. **Cards:** AX, DC, DS, MC, VI. **Special Amenities:** free continental breakfast and free local telephone calls. *(See color ad card insert)*

SOME UNITS

HOLIDAY INN EXPRESS
Phone: (309)343-7100

Motel

All Year [ECP] 1P: $69-$114 2P: $75-$114 XP: $6 F19
Location: I-74, exit 48A (US 150), just w to Michigan Ave, just s to Washington St, then just e. 2285 Washington St 61401. Fax: 309/343-7340. **Facility:** 73 one-bedroom standard units. 3 stories, interior corridors. *Bath:* combo or shower only. **Parking:** on-site, winter plug-ins. **Terms:** pets (in smoking units). **Amenities:** extended cable TV, irons, hair dryers. **Pool(s):** heated indoor. **Leisure Activities:** whirlpool. **Guest Services:** valet and coin laundry. **Business Services:** meeting rooms. **Cards:** AX, CB, DC, DS, MC, VI.

SOME UNITS

JUMER'S CONTINENTAL INN
Phone: (309)343-7151

[AAA] [SAVE]

Motor Inn

All Year 1P: $63-$71 2P: $72-$80 XP: $9 F18
Location: I-74, exit 48 (Main St), just e, then just s. 260 S Soangetaha Rd 61401. Fax: 309/343-7151. **Facility:** 117 one-bedroom standard units, some with whirlpools. 2 stories, interior corridors. **Parking:** on-site, winter plug-ins. **Terms:** package plans, pets ($25 deposit). **Amenities:** video games, voice mail. **Dining:** entertainment. **Pool(s):** indoor. **Leisure Activities:** whirlpool, putting green, game field with 27 stations. **Guest Services:** valet and coin laundry, area transportation. **Business Services:** conference facilities. **Cards:** AX, CB, DC, DS, MC, VI. **Special Amenities:** free local telephone calls and free newspaper.

SOME UNITS

──────── **WHERE TO DINE** ────────

LANDMARK CAFE & CREPERIE   Historical   **Lunch:** $6-$9   **Dinner:** $6-$9   **Phone:** 309/343-5376
▼▼▼ ▼▼▼   **Location:** Downtown; in historic district. 62 S Seminary St 61401. **Hours:** 11 am-9 pm, Fri-10 pm, Sat 9 am-10
      pm, Sun 9 am-9 pm. Closed major holidays. **Reservations:** accepted. **Features:** casual dress; children's
American   menu; carryout; cocktails; a la carte. Housed in Galesburg's first commercial building to be accorded
landmark status, the Landmark Cafe & Creperie has elevated the crepe to a place or prominence on its
menu. Although many other options are offered, you can order crepe entrees and crepe desserts of several types. Smoke free
premises. **Parking:** street. **Cards:** AX, DC, DS, MC, VI.   ⊠

NEW CHINA CAFE   **Lunch:** $5-$11   **Dinner:** $5-$11   **Phone:** 309/342-3218
▼▼   **Location:** Between Seminary and Kellogg. 329 E Main St 61401. **Hours:** 9 am-8 pm, Sat 7 am-9 pm, Sun from 8
      am. Closed: 7/4, 12/25; also Wed. **Reservations:** accepted. **Features:** casual dress; carryout; a la carte.
Chinese   In business since 1928, this is a rare find, a Chinese restaurant with a slew of American favorites.
Authentic Cantonese cuisine, such as moo goo gai kew, is fresh and flavorful. Painted walls and tile floors
lend to the casual atmosphere. **Parking:** street.   ⊠

THE PACKINGHOUSE DINING COMPANY   Historical   **Lunch:** $5-$10   **Dinner:** $15-$20   **Phone:** 309/342-6868
▼▼▼ ▼▼▼   **Location:** 2 mi off I-74; in downtown historic district; just s of Main St via Seminary St. 441 Mulberry St 61401.
      Hours: 11 am-2 & 5-9 pm, Fri & Sat-10 pm, Sun noon-8 pm. Closed major holidays.
Steak & Seafood   **Reservations:** suggested. **Features:** casual dress; children's menu; carryout; salad bar; cocktails; a la
      carte. Built in 1912 to be a meat processing plant, the building which houses The Packinghouse Dining
Company is now home to a restaurant known for steak, seafood and prime rib. Much of the original equipment of the packing
plant was retained and provides authentic ambience. **Parking:** street. **Cards:** AX, CB, DC, DS, MC, VI.   ⊠

GENESEO pop. 6,000

──────── **WHERE TO DINE** ────────

THE CELLAR   **Dinner:** $9-$29   **Phone:** 309/944-2177
ⒶⒶⒶ   **Location:** I-80, exit 19 (US 6/SR 82), 1.5 mi n to State St, then 0.3 mi n. 137 S State & 2nd sts 61254. **Hours:** 5
▼▼▼ ▼▼▼   pm-9 pm, Fri & Sat-10 pm, Sun 11:30 am-9 pm. Closed: 12/24, 12/25; also Mon.
American   **Reservations:** suggested. **Features:** casual dress; children's menu; carryout; cocktails & lounge. The
      Cellar restaurant is in a dining room a short flight of stairs below street-level in downtown Geneseo.
      Charcoal grilled steak, chops, chicken and seafood are the specialties. The menu includes combination
      plates so you can sample more than one of the charcoal broiled features. **Parking:** off-site. **Cards:** AX,
CB, DC, DS, MC, VI.   ⊠

GENEVA —See Chicago p. 340.

GILMAN pop. 1,800

──────── **WHERE TO STAY** ────────

SUPER 8 OF GILMAN   **Phone:** (815)265-7000
ⒶⒶⒶ SAVE   All Year [ECP]   1P: $52-$57   2P: $57-$69   XP: $5   F15
▼▼▼ ▼▼▼   **Location:** I-57, exit 283, 0.3 mi e. 1301 S Crescent St 60938. Fax: 815/265-7000. **Facility:** 52 one-bedroom stan-
      dard units, some with whirlpools. 2 stories, interior corridors. **Parking:** on-site. **Terms:** 7 day cancellation
Motel   notice-fee imposed, small pets only. **Amenities:** extended cable TV, video tape library (fee). **Leisure Activi-
      ties:** whirlpool. **Guest Services:** coin laundry. **Cards:** AX, CB, DC, DS, MC, VI. **Special Amenities:** free
      continental breakfast and free local telephone calls.

SOME UNITS
Ⓢ Ⓓ 🐾 🏋 🍽 📺 🎦 [DATA PORT] 📠 / ⊠ [VCR] 🔌 📠 /
FEE

TRAVEL INN
AAA [SAVE]
♦♦♦♦ ♦♦♦♦
Motel

All Year   1P: $45   2P: $50   XP: $5   F11
Location: I-57, exit 283, just e. 834 Hwy 24 W 60938. Fax: 815/265-7290. **Facility:** 38 one-bedroom standard units, some with whirlpools. 1-2 stories, interior/exterior corridors. **Parking:** on-site. **Terms:** 4 day cancellation notice, [ECP] meal plan available, pets ($4 extra charge). **Amenities:** extended cable TV. *Some:* hair dryers. **Pool(s):** small heated indoor. **Leisure Activities:** whirlpool. **Guest Services:** coin laundry. **Cards:** AX, CB, DC, DS, MC, VI. **Special Amenities:** free continental breakfast and free local telephone calls.

SOME UNITS
Phone: (815)265-7283

(🅂📶) (🐕) (📶🚪) (🏊) (🎥) (DATA PORT) / (⊠) /

GLEN CARBON pop. 7,800

------ WHERE TO DINE ------

GLENWOOD MANOR HOUSE   Lunch: $6-$7   Phone: 618/288-1932
♦♦♦♦ ♦♦♦♦   **Location:** I-270, exit 9 (SR 157), 0.6 mi s. 3506 SR 157 62034. **Hours:** 11 am-3 pm. Closed major holidays.
American   **Reservations:** suggested. **Features:** casual dress; carryout; buffet. This 1897 Greek Revival mansion commands a cheerful, intimate dining room and well-stocked gift shops for patrons to enjoy. Soup, salad, sandwiches, herbal tea and flavored coffee dominate the menu and are served by a casual and friendly service staff. Smoke free premises. **Parking:** on-site. **Cards:** DC, MC, VI.

(⊠)

GLEN ELLYN —See Chicago p. 341.

GLENVIEW —See Chicago p. 341.

GRAFTON pop. 900

------ WHERE TO STAY ------

RUEBEL HOTEL & SALOON   Phone: 618/786-2315
♦♦♦♦ ♦♦♦♦   All Year [CP]   1P: $59-$89   2P: $59-$89   XP: $8   F6
Motel   **Location:** I-270, exit SR 367 N to 100 W. 217 E Main St 62037. Fax: 618/786-2325. **Facility:** 35 units. 25 one-bedroom standard units, some with whirlpools. 10 one-bedroom vacation rentals ($119-$149) with whirlpools. 2 stories. *Bath:* combo or shower only. **Parking:** on-site. **Terms:** check-in 4 pm, 7 day cancellation notice. **Amenities:** extended cable TV. **Leisure Activities:** hiking trails, horseback riding, playground. **Cards:** MC, VI.

SOME UNITS
(🍴) (⊠) (⊠) (🖨) / (DATA PORT) (🔒) (📦) (💻) /

GRAYSLAKE —See Chicago p. 342.

GRAYVILLE pop. 2,000

------ WHERE TO STAY ------

BEST WESTERN WINDSOR OAKS INN   Phone: (618)375-7930
AAA [SAVE]   5/1-8/31 [ECP]   1P: $70-$90   2P: $75-$95   XP: $5   F17
              4/1-4/30 & 9/1-3/31 [ECP] 1P: $65-$84   2P: $70-$89   XP: $5   F17
♦♦♦♦ ♦♦♦♦   **Location:** I-64, exit 130 (SR 1), just n. 2200 S Court St 62844. Fax: 618/375-7339. **Facility:** 60 one-bedroom standard units. 2 stories, interior corridors. **Parking:** on-site, winter plug-ins. **Amenities:** extended cable TV,
Motor Inn   irons, hair dryers. *Some:* safes. **Dining:** 2 restaurants, 11 am-9 pm, Sun 10:30 am-8 pm, $6-$16, cocktails. **Pool(s):** heated indoor. **Leisure Activities:** whirlpool, exercise room. **Guest Services:** valet laundry. **Business Services:** meeting rooms, fax. **Cards:** AX, CB, DC, DS, MC, VI. **Special Amenities:** free continental breakfast and free local telephone calls.

SOME UNITS
(🅂📶) (🍴) (🍸) (🚭) (🏊) (🎥) (DATA PORT) (💻) (🖨) / (⊠) (🔒) (📦) /
                                                              FEE   FEE FEE

GREENVILLE pop. 4,800

------ WHERE TO STAY ------

BUDGET HOST INN   Phone: (618)664-1950
AAA [SAVE]   4/1-9/30 [CP]   1P: $32-$36   2P: $36-$47   XP: $5   F10
              10/1-3/31 [CP]   1P: $28-$35   2P: $30-$45   XP: $5   F10
♦♦♦♦ ♦♦♦♦   **Location:** I-70, exit 45, 0.3 mi n. 1525 S SR 127 62246. Fax: 618/664-1960. **Facility:** 48 one-bedroom standard
Motel   units, some with whirlpools. 2 stories, exterior corridors. **Parking:** on-site. **Terms:** 3 day cancellation notice, pets ($5 extra charge). **Amenities:** extended cable TV. **Pool(s):** heated outdoor. **Guest Services:** coin laundry. **Business Services:** fax (fee). **Cards:** AX, DS, MC, VI. *(See color ad p 269)*

SOME UNITS
(🅂📶) (🐕) (📶🚪) (🏊) (🎥) (💻) / (⊠) (🔒) (📦) /

SUPER 8 MOTEL-GREENVILLE   Phone: (618)664-0800
♦♦♦♦ ♦♦♦♦   4/1-9/30 [CP]   1P: $43-$48   2P: $47-$52   XP: $5   F17
              10/1-3/31 [CP]   1P: $39-$43   2P: $44-$48   XP: $5   F17
Motel   **Location:** I-70, exit 45, just n. 1700 Rt 127 S 62246 (221 W College Ave). Fax: 618/664-0845. **Facility:** 43 one-bedroom standard units. 2 stories, interior corridors. **Parking:** on-site, winter plug-ins. **Terms:** check-in 4 pm. **Amenities:** extended cable TV. **Guest Services:** coin laundry. **Business Services:** fax (fee). **Cards:** AX, DS, MC, VI.

SOME UNITS
(ASK) (🅂📶) (📶🚪) (🎥) / (⊠) (VCR) (🔒) (📦) /

GURNEE —See Chicago p. 342.

HARVARD —*See Chicago p. 343.*

HARVEY —*See Chicago p. 344.*

HIGHLAND pop. 7,500

——— WHERE TO STAY ———

HOLIDAY INN EXPRESS
Phone: (618)651-1100
(AAA) [SAVE]
All Year [ECP]   1P: $66-$76   2P: $66-$76   XP: $5   F18
Location: I-70, exit 24 (SR 143), 4 mi s. 20 Central Blvd 62249. Fax: 618/651-1101. **Facility:** 60 units. 58 one-bedroom standard units. 2 one-bedroom suites ($86-$131) with whirlpools. 3 stories, interior corridors. *Bath:* combo or shower only. **Parking:** on-site, winter plug-ins. **Amenities:** extended cable TV, dual phone lines, voice mail, irons, hair dryers. **Pool(s):** small heated indoor. **Leisure Activities:** exercise room. *Fee:* game room. **Guest Services:** valet laundry. **Business Services:** fax. **Cards:** AX, CB, DC, DS, JC, MC, VI.
Motel
Special Amenities: free continental breakfast and free local telephone calls.
SOME UNITS

MICHAEL'S SWISS INN
Phone: (618)654-8646
All Year   1P: $50-$70   2P: $60-$70   XP: $10   F10
Location: On SR 160, 1.8 mi s of jct US 40/SR 143. 425 Broadway 62249. Fax: 618/654-6545. **Facility:** 20 one-bedroom standard units. 2 stories, exterior corridors. **Parking:** on-site. **Amenities:** extended cable TV.
Motor Inn
Leisure Activities: whirlpool. **Cards:** AX, CB, DC, DS, MC, VI.
SOME UNITS

HIGHLAND PARK —*See Chicago p. 344.*

HILLSBORO pop. 4,400

——— WHERE TO DINE ———

CHURCH STREET PUB   Historical   **Lunch:** $5-$8   **Dinner:** $9-$20   **Phone:** 217/532-6060
Location: At the corner of Church and Broad sts, just se from town square. 202 S Broad St 62049. **Hours:** 11 am-2 & 5-9 pm, Sun 11:30 am-3:30 pm. Closed major holidays; also Tues. **Reservations:** suggested; weekends.
American
Features: casual dress; Sunday brunch; cocktails & lounge; a la carte. Located in a 1903 former church building, this restaurant offers gourmet cuisine in an upscale but comfortably casual setting. Try the superb pub salmon en papillote (cooked in a paper bag) with delightful baby shrimp, aromatic vegetables and herb sauce. **Parking:** on-site. **Cards:** DS, MC, VI.

HILLSIDE —*See Chicago p. 344.*

HINSDALE —*See Chicago p. 344.*

HOFFMAN ESTATES —*See Chicago p. 345.*

ITASCA —*See Chicago p. 346.*

JACKSONVILLE pop. 19,300

——— WHERE TO STAY ———

AMERIHOST INN-JACKSONVILLE
Phone: (217)245-4500
(AAA) [SAVE]
All Year [CP]   1P: $62   2P: $68   XP: $10   F18
Location: On US 67/SR 104, 1.3 mi w of jct SR 78 (Main St). 1709 W Morton Ave 62650. Fax: 217/245-0411.
Facility: 60 one-bedroom standard units. 2 stories, interior corridors. *Bath:* combo or shower only. **Parking:** on-site. **Amenities:** extended cable TV, safes (fee), irons, hair dryers. **Pool(s):** indoor. **Leisure Activities:** sauna, whirlpool, exercise room. **Business Services:** meeting rooms. **Cards:** AX, DC, DS, MC, VI.
Motel
Special Amenities: free continental breakfast and free newspaper.
SOME UNITS

STAR LITE MOTEL
Phone: (217)245-7184
(AAA) [SAVE]
All Year   1P: $38-$42   2P: $42-$48   XP: $3   F12
Location: On US 67/SR 104, 1.8 mi w. 1910 W Morton Ave 62650. Fax: 217/243-1649. **Facility:** 32 one-bedroom standard units. 1 story, exterior corridors. **Parking:** on-site, winter plug-ins. **Terms:** 10 day cancellation notice, pets ($5 extra charge). **Amenities:** extended cable TV. **Leisure Activities:** playground. **Guest Services:** valet laundry. **Cards:** AX, DS, MC, VI. **Special Amenities:** early check-in/late check-out and free local telephone calls.
Motel
SOME UNITS

SUPER 8 MOTEL
Phone: (217)479-0303
All Year [CP]   1P: $49-$79   2P: $49-$79   XP: $5   F12
Location: On US 67, 0.9 mi w. 1003 W Morton Ave 62650. Fax: 217/479-0303. **Facility:** 43 one-bedroom standard units. 2 stories, interior corridors. **Parking:** on-site. **Terms:** pets ($10-$25 deposit). **Amenities:** extended cable TV, safes. **Cards:** AX, CB, DC, DS, MC, VI.
Motel
SOME UNITS

JERSEYVILLE pop. 7,400

—————— WHERE TO STAY ——————

SUPER 8 MOTEL
AAA [SAVE]
▼▼▼▼
Motel

All Year [CP]   1P: $46-$60   2P: $52-$65   XP: $6   F12
Location: SR 109, 0.6 mi s of SR 67. 1281 McClusky Rd 62052. Fax: 618/498-4999. **Facility:** 40 one-bedroom standard units. 1-2 stories, interior corridors. *Bath:* combo or shower only. **Parking:** on-site, winter plug-ins **Terms:** cancellation fee imposed. **Business Services:** meeting rooms. **Cards:** AX, DC, DS, MC, VI **Special Amenities:** free continental breakfast and free local telephone calls.

Phone: (618)498-7888

SOME UNITS

[S] [&M] [⚙] [📞] [DATA PORT] [📠] / [✕] [🛏] /

JOLIET —See Chicago p. 346.

KANKAKEE pop. 27,500

—————— WHERE TO DINE ——————

UNCLE JOHNNIS RESTAURANT & PANCAKE HOUSE   **Lunch:** $5-$16   **Dinner:** $6-$16   **Phone:** 815/933-1022
▼
American

Location: I-57, exit 312, just w on SR 17. 1940 E Court St 60901. **Hours:** 5 am-midnight, Sat & Sun-1 am **Reservations:** accepted. **Features:** casual dress; children's menu; carryout; cocktails. The casual restaurant features a 300-item breakfast menu, as well as lunch and dinner menus that include an extensive selection of sandwiches, salads, steaks, chops, chicken and seafood. Service is friendly, and the value is excellent. **Parking:** on-site. **Cards:** AX, DC, DS, MC, VI.

[✕]

KEWANEE pop. 13,000

—————— WHERE TO STAY ——————

SUPER 8 MOTEL
▼▼
Motel

All Year [CP]   1P: $59-$74   2P: $59-$74   XP: $5   F12
Location: SR 78, 1.9 mi s of jct US 34 and SR 78. 901 S Tenney St 61443. Fax: 309/856-5319. **Facility:** 41 one-bedroom standard units, some with whirlpools. 2 stories, interior corridors. **Parking:** on-site, winter plug-ins **Amenities:** extended cable TV. **Leisure Activities:** sauna, exercise room. **Business Services:** meeting rooms. **Cards:** AX, CB, DC, DS, JC, MC, VI.

Phone: (309)853-8800

SOME UNITS

[ASK] [S] [&M] [📷] [DATA PORT] [📠] / [✕] [▭]

KICKAPOO

—————— WHERE TO DINE ——————

JUBILEE CAFE
▼
American
Parking: on-site.

          Lunch: $4-$8   **Dinner:** $4-$8   **Phone:** 309/691-7778
Location: I-74, exit 82, just n. CR 18 61528. **Hours:** 6 am-9 pm. Closed: 11/28, 12/25. **Features:** casual dress; children's menu; carryout; a la carte. The prices are right on the restaurant's great tasting, family friendly comfort foods: plate dinners, salad, sandwiches and such pies as a tart and sweet strawberry-rhubarb. An area medical center provides a nutritional analysis of some healthy choices. Smoke free premises

[✕] [🅰️]

LAKE FOREST —See Chicago p. 349.

LAKE ZURICH —See Chicago p. 349.

LANSING —See Chicago p. 349.

LA SALLE pop. 9,700

—————— WHERE TO DINE ——————

UPTOWN GRILL
▼▼▼
American

          Lunch: $5-$23   **Dinner:** $9-$23   **Phone:** 815/224-4545
Location: Jct SR 351 and US 6, just s to First St, then just w. 601 First St 61301. **Hours:** 11 am-11 pm, Sun noon-10 pm. Closed: 11/28, 12/25. **Features:** casual dress; children's menu; carryout; cocktails & lounge; a la carte. Two blocks north of the Illinois and Michigan Canal in a busy commercial area, the grill offers a wide variety of palate-pleasing dishes. Homemade fried four-cheese ravioli, in which the little pouches are in marked contrast to the mass-produced envelopes served in many places, is a particular delight. While the location is uptown and the setting is upscale, the service is down home. The wait staff is casually dressed and uniformly friendly. **Parking:** street **Cards:** AX, DC, DS, MC, VI.

[✕]

LIBERTYVILLE —See Chicago p. 350.

LINCOLN pop. 15,400

—————— WHERE TO STAY ——————

HOLIDAY INN EXPRESS
Motel
All Year [ECP]　　　1P: $72-$125　　2P: $72-$125　　XP: $6　　　F19
Phone: (217)735-5800
Location: I-55, exit 126 (US 121), just e to Heitman Dr, just w to Olson Dr, then just n. 130 Olson Dr 62656. **Fax:** 217/732-6168. **Facility:** 71 one-bedroom standard units. 3 stories, interior corridors. *Bath:* combo or shower only. **Parking:** on-site, winter plug-ins. **Amenities:** extended cable TV, irons, hair dryers. **Pool(s):** indoor. **Leisure Activities:** whirlpool. **Guest Services:** valet and coin laundry. **Business Services:** meeting rooms. **Cards:** AX, CB, DC, DS, JC, MC, VI.

SOME UNITS

LINCOLNSHIRE —*See Chicago p. 351.*

LISLE —*See Chicago p. 351.*

LITCHFIELD pop. 6,900

—————— WHERE TO STAY ——————

BAYMONT INN OF LITCHFIELD
Motel
All Year [ECP]　　　1P: $63-$73　　2P: $69-$79　　XP: $7　　　F18
Phone: (217)324-4556
Location: I-55, exit 52 (SR 16), just e to Ohren Ln, just s to W Hudson Dr, then just w. 1405 W Hudson Dr 62056. **Fax:** 217/324-4514. **Facility:** 64 one-bedroom standard units, some with whirlpools. 3 stories, interior corridors. *Bath:* combo or shower only. **Parking:** on-site. **Terms:** 7 day cancellation notice. **Amenities:** video games, voice mail, irons, hair dryers. **Pool(s):** small heated indoor. **Leisure Activities:** whirlpool. **Guest Services:** valet and coin laundry. **Business Services:** meeting rooms. **Cards:** AX, CB, DC, DS, MC, VI. **Special Amenities: free continental breakfast and free newspaper.**

SOME UNITS

LITCHFIELD COMFORT INN
Motel
5/1-9/30　　　1P: $61　　　2P: $66　　　XP: $5　　　F18
4/1-4/30 & 10/1-3/31　1P: $57　　2P: $61　　XP: $5　　F18
Phone: (217)324-9260
Location: I-55, exit 52 (SR 16), 0.7 mi e to Old SR 66, then 0.3 mi n. 1010 E Columbian Blvd N 62056. **Fax:** 217/324-3757. **Facility:** 61 units. 59 one-bedroom standard units. 2 one-bedroom suites ($73-$77). 3 stories, interior corridors. *Bath:* combo, shower or tub only. **Parking:** on-site. **Terms:** 3 day cancellation notice, pets ($10 extra charge). **Amenities:** extended cable TV. *Some:* irons, hair dryers. **Pool(s):** small heated indoor. **Leisure Activities:** whirlpool. **Guest Services:** valet laundry. **Business Services:** fax (fee). **Cards:** AX, CB, DC, DS, JC, MC, VI.

SOME UNITS

—————— WHERE TO DINE ——————

ARISTAN CAFE
American
Lunch: $7-$18　　**Dinner:** $7-$18　　**Phone:** 217/324-2023
Location: I-55, exit 52 (SR 16), 0.3 mi e. South Old Rt 66 62056. **Hours:** 11 am-10 pm, Sat from 4 pm, Sun-9 pm. Closed major holidays. **Features:** Sunday brunch; children's menu; carryout; salad bar; cocktails; buffet. Off old Route 66, this family owned and operated eatery offers polite, friendly staff and comfortable casual surroundings. **Parking:** on-site. **Cards:** AX, DC, DS, MC, VI.

LOCKPORT —*See Chicago p. 352.*

LOMBARD —*See Chicago p. 352.*

MACOMB pop. 20,000

—————— WHERE TO STAY ——————

AMERIHOST INN-MACOMB
Motel
All Year　　　1P: $65-$80　　2P: $71-$81　　XP: $6　　　F18
Phone: (309)837-2220
Location: Jct SR 67/136, 1.9 mi n on SR 67. 1646 N Lafayette St 61455. **Fax:** 309/837-1720. **Facility:** 60 one-bedroom standard units. 2 stories, interior corridors. *Bath:* combo or shower only. **Parking:** on-site, winter plug-ins. **Terms:** 7 day cancellation notice. **Amenities:** extended cable TV, safes (fee), irons, hair dryers. **Pool(s):** heated indoor. **Leisure Activities:** sauna, whirlpool, exercise room. **Guest Services:** valet laundry. **Business Services:** meeting rooms. **Cards:** AX, CB, DC, DS, JC, MC, VI. **Special Amenities: free continental breakfast and free newspaper.**

SOME UNITS

DAYS INN
Motor Inn
5/22-7/31　　　1P: $79-$85　　2P: $85-$91　　XP: $6　　F11
4/1-5/21 & 8/1-10/31　1P: $57-$63　　2P: $63-$69　　XP: $6　　F11
11/1-3/31　　　1P: $51-$56　　2P: $57-$63　　XP: $6　　F11
Phone: 309/833-5511
Location: Jct SR 67/136, 1.3 mi n. 1400 N Lafayette St 61455. **Fax:** 309/836-2926. **Facility:** 144 one-bedroom standard units, some with whirlpools. 2 stories, exterior corridors. *Bath:* combo or shower only. **Parking:** on-site, winter plug-ins. **Terms:** 7 day cancellation notice. **Amenities:** extended cable TV. *Some:* irons, hair dryers. **Pool(s):** outdoor. **Guest Services:** coin laundry. **Business Services:** meeting rooms. **Cards:** AX, CB, DC, DS, JC, MC, VI.

SOME UNITS

SUPER 8 MOTEL

Motel

All Year [CP]   1P: $45-$75   2P: $45-$75   XP: $5   F1
Phone: (309)836-8888
Location: 1.1 mi n on SR 67 to University Ave, 0.5 mi w. 313 University Dr 61455. Fax: 309/833-2646. **Facility:** 4
one-bedroom standard units. 2 stories, interior corridors. **Parking:** on-site. **Amenities:** extended cable TV
Cards: AX, CB, DC, DS, MC, VI.

SOME UNITS

------ **WHERE TO DINE** ------

GREAT WALL BUFFETT

Chinese

Lunch: $5   **Dinner: $8**   **Phone:** 309/836-9998
Location: 1625 W Jackson St 61455. **Hours:** 11 am-10 pm. **Features:** casual dress; Sunday brunch
children's menu; carryout; salad bar; buffet, a la carte. Most people come for the extensive buffet o
traditional Cantonese, Szechwan and Hunan favorites, and few leave disappointed. Three serving lines la
out soups, appetizers, salads, desserts and numerous main dishes. Service is attentive and friendly
Smoke free premises. **Parking:** on-site. **Cards:** MC, VI.

MACOMB DINING COMPANY   Historical

American

Lunch: $5-$7   **Dinner: $11-$20**   **Phone:** 309/833-3000
Location: Center; facing Chandler Park. 127 E Carroll St 61455. **Hours:** 11 am-2 & 5-9 pm, Fri-10 pm, Sat 1
pm-10 pm. Closed major holidays; also Sun. **Reservations:** suggested; weekends. **Features:** casua
dress; children's menu; carryout; salad bar; cocktails & lounge. You can't go wrong when choosing any one
of this restaurant's house specials of black Angus beef, prime rib, orange roughy, honey mustard chicker
and spinach bisque. Your surroundings are spacious and inviting and accented by antiques and tin ceilings. **Parking:** street
Cards: AX, DS, MC, VI.

SUNRISE FAMILY RESTAURANT

American

Lunch: $5-$11   **Dinner: $5-$12**   **Phone:** 309/836-2938
Location: 1.1 mi n on SR 67 to University Ave, 0.4 mi w. 307 University Dr 61455. **Hours:** 6 am-9 pm
Features: casual dress; children's menu; carryout; a la carte. This is a casual family restaurant featuring
comfort foods at a good value. The service tends to be welcoming and informal. Smoke free premises
Parking: on-site. **Cards:** MC, VI.

MAEYSTOWN pop. 100

------ **WHERE TO STAY** ------

CORNER GEORGE INN

Classic Bed &
Breakfast

All Year   1P: $72-$162   2P: $79-$169   XP: $15   F5
Phone: (618)458-6660
Location: Corner of Main and Mill sts. 1101 Main St 62256 (PO Box 103). Fax: 618/458-7770. **Facility:** Historic. An
chored by a restored 1884 hotel and saloon, this historic complex also has a rock house, a brick-and-stone
summer kitchen and an 1860s log cabin. Smoke free premises. 7 one-bedroom standard units, some with
whirlpools. 1-2 stories, interior/exterior corridors. **Bath:** combo, shower or tub only. **Parking:** street
Terms: check-in 4 pm, 7 day cancellation notice-fee imposed. **Guest Services:** gift shop. **Business Services:** meeting rooms
Cards: AX, DS, MC, VI.

SOME UNITS

MANTENO pop. 3,500

------ **WHERE TO STAY** ------

COMFORT INN

SAVE

Motel

All Year   1P: $68-$72   2P: $76-$86   XP: $10   F1
Phone: 815/468-8657
Location: I-57, exit 322. 157 Cypress 60950. Fax: 815/468-2532. **Facility:** 57 one-bedroom standard units, some
with whirlpools. 2 stories, interior corridors. **Parking:** on-site. **Terms:** package plans. **Amenities:** extended
cable TV, safes (fee). Some: irons, hair dryers. **Pool(s):** heated indoor. **Leisure Activities:** whirlpool. **Gues**
Services: coin laundry. **Business Services:** meeting rooms. **Cards:** AX, CB, DC, DS, JC, MC, VI.

SOME UNITS

FEE   FEE

MARION pop. 14,500

------ **WHERE TO STAY** ------

BEST INNS OF AMERICA

AAA SAVE

Motel

All Year   1P: $40-$55   2P: $47-$63
Phone: (618)997-9421
Location: I-57, exit 54B (SR 13), just w. 2700 W DeYoung 62959. Fax: 618/997-1581. **Facility:** 104 one-bedroom
standard units. 2 stories, exterior corridors. **Parking:** on-site, winter plug-ins. **Terms:** small pets only
Amenities: extended cable TV. **Pool(s):** outdoor. **Guest Services:** valet laundry. **Business Services:** fax
(fee). **Cards:** AX, CB, DC, DS, MC, VI. **Special Amenities:** free continental breakfast and free local tele
phone calls.

SOME UNITS

COMFORT INN

SAVE

Motel

All Year [ECP]   1P: $48-$63   2P: $50-$68   XP: $5
Phone: (618)993-6221
Location: I-57, exit 53 (Main St), just w. 2600 W Main St 62959 (PO Box 70). Fax: 618/993-8964. **Facility:** 124 one
bedroom standard units, some with whirlpools. 2 stories, interior corridors. **Parking:** on-site, winter plug-ins
Amenities: extended cable TV. Some: video games, irons, hair dryers. **Leisure Activities:** exercise room
Guest Services: valet laundry. **Business Services:** meeting rooms. **Cards:** AX, CB, DC, DS, JC, MC, VI.

SOME UNITS

FEE

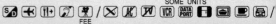

COMFORT SUITES

Phone: (618)997-9133

SAVE

All Year [ECP]   1P: $61-$73   2P: $66-$68   XP: $6   F18
Location: I-57, exit 53 (Main St), just w, then just n. 2608 W Main St 62959 (PO Box 70). Fax: 618/997-1005.
Facility: 64 one-bedroom standard units, some with whirlpools. 2 stories, interior corridors. *Bath:* combo or
shower only. **Parking:** on-site, winter plug-ins. **Amenities:** extended cable TV, video tape library (fee), irons.
Some: hair dryers. **Pool(s):** heated indoor. **Guest Services:** valet and coin laundry. **Business Services:**
meeting rooms, business center, PC, fax (fee). **Cards:** AX, CB, DC, DS, JC, MC, VI.

Motel

SOME UNITS

DRURY INN-MARION

Phone: (618)997-9600

All Year [ECP]   1P: $52-$92   2P: $52-$92   XP: $10
Location: I-57, exit 54 (SR 13), 0.5 mi w. 2706 W DeYoung St 62959. Fax: 618/997-9600. **Facility:** 156 units. 131
one-bedroom standard units. 25 one-bedroom suites ($77-$105). 5 stories, interior corridors. *Bath:* combo or
shower only. **Parking:** on-site. **Amenities:** *Some:* voice mail, irons, hair dryers. **Pool(s):** heated indoor.
Leisure Activities: whirlpool, exercise room. **Guest Services:** complimentary evening beverages: Mon-Thurs, valet and coin
laundry. **Business Services:** meeting rooms. **Cards:** AX, CB, DC, DS, MC, VI. *(See color ad p 5)*

Motel

SOME UNITS

FEE FEE

HAMPTON INN-MARION

Phone: (618)998-9900

SAVE

All Year [ECP]   1P: $59-$71   2P: $64-$76
Location: I-57, exit 54B (SR 13), 0.7 mi w to Williamson County Pkwy, just n to DeYoung St, then just e. 2710 W DeY-
oung St 62959. Fax: 618/997-8684. **Facility:** 64 one-bedroom standard units. 3 stories, interior corridors. *Bath:*
combo or shower only. **Parking:** on-site. **Terms:** cancellation fee imposed. **Amenities:** extended cable TV,
irons, hair dryers. **Pool(s):** heated indoor. **Guest Services:** valet laundry. **Business Services:** fax (fee).
Cards: AX, CB, DC, DS, JC, MC, VI.

Motel

SOME UNITS

HOLIDAY INN EXPRESS

Phone: (618)998-1220

All Year [ECP]   1P: $59-$79   2P: $59-$79   XP: $7   F19
Location: I-57, exit 53 (Main St), just nw. 400 Comfort Dr 62959 (PO Box 70). Fax: 618/998-0212. **Facility:** 79 one-
bedroom standard units. 3 stories, interior corridors. *Bath:* combo or shower only. **Parking:** on-site, winter
plug-ins. **Amenities:** extended cable TV, video games, dual phone lines, voice mail, irons, hair dryers.
Pool(s): heated indoor. **Leisure Activities:** whirlpool. **Guest Services:** valet and coin laundry. **Business Services:** fax (fee).
Cards: AX, CB, DC, DS, JC, MC, VI.

Motel

SOME UNITS

FEE   FEE

MOTEL 6 #1174

Phone: 618/993-2631

5/23-3/31   1P: $36   2P: $42   XP: $3   F17
4/1-5/22   1P: $33   2P: $39   XP: $3   F17
Location: I-57, exit 54B (SR 13), 0.3 mi w. 1008 Halfway Rd 62959. Fax: 618/993-2719. **Facility:** 79 one-bedroom
standard units. 2 stories, exterior corridors. *Bath:* combo or shower only. **Parking:** on-site. **Terms:** small pets
only. **Cards:** AX, CB, DC, DS, MC, VI.

Motel

SOME UNITS

SUPER 8 MOTEL

Phone: 618/993-5577

All Year [ECP]   1P: $47-$67   2P: $56-$76   XP: $6   F12
Location: I-57, exit 54B (SR 13), just w. 2601 W DeYoung St 62959. Fax: 618/997-6779. **Facility:** 63 one-bedroom
standard units. 3 stories (no elevator), interior corridors. **Parking:** on-site. **Terms:** pets (with prior approval).
Amenities: extended cable TV, safes. **Cards:** AX, CB, DC, DS, MC, VI.

Motel

SOME UNITS

FEE

——— WHERE TO DINE ———

20'S HIDEOUT STEAKHOUSE & BAR   **Dinner:** $9-$18   Phone: 618/997-8325
Location: I-57, exit 53 (Main St), 0.5 mi w, then just n. 2606 W Main St 62959. **Hours:** 4 pm-10 pm, Fri-11 pm,
Sat 3:30 pm-11 pm, Sun 11 am-8 pm. Closed: 11/28, 12/25. **Features:** casual dress; children's menu;
carryout; cocktails & lounge. Flavorful steak, chicken, pasta and Mexican dishes and homemade dessert
reign supreme here in this 1920s, gangster themed restaurant. The tiled ceiling, numerous windows and
overhead lighting complement walls covered with pictures of famous thugs. **Parking:** on-site. **Cards:** AX, CB, DC, DS, MC, VI.

American

COLLECTOR'S CHOICE & COURT STREET TEA ROOM   Historical **Lunch:** $6-$8 **Dinner:** $10-$12 **Phone:** 618/997-4883
Location: I-57, exit 53 (Main St), 1.5 mi e, 0.3 mi s on SR 37. 500 S Court St 62959. **Hours:** 11 am-2 pm. Closed
major holidays; also Sun. **Reservations:** suggested. **Features:** casual dress; children's menu; carryout.
Step through the front door, and slip into another era. The Victorian Federal style house, circa 1882, is
appointed with antiques, collectibles and crafts. Soup, salad, sandwiches and light fare is best enjoyed with
flavored teas and gourmet coffees. **Parking:** on-site. **Cards:** DS, MC, VI.

Traditional
Continental

HONEYBAKERS   **Lunch:** $5-$9   **Dinner:** $7-$12   Phone: 618/997-0992
Location: I-57, exit 54A (SR 13), 0.5 mi e; in Town and Country Center. 1131 N Carbon 62959. **Hours:** 11 am-4 pm,
Fri & Sat-8 pm, Sun 11 am-2 pm. Closed major holidays. **Features:** casual dress; children's menu;
carryout. The down home restaurant serves up Southern food with style. Homemade specialties, such as
chicken and dumplings and the apple dumplings dessert, taste great with flavored coffee. Stop by the
on-premises bakery to catch a whiff of wonderful desserts. Smoke free premises. **Parking:** on-site. **Cards:** DS, MC, VI.

American

MARKHAM —See Chicago p. 353.

MATTESON —See Chicago p. 354.

MATTOON pop. 18,400

—————— WHERE TO STAY ——————

COMFORT SUITES
SAVE

Motel

Phone: (217)235-6745

4/1-10/31 [ECP]	1P: $70-$74	2P: $75-$79
11/1-3/31 [ECP]	1P: $68-$73	2P: $72-$77

Location: I-57, exit 190B, just w. 1408 E Broadway 61938. Fax: 217/235-0256. **Facility:** 70 units. 35 one-bedroom standard units, some with whirlpools. 35 one-bedroom suites. 3 stories, interior corridors. *Bath:* combo or shower only. **Parking:** on-site. **Amenities:** extended cable TV, dual phone lines, irons, hair dryers. **Pool(s):** heated indoor. **Leisure Activities:** whirlpool, exercise room. **Guest Services:** valet and coin laundry. **Business Services:** meeting rooms, business center, PC, fax (fee). **Cards:** AX, CB, DC, DS, MC, VI.

SOME UNITS

FAIRFIELD INN BY MARRIOTT
AAA **SAVE**
Motel

Phone: (217)234-2420

All Year [ECP]	1P: $60-$90	2P: $65-$95	XP: $18

F18

Location: I-57, exit 190B, just w. 206 McFall Rd 61938. Fax: 217/234-2420. **Facility:** 63 one-bedroom standard units. 3 stories, interior corridors. **Parking:** on-site, winter plug-ins. **Terms:** 14 day cancellation notice-fee imposed. **Amenities:** extended cable TV, irons, hair dryers. **Pool(s):** heated indoor. **Leisure Activities:** whirlpool. **Guest Services:** valet laundry. **Cards:** AX, DC, DS, MC, VI. **Special Amenities:** free continental breakfast and free local telephone calls. *(See color ad card insert)*

SOME UNITS

HAMPTON INN
SAVE
Motel

Phone: (217)234-4267

All Year [CP]	1P: $63-$71	2P: $80

Location: I-57, exit 190B, just w. 1416 Broadway Ave E 61938. Fax: 217/235-4267. **Facility:** 61 one-bedroom standard units. 3 stories, interior corridors. *Bath:* combo or shower only. **Parking:** on-site, winter plug-ins. **Terms:** 30 day cancellation notice-fee imposed. **Amenities:** extended cable TV. **Pool(s):** heated indoor. **Guest Services:** valet laundry. **Business Services:** meeting rooms, fax (fee). **Cards:** AX, DC, DS, MC, VI.

SOME UNITS

—————— WHERE TO DINE ——————

ALAMO STEAK HOUSE & SALOON
Steak House

Dinner: $10-$20   Phone: 217/234-7337

Location: I-57, exit 190B, 1 mi w; at Cross County Mall. 700 E Broadway Ave 61938. **Hours:** 4 pm-9 pm, Fri & Sat-10 pm. Closed: 1/1, 7/4, 12/24, 12/25. **Reservations:** suggested. **Features:** casual dress; children's menu; carryout; cocktails & lounge. This locally popular, bustling restaurant sports a relaxed dining area where visitors feast on steak, seafood, chicken and a house specialty of blackened meatloaf with vegetables and garlic potatoes. Outside dining on the deck is available. **Parking:** on-site. **Cards:** AX, CB, DC, DS, MC, VI.

CODY'S ROAD HOUSE
Steak House

Lunch: $5-$17   **Dinner:** $5-$17   Phone: 217/235-1200

Location: I-57, exit 190B, just w. 1320 Broadway Ave E 61938. **Hours:** 11 am-10 pm. Closed: 11/28, 12/25. **Features:** casual dress; children's menu; carryout; cocktails & lounge. Casual dining is the norm here with pails of peanuts on the tables and the shells surrounding you on the floor. The mouthwatering steak and lightly smoked, thick center-cut pork chops are highlights. The portions are huge, so bring a hearty appetite. **Parking:** on-site. **Cards:** AX, DC, DS, MC, VI.

COMMON GROUNDS
American

Lunch: $5-$7   **Dinner:** $5-$7   Phone: 217/235-2326

Location: At 17th St. 1612 Charleston Ave 61938. **Hours:** 6 am-9 pm, Fri-11 pm, Sat 7 am-11 pm. Closed major holidays; also Sun. **Features:** casual dress; carryout; a la carte. New York-style freshly baked bagels, high-quality cold cuts, cheese and homemade cookies, muffins and pastries are a few reasons to patronize this casual downtown deli. The restaurant is known for its gourmet offerings. Smoke free premises. **Parking:** on-site. **Cards:** MC, VI.

METROPOLIS pop. 6,700

—————— WHERE TO STAY ——————

AMERIHOST INN-PLAYERS
AAA **SAVE**
Motel

Phone: (618)524-5678

All Year	1P: $90	2P: $100	XP: $10

F18

Location: I-24, exit 37, just s from downtown. 203 E Front St 62960. Fax: 618/524-2225. **Facility:** 120 one-bedroom standard units, some with whirlpools. 2 stories, interior corridors. *Bath:* combo or shower only. **Parking:** on-site, winter plug-ins. **Terms:** 30 day cancellation notice, [ECP] meal plan available, package plans. **Amenities:** extended cable TV, voice mail, safes (fee), irons, hair dryers. **Pool(s):** heated indoor. **Leisure Activities:** sauna, whirlpool, exercise room. **Guest Services:** valet laundry. **Business Services:** meeting rooms, fax. **Cards:** AX, CB, DC, DS, JC, MC, VI. **Special Amenities:** free continental breakfast and free newspaper.

SOME UNITS

FEE

ISLE OF VIEW BED & BREAKFAST

Phone: (618)524-5838

▼▼▼
Historic Bed
& Breakfast

All Year   1P: $42-$135   2P: $70-$135   XP: $15

Location: I-24, exit 37, 3 mi w, 0.3 mi s of US 45. 205 Metropolis St 62960. **Fax:** 618/524-2978. **Facility:** Near a river and casino boat, this 1889 Victorian house offers gas fireplaces in some guest rooms. 5 one-bedroom standard units, some with whirlpools. 2 stories, interior corridors. **Parking:** street. **Terms:** age restrictions may apply, 7 day cancellation notice, pets (cat on premises). **Amenities:** extended cable TV. **Business Services:** fax. **Cards:** AX, CB, DC, DS, MC, VI.

SUPER 8

Phone: (618)524-8200

▼▼▼
Motel

4/1-10/31   1P: $49-$63   2P: $56-$70   XP: $7   F12
11/1-3/31   1P: $45-$58   2P: $52-$65   XP: $7   F12

Location: I-24, exit 37, just w. 2055 E 5th St 62960. **Fax:** 618/524-8200. **Facility:** 63 one-bedroom standard units, some with whirlpools. 2 stories, interior corridors. *Bath:* combo or shower only. **Parking:** on-site, winter plug-ins. **Terms:** small pets only. **Amenities:** extended cable TV. *Some:* hair dryers. **Leisure Activities:** whirlpool. **Cards:** AX, CB, DC, DS, MC, VI.

SOME UNITS

MOLINE pop. 43,200—*See QUAD CITIES.*

MONTICELLO pop. 4,500

——— WHERE TO STAY ———

BEST WESTERN MONTICELLO GATEWAY INN

Phone: (217)762-9436

AAA SAVE
▼▼▼
Motel

All Year [ECP]   1P: $61-$81   2P: $68-$88   XP: $7   F17

Location: I-72, exit 166, just s. 805 Iron Horse Pl 61856. **Fax:** 217/762-3202. **Facility:** 41 one-bedroom standard units, some with whirlpools. 2 stories, interior/exterior corridors. **Parking:** on-site. **Terms:** pets ($100 deposit). **Amenities:** irons, hair dryers. **Pool(s):** heated indoor. **Leisure Activities:** whirlpool. **Guest Services:** valet laundry. **Business Services:** fax (fee). **Cards:** AX, CB, DC, DS, JC, MC, VI. **Special Amenities:** free continental breakfast and free local telephone calls.

SOME UNITS
FEE

MORRIS pop. 10,300

——— WHERE TO STAY ———

BEST WESTERN OF MORRIS

Phone: 815-942-9000

▼▼ ▼▼
Motel

All Year   1P: $55   2P: $55   XP: $5   F18

Location: I-80, exit 112, just n. 80 Hampton Rd 60450. **Fax:** 815/942-9000. **Facility:** 67 one-bedroom standard units, some with whirlpools. 3 stories, interior corridors. *Bath:* combo or shower only. **Parking:** on-site. **Terms:** [CP] meal plan available, small pets only. **Amenities:** extended cable TV, irons. **Pool(s):** small heated indoor. **Leisure Activities:** whirlpool, limited exercise equipment. **Guest Services:** coin laundry. **Business Services:** meeting rooms. **Cards:** AX, CB, DC, DS, MC, VI.

SOME UNITS

COMFORT INN

Phone: (815)942-1433

SAVE
▼▼ ▼▼
Motel

4/1-9/30 [ECP]   1P: $64-$89   2P: $69-$94   XP: $5   F18
10/1-3/31 [ECP]   1P: $59-$89   2P: $64-$94   XP: $5   F18

Location: I-80, exit 112, 0.3 mi nw. 70 Gore Rd W 60450. **Fax:** 815/942-1433. **Facility:** 50 one-bedroom standard units. 2 stories, interior corridors. **Parking:** on-site. **Terms:** package plans - in winter, pets (in smoking units). **Amenities:** *Some:* irons, hair dryers. **Pool(s):** small heated indoor. **Leisure Activities:** whirlpool. **Cards:** AX, CB, DC, DS, JC, MC, VI.

SOME UNITS
FEE   FEE FEE

HOLIDAY INN

Phone: (815)942-6600

▼▼ ▼▼
Motor Inn

All Year   1P: $75-$85   2P: $81-$91   XP: $6   F19

Location: I-80, exit 112, 0.3 mi nw. 200 Gore Rd 60450. **Fax:** 815/942-8255. **Facility:** 119 one-bedroom standard units. 2 stories, interior corridors. *Bath:* combo or shower only. **Parking:** on-site. **Terms:** package plans, pets (in smoking units). **Amenities:** extended cable TV, irons, hair dryers. **Pool(s):** small heated indoor. **Leisure Activities:** whirlpool. **Guest Services:** valet and coin laundry. **Business Services:** meeting rooms. **Cards:** AX, DC, DS, MC, VI.

SOME UNITS
FEE   FEE

——— WHERE TO DINE ———

THE ROCKWELL INN

Lunch: $7-$15   **Dinner: $11-$29**   **Phone: 815-942-6224**

▼▼▼
American

Location: I-80, exit 112, 0.8 mi s on SR 47, then 2.3 mi w. 2400 Rt 6 W 60450. **Hours:** 11 am-close. **Closed:** 12/25. **Reservations:** suggested; weekends. **Features:** casual dress; Sunday brunch; children's menu; early bird specials; carryout; salad bar; cocktails & lounge. Victorian ambience exudes from the restaurant's rural setting. Half-portion dinners are available at reduced prices. **Parking:** on-site. **Cards:** AX, DC, DS, MC, VI.

MORRISON pop. 4,400

------ **WHERE TO STAY** ------

HILLENDALE BED & BREAKFAST
▼▼▼
Historic Bed & Breakfast
All Year [BP]   2P: $70-$135   XP: $15
Phone: (815)772-3454
Location: US 30, 0.4 mi w from jct SR 78 S. 600 W Lincolnway 61270. Fax: 815/772-7023. **Facility:** Adjacent to an authentic Japanese teahouse, this B&B offers themed guest rooms; a fountain and reflecting pool are on the grounds. Smoke free premises. 10 units. 9 one-bedroom standard units, some with whirlpools. 1 one-bedroom suite ($150-$170) with whirlpool. 1-3 stories (no elevator), interior/exterior corridors. *Bath:* combo or shower only. **Parking:** on-site. **Terms:** age restrictions may apply, 3 day cancellation notice. **Amenities:** extended cable TV. *Some:* hair dryers. **Leisure Activities:** exercise room. **Guest Services:** gift shop. **Cards:** AX, CB, DC, DS, VI.
SOME UNITS
⊠ 🖨 / 🕅 VCR 💻 /

MORTON pop. 13,800

------ **WHERE TO STAY** ------

BEST WESTERN ASHLAND HOUSE & CONFERENCE CENTER
AAA SAVE
▼▼▼▼
Motel
4/1-11/30 & 3/1-3/31   1P: $59-$89   2P: $64-$99   XP: $5   F15
12/1-2/28   1P: $55-$79   2P: $60-$85   XP: $5   F15
Phone: (309)263-5116
Location: I-74, exit 102, 0.3 mi ne. 201 E Ashland St 61550. Fax: 309/263-4456. **Facility:** 99 one-bedroom standard units. 3 stories, interior/exterior corridors. **Parking:** on-site. **Terms:** 30 day cancellation notice. **Amenities:** extended cable TV, high-speed Internet, voice mail, irons, hair dryers. **Pool(s):** heated indoor. **Leisure Activities:** whirlpool, putting green, playground, exercise room. *Fee:* game room. **Guest Services:** coin laundry. **Business Services:** conference facilities, business center. **Cards:** AX, CB, DC, DS, JC, MC, VI. **Special Amenities:** free continental breakfast and free local telephone calls.
SOME UNITS
[S✦] ✈ 📺 🏊 ✕ 🎥 DATA PORT 🔒 💻 🖨 / ✕ 🖨 /

COMFORT INN
SAVE
▼▼▼
Motel
6/1-8/31 [ECP]   1P: $60-$70   2P: $70-$75   XP: $5   F18
4/1-5/31 & 9/1-3/31 [ECP]   1P: $55-$65   2P: $70-$75   XP: $5   F18
Phone: (309)266-8888
Location: I-74, exit 102, 0.4 mi ne. 210 E Ashland St 61550. Fax: 309/266-8989. **Facility:** 50 one-bedroom standard units, some with whirlpools. 2 stories, interior corridors. **Parking:** on-site, winter plug-ins. **Terms:** cancellation fee imposed. **Amenities:** extended cable TV, hair dryers. *Some:* irons. **Pool(s):** indoor. **Cards:** AX, CB, DC, DS, JC, MC, VI.
SOME UNITS
[S✦] 🍴 🏊 🎥 DATA PORT 🖨 / ✕ 🔒 🖨 💻 /

HOLIDAY INN EXPRESS
▼▼▼
Motel
All Year   1P: $65-$85   2P: $70-$90   XP: $5   F18
Phone: (309)266-8310
Location: I-74, exit 102B, just w. 115 E Ashland 61550. Fax: 309/266-8312. **Facility:** 48 one-bedroom standard units. 2 stories, interior/exterior corridors. **Parking:** on-site. **Terms:** 30 day cancellation notice. **Amenities:** extended cable TV, irons, hair dryers. **Guest Services:** coin laundry. **Business Services:** meeting rooms. **Cards:** AX, CB, DC, DS, MC, VI.
SOME UNITS
ASK [S✦] 🎥 DATA PORT 🖨 / ✕ 🔒 🖨 💻 /

WELK-UM INN
▼▼
Motel
All Year   1P: $45-$59   2P: $48-$65   XP: $5   F16
Phone: (309)266-1600
Location: I-74, exit 102, 0.3 mi ne. 101 E Ashland St 61550. Fax: 309/263-4456. **Facility:** 48 one-bedroom standard units. 2 stories, interior/exterior corridors. *Bath:* combo or shower only. **Parking:** on-site. **Terms:** 30 day cancellation notice. **Amenities:** extended cable TV. **Leisure Activities:** putting green, horseshoes. **Guest Services:** coin laundry. **Cards:** AX, CB, DC, DS, JC, MC, VI.
SOME UNITS
ASK [S✦] ♿ 🎥 DATA PORT 🖨 / ✕ /

MOUNT PROSPECT —See Chicago p. 354.

MOUNT VERNON pop. 17,000

------ **WHERE TO STAY** ------

BEST INNS OF AMERICA
▼▼
Motel
All Year [ECP]   1P: $38-$45   2P: $45-$51   XP: $5   F18
Phone: (618)244-4343
Location: I-57/64, exit 95 (SR 15), just e to 44th, then just s. 222 S 44th St 62864. Fax: 618/244-4343. **Facility:** 153 one-bedroom standard units. 2 stories, exterior corridors. **Parking:** on-site, winter plug-ins. **Terms:** package plans, small pets only ($10 extra charge). **Amenities:** extended cable TV. **Pool(s):** outdoor. **Business Services:** fax (fee). **Cards:** AX, CB, DC, DS, MC, VI.
SOME UNITS
ASK [S✦] 🐾 🏊 🎥 🖨 / ✕ DATA PORT 🔒 🖨 💻 /

DRURY INN-MOUNT VERNON
▼▼
Motel
5/16-9/3 [ECP]   1P: $58-$94   2P: $58-$94   XP: $7   F18
4/1-5/15 & 9/4-3/31 [ECP]   1P: $48-$91   2P: $48-$91   XP: $7   F18
Phone: (618)244-4550
Location: I-57/64, exit 95 (SR 15), just e, then just n (entry through restaurant parking lot). 145 N 44th St 62864-0805. Fax: 618/244-4550. **Facility:** 81 one-bedroom standard units. 3 stories, interior corridors. **Parking:** on-site, winter plug-ins. **Amenities:** extended cable TV, voice mail, irons, hair dryers. **Pool(s):** outdoor. **Guest Services:** complimentary evening beverages: Mon-Thurs, valet laundry. **Business Services:** meeting rooms. **Cards:** AX, CB, DC, DS, MC, VI.
(See color ad p 5)
SOME UNITS
🐾 🍴 📷 🏊 ♿ 🎥 DATA PORT 💻 🖨 / ✕ 🔒 🖨 /
FEE FEE

HAMPTON INN

Phone: (618)244-2323

SAVE

Motel

All Year [ECP]   1P: $66-$75   2P: $73-$82
Location: I-57/64, exit 95 (SR 15), just w to Potomac Blvd, then just n. 221 Potomac Blvd 62864. Fax: 618/244-9948. **Facility:** 101 units. 98 one-bedroom standard units, some with whirlpools. 3 one-bedroom suites ($89-$109) with whirlpools. 4 stories, interior corridors. *Bath:* combo or shower only. **Parking:** on-site, winter plug-ins. **Terms:** cancellation fee imposed. **Amenities:** extended cable TV, voice mail, irons, hair dryers. **Pool(s):** heated indoor. **Leisure Activities:** whirlpool, limited exercise equipment. **Guest Services:** valet laundry. **Business Services:** meeting rooms, fax (fee). **Cards:** AX, CB, DC, DS, JC, MC, VI.

SOME UNITS

HOLIDAY INN

Phone: (618)244-7100

Hotel

All Year   1P: $71-$170
Location: I-57/64, exit 95 (SR 15), just w to Potomac Blvd, then just n. 222 Potomac Blvd 62864 (PO Box 2148). Fax: 618/242-8876. **Facility:** 236 units. 234 one-bedroom standard units, some with whirlpools. 2 one-bedroom suites. 5 stories, interior corridors. **Parking:** on-site, winter plug-ins. **Terms:** [BP] meal plan available. **Amenities:** extended cable TV, dual phone lines, voice mail, irons, hair dryers. **Leisure Activities:** saunas, whirlpool, exercise room. **Guest Services:** valet laundry. **Business Services:** conference facilities, PC, fax (fee). **Cards:** AX, CB, DC, DS, JC, MC, VI.

SOME UNITS
FEE

MOTEL 6-1180

Phone: 618/244-2383

Motel

5/23-8/31	1P: $35-$45	2P: $41-$51	XP: $3	F17
9/1-10/12	1P: $33-$43	2P: $39-$49	XP: $3	F17
10/13-3/31	1P: $31-$41	2P: $37-$47	XP: $3	F17
4/1-5/22	1P: $29-$39	2P: $35-$45	XP: $3	F17

Location: I-57/64, exit 95 (SR 15), just e to Mateer Dr, then 0.4 mi s. 333 S 44th St 62864. Fax: 618/244-1697. **Facility:** 78 one-bedroom standard units. 2 stories, exterior corridors. *Bath:* combo or shower only. **Parking:** on-site. **Amenities:** extended cable TV. **Pool(s):** outdoor. **Guest Services:** coin laundry. **Business Services:** fax (fee). **Cards:** AX, DC, DS, MC, VI.

SOME UNITS

SUPER 8 MOTEL

Phone: (618)242-8800

Motel

All Year [ECP]   1P: $46-$66   2P: $49-$69   XP: $6   F12
Location: I-57/64, exit 95 (SR 15), just e, then just s. 401 S 44th St 62864. Fax: 618/242-8247. **Facility:** 63 one-bedroom standard units. 3 stories (no elevator), interior corridors. **Parking:** on-site. **Amenities:** extended cable TV, safes (fee). **Cards:** AX, CB, DC, DS, MC, VI.

SOME UNITS
FEE

THRIFTY INN-MT. VERNON

Phone: (618)244-7750

Motel

All Year [CP]   1P: $40-$66   2P: $40-$66   XP: $10   F18
Location: I-57/64, exit 95 (SR 15), just e. 100 N 44th St 62864. Fax: 618/244-7750. **Facility:** 41 one-bedroom standard units. 3 stories (no elevator), exterior corridors. **Parking:** on-site, winter plug-ins. **Amenities:** extended cable TV. **Leisure Activities:** pool privileges. **Guest Services:** valet laundry. **Cards:** AX, CB, DC, DS, MC, VI. *(See color ad p 5)*

SOME UNITS

WHERE TO DINE

TRIPLE-E BBQ

Phone: 618/244-7500

Regional American

Lunch: $3-$6   Dinner: $6-$12
Location: I-57/64, exit 95 (SR 15), just e to 44th St, then 0.4 mi s. 37 Mateer Dr 62864. **Hours:** 10 am-9 pm. Closed major holidays. **Features:** casual dress; children's menu; carryout; a la carte. Don't let the modest building mislead you. The portions and flavors here are far from ordinary. The restaurant is known for house-smoked prime rib, all-you-can-eat catfish filets, shrimp and barbecue rib tips. Service is casual and friendly. **Parking:** on-site. **Cards:** DS, MC, VI.

MUNDELEIN —*See Chicago p. 354.*

NAPERVILLE —*See Chicago p. 355.*

NASHVILLE pop. 3,200

WHERE TO STAY

BEST WESTERN U S INN

Phone: (618)478-5341

AAA SAVE

Motel

All Year   1P: $40-$50   2P: $50-$60   XP: $7   F17
Location: I-64, exit 50 (SR 127), 0.3 mi s. 11640 SR 127 62263. Fax: 618/478-5341. **Facility:** 50 one-bedroom standard units. 2 stories, interior corridors. *Bath:* combo or shower only. **Parking:** on-site, winter plug-ins. **Terms:** 7 day cancellation notice, pets ($20 deposit, in smoking units). **Amenities:** extended cable TV, irons, hair dryers. **Guest Services:** coin laundry. **Business Services:** fax (fee). **Cards:** AX, DC, DS, MC, VI. **Special Amenities:** early check-in/late check-out and free local telephone calls.

SOME UNITS
FEE

NAUVOO pop. 1,100

———— WHERE TO STAY ————

HOTEL NAUVOO
AAA [SAVE]
◆◆ ◆◆
Classic Country Inn

Phone: (217)453-2211
All Year   1P: $54-$74   2P: $54-$74   XP: $7   F7
Location: Downtown. 1290 Mulholland St 62354 (PO Box 398). Fax: 217/453-6100. **Facility:** Historic. Designated smoking area. 8 one-bedroom standard units. 2 stories, interior corridors. **Parking:** on-site. **Terms:** cancellation fee imposed. **Amenities:** extended cable TV. **Dining:** dining room, see separate listing. **Business Services:** meeting rooms. **Special Amenities:** free local telephone calls and preferred room (subject to availability with advanced reservations).

⊞ ⊠ 🖨

MOTEL NAUVOO
◆◆ ◆◆
Motel

Phone: 217/453-2219
4/1-11/15   1P: $43-$55   2P: $43-$55   XP: $7   F12
Location: SR 96, 0.4 mi n. 1610 Mulholland St 62354 (PO Box 398). **Facility:** Smoke free premises. 12 one-bedroom standard units. 1 story, exterior corridors. **Bath:** combo or shower only. **Parking:** on-site. **Terms:** open 4/1-11/15, check-in 4 pm, 3 day cancellation notice-fee imposed. **Amenities:** extended cable TV. **Cards:** AX, DS, MC, VI.

⊠ 🖨

———— WHERE TO DINE ————

GRANDPA JOHN'S CAFE Historical
AAA
◆
American

Lunch: $3-$7   **Phone:** 217/453-2310
Location: Downtown. 1255 Mulholland St 62354. **Hours:** Open 4/1-12/25 & 3/1-3/31; 7 am-6:30 pm. Closed: 11/28, 12/24. **Features:** casual dress; carryout. Up and running since 1912, the charming restaurant is a favorite of locals and tourists alike. Step up to the old-fashioned soda fountain to enjoy homemade ice cream that melts in your mouth. Also on the menu are sandwiches, pies and breakfast foods. Smoke free premises. **Parking:** street.

⊠

HOTEL NAUVOO
◆◆ ◆◆
American

Dinner: $12-$17   **Phone:** 217/453-2211
Location: Downtown; in Hotel Nauvoo. 1290 Mulholland St (SR 96) 62354. **Hours:** Open 4/1-11/15 & 3/15-3/31; 5 pm-8:30 pm, Fri & Sat-9 pm, Sun 11 am-3 pm. Closed: Mon. **Reservations:** suggested. **Features:** casual dress; Sunday brunch; children's menu; salad bar; cocktails & lounge; buffet. Pioneer Mormon architecture, circa 1840, surrounds visitors as they dine on a plentiful buffet made up of more than 40 tasty items. Among the house favorites are various fresh breads, wild rice dressing, blueberry muffins and cinnamon rolls. Smoke free premises. **Parking:** on-site.

⊠

NILES —See Chicago p. 357.

NORMAL pop. 40,000

———— WHERE TO STAY ————

BEST WESTERN UNIVERSITY INN
AAA [SAVE]
◆◆◆◆
Motel

Phone: (309)454-4070
All Year [ECP]   1P: $69   2P: $74   XP: $5   F18
Location: I-55, exit 165A (US 51), just s, then return on frontage road. 6 Traders Cir 61761. Fax: 309/888-4505. **Facility:** 102 one-bedroom standard units. 2 stories, interior corridors. **Parking:** on-site. **Terms:** cancellation fee imposed. **Amenities:** extended cable TV, irons, hair dryers. **Pool(s):** small heated indoor. **Leisure Activities:** sauna. **Guest Services:** valet laundry, area transportation-within city limits. **Business Services:** meeting rooms. **Cards:** AX, DC, DS, MC, VI. **Special Amenities:** free continental breakfast and free local telephone calls.

SOME UNITS
[S⊘] [✦] [🛏] [🍴] [∅] [⇆] [♨] [📷] [🖨] / [⊠] [DATA PORT] [▮] [▦]
         FEE FEE   FEE FEE

BLOOMINGTON/NORMAL COURTYARD BY MARRIOTT
AAA [SAVE]
◆◆◆◆
Motel

Phone: (309)862-1166
All Year [BP]   1P: $74-$94   2P: $79-$99
Location: I-55, exit 167, follow I-55 business route (Veterans Pkwy) 1.3 mi s; at Fort Jesse Rd intersection. 310 A Greenbriar Dr 61761. Fax: 309/862-1166. **Facility:** 78 units. 75 one-bedroom standard units. 3 one-bedroom suites ($109-$119). 3 stories, interior corridors. **Bath:** combo or shower only. **Parking:** on-site. **Amenities:** extended cable TV, dual phone lines, voice mail, irons, hair dryers. **Dining:** coffee shop, 6:30-9:30 am, Sat & Sun 7-11 am. **Pool(s):** small heated indoor. **Leisure Activities:** whirlpool, sun deck, exercise room. **Guest Services:** valet and coin laundry. **Business Services:** meeting rooms. **Cards:** AX, CB, DC, DS, MC, VI. *(See color ad card insert)*

SOME UNITS
[🍴] [Y] [🐄] [⇆] [⊠] [📷] [DATA PORT] [▯] [🖨] / [⊠] [▮] [▦] /
                          FEE   FEE FEE

COMFORT SUITES OF BLOOMINGTON
[SAVE]
◆◆◆◆
Motel

Phone: (309)452-8588
All Year   1P: $70-$90   2P: $75-$95   XP: $5   F18
Location: I-55, exit 167, follow I-55 business route (Veterans Pkwy) 1.3 mi s; at Fort Jesse Rd intersection. 310 B Greenbriar Dr 61761. Fax: 309/452-8588. **Facility:** 60 one-bedroom standard units. 3 stories, interior corridors. **Bath:** combo or shower only. **Parking:** on-site, winter plug-ins. **Terms:** 7 day cancellation notice, package plans, pets ($20 extra charge, in smoking units). **Amenities:** extended cable TV, safes (fee), irons, hair dryers. **Pool(s):** small heated indoor. **Leisure Activities:** whirlpool. **Guest Services:** valet and coin laundry. **Cards:** AX, CB, DC, DS, JC, MC, VI.

SOME UNITS
[S⊘] [🐄] [⚕M] [🐄] [⇆] [♨] [📷] [DATA PORT] [▮] [🖨] [▯] [🖨] / [⊠] /
                          FEE

FAIRFIELD INN BY MARRIOTT

AAA **SAVE**
♦♦ ♦♦
Motel

Phone: (309)454-6600

	1P: $78	2P: $78
4/1-11/16 [ECP]	1P: $78	2P: $78
11/17-3/31 [ECP]	1P: $69	2P: $69

Location: I-55, exit 167, follow I-55 business route (Veterans Pkwy) 1.3 mi s. 202 Landmark Dr 61761. **Fax:** 309/454-6600. **Facility:** 128 one-bedroom standard units. 3 stories, interior/exterior corridors. *Bath:* combo or shower only. **Parking:** on-site. **Amenities:** irons, hair dryers. **Pool(s):** heated outdoor. **Guest Services:** valet laundry. **Business Services:** meeting rooms. **Cards:** AX, CB, DC, DS, MC, VI. **Special Amenities:** free continental breakfast and free local telephone calls. *(See color ad card insert)*

SOME UNITS

⬚⬚⬚ ⬚⬚⬚ ⬚⬚⬚ ⬚⬚⬚ ⬚⬚⬚ ⬚⬚⬚ ⬚⬚⬚ ⬚⬚⬚ ⬚⬚⬚ / ⬚⬚⬚ ⬚⬚⬚ ⬚⬚⬚ /
FEE

HOLIDAY INN BLOOMINGTON-NORMAL

♦♦ ♦♦
Motor Inn

Phone: (309)452-8300

All Year [BP]	1P: $96	2P: $106

Location: I-55, exit 165A, 0.5 mi e, return on service road. 8 Traders Cir 61761. **Fax:** 309/454-6722. **Facility:** 160 units. 159 one-bedroom standard units. 1 one-bedroom suite. 5 stories, interior corridors. **Parking:** on-site, winter plug-ins. **Terms:** package plans, pets ($15 extra charge). **Amenities:** high-speed Internet (fee), voice mail, irons, hair dryers. **Pool(s):** heated indoor. **Leisure Activities:** sauna, whirlpool, exercise room. *Fee:* game room. **Guest Services:** valet and coin laundry. **Business Services:** conference facilities. **Cards:** AX, CB, DC, DS, JC, MC, VI.

SOME UNITS

⬚⬚⬚ ⬚⬚⬚ ⬚⬚⬚ ⬚⬚⬚ ⬚⬚⬚ ⬚⬚⬚ ⬚⬚⬚ ⬚⬚⬚ ⬚⬚⬚ ⬚⬚⬚ ⬚⬚⬚ ⬚⬚⬚ / ⬚⬚⬚ ⬚⬚⬚ ⬚⬚⬚ /
FEE FEE

HOLIDAY INN EXPRESS HOTEL & SUITES

♦♦ ♦♦
Motel

Phone: (309)862-1600

All Year	1P: $69-$99	2P: $99

Location: I-55, exit 167, follow I-55 business route (Veterans Pkwy), 1.7 mi s to Parkway Plaza Dr, then just e. 1715 Parkway Plaza Dr 61761. **Fax:** 309/862-4477. **Facility:** 86 units. 68 one-bedroom standard units. 18 one-bedroom suites, some with whirlpools. 3 stories, interior corridors. *Bath:* combo or shower only. **Parking:** on-site. **Terms:** [ECP] meal plan available, package plans, small pets ($15 fee, with prior approval, in limited units). **Amenities:** dual phone lines, voice mail, irons, hair dryers. *Fee:* video games, high-speed Internet. *Some:* CD players. **Pool(s):** heated indoor. **Leisure Activities:** whirlpool, exercise room. **Guest Services:** complimentary evening beverages: Tues-Thurs, valet and coin laundry. **Business Services:** meeting rooms, PC, fax. **Cards:** AX, CB, DC, DS, JC, MC, VI.

SOME UNITS

⬚⬚⬚ ⬚⬚⬚ ⬚⬚⬚ ⬚⬚⬚ ⬚⬚⬚ ⬚⬚⬚ ⬚⬚⬚ ⬚⬚⬚ ⬚⬚⬚ ⬚⬚⬚ ⬚⬚⬚ / ⬚⬚⬚ ⬚⬚⬚ ⬚⬚⬚ ⬚⬚⬚ /
FEE FEE

SIGNATURE INN-NORMAL

♦♦ ♦♦
Motel

Phone: (309)454-4044

All Year [CP]	1P: $69-$79	2P: $69-$79

Location: I-55, exit 167, follow I-55 business route 55 Veteran's Pkwy 1.5 mi s. 101 S Verteran's Pkwy 61761. **Fax:** 309/454-4044. **Facility:** 124 one-bedroom standard units, some with whirlpools. 3 stories, interior corridors. **Parking:** on-site. **Amenities:** extended cable TV, voice mail, irons, hair dryers. **Pool(s):** outdoor. **Leisure Activities:** exercise room. **Guest Services:** valet laundry. **Business Services:** meeting rooms, business center, PC, fax. **Cards:** AX, DC, DS, MC, VI.

SOME UNITS

⬚⬚⬚ ⬚⬚⬚ ⬚⬚⬚ ⬚⬚⬚ ⬚⬚⬚ ⬚⬚⬚ ⬚⬚⬚ ⬚⬚⬚ ⬚⬚⬚ ⬚⬚⬚ ⬚⬚⬚ / ⬚⬚⬚ ⬚⬚⬚ /
FEE

——— **WHERE TO DINE** ———

MANDARIN GARDEN HOUSE

♦♦ ♦♦
Regional Chinese

Lunch: $5-$7   **Dinner:** $8-$15   **Phone:** 309/454-1118

Location: I-55, exit 167, follow I-55 business route (Veterans Pkwy) 1.5 mi s, just n of College Hills Mall. 106 S Mall Dr 61761. **Hours:** 11:30 am-2 & 4:30-10 pm, Fri & Sat-10:30 pm, Sun 11 am-9 pm. Closed major holidays. **Reservations:** accepted. **Features:** casual dress; Sunday brunch; carryout; cocktails & lounge; a la carte. Patrons dine amid light-wood columns, a vaulted ceiling, deep-red banquettes and lovely Chinese artwork. Mandarin and Szechwan cuisine dominate the creative menu. Mongolian beef served with crispy rice noodles is excellent. **Parking:** on-site. **Cards:** AX, DC, DS, MC, VI.

⬚⬚⬚

NORTH AURORA —*See Chicago p. 358.*

NORTHBROOK —*See Chicago p. 358.*

NORTH CHICAGO —*See Chicago p. 359.*

NORTHLAKE —*See Chicago p. 359.*

OAK BROOK —*See Chicago p. 359.*

OAKBROOK TERRACE —*See Chicago p. 360.*

OAK LAWN —*See Chicago p. 361.*

OAK PARK —*See Chicago p. 361.*

O'FALLON pop. 16,100

——— WHERE TO STAY ———

COMFORT INN   Phone: (618)624-6060
AAA **SAVE**
| | 5/1-9/15 [BP] | 1P: $69-$89 | 2P: $69-$89 | XP: $8 | F18 |
| | 4/1-4/30 & 9/16-3/31 [BP] | 1P: $65-$75 | 2P: $65-$75 | XP: $8 | F18 |

Motel   **Location:** I-64, exit 19B (SR 158), 0.5 mi n, then just sw. 1100 Eastgate Dr 62269 (P O Box 698). Fax: 618/624-1753. **Facility:** 96 one-bedroom standard units, some with whirlpools. 2 stories, interior corridors. **Parking:** on-site. **Terms:** pets ($50 deposit). **Amenities:** extended cable TV, irons, hair dryers. **Pool(s):** outdoor. **Leisure Activities:** whirlpool. **Guest Services:** coin laundry. **Business Services:** meeting rooms, fax (fee). **Cards:** AX, CB, DC, DS, JC, MC, VI.

SOME UNITS

ECONO LODGE   Phone: (618)628-8895
SAVE
	5/24-9/30	1P: $64-$69	2P: $64-$69	XP: $5	F18
	10/1-3/31	1P: $60	2P: $60	XP: $5	F18
	4/1-5/23	1P: $58	2P: $58	XP: $5	F18

Motel   **Location:** I-64, exit 14 (US 50), 0.4 mi w. 1409 W Hwy 50 62269. Fax: 618/628-9495. **Facility:** 50 one-bedroom standard units. 2 stories, interior corridors. *Bath:* some combo or shower only. **Parking:** on-site. **Terms:** pets ($50 deposit). **Amenities:** *Some:* irons. **Pool(s):** small heated indoor. **Leisure Activities:** whirlpool, exercise room. **Guest Services:** coin laundry. **Business Services:** meeting rooms. **Cards:** AX, CB, DC, DS, JC, MC, VI.

SOME UNITS

OGLESBY pop. 3,600

——— WHERE TO STAY ———

HOLIDAY INN EXPRESS   Phone: (815)883-3535
| | All Year | 1P: $59-$64 | 2P: $59-$64 | XP: $6 | F19 |

Motel   **Location:** I-39, exit 54, just e. 900 Holiday St 61348. Fax: 815/883-8050. **Facility:** 69 one-bedroom standard units, some with whirlpools. 2 stories, interior corridors. **Parking:** on-site. **Terms:** cancellation fee imposed, pets (in smoking units). **Amenities:** extended cable TV, irons, hair dryers. **Pool(s):** small heated indoor. **Leisure Activities:** whirlpool. **Guest Services:** valet and coin laundry. **Business Services:** meeting rooms. **Cards:** AX, CB, DC, DS, JC, MC, VI.

SOME UNITS

ORLAND PARK —See Chicago p. 362.

OSWEGO pop. 3,900

——— WHERE TO STAY ———

HOLIDAY INN EXPRESS HOTEL & SUITES   Phone: (630)844-4700
| | All Year [ECP] | 1P: $80-$90 | 2P: $80-$90 | XP: $5 | F19 |

Motel   **Location:** Jct US 30 and 34, 0.6 mi w on US 30 to 5th St, just s to Weisbrook Dr, then just e. 2055 Weisbrook Dr 60543. Fax: 630/844-3408. **Facility:** 64 units. 57 one-bedroom standard units, some with whirlpools. 7 one-bedroom suites ($105-$120). 3 stories, interior corridors. *Bath:* combo or shower only. **Parking:** on-site. **Terms:** 7 day cancellation notice. **Amenities:** extended cable TV, dual phone lines, voice mail, irons, hair dryers. **Pool(s):** small heated indoor. **Leisure Activities:** whirlpool, limited exercise equipment. **Guest Services:** valet and coin laundry. **Business Services:** meeting rooms, business center, fax (fee). **Cards:** AX, CB, DC, DS, JC, MC, VI.

SOME UNITS

OTTAWA pop. 17,500

——— WHERE TO STAY ———

HOLIDAY INN EXPRESS   Phone: (815)433-0029
| | All Year [CP] | 1P: $73-$83 | 2P: $73-$83 | XP: $6 | F18 |

Motel   **Location:** I-80, exit 90 (SR 23), just n. 120 W Stevenson Rd 61350. Fax: 815/433-0382. **Facility:** 70 one-bedroom standard units, some with whirlpools. 3 stories, interior corridors. **Parking:** on-site. **Terms:** pets (in smoking units). **Amenities:** extended cable TV, irons, hair dryers. **Pool(s):** small heated indoor. **Leisure Activities:** whirlpool. **Guest Services:** valet and coin laundry. **Business Services:** meeting rooms. **Cards:** AX, DC, DS, MC, VI.

SOME UNITS

PALATINE —See Chicago p. 362.

PARIS pop. 9,000

——— WHERE TO STAY ———

PINNELL MOTOR INN   Phone: (217)465-6441
AAA **SAVE**
| | All Year | 1P: $45-$55 | 2P: $55-$70 | XP: $3 |

Motel   **Location:** 2 mi n on US 150 and SR 1. 11639 Hwy 1 61944 (PO Box 313). Fax: 217/465-5507. **Facility:** 26 one-bedroom standard units. 1 story, exterior corridors. *Bath:* shower only. **Parking:** on-site, winter plug-ins. **Amenities:** extended cable TV. **Guest Services:** gift shop. **Cards:** AX, DS, MC, VI. **Special Amenities:** free local telephone calls and preferred room (subject to availability with advanced reservations).

SOME UNITS

PEKIN pop. 32,300

——— WHERE TO STAY ———

COMFORT INN
SAVE

			Phone: (309)353-4047
7/1-12/31 [CP]	1P: $65-$75	2P: $75-$85	XP: $7 F12
4/1-6/30 & 1/1-3/31 [CP]	1P: $56-$66	2P: $62-$72	XP: $7 F12

Motel

Location: Just n of SR 9, 3 mi e from jct SR 29. 3240 Vandever Ave 61554. Fax: 309/353-5450. **Facility:** 48 one-bedroom standard units, some with whirlpools. 2 stories, interior corridors. **Parking:** on-site. **Terms:** package plans, pets ($10 extra charge, in smoking units). **Amenities:** extended cable TV. *Some:* irons, hair dryers. **Pool(s):** small heated indoor. **Leisure Activities:** whirlpool. **Guest Services:** valet and coin laundry.
Cards: AX, CB, DC, DS, JC, MC, VI.

SOME UNITS

CONCORDE INN & SUITES

			Phone: (309)347-5533
All Year [CP]	1P: $44-$54	2P: $49-$72	

Motel

Location: 2.5 mi e on SR 9 from jct SR 29. 2801 E Court St 61554. Fax: 309/347-4222. **Facility:** 124 units. 119 one-bedroom standard units. 5 one-bedroom suites. 2-4 stories, exterior corridors. *Bath:* combo or shower only. **Parking:** on-site. **Terms:** [AP] meal plan available, package plans, pets ($25 deposit). **Amenities:** extended cable TV. *Some:* irons. **Pool(s):** outdoor. **Leisure Activities:** exercise room. **Guest Services:** valet and coin laundry. **Business Services:** meeting rooms, PC. **Cards:** AX, CB, DC, DS, MC, VI.

SOME UNITS

HOLIDAY INN EXPRESS HOTEL & SUITES

			Phone: (309)353-3305
All Year [CP]	1P: $65-$100	2P: $65-$100	XP: $5 F19

Motel

Location: Jct SR 9 and 29, 3.8 mi e on SR 9. 3615 Kelly Ave 61554. Fax: 309/353-3308. **Facility:** 70 one-bedroom standard units, some with whirlpools. 3 stories, interior corridors. *Bath:* combo or shower only. **Parking:** on-site. **Terms:** 14 day cancellation notice, package plans. **Amenities:** dual phone lines, voice mail, irons, hair dryers. **Pool(s):** small heated indoor. **Leisure Activities:** whirlpool, limited exercise equipment. **Guest Services:** valet laundry. **Business Services:** meeting rooms, business center, fax. **Cards:** AX, CB, DC, DS, JC, MC, VI.

SOME UNITS

SUPER 8 MOTEL
AAA **SAVE**

			Phone: 309/347-8888
All Year [CP]	1P: $50	2P: $60	XP: $5 F12

Motel

Location: 3.8 mi e on SR 9 from jct SR 29. 3830 Kelly Ave 61554. Fax: 309/347-8888. **Facility:** 42 one-bedroom standard units, some with whirlpools. 2 stories, interior corridors. **Parking:** on-site, winter plug-ins. **Amenities:** extended cable TV, hair dryers. **Pool(s):** small heated indoor. **Leisure Activities:** whirlpool. **Guest Services:** coin laundry. **Business Services:** meeting rooms. **Cards:** AX, CB, DC, DS, MC, VI. **Special Amenities:** free continental breakfast and free local telephone calls.

SOME UNITS

——— WHERE TO DINE ———

KELLY AVENUE GRILL

	Lunch: $7-$17	**Dinner:** $7-$17	**Phone:** 309/346-4102

American

Location: Jct SR 29, 3.8 mi e on SR 9. 3610 Kelly Ave 61554. **Hours:** 11 am-9 pm, Fri & Sat-10 pm. **Features:** casual dress; children's menu; early bird specials; carryout; cocktails & lounge; a la carte. Buffalo wings and homemade chili are among favorite offerings at the laid back restaurant. The menu also comprises three fettuccine dishes, lots of fried appetizers and traditional sandwiches, such as spicy chicken breast and fish fillet. **Parking:** on-site. **Cards:** AX, DS, MC, VI.

PEORIA pop. 113,500—See also EAST PEORIA.

——— WHERE TO STAY ———

AMERICINN OF PEORIA

			Phone: (309)692-9200
All Year [ECP]	1P: $90-$150	2P: $90-$150	XP: $6 F12

Motel

Location: SR 6, exit 6, just n. 9106 N Lindbergh Dr 61615. Fax: 309/692-9262. **Facility:** 61 one-bedroom standard units. 3 stories, interior corridors. *Bath:* combo or shower only. **Parking:** on-site. **Amenities:** extended cable TV, hair dryers. *Some:* irons. **Pool(s):** heated indoor. **Leisure Activities:** whirlpool, exercise room. *Fee:* game room. **Guest Services:** coin laundry. **Business Services:** meeting rooms. **Cards:** AX, CB, DC, DS, JC, MC, VI.

SOME UNITS

AMERISUITES (PEORIA/WESTLAKE)
AAA **SAVE**

			Phone: (309)681-2700
All Year [ECP]	1P: $99	2P: $99	

Motel

Location: I-74, exit 89 (War Memorial Dr) eastbound, 0.9 mi w to Scenic Dr, just s to Sterling Dr, 0.4 mi e to W Lake Ave, then just s; exit 90 (Gale Ave) westbound, just w to Sterling Dr, just n to W Lake Ave, then just s. 2701 W Lake Ave 61615. Fax: 309/681-2701. **Facility:** 124 one-bedroom standard units. 5 stories, interior corridors. *Bath:* combo or shower only. **Parking:** on-site. **Terms:** 3 day cancellation notice. **Amenities:** video games, high-speed Internet, dual phone lines, voice mail, irons, hair dryers. **Pool(s):** heated indoor. **Leisure Activities:** whirlpool, exercise room. **Guest Services:** coin laundry. **Business Services:** meeting rooms, business center, PC, fax (fee). **Cards:** AX, CB, DC, DS, JC, MC, VI. **Special Amenities:** free continental breakfast and free newspaper. *(See color ad p 406)*

SOME UNITS

COMFORT SUITES
SAVE
Motel

Phone: (309)688-3800

6/1-8/31	1P: $80-$90	2P: $85-$95	XP: $5	F18
9/1-3/31	1P: $70-$90	2P: $75-$95	XP: $5	F18
4/1-5/31	1P: $70-$80	2P: $75-$85	XP: $5	F18

Location: I-74, exit 89 (War Memorial Dr/US 150), just e, then just s. 4021 N War Memorial Dr 61614. Fax: 309/688-3800. **Facility:** 66 one-bedroom standard units. 2 stories, interior corridors. **Parking:** on-site, winter plug-ins. **Terms:** small pets only ($15 extra charge). **Amenities:** extended cable TV. *Some:* irons, hair dryers. **Pool(s):** heated indoor. **Leisure Activities:** whirlpool. **Guest Services:** valet laundry. **Cards:** AX, CB, DC, DS, MC, VI.

SOME UNITS

COURTYARD BY MARRIOTT
AAA **SAVE**
Motel

Phone: (309)686-1900

All Year [BP]   1P: $89   2P: $94

Location: I-74, exit 89 (US 150/War Memorial Dr), just n; enter through Northwoods Mall. 4125 N War Memorial Dr 61614. Fax: 309/686-1900. **Facility:** 78 units. 75 one-bedroom standard units. 3 one-bedroom suites ($119-$149). 3 stories, interior corridors. *Bath:* combo or shower only. **Parking:** on-site. **Amenities:** extended cable TV, dual phone lines, voice mail, irons, hair dryers. **Dining:** coffee shop, 6:30-10 am, Sat & Sun 7-11 am. **Pool(s):** small heated indoor. **Leisure Activities:** whirlpool, sun deck, exercise room. **Guest Services:** valet and coin laundry. **Business Services:** meeting rooms. **Cards:** AX, CB, DC, DS, JC, MC, VI. *(See color ad card insert)*

SOME UNITS

FAIRFIELD INN BY MARRIOTT
AAA **SAVE**
Motel

Phone: (309)686-7600

All Year   1P: $60-$69

Location: I-74, exit 89 (US 150/War Memorial Dr), just n; enter through Northwoods Mall. 4203 N War Memorial Dr 61614. Fax: 309/686-0686. **Facility:** 135 one-bedroom standard units. 3 stories, interior/exterior corridors. *Bath:* combo or shower only. **Parking:** on-site, winter plug-ins. **Terms:** 30 day cancellation notice-fee imposed. **Amenities:** irons, hair dryers. **Pool(s):** heated outdoor. **Guest Services:** valet laundry. **Cards:** AX, CB, DC, DS, MC, VI. **Special Amenities: free continental breakfast and free local telephone calls.**

(See color ad card insert)

SOME UNITS

HOLIDAY INN-BRANDYWINE
Motor Inn

Phone: (309)686-8000

All Year   1P: $79

Location: I-74, exit 89 (US 150/War Memorial Dr), just nw. 4400 N Brandywine Dr 61614. Fax: 309/682-8237. **Facility:** 249 units. 247 one-bedroom standard units. 2 one-bedroom suites ($100-$150). 3-4 stories, interior corridors. **Parking:** on-site, winter plug-ins. **Terms:** check-in 4 pm, package plans, pets ($30 deposit). **Amenities:** dual phone lines, voice mail, irons, hair dryers. **Pool(s):** heated indoor. **Leisure Activities:** sauna, whirlpool, exercise room. **Guest Services:** gift shop, valet and coin laundry. **Business Services:** conference facilities, business center, fax. **Cards:** AX, CB, DC, DS, JC, MC, VI.

SOME UNITS

JUMER HOTELS-CASTLE LODGE
AAA **SAVE**
Hotel

Phone: (309)673-8040

All Year   1P: $79-$149   2P: $79-$149   XP: $10   F

Location: I-74, exit 91 (University South), 1 mi s to Moss, 0.7 mi w. 117 N Western Ave 61604. Fax: 309/673-9782. **Facility:** 175 units. 168 one-bedroom standard units. 7 one-bedroom suites. 4 stories, interior corridors. **Parking:** on-site. **Terms:** package plans, small pets only ($25 deposit). **Amenities:** video games (fee), voice mail, irons, hair dryers. **Dining:** Jumer's Restaurant, see separate listing. **Pool(s):** heated indoor. **Leisure Activities:** saunas, whirlpool, exercise room. **Guest Services:** gift shop, valet laundry, area transportation-within 10 mi. **Business Services:** conference facilities. **Cards:** AX, CB, DC, DS, MC, VI. **Special Amenities: free local telephone calls and free newspaper.**

SOME UNITS

MARK TWAIN HOTEL
Hotel

All Year [BP]   1P: $109-$129   XP: $15   F13
Phone: (309)676-3600

Location: I-74, exit 98B (Adams St), just w; exit 93 eastbound. 225 NE Adams St 61602. Fax: 309/636-6259. **Facility:** 110 one-bedroom standard units. 9 stories, interior corridors. **Parking:** on-site. **Terms:** pets ($50 deposit). **Amenities:** extended cable TV, high-speed Internet, dual phone lines, voice mail, irons, hair dryers. *Some:* DVD players, CD players. **Leisure Activities:** exercise room. **Guest Services:** valet laundry. **Business Services:** conference facilities. **Cards:** AX, CB, DC, DS, MC, VI.

SOME UNITS

RED ROOF INN
Motel

	1P	2P	XP	
5/1-9/2	1P: $45-$57	2P: $50-$62	XP: $5	F18
9/3-3/31	1P: $39-$55	2P: $44-$60	XP: $5	F18
4/1-4/30	1P: $39-$54	2P: $44-$59	XP: $5	F18

Phone: (309)685-3911

Location: I-74, exit 89 (US 150/War Memorial Dr), just e. 4031 N War Memorial Dr 61614. Fax: 309/685-3941. **Facility:** 108 one-bedroom standard units. 2 stories, exterior corridors. *Bath:* combo or shower only. **Parking:** on-site. **Terms:** small pets only. **Amenities:** video games (fee), voice mail. **Guest Services:** valet laundry. **Cards:** AX, CB, DC, DS, MC, VI. **Special Amenities:** free local telephone calls and free newspaper.

SOME UNITS

RESIDENCE INN BY MARRIOTT
Apartment

All Year [BP]   1P: $129-$149
Phone: (309)681-9000

Location: I-74, exit 89 (US 150/War Memorial Dr), just n; enter through Northlands Mall. 4201 N War Memorial Dr 61614. Fax: 309/681-9000. **Facility:** 66 units. 18 one-bedroom standard units with kitchens. 36 one- and 12 two-bedroom suites ($149-$179) with kitchens. 3 stories, interior corridors. *Bath:* combo or shower only. **Parking:** on-site, winter plug-ins. **Terms:** pets ($25 fee, $10 extra charge). **Amenities:** extended cable TV, voice mail, irons, hair dryers. **Pool(s):** small heated indoor. **Leisure Activities:** whirlpool, exercise room, sports court. **Guest Services:** valet and coin laundry. **Business Services:** meeting rooms. **Cards:** AX, CB, DC, DS, JC, MC, VI.
(See color ad card insert)

SOME UNITS

SIGNATURE INN PEORIA
Motel

All Year [CP]   1P: $60-$69   2P: $60-$69
Phone: (309)685-2556

Location: I-74, exit 89 (US 150/War Memorial Dr), just e, then just n. 4112 N Brandywine Dr 61614. Fax: 309/685-2556. **Facility:** 124 one-bedroom standard units. 3 stories, interior corridors. **Parking:** on-site, winter plug-ins. **Amenities:** extended cable TV, voice mail, irons, hair dryers. **Pool(s):** outdoor. **Leisure Activities:** exercise room. **Guest Services:** valet laundry. **Business Services:** meeting rooms, business center, PC. **Cards:** AX, DC, DS, MC, VI.

SOME UNITS

SLEEP INN & SUITES
Motel

All Year   1P: $58-$89   2P: $63-$89   XP: $6   F18
Phone: (309)682-3322

Location: I-74, exit 89 (US 150/Memorial Dr), just w to Brandywine Dr, then just ne. 4244 Brandywine Dr 61614. Fax: 309/682-3031. **Facility:** 72 one-bedroom standard units, some with whirlpools. 3 stories, interior corridors. *Bath:* combo or shower only. **Parking:** on-site. **Amenities:** extended cable TV, voice mail, safes (fee). *Some:* dual phone lines, irons, hair dryers. **Pool(s):** small heated indoor. **Leisure Activities:** limited exercise equipment. **Guest Services:** valet and coin laundry. **Business Services:** business center, PC, fax (fee). **Cards:** AX, CB, DC, DS, JC, MC, VI.

SOME UNITS

STAYBRIDGE SUITES PEORIA-DOWNTOWN
Motel

All Year [ECP]   1P: $99-$159   2P: $99-$159
Phone: 309/673-7829

Location: I-74, exit 92 (Glendale Ave), 0.5 mi w via William Kumpf St to Fourth Ave, then just w. 300 W Romeo B Garrett Ave 61605. Fax: 309/673-8014. **Facility:** 106 one-bedroom standard units. 3 stories, interior corridors. *Bath:* combo or shower only. **Parking:** on-site, winter plug-ins. **Amenities:** extended cable TV, dual phone lines, voice mail, irons, hair dryers. **Pool(s):** heated indoor. **Leisure Activities:** whirlpool, exercise room, sports court. **Guest Services:** gift shop, complimentary evening beverages: Tues-Thurs, complimentary laundry. **Business Services:** meeting rooms, business center, PC, fax. **Cards:** AX, CB, DC, DS, JC, MC, VI.

SOME UNITS

SUPER 8 MOTEL OF PEORIA
Motel

All Year [ECP]   1P: $48-$68   2P: $54-$76   XP: $6   F12
Phone: (309)688-8074

Location: I-74, exit 89 (US 150/War Memorial Dr), just e. 4025 N War Memorial Dr 61614. Fax: 309/688-8284. **Facility:** 70 one-bedroom standard units. 3 stories, interior corridors. **Parking:** on-site. **Terms:** pets (in smoking units). **Amenities:** extended cable TV, safes (fee). **Guest Services:** coin laundry. **Cards:** AX, CB, DC, DS, MC, VI.

SOME UNITS

—— WHERE TO DINE ——

FAIRVIEW FARMS RESTAURANT
American

Dinner: $6-$15
Phone: 309/697-4111

Location: I-74, exit 3A (SR 116), 0.6 mi w to Maxwell Rd, 1.2 mi s to Heuermann Rd, then just e. 5911 Heuermann Rd 61607. **Hours:** 5 pm-8 pm, Fri & Sat-9 pm, Sun noon-5 pm. Closed major holidays; also Mon. **Reservations:** suggested. **Features:** casual dress; children's menu; carryout. The family-oriented menu includes such dishes as Swiss steak and smoked pork chops. Smoke free premises. **Parking:** on-site. **Cards:** DS, MC, VI.

FISH HOUSE RESTAURANT   **Dinner:** $11-$28   **Phone:** 309/691-9358

Seafood

Location: I-74, exit 91B (University St), 2.8 mi n. 4919 N University St 61614. **Hours:** 4 pm-10 pm, Fri & Sat-11 pm. Closed major holidays. **Features:** casual dress; children's menu; early bird specials; carryout; cocktails & lounge. Subdued lighting, a nautical decor and the freshest seafood available await you at Fish House Restaurant. The varied menu features shrimp, tuna, salmon, orange roughie, halibut, talapia and more. Most are offered fried, grilled or charbroiled according to your pleasure. Beef and chicken are also served so you may select a combination platter if you wish. **Parking:** on-site. **Cards:** AX, MC, VI.

THE GRILL ON FULTON   **Lunch:** $6-$12   **Dinner:** $13-$35   **Phone:** 309/674-6870

American

Location: Center; on Fulton at Madison; opposite City Hall. 456 Fulton St 61602. **Hours:** 11 am-10 pm, Fri-11 pm, Sat 5 pm-11 pm. Closed: 11/28, 12/25; also Sun. **Reservations:** suggested. **Features:** dressy casual; carryout; cocktails & lounge; entertainment. There is a classic feel to this downtown restaurant. The location and decor of the Grill on Fulton contribute to this because diners can sit near the street-level windows and watch the bustle of the city outside. The menu is also classic with pasta, seafood, steak and chops. Even the service is classic since the wait staff is dressed in traditional black slacks and white dress shirts and they are very professional in their interaction with the diners. **Parking:** on-site. **Cards:** AX, CB, DC, DS, MC, VI.

LINDSAY'S ON LIBERTY   Historical   **Lunch:** $8-$13   **Dinner:** $14-$25   **Phone:** 309/497-3300

American

Location: Downtown; just s from SW Jefferson. 330 Liberty St 61602. **Hours:** 11 am-2 & 5-9 pm, Fri-10 pm, Sat 5 pm-10 pm, Sun 4 pm-8 pm. Closed major holidays. **Reservations:** suggested. **Features:** dressy casual; cocktails & lounge. Housed downtown in a 1902 red brick building, the quaint restaurant serves meals that are as appealing to the eye as they are to the palate. Entrees are garnished with edible flowers. The crab cake appetizer is especially popular, as are the grilled marinated pork medallions, which are served in a distinctive and flavorful stone ground mustard sauce. Smoke free premises. **Parking:** street. **Cards:** AX, DS, MC, VI.

NED KELLY'S STEAKHOUSE   **Lunch:** $7-$12   **Dinner:** $11-$20   **Phone:** 309/685-1033

American

Location: I-74, exit 89 (US 150/War Memorial Dr), just e, then just n. 4114 N Brandywine 61614. **Hours:** 11 am-10 pm, Fri & Sat-11 pm, Sun-9 pm. Closed: 12/25. **Reservations:** suggested. **Features:** casual dress; children's menu; early bird specials; cocktails & lounge. It would be a crime at this restaurant—named for a legendary Australian cattle rustler and bank robber—to not try the outstanding mild and creamy onion and curry house salad dressing. "Down under" overtones are evident on the menu and in the decor with a full size jeep just inside the front door and galvanized metal table tops. Fine steaks, prime rib, pork chops, ribs, pasta and seafood available along with various unique chicken offerings. **Parking:** on-site. **Cards:** AX, CB, DC, DS, MC, VI.

VONACHEN'S OLD PLACE   **Lunch:** $6-$17   **Dinner:** $7-$17   **Phone:** 309/692-7033

American

Location: I-74, exit 89 (US 150/War Memorial Dr), 1.5 mi e, then 1.8 mi n on SR 48; in Junction City Shopping Center. 5934 N Knoxville Ave 61614. **Hours:** 11 am-10 pm, Fri & Sat-11 pm, Sun 9 am-9 pm. Closed: 12/25. **Reservations:** suggested. **Features:** dressy casual; Sunday brunch; children's menu; early bird specials; carryout; cocktails & lounge. The three dining rooms at Vonachen's are built around restored 19th-century railroad cars. If you reserve early, you may be able to dine in one of the cars. Since 1975, this setting has been the place of choice for many in the area who have wanted to go to a special place to celebrate special occasions. **Parking:** on-site. **Cards:** AX, DC, DS, MC, VI.

——————— *The following restaurant has not been evaluated by AAA* ———————
but is listed for your information only.

JUMER'S RESTAURANT   **Phone:** 309/673-8181

[fyi]

Not evaluated. Location: I-74, exit 91 (University South), 1 mi s to Moss, 0.7 mi w; in Jumer Hotels-Castle Lodge. 117 N Western Ave 61604. Seven dining rooms decorated in a Bavarian theme make up the casually upscale restaurant, a favorite spot for traditional German favorites and Continental options. The sweet, signature cinnamon rolls alone are worth a visit.

PEORIA HEIGHTS pop. 6,900

——————— WHERE TO DINE ———————

PAPARAZZI   **Dinner:** $6-$12   **Phone:** 309/682-5205

Italian

Location: I-74, exit 89 (US 150/War Memorial Dr), 2.8 mi e to Prospect Rd, then 0.3 mi n to Lake, just e, then just n. 4315 Voss 61614. **Hours:** 5:30 pm-9:30 pm, Fri & Sat-10:30 pm. Closed major holidays; also 12/24, Sun & Mon. **Reservations:** suggested. **Features:** casual dress; beer & wine only; a la carte. In a little dining room on a little street in the little community of Peoria Heights, Paparazzi serves up traditional Italian meals that are big on taste. Many of these dishes are based on old family recipes. Smoke free premises. **Parking:** on-site. **Cards:** AX, DC, DS, MC, VI.

PERU pop. 9,300

——————— WHERE TO STAY ———————

RAMADA LIMITED   **Phone:** 815/224-9000

Motel

		1P:	2P:	XP:	
6/2-9/30 [ECP]		1P: $74-$99	2P: $74-$99	XP: $6	F18
4/1-6/1 & 10/1-3/31 [ECP]		1P: $69-$74	2P: $69-$74	XP: $6	F18

Location: I-80, exit 75 (SR 251), 0.5 mi s to 38th St, just w to Venture Dr, 0.9 mi nw. 4389 Venture Dr 61354. **Fax:** 815/224-9100. **Facility:** 63 one-bedroom standard units, some with whirlpools. 3 stories, interior corridors. *Bath:* combo or shower only. **Parking:** on-site, winter plug-ins. **Terms:** pets (in smoking units). **Amenities:** extended cable TV, video games, voice mail, irons, hair dryers. **Pool(s):** small heated indoor. **Leisure Activities:** whirlpool, exercise room. *Fee:* game room. **Guest Services:** valet and coin laundry. **Business Services:** meeting rooms. **Cards:** AX, DC, DS, MC, VI.

SOME UNITS
ASK [symbols] FEE

——— **WHERE TO DINE** ———

THE RED DOOR INN
▽▽ ▽▽
American

Lunch: $7-$14   **Dinner:** $10-$22   **Phone:** 815/223-2500
Location: Jct US 6, 0.3 mi s on Putnam St. 1701 Water St 61354. **Hours:** 11 am-2 & 5-9 pm, Sat 4 pm-10 pm, Sun 4 pm-8 pm. Closed: 1/1, 12/25. **Reservations:** suggested. **Features:** dressy casual; Sunday brunch; children's menu; carryout; salad bar; cocktails & lounge; a la carte. Overlooking the Illinois River, the eatery features an 1850s-style lounge with brick walls, ornate light fixtures and the original tin ceiling. Nicely prepared steaks, prime rib, chops and seafood make up the menu. Peach flambe, bananas Foster and cherries jubilee are just a few of the tantalizing desserts. **Parking:** on-site. **Cards:** AX, MC, VI.   ⊠

PIERRON pop. 600

——— **WHERE TO DINE** ———

BLUE SPRINGS CAFE
▽▽
American

Lunch: $6-$10   **Dinner:** $9-$11   **Phone:** 618/654-5788
Location: I-70, exit 30 (US 40). 3505 George St 62249. **Hours:** 11 am-9 pm. **Reservations:** accepted. **Features:** casual dress; children's menu; carryout; cocktails; also prix fixe. Formerly a roadside gift and snack shop, the building now serves as a quaint little eating establishment with a fresh and homey atmosphere. This place is a local favorite with basic comfort food and side dishes, but its specialties—as the sign proclaims—are "mile-hi pies," which come out of the oven fresh daily and are the main reason for stopping. Smoke free premises. **Parking:** on-site.   ⊠

PIKE

——— **WHERE TO DINE** ———

LIGHTHOUSE INN RESTAURANT & CAPTAIN'S LOUNGE   **Lunch:** $7-$14   **Dinner:** $7-$14   **Phone:** 217/437-2500
▽▽
American

Location: US 54; at Mississippi River Bridge. 1 Marina Dr 62370. **Hours:** 11 am-9 pm, Fri-Sun to 10 pm. Closed major holidays. **Reservations:** accepted. **Features:** casual dress; Sunday brunch; carryout; cocktails & lounge; a la carte, buffet. Diners seated on the west side of the casual dining room can watch commercial barge traffic mingling with recreational watercraft on the mighty Mississippi, which flows below the restaurant's large windows. The friendly, attentive staff serves such offerings as fresh catfish and buffalo fish or traditional dishes including steak, chicken and chops. **Parking:** on-site. **Cards:** MC, VI.   ⊠

PITTSFIELD pop. 4,400

——— **WHERE TO DINE** ———

——— *The following restaurant has not been evaluated by AAA* ———
but is listed for your information only.

RED DOME INN AND LOUNGE   **Phone:** 217/285-6502
[fyi]
Not evaluated. **Location:** 109 N Madison 62363. A good selection of wines complements prime rib and other nightly specials.

PONTIAC pop. 11,400

——— **WHERE TO STAY** ———

HOLIDAY INN EXPRESS   **Phone:** 815/844-4444
▽▽▽▽
Motel

| | All Year | 1P: $69-$110 | 2P: $69-$110 | XP: $5 | F18 |

Location: I-55, exit 197, just e on SR 116. 1823 W Reynolds St 61764. Fax: 815/844-4441. **Facility:** 54 one-bedroom standard units, some with whirlpools. 2 stories, interior corridors. *Bath:* combo or shower only. **Parking:** on-site. **Terms:** 14 day cancellation notice. **Amenities:** extended cable TV, irons, hair dryers. **Leisure Activities:** exercise room. **Guest Services:** coin laundry. **Cards:** AX, CB, DC, DS, JC, MC, VI.

SOME UNITS
(ASK) (SⒹ) (🎥) (DATA PORT) (🖨) / ⊠ (📱) (📺) /

PONTOON BEACH pop. 4,000

——— **WHERE TO STAY** ———

BEST WESTERN CAMELOT INN   **Phone:** (618)931-2262
(AAA) (SAVE)
▽▽ ▽▽
Motel

	4/16-9/15	1P: $53-$69	2P: $59-$75	XP: $6	F12
	9/16-2/28	1P: $45-$53	2P: $54-$69	XP: $6	F12
	3/1-4/15	1P: $45-$49	2P: $54-$64	XP: $6	F12

Location: I-270, exit 6B (SR 111), just n. 1240 E Old Chain of Rocks Rd 62040. Fax: 618/931-2011. **Facility:** 54 one-bedroom standard units. 2 stories, interior corridors. **Parking:** on-site, winter plug-ins. **Terms:** 7 day cancellation notice, small pets only ($10 extra charge). **Amenities:** irons, hair dryers. **Pool(s):** small heated indoor. **Leisure Activities:** whirlpool. **Guest Services:** coin laundry. **Business Services:** fax (fee). **Cards:** AX, DC, DS, MC, VI. **Special Amenities:** early check-in/late check-out and free continental breakfast.

SOME UNITS
(SⒹ) (🐾) (🍴) (🛥) (🎥) (DATA PORT) (📱) (🖨) / ⊠ (📱) (📺) /

HOLIDAY INN EXPRESS HOTEL & SUITES   **Phone:** (618)797-1200
▽▽▽▽
Motel

| | All Year | 1P: $62-$69 | 2P: $66-$74 | XP: $5 | |

Location: I-270, exit 6A (SR 111), just n. 1240 Regency Pkwy 62040. Fax: 618/797-1207. **Facility:** 65 one-bedroom standard units, some with whirlpools. 3 stories, interior corridors. *Bath:* combo or shower only. **Parking:** on-site. **Terms:** cancellation fee imposed. **Amenities:** video tape library, dual phone lines, voice mail, irons, hair dryers. **Leisure Activities:** whirlpool, playground. **Guest Services:** coin laundry. **Business Services:** fax (fee). **Cards:** AX, CB, DC, DS, JC, MC, VI.

SOME UNITS
(ASK) (SⒹ) (Ⓜ) (🐾) (🎥) (DATA PORT) (📱) (📺) (📱) (🖨) / ⊠ (VCR) /

PROSPECT HEIGHTS —*See Chicago p. 362.*

QUAD CITIES —See also MOLINE.

The unique community known collectively as the Quad Cities unites the states of Illinois and Iowa. Moline and Rock Island, Illinois, and Bettendorf and Davenport, Iowa, combine to create a major commercial and manufacturing complex on the Mississippi River.

✈ Airport Accommodations

OA	QUAD CITY INTERNATIONAL	Diamond Rating	Rate Range High Season	Listing Page
◔◔◔	Best Western Airport Inn, 1 mi ne of main terminal	▽▽▽	$60-$95 SAVE	410
◔◔◔	Country Inn & Suites by Carlson, 0.4 mi e of entrance	▽▽▽	$80-$90 SAVE	411
◔◔◔	Exel Inn of Moline, 1 mi ne of main terminal	▽▽	$37-$55 SAVE	412
	Hampton Inn-Airport, 0.5 mi e of main terminal	▽▽▽	$71-$87	412
	Holiday Inn-Airport Convention Center, 0.3 mi e of terminal	▽▽▽	$78-$98	413
◔◔◔	La Quinta Inn, 0.3 mi e of entrance	▽▽▽	$56-$79 SAVE	414

─── WHERE TO STAY ───

THE ABBEY HOTEL
◔◔◔ SAVE
▽▽ ▽▽
Classic Country Inn
Phone: (563)355-0291
All Year [ECP]   1P:$99-$129   2P:$99-$129   XP:$10
Location: In Bettendorf, IA; just n of Riverfront at 14th St and Central Ave; I-74, exit 4, to 14th St N. 1401 Central Ave 52722. Fax: 563/355-7647. **Facility:** Historic. Perched on a bluff with a view of the city and Mississippi River below, this Romanesque Revival hotel is named in accord with its past as a monastery. 19 units. 18 one-bedroom standard units. 1 one-bedroom suite ($149). 3 stories, interior corridors. **Parking:** on-site. **Terms:** cancellation fee imposed. **Amenities:** extended cable TV, video tape library, dual phone lines, voice mail, irons, hair dryers. **Pool(s):** small outdoor. **Leisure Activities:** exercise room. **Guest Services:** valet laundry, area transportation-within 5 mi. **Business Services:** conference facilities. **Cards:** AX, DC, DS, MC, VI.

✈ 🛍 ✕ VCR 📷 PORT 🖨

BAYMONT INN & SUITES-DAVENPORT
◔◔◔ SAVE
▽▽▽
Motel
Phone: (563)386-1600
All Year   1P:$64-$79   2P:$64-$79
Location: In Davenport, IA; I-80, exit 295A (US 61), just s to 65th St, 0.5 mi ne on frontage road. 400 Jason Way Ave 52807. Fax: 563/386-2222. **Facility:** 102 units. 99 one-bedroom standard units. 3 one-bedroom suites ($79-$129). 4 stories, interior corridors. **Bath:** combo or shower only. **Parking:** on-site, winter plug-ins. **Terms:** pets (in smoking units). **Amenities:** video games (fee), voice mail, irons, hair dryers. **Leisure Activities:** whirlpool. **Guest Services:** valet and coin laundry. **Business Services:** meeting rooms. **Cards:** AX, CB, DC, DS, MC, VI. **Special Amenities:** free continental breakfast and free newspaper.

SOME UNITS
SD 🐾 🍴 🛗 🚭 📷 PORT 💻 🖨 / ✕ 📶 🖨 /
FEE

BEST WESTERN AIRPORT INN
◔◔◔ SAVE
▽▽▽
Motel
Phone: (309)762-9191
All Year   1P:$60-$90   2P:$65-$95   XP:$5   F17
Location: In Moline, IL; I-280/74, exit 5B westbound; I-280, exit 18A eastbound, just s on US 6 and 150 to traffic light, 0.5 mi w, then n on 27th St. 2550 52nd Ave 61265. Fax: 309/762-9191. **Facility:** 50 one-bedroom standard units. 2 stories, interior corridors. **Parking:** on-site. **Terms:** 3 day cancellation notice, [CP] meal plan available. **Amenities:** extended cable TV, irons, hair dryers. **Pool(s):** heated indoor. **Leisure Activities:** whirlpool. **Guest Services:** valet laundry. **Cards:** AX, CB, DC, DS, JC, MC, VI. **Special Amenities:** free continental breakfast and free newspaper.

SOME UNITS
SD 🛍 📷 PORT 📶 🖨 💻 🖨 / ✕ /
FEE

BEST WESTERN STEEPLEGATE INN
◔◔◔ SAVE
▽▽▽
Motor Inn
Phone: (563)386-6900
All Year [BP]   1P:$85-$159
Location: In Davenport, IA; I-80, exit 295A (US 61), just s to 65th St and frontage road entrance. 100 W 76th St 52806. Fax: 563/388-9955. **Facility:** 121 one-bedroom standard units, some with whirlpools. 2 stories, interior corridors. **Parking:** on-site, winter plug-ins. **Terms:** pets ($10 extra charge). **Amenities:** video games (fee), voice mail, irons, hair dryers. **Dining:** restaurant, 6 am-9 pm, Fri & Sat-10 pm, $8-$19, cocktails, entertainment. **Pool(s):** small heated indoor. **Leisure Activities:** whirlpool, exercise room, indoor recreation area. *Fee:* game room, billiards. **Guest Services:** valet and coin laundry. **Business Services:** conference facilities. **Cards:** AX, CB, DC, DS, JC, MC, VI. **Special Amenities:** free continental breakfast and free local telephone calls.

SOME UNITS
SD ✈ 🛍 🍴 🍷 🚭 ✕ 📷 PORT 💻 🖨 / ✕ VCR 📶 🖨 /
FEE

COMFORT INN
SAVE
▽▽▽
Motel
Phone: (309)762-7000
6/1-9/30 [ECP]   1P:$64-$94   2P:$69-$99   XP:$5   F18
4/1-5/31 & 10/1-3/31 [ECP]   1P:$59-$84   2P:$64-$89   XP:$5   F18
Location: In Moline, IL; I-280/74, exit 5B westbound; I-280, exit 18A eastbound, just s to traffic light, then 0.5 mi w, n on 27th St. 2600 52nd Ave 61265. Fax: 309/762-7000. **Facility:** 62 one-bedroom standard units. 2 stories, interior corridors. **Parking:** on-site, winter plug-ins. **Terms:** pets (in smoking units). **Amenities:** extended cable TV. *Some:* irons, hair dryers. **Pool(s):** heated indoor. **Leisure Activities:** whirlpool. **Guest Services:** valet laundry. **Cards:** AX, DC, DS, JC, MC, VI.

SOME UNITS
SD 🛍 🍴 🛗 🚭 📷 PORT 🖨 / ✕ 📶 🖨 💻 /
FEE

COUNTRY INN & SUITES BY CARLSON
Phone: (563)388-6444

▼▼▼

Motel

6/1-10/31 [ECP]	1P: $69-$99	2P: $74-$109	XP: $5	F18
4/1-5/31 & 11/1-3/31 [ECP]	1P: $64-$89	2P: $69-$99	XP: $5	F18

Location: In Davenport, IA; I-80, exit 295A (US 61), 1.4 mi s. 140 E 55th St 52806. Fax: 563/388-6444. **Facility:** 64 units. 54 one-bedroom standard units. 10 one-bedroom suites ($69-$129). 3 stories, interior corridors. *Bath:* combo or shower only. **Parking:** on-site, winter plug-ins. **Terms:** pets (in smoking units). **Amenities:** extended cable TV, voice mail, irons, hair dryers. **Pool(s):** small heated indoor. **Leisure Activities:** whirlpool. **Guest Services:** valet laundry. **Cards:** AX, DC, DS, MC, VI.

SOME UNITS

COUNTRY INN & SUITES BY CARLSON
Phone: (309)797-4249

Ⓐ SAVE
▼▼▼

Motel

1/1-3/31 [CP]	1P: $80-$90	2P: $80-$90	XP: $8	F18
5/1-9/30 [CP]	1P: $79-$89	2P: $79-$89	XP: $8	F18
10/1-12/31 [CP]	1P: $75-$85	2P: $75-$85	XP: $8	F18
4/1-4/30 [CP]	1P: $74-$84	2P: $74-$84	XP: $8	F18

Location: In Moline, IL; I-280/74, exit 5B westbound; I-280, exit 18A eastbound, just s on US 6 and 150, then just nw. 2721 69th Ave Ct 61265. Fax: 309/797-4253. **Facility:** 61 units. 46 one-bedroom standard units, some with whirlpools. 15 one-bedroom suites ($79-$159). 3 stories, interior corridors. *Bath:* combo or shower only. **Parking:** on-site. **Terms:** 14 day cancellation notice. **Amenities:** extended cable TV, dual phone lines, voice mail, irons, hair dryers. **Pool(s):** small heated indoor. **Leisure Activities:** whirlpool, exercise room. **Guest Services:** valet and coin laundry. **Cards:** AX, DC, DS, MC, VI. **Special Amenities:** free continental breakfast and free newspaper. *(See color ad p 322)*

SOME UNITS

COURTYARD BY MARRIOTT-BETTENDORF
Phone: (563)355-3999

Ⓐ SAVE
▼▼▼

Motor Inn

All Year   1P: $49-$79   2P: $49-$89

Location: In Bettendorf, IA; I-74, exit 2, just e, then n on Utica Ridge, then just w. 895 Golden Valley Dr 52722. Fax: 563/355-0308. **Facility:** 108 units. 102 one-bedroom standard units. 6 one-bedroom suites ($89-$129). 3 stories, interior corridors. **Parking:** on-site. **Amenities:** voice mail, irons, hair dryers. **Dining:** coffee shop, 6 am-9:30 & 5-9 pm, Fri-9:30 am, Sat & Sun 7-11 am, $6-$13. **Pool(s):** small heated indoor. **Leisure Activities:** whirlpool, exercise room. **Guest Services:** valet and coin laundry. **Business Services:** meeting rooms. **Cards:** AX, CB, DC, DS, MC, VI.

SOME UNITS

DAVENPORT HOLIDAY INN
Phone: (563)391-1230

▼▼▼

Motor Inn

5/1-9/30	1P: $140-$150	2P: $140-$150
10/1-3/31	1P: $120-$130	2P: $120-$130
4/1-4/30	1P: $100-$110	2P: $100-$110

Location: In Davenport, IA; I-80, exit 295A (US 61), 1.6 mi s. 5202 Brady St 52806. Fax: 563/391-6715. **Facility:** 287 units. 280 one-bedroom standard units, some with whirlpools. 7 one-bedroom suites ($104-$150) with whirlpools. 3 stories, interior corridors. *Bath:* combo or shower only. **Parking:** on-site, winter plug-ins. **Terms:** package plans. **Amenities:** extended cable TV, video games (fee), voice mail, irons, hair dryers. **Pool(s):** small heated indoor. **Leisure Activities:** sauna, whirlpool, miniature golf, exercise room. *Fee:* game room. **Guest Services:** valet and coin laundry. **Business Services:** conference facilities. **Cards:** AX, CB, DC, DS, JC, MC, VI.

SOME UNITS

DAVENPORT SUPER 8 MOTEL
Phone: 563/388-9810

Ⓐ SAVE
▼▼ ▼

Motel

4/1-9/30 [ECP]	1P: $55-$85	2P: $55-$85	XP: $5	F10
10/1-3/31 [ECP]	1P: $45-$65	2P: $45-$65	XP: $5	F10

Location: In Davenport, IA; I-80, exit 295A (US 61), just e. 410 E 65th St 52807. Fax: 563/388-4705. **Facility:** 61 one-bedroom standard units. 2 stories, interior corridors. **Parking:** on-site, winter plug-ins. **Terms:** 7 day cancellation notice, small pets only (dogs & cats only). **Amenities:** safes (fee). **Guest Services:** coin laundry. **Cards:** AX, CB, DC, DS, MC, VI. **Special Amenities:** free continental breakfast and free local telephone calls.

SOME UNITS

DAYS INN OF DAVENPORT
Phone: (563)355-1190

SAVE
▼▼

Motel

6/1-9/30 [ECP]	1P: $54-$79	2P: $59-$84	XP: $5	F18
4/1-5/31 & 10/1-3/31 [ECP]	1P: $49-$69	2P: $54-$74	XP: $5	F18

Location: In Davenport, IA; I-74, exit 2, just w. 3202 E Kimberly Rd 52807. Fax: 563/355-1190. **Facility:** 65 one-bedroom standard units, some with whirlpools. 2 stories, interior corridors. **Parking:** on-site, winter plug-ins. **Terms:** pets ($5 extra charge). **Amenities:** extended cable TV, hair dryers. *Some:* irons. **Pool(s):** small heated indoor. **Leisure Activities:** whirlpool. **Guest Services:** valet laundry. **Cards:** AX, DC, DS, MC, VI.

SOME UNITS

ECONO LODGE
Phone: (563)355-6471

Ⓐ SAVE
▼ ▼

Motel

4/1-9/30	1P: $45-$75	2P: $45-$80	XP: $4	F12
10/1-3/31	1P: $45-$65	2P: $45-$70	XP: $4	F12

Location: In Bettendorf, IA; I-74, exit 3, 0.3 mi w, then 0.5 mi n. 2205 Kimberly Rd 52722. Fax: 563/359-0559. **Facility:** 65 one-bedroom standard units. 1-2 stories, exterior corridors. *Bath:* combo or shower only. **Parking:** on-site. **Terms:** [BP] & [ECP] meal plans available. **Amenities:** extended cable TV. **Pool(s):** small outdoor. **Guest Services:** coin laundry. **Business Services:** meeting rooms. **Cards:** AX, DC, DS, MC, VI. **Special Amenities:** free continental breakfast and free newspaper.

SOME UNITS

EXEL INN OF DAVENPORT

Phone: (563)386-6350

AAA SAVE

6/1-9/30 [CP]	1P: $36-$56	2P: $42-$62	XP: $6	F18
4/1-5/31 & 10/1-3/31 [CP]	1P: $36-$48	2P: $42-$54	XP: $6	F18

Motel

Location: In Davenport, IA; I-80, exit 295A (US 61), 0.5 mi s. 6310 N Brady St 52806. Fax: 563/388-1548. **Facility:** 103 one-bedroom standard units, some with whirlpools. 2 stories, interior corridors. **Parking:** on-site. **Terms:** small pets only (in smoking units). **Amenities:** extended cable TV. *Some:* hair dryers. **Guest Services:** coin laundry. **Cards:** AX, CB, DC, DS, MC, VI. **Special Amenities:** early check-in/late check-out and free continental breakfast.

SOME UNITS

EXEL INN OF MOLINE

Phone: (309)797-5580

AAA SAVE

All Year [CP]	1P: $37-$49	2P: $43-$55	XP: $6	F18

Motel

Location: In Moline, IL; I-280/74, exit 5B westbound; I-280, exit 18A eastbound, just s on US 6 and 150, then 1 mi nw on 27th St. 2501 52nd Ave 61265. Fax: 309/797-1561. **Facility:** 102 one-bedroom standard units. 2 stories, interior corridors. **Parking:** on-site. **Terms:** small pets only. **Amenities:** extended cable TV. *Some:* irons, hair dryers. **Leisure Activities:** Fee: game room. **Guest Services:** coin laundry. **Cards:** AX, CB, DC, DS, MC, VI. **Special Amenities:** early check-in/late check-out and free continental breakfast. *(See color ad p 318)*

SOME UNITS

FAIRFIELD INN BY MARRIOTT

Phone: (309)762-9083

AAA SAVE

6/1-9/30 [ECP]	1P: $69-$99	2P: $74-$104	XP: $5	F18
4/1-5/31 & 10/1-3/31 [ECP]	1P: $64-$94	2P: $69-$99	XP: $5	F18

Motel

Location: In Moline, IL; I-280/74, exit 5B westbound; I-280, exit 18A eastbound, just s on US 6 to traffic light, 0.5 mi w, n on 27th St. 2705 48th Ave 61265. Fax: 309/762-9083. **Facility:** 63 one-bedroom standard units. 3 stories, interior corridors. **Parking:** on-site, winter plug-ins. **Amenities:** extended cable TV, irons. **Leisure Activities:** whirlpool. **Guest Services:** valet laundry. **Cards:** AX, CB, DC, DS, MC, VI. **Special Amenities:** free continental breakfast and free local telephone calls. *(See color ad card insert)*

SOME UNITS

FAIRFIELD INN BY MARRIOTT-DAVENPORT

Phone: (563)355-2264

AAA SAVE

6/1-10/31 [ECP]	1P: $69-$99	2P: $74-$109	XP: $5	F18
11/1-3/31 [ECP]	1P: $64-$89	2P: $69-$99	XP: $5	F18
4/1-5/31 [ECP]	1P: $64-$89	2P: $69-$94	XP: $5	F18

Motel

Location: In Davenport, IA; I-74, exit 2, just w. 3206 E Kimberly Rd 52807. Fax: 563/355-2264. **Facility:** 62 one-bedroom standard units. 3 stories, interior corridors. **Parking:** on-site. **Amenities:** extended cable TV, irons. **Pool(s):** small heated indoor. **Leisure Activities:** whirlpool. **Guest Services:** valet laundry. **Business Services:** meeting rooms. **Cards:** AX, DC, DS, MC, VI. **Special Amenities:** free continental breakfast and free local telephone calls.

SOME UNITS

FOUR POINTS BY SHERATON

Phone: (309)794-1212

AAA SAVE

All Year	1P: $69	2P: $69	XP: $10	F15

Hotel

Location: In Rock Island, IL; just e of Centennial Bridge, at 3rd Ave and 17th St. 226 17th St 61201-8723. Fax: 309/794-0852. **Facility:** 175 one-bedroom standard units. 8 stories, interior corridors. **Parking:** on-site. **Terms:** package plans. **Amenities:** extended cable TV, video games, voice mail, irons, hair dryers. *Some:* safes. **Dining:** restaurant, 6:30 am-10 pm, $8-$17, cocktails. **Pool(s):** indoor. **Leisure Activities:** saunas, whirlpools. *Fee:* tanning beds. **Guest Services:** massage (fee), valet laundry, area transportation-The Rock Island Asenal. **Business Services:** conference facilities, business center, PC, fax. **Cards:** AX, CB, DC, DS, JC, MC, VI. **Special Amenities:** early check-in/late check-out and free newspaper.

SOME UNITS

HAMPTON INN-AIRPORT

Phone: (309)762-1711

SAVE

6/1-9/30 [ECP]	1P: $71-$77	2P: $81-$87
10/1-3/31 [ECP]	1P: $69-$73	2P: $79-$83
4/1-5/31 [ECP]	1P: $69-$71	2P: $79-$81

Motel

Location: In Moline, IL; I-280/74, exit 5B westbound; I-280, exit 18A eastbound, just s on US 6 and 150, then just nw. 6920 27th St 61265. Fax: 309/762-1788. **Facility:** 138 units. 136 one-bedroom standard units, some with whirlpools. 2 one-bedroom suites ($125-$200) with whirlpools. 2 stories, interior corridors. **Parking:** on-site. **Terms:** small pets only. **Amenities:** extended cable TV, video games (fee), voice mail, irons. **Pool(s):** heated outdoor. **Guest Services:** valet laundry. **Cards:** AX, CB, DC, DS, MC, VI.

SOME UNITS

HAMPTON INN-DAVENPORT

Phone: (563)359-3921

SAVE

4/1-9/23 [ECP]	1P: $69	2P: $69
9/24-3/31 [ECP]	1P: $65	2P: $65

Motel

Location: In Davenport, IA; I-74, exit 2, just w, then just s. 3330 E Kimberly Rd 52807. Fax: 563/359-1912. **Facility:** 130 units. 128 one-bedroom standard units, some with whirlpools. 2 one-bedroom suites ($125-$225) with whirlpools. 2 stories, interior corridors. **Parking:** on-site. **Terms:** cancellation fee imposed. **Amenities:** extended cable TV, video games (fee), voice mail, irons. **Pool(s):** small heated indoor. **Leisure Activities:** sauna, whirlpool, steamroom, exercise room. **Guest Services:** valet and coin laundry. **Business Services:** conference facilities. **Cards:** AX, CB, DC, DS, JC, MC, VI.

SOME UNITS

HEARTLAND INN

Phone: (563)386-8336

WWWW WW

Motel

All Year [ECP] 1P: $65-$155 2P: $65-$155 XP: $5 F16
Location: In Davenport, IA; I-80, exit 295A (US 61), just se. 6605 Brady St 52806. Fax: 563/386-6005. **Facility:** 86 one-bedroom standard units, some with whirlpools. 3 stories, interior corridors. **Parking:** on-site, winter plug-ins. **Amenities:** extended cable TV. **Pool(s):** small heated indoor. **Leisure Activities:** sauna. *Fee:* game room. **Guest Services:** valet laundry. **Cards:** AX, CB, DC, DS, JC, MC, VI.

SOME UNITS

HEARTLAND INN-BETTENDORF

Phone: (563)355-6336

WWWW WW

Motel

All Year [ECP] 1P: $65-$155 2P: $65-$155 XP: $5 F16
Location: In Bettendorf, IA; I-74, exit 2, just e, just n on Utica Ridge Rd, then w. 815 Golden Valley Dr 52722. Fax: 563/355-0039. **Facility:** 86 one-bedroom standard units, some with whirlpools. 3 stories, interior corridors. **Parking:** on-site. **Amenities:** extended cable TV. **Pool(s):** small heated indoor. **Leisure Activities:** sauna. *Fee:* game room. **Guest Services:** valet and coin laundry. **Cards:** AX, CB, DC, DS, JC, MC, VI.

SOME UNITS

HOLIDAY INN-AIRPORT CONVENTION CENTER

Phone: (309)762-8811

WWWW WW

Motor Inn

5/1-8/31 1P: $78-$98 2P: $78-$98
4/1-4/30 & 9/1-3/31 1P: $69-$89 2P: $69-$89
Location: In Moline, IL; I-280/74, exit 5B westbound; I-280, exit 18A eastbound, just s on US 6 and 150, then just nw. 6902 27th St 61265. Fax: 309/762-3393. **Facility:** 216 one-bedroom standard units. 2 stories, interior corridors. *Bath:* combo or shower only. **Parking:** on-site. **Terms:** cancellation fee imposed. **Amenities:** extended cable TV, video games, voice mail, irons, hair dryers. **Pool(s):** 2 indoor. **Leisure Activities:** sauna, whirlpool, miniature golf, exercise room. **Guest Services:** valet and coin laundry. **Business Services:** conference facilities. **Cards:** AX, CB, DC, DS, JC, MC, VI.

SOME UNITS

FEE FEE FEE

HOLIDAY INN EXPRESS-MOLINE AIRPORT

Phone: (309)762-8300

WWWW WW

Motel

All Year 1P: $67 2P: $72
Location: In Moline, IL; I-280/74, exit 5B westbound; I-280, exit 18A eastbound, just s on US 6 and 150, then just nw. 6910 27th St 61265. Fax: 309/762-9922. **Facility:** 110 units. 109 one-bedroom standard units. 1 one-bedroom suite ($140-$160) with whirlpool. 2 stories, interior corridors. *Bath:* combo or shower only. **Parking:** on-site. **Terms:** package plans. **Amenities:** extended cable TV, voice mail, irons, hair dryers. **Guest Services:** valet laundry. **Business Services:** meeting rooms. **Cards:** AX, CB, DC, DS, JC, MC, VI.

SOME UNITS

FEE FEE FEE

HOLIDAY INN HOTEL & SUITES-BETTENDORF

Phone: (563)355-4761

AAA SAVE

WWWW WW

Motor Inn

All Year 1P: $75-$99 2P: $75-$99
Location: In Bettendorf, IA; I-74, exit 3, just w. 909 Middle Rd 52722. Fax: 563/355-5572. **Facility:** 150 units. 144 one-bedroom standard units. 6 one-bedroom suites ($119-$179) with whirlpools. 2 stories, interior corridors. *Bath:* combo or shower only. **Parking:** on-site. **Terms:** 30 day cancellation notice, package plans, small pets only ($50 deposit). **Amenities:** extended cable TV, video games (fee), dual phone lines, voice mail, irons, hair dryers. **Dining:** restaurant, 6:30 am-11 pm, Fri-midnight, Sat 7:30-midnight, Sun 8 am-9 pm, $5-$15, cocktails. **Pool(s):** small heated indoor. **Leisure Activities:** sauna, whirlpool, exercise room. *Fee:* game room. **Guest Services:** valet and coin laundry. **Business Services:** conference facilities, business center, PC. **Cards:** AX, CB, DC, DS, JC, MC, VI. **Special Amenities:** early check-in/late check-out and free local telephone calls.

SOME UNITS

FEE

ISLE OF CAPRI CASINO AND HOTEL

Phone: (563)359-7280

WWWW WW

Hotel

All Year 1P: $84-$125 2P: $84-$125 XP: $10
Location: In Bettendorf, IA; I-74, exit 4 (US 67/State St), just e on State St, then just s. 1777 Isle Pkwy 52722 (PO Box 1166, BETTENDORF, IA). Fax: 563/359-7580. **Facility:** 256 units. 221 one-bedroom standard units. 35 one-bedroom suites, some with whirlpools. 8 stories, interior corridors. *Bath:* combo or shower only. **Parking:** on-site and valet. **Terms:** check-in 4 pm, package plans. **Amenities:** extended cable TV, video games (fee), dual phone lines, voice mail, hair dryers. **Pool(s):** small heated indoor. **Leisure Activities:** whirlpool, exercise room, horseshoes, shuffleboard. **Guest Services:** gift shop, valet laundry. **Business Services:** conference facilities. **Cards:** AX, DS, MC, VI.

SOME UNITS

FEE

JUMER'S CASTLE LODGE-BETTENDORF

Phone: (563)359-7141

AAA SAVE

WWWW WW

Hotel

All Year 1P: $75-$85 2P: $81-$96 XP: $9 F18
Location: In Bettendorf, IA; I-74, exit 2, just e, 3 mi s of jct I-74 and 80. 900 Spruce Hills Dr 52722. Fax: 563/359-7141. **Facility:** 210 units. 207 one-bedroom standard units. 3 one-bedroom suites ($96-$137). 4-9 stories, interior corridors. **Parking:** on-site, winter plug-ins. **Terms:** cancellation fee imposed, [AP] meal plan available, package plans, pets ($25 deposit). **Amenities:** video games (fee), voice mail, irons, hair dryers. **Dining:** Jumer's Restaurant, see separate listing. **Pool(s):** small heated indoor, small heated indoor. **Leisure Activities:** saunas, whirlpool, putting green, playground, exercise room. *Fee:* tennis privileges, game room. **Guest Services:** gift shop, valet laundry, area transportation. **Business Services:** conference facilities. **Cards:** AX, CB, DC, DS, MC, VI. **Special Amenities:** free local telephone calls and free room upgrade (subject to availability with advanced reservations).

SOME UNITS

FEE FEE

LA QUINTA INN

Phone: (309)762-9008

(AAA) [SAVE]
▽▽▽
Motel

All Year — 1P: $56-$79 — 2P: $56-$76
Location: In Moline, IL; I-280/74, exit 5B westbound; I-280, exit 18A eastbound, just s on US 6 and 150 to traffic light, just n, then w on 27th St. 5450 27th St 61265. Fax: 309/762-2455. **Facility:** 126 one-bedroom standard units. 2 stories, interior corridors. **Parking:** on-site, winter plug-ins. **Terms:** pets (in smoking units). **Amenities:** video games, dual phone lines, voice mail, irons, hair dryers. **Guest Services:** valet and coin laundry, area transportation. **Business Services:** meeting rooms. **Cards:** AX, CB, DC, DS, MC, VI. **Special Amenities:** free continental breakfast and free local telephone calls.

RADISSON ON JOHN DEERE COMMONS

Phone: (309)764-1000

(AAA) [SAVE]
▽▽▽
Hotel

All Year [ECP] — 1P: $99-$279 — 2P: $99-$279
Location: In Moline, IL; 0.4 mi w of I-74. 1415 River Dr 61265. Fax: 309/764-1710. **Facility:** 163 units. 109 one-bedroom standard units, some with whirlpools. 54 one-bedroom suites, some with whirlpools. 6 stories, interior corridors. *Bath:* combo or shower only. **Parking:** on-site. **Terms:** package plans. **Amenities:** extended cable TV, dual phone lines, voice mail, irons, hair dryers. **Dining:** restaurant, 11 am-10 pm, $7-$16, cocktails. **Pool(s):** small heated indoor. **Leisure Activities:** whirlpool, boat dock, exercise room, adjacent to 26 mile jogging path. **Guest Services:** valet laundry, area transportation-within 5 mi. **Business Services:** meeting rooms. **Cards:** AX, CB, DC, DS, JC, MC, VI. **Special Amenities:** free continental breakfast and free local telephone calls.

RADISSON QUAD CITY PLAZA HOTEL

Phone: (563)322-2200

(AAA) [SAVE]
▽▽▽
Hotel

All Year — 1P: $99-$109 — 2P: $99-$109 — XP: $15 — F17
Location: In Davenport, IA; I-80, exit 295A (US 61), downtown. 111 E 2nd St 52801. Fax: 563/322-9939. **Facility:** 221 units. 203 one-bedroom standard units. 18 one-bedroom suites ($159). 6 stories, interior corridors. *Bath:* combo or shower only. **Parking:** *Fee:* on-site and valet. **Terms:** package plans. **Amenities:** dual phone lines, voice mail, irons, hair dryers. *Fee:* video games, high-speed Internet. **Dining:** restaurant, 6 am-2 & 5-10 pm, Sat & Sun 7 am-10 pm, $9-$24, cocktails. **Pool(s):** heated indoor. **Leisure Activities:** sauna, whirlpool, sun deck, exercise room, billiards. **Guest Services:** gift shop, valet laundry. **Business Services:** conference facilities, business center, PC, fax (fee). **Cards:** AX, CB, DC, DS, MC, VI. **Special Amenities:** free newspaper.

RESIDENCE INN BY MARRIOTT

Phone: (563)391-8877

(AAA) [SAVE]
▽▽▽
Suite Motel

All Year [ECP] — 1P: $85-$95 — 2P: $85-$95
Location: In Davenport, IA; I-80, exit 295 (US 61), 1.4 mi s. 120 E 55th St 52806. Fax: 563/391-8877. **Facility:** 78 units. 18 one-bedroom standard units with efficiencies. 48 one- and 12 two-bedroom suites, some with efficiencies or kitchens. 3 stories, interior corridors. *Bath:* combo or shower only. **Parking:** on-site. **Terms:** 7 day cancellation notice, pets ($100 extra charge). **Amenities:** extended cable TV, voice mail, irons, hair dryers. **Pool(s):** small heated indoor. **Leisure Activities:** whirlpool, exercise room, sports court. **Guest Services:** complimentary evening beverages: Mon-Thurs, valet and coin laundry. **Business Services:** meeting rooms. **Cards:** AX, DC, DS, MC, VI.

RHYTHM CITY

Phone: 563/328-6000

(AAA) [SAVE]
▽▽▽
Historic Hotel

All Year — 1P: $75-$95 — 2P: $75-$95 — XP: $10 — F18
Location: In Davenport, IA; downtown; connected to River Center Convention Center, at 3rd and Perry sts. 200 E 3rd St 52801. Fax: 563/328-6047. **Facility:** 191 units. 154 one-bedroom standard units, some with whirlpools. 34 one- and 3 two-bedroom suites ($105-$175), some with kitchens and/or whirlpools. 11 stories, interior corridors. **Parking:** on-site. **Terms:** cancellation fee imposed, package plans, pets ($50 deposit). **Amenities:** video games (fee), voice mail, hair dryers. *Some:* safes, irons. **Dining:** High Note, see separate listing, entertainment. **Leisure Activities:** sauna, exercise room. **Guest Services:** valet and coin laundry. **Business Services:** conference facilities. **Cards:** AX, DC, DS, MC, VI. **Special Amenities:** free newspaper.

SIGNATURE INN BETTENDORF

Phone: (563)355-7575

▽▽▽
Motel

All Year [CP] — 1P: $66-$76 — 2P: $66-$76
Location: In Bettendorf, IA; I-74, exit 2, just e. 3020 Utica Ridge Rd 52722. Fax: 563/355-7575. **Facility:** 119 units. 115 one-bedroom standard units, some with whirlpools. 4 one-bedroom suites. 3 stories, interior corridors. **Parking:** on-site. **Amenities:** extended cable TV, voice mail, irons, hair dryers. **Pool(s):** small heated outdoor. **Leisure Activities:** exercise room. **Guest Services:** valet laundry. **Business Services:** meeting rooms, PC. **Cards:** AX, DC, DS, MC, VI.

VICTORIAN INN BED & BREAKFAST

Phone: 309/788-7068

▽▽▽
Historic Bed
& Breakfast

All Year — 1P: $75-$150 — 2P: $75-$150 — XP: $20 — F5
Location: In Rock Island, IL; SR 92 at Rock Island Riverfront, 0.4 mi s. 702 20th St 61201. Fax: 309/788-7086. **Facility:** Seven fireplaces are featured in this elegant 19th-century Victorian B&B; the innkeeper/owner grew up in the house. Smoke free premises. 5 one-bedroom standard units. 3 stories (no elevator), interior corridors. *Bath:* combo or shower only. **Parking:** on-site. **Terms:** package plans. **Amenities:** extended cable TV. **Guest Services:** gift shop. **Cards:** AX, MC, VI.

—— **WHERE TO DINE** ——

BIAGGI'S RISTORANTE ITALIANO

Lunch: $6-$17 — Dinner: $8-$25 — **Phone:** 319/344-2103

▽▽▽
Italian

Location: In Davenport, IA; I-74, exit 1, just e. 5195 Utica Ridge Rd 52807. **Hours:** 11 am-10 pm, Fri & Sat-11 pm, Sun-9 pm. **Features:** casual dress; carryout; cocktails & lounge; a la carte. **Parking:** on-site. **Cards:** AX, DC, DS, MC, VI.

BISHOP BUFFET

American

Lunch: $6   **Dinner:** $7   **Phone:** 563/355-1831
Location: In Bettendorf, IA; I-74, exit 3, just w; west side of Duck Creek Plaza Mall. 852 Middle Rd 52722. **Hours:** 11 am-8 pm, Sun-7:30 pm. Closed: 12/25. **Features:** casual dress; children's menu; buffet, a la carte. The popular restaurant has a good variety of chicken, seafood and roast beef offerings as well as freshly made desserts. **Parking:** on-site. **Cards:** MC, VI.

BUD'S SKYLINE INN

American

Dinner: $8-$21   **Phone:** 309/764-9128
Location: In Moline, IL; I-280/74, exit 5B westbound; I-280, exit 18A eastbound, just s on US 6. 2621 Airport Rd 61265. **Hours:** 4 pm-10 pm, Fri & Sat-11 pm, Sun 4 pm-9 pm. **Reservations:** accepted. **Features:** casual dress; children's menu; carryout; salad bar; cocktails. With a location adjacent to the main runway of the Quad Cities International Airport, at Bud's Skyline Inn you can enjoy excellent views of local air traffic from the dining room's panoramic windows or, in season, from the patio tables. **Parking:** on-site. **Cards:** AX, MC, VI.

CHEF CHARLES' DUCK CITY BISTRO

Continental

Dinner: $14-$22   **Phone:** 319/322-3825
Location: In Davenport, IA; between Brady and Perry sts. 115 E 3rd St 52801. **Hours:** 5 pm-midnight. Closed: 11/28, 12/25; also Sun. **Reservations:** suggested. **Features:** casual dress; children's menu; cocktails & lounge; a la carte. You'll enjoy an excellent dining adventure in a relaxed, casual environment at this bistro. Very well-prepared entrees featuring chicken, pork chops, fresh seafood and pasta are featured on the menu. Outdoor patio dining overlooks the park. **Parking:** street. **Cards:** AX, DS, MC, VI.

FORTUNE GARDEN

Chinese

Lunch: $4-$6   **Dinner:** $7-$18   **Phone:** 563/355-7878
Location: In Bettendorf, IA; jct I-74 and US 67, exit 3, 0.3 mi w to Kimberly Rd, then 0.5 mi n. 2211 Kimberly Rd 52722. **Hours:** 11 am-9 pm, Fri & Sat-10 pm. Closed: Sun. **Reservations:** suggested. **Features:** casual dress; children's menu; carryout; cocktails & lounge. Mongolian-style barbecue and Mandarin, Hunan and Szechwan selections are prepared in hearty portions. **Parking:** on-site. **Cards:** AX, CB, DC, DS, MC, VI.

HIGH NOTE

Steak & Seafood

Dinner: $12-$40   **Phone:** 563/328-6000
Location: In Davenport, IA; downtown; connected to River Center Convention Center, at 3rd and Perry sts; in Rhythm City. 200 E 3rd St 52801. **Hours:** 5 pm-10 pm, Sat-11 pm. **Reservations:** suggested. **Features:** casual dress; cocktails; a la carte. Located on the top floor of the casino/hotel, this restaurant offers breathtaking views of the Mississippi River. Guests can enjoy creative gourmet cuisine such as jerked chicken tamales or Cajun salmon. **Parking:** on-site. **Cards:** AX, DC, DS, MC, VI.

IOWA MACHINE SHED RESTAURANT

American

Lunch: $6-$12   **Dinner:** $9-$19   **Phone:** 319/391-2427
Location: In Davenport, IA; I-80, exit 292, 0.3 mi s. 7250 Northwest Blvd 52806. **Hours:** 6 am-10 pm, Sun 7 am-9 pm. Closed: 1/1, 11/28, 12/25; also 12/24 for dinner. **Features:** casual dress; children's menu; carryout; salad bar; cocktails & lounge. From the antique tractors and farm equipment at the entrance through the agriculture-inspired souveniers in the gift shop, to the overall-clad servers, this restuarant is a tribute to the Midwestern farmer and a credit to the farmer, too as regional farm produce is selected, prepared and served. **Parking:** on-site. **Cards:** AX, CB, DC, DS, MC, VI.

JUMER'S RESTAURANT

American

Lunch: $6-$9   **Dinner:** $9-$20   **Phone:** 563/359-1607
Location: In Bettendorf, IA; I-74, exit 2, just e, 3 mi s of jct I-74 and 80; in Jumer's Castle Lodge-Bettendorf. 900 Spruce Hills Dr 52722. **Hours:** 6 am-10 pm, Sat & Sun 6:30 am-11 pm. **Reservations:** suggested. **Features:** casual dress; children's menu; early bird specials; cocktails & lounge; entertainment; a la carte, buffet. An Old World hunting lodge motif punctuates the elegant dining room. The menu highlights German dishes but also lists American and Continental favorites. **Parking:** on-site. **Cards:** AX, CB, DC, DS, MC, VI.

MISS MAMIE'S NEW ORLEANS GRILLE

Cajun

Lunch: $6-$9   **Dinner:** $9-$14   **Phone:** 319/445-0684
Location: In Davenport, IA; I-80, exit 295A (US 61), 1.7 mi s. 4830 N Brady St 52806. **Hours:** 11 am-9:45 pm, Fri & Sat-10:15 pm, Sun-9 pm. Closed major holidays. **Features:** casual dress; children's menu; carryout; cocktails & lounge. With a menu featuring New Orleans favorites, popular Southern dishes, Midwestern cuisine, seafood and pasta, this place offers something for everyone. The attractively decorated dining room and professional, polished servers contribute to a delightful dining experience. **Parking:** on-site. **Cards:** AX, DS, MC, VI.

MONTANA JACKS AMERICAN CAFE

American

Lunch: $6-$16   **Dinner:** $7-$20   **Phone:** 319/359-4411
Location: In Davenport, IA; I-74, exit 2, just w. 1720 E Kimberly Rd 52807. **Hours:** 11 am-2 & 5-10 pm, Fri & Sat-11 pm, Sun 4 pm-9 pm. **Features:** casual dress; carryout; cocktails & lounge. **Parking:** on-site. **Cards:** AX, DC, DS, MC, VI.

PLANTED EARTH CAFE

American

Lunch: $9-$16   **Dinner:** $11-$21   **Phone:** 309/736-0100
Location: In Moline, IL; I-74, exit 1 (River Dr), 0.4 mi w. 1300 River Dr 61265. **Hours:** 11 am-9 pm, Fri & Sat-10 pm, Sun 8:30 am-9 pm. Closed: 12/25. **Reservations:** accepted. **Features:** casual dress; Sunday brunch; children's menu; carryout; cocktails; a la carte. Located at John Deere Commons, the invigorating and inviting eatery uses fresh regional produce in its innovative food. Superb preparations, including some unusual choices, are described with a dash of humor on the menu. Smoke free premises. **Parking:** on-site. **Cards:** AX, DC, DS, MC, VI.

REXIE'S GOURMET HOUSE

American

Dinner: $10-$39   **Phone:** 309/794-0244
Location: In Rock Island, IL; jct I-280 and SR 92 E, exit 11B, 2.7 mi e to exit 7th Ave, 1.1 mi n to 17th St, just w. 623 17th St 61201. **Hours:** 4 pm-9 pm, Fri & Sat-10 pm, Sun-8 pm. Closed major holidays; also Mon. **Reservations:** suggested. **Features:** casual dress; early bird specials; cocktails & lounge. Located in the downtown area of Rock Island, Rexie's offers an unpretentious yet diverse menu including such interesting entrees as slipper lobster in which chunks of lobster meat are batter-dipped and deep-fried. The atmosphere is casual and relaxed and the service is friendly. **Parking:** on-site. **Cards:** AX, DS, MC, VI.

ROSS' RESTAURANT

Lunch: $3-$8	**Dinner:** $3-$11	**Phone:** 563/355-7573

(AAA)

American

Location: In Bettendorf, IA; I-74, exit 4 southbound, just s to Grant, then just e; exit 4 northbound, just n. 430 14th St 52722. **Hours:** 24 hours. **Closed:** 12/25; also 12/24 from 8 pm. **Features:** casual dress; children's menu; carryout. The restaurant features 24-hour breakfast as well as home-style dishes that range from sandwiches to steak. The signature Magic Mountain sandwich is a popular choice. **Parking:** on-site. **Cards:** MC, VI.

THUNDER BAY GRILLE

Lunch: $6-$11	**Dinner:** $6-$17	**Phone:** 563/386-2722

American

Location: In Davenport, IA; I-80, exit 295A (US 61), 0.5 mi s, at 65th St. 6511 N Brady St 52806. **Hours:** 11 am-10 pm, Fri & Sat-11 pm, Sun 8 am-9 pm. **Closed:** 1/1, 11/28, 12/25; also 12/24 for dinner. **Features:** casual dress; Sunday brunch; children's menu; carryout; cocktails & lounge. Steaks, seafood, pasta, chicken and homemade desserts are among menu offerings. **Parking:** on-site. **Cards:** AX, CB, DC, DS, MC, VI.

QUINCY pop. 39,700

────── WHERE TO STAY ──────

COMFORT INN

SAVE

Motel

4/1-10/31	1P: $58-$78	2P: $63-$84	XP: $5	F18
11/1-10/31	1P: $58-$68	2P: $58-$68	XP: $5	F18

Phone: (217)228-2700

Location: I-172, exit 14 (SR 104), 1.3 mi w. 4122 Broadway 62305. **Fax:** 217/228-2700. **Facility:** 58 one-bedroom standard units. 3 stories, interior corridors. **Parking:** on-site. **Terms:** pets ($10 extra charge). **Amenities:** extended cable TV. *Some:* irons, hair dryers. **Pool(s):** heated indoor. **Leisure Activities:** whirlpool. **Guest Services:** valet laundry. **Cards:** AX, DC, DS, MC, VI.

SOME UNITS

FAIRFIELD INN BY MARRIOTT

(AAA) **SAVE**

Motel

4/1-10/31	1P: $60-$80	2P: $65-$85	XP: $5	F18
11/1-3/31	1P: $56-$80	2P: $61-$85	XP: $5	F18

Phone: (217)223-5922

Location: I-172, exit 14 (SR 104), 1.1 mi w. 4315 Broadway 62305. **Fax:** 217/223-5922. **Facility:** 63 one-bedroom standard units. 3 stories, interior corridors. *Bath:* combo or shower only. **Parking:** on-site, winter plug-ins. **Amenities:** extended cable TV, irons. *Some:* hair dryers. **Pool(s):** heated indoor. **Leisure Activities:** whirlpool. **Guest Services:** valet laundry. **Business Services:** meeting rooms. **Cards:** AX, CB, DC, DS, JC, MC, VI. **Special Amenities:** free continental breakfast and free local telephone calls. *(See color ad card insert)*

SOME UNITS

HOLIDAY INN-QUINCY

Hotel

All Year [BP]	1P: $72-$82	2P: $72-$82	XP: $10

Phone: (217)222-2666

Location: 0.3 mi s on SR 57 from jct SR 104. 201 S 3rd St 62301. **Fax:** 217/222-3238. **Facility:** 152 one-bedroom standard units. 4 stories, interior corridors. **Parking:** on-site, winter plug-ins. **Amenities:** extended cable TV, high-speed Internet, irons, hair dryers. **Pool(s):** heated indoor. **Leisure Activities:** sauna, whirlpool, exercise room. *Fee:* game room. **Guest Services:** coin laundry. **Business Services:** conference facilities. **Cards:** AX, CB, DC, DS, JC, MC, VI.

SOME UNITS

SUPER 8 MOTEL

Motel

All Year	1P: $43	2P: $47	XP: $6	F12

Phone: (217)228-8808

Location: I-172, exit 14 (SR 104), 1.8 mi w, then just s. 224 N 36th St 62301. **Fax:** 217/228-8808. **Facility:** 59 one-bedroom standard units, some with kitchens. 3 stories, interior corridors. **Parking:** on-site. **Terms:** pets (with prior approval). **Amenities:** extended cable TV. **Cards:** AX, CB, DC, DS, MC, VI.

SOME UNITS

────── WHERE TO DINE ──────

THE PATIO

Dinner: $8-$21	**Phone:** 217/222-1281

Steak House

Location: At 4th and Jersey sts. 133 S 4th St 62301. **Hours:** 4 pm-10 pm, Fri & Sat-11 pm. **Closed:** 1/1, 11/28, 12/25. **Reservations:** suggested; weekends. **Features:** children's menu; carryout; cocktails. A few steps below street level, the dining room, decorated with silk plants and furnished with wrought iron chairs, evokes the feeling of an enclosed garden. Among specialties are the patio pork chop, prime rib, steaks and seafood. **Parking:** on-site. **Cards:** AX, CB, DC, DS, MC, VI.

THE PLAZA

Lunch: $4-$8	**Dinner:** $7-$25	**Phone:** 217/222-0690

American

Location: 7 blks n; at 12th and Lind sts. 900 N 12th St 62301. **Hours:** 11 am-9:30 pm, Fri & Sat-10:30 pm. **Closed:** 12/25. **Reservations:** suggested; weekends. **Features:** casual dress; children's menu; carryout; salad bar; cocktails. Hearty, flavorful portions of house specialties such as beef tenderloin, pork fillet and stir-fried dishes are served in The Plaza's friendly, casual and comfortable atmosphere with subdued lighting. A buffet lunch spread is also presented on Sunday. **Parking:** on-site. **Cards:** AX, CB, DC, DS, MC, VI.

THE RITZ

Lunch: $5-$7	**Dinner:** $6-$14	**Phone:** 217/222-8122

American

Location: 0.3 mi s on SR 57 from jct SR 104. 222 S 3rd St 62301. **Hours:** 11 am-10 pm. Closed major holidays. **Reservations:** suggested. **Features:** casual dress; salad bar; cocktails & lounge. Barbecue is the specialty, and ribs are the feature. However, the menu offers a little something for everyone with its eclectic collection of familiar favorites, ranging from egg rolls and breadsticks to Midwestern fried chicken and fettuccine Alfredo. **Parking:** on-site. **Cards:** MC, VI.

The following restaurants have not been evaluated by AAA
but are listed for your information only.

LAKEVIEW RESTAURANT & PATIO BAR
Phone: 217/222-9825
[fyi] Not evaluated. **Location:** 4403 Broadway 62301. Pasta, sandwiches and stir-fry are served in a casual atmosphere.

THE PIER
Phone: 217/221-0020
[fyi] Not evaluated. **Location:** 401 Bayview Dr 62301. Comfort foods, a full-service bar and great river views are available at this restaurant.

TIRAMISU RISTORANTE ITALIANO
Phone: 217/222-9560
[fyi] Not evaluated. **Location:** 137 N Third St 62301. Distinctive Italian cuisine is served in a historic riverfront brick building.

RANTOUL pop. 17,200

------ WHERE TO STAY ------

BEST WESTERN HERITAGE INN
Phone: (217)892-9292
(AAA) [SAVE]   All Year [CP]   1P: $45-$50   XP: $5   F12
[WWW] **Location:** I-57, exit 250 (US 136), 0.5 mi e to Murray Rd, then just s. 420 S Murray Rd 61866. Fax: 217/892-4318.
Motel **Facility:** 47 one-bedroom standard units. 2 stories, exterior corridors. **Parking:** on-site, winter plug-ins. **Amenities:** extended cable TV, irons, hair dryers. **Pool(s):** heated outdoor. **Leisure Activities:** sauna, whirlpool. **Guest Services:** coin laundry. **Business Services:** fax (fee). **Cards:** AX, CB, DC, DS, JC, MC, VI. **Special Amenities:** free continental breakfast and free local telephone calls.

SOME UNITS
[icons] /

RICHMOND —See Chicago p. 362.

RIVERWOODS —See Chicago p. 363.

ROBINSON pop. 6,700

------ WHERE TO STAY ------

BEST WESTERN ROBINSON INN
Phone: (618)544-8448
[WWW] All Year [CP]   1P: $53-$65   2P: $59-$65   XP: $6   F17
Motel **Location:** 1 mi w on SR 33. 1500 W Main St 62454. Fax: 618/544-8710. **Facility:** 64 one-bedroom standard units, some with whirlpools. 2 stories, interior corridors. *Bath:* combo or shower only. **Parking:** on-site. **Terms:** pets ($5 extra charge). **Amenities:** extended cable TV, safes, irons, hair dryers. **Guest Services:** coin laundry.
Business Services: meeting rooms, fax (fee). **Cards:** AX, CB, DC, DS, JC, MC, VI.

SOME UNITS
[icons] /
FEE FEE

ROCHELLE pop. 8,800

------ WHERE TO STAY ------

AMERIHOST INN-ROCHELLE
Phone: (815)562-9530
(AAA) [SAVE]   All Year   1P: $68-$72   2P: $72-$77   XP: $6   F18
[WWW] **Location:** I-39, exit 99 (SR 38), 1 mi w. 567 E Hwy 38 61068. Fax: 815/562-9696. **Facility:** 61 one-bedroom standard units, some with whirlpools. 2 stories, interior corridors. *Bath:* combo or shower only. **Parking:** on-site.
Motel **Terms:** [ECP] meal plan available, package plans. **Amenities:** extended cable TV, voice mail, safes (fee), irons, hair dryers. **Pool(s):** heated indoor. **Leisure Activities:** sauna, whirlpool, exercise room. **Guest Services:** valet laundry. **Business Services:** meeting rooms. **Cards:** AX, CB, DC, DS, JC, MC, VI.
Special Amenities: free continental breakfast and free newspaper.

SOME UNITS
[icons] /
FEE   FEE FEE FEE

COMFORT INN & SUITES
Phone: (815)562-5551
(AAA) [SAVE]   All Year [ECP]   1P: $60-$180   2P: $65-$185   XP: $5   F18
[WWW] **Location:** I-39, exit 99 (SR 38), 2.5 mi w; at jct of SR 38 and 251. 1131 N 7th St 61068. Fax: 815/562-3911.
Hotel **Facility:** 93 units. 70 one-bedroom standard units, some with whirlpools. 14 one- and 9 two-bedroom suites ($80-$180), some with efficiencies (no utensils) and/or whirlpools. 8 stories, interior corridors. *Bath:* combo or shower only. **Parking:** on-site. **Terms:** check-in 4 pm, 30 day cancellation notice, pets ($15 extra charge). **Amenities:** video games (fee), voice mail, irons, hair dryers. **Dining:** restaurant, 5 pm-10 pm; closed Sun, $6-$16, cocktails. **Pool(s):** outdoor, heated indoor. **Leisure Activities:** sauna, whirlpool. *Fee:* game room. **Guest Services:** valet laundry. **Business Services:** conference facilities. **Cards:** AX, CB, DC, DS, JC, MC, VI. **Special Amenities: free continental breakfast and free newspaper.**

SOME UNITS
[icons] /
FEE   FEE FEE

ROCHESTER pop. 2,700

------ WHERE TO STAY ------

COUNTRY DREAMS BED & BREAKFAST
Phone: 217/498-9210
[WWW] All Year [ECP]   1P: $75-$160   2P: $75-$160   XP: $25
Bed & Breakfast **Location:** SR 29, just n on Walnut, 3.5 mi e on E Main/Burhard Rd. 3410 Park Ln 62563. Fax: 217/498-8178. **Facility:** This modern home in a quiet, rural setting offers desks and phones in its business-class rooms. Smoke free premises. 4 one-bedroom standard units. 2 stories, interior corridors. *Bath:* combo or shower only. **Parking:** on-site, winter plug-ins. **Terms:** check-in 4 pm, age restrictions may apply, 10 day cancellation notice-fee imposed, [BP] meal plan available. **Amenities:** *Some:* CD players, hair dryers. **Leisure Activities:** fishing, hiking trails. **Guest Services:** complimentary laundry. **Cards:** AX, DS, MC, VI.

[icons]

ROCKDALE —See Chicago p. 363.

ROCK FALLS pop. 9,700

——— WHERE TO STAY ———

COUNTRY INN & SUITES BY CARLSON
Phone: (815)625-3200
All Year [ECP]   1P: $66   2P: $71   XP: $5   F18
Motel
Location: I-88, exit 41 (SR 40), just n. 2106 First Ave 61071. **Fax:** 815/626-3575. **Facility:** 80 units. 55 one-bedroom standard units, some with whirlpools. 25 one-bedroom suites ($89-$94), some with whirlpools. 3 stories, interior corridors. *Bath:* combo or shower only. **Parking:** on-site. **Terms:** cancellation fee imposed.
Amenities: extended cable TV, voice mail, irons, hair dryers. **Pool(s):** small heated indoor. **Leisure Activities:** sauna, whirlpool, exercise room. *Fee:* game room. **Guest Services:** coin laundry. **Business Services:** meeting rooms. **Cards:** AX, DC, DS, MC, VI. *(See color ad p 322)*

SOME UNITS

HOLIDAY INN
Phone: 815/626-5500
All Year   1P: $65-$70   2P: $65-$70
Motor Inn
Location: I-88, exit 41 (SR 40), 0.4 mi n. 2105 First Ave 61071. **Fax:** 815/626-5501. **Facility:** 118 one-bedroom standard units. 2 stories, interior corridors. *Bath:* combo or shower only. **Parking:** on-site. **Terms:** [BP] meal plan available, package plans, pets ($20 extra charge). **Amenities:** voice mail, irons, hair dryers. *Fee:* video games, Web TV. **Pool(s):** heated indoor. **Leisure Activities:** whirlpool, exercise room. *Fee:* game room. **Guest Services:** valet and coin laundry. **Business Services:** conference facilities. **Cards:** AX, CB, DC, DS, JC, MC, VI.

SOME UNITS

ROCK FALLS SUPER 8
Phone: (815)626-8800
All Year   1P: $46-$48   2P: $55-$57
Motel
Location: I-88, exit 41 (SR 40), 0.3 mi n, just w on W 21st St. 2100 First Ave 61071. **Fax:** 815/626-9522. **Facility:** 63 one-bedroom standard units. 2 stories, interior corridors. **Parking:** on-site, winter plug-ins. **Terms:** small pets only (with prior approval). **Amenities:** extended cable TV, safes (fee). **Cards:** AX, CB, DC, DS, MC, VI.

SOME UNITS

ROCKFORD pop. 139,400

——— WHERE TO STAY ———

BAYMONT INN & SUITES
Phone: (815)229-8200
6/1-9/2   1P: $80   2P: $86   XP: $6   F18
4/1-5/31 & 9/3-3/31   1P: $60   2P: $66   XP: $6   F18
Motel
Location: I-90, exit US 20 business route, just e, then just n. 662 N Lyford Rd 61107. **Fax:** 815/229-8220. **Facility:** 88 one-bedroom standard units, some with whirlpools. 4 stories, interior corridors. *Bath:* combo or shower only. **Parking:** on-site. **Terms:** check-in 4 pm, pets ($15 extra charge). **Amenities:** extended cable TV, video games (fee), dual phone lines, voice mail, irons, hair dryers. **Leisure Activities:** whirlpool. **Guest Services:** valet and coin laundry. **Business Services:** meeting rooms. **Cards:** AX, DC, DS, MC, VI. **Special Amenities:** free continental breakfast and free newspaper.

SOME UNITS

BEST SUITES
Phone: (815)227-1300
All Year   1P: $65-$99   2P: $75-$99   XP: $10   F17
Suite Motel
Location: I-90, exit US 20 business route, just w to Bell School Rd, then just s. 7401 Walton St 61108. **Fax:** 815/227-9231. **Facility:** 95 units. 37 one-bedroom standard units. 58 one-bedroom suites ($150-$200), some with whirlpools. 4 stories, interior corridors. *Bath:* combo or shower only. **Parking:** on-site. **Terms:** check-in 4 pm, package plans, small pets only. **Amenities:** extended cable TV, voice mail, irons, hair dryers. **Pool(s):** small heated indoor. **Leisure Activities:** whirlpool, exercise room, sundries shop. **Guest Services:** complimentary evening beverages, valet and coin laundry. **Business Services:** meeting rooms. **Cards:** AX, CB, DC, DS, MC, VI. **Special Amenities:** free continental breakfast and free local telephone calls.

SOME UNITS

BEST WESTERN CLOCK TOWER RESORT & CONFERENCE CENTER
Phone: (815)398-6000
All Year   1P: $119   2P: $119   XP: $10   F18
Resort
Location: I-90, exit US 20 business route, just e. 7801 E State St 61108 (PO Box 5285, 61125). **Fax:** 815/398-8062. **Facility:** Recreational and entertainment facilities abound at this hotel, which offers accommodations of varied decor and design. 246 one-bedroom standard units, some with whirlpools. 2 stories, interior corridors. **Parking:** on-site, winter plug-ins. **Terms:** check-in 4 pm, package plans. **Amenities:** extended cable TV, video games (fee), voice mail, irons, hair dryers. *Some:* safes. **Pool(s):** 2 heated outdoor, heated indoor, 2 wading. **Leisure Activities:** sauna, whirlpools, playground, sports court. *Fee:* 9 tennis courts (7 indoor, 7 lighted), racquetball courts. **Guest Services:** gift shop, massage (fee), valet and coin laundry. **Business Services:** conference facilities. **Cards:** AX, CB, DC, DS, MC, VI. *(See ad p 419)*

SOME UNITS

BEST WESTERN COLONIAL INN
Phone: (815)398-5050
5/1-8/31 [CP]   1P: $78-$170   2P: $78-$170
4/1-4/30 & 9/1-3/31 [CP]   1P: $49-$120   2P: $49-$120
Motel
Location: I-90, exit US 20 business route, 3.5 mi w. 4850 E State St 61108. **Fax:** 815/398-8180. **Facility:** 84 units. 80 one-bedroom standard units. 4 one-bedroom suites ($99-$150) with whirlpools. 3 stories, interior corridors. **Parking:** on-site, winter plug-ins. **Terms:** pets ($25 extra charge). **Amenities:** extended cable TV, video tape library (fee), irons, hair dryers. **Pool(s):** small heated indoor. **Leisure Activities:** whirlpool, exercise room. **Guest Services:** valet and coin laundry. **Business Services:** meeting rooms. **Cards:** AX, CB, DC, DS, JC, MC, VI. **Special Amenities:** free continental breakfast and free newspaper.

SOME UNITS

CANDLEWOOD SUITES   Phone: (815)229-9300

▼▼▼   4/1-9/30   1P: $72-$80   2P: $72-$80
             10/1-3/31   1P: $63-$70   2P: $63-$70
Extended Stay   **Location:** I-90, exit US 20 business route, 0.3 mi e to Bell School Rd, just s to Walton St, then just e. 7555 Walton St
Motel   61108. Fax: 815/229-9323. **Facility:** 67 one-bedroom standard units with efficiencies. 3 stories, interior corridors. *Bath:* combo or shower only. **Parking:** on-site. **Amenities:** extended cable TV, video tape library, CD
players, dual phone lines, voice mail, irons, hair dryers. **Leisure Activities:** exercise room. **Guest Services:** complimentary
laundry. **Cards:** AX, DC, DS, MC, VI.

SOME UNITS

(ASK) (S/D) (♿) (VCR) (🎥) (DATA PORT) (🔌) (🍴) (🖥) (🖨) / (✕) /

COURTYARD BY MARRIOTT   Phone: (815)397-6222

(AAA) (SAVE)   6/30-3/31   1P: $99-$109   2P: $109-$119
             4/1-6/29   1P: $89-$99   2P: $99-$109
▼▼▼   **Location:** I-90, exit US 20 business route, just nw. 7676 E State St 61108. Fax: 815/397-6254. **Facility:** 147 units.
Motel   133 one-bedroom standard units. 14 one-bedroom suites. 2-3 stories, interior corridors. *Bath:* combo or
shower only. **Parking:** on-site. **Terms:** package plans. **Amenities:** dual phone lines, voice mail, irons, hair
dryers. **Dining:** coffee shop, 6:30-10:30 am, Sat 7-11 am, Sun 7-11:30 am. **Pool(s):** small heated indoor.
Leisure Activities: whirlpool, exercise room. **Guest Services:** valet and coin laundry. **Business Services:** meeting rooms.
Cards: AX, DC, DS, MC, VI. *(See ad p 299 & color ad card insert & ad below)*

SOME UNITS

(S/D) (🍴) (🏋M) (♿) (🏊) (🎥) (DATA PORT) (🖥) (🖨) / (✕) (🔌) (🖥) /
                                       FEE

EXEL INN OF ROCKFORD   Phone: (815)332-4915

(AAA) (SAVE)   6/1-10/31 [CP]   1P: $43-$55   2P: $49-$65   XP: $6   F18
             4/1-5/31 & 11/1-3/31 [CP] 1P: $38-$46   2P: $44-$52   XP: $6   F18
▼▼▼   **Location:** I-90, exit US business route 20, just e, then just s. 220 S Lyford Rd 61108. Fax: 815/332-4843.
Motel   **Facility:** 100 units. 99 one-bedroom standard units, some with whirlpools. 1 one-bedroom suite with kitchen.
2 stories, interior corridors. **Parking:** on-site, winter plug-ins. **Terms:** small pets only ($100 extra charge for
weekly stays). **Amenities:** irons, hair dryers. **Leisure Activities:** exercise room. **Guest Services:** coin
laundry. **Cards:** AX, CB, DC, DS, MC, VI. **Special Amenities:** early check-in/late check-out and free continental breakfast. *(See color ad p 318)*

SOME UNITS

(S/D) (🐕) (🖥) (🎥) (DATA PORT) (🖥) (🖨) / (✕) (🔌) (🖥) /
                      FEE   FEE FEE

FAIRFIELD INN BY MARRIOTT

AAA [SAVE]

◆◆◆

Motel

Phone: 815/397-8000

4/1-10/1	1P: $59-$89	2P: $59-$89
10/2-3/31	1P: $49-$69	2P: $49-$69

Location: I-90, exit US 20 business route, just nw. 7712 Potawatomi Tr 61107. Fax: 815/397-8183. **Facility:** 135 one-bedroom standard units. 3 stories, interior/exterior corridors. *Bath:* combo or shower only. **Parking:** on-site. **Terms:** 14 day cancellation notice. **Amenities:** *Some:* irons. **Pool(s):** heated outdoor. **Guest Services:** valet laundry. **Cards:** AX, CB, DC, DS, MC, VI. **Special Amenities:** free continental breakfast and free local telephone calls. *(See color ad card insert)*

SOME UNITS

[icons] FEE

HAMPTON INN

[SAVE]

◆◆◆

Motel

Phone: (815)229-0404

4/16-10/1	1P: $84-$94	2P: $94-$104
4/1-4/15 & 10/2-3/31	1P: $64-$74	2P: $74-$84

Location: I-90, exit US 20 business route, just nw. 615 Clark Dr 61107-5816. Fax: 815/229-0175. **Facility:** 122 one-bedroom standard units. 4 stories, interior corridors. **Parking:** on-site. **Amenities:** extended cable TV, video games (fee), irons, hair dryers. **Pool(s):** small heated indoor. **Leisure Activities:** whirlpool, exercise room. **Guest Services:** valet laundry. **Business Services:** meeting rooms. **Cards:** AX, CB, DC, DS, MC, VI.

SOME UNITS

[icons] FEE FEE FEE

RAMADA SUITES & ROCKFORD CONFERENCE CENTER

AAA [SAVE]

◆◆◆

Motor Inn

Phone: (815)226-2100

6/2-10/1 [ECP]	1P: $76-$99	2P: $76-$99	XP: $10 F18
4/1-6/1 & 10/2-3/31 [ECP]	1P: $67-$99	2P: $67-$99	XP: $10 F18

Location: I-90, exit US 20 business route, 0.3 mi w to Bell School Rd, just s to Walton St, then just e. 200 S Bell School Rd 61108. Fax: 815/229-3070. **Facility:** 114 units. 109 one-bedroom standard units, some with whirlpools. 5 one-bedroom suites ($89-$175) with whirlpools. 3 stories, interior corridors. *Bath:* combo or shower only. **Parking:** on-site. **Terms:** cancellation fee imposed, package plans. **Amenities:** voice mail, irons, hair dryers. *Some:* dual phone lines. **Dining:** restaurant, 5 pm-10 pm, $9-$19, cocktails. **Pool(s):** small heated indoor. **Leisure Activities:** whirlpool, limited exercise equipment. **Guest Services:** valet laundry. **Business Services:** conference facilities, PC. **Cards:** AX, CB, DC, DS, MC, VI. **Special Amenities:** free continental breakfast and free newspaper.

SOME UNITS

[icons] / [icon] /

RED ROOF INN

AAA [SAVE]

◆◆◆

Motel

Phone: (815)398-9750

5/26-9/8	1P: $51-$71	2P: $56-$76	XP: $5 F18
9/9-9/30	1P: $46-$61	2P: $51-$66	XP: $5 F18
4/1-5/25	1P: $41-$61	2P: $46-$66	XP: $5 F18
10/1-3/31	1P: $38-$48	2P: $43-$53	XP: $5 F18

Location: I-90, exit US 20 business route, just w. 7434 E State St 61108. Fax: 815/398-9761. **Facility:** 108 one-bedroom standard units. 2 stories, exterior corridors. **Parking:** on-site. **Terms:** small pets only. **Amenities:** voice mail. **Cards:** AX, CB, DC, DS, MC, VI. **Special Amenities:** free local telephone calls and free newspaper.

SOME UNITS

[icons] FEE / [icons] /

RESIDENCE INN BY MARRIOTT

AAA [SAVE]

◆◆◆

Apartment

Phone: (815)227-0013

All Year [ECP]	1P: $86-$144

Location: I-90, exit US 20 business route, just w. 7542 Colosseum Dr 61107. Fax: 815/227-0013. **Facility:** 94 units. 37 one-bedroom standard units with efficiencies. 42 one- and 15 two-bedroom suites ($86-$144) with kitchens. 3 stories, interior corridors. **Parking:** on-site. **Terms:** pets ($100 fee, $5 extra charge). **Amenities:** extended cable TV, dual phone lines, voice mail, irons, hair dryers. **Pool(s):** small heated indoor. **Leisure Activities:** whirlpool, exercise room, sports court. **Guest Services:** valet and coin laundry. **Business Services:** meeting rooms. **Cards:** AX, CB, DC, DS, JC, MC, VI. *(See color ad card insert)*

SOME UNITS

[icons] FEE / [icons] [VCR]

SLEEP INN-ROCKFORD

AAA **SAVE**

Motel

Phone: (815)398-8900

5/24-9/1 [ECP]	1P: $65-$80	2P: $69-$99	XP: $5 F18
4/1-5/23 & 9/2-3/31 [ECP]	1P: $55-$70	2P: $59-$75	XP: $5 F18

Location: I-90, exit US 20 business route, just w to Bell School Rd, just n to Clark Dr, then 0.4 mi ne. 725 Clark Dr 61107. Fax: 815/398-4399. **Facility:** 72 one-bedroom standard units. 3 stories, interior corridors. *Bath:* combo or shower only. **Parking:** on-site. **Terms:** pets ($15 fee). **Amenities:** extended cable TV, dual phone lines, voice mail. *Some:* irons, hair dryers. **Leisure Activities:** exercise room. **Guest Services:** valet laundry. **Business Services:** meeting rooms. **Cards:** AX, CB, DC, DS, JC, MC, VI. **Special Amenities: free continental breakfast and free local telephone calls.**

SOME UNITS

SWEDEN HOUSE LODGE

AAA **SAVE**

Motel

Phone: (815)398-4130

5/1-9/30 [CP]	1P: $55-$90	2P: $70-$90	XP: $10 F18
4/1-4/30 & 10/1-3/31 [CP]	1P: $50-$80	2P: $65-$80	XP: $10 F18

Location: I-90, exit US 20 business route, 4 mi w. 4605 E State St 61108. Fax: 815/398-9203. **Facility:** 105 one-bedroom standard units, some with efficiencies. 2-3 stories, interior/exterior corridors. *Bath:* combo or shower only. **Parking:** on-site. **Terms:** package plans. **Amenities:** extended cable TV, safes (fee). **Pool(s):** heated indoor. **Leisure Activities:** whirlpool, exercise room. *Fee:* game room, billiards. **Guest Services:** valet and coin laundry. **Business Services:** meeting rooms. **Cards:** AX, DC, DS, MC, VI. **Special Amenities: early check-in/late check-out and free continental breakfast.** *(See color ad p 420)*

SOME UNITS
FEE FEE

VILLAGER LODGE

AAA **SAVE**

Motel

Phone: 815/399-1890

All Year	1P: $57-$65	2P: $57-$65	XP: $10 F18

Location: I-90, exit US 20 business route, 4 mi w; at jct Alpine Rd and E State St. 4404 E State St 61108. Fax: 815/399-1898. **Facility:** 106 one-bedroom standard units. 1-2 stories, exterior corridors. **Parking:** on-site. **Terms:** package plans. **Amenities:** extended cable TV, safes (fee). **Leisure Activities:** exercise room. **Guest Services:** coin laundry. **Cards:** AX, DC, DS, MC, VI. **Special Amenities: early check-in/late check-out and free continental breakfast.** *(See color ad p 420)*

SOME UNITS

─────── **WHERE TO DINE** ───────

BACCHUS WINE BAR AND RESTAURANT

Northern American

Dinner: $11-$25   **Phone: 815/968-9463**

Location: Downtown; between 2nd and 3rd sts. 515 E State St 61104. **Hours:** 5 pm-9 pm, Fri & Sat-10:30 pm. Closed major holidays; also Sun & Mon. **Reservations:** suggested. **Features:** dressy casual; carryout; cocktails & lounge. The azure blue ceiling and art nouveau theme of the dining room create a certain sense of wow and wonder when you enter Bacchus but be aware that the food stands up to the decor. You will find the menu to be varied, the recipes to be creative, the ingredients to be prime and the dishes to be as appealing to the eye as they are to the palate. **Parking:** street. **Cards:** AX, DC, DS, MC, VI.

CAFE PATOU

French

Lunch: $6-$15   **Dinner: $9-$29**   **Phone: 815/227-4100**

Location: Jct US 20 bypass and Alpine Rd, 2.1 mi n to Broadway, then just w. 3929 Broadway 61108. **Hours:** 11:30 am-2 & 5:30-11 pm, Mon from 5:30 pm, Fri-1 am, Sat 5:30 pm-1 am. Closed major holidays; also Sun. **Reservations:** suggested. **Features:** casual dress; carryout; cocktails & lounge; entertainment. With a wine list representing several regions and vintages, Cafe Patou offers an ever-changing menu anchored by such classic dishes as shrimp thermidore, marinated rack of lamb and veal Milanese. A recent menu also featured a number of "Camp Fire" dishes in which lamb, chicken, shrimp or pork tenderloin were served in a rich meat broth along with selected seasonal vegetables. **Parking:** on-site. **Cards:** AX, CB, DC, DS, MC, VI.

CLIFFBREAKERS RIVER RESTAURANT & CONVENTION CENTER

American

Lunch: $7-$12   **Dinner: $13-$25**   **Phone: 815/282-3033**

Location: 0.7 mi w of SR 251. 700 W Riverside Blvd 61103. **Hours:** 11:30 am-2 & 5-9 pm, Sun 10:30 am-1 & 5-8 pm. Closed: 12/24, 12/25. **Reservations:** suggested. **Features:** dressy casual; Sunday brunch; children's menu; cocktails & lounge. Overlooking the Rock River, the elegant, intimate restaurant boasts a Victorian feel. Chicken Oscar stands out on a menu that includes French, Italian and English options. The Friday night seafood buffet is popular, as is the Sunday brunch. **Parking:** on-site. **Cards:** AX, CB, DC, DS, MC, VI.

GIOVANNI'S RESTAURANT OF ROCKFORD

Continental

Lunch: $8-$12   **Dinner: $17-$35**   **Phone: 815/398-6411**

Location: I-90, exit US 20 business route, just w. 610 N Bell School Rd 61107. **Hours:** 11:30 am-2 & 5:30-10 pm, Sat from 5 pm. Closed major holidays; also Sun. **Reservations:** suggested. **Features:** casual dress; children's menu; carryout; cocktails. The sophisticated dining room boasts dark-wood walls, white tablecloths and lovely artwork. The menu lists fine Continental and Italian dishes with fine desserts made by the resident pastry chef. An attractive mural shows famous actors and actresses from the 1940s and '50s. **Parking:** on-site. **Cards:** AX, DC, DS, MC, VI.

ILLINOIS MACHINE SHED RESTAURANT

American

Lunch: $6-$12   **Dinner: $8-$21**   **Phone: 815/229-3276**

Location: I-90, exit US 20 business route, just w. 7475 E State St 61108. **Hours:** 6 am-10 pm, Sun 7 am-9 pm. Closed: 1/1, 11/28, 12/25. **Features:** casual dress; children's menu; carryout; cocktails & lounge. Home-style food, such as soups and pork entrees, fits in with the down-home, family-oriented mood of the busy restaurant. Farm antiques and tractors decorate the dining room. For dessert, guests can dig their forks into a big, mouthwatering slice of homemade pie. Service is attentive and friendly. **Parking:** on-site. **Cards:** AX, DC, DS, MC, VI.

JMK NIPPON

Japanese

Lunch: $7-$12   **Dinner: $10-$24**   **Phone: 815/877-0505**

Location: I-90, exit US 20 business route, 0.7 mi w to Perryville Rd, then 1.9 mi n. 2551 N Perryville Rd 61107. **Hours:** 11:30 am-2 & 5-10:30 pm, Mon from 5 pm, Fri-11 pm, Sat 4:30 pm-11 pm, Sun 4:30 pm-9:30 pm. Closed: 7/4, 11/28, 12/25. **Reservations:** suggested. **Features:** casual dress; children's menu; carryout; cocktails & lounge; a la carte. The sleek, modern design of the large dining areas sets the stage for fine teppanyaki dining, in which guests are seated around a common table while the chef prepares the food before them. Fresh vegetables, fine seafood and steak are just some of the excellent menu choices. **Parking:** on-site. **Cards:** AX, DC, DS, MC, VI.

JOHN'S RESTAURANT & PIZZERIA   Lunch: $6-$14   Dinner: $8-$19   Phone: 815/398-4044
Italian   **Location:** Jct US 20 and SR 251, 1 mi n. 2914 11th St 61109. **Hours:** 4 pm-11 pm, Wed & Thurs-midnight, Fri & Sat 11 am-midnight. Closed: 11/28, 12/25. **Reservations:** suggested; weekends. **Features:** casual dress; children's menu; carryout; cocktails & lounge; a la carte. Steaks and lobster are on the menu, but pasta and pizza are the big draw to families visiting the restaurant. The atmosphere is decidedly laid-back, and the dining room has an almost rustic feel. The wine list offers several nice selections. **Parking:** on-site. **Cards:** AX, MC, VI.

THUNDER BAY GRILLE   Lunch: $6-$13   Dinner: $7-$25   Phone: 815/397-4800
American   **Location:** I-90, exit US 20 business route (MM 63 1/2), just w. 7652 Potawatomi Tr 61107. **Hours:** 11 am-10 pm, Sun 8 am-9 pm. Closed major holidays. **Reservations:** accepted. **Features:** casual dress; Sunday brunch; children's menu; carryout; cocktails. Thunder Bay Grille recreates the charm of a camping or fishing lodge in the northwoods with its plank walls, vaulted wood ceiling with heavy exposed beams and its chairs framed from tree branches. The menu is diverse and creative with such offerings as pickled northern pike, Margherita pizza, bouillabasse and chicken pot pie. **Parking:** on-site. **Cards:** AX, CB, DC, DS, MC, VI.

ROCK ISLAND —See *QUAD CITIES*.

ROLLING MEADOWS —*See Chicago p. 363.*

ROMEOVILLE —*See Chicago p. 363.*

ROSEMONT —*See Chicago p. 363.*

ST. CHARLES —*See Chicago p. 366.*

SALEM pop. 7,500

——— WHERE TO STAY ———

SUPER 8 MOTEL OF SALEM   Phone: (618)548-5882
All Year [ECP]   1P: $52-$72   2P: $58-$78   XP: $6   F12
Motel   **Location:** I-57, exit 116 (US 50), just w. 118 Woods Ln 62881. Fax: 618/548-1167. **Facility:** 57 one-bedroom standard units. 3 stories (no elevator), interior/exterior corridors. **Parking:** on-site, winter plug-ins. **Amenities:** extended cable TV, safes (fee). **Guest Services:** coin laundry. **Business Services:** fax (fee). **Cards:** AX, CB, DC, DS, MC, VI.

SOME UNITS

——— WHERE TO DINE ———

FIVE BROTHERS CAFE   Lunch: $6-$12   Dinner: $6-$12   Phone: 618/548-8973
American   **Location:** I-57, exit 116 (US 50), 1.6 mi w. 2053 W Main 62881. **Hours:** 5 am-10 pm. **Features:** casual dress; children's menu; carryout. Casual dining in an unpretentious but comfortable restaurant in a semi-rural setting. Comfort food presented by friendly and attentive servers. Portions are quite generous and taste is quite good. Locally popular, particularly at breakfast. **Parking:** on-site. **Cards:** MC, VI.

SAVOY pop. 2,700

——— WHERE TO STAY ———

BEST WESTERN PARADISE INN MOTEL   Phone: (217)356-1824
All Year [ECP]   1P: $55-$65   2P: $65-$75   XP: $5   F18
Motel   **Location:** I-57, exit 229, 1 mi e to US 45, then 2.5 mi n. 1001 N Dunlap 61874. Fax: 217/356-1824. **Facility:** 62 units. 60 one-bedroom standard units. 2 one-bedroom suites ($85-$125). 1-2 stories, exterior corridors. **Parking:** on-site. **Terms:** 7 day cancellation notice-fee imposed, small pets only ($5 extra charge). **Amenities:** extended cable TV. **Pool(s):** outdoor, wading. **Leisure Activities:** playground, exercise room. **Guest Services:** coin laundry. **Business Services:** meeting rooms. **Cards:** AX, DC, DS, MC, VI. **Special Amenities:** free continental breakfast and free local telephone calls.

SOME UNITS

SCHAUMBURG —*See Chicago p. 367.*

SCHILLER PARK —*See Chicago p. 370.*

SHELBYVILLE pop. 4,900

——— WHERE TO STAY ———

THE SHELBY HISTORIC HOUSE & INN   Phone: (217)774-3991
4/1-9/30   1P: $45-$65   2P: $63-$85
10/1-3/31   1P: $42-$65   2P: $59-$79
Motel   **Location:** SR 16, just e from SR 128. 816 W Main St 62565. Fax: 217/774-4284. **Facility:** 41 one-bedroom standard units. 1-2 stories, exterior corridors. **Parking:** on-site, winter plug-ins. **Amenities:** extended cable TV, voice mail. **Cards:** AX, CB, DC, DS, MC, VI. **Special Amenities:** free continental breakfast and free local telephone calls.

SOME UNITS

SKOKIE —See Chicago p. 371.

SOUTH HOLLAND —See Chicago p. 371.

SOUTH JACKSONVILLE

——— WHERE TO STAY ———

COMFORT INN-SOUTH JACKSONVILLE
SAVE

Motel

DS, MC, VI.

Phone: (217)245-8372

All Year [ECP]	1P: $75-$85	2P: $75-$85	XP: $10	F18

Location: I-72, exit 64, just n. 200 Whewell Dr 62650. Fax: 217/245-9502. **Facility:** 70 one-bedroom standard units, some with whirlpools. 3 stories, interior corridors. *Bath:* combo or shower only. **Parking:** on-site. **Terms:** 14 day cancellation notice, pets ($50 deposit). **Amenities:** extended cable TV, dual phone lines, voice mail, irons, hair dryers. **Pool(s):** indoor. **Leisure Activities:** whirlpool, exercise room. **Guest Services:** valet and coin laundry. **Business Services:** meeting rooms, business center, PC, fax. **Cards:** AX, CB, DC,

FEE

SPRINGFIELD pop. 105,400

——— WHERE TO STAY ———

BAYMONT INN
(AAA) SAVE

Motel

Phone: (217)529-6655

All Year [CP]	1P: $65-$70	2P: $72-$77	XP: $7	F12

Location: I-55, exit 90 (Toronto Rd), just e to 6th St, then just n. 5871 S 6th St 62703. Fax: 217/529-6510. **Facility:** 76 one-bedroom standard units, some with whirlpools. 3 stories, interior corridors. *Bath:* combo or shower only. **Parking:** on-site, winter plug-ins. **Terms:** cancellation fee imposed, small pets only. **Amenities:** video games, voice mail, irons, hair dryers. **Pool(s):** indoor. **Leisure Activities:** whirlpool, exercise room. **Guest Services:** valet and coin laundry. **Business Services:** meeting rooms. **Cards:** AX, CB, DC, DS, MC, VI.
Special Amenities: free continental breakfast and free newspaper.

SOME UNITS

FEE

BEST INNS
(AAA) SAVE

Motel

Phone: (217)522-1100

3/1-3/31	1P: $65-$92	2P: $75-$97	XP: $10	F18
4/1-9/30	1P: $62-$87	2P: $72-$97	XP: $10	F18
10/1-2/28	1P: $60-$85	2P: $70-$95	XP: $10	F18

Location: Just n of Capitol; at 1st St and Carpenter. 500 N 1st St 62702. Fax: 217/753-8589. **Facility:** 90 one-bedroom standard units. 2 stories, interior corridors. **Parking:** on-site, winter plug-ins. **Terms:** 30 day cancellation notice, [ECP] meal plan available, small pets only ($10 extra charge). **Amenities:** extended cable TV, irons. **Pool(s):** outdoor. **Guest Services:** valet and coin laundry. **Cards:** AX, DC, DS, MC, VI. **Special Amenities: free continental breakfast and free local telephone calls.**

SOME UNITS

COMFORT INN
SAVE

Motel

MC, VI.

Phone: (217)787-2250

5/1-10/31	1P: $74-$89	2P: $79-$94	XP: $5	F18
4/1-4/30 & 11/1-3/31	1P: $72-$82	2P: $77-$87	XP: $5	F18

Location: I-72, exit 93 (Veterans Pkwy), 0.7 mi n to Lindbergh Blvd, just w to Freedom Dr, then just s. 3442 Freedom Dr 62704. Fax: 217/787-2250. **Facility:** 66 one-bedroom standard units. 2 stories, interior corridors. **Parking:** on-site. **Amenities:** extended cable TV. *Some:* irons, hair dryers. **Pool(s):** indoor. **Leisure Activities:** whirlpool. **Guest Services:** valet laundry. **Business Services:** meeting rooms. **Cards:** AX, CB, DC, DS, JC,

SOME UNITS

FEE

COMFORT SUITES
SAVE

Motel

Phone: (217)753-4000

8/8-9/30 [ECP]	1P: $79-$109	2P: $79-$109	XP: $10
4/1-8/7 [ECP]	1P: $79-$89	2P: $89-$99	XP: $10
10/1-3/31 [ECP]	1P: $69-$79	2P: $79-$89	XP: $10

Location: I-55, exit 94 (Stevenson Dr), just w to Dirksen Pkwy, then 0.4 mi n. 2620 S Dirksen Pkwy 62703. Fax: 217/753-4166. **Facility:** 91 one-bedroom standard units, some with whirlpools. 3 stories, interior corridors. *Bath:* combo or shower only. **Parking:** on-site, winter plug-ins. **Amenities:** voice mail. *Some:* irons, hair dryers. **Pool(s):** small heated indoor. **Leisure Activities:** exercise room. **Guest Services:** valet and coin laundry. **Business Services:** meeting rooms. **Cards:** AX, CB, DC, DS, JC, MC, VI.

SOME UNITS

FEE

COURTYARD BY MARRIOTT
(AAA) SAVE

Motel

Phone: (217)793-5300

4/1-9/15	1P: $94-$109	2P: $99-$109
9/16-3/31	1P: $79-$84	2P: $84-$89

Location: I-72, exit 93 (Veterans Pkwy), 0.7 mi n to Lindbergh Blvd, just w to Freedom Dr, then just s. 3462 Freedom Dr 62704. Fax: 217/793-5300. **Facility:** 78 units. 75 one-bedroom standard units. 3 one-bedroom suites. 3 stories, interior corridors. *Bath:* combo or shower only. **Parking:** on-site. **Terms:** 5 day cancellation notice. **Amenities:** dual phone lines, voice mail, irons, hair dryers. **Dining:** coffee shop, 6:30-9:30 am, Sat & Sun 7-11 am. **Pool(s):** small heated indoor. **Leisure Activities:** whirlpool, exercise room. **Guest Services:** valet and coin laundry. **Business Services:** meeting rooms. **Cards:** AX, CB, DC, DS, JC, MC, VI. *(See color ad card insert)*

SOME UNITS

FEE FEE

CROWNE PLAZA HOTEL

Phone: (217)529-7777

(AAA) [SAVE]

All Year — 1P: $89-$139 — 2P: $89-$139 — XP: $15 — F19

Hotel

Location: I-55, exit 94 (Stevenson Dr), just w to S Dirksen Pkwy, then 0.5 mi n. 3000 S Dirksen Pkwy 62703. Fax: 217/529-6666. **Facility:** 288 units. 278 one-bedroom standard units, some with whirlpools. 10 one-bedroom suites ($360) with whirlpools. 13 stories, interior corridors. *Bath:* combo or shower only. **Parking:** on-site and valet. **Terms:** check-in 4 pm, [BP] meal plan available, package plans. **Amenities:** extended cable TV, voice mail, safes (fee), honor bars, irons, hair dryers. *Some:* dual phone lines. **Dining:** restaurant, 6:30 am-2 & 5-10 pm, $10-$20, cocktails. **Pool(s):** heated outdoor. **Leisure Activities:** sauna, whirlpool, exercise room. **Guest Services:** gift shop, massage (fee), valet laundry, area transportation-train & bus stations. **Business Services:** conference facilities, business center. *Fee:* administrative services, PC, fax. **Cards:** AX, CB, DC, DS, MC, VI. *(See color ad p 425)*

DAYS INN

Phone: (217)529-0171

[SAVE]

5/25-3/31 [CP] — 1P: $55-$75 — 2P: $65-$85 — XP: $5 — F12
4/1-5/24 [CP] — 1P: $54-$74 — 2P: $64-$84 — XP: $5 — F12

Motel

Location: I-55, exit 94 (Stevenson Dr), just w. 3000 Stevenson Dr 62703. Fax: 217/529-9431. **Facility:** 153 one-bedroom standard units. 2 stories, exterior corridors. **Parking:** on-site. **Terms:** 3 day cancellation notice, pets ($5 extra charge). **Amenities:** extended cable TV, hair dryers. *Some:* irons. **Pool(s):** outdoor. **Guest Services:** valet laundry. **Business Services:** meeting rooms. **Cards:** AX, CB, DC, DS, JC, MC, VI.

DRURY INN & SUITES-SPRINGFIELD

Phone: (217)529-3900

Motel

All Year [ECP] — 1P: $72-$102 — 2P: $72-$102 — XP: $10 — F18

Location: I-55, exit 94 (Stevenson Dr), just w to Dirksen Pkwy, then just n. 3180 S Dirksen Pkwy 62703. Fax: 217/529-3900. **Facility:** 118 one-bedroom standard units. 5 stories, interior corridors. *Bath:* combo or shower only. **Parking:** on-site. **Terms:** package plans, small pets only. **Amenities:** extended cable TV, irons, hair dryers. **Pool(s):** indoor. **Leisure Activities:** whirlpool, exercise room. **Guest Services:** complimentary evening beverages: Mon-Thurs, valet laundry. **Business Services:** meeting rooms. **Cards:** AX, CB, DC, DS, MC, VI. *(See color ad p 5)*

FAIRFIELD INN BY MARRIOTT

Phone: (217)793-9277

(AAA) [SAVE]

4/1-9/30 — 1P: $64-$89 — 2P: $69-$94 — XP: $5 — F18
10/1-3/31 — 1P: $64-$69 — 2P: $69-$74 — XP: $5 — F18

Motel

Location: I-72, exit 93 (Veterans Pkwy), 0.7 mi n to Lindbergh Blvd, just w to Freedom Dr, then just s. 3446 Freedom Dr 62704. Fax: 217/793-9277. **Facility:** 63 one-bedroom standard units. 3 stories, interior corridors. **Parking:** on-site. **Amenities:** extended cable TV, irons. **Pool(s):** indoor. **Leisure Activities:** whirlpool. **Guest Services:** valet laundry. **Cards:** AX, CB, DC, DS, MC, VI. **Special Amenities:** free continental breakfast and free local telephone calls. *(See color ad card insert)*

HAMPTON INN OF SPRINGFIELD

Phone: (217)529-1100

[SAVE]

All Year [ECP] — 1P: $69-$74 — 2P: $69-$74

Motel

Location: I-55, exit 94 (Stevenson Dr), just w. 3185 S Dirksen Pkwy 62703. Fax: 217/529-1105. **Facility:** 124 one-bedroom standard units, some with whirlpools. 4 stories, interior corridors. **Parking:** on-site. **Amenities:** extended cable TV, high-speed Internet, voice mail, irons, hair dryers. **Pool(s):** heated indoor. **Leisure Activities:** whirlpool, exercise room. **Guest Services:** valet laundry. **Business Services:** meeting rooms. **Cards:** AX, CB, DC, DS, MC, VI.

HILTON SPRINGFIELD

Phone: (217)789-1530

[SAVE]

All Year — 1P: $89-$159 — 2P: $94-$174 — XP: $15 — F18

Hotel

Location: Just e of the Old Capitol Building; at 7th and Adams sts. 700 E Adams St 62701. Fax: 217/789-0709. **Facility:** 366 one-bedroom standard units. 29 stories, interior corridors. *Bath:* combo or shower only. **Parking:** *Fee:* on-site and valet. **Terms:** cancellation fee imposed, package plans. **Amenities:** dual phone lines, voice mail, safes, irons, hair dryers. **Dining:** Gumbo Ya Ya's Restaurant, see separate listing. **Pool(s):** heated indoor. **Leisure Activities:** exercise room. **Guest Services:** gift shop, valet laundry. **Business Services:** conference facilities, business center, PC, fax (fee). **Cards:** AX, CB, DC, DS, JC, MC, VI.

HOLIDAY INN EXPRESS & SUITES

Phone: (217)529-7771

(AAA) [SAVE]

All Year [ECP] — 1P: $69-$85 — 2P: $69-$85 — XP: $10 — F19

Motel

Location: I-55, exit 94 (Stevenson Pkwy), then 0.4 mi n. 3050 S Dirksen Pkwy 62703. Fax: 217/529-1777. **Facility:** 138 units. 134 one-bedroom standard units. 4 one-bedroom suites ($115). 4 stories, interior corridors. *Bath:* some combo or shower only. **Parking:** on-site. **Amenities:** extended cable TV, dual phone lines, voice mail, irons, hair dryers. **Leisure Activities:** exercise room. *Fee:* game room. **Guest Services:** valet and coin laundry, area transportation-train & bus stations. **Business Services:** meeting rooms. **Cards:** AX, CB, DC, DS, MC, VI. **Special Amenities:** free continental breakfast and free local telephone calls. *(See color ad p 425)*

HOWARD JOHNSON INN & SUITES

▼▼▼

Motel

Phone: (217)541-8762

8/8-8/19	1P: $89-$107	2P: $94-$111	XP: $5	F16
4/1-8/7	1P: $55-$69	2P: $60-$78	XP: $5	F16
8/20-10/31	1P: $57-$71	2P: $62-$75	XP: $5	F16
11/1-3/31	1P: $55-$69	2P: $60-$73		

Location: 1.5 mi n of Capital Airport on SR 29; opposite west entrance to Lincoln's tomb. 1701 J David Jones Pkwy 62702. Fax: 217/541-8774. **Facility:** 78 one-bedroom standard units. 2 stories, exterior corridors. *Bath:* combo or shower only. **Parking:** on-site. **Amenities:** extended cable TV, voice mail, safes, hair dryers. *Some:* irons. **Pool(s):** outdoor. **Leisure Activities:** exercise room. **Guest Services:** coin laundry. **Business Services:** meeting rooms. **Cards:** AX, CB, DC, DS, MC, VI.

SOME UNITS

(ASK) (SD) (+) (🐕) (🐾) (📷) (DATA PORT) (💻) (🖨) / (✕) (🛏) (🖥) /

THE INN AT 835

▼▼▼

Historic Bed
& Breakfast

Phone: (217)523-4466

All Year   1P: $99-$179   2P: $109-$189   XP: $10

Location: Between E Cannedy and E Lawrence. 835 S Second St 62704. Fax: 217/523-4468. **Facility:** Built as a luxury apartment building in 1909, this inn offers handsome rooms, expansive public areas and attentive service. Designated smoking area. 10 one-bedroom standard units, some with whirlpools. 3 stories, interior corridors. **Parking:** on-site. **Terms:** age restrictions may apply, 14 day cancellation notice-fee imposed. **Amenities:** extended cable TV, voice mail, irons, hair dryers. *Some:* CD players. **Leisure Activities:** bicycles. **Guest Services:** valet laundry. **Business Services:** meeting rooms, business center, PC. **Cards:** AX, CB, DC, DS, MC, VI.

SOME UNITS

(✕) (VCR) (🖨) / (🛏) /

MANSION VIEW INN & SUITES

(AAA) (SAVE)

▼▼▼

Motel

Phone: (217)544-7411

All Year [CP]   1P: $79-$129   2P: $79-$129   XP: $10   F16

Location: I-55, exit 92 (6th St), 3.9 mi n to Edwards St, just w on Edwards St, follow signs. 529 S 4th St 62701. Fax: 217/544-6211. **Facility:** 93 one-bedroom standard units, some with whirlpools. 2-4 stories, interior/exterior corridors. *Bath:* combo or shower only. **Parking:** on-site. **Terms:** package plans. **Amenities:** extended cable TV. *Some:* hair dryers. **Guest Services:** valet and coin laundry. **Business Services:** meeting rooms. **Cards:** AX, DC, DS, MC, VI. **Special Amenities:** free continental breakfast and free local telephone calls.

SOME UNITS

(SD) (+) (🍽) (🛋) (🐾) (📷) (DATA PORT) (💻) (🖨) / (✕) (🛏) (🖥) /
FEE FEE

PEAR TREE INN BY DRURY

▼▼▼

Motel

Phone: (217)529-9100

All Year [CP]   1P: $50-$76   2P: $50-$76   XP: $10   F18

Location: I-55, exit 94 (Stevenson Dr), just w. 3190 S Dirksen Pkwy 62703. Fax: 217/529-9100. **Facility:** 52 one-bedroom standard units. 2 stories, interior corridors. *Bath:* combo or shower only. **Parking:** on-site. **Terms:** small pets only. **Amenities:** extended cable TV. **Guest Services:** valet laundry. **Cards:** AX, CB, DC, DS, MC, VI. *(See color ad p 5)*

SOME UNITS

(🛏) (🍽) (🛋) (📷) (DATA PORT) (🖨) / (✕) /

RAMADA LIMITED NORTH

▼▼▼

Motel

Phone: (217)523-4000

All Year [ECP]   1P: $66-$89   2P: $71-$89   XP: $6   F18

Location: I-55, exit 100B (Sangamon Ave), 0.4 mi w to Dirksen Pkwy, just n to Northfield Dr, then just e. 3281 Northfield Dr 62702. Fax: 217/523-4080. **Facility:** 97 one-bedroom standard units. 2 stories, interior corridors. *Bath:* combo or shower only. **Parking:** on-site. **Amenities:** extended cable TV, irons, hair dryers. **Pool(s):** indoor. **Leisure Activities:** fishing, jogging, exercise room. **Guest Services:** coin laundry. **Business Services:** meeting rooms. **Cards:** AX, CB, DC, DS, JC, MC, VI.

SOME UNITS

(ASK) (SD) (+) (🛋) (🏊) (🐾) (✕) (📷) (💻) (🖨) / (✕) (🛏) (🖥) /
FEE

RAMADA LIMITED (SOUTH)

▼▼

Motel

Phone: (217)529-1410

All Year   1P: $59-$69   2P: $69-$79   XP: $6   F16

Location: I-55, exit 90, 0.3 mi e. 5970 S 6th St 62703. Fax: 217/529-1439. **Facility:** 47 one-bedroom standard units. 2 stories, interior corridors. **Parking:** on-site. **Terms:** [CP] meal plan available, pets ($10 extra charge). **Amenities:** voice mail. **Pool(s):** indoor. **Guest Services:** valet laundry. **Cards:** AX, CB, DC, DS, JC, MC, VI.

SOME UNITS

(ASK) (SD) (🐕) (🐾) (📷) (💻) (🖨) / (✕) (🛏) /
FEE

RED ROOF INN

(AAA) (SAVE)

▼▼ ▼▼

Motel

Phone: (217)753-4302

5/25-9/2	1P: $42-$54	2P: $47-$59	XP: $5	F18
9/3-3/31	1P: $40-$53	2P: $45-$58	XP: $5	F18
4/1-5/24	1P: $40-$50	2P: $45-$55	XP: $5	F18

Location: I-55, exit 96B, just w. 3200 Singer Ave 62703. Fax: 217/753-4391. **Facility:** 108 one-bedroom standard units. 2 stories, exterior corridors. **Parking:** on-site. **Terms:** small pets only. **Amenities:** video games, voice mail. **Cards:** AX, CB, DC, DS, MC, VI. **Special Amenities:** free local telephone calls and free newspaper.

SOME UNITS

(🐾) (📷) (✕) (💻) (🖨) / (✕) (🛏) (DATA PORT) /
FEE

SIGNATURE INN & CONFERENCE CENTER

▼▼▼

Motel

Phone: (217)529-6611

All Year [CP]   1P: $66-$76   2P: $66-$76

Location: I-55, exit 94 (Stevenson Dr), just w. 3090 Stevenson Dr 62703. Fax: 217/529-6611. **Facility:** 124 one-bedroom standard units. 2 stories, interior corridors. *Bath:* combo or shower only. **Parking:** on-site. **Amenities:** extended cable TV, voice mail, irons, hair dryers. **Pool(s):** indoor. **Leisure Activities:** exercise room. **Guest Services:** valet and coin laundry. **Business Services:** conference facilities. **Cards:** AX, DC, DS, MC, VI.

SOME UNITS

(ASK) (SD) (+) (🍽) (🛋M) (🛋) (🏊) (🐾) (📷) (DATA PORT) (🛏) (💻) (🖥) (🖨) / (✕) /

SLEEP INN

SAVE

♦♦ ♦♦

Motel

| | 4/1-9/30 | 1P: $64-$89 | 2P: $69-$94 | XP: $5 | F18 |
| | 10/1-3/31 | 1P: $59-$64 | 2P: $64-$69 | XP: $5 | F18 |

Phone: (217)787-6200

Location: I-72, exit 93 (Veterans Pkwy), 0.7 mi n to Lindbergh Blvd, just w to Freedom Dr, then just s. 3470 Freedom Dr 62704. Fax: 217/787-6200. **Facility:** 62 one-bedroom standard units. 3 stories, interior corridors. *Bath:* combo or shower only. **Parking:** on-site. **Terms:** 7 day cancellation notice, small pets only ($25 extra charge). **Amenities:** *Some:* irons, hair dryers. **Guest Services:** valet laundry. **Cards:** AX, CB, DC, DS, JC, MC, VI.

SOME UNITS

🅂🄳 🐾 🍴 ♿ 🎦 📶 🏋 📠 / ✕ 🅿 📺 💻 /
FEE   FEE FEE

SUPER 8 SPRINGFIELD SOUTH

♦♦ ♦♦

Motel

All Year   1P: $55   2P: $65   XP: $10   F12

Phone: (217)529-8898

Location: I-55, exit 92A (Business US 55), just n to Hazel Bell, just w to Access Rd, then just n. 3675 S 6th St 62703. Fax: 217/529-4354. **Facility:** 122 one-bedroom standard units, some with whirlpools. 3 stories, interior corridors. **Parking:** on-site, winter plug-ins. **Terms:** 7 day cancellation notice, [CP] meal plan available, pets ($25 deposit). **Amenities:** extended cable TV, safes (fee). **Guest Services:** coin laundry. **Business Services:** meeting rooms. **Cards:** AX, CB, DC, DS, JC, MC, VI.

SOME UNITS

ASK 🅂🄳 🐾 🏋 / ✕ 🅿 📺 💻 📠 /
FEE   FEE FEE

——— WHERE TO DINE ———

20'S HIDEOUT STEAKHOUSE & BAR   Dinner: $6-$19   Phone: 217/753-0200

♦♦ ♦♦

American

Location: I-55, exit 94 (Stevenson Dr), just w to Dirksen Pkwy, then 0.7 mi n. 2660 S Dirksen Pkwy 62703. **Hours:** 4 pm-10 pm, Fri-11 pm, Sat 3 pm-11 pm, Sun 11:30 am-9 pm. Closed major holidays. **Features:** casual dress; children's menu; carryout; cocktails & lounge; a la carte. Creatively named dishes, such as "shakedown," a.k.a. pasta primavera, add humor to the family restaurant's varied menu of steaks, sandwiches, chops and seafood. Framed newspaper articles, photographs and period decorations lend authenticity to the 1920s theme. **Parking:** on-site. **Cards:** AX, CB, DC, DS, MC, VI. ✕

AUGIE'S FRONT BURNER   Lunch: $5-$9   Dinner: $13-$21   Phone: 217/544-6979

◈◈◈

♦♦ ♦♦

American

Location: Center; on Fifth, between Washington and Adams. 2 W Old State Capital Plaza 62701. **Hours:** 11 am-4 & 5-10 pm, Sat from 5 pm. Closed major holidays; also Sun. **Reservations:** suggested. **Features:** casual dress; carryout; cocktails. Just across the street from the historic Old State Capitol, the restaurant occupies a brick storefront location with a bright red awning and trendy art nouveau interior. The lunch hour is geared for busy professionals on a limited time schedule, but at dinner, the kitchen takes the time to be more creative. The result is cuisine that has been called "American with an attitude." A little sassy and a lot saucy, the food is an eclectic blend of several influences. **Parking:** street. **Cards:** AX, CB, DC, DS, MC, VI. ✕

CHESAPEAKE SEAFOOD HOUSE Lunch: $6 Dinner: $9-$20 Phone: 217/522-5220
AAA
WWW WWW
Seafood

Location: I-55, exit 98B (Clear Lake Ave), 0.8 mi w; 2.3 mi e of downtown, on SR 97 and 29. 3045 Clearlake Ave 62708. **Hours:** 11 am-2 & 4-10 pm. **Closed:** 12/25; also Sun. **Reservations:** suggested. **Features:** casual dress; children's menu; early bird specials; cocktails & lounge. Barbecue ribs, beef and pork are menu mainstays along with the seafood from which this restaurant derives its name. Three notable house specials: a bay platter of scallops, orange roughy and shrimp scampi; rainbow trout; and catfish. Chesapeake, located inside a vintage restored home, is bustling on weekends. **Parking:** on-site.
Cards: AX, DC, DS, MC, VI. ⊠

FOX RUN RESTAURANT & LOUNGE Lunch: $7-$17 Dinner: $10-$22 Phone: 217/698-0990
WWW WWW
American

Location: I-72, exit 93, just n. 3317 Robbins Rd 62704. **Hours:** 11 am-1 am, Sun-3 pm. **Features:** casual dress; carryout; cocktails. You'll enjoy a log cabin atmosphere with fine spirits and food. This rustic new restaurant offers much in the way of ambience in just the aroma of the setting. **Parking:** on-site. **Cards:** AX, DS, MC, VI. ⊠

GABATONI'S Lunch: $8-$17 Dinner: $10-$25 Phone: 217/528-9629
WWW WWW
Italian

Location: I-55/72, exit 96B, 2.1 mi w on S Grand Ave, 1 blk s on 6th St to Laurel, then just w. 300 E Laurel St 62703. **Hours:** 11 am-1 am, Sun from noon. **Features:** casual dress; carryout; cocktails. This is a family-run Italian restaurant with wonderful food and friendly service. Homespun ambience prevails. Ask for one of the house specialties, the Horseshoes. A large bar/wait area with pictures and prints adorning the walls complements this cozy restaurant. Smoke free premises. **Parking:** on-site. **Cards:** AX, DS, MC, VI. ⊠

GUMBO YA YA'S RESTAURANT Dinner: $8-$18 Phone: 217/789-1530
WWW WWW
Regional Ethnic

Location: Just e of the Old Capitol Building, at 7th and Adams sts; in Hilton Springfield. 700 E Adams St 62702. **Hours:** 5 pm-10 pm. **Closed:** 12/25; also Sun. **Reservations:** suggested. **Features:** casual dress; children's menu; cocktails & lounge; also prix fixe. You'll take in beautiful views from the 30th floor of Springfield's tallest building and enjoy food rather atypical for Central Illinois. Jambalaya, shrimp etouffee and steak Creole are just a handful of the many Creole menu items you have to choose from. **Parking:** on-site and valet (fee).
Cards: AX, CB, DC, DS, JC, MC, VI. ⊠

MALDANER'S Lunch: $5-$10 Dinner: $10-$24 Phone: 217/522-4313
WWW WWW
Nouvelle American

Location: Just s of Old State Capitol, at jct Monroe St. 222 S 6th St 62701. **Hours:** 11 am-2:30 & 5-10 pm, Mon-2:30 pm, Fri & Sat-10 pm. **Closed:** major holidays; also Sun. **Reservations:** suggested. **Features:** dressy casual; cocktails & lounge; a la carte. Maldaner's is known for its contemporary, bistro-style menu that employs fresh local and seasonal ingredients. Striking, artful plate presentations, a casual yet sophisticated decor and a prime downtown location make it truly an Epicurean standout. **Parking:** street.
Cards: AX, MC, VI. ⊠

PARKWAY CAFE Lunch: $5-$13 Dinner: $5-$13 Phone: 217/544-2233
WWW
American

Location: I-55, exit Sangamon Ave, 0.4 mi w to Dirksen Pkwy, then 1.7 mi n. 2715 N Dirksen Pkwy 62702. **Hours:** 6 am-8 pm, Fri-10 pm. **Features:** casual dress; carryout; salad bar. Casual dining and comfort food are the hallmarks of this pleasant, unpretentious cafe. Breakfast is served at any time, and other tasty dishes are made to order. The staff is friendly and attentive. **Parking:** on-site. **Cards:** DS, MC, VI. ⊠

TOKYO OF JAPAN Lunch: $6-$12 Dinner: $10-$20 Phone: 217/585-0088
WWW WWW
Japanese

Location: I-55, exit 94 (Stevenson Dr), 0.8 mi w. 2225 Stevenson Dr 62703. **Hours:** 11:30 am-2 & 5-10:30 pm, Fri-11 pm, Sat & Sun 4:30 pm-9:30 pm. **Closed:** major holidays; also Mon. **Reservations:** suggested. **Features:** casual dress; children's menu; carryout; cocktails; prix fixe, a la carte. Dine at a teppan table, where you can watch the show as trained chefs slice, dice and spice traditional Japanese cuisine in a flurry of food and cutlery. Those who prefer a more relaxed experience can opt to be seated at individual tables and have their food prepared in the kitchen and served by the wait staff. **Parking:** on-site. **Cards:** AX, DC, DS, MC, VI.

STAUNTON pop. 4,800

—— WHERE TO STAY ——

STAUNTON SUPER 8 Phone: (618)635-5353
WWW WWW
Motel

All Year [CP] 1P: $50-$58 2P: $60-$70 XP: $6 F13
Location: I-55, exit 41, 0.3 mi w. 1527 Herman Rd 62088. Fax: 618/635-8255. **Facility:** 52 one-bedroom standard units. 2 stories, interior corridors. *Bath:* combo or shower only. **Parking:** on-site, winter plug-ins. **Terms:** 7 day cancellation notice-fee imposed. **Amenities:** extended cable TV, video tape library (fee). **Guest Services:** coin laundry. **Business Services:** meeting rooms. **Cards:** AX, DS, MC, VI.

SOME UNITS
(ASK) 🛏 🐕 📶 🖥 / ⊠ VCR 🔌 /
FEE

SYCAMORE pop. 9,700

—— WHERE TO STAY ——

AMERIHOST INN-SYCAMORE Phone: (815)895-4979
AAA (SAVE)
WWW WWW
Motel

5/15-9/1 1P: $78-$87 2P: $78-$87 XP: $6 F17
4/1-5/14 & 9/2-3/31 1P: $75-$84 2P: $75-$84 XP: $6 F17
Location: Jct SR 23 and Peace Rd. 1475 S Peace Rd 60178. Fax: 815/895-5069. **Facility:** 60 one-bedroom standard units, some with whirlpools. 2 stories, interior corridors. *Bath:* combo or shower only. **Parking:** on-site. **Terms:** 3 day cancellation notice, package plans. **Amenities:** extended cable TV, voice mail, safes (fee), irons, hair dryers. **Leisure Activities:** sauna, whirlpool, exercise room. **Guest Services:** valet laundry. **Business Services:** meeting rooms. **Cards:** AX, CB, DC, DS, MC, VI. **Special Amenities:** free continental breakfast and free newspaper.

SOME UNITS
🛏 🔐 📺 ⊠ 🐕 📶 🖥 🖥 / 🔌 🔌 📶 /
FEE

COUNTRY INN & SUITES BY CARLSON

▼▼▼▼ All Year [ECP]   1P: $79-$85   **Phone:** (815)895-8686   XP: $10   F18

Motel   **Location:** Jct SR 23 and Peace Rd. 1450 S Peace Rd 60178. Fax: 815/895-8685. **Facility:** 73 units. 35 one-bedroom standard units, some with whirlpools. 38 one-bedroom suites ($95-$249). 3 stories, interior corridors. *Bath:* combo or shower only. **Parking:** on-site. **Terms:** [MAP] meal plan available, package plans. **Amenities:** extended cable TV, dual phone lines, voice mail, irons, hair dryers. **Pool(s):** heated indoor. **Leisure Activities:** whirlpool, exercise room. **Guest Services:** valet and coin laundry. **Business Services:** business center, PC, fax (fee). **Cards:** AX, CB, DC, DS, JC, MC, VI. *(See color ad p 322)*

(ASK) (S🐕/D) (⬇M) (♿) (📷) (🏊) (📹) (DATA PORT) (💻) (📠) / (✕) (🛏) (🔲) /   SOME UNITS   FEE

HOLIDAY INN EXPRESS HOTEL & SUITES

▼▼▼ All Year   1P: $84   2P: $84   **Phone:** (815)748-7400   XP: $8   F18

Motel   **Location:** On SR 23, 1 mi s of Peace Rd; between DeKalb and Sycamore aves. 1935 DeKalb Ave 60178. Fax: 815/748-7400. **Facility:** 69 one-bedroom standard units, some with whirlpools. 3 stories, interior corridors. *Bath:* combo or shower only. **Parking:** on-site. **Amenities:** extended cable TV, dual phone lines, voice mail, irons, hair dryers. **Pool(s):** small heated outdoor. **Leisure Activities:** exercise room. **Guest Services:** valet laundry. **Business Services:** meeting rooms, business center, fax. **Cards:** AX, CB, DC, DS, JC, MC, VI.

(ASK) (S🐕/D) (🍴↑) (♿) (🏊) (📹) (DATA PORT) (💻) (📠) / (✕) (🛏) /   SOME UNITS   FEE FEE

STRATFORD INN

▼▼▼ All Year [ECP]   1P: $68-$139   2P: $68-$139   **Phone:** (815)895-6789   XP: $7   F12

Classic Country Inn   **Location:** Downtown; at jct California St, on SR 64. 355 W State St 60178. Fax: 815/895-6563. **Facility:** This home-like inn, part of the quiet downtown district, has a country theme with oak wainscoting, fabric wallcoverings and antiques. 39 units. 37 one-bedroom standard units, some with whirlpools. 2 one-bedroom suites ($110-$139) with whirlpools. 3 stories, interior corridors. **Parking:** on-site. **Terms:** package plans. **Amenities:** irons. **Guest Services:** valet laundry. **Business Services:** conference facilities. **Cards:** AX, CB, DC, DS, MC, VI.

(ASK) (S🐕/D) (🍴) (🍸) (♿↑) (📹) (DATA PORT) (💻) (📠) / (✕) (🛏) /   SOME UNITS   FEE

——— WHERE TO DINE ———

THE COUNTRY INN

♦   **Lunch:** $6-$14   **Dinner:** $6-$14   **Phone:** 815-756-8110

American   **Location:** On SR 23, 1 mi s of jct Peace Rd; between DeKalb and Sycamore aves. 2496 DeKalb Ave 60178. **Hours:** 11 am-2 & 5-8:30 pm, Fri-9 pm, Sat 5 pm-9 pm, Sun 10 am-3 pm. Closed: 12/24, 12/25; also Mon. **Reservations:** suggested; weekends. **Features:** casual dress; Sunday brunch; children's menu; carryout; salad bar; beer & wine only; buffet. The buffet line, stocked with such comfort staples as meatloaf, spicy boneless chicken and roast beef, is the restaurant's big draw. Country decor in the ranch-style building includes folksy art and blue-painted walls. Servers are attentive and steady. Smoke free premises. **Parking:** on-site. **Cards:** AX, DS, MC, VI.   (✕)

JOHNNY'S CHARHOUSE

♦♦   **Lunch:** $8-$15   **Dinner:** $9-$19   **Phone:** 815-756-1155

Steak & Seafood   **Location:** On SR 23, 1 mi s of Peace Rd. 1950 Dekalb Ave 60178. **Hours:** 11 am-10 pm, Fri & Sat-11 pm. Closed: 12/25. **Reservations:** accepted. **Features:** casual dress; children's menu; carryout; cocktails & lounge. Set in a quiet, commercial area, the sleek, casual steakhouse features glistening, light-wood floors and a thick wood-beam ceiling. Fine steaks are the specialty on a menu that also includes Italian specialties and fresh seafood. The limited lunch menu focuses mostly on sandwiches. **Parking:** on-site. **Cards:** AX, MC, VI.   (✕)

TAYLORVILLE pop. 11,100

——— WHERE TO STAY ———

MARKET STREET INN BED & BREAKFAST

▼▼♦♦ All Year [BP]   1P: $85-$135   2P: $85-$135   **Phone:** (217)824-7220   XP: $15   D15

Historic Bed & Breakfast   **Location:** Just e of south side of town square. 220 E Market St 62568. Fax: 217/824-7229. **Facility:** Ornate woodwork adds interest to this charming Victorian house located in a residential area. Smoke free premises. 8 one-bedroom standard units, some (no elevator), interior corridors. *Bath:* combo or shower only. **Parking:** street. **Terms:** check-in 4 pm, 3 day cancellation notice. **Amenities:** extended cable TV, dual phone lines, voice mail. **Leisure Activities:** bicycles. **Business Services:** meeting rooms. **Cards:** AX, MC, VI.

(✕) (DATA PORT) (📠) / (VCR) /   SOME UNITS

TINLEY PARK —See Chicago p. 371.

TROY pop. 6,000

——— WHERE TO STAY ———

RAMADA LIMITED & SUITES

▼▼▼

3/1-3/31	1P: $96-$116	2P: $101-$121	XP: $5 F17
4/1-1/1	1P: $86-$106	2P: $91-$111	XP: $5 F17
1/2-2/28	1P: $76-$86	2P: $81-$91	XP: $5 F17

Phone: 618/667-9200

Motel   **Location:** I-55/70, exit 18, just w. 2020 Formosa Dr 62294 (116 Regency Park, O'FALLON, 62269). Fax: 618/667-9229. **Facility:** 65 one-bedroom standard units. 3 stories, interior corridors. *Bath:* combo or shower only. **Parking:** on-site. **Amenities:** extended cable TV, dual phone lines, voice mail, irons, hair dryers. **Leisure Activities:** whirlpool, playground, exercise room. **Business Services:** meeting rooms, fax (fee). **Cards:** AX, MC.

(⬇M) (♿) (✕) (📹) (DATA PORT) (🛏) (🔲) (💻) (📠) / (✕) (VCR) /   SOME UNITS

SUPER 8 MOTEL

			Phone: (618)667-8888
5/26-9/4	1P: $55	2P: $60	XP: $5
4/1-5/25 & 9/5-3/31	1P: $45	2P: $50	

Motel

Location: I-55/70, exit 18, just w. 910 Edwardsville Rd 62294. Fax: 618/667-1090. **Facility:** 61 one-bedroom standard units. 2 stories, interior corridors. *Bath:* combo or shower only. **Parking:** on-site, winter plug-ins. **Amenities:** extended cable TV. **Pool(s):** small heated indoor. **Leisure Activities:** whirlpool. **Business Services:** fax (fee). **Cards:** AX, DC, DS, MC, VI.

SOME UNITS

TUSCOLA pop. 4,200

―――― WHERE TO STAY ――――

AMERIHOST INN-TUSCOLA

			Phone: (217)253-3500
1/1-3/31 [CP]	1P: $69-$77	2P: $77-$79	XP: $6 F18
4/1-12/31 [CP]	1P: $67-$75	2P: $75-$77	XP: $6 F18

Motel

Location: I-57, exit 212 (US 36), 0.3 mi w. 1006 Southline Rd 61953. Fax: 217/253-2773. **Facility:** 59 one-bedroom standard units, some with whirlpools. 2 stories, interior corridors. *Bath:* combo or shower only. **Parking:** on-site. **Amenities:** extended cable TV, safes (fee), irons, hair dryers. **Pool(s):** heated indoor. **Leisure Activities:** sauna, whirlpool, exercise equipment by pool. **Guest Services:** valet laundry. **Business Services:** meeting rooms, fax (fee). **Cards:** AX, DC, DS, MC, VI. **Special Amenities:** early check-in/late check-out and free continental breakfast.

SOME UNITS

HOLIDAY INN EXPRESS

			Phone: (217)253-6363
All Year [CP]	1P: $70-$80	2P: $70-$80	XP: $6 F19

Motel

Location: I-57, exit 212 (US 36), 0.3 mi w to Progress Blvd, just s to Tuscola Blvd, then 0.4 mi se. 1201 Tuscola Blvd 61953. Fax: 217/253-6655. **Facility:** 82 one-bedroom standard units. 3 stories, interior corridors. **Parking:** on-site. **Terms:** pets (in smoking units). **Amenities:** extended cable TV, irons, hair dryers. **Pool(s):** heated indoor. **Leisure Activities:** whirlpool. **Guest Services:** valet and coin laundry. **Business Services:** meeting rooms, fax (fee). **Cards:** AX, CB, DC, DS, MC, VI.

SOME UNITS

SUPER 8 MOTEL-TUSCOLA

			Phone: (217)253-5488
4/1-8/31	1P: $50-$65	2P: $55-$70	XP: $5 F17
9/1-12/31	1P: $45-$60	2P: $50-$65	XP: $5 F17
1/1-3/31	1P: $40-$55	2P: $45-$60	XP: $5 F17

Motel

Location: I-57, exit 212 (US 36), 0.4 mi w. 1007 E Hwy 36 61953 (PO Box 202). Fax: 217/253-5488. **Facility:** 63 one-bedroom standard units. 2 stories, interior corridors. **Parking:** on-site. **Terms:** cancellation fee imposed. **Amenities:** extended cable TV. *Some:* irons, hair dryers. **Guest Services:** coin laundry. **Cards:** AX, DC, DS, MC, VI.

SOME UNITS

URBANA pop. 36,300—See also CHAMPAIGN.

―――― WHERE TO STAY ――――

RAMADA LIMITED-URBANA/CHAMPAIGN

			Phone: (217)328-4400
All Year [ECP]	1P: $70	2P: $85	XP: $10 F17

Motel

Location: I-74, exit 183 (Lincoln Ave), just s to Killarney St, then just w. 902 W Killarney St 61801. Fax: 217/328-6623. **Facility:** 73 one-bedroom standard units. 2 stories, interior corridors. **Parking:** on-site, winter plug-ins. **Terms:** 3 day cancellation notice, pets ($50 deposit). **Amenities:** extended cable TV, video tape library (fee), voice mail, irons, hair dryers. **Pool(s):** small heated indoor. **Leisure Activities:** whirlpool. **Guest Services:** valet and coin laundry. **Business Services:** fax (fee). **Cards:** AX, CB, DC, DS, MC, VI. **Special Amenities:** free continental breakfast and free local telephone calls.

SOME UNITS

SLEEP INN

			Phone: (217)367-6000
All Year	1P: $62-$99	2P: $69-$109	XP: $7 F16

Motel

Location: I-74, exit 183 (Lincoln Ave), 0.5 mi s. 1908 N Lincoln Ave 61801. Fax: 217/367-6000. **Facility:** 65 one-bedroom standard units. 3 stories, interior corridors. *Bath:* combo or shower only. **Parking:** on-site. **Terms:** pets ($5 fee). **Amenities:** extended cable TV. *Some:* irons, hair dryers. **Leisure Activities:** exercise room. **Guest Services:** valet and coin laundry. **Business Services:** meeting rooms. **Cards:** AX, DC, DS, JC, MC, VI.

SOME UNITS

―――― WHERE TO DINE ――――

KENNEDY'S

Lunch: $5-$8	Dinner: $11-$23	Phone: 217/384-8111

American

Location: I-74, exit 183 (Lincoln Ave), 4 mi s to Windsor Rd, then 2.8 mi e to Stone Creek Blvd, just e. 2560 S Stone Creek Blvd 61802. **Hours:** 10 am-10 pm, Sun-8 pm. Closed major holidays. **Reservations:** suggested. **Features:** dressy casual; Sunday brunch; children's menu; early bird specials; carryout; cocktails & lounge. Casually classy with low lighting, the intimate restaurant is appointed with wood decor and attractive artwork. Innovative, contemporary preparations of fresh seafood are the menu's greatest strength. The chocolate mousse torte is scrumptious. **Parking:** on-site. **Cards:** AX, CB, DC, DS, MC, VI.

NED KELLY'S STEAKHOUSE   Lunch: $5-$10   Dinner: $10-$22   Phone: 217/344-8201

Steak House
Location: I-74, exit 184A (Cunningham Ave), 0.7 mi s. 1601 N Cunningham Ave 61802. **Hours:** 11 am-10 pm, Fri & Sat-11 pm, Sun-9 pm. Closed: 11/28, 12/25. **Reservations:** suggested. **Features:** casual dress; children's menu; early bird specials; carryout; cocktails & lounge. It would be a crime at this restaurant, named for a legendary Australian cattle rustler and bank robber, to not try the outstanding mild and creamy onion and curry house salad dressing. "Down under" overtones are evident on the menu and in the decor. **Parking:** on-site. **Cards:** AX, DC, DS, MC, VI.

SILVERCREEK   Lunch: $6-$9   Dinner: $10-$19   Phone: 217/328-3402

American
Location: Just n from University. 402 N Race 61801. **Hours:** 11 am-10 pm, Fri & Sat-11 pm, Sun 10:30 am-3 & 4:30-10 pm. Closed major holidays. **Reservations:** suggested. **Features:** dressy casual; Sunday brunch; cocktails & lounge. While the lunch menu lists more than 15 sandwiches and the dinner menu presents a tempting variety of sophisticated entrees, the Nicoise salad is an option not to be missed. The beautiful dining room features a vaulted ceiling and exposed beams. Smoke free premises. **Parking:** on-site. **Cards:** AX, DS, MC, VI.

UTICA

──── WHERE TO STAY ────

THE BRIGHTWOOD INN   Phone: 815/667-4600
All Year   1P: $75-$235   2P: $100-$235   XP: $25

Country Inn
Location: I-80, exit 81 (SR 178), 6.2 mi s. 2407 N Illinois (Rt 178) 61348 (2407 N Illinois (Rt 178), OGLESBY). **Fax:** 815/667-4727. **Facility:** Every guest room has a fireplace in this newer, rural-area property designed to feel like a traditional farmhouse. Smoke free premises. 8 units. 7 one-bedroom standard units, some with whirlpools. 1 one-bedroom suite ($200-$235) with whirlpool. 3 stories, interior corridors. *Bath:* combo or shower only. **Parking:** on-site. **Terms:** age restrictions may apply, 7 day cancellation notice-fee imposed, package plans. **Amenities:** video tape library, hair dryers. **Guest Services:** gift shop. **Business Services:** meeting rooms. **Cards:** AX, DS, MC, VI.

SOME UNITS

VANDALIA pop. 6,100

——— WHERE TO STAY ———

DAYS INN
AAA SAVE
Motel
5/24-9/9 [ECP]   1P: $50-$89   2P: $54-$89   XP: $6   F17
4/1-5/23 & 9/10-3/31 [ECP]   1P: $47-$87   2P: $51-$87   XP: $6   F17
Phone: (618)283-4400
Location: I-70, exit 63 (US 51), 0.6 mi n, on US 51. 1920 Kennedy Blvd 62471. Fax: 618/283-4240. **Facility:** 93 units. 92 one-bedroom standard units. 1 one-bedroom suite with whirlpool. 2 stories, exterior corridors. **Parking:** on-site. **Terms:** 14 day cancellation notice, pets ($10 deposit). **Amenities:** extended cable TV, hair dryers. *Some:* irons. **Pool(s):** outdoor. **Business Services:** meeting rooms, fax (fee). **Cards:** AX, CB, DC, DS, MC, VI. **Special Amenities: early check-in/late check-out and preferred room (subject to availability with advanced reservations).**

SOME UNITS

JAY'S INN
AAA SAVE
Motel
All Year   1P: $36-$45   2P: $46-$58
Phone: (618)283-1200
Location: I-70, exit 63 (US 51), just s. 720 Gochenour St 62471. Fax: 618/283-4588. **Facility:** 21 one-bedroom standard units. 2 stories, exterior corridors. **Parking:** on-site, winter plug-ins. **Amenities:** extended cable TV, hair dryers. **Business Services:** fax (fee). **Cards:** AX, DS, MC, VI. **Special Amenities: early check-in/late check-out and free local telephone calls.**

SOME UNITS

RAMADA LIMITED VANDALIA
AAA SAVE
Motel
All Year [ECP]   1P: $50   2P: $58   XP: $8   F18
Phone: (618)283-1400
Location: I-70, exit 61, just s. 2707 Veterans Ave 62471 (PO Box 316). Fax: 618/283-3465. **Facility:** 60 one-bedroom standard units. 2 stories, interior corridors. **Parking:** on-site, winter plug-ins. **Terms:** 30 day cancellation notice, pets ($10 deposit in smoking units). **Amenities:** extended cable TV, voice mail, irons, hair dryers. **Pool(s):** outdoor. **Leisure Activities:** exercise room. **Guest Services:** valet laundry. **Business Services:** meeting rooms, fax (fee). **Cards:** AX, CB, DC, DS, MC, VI. **Special Amenities: free continental breakfast and free newspaper.**

SOME UNITS

FEE

TRAVELODGE OF VANDALIA
AAA SAVE
Motel
4/1-10/31 [CP]   1P: $40-$45   2P: $50-$55   XP: $5   F17
11/1-3/31 [CP]   1P: $36-$39   2P: $45-$50   XP: $5   F17
Phone: (618)283-2363
Location: I-70, exit 63 (US 51), just s. 1500 N 6th St 62471. Fax: 618/283-2363. **Facility:** 45 one-bedroom standard units. 2 stories, exterior corridors. **Parking:** on-site, winter plug-ins. **Terms:** 5 day cancellation notice-fee imposed, pets ($3 extra charge). **Amenities:** extended cable TV. **Pool(s):** outdoor. **Leisure Activities:** playground. **Business Services:** fax (fee). **Cards:** AX, CB, DC, DS, MC, VI. **Special Amenities: free continental breakfast and free newspaper.**

SOME UNITS

FEE   FEE

——— WHERE TO DINE ———

THE DEPOT   Historical   **Lunch:** $4-$7   **Dinner:** $6-$14   **Phone:** 618/283-1918
American
Location: Just n from SR 140, 0.3 mi w of US 51/40. 107 S Sixth St 62471. **Hours:** 11 am-9:30 pm, Fri & Sat-10 pm. **Reservations:** suggested. **Features:** casual dress; children's menu; carryout; cocktails & lounge; entertainment. The historic train station, which dates back to the early 20th-century, is converted to a charming dining room, decorated in rich greens and attractive linens. Steak and seafood make up the bulk of the menu although Cajun selections are interesting. **Parking:** on-site. **Cards:** AX, MC, VI.

VERNON HILLS —*See Chicago p. 372.*

WADSWORTH —*See Chicago p. 373.*

WARRENVILLE —*See Chicago p. 373.*

WASHINGTON pop. 10,100

——— WHERE TO STAY ———

SUPER 8 MOTEL
Motel
All Year   1P: $46-$53   XP: $5   F18
Phone: (309)444-8881
Location: On Business SR 24, 1.5 mi w. 1884 Washington Rd 61571. Fax: 309/444-8881. **Facility:** 47 one-bedroom standard units. 2 stories, interior corridors. **Parking:** on-site. **Amenities:** extended cable TV. **Business Services:** meeting rooms. **Cards:** AX, DC, DS, MC, VI.

SOME UNITS

FEE

WATSEKA pop. 5,400

—— WHERE TO STAY ——

SUPER 8 MOTEL
(AAA) (SAVE)
▼▼▼ ▼▼
Motel

All Year [ECP]   1P: $52-$57   2P: $57-$69   XP: $5   F15   **Phone:** (815)432-6000
Location: On US 24; in center of town. 710 W Walnut 60970. Fax: 815/432-6000. **Facility:** 42 one-bedroom standard units, some with whirlpools. 2 stories, interior corridors. **Parking:** on-site, winter plug-ins. **Terms:** 7 day cancellation notice-fee imposed, pets ($3 extra charge, in smoking units). **Amenities:** extended cable TV. **Leisure Activities:** whirlpool. **Guest Services:** coin laundry. **Business Services:** meeting rooms. **Cards:** AX, CB, DC, DS, MC, VI. **Special Amenities:** free continental breakfast and preferred room (subject to availability with advanced reservations).

SOME UNITS
(S🅓) (🛏) (🍴➕) (📺) (📷) (DATA PORT) (🖨) / (✕) (🔌) (🖥) /

WAUKEGAN —See Chicago p. 373.

WESTCHESTER —See Chicago p. 375.

WEST CITY pop. 700

—— WHERE TO STAY ——

DAYS INN BENTON
(AAA) (SAVE)
▼▼▼ ▼▼
Motor Inn

4/1-11/30   1P: $50   2P: $54   XP: $5   F18   **Phone:** (618)439-3183
12/1-3/31   1P: $45   2P: $49   XP: $5   F18
Location: I-57, exit 71, just e. 711 W Main St 62812. Fax: 618/439-3183. **Facility:** 57 one-bedroom standard units, some with whirlpools. 2 stories, interior corridors. *Bath:* combo or shower only. **Parking:** on-site, winter plug-ins. **Terms:** 10 day cancellation notice, pets ($5 extra charge, in smoking units). **Amenities:** extended cable TV, hair dryers. **Dining:** restaurant, 6 am-9 pm, $4-$13, cocktails. **Guest Services:** coin laundry. **Business Services:** meeting rooms, fax (fee). **Cards:** AX, DC, DS, MC, VI. **Special Amenities:** free local telephone calls and free newspaper.

SOME UNITS
(S🅓) (🛏) (🍴) (🍸) (🖥) (📷) / (✕) (VCR) (🔌) (🖥) (🖨) /
     FEE FEE

SUPER 8 MOTEL OF BENTON/WEST CITY
▼▼ ▼▼
Motel

4/1-12/1 [CP]   1P: $50-$60   2P: $60-$70   XP: $5   F18   **Phone:** (618)438-8205
12/2-3/31 [CP]   1P: $40-$50   2P: $50-$60   XP: $5   F18
Location: I-57, exit 71 (SR 14), just e. 711 1/2 W Main St 62812. Fax: 618/439-3183. **Facility:** 54 one-bedroom standard units. 2 stories, interior corridors. *Bath:* combo or shower only. **Parking:** on-site, winter plug-ins. **Terms:** 10 day cancellation notice, small pets only. **Amenities:** extended cable TV. **Cards:** AX, DC, DS, MC, VI.

SOME UNITS
(ASK) (S🅓) (🛏) (🍴➕) (🖥) (📷) (DATA PORT) (🖨) / (✕) (VCR) (🔌) /
                    FEE FEE

WEST DUNDEE —See Chicago p. 375.

WESTMONT —See Chicago p. 375.

WHEATON —See Chicago p. 376.

WHEELING —See Chicago p. 376.

WHITTINGTON pop. 200

—— WHERE TO STAY ——

SEASONS LODGE AT REND LAKE GOLF COURSE
▼▼▼▼▼
Resort

Property failed to provide current rates   **Phone:** 618/629-2600
Location: I-57, exit 77 (SR 154), 0.3 mi w to Larry Foster Pkwy, just s to Golf Course Dr, then just w. 12575 Golf Course Rd 62897. Fax: 618/629-2365. **Facility:** A large front porch and covered back patio look out onto well-kept landscaping at this lodge, which has a charming design and decor. 46 one-bedroom standard units, some with whirlpools. 2 stories, interior corridors. **Parking:** on-site, winter plug-ins. **Terms:** package plans. **Amenities:** video games, Web TV (fee), voice mail. **Dining:** Seasons on the Green, see separate listing. **Pool(s):** outdoor. **Leisure Activities:** whirlpool, golf-27 holes, bicycles, playground, exercise room. **Business Services:** meeting rooms. **Cards:** AX, CB, DC, DS, MC, VI.

SOME UNITS
(🍴) (🍸) (🏊) (✕) (📷) (DATA PORT) (🖥) (🖨) / (✕) (VCR) (🔌) /
                    FEE

—— WHERE TO DINE ——

SEASONS ON THE GREEN
▼▼▼ ▼▼
American

Lunch: $4-$7   **Dinner:** $9-$25   **Phone:** 618/629-2454
Location: I-57, exit 77 (SR 154), 0.3 mi w to Larry Foster Pkwy, just s to Golf Course Dr, then just w; in Seasons Lodge at Rend Lake Golf Course. 12476 Golf Course Rd 62897. **Hours:** 6 am-10 pm; 10 am-9 pm in winter. Closed: 11/28, 12/25. **Reservations:** accepted. **Features:** casual dress; Sunday brunch; children's menu; carryout; salad bar; cocktails & lounge; buffet. On the grounds of Rend Lake Resort, the restaurant and its outdoor dining area look out onto the golf course. Steak, seafood and Italian buffets alternate nightly throughout the week. The popular Sunday brunch also is served buffet-style. **Parking:** on-site. **Cards:** AX, DC, DS, MC, VI.

(✕)

WINDOWS AT REND LAKE RESORT   Lunch: $4-$7   Dinner: $8-$25   Phone: 618/629-256?
Location: I-57, exit 77 (SR 154), 2 mi w to Fitzgerrel Park Dr, 2.9 mi n; in Wayne Fitzgerrel State Park. 11712 E Windy Lane 62897. **Hours:** 8 am-9 pm, Sun-8 am; 7 am-9 pm, Fri & Sat-10 pm 4/1-10/1. Closed: 1/1, 12/25.
Steak & Seafood   **Reservations:** suggested; weekends. **Features:** casual dress; Sunday brunch; children's menu; carryout; cocktails & lounge; buffet. Casual lakeside dining in Wayne Fitzgerrel State Park makes this a popula stop. The menu is varied with baked halibut, shrimp scampi, steak and Mexican entrees topping the list of favorites. Outdoor dining is available and perfect for sunset watching. **Parking:** on-site. **Cards:** AX, DC, DS, MC, VI.

WILLOWBROOK —See Chicago p. 377.

WILMETTE —See Chicago p. 377.

WOOD DALE —See Chicago p. 377.

WOODHULL pop. 800

——— WHERE TO DINE ———

THE HOMESTEAD RESTAURANT   Lunch: $3-$7   Dinner: $8-$13   Phone: 309/334-2844
Location: Jct I-74 and SR 17, exit 32. SR 17 W 61490. **Hours:** 6 am-8:30 pm, Fri & Sat-9:30 pm. Closed: 1/1 12/25. **Reservations:** accepted. **Features:** casual dress; Sunday brunch; children's menu; carryout; cocktails & lounge. Casual dining and friendly service are the hallmarks of this family restaurant. Tradition American comfort foods are augmented by Italian favorites, which are flavored with sauces created according to cherished family recipes. Crafts decorate the foyer. **Parking:** on-site.

WOODSTOCK —See Chicago p. 378.

Indiana

ANDERSON —*See Indianapolis p. 488.*

ANGOLA pop. 5,800

——— **WHERE TO STAY** ———

BEST WESTERN ANGOLA INN
Phone: **(260)665-9561**
Motel
All Year [CP]   1P: $65-$75   2P: $75-$85   XP: $5   F18
Location: I-69, exit 148 (US 20). 3155 US 20 46703. Fax: 260/665-9564. **Facility:** 93 one-bedroom standard units. 2 stories, exterior corridors. **Parking:** on-site, winter plug-ins. **Terms:** 5 day cancellation notice, small pets only ($7 extra charge). **Amenities:** extended cable TV, dual phone lines. **Guest Services:** coin laundry.
Cards: AX, CB, DC, DS, MC, VI.
SOME UNITS

POTAWATOMI INN & CONFERENCE CENTER
Phone: **(260)833-1077**
Resort
All Year   1P: $59-$89   2P: $59-$89
Location: I-69, exit 154, just w to Pokagon State Park, 0.5 mi inside park. 6 Lane 100A, Lake James 46703. Fax: 260/833-4087. **Facility:** This inn and conference center dating from 1926 offers small, rustic rooms in its older wing and larger, more modern rooms and cabins elsewhere. 140 units. 135 one-bedroom standard units. 5 one-bedroom suites ($89-$129). 2 stories, interior corridors. *Bath:* combo or shower only. **Parking:** on-site. **Terms:** check-in 4 pm, 4 day cancellation notice. **Amenities:** *Some:* hair dryers. **Leisure Activities:** sauna, whirlpool, rental paddleboats, boat dock, fishing, cross country skiing, ice skating, children's program, nature program & trails, social program, hiking trails, playground, exercise room. *Fee:* tobogganing, horseback riding. **Guest Services:** gift shop, coin laundry. **Business Services:** conference facilities. **Cards:** AX, DS, MC, VI.
SOME UNITS
FEE

RAMADA INN
Phone: **(260)665-9471**
Motor Inn
JC, MC, VI.
6/2-8/31 [ECP]   1P: $94-$119   2P: $94-$119
4/1-6/1 & 9/1-3/31 [ECP]   1P: $89-$119   2P: $89-$119
Location: I-69, exit 154, follow signs. 3855 N SR 127 46703. Fax: 260/665-5899. **Facility:** 149 one-bedroom standard units. 2 stories, interior corridors. **Parking:** on-site. **Terms:** package plans. **Amenities:** extended cable TV, voice mail, irons, hair dryers. **Dining:** restaurant, 6 am-2 & 5-9 pm, Fri & Sat 6 am-9 pm, $6-$16, cocktails. **Leisure Activities:** exercise room. **Business Services:** conference facilities. **Cards:** AX, CB, DC, DS,
SOME UNITS
FEE FEE

——— **WHERE TO DINE** ———

THE HATCHERY
Lunch: $5-$10   Dinner: $15-$25   Phone: 260/665-9957
American
Location: Just sw of center monument, corner Elizabeth and Gale sts. 118 S Elizabeth St 46703. **Hours:** 5 pm-9 pm, Fri & Sat-10 pm. Closed major holidays; also Sun. **Reservations:** suggested. **Features:** casual dress; carryout; cocktails & lounge; a la carte, a la carte. A stately low-lit dining room with cloth covered tables, plush royal blue high back chairs and lighted artwork set the stage for a fine dining experience. Try the delicious grilled salmon that is served with a juicy peach topping in a rich hazelnut cream, accompanied by red potatoes, carrots and asparagus. **Parking:** on-site. **Cards:** AX, CB, DC, DS, MC, VI.

ATLANTA —*See Indianapolis p. 489.*

AUBURN pop. 9,400

——— **WHERE TO STAY** ———

COUNTRY HEARTH INN
Phone: **(260)925-1316**
Motel
All Year [CP]   1P: $39-$79   2P: $39-$79   XP: $6   F17
Location: I-69, exit 129, 0.5 mi e on SR 8. 1115 W 7th St 46706. Fax: 260/927-8012. **Facility:** 77 one-bedroom standard units, some with whirlpools. 2 stories, exterior corridors. **Parking:** on-site. **Amenities:** extended cable TV. **Guest Services:** complimentary evening beverages: Tues-Thurs, valet laundry. **Business Services:** meeting rooms. **Cards:** AX, CB, DC, DS, MC, VI.
SOME UNITS

HOLIDAY INN EXPRESS
Phone: (260)925-1900

Motel

All Year   1P: $75   2P: $81   XP: $6   F18
Location: I-69, exit 129, just e off SR 8. 404 Touring Dr 46706. **Fax:** 260/927-1138. **Facility:** 70 one-bedroom standard units, some with whirlpools. 3 stories, interior corridors. *Bath:* combo or shower only. **Parking:** on-site. **Terms:** cancellation fee imposed, pets (in smoking units). **Amenities:** extended cable TV, voice mail, irons, hair dryers. **Guest Services:** valet and coin laundry. **Business Services:** meeting rooms. **Cards:** AX, CB, DC, DS, JC, MC, VI.

RAMADA LIMITED & SUITES & CONFERENCE CENTER
Phone: (260)920-1900

Motel

All Year   1P: $75-$105   2P: $81-$105   XP: $6   F18
Location: I-69, exit 129, 0.5 mi e on SR 8. 306 Touring Dr 46706. **Fax:** 260/920-1992. **Facility:** 66 units. 64 one-bedroom standard units, some with whirlpools. 2 one-bedroom suites with whirlpools. 3 stories, interior corridors. *Bath:* combo or shower only. **Parking:** on-site. **Terms:** cancellation fee imposed, pets (in smoking units). **Amenities:** voice mail, irons, hair dryers. **Leisure Activities:** whirlpool. **Guest Services:** valet and coin laundry. **Business Services:** meeting rooms, business center, PC. **Cards:** AX, CB, DC, DS, MC, VI.

BATESVILLE —*See Cincinnati p. 588.*

BEDFORD pop. 13,800

——— WHERE TO STAY ———

HOLIDAY INN EXPRESS
Phone: (812)279-1206

Motel

All Year   1P: $74-$84   2P: $80-$90   XP: $6   F17
Location: On US 50/SR 37, 1.4 mi s from jct SR 450. 2800 Express Ln 47421. **Fax:** 812/279-1496. **Facility:** 64 one-bedroom standard units, some with whirlpools. 3 stories, interior corridors. *Bath:* combo or shower only. **Parking:** on-site. **Terms:** check-in 4 pm, cancellation fee imposed, [CP] meal plan available, pets ($10 extra charge). **Amenities:** extended cable TV, dual phone lines, voice mail, irons, hair dryers. **Pool(s):** heated indoor. **Leisure Activities:** sauna, whirlpool, limited exercise equipment. **Guest Services:** valet laundry. **Business Services:** meeting rooms, business center, PC, fax. **Cards:** AX, CB, DC, DS, JC, MC, VI.

BERNE pop. 3,600

——— WHERE TO STAY ———

BLACK BEAR INN & SUITES
Phone: (260)589-8955

Motel

All Year   1P: $50-$55   2P: $55-$60   XP: $5   F12
Location: 1 mi n. 1335 US 27 N 46711. **Fax:** 260/589-8698. **Facility:** 45 units. 42 one-bedroom standard units, some with whirlpools. 3 one-bedroom suites ($79-$124) with whirlpools, some with kitchens. 2 stories, interior corridors. **Parking:** on-site. **Terms:** 7 day cancellation notice-fee imposed, package plans. **Amenities:** extended cable TV, hair dryers. **Pool(s):** small heated indoor. **Leisure Activities:** whirlpool. **Business Services:** meeting rooms, fax (fee). **Cards:** AX, CB, DC, DS, JC, MC, VI. **Special Amenities:** free continental breakfast and free local telephone calls.

BLOOMINGTON pop. 60,600

——— WHERE TO STAY ———

CENTURY SUITES HOTEL
Phone: (812)336-7777

Suite Motel

All Year   1P: $85-$155
Location: SR 446, just s of jct SR 46, 1 mi e of College Mall. 300 SR 446 47401. **Fax:** 812/336-0436. **Facility:** 21 one-bedroom suites ($165-$185) with kitchens and whirlpools. 1-2 stories, exterior corridors. **Parking:** on-site. **Terms:** 30 day cancellation notice-fee imposed. **Amenities:** extended cable TV, irons, hair dryers. **Business Services:** meeting rooms, fax (fee). **Cards:** AX, DC, DS, MC, VI.

COURTYARD BY MARRIOTT
Phone: (812)335-8000

Motor Inn

All Year [BP]   1P: $84-$109   2P: $84-$109
Location: SR 48, 0.3 mi s of courthouse. 310 S College Ave 47403. **Fax:** 812/336-9997. **Facility:** 117 units. 112 one-bedroom standard units. 5 one-bedroom suites ($129-$199) with whirlpools. 5 stories, interior corridors. *Bath:* combo or shower only. **Parking:** on-site. **Amenities:** extended cable TV, voice mail, irons, hair dryers. **Dining:** coffee shop, 6:30-10 am, Sat & Sun 7-11 am. **Pool(s):** heated indoor. **Leisure Activities:** whirlpool, limited exercise equipment. **Guest Services:** valet and coin laundry. **Business Services:** meeting rooms, fax (fee). **Cards:** AX, DC, DS, MC, VI. *(See color ad card insert)*

FAIRFIELD INN BY MARRIOTT

Phone: (812)331-1122

8/1-11/30 [ECP]	1P: $89-$149	2P: $99-$149
5/24-7/31 [ECP]	1P: $79-$99	2P: $89-$109
4/1-5/23 [ECP]	1P: $74-$99	2P: $84-$109
12/1-3/31 [ECP]	1P: $69-$89	2P: $79-$99

Motel

Location: Just w from SR 37 at Third St. 120 Fairfield Dr 47404. Fax: 812/323-1133. **Facility:** 105 one-bedroom standard units. 3 stories, interior corridors. *Bath:* combo or shower only. **Parking:** on-site, winter plug-ins. **Terms:** 7 day cancellation notice. **Amenities:** extended cable TV, irons. *Some:* hair dryers. **Pool(s):** heated indoor. **Leisure Activities:** whirlpool, exercise room. **Guest Services:** valet and coin laundry. **Business Services:** meeting rooms, fax (fee). **Cards:** AX, DC, DS, MC, VI. **Special Amenities:** free continental breakfast and free local telephone calls. *(See color ad card insert)*

SOME UNITS

HAMPTON INN

Phone: (812)334-2100

6/16-11/2 [ECP]	1P: $74-$89	2P: $84-$99	XP: $10	F18
4/1-6/15 & 11/3-3/31 [ECP]	1P: $69-$79	2P: $79-$89	XP: $10	F18

Motel

Location: 1 mi e of jct SR 37 on SR 45/46 Bypass, just s on College Ave/Walnut St. 2100 N Walnut St 47404. Fax: 812/334-8433. **Facility:** 130 units. 126 one-bedroom standard units, some with whirlpools. 4 one-bedroom suites ($129-$169), some with whirlpools. 4 stories, interior corridors. *Bath:* combo or shower only. **Parking:** on-site. **Amenities:** extended cable TV, dual phone lines, voice mail, irons. *Some:* hair dryers. **Pool(s):** outdoor. **Leisure Activities:** exercise room. **Guest Services:** valet laundry. **Business Services:** meeting rooms, fax (fee). **Cards:** AX, CB, DC, DS, MC, VI.

SOME UNITS

FEE   FEE   FEE   FEE

QUALITY INN

Phone: (812)323-2222

All Year [ECP]	1P: $50-$150	2P: $50-$150

Motel

Location: 0.5 mi e of jct SR 37 and 45/46 Bypass. 1100 W Rappel Dr 47404. Fax: 812/323-8846. **Facility:** 47 units. 46 one-bedroom standard units, some with whirlpools. 1 one-bedroom suite with whirlpool. 2-3 stories, interior corridors. *Bath:* combo or shower only. **Parking:** on-site. **Amenities:** extended cable TV, hair dryers. *Some:* irons. **Pool(s):** small heated indoor. **Leisure Activities:** whirlpool, limited exercise equipment. **Guest Services:** valet and coin laundry. **Business Services:** fax (fee). **Cards:** AX, CB, DC, DS, JC, MC, VI.

SOME UNITS

FEE   FEE

TOWNEPLACE SUITES BY MARRIOTT

Phone: (812)334-1234

All Year   1P: $84-$124

Extended Stay Motel

Location: Just w from SR 37 at Third St, 0.3 mi n. 105 S Franklin Rd 47404. Fax: 812/334-1995. **Facility:** 84 units. 62 one-bedroom standard units with efficiencies. 4 one- and 18 two-bedroom suites with kitchens. 3 stories, interior corridors. *Bath:* combo or shower only. **Parking:** on-site. **Terms:** pets ($75 extra charge). **Amenities:** extended cable TV, dual phone lines, voice mail, irons, hair dryers. **Pool(s):** outdoor. **Leisure Activities:** limited exercise equipment. **Guest Services:** valet and coin laundry. **Business Services:** business center, PC, fax (fee). **Cards:** AX, CB, DC, DS, JC, MC, VI. **Special Amenities:** free local telephone calls. *(See color ad card insert)*

SOME UNITS

WHERE TO DINE

CHAPMAN'S RESTAURANT

Lunch: $6-$8   **Dinner:** $11-$21   **Phone:** 812/337-9999

American

Location: At jct SR 46; 1 mi e of College Mall adjoining Century Suites. 300 SR 446 47401. **Hours:** 11:30 am-1:30 & 5-9 pm, Fri & Sat-10 pm, Sun 10:30 am-1:30 & 5-9 pm. Closed major holidays. **Reservations:** suggested; weekends. **Features:** casual dress; Sunday brunch; children's menu; cocktails. Duck, rack of lamb and peppercorn filet are among house specialties at the Colonial restaurant, a nice spot for a romantic evening out. For dessert, savor cherries jubilee. **Parking:** on-site. **Cards:** AX, CB, DC, DS, MC, VI.

ENCORE CAFE

Lunch: $5-$9   **Dinner:** $5-$9   **Phone:** 812/333-7312

American

Location: At Madison St. 316 W 6th St 47404. **Hours:** 11 am-10 pm, Fri & Sat-midnight, Sun 10 am-10 pm. Closed major holidays. **Reservations:** accepted. **Features:** casual dress; Sunday brunch; children's menu; carryout; beer & wine only; cafeteria. The popular cafeteria, which includes a lively coffee bar, bustles with activity. Comfort foods—lots of salads, sandwiches and desserts, as well as several entree choices—are the name of the game. Smoke free premises. **Parking:** on-site. **Cards:** AX, MC, VI.

MICHAEL'S UPTOWN CAFE

Lunch: $4-$8   **Dinner:** $8-$20   **Phone:** 812/339-0900

Nouvelle American

Location: In city center at southeast corner of Courthouse Square. 102 E Kirkwood Ave 47408. **Hours:** 7 am-9 pm, Wed-Fri to 10 pm, Sat 8 am-10 pm, Sun 9 am-2 pm. Closed: 11/28, 12/25. **Reservations:** accepted. **Features:** casual dress; Sunday brunch; children's menu; carryout; beer & wine only; a la carte. Not your typical Midwestern restaurant, Michael's has drawn upon Cajun, Cuban, Creole and continental influences to create its own particular cooking style. Try the persimmon pudding for a dessert out of the ordinary. **Parking:** street. **Cards:** AX, CB, DC, DS, MC, VI.

PUCCINI'S LA DOLCE VITA

Lunch: $5-$8   **Dinner:** $9-$24   **Phone:** 812/333-5522

Italian

Location: Just n from SR 48, 0.4 mi e of downtown square. 420 E 4th St 47408. **Hours:** 11 am-2 & 5-9 pm, Fri & Sat-10 pm. Closed: 12/24, 12/25. **Reservations:** suggested. **Features:** casual dress; cocktails; a la carte. The varied menu lists traditional Italian dishes, such as the favorite chicken Marsala. An attractive waterfall decorates the atrium, which separates the four cozy dining rooms. The wine list includes American, French and Italian choices. **Parking:** street. **Cards:** AX, MC, VI.

SAMIRA
▽▽▽ ▽▽▽
Afghan

Lunch: $7-$8   **Dinner:** $11-$14   **Phone:** 812/331-3761
Location: At Walnut St; on northeast corner of town square. 100 W 6th St 47404. **Hours:** 11 am-2 & 5-9 pm, Fri-10 pm, Sat 5 pm-10 pm. Closed major holidays; also Sun. **Reservations:** suggested; weekends. **Features:** casual dress; carryout; beer & wine only; a la carte. Subtle, delicate flavors distinguish authentic Afghan food, which is divided into kebabs—which include beef, lamb, chicken, Cornish game hen and shrimp—and other entrees. Plate presentations are simple but logical and balanced. Smoke free premises. **Parking:** street.
Cards: AX, MC, VI.

BLUFFTON pop. 9,000

——— WHERE TO STAY ———

BUDGET INN
▽
Motel
MC, VI.

Phone: (260)824-0820
All Year   1P: $35-$38   2P: $39-$45   XP: $4   F11
Location: Jct SR 1 and 116; north side of town. 1090 N Main St 46714. Fax: 260/824-0820. **Facility:** 20 one-bedroom standard units, some with efficiencies. 1 story, exterior corridors. *Bath:* combo or shower only. **Parking:** on-site. **Terms:** small pets only ($5 extra charge). **Business Services:** fax (fee). **Cards:** AX, DS,

SOME UNITS

HOLIDAY INN EXPRESS
▽▽▽ ▽▽▽
Motel

Phone: (260)824-4455
All Year [CP]   1P: $72   2P: $72   XP: $7   F14
Location: 0.8 mi n of jct SR 116 and 124, on SR 1 (Main St). 1782 N Main St 46714. Fax: 260/824-4411. **Facility:** 54 units. 53 one-bedroom standard units, some with whirlpools. 1 two-bedroom suite ($95). 2 stories, interior corridors. *Bath:* combo or shower only. **Parking:** on-site, winter plug-ins. **Amenities:** extended cable TV, irons, hair dryers. **Pool(s):** heated indoor. **Leisure Activities:** whirlpool, limited exercise equipment. **Guest Services:** valet and coin laundry. **Business Services:** meeting rooms, fax (fee). **Cards:** AX, DC, DS, JC, MC, VI.

SOME UNITS

BRISTOL pop. 1,100

——— WHERE TO STAY ———

RUST HOLLAR BED & BREAKFAST
▽▽▽ ▽▽▽
Bed & Breakfast

Phone: 574/825-1111
All Year [BP]   1P: $59   2P: $79   XP: $20   D10
Location: 2.5 mi e of jct US 20 and SR 15, 1.7 mi n. 55238 CR 31 46507-9569. Fax: 574/825-4614. **Facility:** A rustic log home located in a quiet wooded setting just a few miles from Bonneyville Mill Park and in the heart of Amish country. The perfect get-away place with plenty of space in common areas to relax. Smoke free premises. 4 one-bedroom standard units. 2 stories, interior corridors. *Bath:* combo or shower only. **Parking:** on-site. **Terms:** check-in 4 pm, 10 day cancellation notice-fee imposed. **Amenities:** extended cable TV. **Guest Services:** TV in common area. **Business Services:** meeting rooms. **Cards:** AX, DS, MC, VI.

SOME UNITS

BROWNSBURG —See Indianapolis p. 489.

BRYANT

——— WHERE TO DINE ———

BEARCREEK FARMS
▽▽ ▽▽
American

Lunch: $6-$8   **Dinner:** $7-$14   **Phone:** 260/997-6822
Location: Jct US 27 and SR 67 (SR 18), 1.6 mi e; jct SR 67 and CR 350 E, 1 mi n to CR 800 N, 0.4 mi e on CR 800 N to CR 400 E, just n. 8329 North 400 E 47326. **Hours:** Open 4/1-12/23 & 2/8-3/31; 11 am-7 pm, Fri & Sat-8 pm, Sun-4 pm, also open Mon 11 am-7 pm, 5/27-9/2. Closed: 11/28, 12/24, 12/25. **Features:** casual dress; children's menu; carryout. Truly in the country, the off-the-beaten-path complex, which includes a restaurant, theater, cabins and RV parking, likely will require unfamiliar patrons to track down a map or get directions. The specialty is home-cooked food served in portions large enough to get diners through a day of working on the farm. The restaurant prides itself on down-home, friendly service. Smoke free premises. **Parking:** on-site. **Cards:** DS, MC, VI.

CARMEL —See Indianapolis p. 489.

CEDAR LAKE pop. 8,900

——— WHERE TO STAY ———

CRESTVIEW INN & SUITES
ⒶⒶⒶ SAVE
▽▽ ▽▽
Motel

Phone: (219)374-5434
All Year   1P: $55-$225   2P: $55-$225   XP: $5   F12
Location: US 41, 6.8 mi s of jct US 30; 2 mi s of jct US 231. 12551 Wicker Ave 46303. Fax: 219/374-7513. **Facility:** 27 one-bedroom standard units, some with efficiencies and/or whirlpools. 2 stories, exterior corridors. *Bath:* combo or shower only. **Parking:** on-site, winter plug-ins. **Terms:** cancellation fee imposed, package plans. **Amenities:** hair dryers. *Some:* CD players. **Leisure Activities:** fishing, playground. **Guest Services:** coin laundry. **Cards:** AX, CB, DC, DS, MC, VI.

SOME UNITS
FEE

CENTERVILLE pop. 2,400

—————— WHERE TO STAY ——————

HISTORIC LANTZ HOUSE INN
Phone: (765)855-2936
All Year [BP]   1P: $72-$92   2P: $77-$97   XP: $15   D18
Historic Bed & Breakfast   **Location:** I-70, exit 145, 3 mi s to US 40 (W Main), just w. 214 W Main St 47330. Fax: 765/855-3192. **Facility:** Flower beds and nearby hiking trails make this inn with simple surroundings well suited to nature lovers. Designated smoking area. 5 one-bedroom standard units, some with whirlpools. 2 stories, interior/exterior corridors. *Bath:* combo or shower only. **Parking:** street. **Terms:** 7 day cancellation notice-fee imposed, package plans. **Guest Services:** TV in common area. **Cards:** AX, MC, VI.

CHESTERFIELD —See Indianapolis p. 489.

CHESTERTON pop. 9,100

—————— WHERE TO STAY ——————

GRAY GOOSE INN
Phone: (219)926-5781
All Year [BP]   1P: $90-$125   2P: $90-$125
Bed & Breakfast   **Location:** I-94, exit 26A, 0.4 mi s to Indian Boundary Rd, then just w. 350 Indian Boundary Rd 46304. Fax: 219/926-4845. **Facility:** A picturesque, wooded, lake-view setting gives this inn appeal; some large rooms feature fireplaces. Designated smoking area. 8 units. 7 one-bedroom standard units, some with whirlpools. 1 one-bedroom suite ($150-$185). 2 stories, interior corridors. *Bath:* combo or shower only. **Parking:** on-site. **Terms:** age restrictions may apply, 10 day cancellation notice. **Amenities:** video tape library, dual phone lines, hair dryers. **Leisure Activities:** paddleboats. **Guest Services:** gift shop, valet laundry. **Business Services:** fax (fee). **Cards:** AX, DS, MC, VI.

SUPER 8 MOTEL
Phone: (219)929-5549
All Year [CP]   1P: $53-$57   2P: $59-$64
Motel   **Location:** I-94, exit 26A, 0.5 mi s; I-80/90, exit 31, 3 mi n on SR 49, just se. 418 Council Dr 46304. Fax: 219/929-5549. **Facility:** 49 one-bedroom standard units, some with whirlpools. 2 stories, interior corridors. **Parking:** on-site, winter plug-ins. **Terms:** pets ($10 fee). **Amenities:** extended cable TV. **Cards:** AX, DC, DS, MC, VI.

CICERO —See Indianapolis p. 490.

CLARKSVILLE pop. 19,800

—————— WHERE TO STAY ——————

BEST WESTERN GREEN TREE INN
Phone: (812)288-9281
6/1-3/31 [ECP]   1P: $69-$79   2P: $79-$89
4/1-5/31 [ECP]   1P: $59-$69   2P: $69-$79
Motel   **Location:** I-65, exit 4, just w. 1425 Broadway 47129. Fax: 812/288-9281. **Facility:** 103 units. 102 one-bedroom standard units. 1 one-bedroom suite. 1 story, exterior corridors. **Parking:** on-site. **Terms:** small pets only ($20 fee for dog show, no cats). **Amenities:** voice mail, irons, hair dryers. **Pool(s):** heated outdoor. **Guest Services:** coin laundry. **Cards:** AX, CB, DC, DS, JC, MC, VI.

HAMPTON INN LOUISVILLE NORTH
Phone: (812)280-1501
SAVE
All Year [CP]   1P: $76-$89   2P: $79-$94
Motel   **Location:** I-65, exit 4, just w. 1501 Broadway St 47129. Fax: 812/280-8901. **Facility:** 120 one-bedroom standard units. 4 stories, interior corridors. *Bath:* combo or shower only. **Parking:** on-site. **Terms:** 3 day cancellation notice. **Amenities:** dual phone lines, voice mail, irons, hair dryers. **Pool(s):** outdoor. **Guest Services:** valet laundry. **Business Services:** meeting rooms. **Cards:** AX, CB, DC, DS, JC, MC, VI.

CLOVERDALE pop. 3,100

—————— WHERE TO STAY ——————

HOLIDAY INN EXPRESS
Phone: (765)795-5050
All Year [ECP]   1P: $79-$89   2P: $89-$90
Motel   **Location:** I-70, exit 41. 1017 N Main St 46120. Fax: 765/795-5757. **Facility:** 60 one-bedroom standard units, some with whirlpools. 2 stories, interior corridors. *Bath:* combo or shower only. **Parking:** on-site. **Terms:** 30 day cancellation notice, pets ($25 deposit, in designated units). **Amenities:** irons, hair dryers. **Pool(s):** heated indoor. **Leisure Activities:** whirlpool, exercise room. **Guest Services:** coin laundry. **Business Services:** meeting rooms. **Cards:** AX, CB, DC, DS, JC, MC, VI.

COLUMBIA CITY pop. 5,700

——— WHERE TO STAY ———

AMERIHOST INN

Phone: (260)248-4551

(AAA) [SAVE]

8/29-9/2   1P: $79-$149   2P: $79-$149   XP: $7
4/1-8/28 & 9/3-3/31   1P: $64-$149   2P: $69-$149   XP: $7

Location: Jct SR 9 and 109, 1 mi w, just off US 30. 701 Connexion Way 46725. Fax: 260/248-4559. **Facility:** 60 one-bedroom standard units, some with whirlpools. 2 stories, interior corridors. *Bath:* combo or shower only.

Motel   **Parking:** on-site. **Amenities:** extended cable TV, voice mail, safes (fee), irons, hair dryers. **Pool(s):** heated indoor. **Leisure Activities:** whirlpool, exercise room. **Business Services:** meeting rooms. **Cards:** AX, CB, DC, DS, JC, MC, VI. **Special Amenities:** free continental breakfast and free newspaper.

SOME UNITS

[icons]

COLUMBUS pop. 31,800

——— WHERE TO STAY ———

THE COLUMBUS INN BED & BREAKFAST

Phone: 812/378-4289

(AAA) [SAVE]

All Year   1P: $119-$235   2P: $129-$245   XP: $10   F18

Location: I-65, exit 68, 2.5 mi e on SR 46; at 5th and Franklin sts. 445 5th St 47201. Fax: 812/378-4289. **Facility:** Built in 1895 as the Columbus City Hall, the property is now restored with many antique furnishings, attractively appointed units and public areas. 34 units. 32 one-bedroom standard units. 2 one-bedroom suites

Historic Bed & Breakfast   ($139-$235). 3 stories, interior corridors. *Bath:* combo or shower only. **Parking:** on-site. **Terms:** 21 day cancellation notice. **Amenities:** extended cable TV, voice mail, irons, hair dryers. **Guest Services:** afternoon tea, valet laundry. **Business Services:** meeting rooms, fax (fee). **Cards:** AX, CB, DC, DS, JC, MC, VI.

Special Amenities: free continental breakfast and preferred room (subject to availability with advanced reservations).

SOME UNITS

[icons]

COURTYARD BY MARRIOTT

Phone: (812)342-8888

(AAA) [SAVE]

All Year [BP]   1P: $80-$129   2P: $80-$129

Location: I-65, exit 68, 0.5 mi w on SR 46, just s on Goeller Blvd. 3888 Mimosa Dr 47201. Fax: 812/342-4892. **Facility:** 90 units. 87 one-bedroom standard units. 3 one-bedroom suites ($125-$179). 3 stories, interior cor-

Motel   ridors. *Bath:* combo or shower only. **Parking:** on-site. **Terms:** 3 day cancellation notice-fee imposed. **Amenities:** extended cable TV, voice mail, irons, hair dryers. **Dining:** coffee shop, 6:30-10 am, Sat & Sun 7-11 am. **Pool(s):** heated indoor. **Leisure Activities:** whirlpool, exercise room. **Guest Services:** valet and coin laundry. **Business Services:** meeting rooms, PC, fax. **Cards:** AX, CB, DC, DS, MC, VI. *(See color ad card insert)*

SOME UNITS

[icons]

DAYS INN COLUMBUS

Phone: 812/376-9951

(AAA) [SAVE]

All Year   1P: $49-$59

Location: I-65, exit 68, just w. 3445 Jonathan Moore Pike 47201. Fax: 812/376-6183. **Facility:** 115 one-bedroom standard units. 2 stories, interior corridors. **Parking:** on-site. **Terms:** check-in 4 pm, [CP] meal plan available,

Motel   small pets only. **Amenities:** hair dryers. **Pool(s):** outdoor. **Leisure Activities:** limited exercise equipment, video games in vending area. **Guest Services:** valet laundry. **Business Services:** meeting rooms, fax (fee). **Cards:** AX, CB, DC, DS, MC, VI. **Special Amenities:** free continental breakfast and free local telephone calls. *(See color ad below)*

SOME UNITS

[icons]

HOLIDAY INN COLUMBUS-CONFERENCE CENTER

Phone: (812)372-1541

AAA SAVE

Motor Inn

10/1-10/31	1P: $90-$120
4/1-9/30 & 11/1-3/31	1P: $80-$110

Location: I-65, exit 68, just e on SR 46. 2480 Jonathan Moore Pike 47201. Fax: 812-378-9049. **Facility:** 253 units. 249 one-bedroom standard units. 4 one-bedroom suites ($150-$175). 7 stories, interior/exterior corridors. **Parking:** on-site. **Terms:** check-in 4 pm, 3 day cancellation notice, package plans, small pets only (in exterior units). **Amenities:** extended cable TV, voice mail, irons, hair dryers. **Dining:** restaurant, 6 am-10 pm, $9-$16, cocktails. **Pool(s):** heated indoor. **Leisure Activities:** saunas, whirlpool, putting green, jogging, exercise room, hair salon, indoor recreation area. **Fee:** game room. **Guest Services:** gift shop, valet laundry. **Business Services:** conference facilities. **Cards:** AX, CB, DC, DS, JC, MC, VI. **Special Amenities: free local telephone calls.**

SOME UNITS

RAMADA INN & PLAZA HOTEL CONFERENCE CENTER

Phone: (812)376-3051

AAA SAVE

Motor Inn

All Year [BP]	1P: $75-$115	2P: $85-$125	XP: $10 F18

Location: I-65, exit 68, just e on SR 46. 2485 Jonathan Moore Pike 47201. Fax: 812/376-0949. **Facility:** 166 units. 158 one-bedroom standard units, some with whirlpools. 8 one-bedroom suites ($150-$250), some with efficiencies. 2-3 stories, interior corridors. **Parking:** on-site. **Terms:** package plans, pets ($25 deposit). **Amenities:** video games, voice mail, safes, hair dryers. *Some:* irons. **Dining:** restaurant, 6 am-2 & 5-9 pm, Fri-10 pm, Sat 7 am-11 & 5-10 pm, Sun 7 am-11 & 5-9 pm, $8-$20, cocktails, nightclub. **Pool(s):** heated outdoor, heated indoor. **Leisure Activities:** whirlpool, fishing, 2 lighted tennis courts, exercise room, basketball. **Fee:** game room. **Guest Services:** valet laundry, airport transportation-Columbus Regional Airport. **Business Services:** conference facilities, business center, PC, fax. **Cards:** AX, CB, DC, DS, JC, MC, VI. **Special Amenities: free continental breakfast and free local telephone calls.**

SOME UNITS

─── WHERE TO DINE ───

SMITH'S ROW FOOD & SPIRITS

Lunch: $5-$8 **Dinner:** $12-$23 **Phone:** 812/373-9382

American

Location: I-65, exit 68, 2.5 mi e on SR 46, just ne at 4th and Washington sts. 418 Fourth St 47201. **Hours:** 11 am-2 & 5-10 pm, Sat & Sun from 5 pm. Closed: 1/1, 11/28, 12/25. **Reservations:** accepted. **Features:** dressy casual; cocktails; a la carte. Frequented by locals, the bustling downtown restaurant offers a relaxed atmosphere and quick service for the time-conscious diner. The surroundings are casually upscale. On the menu is a great variety of reasonably priced dishes that range from burgers to entrees of Continental flavor. Treat yourself to one of the eye-pleasing desserts. Smoke free premises. **Parking:** street. **Cards:** AX, CB, DS, MC, VI.

CORYDON pop. 2,700

─── WHERE TO STAY ───

BAYMONT INN

Phone: 812/738-1500

AAA SAVE

Motel

All Year	1P: $59	2P: $66	XP: $7 F21

Location: I-64, exit 105, just s. 2455 Landmark Ave NE 47112. Fax: 812/738-1503. **Facility:** 81 units. 80 one-bedroom standard units. 1 one-bedroom suite ($75-$99) with kitchen. 3 stories, interior corridors. **Parking:** on-site. **Amenities:** video games, voice mail, irons, hair dryers. **Guest Services:** valet and coin laundry. **Business Services:** fax. **Cards:** AX, CB, DC, DS, MC, VI. **Special Amenities: free continental breakfast and free newspaper.**

SOME UNITS

HAMPTON INN

Phone: (812)738-6688

SAVE

Motel

11/16-3/31	1P: $79	2P: $79
4/1-11/15	1P: $74	2P: $74

Location: I-64, exit 105, just s. 2455 Landmark Ave 47112. Fax: 812/738-6699. **Facility:** 69 one-bedroom standard units, some with whirlpools. 3 stories, interior corridors. *Bath:* combo or shower only. **Parking:** on-site. **Terms:** 15 day cancellation notice-fee imposed. **Amenities:** extended cable TV, voice mail, irons. *Some:* hair dryers. **Pool(s):** heated indoor. **Leisure Activities:** whirlpool, exercise room. **Guest Services:** valet and coin laundry. **Business Services:** meeting rooms, PC. **Cards:** AX, CB, DC, DS, MC, VI.

SOME UNITS

HOLIDAY INN EXPRESS

Phone: (812)738-1623

AAA SAVE

Motel

All Year [ECP]	1P: $69-$79	2P: $69-$79	XP: $10 F18

Location: I-64, exit 105, 0.6 mi s, then just w. 249 Federal Dr 47112. Fax: 812/738-4858. **Facility:** 57 units. 53 one-bedroom standard units. 4 one-bedroom suites ($129-$199). 3 stories, interior corridors. *Bath:* combo or shower only. **Parking:** on-site. **Terms:** cancellation fee imposed. **Amenities:** extended cable TV, voice mail, irons, hair dryers. **Pool(s):** heated indoor. **Leisure Activities:** whirlpool, limited exercise equipment. **Guest Services:** valet and coin laundry. **Business Services:** meeting rooms, business center, PC, fax. **Cards:** AX, CB, DC, DS, JC, MC, VI. **Special Amenities: early check-in/late check-out and free continental breakfast.**

SOME UNITS

KINTNER HOUSE INN

Phone: 812/738-2020

AAA SAVE

Historic Bed & Breakfast

All Year	2P: $59-$99

Location: In historic downtown; at Capitol and Chestnut (SR 62 and 337), just off main square. 101 S Capitol Ave 47112. Fax: 812/738-7181. **Facility:** This 1873 house, which has been restored, is decorated with antiques; guests are allowed kitchen privileges. Smoke free premises. 15 one-bedroom standard units. 3 stories (no elevator), interior corridors. *Bath:* combo or shower only. **Parking:** on-site. **Terms:** 3 day cancellation notice. **Amenities:** extended cable TV. **Cards:** AX, DS, MC, VI.

SOME UNITS

------- WHERE TO DINE -------

MAGDALENA'S RESTAURANT   Lunch: $5-$7   Dinner: $8-$15   Phone: 812/738-8075
▼▼   **Location:** In historic downtown; on the square, at Capitol and Beaver sts. 103 E Chestnut 47112. **Hours:** 10:30
        am-9:30 pm, Fri & Sat-10:30 pm. Closed major holidays. **Reservations:** accepted. **Features:** casual dress;
American   children's menu; carryout; wine only. Gracing one side of a tree-lined, historical town square, the decidedly
efficient. **Parking:** on-site. **Cards:** AX, DC, DS, MC, VI.   casual restaurant presents Angus steaks and seafood, pasta and chicken entrees. Service is prompt and   ✕

COVINGTON pop. 2,700

------- WHERE TO DINE -------

BEEF HOUSE   Lunch: $5-$10   Dinner: $12-$30   Phone: 765/793-4770
▼▼   **Location:** I-74, exit 4, just n. 16501 N SR 63 47932. **Hours:** 8 am-10 pm, Sat 2:30 pm-10:30 pm, Sun 11 am-9
        pm. Closed: 7/4, 11/28, 12/25. **Reservations:** accepted; except Sat. **Features:** casual dress; early bird
American   specials; carryout; salad bar; cocktails. The popular, casual establishment is known for delicious rolls and
        high-quality meat, most of which is charcoal grilled on an open hearth. Combination platters match steak
with chicken, shrimp or crab legs. Service is prompt and cordial. **Parking:** on-site. **Cards:** AX, DC, DS, MC, VI.   ✕

CRAWFORDSVILLE pop. 13,600

------- WHERE TO STAY -------

COMFORT INN   Phone: (765)361-0665
ⒶⒶⒶ [SAVE]   All Year [ECP]   1P: $74-$125   2P: $79-$125   XP: $7   F18
▼▼▼   **Location:** I-74, exit 34, just s on US 231. 2991 N Gandhi Dr 47933. Fax: 765/361-1328. **Facility:** 72 one-bedroom
        standard units, some with efficiencies and/or whirlpools. 3 stories, interior corridors. **Bath:** combo or shower
Motel   only. **Parking:** on-site. **Terms:** pets ($10 extra charge). **Amenities:** extended cable TV, voice mail, irons, hair
        dryers. **Pool(s):** heated indoor. **Leisure Activities:** exercise room. **Guest Services:** coin laundry. **Cards:** AX,
CB, DC, DS, JC, MC, VI. **Special Amenities:** free continental breakfast and free local telephone calls.

SOME UNITS
[⒮Ⓓ] [🛏] [🏊] [📷] [DATA PORT] [💻] [🖨] / [✕] [🔋] [📠] /

Look for a SAVE Place to Stay!

When selecting a AAA Approved lodging, look for properties that participate in our SAVE programs. These properties understand the value of AAA business and many offer discounts to AAA members.

• A red [SAVE] icon in their TourBook® guide listing indicates an **Official Appointment** property that offers a minimum 10% discount off published TourBook standard room rates or the lowest public standard room rate, at the time of booking, for the dates of stay.

• A black [SAVE] icon indicates a chain hotel that participates in the **Show Your Card & Save®** program. These properties offer a satisfaction guarantee and AAA's best rates for your dates of stay. Please refer to page 22 in the TourBook Navigator section for complete details and a list of participating hotel chains or call AAA/CAA's exclusive toll-free reservation number **866-AAA-SAVE** to make a reservation.

HOLIDAY INN-CRAWFORDSVILLE
Phone: (765)362-8700

Motor Inn

All Year 1P: $74-$79 2P: $74-$79 XP: $6 F19
Location: I-74, exit 34, 0.3 mi s on US 231. 2500 N Lafayette Rd 47933. **Fax:** 765/362-8700. **Facility:** 148 units. 145 one-bedroom standard units, some with whirlpools. 3 one-bedroom suites ($109-$135). 2 stories, exterior corridors. **Parking:** on-site, winter plug-ins. **Terms:** cancellation fee imposed, package plans, small pets only. **Amenities:** dual phone lines, voice mail, irons, hair dryers. **Pool(s):** heated outdoor. **Leisure Activities:** exercise room. *Fee:* game room. **Guest Services:** valet and coin laundry. **Business Services:** conference facilities. **Cards:** AX, CB, DC, DS, JC, MC, VI.

SOME UNITS

——— WHERE TO DINE ———

THE BUNGALOW

American

Lunch: $4-$16 Dinner: $4-$16 Phone: 765/362-2596
Location: Just e on Pike St from jct US 231. 210 E Pike St 47933. **Hours:** 11 am-2 & 4:30-midnight, Fri-2 am, Sat 5 pm-2 am. Closed major holidays; also Sun & Tues for dinner. **Reservations:** suggested; weekends. **Features:** casual dress; carryout; cocktails & lounge. You'll be asked to choose a teacup to use during your meal from a colorful collection at the entrance to this small, converted bungalow-style home. Year-round this eatery grills its fresh fare of steak, chicken and fish outdoors for a distinctive flavor. **Parking:** street. **Cards:** AX, DC, MC, VI.

CULVER pop. 1,400

——— WHERE TO STAY ———

CULVER COVE RESORT & CONFERENCE CENTER
Phone: (574)842-2683

Motor Inn

5/15-10/31 [BP] 1P: $149-$219 2P: $179-$239 XP: $10
4/1-5/14 & 11/1-3/31 [BP] 1P: $104-$119 2P: $119-$149 XP: $10
Location: Just e of jct Main St. 319 E Jefferson St 46511. **Fax:** 574/842-2821. **Facility:** Designated smoking area. 65 units. 33 one- and 32 two-bedroom suites with kitchens, some with whirlpools. 2 stories, interior corridors. *Bath:* combo or shower only. **Parking:** on-site. **Terms:** check-in 4 pm, 30 day cancellation notice-fee imposed, package plans. **Pool(s):** heated indoor. **Leisure Activities:** sauna, whirlpool, 2 tennis courts, exercise room. *Fee:* boat dock, bicycles. **Guest Services:** coin laundry. **Business Services:** conference facilities. **Cards:** AX, DC, DS, MC, VI.

SOME UNITS

DALE pop. 1,600

——— WHERE TO STAY ———

BAYMONT INN & SUITES
Phone: (812)937-7000

Motel

7/4-9/1 [ECP] 1P: $70-$120
6/14-7/3 [ECP] 1P: $70-$90
4/1-6/13 & 9/2-3/31 [ECP] 1P: $60-$80
Location: I-64, exit 57 (US 231), just s. 20857 N US 231 47523 (PO Box 467). **Fax:** 812/937-7030. **Facility:** 75 units. 72 one-bedroom standard units, some with whirlpools. 3 one-bedroom suites ($99-$179). 3 stories, interior corridors. *Bath:* combo or shower only. **Parking:** on-site, winter plug-ins. **Terms:** check-in 4 pm, pets ($50 deposit). **Amenities:** video games, voice mail, irons, hair dryers. **Pool(s):** heated indoor. **Leisure Activities:** whirlpool, exercise room. **Guest Services:** valet and coin laundry. **Cards:** AX, DC, DS, MC, VI. **Special Amenities:** free continental breakfast and free newspaper.

SOME UNITS

STONE'S BUDGET HOST MOTEL
Phone: (812)937-4448

Motor Inn

All Year 1P: $33-$39 2P: $35-$41 XP: $2
Location: I-64, exit 57 (US 231), 2 mi s. 410 S Washington St 47523. **Facility:** 23 one-bedroom standard units. 1-2 stories, exterior corridors. **Parking:** on-site, winter plug-ins. **Amenities:** extended cable TV. **Cards:** AX, DC, DS, MC, VI. *(See color ad p 436)*

SOME UNITS

DECATUR pop. 8,600

——— WHERE TO STAY ———

AMERIHOST INN DECATUR
Phone: (260)728-4600

Motel

All Year 1P: $64-$79 2P: $75-$159 XP: $6 F18
Location: On US 27 and 33, 1 mi s of jct US 224. 1201 S 13th St 46733. **Fax:** 260/728-4611. **Facility:** 60 one-bedroom standard units, some with whirlpools. 2 stories, interior corridors. *Bath:* combo or shower only. **Parking:** on-site. **Terms:** 7 day cancellation notice-fee imposed, package plans. **Amenities:** voice mail, safes, irons, hair dryers. **Pool(s):** indoor. **Leisure Activities:** whirlpool, exercise room. **Business Services:** meeting rooms. **Cards:** AX, DC, DS, MC, VI. **Special Amenities:** free continental breakfast and free newspaper.

SOME UNITS

DAYS INN
Phone: (260)728-2196

Motel

All Year [CP] 1P: $46-$49 2P: $49-$52 XP: $7 F12
Location: On US 27 and 33, 0.5 mi n of jct US 224. 1033 N 13th St 46733. **Fax:** 260/724-8014. **Facility:** 42 one-bedroom standard units, some with whirlpools. 1 story, interior/exterior corridors. **Parking:** on-site, winter plug-ins. **Terms:** small pets only ($5 extra charge). **Amenities:** hair dryers. *Some:* irons. **Pool(s):** heated outdoor. **Guest Services:** coin laundry. **Cards:** AX, CB, DC, DS, MC, VI. **Special Amenities:** free continental breakfast and free local telephone calls.

SOME UNITS

SUPER 8 MOTEL

◆◆◆◆ ◆◆ ◆ (diamond icons)

Motel

All Year   1P: $52-$57   2P: $52-$57   XP: $5   F18
Location: 1 mi s on US 27 and 33. 1302 S 13th St 46733. Fax: 260/724-8888. **Facility:** 62 one-bedroom standard units, some with whirlpools. 2 stories, interior corridors. *Bath:* combo or shower only. **Parking:** on-site. **Terms:** 7 day cancellation notice. **Pool(s):** heated indoor. **Leisure Activities:** whirlpool. **Guest Services:** coin laundry. **Business Services:** meeting rooms. **Cards:** AX, CB, DC, DS, MC, VI.

SOME UNITS

(icons: ASK, SD, TI+, wheelchair/M, hand, swim, camera, FEE, DATA PORT, TV, printer, / X, FEE, icon, FEE /)

--------- **WHERE TO DINE** ---------

BACK FORTY JUNCTION

◆◆◆◆ ◆◆ (diamond icons)

American

Lunch: $7-$9   **Dinner:** $11-$18   **Phone:** 260/724-3355
Location: On US 27 and 33, 0.5 mi n of jct US 224. 1011 N 13th St 46733. **Hours:** 11 am-9 pm, Fri & Sat-9:30 pm, Sun-7 pm. Closed: 12/25. **Reservations:** suggested; weekends. **Features:** casual dress; salad bar; cocktails; buffet. The Back Fourty Junction is conveniently located on the north side of Decatur. They feature an extensive selection of salad, entrees, bread and dessert available on several buffet lines. Don't forget to take a minute to look at the selection of merchandise reminiscent of an old country store complete with old time candy jars, toys and "nick-nacks". **Parking:** on-site. **Cards:** AX, CB, DC, DS, MC, VI.

(icon: X)

EDINBURGH —*See Indianapolis p. 490.*

ELKHART pop. 43,600

--------- **WHERE TO STAY** ---------

BEST WESTERN INN & SUITES

AAA SAVE
◆◆◆◆ ◆◆ ◆ (diamond icons)

Motel

All Year   1P: $60-$80   2P: $60-$80   XP: $10   F16
Location: I-80/90, exit 92, 0.3 mi n. 3326 Cassopolis St 46514. Fax: 574/266-8984. **Facility:** 60 one-bedroom standard units, some with whirlpools. 3 stories, interior corridors. *Bath:* combo or shower only. **Parking:** on-site. **Terms:** 30 day cancellation notice, [CP] meal plan available. **Amenities:** extended cable TV, dual phone lines, voice mail. **Pool(s):** small indoor. **Leisure Activities:** exercise room. **Guest Services:** valet laundry. **Business Services:** meeting rooms. **Cards:** AX, CB, DC, DS, MC, VI. **Special Amenities:** free continental breakfast and free local telephone calls.

SOME UNITS

(icons: SD, TI+, wheelchair/M, hand, swim, camera, DATA PORT, printer, / X, icon, icon)

DIPLOMAT MOTEL

AAA SAVE
◆◆ (diamond icon)

Motel

4/1-9/30   1P: $32-$38   2P: $40-$45   XP: $5   D12
10/1-3/31   1P: $25-$30   2P: $32-$36   XP: $5   D12
Location: I-80/90, exit 92, just n. 3300 Cassopolis St 46514. **Facility:** 20 one-bedroom standard units. 1 story, exterior corridors. *Bath:* combo or shower only. **Parking:** on-site, winter plug-ins. **Terms:** cancellation fee imposed, small pets only ($5 extra charge). **Cards:** AX, DS, MC, VI. **Special Amenities:** free local telephone calls and free room upgrade (subject to availability with advanced reservations).

SOME UNITS

(icons: hand, TI+, camera, / X, icon /)

ECONO LODGE

AAA SAVE
◆◆◆◆ ◆◆ (diamond icons)

Motel

4/1-9/30 [CP]   1P: $34-$42   2P: $40-$49   XP: $5   F11
10/1-3/31 [CP]   1P: $25-$30   2P: $34-$39   XP: $5   F11
Location: I-80/90, exit 92, 0.3 mi n. 3440 Cassopolis St 46514. Fax: 574/262-0540. **Facility:** 35 one-bedroom standard units, some with whirlpools. 2 stories, exterior corridors. **Parking:** on-site, winter plug-ins. **Terms:** cancellation fee imposed, small pets only ($5 extra charge). **Amenities:** extended cable TV. **Guest Services:** coin laundry. **Cards:** AX, CB, DC, DS, JC, MC, VI. **Special Amenities:** free continental breakfast and free local telephone calls.

SOME UNITS

(icons: SD, hand, TI+, camera, DATA PORT, / X, VCR, icon, icon, icon /, FEE)

THE FAIRWAY INN

◆◆◆◆ ◆◆ (diamond icons)

Motel

All Year [CP]   1P: $56   2P: $61   XP: $5   F18
Location: I-80/90, exit 92, just n. 115 N Pointe Blvd 46514. Fax: 574/266-1940. **Facility:** 61 one-bedroom standard units. 2 stories, interior corridors. **Parking:** on-site, winter plug-ins. **Terms:** 14 day cancellation notice. **Amenities:** extended cable TV, safes. **Guest Services:** coin laundry. **Cards:** AX, CB, DC, DS, MC, VI.

SOME UNITS

(icons: ASK, SD, TI+, camera, DATA PORT, printer, / X, icon, icon, icon /, FEE FEE)

HOLIDAY INN EXPRESS

◆◆◆◆ ◆◆ (diamond icons)

Motel

All Year   1P: $84-$149   2P: $89-$154   XP: $5
Location: I-80/90, exit 92. 330 N Pointe Blvd 46514. Fax: 574/262-0662. **Facility:** 62 one-bedroom standard units, some with whirlpools. 3 stories, interior corridors. *Bath:* combo or shower only. **Parking:** on-site, winter plug-ins. **Amenities:** extended cable TV, dual phone lines, voice mail, irons, hair dryers. **Pool(s):** small indoor. **Leisure Activities:** whirlpool, exercise room. **Guest Services:** valet laundry. **Business Services:** meeting rooms. **Cards:** AX, CB, DC, DS, JC, MC, VI.

SOME UNITS

(icons: ASK, SD, TI+, wheelchair/M, hand, swim, camera, DATA PORT, TV, printer, / X, VCR, icon, icon /, FEE FEE)

QUALITY INN & SUITES

SAVE
◆◆◆◆ ◆◆ (diamond icons)

Motel

4/1-8/31 [ECP]   1P: $79-$169   2P: $79-$169   XP: $10   F16
9/1-3/31 [ECP]   1P: $69-$169   2P: $69-$169   XP: $10   F16
Location: I-80/90, exit 92, just n. 3321 Plaza Ct 46514. Fax: 574/264-5108. **Facility:** 70 units. 58 one-bedroom standard units, some with whirlpools. 12 one-bedroom suites ($85-$169). 2 stories, interior corridors. *Bath:* combo or shower only. **Parking:** on-site. **Terms:** 30 day cancellation notice, small pets only ($25 deposit). **Amenities:** extended cable TV, irons, hair dryers. **Pool(s):** small indoor. **Leisure Activities:** exercise room. **Guest Services:** coin laundry. **Business Services:** meeting rooms. **Cards:** AX, CB, DC, DS, MC, VI.

SOME UNITS

(icons: SD, hand, TI+, swim, camera, DATA PORT, TV, printer, / X, icon, icon /)

RED ROOF INN-ELKHART

AAA SAVE

Motel

6/23-10/26	1P: $55-$66	2P: $60-$71	XP: $5 F18
4/28-6/22	1P: $51-$66	2P: $56-$71	XP: $5 F18
4/1-4/27 & 10/27-3/31	1P: $39-$66	2P: $44-$71	XP: $5 F18

Phone: (574)262-3691

Location: I-80/90, exit 92, 0.5 mi s. 2902 Cassopolis St 46514. Fax: 574/262-3695. **Facility:** 80 one-bedroom standard units. 2 stories, exterior corridors. *Bath:* combo or shower only. **Parking:** on-site. **Terms:** small pets only. **Amenities:** video games, voice mail. **Cards:** AX, CB, DC, DS, MC, VI. **Special Amenities:** free local telephone calls and free newspaper.

SOME UNITS
FEE / FEE FEE

SIGNATURE INN ELKHART

Motel

All Year [CP]   1P: $72-$83   2P: $72-$83

Phone: (574)264-7222

Location: I-80/90, exit 92, 0.3 mi s. 3010 Brittany Ct 46514. Fax: 574/264-7222. **Facility:** 125 one-bedroom standard units, some with whirlpools. 2 stories, interior corridors. **Parking:** on-site. **Amenities:** extended cable TV, voice mail, irons, hair dryers. **Pool(s):** outdoor. **Guest Services:** valet laundry. **Business Services:** meeting rooms. **Cards:** AX, DC, DS, MC, VI.

SOME UNITS
ASK /

SUPER 8 MOTEL-ELKHART

Motel

9/1-3/31 [CP]	1P: $45-$119	2P: $45-$139	XP: $5 F17
4/1-8/31 [CP]	1P: $45-$55	2P: $47-$57	XP: $5 F17

Phone: (574)264-4457

Location: I-80/90, exit 92, just s. 345 Windsor Ave 46514. Fax: 574/264-4457. **Facility:** 62 one-bedroom standard units. 2 stories, interior corridors. **Parking:** on-site. **Terms:** 7 day cancellation notice, package plans, small pets only ($2 extra charge). **Amenities:** extended cable TV, safes. *Some:* irons, hair dryers. **Cards:** AX, CB, DC, DS, MC, VI.

SOME UNITS
ASK / FEE FEE

TURNPIKE MOTEL

AAA SAVE

Motel

4/1-9/30	1P: $32-$38	2P: $38-$44	XP: $5 F11
10/1-3/31	1P: $24-$30	2P: $32-$36	XP: $5 F11

Phone: 574/264-1108

Location: I-80/90, exit 92, 0.3 mi n. 3500 Cassopolis St 46514. Fax: 574/264-1108. **Facility:** 18 one-bedroom standard units. 1 story, exterior corridors. **Parking:** on-site. **Terms:** cancellation fee imposed, small pets only ($3 extra charge). **Amenities:** extended cable TV. **Cards:** AX, CB, DC, DS, JC, MC, VI. **Special Amenities:** free local telephone calls and preferred room (subject to availability with advanced reservations).

SOME UNITS
/ FEE FEE

------- **WHERE TO DINE** -------

D'ANTINI

American

Dinner: $13-$22

Phone: 574/262-0683

Location: I-80/90, exit 92, just nw on SR 19. 3421 Plaza Ct 46514. **Hours:** 5 pm-10 pm. Closed major holidays; also Sun. **Reservations:** suggested. **Features:** casual dress; cocktails & lounge. Before you fill up while nibbling on the well-prepared appetizers, keep in mind that large portions of attractively prepared entrees are yet to come. Prime rib is the signature dish, but plenty of samplings of Italian cuisine also make up the menu. **Parking:** on-site. **Cards:** AX, MC, VI.

HACIENDA MEXICAN RESTAURANT

Mexican

Lunch: $4-$10   Dinner: $4-$10

Phone: 574/294-6597

Location: 0.3 mi e of Main St on Jackson Blvd. 186 Shopping Place 46515. **Hours:** 11 am-10 pm, Fri & Sat-11 pm. Closed: 12/25. **Reservations:** accepted. **Features:** casual dress; children's menu; carryout; cocktails & lounge; a la carte. "Wet burritos" are the house specialty at the colorful, upbeat restaurant. The menu includes huge helpings of standard favorites, such as tacos, chimichangas and enchiladas, as well as two types of chili. Antique Mexican photographs decorate the walls. **Parking:** on-site. **Cards:** AX, MC, VI.

THE MATTERHORN RESTAURANT

American

Lunch: $6-$14   Dinner: $10-$26

Phone: 574/262-1509

Location: I-80/90, exit 92, 1 mi s on SR 19. 2041 Cassopolis St 46514. **Hours:** 11 am-2 & 5-10 pm, Sat from 5 pm, Sun 10 am-2 pm. Closed major holidays. **Reservations:** suggested. **Features:** casual dress; Sunday brunch; children's menu; carryout; cocktails & lounge. An overall elegant decor punctuates the dining room, which is appointed with brass chandeliers and sconces, metal-framed artwork and dark, patterned wallpaper. An extensive selection of California wines complements entrees of steak, seafood and pasta. **Parking:** on-site. **Cards:** AX, DC, DS, MC, VI.

EVANSVILLE pop. 126,300

------- **WHERE TO STAY** -------

CASINO AZTAR HOTEL

AAA SAVE

Hotel

All Year   1P: $69-$115   2P: $69-$115   XP: $10 F12

Phone: (812)433-4000

Location: SR 62 (Lloyd Expwy), just s on Fulton. 421 NW Riverside Dr 47708. Fax: 812/433-4384. **Facility:** 251 units. 244 one-bedroom standard units, some with whirlpools. 7 one-bedroom suites ($129-$325) with whirlpools. 11 stories, interior corridors. *Bath:* combo or shower only. **Parking:** on-site and valet. **Terms:** small pets only ($300 deposit). **Amenities:** extended cable TV, voice mail, hair dryers. **Dining:** dining room, 3 restaurants, coffee shop, 24 hours, $14-$28, cocktails, entertainment. **Leisure Activities:** exercise room. **Guest Services:** valet laundry. **Business Services:** conference facilities, business center, PC, fax (fee). **Cards:** AX, CB, DC, DS, MC, VI. *(See color ad p 447)*

SOME UNITS
FEE /

COMFORT INN

SAVE

▼▼▼▼
Motel

Phone: (812)477-2211

All Year 1P: $54-$64 2P: $59-$69 XP: $5 F18
Location: I-164, exit 9, 1.5 mi w on SR 62. 5006 Morgan Ave 47715. Fax: 812/477-2211. **Facility:** 52 one-bedroom standard units. 3 stories, interior corridors. **Parking:** on-site, winter plug-ins. **Terms:** small pets only. **Amenities:** extended cable TV. *Some:* irons, hair dryers. **Pool(s):** heated indoor. **Leisure Activities:** whirlpool. **Guest Services:** valet laundry. **Cards:** AX, DC, DS, JC, MC, VI.

SOME UNITS

🆘 🐕 🛠️ 🚫 🏊 ➕ 📶 DATA PORT 🖨️ / ✕ 🛏️ 📷 📺 /
FEE FEE

COMFORT INN EVANSVILLE

SAVE

▼▼▼▼
Motel

Phone: (812)476-3600

All Year 1P: $50 2P: $55
Location: I-164, exit 7B (SR 66/Lloyd Expwy), 0.5 mi w to Eagle Crest Blvd, 0.3 mi se to Fuquay, just s to Walnut, then 0.4 mi e. 8331 E Walnut St 47715. Fax: 812/476-3648. **Facility:** 115 units. 113 one-bedroom standard units. 2 one-bedroom suites. 3 stories, interior corridors. *Bath:* combo or shower only. **Parking:** on-site. **Terms:** [ECP] meal plan available. **Amenities:** extended cable TV, irons, hair dryers. **Pool(s):** heated outdoor. **Leisure Activities:** exercise room. **Guest Services:** valet laundry. **Business Services:** meeting rooms, fax. **Cards:** AX, DC, DS, MC, VI.

SOME UNITS

🆘 🐕 🚹 🛠️ 🚫 🏊 📶 DATA PORT 📺 🖨️ / ✕ 🛏️ 📷 /

COUNTRY INN & SUITES BY CARLSON

▼▼▼▼
Motel

Phone: (812)471-8399

4/1-10/31 [BP] 1P: $59-$99 2P: $59-$99 XP: $10 F18
11/1-3/31 [BP] 1P: $54-$69 2P: $54-$69 XP: $10 F18
Location: I-164, exit 7B (SR 66/Lloyd Expwy), 0.5 mi to Cross Pointe Blvd, just n, just n to Division St, then just 0.5 mi e. 301 Circle Front Dr 47715. Fax: 812/471-3133. **Facility:** 69 units. 45 one-bedroom standard units. 24 one-bedroom suites ($80-$150), some with whirlpools. 4 stories, interior corridors. *Bath:* combo or shower only. **Parking:** on-site, winter plug-ins. **Terms:** [ECP] meal plan available. **Amenities:** extended cable TV, voice mail, irons, hair dryers. *Some:* dual phone lines. **Leisure Activities:** exercise room. **Guest Services:** valet and coin laundry. **Business Services:** meeting rooms. **Cards:** AX, CB, DC, DS, MC, VI. *(See color ad p 476)*

SOME UNITS

ASK 🛠️ 🚫 📶 DATA PORT 📺 🖨️ / ✕ VCR 🛏️ 📷 /

DRURY INN & SUITES EVANSVILLE EAST

▼▼▼▼
Motel

Phone: (812)471-3400

All Year [ECP] 1P: $57-$92 2P: $57-$92 XP: $10 F18
Location: I-164, exit 7B (SR 66/Lloyd Expwy), 0.5 mi w. 100 Cross Pointe Blvd 47715. Fax: 812/471-3400. **Facility:** 150 units. 136 one-bedroom standard units. 14 one-bedroom suites ($82-$107). 6 stories, interior corridors. *Bath:* combo or shower only. **Parking:** on-site. **Amenities:** extended cable TV, irons, hair dryers. **Pool(s):** heated indoor. **Leisure Activities:** whirlpool, exercise room. **Guest Services:** complimentary evening beverages: Mon-Thurs, valet and coin laundry. **Business Services:** meeting rooms, fax. **Cards:** AX, CB, DC, DS, MC, VI. *(See color ad p 5)*

SOME UNITS

🐕 🚹 🚫 📶 DATA PORT 📺 🖨️ / ✕ 🛏️ 📷 /

DRURY INN-EVANSVILLE NORTH

▼▼▼
Motel

Phone: (812)423-5818

All Year [ECP] 1P: $60-$92 2P: $60-$92 XP: $10 F18
Location: US 41, 2.5 mi n of jct SR 62 and 66 (Lloyd Expwy), 3.3 mi sw of Regional Airport entrance. 3901 US 41 N 47711. Fax: 812/423-5818. **Facility:** 151 units. 150 one-bedroom standard units. 1 one-bedroom suite. 4 stories, interior corridors. **Parking:** on-site. **Amenities:** voice mail, irons, hair dryers. **Pool(s):** indoor. **Leisure Activities:** whirlpool, exercise room. **Guest Services:** complimentary evening beverages: Mon-Thurs, valet and coin laundry. **Business Services:** meeting rooms, fax. **Cards:** AX, CB, DC, DS, MC, VI. *(See color ad p 5)*

SOME UNITS

🐕 🚹 🚫 📶 DATA PORT 📺 🖨️ / ✕ 🛏️ 📷 /

EVANSVILLE AIRPORT MARRIOTT

AAA **SAVE**

▼▼▼▼
Hotel

Phone: (812)867-7999

All Year 1P: $79-$154 2P: $79-$154 XP: $10 F
Location: US 41, 4.3 mi n of jct SR 62 and 66, (Lloyd Expwy). 7101 US 41 N 47725. Fax: 812/867-0241. **Facility:** 199 one-bedroom standard units. 5 stories, interior corridors. **Parking:** on-site, winter plug-ins. **Terms:** check-in 4 pm, [BP] meal plan available, package plans. **Amenities:** voice mail, irons, hair dryers. **Dining:** restaurant, 6 am-2 & 5-10 pm, $12-$18, cocktails. **Pool(s):** heated indoor. **Leisure Activities:** whirlpool, exercise room. *Fee:* game room. **Guest Services:** valet laundry. **Business Services:** meeting rooms, business center, PC, fax (fee). **Cards:** AX, CB, DC, DS, JC, MC, VI. *(See color ad card insert)*

SOME UNITS

🆘 ✈️ 🚹 🍽️ 🚫 🏊 ✕ 📶 DATA PORT 📺 🖨️ / ✕ 🛏️ /
FEE

FAIRFIELD INN BY MARRIOTT EAST

Phone: (812)471-7000

(AAA) (SAVE)

Motel

All Year [CP]   1P: $59-$79   2P: $66-$86   XP: $7   F
Location: I-164, exit 7B (SR 66/Lloyd Expwy), 0.5 mi w to Eagle Creek Blvd, 0.5 mi s, then just e. 7879 Eagle Crest Blvd 47715. Fax: 812/471-7007. **Facility:** 118 one-bedroom standard units. 3 stories, interior corridors. *Bath:* combo or shower only. **Parking:** on-site. **Amenities:** extended cable TV, irons, hair dryers. **Pool(s):** heated outdoor. **Leisure Activities:** exercise room. **Guest Services:** valet laundry. **Business Services:** meeting rooms, fax. **Cards:** AX, CB, DC, DS, VI. **Special Amenities:** free continental breakfast and free local telephone calls. *(See color ad card insert)*

SOME UNITS

FAIRFIELD INN-WEST

Phone: (812)429-0900

(AAA) (SAVE)

Motel

All Year [ECP]   1P: $59-$68   2P: $66-$75
Location: 5 mi w of US 41 on SR 62 (Lloyd Expwy), at Lloyd Expwy and Red Bank Rd. 5400 Weston Rd 47712. Fax: 812/429-0900. **Facility:** 110 units. 106 one-bedroom standard units. 4 one-bedroom suites. 4 stories, interior corridors. *Bath:* combo or shower only. **Terms:** 3 day cancellation notice. **Amenities:** extended cable TV, irons, hair dryers. **Pool(s):** heated indoor. **Leisure Activities:** exercise room. **Guest Services:** valet laundry. **Business Services:** meeting rooms, fax. **Cards:** AX, DC, DS, MC, VI. **Special Amenities:** free continental breakfast and free local telephone calls. *(See color ad card insert)*

SOME UNITS

HAMPTON INN

Phone: (812)473-5000

(SAVE)

Motel

All Year [ECP]   1P: $63-$75   2P: $70-$82
Location: I-164, exit 7B (SR 66/Lloyd Expwy), 0.5 mi w to Eagle Crest Blvd, 0.5 mi s, then just e. 8000 Eagle Crest Blvd 47715. Fax: 812/479-1664. **Facility:** 141 one-bedroom standard units. 5 stories, interior corridors. **Parking:** on-site, winter plug-ins. **Terms:** 14 day cancellation notice. **Amenities:** extended cable TV, dual phone lines, voice mail, irons, hair dryers. **Pool(s):** heated indoor. **Leisure Activities:** hiking trails, jogging, exercise room. **Guest Services:** valet laundry. **Business Services:** meeting rooms, fax. **Cards:** AX, CB, DC, DS, MC, VI.

SOME UNITS
FEE

HOLIDAY INN EVANSVILLE CONFERENCE CENTER

Phone: (812)424-6400

Motor Inn

All Year   1P: $59-$99   2P: $59-$99
Location: US 41, 2.5 mi n of jct SR 66 and 62 (Lloyd Expwy). 4101 US 41 N 47711. Fax: 812/424-6409. **Facility:** 198 one-bedroom standard units. 2 stories, interior corridors. **Parking:** on-site. **Amenities:** video games, voice mail, irons, hair dryers. **Pool(s):** heated indoor, wading. **Leisure Activities:** whirlpool, playground, exercise room. **Guest Services:** complimentary laundry. **Business Services:** meeting rooms, business center, PC, fax. **Cards:** AX, DC, DS, JC, MC, VI.

SOME UNITS
FEE

HOLIDAY INN EXPRESS EAST

Phone: (812)473-0171

Motel

All Year [ECP]   1P: $59-$72   2P: $64-$77   XP: $5   F18
Location: I-164, exit 7B (SR 66/Lloyd Expwy), 2 mi w. 100 S Green River Rd 47715. Fax: 812/473-5021. **Facility:** 102 one-bedroom standard units, some with whirlpools. 2 stories, exterior corridors. *Bath:* combo or shower only. **Parking:** on-site, winter plug-ins. **Amenities:** extended cable TV, irons, hair dryers. **Pool(s):** heated outdoor. **Guest Services:** complimentary evening beverages: Mon-Thurs, valet laundry. **Business Services:** PC, fax. **Cards:** AX, CB, DC, DS, JC, MC, VI.

SOME UNITS

RESIDENCE INN HOTEL

Phone: (812)471-7191

(AAA) (SAVE)

Apartment

All Year   1P: $96   2P: $96
Location: I-164, exit 7B (SR 66/Lloyd Expwy), 0.5 mi w to Eagle Crest Blvd, 0.3 mi se to Fuquay St, then 0.3 mi e. 8283 E Walnut St 47715. Fax: 812/471-2902. **Facility:** 78 units. 45 one-bedroom standard units with kitchens. 24 one- and 9 two-bedroom suites ($156) with kitchens. 3 stories, interior corridors. *Bath:* combo or shower only. **Parking:** on-site. **Terms:** 14 day cancellation notice, pets ($200 extra charge). **Amenities:** extended cable TV, dual phone lines, voice mail, irons, hair dryers. **Pool(s):** heated indoor. **Leisure Activities:** whirlpool, jogging, exercise room, sports court. **Guest Services:** complimentary evening beverages: Mon-Thurs, valet and coin laundry. **Business Services:** meeting rooms, fax (fee). **Cards:** AX, CB, DC, DS, JC, MC, VI. *(See color ad card insert)*

SOME UNITS

SIGNATURE INN EVANSVILLE

Phone: (812)476-9626

Motel

All Year [CP]   1P: $56-$65   2P: $56-$65
Location: 0.8 mi n of jct SR 66 (Lloyd Expwy), 0.3 mi s of jct SR 62 E (Morgan Ave). 1101 N Green River Rd 47715. Fax: 812/476-9626. **Facility:** 125 one-bedroom standard units, some with whirlpools. 2 stories, interior corridors. **Parking:** on-site, winter plug-ins. **Amenities:** extended cable TV, voice mail, irons, hair dryers. **Pool(s):** outdoor. **Guest Services:** valet laundry. **Business Services:** meeting rooms, business center, PC, fax. **Cards:** AX, DC, DS, MC, VI.

SOME UNITS
FEE

SUPER 8 MOTEL

Phone: (812)476-4008

Motel

All Year   1P: $40-$45   XP: $5   F18
Location: I-164, exit 9 (SR 62 E/Morgan Ave), 1.7 mi w on SR 62. 4600 Morgan Ave 47715. Fax: 812/476-4008. **Facility:** 62 one-bedroom standard units. 3 stories, interior corridors. **Parking:** on-site, winter plug-ins. **Terms:** small pets only. **Amenities:** extended cable TV. **Guest Services:** valet laundry. **Cards:** AX, CB, DC, DS, MC, VI.

SOME UNITS
FEE

──────── **WHERE TO DINE** ────────

HACIENDA MEXICAN RESTAURANT **Lunch:** $4-$10 **Dinner:** $4-$10 **Phone:** 812/423-6355
◆◆ ◆◆ **Location:** 0.5 mi n of SR 66 (Lloyd Expwy). 711 N First St 47710. **Hours:** 10:30 am-10 pm, Fri & Sat-11 pm.
Mexican Closed major holidays. **Reservations:** accepted. **Features:** casual dress; children's menu; carryout; cocktails; a la carte. "Wet burritos" are the house specialty at the colorful, upbeat restaurant. The menu includes huge helpings of standard favorites, such as tacos, chimichangas and enchiladas, as well as two types of chili. Antique Mexican photographs decorate the walls. **Parking:** on-site. **Cards:** AX, MC, VI.

HACIENDA MEXICAN RESTAURANT **Lunch:** $4-$10 **Dinner:** $4-$10 **Phone:** 812/474-1635
◆◆ ◆◆ **Location:** 1 mi s from SR 66 (Lloyd Expwy), at Washington St. 990 S Green River Rd 47715. **Hours:** 10:30 am-11
Mexican pm, Sun 11 am-10 pm. Closed major holidays. **Features:** casual dress; children's menu; carryout; cocktails & lounge; a la carte. "Wet burritos" are the house specialty at the colorful, upbeat restaurant. The menu includes huge helpings of standard favorites, such as tacos, chimichangas and enchiladas, as well as two types of chili. Antique Mexican photographs decorate the walls. **Parking:** on-site. **Cards:** AX, MC, VI.

WESTERN RIB-EYE & RIBS **Lunch:** $7-$19 **Dinner:** $12-$19 **Phone:** 812/476-5405
◆◆ ◆◆ **Location:** 1 mi n of jct SR 66 (Lloyd Expwy). 1401 N Boeke Rd 47711. **Hours:** 11 am-10 pm, Fri-11 pm, Sat 4
American pm-11 pm, Sun 11 am-9 pm. Closed major holidays. **Reservations:** accepted. **Features:** casual dress; children's menu; carryout; salad bar; cocktails. You'll enjoy the informal family atmosphere where certified Angus beef, steak, chicken, seafood and a large salad bar top the menu of well-prepared fare. A wide variety of specialty coffees round out the desert menu. The service is friendly and prompt. **Parking:** on-site. **Cards:** AX, DC, DS, MC, VI.

WOLF'S BAR-B-Q RESTAURANT **Lunch:** $6-$15 **Dinner:** $6-$17 **Phone:** 812/424-8891
◆◆ ◆◆ **Location:** SR 62 (Lloyd Expwy), 7.6 mi n. 6600 First Ave N 47710-4458. **Hours:** 10 am-9 pm, Fri-Sat to 10 pm.
Regional American Closed major holidays. **Features:** casual dress; children's menu; carryout; a la carte. A bright, fresh, inviting decor and traditional barbecue fare combined with casual, friendly service greets diners at Wolf's, a family-owned eatery. Regulars enjoy the hickory-smoked ribs, pork and chicken and flavorfully sweet coconut cream pie. **Parking:** on-site. **Cards:** AX, DS, MC, VI.

FISHERS —See Indianapolis p. 490.

FORT WAYNE pop. 173,000

✈ **Airport Accommodations**			
FORT WAYNE INTERNATIONAL	Diamond Rating	Rate Range High Season	Listing Page
Airport Plaza, at the terminal	◆◆	$73	449

──────── **WHERE TO STAY** ────────

AIRPORT PLAZA **Phone:** (260)747-9171
◆◆ ◆◆ All Year 1P: $73 2P: $73
Motor Inn **Location:** Across from terminal at Fort Wayne International Airport. 3939 Ferguson Rd 46809. Fax: 260/747-1848. **Facility:** 146 one-bedroom standard units. 2 stories, interior corridors. **Parking:** on-site. **Terms:** [MAP] meal plan available. **Amenities:** video games. **Leisure Activities:** sauna, exercise room, volleyball. **Guest Services:** valet laundry. **Business Services:** meeting rooms. **Cards:** AX, DC, DS, MC, VI. SOME UNITS

AMERICINN MOTEL & SUITES **Phone:** (260)490-7950
◆◆ ◆◆ All Year [ECP] 1P: $80-$120 2P: $80-$120 XP: $6 F16
Motel **Location:** I-69, exit 116. 2902 E Dupont Rd 46825. Fax: 260/490-8741. **Facility:** 78 units. 65 one-bedroom standard units, some with whirlpools. 13 one-bedroom suites ($110-$130), some with whirlpools. 3 stories, interior corridors. *Bath:* combo or shower only. **Parking:** on-site. **Amenities:** extended cable TV, safes, hair dryers. **Pool(s):** heated indoor. **Guest Services:** coin laundry. **Business Services:** meeting rooms. **Cards:** AX, CB, DC, DS, JC, MC, VI. SOME UNITS

AMERISUITES (FT WAYNE) **Phone:** (260)471-8522
🔺🔺🔺 SAVE All Year [ECP] 1P: $89 2P: $89 XP: $10 F18
◆◆ ◆◆ **Location:** I-69, exit 112A, just w of Coldwater Rd. 111 W Washington Center Rd 46825. Fax: 260/471-9223.
Motel **Facility:** 122 one-bedroom standard units. 5 stories, interior corridors. **Parking:** on-site. **Terms:** cancellation fee imposed, package plans, small pets only. **Amenities:** extended cable TV, high-speed Internet, dual phone lines, voice mail, irons, hair dryers. **Leisure Activities:** exercise room. **Guest Services:** valet and coin laundry. **Business Services:** meeting rooms. **Cards:** AX, CB, DC, DS, MC, VI. **Special Amenities:** free continental breakfast and free newspaper. *(See color ad p 450)* SOME UNITS

BAYMONT INN
AAA SAVE
◇◇◇
Motel

All Year [ECP]   1P: $62-$69   2P: $67-$74

Phone: (260)489-2220
XP: $5   F17

Location: I-69, exit 111B, 0.5 mi e. 1005 W Washington Center Rd 46825. Fax: 260/489-4579. **Facility:** 101 one-bedroom standard units. 3 stories, interior corridors. **Parking:** on-site. **Terms:** 3 day cancellation notice, pets ($10 deposit). **Amenities:** extended cable TV, video games, voice mail, irons, hair dryers. **Guest Services:** valet laundry. **Business Services:** meeting rooms. **Cards:** AX, DC, DS, MC, VI. **Special Amenities: free continental breakfast and free newspaper.**

SOME UNITS

BEST INN
AAA SAVE
◇◇
Motel

5/1-10/31 [ECP]   1P: $46-$53   2P: $53-$60
4/1-4/30 & 11/1-3/31 [ECP] 1P: $43-$50   2P: $50-$57

Phone: (260)483-0091
XP: $7   F18
XP: $7   F18

Location: I-69, exit 109A, just s, then just w. 3017 W Coliseum Blvd 46808. Fax: 260/483-1591. **Facility:** 105 one-bedroom standard units. 2 stories, interior corridors. **Parking:** on-site. **Terms:** 3 day cancellation notice, pets ($10 fee). **Amenities:** extended cable TV. **Cards:** AX, CB, DC, DS, MC, VI. **Special Amenities: free continental breakfast and free local telephone calls.**

SOME UNITS

BEST WESTERN LUXBURY INN
AAA SAVE
◇◇◇
Motel

All Year [ECP]   1P: $74-$76   2P: $81-$83

Phone: (260)436-0242
XP: $7   F18

Location: I-69, exit 102. 5501 Coventry Ln 46804. Fax: 260/436-2256. **Facility:** 98 one-bedroom standard units, some with whirlpools. 3 stories, interior corridors. **Parking:** on-site. **Terms:** 3 day cancellation notice, package plans. **Amenities:** video games, irons, hair dryers. **Guest Services:** valet and coin laundry. **Business Services:** meeting rooms. **Cards:** AX, CB, DC, DS, MC, VI. **Special Amenities: free continental breakfast and free local telephone calls.**

SOME UNITS

COMFORT SUITES-SOUTH
AAA SAVE
◇◇◇
Suite Motel

All Year   1P: $85-$125   2P: $85-$125

Phone: (260)436-4300
XP: $5   F18

Location: I-69, exit 102, just w. 5775 Coventry Ln 46804. Fax: 260/436-2030. **Facility:** 128 one-bedroom standard units, some with whirlpools. 3 stories, interior corridors. **Bath:** combo or shower only. **Parking:** on-site. **Terms:** check-in 4 pm, [CP] meal plan available, package plans. **Amenities:** dual phone lines, irons, hair dryers. **Leisure Activities:** sauna, whirlpool, exercise room. **Guest Services:** valet and coin laundry. **Business Services:** meeting rooms, business center, PC, fax. **Cards:** AX, CB, DC, DS, MC, VI. **Special Amenities: free continental breakfast and free local telephone calls.**

SOME UNITS

COURTYARD BY MARRIOTT
AAA SAVE
◇◇◇
Motel

(See color ad card insert)

All Year [BP]   1P: $69-$109   2P: $69-$109

Phone: (260)489-1500

Location: I-69, exit 111B, just w on SR 3, then just s. 1619 W Washington Center Rd 46818. Fax: 260/489-3273. **Facility:** 142 one-bedroom standard units, some with whirlpools. 2 stories, interior corridors. **Parking:** on-site. **Amenities:** video games, dual phone lines, voice mail, irons, hair dryers. **Dining:** coffee shop, 6-9:30 am, Sat & Sun 7-11 am. **Leisure Activities:** whirlpool, exercise room. **Guest Services:** valet and coin laundry. **Business Services:** meeting rooms, business center, PC, fax. **Cards:** AX, CB, DC, DS, MC, VI.

SOME UNITS

DON HALL'S GUESTHOUSE
◇◇◇
Motor Inn

All Year   1P: $79   2P: $89

Phone: (260)489-2524
XP: $10   F18

Location: I-69, exit 111B, just n on SR 3, then 0.3 mi e. 1313 Washington Center Rd 46825. Fax: 260/489-7067. **Facility:** 130 one-bedroom standard units. 2 stories, interior/exterior corridors. **Parking:** on-site. **Terms:** package plans. **Amenities:** extended cable TV, high-speed Internet, voice mail, irons. *Some:* hair dryers. **Dining:** Mallory's, see separate listing. **Leisure Activities:** whirlpool, exercise room. *Fee:* game room. **Guest Services:** valet laundry. **Business Services:** conference facilities. **Cards:** AX, DC, DS, MC, VI. *(See color ad p 451)*

SOME UNITS

ECONO LODGE

SAVE

Motel

All Year [CP]   1P: $44-$50   2P: $44-$50   XP: $5
Phone: (260)484-6262   F18
Location: I-69, exit 109A, 0.3 mi s of jct US 30 and 33. 2908 Goshen Rd 46808. Fax: 260/482-8463. **Facility:** 52 one-bedroom standard units, some with whirlpools. 2 stories, interior corridors. **Parking:** on-site, winter plug-ins. **Terms:** pets ($25 deposit). **Amenities:** extended cable TV. *Some:* irons, hair dryers. **Cards:** AX, CB, DC, DS, JC, MC, VI.

SOME UNITS

FAIRFIELD INN

SAVE

Motel

6/1-9/15   1P: $61   2P: $61
4/1-5/31 & 9/16-3/31   1P: $59   2P: $59
Phone: (260)489-0050
Location: I-69, exit 111B. 5710 Challenger Pkwy 46818. Fax: 260/489-0050. **Facility:** 105 one-bedroom standard units. 3 stories, interior/exterior corridors. **Parking:** on-site. **Amenities:** voice mail, irons. **Guest Services:** valet laundry. **Cards:** AX, DC, DS, MC, VI. **Special Amenities:** free continental breakfast and free local telephone calls. *(See color ad card insert)*

SOME UNITS

FORT WAYNE HILTON AT THE CONVENTION CENTER

SAVE

Hotel

All Year   1P: $89   2P: $99   XP: $10
Phone: (260)420-1100   F18
Location: Center. 1020 S Calhoun St 46802 (PO Box 12049). Fax: 260/424-7775. **Facility:** 250 units. 245 one-bedroom standard units. 5 one-bedroom suites ($99-$109). 9 stories, interior corridors. *Bath:* combo or shower only. **Terms:** [AP] meal plan available, package plans. **Amenities:** dual phone lines, voice mail, irons, hair dryers. **Dining:** dining room, restaurant, 6 am-11 pm, $8-$21, cocktails. **Leisure Activities:** whirlpool, exercise room. **Guest Services:** gift shop, valet laundry, area transportation-within 4 mi. **Business Services:** conference facilities, fax. **Cards:** AX, CB, DC, DS, JC, MC, VI.

SOME UNITS

FORT WAYNE MARRIOTT

SAVE

Hotel

All Year   1P: $135-$165   2P: $145-$175   XP: $10
Phone: (260)484-0411   F18
Location: I-69, exit 112A (Coldwater Rd). 305 E Washington Center Rd 46825. Fax: 260/483-2892. **Facility:** 223 one-bedroom standard units. 2-6 stories, interior corridors. **Parking:** on-site. **Terms:** package plans, small pets only. **Amenities:** *Some:* video games, voice mail, irons, hair dryers. **Dining:** restaurant, 6 am-11 pm, $8-$21, cocktails. **Leisure Activities:** whirlpool, putting green, exercise room. **Guest Services:** gift shop, valet and coin laundry. **Business Services:** conference facilities. **Cards:** AX, CB, DC, DS, JC, MC, VI.
(See color ad card insert)

SOME UNITS

HAMPTON INN & SUITES

SAVE

Motel

7/1-9/1   1P: $79   2P: $84
4/1-6/30 & 9/2-3/31   1P: $69   2P: $74
Phone: (260)489-0908
Location: I-69, exit 111B, off Washington Center Rd. 5702 Challenger Pkwy 46818. Fax: 260/489-9295. **Facility:** 90 units. 62 one-bedroom standard units. 28 one-bedroom suites ($89-$119). 4 stories, interior corridors. *Bath:* combo or shower only. **Parking:** on-site. **Terms:** 14 day cancellation notice, [ECP] meal plan available, small pets only. **Amenities:** extended cable TV, voice mail, irons. **Leisure Activities:** whirlpool, exercise room. **Guest Services:** valet and coin laundry. **Business Services:** meeting rooms. **Cards:** AX, CB, DC, DS, MC, VI.

SOME UNITS

HAMPTON INN SW

SAVE

Motel

All Year [ECP]   1P: $74-$164   XP: $5
Phone: (260)459-1999   F18
Location: I-69, exit 102. 8219 W Jefferson Blvd 46804. Fax: 260/432-4087. **Facility:** 119 units. 118 one-bedroom standard units, some with whirlpools. 1 one-bedroom suite with kitchen. 4 stories, interior corridors. *Bath:* combo or shower only. **Parking:** on-site. **Amenities:** extended cable TV, irons, hair dryers. **Leisure Activities:** whirlpool, sun deck, exercise room. **Guest Services:** valet laundry. **Business Services:** meeting rooms. **Cards:** AX, CB, DC, DS, JC, MC, VI.

SOME UNITS

HOLIDAY INN HOTEL & SUITES

Phone: (260)422-5511

AAA SAVE

Hotel

All Year   1P: $99-$149   2P: $99-$149

Location: Downtown; corner of Lafayette and Jefferson sts. 300 E Washington Blvd 46802. Fax: 260/424-1511. **Facility:** 208 units. 180 one-bedroom standard units. 28 one-bedroom suites. 14 stories, interior corridors. *Bath:* combo or shower only. **Parking:** on-site. **Terms:** cancellation fee imposed, package plans. **Amenities:** extended cable TV, dual phone lines, voice mail, irons, hair dryers. **Dining:** coffee shop, 6 am-11 & 5-9 pm, $10-$17, cocktails. **Leisure Activities:** whirlpool, exercise room. **Guest Services:** valet and coin laundry. **Business Services:** conference facilities. **Cards:** AX, CB, DC, DS, JC, MC, VI.

SOME UNITS

HOLIDAY INN-NORTHWEST

Phone: (260)484-7711

AAA SAVE

Motor Inn

| All Year | 1P: $99-$114 | 2P: $99-$114 | XP: $6 | F19 |

Location: I-69, exit 109A, just s to Coliseum Blvd, then 0.4 mi w. 3330 W Coliseum Blvd 46808. Fax: 260/482-7429. **Facility:** 255 units. 251 one-bedroom standard units. 4 one-bedroom suites ($239-$299). 2 stories, interior corridors. **Parking:** on-site, winter plug-ins. **Terms:** check-in 4:30 pm, package plans. **Amenities:** voice mail, safes, irons, hair dryers. **Dining:** restaurant, 6:30 am-2 & 5-10 pm, Sat from 7 am, Sun 7 am-noon, $9-$15, cocktails. **Pool(s):** wading. **Leisure Activities:** sauna, whirlpool, exercise room, indoor recreation area. *Fee:* game room. **Guest Services:** coin laundry. **Business Services:** conference facilities. **Cards:** AX, CB, DC, DS, JC, MC, VI. **Special Amenities:** free newspaper.

SOME UNITS

FEE   FEE FEE

LEES INN & SUITES

Phone: (260)489-8888

Motel

| All Year [BP] | 1P: $69-$199 | 2P: $79-$199 | XP: $10 | F18 |

Location: I-69, exit 111B. 5707 Challenger Pkwy 46818. Fax: 260/489-4354. **Facility:** 68 units. 62 one-bedroom standard units, some with whirlpools. 6 one-bedroom suites ($129-$199). 2 stories, interior corridors. **Parking:** on-site. **Terms:** 7 day cancellation notice, [ECP] meal plan available, small pets only. **Amenities:** extended cable TV, irons, hair dryers. **Guest Services:** valet laundry. **Business Services:** meeting rooms. **Cards:** AX, DC, DS, JC, MC, VI.

SOME UNITS

RED ROOF INN-FORT WAYNE

Phone: (260)484-8641

Motel

4/29-9/29	1P: $44-$64	2P: $50-$70	XP: $6	F18
9/30-12/31	1P: $39-$60	2P: $45-$66	XP: $6	F18
1/1-3/31	1P: $35-$59	2P: $41-$66	XP: $6	F18
4/1-4/28	1P: $35-$54	2P: $41-$60	XP: $6	F18

Location: I-69, exit 109A, at jct US 30 Bypass. 2920 Goshen Rd 46808. Fax: 260/484-3441. **Facility:** 79 one-bedroom standard units. 2 stories, exterior corridors. *Bath:* combo or shower only. **Parking:** on-site. **Terms:** small pets only. **Amenities:** video games, voice mail. **Cards:** AX, CB, DC, DS, MC, VI. **Special Amenities:** free local telephone calls and free newspaper.

SOME UNITS

FEE

RESIDENCE INN BY MARRIOTT

Phone: (260)484-4700

AAA SAVE

Apartment

All Year [ECP]   1P: $99-$159

Location: I-69, exit 111A, just s. 4919 Lima Rd 46808. Fax: 260/484-9772. **Facility:** 80 one-bedroom standard units. 2 stories, exterior corridors. **Parking:** on-site. **Terms:** 5 day cancellation notice, pets ($50-$100 extra charge). **Amenities:** extended cable TV, voice mail, irons, hair dryers. **Leisure Activities:** whirlpool, playground, sports court. **Guest Services:** valet and coin laundry. **Cards:** AX, CB, DC, DS, JC, MC, VI.

(See color ad card insert)

SOME UNITS

SIGNATURE INN FORT WAYNE

Phone: (260)489-5554

Motel

All Year [CP]   1P: $64-$74   2P: $64-$74

Location: I-69, exit 111B. 1734 W Washington Center Rd 46818. Fax: 260/489-5554. **Facility:** 102 one-bedroom standard units, some with whirlpools. 2 stories, interior corridors. **Parking:** on-site. **Amenities:** extended cable TV, voice mail, irons, hair dryers. **Guest Services:** valet laundry. **Business Services:** meeting rooms, business center, PC. **Cards:** AX, DC, DS, MC, VI.

SOME UNITS

SUPER 8 MOTEL

Phone: (260)484-8326

Motel

| All Year | 1P: $51-$57 | 2P: $57-$63 | XP: $6 | F12 |

Location: I-69, exit 112A, 0.8 mi s to jct US 30 Bypass. 522 Coliseum Blvd E 46805. Fax: 260/484-8326. **Facility:** 44 one-bedroom standard units. 3 stories, interior corridors. **Parking:** on-site. **Cards:** AX, CB, DC, DS, MC, VI.

SOME UNITS

FEE

———— WHERE TO DINE ————

CAFE JOHNELL

Dinner: $17-$30   **Phone: 260/456-1939**

Continental

Location: 1.8 mi s. 2529 S Calhoun St 46807. **Hours:** 6 pm-9 pm, Sat 5 pm-10 pm. Closed major holidays; also Sun & Mon. **Reservations:** suggested. **Features:** dressy casual; cocktails & lounge. The Cafe Johnell is located near downtown Fort Wayne and the business district. The restaurant offers a wide selection of fish, beef, poultry and veal dishes cooked in a variety of ways to please your palate. Elaborate artwork adorns the walls throughout the restaurant. They offer table seating as well as the more romantic red velvet banquettes. The restaurant has been in the same family since 1956. Smoke free premises. **Parking:** on-site and valet. **Cards:** AX, CB, DC, MC, VI.

DON HALL'S FACTORY STEAKHOUSE

Lunch: $6-$9   **Dinner: $8-$16**   **Phone: 260/484-8693**

American

Location: I-69, exit 112A, 0.3 mi s. 5811 Coldwater Rd 46825. **Hours:** 11 am-10:30 pm, Fri & Sat-midnight, Sun-9:30 pm. Closed major holidays. **Reservations:** accepted. **Features:** casual dress; children's menu; carryout; cocktails & lounge. Prime rib reigns supreme and keeps good company with other reasonably priced menu selections such as beef, chicken and seafood. Try the tasty and cooked-to-order beef tenderloin with potatoes or any of the smoked meat choices. The service staff is consistently prompt and attentive. **Parking:** on-site. **Cards:** AX, DC, DS, MC, VI.

GOLDEN CHINA Lunch: $4-$7 Dinner: $7-$15 Phone: 260/489-6725
Chinese
Location: I-69, exit 111B, at jct with SR 3. 1738 W Washington Center Rd 46818. **Hours:** 11:30 am-9:30 pm, Fri & Sat-10:30 pm, Sun 11:30 am-9 pm. Closed: 11/28. **Reservations:** suggested. **Features:** casual dress; carryout; beer & wine only. Flavorful food is the highlight at the casual restaurant. The extensive menu samples beef, pork, seafood, chicken, duck, vegetable, noodle and rice selections. Portions are large, and prices are a great value. Service is friendly and consistent. **Parking:** on-site. **Cards:** AX, DC, DS, MC, VI.

HOUSE OF HUNAN Lunch: $4-$7 Dinner: $7-$25 Phone: 260/482-9402
Chinese
Location: I-69, exit 112A, 0.3 mi se. 5626 Coldwater Rd 46825. **Hours:** 11:30 am-10 pm, Fri & Sat-10:30 pm, Sun 11:30 am-9:30 pm. Closed: 11/28. **Reservations:** accepted. **Features:** casual dress; Sunday brunch; carryout; beer & wine only; a la carte. Ample portions of cleverly garnished dishes, mostly of the Hunan variety, make up the restaurant's extensive menu. Oriental prints in large metal frames, ceramic statues and wood latticework are among tasteful decorations in the charming dining room. **Parking:** on-site. **Cards:** AX, DC, DS, MC, VI.

MALLORY'S Dinner: $15-$24 Phone: 260/489-5583
American
Location: I-69, exit 111B, just n on SR 3, then 0.3 mi e; in Don Hall's Guesthouse. 1313 Washington Center Rd 46825. **Hours:** 5:30 pm-9 pm. Closed major holidays; also Sun. **Reservations:** suggested. **Features:** dressy casual; cocktails. A seasonally changing menu of eclectic and imaginative American cuisine includes such dishes as sweet potato-crusted sea bass on a bed of black pepper linguine. Most desserts, including the sinful chocolate cheesecake, are made on the premises. **Parking:** on-site. **Cards:** AX, CB, DC, DS, MC, VI.

OLD GAS HOUSE RESTAURANT Lunch: $4-$8 Dinner: $8-$20 Phone: 260/426-3411
American
Location: Just ne. 305 E Superior 46802. **Hours:** 11 am-10:30 pm, Fri & Sat-11 pm, Sun 11:30 am-8:30 pm. Closed major holidays. **Reservations:** accepted. **Features:** casual dress; children's menu; salad bar; cocktails & lounge; buffet. Steak and seafood dishes are the forte, with several daily specials. The dining room is comfortable, with a slightly more upscale feel at dinner. Several freshly made desserts top off a filling meal. Service is unobtrusive, friendly and prompt. **Parking:** on-site. **Cards:** AX, DC, DS, MC, VI.

PARK PLACE GRILL Lunch: $6-$12 Dinner: $12-$22 Phone: 260/420-7275
American
Location: Corner of Barr and Main sts, just e of Clinton St. 200 E Main St 46802. **Hours:** 11 am-2 & 5-9 pm, Fri-10 pm, Sat 5 pm-10 pm. Closed major holidays; also Sun. **Reservations:** accepted. **Features:** casual dress; carryout; cocktails & lounge. The Park Place Grill is conveniently located near the business district in downtown Fort Wayne. The cuisine is American with a Southwestern flair. You will find a good selection of sandwiches and salad served at lunch. The evening menu offers you more wider choice of selections. **Parking:** on-site. **Cards:** AX, CB, DC, DS, MC, VI.

FRANKFORT pop. 14,800

——— **WHERE TO STAY** ———

HOLIDAY INN EXPRESS All Year 1P: $58 2P: $58 Phone: (765)659-4400
Motel
Location: I-65, exit 158, 6.1 mi e; jct US 421/SR 38/39, 1.8 mi w. 592 S CR Rd 200 W 46041. Fax: 765/659-4064. **Facility:** 63 one-bedroom standard units, some with whirlpools. 2 stories, interior corridors. *Bath:* combo or shower only. **Parking:** on-site. **Terms:** pets (in smoking units). **Amenities:** extended cable TV, voice mail, irons, hair dryers. **Pool(s):** heated indoor. **Leisure Activities:** whirlpool. **Guest Services:** valet and coin laundry. **Business Services:** meeting rooms, fax. **Cards:** AX, CB, DC, DS, JC, MC, VI.
SOME UNITS

SUPER 8 MOTEL Property failed to provide current rates Phone: 765/654-0088
Motel
Location: I-65, exit 158, 6.4 mi e; jct US 421/SR 38/39, 1.6 mi w. 1875 W SR 28 46041. Fax: 765/654-0461. **Facility:** 41 one-bedroom standard units, some with whirlpools. 2 stories, interior corridors. **Parking:** on-site. **Terms:** small pets only ($5 extra charge). **Amenities:** extended cable TV. **Pool(s):** heated indoor. **Cards:** AX, DC, DS, MC, VI.
SOME UNITS

FRANKLIN —See Indianapolis p. 491.

FREMONT pop. 1,400

——— **WHERE TO STAY** ———

HAMPTON INN All Year [ECP] 1P: $84-$139 2P: $84-$139 Phone: (260)495-9770
Hotel
Location: I-69, exit 157, off the Indiana Toll road, I-80/90 follow SR 120 on left. 271 W SR 120 46737. Fax: 260/495-9880. **Facility:** 75 one-bedroom standard units, some with whirlpools. 3 stories, interior corridors. *Bath:* combo or shower only. **Parking:** on-site. **Amenities:** extended cable TV, high-speed Internet, dual phone lines, voice mail, irons, hair dryers. **Pool(s):** heated indoor. **Leisure Activities:** exercise room. **Guest Services:** coin laundry. **Cards:** AX, CB, DC, DS, JC, MC, VI.
SOME UNITS

HOLIDAY INN EXPRESS

(AAA) (SAVE)

Motel

Phone: (260)833-6464

All Year [ECP]   1P: $89-$299

Location: Just off SR 120, 0.3 mi n on Old SR 27; just s of I-80/90, exit 144; I-69, exit 157. 6245 N Old 27, Suite 400 46737. Fax: 260/833-6464. **Facility:** 61 units. 60 one-bedroom standard units, some with whirlpools. 1 one-bedroom suite ($155-$299). 2 stories, interior corridors. **Parking:** on-site, winter plug-ins. **Terms:** 30 day cancellation notice. **Amenities:** extended cable TV, irons, hair dryers. **Leisure Activities:** exercise room. **Guest Services:** valet laundry. **Business Services:** meeting rooms. **Cards:** AX, CB, DC, DS, JC, MC, VI.
Special Amenities: free continental breakfast and free local telephone calls.

SOME UNITS

LAKE GEORGE INN

(AAA) (SAVE)

Motel

Phone: 260/495-2243

All Year   1P: $40-$50   2P: $45-$55   F12

Location: I-69, exit 157; I-80/90, 1 mi n via I-69 and Lake George exit. 7267 N Baker Rd 46737. **Facility:** 24 one-bedroom standard units. 1 story, exterior corridors. **Parking:** on-site. **Cards:** AX, DC, DS, MC, VI.
Special Amenities: early check-in/late check-out and free local telephone calls.

SOME UNITS

FRENCH LICK pop. 2,100

—————— WHERE TO STAY ——————

FRENCH LICK SPRINGS RESORT & SPA

(AAA) (SAVE)

Classic Resort

Phone: (812)936-9300

4/1-10/31	1P: $119-$179	2P: $119-$179	XP: $10 F18
11/1-3/31	1P: $89-$179	2P: $89-$179	XP: $10 F18

Location: On SR 56 at SR 145. 8670 W SR 56 47432. Fax: 812/936-2100. **Facility:** Historic. Once so popular for its three mineral springs that it had its own train station, this 1834 resort is still appealing. 470 units. 443 one-bedroom standard units. 17 one-, 8 two- and 2 three-bedroom suites ($179-$799). 6-7 stories, interior corridors. **Bath:** combo or shower only. **Parking:** on-site, winter plug-ins. **Terms:** check-in 4 pm, 3 day cancellation notice-fee imposed, [AP], [BP] & [MAP] meal plans available, package plans. **Amenities:** voice mail. **Dining:** dining room, 2 restaurants, coffee shop, 6:30 am-midnight, $25-$30, cocktails. **Pool(s):** outdoor, heated indoor. **Leisure Activities:** sauna, whirlpool, steamroom, 18 tennis courts (8 indoor, 18 lighted), children's program, nature program, recreation program, hiking trails, playground, basketball, horseshoes, volleyball, badminton. Fee: golf-36 holes, miniature golf, bicycles, horseback riding, archery, billiards, bowling, croquet, surrey rides. **Guest Services:** gift shop, massage (fee), valet and coin laundry, airport transportation-French Lick Airport. **Business Services:** conference facilities. Fee: administrative services, fax. **Cards:** AX, CB, DC, DS, MC, VI. *(See color ad below)*

SOME UNITS

FEE   FEE   FEE

GARY pop. 116,600

―――― **WHERE TO DINE** ――――

MILLER BAKERY CAFE   **Lunch:** $8-$14   **Dinner:** $12-$26   **Phone:** 219/938-2229
♦♦♦ ♦♦♦ **Location:** I-90, exit 17, follow US 12 and 20 signs e, then 2 mi e on US 12 to S Lake St, just n; I-65, to end then 2 mi
e on US 12 to S Lake St, just n. 555 S Lake St 46403. **Hours:** 11:30 am-2 & 5-10 pm, Sat from 5 pm, Sun 4
International pm-8 pm. Closed: Mon. **Reservations:** suggested. **Features:** dressy casual; carryout; beer & wine only; a
la carte. The exterior is modest, but the surprises inside make the quaint, cozy cafe a diamond in the
rough. The menu features imaginative preparations of globally influenced cuisine, such as Midwestern duck breast with wild
mushroom risotto, New Zealand lamb rack and osso buco with oven-roasted veal. Smoke free premises. **Parking:** street.
Cards: AX, DC, DS, MC, VI. ⊠

GENEVA pop. 1,000

―――― **WHERE TO DINE** ――――

ESSEN PLATZ (AT AMISHVILLE USA)   **Lunch:** $4-$8   **Dinner:** $4-$10   **Phone:** 260/589-3536
♦ **Location:** Just n on US 27, 2.5 mi e on CR 950 S, follow signs. 844 E 900 S 46740. **Hours:** Open 4/1-12/20; 11
am-7 pm, Fri & Sat-8 pm. Closed: 11/28. **Features:** casual dress; children's menu; carryout; salad bar.
American Amish style restaurant in a rural setting offers many delicious and hearty home-style cooked offerings.
House speciality is the "Broasted Chicken", but you'll be happy with any of the many fine tasting foods
here. Try the fresh baked "Amish Bread" and pie. Smoke free premises. **Parking:** on-site. **Cards:** DS, MC, VI. ⊠

GOSHEN pop. 23,800

―――― **WHERE TO STAY** ――――

BEST WESTERN INN   **Phone:** (574)533-0408
⑭ SAVE All Year [CP]   1P: $59-$65   2P: $64-$67   XP: $3   F12
♦♦♦ ♦♦ **Location:** 1 mi se on US 33. 900 Lincolnway E 46526. **Fax:** 574/533-0408. **Facility:** 77 one-bedroom standard
units. 2 stories, exterior corridors. **Parking:** on-site, winter plug-ins. **Terms:** small pets only. **Amenities:** ex-
Motel tended cable TV, irons, hair dryers. **Leisure Activities:** limited exercise equipment. **Business Services:**
meeting rooms, fax (fee). **Cards:** AX, CB, DC, DS, MC, VI. **Special Amenities:** free local telephone calls
and free newspaper.

SOME UNITS
🛎️ 🐾 🍴➕ 🎥 📠 🖥️ 🖨️ / ⊠ VCR /
FEE

COURTYARD BY MARRIOTT   **Phone:** (574)534-3133
⑭ SAVE 4/1-10/1   1P: $89-$159   2P: $89-$159
♦♦♦ ♦♦ 10/2-3/31   1P: $79-$129   2P: $79-$129
Location: 2.5 mi se on US 33. 1930 Lincolnway E 46526. **Fax:** 574/534-6929. **Facility:** 91 units. 90 one-bedroom
Motel standard units, some with whirlpools. 1 one-bedroom suite ($99-$159) with whirlpool. 2 stories, interior corridors. **Parking:** on-site. **Terms:** 7 day cancellation notice, package plans. **Amenities:** video games (fee),
voice mail, irons, hair dryers. **Pool(s):** heated indoor/outdoor. **Leisure Activities:** whirlpool, limited exercise
equipment. **Guest Services:** valet and coin laundry. **Business Services:** meeting rooms, fax (fee). **Cards:** AX, DC, DS,
MC, VI. *(See color ad card insert)*

SOME UNITS
🛎️ 🏊 ⛱️ 🎥 📠 🖥️ 🖨️ / ⊠ 🔌 🖨️ /
FEE   FEE   FEE

HOLIDAY INN EXPRESS
Phone: (574)533-0200

Motel

All Year — 1P: $66-$89 — 2P: $66-$89 — XP: $5 — F18
Location: 3 mi se on US 33. 2309 Lincolnway E 46526. Fax: 574/533-1528. **Facility:** 74 one-bedroom standard units, some with whirlpools. 3 stories, interior corridors. *Bath:* combo or shower only. **Parking:** on-site. **Terms:** cancellation fee imposed. **Amenities:** extended cable TV, dual phone lines, voice mail, irons, hair dryers. **Pool(s):** small heated indoor. **Leisure Activities:** whirlpool, limited exercise equipment. **Guest Services:** valet laundry. **Business Services:** meeting rooms, fax (fee). **Cards:** AX, CB, DC, DS, JC, MC, VI.

SOME UNITS

INDIAN CREEK BED & BREAKFAST
Phone: (574)875-6606

Bed & Breakfast

All Year [BP] — 1P: $69-$89 — 2P: $79-$99 — XP: $20 — F12
Location: I-80/90, exit 96, 5.5 mi s on CR 17, 1.6 mi e. 20300 CR 18 46528. Fax: 574/875-8396. **Facility:** Set in Amish country, this new-construction, Victorian-style B&B offers a large deck, a cobblestone fishpond and quaint yet modern furnishings. Smoke free premises. 4 one-bedroom standard units. 2 stories, interior corridors. *Bath:* combo or shower only. **Parking:** on-site. **Terms:** check-in 4 pm, 10 day cancellation notice-fee imposed, [ECP] meal plan available. **Amenities:** hair dryers. **Business Services:** fax (fee). **Cards:** AX, DS, MC, VI.

RAMADA INN & CONFERENCE CENTER
Phone: (574)533-9551

Motor Inn

5/12-9/7 — 1P: $76-$99 — 2P: $76-$99
9/8-11/9 — 1P: $69-$99 — 2P: $69-$99
4/1-5/11 & 11/10-3/31 — 1P: $65-$99 — 2P: $65-$99
Location: 1.3 mi se on US 33. 1375 Lincolnway E 46526. Fax: 574/533-2840. **Facility:** 207 units. 205 one-bedroom standard units, some with whirlpools. 2 one-bedroom suites ($129) with whirlpools. 2 stories, interior corridors. *Bath:* combo or shower only. **Parking:** on-site, winter plug-ins. **Terms:** package plans. **Amenities:** extended cable TV. **Pool(s):** heated indoor. **Leisure Activities:** sauna, whirlpool, putting green, exercise room. *Fee:* game room. **Guest Services:** valet and coin laundry. **Business Services:** conference facilities, fax (fee). **Cards:** AX, CB, DC, DS, MC, VI.

SOME UNITS

---- **WHERE TO DINE** ----

HACIENDA MEXICAN RESTAURANT
Lunch: $4-$10 — **Dinner:** $4-$10 — **Phone:** 574/534-9590

Mexican

Location: 0.5 mi w of US 33. 618 W Lincoln Ave 46526. **Hours:** 11 am-10 pm, Fri & Sat-11 pm. Closed: 11/28, 12/25. **Reservations:** accepted; weekdays. **Features:** casual dress; children's menu; carryout; cocktails & lounge; a la carte. "Wet burritos" are the house specialty at the colorful, upbeat restaurant. The menu includes huge helpings of standard favorites, such as tacos, chimichangas and enchiladas, as well as two types of chili. Antique Mexican photographs decorate the walls. **Parking:** on-site. **Cards:** AX, MC, VI.

GREENCASTLE pop. 9,000

---- **WHERE TO STAY** ----

COLLEGE INN
Phone: (765)653-4167

Motel

All Year — 1P: $30-$38 — 2P: $38-$48 — XP: $8 — F5
Location: I-70, exit 41, 8 mi n on US 231. 315 Bloomington St 46135. **Facility:** 20 one-bedroom standard units. 1 story, exterior corridors. **Parking:** on-site, winter plug-ins. **Terms:** cancellation fee imposed, small pets only ($10 extra charge). **Amenities:** extended cable TV. **Cards:** AX, DC, DS, MC, VI. **Special Amenities:** free local telephone calls.

SOME UNITS

WALDEN INN
Phone: (765)653-2761

Country Inn

All Year — 1P: $70-$120 — 2P: $90-$150 — XP: $10 — F12
Location: I-70, exit 41, 8.3 mi n on US 231, 0.3 mi w; center, corner of Seminary St and Vine, on Seminary St. 2 Seminary Sq 46135 (PO Box 490). Fax: 765/653-4833. **Facility:** A library with a fireplace and plush sofas is among the appealing common areas in this Amish-themed downtown inn near the university. 55 units. 54 one-bedroom standard units. 1 one-bedroom suite ($120-$135). 3 stories, interior corridors. *Bath:* combo or shower only. **Parking:** on-site. **Terms:** check-in 4 pm. **Business Services:** meeting rooms. **Cards:** AX, CB, DC, DS, MC, VI.

SOME UNITS

GREENFIELD —See Indianapolis p. 491.

GREENSBURG pop. 9,300

---- **WHERE TO STAY** ----

BEST WESTERN PINES INN
Phone: (812)663-6055

Motel

5/16-8/31 [CP] — 1P: $64-$84 — 2P: $69-$89 — XP: $5 — F13
9/1-11/30 [CP] — 1P: $64-$74 — 2P: $69-$79 — XP: $5 — F13
4/1-5/15 & 12/1-3/31 [CP] — 1P: $59-$69 — 2P: $69-$79 — XP: $5 — F13
Location: I-74, exit 134A. 2317 N SR 3 47240. Fax: 812/663-6264. **Facility:** 74 one-bedroom standard units, some with efficiencies. 2 stories, interior corridors. **Parking:** on-site. **Terms:** 7 day cancellation notice, pets ($5 extra charge). **Amenities:** extended cable TV, hair dryers. **Pool(s):** heated indoor. **Leisure Activities:** sauna, whirlpool, exercise room. **Guest Services:** valet laundry. **Business Services:** meeting rooms, fax (fee). **Cards:** AX, CB, DC, DS, JC, MC, VI. **Special Amenities:** free continental breakfast and free newspaper.

SOME UNITS

GREENWOOD —See Indianapolis p. 491.

HAMMOND pop. 84,200

──────── WHERE TO STAY ────────

AMERIHOST INN-HAMMOND　　　　　　　　　　　　　　　　　Phone: (219)845-4678
(AAA) SAVE　　5/26-9/3 [ECP]　　　　　1P: $89-$99　　　2P: $89-$99　　　XP: $10　　　F18
　　　　　　4/1-5/25 & 9/4-3/31 [ECP]　1P: $79-$89　　　2P: $79-$89　　　XP: $10　　　F18
Motel　　**Location:** I-80/94, exit 2A, just s. 7813 Indianapolis Blvd 46324. Fax: 219/845-4074. **Facility:** 86 one-bedroom standard units, some with whirlpools. 4 stories, interior corridors. *Bath:* combo or shower only. **Parking:** on-site. **Amenities:** voice mail, safes, irons, hair dryers. **Pool(s):** heated indoor. **Leisure Activities:** sauna, whirlpool, exercise room. **Guest Services:** valet and coin laundry. **Business Services:** meeting rooms. **Cards:** AX, CB, DC, DS, MC, VI. **Special Amenities: free continental breakfast and free newspaper.**

SOME UNITS

COURTYARD BY MARRIOTT　　　　　　　　　　　　　　　　Phone: (219)845-6350
(AAA) SAVE　　All Year　　　　　　　1P: $89-$99　　　2P: $89-$99
Motel　　**Location:** I-80/94, exit 3 (Kennedy Ave S). 7730 Corinne Dr 46323. Fax: 219/845-5265. **Facility:** 85 units. 82 one-bedroom standard units, some with whirlpools. 3 one-bedroom suites. 3 stories, interior corridors. *Bath:* combo or shower only. **Terms:** cancellation fee imposed. **Amenities:** extended cable TV, video games, dual phone lines, voice mail, irons, hair dryers. **Dining:** coffee shop, 6-10 am, 7-11 am weekends. **Pool(s):** small heated indoor. **Leisure Activities:** whirlpool, sun deck, exercise room. **Guest Services:** valet and coin laundry. **Business Services:** meeting rooms. **Cards:** AX, DC, DS, MC, VI. *(See color ad card insert)*

SOME UNITS

FAIRFIELD INN BY MARRIOTT　　　　　　　　　　　　　　Phone: (219)845-6950
(AAA) SAVE　　All Year　　　　　　　1P: $79-$129　　　2P: $79-$129
Motel　　**Location:** I-80/94, exit 3 (Kennedy Ave S). 7720 Corinne Dr 46323. Fax: 219/845-7655. **Facility:** 94 one-bedroom standard units, some with whirlpools. 4 stories, interior corridors. *Bath:* combo or shower only. **Parking:** on-site. **Terms:** [CP] meal plan available. **Amenities:** extended cable TV, irons, hair dryers. **Pool(s):** small heated indoor. **Leisure Activities:** whirlpool, exercise room. **Guest Services:** valet and coin laundry. **Cards:** AX, CB, DC, DS, MC, VI. **Special Amenities: free continental breakfast and free local telephone calls.** *(See color ad card insert)*

SOME UNITS

HOLIDAY INN CHICAGO SOUTHEAST/HAMMOND　　　　　　Phone: (219)844-2140
Motor Inn　　All Year　　　　　　　1P: $86
Location: I-80/94, exit Cline Ave, 0.6 mi s to frontage road, 0.6 mi n. 3830 179th St 46323. Fax: 219/845-7760. **Facility:** 152 one-bedroom standard units. 4 stories, interior corridors. **Parking:** on-site. **Terms:** check-in 4 pm, 7 day cancellation notice, package plans, small pets only ($20 deposit). **Amenities:** safes (fee), irons, hair dryers. **Leisure Activities:** exercise room. **Guest Services:** valet and coin laundry. **Business Services:** meeting rooms. **Cards:** AX, CB, DC, DS, JC, MC, VI.

SOME UNITS

RAMADA INN & CONFERENCE CENTER - HAMMOND　　　　Phone: (219)933-0500
Motel　　All Year [ECP]　　　　1P: $72-$76　　　2P: $82-$86
Location: I-80/94, exit Calumet Ave, then 4.5 mi n; I-90, exit 5. 4141 Calumet Ave 46320-1132. Fax: 219/933-0506. **Facility:** 100 units. 82 one-bedroom standard units, some with whirlpools. 18 one-bedroom suites ($99-$154). 1-2 stories, interior corridors. *Bath:* combo or shower only. **Parking:** on-site. **Terms:** package plans. **Amenities:** extended cable TV, voice mail, irons, hair dryers. **Pool(s):** heated outdoor. **Leisure Activities:** whirlpool. **Guest Services:** coin laundry. **Business Services:** conference facilities, business center, PC, fax. **Cards:** AX, CB, DC, DS, MC, VI.

SOME UNITS

RESIDENCE INN BY MARRIOTT　　　　　　　　　　　　Phone: (219)844-8440
(AAA) SAVE　　All Year [ECP]　　　　1P: $129-$189
Extended Stay Apartment　　**Location:** I-80/94, exit 3 (Kennedy Ave S). 7740 Corinne Dr 46323. Fax: 219/844-8454. **Facility:** 78 units. 18 one-bedroom standard units with kitchens. 48 one- and 12 two-bedroom suites with kitchens. 3 stories, interior corridors. *Bath:* combo or shower only. **Parking:** on-site, winter plug-ins. **Terms:** pets ($75 fee, $5 extra charge). **Amenities:** extended cable TV, video games, dual phone lines, voice mail, irons, hair dryers. **Pool(s):** heated indoor. **Leisure Activities:** whirlpool, exercise room, sports court. **Guest Services:** complimentary evening beverages: Mon-Thurs, valet and coin laundry. **Cards:** AX, CB, DC, DS, JC, MC, VI. *(See color ad card insert)*

SOME UNITS

──────── WHERE TO DINE ────────

FREDDY'S STEAK HOUSE　　　**Lunch:** $9-$17　　　**Dinner:** $12-$23　　　Phone: 219/844-1500
Steak & Seafood　　**Location:** I-80/94, exit 3 (Kennedy Ave N), 1.4 mi n, at jct Kennedy Ave and 165th St. 6442 Kennedy Ave 46323. **Hours:** 11 am-10 pm, Fri & Sat-11 pm. Closed major holidays; also Sun. **Reservations:** accepted. **Features:** casual dress; carryout; cocktails & lounge. The long-established steak and seafood restaurant follows a rustic, Viking theme throughout its various dining rooms. A large variety of fresh seafood dishes and fine steaks lines the casual eatery's menu. **Parking:** on-site. **Cards:** AX, MC, VI.

PHIL SMIDT & SON
Lunch: $8-$14   **Dinner:** $12-$27   **Phone:** 219/659-0025

Seafood

Location: Just n of jct US 12, 20 and 41; use Indiana Toll Rd, West Point exit. 1205 N Calumet Ave 46320. **Hours:** 11:15 am-9 pm, Fri & Sat-9:30 pm, Sun 1 pm-7:30 pm. Closed major holidays; also Mon. **Reservations:** accepted. **Features:** casual dress; children's menu; carryout; cocktails & lounge. Lake perch and original seafood chowder are a hallmark at this well-established restaurant adjacent to a popular port and boat ride venue. Try the tasty and well-seasoned stuffed snapper and a nicely-presented cheesecake with strawberry sauce. **Parking:** on-site. **Cards:** AX, CB, DC, MC, VI.

HAUBSTADT pop. 1,500

—— WHERE TO STAY ——

BAYMONT INN & SUITES
Phone: (812)768-5878

Motel

All Year	1P: $64-$90	2P: $71-$97	XP: $7	F18

Location: I-64, exit 25B, 0.4 mi n to Warrenton Rd, just w to frontage road, then 0.3 mi s. RR 1 Box 252 47639. **Fax:** 812/768-5848. **Facility:** 74 units. 71 one-bedroom standard units, some with whirlpools. 3 one-bedroom suites ($79-$140). 3 stories, interior corridors. *Bath:* combo or shower only. **Parking:** on-site. **Terms:** 14 day cancellation notice, pets ($50 deposit). **Amenities:** video games, voice mail, safes, irons, hair dryers. *Some:* dual phone lines. **Pool(s):** heated indoor. **Leisure Activities:** whirlpool, exercise room. **Guest Services:** valet and coin laundry. **Cards:** AX, CB, DC, DS, JC, MC, VI. **Special Amenities:** free continental breakfast and free newspaper.

SOME UNITS

—— WHERE TO DINE ——

HAUB STEAK HOUSE
Dinner: $9-$25   **Phone:** 812/768-6462

Steak House

Location: US 41, 1.5 mi w on SR 68, just n. 103 Main St 47639. **Hours:** 4 pm-10 pm. Closed major holidays; also Sun. **Reservations:** suggested; weekends. **Features:** casual dress; early bird specials; carryout; cocktails & lounge; a la carte. This brick building, erected in 1900 to be a grain warehouse, now houses a fine dining restaurant. The Haub Steak House is known for the quality of its beef which is aged in its own locker then hand-cut and trimmed. Service can be a bit ragged but the food and the decor make this a worthy choice for family or special occasion dining. **Parking:** on-site. **Cards:** AX, DC, DS, MC, VI.

HEBRON

—— WHERE TO STAY ——

SUPER 8 MOTEL HEBRON/LOWELL
Phone: 219/696-8888

Motel

4/1-10/31	1P: $50-$70	2P: $55-$75	XP: $5
11/1-3/31	1P: $45-$65	2P: $50-$70	XP: $5

Location: I-65, exit 240, 0.5 mi e. 3423 E SR 2 46341. **Fax:** 219/696-8888. **Facility:** 72 one-bedroom standard units, some with whirlpools. 2 stories, interior corridors. *Bath:* combo or shower only. **Parking:** on-site. **Guest Services:** coin laundry. **Cards:** AX, CB, DC, DS, MC, VI.

SOME UNITS

HOBART pop. 21,800

—— WHERE TO STAY ——

COMFORT INN
Phone: (219)947-7677

Motel

4/1-9/15 [CP]	1P: $89-$99	2P: $94-$104	XP: $5	F18
9/16-3/31 [CP]	1P: $75-$79	2P: $84-$89	XP: $5	F18

Location: I-65, exit 255 (61st St), then just e. 1915 S Mississippi St 46342. **Fax:** 219/947-7677. **Facility:** 61 units. 60 one-bedroom standard units, some with whirlpools. 1 one-bedroom suite with whirlpool. 3 stories, interior corridors. *Bath:* combo or shower only. **Parking:** on-site, winter plug-ins. **Terms:** package plans, small pets only ($50 deposit). **Amenities:** extended cable TV. *Some:* irons, hair dryers. **Pool(s):** small heated indoor. **Leisure Activities:** whirlpool. **Guest Services:** valet laundry. **Cards:** AX, DC, DS, MC, VI. **Special Amenities:** free continental breakfast and free local telephone calls.

SOME UNITS

HOWE pop. 600

—— WHERE TO STAY ——

HOLIDAY INN EXPRESS-HOWE/STURGIS
Phone: (260)562-3660

Motel

4/1-10/31 [ECP]	1P: $89-$99	2P: $89-$99	XP: $10	F18
11/1-3/31 [ECP]	1P: $79	2P: $79	XP: $10	F18

Location: I-80/90, exit 121. 0045 W 750 N 46746. **Fax:** 260/562-3660. **Facility:** 66 units. 65 one-bedroom standard units, some with whirlpools. 1 one-bedroom suite ($119-$129). 3 stories, interior corridors. *Bath:* combo or shower only. **Parking:** on-site. **Terms:** package plans. **Amenities:** dual phone lines, voice mail, irons, hair dryers. **Pool(s):** small indoor. **Leisure Activities:** exercise room. **Guest Services:** complimentary evening beverages: Mon-Thurs, valet laundry. **Cards:** AX, CB, DC, DS, JC, MC, VI. **Special Amenities:** free continental breakfast and free local telephone calls.

SOME UNITS

SUPER 8 MOTEL

AAA SAVE
◈◈
Motel

					Phone: (260)562-2828
	5/1-9/30 [ECP]	1P: $65-$75	2P: $75-$85		XP: $10	F12
	4/1-4/30 & 10/1-3/31 [ECP]	1P: $55-$65	2P: $65-$75		XP: $10	F12

Location: I-80/90, exit 121, 0.5 mi s. 7333 N SR 9 46746. **Fax:** 260/562-2815. **Facility:** 77 one-bedroom standard units, some with whirlpools. 2 stories, interior corridors. *Bath:* combo or shower only. **Parking:** on-site. **Terms:** 3 day cancellation notice, small pets only. **Amenities:** *Some:* irons, hair dryers. **Guest Services:** coin laundry. **Business Services:** meeting rooms. **Cards:** AX, CB, DC, DS, MC, VI. **Special Amenities:** free continental breakfast and free local telephone calls.

SOME UNITS

HUNTINGBURG pop. 5,200

------ WHERE TO STAY ------

VILLAGER LODGE DUTCHMAN INN

AAA SAVE
◈◈
Motor Inn

					Phone: (812)683-2334
	6/15-9/30 [CP]	1P: $79-$89	2P: $89-$99		XP: $10	F18
	4/1-6/14 & 10/1-3/31 [CP]	1P: $49-$59	2P: $49-$59		XP: $10	F18

Location: On US 231, 1.5 mi n of jct SR 64. 406 E 22nd St 47542. **Fax:** 812/683-8474. **Facility:** 88 one-bedroom standard units. 2 stories, exterior corridors. **Parking:** on-site, winter plug-ins. **Terms:** cancellation fee imposed, weekly rates available, package plans. **Amenities:** extended cable TV. **Dining:** restaurant, 11 am-10 pm, $5-$15, cocktails. **Pool(s):** heated outdoor, wading. **Business Services:** meeting rooms. **Cards:** AX, DC, DS, MC, VI.

SOME UNITS

HUNTINGTON pop. 16,400

------ WHERE TO STAY ------

AMERIHOST INN HUNTINGTON

AAA SAVE
◈◈◈
Motel

					Phone: (260)359-9000
	All Year	1P: $63-$103	2P: $63-$103		XP: $10	F19

Location: 0.6 mi nw of jct US 24/224 and SR 5. 2820 Hotel Ave 46750. **Fax:** 260/359-9100. **Facility:** 62 one-bedroom standard units, some with whirlpools. 2 stories, interior corridors. *Bath:* combo or shower only. **Parking:** on-site. **Terms:** package plans. **Amenities:** voice mail, safes, irons, hair dryers. **Pool(s):** heated indoor. **Leisure Activities:** whirlpool, exercise room. **Guest Services:** valet laundry. **Business Services:** meeting rooms. **Cards:** AX, CB, DC, DS, MC, VI. **Special Amenities:** free continental breakfast and free newspaper.

SOME UNITS

COMFORT INN

AAA SAVE
◈◈◈
Motel

					Phone: (260)356-3434
	All Year	1P: $69-$109	2P: $69-$129		XP: $7	F16

Location: Jct US 24/224 and SR 5. 2205 N Jefferson 46750. **Fax:** 260/356-3839. **Facility:** 62 one-bedroom standard units, some with whirlpools. 2 stories, interior corridors. *Bath:* combo or shower only. **Parking:** on-site. **Amenities:** extended cable TV, irons, hair dryers. **Pool(s):** heated indoor. **Leisure Activities:** whirlpool, exercise room. **Guest Services:** coin laundry. **Business Services:** meeting rooms, fax (fee). **Cards:** AX, CB, DC, DS, JC, MC, VI.

SOME UNITS

Destination Indianapolis
pop. 731,300

Culture-seekers will find Indianapolis abloom with the arts. It has a wide selection of opera, dance and theater, and its symphony orchestra is led by one of the world's best.

Indianapolis skyline. It's a city that has everything: peaceful, well-kept parks as well as towering skyscrapers.

For those who would rather don sweats and head for the great outdoors, 113 city parks provide recreational opportunities from golfing to cross-country skiing.

Broad Ripple, Indianapolis. About 15 minutes from downtown, this shopping area has eateries and eclectic boutiques in old restored houses. (See mention page 144)

Indianapolis Symphony Orchestra. Conducted by Raymond Leppard, the orchestra performs in the Hilbert Circle Theatre September through May. (See mention page 146)

Indianapolis

See Vicinity map page 463

See Downtown map page 463

The Indianapolis Artsgarden. This unusual glass-domed structure in the Circle Centre Mall houses local artwork. (See mention page 146)

Places included in this AAA Destination City:

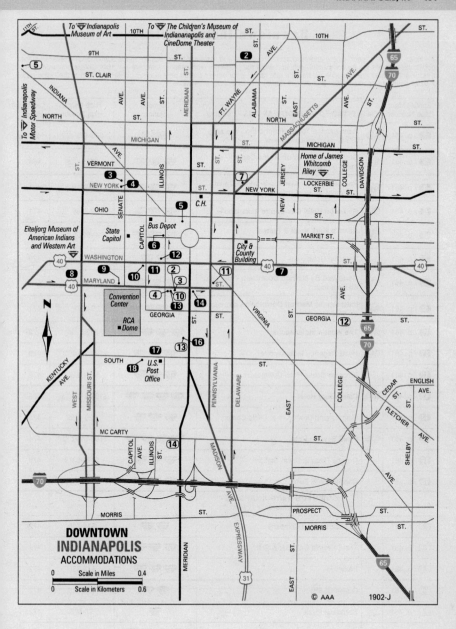

DOWNTOWN INDIANAPOLIS ACCOMMODATIONS

Scale in Miles 0 — 0.4
Scale in Kilometers 0 — 0.6

© AAA   1902-J

Downtown Indianapolis

This index helps you "spot" where approved accommodations and restaurants are located on the corresponding detailed maps. Lodging rate ranges are for comparison only and show the property's high season; rates are per night, unless only weekly (W) or monthly (M) rates are available. Restaurant rate range is for dinner, unless only lunch (L) is served. Turn to the listing page for more detailed rate information and consult display ads for special promotions.

Spotter/Map Page Number	OA	DOWNTOWN INDIANAPOLIS - Lodgings	Diamond Rating	Rate Range High Season	Listing Page
2 / p. 461	AAA	Renaissance Tower Historic Inn - see ad p 471 & color ad card insert	◆◆	$85-$95 SAVE	471
3 / p. 461	AAA	Courtyard by Marriott-At the Capitol - see color ad card insert	◆◆◆	$129 SAVE	469
4 / p. 461	AAA	Residence Inn Indianapolis on the Canal - see color ad card insert	◆◆◆	$129-$199 SAVE	471
5 / p. 461	AAA	Radisson Hotel City Centre Indianapolis	◆◆◆	$129-$189 SAVE	471
6 / p. 461	AAA	Adam's Mark Hotel & Suites Indianapolis-Downtown	◆◆◆	$99-$224 SAVE	468
7 / p. 461		Days Inn Downtown	◆◆	$69-$90	470
8 / p. 461	AAA	Courtyard By Marriott-Downtown - see color ad card insert	◆◆◆	$139-$199 SAVE	469
9 / p. 461	AAA	Indianapolis Marriott Downtown - see color ad card insert	◆◆◆	$159-$279 SAVE	471
10 / p. 461	AAA	The Westin Indianapolis	◆◆◆	$135 SAVE	472
11 / p. 461	AAA	Hyatt Regency Indianapolis	◆◆◆	$120-$220 SAVE	470
12 / p. 461		Embassy Suites Hotel-Downtown	◆◆◆	$157-$173	470
13 / p. 461	AAA	Canterbury Hotel	◆◆◆◆	$155-$190 SAVE	469
14 / p. 461		Hampton Inn Downtown at Circle Center	◆◆◆	$99-$129	470
16 / p. 461	AAA	Omni Severin Hotel	◆◆◆◆	$100-$199 SAVE	471
17 / p. 461		Crowne Plaza at Union Station	◆◆◆	$179-$279	470
18 / p. 461		Comfort Inn & Suites City Centre	◆◆◆	$119-$350	469
		DOWNTOWN INDIANAPOLIS - Restaurants			
2 / p. 461		Alcatraz Brewing Company	◆◆	$12-$20	472
3 / p. 461		The California Cafe Bar & Grill	◆◆◆	$12-$25	472
4 / p. 461		Palomino	◆◆◆	$14-$30	472
5 / p. 461		Queen Of Sheba	◆◆	$10-$15	472
7 / p. 461		Bazbeaux Pizza	◆	$5-$20	472
10 / p. 461		The Restaurant at The Canterbury Hotel	◆◆◆◆	$15-$25	473
11 / p. 461		The Majestic Restaurant	◆◆◆	$13-$39	472
12 / p. 461		The Milano Inn Restaurant	◆◆	$9-$17	472
13 / p. 461		40 West Coffee Cafe	◆	$4-$10(L)	472
14 / p. 461		Shapiro's Delicatessen & Cafeteria	◆	$5-$10	473

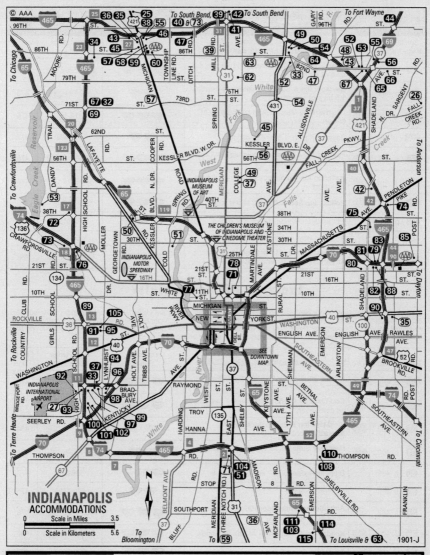

INDIANAPOLIS
ACCOMMODATIONS

Scale in Miles 0 — 3.5
Scale in Kilometers 0 — 5.6

1901-J

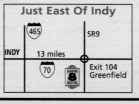

✈ Airport Accommodations

Spotter/Map Page Number	OA	INDIANAPOLIS INT'L	Diamond Rating	Rate Range High Season	Listing Page
99 / p. 463	AAA	Adam's Mark Hotel Indianapolis Airport, 0.5 mi e of airport	▼▼▼	$145-$209 SAVE	473
97 / p. 463	AAA	Baymont Inn & Suites Indianapolis-Airport, 1.5 mi e of airport	▼▼	$69-$84 SAVE	473
102 / p. 463	AAA	Courtyard by Marriott-Airport, 1.5 mi e of airport	▼▼▼	$119 SAVE	475
100 / p. 463		Days Inn Airport, 1.5 mi e of airport	▼▼	$65-$80	477
96 / p. 463	AAA	Fairfield Inn by Marriott/Indianapolis Airport, 1.5 mi e from airport	▼▼▼	$79-$119 SAVE	478
101 / p. 463	AAA	Hampton Inn-Indianapolis Airport, 1.5 mi e of airport	▼▼▼	$84-$114 SAVE	478
93 / p. 463	AAA	Holiday Inn Select Airport, at the airport	▼▼▼	$179 SAVE	480
98 / p. 463		La Quinta Inn-Airport, 1.5 mi e of airport	▼▼▼	$90-$122	480
92 / p. 463		Radisson Hotel Indianapolis Airport, airport	fyi	$159-$350	485
94 / p. 463	AAA	Residence Inn by Marriott/Indianapolis Airport, 1.5 mi e of terminal	▼▼▼	$119-$139 SAVE	482

Indianapolis and Vicinity

This index helps you "spot" where approved accommodations and restaurants are located on the corresponding detailed maps. Lodging rate ranges are for comparison only and show the property's high season; rates are per night, unless only weekly (W) or monthly (M) rates are available. Restaurant rate range is for dinner, unless only lunch (L) is served. Turn to the listing page for more detailed rate information and consult display ads for special promotions.

Spotter/Map Page Number	OA	INDIANAPOLIS - Lodgings	Diamond Rating	Rate Range High Season	Listing Page
25 / p. 463		Country Inn & Suites By Carlson-Indianapolis North - see color ad p 476	▼▼▼	$78-$159	475
32 / p. 463	AAA	Courtyard by Marriott-Northwest - see color ad card insert	▼▼▼	$95 SAVE	476
33 / p. 463	AAA	Wellesley Inn & Suites (Indianapolis Airport/Marion)	▼▼	$79-$109 SAVE	484
34 / p. 463	AAA	MainStay Suites-Indianapolis - See color ad p 468	▼▼	$79-$99 SAVE	481
35 / p. 463		Drury Inn-Indianapolis - see color ad p 5	▼▼▼	$62-$95	477
36 / p. 463		Comfort Inn-North	▼▼	$70-$129	475
37 / p. 463	AAA	AmeriSuites (Indianapolis/Airport) - see color ad p 468	▼▼▼	$89-$235 SAVE	473
38 / p. 463	AAA	Holiday Inn-Select North At The Pyramids	▼▼▼	$159-$199 SAVE	480
39 / p. 463		Doubletree Guest Suites - see ad p 477	▼▼▼	$99-$109	477
40 / p. 463	AAA	Courtyard by Marriott-Indianapolis North/Carmel - see color ad card insert	▼▼▼	$69-$104 SAVE	476
41 / p. 463		Signature Inn Carmel	▼▼	$81-$92	483
42 / p. 463	AAA	Wyndham Hotel Indianapolis	▼▼▼	$89-$129 SAVE	484
43 / p. 463	AAA	Wellesley Inn & Suites (Indianapolis/North)	▼▼▼	$61-$81 SAVE	484
44 / p. 463	AAA	Residence Inn by Marriott Indianapolis/Fishers - see color ad card insert	▼▼▼	$119-$129 SAVE	482
45 / p. 463		Signature Inn & Suites-Northwest	▼▼▼	$62-$72	483
46 / p. 463	AAA	Fairfield Inn by Marriott-College Park - see color ad card insert	▼▼▼	$49-$149 SAVE	478

Spotter/Map Page Number	OA	INDIANAPOLIS - Lodgings (continued)	Diamond Rating	Rate Range High Season	Listing Page
47 / p. 463	AAA	Pickwick Farms Short-Term Furnished Apartments - see ad p 471	◆◆	$35-$90 SAVE	482
49 / p. 463		Sheraton Indianapolis Hotel & Suites	◆◆◆	$149-$159	483
50 / p. 463	AAA	AmeriSuites (Indianapolis/Keystone) - see color ad p 468	◆◆◆	$99-$109 SAVE	473
51 / p. 463	AAA	Holiday Inn Express South	◆◆◆	$89-$109 SAVE	479
52 / p. 463	AAA	Best Western Castleton Inn	◆◆	$69-$96 SAVE	474
53 / p. 463		Days Inn & Suites	◆◆	$59-$64	477
54 / p. 463	AAA	Indianapolis Marriott North - see color ad card insert	◆◆◆	$129-$159 SAVE	480
55 / p. 463	AAA	Fairfield Inn by Marriott-Castleton - see color ad card insert	◆◆◆	$44-$64 SAVE	478
56 / p. 463		Super 8 Castleton-Northeast	◆◆	$59-$150	484
57 / p. 463		Embassy Suites Hotel-North	◆◆◆	$119-$214	477
58 / p. 463	AAA	Quality Inn & Suites At The Pyramids - see color ad p 468	◆◆◆	$45-$220 SAVE	482
59 / p. 463		Extended Stay America Northwest	◆◆	Failed to provide	477
60 / p. 463	AAA	Residence Inn by Marriott Indianapolis North - see color ad card insert	◆◆◆	$69-$105 SAVE	483
63 / p. 463		The Inn at St. Francis	◆◆◆	$70	480
64 / p. 463		Signature Inn-Castleton	◆◆	$69-$79	483
65 / p. 463		Hampton Inn-Northeast - see ad p 479	◆◆◆	$79-$225	478
66 / p. 463	AAA	Omni Indianapolis North Hotel - see ad p 481	◆◆◆	$89 SAVE	481
67 / p. 463		Hampton Inn-Northwest	◆◆◆	$82-$97	479
69 / p. 463	AAA	Clarion Inn & Suites	◆◆◆	$76-$92 SAVE	475
71 / p. 463		The Looking Glass Inn	◆◆◆	$105-$135	481
72 / p. 463		Signature Inn-Indianapolis West	◆◆	$76-$87	483
73 / p. 463	AAA	Best Western Waterfront Plaza Hotel	◆◆	$58-$125 SAVE	475
74 / p. 463	AAA	Four Points by Sheraton Indianapolis East	◆◆◆	$69-$99 SAVE	478
75 / p. 463		Quality Inn East	◆◆	$55-$275	482
76 / p. 463	AAA	Red Roof Inn-Speedway	◆◆	$39-$61 SAVE	482
77 / p. 463	AAA	University Place Hotel & Conference Center	◆◆◆	$245 SAVE	484
78 / p. 463		Stone Soup Inn	◆◆◆	$85-$135	484
79 / p. 463		Comfort Inn-East	◆◆◆	$75-$250	475
80 / p. 463	AAA	Holiday Inn East	◆◆◆	$129 SAVE	479
81 / p. 463		Hampton Inn-East	◆◆◆	$82-$97	478
82 / p. 463	AAA	Indianapolis Marriott East - see color ad card insert	◆◆◆	$100 SAVE	480
83 / p. 463		Hawthorn Suites East	◆◆◆	$79-$260	479
85 / p. 463	AAA	Baymont Inn & Suites-Indianapolis East - see color ad opposite title page	◆◆	$79-$89 SAVE	474
88 / p. 463	AAA	La Quinta Inn-East	◆◆◆	$60-$86 SAVE	481
89 / p. 463	AAA	Pickwick Farms Airport - see ad p 471	◆◆	$38-$85 SAVE	481

Spotter/Map Page Number	OA	INDIANAPOLIS - Lodgings (continued)	Diamond Rating	Rate Range High Season	Listing Page
90 / p. 463		Signature Inn-Indianapolis East	◆◆◆	$71-$81	483
91 / p. 463	AAA	Comfort Inn-West	◆◆◆	$97-$99 SAVE	475
92 / p. 463		Radisson Hotel Indianapolis Airport	fyi	$159-$350	485
93 / p. 463	AAA	Holiday Inn Select Airport	◆◆◆	$179 SAVE	480
94 / p. 463	AAA	Residence Inn by Marriott/Indianapolis Airport - see color ad card insert	◆◆◆	$119-$139 SAVE	482
95 / p. 463	AAA	Sleep Inn West	◆◆	$81-$87 SAVE	483
96 / p. 463	AAA	Fairfield Inn by Marriott/Indianapolis Airport - see color ad card insert	◆◆◆	$79-$119 SAVE	478
97 / p. 463	AAA	Baymont Inn & Suites Indianapolis-Airport - see color ad opposite title page	◆◆	$69-$84 SAVE	473
98 / p. 463		La Quinta Inn-Airport	◆◆◆	$90-$122	480
99 / p. 463	AAA	Adam's Mark Hotel Indianapolis Airport	◆◆◆	$145-$209 SAVE	473
100 / p. 463		Days Inn Airport	◆◆	$65-$80	477
101 / p. 463	AAA	Hampton Inn-Indianapolis Airport - see color ad p 470	◆◆◆	$84-$114 SAVE	478
102 / p. 463	AAA	Courtyard by Marriott-Airport - see color ad card insert	◆◆◆	$119 SAVE	475
103 / p. 463	AAA	Hampton Inn South	◆◆◆	$63-$84 SAVE	479
104 / p. 463		Best Inns	◆◆	$45-$65	474
105 / p. 463		Wingate Inn-Airport	◆◆◆	$85-$225	484
108 / p. 463	AAA	Red Roof Inn-South	◆◆	$39-$64 SAVE	482
110 / p. 463		Holiday Inn-Southeast	◆◆	$89-$250	480
111 / p. 463		Signature Inn-South	◆◆	$60-$69	483
114 / p. 463	AAA	Courtyard by Marriott Indianapolis South - see color ad card insert	◆◆◆	$69-$94 SAVE	476
115 / p. 463	AAA	Best Western South	◆◆◆	$79-$99 SAVE	474
		INDIANAPOLIS - Restaurants			
26 / p. 463		The Heron Restaurant	◆◆	$15-$30	486
27 / p. 463	AAA	Chanteclair	◆◆◆	$25-$40	485
33 / p. 463		Keystone Grill	◆◆◆	$17-$27	486
35 / p. 463		Grindstone Charley's Restaurant & Pub	◆◆	$9-$16	485
36 / p. 463		Acropolis	◆◆	$8-$15	485
37 / p. 463		Aristocrat Pub & Restaurant	◆◆	$7-$22	485
39 / p. 463		Bacco	◆◆◆	$12-$22	485
42 / p. 463		Cafe Europa	◆◆	$12-$20	485
43 / p. 463		Don Hall's Castleton Grill	◆◆	$9-$15	485
45 / p. 463		The Jazz Cooker	◆◆	$12-$22	486
47 / p. 463		Malibu Grill	◆◆	$11-$21	486
48 / p. 463		Mediterrano Cafe	◆◆	$8-$15	486
49 / p. 463		Midtown Grill	◆◆◆	$13-$25	487

Spotter/Map Page Number	OA	INDIANAPOLIS - Restaurants (continued)	Diamond Rating	Rate Range High Season	Listing Page
50 / p. 463		New China Buffet	◆	$7	487
51 / p. 463		Iron Skillet Restaurant & Gift Shop	◆◆	$14-$18	486
52 / p. 463		Peter's A Restaurant & Bar	◆◆◆	$22-$32	487
53 / p. 463		Rick's Boatyard	◆◆	$7-$37	487
54 / p. 463		Sakura Japanese Restaurant	◆	$10-$15	487
55 / p. 463		San Remo Grille	◆◆	$15-$25	487
56 / p. 463		Shaffer's Restaurant	◆◆	$14-$25	487
57 / p. 463		Thien Huong Sizzling Wok	◆◆	$6-$12	487
59 / p. 463		Vito Provolone's	◆◆	$9-$15	487
62 / p. 463		Hollyhock Hill	◆◆	$14-$18	486
63 / p. 463		Il Gargano	◆◆◆	$13-$23	486
67 / p. 463		Charleston's Restaurant	◆◆	$9-$17	485
71 / p. 463	AAA	**Heritage House Smorgasbord**	◆	$8-$9	486
		CARMEL - Restaurant			
73 / p. 463		Illusions Restaurant	◆◆	$12-$30	489

DOWNTOWN INDIANAPOLIS   (See map p. 461; index p. 462)

──────── WHERE TO STAY ────────

ADAM'S MARK HOTEL & SUITES INDIANAPOLIS-DOWNTOWN   **Phone:** (317)972-0600   **6**
All Year   1P: $99-$199   2P: $124-$224   XP: $25   F18
Location: Jct Illinois and Market sts. 120 W Market St 46204. Fax: 317/972-0660. **Facility:** 332 units. 248 one-bedroom standard units. 84 one-bedroom suites ($119-$699). 20 stories, interior corridors. *Bath:* combo or shower only. **Parking:** *Fee:* on-site and valet. **Terms:** cancellation fee imposed, package plans. **Amenities:** video games, Web TV, high-speed Internet, dual phone lines, voice mail, irons, hair dryers. **Dining:** restaurant, 6 am-11 pm, $7-$20, cocktails. **Pool(s):** heated indoor. **Leisure Activities:** whirlpool, exercise room. **Guest Services:** gift shop, valet and coin laundry. **Business Services:** conference facilities, business center. *Fee:* PC, fax. **Cards:** AX, CB, DC, DS, MC, VI. **Special Amenities:** early check-in/late check-out and preferred room (subject to availability with advanced reservations).

SOME UNITS

(See map p. 461)

CANTERBURY HOTEL

Classic Hotel

Phone: (317)634-3000   **13** F

All Year   1P: $155-$190   2P: $155-$190   XP: $25

Location: Downtown; between Georgia and Maryland sts. 123 S Illinois St 46225. Fax: 317/685-2519. **Facility:** Historic. The guest rooms in this restored European-style hotel, which offers private access to a shopping mall, are inviting, though some are small. 99 units. 89 one-bedroom standard units, some with whirlpools. 10 one-bedroom suites ($305-$595), some with whirlpools. 12 stories, interior corridors. *Bath:* combo or shower only. **Parking:** *Fee:* on-site and valet. **Terms:** 90 day cancellation notice-fee imposed, [ECP] meal plan available, package plans. **Amenities:** extended cable TV, video games, voice mail, honor bars, hair dryers. *Some:* dual phone lines, irons. **Dining:** The Restaurant at The Canterbury Hotel, see separate listing. **Leisure Activities:** exercise equipment available. **Guest Services:** afternoon tea, valet laundry. **Business Services:** meeting rooms, fax (fee). **Cards:** AX, CB, DC, DS, JC, MC, VI. **Special Amenities:** free continental breakfast and free newspaper. Affiliated with A Preferred Hotel.

SOME UNITS

[icons] FEE / FEE

COMFORT INN & SUITES CITY CENTRE

Motel

MC, VI.

Phone: (317)631-9000   **18**

All Year [ECP]   1P: $119-$350   2P: $119-$350

Location: Downtown; just s of South St; across from RCA Dome. 530 S Capitol Ave 46225. Fax: 317/631-9999. **Facility:** 143 one-bedroom standard units, some with whirlpools. 4-5 stories, interior corridors. **Parking:** on-site. **Terms:** 4 day cancellation notice, [CP] meal plan available, small pets only. **Amenities:** video games, irons, hair dryers. *Some:* voice mail. **Pool(s):** indoor. **Leisure Activities:** whirlpool, exercise room. **Guest Services:** coin laundry. **Business Services:** meeting rooms, fax (fee). **Cards:** AX, CB, DC, DS, JC,

SOME UNITS

[icons] FEE / FEE FEE

COURTYARD BY MARRIOTT-AT THE CAPITOL

Motel

Phone: (317)684-7733   **3**

All Year   1P: $129   2P: $129

Location: Downtown; corner of New York and Senate aves. 320 N Senate Ave 46204. Fax: 317/684-7734. **Facility:** 124 one-bedroom standard units, some with whirlpools. 4 stories, interior corridors. *Bath:* combo or shower only. **Parking:** on-site. **Terms:** cancellation fee imposed, [BP] meal plan available. **Amenities:** video games, voice mail, irons, hair dryers. **Dining:** coffee shop, 6:30-10 am, Sat & Sun 7-11 am. **Pool(s):** heated indoor. **Leisure Activities:** whirlpool, sun deck, exercise room. **Guest Services:** coin laundry. **Business Services:** meeting rooms, business center, PC, fax (fee). **Cards:** AX, DC, DS, MC, VI. *(See color ad card insert)*

SOME UNITS

[icons] FEE /

COURTYARD BY MARRIOTT-DOWNTOWN

Hotel

Phone: (317)635-4443   **8**

All Year   1P: $139-$199   2P: $139-$199

Location: Downtown; at W Washington and West sts, facing the Eiteljorg Museum. 501 W Washington St 46204. Fax: 317/687-0029. **Facility:** 235 one-bedroom standard units. 3-8 stories, interior corridors. **Parking:** on-site (fee). **Terms:** [AP] meal plan available, package plans. **Amenities:** extended cable TV, dual phone lines, voice mail, irons, hair dryers. **Dining:** restaurant, 6:30 am-midnight, Fri & Sat-1 am, Sun-11 pm, $7-$18, cocktails. **Pool(s):** heated outdoor. **Leisure Activities:** playground, exercise room. **Guest Services:** gift shop, coin laundry. **Business Services:** meeting rooms, fax (fee). **Cards:** AX, CB, DC, DS, MC, VI. *(See color ad card insert)*

SOME UNITS

[icons] FEE / /

(See map p. 461)

CROWNE PLAZA AT UNION STATION

Hotel

Phone: (317)631-2221 **17**

All Year   1P: $179-$279
Location: Downtown; in Union Station at Capitol and Louisiana sts; opposite RCA Dome and Convention Center. 123 W Louisiana St 46225. Fax: 317/236-7474. **Facility:** 275 units. 273 one-bedroom standard units. 2 one-bedroom suites. 3 stories, interior corridors. **Parking:** *Fee:* on-site and valet. **Terms:** check-in 4 pm, package plans. **Amenities:** video games, voice mail, irons, hair dryers. **Pool(s):** heated indoor. **Leisure Activities:** whirlpool, exercise room. **Guest Services:** valet laundry. **Business Services:** conference facilities, business center. *Fee:* PC, fax. **Cards:** AX, CB, DC, DS, JC, MC, VI.

SOME UNITS

DAYS INN DOWNTOWN

SAVE

Motel

Phone: (317)637-6464 **7**

All Year [ECP]   1P: $69-$80   2P: $74-$90   XP: $10   F18
Location: Corner of Washington and New Jersey sts, just s of Market Square Arena. 401 E Washington St 46204. Fax: 317/637-0242. **Facility:** 100 one-bedroom standard units. 3 stories, interior corridors. **Terms:** 10 day cancellation notice. **Amenities:** voice mail, safes (fee), hair dryers. *Some:* irons. **Leisure Activities:** exercise room. **Business Services:** fax (fee). **Cards:** AX, DC, DS, MC, VI.

SOME UNITS

EMBASSY SUITES HOTEL-DOWNTOWN

SAVE

Suite Hotel

Phone: (317)236-1800 **12**

All Year   1P: $157-$173   2P: $157-$173   XP: $15   F18
Location: Downtown; at Illinois St. 110 W Washington St 46204. Fax: 317/972-9579. **Facility:** 360 units. 359 one- and 1 two-bedroom suites, some with whirlpools. 18 stories, interior corridors. **Parking:** on-site (fee). **Terms:** check-in 4 pm, cancellation fee imposed, [BP] meal plan available, package plans. **Amenities:** video games, dual phone lines, voice mail, irons, hair dryers. **Pool(s):** heated indoor. **Leisure Activities:** sauna, whirlpools, exercise room. **Guest Services:** gift shop, complimentary evening beverages, valet laundry. **Business Services:** conference facilities, business center, PC (fee), fax. **Cards:** AX, CB, DC, DS, MC, VI.

SOME UNITS

HAMPTON INN DOWNTOWN AT CIRCLE CENTER

SAVE

Motor Inn

Phone: (317)261-1200 **14**

All Year   1P: $99-$119   2P: $106-$129   XP: $10   F18
Location: Downtown; at Maryland St. 105 S Meridian St 46225. Fax: 317/261-1030. **Facility:** 180 units. 162 one-bedroom standard units, some with whirlpools. 18 one-bedroom suites ($169-$179). 9 stories, interior corridors. *Bath:* combo or shower only. **Parking:** *Fee:* on-site and valet. **Terms:** 3 day cancellation notice, [CP] meal plan available, package plans. **Amenities:** extended cable TV, video games, voice mail, irons, hair dryers. **Leisure Activities:** exercise room. **Guest Services:** coin laundry. **Business Services:** meeting rooms, business center, fax (fee). **Cards:** AX, CB, DC, DS, MC, VI.

SOME UNITS

HYATT REGENCY INDIANAPOLIS

AAA SAVE

Hotel

Phone: (317)632-1234 **11**

All Year   1P: $120-$195   2P: $145-$220   XP: $25   F18
Location: Just w; opposite RCA Dome. 1 S Capitol Ave 46204. Fax: 317/616-6079. **Facility:** 500 units. 480 one-bedroom standard units. 20 one-bedroom suites. 20 stories, interior corridors. *Bath:* combo or shower only. **Parking:** *Fee:* on-site and valet. **Terms:** cancellation fee imposed, package plans. **Amenities:** high-speed Internet, dual phone lines, voice mail, irons, hair dryers. *Some:* fax. **Dining:** dining room, restaurant, coffee shop, 6 am-11 pm, $8-$28, cocktails. **Pool(s):** heated indoor. **Leisure Activities:** sauna, whirlpool, steamroom. **Guest Services:** gift shop, massage (fee), valet laundry. **Business Services:** conference facilities, business center. *Fee:* PC, fax. **Cards:** AX, CB, DC, DS, JC, MC, VI.

SOME UNITS

(See map p. 461)

INDIANAPOLIS MARRIOTT DOWNTOWN   Phone: (317)822-3500   **9**
(AAA) (SAVE)   All Year   1P: $159-$259   2P: $179-$279   XP: $20   F16
♦♦♦♦ ♦♦♦♦   **Location:** Opposite the Convention Center. 350 W Maryland St 46225. Fax: 317/822-1002. **Facility:** Full service,
            convention hotel conveniently located opposite the convention center and near the Capitol. Spacious well-
Hotel   appointed public areas. 615 units. 587 one-bedroom standard units. 28 one-bedroom suites ($350-$1000).
            19 stories, interior corridors. *Bath:* combo or shower only. **Parking:** *Fee:* on-site and valet. **Terms:** check-in
4 pm, cancellation fee imposed. **Amenities:** extended cable TV, dual phone lines, voice mail, safes, irons,
hair dryers. *Fee:* video games, Web TV. *Some:* DVD players, CD players. **Dining:** 2 restaurants, 6:30 am-1 am, $7-$29, cocktails. **Pool(s):** heated indoor. **Leisure Activities:** whirlpool, exercise room. **Guest Services:** gift shop, valet and coin laundry.
Business Services: conference facilities, business center. *Fee:* PC, fax. **Cards:** AX, CB, DC, DS, JC, MC, VI.
(See color ad card insert)

SOME UNITS
[icons] FEE ... FEE ... / [icons]

OMNI SEVERIN HOTEL   Phone: (317)634-6664   **16**
(AAA) (SAVE)   9/4-3/31   1P: $100-$179   2P: $120-$199   XP: $20   F18
           4/1-9/3   1P: $95-$170   2P: $115-$190   XP: $20   F18
♦♦♦♦ ♦♦♦♦   **Location:** Opposite Union Station. 40 W Jackson Pl 46225. Fax: 317/687-3612. **Facility:** A mix of traditional and
Hotel   contemporary decor elements creates a pleasant ambience at this hotel. 424 units. 413 one-bedroom stan-
            dard units. 11 one-bedroom suites ($225-$800). 13 stories, interior corridors. *Bath:* combo or shower only.
            Parking: *Fee:* on-site and valet. **Amenities:** extended
cable TV, dual phone lines, voice mail, honor bars, irons, hair dryers. *Fee:* video games, Web TV. **Dining:** dining room, 6:30
am-11 pm, $11-$25, cocktails, also, 40 West Coffee Cafe, see separate listing. **Pool(s):** small heated indoor/outdoor. **Leisure
Activities:** exercise room. **Guest Services:** gift shop, valet laundry. **Business Services:** conference facilities, business center.
Fee: PC, fax. **Cards:** AX, CB, DC, DS, JC, MC, VI. **Special Amenities:** free newspaper and preferred room (subject to availability with advanced reservations).

SOME UNITS
[icons] FEE ... / [icons] FEE FEE /

RADISSON HOTEL CITY CENTRE INDIANAPOLIS   Phone: (317)635-2000   **5**
(AAA) (SAVE)   All Year   1P: $129-$189   2P: $129-$189   XP: $20
♦♦♦♦ ♦♦♦♦   **Location:** Meridan and Ohio sts; just n of Monument Cir. 31 W Ohio St 46204. Fax: 317/638-0782. **Facility:** 374
           units. 333 one-bedroom standard units. 41 one-bedroom suites ($159-$249). 21 stories, interior corridors.
Hotel   *Bath:* combo or shower only. **Parking:** on-site (fee). **Terms:** 7 day cancellation notice. **Amenities:** extended
           cable TV, dual phone lines, voice mail, irons, hair dryers. **Dining:** dining room, coffee shop, 6:30 am-2 & 5-9
pm, Sat from 7 am, Sun 7 am-2 pm, $10-$24, cocktails. **Pool(s):** outdoor. **Leisure Activities:** exercise room.
Guest Services: gift shop, valet laundry. **Business Services:** conference facilities, business center. *Fee:* PC, fax. **Cards:** AX,
CB, DC, DS, JC, MC, VI. **Special Amenities:** free room upgrade and preferred room (each subject to availability with advanced reservations).

SOME UNITS
[icons] FEE ... / [icons]

RENAISSANCE TOWER HISTORIC INN   Phone: (317)261-1652   **2**
(AAA) (SAVE)   All Year [CP]   1P: $85   2P: $95   XP: $10   F12
♦♦♦ ♦♦   **Location:** Downtown; between Alabama and Delaware sts. 230 E 9th St 46204. Fax: 317/262-8648. **Facility:** 79
            one-bedroom standard units with kitchens. 6 stories, interior corridors. **Parking:** on-site. **Terms:** 3 day can-
            cellation notice-fee imposed. **Amenities:** voice mail, irons. **Guest Services:** coin laundry. **Business Serv-**
Historic Apartment **ices:** fax (fee). **Cards:** AX, DC, DS, MC, VI. *(See ad below & color ad card insert)*

SOME UNITS
[icons] / [icons] /

RESIDENCE INN INDIANAPOLIS ON THE CANAL   Phone: (317)822-0840   **4**
(AAA) (SAVE)   All Year [ECP]   1P: $129-$199
♦♦♦ ♦♦   **Location:** Downtown; at New York St and Senate Ave. 350 W New York St 46202. Fax: 317/822-0848. **Facility:** 134
            units. 58 one-bedroom standard units. 63 one- and 13 two-bedroom suites ($199-$289). 5 stories, interior
Extended Stay corridors. *Bath:* combo or shower only. **Parking:** on-site (fee). **Terms:** check-in 4 pm, pets ($50 fee, $5 extra
Apartment   charge). **Amenities:** extended cable TV, video games, voice mail, irons, hair dryers. **Pool(s):** heated indoor.
            Leisure Activities: whirlpool, exercise room, billiards and poker table. **Guest Services:** complimentary
            evening beverages: Mon-Thurs, coin laundry. **Business Services:** meeting rooms, fax (fee). **Cards:** AX, CB,
DC, DS, JC, MC, VI. *(See color ad card insert)*

SOME UNITS
[icons] FEE ... / [icons]

(See map p. 461)

THE WESTIN INDIANAPOLIS

[AAA] [SAVE]

▼▼▼▼

Hotel

All Year | 1P: $135 | 2P: $135 | XP: $30 | Phone: (317)262-8100 [10] F18

Location: At Washington, Maryland and Capitol aves; adjacent to Hoosier Dome and Convention Center. 50 S Capitol Ave 46204. Fax: 317/231-3928. **Facility:** Modern full service hotel convenient to the Capitol, convention center and shopping. Upscale public areas and guest rooms. 573 units. 541 one-bedroom standard units. 32 one-bedroom suites ($215-$1000), some with whirlpools. 15 stories, interior corridors. *Bath:* combo or shower only. **Parking:** *Fee:* on-site and valet. **Terms:** package plans. **Amenities:** dual phone lines, voice mail, safes, irons, hair dryers. *Some:* CD players, fax, honor bars. **Dining:** restaurant, 6:30 am-2 & 5-10:30 pm, Fri & Sat-11 pm, $25-$50, cocktails. **Pool(s):** heated indoor. **Leisure Activities:** whirlpool, exercise room. **Guest Services:** gift shop, valet laundry. **Business Services:** conference facilities, business center. *Fee:* PC, fax. **Cards:** AX, CB, DC, DS, JC, MC, VI. **Special Amenities:** early check-in/late check-out and free newspaper.

SOME UNITS

[icons] 🍴 24🛎 🍸 🏋 🖇 ✏ 🌊 🐾 🛎 DATA PORT 💻 🖨 / ✕ 🖪 /
FEE   FEE   FEE

─────── **WHERE TO DINE** ───────

40 WEST COFFEE CAFE

▼▼▼

American

Lunch: $4-$10 | Phone: 317/686-1414 [13]

Location: Opposite Union Station; in Omni Severin Hotel. 40 W Jackson Place 46225. **Hours:** 6 am-6 pm, Sun-noon. **Features:** casual dress; carryout. Get comfortable in the casual atmosphere of the trendy cafe, and enjoy gourmet coffees, including cappuccino, latte, mocha and espresso. The menu lists a delicious array of meatless choices mingled with salads, sandwiches, breads and desserts. **Parking:** on-site. **Cards:** AX, CB, DC, DS, MC, VI.

✕

ALCATRAZ BREWING COMPANY

◈◈ ◈◈
▼▼ ▼▼

American

Lunch: $7-$10 | Dinner: $12-$20 | Phone: 317/488-1230 [2]

Location: In Circle Centre Mall. 49 W Maryland St 46204. **Hours:** 11 am-11 pm, Fri & Sat-midnight, Sun 11 am-8 pm. Closed: 11/28, 12/25. **Reservations:** accepted. **Features:** casual dress; cocktails & lounge; a la carte. Seafood, gourmet pasta, sandwiches and salad are complimented with many home brews. The hard, stark prison environment with sheet metal tables and bars on the booths is contrasted with bright neon and lively background music. Trendy Southwest cuisine with California influences include organic salad with beer-mustard dressing, blacken chicken caesar salad, crab cakes, and football sized calzone. Located at street entrance to Circle Centre Mall. **Parking:** on-site (fee). **Cards:** AX, DC, DS, MC, VI.

✕

BAZBEAUX PIZZA

▼▼▼

Italian

Lunch: $5-$20 | Dinner: $5-$20 | Phone: 317/636-7662 [7]

Location: Downtown; just w of 5 points. 334 Massachusetts Ave 46202. **Hours:** 11 am-10 pm, Fri & Sat-11 pm, Sun 4:30 pm-10 pm. Closed major holidays. **Features:** carryout; beer & wine only. Specialty pizza in the theatre district. Visitors are greeted with unique hand painted murals, and mannequins in fish-net stockings. Specialty pizza, tchoupitoulas, mufalettas, baguettes. Unique ingredients. Located in an area of quaint shops just a few blocks north of downtown. **Parking:** street. **Cards:** MC, VI.

✕

THE CALIFORNIA CAFE BAR & GRILL

▼▼▼▼

West American

Lunch: $7-$14 | Dinner: $12-$25 | Phone: 317/488-8686 [3]

Location: In Circle Centre Mall. 49 W Maryland St 46204. **Hours:** 11 am-4 & 5-10 pm, Fri 5 pm-10:30 pm, Sat 4 pm-10:30 pm, Sun 11 am-8 pm. Closed: 11/28, 12/25. **Reservations:** accepted. **Features:** casual dress; Sunday brunch; carryout; cocktails & lounge; a la carte. Here, members will find Californian cuisine with Mediterranean influences served in a modern and bright setting. The restaurant has high ceilings, soft white drapes and contemporary artsy decor. Wide ranging selections include roasted garlic appetizers, buffalo bratwurst, osterich burgers, gourmet pizza and a wide selection of wine. Located on the third level of the Circle Center Mall adjacent to the food court. Smoke free premises. **Parking:** on-site (fee). **Cards:** AX, DC, DS, MC, VI.

✕

THE MAJESTIC RESTAURANT   Historical

▼▼▼▼

Seafood

Lunch: $8-$18 | Dinner: $13-$39 | Phone: 317/636-5418 [11]

Location: Downtown; at Pennsylvania and Maryland sts. 47 S Pennsylvania St 46204. **Hours:** 11 am-2 & 5-9:30 pm, Sat from 5 pm. Closed major holidays; also Sun. **Reservations:** accepted. **Features:** dressy casual; cocktails. The 1895 Romanesque former office building was the first skyscraper in Indianapolis. The decor and ambience evoke the feel of the early 1900s. An extensive list of wines and cordials complements thoughtful preparations of seafood and steak. **Parking:** on-site (fee). **Cards:** AX, CB, DC, DS, MC, VI.

✕

THE MILANO INN RESTAURANT

▼▼▼▼

Italian

Lunch: $5-$8 | Dinner: $9-$17 | Phone: 317/264-3585 [12]

Location: Downtown; between Louisiana and Georgia sts. 231 S College Ave 46202. **Hours:** 11 am-10 pm, Fri & Sat-11 pm, Sun 4 pm-9 pm. Closed major holidays. **Reservations:** suggested. **Features:** casual dress; children's menu; carryout; cocktails & lounge. The long-established restaurant with an easygoing atmosphere delivers a menu of traditional pasta, chicken and veal dishes. Several American choices, mostly sandwiches, are also good. Some desserts, including the must try cheesecake, are made in-house. **Parking:** on-site. **Cards:** AX, DC, DS, MC, VI.

✕

PALOMINO

▼▼▼▼

Continental

Lunch: $7-$16 | Dinner: $14-$30 | Phone: 317/974-0400 [4]

Location: At jct Maryland and Illinois sts. 49 W Maryland, #189 46203. **Hours:** 11:15 am-2:30 & 5-10 pm, Fri & Sat noon-3 & 5-11 pm. Closed major holidays; also Sun. **Reservations:** accepted. **Features:** dressy casual; children's menu; carryout; cocktails & lounge; a la carte. Hand-blown glass, dark wood millwork and Italian marble decorate the trendy dining spot. Mediterranean influences infuse dishes of Italian, Spanish and French cuisine. The applewood-grilled king salmon is served with artichoke tartar and fresh greens. **Parking:** street. **Cards:** AX, CB, DC, DS, MC, VI.

✕

QUEEN OF SHEBA

▼▼ ▼▼

Ethiopian

Lunch: $10-$15 | Dinner: $10-$15 | Phone: 317/638-8426 [5]

Location: At Blake St, just s of 10th St and Indiana University Medical Center. 936 Indiana Ave 46202. **Hours:** 11 am-2 & 5-9:30 pm, Fri-10 pm, Sat 4 pm-10 pm. Closed: Sun & Mon. **Reservations:** suggested. **Features:** casual dress; carryout; beer & wine only. An attentive staff of servers in cultural clothing deliver rich East African entrees of chicken, beef and lamb, served in the traditional style on low tables and chairs. All meals, which are served with thin, rolled-up bread, are eaten as finger foods. **Parking:** on-site. **Cards:** AX, DS, MC, VI.

✕

(See map p. 461)

THE RESTAURANT AT THE CANTERBURY HOTEL   **Lunch:** $7-$13   **Dinner:** $15-$25   **Phone:** 317/634-3000   ⑩
▼▲▼▲▼ ▼▲▼▲▼   **Location:** Downtown; between Georgia and Maryland sts; in Canterbury Hotel. 123 S Illinois St 46225.
Hours: 7-10:30 am, 11-2 & 5-10 pm, Fri & Sat 5 pm-11 pm. **Reservations:** suggested; for dinner.
Continental   **Features:** dressy casual; Sunday brunch; cocktails & lounge; a la carte. This is a cozy, intimate and refined restaurant with an exciting menu. Highlights include oven baked Pacific white bass with grilled duck and seville orange sausage, bouillabaisee with seafood, shellfish, garlic, safron and vermouth. Like a classic English dining room, the walls are covered in rich woods and framed art. The tables have starched white linens, elegant stemware, candles, flowers and brilliant ceramic china. Smoke free premises. **Parking:** on-site (fee) and valet. **Cards:** AX, CB, DC, DS, JC, MC, VI.   ⊗

SHAPIRO'S DELICATESSEN & CAFETERIA   **Lunch:** $5-$10   **Dinner:** $5-$10   **Phone:** 317/631-4041   ⑭
▼▲▼   **Location:** I-70, exit 79B (McCarty St), then w; at S Meridian and McCarty sts. 808 S Meridian St 46225. **Hours:** 6:30
American   am-8:30 pm. **Features:** casual dress; carryout; beer only; a la carte. Baked chicken, meatloaf and corned beef and cabbage are among familiar homemade favorites at the exceptionally popular cafeteria style restaurant, which boasts an equally bustling delicatessen. Prices are reasonable and serving sizes are plentiful. **Parking:** on-site.   ⊗

———— *The following restaurants have not been evaluated by AAA* ————
but are listed for your information only.

RATHSKELLER   **Phone:** 317/636-0396
ⓕⓨⓘ   Not evaluated. **Location:** In the Athenaeum Building. 401 E Michigan St 46204. German and American cuisines are served in the historic Athenaeum Building.

ST. ELMO STEAK HOUSE   **Phone:** 317/637-1811
ⓕⓨⓘ   Not evaluated. **Location:** 127 S Illinois St. The turn-of-the-20th-century-themed restaurant specializes in steak and fresh seafood.

INDIANAPOLIS pop. 731,300   (See map p. 463; index p. 464)

———— **WHERE TO STAY** ————

ADAM'S MARK HOTEL INDIANAPOLIS AIRPORT   **Phone:** (317)248-2481   ⑨⑨
ⒶⒶ Ⓢ̲Ⓐ̲V̲E̲   All Year   1P: $145-$189   2P: $165-$209   XP: $20   F17
▼▲▼ ▼▲▼   **Location:** I-465, exit 11B, just e on Airport Expwy at Executive Dr exit. 2544 Executive Dr 46241. **Fax:** 317/381-6159.
Hotel   **Facility:** 407 one-bedroom standard units. 6 stories, interior corridors. *Bath:* combo or shower only. **Parking:** on-site. **Terms:** check-in 4 pm, cancellation fee imposed, package plans. **Amenities:** voice mail, irons, hair dryers. *Fee:* video games, Web TV. **Dining:** dining room, restaurant, 6 am-midnight, $7-$26, cocktails, entertainment. **Pool(s):** heated outdoor. **Leisure Activities:** limited exercise equipment. **Guest Services:** gift shop, valet and coin laundry. **Business Services:** conference facilities, business center. *Fee:* PC, fax. **Cards:** AX, CB, DC, DS, MC, VI. **Special Amenities: early check-in/late check-out and preferred room (subject to availability with advanced reservations).**
SOME UNITS
Ⓢ̲D̲ ⊹⊱ ⑪ Ⓨ ⊕ ⊘ ➳ 🕭 🄳🄰🅃🄰🄿🄾🅁🅃 ▢ 🖨 / ⊗ 🛢 /
FEE

AMERISUITES (INDIANAPOLIS/AIRPORT)   **Phone:** (317)227-0950   ㊲
ⒶⒶ Ⓢ̲Ⓐ̲V̲E̲   All Year   1P: $89-$235   2P: $89-$235
▼▲▼ ▼▲▼   **Location:** I-465, exit 11A, 0.3 mi e on Airport Expwy to Executive Dr exit. 5500 Bradbury Ave 46241.
Motel   **Fax:** 317/227-0952. **Facility:** 135 one-bedroom standard units. 6 stories, interior corridors. **Parking:** on-site. **Terms:** package plans, small pets only. **Amenities:** extended cable TV, dual phone lines, voice mail, irons, hair dryers. **Pool(s):** heated outdoor. **Leisure Activities:** exercise room. **Guest Services:** valet and coin laundry, area transportation-within 5 mi. **Business Services:** conference facilities, fax (fee). **Cards:** AX, CB, DC, DS, MC, VI. **Special Amenities: free continental breakfast and free newspaper.** *(See color ad p 468)*
SOME UNITS
Ⓢ̲D̲ ⊹⊱ 🛏 ⓜ ⊘ ➳ 🕭 🄳🄰🅃🄰🄿🄾🅁🅃 🛢 🖨 ▢ 🖨 / ⊗ /

AMERISUITES (INDIANAPOLIS/KEYSTONE)   **Phone:** (317)843-0064   ㊼
ⒶⒶ Ⓢ̲Ⓐ̲V̲E̲   All Year   1P: $99-$109   2P: $99-$109   XP: $10   F18
▼▲▼ ▼▲▼   **Location:** I-465, exit 33, 0.5 mi s on SR 431, just e on 86th St, then 0.5 mi n. 9104 Keystone Crossing 46240.
Suite Motel   **Fax:** 317/843-1851. **Facility:** 126 one-bedroom suites with efficiencies. 6 stories, interior corridors. *Bath:* combo or shower only. **Parking:** on-site. **Terms:** package plans, small pets only. **Amenities:** high-speed Internet (fee), voice mail, irons, hair dryers. *Some:* dual phone lines. **Pool(s):** heated outdoor. **Leisure Activities:** exercise room. **Guest Services:** valet and coin laundry. **Business Services:** meeting rooms, business center. *Fee:* PC, fax. **Cards:** AX, CB, DC, DS, JC, MC, VI. **Special Amenities: free continental breakfast and free newspaper.** *(See color ad p 468)*
SOME UNITS
Ⓢ̲D̲ 🛏 ⑪ ⊕ ⊘ ➳ Ⓥ̲C̲R̲ 🕭 🄳🄰🅃🄰🄿🄾🅁🅃 🛢 🖨 ▢ 🖨 / ⊗ /

BAYMONT INN & SUITES INDIANAPOLIS-AIRPORT   **Phone:** (317)244-8100   �97
Ⓐ Ⓢ̲Ⓐ̲V̲E̲   All Year   1P: $69-$84   2P: $69-$84
▼▲▼ ▼▲▼   **Location:** I-465, exit 11, 0.3 mi e. 2650 Executive Dr 46241. **Fax:** 317/241-5136. **Facility:** 97 units. 94 one-
Motel   bedroom standard units. 3 one-bedroom suites ($84-$134), some with kitchens. 3 stories, interior corridors. **Parking:** on-site. **Terms:** pets ($50 deposit). **Amenities:** video games (fee), voice mail, irons, hair dryers. **Leisure Activities:** limited exercise equipment. **Guest Services:** valet laundry. **Business Services:** meeting rooms, fax (fee). **Cards:** AX, CB, DC, DS, MC, VI. **Special Amenities: free continental breakfast and free newspaper.** *(See color ad opposite title page)*
SOME UNITS
Ⓢ̲D̲ 🛏 ⑪ ⊘ 🕭 🄳🄰🅃🄰🄿🄾🅁🅃 ▢ 🖨 / ⊗ 🛢 🖨 /
FEE

(See map p. 463)

BAYMONT INN & SUITES-INDIANAPOLIS EAST   Phone: (317)897-2300   85
AAA SAVE   All Year   1P: $79-$89   2P: $79-$89
       Location: I-70, exit 91 (Post Rd), just n. 2349 Post Dr 46219. Fax: 317/897-2266. Facility: 102 units. 99 one-
              bedroom standard units, some with kitchens. 3 one-bedroom suites ($89-$144). 4 stories, interior corridors.
Motel   Bath: combo or shower only. Parking: on-site. Terms: small pets only ($50 deposit). Amenities: video
              games (fee), voice mail, irons, hair dryers. Guest Services: valet and coin laundry. Business Services:
              meeting rooms, fax (fee). Cards: AX, CB, DC, DS, MC, VI. Special Amenities: free continental breakfast
and free newspaper. (See color ad opposite title page)
                                                                                         SOME UNITS

BEST INNS   Phone: (317)788-0811   104
              All Year   1P: $45-$65   2P: $45-$65
Motel   Location: I-465, exit 2B. 450 Bixler Rd 46227. Fax: 317/788-0143. Facility: 103 one-bedroom standard units. 2
              stories, interior corridors. Parking: on-site. Terms: 14 day cancellation notice, pets ($10 fee).
              Amenities: video games (fee). Some: dual phone lines. Pool(s): outdoor, wading. Guest Services: coin
laundry. Business Services: meeting rooms, fax (fee). Cards: AX, CB, DC, DS, MC, VI.
                                                                                         SOME UNITS

BEST WESTERN CASTLETON INN   Phone: (317)842-9190   52
AAA SAVE   All Year   1P: $69-$89   2P: $76-$96   XP: $7   F17
              Location: I-69, exit 1, 0.5 mi w to Craig St, then just n. 8300 Craig St 46250. Fax: 317/577-1599. Facility: 114 one-
              bedroom standard units. 3 stories, interior corridors. Parking: on-site. Terms: 10 day cancellation notice,
Motel   pets ($25 fee). Amenities: video games (fee), irons, hair dryers. Pool(s): outdoor. Guest Services: valet
              laundry. Business Services: meeting rooms, fax (fee). Cards: AX, CB, DC, DS, MC, VI. Special Amenities:
              free continental breakfast and free local telephone calls.
                                                                                         SOME UNITS

BEST WESTERN SOUTH   Phone: (317)888-5588   115
AAA SAVE   All Year   1P: $79-$99   2P: $79-$99
              Location: I-65, exit 103, just w. 4450 Southport Crossing Dr 46237. Fax: 317/888-5588. Facility: 65 one-bedroom
Motel   standard units, some with whirlpools. 2 stories, interior corridors. Bath: combo or shower only. Parking: on-
              site. Terms: package plans. Amenities: extended cable TV, hair dryers. Some: irons. Pool(s): heated indoor.
              Leisure Activities: limited exercise equipment. Business Services: fax (fee). Cards: AX, CB, DC, DS,
              MC, VI. Special Amenities: free continental breakfast and free local telephone calls.
                                                                                         SOME UNITS

(See map p. 463)

BEST WESTERN WATERFRONT PLAZA HOTEL   Phone: (317)299-8400   [73]
(AAA) [SAVE]   4/1-10/31   1P: $58-$125   2P: $58-$125   XP: $6   F18
               1/1-3/31   1P: $60-$110   2P: $60-$110   XP: $6   F18
◆◆◆ ◆◆   11/1-12/31   1P: $56-$99   2P: $56-$99   XP: $6   F18
Motel   **Location:** I-465, exit 16A, 0.3 mi se, 0.8 mi w on US 136. 2930 Waterfront Pkwy W Dr 46214. **Fax:** 317/299-9257. **Facility:** 143 one-bedroom standard units. 2-3 stories, interior corridors. **Parking:** on-site. **Terms:** [BP] & [ECP] meal plans available. **Amenities:** voice mail, irons, hair dryers. **Dining:** coffee shop, 6:30-10:30 am, Sat & Sun from 7 am. **Pool(s):** heated indoor. **Leisure Activities:** whirlpool. **Guest Services:** valet laundry. **Business Services:** conference facilities, business center, PC, fax (fee). **Cards:** AX, DC, DS, MC, VI. **Special Amenities:** free local telephone calls and free newspaper.

SOME UNITS

CLARION INN & SUITES   Phone: (317)298-3700   [69]
(AAA) [SAVE]   All Year [ECP]   1P: $76-$85   2P: $83-$92   XP: $7   F18
◆◆◆ ◆◆   **Location:** I-465, exit 21, just se. 7001 Corporate Dr 46278. **Fax:** 317/298-9080. **Facility:** 67 units. 65 one-bedroom standard units, some with whirlpools. 2 one-bedroom suites ($102-$200) with whirlpools. 2 stories, interior corridors. **Bath:** combo or shower only. **Parking:** on-site. **Terms:** [CP] meal plan available, package plans.
Motel   **Amenities:** voice mail, irons, hair dryers. **Pool(s):** small heated indoor. **Leisure Activities:** whirlpool, exercise room. **Guest Services:** valet and coin laundry. **Business Services:** meeting rooms, business center, PC, fax (fee). **Cards:** AX, CB, DC, DS, JC, MC, VI. **Special Amenities:** free continental breakfast and free local telephone calls.

SOME UNITS

COMFORT INN-EAST   Phone: (317)359-9999   [79]
[SAVE]   All Year [ECP]   1P: $75-$250   2P: $85-$250   XP: $10   F17
◆◆◆ ◆◆   **Location:** I-70, exit 89, 0.5 mi w of jct I-465. 7015 Western Select Dr 46219. **Fax:** 317/359-3115. **Facility:** 73 one-bedroom standard units. 4 stories, interior corridors. **Bath:** combo or shower only. **Parking:** on-site.
Motel   **Terms:** 15 day cancellation notice. **Amenities:** Some: irons, hair dryers. **Pool(s):** small heated indoor. **Business Services:** fax (fee). **Cards:** AX, CB, DC, DS, JC, MC, VI.

SOME UNITS

COMFORT INN-NORTH   Phone: (317)872-3100   [36]
[SAVE]   4/1-10/15 [CP]   1P: $70-$129   2P: $70-$129   XP: $5   F17
◆◆◆ ◆◆   10/16-3/31 [CP]   1P: $50-$99   2P: $50-$99   XP: $5   F17
Motel   **Location:** I-465, exit 27, just s. 3880 W 92nd St 46268. **Fax:** 317/872-3100. **Facility:** 58 one-bedroom standard units. 3 stories, interior corridors. **Parking:** on-site. **Terms:** 30 day cancellation notice-fee imposed, small pets only ($10 fee). **Amenities:** extended cable TV. **Pool(s):** small heated indoor. **Leisure Activities:** whirlpool. **Guest Services:** valet laundry. **Business Services:** fax (fee). **Cards:** AX, DC, DS, MC, VI.

SOME UNITS
FEE

COMFORT INN-WEST   Phone: (317)487-9800   [91]
(AAA) [SAVE]   All Year [ECP]   1P: $97-$99   2P: $97-$99   XP: $5   F18
◆◆◆ ◆◆   **Location:** I-465, exit 13A, just e. 5855 Rockville Rd 46224. **Fax:** 317/487-1125. **Facility:** 94 units. 82 one-bedroom standard units, some with whirlpools. 12 one-bedroom suites ($125-$200) with whirlpools. 4 stories, interior corridors. **Bath:** combo or shower only. **Parking:** on-site. **Terms:** package plans. **Amenities:** voice mail, irons. Some: hair dryers. **Pool(s):** heated indoor. **Leisure Activities:** whirlpool, play room for small children, exercise room. **Guest Services:** valet and coin laundry. **Business Services:** meeting rooms, fax (fee).
Motel   **Cards:** AX, CB, DC, DS, JC, MC, VI. **Special Amenities:** free continental breakfast and free local telephone calls.

SOME UNITS
FEE

COUNTRY INN & SUITES BY CARLSON-INDIANAPOLIS NORTH   Phone: (317)876-0333   [25]
◆◆◆ ◆◆   All Year   1P: $78-$159   2P: $78-$159   XP: $6   F18
Motel   **Location:** I-465, exit 27, 0.3 mi n on US 421. 46032 N Michigan Rd (9797 N Michigan Rd, CARMEL). **Fax:** 317/876-1312. **Facility:** 66 units. 51 one-bedroom standard units, some with whirlpools. 15 one-bedroom suites ($89-$159). 3 stories, interior corridors. **Bath:** combo or shower only. **Parking:** on-site. **Terms:** small pets only ($25 extra charge). **Amenities:** voice mail, irons, hair dryers. **Pool(s):** small heated indoor. **Leisure Activities:** whirlpool, limited exercise equipment. **Guest Services:** valet and coin laundry. **Business Services:** meeting rooms, fax (fee). **Cards:** AX, CB, DC, DS, MC, VI. *(See color ad p 476)*

SOME UNITS
FEE

COURTYARD BY MARRIOTT-AIRPORT   Phone: (317)248-0300   [102]
(AAA) [SAVE]   8/11-12/7   1P: $119   2P: $119
               4/1-8/10   1P: $114   2P: $114
◆◆◆ ◆◆   12/8-3/31   1P: $109   2P: $109
Motor Inn   **Location:** I-465, exit 11A, 0.3 mi e on Airport Expwy to Executive Dr exit. 5525 Fortune Cir E 46241. **Fax:** 317/248-1834. **Facility:** 151 units. 141 one-bedroom standard units. 10 one-bedroom suites ($139-$169). 4 stories, interior corridors. **Bath:** combo or shower only. **Parking:** on-site. **Terms:** package plans.
Amenities: high-speed Internet (fee), dual phone lines, voice mail, irons, hair dryers. **Dining:** coffee shop, 6-10 am, 11-2 & 4:30-9:30 pm, Fri 6 am-10 & 11-2 pm, Sat 7-11 am, Sun 7 am-11 & 4:30-9:30 pm, cocktails. **Pool(s):** heated indoor. **Leisure Activities:** whirlpool, exercise room. **Guest Services:** valet and coin laundry. **Business Services:** meeting rooms, fax (fee). **Cards:** AX, CB, DC, DS, MC, VI. *(See color ad card insert)*

SOME UNITS
FEE

(See map p. 463)

COURTYARD BY MARRIOTT-INDIANAPOLIS NORTH/CARMEL   Phone: (317)571-1110 🟠40

AAA SAVE All Year   1P: $69-$104   2P: $69-$104

▽▽▽▽ **Location:** I-465, exit 31 (Meridian St), 0.3 mi n on US 31. 10290 N Meridian St 46290. Fax: 317/571-0416.
Facility: 149 units. 137 one-bedroom standard units. 12 one-bedroom suites ($109-$139). 4 stories, interior

Motel   corridors. *Bath:* combo or shower only. **Parking:** on-site. **Terms:** package plans. **Amenities:** high-speed Internet, voice mail, irons, hair dryers. **Dining:** coffee shop, 6-10 am, Sat & Sun 7 am-noon. **Pool(s):** heated indoor. **Leisure Activities:** whirlpool, sun deck, exercise room. **Guest Services:** gift shop, coin laundry.
Business Services: meeting rooms, business center, fax (fee). **Cards:** AX, DC, DS, MC, VI. *(See color ad card insert)*

SOME UNITS

🆂🅳 🍴 🍸 📶 🐾 🏊 ✖ 🎥 | 📠 📇 / ✖ 🆅🅲🆁 🔌 🖥 /
                    FEE

COURTYARD BY MARRIOTT INDIANAPOLIS SOUTH   Phone: 317/885-9799 🟠114

AAA SAVE All Year   1P: $69-$94   2P: $69-$94

▽▽▽▽ **Location:** I-65, exit 103. 4650 Southport Crossing Dr 46237. Fax: 317/885-3982. **Facility:** 83 units. 80 one-bedroom standard units, some with whirlpools. 3 one-bedroom suites ($89-$139). 3 stories, interior corridors.

Motel   *Bath:* combo or shower only. **Parking:** on-site. **Amenities:** voice mail, irons, hair dryers. *Fee:* video games, high-speed Internet. **Dining:** coffee shop, 6:30-9:30 am, Sat & Sun 7-10 am.
Pool(s): heated indoor. **Leisure Activities:** whirlpool, limited exercise equipment. **Guest Services:** coin laundry. **Business Services:** meeting rooms, fax (fee). **Cards:** AX, CB, DC, DS, JC, MC, VI. *(See color ad card insert)*

SOME UNITS

🆂🅳 🍴 🍸 📶 📶 📶 🐾 🏊 ✖ 🎥 🔌 🖥 📠 / ✖ 🔌 🖥 /
                    FEE

COURTYARD BY MARRIOTT-NORTHWEST   Phone: (317)297-7700 🟠32

AAA SAVE All Year   1P: $95   2P: $95

▽▽▽▽ **Location:** I-465, exit 21. 7226 Woodland Dr 46278. Fax: 317/387-1628. **Facility:** 90 units. 87 one-bedroom standard units, some with whirlpools. 3 one-bedroom suites ($135). 3 stories, interior corridors. **Parking:** on-site.
Amenities: video games (fee), dual phone lines, voice mail, irons, hair dryers. **Dining:** coffee shop, 6:30-10

Motel   am, Sat & Sun 7-11 am. **Leisure Activities:** whirlpool, limited exercise equipment. **Guest Services:** valet and coin laundry. **Business Services:** meeting rooms, fax (fee). **Cards:** AX, DC, DS, MC, VI.

(See color ad card insert)

SOME UNITS

🆂🅳 🍴 📶 📶 📶 🐾 🎥 🔌 🖥 📠 / ✖ 🔌 🖥 /
                    FEE   FEE FEE

(See map p. 463)

DAYS INN AIRPORT

SAVE

Motor Inn

Phone: (317)248-0621 [100]

| | | | | F18 |
All Year   1P: $65-$75   2P: $70-$80   XP: $5

Location: I-465, exit 11A, 0.3 mi e on Airport Expwy to Executive Dr exit. 5860 Fortune Cir W 46241. Fax: 317/247-7637. **Facility:** 238 units. 237 one-bedroom standard units. 1 one-bedroom suite. 7 stories, interior corridors. **Parking:** on-site. **Terms:** package plans. **Amenities:** hair dryers. **Pool(s):** outdoor. **Leisure Activities:** limited exercise equipment. **Guest Services:** valet and coin laundry. **Business Services:** meeting rooms, fax (fee). **Cards:** AX, CB, DC, DS, MC, VI.

SOME UNITS

DAYS INN & SUITES

SAVE

Motel

Phone: (317)841-9700 [53]

All Year   1P: $59   2P: $64   XP: $5   F12

Location: I-69, exit 1, 0.5 mi w to Craig St, then just n. 8275 Craig St 46250. Fax: 317/576-0795. **Facility:** 161 units. 132 one-bedroom standard units. 29 one-bedroom suites ($85-$105). 2 stories, interior corridors. **Parking:** on-site. **Terms:** [ECP] meal plan available, small pets only ($25 fee). **Amenities:** extended cable TV, safes (fee), hair dryers. **Leisure Activities:** limited exercise equipment. **Guest Services:** coin laundry. **Business Services:** meeting rooms, fax (fee). **Cards:** AX, CB, DC, DS, MC, VI.

SOME UNITS

DOUBLETREE GUEST SUITES

AAA SAVE

Suite Motor Inn

Phone: (317)844-7994 [39]

| | | |
4/1-10/31   1P: $99   2P: $109   XP: $10
11/1-3/31   1P: $89   2P: $99   XP: $10

Location: I-465, exit 31, 1 mi n. 11355 N Meridian St 46032. Fax: 317/844-2118. **Facility:** 137 one-bedroom suites. 3 stories, interior corridors. *Bath:* combo or shower only. **Parking:** on-site, winter plug-ins. **Terms:** cancellation fee imposed, package plans. **Amenities:** voice mail, irons, hair dryers. **Pool(s):** heated indoor/outdoor. **Leisure Activities:** whirlpool, exercise room. **Guest Services:** coin laundry. **Business Services:** meeting rooms, fax (fee). **Cards:** AX, CB, DC, DS, MC, VI. *(See ad below)*

SOME UNITS

DRURY INN-INDIANAPOLIS

Motel

Phone: (317)876-9777 [35]

All Year [ECP]   1P: $62-$95   2P: $62-$95   XP: $10   F18

Location: I-465, exit 27, just s. 9320 N Michigan Rd 46268. Fax: 317/876-9777. **Facility:** 110 one-bedroom standard units. 4 stories, interior corridors. **Parking:** on-site. **Amenities:** voice mail, irons, hair dryers. **Pool(s):** outdoor. **Guest Services:** complimentary evening beverages: Mon-Thurs, valet and coin laundry. **Business Services:** meeting rooms, fax (fee). **Cards:** AX, CB, DC, DS, MC, VI. *(See color ad p 5)*

SOME UNITS

EMBASSY SUITES HOTEL-NORTH

SAVE

Suite Hotel

Phone: (317)872-7700 [57]

All Year [BP]   1P: $119-$199   2P: $119-$214   XP: $15   F18

Location: I-465, exit 27, 0.5 mi s of US 421, then just w. 3912 Vincennes Rd 46268-3024. Fax: 317/872-2974. **Facility:** 221 one-bedroom suites. 8 stories, interior corridors. **Parking:** on-site. **Terms:** cancellation fee imposed, package plans. **Amenities:** video games (fee), voice mail, irons, hair dryers. **Pool(s):** heated indoor. **Leisure Activities:** sauna, whirlpool, limited exercise equipment. **Guest Services:** complimentary evening beverages, valet laundry. **Business Services:** conference facilities, business center, PC (fee), fax. **Cards:** AX, CB, DC, DS, JC, MC, VI.

SOME UNITS

EXTENDED STAY AMERICA NORTHWEST

Extended Stay Motel

Phone: 317/872-3090 [59]

Property failed to provide current rates

Location: I-465, exit 27, s on US 421. 9030 Wesleyan Rd 46268. Fax: 317/471-6262. **Facility:** 72 one-bedroom standard units with efficiencies. 3 stories, interior corridors. **Parking:** on-site. **Amenities:** extended cable TV, voice mail. **Guest Services:** coin laundry. **Business Services:** fax (fee). **Cards:** AX, CB, DC, DS, JC, MC, VI.

SOME UNITS

(See map p. 463)

FAIRFIELD INN BY MARRIOTT-CASTLETON
Phone: (317)577-0455   **55**

AAA SAVE   All Year [CP]   1P: $44-$64   2P: $44-$64
◇◇◇   **Location:** I-69, exit 1, just w. 8325 Bash Rd 46250. Fax: 317/577-0455. **Facility:** 132 one-bedroom standard
Motel   units. 3 stories, interior/exterior corridors. *Bath:* combo or shower only. **Parking:** on-site. **Amenities:** irons.
Pool(s): heated outdoor. **Guest Services:** valet laundry. **Business Services:** fax (fee). **Cards:** AX, CB, DC,
DS, MC, VI. **Special Amenities: free continental breakfast and free local telephone calls.**
(See color ad card insert)

SOME UNITS

[icons]   FEE   FEE

FAIRFIELD INN BY MARRIOTT-COLLEGE PARK
Phone: (317)879-9100   **46**

AAA SAVE   All Year   1P: $49-$149
◇◇◇   **Location:** I-465, exit 27, just s, then just e on Depaw Blvd. 9251 Wesleyan Rd 46268. Fax: 317/879-0016.
  Facility: 132 one-bedroom standard units. 3 stories, interior/exterior corridors. *Bath:* combo or shower only.
Motel   **Parking:** on-site. **Amenities:** irons. **Pool(s):** heated outdoor. **Guest Services:** valet laundry. **Business
Services:** fax (fee). **Cards:** AX, DC, DS, MC, VI. **Special Amenities: free continental breakfast and free
local telephone calls.** *(See color ad card insert)*

SOME UNITS

[icons]   FEE

FAIRFIELD INN BY MARRIOTT/INDIANAPOLIS AIRPORT
Phone: 317/244-1600   **96**

AAA SAVE   4/1-11/15   1P: $79-$119
◇◇◇   11/16-3/31   1P: $49-$119
  Location: I-465, exit 11B, 0.5 mi e on Airport Expwy to Lynhurst Dr exit. 5220 W Southern Ave 46241.
  Fax: 317/241-2136. **Facility:** 86 one-bedroom standard units, some with whirlpools. 3 stories, interior corri-
Motel   dors. *Bath:* combo or shower only. **Parking:** on-site. **Amenities:** video games (fee), irons. *Some:* hair dryers.
Pool(s): heated indoor. **Leisure Activities:** limited exercise equipment. **Guest Services:** valet and coin
laundry. **Business Services:** fax (fee). **Cards:** AX, CB, DC, DS, MC, VI. **Special Amenities: free continental breakfast and
free local telephone calls.** *(See color ad card insert)*

SOME UNITS

[icons]   FEE

FOUR POINTS BY SHERATON INDIANAPOLIS EAST
Phone: (317)897-4000   **74**

AAA SAVE   All Year   1P: $69-$99   2P: $69-$99   XP: $10   F12
◇◇◇   **Location:** I-465, exit 42 (Pendleton Pike), just e. 7701 E 42nd St 46226. Fax: 317/897-8100. **Facility:** 190 one-
  bedroom standard units, some with whirlpools. 2 stories, interior corridors. *Bath:* combo or shower only.
Motor Inn   **Parking:** on-site. **Terms:** package plans, small pets only. **Amenities:** extended cable TV, voice mail, irons,
hair dryers. *Fee:* video games, Web TV. *Some:* dual phone lines. **Dining:** restaurant, 6:30 am-midnight, Fri
& Sat-1 am, $9-$15, cocktails. **Pool(s):** outdoor, heated indoor. **Leisure Activities:** sauna, whirlpool, exercise room. **Guest Services:** valet and coin laundry. **Business Services:** conference facilities, business center, PC, fax.
Cards: AX, CB, DC, DS, MC, VI. **Special Amenities: early check-in/late check-out and free newspaper.**

SOME UNITS

[icons]   FEE

HAMPTON INN-EAST
Phone: (317)359-9900   **81**

SAVE   7/1-3/31   1P: $82-$92   2P: $87-$97
◇◇◇   4/1-6/30   1P: $80-$90   2P: $85-$95
Motel   **Location:** I-70, exit 89; 0.5 mi w of jct I-465. 2311 N Shadeland Ave 46219. Fax: 317/359-1376. **Facility:** 123 one-
  bedroom standard units. 4 stories, interior corridors. **Parking:** on-site. **Amenities:** voice mail, irons, hair
dryers. **Pool(s):** heated indoor. **Leisure Activities:** whirlpool, limited exercise equipment, game room. **Guest
Services:** valet laundry. **Business Services:** meeting rooms, fax (fee). **Cards:** AX, CB, DC, DS, MC, VI.

SOME UNITS

[icons]   FEE

HAMPTON INN-INDIANAPOLIS AIRPORT
Phone: (317)244-1221   **101**

AAA SAVE   All Year [CP]   1P: $84-$114   2P: $84-$114
◇◇◇   **Location:** I-465, exit 11A, 0.3 mi e on Airport Expwy to Executive Dr exit. 5601 Fortune Cir W 46241.
  Fax: 317/247-4573. **Facility:** 131 units. 125 one-bedroom standard units. 6 one-bedroom suites ($124-$199).
Motel   4 stories, interior corridors. *Bath:* combo or shower only. **Parking:** on-site. **Terms:** 14 day cancellation no-
tice. **Amenities:** voice mail, irons, hair dryers. **Leisure Activities:** limited exercise equipment. **Guest Serv-
ices:** valet laundry. **Business Services:** meeting rooms, fax (fee). **Cards:** AX, CB, DC, DS, MC, VI.
Special Amenities: free continental breakfast and free local telephone calls. *(See color ad p 470)*

SOME UNITS

[icons]   FEE

HAMPTON INN-NORTHEAST
Phone: (317)576-0220   **65**

SAVE   All Year [CP]   1P: $79-$225   2P: $89-$225   XP: $10   F
◇◇◇   **Location:** I-69, exit 1, just w. 6817 E 82nd St 46250. Fax: 317/849-4338. **Facility:** 129 units. 123 one-bedroom
Motel   standard units. 6 one-bedroom suites ($129-$229). 4 stories, interior corridors. **Parking:** on-site. **Terms:** 30
day cancellation notice-fee imposed. **Amenities:** video games, voice mail, irons, hair dryers. **Pool(s):** heated
indoor. **Guest Services:** valet laundry. **Business Services:** meeting rooms, fax (fee). **Cards:** AX, DC, DS,
MC, VI. *(See ad p 479)*

SOME UNITS

[icons]   FEE

(See map p. 463)

HAMPTON INN-NORTHWEST　　　　　　　　　　　Phone: (317)290-1212　67

[SAVE] ▼▼▼▼
Motel

7/1-3/31　　1P: $82-$92　　2P: $87-$97
4/1-6/30　　1P: $81-$91　　2P: $86-$96
Location: I-465, exit 21. 7220 Woodland Dr 46278. Fax: 317/291-1579. **Facility:** 121 one-bedroom standard units. 4 stories, interior corridors. **Parking:** on-site. **Amenities:** voice mail, irons, hair dryers. **Pool(s):** heated indoor. **Leisure Activities:** whirlpool, limited exercise equipment. *Fee:* game room. **Guest Services:** valet laundry. **Business Services:** meeting rooms, fax (fee). **Cards:** AX, DC, DS, MC, VI.

SOME UNITS

HAMPTON INN SOUTH　　　　　　　　　　　　　Phone: (317)889-0722　103

AAA [SAVE] ▼▼▼▼
Motel

5/1-10/1　　　　　1P: $63-$75　　2P: $72-$84
4/1-4/30 & 10/2-3/31　1P: $54-$66　　2P: $63-$75
Location: I-65, exit 103. 7045 McFarland Blvd 46237. Fax: 317/889-5463. **Facility:** 112 one-bedroom standard units. 4 stories, interior corridors. **Parking:** on-site. **Amenities:** extended cable TV, irons. **Pool(s):** heated indoor. **Leisure Activities:** limited exercise equipment. **Guest Services:** valet laundry. **Business Services:** meeting rooms, fax (fee). **Cards:** AX, CB, DC, DS, JC, MC, VI. **Special Amenities:** free continental breakfast and free local telephone calls.

SOME UNITS

HAWTHORN SUITES EAST　　　　　　　　　　　Phone: (317)322-0011　83

▼▼▼
Motel

All Year [BP]　　1P: $79-$250　　2P: $89-$260　　XP: $10　F17
Location: I-70, exit 89; 0.5 mi w of jct I-465. 7035 Western Select Dr 46219. Fax: 317/322-0033. **Facility:** 90 one-bedroom standard units, some with efficiencies and/or whirlpools. 5 stories, interior corridors. *Bath:* combo or shower only. **Parking:** on-site. **Terms:** small pets only ($150 fee). **Amenities:** video tape library (fee), dual phone lines, voice mail, irons, hair dryers. **Pool(s):** heated indoor. **Leisure Activities:** exercise room, sports court. **Guest Services:** complimentary evening beverages, valet and coin laundry. **Business Services:** meeting rooms, business center, fax (fee). **Cards:** AX, CB, DC, DS, JC, MC, VI.

SOME UNITS

HOLIDAY INN EAST　　　　　　　　　　　　　　Phone: (317)359-5341　80

AAA [SAVE] ▼▼▼▼
Motor Inn

All Year　　1P: $129
Location: I-70, exit 89; 0.5 mi w of jct I-465. 6990 E 21st St 46219. Fax: 317/351-1666. **Facility:** 184 one-bedroom standard units. 6 stories, interior corridors. **Parking:** on-site. **Terms:** 3 day cancellation notice, package plans, small pets only. **Amenities:** video games (fee), voice mail, irons, hair dryers. **Dining:** restaurant, 6 am-11 pm, Fri & Sat-midnight, $6-$18, cocktails. **Leisure Activities:** whirlpool, limited exercise equipment. **Guest Services:** valet and coin laundry. **Business Services:** meeting rooms, fax (fee). **Cards:** AX, CB, DC, DS, MC, VI. **Special Amenities:** free local telephone calls and free newspaper.

SOME UNITS

HOLIDAY INN EXPRESS SOUTH　　　　　　　　Phone: 317/783-5151　51

AAA [SAVE] ▼▼▼▼
Motel

All Year [ECP]　　1P: $89-$109　　2P: $89-$109
Location: I-465, exit 2B, 0.3 mi s. 5151 S East St 46227. Fax: 317/782-4793. **Facility:** 118 one-bedroom standard units, some with whirlpools. 4 stories, interior corridors. *Bath:* combo or shower only. **Parking:** on-site. **Terms:** 7 day cancellation notice, package plans. **Amenities:** video games (fee), voice mail, irons, hair dryers. **Pool(s):** heated indoor. **Leisure Activities:** whirlpool, limited exercise equipment. **Guest Services:** complimentary evening beverages: Tues-Thurs, valet laundry. **Business Services:** meeting rooms, fax (fee). **Cards:** AX, CB, DC, DS, JC, MC, VI. **Special Amenities:** free continental breakfast and free local telephone calls.

SOME UNITS

(See map p. 463)

HOLIDAY INN SELECT AIRPORT
Phone: (317)244-6861 **93**

(AAA) (SAVE)

Hotel

9/19-3/31 [BP]	1P: $179	2P: $179
4/1-9/18 [BP]	1P: $169	2P: $169

Location: I-465, exit 11B; at Indianapolis International Airport. 2501 S High School Rd 46241. Fax: 317/243-1059. **Facility:** 274 units. 268 one-bedroom standard units, some with whirlpools. 6 one-bedroom suites ($199-$229) with whirlpools. 5 stories, interior corridors. **Parking:** on-site. **Terms:** package plans. **Amenities:** video games (fee), voice mail, irons, hair dryers. **Dining:** dining room, restaurant, 6 am-10 pm, Fri & Sat-11 pm, $7-$20, cocktails, also, Chanteclair, see separate listing. **Pool(s):** heated indoor. **Leisure Activities:** saunas, whirlpool, exercise room. **Guest Services:** gift shop, valet laundry. **Business Services:** conference facilities, business center. *Fee:* PC, fax. **Cards:** AX, CB, DC, DS, JC, MC, VI. **Special Amenities: free continental breakfast and free newspaper.**

SOME UNITS

HOLIDAY INN-SELECT NORTH AT THE PYRAMIDS
Phone: (317)872-9790 **38**

(AAA) (SAVE)

Motor Inn

1/1-3/31	1P: $159-$199	2P: $159-$199
4/1-12/31	1P: $149-$185	2P: $149-$185

Location: I-165, exit 27, just s. 3850 De Pauw Blvd 46268. Fax: 317/871-5608. **Facility:** 344 one-bedroom standard units, some with whirlpools. 4-5 stories, interior corridors. **Parking:** on-site. **Terms:** check-in 4 pm, package plans. **Amenities:** video games (fee), voice mail, irons, hair dryers. **Dining:** restaurant, 6 am-2 & 5-10 pm, $15-$24, cocktails, also, San Remo Grille, see separate listing. **Pool(s):** heated indoor. **Leisure Activities:** saunas, whirlpool, putting green, limited exercise equipment, indoor recreation area. **Guest Services:** valet and coin laundry. **Business Services:** conference facilities, business center, PC, fax (fee). **Cards:** AX, CB, DC, DS, JC, MC, VI. **Special Amenities: free local telephone calls and free newspaper.**

SOME UNITS

HOLIDAY INN-SOUTHEAST
Phone: (317)783-7751 **110**

Motor Inn

8/2-10/1	1P: $89-$250	2P: $89-$250	XP: $6	F18
4/1-8/1 & 10/2-3/31	1P: $89-$129	2P: $89-$129	XP: $6	F18

Location: I-465, exit 52 (Emerson Ave). 5120 Victory Dr 46203. Fax: 317/787-1545. **Facility:** 140 one-bedroom standard units. 6 stories, interior corridors. *Bath:* combo or shower only. **Parking:** on-site. **Terms:** 30 day cancellation notice-fee imposed, small pets only. **Amenities:** video games (fee), voice mail, irons, hair dryers. **Pool(s):** heated outdoor. **Leisure Activities:** limited exercise equipment. **Guest Services:** valet and coin laundry. **Business Services:** meeting rooms, fax (fee). **Cards:** AX, CB, DC, DS, JC, MC, VI.

SOME UNITS

INDIANAPOLIS MARRIOTT EAST
Phone: (317)352-1231 **82**

(AAA) (SAVE)

Hotel

All Year	1P: $100	2P: $100	XP: $10	F

Location: I-70, exit 89 (Shadeland Ave), 0.3 mi se; 0.5 mi w of jct I-465. 7202 E 21st St 46219. Fax: 317/352-9775. **Facility:** 253 units. 250 one-bedroom standard units, some with whirlpools. 3 one-bedroom suites ($175-$300) with whirlpools. 3-5 stories, interior corridors. **Parking:** on-site. **Terms:** check-in 4 pm, 3 day cancellation notice-fee imposed, package plans, small pets only (with prior approval). **Amenities:** Web TV (fee), high-speed Internet, voice mail, irons, hair dryers. **Dining:** dining room, 6:30 am-10 pm, $9-$22, cocktails. **Pool(s):** heated indoor/outdoor, wading. **Leisure Activities:** whirlpool, putting green, exercise room. **Guest Services:** gift shop, valet and coin laundry. **Business Services:** conference facilities, business center. *Fee:* PC, fax. **Cards:** AX, CB, DC, DS, JC, MC, VI. *(See color ad card insert)*

SOME UNITS

INDIANAPOLIS MARRIOTT NORTH
Phone: (317)705-0000 **54**

(AAA) (SAVE)

Hotel

All Year	1P: $129-$159	2P: $129-$159

Location: I-465, exit 33, just s to 86th St, then just e; rear of Keystone Mall. 3645 River Crossing Pkwy 46240. Fax: 317/819-1099. **Facility:** 315 one-bedroom standard units. 11 stories, interior corridors. *Bath:* combo or shower only. **Parking:** on-site. **Amenities:** high-speed Internet (fee), dual phone lines, voice mail, irons, hair dryers. **Dining:** restaurant, 6:30 am-2 & 5-10:30 pm, $12-$28, cocktails. **Pool(s):** heated indoor. **Leisure Activities:** whirlpool, exercise room. **Guest Services:** valet laundry. **Business Services:** conference facilities, business center. *Fee:* PC, fax. **Cards:** AX, DC, DS, MC, VI. *(See color ad card insert)*

SOME UNITS

THE INN AT ST. FRANCIS
Phone: 317/865-5575 **63**

Suite Motel

All Year [CP]	1P: $70	2P: $70

Location: I-65, exit 103, just e to Emerson Ave, 1.2 mi s; in St. Francis Hospital Complex. 8111 S Emerson Ave 46237. Fax: 317/865-5584. **Facility:** Smoke free premises. 27 one-bedroom suites ($70). 4 stories, interior corridors. *Bath:* combo or shower only. **Parking:** on-site. **Terms:** check-in 4 pm. **Amenities:** extended cable TV, voice mail, hair dryers. **Business Services:** fax (fee). **Cards:** AX, DS, MC, VI.

SOME UNITS

LA QUINTA INN-AIRPORT
Phone: (317)247-4281 **98**

(SAVE)

Motel

All Year	1P: $90-$112	2P: $100-$122	XP: $10	F18

Location: I-465, exit 11A, 0.5 mi e on Airport Expwy to Lynhurst Dr exit. 5316 W Southern Ave 46241-5510. Fax: 317/247-0576. **Facility:** 121 one-bedroom standard units. 2 stories, interior corridors. **Parking:** on-site. **Terms:** small pets only. **Amenities:** video games (fee), voice mail, irons, hair dryers. **Pool(s):** outdoor. **Guest Services:** valet and coin laundry. **Business Services:** meeting rooms, fax (fee). **Cards:** AX, CB, DC, DS, MC, VI.

SOME UNITS

(See map p. 463)

LA QUINTA INN-EAST
AAA SAVE
△▽△▽△▽
Motel

Phone: (317)359-1021 **88**
All Year 1P: $60-$80 2P: $66-$86 XP: $6 F18
Location: I-70, exit 89 (Shadeland Ave), just s, then just e; 0.5 mi w of jct I-465. 7304 E 21st St 46219. Fax: 317/359-0578. **Facility:** 122 units. 120 one-bedroom standard units. 2 one-bedroom suites ($90-$116). 2 stories, interior corridors. **Parking:** on-site. **Terms:** package plans, small pets only. **Amenities:** video games (fee), voice mail, irons, hair dryers. **Pool(s):** heated outdoor. **Guest Services:** valet and coin laundry. **Business Services:** fax (fee). **Cards:** AX, CB, DC, DS, MC, VI. **Special Amenities:** free continental breakfast and free local telephone calls.

SOME UNITS
[🅂🅓] [🛏] [📶] [🏐] [🐾] [🍴] [DATA PORT] [💻] [🖨] / [✕] /
FEE

THE LOOKING GLASS INN
△▽△▽△▽
Historic Bed
& Breakfast

Phone: 317/639-9550 **71**
All Year 2P: $105-$135 XP: $25 F5
Location: Just n of 13th St; between Delaware and N Central Ave. 1319 N New Jersey St 46202. Fax: 317/684-9536. **Facility:** In a historic neighborhood near downtown, this restored 1905 mansion is notable for its grand foyer, white crown molding and well-decorated rooms. Smoke free premises. 6 units. 5 one-bedroom standard units, some with kitchens and/or whirlpools. 1 one-bedroom suite. 3 stories (no elevator), interior corridors. *Bath:* combo or shower only. **Parking:** on-site. **Terms:** check-in 4 pm, 7 day cancellation notice-fee imposed, [BP] meal plan available, package plans. **Amenities:** extended cable TV, video tape library, CD players, voice mail, irons, hair dryers. **Business Services:** conference facilities. **Cards:** AX, DS, MC, VI.

SOME UNITS
[✕] [VCR] [🎥] [🖨] / [DATA PORT] [📞] [🖨] [💻] /

MAINSTAY SUITES-INDIANAPOLIS
AAA SAVE
△▽△▽
Extended Stay
Motel

Phone: (317)334-7829 **34**
All Year 1P: $79-$99
Location: I-465, exit 23, just e. 8520 Northwest Blvd 46278. Fax: 317/334-0267. **Facility:** 88 units. 64 one-bedroom standard units with efficiencies. 24 one-bedroom suites with efficiencies. 3 stories, interior corridors. *Bath:* combo or shower only. **Parking:** on-site. **Terms:** cancellation fee imposed, pets ($25 fee). **Amenities:** video games (fee), dual phone lines, voice mail, irons, hair dryers. **Pool(s):** heated indoor. **Leisure Activities:** limited exercise equipment. **Guest Services:** complimentary evening beverages: Mon-Wed, valet and coin laundry. **Business Services:** fax (fee). **Cards:** AX, CB, DC, DS, JC, MC, VI. **Special Amenities:** early check-in/late check-out. *(See color ad p 468)*

SOME UNITS
[🅂🅓] [🛏] [📶] [🅜] [🔑] [🏐] [🐾] [🍴] [DATA PORT] [📞] [🖨] [💻] [🖨] / [✕] /
FEE

OMNI INDIANAPOLIS NORTH HOTEL
AAA SAVE
△▽△▽△▽
Hotel

Phone: (317)849-6668 **66**
All Year 1P: $89 2P: $89 XP: $10 F18
Location: I-69, exit 1, just e. 8181 N Shadeland Ave 46250. Fax: 317/849-4936. **Facility:** 215 one-bedroom standard units, some with whirlpools. 6 stories, interior corridors. *Bath:* combo or shower only. **Parking:** on-site. **Terms:** package plans, pets ($50 deposit). **Amenities:** extended cable TV, voice mail, irons, hair dryers. **Dining:** dining room, 6 am-10 pm, Sat & Sun from 7 am, $8-$22, cocktails. **Pool(s):** heated indoor. **Leisure Activities:** sauna, exercise room. *Fee:* game room. **Guest Services:** valet and coin laundry, area transportation-within 5 mi. **Business Services:** conference facilities, fax. **Cards:** AX, CB, DC, DS, JC, MC, VI. **Special Amenities:** early check-in/late check-out. *(See ad below)*

SOME UNITS
[🅂🅓] [🛏] [🍴] [🍸] [🔑] [🏐] [🐾] [✕] [🍴] [DATA PORT] [💻] [🖨] / [✕] [📞] /
FEE

PICKWICK FARMS AIRPORT
AAA SAVE
△▽△▽
Suite Apartment

Phone: (317)240-3567 **89**
All Year 1P: $38-$85 2P: $38-$85
Location: I-465, exit 13A, just ne. 25 Beachway Dr 46224. Fax: 317/240-3568. **Facility:** 124 units. 48 one- and 76 two-bedroom suites ($38-$85) with kitchens. 2 stories, exterior corridors. **Parking:** on-site. **Terms:** 30 day cancellation notice-fee imposed, pets ($50 fee, $100 deposit, $1.50 extra charge). **Amenities:** extended cable TV, voice mail, irons. **Pool(s):** outdoor. **Leisure Activities:** limited exercise equipment. **Guest Services:** coin laundry. **Business Services:** fax (fee). **Cards:** AX, DC, DS, MC, VI. **Special Amenities:** early check-in/late check-out and free local telephone calls. *(See ad p 471)*

SOME UNITS
[🅂🅓] [🛏] [📶] [🐾] [📞] [🖨] [💻] [🖨] / [VCR] /
FEE

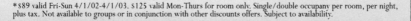

(See map p. 463)

PICKWICK FARMS SHORT-TERM FURNISHED APARTMENTS
Phone: (317)872-6506 **47**

(AAA) SAVE

Extended Stay
Apartment

All Year   1P: $35-$90   2P: $35-$90
Location: I-465, exit 31, just s to 96th St, 1.5 mi w to N Ditch Rd, then just s. 9300 N Ditch Rd 46260. Fax: 317/879-7380. **Facility:** 350 units. 194 one-, 143 two- and 13 three-bedroom suites ($35-$90). 2 stories, exterior corridors. **Parking:** on-site. **Terms:** check-in 4 pm, 30 day cancellation notice-fee imposed, pets ($150 fee, $1.25 extra charge). **Amenities:** extended cable TV, voice mail, irons. **Leisure Activities:** 2 lighted tennis courts, racquetball courts, playground, exercise room. **Guest Services:** coin laundry. **Business Services:** meeting rooms, fax (fee). **Cards:** AX, CB, DC, DS, MC, VI. **Special Amenities:** early check-in/late check-out and free local telephone calls. *(See ad p 471)*

QUALITY INN & SUITES AT THE PYRAMIDS
Phone: (317)875-7676 **58**

(AAA) SAVE

Motel

All Year [ECP]   1P: $45-$220   2P: $49-$220   XP: $10   F18
Location: I-465, exit 27, just s to De Pauw Blvd, just e, then just s. 9090 Wesleyan Rd 46268. Fax: 317/875-9051. **Facility:** 116 units. 110 one-bedroom standard units, some with whirlpools. 6 one-bedroom suites. 3 stories, interior corridors. **Parking:** on-site. **Amenities:** extended cable TV, video games (fee), irons, hair dryers. **Pool(s):** valet laundry. **Guest Services:** meeting rooms, fax (fee). **Cards:** AX, CB, DC, DS, JC, MC, VI. **Special Amenities:** early check-in/late check-out. *(See color ad p 468)*

SOME UNITS

QUALITY INN EAST
Phone: (317)549-2222 **75**

SAVE

Motor Inn

8/19-9/30	1P: $55-$275	2P: $60-$275	XP: $5 F18
4/1-8/18	1P: $60-$200	2P: $65-$205	XP: $5 F18
10/1-3/31	1P: $50-$100	2P: $55-$105	XP: $5 F18

Location: I-70, exit 89, 1.5 mi n. 3525 N Shadeland Ave 46226. Fax: 317/549-2222. **Facility:** 123 one-bedroom standard units with whirlpools. 2 stories, interior/exterior corridors. **Parking:** on-site. **Amenities:** video games (fee), voice mail, irons, hair dryers. **Pool(s):** heated indoor. **Leisure Activities:** whirlpools, limited exercise equipment, game room. **Guest Services:** valet and coin laundry. **Business Services:** conference facilities. *Fee:* PC, fax. **Cards:** AX, CB, DC, DS, JC, MC, VI.

SOME UNITS

RED ROOF INN-SOUTH
Phone: (317)788-9551 **108**

(AAA) SAVE

Motel

4/1-9/28	1P: $39-$59	2P: $44-$64	XP: $5 F18
9/29-3/31	1P: $33-$59	2P: $38-$64	XP: $5 F18

Location: I-465/74, exit 52 (Emerson Ave). 5221 Victory Dr 46203. Fax: 317/788-0132. **Facility:** 107 one-bedroom standard units. 2 stories, exterior corridors. *Bath:* combo or shower only. **Parking:** on-site. **Terms:** package plans. **Amenities:** video games (fee), voice mail. **Business Services:** fax (fee). **Cards:** AX, CB, DC, DS, MC, VI. **Special Amenities:** free local telephone calls and free newspaper.

SOME UNITS

RED ROOF INN-SPEEDWAY
Phone: (317)293-6881 **76**

(AAA) SAVE

Motel

4/23-10/7	1P: $39-$56	2P: $44-$61	XP: $5 F18
4/1-4/22	1P: $34-$52	2P: $39-$59	XP: $5 F18
10/8-3/31	1P: $34-$49	2P: $39-$54	XP: $5 F18

Location: I-465, exit 16A, just se of jct US 136. 6415 Debonair Ln 46224. Fax: 317/293-9892. **Facility:** 108 one-bedroom standard units. 2 stories, exterior corridors. **Parking:** on-site. **Terms:** small pets only. **Amenities:** video games (fee), voice mail. **Business Services:** fax (fee). **Cards:** AX, CB, DC, DS, JC, MC, VI. **Special Amenities:** free local telephone calls and free newspaper.

SOME UNITS

RESIDENCE INN BY MARRIOTT/INDIANAPOLIS AIRPORT
Phone: (317)244-1500 **94**

(AAA) SAVE

Extended Stay
Apartment

4/1-10/31	1P: $119-$139	2P: $119-$139
11/1-3/31	1P: $109-$139	2P: $109-$139

Location: I-465, exit 11A, 0.5 mi e on Airport Expwy to Lynhurst Dr exit. 5224 W Southern Ave 46241. Fax: 317/244-4486. **Facility:** 95 units. 37 one-bedroom standard units with efficiencies. 42 one- and 16 two-bedroom suites ($149-$179), some with efficiencies or kitchens. 3 stories, interior corridors. *Bath:* combo or shower only. **Parking:** on-site. **Terms:** pets ($75 fee, $5 extra charge). **Amenities:** video games (fee), dual phone lines, voice mail, irons, hair dryers. **Pool(s):** heated indoor. **Leisure Activities:** whirlpool, exercise room, sports court. **Guest Services:** complimentary evening beverages: Mon-Thurs, valet and coin laundry. **Business Services:** meeting rooms, fax (fee). **Cards:** AX, CB, DC, DS, JC, MC, VI. *(See color ad card insert)*

SOME UNITS

RESIDENCE INN BY MARRIOTT INDIANAPOLIS/FISHERS
Phone: (317)842-1111 **44**

(AAA) SAVE

Extended Stay
Apartment

4/1-11/30 [BP]	1P: $119-$129
12/1-3/31 [BP]	1P: $99-$109

Location: I-69, exit 3, just nw. 9765 Crosspoint Blvd 46256. Fax: 317/842-0462. **Facility:** 78 units. 18 one-bedroom standard units with efficiencies. 48 one- and 12 two-bedroom suites, some with efficiencies or kitchens. 3 stories, interior corridors. *Bath:* combo or shower only. **Parking:** on-site. **Terms:** pets ($75-$100 extra charge). **Amenities:** video games, dual phone lines, voice mail, irons, hair dryers. **Pool(s):** heated indoor. **Leisure Activities:** whirlpool, exercise room, sports court. **Guest Services:** complimentary evening beverages: Mon-Thurs, coin laundry. **Business Services:** fax (fee). **Cards:** AX, CB, DC, DS, JC, MC, VI. *(See color ad card insert)*

SOME UNITS

(See map p. 463)

RESIDENCE INN BY MARRIOTT INDIANAPOLIS NORTH
Phone: (317)872-0462   **60**

AAA SAVE
Extended Stay Apartment

All Year [BP]   1P: $69-$105
Location: I-465, exit 27, 1 mi s. 3553 Founders Rd 46268. Fax: 317/876-8829. **Facility:** 88 one-bedroom standard units with efficiencies. 2 stories, exterior corridors. **Parking:** on-site. **Terms:** cancellation fee imposed, pets ($50 fee, $7 extra charge). **Amenities:** extended cable TV, voice mail, irons, hair dryers. **Pool(s):** outdoor. **Leisure Activities:** whirlpool, sports court. **Guest Services:** valet and coin laundry. **Business Services:** PC, fax (fee). **Cards:** AX, CB, DC, DS, JC, MC, VI. *(See color ad card insert)*   SOME UNITS

SHERATON INDIANAPOLIS HOTEL & SUITES
Phone: (317)846-2700   **49**

Hotel

1/1-3/31   1P: $149   2P: $159   XP: $10   F18
4/1-12/31   1P: $139   2P: $149   XP: $10   F18
Location: I-465, exit 33, at jct SR 431; connected to the Fashion Mall. 8787 Keystone Crossing 46240. Fax: 317/574-6775. **Facility:** 560 units. 401 one-bedroom standard units. 159 one-bedroom suites ($179-$199) with efficiencies (no utensils). 12 stories, interior corridors. *Bath:* some combo or shower only. **Parking:** on-site and valet (fee). **Terms:** cancellation fee imposed, package plans, pets ($75 deposit). **Amenities:** dual phone lines, voice mail, irons, hair dryers. *Some:* fax, safes. **Pool(s):** heated indoor. **Leisure Activities:** saunas, whirlpool, sun deck. **Guest Services:** gift shop, valet laundry. **Business Services:** conference facilities, business center. *Fee:* PC, fax. **Cards:** AX, CB, DC, DS, JC, MC, VI.   SOME UNITS

SIGNATURE INN & SUITES-NORTHWEST
Phone: (317)875-5656   **45**

Motel

All Year [CP]   1P: $62-$72   2P: $62-$72
Location: I-465, exit 27, just s. 3910 Payne Branch Rd 46268. Fax: 317/875-5656. **Facility:** 137 units. 136 one-bedroom standard units, some with whirlpools. 1 one-bedroom suite. 2 stories, interior corridors. **Parking:** on-site, winter plug-ins. **Amenities:** extended cable TV, voice mail, irons, hair dryers. **Pool(s):** heated indoor. **Leisure Activities:** whirlpool, exercise room. **Guest Services:** coin laundry. **Business Services:** meeting rooms, fax (fee). **Cards:** AX, DC, DS, MC, VI.   SOME UNITS

SIGNATURE INN CARMEL
Phone: (317)816-1616   **41**

Motel

All Year [CP]   1P: $81-$92   2P: $81-$92
Location: I-465, exit 31, just n on US 31. 10201 N Meridian St 46280. Fax: 317/816-1616. **Facility:** 81 one-bedroom standard units, some with whirlpools. 3 stories, interior corridors. **Parking:** on-site. **Amenities:** voice mail, irons, hair dryers. **Pool(s):** heated indoor. **Leisure Activities:** whirlpool, sun deck, exercise room. **Guest Services:** valet laundry. **Business Services:** meeting rooms. **Cards:** AX, DC, DS, MC, VI.   SOME UNITS

SIGNATURE INN-CASTLETON
Phone: (317)849-8555   **64**

Motel

All Year [CP]   1P: $69-$79   2P: $69-$79
Location: I-465, exit 35 (Allisonville Rd). 8380 Kelly Ln 46250. Fax: 317/849-8555. **Facility:** 125 one-bedroom standard units, some with whirlpools. 2 stories, interior corridors. **Parking:** on-site. **Terms:** package plans. **Amenities:** extended cable TV, voice mail, irons, hair dryers. **Pool(s):** outdoor. **Guest Services:** valet laundry. **Business Services:** meeting rooms, fax (fee). **Cards:** AX, DC, DS, MC, VI.   SOME UNITS

SIGNATURE INN-INDIANAPOLIS EAST
Phone: (317)353-6966   **90**

Motel

All Year [CP]   1P: $71-$81   2P: $71-$81
Location: I-465, exit 46, just sw. 7610 Old Trails Rd 46219. Fax: 317/353-6966. **Facility:** 101 one-bedroom standard units, some with whirlpools. 2 stories, interior corridors. **Parking:** on-site. **Amenities:** extended cable TV, voice mail, irons, hair dryers. **Pool(s):** outdoor. **Guest Services:** valet laundry. **Business Services:** meeting rooms, business center, PC, fax (fee). **Cards:** AX, DC, DS, MC, VI.   SOME UNITS

SIGNATURE INN-INDIANAPOLIS WEST
Phone: (317)299-6165   **72**

Motel

All Year [CP]   1P: $76-$87   2P: $76-$87
Location: I-465, exit 17, just w on 38th St. 3850 Eagle View Dr 46254. Fax: 317/299-6165. **Facility:** 101 one-bedroom standard units, some with whirlpools. 2 stories, interior corridors. **Parking:** on-site. **Amenities:** extended cable TV, voice mail, irons, hair dryers. **Pool(s):** outdoor. **Guest Services:** valet laundry. **Business Services:** meeting rooms, fax (fee). **Cards:** AX, DC, DS, MC, VI.   SOME UNITS

SIGNATURE INN-SOUTH
Phone: (317)784-7006   **111**

Motel

All Year [CP]   1P: $60-$69   2P: $60-$69
Location: I-65, exit 103. 4402 E Creekview Dr 46237. Fax: 317/784-7006. **Facility:** 101 one-bedroom standard units, some with whirlpools. 2 stories, interior corridors. **Parking:** on-site. **Amenities:** extended cable TV, voice mail, irons, hair dryers. **Pool(s):** outdoor. **Guest Services:** valet laundry. **Business Services:** meeting rooms, PC. **Cards:** AX, DC, DS, MC, VI.   SOME UNITS

SLEEP INN WEST
Phone: (317)247-4100   **95**

AAA SAVE
Motel

All Year [ECP]   1P: $81-$87   2P: $81-$87   XP: $5   F18
Location: I-465, exit 13A, just e. 5845 Rockville Rd 46224. Fax: 317/247-1559. **Facility:** 63 one-bedroom standard units. 3 stories, interior corridors. *Bath:* combo or shower only. **Parking:** on-site. **Amenities:** voice mail. *Some:* irons, hair dryers. **Guest Services:** valet laundry. **Business Services:** fax (fee). **Cards:** AX, CB, DC, DS, JC, MC, VI. **Special Amenities:** free continental breakfast and free local telephone calls.   SOME UNITS

(See map p. 463)

STONE SOUP INN
Historic Bed & Breakfast

Phone: 317/639-9550   [78]

All Year   2P: $85-$135   XP: $25   F10
Location: Corner of 13th and N Central Ave. 1304 N Central Ave 46202. Fax: 317/684-9536. **Facility:** This quiet, spacious B&B near downtown is in a restored 1901 home with decoratively painted walls, antique furniture and down comforters. Smoke free premises. 8 one-bedroom standard units, some with kitchens and/or whirlpools. 3 stories (no elevator), interior corridors. *Bath:* some shared or private, combo or shower only.
Parking: on-site. **Terms:** check-in 4 pm, 7 day cancellation notice-fee imposed, package plans. **Amenities:** extended cable TV, video tape library, CD players, voice mail, hair dryers. *Some:* irons. **Business Services:** fax (fee). **Cards:** AX, DS, MC, VI.

SOME UNITS

SUPER 8 CASTLETON-NORTHEAST
Motel

Phone: (317)841-8585   [56]

4/1-10/31 [CP]   1P: $59-$150   2P: $59-$150   XP: $6   F
11/1-3/31 [CP]   1P: $55-$150   2P: $55-$150   XP: $6   F
Location: I-69, exit 1, 0.3 mi e to Clear Vista, just n, then just w on Clear Vista Ln. 7202 E 82nd St 46256. Fax: 317/577-1731. **Facility:** 75 units. 55 one-bedroom standard units, some with whirlpools. 20 one-bedroom suites ($79-$99). 2 stories, exterior corridors. *Bath:* combo or shower only. **Parking:** on-site. **Amenities:** extended cable TV. **Pool(s):** outdoor. **Leisure Activities:** limited exercise equipment. **Business Services:** meeting rooms. **Cards:** AX, DC, DS, MC, VI.

SOME UNITS

UNIVERSITY PLACE HOTEL & CONFERENCE CENTER
Hotel

Phone: (317)269-9000   [77]

All Year   1P: $245   2P: $245
Location: Just w on campus of Indiana University and Purdue University at Indianapolis. 850 W Michigan St 46206-6044 (PO Box 6044, 46206). Fax: 317/231-5168. **Facility:** 278 units. 276 one-bedroom standard units. 2 one-bedroom suites ($209-$394). 10 stories, interior corridors. *Bath:* combo or shower only. **Parking:** on-site (fee). **Terms:** check-in 4 pm, package plans. **Amenities:** Web TV (fee), dual phone lines, voice mail, irons, hair dryers. **Dining:** 2 restaurants, 6 am-midnight, $10-$22, cocktails. **Leisure Activities:** Fee: sports complex privileges. **Guest Services:** gift shop, valet and coin laundry, area transportation-within 3 mi. **Business Services:** conference facilities, business center. *Fee:* PC, fax. **Cards:** AX, DC, DS, MC, VI. Affiliated with Doubletree Hotels.

SOME UNITS
FEE   FEE   FEE

WELLESLEY INN & SUITES (INDIANAPOLIS AIRPORT/MARION)
Extended Stay Motel

Phone: (317)241-0700   [33]

All Year [ECP]   1P: $79-$109   2P: $79-$109   XP: $10   F18
Location: I-465, exit 11A, just e to Lynhurst St, just s, then just w. 5350 W Southern Ave 46241. Fax: 317/241-0746. **Facility:** 121 units. 96 one-bedroom standard units with efficiencies. 25 one-bedroom suites ($89-$109), some with efficiencies or kitchens. 3 stories, interior corridors. *Bath:* combo or shower only. **Parking:** on-site. **Terms:** 14 day cancellation notice, package plans, small pets only. **Amenities:** video games (fee), voice mail, irons, hair dryers. **Pool(s):** heated outdoor. **Leisure Activities:** limited exercise equipment. **Guest Services:** valet and coin laundry. **Business Services:** meeting rooms, fax (fee). **Cards:** AX, CB, DC, DS, JC, MC, VI.
Special Amenities: free continental breakfast and free newspaper. *(See color ad p 469)*

SOME UNITS
FEE

WELLESLEY INN & SUITES (INDIANAPOLIS/NORTH)
Extended Stay Motel

Phone: (317)471-0700   [43]

All Year [ECP]   1P: $61-$71   2P: $71-$81   XP: $10   F18
Location: I-465, exit 27, just s to 92nd St, just w to Waldemar Rd, 0.3 mi n. 9370 Waldemar Rd 46268. Fax: 317/471-0701. **Facility:** 139 one-bedroom standard units with efficiencies. 3 stories, interior corridors. *Bath:* combo or shower only. **Parking:** on-site. **Terms:** package plans, small pets only. **Amenities:** video games, high-speed Internet, dual phone lines, voice mail, irons, hair dryers. **Leisure Activities:** exercise room. **Guest Services:** valet and coin laundry. **Business Services:** meeting rooms. **Cards:** AX, CB, DC, DS, JC, MC, VI. **Special Amenities: free continental breakfast and free newspaper.** *(See color ad p 469)*

SOME UNITS
FEE

WINGATE INN-AIRPORT
Motel

Phone: (317)243-8310   [105]

All Year [ECP]   1P: $85-$225   2P: $85-$225   XP: $10   F18
Location: I-465, exit 13A, just e. 5797 Rockville Rd 46224. Fax: 317/243-8315. **Facility:** 96 units. 83 one-bedroom standard units, some with whirlpools. 13 one-bedroom suites ($150-$300) with whirlpools. 3 stories, interior corridors. *Bath:* combo or shower only. **Amenities:** dual phone lines, voice mail, safes, irons, hair dryers. *Fee:* video games, high-speed Internet. **Pool(s):** heated outdoor. **Leisure Activities:** whirlpool, limited exercise equipment. **Guest Services:** valet and coin laundry. **Cards:** AX, CB, DC, DS, JC, MC, VI.

SOME UNITS
FEE

WYNDHAM HOTEL INDIANAPOLIS
Motor Inn

Phone: (317)574-4600   [42]

All Year   1P: $89-$119   2P: $99-$129   XP: $10   F18
Location: I-465, exit 31, 0.5 mi n on US 31, 0.5 mi se via 103rd St, follow signs. 251 E Pennsylvania Pkwy 46280. Fax: 317/574-4633. **Facility:** 171 units. 160 one-bedroom standard units. 11 one-bedroom suites. 6 stories, interior corridors. **Parking:** on-site. **Terms:** cancellation fee imposed, package plans. **Amenities:** video games, Web TV, high-speed Internet, dual phone lines, voice mail, irons, hair dryers. *Some:* CD players. **Dining:** restaurant, 6:30 am-10 pm, $7-$22, cocktails. **Pool(s):** heated indoor. **Leisure Activities:** whirlpool, exercise room. **Guest Services:** coin laundry. **Business Services:** conference facilities, fax (fee). **Cards:** AX, CB, DC, DS, JC, MC, VI.

SOME UNITS
FEE   FEE

(See map p. 463)

─────── *The following lodging was either not evaluated or did not* ───────
meet AAA rating requirements but is listed for your information only.

RADISSON HOTEL INDIANAPOLIS AIRPORT   **Phone:** (317)244-3361   [92]
[fyi]   All Year   1P: $159-$350   2P: $159-$350   XP: $15   F17
                      Under major renovation, scheduled to be completed December 2001. **Last rated:** ♦♦ **Location:** I-465, exit
Motor Inn   11B; at Indianapolis International Airport. 2500 S High School Rd 46241. Fax: 317/241-9202. **Facility:** 261 units. 226
              one-bedroom standard units. 35 one-bedroom suites ($200-$450). 3-6 stories, interior corridors. *Bath:* combo
or shower only. **Parking:** on-site. **Terms:** 3 day cancellation notice, package plans. **Amenities:** dual phone lines, voice mail,
irons, hair dryers. **Leisure Activities:** limited exercise equipment. **Guest Services:** valet laundry. **Business Services:** meeting
rooms. **Cards:** AX, CB, DC, DS, JC, MC, VI.

SOME UNITS

(ASK) 🆂🎄 ➕ 🍽️ 🍸 🖉 🎥 📶 💻 🖨️ / ✕ 🛏️ 🖥️ /

─────── **WHERE TO DINE** ───────

ACROPOLIS   **Lunch:** $4-$8   **Dinner:** $8-$15   **Phone:** 317/787-8883   [36]
♦♦   **Location:** I-65, exit 103, 2 mi w. 1625 E Southport Rd 46227. **Hours:** 11 am-9:30 pm, Fri & Sat-10 pm. Closed
            major holidays; also Sun. **Reservations:** accepted. **Features:** casual dress; children's menu; carryout;
Greek   cocktails & lounge; entertainment. On weekend evenings, it's hard to determine the bigger attraction: the
            belly dancers or the food. Robust flavors leap from traditional Greek dishes, such as gyros, moussaka,
dolmades and spanakopita, which are served in large portions. The staff is friendly and efficient. **Parking:** on-site. **Cards:** DC,
DS, MC, VI.
                                                                                                                    ✕

ARISTOCRAT PUB & RESTAURANT   **Lunch:** $7-$10   **Dinner:** $7-$22   **Phone:** 317/283-7388   [37]
♦♦   **Location:** Jct 52nd St. 5212 N College Ave 46220. **Hours:** 11 am-11 pm, Fri & Sat-1 am, Sun 10 am-10 pm.
            Closed: 1/1, 11/28, 12/25. **Features:** casual dress; Sunday brunch; children's menu; carryout; cocktails &
American   lounge. Decorated in a pub-like style with dark woods and yesteryear farm pictures, the restaurant
            presents a far-ranging menu with salads, sandwiches, pasta dishes and several boutique martinis,
including peanut butter and white and dark chocolate martinis. Seating can be requested at tables or booths or on the patio.
Parking: on-site. **Cards:** AX, DC, DS, MC, VI.
                                                                                                                    ✕

BACCO   **Dinner:** $12-$22   **Phone:** 317/582-1362   [39]
♦♦♦   **Location:** 1.3 mi w of jct US 31; in Old Town Shoppes Strip Mall. 1260 W 86th St 46260. **Hours:** 11 am-2:30 & 5-9
            pm, Fri-10 pm, Sat from 5 pm. Closed major holidays; also Sun. **Reservations:** suggested.
Italian   **Features:** casual dress; cocktails. The well-executed menu includes artfully prepared, Northern Italian
            dishes, such as the abundantly seasoned chicken cacciatore. Low lighting adds to the romantic charm of
the dining room. The delicious custard is served with honey and pine nuts. **Parking:** on-site. **Cards:** AX, DC, DS, MC, VI. ✕

CAFE EUROPA   **Lunch:** $7-$10   **Dinner:** $12-$20   **Phone:** 317/547-4474   [42]
♦♦   **Location:** Just n of jct 46th St; in "The D'Liteful Shoppes" Center. 4709 N Shadeland Ave 46226. **Hours:** 11
            am-2:30 & 5-8:30 pm, Sun 10 am-3 pm. Closed major holidays; also Mon. **Reservations:** accepted.
German   **Features:** casual dress; children's menu; carryout; beer & wine only. German knick-knacks, as well as lace
            curtains and other quaint appointments, decorate this cozy dining room in a small shopping plaza.
Well-prepared dishes, such as wursts and Wiener schnitzel, burst with hearty flavor. Splurge on the rich German chocolate
cake. Smoke free premises. **Parking:** on-site. **Cards:** AX, DS, MC, VI.
                                                                                                                    ✕

CHANTECLAIR   **Dinner:** $25-$40   **Phone:** 317/243-1040   [27]
🔺🔺🔺   **Location:** I-465, exit 11B; at Indianapolis International Airport; in Holiday Inn Select Airport. 2501 S High School Rd
            46241. **Hours:** 6 pm-10 pm, Fri & Sat-11 pm. Closed major holidays; also Sun. **Reservations:** suggested.
♦♦♦♦   **Features:** semi-formal attire; cocktails & lounge; entertainment; a la carte. Guests who pass through
Continental frosted-glass doors enter a classic French dining room with crisp, white linen tablecloths, candles and
            elegant stemware. Special touches include an ample wine list, a strolling violinist, tuxedo-clad staff and
            freshly baked bread wrapped in linen and presented on a sterling tray. Memorable selections include
escargots au Pernod on mushroom caps, saumon fume, veal Oscar and oysters Rockefeller. Dishes are finished and plated
tableside. **Parking:** on-site. **Cards:** AX, CB, DC, DS, JC, MC, VI.
                                                                                                                    ✕

CHARLESTON'S RESTAURANT   **Lunch:** $6-$15   **Dinner:** $9-$17   **Phone:** 317/841-0442   [67]
♦♦   **Location:** I-69, exit 1, just w. 6815 E 82nd St 46250. **Hours:** 11 am-10 pm, Fri & Sat-11 pm. Closed: 11/28,
            12/25. **Reservations:** accepted. **Features:** casual dress; children's menu; carryout; cocktails & lounge. A
American   favorite with the local crowd, the casual dining spot boasts a friendly, clublike atmosphere. Fine steak and
            seafood, as well as hickory-grilled dishes, are at the heart of the menu. The noteworthy potato soup is rich,
with onions and bacon bits. **Parking:** on-site. **Cards:** AX, DC, DS, MC, VI.
                                                                                                                    ✕

DON HALL'S CASTLETON GRILL   **Lunch:** $5-$10   **Dinner:** $9-$15   **Phone:** 317/577-2340   [43]
♦♦♦   **Location:** I-69, exit 1, 1 mi w; at Castleton Square Mall entrance. 6010 E 82nd St 46250. **Hours:** 11 am-10 pm,
            Fri-11 pm, Sat 9 am-11 pm, Sun 9 am-9 pm. Closed: 1/1, 11/28, 12/25. **Reservations:** accepted.
American   **Features:** casual dress; children's menu; carryout; cocktails & lounge. This is a comfortable family
            restaurant with plenty of menu options. This is a large modern family restaurant with table/booth seating,
stained glass lamps and a small bar. This restaurant offers broiled portabellas, hickory fired salmon, burgers, ruebens, pasta
and USDA choice grade steak. This grill is located at the entrance to Castleton Square Mall entrance facing 82nd Street.
Parking: on-site. **Cards:** AX, DS, MC, VI.
                                                                                                                    ✕

GRINDSTONE CHARLEY'S RESTAURANT & PUB   **Lunch:** $6-$8   **Dinner:** $9-$16   **Phone:** 317/897-3415   [35]
♦♦   **Location:** I-465, exit 46, 0.3 me e on US 40. 8009 E Washington St 46219. **Hours:** 11 am-11 pm, Fri &
            Sat-midnight, Sun-10 pm. Closed: 11/28, 12/25. **Features:** casual dress; children's menu; carryout;
American   cocktails & lounge. The ultra-casual dining spot serves a good variety of traditional American entrees and
            sandwiches. Although the specialty barbecue pork ribs are a clear favorite, the steaks are also a tempting
choice. **Parking:** on-site. **Cards:** AX, DC, DS, MC, VI.
                                                                                                                    ✕

(See map p. 463)

HERITAGE HOUSE SMORGASBORD   **Lunch:** $6-$7   **Dinner:** $8-$9   **Phone:** 317/783-9388   71

American

Location: I-465, exit 2B, just s on US 31 S. 4990 US 31 S 46227. **Hours:** 8 am-8:30 pm, Fri & Sat-9 pm. Closed: 12/24, 12/25. **Features:** casual dress; children's menu; carryout. The longtime smorgasbord lays out an extensive selection of family favorites. **Parking:** on-site. **Cards:** MC, VI.

THE HERON RESTAURANT   **Lunch:** $7-$11   **Dinner:** $15-$30   **Phone:** 317/845-8899   26

American

Location: I-69, exit 3, 2 mi e, then 1 mi n. 11699 Fall Creek Rd 46236. **Hours:** 11 am-10 pm, Fri & Sat-11 pm, Sun-9 pm, Mon 4 pm-10 pm. Closed: 11/28, 12/25. **Reservations:** suggested. **Features:** casual dress; Sunday brunch; children's menu; carryout; cocktails & lounge; a la carte. Gaze out on the lake as you dine on a variety of pasta, seafood, sandwiches and steak. The dining room features large glass windows, some nautical decor accents, a high loft and a complete bar. House specialties include bourbon chicken and Jamaican honey-slazed shrimp. This restaurant is located in the marina of Geist Lake. Smoke free premises. **Parking:** on-site. **Cards:** AX, DC, DS, MC, VI.

HOLLYHOCK HILL   **Lunch:** $10-$12   **Dinner:** $14-$18   **Phone:** 317/251-2294   62

American

Location: I-465, exit 31, 1.3 mi s on US 31 (Meridian St), 0.5 mi e on 86th St, then 0.5 mi s. 8110 N College Ave 46240. **Hours:** 5 pm-8 pm, Sun noon-7:30 pm. Closed: 7/4, 12/24, 12/25; also Mon. **Reservations:** suggested. **Features:** children's menu; carryout; cocktails. Family dining with attentive, fast paced service. Upscale country style decor with candles, ruffled windows and decorative walls. Select your entree of fried chicken, fish or steak and it will come with potatoes, gravy, relish/pickle tray, vegetables and rolls. Located in quiet residential area. **Parking:** on-site. **Cards:** AX, MC, VI.

IL GARGANO   **Dinner:** $13-$23   **Phone:** 317/843-0226   63

Italian

Location: Jct US 31, 1 mi e on 86th St; in Nora Plaza. 1300 E 86th St, 30-B 46240. **Hours:** 5 pm-9 pm, Fri & Sat-10 pm. Closed major holidays; also Mon. **Reservations:** suggested; weekends. **Features:** dressy casual; cocktails. The menu centers on attractively presented dishes of pasta, veal and chicken. Delicious veal Marsala swims in a sweet, but subtle, sauce. Soups are well-seasoned, and the wine list includes a number of fine choices. **Parking:** on-site. **Cards:** AX, DC, DS, MC, VI.

IRON SKILLET RESTAURANT & GIFT SHOP   **Dinner:** $14-$18   **Phone:** 317/923-6353   51

American

Location: I-65, exit 116, 2 mi w between Riverside and Coffin golf courses; 1.1 mi e of US 52. 2489 W 30th St 46222. **Hours:** 5 pm-8:30 pm, Sun noon-7:30 pm. Closed: 1/1, 7/4, 12/24, 12/25; also Mon & Tues. **Reservations:** suggested. **Features:** children's menu; cocktails. Relaxing atmosphere serving steaks, seafood and chicken dishes family style with homestyle vegetables. **Parking:** on-site. **Cards:** AX, CB, DC, DS, MC, VI.

THE JAZZ COOKER   **Dinner:** $12-$22   **Phone:** 317/253-2883   45

Creole

Location: On Keystone Ave, 1.1 mi w on 62nd St (Broad Ripple Ave) to Winthrop, just n; in Broad Ripple Village. 925 E Westfield Blvd 46220. **Hours:** 5 pm-9:30 pm, Fri & Sat-10 pm. Closed: 1/1, 12/25. **Reservations:** suggested; weekends. **Features:** casual dress; children's menu; carryout; cocktails & lounge. The busy, casual restaurant is known for Cajun, Creole and Southern style dishes, such as peel-and-eat shrimp in a piquant dipping sauce and crab cakes with rice. Strains of live jazz drift through the indoor and outdoor dining areas Thursday through Saturday. **Parking:** street. **Cards:** AX, CB, DC, DS, MC, VI.

KEYSTONE GRILL   **Lunch:** $7-$13   **Dinner:** $17-$27   **Phone:** 317/848-5202   33

American

Location: I-465, exit 33, s to 86th St exit, e to Keystone Crossing. 8650 Keystone at the Crossing 46240. **Hours:** 11 am-3 & 5-11 pm, Fri & Sat-midnight, Sun 10 am-1:30 & 3-10 pm. Closed: 12/25. **Reservations:** suggested. **Features:** casual dress; Sunday brunch; cocktails & lounge; a la carte. This is a modern dining room with plush carpeting, rich woods, soft music, white linens, elegant stemware and celebrity tables with name plates. Framed art work features racing memorabilia. Libations include Remy Martin Louis XIII cognac and an ample wine list. Age restrictions may apply. **Parking:** on-site. **Cards:** AX, DC, DS, MC, VI.

MALIBU GRILL   **Lunch:** $7-$11   **Dinner:** $11-$21   **Phone:** 317/845-4334   47

California

Location: Jct Alisonville Rd, 0.5 mi w. 4503 E 82nd St 46250. **Hours:** 11:30 am-2 & 5:30-10 pm, Fri-11 pm, Sat 11:30 am-11 pm, Sun noon-9 pm. Closed major holidays. **Reservations:** accepted; Sun-Thurs. **Features:** casual dress; children's menu; carryout; cocktails & lounge; a la carte. The friendly, laid-back restaurant invites you to settle in, relax and enjoy a filling meal, California style. The menu centers on flavorful pizza, heaping plates of pasta and juicy steak. The service staff shows good knowledge and great follow up. **Parking:** on-site. **Cards:** AX, DC, DS, MC, VI.

MEDITERRANO CAFE   **Lunch:** $5-$7   **Dinner:** $8-$15   **Phone:** 317/595-0399   48

Greek

Location: Jct Allisonville Rd; behind the mall at The Pavilion at Castleton. 5941 E 86th St 46250. **Hours:** 11 am-2 & 5-9 pm, Fri-10 pm, Sat noon-10 pm. Closed major holidays; also Sun. **Reservations:** suggested. **Features:** casual dress; carryout. This Greek restaurant is reminiscent of a bustling Mediterranean bazar, beckoning with rythmic sounds, fragrances of exotic spices and colorful dishes. Journey to culinary Greece with appetizers of homous, baba ghanof and lentil or cracked wheat soup. The lamb kabobs are moist, tender, flavorful and served with long grain India rice. Several vegetarian dishes are also available. The restaurant is simple and unassuming with cozy tables, Greek framed artworks and Greek background music. Smoke free premises. **Parking:** on-site. **Cards:** MC, VI.

(See map p. 463)

MIDTOWN GRILL
Continental
Lunch: $8-$11 **Dinner:** $13-$25 **Phone:** 317/253-1141 ㊾
Location: Just n of Broad Ripple Ave (62nd St) off College Ave; in Broad Ripple Village. 815 E Westfield Blvd 46220.
Hours: 11 am-2 & 5-10 pm, Fri & Sat-11 pm, Sun 5 pm-9 pm. Closed: 1/1, 11/28, 12/25.
Reservations: accepted. **Features:** casual dress; carryout; cocktails; a la carte. The popular restaurant is decorated with art deco stylings. Innovative combinations of foods and preparation styles make for an interesting menu. The tomato dill soup is rich and fresh. The artfully presented grilled chicken penne is wonderfully seasoned. **Parking:** on-site. **Cards:** AX, DC, DS, MC, VI.

NEW CHINA BUFFET
Chinese
Lunch: $6 **Dinner:** $7 **Phone:** 317/388-8833 ㊿
Location: I-465, exit 17, 1.8 mi e at jct of Georgetown Rd; in Lafayette Shoppes Strip Mall. 4720 W 38th St 46254.
Hours: 11 am-9 pm, Fri & Sat-10 pm. Closed: 11/28. **Features:** casual dress; buffet. The buffet-style eatery lays out a selection of value-priced Chinese favorites. Service is limited but friendly. **Parking:** on-site. **Cards:** DS, MC, VI.

PETER'S A RESTAURANT & BAR
Continental
Dinner: $22-$32 **Phone:** 317/465-1155 ㊷
Location: I-465, exit 37, just s to 86th St, then just e; across from mall. 8505 Keystone Crossing Blvd 46240.
Hours: 5 pm-10 pm, Fri & Sat-10:30 pm. Closed major holidays. **Reservations:** suggested. **Features:** semi-formal attire; early bird specials; cocktails; a la carte. Even though this restaurant is located in a strip mall, you will still see a fresh garden producing tomatoes and the exotic herbs utilized in the complex dish preparations. Feast on house specialties such as four day marinated Colorado lamb, quali, pheasant, duck/truffle pate, and a shrimp/blue crab stack. **Parking:** on-site. **Cards:** AX, DC, MC, VI.

RICK'S BOATYARD
American
Lunch: $7-$37 **Dinner:** $7-$37 **Phone:** 317/290-9300 ㊳
Location: I-465, exit 17, 1 mi w on 38th St, just n, follow signs. 4050 Dandy Tr 46254. **Hours:** 11 am-10 pm, Fri & Sat-11 pm, Sun from 10 am. Closed: 12/25. **Features:** casual dress; Sunday brunch; children's menu; carryout; cocktails & lounge; entertainment. Overlooking Eagle Creek Reservoir, the charming, waterfront restaurant delivers an interesting combination of menu items, ranging from steaks and seafood to pasta, pizza, sandwiches and salads. Guests can unwind in the festive, laid-back atmosphere. Brunch is an option on Saturday and Sunday. Reservations accepted except weekends 3/1-10/31. **Parking:** on-site. **Cards:** AX, DC, DS, MC, VI.

SAKURA JAPANESE RESTAURANT
Japanese
Lunch: $6-$8 **Dinner:** $10-$15 **Phone:** 317/259-4171 ㊴
Location: I-465, exit 33, 2.5 mi s on SR 431 (Keystone Ave), just n of jct 71st St. 7201 N Keystone Ave 46240.
Hours: 11:30 am-2:30 & 5-10 pm, Fri & Sat-11 pm, Sun 5 pm-9:30 pm. Closed major holidays. **Reservations:** accepted. **Features:** casual dress; carryout; beer & wine only. The simple appearance of this neighborhood restaurant belies flavorful and unusual dishes. The menu offers a wide variety of authentic Japanese fare. What looks like a simple salad is a special treat with its intriguing ginger/sesame dressing. A tantalizing selection of sushi and sushimi is also offered. The decor is simple and unassuming with table/booth seating, rows of framed accolades and a large sushi bar. The classical background music is a suprise. **Parking:** on-site. **Cards:** AX, DS, MC, VI.

SAN REMO GRILLE
Italian
Dinner: $15-$25 **Phone:** 317/871-5630 ㊵
Location: I-465, exit 27, just s; in Holiday Inn-Select North At The Pyramids. 3850 De Pauw Blvd 46268. **Hours:** 5:30 pm-10 pm, Fri & Sat-11 pm. Closed major holidays; also Sun. **Reservations:** suggested. **Features:** dressy casual; cocktails. A thorough wine list with Italian, French and domestic choices complements a thoughtful menu of seafood, beef and chicken entrees, including many fine Italian dishes. The award-winning vanilla custard with strawberries is served in a cocktail glass. **Parking:** on-site. **Cards:** AX, CB, DC, DS, MC, VI.

SHAFFER'S RESTAURANT
American
Lunch: $4-$8 **Dinner:** $14-$25 **Phone:** 317/253-1404 ㊶
Location: I-465, exit 33, 2 mi s; across from Glendale Shopping Center. 6125 Hillside 46220. **Hours:** 11 am-2 & 5-9 pm. Closed major holidays. **Features:** cocktails & lounge. The simple exterior of this restaurant belies the intriguing menu selections and attentive personal service that you will experience. The decor is a journey back in time. Hardwood floors match the hardwood tables but don't look up! The menu offers egg rolls, escargot, fried ravioli and state fair pork loin chops. Tucked into a side street, it's worth the effort to search for this restaurant. **Parking:** on-site. **Cards:** AX, DS, MC, VI.

THIEN HUONG SIZZLING WOK
Vietnamese
Lunch: $4-$6 **Dinner:** $6-$12 **Phone:** 317/298-9001 ㊸
Location: Jct 71st St. 7280 N Michigan Rd 46268. **Hours:** 11 am-10 pm, Sun-9 pm. Closed: 11/28, 12/25. **Features:** casual dress; carryout; beer & wine only; a la carte. Attractive straw ceiling fans with matching drop-down lights are among decorative touches in the divided dining area. Chinese and Vietnamese specialties, such as the sizzling wok seafood combination, are a real treat. Servers are knowledgeable. **Parking:** on-site. **Cards:** MC, VI.

VITO PROVOLONE'S
Italian
Dinner: $9-$15 **Phone:** 317/888-4867 ㊹
Location: Jct Meridian School Rd; in South Meridian Shoppes. 8031 S Meridian St 46217. **Hours:** 4 pm-10 pm, Fri & Sat-11 pm, Sun-9 pm. Closed major holidays. **Reservations:** accepted. **Features:** casual dress; children's menu; carryout; beer & wine only. Lace-curtained windows add to the storefront appeal of the popular, quaint restaurant. The menu offers all of your traditional Italian favorites, including all kinds of pasta and gourmet pizza, as well as an exceptionally flavorful Italian salad dressing. **Parking:** on-site. **Cards:** AX, DS, MC, VI.

The following restaurants have not been evaluated by AAA but are listed for your information only.

AGIO
[fyi]
Phone: 317/488-0359
Not evaluated. **Location:** 635 Massachusetts Ave 46204. This fine-dining establishment features Italian cuisine, including cioppino.

(See map p. 463)

ARTUROS
Phone: 317/257-4806

fyi   Not evaluated. **Location:** 2727 E 86th St 46240. A chef's table is available at the eatery, which offers Italian cuisine.

BUCA DI BEPPO
Phone: 317/632-2822

fyi   Not evaluated. **Location:** 35 N Illinois St 46225. Tremendous portions of traditional Italian favorites are emphasized.

DUNAWAY'S PALAZZO OSSIGENO
Phone: 317/638-7663

fyi   Not evaluated. **Location:** 351 S East St 46225. The elegant restaurant features fine Italian cuisine, including many appetizers.

GEORGE'S PLACE
Phone: 317/255-7064

fyi   Not evaluated. **Location:** 2727 E 86th St 46240. Steaks and fresh seafood are menu offerings at this fairly expensive restaurant.

G.T. SOUTH'S RIB HOUSE
Phone: 317/849-6997

fyi   Not evaluated. **Location:** 5711 E 71st St 46220. Reasonably priced barbecue and hickory-smoked ribs are offered at this restaurant.

MURPHY'S STEAKHOUSE
Phone: 317/545-3707

fyi   Not evaluated. **Location:** 4189 N Keystone Ave 46205. Tender steaks and the blackberry cobbler dessert are signature dishes here.

PETERSON'S
Phone: 317/598-8863

fyi   Not evaluated. **Location:** 7690 96th St. Seafood and steak are emphasized on a menu of innovative American cuisine.

SALVATORO'S RISTORANTE
Phone: 317/844-9144

fyi   Not evaluated. **Location:** 1268 W 86th St 46260. Salvatoro's serves fine Italian offerings, including the signature cataplana, made for two.

The Indianapolis Vicinity

ANDERSON pop. 59,500

—— **WHERE TO STAY** ——

BEST INNS
Phone: (765)644-2000

AAA SAVE Motel

All Year [ECP]   1P: $34-$58   2P: $49-$63
Location: I-69, exit 26, on SR 9. 5706 Scatterfield Rd 46013. Fax: 765/683-1747. **Facility:** 93 one-bedroom standard units. 2 stories, interior corridors. **Parking:** on-site, winter plug-ins. **Terms:** small pets only. **Amenities:** *Some:* irons. **Business Services:** fax (fee). **Cards:** AX, CB, DC, DS, MC, VI. **Special Amenities: free continental breakfast and free local telephone calls.**

SOME UNITS

COMFORT INN-ANDERSON
Phone: (765)644-4422

SAVE Motel

4/1-9/1 [CP]	1P: $59-$64	2P: $64-$69	XP: $5 F17
9/2-3/31 [CP]	1P: $55-$59	2P: $59-$64	XP: $5 F17

Location: I-69, exit 26, on SR 9. 2205 E 59th St 46013. Fax: 765/644-4422. **Facility:** 56 one-bedroom standard units. 2 stories, interior corridors. **Parking:** on-site, winter plug-ins. **Terms:** small pets only ($15 fee). **Amenities:** *Some:* hair dryers. **Pool(s):** small indoor. **Leisure Activities:** whirlpool. **Guest Services:** valet laundry. **Business Services:** fax (fee). **Cards:** AX, CB, DC, DS, MC, VI.

SOME UNITS
FEE

HAMPTON INN
Phone: (765)622-0700

SAVE Motel

All Year [ECP]   1P: $64-$74   2P: $64-$74
Location: I-69, exit 26. 2312 Hampton Dr 46013. Fax: 765/622-0707. **Facility:** 99 one-bedroom standard units, some with whirlpools. 4 stories, interior corridors. *Bath:* combo or shower only. **Parking:** on-site. **Amenities:** voice mail, irons, hair dryers. **Pool(s):** small heated indoor. **Leisure Activities:** whirlpool, exercise room. **Guest Services:** valet laundry. **Business Services:** meeting rooms, fax (fee). **Cards:** AX, DC, DS, MC, VI.

SOME UNITS

HAWTHORN INN & SUITES
Phone: (765)641-9980

Motel

All Year [BP]   1P: $65-$85   2P: $65-$85
Location: I-69, exit 26. 1836 E 64th St 46013. Fax: 765/641-7984. **Facility:** 49 one-bedroom standard units, some with whirlpools. 3 stories, interior corridors. *Bath:* combo or shower only. **Parking:** on-site. **Amenities:** irons, hair dryers. **Pool(s):** small indoor. **Leisure Activities:** whirlpool. **Guest Services:** coin laundry. **Business Services:** fax (fee). **Cards:** AX, CB, DC, DS, MC, VI.

SOME UNITS

HOLIDAY INN
▼▼▼
Motor Inn

All Year   1P: $79-$150   Phone: (765)644-2581
Location: I-69, exit 26. 5920 S Scatterfield Rd 46013. Fax: 765/642-8545. **Facility:** 157 units. 155 one-bedroom standard units. 2 one-bedroom suites ($150) with whirlpools. 2 stories, interior/exterior corridors. **Parking:** on-site. **Amenities:** video games, irons, hair dryers. **Pool(s):** heated outdoor, heated indoor. **Leisure Activities:** sauna, whirlpool, exercise room. **Guest Services:** coin laundry. **Business Services:** conference facilities, fax (fee). **Cards:** AX, CB, DC, DS, JC, MC, VI.

SOME UNITS

LEES INN & SUITES
▼▼▼
Motel

All Year [BP]   1P: $69-$250   2P: $79-$260   XP: $10   F18
Location: I-69, exit 26, on SR 9. 2114 E 59th St 46013. Fax: 765/643-0349. **Facility:** 67 units. 61 one-bedroom standard units. 6 one-bedroom suites ($129-$250). 2 stories, interior corridors. **Parking:** on-site. **Terms:** 7 day cancellation notice, [ECP] meal plan available, small pets only (in smoking units). **Amenities:** extended cable TV, irons, hair dryers. **Leisure Activities:** exercise room. **Guest Services:** complimentary evening beverages: Mon-Thurs, valet and coin laundry. **Business Services:** meeting rooms, fax (fee). **Cards:** AX, DC, DS, JC, MC, VI.

SOME UNITS

ATLANTA pop. 700

──── **WHERE TO DINE** ────

FLETCHER'S OF ATLANTA
▼▼▼
American

Dinner: $14-$29   Phone: 765/292-2777
Location: Jct Walnut. 185 W Main St 46031. **Hours:** 5 pm-9:30 pm; closing hours may vary. Closed major holidays; also Sun & Mon. **Reservations:** suggested. **Features:** casual dress; cocktails. High-quality, locally grown produce infuses great flavor into dishes of steak, seafood and game. Preparations are artful, with colorful garnishes. The wine list is surprisingly extensive for such a remote location. The service staff gets high marks. **Parking:** on-site. **Cards:** MC, VI.

BROWNSBURG pop. 7,600

──── **WHERE TO STAY** ────

COMFORT SUITES-BROWNSBURG
AAA SAVE
▼▼▼
Motel

5/2-10/31   1P: $72-$79   2P: $81-$88   XP: $7   F18
4/1-5/1   1P: $67-$70   2P: $74-$77   XP: $7   F18
11/1-3/31   1P: $69   2P: $76   XP: $7   F18
Phone: (317)852-2000
Location: I-74, exit 66, just s, then 0.4 mi w. 500 W Northfield Dr 46112. Fax: 317/852-2112. **Facility:** 70 units. 69 one-bedroom standard units, some with whirlpools. 1 one-bedroom suite with whirlpool. 3 stories, interior corridors. *Bath:* combo or shower only. **Parking:** on-site. **Terms:** cancellation fee imposed, [ECP] meal plan available. **Amenities:** safes (fee), irons, hair dryers. **Pool(s):** small heated indoor. **Leisure Activities:** limited exercise equipment. **Guest Services:** valet and coin laundry. **Business Services:** meeting rooms, fax (fee). **Cards:** AX, CB, DC, DS, JC, MC, VI. **Special Amenities:** free continental breakfast and free local telephone calls.

SOME UNITS

──── **WHERE TO DINE** ────

BOULDER CREEK DINING COMPANY
▼▼▼ ▼▼▼
American

Lunch: $7-$10   Dinner: $11-$16   Phone: 317/858-8100
Location: I-74, exit 66, 0.4 mi n. 1551 N Green St 46112. **Hours:** 11 am-10 pm, Fri & Sat-11 pm, Sun-9 pm. Closed major holidays. **Features:** casual dress; children's menu; carryout; cocktails & lounge. Although the menu features sandwiches, burgers, beef tenderloin, seafood and pizzas cooked in a wood oven, the restaurant is known for its succulent ribs. Portions are plentiful, and the atmosphere is laid-back, especially on the breezy patio. **Parking:** on-site. **Cards:** AX, CB, DC, DS, MC, VI.

CARMEL pop. 25,400 (See map p. 463; index p. 467)

──── **WHERE TO DINE** ────

ILLUSIONS RESTAURANT
▼▼▼
American

Dinner: $12-$30   Phone: 317/575-8312   [73]
Location: I-465 N, exit 431 (Keystone), 1.7 mi n to Carmel Dr, just w. 969 Keystone Way 46032. **Hours:** 5 pm-9:30 pm, Fri-10 pm, Sat 4:30 pm-10 pm. Closed: Sun. **Reservations:** accepted. **Features:** casual dress; cocktails & lounge. Here you will find a magical, mystery tour for the family. The dining rooms entrance is through a mysterious gateway that traps you. Pulling the sword from the rock will reveal the passage way to the inner sanctum. Search for your menu by waving your hand through a seemingly empty hat. Then your waiter waves a magic wand and presto! your menu mysteriously appears. A wandering magician strolls by your table performing sleight-of-hand and other magic tricks. **Parking:** on-site. **Cards:** MC, VI.

CHESTERFIELD pop. 2,700

──── **WHERE TO STAY** ────

SUPER 8 MOTEL
▼▼▼
Motel

All Year   1P: $43-$53   2P: $47-$57   XP: $4   F12
Phone: 765/378-0888
Location: I-69, exit 34. (15701 W Commerce Rd, DALEVILLE, 47334). Fax: 765/378-0888. **Facility:** 43 one-bedroom standard units. 2 stories, interior/exterior corridors. **Parking:** on-site. **Terms:** 7 day cancellation notice, [ECP] meal plan available, pets ($25 deposit). **Amenities:** extended cable TV. **Guest Services:** coin laundry. **Business Services:** fax (fee). **Cards:** AX, DC, DS, MC, VI.

SOME UNITS

CICERO pop. 3,300

------ **WHERE TO DINE** ------

THE ANVIL INN   **Dinner:** $10-$20   **Phone:** 317/984-4533
◆◆◆   **Location:** Jct SR 19 and Jackson St, just e. 29 E Jackson St 46034. **Hours:** 5 pm-9 pm, Fri & Sat-10 pm.
American   Closed: Sun-Tues. **Features:** casual dress; cocktails & lounge. In a historic blacksmith's shop, the restaurant provides an intimate, down-home atmosphere. The distinctive decor incorporates framed photographs from yesteryear Indiana, tools of the blacksmithing trade, antique clocks and charming china.
Steak, seafood and pork chops are at the heart of the menu. **Parking:** on-site. **Cards:** MC, VI.

EDINBURGH pop. 4,500

------ **WHERE TO STAY** ------

BEST WESTERN HORIZON INN   **Phone:** (812)526-9883
◆◆◆ SAVE   All Year [ECP]   1P: $49-$129   2P: $59-$139   XP: $10   F17
◆◆ ◆◆   **Location:** I-65, exit 76B, just n. 11780 N US 31 46124. **Fax:** 812/526-2855. **Facility:** 57 one-bedroom standard
Motel   units, some with whirlpools. 2 stories, interior corridors. **Parking:** on-site, winter plug-ins. **Terms:** pets ($10 extra charge). **Amenities:** irons, hair dryers. **Pool(s):** heated indoor. **Cards:** AX, CB, DC, DS, JC, MC, VI.
Special Amenities: free continental breakfast and free local telephone calls.

SOME UNITS
[icons]

HAMPTON INN COLUMBUS/TAYLORSVILLE   **Phone:** 812/526-5100
SAVE   All Year [ECP]   1P: $69-$125   2P: $75-$131
◆◆ ◆◆   **Location:** I-65, exit 76B, just n. 12161 N US 31 46124. **Fax:** 812/526-3818. **Facility:** 94 one-bedroom standard
Motel   units, some with whirlpools. 4 stories, interior corridors. **Parking:** on-site. **Terms:** cancellation fee imposed.
Amenities: extended cable TV, dual phone lines, voice mail, irons, hair dryers. **Pool(s):** heated indoor.
Leisure Activities: exercise room. **Guest Services:** complimentary evening beverages: Mon-Thurs, valet and coin laundry. **Business Services:** meeting rooms, fax (fee). **Cards:** AX, CB, DC, DS, JC, MC, VI.

SOME UNITS
[icons]

HOLIDAY INN EXPRESS   **Phone:** (812)526-9899
◆◆ ◆◆   All Year   1P: $69-$79
Motel   **Location:** I-65, exit 76B, just n. 11711 US 31 46124. **Fax:** 812/526-9899. **Facility:** 62 one-bedroom standard units, some with whirlpools. 2 stories, interior corridors. **Parking:** on-site. **Terms:** [CP] meal plan available.
Amenities: extended cable TV, dual phone lines, voice mail, irons, hair dryers. **Pool(s):** heated indoor.
Leisure Activities: exercise room. **Guest Services:** valet and coin laundry. **Business Services:** meeting rooms, fax (fee).
Cards: AX, CB, DC, DS, JC, MC, VI.

SOME UNITS
[icons]

FISHERS pop. 7,500

------ **WHERE TO STAY** ------

FREDERICK-TALBOTT INN   **Phone:** (317)578-3600
◆◆◆◆   All Year [ECP]   2P: $124-$199   XP: $10
Bed & Breakfast   **Location:** I-465, exit 35 (Allisonville Rd), 6.2 mi n; I-69, exit 5, 1.5 mi w on 116th St to Allisonville Rd, then 2 mi n. 13805 Allisonville Rd 46038. **Fax:** 317/578-3600. **Facility:** The well-appointed guest rooms in this renovated historic house all feature hair dryers. Designated smoking area. 10 one-bedroom standard units, some with whirlpools. 2 stories, interior corridors. *Bath:* combo or shower only. **Parking:** on-site. **Terms:** check-in 4 pm, 7 day cancellation notice-fee imposed, [BP] meal plan available, package plans. **Amenities:** extended cable TV, hair dryers. **Leisure Activities:** horseshoes. **Business Services:** meeting rooms, fax (fee). **Cards:** AX, DC, DS, MC, VI.

SOME UNITS
[icons]

HOLIDAY INN EXPRESS-FISHERS   **Phone:** (317)578-2000
◆◆◆◆   All Year [ECP]   1P: $84-$95   2P: $84-$95   XP: $6   F18
Motel   **Location:** I-69, exit 3, just ne. 9790 North by Northeast Blvd 46038. **Fax:** 317/578-1111. **Facility:** 140 units. 128 one-bedroom standard units, some with whirlpools. 12 one-bedroom suites ($104-$154) with whirlpools. 2 stories, interior corridors. *Bath:* combo or shower only. **Parking:** on-site. **Amenities:** voice mail, irons, hair dryers. **Pool(s):** outdoor. **Leisure Activities:** limited exercise equipment. **Guest Services:** valet and coin laundry. **Business Services:** meeting rooms, fax (fee). **Cards:** AX, CB, DC, DS, MC, VI.

SOME UNITS
[icons]

HOLIDAY INN-INDIANAPOLIS NORTHEAST   **Phone:** (317)578-9000
◆◆◆   All Year   1P: $84-$99   2P: $84-$99
Motor Inn   **Location:** I-69, exit 3, just ne. 9780 North by Northeast Blvd 46038. **Fax:** 317/578-9999. **Facility:** 78 units. 70 one-bedroom standard units. 8 one-bedroom suites with whirlpools. 3 stories, interior corridors. *Bath:* combo or shower only. **Parking:** on-site. **Terms:** cancellation fee imposed, package plans. **Amenities:** voice mail, irons, hair dryers. **Pool(s):** small heated indoor. **Leisure Activities:** whirlpool, exercise room. **Guest Services:** valet and coin laundry. **Business Services:** meeting rooms, fax (fee). **Cards:** AX, CB, DC, DS, JC, MC, VI.

SOME UNITS
[icons]

STAYBRIDGE SUITES INDIANAPOLIS-FISHERS

Phone: (317)577-9500

▼▼▼▼

5/1-10/31 [ECP]   1P: $99-$119   2P: $119-$169
4/1-4/30 & 11/1-3/31 [ECP]   1P: $89-$109   2P: $109-$159

Extended Stay
Motel

Location: I-69, exit 3, just nw. (9780 Crosspoint Blvd, INDIANAPOLIS, 46256). Fax: 317/712-5200. **Facility:** 146 units. 55 one-bedroom standard units with efficiencies. 62 one- and 29 two-bedroom suites ($89-$169) with efficiencies. 5 stories, interior corridors. **Bath:** combo or shower only. **Parking:** on-site. **Terms:** 30 day cancellation notice-fee imposed, small pets only ($75 fee). **Amenities:** extended cable TV, dual phone lines, voice mail, irons, hair dryers. **Fee:** video tape library, high-speed Internet. **Pool(s):** small heated indoor. **Leisure Activities:** whirlpool, limited exercise equipment, sports court. **Guest Services:** complimentary evening beverages: Tues-Thurs, valet and coin laundry. **Business Services:** meeting rooms, business center, PC, fax (fee). **Cards:** AX, CB, DC, DS, JC, MC, VI.

FRANKLIN pop. 12,900

——— WHERE TO STAY ———

CARLTON LODGE-FRANKLIN

Phone: (317)736-0480

AAA SAVE
▼▼▼▼

5/16-10/31 [BP]   1P: $89-$99   2P: $89-$99   XP: $10   F18
4/1-5/15 & 11/1-3/31 [BP]   1P: $79-$89   2P: $79-$89   XP: $10   F18

Motel

Location: I-65, exit 90, just w. 2122 Holiday Ln 46131. Fax: 317/736-0480. **Facility:** 71 units. 69 one-bedroom standard units, some with whirlpools. 2 one-bedroom suites ($129-$159), some with whirlpools. 2 stories, interior corridors. **Bath:** combo or shower only. **Parking:** on-site. **Terms:** package plans. **Amenities:** extended cable TV, high-speed Internet, voice mail, irons, hair dryers. **Some:** dual phone lines. **Pool(s):** heated indoor. **Leisure Activities:** exercise room. **Guest Services:** complimentary evening beverages: Mon-Thurs, valet laundry. **Business Services:** meeting rooms, fax (fee). **Cards:** AX, CB, DC, DS, JC, MC, VI. **Special Amenities:** free continental breakfast and free local telephone calls.

SOME UNITS

QUALITY INN

Phone: (317)346-6444

SAVE
▼▼▼

All Year   1P: $48-$53   2P: $53-$59   XP: $10   F12

Motel

Location: I-65, exit 90, just w. 150 Lovers Ln 46131. Fax: 317/346-6445. **Facility:** 46 units. 42 one-bedroom standard units. 3 one- and 1 two-bedroom suites ($116-$150), some with kitchens and/or whirlpools. 2 stories, interior corridors. **Parking:** on-site. **Terms:** [CP] meal plan available. **Amenities:** extended cable TV. **Some:** hair dryers. **Pool(s):** small heated indoor. **Leisure Activities:** limited exercise equipment. **Guest Services:** coin laundry. **Business Services:** fax. **Cards:** AX, CB, DC, DS, JC, MC, VI.

SOME UNITS

GREENFIELD pop. 11,700

——— WHERE TO STAY ———

COMFORT INN-GREENFIELD/INDIANAPOLIS

Phone: (317)467-9999

SAVE
▼▼ ◆◆◆

4/1-10/31 [CP]   1P: $59-$189   2P: $69-$199   XP: $4   F12
11/1-3/31 [CP]   1P: $57-$189   2P: $66-$199   XP: $4   F12

Motel

Location: I-70, exit 104. 178 E Martindale Dr 46140. Fax: 317/467-9999. **Facility:** 60 one-bedroom standard units, some with whirlpools. 3 stories, interior corridors. **Bath:** combo or shower only. **Parking:** on-site. **Terms:** small pets only ($5 extra charge, must be caged). **Amenities:** extended cable TV, irons, hair dryers. **Pool(s):** small heated indoor. **Business Services:** fax (fee). **Cards:** AX, CB, DC, DS, JC, MC, VI.

SOME UNITS

LEES INN

Phone: (317)462-7112

▼▼◆▼

All Year [ECP]   1P: $59-$250   2P: $69-$260   XP: $10   F18

Motel

Location: I-70, exit 104. 2270 N State St 46140. Fax: 317/462-9801. **Facility:** 100 units. 92 one-bedroom standard units, some with whirlpools. 8 one-bedroom suites ($99-$260). 2 stories, interior corridors. **Parking:** on-site. **Terms:** 7 day cancellation notice. **Amenities:** irons, hair dryers. **Business Services:** meeting rooms, fax (fee). **Cards:** AX, DC, DS, JC, MC, VI.

SOME UNITS

SUPER 8 MOTEL

Phone: (317)462-8899

▼▼▼ ◆◆◆

All Year [CP]   1P: $45-$65   2P: $50-$65   XP: $4   F12

Motel

Location: I-70, exit 104, just s. 2100 N State St 46140. Fax: 317/462-8899. **Facility:** 80 one-bedroom standard units. 2 stories, interior corridors. **Parking:** on-site, winter plug-ins. **Terms:** package plans. **Amenities:** extended cable TV. **Pool(s):** small heated indoor. **Leisure Activities:** whirlpool. **Business Services:** meeting rooms, fax (fee). **Cards:** AX, CB, DC, DS, MC, VI. *(See color ad p 463)*

SOME UNITS

GREENWOOD pop. 26,300

——— WHERE TO STAY ———

COMFORT INN GREENWOOD

Phone: (317)887-1515

SAVE
▼▼ ◆▼

All Year   1P: $49-$200   2P: $54-$200   XP: $5   F18

Motel

Location: I-65, exit 99. 110 Sheek Rd 46143 (PO Box 901). Fax: 317/887-1515. **Facility:** 74 one-bedroom standard units, some with whirlpools. 2 stories, exterior corridors. **Parking:** on-site. **Terms:** 30 day cancellation notice-fee imposed, [ECP] meal plan available, small pets only ($5 extra charge). **Pool(s):** outdoor. **Business Services:** fax (fee). **Cards:** AX, CB, DC, DS, JC, MC, VI.

SOME UNITS

LEES INN & SUITES

Motel

All Year [ECP]   1P: $69-$450   2P: $79-$500   XP: $10   F18

Phone: (317)865-0100

Location: I-65, exit 99. 1281 S Park Dr 46143. Fax: 317/885-8376. **Facility:** 81 units. 76 one-bedroom standard units, some with whirlpools. 5 one-bedroom suites ($119-$450). 3 stories, interior corridors. *Bath:* combo or shower only. **Parking:** on-site. **Terms:** 7 day cancellation notice, small pets only (1st floor units, with signed waiver). **Amenities:** irons, hair dryers. **Pool(s):** small heated indoor. **Leisure Activities:** whirlpool, limited exercise equipment. **Guest Services:** valet laundry. **Business Services:** meeting rooms, fax (fee). **Cards:** AX, DC, DS, JC, MC, VI.

SOME UNITS

[ASK] [S/D] [🐕] [🍴] [&M] [⬩] [🌀] [🏊] [🎬] [DATA PORT] [🔌] [💻] [🖨] / [✕] /

─────── **WHERE TO DINE** ───────

─────── *The following restaurant has not been evaluated by AAA* ───────
but is listed for your information only.

CARVER'S STEAK & CHOPS

[fyi]

Phone: 317/887-6380

Not evaluated. **Location:** 780 US 31 N 46142. Corn-fed, Midwestern beef and an extensive wine list are offered at this restaurant.

LEBANON pop. 12,100

─────── **WHERE TO STAY** ───────

COMFORT INN

[AAA] [SAVE]

Motel

5/1-10/31 [ECP]	1P: $69-$205	2P: $76-$205	XP: $7 F18
11/1-3/31 [ECP]	1P: $65-$205	2P: $68-$205	XP: $7 F18
4/1-4/30 [ECP]	1P: $62-$205	2P: $67-$205	XP: $7 F18

Phone: (765)482-4800

Location: I-65, exit 140. 210 Sam Ralston Rd 46052. Fax: 765/482-4850. **Facility:** 57 one-bedroom standard units, some with whirlpools. 2 stories, interior corridors. **Parking:** on-site, winter plug-ins. **Amenities:** safes. *Some:* irons, hair dryers. **Pool(s):** small indoor. **Leisure Activities:** exercise room. **Guest Services:** valet laundry. **Business Services:** meeting rooms, fax (fee). **Cards:** AX, CB, DC, DS, JC, MC, VI. **Special Amenities: free continental breakfast and free local telephone calls.**

SOME UNITS

[S/D] [🍴] [🏊] [🎬] [DATA PORT] [🖨] / [✕] [🔌] [💻] [💻] /
FEE

SUPER 8 MOTEL

Motel

Property failed to provide current rates

Phone: 765/482-9999

Location: I-65, exit 140, just w. 405 N Mount Zion Rd 46052. Fax: 765/482-9999. **Facility:** 55 one-bedroom standard units, some with whirlpools. 1-2 stories, interior corridors. *Bath:* combo or shower only. **Parking:** on-site, winter plug-ins. **Terms:** pets ($10 extra charge). **Amenities:** extended cable TV. **Pool(s):** small indoor. **Guest Services:** coin laundry. **Cards:** AX, DS, MC, VI.

SOME UNITS

[🐕] [🍴] [⬩] [🏊] [🎬] / [✕] [🔌] [🖨]

─────── **WHERE TO DINE** ───────

USA ALL-STAR CAFE

American

Lunch: $6-$14   **Dinner:** $9-$17   **Phone:** 765/483-0400

Location: I-65, exit 140, 0.5 mi e. 100 S Smith St 46052. **Hours:** 11 am-10 pm. Closed major holidays; also Sun. **Features:** casual dress; carryout; cocktail lounge. A sports theme cafe located in a lovely brick building that was formerly a railroad station. The USA All Star-Cafe features pasta, steak, chicken and surf and turf. **Parking:** on-site. **Cards:** MC, VI.

[✕]

MARTINSVILLE pop. 11,700

─────── **WHERE TO STAY** ───────

COMFORT INN MARTINSVILLE

[SAVE]

Motel

All Year [CP]   1P: $60-$80   2P: $60-$80   XP: $5   F17

Phone: (765)342-1842

Location: Jct SR 37 and Ohio St, just w. 50 Bill's Blvd 46151. Fax: 765/342-2734. **Facility:** 49 one-bedroom standard units, some with whirlpools. 2 stories, interior corridors. **Parking:** on-site. **Terms:** 7 day cancellation notice, pets ($10 fee). **Amenities:** irons, hair dryers. **Leisure Activities:** limited exercise equipment. **Business Services:** meeting rooms. **Cards:** AX, DC, DS, MC, VI.

SOME UNITS

[S/D] [🐕] [🍴] [🎬] [💻] [🖨] / [✕] [🔌] [🖨] /

MOORESVILLE pop. 5,500

─────── **WHERE TO DINE** ───────

CHEZ JEAN

French

Dinner: $22-$45   **Phone:** 317/831-0870

Location: I-465, exit 8, 6.1 mi sw. 8821 S SR 67 46113. **Hours:** 6 pm-10 pm. Closed major holidays; also Sun & Mon. **Reservations:** suggested; weekends. **Features:** casual dress; cocktails & lounge. The cozy restaurant, away from the bustle of the city, is a quiet spot for dinner for two. Classic French creations are served in a country farmhouse setting. Dishes are prepared from scratch with high quality ingredients. The service staff is attentive. **Parking:** on-site. **Cards:** AX, MC, VI.

[✕]

NOBLESVILLE pop. 17,700

———— WHERE TO DINE ————

ALEXANDER'S ON THE SQUARE
    Lunch: $4-$7   **Dinner:** $4-$7   **Phone:** 317/773-9177
Location: Downtown. 864 Logan St 46060. **Hours:** 9 am-9 pm, Sat from 10 am; Sun from 11 am in summer.
Features: casual dress; a la carte. This 1950s soda shop-style eatery scoops up 36 flavors of hand-dipped
ice cream and an array of tasty sandwiches, salad and soup. The atmosphere is fun, festive and typical of
the old-fashioned ambience that fits nicely inside Alexander's historic digs. **Parking:** street.

American

CARRIGAN CROSSING
    Lunch: $7-$10   **Dinner:** $12-$25   **Phone:** 317/984-4477
Location: Jct SR 32, 3 mi n on SR 19, 1 mi w on 206th St, just n; in Morse Lake Marina. 20999 Hague Rd 46060.
Hours: 11 am-11 pm, Fri & Sat-midnight, Sun 10 am-10 pm. **Reservations:** accepted. **Features:** casual
dress; carryout; cocktails & lounge. A casual eatery located in a quiet marina setting overlooking Morse
Lake. Carrigan Crossing serves up a variety of very well prepared fresh seafood and the finest hand-cut
steak. The Cajun chicken pasta is colorfully presented in a large bowl and delicious. **Parking:** on-site. **Cards:** DS, MC, VI.

American

PLAINFIELD pop. 10,400

———— WHERE TO STAY ————

AMERIHOST INN-PLAINFIELD/INDIANAPOLIS
    Phone: (317)838-9300
All Year [ECP]   1P: $71-$149   2P: $76-$149   XP: $6   F18
Location: I-70, exit 66, just n. 6105 Cambridge Way 46168. Fax: 317/838-7018. **Facility:** 59 one-bedroom stan-
dard units, some with whirlpools. 2 stories, interior corridors. *Bath:* combo or shower only. **Parking:** on-site.
Terms: 30 day cancellation notice, package plans. **Amenities:** voice mail, safes (fee), irons, hair dryers.
Pool(s): heated indoor. **Leisure Activities:** whirlpool, limited exercise equipment. **Business Services:**
meeting rooms, fax (fee). **Cards:** AX, DC, DS, MC, VI. **Special Amenities:** free continental breakfast and
free newspaper.

Motel

SOME UNITS

COMFORT INN-INDIANAPOLIS/PLAINFIELD
    Phone: (317)839-9600
6/1-10/31 [ECP]   1P: $55-$275   2P: $55-$275   XP: $10   F18
4/1-5/31 & 11/1-3/31 [ECP]   1P: $55-$200   2P: $55-$225   XP: $10   F18
Location: I-70, exit 66, just n. 6107 Cambridge Way 46168. Fax: 317/839-7455. **Facility:** 66 one-bedroom standard units, some with whirlpools. 3 stories, interior corridors. *Bath:* combo or shower only. **Parking:** on-site.
Terms: package plans. **Amenities:** extended cable TV, voice mail, irons, hair dryers. **Pool(s):** small heated
indoor. **Leisure Activities:** limited exercise equipment. **Guest Services:** coin laundry. **Business Services:**
meeting rooms, fax (fee). **Cards:** AX, CB, DC, DS, MC, VI. **Special Amenities:** free continental breakfast and free local telephone calls.

Motel

SOME UNITS

DAYS INN-PLAINFIELD/INDIANAPOLIS
    Phone: (317)839-5000
All Year [ECP]   1P: $54-$225   2P: $73-$225   XP: $10   F18
Location: I-70, exit 66. 2245 Hadley Rd 46168. Fax: 317/839-9530. **Facility:** 63 one-bedroom standard units. 2
stories, exterior corridors. **Parking:** on-site. **Terms:** 30 day cancellation notice. **Amenities:** safes (fee), hair
dryers. **Cards:** AX, CB, DC, DS, MC, VI. **Special Amenities:** free continental breakfast and free room
upgrade (subject to availability with advanced reservations).

Motel

SOME UNITS

HAMPTON INN PLAINFIELD
    Phone: (317)839-9993
4/1-10/31 [ECP]   1P: $79-$99   2P: $85-$99
11/1-3/31 [ECP]   1P: $69-$99   2P: $69-$99
Location: I-70, exit 66, just n. 2244 Hadley Rd 46168. Fax: 317/839-0460. **Facility:** 79 units. 78 one- and 1 two-
bedroom standard units, some with whirlpools. 3 stories, interior corridors. *Bath:* combo or shower only.
Parking: on-site. **Terms:** check-in 4 pm, 3 day cancellation notice. **Amenities:** extended cable TV, dual
phone lines, voice mail, safes, irons, hair dryers. **Pool(s):** small heated indoor. **Leisure Activities:** limited
exercise equipment. **Guest Services:** valet laundry. **Business Services:** meeting rooms, business center, PC, fax. **Cards:** AX,
CB, DC, DS, JC, MC, VI.

Motel

SOME UNITS

HOLIDAY INN EXPRESS
    Phone: 317/839-9000
9/2-12/31 [ECP]   1P: $89-$300   2P: $89-$300   XP: $10   F18
4/1-9/1 [ECP]   1P: $99-$200   2P: $99-$200   XP: $10   F18
1/1-3/31 [ECP]   1P: $89-$109   2P: $89-$109   XP: $10   F18
Location: I-70, exit 66, just n. 6296 Cambridge Way 46168. Fax: 317/838-0000. **Facility:** 76 one-bedroom standard units, some with whirlpools. 3 stories, interior corridors. *Bath:* combo or shower only. **Parking:** on-site. **Terms:** 30 day cancellation notice, small pets only (must be caged). **Amenities:** voice mail, irons, hair dryers. **Pool(s):** heated outdoor. **Guest
Services:** valet and coin laundry. **Business Services:** meeting rooms, fax (fee). **Cards:** AX, CB, DC, DS, JC, MC, VI.

Motel

SOME UNITS

LEES INN & SUITES
    Phone: (317)837-9000
All Year [ECP]   1P: $69-$399   2P: $79-$409   XP: $10   F18
Location: I-70, exit 66, just n. 6010 Gateway Dr 46168. Fax: 317/837-1100. **Facility:** 81 units. 75 one-bedroom
standard units, some with whirlpools. 6 one-bedroom suites ($119-$409), some with whirlpools. 3 stories, interior corridors. *Bath:* combo or shower only. **Parking:** on-site. **Terms:** 7 day cancellation notice, small pets
only (1st floor units, with signed waiver). **Amenities:** irons, hair dryers. **Pool(s):** heated indoor. **Leisure Activities:** whirlpool,
limited exercise equipment. **Guest Services:** valet laundry. **Business Services:** meeting rooms, fax (fee). **Cards:** AX, DC, DS,
MC, VI.

Motel

SOME UNITS

SHELBYVILLE pop. 15,300

———— WHERE TO STAY ————

COMFORT INN

SAVE

◆◆ ◆◆

Motel

Phone: (317)398-8044

All Year [ECP]   1P: $65-$150   2P: $75-$175   XP: $7   F18
Location: I-74, exit 113. 36 W Rampart Dr 46176. Fax: 317/398-8442. **Facility:** 58 one-bedroom standard units, some with whirlpools. 3 stories, interior corridors. *Bath:* combo or shower only. **Parking:** on-site. **Terms:** 7 day cancellation notice, pets (in limited units). **Amenities:** irons, hair dryers. **Pool(s):** small heated indoor. **Guest Services:** valet laundry. **Business Services:** meeting rooms. **Cards:** AX, CB, DC, DS, MC, VI.

SOME UNITS

🆂🅳 🐾 🍴 🚿 ♿ 🏊 ♨ 📷 📶 💻 📠 / ⊠ 🔌 /
FEE

HOLIDAY INN EXPRESS

◆◆◆

Motel

Phone: 317/398-0472

4/1-10/31   1P: $74-$250   2P: $74-$250   XP: $7   F18
11/1-3/31   1P: $69-$250   2P: $69-$250   XP: $7   F18
Location: I-74, exit 113. 68 E Rampart St 46176. Fax: 317/398-0472. **Facility:** 50 one-bedroom standard units, some with whirlpools. 2 stories, interior corridors. *Bath:* combo, shower or tub only. **Parking:** on-site.
Terms: 7 day cancellation notice. **Amenities:** irons, hair dryers. **Pool(s):** small heated indoor. **Guest Services:** valet laundry.
Business Services: meeting rooms, fax (fee). **Cards:** AX, DC, DS, MC, VI.

SOME UNITS

ASK 🍴 ♿ 🏊 ♨ 📷 📶 💻 📠 / ⊠ 🔌 🖥 /

LEES INN

◆◆◆

Motel

Phone: (317)392-2299

All Year [ECP]   1P: $61-$250   2P: $71-$260   XP: $10   F18
Location: I-74, exit 116. 111 Lee Blvd 46176. Fax: 317/392-3575. **Facility:** 72 units. 61 one-bedroom standard units, some with whirlpools. 11 one-bedroom suites ($99-$260). 2 stories, interior corridors. **Parking:** on-site.
Terms: 7 day cancellation notice. **Amenities:** extended cable TV, irons, hair dryers. **Guest Services:** valet laundry. **Business Services:** meeting rooms, fax (fee). **Cards:** AX, DC, DS, JC, MC, VI.

SOME UNITS

ASK 🆂🅳 🐾 🍴 🌀 ♨ 📷 💻 📠 / ⊠ 📶 🔌 /

ZIONSVILLE pop. 5,300

———— WHERE TO DINE ————

ADAMS RIB & SEAFOOD HOUSE

◆◆

Steak & Seafood

Lunch: $7-$10   **Dinner:** $11-$20   **Phone:** 317/873-3301
Location: Center. 40 S Main St 46077. **Hours:** 11:30 am-2 & 5:30-9 pm. Closed major holidays; also Sun & Mon. **Reservations:** suggested; weekends. **Features:** casual dress; children's menu; cocktails; a la carte. In business since the early 1970s, the rustic restaurant is in a historic building with a warm, cozy fireplace. Upscale surf and turf, prime rib, barbecue ribs and such seafood choices as pike, salmon and swordfish, makes up a tempting menu. **Parking:** on-site. **Cards:** AX, DS, MC, VI.

⊠

This ends listings for the Indianapolis Vicinity.
The following page resumes the alphabetical listings of
cities in Indiana.

JASPER pop. 10,000

—— WHERE TO STAY ——

DAYS INN JASPER
SAVE

Motor Inn

DC, DS, MC, VI.

All Year [BP]   1P: $65-$79   2P: $65-$79   XP: $6   F18
Location: On SR 162 and 164, 0.5 mi e of jct US 231. 272 Brucke Strasse 47546 (PO Box 762). Fax: 812/482-7207. **Facility:** 84 units. 83 one-bedroom standard units. 1 one-bedroom suite. 2 stories, interior/exterior corridors. **Parking:** on-site, winter plug-ins. **Terms:** check-in 4 pm, small pets only ($5 extra charge). **Amenities:** extended cable TV, voice mail, hair dryers. *Some:* irons. **Leisure Activities:** miniature golf, playground, exercise room. **Guest Services:** valet and coin laundry. **Business Services:** meeting rooms. **Cards:** AX, CB,

Phone: (812)482-6000

HAMPTON INN
SAVE
Motel

5/25-9/1 [ECP]   1P: $83-$95   2P: $89-$101   XP: $5   F18
9/2-3/31 [ECP]   1P: $69-$79   2P: $74-$84   XP: $5   F18
4/1-5/24 [ECP]   1P: $69   2P: $74   XP: $5   F18
Location: On SR 162, just n from jct with SR 164. 355 3rd Ave 47546. Fax: 812/481-1811. **Facility:** 73 one-bedroom standard units. 3 stories, interior corridors. *Bath:* combo or shower only. **Parking:** on-site, winter plug-ins. **Amenities:** extended cable TV, dual phone lines, voice mail, irons, hair dryers. **Pool(s):** heated indoor. **Leisure Activities:** whirlpool, exercise room. **Guest Services:** valet and coin laundry. **Business Services:** meeting rooms. **Cards:** AX, CB, DC, DS, JC, MC, VI.

Phone: (812)481-1888

SLEEP INN
SAVE
Motel

5/25-9/1 [ECP]   1P: $70-$75   2P: $75-$80   XP: $5   F18
4/1-5/24 [ECP]   1P: $70-$70   2P: $70-$75   XP: $5   F18
9/2-3/31 [ECP]   1P: $65-$70   2P: $70-$75   XP: $5   F18
Location: On US 231, just s of jct SR 56 and 6th St. 75 Indiana St 47546. Fax: 812/634-2338. **Facility:** 56 one-bedroom standard units. 3 stories, interior corridors. *Bath:* combo or shower only. **Parking:** on-site, winter plug-ins. **Amenities:** extended cable TV. *Some:* irons, hair dryers. **Pool(s):** heated outdoor. **Guest Services:** valet laundry. **Business Services:** meeting rooms. **Cards:** AX, CB, DC, DS, JC, MC, VI.

Phone: (812)481-2008

—— WHERE TO DINE ——

SCHNITZELBANK
Traditional
German

Lunch: $7-$10   **Dinner:** $12-$22   **Phone:** 812/482-2640
Location: On SR 162, just s of jct SR 164. 393 3rd Ave 47546. **Hours:** 8 am-10 pm. Closed major holidays; also Sun. **Reservations:** suggested. **Features:** casual dress; children's menu; early bird specials; carryout; salad bar; cocktails & lounge. Traditional German fare, such as goulash, sauerbraten, Wiener schnitzel, knockwurst and kassler rippchen, is delivered in the light-hearted restaurant. Servers clad in Bavarian attire American entrees also serve entrees of steak and seafood. **Parking:** on-site. **Cards:** DS, MC, VI.

JEFFERSONVILLE pop. 22,000

—— WHERE TO STAY ——

FAIRFIELD INN LOUISVILLE NORTH
AAA **SAVE**
Motel

telephone calls.

All Year [ECP]   1P: $69-$149   2P: $69-$149
Location: I-65, exit 0, just w. 619 N Shore Dr 47130. Fax: 812/280-8211. **Facility:** 78 one-bedroom standard units, some with whirlpools. 3 stories, interior corridors. *Bath:* combo or shower only. **Parking:** on-site. **Amenities:** extended cable TV, dual phone lines, voice mail, irons, hair dryers. **Pool(s):** heated outdoor. **Leisure Activities:** whirlpool. **Guest Services:** valet and coin laundry. **Business Services:** meeting rooms, fax. **Cards:** AX, CB, DC, DS, JC, MC, VI. **Special Amenities:** free continental breakfast and free local

Phone: (812)280-8220

KENDALLVILLE pop. 7,800

—— WHERE TO STAY ——

BEST WESTERN KENDALLVILLE INN
AAA **SAVE**
Motel

All Year [ECP]   1P: $61-$69   2P: $61-$69   XP: $5   F17
Location: 1 mi e on US 6. 621 Professional Way 46755 (Box 769). Fax: 260/347-5263. **Facility:** 87 one-bedroom standard units, some with whirlpools. 2 stories, interior corridors. **Parking:** on-site. **Terms:** package plans. **Amenities:** irons, hair dryers. **Leisure Activities:** whirlpool. *Fee:* game room. **Guest Services:** valet and coin laundry. **Business Services:** meeting rooms. **Cards:** AX, CB, DC, DS, JC, MC, VI. **Special Amenities:** free continental breakfast and free local telephone calls.

Phone: (260)347-5263

KOKOMO pop. 45,000

─── WHERE TO STAY ───

COMFORT INN

SAVE

Motel

Phone: (765)452-5050

4/1-10/31 [CP]	1P: $62-$85	2P: $68-$95	XP: $6	F17
11/1-3/31 [CP]	1P: $66-$75	2P: $66-$83	XP: $6	F17

Location: US 31, just n of jct US 35. 522 Essex Dr 46901. Fax: 765/452-5050. **Facility:** 63 one-bedroom standard units. 2 stories, interior corridors. **Parking:** on-site, winter plug-ins. **Terms:** small pets only ($15 fee, in smoking units). **Amenities:** extended cable TV. *Some:* irons, hair dryers. **Pool(s):** small indoor. **Leisure Activities:** whirlpool. **Guest Services:** valet laundry. **Cards:** AX, DC, DS, MC, VI.

SOME UNITS

COURTYARD BY MARRIOTT

AAA SAVE

Motel

Phone: (765)453-0800

All Year	1P: $69-$89	2P: $69-$89

Location: US 31, 3 mi s of jct US 35. 411 Kentucky Dr 46902. Fax: 765/455-2075. **Facility:** 90 units. 87 one-bedroom standard units. 3 one-bedroom suites ($129-$149). 3 stories, interior corridors. **Bath:** combo or shower only. **Parking:** on-site. **Terms:** cancellation fee imposed. **Amenities:** video games, dual phone lines, voice mail, irons, hair dryers. **Pool(s):** heated indoor. **Leisure Activities:** whirlpool, exercise room. **Guest Services:** valet and coin laundry. **Business Services:** meeting rooms, fax (fee). **Cards:** AX, CB, DC, DS, JC, MC, VI. *(See color ad card insert)*

SOME UNITS

DAYS INN & SUITES

SAVE

Motor Inn

Phone: (765)453-7100

All Year [CP]	1P: $52-$82	2P: $57-$82	XP: $7	F17

Location: US 31, 2.8 mi s of US 35. 264 US 31 S 46902. Fax: 765/453-7101. **Facility:** 79 one-bedroom standard units. 2 stories, exterior corridors. **Parking:** on-site. **Terms:** 7 day cancellation notice. **Amenities:** extended cable TV, hair dryers. *Some:* irons. **Guest Services:** coin laundry. **Cards:** AX, CB, DC, DS, MC, VI.

SOME UNITS

HAMPTON INN & SUITES

SAVE

Motel

Phone: (765)455-2900

All Year [ECP]	1P: $79-$159	2P: $86-$159

Location: US 31, 2 mi s of jct US 35. 2920 S Reed Rd (US Hwy 31) 46902. Fax: 765/455-2800. **Facility:** 105 units. 78 one-bedroom standard units, some with whirlpools. 27 one-bedroom suites with efficiencies. 5 stories, interior corridors. **Bath:** combo or shower only. **Parking:** on-site. **Amenities:** video games, voice mail, irons. *Some:* dual phone lines, hair dryers. **Leisure Activities:** whirlpool, exercise room. **Guest Services:** coin laundry. **Business Services:** meeting rooms, fax (fee). **Cards:** AX, CB, DC, DS, JC, MC, VI.

SOME UNITS

HOLIDAY INN EXPRESS
Phone: (765)453-2222

▼▼▼▼

Motel

All Year [ECP]   1P: $88

Location: US 31, 2.8 mi s of jct US 35. 511 Albany Dr 46902. Fax: 765/453-4398. **Facility:** 79 units. 75 one-bedroom standard units. 4 one-bedroom suites. 3 stories, interior corridors. *Bath:* combo or shower only. **Parking:** on-site. **Terms:** 14 day cancellation notice. **Amenities:** extended cable TV, dual phone lines, voice mail, irons, hair dryers. **Pool(s):** small indoor. **Leisure Activities:** exercise room. **Guest Services:** complimentary evening beverages: Mon-Thurs, valet and coin laundry. **Business Services:** meeting rooms, fax (fee). **Cards:** AX, CB, DC, DS, JC, MC, VI.

SOME UNITS

(ASK) (S/D) (⊞•) (&M) (⊙) (⊘) (➔) (※) (DATA PORT) (□) (▤) (◻) (➗) / (✕) (VCR) /

KOKOMO FAIRFIELD INN
Phone: (765)453-8822

◆◆◆ SAVE

▼▼ ▼▼▼

Motel

4/1-9/30 [CP]   1P: $59-$149   2P: $59-$149
10/1-3/31 [CP]   1P: $55-$85   2P: $55-$85

Location: US 31, 2 mi s of jct US 35. 1717 E Lincoln Rd 46902. Fax: 765/453-8822. **Facility:** 61 one-bedroom standard units. 3 stories, interior corridors. **Parking:** on-site, winter plug-ins. **Amenities:** extended cable TV, irons. **Pool(s):** small heated indoor. **Leisure Activities:** whirlpool. **Guest Services:** valet laundry. **Business Services:** meeting rooms, fax (fee). **Cards:** AX, DC, DS, MC, VI. **Special Amenities: free continental breakfast and free local telephone calls.** *(See color ad card insert)*

SOME UNITS

(S/D) (⊞•) (➔) (※) (DATA PORT) (➗) / (✕) (□) (▤) /
FEE

SIGNATURE INN-KOKOMO
Phone: (765)455-1000

▼▼ ▼▼▼

Motel

All Year [CP]   1P: $61-$72   2P: $61-$70

Location: US 31, 2.5 mi s of jct US 35. 4021 S LaFountain St 46902. Fax: 765/455-1000. **Facility:** 101 one-bedroom standard units, some with whirlpools. 2 stories, interior corridors. **Parking:** on-site. **Amenities:** extended cable TV, voice mail, irons, hair dryers. **Pool(s):** heated indoor. **Leisure Activities:** whirlpool, sun deck, exercise room. **Guest Services:** valet laundry. **Business Services:** meeting rooms, business center, PC. **Cards:** AX, DC, DS, MC, VI.

SOME UNITS

(ASK) (S/D) (⊞•) (⊘) (➔) (✕) (※) (DATA PORT) (□) (▤) (◻) (➗) / (✕) /

SUPER 8 MOTEL
Phone: 765/455-3288

▼▼ ▼▼▼

Motel

All Year   1P: $53   2P: $58   XP: $8   F17

Location: US 31, 2.8 mi s of jct US 35. 5110 Clinton Dr 46902. Fax: 765/455-3288. **Facility:** 56 units. 55 one-bedroom standard units, some with whirlpools. 1 one-bedroom suite. 2 stories, interior corridors. *Bath:* combo or shower only. **Parking:** on-site. **Terms:** small pets only ($50 deposit). **Amenities:** extended cable TV. **Pool(s):** small indoor. **Guest Services:** valet laundry. **Cards:** AX, CB, DC, DS, JC, MC, VI.

SOME UNITS

(ASK) (S/D) (🐾) (⊞•) (&) (➔) (※) (DATA PORT) / (✕) (□) (▤) (◻) /

——— **WHERE TO DINE** ———

HACIENDA MEXICAN RESTAURANT   Lunch: $6-$12   Dinner: $6-$12   Phone: 765/452-8231

▼▼ ▼▼▼

Mexican

Location: US 31, 0.4 mi w on Boulevard St, just n. 2006 S Plate St 46902. **Hours:** 11 am-10 pm, Fri & Sat-11 pm. Closed major holidays. **Features:** casual dress; carryout; cocktails & lounge; a la carte. "Wet burritos" are the house specialty at the colorful, upbeat restaurant. The menu includes huge helpings of standard favorites, such as tacos, chimichangas and enchiladas, as well as two types of chili. Antique Mexican photographs decorate the walls. **Parking:** on-site. **Cards:** AX, MC, VI.

(✕)

LADOGA pop. 1,100

——— **WHERE TO STAY** ———

RENAISSANCE GALLERY AND TOWERS
Phone: (765)942-2108

◆◆◆ SAVE

▼▼ ▼▼▼

Historic Bed
& Breakfast

All Year [ECP]   1P: $75-$110   2P: $110-$250   XP: $35   D12

Location: Center. 102 E Main 47954. Fax: 765/942-2110. **Facility:** This restored 1876 building in the heart of a small town features a first floor art gallery. Bedrooms are themed in the names of Renaissance artists. Smoke free premises. 5 one-bedroom standard units. 2 stories, interior corridors. *Bath:* combo or shower only. **Parking:** street. **Terms:** check-in 4 pm, 14 day cancellation notice-fee imposed. **Business Services:** meeting rooms. **Cards:** AX, DC, DS, MC, VI. *(See color ad card insert)*

SOME UNITS

(⊞•) (✕) / (□) /

LAFAYETTE pop. 43,800—*See also WEST LAFAYETTE.*

——— **WHERE TO STAY** ———

BAYMONT INN
Phone: (765)446-2400

◆◆◆ SAVE

▼▼ ▼▼▼

Motel

All Year [ECP]   1P: $67-$77   2P: $72-$82

Location: I-65, exit 172. 312 Meijer Dr 47905. Fax: 765/446-2401. **Facility:** 77 one-bedroom standard units. 3 stories, interior corridors. *Bath:* combo or shower only. **Parking:** on-site. **Terms:** 7 day cancellation notice. **Amenities:** extended cable TV, video games, voice mail, irons, hair dryers. **Pool(s):** small heated indoor. **Leisure Activities:** whirlpool, sun deck, patio. **Guest Services:** valet and coin laundry. **Cards:** AX, DC, DS, MC, VI. **Special Amenities: free continental breakfast and free newspaper.**

SOME UNITS

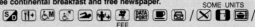
(S/D) (⊞•) (&M) (&) (➔) (↔) (※) (DATA PORT) (□) (▤) (◻) / (✕) (□) (▤) /
FEE

BUDGET INN OF AMERICA

Phone: (765)447-7566

AAA SAVE

All Year [CP] 1P: $45-$75 2P: $49-$79 XP: $5 F16
Location: I-65, exit 172. 139 Frontage Rd 47905. Fax: 765/448-2833. **Facility:** 94 one-bedroom standard units. 2 stories, exterior corridors. **Parking:** on-site. **Terms:** small pets only. **Amenities:** extended cable TV. **Guest Services:** coin laundry. **Cards:** AX, CB, DC, DS, MC, VI. **Special Amenities:** free continental breakfast.

Motel *(See ad below)*

SOME UNITS
 / FEE

COMFORT SUITES

Phone: (765)447-0016

AAA SAVE

All Year 1P: $79-$185 2P: $85-$185 XP: $6 F18
Location: I-65, exit 172, just e. 31 Frontage Rd 47905. Fax: 765/447-9980. **Facility:** 62 one-bedroom standard units, some with whirlpools. 2 stories, interior corridors. *Bath:* combo or shower only. **Parking:** on-site. **Terms:** 14 day cancellation notice, small pets only ($10 extra charge, in smoking units). **Amenities:** extended cable TV, dual phone lines, irons, hair dryers. **Pool(s):** heated indoor. **Leisure Activities:** sauna, outdoor spa, exercise room. **Guest Services:** valet and coin laundry. **Business Services:** meeting rooms.

Motel

Cards: AX, DC, DS, JC, MC, VI. **Special Amenities:** free continental breakfast and free local telephone calls.
(See ad below)

SOME UNITS
/ FEE

FAIRFIELD INN

Phone: (765)449-0083

AAA SAVE

10/1-3/31 [CP] 1P: $75-$104 2P: $75-$104
4/1-9/30 [CP] 1P: $70-$99 2P: $70-$99
Location: I-65, exit 172, 0.5 mi w. 4000 SR 26 E 47905. Fax: 765/449-0083. **Facility:** 79 one-bedroom standard units. 3 stories, interior corridors. *Bath:* combo or shower only. **Parking:** on-site. **Terms:** 31 day cancellation notice. **Amenities:** extended cable TV, irons. **Pool(s):** heated indoor. **Leisure Activities:** whirlpool. **Guest Services:** valet laundry. **Business Services:** meeting rooms. **Cards:** AX, CB, DC, DS, MC, VI.

Motel

Special Amenities: free continental breakfast and free local telephone calls. *(See color ad card insert)*

SOME UNITS
/ FEE

HAMPTON INN

Phone: (765)447-1600

SAVE

All Year [ECP] 1P: $79-$125 2P: $87-$125 XP: $8 F18
Location: I-65, exit 172, 0.8 mi w. 3941 SR 26 E 47905. Fax: 765/449-9963. **Facility:** 62 one-bedroom standard units, some with efficiencies and/or whirlpools. 3 stories, interior corridors. *Bath:* combo or shower only. **Parking:** on-site. **Terms:** package plans. **Amenities:** video games, dual phone lines, voice mail, irons, hair dryers. **Pool(s):** heated indoor. **Leisure Activities:** whirlpool. **Guest Services:** valet laundry. **Cards:** AX, CB, DC, DS, MC, VI.

Motel

SOME UNITS
/ FEE

HOLIDAY INN EXPRESS
Phone: 765/449-4808
AAA SAVE
WWW
Motel
All Year [ECP] 1P: $65-$220 2P: $65-$220
Location: I-65, exit 172. 201 Frontage Rd 47905. Fax: 765/448-1939. **Facility:** 63 units. 62 one-bedroom standard units, some with whirlpools. 1 one-bedroom suite. 3 stories, interior corridors. *Bath:* combo or shower only. **Parking:** on-site. **Terms:** 30 day cancellation notice. **Amenities:** extended cable TV, irons, hair dryers. **Guest Services:** valet laundry. **Cards:** AX, CB, DC, DS, JC, MC, VI. **Special Amenities:** free newspaper and free room upgrade (subject to availability with advanced reservations). *(See ad below)*

SOME UNITS
(S D) (🐕) (🍴) (🛁) (❄) (DATA PORT) (☕) / (✕) (🔌) /
FEE   FEE

HOMEWOOD SUITES
Phone: (765)448-9700
SAVE
WWW
Suite Motel
All Year [ECP] 1P: $99-$179 2P: $99-$179
Location: I-65, exit 172, 0.8 mi w. 3939 SR 26 E 47905. Fax: 765/449-1297. **Facility:** 84 units. 76 one- and 8 two-bedroom suites with efficiencies. 3 stories, interior/exterior corridors. **Parking:** on-site. **Terms:** package plans, pets ($50 extra charge). **Amenities:** extended cable TV, video tape library (fee), dual phone lines, voice mail, irons, hair dryers. **Pool(s):** heated outdoor. **Leisure Activities:** sauna, whirlpool, exercise room, basketball. **Guest Services:** gift shop, complimentary evening beverages, valet and coin laundry. **Business Services:** meeting rooms, business center, PC. **Cards:** AX, CB, DC, DS, JC, MC, VI.

SOME UNITS
(✈) (🐕) (🍴) (🅿) (🛌) (✕) (VCR) (DATA PORT) (🔌) (☕) (☕) / (✕) /

KNIGHTS INN
Phone: 765/447-5611
WWW
Motel
Property failed to provide current rates
Location: I-65, exit 172, 0.3 mi w. 4110 SR 26 E 47905. Fax: 765/449-4996. **Facility:** 108 one-bedroom standard units. 1 story, exterior corridors. **Parking:** on-site. **Terms:** check-in 4 pm, pets ($15 fee, in smoking units). **Amenities:** extended cable TV, safes (fee). **Pool(s):** small outdoor. **Cards:** AX, CB, DC, DS, MC, VI.

SOME UNITS
(🐕) (🍴) (🛌) (DATA PORT) / (✕) (🔌) (☕) (☕) /

LEES INN & SUITES
Phone: (765)447-3434
WWW
Motel
All Year [ECP] 1P: $69-$249 2P: $79-$300 XP: $10 F18
Location: I-65, exit 172, just e on SR 26. 4701 Meijer Ct 47905. Fax: 765/448-6105. **Facility:** 81 units. 75 one-bedroom standard units, some with whirlpools. 6 one-bedroom suites ($119-$300), some with whirlpools. 3 stories, interior corridors. *Bath:* combo or shower only. **Parking:** on-site. **Terms:** 7 day cancellation notice, small pets only. **Amenities:** extended cable TV, irons, hair dryers. **Pool(s):** heated indoor. **Leisure Activities:** whirlpool, exercise room. **Guest Services:** valet laundry. **Business Services:** meeting rooms. **Cards:** AX, DC, DS, JC, MC, VI.

SOME UNITS
(ASK) (S D) (🐕) (🍴) (🛎) (🅿) (🛌) (📹) (DATA PORT) (🔌) (☕) (☕) / (✕) /

LOEB HOUSE INN
Phone: (765)420-7737
WWW
Historic Bed
& Breakfast
All Year [BP] 1P: $89-$175 2P: $89-$175 XP: $20 F8
Location: SR 38, 0.4 mi n on 9th St, just w. 708 Cincinnati St 47901. Fax: 765/420-7805. **Facility:** Antiques-furnished and elegantly appointed public areas distinguish this restored 1822 home, which has fireplaces in some guest rooms. Smoke free premises. 5 one-bedroom standard units, some with whirlpools. 3 stories, interior corridors. **Parking:** on-site. **Terms:** check-in 4 pm, age restrictions may apply, 4 day cancellation notice, package plans. **Amenities:** extended cable TV. **Guest Services:** complimentary evening beverages. **Business Services:** meeting rooms. **Cards:** AX, MC, VI.

(ASK) (🍴) (❄) (✕)

RADISSON INN-LAFAYETTE
Phone: (765)447-0575
AAA SAVE
WWW
Motor Inn
All Year 1P: $78-$199 XP: $10 F18
Location: I-65, exit 172, 0.3 mi n. 4343 SR 26 E 47905. Fax: 765/447-0901. **Facility:** 124 one-bedroom standard units, some with whirlpools. 6 stories, interior corridors. *Bath:* combo or shower only. **Parking:** on-site. **Terms:** 30 day cancellation notice, package plans, small pets only ($15 extra charge). **Amenities:** video games, voice mail, irons, hair dryers. **Dining:** restaurant, 6:30 am-2 & 5-9:30 pm, Sat 7 am-2 & 5-10 pm, Sun-9 pm, $12-$28, cocktails. **Pool(s):** small heated indoor. **Leisure Activities:** sauna, whirlpool. **Guest Services:** valet and coin laundry, airport transportation-Purdue Airport, area transportation-local businesses. **Business Services:** conference facilities. **Cards:** AX, DC, DS, JC, MC, VI. **Special Amenities:** free local telephone calls and free newspaper.

SOME UNITS
(S D) (✈) (🐕) (🛌) (🍴) (🍽) (🛎) (🅿) (🛌) (❄) (🎬) (DATA PORT) (🔌) (☕) (☕) / (✕) (VCR) (☕) /
FEE   FEE

RAMADA INN-LAFAYETTE

Phone: (765)447-9460

AAA SAVE

Motor Inn

All Year [ECP]   1P: $75-$169   2P: $82-$169   XP: $7   F18
Location: I-65, exit 172, 0.3 mi w. 4221 SR 26 E 47905. **Fax:** 765/447-4905. **Facility:** 144 one-bedroom standard units, some with whirlpools. 4 stories, interior corridors. **Parking:** on-site. **Terms:** small pets only. **Amenities:** extended cable TV, voice mail, safes. **Dining:** restaurant, 11 am-midnight, Fri & Sat-1 am, $8-$17, cocktails. **Pool(s):** outdoor. **Leisure Activities:** exercise room. **Guest Services:** valet and coin laundry. **Business Services:** meeting rooms. **Cards:** AX, CB, DC, DS, JC, MC, VI. **Special Amenities:** free continental breakfast and free local telephone calls.

SOME UNITS

RED ROOF INN-LAFAYETTE

Phone: (765)448-4671

AAA SAVE

Motel

4/28-11/16   1P: $41-$59   2P: $47-$65   XP: $6   F18
11/17-3/31   1P: $38-$57   2P: $44-$63   XP: $6   F18
4/1-4/27   1P: $36-$55   2P: $42-$61   XP: $6   F18
Location: I-65, exit 72, 0.3 mi w. 4201 SR 26 E 47905. **Fax:** 765/448-9726. **Facility:** 80 one-bedroom standard units. 2 stories, exterior corridors. *Bath:* combo or shower only. **Parking:** on-site. **Amenities:** extended cable TV, video games, voice mail. **Cards:** AX, CB, DC, DS, MC, VI. **Special Amenities:** free local telephone calls and free newspaper.

SOME UNITS

FEE

SIGNATURE INN LAFAYETTE

Phone: (765)447-4142

Motel

All Year [CP]   1P: $61   2P: $61-$70
Location: I-65, exit 172. 4320 SR 26 E 47905. **Fax:** 765/447-4142. **Facility:** 121 one-bedroom standard units, some with whirlpools. 2 stories, interior corridors. **Parking:** on-site. **Terms:** package plans. **Amenities:** extended cable TV, voice mail, irons, hair dryers. **Pool(s):** heated outdoor. **Guest Services:** valet laundry. **Business Services:** meeting rooms, business center, PC, fax. **Cards:** AX, CB, DC, DS, MC, VI.

SOME UNITS

——— WHERE TO DINE ———

SPAGEDDIES ITALIAN KITCHEN

Lunch: $5-$10   **Dinner:** $8-$13   **Phone:** 765/449-0773

Italian

Location: I-65, exit 172, 0.8 mi w. 3990 SR 26 E 47905. **Hours:** 11 am-10 pm, Fri & Sat-11 pm. Closed: 11/28, 12/25. **Reservations:** accepted. **Features:** casual dress; children's menu; carryout; cocktails & lounge; a la carte. The casual Italian eatery features an open kitchen in which a variety of pasta dishes are nicely prepared. Seafood also makes the menu here. Penne pasta with chicken in a four-cheese sauce is delightful. **Parking:** on-site. **Cards:** AX, DC, DS, MC, VI.

LAPORTE pop. 21,500

——— WHERE TO STAY ———

RAMADA INN

Phone: (574)362-4585

Motor Inn

All Year [BP]   1P: $69-$129   2P: $69-$129   XP: $10   F17
Location: 1.5 mi n on US 35. 444 Pine Lake Ave 46350. **Fax:** 574/324-6993. **Facility:** 140 one-bedroom standard units. 4 stories, interior corridors. **Parking:** on-site. **Terms:** check-in 4 pm, 14 day cancellation notice, package plans, small pets only ($25 extra charge). **Amenities:** voice mail, safes (fee), irons, hair dryers. **Pool(s):** heated indoor/outdoor. **Leisure Activities:** whirlpool, putting green, playground, exercise room. **Guest Services:** gift shop, valet and coin laundry. **Business Services:** conference facilities. **Cards:** AX, DC, DS, MC, VI.

SOME UNITS

LAWRENCEBURG —*See Cincinnati p. 589.*

LEAVENWORTH pop. 300

——— WHERE TO STAY ———

THE LEAVENWORTH INN

Phone: 812/739-2120

AAA SAVE

Historic Bed
& Breakfast

1/1-3/31 [BP]   1P: $79-$99   2P: $79-$99   XP: $10   F12
9/15-10/31 [BP]   1P: $99   2P: $99   XP: $10   F12
4/1-9/14 [BP]   1P: $74-$94   2P: $74-$94   XP: $10   F12
11/1-12/31 [BP]   1P: $79   2P: $79   XP: $10   F12
Location: I-64, exit 92, 3 mi s on SR 66, then 0.5 mi e. 930 W SR 62 47137 (PO Box 9). **Fax:** 812/739-2012. **Facility:** This restored white-frame 1890s farmhouse has an inviting front porch, pine-plank floors and spacious rooms and baths. Smoke free premises. 10 units. 9 one-bedroom standard units. 1 one-bedroom suite ($94-$119) with whirlpool. 2 stories, interior corridors. **Parking:** on-site. **Terms:** check-in 4 pm, 5 day cancellation notice-fee imposed, package plans. **Amenities:** extended cable TV, hair dryers. **Leisure Activities:** tennis court, bicycles, jogging, exercise room, horseshoes. **Business Services:** PC. **Cards:** AX, DC, DS, MC, VI. **Special Amenities:** free local telephone calls and preferred room (subject to availability with advanced reservations).

LEBANON —*See Indianapolis p. 492.*

LEESBURG

─── WHERE TO STAY ───

PRAIRIE HOUSE BED & BREAKFAST   **Phone:** 574/658-9211

▽▽▽▽   All Year [BP]   1P: $45   2P: $60-$65

Bed & Breakfast   **Location:** Jct SR 15, 1 mi e. 495 E 900 N 46538. **Fax:** 574/453-4787. **Facility:** A charming B&B located in a quiet farmland setting that is surrounded by mature trees and brilliantly colored wild flowers. The B&B features a warm country decor throughout the common areas and rooms. Smoke free premises. 4 one-bedroom standard units. 2 stories, interior corridors. *Bath:* some shared or private, shower only. **Parking:** on-site. **Terms:** check-in 4 pm, age restrictions may apply, 5 day cancellation notice-fee imposed. **Guest Services:** TV in common area. **Cards:** MC, VI.

SOME UNITS
(ASK) ✈ ✕ 𝓦 / (VCR) /

LOGANSPORT pop. 16,800

─── WHERE TO STAY ───

HOLIDAY INN   **Phone:** (574)753-6351

▽▽▽▽   6/2-8/20 [ECP]   1P: $90   XP: $6   F18
         4/1-6/1 & 8/21-3/31 [ECP] 1P: $80   XP: $6   F18

Motor Inn   **Location:** 2.5 mi e on US 24. 3550 E Market St 46947-0813 (PO Box 813). **Fax:** 574/722-1568. **Facility:** 92 units. 91 one-bedroom standard units. 1 one-bedroom suite ($110-$140) with whirlpool. 2 stories, interior corridors.
Parking: on-site. **Terms:** 30 day cancellation notice, package plans. **Amenities:** extended cable TV, voice mail, irons, hair dryers. **Pool(s):** outdoor. **Leisure Activities:** exercise room. **Guest Services:** valet laundry. **Business Services:** conference facilities. **Cards:** AX, DC, DS, MC, VI.

SOME UNITS
(ASK) (S/D) 🛏 🍴 ⛾ (&M) 🏊 ☎ (DATA PORT) 🖥 🖨 / ✕ 🔋 🖨 /
                    FEE   FEE FEE

MADISON pop. 12,000

─── WHERE TO STAY ───

CARRIAGE HOUSE BED & BREAKFAST   **Phone:** (812)265-6892

◈◈ ◈◈   5/1-10/31 [BP]   1P: $90-$100   2P: $90-$100   XP: $25   F6

Historic Bed   **Location:** In historic district; just s of Main St (SR 56), between Poplar and Broadway sts. 308 W 2nd St 47250.
& Breakfast   **Facility:** Designated smoking area. 1 one-bedroom standard unit. 2 stories, exterior corridors. *Bath:* tub only.
Parking: street. **Terms:** open 5/1-10/31, 7 day cancellation notice. **Amenities:** hair dryers.

✕ (VCR) 🔋 🖥 🖨 🖨

MARION pop. 32,600

─── WHERE TO STAY ───

COMFORT SUITES   **Phone:** (765)651-1006

(AAA) (SAVE)   All Year [ECP]   1P: $79-$125   2P: $79-$125   XP: $5   F18

▽▽▽▽   **Location:** On SR 9, 1.5 mi n of SR 18. 1345 N Baldwin Ave 46952. **Fax:** 765/651-0145. **Facility:** 62 units. 61 one-
Motel   bedroom standard units, some with whirlpools. 1 one-bedroom suite. 2 stories, interior corridors. *Bath:* combo or shower only. **Parking:** on-site. **Terms:** 3 day cancellation notice, pets ($10 extra charge, in smoking units). **Amenities:** irons, hair dryers. **Pool(s):** heated indoor. **Leisure Activities:** sauna, whirlpool, sun deck, exercise room. **Guest Services:** coin laundry. **Business Services:** meeting rooms. **Cards:** AX, CB, DC, DS, JC, MC, VI. **Special Amenities: free continental breakfast and free local telephone calls.**

SOME UNITS
(S/D) 🛏 🍴 ⛾ 🚲 🏊 ✕ ☎ (DATA PORT) 🔋 🖥 🖨 🖨 / ✕ /

HAMPTON INN   **Phone:** 765/662-6656

(AAA) (SAVE)   All Year [ECP]   1P: $79-$129   2P: $79-$129

▽▽▽▽   **Location:** On SR 9, 1.5 mi n of SR 18. 1502 N Baldwin Ave 46952. **Fax:** 765/662-6653. **Facility:** 73 one-bedroom
Motel   standard units, some with whirlpools. 3 stories, interior corridors. *Bath:* combo or shower only. **Parking:** on-site. **Amenities:** extended cable TV, high-speed Internet, dual phone lines, voice mail, irons, hair dryers. **Pool(s):** heated indoor. **Leisure Activities:** exercise room. **Guest Services:** coin laundry. **Business Services:** meeting rooms. **Cards:** AX, CB, DC, DS, JC, MC, VI. **Special Amenities: free continental breakfast and free local telephone calls.**

SOME UNITS
(S/D) 🍴 (&M) 🏊 ☎ (DATA PORT) 🔋 🖥 🖨 🖨 / ✕ /

HOLIDAY INN-MARION   **Phone:** (765)668-8801

▽▽ ▽▽   All Year [BP]   1P: $66   XP: $6   F18

Motor Inn   **Location:** On SR 18, at corner of 4th and Shunk sts. 501 E 4th St 46952. **Fax:** 765/662-6827. **Facility:** 121 one-
bedroom standard units. 5 stories, interior corridors. **Parking:** on-site. **Terms:** 3 day cancellation notice, package plans. **Amenities:** extended cable TV, irons, hair dryers. **Pool(s):** heated outdoor. **Leisure Activities:** exercise room. **Guest Services:** valet and coin laundry. **Business Services:** meeting rooms. **Cards:** AX, CB, DC, DS, JC, MC, VI.

SOME UNITS
(ASK) (S/D) 🛏 🍴 ⛾ 🏊 ☎ (DATA PORT) 🖥 🖨 / ✕ 🔋 🖨 /

SUPER 8 MOTEL GAS CITY   **Phone:** (765)998-6800

▽▽ ▽▽   4/1-10/31   1P: $45-$55   2P: $45-$65   XP: $5   F18
         11/1-3/31   1P: $45-$50   2P: $45-$60   XP: $5   F18

Motel   **Location:** I-69, exit 59. 5172 S Kaybee Dr 46953. **Fax:** 765/998-6810. **Facility:** 45 one-bedroom standard units. 2 stories, interior corridors. *Bath:* combo or shower only. **Parking:** on-site, winter plug-ins. **Terms:** 3 day cancellation notice, package plans, small pets only ($15 extra charge). **Guest Services:** coin laundry. **Business Services:** fax (fee). **Cards:** AX, DC, DS, MC, VI.

SOME UNITS
(ASK) (S/D) 🛏 ⛾ 🥽 (DATA PORT) 🖨 / ✕ /

MARKLE

―――― **WHERE TO STAY** ――――

SLEEP INN
AAA SAVE
▼▼▼
Motel

Phone: (260)758-8111
All Year [CP]   1P: $54-$130   2P: $59-$130   XP: $5   F19
Location: I-69, exit 86. 730 W Logan St 46770. Fax: 260/758-9702. **Facility:** 50 one-bedroom standard units, some with whirlpools. 3 stories, interior corridors. *Bath:* combo or shower only. **Parking:** on-site. **Terms:** pets ($7 fee, in designated units). **Amenities:** *Some:* irons, hair dryers. **Business Services:** fax (fee). **Cards:** AX, CB, DC, DS, MC, VI. **Special Amenities:** free continental breakfast and free local telephone calls.

SOME UNITS
[icons] FEE FEE

SUPER 8 MOTEL FORT WAYNE SOUTH/MARKLE
▼▼ ▼▼
Motel

Phone: (260)758-8888
All Year [ECP]   1P: $47   2P: $52   XP: $5   F12
Location: I-69, exit 86. 610 Annette Dr 46770. Fax: 260/758-8888. **Facility:** 30 one-bedroom standard units, some with whirlpools. 2 stories, interior corridors. **Parking:** on-site, winter plug-ins. **Terms:** small pets only ($7 fee). **Amenities:** extended cable TV. **Business Services:** fax (fee). **Cards:** AX, DS, MC, VI.

SOME UNITS
[icons]

MARTINSVILLE —See Indianapolis p. 492.

MERRILLVILLE pop. 27,300

―――― **WHERE TO STAY** ――――

COURTYARD BY MARRIOTT
AAA SAVE
▼▼▼
Motel

Phone: (219)756-1600
All Year   1P: $89-$109
Location: I-65, exit 253B (US 30), 0.3 mi nw. 7850 Rhode Island Ave 46410. Fax: 219/756-2080. **Facility:** 112 units. 110 one-bedroom standard units, some with whirlpools. 2 one-bedroom suites. 2 stories, interior corridors. **Parking:** on-site. **Amenities:** extended cable TV, dual phone lines, voice mail, irons, hair dryers. **Dining:** coffee shop, 6-10 am, Sat & Sun 7-11 am. **Pool(s):** heated indoor. **Leisure Activities:** whirlpool, exercise room, sports court. **Guest Services:** valet and coin laundry. **Business Services:** meeting rooms.
Cards: AX, DC, DS, MC, VI. *(See color ad card insert)*

SOME UNITS
[icons] FEE

FAIRFIELD INN
AAA SAVE
▼▼▼
Motel

Phone: (219)736-0500
6/1-10/31 [ECP]   1P: $69-$99   2P: $69-$99
4/1-5/31 & 11/1-3/31 [ECP]   1P: $59-$89   2P: $59-$89
Location: I-65, exit 253B (US 30), 0.3 mi sw. 8375 Georgia St 46410. Fax: 219/736-5116. **Facility:** 132 one-bedroom standard units. 3 stories, interior corridors. **Parking:** on-site. **Terms:** 7 day cancellation notice. **Amenities:** extended cable TV, video games, irons, hair dryers. **Guest Services:** valet laundry. **Cards:** AX, DC, DS, MC, VI. **Special Amenities:** free continental breakfast and free local telephone calls.
(See color ad card insert)

SOME UNITS
[icons] FEE

HAMPTON INN
SAVE
▼▼▼
Motel

Phone: (219)736-7600
All Year [ECP]   1P: $79-$119   2P: $79-$119
Location: I-65, exit 253B (US 30), 0.3 mi sw. 8353 Georgia St 46410. Fax: 219/736-7676. **Facility:** 64 one-bedroom standard units, some with whirlpools. 3 stories, interior corridors. *Bath:* combo or shower only. **Parking:** on-site. **Amenities:** irons, hair dryers. **Pool(s):** small heated indoor. **Leisure Activities:** exercise room. **Guest Services:** valet laundry. **Cards:** AX, CB, DC, DS, MC, VI.

SOME UNITS
[icons] FEE

HOLIDAY INN EXPRESS
▼▼▼
Motel

Phone: 219/795-9500
All Year   1P: $79-$109
Location: I-65, exit 253B (US 30), 0.3 mi sw. 8375 Georgia St 46410. Fax: 219/795-9595. **Facility:** 62 units. 60 one-bedroom standard units, some with whirlpools. 2 one-bedroom suites ($109-$149) with kitchens. 3 stories, interior corridors. *Bath:* combo or shower only. **Parking:** on-site. **Terms:** cancellation fee imposed. [CP] meal plan available. **Amenities:** irons, hair dryers. **Pool(s):** small heated indoor. **Leisure Activities:** exercise room. **Guest Services:** valet laundry. **Business Services:** meeting rooms. **Cards:** AX, CB, DC, DS, MC, VI.

SOME UNITS
[icons] FEE

KNIGHTS INN
AAA SAVE
▼▼
Motel

Phone: (219)736-5100
5/15-10/31   1P: $45-$65   2P: $45-$65   XP: $6   F18
11/1-3/31   1P: $40-$45   2P: $45-$60   XP: $6   F18
4/1-5/14   1P: $39-$45   2P: $45-$50   XP: $6   F18
Location: I-65, exit 253A (US 30), 0.5 mi se. 8250 Louisiana St 46410. Fax: 219/736-8360. **Facility:** 129 one-bedroom standard units, some with efficiencies (no utensils). 1 story, exterior corridors. **Parking:** on-site. **Terms:** [CP] meal plan available, pets ($10 fee, in smoking units). **Guest Services:** coin laundry. **Cards:** AX, DC, DS, MC, VI. **Special Amenities:** free continental breakfast and free local telephone calls.

SOME UNITS
[icons]

LA QUINTA INN

AAA SAVE

Motel

Phone: (219)738-2870
All Year   1P: $60-$72   2P: $67-$79   XP: $7   F18
Location: I-65, exit 253A (US 30), 0.3 mi se. 8210 Louisiana St 46410. Fax: 219/738-1858. **Facility:** 121 units. 120 one-bedroom standard units. 1 one-bedroom suite ($89-$109). 2 stories, interior corridors. **Parking:** on-site. **Amenities:** video games, voice mail, irons, hair dryers. **Pool(s):** heated outdoor. **Guest Services:** valet and coin laundry. **Business Services:** meeting rooms. **Cards:** AX, CB, DC, DS, MC, VI. **Special Amenities:** free continental breakfast and free local telephone calls.

SOME UNITS
[icons] FEE

LEES INN & SUITES

Motel

Phone: (219)942-8555
All Year [BP]   1P: $79-$249   2P: $89-$259   XP: $10   F18
Location: I-65, exit 255 (61st Ave), 0.3 mi e. 6201 Opportunity Ln 46410. Fax: 219/942-6223. **Facility:** 70 units. 62 one-bedroom standard units, some with whirlpools. 8 one-bedroom suites ($129-$249). 2 stories, interior corridors. **Parking:** on-site. **Terms:** 7 day cancellation notice, [ECP] meal plan available, package plans, small pets only (in designated units). **Amenities:** extended cable TV, irons, hair dryers. **Pool(s):** heated indoor. **Leisure Activities:** exercise room. **Guest Services:** complimentary evening beverages: Mon-Thurs, valet and coin laundry. **Business Services:** meeting rooms. **Cards:** AX, CB, DC, DS, JC, MC, VI.

SOME UNITS
[icons]

RADISSON HOTEL AT STAR PLAZA

AAA SAVE

Hotel

Phone: (219)769-6311
All Year   1P: $119   2P: $119   XP: $10   F18
Location: I-65, exit 253B (US 30). 800 E 81st Ave 46410. Fax: 219/769-1462. **Facility:** 347 units. 342 one-bedroom standard units. 5 one-bedroom suites ($159-$1000). 4 stories, interior corridors. *Bath:* combo or shower only. **Parking:** on-site and valet. **Terms:** check-in 4 pm, package plans, pets ($25 deposit). **Amenities:** video games (fee), dual phone lines, voice mail, irons, hair dryers. **Dining:** restaurant, 6 am-11 pm, $9-$20, cocktails, also, J Ginger's, see separate listing, nightclub. **Pool(s):** heated outdoor, heated indoor. **Leisure Activities:** sauna, whirlpools, putting green, playground, exercise room, indoor recreation area. **Guest Services:** gift shop, valet and coin laundry. **Business Services:** conference facilities. **Cards:** AX, CB, DC, DS, JC, MC, VI.

SOME UNITS
[icons] FEE

RED ROOF INN-MERRILLVILLE

AAA SAVE

Motel

Phone: (219)738-2430
5/26-8/31   1P: $45-$71   2P: $50-$71   XP: $5   F18
4/1-5/25   1P: $35-$61   2P: $40-$61   XP: $5   F18
9/1-12/31   1P: $41-$58   2P: $46-$58   XP: $5   F18
1/1-3/31   1P: $37-$56   2P: $42-$56   XP: $5   F18
Location: I-65, exit 253A (US 30), 0.3 mi sw. 8290 Georgia St 46410. Fax: 219/738-2436. **Facility:** 108 one-bedroom standard units. 2 stories, exterior corridors. *Bath:* combo or shower only. **Parking:** on-site. **Amenities:** video games, voice mail. **Cards:** AX, CB, DC, DS, MC, VI. **Special Amenities:** free local telephone calls and free newspaper.

SOME UNITS
[icons] FEE

RESIDENCE INN BY MARRIOTT

AAA SAVE

Apartment

Phone: (219)791-9000
All Year   1P: $89-$129   2P: $89-$129
Location: I-65, exit 253B (US 30). 8018 Delaware Place 46410. Fax: 219/791-9777. **Facility:** 78 units. 18 one-bedroom standard units. 48 one- and 12 two-bedroom suites ($129-$139). 3 stories, interior corridors. *Bath:* combo or shower only. **Parking:** on-site. **Terms:** [ECP] meal plan available, pets ($50 fee, $5 extra charge). **Amenities:** extended cable TV, video games, dual phone lines, voice mail, irons, hair dryers. **Pool(s):** small heated indoor. **Leisure Activities:** whirlpool, exercise room, sports court. **Guest Services:** valet and coin laundry. **Business Services:** meeting rooms. **Cards:** AX, CB, DC, DS, JC, MC, VI. *(See color ad card insert)*

SOME UNITS
[icons] FEE

SUPER 8 MOTEL

AAA SAVE

Motel

Phone: (219)736-8383
6/2-9/30 [CP]   1P: $53-$59   2P: $58-$64   XP: $4   F12
4/1-6/1 [CP]   1P: $45   2P: $50   XP: $4   F12
10/1-3/31 [CP]   1P: $37-$42   2P: $42-$47   XP: $4   F12
Location: I-65, exit 253A (US 30), 0.5 mi se. 8300 Louisiana St 46410. Fax: 219/736-8383. **Facility:** 59 one-bedroom standard units. 2 stories, interior corridors. **Parking:** on-site. **Terms:** 8 day cancellation notice. **Guest Services:** coin laundry. **Business Services:** meeting rooms. **Cards:** AX, CB, DC, DS, MC, VI. **Special Amenities:** free continental breakfast and free local telephone calls.

SOME UNITS
[icons] FEE   FEE FEE

------- WHERE TO DINE -------

J GINGER'S

American

Dinner: $13-$27   **Phone:** 219/769-6311
Location: I-65, exit 253B (US 30); in Radisson Hotel at Star Plaza. 800 E 81st Ave 46410. **Hours:** 5 pm-10 pm, Fri & Sat-11 pm. **Reservations:** suggested. **Features:** casual dress; cocktails & lounge. Nautical decor punctuates the upscale casual setting. Prime beef, such as the nicely prepared filet mignon, mingles with such complements as the house salad, which is served with baby shrimp, mandarin orange slices, coconut and avocado dressing. **Parking:** on-site. **Cards:** AX, CB, DC, DS, JC, MC, VI.

[icon]

NEW MOON RESTAURANT

Chinese

Lunch: $4-$6   **Dinner:** $8-$12   **Phone:** 219/738-2666
Location: I-65, exit 253B, 0.3 mi sw on US 30. 761 E 81st Ave 46410. **Hours:** 11 am-9:30 pm, Fri-11 pm, Sat 11:30 am-11 pm, Sun noon-10 pm. **Closed:** 11/28. **Reservations:** accepted. **Features:** casual dress; carryout; cocktails & lounge; a la carte, buffet. The popular restaurant serves well-prepared Chinese cuisine in a lovely dining room that features traditional Oriental decor. Lunch and dinner buffets are the draw here, and some vegetarian dishes are available. **Parking:** on-site. **Cards:** AX, DC, MC, VI.

[icon]

--------- *The following restaurant has not been evaluated by AAA but is listed for your information only.* ---------

CAFE VENEZIA
[fyi]
Phone: 219/736-2203
Not evaluated. **Location:** I-65, exit 253B, 1.2 mi w on US 30; in the Ross Plaza. 405 W 81st Ave 46410. Traditional Italian cuisine and desserts made in house are served in the cozy dining room.

MICHIGAN CITY pop. 33,800

--------- **WHERE TO STAY** ---------

AL & SALLY'S MOTEL
AAA SAVE
◇◇◇
Motel

Phone: 219/872-9131

5/1-9/30	1P: $45-$55	2P: $60-$70	XP: $5
4/1-4/30 & 10/1-3/31	1P: $40-$45	2P: $50-$55	XP: $5

Location: 3.5 mi w on US 12. 3221 W Dunes Hwy 46360. Fax: 219/872-9132. **Facility:** 16 one-bedroom standard units, some with whirlpools. 1 story, exterior corridors. *Bath:* combo or shower only. **Parking:** on-site. **Terms:** 3 day cancellation notice-fee imposed. **Amenities:** extended cable TV. **Pool(s):** outdoor. **Leisure Activities:** lighted tennis court, playground. **Cards:** AX, DS, MC, VI.

SOME UNITS

COMFORT INN
AAA SAVE
◇◇ ◇◇
Motel

Phone: (219)879-9190

4/1-9/10 [ECP]	1P: $80-$90	2P: $90-$94	XP: $6 F18
9/11-12/31 [ECP]	1P: $60-$80	2P: $80-$94	XP: $6 F18
1/1-3/31 [ECP]	1P: $55-$75	2P: $60-$85	XP: $6 F18

Location: I-94, exit 34B. 3801 N Frontage Rd 46360. Fax: 219/879-0373. **Facility:** 50 one-bedroom standard units, some with whirlpools. 2 stories, interior corridors. **Parking:** on-site. **Terms:** cancellation fee imposed. **Amenities:** extended cable TV, hair dryers. *Some:* irons. **Pool(s):** small indoor. **Guest Services:** valet and coin laundry. **Business Services:** meeting rooms. **Cards:** AX, CB, DC, DS, JC, MC, VI. **Special Amenities:** free continental breakfast and free local telephone calls.

SOME UNITS
FEE   FEE FEE

CREEKWOOD INN
◇◇◇◇
Country Inn

Phone: 219/872-8357

4/1-1/1 & 1/10-3/31 [ECP]	1P: $130-$185	2P: $145-$195	XP: $16

Location: I-94, exit 40B, 0.3 mi n on US 20 and 35, follow signs at I-94. 5727 600 W 46360. Fax: 219/872-6986. **Facility:** An outstanding element at this secluded English-country-style inn is the two-story conservatory, which includes a piano. Smoke free premises. 13 one-bedroom standard units. 2 stories, interior corridors. *Bath:* combo or shower only. **Parking:** on-site. **Terms:** open 4/1-1/1 & 1/10-3/31, check-in 4 pm, 14 day cancellation notice-fee imposed, package plans - off season. **Amenities:** hair dryers. **Leisure Activities:** whirlpool, cross country skiing, nature trails, bicycles. **Business Services:** meeting rooms. **Cards:** AX, DC, MC, VI.

SOME UNITS
FEE

HAMPTON INN
SAVE
◇◇◇
Motel

Phone: (219)879-9994

All Year	1P: $79-$99	2P: $79-$99

Location: I-94, exit 34B, 1 mi n on US 421. 4128 S Franklin St 46360. Fax: 219/874-9640. **Facility:** 107 units. 106 one-bedroom standard units. 1 one-bedroom suite. 2 stories, interior corridors. **Parking:** on-site. **Terms:** check-in 4 pm, package plans. **Amenities:** extended cable TV, voice mail, irons, hair dryers. **Pool(s):** heated indoor. **Leisure Activities:** whirlpool, exercise room. **Guest Services:** valet and coin laundry. **Business Services:** meeting rooms. **Cards:** AX, CB, DC, DS, MC, VI.

SOME UNITS

HOLIDAY INN
◇◇◇
Motor Inn

Phone: (219)879-0311

All Year	1P: $89-$119	2P: $89-$119

Location: I-94, exit 34B, 0.3 mi n on US 421. 5820 S Franklin St 46360. Fax: 219/879-2536. **Facility:** 164 units. 153 one-bedroom standard units. 11 one-bedroom suites ($130-$190), some with whirlpools. 2-3 stories, interior/exterior corridors. **Parking:** on-site. **Terms:** check-in 4 pm, package plans. **Amenities:** extended cable TV, voice mail, irons, hair dryers. **Pool(s):** heated indoor. **Leisure Activities:** sauna, whirlpool, exercise room. **Guest Services:** valet and coin laundry. **Business Services:** conference facilities. **Cards:** AX, CB, DC, DS, JC, MC, VI.

SOME UNITS

KNIGHTS INN
AAA SAVE
◇◇
Motel

Phone: (219)874-9500

4/1-10/31	1P: $45-$150	2P: $45-$150	XP: $7 F18
11/1-3/31	1P: $35-$99	2P: $35-$99	XP: $7 F18

Location: I-94, exit 34B, 0.3 mi n on US 421. 201 W Kieffer Rd 46360. Fax: 219/874-5122. **Facility:** 103 one-bedroom standard units, some with whirlpools. 1 story, exterior corridors. **Parking:** on-site. **Terms:** check-in 4 pm, small pets only ($10 fee). **Amenities:** dual phone lines. **Pool(s):** small outdoor. **Business Services:** meeting rooms. **Cards:** AX, CB, DC, DS, MC, VI. **Special Amenities:** free local telephone calls.

SOME UNITS

RED ROOF INN-MICHIGAN CITY
AAA SAVE
◇◇ ◇◇
Motel

Phone: (219)874-5251

5/12-6/22	1P: $47-$71	2P: $53-$71	XP: $6 F18
6/23-9/7	1P: $54-$66	2P: $60-$66	XP: $6 F18
9/8-3/31	1P: $42-$59	2P: $48-$59	XP: $6 F18
4/1-5/11	1P: $37-$59	2P: $43-$59	XP: $6 F18

Location: I-94, exit 34B, 0.3 mi n on US 421. 110 W Kieffer Rd 46360. Fax: 219/874-5287. **Facility:** 79 one-bedroom standard units. 2 stories, exterior corridors. *Bath:* combo or shower only. **Parking:** on-site. **Terms:** small pets only. **Amenities:** video games, voice mail. **Cards:** AX, CB, DC, DS, MC, VI. **Special Amenities:** free local telephone calls and free newspaper.

SOME UNITS
FEE

─────── **WHERE TO DINE** ───────

HACIENDA MEXICAN RESTAURANT   **Lunch:** $3-$10   **Dinner:** $3-$10   **Phone:** 219/879-4404
Mexican   **Location:** US 35, 2.4 mi e on US 12 to Karwick Rd, 0.3 mi n. 1099 N Karwick Rd 46360. **Hours:** 11 am-10 pm, Fri & Sat-11 pm. **Closed:** 11/28, 12/25. **Reservations:** accepted. **Features:** casual dress; children's menu; carryout; cocktails & lounge; a la carte. "Wet burritos" are the house specialty at the colorful, upbeat restaurant. The menu includes huge helpings of standard favorites, such as tacos, chimichangas and enchiladas, as well as two types of chili. Antique Mexican photographs decorate the walls. **Parking:** on-site. **Cards:** AX, MC, VI.

PUMPS ON 12   **Lunch:** $6-$10   **Dinner:** $8-$17   **Phone:** 219/874-6201
American   **Location:** 3 mi w on US 12. 3085 W Dunes Hwy 46360. **Hours:** 11 am-10 pm, Fri & Sat-10:30, Sun noon-9 pm. **Reservations:** accepted. **Features:** casual dress; children's menu; carryout; cocktails & lounge. Steak, seafood and pizza are served in a casual roadhouse atmosphere of automobile memorabilia and license plates. But keep your eyes on the menu for distinctive pasta dishes, sandwiches, salad, steak, fresh fish and homemade thin-crust pizza. **Parking:** on-site. **Cards:** AX, DS, MC, VI.

MIDDLEBURY pop. 2,000

─────── **WHERE TO STAY** ───────

1898 VARNES GUEST HOUSE   **Phone:** 574/825-9666
| | 4/1-11/1 [BP] | 1P: $79-$99 | 2P: $89-$109 | XP: $15 | F12 |
| | 11/2-3/31 [BP] | 1P: $59-$69 | 2P: $69-$89 | XP: $15 | F12 |

Bed & Breakfast   **Location:** Center; on SR 13. 205 S Main St 46540 (PO Box 93). **Facility:** An English garden, teahouse and outdoor fireplace are special features at this nicely furnished, restored 1898 home. 5 one-bedroom standard units, some with whirlpools. 3 stories, interior corridors. *Bath:* combo or shower only. **Parking:** on-site. **Terms:** 10 day cancellation notice, package plans. **Amenities:** extended cable TV. **Cards:** MC, VI.

SOME UNITS

THE COUNTRY VICTORIAN BED & BREAKFAST   **Phone:** (574)825-2568
| | All Year [BP] | 1P: $69-$129 | 2P: $69-$129 | XP: $10 | F |

Historic Bed & Breakfast   **Location:** 4 blks s on SR 13. 435 S Main St 46540. Fax: 574/825-3411. **Facility:** Guest rooms at this 1894 house are well appointed. Smoke free premises. 5 one-bedroom standard units, some with whirlpools. 2 stories, interior corridors. *Bath:* combo or shower only. **Parking:** on-site. **Terms:** check-in 4 pm, 10 day cancellation notice. **Cards:** AX, DS, MC, VI.

ESSENHAUS COUNTRY INN   **Phone:** 574/825-9447
| | All Year [CP] | 1P: $75 | 2P: $75-$87 | XP: $10 | F12 |

Country Inn   **Location:** US 20, 1 mi w of jct SR 13. 240 US 20 46540 (PO Box 1217). Fax: 574/825-1303. **Facility:** Handcrafted furniture and other country touches are evident in this restored farmhouse; light breakfasts are served in-room. Smoke free premises. 40 one-bedroom standard units, some with whirlpools. 3 stories (no elevator), interior corridors. **Parking:** on-site. **Terms:** cancellation fee imposed, package plans - off season. **Amenities:** voice mail. **Dining:** Das Dutchman Essenhaus, see separate listing. **Leisure Activities:** playground. **Guest Services:** gift shop. **Business Services:** meeting rooms. **Cards:** AX, DS, MC, VI.

SOME UNITS

─────── **WHERE TO DINE** ───────

DAS DUTCHMAN ESSENHAUS   **Lunch:** $6-$12   **Dinner:** $7-$15   **Phone:** 574/825-9471
American   **Location:** US 20, 1 mi w of jct SR 13; in Essenhaus Country Inn. 240 US 20 46540. **Hours:** 6 am-8 pm, Fri & Sat-9 pm. **Closed:** 1/1, 11/28, 12/25; also Sun. **Features:** casual dress; children's menu; carryout; buffet. The Amish-style atmosphere provides a pleasant surprise in the country. Diners are treated to such dishes as broasted chicken and real mashed potatoes with gravy. The outstanding home-baked desserts are prepared daily. Smoke free premises. **Parking:** on-site. **Cards:** DS, MC, VI.

PATCHWORK QUILT COUNTRY INN RESTAURANT   **Lunch:** $7   **Dinner:** $11   **Phone:** 574/825-2417
American   **Location:** I-80/90 (Indiana Toll Rd), exit 107, 0.3 mi ne on SR 13, 1 mi w on CR 2; in Patchwork Quilt Country Inn. 11748 CR 2 46540. **Hours:** Open 4/1-12/31 & 3/1-3/31; 11 am-8 pm; from 4 pm 2/1-3/31. Closed major holidays; also Sun & Mon. **Reservations:** suggested. **Features:** casual dress; buffet. Very well-prepared fare is displayed at both the lunch and dinner buffets and served in a charmingly rustic and relaxing dining room. Peruse an array of soup, salad and entree offerings that includes one notable house specialty: buttermilk pecan chicken. Smoke free premises. **Parking:** on-site. **Cards:** MC, VI.

MISHAWAKA pop. 42,600

─────── **WHERE TO STAY** ───────

BEST WESTERN INN & SUITES   **Phone:** (574)247-4000
| | 4/1-8/31 [ECP] | 1P: $89 | 2P: $89 | XP: $15 | F18 |
| | 9/1-3/31 [ECP] | 1P: $79 | 2P: $79 | XP: $15 | F18 |

Motel   **Location:** I-80/90, exit 83 to SR 23, 1.6 mi sw to Main St, 0.8 mi s. 5640 N Main St 46545. Fax: 574/247-4011. **Facility:** 73 one-bedroom standard units, some with whirlpools. 3 stories, interior corridors. *Bath:* combo or shower only. **Parking:** on-site. **Terms:** cancellation fee imposed. **Amenities:** extended cable TV, dual phone lines, voice mail, irons, hair dryers. **Pool(s):** indoor. **Leisure Activities:** exercise room. **Guest Services:** coin laundry. **Business Services:** meeting rooms. **Cards:** AX, CB, DC, DS, JC, MC, VI.

SOME UNITS

CARLTON LODGE-MISHAWAKA
Phone: (574)277-2520

AAA SAVE
WVWVW
Motel

All Year [ECP]   1P: $89-$275   2P: $89-$275
Location: I-80/90, exit 83 to SR 23, 1.6 mi sw to Main St, just s to University Dr, then just w. 420 W University Dr 46545.
Fax: 574/277-2520. **Facility:** 80 units. 76 one-bedroom standard units, some with whirlpools. 4 one-bedroom
suites. 2 stories, interior corridors. *Bath:* combo or shower only. **Parking:** on-site. **Terms:** cancellation fee
imposed, package plans. **Amenities:** extended cable TV, dual phone lines, voice mail, irons, hair dryers.
Leisure Activities: exercise room. **Guest Services:** valet laundry. **Business Services:** meeting rooms.
Cards: AX, CB, DC, DS, JC, MC, VI. **Special Amenities:** free continental breakfast and free local telephone calls.

SOME UNITS

COURTYARD BY MARRIOTT-MISHAWAKA
Phone: (574)273-9900

AAA SAVE
WVWVW
Motel

All Year   1P: $99-$149
Location: I-80/90, exit 83 to SR 23, 1.6 mi sw, then 1.2 mi s. 4825 N Main St 46545. Fax: 574/272-0143. **Facility:** 78
one-bedroom standard units, some with whirlpools. 3 stories, interior corridors. *Bath:* combo or shower only.
Parking: on-site. **Terms:** 30 day cancellation notice-fee imposed, [BP] meal plan available, package plans.
Amenities: video games, dual phone lines, voice mail, irons, hair dryers. **Dining:** coffee shop, 6:30-9:30 am,
Sat & Sun 7-11 am. **Pool(s):** heated indoor. **Leisure Activities:** whirlpool, exercise room. **Guest Services:**
valet and coin laundry. **Business Services:** meeting rooms. **Cards:** AX, DC, DS, MC, VI. *(See color ad card insert)*

SOME UNITS
FEE

FAIRFIELD INN BY MARRIOTT
Phone: (574)273-2202

AAA SAVE
WVWVW
Motel

5/2-10/1 [CP]   1P: $75-$79   2P: $79-$85
10/2-3/31 [CP]   1P: $74-$79   2P: $79-$84
4/1-5/1 [CP]   1P: $69-$75   2P: $75-$79
Location: I-80/90, exit 83 to SR 23, 1.6 mi sw to Main St, just s to University Dr, then just w. 425 University Dr 46545.
Fax: 574/273-2202. **Facility:** 62 one-bedroom standard units. 3 stories, interior corridors. *Bath:* combo or
shower only. **Parking:** on-site. **Terms:** 30 day cancellation notice-fee imposed. **Amenities:** irons. **Pool(s):**
small indoor. **Leisure Activities:** whirlpool. **Guest Services:** valet laundry. **Cards:** AX, DC, DS, MC, VI. **Special Amenities:** free
continental breakfast and free local telephone calls. *(See color ad card insert)*

SOME UNITS
FEE   FEE FEE

HAMPTON INN
Phone: (574)273-2309

SAVE
WVWVW
Motel

9/2-11/22 [CP]   1P: $74-$199   2P: $74-$199   XP: $10   F17
4/1-9/1 & 11/23-3/31 [CP]   1P: $74-$86   2P: $74-$86   XP: $10   F17
Location: I-80/90, exit 83 to SR 23, 1.6 mi sw to Main St, just s to University Dr, then just w. 445 University Dr 46545.
Fax: 574/273-0258. **Facility:** 62 one-bedroom standard units. 3 stories, interior corridors. *Bath:* combo or
shower only. **Parking:** on-site. **Terms:** 21 day cancellation notice-fee imposed. **Amenities:** voice mail, irons.
Pool(s): small indoor. **Leisure Activities:** whirlpool. **Guest Services:** valet laundry. **Cards:** AX, DC, DS,
MC, VI.

SOME UNITS
FEE FEE   FEE FEE

HOLIDAY INN EXPRESS
Phone: (574)271-1700

WVWVW
Motel

5/16-10/31 [ECP]   1P: $99-$109   2P: $99-$109   XP: $10   F18
4/1-5/15 & 11/1-3/31 [ECP]   1P: $89-$99   2P: $89-$99   XP: $10   F18
Location: I-80/90, exit 83 to SR 23, 1.6 mi sw to Main St, then just s. 6701 N Main St 46530. Fax: 574/243-1432.
Facility: 62 one-bedroom standard units, some with whirlpools. 2 stories, interior corridors. *Bath:* combo or
shower only. **Parking:** on-site. **Terms:** package plans. **Amenities:** extended cable TV, dual phone lines, voice mail, irons, hair
dryers. **Pool(s):** indoor. **Guest Services:** valet laundry. **Business Services:** meeting rooms. **Cards:** AX, CB, DC, DS, MC, VI.

SOME UNITS
FEE FEE

SPRINGHILL SUITES BY MARIOTT-MISHAWAKA
Phone: 574/271-0832

AAA SAVE
WVWVW
Motel

4/1-9/30   1P: $99   2P: $99
10/1-3/31   1P: $89   2P: $89
Location: I-80/90, exit 83 to SR 23, 1.6 mi sw, then 1.2 mi s. 5225 Edison Lakes Pkwy 46545. Fax: 574/271-0843.
Facility: 87 one-bedroom standard units. 3 stories, interior corridors. *Bath:* combo or shower only. **Parking:**
on-site. **Amenities:** dual phone lines, voice mail, irons, hair dryers. **Pool(s):** small indoor. **Leisure Activities:** exercise room. **Guest Services:** coin laundry. **Business Services:** meeting rooms. **Cards:** AX, DC,
DS, MC, VI. **Special Amenities:** free continental breakfast and free local telephone calls. *(See color ad card insert)*

SOME UNITS
FEE

SUPER 8 MOTEL
Phone: (574)247-0888

WVWVW
Motel

4/1-10/31 [CP]   1P: $54-$62   2P: $60-$67   XP: $5   F13
11/1-3/31 [CP]   1P: $52-$59   2P: $54-$61   XP: $5   F13
Location: I-80/90, exit 83 to SR 23, 1.6 mi sw to Main St, just s, then just w. 535 W University Dr 46545.
Fax: 574/247-0889. **Facility:** 66 one-bedroom standard units. 2 stories, interior corridors. *Bath:* combo or
shower only. **Parking:** on-site. **Terms:** 3 day cancellation notice, pets ($25 deposit). **Amenities:** extended cable TV. **Guest Serv-
ices:** coin laundry. **Cards:** AX, DC, DS, MC, VI.

SOME UNITS

─────── WHERE TO DINE ───────

HACIENDA MEXICAN RESTAURANT   **Lunch:** $6-$12   **Dinner:** $6-$12   **Phone:** 574/277-1318
▼▼ ▼▼
Mexican

Location: I-80/90, exit 83 to SR 23 S, 2 mi s to Grape Rd, 0.6 mi e; in Indian Ridge Plaza. 5836 Grape Rd 46545. **Hours:** 11 am-11 pm, Fri & Sat-midnight, Sun-10 pm. Closed major holidays. **Features:** casual dress; children's menu; carryout; cocktails & lounge; a la carte. "Wet burritos" are the house specialty at the colorful, upbeat restaurant. The menu includes huge helpings of standard favorites, such as tacos, chimichangas and enchiladas, as well as two types of chili. Antique Mexican photographs decorate the walls. **Parking:** on-site. **Cards:** AX, MC, VI.

⊠

MONTGOMERY pop. 400

─────── WHERE TO STAY ───────

GASTHOF VILLAGE INN   **Phone:** (812)486-2600
▼▼▼
Motel

5/1-10/31	1P: $70-$100
4/1-4/30 & 11/1-3/31	1P: $60-$90

Location: US 50, 1 mi n on CR 650 E, PO Box 60 47558. Fax: 812/486-4999. **Facility:** 82 units. 80 one-bedroom standard units. 2 one-bedroom suites ($90-$100). 3 stories, interior corridors. *Bath:* combo or shower only. **Parking:** on-site, winter plug-ins. **Terms:** [ECP] meal plan available, package plans, small pets only ($50 deposit). **Amenities:** video games. *Some:* irons, hair dryers. **Pool(s):** heated outdoor. **Leisure Activities:** fishing, volleyball. **Business Services:** meeting rooms. **Cards:** AX, CB, DC, DS, MC, VI.

SOME UNITS
(ASK) 🐕 🍽️ 🚗 ♿ 🐾 ⛟ 🎾 🖨️ / ⊠ 📶 🛏️ 🖵 /
FEE

MOORESVILLE —*See Indianapolis p. 492.*

MOUNT VERNON pop. 7,200

─────── WHERE TO STAY ───────

FOUR SEASONS MOTEL   **Phone:** (812)838-4821
▼▼▼
Motel

All Year	1P: $50-$89	2P: $62-$95	XP: $5 F12

Location: SR 62, 1.8 mi w of jct SR 69 N. 70 Hwy 62 W 47620. Fax: 812/838-4287. **Facility:** 44 units. 40 one-bedroom standard units. 4 one-bedroom suites ($89-$95). 1 story, exterior corridors. **Parking:** on-site. **Terms:** cancellation fee imposed, pets ($25 deposit). **Amenities:** extended cable TV. *Some:* irons. **Pool(s):** outdoor. **Guest Services:** valet and coin laundry. **Business Services:** meeting rooms. **Cards:** AX, CB, DC, DS, MC, VI.

SOME UNITS
(ASK) 🅂🄳 🐕 🚗 ♿ 🎾 (DATA PORT) 🛏️ 🖵 🖨️ / ⊠ (VCR)
FEE   FEE

SUPER 8 MOTEL   **Phone:** (812)838-8888
▼▼▼
Motel

All Year [CP]	1P: $51-$56	2P: $56-$61	XP: $7 F12

Location: On SR 69 Bypass, just n from SR 62. 6225 Hwy 69 S 47620. Fax: 812/838-8888. **Facility:** 44 units. 40 one-bedroom standard units, some with whirlpools. 2 stories, interior corridors. **Parking:** on-site. **Terms:** pets ($5 extra charge). **Pool(s):** heated indoor. **Business Services:** meeting rooms. **Cards:** AX, CB, DC, DS, MC, VI.

SOME UNITS
(ASK) 🅂🄳 🐕 🚗 🎾 (DATA PORT) 🖨️ / ⊠ (VCR) 🛏️ 🖵 /

MUNCIE pop. 71,000

─────── WHERE TO STAY ───────

BEST WESTERN-MUNCIE   **Phone:** (765)282-0600
🅰🅰🅰 (SAVE)

▼▼▼▼
Motel

All Year	1P: $54-$64	2P: $58-$68	XP: $5 F17

Location: I-69, exit 41, 6.4 mi e on SR 332, 0.5 mi s on Tillotson, then just w. 3011 W Bethel Ave 47304. Fax: 765/282-0377. **Facility:** 60 one-bedroom standard units, some with whirlpools. 2 stories, interior corridors. *Bath:* combo or shower only. **Parking:** on-site. **Terms:** [CP] meal plan available. **Amenities:** extended cable TV, hair dryers. **Pool(s):** heated indoor. **Leisure Activities:** sauna, whirlpool, sun deck, limited exercise equipment. **Guest Services:** valet laundry. **Business Services:** fax (fee). **Cards:** AX, CB, DC, DS, JC, MC, VI. **Special Amenities:** free continental breakfast and free local telephone calls.

SOME UNITS
🅂🄳 🍽️ 🗡️ ♿ 🐾 🚗 ⊠ 🎾 (DATA PORT) 🖵 🖨️ / ⊠ 🛏️ 🖵 /

COMFORT INN   **Phone:** (765)282-6666
(SAVE)

▼▼ ▼▼
Motel

4/1-9/30 [CP]	1P: $59-$66	2P: $64-$69	XP: $5 F17
10/1-3/31 [CP]	1P: $54-$61	2P: $59-$64	XP: $5 F17

Location: I-69, exit 41, 6.3 mi e on SR 332, just n. 4011 W Bethel Ave 47304. Fax: 765/282-6666. **Facility:** 66 one-bedroom standard units. 2 stories, interior corridors. **Parking:** on-site, winter plug-ins. **Terms:** small pets only ($15 extra charge). **Amenities:** extended cable TV. *Some:* irons, hair dryers. **Pool(s):** small heated indoor. **Leisure Activities:** whirlpool. **Business Services:** fax (fee). **Cards:** AX, DC, DS, MC, VI.

SOME UNITS
🅂🄳 🐕 🍽️ 🚗 ♿ 🎾 (DATA PORT) 🖨️ / ⊠ 🛏️ 🖵 🖵 /
FEE

HOLIDAY INN EXPRESS HOTEL & SUITES   **Phone:** (765)289-4678
▼▼ ▼▼
Motel

All Year	1P: $65	2P: $65	XP: $10 F

Location: I-69, exit 41, 6.3 mi e on SR 332, then just n. 4201 W Bethel Ave 47304. Fax: 765/289-0533. **Facility:** 76 units. 74 one-bedroom standard units. 2 one-bedroom suites ($99-$125) with whirlpools. 3 stories, interior corridors. *Bath:* combo or shower only. **Parking:** on-site. **Amenities:** voice mail, irons, hair dryers. **Pool(s):** heated indoor. **Leisure Activities:** whirlpool. **Guest Services:** coin laundry. **Business Services:** meeting rooms. **Cards:** AX, CB, DC, DS, MC, VI.

SOME UNITS
(ASK) 🅂🄳 🍽️ ♿ 🚗 🎾 (DATA PORT) 🖵 🖨️ / ⊠ 🛏️ 🖵 /

MUNCIE DAYS INN

[SAVE]

Motel

	4/1-9/30 [ECP]	1P: $50-$68	2P: $56-$72	XP: $5	F17
	3/1-3/31 [ECP]	1P: $41-$68	2P: $46-$72	XP: $5	F17
	10/1-2/28 [ECP]	1P: $41-$56	2P: $46-$59	XP: $5	F17

Phone: (765)288-2311

Location: I-69, exit 41, 6.3 mi e on SR 332, just n. 3509 N Everbrook Ln 47304. **Fax:** 765/288-0485. **Facility:** 62 one-bedroom standard units. 2 stories, interior corridors. **Parking:** on-site, winter plug-ins. **Terms:** small pets only ($10-$15 extra charge). **Amenities:** extended cable TV, safes (fee), irons, hair dryers. **Business Services:** fax (fee). **Cards:** AX, DC, DS, MC, VI.

SOME UNITS

RADISSON HOTEL ROBERTS

[AAA] [SAVE]

Historic Hotel

All Year   1P: $110-$250   XP: $10   F18

Phone: (765)741-7777

Location: Opposite Horizon Convention Center. 420 S High St 47305. **Fax:** 765/747-0067. **Facility:** 130 units. 94 one-bedroom standard units. 36 one-bedroom suites ($129-$250), some with whirlpools. 7 stories, interior corridors. **Terms:** package plans, pets ($25 deposit). **Amenities:** irons, hair dryers. **Dining:** restaurant, 6:30 am-9 pm, Fri & Sat-10 pm, $10-$20, (cocktails). **Pool(s):** heated indoor. **Leisure Activities:** whirlpool. **Guest Services:** valet laundry, airport transportation-Delaware County Municipal Airport, area transportation-within 10 mi. **Business Services:** conference facilities, fax (fee). **Cards:** AX, CB, DC, DS, MC, VI. **Special Amenities:** free local telephone calls and free newspaper.

SOME UNITS

SIGNATURE INN-MUNCIE

Motel

All Year [CP]   1P: $61-$70   2P: $61-$70

Phone: (765)284-4200

Location: I-69, exit 41, 6.3 mi e on SR 332. 3400 N Chadam Ln 47304. **Fax:** 765/284-4200. **Facility:** 101 one-bedroom standard units, some with whirlpools. 2 stories, interior corridors. **Parking:** on-site, winter plug-ins. **Amenities:** extended cable TV, voice mail, irons, hair dryers. **Pool(s):** heated indoor. **Leisure Activities:** whirlpool, exercise room. **Guest Services:** valet laundry. **Business Services:** meeting rooms, business center, PC. **Cards:** AX, DC, DS, MC, VI.

SOME UNITS

SUPER 8 MOTEL

Motel

All Year   1P: $46-$65   2P: $46-$70   XP: $5   F12

Phone: 765/286-4333

Location: I-69, exit 41, 6.3 mi e on SR 332. 3601 W Fox Ridge Ln 47304. **Fax:** 765/286-4333. **Facility:** 63 one-bedroom standard units. 2 stories, interior corridors. **Parking:** on-site, winter plug-ins. **Terms:** small pets only ($10 fee). **Amenities:** extended cable TV, safes (fee). **Cards:** AX, CB, DC, DS, MC, VI.

SOME UNITS

——— **WHERE TO DINE** ———

FOXFIRE'S

American

Dinner: $10-$32

Phone: 765/284-5235

Location: I-69, exit 41, 6 mi e on SR 332, 3.5 mi nw. 3300 Chadam Ln 47304. **Hours:** 5 pm-11 pm. Closed major holidays; also Sun. **Reservations:** suggested. **Features:** casual dress; children's menu; cocktails. The Foxfire's location is convenient to the major motel accomodations on the west side of Muncie. You will need to look closely for their sign as it is somewhat hard to see. The food and presentation is on the upscale side, but not yet so formal to be "stuffy". You might wonder about the Garfield the Cat artwork on the walls, the owner is the creator of the cartoon series. The Foxfire staff is efficient, friendly and make every effort to see that your dining experience is a memorable one. **Parking:** on-site. **Cards:** AX, CB, DC, DS, MC, VI.

J R BROOK'S

American

Lunch: $6-$8   Dinner: $9-$13   Phone: 765/282-1321

Location: I-69, exit 41, 7.2 mi e on SR 332 (W McGalliard Rd). 1101 W McGalliard Rd 47303. **Hours:** 11 am-8:30 pm, Fri & Sat-9:30 pm. Closed: 12/25. **Reservations:** accepted. **Features:** casual dress; children's menu; carryout; cocktails. Large portions of familiar, simply prepared food, such as chicken, fish, steak and lots of sandwiches, make the restaurant a favorite of families. Attractive artwork and mirrored wall sections distinguish the dining room. The casual wait staff is efficient. **Parking:** on-site. **Cards:** AX, DC, DS, MC, VI.

NAPPANEE pop. 5,500

——— **WHERE TO STAY** ———

HOMESPUN COUNTRY INN

Bed & Breakfast

| | 5/1-12/31 [BP] | 1P: $59-$79 | 2P: $59-$79 | XP: $10 | F12 |
| | 4/1-4/30 & 1/1-3/31 [BP] | 1P: $59 | 2P: $59 | XP: $10 | F12 |

Phone: (574)773-2034

Location: On SR 19, just n of SR 6. 302 N Main St 46550. **Fax:** 574/773-3456. **Facility:** Guests of this Queen Anne-style 1902 inn may attend a traditional Amish dinner at a local Amish home; reservations are required. Smoke free premises. 5 one-bedroom standard units. 3 stories, interior corridors. **Bath:** shower only. **Parking:** on-site. **Terms:** check-in 4 pm, 7 day cancellation notice-fee imposed, package plans. **Amenities:** extended cable TV. **Cards:** DS, MC, VI.

THE INN AT AMISH ACRES

[AAA] [SAVE]

Motel

| | 5/1-10/31 [CP] | 1P: $89-$135 | 2P: $94-$145 | XP: $10 | F17 |
| | 4/1-4/30 & 11/1-3/31 [CP] | 1P: $74-$94 | 2P: $79-$99 | XP: $10 | F17 |

Phone: (574)773-2011

Location: On US 6, 0.5 mi w. 1234 W Market St 46550. **Fax:** 574/773-2078. **Facility:** 64 one-bedroom standard units, some with whirlpools. 2 stories, interior corridors. **Parking:** on-site, winter plug-ins. **Terms:** cancellation fee imposed, [ECP] meal plan available, package plans. **Amenities:** extended cable TV, irons. **Pool(s):** small outdoor. **Leisure Activities:** Fee: bicycles. **Guest Services:** gift shop, massage (fee). **Business Services:** meeting rooms. **Cards:** AX, DC, DS, MC, VI. **Special Amenities:** free continental breakfast and free local telephone calls.

SOME UNITS

THE NAPPANEE INN
Phone: (574)773-5999

🔵🔵🔵 SAVE
▽▽▽▽▽
Motel

5/1-3/31 [CP]   1P: $79-$135   2P: $84-$135   XP: $10   F17
Location: 1 mi w on US 6. 2004 W Market St 46550. Fax: 574/773-5988. **Facility:** 66 one-bedroom standard units. 2 stories, interior corridors. *Bath:* combo or shower only. **Parking:** on-site. **Terms:** open 5/1-3/31, cancellation fee imposed, [ECP] meal plan available, package plans. **Amenities:** extended cable TV. **Pool(s):** small outdoor. **Leisure Activities:** Fee: bicycles. **Guest Services:** gift shop, massage (fee). **Cards:** AX, DC, DS, MC, VI. **Special Amenities:** free continental breakfast and free local telephone calls.

SOME UNITS

🛇🔲 🛗 ᕦ🅜 ᕦ⌨ 🖃 🏊 🖥 / 🗙 /

OLDE BUFFALO INN BED AND BREAKFAST
Phone: 574/773-2223

▽▽▽▽▽
Bed & Breakfast

All Year   1P: $69-$149   2P: $79-$159   XP: $35   D10
Location: 0.7 mi n on SR 19 to Heritage Pkwy, then 0.4 mi e. 1061 Parkwood Dr 46550. Fax: 574/773-4275. **Facility:** A replica of a Williamsburg tavern sits in the basement of this renovated and expanded 1840s farmhouse. Smoke free premises. 7 one-bedroom standard units. 2 stories, interior corridors. *Bath:* combo or shower only. **Parking:** on-site. **Terms:** check-in 4 pm, 10 day cancellation notice-fee imposed. **Amenities:** extended cable TV. **Leisure Activities:** bicycles. **Guest Services:** gift shop. **Cards:** DS, MC, VI.

🗙 📷 🖨

VICTORIAN GUEST HOUSE
Phone: 574/773-4383

▽▽▽▽▽
Historic Bed
& Breakfast

All Year [BP]   1P: $79   2P: $79-$159   XP: $30
Location: Jct US 6 and SR 19, just e. 302 E Market St 46550. Fax: 574/773-4145. **Facility:** A stately Victorian style home built in 1887 that features stained glass windows and an abundance of exceptional antique furniture throughout the home. Smoke free premises. 6 one-bedroom standard units. 3 stories, interior corridors. *Bath:* combo or shower only. **Parking:** on-site. **Terms:** check-in 4 pm, age restrictions may apply, 30 day cancellation notice-fee imposed, package plans. **Amenities:** extended cable TV. **Guest Services:** gift shop. **Cards:** DS, MC, VI.

🗙 📷 🖨

——————— WHERE TO DINE ———————

AMISH ACRES RESTAURANT
Lunch: $15   **Dinner:** $15   **Phone:** 574/773-4188

🔵🔵🔵
▽▽▽▽▽
American

Location: 1 mi w on US 6. 1600 W Market St 46550. **Hours:** Open 4/1-12/30 & 3/1-3/31; 11 am-7 pm, Sun-6 pm. **Closed:** 12/25. **Reservations:** accepted. **Features:** casual dress. Melt-in-the-mouth country-baked chicken, roast beef and shoo-fly pie are just three good reasons to like the casual restaurant. Threshers dinner is served family-style with a large selection of meat. Theme buffets are presented on certain Fridays before live theater. Smoke free premises. **Parking:** on-site. **Cards:** DC, DS, MC, VI.

🗙

NASHVILLE pop. 900

——————— WHERE TO STAY ———————

ARTISTS COLONY INN & RESTAURANT
Phone: 812/988-0600

▽▽◇▽▽
Country Inn

6/1-12/31   2P: $90-$170   XP: $10   F18
4/1-5/31   2P: $80-$110   XP: $10   F18
1/1-3/31   2P: $70-$100   XP: $10   F18
Location: On SR 135 (Van Buren) at Franklin St. 105 Van Buren St 47448 (PO Box 1099). Fax: 812/988-9023. **Facility:** This 19th-century inn has a rooftop whirlpool; the inn is furnished with Shaker-style pieces made by local craftsmen. 23 units. 20 one-bedroom standard units. 3 one-bedroom suites ($120-$220) with whirlpools. 3 stories, interior corridors. **Parking:** on-site. **Terms:** check-in 4 pm, 14 day cancellation notice-fee imposed. **Amenities:** extended cable TV, voice mail, hair dryers. *Some:* irons. **Leisure Activities:** whirlpool. **Guest Services:** gift shop. **Business Services:** meeting rooms, fax (fee). **Cards:** AX, MC, VI.

SOME UNITS

🍴 📶 🖨 / 🗙 VCR 🔲 🖥 💻 /

COMFORT INN
Phone: (812)988-6118

SAVE
▽▽▽▽▽
Motel

4/1-11/15   1P: $80-$195   2P: $80-$195   XP: $6   F18
3/16-3/31   1P: $82-$195   2P: $82-$192   XP: $6   F18
11/16-3/15   1P: $65-$125   2P: $65-$125   XP: $6   F18
Location: SR 46, just w of SR 136. 75 W Chestnut St 47448 (PO Box 1785). Fax: 812/988-6118. **Facility:** 55 one-bedroom standard units, some with whirlpools. 2 stories, interior corridors. **Parking:** on-site, winter plug-ins. **Terms:** cancellation fee imposed. **Amenities:** extended cable TV, hair dryers. *Some:* irons. **Pool(s):** heated indoor. **Leisure Activities:** exercise room. *Fee:* game room. **Business Services:** meeting rooms. **Cards:** AX, CB, DC, DS, MC, VI.

SOME UNITS

🛇🔲 🏊 📷 📶 💻 🖨 / 🗙 🔲 🖥 /

THE SEASONS LODGE
Phone: (812)988-2284

▽▽ ▽▽▽
Motor Inn

10/1-10/31   1P: $89-$125   2P: $89-$125   XP: $5   F18
6/1-9/30   1P: $85-$120   2P: $85-$120   XP: $5   F18
4/1-5/31   1P: $69-$120   2P: $69-$120   XP: $5   F18
11/1-3/31   1P: $59-$115   2P: $59-$115   XP: $5   F18
Location: SR 46, 0.3 mi e of jct SR 135. 560 E SR 46 47448 (PO Box 187). Fax: 812/988-7510. **Facility:** 80 one-bedroom standard units. 2 stories, interior corridors. **Parking:** on-site. **Terms:** check-in 4 pm, 3 day cancellation notice. **Amenities:** extended cable TV, hair dryers. **Pool(s):** heated indoor. **Leisure Activities:** basketball, volleyball. **Guest Services:** valet laundry. **Business Services:** conference facilities, PC, fax (fee). **Cards:** AX, DC, DS, MC, VI.

SOME UNITS

ASK 🛇🔲 🍴 🍸 🏊 📶 💻 🖨 / 🗙 VCR
FEE

——————— WHERE TO DINE ———————

THE ORDINARY
Lunch: $6-$16   **Dinner:** $10-$16   **Phone:** 812/988-6166

▽▽
American

Location: On SR 135, just s of Main St. Van Buren St 47448. **Hours:** 11:30 am-8 pm, Fri & Sat-10 pm. Closed major holidays; also Mon 11/1-9/30 & Tues 11/1-10/31. **Reservations:** accepted. **Features:** casual dress; children's menu; cocktails & lounge. The multilevel, old-fashioned dining room, with cathedral ceilings and a cozy fireplace, evokes the feel of a Colonial tavern. American staples, such as barbecue ribs, smoked pork chops, steaks, chicken and homemade fruit cobblers, comprise the menu. **Parking:** street. **Cards:** DS, MC, VI.

🗙

NEW ALBANY pop. 36,300

———— WHERE TO STAY ————

HOLIDAY INN EXPRESS LOUISVILLE NORTHWEST   **Phone:** 812/945-2771
All Year [ECP]   1P: $69-$99   2P: $69-$99
Motel   **Location:** I-64, exit 123. 411 W Spring St 47150. Fax: 812/949-7937. **Facility:** 134 one-bedroom standard units. 5 stories, interior corridors. *Bath:* combo or shower only. **Parking:** on-site. **Terms:** 14 day cancellation notice-fee imposed, small pets only. **Amenities:** voice mail, irons, hair dryers. **Pool(s):** heated indoor. **Leisure Activities:** exercise room. *Fee:* game room. **Guest Services:** valet and coin laundry. **Business Services:** meeting rooms, business center, PC, fax (fee). **Cards:** AX, CB, DC, DS, JC, MC, VI.

SOME UNITS

NEW ALSACE —*See Cincinnati p. 589.*

NEW CASTLE pop. 17,800

———— WHERE TO STAY ————

BEST WESTERN RAINTREE INN   **Phone:** 765/521-0100
All Year   1P: $58-$71   2P: $58-$71
Motor Inn   **Location:** I-70, exit 123, 2.5 mi n. 2836 S SR 3 47362. Fax: 765/521-3157. **Facility:** 104 units. 101 one-bedroom standard units. 3 one-bedroom suites ($91-$131) with whirlpools. 2 stories, interior/exterior corridors. *Bath:* combo or shower only. **Parking:** on-site, winter plug-ins. **Terms:** small pets only ($20 deposit). **Amenities:** extended cable TV, video games (fee), irons, hair dryers. **Dining:** dining room, 6 am-9 pm, $5-$15, cocktails. **Pool(s):** heated indoor. **Leisure Activities:** whirlpool, limited exercise equipment. *Fee:* game room. **Guest Services:** valet and coin laundry. **Business Services:** meeting rooms. **Cards:** AX, CB, DC, DS, MC, VI. **Special Amenities:** free local telephone calls and free newspaper.

SOME UNITS

HOLIDAY INN EXPRESS   **Phone:** 765/529-0345
All Year [CP]   1P: $82-$87   2P: $87-$93
Motel   **Location:** I-70, exit 123, 2 mi n. 24 E Executive Dr 47362. Fax: 765/529-4880. **Facility:** 48 one-bedroom standard units, some with whirlpools. 2 stories, interior corridors. **Parking:** on-site. **Terms:** small pets only. **Amenities:** voice mail, irons, hair dryers. *Some:* dual phone lines. **Pool(s):** small heated indoor/outdoor. **Leisure Activities:** whirlpool. **Business Services:** fax (fee). **Cards:** AX, DC, DS, MC, VI. **Special Amenities:** free continental breakfast and free local telephone calls.

SOME UNITS

NEW HARMONY pop. 800

———— WHERE TO DINE ————

RED GERANIUM   **Lunch:** $6-$12   **Dinner:** $16-$25   **Phone:** 812/682-4431
American   **Location:** Just ne of jct SR 66 and 69; at The New Harmony Inn. 504 North St 47631. **Hours:** 11 am-10 pm, Fri & Sat-11 pm, Sun-8 pm; from 4 pm 1/1-3/31. Closed: 1/1, 7/4, 12/24, 12/25; also Mon. **Reservations:** suggested. **Features:** dressy casual; children's menu; cocktails; a la carte. Caesar steak and prime rib are two of the quiet restaurant's best offerings. Two others are the luscious Shaker lemon pie and heaven cake. Each dining room, decorated with artwork and furnishings along a particular theme, evokes a different feel. **Parking:** on-site. **Cards:** AX, DC, DS, MC, VI.

NEW HAVEN pop. 9,300

———— WHERE TO STAY ————

HOLIDAY INN EXPRESS-FT WAYNE, EAST   **Phone:** 260/748-6767
All Year [ECP]   1P: $89-$149   2P: $89-$149   XP: $6   F18
Motel   **Location:** I-469, exit 19B. 11205 Isabelle Dr 46774. Fax: 260/748-7448. **Facility:** 61 units. 59 one-bedroom standard units. 2 one-bedroom suites ($99-$149). 3 stories, interior corridors. *Bath:* combo or shower only. **Parking:** on-site. **Terms:** 3 day cancellation notice-fee imposed. **Amenities:** extended cable TV, dual phone lines, voice mail, irons, hair dryers. **Leisure Activities:** exercise room. **Business Services:** meeting rooms. **Cards:** AX, CB, DC, DS, MC, VI.

SOME UNITS

NOBLESVILLE —*See Indianapolis p. 493.*

NORTH VERNON pop. 5,300

———— WHERE TO STAY ————

COMFORT INN   **Phone:** (812)352-9999
All Year [ECP]   1P: $74-$84   2P: $94   XP: $10   F
Motel   **Location:** Jct US 50, 0.6 mi n on SR 7. 150 FDR Dr 47265. Fax: 812/352-9999. **Facility:** 60 units. 59 one-bedroom standard units, some with whirlpools. 1 one-bedroom suite ($120-$150) with kitchen. 2 stories, interior corridors. *Bath:* combo or shower only. **Parking:** on-site. **Terms:** 14 day cancellation notice. **Amenities:** extended cable TV. *Some:* irons, hair dryers. **Pool(s):** heated indoor. **Business Services:** meeting rooms. **Cards:** AX, DC, DS, MC, VI.

SOME UNITS

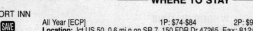

NOTRE DAME pop. 10,700—*See also SOUTH BEND.*

──────── WHERE TO STAY ────────

THE MORRIS INN
▼▼▼
Motor Inn

7/1-12/18 [BP]	1P: $102-$116	2P: $122-$134	XP: $20	F11
1/6-3/31 [BP]	1P: $102-$116	2P: $120-$134	XP: $20	F11
4/1-6/30 [BP]	1P: $98-$112	2P: $116-$130	XP: $18	F11

Phone: 574/631-2000

Location: Campus of University of Notre Dame. N Notre Dame Ave 46556 (PO Box 1085). Fax: 574/631-2340. **Facility:** 92 units. 89 one-bedroom standard units. 3 one-bedroom suites. 3 stories, interior corridors. **Parking:** on-site. **Terms:** open 4/1-12/18 & 1/6-3/31. **Amenities:** extended cable TV, high-speed Internet, dual phone lines, voice mail, honor bars, irons, hair dryers. **Leisure Activities:** Fee: golf-18 holes. **Guest Services:** gift shop, valet laundry. **Business Services:** conference facilities, fax (fee). **Cards:** AX, CB, DC, DS, MC, VI.

SOME UNITS

──────── WHERE TO DINE ────────

The following restaurant has not been evaluated by AAA but is listed for your information only.

SORIN'S
[fyi]

Phone: 574/631-2000

Not evaluated. **Location:** N Notre Dame Ave 46556. An upscale eatery that features a seasonal menu with very well-prepared American cuisine.

PLAINFIELD —*See Indianapolis p. 493.*

PLYMOUTH pop. 8,300

──────── WHERE TO STAY ────────

RAMADA INN
▼▼ ▼▼▼
Motor Inn

4/1-9/30	1P: $70-$73	2P: $70-$73	XP: $5	F17
10/1-3/31	1P: $60-$73	2P: $60-$73	XP: $5	F17

Phone: (574)936-4013

Location: Jct US 30, 0.5 mi n on SR 17. 2550 N Michigan St 46563. Fax: 574/936-4553. **Facility:** 108 one-bedroom standard units. 2 stories, exterior corridors. **Parking:** on-site. **Terms:** small pets only ($10 extra charge). **Amenities:** extended cable TV, voice mail, irons, hair dryers. **Pool(s):** outdoor. **Guest Services:** coin laundry. **Business Services:** conference facilities. **Cards:** AX, CB, DC, DS, JC, MC, VI.

SOME UNITS
FEE

SUPER 8 MOTEL
ⒶⒶⒶ [SAVE]
◆◆ ◆◆
Motel

Phone: 574/936-8856

All Year [ECP]	1P: $55-$120	2P: $65-$120

Location: Just off US 30. 2160 N Oak Rd 46563. Fax: 574/936-2569. **Facility:** 59 one-bedroom standard units, some with whirlpools. 2 stories, interior corridors. **Parking:** on-site. **Terms:** small pets only. **Amenities:** extended cable TV, voice mail. **Pool(s):** small heated indoor. **Leisure Activities:** whirlpool. **Cards:** AX, CB, DC, DS, MC, VI. **Special Amenities:** free newspaper and free room upgrade (subject to availability with advanced reservations).

SOME UNITS
FEE

PORTAGE pop. 29,100

──────── WHERE TO STAY ────────

COMFORT INN
[SAVE]
◆◆ ◆◆
Motel

Phone: (219)763-7177

All Year [ECP]	1P: $60-$129	2P: $60-$129	XP: $10
			F18

Location: I-80/90, exit 23; I-94, exit 19, 1.5 mi s. 2300 Willow Creek Rd 46368. Fax: 219/763-2068. **Facility:** 52 units. 48 one-bedroom standard units, some with whirlpools. 4 one-bedroom suites. 2 stories, interior corridors. **Parking:** on-site. **Terms:** 7 day cancellation notice-fee imposed, small pets only. **Amenities:** extended cable TV, irons, hair dryers. **Guest Services:** valet laundry. **Business Services:** meeting rooms. **Cards:** AX, DC, DS, MC, VI.

SOME UNITS
FEE   FEE   FEE

HAMPTON INN-PORTAGE
[SAVE]
◆◆ ◆◆
Motel

Phone: (219)764-1919

All Year [ECP]	1P: $89-$99	2P: $89-$99

Location: I-94, exit 19, 0.3 mi s, just e on US 20. 6353 Melton Rd 46368. Fax: 219/764-0020. **Facility:** 60 one-bedroom standard units, some with whirlpools. 3 stories, interior corridors. *Bath:* combo or shower only. **Parking:** on-site. **Terms:** package plans. **Amenities:** extended cable TV, voice mail, irons. **Leisure Activities:** sun deck, exercise room. **Guest Services:** valet and coin laundry. **Business Services:** meeting rooms. **Cards:** AX, CB, DC, DS, JC, MC, VI.

SOME UNITS
FEE

SUPER 8 MOTEL
◆◆ ◆◆
Motel

Phone: (219)762-8857

All Year	1P: $49-$59	2P: $55-$65	XP: $6
			F12

Location: I-94, exit 19, 0.5 mi w on US 20. 6118 Melton Rd 46368. Fax: 219/763-2355. **Facility:** 68 one-bedroom standard units, some with whirlpools. 3 stories, interior corridors. **Parking:** on-site. **Terms:** package plans. **Guest Services:** coin laundry. **Cards:** AX, CB, DC, DS, MC, VI.

SOME UNITS
FEE

PORTER pop. 3,100

—————— WHERE TO STAY ——————

SPRING HOUSE INN
Phone: (219)929-4600

Motel

All Year [ECP]   1P: $79-$149   2P: $79-$149
Location: I-94, exit 22B, 1.5 mi ne on SR 20, follow signs. 303 N Mineral Springs Rd 46304. Fax: 219/926-8258. **Facility:** 50 one-bedroom standard units, some with whirlpools. 3 stories, interior corridors. **Parking:** on-site. **Terms:** package plans - seasonal. **Amenities:** extended cable TV, irons, hair dryers. **Pool(s):** small heated indoor. **Leisure Activities:** sauna, whirlpool, exercise room. **Guest Services:** complimentary evening beverages: Mon-Thurs, valet and coin laundry. **Business Services:** meeting rooms. **Cards:** AX, CB, DC, DS, MC, VI.

SOME UNITS

PORTLAND pop. 6,500

—————— WHERE TO STAY ——————

HOOSIER INN
Phone: (260)726-7113

Motel

4/1-11/30   1P: $42-$45   2P: $45-$50   XP: $5   F10
12/1-3/31   1P: $38-$45   2P: $42-$50
Location: 0.5 mi n on US 27. 1620 Meridian St 47371. Fax: 260/726-7113. **Facility:** 25 one-bedroom standard units. 2 stories, exterior corridors. **Parking:** on-site, winter plug-ins. **Terms:** 7 day cancellation notice. **Amenities:** extended cable TV, hair dryers. **Guest Services:** coin laundry. **Business Services:** fax (fee). **Cards:** AX, DC, DS, MC, VI.

SOME UNITS

SUPER 8 MOTEL
Phone: 260/726-8888

Motel

All Year [ECP]   1P: $55-$120   2P: $60-$140   XP: $10   F12
Location: 1 mi n on US 27. 1147 US 27 N 47371. Fax: 260/726-8888. **Facility:** 40 units. 38 one-bedroom standard units, some with whirlpools. 2 one-bedroom suites ($85-$115). 2 stories, interior corridors. *Bath:* combo or shower only. **Parking:** on-site. **Terms:** 7 day cancellation notice. **Amenities:** extended cable TV, hair dryers. **Pool(s):** small heated indoor. **Business Services:** fax (fee). **Cards:** AX, DS, MC, VI.

SOME UNITS

PRINCETON pop. 8,100

—————— WHERE TO STAY ——————

FAIRFIELD INN BY MARRIOTT
Phone: (812)385-4300

Motel

All Year [ECP]   1P: $51   2P: $58
Location: Jct US 41 and SR 64, 0.3 mi w. 2828 Dixon St 47670. Fax: 812/385-4300. **Facility:** 73 one-bedroom standard units. 3 stories, interior corridors. *Bath:* combo or shower only. **Terms:** 3 day cancellation notice. **Amenities:** extended cable TV. **Pool(s):** heated indoor. **Leisure Activities:** whirlpool, sun deck. **Guest Services:** valet laundry. **Cards:** AX, CB, DC, DS, MC, VI. **Special Amenities:** free continental breakfast and free local telephone calls.

(See color ad card insert)

SOME UNITS

HAMPTON INN
Phone: (812)385-2400

Motel

All Year [ECP]   1P: $59-$129   2P: $66-$136
Location: Jct US 41 and SR 64, 0.3 mi e. 107 S Richland Creek Dr 47670. Fax: 812/386-5096. **Facility:** 101 units. 99 one-bedroom standard units, some with whirlpools. 2 one-bedroom suites ($129-$136) with whirlpools. 3 stories, interior corridors. *Bath:* combo or shower only. **Parking:** on-site, winter plug-ins. **Amenities:** extended cable TV, irons, hair dryers. **Pool(s):** heated indoor. **Leisure Activities:** whirlpool, exercise room. **Guest Services:** valet and coin laundry. **Business Services:** meeting rooms, fax (fee). **Cards:** AX, CB, DC, DS, JC, MC, VI.

SOME UNITS

REMINGTON pop. 1,200

—————— WHERE TO STAY ——————

SUPER 8 MOTEL-REMINGTON
Phone: 219/261-2883

Motel

5/1-10/31   1P: $60-$72   2P: $65-$77   XP: $5
4/1-4/30 & 11/1-3/31   1P: $58-$69   2P: $63-$72   XP: $5
Location: I-65, exit 201, just w. 4278 W US 24 47977. Fax: 219/261-3742. **Facility:** 47 one-bedroom standard units, some with whirlpools. 2 stories, interior corridors. *Bath:* combo or shower only. **Parking:** on-site. **Amenities:** extended cable TV, hair dryers. **Pool(s):** heated indoor. **Leisure Activities:** whirlpool. **Cards:** AX, DS, MC, VI.

SOME UNITS

RENSSELAER pop. 5,000

——— WHERE TO STAY ———

HOLIDAY INN EXPRESS
Phone: (219)866-7111

AAA [SAVE]

▽▽▽▽

Motel

All Year [ECP]   1P: $77-$87   2P: $77-$87   XP: $6   F18
Location: I-65, exit 215, just e. 4788 Nesbitt Dr 47978 (PO Box 8). Fax: 219/866-7232. **Facility:** 69 one-bedroom standard units. 3 stories, interior corridors. *Bath:* combo or shower only. **Parking:** on-site. **Terms:** small pets only. **Amenities:** extended cable TV, irons, hair dryers. **Leisure Activities:** Fee: off-site golf privileges, game room. **Guest Services:** valet and coin laundry. **Business Services:** meeting rooms. **Cards:** AX, CB, DC, DS, MC, VI. **Special Amenities:** free continental breakfast and free newspaper.

SOME UNITS

RICHMOND pop. 38,700

——— WHERE TO STAY ———

BEST WESTERN IMPERIAL MOTOR LODGE
Phone: (765)966-1505

AAA [SAVE]

▽▽▽▽

Motel

5/1-10/31 [CP]	1P: $44-$55	2P: $48-$60	XP: $5	F12
11/1-3/31 [CP]	1P: $40	2P: $45-$50	XP: $5	F12
4/1-4/30 [CP]	1P: $38	2P: $42-$46	XP: $5	F12

Location: I-70, exit 156A, 2 mi w. 3020 E Main St 47374. Fax: 765/935-1426. **Facility:** 44 one-bedroom standard units, some with efficiencies (no utensils). 2 stories, exterior corridors. **Parking:** on-site. **Terms:** small pets only ($5 extra charge). **Amenities:** extended cable TV, irons, hair dryers. **Cards:** AX, DC, DS, MC, VI.
Special Amenities: free continental breakfast and free local telephone calls.

SOME UNITS

COMFORT INN
Phone: (765)935-4766

AAA [SAVE]

▽▽▽▽

Motel

All Year [ECP]   1P: $52-$89   2P: $52-$89   XP: $5   F18
Location: I-70, exit 151A. 912 Mendelson Dr 47374. Fax: 765/935-4766. **Facility:** 52 one-bedroom standard units. 2 stories, interior corridors. **Parking:** on-site, winter plug-ins. **Terms:** 30 day cancellation notice. **Amenities:** extended cable TV. *Some:* irons, hair dryers. **Pool(s):** heated indoor. **Leisure Activities:** whirlpool. **Cards:** AX, DC, DS, MC, VI. **Special Amenities:** free continental breakfast and free room upgrade (subject to availability with advanced reservations).

SOME UNITS

FEE

HOLIDAY INN-RICHMOND
Phone: (765)966-7511

▽▽▽▽

Hotel

All Year [BP]   1P: $86-$325   2P: $86-$325
Location: I-70, exit 156A, 0.3 mi w. 5501 National Rd E 47374. Fax: 765/966-4612. **Facility:** 135 units. 130 one-bedroom standard units, some with whirlpools. 5 one-bedroom suites ($135-$325) with whirlpools. 4 stories, interior corridors. *Bath:* combo or shower only. **Parking:** on-site. **Terms:** package plans, small pets only ($15 fee). **Amenities:** extended cable TV, video games (fee), voice mail, irons, hair dryers. **Pool(s):** heated indoor. **Leisure Activities:** whirlpool, exercise room. **Guest Services:** gift shop, valet laundry. **Business Services:** meeting rooms, fax (fee). **Cards:** AX, DC, DS, JC, MC, VI.

SOME UNITS

FEE   FEE FEE

LEES INN & SUITES
Phone: (765)966-6559

▽▽▽▽

Motel

All Year [BP]   1P: $69-$199   2P: $79-$209   XP: $10   F18
Location: I-70, exit 156A, jct SR 40. 6030 National Rd E 47374. Fax: 765/966-7732. **Facility:** 86 units. 84 one-bedroom standard units, some with whirlpools. 2 one-bedroom suites ($99-$209). 2 stories, interior corridors. **Parking:** on-site. **Terms:** 7 day cancellation notice, [ECP] meal plan available, package plans. **Amenities:** extended cable TV, irons, hair dryers. **Pool(s):** heated indoor. **Leisure Activities:** whirlpool, exercise room. **Guest Services:** complimentary evening beverages: Mon-Thurs, valet and coin laundry. **Business Services:** meeting rooms. **Cards:** AX, DC, DS, JC, MC, VI.

SOME UNITS

FEE FEE

PHILIP W SMITH BED & BREAKFAST
Phone: (765)966-8972

▽▽▽▽

Bed & Breakfast

All Year [BP]   1P: $79-$99   2P: $99   XP: $10   D18
Location: I-70, exit 156A, 3 mi w on National Rd (E Main St); at corner 21st St. 2039 E Main St 47374. **Facility:** Each room is decorated individually at this stately 1890 Victorian home. Smoke free premises. 4 one-bedroom standard units. 2 stories, interior corridors. *Bath:* shower or tub only. **Parking:** street. **Terms:** check-in 4 pm, 5 day cancellation notice-fee imposed, package plans. **Guest Services:** complimentary evening beverages. **Cards:** AX, MC, VI.

SOME UNITS

——— WHERE TO DINE ———

BUD KING'S "TASTE OF THE TOWN"
Lunch: $5-$7   Dinner: $8-$16   Phone: 765/935-5464

AAA

▽▽▽▽

American

Location: I-70, exit 156, 4 mi w on US 40. 1616 E Main St 47374. **Hours:** 11 am-10 pm, Sat from 4 pm. Closed major holidays; also Sun. **Reservations:** accepted. **Features:** casual dress; children's menu; carryout; salad bar; cocktails. Bud King's "Taste of the Town" is located on E Main Street close to the downtown business district of Richmond. The food is simple, but wholesome and the portions are quite large. The cuisine is primarily American, but you can get a few of your Italian favorites like lasagna and chicken alfredo. The conscientious staff provides you with friendly and efficient service. **Parking:** on-site.
Cards: AX, DC, DS, MC, VI.

THE OLDE RICHMOND INN   Lunch: $5-$8   Dinner: $10-$18   Phone: 765/962-2247

(AAA)

♦♦♦ ♦♦♦

American

Location: S 5th and B sts. 138 S 5th St 47374. **Hours:** 11 am-9 pm, Fri & Sat-10 pm, Sun-8 pm. Closed: 1/1, 12/25. **Reservations:** suggested; weekends. **Features:** dressy casual; children's menu; carryout; cocktails & lounge. The restaurant is located close to downtown in the historic area of Richmond. The cuisine is primarily American, but you can also get some of your favorite Italian dishes as well. They offer a very good selection of fresh seafood, steak, poultry and pasta. The renovated turn-of-the-century house resembles a true country home with its wood wainscotting, colorful print wallpaper, fireplaces and antique stained glass windows. **Parking:** on-site. **Cards:** MC, VI.

[X]

RISING SUN —See Cincinnati p. 589.

ROCHESTER pop. 6,000

——— WHERE TO STAY ———

COMFORT INN   Phone: (574)223-7300

[SAVE]

♦♦♦ ♦♦♦

Motel

| | 1/1-3/31 [ECP] | 1P: $70-$97 | 2P: $77-$103 | XP: $7 | F18 |
| | 4/1-12/31 [ECP] | 1P: $68-$95 | 2P: $75-$101 | XP: $7 | F18 |

Location: Just off SR 25, 0.5 mi n of jct US 31. 289 McDonald Dr 46975. Fax: 574/223-7300. **Facility:** 60 one-bedroom standard units, some with whirlpools. 2 stories, interior corridors. **Parking:** on-site, winter plug-ins. **Amenities:** extended cable TV, hair dryers. **Pool(s):** small outdoor. **Guest Services:** coin laundry. **Business Services:** meeting rooms. **Cards:** AX, CB, DC, DS, MC, VI.

SOME UNITS

[S▣] [¶†⋅] [⇋] [✦] [DATA PORT] [🖨] / [X] [VCR] [🔒] [🖳] [🖵] /

ROSE-DALE MOTEL   Phone: 574/223-3185

(AAA) [SAVE]

♦♦♦

Motel

| | All Year | 1P: $38 | 2P: $42-$48 | XP: $3 | F12 |

Location: 1 mi n on Old SR 31. 2147 S Southway 46975. **Facility:** 14 one-bedroom standard units. 1 story, exterior corridors. *Bath:* shower only. **Parking:** on-site, winter plug-ins. **Terms:** cancellation fee imposed. **Amenities:** extended cable TV. **Cards:** AX, DS, MC, VI. **Special Amenities:** free local telephone calls and **preferred room (subject to availability with advanced reservations).**

SOME UNITS

[✦] / [X] /

ROCKVILLE pop. 2,700

——— WHERE TO STAY ———

BILLIE CREEK VILLAGE & INN   Phone: (765)569-3430

(AAA) [SAVE]

♦♦♦ ♦♦♦

Motel

	5/24-8/31 [ECP]	1P: $69-$99	2P: $69-$99
	9/1-11/9 [ECP]	1P: $59-$89	2P: $59-$89
	4/1-5/23 & 11/10-3/31 [ECP]	1P: $49-$79	2P: $49-$79

Location: 1.4 mi e on US 36. Billie Creek Dr 47872 (RR 2, Box 27). Fax: 765/569-3582. **Facility:** 31 one-bedroom standard units, some with whirlpools. 2 stories, interior corridors. **Parking:** on-site. **Terms:** 3 day cancellation notice, package plans, pets ($10 extra charge, in designated units). **Amenities:** extended cable TV, video tape library. **Pool(s):** heated outdoor. **Guest Services:** valet laundry. **Business Services:** meeting rooms. **Cards:** AX, DS, MC, VI. **Special Amenities: free continental breakfast and free local telephone calls.**

SOME UNITS

[🛏] [&M] [⇋] [🖨] / [X] [VCR] [🔒] /
                                                     FEE   FEE

PARKE BRIDGE MOTEL   Phone: 765/569-3525

♦♦♦ ♦♦♦

Motel

| | 5/1-10/31 | 1P: $33-$51 | 2P: $40-$60 | XP: $5 |
| | 4/1-4/30 & 11/1-3/31 | 1P: $30-$43 | 2P: $35-$45 | XP: $5 |

Location: US 36, just e of center, 0.5 mi e of jct US 41. 304 E Ohio St 47872. Fax: 765/569-0317. **Facility:** 10 one-bedroom standard units. 1 story, exterior corridors. *Bath:* combo or shower only. **Parking:** on-site, winter plug-ins. **Amenities:** extended cable TV, video tape library. **Cards:** AX, DS, MC, VI.

SOME UNITS

[🖨] / [VCR]
                                                     FEE

ROSELAND pop. 700—See also SOUTH BEND.

——— WHERE TO STAY ———

BEST INNS OF AMERICA/SOUTH BEND   Phone: (574)277-7700

(AAA) [SAVE]

♦♦♦ ♦♦♦

Motel

	4/1-10/31 [CP]	1P: $57-$63	2P: $57-$63
	1/1-3/31 [CP]	1P: $48-$61	2P: $48-$61
	11/1-12/31 [CP]	1P: $46-$57	2P: $56-$57

Location: I-80/90, exit 77, 0.8 mi n on US 933. 425 Dixie Hwy N 46637. Fax: 574/277-2490. **Facility:** 93 one-bedroom standard units. 2 stories, interior corridors. **Parking:** on-site, winter plug-ins. **Terms:** 31 day cancellation notice-fee imposed, small pets only. **Amenities:** extended cable TV. **Cards:** AX, CB, DC, DS, MC, VI. **Special Amenities: early check-in/late check-out and preferred room (subject to availability with advanced reservations).**

SOME UNITS

[S▣] [🛏] [¶†⋅] [✦] [DATA PORT] [🖳] [🖨] / [X] /

HAMPTON INN & SUITES - SOUTH BEND   Phone: (574)277-9373

[SAVE]

♦♦♦ ♦♦♦

Motel

| | 4/1-10/31 & 3/1-3/31 [ECP] | 1P: $84-$125 | 2P: $94-$125 |
| | 11/1-2/28 [ECP] | 1P: $74-$125 | 2P: $84-$125 |

Location: I-80/90, exit 77, 1 mi n on US 933. (52709 US 31 N, SOUTH BEND, 46637). Fax: 574/243-0128. **Facility:** 117 units. 90 one-bedroom standard units. 27 one-bedroom suites ($115-$125) with efficiencies. 3 stories, interior corridors. *Bath:* combo or shower only. **Parking:** on-site. **Amenities:** dual phone lines, voice mail, irons, hair dryers. **Pool(s):** small indoor. **Leisure Activities:** whirlpool, exercise room. **Guest Services:** coin laundry. **Business Services:** meeting rooms. **Cards:** AX, CB, DC, DS, MC, VI.

SOME UNITS

[¶†⋅] [&M] [&] [📷] [⇋] [✦] [DATA PORT] [🖳] [🖨] / [X] [VCR] [🔒] [🖵] /
                                             FEE

HOLIDAY INN-UNIVERSITY AREA

▼▼ ▼▼
Motor Inn

9/1-11/30	1P: $94-$214	2P: $94-$214	
4/1-8/31	1P: $104-$124	2P: $104-$124	
12/1-3/31	1P: $94-$104	2P: $94-$104	

Phone: (574)272-6600

Location: I-80/90, exit 77, on US 31 and 933, 0.8 mi n. (515 Dixie Way N, SOUTH BEND, 46637). Fax: 574/272-5553. Facility: 228 one-bedroom standard units. 2 stories, interior/exterior corridors. Bath: combo or shower only. Parking: on-site. Terms: cancellation fee imposed, package plans. Amenities: voice mail, irons, hair dryers. Pool(s): heated indoor, wading. Leisure Activities: exercise room. Guest Services: valet and coin laundry. Business Services: conference facilities. Cards: AX, CB, DC, DS, JC, MC, VI. (See color ad p 518)

SOME UNITS
(ASK) (SD) (✈) (†¶) (Y) (&) (➡) (♥) (DATA PORT) (■) (▤) / (✕) /
FEE

HOWARD JOHNSON INN

AAA (SAVE)
▼▼
Motel

All Year   1P: $40-$65   2P: $50-$75   XP: $5   F18

Phone: (574)272-7900

Location: I-80/90, exit 77, just n on US 933. 130 Dixie Way S 46637. Fax: 574/272-7944. Facility: 129 one-bedroom standard units, some with whirlpools. 2 stories, interior/exterior corridors. Bath: combo or shower only. Terms: 14 day cancellation notice, [CP] meal plan available. Amenities: extended cable TV. Pool(s): small indoor. Business Services: meeting rooms. Cards: AX, CB, DC, DS, JC, MC, VI. Special Amenities: free continental breakfast and free newspaper.

SOME UNITS
(SD) (†¶) (➡) (♥) (DATA PORT) (▤) / (✕) /

SIGNATURE INN SOUTH BEND

▼▼▼▼
Motel

All Year [CP]   1P: $76-$87   2P: $76-$87

Phone: (574)277-3211

Location: I-80/90, exit 77, just n on US 933. 215 Dixie Way S 46637. Fax: 574/277-3211. Facility: 123 one-bedroom standard units, some with whirlpools. 2 stories, interior corridors. Parking: on-site. Amenities: extended cable TV, voice mail, irons, hair dryers. Pool(s): heated indoor. Leisure Activities: sauna, whirlpool, exercise room. Guest Services: valet laundry. Business Services: meeting rooms, PC. Cards: AX, DC, DS, MC, VI.

SOME UNITS
(ASK) (SD) (†¶) (⌧) (➡) (✕) (♥) (DATA PORT) (■) (▤) (▤) (▤) / (✕) /

RUSHVILLE pop. 5,500

——— WHERE TO STAY ———

HOLIDAY INN EXPRESS

▼▼ ▼▼
Motel

All Year [ECP]   1P: $69   2P: $76   XP: $10   F18

Phone: (765)932-2999

Location: Just e of SR 3. 320 Conrad Harcourt Way 46173. Fax: 765/932-2999. Facility: 58 one-bedroom standard units, some with whirlpools. 2 stories, interior corridors. Bath: combo or shower only. Parking: on-site, winter plug-ins. Terms: 30 day cancellation notice. Amenities: video tape library (fee), irons, hair dryers. Leisure Activities: exercise room. Guest Services: coin laundry. Business Services: meeting rooms, fax (fee). Cards: AX, DC, DS, JC, MC, VI.

SOME UNITS
(ASK) (SD) (&) (♥) (DATA PORT) (▤) (▤) / (✕) (VCR) (■) (▤) /

SCHERERVILLE pop. 19,900

——— WHERE TO STAY ———

BEST WESTERN CROSSROADS INN

AAA (SAVE)
▼▼▼▼
Motel

10/1-12/31 [ECP]	1P: $79-$150	2P: $79-$150	XP: $10	F15
5/30-9/30 [ECP]	1P: $89-$119	2P: $89-$119	XP: $10	F15
1/1-3/31 [ECP]	1P: $89-$99	2P: $89-$99	XP: $10	F15
4/1-5/29 [ECP]	1P: $69-$89	2P: $69-$89	XP: $10	F15

Phone: (219)865-3400

Location: I-65, exit 253, 7 mi w to US 41, then just s, set back east of road. 1905 Harder Ct 46375. Fax: 219/865-2800. Facility: 57 one-bedroom standard units, some with whirlpools. 2 stories, interior corridors. Bath: combo or shower only. Parking: on-site, winter plug-ins. Terms: 7 day cancellation notice. Amenities: irons, hair dryers. Pool(s): heated outdoor. Leisure Activities: limited exercise equipment. Business Services: meeting rooms, fax (fee). Cards: AX, CB, DC, DS, JC, MC, VI. Special Amenities: free continental breakfast and free local telephone calls.

SOME UNITS
(SD) (†¶) (&M) (&) (➡) (♥) (DATA PORT) (▤) (▤) / (✕) (■) (▤) /

SCOTTSBURG pop. 5,300

——— WHERE TO STAY ———

BEST WESTERN SCOTTSBURG INN

AAA (SAVE)
▼▼ ▼▼
Motor Inn

5/3-8/8 [BP]	1P: $62	2P: $69	XP: $7	F17
4/1-5/2 & 8/9-3/31 [BP]	1P: $60	2P: $67	XP: $7	F17

Phone: (812)752-2212

Location: I-65, exit 29, just w. 1525 West McClain St 47170 (PO Box 129). Fax: 812/752-5599. Facility: 96 one-bedroom standard units. 2 stories, interior corridors. Parking: on-site. Terms: cancellation fee imposed, [AP] meal plan available, small pets only. Amenities: extended cable TV, irons, hair dryers. Dining: restaurant, 6 am-9 pm, $6-$15, cocktails. Guest Services: valet laundry. Business Services: meeting rooms. Cards: AX, CB, DC, DS, MC, VI. Special Amenities: free continental breakfast and free local telephone calls.

SOME UNITS
(SD) (☎) (†¶) (Y) (⌧) (♥) (DATA PORT) (▤) (▤) / (✕) (■) (▤) /

HAMPTON INN AND SUITES

(SAVE)
▼▼▼▼
Motel

All Year   1P: $60-$70   2P: $70-$80

Phone: (812)752-1999

Location: I-65, exit 29, just w. 1535 McClain Ave 47170. Fax: 812/752-5572. Facility: 86 units. 59 one-bedroom standard units. 27 one-bedroom suites ($90-$110) with kitchens. 4 stories, interior corridors. Bath: combo or shower only. Parking: on-site. Terms: [CP] meal plan available. Amenities: extended cable TV, voice mail, irons, hair dryers. Some: dual phone lines. Pool(s): heated indoor. Leisure Activities: whirlpool, exercise room. Guest Services: valet and coin laundry. Business Services: meeting rooms. Cards: AX, DC, DS, JC, MC, VI.

SOME UNITS
(SD) (†¶) (&) (➡) (♥) (DATA PORT) (▤) (▤) / (✕) (VCR) (■) (▤) /

MARIANN TRAVEL INN
AAA SAVE
WWW WWW
Motor Inn

All Year   1P: $44-$47   2P: $55-$58   XP: $4   F12
Phone: (812)752-3396
Location: I-65, exit 29, just e. SR 56 47170 (PO Box 36). Fax: 812/752-2259. **Facility:** 94 one-bedroom standard units. 2 stories, exterior corridors. **Parking:** on-site. **Terms:** small pets only. **Amenities:** extended cable TV. **Dining:** restaurant, 6 am-9 pm, $7-$10, beer only. **Pool(s):** heated outdoor. **Leisure Activities:** playground, shuffleboard. **Guest Services:** valet and coin laundry. **Cards:** AX, CB, DC, DS, MC, VI. **Special Amenities:** early check-in/late check-out and free local telephone calls.
SOME UNITS

───── **WHERE TO DINE** ─────

JEEVES & COMPANY
WWW WWW
American

Lunch: $4-$8   Dinner: $9-$23   Phone: 812/752-6559
Location: I-65, exit 29, 1 mi e; in downtown square at McClain and Main sts. 64 S Main 47170. **Hours:** 9 am-8 pm, Mon-2 pm, Fri & Sat-9 pm, Sun 11 am-2 pm. Closed major holidays. **Reservations:** accepted. **Features:** casual dress; children's menu; carryout; beer & wine only; a la carte. You'll experience casual dining in this old downtown store-turned-restaurant, where sandwiches, salad, soup, steak, pasta and bourbon pecan chicken are offered, but whose specialties spotlight a bounty of fabulous dessert creations and muffins. **Parking:** on-site. **Cards:** AX, DC, DS, MC, VI.

ROADHOUSE USA
WWW WWW
Steak House

Lunch: $4-$17   Dinner: $4-$17   Phone: 812/752-9272
Location: I-65, exit 29, just w. 519 Beatrice Ave 47170. **Hours:** 11 am-11 pm. Closed major holidays. **Features:** casual dress; cocktails & lounge. Diners who enter the woodsy interior are greeted by an attentive staff that's well-trained in the art of follow up. Menu selections reach from hoof to stream and also include lighter fare for smaller appetites. A small but select array of desserts is offered. No one goes hungry here. **Parking:** on-site. **Cards:** AX, DS, MC, VI.

SELLERSBURG pop. 5,700

───── **WHERE TO STAY** ─────

COMFORT INN
SAVE
WWW WWW
Motel

All Year   1P: $65-$250   2P: $75-$250   XP: $7   F
Phone: 812/246-1200
Location: I-65, exit 9, just nw. 111 Enterprise Way 47172. Fax: 812/246-5948. **Facility:** 77 one-bedroom standard units, some with whirlpools. 3 stories, interior corridors. **Parking:** on-site. **Terms:** package plans. **Amenities:** voice mail. Some: dual phone lines. **Pool(s):** heated indoor. **Leisure Activities:** exercise room. **Guest Services:** coin laundry. **Business Services:** meeting rooms, fax (fee). **Cards:** AX, DC, DS, MC, VI.
SOME UNITS
FEE

DAYS INN LOUISVILLE NORTH
SAVE
WWW WWW
Motel

All Year [CP]   1P: $54-$79   2P: $59-$99   XP: $5   F17
Phone: 812/246-4451
Location: I-65, exit 7, just nw. 7618 Old SR 60 47172. Fax: 812/246-2200. **Facility:** 105 units. 101 one-bedroom standard units, some with whirlpools. 4 one-bedroom suites ($79-$199), some with whirlpools. 2 stories, exterior corridors. Bath: combo or shower only. **Parking:** on-site. **Terms:** cancellation fee imposed, package plans. **Amenities:** extended cable TV, hair dryers. Some: irons. **Pool(s):** outdoor. **Leisure Activities:** playground. **Business Services:** meeting rooms, fax (fee). **Cards:** AX, CB, DC, DS, JC, MC, VI.
SOME UNITS

SEYMOUR pop. 15,600

───── **WHERE TO DINE** ─────

THE CHEF'S TABLE
WWW WWW WWW
Nouvelle Italian

Lunch: $5-$9   Dinner: $8-$18   Phone: 812/524-7495
Location: Center; corner of Chestnut St. 114 W 2nd St 47274. **Hours:** 11 am-9:30 pm, Sat from 4 pm, Sun 10:30 am-3 pm. Closed: 11/28, 12/25. **Reservations:** suggested; weekend dinner. **Features:** casual dress; Sunday brunch; children's menu; carryout; cocktails & lounge; a la carte. **Parking:** street. **Cards:** AX, DS, MC, VI.

SHELBYVILLE —See Indianapolis p. 494.

SHIPSHEWANA pop. 500

───── **WHERE TO STAY** ─────

COUNTRY INN & SUITES BY CARLSON
AAA SAVE
WWW WWW
Motel

4/1-11/30 [ECP]   1P: $89-$99   2P: $89-$99   XP: $10   F18
12/1-3/31 [ECP]   1P: $69-$99   2P: $69-$99   XP: $10   F18
Phone: (260)768-7780
Location: 0.5 mi n. 3440 N SR 5 46565 (PO Box 428). Fax: 260/768-9103. **Facility:** 44 units. 39 one-bedroom standard units. 5 one-bedroom suites ($89-$139), some with whirlpools. 2 stories, interior corridors. Bath: combo or shower only. **Parking:** on-site. **Terms:** check-in 4 pm. **Amenities:** extended cable TV, irons, hair dryers. **Pool(s):** heated indoor. **Guest Services:** coin laundry. **Cards:** AX, DC, DS, MC, VI. **Special Amenities:** free continental breakfast and free newspaper. (See color ad p 476)
SOME UNITS
FEE

SUPER 8 MOTEL

Phone: (260)768-4004

5/1-9/30	1P: $65-$89	2P: $65-$89	XP: $5	F12
1/1-3/31	1P: $65-$80	2P: $65-$80	XP: $5	F12
4/1-4/30	1P: $60-$80	2P: $60-$80	XP: $5	F12
10/1-12/31	1P: $59-$75	2P: $59-$75	XP: $5	F12

Motel

Location: US 20, 0.8 mi n on SR 5. 740 S Van Buren 46565. Fax: 260/768-7498. **Facility:** 46 one-bedroom standard units. 2 stories, interior corridors. **Parking:** on-site. **Terms:** 14 day cancellation notice, pets ($8 fee). **Guest Services:** coin laundry. **Cards:** AX, DC, DS, JC, MC, VI.

SOME UNITS

FEE

SMITHVILLE pop. 300

——— WHERE TO STAY ———

FOURWINDS RESORT & MARINA

Phone: (812)824-9904

SAVE

Motor Inn

All Year   1P: $60-$170   XP: $10   F15

Location: SR 37 S, 6 mi se off Smithville Rd exit; SR 37 N, 5 mi ne off Monroe Reservoir exit; in Fairfax Recreation area. 9301 S Fairfax Rd 47401 (9301 S Fairfax Rd, BLOOMINGTON). Fax: 812/824-9816. **Facility:** 123 units. 120 one-bedroom standard units. 3 one-bedroom suites. 1-3 stories (no elevator), interior corridors. **Parking:** on-site. **Terms:** check-in 4 pm, 3 day cancellation notice, package plans. **Amenities:** voice mail, irons, hair dryers. **Pool(s):** heated indoor/outdoor. **Leisure Activities:** sauna, whirlpool, rental boats, marina, fishing, putting green, miniature golf, 3 tennis courts, playground, sports court, horseshoes, shuffleboard, volleyball. **Fee:** bicycles, game room. **Guest Services:** coin laundry. **Business Services:** meeting rooms, fax (fee). **Cards:** AX, DC, DS, MC, VI. Affiliated with Clarion Hotels.

SOME UNITS

FEE   FEE

SOUTH BEND pop. 105,500—See also NOTRE DAME & ROSELAND.

——— WHERE TO STAY ———

BOOK INN B & B

Phone: (574)288-1990

AAA SAVE

Historic Bed & Breakfast

All Year [BP]   1P: $95-$160   2P: $100-$160

Location: 0.4 mi w of Business US 31. 508 W Washington St 46601. Fax: 574/234-2338. **Facility:** Antiques abound in this restored 1872 mansion, which has well-appointed rooms. Smoke free premises. 5 one-bedroom standard units. 2 stories, interior corridors. **Bath:** combo or shower only. **Parking:** on-site. **Terms:** 14 day cancellation notice-fee imposed. **Amenities:** CD players. **Guest Services:** valet laundry. **Cards:** AX, MC, VI. **Special Amenities:** free local telephone calls and free newspaper.

SOME UNITS

DAYS INN OF SOUTH BEND

Phone: (574)277-0510

AAA SAVE

Motel

All Year [CP]   1P: $59-$99   2P: $59-$99   XP: $10   F12

Location: I-80/90, exit 77, 1 mi n. 52757 SR 933 46637. Fax: 574/277-9316. **Facility:** 180 one-bedroom standard units. 3 stories, exterior corridors. **Parking:** on-site. **Terms:** 30 day cancellation notice-fee imposed. **Amenities:** extended cable TV, safes (fee), hair dryers. **Pool(s):** outdoor. **Guest Services:** valet laundry. **Cards:** AX, DC, DS, MC, VI. **Special Amenities:** free continental breakfast and free local telephone calls.

SOME UNITS

THE ENGLISH ROSE INN BED & BREAKFAST

Phone: 574/289-2114

Historic Bed & Breakfast

All Year   1P: $65-$155   2P: $75-$155   XP: $10   D12

Location: Business US 31, just w on Washington St to Taylor, just s. 116 S Taylor 46601. Fax: 574/287-1311. **Facility:** Four-poster beds and fine antique furniture warm this rose-and-plum-toned 1892 Victorian home in South Bend's historic district. Smoke free premises. 6 one-bedroom standard units, some with whirlpools. 3 stories, interior corridors. **Bath:** some combo or shower only. **Parking:** on-site. **Terms:** check-in 4 pm, age restrictions may apply, 14 day cancellation notice, package plans. **Amenities:** extended cable TV. **Cards:** AX, MC, VI.

HOLIDAY INN CITY CENTER

Phone: (574)232-3941

Hotel

All Year   1P: $95

Location: Center. 213 W Washington St 46601. Fax: 574/284-3715. **Facility:** 176 units. 174 one-bedroom standard units. 2 one-bedroom suites ($115). 16 stories, interior corridors. **Parking:** on-site (fee). **Terms:** check-in 4 pm, package plans. **Amenities:** voice mail, irons, hair dryers. **Pool(s):** indoor. **Leisure Activities:** exercise room. **Guest Services:** valet laundry. **Business Services:** conference facilities, business center, PC, fax (fee). **Cards:** AX, CB, DC, DS, JC, MC, VI.

SOME UNITS

FEE   FEE FEE

THE INN AT SAINT MARY'S

Phone: (574)232-4000

AAA SAVE

Motel

All Year [ECP]   1P: $89   2P: $98   XP: $10   F17

Location: I-80/90, exit 77. 53993 US 31-33 N 46637. Fax: 574/289-0986. **Facility:** 150 units. 120 one-bedroom standard units. 30 one-bedroom suites ($119-$189), some with kitchens. 3 stories, interior corridors. **Bath:** combo or shower only. **Parking:** on-site. **Terms:** 7 day cancellation notice. **Amenities:** extended cable TV, video games, high-speed Internet, dual phone lines, voice mail, irons, hair dryers. **Leisure Activities:** sauna, whirlpool, exercise room, 9 units with exercise equipment. **Guest Services:** gift shop, valet and coin laundry, area transportation-within 10 mi. **Business Services:** meeting rooms, business center, fax. **Cards:** AX, CB, DC, DS, MC, VI. **Special Amenities:** free continental breakfast and free newspaper.

SOME UNITS

FEE

THE OLIVER INN BED & BREAKFAST

Phone: (574)232-4545

WWW

Historic Bed
& Breakfast

All Year [BP]   1P: $95-$165   2P: $95-$165   XP: $20   F5
Location: 0.3 mi w of US 31. 630 W Washington St 46601. Fax: 574/288-9788. **Facility:** Manicured grounds surround this restored 1880s house; featured are a cozy library, an automated baby-grand piano and candlelit breakfasts. Smoke free premises. 9 one-bedroom standard units, some with whirlpools. 3 stories, interior corridors. *Bath:* some shared or private. **Parking:** on-site. **Terms:** check-in 4 pm, 14 day cancellation notice-fee imposed, package plans. **Amenities:** hair dryers. *Some:* CD players. **Cards:** AX, DS, MC, VI.

QUALITY INN & SUITES

Phone: (574)288-3800

SAVE

WWW
Motel

All Year [ECP]   1P: $69-$119   2P: $79-$129   XP: $10   F18
Location: I-80/90, exit 72, follow US 31 S to South Bend Airport exit, follow signs to airport, 1.8 mi e to US 20. 4124 Lincoln Way West 46628. Fax: 574/288-3810. **Facility:** 64 units. 58 one-bedroom standard units. 6 one-bedroom suites ($109-$149). 3 stories, interior corridors. *Bath:* combo or shower only. **Parking:** on-site. **Terms:** 30 day cancellation notice-fee imposed. **Amenities:** extended cable TV, dual phone lines, voice mail, irons, hair dryers. **Pool(s):** small indoor. **Leisure Activities:** whirlpool, exercise room. **Guest Services:** valet laundry. **Business Services:** meeting rooms. **Cards:** AX, CB, DC, DS, MC, VI.

SOME UNITS
FEE   FEE

QUEEN ANNE INN

Phone: (574)234-5959

WWW

Historic Bed
& Breakfast

All Year [BP]   1P: $70-$109   2P: $75-$119   XP: $20   F6
Location: Just w of US 31; at jct William and Washington sts. 420 W Washington St 46601. Fax: 574/234-4324. **Facility:** Smoke free premises. 6 one-bedroom standard units. 3 stories, interior corridors. *Bath:* combo or shower only. **Parking:** on-site. **Terms:** check-in 4 pm, 7 day cancellation notice, package plans. **Guest Services:** afternoon tea. **Cards:** AX, DS, MC, VI.

RAMADA INN

Phone: (574)272-5220

AAA SAVE
WWW
Motor Inn

4/1-11/1 [BP]   1P: $75   2P: $75
11/2-3/31 [BP]   1P: $60   2P: $60
Location: I-80/90, exit 77, 1 mi n on US 933. 52890 SR 933 N 46637 (52890 SR 933 N). Fax: 574/272-3956. **Facility:** 200 one-bedroom standard units, some with kitchens and/or whirlpools. 2 stories, interior/exterior corridors. **Parking:** on-site. **Terms:** 21 day cancellation notice. **Amenities:** video games, voice mail, irons, hair dryers. **Dining:** restaurant, 6 am-1 & 5-9 pm, $7-$15, cocktails. **Pool(s):** outdoor, indoor. **Leisure Activities:** whirlpools, exercise room. **Guest Services:** valet and coin laundry, airport transportation-South Bend Regional Airport. **Business Services:** conference facilities. **Cards:** AX, CB, DC, DS, MC, VI. **Special Amenities:** free local telephone calls and free newspaper. *(See color ad below)*

SOME UNITS
FEE

RESIDENCE INN BY MARRIOTT

Phone: (574)289-5555

AAA SAVE

8/2-11/30 [BP]	1P: $99-$349	2P: $99-$449
4/1-8/1 & 12/1-3/31 [BP]	1P: $99-$199	2P: $99-$199

WWWW

Apartment

Location: US 33, just e on Northshore Ave, 0.4 mi s. 716 N Niles Ave 46617. Fax: 574/288-4531. **Facility:** 80 one-bedroom standard units with kitchens. 2 stories, exterior corridors. **Parking:** on-site. **Terms:** pets ($100 fee). **Amenities:** extended cable TV, dual phone lines, voice mail, irons, hair dryers. **Pool(s):** small outdoor. **Leisure Activities:** exercise room, sports court. **Guest Services:** complimentary evening beverages: Mon-Thurs, valet and coin laundry. **Business Services:** meeting rooms, fax. **Cards:** AX, CB, DC, DS, JC, MC, VI.
(See color ad card insert)

SOME UNITS

🛎️ 🐕 🈯 ⛲ DATA PORT 📧 🖥️ 💻 🖨️ / ⊠ /
                    FEE

SOUTH BEND MARRIOTT HOTEL

Phone: 574/234-2000

AAA SAVE

9/6-11/24	1P: $69-$369
4/1-9/5 & 11/25-3/31	1P: $69-$159

WWWW

Hotel

Location: Center; at jct US 20/31/33. 123 N St Joseph St 46601. Fax: 574/234-2252. **Facility:** 298 one-bedroom standard units. 9 stories, interior corridors. **Parking:** on-site (fee). **Terms:** 45 day cancellation notice-fee imposed, package plans. **Amenities:** high-speed Internet, dual phone lines, voice mail, irons, hair dryers. **Dining:** restaurant, 6:30 am-10:30 pm, Sat & Sun from 7 am, $9-$21, cocktails. **Pool(s):** small heated indoor. **Leisure Activities:** sauna, whirlpool, exercise room. **Business Services:** conference facilities, business center. *Fee:* PC, fax. **Cards:** AX, CB, DC, DS, JC, MC, VI. *(See color ad card insert)*

SOME UNITS

🈯 🍽️ 🍸 👨‍💼 🐾 🈯 ⊠ ⛲ DATA PORT 💻 🖨️ / ⊠ 📧 🖥️ /
FEE   FEE   FEE FEE

WHERE TO DINE

THE CARRIAGE HOUSE

Dinner: $18-$32   **Phone:** 574/272-9220

AAA

WWW

Continental

Location: I-80/90, exit 72, n on US 31 Bypass to Brick Rd exit, 0.3 mi w to Orange Rd, then 1 mi n, follow signs. 24460 Adams Rd 46628. **Hours:** 5 pm-9:30 pm. Closed: Sun, Mon & 1/1-1/15. **Reservations:** suggested. **Features:** dressy casual; cocktails & lounge; a la carte. A rural location in a converted 1850s church is a memorable spot for elegant dining. Well-prepared, artistically presented cuisine uses only the finest ingredients. Selections on both the menu and wine list are extensive. Be prepared to be pampered by the welcoming staff. **Parking:** on-site. **Cards:** AX, CB, DC, MC, VI.

⊠

HACIENDA MEXICAN RESTAURANT

Lunch: $4-$10   **Dinner:** $4-$10   **Phone:** 574/291-2566

WW WW

Mexican

Location: Jct US 31/20, 0.9 mi e on Ireland Rd to Miami Ave, just s. 1290 Scottsdale Mall, Suite 2000 46614. **Hours:** 11 am-10 pm, Fri & Sat-11 pm, Sun-9 pm. **Reservations:** accepted. **Features:** casual dress; children's menu; carryout; cocktails & lounge; a la carte. "Wet burritos" are the house specialty at the colorful, upbeat restaurant. The menu includes huge helpings of standard favorites, such as tacos, chimichangas and enchiladas, as well as two types of chili. Antique Mexican photographs decorate the walls. **Parking:** on-site. **Cards:** AX, MC, VI.

👨‍💼 ⊠

LASALLE GRILL

Dinner: $20-$29   **Phone:** 574/288-1155

AAA

WWW WWW

American

Location: Between Michigan (US 31 and 33) and Main sts. 115 W Colfax 46601. **Hours:** 5 pm-10 pm, Fri & Sat-11 pm. Closed major holidays; also Sun. **Reservations:** suggested. **Features:** dressy casual; cocktails; a la carte. A fashionable, locally popular dining spot featuring contemporary American cuisine that is exceptionally well prepared. Grilling is the primary preparation and they do it to perfection. Prime steaks are the signature, but the fresh seafood, trout, lamb, Amish chicken, pasta and pork chops are also excellent. The dining room is comfortably small featuring six white columns, crisp white linen covered tables and a fine view of the street through the large windows that line the front of the room. **Parking:** street. **Cards:** AX, CB, DC, DS, MC, VI.

⊠

TIPPECANOE PLACE

Historical   **Lunch:** $7-$10   **Dinner:** $14-$22   **Phone:** 574/234-9077

WWW

American

Location: US 31, 0.3 mi w. 620 W Washington St 46601. **Hours:** 11:30 am-2 & 5-10 pm, Fri-10:30 pm, Sat 4:30 pm-10:30 pm, Sun 9 am-2 & 4-9 pm. **Reservations:** suggested. **Features:** dressy casual; Sunday brunch; cocktails & lounge. Fine dining is what you'll discover in the restored 1888 Studebaker Mansion, resplendent in antique and period furnishings. Prime rib, steak, beef tenderloin medallions, and seafood are served, along with an amply portioned and colorfully presented shrimp and scallop stir fry. **Parking:** on-site. **Cards:** AX, DC, DS, MC, VI.

⊠

STACER

WHERE TO STAY

HOLIDAY INN EXPRESS

Phone: (812)867-1100

WWW

Motel

All Year [ECP]   1P: $58   2P: $58   XP: $5   F19

Location: I-64, exit 25A (US 41), just s. (19600 Elpers Rd, EVANSVILLE, 47725). Fax: 812/867-2170. **Facility:** 99 one-bedroom standard units, some with whirlpools. 3 stories, interior corridors. *Bath:* combo or shower only. **Parking:** on-site, winter plug-ins. **Terms:** check-in 4 pm, cancellation fee imposed. **Amenities:** irons, hair dryers. **Pool(s):** heated indoor. **Leisure Activities:** whirlpool, exercise room. **Guest Services:** valet and coin laundry. **Business Services:** meeting rooms, fax. **Cards:** AX, CB, DC, DS, JC, MC, VI.

SOME UNITS

ASK 🈯 🍽️ 👨‍💼 🈯 🐾 ⛲ DATA PORT 💻 🖨️ / ⊠ 📧 🖥️ /
                  FEE   FEE

STORY

------ **WHERE TO DINE** ------

THE STORY INN Historical — **Lunch:** $6-$8 — **Dinner:** $20-$25 — **Phone:** 812/988-2273
(AAA) **Location:** 9.5 mi s of jct SR 135 and 46. 6404 S SR 135 47448. **Hours:** 9 am-2 & 5-8 pm, Sat & Sun from 8 am.
Closed: 12/24, 12/25; also Mon. **Reservations:** suggested; for dinner. **Features:** casual dress; cocktails; a
la carte. An 1850s mercantile theme is carried out in the charming restaurant, a favorite place for couples.
Stunning plate presentation sets the gourmet cuisine apart. Hand-cut steaks and the delicious
Nouvelle American banana-walnut pancakes are specialties of the house. Smoke free premises. **Parking:** on-site.
Cards: MC, VI.   [X]

TAYLORSVILLE pop. 1,000

------ **WHERE TO STAY** ------

COMFORT INN — **Phone:** (812)526-9747
[SAVE] All Year [ECP] — 1P: $53-$175 — 2P: $58-$200 — XP: $5 — F18
Location: I-65, exit 76A, just s. 10330 US 31 47280 (PO Box 506). Fax: 812/526-9747. **Facility:** 56 one-bedroom
standard units, some with whirlpools. 1-2 stories, exterior corridors. **Parking:** on-site. **Terms:** 14 day cancel-
Motel lation notice, pets ($5 extra charge). **Amenities:** extended cable TV. *Some:* irons. **Pool(s):** outdoor.
Cards: AX, CB, DC, DS, JC, MC, VI.

SOME UNITS
[Sᴅ] [🛏] [➔] [📺] [DATA PORT] [🖨] / [X] [🛁] [🖥] [🗒] /

TELL CITY pop. 8,100

------ **WHERE TO STAY** ------

RAMADA LIMITED — **Phone:** (812)547-3234
All Year — 1P: $60 — 2P: $60 — XP: $7 — F17
Location: Just off SR 66, 1.7 mi se of jct SR 37. 235 Orchard Hill Dr 47586. Fax: 812/547-3216. **Facility:** 58 one-
Motel bedroom standard units. 2 stories, interior corridors. *Bath:* combo or shower only. **Parking:** on-site, winter
plug-ins. **Terms:** pets ($50 deposit). **Amenities:** extended cable TV, irons, hair dryers. **Pool(s):** outdoor.
Leisure Activities: exercise room. **Guest Services:** valet and coin laundry. **Cards:** AX, CB, DC, DS, JC, MC, VI.

SOME UNITS
[ASK] [Sᴅ] [🛏] [Y] [&M] [☕] [➔] [📺] [DATA PORT] [🛁] [🖥] [🗒] [🖨] / [X] /

TERRE HAUTE pop. 55,400

──── **WHERE TO STAY** ────

COMFORT SUITES
SAVE

Phone: (812)235-1770

Motel

All Year   1P: $60-$125   2P: $65-$125   XP: $5   F18
Location: I-70, exit 7 (US 41/150), just ne. 501 E Margaret Ave 47802. Fax: 812/235-1770. **Facility:** 60 one-bedroom standard units. 3 stories, interior corridors. **Bath:** combo or shower only. **Parking:** on-site, winter plug-ins. **Terms:** pets ($10 extra charge, in smoking units). **Amenities:** extended cable TV. *Some:* irons, hair dryers. **Pool(s):** heated indoor. **Leisure Activities:** whirlpool. **Guest Services:** valet laundry. **Business Services:** meeting rooms. **Cards:** AX, DC, DS, JC, MC, VI.

SOME UNITS

DRURY INN-TERRE HAUTE

Phone: (812)238-1206

Motel

All Year [ECP]   1P: $64-$98   2P: $64-$98   XP: $10   F18
Location: I-70, exit 7 (US 41/150), just ne. 3040 Hwy 41 S 47802. Fax: 812/238-1206. **Facility:** 152 units. 150 one-bedroom standard units. 2 one-bedroom suites ($84-$108). 7 stories, interior corridors. *Bath:* combo or shower only. **Parking:** on-site. **Amenities:** extended cable TV, voice mail, irons, hair dryers. **Pool(s):** heated indoor. **Leisure Activities:** whirlpool, exercise room. **Guest Services:** complimentary evening beverages: Mon-Thurs, valet and coin laundry. **Business Services:** meeting rooms. **Cards:** AX, CB, DC, DS, MC, VI. *(See color ad p 5)*

SOME UNITS

FAIRFIELD INN BY MARRIOTT
SAVE

Phone: (812)235-2444

Motel

All Year [ECP]   1P: $54-$84   2P: $60-$90   XP: $6   F18
Location: I-70, exit 7 (US 41/150), just ne. 475 E Margaret Dr 47802. Fax: 812/235-2444. **Facility:** 62 one-bedroom standard units. 3 stories, interior corridors. *Bath:* combo or shower only. **Parking:** on-site. **Terms:** 7 day cancellation notice. **Amenities:** extended cable TV, irons. **Pool(s):** heated indoor. **Leisure Activities:** whirlpool. **Guest Services:** valet laundry. **Cards:** AX, CB, DC, DS, MC, VI. **Special Amenities:** free continental breakfast and free local telephone calls. *(See color ad card insert)*

SOME UNITS

FARRINGTON BED & BREAKFAST
SAVE

Phone: (812)238-0524

Historic Bed
& Breakfast

All Year   1P: $85   2P: $85   XP: $10   F12
Location: I-70, exit 7 (US 41/150), 1.9 mi n to Farrington St, 0.4 mi e to S 7th St, then just n. 931 S 7th St 47807. Fax: 812/242-8335. **Facility:** Victorian charm and elegance are abundant in this stately turn-of-the-20th-century home, which is located in a residential neighborhood. Designated smoking area. 5 one-bedroom standard units. 2 stories, interior corridors. *Bath:* some shared or private, combo or shower only. **Parking:** on-site, winter plug-ins. **Terms:** cancellation fee imposed. **Amenities:** extended cable TV. **Business Services:** meeting rooms. **Cards:** DS, MC, VI. **Special Amenities:** free local telephone calls and preferred room (subject to availability with advanced reservations).

SOME UNITS

/ VCR /

HOLIDAY INN
SAVE

Phone: (812)232-6081

Motor Inn

All Year   1P: $109   2P: $109   XP: $8   F18
Location: I-70, exit 7 (US 41/150), just s. 3300 US 41 S 47802. Fax: 812/238-9934. **Facility:** 227 units. 223 one-bedroom standard units. 4 one-bedroom suites. 2-5 stories, interior/exterior corridors. **Parking:** on-site. **Terms:** check-in 4 pm, small pets only. **Amenities:** extended cable TV, video games, voice mail, irons, hair dryers. **Dining:** dining room, restaurant, 6:30 am-2 & 5-10 pm, Sun-9 pm, $13-$26, cocktails, also, The Apple Club, see separate listing, entertainment. **Pool(s):** heated indoor. **Leisure Activities:** saunas, whirlpool, exercise room, board games, table tennis. *Fee:* game room, billiards. **Guest Services:** complimentary laundry. **Business Services:** conference facilities, business center, PC, fax (fee). **Cards:** AX, CB, DC, DS, JC, MC, VI. **Special Amenities:** free local telephone calls and free newspaper.

SOME UNITS

KNIGHTS INN

Phone: (812)234-9931

Motel

All Year [CP]   1P: $44-$57   2P: $44-$57
Location: I-70, exit 7 (US 41/150), just n to Margaret Dr, then e. 401 E Margaret Dr 47802. Fax: 812/234-0890. **Facility:** 125 one-bedroom standard units, some with efficiencies. 1 story, exterior corridors. **Parking:** on-site. **Amenities:** extended cable TV. **Pool(s):** outdoor. **Guest Services:** valet laundry. **Business Services:** meeting rooms. **Cards:** AX, DC, DS, MC, VI.

SOME UNITS

PEAR TREE INN BY DRURY

Phone: (812)234-4268

Motel

All Year [CP]   1P: $50-$88   2P: $50-$88   XP: $10   F18
Location: I-70, exit 7 (US 41/150), just n. 3050 US 41 S 47802. Fax: 812/234-4268. **Facility:** 64 one-bedroom standard units. 4 stories, interior corridors. *Bath:* combo or shower only. **Parking:** on-site. **Amenities:** extended cable TV. **Guest Services:** valet laundry. **Cards:** AX, CB, DC, DS, MC, VI. *(See color ad p 5)*

SOME UNITS

SIGNATURE INN-TERRE HAUTE

Phone: (812)238-1461

Motel

All Year [CP]   1P: $56-$65   2P: $56-$65
Location: I-70, exit 7 (US 41/150), just n. 3053 US 41 S 47802. Fax: 812/238-1461. **Facility:** 150 units. 143 one-bedroom standard units, some with whirlpools. 7 one-bedroom suites. 3 stories, interior corridors. **Parking:** on-site. **Amenities:** extended cable TV, voice mail, irons, hair dryers. **Pool(s):** outdoor. **Leisure Activities:** exercise room. **Guest Services:** valet and coin laundry. **Business Services:** meeting rooms. **Cards:** AX, CB, DC, DS, MC, VI.

SOME UNITS

SUPER 8 LODGE
Motel

All Year   1P: $43-$80   2P: $48-$85   XP: $5   F16
Phone: (812)232-4890
Location: I-70, exit 7 (US 41/150), just nw. 3089 S 1st St 47802. Fax: 812/232-4890. **Facility:** 118 one-bedroom standard units. 3 stories, interior corridors. **Parking:** on-site. **Terms:** small pets only. **Amenities:** extended cable TV, safes (fee). **Cards:** AX, CB, DC, DS, MC, VI.

SOME UNITS

——— WHERE TO DINE ———

THE APPLE CLUB
American

Dinner: $16-$25   Phone: 812/232-6081
Location: I-70, exit 7 (US 41/150), just s; in Holiday Inn. 3300 US 41 S 47802. **Hours:** 5 pm-10 pm. Closed major holidays; also Sun & Mon. **Reservations:** accepted. **Features:** dressy casual; cocktails & lounge. Combining a casual atmosphere and upscale dining features, the restaurant offers diners an opportunity to enjoy polished service and creative American classic and innovative cuisine in an environment that is neither stuffy nor pretentious. The open-plan kitchen affords views of the chef at work, preparing such dishes as the signature grilled yellow-fin tuna served with wasabi on a bed of pickled ginger. **Parking:** on-site. **Cards:** AX, CB, DC, DS, MC, VI.

GERHARDT'S BIERSTUBE
German

Lunch: $5-$8   Dinner: $5-$16   Phone: 812/466-9249
Location: I-70, exit 7 (US 41/150), 5.5 mi n, 1.1 mi e on Harrison Rd, then just s. 1724 Lafayette Ave 47802. **Hours:** 11 am-2 & 4-9 pm, Fri-10 pm, Sat 4 pm-10 pm, Sun 4 pm-9 pm. Closed major holidays; also Mon. **Reservations:** accepted. **Features:** casual dress; children's menu; carryout; cocktails. A handful of American choices mingle with mostly German cuisine: Wiener schnitzel and such delicious desserts as apple strudel and Black Forest cake. The ambience is informal, with a cozy fireplace and Bavarian appointments. **Parking:** on-site. **Cards:** DS, MC, VI.

HAPPY DRAGON
Chinese

Lunch: $5-$6   Dinner: $7-$8   Phone: 812/235-8038
Location: I-70, exit 7 (US 41/150), 1.6 mi n. 920 S 3rd St 47807. **Hours:** 11 am-10 pm. **Reservations:** suggested. **Features:** children's menu; carryout; cocktails; buffet, a la carte. Most diners opt for the buffet, which lays out an extensive selection of traditional Chinese offerings. The dining rooms, appointed in tasteful and subtle Oriental decor, are spacious and comfortable. **Parking:** on-site. **Cards:** AX, CB, DC, DS, MC, VI.

M. MOGGER'S BREWERY, RESTAURANT & PUB   Historical
American

Lunch: $5-$15   Dinner: $5-$15   Phone: 812/234-9202
Location: I-70, exit 7 (US 41/150), 2.1 mi n to Poplar St, then 0.5 mi e. 908 Poplar St 47807. **Hours:** 11 am-10 pm, Fri & Sat-11 pm, Sun-9 pm. Closed major holidays. **Features:** casual dress; children's menu; carryout; cocktails. Housed in a brewery built in 1837, the lively restaurant is named for one of the founders of the former Terre Haute Brewing Co. Equipment from the facility, as well as other artifacts, decorates the dining room. The barbecue pork loin sandwich is yummy, as is the "drunken cod", beer-battered white fish chunks. Mogger's also offers one of the largest selections of beers in the area, including popular domestic brands, imports and microbrews. **Parking:** on-site. **Cards:** AX, DC, DS, MC, VI.

ROSE OF INDIA
Indian

Dinner: $8-$13   Phone: 812/235-0909
Location: I-70, exit 7, 1.3 mi n on US 41/150. 1936 S Third St 47802. **Hours:** 5 pm-9 pm. Closed: 12/25; also Sun & Mon. **Reservations:** suggested; weekends. **Features:** casual dress; carryout; wine only. Pungent aromas of spicy Indian cuisine punctuate the air as you enter the bright, spacious dining room. Traditional preparations of chicken, seafood, lamb and freshly baked bread are delicious and flavorful, as are the pistachio and mango ice creams. **Parking:** on-site. **Cards:** AX, DS, MC, VI.

SYCAMORE FARM TEA ROOMS   Historical
American

Lunch: $7-$9   Phone: 812/877-9288
Location: I-70, exit 11 (SR 46), 2.2 mi n to Poplar Dr, then 0.4 mi w. 5001 E Poplar Dr 47803. **Hours:** 11 am-2 pm. Closed major holidays; also Sat & Sun. **Reservations:** suggested. **Features:** casual dress; wine only. Tea rooms furnished with period pieces make up the charming 1860s farmhouse. The signature sycamore Wellington is a chicken breast stuffed with wild rice and baked in a puffed pastry topped with marinade. Baked fudge is a specialty dessert. Smoke free premises. **Parking:** on-site. **Cards:** MC, VI.

WESTERN RIB-EYE
Steak & Seafood

Lunch: $8-$14   Dinner: $10-$18   Phone: 812/232-5591
Location: US 41, 3 mi e on Wabash Ave, just s. 100 S Fruitridge Ave 47803. **Hours:** 11 am-9 pm, Fri-10 pm, Sat 4 pm-10 pm, Sun 11 am-6 pm. Closed major holidays; also Mon. **Reservations:** accepted. **Features:** casual dress; children's menu; carryout; salad bar; cocktails & lounge. The attractive rustic barn-style decor complements the varied menu featuring beef and some seafood entrees. Choose from such specialties as marinated chicken breast, prime rib or rib eye, then top off your meal with a sweet slice of peanut butter pie. **Parking:** on-site. **Cards:** AX, DC, DS, MC, VI.

VALPARAISO pop. 24,400

——— WHERE TO STAY ———

COURTYARD BY MARRIOTT
Motel

All Year   1P: $89-$109
Phone: (219)465-1700
Location: US 30, w of jct SR 49 Bypass. 2301 E Morthland Dr 46383. Fax: 219/477-2430. **Facility:** 111 units. 110 one-bedroom standard units, some with whirlpools. 1 one-bedroom suite ($109-$159) with whirlpool. 2 stories, interior corridors. **Parking:** on-site. **Terms:** 4 day cancellation notice. **Amenities:** video games (fee), dual phone lines, voice mail, irons, hair dryers. **Dining:** coffee shop, 6-10 am, Sat & Sun 7-11 am. **Pool(s):** heated indoor/outdoor. **Leisure Activities:** whirlpool, exercise room. **Guest Services:** valet and coin laundry. **Business Services:** meeting rooms. **Cards:** AX, DC, DS, MC, VI. *(See color ad card insert)*

SOME UNITS
FEE

FAIRFIELD INN BY MARRIOTT

Motel

(See color ad card insert)

Phone: (219)465-6225

All Year [ECP]   1P: $69-$99   2P: $69-$99   XP: $10   F18
Location: US 30, 0.3 mi w of jct SR 49 Bypass. 2101 E Morthland Dr 46383. Fax: 219/464-9590. **Facility:** 63 one-bedroom standard units, some with whirlpools. 3 stories, interior corridors. *Bath:* combo or shower only. **Parking:** on-site. **Amenities:** irons, hair dryers. **Pool(s):** small heated indoor. **Leisure Activities:** whirlpool, limited exercise equipment. **Guest Services:** valet and coin laundry. **Cards:** AX, DC, DS, MC, VI. **Special Amenities:** free continental breakfast and free local telephone calls.

SOME UNITS

HOLIDAY INN EXPRESS

Motel

Phone: (219)464-8555

All Year [ECP]   1P: $89-$119   2P: $89-$119
Location: 0.8 mi e on US 30. 760 Morthland Dr 46385. Fax: 219/477-2492. **Facility:** 54 one-bedroom standard units. 4 stories, interior/exterior corridors. *Bath:* combo or shower only. **Parking:** on-site. **Terms:** small pets only ($10 fee). **Amenities:** irons, hair dryers. **Leisure Activities:** exercise room. **Guest Services:** complimentary evening beverages: Mon-Thurs, valet laundry. **Business Services:** meeting rooms. **Cards:** AX, CB, DC, DS, JC, MC, VI. **Special Amenities:** free continental breakfast and free local telephone calls.

SOME UNITS
FEE FEE

THE INN AT ABERDEEN

Bed & Breakfast

Phone: 219/465-3753

All Year [BP]   2P: $99-$137   XP: $20   F12
Location: Jct US 30 and SR 2, 2.7 mi s. 3158 S SR 2 46385. Fax: 219/465-9227. **Facility:** A lovely restored 1895 farmhouse with Queen Anne decor with fireplace and whirlpool in each room and a library and two-story solarium in which to sit. Smoke free premises. 11 units. 9 one-bedroom standard units with whirlpools. 2 one-bedroom suites ($148-$172) with whirlpools, some with kitchens. 3 stories (no elevator), interior corridors. **Parking:** on-site. **Terms:** check-in 4 pm, package plans. **Amenities:** extended cable TV, video tape library, hair dryers. **Guest Services:** gift shop. **Business Services:** meeting rooms. **Cards:** AX, CB, DC, DS, MC, VI. **Special Amenities:** free local telephone calls and preferred room (subject to availability with advanced reservations).

SOME UNITS
FEE

SUPER 8 MOTEL

Motel

Phone: 219/464-9840

All Year   1P: $62-$73   2P: $69-$77   XP: $2   F17
Location: SR 2, just w of jct SR 49. 3005 John Howell Dr 46383. Fax: 219/464-9840. **Facility:** 58 one-bedroom standard units, some with whirlpools. 2 stories, interior corridors. *Bath:* combo or shower only. **Parking:** on-site. **Pool(s):** small heated indoor. **Guest Services:** coin laundry. **Cards:** AX, CB, DC, DS, MC, VI.

SOME UNITS

Hungry? Look for the RED AAA Logo

*N*ext time you look through a AAA TourBook® guide in search of a place to dine, take note of the bright red AAA logo just under a select group of restaurant names! These Official Appointment restaurants place a high value on the business they receive from dedicated AAA travelers.

As a member, you already turn to TourBooks for quality travel information. Now look for restaurants that display the bright red AAA logo in their listing for dining experiences you'll long remember!

─── **WHERE TO DINE** ───

SOLE AT ONE FIVE SEVEN

▼▼▼

International

Lunch: $7-$13 **Dinner:** $14-$24 **Phone:** 219/462-0992
Location: Downtown; just w of jct Lafayette and Lincolnway. 157 W Lincolnway 46383. **Hours:** 11 am-2 & 5-9 pm, Sat 5 pm-10 pm, Sun 4 pm-8 pm. Closed major holidays; also Mon. **Reservations:** suggested. **Features:** casual dress; carryout; beer & wine only; a la carte. Complete with white linen tablecloths, a brick accent wall and colorful eclectic artwork, the stylish dining room is the perfect setting for superbly prepared cuisine. Creative, globally influenced dishes include duck breast, beef tenderloin, lamb shank, veal medallions, chicken breast, fresh shellfish, seafood and risotto. Smoke free premises. **Parking:** street. **Cards:** AX, DS, MC, VI. ☒

STRONGBOW INN

🆑

▼▼ ▼▼

American

Lunch: $6-$12 **Dinner:** $10-$23 **Phone:** 219/462-5121
Location: On US 30 at jct SR 49 Bypass. 2405 US 30 E 46383. **Hours:** 11 am-9 pm, Fri & Sat-10 pm, Sun-8 pm. Closed: 1/1, 11/28, 12/24-12/26. **Reservations:** suggested. **Features:** casual dress; Sunday brunch; children's menu; carryout; cocktails & lounge. Fresh turkey dishes are served in attractive country dining rooms by an attentive wait staff. You won't be disappointed when ordering the delicious open-faced turkey sandwich. If turkey's not your bag, there's also beef tenderloin, venison and seafood. Be sure to try the pecan pie or any of the in-house prepared desserts. **Parking:** on-site. **Cards:** AX, DC, DS, MC, VI. ☒

VINCENNES pop. 19,900

─── **WHERE TO STAY** ───

COMFORT SUITES

🆑 SAVE

▼▼▼

Motel

Phone: (812)882-2244
All Year   1P: $59-$79   2P: $69-$89   XP: $10   F17
Location: Jct US 41 Bypass and Hart St, just se. 2555 Hart St 47591. **Fax:** 812/886-9137. **Facility:** 63 one-bedroom standard units, some with whirlpools. 3 stories, interior corridors. *Bath:* combo or shower only. *Some:* irons. **Pool(s):** heated indoor. **Leisure Activities:** exercise room. **Business Services:** meeting rooms, fax (fee). **Cards:** AX, DC, DS, MC, VI. **Special Amenities: free continental breakfast and free local telephone calls.**

SOME UNITS

WABASH pop. 12,100

─── **WHERE TO STAY** ───

HOLIDAY INN EXPRESS HOTEL & SUITES

🆑 SAVE

▼▼▼

Motel

Phone: (260)569-1189
All Year   1P: $74-$125   2P: $74-$125   XP: $7   F18
Location: Jct SR 15 and US 24; entrance off SR 15 through Wabash Village Shopping Plaza. 1311 N Cass St 46992. **Fax:** 260/569-0228. **Facility:** 60 one-bedroom standard units, some with efficiencies and/or whirlpools. 3 stories, interior corridors. *Bath:* combo or shower only. **Parking:** on-site. **Terms:** cancellation fee imposed. **Amenities:** extended cable TV, irons, hair dryers. **Pool(s):** heated indoor. **Leisure Activities:** whirlpool, exercise room. **Guest Services:** valet and coin laundry. **Business Services:** meeting rooms. **Cards:** AX, DC, DS, MC, VI. **Special Amenities: free local telephone calls and free newspaper.**

SOME UNITS

─── **WHERE TO DINE** ───

MARKET STREET GRILL

🆑

▼▼▼

American

Dinner: $9-$20 **Phone:** 260/563-7779
Location: SR 15, just e. 90 W Market St 46992. **Hours:** 5 pm-9:30 pm, Fri & Sat-10:30 pm. Closed: Mon & Tues. **Features:** casual dress; carryout; cocktails. Market Street Grill is located in the historic downtown area and has created for their guests a festive and friendly environment in which to dine. The food is well prepared and features steak, prime rib, seafood and barbecued items. The Wild Bills World Famous Indiana Red Chili is excellent and all would expect from the name. **Parking:** street. **Cards:** DS, MC, VI.

☒

WARREN pop. 1,200

─── **WHERE TO STAY** ───

RAMADA LIMITED WARREN

▼▼▼

Motel

Phone: (260)375-4800
All Year [ECP]   1P: $55-$89   2P: $61-$89   XP: $6   F18
Location: I-69, exit 78, just n. 7275 S CR 75 E 46792. **Fax:** 260/375-4114. **Facility:** 66 one-bedroom standard units, some with whirlpools. 3 stories, interior corridors. *Bath:* combo or shower only. **Parking:** on-site. **Terms:** pets (in smoking units). **Amenities:** voice mail, irons, hair dryers. **Pool(s):** heated indoor. **Leisure Activities:** whirlpool. **Guest Services:** coin laundry. **Business Services:** meeting rooms, fax (fee). **Cards:** AX, DC, DS, MC, VI.

SOME UNITS

SUPER 8 MOTEL

Phone: (260)375-4688

| | 4/1-9/30 | 1P: $40-$44 | 2P: $49-$54 | XP: $5 | F12 |
| Motel | 10/1-3/31 | 1P: $40 | 2P: $44 | XP: $5 | F12 |

Location: I-69, exit 78. 7281 S 75 E 46792. Fax: 260/375-4695. **Facility:** 47 one-bedroom standard units. 2 stories, interior corridors. **Parking:** on-site, winter plug-ins. **Terms:** 3 day cancellation notice. **Amenities:** extended cable TV. **Cards:** AX, DS, MC, VI.

SOME UNITS

WARRENTON

------ **WHERE TO DINE** ------

THE LOG INN Historical

Dinner: $9-$12

Phone: 812/867-3216

American

Location: I-64, exit 25B, just n, then 1 mi e. Old State Rd 47639. **Hours:** Open 4/1-12/31 & 1/21-3/31; 4 pm-9 pm, Fri & Sat-10 pm. Closed major holidays; also Sun & Mon. **Reservations:** accepted. **Features:** casual dress; children's menu; carryout; cocktails; a la carte. In the hospitality business continuously since 1825, the cozy inn has brick floors, rough-hewn log walls and a wooden-plank ceiling. The menu centers on country comfort foods: fried chicken, fried catfish, country ham, roast beef and the like. **Parking:** on-site.

WARSAW pop. 11,000

------ **WHERE TO STAY** ------

HAMPTON INN & SUITES

Phone: (574)269-6655

| | All Year [ECP] | 1P: $62-$114 | 2P: $67-$120 |

Motel

Location: 2.8 mi e of SR 15, on US 30. 3328 E Center St 46580. Fax: 574/268-9952. **Facility:** 71 units. 53 one-bedroom standard units. 18 one-bedroom suites, some with whirlpools. 3 stories, interior corridors. *Bath:* combo or shower only. **Parking:** on-site. **Amenities:** dual phone lines, voice mail, irons, hair dryers. **Pool(s):** small indoor. **Leisure Activities:** sauna, whirlpool, sun deck, exercise room. **Guest Services:** valet and coin laundry. **Business Services:** meeting rooms. **Cards:** AX, CB, DC, DS, MC, VI. **Special Amenities:** free continental breakfast and free local telephone calls.

SOME UNITS
FEE   FEE   FEE

RAMADA PLAZA HOTEL OF WARSAW

Phone: (574)269-2323

| | 6/1-10/31 | 1P: $95 | 2P: $101 | XP: $6 | F18 |
| Motor Inn | 4/1-5/31 & 11/1-3/31 | 1P: $91 | 2P: $97 | XP: $6 | F18 |

Location: 2.8 mi e of SR 15 on US 30, just s. 2519 E Center St 46580. Fax: 574/269-2432. **Facility:** 155 units. 154 one-bedroom standard units, some with whirlpools. 1 one-bedroom suite ($109-$199). 4 stories, interior corridors. **Parking:** on-site. **Terms:** cancellation fee imposed, package plans. **Amenities:** voice mail, safes, irons, hair dryers. **Dining:** dining room, 6:30 am-midnight, Fri & Sat 7 am-2 am, Sun 8 am-midnight, $8-$22, cocktails. **Pool(s):** heated outdoor, heated indoor. **Leisure Activities:** sauna, whirlpool, exercise room. *Fee:* game room, theatre. **Guest Services:** valet and coin laundry. **Business Services:** meeting rooms, business center, PC, fax. **Cards:** AX, CB, DC, DS, JC, MC, VI.

SOME UNITS
FEE   FEE   FEE   FEE

SUPER 8 MOTEL

Phone: 574/268-2888

| | All Year [CP] | 1P: $60-$88 | 2P: $60-$88 |

Motel

Location: 2.8 mi e of SR 15, on US 30. 3014 Frontage Rd 46580. Fax: 574/268-2888. **Facility:** 56 one-bedroom standard units, some with whirlpools. 2 stories, interior corridors. *Bath:* combo or shower only. **Parking:** on-site. **Amenities:** extended cable TV. **Pool(s):** small indoor. **Cards:** AX, CB, DC, DS, JC, MC, VI.

SOME UNITS

------ **WHERE TO DINE** ------

HACIENDA MEXICAN RESTAURANT

Lunch: $4-$7   **Dinner:** $4-$12   **Phone:** 574/269-4711

Mexican

Location: Off US 30. 3805 Lake City Hwy 46580. **Hours:** 11 am-11 pm, Fri & Sat-midnight. Closed: 11/28, 12/25. **Features:** casual dress; children's menu; carryout; cocktails & lounge. A nice selection of Mexican and American dishes are served here in an atmosphere of bustling activity. Several favorites are offered in combination so the diner can get a taste of several different dishes in one setting. Signature items are "Wet Burrito" and the "Arriba Margherita". **Parking:** on-site. **Cards:** AX, MC, VI.

WASHINGTON pop. 10,800

------ **WHERE TO STAY** ------

BAYMONT INN & SUITES

Phone: (812)254-7000

| | All Year [ECP] | 1P: $64-$94 | 2P: $64-$94 |

Motel

Location: Just ne of jct US 50 and SR 57. 7 Cumberland Dr 47501. Fax: 812/254-7099. **Facility:** 68 one-bedroom standard units, some with whirlpools. 2 stories, interior corridors. *Bath:* combo or shower only. **Parking:** on-site, winter plug-ins. **Terms:** pets ($50 deposit). **Amenities:** video games, voice mail, irons, hair dryers. **Pool(s):** heated indoor. **Leisure Activities:** whirlpool, fishing. **Guest Services:** coin laundry. **Business Services:** meeting rooms. **Cards:** AX, CB, DC, DS, MC, VI. **Special Amenities:** free continental breakfast and free newspaper.

SOME UNITS
FEE

HOLIDAY INN EXPRESS

Phone: (812)254-6666

	2/1-3/31 [ECP]	1P: $68-$120	2P: $75-$127	XP: $7	F18
Motel	4/1-10/31 [ECP]	1P: $66-$118	2P: $73-$125	XP: $7	F18
	11/1-1/31 [ECP]	1P: $62-$114	2P: $69-$121	XP: $7	F18

Location: On US 50 business route, 0.4 mi e of SR 257. 1808 E National Hwy 47501. Fax: 812/254-9730. **Facility:** 60 one-bedroom standard units, some with whirlpools. 3 stories, interior corridors. *Bath:* combo or shower only. **Parking:** on-site. **Terms:** 3 day cancellation notice. **Amenities:** extended cable TV, dual phone lines, voice mail, irons, hair dryers. **Pool(s):** small heated indoor. **Leisure Activities:** exercise room. **Guest Services:** valet and coin laundry. **Business Services:** meeting rooms. **Cards:** AX, CB, DC, DS, MC, VI.

SOME UNITS

WEST LAFAYETTE pop. 25,900—See also LAFAYETTE.

———— WHERE TO STAY ————

DAYS INN

Phone: (765)567-2131

| | All Year | 1P: $69 | 2P: $69 |

Motor Inn

Location: I-65, exit 178. 5600 SR 43 N 47906. Fax: 765/567-2511. **Facility:** 150 one-bedroom standard units. 4 stories, interior corridors. *Bath:* combo or shower only. **Parking:** on-site. **Amenities:** extended cable TV, irons, hair dryers. **Dining:** restaurant, 6 am-2 & 5-10 pm, Sat & Sun from 7 am, $8-$16, cocktails. **Pool(s):** heated indoor. **Leisure Activities:** saunas, exercise room, volleyball, ping pong. *Fee:* game room, pool table. **Guest Services:** complimentary laundry. **Business Services:** conference facilities. **Cards:** AX, CB, DC, DS, JC, MC, VI. **Special Amenities:** free local telephone calls and free newspaper.

SOME UNITS

SUPER 8 MOTEL-WEST LAFAYETTE

Phone: (765)567-7100

| | All Year | 1P: $53-$110 | 2P: $53-$110 | XP: $7 | F12 |

Motel

Location: I-65, exit 178, just n on SR 43. 2030 Northgate Dr 47906. Fax: 765/567-7100. **Facility:** 52 units. 51 one-bedroom standard units. 1 one-bedroom suite. 2 stories, interior corridors. *Bath:* combo or shower only. **Parking:** on-site. **Terms:** pets ($15 fee, in smoking units). **Amenities:** extended cable TV. **Cards:** AX, CB, DC, DS, MC, VI.

SOME UNITS

ZIONSVILLE —See Indianapolis p. 494.

Ohio

Major destinations are color-coded to index boxes, which display vicinity communities
you will find listed within that destination's section of the book. Cities outside major
destination vicinities are listed in alphabetical order throughout the book. Use the
Comprehensive City Index at the back of this book to find every city's listing locations.

AKRON pop. 223,000

──────── **WHERE TO STAY** ────────

BEST WESTERN EXECUTIVE INN   **Phone:** (330)794-1050

(AAA) [SAVE]   5/24-9/9   1P: $61-$64   2P: $73-$76   XP: $6   F16
              4/1-5/23 & 9/10-3/31   1P: $58-$61   2P: $70-$73   XP: $6   F16
▼▼▼   **Location:** I-76, exit 27 (SR 91). 2677 Gilchrist Rd 44305. **Fax:** 330/794-8495. **Facility:** 120 one-bedroom standard
Motor Inn   units, some with whirlpools. 3 stories, interior corridors. **Parking:** on-site. **Terms:** 7 day cancellation notice.
            Amenities: *Some:* hair dryers. **Dining:** dining room, 6 am-10 pm, $8-$14, cocktails. **Pool(s):** heated outdoor.
            Leisure Activities: exercise room. **Guest Services:** valet laundry. **Business Services:** meeting rooms.
Cards: AX, CB, DC, DS, JC, MC, VI. **Special Amenities:** free local telephone calls and free newspaper.

SOME UNITS

COMFORT INN   **Phone:** (330)645-1100

(AAA) [SAVE]   6/1-8/31 [CP]   1P: $59-$149   2P: $67-$149   XP: $8   F18
              4/1-5/31 & 9/1-10/31 [CP]   1P: $49-$99   2P: $55-$99   XP: $8   F18
▼▼▼▼   11/1-3/31 [CP]   1P: $45-$89   2P: $52-$89   XP: $8   F18
Motel   **Location:** I-77, exit 120, just n. 2873 S Arlington Rd 44312. **Fax:** 330/645-1101. **Facility:** 60 one-bedroom stan-
            dard units, some with whirlpools. 3 stories, interior corridors. *Bath:* combo or shower only. **Parking:** on-site.
            Amenities: extended cable TV, hair dryers. *Some:* irons. **Leisure Activities:** whirlpool, exercise room.
Cards: AX, DC, DS, MC, VI. **Special Amenities:** free continental breakfast and free local telephone calls.

SOME UNITS

CROWNE PLAZA QUAKER SQUARE

	6/1-8/31 [CP]	1P: $89-$109	2P: $99-$119	XP: $10	F18
	4/1-5/31 & 9/1-3/31 [CP]	1P: $89-$99	2P: $99-$109	XP: $10	F18

Phone: (330)253-5970

Classic Hotel

Location: I-76 and 77, exit Main-Broadway, n to Mill St. 135 S Broadway 44308. Fax: 330/253-7021. **Facility:** Historic. 190 one-bedroom standard units. 8 stories, interior corridors. **Parking:** on-site (fee). **Terms:** [AP] & [BP] meal plans available, package plans - weekends. **Amenities:** voice mail, irons, hair dryers. **Dining:** Trackside Grille, Mill Street Tavern, see separate listing. **Pool(s):** heated indoor. **Leisure Activities:** exercise room. **Guest Services:** gift shop, valet laundry. **Business Services:** conference facilities, business center, fax. **Cards:** AX, DC, DS, MC, VI. *(See color ad below)*

SOME UNITS

ASK SD ⊓|⊺ ☏ ⇌ ▣ DATA PORT ▣ 🖨 / ☒ VCR 🔋 /
                                    FEE   FEE

DAYS INN AKRON SOUTH/AIRPORT

SAVE

5/16-9/6	1P: $50-$60	2P: $60-$70	XP: $7	F
4/1-5/15 & 1/1-3/31	1P: $45-$50	2P: $50-$60	XP: $7	F
9/7-12/31	1P: $45-$50	2P: $50-$60	XP: $10	F

Phone: (330)644-1204

Motel

Location: I-77, exit 120, just s. 3237 S Arlington Rd 44312. Fax: 330/644-8426. **Facility:** 80 one-bedroom standard units, some with whirlpools. 1 story, exterior corridors. **Parking:** on-site. **Terms:** 14 day cancellation notice, pets ($5 fee). **Amenities:** *Some:* hair dryers. **Pool(s):** outdoor. **Cards:** AX, DC, DS, MC, VI.

SOME UNITS

SD 🐾 ⊓|⊺ ⇌ ▣ / ☒ 🔋 🖨 /

ECONO LODGE

SAVE

Motel

Phone: (330)644-1847

	1P:	2P:	XP:	
5/16-9/6	1P: $50-$60	2P: $60-$70	XP: $7	F17
4/1-5/15 & 9/7-3/31	1P: $40-$45	2P: $45-$50	XP: $7	F17

Location: I-77, exit 120, just s. 3237 1/2 S Arlington 44312. Fax: 330/644-8426. **Facility:** 39 one-bedroom standard units, some with efficiencies and/or whirlpools. 1 story, exterior corridors. **Parking:** on-site. **Terms:** 14 day cancellation notice, pets ($5 fee). **Amenities:** hair dryers. **Leisure Activities:** pool privileges. **Cards:** AX, DC, DS, MC, VI.

SOME UNITS

HOLIDAY INN EXPRESS AKRON SOUTH

SAVE

Motel

Phone: (330)644-7126

	1P:	2P:
5/31-6/8 [ECP]	1P: $99-$119	2P: $99-$119
6/9-9/1 [ECP]	1P: $89-$109	2P: $89-$109
4/1-5/30 & 9/2-3/31 [ECP]	1P: $79-$89	2P: $79-$89

Location: I-77, exit 120, just n. 2940 Chenoweth Rd 44312. Fax: 330/644-1776. **Facility:** 129 one-bedroom standard units, some with whirlpools. 2 stories, interior corridors. **Parking:** on-site. **Terms:** 3 day cancellation notice-fee imposed. **Amenities:** video games, voice mail, irons, hair dryers. **Pool(s):** heated outdoor. **Guest Services:** valet laundry. **Business Services:** conference facilities. **Cards:** AX, CB, DC, DS, JC, MC, VI.

SOME UNITS

FEE

THE O'NEIL HOUSE BED & BREAKFAST

Bed & Breakfast

Phone: 330/867-2650

	1P:	2P:
All Year	1P: $70-$85	2P: $100-$150

Location: I-77, exit Mull Ave, 1 mi n, then just w. 1290 W Exchange 44313. Fax: 330/867-2650. **Facility:** Built as a home for the founder of the General Tire Company in 1923, this Tudor mansion has spacious rooms. Smoke free premises. 4 one-bedroom standard units. 3 stories, interior corridors. *Bath:* combo or shower only. **Parking:** on-site. **Terms:** check-in 4 pm, age restrictions may apply, 4 day cancellation notice-fee imposed. **Business Services:** meeting rooms. **Cards:** DS, MC, VI.

SOME UNITS

/ VCR /

RADISSON HOTEL AKRON CITY CENTRE

SAVE

Motor Inn

Phone: (330)384-1500

	1P:	2P:
All Year	1P: $125	2P: $125

Location: Downtown; by Cascade Plaza. 20 W Mill St 44308. Fax: 330/253-8863. **Facility:** 287 one-bedroom standard units, some with efficiencies (no utensils) and/or whirlpools. 20 stories, interior corridors. *Bath:* combo or shower only. **Parking:** on-site. **Terms:** cancellation fee imposed, [ECP] meal plan available, package plans. **Amenities:** extended cable TV, dual phone lines, voice mail, irons, hair dryers. **Dining:** City Beat, see separate listing. **Pool(s):** heated indoor. **Leisure Activities:** exercise room. **Guest Services:** valet laundry. **Business Services:** conference facilities, business center. **Cards:** AX, CB, DC, DS, JC, MC, VI. **Special Amenities:** early check-in/late check-out and free newspaper.

SOME UNITS

FEE   FEE

RED ROOF INN-AKRON SOUTH

SAVE

Motel

Phone: (330)644-7748

	1P:	2P:	XP:	
5/24-9/1	1P: $49-$59	2P: $55-$65	XP: $6	F18
9/2-10/12	1P: $41-$53	2P: $46-$59	XP: $6	F18
4/1-5/23 & 10/13-3/31	1P: $35-$49	2P: $41-$55	XP: $6	F18

Location: I-77, exit 120, just n. 2939 S Arlington Rd 44312. **Facility:** 121 one-bedroom standard units. 3 stories. **Parking:** on-site. **Terms:** small pets only. **Amenities:** video games, voice mail. **Cards:** AX, CB, DC, DS, MC, VI. **Special Amenities:** free local telephone calls and free newspaper.

SOME UNITS

-------- WHERE TO DINE --------

ANTHE'S AT THE LAKES

American

Lunch: $6-$10   **Dinner:** $12-$25   **Phone:** 330/644-2239

Location: SR 93, 3 mi s of jct I-277 and US 224; n of SR 619. 4315 Manchester Rd 44319. **Hours:** 11 am-10 pm, Fri & Sat-11 pm, Sun-8 pm. Closed major holidays. **Reservations:** suggested. **Features:** early bird specials; carryout; cocktails & lounge; minimum charge-$5. The menu is varied, steak, seafood, pasta, chicken and the homemade dessert offerings similarly so. Favorites include "ho ho" cake and "death by chocolate." Anthe's lounge has a nice view of the gardens and complements the warm, casual atmosphere. **Parking:** on-site. **Cards:** AX, DC, MC, VI.

CITY BEAT

American

Lunch: $6-$9   **Dinner:** $8-$18   **Phone:** 330/384-1500

Location: Downtown; by Cascade Plaza; in Radisson Hotel Akron City Centre. 20 W Mill St 44308. **Hours:** 11 am-midnight. **Features:** casual dress; carryout; cocktails & lounge. Nestled in bustling Cascade Plaza is this lively sports bar-like eatery whose menu hits a home run every time. Tender New York strip steak, spicy buffalo wings and a slice of delectable walnut carrot cake make for a tasty and memorable meal. **Parking:** on-site (fee). **Cards:** AX, DC, DS, MC, VI.

GUS' CHALET RESTAURANT & LOUNGE

Continental

Lunch: $4-$8   **Dinner:** $7-$16   **Phone:** 330/633-2322

Location: SR 8, 1.5 mi e. 938 E Tallmadge Ave 44310. **Hours:** 11 am-11 pm. Closed major holidays; also Sun. **Reservations:** suggested. **Features:** casual dress; children's menu; early bird specials; carryout; cocktails & lounge. There's a nice variety, and some creativity, in menu selections, mostly steak, chops and seafood. Horseradish lends a distinct flavor to the sauerkraut balls. The dining room is airy and comfortable. The wait staff provides friendly, prompt service. **Parking:** on-site. **Cards:** AX, DC, DS, MC, VI.

KEN STEWART'S GRILL **Lunch:** $7-$15 **Dinner:** $16-$35 **Phone:** 330/867-2555

▼▼▼▼ **Location:** Corner of Pershing and W Market St, on SR 18. 1970 W Market St 44313. **Hours:** 11 am-10 pm, Fri & Sat-11 pm. Closed major holidays; also Sun. **Reservations:** suggested. **Features:** semi-formal attire; children's menu; early bird specials; carryout; cocktails & lounge; a la carte. The trendy restaurant, a popular spot for the "in" crowd, is sophisticated in its Southwestern decor, with Indian and cowboy caricatures. Creative preparations of seafood, steak, chicken, lamb, veal and pasta are a big reason why this place bustles. Smoke free premises. **Parking:** on-site. **Cards:** AX, DC, DS, MC, VI.

Continental

❌

MENCHES BROS **Lunch:** $5-$8 **Dinner:** $6-$12 **Phone:** 330/375-1717

▼ **Location:** Downtown; overlooks Canal Park. 300 R S Main St 44308. **Hours:** 11 am-3 pm; 11 am-10 pm on Aero's baseball game nights. Closed major holidays; also Sun. **Reservations:** suggested; baseball games. **Features:** casual dress; children's menu; carryout; cocktails. Original creators of the hamburger and ice cream cone, this restaurant still uses the original recipes and high quality ingredients today. Specialty sandwiches and homemade soups available daily. Smoke free premises. **Parking:** on-site. **Cards:** AX, DS, MC, VI.

American

❌

MILL STREET TAVERN Historical **Lunch:** $5-$8 **Dinner:** $12-$20 **Phone:** 330/762-9333

▼▼ **Location:** I-76 and 77, exit Main-Broadway, n to Mill St; in Crowne Plaza Quaker Square. 135 S Broadway St 44308. **Hours:** 11:30 am-2 & 5-10 pm, Fri & Sat-midnight. Closed major holidays; also Sun. **Reservations:** suggested. **Features:** casual dress; children's menu; carryout; cocktails & lounge. Much of the original 1800s decor is preserved in what was once the Quaker Oats building, but the fare is anything but old-fashioned. Prime rib, horseradish-crusted salmon, tavern chicken and seafood top the list of house specials. **Parking:** on-site. **Cards:** AX, DC, DS, MC, VI. *(See color ad p 530)*

American

❌

THE PIE FACTORY **Lunch:** $4-$7 **Dinner:** $4-$9 **Phone:** 330/252-0552

▼ **Location:** Just n on Mill St; at Quaker Square. 135 S Broadway St 44308. **Hours:** 11 am-11 pm. **Features:** casual dress; carryout. Not only can diners here indulge in delicious sweets, they can watch as they are created through a glassed-in bakery. Smoke free premises. **Parking:** on-site. **Cards:** AX, DC, DS, MC, VI.

American

❌

TANGIER RESTAURANT & CABARET **Lunch:** $9-$15 **Dinner:** $9-$22 **Phone:** 330/376-7171

▼▼▼ **Location:** 2.5 mi w on SR 18. 532 W Market St 44303. **Hours:** 11:30 am-3 & 5-9 pm, Fri-10 pm, Sat 5 pm-10 pm. Closed major holidays; also Sun. **Reservations:** suggested. **Features:** dressy casual; carryout; cocktails & lounge; entertainment. This locally family owned restaurant has the brilliant purple, red and gold color schemes and decor of the Mid-East. Their menu includes steak, seafood, pasta, dessert and bread from their in house bakery. They are well known for their Rack of Lamb Phoenicia and the Mid-East Sampler and authentic Mediterranean feast are two local favorites. Las Vegas style entertainment is available in their 300 seat Cabaret with close up views of stars from all seats. **Parking:** on-site. **Cards:** AX, DC, DS, MC, VI.

Ethnic

❌

TRACKSIDE GRILLE **Lunch:** $4-$8 **Dinner:** $7-$14 **Phone:** 330/253-5970

▼ **Location:** I-76 and 77, exit Main-Broadway, n to Mill St; in Crowne Plaza Quaker Square. 135 S Broadway St 44308. **Hours:** 11 am-10 pm. **Features:** casual dress; children's menu; carryout; cocktails & lounge. As the restaurant's name might suggest, trains are a focal point, and you'll find them throughout the family-friendly restaurant. Familiar favorites, steak, chicken and burgers anchor the menu. The atmosphere is particularly lively on weekends. **Parking:** on-site. **Cards:** AX, DC, DS, MC, VI. *(See color ad p 530)*

American

❌

The following restaurants have not been evaluated by AAA but are listed for your information only.

DIAMOND GRILL **Phone:** 330/253-0041

[fyi] Not evaluated. **Location:** Downtown; just w. 77 W Market St 44308. In an easily accessible location near downtown, the restaurant is popular for its steak and seafood.

EL RINCON **Phone:** 330/785-3724

[fyi] Not evaluated. **Location:** 1485 S Arlington Rd. Authentic Mexican cuisine.

HICKORY CREEK WOOD FIRED STEAKS **Phone:** 330/644-7649

[fyi] Not evaluated. **Location:** 2380 S Arlington 44312. Wood cooking is employed to flavor prime cuts of steak.

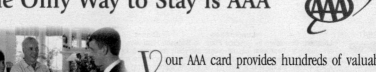

MARIACHI LOCO'S

(fyi) Not evaluated. **Location:** 3430 Arlington Rd 44312. A lively atmosphere hangs in the air of the restaurant, which offers a menu of creative local favorites.

Phone: 330/864-8186

ALLIANCE pop. 23,400

—— WHERE TO STAY ——

HOLIDAY INN EXPRESS HOTEL & SUITES

Phone: (330)821-6700

(AAA) (SAVE)

4/1-10/31	1P: $80-$109	2P: $80-$109
11/1-3/31	1P: $75-$99	2P: $75-$99

Motel

Location: 2 mi w on US 62. 2341 W State St 44601. Fax: 330/821-6700. **Facility:** 70 one-bedroom standard units, some with whirlpools. 3 stories, interior corridors. *Bath:* combo or shower only. **Parking:** on-site. **Terms:** small pets only ($10 fee). **Amenities:** extended cable TV, dual phone lines, voice mail, safes, irons, hair dryers. **Pool(s):** heated indoor. **Leisure Activities:** whirlpool, exercise room. **Guest Services:** coin laundry. **Business Services:** meeting rooms. **Cards:** AX, CB, DC, DS, JC, MC, VI. **Special Amenities:** free continental breakfast and free local telephone calls.

SOME UNITS

🅂🄳 🐕 🖥️ 🌊 📺 [DATA PORT] 💻 🖨️ / ✕ 🛄 📷 /
FEE

SUPER 8 MOTEL

Phone: (330)821-5688

(AAA) (SAVE)

6/1-8/31	1P: $48-$62	2P: $53-$67	XP: $5	F12
4/1-5/31	1P: $46-$51	2P: $51-$54	XP: $5	F12
9/1-3/31	1P: $44-$49	2P: $49-$53	XP: $5	F12

Motel

Location: 2 mi w on US 62. 2330 W State St 44601. Fax: 330/821-5688. **Facility:** 46 one-bedroom standard units. 1 story, exterior corridors. *Bath:* combo or shower only. **Parking:** on-site. **Terms:** pets ($5 extra charge). **Amenities:** extended cable TV. **Pool(s):** outdoor. **Business Services:** meeting rooms. **Cards:** AX, CB, DC, DS, JC, MC, VI. **Special Amenities:** free continental breakfast and free local telephone calls.

SOME UNITS

🅂🄳 🐕 🍴 🖥️ 🌊 📺 [DATA PORT] 🖨️ / ✕ /

AMHERST pop. 10,300

—— WHERE TO STAY ——

COUNTRY HEARTH INN

Phone: (440)985-1428

♦♦♦ ♦♦♦

Motel

All Year [CP]	1P: $55-$85	2P: $55-$85	F17

Location: SR 58, 0.3 mi n of SR 2. 934 N Leavitt Rd 44001. Fax: 440/985-1540. **Facility:** 88 one-bedroom standard units. 2 stories, interior/exterior corridors. **Parking:** on-site. **Amenities:** extended cable TV, safes (fee). **Pool(s):** outdoor. **Business Services:** meeting rooms. **Cards:** AX, CB, DC, DS, MC, VI.

SOME UNITS

(ASK) 🅂🄳 🍴 🌊 📺 [DATA PORT] 💻 🖨️ / ✕ 🛄 📷 /
FEE

ARCHBOLD pop. 3,400

—— WHERE TO STAY ——

SAUDER HERITAGE INN

Phone: 419/445-6408

(AAA) (SAVE)

♦♦♦ ♦♦♦

Motel

All Year [ECP]	1P: $98	2P: $98	XP: $10	F18

Location: Just e from jct SR 2 and 66. 22611 Rt 2 43502 (PO Box 235, Rt 2). Fax: 419/445-2609. **Facility:** Smoke free premises. 35 units. 34 one-bedroom standard units. 1 one-bedroom suite ($129-$149) with kitchen. 3 stories, interior corridors. **Parking:** on-site. **Terms:** package plans. **Amenities:** extended cable TV, video tape library (fee), voice mail. **Leisure Activities:** limited exercise equipment, shuffleboard. *Fee:* game room. **Guest Services:** coin laundry. **Business Services:** conference facilities, fax (fee). **Cards:** AX, MC, VI. **Special Amenities:** free continental breakfast and free local telephone calls. *(See color ad p 184)*

SOME UNITS

🍴 🐧M 🗂️ ✕ ✕ [DATA PORT] 🛄 💻 🖨️ / [VCR] /
FEE

—— WHERE TO DINE ——

BARN RESTAURANT

Lunch: $8-$12   **Dinner:** $9-$20   **Phone:** 419/445-2231

(AAA)

♦♦♦

American

Location: 1.8 mi ne. SR 2 43502. **Hours:** 11 am-8 pm, Sun-2 pm. Closed: 1/1, 11/28, 12/24, 12/25. **Features:** casual dress; Sunday brunch; children's menu; carryout; salad bar; buffet. The Barn's most popular dishes are broasted chicken and roast beef, both accompanied by homemade mashed potatoes. Hand-hewn beams, wagon wheel lights and a hay sling set the mood for an enjoyable meal in this restored barn. A buffet is offered on Sun. Smoke free premises. **Parking:** on-site. **Cards:** AX, MC, VI.
(See color ad p 184)

✕

ASHLAND pop. 20,100

—— WHERE TO STAY ——

AMERIHOST INN-ASHLAND

Phone: (419)281-8090

(AAA) (SAVE)

♦♦♦ ♦♦♦

Motel

All Year [ECP]	1P: $69	2P: $99

Location: I-71, exit 186, 0.5 mi w. 741 US 250 E 44805. Fax: 419/281-9809. **Facility:** 62 one-bedroom standard units, some with whirlpools. 2 stories, interior corridors. *Bath:* combo or shower only. **Parking:** on-site. **Terms:** 3 day cancellation notice. **Amenities:** extended cable TV, voice mail, safes (fee), irons, hair dryers. **Pool(s):** heated indoor. **Leisure Activities:** whirlpool, exercise room. **Guest Services:** valet laundry. **Business Services:** meeting rooms. **Cards:** AX, CB, DC, DS, JC, MC, VI. **Special Amenities:** free continental breakfast and free newspaper.

SOME UNITS

🅂🄳 🍴 🖥️ 🗂️ 🌊 📺 [DATA PORT] 💻 🖨️ / ✕ 🛄 📷 /

DAYS INN

AAA **SAVE**
Motel

Phone: (419)289-0101

6/1-10/31		1P: $50-$58	2P: $62-$70
4/1-5/31		1P: $45-$55	2P: $52-$62
11/1-3/31		1P: $39-$45	2P: $45-$50

Location: I-71, exit 186, just w. 1423 CR 1575 44805. Fax: 419/281-7515. **Facility:** 61 one-bedroom standard units, some with whirlpools. 2 stories, exterior corridors. **Parking:** on-site. **Terms:** cancellation fee imposed, pets ($25 fee). **Amenities:** extended cable TV, hair dryers. **Pool(s):** outdoor. **Cards:** AX, DC, DS, MC, VI.
Special Amenities: free continental breakfast and free local telephone calls.

SOME UNITS
🛏 🎙 🏊 📺 DATA PORT 💻 🖨 / ✕ 🗄 🖥 /

HOLIDAY INN EXPRESS HOTEL & SUITES-ASHLAND

Motel

Phone: (419)281-2900

All Year [ECP]   1P: $79-$139

Location: I-71, exit 186, 0.5 mi w. 1392 Montgomery Township Rd 743 44805 (1392 Enterprise Pkwy). Fax: 419/281-5754. **Facility:** 89 units. 83 one-bedroom standard units, some with whirlpools. 6 one-bedroom suites ($99-$159) with efficiencies (no utensils) and whirlpools. 4 stories, interior corridors. *Bath:* combo or shower only. **Parking:** on-site. **Terms:** pets ($35 deposit). **Amenities:** extended cable TV, dual phone lines, voice mail, irons, hair dryers. **Pool(s):** heated indoor. **Leisure Activities:** whirlpool, exercise room. **Guest Services:** coin laundry. **Business Services:** meeting rooms, business center. **Cards:** AX, CB, DC, DS, JC, MC, VI.

SOME UNITS
ASK SD 🛏 🏊 📺 DATA PORT 🖨 / ✕ 🗄 🖥 💻 /

--------- WHERE TO DINE ---------

The following restaurants have not been evaluated by AAA but are listed for your information only.

CASA FIESTA

[fyi]

Phone: 419/281-9319

Not evaluated. **Location:** 1202 E Main St 44805. Serving authentic Mexican cuisine since 1962, the restaurant features strolling mariachi singers on Friday and Saturday.

CODY'S FAMILY RESTAURANT

[fyi]

Phone: 419/281-7158

Not evaluated. **Location:** 810 E Main St 44805. Reasonably priced homemade soups and sandwiches are on the menu of the neighborhood favorite.

ASHTABULA pop. 21,600

--------- WHERE TO STAY ---------

CEDARS MOTEL

AAA **SAVE**
Motel

Phone: 440/992-5406

All Year	1P: $50-$60	2P: $70-$80	XP: $10 F9

Location: Jct SR 11, 3 mi w on US 20. 2015 W Prospect Rd 44004. **Facility:** 16 one-bedroom standard units. 1 story, exterior corridors. *Bath:* shower only. **Parking:** on-site. **Terms:** pets ($5 extra charge). **Amenities:** extended cable TV. **Guest Services:** coin laundry. **Cards:** AX, DS, MC, VI. **Special Amenities:** early check-in/late check-out and free local telephone calls.

SOME UNITS
🛏 📺 DATA PORT / ✕ /

HO HUM MOTEL

AAA **SAVE**
Motel

Phone: 440/969-1136

All Year	1P: $45-$60	2P: $55-$80	XP: $10 F12

Location: I-90, exit 223, 3 mi n on SR 45, 1 mi e on SR 20. 3801 N Ridge West 44004. **Facility:** 10 one-bedroom standard units. **Parking:** on-site. **Terms:** cancellation fee imposed, pets ($5 extra charge). **Amenities:** extended cable TV. **Cards:** AX, DS, MC, VI. **Special Amenities:** free local telephone calls and preferred room (subject to availability with advanced reservations).

SOME UNITS
SD 🛏 📺 / ✕ DATA PORT 🗄 🖥 /

--------- WHERE TO DINE ---------

CASA CAPELLI

Italian

Lunch: $5-$8	**Dinner:** $7-$14	Phone: 440/992-3700

Location: Downtown. 4641 Main Ave 44004. **Hours:** 11 am-9 pm, Sat 2 pm-10 pm, Sun 11 am-8 pm. Closed major holidays. **Reservations:** suggested. **Features:** casual dress; children's menu; carryout; cocktails & lounge. In the historic district, the interesting former bank boasts stained glass, an arched ceiling and a vault that now functions as a private dining room. Although the menu centers on Italian fare, it also includes seafood, steaks and Mexican choices. **Parking:** on-site. **Cards:** AX, DS, MC, VI.

✕

ATHENS pop. 21,300

--------- WHERE TO STAY ---------

AMERIHOST INN & SUITES-ATHENS

AAA **SAVE**
Motel

Phone: (740)594-3000

1/1-3/31 [CP]	1P: $95-$135	2P: $95-$135	XP: $6 F18
4/1-12/31 [CP]	1P: $90-$130	2P: $90-$130	XP: $6 F18

Location: At US 33 Bypass, exit State St. 20 Home St 45701. Fax: 740/594-5546. **Facility:** 100 one-bedroom standard units, some with whirlpools. 2 stories, interior corridors. *Bath:* combo or shower only. **Parking:** on-site. **Amenities:** extended cable TV, voice mail, safes (fee), irons, hair dryers. **Pool(s):** heated indoor. **Leisure Activities:** whirlpool, exercise room. **Guest Services:** valet laundry. **Business Services:** meeting rooms. **Cards:** AX, CB, DC, DS, JC, MC, VI. **Special Amenities:** free continental breakfast and free newspaper.

SOME UNITS

SD 🎙 📺 🏊 DATA PORT 💻 🖨 / ✕ 🗄 🖥 /
FEE

BUDGET HOST-COACH INN

AAA [SAVE]
▼ Motel

All Year   1P: $37-$50   2P: $41-$85

Phone: (740)594-2294
XP: $5   F12

Location: US 50 W, just past Richland Ave exit; US 50 E, e on Township Rd 60. 100 Albany Rd (Hwy 50 W) 45701. Fax: 740/594-2295. **Facility:** 29 one-bedroom standard units. 1-2 stories, exterior corridors. **Parking:** on-site. **Terms:** [CP] meal plan available. **Amenities:** extended cable TV. **Cards:** AX, DS, MC, VI. **Special Amenities: free local telephone calls.** *(See color ad p 529)*

SOME UNITS

DAYS INN-ATHENS

AAA [SAVE]
▼▼ ▼▼
Motel

All Year [CP]   1P: $62-$75   2P: $69-$85

Phone: (740)592-4000
XP: $6   F17

Location: Jct US 33, SR 550 and 13. 330 Columbus Rd 45701. Fax: 740/593-7687. **Facility:** 60 one-bedroom standard units. 2 stories, exterior corridors. **Parking:** on-site. **Terms:** 6 day cancellation notice, pets ($5 extra charge). **Amenities:** extended cable TV, safes (fee). **Guest Services:** valet laundry. **Cards:** AX, CB, DC, DS, MC, VI. **Special Amenities: free continental breakfast and free newspaper.**

SOME UNITS

FEE

THE OHIO UNIVERSITY INN & CONFERENCE CENTER

AAA [SAVE]
▼▼▼▼
Motor Inn

MC, VI.

All Year   1P: $99-$109   2P: $99-$109

Phone: (740)593-6661

Location: 1 mi s on US 33 and 50; adjacent to campus. 331 Richland Ave 45701. Fax: 740/592-5139. **Facility:** 139 one-bedroom standard units. 3 stories, interior corridors. *Bath:* combo or shower only. **Parking:** on-site. **Amenities:** extended cable TV, voice mail, irons, hair dryers. **Dining:** dining room, 6:30 am-2 & 5-10 pm, Sat & Sun from 7 am, $10-$17, cocktails. **Pool(s):** outdoor. **Leisure Activities:** exercise room. **Guest Services:** valet laundry. **Business Services:** conference facilities, business center, PC. **Cards:** AX, CB, DC, DS, JC,

SOME UNITS

FEE   FEE FEE

─────── **WHERE TO DINE** ───────

LUI-LUI RESTAURANT

▼▼ ▼▼
Thai

Lunch: $7-$9   **Dinner:** $8-$16   **Phone:** 740/594-8905

Location: 0.5 mi w on Union St. 8 Station St 45701. **Hours:** 11:30 am-9:30 pm, Fri-10 pm, Sat noon-10 pm, Sun noon-9:30 pm. Closed major holidays. **Features:** casual dress; carryout. The menu of the eclectic restaurant samples a broad range of cuisines, ranging from Thai and Chinese to Italian. Pizzas and calzone are baked in a brick oven. The spiciness of the dishes varies widely, from mild to knock-your-socks-off hot. Smoke free premises. **Parking:** on-site. **Cards:** AX, DS, MC, VI.

TOSCANO'S CUCINA ITALIA

▼▼ ▼▼
Italian

Lunch: $8-$12   **Dinner:** $12-$22   **Phone:** 740/594-3484

Location: 0.5 mi w on Union St. 4 Depot St 45701. **Hours:** 11:30 am-2 & 5-9 pm, Sun 11 am-7 pm. Closed major holidays; also Sun. **Reservations:** accepted. **Features:** casual dress; children's menu; carryout; cocktails. The comfortable special occasion restaurant is divided into five quiet dining rooms. Excellent selections of seafood and Italian cuisine, such as the well-presented manicotti, are made from scratch. The delicious cheesecakes come in many varieties. **Parking:** on-site. **Cards:** AX, MC, VI.

ZACHARAY'S SPECIALTY DELICATESSEN

▼▼
Deli/Subs/
Sandwiches

Lunch: $6-$10   **Dinner:** $6-$10   **Phone:** 740/592-2000

Location: Just n. 30 N Court St 45701. **Hours:** 11 am-8 pm, Fri & Sat-9 pm, Sun 11 am-7 pm. Closed major holidays. **Features:** casual dress; children's menu; carryout; cocktails; a la carte. Delicatessen sandwiches are made with high-quality ingredients, including cooked meats. Microbrewed beer, fresh salad and rich cheesecake are other menu favorites. Hardwood floors and brick walls add to the relaxed, welcoming atmosphere. Smoke free premises. **Parking:** street. **Cards:** DS, MC, VI.

───── *The following restaurant has not been evaluated by AAA* ─────
but is listed for your information only.

7 SAUCES

[fyi]

Phone: 614/592-5555

Not evaluated. **Location:** 66 N Court St 45701. The downtown restaurant serves popular renditions of American cuisine.

AURORA pop. 9,200   (See map p. 600; index p. 605)

───── **WHERE TO STAY** ─────

AURORA INN OF MARIO'S INTERNATIONAL

▼▼▼▼
Country Inn

6/14-9/2   1P: $159-$225   2P: $159-$225
4/1-6/13 & 9/3-3/31   1P: $125-$175   2P: $125-$175

Phone: (330)562-6121   [114]

Location: Jct SR 82 and 306. 30 Shawnee Tr 44202. Fax: 330/562-5249. **Facility:** Colonial-style decor gives the property a country-inn ambience. 69 one-bedroom standard units, some with whirlpools. 2 stories, interior corridors. **Parking:** on-site. **Terms:** check-in 4 pm, 3 day cancellation notice-fee imposed, package plans. **Amenities:** extended cable TV, voice mail, irons. *Some:* hair dryers. **Pool(s):** heated indoor, wading. **Leisure Activities:** saunas, whirlpool, 2 tennis courts. **Guest Services:** valet laundry. **Business Services:** meeting rooms. **Cards:** AX, CB, DC, DS, MC, VI.

SOME UNITS

(See map p. 600)

THE BERTRAM INN & CONFERENCE CENTER

Phone: (330)995-0200   **112**

(AAA) (SAVE)

◊◊◊

Motor Inn

6/16-8/31	1P: $159-$189	XP: $15	F18
9/1-3/31	1P: $90-$99	XP: $15	F18
4/1-6/15	1P: $99	XP: $15	F18

Location: 1.5 mi n of SR 82. 600 N Aurora Rd 44202. Fax: 330/562-9163. **Facility:** 156 units. 150 one-bedroom standard units. 6 one-bedroom suites ($140-$290). 3 stories, interior corridors. **Parking:** on-site. **Terms:** cancellation fee imposed. **Amenities:** video games, Web TV, high-speed Internet, dual phone lines, voice mail, honor bars, irons, hair dryers. **Dining:** restaurant, 6:30 am-11 pm, $10-$38, cocktails. **Pool(s):** heated outdoor. **Leisure Activities:** exercise room. **Guest Services:** gift shop, valet laundry. **Business Services:** conference facilities, business center, PC, fax. **Cards:** AX, DC, DS, MC, VI. *(See color ad below)*

SOME UNITS

🛎️ 🍴 🍸 🏊 📷 [DATA PORT] 📻 🖨️ / ✕ /
FEE

SIX FLAGS HOTEL OF OHIO

Phone: (330)562-9151   **113**

(AAA) (SAVE)

◊◊◊

Motor Inn

5/24-9/2 [BP]   1P: $185-$275

Location: SR 43, 2 mi n of SR 82. 800 N Aurora Rd 44202. Fax: 330/562-5701. **Facility:** 145 one-bedroom standard units. 2 stories, interior corridors. *Bath:* combo or shower only. **Parking:** on-site. **Terms:** open 5/24-9/2, cancellation fee imposed, package plans. **Amenities:** extended cable TV, voice mail. *Some:* irons, hair dryers. **Dining:** dining room, restaurant, 7 am-1 & 5-10 pm, $10-$16, cocktails. **Pool(s):** heated indoor, wading. **Leisure Activities:** exercise room, shuffleboard, volleyball, large seasonal family center. **Guest Services:** gift shop, valet and coin laundry, area transportation-major attractions. **Business Services:** conference facilities. **Cards:** AX, CB, DC, DS, MC, VI. **Special Amenities:** free room upgrade (subject to availability with advanced reservations).

SOME UNITS

🛎️ 🍴 🔧 🏊 ✕ 📷 [DATA PORT] 🖨️ / ✕ 📻 🖥️ 📻 /

WALDEN COUNTRY INN & STABLES

Phone: (330)562-5508   **115**

(AAA) (SAVE)

◊◊◊ ◊◊◊

Complex

All Year [BP]   2P: $220-$345   XP: $50

Location: 3 mi s on SR 43, 0.8 mi w on Mennonite Rd. 1119 Aurora Hudson Rd 44202. Fax: 330/562-8001. **Facility:** Skylights and walls of windows bring the outdoors in to this stylish modern inn set amid horse pastures in a private community. Smoke free premises. 25 units. 24 one-bedroom standard units, some with kitchens and/or whirlpools. 1 one-bedroom vacation rental. 2 stories, interior/exterior corridors. *Bath:* combo or shower only. **Parking:** on-site. **Terms:** 10 day cancellation notice-fee imposed. **Amenities:** extended cable TV, video tape library, dual phone lines, voice mail, irons, hair dryers. *Some:* honor bars. **Dining:** restaurant, 6 am-9 pm, $10-$20. **Leisure Activities:** country club privileges. *Fee:* golf-18 holes, horseback riding. **Guest Services:** massage (fee), valet laundry. **Business Services:** meeting rooms, fax. **Cards:** AX, DC, DS, MC, VI. **Special Amenities:** free continental breakfast and free newspaper.

SOME UNITS

🛎️ 🍴 🍸 ✕ ✕ [VCR] [DATA PORT] 🖥️ 🖨️ / 📻 🖥️ /

(See map p. 600)

------ **WHERE TO DINE** ------

AURORA'S AMISH STYLE RESTAURANT & BAKERY   **Lunch:** $5-$8   **Dinner:** $7-$12   **Phone:** 330/562-3554   (65)
Location: Located in Aurora Premium Outlets, 1 mi s of SR 82 on SR 43. 549 S Chillicothe Rd 44202. **Hours:** 10 am-9 pm, Sat 9 am-9 pm, Sun 9 am-7 pm. Closed: 11/28, 12/25. **Features:** casual dress; children's menu; carryout; beer & wine only. Smoke free premises. **Parking:** on-site. **Cards:** AX, DS, MC, VI.

American

AUSTINBURG pop. 500

------ **WHERE TO STAY** ------

ASHTABULA AUSTINBURG TRAVELODGE   **Phone:** (440)275-2011

4/1-9/30	1P: $68	2P: $88	XP: $10 F17
10/1-3/31	1P: $58	2P: $68	XP: $10 F17

Location: I-90, exit 223, just n. 2352 SR 45 N 44010. Fax: 440/275-1253. **Facility:** 47 one-bedroom standard units, some with whirlpools. 2 stories, interior/exterior corridors. *Bath:* combo or shower only. **Parking:** on-site. **Amenities:** extended cable TV. *Some:* hair dryers. **Pool(s):** outdoor. **Leisure Activities:** whirlpool. **Guest Services:** valet laundry. **Cards:** AX, CB, DC, DS, MC, VI. **Special Amenities:** free continental breakfast and free local telephone calls.

Motel

SOME UNITS

COMFORT INN-ASHTABULA   **Phone:** (440)275-2711

6/28-8/24 [ECP]	1P: $91-$135	2P: $91-$135	XP: $8 F18
4/1-6/27 & 8/25-3/31 [ECP]	1P: $78-$135	2P: $78-$135	XP: $8 F18

Location: I-90, exit 223, just n. 1860 Austinburg Rd 44010. Fax: 440/275-7314. **Facility:** 119 one-bedroom standard units, some with whirlpools. 2 stories, interior corridors. **Parking:** on-site. **Terms:** small pets only ($8 fee). **Amenities:** extended cable TV, voice mail, hair dryers. *Some:* irons. **Pool(s):** heated outdoor. **Leisure Activities:** exercise room. **Guest Services:** coin laundry. **Business Services:** meeting rooms. **Cards:** AX, CB, DC, DS, JC, MC, VI.

Motor Inn

SOME UNITS

FEE

HAMPTON INN   **Phone:** 440/275-2000

All Year [ECP]	1P: $88-$110	2P: $95-$129

Location: I-90, exit 223, just s on SR 45. 2900 GH Dr 44010. Fax: 440/275-1926. **Facility:** 71 one-bedroom standard units, some with whirlpools. 3 stories, interior corridors. *Bath:* combo or shower only. **Parking:** on-site. **Terms:** 3 day cancellation notice. **Amenities:** extended cable TV, voice mail, irons. **Pool(s):** heated indoor. **Leisure Activities:** exercise room. **Guest Services:** valet laundry. **Business Services:** meeting rooms. **Cards:** AX, DC, DS, MC, VI.

Motel

SOME UNITS

HOLIDAY INN EXPRESS HOTEL & SUITES   **Phone:** (440)275-2020

All Year	1P: $89	2P: $109	XP: $15 F16

Location: I-90, exit 223, just n. 1831 Austinburg Rd 44010. Fax: 440/275-3221. **Facility:** 77 one-bedroom standard units, some with whirlpools. 3 stories, interior corridors. *Bath:* combo or shower only. **Parking:** on-site. **Terms:** cancellation fee imposed. **Amenities:** voice mail, irons, hair dryers. **Pool(s):** heated indoor. **Leisure Activities:** sauna, whirlpool, exercise room. **Guest Services:** coin laundry. **Business Services:** meeting rooms, business center. **Cards:** AX, DC, DS, JC, MC, VI.

Motel

SOME UNITS

FEE

Look for our Partners in Savings!

When selecting a AAA Approved lodging, look for properties that participate in our advertising, **Official Appointment**, and **Show Your Card & Save®** programs. In addition to understanding the value of AAA business, they offer discounts off published TourBook® guide standard room rates or the lowest public standard room rate, at the time of booking, for the dates of stay.

Official Appointment properties are indicated with a red SAVE icon in the TourBook listings and SYC&S partners are indicated with a black SAVE icon. For a complete list of SYC&S participating hotel chains, please refer to page 22 of the TourBook Navigator section or call **866-AAA-SAVE** to make a reservation.

AUSTINTOWN pop. 22,700

——— WHERE TO STAY ———

BEST WESTERN MEANDER INN
AAA **SAVE**
▼▼▼ ▼▼▼
Motor Inn

Phone: (330)544-2378

4/1-11/1 [ECP]	1P: $65-$89	2P: $70-$90	XP: $5 F17
11/2-3/31 [ECP]	1P: $54-$65	2P: $60-$65	XP: $5 F17

Location: I-80, exit 223, 0.3 mi s on SR 46. 870 N Canfield-Niles Rd 44515. Fax: 330/544-7926. **Facility:** 57 one-bedroom standard units, some with whirlpools. 2 stories, interior corridors. *Bath:* combo or shower only. **Parking:** on-site. **Terms:** pets ($6 extra charge). **Amenities:** extended cable TV, irons, hair dryers. **Dining:** restaurant, 4 pm-10 pm, $8-$14. **Pool(s):** outdoor. **Guest Services:** coin laundry. **Business Services:** meeting rooms. **Cards:** AX, DC, DS, JC, MC, VI. **Special Amenities:** free continental breakfast and free newspaper.

SOME UNITS
[icons] FEE

ECONO LODGE
AAA **SAVE**
▼▼▼ ▼▼▼
Motel

Phone: (330)270-2865

All Year [CP]	1P: $45-$80	2P: $50-$80	XP: $6 F18

Location: I-80, exit 223, just s on SR 46. (5431 1/2 Seventy-Six Dr, YOUNGSTOWN, 44515). Fax: 330/270-5416. **Facility:** 45 one-bedroom standard units, some with whirlpools. 1 story, exterior corridors. **Parking:** on-site. **Amenities:** extended cable TV. *Some:* hair dryers. **Leisure Activities:** pool privileges. **Guest Services:** complimentary laundry. **Cards:** AX, DS, MC, VI. **Special Amenities:** free continental breakfast and free local telephone calls.

SOME UNITS
[icons]

HAMPTON INN YOUNGSTOWN WEST
AAA **SAVE**
▼▼▼ ◆
Motel

Phone: 330/544-0660

4/1-10/31	1P: $79	2P: $89
11/1-3/31	1P: $72	2P: $84

Location: I-80, exit 223, 0.3 mi s on SR 46. 880 N Canfield-Niles Rd 44515. Fax: 330/652-7800. **Facility:** 83 one-bedroom standard units. 3 stories, interior corridors. *Bath:* combo or shower only. **Parking:** on-site. **Amenities:** extended cable TV, voice mail, irons, hair dryers. **Pool(s):** heated indoor. **Leisure Activities:** exercise room. **Guest Services:** valet laundry. **Business Services:** meeting rooms. **Cards:** AX, CB, DC, DS, JC, MC, VI. *(See color ad p 777)*

SOME UNITS
[icons]

HOWARD JOHNSON EXPRESS INN
▼▼▼
Motel

Phone: (330)792-9740

5/1-9/5 [ECP]	1P: $79	2P: $79
4/1-4/30 [ECP]	1P: $59-$69	2P: $59-$69
9/6-3/31 [ECP]	1P: $69	2P: $69

Location: I-80, exit 223B, just n. 5425 Clarkins Dr 44515. Fax: 330/793-7199. **Facility:** 119 one-bedroom standard units. 2 stories. *Bath:* combo or shower only. **Parking:** on-site. **Terms:** 3 day cancellation notice. **Amenities:** extended cable TV, voice mail. *Some:* dual phone lines, irons, hair dryers. **Pool(s):** outdoor. **Leisure Activities:** exercise room. **Guest Services:** coin laundry. **Business Services:** meeting rooms, business center. **Cards:** AX, CB, DC, DS, MC, VI.

SOME UNITS
[icons]

MOTEL 6 - 4066
AAA **SAVE**
▼▼▼ ▼▼▼
Motel

Phone: (330)793-9305

5/25-10/23	1P: $50-$55	2P: $50-$70	XP: $5 F18
4/1-5/24 & 10/24-3/31	1P: $45-$50	2P: $50-$55	XP: $5 F18

Location: I-80, exit 223, just s on SR 46. 5431 Seventy Six Dr 44515. Fax: 330/793-2584. **Facility:** 79 one-bedroom standard units. 1 story, exterior corridors. **Parking:** on-site. **Amenities:** extended cable TV. **Pool(s):** outdoor. **Guest Services:** coin laundry. **Cards:** AX, DS, MC, VI.

SOME UNITS
[icons]

SLEEP INN
AAA **SAVE**
▼▼▼ ▼▼▼
Motel

Phone: (330)544-5555

6/1-9/30	1P: $70-$80	2P: $70-$80
4/1-5/31	1P: $60-$65	2P: $60-$65
10/1-3/31	1P: $56-$60	2P: $56-$60

Location: I-80, exit 223, just s on SR 46. 5555 Interstate Blvd 44515. Fax: 330/544-7454. **Facility:** 57 one-bedroom standard units, some with whirlpools. 3 stories, interior corridors. *Bath:* shower or tub only. **Parking:** on-site. **Terms:** [ECP] meal plan available. **Amenities:** extended cable TV. *Some:* irons, hair dryers. **Pool(s):** heated indoor. **Leisure Activities:** whirlpool. **Cards:** AX, CB, DC, DS, JC, MC, VI. **Special Amenities:** free continental breakfast and free local telephone calls.

SOME UNITS
[icons]

——— WHERE TO DINE ———

THE SANDWICH FACTORY
◆
American

Lunch: $4-$7   **Dinner:** $5-$9   **Phone:** 330/793-4084

Location: I-80, exit 223, 1 mi s on SR 46. 15 N Canfield-Niles Rd 44515. **Hours:** 10 am-10 pm, Thurs-Sat to 11 pm, Sun from 11 am. Closed major holidays. **Features:** casual dress; carryout. This local landmark has been known for their made-to-order sandwiches for years. The large size along with fresh ingredients and quick service are their trademark. **Parking:** on-site.

——— ***The following restaurant has not been evaluated by AAA***
but is listed for your information only. ———

THE ORIGINAL ROADHOUSE
[fyi]

Phone: 330/544-3990

Not evaluated. **Location:** I-80, exit 223. 920 N Canfield-Niles Rd 44515. Easy access off the interstate and reasonable prices make the steakhouse a good place for family and friends to meet.

BATAVIA —See Cincinnati p. 572.

BEACHWOOD —*See Cleveland p. 617.*

BEAVER CREEK

——— WHERE TO STAY ———

——— *The following lodging was either not evaluated or did not*
meet AAA rating requirements but is listed for your information only. ———

COURTYARD BY MARRIOTT DAYTON/BEAVER CREEK			Phone: 937/429-5203	
[fyi]	7/1-10/31	1P: $94-$139	2P: $99-$144	XP: $5	F16
	4/1-6/30 & 11/1-3/31	1P: $89-$129	2P: $94-$134	XP: $5	F16
Motel	Too new to rate, opening scheduled for March 2002. **Location:** I-675, exit 17. 2777 Fairfield Commons 45432. Fax: 937/429-5203. **Amenities:** radios, coffeemakers, pool. **Cards:** AX, DC, DS, MC, VI.				

BEDFORD —*See Cleveland p. 619.*

BELLBROOK pop. 6,500   (See map p. 672; index p. 675)

——— WHERE TO DINE ———

GARSTKA'S CAFE   **Lunch:** $6-$8   **Dinner:** $12-$22   **Phone:** 937/848-2226   [62]
▼▼ ▼▼   **Location:** I-675, exit 8, 1.3 mi s on Dayton Wilmington Pike, then 2 mi e on SR 725. 129 W Franklin St 45305.
Hours: 11 am-9 pm, Fri & Sat-10 pm. Closed major holidays. **Features:** casual dress; children's menu;
Polish   carryout; cocktails & lounge. Garstka means "handful" in Polish, and diners should be prepared to stuff
themselves with generous portions of home-style food. The diverse menu includes Greek specialties,
cabbage rolls, tempura vegetables, chicken pot pie and peach cobbler. **Parking:** on-site. **Cards:** AX, DS, MC, VI.   ⊠

BELLEFONTAINE pop. 12,100

——— WHERE TO STAY ———

BEST HOTEL   **Phone:** (937)593-8515
▼▼ ▼▼   All Year [ECP]   1P: $69-$119   2P: $69-$119   XP: $5   F14
Location: Jct US 33 and SR 68. 1134 N Main St 43311. Fax: 937/593-4802. **Facility:** 103 one-bedroom standard
Motor Inn   units. 2 stories, interior/exterior corridors. **Parking:** on-site. **Terms:** 15 day cancellation notice, pets ($10
extra charge). **Amenities:** extended cable TV, irons, hair dryers. **Pool(s):** heated indoor. **Leisure Activi-**
ties: exercise room. **Guest Services:** coin laundry. **Business Services:** meeting rooms. **Cards:** AX, CB, DC, DS, JC, MC, VI.

SOME UNITS
(ASK) (S/D) 🛏 📺 ➤ 🐾 (DATA PORT) 🖥 🖨 / ⊠ 🚻 📷 /

SUPER 8 MOTEL   **Phone:** 937/599-5300
(AAA) (SAVE)   All Year   1P: $60-$80   2P: $65-$85   XP: $8   F11
▼▼ ▼▼   **Location:** Jct US 33 and SR 68. 1117 N Main St 43311. Fax: 937/599-4433. **Facility:** 40 one-bedroom standard
units, some with whirlpools. 2 stories, interior corridors. **Parking:** on-site. **Amenities:** extended cable TV,
Motel   irons, hair dryers. **Leisure Activities:** whirlpool, exercise room. **Guest Services:** valet laundry. **Business**
Services: meeting rooms. **Cards:** AX, DC, DS, MC, VI.

SOME UNITS
(S/D) 📺 🐾 🐾 (DATA PORT) 🖨 / ⊠ (VCR) 🚻 📷 /

——— WHERE TO DINE ———

HOUSE OF SZECHWAN RESTAURANT   **Lunch:** $6-$8   **Dinner:** $8-$16   **Phone:** 937/592-0767
▼▼ ▼▼   **Location:** Downtown; at jct Main St and Columbus Ave, just w. 137 W Columbus Ave 43311. **Hours:** 11 am-9:30
pm, Fri-10 pm, Sat 11:30 am-10 pm, Sun 11:30 am-9 pm. Closed: 7/4, 11/28, 12/25. **Features:** casual
Chinese   dress; carryout; cocktails & lounge; buffet. Cuisine from all major regions of China make up an extensive
menu that highlights such specialties as orange beef and General Tso's chicken. The fried banana and
apple is a light, sweet treat. Oriental appointments decorate the intimate dining room. Dinner buffet on Friday and Saturday
nights, as well as Sunday from 11:30 am-3:00 pm. **Parking:** street. **Cards:** AX, DS, MC, VI.   ⊠

RED LANTERN RESTAURANT   **Lunch:** $5-$6   **Dinner:** $5-$9   **Phone:** 937/592-7826
(AAA)   **Location:** Jct US 33, 0.3 mi s on US 68. 125 Dowell Ave 43311. **Hours:** 5:30 am-9 pm, Fri & Sat-10 pm, Sun 7
am-3 pm. Closed major holidays. **Reservations:** suggested; weekends. **Features:** casual dress; children's
American   menu; carryout; cocktails; a la carte. Fried chicken is always fresh at the family-oriented restaurant that
also delivers nacho platters, hot wings, pepper steak and prime rib. For dessert, nibble on a homemade
pie or a sweet roll. Stop by on the weekend for the breakfast buffet. **Parking:** on-site. **Cards:** DS, MC, VI.   ⊠

BELLEVUE pop. 8,100

——— WHERE TO STAY ———

BEST WESTERN BELLEVUE INN				Phone: (419)483-5740	
(AAA) (SAVE)	6/1-9/4 [CP]	1P: $60-$199	2P: $60-$199		
	5/1-5/31 [CP]	1P: $60-$120	2P: $60-$120		
▼▼ ▼▼	9/5-3/31 [CP]	1P: $38-$60	2P: $60-$120		
	4/1-4/30 [CP]	1P: $38-$60	2P: $42-$49	XP: $4	F18
Motel	**Location:** 1 mi e on US 20. 1120 E Main St 44811. Fax: 419/483-5566. **Facility:** 71 one- and 12 two-bedroom standard units, some with kitchens and/or whirlpools. 2 stories, interior/exterior corridors. **Parking:**				

on-site. **Terms:** cancellation fee imposed. **Amenities:** *Some:* irons, hair dryers. **Pool(s):** outdoor, heated indoor. **Leisure Activi-**
ties: whirlpool. **Guest Services:** complimentary laundry. **Business Services:** meeting rooms. **Cards:** AX, CB, DC, DS, MC, VI.
Special Amenities: free local telephone calls. *(See color ad p 738)*

SOME UNITS
(S/D) 📺 🍽 🛢 ➤ 🐾 (DATA PORT) / ⊠ 🚻 📷 /

BELLVILLE pop. 1,600

------ **WHERE TO STAY** ------

COMFORT INN SOUTH　　　　　　　　　　　　　　　　　　　　　　Phone: (419)886-4000

AAA SAVE　All Year　　　　　　1P: $65-$99　　　2P: $69-$110　　　XP: $6　　　　　F18
♦♦♦　**Location:** I-71, exit 165, 0.3 mi e on SR 97. 855 Comfort Plaza Dr 44813. **Fax:** 419/886-3813. **Facility:** 100 one-
Motel　bedroom standard units, some with efficiencies (no utensils) and/or whirlpools. 2 stories, interior corridors. **Parking:** on-site. **Terms:** package plans. **Amenities:** extended cable TV. *Some:* irons, hair dryers. **Pool(s):** heated indoor. **Leisure Activities:** whirlpool, exercise room. *Fee:* bicycles. **Guest Services:** gift shop, valet and coin laundry. **Business Services:** meeting rooms. **Cards:** AX, CB, DC, DS, JC, MC, VI.
Special Amenities: free continental breakfast and free local telephone calls. *(See color ad p 706)*

SOME UNITS

RAMADA LIMITED　　　　　　　　　　　　　　　　　　　　　　Phone: (419)886-7000

AAA SAVE　All Year　　　　　　1P: $69-$89　　　2P: $74-$99　　　XP: $5　　　　　F18
♦♦♦　**Location:** I-71, exit 165, 0.3 mi e on SR 97. 1000 Comfort Plaza 44813. **Fax:** 419/886-9943. **Facility:** 66 one-
Motel　bedroom standard units, some with whirlpools. 3 stories, interior corridors. *Bath:* combo or shower only. **Parking:** on-site. **Amenities:** extended cable TV, voice mail, hair dryers. **Pool(s):** heated indoor. **Leisure Activities:** whirlpool, exercise room. *Fee:* bicycles. **Guest Services:** valet and coin laundry. **Business Services:** meeting rooms. **Cards:** AX, CB, DC, DS, JC, MC, VI. **Special Amenities: free continental breakfast and free local telephone calls.** *(See color ad p 706)*

SOME UNITS

------ **WHERE TO DINE** ------

DER DUTCHMAN　　　**Lunch:** $5-$8　　　**Dinner:** $7-$14　　　**Phone:** 419/886-7070
♦♦　**Location:** I-71, exit 165, 0.5 mi e. 720 SR 97 W 44813. **Hours:** 7 am-8 pm, Fri & Sat-9 pm. Closed major
American　holidays; also Sun. **Features:** casual dress; children's menu; carryout; salad bar. Roasted chicken and roast beef baked in natural juices are among the Amish-style specialties of this charming, family-oriented restaurant. A trip through the pastry shop reveals a tempting array of fresh-baked pies. Service is friendly and attentive. Smoke free premises. **Parking:** on-site. **Cards:** DS, MC, VI.

------ **The following restaurant has not been evaluated by AAA** ------
but is listed for your information only.

DOC'S RESTAURANT & LOUNGE　　　　　　　　　　　　　　Phone: 419/886-4505
fyi　Not evaluated. **Location:** 844 SR 97 44813. Large portions of home cooking, including daily specials, are served daily at the family-friendly eatery.

Look for a SAVE Place to Stay!

When selecting a AAA Approved lodging, look for properties that participate in our SAVE programs. These properties understand the value of AAA business and many offer discounts to AAA members.

• A red SAVE icon in their TourBook® guide listing indicates an **Official Appointment** property that offers a minimum 10% discount off published TourBook standard room rates or the lowest public standard room rate, at the time of booking, for the dates of stay.

• A black SAVE icon indicates a chain hotel that participates in the **Show Your Card & Save®** program. These properties offer a satisfaction guarantee and AAA's best rates for your dates of stay. Please refer to page 22 in the TourBook Navigator section for complete details and a list of participating hotel chains or call AAA/CAA's exclusive toll-free reservation number **866-AAA-SAVE** to make a reservation.

BEREA —See Cleveland p. 619.

BERLIN pop. 100

———— WHERE TO STAY ————

BERLIN VILLAGE INN
Phone: 330/893-2861
Motel

All Year [CP]   1P: $40-$85   2P: $40-$85   XP: $10   F16
Location: 0.5 mi w. 5135 SR 39 44610. Fax: 330/893-2530. **Facility:** 22 one-bedroom standard units. 2 stories, exterior corridors. **Parking:** on-site. **Amenities:** extended cable TV. **Cards:** AX, DS, MC, VI.

SOME UNITS
/ ⊠ /

BEXLEY —See Columbus p. 657.

BLUE ASH —See Cincinnati p. 573.

BLUFFTON pop. 3,400

———— WHERE TO STAY ————

COMFORT INN
Phone: (419)358-6000
Motel

All Year   1P: $50-$100   2P: $50-$100
Location: I-75, exit 142, just w on SR 103. 117 Commerce Ln 45817. Fax: 419/358-6015. **Facility:** 63 one-bedroom standard units, some with whirlpools. 3 stories, interior corridors. *Bath:* combo or shower only. **Parking:** on-site. **Terms:** pets ($15 extra charge). **Amenities:** extended cable TV, voice mail, safes (fee), irons, hair dryers. **Pool(s):** heated indoor. **Leisure Activities:** whirlpool. **Guest Services:** coin laundry. **Business Services:** meeting rooms, fax (fee). **Cards:** AX, DC, DS, JC, MC, VI. **Special Amenities: free continental breakfast and free newspaper.** *(See color ad below)*

SOME UNITS
🅂🄳 🐾 ♿ 🏷 🛶 🎬 DATA PORT 💻 🖨 / ⊠ 📶 📷 /

BOARDMAN pop. 38,500

———— WHERE TO STAY ————

DAYS INN
Phone: (330)758-2371
Motel

	1P	2P	XP	
5/26-9/5 [CP]	1P: $49-$85	2P: $49-$85	XP: $5	F12
4/1-5/25 [CP]	1P: $40-$65	2P: $40-$65	XP: $5	F12
9/6-11/30 [CP]	1P: $40-$55	2P: $40-$55	XP: $5	F12
12/1-3/31 [CP]	1P: $36-$50	2P: $36-$50	XP: $5	F12

Location: I-76 (Ohio Tpke), exit 232, 1.8 mi n on SR 7. 8392 Market St 44512. Fax: 330/758-2371. **Facility:** 50 one-bedroom standard units, some with whirlpools. 1 story, exterior corridors. **Parking:** on-site. **Terms:** 7 day cancellation notice, pets ($5 extra charge). **Amenities:** extended cable TV, hair dryers. **Pool(s):** outdoor. **Cards:** AX, CB, DC, DS, JC, MC, VI. **Special Amenities: free continental breakfast and free local telephone calls.**

SOME UNITS
🅂🄳 🐾 🛶 🎬 🖨 / ⊠ VCR 📶 /
FEE FEE

HOLIDAY INN-BOARDMAN
Phone: (330)726-1611
Motor Inn

	1P	2P
6/1-3/31	1P: $109-$125	2P: $109-$125
4/1-5/31	1P: $99-$115	2P: $99-$115

Location: Jct I-680 and US 224, 0.3 mi w. 7410 South Ave 44512. Fax: 330/726-0717. **Facility:** 133 units. 126 one-bedroom standard units. 7 one-bedroom suites ($175-$225), some with whirlpools. 6 stories, interior corridors. **Parking:** on-site. **Amenities:** extended cable TV, voice mail, irons, hair dryers. *Some:* dual phone lines. **Pool(s):** heated indoor. **Leisure Activities:** whirlpool, exercise room. **Guest Services:** coin laundry. **Business Services:** meeting rooms. **Cards:** AX, CB, DC, DS, JC, MC, VI. *(See color ad p 777)*

SOME UNITS
ASK 🅂🄳 🍴 🎧 🛶 🎬 DATA PORT 💻 🖨 / ⊠ VCR 📶 📷 /
FEE

MICROTEL INN YOUNGSTOWN   Phone: (330)758-1816

◇ (diamond)

1/1-3/31	1P: $40-$50	2P: $50-$60	XP: $10 F18
4/1-12/31	1P: $30	2P: $40	XP: $10 F18

Motel   **Location:** Jct I-680 and US 224, 0.3 mi w. 7393 South Ave 44512. Fax: 330/758-8117. **Facility:** 92 one-bedroom standard units. 2 stories, interior corridors. *Bath:* combo or shower only. **Parking:** on-site. **Terms:** 7 day cancellation notice, [CP] meal plan available, pets ($25 fee). **Amenities:** extended cable TV, video games, safes (fee). **Business Services:** meeting rooms. **Cards:** AX, CB, DC, DS, MC, VI.

SOME UNITS
🛏 🎮 ♿ 🐾 📺 [DATA PORT] 🖨 / ⊠ /

RAMADA LIMITED INN & SUITES   Phone: (330)549-0157

🔺🔺🔺 [SAVE]
◇◇ ◇◇

6/1-8/31	1P: $60	2P: $70	
4/1-5/31 & 9/1-10/31	1P: $50	2P: $60	
11/1-3/31	1P: $40	2P: $50	

Motel   **Location:** I-76 (Ohio Tpke), exit 232, 0.5 mi n on SR 7. 9988 Market St 44452 (PO Box 264, NORTH LIMA). Fax: 330/549-9995. **Facility:** 82 one-bedroom standard units, some with efficiencies (no utensils). 3 stories, interior corridors. *Bath:* combo or shower only. **Parking:** on-site. **Terms:** [ECP] meal plan available, pets ($12 fee). **Amenities:** extended cable TV, voice mail. **Cards:** AX, DC, DS, MC, VI. **Special Amenities:** free continental breakfast and free local telephone calls.

SOME UNITS
[S/D] 🛏 📺 [DATA PORT] 🖨 / ⊠ 🍴 📦 💻 /

━━━━━━ **WHERE TO DINE** ━━━━━━

ALADDIN'S EATERY   **Lunch:** $4-$6   **Dinner:** $4-$8   Phone: 330/629-6450

🔺🔺◇

Ethnic   **Location:** Jct I-680 and US 224, 0.3 mi w on US 224; across from Holiday Inn. 7325 S Ave Extension 44512. **Hours:** 11 am-10:30 pm, Fri & Sat-11:30 pm, Sun-10 pm. **Features:** casual dress; carryout; beer & wine only. Traditional, natural foods of the Middle East, many of which appeal to the health conscious crowd, are the restaurant's big draw. Stop in for homemade soup, juice or specialty coffee, or enjoy the entertaining belly dancer who performs at certain times during the summer. Smoke free premises. **Parking:** on-site. **Cards:** MC, VI.   ⊠

━━━━━ ***The following restaurant has not been evaluated by AAA*** ━━━━━
but is listed for your information only.

ARMADILLO'S   Phone: 330/758-5250

[fyi]   Not evaluated. **Location:** 3031 Mahoning Ave 44514. The menu centers on tried-and-true barbecue favorites.

BOLIVAR pop. 900

━━━━━━ **WHERE TO STAY** ━━━━━━

SLEEP INN   Phone: (330)874-3435

[SAVE]

◇◇◇ ◇

5/2-9/1 [CP]	1P: $75-$85	2P: $80-$90	XP: $5 F18
4/1-5/1 [CP]	1P: $65-$70	2P: $70-$75	XP: $5 F18
9/2-10/1 [CP]	1P: $55-$60	2P: $60-$65	XP: $5 F18
10/2-3/31 [CP]	1P: $50-$55	2P: $55-$60	XP: $5 F18

Motel   **Location:** I-77, exit 93, 0.5 mi e. 11155 SR 212 NE 44612. Fax: 330/874-2412. **Facility:** 59 one-bedroom standard units. 3 stories, interior corridors. *Bath:* shower only. **Parking:** on-site. **Amenities:** extended cable TV, safes (fee), hair dryers. *Some:* irons. **Pool(s):** heated indoor. **Leisure Activities:** whirlpool. **Guest Services:** coin laundry. **Business Services:** meeting rooms. **Cards:** AX, DC, DS, MC, VI.

SOME UNITS
[S/D] 🍴 ♿ 🐾 📺 [DATA PORT] 🖨 / ⊠ 🍴 📦 💻 /

━━━━━━ **WHERE TO DINE** ━━━━━━

DER DUTCHMAN OF BOLIVAR   **Lunch:** $5-$8   **Dinner:** $8-$14   Phone: 330/874-1041

🔺🔺🔺
◇◇ ◇

American   **Location:** I-77, exit 93, 0.6 mi e. 10911 SR 212 NE 44612. **Hours:** 7 am-8 pm. Closed major holidays; also Sun. **Features:** casual dress; children's menu; carryout; salad bar. Broasted chicken and roast beef baked in natural juices are among the Amish-style specialties of the charming, family-oriented restaurant. A tempting array of fresh-baked pies lets you give in to your sweet tooth. Service is friendly and attentive. Smoke free premises. **Parking:** on-site. **Cards:** DS, MC, VI.   ⊠ 🍴

BOSTON HEIGHTS pop. 700   (See map p. 600; index p. 606)

━━━━━━ **WHERE TO STAY** ━━━━━━

COMFORT INN   Phone: (330)650-2040   [143]

🔺🔺🔺 [SAVE]
◇◇◇ ◇

5/24-9/1	1P: $99-$159	2P: $109-$179	XP: $10 F17
11/1-3/31	1P: $79-$99	2P: $79-$129	XP: $7 F17
9/2-10/31	1P: $79-$109	2P: $79-$119	XP: $7 F17
4/1-5/23	1P: $79-$109	2P: $79-$119	XP: $7 F17

Motel   **Location:** I-80/90 (Ohio Tpke), exit 180, 0.3 mi n on SR 8. (6731 Industrial Pkwy, 44236). Fax: 330/650-6925. **Facility:** 58 one-bedroom standard units, some with whirlpools. 2 stories, interior corridors. *Bath:* combo or shower only. **Parking:** on-site. **Terms:** 7 day cancellation notice, package plans. **Amenities:** voice mail, irons, hair dryers. *Some:* dual phone lines. **Pool(s):** heated indoor. **Leisure Activities:** whirlpool, exercise room. **Guest Services:** valet laundry. **Business Services:** meeting rooms. **Cards:** AX, CB, DC, DS, JC, MC, VI. **Special Amenities:** free continental breakfast and free local telephone calls.

SOME UNITS
[S/D] ♿ 🐾 🐾 📺 [DATA PORT] 🖨 / ⊠ [VCR] 🍴 📦 💻 /
FEE

(See map p. 600)

HOLIDAY INN

Motor Inn

6/1-8/31	1P: $129-$159	2P: $129-$159
4/1-5/31 & 9/1-3/31	1P: $99-$109	2P: $99-$109

Phone: (330)653-9191 [142]

Location: I-80/90 (Ohio Tpke), exit 180, 0.3 mi n on SR 8. (240 Hines Hill Rd, HUDSON, 44236). Fax: 330/656-0048. **Facility:** 288 units. 286 one-bedroom standard units. 2 one-bedroom suites ($179). 2 stories, interior corridors. *Bath:* combo or shower only. **Parking:** on-site. **Terms:** check-in 4 pm, package plans. **Amenities:** video games, high-speed Internet, voice mail, irons, hair dryers. **Pool(s):** heated outdoor, heated indoor. **Leisure Activities:** sauna, whirlpool, 2 tennis courts, exercise room. **Guest Services:** gift shop, coin laundry. **Business Services:** conference facilities. **Cards:** AX, CB, DC, DS, JC, MC, VI. *(See color ad p 613)*

SOME UNITS

BOTKINS pop. 1,300

———— **WHERE TO STAY** ————

BUDGET HOST WESTERN OHIO INN

Motor Inn

All Year	1P: $32-$38	2P: $37-$43	XP: $5 F13

Phone: (937)693-6911

Location: I-75, exit 104 (SR 219), just w. 505 E State St 45306 (PO Box 478). Fax: 937/693-8200. **Facility:** 50 one-bedroom standard units. 2 stories, exterior corridors. **Terms:** 14 day cancellation notice-fee imposed. **Amenities:** extended cable TV. **Dining:** restaurant, 5 pm-10 pm, $5-$10. **Pool(s):** outdoor. **Leisure Activities:** tennis court, basketball. **Guest Services:** coin laundry. **Business Services:** meeting rooms. **Cards:** AX, DS, MC, VI. **Special Amenities:** early check-in/late check-out and free continental breakfast. *(See color ad p 529)*

SOME UNITS

BOWLING GREEN pop. 28,200

———— **WHERE TO STAY** ————

BEST WESTERN FALCON PLAZA

Motel

6/1-3/31 [ECP]	1P: $72-$102	2P: $77-$102	XP: $5 F12
4/1-5/31 [ECP]	1P: $69-$99	2P: $74-$99	XP: $5 F12

Phone: (419)352-4671

Location: I-75, exit 181, just w. 1450 E Wooster St 43402. Fax: 419/352-5351. **Facility:** 87 one-bedroom standard units, some with whirlpools. 2 stories, exterior corridors. **Parking:** on-site, winter plug-ins. **Terms:** 3 day cancellation notice. **Amenities:** extended cable TV, irons, hair dryers. *Some:* dual phone lines. **Leisure Activities:** whirlpool, exercise room. **Guest Services:** valet laundry. **Business Services:** meeting rooms, business center, PC. **Cards:** AX, CB, DC, DS, MC, VI. **Special Amenities:** free continental breakfast and free local telephone calls. *(See color ad below)*

SOME UNITS
FEE

DAYS INN

Motel

All Year [ECP]	1P: $51-$129	2P: $56-$129	XP: $6 F17

Phone: (419)352-5211

Location: I-75, exit 181, just w. 1550 E Wooster St 43402. Fax: 419/354-8030. **Facility:** 100 one-bedroom standard units, some with whirlpools. 2 stories, exterior corridors. **Parking:** on-site. **Terms:** 7 day cancellation notice, pets ($10 fee). **Amenities:** safes (fee), hair dryers. **Guest Services:** coin laundry. **Business Services:** meeting rooms. **Cards:** AX, CB, DC, DS, JC, MC, VI. **Special Amenities:** free continental breakfast and free newspaper.

SOME UNITS
FEE   FEE FEE

QUALITY INN & SUITES

Motor Inn

8/16-3/31	1P: $85-$169
5/11-8/15	1P: $75-$169
4/1-5/10	1P: $65-$149

Phone: (419)352-2521

Location: I-75, exit 181, just w. 1630 E Wooster St 43402. Fax: 419/353-5975. **Facility:** 101 one-bedroom standard units, some with whirlpools. 2 stories, interior corridors. **Parking:** on-site, winter plug-ins. **Amenities:** irons, hair dryers. **Pool(s):** heated indoor. **Leisure Activities:** whirlpool. **Business Services:** meeting rooms. **Cards:** AX, DC, DS, MC, VI.

SOME UNITS

——— WHERE TO DINE ———

FRICKER'S

American

Lunch: $6-$8   **Dinner:** $7-$13   **Phone:** 419/354-2000

Location: I-75, exit 181, just w. 1720 E Wooster St 43402. **Hours:** 11 am-2:30 am. Closed: 12/25 5 pm-1:30 am. **Features:** casual dress; carryout; cocktails & lounge; a la carte. Televisions broadcasting sporting events are spread out throughout the boisterous restaurant, which is decorated with sports memorabilia. The food, such as chicken wings, sandwiches and ribs, is familiar and filling. Service is casual and attentive. **Parking:** on-site. **Cards:** AX, DS, MC, VI.

——— *The following restaurants have not been evaluated by AAA* ——— *but are listed for your information only.*

EASYSTREET CAFE

[fyi]

Phone: 419/353-0988

Not evaluated. **Location:** 104 S Main 43402. The casual restaurant offers reasonably priced, wholesome fare and friendly, efficient service.

JUNCTION BAR & GRILLE

[fyi]

Phone: 419/382-9222

Not evaluated. **Location:** 110 N Main 43402. This is a favorite gathering place for locals and features daily specials and reasonable prices.

KAUFMAN'S AT THE LODGE

[fyi]

Phone: 419/354-2535

Not evaluated. **Location:** 168 E Wooster St 43402. Friendly servers at the downtown establishment deliver selections from a varied menu.

SAM B'S RESTAURANT

[fyi]

Phone: 419/353-2277

Not evaluated. **Location:** 146 N Main 43402. The relaxed restaurant's diverse menu offerings are prepared in heaping portions.

BRECKSVILLE —See Cleveland p. 619.

BRIDGEPORT

——— WHERE TO DINE ———

——— *The following restaurant has not been evaluated by AAA* ——— *but is listed for your information only.*

STEVE'S GRILL & TAVERN

[fyi]

Phone: 740/633-3700

Not evaluated. **Location:** 223 N Lincoln Ave 43912. Steak, pasta and hamburgers are among offerings at this restaurant.

BROADVIEW HEIGHTS —See Cleveland p. 619.

BROOK PARK —See Cleveland p. 620.

BROOKVILLE pop. 4,600   (See map p. 672; index p. 674)

——— WHERE TO STAY ———

BROOKVILLE DAYS INN

[AAA] [SAVE]

Motel

All Year   1P: $50-$70   2P: $50-$70   **Phone:** (937)833-4003   **51**
                                          XP: $5

Location: I-70, exit 21. 100 Parkview Dr 45309. Fax: 937/833-4681. **Facility:** 62 one-bedroom standard units. 2 stories, exterior corridors. **Parking:** on-site. **Terms:** 30 day cancellation notice, pets ($10 extra charge). **Amenities:** extended cable TV. **Pool(s):** outdoor. **Cards:** AX, DC, DS, MC, VI. **Special Amenities:** free continental breakfast and free newspaper.

SOME UNITS

——— WHERE TO DINE ———

ROB'S FAMILY DINING

American

Lunch: $7-$11   **Dinner:** $7-$11   **Phone:** 937/833-3310   **28**

Location: I-70, exit 21, just s. 705 Arlington Rd 45309. **Hours:** 7 am-9 pm, Sun-8 pm. Closed: 12/25. **Features:** casual dress; children's menu; carryout; buffet. The simple, home-style menu and extensive dinner buffet are geared toward the family crowd. Booths and pedestal tables are spaced throughout the comfortable, well-maintained dining room. The uniformed wait staff provides friendly, upbeat service. **Parking:** on-site. **Cards:** AX, DS, MC, VI.

BRUNSWICK pop. 28,200

——— WHERE TO STAY ———

HOWARD JOHNSON EXPRESS

Motel

All Year   1P: $55-$65   2P: $65-$75   **Phone:** (330)225-9161
                                          XP: $10   F17

Location: I-71, exit 226, just w. 1385 S Carpenter Rd 44212 (PO Box 148). Fax: 330/273-1638. **Facility:** 25 one-bedroom standard units. 2 stories, interior corridors. **Parking:** on-site. **Cards:** AX, CB, DC, DS, JC, MC, VI.

SOME UNITS

SLEEP INN

[SAVE]

◆◆ ◆◆

Motel

| 4/1-10/31 | 1P: $65-$75 | 2P: $75-$80 | XP: $10 | F12 |
| 11/1-3/31 | 1P: $60-$65 | 2P: $65-$75 | XP: $10 | F12 |

Phone: (330)273-1112

Location: I-71, exit 226, just w. 1435 S Carpenter Rd 44212. Fax: 330/225-0639. **Facility:** 65 one-bedroom standard units, some with whirlpools. 2 stories, exterior corridors. *Bath:* shower or tub only. **Parking:** on-site. **Terms:** 7 day cancellation notice, pets ($10-$20 extra charge). **Amenities:** extended cable TV, irons, hair dryers. **Pool(s):** heated outdoor. **Business Services:** meeting rooms. **Cards:** AX, DC, DS, JC, MC, VI.

SOME UNITS

⬛ 🛏 ➿ 🕿 [DATA PORT] ▭ 🖨 / ✕ 🔲 🖼 /
FEE

──────── WHERE TO DINE ────────

JOHNNY'S BAR & GRILLE

◆◆ ◆◆

American

Lunch: $5-$8   **Dinner:** $8-$16   Phone: 330/225-6900

Location: Jct SR 303 and 42, 1.5 mi s on SR 42. 1813 Pearl Rd 44212. **Hours:** 11 am-10 pm. Closed major holidays. **Features:** casual dress; carryout; cocktails. Outdoor deck and patio for summer dining, family owned and operated, many homemade recipes. **Parking:** on-site. **Cards:** AX, DS, MC, VI.   ✕

MAPLESIDE FARMS

◆◆ ◆◆

American

Lunch: $7-$9   **Dinner:** $10-$16   Phone: 330/225-5576

Location: 2 mi n of SR 303. 294 Pearl Rd 44212. **Hours:** 11 am-8:30 pm, Fri & Sat-9:30 pm, Sun 10 am-7 pm. Closed: Mon. **Reservations:** suggested. **Features:** casual dress; Sunday brunch; children's menu; carryout; cocktails. Overlooking the apple orchards in the valley, the rustic, beamed restaurant serves such diverse offerings as apple butter barbecue ribs, stuffed chicken breast salad and sandwiches. Families are welcomed. Smoke free premises. **Parking:** on-site. **Cards:** AX, DC, DS, MC, VI.   ✕

BRYAN pop. 8,300

──────── WHERE TO STAY ────────

COLONIAL MANOR MOTEL

◆◆◆◆

Motel

| All Year | 1P: $50-$80 | 2P: $54-$84 | XP: $4 | F12 |

Phone: 419/636-3123

Location: US 127, 0.8 mi e on SR 2/34. 924 E High St 43506. Fax: 419/636-3991. **Facility:** 52 one-bedroom standard units. 1 story, exterior corridors. *Bath:* combo or shower only. **Parking:** on-site. **Amenities:** extended cable TV. **Guest Services:** valet and coin laundry. **Cards:** AX, DS, MC, VI.

SOME UNITS

🍽 🍸 🖖 [DATA PORT] 🖨 / ✕ 🔲 🖼 /

PLAZA MOTEL

[AAA] [SAVE]

◆◆◆

Motel

| All Year | 1P: $38-$85 | 2P: $47-$95 | XP: $10 | F7 |

Phone: 419/636-3159

Location: 1.3 mi s on US 127 and SR 15. 1604 S Main St 43506. Fax: 419/636-7574. **Facility:** 23 one-bedroom standard units. 1 story, exterior corridors. *Bath:* combo or shower only. **Parking:** on-site. **Terms:** 7 day cancellation notice. **Amenities:** extended cable TV, voice mail. *Some:* high-speed Internet. **Guest Services:** valet and coin laundry. **Business Services:** PC. **Cards:** AX, CB, DC, DS, MC, VI. **Special Amenities:** early check-in/late check-out.

SOME UNITS

⬛ 🎥 [DATA PORT] ▭ / ✕ 🔲 🖼 /

BUCYRUS pop. 13,500

──────── WHERE TO STAY ────────

HIDEAWAY BED & BREAKFAST

◆◆◆◆

Bed & Breakfast

| All Year [BP] | 1P: $127-$257 | 2P: $127-$257 | XP: $20 | F5 |

Phone: 419/562-3013

Location: 4.5 mi s on SR 4. 1601 SR 4 44820. Fax: 419/562-3003. **Facility:** Designated smoking area. 11 one-bedroom standard units, some with whirlpools. 2 stories, interior corridors. **Parking:** on-site. **Terms:** check-in 4 pm, 14 day cancellation notice, package plans. **Amenities:** extended cable TV, video tape library, CD players, high-speed Internet, dual phone lines, voice mail, irons, hair dryers. **Pool(s):** heated outdoor. **Leisure Activities:** exercise room. **Guest Services:** valet laundry. **Business Services:** meeting rooms. **Cards:** DS, MC, VI.

SOME UNITS

⬛ ➿ ✕ 🖖 [DATA PORT] ▭ 🖨 / 📺 [VCR] 🔲 🖼 /
FEE

BURTON pop. 1,300

──────── WHERE TO STAY ────────

RED MAPLE INN

[AAA] [SAVE]

◆◆◆◆

Bed & Breakfast

| 4/1-10/31 | 1P: $109-$179 | 2P: $109-$179 | XP: $10 | F12 |
| 11/1-3/31 | 1P: $99-$179 | 2P: $99-$179 | XP: $10 | F12 |

Phone: 440/834-8334

Location: Just e of Park Cir, on SR 168 and 700. 14707 S Cheshire St 44021. Fax: 440/834-8356. **Facility:** The inn, which is in Amish country surrounded by hills, is accented with cherry woodwork and features a fireplace and a library. Smoke free premises. 18 units. 17 one-bedroom standard units. 1 one-bedroom suite ($175-$225). 2 stories, interior corridors. **Parking:** on-site. **Terms:** 7 day cancellation notice, [BP] meal plan available, package plans. **Amenities:** extended cable TV, dual phone lines, irons, hair dryers. **Leisure Activities:** small outdoor putting green, exercise room. **Business Services:** meeting rooms. **Cards:** AX, DC, DS, JC, MC, VI. **Special Amenities:** free continental breakfast and free newspaper.

SOME UNITS

✕ 🖖 [DATA PORT] ▭ 🖨 / 🔲 🖼 /

CALDWELL pop. 1,800

—————— WHERE TO STAY ——————

BEST WESTERN CALDWELL INN
Phone: (740)732-7599

(AAA) [SAVE]
All Year [CP] 1P: $40-$65 2P: $45-$70 XP: $5 F17

Motel
Location: I-77, exit 25, just e. 44128 Fairground Rd 43724. **Fax:** 740/732-7599. **Facility:** 53 one-bedroom standard units, some with whirlpools. 2 stories, interior corridors. *Bath:* combo or shower only. **Parking:** on-site. **Amenities:** extended cable TV, irons, hair dryers. **Pool(s):** heated indoor. **Leisure Activities:** sauna, whirlpool, exercise room. **Business Services:** meeting rooms. **Cards:** AX, DC, DS, JC, MC, VI. **Special Amenities:** free continental breakfast and free local telephone calls.

—————— WHERE TO DINE ——————

LORI'S FAMILY RESTAURANT
Lunch: $6-$9   **Dinner:** $6-$9   **Phone:** 740/732-4711

American
Location: I-77, exit 25, just e. 17020 SR 78 43724. **Hours:** 6 am-9 pm, Sun from 7 am. **Closed:** 11/28, 12/25. **Features:** casual dress; children's menu; carryout; salad bar; a la carte. The roadside diner is a popular spot for home-style cooking, such as sliced roast beef and mashed potatoes. Well-maintained with simple furnishings, the dining area is bright, comfortable and friendly to families. Service is prompt and attentive. **Parking:** on-site.

CAMBRIDGE pop. 11,700

—————— WHERE TO STAY ——————

AMERIHOST INN CAMBRIDGE
Phone: (740)439-1505

(AAA) [SAVE]
5/1-10/31 [ECP] 1P: $81-$145 2P: $81-$145 XP: $6 F17
4/1-4/30 & 11/1-3/31 [ECP] 1P: $79-$145 2P: $79-$145 XP: $6 F17

Motel
Location: I-70, exit 178, just s on SR 209. 61595 Southgate Pkwy 43725. **Fax:** 740/439-0143. **Facility:** 72 one-bedroom standard units, some with whirlpools. 2 stories, interior corridors. *Bath:* combo or shower only. **Parking:** on-site. **Amenities:** extended cable TV, voice mail, safes (fee), irons, hair dryers. **Pool(s):** heated indoor. **Leisure Activities:** whirlpool, exercise room. **Guest Services:** valet laundry. **Business Services:** meeting rooms. **Cards:** AX, CB, DC, DS, JC, MC, VI. **Special Amenities:** free continental breakfast and free newspaper.

BEST WESTERN CAMBRIDGE
Phone: (740)439-3581

6/1-9/30 1P: $49-$79 2P: $49-$79 XP: $5 F18
4/1-5/31 & 10/1-3/31 1P: $39-$59 2P: $39-$59 XP: $5 F18

Motel
Location: I-70, exit 178, 0.3 mi n on SR 209. 1945 Southgate Pkwy 43725. **Fax:** 740/439-1824. **Facility:** 95 one-bedroom standard units. 2 stories, exterior corridors. *Bath:* combo or shower only. **Parking:** on-site. **Terms:** 3 day cancellation notice, small pets only. **Amenities:** extended cable TV, safes. **Pool(s):** outdoor. **Leisure Activities:** playground. **Guest Services:** valet laundry. **Cards:** AX, CB, DC, DS, MC, VI. *(See ad below)*

BUDGET HOST DEER CREEK MOTEL
Phone: 740/432-6391

5/1-11/30 1P: $35-$55 2P: $39-$59 XP: $5 F12
4/1-4/30 1P: $32-$45 2P: $35-$55 XP: $5 F12
12/1-3/31 1P: $32-$35 2P: $35-$42 XP: $5 F12

Motel
Location: I-70, exit 178, just n on SR 209. 2321 Southgate Pkwy 43725. **Fax:** 740/439-3425. **Facility:** 90 one-bedroom standard units. 1 story, exterior corridors. **Parking:** on-site. **Terms:** [CP] meal plan available, pets ($5 extra charge). **Amenities:** extended cable TV. **Pool(s):** heated indoor. **Business Services:** meeting rooms. **Cards:** AX, DC, DS, MC, VI. *(See color ad p 529)*

BUDGET INN
△△△ [SAVE]
▽▽▽
Motel

All Year   1P: $30-$40   2P: $30-$50   XP: $5   F12   **Phone:** (740)432-2304
Location: I-70, exit 176, e on US 40. 6405 Glenn Hwy 43725. **Facility:** 19 one-bedroom standard units. 2 stories, interior/exterior corridors. *Bath:* combo or shower only. **Parking:** on-site, winter plug-ins. **Terms:** small pets only. **Amenities:** extended cable TV. **Cards:** AX, DS, MC, VI. **Special Amenities:** free local telephone calls and free newspaper.

SOME UNITS

COLONEL TAYLOR INN BED & BREAKFAST
▽▽▽ ▽▽▽
Historic Bed
& Breakfast
MC, VI.

All Year   2P: $105-$125   **Phone:** 740/432-7802
Location: I-70, exit 178, w on SR 209 to downtown at Courthouse; 2 blks w on SR 40, n on N 6th St, 8 blks e on Sherman, just s on N 7th, then w. 633 Upland Rd 43725. Fax: 740/435-3152. **Facility:** Smoke free premises. 4 units. 3 one- and 1 two-bedroom standard units, some with whirlpools. 3 stories, interior corridors. *Bath:* combo or shower only. **Parking:** on-site. **Terms:** 14 day cancellation notice-fee imposed. **Cards:** AX, DS,

---

COMFORT INN
△△△ [SAVE]
▽▽▽▽▽
Motel

4/1-10/31   1P: $79-$109   2P: $84-$114   XP: $5   F18
11/1-3/31   1P: $69-$99   2P: $74-$104   XP: $5   F18
Phone: (740)435-3200
Location: I-70, exit 178, just n on SR 209. 2327 Southgate Pkwy 43725. Fax: 740/435-3200. **Facility:** 71 one-bedroom standard units, some with whirlpools. 3 stories, interior corridors. *Bath:* combo or shower only. **Parking:** on-site. **Terms:** pets ($10 fee, in smoking units). **Amenities:** extended cable TV, dual phone lines, safes, hair dryers. **Pool(s):** heated indoor. **Leisure Activities:** whirlpool. **Guest Services:** coin laundry. **Business Services:** meeting rooms. **Cards:** AX, DC, DS, MC, VI. **Special Amenities:** free continental breakfast and free local telephone calls.

SOME UNITS

DAYS INN-CAMBRIDGE
[SAVE]
▽▽▽
Motel

6/1-10/31   1P: $69-$89   2P: $71-$99   XP: $6   F12
4/1-5/31 & 11/1-3/31   1P: $62-$79   2P: $69-$89   XP: $6   F12
Phone: (740)432-5691
Location: I-70, exit 178, just n on SR 209. 2328 Southgate Pkwy 43725. Fax: 740/432-3526. **Facility:** 103 one-bedroom standard units. 2 stories, interior corridors. **Parking:** on-site. **Amenities:** extended cable TV, safes, hair dryers. *Some:* irons. **Pool(s):** outdoor. **Guest Services:** valet laundry. **Business Services:** meeting rooms. **Cards:** AX, CB, DC, DS, MC, VI. *(See ad p 546)*

SOME UNITS

HOLIDAY INN CAMBRIDGE/SALT FORK AREA
▽▽▽
Motor Inn

5/16-9/15 [BP]   1P: $59-$65   2P: $65-$79
4/1-5/15 & 9/16-3/31 [BP]   1P: $49-$55   2P: $55-$69
Phone: (740)432-7313
Location: I-70, exit 178, just n on SR 209. 2248 Southgate Pkwy 43725 (PO Box 1270). Fax: 740/432-2337. **Facility:** 109 one-bedroom standard units. 2 stories, interior corridors. **Parking:** on-site. **Terms:** package plans, small pets only. **Amenities:** extended cable TV, voice mail, irons, hair dryers. **Pool(s):** wading. **Guest Services:** valet and coin laundry. **Business Services:** meeting rooms, PC, fax. **Cards:** AX, CB, DC, DS, JC, MC, VI.

SOME UNITS

MISTY MEADOW FARM BED & BREAKFAST
▽▽▽
Bed & Breakfast

All Year [BP]   2P: $130   **Phone:** 740/439-5135
Location: I-77, exit 46 southbound; exit 46A northbound, just e on SR 40, 1 mi n. 64878 Slaughter Hill Rd 43725 (PO Box 1633). Fax: 740/439-5408. **Facility:** Guests share this 150-acre farm with three pet goats and a horse; the grounds include meadows, orchards and a spring-fed pond with bass and panfish. Smoke free premises. 4 one-bedroom standard units, some with whirlpools. 1 story, interior corridors. *Bath:* combo or shower only. **Parking:** on-site. **Terms:** 2 night minimum stay - in cottage, age restrictions may apply, 14 day cancellation notice, no pets allowed (pets on premises). **Amenities:** extended cable TV, hair dryers. *Some:* irons. **Pool(s):** outdoor. **Leisure Activities:** sauna, whirlpool, paddleboats, fishing, hiking trails. **Business Services:** meeting rooms. **Cards:** DS, MC, VI.

SOME UNITS

──────── **WHERE TO DINE** ────────

THE FORUM
▽▽ ▽▽
American

Lunch: $4-$10   Dinner: $5-$17   **Phone:** 740/439-2777
Location: I-70, exit 178, just n on SR 209. 2205 Southgate Pkwy 43725. **Hours:** 11 am-10 pm, Fri & Sat-11 pm. Closed major holidays. **Reservations:** accepted; weekdays. **Features:** casual dress; children's menu; carryout; cocktails & lounge. Varied American fare, seafood, steak, chops, chicken and pizza. Also some Mexican, Italian and Greek dishes. A small selection of California wines available to complement the varied menu. **Parking:** on-site. **Cards:** AX, DS, MC, VI.

THEO'S CONEY ISLAND RESTAURANT
▽▽
American

Lunch: $5-$6   Dinner: $5-$10   **Phone:** 740/432-3878
Location: Downtown; between N 6th and S 7th sts. 632 Wheeling Ave 43725. **Hours:** 9 am-9 pm. Closed major holidays; also Sun. **Features:** casual dress; children's menu; carryout; cocktails. The laid-back, diner-style restaurant—family owned since 1931, delivers chicken, chops, Coney Island hot dogs, steaks and sandwiches, with a few Greek and Italian dishes thrown in for good measure. The homemade pie are particularly tasty. **Parking:** on-site. **Cards:** DS, MC, VI.

──────── *The following restaurants have not been evaluated by AAA* ────────
but are listed for your information only.

HOUSE OF HUNAN
[fyi]

Phone: 740/439-5252
Not evaluated. **Location:** 2301 E Wheeling Ave 43725. The small Chinese restaurant offers a varied lunch and dinner buffet.

LAREDO MEXICAN RESTAURANT   Phone: 740/439-0606
(fyi)   Not evaluated. **Location:** I-70, exit 178, 1 mi n on SR 209. 1228 Southgate Pkwy 43725. Mexican specialties include steak and chicken dishes.

CANAL WINCHESTER —See Columbus p. 657.

CANTON pop. 84,200—See also NORTH CANTON.

——— WHERE TO STAY ———

BEST SUITES OF AMERICA   Phone: (330)499-1011
(AAA) (SAVE)   All Year   1P: $63-$117   2P: $73-$127   XP: $10   F18
▽▽▽   **Location:** I-77, exit 109, 1 mi w. 4914 Everhard Rd 44718. Fax: 330/499-3175. **Facility:** 102 one-bedroom standard units with efficiencies, some with whirlpools. 3 stories, interior corridors. **Parking:** on-site. **Terms:** 14 day cancellation notice, small pets only. **Amenities:** extended cable TV, irons, hair dryers. **Pool(s):** heated indoor. **Leisure Activities:** whirlpools, exercise room. **Guest Services:** complimentary evening beverages, coin laundry. **Business Services:** meeting rooms. **Cards:** AX, CB, DC, DS, JC, MC, VI. **Special Amenities:** free continental breakfast and free local telephone calls.

Suite Motel

SOME UNITS

(S/D) (🐾) (🍴) (📶) (🏊) (VCR) (🐶) (DATA PORT) (🛗) (📺) (📹) (🖨) / (🚫✕) /

COMFORT INN-HALL OF FAME   Phone: (330)492-1331
(AAA) (SAVE)   6/16-8/17   1P: $90   2P: $100   XP: $10   F18
▽▽▽   4/1-6/15 & 8/18-10/5   1P: $80   2P: $90   XP: $10   F18
    10/6-3/31   1P: $70   2P: $80   XP: $10   F18
Motel   **Location:** I-77, exit 109, 0.5 mi w on Everhard Rd. 5345 Broadmoor Cir NW 44709. Fax: 330/492-9093. **Facility:** 124 one-bedroom standard units, some with whirlpools. 3 stories, interior corridors. **Parking:** on-site. **Terms:** 3 day cancellation notice, [ECP] meal plan available, package plans. **Amenities:** extended cable TV, video games, voice mail, irons, hair dryers. *Some:* dual phone lines. **Pool(s):** outdoor. **Guest Services:** valet laundry. **Business Services:** meeting rooms, business center. **Cards:** AX, CB, DC, DS, JC, MC, VI. **Special Amenities:** early check-in/late check-out and free room upgrade (subject to availability with advanced reservations). *(See color ad below)*

SOME UNITS

(S/D) (📶) (🏊) (🐶) (DATA PORT) (📺) (🖨) / (🚫✕) (🛗) (📹) /
FEE

FAIRFIELD INN   Phone: (330)493-7373
(AAA) (SAVE)   All Year [CP]   1P: $69-$89   2P: $69-$89   XP: $6   F17
▽▽▽   **Location:** I-77, exit 109, 0.5 mi e on Everhard Rd. 5335 Broadmoor Cir NW 44709. Fax: 330/493-7373. **Facility:** 62 one-bedroom standard units. 3 stories, interior corridors. **Parking:** on-site. **Terms:** 5 day cancellation notice. **Amenities:** extended cable TV, irons. **Pool(s):** heated indoor. **Leisure Activities:** whirlpool. **Guest Services:** valet laundry. **Cards:** AX, CB, DC, DS, MC, VI. **Special Amenities:** free continental breakfast and free local telephone calls. *(See color ad card insert)*

Motel

SOME UNITS

(S/D) (🏊) (🐶) (DATA PORT) (🖨) / (🚫✕) (🛗) (📹) (📺) /
FEE

FOUR POINTS BY SHERATON CANTON   Phone: (330)494-6494
▽▽▽   4/1-10/31   1P: $80   2P: $80
    11/1-3/31   1P: $70   2P: $70
Motor Inn   **Location:** I-77, exit 109, just w on Everhard Rd, then just n on Dressler Rd. 4375 Metro Cir NW 44720. Fax: 330/494-7129. **Facility:** 152 one-bedroom standard units. 6 stories, interior corridors. **Parking:** on-site. **Terms:** cancellation fee imposed. **Amenities:** video games, high-speed Internet, voice mail, irons, hair dryers. **Pool(s):** heated indoor/outdoor. **Leisure Activities:** sauna, whirlpool, exercise room. **Guest Services:** massage (fee), valet laundry. **Business Services:** meeting rooms. **Cards:** AX, CB, DC, DS, JC, MC, VI.

SOME UNITS

(ASK) (S/D) (✈) (🍴) (📶) (🏊) (✕) (🐶) (DATA PORT) (📺) (🖨) / (🚫✕) (🛗) (📹) /
FEE

HAMPTON INN   Phone: (330)492-0151
(AAA) (SAVE)   All Year [CP]   1P: $79-$89   2P: $85-$95
▽▽▽   **Location:** I-77, exit 109, 0.5 mi e on Everhard Rd. 5335 Broadmoor Cir 44709. Fax: 330/492-7523. **Facility:** 107 one-bedroom standard units. 4 stories, interior corridors. **Parking:** on-site. **Amenities:** extended cable TV, video games, voice mail, irons, hair dryers. **Guest Services:** valet laundry. **Business Services:** meeting rooms. **Cards:** AX, DC, DS, MC, VI.

Motel

SOME UNITS

(S/D) (📶) (🏊) (🐶) (DATA PORT) (📺) (🖨) / (🚫✕) (🛗) /
FEE

THE HILTON CANTON

Phone: (330)454-5000

All Year	1P: $89-$129	2P: $99-$139	XP: $10	F18

Location: I-77, exit 105B (Tuscarawas St), 1.5 mi e, then just s. 320 Market Ave S 44702. Fax: 330/454-5494. **Facility:** 170 one-bedroom standard units. 8 stories, interior corridors. *Bath:* combo or shower only. **Parking:** on-site. **Terms:** package plans. **Amenities:** video games, dual phone lines, voice mail, irons, hair dryers. **Pool(s):** heated indoor. **Leisure Activities:** sauna, whirlpool, exercise room. *Fee:* game room. **Guest Services:** valet laundry. **Business Services:** conference facilities, fax. **Cards:** AX, CB, DC, DS, JC, MC, VI.

Hotel

SOME UNITS

RED ROOF INN

Phone: (330)499-1970

5/24-9/7	1P: $49-$62	2P: $55-$68	XP: $6	F18
9/8-11/2	1P: $39-$51	2P: $45-$57	XP: $6	F18
4/1-5/23	1P: $36-$51	2P: $42-$57	XP: $6	F18
11/3-3/31	1P: $37-$49	2P: $43-$55	XP: $6	F18

Location: I-77, exit 109, just w on Everhard Rd. 5353 Inn Circle Ct NW 44720. Fax: 330/499-1975. **Facility:** 108 one-bedroom standard units. 2 stories, exterior corridors. *Bath:* combo or shower only. **Parking:** on-site. **Terms:** small pets only. **Amenities:** video games, voice mail. **Cards:** AX, CB, DC, DS, MC, VI. **Special Amenities:** free local telephone calls and free newspaper.

Motel

SOME UNITS

RESIDENCE INN BY MARRIOTT

Phone: (330)493-0004

5/16-9/15 [ECP]	1P: $96	2P: $96
4/1-5/15 [ECP]	1P: $76	2P: $76
9/16-3/31 [ECP]	1P: $68	2P: $68

Location: I-77, exit 109, 0.5 mi e on Everhard Rd. 5325 Broadmoor Cir NW 44709. Fax: 330/493-0004. **Facility:** 66 units. 54 one- and 12 two-bedroom standard units. 3 stories, interior corridors. **Parking:** on-site. **Terms:** cancellation fee imposed, pets ($100 fee, $5 extra charge). **Amenities:** extended cable TV, voice mail, irons, hair dryers. **Pool(s):** heated indoor. **Leisure Activities:** whirlpool, exercise room, sports court. **Guest Services:** coin laundry. **Business Services:** meeting rooms. **Cards:** AX, DC, DS, MC, VI. *(See color ad card insert)*

Extended Stay Apartment

SOME UNITS

FEE

———— **WHERE TO DINE** ————

BENDER'S RESTAURANT Historical

Lunch: $5-$8 Dinner: $13-$24 Phone: 330/453-8424

Location: I-77, exit 105B (Tuscarawas St), 1.2 mi e, just s on Market Ave, then just w on 2nd St. 137 Court Ave SW 44702. **Hours:** 11 am-9:30 pm, Fri & Sat-10:30 pm. Closed major holidays; also Sun. **Reservations:** suggested; for dinner. **Features:** dressy casual; children's menu; carryout; cocktails & lounge. Originally a saloon, livery stable and hotel, the 1899 building now houses the friendly restaurant, which was started in 1906. The diverse menu includes plenty of seafood selections as well as lamb chops, steaks, pork chops and chicken marsala. **Parking:** on-site. **Cards:** AX, DC, DS, MC, VI.

American

PAPA BEAR'S

Lunch: $5-$9 Dinner: $8-$16 Phone: 330/493-0714

Location: Just s of Beldon Village Mall. 4990 Dressler Rd NW 44718. **Hours:** 11 am-11 pm, Fri & Sat-midnight. Closed: 11/28, 12/25. **Features:** casual dress; carryout; beer & wine only. Near a large mall, the local favorite has good variety in menu selections of chicken, seafood and beef. Parking space is ample, and the staff is friendly and efficient. **Parking:** on-site. **Cards:** AX, DS, MC, VI.

Italian

RICKY LY'S CHINESE GOURMET

Lunch: $4-$7 Dinner: $7-$24 Phone: 330/492-5905

Location: I-77, exit 109, 0.3 mi w on Everhard, 0.8 mi s; in Thursday's Plaza. 4695 Dressler Rd NW 44718. **Hours:** 11:30 am-10:30 pm, Fri-11:30 pm, Sat noon-11:30 pm, Sun 11 am-9:30 pm. Closed major holidays. **Reservations:** accepted. **Features:** dressy casual; Sunday brunch; carryout; cocktails & lounge. The eclectic menu lists many Thai entrees, some American fare, sushi bar offerings and Mandarin, Szechwan, Hunan and Cantonese selections. The prompt, attentive staff contributes to an elegant dining experience. Patio dining is available, weather permitting. **Parking:** on-site. **Cards:** AX, CB, DC, DS, MC, VI.

Chinese

THE STABLES

Lunch: $5-$10 Dinner: $8-$15 Phone: 330/452-1230

Location: I-77, exit 13th St, just w. 2317 13th St NW 44708. **Hours:** 10 am-10 pm, Fri & Sat-11 pm, Sun-9 pm. Closed: 12/25. **Features:** casual dress; Sunday brunch; children's menu; carryout; cocktails. Dating to the 1900s, the converted horse barn is decorated with football memorabilia. **Parking:** on-site. **Cards:** AX, DS, MC, VI.

American

———— *The following restaurant has not been evaluated by AAA but is listed for your information only.* ————

ROLANDO'S

Phone: 330/477-5934

[fyi] Not evaluated. **Location:** 2433 Whipple Ave NW 44718. A good variety of reasonably priced dishes is presented at the casual establishment.

CARROLLTON pop. 3,000

———— **WHERE TO STAY** ————

CARROLLTON DAYS INN

Phone: (330)627-9314

All Year	1P: $59-$89	2P: $69-$99	XP: $5	F17

Location: On SR 43, 0.5 mi n of SR 39. 1111 Canton Rd 44615. Fax: 330/627-9214. **Facility:** 43 one-bedroom standard units, some with whirlpools. 3 stories, interior corridors. **Parking:** on-site. **Terms:** check-in 4 pm, 7 day cancellation notice, package plans, small pets only ($50 deposit). **Amenities:** extended cable TV, dual phone lines, irons, hair dryers. **Pool(s):** heated indoor. **Leisure Activities:** whirlpool, exercise room. **Guest Services:** coin laundry. **Business Services:** meeting rooms. **Cards:** AX, DC, DS, MC, VI.

Motel

SOME UNITS

CELINA pop. 9,700

——— WHERE TO STAY ———

COMFORT INN

(AAA) (SAVE)

Motel

All Year   1P: $59-$159   2P: $59-$159   XP: $10   F18
Location: Jct SR 29 and 703. 1421 SR 703 E 45822. Fax: 419/586-4152. **Facility:** 40 units. 39 one-bedroom standard units, some with whirlpools. 1 one-bedroom suite ($159-$199). 2 stories, exterior corridors. **Parking:** on-site. **Terms:** 24 day cancellation notice. **Amenities:** extended cable TV. *Some:* hair dryers. **Cards:** AX, DC, DS, MC, VI.
Phone: (419)586-4656

SOME UNITS

HOLIDAY INN EXPRESS-CELINA

Motel

All Year   1P: $69-$84   2P: $69-$84   XP: $5   F18
Location: Jct Haveman Rd and SR 29, just n; e of downtown. 2020 Holiday Dr 45822. Fax: 419/586-4919. **Facility:** 52 one-bedroom standard units, some with whirlpools. 2 stories, interior corridors. *Bath:* combo or shower only. **Parking:** on-site, winter plug-ins. **Terms:** 7 day cancellation notice. **Amenities:** extended cable TV, voice mail, safes, irons, hair dryers. **Pool(s):** heated indoor. **Leisure Activities:** whirlpool, exercise room. **Guest Services:** valet laundry. **Business Services:** meeting rooms. **Cards:** AX, CB, DC, DS, JC, MC, VI.
Phone: (419)586-4919

SOME UNITS

FEE

——— WHERE TO DINE ———

C. J.'S HIGHMARKS   **Lunch:** $6-$8   **Dinner:** $8-$16   **Phone:** 419/586-5552

American

Location: Jct Haveman Rd and US 33, just n; e of downtown. 1211 Irmscher Blvd 45822. **Hours:** 11 am-10 pm, Fri & Sat-11 pm. Closed: 11/28, 12/25. **Features:** casual dress; children's menu; carryout; cocktails & lounge. The upbeat family restaurant reflects the mood and stylings of a schoolhouse, with hanging plastic crayons, a gymnasium-themed bar and lots of books and pencils. The menu, which resembles a folder, lists steak, seafood and specialty salads. **Parking:** on-site. **Cards:** AX, DS, MC, VI.

WELCH'S RESTAURANT   **Lunch:** $6-$9   **Dinner:** $8-$15   **Phone:** 419/586-2579

American

Location: US 127/703 (S Main St), 0.5 mi e. 1081 W Bank Rd 45822. **Hours:** 11 am-1 & 5-8:45 pm, Fri-9:45 pm, Sat 4:30 pm-9:45 pm, Sun 11 am-7:30 pm. Closed major holidays. **Features:** casual dress; Sunday brunch; children's menu; carryout; salad bar; cocktails & lounge; a la carte. Lots of windows overlook the lovely lake next to the quiet, comfortable restaurant. Offerings of surf and turf join pasta and sandwiches. The homemade pies, in mouthwatering varieties such as coconut cream and chocolate peanut butter, shouldn't be missed. **Parking:** on-site. **Cards:** AX, DC, DS, MC, VI.

CENTERVILLE pop. 21,100   (See map p. 672; index p. 675)

——— WHERE TO DINE ———

AMAR INDIA RESTAURANT   **Lunch:** $6-$8   **Dinner:** $10-$15   **Phone:** 937/439-9005   49

(AAA)

Ethnic

Location: I-75, exit 44, just e on SR 725; I-675, exit 2, just w on SR 725; in Mad River Station. 2759 Miamisburg-Centerville Rd 45459. **Hours:** 11:30 am-2 & 5-10 pm, Sun noon-3 & 4:30-9 pm. Closed: 11/28, 12/25. **Features:** casual dress; carryout; cocktails; buffet. Savory tandoori dishes and chicken makhani are among the traditional Indian favorites on a menu full of piquant temptations. Crystal chandeliers, lots of windows and cultural artwork gives the dining room a friendly, comfortable atmosphere. Smoke free premises. **Parking:** on-site. **Cards:** AX, DC, DS, MC, VI.

THE CHOP HOUSE   **Lunch:** $6-$13   **Dinner:** $8-$21   **Phone:** 937/291-1661   51

Steak & Seafood

Location: I-675, exit 2, just e on SR 725; in Washington Village Plaza. 7727 Washington Village 45459. **Hours:** 11 am-10 pm, Fri & Sat-11 pm. Closed: 11/28, 12/25. **Reservations:** suggested. **Features:** casual dress; children's menu; cocktails & lounge. Hickory-smoked and chargrilled specialties, such as pork chops and prime rib, are well-seasoned and filling. A stonework fireplace is the cozy centerpiece of the quiet dining room, which resembles a modern tavern. Service is friendly and attentive. **Parking:** on-site. **Cards:** AX, DC, DS, MC, VI.

COZYMEL'S COASTAL MEXICAN GRILL   **Lunch:** $7-$16   **Dinner:** $7-$16   **Phone:** 937/434-1855   50

Mexican

Location: I-675, exit 2, just e on SR 725. 1060 Miamisburg-Centerville Rd 45459. **Hours:** 11 am-10 pm, Fri & Sat-11 pm. Closed: 11/28, 12/24, 12/25. **Reservations:** suggested. **Features:** casual dress; children's menu; carryout; cocktails & lounge. Latin artwork and splashes of vivid color add to the restaurant's lively mood, which reflects a market and cantina feel. Fresh ingredients flavor traditional selections, such as burritos and tacos, in addition to coastal seafood preparations. **Parking:** on-site. **Cards:** AX, DC, DS, MC, VI.

J ALEXANDER'S RESTAURANT   **Lunch:** $6-$17   **Dinner:** $8-$20   **Phone:** 937/435-4441   54

Steak & Seafood

Location: I-675, exit 2, just e on SR 725; in Washington Square Village Shopping Plaza. 7970 Washington Village Dr 45459. **Hours:** 11 am-11 pm, Fri & Sat-midnight, Sun-10 pm. Closed: 11/28, 12/25. **Features:** casual dress; children's menu; cocktails & lounge. Redwood beams and dim lighting contribute to the restaurant's rustic tavern ambience. Freshly prepared steak, chops, ribs and seafood are offerings on the varied menu. The scrumptious in-house desserts make this place popular with the locals. **Parking:** on-site. **Cards:** AX, DC, DS, MC, VI.

(See map p. 672)

THE PARAGON CLUB   **Dinner: $12-$22**   **Phone: 937/433-1234**   52

▼▽▼▽   **Location:** I-675, exit 4, 1 mi e. 797 Miamisburg-Centerville Rd 45459. **Hours:** 5 pm-9 pm, Fri & Sat-10 pm.
     Closed major holidays. **Features:** dressy casual; cocktails & lounge; a la carte. Specializing in filets,
American   seafood and dry-aged New York strip steak, the restaurant is decorated in wood, brick and brass. The
     Paragon Supreme is a scrumptious after-dinner drink that melds cream, mint, chocolate and peanut butter
flavors. **Parking:** on-site. **Cards:** DC, DS, MC, VI.   ⊠

**The following restaurants have not been evaluated by AAA
but are listed for your information only.**

BALI CAFE   **Phone: 937/428-9933**
[fyi]   Not evaluated. **Location:** 8971 Kingsridge Dr 45358. Both Indonesian and Thai entrees are offered here.

FOX AND HOUND ENGLISH PUB & GRILLE   **Phone: 937/432-9904**
[fyi]   Not evaluated. **Location:** 671 Lyons Rd 45459. English pub and ambience featuring popular American cuisine.

LAS PIRAMIDES   **Phone: 937/291-0900**
[fyi]   Not evaluated. **Location:** 101 W Franklin St 45459. The restaurant features traditional Mexican fare.

SHELL'S SEAFOOD   **Phone: 937/432-0056**
[fyi]   Not evaluated. **Location:** 1516 Centerville Rd 45459. True to its name, the restaurant offers a variety of fresh
     seafood entrees.

WRAPSOPY   **Phone: 937/435-1900**
[fyi]   Not evaluated. **Location:** 298 N Main St 45459. American and International cuisine offered at this popular
     establishment.

CHARM pop. 200

--- **WHERE TO STAY** ---

GUGGISBERG SWISS INN   **Phone: (330)893-3600**

▼▽▼▽	6/1-10/31 [ECP]	1P: $88-$96	2P: $88-$96	XP: $9	F12
	4/1-5/31 [ECP]	1P: $70-$80	2P: $70-$80	XP: $9	F12
Motel	11/1-3/31 [ECP]	1P: $59-$69	2P: $59-$69	XP: $9	F12

Location: 1 mi n. 5025 SR 557 44617 (PO Box 1). Fax: 330/893-2810. **Facility:** Smoke free premises. 24 units.
23 one-bedroom standard units. 1 one-bedroom suite ($128-$160) with whirlpool. 2 stories, interior/exterior corridors. **Parking:**
on-site. **Terms:** package plans. **Amenities:** video tape library, irons.   SOME UNITS

(ASK) (🍴) (∅) (VCR) (📷) (💻) (📠) / (⊠) (🛏) (📷) /

HOLMES WITH A VIEW   **Phone: 330/893-2390**

AAA (SAVE)   All Year [CP]   1P: $200-$250   2P: $200-$250
▼▽▼▽   **Location:** N on SR 557, just s on CR 154. 3672 Twp Rd 154 44654. Fax: 330/893-4154. **Facility:** Smoke free prem-
     ises. 6 units. 4 one-bedroom standard units, some with kitchens and/or whirlpools. 2 two-bedroom suites with
Cottage   kitchens. 1 story, exterior corridors. **Parking:** on-site. **Terms:** 10 day cancellation notice-fee imposed.
     Amenities: extended cable TV, video tape library, CD players, irons. *Some:* DVD players. **Business Serv-
ices:** fax. **Cards:** DS, MC, VI.   SOME UNITS

(S🄳) (⊠) (📷) (DATA PORT) (🛏) (📷) (💻) (📠) / (VCR) /

CHERRY GROVE —See Cincinnati p. 575.

CHILLICOTHE pop. 21,900

--- **WHERE TO STAY** ---

CHILLICOTHE INN   **Phone: (740)774-2512**

AAA (SAVE)   All Year   1P: $33-$47   2P: $38-$49   XP: $5   F12
▼▽   **Location:** Jct US 50, just n on US 23 business route. 24 N Bridge St 45601. Fax: 740/773-7958. **Facility:** 40 one-
     bedroom standard units. 1-2 stories, interior/exterior corridors. *Bath:* combo or shower only. **Parking:** on-site.
Motel   **Terms:** cancellation fee imposed. **Amenities:** extended cable TV. **Cards:** AX, DS, MC, VI.
     **Special Amenities: early check-in/late check-out and preferred room (subject to availability with ad-
vanced reservations).**   SOME UNITS

(DATA PORT) / (⊠) /

CHRISTOPHER INN   **Phone: (740)774-6835**

AAA (SAVE)   All Year [ECP]   1P: $59-$79
▼▽▼▽   **Location:** US 35, exit Bridge St. 30 N Plaza Blvd 45601. Fax: 740/774-2001. **Facility:** 61 units. 56 one-bedroom
     standard units. 5 one-bedroom suites ($71-$99), some with whirlpools. 2 stories, interior corridors. *Bath:*
Motel   combo or shower only. **Parking:** on-site. **Terms:** package plans, small pets only. **Amenities:** extended cable
     TV. *Some:* irons, hair dryers. **Pool(s):** heated indoor. **Leisure Activities:** sauna, whirlpool. **Guest Services:**
     complimentary evening beverages: Mon-Thurs, winter, valet and coin laundry. **Cards:** AX, CB, DC, DS, JC,
MC, VI. **Special Amenities: free continental breakfast and free local telephone calls.**   SOME UNITS

(S🄳) (🐕) (🍴) (🎣) (🏊) (↔) (📷) (DATA PORT) (💻) / (⊠) (VCR) (🛏) (📷) /
     FEE

COMFORT INN

AAA SAVE

◈◈◈ ▽▽▽

Motel

| | 7/1-10/30 | 1P: $59-$79 | 2P: $59-$79 | XP: $10 | F17 |
| | 4/1-6/30 & 10/31-3/31 | 1P: $49-$69 | 2P: $49-$69 | XP: $10 | F17 |

Phone: (740)775-3500

Location: Jct US 35 and US 23 business route. 20 N Plaza Blvd 45601. **Fax:** 740/775-3588. **Facility:** 106 units. 97 one-bedroom standard units. 9 one-bedroom suites ($69-$89), some with kitchens and/or whirlpools. 2 stories, interior corridors. **Parking:** on-site. **Terms:** package plans, small pets only. **Amenities:** extended cable TV, voice mail. *Some:* irons, hair dryers. **Pool(s):** heated outdoor. **Guest Services:** valet and coin laundry. **Business Services:** conference facilities, fax (fee). **Cards:** AX, DC, DS, MC, VI. **Special Amenities:** free continental breakfast and free local telephone calls.

SOME UNITS

⊞ ☎ ⊞ ⊞ ⊞ ⊘ ⊠ ⊞ ⊞ DATA PORT ⊞ ⊞ / ⊠ VCR ⊞ ⊞ /

COUNTRY HEARTH INN

◈◈◈ ▽▽▽

Motel

| | All Year [CP] | 1P: $45-$75 | 2P: $45-$75 | XP: $6 | F17 |

Phone: (740)775-2500

Location: Jct US 35 and 50. 1135 E Main St 45601. **Fax:** 740/775-2500. **Facility:** 58 one-bedroom standard units. 1-2 stories, interior/exterior corridors. **Parking:** on-site. **Terms:** pets ($20 deposit). **Amenities:** extended cable TV. **Pool(s):** outdoor. **Business Services:** fax. **Cards:** AX, CB, DC, DS, MC, VI.

SOME UNITS

ASK ⊞ ☎ ⊞ ⊞ ⊞ ⊞ ⊞ / ⊠ DATA PORT ⊞ ⊞ /
FEE

DAYS INN CHILLICOTHE

AAA SAVE

◈◈◈ ▽▽▽

Motel

| | All Year [ECP] | 1P: $50-$62 | 2P: $50-$62 |

Phone: (740)775-7000

Location: US 35, exit Bridge St, 0.8 mi n. 1250 N Bridge St 45601. **Fax:** 740/773-1622. **Facility:** 42 one-bedroom standard units, some with whirlpools. 2 stories, interior corridors. **Parking:** on-site. **Terms:** 3 day cancellation notice, pets ($5 extra charge). **Amenities:** extended cable TV, video tape library, hair dryers. **Pool(s):** heated outdoor. **Guest Services:** valet laundry. **Business Services:** meeting rooms. **Cards:** AX, CB, DC, DS, MC, VI. **Special Amenities:** free continental breakfast and free local telephone calls.

SOME UNITS

⊞ ☎ ⊞ ⊞ ⊞ DATA PORT ⊞ ⊞ / ⊠ ⊞ ⊞ /

THE GREENHOUSE BED & BREAKFAST

◈◈◈ ▽▽▽

Historic Bed & Breakfast

| | 4/1-12/20 & 1/3-3/31 [BP] | 1P: $70 | 2P: $80 | XP: $15 | F5 |

Phone: 740/775-5313

Location: Just e of Paint St. 47 E 5th St 45601. **Facility:** Beyond the black, wrought iron entry fence, each room of this 1894 Victorian house is decorated in a period theme featuring artifacts and antiques. 4 one-bedroom standard units. 3 stories (no elevator), interior corridors. *Bath:* combo or shower only. **Parking:** street. **Terms:** open 4/1-12/20 & 1/3-3/31. **Amenities:** extended cable TV. **Business Services:** meeting rooms. **Cards:** AX, DS, MC, VI.

⊠ ⊞

HAMPTON INN & SUITES

AAA SAVE

◈◈◈ ▽▽▽

Motel

| | All Year | 1P: $79-$89 |

Phone: (740)773-1616

Location: US 35, exit Bridge St. 100 N Plaza Blvd 45601. **Fax:** 740/773-1770. **Facility:** 71 units. 49 one-bedroom standard units. 22 one-bedroom suites ($99-$119) with kitchens. 3 stories, interior corridors. *Bath:* combo or shower only. **Parking:** on-site. **Terms:** 3 day cancellation notice-fee imposed, package plans, small pets only. **Amenities:** extended cable TV, dual phone lines, voice mail, irons. **Pool(s):** small heated outdoor. **Leisure Activities:** sauna, whirlpool, exercise room. **Guest Services:** valet and coin laundry. **Business Services:** meeting rooms, business center, PC, fax. **Cards:** AX, CB, DC, DS, JC, MC, VI. **Special Amenities:** free continental breakfast and free local telephone calls.

SOME UNITS

⊞ ☎ ⊞ ⊞ GM ⊞ ⊞ ⊠ ⊞ DATA PORT ⊞ ⊞ / ⊠ VCR ⊞ ⊞ /
FEE

——— WHERE TO DINE ———

NEW YORK NEW YORK GRILL

AAA

◈◈◈ ▽▽▽

American

| Dinner: $8-$20 |

Phone: 740/773-2100

Location: US 35, just n on US 23 business route. 200 N Plaza Blvd 45601. **Hours:** 4:30 pm-9:30 pm, Fri & Sat-10:30 pm. Closed: 1/1, 11/28, 12/25; also Sun. **Reservations:** suggested. **Features:** dressy casual; children's menu; carryout; cocktails & lounge; a la carte. The cosmopolitan atmosphere is an oasis of tranquil dining with some formality. Cooks attired in berets prepare food in the open cooking area. Tantalizing items include home favorites of fresh seafood and pasta and such distinctive offerings as blackberry-glazed pork tenderloin. Key lime pie is a tart treat. The staff is knowledgeable. **Parking:** on-site. **Cards:** AX, DS, MC, VI.

⊠

SUNNYBROOK CAFE

▽▽▽

American

| Lunch: $5-$6 | Dinner: $5-$6 |

Phone: 740/773-3354

Location: Jct Main and Paint sts, 0.4 mi n. 85 N Paint St 45601. **Hours:** 10:30 am-3 & 5-9 pm, Mon-Wed to 3 pm. Closed major holidays; also Sun. **Reservations:** suggested; weekends. **Features:** casual dress; carryout; cocktails & lounge; a la carte. In an attractive, three-story, brick building in the center of the historic city, the cafe serves deli-style sandwiches, pork barbecue, hamburgers and salads. Different homemade soups are prepared daily along with a limited selection of desserts. **Parking:** street. **Cards:** AX, DS, MC, VI. ⊠

CHIPPEWA LAKE pop. 300

——— WHERE TO DINE ———

THE OAKS LODGE

◈◈ ▽▽

American

| Dinner: $16-$32 |

Phone: 330/769-2601

Location: 4 mi s on SR 3, 2 mi w on CR 50, 0.8 mi sw on CR 19 (Lake Rd), follow signs. 5878 Longacre Dr 44215. **Hours:** 5 pm-10 pm, Fri & Sat-11 pm, Sun 11 am-9 pm; hours vary 12/1-12/31. Closed: 1/1, 12/25. **Reservations:** suggested; weekends. **Features:** dressy casual; Sunday brunch; cocktails. This landmark restaurant is located on the beautiful shores of Chippewa Lake with here after performing in the nearby ballroom. The menu is creative and the Sunday brunch is a local favorite. Outside patio dining when weather permits. Big Band leaders Lawrence Welk and Glen Miller used to dine here. **Parking:** on-site. **Cards:** AX, DC, MC, VI.

By Highway or Byway ... Turn to the AAA Road Atlas

Whether you prefer the direct route or scenic diversions, you'll stay on track by keeping the AAA Road Atlas in reach. With annual updates from AAA road travel experts, you can rely on this accurate atlas to help you navigate every stretch of North America:

- New design, larger-format
- Large-scale maps with same-page distance charts
- Driving-time chart
- Top scenic byways
- Recreational, city, and national park maps
- More roads, towns, cities than any other road atlas

Receive the special discounted price for AAA members.

Available at participating AAA club offices aaa.com or by calling 1-877-AAA-BOOK.

Destination Cincinnati
pop. 364,000

Cincinnati Skyline.
For more than 2 centuries the skyline of Cincinnati has risen dramatically above the banks of the Ohio River.

Don't let the beauty of this sophisticated city built on the hills and in the valleys along the Ohio River fool you into thinking its pastimes are pastoral.

The atmosphere is charged with energy waiting to be released during celebrations of its river heritage, ethnic festivals, and at Reds' and Bengals' home games. Cincinnati is alive and enjoying life!

River Downs Racetrack, Cincinnati. After furlongs of cheering, fans prepare to say "So long" to their $2 bets as the Thoroughbreds cross the finish line. (See mention page 200)

*P*laces included in this AAA Destination City:

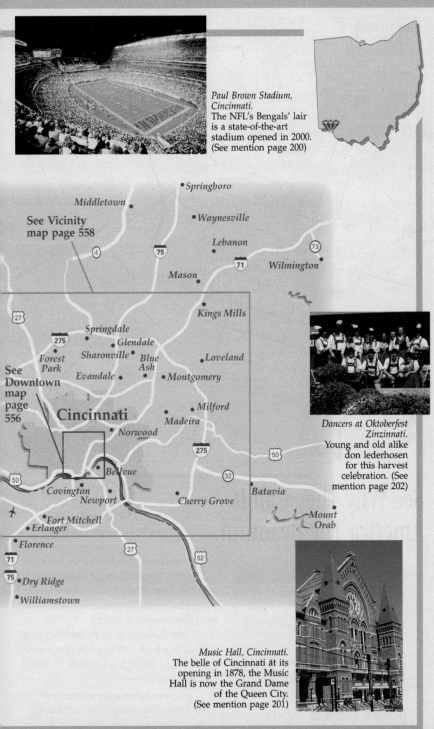

Paul Brown Stadium, Cincinnati.
The NFL's Bengals' lair is a state-of-the-art stadium opened in 2000. (See mention page 200)

Springboro

Middletown

See Vicinity map page 558

Waynesville

Lebanon

75

4

73

Wilmington

71

Mason

27

Kings Mills

275

Springdale

Glendale

Sharonville   *Blue Ash*

Forest Park

Loveland

Evandale

Montgomery

See Downtown map page 556

Cincinnati

Milford

Madeira

Norwood

275

50

32

Batavia

50

Bellvue

Covington

Newport

Cherry Grove

Mount Orab

Fort Mitchell
Erlanger

Florence

71

27

52

75 *Dry Ridge*

Williamstown

Dancers at Oktoberfest Zinzinnati.
Young and old alike don lederhosen for this harvest celebration. (See mention page 202)

Music Hall, Cincinnati.
The belle of Cincinnati at its opening in 1878, the Music Hall is now the Grand Dame of the Queen City. (See mention page 201)

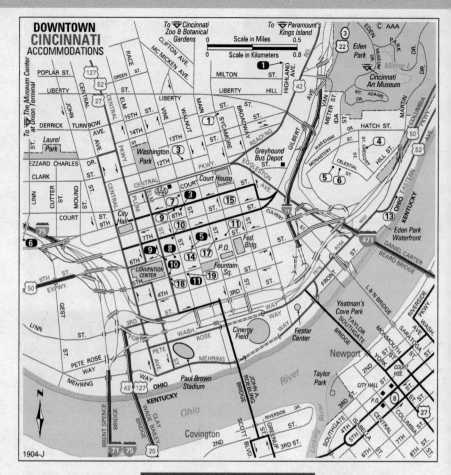

DOWNTOWN
CINCINNATI
ACCOMMODATIONS

1904-J

See Why They Call It
America The Beautiful.

Travel

Travel With Someone You Trust®

*T*rafalgar's exciting selection of escorted tours lets you discover the magnificence and grandeur of the USA and Canada. These vacations include first-class accommodations, touring by luxury motorcoach, many meals and the service of a professional tour director.

AAA members who book an escorted motorcoach tour to the USA or Canada with a AAA Travel Agency also receive an exclusive AAA member benefit value of at least $30. See your AAA Travel professional for details.

For more information, contact your AAA Travel Office or log on to www.aaa.com.

* Discount vouchers available on select motorcoach tours only. Ask your AAA Travel Agency for details.

TRAFALGAR TOURS
THE WORLD'S BEST SELLING ESCORTED TOURS

Downtown Cincinnati

This index helps you "spot" where approved accommodations and restaurants are located on the corresponding detailed maps. Lodging rate ranges are for comparison only and show the property's high season; rates are per night, unless only weekly (W) or monthly (M) rates are available. Restaurant rate range is for dinner, unless only lunch (L) is served. Turn to the listing page for more detailed rate information and consult display ads for special promotions.

Spotter/Map Page Number	OA	DOWNTOWN CINCINNATI - Lodgings	Diamond Rating	Rate Range High Season	Listing Page
1 / p. 556		The Phuntsok House B&B	◆◆◆	$150-$300	567
3 / p. 556	AAA	**Garfield Suites Hotel**	◆◆◆	$129-$600 SAVE	566
5 / p. 556	AAA	**The Cincinnatian Hotel**	◆◆◆◆	$225-$1500 SAVE	565
6 / p. 556	AAA	**Holiday Inn-Downtown**	◆◆◆	$79-$89 SAVE	567
8 / p. 556		Crowne Plaza Hotel Cincinnati	◆◆◆	$155-$175	565
9 / p. 556		Millennium Hotel Cincinnati	◆◆◆	$127-$135	567
10 / p. 556	AAA	**Four Points by Sheraton Cincinnati Downtown**	◆◆◆	$70-$118 SAVE	566
11 / p. 556	AAA	**Omni Netherland Plaza**	◆◆◆	$119-$159 SAVE	567
		DOWNTOWN CINCINNATI - Restaurants			
1 / p. 556		Nicola's Ristorante Italiano	◆◆	$16-$24	568
3 / p. 556		Barrel House Brewing Company	◆◆	$7-$10(L)	567
4 / p. 556		Mt. Adams Fish House	◆◆◆	$8-$25	568
5 / p. 556	AAA	**Celestial Restaurant**	◆◆◆◆	$33-$40	567
6 / p. 556		The Rookwood Pottery Restaurant	◆◆	$6-$17	568
7 / p. 556		Scotti's Italian Restaurant	◆◆	$13-$23	569
9 / p. 556		LeBoxx Cafe	◆◆	$5-$9(L)	568
10 / p. 556		RedFish	◆◆	$12-$17	568
11 / p. 556		La Normandie Tavern & Chop House	◆◆◆	$18-$30	568
13 / p. 556		Montgomery Inn at the Boathouse	◆◆	$11-$24	568
14 / p. 556	AAA	**The Palace Restaurant**	◆◆◆◆	$12-$33	568
15 / p. 556		Arnold's	◆	$8-$16	567
17 / p. 556		Maisonette	◆◆◆◆	$28-$44	568
18 / p. 556		Champs-Italian Chop House	◆◆	$16-$26	567
19 / p. 556	AAA	**The Palm Court Restaurant**	◆◆◆	$10-$30	568

Stop! Savings Ahead

When you see the red SAVE icon next to lodging listings in this book, you know these establishments offer great room rates to AAA members!

So, as you're turning the pages, remember to stop when you see SAVE. **It's your guarantee of savings.**

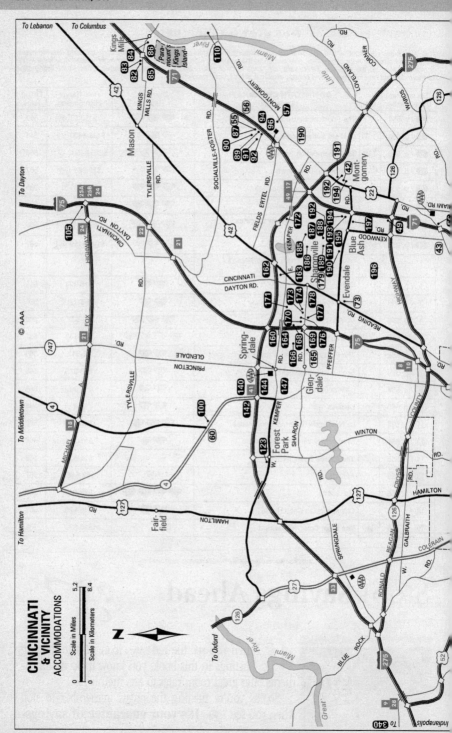

CINCINNATI
& VICINITY
ACCOMMODATIONS

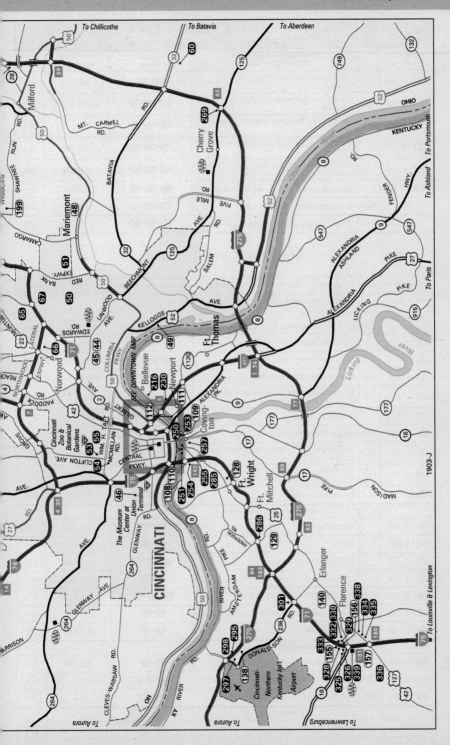

✈ Airport Accommodations

Spotter/Map Page Number	OA	CINCINNATI-NORTHERN KENTUCKY INT'L	Diamond Rating	Rate Range High Season	Listing Page
301 / p. 558		Comfort Inn-Cincinnati Airport, 3 mi e of entrance	▽▽	$69-$88	592
298 / p. 558	AAA	Holiday Inn-Cincinnati Airport, 3 mi e of entrance	▽▽▽	$98-$129 SAVE	592
329 / p. 558	AAA	Courtyard by Marriott Florence, 3.5 mi e of terminal	▽▽▽	$70-$90 SAVE	593
328 / p. 558		Hampton Inn-Cincinnati Airport, 3.5 mi e of entrance	▽▽▽	$94-$99	594
325 / p. 558		Hilton Greater Cincinnati Airport, 3.5 mi e of entrance	▽▽▽	$94-$154	594
330 / p. 558		Signature Inn Florence, 5 mi e of entrance	▽▽▽	$65-$71	594
N/A	AAA	Cincinnati Airport Marriott, 1.3 mi e	▽▽▽	$149-$179 SAVE	596
N/A		Radisson Hotel Cincinnati Airport, at the airport	▽▽▽	$85-$139	596

Cincinnati and Vicinity

This index helps you "spot" where approved accommodations and restaurants are located on the corresponding detailed maps. Lodging rate ranges are for comparison only and show the property's high season; rates are per night, unless only weekly (W) or monthly (M) rates are available. Restaurant rate range is for dinner, unless only lunch (L) is served. Turn to the listing page for more detailed rate information and consult display ads for special promotions.

Spotter/Map Page Number	OA	CINCINNATI - Lodgings	Diamond Rating	Rate Range High Season	Listing Page
49 / p. 558		Hannaford Suites Hotel - see color ad p 580	▽▽▽	$99-$129	570
50 / p. 558		The Victoria Inn of Hyde Park	▽▽▽	$99-$189	571
51 / p. 558	AAA	Best Western Mariemont Inn - see ad p 569	▽▽▽	$69-$86 SAVE	569
53 / p. 558	AAA	Marriott Kingsgate Conference Center - see color ad card insert	▽▽▽	$89-$149 SAVE	571
54 / p. 558		The Parker House	▽▽▽	$75-$115	571
55 / p. 558	AAA	Vernon Manor Hotel	▽▽▽	$89-$185 SAVE	571
56 / p. 558	AAA	Four Points by Sheraton North East - see color ad p 570	▽▽▽	$65 SAVE	569
57 / p. 558	AAA	TownePlace Suites by Marriott - see color ad card insert	▽▽▽	$80 SAVE	571
60 / p. 558		Comfort Inn & Suites	▽▽▽	$60-$90	569
		CINCINNATI - Restaurants			
42 / p. 558		Montgomery Inn	▽▽	$12-$23	572
43 / p. 558		Trio	▽▽	$12-$25	572
44 / p. 558		J's Fresh Seafood Restaurant	▽▽▽	$14-$25	571
45 / p. 558		Chateau Pomije	▽▽	$10-$22	571
46 / p. 558		Primavista	▽▽▽	$15-$28	572
48 / p. 558		Heritage Restaurant, Stein & Vine Pub	▽▽	$17-$24	571
49 / p. 558		Michael G's Restaurant & Banquet Facility	▽▽	$14-$30	572
		NORWOOD - Lodgings			
65 / p. 558		Howard Johnson East - see color ad p 583	▽▽	$70-$80	583
66 / p. 558	AAA	Quality Hotel & Suites - see color ad p 583	▽▽▽	$95-$130 SAVE	584
67 / p. 558	AAA	Red Roof Inn Cincinnati Central (Norwood)	▽▽	$51-$56 SAVE	584
		MASON - Lodgings			
82 / p. 558	AAA	Microtel Inn & Suites	▽▽	$38-$130 SAVE	580

Spotter/Map Page Number	OA	MASON - Lodgings (continued)	Diamond Rating	Rate Range High Season	Listing Page
83 / p. 558	⟨AAA⟩	**Hampton Inn Kings Island**	◇◇◇	$99-$179 SAVE	578
84 / p. 558	⟨AAA⟩	**Kings Island Resort & Conference Center -** see color ad p 579	◇◇◇	$69-$199 SAVE	579
85 / p. 558	⟨AAA⟩	**Holiday Inn Express Kings Island -** see color ad p 566	◇◇◇	$99-$275 SAVE	579
86 / p. 558	⟨AAA⟩	**Comfort Suites-Kings Island -** see color ad p 578	◇◇◇	$75-$200 SAVE	578
87 / p. 558	⟨AAA⟩	**Marriott Northeast -** see color ad card insert, p 579	◇◇◇	$89-$155 SAVE	579
89 / p. 558	⟨AAA⟩	**Hannaford Inn & Suites -** see color ad p 580	◇◇	$69-$129 SAVE	580
90 / p. 558	⟨AAA⟩	**AmeriSuites (Cincinnati/Deerfield Crossing)** - see color ad p 565	◇◇◇	$129 SAVE	577
91 / p. 558	⟨AAA⟩	**Country Hearth Inn Cincinnati NE**	◇◇◇	$49-$109 SAVE	578
92 / p. 558	⟨AAA⟩	**Baymont Inn & Suites Cincinnati-Mason/near Kings Island -** see color ad opposite title page	◇◇◇	$64-$74 SAVE	577
93 / p. 558		Red Roof Inn-Kings Island	◇◇	$55-$125	580
94 / p. 558	⟨AAA⟩	**Comfort Inn Cincinnati NE -** see color ad p 578	◇◇◇	$65-$175 SAVE	578
96 / p. 558		Signature Inn Cincinnati NE	◇◇◇	$61-$70	580
		MASON - Restaurants			
55 / p. 558		River City Grille	◇◇	$10-$22	580
56 / p. 558		Grand Oriental Chinese Restaurant	◇◇	$9-$19	580
		FAIRFIELD - Lodgings			
100 / p. 558		Holiday Inn Express	◇◇◇	$89	686
		FAIRFIELD - Restaurant			
60 / p. 558		Pedro's Steakhouse Restaurant	◇◇	$7-$18	687
		WEST CHESTER - Lodgings			
105 / p. 558	⟨AAA⟩	**Cincinnati Marriott North -** see color ad card insert	◇◇◇	$134-$152 SAVE	772
		KINGS MILLS - Lodgings			
110 / p. 558		Kings Manor Inn Bed & Breakfast	◇◇◇	$70-$90	576
		FOREST PARK - Lodgings			
123 / p. 558		Lees Inn & Suites Cincinnati	◇◇◇	$89-$129	575
		SPRINGDALE - Lodgings			
140 / p. 558	⟨AAA⟩	**Baymont Inn & Suites-Cincinnati North -** see color ad opposite title page	◇◇	$59-$69 SAVE	587
142 / p. 558	⟨AAA⟩	**Best Western Springdale Hotel & Conference Centre -** see ad p 569	◇◇◇	$59-$99 SAVE	587
144 / p. 558	⟨AAA⟩	**Cross Country Inn**	◇◇	$42-$56 SAVE	587
147 / p. 558	⟨AAA⟩	**The Hampshire House Hotel & Conference Center**	◇◇	$58-$85 SAVE	587
		SHARONVILLE - Lodgings			
160 / p. 558	⟨AAA⟩	**Residence Inn by Marriott -** see color ad card insert	◇◇◇	$99-$109 SAVE	586
162 / p. 558		Holiday Inn-I-275 North - see color ad p 570	◇◇◇	$94-$124	585
163 / p. 558		Days Inn Cincinnati/Sharonville	◇◇	$45-$145	584
164 / p. 558	⟨AAA⟩	**Red Roof Inn Chester Rd**	◇◇	$44-$64 SAVE	586
166 / p. 558		Signature Inn Cincinnati North	◇◇◇	$61-$70	586
168 / p. 558	⟨AAA⟩	**Hilton Garden Inn Cincinnati/Sharonville**	◇◇◇	$98 SAVE	585

Spotter/Map Page Number	OA	SHARONVILLE - Lodgings (continued)	Diamond Rating	Rate Range High Season	Listing Page
169 / p. 558	AAA	Radisson Hotel Cincinnati - see ad p 586	◆◆◆	$70-$95 SAVE	585
170 / p. 558	AAA	Best Western Inn & Suites	◆◆◆	$59-$99 SAVE	584
171 / p. 558		Homewood Suites by Hilton-Cincinnati North - see ad 585	◆◆◆	$119-$129	585
172 / p. 558	AAA	Doubletree Guest Suites	◆◆◆	$89-$149 SAVE	584
173 / p. 558	AAA	Woodfield Suites	◆◆◆	$99-$199 SAVE	587
174 / p. 558	AAA	Fairfield Inn by Marriott-Sharonville - see color ad card insert	◆◆	$69-$79 SAVE	584
176 / p. 558	AAA	Country Inn & Suites By Carlson-Cincinnati-North - see color ad p 646	◆◆◆	$69-$129 SAVE	584
177 / p. 558	AAA	Red Roof Inn-Sharon Road	◆◆	$44-$64 SAVE	586
178 / p. 558	AAA	Hampton Inn-Cincinnati North	◆◆◆	$70-$80 SAVE	585
		SHARONVILLE - Restaurant			
73 / p. 558		Anand India Restaurant	◆◆	$8-$14	587
		BLUE ASH - Lodgings			
185 / p. 558	AAA	AmeriSuites (Cincinnati/Blue Ash) - see color ad p 565	◆◆◆	$99-$119 SAVE	573
186 / p. 558	AAA	Comfort Suites	◆◆◆	$85 SAVE	573
187 / p. 558	AAA	Residence Inn by Marriott-Blue Ash - see color ad card insert	◆◆◆	$129 SAVE	574
188 / p. 558		Wingate Inn-Cincinnati/Blue Ash	◆◆◆	$99-$109	575
189 / p. 558		Holiday Inn Express Hotel & Suites	◆◆◆	$79-$109	574
190 / p. 558	AAA	Hampton Inn	◆◆◆	$79-$99 SAVE	574
191 / p. 558	AAA	MainStay Suites-Blue Ash - see color ad p 565	◆◆◆	$55-$95 SAVE	574
192 / p. 558	AAA	TownePlace Suites by Marriott Blue Ash - see color ad card insert	◆◆◆	$89 SAVE	575
193 / p. 558	AAA	Red Roof Inn Northeast (Blue Ash)	◆◆	$51-$76 SAVE	574
194 / p. 558	AAA	Courtyard By Marriott-Blue Ash - see color ad card insert	◆◆◆	$74-$109 SAVE	573
195 / p. 558		Embassy Suites Hotel-Cincinnati Northeast	◆◆◆	$109-$199	574
196 / p. 558		Extended Stay America-Blue Ash	◆◆	Failed to provide	574
197 / p. 558	AAA	Clarion Hotel and Suites Cincinnati	◆◆◆	$89-$149 SAVE	573

Nearby Kentucky

Spotter/Map Page Number	OA		Diamond Rating	Rate Range High Season	Listing Page
		BELLEVUE, KY - Lodgings			
216 / p. 558		Cincinnati's Weller Haus Bed & Breakfast	◆◆◆	$89-$168	589
		NEWPORT, KY - Lodgings			
230 / p. 558		Comfort Suites Riverfront	◆◆◆	$84-$114	596
		COVINGTON, KY - Lodgings			
250 / p. 558	AAA	Cincinnati Marriott at RiverCenter - see color ad card insert	◆◆◆◆	$129-$169 SAVE	590
251 / p. 558		Radisson Cincinnati Riverfront Hotel	◆◆◆	$109-$119	591
253 / p. 558	AAA	Holiday Inn Riverfront	◆◆◆	$89-$107 SAVE	591
254 / p. 558		Hampton Inn Cincinnati Riverfront	◆◆◆	$84-$94	591
255 / p. 558		Embassy Suites Cincinnati RiverCenter	◆◆	$109-$169	590

Spotter/Map Page Number	OA	COVINGTON, KY - Lodgings (continued)	Diamond Rating	Rate Range High Season	Listing Page
257 / p. 558	AAA	Amos Shinkle Townhouse Bed & Breakfast	◆◆◆	$85-$165 SAVE	590
		COVINGTON, KY - Restaurants			
108 / p. 558	AAA	Riverview Restaurant	◆◆◆	$17-$25	591
109 / p. 558		Chez Nora Restaurant	◆	$11-$25	591
110 / p. 558		Zebo's Bistro	◆◆◆	$15-$25	591
111 / p. 558		Mike Fink	◆◆	$14-$25	591
112 / p. 558		BB Riverboats	◆◆	$30-$36	591
		CHERRY GROVE, KY - Lodgings			
269 / p. 558	AAA	Red Roof Inn Cincinnati East	◆◆	$49-$79 SAVE	575
		FORT MITCHELL, KY - Lodgings			
285 / p. 558	AAA	Holiday Inn Fort Mitchell/I-75/Greater Cincinnati Area	◆◆◆	$59-$89 SAVE	595
286 / p. 558	AAA	Cross Country Inn	◆◆	$40-$54 SAVE	595
		FORT MITCHELL, KY - Restaurants			
128 / p. 558		Greyhound Tavern	◆◆	$7-$20	595
129 / p. 558		Oriental Wok	◆◆	$8-$17	596
		ERLANGER, KY - Lodgings			
295 / p. 558	AAA	Baymont Inn & Suites Cincinnati-Airport (Erlanger, KY) - see color ad opposite title page	◆◆◆	$69-$89 SAVE	592
297 / p. 558	AAA	Residence Inn by Marriott, Cincinnati Airport - see color ad card insert	◆◆◆	$109-$179 SAVE	593
298 / p. 558	AAA	Holiday Inn-Cincinnati Airport	◆◆◆	$98-$129 SAVE	592
301 / p. 558		Comfort Inn-Cincinnati Airport	◆◆	$69-$88	592
		ERLANGER, KY - Restaurants			
138 / p. 558		Jo An Japanese Cuisine	◆◆	$9-$20	593
140 / p. 558	AAA	Colonial Cottage Inn	◆◆	$6-$12	593
		FLORENCE, KY - Lodgings			
325 / p. 558		Hilton Greater Cincinnati Airport	◆◆◆	$94-$154	594
326 / p. 558	AAA	AmeriSuites (Cincinnati Airport) - see color ad p 565	◆◆◆	$99-$109 SAVE	593
328 / p. 558		Hampton Inn-Cincinnati Airport	◆◆◆	$94-$99	594
329 / p. 558	AAA	Courtyard by Marriott Florence	◆◆◆	$70-$90 SAVE	593
330 / p. 558		Signature Inn Florence	◆◆◆	$65-$71	594
332 / p. 558	AAA	Fairfield Inn by Marriott-Florence Kentucky	◆◆	$49-$75 SAVE	594
333 / p. 558	AAA	Best Western Inn Florence	◆◆◆	$70-$150 SAVE	593
334 / p. 558	AAA	Cross Country Inn Florence	◆◆	$40-$54 SAVE	594
335 / p. 558	AAA	Florence Super 8	◆◆	$56-$67 SAVE	594
336 / p. 558	AAA	Holiday Inn Florence	◆◆◆	$79-$109 SAVE	594
338 / p. 558	AAA	Knights Inn Florence	◆◆	$30-$99 SAVE	594
339 / p. 558		Ashley Quarters	◆◆◆	$343-$534	593
		FLORENCE, KY - Restaurants			
155 / p. 558		Karlo's Bistro Italia	◆◆	$10-$16	595

Spotter/Map Page Number	OA	FLORENCE, KY - Restaurants (continued)	Diamond Rating	Rate Range High Season	Listing Page
(156) / p. 558		Chung Gi Wha Sushi & Korean BBQ	◇◇	$25	595
(157) / p. 558		Cathay Kitchen Chinese Restaurant	◇◇	$7-$15	595
		HARRISON, KY - Lodgings			
(340) / p. 558		Quality Inn	◇◇	$70-$75	576
		MILFORD, KY - Lodgings			
(347) / p. 558	AAA	Holiday Inn Express Hotel & Suites - see color ad p 582	◇◇◇	$100-$110 [SAVE]	582
		GLENDALE, KY - Restaurant			
(165) / p. 558		The Iron Horse Inn	◇◇	$15-$23	575
		EVENDALE, KY - Restaurant			
(179) / p. 558		Evendale Buffet	◇	$8	575
		MONTGOMERY, KY - Restaurants			
(190) / p. 558		de Sha's American Tavern	◇◇	$10-$23	582
(191) / p. 558		Chester's Road House	◇◇◇	$16-$29	582
(192) / p. 558		Germano's	◇◇◇	$14-$28	582
(194) / p. 558		Pacific Moon Cafe	◇◇	$10-$20	583
		MADEIRA, KY - Restaurant			
(199) / p. 558		Ferrari's Little Italy and Bakery	◇◇	$10-$25	577

Look for the Signs Along the Way

*W*hen selecting a place to dine while traveling, look for Official Appointment restaurants that display the AAA Approved sign. It's the only sign you need to be assured of an enjoyable dining experience.

As a member, you already know the AAA sign indicates quality establishments. So, when you don't have advance dining reservations, look for the AAA Approved sign along the way, for a meal you'll long remember!

DOWNTOWN CINCINNATI   (See map p. 556; index p. 557)

── WHERE TO STAY ──

THE CINCINNATIAN HOTEL
(AAA) SAVE
▼▼▼▼ ▼▼▼▼
Hotel

Phone: (513)381-3000   **5**
All Year   1P: $225-$1500   XP: $25   F16
Location: Corner of 6th and Vine sts; entrance on 6th St. 601 Vine St 45202. Fax: 513/651-0256. **Facility:** This historic hotel, built in 1882, has been elegantly restored with contemporary amenities. 146 one-bedroom standard units, some with whirlpools. 8 stories, interior corridors. *Bath:* combo or shower only. **Parking:** on-site and valet (fee). **Terms:** package plans - weekends. **Amenities:** high-speed Internet (fee), voice mail, safes, honor bars, irons, hair dryers. *Some:* CD players. **Dining:** dining room, 6:30 am-1:30 & 5-9 pm, $12-$33, also, The Palace Restaurant, see separate listing. **Leisure Activities:** sauna, exercise room. *Fee:* internet access. **Guest Services:** afternoon tea, valet laundry. **Business Services:** meeting rooms, PC, fax. **Cards:** AX, CB, DS, JC, MC, VI.
Special Amenities: free newspaper. Affiliated with A Preferred Hotel.

SOME UNITS

[⑪] [24⑪] [📺] [🛏M] [🐾] [⊠] [📷] [DATA PORT] [🖨] / [⊠] [VCR] FEE

CROWNE PLAZA HOTEL CINCINNATI
▼▼▼▼
Hotel

Phone: (513)381-4000   **8**
All Year   1P: $155-$175
Location: I-75, exit 5th St to Vine St. 15 W 6th St 45202. Fax: 513/381-5158. **Facility:** 326 one-bedroom standard units. 20 stories, interior corridors. *Bath:* combo or shower only. **Parking:** *Fee:* on-site and valet. **Amenities:** high-speed Internet, voice mail, irons, hair dryers. **Leisure Activities:** exercise room. **Guest Services:** valet laundry. **Business Services:** conference facilities. **Cards:** AX, CB, DC, DS, JC, MC, VI.

SOME UNITS

[A$K] [S/D] [⑪] [📺] [🛏] [🐾] [📷] [DATA PORT] FEE [💻] [🖨] / [⊠] [🔌] FEE [📠] FEE /

Minutes from Kings Island...MainStay Suites in Blue Ash.
From the People Who Brought You Comfort Inn

- Full Kitchens, Continental Breakfast (M-F)
- Condo Privacy With Full Hotel Amenities
- Guest Exercise Room & Laundry
- Guest Barbecue, Social Hours & Outdoor Pool

see full listing: Blue Ash, OH

(800) 660-MAIN
(800) 660-6246

4630 Creek Road • Blue Ash, OH 45242 • I-71 & I-275
(513) 985-9992   ▼▼▼ Ask for the LAAA Promotional Rate

$59⁹⁵ Queen Suite
1-4 people, plus tax.
Subject to availability.

MainStay Suites
Stay longer for less.

Don't Downsize. AMERISIZE℠

AAA travelers don't downsize, they AmeriSize!℠ Stay at AmeriSuites,® and you'll enjoy a suite for the price of an ordinary room, our FREE Bountiful Breakfast Buffet,℠ plus **10% off*** for AAA members. Earn points with our frequent traveler program!

All AmeriSuites are AAA official appointment hotels and are ◆◆◆ rated properties.

AMERISUITES®
AMERICA'S AFFORDABLE ALL-SUITE HOTEL
1-800-833-1516
www.amerisuites.com

(AAA) Approved

CINCINNATI/Airport • 300 Meijer Drive • Florence, KY 41042 • 859-647-1170
CINCINNATI/Blue Ash • 11435 Reed Hartman Highway • Blue Ash, OH 45241 • 513-489-3666
CINCINNATI/Deerfield Crossing • 5070 Natorp Boulevard • Mason, OH 45040 • 513-754-0003
CINCINNATI/North • 12001 Chase Plaza Drive • Forest Park, OH 45240 • 513-825-9035

*Discount off published rates.   ©2001 Prime Hospitality Corp.

(See map p. 556)

FOUR POINTS BY SHERATON CINCINNATI DOWNTOWN

Phone: (513)357-5800 [10]

AAA [SAVE]

7/1-10/31	1P: $70-$118	2P: $70-$118	XP: $10	F18
4/1-6/30	1P: $65-$110	2P: $65-$110	XP: $10	F18
1/1-3/31	1P: $55-$93	2P: $55-$93	XP: $10	F18
11/1-12/31	1P: $50-$84	2P: $50-$84	XP: $10	F18

Motor Inn   **Location:** Opposite Convention Hall; between Elm and Race sts. 150 W 5th St 45202. Fax: 513/357-5810. **Facility:** 450 one-bedroom standard units. 21 stories, interior corridors. **Bath:** combo or shower only. **Parking:** on-site and valet (fee). **Terms:** check-in 4 pm, cancellation fee imposed. **Amenities:** extended cable TV, voice mail, irons, hair dryers. **Dining:** dining room, restaurant, 6:30 am-11 pm, $9-$18, cocktails. **Leisure Activities:** exercise room. **Guest Services:** gift shop, valet laundry. **Business Services:** conference facilities, business center, PC, fax. **Cards:** AX, CB, DC, DS, MC, VI.

SOME UNITS

[ICONS] / [✕] /

GARFIELD SUITES HOTEL

Phone: (513)421-3355 [3]

AAA [SAVE]

All Year	1P: $129-$600	2P: $149-$600	XP: $25	F18

Cottage   **Location:** Corner of Vine and 8th sts. 2 Garfield Pl 45202. Fax: 513/421-3729. **Facility:** 152 units. 80 one- and 70 two-bedroom standard units. 2 three-bedroom suites. 16 stories, interior corridors. **Parking:** Fee: on-site and valet. **Terms:** check-in 4 pm, package plans, pets ($100 extra charge). **Amenities:** video games, voice mail, safes, irons, hair dryers. Some: CD players. **Dining:** deli, 6:30 am-7 pm, Sun-11 am, $4-$13. **Guest Services:** valet and coin laundry. **Business Services:** meeting rooms, fax. **Cards:** AX, CB, DC, DS, MC, VI.

SOME UNITS

[ICONS] FEE FEE ... / [✕] / [VCR] FEE

SAVE Yourself From Paying Full Room Rates

When selecting a AAA Approved lodging, look for the [SAVE] or the [SAVE] icons in TourBook® guide listings, and save money on your travel expenses. These properties actively solicit AAA business and offer members great room rates. See the TourBook Navigator section, pages 16 and 22, for details.

(See map p. 556)

HOLIDAY INN-DOWNTOWN
Phone: (513)241-8660   **6**

AAA SAVE

Motor Inn

6/1-10/31	1P: $79-$89	2P: $79-$89
4/1-5/31 & 11/1-3/31	1P: $69-$79	2P: $69-$79

Location: I-75, exit 1G; entrance on 8th St. 800 W 8th St 45203. Fax: 513/241-9057. **Facility:** 242 one-bedroom standard units. 12 stories, interior corridors. *Bath:* combo or shower only. **Parking:** on-site. **Terms:** package plans. **Amenities:** voice mail, irons, hair dryers. **Dining:** dining room, 6:30 am-10:30 & 5:30-10 pm, Sat & Sun 7-11 am, $9-$18, cocktails. **Pool(s):** outdoor. **Leisure Activities:** exercise room. **Guest Services:** valet and coin laundry. **Business Services:** meeting rooms. **Cards:** AX, CB, DC, DS, MC, VI.

SOME UNITS

MILLENNIUM HOTEL CINCINNATI
Phone: (513)352-2100   **9**

Motor Inn

7/1-10/31	1P: $127-$135	2P: $127-$135	XP: $10	F18
4/1-6/30	1P: $101-$119	2P: $101-$119	XP: $10	F18
11/1-12/31	1P: $95-$103	2P: $95-$103	XP: $10	F18
1/1-3/31	1P: $87-$95	2P: $87-$95	XP: $10	F18

Location: Between Elm and Rale sts; opposite Convention Hall. 142 W Sixth St 45202. Fax: 513/352-2248. **Facility:** 422 one-bedroom standard units. 32 stories, interior corridors. *Bath:* combo or shower only. **Parking:** on-site and valet. **Terms:** check-in 4 pm, cancellation fee imposed. **Amenities:** extended cable TV, voice mail, irons, hair dryers. **Pool(s):** outdoor. **Leisure Activities:** exercise room. **Guest Services:** gift shop, coin laundry. **Business Services:** conference facilities, business center, PC, fax. **Cards:** AX, CB, DC, DS, JC, MC, VI.

SOME UNITS

OMNI NETHERLAND PLAZA
Phone: (513)421-9100   **11**

AAA SAVE

Historic Hotel

All Year   1P: $119-$159   2P: $119-$159

Location: 5th and Race sts; entrance on Race St. 35 W 5th St 45202. Fax: 513/421-4291. **Facility:** 621 one-bedroom standard units. 31 stories, interior corridors. *Bath:* combo or shower only. **Parking:** *Fee:* on-site and valet. **Terms:** cancellation fee imposed, package plans. **Amenities:** high-speed Internet, voice mail, irons, hair dryers. *Some:* fax, safes, honor bars. **Dining:** dining room, 6:30 am-2 & 5-10 pm, Fri & Sat-11 pm; Sunday brunch, $10-$20, cocktails, also, The Palm Court Restaurant, see separate listing, entertainment. **Guest Services:** gift shop, valet laundry. **Business Services:** conference facilities, business center, PC, fax. **Cards:** AX, CB, DC, DS, JC, MC, VI. **Special Amenities:** early check-in/late check-out and free newspaper.

SOME UNITS

THE PHUNTSOK HOUSE B&B
Phone: (513)961-6455   **1**

Historic Bed & Breakfast

All Year [BP]   1P: $150-$275   2P: $275-$300   XP: $25

Location: I-71, exit 3 (Taft Rd), 0.5 mi w, then just n. 2641 Highland Ave 45219 (PO Box 19236, CINCINNATI). **Facility:** Property policy is to remove shoes at entry. Public areas and rooms with Tibetan Buddhist themes and decorations. 4 one-bedroom standard units. 3 stories, interior corridors. *Bath:* shower or tub only. **Parking:** on-site. **Terms:** check-in 4 pm, age restrictions may apply, 30 day cancellation notice-fee imposed. **Business Services:** business center. **Cards:** AX, CB, DC, DS, JC, MC, VI.

——— WHERE TO DINE ———

ARNOLD'S
Lunch: $5-$10   Dinner: $8-$16   Phone: 513/421-6234   **15**

American

Location: Between Main and Sycamore sts. 210 E 8th St 45202. **Hours:** 11 am-10 pm, Fri-11 pm, Sat 4 pm-11 pm. Closed major holidays; also Sun. **Reservations:** accepted. **Features:** casual dress; carryout; cocktails & lounge; entertainment. Operated since 1861, the former barroom was converted to a restaurant during Prohibition. Greek and Italian influences show in a diverse menu of seafood and vegetarian selections. The courtyard is a departure from the dining room's bustling atmosphere. **Parking:** street. **Cards:** AX, MC, VI.

BARREL HOUSE BREWING COMPANY
Lunch: $7-$10   Phone: 513/421-2337   **3**

American

Location: Between Vine and Walnut sts. 22 E 12th St 45210. **Hours:** 11 am-11 pm, Sat noon-midnight. Closed: 11/28, 12/25; also Sun & Mon. **Reservations:** suggested; weekends. **Features:** casual dress; cocktails; entertainment. Freshly brewed beers nicely accompany brew-pub fare, which includes appetizers, sandwiches and creative pizzas. **Parking:** on-site (fee). **Cards:** AX, CB, DC, DS, MC, VI.

CELESTIAL RESTAURANT
Dinner: $33-$40   Phone: 513/241-4455   **5**

AAA

Continental

Location: 0.5 mi e, at top of Mt Adams; on 1st floor of Highland Towers. 1071 Celestial St 45202. **Hours:** 5:30 pm-9 pm, Fri-10 pm, Sat 5:30 pm-10 pm. Closed: 1/1, 7/4, 12/25; also Sun & Mon. **Reservations:** suggested; weekends. **Features:** semi-formal attire; cocktails & lounge. Atop Mt Adams sits this restaurant with a panoramic view of Cincinnati below as aloft eagles wings. Greeted and served by a formally attired staff for a very relaxing elegant experience. Enjoy the basics of steak, chicken and seafood with some speciality choices of duck or Australian lamb. Great dessert selections, as an example, being creme brulee or Graeters ice cream a locally produced product. Jackets are required for gentleman diners. Smoke free premises. **Parking:** on-site and valet. **Cards:** AX, CB, DC, MC, VI.

CHAMPS-ITALIAN CHOP HOUSE
Lunch: $7-$12   Dinner: $16-$26   Phone: 513/579-1234   **18**

Italian

Location: Center; Hyatt-Saks Square on 5th St; in Hyatt Regency Cincinnati. 151 W 5th St 45202. **Hours:** 11:30 am-2 & 5:30-10 pm; Sat & Sun 5:30 pm. **Reservations:** suggested; Fri & Sat. **Features:** dressy casual; cocktails; a la carte. Dine on steak, chops, pasta and seafood in Champs' relaxed atmosphere with a view of the open kitchen. Notable accompaniments include fresh, plentiful salad and tasty bread served by a friendly and prompt staff. For dessert is a distinctive tiramisu. **Parking:** on-site (fee) and valet. **Cards:** AX, DC, DS, JC, MC, VI.

(See map p. 556)

LA NORMANDIE TAVERN & CHOP HOUSE **Lunch:** $7-$12 **Dinner:** $18-$30 **Phone:** 513/721-2761 ⑪
Steak House
Location: I-71, exit 1D (Main St), just n, then just w. 114 E 6th St 45202. **Hours:** 11 am-2:30 & 5-10 pm, Fri-11 pm, Sat 5 pm-11 pm. Closed major holidays; also Sun. **Reservations:** accepted. **Features:** casual dress; children's menu; cocktails & lounge. Playbills from local Broadway shows that appeared in the city hang on the walls of the intimate dining room, which reflects an Old English tavern decor. Hand-cut steak and fresh fish make up the menu. The white and dark chocolate mousse is sinful. **Parking:** on-site and valet (fee). **Cards:** AX, CB, DC, DS, MC, VI.

LEBOXX CAFE **Lunch:** $5-$9 **Phone:** 513/721-5638 ⑨
American
Location: 819 Vine St 45202. **Hours:** 11 am-2:30 pm. Closed major holidays; also Sat & Sun. **Features:** casual dress; carryout; cocktails. A great spot for lunch, the restaurant features American fare, including burgers, meatloaf. **Parking:** on-site (fee). **Cards:** AX, DC, DS, MC, VI.

MAISONETTE **Lunch:** $15-$22 **Dinner:** $28-$44 **Phone:** 513/721-2260 ⑰
French
Location: Downtown; between Walnut and Main sts. 114 E 6th St 45202. **Hours:** noon-2 & 6-10:30 pm, Sat 5:30 pm-10 pm. Closed major holidays; also Sun & for lunch Mon & Sat. **Reservations:** suggested. **Features:** semi-formal attire; cocktails & lounge; a la carte, also prix fixe. The quiet, upscale dining environment is decorated with illuminated art, fresh roses on the tables and high-quality table settings. High-quality, fresh ingredients go into the well-prepared and attractive dishes. Service is professional and formal. Smoke free premises. **Parking:** on-site and valet (fee). **Cards:** AX, DC, DS, MC, VI.

MONTGOMERY INN AT THE BOATHOUSE **Lunch:** $7-$13 **Dinner:** $11-$24 **Phone:** 513/721-7427 ⑬
American
Location: I-71, exit 1B, 1.1 mi s on Pete Rose Way and Eastern Ave. 925 Eastern Ave 45202. **Hours:** 11 am-10:30 pm, Fri-11 pm, Sat 3 pm-11 pm, Sun 3 pm-10 pm. Closed major holidays. **Reservations:** accepted; except Sat. **Features:** casual dress; children's menu; carryout; cocktails. Famous for barbecue ribs served in a flavorful tomato-based sauce, the comfortable restaurant also delivers barbecue duck, chicken, sandwiches and seafood. Walls are festooned top to bottom with memorabilia from sports and entertainment legends. **Parking:** on-site and valet (fee). **Cards:** AX, DC, DS, MC, VI.

MT. ADAMS FISH HOUSE **Lunch:** $7-$15 **Dinner:** $8-$25 **Phone:** 513/421-3250 ④
Seafood
Location: 0.5 mi e; at top of Mt. Adams. 940 Pavilion 45202. **Hours:** 11:30 am-2 & 5-10 pm, Sat 5 pm-11 pm, Sun 5 pm-9 pm. Closed major holidays. **Features:** casual dress; cocktails & lounge; a la carte. In the historic Mount Adams neighborhood, the restaurant prepares many selections, including blackened salmon and various sushi offerings. Smoke free premises. **Parking:** on-site. **Cards:** AX, CB, DC, DS, MC, VI.

NICOLA'S RISTORANTE ITALIANO **Lunch:** $9-$12 **Dinner:** $16-$24 **Phone:** 513/721-6200 ①
Italian
Location: 0.5 mi n of US 42 (Central Pkwy). 1420 Sycamore St 45210. **Hours:** 11:30 am-2 & 5:30-10 pm, Fri & Sat-11 pm. Closed major holidays; also Sun. **Reservations:** suggested; Fri & Sat. **Features:** dressy casual; children's menu; cocktails; a la carte. Along the streets and a short distance from downtown sits this Italian eatery. Don't let the unpretentious outside fool you, it is a gem inside with a modern industrial exposed ceiling, vibrant colors and textures, and paintings for sale all over the walls. Common Italian dishes, which unite sauces and spices into tantalizing flavors, reflect some Tuscan and Mediterranean influences. Among the more unusual dishes are preparations of lobster, swordfish and lamb. **Parking:** on-site (fee). **Cards:** AX, DC, DS, MC, VI.

THE PALACE RESTAURANT **Lunch:** $15-$24 **Dinner:** $12-$33 **Phone:** 513/381-6006 ⑭
AAA
American
Location: Corner of 6th and Vine sts; entrance on 6th St; in The Cincinnatian Hotel. 601 Vine St 45202. **Hours:** 6:30 am-1:30 & 6-10 pm, Sun 6:30 am-noon & 6-10 pm. Closed: 1/1, 12/25. **Reservations:** required. **Features:** semi-formal attire; cocktails & lounge; a la carte. Waiting for you inside an elegant boutique hotel awaits an adventure of a tapestry of aromas, flavors and eye dazzling treats starting with appetizers and ending with a finale of sweet tantalizing desserts with matching domestic choices of wines and some imports. Relax, the staff is there for your pleasure and while awaiting the next course you will have a choice of reading material to your interludes of dining extravaganza with the skilled team of wait staff at your beck and call. Smoke free premises. **Parking:** on-site and valet (fee). **Cards:** AX, CB, DC, DS, JC, MC, VI.

THE PALM COURT RESTAURANT **Lunch:** $7-$11 **Dinner:** $10-$30 **Phone:** 513/564-6465 ⑲
AAA
American
Location: 5th and Race sts; entrance on Race St; in Omni Netherland Plaza. 35 W 5th St 45202. **Hours:** 6:30-10:30 am, 11:30-1:30 & 5-9:30 pm. **Reservations:** suggested. **Features:** dressy casual; Sunday brunch; cocktails & lounge; entertainment; a la carte. Exceptionally elegant, the dining room is appointed with lavish furnishings and French art deco touches. Flavorful sauces enhance thoughtful menu preparations. The irresistible dessert cart beckons with such enticements as macadamia-crusted key lime pie. Smoke free premises. **Parking:** Fee: on-site and valet. **Cards:** AX, DC, DS, JC, MC, VI.

REDFISH **Lunch:** $6-$8 **Dinner:** $12-$17 **Phone:** 513/929-4700 ⑩
Cajun
Location: I-71, exit 1, just e on W 5th St, then just n on US 22. 700 Race St 45202. **Hours:** 11 am-10 pm, Fri-11 pm, Sat noon-11 pm, Sun 4 pm-9 pm. Closed: 11/28, 12/25. **Reservations:** suggested. **Features:** casual dress; cocktails. The menu has a New Orleans influence, and the staff is known for warm, professional service. Try the fried seafood and barbecue. **Parking:** Fee: on-site and valet. **Cards:** AX, DC, DS, MC, VI.

THE ROOKWOOD POTTERY RESTAURANT **Lunch:** $6-$17 **Dinner:** $6-$17 **Phone:** 513/721-5456 ⑥
American
Location: 0.5 mi e; at top of Mt Adams. 1077 Celestial St 45202. **Hours:** 11:30 am-9:30 pm, Fri & Sat-11:30 pm. Closed: 5/27, 11/28, 12/25. **Features:** casual dress; children's menu; carryout; cocktails; a la carte. In the former Rookwood pottery factory, the restaurant has its dining room inside brick kilns. A wide variety of jumbo hamburgers are at the heart of the menu, but other selections, such as steak, chops and salmon are listed. Microbrewed beers are plentiful. **Parking:** on-site. **Cards:** AX, DC, MC, VI.

(See map p. 556)

SCOTTI'S ITALIAN RESTAURANT
Lunch: $6-$9   **Dinner:** $13-$23   **Phone:** 513/721-9484   ⑦

Italian

Location: Jct Vine and Court sts. 919 Vine St 45202. **Hours:** Open 4/1-7/31 & 9/1-3/31; 11:30 am-1:30 & 5-8:15 pm. Closed: 12/25-12/31; also Sun and Mon. **Reservations:** accepted. **Features:** casual dress; beer & wine only; a la carte. Scotti's has been serving traditional, Italian cuisine since 1912. The restaurant takes its name from famed Italian singer, Antonio Scotti. **Parking:** on-site. **Cards:** MC, VI.

CINCINNATI pop. 364,000   (See map p. 558; index p. 560)

——— WHERE TO STAY ———

BEST WESTERN MARIEMONT INN
AAA **SAVE**

Historic Motor Inn

Phone: (513)271-2100   🛇 F17
All Year   1P: $69-$79   2P: $76-$86   XP: $7
Location: I-71, exit 9, 2 mi s on Red Bank Rd, then 1.5 mi e on US 50 E. 6880 Wooster Pike 45227. Fax: 513/271-1057. **Facility:** 60 one-bedroom standard units. 3 stories, interior corridors. *Bath:* combo, shower or tub only. **Parking:** on-site. **Amenities:** voice mail, irons, hair dryers. **Dining:** dining room, 7 am-10 pm, Fri & Sat-10:30 pm, Sun-9 pm, $12-$20, cocktails. **Guest Services:** valet and coin laundry. **Business Services:** meeting rooms. **Cards:** AX, CB, DC, DS, JC, MC, VI. **Special Amenities:** free local telephone calls and free newspaper. *(See ad below)*

SOME UNITS
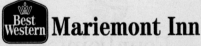

COMFORT INN & SUITES
SAVE

Motel

Phone: (513)947-0100   🛇 F18
All Year [ECP]   1P: $60   2P: $90   XP: $5
Location: I-275, exit 63B, just e. 4421 Aicholtz Rd 45245. Fax: 513/943-2991. **Facility:** 72 one-bedroom standard units. 3 stories, interior corridors. *Bath:* combo or shower only. **Parking:** on-site. **Amenities:** extended cable TV, voice mail, irons, hair dryers. **Pool(s):** heated indoor. **Guest Services:** coin laundry. **Business Services:** meeting rooms. **Cards:** AX, CB, DC, DS, JC, MC, VI.

SOME UNITS

FOUR POINTS BY SHERATON NORTH EAST
AAA **SAVE**

Motor Inn

Phone: (513)793-4300   🛇 F18
All Year   1P: $65   2P: $65   XP: $10
Location: I-71, exit 12, just se on US 22. 8020 Montgomery Rd 45236. Fax: 513/793-1413. **Facility:** 152 one-bedroom standard units. 2 stories, interior corridors. *Bath:* combo or shower only. **Parking:** on-site. **Terms:** [AP] meal plan available, package plans. **Amenities:** video games, dual phone lines, voice mail, irons, hair dryers. **Dining:** restaurant, 6:30 am-9:30 & 4-10 pm, Sat 7 am-10:30 & 5-10 pm, Sun 7 am-3 & 5-10 pm, $8-$17, cocktails. **Pool(s):** outdoor, heated indoor. **Leisure Activities:** sauna, whirlpool, 2 lighted tennis courts, exercise room, volleyball. **Guest Services:** valet laundry, area transportation-within 5 mi. **Business Services:** conference facilities, business center, PC. **Cards:** AX, CB, DC, DS, MC, VI. **Special Amenities:** early check-in/late check-out and free newspaper. *(See color ad p 570)*

SOME UNITS
FEE   FEE FEE

(See map p. 558)

HANNAFORD SUITES HOTEL   **Phone:** (513)936-0525   **49**

	7/4-7/29 [ECP]	1P: $99-$129	2P: $99-$129	F18
	4/1-7/3 & 7/30-9/3 [ECP]	1P: $89-$119	2P: $89-$119	F18
Motel	9/4-3/31 [ECP]	1P: $79-$109	2P: $79-$109	F18

Location: I-71, exit 12, just w. 5900 E Galbraith Rd 45236. Fax: 513/936-0087. **Facility:** 79 one-bedroom standard units. 4 stories, interior corridors. *Bath:* combo or shower only. **Parking:** on-site. **Terms:** cancellation fee imposed, small pets only. **Amenities:** extended cable TV, high-speed Internet, voice mail, irons, hair dryers. **Pool(s):** outdoor. **Leisure Activities:** exercise room. **Guest Services:** coin laundry. **Business Services:** meeting rooms, business center. **Cards:** AX, CB, DC, DS, JC, MC, VI. *(See color ad p 580)*

SOME UNITS

(See map p. 558)

MARRIOTT KINGSGATE CONFERENCE CENTER
Phone: (513)487-3800   53

(AAA) [SAVE]
▼▼▼▼
Motor Inn

All Year   1P: $89-$149   2P: $89-$149
Location: I-75, exit 3, 1.3 mi e on Martin Luther King to Eden St, then just n at University of Cincinnati; I-71, exit 3 (Taft Rd), 0.6 mi w, 0.4 mi n on N Vine St. 151 Goodman Dr 45219. Fax: 513/487-3810. **Facility:** 206 one-bedroom standard units. 8 stories, interior corridors. *Bath:* combo or shower only. **Parking:** *Fee:* on-site and valet. **Terms:** cancellation fee imposed, package plans. **Amenities:** high-speed Internet, voice mail, irons, hair dryers. **Dining:** restaurant, 6:30 am-2:30 & 5-10 pm, $9-$19, cocktails. **Leisure Activities:** exercise room, sundries shop. **Guest Services:** valet and coin laundry. **Business Services:** conference facilities, business center, PC, fax.
Cards: AX, CB, DC, DS, JC, MC, VI. *(See color ad card insert)*

SOME UNITS
[icons] FEE / FEE

THE PARKER HOUSE
Phone: 513/579-8236   54

▼▼▼
Historic Bed & Breakfast

All Year [BP]   1P: $75-$95   2P: $95-$115   XP: $20
Location: 2 mi n on Vine, just w on Calhoun to Ohio Ave, then just s. 2323 Ohio Ave 45219. **Facility:** Unusual mural ceilings and reproduction wall coverings distinguish this restored 1870s residence, which is decorated with antique furnishings. Designated smoking area. 3 one-bedroom standard units. 3 stories (no elevator), interior corridors. *Bath:* some shared or private. **Parking:** on-site. **Terms:** 3 day cancellation notice-fee imposed.
Amenities: extended cable TV. **Business Services:** meeting rooms. **Cards:** MC, VI.

[icons]

TOWNEPLACE SUITES BY MARRIOTT
Phone: (513)774-0610   57

(AAA) [SAVE]
▼▼▼
Motel

7/5-8/30   1P: $80   2P: $80
5/2-7/4   1P: $71   2P: $71
4/1-5/1 & 8/31-3/31   1P: $58   2P: $58
Location: I-71, exit 19, just e. 9369 Waterstone Blvd 45249. Fax: 513/774-0710. **Facility:** 95 units. 73 one- and 22 two-bedroom standard units with kitchens. 3 stories, interior corridors. *Bath:* combo or shower only. **Parking:** on-site. **Terms:** 7 day cancellation notice-fee imposed. **Amenities:** extended cable TV, video games, voice mail, irons, hair dryers. **Pool(s):** outdoor. **Leisure Activities:** exercise room. **Guest Services:** coin laundry. **Business Services:** business center. **Cards:** AX, CB, DC, DS, JC, MC, VI. **Special Amenities:** free local telephone calls.
(See color ad card insert)

SOME UNITS
[icons] /

VERNON MANOR HOTEL
Phone: (513)281-3300   55

(AAA) [SAVE]
▼▼▼
Historic Hotel

All Year   1P: $89-$160   2P: $185   XP: $15   F18
Location: I-71, exit 2 (Reading Rd), 1 mi n; exit 3 (Taft Rd), w on Reading, then n. 400 Oak St 45219. Fax: 513/281-8933. **Facility:** 177 units. 166 one- and 11 two-bedroom standard units. 7 stories, interior corridors. *Bath:* combo or shower only. **Parking:** on-site and valet. **Terms:** package plans. **Amenities:** extended cable TV, video games, Web TV, voice mail, irons, hair dryers. **Dining:** dining room, 6:30 am-10 pm, Sat from 7 am, Sun from 8 am, $14-$21, cocktails. **Leisure Activities:** exercise room. **Guest Services:** coin laundry, area transportation-within 5 mi. **Business Services:** conference facilities, business center, PC, fax. **Cards:** AX, CB, DC, DS, JC, MC, VI. **Special Amenities:** free newspaper.

SOME UNITS
[icons] FEE / FEE / FEE

THE VICTORIA INN OF HYDE PARK
Phone: 513/321-3567   50

▼▼▼
Historic Bed & Breakfast

All Year [ECP]   1P: $99-$189   2P: $99-$189
Location: Just e of Hyde Park Square. 3567 Shaw Ave 45208. Fax: 513/533-2944. **Facility:** Feather beds and private phone lines complement antique appointments in this service-oriented 1909 home. Smoke free premises. 4 one-bedroom standard units, some with whirlpools. 3 stories (no elevator), interior corridors. *Bath:* combo or shower only. **Parking:** on-site. **Terms:** age restrictions may apply. **Amenities:** extended cable TV.
Some: CD players. **Pool(s):** outdoor. **Cards:** AX, MC, VI.

SOME UNITS
[icons] / [VCR]

--------- WHERE TO DINE ---------

CHATEAU POMIJE
Lunch: $7-$9   **Dinner:** $10-$22   **Phone:** 513/871-8788   45

▼▼▼
Provincial American

Location: I-71, exit 5, 0.5 mi e on Dana Ave, 0.5 mi s. 2019 Madison Rd 45208. **Hours:** 11 am-2:30 & 5:30-9:30 pm, Fri & Sat-10:30 pm. Closed major holidays; also Sun. **Features:** casual dress; carryout; beer & wine only. Guests can take a seat in the cozy dining room or on the outdoor deck and order from a menu of pasta, chicken, salad and sandwiches. Contributing to the intimate atmosphere are wood appointments and local artwork. Specials include chateau chicken, cioppino, Arctic char, duck and New York strip. Smoke free premises. **Parking:** on-site. **Cards:** DS, MC, VI.

[icon]

HERITAGE RESTAURANT, STEIN & VINE PUB   Historical   **Dinner:** $17-$24   **Phone:** 513/561-9300   48

▼▼▼
American

Location: 1 mi e on US 50 from downtown Mariemont. 7664 Wooster Pike 45227. **Hours:** 5 pm-9:30 pm, Fri & Sat-10 pm, Sun 10:30 am-2 & 5-9 pm. Closed major holidays; also 12/24. **Reservations:** accepted. **Features:** dressy casual; Sunday brunch; children's menu; cocktails. This eatery is located in the historic village of Mariemont in an 1827 farmhouse. Food is influenced by their Cajun and southwestern cuisine and flavored by their extensive on-site herb garden. Diners have the option of dining in the colonial formal dining room, the pub, or outside under umbrella tables. Special requests don't upset the attentive staff that is willing to accommodate your dining needs. Desserts are made from scratch. **Parking:** on-site. **Cards:** AX, DC, DS, MC, VI.

[icon]

J'S FRESH SEAFOOD RESTAURANT
Lunch: $8-$15   **Dinner:** $14-$25   **Phone:** 513/871-2888   44

▼▼▼
Seafood

Location: I-71, exit 5, 0.5 mi e on Duck Creek to Dana, just se; I-75, exit 5, 0.3 mi se. 2444 Madison Rd 45208. **Hours:** 11:30 am-2 & 5:30-10 pm, Fri-11 pm, Sat 5 pm-11 pm, Sun 5 pm-9 pm. Closed major holidays; also Mon. **Reservations:** suggested; except Sat. **Features:** casual dress; children's menu; carryout; cocktails & lounge; a la carte. The market-fresh fish is first rate, and the pasta preparations, such as fusilli with mascarpone, chicken sausage and shrimp, are flavorful at the busy restaurant. A logically presented wine list shows many selections available by the glass. **Parking:** on-site and valet. **Cards:** AX, CB, DC, DS, MC, VI.

[icon]

(See map p. 558)

MICHAEL G'S RESTAURANT & BANQUET FACILITY   Lunch: $4-$9   Dinner: $14-$30   Phone: 513/533-3131   (49)
⬥⬥ ⬥⬥   **Location:** I-275, exit 72, 2.5 mi w. 4601 Kellogg Ave 45226. **Hours:** 11 am-2 & 5-9 pm, Fri-11 pm, Sat 5 pm-11
Seafood   pm, Sun 10:30 am-2 & 5-9 pm. Closed major holidays. **Reservations:** suggested. **Features:** dressy
casual; Sunday brunch; children's menu; early bird specials; carryout; cocktails & lounge. Fish is the
mainstay of the menu here: 12 types of fish are flown in daily, cooked well and served simply, unsauced
and unadorned. Also of note are chicken fettuccine Alfredo, rack of lamb and steak. A jazz trio performs on weekend evenings.
Parking: on-site. **Cards:** AX, MC, VI.
☒

MONTGOMERY INN   Lunch: $5-$9   Dinner: $12-$23   Phone: 513/791-3482   (42)
⬥⬥ ⬥⬥   **Location:** I-71, exit 12, 2 mi n on US 22 and SR 3; downtown Montgomery. 9440 Montgomery Rd 45242. **Hours:** 11
American   am-11 pm, Fri-midnight, Sat 3 pm-midnight, Sun 3 pm-9:30 pm. Closed major holidays. **Reservations:** suggested; except Sat. **Features:** casual dress; children's menu; carryout; cocktails &
lounge. Famous for barbecue ribs served in a flavorful tomato-based sauce, the comfortable restaurant
also delivers barbecue duck, chicken, sandwiches and seafood. Walls are festooned from top to bottom with memorabilia from
sports and entertainment legends, especially Bob Hope and Pete Rose. One of the city's most popular eateries, this place is
usually crowded. **Parking:** on-site and valet (fee). **Cards:** AX, DC, DS, MC, VI.
☒

PRIMAVISTA   Dinner: $15-$28   Phone: 513/251-6467   (46)
⬥⬥⬥⬥   **Location:** Queen's Tower, Price Ave; in Price Hill. 810 Matson Pl 45204. **Hours:** 5:30 pm-9:30 pm, Fri-10 pm, Sat
5 pm-11 pm, Sun 5 pm-9 pm. Closed major holidays; also 12/24. **Reservations:** accepted.
Italian   **Features:** dressy casual; carryout; cocktails & lounge. Diners enjoy Northern Italian entrees with an
emphasis on fresh fish and veal dishes while surrounded by a spectacular view of the river and city. Amid
a simple but elegant setting, the knowledgeable staff serves visitors promptly and with a smile. **Parking:** on-site. **Cards:** AX,
DC, DS, MC, VI.
☒

TRIO   Lunch: $8-$12   Dinner: $12-$25   Phone: 513/984-1905   (43)
⬥⬥ ⬥⬥   **Location:** I-71, exit 12, 0.3 mi w on Montgomery, just n. 7565 Kenwood Rd 45236. **Hours:** 11 am-10 pm, Fri &
American   Sat-11 pm. Closed: 7/4, 11/28, 12/25. **Reservations:** accepted. **Features:** dressy casual; carryout;
cocktails. There's something for everyone on the varied menu of pizza, pasta dishes, wood-grilled chicken
and seafood. House specials run the gamut of Moroccan chicken, grilled Norwegian salmon and banana
cream pie. An extensive wine list is available. **Parking:** on-site. **Cards:** AX, CB, DC, DS, MC, VI.
♿M ☒

The Cincinnati Vicinity

BATAVIA pop. 1,700

──── **WHERE TO STAY** ────

HAMPTON INN-CINCINNATI EASTGATE   Phone: (513)752-8584
[SAVE]   7/1-8/31 [ECP]   1P: $79-$109   2P: $79-$109
4/1-6/30 [ECP]   1P: $71-$99   2P: $71-$99
⬥⬥ ⬥⬥   9/1-10/31 [ECP]   1P: $75-$91   2P: $75-$91
11/1-3/31 [ECP]   1P: $73-$91   2P: $73-$91
Motel   **Location:** I-275, exit 63B (SR 32). 858 Eastgate North Dr 45245. Fax: 513/752-8488. **Facility:** Designated smoking
area. 120 one-bedroom standard units. 4 stories, interior corridors. **Parking:** on-site. **Terms:** small pets only.
Amenities: voice mail, irons. **Pool(s):** outdoor. **Leisure Activities:** exercise room. **Guest Services:** valet laundry. **Business
Services:** meeting rooms. **Cards:** AX, CB, DC, DS, MC, VI. *(See color ad below)*   SOME UNITS
[amenity icons] DATA PORT / ☒ VCR /
FEE

HOLIDAY INN-CINCINNATI EASTGATE

AAA SAVE

Motor Inn

All Year   1P: $79-$119   2P: $79-$119

Phone: (513)752-4400
XP: $12   F18

Location: I-275, exit 63B (SR 32) to Eastgate Mall exit. 4501 Eastgate Blvd 45245. Fax: 513/753-3178. **Facility:** 247 one-bedroom standard units. 6 stories, interior corridors. **Parking:** on-site. **Terms:** [BP] meal plan available, package plans. **Amenities:** dual phone lines, voice mail, irons, hair dryers. **Dining:** dining room, 6:30 am-2 & 5-11 pm, Sun-10 pm, $12-$20, cocktails. **Pool(s):** heated indoor. **Leisure Activities:** whirlpool, exercise room. **Guest Services:** gift shop, valet laundry. **Business Services:** conference facilities, business center, fax. **Cards:** AX, CB, DC, DS, JC, MC, VI.

SOME UNITS

BLUE ASH pop. 11,900   (See map p. 558; index p. 562)

—— WHERE TO STAY ——

AMERISUITES (CINCINNATI/BLUE ASH)

AAA SAVE

Motor

6/1-8/20   1P: $99-$119   2P: $99-$119   XP: $10   F18
4/1-5/31   1P: $79-$119   2P: $79-$119   XP: $10   F18
8/21-3/31   1P: $79-$99   2P: $79-$99   XP: $10   F18

Phone: (513)489-3666   185

Location: I-275, exit 47, 0.8 mi s. 11435 Reed-Hartman Hwy 45241. Fax: 513/489-4187. **Facility:** 127 one-bedroom standard units. 6 stories, interior corridors. **Parking:** on-site. **Terms:** [ECP] meal plan available, package plans. **Amenities:** high-speed Internet, voice mail, irons, hair dryers. *Some:* dual phone lines. **Pool(s):** heated outdoor. **Leisure Activities:** exercise room. **Guest Services:** valet and coin laundry, airport transportation-local, area transportation-within 5 mi. **Business Services:** meeting rooms, business center, PC. **Cards:** AX, CB, DC, DS, JC, MC, VI. **Special Amenities:** free continental breakfast and free newspaper. *(See color ad p 565)*

SOME UNITS

CLARION HOTEL AND SUITES CINCINNATI

AAA SAVE

Motor Inn

6/1-8/24   1P: $89-$149   2P: $89-$149   XP: $10   F18
8/25-3/31   1P: $69-$119   2P: $69-$119   XP: $10   F18
4/1-5/31   1P: $69-$119   2P: $69-$119   XP: $10   F18

Phone: (513)793-4500   197

Location: I-71, exit 15, just w. 5901 Pfieffer Rd 45242. Fax: 513/793-6355. **Facility:** 177 units. 127 one-bedroom standard units. 5 one- and 45 two-bedroom suites. 2-6 stories, interior corridors. *Bath:* combo or shower only. **Parking:** on-site. **Terms:** cancellation fee imposed, package plans, small pets only. **Amenities:** video games, voice mail, hair dryers. *Some:* irons. **Dining:** restaurant, 7 am-2 & 5-10 pm; Sunday brunch, $8-$17, cocktails. **Pool(s):** heated indoor. **Leisure Activities:** exercise room. *Fee:* game room. **Guest Services:** valet laundry, area transportation-within 5 mi. **Business Services:** conference facilities, business center. **Cards:** AX, CB, DC, DS, JC, MC, VI.

SOME UNITS

COMFORT SUITES

AAA SAVE

Motor Inn

5/1-9/5   1P: $85   2P: $85   XP: $6   F17
4/1-4/30 & 9/6-3/31   1P: $74   2P: $77   XP: $6   F17

Phone: (513)530-5999   186

Location: I-275, exit 47, 1 mi s. 11349 Reed Hartman Hwy 45241. Fax: 513/530-0179. **Facility:** 50 one-bedroom standard units. 3 stories, interior corridors. **Parking:** on-site. **Terms:** cancellation fee imposed, [ECP] meal plan available, package plans. **Amenities:** extended cable TV, voice mail, irons, hair dryers. **Dining:** restaurant, 11 am-10 pm, Sat & Sun from 4 pm, $10-$20. **Pool(s):** outdoor. **Leisure Activities:** steamroom, exercise room. **Guest Services:** valet laundry. **Business Services:** meeting rooms. **Cards:** AX, CB, DC, DS, MC, VI. **Special Amenities:** free continental breakfast and free local telephone calls.

SOME UNITS

COURTYARD BY MARRIOTT-BLUE ASH

AAA SAVE

Motor

All Year   1P: $74-$99   2P: $84-$109

Phone: (513)733-4334   194

Location: I-275, exit 47, 2.4 mi s; I-71, exit 15, 1 mi w on Pfeiffer Rd. 4625 Lake Forest Dr 45242. Fax: 513/733-5711. **Facility:** 149 units. 138 one-bedroom standard units. 11 one-bedroom suites ($109-$139). 2-3 stories, interior corridors. *Bath:* combo or shower only. **Parking:** on-site. **Amenities:** dual phone lines, voice mail, irons, hair dryers. **Pool(s):** heated indoor. **Leisure Activities:** whirlpool, exercise room. **Guest Services:** valet and coin laundry. **Business Services:** meeting rooms. **Cards:** AX, DC, DS, MC, VI. *(See color ad card insert)*

SOME UNITS

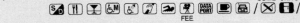

(See map p. 558)

EMBASSY SUITES HOTEL-CINCINNATI NORTHEAST   Phone: (513)733-8900 [195]

[SAVE]

Motor Inn

All Year   1P: $109-$199   2P: $109-$199
Location: I-275, exit 47, 2.5 mi s; I-71, exit 15, 1 mi w on Pfeiffer Rd. 4554 Lake Forest Dr 45242. Fax: 513/733-3720. **Facility:** 235 one-bedroom suites. 5 stories, interior corridors. *Bath:* combo or shower only. **Parking:** on-site. **Amenities:** extended cable TV, video games, high-speed Internet, dual phone lines, voice mail, irons, hair dryers. **Pool(s):** heated indoor. **Leisure Activities:** sauna, whirlpool, exercise room. **Guest Services:** gift shop, complimentary evening beverages, valet and coin laundry. **Business Services:** conference facilities, PC, fax. **Cards:** AX, CB, DC, DS, MC, VI.

SOME UNITS

[icons] SD ¶ ☂ 🎿 📶 ⊠ 🎥 DATA/PORT ♨ 📺 💻 🖨 / ⊠ /
                                   FEE

EXTENDED STAY AMERICA-BLUE ASH   Phone: 513/793-6750 [196]

Extended Stay
Motel

Property failed to provide current rates
Location: I-71, exit 15, 0.8 mi w on Pfeiffer Rd, 2 mi s on Reed-Hartman Hwy, just e. 4260 Hunt Rd 45242. Fax: 513/792-6037. **Facility:** 72 one-bedroom standard units with kitchens. 3 stories (no elevator), interior corridors. **Parking:** on-site. **Amenities:** extended cable TV, voice mail. *Some:* irons. **Pool(s):** outdoor. **Guest Services:** valet and coin laundry. **Business Services:** fax. **Cards:** AX, CB, DC, DS, MC, VI.

SOME UNITS

[icons] ¶✦ 📶 🎥 DATA/PORT ♨ 📺 💻 🖨 / ⊠ /

HAMPTON INN   Phone: (513)791-2822 [190]

[AAA] [SAVE]

Motel

All Year [CP]   1P: $79-$99   2P: $79-$99
Location: I-275, exit 47, 2.3 mi s, just e, behind MainStay Suites. 4640 Creek Rd 45242. Fax: 513/791-2842. **Facility:** 82 one-bedroom standard units. 3 stories, interior corridors. *Bath:* combo or shower only. **Parking:** on-site. **Terms:** 7 day cancellation notice. **Amenities:** extended cable TV, voice mail, irons. **Pool(s):** heated indoor. **Leisure Activities:** whirlpool. **Guest Services:** valet laundry. **Cards:** AX, CB, DC, DS, MC, VI.

SOME UNITS

[icons] SD 🔥M 📶 🎿 📶 🎥 DATA/PORT 💻 🖨 / ⊠ ♨ 📺 /
                                   FEE

HOLIDAY INN EXPRESS HOTEL & SUITES   Phone: (513)985-9035 [189]

Motel

All Year   1P: $79-$99   2P: $79-$109   XP: $7   F18
Location: I-275, exit 47, 2.3 mi s on Reed-Hartman Hwy, just e. 4660 Creek Rd 45242. Fax: 513/985-9034. **Facility:** 69 one-bedroom standard units, some with whirlpools. 3 stories, interior corridors. *Bath:* combo or shower only. **Parking:** on-site. **Terms:** [ECP] meal plan available. **Amenities:** extended cable TV, high-speed Internet, voice mail, irons, hair dryers. **Pool(s):** heated indoor. **Leisure Activities:** exercise room. **Guest Services:** coin laundry. **Business Services:** meeting rooms. **Cards:** AX, CB, DC, DS, JC, MC, VI.

SOME UNITS

[icons] SD 🎿 📶 🎥 DATA/PORT ♨ 📺 💻 🖨 / ⊠ /

MAINSTAY SUITES-BLUE ASH   Phone: (513)985-9992 [191]

[AAA] [SAVE]

Extended Stay
Motel

All Year [ECP]   1P: $55-$85   2P: $65-$95
Location: I-275, exit 47, 2.3 mi s on Reed-Hartman Hwy, just e. 4630 Creek Rd 45242. Fax: 513/985-0919. **Facility:** 100 units. 68 one-bedroom standard units with kitchens. 32 one-bedroom suites with kitchens. 3 stories, interior corridors. *Bath:* combo or shower only. **Parking:** on-site. **Terms:** pets ($100 deposit, $5 extra charge). **Amenities:** video games, dual phone lines, voice mail, irons, hair dryers. **Pool(s):** heated outdoor. **Leisure Activities:** limited exercise equipment. **Guest Services:** complimentary evening beverages: Mon-Wed, valet and coin laundry. **Business Services:** fax. **Cards:** AX, CB, DC, DS, MC, VI. **Special Amenities:** early check-in/late check-out. *(See color ad p 565)*

SOME UNITS

[icons] SD 🐾 🎿 📶 ⊠ 🎥 DATA/PORT ♨ 📺 💻 🖨 / ⊠ /
                                   FEE

RED ROOF INN NORTHEAST (BLUE ASH)   Phone: (513)793-8811 [193]

[AAA] [SAVE]

Motel

6/4-9/1	1P: $51-$71	2P: $56-$76	XP: $5 F18
9/2-10/20	1P: $46-$56	2P: $51-$61	XP: $5 F18
10/21-3/31	1P: $41-$56	2P: $46-$61	XP: $5 F18
4/1-6/3	1P: $44-$54	2P: $49-$59	XP: $5 F18

Location: I-71, exit 15, just w. 5900 Pfeiffer Rd 45242. Fax: 513/793-8930. **Facility:** 108 one-bedroom standard units. 2 stories, exterior corridors. *Bath:* combo or shower only. **Parking:** on-site. **Terms:** small pets only. **Amenities:** video games, voice mail. **Cards:** AX, CB, DC, DS, MC, VI. **Special Amenities:** free local telephone calls and free newspaper.

SOME UNITS

[icons] 🐾 ¶✦ 🔥M 🎿 📶 🎥 DATA/PORT 🖨 / ⊠ ♨ 📺 /
                              FEE FEE

RESIDENCE INN BY MARRIOTT-BLUE ASH   Phone: (513)530-5060 [187]

[AAA] [SAVE]

Suite Motel

5/29-10/14   1P: $129   2P: $129
4/1-5/28 & 10/15-3/31   1P: $119   2P: $119
Location: I-275, exit 47, 0.8 mi s. 11401 Reed-Hartman Hwy 45241. Fax: 513/530-0133. **Facility:** 118 units. 90 one-bedroom standard units. 28 two-bedroom suites. 2 stories, exterior corridors. *Bath:* combo or shower only. **Parking:** on-site. **Terms:** pets ($75-$95 extra charge). **Amenities:** voice mail, irons, hair dryers. *Some:* dual phone lines. **Pool(s):** heated outdoor. **Leisure Activities:** whirlpool, exercise room, sports court, basketball. **Guest Services:** complimentary evening beverages: Mon-Thurs, valet and coin laundry. **Business Services:** meeting rooms. **Cards:** AX, CB, DC, DS, JC, MC, VI. *(See color ad card insert)*

SOME UNITS

[icons] SD 🐾 🔥M 🎿 📶 ⊠ 🎥 DATA/PORT ♨ 📺 💻 🖨 / ⊠ ♨ VCR /
                                   FEE   FEE

(See map p. 558)

TOWNEPLACE SUITES BY MARRIOTT BLUE ASH   Phone: (513)469-8222   `192`

AAA SAVE   5/2-11/17   1P: $89
▽▽▽▽   4/1-5/1 & 11/18-3/31   1P: $79
Location: I-275, exit 47, 0.9 mi s on Reed-Hartman Hwy, just w. 4650 Cornell Rd 45241. Fax: 513/469-8333.
Motel   **Facility:** 95 units. 73 one- and 22 two-bedroom standard units with kitchens. 3 stories, interior corridors. *Bath:* combo or shower only. **Parking:** on-site. **Amenities:** extended cable TV, voice mail, irons, hair dryers. **Pool(s):** outdoor. **Guest Services:** coin laundry. **Business Services:** meeting rooms. **Cards:** AX, CB, DC, DS, JC, MC, VI. **Special Amenities:** free local telephone calls. *(See color ad card insert)*

SOME UNITS

WINGATE INN-CINCINNATI/BLUE ASH   Phone: (513)733-1142   `188`

▽▽▽▽   6/21-9/3 [ECP]   1P: $99   2P: $109   XP: $10
   9/4-12/31 [ECP]   1P: $79-$89   2P: $89-$99   XP: $10
Motel   4/1-6/20 [ECP]   1P: $89   2P: $99   XP: $10
   1/1-3/31 [ECP]   1P: $89   2P: $89   XP: $10
Location: I-71, exit 15, 1.2 mi w; I-75, exit 14, 3 mi e. 4320 Glendale-Milford Rd 45242. Fax: 513/733-1146. **Facility:** 85 one-bedroom standard units. 4 stories, interior corridors. *Bath:* combo or shower only. **Amenities:** extended cable TV, video games, high-speed Internet, voice mail, safes, irons, hair dryers. **Pool(s):** indoor. **Leisure Activities:** sauna, whirlpool, exercise room. **Guest Services:** coin laundry. **Business Services:** meeting rooms, business center. **Cards:** AX, CB, DC, DS, JC, MC, VI.

SOME UNITS

CHERRY GROVE pop. 5,000   (See map p. 558; index p. 563)

─────── WHERE TO STAY ───────

RED ROOF INN CINCINNATI EAST   Phone: (513)528-2741   `269`

AAA SAVE   6/2-8/31   1P: $49-$74   2P: $54-$79   XP: $5   F18
   9/1-11/2   1P: $44-$56   2P: $49-$63   XP: $5   F18
▽▽   4/1-6/1   1P: $44-$56   2P: $49-$61   XP: $5   F18
Motel   11/3-3/31   1P: $39-$51   2P: $44-$53   XP: $5   F18
Location: I-275, exit 65. 4035 Mt Carmel-Tobasco Rd 45255. Fax: 513/528-2965. **Facility:** 108 one-bedroom standard units. 2 stories, exterior corridors. *Bath:* combo or shower only. **Parking:** on-site. **Amenities:** video games, voice mail. **Guest Services:** coin laundry. **Business Services:** fax (fee). **Cards:** AX, CB, DC, DS, MC, VI. **Special Amenities:** free local telephone calls and free newspaper.

SOME UNITS
FEE

EVENDALE pop. 3,200   (See map p. 558; index p. 564)

─────── WHERE TO DINE ───────

EVENDALE BUFFET   **Lunch:** $5   **Dinner:** $8   Phone: 513/733-9595   `179`
▽▽   **Location:** I-275, exit 46, 2.2 mi s on US 42. 10784 Reading Rd 45241. **Hours:** 11:15 am-2:30 & 5-8 pm, Fri-9 pm, Sat 4 pm-9 pm, Sun 11:15 am-8 pm. Closed major holidays; also for lunch 5/31 & Mon.
American   **Features:** casual dress; salad bar; cocktails & lounge; buffet. Separate buffet lines for salad, entrees and dessert offer an extensive selection of items and fresh ingredients to please every taste preference. Tender hand-carved roast beef and peach cobbler with vanilla ice cream are the house specialties. **Parking:** on-site. **Cards:** CB, DC, DS, MC, VI.

FOREST PARK pop. 18,600   (See map p. 558; index p. 561)

─────── WHERE TO STAY ───────

LEES INN & SUITES CINCINNATI   Phone: (513)825-9600   `123`
▽▽▽▽   All Year [ECP]   1P: $89-$119   2P: $99-$129   XP: $10   F18
Location: I-275, exit 39, just s on Winton Rd. 11967 Chase Plaza Dr 45240. Fax: 513/825-8369. **Facility:** 81 units. 76 one-bedroom standard units, some with whirlpools. 5 one-bedroom suites ($139-$299). 3 stories, interior
Motel   corridors. *Bath:* some combo or shower only. **Parking:** on-site. **Terms:** 7 day cancellation notice, small pets only (1st floor units). **Amenities:** video games, voice mail, irons, hair dryers. **Pool(s):** heated outdoor. **Leisure Activities:** whirlpool, limited exercise equipment. **Guest Services:** valet laundry. **Business Services:** meeting rooms, fax (fee). **Cards:** AX, DC, DS, MC, VI.

SOME UNITS
FEE

GLENDALE pop. 2,400   (See map p. 558; index p. 564)

─────── WHERE TO DINE ───────

THE IRON HORSE INN   **Lunch:** $8-$10   **Dinner:** $15-$23   Phone: 513/771-4787   `165`
▽▽▽▽   **Location:** I-75, exit 15, 1 mi w. 40 Village Sq 45246. **Hours:** 11 am-10 pm. Closed major holidays.
   Reservations: suggested; weekends. **Features:** casual dress; Sunday brunch; early bird specials;
American   cocktails & lounge; a la carte. Highlighted on the menu are boldly flavored contemporary dishes, a house specialty of sea bass and delicious bread pudding, one of a selection of made-from-scratch desserts. The menu includes some vegetarian choices and a few pasta selections. Depending on the timing and seating, dining experiences can be casual or formal. The seasonal patio is a favorite place to unwind. Smoke free premises. **Parking:** on-site. **Cards:** AX, DC, DS, MC, VI.

GRANDVIEW

——— WHERE TO DINE ———

——— *The following restaurant has not been evaluated by AAA* ———
but is listed for your information only.

BRADDOCK'S GRANDVIEW   Phone: 614/487-0077
[fyi] Not evaluated. **Location:** Corner of Grandview and Ida aves. 1470 Grandview Ave 43212. Southern Low Country food, grits and fried shrimp are served here.

HARRISON pop. 7,500 (See map p. 558; index p. 564)

——— WHERE TO STAY ———

QUALITY INN   Phone: (513)367-5200   **340**
[SAVE] All Year   1P: $70   2P: $75   XP: $5   F18
Location: I-74, exit 1, just s. 10900 New Haven Rd 45030 (PO Box 208). Fax: 513/367-5801. **Facility:** 108 one-
Motor Inn bedroom standard units. 2 stories, interior corridors. **Parking:** on-site. **Terms:** 3 day cancellation notice. [CP]
meal plan available. **Amenities:** irons, hair dryers. **Pool(s):** outdoor. **Guest Services:** valet and coin laundry.
Business Services: meeting rooms, fax (fee). **Cards:** AX, CB, DC, DS, JC, MC, VI.

SOME UNITS

KINGS MILLS pop. 700 (See map p. 558; index p. 561)

——— WHERE TO STAY ———

KINGS MANOR INN BED & BREAKFAST   Phone: (513)459-9959   **110**
All Year [BP]   1P: $70-$80   2P: $80-$90   XP: $10
Location: I-71, exit 25A southbound; exit 25 northbound, 1 mi e on Kings Mills Rd, then just w. 1826 Church St 45034
Bed & Breakfast (PO Box 312). Fax: 513/984-2077. **Facility:** Built by town founders, this century-old frame house has a front
porch, attractive grounds, vintage furnishings and a portrait of the King family. Designated smoking area. 4
one-bedroom standard units, some with whirlpools. 3 stories, interior corridors. *Bath:* combo or shower only. **Parking:** on-site.
Terms: 7 day cancellation notice. **Amenities:** extended cable TV. **Guest Services:** complimentary evening beverages. **Business Services:** meeting rooms. **Cards:** AX, DS, MC, VI.

SOME UNITS

LEBANON pop. 10,500

——— WHERE TO STAY ———

BUDGET INN   Phone: (513)932-1966
[AAA] [SAVE] 4/1-9/30   1P: $50-$55   2P: $55-$62   XP: $10   F
10/1-3/31   1P: $38-$45   2P: $42   XP: $10   F
Motel **Location:** Center; on US 42. 115 N Broadway 45036. Fax: 513/932-1966. **Facility:** 16 one-bedroom standard
units. 1-2 stories, interior/exterior corridors. *Bath:* combo or shower only. **Parking:** on-site. **Terms:** 3 day cancellation notice. **Amenities:** hair dryers. **Cards:** AX, DS, MC, VI.

SOME UNITS

THE GOLDEN LAMB INN   Phone: (513)932-5065
All Year   1P: $77-$87   2P: $88-$115   XP: $10   F10
Location: Jct SR 63 and 123, on US 42. 27 S Broadway 45036 (PO Box 28). Fax: 513/934-3049. **Facility:** 18 one-
Historic Country bedroom standard units. 4 stories (no elevator), interior corridors. *Bath:* combo or shower only. **Parking:** on-
Inn site. **Terms:** 3 day cancellation notice-fee imposed, package plans. **Dining:** dining room, see separate listing.
Guest Services: gift shop. **Business Services:** meeting rooms, fax (fee). **Cards:** AX, DC, DS, MC, VI.

SOME UNITS

SHAKER INN   Phone: 513/932-7575
[AAA] [SAVE] 5/24-9/3   1P: $54-$56   2P: $62-$64   XP: $10   F12
4/1-5/23 & 9/4-10/31 1P: $43-$45   2P: $49-$51   XP: $10   F12
Motel 11/1-3/31   1P: $38-$40   2P: $43-$45   XP: $10   F12
Location: 1 mi s on US 42. 600 Cincinnati Ave 45036. Fax: 513/934-0666. **Facility:** 21 one-bedroom standard
units, some with efficiencies. 1 story, exterior corridors. *Bath:* combo or shower only. **Parking:** on-site.
Terms: cancellation fee imposed. **Amenities:** extended cable TV. **Pool(s):** outdoor. **Cards:** AX, DS, MC, VI.
Special Amenities: free local telephone calls and preferred room (subject to availability with advanced reservations).

SOME UNITS

FEE

——— WHERE TO DINE ———

THE BEST CAFE   Lunch: $6-$8   Dinner: $9-$16   Phone: 513/932-4400
Location: From Broadway, just e. 17 E Mulberry St 45036. **Hours:** 11 am-3 pm, Wed & Thurs-8:30 pm, Fri &
American Sat-9 pm. Closed major holidays; also Sun. **Reservations:** suggested; except festival. **Features:** casual
dress; children's menu; carryout; cocktails; a la carte. On a quiet side street, the comfortable, two-room
cafe offers a good selection of salads, soups and hot and cold sandwiches. The dinner menu lists some
vegetarian dishes, as well as a smattering of foods from around eastern Europe, including goulash, sauerbraten and schnitzel.
Parking: street. **Cards:** AX, DS, MC, VI.

THE GOLDEN LAMB DINING ROOM Historical **Lunch:** $9-$12 **Dinner:** $11-$20 **Phone:** 513/932-5065
▼▼▼ **Location:** Jct SR 63 and 123, on US 42; in The Golden Lamb Inn. 27 S Broadway 45036. **Hours:** 11 am-3 & 5-9
pm, Sun noon-3 & 4-8 pm. Closed: 12/25. **Features:** dressy casual; children's menu; cocktails & lounge;
American minimum charge-lunch $5, dinner $7. This very popular eatery, founded in 1803 and one the oldest Ohio
inns, serves attractively presented, traditional family-style dinners, including roast leg of lamb, a house
specialty. Of note is the grilled salmon served with green beans and asparagus. **Parking:** on-site. **Cards:** AX, CB, DC, DS,
MC, VI.

LOVELAND pop. 10,000

——— WHERE TO STAY ———

HILTON GARDEN INN CINCINNATI NORTHEAST **Phone:** (513)576-6999
AAA SAVE All Year 1P: $99 2P: $99 XP: $10 F18
▼▼▼▼ **Location:** I-275, exit 54, just w. 6288 Tri-Ridge Blvd 45140. Fax: 513/576-1150. **Facility:** 84 one-bedroom standard
units. 3 stories, interior corridors. *Bath:* combo or shower only. **Parking:** on-site. **Terms:** 10 day cancellation
Motel notice, package plans. **Amenities:** video games, high-speed Internet, dual phone lines, voice mail, irons, hair
dryers. **Dining:** coffee shop, 6:30-10 am. **Pool(s):** small heated indoor. **Leisure Activities:** whirlpool, exercise room. **Guest Services:** valet and coin laundry. **Business Services:** meeting rooms, business center,
PC, fax. **Cards:** AX, CB, DC, DS, JC, MC, VI. **Special Amenities:** free newspaper and preferred room (subject to availability
with advanced reservations). *(See ad below)* SOME UNITS

MADEIRA pop. 9,100 (See map p. 558; index p. 564)

——— WHERE TO DINE ———

FERRARI'S LITTLE ITALY AND BAKERY **Lunch:** $5-$9 **Dinner:** $10-$25 **Phone:** 513/272-2220 (199)
▼▼▼ **Location:** Jct Miami Ave and Goff Terrace. 7677 Goff Terrace 45243. **Hours:** 11:30 am-2:30 & 5-10 pm, Fri-11
pm, Sat 5 pm-11 pm, Sun 4 pm-9 pm. Closed major holidays. **Reservations:** accepted. **Features:** casual
Italian dress; children's menu; early bird specials; carryout; cocktails & lounge; a la carte. Sharing is encouraged
at this casual, family-owned restaurant where hefty portions are served. Good choices are fungi al forno,
Caesar aromatico, pollo parmesan, torta a la sonna and Ferrari's salad (mixed greens, pine nuts, gorgonzola and cranberries).
Parking: on-site. **Cards:** AX, CB, DC, DS, MC, VI.

MASON pop. 11,500 (See map p. 558; index p. 560)

——— WHERE TO STAY ———

AMERISUITES (CINCINNATI/DEERFIELD CROSSING) **Phone:** (513)754-0003 90
AAA SAVE 4/1-9/2 1P: $129
9/3-3/31 1P: $109
▼▼▼▼ **Location:** I-71, exit 19, 0.5 mi w. 5070 Natorp Blvd 45040. Fax: 513/754-0039. **Facility:** 128 one-bedroom stan-
dard units. 6 stories, interior corridors. *Bath:* combo or shower only. **Parking:** on-site. **Terms:** cancellation fee
Motel imposed, [ECP] meal plan available, package plans, small pets only. **Amenities:** video games, high-speed
Internet, voice mail, irons, hair dryers. *Some:* dual phone lines. **Pool(s):** heated indoor. **Leisure Activi-
ties:** exercise room. **Guest Services:** valet and coin laundry. **Business Services:** meeting rooms, business center. **Cards:** AX,
CB, DC, DS, JC, MC, VI. **Special Amenities:** free continental breakfast and free newspaper. *(See color ad p 565)*
SOME UNITS

BAYMONT INN & SUITES CINCINNATI-MASON/NEAR KINGS ISLAND **Phone:** (513)459-1111 92
AAA SAVE All Year 1P: $64-$74 2P: $64-$74
▼▼▼ **Location:** I-71, exit 19, just w, then just s. 9918 Escort Dr 45040. Fax: 513/459-1168. **Facility:** 88 units. 84 one-
bedroom standard units. 4 one-bedroom suites ($74-$109). 4 stories, interior corridors. *Bath:* combo or
shower only. **Parking:** on-site. **Terms:** pets ($50 deposit). **Amenities:** video games, voice mail, irons, hair
Motel dryers. *Some:* Web TV, high-speed Internet. **Pool(s):** heated indoor. **Leisure Activities:** whirlpool. **Guest
Services:** valet and coin laundry. **Business Services:** meeting rooms, fax (fee). **Cards:** AX, CB, DC, DS,
MC, VI. **Special Amenities:** free continental breakfast and free newspaper. *(See color ad opposite title page)*
SOME UNITS

(See map p. 558)

COMFORT INN CINCINNATI NE   Phone: (513)683-9700   94

(AAA) (SAVE)

◇◇◇◇◇◇

Motel

7/2-8/20	1P: $65-$175	2P: $65-$175	XP: $10	F17
8/21-10/31	1P: $50-$120	2P: $50-$120	XP: $10	F17
4/1-7/1	1P: $40-$120	2P: $40-$120	XP: $10	F17
11/1-3/31	1P: $45-$80	2P: $45-$80	XP: $10	F17

Location: I-71, exit 19, just e. 9011 Fields-Ertel Rd 45249. Fax: 513/683-1284. **Facility:** 113 one-bedroom standard units. 3 stories, interior corridors. **Parking:** on-site. **Terms:** 14 day cancellation notice-fee imposed. **Amenities:** safes (fee), hair dryers. *Some:* irons. **Pool(s):** outdoor. **Guest Services:** valet and coin laundry. **Business Services:** meeting rooms, fax (fee). **Cards:** AX, CB, DC, DS, MC, VI. **Special Amenities:** free continental breakfast and free local telephone calls. *(See color ad below)*

SOME UNITS
[icons] FEE

COMFORT SUITES-KINGS ISLAND   Phone: (513)336-9000   86

(AAA) (SAVE)

◇◇◇◇◇◇

Motel

7/1-9/3 [CP]	1P: $75-$200	2P: $75-$200
4/1-6/30 & 9/4-3/31 [CP]	1P: $55-$150	2P: $55-$150

Location: I-71, exit 25, just e. 5457 Kings Center Dr 45040. Fax: 513/336-9007. **Facility:** 78 one-bedroom standard units, some with kitchens and/or whirlpools. 3 stories, interior corridors. *Bath:* combo or shower only. **Parking:** on-site. **Terms:** 14 day cancellation notice-fee imposed. **Amenities:** voice mail, safes (fee), hair dryers. *Some:* irons. **Pool(s):** small heated indoor. **Guest Services:** valet and coin laundry. **Business Services:** meeting rooms, fax (fee). **Cards:** AX, CB, DC, DS, JC, MC, VI. **Special Amenities:** free continental breakfast and free local telephone calls. *(See color ad below)*

SOME UNITS
[icons]

COUNTRY HEARTH INN CINCINNATI NE   Phone: (513)336-7911   91

(AAA) (SAVE)

◇◇◇◇◇◇

Motel

All Year [CP]	1P: $49-$109	2P: $49-$109	XP: $6	F17

Location: I-71, exit 19, 0.4 mi w. 9665 Mason-Montgomery Rd 45040. Fax: 513/336-8873. **Facility:** 92 units. 86 one-bedroom standard units. 6 one-bedroom suites. 3 stories, interior corridors. *Bath:* combo or shower only. **Parking:** on-site. **Amenities:** video games, dual phone lines, voice mail, safes (fee), hair dryers. **Pool(s):** small heated indoor. **Leisure Activities:** whirlpool. **Guest Services:** valet laundry. **Business Services:** meeting rooms, fax (fee). **Cards:** AX, DC, DS, MC, VI. **Special Amenities:** free continental breakfast and free newspaper.

SOME UNITS
[icons] FEE

HAMPTON INN KINGS ISLAND   Phone: (513)459-8900   83

(AAA) (SAVE)

◇◇◇◇◇◇

Motel

5/24-9/2 [ECP]	1P: $99-$179	2P: $99-$179
4/19-5/23 & 9/3-3/31 [ECP]	1P: $59-$149	2P: $59-$149
4/1-4/18 [ECP]	1P: $59-$99	2P: $59-$99

Location: I-71, exit 25, just nw. 5323 Beach Blvd 45040. Fax: 513/459-8850. **Facility:** 90 one-bedroom standard units, some with kitchens. 3 stories, interior corridors. *Bath:* combo or shower only. **Parking:** on-site. **Terms:** 30 day cancellation notice. **Amenities:** extended cable TV, voice mail, irons. *Some:* hair dryers. **Pool(s):** small heated indoor. **Leisure Activities:** exercise room. **Guest Services:** valet and coin laundry. **Business Services:** meeting rooms, fax (fee). **Cards:** AX, CB, DC, DS, MC, VI. **Special Amenities:** free continental breakfast and free local telephone calls.

SOME UNITS
[icons]

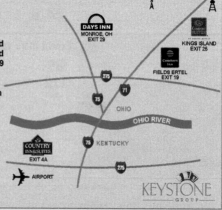

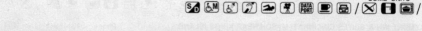

(See map p. 558)

HOLIDAY INN EXPRESS KINGS ISLAND   Phone: (513)398-8075   [85]

(AAA) [SAVE]

6/1-9/8 [ECP]	2P: $99-$275	XP: $8	F17
4/1-5/31 & 9/9-10/31 [ECP]	2P: $59-$225	XP: $8	F17
11/1-3/31 [ECP]	2P: $59-$175	XP: $8	F17

Motel

Location: I-71, exit 25, just w, then just s. 5589 Kings Mills Rd 45034-0425. Fax: 513/459-1043. **Facility:** 194 units. 182 one-bedroom standard units. 12 one-bedroom suites, some with whirlpools. 2 stories, exterior corridors. *Bath:* combo or shower only. **Parking:** on-site. **Terms:** package plans - seasonal, small pets only ($20 deposit). **Amenities:** voice mail, irons, hair dryers. **Pool(s):** heated outdoor. **Leisure Activities:** fishing, playground, exercise room. *Fee:* game room. **Guest Services:** valet and coin laundry, area transportation-Kings Island, Beach Water Park. **Business Services:** conference facilities, fax. **Cards:** AX, CB, DC, DS, MC, VI. **Special Amenities:** free continental breakfast and free local telephone calls. *(See color ad p 566)*

SOME UNITS

[icons]

KINGS ISLAND RESORT & CONFERENCE CENTER   Phone: (513)398-0115   [84]

(AAA) [SAVE]

4/1-9/1	1P: $69-$199	2P: $69-$199	XP: $10	F17
9/2-3/31	1P: $49-$169	2P: $49-$169	XP: $10	F17

Motor Inn

Location: I-71, exit 25, exit 25 northbound; exit 25A southbound, at jct Kings Mills Rd; in King's Island Amusement Center. 5691 Kings Island Dr 45034. Fax: 513/398-1095. **Facility:** 288 one-bedroom standard units. 2 stories, interior/exterior corridors. *Some:* dual phone lines. **Dining:** dining room, 6:30 am-9 pm, Sat & Sun 7:30 am-9:30 pm, $8-$20, cocktails. **Pool(s):** outdoor, heated indoor. **Leisure Activities:** whirlpool, fishing, 2 tennis courts, playground, exercise room, basketball, horseshoes, shuffleboard, volleyball, tetherball. *Fee:* game room. **Guest Services:** valet and coin laundry, area transportation-Kings Island. **Business Services:** business center. **Cards:** AX, CB, DC, DS, MC, VI. **Special Amenities:** free local telephone calls. *(See color ad below)*

SOME UNITS

[icons] FEE

MARRIOTT NORTHEAST   Phone: (513)459-9800   [87]

(AAA) [SAVE]

All Year	1P: $89-$155	2P: $89-$155

Hotel

Location: I-71, exit 19, just w. 9664 Mason-Montgomery Rd 45040. Fax: 513/459-9808. **Facility:** 302 units. 295 one-bedroom standard units. 7 one-bedroom suites ($225) with whirlpools. 6 stories, interior corridors. *Bath:* combo or shower only. **Parking:** on-site. **Terms:** package plans. **Amenities:** dual phone lines, voice mail, irons, hair dryers. **Dining:** River City Grille, see separate listing. **Pool(s):** heated outdoor, heated indoor. **Leisure Activities:** exercise room. **Guest Services:** gift shop, valet laundry. **Business Services:** conference facilities, business center, PC, fax. **Cards:** AX, CB, DC, DS, JC, MC, VI. *(See color ad card insert & below)*

SOME UNITS

[icons] FEE

(See map p. 558)

MICROTEL INN & SUITES
Phone: (513)754-1500 [82]

AAA SAVE
Motel

All Year   1P: $38-$130
Location: I-71, exit 25, just nw. 5324 Beach Blvd 45040. Fax: 513/754-1550. **Facility:** 52 one-bedroom standard units. 2 stories, interior corridors. **Parking:** on-site. **Terms:** [CP] meal plan available. **Amenities:** *Some:* hair dryers. **Guest Services:** valet and coin laundry. **Business Services:** fax. **Cards:** AX, CB, DC, DS, MC, VI.

SOME UNITS

RAMADA INN-KINGS ISLAND
Phone: (513)398-8015 [89]

AAA SAVE
Motor Inn

5/1-9/3   1P: $69-$129
4/1-4/30 & 9/4-3/31   1P: $49-$79
Location: I-71, exit 19, just w. 9845 Escort Dr 45040. Fax: 513/398-0822. **Facility:** 101 one-bedroom standard units. 2 stories, interior corridors. **Parking:** on-site. **Terms:** package plans, pets ($10 fee). **Amenities:** *Some:* irons. **Dining:** restaurant, 11 am-10:30 pm, Fri & Sat-11:30 pm, $7-$10. **Pool(s):** outdoor. **Guest Services:** valet laundry. **Business Services:** meeting rooms, PC, fax. **Cards:** AX, DC, DS, MC, VI. **Special Amenities:** free continental breakfast and free local telephone calls. *(See color ad below)*

SOME UNITS
FEE FEE

RED ROOF INN-KINGS ISLAND
Phone: (513)398-3633 [93]

Motel

5/31-9/3 [CP]   1P: $55-$105   2P: $55-$125
4/1-5/30 [CP]   1P: $35-$65   2P: $35-$75
9/4-3/31 [CP]   1P: $35-$65   2P: $35-$65
Location: I-71, exit 19, just w. 9847 Bards Rd 45040. Fax: 513/398-3633. **Facility:** 124 one-bedroom standard units. 2 stories, exterior corridors. *Bath:* combo or shower only. **Parking:** on-site. **Terms:** 10 day cancellation notice, small pets only ($10 fee). **Amenities:** video games. *Fee:* high-speed Internet, safes. *Some:* irons. **Pool(s):** outdoor. **Guest Services:** valet laundry. **Business Services:** fax. **Cards:** AX, CB, DC, DS, MC, VI.

SOME UNITS
FEE

SIGNATURE INN CINCINNATI NE
Phone: (513)683-3086 [96]

Motel

All Year [CP]   1P: $61-$70   2P: $61-$70
Location: I-71, exit 19, just se. 8870 Governor's Hill Dr 45249. Fax: 513/683-3086. **Facility:** 99 one-bedroom standard units, some with whirlpools. 2 stories, interior corridors. **Parking:** on-site. **Amenities:** extended cable TV, voice mail, irons, hair dryers. **Pool(s):** outdoor. **Guest Services:** valet laundry. **Business Services:** meeting rooms, business center, PC. **Cards:** AX, DC, DS, MC, VI.

SOME UNITS

———— **WHERE TO DINE** ————

GRAND ORIENTAL CHINESE RESTAURANT   **Lunch:** $5-$5   **Dinner:** $9-$19   Phone: 513/677-3388 [56]

Chinese

Location: I-71, exit 19, just e; in south end of Kings Mall. 4800 Fields-Ertel Rd 45249. **Hours:** 11:30 am-10 pm, Fri-10:30 pm, Sat 4 pm-10:30 pm, Sun 10 am-2:30 & 4-10 pm. Closed: 11/28. **Reservations:** suggested; weekends. **Features:** casual dress; children's menu; carryout; cocktails; a la carte, buffet. In a suburban strip mall, the casual restaurant offers excellent value and a comfortable environment. Elaborate red and gold touches decorate the walls and ceiling of the traditional, comfortable dining room. The extensive menu lists such favorites as seafood and bean curd soup and twice-cooked pork. Brunch is served on the weekends. **Parking:** on-site. **Cards:** AX, DC, DS, JC, MC, VI.

RIVER CITY GRILLE   **Lunch:** $8-$10   **Dinner:** $10-$22   Phone: 513/459-9800 [55]

American

Location: I-71, exit 19, just w; in Marriott Northeast. 9664 Mason-Montgomery Rd 45040. **Hours:** 6:30 am-2 & 5-10:30 pm, Sat & Sun 7 am-midnight. Closed: 12/25. **Reservations:** accepted. **Features:** casual dress; children's menu; cocktails. Behind a splashing fountain in the lobby of the Cincinnati Marriott Northeast, the relaxed restaurant offers hotel guests and other diners an assortment of steak, pasta and seafood dishes. Signature items include San Francisco stir-fry scallops, coconut shrimp, herb-crusted pork loin and sesame-crusted yellowfin tuna. Noteworthy desserts include apple tarts, lemon tarts and Graeters ice cream. **Parking:** on-site. **Cards:** AX, CB, DC, DS, JC, MC, VI.

MIDDLETOWN pop. 46,000

—— WHERE TO STAY ——

COMFORT INN MIDDLETOWN
SAVE
Motel

Phone: (513)420-9378

5/1-8/31	1P: $69-$89	2P: $69-$89	XP: $5 F18
4/1-4/30 & 9/1-3/31	1P: $59-$79	2P: $59-$79	XP: $5 F18

Location: I-75, exit 32, just e, then just n. 3458 Commerce Dr 45005. Fax: 513/422-4387. **Facility:** 54 one-bedroom standard units. 2 stories, interior corridors. **Parking:** on-site. **Amenities:** extended cable TV, irons, hair dryers. **Pool(s):** heated outdoor. **Guest Services:** valet laundry. **Cards:** AX, CB, DC, DS, JC, MC, VI.

SOME UNITS

FAIRFIELD INN MIDDLETOWN
AAA **SAVE**
Motel

Phone: (513)424-5444

4/1-9/15 [CP]	1P: $69-$72	2P: $74-$77	XP: $5 F17
9/16-3/31 [CP]	1P: $66-$69	2P: $71-$74	XP: $5 F17

Location: I-75, exit 32, 0.5 mi w on SR 122. 6750 Roosevelt Pkwy 45044. Fax: 513/424-5444. **Facility:** 57 one-bedroom standard units. 3 stories, interior corridors. *Bath:* combo or shower only. **Parking:** on-site. **Terms:** 14 day cancellation notice. **Amenities:** extended cable TV, irons. **Pool(s):** heated indoor. **Leisure Activities:** whirlpool. **Guest Services:** valet laundry. **Business Services:** meeting rooms. **Cards:** AX, DC, DS, MC, VI. **Special Amenities:** free continental breakfast and free local telephone calls. *(See color ad card insert)*

SOME UNITS
FEE

HOLIDAY INN EXPRESS
Motel

Phone: (513)727-8440

All Year [CP]   1P: $79-$99   2P: $79-$99

Location: I-75, exit 32, 0.5 mi w on SR 122. 6575 Terhune Dr 45044. Fax: 513/727-8440. **Facility:** 64 one-bedroom standard units. 3 stories, interior corridors. *Bath:* combo or shower only. **Parking:** on-site. **Terms:** 10 day cancellation notice. **Amenities:** extended cable TV, dual phone lines, voice mail, irons, hair dryers. **Pool(s):** heated indoor. **Leisure Activities:** whirlpool. **Guest Services:** valet laundry. **Business Services:** meeting rooms. **Cards:** AX, CB, DC, DS, MC, VI.

SOME UNITS
FEE

THE MANCHESTER INN & CONFERENCE CENTER
Historic Hotel

Phone: (513)422-5481

All Year   1P: $74   2P: $82   XP: $8 F17

Location: Just w of SR 4 and 73; at Middletown Civic Center. 1027 Manchester Ave 45042. Fax: 513/422-4615. **Facility:** 76 units. 66 one-bedroom standard units. 10 one-bedroom suites ($99-$150). 5 stories, interior corridors. *Bath:* combo or shower only. **Parking:** on-site. **Terms:** package plans, small pets only. **Amenities:** extended cable TV. *Some:* irons, hair dryers. **Dining:** dining room, see separate listing. **Guest Services:** valet laundry. **Business Services:** conference facilities, fax. **Cards:** AX, CB, DC, DS, MC, VI. *(See color ad below)*

SOME UNITS

RAMADA INN MIDDLETOWN
AAA **SAVE**
Motel

Phone: (513)424-1201

All Year [ECP]   1P: $79-$129   2P: $89-$139   XP: $10 F12

Location: I-75, exit 32, just e. (6147 W SR 122, FRANKLIN, 45005). Fax: 513/425-9681. **Facility:** 120 one-bedroom standard units, some with whirlpools. 2 stories, interior corridors. **Parking:** on-site. **Terms:** [MAP] meal plan available, package plans. **Amenities:** voice mail, safes (fee), irons, hair dryers. **Dining:** restaurant, 6 am-2 & 5-10 pm, $6-$8. **Guest Services:** valet laundry. **Business Services:** meeting rooms. **Cards:** AX, CB, DC, DS, JC, MC, VI. **Special Amenities:** free continental breakfast and free local telephone calls.

SOME UNITS

SUPER 8 MOTEL
Motel

Phone: (513)422-4888

5/1-8/31	1P: $59-$79	2P: $59-$79	XP: $5 F18
4/1-4/30 & 9/1-3/31	1P: $49-$69	2P: $49-$69	XP: $5 F18

Location: I-75, exit 32, just e, then just n. 3553 Commerce Dr 45005 (3553 Commerce Dr, FRANKLIN). Fax: 513/420-9599. **Facility:** 49 one-bedroom standard units, some with whirlpools. 2 stories, interior corridors. **Parking:** on-site. **Amenities:** extended cable TV. **Guest Services:** valet laundry. **Cards:** AX, CB, DC, DS, MC, VI.

SOME UNITS
FEE

WHERE TO DINE

THE MANCHESTER ROOM

American

Lunch: $6-$10   **Dinner:** $9-$21   **Phone:** 513/423-2877
Location: Just w of SR 4 and 73; at Middleton Civic Center; in The Manchester Inn & Conference Center. 1027 Manchester Ave 45042. **Hours:** 6:30-11 am, 11-2 & 5-10 pm, Sat 8 am-2 & 5-11 pm, Sun 8-10:30 am, 11-2 & 5-9 pm. **Reservations:** suggested; weeekends. **Features:** casual dress; Sunday brunch; children's menu; carryout; salad bar; cocktails; buffet. Prime rib is a house specialty on a menu that samples a wide selection of traditional favorites such as steak, shrimp and chicken. Food is simple in concept and prepared with quality ingredients. The restaurant is inside a historic downtown hotel. **Parking:** on-site. **Cards:** AX, CB, DC, DS, MC, VI.

MILFORD pop. 5,700   (See map p. 558; index p. 564)

WHERE TO STAY

HOLIDAY INN EXPRESS HOTEL & SUITES   **Phone:** (513)831-7829   347
Motel

	5/1-8/31 [CP]	1P: $100-$110	2P: $100-$110	XP: $10	F18
	4/1-4/30 & 9/1-10/31 [CP]	1P: $90-$100	2P: $90-$100	XP: $10	F18
	11/1-3/31 [CP]	1P: $80-$90	2P: $80-$90	XP: $10	F18

Location: I-275, exit 57, just sw. 301 Old Bank Rd 45150. Fax: 513/831-8829. **Facility:** 79 one-bedroom standard units, some with whirlpools. 3 stories, interior corridors. *Bath:* combo or shower only. **Parking:** on-site. **Amenities:** video games, dual phone lines, voice mail, irons, hair dryers. **Pool(s):** small heated indoor. **Leisure Activities:** exercise room. **Guest Services:** valet and coin laundry. **Business Services:** meeting rooms, business center, PC, fax (fee). **Cards:** AX, CB, DC, DS, JC, MC, VI. **Special Amenities:** free continental breakfast and free local telephone calls. *(See color ad below)*

SOME UNITS

MONTGOMERY pop. 9,800   (See map p. 558; index p. 564)

WHERE TO DINE

CHESTER'S ROAD HOUSE
American

Lunch: $8-$10   **Dinner:** $16-$29   **Phone:** 513/793-8700   191
Location: I-71, exit 12, 2.5 mi n; at jct US 22 and SR 3. 9678 Montgomery Rd 45242. **Hours:** 11:30 am-2:30 & 5-10 pm, Sat 5 pm-11 pm, Sun 5 pm-9 pm. Closed: 1/1, 7/4, 12/25; also Super Bowl Sun. **Reservations:** suggested. **Features:** casual dress; children's menu; carryout; cocktails; lounge; a la carte. A Southwestern flair punctuates such American dishes as rack of lamb and chili-lime-marinated chicken. The atrium dining room has the comfortable feel of an old farmhouse, with casually elegant appointments and a tree as the room's focal point. Smoke free premises. **Parking:** on-site. **Cards:** AX, CB, DC, DS, MC, VI.

DE SHA'S AMERICAN TAVERN
American

Lunch: $7-$12   **Dinner:** $10-$23   **Phone:** 513/247-9933   190
Location: I-275, exit 50, 0.7 mi n. 11320 Montgomery Rd 45249. **Hours:** 11 am-10 pm, Fri & Sat-11 pm, Sun 10 am-2 & 4-8 pm. Closed: 1/1, 12/25. **Reservations:** suggested. **Features:** casual dress; Sunday brunch; children's menu; carryout; cocktails & lounge. Steak, seafood, pasta, rainbow trout and stuffed mushrooms top the list of notable house specials served in this lively, tavern-like restaurant, located in an upscale suburban neighborhood. There's a separate menu available in the sports bar. **Parking:** on-site. **Cards:** AX, CB, DC, DS, MC, VI.

GERMANO'S
Italian

Lunch: $7-$13   **Dinner:** $14-$28   **Phone:** 513/794-1155   192
Location: I-71, exit 14 (Ronald Reagan Cross County Hwy), just e, then just n. 9415 Montgomery Rd 45242. **Hours:** 11:30 am-2:30 & 5:30-9:30 pm, Fri-10 pm, Sat 5 pm-10 pm. Closed major holidays; also Sun. **Reservations:** suggested. **Features:** dressy casual; carryout; cocktails; a la carte. The emphasis is on fresh seafood, pasta, veal, chicken and homemade desserts, including a delectable raspberry pie. The decor is reminiscent of an Italian villa, with mural and tapestry accents. The building blends in with the upscale village location. Smoke free premises. **Parking:** on-site. **Cards:** AX, DS, MC, VI.

(See map p. 558)

PACIFIC MOON CAFE   **Lunch:** $6-$10   **Dinner:** $10-$20   **Phone:** 513/891-0091   194
◆◆◆   **Location:** I-275, exit 50, 1.8 mi sw on Montgomery Rd. 8300 Market Place Ln 45242. **Hours:** 11 am-10 pm, Fri-11
Asian   pm, Sat 10 am-11 pm, Sun 10 am-9:30 pm. **Reservations:** suggested; weekends. **Features:** casual dress;
carryout; cocktails & lounge; a la carte. The extensive menu offers selections of Cantonese, Hunan,
Szechwan and south Asian dishes built around a foundation of seafood, pork, duck and chicken. The
dumplings come highly recommended and with good reason. Vegetarian entrees also are available. **Parking:** on-site.
Cards: AX, DC, DS, MC, VI.   ☒

MOUNT ORAB pop. 1,900

——— **WHERE TO STAY** ———

HOLIDAY INN EXPRESS-MT. ORAB   **Phone:** (937)444-6666
◆◆◆   6/1-9/1 [ECP]   1P: $84-$169   2P: $84-$169   XP: $10   F19
           4/1-5/31 & 9/2-3/31 [ECP]   1P: $79-$159   2P: $79-$159   XP: $10   F19
Motel   **Location:** Jct SR 32 and US 68, just n on US 68. 100 Leininger St 45154 (PO Box 100). **Fax:** 937/444-7377.
Facility: 51 one-bedroom standard units, some with whirlpools. 2 stories, interior corridors. *Bath:* combo or
shower only. **Parking:** on-site. **Terms:** 15 day cancellation notice, package plans, pets (with prior approval). **Amenities:** extended cable TV, dual phone lines, voice mail, irons, hair dryers. **Pool(s):** small heated indoor. **Leisure Activities:** whirlpool. *Fee:*
game room. **Guest Services:** valet and coin laundry. **Business Services:** meeting rooms, fax (fee). **Cards:** AX, CB, DC, DS,
JC, MC, VI.   SOME UNITS

ASK ☒ 🐾 ⚒ ➔ 🎦 DATA PORT 🖨 / ☒ ▤ 🖵 /

NORWOOD pop. 23,700   (See map p. 558; index p. 560)

——— **WHERE TO STAY** ———

HOWARD JOHNSON EAST   **Phone:** (513)631-8500   65
◆◆   6/7-9/2   1P: $70-$80   2P: $70-$80
           4/1-6/6 & 9/3-3/31   1P: $58-$68   2P: $58-$68
Motel   **Location:** I-71, exit 8 southbound; exit 8B northbound, 4 mi nw. 5410 Ridge Rd 45213. **Fax:** 513/631-9293.
Facility: 121 one-bedroom standard units, some with whirlpools. 2 stories, interior corridors. *Bath:* combo or
shower only. **Parking:** on-site. **Terms:** 14 day cancellation notice, small pets only. **Pool(s):** outdoor. **Guest Services:** valet and
coin laundry. **Business Services:** meeting rooms. **Cards:** AX, CB, DC, DS, MC, VI. **(See color ad below)**
                                                        SOME UNITS

ASK ☒ 🐾 🍴 ⛲ ➔ ✚ 🎦 DATA PORT ▭ 🖨 / ☒ ▤ 🖵 /
                               FEE

(See map p. 558)

QUALITY HOTEL & SUITES

Phone: (513)351-6000 [66]

(AAA) [SAVE]
▼▼▼▼

Hotel

All Year [BP] 1P: $95-$130 2P: $95-$130 XP: $5 F17
Location: I-71, exit 7, 1 mi w on SR 562, exit Montgomery Rd, just w, then just s; I-75, exit 7, 1.5 mi e on SR 562, exit Montgomery Rd. (4747 Montgomery Rd, CINCINNATI, 45212). Fax: 513/351-0215. **Facility:** 148 one-bedroom standard units. 8 stories, interior corridors. *Bath:* combo or shower only. **Parking:** on-site. **Terms:** cancellation fee imposed, package plans. **Amenities:** video games, voice mail, irons, hair dryers. **Dining:** restaurant, 11 am-10 pm, Sat from 4 pm, Sun 4 pm-9 pm, $10-$12, cocktails. **Pool(s):** heated outdoor. **Guest Services:** valet laundry. **Business Services:** conference facilities, business center. **Cards:** AX, CB, DC, DS, JC, MC, VI. **Special Amenities:** free local telephone calls. *(See color ad p 583)*

SOME UNITS

[icons] FEE

RED ROOF INN CINCINNATI CENTRAL (NORWOOD)

Phone: (513)531-6589 [67]

(AAA) [SAVE]
▼▼▼

Motel

6/2-8/31	1P: $51	2P: $56	XP: $5	F18
9/1-11/2	1P: $46	2P: $51	XP: $5	F18
4/1-6/1	1P: $44	2P: $49	XP: $5	F18
11/3-3/31	1P: $39	2P: $44	XP: $5	F18

Location: I-71, exit 8 southbound; exit 8B northbound; corner of Highland. 5300 Kennedy Ave 45213. Fax: 513/531-6681. **Facility:** 80 one-bedroom standard units. 2 stories, exterior corridors. *Bath:* combo or shower only. **Parking:** on-site. **Terms:** small pets only. **Amenities:** video games, voice mail. **Cards:** AX, CB, DC, DS, MC, VI. **Special Amenities:** free local telephone calls and free newspaper.

SOME UNITS

[icons] FEE

SHARONVILLE pop. 13,200 (See map p. 558; index p. 561)

——— WHERE TO STAY ———

BEST WESTERN INN & SUITES

Phone: (513)771-9080 [170]

(AAA) [SAVE]
▼▼▼

Motel

All Year [ECP] 1P: $59-$89 2P: $69-$99
Location: I-75, exit 15, just ne of jct Sharon Rd. 11160 Dowlin Dr 45241. Fax: 513/771-0043. **Facility:** 74 units. 59 one-bedroom standard units, some with whirlpools. 15 one-bedroom suites ($99-$200). 3 stories, interior corridors. *Bath:* combo or shower only. **Parking:** on-site. **Terms:** 2 night minimum stay, package plans. **Amenities:** high-speed Internet, voice mail, irons, hair dryers. **Pool(s):** heated indoor. **Leisure Activities:** whirlpool, exercise room. **Guest Services:** valet and coin laundry. **Business Services:** meeting rooms. **Cards:** AX, DC, DS, MC, VI. **Special Amenities:** early check-in/late check-out and free continental breakfast.

SOME UNITS

[icons] [VCR]

COUNTRY INN & SUITES BY CARLSON-CINCINNATI-NORTH

Phone: (513)771-9309 [176]

(AAA) [SAVE]
▼▼▼

Motel

4/1-10/31	1P: $69-$129	2P: $69-$129	XP: $10	F17
11/1-3/31	1P: $49-$99	2P: $49-$99	XP: $10	F17

Location: I-75, exit 15. 2463 E Sharon Rd 45241. Fax: 513/771-9310. **Facility:** 60 one-bedroom standard units. 3 stories, interior corridors. *Bath:* combo or shower only. **Parking:** on-site. **Terms:** 3 day cancellation notice. **Amenities:** extended cable TV, high-speed Internet, voice mail, irons, hair dryers. **Pool(s):** heated indoor. **Leisure Activities:** whirlpool, exercise room. **Guest Services:** coin laundry. **Business Services:** meeting rooms. **Cards:** AX, CB, DC, DS, JC, MC, VI. **Special Amenities:** free continental breakfast and free local telephone calls. *(See color ad p 646)*

SOME UNITS

[icons]

DAYS INN CINCINNATI/SHARONVILLE

Phone: (513)554-1400 [163]

[SAVE]
▼▼▼

Motel

All Year [CP] 2P: $45-$145 XP: $5 F12
Location: I-275, exit 46, just s. 11775 Lebanon Rd 45241. Fax: 513/554-1926. **Facility:** 142 one-bedroom standard units. 2 stories, interior/exterior corridors. **Parking:** on-site. **Terms:** cancellation fee imposed, small pets only. **Amenities:** high-speed Internet (fee), dual phone lines, safes, hair dryers. **Pool(s):** outdoor. **Leisure Activities:** Fee: game room. **Guest Services:** valet laundry. **Business Services:** meeting rooms. **Cards:** AX, CB, DC, DS, MC, VI.

SOME UNITS

[icons]

DOUBLETREE GUEST SUITES

Phone: (513)489-3636 [172]

(AAA) [SAVE]
▼▼▼

Suite Motor Inn

All Year 1P: $89-$149
Location: I-275, exit 47, just s, then just e. 6300 E Kemper Rd 45241. Fax: 513/489-8231. **Facility:** 152 one-bedroom suites. 3 stories, interior corridors. *Bath:* combo or shower only. **Parking:** on-site. **Terms:** package plans. **Amenities:** CD players, dual phone lines, voice mail, honor bars, irons, hair dryers. **Dining:** restaurant, 6:30 am-2 & 5-midnight, $10-$20, cocktails. **Pool(s):** heated outdoor. **Leisure Activities:** whirlpool, exercise room. **Guest Services:** valet and coin laundry. **Business Services:** meeting rooms, business center, PC. **Fee:** administrative services, fax. **Cards:** AX, CB, DC, DS, JC, MC, VI.

SOME UNITS

[icons] FEE

FAIRFIELD INN BY MARRIOTT-SHARONVILLE

Phone: (513)772-4114 [174]

(AAA) [SAVE]
▼▼▼

Motel

6/1-8/31 [CP]	1P: $69-$79	2P: $69-$79
4/1-5/31 & 9/1-10/31 [CP]	1P: $59-$69	2P: $69-$69
11/1-3/31 [CP]	1P: $49-$59	2P: $49-$59

Location: I-75, exit 15, just e, then just w. 11171 Dowlin Dr 45241. Fax: 513/772-8092. **Facility:** 135 one-bedroom standard units. 3 stories, interior/exterior corridors. **Parking:** on-site. **Terms:** 21 day cancellation notice. **Amenities:** voice mail, irons. **Pool(s):** heated outdoor. **Guest Services:** valet laundry. **Business Services:** meeting rooms. **Cards:** AX, DC, DS, MC, VI. **Special Amenities:** free continental breakfast and free local telephone calls. *(See color ad card insert)*

SOME UNITS

[icons] FEE

(See map p. 558)

HAMPTON INN-CINCINNATI NORTH
Phone: 513/771-6888 **178**

(AAA) (SAVE)

Motel

4/27-10/25	1P: $70-$80	2P: $70-$80
10/26-3/31	1P: $65-$75	2P: $65-$75
4/1-4/26	1P: $63-$70	2P: $63-$70

Location: I-75, exit 15, just e. 10900 Crowne Point Dr 45241. Fax: 513/771-5768. **Facility:** 130 one-bedroom standard units. 4 stories, interior corridors. **Parking:** on-site. **Amenities:** voice mail, irons. **Pool(s):** outdoor. **Leisure Activities:** driving range, billiard room. *Fee:* game room. **Guest Services:** valet laundry. **Business Services:** meeting rooms, administrative services (fee). **Cards:** AX, CB, DC, DS, MC, VI.

SOME UNITS

HILTON GARDEN INN CINCINNATI/SHARONVILLE
Phone: (513)772-2837 **168**

(AAA) (SAVE)

Motel

7/1-9/30	1P: $98	2P: $98	XP: $9	F18
4/1-6/30 & 10/1-3/31	1P: $71	2P: $71	XP: $9	F18

Location: I-75, exit 15, just e, then just w. 11149 Dowlin Dr 45241 (11149 Dowlin Dr, CINCINNATI). Fax: 513/772-2885. **Facility:** 90 one-bedroom standard units. 3 stories. *Bath:* combo or shower only. **Parking:** on-site. **Terms:** 14 day cancellation notice. **Amenities:** extended cable TV, video games, voice mail, irons, hair dryers. **Pool(s):** heated indoor. **Leisure Activities:** whirlpool, exercise room. **Guest Services:** coin laundry. **Business Services:** meeting rooms, business center. **Cards:** AX, CB, DC, DS, JC, MC, VI.

SOME UNITS

HOLIDAY INN-I-275 NORTH
Phone: (513)563-8330 **162**

Hotel

6/9-9/1	1P: $94-$124	2P: $94-$124
4/28-6/8	1P: $89-$114	2P: $89-$114
9/2-3/31	1P: $79-$114	2P: $79-$114
4/1-4/27	1P: $79-$109	2P: $79-$109

Location: I-275, exit 46, just n. 3855 Hauck Rd 45241. Fax: 513/563-9679. **Facility:** 275 units. 274 one-bedroom standard units. 1 one-bedroom suite ($150). 12 stories, interior corridors. *Bath:* combo or shower only. **Parking:** on-site. **Terms:** check-in 4 pm, package plans. **Amenities:** video games, dual phone lines, voice mail, irons, hair dryers. **Pool(s):** outdoor, heated indoor, wading. **Leisure Activities:** lighted tennis court, exercise room, basketball, volleyball. *Fee:* game room. **Guest Services:** valet and coin laundry. **Business Services:** conference facilities, business center, administrative services (fee), PC, fax. **Cards:** AX, CB, DC, DS, MC, VI. *(See color ad p 570)*

SOME UNITS

HOMEWOOD SUITES BY HILTON-CINCINNATI NORTH
Phone: (513)772-8888 **171**

(SAVE)

Apartment

5/1-8/31 [ECP]	1P: $119-$129	2P: $119-$129
4/1-4/30 & 9/1-3/31 [ECP]	1P: $109-$119	2P: $109-$119

Location: I-275, exit 44, jct Mosteller Rd. 2670 E Kemper Rd 45241. Fax: 513/772-8737. **Facility:** 111 units. 12 one-bedroom standard units. 99 one-bedroom suites with efficiencies. 3 stories, interior corridors. *Bath:* some combo or shower only. **Parking:** on-site. **Terms:** [MAP] meal plan available, package plans, small pets only ($8 extra charge). **Amenities:** extended cable TV, video tape library, video games, dual phone lines, voice mail, irons, hair dryers. **Pool(s):** outdoor. **Leisure Activities:** whirlpool, exercise room, sports court. **Guest Services:** gift shop, complimentary evening beverages: Mon-Thurs, valet and coin laundry. **Business Services:** meeting rooms, business center, PC, fax. **Cards:** AX, CB, DC, DS, JC, MC, VI. *(See ad below)*

SOME UNITS

RADISSON HOTEL CINCINNATI
Phone: (513)772-1720 **169**

(AAA) (SAVE)

Hotel

All Year	1P: $70-$85	2P: $95	XP: $10	F18

Location: I-75, exit 15, 0.3 mi w on Sharon Rd, 0.5 mi n. 11320 Chester Rd 45246. Fax: 513/772-6466. **Facility:** 350 units. 347 one-bedroom standard units. 3 one-bedroom suites, some with whirlpools. 3-14 stories, interior corridors. *Bath:* combo or shower only. **Parking:** on-site. **Terms:** 3 day cancellation notice, package plans, pets ($50 deposit). **Amenities:** video games, high-speed Internet, dual phone lines, voice mail, irons, hair dryers. **Dining:** dining room, 6:30 am-11 pm, $10-$17, cocktails. **Pool(s):** heated indoor/outdoor. **Leisure Activities:** exercise room. **Guest Services:** massage (fee), valet laundry. **Business Services:** conference facilities, business center, PC, fax. **Cards:** AX, DC, DS, MC, VI. **Special Amenities:** free newspaper. *(See ad p 586)*

SOME UNITS

(See map p. 558)

RED ROOF INN CHESTER RD   Phone: (513)771-5141 164

AAA SAVE
6/2-8/24   1P: $44-$59   2P: $49-$64   XP: $5   F18
8/25-3/31   1P: $41-$59   2P: $46-$64   XP: $5   F18
4/1-6/1   1P: $39-$49   2P: $44-$54   XP: $5   F18

Motel
Location: I-75, exit 15, 0.3 mi w on Sharon Rd, 0.5 mi n. 11345 Chester Rd 45246. **Fax:** 513/771-0812. **Facility:** 108 one-bedroom standard units. 2 stories, exterior corridors. *Bath:* combo or shower only. **Parking:** on-site. **Amenities:** video games, voice mail. **Business Services:** fax (fee). **Cards:** AX, CB, DC, DS, MC, VI. **Special Amenities:** free local telephone calls and free newspaper.

SOME UNITS

[icons] FEE / [icons] /

RED ROOF INN-SHARON ROAD   Phone: (513)771-5552 177

AAA SAVE
6/2-8/24   1P: $44-$59   2P: $49-$64   XP: $5   F18
8/25-3/31   1P: $41-$59   2P: $46-$64   XP: $5   F18
4/1-6/1   1P: $39-$54   2P: $44-$59   XP: $5   F18

Motel
Location: I-75, exit 15, just e. 2301 E Sharon Rd 45241. **Fax:** 513/771-5689. **Facility:** 108 one-bedroom standard units. 3 stories, exterior corridors. **Parking:** on-site. **Terms:** small pets only. **Amenities:** video games, voice mail. **Guest Services:** coin laundry. **Cards:** AX, CB, DC, DS, MC, VI. **Special Amenities:** free local telephone calls and free newspaper.

SOME UNITS

[icons] FEE / [icons] FEE FEE

RESIDENCE INN BY MARRIOTT   Phone: (513)771-2525 160

AAA SAVE
All Year [BP]   1P: $99-$109

Extended Stay Apartment
Location: I-75, exit 15, 0.3 mi w on Sharon Rd, 1 mi n. 11689 Chester Rd 45246. **Fax:** 513/771-3444. **Facility:** 144 units. 108 one-bedroom standard units with kitchens. 36 one-bedroom suites ($99-$149) with kitchens. 2 stories, exterior corridors. *Bath:* combo or shower only. **Parking:** on-site. **Terms:** pets ($100-$125 fee, $6 extra charge). **Amenities:** extended cable TV, voice mail, irons, hair dryers. **Pool(s):** heated outdoor. **Leisure Activities:** whirlpool, sports court. **Guest Services:** complimentary evening beverages: Mon-Thurs, valet and coin laundry. **Cards:** AX, DC, DS, MC, VI. *(See color ad card insert)*

SOME UNITS

[icons] FEE / [icons] /

SIGNATURE INN CINCINNATI NORTH   Phone: (513)772-7877 166

All Year [CP]   1P: $61-$70   2P: $61-$70

Motel
Location: I-75, exit 15, just w on Sharon Rd, 0.5 mi n. 11385 Chester Rd 45246. **Fax:** 513/772-7877. **Facility:** 130 one-bedroom standard units, some with whirlpools. 3 stories, interior corridors. *Bath:* combo or shower only. **Parking:** on-site. **Amenities:** voice mail, irons, hair dryers. **Guest Services:** valet laundry. **Business Services:** meeting rooms, business center. **Cards:** AX, DC, DS, MC, VI.

SOME UNITS

[icons] /

(See map p. 558)

WOODFIELD SUITES

AAA SAVE
▽▽▽▽

Motel

Phone: (513)771-0300   **173**
F17

All Year [ECP]   1P: $99-$199   2P: $99-$199   XP: $10
Location: I-75, exit 15, just e. 11029 Dowlin Dr 45241. Fax: 513/771-6411. **Facility:** 151 units. 101 one-bedroom standard units. 50 one-bedroom suites, some with kitchens and/or whirlpools. 8 stories, interior corridors. *Bath:* combo or shower only. **Parking:** on-site. **Terms:** check-in 4 pm, package plans, pets ($50 deposit). **Amenities:** video games, dual phone lines, voice mail, irons, hair dryers. **Pool(s):** heated outdoor. **Leisure Activities:** whirlpool, playground, exercise room, billiards room. **Guest Services:** complimentary evening beverages, valet and coin laundry. **Business Services:** conference facilities, administrative services (fee), PC, fax. **Cards:** AX, CB, DC, DS, MC, VI. **Special Amenities:** free local telephone calls and free newspaper.

SOME UNITS

[icons] / [icons] VCR /
FEE

——— WHERE TO DINE ———

ANAND INDIA RESTAURANT
▽▽▽▽

Indian

Lunch: $6-$8   **Dinner:** $8-$14   Phone: 513/554-4040   **73**
Location: Just se of Shanon Ave. 10890 Reading Rd 45241. **Hours:** 11 am-2 & 5-10 pm, Sat 11 am-10 pm, Sun noon-9 pm. Closed: 11/28, 12/25. **Features:** casual dress; a la carte. Affordable Indian cuisine is served in elegant surroundings. On the menu, as well as the daily lunch buffet, is a wide variety of appetizers, breads, tandoori specialties and rice, plus vegetarian, chicken and lamb dishes that employ varied cooking techniques. Dessert and drink choices are interesting. Try the mango lassi. Smoke free premises. **Parking:** on-site.
Cards: AX, DS, MC, VI.

[icon]

SPRINGBORO pop. 6,600

——— WHERE TO STAY ———

HOLIDAY INN EXPRESS
▽▽▽▽

Motel

Phone: (937)746-0151
4/1-10/30   1P: $79   2P: $79   XP: $6   F18
10/31-3/31   1P: $69   2P: $69   XP: $6   F18
Location: I-75, exit 38, just e. 15 Sharts Rd 45066. Fax: 937/746-3138. **Facility:** 53 one-bedroom standard units, some with whirlpools. 3 stories, interior corridors. **Parking:** on-site. **Amenities:** extended cable TV, irons, hair dryers. *Some:* dual phone lines. **Leisure Activities:** limited exercise equipment. **Guest Services:** valet laundry. **Business Services:** fax. **Cards:** AX, CB, DC, DS, JC, MC, VI.

SOME UNITS

[icons] / [icons] VCR [icon] /

SPRINGDALE pop. 10,600   (See map p. 558; index p. 561)

——— WHERE TO STAY ———

BAYMONT INN & SUITES-CINCINNATI NORTH

AAA SAVE
▽▽▽▽

Motel

Phone: (513)671-2300   **140**

All Year   1P: $59-$69   2P: $59-$69
Location: I-275, exit 41, just n. 12150 Springfield Pike 45246. Fax: 513/671-7324. **Facility:** 101 units. 99 one-bedroom standard units. 2 one-bedroom suites ($69-$114). 3 stories, interior corridors. **Parking:** on-site. **Terms:** pets ($50 deposit). **Amenities:** video games, voice mail, irons, hair dryers. **Guest Services:** valet laundry. **Business Services:** meeting rooms, fax (fee). **Cards:** AX, CB, DC, DS, MC, VI. **Special Amenities:** free continental breakfast and free newspaper. *(See color ad opposite title page)*

SOME UNITS

[icons] / [icons] /
FEE

BEST WESTERN SPRINGDALE HOTEL & CONFERENCE CENTRE

AAA SAVE
▽▽▽▽

Motor Inn

Phone: (513)671-6600   **142**

All Year   1P: $59-$99   2P: $59-$99
Location: I-275, exit 41, just nw on SR 4. 11911 Sheraton Ln 45246. Fax: 513/671-0507. **Facility:** 267 one-bedroom standard units. 10 stories, interior corridors. **Parking:** on-site. **Terms:** cancellation fee imposed, package plans, pets ($25 extra charge). **Amenities:** video games, voice mail, irons, hair dryers. **Dining:** restaurant, 6:30 am-2 & 5-10 pm, Sat & Sun from 7 am, $12-$20, cocktails. **Leisure Activities:** whirlpool, limited exercise equipment. *Fee:* game room. **Guest Services:** valet and coin laundry. **Business Services:** conference facilities, fax (fee). **Cards:** AX, DC, DS, MC, VI. **Special Amenities:** free continental breakfast and free room upgrade (subject to availability with advanced reservations). *(See ad p 569)*

SOME UNITS

[icons] / [icon] /
FEE

CROSS COUNTRY INN

AAA SAVE
▽▽

Motel

Phone: (513)671-0556   **144**
F17

All Year   1P: $42-$49   2P: $49-$56   XP: $2
Location: I-275, exit 41, just s, then just e. 330 Glensprings Dr 45246. Fax: 513/671-4953. **Facility:** 120 one-bedroom standard units. 2 stories, exterior corridors. *Bath:* combo or shower only. **Parking:** on-site. **Amenities:** video games, voice mail. **Pool(s):** heated outdoor. **Business Services:** meeting rooms, fax (fee). **Cards:** AX, CB, DC, DS, MC, VI. **Special Amenities:** free local telephone calls and preferred room (subject to availability with advanced reservations).

SOME UNITS

[icons] / [icon] /
FEE

THE HAMPSHIRE HOUSE HOTEL & CONFERENCE CENTER

AAA SAVE
▽▽▽▽

Motor Inn

Phone: (513)772-5440   **147**

6/14-9/2 [ECP]   1P: $58-$85   2P: $58-$85   XP: $6   F17
4/1-6/13 & 9/3-12/31 [ECP]   1P: $53-$69   2P: $53-$69   XP: $6   F17
1/1-3/31 [ECP]   1P: $44-$65   2P: $44-$65   XP: $6   F17
Location: I-275, exit 42, 0.8 mi s on SR 747, then just w. 30 Tri County Pkwy 45246. Fax: 513/772-1611. **Facility:** 150 units. 147 one-bedroom standard units. 3 one-bedroom suites ($125-$150), some with whirlpools. 4 stories, interior corridors. **Parking:** on-site. **Terms:** 3 day cancellation notice, package plans. **Amenities:** extended cable TV, high-speed Internet, voice mail, irons, hair dryers. **Dining:** restaurant, 6:30 am-2 & 5-10 pm, Sat & Sun 7 am-midnight, $6-$20, cocktails. **Pool(s):** heated indoor. **Leisure Activities:** sauna, whirlpool, exercise room. **Guest Services:** valet laundry. **Business Services:** conference facilities, fax (fee). **Cards:** AX, CB, DC, DS, MC, VI. **Special Amenities:** free continental breakfast and free local telephone calls.

SOME UNITS

[icons] / [icons] /
FEE

WAYNESVILLE pop. 1,900

-------- WHERE TO STAY --------

CREEKWOOD MOTEL
♦♦♦

Motel

			Phone: 513/897-1000
5/1-10/31	1P: $55	2P: $60	XP: $5 F12
4/1-4/30 & 11/1-3/31	1P: $45	2P: $50	XP: $5 F12

Location: Jct US 42 and SR 73. 401 S Main St 45068 (PO Box 636). Fax: 513/897-1446. **Facility:** 18 one-bedroom standard units. 2 stories, exterior corridors. **Parking:** on-site. **Terms:** cancellation fee imposed. **Business Services:** fax (fee). **Cards:** DS, MC, VI.

SOME UNITS
ASK S/D ⊤†⊢ DATA PORT / ⊠ /

-------- WHERE TO DINE --------

DER DUTCHMAN RESTAURANT
♦♦

American

Smoke free premises.

Lunch: $5-$13   **Dinner:** $8-$13   **Phone:** 513/897-4716
Location: 1 mi n on US 42. 230 N SR 42 45068. **Hours:** 7 am-8 pm, Fri & Sat-9 pm. Closed major holidays; also Sun. **Features:** casual dress; children's menu; carryout; salad bar. You'll be hard-pressed not to find something to satisfy your appetite from the varied selection of Amish family-style dinners such as roast beef, pot roast, homemade bread, doughnuts, cookies and pie. A large, generous salad bar also is notable. **Parking:** on-site. **Cards:** DS, MC, VI.

⊠

WILMINGTON pop. 11,200

-------- WHERE TO STAY --------

AMERIHOST INN & SUITES
AAA SAVE
♦♦♦

Motel

			Phone: (937)383-3950
All Year [ECP]	1P: $82	2P: $92	XP: $6 F18

Location: Jct US 68 and 22, 1.5 mi e on US 22. 201 Carrie Dr 45177. Fax: 937/383-1693. **Facility:** 61 one-bedroom standard units, some with kitchens. 2 stories, interior corridors. *Bath:* combo or shower only. **Parking:** on-site. **Amenities:** voice mail, safes (fee), irons, hair dryers. **Pool(s):** heated indoor. **Leisure Activities:** sauna, whirlpool, exercise room. **Guest Services:** valet laundry. **Business Services:** meeting rooms, fax (fee). **Cards:** AX, DC, DS, MC, VI. **Special Amenities:** free continental breakfast and free newspaper.

SOME UNITS
S/D ⊤†⊢ 🚫 🏊 ⊠ 🎥 DATA PORT ▭ 🖨 / ⊠ 🔒 🖵 /
FEE

HOLIDAY INN EXPRESS
AAA SAVE
♦♦♦

Motel

		Phone: 937/382-5858
All Year [ECP]	1P: $79	2P: $79

Location: 1.6 mi e on US 22. 155 Holiday Dr 45177. Fax: 937/382-0457. **Facility:** 75 one-bedroom standard units, some with whirlpools. 3 stories, interior corridors. *Bath:* combo or shower only. **Parking:** on-site. **Terms:** cancellation fee imposed, small pets only. **Amenities:** extended cable TV, dual phone lines, voice mail, irons, hair dryers. **Pool(s):** small heated indoor. **Leisure Activities:** whirlpool, exercise room. *Fee:* game room. **Guest Services:** valet and coin laundry. **Business Services:** meeting rooms, fax. **Cards:** AX, CB, DC, DS, JC, MC, VI. **Special Amenities:** free continental breakfast and free local telephone calls.

SOME UNITS
S/D 🐕 ⊤†⊢ 🚫M 🚫 🗘 🏊 ⊠ 🎥 DATA PORT ▭ 🖨 / ⊠ 🔒 🖵 /

Nearby Indiana

BATESVILLE pop. 4,700

-------- WHERE TO STAY --------

COMFORT INN
SAVE
♦♦

Motel

			Phone: (812)934-6185
All Year [CP]	1P: $57-$70	2P: $57-$70	XP: $5 F16

Location: I-74, exit 149, just se. 112 SR 46 E 47006. Fax: 812/934-6243. **Facility:** 56 one-bedroom standard units, some with whirlpools. 2 stories, interior corridors. **Parking:** on-site. **Amenities:** extended cable TV, hair dryers. *Some:* irons. **Pool(s):** heated indoor. **Business Services:** meeting rooms. **Cards:** AX, CB, DC, DS, MC, VI.

SOME UNITS
S/D ⊤†⊢ 🏊 🎥 DATA PORT / ⊠ 🔒 🖵 ▭ /

HAMPTON INN BATESVILLE
AAA SAVE
♦♦♦

Motel

calls.

			Phone: (812)934-6262
All Year [ECP]	1P: $69-$125	2P: $69-$125	

Location: I-74, exit 149, just n. 1030 SR 229 N 47006. Fax: 812/934-4546. **Facility:** 100 units. 98 one-bedroom standard units. 2 one-bedroom suites ($125). 2 stories, interior corridors. *Bath:* combo or shower only. **Parking:** on-site. **Amenities:** voice mail, irons. **Pool(s):** heated indoor. **Leisure Activities:** whirlpool, exercise room. **Guest Services:** valet and coin laundry. **Business Services:** meeting rooms, fax (fee). **Cards:** AX, CB, DC, DS, MC, VI. **Special Amenities:** free continental breakfast and free local telephone

SOME UNITS
S/D ⊤†⊢ 🚫M 🚫 🗘 🏊 🎥 DATA PORT ▭ 🖨 / ⊠ 🔒 🖵 /

THE SHERMAN HOUSE

AAA SAVE

Historic Country Inn

All Year   1P: $53-$69   2P: $59-$79   Phone: 812/934-1000

Location: I-74, exit 149, 0.8 mi s on SR 229. 35 S Main St 47006. Fax: 812/934-8339. **Facility:** 23 units. 19 one-bedroom standard units. 4 one-bedroom suites, some with efficiencies. 2 stories, interior corridors. *Bath:* combo or shower only. **Parking:** on-site. **Terms:** [ECP] meal plan available, package plans. **Amenities:** extended cable TV. **Dining:** dining room, see separate listing. **Leisure Activities:** pool tables. **Guest Services:** valet laundry. **Business Services:** conference facilities, fax. **Cards:** AX, CB, DC, MC, VI. **Special Amenities:** free continental breakfast and free local telephone calls.

SOME UNITS

——— WHERE TO DINE ———

SHERMAN HOUSE Historical   **Lunch:** $6-$8   **Dinner:** $12-$17   **Phone:** 812/934-2407

German

Location: I-74, exit 149, 0.8 mi s; in The Sherman House. 35 S Main St 47006. **Hours:** 6:30 am-8:45 pm, Fri & Sat-9:45 pm, Sun-7:45 pm. **Closed:** 1/1, 12/25. **Reservations:** suggested. **Features:** dressy casual; Sunday brunch; children's menu; salad bar; cocktails & lounge; buffet. German cuisine aficionados will delight in the old European ambience and fare served in this inn, parts of which date from 1852. All your favorites are served from sauerbraten and sausage and 'kraut to German chocolate cake. Fresh lobster is served daily. **Parking:** on-site. **Cards:** AX, CB, DC, MC, VI.

LAWRENCEBURG pop. 4,400

——— WHERE TO STAY ———

RIVERSIDE INN

Motel

All Year   1P: $49   2P: $59   XP: $5   F12   Phone: 812/537-4441

Location: On US 50; 1 mi sw of jct I-275. 515 Eads Pkwy E 47025. Fax: 812/537-6341. **Facility:** 109 units. 106 one-bedroom standard units. 3 two-bedroom suites ($62-$110) with kitchens. 2 stories, interior corridors. **Parking:** on-site. **Amenities:** extended cable TV, voice mail. **Guest Services:** valet laundry. **Business Services:** meeting rooms. **Cards:** AX, MC, VI.

SOME UNITS

NEW ALSACE pop. 200

——— WHERE TO DINE ———

CHATEAU POMIJE WINERY & RESTAURANT   **Lunch:** $5-$9   **Dinner:** $13-$21   **Phone:** 812/623-3332

American

Location: I-74, exit 164, 2.8 mi s on SR 1 to Dover, then 2.8 mi w on N Dearborn Rd, follow signs. 25043 Jacobs Rd 47022. **Hours:** 4 pm-8 pm, Fri & Sat-9:30 pm, Sun noon-8 pm. Closed major holidays; also Mon & Tues. **Reservations:** suggested; for dinner wknd. **Features:** casual dress; carryout; cocktails. A winery operates below the comfortable restaurant, a reconstructed 1861 barn. A stone fireplace is the centerpiece of the rustic dining area, which looks out over the vineyards. Country-style cuisine includes such offerings as ribs and pork tenderloin. **Parking:** on-site. **Cards:** MC, VI.

RISING SUN pop. 2,300

——— WHERE TO STAY ———

MULBERRY INN & GARDENS BED & BREAKFAST   Phone: (812)438-2206

Bed & Breakfast

All Year [BP]   2P: $79-$125   XP: $20

Location: Downtown; just w of jct SR 56 off SR 262. 118 S Mulberry St 47040. Fax: 812/438-2206. **Facility:** In a garden setting. Cozy rooms with antique style furnishings. Free casino passes available. Designated smoking area. 6 one-bedroom standard units, some with whirlpools. 2 stories, interior corridors. *Bath:* combo or shower only. **Parking:** on-site. **Terms:** age restrictions may apply, 7 day cancellation notice-fee imposed, package plans. **Amenities:** extended cable TV. **Cards:** CB, DC, DS, MC, VI.

Nearby Kentucky

BELLEVUE pop. 7,000 (See map p. 558; index p. 562)

——— WHERE TO STAY ———

CINCINNATI'S WELLER HAUS BED & BREAKFAST   Phone: (859)431-6829   216

Historic Bed & Breakfast

All Year [BP]   1P: $89-$168   2P: $89-$168   XP: $25

Location: I-471, exit 5, 0.5 mi e on SR 8, just s on Washington St, then just w. 319 Poplar St 41073. Fax: 859/431-4332. **Facility:** This family-oriented B&B features two 1880s Gothic Revival homes; a shared refrigerator and microwave are provided. Smoke free premises. 5 one-bedroom standard units, some with whirlpools. 2 stories, interior corridors. *Bath:* combo or shower only. **Parking:** street. **Terms:** check-in 4 pm, 7 day cancellation notice-fee imposed. **Business Services:** meeting rooms. **Cards:** AX, CB, DC, DS, MC, VI.

SOME UNITS

CARROLLTON pop. 3,700

------ **WHERE TO STAY** ------

DAYS INN CARROLLTON
(AAA) (SAVE)
▽▽▽ ▽▽▽
Motor Inn

All Year   1P: $55-$99   2P: $55-$99   Phone: (502)732-9301
XP: $6   F17
Location: I-71, exit 44, just nw. 61 Inn Rd 41008. Fax: 502/732-5596. **Facility:** 84 one-bedroom standard units. 2 stories, interior corridors. **Parking:** on-site. **Terms:** 7 day cancellation notice, package plans, small pets only. **Amenities:** extended cable TV. **Pool(s):** outdoor. **Business Services:** meeting rooms. **Cards:** AX, CB, DC, DS, MC, VI. **Special Amenities:** free continental breakfast and free local telephone calls.

SOME UNITS
⑤D 🐾 🛏 🍽 📷 DATA PORT / ⊠ 🔌 📖 /
FEE   FEE

HOLIDAY INN EXPRESS
▽▽▽ ▽▽▽
Motel

All Year   1P: $59-$109   2P: $59-$109   Phone: (502)732-6661
XP: $6   F17
Location: I-71, exit 44, just nw. 141 Inn Rd 41008. Fax: 502/732-6661. **Facility:** 62 one-bedroom standard units. 2 stories, interior corridors. **Parking:** on-site. **Terms:** [ECP] meal plan available, package plans, small pets only. **Amenities:** extended cable TV. **Leisure Activities:** off-site pool privileges. **Guest Services:** valet laundry. **Business Services:** meeting rooms. **Cards:** AX, CB, DC, DS, JC, MC, VI.

SOME UNITS
(ASK) ⑤D 🐾 📷 DATA PORT 🖨 / ⊠ 🔌 📖 /
FEE   FEE

SUPER 8 CARROLLTON
▽▽▽ ▽▽
Motel

All Year   1P: $49-$99   2P: $49-$99   Phone: (502)732-0252
XP: $6   F17
Location: I-71, exit 44, just nw. 130 Slumber Ln 41008. Fax: 502/732-0252. **Facility:** 46 one-bedroom standard units. 2 stories, interior corridors. **Parking:** on-site. **Terms:** 7 day cancellation notice, small pets only. **Amenities:** extended cable TV. **Guest Services:** coin laundry. **Cards:** AX, CB, DC, DS, MC, VI.

SOME UNITS
(ASK) ⑤D 🐾 🍽 📷 🖨 / ⊠ 🔌 📖 /
FEE   FEE

------ **WHERE TO DINE** ------

THE DINING ROOM AT GENERAL BUTLER
STATE RESORT PARK
▽▽▽ ▽▽▽
American

Lunch: $6-$7   Dinner: $8-$13   Phone: 502/732-4384
Location: I-74, exit 44, 1.5 mi nw on US 227; in General Butler Resort Park. 1608 Hwy 227 41008. **Hours:** 7-10:30 am, 11:30-4 & 5-8 pm, Fri & Sat-9 pm; to 9 pm in summer. Closed: 12/23-12/30. **Features:** casual dress; Sunday brunch; children's menu; carryout; salad bar; buffet. This state park lodge serves up value-priced, generous portions of such standard fare as fried chicken and stewed apples as well as such regional specialties as hot brown. The walls are lined with handsome native stone. The service is friendly and casual. **Parking:** on-site. **Cards:** AX, DC, DS, MC, VI.

⊠

COVINGTON pop. 43,300 (See map p. 558; index p. 562)

------ **WHERE TO STAY** ------

AMOS SHINKLE TOWNHOUSE BED & BREAKFAST
(AAA) (SAVE)
▽▽▽ ▽▽▽
Historic Bed
& Breakfast

All Year [BP]   1P: $85-$155   2P: $95-$165   Phone: (859)431-2118   257
XP: $15   F6
Location: I-71/75, exit 192, 0.8 mi e on 5th St, just n. 215 Garrard St 41011-1715. Fax: 859/491-4551. **Facility:** An ornately decorated 1854 home and a carriage house at this property are set behind a black-iron, columned fence. Designated smoking area. 7 one-bedroom standard units, some with whirlpools. 2 stories, interior corridors. **Parking:** on-site. **Terms:** 4 day cancellation notice. **Business Services:** meeting rooms. **Cards:** AX, DC, DS, MC, VI.

⑤D ⊠ 🖨

CINCINNATI MARRIOTT AT RIVERCENTER
(AAA) (SAVE)
▽▽▽ ▽▽▽ ▽▽
Hotel

4/1-10/31   1P: $129-$169   2P: $129-$169   Phone: (859)261-2900   250
11/1-3/31   1P: $119-$159   2P: $119-$159
Location: I-71/75, exit 192, 0.8 mi e on 5th Ave, 0.3 mi n on Madison. 10 W River Center Blvd 41011. Fax: 859/261-0900. **Facility:** 326 one-bedroom standard units. 14 stories, interior corridors. *Bath:* combo or shower only. **Parking:** on-site and valet (fee). **Terms:** check-in 4 pm, package plans. **Amenities:** video games, dual phone lines, voice mail, irons, hair dryers. *Some:* honor bars. **Dining:** Zebo's Bistro, see separate listing. **Pool(s):** heated indoor. **Leisure Activities:** sauna, whirlpool. **Guest Services:** gift shop, massage (fee), valet laundry, area transportation-downtown. **Business Services:** conference facilities, business center, PC, fax. **Cards:** AX, CB, DC, DS, JC, MC, VI. *(See color ad card insert)*

SOME UNITS
⑤D 🔌 🍽 ♿M ♿ 🐾 🛏 📷 DATA PORT 📠 🖨 / ⊠ VCR 🔌 📖 /
FEE   FEE   FEE

EMBASSY SUITES CINCINNATI RIVERCENTER
(SAVE)
▽▽▽ ▽▽
Suite Hotel

All Year [BP]   1P: $109-$169   2P: $109-$169   Phone: (859)261-8400   255
XP: $10   F18
Location: I-75, exit 192, 0.8 mi e on 5th Ave, 0.3 mi n on Madison. 10 E River Center Blvd 41011. Fax: 859/261-8486. **Facility:** 226 units. 221 one- and 5 two-bedroom standard units. 8 stories, interior corridors. **Parking:** on-site and valet (fee). **Terms:** cancellation fee imposed, package plans, small pets only. **Amenities:** voice mail, irons, hair dryers. **Pool(s):** heated indoor. **Leisure Activities:** sauna, whirlpool, sun deck, exercise room. **Guest Services:** gift shop, complimentary evening beverages, valet and coin laundry. **Business Services:** conference facilities, PC, fax. **Cards:** AX, CB, DC, DS, JC, MC, VI.

SOME UNITS
⑤D 🔌 🐾 🍽 ♿M 🛏 ⊠ 📷 DATA PORT 🔌 📖 📠 🖨 / ⊠ VCR /
FEE

(See map p. 558)

HAMPTON INN CINCINNATI RIVERFRONT
[SAVE]

Phone: (859)581-7800 [254]

Motel

| 3/1-10/31 | 1P: $84 | 2P: $94 |
| 12/1-2/28 & 11/1-11/30 | 1P: $79 | 2P: $89 |

Location: I-71/75, exit 192, 0.6 mi nw. 200 Crescent Ave 41011. Fax: 859/581-8282. **Facility:** 151 one-bedroom standard units. 6 stories, interior corridors. *Bath:* combo or shower only. **Parking:** on-site. **Amenities:** voice mail, irons, hair dryers. **Pool(s):** heated outdoor. **Leisure Activities:** exercise room. **Guest Services:** valet laundry. **Business Services:** meeting rooms. **Cards:** AX, CB, DC, DS, JC, MC, VI.

SOME UNITS

HOLIDAY INN RIVERFRONT
(AAA) [SAVE]

Phone: (859)291-4300 [253]

Motor Inn

| 4/30-9/30 | 1P: $89 | 2P: $107 |
| 12/1-4/29 & 10/1-11/30 | 1P: $80 | |

Location: I-71/75, exit 192, 0.4 mi ne on SR 8. 600 W 3rd St 41011. Fax: 859/491-2331. **Facility:** 156 one-bedroom standard units. 4 stories, interior corridors. **Parking:** on-site. **Terms:** cancellation fee imposed, [CP] meal plan available, package plans. **Amenities:** dual phone lines, voice mail, irons, hair dryers. **Dining:** restaurant, 6:30 am-2 & 5-10 pm, $6-$16, cocktails. **Pool(s):** outdoor. **Leisure Activities:** exercise room. **Guest Services:** valet laundry. **Business Services:** meeting rooms, business center, fax. **Cards:** AX, CB, DS, MC, VI.

SOME UNITS

RADISSON CINCINNATI RIVERFRONT HOTEL

Phone: (859)491-1200 [251]

Hotel

| All Year | 1P: $109-$119 | 2P: $109-$119 | XP: $10 | F |

Location: I-71/75, exit 192. 668 W 5th St 41011. Fax: 859/491-0326. **Facility:** 236 units. 232 one-bedroom standard units. 4 one-bedroom suites ($250-$275) with whirlpools. 18 stories, interior corridors. *Bath:* combo or shower only. **Parking:** on-site. **Terms:** package plans, small pets only. **Amenities:** video games, voice mail, irons, hair dryers. **Dining:** Riverview Restaurant, see separate listing. **Pool(s):** heated indoor. **Leisure Activities:** whirlpool, exercise room, basketball. **Guest Services:** valet and coin laundry. **Business Services:** conference facilities. **Cards:** AX, CB, DC, DS, MC, VI.

SOME UNITS

--------- WHERE TO DINE ---------

BB RIVERBOATS

American

| Lunch: $25 | Dinner: $30-$36 | Phone: 859/261-8500 [112] |

Location: I-75, exit 192, 1 mi e on 5th St, just n; at Covington Landing on the Ohio River. 1 Madison Ave 41011. **Hours:** noon-2 & 7-10 pm, Sun-7 pm; winter hours may vary, call in advance. Closed: 12/25. **Reservations:** required. **Features:** casual dress; cocktails; entertainment; buffet. Step onto the enclosed deck of this riverboat to enjoy a buffet-style luncheon or dinner while cruising on the Ohio River. Fill up on chicken, prime rib, pasta, roast beef, vegetables, salad and a choice of dessert. The views are outstanding from the upper deck. Smoke free premises. **Parking:** *Fee:* off-site and valet. **Cards:** AX, DC, DS, MC, VI.

CHEZ NORA RESTAURANT

American

| Lunch: $6-$9 | Dinner: $11-$25 | Phone: 859/491-8027 [109] |

Location: I-71/75, exit 192, just se. 530 Main St 41011. **Hours:** 11 am-11 pm. Closed major holidays. **Reservations:** accepted. **Features:** casual dress; Sunday brunch; cocktails; a la carte. Visit this corner pub located in a historic district. Good variety with a few Cajun choices, seasonal outdoor dining, pizza, wraps and an interesting choice of salad. Very eclectic interior with display of menu items on chalkboard. Daily specials. **Parking:** street. **Cards:** AX, DS, MC, VI.

MIKE FINK

Seafood

| Lunch: $7-$11 | Dinner: $14-$25 | Phone: 859/261-4212 [111] |

Location: Just n at the foot of Greenup St, on the Ohio River. 100 Greenup St 41011. **Hours:** 11 am-10 pm, Fri & Sat-11 pm, Sun 10 am-9 pm. **Reservations:** suggested. **Features:** casual dress; children's menu; carryout; cocktails & lounge; a la carte. An informal atmosphere marks the riverboat restaurant, which boasts a clear view of downtown Cincinnati from many tables. Broiled salmon, fettuccine Alfredo and fried breaded shrimp are among the menu choices, or sample from the raw seafood bar. **Parking:** on-site. **Cards:** AX, DC, DS, MC, VI.

RIVERVIEW RESTAURANT
(AAA)

Seafood

| Lunch: $5-$12 | Dinner: $17-$25 | Phone: 859/491-5300 [108] |

Location: I-71/75, exit 192; in the Radisson Cincinnati Riverfront Hotel. 668 5th St 41011. **Hours:** 11:30 am-2 & 5-9:30 pm, Fri & Sat 5 pm-10 pm, Sun 9:30 am-2:30 & 5-9:30 pm. Closed: 12/25. **Reservations:** suggested. **Features:** casual dress; Sunday brunch; children's menu; cocktails; a la carte. Perched atop a high-rise hotel, the circular, revolving restaurant affords outstanding panoramas of the Ohio River and Cincinnati skyline. The atmosphere is decidedly upscale, as are such artfully prepared entrees as the succulent pork tenderloin. Fresh seafood is prepared in a variety of ways. Several namesake selections are offered alongside native Kentucky classics. **Parking:** on-site. **Cards:** AX, DC, DS, JC, MC, VI.

ZEBO'S BISTRO

Regional American

| Lunch: $7-$13 | Dinner: $15-$25 | Phone: 859/392-3750 [110] |

Location: I-71/75, exit 192, 0.8 mi e on 5th Ave, 0.3 mi n on Madison; in Cincinnati Marriott at RiverCenter. 10 W River Center Blvd 41011. **Hours:** 6:30-10 am, 11-2:30 & 5-10 pm, Fri-11 pm, Sat 7 am-11 pm, Sun 7 am-10 pm. Closed: 12/25. **Reservations:** suggested. **Features:** dressy casual; carryout; cocktails; a la carte. Featuring a friendly, uniformed staff and a smartly appointed dining room overlooking the Ohio River, Zebo's specializes in seafood prepared at the discretion of the diner with many options: blackened, sauteed with feta cheese or grilled and served with spaetzle. Diners can salivate over desserts on display at the entry, as well as displayed tableside after the meal. Smoke free premises. **Parking:** on-site and valet (fee). **Cards:** AX, CB, DC, DS, JC, MC, VI.

DRY RIDGE pop. 1,600

──────── WHERE TO STAY ────────

HAMPTON INN
[SAVE]
▼▼▼▼
Motel

All Year   1P: $62-$89   2P: $67-$94   XP: $5   F18
Location: I-75, exit 159, just nw. 1200 Cull Rd 41035. Fax: 859/823-0009. **Facility:** 62 units. 60 one-bedroom standard units, some with whirlpools. 2 one-bedroom suites ($87-$120) with whirlpools. 4 stories, interior corridors. *Bath:* combo or shower only. **Parking:** on-site. **Terms:** package plans. **Amenities:** extended cable TV, dual phone lines, voice mail, irons. **Pool(s):** heated indoor. **Leisure Activities:** exercise room. **Cards:** AX, CB, DC, DS, MC, VI.

Phone: (859)823-7111

HOLIDAY INN EXPRESS
▼▼▼▼
Motel

All Year   1P: $69-$89   2P: $89
Location: I-75, exit 159, just nw. 1050 Fashion Ridge Rd 41035. Fax: 859/824-7430. **Facility:** 62 one-bedroom standard units, some with whirlpools. 3 stories, interior corridors. *Bath:* combo or shower only. **Parking:** on-site. **Terms:** pets ($20 deposit). **Amenities:** extended cable TV, irons, hair dryers. **Guest Services:** valet and coin laundry. **Business Services:** meeting rooms. **Cards:** AX, DC, DS, MC, VI.

Phone: 859/824-7121

MICROTEL INN AND SUITES
▼▼
Motel
DS, MC, VI.

All Year   1P: $39-$78   2P: $44-$83   XP: $5   F18
Location: I-75, exit 159, just ne. 79 Blackburn Ln 41035. Fax: 859/824-1329. **Facility:** 55 one-bedroom standard units, some with whirlpools. 3 stories, interior corridors. *Bath:* combo or shower only. **Parking:** on-site. **Terms:** [CP] meal plan available, pets ($10 extra charge). **Amenities:** extended cable TV. **Cards:** AX, DC,

Phone: 859/824-2000

──────── WHERE TO DINE ────────

THE COUNTRY GRILL
▼▼
American

Lunch: $6-$15   **Dinner:** $6-$15   **Phone:** 859/824-6000
Location: I-75, exit 159, 0.5 mi w on SR 22. 21 Taft Hwy 41035. **Hours:** 9 am-9 pm, Fri & Sat 8 am-10 pm. Closed major holidays. **Reservations:** suggested. **Features:** casual dress; children's menu; carryout. Serving an assortment of plump burgers, juicy steak and homemade dessert, this cheerful cafe boasts a country theme complete with folk art on the walls and antiques scattered about. A cordial wait staff meets your needs. **Parking:** on-site. **Cards:** AX, DS, MC, VI.

ERLANGER pop. 16,000 (See map p. 558; index p. 563)

──────── WHERE TO STAY ────────

BAYMONT INN & SUITES CINCINNATI-AIRPORT (ERLANGER, KY)
(AAA) [SAVE]
▼▼▼▼
Motel

1P: $69-$89   2P: $69-$89   [295]
All Year
Location: I-275, exit 2. 1805 Airport Exchange Blvd 41018. Fax: 859/746-0305. **Facility:** 110 one-bedroom standard units. 4 stories, interior corridors. *Bath:* combo or shower only. **Parking:** on-site. **Terms:** pets ($50 deposit). **Amenities:** video games, Web TV (fee), voice mail, irons, hair dryers. *Some:* high-speed Internet. **Pool(s):** outdoor. **Leisure Activities:** exercise room. **Guest Services:** valet and coin laundry. **Business Services:** meeting rooms. **Cards:** AX, DC, DS, MC, VI. **Special Amenities:** free continental breakfast and free newspaper. *(See color ad opposite title page)*

Phone: (859)746-0300

COMFORT INN-CINCINNATI AIRPORT
[SAVE]
▼▼▼▼
Motel

5/1-8/31   1P: $69-$79   2P: $76-$88
9/1-11/30   1P: $59-$69   2P: $69-$81
12/1-4/30   1P: $59-$69   2P: $69-$81   XP: $7
Location: I-71/75, exit 184, off SR 236 southbound; exit 184B northbound. 630 Donaldson Rd 41018. Fax: 859/727-1378. **Facility:** 145 one-bedroom standard units. 4 stories, interior corridors. **Parking:** on-site. **Terms:** cancellation fee imposed, package plans. **Amenities:** dual phone lines, irons, hair dryers. **Pool(s):** outdoor. **Leisure Activities:** exercise room. **Guest Services:** valet and coin laundry. **Business Services:** meeting rooms. **Cards:** AX, CB, DC, DS, MC, VI.

Phone: 859/727-3400   [301]

HOLIDAY INN-CINCINNATI AIRPORT
(AAA) [SAVE]
▼▼▼▼
Motor Inn

All Year   1P: $98-$129   2P: $98-$129
Location: I-275, exit 2. 1717 Airport Exchange Blvd 41018. Fax: 859/371-5002. **Facility:** 305 one-bedroom standard units, some with whirlpools. 2-6 stories, interior corridors. **Parking:** on-site. **Terms:** package plans. **Amenities:** dual phone lines, voice mail, irons, hair dryers. **Dining:** dining room, 6 am-11 pm, $6-$22, cocktails. **Pool(s):** heated indoor. **Leisure Activities:** sauna, whirlpool, jogging, exercise room. **Guest Services:** gift shop, valet and coin laundry, area transportation-within 10 mi. **Business Services:** conference facilities, business center, PC, fax. **Cards:** AX, CB, DC, DS, JC, MC, VI.

Phone: (859)371-2233   [298]

(See map p. 558)

RESIDENCE INN BY MARRIOTT, CINCINNATI AIRPORT

Phone: (859)282-7400   **297**

All Year   1P: $109-$179   2P: $109-$179

Location: I-275, exit 2. 2811 Circleport Dr 41018. Fax: 859/282-1790. **Facility:** 150 units. 126 one- and 24 two-bedroom standard units with kitchens. 3 stories, interior corridors. *Bath:* combo or shower only. **Parking:** on-site. **Terms:** package plans, pets ($100 fee). **Amenities:** extended cable TV, high-speed Internet, dual phone lines, voice mail, irons, hair dryers. **Pool(s):** heated outdoor. **Leisure Activities:** whirlpool, exercise room, sports court. **Guest Services:** complimentary evening beverages: Mon-Thurs, valet and coin laundry. **Business Services:** meeting rooms. **Cards:** AX, CB, DC, DS, MC, VI. *(See color ad card insert)*

Extended Stay
Apartment

SOME UNITS

——— WHERE TO DINE ———

COLONIAL COTTAGE INN

Lunch: $5-$7   **Dinner:** $6-$12   Phone: 859/341-4498   **140**

Location: I-71/75, exit 184, 0.8 mi e on Commonwealth Ave, then 0.5 mi n. 3140 Dixie Hwy 41018. **Hours:** 6 am-9 pm, Sun from 7 am. Closed: 11/27, 12/25; also half day on 12/24. **Reservations:** accepted; weekends. **Features:** casual dress; carryout; beer only; a la carte. A boisterous wait staff serves delicious, old-fashioned diner food at this popular eatery. Try the tasty homemade meatloaf and hot turkey sandwiches smothered in creamy brown gravy. Daily specials are offered. **Parking:** on-site. **Cards:** MC, VI.

American

JO AN JAPANESE CUISINE

Lunch: $8-$16   **Dinner:** $9-$20   Phone: 859/746-2634   **138**

Location: I-275, exit 2, just nw. 3940 Olympic Blvd Suite 135 41018. **Hours:** 11:30 am-1:30 & 5:30-10 pm, Sat from 5:30 pm. Closed: 5/26; also Sun. **Features:** dressy casual; a la carte. An artsy flair envelops the cozy restaurant, from its neatly contemporary setting to its chefs, who use their creative skills masterfully at the sit-down sushi bar. The lengthy menu reveals many small entree items, including exotic choices-such as duck, soybean, tuna, shellfish and eel is sure to please the adventurer. The staff is attentive. **Parking:** on-site. **Cards:** AX, DC, MC, VI.

Japanese

FLORENCE pop. 18,600   (See map p. 558; index p. 563)

——— WHERE TO STAY ———

AMERISUITES (CINCINNATI AIRPORT)

Phone: (859)647-1170   **326**

6/1-8/31 [ECP]   1P: $99-$109   2P: $99-$109   XP: $10   F18
12/1-5/31 & 9/1-11/30 [ECP]   1P: $89-$99   2P: $89-$99   XP: $10   F18

Location: I-75, exit 182, 0.4 mi sw. 300 Meijer Dr 41042. Fax: 859/647-1179. **Facility:** 128 one-bedroom standard units. 6 stories, interior corridors. *Bath:* combo or shower only. **Parking:** on-site. **Terms:** 30 day cancellation notice, package plans, small pets only. **Amenities:** high-speed Internet (fee), voice mail, irons, hair dryers. *Some:* dual phone lines. **Pool(s):** heated indoor. **Leisure Activities:** exercise room. **Guest Services:** valet and coin laundry, area transportation-within 2 mi. **Business Services:** meeting rooms, business center, PC, fax. **Cards:** AX, CB, DC, DS, JC, MC, VI. **Special Amenities:** free continental breakfast and free newspaper. *(See color ad p 565)*

Motel

SOME UNITS

ASHLEY QUARTERS

Phone: (859)525-9997   **339**

All Year   1P: $343-$499   2P: $378-$534   XP: $5   F12

Location: I-75, exit 182, 0.6 mi w on Turfway and Houston rds. 4880 Houston Rd 41042. Fax: 859/525-9980. **Facility:** 70 one-bedroom standard units with kitchens, some with whirlpools. 3 stories (no elevator), interior corridors. *Bath:* combo or shower only. **Parking:** on-site. **Terms:** check-in 5 pm, small pets only ($20 extra charge). **Amenities:** extended cable TV, voice mail, irons, hair dryers. *Some:* dual phone lines. **Pool(s):** outdoor. **Guest Services:** valet and coin laundry. **Business Services:** meeting rooms. **Cards:** AX, CB, DC, MC, VI.

Extended Stay
Motel

SOME UNITS

BEST WESTERN INN FLORENCE

Phone: (859)525-0090   **333**

7/1-10/31   1P: $70-$150   2P: $80-$150   XP: $5   F12
4/1-6/30   1P: $55-$65   2P: $60-$70   XP: $5   F12
12/1-3/31 & 11/1-11/30   1P: $50-$60   2P: $55-$65   XP: $5   F12

Location: I-75, exit 181, just ne. 7821 Commerce Dr 41042. Fax: 859/525-6743. **Facility:** 51 one-bedroom standard units, some with whirlpools. 3 stories, interior corridors. *Bath:* combo or shower only. **Parking:** on-site. **Terms:** 7 day cancellation notice-fee imposed, [CP] meal plan available, pets ($5 extra charge). **Amenities:** extended cable TV, hair dryers. **Pool(s):** outdoor. **Leisure Activities:** whirlpool, exercise room. **Cards:** AX, DC, DS, MC, VI. **Special Amenities:** free continental breakfast and free newspaper.

Motel

SOME UNITS

COURTYARD BY MARRIOTT FLORENCE

Phone: (859)371-6464   **329**

All Year   1P: $70-$90   2P: $70-$90   XP: $5   F18

Location: I-75, exit 182, 0.4 mi se. 46 Cavalier Blvd 41042. Fax: 859/371-3443. **Facility:** 78 units. 75 one-bedroom standard units, some with whirlpools. 3 one-bedroom suites ($159-$169). 3 stories, interior corridors. **Parking:** on-site. **Terms:** [BP] meal plan available. **Amenities:** voice mail, irons, hair dryers. **Dining:** coffee shop, 6:30-10 am, Sat & Sun 7-11 am. **Pool(s):** heated indoor. **Leisure Activities:** whirlpool, exercise room. **Guest Services:** valet and coin laundry. **Business Services:** meeting rooms. **Cards:** AX, DC, DS, MC, VI.

Motel

SOME UNITS

(See map p. 558)

CROSS COUNTRY INN FLORENCE
Phone: (859)283-2030   334

(AAA) (SAVE)   Motel

All Year   1P: $40-$47   2P: $47-$54   XP: $2   F17
Location: I-71/75, exit 181, just ne. 7810 Commerce Dr 41042. Fax: 859/283-0171. **Facility:** 112 one-bedroom standard units. 2 stories, exterior corridors. *Bath:* combo or shower only. **Parking:** on-site. **Amenities:** voice mail. **Pool(s):** small heated outdoor. **Cards:** AX, CB, DC, DS, MC, VI. **Special Amenities:** free local telephone calls and preferred room (subject to availability with advanced reservations).

SOME UNITS

FAIRFIELD INN BY MARRIOTT-FLORENCE KENTUCKY
Phone: (859)371-4800   332

(AAA) (SAVE)   Motel

All Year   1P: $49-$75   2P: $49-$75
Location: I-71/75, exit 182, 0.5 mi se. 50 Cavalier Blvd 41042. Fax: 859/371-4998. **Facility:** 135 one-bedroom standard units. 3 stories, interior/exterior corridors. **Parking:** on-site. **Terms:** [ECP] meal plan available. **Amenities:** voice mail, irons. **Pool(s):** heated outdoor. **Guest Services:** valet laundry. **Business Services:** meeting rooms. **Cards:** AX, DC, DS, MC, VI. **Special Amenities:** free continental breakfast and free local telephone calls.

SOME UNITS

FLORENCE SUPER 8
Phone: 859/283-1221   335

(AAA) (SAVE)   Motel

All Year   1P: $56-$59   2P: $64-$67   XP: $4   F18
Location: I-75, exit 180, just e on US 42, just n. 7928 Dream St 41042 (3280 Olive St, LEMON GROVE, CA, 91945). Fax: 859/283-1490. **Facility:** 91 one-bedroom standard units, some with whirlpools. 2 stories, interior corridors. **Parking:** on-site. **Terms:** [CP] meal plan available, small pets only ($5 extra charge). **Amenities:** extended cable TV. **Guest Services:** coin laundry. **Cards:** AX, CB, DC, DS, MC, VI. **Special Amenities:** free continental breakfast and free newspaper.

SOME UNITS

HAMPTON INN-CINCINNATI AIRPORT
Phone: (859)283-1600   328

(SAVE)   Motel

All Year   1P: $94-$99   2P: $94-$99
Location: I-71/75, exit 182, 0.4 mi sw. 7393 Turfway Rd 41042. Fax: 859/283-0680. **Facility:** 117 one-bedroom standard units. 4 stories, interior corridors. **Parking:** on-site. **Terms:** 14 day cancellation notice. **Amenities:** irons, hair dryers. **Pool(s):** outdoor. **Guest Services:** valet laundry. **Business Services:** meeting rooms. **Cards:** AX, CB, DC, DS, MC, VI.

SOME UNITS

HILTON GREATER CINCINNATI AIRPORT
Phone: (859)371-4400   325

(SAVE)   Motor Inn   DC, DS, MC, VI.

All Year   1P: $94-$144   2P: $94-$154   XP: $10   F18
Location: I-71/75, exit 182, 0.4 mi sw. 7373 Turfway Rd 41042. Fax: 859/371-3361. **Facility:** 306 units. 304 one-bedroom standard units, some with whirlpools. 2 one-bedroom suites ($169-$219). 5 stories, interior corridors. *Bath:* combo or shower only. **Parking:** on-site. **Terms:** package plans. **Amenities:** dual phone lines, voice mail, irons, hair dryers. **Pool(s):** heated indoor. **Leisure Activities:** sauna, exercise room. **Guest Services:** gift shop, valet laundry. **Business Services:** meeting rooms, business center, PC, fax. **Cards:** AX, CB,

SOME UNITS

HOLIDAY INN FLORENCE
Phone: (859)371-2700   336

(AAA) (SAVE)   Motor Inn

All Year   1P: $79-$109   2P: $79-$109   XP: $10   F
Location: I-71/75, exit 180, just sw. 8050 Holiday Place (US 42) 41042. Fax: 859/283-9577. **Facility:** 105 one-bedroom standard units. 2 stories, interior corridors. *Bath:* combo or shower only. **Parking:** on-site. **Terms:** package plans. **Amenities:** extended cable TV, voice mail, irons, hair dryers. **Dining:** restaurant, 6 am-11 & 5:30-10 pm, Sun from 7 am, $5-$10, cocktails. **Pool(s):** outdoor. **Guest Services:** valet laundry, area transportation-within 5 mi. **Business Services:** meeting rooms. **Cards:** AX, CB, DC, DS, JC, MC, VI.

SOME UNITS

KNIGHTS INN FLORENCE
Phone: (859)371-9711   338

(AAA) (SAVE)   Motel

6/1-9/1   1P: $30-$99   2P: $40-$99   XP: $6   F17
3/1-5/31   1P: $30-$50   2P: $36-$60   XP: $6   F17
12/1-2/28 & 9/2-11/30   1P: $30-$39   2P: $33-$46   XP: $6   F17
Location: I-71/75, exit 180, just e on US 42, then just n. 8049 Dream St 41042. Fax: 859/371-4325. **Facility:** 115 one-bedroom standard units, some with efficiencies (no utensils). 1 story, exterior corridors. **Parking:** on-site. **Terms:** package plans, pets ($10 extra charge). **Amenities:** extended cable TV, high-speed Internet (fee), dual phone lines. **Pool(s):** outdoor. **Guest Services:** coin laundry. **Cards:** AX, DS, MC, VI.

SOME UNITS

SIGNATURE INN FLORENCE
Phone: (859)371-0081   330

Motel

All Year [ECP]   1P: $65-$71
Location: I-71/75, exit 182, just se. 30 Cavalier Ct 41042. Fax: 859/371-0081. **Facility:** 125 one-bedroom standard units, some with whirlpools. 2 stories, interior corridors. **Parking:** on-site. **Amenities:** extended cable TV, voice mail, irons, hair dryers. **Pool(s):** outdoor. **Guest Services:** valet laundry. **Business Services:** meeting rooms. **Cards:** AX, CB, DC, DS, MC, VI.

SOME UNITS

(See map p. 558)

———— WHERE TO DINE ————

CATHAY KITCHEN CHINESE RESTAURANT Lunch: $5-$8 Dinner: $7-$15 Phone: 859/282-0770 157
Chinese
Location: I-71/75, exit 180A (Mall Rd). 8049 Connector Dr 41042. **Hours:** 11 am-10 pm, Fri & Sat-10:30 pm, Sun-9 pm. Closed major holidays. **Reservations:** suggested. **Features:** casual dress; carryout; cocktails; a la carte. This bright and modern Chinese restaurant specializes in authentic Cantonese and not-so-spicy Szechuan cuisine. Fresh seafood and noodle menu. Try the crispy aromatic duck or walnut shrimp Hong Kong style. **Parking:** on-site. **Cards:** AX, DC, DS, MC, VI. ⊠

CHUNG GI WHA SUSHI & KOREAN BBQ Lunch: $7-$9 Dinner: $25 Phone: 859/525-9978 156
Sushi
Location: I-75, exit 181, just ne. 7800 Commerce 41042. **Hours:** 11:30 am-2:30 & 5-10 pm, Sat & Sun 3 pm-10 pm. Closed: 11/27, 12/25. **Features:** casual dress; beer & wine only; a la carte. An adventure for the palate, the restaurant offers opportunities for self-cooking at the evening buffet. Each table has a charcoal barbecue, tongs and scissors, and the friendly staff provides assistance, when needed. The evening buffet is divided into different meats, fowl and seafood—including such unusual choices as octopus and squid—and nicely displayed sushi rolls. A menu is provided for those not partaking of the buffet and for lunch patrons. **Parking:** on-site.

KARLO'S BISTRO ITALIA Lunch: $7-$10 Dinner: $10-$16 Phone: 859/282-8282 155
Italian
Location: I-75, exit 182. 4911 Houston Rd 41042. **Hours:** 11 am-10 pm, Fri-11 pm, Sat noon-11 pm. Closed: 11/27, 12/25. **Reservations:** suggested. **Features:** casual dress; children's menu; carryout; cocktails; a la carte. Indulge in multi-regional Italian cuisine at this classic restaurant decorated with artifacts and old-time photos of Italian families. Start your meal with minestrone soup and crusty bread served with olive oil and a vinaigrette. **Parking:** on-site. **Cards:** AX, DC, DS, MC, VI. ⊠

FORT MITCHELL pop. 7,400 (See map p. 558; index p. 563)

———— WHERE TO STAY ————

CROSS COUNTRY INN Phone: (859)341-2090 286
Motel
All Year 1P: $40-$47 2P: $47-$54 XP: $2 F17
Location: I-71/75, exit 186, off Buttermilk Pike. 2350 Royal Dr 41017. Fax: 859/341-3371. **Facility:** 106 one-bedroom standard units. 3 stories, exterior corridors. *Bath:* combo or shower only. **Parking:** on-site. **Amenities:** video games, voice mail. **Pool(s):** small heated outdoor. **Business Services:** meeting rooms. **Cards:** AX, CB, DC, DS, MC, VI. **Special Amenities:** free local telephone calls and preferred room (subject to availability with advanced reservations).
SOME UNITS
🅂🄳 📶 🄵 🏊 🎥 🖥 / ⊠ /
FEE

HOLIDAY INN FORT MITCHELL/I-75/GREATER CINCINNATI AREA Phone: (859)331-1500 285
Motor Inn
All Year 1P: $59-$89 2P: $59-$89 XP: $5 F17
Location: I-71/75, exit 188, just w. 2100 Dixie Hwy 41011. Fax: 859/331-2259. **Facility:** 214 units. 213 one-bedroom standard units. 1 one-bedroom suite. 2 stories, interior/exterior corridors. *Bath:* combo or shower only. **Parking:** on-site. **Terms:** check-in 4 pm, package plans. **Amenities:** voice mail, irons, hair dryers. **Dining:** dining room, 6 am-11 & 5-10 pm, $8-$15, cocktails. **Pool(s):** heated indoor. **Leisure Activities:** whirlpool, exercise room, indoor recreation area. **Guest Services:** valet laundry, area transportation-within 10 mi. **Business Services:** meeting rooms. **Cards:** AX, DC, DS, JC, MC, VI.
SOME UNITS
🅂🄳 ✈ 🍽 🄶🄼 🄵 🏊 ⊠ 🎥 📠 🖥 🖨 / ⊠ 📞 /
FEE FEE

———— WHERE TO DINE ————

GREYHOUND TAVERN Lunch: $5-$7 Dinner: $7-$20 Phone: 859/331-3767 128
Regional American
Location: At jct Buttermilk Pike and Dixie Hwy. 2500 Dixie Hwy 41017. **Hours:** 11:30 am-11 pm, Fri & Sat-midnight, Sun 10 am-10 pm. Closed major holidays. **Reservations:** suggested. **Features:** dressy casual; Sunday brunch; children's menu; carryout; cocktails & lounge; a la carte. Located in a rambling white-frame house, this popular neighborhood restaurant features traditional favorites like crispy fried chicken, juicy Kentucky ham and mashed potatoes overflowing with gravy. For dessert, try a sliver of warm apple pie. **Parking:** on-site. **Cards:** AX, MC, VI. ⊠

(See map p. 558)

ORIENTAL WOK   Lunch: $6-$7   Dinner: $8-$17   Phone: 859/331-3000   [129]
▼▼ ▼▼   **Location:** I-71/75, exit 186, just e. 317 Buttermilk Pike 41017. **Hours:** 11 am-10 pm, Fri-11 pm, Sat 4 pm-11 pm.
          Closed: 7/4, 11/27, 12/25. **Reservations:** accepted. **Features:** casual dress; Sunday brunch; children's
Chinese   menu; carryout; cocktails; a la carte. Although the spacious restaurant, decorated in a contemporary
          American motif with large picture windows, which focus on entrees that reflect the owner's southern
Chinese roots, it does offer pleasing surprises, such as a curried noodle dish from Singapore. **Parking:** on-site. **Cards:** AX,
DC, DS, MC, VI.
                                                                                                              ⊠

HEBRON pop. 5,600

———— **WHERE TO STAY** ————

CINCINNATI AIRPORT MARRIOTT   **Phone:** (859)586-0166
AAA SAVE   All Year   1P: $149-$179
▼▼▼▼   **Location:** I-275, exit 4A, 0.4 mi e. 2395 Progress Dr 41048. **Fax:** 859/586-0266. **Facility:** 295 units. 291 one-
          bedroom standard units. 4 one-bedroom suites ($255-$300), some with whirlpools. 8 stories, interior corri-
Motel   dors. *Bath:* combo or shower only. **Parking:** on-site. **Terms:** package plans. **Amenities:** video games, dual
          phone lines, voice mail, irons, hair dryers. **Dining:** restaurant, 6 am-2 & 5-11 pm, $10-$20. **Pool(s):** heated
          indoor. **Leisure Activities:** exercise room. **Guest Services:** valet and coin laundry. **Business Services:**
conference facilities, business center, PC. **Cards:** AX, DC, DS, MC, VI. *(See color ad card insert)*
                                                                                                SOME UNITS
                        [S] [✈] [¶] [⇆] [♨] [DATA PORT] [▢] [🖨] / [⊠] [▯] /
                                                       FEE

RADISSON HOTEL CINCINNATI AIRPORT   **Phone:** (859)371-6166
▼▼▼▼   All Year   1P: $85-$129   2P: $89-$139   XP: $10   F17
Motor Inn **Location:** 4 mi w of I-71 and 75 via I-275, exit 4B from I-275 (SR 212), 1.3 mi w on SR 212. Cincinnati N KY Airport
          41048 (PO Box 75108, CINCINNATI, 45275). **Fax:** 859/371-9863. **Facility:** 214 units. 211 one-bedroom standard
          units. 2 one- and 1 two-bedroom suites ($139-$199). 2-8 stories, interior corridors. **Parking:** on-site.
Terms: package plans, small pets only. **Amenities:** voice mail, irons, hair dryers. **Pool(s):** heated indoor. **Leisure Activities:** whirlpool, limited exercise equipment. **Guest Services:** gift shop, valet laundry. **Business Services:** conference facilities,
fax. **Cards:** AX, CB, DC, DS, JC, MC, VI.
                                                                                                SOME UNITS
             [ASK] [S] [✈] [🐾] [¶] [∅] [⇆] [♨] [DATA PORT] [▢] [🖨] / [⊠] [VCR] [▯]
                                                   FEE   FEE FEE

———— *The following lodging was either not evaluated or did not* ————
meet AAA rating requirements but is listed for your information only.

COUNTRY INN AND SUITES-CINCINNATI AIRPORT   **Phone:** 859/689-0700
[fyi]   4/1-6/30 & 10/1-11/30 [ECP]   1P: $89   2P: $89   XP: $10   F17
           12/1-3/31 & 7/1-9/30 [ECP]   1P: $79   2P: $79   XP: $10   F17
Motel   Too new to rate. **Location:** I-275, exit 4A, just off exit, on the right. 759 Petersburg Rd 41048. **Fax:** 859/389-1777.
           Amenities: radios, coffeemakers, microwaves, refrigerators, pool. **Terms:** 5 day cancellation notice.
Cards: AX, CB, DC, DS, JC, MC, VI. *(See color ad p 578)*

NEWPORT pop. 18,900   (See map p. 558; index p. 562)

———— **WHERE TO STAY** ————

COMFORT SUITES RIVERFRONT   **Phone:** (859)291-6700   [230]
SAVE   All Year   1P: $84-$114   2P: $84-$114   XP: $10   F18
▼▼▼   **Location:** I-471, exit 5, just e on SR 8. 420 Riverboat Row 41071. **Fax:** 859/291-6702. **Facility:** 124 units. 115 one-
Motel   bedroom standard units. 9 one-bedroom suites ($155-$199) with whirlpools. 6 stories, interior corridors. *Bath:*
          combo or shower only. **Parking:** on-site. **Terms:** check-in 4 pm. **Amenities:** extended cable TV, dual phone
          lines, voice mail, safes (fee), irons, hair dryers. **Leisure Activities:** exercise room. **Business Services:**
          meeting rooms. **Cards:** AX, CB, DC, DS, JC, MC, VI.
                                                                                                SOME UNITS
                   [S] [✈] [⊪] [∅M] [♨] [DATA PORT] [▯] [🖙] [▢] [🖨] / [⊠] /
                                                    FEE

WILLIAMSTOWN pop. 3,000

———— **WHERE TO STAY** ————

DAYS INN   **Phone:** (859)824-5025
AAA SAVE   All Year [CP]   1P: $45-$56   2P: $49-$66   XP: $5
▼▼ ▼▼   **Location:** I-75, exit 154, just n. 211 SR 36 W 41097. **Fax:** 859/824-5028. **Facility:** 51 one-bedroom standard units.
Motel   1-2 stories, exterior corridors. **Parking:** on-site. **Terms:** small pets only ($5 extra charge). **Amenities:** ex-
          tended cable TV, hair dryers. *Some:* irons. **Pool(s):** outdoor. **Cards:** AX, CB, DC, DS, JC, MC, VI.
          Special Amenities: early check-in/late check-out and free local telephone calls.
                                                                                                SOME UNITS
                      [S] [🐾] [⊪] [⇆] [♨] [🖨] / [⊠] [▯] [🖙] [▢] /

The previous listings were for the Cincinnati Vicinity.
The following resumes the alphabetical listings
of cities in Ohio.

CIRCLEVILLE —See Columbus p. 657.

Destination Cleveland
pop. 505,600

Cleveland is a vibrant city that knows how to indulge itself. The Metroparks system offers recreational opportunities ranging from golfing to cross-country skiing.

One of the country's largest consumer markets, shopping here is a pleasure. Don't pass up a trip to The Arcade, an indoor mall built in the late 19th century.

Dining along the waterfront, Cleveland. Sidewalk dining makes a refreshing break in a hectic sightseeing and shopping schedule.

Cleveland Browns Stadium. In 1999, after a 4-year hiatus, the NFL's Browns returned to their hometown and their home stadium. (See mention page 217)

Cleveland Skyline. The city's diverse architecture includes such landmarks as the Art Deco Terminal Tower (far right) and the ultramodern Rock and Roll Hall of Fame and Museum (foreground).

See Downtown map page 598

Cleveland

Rocky River · Lakewood · Cleveland Heights · Mayfield · Mayfield Heights · Beachwood · Westlake · Shaker Heights · Moreland Hills · North Olmstead · Brook Park · Independence · Bedford · Berea · Middleburg Heights · Solon · Strongsville · Broadview Heights · Brecksville · Medina

***P**laces included in this AAA Destination City:*

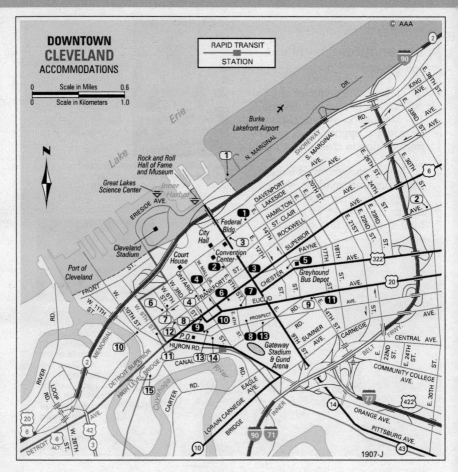

© AAA

DOWNTOWN CLEVELAND ACCOMMODATIONS

RAPID TRANSIT ▪ STATION

Scale in Miles 0 — 0.6
Scale in Kilometers 0 — 1.0

1907-J

Downtown Cleveland

This index helps you "spot" where approved accommodations and restaurants are located on the corresponding detailed maps. Lodging rate ranges are for comparison only and show the property's high season; rates are per night, unless only weekly (W) or monthly (M) rates are available. Restaurant rate range is for dinner, unless only lunch (L) is served. Turn to the listing page for more detailed rate information and consult display ads for special promotions.

Spotter/Map Page Number	OA	DOWNTOWN CLEVELAND - Lodgings	Diamond Rating	Rate Range High Season	Listing Page
❶ / above	AAA	Holiday Inn Select-City Centre Lakeshore - see color ad p 608	◈◈◈	$119-$139 SAVE	608
❷ / above	AAA	Sheraton Cleveland City Centre	◈◈◈	$169 SAVE	610
❸ / above	AAA	Hampton Inn Cleveland-Downtown - see ad p 608	◈◈◈	$99-$119 SAVE	607
❹ / above	AAA	Cleveland Marriott Downtown at Key Center - see color ad card insert	◈◈◈	$99-$239 SAVE	607
❺ / above	AAA	Embassy Suites-Cleveland Downtown - see ad p 607	◈◈◈	$169-$259 SAVE	607
❻ / above	AAA	Hyatt Regency Cleveland at the Arcade - see ad p 609	◈◈◈	$109-$261 SAVE	609
❼ / above	AAA	Holiday Inn Express Hotel & Suites	◈◈◈	$99-$129 SAVE	607

Spotter/Map Page Number	OA	DOWNTOWN CLEVELAND - Lodgings (continued)	Diamond Rating	Rate Range High Season	Listing Page
8 / p. 598	AAA	Residence Inn by Marriott - see color ad card insert	◈◈◈	$79-$199 SAVE	610
9 / p. 598	AAA	Renaissance Cleveland Hotel - see color ad card insert	◈◈◈	$99-$239 SAVE	609
10 / p. 598		The Ritz-Carlton, Cleveland	◈◈◈◈	$269	610
11 / p. 598	AAA	Wyndham Cleveland at Playhouse Square	◈◈◈	$109-$169 SAVE	610
13 / p. 598	AAA	Radisson Hotel at Gateway-Cleveland - see color ad p 609	◈◈◈	$129-$149 SAVE	609
		DOWNTOWN CLEVELAND - Restaurants			
1 / p. 598	AAA	Hornblower's Barge & Grill	◈◈	$13-$25	611
2 / p. 598		Li Wah	◈◈	$8-$15	611
3 / p. 598		Cafe Sausalito	◈◈	$10-$20	610
4 / p. 598		John Q's Steakhouse	◈◈	$16-$30	611
6 / p. 598		Blue Point Grille	◈◈◈	$15-$30	610
7 / p. 598		Greek Isles	◈◈	$13-$30	610
8 / p. 598	AAA	Sans Souci	◈◈◈	$11-$27	611
9 / p. 598		Hickerson's At The Hanna	◈◈	$15-$30	611
10 / p. 598	AAA	Watermark Restaurant	◈◈◈	$17-$38	611
11 / p. 598		Mallorca	◈◈◈	$15-$28	611
12 / p. 598		Johnny's Downtown	◈◈◈	$18-$34	611
13 / p. 598		Century	◈◈◈◈	$20-$35	610
14 / p. 598		Hyde Park Chop House	◈◈	$14-$36	611
15 / p. 598		Lola	◈◈◈	$16-$23	611

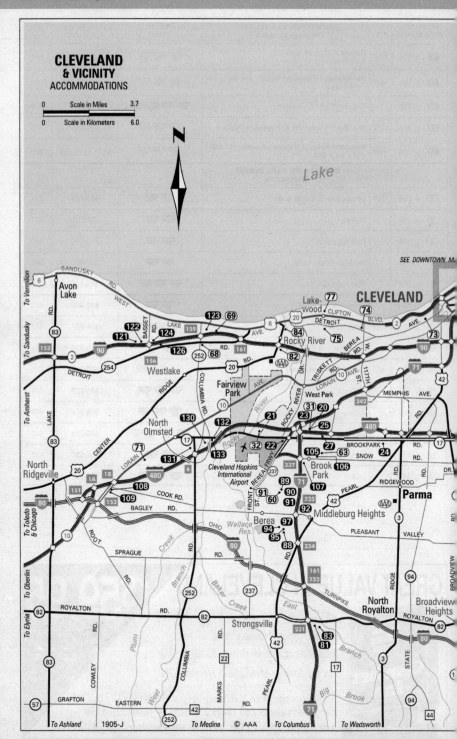

CLEVELAND
& VICINITY
ACCOMMODATIONS

0 Scale in Miles 3.7

0 Scale in Kilometers 6.0

✈ Airport Accommodations

Spotter/Map Page Number	OA	CLEVELAND-HOPKINS INT'L	Diamond Rating	Rate Range High Season	Listing Page
105 / p. 600	AAA	Fairfield Inn by Marriott-Brook Park, 1.5 mi e of airport	▽▽	$79 SAVE	620
23 / p. 600	AAA	Baymont Inn & Suites Cleveland-Airport, 3.5 mi ne of airport	▽▽▽	$74-$84 SAVE	612
24 / p. 600	AAA	Budget Inn Cleveland Airport, 2.3 mi e of airport	▽	$62 SAVE	612
21 / p. 600	AAA	Hilton Garden Inn Cleveland Airport, 1.5 mi n of airport	▽▽▽	$89-$119 SAVE	614
20 / p. 600	AAA	Holiday Inn-Cleveland Airport, 3.5 mi ne of airport	▽▽▽	$69-$139 SAVE	615
27 / p. 600	AAA	Ramada Inn-Cleveland Airport, 2.3 mi e of airport	▽	$99-$109 SAVE	615
22 / p. 600		Sheraton Airport Hotel Cleveland, at the airport	▽▽▽	$180-$200	615
90 / p. 600	AAA	Comfort Inn-Cleveland Airport, 3.5 mi s of airport	▽▽▽	$60-$150 SAVE	626
88 / p. 600	AAA	Courtyard by Marriott, 3.5 mi se of airport	▽▽▽	$99-$119 SAVE	626
95 / p. 600	AAA	Cross Country Inn, 3.5 mi se of airport	▽▽	$46-$60 SAVE	626
94 / p. 600	AAA	Radisson-Hotel Cleveland Southwest, 3.5 mi se	▽▽▽	$109-$139 SAVE	626
97 / p. 600	AAA	Red Roof Inn-Middleburg Heights, 3.5 mi se	▽	$57-$73 SAVE	626
91 / p. 600	AAA	Residence Inn by Marriott, 3.5 mi s of airport	▽▽▽	$79-$119 SAVE	627

Cleveland and Vicinity

This index helps you "spot" where approved accommodations and restaurants are located on the corresponding detailed maps. Lodging rate ranges are for comparison only and show the property's high season; rates are per night, unless only weekly (W) or monthly (M) rates are available. Restaurant rate range is for dinner, unless only lunch (L) is served. Turn to the listing page for more detailed rate information and consult display ads for special promotions.

Spotter/Map Page Number	OA	WILLOUGHBY - Lodgings	Diamond Rating	Rate Range High Season	Listing Page
10 / p. 600	AAA	Red Roof Inn-East	▽▽	$56-$72 SAVE	774
11 / p. 600		Days Inn-Willoughby	▽▽	$58	773
12 / p. 600	AAA	Fairfield Inn by Marriott-Willoughby - see color ad card insert	▽▽▽	$65-$89 SAVE	774
13 / p. 600	AAA	Courtyard by Marriott - see color ad card insert	▽▽▽	$79-$119 SAVE	773
14 / p. 600	AAA	Ramada Inn Cleveland East - see color ad p 615	▽▽	$50-$60 SAVE	774
		WILLOUGHBY - Restaurant			
24 / p. 600		Gavi's Italian Cuisine	▽▽▽	$10-$20	774
		WICKLIFFE - Lodgings			
16 / p. 600		Hampton Inn-Cleveland/Wickliffe	▽▽▽	$89-$99	773
17 / p. 600		Four Points by Sheraton Cleveland East	▽▽▽	$99-$139	773
18 / p. 600	AAA	Holiday Inn North East	▽▽▽	$105-$135 SAVE	773
		CLEVELAND - Lodgings			
19 / p. 600		Inter-Continental Suite Hotel	▽▽▽	Failed to provide	615
20 / p. 600	AAA	Holiday Inn-Cleveland Airport	▽▽▽	$69-$139 SAVE	615
21 / p. 600	AAA	Hilton Garden Inn Cleveland Airport	▽▽▽	$89-$119 SAVE	614
22 / p. 600		Sheraton Airport Hotel Cleveland	▽▽▽	$180-$200	615
23 / p. 600	AAA	Baymont Inn & Suites Cleveland-Airport - see color ad opposite title page	▽▽▽	$74-$84 SAVE	612

Spotter/Map Page Number	OA	CLEVELAND - Lodgings (continued)	Diamond Rating	Rate Range High Season	Listing Page
24 / p. 600	AAA	Budget Inn Cleveland Airport	◈	$62 SAVE	612
25 / p. 600	AAA	Cleveland Airport Marriott - see color ad card insert	◈◈◈	$89-$169 SAVE	612
26 / p. 600	AAA	Glidden House - see color ad p 614	◈◈◈	$159-$179 SAVE	613
27 / p. 600	AAA	Ramada Inn-Cleveland Airport	◈	$99-$109 SAVE	615
		CLEVELAND - Restaurants			
28 / p. 600		The Baricelli Inn	◈◈◈◈	$18-$40	616
31 / p. 600		Somer's Place	◈◈	$7-$14	616
32 / p. 600	AAA	100th Bomb Group-A Restaurant	◈	$13-$25	616
33 / p. 600	AAA	Guarino's	◈◈	$11-$17	616
37 / p. 600		Salvatore's Ristorante	◈◈	$7-$14	616
39 / p. 600		Sergio's in University Circle	◈◈◈	$12-$22	616
		BEACHWOOD - Lodgings			
29 / p. 600		Hilton Cleveland East/Beachwood - see ad p 614	◈◈◈	$109-$159	617
30 / p. 600	AAA	Holiday Inn-Beachwood	◈◈◈	$85-$119 SAVE	617
31 / p. 600	AAA	Ramada Inn & Conference Center - see color ad p 617	◈◈◈	$69-$119 SAVE	617
32 / p. 600		Homestead Studio Suites-Cleveland/Beachwood	◈◈	$89-$104	617
33 / p. 600	AAA	Residence Inn by Marriot Cleveland-Beachwood - see color ad card insert	◈◈◈	$155-$165 SAVE	618
34 / p. 600		Embassy Suites - see ad p 607	◈◈◈	$159-$209	617
		BEACHWOOD - Restaurants			
41 / p. 600		Napa Valley Grille-in Beachwood Place	◈◈◈	$12-$20	618
42 / p. 600		Ho Wah Restaurant	◈◈	$9-$16	618
43 / p. 600		Moxie Restaurant	◈◈	$9-$26	618
44 / p. 600		Shuhei	◈◈	$14-$30	618
45 / p. 600		J Gilbert's	◈◈	$12-$20	618
46 / p. 600		Charley's Crab	◈◈	$13-$32	618
47 / p. 600		Cafe 56 Grill	◈◈	$10-$15	618
49 / p. 600		Ristorante Giovanni's	◈◈◈◈	$19-$35	618
		TWINSBURG - Lodgings			
35 / p. 600		Hilton Garden Inn Cleveland/Twinsburg - see ad p 751	◈◈◈	$79-$169	764
36 / p. 600		Twinsburg Super 8 Motel	◈◈	$80-$85	764
		TWINSBURG - Restaurant			
53 / p. 600		Mac Laren's	◈◈◈	$12-$25	765
		MACEDONIA - Lodgings			
38 / p. 600	AAA	Cleveland/Akron Travelodge - see color ad p 613	◈	$65-$100 SAVE	704
39 / p. 600		Country Inn & Suites By Carlson - see color ad p 646	◈◈◈	$129	705
40 / p. 600	AAA	Baymont Inn & Suites Cleveland-Macedonia - see color ad opposite title page	◈◈◈	$99-$119 SAVE	704
41 / p. 600		Knights Inn-Cleveland/Macedonia	◈	$57-$79	705

Spotter/Map Page Number	OA	RICHFIELD - Lodgings	Diamond Rating	Rate Range High Season	Listing Page
44 / p. 600		Super 8 Motel	◆◆◆	$60-$82	732
45 / p. 600	AAA	Holiday Inn-Richfield	◆◆◆	$84 (SAVE)	732
		BROADVIEW HEIGHTS - Lodgings			
51 / p. 600		Tallyho-tel	◆	$50-$85	619
		INDEPENDENCE - Lodgings			
59 / p. 600		Cleveland/Independence Days Inn - see ad p 621	◆◆	$69-$109	621
60 / p. 600	AAA	Residence Inn by Marriott - see color ad card insert	◆◆◆	$98-$134 (SAVE)	623
61 / p. 600	AAA	Courtyard by Marriott - see color ad card insert	◆◆◆	$69-$129 (SAVE)	621
62 / p. 600	AAA	Amerisuites (Cleveland So/Independence)	◆◆◆	$89-$119 (SAVE)	621
63 / p. 600		Holiday Inn-Independence/Rockside I-77	◆◆◆	$69-$129	622
64 / p. 600	AAA	Four Points By Sheraton Cleveland South - see color ad p 622	◆◆◆	$79-$169 (SAVE)	622
65 / p. 600	AAA	Red Roof Inn	◆◆	$61-$67 (SAVE)	622
66 / p. 600	AAA	Baymont Inn & Suites Cleveland-Independence - see color ad opposite title page	◆◆	$74-$84 (SAVE)	621
68 / p. 600		Hilton Cleveland South	◆◆◆	$109-$199	622
69 / p. 600		Comfort Inn	◆◆◆	$69-$89	621
70 / p. 600		Hampton Inn & Suites	◆◆◆	$85-$97	622
		INDEPENDENCE - Restaurants			
55 / p. 600		Harry's Steakhouse	◆◆	$9-$18	623
56 / p. 600		Aladdin's Eatery	◆◆	$4-$10	623
57 / p. 600		Zayda's	◆	$8-$15	623
		BEDFORD - Lodgings			
72 / p. 600		Holiday Inn Express	◆◆◆	$99-$119	619
		SOLON - Lodgings			
76 / p. 600	AAA	Days Inn Six Flags	◆	$98-$119 (SAVE)	629
77 / p. 600		Hampton Inn	◆◆◆	$129-$139	629
		SOLON - Restaurant			
58 / p. 600		43 Bistro	◆◆◆	$15-$25	629
		STRONGSVILLE - Lodgings			
81 / p. 600	AAA	Holiday Inn Select-Strongsville	◆◆◆	$99-$109 (SAVE)	629
83 / p. 600	AAA	Red Roof Inn-Strongsville	◆	$49-$65 (SAVE)	629
		EASTLAKE - Lodgings			
87 / p. 600	AAA	Radisson Hotel & Conference Cleveland-Eastlake	◆◆◆	$106-$129 (SAVE)	682
		MIDDLEBURG HEIGHTS - Lodgings			
88 / p. 600	AAA	Courtyard by Marriott - see color ad card insert	◆◆◆	$99-$119 (SAVE)	626
89 / p. 600		Hampton Inn & Suites	◆◆◆	$89	626
90 / p. 600	AAA	Comfort Inn-Cleveland Airport - see color ad p 599	◆◆◆	$60-$150 (SAVE)	626

Spotter/Map Page Number	OA	MIDDLEBURG HEIGHTS - Lodgings (continued)	Diamond Rating	Rate Range High Season	Listing Page
91 / p. 600	◈	Residence Inn by Marriott - see color ad card insert	◇◇◇	$79-$119 SAVE	627
92 / p. 600	◈	Clarion Cleveland Airport West - see color ad p 625	◇◇◇	$80-$90 SAVE	625
94 / p. 600	◈	Radisson-Hotel Cleveland Southwest - see ad p 626	◇◇◇	$109-$139 SAVE	626
95 / p. 600	◈	Cross Country Inn	◇◇	$46-$60 SAVE	626
97 / p. 600	◈	Red Roof Inn-Middleburg Heights	◇	$57-$73 SAVE	626
		MIDDLEBURG HEIGHTS - Restaurant			
60 / p. 600	.	Hong Kong Palace	◇◇	$8-$16	627
		MAYFIELD HEIGHTS - Lodgings			
100 / p. 600	◈	Baymont Inn & Suites-Cleveland NE (Mayfield Heights)	◇◇	$85-$95 SAVE	624
		BROOK PARK - Lodgings			
105 / p. 600	◈	Fairfield Inn by Marriott-Brook Park - see ad p 612 & color ad card insert	◇◇	$79 SAVE	620
106 / p. 600	◈	Holiday Inn Express/Brookpark-Cleveland Hopkins Airport	◇◇◇	$99-$119 SAVE	620
107 / p. 600		Best Western Airport Inn & Suites	◇◇◇	$79-$109	620
		BROOK PARK - Restaurant			
63 / p. 600		El Rincon	◇◇	$6-$12	620
		NORTH RIDGEVILLE - Lodgings			
108 / p. 600	◈	Travelodge North Ridgeville	◇	$41-$66 SAVE	722
109 / p. 600		Super 8 Motel - see color ad p 739	◇	$56-$89	722
		AURORA - Lodgings			
112 / p. 600	◈	The Bertram Inn & Conference Center - see color ad p 536	◇◇◇	$159-$189 SAVE	536
113 / p. 600	◈	Six Flags Hotel of Ohio	◇◇◇	$185-$275 SAVE	536
114 / p. 600		Aurora Inn of Mario's International	◇◇◇	$159-$225	535
115 / p. 600	◈	Walden Country Inn & Stables	◇◇◇	$220-$345 SAVE	536
		AURORA - Restaurant			
65 / p. 600	◈	Aurora's Amish Style Restaurant & Bakery	◇	$7-$12	537
		WESTLAKE - Lodgings			
121 / p. 600	◈	Residence Inn by Marriott - see color ad card insert	◇◇◇	$109-$119 SAVE	630
122 / p. 600	◈	Holiday Inn Westlake	◇◇◇	$79-$129 SAVE	630
123 / p. 600	◈	Cross Country Inn	◇◇	$44-$58 SAVE	630
124 / p. 600	◈	Red Roof Inn-Westlake	◇◇	$59-$76 SAVE	630
126 / p. 600	◈	Hampton Inn	◇◇	$70-$96 SAVE	630
		WESTLAKE - Restaurants			
68 / p. 600		Le Bistro du Beaujolais Restaurant	◇◇◇	$8-$15	631
69 / p. 600		Big Fish Seafood Bistro	◇◇◇	$9-$20	630
		NORTH OLMSTED - Lodgings			
130 / p. 600	◈	Radisson Inn Cleveland Airport - see ad p 614	◇◇◇	$129 SAVE	628
131 / p. 600	◈	Hampton Inn	◇◇	$79-$95 SAVE	627
132 / p. 600	◈	Courtyard by Marriott - see color ad card insert	◇◇◇	$109 SAVE	627

Spotter/Map Page Number	OA	NORTH OLMSTED - Lodgings (continued)	Diamond Rating	Rate Range High Season	Listing Page
133 / p. 600		Homestead Studio Suites-Cleveland/Airport/North Olmsted	◆◆	$54-$69	627
		NORTH OLMSTED - Restaurant			
71 / p. 600		El Charro	◆	$6-$12	628
		BOSTON HEIGHTS - Lodgings			
142 / p. 600		Holiday Inn - see color ad p 613	◆◆◆	$129-$159	543
143 / p. 600	AAA	Comfort Inn	◆◆◆	$99-$179 SAVE	542
		LAKEWOOD - Restaurants			
73 / p. 600		Aladdin's Eatery	◆◆	$7-$12	623
74 / p. 600		Maria's Roman Room	◆◆	$9-$16	623
75 / p. 600		Players	◆◆	$13-$20	623
77 / p. 600		Pier W	◆◆	$22	623
		MORELAND HILLS - Restaurant			
80 / p. 600		Wards' Inn	◆◆◆	$17-$30	627
		ROCKY RIVER - Restaurants			
82 / p. 600		King Wah Restaurant	◆◆	$6-$10	628
84 / p. 600		Gamekeeper's Lodge	◆◆	$15-$25	628
		CLEVELAND HEIGHTS - Restaurants			
86 / p. 600		Lemon Grass	◆◆	$7-$13	620
87 / p. 600		Cafe Tandoor	◆◆	$9-$20	620
		BEREA - Restaurant			
91 / p. 600		Pufferbelly Ltd	◆◆	$10-$17	619
		SHAKER HEIGHTS - Restaurant			
99 / p. 600		Eddie Sand's Blueline Cafe	◆	$6-$14	628
		BRECKSVILLE - Restaurant			
110 / p. 600		Marco Polo's	◆◆◆	$11-$20	619

DOWNTOWN CLEVELAND   (See map p. 598; index p. 598)

——— WHERE TO STAY ———

CLEVELAND MARRIOTT DOWNTOWN AT KEY CENTER   Phone: (216)696-9200   **4**

(AAA) (SAVE)
Hotel

4/1-10/26	1P: $99-$239
10/27-3/31	1P: $89-$199

Location: Northeast corner of Public Square (W Mall Dr). 127 Public Sq 44114-1305. Fax: 216/696-0966. **Facility:** 400 units. 386 one-bedroom standard units. 14 one-bedroom suites ($299-$750). 25 stories, interior corridors. *Bath:* combo or shower only. **Parking:** *Fee:* off-site and valet. **Terms:** check-in 4 pm, package plans. **Amenities:** high-speed Internet (fee), dual phone lines, voice mail, safes, irons, hair dryers. *Some:* CD players. **Dining:** dining room, restaurant, deli, 6:30 am-midnight, $14-$28, cocktails. **Pool(s):** heated indoor. **Leisure Activities:** sauna, whirlpool, exercise room. **Guest Services:** valet and coin laundry. **Business Services:** conference facilities, business center. *Fee:* PC, fax. **Cards:** AX, CB, DC, DS, JC, MC, VI. *(See color ad card insert)*

SOME UNITS

🅢🅓 📶 🍴 🍸 🉐 🏊 ✕ 📺 [DATA PORT] 🔌 🍽 💻 📠 / ✕ /
　　　　　　　　　　　　FEE

EMBASSY SUITES-CLEVELAND DOWNTOWN   Phone: (216)523-8000   **5**

(AAA) (SAVE)
Suite Hotel

6/1-8/31	1P: $169-$259	2P: $169-$259	XP: $20 F17
4/1-5/31 & 9/1-3/31	1P: $149-$259	2P: $149-$259	XP: $20 F17

Location: In Reserve Square Complex. 1701 E 12th St 44114. Fax: 216/523-1698. **Facility:** 268 units. 263 one- and 5 two-bedroom suites ($149-$259). 13 stories, interior corridors. **Terms:** [BP] meal plan available. **Amenities:** video games, voice mail, irons, hair dryers. **Dining:** restaurant, 11:30 am-11 pm, $10-$25, cocktails. **Pool(s):** heated indoor. **Leisure Activities:** sauna, lighted tennis court. **Guest Services:** complimentary evening beverages, valet and coin laundry. **Business Services:** meeting rooms. **Cards:** AX, CB, DC, DS, JC, MC, VI. **Special Amenities:** free continental breakfast and free newspaper. *(See ad below)*

SOME UNITS

🅢🅓 📶 🍴 🍸 🉐 🏊 📡 📺 [DATA PORT] 🔌 🍽 💻 📠 / ✕ /
　　　　　　　　　　　　FEE

HAMPTON INN CLEVELAND-DOWNTOWN   Phone: (216)241-6600   **3**

(AAA) (SAVE)
Motel

10/1-3/31 [CP]	1P: $99-$109	2P: $99-$119	
4/1-9/30 [CP]	1P: $99-$109	2P: $99-$109	XP: $10 F18

Location: Downtown; jct of E 9th St and Superior. 1460 E 9th St 44114. Fax: 216/241-8811. **Facility:** 194 units. 185 one-bedroom standard units. 9 one-bedroom suites ($109-$129). 14 stories, interior corridors. *Bath:* combo or shower only. **Parking:** on-site (fee). **Amenities:** dual phone lines, voice mail, irons, hair dryers. **Leisure Activities:** exercise room. **Guest Services:** valet laundry. **Business Services:** meeting rooms, fax. **Cards:** AX, DC, DS, MC, VI. **Special Amenities:** free continental breakfast and free local telephone calls. *(See ad p 608)*

SOME UNITS

🅛🅜 🉐 📺 [DATA PORT] 💻 📠 / ✕ /
　　　　　　　FEE

HOLIDAY INN EXPRESS HOTEL & SUITES   Phone: (216)443-1000   **7**

(AAA) (SAVE)
Motel

7/1-3/31	1P: $99-$129	2P: $99-$129	XP: $10 F18
4/1-6/30	1P: $79-$119	2P: $79-$119	XP: $10 F18

Location: Jct E 9th St and Euclid Ave. 629 Euclid Ave 44114. Fax: 216/443-1722. **Facility:** 141 one-bedroom standard units, some with efficiencies (no utensils) and/or whirlpools. 16 stories, interior corridors. *Bath:* combo or shower only. **Parking:** *Fee:* off-site and valet. **Terms:** cancellation fee imposed, [ECP] meal plan available. **Amenities:** video games, dual phone lines, voice mail, irons, hair dryers. **Leisure Activities:** exercise room. *Fee:* game room. **Guest Services:** valet and coin laundry. **Business Services:** meeting rooms, business center. **Cards:** AX, DC, DS, MC, VI.

SOME UNITS

🅢🅓 ✈ 🉐 📺 [DATA PORT] 💻 📠 / ✕ 🔌 🍽 /
　FEE　　　　FEE

(See map p. 598)

HOLIDAY INN SELECT-CITY CENTRE LAKESHORE   Phone: (216)241-5100

Motor Inn

4/1-10/31   1P: $119-$139
11/1-3/31   1P: $109-$129

Location: Jct E 12th St and Lakeside Ave. 1111 Lakeside Ave 44114. Fax: 216/241-1831. **Facility:** 381 units. 379 one-bedroom standard units. 2 one-bedroom suites. 18 stories, interior corridors. *Bath:* some combo or shower only. **Parking:** on-site (fee). **Terms:** cancellation fee imposed, package plans. **Amenities:** CD players, dual phone lines, irons, hair dryers. *Some:* voice mail. **Dining:** restaurant, 6 am-10 pm, $10-$18. cocktails. **Pool(s):** heated indoor. **Leisure Activities:** whirlpool, exercise room. **Guest Services:** gift shop, valet and coin laundry, area transportation-within 5 mi. **Business Services:** conference facilities, business center, PC, fax. **Cards:** AX, CB, DC, DS, JC, MC, VI. **Special Amenities:** free room upgrade and preferred room (each subject to availability with advanced reservations). *(See color ad below)*

SOME UNITS

(See map p. 598)

HYATT REGENCY CLEVELAND AT THE ARCADE   Phone: (216)575-1234   **6**

(AAA) (SAVE)   All Year   1P: $109-$261   XP: $25   F18

Hotel

Location: Downtown; just e of Public Square. 420 Superior Ave 44114. Fax: 216/575-1690. **Facility:** 293 units. 289 one-bedroom standard units. 4 one-bedroom suites ($495-$995). 9 stories, interior corridors. *Bath:* combo or shower only. **Parking:** on-site and valet (fee). **Terms:** cancellation fee imposed, [AP], [BP] & [CP] meal plans available. **Amenities:** dual phone lines, voice mail, safes, irons, hair dryers. **Dining:** restaurant, 6:30 am-10 pm, $17-$24, cocktails. **Leisure Activities:** exercise room. **Guest Services:** valet laundry. **Business Services:** conference facilities, business center, PC, fax. **Cards:** AX, CB, DC, DS, MC, VI. *(See ad below)*

SOME UNITS

FEE   FEE FEE FEE

RADISSON HOTEL AT GATEWAY-CLEVELAND   Phone: (216)377-9000   **13**

(AAA) (SAVE)   4/1-9/3   1P: $129   2P: $149   XP: $15   F18
             9/4-3/31   1P: $119   2P: $139   XP: $15   F18

Hotel

Location: North side of Jacob's Field. 651 Huron Rd 44115. Fax: 216/377-9001. **Facility:** 142 units. 138 one-bedroom standard units. 4 one-bedroom suites. 5-8 stories, interior corridors. *Bath:* combo or shower only. **Parking:** on-site (fee). **Terms:** cancellation fee imposed, small pets only. **Amenities:** video games, dual phone lines, voice mail, irons, hair dryers. **Dining:** restaurant, 6:30 am-10:30 pm, Sat & Sun from 7 am, $7-$19, cocktails. **Leisure Activities:** exercise room. **Guest Services:** valet laundry. **Business Services:** meeting rooms, PC, fax. **Cards:** AX, DC, DS, MC, VI. **Special Amenities:** early check-in/late check-out and free newspaper. *(See color ad below)*

SOME UNITS

FEE   FEE FEE

RENAISSANCE CLEVELAND HOTEL   Phone: (216)696-5600   **9**

(AAA) (SAVE)   4/1-10/26   1P: $99-$239
             10/27-3/31   1P: $89-$199

Historic Hotel

Location: At Superior and West 3rd St. 24 Public Sq 44113. Fax: 216/696-3102. **Facility:** 391 units. 364 one-bedroom standard units. 27 one-bedroom suites ($269-$900), some with whirlpools. 15 stories, interior corridors. *Bath:* combo or shower only. **Parking:** *Fee:* on-site and valet. **Dining:** 2 restaurants, 6 am-2 & 4-10 pm, $11-$27, cocktails, also, Sans Souci, see separate listing, entertainment. **Pool(s):** heated indoor. **Leisure Activities:** sauna, exercise room. **Guest Services:** gift shop, massage (fee), valet laundry. **Business Services:** conference facilities, business center, fax. **Cards:** AX, CB, DC, DS, JC, MC, VI. *(See color ad card insert)*

SOME UNITS

FEE

(See map p. 598)

RESIDENCE INN BY MARRIOTT
Phone: (216)443-9043   8

AAA SAVE
Suite Motel

All Year   1P: $79-$199   2P: $79-$199
Location: Downtown; across from Gund Arena/Jacob's Field. 527 Prospect Ave 44115. Fax: 216/443-9843. **Facility:** 174 units. 96 one-bedroom standard units with efficiencies. 63 one- and 15 two-bedroom suites with kitchens, some with whirlpools. 7 stories, interior corridors. *Bath:* combo or shower only. **Parking:** on-site and valet (fee). **Amenities:** *Some:* high-speed Internet (fee). **Leisure Activities:** billiard room. **Guest Services:** valet and coin laundry, area transportation-within 5 mi. **Business Services:** meeting rooms, fax. **Cards:** AX, CB, DC, MC, VI. *(See color ad card insert)*

SOME UNITS

THE RITZ-CARLTON, CLEVELAND
Phone: (216)623-1300 10

Hotel

9/8-3/31	1P: $269	2P: $269	XP: $50 F18
4/8-9/7	1P: $259	2P: $259	XP: $50 F18
4/1-4/7	1P: $249	2P: $249	XP: $50 F18

Location: In Tower City Center (3rd St side). 1515 W 3rd St 44113. Fax: 216/623-0515. **Facility:** This outpost of the national chain offers stately elegance in a service-oriented atmosphere. 206 units. 184 one-bedroom standard units. 22 one-bedroom suites, some with whirlpools. 14 stories, interior corridors. *Bath:* some combo or shower only. **Parking:** *Fee:* on-site and valet. **Terms:** cancellation fee imposed, small pets only ($30 deposit). **Amenities:** *Some:* CD players. **Dining:** Century, see separate listing. **Pool(s):** heated indoor. **Leisure Activities:** sauna, whirlpool, exercise room. **Guest Services:** massage (fee), afternoon tea, valet laundry. **Business Services:** conference facilities, business center, PC, fax (fee). **Cards:** AX, CB, DC, DS, JC, MC, VI.

SOME UNITS

SHERATON CLEVELAND CITY CENTRE
Phone: (216)771-7600 2

AAA SAVE
Hotel

6/16-10/31	1P: $169	2P: $169	XP: $20 F18
4/1-6/15	1P: $159	2P: $159	XP: $20 F18
11/1-3/31	1P: $149	2P: $149	XP: $20 F18

Location: E 6th and St Clair Ave; opposite the Convention Center. 777 St Clair Ave 44114. Fax: 216/566-0736. **Facility:** 470 units. 439 one-bedroom standard units. 31 one-bedroom suites ($189-$209). 22 stories, interior corridors. *Bath:* combo or shower only. **Parking:** *Fee:* on-site and valet. **Terms:** cancellation fee imposed, package plans. **Amenities:** video games, voice mail, irons, hair dryers. *Some:* fax. **Dining:** restaurant, 6:30 am-2 & 5-10 pm, Sun from 7 am, $17-$25, cocktails. **Leisure Activities:** exercise room. **Guest Services:** gift shop, valet laundry. **Business Services:** conference facilities, fax. **Cards:** AX, DC, DS, MC, VI.

SOME UNITS

WYNDHAM CLEVELAND AT PLAYHOUSE SQUARE
Phone: (216)615-7500 11

AAA SAVE
Hotel

9/3-3/31	1P: $109-$169	2P: $109-$169	XP: $10 F18
4/1-9/2	1P: $119-$165	2P: $119-$165	XP: $10 F18

Location: Jct Euclid and E 14th St; downtown. 1260 Euclid Ave 44115. Fax: 216/615-3355. **Facility:** 205 one-bedroom standard units. 14 stories, interior corridors. *Bath:* combo or shower only. **Parking:** on-site and valet (fee). **Terms:** cancellation fee imposed, package plans. **Amenities:** high-speed Internet, voice mail, irons, hair dryers. **Dining:** restaurant, 6:30 am-10:30 pm, $13-$29, cocktails. **Leisure Activities:** sauna, whirlpool, exercise room. **Guest Services:** valet laundry, area transportation-within 5 mi. **Business Services:** conference facilities, fax. **Cards:** AX, CB, DC, DS, JC, MC, VI.

SOME UNITS

————— **WHERE TO DINE** —————

BLUE POINT GRILLE
Seafood

Lunch: $7-$14   **Dinner:** $15-$30   **Phone:** 216/875-7827 6
Location: Just w of town square. 700 W St Clair Ave 44113. **Hours:** 11:30 am-3 & 5-10:30 pm, Fri-11:30 pm, Sat 4 pm-11:30 pm, Sun 4 pm-9 pm. Closed major holidays. **Reservations:** suggested. **Features:** dressy casual; cocktails. The upscale grill in the warehouse district delivers fresh seafood, which is flown in daily. A nice wine selection complements the dishes. The attractive decor features slate tile squares, brick walls, wood ceiling beams and exposed pipes. **Parking:** on-site and valet (fee). **Cards:** AX, DC, DS, MC, VI.

CAFE SAUSALITO
American

Lunch: $6-$12   **Dinner:** $10-$20   **Phone:** 216/696-2233 3
Location: In the Galleria at Erieview, second level. 1301 E 9th St 44114. **Hours:** 11:30 am-8 pm, Fri & Sat noon-9 pm. Closed major holidays; also Sun. **Reservations:** suggested. **Features:** casual dress; carryout; cocktails & lounge. Good food at reasonable prices pervades the lively atmosphere at Cafe Sausalito, located within walking distance of several entertainment venues. Signature dishes include a variety of fresh seafood and pasta. The piano bar is open on Fri and Sat evenings. **Parking:** street. **Cards:** AX, DC, DS, MC, VI.

CENTURY
American

Lunch: $20-$35   **Dinner:** $20-$35   **Phone:** 216/902-5255 13
Location: In Tower City Center (3rd St side); in The Ritz-Carlton, Cleveland. 1515 W 3rd St 44113. **Hours:** 6:30 am-midnight. **Reservations:** suggested. **Features:** dressy casual; Sunday brunch; cocktails & lounge. The Ritz Carlton tradition of excellent cuisine and impeccable service is continued here. Seafood specialties and sushi are featured with innovative selections and Bento box offerings daily. The decor is inspired by the Twentieth Century Limited, the fabled train car that ran from Chicago to New York in record time from 1902 to 1967. **Parking:** on-site and valet. **Cards:** AX, CB, DC, DS, MC, VI.

GREEK ISLES
Greek

Lunch: $9-$18   **Dinner:** $13-$30   **Phone:** 216/861-1919 7
Location: In the warehouse district; at jct 6 St. 500 W St Clair 44114. **Hours:** 11 am-10 pm, Fri & Sat-midnight. Closed major holidays. **Reservations:** suggested. **Features:** casual dress; cocktails. A Mediterranean influence is evident in such dishes as calamari, flaming saganaki cheese and grilled seafood. **Parking:** street. **Cards:** AX, DC, DS, MC, VI.

(See map p. 598)

HICKERSON'S AT THE HANNA   **Lunch:** $7-$12   **Dinner:** $15-$30   **Phone:** 216/771-1818   ⑨
Continental
Location: From E 9th St. just e. 1422 Euclid Ave 44115. **Hours:** 11:30 am-2:30 & 5-10 pm, closing hours may vary. Closed major holidays; also Sun. **Reservations:** suggested. **Features:** dressy casual; carryout; cocktails & lounge. Red meat classics, such as chateaubriand and prime rib, share the bill with a long list of seafood and pasta selections. The restaurant sits in the heart of the theater district. Dark woodwork and minimal lighting characterize the relaxed dining room. **Parking:** on-site. **Cards:** AX, DC, MC, VI.   ⊠

HORNBLOWER'S BARGE & GRILL   **Lunch:** $6-$12   **Dinner:** $13-$25   **Phone:** 216/363-1151   ①
Seafood
Location: 0.3 mi e of E 9th St. 1151 N Marginal Rd 44114. **Hours:** 11:30 am-3:15 & 4:30-9 pm, Fri & Sat-10 pm, Sun 10:30 am-2 & 4:30-9 pm. Closed major holidays. **Reservations:** suggested; in summer. **Features:** casual dress; Sunday brunch; children's menu; carryout; cocktails. Named after fictional character Captain Horatio Hornblower, this popular restaurant is a converted barge that is moored and floats on the waterfront of Lake Erie. You can sit on the deck and get spectacular views of the city's skyline while enjoying a menu of seafood, steak and pasta. **Parking:** on-site. **Cards:** AX, DC, DS, MC, VI.   ⊠

HYDE PARK CHOP HOUSE   **Lunch:** $9-$15   **Dinner:** $14-$36   **Phone:** 216/344-2444   ⑭
Steak House
Location: W 2nd St. 123 Prospect Ave 44113. **Hours:** 11:30 am-2 & 5:30-10 pm, Fri-11 pm, Sat 5 pm-11 pm, Sun 4 pm-9 pm. Closed major holidays. **Reservations:** suggested. **Features:** dressy casual; carryout; cocktails. The menu blends hearty entrees—USDA prime, dry-aged steaks, chops and preparations of lamb, veal and fresh seafood—with a great selection of appetizers, salads and sides. The clublike, wood-paneled setting is warm and inviting. **Parking:** *Fee:* on-site and valet. **Cards:** AX, DC, DS, MC, VI.   ⊠

JOHNNY'S DOWNTOWN   **Lunch:** $8-$16   **Dinner:** $18-$34   **Phone:** 216/623-0055   ⑫
Northern Italian
Location: Corner of W 6th and Frankfort sts. 1406 W 6th St 44113. **Hours:** 11:30 am-3 & 5-10:30 pm, Fri-11:30 pm, Sat 5 pm-11:30 pm, Sun 4 pm-9 pm. Closed major holidays. **Reservations:** required; weekends. **Features:** dressy casual; carryout; cocktails. You'll enjoy this popular downtown restaurant that boasts a variety of appetizers and entrees including a creative grilled tuna with yellow and red sauces, accompanied by risotto and fresh summer squash. Free valet parking is offered evenings. **Parking:** street and valet. **Cards:** AX, DC, MC, VI.   ⊠

JOHN Q'S STEAKHOUSE   **Lunch:** $7-$15   **Dinner:** $16-$30   **Phone:** 216/861-0900   ④
Steak House
Location: Corner of W Third and Frankfort sts; across from the Renaissance Hotel. 55 Public Sq 44113. **Hours:** 11:30 am-10 pm, Fri-11 pm, Sat 4 pm-11 pm, Sun 4 pm-10 pm. Closed major holidays. **Reservations:** suggested. **Features:** dressy casual; children's menu; carryout; cocktails & lounge. A tasty meal might start with the black pepper strip steak or porterhouse and end with a nice chocolate mousse, all served in one of the eatery's intimate dining areas. Those preferring something other than steak and chops might enjoy the grilled salmon or pan-fried walleye. **Parking:** off-site. **Cards:** AX, CB, DC, DS, MC, VI.   ⊠

LI WAH   **Lunch:** $5-$7   **Dinner:** $8-$15   **Phone:** 216/696-6556   ②
Chinese
Location: Between E 27th and E 30th sts; in Asia Plaza. 2999 Payne Ave 44114. **Hours:** 10 am-2 am. **Reservations:** suggested. **Features:** casual dress; carryout; cocktails; a la carte. People of Oriental heritage frequent the restaurant because they can find authentic dishes that aren't offered elsewhere. Dim sum is served, as are traditional Chinese preparations of beef, poultry and seafood. The dining room is spacious and attractive. **Parking:** on-site. **Cards:** AX, DC, DS, MC, VI.   ⊠

LOLA   **Dinner:** $16-$23   **Phone:** 216/771-5652   ⑮
American
Location: At jct Professor Rd; in the Tremont neighborhood. 900 Literary Rd 44118. **Hours:** 4 pm-1 am, Fri & Sat-2 am, Sun 4 pm-11 pm. Closed major holidays; also Mon. **Reservations:** suggested. **Features:** casual dress; cocktails; a la carte. Midwestern fare goes gourmet in such dishes as crab pierogies, herb-roasted walleye and the signature mac 'n' cheese with goat cheese. **Parking:** on-site and valet (fee). **Cards:** AX, DC, DS, MC, VI.   ⊠

MALLORCA   **Lunch:** $7-$15   **Dinner:** $15-$28   **Phone:** 216/687-9494   ⑪
Spanish
Location: In the warehouse district; between Superior and St Clair Ave. 1390 W 9th St 44113. **Hours:** 11:30 am-10:30 pm, Fri & Sat-11:30 pm. Closed: 12/25. **Reservations:** suggested; weekends. **Features:** casual dress; cocktails. Spanish and Portuguese cuisine is presented with Old World service. **Parking:** street. **Cards:** AX, DC, MC, VI.   ⊠ ⑭

SANS SOUCI   **Lunch:** $8-$14   **Dinner:** $11-$27   **Phone:** 216/696-5600   ⑧
Provincial French
Location: At Superior and West 3rd St; in Renaissance Cleveland Hotel. 24 Public Sq 44113. **Hours:** 11:30 am-2:30 & 5:30-10 pm, Fri-11 pm, Sat 5:30 pm-11 pm, Sun 5:30 pm-10 pm. Closed: 1/1, 12/25. **Reservations:** suggested. **Features:** dressy casual; cocktails & lounge; a la carte. French Provencal touches lend a casually elegant atmosphere to the dining room. Regional Mediterranean cuisine, such as smoked salmon with potato pancakes, is infused with robust flavors and piquant seasonings. Desserts are attractive and delicious. **Parking:** on-site and valet (fee). **Cards:** AX, DC, DS, JC, MC, VI.   ⊠

WATERMARK RESTAURANT   **Lunch:** $8-$10   **Dinner:** $17-$38   **Phone:** 216/241-1600   ⑩
Seafood
Location: In the Flats section. 1250 Old River Rd 44113. **Hours:** 11:30 am-10 pm, Fri & Sat-11 pm, Sun 10 am-2:30 & 5-10 pm. Closed: 1/1, 11/28, 12/25. **Reservations:** suggested. **Features:** Sunday brunch; carryout; cocktails. Especially at night, diners are treated to breathtaking views of boats and barges coasting down the river and sometimes docking to unload other restaurant patrons. House specialties include Lake Erie walleye and sea bass with Moroccan salsa. Exceptional appetizers, pasta and desserts also can be had. **Parking:** on-site and valet. **Cards:** AX, DC, DS, MC, VI.   ⊠

CLEVELAND pop. 505,600 (See map p. 600; index p. 602)

──── WHERE TO STAY ────

BAYMONT INN & SUITES CLEVELAND-AIRPORT   **Phone:** (216)251-8500   23

AAA SAVE   All Year   1P: $74-$84   2P: $74-$84
♦♦♦♦   **Location:** I-71, exit 240, just n. 4222 W 150th St 44135. **Fax:** 216/251-4117. **Facility:** 116 one-bedroom standard
Motel   units. 4 stories, interior corridors. **Parking:** on-site. **Amenities:** video games, voice mail, irons, hair dryers.
Leisure Activities: exercise room. **Guest Services:** coin laundry. **Business Services:** meeting rooms.
Cards: AX, CB, DC, DS, MC, VI. **Special Amenities:** free continental breakfast and free newspaper.
(See color ad opposite title page)

SOME UNITS
[icons] FEE

BUDGET INN CLEVELAND AIRPORT   **Phone:** (216)267-2350   24

AAA SAVE   All Year   1P: $62   2P: $62   XP: $10   F18
♦   **Location:** 1 mi e from 150th St, on SR 17. 14043 Brookpark Rd 44142. **Fax:** 216/267-9237. **Facility:** 126 one-
Hotel   bedroom standard units. 5 stories, interior corridors. **Parking:** on-site. **Amenities:** extended cable TV.
Leisure Activities: exercise room. **Guest Services:** coin laundry. **Business Services:** meeting rooms.
Cards: AX, CB, DC, DS, JC, MC, VI. **Special Amenities:** early check-in/late check-out and preferred
room (subject to availability with advanced reservations).

SOME UNITS
[icons] FEE

CLEVELAND AIRPORT MARRIOTT   **Phone:** (216)252-5333   25

AAA SAVE   5/25-9/6   1P: $89-$169   2P: $89-$169   XP: $10   F17
♦♦♦♦   4/1-5/24   1P: $69-$164   2P: $69-$164   XP: $10   F17
Hotel   9/7-11/15   1P: $89-$149   2P: $59-$149   XP: $10   F17
11/16-3/31   1P: $59-$149   2P: $59-$149   XP: $10   F17
Location: I-71, exit 240, just s. 4277 W 150th St 44135. **Fax:** 216/251-1508. **Facility:** 370 units. 366 one-bedroom
standard units. 4 one-bedroom suites ($250-$350). 4-9 stories, interior corridors. **Bath:** combo or shower
only. **Parking:** on-site. **Terms:** package plans, pets ($50 fee). **Amenities:** high-speed Internet, voice mail, irons, hair dryers.
Dining: dining room, restaurant, 6 am-10 pm, $14-$22, cocktails. **Pool(s):** heated indoor. **Leisure Activities:** whirlpool, exercise
room. **Guest Services:** gift shop, valet laundry. **Business Services:** conference facilities, business center. **Cards:** AX, CB, DC,
DS, JC, MC, VI. *(See color ad card insert)*

SOME UNITS
[icons] FEE

Special People Get
Special Treatment

Want to be sure you'll be treated right
on your next travel adventure?

*L*ook for establishments that advertise in the AAA TourBook®
guides. These are the businesses that cater to AAA members. They
value the business they receive from AAA members, and are willing to go
the extra mile to get it. And in turn, they pass value on to you.

(See map p. 600)

GLIDDEN HOUSE

Phone: (216)231-8900   **26 F18**

Motor Inn

All Year [ECP]   1P: $159-$179   XP: $10
Location: I-90 E, exit 173B (Chester Ave), to Euclid Ave, 0.7 mi e to Ford Dr, then just n; in University Circle. 1901 Ford Dr 44106. Fax: 216/231-2130. **Facility:** 60 units. 52 one-bedroom standard units. 8 one-bedroom suites ($189-$229). 3 stories, interior corridors. **Parking:** on-site. **Terms:** check-in 4 pm, cancellation fee imposed. **Amenities:** voice mail, irons, hair dryers. **Dining:** 5 pm-9 pm, Fri & Sat-11 pm, $8-$25, cocktails. **Guest Services:** valet laundry. **Business Services:** meeting rooms, fax. **Cards:** AX, DC, DS, MC, VI.
Special Amenities: free continental breakfast and free local telephone calls. *(See color ad p 614)*

SOME UNITS

(See map p. 600)

HILTON GARDEN INN CLEVELAND AIRPORT

			Phone: (216)898-1898	21
(AAA) SAVE	5/1-9/1	1P: $89-$119	2P: $89-$119	XP: $10
▼▼▼▼	9/2-3/31	1P: $69-$119	2P: $69-$119	XP: $10
	4/1-4/30	1P: $69-$109	2P: $69-$109	XP: $10

Motor Inn

Location: I-480, exit Grayton Rd, just n. 4900 Emerald Ct SW 44135. Fax: 216/898-1498. **Facility:** 168 one-bedroom standard units. 7 stories, interior corridors. *Bath:* combo or shower only. **Parking:** on-site. **Terms:** package plans - weekends. **Amenities:** extended cable TV, video games, high-speed Internet, dual phone lines, voice mail, irons, hair dryers. **Dining:** restaurant, 6-10:30 am, 11:30-1:30, 5-10 pm, Sat & Sun 6:30-11 am, 11:30-1:30 & 5-10 pm, $7-$15, cocktails. **Pool(s):** heated indoor. **Leisure Activities:** whirlpool, exercise room. **Guest Services:** coin laundry. **Business Services:** meeting rooms, business center. **Cards:** AX, CB, DC, DS, JC, MC, VI. **Special Amenities:** free newspaper.

SOME UNITS

[icons] SD / FEE / X /

(See map p. 600)

HOLIDAY INN-CLEVELAND AIRPORT
Phone: (216)252-7700 ② F18

Motor Inn

All Year   1P: $69-$129   2P: $69-$139   XP: $10
Location: I-71, exit 240, just n. 4181 W 150th St 44135. **Fax:** 216/252-3850. **Facility:** 146 one-bedroom standard units. 6 stories, interior corridors. **Parking:** on-site. **Terms:** 7 day cancellation notice-fee imposed, package plans. **Amenities:** extended cable TV, video games, dual phone lines, voice mail, irons, hair dryers. **Dining:** restaurant, 6:30 am-2 & 5-10 pm, $7-$16, cocktails. **Pool(s):** heated indoor. **Leisure Activities:** exercise room. **Guest Services:** valet laundry, area transportation-within 5 mi. **Business Services:** meeting rooms. **Cards:** AX, CB, DC, DS, JC, MC, VI. **Special Amenities:** free newspaper and free room upgrade (subject to availability with advanced reservations).

SOME UNITS

INTER-CONTINENTAL SUITE HOTEL
Phone: 216/707-4300 ⑲

Suite Hotel

Property failed to provide current rates
Location: I-90, exit 172C, 0.7 mi e to E 88th St, 1 blk n, then just e. 8800 Euclid Ave 44106. **Fax:** 216/707-4301. **Facility:** 163 one-bedroom suites. 8 stories, interior corridors. **Bath:** combo or shower only. **Parking:** off-site (fee). **Terms:** package plans. **Amenities:** video games, dual phone lines, voice mail, safes, irons, hair dryers. **Guest Services:** valet laundry. **Business Services:** fax. **Cards:** AX, CB, DC, DS, JC, MC, VI.

SOME UNITS

RAMADA INN-CLEVELAND AIRPORT
Phone: (216)267-5700 ㉗

Motor Inn

5/1-8/31   1P: $99   2P: $109   XP: $10   F18
4/1-4/30 & 9/1-3/31   1P: $89   2P: $99   XP: $10   F18
Location: 1 mi e from 150th St, on SR 17. 13930 Brookpark Rd 44135. **Fax:** 216/267-1609. **Facility:** 154 one-bedroom standard units. 2 stories, interior corridors. **Parking:** on-site. **Amenities:** video games, voice mail, irons, hair dryers. **Dining:** restaurant, 11:30 am-midnight, $9-$15, cocktails. **Leisure Activities:** exercise room. **Guest Services:** coin laundry. **Business Services:** meeting rooms. **Cards:** AX, DC, DS, JC, MC, VI. **Special Amenities:** free continental breakfast and free newspaper.

SOME UNITS

SHERATON AIRPORT HOTEL CLEVELAND
Phone: (216)267-1500 ㉒

Hotel

All Year   1P: $180-$200   2P: $180-$200
Location: On SR 237. 5300 Riverside Dr 44135. **Fax:** 216/265-3177. **Facility:** 288 one-bedroom standard units, some with whirlpools. 2-9 stories, interior corridors. **Parking:** on-site. **Terms:** package plans. **Amenities:** video games, dual phone lines, voice mail, irons, hair dryers. *Some:* fax. **Pool(s):** heated indoor. **Leisure Activities:** sauna, whirlpool, exercise room. **Guest Services:** gift shop, valet laundry. **Business Services:** conference facilities, business center, fax. **Cards:** AX, CB, DC, DS, JC, MC, VI.

SOME UNITS

(See map p. 600)

———— *The following lodging was either not evaluated or did not* ————
meet AAA rating requirements but is listed for your information only.

HILTON GARDEN INN CLEVELAND GATEWAY   **Phone:** 216/658-6400
   [fyi]   5/1-10/31   1P: $89-$179   2P: $89-$189   XP: $10   F18
                11/1-3/31   1P: $79-$179   2P: $79-$189   XP: $10   F18
   Motor Inn   4/1-4/30   1P: $79-$139   2P: $79-$139   XP: $10   F18
                Too new to rate, opening scheduled for February 2002. **Location:** I-71/77, exit E 9th St. 1100 Carnegie Ave 44115
(1022 Carnegie Ave). **Fax:** 216/658-6405. **Amenities:** radios, coffeemakers, microwaves, refrigerators, pool. **Cards:** AX, CB, DC,
DS, JC, MC, VI. *(See ad p 615)*

———— **WHERE TO DINE** ————

100TH BOMB GROUP-A RESTAURANT   **Lunch:** $6-$12   **Dinner:** $13-$25   **Phone:** 216/267-1010   ③②
   ⒶⒶⒶ   **Location:** I-480, exit Grayton Rd. 20000 Brookpark Rd 44135. **Hours:** 11 am-3 & 4:30-11 pm, Sat 11 am-2:30 &
   ▽▽▽   4:30-11 pm, Sun 9:30 am-2:30 & 4:30-10 pm. **Reservations:** suggested. **Features:** casual dress; Sunday
   American   brunch; children's menu; early bird specials; cocktails & lounge. A World War II aviation theme weaves
             through the 1940s French farmhouse, appointed with artifacts from that period in history. Bombed-out
             sections of the comfortable patio further develop that theme. Prime rib and American fare makes up the
             menu. **Parking:** on-site. **Cards:** AX, DC, DS, MC, VI.   ✕

THE BARICELLI INN Country Inn   **Dinner:** $18-$40   **Phone:** 216/791-6500   ②⑧
   ▽▽▽ ▽▽▽   **Location:** Jct Euclid and Mayfield Rd; 1 mi se on Mayfield Rd to Murray Hill Rd, 0.5 mi s. 2203 Cornell Rd 44106.
   Continental **Hours:** 5:30 pm-9:30 pm, Fri & Sat-10:30 pm. Closed Sun. **Reservations:** suggested. **Features:** semi-formal attire; cocktails & lounge; a la carte. The brownstone, turn-of-the-20th-century inn is
             a charming spot for elegant dining. The seasonally changing menu is strongly influenced by fine
restaurants in Europe although the ingredients, preparation and presentation style are decidedly American. Smoke free
premises. **Parking:** on-site and valet. **Cards:** AX, DC, MC, VI.   ✕

GUARINO'S   **Lunch:** $7-$9   **Dinner:** $11-$17   **Phone:** 216/231-3100   ③③
   ⒶⒶⒶ   **Location:** On US 322; in Little Italy (University Circle area). 12309 Mayfield Rd 44106. **Hours:** 11:30 am-9:30 pm,
   ▽▽▽ ▽▽▽   Thurs-10 pm, Fri & Sat-11:30 pm, Sun 1 pm-8 pm. Closed major holidays. **Reservations:** suggested.
   Italian   **Features:** cocktails. Victorian touches of lace and antiques grace Guarino's. Billed as the oldest restaurant
             in Cleveland, it's considered a great place for a casual meal before or after wandering the historic
             neighborhood. Southern Italian fare is served in a "famiglia" atmosphere. **Parking:** on-site. **Cards:** AX, DC,
             DS, MC, VI.   ✕

SALVATORE'S RISTORANTE   **Dinner:** $7-$14   **Phone:** 216/231-7670   ③⑦
   ▽▽▽ ▽▽▽   **Location:** Cornell Ave and Murray Hill Rd. 2181 Murray Hill Rd 44106. **Hours:** 5 pm-10 pm. Closed major
   Italian   holidays; also Mon. **Reservations:** accepted. **Features:** casual dress; cocktails. Food, prepared from
             scratch with fresh ingredients, is the restaurant's strength. The veal scaloppine is delicious, with tender
             meat over sourdough bread coated in a zesty sauce with melted cheese. A spicy marinara sauce blankets
the seafood linguine. Smoke free premises. **Parking:** on-site. **Cards:** AX, DC, DS, MC, VI.   ✕

SERGIO'S IN UNIVERSITY CIRCLE   **Lunch:** $6-$12   **Dinner:** $12-$22   **Phone:** 216/231-1234   ③⑨
   ▽▽▽ ▽▽▽   **Location:** Adjacent to Glidden House on the Case Western Reserve University campus; in University Circle. 1903
   Continental Ford Dr 44106. **Hours:** 11:30 am-2:30 & 5:30-9:30 pm, Fri-11 pm, Sat noon-11 pm, Sun 4 pm-9 pm. Closed
             major holidays. **Reservations:** suggested. **Features:** casual dress; children's menu; carryout; cocktails;
             entertainment. The chef/owner draws on an international culinary palate to create inspired cross-cultural
offerings. The Brazilian influence is particularly strong. Eclectic decorations enliven the comfortable dining room, which
constantly bustles with activity. Smoke free premises. **Parking:** on-site. **Cards:** AX, DC, DS, MC, VI.   ✕

SOMER'S PLACE   **Lunch:** $5-$10   **Dinner:** $7-$14   **Phone:** 216/671-4200   ③①
   ▽▽▽ ▽▽▽   **Location:** I-71, exit 240, just n. 4197 W 150th St 44135. **Hours:** 5:30 am-11 pm, Sun 6 am-9 pm.
   Mediterranean **Features:** casual dress; carryout. In a convenient highway location, the family-oriented restaurant offers a
             menu of authentic Lebanese and Greek selections. Portion sizes are hearty, and servers are friendly and
             attentive. **Parking:** on-site. **Cards:** AX, DC, DS, MC, VI.   ✕

———— *The following restaurants have not been evaluated by AAA* ————
but are listed for your information only.

JIMMY C'S   **Phone:** 216/671-7167
   [fyi]   Not evaluated. **Location:** 15024 Puritas Ave 44135. Budget-friendly homemade soups and sandwiches are on the
            menu of the popular neighborhood haunt.

STERLE'S SLOVENIAN COUNTRY HOUSE   **Phone:** 216/881-4181
   [fyi]   Not evaluated. **Location:** 1401 E 55th St. The restaurant features authentic Slovenian cuisine and live polka music
            on Friday and Saturday nights.

The Cleveland Vicinity

BEACHWOOD pop. 10,700   (See map p. 600; index p. 603)

──────── **WHERE TO STAY** ────────

EMBASSY SUITES   Phone: (216)765-8066   **34**
SAVE
  5/17-9/2   1P: $159-$209   2P: $159-$209   XP: $15   F18
  4/1-5/16 & 9/3-3/31   1P: $139-$169   2P: $139-$169   XP: $15   F18
Suite Hotel   **Location:** I-271, exit Chagrin Blvd, just w. 3775 Park East Dr 44122. Fax: 216/765-0930. **Facility:** 216 one-bedroom standard units with efficiencies. 4 stories, interior corridors. **Parking:** on-site. **Terms:** package plans. **Amenities:** video games, dual phone lines, voice mail, irons, hair dryers. **Pool(s):** heated indoor. **Leisure Activities:** sauna, whirlpool, exercise room. **Guest Services:** gift shop, coin laundry. **Business Services:** meeting rooms. **Cards:** AX, CB, DC, DS, JC, MC, VI. *(See ad p 607)*

SOME UNITS

HILTON CLEVELAND EAST/BEACHWOOD   Phone: (216)464-5950   **29**
SAVE
  6/1-8/31   1P: $109-$159   XP: $15   F18
  4/1-5/31 & 9/1-3/31   1P: $79-$139   XP: $15   F18
Hotel   **Location:** I-271, exit Chagrin Blvd, just w. 3663 Park East Dr 44122. Fax: 216/464-6539. **Facility:** 403 one-bedroom standard units. 4-7 stories, interior corridors. *Bath:* combo or shower only. **Parking:** on-site. **Terms:** package plans. **Amenities:** video games, dual phone lines, voice mail, irons, hair dryers. **Pool(s):** heated indoor. **Leisure Activities:** sauna, whirlpool. **Guest Services:** gift shop, massage (fee), coin laundry. **Business Services:** conference facilities, business center. **Cards:** AX, CB, DC, DS, JC, MC, VI. *(See ad p 614)*

SOME UNITS

HOLIDAY INN-BEACHWOOD   Phone: (216)831-3300   **30**
AAA SAVE
  All Year   1P: $85-$119   2P: $85-$119
Motor Inn   **Location:** I-271, exit Chagrin Blvd, just e. 3750 Orange Pl 44122. Fax: 216/831-0486. **Facility:** 171 one-bedroom standard units. 4 stories, interior corridors. *Bath:* combo or shower only. **Parking:** on-site. **Amenities:** video games, high-speed Internet (fee), voice mail, irons, hair dryers. **Dining:** restaurant, 7 am-11 pm, $8-$16, cocktails. **Pool(s):** heated outdoor, heated indoor. **Leisure Activities:** saunas, exercise room. **Guest Services:** coin laundry. **Business Services:** meeting rooms. **Cards:** AX, CB, DC, DS, JC, MC, VI.

SOME UNITS

HOMESTEAD STUDIO SUITES-CLEVELAND/BEACHWOOD   Phone: (216)896-5555   **32**
  All Year   1P: $89-$99   2P: $94-$104
Extended Stay Motel   **Location:** I-271, exit Chagrin Blvd, just w. 3625 Orange Pl 44122. Fax: 216/896-9021. **Facility:** 142 one-bedroom standard units with efficiencies. 3 stories, interior corridors. *Bath:* combo or shower only. **Parking:** on-site. **Terms:** small pets only ($75 fee). **Amenities:** voice mail, irons. **Guest Services:** coin laundry. **Cards:** AX, CB, DC, DS, JC, MC, VI.

SOME UNITS

RAMADA INN & CONFERENCE CENTER   Phone: (216)831-5150   **31**
AAA SAVE
  6/16-8/25   1P: $69-$119   2P: $69-$119   XP: $10   F18
  4/1-6/15 & 8/26-3/31 1P: $59-$99   2P: $59-$109   XP: $10   F18
Motor Inn   **Location:** I-271, exit Chagrin Blvd, just w. 26300 Chagrin Blvd 44122. Fax: 216/765-1156. **Facility:** 196 one-bedroom standard units, some with whirlpools. 4 stories, interior corridors. **Parking:** on-site. **Terms:** 3 day cancellation notice. **Amenities:** video games, high-speed Internet, dual phone lines, voice mail, irons, hair dryers. **Dining:** dining room, 6:30 am-10 pm, Fri-11 pm, Sat 7 am-11 pm, Sun 7 am-9 pm, $10-$20, cocktails. **Pool(s):** heated outdoor. **Leisure Activities:** exercise room. **Guest Services:** gift shop, valet laundry, area transportation-within 5 mi. **Business Services:** meeting rooms. **Cards:** AX, CB, DC, DS, JC, MC, VI. *(See color ad below)*

SOME UNITS

(See map p. 600)

RESIDENCE INN BY MARRIOT CLEVELAND-BEACHWOOD   Phone: (216)831-3030   33

◬◬◬ SAVE	6/1-8/31 [ECP]	1P: $155-$165	2P: $155-$165
	12/31-3/31 [ECP]	1P: $139-$159	2P: $139-$159
▽▽▽▽	4/1-5/31 [ECP]	1P: $129-$149	2P: $129-$149
	9/1-12/30 [ECP]	1P: $129-$139	2P: $129-$139

Apartment   **Location:** Jct US 422 and I-271, exit Chagrin Blvd, just w. 3628 Park East Dr 44122. Fax: 216/831-3232. **Facility:** 174 units. 77 one-bedroom standard units. 53 one- and 44 two-bedroom suites, some with efficiencies or kitchens. 4 stories, interior corridors. *Bath:* combo or shower only. **Parking:** on-site. **Terms:** cancellation fee imposed, pets ($250 fee). **Amenities:** extended cable TV, video games, dual phone lines, voice mail, irons, hair dryers. **Pool(s):** heated outdoor. **Leisure Activities:** whirlpool, exercise room, sports court. **Guest Services:** complimentary evening beverages: Mon-Thurs, valet laundry. **Business Services:** meeting rooms. **Cards:** AX, CB, DC, DS, JC, MC, VI. *(See color ad card insert)*

SOME UNITS

⟨S⟩ 🐾 🏋️ ⟨M⟩ ♿ 🛏️ 🐕 ✕ 🚪 DATA PORT 🔌 📺 💻 🖨️ / ✕ VCR /
                                      FEE   FEE

------ **WHERE TO DINE** ------

CAFE 56 GRILL   Lunch: $5-$8   Dinner: $10-$15   Phone: 216/464-3090   47
▽▽▽ ▽▽   **Location:** I-271, exit Chagrin Blvd, 1 mi w. 23230 Chagrin Blvd, Bldg 3 44122. **Hours:** 11:30 am-7 pm, Fri & Sat-7:30 pm. Closed: 11/28, 12/25; also Sun. **Reservations:** suggested. **Features:** casual dress; children's menu; carryout; cocktails & lounge. The restaurant gets its name from its 56 variations of fresh salad.
American   Guests can request seating on the seasonal patio or in the two-tiered dining room, each decorated with a variety of plants. The pretzel bread and bagels shouldn't be missed. **Parking:** on-site. **Cards:** AX, DC, DS, MC, VI.   ✕

CHARLEY'S CRAB   Lunch: $7-$20   Dinner: $13-$32   Phone: 216/831-8222   46
▽▽▽ ▽▽▽   **Location:** I-271, exit Chagrin Blvd, 0.3 mi w. 25765 Chagrin Blvd 44122. **Hours:** 11 am-10 pm, Fri & Sat 11 am-3 & 4-10:30 pm, Sun 4 pm-10 pm. Closed major holidays. **Reservations:** suggested. **Features:** dressy
Seafood   casual; children's menu; early bird specials; carryout; cocktails. Creativity and innovation punctuate the varied menu, which offers such seafood temptations as lobster bisque, crab cakes, yellowfin tuna and salmon burger with red and green peppers. Excellent desserts include the tart key lime pie and the creme brulee. Smoke free premises. **Parking:** on-site and valet. **Cards:** AX, DC, DS, MC, VI.   ✕

HO WAH RESTAURANT   Lunch: $6-$12   Dinner: $9-$16   Phone: 216/831-2327   42
▽▽ ▽   **Location:** Southeast corner of Cedar and Richmond Rd; in Le Place Centre. 2101 Richmond Rd 44122. **Hours:** 11 am-10:30 pm, Fri-Sat to 11:30 pm, Sun noon-9:30 pm. Closed: 11/28. **Reservations:** suggested;
Chinese   weekends. **Features:** casual dress; carryout; cocktails. The broad menu features an extensive selection of gourmet items as well as daily chef specials. All dinners can be prepared family style. **Parking:** on-site.
Cards: AX, DC, DS, MC, VI.   ✕

J GILBERT'S   Lunch: $7-$12   Dinner: $12-$20   Phone: 216/464-7544   45
▽▽▽▽   **Location:** I-271, exit Chagrin Blvd, 1 mi w. 24103 Chagrin Blvd 44122. **Hours:** 11:30 am-2:30 & 4:30-10 pm, Fri & Sat-11 am. Closed: 1/1, 11/28, 12/25; also Sun. **Reservations:** suggested. **Features:** casual dress;
Steak House   carryout; cocktails. A sophisticated interior with dark, mahogany woodwork and some brick wall accents characterizes the restaurant's booth and table seating. The lounge is cozy and private with comfortable seating. Southwestern-influenced menu selections are made with prime-grade aged beef on a mesquite grill. Servers are personable, informative and attentive. **Parking:** on-site. **Cards:** AX, DC, DS, MC, VI.   ✕

MOXIE RESTAURANT   Lunch: $6-$15   Dinner: $9-$26   Phone: 216/831-5599   43
▽▽ ▽   **Location:** I-271, exit Chagrin Blvd, 0.3 mi w. 3355 Richmond Rd 44122. **Hours:** 11:30 am-9 pm, Fri & Sat-11 pm. Closed: 7/4, 12/25. **Features:** casual dress; carryout; cocktails & lounge. Design elements of the trendy
American   new bistro—such as an open kitchen, wall murals and a waiting area with the air of a coffeehouse—reflect current restaurant trends. Casual attire is perfectly acceptable in this upscale setting, but a majority of young professionals who frequent the spot favor businesswear. Don't miss the fresh bread, served on a spiral holder. It comes out warm and has a wonderful aroma. **Parking:** on-site and valet (fee). **Cards:** AX, DS, MC, VI.   ✕

NAPA VALLEY GRILLE-IN BEACHWOOD PLACE   Lunch: $7-$12   Dinner: $12-$20   Phone: 216/514-8686   41
▽▽▽▽   **Location:** I-271, exit Cedar/Brainard Rd, 0.5 mi w to Beachwood Place Mall. 2630 Cedar Rd 44122. **Hours:** 11:30 am-4 & 5-10 pm, Fri & Sat-10:30 pm, Sun 4:30 pm-8:30 pm. Closed major holidays.
California   **Reservations:** suggested. **Features:** casual dress; Sunday brunch; children's menu; carryout; cocktails. In the upscale Beachwood Place Mall, the restaurant reflects a California theme in both its creative cuisine and domestic wine list, which includes more than 300 selections. Menu items are prepared with high-quality ingredients and are artfully presented. The wait staff is knowledgeable and helpful without appearing stuffy. **Parking:** on-site. **Cards:** AX, DC, DS, MC, VI.   ✕

RISTORANTE GIOVANNI'S   Lunch: $10-$16   Dinner: $19-$35   Phone: 216/831-8625   49
▽▽▽▽ ▽▽▽▽   **Location:** I-271, exit Chagrin Blvd, 0.3 mi w; in Chagrin Richmond Building. 25550 Chagrin Blvd 44122. **Hours:** 11:30 am-2:30 & 5:30-9:30 pm, Sat 5:30 pm-10:30 pm. Closed major holidays; also Sun. **Reservations:** suggested. **Features:** semi-formal attire; carryout; cocktails & lounge. The upscale
Northern Italian   restaurant, which re-creates the casual elegance of old Italy, doesn't offer a typical Italian flavor. Fresh vegetables, flavorful sauces and eye-catching presentation combine in excellent selections of pasta, veal, seafood, chicken and beef. **Parking:** on-site and valet. **Cards:** AX, CB, DC, DS, MC, VI.   ✕

SHUHEI   Lunch: $7-$17   Dinner: $14-$30   Phone: 216/464-1720   44
▽▽ ▽   **Location:** I-271, exit Chagrin Blvd, 1.4 mi w. 23360 Chagrin Blvd 44122. **Hours:** 11:30 am-2:30 & 5:30-10 pm, Fri & Sat-11 pm, Sun 5 pm-9 pm. Closed major holidays. **Features:** casual dress; carryout; cocktails & lounge.
Japanese   Restaurant offerings include traditional Japanese cuisine, a sushi bar and an elegant atmosphere. Female servers in kimonos and male servers in vests and slacks and friendly and accommodating. **Parking:** on-site. **Cards:** AX, DC, DS, MC, VI.   ✕

(See map p. 600)

─────── *The following restaurants have not been evaluated by AAA* ───────
but are listed for your information only.

JASMINE'S   Phone: 216/514-8184
[fyi]   Not evaluated. **Location:** In Beachwood Place. 2680 Cedar Rd 44122. On the lower level of the upscale Beachwood
             Place Mall, the contemporary outlet has a varied menu and attentive servers.

TONY'S AM GRILLE   Phone: 216/595-6950
[fyi]   Not evaluated. **Location:** 3690 Orange Pl 44122. A local favorite, the convenient restaurant offers friendly service
             and a diverse menu.

BEDFORD pop. 14,800   (See map p. 600; index p. 604)

─────── **WHERE TO STAY** ───────

HOLIDAY INN EXPRESS   Phone: (440)786-1998   [72]
              5/24-9/2   1P: $99-$119   2P: $99-$119   XP: $10   F19
▽▽▽▽   4/1-5/23 & 9/3-3/31 1P: $65-$79   2P: $65-$79   XP: $10   F19
  Motel   **Location:** I-271, exit 23, just e on Broadway. (23303 Oakwood Commons, OAKWOOD VILLAGE, 44146).
              Fax: 440/786-2779. **Facility:** 60 one-bedroom standard units, some with whirlpools. 2 stories, interior corri-
dors. *Bath:* combo or shower only. **Parking:** on-site. **Terms:** check-in 4 pm, package plans. **Amenities:** extended cable TV, voice
mail, irons, hair dryers. **Pool(s):** heated indoor. **Leisure Activities:** sauna, whirlpool. **Guest Services:** complimentary laundry.
Business Services: meeting rooms. **Cards:** AX, CB, DC, DS, JC, MC, VI.
                                                                          SOME UNITS
(ASK) (SD) (&) (🏊) (🎥) (DATA PORT) (🛏) (🖥) (🖨) / (✕) /

BEREA pop. 19,100   (See map p. 600; index p. 606)

─────── **WHERE TO DINE** ───────

PUFFERBELLY LTD   **Lunch:** $5-$10   **Dinner:** $10-$17   Phone: 440/234-1144   [91]
▽▽▽ ▽▽   **Location:** I-71, exit 235 (Bagley Rd), 1.7 mi w, then 0.6 mi n on Front St. 30 Depot St 44017. **Hours:** 11 am-9 pm,
                Wed & Thurs-10 pm, Fri & Sat-11 pm. Closed major holidays. **Reservations:** suggested; weekends.
  American   **Features:** casual dress; Sunday brunch; children's menu; carryout; cocktails & lounge; a la carte. Antiques
                hang on the walls and candles sit on the tables in the quaint former train station, now a bustling, upbeat
spot for family dining. The specialty chicken Pufferbelly consists of a pan-fried chicken breast served over fettuccine
primavera. **Parking:** on-site. **Cards:** AX, DS, MC, VI.   (✕)

─────── *The following restaurant has not been evaluated by AAA* ───────
but is listed for your information only.

ENCORE BAR & GRILLE   Phone: 440/234-4252
[fyi]   Not evaluated. **Location:** 826 Front St 44017. Signature pizzas, steaks, seafood and pasta are seared in
             wood-burning ovens.

BRECKSVILLE pop. 11,800   (See map p. 600; index p. 606)

─────── **WHERE TO DINE** ───────

MARCO POLO'S   **Lunch:** $6-$9   **Dinner:** $11-$20   Phone: 216/526-6130   [110]
▽▽▽▽   **Location:** I-77, exit Rockside Rd, 0.7 mi e to Brecksville Rd, 3.5 mi s. 8188 Brecksville Rd 44141. **Hours:** 11:30
  Italian   am-10 pm, Fri & Sat-11 pm, Sun 10:30 am-3 & 4-9 pm. Closed major holidays. **Reservations:** suggested.
                Features: casual dress; Sunday brunch; children's menu; early bird specials; carryout; cocktails. Enjoy a
                meal in this time capsule of a restaurant. Having been there since the 1820s with some additions and
changes, this place boasts of a history being everything from a one-room schoolhouse to a dance hall, a tavern, a gambling
hall and even a bordello. Not only having history, families can sup on some of the finest meals in Brecksville with everything
from seafood and steak to pasta and some wonderful desserts. **Parking:** on-site. **Cards:** AX, DC, DS, MC, VI.   (✕)

BROADVIEW HEIGHTS pop. 12,200   (See map p. 600; index p. 604)

─────── **WHERE TO STAY** ───────

TALLYHO-TEL   Phone: 440/526-0640   [51]
              5/1-9/30   1P: $50-$80   2P: $55-$85   XP: $5
▽   4/1-4/30 & 1/1-3/31 1P: $40-$70   2P: $45-$75   XP: $5
  Motel   10/1-12/31   1P: $45-$65   2P: $50-$70   XP: $5
              Location: I-77, exit 149B southbound; exit 149 northbound. 4501 E Royalton Rd 44147. Fax: 440/526-9512.
Facility: 109 one-bedroom standard units, some with efficiencies (no utensils). 1 story, exterior corridors. **Parking:** on-site.
Terms: check-in 4 pm. **Pool(s):** outdoor. **Business Services:** meeting rooms. **Cards:** AX, DC, DS, MC, VI.
                                                                          SOME UNITS
(🛗) (🏊) (🎥) (DATA PORT) / (✕) (🛏) (🖥) /

BROOK PARK pop. 22,900 (See map p. 600; index p. 605)

──────── WHERE TO STAY ────────

BEST WESTERN AIRPORT INN & SUITES   Phone: (216)267-9364   107

4/1-9/30 [ECP]	1P: $79-$99	2P: $89-$109	XP: $10	F18
10/1-3/31 [ECP]	1P: $69-$79	2P: $79-$89	XP: $10	F18

Motel   **Location:** I-71, exit 237, just e. 16501 Snow Rd 44142. Fax: 216/267-9365. **Facility:** 64 one-bedroom standard units. 3 stories, interior corridors. *Bath:* combo or shower only. **Parking:** on-site, winter plug-ins. **Terms:** check-in 4 pm, 14 day cancellation notice. **Amenities:** extended cable TV, irons, hair dryers. **Pool(s):** heated indoor. **Leisure Activities:** whirlpool, exercise room. **Guest Services:** coin laundry. **Cards:** AX, CB, DC, DS, MC, VI.

SOME UNITS

(ASK) (SD) (+K) (&) (~) (🏃) (DATA PORT) (💻) (🖨) / (✕) (🛢) (📠) /
               FEE

FAIRFIELD INN BY MARRIOTT-BROOK PARK   Phone: (216)676-5200   105

(AAA) (SAVE)   All Year [CP]   1P: $79

Location: I-71, exit 237, just e. 16644 Snow Rd 44142. Fax: 216/676-5200. **Facility:** 135 one-bedroom standard units. 3 stories, interior/exterior corridors. *Bath:* combo or shower only. **Parking:** on-site. **Amenities:** irons. **Pool(s):** outdoor. **Guest Services:** valet laundry. **Cards:** AX, CB, DC, DS, MC, VI. **Special Amenities:** free continental breakfast and free local telephone calls. *(See ad p 612 & color ad card insert)*

Motel

SOME UNITS

(&) (📶) (~) (🏃) (DATA PORT) (🖨) / (✕) (🛢) (📠) /

HOLIDAY INN EXPRESS/BROOKPARK-CLEVELAND HOPKINS AIRPORT   Phone: (216)433-0004   106

(AAA) (SAVE)   6/1-8/31 [ECP]   1P: $99-$119
          4/1-5/31 & 9/1-3/31 [ECP]   1P: $89-$119

Motel   **Location:** I-71, exit 237, just e. 16330 Snow Rd 44142. Fax: 216/433-1936. **Facility:** 67 one-bedroom standard units, some with whirlpools. 2 stories, interior corridors. *Bath:* combo or shower only. **Parking:** on-site. **Amenities:** extended cable TV, voice mail, irons, hair dryers. **Pool(s):** heated indoor. **Leisure Activities:** whirlpool, exercise room. **Guest Services:** coin laundry. **Cards:** AX, CB, DC, DS, JC, MC, VI. **Special Amenities:** free continental breakfast and free local telephone calls.

SOME UNITS

(SD) (+K) (~) (🏃) (DATA PORT) (🛢) (📠) (💻) (🖨) / (✕) /

──────── WHERE TO DINE ────────

EL RINCON   **Lunch:** $5-$8   **Dinner:** $6-$12   Phone: 216/676-6771   63

Mexican   **Location:** I-71, exit 237, 1 mi e on Snow Rd; in plaza. 5843 Smith Rd 44142. **Hours:** 11 am-10 pm, Fri & Sat-10:30 pm, Sun noon-8 pm. Closed major holidays. **Features:** casual dress; carryout; cocktails & lounge. Traditional, authentic Mexican food is served in a homey atmosphere. Homemade items are prepared fresh daily. Those unfamiliar with Mexican dishes can peruse food descriptions on the back of the menu. **Parking:** on-site. **Cards:** DS, MC, VI.

(✕)

──────── *The following restaurant has not been evaluated by AAA* ────────
but is listed for your information only.

MEXICAN PALACE RESTAURANTE   Phone: 216/875-5330

(fyi)   Not evaluated. **Location:** 1409 Brookpark Rd 44135. Serving authentic Mexican cuisine since 1962, the restaurant features strolling mariachi singers on Friday and Saturday.

CLEVELAND HEIGHTS pop. 54,100 (See map p. 600; index p. 606)

──────── WHERE TO DINE ────────

CAFE TANDOOR   **Lunch:** $6-$9   **Dinner:** $9-$20   Phone: 216/371-8500   87

Ethnic   **Location:** I-71, exit 172D (Carnegie), 6 mi e to Taylor Rd, just n. 2096 S Taylor Rd 44118. **Hours:** 11:30 am-2 & 5:30-10 pm, Sun 3 pm-9 pm. Closed: 11/28, 12/24-12/26. **Reservations:** suggested. **Features:** casual dress; carryout; cocktails & lounge. Smoky, exotic Indian cooking featuring such items as chicken tikka roasted in the tandoori oven make Cafe Tandoor memorable. Also served are batter-fried pakoras, samosas (spicy, delicate pastry dumplings) and vegetarian and non-vegetarian sampler plates. Great background music that is very soothing and enhancing to the dining experience. Smoke free premises. **Parking:** on-site. **Cards:** AX, DC, DS, MC, VI.

(✕)

LEMON GRASS   **Lunch:** $5-$8   **Dinner:** $7-$13   Phone: 216/321-0210   86

Thai   **Location:** Just s of Cedar Rd. 2179 Lee Rd 44118. **Hours:** 11:30 am-2:30 & 5-11 pm, Fri-11 pm, Sat 5 pm-11 pm. Closed major holidays; also Sun. **Reservations:** accepted; weekends. **Features:** casual dress; carryout; cocktails. Select from signature dishes that can be customized to taste with various meats, crispy vegetables and spice-infused sauces. The beef with macadamia nuts is particularly flavorful. Homemade coconut ice cream gives your palate a special treat. **Parking:** on-site. **Cards:** AX, DC, MC, VI.

(✕)

INDEPENDENCE pop. 6,500   (See map p. 600; index p. 604)

──── WHERE TO STAY ────

AMERISUITES (CLEVELAND SO/INDEPENDENCE)
AAA SAVE

Suite Motel

Phone: (216)328-1060   **62**   F18

All Year [ECP]   1P: $89-$109   2P: $99-$119   XP: $10   **Location:** I-77, exit Rockside Rd, just w to W Creek Rd, then just n. 6025 Jefferson Dr 44131. Fax: 216/328-1071. **Facility:** 128 one-bedroom standard units. 6 stories, interior corridors. *Bath:* combo or shower only. **Parking:** on-site. **Terms:** pets ($25 fee). **Amenities:** high-speed Internet (fee), voice mail, irons, hair dryers. *Some:* dual phone lines. **Pool(s):** heated indoor. **Leisure Activities:** exercise room. **Guest Services:** valet and coin laundry, area transportation-within 2 mi. **Business Services:** meeting rooms, business center, PC, fax. **Cards:** AX, CB, DC, DS, MC, VI. **Special Amenities:** free continental breakfast and free newspaper.

SOME UNITS

(icons) FEE

BAYMONT INN & SUITES CLEVELAND-INDEPENDENCE
AAA SAVE

Motel

Phone: (216)447-1133   **66**

All Year   1P: $74-$84   2P: $74-$84   **Location:** I-77, exit Rockside Rd, just e. 6161 Quarry Ln 44131. Fax: 216/447-0135. **Facility:** 101 units. 99 one-bedroom standard units. 2 one-bedroom suites ($84-$134). 3 stories, interior corridors. **Parking:** on-site. **Amenities:** extended cable TV, video games, voice mail, irons, hair dryers. **Guest Services:** valet laundry. **Business Services:** meeting rooms. **Cards:** AX, CB, DC, DS, MC, VI. **Special Amenities:** free continental breakfast and free newspaper. *(See color ad opposite title page)*

SOME UNITS

(icons) FEE

CLEVELAND/INDEPENDENCE DAYS INN
SAVE

Motel

Phone: (216)524-3600   **59**

6/1-9/30   1P: $69-$109   XP: $5   4/1-5/31 & 10/1-3/31   1P: $49-$79   XP: $5   **Location:** I-77, exit 157, just s. 5555 Brecksville Rd 44131. Fax: 216/901-1844. **Facility:** 80 one-bedroom standard units, some with whirlpools. 5 stories, interior corridors. **Parking:** on-site. **Terms:** 7 day cancellation notice. **Amenities:** extended cable TV, dual phone lines, voice mail, irons, hair dryers. **Business Services:** meeting rooms. **Cards:** AX, DC, DS, MC, VI. *(See ad below)*

SOME UNITS

(icons)

COMFORT INN
SAVE

Motel

Phone: (216)328-7777   **69**   F18

All Year [ECP]   1P: $69-$79   2P: $69-$89   XP: $8   **Location:** I-77, exit Rockside Rd, just e. 6191 Quarry Ln 44131. Fax: 216/328-7777. **Facility:** 89 one-bedroom standard units, some with whirlpools. 3 stories, interior corridors. **Parking:** on-site. **Terms:** check-in 4 pm, cancellation fee imposed, package plans. **Amenities:** extended cable TV, irons, hair dryers. **Pool(s):** outdoor. **Guest Services:** valet laundry. **Business Services:** meeting rooms, fax. **Cards:** AX, DC, DS, MC, VI.

SOME UNITS

(icons)

COURTYARD BY MARRIOTT
AAA SAVE

Motel

Phone: (216)901-9988   **61**

All Year   1P: $69-$119   2P: $79-$129   **Location:** I-77, exit Rockside Rd, 0.3 mi w to W Creek Rd, then 0.3 mi n. 5051 W Creek Rd 44131. Fax: 216/901-9989. **Facility:** 154 units. 149 one-bedroom standard units, some with whirlpools. 5 one-bedroom suites. 5 stories, interior corridors. *Bath:* combo or shower only. **Parking:** on-site. **Terms:** 7 day cancellation notice. **Amenities:** voice mail, irons, hair dryers. **Pool(s):** heated indoor. **Leisure Activities:** whirlpool, exercise room. **Guest Services:** coin laundry. **Business Services:** meeting rooms, fax. **Cards:** AX, DC, DS, MC, VI. *(See color ad card insert)*

SOME UNITS

(icons) FEE   FEE

(See map p. 600)

FOUR POINTS BY SHERATON CLEVELAND SOUTH　　　　　　Phone: (216)524-0700　64

AAA SAVE

WWW

Hotel

All Year　　　　　1P: $79-$169　　　2P: $79-$169

Location: I-77, exit Rockside Rd. 5300 Rockside Rd 44131. Fax: 216/524-6477. **Facility:** 179 one-bedroom standard units, some with whirlpools. 5 stories, interior corridors. **Parking:** on-site. **Terms:** cancellation fee imposed, package plans. **Amenities:** video games, dual phone lines, voice mail, safes (fee), irons, hair dryers. **Dining:** dining room, 6:30 am-10 pm, $12-$18, cocktails. **Pool(s):** heated outdoor, heated indoor. **Leisure Activities:** saunas, whirlpool, 2 lighted tennis courts, exercise room. **Guest Services:** valet laundry, area transportation-within 5 mi. **Business Services:** conference facilities, business center, PC, fax. **Cards:** AX, CB, DC, DS, JC, MC, VI. *(See color ad below)*

SOME UNITS

🅢🄳 ✈ 🍴 🍸 👤 🏊 ✕🔲 📷 DATA PORT 🔲 🖨 / ✕ 🗋 /
　　　　　　　　　　　FEE　　　　　　　FEE

HAMPTON INN & SUITES　　　　　　　　　　　　　　Phone: (216)520-2020　70

SAVE

WWW

Motel

All Year　　　　　1P: $85-$91　　　2P: $90-$97

Location: I-77, exit Rockside Rd, just w to W Creek Rd, then just n. 6020 Jefferson Dr 44131. Fax: 216/674-7917. **Facility:** 103 units. 69 one-bedroom standard units, some with whirlpools. 34 one-bedroom suites ($103-$120) with kitchens, some with whirlpools. 3 stories, interior corridors. **Parking:** on-site. **Terms:** check-in 4 pm, [ECP] meal plan available. **Amenities:** extended cable TV, voice mail, irons. **Pool(s):** heated outdoor. **Leisure Activities:** exercise room. **Guest Services:** coin laundry. **Business Services:** meeting rooms, fax. **Cards:** AX, DC, DS, JC, MC, VI.

SOME UNITS

🅖🄼 🏊 🏊 📷 DATA PORT 🔲 🖨 / ✕ VCR 🗋 🖨 /

HILTON CLEVELAND SOUTH　　　　　　　　　　　　　Phone: (216)447-1300　68

SAVE

WWW

Motor Inn

All Year　　　　　1P: $109-$199　　2P: $109-$199　　XP: $10　　F18

Location: I-77, exit Rockside Rd. 6200 Quarry Ln 44131. Fax: 216/642-9334. **Facility:** 193 units. 190 one-bedroom standard units. 3 one-bedroom suites. 5 stories, interior corridors. *Bath:* combo or shower only. **Parking:** on-site. **Terms:** package plans. **Amenities:** extended cable TV. **Pool(s):** heated indoor/outdoor. **Leisure Activities:** sauna, whirlpool, exercise room. **Guest Services:** gift shop, valet laundry. **Business Services:** conference facilities, business center, PC. **Cards:** AX, CB, DC, DS, JC, MC, VI.

SOME UNITS

🅢🄳 ✈ 🍴 🍸 👤 🏊 ✕🔲 📷 DATA PORT 🔲 🖨 / ✕ 🗋 /
　　　　　　　FEE　　　　　　　　　　　　　FEE

HOLIDAY INN-INDEPENDENCE/ROCKSIDE I-77　　　　　Phone: (216)524-8050　63

WWW

Hotel

All Year　　　　　1P: $69-$129　　　2P: $69-$129

Location: I-77, exit Rockside Rd, just e. 6001 Rockside Rd 44131. Fax: 216/524-9280. **Facility:** 364 one-bedroom standard units. 5 stories, interior corridors. *Bath:* combo or shower only. **Parking:** on-site. **Terms:** check-in 4 pm, package plans. **Amenities:** dual phone lines, voice mail, irons, hair dryers. **Pool(s):** heated indoor. **Leisure Activities:** sauna, exercise room. **Guest Services:** gift shop, coin laundry. **Business Services:** conference facilities, business center, PC (fee), fax. **Cards:** AX, CB, DC, DS, JC, MC, VI.

SOME UNITS

ASK 🅢🄳 ✈ 🍴 🍸 👤 🏊 ✕🔲 📷 DATA PORT 🔲 🖨 / ✕ 🗋 /
　　　　　　　　　　　　FEE　　　　　　　　　　　FEE

RED ROOF INN　　　　　　　　　　　　　　　　　　Phone: (216)447-0030　65

AAA SAVE

WWW

Motel

5/24-9/7	1P: $61	2P: $67	XP: $6	F18
9/8-11/2	1P: $55	2P: $61	XP: $6	F18
4/1-5/23	1P: $49	2P: $55	XP: $6	F18
11/3-3/31	1P: $49	2P: $53	XP: $6	F18

Location: I-77, exit Rockside Rd, just e. 6020 Quarry Ln 44131. Fax: 216/447-0092. **Facility:** 108 one-bedroom standard units. 2 stories, exterior corridors. *Bath:* combo or shower only. **Parking:** on-site. **Terms:** small pets only. **Amenities:** extended cable TV, video games, voice mail. **Guest Services:** valet laundry. **Business Services:** fax. **Cards:** AX, CB, DC, DS, MC, VI. **Special Amenities:** free local telephone calls and free newspaper.

SOME UNITS

🛏 🍴 🅖 📷 DATA PORT 🖨 / ✕ /
　　　　　　　FEE

(See map p. 600)

RESIDENCE INN BY MARRIOTT   Phone: (216)520-1450   60

AAA SAVE   All Year   1P: $98-$107   2P: $125-$134
            Location: I-77, exit Rockside Rd, just w to W Creek Rd, then just n. 5101 W Creek Rd 44131. Fax: 216/642-9830.
Suite Motel **Facility:** 118 units. 90 one-bedroom standard units with efficiencies. 28 two-bedroom suites with kitchens. 2
            stories, exterior corridors. **Bath:** combo or shower only. **Parking:** on-site. **Terms:** pets ($200-$250 fee).
            Amenities: extended cable TV, video games, voice mail, irons, hair dryers. **Pool(s):** outdoor. **Leisure Ac-**
            tivities: whirlpool, exercise room, sports court. **Guest Services:** coin laundry. **Business Services:** meeting
rooms, fax. **Cards:** AX, DC, DS, JC, MC, VI. *(See color ad card insert)*

SOME UNITS

———— WHERE TO DINE ————

ALADDIN'S EATERY   **Lunch:** $4-$8   **Dinner:** $4-$10   **Phone:** 216/642-7550   56
                        Location: I-77, exit Rockside Rd, 0.6 mi e; in Rockside Corners Plaza. 6901 Rockside Rd 44131. **Hours:** 11 am-10
Ethnic   pm, Sun-8 pm. Closed major holidays. **Features:** casual dress; carryout. Natural foods with a distinctive
                        Mediterranean influence make Aladdin's a popular spot. Plenty of healthy selections grace the menu
                        including fresh foods of the Middle East such as hummos, tabouli, falaffel and great pita pockets. Smoke
free premises. **Parking:** on-site. **Cards:** AX, MC, VI.

HARRY'S STEAKHOUSE   **Lunch:** $5-$8   **Dinner:** $9-$18   **Phone:** 216/524-5300   55
                        Location: I-77, exit Rockside Rd, 0.5 mi e on Rockside, 0.7 mi n on SR 21. 5664 Brecksville Rd 44131. **Hours:** 4
Steak House   pm-10:30 pm, Fri-midnight, Sat 3 pm-midnight, Sun noon-10 pm. Closed: 11/28, 12/25. **Features:** casual
                        dress; children's menu; early bird specials; carryout; cocktails. This local favorite is known for their friendly
                        service and reasonable prices. Only prime grade cuts selected and cut daily are used in their steaks and
slow roasted prime rib. **Parking:** on-site. **Cards:** AX, MC, VI.

ZAYDA'S   **Lunch:** $5-$8   **Dinner:** $8-$15   **Phone:** 216/642-4341   57
                        Location: I-77, exit Rockside Rd, 0.5 mi e, then just n on SR 21. 6080 Brecksville Rd 44131. **Hours:** 11 am-9 pm.
American   Closed major holidays; also Sun. **Features:** casual dress; children's menu; carryout; cocktails. The warm,
                        friendly restaurant has a lively, fast-paced atmosphere. The menu comprises deli sandwiches, Angus
                        steaks, fresh salads and preparations of chicken, pasta and seafood. Desserts are simply wonderful, from
the tortes to the eclairs. **Parking:** on-site. **Cards:** AX, DC, DS, MC, VI.

LAKEWOOD pop. 59,700   (See map p. 600; index p. 606)

———— WHERE TO DINE ————

ALADDIN'S EATERY   **Lunch:** $4-$7   **Dinner:** $7-$12   **Phone:** 216/521-4005   73
                        Location: 2 blks e of Warren. 14536 Detroit Ave 44107. **Hours:** 11 am-10:30 pm, Fri & Sat-11:30 pm. Closed:
Middle Eastern   11/28, 12/25. **Features:** casual dress; children's menu; carryout; beer & wine only. Natural foods with a
                        distinctive Mediterranean influence make Aladdins a popular spot. Plenty of healthy selections grace the
                        menu, including fresh foods of the Middle East such as hummus, tabbouleh, falafel and great pita pockets.
Smoke free premises. **Parking:** on-site. **Cards:** AX, MC, VI.

MARIA'S ROMAN ROOM   **Lunch:** $5-$8   **Dinner:** $9-$16   **Phone:** 216/226-5875   74
                        Location: Just w of W 117th St. 11822 Detroit Ave 44107. **Hours:** 11 am-10 pm, Sat-11 pm. Closed: 1/1, 11/28,
Italian   12/25. **Reservations:** accepted. **Features:** casual dress; carryout; cocktails. Generous portions of
                        homemade thick-cut pasta dominate the menu and afford a tasty dining experience. Of note are the baked
                        lasagna, chicken marsala, veal parmigiana and pizza. Be sure to try the chocolate salami log for a sweet
ending to your meal. **Parking:** on-site. **Cards:** AX, MC, VI.

PIER W   **Lunch:** $7-$13   **Dinner:** $22   **Phone:** 216/228-2250   77
                        Location: I-90, exit 166, 1.5 n on W 117th St, then 0.5 mi w. 12700 Lake Ave at Winton Pl 44107. **Hours:** 11:30
Seafood   am-3 & 5:30-10 pm, Fri-11 pm, Sat 5 pm-11 pm, Sun 9:30 am-2:30 & 4:30-9 pm. Closed: 12/25.
                        Reservations: suggested. **Features:** casual dress; Sunday brunch; children's menu; carryout; cocktails &
                        lounge. Tasty selections of fresh seafood, such as walleye and clam chowder, are the menu's big focus.
The dining room's draw is its spectacular view of Lake Erie and the Cleveland skyline. Angle for a table by a window. Servers
are friendly and thoughtful. **Parking:** on-site and valet. **Cards:** AX, DC, DS, MC, VI.

PLAYERS   **Dinner:** $13-$20   **Phone:** 216/226-5200   75
                        Location: 1.4 mi w of 117th St. 14523 Madison 44107. **Hours:** 5 pm-10 pm, Fri & Sat-11 pm. Closed major
Italian   holidays. **Reservations:** suggested. **Features:** dressy casual; carryout; cocktails; a la carte. The restaurant
                        serves gourmet pizza and pasta with contemporary Italian cuisine entrees. The specialty penne ala vodka
                        blends Gulf shrimp, roasted shallots, spinach and sun-dried tomato vodka cream sauce. Try the spring rolls
appetizer, filled with chicken, corn and baby spinach. **Parking:** on-site. **Cards:** AX, DC, DS, MC, VI.

———— The following restaurant has not been evaluated by AAA ————
but is listed for your information only.

BARNACLE BILL'S CRAB HOUSE   **Phone:** 216/521-2722
fyi   Not evaluated. **Location:** 14810 Detroit Ave 44107. This local landmark offers a wide variety of seafood dishes.

MAYFIELD pop. 3,500

—— WHERE TO STAY ——

HOLIDAY INN-MAYFIELD   Phone: (440)461-9200
AAA SAVE   6/1-8/31   1P: $109
▼▼▼▼   4/1-5/31 & 9/1-3/31   1P: $89
           Location: I-271, exit 36, just e. 780 Beta Dr 44143. Fax: 440/461-7564. **Facility:** 115 one-bedroom standard units.
Motor Inn   4 stories, interior corridors. **Parking:** on-site. **Terms:** 18% service charge. **Amenities:** extended cable TV,
           video games, dual phone lines, voice mail, irons, hair dryers. **Dining:** restaurant, deli, 7 am-10:30 & 11:30-10
           pm, Sat & Sun 8 am-11:30 & noon-10 pm, $9-$17. **Pool(s):** heated indoor/outdoor. **Leisure Activi-**
ties: sauna, exercise room. **Guest Services:** coin laundry. **Business Services:** conference facilities. **Cards:** AX, CB, DC, DS,
JC, MC, VI.

SOME UNITS

MAYFIELD HEIGHTS pop. 19,800   (See map p. 600; index p. 605)

—— WHERE TO STAY ——

BAYMONT INN & SUITES-CLEVELAND NE (MAYFIELD HEIGHTS)   Phone: (440)442-8400   [100]
AAA SAVE   All Year   1P: $85-$95
▼▼ ▼▼   **Location:** I-271, exit Mayfield exit, 0.3 mi w off US 322. 1421 Golden Gate Blvd 44124. Fax: 440/442-0327.
           Facility: 99 one-bedroom standard units. 3 stories, interior corridors. **Parking:** on-site. **Terms:** pets ($50 de-
Motel   posit). **Amenities:** extended cable TV, video games, voice mail, irons, hair dryers. **Guest Services:** coin
           laundry. **Cards:** AX, CB, DC, DS, MC, VI. **Special Amenities: free continental breakfast and free news-**
           paper.

SOME UNITS

MEDINA pop. 19,200

—— WHERE TO STAY ——

BEST WESTERN MEDINA INN   Phone: (330)725-4571
AAA SAVE   All Year   1P: $42-$69   2P: $46-$79   XP: $5   F12
▼▼▼▼   **Location:** I-71, exit 218, just e. 2875 Medina Rd 44256. Fax: 330/725-5926. **Facility:** 135 one-bedroom standard
           units, some with whirlpools. 2 stories, interior corridors. **Parking:** on-site. **Amenities:** extended cable TV,
Motor Inn   voice mail, irons, hair dryers. **Dining:** dining room, 7 am-2 & 5-9 pm, Sun 8 am-2 pm, Fri & Sat-10 pm, $6-
           $15, cocktails. **Pool(s):** outdoor. **Business Services:** meeting rooms. **Cards:** AX, DC, DS, MC, VI.
           Special Amenities: free local telephone calls and free newspaper.

SOME UNITS

CROSS COUNTRY INN   Phone: (330)725-1395
AAA SAVE   All Year   1P: $39-$46   2P: $46-$53   XP: $2   F17
▼▼ ▼   **Location:** I-71, exit 218, just w. 5021 Eastpointe Dr 44256. Fax: 330/722-5099. **Facility:** 120 one-bedroom stan-
           dard units. 2 stories, exterior corridors. **Parking:** on-site. **Amenities:** video games, voice mail. **Pool(s):**
Motel   heated outdoor. **Cards:** AX, CB, DC, DS, MC, VI. **Special Amenities: free local telephone calls and pre-**
           ferred room (subject to availability with advanced reservations).

SOME UNITS

DAYS INN MEDINA   Phone: (330)722-4335
AAA SAVE   All Year [CP]   1P: $32-$79   2P: $38-$85   XP: $6   F17
▼▼   **Location:** I-71, exit 218, just e. 5200 Montville Dr 44256. Fax: 330/725-6101. **Facility:** 116 one-bedroom standard
           units, some with efficiencies. 1 story, exterior corridors. **Parking:** on-site. **Terms:** check-in 4 pm, 14 day can-
Motel   cellation notice-fee imposed, pets ($25 deposit). **Amenities:** extended cable TV, hair dryers. **Pool(s):** small
           outdoor. **Guest Services:** coin laundry. **Business Services:** meeting rooms. **Cards:** AX, CB, DC, DS, JC,
           MC, VI. **Special Amenities: free continental breakfast and free newspaper.** *(See color ad below)*

SOME UNITS

HAMPTON INN

Phone: 330/721-8955

(AAA) (SAVE)
▼▼▼▼
Motel

All Year [ECP]   1P: $79-$99   2P: $89-$99
Location: I-71, exit 218, just w. 3073 E Pointe Dr 44256. Fax: 330/721-8954. **Facility:** 78 one-bedroom standard units. 3 stories, interior corridors. *Bath:* combo or shower only. **Parking:** on-site. **Terms:** check-in 4 pm, cancellation fee imposed. **Amenities:** extended cable TV, dual phone lines, voice mail, irons, hair dryers. **Pool(s):** heated indoor. **Leisure Activities:** sauna, whirlpool, exercise room. **Guest Services:** valet and coin laundry. **Business Services:** meeting rooms, business center. **Cards:** AX, DC, DS, MC, VI.
Special Amenities: free continental breakfast and free local telephone calls.

SOME UNITS

⬛ ⬛ ⬛ ⬛ ⬛ ⬛ ⬛ ⬛ / ⬛ /

HOLIDAY INN EXPRESS

Phone: (330)723-4994

(AAA) (SAVE)
▼▼▼▼
Motel

5/1-8/31   1P: $72   2P: $72
4/1-4/30 & 9/1-3/31   1P: $63   2P: $63
Location: I-71, exit 218, just e. 2850 Medina Rd 44256. Fax: 330/723-3469. **Facility:** 79 one-bedroom standard units, some with whirlpools. 2 stories, interior corridors. **Parking:** on-site. **Amenities:** extended cable TV, voice mail, irons, hair dryers. **Pool(s):** heated indoor. **Leisure Activities:** sauna, exercise room. **Guest Services:** coin laundry. **Business Services:** meeting rooms. **Cards:** AX, DS, MC, VI. **Special Amenities: early check-in/late check-out and free continental breakfast.**

SOME UNITS

⬛ ⬛ ⬛ ⬛ ⬛ ⬛ ⬛ / ⬛ ⬛ ⬛ /

MOTEL 6 4112

Phone: 330/723-3322

▼▼
Motel

4/1-9/3	1P: $53-$59	2P: $59-$65	XP: $3	F17
9/4-10/31	1P: $43-$49	2P: $49-$55	XP: $3	F17
11/1-2/28	1P: $38-$44	2P: $44-$50	XP: $3	F17
3/1-3/31	1P: $38-$44	2P: $44-$50	XP: $36	F17

Location: I-71, exit 218, just w. 3122 E Pointe Dr 44256. Fax: 330/723-3321. **Facility:** 63 one-bedroom standard units. 3 stories, interior corridors. *Bath:* combo or shower only. **Parking:** on-site. **Terms:** 3 day cancellation notice. **Amenities:** extended cable TV, voice mail. **Pool(s):** heated indoor. **Leisure Activities:** whirlpool. **Cards:** AX, DC, DS, MC, VI.

SOME UNITS

(ASK) ⬛ ⬛ ⬛ ⬛ ⬛ / ⬛ /

——— WHERE TO DINE ———

ON TAP

▼▼
American

Lunch: $5-$8   **Dinner:** $7-$14   **Phone:** 330/725-1972
Location: I-71, exit 218, just e. 2905 Medina Rd 44256. **Hours:** 11 am-11 pm, Fri & Sat-midnight, Sun noon-10 pm. Closed: 11/28, 12/25. **Features:** casual dress; children's menu; carryout; cocktails. Juicy, half-pound hamburgers are what give the friendly restaurant a devoted local following. Nibble on fresh popcorn as you await a good-sized portion of wings, a hearty sandwich or one of the daily specials. Service is prompt and attentive. **Parking:** on-site. **Cards:** AX, MC, VI.

⬛

——— *The following restaurant has not been evaluated by AAA* ———
but is listed for your information only.

ALEXANDRIS RESTAURANT

Phone: 330/722-4139

(fyi)   Not evaluated. **Location:** 2835 Medina Rd 44256. Conveniently accessible from the interstate, the casual restaurant serves reasonably priced food.

MIDDLEBURG HEIGHTS pop. 14,700   (See map p. 600; index p. 604)

——— WHERE TO STAY ———

CLARION CLEVELAND AIRPORT WEST

Phone: (440)243-5200   (92)

(AAA) (SAVE)
▼▼▼▼
Motor Inn

All Year   1P: $80-$90   2P: $80-$90
Location: I-71, exit 235, just e. 17000 Bagley Rd 44130. Fax: 440/243-5244. **Facility:** 238 one-bedroom standard units, some with whirlpools. 2 stories, interior corridors. *Bath:* combo or shower only. **Parking:** on-site, winter plug-ins. **Terms:** check-in 4 pm. **Amenities:** voice mail, safes (fee), irons, hair dryers. **Dining:** restaurant, 6:30 am-2 & 5-10 pm, $10-$15, cocktails. **Pool(s):** heated outdoor, heated indoor, wading. **Leisure Activities:** saunas, exercise room. **Guest Services:** valet and coin laundry. **Business Services:** conference facilities. **Cards:** AX, CB, DC, DS, JC, MC, VI. **Special Amenities: free newspaper and preferred room (subject to availability with advanced reservations).** *(See color ad below)*

SOME UNITS

⬛ ⬛ ⬛ ⬛ ⬛ ⬛ ⬛ ⬛ ⬛ ⬛ / ⬛ ⬛ /
FEE

(See map p. 600)

COMFORT INN-CLEVELAND AIRPORT
Phone: (440)234-3131   **90**

AAA **SAVE**   ♦♦♦   Motel

All Year [ECP]   1P: $60-$140   2P: $70-$150   XP: $10   F16
Location: I-71, exit 235, 0.3 mi w to Engle Rd, then 0.3 mi n. 17550 Rosbough Dr 44130. Fax: 440/234-6111. **Facility:** 136 one-bedroom standard units, some with whirlpools. 3 stories, interior corridors. **Parking:** on-site. **Terms:** package plans, pets ($25 fee). **Amenities:** video games, voice mail, irons. *Some:* dual phone lines, hair dryers. **Pool(s):** outdoor. **Guest Services:** valet laundry, area transportation-within 5 mi. **Business Services:** meeting rooms. **Cards:** AX, DC, DS, JC, MC, VI. **Special Amenities:** early check-in/late check-out and free room upgrade (subject to availability with advanced reservations). *(See color ad p 599)*

SOME UNITS

COURTYARD BY MARRIOTT
Phone: (440)243-8785   **88**

AAA **SAVE**   ♦♦♦   Motel

All Year   1P: $99-$119
Location: I-71, exit 235, just w on Bagley, just s. 7345 Engle Rd. Fax: 440/243-8835. **Facility:** 154 one-bedroom standard units, some with whirlpools. 5 stories, interior corridors. *Bath:* combo or shower only. **Parking:** on-site. **Amenities:** high-speed Internet, dual phone lines, voice mail, irons, hair dryers. **Pool(s):** heated indoor. **Leisure Activities:** whirlpool, exercise room. **Guest Services:** valet and coin laundry. **Business Services:** meeting rooms. **Cards:** AX, DC, DS, MC, VI. *(See color ad card insert)*

SOME UNITS
FEE

CROSS COUNTRY INN
Phone: (440)243-2277   **95**

AAA **SAVE**   ♦♦   Motel

All Year   1P: $46-$53   2P: $53-$60   XP: $2   F17
Location: I-71, exit 235, just w. 7233 Engle Rd 44130. Fax: 440/243-9852. **Facility:** 112 one-bedroom standard units. 2 stories, exterior corridors. *Bath:* combo or shower only. **Parking:** on-site. **Amenities:** video games, voice mail. **Pool(s):** heated outdoor. **Business Services:** meeting rooms. **Cards:** AX, CB, DC, DS, MC, VI. **Special Amenities:** free local telephone calls and preferred room (subject to availability with advanced reservations).

SOME UNITS
FEE

HAMPTON INN & SUITES
Phone: (440)234-0206   **89**

SAVE   ♦♦♦   Motel

All Year [ECP]   1P: $89
Location: I-71, exit 235, just w on Bagley Rd. 7074 Engle Rd 44130. Fax: 440/234-0208. **Facility:** 97 one-bedroom standard units, some with whirlpools. 4 stories, interior corridors. *Bath:* combo or shower only. **Parking:** on-site. **Amenities:** extended cable TV, dual phone lines, voice mail, irons, hair dryers. **Pool(s):** heated indoor. **Leisure Activities:** whirlpool, exercise room. **Guest Services:** coin laundry. **Business Services:** meeting rooms. **Cards:** AX, CB, DC, DS, MC, VI.

SOME UNITS
FEE

RADISSON-HOTEL CLEVELAND SOUTHWEST
Phone: (440)243-4040   **94**

AAA **SAVE**   ♦♦♦   Motor Inn

All Year   1P: $109-$139   2P: $109-$139   XP: $10   F18
Location: I-71, exit 235, just w on Bagley Rd. 7230 Engle Rd 44130. Fax: 440/243-5319. **Facility:** 237 one-bedroom standard units. 5 stories, interior corridors. **Parking:** on-site. **Terms:** package plans. **Amenities:** video games, voice mail, irons, hair dryers. *Some:* dual phone lines. **Dining:** dining room, 6:30 am-2:30 & 5-10 pm, Sat & Sun from 7 am, $10-$20, cocktails. **Pool(s):** heated indoor/outdoor. **Leisure Activities:** sauna, whirlpool, exercise room. **Guest Services:** valet laundry, area transportation-within 5 mi. **Business Services:** conference facilities. **Cards:** AX, CB, DC, DS, JC, MC, VI. **Special Amenities:** free newspaper. *(See ad below)*

SOME UNITS
FEE

RED ROOF INN-MIDDLEBURG HEIGHTS
Phone: (440)243-2441   **97**

AAA **SAVE**   ♦   Motel

6/21-9/8	1P: $57-$67	2P: $63-$73	XP: $6	F18
5/17-6/20	1P: $49-$59	2P: $56-$65	XP: $6	F18
9/9-3/31	1P: $49-$59	2P: $55-$65	XP: $6	F18
4/1-5/16	1P: $45-$55	2P: $51-$61	XP: $6	F18

Location: I-71, exit 235, just w. 17555 Bagley Rd 44130. Fax: 440/243-2474. **Facility:** 117 one-bedroom standard units. 3 stories, interior/exterior corridors. **Parking:** on-site. **Terms:** small pets only. **Amenities:** video games, voice mail. **Cards:** AX, CB, DC, DS, MC, VI. **Special Amenities:** free local telephone calls and free newspaper.

SOME UNITS

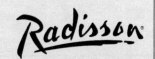

(See map p. 600)

RESIDENCE INN BY MARRIOTT
AAA (SAVE)
▼▼▼▼▼
Apartment

Phone: (440)234-6688 [91]

6/1-8/31 [BP]   1P: $79-$119
4/1-5/31 & 9/1-3/31 [BP]   1P: $69-$109

Location: I-71, exit 235, just w on Bagley Rd, just n on Engle Rd. 17525 Rosbough Dr 44130. Fax: 440/234-3459. **Facility:** 316 units. 158 one-bedroom standard units. 134 one- and 24 two-bedroom suites with kitchens. 2-3 stories, interior/exterior corridors. *Bath:* combo or shower only. **Parking:** on-site. **Terms:** cancellation fee imposed, pets ($200-$250 fee). **Amenities:** extended cable TV. *Some:* video games, voice mail, irons, hair dryers. **Leisure Activities:** whirlpool, exercise room, sports court. **Guest Services:** complimentary evening beverages: Mon-Thurs, coin laundry. **Business Services:** meeting rooms. **Cards:** AX, DC, DS, JC, MC, VI. *(See color ad card insert)*

SOME UNITS
✈ 🐕 🍽 ⚙ ☒ 📹 / ☒ 🅺 🆆 (DATA PORT) ⬛ 🖥 ▭ 🖨 /

─────── WHERE TO DINE ───────

HONG KONG PALACE
▼▼ ▼▼
Chinese

Lunch: $5-$9   **Dinner: $8-$16**   **Phone: 440/234-1668** [60]

Location: I-71, exit 235, just w on Bagley Rd. 7080B Engle Rd 44130. **Hours:** 11 am-10 pm, Fri-11 pm, Sat noon-11 pm, Sun noon-9 pm. Closed: 7/4, 11/28. **Features:** casual dress; carryout. Traditional Chinese cuisine reflects a Cantonese flair. The family-run establishment takes special care in preparing meals with distinctive sauces you won't find at most Asian restaurants. The dining room incorporates design elements that make it clear that this is no fast-food joint. **Parking:** on-site. **Cards:** AX, DC, DS, MC, VI.

☒ 🅺

─────── *The following restaurant has not been evaluated by AAA* ───────
but is listed for your information only.

AMAZON TRAIL
(fyi)

Phone: 440/234-6050

Not evaluated. **Location:** Corner of Eastland and Sheldon rds. 6611 Eastland Rd 44130. Fried bananas and fresh fish and seafood are favorites at the restaurant, which transports guests to the Amazon rain forest.

MORELAND HILLS pop. 3,400   (See map p. 600; index p. 606)

─────── WHERE TO DINE ───────

WARDS' INN
▼▼ ▼
American

Dinner: $17-$30   **Phone: 216/595-1954** [80]

Location: Jct Chagrin Blvd and SR 91. 34105 Chagrin Blvd 44022. **Hours:** 5 pm-10 pm, Fri & Sat-11 pm. Closed major holidays; also Sun. **Reservations:** suggested. **Features:** semi-formal attire; carryout; cocktails & lounge; a la carte. The cuisine revolves around the seasons, with innovative preparations of game prevailing in the fall and winter. Richly seasoned sauces perk up menu choices, and a warm Old English ambience adds life and charm to the cozy, intimate dining room. **Parking:** on-site and valet. **Cards:** AX, DC, DS, MC, VI. ☒

NORTH OLMSTED pop. 34,200   (See map p. 600; index p. 605)

─────── WHERE TO STAY ───────

COURTYARD BY MARRIOTT
AAA (SAVE)
▼▼▼▼
Motel

Phone: (440)716-9977 [132]

4/22-12/31   1P: $109   2P: $109
4/1-4/21 & 1/1-3/31   1P: $99   2P: $99

Location: I-480, exit 6B, just n. 24901 Country Club Blvd 44070. Fax: 440/716-1995. **Facility:** 121 one-bedroom standard units, some with whirlpools. 3 stories, interior corridors. *Bath:* combo or shower only. **Parking:** on-site. **Terms:** [BP] meal plan available. **Amenities:** high-speed Internet, voice mail, irons, hair dryers. **Pool(s):** heated indoor. **Leisure Activities:** whirlpool, exercise room. **Guest Services:** coin laundry. **Business Services:** meeting rooms. **Cards:** AX, CB, DC, DS, MC, VI. *(See color ad card insert)*

SOME UNITS
(S/D) ✈ 🍽 ⚙ 🕐 🏊 📹 (DATA PORT) ▭ 🖨 / ☒ ⬛ 🖥 /
FEE

HAMPTON INN
AAA (SAVE)
▼▼▼ ▼
Motel

Phone: (440)734-4477 [131]

6/1-8/31 [ECP]   1P: $79-$95   2P: $79-$95
4/1-5/31 & 9/1-3/31 [ECP]   1P: $69-$85   2P: $69-$85

Location: I-480, exit 6B, just n on SR 252. 25105 Country Club Blvd 44070. Fax: 440/734-0836. **Facility:** 111 one-bedroom standard units. 5 stories, interior corridors. **Parking:** on-site. **Terms:** cancellation fee imposed, pets ($50 fee). **Amenities:** extended cable TV, video games, irons, hair dryers. **Leisure Activities:** exercise room. **Guest Services:** valet laundry. **Business Services:** meeting rooms. **Cards:** AX, DC, DS, MC, VI.

SOME UNITS
(S/D) ✈ 🐕 📹 📹 (DATA PORT) ▭ 🖨 / ☒ /

HOMESTEAD STUDIO SUITES-CLEVELAND/AIRPORT/NORTH OLMSTED
▼▼ ▼▼
Extended Stay Motel

Phone: (440)777-8585 [133]

All Year   1P: $54-$64   2P: $59-$69   XP: $5   F12

Location: I-480, exit 6B, just n on SR 252. 24851 Country Club Blvd 44070. Fax: 440/777-5807. **Facility:** 136 one-bedroom standard units. 3 stories, exterior corridors. *Bath:* combo or shower only. **Parking:** on-site. **Terms:** cancellation fee imposed, pets ($75 fee). **Amenities:** voice mail, irons. **Guest Services:** coin laundry.

SOME UNITS
(ASK) 🐕 📹 🍽 📹 (DATA PORT) ⬛ 🖥 ▭ 🖨 / ☒ /

(See map p. 600)

RADISSON INN CLEVELAND AIRPORT　　　　　　　　　　Phone: (440)734-5060　130
　AAA SAVE　　All Year　　　　　　　1P: $129　　　　　2P: $129　　　　XP: $10　　　F18
　▽▽▽▽　　**Location:** I-480, exit 6B, just n on SR 252. 25070 Country Club Blvd 44070. Fax: 440/734-5471. **Facility:** 139 one-
　Hotel　　bedroom standard units, some with whirlpools. 6 stories, interior corridors. **Parking:** on-site. **Terms:** package
plans. **Amenities:** video games, voice mail, irons, hair dryers. **Dining:** dining room, 6:30 am-2 & 5-10 pm,
Sun from 7 am, $8-$16, cocktails. **Pool(s):** heated indoor. **Leisure Activities:** sauna, whirlpool, exercise
room. **Guest Services:** valet laundry. **Business Services:** conference facilities. **Cards:** AX, CB, DC, DS, JC,
MC, VI. **Special Amenities:** early check-in/late check-out and free newspaper. (See ad p 614)

———— **WHERE TO DINE** ————

EL CHARRO　　　　　　　　**Lunch:** $5-$8　　　　**Dinner:** $6-$12　　　　Phone: 440/779-9200　71
　▽　　　**Location:** I-480, exit 6B, 0.5 mi n, then 2.5 mi w. 30111 Lorain Rd 44070. **Hours:** 11 am-10 pm, Fri & Sat-11 pm,
　Mexican　Sun 4 pm-9 pm. Closed major holidays; also Mon. **Features:** casual dress; children's menu; carryout;
cocktails. This casual, friendly restaurant features over 28 types of margaritas. Daily specials and sampler
combos are offered. Service is laid back, yet attentive. **Parking:** on-site. **Cards:** AX, DC, DS, MC, VI.

———— *The following restaurant has not been evaluated by AAA* ————
but is listed for your information only.

WEIA TEIA　　　　　　　　　　　　　　　　　　　　　　　Phone: 440/716-8241
　[fyi]　　Not evaluated. **Location:** 140 Great Northern Mall 44070. Home to the latest trend in contemporary cuisine, the
restaurant boasts a variety of innovative dishes.

PARMA pop. 87,900

———— **WHERE TO DINE** ————

———— *The following restaurant has not been evaluated by AAA* ————
but is listed for your information only.

COLONIAL EATERY　　　　　　　　　　　　　　　　　　　Phone: 216/749-2310
　[fyi]　　Not evaluated. **Location:** 5222 Ridge Rd 44136. Among restaurant offerings are daily homemade specials, large
salads and a good variety of sandwiches, seafood and pasta.

ROCKY RIVER pop. 20,400　(See map p. 600; index p. 606)

———— **WHERE TO DINE** ————

GAMEKEEPER'S LODGE　　　　　**Lunch:** $6-$10　　　**Dinner:** $15-$25　　Phone: 440/333-8505　84
　▽▽▽　▽▽　　**Location:** West of bridge; in Beachcliff Market Square. 19300 Detroit Rd 44116. **Hours:** 11:30 am-10 pm, Fri &
　American　Sat-11 pm, Sun 4 pm-9 pm. Closed major holidays. **Reservations:** suggested. **Features:** casual dress;
carryout; cocktails & lounge; a la carte. Specialties include such items as sauteed ostrich filet, elk strip loin
and herb-crusted pork chops. **Parking:** on-site. **Cards:** AX, DC, DS, MC, VI.

KING WAH RESTAURANT　　　　　**Lunch:** $4-$7　　　　**Dinner:** $6-$10　　Phone: 440/331-0330　82
　▽▽▽　▽▽　　**Location:** Just e of 210th St. 20668 Center Ridge 44126. **Hours:** 11 am-10:30 pm, Fri-11:30 pm, Sat 11:30
　Chinese　am-11:30 pm, Sun 11:30 am-10 pm. Closed: 11/28. **Features:** casual dress; carryout; cocktails. Traditional
Chinese cuisine is the focus of the modern restaurant, a fixture in the area since the mid-1970s. The menu
also dabbles in a handful of gourmet Asian-fusion dishes. The atmosphere is decidedly relaxed, with
Oriental decor and a cozy patio. **Parking:** on-site. **Cards:** AX, DC, DS, MC, VI.

———— *The following restaurant has not been evaluated by AAA* ————
but is listed for your information only.

SALMON DAVE'S　　　　　　　　　　　　　　　　　　　　Phone: 440/331-2739
　[fyi]　　Not evaluated. **Location:** 19015 Old Lake Rd 44116. The restaurant employs creativity in its entree offerings.

SHAKER HEIGHTS pop. 30,800　(See map p. 600; index p. 606)

———— **WHERE TO DINE** ————

EDDIE SAND'S BLUELINE CAFE　　**Lunch:** $4-$8　　　**Dinner:** $6-$14　　Phone: 216/561-5050　99
　▽　　　**Location:** Jct Warrensville Rd and Van Aken Blvd; in the Van Aken Shopping Center. 20255 Van Aken Blvd 44122.
　Traditional　**Hours:** 7 am-10 pm, Fri & Sat-10:45 pm, Sun 7:30 am-9 pm. Closed: 11/28, 12/25. **Features:** casual
　American　dress; Sunday brunch; children's menu; carryout; cocktails & lounge. Eddie Sand's is a great stop for a bite
to eat and a bit of people watching before or after a day of shopping the city's upscale stores. You're
greeted by an eclectic decor and a menu of roast chicken, deli sandwiches, fresh bread and vegetarian
specials. **Parking:** on-site. **Cards:** AX, DC, DS, MC, VI.

(See map p. 600)

──────── *The following restaurant has not been evaluated by AAA* ────────
but is listed for your information only.

LARCHMERE TAVERN   **Phone:** 216/721-1111
[fyi]   Not evaluated. **Location:** 13051 Larchmere Blvd. Golfers frequent the traditional American tavern.

SOLON pop. 18,500   (See map p. 600; index p. 604)

──────── **WHERE TO STAY** ────────

DAYS INN SIX FLAGS   **Phone:** (440)248-3110   **76**
AAA [SAVE]   6/16-9/1   1P: $98-$119   2P: $98-$119
              4/1-6/15   1P: $54-$78   2P: $54-$78
▽▽▽   9/2-3/31   1P: $54-$68
Motel   **Location:** Jct SR 422 and 91. 6110 Som Center Rd 44139. Fax: 440/248-6687. **Facility:** 137 one-bedroom stan-
              dard units. 2 stories, exterior corridors. **Parking:** on-site. **Terms:** package plans. **Amenities:** voice mail, hair
rooms. **Cards:** AX, DC, DS, MC, VI.   dryers. *Some:* irons. **Pool(s):** heated outdoor. **Guest Services:** coin laundry. **Business Services:** meeting

SOME UNITS
[icons]

HAMPTON INN   **Phone:** (440)542-0400   **77**
[SAVE]   6/15-9/2 [ECP]   1P: $129   2P: $139
              5/24-6/14 [ECP]   1P: $109   2P: $119
▽▽▽▽▽   4/1-5/23 & 9/3-3/31 [ECP]   1P: $92   2P: $102
Motel   **Location:** SR 442, exit Harper Rd, 0.6 mi s, 0.4 mi e. 6035 Enterprise Pkwy 44139. Fax: 440/542-0353. **Facility:** 103
              one-bedroom standard units, some with whirlpools. 4 stories, interior corridors. *Bath:* combo or shower only.
              Parking: on-site. **Terms:** check-in 4 pm, 7 day cancellation notice. **Amenities:** extended cable TV, video
games, dual phone lines, voice mail, irons, hair dryers. **Pool(s):** heated indoor. **Leisure Activities:** exercise room. **Guest Services:** valet laundry. **Business Services:** meeting rooms. **Cards:** AX, CB, DC, DS, JC, MC, VI.

SOME UNITS
[icons]
FEE

──────── **WHERE TO DINE** ────────

43 BISTRO   **Lunch:** $7-$12   **Dinner:** $15-$25   **Phone:** 440/248-4343   **58**
▽▽▽▽   **Location:** SR 91, exit SR 422, just n to Aurora Rd, then just w; in plaza. 33587 Aurora Rd 44139. **Hours:** 11 am-10
              pm, Fri & Sat-11 pm, Sun 5 pm-9 pm. Closed major holidays. **Reservations:** suggested. **Features:** casual
American   dress; children's menu; cocktails. Creative, sophisticated dishes—such as chicken paprikash, lamb ragout
              and Carolina catfish—are prepared by a member of the 1992 Olympic team. Because space is limited,
reservations are suggested. **Parking:** on-site. **Cards:** AX, DC, MC, VI.   [icon]

──────── *The following restaurants have not been evaluated by AAA* ────────
but are listed for your information only.

FAT FISH BLUE   **Phone:** 440/542-0410
[fyi]   Not evaluated. **Location:** 6025 Kruse Dr 44139. The Creole owners use plenty of spices to prepare crawfish platters,
              mumbo jambalaya and sweet potato pancakes.

JIMMY DADDONA'S   **Phone:** 440/248-2444
[fyi]   Not evaluated. **Location:** Harper Rd, exit off SR 442, 0.6 mi s, then 0.4 mi e. 5610 Enterprise Pkwy 44139. On the
              menu are reasonably priced preparations of Italian fare.

STRONGSVILLE pop. 35,300   (See map p. 600; index p. 604)

──────── **WHERE TO STAY** ────────

HOLIDAY INN SELECT-STRONGSVILLE   **Phone:** (440)238-8800   **81**
AAA [SAVE]   7/1-9/30   1P: $99-$109
              4/1-6/30 & 10/1-3/31   1P: $89-$99
▽▽▽▽   **Location:** I-71, exit 231A, just e; I-76 (Ohio Tpke), exit 161, 1 mi s. 15471 Royalton Rd 44136. Fax: 440/238-0273.
              Facility: 302 one-bedroom standard units. 6 stories, interior corridors. **Parking:** on-site. **Terms:** check-in 4
Motor Inn   pm, package plans. **Amenities:** video games, voice mail, irons, hair dryers. **Dining:** dining room, 6:30 am-11
              pm, Sat & Sun from 7 am, $8-$15, cocktails. **Pool(s):** heated indoor. **Leisure Activities:** sauna, exercise
room. **Guest Services:** gift shop, valet and coin laundry. **Business Services:** conference facilities, business center. **Cards:** AX,
CB, DC, DS, JC, MC, VI.

SOME UNITS
[icons]
FEE

RED ROOF INN-STRONGSVILLE   **Phone:** (440)238-0170   **83**
AAA [SAVE]   6/28-9/1   1P: $49-$65   2P: $55-$65   XP: $6   F18
              9/2-11/9   1P: $46-$56   2P: $52-$62   XP: $6   F18
▽▽   11/10-3/31   1P: $39-$51   2P: $45-$57   XP: $6   F18
Motel   4/1-6/27   1P: $39-$49   2P: $45-$55   XP: $6   F18
              Location: I-71, exit 231A, just e; I-76 (Ohio Tpke), exit 161, 1 mi s. 15385 Royalton Rd 44136. Fax: 440/238-1097.
              Facility: 108 one-bedroom standard units. 2 stories, exterior corridors. *Bath:* combo or shower only. **Parking:**
on-site. **Terms:** small pets only. **Amenities:** video games, voice mail. **Cards:** AX, CB, DC, DS, MC, VI. **Special Amenities:** free
local telephone calls and free newspaper.

SOME UNITS
[icons]

(See map p. 600)

------ **WHERE TO DINE** ------

------ *The following restaurant has not been evaluated by AAA* ------
but is listed for your information only.

THE MAD CRAB   **Phone:** 440/238-4677
[fyi]   Not evaluated. **Location:** 12492 Prospect Rd 44136. The seasonally changing menu centers on fresh seafood, which
             matches well with selections from the microbrewery.

WESTLAKE pop. 27,000 (See map p. 600; index p. 605)

------ **WHERE TO STAY** ------

CROSS COUNTRY INN   **Phone:** (440)871-3993 [123]
(AAA) [SAVE]   All Year   1P: $44-$51   2P: $51-$58   XP: $2   F17
▽▽▽▽   **Location:** I-90, exit 159, just n. 25200 Sperry Dr 44145. Fax: 440/871-3917. **Facility:** 115 one-bedroom standard
            units. 2 stories, exterior corridors. **Parking:** on-site. **Amenities:** video games, voice mail. **Pool(s):** heated
Motel   outdoor. **Cards:** AX, CB, DC, DS, JC, MC, VI. **Special Amenities:** free local telephone calls and preferred
            room (subject to availability with advanced reservations).
                                                                              SOME UNITS
                                                                    [S/D] [🛏] [📺] [🖨] / [✕] /
                                                                          FEE

HAMPTON INN   **Phone:** (440)892-0333 [126]
(AAA) [SAVE]   All Year [ECP]   1P: $70-$91   2P: $76-$96   XP: $6   F18
▽▽▽▽   **Location:** I-90, exit 156, just s to Detroit Rd, then just e. 29690 Detroit Rd 44145. Fax: 440/892-7911. **Facility:** 123
            one-bedroom standard units. 5 stories, interior corridors. **Parking:** on-site. **Amenities:** video games, voice
Motel   mail, irons, hair dryers. **Guest Services:** valet laundry. **Business Services:** meeting rooms. **Cards:** AX, CB,
            DC, DS, JC, MC, VI. **Special Amenities:** free continental breakfast and free local telephone calls.
                                                                              SOME UNITS
                                                        [S/D] [🍴] [📞] [📺] [DATA PORT] [💻] [🖨] / [✕] /
                                                                          FEE

HOLIDAY INN WESTLAKE   **Phone:** (440)871-6000 [122]
(AAA) [SAVE]   All Year   1P: $79-$129   2P: $79-$129   XP: $10   F18
▽▽▽▽   **Location:** I-90, exit 156, just n. 1100 Crocker Rd 44145. Fax: 440/835-1768. **Facility:** 266 one-bedroom standard
            units. 5 stories, interior corridors. **Parking:** on-site. **Terms:** [BP] & [CP] meal plans available, package plans.
Hotel   **Amenities:** video games, dual phone lines, voice mail, irons, hair dryers. **Dining:** dining room, coffee shop,
            6:30 am-2 & 5-10 pm, $10-$18, cocktails, entertainment. **Pool(s):** heated indoor, wading. **Leisure Activi-
            ties:** sauna, whirlpool, exercise room. **Guest Services:** gift shop, coin laundry. **Business Services:** confer-
ence facilities, fax. **Cards:** AX, CB, DC, DS, MC, VI.
                                                                              SOME UNITS
                                              [S/D] [🏊] [🍴] [📞] [🛏] [✕] [📺] [DATA PORT] [💻] [🖨] / [✕] [🖥] [🖨] /
                                                                          FEE

RED ROOF INN-WESTLAKE   **Phone:** (440)892-7920 [124]
(AAA) [SAVE]   6/28-9/1   1P: $59-$71   2P: $64-$76   XP: $5   F18
▽▽▽▽   5/3-6/27   1P: $51-$62   2P: $56-$67   XP: $5   F18
            9/2-3/31   1P: $47-$61   2P: $52-$66   XP: $5   F18
            4/1-5/2   1P: $42-$54   2P: $47-$59   XP: $5   F18
Motel   **Location:** I-90, exit 156, just n. 29595 Clemens Rd 44145. Fax: 440/892-7925. **Facility:** 99 one-bedroom standard
            units. 2 stories, exterior corridors. **Parking:** on-site. **Terms:** small pets only. **Amenities:** video games, voice
mail. **Guest Services:** valet laundry. **Cards:** AX, CB, DC, DS, MC, VI. **Special Amenities:** free local telephone calls and free
newspaper.
                                                                              SOME UNITS
                                                        [🛏] [📞] [📺] [DATA PORT] [🖨] / [✕] [🖥] [🖨] /

RESIDENCE INN BY MARRIOTT   **Phone:** (440)892-2254 [121]
(AAA) [SAVE]   5/5-11/17   1P: $109-$119
            4/1-5/4 & 11/18-3/31 1P: $99
▽▽▽▽   **Location:** I-90, exit 156, just n. 30100 Clemens Rd 44145. Fax: 440/892-3709. **Facility:** 104 one-bedroom stan-
            dard units. 3 stories, exterior corridors. **Parking:** on-site. **Terms:** cancellation fee imposed, small pets only
Extended Stay ($200-$250 fee). **Amenities:** extended cable TV, video games, voice mail, irons, hair dryers. **Pool(s):** heated
Apartment   indoor. **Leisure Activities:** whirlpool, sports court. **Guest Services:** complimentary laundry. **Business Serv-
            ices:** meeting rooms. **Cards:** AX, CB, DC, DS, JC, MC, VI. *(See color ad card insert)*
                                                                              SOME UNITS
                                [S/D] [🏊] [🐕] [🍴] [📞] [🛏] [👶] [📺] [DATA PORT] [🖥] [🖨] [💻] [🖨] / [✕] /

------ **WHERE TO DINE** ------

BIG FISH SEAFOOD BISTRO   **Lunch:** $6-$10   **Dinner:** $9-$20   **Phone:** 440/892-5151 [69]
▽▽▽   **Location:** I-90, exit 159, just n. 24940 Sperry Dr 44145. **Hours:** 11 am-10:30 pm, Fri & Sat-11:30 pm, Sun-10
             pm. **Closed:** 12/25. **Features:** casual dress; Sunday brunch; children's menu; carryout; cocktails. For
Seafood   delicious, budget-friendly food in a distinctive atmosphere, give this restaurant a try. Clam chowder and
             Maryland crab cakes are favorites on a menu of tempting and imaginative dishes that can't be found
elsewhere, including pasta and steak selections. Everything is prepared in house. The open and spacious dining room offers
both booth and table seating. **Parking:** on-site. **Cards:** AX, DC, DS, MC, VI.
                                                                                          [✕]

(See map p. 600)

LE BISTRO DU BEAUJOLAIS RESTAURANT   **Lunch:** $6-$10   **Dinner:** $8-$15   **Phone:** 440/871-7880   68

French
Location: I-90, exit 159, just s, then 0.6 mi e. 24481 Detroit Rd 44145. **Hours:** 11:30 am-2:30 & 5-10 pm, Sat from 5 pm. Closed major holidays; also Sun & Mon. **Reservations:** required; after 9 pm. **Features:** casual dress; children's menu; carryout; cocktails & lounge. Fresh, high-quality ingredients go into traditional French dishes at the cozy bistro. **Parking:** on-site. **Cards:** AX, DC, DS, MC, VI.

The following restaurant has not been evaluated by AAA but is listed for your information only.

CARRABBA'S   **Phone:** 440/250-0880
[fyi]
Not evaluated. **Location:** 25054 Sperry Dr 44145. The attractive restaurant has ample parking, easy access off the interstate and a variety of classic and traditional Italian dishes.

The previous listings were for the Cleveland Vicinity. The following resumes the alphabetical listings of cities in Ohio.

CLEVELAND HEIGHTS —See Cleveland p. 620.

CLIFTON pop. 200

——— WHERE TO DINE ———

CLIFTON MILL   **Lunch:** $5-$10   **Phone:** 937/767-5501

American
Location: I-70, exit 54, left on SR 72, 7 mi on left. 75 Water St 45316. **Hours:** 9 am-2 pm, Sat & Sun 8 am-5 pm. Closed: 11/28, 12/25. **Features:** casual dress; children's menu; carryout; wine only. Built in 1802, the grist mill restaurant presents a menu of home-style American favorites, including sandwich platters and homemade soups. Smoke free premises. **Parking:** on-site. **Cards:** MC, VI.

CLYDE pop. 5,800

——— WHERE TO STAY ———

RED ROOF INN   **Phone:** 419/547-6660

5/25-9/1 [ECP]	1P: $49-$98	2P: $59-$109	XP: $5	F17
4/1-5/24 & 9/2-3/31 [ECP]	1P: $49-$59	2P: $49-$69	XP: $5	F17

Motel
Location: 1 mi w on SR 20. 1363 W McPherson Hwy 43410 (2027 Cleveland Rd, SANDUSKY, 44870). Fax: 419/547-6660. **Facility:** 68 units. 65 one-bedroom standard units. 3 two-bedroom suites ($79-$179). 3 stories, interior corridors. *Bath:* combo or shower only. **Parking:** on-site. **Terms:** 3 day cancellation notice, pets ($50 deposit). **Amenities:** hair dryers. **Pool(s):** heated indoor. **Leisure Activities:** whirlpool, exercise room. **Guest Services:** coin laundry. **Business Services:** meeting rooms. **Cards:** AX, DC, DS, MC, VI.

SOME UNITS
FEE

COLUMBIANA pop. 5,000

——— WHERE TO STAY ———

DUTCH VILLAGE INN   **Phone:** 330/482-5050

All Year [ECP]	1P: $99-$119	2P: $99-$119	XP: $10	F21

Country Inn
Location: Jct SR 164 and 14, just e. 150 E SR 14 44408. Fax: 330/482-4141. **Facility:** Smoke free premises. 52 units. 46 one-bedroom standard units, some with efficiencies and/or whirlpools. 6 one-bedroom suites ($159-$249) with efficiencies and whirlpools. 3 stories, interior corridors. **Parking:** on-site. **Amenities:** high-speed Internet (fee), voice mail, irons, hair dryers. **Leisure Activities:** exercise room. **Guest Services:** coin laundry. **Business Services:** meeting rooms. **Cards:** AX, DC, DS, MC, VI. **Special Amenities:** free continental breakfast and preferred room (subject to availability with advanced reservations).

SOME UNITS

Destination Columbus
pop. 632,900

*A*lthough Columbus is down-to-earth, its tastes are wide ranging. The repertoires of its musical groups range from jazz to chamber. Shopping ranges from standard malls to restored 19th-century districts. And cuisines range from Caribbean to Old World German.

*B*ut for residents, sports means just one thing—the Ohio State University Buckeyes.

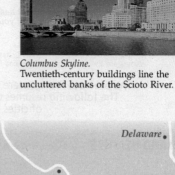

Columbus Skyline.
Twentieth-century buildings line the uncluttered banks of the Scioto River.

Jazz and Ribfest, Columbus.
Jazz musicians feed the souls while barbecuers feed the body during the July Jazz and Ribfest.

See Downtown map page 634

See Vicinity map page 636

*P*laces included in this AAA Destination City:

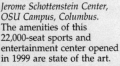

Jerome Schottenstein Center, OSU Campus, Columbus. The amenities of this 22,000-seat sports and entertainment center opened in 1999 are state of the art.

• *Sunbury*

Columbus

Granville

Newark

16

Gahanna

16

Heath

✈
Bexley   • *Reynoldsburg*   *Hebron*

70

Pickerington

270

Canal Winchester   33

22

Lancaster

159   33

German Village, Columbus. Book lovers, antiques hunters and seekers after the ultimate bakery visit the German Village. (See listing page 223)

© AAA

DOWNTOWN
COLUMBUS
ACCOMMODATIONS

1909-J

Look For Savings

When you pick up a AAA TourBook® guide, look for establishments that display a bright red AAA logo, [SAVE] icon, and Diamond rating in their listing. These Official Appointment establishments place a high value on the patronage they receive from AAA members. And, by offering members great room rates*, they are willing to go the extra mile to get your business.

So, when you turn to the AAA TourBook guide to make your travel plans, look for the establishments that will give you the special treatment you deserve.

See TourBook Navigator section, page 16, for complete details.

Downtown Columbus

This index helps you "spot" where approved accommodations and restaurants are located on the corresponding detailed maps. Lodging rate ranges are for comparison only and show the property's high season; rates are per night, unless only weekly (W) or monthly (M) rates are available. Restaurant rate range is for dinner, unless only lunch (L) is served. Turn to the listing page for more detailed rate information and consult display ads for special promotions.

Spotter/Map Page Number	OA	DOWNTOWN COLUMBUS - Lodgings	Diamond Rating	Rate Range High Season	Listing Page
❶ / p. 634		50 Lincoln Inn	▼▼▼	$99-$149	642
❷ / p. 634	AAA	Hyatt Regency Columbus - see ad p 643	▼▼▼	$99-$200 SAVE	644
❸ / p. 634		The Lofts Hotel	▼▼▼	$199-$259	644
❹ / p. 634	AAA	Crowne Plaza Hotel	▼▼▼	$169-$189 SAVE	643
❺ / p. 634	AAA	Courtyard by Marriott Downtown Columbus - see color ad card insert	▼▼▼	$89-$139 SAVE	642
❻ / p. 634	AAA	Doubletree Guest Suites	▼▼▼	$89-$139 SAVE	643
❽ / p. 634	AAA	Adam's Mark Columbus - see ad p 642	▼▼▼	$129 SAVE	642
❾ / p. 634	AAA	Hyatt on Capitol Square - see ad p 643	▼▼▼▼	$99-$224 SAVE	644
⓫ / p. 634	AAA	Holiday Inn City Center	▼▼	$89-$119 SAVE	643
⓭ / p. 634	AAA	The Westin Great Southern Columbus	▼▼▼▼	$205-$215 SAVE	644
		DOWNTOWN COLUMBUS - Restaurants			
③ / p. 634		Rigsby's Cuisine Volatile	▼▼▼	$12-$24	645
④ / p. 634		Tapatio Restaurant	▼▼	$9-$18	645
⑤ / p. 634		Japanese Steak House	▼▼	$12-$25	644
⑥ / p. 634		Strada World Cuisine	▼▼▼	$11-$19	645
⑦ / p. 634		R J Snappers	▼▼▼	$16-$23	645
⑧ / p. 634		Saigon Palace	▼	$7-$12	645
⑨ / p. 634		The Plaza Restaurant	▼▼▼	$17-$24	645
⑩ / p. 634		Handke's Cuisine	▼▼▼	$10-$26	644
⑪ / p. 634		Schmidt's Restaurant and Sausage Haus	▼▼	$7-$12	645
⑫ / p. 634		The Clarmont	▼▼▼	$13-$24	644
⑬ / p. 634		Mitchell's Steakhouse	▼▼▼	$35-$55	645
⑭ / p. 634		The Columbus Brewing Company	▼▼	$8-$18	644

Camper Sweet Camper

*I*f camping is where your heart is, then **AAA CampBook® guides** are for you. With information about campgrounds throughout North America, **CampBooks** provide campers valuable details on camping facilities. From rate information to site descriptions to recreational activities, these guides give campers all the information they need before hitting the trail.

*To get your **CampBook** guide, call or visit your local AAA office today.*

Travel With Someone You Trust®

COLUMBUS
ACCOMMODATIONS

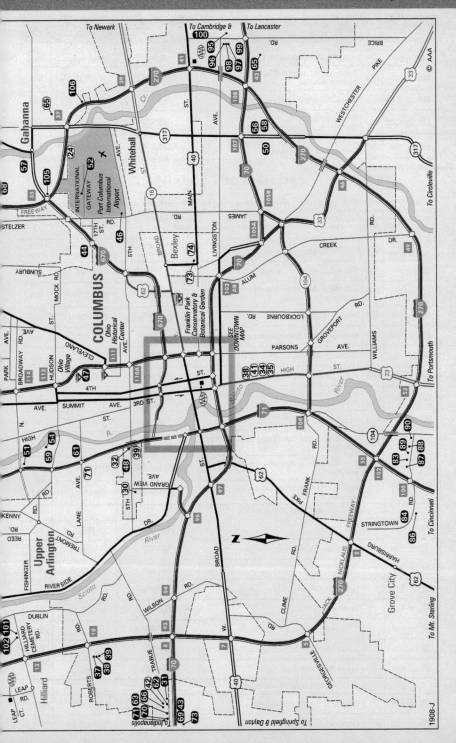

✈ Airport Accommodations

Spotter/Map Page Number	OA	PORT COLUMBUS INTERNATIONAL	Diamond Rating	Rate Range High Season	Listing Page
57 / p. 636	AAA	**Courtyard By Marriott-Columbus Airport**, 1.5 mi from terminal	▽▽▽	$79-$129 SAVE	648
52 / p. 636	AAA	**Cross Country Inn Airport**, at the airport	▽▽	$59-$73 SAVE	648
46 / p. 636		Holiday Inn-Columbus Airport, 2 mi e of terminal	▽▽	$109-$139	651
44 / p. 636	AAA	**Radisson Airport Hotel & Conference Center**, 1 mi from entrance	▽▽▽	$94-$155 SAVE	653

Columbus and Vicinity

This index helps you "spot" where approved accommodations and restaurants are located on the corresponding detailed maps. Lodging rate ranges are for comparison only and show the property's high season; rates are per night, unless only weekly (W) or monthly (M) rates are available. Restaurant rate range is for dinner, unless only lunch (L) is served. Turn to the listing page for more detailed rate information and consult display ads for special promotions.

Spotter/Map Page Number	OA	DUBLIN - Lodgings	Diamond Rating	Rate Range High Season	Listing Page
14 / p. 636	AAA	**Hilton Garden Inn** - see color ad p 659	▽▽▽	$99-$179 SAVE	659
15 / p. 636	AAA	**Columbus Marriott Northwest** - see color ad card insert	▽▽▽	$159-$179 SAVE	659
16 / p. 636	AAA	**Wyndham Dublin**	▽▽▽	$99-$154 SAVE	660
17 / p. 636	AAA	**Wellesley Inn & Suites (Columbus/Dublin)**	▽▽▽	$69-$99 SAVE	660
18 / p. 636		Woodfin Suites Hotel	▽▽▽	$99-$150	660
19 / p. 636	AAA	**Cross Country Inn Northwest**	▽▽	$39-$53 SAVE	659
20 / p. 636	AAA	**Baymont Inn & Suites Columbus-Dublin** - see color ad opposite title page	▽▽	$74-$84 SAVE	659
21 / p. 636	AAA	**Red Roof Inn-Dublin**	▽▽	$49-$73 SAVE	660
22 / p. 636	AAA	**Courtyard by Marriott-Dublin** - see color ad card insert	▽▽▽	$112 SAVE	659
23 / p. 636	AAA	**Residence Inn by Marriott** - see color ad card insert	▽▽▽	$119-$149 SAVE	660
24 / p. 636	AAA	**AmeriSuites-Columbus/Dublin** - see color ad p 642	▽▽▽	$98-$108 SAVE	658
		DUBLIN - Restaurants			
13 / p. 636		Thai Orchid	▽▽	$8-$13	661
14 / p. 636		The Morgan House Restaurant	▽▽	$6-$8(L)	661
15 / p. 636		Oscar's of Dublin	▽▽	$11-$18	661
16 / p. 636		Hyde Park Grille	▽▽▽	$14-$29	661
17 / p. 636		Moretti's Cafe	▽▽	$9-$15	661
18 / p. 636		Chile Verde Cafe	▽▽	$7-$16	660
19 / p. 636		Bravo! Italian Kitchen	▽▽	$10-$18	660
21 / p. 636		Anna's Restaurant	▽▽	$10-$17	660
		COLUMBUS - Lodgings			
25 / p. 636		Wingate Inn - see color ad p 654	▽▽▽	$89-$109	655
26 / p. 636	AAA	**Cross Country Inn at the Continent**	▽▽	$37-$55 SAVE	648

Spotter/Map Page Number	OA	COLUMBUS - Lodgings (continued)	Diamond Rating	Rate Range High Season	Listing Page
27 / p. 636	AAA	The Residence Inn by Marriott-Columbus North - see color ad card insert	◈◈◈	$109 SAVE	653
28 / p. 636	AAA	Cross Country Inn-Sinclair Rd	◈◈	$37-$51 SAVE	649
29 / p. 636		Holiday Inn Express North	◈◈◈	$76-$89	651
30 / p. 636	AAA	Best Western Columbus North - see color ad p 646	◈◈◈	$60-$65 SAVE	646
31 / p. 636	AAA	Fairfield Inn Columbus West - see color ad card insert	◈◈◈	$55-$65 SAVE	650
34 / p. 636	AAA	Columbus Marriott North - see color ad card insert	◈◈◈	$64-$125 SAVE	647
35 / p. 636		Sheraton Suites Columbus	◈◈◈	$79-$189	654
36 / p. 636	AAA	Wellesley Inn & Suites (Columbus/Polaris)	◈◈◈	$79-$109 SAVE	655
37 / p. 636		Royal Inn Motel	◈◈	$45-$59	654
38 / p. 636		Super 8 Motel	◈◈	$65-$89	654
39 / p. 636		Holiday Inn Columbus West	◈◈◈	$99-$118	651
40 / p. 636		Signature Inn Columbus North	◈◈◈	$68-$78	654
41 / p. 636	AAA	Embassy Suites Hotel	◈◈◈	$119-$149 SAVE	649
42 / p. 636	AAA	Homewood Suites	◈◈◈	$115-$145 SAVE	652
43 / p. 636	AAA	Best Western Suites-Columbus West	◈◈◈	$80-$180 SAVE	646
44 / p. 636	AAA	Radisson Airport Hotel & Conference Center	◈◈◈	$94-$155 SAVE	653
45 / p. 636	AAA	Holiday Inn-Columbus/Worthington Area	◈◈◈	$79-$109 SAVE	651
46 / p. 636		Holiday Inn-Columbus Airport	◈◈	$109-$139	651
47 / p. 636	AAA	Days Inn Fairgrounds	◈◈	$70-$75 SAVE	649
48 / p. 636	AAA	Cross Country Inn-OSU South	◈◈	$49-$63 SAVE	649
49 / p. 636	AAA	Fairfield Inn by Marriott - see color ad card insert	◈◈	$59-$72 SAVE	650
50 / p. 636	AAA	Knights Inn-Columbus East	◈◈	$50-$90 SAVE	652
51 / p. 636	AAA	Cross Country Inn Olentangy, OSU North	◈◈	$43-$57 SAVE	648
52 / p. 636	AAA	Cross Country Inn Airport - see color ad p 648	◈◈	$59-$73 SAVE	648
53 / p. 636	AAA	Courtyard by Marriott Worthington - see color ad card insert	◈◈◈	$109-$119 SAVE	648
54 / p. 636	AAA	The University Plaza Hotel & Conference Center	◈◈◈	$99-$149 SAVE	654
55 / p. 636	AAA	Residence Inn by Marriott - see color ad card insert	◈◈◈	$109 SAVE	653
56 / p. 636		Holiday Inn East I-70 - see color ad p 651	◈◈◈	$109	651
57 / p. 636	AAA	Courtyard By Marriott-Columbus Airport - see color ad card insert	◈◈◈	$79-$129 SAVE	648
58 / p. 636	AAA	Residence Inn by Marriott-Columbus Southeast - see color ad card insert	◈◈◈	$59-$149 SAVE	654
59 / p. 636	AAA	Red Roof Inn-OSU	◈◈	$59-$69 SAVE	653
60 / p. 636	AAA	AmeriSuites (Columbus/Worthington) - see color ad p 642	◈◈◈	$79-$114 SAVE	645

Spotter/Map Page Number	OA	COLUMBUS - Lodgings (continued)	Diamond Rating	Rate Range High Season	Listing Page
61 / p. 636	AAA	Holiday Inn on the Lane - see color ad p 652	◆◆◆	$99-$119 SAVE	652
62 / p. 636	AAA	Cross Country Inn-Columbus West	◆◆	$42-$56 SAVE	648
63 / p. 636	AAA	Red Roof Inn-West	◆◆	$47-$75 SAVE	653
64 / p. 636		Microtel Inn-North	◆	$49-$59	652
65 / p. 636	AAA	Comfort Suites	◆◆◆	$84-$94 SAVE	647
66 / p. 636		Hampton Inn Columbus West	◆◆◆	$74-$115	650
67 / p. 636	AAA	Red Roof Inn Columbus North	◆◆	$41-$68 SAVE	653
68 / p. 636	AAA	Hilton Columbus	◆◆◆◆	$179-$219 SAVE	650
69 / p. 636	AAA	Country Inn & Suites By Carlson Columbus West - see color ad p 646	◆◆◆	$77 SAVE	647
70 / p. 636	AAA	Hawthorn Suites Ltd - see color ad p 650	◆◆◆	$89-$159 SAVE	650
71 / p. 636		Comfort Suites-Columbus	◆◆◆	$79-$125	647
72 / p. 636	AAA	Ramada Limited North	◆◆	$47-$109 SAVE	653
73 / p. 636	AAA	Microtel Inn & Suites (West)	◆◆	$60-$80 SAVE	652
		COLUMBUS - Restaurants			
23 / p. 636	AAA	The Refectory	◆◆◆◆	$23-$28	656
24 / p. 636		94th Aero Squadron	◆◆	$15-$25	655
25 / p. 636		Otani Japanese Restaurant and Sushi Bar	◆◆	$9-$25	656
28 / p. 636		Sapporo Wind	◆◆	$8-$22	656
30 / p. 636		Spagio	◆◆◆	$10-$25	657
32 / p. 636		Buckeye Hall of Fame Cafe	◆◆◆	$8-$21	655
33 / p. 636		Siam Restaurant	◆◆	$9-$12	656
34 / p. 636		Lindey's	◆◆◆	$13-$28	656
35 / p. 636		Old Mohawk Restaurant	◆◆	$6-$9	656
38 / p. 636		Engine House No. 5	◆◆◆	$12-$32	656
39 / p. 636		Cap City Fine Diner & Bar	◆◆	$10-$15	656
40 / p. 636		Brio Tuscan Grille	◆◆◆	$10-$23	655
41 / p. 636		Barcelona	◆◆◆	$9-$18	655
42 / p. 636		Salvi's Bistro	◆◆	$10-$18	656
		WORTHINGTON - Lodgings			
78 / p. 636	AAA	Red Roof Inn-Worthington	◆◆	$45-$63 SAVE	669
80 / p. 636	AAA	The Worthington Inn	◆◆◆	$150 SAVE	669
81 / p. 636		Clarion Hotel Worthington	◆◆	$79	669
		WORTHINGTON - Restaurants			
49 / p. 636		Cameron's Contemporary American Cuisine	◆◆	$8-$22	669
52 / p. 636	AAA	Seven Stars at The Worthington Inn	◆◆	$13-$26	669

Spotter/Map Page Number	OA	GROVE CITY - Lodgings	Diamond Rating	Rate Range High Season	Listing Page
83 / p. 636		Hampton Inn Columbus South	◆◆◆	$71-$80	662
84 / p. 636	AAA	Red Roof Inn-South Columbus	◆◆	$47-$74 SAVE	662
86 / p. 636	AAA	Comfort Inn	◆◆◆	$60-$119 SAVE	662
87 / p. 636	AAA	Cross Country Inn Southwest	◆◆	$43-$56 SAVE	662
88 / p. 636	AAA	Super 8 Motel - see ad p 662	◆◆◆	$50-$80 SAVE	663
89 / p. 636	AAA	Best Western Executive Inn	◆◆	$62-$72 SAVE	662
90 / p. 636	AAA	Hilton Garden Inn Columbus/Grove City	◆◆◆	$59-$99 SAVE	662
		WESTERVILLE - Lodgings			
92 / p. 636	AAA	Cross Country Inn Westerville	◆◆	$43-$57 SAVE	668
93 / p. 636		Knights Inn-Columbus/Westerville	◆	$50-$60	668
		REYNOLDSBURG - Lodgings			
95 / p. 636	AAA	Best Western Columbus East - see color ad p 646	◆◆	$57-$65 SAVE	666
96 / p. 636	AAA	Cross Country Inn East	◆◆	$45-$55 SAVE	667
97 / p. 636	AAA	La Quinta Inn	◆◆◆	$56-$72 SAVE	667
98 / p. 636		Extended Stay America East	◆◆	$39-$59	667
99 / p. 636	AAA	Red Roof Inn-East	◆◆	$49-$69 SAVE	668
100 / p. 636		Country Inn & Suites By Carlson-Columbus East - see color ad p 646	◆◆◆	$75-$90	667
		HILLIARD - Lodgings			
101 / p. 636		Comfort Suites	◆◆◆	$88-$98	663
102 / p. 636		Homewood Suites by Hilton-Columbus/Hilliard	◆◆◆	$109-$149	663
		GAHANNA - Lodgings			
105 / p. 636	AAA	SpringHill Suites by Marriott - see color ad card insert	◆◆◆	$89-$115 SAVE	661
106 / p. 636	AAA	TownePlace Suites by Marriott - see color ad card insert	◆◆	$109-$129 SAVE	661
		GAHANNA - Restaurant			
65 / p. 636		Montana Mining Company Steakhouse & Saloon	◆	$7-$14	661
		UPPER ARLINGTON - Restaurant			
71 / p. 636		China Dynasty	◆◆	$8-$16	668
		BEXLEY - Restaurants			
73 / p. 636		Fisherman's Wharf	◆◆	$12-$18	657
74 / p. 636		Bexley's Monk	◆◆◆	$9-$22	657

DOWNTOWN COLUMBUS   (See map p. 634; index p. 635)

——— WHERE TO STAY ———

50 LINCOLN INN

▼▼▼▼
Historic Bed & Breakfast

Phone: 614/291-5056   **1**

All Year   1P: $99   2P: $149
Location: Downtown; 1 mi n on High St, just e. 50 E Lincoln St 43215. Fax: 614/291-4924. **Facility:** Located in the Italian Village part of town, this restored brick 1917 manor features a mixture of antique and contemporary furnishings. Smoke free premises. 8 one-bedroom standard units. 3 stories (no elevator), interior corridors. **Parking:** on-site. **Terms:** check-in 4 pm, 4 day cancellation notice. **Amenities:** extended cable TV. **Business Services:** meeting rooms. **Cards:** MC, VI.

ADAM'S MARK COLUMBUS

AAA [SAVE]
▼▼▼▼
Hotel

Phone: (614)228-5050   **8**

4/1-11/22 & 1/1-3/31	1P: $129	2P: $129	XP: $20	F12
11/23-12/31	1P: $109	2P: $109	XP: $20	F12

Location: Corner of Third and Gay sts. 50 N Third St 43215. Fax: 614/228-2525. **Facility:** 415 units. 412 one-bedroom standard units. 3 one-bedroom suites. 22 stories, interior corridors. *Bath:* combo or shower only. **Parking:** *Fee:* on-site and valet. **Terms:** package plans. **Amenities:** video games, high-speed Internet, dual phone lines, voice mail, irons, hair dryers. *Some:* DVD players (fee), CD players. **Dining:** dining room, 6 am-2 & 5-11 pm, $10-$24. **Pool(s):** heated outdoor. **Leisure Activities:** sauna, whirlpool, exercise room. **Guest Services:** gift shop, valet and coin laundry, area transportation (fee). **Business Services:** conference facilities, business center, fax. **Cards:** AX, CB, DC, DS, MC, VI. **Special Amenities:** early check-in/late check-out and preferred room (subject to availability with advanced reservations). *(See ad below)*

COURTYARD BY MARRIOTT DOWNTOWN COLUMBUS

AAA [SAVE]
▼▼▼
Motel

Phone: (614)228-3200   **5**

All Year   1P: $89-$139   2P: $89-$139
Location: Downtown; corner of Front and Spring sts. 35 W Spring St 43215. Fax: 614/228-6752. **Facility:** 149 units. 145 one-bedroom standard units, some with efficiencies and/or whirlpools. 4 one-bedroom suites ($119-$149). 5 stories, interior corridors. *Bath:* combo or shower only. **Parking:** *Fee:* on-site and valet. **Terms:** package plans. **Amenities:** extended cable TV, video games, dual phone lines, voice mail, irons, hair dryers. **Dining:** restaurant, 6:30-10 am, Sat & Sun 7 am-noon. **Pool(s):** heated indoor. **Leisure Activities:** whirlpool, exercise room. **Guest Services:** valet and coin laundry. **Business Services:** meeting rooms, fax. **Cards:** AX, DC, DS, MC, VI. *(See color ad card insert)*

(See map p. 634)

CROWNE PLAZA HOTEL
 (AAA) (SAVE)

▼▼▼▼

Hotel

Phone: (614)461-4100   **4**

All Year   1P: $169-$189   2P: $169-$189   XP: $10   F18
Location: 0.3 mi n off US 23; opposite Ohio Center, corner of N High St and Nationwide Blvd. 33 Nationwide Blvd 43215. **Fax:** 614/461-5828. **Facility:** 384 units. 383 one-bedroom standard units. 1 one-bedroom suite. 11-12 stories, interior corridors. **Bath:** combo or shower only. **Parking:** Fee: on-site and valet. **Terms:** package plans. **Amenities:** extended cable TV, video games, dual phone lines, voice mail, irons, hair dryers. **Dining:** restaurant, coffee shop, deli, 6:30 am-11 pm, $11-$25, cocktails. **Pool(s):** heated indoor. **Leisure Activities:** sauna, exercise room. **Guest Services:** valet and coin laundry, area transportation-downtown. **Business Services:** conference facilities, business center, PC, fax. **Cards:** AX, CB, DC, DS, JC, MC, VI.

SOME UNITS

[icons]

DOUBLETREE GUEST SUITES
(AAA) (SAVE)

▼▼▼▼

Suite Hotel

Phone: (614)228-4600   **6**

All Year   1P: $89-$139   2P: $89-$139
Location: Downtown; corner of Front and State sts, just n. 50 S Front St 43215. **Fax:** 614/228-0297. **Facility:** 194 one-bedroom suites. 10 stories, interior corridors. **Parking:** on-site (fee). **Terms:** cancellation fee imposed, package plans, small pets only ($50 fee). **Amenities:** voice mail, irons, hair dryers. **Dining:** dining room, 6 am-11 pm, Sat & Sun from 7 am, $13-$19, cocktails. **Guest Services:** valet laundry, area transportation-within 3 mi. **Business Services:** meeting rooms, PC, fax. **Cards:** AX, CB, DC, DS, JC, MC, VI.

SOME UNITS

[icons]

HOLIDAY INN CITY CENTER
(AAA) (SAVE)

▼▼▼

Motor Inn

Phone: (614)221-3281   **11**

All Year   1P: $89-$119
Location: At 4th and E Town sts. 175 E Town St 43215. **Fax:** 614/221-2667. **Facility:** 240 one-bedroom standard units. 12 stories, interior corridors. **Bath:** combo or shower only. **Parking:** on-site (fee). **Terms:** cancellation fee imposed, pets ($20 fee). **Amenities:** voice mail, irons, hair dryers. **Dining:** restaurant, 6:30 am-2 & 5-9 pm, $15-$23, cocktails. **Pool(s):** outdoor. **Guest Services:** valet laundry, area transportation-within 2 mi. **Business Services:** meeting rooms. **Cards:** AX, CB, DC, DS, MC, VI.

SOME UNITS

[icons]

(See map p. 634)

HYATT ON CAPITOL SQUARE
Phone: (614)228-1234 **9**

(AAA) [SAVE]

▽▽▽▽ ▽▽▽▽

Hotel

All Year   1P: $99-$199   2P: $124-$224   XP: $25   F18
Location: Corner of State and Third sts. 75 E State St 43215. Fax: 614/469-9664. **Facility:** This hotel next to a shopping mall offers spacious rooms featuring cherry-veneer furniture. 400 units. 398 one-bedroom standard units. 2 one-bedroom suites with whirlpools. 22 stories, interior corridors. *Bath:* combo or shower only.
Parking: *Fee:* on-site and valet. **Terms:** cancellation fee imposed, package plans. **Amenities:** extended cable TV, voice mail, fax, irons, hair dryers. *Some:* CD players, safes. **Dining:** The Plaza Restaurant, see separate listing. **Leisure Activities:** sauna, exercise room. **Guest Services:** massage (fee), valet laundry, area transportation-within 3 mi. **Business Services:** conference facilities, business center, PC, fax. **Cards:** AX, CB, DC, DS, JC, MC, VI.
(See ad p 643)

SOME UNITS
[icons] FEE

HYATT REGENCY COLUMBUS
Phone: (614)463-1234 **2**

(AAA) [SAVE]

▽▽▽▽

Hotel

All Year   1P: $99-$175   2P: $124-$200   XP: $25   F18
Location: 0.3 mi n on US 23; at Ohio Center. 350 N High St 43215. Fax: 614/280-3034. **Facility:** 631 one-bedroom standard units. 20 stories, interior corridors. *Bath:* combo or shower only. **Parking:** on-site and valet (fee).
Terms: cancellation fee imposed, package plans. **Amenities:** voice mail, safes, irons, hair dryers. *Some:* dual phone lines. **Dining:** restaurant, deli, 6:30 am-2 & 5-11 pm, $11-$21, cocktails. **Pool(s):** heated indoor.
Leisure Activities: sun deck, exercise room. **Guest Services:** valet laundry. **Business Services:** conference facilities, business center, PC, fax. **Cards:** AX, CB, DC, DS, JC, MC, VI. *(See ad p 643)*

SOME UNITS
[icons] FEE   FEE FEE FEE

THE LOFTS HOTEL
Phone: (614)461-2663 **3**

▽▽▽▽

Hotel

All Year [ECP]   1P: $199-$259   2P: $199-$259
Location: 0.3 mi n off US 23; opposite Ohio Center, corner of N High St and Nationwide Blvd. 55 E Nationwide Blvd 43215. Fax: 614/461-2630. **Facility:** 44 units. 22 one-bedroom standard units. 22 one-bedroom suites. 5 stories, interior corridors. **Parking:** *Fee:* on-site and valet. **Terms:** package plans. **Amenities:** extended cable TV, video games, high-speed Internet, dual phone lines, voice mail, safes, honor bars, irons, hair dryers. **Pool(s):** heated indoor.
Leisure Activities: sauna, exercise room. **Guest Services:** valet laundry. **Business Services:** meeting rooms, business center, PC, fax. **Cards:** AX, CB, DC, DS, JC, MC, VI.

SOME UNITS
[ASK] [icons] FEE   [icons] FEE

THE WESTIN GREAT SOUTHERN COLUMBUS
Phone: (614)228-3800 **13**

(AAA) [SAVE]

▽▽▽▽ ▽▽▽▽

Classic Hotel

All Year   1P: $205   2P: $215   XP: $10   F18
Location: Downtown; corner of Main and High sts. 310 S High St 43215. Fax: 614/228-7666. **Facility:** Historic. Ornate public areas decorated with changing art exhibits, including some by former resident James Thurber, are a draw at this restored 1897 hotel. Designated smoking area. 196 units. 185 one-bedroom standard units. 11 one-bedroom suites ($235-$800), some with whirlpools. 7 stories, interior corridors. *Bath:* combo or shower only. **Parking:** *Fee:* on-site and valet. **Terms:** package plans, pets ($50 deposit). **Amenities:** extended cable TV, video games, dual phone lines, voice mail, safes, honor bars, irons, hair dryers. *Some:* CD players. **Dining:** dining room, 6 am-2:30 & 5-11 pm, Sat & Sun from 7 am, $15-$27, cocktails. **Leisure Activities:** exercise room, adjacent restored Victorian era theater performing a variety of stage productions. **Guest Services:** valet laundry, area transportation-downtown. **Business Services:** conference facilities, administrative services, fax. **Cards:** AX, CB, DC, DS, JC, MC, VI.
Special Amenities: free newspaper.

SOME UNITS
[icons] FEE   [icons] FEE

――――― WHERE TO DINE ―――――

THE CLARMONT
Lunch: $6-$15   Dinner: $13-$24   Phone: 614/443-1125 **12**

▽▽▽ ▽▽▽

Steak & Seafood

Location: I-70, exit 100A, 0.5 mi s. 684 High St 43215. **Hours:** 7 am-2:30 & 5-10 pm, Fri & Sat 7 am-11 pm, Sun 4 pm-9 pm. Closed major holidays; also Super Bowl Sun. **Reservations:** suggested. **Features:** dressy casual; carryout; cocktails & lounge; a la carte. Locally popular as a destination for politicos, bankers, brokers and other downtown business people, The Clarmont serves seafood, steak and the house-favorite, chicken in a clay pot. Relax in the club-like atmosphere where the lounge boasts a humidor. **Parking:** on-site. **Cards:** AX, CB, DC, MC, VI.

[icon]

THE COLUMBUS BREWING COMPANY
Lunch: $7-$11   Dinner: $8-$18   Phone: 614/464-2739 **14**

▽▽▽ ▽▽▽

American

Location: Jct of Liberty and Short St. 525 Short St 43215. **Hours:** 11:30 am-4 pm, Sat 5 pm-11 pm. Closed: Sun. **Features:** casual dress; children's menu; carryout; cocktails & lounge; a la carte. Microbrewed beer and pizza baked in a wood-fired oven are restaurant signatures. **Parking:** on-site. **Cards:** AX, DC, DS, MC, VI.

HANDKE'S CUISINE
Dinner: $10-$26   Phone: 614/621-2500 **10**

▽▽▽▽ ▽▽▽▽

American

Location: I-70, exit 100B, just s on High St, just e on Beck St, then just n. 520 S Front St 43215. **Hours:** 5:30 pm-10 pm. Closed major holidays; also Sun. **Reservations:** suggested. **Features:** dressy casual; cocktails & lounge; a la carte. Located in a historic district below street level in a remodeled brewery, painted arched ceilings and elegantly set tables give an intimate romantic feeling for those special evenings for couples. Some specialties are the Amish chicken, Chilean sea bass, duck and lamb done in some uncharacteristic creativity with memorable flavors to savor. **Parking:** on-site and valet. **Cards:** AX, DC, DS, MC, VI.

[icon]

JAPANESE STEAK HOUSE
Lunch: $7-$10   Dinner: $12-$25   Phone: 614/228-3030 **5**

▽▽▽ ▽▽▽

Japanese

Location: Corner of Broad and High sts; 0.6 mi n. 479 N High St 43215. **Hours:** 11:30 am-1:15 & 5:30-9 pm, Fri-10 pm, Sat 5:30 pm-10 pm. Closed major holidays; also Sun. **Reservations:** suggested. **Features:** casual dress; children's menu; cocktails; a la carte. Service is quick and professional at the friendly restaurant, a favorite for table-side preparations of steak, seafood and chicken, including some tempura dishes. Group seatings bring together several different parties around a common grill. **Parking:** on-site. **Cards:** AX, DC, DS, MC, VI.

[icon]

(See map p. 634)

MITCHELL'S STEAKHOUSE   **Lunch:** $8-$15   **Dinner:** $35-$55   **Phone:** 614/621-2333   13
American   **Location:** Corner of Broad and Third sts. 45 N Third St 43215. **Hours:** 11:30 am-2:30 & 5-10 pm, Fri & Sat-11 pm, Sun-9 pm. Closed: 1/1, 11/28, 12/25. **Features:** casual dress; carryout; cocktails & lounge; a la carte. Entrees include steak, seafood and salads. **Parking:** on-site and valet. **Cards:** AX, DC, DS, MC, VI.

THE PLAZA RESTAURANT   **Lunch:** $8-$16   **Dinner:** $17-$24   **Phone:** 614/365-4550   9
American   **Location:** Corner of State and Third sts; in Hyatt on Capitol Square. 75 E State St 43215. **Hours:** 5:30 am-10 pm, Fri & Sat-11 pm. **Reservations:** suggested. **Features:** casual dress; Sunday brunch; children's menu; cocktails; entertainment; a la carte. A broad selection of seafood, beef and pasta dishes takes center stage on the seasonal menu with barbecued salmon, New York strip steak and penne pasta deemed house favorites. Opt for a seat near the fountain or the terrace which offers a garden view. Newspapers and other reading materials for patrons. Spacious dining area with superior downtown views. **Parking:** on-site and valet. **Cards:** AX, CB, DC, DS, JC, MC, VI.

RIGSBY'S CUISINE VOLATILE   **Lunch:** $8-$15   **Dinner:** $12-$24   **Phone:** 614/461-7888   3
American   **Location:** 1 mi n, just s of Lincoln. 698 N High St 43215. **Hours:** 11 am-11 pm. Closed major holidays; also Sun. **Reservations:** suggested. **Features:** dressy casual; carryout; cocktails; entertainment; a la carte. Musicians perform on some weekday evenings to infuse the cozy restaurant with a romantic charm. Sophisticated, imaginative preparations of pasta, chicken and seafood, such as fresh swordfish, show superior presentation. Try the wonderful desserts. **Parking:** on-site and valet. **Cards:** AX, DC, DS, MC, VI.

R J SNAPPERS   **Dinner:** $16-$23   **Phone:** 614/280-1070   7
Seafood   **Location:** I-70, exit 100B (SR 23), 1.4 mi n on 4th St, just w on Goodale, then just n; at jct Lincoln St in Short North. 700 N High St 43215. **Hours:** 5 pm-10 pm, Fri & Sat-11 pm, Sun-9 pm. Closed major holidays. **Reservations:** suggested. **Features:** dressy casual; children's menu; cocktails; a la carte. The two-story brick building offers romantic dining in a cozy, dimly lit dining room that's painted to resemble a Mediterranean fishing village. Fish and shellfish, such as lobster Savannah, are the restaurant's focus. The banana cream pie is luscious. **Parking:** valet only. **Cards:** AX, DC, DS, MC, VI.

SAIGON PALACE   **Lunch:** $6-$8   **Dinner:** $7-$12   **Phone:** 614/464-3325   8
Vietnamese   **Location:** Downtown; corner of Front and Long. 114 N Front St 43215. **Hours:** 11 am-3 & 5-9 pm, Sat from 5 pm. Closed major holidays; also Sun & 12/24-1/3. **Features:** casual dress; children's menu; carryout; beer only; a la carte. The small storefront restaurant delivers rice and noodle dishes with shrimp, beef, pork and chicken—plus a number of vegetarian selections. Portions are plentiful, especially the Pad Thai. Vietnamese pictures hang from the dining room walls. **Parking:** on-site (fee). **Cards:** DC, DS, MC, VI.

SCHMIDT'S RESTAURANT AND SAUSAGE HAUS   Historical   **Lunch:** $7-$12   **Dinner:** $7-$12   **Phone:** 614/444-6808   11
German   **Location:** I-71, exit 100A, 0.5 mi s on High St, 0.3 mi e. 240 E Kossuth St 43206. **Hours:** 11 am-9 pm, Tues-Thurs to 10 pm, Fri & Sat-11 pm. Closed: 11/28, 12/25. **Features:** casual dress; children's menu; carryout; cocktails & lounge; buffet. Cabbage rolls, spaetzle and schnitzel are samplings of the German cuisine served up by the quaint restaurant. The decor is reminiscent of the late 19th century. The selection of beer is varied, as is the assortment of strudel, pie and cream puffs. **Parking:** on-site. **Cards:** AX, DC, DS, MC, VI.

STRADA WORLD CUISINE   **Lunch:** $5-$12   **Dinner:** $11-$19   **Phone:** 614/228-8244   6
American   **Location:** I-670, exit Neil St. 106 Vine St 43215. **Hours:** 11 am-10 pm, Fri-midnight, Sat 5 pm-midnight, Sun 4:30 pm-9:30 pm. **Reservations:** suggested. **Features:** casual dress; carryout; cocktails; a la carte. Fusion cuisine reflects Asian, European and Mediterranean influences. **Parking:** on-site and valet.

TAPATIO RESTAURANT   **Lunch:** $7-$9   **Dinner:** $9-$18   **Phone:** 614/221-1085   4
Mexican   **Location:** Corner of Park and Spruce sts. 491 N Park St 43215. **Hours:** 11:30 am-10 pm, Fri & Sat-11 pm, Sun from 5 pm. Closed: 12/25. **Reservations:** suggested. **Features:** casual dress; carryout; cocktails; a la carte. Among the offerings of imaginative and creative cuisine are black bean hummus, shrimp with chipotle butter and crab cakes with red pepper sauce. Caribbean and South American foods have a strong presence. The patio is pleasant during season. **Parking:** on-site. **Cards:** AX, DC, DS, MC, VI.

COLUMBUS   pop. 632,900   (See map p. 636; index p. 638)

———— **WHERE TO STAY** ————

AMERISUITES (COLUMBUS/WORTHINGTON)   **Phone:** (614)846-4355   60
AAA SAVE   All Year   1P: $79-$114   2P: $79-$114   XP: $5   F
Suite Motel   **Location:** I-270, exit 23 (US 23 N), just ne. 7490 Vantage Dr 43235. Fax: 614/846-4493. **Facility:** 126 one-bedroom standard units. 6 stories, interior corridors. **Bath:** combo or shower only. **Parking:** on-site. **Terms:** small pets only. **Amenities:** voice mail, irons, hair dryers. **Some:** dual phone lines. **Pool(s):** outdoor. **Leisure Activities:** exercise room. **Guest Services:** complimentary evening beverages. Wed, valet and coin laundry. **Business Services:** meeting rooms, business center, PC, fax. **Cards:** AX, CB, DC, DS, JC, MC, VI.
Special Amenities: free continental breakfast and free newspaper. *(See color ad p 642)*

SOME UNITS

(See map p. 636)

BEST WESTERN COLUMBUS NORTH
Phone: (614)888-8230 [30]

⬥⬥ SAVE All Year 1P: $60-$65 2P: $60-$65

▽▽◇▽▽ **Location:** I-71, exit 117, 0.5 mi w on SR 161. 888 E Dublin-Granville Rd 43229. Fax: 614/888-8223. **Facility:** 180 one-bedroom standard units. 2 stories, interior corridors. *Bath:* combo or shower only. **Parking:** on-site.
Motor Inn **Amenities:** extended cable TV, voice mail, irons, hair dryers. **Dining:** dining room, 7-10 am, 11-2 & 5-11 pm, $12-$18, cocktails. **Pool(s):** outdoor, heated indoor. **Leisure Activities:** saunas, whirlpool, steamroom, jogging. **Guest Services:** coin laundry. **Business Services:** meeting rooms. **Cards:** AX, CB, DC, DS, MC, VI.
Special Amenities: free local telephone calls. *(See color ad below)*

SOME UNITS

BEST WESTERN SUITES-COLUMBUS WEST
Phone: (614)870-2378 [43]

⬥⬥ SAVE All Year [ECP] 1P: $80-$180 2P: $80-$180

▽▽◇▽▽ **Location:** I-70, exit 91 eastbound; exit 91A westbound, just sw. 1133 Evans Way Ct 43228. Fax: 614/870-9919.
Motel **Facility:** 66 one-bedroom standard units, some with whirlpools. 2 stories, interior corridors. *Bath:* combo or shower only. **Parking:** on-site. **Amenities:** extended cable TV, video tape library (fee), irons, hair dryers.
Pool(s): heated indoor. **Leisure Activities:** sauna, whirlpool, exercise room. **Guest Services:** valet and coin laundry. **Business Services:** meeting rooms. **Cards:** AX, DC, DS, JC, MC, VI. **Special Amenities:** free continental breakfast and free local telephone calls.

SOME UNITS

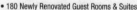

Ohio
Cincinnati–Airport
Cincinnati–Eastgate
Cincinnati–North

Columbus–Airport
Columbus–Airport East
Columbus–East
Columbus–North

Columbus–West
Cuyahoga Falls
Dayton–North
Elyria

(See map p. 636)

COLUMBUS MARRIOTT NORTH Phone: (614)885-1885 **34**

🔺🔺🔺 [SAVE] All Year 1P: $64-$125 2P: $64-$125

🔻🔻🔻🔻 **Location:** I-71, exit 117, 0.3 mi w on SR 161, 0.8 mi on Busch Blvd to Kingsmill Pkwy. 6500 Doubletree Ave 43229. Fax: 614/885-7222. **Facility:** 300 units. 294 one-bedroom standard units. 6 one-bedroom suites ($225). 9

Hotel stories, interior corridors. **Bath:** combo or shower only. **Parking:** on-site. **Terms:** cancellation fee imposed, package plans, pets ($50 fee). **Amenities:** voice mail, irons, hair dryers. **Dining:** dining room, 6:30 am-2 & 5-10 pm, Fri-11 pm, Sat 7 am-11 pm, $12-$22, cocktails. **Pool(s):** heated indoor/outdoor. **Leisure Activities:** sauna, whirlpool, exercise room. **Guest Services:** gift shop, coin laundry. **Business Services:** conference facilities, business center, fax. **Cards:** AX, CB, DC, DS, MC, VI. *(See color ad card insert)*

SOME UNITS

🅢🅓 ✈ ❄ 🍴 🍸 🐾Ⓜ 🐕 📷 🔌 ✕ 📶 / ✕ 📠 📧 /
FEE

COMFORT SUITES Phone: (614)552-2525 **65**

🔺🔺🔺 [SAVE] All Year [ECP] 1P: $84 2P: $94 XP: $10 F16

🔻🔻🔻🔻 **Location:** I-70, exit 110, just s on Brice Rd. 5944 Scarborough Blvd 43232. Fax: 614/552-2526. **Facility:** 66 units. 64 one-bedroom standard units. 2 one-bedroom suites ($169) with whirlpools. 3 stories, interior corridors.

Motel **Bath:** combo or shower only. **Parking:** on-site. **Amenities:** irons, hair dryers. **Pool(s):** heated indoor. **Business Services:** meeting rooms, fax (fee). **Cards:** AX, DC, DS, MC, VI. **Special Amenities:** free continental breakfast and free local telephone calls.

SOME UNITS

🅢🅓 🍴 🔌 🐾 📶 🍸 🔌 📶 🖥 📧 📠 / ✕ /

COMFORT SUITES-COLUMBUS Phone: (614)870-7658 **71**

[SAVE] 4/1-9/30 1P: $79-$125 2P: $79-$125 XP: $10 F16

🔻🔻🔻 10/1-3/31 1P: $69-$115 2P: $69-$115 XP: $10 F16

Motel **Location:** I-70, exit 91B, just n on Renner Rd. 5547 Keim Cir 43228. Fax: 614/878-8366. **Facility:** 71 units. 66 one-bedroom standard units, some with whirlpools. 5 one-bedroom suites, some with whirlpools. 3 stories, interior corridors. **Bath:** combo or shower only. **Parking:** on-site. **Amenities:** extended cable TV, voice mail, irons. *Some:* dual phone lines, hair dryers. **Pool(s):** heated indoor. **Leisure Activities:** whirlpool, limited exercise equipment. **Cards:** AX, DC, DS, MC, VI.

SOME UNITS

🅢🅓 🐾 📶 🔌 📶 🖥 📧 📠 / ✕ 📼 /
FEE

COUNTRY INN & SUITES BY CARLSON COLUMBUS WEST Phone: (614)322-8000 **69**

🔺🔺🔺 [SAVE] All Year [ECP] 1P: $77 2P: $77

🔻🔻🔻🔻 **Location:** I-70, exit 91A, just sw. 1155 Evans Way Ct 43228. Fax: 614/853-2313. **Facility:** 52 units. 41 one-bedroom standard units, some with whirlpools. 11 one-bedroom suites ($94-$149). 3 stories, interior corri-

Motel dors. **Bath:** combo or shower only. **Parking:** on-site. **Amenities:** extended cable TV, voice mail, irons, hair dryers. **Pool(s):** heated indoor. **Leisure Activities:** whirlpool, exercise room. **Guest Services:** valet and coin laundry. **Business Services:** meeting rooms. **Cards:** AX, DC, DS, MC, VI. *(See color ad p 646)*

SOME UNITS

🅢🅓 ♿Ⓜ 🐕 🐾 📼 📶 🔌 📶 🖥 📧 📧 📠 / ✕ /

(See map p. 636)

COURTYARD BY MARRIOTT-COLUMBUS AIRPORT
Phone: (614)475-8530   **57**

(AAA) (SAVE)

Motel

All Year   1P: $79-$129
Location: I-670, exit 9 (Johnstown Rd) eastbound; exit 9 (Cassady Ave) westbound. 2901 Airport Dr 43219. Fax: 614/475-8599. **Facility:** 150 units. 144 one-bedroom standard units, some with whirlpools. 6 one-bedroom suites ($139-$169). 3 stories, interior corridors. *Bath:* combo or shower only. **Parking:** on-site. **Amenities:** video games, dual phone lines, voice mail, irons, hair dryers. *Some:* high-speed Internet (fee). **Dining:** coffee shop, 6-10 am, Sat & Sun 7 am-noon. **Pool(s):** heated indoor. **Leisure Activities:** whirlpool, exercise room. **Guest Services:** coin laundry. **Business Services:** meeting rooms, fax. **Cards:** AX, CB, DC, DS, JC, MC, VI. *(See color ad card insert)*

SOME UNITS

COURTYARD BY MARRIOTT WORTHINGTON
Phone: (614)436-7070   **53**

(AAA) (SAVE)

Motel

All Year   1P: $109-$119   2P: $109-$119
Location: I-270, exit 23, just ne. 7411 Vantage Dr 43235. Fax: 614/436-4970. **Facility:** 145 units. 133 one-bedroom standard units. 12 one-bedroom suites ($115-$139). 4 stories, interior corridors. *Bath:* combo or shower only. **Parking:** on-site. **Amenities:** dual phone lines, voice mail, irons, hair dryers. **Dining:** coffee shop, 6:30-10 am, Sat & Sun 7 am-noon. **Leisure Activities:** whirlpool, exercise room. **Guest Services:** coin laundry. **Business Services:** meeting rooms. **Cards:** AX, DC, DS, MC, VI. *(See color ad card insert)*

SOME UNITS

CROSS COUNTRY INN AIRPORT
Phone: (614)237-3403   **52**

(AAA) (SAVE)

Motel

All Year   1P: $59-$66   2P: $66-$73   XP: $2   F17
Location: At Port Columbus International Airport. 4240 International Gateway 43219. Fax: 614/237-2173. **Facility:** 120 one-bedroom standard units. 2 stories, exterior corridors. *Bath:* combo or shower only. **Parking:** on-site. **Terms:** package plans. **Amenities:** extended cable TV, video games, voice mail. **Pool(s):** outdoor. **Business Services:** fax. **Cards:** AX, CB, DC, DS, MC, VI. **Special Amenities:** free local telephone calls and preferred room (subject to availability with advanced reservations). *(See color ad below)*

SOME UNITS

CROSS COUNTRY INN AT THE CONTINENT
Phone: (614)848-3819   **26**

(AAA) (SAVE)

Motel

All Year   1P: $37-$44   2P: $48-$55   XP: $2   F17
Location: I-71, exit 117, just nw. 6225 Zumstein Dr 43229. Fax: 614/848-6980. **Facility:** 142 one-bedroom standard units. 3 stories, exterior corridors. *Bath:* combo or shower only. **Parking:** on-site. **Pool(s):** heated outdoor. **Business Services:** meeting rooms. **Cards:** AX, CB, DC, DS, MC, VI. **Special Amenities:** free local telephone calls and preferred room (subject to availability with advanced reservations).

SOME UNITS

CROSS COUNTRY INN-COLUMBUS WEST
Phone: (614)870-7090   **62**

(AAA) (SAVE)

Motel

All Year   1P: $42-$49   2P: $49-$56   XP: $2   F17
Location: I-70, exit 91 eastbound; exit 91B westbound. 1313 W St. James Lutheran Ln 43228. Fax: 614/870-8307. **Facility:** 120 one-bedroom standard units. 2 stories, exterior corridors. *Bath:* combo or shower only. **Parking:** not available (no self-parking). **Amenities:** video games, voice mail. **Pool(s):** heated outdoor. **Cards:** AX, CB, DC, DS, MC, VI. **Special Amenities:** free local telephone calls and preferred room (subject to availability with advanced reservations).

SOME UNITS

CROSS COUNTRY INN OLENTANGY, OSU NORTH
Phone: (614)267-4646   **51**

(AAA) (SAVE)

Motel

All Year   1P: $43-$50   2P: $50-$57   XP: $2   F17
Location: SR 315, exit N Broadway, 0.3 mi s. 3246 Olentangy River Rd 43202. Fax: 614/267-1535. **Facility:** 96 one-bedroom standard units. 2 stories, exterior corridors. **Parking:** on-site. **Amenities:** extended cable TV, video games, voice mail. **Pool(s):** heated outdoor. **Cards:** AX, CB, DC, DS, MC, VI. **Special Amenities:** free local telephone calls and preferred room (subject to availability with advanced reservations).

SOME UNITS

(See map p. 636)

CROSS COUNTRY INN-OSU SOUTH
(AAA) (SAVE)

Motel

All Year   1P: $49-$56   2P: $56-$63   Phone: (614)291-2983   **48**
    XP: $2   F17
Location: SR 315, exit King Ave southbound; exit Lane Ave northbound, 1 mi s. 1445 Olentangy River Rd 43212. Fax: 614/291-4082. **Facility:** 120 one-bedroom standard units. 2 stories, exterior corridors. *Bath:* combo or shower only. **Parking:** on-site. **Amenities:** video games, voice mail. **Pool(s):** outdoor. **Business Services:** fax. **Cards:** AX, CB, DC, DS, MC, VI. **Special Amenities:** free local telephone calls and preferred room (subject to availability with advanced reservations).

SOME UNITS
🛎️ ⊡ 🍴 📶 🏊 📹 [DATA PORT] 🖨️ / ✕ [VCR] ▯ 🖥️ 🖥️ 🖥️ /
FEE

CROSS COUNTRY INN-SINCLAIR RD
(AAA) (SAVE)
Motel

All Year   1P: $37-$44   2P: $44-$51   Phone: (614)431-3670   **28**
    XP: $2   F17
Location: I-71, exit 116. 4875 Sinclair Rd 43229. Fax: 614/431-7261. **Facility:** 136 one-bedroom standard units. 2 stories, exterior corridors. *Bath:* combo or shower only. **Parking:** on-site. **Amenities:** video games, voice mail. **Pool(s):** outdoor. **Business Services:** fax. **Cards:** AX, CB, DC, DS, MC, VI. **Special Amenities:** free local telephone calls and preferred room (subject to availability with advanced reservations).

SOME UNITS
🛎️ ⊡ 🏊 📹 [DATA PORT] / ✕ [DATA PORT]
FEE

DAYS INN FAIRGROUNDS
(AAA) (SAVE)
Motel

6/11-8/31 [CP]   1P: $70-$75   2P: $70-$75   XP: $5   F12   **47**
9/1-3/31 [CP]   1P: $50-$75   2P: $50-$75   XP: $5   F12
4/1-6/10 [CP]   1P: $50-$55   2P: $50-$55   XP: $5   F12
Phone: (614)299-4300
Location: I-71, exit 111, just w. 1700 Clara St 43211. Fax: 614/299-0058. **Facility:** 113 one-bedroom standard units. 2 stories, exterior corridors. **Parking:** on-site. **Terms:** small pets only ($20 deposit). **Amenities:** extended cable TV, voice mail, safes (fee), hair dryers. **Pool(s):** outdoor. **Business Services:** meeting rooms. **Cards:** AX, CB, DC, DS, JC, MC, VI. **Special Amenities:** free continental breakfast and free newspaper.

SOME UNITS
🛎️ 🐾 🏊 📹 [DATA PORT] 🖨️ / ✕ 🖥️ 🖥️ 🖥️ /

EMBASSY SUITES HOTEL
(AAA) (SAVE)
Suite Hotel

All Year [BP]   1P: $119-$149   2P: $119-$149   Phone: (614)890-8600   **41**
    XP: $20   F18
Location: I-270, exit 27, just se. 2700 Corporate Exchange Dr 43231. Fax: 614/890-8626. **Facility:** 221 one-bedroom suites. 8 stories, interior corridors. **Parking:** on-site. **Terms:** package plans. **Amenities:** video games, voice mail, irons, hair dryers. **Dining:** dining room, 11 am-2 & 6-10 pm, Sat-11 pm; closed Sun, $11-$21. **Pool(s):** heated indoor/outdoor. **Leisure Activities:** sauna, exercise room. **Guest Services:** complimentary evening beverages, valet laundry, area transportation-within 3 mi. **Business Services:** meeting rooms, business center, PC, fax. **Cards:** AX, CB, DC, DS, MC, VI. **Special Amenities:** early check-in/late check-out and preferred room (subject to availability with advanced reservations).

SOME UNITS
🛎️ ✈️ 🍴 ⊡ [LM] 📶 🏊 📹 [DATA PORT] ▯ 🖥️ 🖥️ 🖨️ / ✕ [VCR] /
FEE   FEE

(See map p. 636)

FAIRFIELD INN BY MARRIOTT

Phone: (614)262-4000 **49**

AAA SAVE
▼▼▼▼
Motel

All Year [CP] 1P: $59-$72 2P: $59-$72
Location: I-71, exit 116, just se. 887 Morse Rd 43229. Fax: 614/262-4000. **Facility:** 135 one-bedroom standard units. 3 stories, interior/exterior corridors. *Bath:* combo or shower only. **Parking:** on-site. **Amenities:** irons, hair dryers. **Pool(s):** outdoor. **Guest Services:** valet laundry. **Business Services:** fax. **Cards:** AX, DC, DS, JC, MC, VI. **Special Amenities:** free continental breakfast and free local telephone calls.
(See color ad card insert)

SOME UNITS

[icons] FEE / ✕ /

FAIRFIELD INN COLUMBUS WEST

Phone: (614)870-2880 **31**

AAA SAVE
▼▼▼▼
Motel

6/2-9/1 [ECP] 1P: $55-$65 2P: $55-$65
4/1-6/1 [ECP] 1P: $51-$61 2P: $51-$61
9/2-12/31 [ECP] 1P: $47-$57 2P: $47-$57
1/1-3/31 [ECP] 1P: $44-$54 2P: $44-$54
Location: I-70, exit 91 eastbound; exit 91B westbound, just ne. 1309 St. James Luthern Ln 43228. Fax: 614/870-2927. **Facility:** 105 one-bedroom standard units. 3 stories, interior/exterior corridors. **Parking:** on-site. **Amenities:** voice mail, irons. **Pool(s):** heated outdoor. **Guest Services:** valet laundry. **Business Services:** meeting rooms. **Cards:** AX, CB, DC, DS, MC, VI. **Special Amenities:** free continental breakfast and free local telephone calls.
(See color ad card insert)

SOME UNITS

[icons] FEE / ✕ /

HAMPTON INN COLUMBUS WEST

Phone: (614)851-5599 **66**

SAVE
▼▼▼▼
Motel

All Year 1P: $74-$115 2P: $81-$115
Location: I-70, exit 91B westbound, just ne. 5625 Trabue Rd 43228. Fax: 614/851-5590. **Facility:** 77 one-bedroom standard units, some with whirlpools. 3 stories, interior corridors. *Bath:* combo or shower only. **Parking:** on-site. **Terms:** 3 day cancellation notice. **Amenities:** extended cable TV, voice mail, irons, hair dryers. **Pool(s):** heated outdoor. **Leisure Activities:** whirlpool, exercise room. **Guest Services:** valet and coin laundry. **Business Services:** meeting rooms. **Cards:** AX, CB, DC, DS, MC, VI.

SOME UNITS

[icons] FEE / ✕ VCR /

HAWTHORN SUITES LTD

Phone: (614)853-6199 **70**
F18

AAA SAVE
▼▼▼▼
Suite Motel

All Year [BP] 1P: $89-$159 2P: $89-$159 XP: $10
Location: I-70, exit 91B, just n on Renner Rd. 5505 Keim Cir 43228. Fax: 614/853-6198. **Facility:** 80 one-bedroom standard units with efficiencies, some with whirlpools. 3 stories, interior corridors. *Bath:* combo or shower only. **Parking:** on-site. **Terms:** 14 day cancellation notice. **Amenities:** voice mail, safes (fee), irons, hair dryers. **Pool(s):** heated indoor. **Leisure Activities:** whirlpool, exercise room. **Guest Services:** complimentary evening beverages: Wed, valet and coin laundry. **Business Services:** meeting rooms. **Cards:** AX, CB, DC, DS, MC, VI. **Special Amenities:** free continental breakfast and free newspaper. *(See color ad below)*

SOME UNITS

[icons] VCR / ✕ /

HILTON COLUMBUS

Phone: (614)414-5000 **68**

AAA SAVE
▼▼▼▼
Hotel

All Year 1P: $179-$219 2P: $179-$219 XP: $20
Location: I-270, exit 33, just e at Easton Town Center. 3900 Chagrin Dr 43219. Fax: 614/414-5100. **Facility:** 313 units. 308 one-bedroom standard units. 5 one-bedroom suites ($239-$344). 7 stories, interior corridors. *Bath:* combo or shower only. **Parking:** on-site and valet (fee). **Amenities:** extended cable TV, video games, dual phone lines, voice mail, irons, hair dryers. *Some:* high-speed Internet (fee). **Dining:** dining room, 6 am-11 pm, cocktails. **Pool(s):** heated indoor. **Leisure Activities:** whirlpool, exercise room. *Fee:* game room. **Guest Services:** valet laundry. **Business Services:** conference facilities, business center, PC, fax. **Cards:** AX, DC, DS, JC, MC, VI.

SOME UNITS

[icons] FEE / ✕ / FEE

(See map p. 636)

HOLIDAY INN-COLUMBUS AIRPORT
Phone: (614)237-6360 46

▼▼▼ ▼▼▼
Motor Inn

4/1-10/31	1P: $109-$129	2P: $119-$139
11/1-3/31	1P: $99-$125	2P: $109-$135

Location: 0.8 mi s of Port Columbus International Airport entrance. 750 Stelzer Rd 43219. Fax: 614/237-2978. **Facility:** 236 one-bedroom standard units. 3 stories, interior corridors. *Bath:* combo or shower only. **Parking:** on-site. **Terms:** package plans. **Amenities:** video games, voice mail, irons, hair dryers. **Pool(s):** heated indoor. **Leisure Activities:** sauna, whirlpool, exercise room. **Guest Services:** valet and coin laundry. **Business Services:** meeting rooms, fax. **Cards:** AX, CB, DC, DS, JC, MC, VI.

SOME UNITS
(ASK) (S/D) (✈) (¶) (&) (⌖) (🏊) (✕) (🎮) (DATA PORT) (▭) (🖨) / (✕) (VCR) (📶) (📷) /
FEE · FEE

HOLIDAY INN COLUMBUS WEST
Phone: (614)771-8999 39

▼▼▼ ▼▼▼
Motor Inn

All Year — 1P: $99-$118

Location: I-270, exit 10, just w. 2350 Westbelt Dr 43228. Fax: 614/771-8857. **Facility:** 150 one-bedroom standard units. 4 stories, interior corridors. *Bath:* combo or shower only. **Parking:** on-site. **Terms:** 3 day cancellation notice, package plans. **Amenities:** voice mail, irons, hair dryers. **Pool(s):** heated indoor. **Leisure Activities:** sauna, whirlpool, children's program, exercise room. **Guest Services:** valet laundry. **Business Services:** meeting rooms, fax. **Cards:** AX, CB, DC, DS, MC, VI.

SOME UNITS
(ASK) (S/D) (¶) (Y) (&M) (&) (⌖) (🏊) (✕) (🎮) (DATA PORT) (▭) (🖨) / (✕) (VCR) (📶) /
FEE · FEE

HOLIDAY INN-COLUMBUS/WORTHINGTON AREA
Phone: (614)885-3334 45

(AAA) (SAVE)
▼▼▼ ▼▼▼
Motor Inn

All Year — 1P: $79-$109

Location: I-270, exit 23, just n of jct US 23 N. 175 Hutchinson Ave 43235. Fax: 614/431-4450. **Facility:** 306 units. 300 one-bedroom standard units. 6 one-bedroom suites ($210-$225) with whirlpools. 6 stories, interior corridors. *Bath:* combo or shower only. **Parking:** on-site. **Terms:** package plans, small pets only. **Amenities:** extended cable TV, voice mail, irons, hair dryers. **Dining:** restaurant, 6 am-2 & 5-11 pm, Sat & Sun from 6:30 am, $11-$20, cocktails. **Pool(s):** heated indoor. **Leisure Activities:** whirlpool, exercise room, sports court. **Guest Services:** gift shop, valet and coin laundry. **Business Services:** conference facilities, business center, PC, fax. **Cards:** AX, CB, DC, DS, JC, MC, VI.

SOME UNITS
(S/D) (🐾) (¶) (&M) (&) (⌖) (🏊) (✕) (🎮) (DATA PORT) (▭) (🖨) / (✕) (📶) /
FEE · FEE

HOLIDAY INN EAST I-70
Phone: (614)868-1380 56

▼▼▼ ▼▼▼
Hotel

All Year — 1P: $109 · 2P: $109

Location: I-70, exit 107. 4560 Hilton Corporate Dr 43232. Fax: 614/863-3210. **Facility:** 278 one-bedroom standard units. 12 stories, interior corridors. *Bath:* combo or shower only. **Parking:** on-site. **Terms:** package plans. **Amenities:** extended cable TV, video games, voice mail, irons, hair dryers. **Leisure Activities:** playground, exercise room. **Guest Services:** valet laundry. **Business Services:** conference facilities, business center, PC. **Cards:** AX, CB, DC, DS, JC, MC, VI. *(See color ad below)*

SOME UNITS
(ASK) (S/D) (✈) (🐾) (¶) (&M) (&) (🎮) (DATA PORT) (▭) (🖨) / (✕) (VCR) (📶) (📷) /
FEE

HOLIDAY INN EXPRESS NORTH
Phone: (614)885-4334 29

▼▼▼ ▼▼▼
Motel

5/1-10/31 [ECP]	1P: $76-$89
4/1-4/30 & 11/1-3/31 [ECP]	1P: $65-$72

Location: I-71, exit 117. 1221 E Dublin Granville Rd 43229. Fax: 614/885-4955. **Facility:** 89 one-bedroom standard units. 2 stories, interior corridors. *Bath:* combo or shower only. **Parking:** on-site. **Amenities:** dual phone lines, voice mail, irons, hair dryers. **Guest Services:** valet laundry. **Business Services:** fax. **Cards:** AX, CB, DC, DS, MC, VI.

SOME UNITS
(ASK) (S/D) (¶→) (&) (🎮) (DATA PORT) (🖨) / (✕) (📶) /

(See map p. 636)

HOLIDAY INN ON THE LANE
Phone: (614)294-4848 61

AAA SAVE
Hotel

All Year 1P: $99-$119
Location: SR 315, exit Lane Ave, 0.5 mi e; opposite Ohio State University. 328 W Lane Ave 43201. Fax: 614/294-3390. **Facility:** 243 one-bedroom standard units. 11 stories, interior corridors. **Parking:** on-site. **Terms:** 7 day cancellation notice-fee imposed, package plans. **Amenities:** video games, dual phone lines, voice mail, irons, hair dryers. **Dining:** dining room, 6 am-2 & 5-10 pm, $10-$29, cocktails. **Pool(s):** heated indoor. **Leisure Activities:** whirlpool, jogging, exercise room. **Guest Services:** gift shop, valet and coin laundry, area transportation-within 3 mi. **Business Services:** conference facilities. **Cards:** AX, CB, DC, DS, JC, MC, VI. **Special Amenities:** free newspaper and free room upgrade (subject to availability with advanced reservations). *(See color ad below)*

SOME UNITS

HOMEWOOD SUITES
Phone: (614)785-0001 42

AAA SAVE
Extended Stay
Motel

4/27-12/31 [ECP] 1P: $115-$145 2P: $115-$145
4/1-4/26 & 1/1-3/31 [ECP] 1P: $109-$139 2P: $109-$139
Location: I-270, exit 23, just ne. 115 Hutchinson Ave 43235. Fax: 614/785-0143. **Facility:** 99 units. 12 one-bedroom standard units. 87 one-bedroom suites with kitchens. 3 stories, interior corridors. **Parking:** on-site. **Terms:** cancellation fee imposed, package plans, pets ($10 extra charge). **Amenities:** voice mail, irons, hair dryers. **Leisure Activities:** whirlpool, exercise room, sports court. **Guest Services:** complimentary evening beverages: Mon-Thurs, coin laundry. **Business Services:** meeting rooms, business center, PC. **Cards:** AX, CB, DC, DS, JC, MC, VI.

SOME UNITS

KNIGHTS INN-COLUMBUS EAST
Phone: (614)864-0600 50

AAA SAVE
Motel

6/1-10/31 1P: $50-$70 2P: $70-$90 XP: $10 F15
11/1-12/31 1P: $50-$53 2P: $53-$55 XP: $10 F15
4/1-5/31 & 1/1-3/31 1P: $47-$50 2P: $50-$55 XP: $10 F15
Location: I-70, exit 107, just sw. 4320 Groves Rd 43232. Fax: 614/864-9352. **Facility:** 105 one-bedroom standard units, some with whirlpools. 1 story, exterior corridors. **Parking:** on-site. **Terms:** check-in 4 pm, pets ($25 deposit). **Amenities:** extended cable TV. **Business Services:** meeting rooms. **Cards:** AX, CB, DC, DS, JC, MC, VI. **Special Amenities:** early check-in/late check-out and free room upgrade (subject to availability with advanced reservations).

SOME UNITS

MICROTEL INN & SUITES (WEST)
Phone: (614)851-1745 73

AAA SAVE
Motel

All Year 1P: $60-$80 2P: $60-$80 XP: $5 F18
Location: I-70, exit 91A, just sw. 5655 Feder Rd 43228. Fax: 614/851-9787. **Facility:** 64 one-bedroom standard units. 3 stories, interior corridors. **Bath:** combo or shower only. **Parking:** on-site. **Amenities:** irons, hair dryers. **Leisure Activities:** exercise room. **Guest Services:** coin laundry. **Cards:** AX, DC, DS, MC, VI. **Special Amenities:** free continental breakfast and free local telephone calls.

SOME UNITS

MICROTEL INN-NORTH
Phone: (614)436-0556 64

Motel

10/1-11/1 [CP] 1P: $49-$59 XP: $5
7/1-9/30 [CP] 1P: $48-$54 XP: $5
4/1-6/30 [CP] 1P: $42-$48 XP: $5
11/2-3/31 [CP] 1P: $37-$42 XP: $5
Location: I-270, exit 23, just n of US 23 N. 7500 Vantage Dr 43235. Fax: 614/436-2205. **Facility:** 99 one-bedroom standard units. 2 stories, interior corridors. **Parking:** on-site. **Terms:** pets ($5 extra charge). **Amenities:** extended cable TV, video games, safes (fee). **Cards:** AX, DC, DS, MC, VI.

SOME UNITS

(See map p. 636)

RADISSON AIRPORT HOTEL & CONFERENCE CENTER Phone: (614)475-7551 **44**

AAA SAVE

12/31-3/31	1P: $94-$155	2P: $94-$155	XP: $10 F17
4/1-12/30	1P: $94-$149	2P: $94-$149	XP: $10 F17

Hotel

Location: I-670, exit 9 (Johnstown Rd) eastbound; exit 9 (Cassady Ave) westbound. 1375 N Cassady Ave 43219. Fax: 614/476-1476. **Facility:** 245 units. 242 one-bedroom standard units. 3 one-bedroom suites with whirlpools. 6 stories, interior corridors. **Parking:** on-site. **Terms:** check-in 4 pm, package plans. **Amenities:** extended cable TV, high-speed Internet (fee), voice mail, irons, hair dryers. **Dining:** dining room, 6 am-2 & 5-11 pm, Sat & Sun from 7 am, $8-$18, cocktails. **Pool(s):** heated indoor. **Leisure Activities:** sauna, whirlpool, exercise room. **Guest Services:** gift shop, valet and coin laundry. **Business Services:** conference facilities, business center, PC. **Cards:** AX, CB, DC, DS, JC, MC, VI.

SOME UNITS

🛬 🍴 🏋 🏊 ✕ 🐕 [DATA PORT] 💻 🖨 / ✕ 🛏 🗄 /
FEE

RAMADA LIMITED NORTH Phone: (614)846-9070 **72**

AAA SAVE

9/30-10/21 [CP]	1P: $47-$109	2P: $53-$109	XP: $5 F18
4/1-9/29 & 10/22-3/31 [CP]	1P: $29-$99	2P: $35-$99	XP: $5 F18

Motel

Location: I-71, exit 117, at jct SR 161. 6121 Zumstein Dr 43229. Fax: 614/436-0875. **Facility:** 92 one-bedroom standard units, some with whirlpools. 2 stories, interior corridors. **Parking:** on-site. **Amenities:** irons. **Guest Services:** valet laundry. **Business Services:** meeting rooms. **Cards:** AX, CB, DC, DS, JC, MC, VI. **Special Amenities:** free continental breakfast and free local telephone calls.

SOME UNITS

[S/D] 🏋 🏋 🎥 [DATA PORT] / ✕ 🛏 💻 /

RED ROOF INN COLUMBUS NORTH Phone: (614)846-8520 **67**

AAA SAVE

6/9-11/2	1P: $41-$61	2P: $48-$68	XP: $7 F18
11/3-3/31	1P: $37-$59	2P: $44-$66	XP: $7 F18
4/1-6/8	1P: $35-$56	2P: $42-$63	XP: $7 F18

Motel

Location: I-71, exit 116. 750 Morse Rd 43229. Fax: 614/846-8526. **Facility:** 107 one-bedroom standard units. 2 stories, exterior corridors. *Bath:* combo or shower only. **Parking:** on-site. **Terms:** small pets only. **Amenities:** video games. **Cards:** AX, CB, DC, DS, MC, VI. **Special Amenities:** free local telephone calls and free newspaper.

SOME UNITS

🐕 [&M] [&] 🎥 [DATA PORT] 🖨 / ✕ /
FEE

RED ROOF INN-OSU Phone: (614)267-9941 **59**

AAA SAVE

4/29-3/31	1P: $59-$69	2P: $64-$69	XP: $5 F18
4/1-4/28	1P: $54-$69	2P: $59-$69	XP: $5 F18

Motel

Location: SR 315, exit Ackerman Rd, 0.3 mi e. 441 Ackerman Rd 43202. Fax: 614/267-5925. **Facility:** 113 one-bedroom standard units. 3 stories, exterior corridors. *Bath:* combo or shower only. **Parking:** on-site. **Terms:** small pets only. **Amenities:** video games, voice mail. **Business Services:** fax. **Cards:** AX, CB, DC, DS, MC, VI. **Special Amenities:** free local telephone calls and free newspaper.

SOME UNITS

🐕 🏋 🎥 [DATA PORT] 🖨 / ✕ /
FEE

RED ROOF INN-WEST Phone: (614)878-9245 **63**

AAA SAVE

5/5-8/31	1P: $47-$69	2P: $53-$75	XP: $6 F18
9/1-11/16	1P: $43-$59	2P: $49-$65	XP: $6 F18
11/17-3/31	1P: $41-$59	2P: $47-$65	XP: $6 F18
4/1-5/4	1P: $39-$52	2P: $45-$58	XP: $6 F18

Motel

Location: I-70, exit 91 eastbound; exit 91B westbound, just nw. 5001 Renner Rd 43228. Fax: 614/878-0142. **Facility:** 79 one-bedroom standard units. 2 stories, exterior corridors. *Bath:* combo or shower only. **Parking:** on-site. **Terms:** small pets only. **Amenities:** video games, voice mail. **Cards:** AX, CB, DC, DS, MC, VI. **Special Amenities:** free local telephone calls and free newspaper.

SOME UNITS

🐕 🏋 [&M] [&] 🎥 [DATA PORT] 🖨 / ✕ 🛏 🗄 /
FEE

RESIDENCE INN BY MARRIOTT Phone: 614/885-0799 **55**

AAA SAVE

All Year [ECP]	1P: $109

Motel

Location: I-270, exit 23, just e of Vantage. 7300 Huntington Park Dr 43235. Fax: 614/885-0953. **Facility:** 104 units. 42 one-bedroom standard units with kitchens. 48 one- and 14 two-bedroom suites with kitchens. 4 stories, interior corridors. *Bath:* combo or shower only. **Parking:** on-site. **Terms:** pets ($100 fee). **Amenities:** extended cable TV, voice mail, irons, hair dryers. *Some:* dual phone lines. **Pool(s):** outdoor. **Leisure Activities:** whirlpool, sports court, basketball. **Guest Services:** valet and coin laundry. **Business Services:** meeting rooms. **Cards:** AX, CB, DC, DS, JC, MC, VI. *(See color ad card insert)*

SOME UNITS

🐕 🏋 [&] 🏊 ✕ 🎥 [DATA PORT] 🛏 🗄 💻 🖨 / ✕ /

THE RESIDENCE INN BY MARRIOTT-COLUMBUS NORTH Phone: (614)431-1819 **27**

AAA SAVE

6/2-10/31 [BP]	1P: $109
4/1-6/1 & 11/1-3/31 [BP]	1P: $99

Apartment

Location: I-71, exit 117, 0.3 mi w on SR 161, 0.4 mi n on Busch Blvd, Shapter, and Mediterranean. 6191 W Zumstein Dr 43229. Fax: 614/431-2477. **Facility:** 96 units. 72 one-bedroom standard units with kitchens. 24 two-bedroom suites with kitchens. 2 stories, exterior corridors. *Bath:* combo or shower only. **Parking:** on-site. **Terms:** cancellation fee imposed, package plans, pets ($100 fee). **Amenities:** extended cable TV, voice mail, irons, hair dryers. **Pool(s):** outdoor. **Leisure Activities:** whirlpool, sports court. **Guest Services:** coin laundry. **Business Services:** fax. **Cards:** AX, CB, DC, DS, JC, MC, VI. *(See color ad card insert)*

SOME UNITS

[S/D] 🐕 🏋 [&] 🏊 ➕ 🎥 [DATA PORT] 🛏 🗄 💻 / ✕ /
FEE

(See map p. 636)

RESIDENCE INN BY MARRIOTT-COLUMBUS SOUTHEAST　　　　　　　**Phone:** (614)864-8844　58

Apartment

All Year [BP]　　　　1P: $59-$149
Location: I-70, exit 107, just e. 2084 S Hamilton Rd 43232. Fax: 614/864-4572. **Facility:** 80 units. 50 one-bedroom standard units with kitchens. 30 one-bedroom suites with kitchens. 2 stories, exterior corridors. *Bath:* combo or shower only. **Parking:** on-site. **Terms:** [MAP] meal plan available, pets ($100 fee, $5 extra charge). **Amenities:** voice mail, irons, hair dryers. **Pool(s):** heated outdoor. **Leisure Activities:** whirlpool, sports court. **Guest Services:** complimentary evening beverages: Mon-Thurs, valet and coin laundry. **Cards:** AX, CB, DC, DS, JC, MC, VI. *(See color ad card insert)*

SOME UNITS

ROYAL INN MOTEL　　　　　　　**Phone:** (614)771-2760　37

Motel

All Year　　　　1P: $45-$49　　　2P: $51-$59　　　XP: $5　　　F15
Location: I-270, exit 10, jct Roberts Rd. 2330 Westbelt Dr 43228. Fax: 614/529-8927. **Facility:** 22 one-bedroom standard units. 1 story, exterior corridors. **Parking:** on-site. **Amenities:** hair dryers. *Some:* irons. **Cards:** AX, DS, MC, VI.

SOME UNITS

SHERATON SUITES COLUMBUS　　　　　　　**Phone:** 614/436-0004　35

Suite Hotel

All Year　　　　1P: $79-$189　　　2P: $79-$189　　　XP: $10　　　F18
Location: I-270, exit 23, just ne. 201 Hutchinson Ave 43235. Fax: 614/436-0926. **Facility:** 261 one-bedroom suites. 9 stories, interior corridors. *Bath:* combo or shower only. **Parking:** on-site. **Terms:** package plans. **Amenities:** video games, voice mail, irons, hair dryers. *Some:* dual phone lines, fax. **Pool(s):** heated outdoor, heated indoor. **Leisure Activities:** whirlpool, exercise room. **Guest Services:** valet laundry. **Business Services:** meeting rooms, business center, PC, fax. **Cards:** AX, CB, DC, DS, JC, MC, VI.

SOME UNITS

FEE

SIGNATURE INN COLUMBUS NORTH　　　　　　　**Phone:** (614)890-8111　40

Motel

All Year [CP]　　　　1P: $68-$78　　　2P: $68-$78
Location: I-270, exit 27, n off Cleveland Ave; enter off Schrock Rd. 6767 Schrock Hill Ct 43229. Fax: 614/890-8111. **Facility:** 125 one-bedroom standard units, some with whirlpools. 2 stories, interior corridors. **Parking:** on-site. **Amenities:** extended cable TV, voice mail, irons, hair dryers. **Pool(s):** outdoor. **Guest Services:** valet laundry. **Business Services:** meeting rooms, business center, PC, fax. **Cards:** AX, DC, DS, MC, VI.

SOME UNITS

FEE

SUPER 8 MOTEL　　　　　　　**Phone:** 614/771-8944　38

Motel

All Year [ECP]　　　　1P: $65-$85　　　2P: $69-$89　　　XP: $5　　　F12
Location: I-270, exit 10 (Roberts Rd). 2340 Westbelt Dr 43228. Fax: 614/771-8940. **Facility:** 51 one-bedroom standard units, some with whirlpools. 3 stories, interior corridors. *Bath:* combo or shower only. **Parking:** on-site. **Amenities:** voice mail, irons, hair dryers. **Leisure Activities:** exercise room. **Business Services:** meeting rooms. **Cards:** AX, DC, DS, MC, VI.

SOME UNITS

THE UNIVERSITY PLAZA HOTEL & CONFERENCE CENTER　　　　　　　**Phone:** (614)267-7461　54

Motor Inn

All Year　　　　1P: $99-$149　　　2P: $99-$149
Location: SR 315, exit N Broadway Rd, 0.5 mi s. 3110 Olentangy River Rd 43202. Fax: 614/263-5299. **Facility:** 243 units. 239 one-bedroom units. 4 one-bedroom suites ($149-$179). 5 stories, interior corridors. **Parking:** on-site. **Terms:** package plans, pets ($25 deposit, $10 extra charge). **Amenities:** voice mail, irons. **Dining:** restaurant, 6:30 am-2 & 5-10 pm, Sat & Sun from 7 am, $8-$16, cocktails. **Pool(s):** outdoor. **Guest Services:** valet laundry, area transportation-within 3 mi. **Business Services:** conference facilities, business center, fax. **Cards:** AX, CB, DC, DS, JC, MC, VI.

SOME UNITS

FEE　　　FEE

(See map p. 636)

WELLESLEY INN & SUITES (COLUMBUS/POLARIS)
Phone: (614)431-5522 〖36〗

(AAA) [SAVE]
▽▽▼▽▽
Motel

All Year [ECP]   1P: $79-$109   2P: $89-$109   XP: $10   F18
Location: I-71, exit 121, just w on Polaris Pkwy. 8555 Lyra Dr 43240. Fax: 614/431-5533. **Facility:** 124 units. 47 one-bedroom standard units, some with efficiencies. 77 one-bedroom suites with efficiencies. 3 stories, interior corridors. *Bath:* combo or shower only. **Parking:** on-site. **Terms:** 3 day cancellation notice, small pets only. **Amenities:** video games, dual phone lines, voice mail, irons, hair dryers. **Pool(s):** heated outdoor. **Leisure Activities:** exercise room. **Guest Services:** coin laundry. **Business Services:** meeting rooms. **Cards:** AX, DC, DS, JC, MC, VI. **Special Amenities:** free continental breakfast and free newspaper. *(See color ad p 643)*

SOME UNITS

[icons] FEE

WINGATE INN
Phone: (614)844-5888 〖25〗

▽▽▼▽▽
Motel

All Year   1P: $89-$109   2P: $89-$109   XP: $10
Location: I-71, exit 121. 8505 Pulsar Place 43240. Fax: 614/781-1985. **Facility:** 100 one-bedroom standard units. 4 stories, interior corridors. *Bath:* combo or shower only. **Parking:** on-site. **Amenities:** video games, Web TV, high-speed Internet, dual phone lines, voice mail, safes, irons, hair dryers. **Leisure Activities:** whirlpool, exercise room. **Guest Services:** valet laundry. **Business Services:** meeting rooms, business center, PC, fax. **Cards:** AX, CB, DC, DS, MC, VI. *(See color ad p 654)*

SOME UNITS

[icons]

---

*The following lodgings were either not evaluated or did not
meet AAA rating requirements but are listed for your information only.*

COUNTRY INN & SUITES BY CARLSON-COLUMBUS AIRPORT EAST
Phone: 614/322-8000

[fyi]
Motel

All Year [CP]   1P: $103   2P: $103   XP: $10   F18
Too new to rate, opening scheduled for November 2001. **Location:** I-270, exit 39, just e. 6305 E Broad St 43213. Fax: 614/322-8001. **Amenities:** pets, radios, coffeemakers. **Terms:** cancellation fee imposed. **Cards:** AX, DC, DS, MC, VI. *(See color ad p 646)*

DRURY INN & SUITES-COLUMBUS NORTHWEST
Phone: 614/798-8802

[fyi]
Motel

Under construction, scheduled to open November 2002. **Location:** I-270, exit 15. 6170 Park Center Cir 43017. Fax: 614/798-8802. **Planned Amenities:** pets, radios, coffeemakers, microwaves, refrigerators, pool.

FAIRFIELD INN & SUITES
Phone: 614/267-1111

[fyi]
Motel

All Year [ECP]   1P: $79-$149   2P: $79-$149
Too new to rate, opening scheduled for December 2001. **Location:** SR 315, exit Ackerman Rd, just e. 3031 Olentangy River Rd 43202. Fax: 614/267-0904. **Amenities:** radios, coffeemakers, microwaves, refrigerators, pool. **Cards:** AX, CB, DC, DS, MC, VI. *(See color ad card insert)*

STAYBRIDGE SUITES BY HOLIDAY INN
Phone: 614/734-9882

[fyi]
Motel

Under construction, scheduled to open May 2002. **Location:** I-270, exit Tuttle Crossing. 6095 Emerald Pkwy 43016. Fax: 614/734-0668. **Planned Amenities:** radios, coffeemakers, microwaves, refrigerators.

--- **WHERE TO DINE** ---

94TH AERO SQUADRON
Lunch: $7-$11   **Dinner: $15-$25**   **Phone: 614/237-8887** 〖24〗

▼▽ ▼▽
Steak House

Location: I-270, exit 37, 1 mi w on SR 317, follow signs; on grounds of Port Columbus International Airport. 5030 Sawyer Rd 43219. **Hours:** 11 am-3 & 4:30-10 pm, Fri & Sat-11 pm, Sun 9 am-2:30 & 4:30-10 pm. **Reservations:** suggested. **Features:** casual dress; Sunday brunch; children's menu; early bird specials; cocktails & lounge. Overlooking airport runways, the dining room at the French farmhouse restaurant reflects a World War I aviation theme. American cuisine includes New York strip steak, seafood and country-market chicken. The upside-down apple walnut pie is delicious. **Parking:** on-site. **Cards:** AX, DC, DS, MC, VI.
[icon]

BARCELONA
Lunch: $8-$10   **Dinner: $9-$18**   **Phone: 614/443-3699** 〖41〗

▽▽▼▽▽
Ethnic

Location: Corner of E Whittier and Jaeger; in German Village. 263 E Whittier St 43206. **Hours:** 11:30 am-5 & 5:30-10 pm, Fri-11 pm, Sat 5:30 pm-11 pm, Sun 5 pm-10 pm. Closed major holidays; also Sun. **Reservations:** suggested. **Features:** dressy casual; carryout; cocktails & lounge. You'll have no trouble finding something on the menu to tickle your taste buds; the multi-ethnic cuisine and exquisite dessert selections served here are varied. Open courtyard seating is available in addition to the eclectic, artsy decor indoors. **Parking:** on-site and valet. **Cards:** AX, CB, DC, DS, MC, VI.
[icon]

BRIO TUSCAN GRILLE
Lunch: $10-$15   **Dinner: $10-$23**   **Phone: 614/416-4745** 〖40〗

▽▽▼▽▽
Northern
Italian

Location: I-270, exit 33, 0.5 mi w. 3993 Easton Station 43081. **Hours:** 11 am-10 pm, Fri & Sat-midnight. Closed: 11/28, 12/25. **Reservations:** accepted. **Features:** dressy casual; children's menu; carryout; cocktails & lounge; a la carte. Near a major shopping mall, the restaurant has a large open kitchen that helps create a brisk, but fun, atmosphere. Hearty Tuscan dishes include steak, pasta and risotto. Lasagna Bolognese is a specialty. **Parking:** on-site. **Cards:** AX, CB, DC, DS, MC, VI.
[icons]

BUCKEYE HALL OF FAME CAFE
Lunch: $6-$11   **Dinner: $8-$21**   **Phone: 614/291-2233** 〖32〗

▼▽▼▽
American

Location: 0.5 mi s of SR 315 at Olentangy River Rd to King Ave. 1421 Olentangy River Rd 43212. **Hours:** 11 am-midnight, Fri & Sat-11 pm, Sun 10 am-10 pm. Closed: 11/28, 12/25. **Features:** casual dress; Sunday brunch; children's menu; carryout; cocktails; a la carte. Ohio State University memorabilia decorates the appropriately named restaurant. **Parking:** on-site. **Cards:** AX, DC, DS, MC, VI.
[icon]

(See map p. 636)

CAP CITY FINE DINER & BAR   Lunch: $6-$8   Dinner: $10-$15   Phone: 614/291-3663   39
American
Location: SR 315, 0.7 mi s. 1299 Olentangy River Rd 43212. **Hours:** 11 am-11 pm, Sun-10 pm. Closed major holidays. **Reservations:** accepted. **Features:** casual dress; Sunday brunch; children's menu; carryout; cocktails; a la carte. Cap City makes an excellent showing of its creative interpretation of traditional diner fare of hearty portions of meatloaf, seafood and sandwiches. Presentation of many of these dishes is magnificent. Some al fresco dining is offered in season. Fun, upbeat and lively atmosphere. Attention to service. **Parking:** on-site. **Cards:** AX, DC, DS, MC, VI.

ENGINE HOUSE NO. 5   Historical   Lunch: $7-$16   Dinner: $12-$32   Phone: 614/443-4877   38
Seafood
Location: Corner of 4th St and Thurman Ave; in German Village. 121 Thurman Ave 43206. **Hours:** 11:30 am-10 pm, Fri-11 pm, Sat 4 pm-11 pm, Sun 4 pm-9 pm; call for hours on major holidays. **Reservations:** suggested. **Features:** casual dress; children's menu; early bird specials; cocktails & lounge. Extensive firefighting memorabilia and historical pictures decorate the 1892 converted firehouse. Good choices include Charly's bucket, with lobster, clams and mussels, and the house-made pasta dishes. Servers slide down the brass pole with cakes to help guests celebrate special events. **Parking:** on-site. **Cards:** AX, CB, DC, DS, JC, MC, VI.

LINDEY'S   Historical   Lunch: $8-$18   Dinner: $13-$28   Phone: 614/228-4343   34
American
Location: Corner of Beck and Mohawk; in German Village. 169 E Beck St 43206. **Hours:** 11 am-10 pm, Thurs-Sat to 11 pm. Closed major holidays; also Super Bowl Sun. **Reservations:** suggested; Thurs-Sat. **Features:** dressy casual; Sunday brunch; carryout; cocktails; a la carte. Enjoy creative American fare in the bustling bistro atmosphere of this renovated mid-19th century building. Bring your appetite for a variety of pasta, sandwiches, steak and seafood all served in ample portions. **Parking:** on-site and valet. **Cards:** AX, DC, DS, MC, VI.

OLD MOHAWK RESTAURANT   Lunch: $6-$9   Dinner: $6-$9   Phone: 614/444-7204   35
American
Location: Corner of Kassuth and Mohawk; in German Village. 819 Mohawk St 43206. **Hours:** 11 am-midnight, Mon-11 pm, Fri-1 am, Sat 9 am-11 pm, Sun 9 am-1 am. Closed: 11/28, 12/25. **Features:** casual dress; cocktails; a la carte. Built in 1933, the historic structure was a speakeasy during Prohibition. Don't be alarmed by the arm sticking out of the building—it serves to give diners an idea of the eclectic feel of the place. Food is an adventure in everything from burgers, sandwiches and wraps to pasta, pizza and vegetarian dishes. Try the signature turtle soup or meatloaf. **Parking:** street. **Cards:** AX, DC, DS, MC, VI.

OTANI JAPANESE RESTAURANT AND SUSHI BAR   Lunch: $6-$13   Dinner: $9-$25   Phone: 614/431-3333   25
Ethnic
Location: Jct SR 161 and I-71, exit 117. 5900 Roche Dr 43229. **Hours:** 11:30 am-2 & 5-10:30 pm, Fri & Sat-2 am. Closed: Sun. **Reservations:** suggested. **Features:** casual dress; children's menu; carryout; cocktails; a la carte. Live jazz music on weekends contributes to the relaxed restaurant's ambience. A wide selection of seafood includes sashimi and fresh, flavorful sushi. Several American-style offerings round out the menu. Uniformed servers are prompt and attentive. **Parking:** on-site. **Cards:** AX, DC, DS, MC, VI.

THE REFECTORY   Dinner: $23-$28   Phone: 614/451-9774   23
AAA
French
Location: SR 315, 0.8 mi w. 1092 Bethel Rd 43220. **Hours:** 5:30 pm-10 pm, Fri & Sat 5 pm-10:30 pm. Closed major holidays; also Sun. **Reservations:** suggested. **Features:** formal attire; cocktails; a la carte, a la carte. This restaurant is located in a historic remodeled converted church and school with charming original log beams and rustic elegance. A seasonally revised menu balances selections of seafood, veal and poultry. An extensive wine list will quench any thirst. Sophisticated and romantic in setting, quality food and a highly trained staff all add up to a wonderful fine dining experience. **Parking:** on-site. **Cards:** AX, DC, DS, JC, MC, VI.

SALVI'S BISTRO   Lunch: $6-$7   Dinner: $10-$18   Phone: 614/870-8788   42
Italian
Location: I-70, exit 91 eastbound; exit 91B westbound. 1323 St James Lutheran Lane 43228. **Hours:** 11 am-10 pm, Fri & Sat-11 pm, Sun from 10:30 am. Closed: 12/25. **Reservations:** accepted; weekdays. **Features:** casual dress; Sunday brunch; children's menu; carryout; cocktails; a la carte. Most dishes are familiar fare, pasta, steaks and sandwiches, although the signature entree, pasta Salvi, shows a with creative flair. The brick and stucco building opens into an airy dining room with attractive black laminate tables topped with flowers. **Parking:** on-site. **Cards:** AX, DC, DS, MC, VI.

SAPPORO WIND   Lunch: $6-$14   Dinner: $8-$22   Phone: 614/895-7575   28
Japanese
Location: I-270, exit 27, just s; in the Corporate Exchange Plaza. 6188 Cleveland Ave 43231. **Hours:** 11:30 am-1:30 & 4:30-10 pm, Sat from 4:30 pm, Sun 5 pm-9 pm. Closed: 1/1, 12/25. **Reservations:** suggested. **Features:** casual dress; children's menu; carryout; cocktails; a la carte. The menu outlines an extensive selection of Japanese seafood, with a handful of beef and vegetable dishes. Among the restaurant's features are a sushi bar with step-up service, small rooms with tatami seating and a tastefully decorated main dining room. **Parking:** on-site. **Cards:** AX, CB, DC, DS, MC, VI.

SIAM RESTAURANT   Lunch: $6-$12   Dinner: $9-$12   Phone: 614/451-1109   33
Ethnic
Location: SR 315, exit Bethel Rd, 0.5 mi w; in Olentangy Plaza. 855 Bethel Rd 43214. **Hours:** 11:30 am-10 pm, Fri-11 pm, Sat noon-11 pm, Sun noon-9 pm. Closed major holidays. **Features:** casual dress; children's menu; carryout; cocktails & lounge; a la carte, buffet. Diners determine the degree of spiciness they prefer in preparations of traditional Thai and Chinese dishes. Paintings decorate the walls, while flowers and candles are a romantic touch on the tables. The overall mood is quiet and relaxed. **Parking:** on-site. **Cards:** AX, DC, DS, MC, VI.

(See map p. 636)

SPAGIO
▼▼▼
American

Lunch: $8-$13   **Dinner:** $10-$25   **Phone:** 614/486-1114   (30)
Location: I-70, exit 96, 1 mi n. 1295 Grandview Ave 43212. **Hours:** 11 am-midnight, Fri & Sat-1:30 am. Closed major holidays; also Mon. **Features:** casual dress; carryout; cocktails; a la carte. A large picture window allows indoor diners the same sidewalk views afforded to those who opt to dine on the patio. Bistro-style food, such as wood-fired oven pizza and pasta with smoked chicken, is prepared from scratch with high-quality ingredients. **Parking:** on-site. **Cards:** AX, MC, VI.

The Columbus Vicinity

BEXLEY pop. 13,100   (See map p. 636; index p. 641)

—— WHERE TO DINE ——

BEXLEY'S MONK
▼▼▼
American

Lunch: $7-$12   **Dinner:** $9-$22   **Phone:** 614/239-6665   (74)
Location: I-70, exit 103A, 0.7 mi n, e on Alan Creek. 2232 E Main St 43209. **Hours:** 11:30 am-2:30 & 5:30-10 pm, Fri-11 pm, Sat 5:30 pm-11 pm, Sun from 5:30 pm. Closed major holidays. **Reservations:** suggested. **Features:** casual dress; carryout; cocktails; entertainment; a la carte. Gourmet pizzas cooked in a wood-burning oven are outstanding at the casual restaurant, which also offers pasta, fresh fish and steak on its menu. Paneled walls are decorated with colorful posters. The resident pastry chef creates sinful desserts. **Parking:** on-site and valet. **Cards:** AX, DC, DS, MC, VI.

FISHERMAN'S WHARF
▼▼ ▼
Seafood

Lunch: $7-$11   **Dinner:** $12-$18   **Phone:** 614/236-0043   (73)
Location: I-70, exit 103A, 1 mi ne. 2143 E Main St 43209. **Hours:** 11:30 am-2 & 5-10 pm, Sat from 5 pm, Sun 1 pm-8 pm. **Reservations:** accepted. **Features:** dressy casual; a la carte. On the menu are poultry, lamb and pasta dishes, as well as center-cut steak and fresh seafood. **Parking:** on-site. **Cards:** AX, DC, DS, MC, VI.

CANAL WINCHESTER pop. 2,600

—— WHERE TO STAY ——

AMERIHOST INN COLUMBUS SOUTHEAST
(AAA) (SAVE)
▼▼▼
Motel

Phone: (614)834-4790
All Year [ECP]   1P: $60-$109   2P: $66-$129   XP: $6   F18
Location: US 33, exit Canal Winchester. 6323 Prentiss School Rd 43110. Fax: 614/834-4797. **Facility:** 60 one-bedroom standard units, some with whirlpools. 2 stories, interior corridors. *Bath:* combo or shower only. **Parking:** on-site. **Amenities:** voice mail, safes (fee), irons, hair dryers. **Pool(s):** heated indoor. **Leisure Activities:** whirlpool, exercise room. **Guest Services:** valet laundry. **Business Services:** meeting rooms. **Cards:** AX, DC, DS, JC, MC, VI. **Special Amenities:** free continental breakfast and free newspaper.

SOME UNITS

FEE

CIRCLEVILLE pop. 11,700

—— WHERE TO STAY ——

COMFORT INN CIRCLEVILLE
(SAVE)
▼▼▼
Motel

Phone: (740)477-6116
All Year   1P: $60-$95   2P: $70-$110   XP: $5   F18
Location: Jct US 22 and 23, 2.0 mi s on US 23. 24517 US 23 S 43113. Fax: 740/477-8419. **Facility:** 60 one-bedroom standard units, some with whirlpools. 2 stories, interior corridors. *Bath:* combo or shower only. **Parking:** on-site. **Amenities:** extended cable TV. *Some:* irons, hair dryers. **Pool(s):** outdoor. **Leisure Activities:** exercise room. **Guest Services:** valet and coin laundry. **Business Services:** meeting rooms, fax. **Cards:** AX, CB, DC, DS, JC, MC, VI.

SOME UNITS
FEE

KNIGHTS INN
(AAA) (SAVE)
▼▼
Motel

Phone: 740/474-6006
All Year   1P: $40   2P: $45   XP: $5
Location: 1.5 mi s. 23897 US 23 S 43113. Fax: 740/474-9250. **Facility:** 70 one-bedroom standard units, some with whirlpools. 1 story, exterior corridors. **Parking:** on-site. **Terms:** pets ($5 extra charge, in limited units). **Amenities:** *Some:* hair dryers. **Business Services:** meeting rooms, fax (fee). **Cards:** AX, CB, DC, DS, MC, VI. **Special Amenities:** early check-in/late check-out and free local telephone calls.

SOME UNITS

PENGUIN CROSSING BED AND BREAKFAST
▼▼▼
Historic Bed
& Breakfast

Phone: 740/477-6222
All Year [ECP]   2P: $125-$225   XP: $20   D10
Location: 4.5 mi w. 3291 SR 56 W 43113. Fax: 740/420-6060. **Facility:** This 1820 Federal style red brick farmhouse is located amidst verdant farmland. Hardwood floors and many antiques recreate an historic atmosphere. Smoke free premises. 5 one-bedroom standard units, some with whirlpools. 2 stories, interior corridors. *Bath:* combo or shower only. **Parking:** on-site. **Terms:** check-in 4 pm, 14 day cancellation notice-fee imposed, package plans. **Amenities:** video tape library, dual phone lines, hair dryers. *Some:* CD players. **Cards:** AX, DS, MC, VI.

SOME UNITS

——— **WHERE TO DINE** ———

J R HOOKS CAFE
▼▼ ▼▼
Regional American
Lunch: $6-$8   **Dinner:** $9-$16   **Phone:** 740/474-2158
Location: Main St, just n on Court St, then just e. 115 Watt St 43113. **Hours:** 11 am-11 pm, Fri & Sat-midnight. Closed major holidays; also Sun. **Reservations:** accepted. **Features:** casual dress; children's menu; early bird specials; carryout; cocktails. Some Cajun cuisine intertwines with selections of prime rib, pasta, steak and seafood. Mirrors, etched glass and art deco stylings, including New Orleans-variety paintings and photographs, add character to the relaxed, hospitable dining room. **Parking:** on-site. **Cards:** AX, DC, MC, VI.   ⊠

DELAWARE pop. 20,000

——— **WHERE TO STAY** ———

AMERIHOST INN & SUITES-DELAWARE
(AAA) [SAVE]
▼▼▼▼
Motel
Phone: (740)363-3510
All Year [CP]   1P: $84   2P: $84
Location: I-270, exit 23, 11 mi n on US 23. 1720 Columbus Pike 43015. Fax: 740/363-1677. **Facility:** 73 one-bedroom standard units, some with whirlpools. 2 stories, interior corridors. **Bath:** combo or shower only. **Parking:** on-site. **Terms:** 10 day cancellation notice. **Amenities:** extended cable TV, voice mail, safes (fee), irons, hair dryers. **Pool(s):** heated indoor. **Leisure Activities:** sauna, whirlpool, exercise room. **Guest Services:** valet laundry. **Business Services:** meeting rooms. **Cards:** AX, CB, DC, DS, JC, MC, VI.
Special Amenities: free continental breakfast and free newspaper.
SOME UNITS
[icons]

BEST WESTERN DELAWARE HOTEL
▼▼ ▼▼
Motor Inn
Phone: (740)363-1262
All Year [CP]   1P: $69-$85   2P: $69-$85   XP: $5
Location: 0.5 mi e. 351 S Sandusky St 43015. Fax: 740/363-4027. **Facility:** 101 one-bedroom standard units. 4 stories, interior corridors. **Parking:** on-site. **Terms:** [BP] meal plan available, package plans, pets ($15-$25 deposit). **Amenities:** extended cable TV. **Leisure Activities:** sauna, whirlpool, exercise room. **Guest Services:** valet and coin laundry. **Business Services:** meeting rooms. **Cards:** AX, DC, DS, MC, VI.
SOME UNITS
[icons]

SUPER 8 MOTEL
▼▼ ▼▼
Motel
Phone: (740)363-8869
All Year   1P: $60   2P: $65   XP: $5   F12
Location: 1.5 mi s on US 23; at Delaware Square Shopping Center. 1251 Columbus Pike 43015. Fax: 740/363-8869. **Facility:** 57 units. 55 one-bedroom standard units. 2 one-bedroom suites ($96-$126) with whirlpools. 3 stories, interior corridors. **Bath:** combo or shower only. **Parking:** on-site. **Terms:** [ECP] meal plan available. **Amenities:** extended cable TV. *Some:* irons, hair dryers. **Pool(s):** heated indoor. **Leisure Activities:** whirlpool. **Business Services:** meeting rooms. **Cards:** AX, CB, DC, DS, MC, VI.
SOME UNITS
[icons]

TRAVELODGE
(AAA) [SAVE]
▼▼
Motel
Phone: 740/369-4421
9/1-9/24   1P: $60-$150   2P: $60-$150   XP: $10   F16
4/1-8/31 & 9/25-3/31   1P: $38-$85   2P: $48-$85   XP: $10   F16
Location: 0.5 mi n of downtown. 1001 US Rt 23 N 43015. Fax: 740/362-9090. **Facility:** 31 one-bedroom standard units. 2 stories, interior/exterior corridors. **Parking:** on-site. **Terms:** cancellation fee imposed, [CP] meal plan available, pets ($10 extra charge). **Amenities:** extended cable TV. **Guest Services:** valet laundry. **Cards:** AX, DC, DS, MC, VI.
SOME UNITS
[icons]

——— **WHERE TO DINE** ———

BUN'S RESTAURANT/BAKERY
(AAA)
▼▼ ▼▼
American
Lunch: $6-$8   **Dinner:** $9-$16   **Phone:** 740/363-3731
Location: Just off US 23 business route. 6 W Winter St 43015. **Hours:** 11 am-7 pm, Fri & Sat-10 pm. Closed major holidays; also Mon. **Reservations:** accepted; for dinner. **Features:** casual dress; children's menu; carryout; cocktails. Established in 1864, the Victorian-flavor restaurant is decorated with fancy chandeliers and attractive carpet. Steaks, ham loaf and meatloaf are representative of menu offerings. Fudge cake and chocolate eclairs are made in the on-premises bakery. **Parking:** on-site. **Cards:** AX, DC, MC, VI.   ⊠

DUBLIN pop. 16,400   (See map p. 636; index p. 638)

——— **WHERE TO STAY** ———

AMERISUITES-COLUMBUS/DUBLIN
(AAA) [SAVE]
▼▼▼▼
Motel
Phone: (614)799-1913   [24]
All Year [ECP]   1P: $98   2P: $108   XP: $10   F17
Location: I-270, exit 15 (Tuttle Crossing), just e. 6161 Park Center Cir 43016. Fax: 614/799-8115. **Facility:** 124 one-bedroom standard units. 6 stories, interior corridors. **Bath:** combo or shower only. **Parking:** on-site. **Terms:** 3 day cancellation notice, package plans, pets ($50 deposit). **Amenities:** extended cable TV, high-speed Internet, dual phone lines, voice mail, irons, hair dryers. **Pool(s):** heated outdoor. **Leisure Activities:** exercise room. **Guest Services:** valet and coin laundry, area transportation-within 5 mi. **Business Services:** meeting rooms. **Cards:** AX, CB, DC, DS, MC, VI. **Special Amenities: free continental breakfast and free newspaper.**
(See color ad p 642)
SOME UNITS
[icons]

(See map p. 636)

BAYMONT INN & SUITES COLUMBUS-DUBLIN

Phone: (614)792-8300 **20**

AAA (SAVE) ♦♦ Motel

All Year 1P: $74-$84 2P: $74-$84
Location: I-270, exit 15 (Tuttle Crossing), just e. 6145 Park Center Cir 43017. Fax: 614/792-3333. **Facility:** 100 one-bedroom standard units. 4 stories, interior corridors. *Bath:* combo or shower only. **Parking:** on-site. **Terms:** pets ($50 deposit). **Amenities:** video games, voice mail, irons, hair dryers. **Leisure Activities:** exercise room. **Guest Services:** valet and coin laundry. **Business Services:** meeting rooms. **Cards:** AX, CB, DC, DS, MC, VI. **Special Amenities:** free continental breakfast and free newspaper.
(See color ad opposite title page)

SOME UNITS

COLUMBUS MARRIOTT NORTHWEST

Phone: (614)791-1000 **15**

AAA (SAVE) ♦♦♦♦ Hotel

5/1-3/31 1P: $159-$179 2P: $159-$179
4/1-4/30 1P: $155-$175 2P: $155-$175
Location: I-270, exit 15 (Tuttle Crossing), 0.3 mi e. 5605 Paul Blazer Memorial Pkwy 43017. Fax: 614/791-1001. **Facility:** 303 units. 297 one-bedroom standard units. 6 one-bedroom suites ($269-$319), some with whirlpools. 7 stories, interior corridors. *Bath:* combo or shower only. **Parking:** on-site. **Terms:** package plans, small pets only. **Amenities:** dual phone lines, voice mail, irons, hair dryers. **Dining:** restaurant, 6:30 am-10:30 pm, $14-$18, cocktails. **Pool(s):** heated indoor. **Leisure Activities:** exercise room. **Guest Services:** valet and coin laundry. **Business Services:** conference facilities, business center, PC, fax. **Cards:** AX, CB, DC, DS, JC, MC, VI.
(See color ad card insert)

SOME UNITS

COURTYARD BY MARRIOTT-DUBLIN

Phone: (614)764-9393 **22**

AAA (SAVE) ♦♦♦ Motel

All Year 1P: $112 2P: $112
Location: I-270, exit 17A, just e. 5175 Post Rd 43017. Fax: 614/764-9825. **Facility:** 147 units. 135 one-bedroom standard units. 12 one-bedroom suites ($140). 2-3 stories, interior corridors. *Bath:* combo or shower only. **Parking:** on-site. **Terms:** [AP] meal plan available. **Amenities:** voice mail, irons, hair dryers. **Dining:** coffee shop, 6:30-10:30 am, Sat & Sun 7 am-noon. **Pool(s):** heated indoor. **Leisure Activities:** whirlpool, exercise room. **Guest Services:** valet and coin laundry. **Business Services:** meeting rooms, fax (fee). **Cards:** AX, DC, DS, MC, VI. *(See color ad card insert)*

SOME UNITS

CROSS COUNTRY INN NORTHWEST

Phone: (614)764-4545 **19** F17

AAA (SAVE) ♦♦ Motel

All Year 1P: $39-$46 2P: $46-$53 XP: $2
Location: I-270, exit 17A, 0.5 mi e to Frantz Rd, 0.3 mi s. 6364 Frantz Rd 43017. Fax: 614/764-0520. **Facility:** 112 one-bedroom standard units. 2 stories, exterior corridors. *Bath:* combo or shower only. **Parking:** on-site. **Amenities:** voice mail. **Pool(s):** heated outdoor. **Business Services:** meeting rooms. **Cards:** AX, CB, DC, DS, MC, VI. **Special Amenities:** free local telephone calls and preferred room (subject to availability with advanced reservations).

SOME UNITS

HILTON GARDEN INN

Phone: (614)766-9900 **14** F17

AAA (SAVE) ♦♦♦ Motor Inn

All Year 1P: $99-$179 2P: $99-$179 XP: $10
Location: I-270, exit 17A, just se. 500 Metro Place N 43017. Fax: 614/766-1889. **Facility:** 100 one-bedroom standard units. 4 stories, interior corridors. *Bath:* combo or shower only. **Parking:** on-site. **Terms:** cancellation fee imposed. **Amenities:** video games, dual phone lines, voice mail, irons, hair dryers. **Dining:** dining room, 6:30 am-10 & 5-9 pm, $6-$15, cocktails. **Pool(s):** heated indoor. **Leisure Activities:** exercise room. **Guest Services:** valet and coin laundry. **Business Services:** meeting rooms, business center, PC, fax. **Cards:** AX, DC, DS, JC, MC, VI. **Special Amenities:** early check-in/late check-out and free newspaper. *(See color ad below)*

SOME UNITS

Kids under 18 stay free in their parents' or grandparents' room. Your valid AAA membership card is required for reservation and at check-in. Rates may not apply to all rooms, groups or other offers and are exclusive of tax and gratuities. Rates based on sgl/dbl occupancy, standard rooms only. Subject to availability. Rates confirmed at time of reservation. ©2002 Hilton Hospitality, Inc.

(See map p. 636)

RED ROOF INN-DUBLIN
Phone: (614)764-3993   **21**

6/30-9/7	1P: $49-$66	2P: $56-$73	XP: $7	F18
4/1-6/29	1P: $45-$69	2P: $56-$69	XP: $7	F18
9/8-3/31	1P: $45-$59	2P: $52-$66	XP: $3	F18

Motel

Location: I-270, exit 17A, just ne. 5125 Post Rd 43017. **Fax:** 614/764-0698. **Facility:** 106 one-bedroom standard units. 2 stories, exterior corridors. *Bath:* combo or shower only. **Parking:** on-site. **Terms:** small pets only. **Amenities:** video games, voice mail. **Guest Services:** valet laundry. **Cards:** AX, CB, DC, DS, MC, VI. **Special Amenities:** free local telephone calls and free newspaper.

SOME UNITS

RESIDENCE INN BY MARRIOTT
Phone: (614)791-0403   **23**

All Year [ECP]   1P: $119-$149

Apartment

Location: I-270, exit 17A, 0.5 mi s to Frantz Rd, 0.5 mi w. 435 Metro Place S 43017. **Fax:** 614/791-9224. **Facility:** 106 units. 82 one-bedroom standard units. 24 one-bedroom suites. 2 stories, interior/exterior corridors. *Bath:* combo or shower only. **Parking:** on-site. **Terms:** package plans, pets ($100 deposit). **Amenities:** extended cable TV, video games, voice mail, irons, hair dryers. **Pool(s):** heated outdoor. **Leisure Activities:** whirlpool, exercise room, sports court. **Guest Services:** valet and coin laundry, area transportation-within 5 mi. **Business Services:** meeting rooms, business center. **Cards:** AX, CB, DC, DS, JC, MC, VI. *(See color ad card insert)*

SOME UNITS

WELLESLEY INN & SUITES (COLUMBUS/DUBLIN)
Phone: (614)760-0245   **17**

All Year   1P: $69-$99   2P: $69-$99

Motel

Location: I-270, exit 15, 0.3 mi w. 5530 Tuttle Crossing Blvd 43016. **Fax:** 614/760-0431. **Facility:** 82 units. 80 one-bedroom standard units with efficiencies (no utensils). 2 one-bedroom suites with efficiencies (no utensils). 3 stories, interior corridors. *Bath:* combo or shower only. **Terms:** [ECP] meal plan available. **Amenities:** video games, dual phone lines, voice mail, irons, hair dryers. **Leisure Activities:** exercise room. **Guest Services:** valet and coin laundry. **Business Services:** meeting rooms. **Cards:** AX, DC, DS, MC, VI. **Special Amenities:** free continental breakfast and free newspaper. *(See color ad p 643)*

SOME UNITS

WOODFIN SUITES HOTEL
Phone: (614)766-7762   **18**

All Year [BP]   1P: $99-$150   XP: $10   F12

Apartment

Location: I-270, exit 20, 0.3 mi s on Sawmill Rd via Dublin Center Dr. 4130 Tuller Rd 43017. **Fax:** 614/761-1906. **Facility:** 88 units. 8 one-bedroom standard units. 72 one- and 8 two-bedroom suites with kitchens. 2 stories, exterior corridors. **Parking:** on-site. **Terms:** check-in 4 pm, package plans, pets ($50 fee). **Amenities:** extended cable TV, video tape library, voice mail, safes, irons, hair dryers. *Some:* CD players. **Pool(s):** heated outdoor. **Leisure Activities:** whirlpool. **Guest Services:** complimentary evening beverages: Mon-Thurs, valet and coin laundry. **Business Services:** meeting rooms, business center, PC, fax. **Cards:** AX, CB, DC, DS, JC, MC, VI.

SOME UNITS

WYNDHAM DUBLIN
Phone: (614)764-2200   **16**

9/3-3/31	1P: $99-$154	2P: $109-$154	XP: $10	F18
4/1-9/2	1P: $99-$149	2P: $109-$149	XP: $10	F18

Motor Inn

Location: I-270, exit 17A, 0.5 mi s, then 0.5 mi nw. 600 Metro Place N 43017. **Fax:** 614/764-1213. **Facility:** 217 units. 216 one-bedroom standard units. 1 one-bedroom suite. 3 stories, interior corridors. **Parking:** on-site. **Terms:** cancellation fee imposed, package plans, pets ($50 fee). **Amenities:** extended cable TV, high-speed Internet, voice mail, irons, hair dryers. **Dining:** dining room, 6:30 am-10 pm, $10-$18, cocktails. **Pool(s):** heated indoor. **Leisure Activities:** exercise room. **Guest Services:** valet laundry, area transportation-within 5 mi. **Business Services:** conference facilities, fax. **Cards:** AX, CB, DC, DS, JC, MC, VI.

SOME UNITS

———— **WHERE TO DINE** ————

ANNA'S RESTAURANT
Lunch: $6-$9   **Dinner:** $10-$17   **Phone:** 614/799-2207   **21**

Greek

Location: I-270, exit 20, 0.5 mi s. 7370 Sawmill Center 43235. **Hours:** 11 am-9 pm. Closed major holidays; also Sun. **Features:** dressy casual; children's menu; carryout; cocktails. A good selection of Greek dishes including appetizers, lamb and chicken entrees, casseroles, gyros and moussaka, is available at Anna's, located inside a small shopping center. The portions are ample and the service staff friendly and prompt. Smoke free premises. **Parking:** on-site. **Cards:** AX, DS, MC, VI.

BRAVO! ITALIAN KITCHEN
Lunch: $8-$13   **Dinner:** $10-$18   **Phone:** 614/791-1245   **19**

Italian

Location: SR 315, 3 mi w on Bethel and Hayden rds. 3000 Hayden Rd 43235. **Hours:** 11 am-10 pm, Fri & Sat-11 pm, Sun-9:30 pm. Closed: 1/1, 11/28, 12/25. **Reservations:** accepted. **Features:** casual dress; children's menu; carryout; cocktails; a la carte. Imagine classic pasta dishes, pizza and wood-grilled meats cooked and served in a bustling atmosphere. Your choice of delicious pizza toppings includes smoked chicken, caramelized onions and feta cheese. Be sure to try the complimentary Italian bread. **Parking:** on-site. **Cards:** AX, CB, DC, DS, MC, VI.

CHILE VERDE CAFE
Lunch: $6-$9   **Dinner:** $7-$16   **Phone:** 614/442-6630   **18**

Regional American

Location: I-270, exit 20, 3 mi s; at corner of Sawmill and Bethel rds. 4852 Sawmill Rd 43235. **Hours:** 11 am-9 pm, Fri-10 pm, Sat noon-10 pm. Closed major holidays; also Sun. **Features:** casual dress; children's menu; carryout; cocktails. Authentic New Mexican cooking, such as blue corn enchiladas, crab cakes, homemade salsa, fajitas and chimichangas with mushroom sauce, attracts the family and young professional crowd. Margaritas are the only cocktails. Smoke free premises. **Parking:** on-site. **Cards:** AX, CB, DC, DS, MC, VI.

(See map p. 636)

HYDE PARK GRILLE
▼▼▼▼
Steak House
Dinner: $14-$29   **Phone: 614/717-2828**   16
Location: I-270, exit 17A, just s. 6360 Frantz Rd 43017. **Hours:** 5 pm-10 pm, Fri & Sat-11 pm. Closed major holidays; also Sun. **Reservations:** suggested. **Features:** dressy casual; carryout; cocktails & lounge; a la carte. Many steaks are named after Ohio State University football stars at the quiet, clublike restaurant, a favorite with the locals. Wood-paneled walls and exposed beams add to the upscale feel of the dining room. Service is prompt and professional. Smoke free premises. **Parking:** on-site and valet. **Cards:** AX, CB, DC, DS, MC, VI. ✕

MORETTI'S CAFE
▼▼ ▼▼
Italian
Dinner: $9-$15   **Phone: 614/717-0400**   17
Location: I-270, exit 20, 1.5 mi s. 5849 Sawmill Rd 43017. **Hours:** 5 pm-10 pm, Fri & Sat-11 pm. Closed major holidays; also Sun. **Reservations:** accepted; weekends. **Features:** casual dress; carryout; cocktails; a la carte. Pasta and veal specialties are offered at this eatery. **Parking:** on-site. **Cards:** AX, MC, VI. ✕

THE MORGAN HOUSE RESTAURANT
▼▼ ▼▼
American
Lunch: $6-$8   **Phone: 614/889-5703**   14
Location: I-270, exit 17A, 1 mi e to SR 745 (N High St/Dublin Rd), 3.5 mi n. 5300 Glick Rd 43017. **Hours:** 11 am-3 pm, Sun noon-3 pm. Closed major holidays. **Features:** casual dress; children's menu; carryout. Two fireplaces add warmth and charm to the cozy restored log cabin, which is decorated in country furnishings. The menu centers on light fare, with soup, salad, quiche and sandwiches. Made from scratch desserts include cheesecake, pie and cobbler. Smoke free premises. **Parking:** on-site. **Cards:** DS, MC, VI. ✕

OSCAR'S OF DUBLIN
▼▼ ▼▼
American
Lunch: $7-$9   **Dinner: $11-$18**   **Phone: 614/792-3424**   15
Location: I-270, exit 17A, 1 mi e on SR 161, just n. 84 N High St 43017. **Hours:** 11:30 am-2:30 & 5-10 pm, Fri & Sat-11 pm. Closed major holidays; also Sun. **Reservations:** suggested. **Features:** dressy casual; carryout; cocktails & lounge; a la carte. Superior ingredients and innovative techniques make this eatery's menu of beef, pork, veal, pasta and seafood a creatively tasty experience. Located in Old Dublin inside a restored house, Oscar's makes dining an art form. California wines are served. **Parking:** on-site. **Cards:** AX, DC, DS, MC, VI. ✕

THAI ORCHID
▼▼ ▼▼
Ethnic
Lunch: $6-$7   **Dinner: $8-$13**   **Phone: 614/792-1112**   13
Location: I-270, exit 20, 1 mi n. 7654 Sawmill Rd 43016. **Hours:** 11 am-2:30 & 4:30-10 pm, Sun 4:30 pm-9 pm. **Reservations:** accepted. **Features:** casual dress; carryout; cocktails & lounge; a la carte. Extensive choices are outlined on a menu that includes piquant Thai and South Chinese dishes of beef, seafood, chicken and pork. A light cucumber-onion sauce is a nice complement to the chicken patty appetizer, fried with minced scallions. Smoke free premises. **Parking:** on-site. **Cards:** AX, DC, DS, MC, VI. ✕

GAHANNA pop. 27,800   (See map p. 636; index p. 641)

———— WHERE TO STAY ————

SPRINGHILL SUITES BY MARRIOTT
AAA SAVE
▼▼▼▼
Motel
Phone: (614)501-4770   105
All Year [ECP]   1P: $89-$115   2P: $89-$115
Location: I-270, exit 37, just se. 665 Taylor Rd 43230. Fax: 614/501-4750. **Facility:** 80 one-bedroom standard units. 3 stories. *Bath:* combo or shower only. **Parking:** on-site. **Amenities:** extended cable TV, voice mail, irons, hair dryers. **Pool(s):** heated indoor. **Leisure Activities:** whirlpool, exercise room. **Guest Services:** valet laundry. **Business Services:** meeting rooms. **Cards:** AX, CB, DC, DS, MC, VI. **Special Amenities:** free continental breakfast and free local telephone calls. *(See color ad card insert)*

SOME UNITS

🛆 🛏 📺 DATAPORT 🍴 🖥 📋 🖨 / ✕ /

TOWNEPLACE SUITES BY MARRIOTT
AAA SAVE
▼▼ ▼▼
Extended Stay
Motel
Phone: (614)861-1400   106
4/28-12/31   1P: $109-$129
4/1-4/27   1P: $95-$115
1/1-3/31   1P: $99-$114
Location: I-270, exit 37, just w to Morrison Rd, just s to Taylor Rd, then just w. 695 Taylor Rd 43230. Fax: 614/861-0067. **Facility:** 95 units. 69 one-bedroom standard units with kitchens. 4 one- and 22 two-bedroom suites with efficiencies. 3 stories, interior corridors. *Bath:* combo or shower only. **Parking:** on-site. **Terms:** pets ($75-$125 extra charge). **Amenities:** extended cable TV, dual phone lines, voice mail, irons, hair dryers. **Leisure Activities:** exercise room. **Guest Services:** coin laundry. **Business Services:** fax. **Cards:** AX, DC, DS, JC, MC, VI. **Special Amenities:** free local telephone calls. *(See color ad card insert)*

SOME UNITS

🅂🄳 🐾 🛆 🍳 📺 DATAPORT 🍴 🖥 📋 🖨 / ✕ VCR / FEE

———— WHERE TO DINE ————

MONTANA MINING COMPANY
STEAKHOUSE & SALOON
▼
Steak House
Lunch: $7-$14   **Dinner: $7-$14**   **Phone: 614/428-2885**   65
Location: I-270, exit 37, just s; at jct of Morrison and Taylor rds. 550 Office Center Place 43230. **Hours:** 11 am-9 pm. Closed major holidays. **Features:** casual dress; carryout; cocktails & lounge. **Parking:** on-site. **Cards:** AX, DC, DS, MC, VI. ✕

GRANVILLE pop. 4,400

———— WHERE TO DINE ————

BUXTON INN-1812   Historical
▼▼ ▼▼
American
Lunch: $6-$8   **Dinner: $13-$23**   **Phone: 740/587-0001**
Location: Town center. 313 E Broadway 43023. **Hours:** 11:30 am-2 & 5:30-9 pm, Fri & Sat-10 pm, Sun 11 am-3 & 4-8 pm. Closed major holidays; also Mon. **Reservations:** suggested. **Features:** dressy casual; Sunday brunch; children's menu; carryout; cocktails. Built in 1812, the former stagecoach tavern sits in the center of the quiet college town. The menu comprises mostly standard fare, seafood, chicken and steak entrees, with a few specialties like roast duck. Courtyard dining is popular in season. **Parking:** on-site. **Cards:** AX, DS, MC, VI. ✕

GROVE CITY   pop. 19,700   (See map p. 636; index p. 641)

—— WHERE TO STAY ——

BEST WESTERN EXECUTIVE INN

AAA SAVE

♦♦♦

Motel

			Phone: (614)875-7770	89
11/1-3/31 [CP]	1P: $62-$68	2P: $68-$72	XP: $5	F12
4/1-10/31 [CP]	1P: $52-$57	2P: $57-$62	XP: $5	F12

Location: I-71, exit 100, just e. 4026 Jackpot Rd 43123. Fax: 614/875-2202. **Facility:** 50 one-bedroom standard units. 2 stories, exterior corridors. **Parking:** on-site. **Terms:** small pets only ($8 extra charge, dogs only). **Amenities:** extended cable TV, irons, hair dryers. **Pool(s):** outdoor. **Leisure Activities:** exercise room. **Guest Services:** coin laundry. **Cards:** AX, CB, DC, DS, MC, VI. **Special Amenities:** free continental breakfast and free local telephone calls.

SOME UNITS

COMFORT INN

AAA SAVE

♦♦♦

Motel

| | | | Phone: 614/539-3500 | 86 |
| All Year [CP] | 1P: $60-$119 | 2P: $68-$119 | XP: $8 | F16 |

Location: I-71, exit 100, just sw. 4197 Marlane Dr 43123. Fax: 614/539-3510. **Facility:** 60 one-bedroom standard units, some with whirlpools. 3 stories, interior corridors. *Bath:* combo or shower only. **Parking:** on-site. **Amenities:** extended cable TV, irons, hair dryers. **Pool(s):** heated indoor. **Leisure Activities:** sauna, whirlpool, exercise room. **Guest Services:** coin laundry. **Business Services:** meeting rooms. **Cards:** AX, CB, DC, DS, JC, MC, VI.

SOME UNITS

CROSS COUNTRY INN SOUTHWEST

AAA SAVE

♦♦♦

Motel

| | | | Phone: (614)871-9617 | 87 |
| All Year | 1P: $43-$50 | 2P: $49-$56 | XP: $2 | F17 |

Location: I-71, exit 100, 1.3 mi s of jct I-270. 4055 Jackpot Rd 43123. Fax: 614/871-0740. **Facility:** 120 one-bedroom standard units. 2 stories, exterior corridors. *Bath:* combo or shower only. **Pool(s):** heated outdoor. **Cards:** AX, CB, DC, DS, MC, VI. **Special Amenities:** free local telephone calls and preferred room (subject to availability with advanced reservations).

SOME UNITS
FEE

HAMPTON INN COLUMBUS SOUTH

SAVE

♦♦♦

Motel

| | | | Phone: 614/539-1177 | 83 |
| All Year [ECP] | 1P: $71 | 2P: $80 | |

Location: I-71, exit 100, 1.3 mi s of jct I-270. 4017 Jackpot Rd 43123. Fax: 614/539-0110. **Facility:** 57 one-bedroom standard units. 2 stories, interior corridors. *Bath:* combo or shower only. **Parking:** on-site. **Amenities:** extended cable TV, video games, dual phone lines, voice mail, irons, hair dryers. **Pool(s):** small heated outdoor. **Leisure Activities:** whirlpool. **Cards:** AX, CB, DC, DS, MC, VI.

SOME UNITS
FEE

HILTON GARDEN INN COLUMBUS/GROVE CITY

AAA SAVE

♦♦♦

Motel

| | | | Phone: (614)539-8944 | 90 |
| All Year | 1P: $59-$99 | 2P: $59-$99 | XP: $10 | F18 |

Location: I-71, exit 100, just e. 3928 Jackpot Rd 43123. Fax: 614/539-8956. **Facility:** 88 one-bedroom standard units. 3 stories, interior corridors. *Bath:* combo or shower only. **Parking:** on-site. **Terms:** cancellation fee imposed. **Amenities:** extended cable TV, video games, dual phone lines, voice mail, irons, hair dryers. **Dining:** coffee shop, 6-10 am. **Pool(s):** heated indoor. **Leisure Activities:** exercise room. **Business Services:** meeting rooms, business center, PC, fax. **Cards:** AX, DC, DS, JC, MC, VI. **Special Amenities:** free local telephone calls and free newspaper.

SOME UNITS
FEE

RED ROOF INN-SOUTH COLUMBUS

AAA SAVE

♦♦♦

Motel

			Phone: (614)875-8543	84
5/5-11/2	1P: $47-$69	2P: $52-$74	XP: $5	F18
11/3-3/31	1P: $41-$58	2P: $46-$63	XP: $5	F18
4/1-5/4	1P: $41-$56	2P: $46-$61	XP: $5	F18

Location: I-71, exit 100, just w. 1900 Stringtown Rd 43123. Fax: 614/875-8585. **Facility:** 106 one-bedroom standard units. 2 stories, exterior corridors. *Bath:* combo or shower only. **Parking:** on-site. **Terms:** small pets only. **Amenities:** video games, voice mail. **Cards:** AX, CB, DC, DS, MC, VI. **Special Amenities:** free local telephone calls and free newspaper.

SOME UNITS
FEE

(See map p. 636)

SUPER 8 MOTEL

Phone: 614/539-6200   [88]

AAA **SAVE**
▽▽▽▽

Motel

All Year [ECP]   1P: $50-$60   2P: $70-$80   XP: $10   F17
Location: I-71, exit 100, just ne. 3962 Jackpot Rd 43123. Fax: 614/539-6211. **Facility:** 60 one-bedroom standard units, some with whirlpools. 3 stories, interior corridors. *Bath:* combo or shower only. **Parking:** on-site. **Terms:** 30 day cancellation notice. **Amenities:** extended cable TV, irons, hair dryers. **Pool(s):** heated indoor. **Leisure Activities:** sauna, whirlpool, exercise room. **Guest Services:** coin laundry. **Business Services:** meeting rooms, business center. **Cards:** AX, CB, DC, DS, MC, VI. **Special Amenities:** free continental breakfast and free local telephone calls. *(See ad p 662)*

SOME UNITS

🅂🄳 🍽️ 🏊 ⊠ 🐾 📠 🚪 🖨️ / ⊠ 🖨️ /
FEE

HEATH pop. 7,200

——— WHERE TO STAY ———

HOLIDAY INN EXPRESS HOTEL & SUITES

Phone: (740)522-0770

▽▽▽▽
Motel

All Year   1P: $99-$139   2P: $109-$169   XP: $10   F16
Location: I-70, exit 129B, 7 mi on SR 79. 773 Hebron Rd 43056. Fax: 740/522-0088. **Facility:** 63 one-bedroom standard units. 4 stories, interior corridors. *Bath:* combo or shower only. **Parking:** on-site. **Terms:** cancellation fee imposed, [BP] meal plan available. **Amenities:** voice mail, irons, hair dryers. **Leisure Activities:** whirlpool, exercise room. **Guest Services:** coin laundry. **Business Services:** business center, PC. **Cards:** AX, DC, DS, JC, MC, VI.

SOME UNITS

🄰🅂🄺 🅂🄳 📠 💻 🖨️ / ⊠ 🆅🄲🆁 🚪 🖨️ /

RAMADA INN NEWARK/HEATH

Phone: (740)522-1165

AAA **SAVE**
▽▽▽▽

Motor Inn

All Year [CP]   1P: $59-$99   2P: $69-$110   XP: $10   F12
Location: I-70, exit 129B, 7 mi n on SR 79. 733 Hebron Rd 43056. Fax: 740/522-6420. **Facility:** 107 one-bedroom standard units. 2 stories, exterior corridors. **Parking:** on-site. **Terms:** 14 day cancellation notice, [AP] meal plan available, small pets only ($5 extra charge). **Amenities:** extended cable TV, voice mail, irons, hair dryers. **Dining:** dining room, 6 am-10 pm, Sat & Sun from 7 am, $6-$15, cocktails. **Pool(s):** heated outdoor. **Leisure Activities:** exercise room. **Guest Services:** valet and coin laundry. **Business Services:** meeting rooms. **Cards:** AX, DC, DS, MC, VI.

SOME UNITS

🅂🄳 🐾 🍽️ 🍸 🏊 🐾 📠 🚪 💻 🖨️ / ⊠ /

HEBRON pop. 3,200

——— WHERE TO STAY ———

AMERIHOST INN & SUITES-NEWARK/HEBRON

Phone: (740)928-1800

AAA **SAVE**
▽▽▽▽

Motel

4/1-10/31 [CP]   1P: $90-$185   2P: $90-$185   XP: $5   F17
11/1-3/31 [CP]   1P: $75-$165   2P: $75-$165   XP: $5   F17
Location: I-70, exit 129B, 1 mi n on US 79. 122 Arrowhead Blvd 43025. Fax: 740/928-1899. **Facility:** 72 one-bedroom standard units, some with whirlpools. 2 stories, interior corridors. *Bath:* combo or shower only. **Parking:** on-site. **Amenities:** extended cable TV, voice mail, safes (fee), irons, hair dryers. **Pool(s):** heated indoor. **Leisure Activities:** whirlpool, exercise room. **Guest Services:** valet laundry. **Business Services:** meeting rooms. **Cards:** AX, CB, DC, DS, JC, MC, VI. **Special Amenities:** free continental breakfast and free newspaper.

SOME UNITS

🅂🄳 🅖🄼 🐾 🏊 🐾 📠 💻 🖨️ / ⊠ 🚪 🖨️ /
FEE

HILLIARD pop. 11,800   (See map p. 636; index p. 641)

——— WHERE TO STAY ———

COMFORT SUITES

Phone: (614)529-8118   [101]

SAVE
▽▽▽▽
Motel

All Year [CP]   1P: $88-$98   2P: $88-$98   XP: $5   F17
Location: I-270, exit 13A northbound; exit 13 southbound. 3831 Park Mill Run Dr 43026. Fax: 614/529-8118. **Facility:** 60 one-bedroom standard units. 3 stories, interior corridors. *Bath:* combo or shower only. **Parking:** on-site. **Terms:** 3 day cancellation notice, pets ($20 extra charge). **Amenities:** extended cable TV. **Pool(s):** heated indoor. **Leisure Activities:** whirlpool. *Fee:* game room. **Guest Services:** valet laundry. **Business Services:** meeting rooms. **Cards:** AX, CB, DC, DS, JC, MC, VI.

SOME UNITS

🅂🄳 🐾 🍽️ 🅖🄼 🚫 🎮 🏊 🐾 📠 🚪 🖨️ 💻 🖨️ / ⊠ /
FEE

HOMEWOOD SUITES BY HILTON-COLUMBUS/HILLIARD

Phone: (614)529-4100   [102]

SAVE
▽▽▽▽

Extended Stay Motel

All Year [ECP]   1P: $109-$129   2P: $129-$149
Location: I-270, exit 13 southbound; exit 13A northbound. 3841 Park Mill Run Dr 43026. Fax: 614/850-9170. **Facility:** 66 units. 58 one- and 8 two-bedroom suites. 3 stories, interior corridors. *Bath:* combo or shower only. **Parking:** on-site. **Terms:** 7 day cancellation notice, package plans, pets ($45 fee, $10 extra charge). **Amenities:** extended cable TV, video games, voice mail, irons, hair dryers. **Pool(s):** heated indoor. **Leisure Activities:** whirlpool, exercise room, sports court. **Guest Services:** gift shop, complimentary evening beverages: Mon-Thurs, coin laundry. **Business Services:** meeting rooms, business center, PC. **Cards:** AX, CB, DC, DS, JC, MC, VI.

SOME UNITS

🅂🄳 🐾 🍽️ 🅖🄼 🚫 🎮 🏊 ⊠ 🆅🄲🆁 🐾 📠 🚪 🖨️ 💻 🖨️ / ⊠ /
FEE

LANCASTER pop. 34,500

——— WHERE TO STAY ———

AMERIHOST INN-LANCASTER
◇◇◇ SAVE
▼▼▼
Motel

All Year [ECP]	1P: $72-$99	2P: $72-$99	XP: $6 F18

Phone: (740)654-5111

Location: 2.5 mi nw on US 33; adjacent to River Valley Mall. 1721 River Valley Cir N 43130. Fax: 740/654-5108. **Facility:** 60 one-bedroom standard units, some with whirlpools. 2 stories, interior corridors. *Bath:* combo or shower only. **Parking:** on-site. **Terms:** 3 day cancellation notice. **Amenities:** extended cable TV, voice mail, safes (fee), irons, hair dryers. **Pool(s):** heated indoor. **Leisure Activities:** whirlpool. **Guest Services:** valet laundry. **Business Services:** meeting rooms. **Cards:** AX, CB, DC, DS, JC, MC, VI. **Special Amenities:** free continental breakfast and free newspaper.

SOME UNITS

BEST WESTERN LANCASTER INN
◇◇◇ SAVE
▼▼ ▼▼
Motor Inn

6/1-8/31 [BP]	1P: $65-$79	2P: $75-$85	XP: $7 F18
9/1-3/31 [BP]	1P: $63-$70	2P: $67-$72	XP: $7 F18
4/1-5/31 [BP]	1P: $63-$70	2P: $65-$70	XP: $7 F18

Phone: (740)653-3040

Location: 2 mi nw on US 33. 1858 N Memorial Dr 43130. Fax: 740/653-1172. **Facility:** 168 one-bedroom standard units. 2 stories, interior/exterior corridors. *Bath:* combo or shower only. **Parking:** on-site. **Terms:** check-in 4 pm, 3 day cancellation notice, [AP] meal plan available, package plans, pets ($10 extra charge). **Amenities:** extended cable TV, irons, hair dryers. **Dining:** restaurant, 6 am-10 pm, $8-$15, cocktails, entertainment. **Pool(s):** outdoor. **Leisure Activities:** putting green. **Guest Services:** valet and coin laundry. **Business Services:** meeting rooms. **Cards:** AX, CB, DC, DS, JC, MC, VI. **Special Amenities:** free local telephone calls and free newspaper.

SOME UNITS

HAMPTON INN LANCASTER
◇◇◇ SAVE
▼▼▼ ▼
Motel

All Year [ECP]	1P: $75	2P: $79

Phone: (740)654-2999

Location: 2.1 mi nw on US 33. 2041 Schorrway Dr 43130. Fax: 740/689-2940. **Facility:** 78 one-bedroom standard units, some with whirlpools. 3 stories, interior corridors. *Bath:* combo or shower only. **Amenities:** extended cable TV, voice mail, irons, hair dryers. **Pool(s):** heated indoor. **Leisure Activities:** whirlpool, exercise room. **Guest Services:** valet and coin laundry. **Business Services:** meeting rooms. **Cards:** AX, DC, DS, MC, VI. **Special Amenities:** free continental breakfast and free local telephone calls.

SOME UNITS

HOLIDAY INN EXPRESS HOTEL & SUITES
◇◇◇ SAVE
▼▼▼ ▼
Motel

All Year [ECP]	1P: $79-$99	2P: $79-$99	XP: $16

Phone: (740)654-4445

Location: 2.5 mi nw on US 33; adjacent to River Valley Mall. 1861 Riverway Dr 43130. Fax: 740/654-5546. **Facility:** 63 one-bedroom units, some with whirlpools. 3 stories, interior corridors. *Bath:* combo or shower only. **Parking:** on-site. **Amenities:** extended cable TV, dual phone lines, voice mail, irons, hair dryers. **Pool(s):** heated indoor. **Leisure Activities:** exercise room. **Guest Services:** valet and coin laundry. **Cards:** AX, CB, DC, DS, MC, VI. **Special Amenities:** free continental breakfast and free local telephone calls.

SOME UNITS

KNIGHTS INN
◇◇◇ SAVE
▼
Motel

4/1-10/31	1P: $73	2P: $73	XP: $6 F17
11/1-3/31	1P: $63	2P: $63	XP: $6 F17

Phone: (740)687-4823

Location: 2 mi nw on US 33; at River Valley Mall entrance. 1327 River Valley Blvd 43130. Fax: 740/687-4823. **Facility:** 60 one-bedroom standard units, some with efficiencies and/or whirlpools. 1 story, exterior corridors. **Parking:** on-site. **Terms:** check-in 4 pm, 3 day cancellation notice. **Amenities:** extended cable TV. *Some:* hair dryers. **Business Services:** meeting rooms. **Cards:** AX, CB, DC, DS, JC, MC, VI. **Special Amenities:** free continental breakfast and free newspaper.

SOME UNITS

SHAW'S RESTAURANT AND INN
▼▼ ▼▼
Motor Inn

All Year [BP]	1P: $65-$210	2P: $78-$223	XP: $13

Phone: 740-654-1842

Location: US 33, just e on E Wheeling St, at corner of Wheeling and Broad sts. 123 N Broad St 43130. Fax: 740/654-7032. **Facility:** 22 one-bedroom standard units, some with whirlpools. 6 stories, interior corridors. *Bath:* combo or shower only. **Parking:** on-site. **Terms:** 15 day cancellation notice, package plans. **Amenities:** extended cable TV, irons, hair dryers. **Dining:** dining room, see separate listing. **Guest Services:** valet laundry. **Business Services:** meeting rooms. **Cards:** MC, VI.

SOME UNITS

——— WHERE TO DINE ———

FOUR REASONS BAKERY & DELI
▼
American

Lunch: $3-$6	**Dinner:** $3-$6	**Phone:** 740-654-2253

Location: Just e of US 33 (town center). 135 W Main St 43130. **Hours:** 6 am-7 pm, Sat & Sun 8 am-5 pm. Closed major holidays. **Features:** casual dress; carryout; a la carte. Box lunches and gift baskets are nice touches at the casual deli, which delivers salad, pastries, ice cream and sandwiches. The specialty Ryckman's Reuben stacks corned beef, sauerkraut, Swiss cheese and Thousand Island dressing on grilled marble rye. Smoke free premises. **Parking:** on-site. **Cards:** AX, DS, MC, VI.

MAUGER'S SEAFOOD

▽▽ ▽▽
Seafood

Lunch: $6-$10   **Dinner:** $10-$20   **Phone:** 740/654-8237
Location: Jct US 33, 0.7 mi e on US 22. 512 E Main St 43130. **Hours:** 11 am-2 & 5-9 pm, Fri-10 pm, Sat 1 pm-9 pm. Closed major holidays; also Sun & Mon. **Reservations:** accepted. **Features:** casual dress; children's menu; early bird specials; carryout; cocktails. This restaurant has been in this community since 1898 and at its present location since 1932. The quaint lounge speaks history and has a vintage cash register and glasses circling overhead. Entering through an archway with a swordfish mounted overhead into a rustic dining area with a touch of elegance with leather like tablecloths. One of their specialties is the turtle soup. Try a different dessert with a piece of Cane Bay Pie. **Parking:** street. **Cards:** MC, VI.   ✕

SHAW'S RESTAURANT & INN

ⒶⒶ
▽▽▽
American

Lunch: $7-$13   **Dinner:** $12-$30   **Phone:** 740/654-1842
Location: US 33, just e on E Wheeling St. 123 N Broad St 43130. **Hours:** 7-10:30 am, 11:30-2:30 & 5-10 pm, Sun 7 am-9 pm. Closed major holidays; also Super Bowl Sun. **Reservations:** suggested; weekends. **Features:** casual dress; Sunday brunch; children's menu; carryout; cocktails & lounge. An extensive list of wines complements selections of seafood and steak. The prime rib is particularly flavorful. Wallpaper and wood contribute to the Victorian mood of the dining room. Classical music plays in the background. **Parking:** on-site. **Cards:** MC, VI.   ✕

MARYSVILLE pop. 9,700

------ **WHERE TO STAY** ------

AMERIHOST INN-MARYSVILLE

ⒶⒶ ⓈⒶⓋⒺ
▽▽▽
Motel

Phone: (937)644-0400
All Year   1P: $66-$99   2P: $72-$105   XP: $6   F18
Location: US 36 at jct US 33. 16420 Allenby Dr 43040. Fax: 937/642-1747. **Facility:** 78 one-bedroom standard units, some with whirlpools. 2 stories, interior corridors. *Bath:* combo or shower only. **Parking:** on-site. **Amenities:** extended cable TV, voice mail, safes (fee), irons, hair dryers. **Pool(s):** heated indoor. **Leisure Activities:** sauna, whirlpool, exercise room. **Guest Services:** valet and coin laundry. **Business Services:** meeting rooms. **Cards:** AX, CB, DC, DS, JC, MC, VI. **Special Amenities:** free continental breakfast and free newspaper.

SOME UNITS
[S🄳] [▯◍] [🛏] [🐾] [⌖] [✕] [📺] [DATA PORT] [💻] [🗄] / [✕] [🗄] [🍽] /
FEE

DAYS INN MARYSVILLE

ⓈⒶⓋⒺ
▽▽
Motel

Phone: (937)644-8821
All Year   1P: $69   2P: $69   XP: $5   F18
Location: Just e of US 36, exit off US 33. 16510 Square Dr 43040. Fax: 937/644-8821. **Facility:** 74 one-bedroom standard units, some with kitchens and/or whirlpools. 2 stories, exterior corridors. **Parking:** on-site. **Terms:** [ECP] meal plan available, small pets only ($10 fee). **Amenities:** extended cable TV. *Some:* hair dryers. **Guest Services:** complimentary evening beverages: Tues-Thurs, valet laundry. **Business Services:** meeting rooms. **Cards:** AX, CB, DC, DS, JC, MC, VI.

SOME UNITS
[S🄳] [🐾] [▯◍] [🛏] [📺] [DATA PORT] [💻] [🗄] / [✕] [VCR] [🗄] [🍽] /
FEE

MOUNT STERLING pop. 1,600

------ **WHERE TO STAY** ------

DEER CREEK RESORT AND CONFERENCE CENTER

ⒶⒶ ⓈⒶⓋⒺ
▽▽▽
Resort

Phone: (740)869-2020
5/1-3/31   1P: $110-$120   2P: $110-$120
4/1-4/30   1P: $108-$113   2P: $108-$113
Location: I-71, exit 84, 3.4 mi e on US 62, 4.2 mi s on SR 207, then 4.7 mi e on Cook-Yankeetown Rd and State Park Rd 20, follow signs. 22300 State Park Rd 20 43143. Fax: 740/869-4059. **Facility:** This state park resort features a limestone lodge set on the shore of a lake. All lodge rooms have either a balcony or a patio. 136 units. 100 one- and 10 two-bedroom standard units. 25 two- and 1 three-bedroom vacation rentals ($135-$1135). 1-2 stories, interior/exterior corridors. *Bath:* combo or shower only. **Parking:** on-site. **Terms:** 14 day cancellation notice, package plans. **Amenities:** extended cable TV, video tape library, dual phone lines, irons, hair dryers. *Some:* voice mail. **Dining:** restaurant, 7 am-9 pm, $10-$24. **Pool(s):** outdoor, heated indoor, wading. **Leisure Activities:** sauna, whirlpool, rental boats, rental canoes, marina, fishing, 2 lighted tennis courts, hiking trails, exercise room, basketball, horseshoes, shuffleboard, volleyball, shooting range, archery. *Fee:* jet skis, golf-18 holes, game room. **Guest Services:** gift shop, coin laundry. **Business Services:** conference facilities, business center, PC, fax (fee). **Cards:** AX, DC, DS, MC, VI.

SOME UNITS
[S🄳] [▯] [🍽] [Ⓜ] [⌖] [🐾] [✕] [📺] [DATA PORT] [💻] [🗄] / [✕] [VCR] [🍽] /

NEWARK pop. 44,400

------ **WHERE TO STAY** ------

CHERRY VALLEY LODGE

▽▽▽
Motor Inn

Phone: (740)788-1200
All Year   1P: $160   2P: $170   XP: $10   F18
Location: 3.5 mi w on SR 16, then 0.3 mi s. 2299 Cherry Valley Rd 43055. Fax: 740/788-8800. **Facility:** 200 units. 184 one-bedroom standard units. 16 one-bedroom suites ($195-$230). 2 stories, interior corridors. *Bath:* combo or shower only. **Parking:** on-site. **Terms:** check-in 4 pm, cancellation fee imposed, package plans. **Amenities:** voice mail, irons, hair dryers. **Pool(s):** heated outdoor, heated indoor. **Leisure Activities:** whirlpool, playground, horseshoes, shuffleboard, volleyball. *Fee:* game room. **Guest Services:** valet laundry. **Business Services:** conference facilities, PC, fax. **Cards:** AX, DC, DS, JC, MC, VI.

SOME UNITS
[ASK] [S🄳] [▯] [🍽] [⌖] [Ⓜ] [🐾] [✕] [VCR] [DATA PORT] [💻] [🗄] / [✕] [🍽] /
FEE

THE PLACE OFF THE SQUARE

Phone: (740)322-6455

4/1-10/31 [ECP]	1P: $98-$108	2P: $98-$108	XP: $10	F17
1/1-3/31 [ECP]	1P: $80-$108	2P: $80-$108	XP: $10	F17
11/1-12/31 [ECP]	1P: $80-$90	2P: $80-$90	XP: $10	F17

Motor Inn

Location: Jct Second St and E Locust. 50 N Second St 43055. **Fax:** 740/322-6267. **Facility:** 117 one-bedroom standard units. 6 stories, interior corridors. **Parking:** on-site. **Terms:** 3 day cancellation notice-fee imposed, package plans. **Amenities:** extended cable TV, voice mail, irons, hair dryers. **Dining:** restaurant, 11 am-3 & 6-9 pm, $7-$13, cocktails. **Pool(s):** heated indoor. **Guest Services:** gift shop, valet and coin laundry. **Business Services:** meeting rooms. **Cards:** AX, DS, MC, VI. **Special Amenities:** free continental breakfast.

SOME UNITS

WHERE TO DINE

NATOMA CAFE

Lunch: $5-$6   **Dinner:** $9-$20   **Phone:** 740/345-7260

American

Location: Downtown; on the square. 10 N Park Pl 43055. **Hours:** 11 am-9:30 pm, Fri-10 pm, Sat 5 pm-10 pm. Closed major holidays; also Sun. **Reservations:** suggested. **Features:** dressy casual; children's menu; cocktails. The established downtown restaurant serves such specialties as beef tenderloin and amaretto cheesecake. **Parking:** street. **Cards:** AX, DC, DS, MC, VI.

PICKERINGTON pop. 5,700

WHERE TO STAY

HAMPTON INN EAST

Phone: (614)864-8383

4/1-9/30 [ECP]	1P: $59-$90	2P: $59-$95	
10/1-3/31 [ECP]	1P: $55-$90	2P: $55-$95	

Motel

Location: I-70, exit 112. 1890 Winderly Ln 43147. **Fax:** 614/864-4884. **Facility:** 76 one-bedroom standard units, some with whirlpools. 3 stories, interior corridors. *Bath:* combo or shower only. **Parking:** on-site. **Amenities:** extended cable TV, dual phone lines, voice mail, irons, hair dryers. **Pool(s):** heated indoor. **Leisure Activities:** whirlpool, exercise room. **Business Services:** meeting rooms. **Cards:** AX, CB, DC, DS, MC, VI. **Special Amenities:** free continental breakfast and free local telephone calls.

SOME UNITS

HAWTHORN SUITES

Phone: (614)860-9804

4/1-9/30 [ECP]	1P: $59-$90	2P: $59-$95	
10/1-3/31 [ECP]	1P: $55-$90	2P: $55-$95	

Motel

Location: I-70, exit 112, just sw. 1899 Winderly Ln 43147. **Fax:** 614/864-9002. **Facility:** 68 one-bedroom standard units, some with whirlpools. 3 stories, interior corridors. *Bath:* some combo or shower only. **Parking:** on-site. **Terms:** cancellation fee imposed. **Amenities:** extended cable TV, voice mail, irons, hair dryers. **Pool(s):** heated indoor. **Leisure Activities:** whirlpool, exercise room. **Guest Services:** valet and coin laundry. **Business Services:** meeting rooms. **Cards:** AX, CB, DC, DS, MC, VI. **Special Amenities:** free continental breakfast and free local telephone calls.

SOME UNITS

WHERE TO DINE

MONTANA MINING COMPANY STEAKHOUSE & SALOON   **Lunch:** $7-$14   **Dinner:** $7-$14   **Phone:** 614/501-8737

Steak House

Location: I-70, exit 112A, 0.5 mi s on SR 256. 1849 Winderly Ln 43147. **Hours:** 11 am-9 pm. Closed major holidays. **Features:** casual dress; carryout; cocktails & lounge. In a shopping plaza, the steakhouse offers tried-and-true American cuisine, including choice steaks, ribs and pasta. The lounge entertains guests with interactive video games and televised sporting events. **Parking:** on-site. **Cards:** AX, DC, DS, MC, VI.

PLAIN CITY pop. 2,300

WHERE TO DINE

DER DUTCHMAN RESTAURANT   **Lunch:** $6-$12   **Dinner:** $6-$12   **Phone:** 614/873-3414

American

Location: 1 mi s on US 42. 445 S Jefferson Ave 43064. **Hours:** 6 am-8 pm, Fri & Sat-9 pm. Closed: 1/1, 11/28, 12/25; also Sun. **Features:** casual dress; children's menu; carryout; salad bar; a la carte. The popularity of Der Dutchman may produce a wait for seating but it's worth it. Amish cooking is the highlight here and includes hearty portions of turkey, chicken, roast beef and ham as well as an array of pies. All-you-can-eat dinners are also offered. Smoke free premises. **Parking:** on-site. **Cards:** DS, MC, VI.

REYNOLDSBURG pop. 25,700   (See map p. 636; index p. 641)

WHERE TO STAY

BEST WESTERN COLUMBUS EAST

Phone: (614)864-1280   **95**

All Year	1P: $57-$59	2P: $61-$65	XP: $10	F18

Motor Inn

Location: I-70, exit 110 westbound; exit 110B eastbound, just n. 2100 Brice Rd 43068. **Fax:** 614/864-1280. **Facility:** 143 one-bedroom standard units. 2 stories, interior corridors. *Bath:* combo or shower only. **Parking:** on-site. **Amenities:** extended cable TV, irons, hair dryers. **Dining:** dining room, 6 am-11 pm, Sun 7 am-9 pm, $6-$12, cocktails. **Guest Services:** valet laundry, area transportation-within 5 mi. **Business Services:** meeting rooms. **Cards:** AX, DC, DS, MC, VI. **Special Amenities:** early check-in/late check-out and free room upgrade (subject to availability with advanced reservations). (See color ad p 646)

SOME UNITS

(See map p. 636)

COUNTRY INN & SUITES BY CARLSON-COLUMBUS EAST   Phone: (614)861-8888   [100]

| | 4/1-10/31 & 2/22-3/31 [ECP] | 1P: $75-$80 | 2P: $80-$90 | XP: $5 | F18 |
| | 11/1-2/21 [ECP] | 1P: $65-$70 | 2P: $70-$75 | XP: $5 | F18 |

Motel   **Location:** I-70, exit 112, just n on SR 256, then e. 2806 Taylor Rd 43068. Fax: 614/861-6381. **Facility:** 81 units. 61 one-bedroom standard units, some with whirlpools. 20 one-bedroom suites ($85-$125). 3 stories, interior corridors. *Bath:* combo or shower only. **Parking:** on-site. **Amenities:** high-speed Internet, dual phone lines, voice mail, irons, hair dryers. **Pool(s):** heated indoor. **Leisure Activities:** whirlpool, exercise room. **Business Services:** meeting rooms. **Cards:** AX, DC, DS, MC, VI. *(See color ad p 646)*

SOME UNITS

CROSS COUNTRY INN EAST   Phone: (614)864-3880   [96]

AAA SAVE   All Year   1P: $45-$52   2P: $48-$55   XP: $2   F17
Motel   **Location:** I-70, exit 110 westbound; exit 110B eastbound. 2055 Brice Rd 43068. Fax: 614/864-2945. **Facility:** 120 one-bedroom standard units. 2 stories, exterior corridors. *Bath:* combo or shower only. **Parking:** on-site. **Amenities:** video games, voice mail. **Pool(s):** heated outdoor. **Business Services:** meeting rooms. **Cards:** AX, CB, DC, DS, MC, VI. **Special Amenities:** free local telephone calls and preferred room (subject to availability with advanced reservations).

SOME UNITS
FEE

EXTENDED STAY AMERICA EAST   Phone: (614)759-1451   [98]
     All Year   1P: $39-$59   2P: $39-$59
Extended Stay Motel   **Location:** I-70, exit 110 westbound; exit 110B eastbound, 0.5 mi n on Brice Rd, just w on Channingway, then just s. 2200 Lake Club Dr 43232. Fax: 614/863-7755. **Facility:** 71 one-bedroom standard units with kitchens. 3 stories (no elevator), interior corridors. **Parking:** on-site. **Amenities:** extended cable TV, voice mail. **Pool(s):** outdoor. **Guest Services:** coin laundry. **Cards:** AX, DC, DS, MC, VI.

SOME UNITS

LA QUINTA INN   Phone: (614)866-6456   [97]
AAA SAVE   All Year   1P: $56-$66   2P: $62-$72   XP: $6   F18
Motel   **Location:** I-70, exit 110 westbound; exit 110B eastbound, 0.3 mi n. 2447 Brice Rd 43068. Fax: 614/866-4522. **Facility:** 122 units. 120 one-bedroom standard units. 2 one-bedroom suites ($76-$116). 2 stories, interior corridors. **Parking:** on-site. **Terms:** small pets only. **Amenities:** extended cable TV, video games, voice mail, irons, hair dryers. **Guest Services:** valet laundry. **Cards:** AX, CB, DC, DS, MC, VI. **Special Amenities:** free continental breakfast and free local telephone calls.

SOME UNITS
FEE

(See map p. 636)

RED ROOF INN-EAST
Phone: (614)864-3683   99

AAA SAVE

| | 6/2-8/25 | 1P: $49-$64 | 2P: $54-$69 | XP: $5 | F18 |
| | 4/1-6/1 & 8/26-3/31 | 1P: $47-$64 | 2P: $52-$69 | XP: $5 | F18 |

Motel

Location: I-70, exit 110 westbound; exit 110B eastbound. 2449 Brice Rd 43068. Fax: 614/864-4296. **Facility:** 108 one-bedroom standard units. 2 stories, exterior corridors. *Bath:* combo or shower only. **Parking:** on-site. **Terms:** small pets only. **Amenities:** video games, voice mail. **Cards:** AX, CB, DC, DS, MC, VI. **Special Amenities:** free local telephone calls and free newspaper.

SOME UNITS

SUNBURY pop. 2,000

──────── **WHERE TO STAY** ────────

DAYS INN OF SUNBURY
Phone: (740)362-6159

AAA SAVE

	9/2-10/1 [CP]	1P: $70	2P: $70	XP: $5	F12
	6/1-9/1 [CP]	1P: $55-$65	2P: $55-$65	XP: $5	F12
	4/1-5/31 & 10/2-3/31 [CP]	1P: $45-$55	2P: $45-$55	XP: $5	F12

Motel

Location: I-71, exit 131, just w. 7323 SR 37 E 43074. Fax: 740/363-1692. **Facility:** 61 one-bedroom standard units. 2 stories, interior corridors. *Bath:* combo or shower only. **Parking:** on-site. **Terms:** pets ($20 extra charge). **Amenities:** voice mail. **Pool(s):** heated indoor. **Cards:** AX, DS, MC, VI. **Special Amenities:** free continental breakfast and free newspaper.

SOME UNITS

HOLIDAY INN EXPRESS HOTEL & SUITES
Phone: (740)362-3036

AAA SAVE

All Year   1P: $69-$90

Motel

Location: I-71, exit 131, just nw. 7301 SR 37 43074. Fax: 740/363-7386. **Facility:** 61 one-bedroom standard units, some with whirlpools. 3 stories, interior corridors. *Bath:* combo or shower only. **Parking:** on-site. **Terms:** cancellation fee imposed, package plans. **Amenities:** voice mail, irons, hair dryers. **Pool(s):** heated indoor. **Leisure Activities:** exercise room. **Guest Services:** valet and coin laundry. **Cards:** AX, DC, DS, MC, VI. **Special Amenities:** free continental breakfast and free local telephone calls.

SOME UNITS

UPPER ARLINGTON pop. 34,100 (See map p. 636; index p. 641)

──────── **WHERE TO DINE** ────────

CHINA DYNASTY
Lunch: $6-$9   **Dinner:** $8-$16   **Phone:** 614/486-7126   71

Chinese

Location: SR 315, 1.2 mi w. 1677 W Lane Ave 43221. **Hours:** 11 am-10 pm, Fri & Sat-10:30 pm, Sun-9 pm. Closed: 7/4, 11/28. **Reservations:** suggested. **Features:** casual dress; Sunday brunch; carryout; cocktails; a la carte. The casually upscale restaurant offers a voluminous selection of mainstream Hunan, Szechuan and Mandarin dishes, many of which are listed as spicy, with chicken, pork, beef and seafood. Portions are generous. The uniformed wait staff provides prompt service. **Parking:** on-site. **Cards:** AX, DC, DS, MC, VI.

──────── *The following restaurant has not been evaluated by AAA but is listed for your information only.* ────────

ALEX'S BISTRO RESTAURANT FRANCAIS
Phone: 614/457-8887

fyi

Not evaluated. **Location:** 4681 Reed Rd 43221. Pan-seared salmon and crepes are among dishes prepared at the restaurant.

WESTERVILLE pop. 30,300 (See map p. 636; index p. 641)

──────── **WHERE TO STAY** ────────

CROSS COUNTRY INN WESTERVILLE
Phone: (614)890-1244   92

AAA SAVE

All Year   1P: $43-$50   2P: $50-$57   XP: $2   F17

Motel

Location: I-270, exit 29, 0.3 mi n on SR 3. 909 S State St 43081. Fax: 614/890-0983. **Facility:** 152 one-bedroom standard units. 2 stories, exterior corridors. *Bath:* combo or shower only. **Parking:** on-site. **Amenities:** video games, voice mail. **Pool(s):** heated outdoor. **Cards:** AX, CB, DC, DS, MC, VI. **Special Amenities:** free local telephone calls and preferred room (subject to availability with advanced reservations).

SOME UNITS

KNIGHTS INN-COLUMBUS/WESTERVILLE
Phone: (614)890-0426   93

All Year [CP]   1P: $50   2P: $60   XP: $10   F18

Motel

Location: I-270, exit 29, 0.3 mi n on SR 3. 32 Heatherdown Dr 43081. Fax: 614/890-1678. **Facility:** 105 one-bedroom standard units. 1 story, exterior corridors. **Parking:** on-site. **Terms:** check-in 4 pm. **Pool(s):** outdoor. **Cards:** AX, CB, DC, DS, MC, VI.

SOME UNITS

WORTHINGTON pop. 14,900   (See map p. 636; index p. 640)

———— WHERE TO STAY ————

CLARION HOTEL WORTHINGTON
Phone: (614)436-0700   **81**
All Year   2P: $79

SAVE

▼▼ ▼▼
Motor Inn

Location: I-270, exit 23, 0.3 mi s on US 23. 7007 N High St 43085. Fax: 614/436-5318. **Facility:** 230 one-bedroom standard units. 3 stories, interior corridors. *Bath:* combo or shower only. **Parking:** on-site. **Terms:** package plans. **Amenities:** extended cable TV, voice mail, safes (fee), irons, hair dryers. **Pool(s):** heated indoor. **Leisure Activities:** exercise room. **Guest Services:** valet and coin laundry. **Business Services:** meeting rooms, fax. **Cards:** AX, CB, DC, DS, JC, MC, VI.

SOME UNITS

FEE   FEE

RED ROOF INN-WORTHINGTON
Phone: (614)846-3001   **78**

AAA **SAVE**

▼▼ ▼▼
Motel

5/20-10/27	1P: $45-$59	2P: $49-$63	XP: $4	F18
4/1-5/19	1P: $39-$59	2P: $47-$63	XP: $4	F18
10/28-3/31	1P: $39-$59	2P: $44-$63	XP: $4	F18

Location: I-270, exit 23, just n. 7474 N High St 43235. Fax: 614/846-4613. **Facility:** 106 one-bedroom standard units. 2 stories, exterior corridors. *Bath:* combo or shower only. **Parking:** on-site. **Terms:** small pets only. **Amenities:** video games, voice mail. **Cards:** AX, CB, DC, DS, MC, VI. **Special Amenities: free local tele-**
phone calls and free newspaper.

SOME UNITS

FEE   FEE FEE

THE WORTHINGTON INN
Phone: (614)885-2600   **80**

AAA **SAVE**

▼▼ ▼▼
Classic Country Inn

All Year   1P: $150   2P: $150   XP: $25   F12

Location: I-270, exit 23, 1.7 mi s on US 23. 649 High St 43085. Fax: 614/885-1283. **Facility:** Historic. -anopy beds and antiques furnish this inn built in the 1830s. Designated smoking area. 23 units. 20 one-bedroom stan-dard units. 3 one-bedroom suites ($215-$260). 3 stories, interior corridors. **Parking:** on-site. **Terms:** cancel-lation fee imposed. **Amenities:** extended cable TV, irons, hair dryers. **Dining:** Seven Stars at The Worthington Inn, see separate listing. **Guest Services:** complimentary evening beverages, valet laundry. **Business Services:** meeting rooms, fax. **Cards:** AX, DS, MC, VI.

———— WHERE TO DINE ————

CAMERON'S CONTEMPORARY AMERICAN CUISINE   **Dinner:** $8-$22   Phone: 614/885-3663   **49**

▼▼ ▼▼
American

Location: Jct US 315 and 161 (Dublin-Granville Rd), 0.6 mi w on SR 161. 2185 W Dublin-Granville Rd 43085. **Hours:** 5 pm-10 pm, Fri & Sat-11 pm, Sun-9 pm. Closed major holidays. **Reservations:** accepted. **Features:** casual dress; children's menu; carryout; cocktails; a la carte. Diners are consistently pleased with Cameron's creative concepts of seafood, pasta and chops, all served in a bustling, informal atmosphere. Of note is the outstanding mushroom-crusted halibut and a fresh fruit, lettuce, gorgonzola and proscuitto salad. **Parking:** on-site. **Cards:** AX, CB, DC, DS, MC, VI.

SEVEN STARS AT THE WORTHINGTON INN   **Lunch:** $7-$11   **Dinner:** $13-$26   **Phone:** 614/885-2600   **52**

AAA

▼▼ ▼▼
American

Location: I-270, exit 23, 1.7 mi s on US 23; in The Worthington Inn. 649 High St 43085. **Hours:** 7-10 am, 11-3 & 5:30-10 pm, Fri & Sat-11 pm, Sun-9 pm. Closed: 1/1, 7/4, 12/25. **Reservations:** suggested. **Features:** dressy casual; children's menu; carryout; cocktails; a la carte. Tasty rack of lamb and pleasant, attentive servers reign supreme at Seven Stars, located in Worthington's historic district. Dining rooms are decorated with local artwork and exude a country inn atmosphere. For dessert, try the triple-layer mousse cake. Smoke free premises. **Parking:** on-site. **Cards:** AX, DS, MC, VI.

This ends listings for the Columbus Vicinity.
The following page resumes the alphabetical listings of cities in Ohio.

CONNEAUT pop. 13,200

------ WHERE TO STAY ------

DAYS INN OF CONNEAUT
Phone: (440)593-6000

AAA [SAVE]

5/24-9/2 [BP]	1P: $85-$150	2P: $85-$150	XP: $5	F17
4/1-5/23 & 1/1-3/31 [ECP]	1P: $70-$100	2P: $70-$100	XP: $5	F17
9/3-12/31 [ECP]	1P: $65-$100	2P: $65-$100	XP: $5	F17

Motel **Location:** I-90, exit 241, 0.3 mi n. 600 Days Blvd 44030. Fax: 440/593-6003. **Facility:** 105 one-bedroom standard units, some with whirlpools. 2 stories, interior corridors. **Parking:** on-site. **Terms:** small pets only. **Amenities:** extended cable TV, irons. *Some:* hair dryers. **Pool(s):** outdoor. **Business Services:** meeting rooms. **Cards:** AX, DC, DS, MC, VI. **Special Amenities:** free continental breakfast and free newspaper.

COSHOCTON pop. 12,200

SOME UNITS

------ WHERE TO STAY ------

COSHOCTON VILLAGE INN & SUITES
Phone: (740)622-9455

AAA [SAVE]

All Year [ECP]	1P: $69-$99	2P: $69-$99	XP: $5	F17

Motel **Location:** SR 16 and 541, just e. 115 N Water St 43812. Fax: 740/623-0873. **Facility:** 64 units. 39 one-bedroom standard units, some with whirlpools. 25 one-bedroom suites ($89-$135) with efficiencies. 3 stories, interior corridors. *Bath:* combo or shower only. **Parking:** on-site. **Terms:** package plans. **Amenities:** extended cable TV, voice mail, hair dryers. *Some:* irons. **Pool(s):** heated indoor. **Leisure Activities:** sauna, whirlpool, exercise room. **Guest Services:** coin laundry. **Business Services:** meeting rooms. **Cards:** AX, DS, MC, VI. **Special Amenities:** free continental breakfast and free local telephone calls.

SOME UNITS

THE INN AT ROSCOE VILLAGE
Phone: (740)622-2222

AAA [SAVE]

5/1-10/31		2P: $89	XP: $8	F18
4/1-4/30 & 11/1-3/31		2P: $75	XP: $8	F18

Motor Inn **Location:** SR 16 and 83, just n; in Roscoe Village. 200 N Whitewoman St 43812. Fax: 740/623-6568. **Facility:** 51 one-bedroom standard units. 4 stories, interior corridors. **Parking:** on-site. **Terms:** package plans. **Amenities:** extended cable TV, irons, hair dryers. **Dining:** dining room, 7-10 am, 11:30-2 & 5-9 pm, Sat from 8 am, Sun 8 am-2 pm, $9-$26, cocktails. **Guest Services:** gift shop, valet laundry. **Business Services:** meeting rooms. **Cards:** AX, DC, DS, MC, VI. *(See color ad below)*

SOME UNITS

SUPER 8 MOTEL
Phone: (740)622-8899

All Year	1P: $60-$65	2P: $65-$70	XP: $5	F12

Motel **Location:** SR 16 and 83, 0.3 mi w of jct SR 541. 70 S Whitewoman St 43812. Fax: 740/622-8899. **Facility:** 48 one-bedroom standard units, some with whirlpools. 2 stories, interior corridors. *Bath:* combo or shower only. **Parking:** on-site. **Terms:** 14 day cancellation notice. **Amenities:** extended cable TV. **Pool(s):** heated indoor. **Leisure Activities:** whirlpool. **Cards:** AX, DC, DS, MC, VI.

SOME UNITS
FEE

------ WHERE TO DINE ------

THE OLD WAREHOUSE RESTAURANT Historical
Lunch: $7-$10   **Dinner:** $9-$17   **Phone:** 740/622-4001

AAA **Location:** SR 16 and 83, just n; in Roscoe Village. 400 N Whitewoman St 43812. **Hours:** 11 am-8 pm. Closed: 11/28, 12/25. **Reservations:** suggested. **Features:** casual dress; children's menu; carryout; cocktails & lounge; a la carte. An Early American feel punctuates the restored 1838 building, which looks like the inside of a canal boat. Prime rib is a specialty, as are the flavorful bean soup and bran muffins. For dessert, treat your palate to bread pudding or apple dumplings. **Parking:** on-site. **Cards:** AX, DC, DS, MC, VI.

American

ROBSON'S RESTAURANT
Lunch: $6-$8   **Dinner:** $9-$22   **Phone:** 740/622-8262

American **Location:** Town center. 442 Main St 43812. **Hours:** 7 am-10 pm, Fri & Sat 6 am-11 pm, Sun 8:30 am-9 pm. Closed major holidays. **Reservations:** accepted. **Features:** casual dress; children's menu; carryout; cocktails & lounge. Entrees include preparations of steak, seafood, chicken and pasta. As desserts go, it's hard to beat the apple pie, which is topped with cinnamon ice cream and caramel sauce. Dark wood, maroon carpet and cream-colored walls decorate the dining room. **Parking:** on-site. **Cards:** AX, DC, DS, MC, VI.

COVINGTON pop. 2,600

------ WHERE TO DINE ------

BUFFALO JACKS Historical **Lunch:** $7-$21 **Dinner:** $7-$21 **Phone:** 937/473-2524
Location: Just n of jct SR 41 and 48. 137 S High St 45318. **Hours:** 6 am-10 pm, Fri & Sat-11 pm, Sun 7 am-8 pm. **Closed:** 11/28, 12/25. **Features:** casual dress; children's menu; carryout; cocktails & lounge; a la carte. Built as a tavern in 1886, the restaurant delivers such exotic game dinners as alligator, rattlesnake, turtle soup and buffalo steaks and burgers. For the less adventurous, steak, chops, chicken, seafood, sandwiches and salad fit the bill. **Parking:** on-site. **Cards:** AX, DS, MC, VI.
American

CUYAHOGA FALLS pop. 49,000

------ WHERE TO STAY ------

AKRON SHERATON SUITES CUYAHOGA FALLS **Phone:** (330)929-3000
4/1-8/31 1P: $140-$179 2P: $140-$179 XP: $15 F18
9/1-3/31 1P: $119-$179 2P: $119-$179 XP: $15 F18
Location: SR 8, exit Broad Blvd, just w. 1989 Front St 44221. **Fax:** 330/929-3031. **Facility:** 214 units. 211 one- and 3 two-bedroom suites, some with efficiencies or kitchens. 5 stories, interior corridors. *Bath:* shower only.
Suite Motor Inn **Parking:** on-site. **Terms:** package plans. **Amenities:** video games, dual phone lines, voice mail, fax, irons, hair dryers. *Some:* honor bars. **Dining:** River Front Restaurant, see separate listing. **Pool(s):** heated indoor.
Leisure Activities: sauna, whirlpool, exercise room. **Guest Services:** gift shop, coin laundry. **Business Services:** conference facilities. **Cards:** AX, DC, DS, JC, MC, VI. **Special Amenities:** free newspaper. *(See color ad p 529)*

COUNTRY INN & SUITES BY CARLSON **Phone:** (330)926-1233
6/1-8/31 [ECP] 1P: $79-$109 2P: $84-$114 XP: $5 F18
4/1-5/31 & 9/1-10/31 [ECP] 1P: $69-$99 2P: $74-$104 XP: $5 F18
11/1-3/31 [ECP] 1P: $59-$89 2P: $64-$94 XP: $5 F18
Location: SR 8, exit Howe Rd, just n. 1420 Main St 44221. **Fax:** 330/926-1218. **Facility:** 79 one-bedroom standard units, some with whirlpools. 4 stories, interior corridors. *Bath:* combo or shower only. **Parking:** on-site.
Suite Motel **Terms:** cancellation fee imposed. **Amenities:** extended cable TV, voice mail, irons, hair dryers. **Pool(s):** heated indoor. **Leisure Activities:** whirlpool, exercise room. **Guest Services:** coin laundry. **Business Services:** meeting rooms, business center. **Cards:** AX, CB, DC, DS, MC, VI. **Special Amenities:** free continental breakfast and free newspaper. *(See color ad p 646)*

------ WHERE TO DINE ------

RIVER FRONT RESTAURANT **Lunch:** $5-$10 **Dinner:** $15-$23 **Phone:** 330/920-7530
Location: SR 8, exit Broad Blvd, just w; in Akron Sheraton Suites Cuyahoga Falls. 1989 Front St 44221. **Hours:** 6:30 am-2 & 5-10:30 pm, Sun from 7 am. **Reservations:** suggested. **Features:** dressy casual; Sunday brunch; children's menu; cocktails & lounge; a la carte. Glass encases the charming restaurant, which extends out over the Cuyahoga River. Hanging lights and globe candles provide soft, romantic illumination in the intimate dining room, while the deck has a more festive feel. The menu changes seasonally. **Parking:** on-site. **Cards:** AX, DC, DS, JC, MC, VI. *(See color ad p 529)*
American

------ *The following restaurant has not been evaluated by AAA but is listed for your information only.* ------

EMIDIO & SONS **Phone:** 330/929-4282
[fyi] Not evaluated. **Location:** 3204 State Rd 44221. Reasonably priced food served in generous portions can be eaten in the dining room or carried out.

DALTON pop. 1,400

------ WHERE TO DINE ------

DAS DUTCH KITCHEN **Lunch:** $4-$7 **Dinner:** $5-$9 **Phone:** 330/683-0530
Location: 2 mi w of Dalton, on US 30. 14278 E Lincolnway (Rt 30) 44618. **Hours:** 7 am-8 pm. **Closed:** 11/28, 12/25; also Sun. **Features:** casual dress; carryout; salad bar. The warm, friendly 1858 Victorian home is appointed with lace curtains and period antiques. Amish cooking includes such family favorites as roast beef, chicken, homemade mashed potatoes, casseroles and a delectable assortment of freshly baked pies. Smoke free premises. **Parking:** on-site. **Cards:** DS, MC, VI.
American

DANVILLE pop. 1,000

------ WHERE TO STAY ------

THE WHITE OAK INN **Phone:** (740)599-6107
All Year [BP] 1P: $75-$85 2P: $85-$165
Location: 3 mi s on US 62, 1.3 mi se on US 36, 2.7 mi e on SR 715. 29683 Walhonding Rd (SR 715) 43014. **Facility:** Three rooms in this quiet, rural inn have fireplaces; telephones and televisions are available on request. Smoke free premises. 10 one-bedroom standard units, some with whirlpools. 3 stories (no elevator), interior corridors. *Bath:* combo or shower only. **Parking:** on-site. **Terms:** age restrictions may apply, 14 day cancellation notice fee imposed, package plans, no pets allowed (pet on premises). **Leisure Activities:** hiking trails. **Guest Services:** complimentary evening beverages. **Business Services:** meeting rooms. **Cards:** AX, DS, MC, VI.
Bed & Breakfast

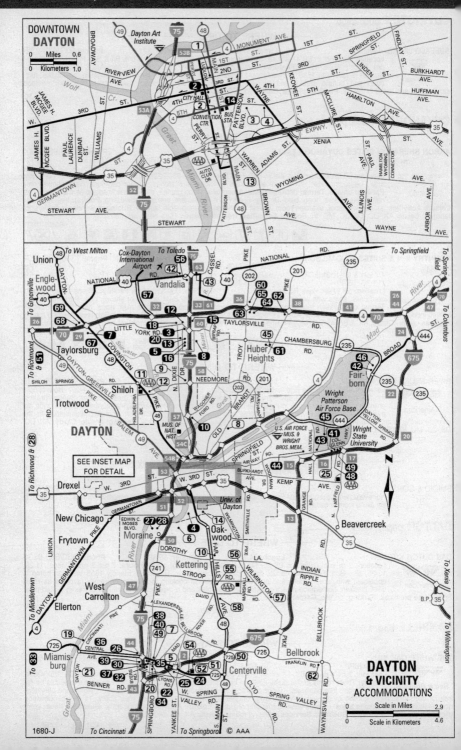

DOWNTOWN DAYTON

DAYTON & VICINITY ACCOMMODATIONS

1680-J
© AAA

Dayton and Vicinity

This index helps you "spot" where approved accommodations and restaurants are located on the corresponding detailed maps. Lodging rate ranges are for comparison only and show the property's high season; rates are per night, unless only weekly (W) or monthly (M) rates are available. Restaurant rate range is for dinner, unless only lunch (L) is served. Turn to the listing page for more detailed rate information and consult display ads for special promotions.

Spotter/Map Page Number	OA	DAYTON - Lodgings	Diamond Rating	Rate Range High Season	Listing Page
2 / p. 672	AAA	**DoubleTree Hotel Dayton Downtown**	◆◆◆	$69-$199 SAVE	676
3 / p. 672		Motel 6 - 603	◆	$37-$53	678
4 / p. 672	AAA	**Dayton Marriott Hotel** - see color ad card insert	◆◆◆	$69-$149 SAVE	676
5 / p. 672		Extended Stay America-Dayton North	◆◆	$49-$74	676
7 / p. 672		Comfort Inn-Englewood	◆◆◆	$70-$165	676
8 / p. 672	AAA	**Residence Inn by Marriott-Dayton North** - see color ad card insert	◆◆◆	$129 SAVE	679
10 / p. 672		Holiday Inn Dayton North	◆◆◆	$76-$85	677
12 / p. 672	AAA	**Red Roof Inn-North**	◆◆	$49-$73 SAVE	679
13 / p. 672	AAA	**Fairfield Inn by Marriott** - see color ad card insert	◆◆◆	$69 SAVE	676
14 / p. 672		Crowne Plaza-Dayton	◆◆◆	$89-$149	676
15 / p. 672		Howard Johnson Express Inn - see color ad p 677	◆◆	$61-$99	677
16 / p. 672	AAA	**Courtyard By Marriott** - see color ad card insert	◆◆◆	$89-$144 SAVE	676
18 / p. 672		Ramada Inn-North	◆◆	$45-$75	678
20 / p. 672		Comfort Inn-Dayton North	◆◆◆	$77-$97	676
22 / p. 672		Quality Inn Dayton-South	◆◆	$59-$89	678
24 / p. 672	AAA	**Hampton Inn-Dayton South**	◆◆◆	$65-$90 SAVE	677
25 / p. 672	AAA	**Fairfield Inn By Marriott Dayton South** - see color ad card insert	◆◆◆	$77-$80 SAVE	677
26 / p. 672	AAA	**Ramada Inn Dayton Mall** - see ad p 678	◆◆◆	$79-$104 SAVE	678
		DAYTON - Restaurants			
1 / p. 672		Olivia's	◆◆◆	$14-$26	680
2 / p. 672		The Spaghetti Warehouse	◆◆	$6-$12	680
3 / p. 672	AAA	**Jay's Restaurant**	◆◆	$12-$28	679
4 / p. 672		The Trolley Shop	◆	$6-$9	680
5 / p. 672		Bravo Cucina Italian Restaurant	◆◆	$9-$22	679
6 / p. 672	AAA	**Neils Restaurant**	◆◆	$10-$25	680
7 / p. 672		India Palace Restaurant	◆	$8-$13	679
8 / p. 672		Elinor's Amber Rose	◆◆	$10-$15	679
9 / p. 672		Ma's Chinese Restaurant	◆◆	$9-$25	680
10 / p. 672		Nanci's Porches	◆◆	$10-$16	680
11 / p. 672		Shuckin Shack	◆◆	$10-$17	680
12 / p. 672		The Barnsider	◆◆	$11-$22	679
13 / p. 672		Benham's	◆◆◆	$17-$24	679
14 / p. 672		The Pine Club	◆◆◆	$10-$25	680

Spotter/Map Page Number	OA	**MORAINE** - Lodgings	Diamond Rating	Rate Range High Season	Listing Page
27 / p. 672		Holiday Inn Hotel & Suites	▽▽▽	$79	717
28 / p. 672		Super 8 Motel-Moraine	▽▽	$49-$99	717
		MIAMISBURG - Lodgings			
30 / p. 672	AAA	**Courtyard by Marriott** - see color ad card insert	▽▽▽	$120-$130 [SAVE]	713
32 / p. 672	AAA	**Residence Inn by Marriott-Dayton South** - see color ad card insert	▽▽▽	$124-$140 [SAVE]	714
33 / p. 672		English Manor Bed & Breakfast	▽▽	$79-$125	713
34 / p. 672		Homewood Suites Hotel-Dayton Mall	▽▽▽	$129-$149	713
35 / p. 672		Doubletree Guest Suites-Dayton Mall	▽▽▽	$179-$194	713
36 / p. 672		Best Western Continental Inn	▽▽	$60-$73	713
37 / p. 672		Signature Inn Dayton South	▽▽▽	$68-$78	714
38 / p. 672		Holiday Inn-Dayton Mall - see color ad p 677	▽▽▽	$98-$107	713
39 / p. 672	AAA	**Red Roof Inn-South**	▽▽	$47-$66 [SAVE]	713
40 / p. 672		Comfort Suites	▽▽▽	$85	713
		MIAMISBURG - Restaurants			
19 / p. 672		Bullwinkles Top Hat Bistro	▽▽	$9-$23	714
20 / p. 672		Steve Kao's Chinese Cuisine	▽▽▽	$10-$16	714
21 / p. 672	AAA	**Peerless Mill Inn**	▽▽▽	$11-$18	714
		FAIRBORN - Lodgings			
41 / p. 672	AAA	**Holiday Inn Conference Center/I-675**	▽▽▽	$109 [SAVE]	686
42 / p. 672	AAA	**Comfort Inn-Wright Patterson**	▽▽▽	$76-$84 [SAVE]	685
43 / p. 672		StudioPlus at Fairborn	▽▽	$65-$115	686
44 / p. 672	AAA	**Red Roof Inn-Fairborn**	▽▽	$56-$74 [SAVE]	686
45 / p. 672	AAA	**Homewood Suites-Fairborn/Dayton**	▽▽▽	$113-$115 [SAVE]	686
46 / p. 672	AAA	**Best Western Wright Patterson**	▽▽▽	$70-$110 [SAVE]	685
48 / p. 672	AAA	**Fairborn Fairfield Inn** - see color ad card insert	▽▽▽	$75-$95 [SAVE]	685
49 / p. 672		Hampton Inn Fairborn	▽▽▽	$66-$96	685
		FAIRBORN - Restaurant			
25 / p. 672		The City Chop House	▽▽▽	$10-$21	686
		BROOKVILLE - Lodgings			
51 / p. 672	AAA	**Brookville Days Inn**	▽▽	$50-$70 [SAVE]	544
		BROOKVILLE - Restaurant			
28 / p. 672		Rob's Family Dining	▽	$7-$11	544
		VANDALIA - Lodgings			
56 / p. 672	AAA	**Cross Country Inn**	▽▽	$40-$54 [SAVE]	766
57 / p. 672	AAA	**Travelodge Dayton Airport** - see ad p 678	▽▽	$55-$90 [SAVE]	766
		VANDALIA - Restaurants			
42 / p. 672	AAA	**Original Rib House**	▽▽	$8-$17	767
43 / p. 672		Fricker's	▽	$7-$14	767
		HUBER HEIGHTS - Lodgings			
60 / p. 672		Super 8 Motel	▽▽	$48-$51	697

Spotter/Map Page Number	OA	HUBER HEIGHTS - Lodgings (continued)	Diamond Rating	Rate Range High Season	Listing Page
61 / p. 672	AAA	Comfort Inn Dayton/Huber Heights	◈◈◈	$70-$75 SAVE	696
62 / p. 672	AAA	Travelodge	◈	$55-$60 SAVE	697
63 / p. 672	AAA	Days Inn-Huber Heights	◈◈◈	$45-$85 SAVE	696
64 / p. 672	AAA	Hampton Inn	◈◈◈	$89-$99 SAVE	696
65 / p. 672	AAA	Holiday Inn Express & Suites	◈◈◈	$79 SAVE	697
		HUBER HEIGHTS - Restaurant			
45 / p. 672		Thai-West Restaurant	◈	$9-$14	697
		ENGLEWOOD - Lodgings			
67 / p. 672	AAA	Cross Country Inn	◈◈	$38-$52 SAVE	684
68 / p. 672	AAA	Hampton Inn, Dayton NW	◈◈◈	$75-$110 SAVE	685
69 / p. 672		Holiday Inn-Dayton Northwest Airport	◈◈◈	$65-$125	685
		CENTERVILLE - Restaurants			
49 / p. 672	AAA	Amar India Restaurant	◈	$10-$15	550
50 / p. 672		Cozymel's Coastal Mexican Grill	◈◈	$7-$16	550
51 / p. 672		The Chop House	◈◈	$8-$21	550
52 / p. 672		The Paragon Club	◈◈◈	$12-$22	551
54 / p. 672		J Alexander's Restaurant	◈◈	$8-$20	550
		KETTERING - Restaurants			
55 / p. 672		Peasant Stock-A Restaurant	◈◈	$11-$18	701
56 / p. 672		Mamma Disalvo's Italian Ristorante	◈◈	$7-$20	701
57 / p. 672		Weltons Restaurant	◈◈◈	$10-$17	701
58 / p. 672		L'Auberge	◈◈◈	$40-$50	701
		BELLBROOK - Restaurant			
62 / p. 672		Garstka's Cafe	◈◈	$12-$22	539

Get on the Right Track

*The **AAA New Car & Truck Buying Guide*** presents unbiased reviews on more than 180 new domestic and imported vehicles. You will find easy-to-read comparison data, ratings of key vehicle features, strong and weak points, specifications, pricing information, and more. Make sure your next vehicle is the right vehicle for you. **Purchase at participating AAA club offices or web sites (aaa.com) or by calling 1-877-AAA-BOOK.**

DAYTON pop. 182,000　(See map p. 672; index p. 673)

———— WHERE TO STAY ————

COMFORT INN-DAYTON NORTH
Phone: (937)890-9995　**20**

SAVE

Motel

	5/1-10/31 [CP]	1P: $77-$87	2P: $87-$97	XP: $5	F17
	4/1-4/30 [CP]	1P: $74-$84	2P: $79-$89	XP: $5	F17
	11/1-3/31 [CP]	1P: $71-$81	2P: $76-$86	XP: $5	F17

Location: I-75, exit 60, at Little York Rd. 7125 Miller Ln 45414. Fax: 937/890-9995. **Facility:** 56 one-bedroom standard units. 2 stories, interior corridors. *Bath:* combo or shower only. **Parking:** on-site, winter plug-ins. **Terms:** 5 day cancellation notice. **Amenities:** extended cable TV. *Some:* irons, hair dryers. **Pool(s):** heated indoor. **Leisure Activities:** whirlpool. **Guest Services:** valet laundry. **Cards:** AX, DC, DS, MC, VI.

SOME UNITS

COMFORT INN-ENGLEWOOD
Phone: (937)836-9400　**7**

SAVE

Motel

All Year　1P: $70-$150　2P: $75-$165　XP: $10　F12

Location: I-70, exit 29. 9305 N Main St 45415. Fax: 937/832-9712. **Facility:** 55 one-bedroom standard units, some with whirlpools. 3 stories, interior corridors. *Bath:* combo or shower only. **Parking:** on-site. **Terms:** 10 day cancellation notice. **Amenities:** extended cable TV, voice mail, irons, hair dryers. **Pool(s):** heated indoor. **Cards:** AX, DC, DS, MC, VI.

SOME UNITS

COURTYARD BY MARRIOTT
Phone: (937)890-6112　**16**

AAA **SAVE**

Motel

	6/1-9/30	1P: $89-$139	2P: $94-$144	XP: $5	F16
	4/1-5/31 & 10/1-11/30	1P: $79-$129	2P: $84-$134	XP: $5	F16
	12/1-3/31	1P: $69-$119	2P: $74-$124	XP: $5	F16

Location: I-75, exit 60, just s. 7087 Miller Ln 45414. Fax: 937/890-6112. **Facility:** 78 units. 75 one-bedroom standard units. 3 one-bedroom suites. 3 stories, interior corridors. *Bath:* combo or shower only. **Parking:** on-site. **Terms:** cancellation fee imposed. **Amenities:** extended cable TV, dual phone lines, voice mail, irons, hair dryers. **Dining:** 6:30-10 am, Sat & Sun 7-11 am. **Pool(s):** heated indoor. **Leisure Activities:** whirlpool, exercise room. **Guest Services:** valet and coin laundry. **Business Services:** meeting rooms. **Cards:** AX, DC, DS, MC, VI. *(See color ad card insert)*

SOME UNITS

CROWNE PLAZA-DAYTON
Phone: (937)224-0800　**14**

Hotel

All Year　1P: $89-$149　2P: $89-$149

Location: Downtown; opposite Dayton Convention Center, Fifth and Jefferson sts. 33 E Fifth St 45402. Fax: 937/224-3913. **Facility:** 283 one-bedroom standard units. 14 stories, interior corridors. **Parking:** on-site and valet (fee). **Terms:** 24 day cancellation notice-fee imposed, package plans. **Amenities:** extended cable TV, video games, voice mail, irons, hair dryers. **Pool(s):** heated outdoor. **Leisure Activities:** exercise room. **Guest Services:** gift shop, valet laundry. **Business Services:** conference facilities, business center, administrative services, PC, fax. **Cards:** AX, CB, DC, DS, JC, MC, VI.

SOME UNITS

DAYTON MARRIOTT HOTEL
Phone: (937)223-1000　**4**

AAA **SAVE**

Hotel

All Year　1P: $69-$149　2P: $69-$149

Location: I-75, exit 51 (Edwin C Moses Blvd), 1 mi e. 1414 S Patterson Blvd 45409. Fax: 937/223-7853. **Facility:** 399 one-bedroom standard units. 6 stories, interior corridors. *Bath:* combo or shower only. **Parking:** on-site. **Terms:** [BP] meal plan available, package plans, small pets only. **Amenities:** Web TV, voice mail, irons, hair dryers. **Dining:** restaurant, 6:30 am-2 & 5-11 pm, Sat & Sun from 7 am, $8-$20, cocktails. **Leisure Activities:** sauna, whirlpool, bicycles, exercise room. **Guest Services:** gift shop, coin laundry. **Business Services:** conference facilities, business center, PC, fax. **Cards:** AX, CB, DC, DS, JC, MC, VI. *(See color ad card insert)*

SOME UNITS

DOUBLETREE HOTEL DAYTON DOWNTOWN
Phone: (937)461-4700　**2**

AAA **SAVE**

Hotel

All Year　1P: $69-$199　2P: $69-$199　XP: $10　D18

Location: Downtown; at Courthouse Square. 11 S Ludlow St 45402. Fax: 937/461-3440. **Facility:** 185 one-bedroom standard units. 12 stories, interior corridors. **Parking:** *Fee:* on-site and valet. **Terms:** package plans. **Amenities:** voice mail, irons, hair dryers. **Dining:** dining room, 6 am-10 pm, Sat & Sun from 7 am, $9-$16, cocktails, entertainment. **Pool(s):** heated indoor. **Leisure Activities:** sauna, whirlpool, exercise room. **Guest Services:** valet laundry. **Business Services:** conference facilities. **Cards:** AX, DC, DS, MC, VI.

SOME UNITS

EXTENDED STAY AMERICA-DAYTON NORTH
Phone: (937)898-9221　**5**

Extended Stay Motel

All Year　1P: $49-$74　2P: $49-$74

Location: I-75, exit 60, just s. 6688 Miller Ln 45414. Fax: 937/898-9227. **Facility:** 104 one-bedroom standard units with efficiencies. 3 stories, interior corridors. *Bath:* combo or shower only. **Parking:** on-site. **Amenities:** voice mail. **Guest Services:** coin laundry. **Cards:** AX, DC, DS, MC, VI.

SOME UNITS

FAIRFIELD INN BY MARRIOTT
Phone: (937)898-1120　**13**

AAA **SAVE**

Motel

All Year　1P: $69

Location: I-75, exit 60, at Little York Rd. 6960 Miller Ln 45414. Fax: 937/898-1120. **Facility:** 135 one-bedroom standard units. 3 stories, interior/exterior corridors. *Bath:* combo or shower only. **Parking:** on-site. **Terms:** [ECP] meal plan available. **Amenities:** irons. **Pool(s):** heated outdoor. **Guest Services:** valet laundry. **Cards:** AX, DC, DS, MC, VI. **Special Amenities:** free continental breakfast and free local telephone calls. *(See color ad card insert)*

SOME UNITS

(See map p. 672)

FAIRFIELD INN BY MARRIOTT DAYTON SOUTH **Phone:** (937)428-7736 [25]

AAA **SAVE**

Motel

| 4/1-10/15 & 3/8-3/31 [CP] | 1P: $77-$80 | 2P: $77-$80 |
| 10/16-3/7 [CP] | 1P: $65-$70 | 2P: $65-$70 |

Location: I-675, exit 2, just e on SR 725. 8035 Washington Village Dr 45458. Fax: 937/428-7736. **Facility:** 82 one-bedroom standard units. 3 stories, interior corridors. *Bath:* combo or shower only. **Parking:** on-site. **Amenities:** extended cable TV, irons. **Pool(s):** heated indoor. **Leisure Activities:** whirlpool. **Guest Services:** valet laundry. **Cards:** AX, DC, DS, MC, VI. **Special Amenities:** free continental breakfast and free local telephone calls. *(See color ad card insert)*

HAMPTON INN-DAYTON SOUTH **Phone:** (937)436-3700 [24]

AAA **SAVE**

Motel

| All Year [CP] | 1P: $65-$85 | 2P: $70-$90 | XP: $5 | F18 |

Location: I-675, exit 2. 8099 Old Yankee St 45458. Fax: 937/436-2995. **Facility:** 130 one-bedroom standard units. 4 stories, interior corridors. **Parking:** on-site. **Amenities:** extended cable TV, voice mail, irons, hair dryers. **Pool(s):** outdoor. **Leisure Activities:** exercise room. **Guest Services:** valet laundry. **Business Services:** meeting rooms. **Cards:** AX, CB, DC, DS, MC, VI. **Special Amenities:** free continental breakfast and free local telephone calls.

HOLIDAY INN DAYTON NORTH **Phone:** (937)278-4871 [10]

Motor Inn

| All Year | 1P: $76-$85 | 2P: $76-$85 |

Location: I-75, exit 57B (Wagner-Ford Rd). 2301 Wagner-Ford Rd 45414. Fax: 937/278-0146. **Facility:** 231 one-bedroom standard units. 2-5 stories, interior corridors. **Terms:** package plans. **Amenities:** voice mail, irons, hair dryers. *Some:* dual phone lines. **Pool(s):** heated indoor. **Leisure Activities:** sauna, whirlpool, exercise room. **Guest Services:** valet laundry. **Business Services:** conference facilities. **Cards:** AX, CB, DC, DS, JC, MC, VI.

HOWARD JOHNSON EXPRESS INN **Phone:** (937)454-0550 [15]

Motel

| All Year [ECP] | 1P: $61-$92 | 2P: $68-$99 | XP: $7 | F18 |

Location: I-75, exit 60 northbound, just n; exit 60 southbound, n on Miller Ln, then n on Little York Rd. 7575 Poe Ave 45414. Fax: 937/454-5566. **Facility:** 120 one-bedroom standard units. 2 stories, interior corridors. **Parking:** on-site. **Terms:** pets ($50 deposit). **Pool(s):** outdoor. **Leisure Activities:** exercise room. **Guest Services:** coin laundry. **Business Services:** meeting rooms. **Cards:** AX, CB, DC, DS, MC, VI. *(See color ad below)*

(See map p. 672)

MOTEL 6 - 603

Motel

	5/23-3/31	1P: $37-$47	2P: $43-$53	Phone: 937/898-3606	**3**
	4/1-5/22	1P: $35-$45	2P: $41-$51	XP: $3	F17
				XP: $3	F17

Location: I-75, exit 60 (Little York Rd). 7130 Miller Ln 45414. Fax: 937/890-3898. **Facility:** 98 one-bedroom standard units. 3 stories, exterior corridors. *Bath:* shower only. **Parking:** on-site. **Terms:** small pets only. **Pool(s):** heated outdoor. **Guest Services:** coin laundry. **Cards:** AX, CB, DC, DS, MC, VI.

SOME UNITS

QUALITY INN DAYTON-SOUTH

SAVE

Motel

Phone: (937)435-1550 **22**

All Year [ECP]   1P: $59-$89   2P: $59-$89   XP: $10   F17

Location: I-675, exit 2, just w of jct SR 725. 1944 Miamisburg-Centerville Rd 45459. Fax: 937/438-1878. **Facility:** 73 one-bedroom standard units. 2 stories, exterior corridors. **Parking:** on-site, winter plug-ins. **Amenities:** extended cable TV, irons, hair dryers. **Pool(s):** indoor. **Guest Services:** coin laundry. **Cards:** AX, CB, DC, DS, JC, MC, VI.

SOME UNITS

FEE

RAMADA INN DAYTON MALL

(AAA) SAVE

Motor Inn

Phone: (937)847-8422 **26**

All Year [ECP]   1P: $79-$99   2P: $84-$104   XP: $10   F17

Location: I-75, exit 2, just w on SR 725. 3555 Miamisburg-Centerville Rd 45449. Fax: 937/847-8862. **Facility:** 215 one-bedroom standard units, some with whirlpools. 2 stories, interior corridors. *Bath:* combo or shower only. **Parking:** on-site. **Terms:** [CP] meal plan available. **Amenities:** extended cable TV, dual phone lines, voice mail, safes, irons, hair dryers. **Dining:** restaurant, 7 am-10 pm, $5-$8, cocktails. **Pool(s):** heated indoor. **Leisure Activities:** sauna, whirlpool, tennis court, exercise room, basketball, shuffleboard, volleyball. *Fee:* game room. **Guest Services:** valet and coin laundry. **Business Services:** meeting rooms. **Cards:** AX, DC, DS, MC, VI. **Special Amenities:** free continental breakfast and free room upgrade (subject to availability with advanced reservations). *(See ad below)*

SOME UNITS

RAMADA INN-NORTH

Motor Inn

Phone: (937)890-9500 **18**

All Year [CP]   1P: $45-$65   2P: $50-$75   XP: $5   F18

Location: I-75, exit 60, 0.5 mi s of jct I-70. 4079 Little York Rd 45414. Fax: 937/890-8525. **Facility:** 136 one-bedroom standard units, some with whirlpools. 2 stories, interior/exterior corridors. **Parking:** on-site. **Terms:** 10 day cancellation notice, pets ($10 extra charge). **Amenities:** extended cable TV, voice mail, irons, hair dryers. **Pool(s):** heated outdoor. **Leisure Activities:** playground, exercise room. **Guest Services:** coin laundry. **Business Services:** meeting rooms. **Cards:** AX, CB, DC, DS, MC, VI.

SOME UNITS

FEE

(See map p. 672)

RED ROOF INN-NORTH   Phone: (937)898-1054   🔢12

AAA SAVE

5/5-8/24	1P: $49-$68	2P: $54-$73	XP: $5	F18
4/1-5/4	1P: $44-$68	2P: $49-$73	XP: $5	F18
8/25-3/31	1P: $44-$63	2P: $49-$73	XP: $5	F18

Motel   **Location:** I-75, exit 60; 0.5 mi s of jct I-70. 7370 Miller Ln 45414. Fax: 937/898-1059. **Facility:** 109 one-bedroom standard units. 2 stories, exterior corridors. *Bath:* combo or shower only. **Parking:** on-site. **Amenities:** video games, voice mail. **Guest Services:** coin laundry. **Cards:** AX, CB, DC, DS, MC, VI. **Special Amenities: free local telephone calls and free newspaper.**

🏨 🅿️ ⚙️ 📶 📺 🔌 DATA PORT 🖨️ / ✕ 🔒 🗄️ 💻 /
FEE

RESIDENCE INN BY MARRIOTT-DAYTON NORTH   Phone: 937/898-7764   🔢8

AAA SAVE

| 4/1-10/31 [BP] | 1P: $129 | 2P: $129 |
| 11/1-3/31 [BP] | 1P: $119 | 2P: $119 |

Apartment   **Location:** I-75, exit 60. 7070 Poe Ave 45414. Fax: 937/890-5891. **Facility:** 64 one-bedroom standard units with kitchens. 2 stories, exterior corridors. *Bath:* combo or shower only. **Parking:** on-site. **Terms:** 7 day cancellation notice-fee imposed, pets ($100-$200 extra charge). **Amenities:** voice mail, irons, hair dryers. **Pool(s):** heated outdoor. **Leisure Activities:** whirlpool, sports court, barbecue grills. **Guest Services:** coin laundry. **Business Services:** meeting rooms. **Cards:** AX, CB, DC, DS, JC, MC, VI. *(See color ad card insert)*

S/D 🏨 🅿️ ⚙️ 📶 🌊 📺 ✕ 🔌 DATA PORT 🔒 🗄️ 💻 🖨️ / ✕ VCR /
SOME UNITS   FEE

———— *The following lodging was either not evaluated or did not* ————
meet AAA rating requirements but is listed for your information only.

EXTENDED STAY AMERICA   Phone: 937/439-2022

[fyi]   Not evaluated. **Location:** I-75, exit 44, just e on SR 725; opposite mall. 7851 Lois Cir 45459. Facilities, services, and decor characterize a mid-range property.

———— **WHERE TO DINE** ————

THE BARNSIDER   Dinner: $11-$22   Phone: 937/277-1332   🔢12

Steak & Seafood   **Location:** I-75, exit 54B, 5 mi nw on SR 48 (N Main St). 5202 N Main St 45415. **Hours:** 5 pm-10 pm, Fri & Sat from 4 pm, Sun noon-10 pm. Closed major holidays. **Reservations:** suggested. **Features:** casual dress; children's menu; carryout; cocktails & lounge. Subtle lighting, candles and background music give the intimate dining room a romantic feel. Prime rib and shrimp are among entrees served with fresh bread. The redskin potatoes are well-seasoned and flavorful. Service is attentive and prompt. **Parking:** on-site. **Cards:** AX, MC, VI.
✕

BENHAM'S   Lunch: $8-$11   Dinner: $17-$24   Phone: 937/228-7041   🔢13

American   **Location:** From Main St/Jefferson, exit off SR 35, 0.3 mi s via Jefferson. 209 Warren St 45402. **Hours:** 11 am-2 pm, also 5:30 pm-8:30 pm Thurs-Sat. Closed major holidays; also Sun. **Reservations:** suggested. **Features:** dressy casual; carryout; cocktails; a la carte. Elegant artwork and historical furnishings decorate the quiet, upscale dining room. The restaurant serves up innovative, well-prepared American cuisine, including an excellent array of homemade desserts. The wait staff is professional and attentive. A few memorable dishes would include wild mushrooms and spinach pasta and sauteed chicken parmesan. Smoke free premises. **Parking:** on-site. **Cards:** AX, MC, VI.
✕

BRAVO CUCINA ITALIAN RESTAURANT   Lunch: $8-$12   Dinner: $9-$22   Phone: 937/439-1398   🔢5

Italian   **Location:** I-675, exit 2, just w on SR 725; near Dayton Mall. 2148 Miamisburg-Centerville Rd 45459. **Hours:** 11 am-10 pm, Fri & Sat-11 pm. Closed major holidays. **Features:** casual dress; children's menu; carryout; cocktails & lounge. Lasagna, chicken scalloppine romano and grilled steaks are among specialties on the restaurant's creative menu. The large, spacious dining room resembles historic Roman ruins. A wood-burning stove serves as the centerpiece of the open kitchen. **Parking:** on-site. **Cards:** AX, DC, DS, MC, VI.
✕

ELINOR'S AMBER ROSE   Historical   Lunch: $7-$10   Dinner: $10-$15   Phone: 937/228-2511   🔢8

East German   **Location:** SR 4, w on Stanley Ave, then 3 blks n. 1400 Valley St 45404. **Hours:** 11 am-9 pm, Mon-2 pm, Fri & Sat 11 am-10 pm. Closed major holidays; also Sun. **Reservations:** suggested. **Features:** casual dress; children's menu; carryout; cocktails & lounge; a la carte. Home-cooked Eastern European cuisine, such as cabbage rolls, sauerbraten and sweet homemade strudel, makes up much of the restaurant's menu. The cozy dining room has the feel of a laid-back deli, with a marble bar, wood flooring and tapestries. **Parking:** on-site. **Cards:** AX, MC, VI.

INDIA PALACE RESTAURANT   Lunch: $4-$6   Dinner: $8-$13   Phone: 937/433-3575   🔢7

Ethnic   **Location:** Jct SR 741 and 725, just s on SR 741; then e behind Dayton Mall. 8990 Kingsridge Dr 45459. **Hours:** 11 am-3 & 5-10 pm, Fri & Sat 11 am-10:30 pm, Sun 11 am-9:30 pm. **Features:** casual dress; carryout; cocktails; buffet. Flavorful teas, tandoori chicken, rice pudding and honey cake are among the authentic specialties of the small, quiet restaurant. Indian-themed artwork adds a nice touch to the overall simple decor. Friendly servers show good follow-up skills. Lunch buffet includes tandoori, chicken, vegetables and Indian bread. Smoke free premises. **Parking:** on-site. **Cards:** DS, MC, VI.
✕

JAY'S RESTAURANT   Historical   Dinner: $12-$28   Phone: 937/222-2892   🔢3

AAA

Seafood   **Location:** In Historical Oregon District. 225 E 6th St 45402. **Hours:** 5 pm-10:30 pm, Fri & Sat-11 pm, Sun-9 pm. Closed major holidays. **Reservations:** suggested; except Sat. **Features:** casual dress; carryout; cocktails; a la carte. Originally an 1862 grist mill, the restaurant has a cozy turn-of-the-20th-century atmosphere. The salmon en croute is wrapped in puff pastry and topped with mushrooms and lobster sauce. The on-premises bakery creates delicious breads and desserts. Other favorite dishes include Atlantic arctic char and crab stuffed sole. **Parking:** on-site. **Cards:** AX, DC, DS, MC, VI.
✕

(See map p. 672)

MA'S CHINESE RESTAURANT

Chinese

Lunch: $7-$9   **Dinner:** $9-$25   **Phone:** 937/898-1466   ⑨

Location: I-75, exit 58 (Needmore Rd), 0.5 mi w. 1875 Needmore Rd 45414. **Hours:** 11 am-2 & 4:30-10 pm, Sat noon-9 pm. Closed: 11/28, 12/25. **Reservations:** suggested. **Features:** casual dress; Sunday brunch; carryout; cocktails & lounge; a la carte, buffet. Szechuan and Mandarin specialties, such as spicy chicken with vegetables and glazed bananas, make up the restaurant's traditional menu. Tables topped with flowers and candles sit in a relaxed dining room decorated with attractive paintings. Popular lunch buffet includes hot and sour soup, crab rangoon and a variety of main dishes. **Parking:** on-site. **Cards:** AX, DC, MC, VI.

NANCI'S PORCHES

American

Lunch: $8-$10   **Dinner:** $10-$16   **Phone:** 937/299-9000   ⑩

Location: Jct E Dorthy Ln and Far Hills Ave, just n. 2600 Far Hills Ave 45419. **Hours:** 11 am-2:30 & 5-10 pm, Fri & Sat-11 pm, Sun 5 pm-9 pm. Closed major holidays; also Mon. **Features:** casual dress; cocktails. Located in the heart of Oakwood, this restaurant serves popular eclectic, classic American cuisine. **Parking:** on-site. **Cards:** AX, DS, MC, VI.

NEILS RESTAURANT

American

Cards: MC, VI.

Lunch: $8-$12   **Dinner:** $10-$25   **Phone:** 937/298-8611   ⑥

Location: I-75, exit 51, 0.8 mi e Edwin C Moses Blvd, e over Stewart St Bridge, then 0.8 mi s on S Patterson Blvd. 2323 W Schantz Ave 45409. **Hours:** 11 am-2 & 5-9 pm, Fri & Sat-10 pm, Sun 11 am-8 pm. Closed major holidays; also Mon. **Reservations:** suggested. **Features:** casual dress; Sunday brunch; children's menu; carryout; cocktails & lounge; a la carte. A local tradition since 1946, the casually upscale restaurant specializes in steak and fresh seafood, such as salmon and broiled scrod. Soft background music adds to the cozy ambience in the two main dining rooms. Sunday brunch is particularly popular. **Parking:** on-site.

OLIVIA'S

Regional American

Lunch: $8-$14   **Dinner:** $14-$26   **Phone:** 937/222-6771   ①

Location: Center; in Kettering Tower lobby. 2nd & Main sts 45402. **Hours:** 11:30 am-2 & 5-10 pm, Mon-2 pm, Sat from 5 pm. Closed major holidays; also Sun. **Reservations:** suggested. **Features:** dressy casual; cocktails & lounge; a la carte. Olivia's takes a fresh, updated approach to haute Midwestern cuisine, capturing the best of seasonally available ingredients. A fine example is the roast pepper duck with black-eyed peas and hominy succotash. An extensive wine list is available. **Parking:** on-site (fee). **Cards:** AX, DC, DS, MC, VI.

THE PINE CLUB

American

Dinner: $10-$25   **Phone:** 937/228-7463   ⑭

Location: Downtown; 3 mi s. 1926 Brown St 45409. **Hours:** 5 pm-midnight, Fri & Sat-1 am. Closed major holidays; also Sun. **Features:** casual dress; cocktails & lounge. The restaurant is known for its creative steak entrees. **Parking:** on-site.

SHUCKIN SHACK

Seafood

Dinner: $10-$17   **Phone:** 937/274-3335   ⑪

Location: I-75, exit 54B, 5.3 mi nw on SR 48 (N Main St). 5515 N Main St 45415. **Hours:** 4 pm-11 pm, Sat 3 pm-midnight, Sun 3 pm-10 pm. Closed major holidays; also Mon. **Features:** casual dress; children's menu; carryout; cocktails & lounge. Appointed with numerous fish tanks and a seafaring theme, the dining room sets the tone for this seafood restaurant. The menu includes fresh oyster stew, Lake Erie smelt, crawfish, pasta and blue crab imperial. Servers are casual and attentive. **Parking:** on-site. **Cards:** AX, DC, DS, MC, VI.

THE SPAGHETTI WAREHOUSE

Italian

Lunch: $6-$9   **Dinner:** $6-$12   **Phone:** 937/461-3913   ②

Location: Downtown; between S Ludlow and Main sts. 36 W Fifth St 45402. **Hours:** 11 am-10 pm, Fri-11 pm, Sat noon-11 pm. Closed: 11/28, 12/25. **Features:** casual dress; children's menu; carryout; cocktails & lounge. Served here are an assortment of American and Italian entrees. **Parking:** on-site. **Cards:** AX, DS, MC, VI.

THE TROLLEY SHOP

American

Lunch: $6-$9   **Dinner:** $6-$9   **Phone:** 937/461-1101   ④

Location: In Historic Oregon District; at jct E Fifth St and Wayne. 530 E Fifth St 45402. **Hours:** 11 am-10 pm. Closed major holidays; also Sun. **Features:** casual dress; carryout; cocktails & lounge. Near downtown, the restaurant serves eclectic, vegetarian dishes. **Parking:** on-site. **Cards:** AX, DC, DS, MC, VI.

The following restaurants have not been evaluated by AAA but are listed for your information only.

BUCKHORN TAVERN   **Phone:** 937/890-3261
[fyi]   Not evaluated. **Location:** I-270, exit 29; 0.5 mi s on SR 48, 0.5 mi s on Heathcliff, just n on Meerer Rd. 8800 Meerer Rd 45415.

CAFE BOULEVARD   **Phone:** 937/824-2722
[fyi]   Not evaluated. **Location:** 329 E Fifth St 45402. Located in the popular Oregon historic district, this eatery prepares French/European dishes.

DUKE'S GOLDEN OX   **Phone:** 937/222-6200
[fyi]   Not evaluated. **Location:** 1202 S Main St 45409. Near the fairgrounds, this eatery prepares steak and Italian specialties.

FUSION GRILL   **Phone:** 937/224-9727
[fyi]   Not evaluated. **Location:** 211 S Main St 45402. The downtown eatery features Caribbean cuisine and popular American fare.

LITTLE SAIGON   **Phone:** 937/258-8010
[fyi]   Not evaluated. **Location:** 1718 Woodman Dr. The modest restaurant presents a menu of inexpensive Vietnamese cuisine.

PACCHIA   **Phone:** 937/341-5050
[fyi]   Not evaluated. **Location:** 410 E Fifth St 45402. The eatery features California bistro-style food and Italian dishes.

(See map p. 672)

PARK ROW SUPPER CLUB   Phone: 937/298-0358
[fyi] Not evaluated. **Location:** 969 Patterson Rd 45419. French cuisine is the specialty at this restaurant.

PEASANT STOCK ON THE RIVER   Phone: 937/224-0535
[fyi] Not evaluated. **Location:** 34 Emmet St 45405. This eatery has a great location overlooking the river.

PEPITOS   Phone: 937/277-1476
[fyi] Not evaluated. **Location:** 2412 Catalpa Dr 45406. Classic Mexican dishes are served at the casual restaurant.

DEFIANCE pop. 16,800

——— WHERE TO STAY ———

COMFORT INN   Phone: 419/784-4900
[SAVE]
Motel
Location: Jct SR 66 and 15. 1068 Hotel Dr 43512. Fax: 419/784-5555. **Facility:** 61 units. 59 one-bedroom standard units, some with whirlpools. 2 one-bedroom suites with whirlpools. 2 stories, interior corridors. *Bath:* combo or shower only. **Parking:** on-site. **Terms:** 15 day cancellation notice. **Amenities:** extended cable TV, irons, hair dryers. **Pool(s):** indoor. **Leisure Activities:** whirlpool, exercise room. **Guest Services:** coin laundry. **Business Services:** meeting rooms. **Fee:** PC, fax. **Cards:** AX, CB, DC, DS, JC, MC, VI.

| | 1P: $66 | 2P: $66 | XP: $5 | F18 |
| All Year | | | | |

SOME UNITS

SUPER 8 MOTEL   Phone: 419/782-8000
Motel
Location: Jct SR 66 and 15. 1053 Hotel Dr 43512. Fax: 419/782-4645. **Facility:** 50 one-bedroom standard units, some with whirlpools. 2 stories, interior corridors. **Parking:** on-site. **Amenities:** extended cable TV. **Guest Services:** coin laundry. **Business Services:** meeting rooms. **Cards:** AX, CB, DC, DS, JC, MC, VI.

| All Year | 1P: $46 | 2P: $52 | XP: $5 | F12 |

SOME UNITS

——— WHERE TO DINE ———

BARNESFOOD.COM   Lunch: $6-$10   Dinner: $8-$14   Phone: 419/782-2891
American
Location: 1.8 mi e of town center. 1940 E Second St 43512. **Hours:** 6:30 am-2 pm, Sat 7-11 am. Closed major holidays; also Mon. **Features:** casual dress; children's menu; carryout; salad bar; buffet. Blue-plate specials, such as meatloaf and Salisbury steak, are filling at the laid-back family restaurant. The buffet-line of rotating items is also an option. Country decorations, with latticework and shades of mauve, adorn the comfortable dining room. The apple dumplings are delicious. **Parking:** on-site. **Cards:** AX, MC, VI.

DELAWARE —*See Columbus p. 658.*

DELLROY pop. 300

——— WHERE TO STAY ———

ATWOOD LAKE RESORT   Phone: (330)735-2211
Resort

	1P	2P	XP	
5/25-9/30	1P: $116-$131	2P: $133-$148	XP: $15	F17
4/1-5/24 & 10/1-11/16	1P: $104-$119	2P: $121-$136	XP: $15	F17
11/17-3/31	1P: $96-$111	2P: $113-$128	XP: $15	F17

Location: 2.5 mi sw on SR 542. 2650 Lodge Rd (Rt 542) 44620 (PO Box 96). Fax: 330/735-2562. **Facility:** 121 units. 104 one-bedroom standard units. 17 three-bedroom vacation rentals ($115-$135). 2 stories, interior corridors. *Bath:* combo or shower only. **Parking:** on-site. **Terms:** check-in 4 pm, 14 day cancellation notice-fee imposed, package plans. **Amenities:** hair dryers. **Dining:** dining room, see separate listing. **Pool(s):** outdoor, heated indoor. **Leisure Activities:** sauna, whirlpool, marina, waterskiing, fishing, cross country skiing, children's program, nature trails, recreation program in summer, hiking trails, playground, exercise room, basketball, horseshoes, shuffleboard, volleyball. **Fee:** golf-18 holes, 2 lighted tennis courts, bicycles, game room. **Guest Services:** gift shop, valet laundry. **Business Services:** conference facilities, fax. **Cards:** AX, DC, DS, MC, VI.

SOME UNITS

FEE

WHISPERING PINES BED & BREAKFAST   Phone: (330)735-2824
Bed & Breakfast
Location: 3 mi n on SR 542. 1268 Magnolia, Rd SW 44620 (PO Box 340). Fax: 330/735-7006. **Facility:** Decorated with Victorian antiques, this lake-view B&B offers proximity to fishing, golf and wildlife-watching areas. Smoke free premises. 5 one-bedroom standard units, some with whirlpools. 2 stories, interior corridors. **Parking:** on-site. **Terms:** 14 day cancellation notice-fee imposed. **Amenities:** CD players, hair dryers. **Cards:** AX, DS, MC, VI.

| All Year [BP] | 1P: $120-$140 | 2P: $130-$195 |

——— WHERE TO DINE ———

DINING ROOM AT ATWOOD RESORT   Lunch: $7-$12   Dinner: $12-$20   Phone: 330/735-2211
American
Location: 2.5 mi sw on SR 542; in Atwood Lake Resort. 2650 Lodge Rd (Rt 542) 44620. **Hours:** 7 am-11, noon-2 & 5-9 pm. **Reservations:** suggested. **Features:** casual dress; Sunday brunch; children's menu; carryout; salad bar; cocktails & lounge; a la carte. You'll enjoy a fine view of Atwood Lake and the varied offering of breakfast, lunch and dinner buffets, including Friday seafood and Saturday prime rib spreads. The restaurant sits on a hill amid plenty of greenery. Vegetarian selections are available. Smoke free premises. **Parking:** on-site. **Cards:** AX, DC, DS, MC, VI.

DELPHOS

─────── WHERE TO DINE ───────

─────── *The following restaurants have not been evaluated by AAA* ───────
but are listed for your information only.

CARRIAGE INN RESTAURANT   **Phone:** 419/692-8866
[fyi]   Not evaluated. **Location:** 1201 E 5th St 45833. The focus of the menu is on Continental cuisine.

TOPP CHALET   **Phone:** 419/692-8888
[fyi]   Not evaluated. **Location:** 229 W 5th St 45833. Diners have come to expect home-style food that appeals to families.

DOVER pop. 11,300

─────── WHERE TO STAY ───────

COMFORT INN   **Phone:** (330)364-8881
(AAA) [SAVE]   5/2-10/31 [ECP]   1P: $65-$125   XP: $5   F18
▽▽▽▽   4/1-5/1 & 11/1-3/31 [ECP]   1P: $65-$100   XP: $5   F18
Motel   **Location:** I-77, exit 83, just w. 2024 SR 39 NW 44622. **Fax:** 330/364-6992. **Facility:** 60 one-bedroom standard units, some with whirlpools. 2 stories, interior corridors. **Parking:** on-site. **Amenities:** extended cable TV. *Some:* irons, hair dryers. **Pool(s):** heated indoor. **Leisure Activities:** whirlpool. **Guest Services:** coin laundry. **Business Services:** meeting rooms. **Cards:** AX, CB, DC, DS, MC, VI. **Special Amenities:** free **continental breakfast and preferred room (subject to availability with advanced reservations).**

SOME UNITS
[S/D] [⊞] [†↓] [⊇] [��] [DATA PORT] [▣] [🖨] / [✕] [🖬] [🖳] /

HOSPITALITY INN   **Phone:** (330)364-7724
▽▽▽   5/1-10/31   1P: $45-$65   2P: $55-$85   XP: $10   F16
Motel   11/1-3/31   1P: $38-$48   2P: $42-$52   XP: $6   F16
4/1-4/30   1P: $35-$45   2P: $40-$50   XP: $6   F16
Location: I-77, exit 83, just e. 889 Commercial Pkwy 44622. **Fax:** 330/364-7728. **Facility:** 100 one-bedroom standard units. 1 story, exterior corridors. **Parking:** on-site. **Terms:** 7 day cancellation notice, small pets only ($10 fee). **Amenities:** extended cable TV, voice mail. **Pool(s):** outdoor. **Guest Services:** valet laundry. **Cards:** AX, DC, DS, MC, VI.

SOME UNITS
[ASK] [S/D] [☞] [†↓] [⊘] [⊇] [🗡] [DATA PORT] / [✕] [🖬]

OLDE WORLD BED & BREAKFAST   **Phone:** 330/343-1333
▽▽▽   4/1-1/1 [BP]   1P: $80-$110   2P: $80-$110   XP: $20
Bed & Breakfast   1/2-3/31 [BP]   1P: $70-$100   2P: $70-$100   XP: $20
Location: I-77, exit 83, 0.3 mi w to SR 516, 1 mi nw. 2982 SR 516 NW 44622. **Fax:** 330/364-8022. **Facility:** Right off the interstate, this quiet B&B has a countryside ambience yet is convenient to attractions; its romance packages include carriage rides. Smoke free premises. 5 one-bedroom standard units. 2 stories, interior corridors. *Bath:* combo, shower or tub only. **Parking:** on-site. **Terms:** 5 day cancellation notice, package plans. **Leisure Activities:** whirlpool. **Cards:** DS, MC, VI.

SOME UNITS
[✕] [🖨] / [W] /

DUBLIN —*See Columbus p. 658.*

EAST CANTON pop. 1,700

─────── WHERE TO DINE ───────

NICOLE'S FAMILY RESTAURANT   **Lunch:** $4-$6   **Dinner:** $5-$8   **Phone:** 330/488-6111
(AAA)   **Location:** 0.5 mi w on US 30 and SR 172. 800 W Nausau St 44730. **Hours:** 6 am-8 pm, Sat from 7 am, Sun 7
▽▽   am-4 pm. Closed major holidays; also Mon. **Features:** children's menu; carryout. Decor reminiscent of the
American   1950s and 60s decorates the relaxed restaurant. Broasted chicken is a favorite on a menu that also includes homemade soup and chili. The food is reasonably priced. **Parking:** on-site. **Cards:** MC, VI.   [✕]

EASTLAKE pop. 21,200   (See map p. 600; index p. 604)

─────── WHERE TO STAY ───────

RADISSON HOTEL & CONFERENCE CLEVELAND-EASTLAKE   **Phone:** (440)953-8000   [87]
(AAA) [SAVE]   5/24-10/31   1P: $106-$129   2P: $106-$129   XP: $10   F17
▽▽▽▽   4/1-5/23 & 11/1-3/31   1P: $86-$116   2P: $86-$116   XP: $10   F17
Hotel   **Location:** Jct SR 2 and 91. 35000 Curtis Blvd 44095. **Fax:** 440/953-1706. **Facility:** 148 units. 136 one-bedroom standard units, some with whirlpools. 2 one- and 10 two-bedroom suites ($99-$289) with kitchens. 5 stories, interior corridors. *Bath:* combo or shower only. **Parking:** on-site. **Amenities:** extended cable TV, video games, voice mail, irons, hair dryers. *Some:* dual phone lines. **Dining:** restaurant, 6:30 am-2 & 5:30-10 pm, $10-$18, cocktails. **Pool(s):** heated indoor. **Leisure Activities:** exercise room. **Guest Services:** valet laundry, area transportation (fee). **Business Services:** conference facilities. **Cards:** AX, CB, DC, DS, MC, VI.

SOME UNITS
[S/D] [†↓] [Y] [⊘] [⊇] [🗡] [DATA PORT] [▣] [🖨] / [✕] [🖬] [🖳]
FEE   FEE FEE

EAST LIVERPOOL pop. 13,700

—————— WHERE TO STAY ——————

AMERIHOST INN & SUITES EAST LIVERPOOL
Phone: (330)386-3800
(AAA) (SAVE)   All Year   1P: $79-$89   2P: $79-$89   XP: $6   F18
WWWW   **Location:** US 30, exit SR 170, 1 mi e, then just s. 15860 St Clair Ave 43920. Fax: 330/386-3854. **Facility:** 66 one-
Hotel   bedroom standard units, some with whirlpools. 2 stories, interior corridors. *Bath:* combo or shower only.
Parking: on-site. **Amenities:** extended cable TV, high-speed Internet, voice mail, safes (fee), irons, hair
dryers. **Pool(s):** heated indoor. **Leisure Activities:** whirlpool, exercise room. **Guest Services:** valet laundry.
Business Services: meeting rooms. **Cards:** AX, CB, DC, DS, JC, MC, VI. **Special Amenities:** free conti-
nental breakfast and free newspaper.

SOME UNITS
[icons]

EAST LIVERPOOL MOTOR LODGE
Phone: (330)386-5858
(AAA) (SAVE)   All Year   1P: $55-$85   2P: $60-$90   XP: $5   F12
WWWW   **Location:** US 30, just n on SR 170 to Dresden Ave (CR 447), 1.3 mi e. 2340 Dresden Ave 43920. Fax: 330/386-6736.
Motor Inn   **Facility:** 69 one-bedroom standard units, some with whirlpools. 2 stories, interior corridors. *Bath:* combo or
shower only. **Parking:** on-site. **Terms:** 7 day cancellation notice. **Amenities:** extended cable TV.
Dining: Frontier Steak & Fish House, see separate listing. **Pool(s):** heated indoor. **Leisure Activi-
ties:** sauna, whirlpool. **Guest Services:** gift shop, coin laundry. **Business Services:** meeting rooms.
Cards: AX, CB, DC, DS, MC, VI.

SOME UNITS
[icons]

—————— WHERE TO DINE ——————

FRONTIER STEAK & FISH HOUSE   **Lunch:** $7   **Dinner:** $7-$17   **Phone:** 330/386-5858
WWWW WWWW   **Location:** US 30, just n on SR 170 to Dresden Ave (CR 447), 1.3 mi e; in East Liverpool Motor Lodge. 2340 Dresden
American   Ave 43920. **Hours:** 4 pm-10 pm, Wed & Fri from 11:30 am, Sat 4 pm-11 pm, Sun 9 am-9 pm. Closed:
12/25. **Reservations:** suggested. **Features:** casual dress; Sunday brunch; children's menu; early bird
specials; carryout; salad bar; cocktails & lounge. This restaurant offers fresh Chilean sea bass, stuffed
shrimp with sage dressing and the signature slow-roasted prime rib of beef. **Parking:** on-site. **Cards:** AX, DC, DS, MC, VI.
[icon]

HOT DOG SHOPPE   **Lunch:** $4-$7   **Dinner:** $4-$8   **Phone:** 330/386-6688
WWW   **Location:** Downtown. 318 Market St. **Hours:** 6:30 am-midnight, Sun 8 am-11 pm. Closed major holidays.
American   **Features:** casual dress; carryout. Quick service and a convenient location are found at this local eatery.
They specialize in hot dogs with burgers, sandwiches and fresh cut french fries also available. Their chili
recipe has been handed down from generation to generation. **Parking:** on-site.
[icon]

EATON pop. 7,400

—————— WHERE TO STAY ——————

ECONO LODGE
Phone: (937)456-5959
(AAA) (SAVE)   All Year [CP]   1P: $40-$45   2P: $49-$55   XP: $5   F18
WW WW   **Location:** I-70, exit 10 (US 127). 6161 Rt 127 N 45320. Fax: 937/456-5959. **Facility:** 51 one-bedroom standard
Motel   units. 1 story, exterior corridors. **Parking:** on-site. **Terms:** pets ($10 extra charge). **Amenities:** *Some:* hair
dryers. **Business Services:** meeting rooms. **Cards:** AX, DS, MC, VI.

SOME UNITS
[icons]

ELYRIA pop. 56,700

—————— WHERE TO STAY ——————

BEST WESTERN INN
Phone: (440)324-5050
(AAA) (SAVE)   6/4-9/17   1P: $90-$110   2P: $90-$110   XP: $5   F17
    9/18-3/31   1P: $60-$90   2P: $60-$100   XP: $5   F17
WWWW   5/15-6/3   1P: $70-$90   2P: $70-$90   XP: $5   F17
Motel   4/1-5/14   1P: $50-$60   2P: $50-$60
Location: I-80, exit 8, 0.3 mi n on SR 57, exit Midway Blvd. 636 Griswold Rd 44035. Fax: 440/324-1788. **Facility:** 56
one-bedroom standard units, some with whirlpools. 2 stories, interior corridors. *Bath:* combo or shower only.
Parking: on-site. **Terms:** 60 day cancellation notice-fee imposed. **Amenities:** extended cable TV, irons, hair dryers. **Pool(s):**
heated indoor. **Leisure Activities:** exercise room. **Business Services:** meeting rooms. **Cards:** AX, DC, DS, MC, VI.
Special Amenities: free continental breakfast and free local telephone calls.

SOME UNITS
[icons]

COMFORT INN
Phone: (440)324-7676
(AAA) (SAVE)   6/15-9/5   1P: $64-$96   2P: $70-$102   XP: $6   F17
    9/6-10/31   1P: $60-$70   2P: $66-$76   XP: $6   F17
WWWW   4/1-6/14 & 11/1-3/31   1P: $54-$70   2P: $60-$76   XP: $6   F17
Motel   **Location:** I-80, exit 8, just n on SR 57. 739 Leona St 44035. Fax: 440/324-4046. **Facility:** 66 one-
bedroom standard units, some with whirlpools. 2 stories, interior corridors. **Parking:** on-site. **Terms:** pets ($6
extra charge). **Amenities:** extended cable TV. *Some:* irons, hair dryers. **Guest Services:** coin laundry. **Business Services:** meeting rooms. **Cards:** AX, CB, DC, DS, JC, MC, VI. **Special Amenities:** free continental breakfast and free
newspaper.

SOME UNITS
[icons]

DAYS INN

SAVE

▼▼▼▼

Motel

7/4-9/1 [ECP]	1P: $74-$96	2P: $82-$104	XP: $10	F12
5/24-7/3 [ECP]	1P: $42-$72	2P: $52-$80	XP: $10	F12
4/1-5/23 & 9/2-3/31 [ECP]	1P: $42-$54	2P: $52-$64	XP: $10	F12

Phone: (440)324-4444

Location: I-80, exit 8, just n on SR 57, exit Midway Blvd. 621 Midway Blvd 44035. Fax: 440/324-2065. **Facility:** 101 one-bedroom standard units, some with whirlpools. 3 stories, interior corridors. **Parking:** on-site. **Amenities:** extended cable TV, hair dryers. **Pool(s):** heated indoor. **Leisure Activities:** sauna, exercise room. **Guest Services:** coin laundry. **Cards:** AX, CB, DC, DS, MC, VI. *(See color ad p 739)*

SOME UNITS

[icons]

ECONO LODGE

SAVE

▼▼▼▼

Motel

7/4-9/1	1P: $65-$87	2P: $73-$94	XP: $10	F12
5/24-7/3	1P: $37-$68	2P: $47-$77	XP: $10	F12
4/1-5/23 & 9/2-3/31	1P: $37-$50	2P: $47-$60	XP: $8	F12

Phone: (440)324-3911

Location: I-80, exit 8, 0.3 mi n on SR 57, exit Midway Blvd. 523 Griswold Rd 44035. Fax: 440/324-3911. **Facility:** 116 one-bedroom standard units, some with whirlpools. 1 story, exterior corridors. **Parking:** on-site. **Amenities:** extended cable TV. **Pool(s):** heated outdoor. **Guest Services:** coin laundry. **Business Services:** meeting rooms. **Cards:** AX, CB, DC, DS, MC, VI. *(See color ad p 739)*

SOME UNITS

[icons]

HOLIDAY INN

▼▼▼

Motor Inn

| 5/25-9/3 | 1P: $107 | 2P: $107 |
| 4/1-5/24 & 9/4-3/31 | 1P: $89 | 2P: $89 |

Phone: (440)324-5411

Location: I-80, exit 145, just n on SR 57, exit Midway Blvd. 1825 Lorain Blvd 44035. Fax: 440/324-2785. **Facility:** 248 one-bedroom standard units. 6 stories, interior corridors. **Parking:** on-site. **Terms:** 30 day cancellation notice, package plans. **Amenities:** video games, voice mail, irons, hair dryers. **Pool(s):** heated outdoor. **Leisure Activities:** exercise room. **Guest Services:** coin laundry. **Business Services:** conference facilities. **Cards:** AX, CB, DC, DS, JC, MC, VI.

SOME UNITS

[icons] FEE

SUPER 8 MOTEL

▼▼▼

Motel

7/4-9/1 [ECP]	1P: $74-$96	2P: $82-$104	XP: $10	F12
5/24-7/3 [ECP]	1P: $42-$72	2P: $52-$90	XP: $10	F12
4/1-5/23 & 9/2-3/31 [ECP]	1P: $42-$54	2P: $52-$64	XP: $8	F12

Phone: (440)323-7488

Location: I-80, exit 8, 0.5 mi s on SR 57. 910 Lorain Blvd 44035. Fax: 440/323-7488. **Facility:** 64 one-bedroom standard units, some with whirlpools. 2 stories, interior corridors. *Bath:* combo or shower only. **Parking:** on-site. **Amenities:** extended cable TV, voice mail. *Some:* hair dryers. **Pool(s):** heated outdoor. **Guest Services:** coin laundry. **Business Services:** meeting rooms. **Cards:** AX, CB, DC, DS, MC, VI. *(See color ad p 739)*

SOME UNITS

[icons]

The following lodging was either not evaluated or did not meet AAA rating requirements but is listed for your information only.

COUNTRY INN & SUITES BY CARLSON

[fyi]

Motel

6/16-9/2 [ECP]	1P: $79-$109	2P: $87-$117	XP: $8	F18
9/3-10/31 [ECP]	1P: $64-$74	2P: $72-$82	XP: $8	F18
4/1-6/15 & 11/1-3/31 [ECP]	1P: $59-$69	2P: $67-$77	XP: $8	F18

Phone: 440/324-0099

Too new to rate, opening scheduled for January 2002. **Location:** I-90, exit 145A, just w of SR 57. 645 Griswold Rd 44035 (739 Leona St). Fax: 440/324-1199. **Amenities:** radios, coffeemakers, microwaves, refrigerators, pool. **Terms:** 7 day cancellation notice. **Cards:** AX, CB, DC, DS, MC, VI. *(See color ad p 646)*

WHERE TO DINE

SORRENTO'S RISTORANTE ITALIANO

▼▼▼ ▼▼

Italian

Lunch: $5-$8   **Dinner:** $7-$12   **Phone:** 440/366-6620

Location: I-90, exit 148, just s to Abbe Rd; in College Plaza, 0.5 mi w. 108 Antioch Dr 44035. **Hours:** 11 am-10:30 pm, Fri & Sat-11:30 pm, Sun 2 pm-10 pm. **Closed:** 1/1, 12/25. **Features:** casual dress; children's menu; carryout; beer & wine only. Owned and operated by an Italian family for more than 10 years, the small eatery serves traditional selections and creative specials that can be ordered for carrying out or eating in. Casual servers are friendly and efficient. **Parking:** on-site. **Cards:** AX, DS, MC, VI.

[icon]

ENGLEWOOD pop. 11,400 (See map p. 672; index p. 675)

WHERE TO STAY

CROSS COUNTRY INN

AAA SAVE

▼▼ ▼▼

Motel

| All Year | 1P: $38-$45 | 2P: $45-$52 | XP: $2 | F17 |

Phone: (937)836-8339 [67]

Location: I-70, exit 29, just s. 9325 N Main St 45415. Fax: 937/836-1772. **Facility:** 120 one-bedroom standard units. 2 stories, exterior corridors. *Bath:* combo or shower only. **Parking:** on-site. **Amenities:** video games, voice mail. **Pool(s):** heated outdoor. **Cards:** AX, CB, DC, DS, MC, VI. **Special Amenities:** free local telephone calls and preferred room (subject to availability with advanced reservations).

SOME UNITS

[icons] FEE

(See map p. 672)

HAMPTON INN, DAYTON NW
Phone: (937)832-2222   68
Motel
All Year [ECP]   1P: $75-$100   2P: $110   XP: $10   F19
Location: I-70, exit 29. 20 Rockridge Rd 45322. **Fax:** 937/832-3859. **Facility:** 130 one-bedroom standard units. 4 stories, interior corridors. **Parking:** on-site. **Terms:** check-in 4 pm, 3 day cancellation notice-fee imposed. **Amenities:** extended cable TV, voice mail, irons, hair dryers. **Leisure Activities:** exercise room. **Guest Services:** valet laundry. **Business Services:** meeting rooms. **Cards:** AX, CB, DC, DS, JC, MC, VI. **Special Amenities:** free continental breakfast and free newspaper.

SOME UNITS

HOLIDAY INN-DAYTON NORTHWEST AIRPORT
Phone: (937)832-1234   69
Motor Inn
All Year   1P: $65-$125   XP: $8   F18
Location: I-70, exit 29. 10 Rockridge Rd 45322. **Fax:** 937/832-3548. **Facility:** 149 one-bedroom standard units. 4 stories, interior corridors. **Parking:** on-site. **Terms:** package plans, pets ($20 deposit). **Amenities:** extended cable TV, voice mail, irons, hair dryers. **Pool(s):** heated indoor. **Guest Services:** coin laundry. **Business Services:** meeting rooms. **Cards:** AX, CB, DC, DS, JC, MC, VI.

SOME UNITS

ERIE

-------- WHERE TO DINE --------

-------- *The following restaurant has not been evaluated by AAA* -------- *but is listed for your information only.*

SALMON RUN
[fyi]
Phone: 419/433-3800
Not evaluated. **Location:** 400 Sawmill 44839. Inside the Sawmill Creek Resort, the themed restaurant prepares daily seafood, beef and poultry specials.

EVENDALE —*See Cincinnati p. 575.*

FAIRBORN pop. 31,300   (See map p. 672; index p. 674)

-------- WHERE TO STAY --------

BEST WESTERN WRIGHT PATTERSON
Phone: (937)879-3920   46
Motor Inn
6/2-8/31 [CP]   1P: $70-$110   2P: $70-$110   XP: $10   F18
4/1-6/1 [CP]   1P: $60-$100   2P: $60-$100   XP: $10   F18
9/1-3/31 [CP]   1P: $55-$100   2P: $55-$100   XP: $10   F18
Location: I-675, exit 24, 1.8 sw on SR 444. 800 N Broad St 45423. **Fax:** 937/879-3896. **Facility:** 149 one-bedroom standard units. 2 stories, interior corridors. **Parking:** on-site. **Amenities:** extended cable TV, irons, hair dryers. **Dining:** restaurant, 11 am-11 pm, $8-$12, cocktails. **Pool(s):** outdoor. **Leisure Activities:** exercise room. **Guest Services:** coin laundry. **Business Services:** meeting rooms. **Cards:** AX, DC, DS, MC, VI. **Special Amenities:** free continental breakfast and free local telephone calls.

SOME UNITS

COMFORT INN-WRIGHT PATTERSON
Phone: (937)879-7666   42
Motel
4/1-9/30   1P: $76-$84   2P: $76-$84
10/1-3/31   1P: $69-$74   2P: $69-$74
Location: I-675, exit 24, 1.8 sw on SR 444. 616 N Broad St 45324. **Fax:** 937/879-7645. **Facility:** 90 one-bedroom standard units, some with whirlpools. 2 stories, interior corridors. **Parking:** on-site. **Terms:** 3 day cancellation notice, pets ($100 deposit). **Amenities:** extended cable TV. *Some:* irons, hair dryers. **Pool(s):** outdoor. **Leisure Activities:** exercise room. **Guest Services:** valet laundry. **Business Services:** meeting rooms. **Cards:** AX, CB, DC, DS, MC, VI. **Special Amenities:** free continental breakfast and free local telephone calls.

SOME UNITS

FAIRBORN FAIRFIELD INN
Phone: (937)427-0800   48
Motel
4/1-9/30 [CP]   1P: $75-$95   2P: $75-$95
10/1-3/31 [CP]   1P: $70-$90   2P: $70-$90
Location: I-675, exit 17 (N Fairfield Rd). 2500 Paramount Pl 45324. **Fax:** 937/427-0800. **Facility:** 63 one-bedroom standard units. 3 stories, interior corridors. *Bath:* combo or shower only. **Parking:** on-site. **Amenities:** extended cable TV, irons. **Pool(s):** small heated indoor. **Leisure Activities:** whirlpool. **Guest Services:** valet laundry. **Business Services:** meeting rooms. **Cards:** AX, CB, DC, DS, JC, MC, VI. **Special Amenities:** free continental breakfast and free local telephone calls. *(See color ad card insert)*

SOME UNITS

HAMPTON INN FAIRBORN
Phone: (937)429-5505   49
Motel
All Year [CP]   1P: $66-$96   2P: $66-$96
Location: I-675, exit 17 (N Fairfield Rd). 2550 Paramount Pl 45324. **Fax:** 937/429-6828. **Facility:** 63 one-bedroom standard units. 3 stories, interior corridors. *Bath:* combo or shower only. **Parking:** on-site. **Amenities:** extended cable TV, voice mail, irons. **Pool(s):** heated indoor. **Leisure Activities:** whirlpool. **Guest Services:** valet laundry. **Cards:** AX, DC, DS, MC, VI.

SOME UNITS

(See map p. 672)

HOLIDAY INN CONFERENCE CENTER/I-675
AAA [SAVE]

All Year   1P: $109   2P: $109   **Phone:** (937)426-7800 **41**

Motor Inn

Location: I-675, exit 17 (N Fairfield Rd). 2800 Presidential Dr 45324. Fax: 937/426-1284. **Facility:** 204 one-bedroom standard units. 6 stories, interior corridors. **Parking:** on-site. **Terms:** package plans. **Amenities:** extended cable TV, video games, voice mail, irons, hair dryers. **Dining:** dining room, restaurant, 6 am-2 & 5-10 pm, Fri & Sat 7 am-2 & 5-11 pm, Sun 7 am-2 & 5-10 pm, $8-$17, cocktails, also, The City Chop House, see separate listing. **Pool(s):** heated indoor. **Leisure Activities:** exercise room. **Guest Services:** valet laundry. **Business Services:** meeting rooms, business center. **Cards:** AX, CB, DC, DS, MC, VI.

SOME UNITS

HOMEWOOD SUITES-FAIRBORN/DAYTON
AAA [SAVE]

All Year [ECP]   1P: $113   2P: $113   **Phone:** (937)429-0600 **45**

Apartment

Location: I-675, exit 17 (N Fairfield Rd). 2750 Presidential Dr 45324. Fax: 937/429-6311. **Facility:** 128 one-bedroom standard units with efficiencies. 3 stories, interior/exterior corridors. **Parking:** on-site. **Terms:** package plans, small pets only ($50 extra charge). **Amenities:** extended cable TV, voice mail, irons, hair dryers. **Pool(s):** outdoor. **Leisure Activities:** exercise room, sports court. **Guest Services:** gift shop, coin laundry. **Business Services:** meeting rooms, business center, PC, fax. **Cards:** AX, CB, DC, DS, MC, VI.

SOME UNITS

RED ROOF INN-FAIRBORN
AAA [SAVE]

5/26-8/24	1P: $56-$69	2P: $61-$74	XP: $5	F18
4/1-5/25	1P: $49-$69	2P: $54-$74	XP: $5	F18
8/25-12/31	1P: $49-$63	2P: $54-$68	XP: $5	F18
1/1-3/31	1P: $47-$63	2P: $52-$68	XP: $5	F18

Phone: (937)426-6116 **44**

Motel

Location: I-675, exit 17 (N Fairfield Rd). 2580 Colonel Glenn Hwy 45324. Fax: 937/426-7575. **Facility:** 109 one-bedroom standard units. 3 stories, exterior corridors. **Parking:** on-site. **Terms:** small pets only. **Amenities:** video games, voice mail. **Guest Services:** coin laundry. **Cards:** AX, CB, DC, DS, MC, VI. **Special Amenities:** free local telephone calls and free newspaper.

SOME UNITS

STUDIOPLUS AT FAIRBORN

All Year   1P: $65-$110   2P: $70-$115   **Phone:** 937/429-0140 **43**

Extended Stay Motel

Location: I-675, exit 17 (N Fairfield Rd), just n, 0.5 mi sw on Colonel Glenn Hwy; opposite Wright State University. 3131 Presidential Dr 45324. Fax: 937/320-4922. **Facility:** 71 one-bedroom standard units with kitchens. 3 stories, interior corridors. *Bath:* combo or shower only. **Parking:** on-site. **Amenities:** extended cable TV, dual phone lines, voice mail, irons. **Pool(s):** outdoor. **Leisure Activities:** exercise room. **Guest Services:** coin laundry. **Cards:** AX, CB, DC, DS, MC, VI.

SOME UNITS

——— *The following lodging was either not evaluated or did not* ———
meet AAA rating requirements but is listed for your information only.

RAMADA LIMITED & SUITES
[fyi]

4/1-10/31 [ECP]	1P: $80-$85	2P: $85-$90
1/1-3/31 [ECP]	1P: $75-$79	2P: $78-$84
11/1-12/31 [ECP]	1P: $75-$80	2P: $77-$82

Phone: 937/490-2000

Motel

Too new to rate. **Location:** I-675, exit 15. 2540 University Blvd 45324. Fax: 937/431-0660. **Amenities:** radios, coffeemakers, microwaves, refrigerators, pool. **Terms:** 7 day cancellation notice. **Cards:** AX, CB, DC, DS, JC, MC, VI.

——— **WHERE TO DINE** ———

THE CITY CHOP HOUSE

Dinner: $10-$21   **Phone:** 937/426-7800 **25**

Steak House

Location: I-675, exit 17 (N Fairfield Rd); in Holiday Inn Conference Center/I-675. 2800 Presidential Dr 45324. **Hours:** 5 pm-10 pm, Fri & Sat-11 pm. Closed: 12/25. **Reservations:** accepted. **Features:** casual dress; children's menu; carryout; cocktails; a la carte. Hearty portions with colorful plate presentation are the norm at The City Chop House, a modern tavern-like restaurant that boasts a knowledgeable, friendly wait staff. Flavorful and tender prime rib is cooked to order and served with a fresh baked potato. Smoke free premises. **Parking:** on-site. **Cards:** AX, DC, DS, MC, VI.

FAIRFIELD pop. 39,700 (See map p. 558; index p. 561)

——— **WHERE TO STAY** ———

HOLIDAY INN EXPRESS

6/1-8/31 [ECP]	1P: $89	2P: $89	XP: $10	F18
4/1-5/31 & 9/1-3/31 [ECP]	1P: $79	2P: $79	XP: $10	F18

Phone: (513)860-2900 **100**

Hotel

Location: I-275, exit 41 (SR 4), 1.5 mi n. 6755 Fairfield Business Park Dr 45014. Fax: 513/860-2924. **Facility:** 80 one-bedroom standard units, some with whirlpools. 3 stories, interior corridors. *Bath:* combo or shower only. **Parking:** on-site. **Amenities:** extended cable TV, voice mail, irons, hair dryers. **Pool(s):** heated indoor. **Leisure Activities:** whirlpool, exercise room. **Guest Services:** coin laundry. **Business Services:** meeting rooms. **Cards:** AX, CB, DC, DS, JC, MC, VI.

SOME UNITS

(See map p. 558)

──────── WHERE TO DINE ────────

PEDRO'S STEAKHOUSE RESTAURANT   **Lunch:** $5-$7   **Dinner:** $7-$18   **Phone:** 513/874-4755
♦♦   **Location:** I-275, exit 41 (SR 4), 1 mi n. 7105 Dixie Hwy 45014. **Hours:** 11 am-11 pm, Fri & Sat-midnight. Closed:
Mexican   11/28, 12/25. **Features:** casual dress; children's menu; carryout; cocktails & lounge. No need to go to the
border and no passport required. A nice selection of Mexican fare with flaming fajitas or try any
combination of chicken or portabello, or steak and many combination choices. A wide array of Certified
Angus beef steak is a bonus. Festive lounge during happy hour or spend time around the fireplace during those cold winter
nights. Transform yourself to another world removed from the day to day distractions. **Parking:** on-site. **Cards:** AX, MC, VI.

FAIRLAWN pop. 5,800

──────── WHERE TO STAY ────────

AKRON SUPER 8 MOTEL   **Phone:** (330)666-8887
[AAA] [SAVE]   5/23-9/8   1P: $42-$85   2P: $42-$85   XP: $5   F17
♦   4/1-5/22 & 9/9-3/31   1P: $35-$65   2P: $35-$65   XP: $5   F17
Motel   **Location:** I-77, exit 137A, just e. 79 Rothrock Rd 44321. **Fax:** 330/666-8887. **Facility:** 58 one-bedroom standard
units. 3 stories, interior corridors. **Parking:** on-site. **Terms:** 5 day cancellation notice. **Amenities:** extended
cable TV, safes (fee). **Guest Services:** coin laundry. **Cards:** AX, DC, DS, MC, VI. **Special Amenities:** free
continental breakfast and free local telephone calls.
                                                                     SOME UNITS

BEST WESTERN INN & SUITES   **Phone:** (330)670-0888
♦♦♦   12/1-3/31 [ECP]   1P: $59-$2009   2P: $59-$2009   XP: $20   F12
5/1-8/31 [ECP]   1P: $69-$799   2P: $69-$799   XP: $20   F12
Motel   4/1-4/30 & 9/1-11/30 [ECP]   1P: $59-$799   2P: $59-$799   XP: $20   F12
Location: I-77, exit 137B, just w. 160 W Montross Ave 44321. **Fax:** 330/668-2926. **Facility:** 54 one-bedroom standard units, some with whirlpools. 4 stories, interior corridors. *Bath:* combo or shower only. **Parking:** on-site. **Terms:** cancellation
fee imposed, pets ($25 deposit). **Amenities:** voice mail, irons, hair dryers. **Pool(s):** heated indoor. **Leisure Activities:** whirlpool,
exercise room. **Guest Services:** coin laundry. **Business Services:** meeting rooms, business center. **Cards:** AX, DC, DS,
MC, VI.
                                                                     SOME UNITS

COMFORT INN-AKRON WEST   **Phone:** (330)666-5050
[SAVE]   4/1-9/30 [ECP]   1P: $63-$129   2P: $63-$129
♦♦   10/1-3/31 [ECP]   1P: $50-$129   2P: $50-$129
Motel   **Location:** I-77, exit 137B, just w on SR 18. 130 W Montrose Ave 44321. **Fax:** 330/668-2550. **Facility:** 132 one-
bedroom standard units, some with whirlpools. 2 stories, interior corridors. **Parking:** on-site. **Terms:** 10 day
cancellation notice. **Amenities:** voice mail, safes (fee). *Some:* irons, hair dryers. **Pool(s):** heated indoor.
Guest Services: coin laundry. **Business Services:** meeting rooms. **Cards:** AX, CB, DC, DS, JC, MC, VI.
                                                                     SOME UNITS

COURTYARD BY MARRIOTT   **Phone:** (330)668-9090
[AAA] [SAVE]   All Year   1P: $77   2P: $82
♦♦♦   **Location:** I-77, exit 137, just e. 100 Springside Dr 44333. **Fax:** 330/668-9090. **Facility:** 78 one-bedroom standard
Motel   units. 3 stories, interior corridors. **Parking:** on-site. **Terms:** [BP] & [ECP] meal
plans available. **Amenities:** extended cable TV, voice mail, irons, hair dryers. **Pool(s):** heated indoor.
Leisure Activities: whirlpool, exercise room. **Guest Services:** valet laundry. **Business Services:** meeting
rooms. **Cards:** AX, CB, DC, DS, MC, VI. *(See color ad card insert)*   SOME UNITS

FAIRFIELD INN BY MARRIOTT   **Phone:** (330)668-2700
[AAA] [SAVE]   5/1-8/31 [CP]   1P: $69-$73
♦♦♦   4/1-4/30 [CP]   1P: $61-$65
Motel   9/1-12/31 [CP]   1P: $55-$58
1/1-3/31 [CP]   1P: $50-$53
Location: I-77, exit 137A, just e. 70 Rothrock Rd 44321. **Fax:** 330/666-9851. **Facility:** 117 one-bedroom standard
units. 3 stories, interior/exterior corridors. **Parking:** on-site. **Amenities:** voice mail, irons. **Pool(s):** heated
outdoor. **Guest Services:** valet laundry. **Cards:** AX, CB, DC, DS, MC, VI. **Special Amenities:** free continental breakfast and
free local telephone calls. *(See color ad card insert)*   SOME UNITS

FOUR POINTS SHERATON AKRON WEST   **Phone:** (330)869-9000
♦♦♦   All Year   1P: $75-$89   2P: $75-$89
Motel   **Location:** I-77, exit 137A, 2 mi e on SR 18. 3150 W Market St 44333. **Fax:** 330/869-8325. **Facility:** 120 one-
bedroom standard units, some with whirlpools. 2 stories, interior corridors. *Bath:* combo or shower only.
Parking: on-site. **Terms:** cancellation fee imposed. **Amenities:** extended cable TV, video games, voice mail,
irons, hair dryers. **Pool(s):** heated indoor. **Leisure Activities:** exercise room. **Guest Services:** coin laundry. **Business Services:**
meeting rooms. **Cards:** AX, DC, DS, MC, VI.
                                                                     SOME UNITS

HAMPTON INN

Phone: (330)666-7361

SAVE

Motel

9/1-3/31 [CP]	1P: $82-$92	2P: $92-$102	XP: $6 F17
4/1-8/31 [CP]	1P: $79-$89	2P: $89-$99	XP: $6 F17

Location: I-77, exit 137, just e. 80 Springside Dr 44333. Fax: 330/665-7673. **Facility:** 64 one-bedroom standard units. 3 stories, interior corridors. *Bath:* combo or shower only. **Parking:** on-site. **Terms:** 7 day cancellation notice. **Amenities:** extended cable TV, voice mail, irons. **Pool(s):** heated indoor. **Leisure Activities:** whirlpool. **Guest Services:** valet laundry. **Cards:** AX, CB, DC, DS, JC, MC, VI.

SOME UNITS

HILTON AKRON/FAIRLAWN

Phone: (330)867-5000

SAVE

Motor Inn

All Year	1P: $96-$159	2P: $96-$159	F18

Location: I-77, exit 137A, 2 mi e on SR 18. (3180 W Market St, AKRON, 44333). Fax: 330/867-1648. **Facility:** 204 units. 174 one-bedroom standard units. 30 one-bedroom suites ($119-$169), some with kitchens and/or whirlpools. 4 stories, interior corridors. *Bath:* combo or shower only. **Parking:** on-site. **Terms:** package plans. **Amenities:** voice mail, irons, hair dryers. **Pool(s):** heated outdoor, heated indoor. **Leisure Activities:** sauna, whirlpool, steamroom, exercise room. **Guest Services:** gift shop, coin laundry. **Business Services:** conference facilities, fax. **Cards:** AX, DC, DS, MC, VI.

SOME UNITS

HOLIDAY INN-AKRON/FAIRLAWN

Phone: (330)666-4131

Motor Inn

6/9-9/5	1P: $99	2P: $99	
4/1-6/8 & 1/1-3/31	1P: $94	2P: $94	
9/6-12/31	1P: $89	2P: $89	

Location: I-77, exit 137, just e. (4073 Medina Rd, AKRON, 44333). Fax: 330/666-7190. **Facility:** 166 one-bedroom standard units. 4 stories, interior corridors. *Bath:* combo or shower only. **Parking:** on-site. **Amenities:** video games, voice mail, irons, hair dryers. **Pool(s):** heated outdoor. **Leisure Activities:** exercise room. **Guest Services:** coin laundry. **Business Services:** meeting rooms. **Cards:** AX, CB, DC, DS, .MC, VI.

SOME UNITS
FEE

RADISSON INN AKRON/BATH/FAIRLAWN

Phone: (330)666-9300

AAA SAVE

Motor Inn

All Year	1P: $90		XP: $10 F17

Location: I-77, exit 137B, just w on SR 18. 200 W Montrose Ave 44321. Fax: 330/668-2270. **Facility:** 130 one-bedroom standard units. 4 stories, interior corridors. **Parking:** on-site. **Amenities:** high-speed Internet (fee), voice mail, irons, hair dryers. **Dining:** dining room, 6 am-1:30 & 5-10 pm, Sat & Sun from 7 am, $10-$18, cocktails. **Pool(s):** heated indoor. **Leisure Activities:** sauna, whirlpool, exercise room. **Guest Services:** valet laundry. **Business Services:** conference facilities. **Cards:** AX, CB, DC, DS, JC, MC, VI. **Special Amenities:** free newspaper and free room upgrade (subject to availability with advanced reservations).
(See color ad p 530)

SOME UNITS
FEE

RED ROOF INN AKRON NORTH

Phone: (330)666-0566

AAA SAVE

Motel

5/24-9/1	1P: $44-$59	2P: $49-$64	XP: $5 F18
4/1-5/23	1P: $34-$54	2P: $39-$59	XP: $5 F18
9/2-11/2	1P: $36-$51	2P: $41-$56	XP: $5 F18
11/3-3/31	1P: $29-$49	2P: $34-$54	XP: $5 F18

Location: I-77, exit 137A, just e. 99 Rothrock Rd 44321. Fax: 330/666-6874. **Facility:** 108 one-bedroom standard units. 2 stories, exterior corridors. **Parking:** on-site. **Terms:** small pets only. **Amenities:** video games, voice mail. **Cards:** AX, CB, DC, DS, MC, VI. **Special Amenities:** free local telephone calls and free newspaper.

SOME UNITS
FEE

THE RESIDENCE INN BY MARRIOTT

Phone: (330)666-4811

AAA SAVE

Apartment

All Year [BP]	1P: $75-$115	2P: $75-$115

Location: I-77, exit 137B, just w. 120 W Montrose Ave 44321. Fax: 330/666-8029. **Facility:** 112 one-bedroom standard units with kitchens. 2 stories, exterior corridors. **Parking:** on-site. **Terms:** [MAP] meal plan available, pets ($75-$150 fee). **Amenities:** video games, voice mail, irons, hair dryers. **Pool(s):** heated outdoor. **Leisure Activities:** whirlpool, sports court. **Guest Services:** coin laundry. **Business Services:** meeting rooms. **Cards:** AX, DC, DS, JC, MC, VI. *(See color ad card insert)*

SOME UNITS
FEE

——— **WHERE TO DINE** ———

ON TAP

Lunch: $5-$8   **Dinner:** $8-$15   **Phone:** 330/668-1116

American

Location: I-77, exit 137B, 0.4 mi e on SR 18. 3997 Medina Rd 44321. **Hours:** 11 am-10 pm, Fri & Sat-11 pm, Sun noon-10 pm. Closed major holidays. **Features:** casual dress; children's menu; carryout; cocktails. When was the last time you had a really good burger? Then it might be time to visit On Tap where burgers are well known as the popular meal of choice. Specialty sandwiches, huge salad fare and pasta round out the varied and distinctive offerings. **Parking:** on-site. **Cards:** AX, MC, VI.

RIZZI'S RISTORANTE

Lunch: $5-$9   **Dinner:** $8-$16   **Phone:** 330/864-2141

Italian

Location: Lower level of Summit Mall; northeast corner. 3265 W Market St. **Hours:** 11:30 am-10 pm, Fri & Sat-11:30 pm, Sun noon-10 pm. Closed major holidays. **Features:** casual dress; children's menu; carryout; cocktails. In a convenient mall location, this restaurant uses family recipes to create its traditional Italian fare and daily specials. Prices are reasonable, and service is friendly in the relaxed atmosphere. **Parking:** on-site. **Cards:** AX, DC, DS, MC, VI.

FINDLAY pop. 35,700

──────── **WHERE TO STAY** ────────

COUNTRY HEARTH INN

Phone: 419/423-4303

Motel

Property failed to provide current rates

Location: I-75, exit 159, just w. 1020 Interstate Ct 45840. Fax: 419/423-3459. **Facility:** 72 one-bedroom standard units, some with whirlpools. 2 stories, exterior corridors. **Parking:** on-site. **Amenities:** extended cable TV, safes (fee). *Some:* hair dryers. **Pool(s):** outdoor. **Leisure Activities:** jogging. **Guest Services:** valet laundry. **Business Services:** meeting rooms. **Cards:** AX, CB, DC, DS, MC, VI.

SOME UNITS

CROSS COUNTRY INN

AAA SAVE

Motel

Phone: (419)424-0466

All Year   1P: $40-$47   2P: $47-$54   XP: $2   F17
Location: I-75, exit 159, 0.5 mi e. 1951 Broad Ave 45840. Fax: 419/424-1043. **Facility:** 120 one-bedroom standard units. 2 stories, exterior corridors. **Parking:** on-site. **Amenities:** video games, voice mail. **Pool(s):** heated outdoor. **Cards:** AX, CB, DC, DS, MC, VI. **Special Amenities:** free local telephone calls and preferred room (subject to availability with advanced reservations).

SOME UNITS

DAYS INN FINDLAY

AAA SAVE

Motel

Phone: (419)423-7171

All Year   1P: $46-$62   2P: $56-$68   XP: $6   F10
Location: I-75, exit 157, just e. 1305 W Main Cross St 45840. Fax: 419/423-8013. **Facility:** 113 one-bedroom standard units, some with whirlpools. 2 stories, interior corridors. **Parking:** on-site. **Terms:** 5 day cancellation notice. **Amenities:** safes, hair dryers. **Dining:** restaurant, 6 am-9 pm, Sat & Sun from 7 am, $10-$18. **Pool(s):** outdoor. **Guest Services:** valet laundry. **Business Services:** meeting rooms. **Cards:** AX, CB, DC, DS, JC, MC, VI. **Special Amenities:** free local telephone calls and free newspaper.

SOME UNITS

FAIRFIELD INN BY MARRIOTT

AAA SAVE

Motel

Phone: (419)424-9940

All Year [CP]   1P: $64-$80   2P: $68-$82   XP: $6   F17
Location: 2.5 mi e on US 224. 2000 Tiffin Ave 45839. Fax: 419/424-9940. **Facility:** 57 one-bedroom standard units. 3 stories, interior corridors. **Parking:** on-site. **Amenities:** extended cable TV, irons. **Pool(s):** heated indoor. **Leisure Activities:** whirlpool. **Guest Services:** valet laundry. **Business Services:** meeting rooms. **Cards:** AX, DC, DS, MC, VI. **Special Amenities:** free continental breakfast and free local telephone calls. *(See color ad card insert)*

SOME UNITS
FEE

HAMPTON INN

SAVE

Motel

Phone: (419)422-5252

All Year [CP]   1P: $70-$80   2P: $75-$85   XP: $6   F17
Location: I-75, exit 159, just w. 921 Interstate Dr 45840. Fax: 419/422-8964. **Facility:** 62 one-bedroom standard units. 2 stories, interior corridors. *Bath:* combo or shower only. **Parking:** on-site. **Amenities:** extended cable TV, voice mail, irons. **Pool(s):** heated indoor. **Leisure Activities:** whirlpool. **Guest Services:** valet laundry. **Cards:** AX, CB, DC, DS, JC, MC, VI.

SOME UNITS
FEE

HAWTHORN SUITES LTD

AAA SAVE

Extended Stay
Motel

Phone: (419)425-9696

All Year   1P: $89-$129
Location: 3 mi e on US 224. 2355 Tiffin Ave 45840. Fax: 419/425-9677. **Facility:** 68 units. 66 one- and 2 two-bedroom standard units with efficiencies. 3 stories, interior corridors. **Parking:** on-site. **Terms:** [BP] meal plan available. **Amenities:** extended cable TV, voice mail, irons, hair dryers. **Pool(s):** heated indoor. **Leisure Activities:** whirlpool, exercise room. **Guest Services:** coin laundry. **Business Services:** meeting rooms. **Cards:** AX, DC, DS, MC, VI. **Special Amenities:** free continental breakfast and free newspaper. *(See color ad below)*

SOME UNITS

HOLIDAY INN EXPRESS HOTEL & SUITES

▼▼▼

Motel

All Year   1P: $89-$99   2P: $89-$99   **Phone:** (419)420-1776

Location: I-75, exit 159, just w. 941 Interstate Dr 45840. **Fax:** 419/420-1777. **Facility:** 74 one-bedroom standard units, some with whirlpools. 3 stories, interior corridors. *Bath:* combo or shower only. **Parking:** on-site. **Pool(s):** heated indoor. **Leisure Activities:** whirlpool, jogging, exercise room. **Guest Services:** coin laundry. **Business Services:** meeting rooms. **Cards:** AX, CB, DC, DS, JC, MC, VI.

SOME UNITS

(ASK) (S🅳) (†|→) (🔥M) (&) (➰) (✕) (📹) (DATA PORT) (💻) (📠) / (✕) (🚿) (📶) (📱) /

RODEWAY INN

(AAA) (SAVE)

▼▼▼

Motel

5/1-8/31   1P: $44-$49   2P: $49-$54   XP: $5   F12
4/1-4/30   1P: $34-$41   2P: $41-$49   XP: $5   F12
9/1-3/31   1P: $33-$39   2P: $39-$45   XP: $5   F12

Location: I-75, exit 159, 0.5 mi e. 1901 Broad Ave 45840. **Fax:** 419/425-9810. **Facility:** 100 one-bedroom standard units, some with efficiencies (no utensils). 1 story, exterior corridors. **Parking:** on-site. **Terms:** 3 day cancellation notice-fee imposed, pets ($10 fee). **Amenities:** extended cable TV. **Pool(s):** outdoor. **Cards:** AX, DC, DS, MC, VI. **Special Amenities:** free continental breakfast and free local telephone calls.

SOME UNITS

(S🅳) (🛏) (†|→) (➰) (📹) / (✕) (📶) (💻) (📠) /

SUPER 8 MOTEL-FINDLAY

▼▼

Motel

4/1-9/15   1P: $45   2P: $51   XP: $6   F12
1/1-3/31   1P: $44   2P: $50   XP: $6   F12
9/16-12/31   1P: $43   2P: $49   XP: $6   F12

Location: I-75, exit 159, just e. 1600 Fox St 45839. **Fax:** 419/422-8863. **Facility:** 62 one-bedroom standard units. 3 stories, interior corridors. **Parking:** on-site. **Amenities:** extended cable TV. *Some:* hair dryers. **Cards:** AX, DC, DS, MC, VI.

SOME UNITS

(ASK) (S🅳) (🛏) (🐾) (📹) (📠) / (✕) (📶) (📱) /
FEE

——— **WHERE TO DINE** ———

BISTRO ON MAIN

▼▼▼

Italian

Lunch: $5-$9   **Dinner:** $10-$17   **Phone:** 419/425-4900

Location: Downtown. 407 S Main St 45840. **Hours:** 11 am-2:30 & 5-10:30 pm, Fri & Sat-11 pm. Closed major holidays. **Reservations:** suggested; weekends. **Features:** casual dress; children's menu; carryout; cocktails. Rosemary chicken, salmon, penne pollo vento and risotto are among flavorful dishes on the restaurant's traditional menu. Brick walls, high ceilings and attractive artwork add to the charm of this relaxed downtown dining spot. **Parking:** on-site. **Cards:** AX, DC, MC, VI.

(✕)

DIAMOND RIVER

▼▼▼

American

Lunch: $5-$10   **Dinner:** $9-$18   **Phone:** 419/425-9205

Location: 3 mi e on US 224. 2215 Tiffin Ave 45840. **Hours:** 11 am-10 pm, Fri & Sat-11 pm, Sun-9 pm. Closed: 11/28, 12/25. **Reservations:** suggested. **Features:** casual dress; Sunday brunch; children's menu; early bird specials; carryout; cocktails. Locals rave about the prime rib, which is among preparations made from hand-cut prime beef and slow roasted for four to five hours. Salmon, pork chops and made-to-order pasta meals are other noteworthy choices. A great stone fireplace flanks both the dining room and the lounge, and Indian artifacts and oil paintings line the walls. The friendly wait staff knowledgeably answers patrons' menu questions. Smoke free premises. **Parking:** on-site. **Cards:** AX, DC, DS, MC, VI.

(✕)

JAPAN WEST

▼▼

Japanese

Lunch: $8-$14   **Dinner:** $15-$25   **Phone:** 419/424-1007

Location: Downtown; s of Court House. 406 S Main St 45840. **Hours:** 11 am-2 & 5-10 pm, Sat from 5 pm. Closed major holidays; also Sun. **Reservations:** suggested. **Features:** casual dress; children's menu; early bird specials; carryout; cocktails. The cuisine found in this downtown restaurant with Japanese owners is authentic and varied. You can opt for a traditional table or join other diners at one of the special grill tables. Here a friendly chef will prepare your meal with skilled showmanship as you watch. Beef, chicken and seafood entrees have accompanying vegetables and rice. A sushi bar is also available. **Parking:** on-site. **Cards:** AX, DS, MC, VI. (✕)

OLER'S BAR & GRILL

▼▼

Mexican

Lunch: $5-$8   **Dinner:** $6-$15   **Phone:** 419/423-2846

Location: 0.8 mi s on Main St, then 0.5 mi w. 708 Lima Ave 45840. **Hours:** 11 am-midnight. Closed major holidays. **Features:** casual dress; carryout; cocktails. The delightfully tacky restaurant is known for its authenticity, not its decor. Diners should come early, as this place is often crowded and doesn't accept weekend reservations. **Parking:** on-site. **Cards:** AX, DC, DS, MC, VI.

(✕)

STEVE'S DAKOTA GRILL

▼▼

Steak House

Lunch: $5-$10   **Dinner:** $10-$20   **Phone:** 419/420-9394

Location: I-75, exit 159, just e. Rt 224 45840. **Hours:** 4 pm-10 pm, Fri-11 pm, Sat 1 pm-11 pm. Closed: 12/25. **Features:** casual dress; carryout; cocktails. Experience the Thrill of the Grill. This taste of the Northwest has hand selected Prime and Choice aged beef, slow roasted prime rib and seafood flown in daily. **Parking:** on-site. **Cards:** AX, DC, DS, MC, VI.

(✕)

WOODLAND RESTAURANT

(AAA)

▼

American

Lunch: $5-$8   **Dinner:** $7-$12   **Phone:** 419/423-4131

Location: Downtown; across from Court House. 317 S Main St 45840. **Hours:** 6 am-8 pm. Closed major holidays; also Sun. **Features:** casual dress; children's menu; early bird specials; carryout; salad bar; a la carte. Generous portions of tried-and-true comfort food, ham steak, mashed potatoes, chicken noodle soup, pie and chocolate, vanilla and tapioca puddings, keep patrons full and happy at the casual restaurant. The atmosphere is friendly to families. **Parking:** on-site.

(✕)

──────── **The following restaurants have not been evaluated by AAA** ────────
but are listed for your information only.

BELLACINO'S GRINDERS   Phone: 419/423-4299
[fyi]   Not evaluated. **Location:** 2320 Tiffin Ave 45840. In the plaza, the cozy eatery offers budget-friendly food and efficient
       service.

BE TRAN EGG ROLL   Phone: 419/424-1721
[fyi]   Not evaluated. **Location:** 124 E Sandusky 45840. Quick and efficient servers deliver both traditional selections and
       daily specials.

THE GATHERING   Phone: 419/422-5930
[fyi]   Not evaluated. **Location:** 114 E Main Cross 45840. Reasonable prices and a friendly, attentive wait staff make this
       local eatery popular.

JANET'S   Phone: 419/422-8335
[fyi]   Not evaluated. **Location:** 3210 N Main St 45840. Lunch and dinner crowds come to the restaurant for its diverse
       menu and daily specials.

KEITHS DUGOUT   Phone: 419/423-7911
[fyi]   Not evaluated. **Location:** 3112 N Main St 45840. Patrons can watch the latest televised sports events and nosh on
       reliable pub fare.

FOREST PARK —*See Cincinnati p. 575.*

FOSTORIA pop. 15,000

──────── **WHERE TO STAY** ────────

DAYS INN   Phone: (419)435-6511
[AAA] [SAVE]   4/1-9/30   1P: $56-$64   2P: $62-$70
              10/1-3/31   1P: $42-$50   2P: $56-$64
[◇]   **Location:** SR 12, 1 mi w of SR 23. 737 Independence Rd 44830. Fax: 419/435-7825. **Facility:** 42 one-bedroom
Motel   standard units, some with whirlpools. 2 stories, exterior corridors. **Parking:** on-site. **Amenities:** extended
              cable TV, hair dryers. **Cards:** AX, CB, DC, DS, JC, MC, VI. **Special Amenities:** free local telephone calls
              and free newspaper.
                                                                       SOME UNITS

HOLIDAY INN EXPRESS   Phone: (419)436-3600
[◇◇◇]   All Year   1P: $64-$69   2P: $64-$69   XP: $5   F18
Motel   **Location:** SR 12, 2 mi n on SR 23. 1690 N County Line Rd 44830. Fax: 419/436-3600. **Facility:** 52 one-bedroom
              standard units, some with whirlpools. 2 stories, interior corridors. *Bath:* combo or shower only. **Parking:** on-
              site. **Terms:** 7 day cancellation notice. **Amenities:** extended cable TV, voice mail, safes, irons, hair dryers.
Pool(s): heated indoor. **Leisure Activities:** exercise room. **Guest Services:** valet laundry. **Business Services:** meeting rooms.
Cards: AX, CB, DC, DS, MC, VI.
                                                                       SOME UNITS

──────── **WHERE TO DINE** ────────

──────── **The following restaurant has not been evaluated by AAA** ────────
but is listed for your information only.

EL PATIO   Phone: 419/435-4110
[fyi]   Not evaluated. **Location:** 737 Indpendence Rd 44830. Reasonably priced traditional dishes and daily specials are
       served by the friendly staff.

FREDERICKSBURG pop. 500

──────── **WHERE TO STAY** ────────

GILEAD'S BALM MANOR   Phone: 330/695-3881
[◇◇◇]   All Year [BP]   1P: $100-$165   2P: $110-$175   XP: $10
Bed & Breakfast **Location:** E on SR 250, 6 mi s on CR 201 44627. **Facility:** Set in a striking Tudor home overlooking
              a two-acre lake, this inn offers six large guests rooms decorated in a romantic Victorian style. Smoke free
              premises. 6 one-bedroom standard units with whirlpools. 2 stories, interior corridors. **Parking:** on-site.
Terms: 7 day cancellation notice. **Amenities:** extended cable TV, video tape library, CD players, hair dryers. **Leisure Activities:** paddleboats, fishing. **Cards:** AX, DS, MC, VI.

FREDERICKTOWN pop. 2,400

──────── **WHERE TO STAY** ────────

HEARTLAND COUNTRY RESORT   Phone: (419)768-9300
[◇◇◇]   All Year [BP]   1P: $105-$195   2P: $105-$195   XP: $25   D5
Bed & Breakfast **Location:** I-71, exit 151, 2 mi e on SR 95, 2 mi s on SR 314, then 1 mi e on SR 179. 2994 Township Rd 190 43019.
              Fax: 419/768-9133. **Facility:** At this resort, a remodeled 1878 farmhouse and three log-home suites share a
              serene country setting amid hills, woods and pastures dotted with barns. Smoke free premises. 7 one-
bedroom standard units, some with whirlpools. 2 stories, interior corridors. *Bath:* combo or shower only. **Parking:** on-site.
Terms: check-in 4 pm, 7 day cancellation notice-fee imposed, [AP] & [MAP] meal plans available, pets ($15 fee, dogs and horses
only). **Amenities:** *Some:* CD players. **Pool(s):** heated outdoor. **Leisure Activities:** Fee: horseback riding. **Guest Services:** gift
shop, massage (fee). **Cards:** AX, DS, MC, VI.
                                                                       SOME UNITS

FREMONT pop. 17,600

—— WHERE TO STAY ——

COMFORT INN & SUITES   Phone: (419)355-9300

AAA SAVE

5/24-8/31	1P: $87-$125	2P: $87-$125
4/1-5/23 & 9/1-3/31	1P: $83-$87	2P: $83-$87

Motel

Location: I-80/90, exit 6, 2 mi s on SR 53. 840 Sean Dr 43420. **Fax:** 419/355-0556. **Facility:** 65 one-bedroom standard units, some with whirlpools. 3 stories, interior corridors. *Bath:* combo or shower only. **Parking:** on-site, winter plug-ins. **Terms:** [ECP] meal plan available, pets ($15 fee). **Amenities:** dual phone lines, voice mail, safes (fee), irons, hair dryers. **Pool(s):** heated indoor. **Leisure Activities:** whirlpool, exercise room. **Guest Services:** coin laundry. **Business Services:** meeting rooms, fax. **Cards:** AX, DC, DS, JC, MC, VI. **Special Amenities:** free continental breakfast and free newspaper. *(See color ad below)*

SOME UNITS

FEE   FEE

DAYS INN   Phone: (419)334-9551

SAVE

5/25-9/2	1P: $68-$128	2P: $78-$128	XP: $8	F16
4/1-5/24 & 9/3-3/31	1P: $48-$68	2P: $48-$78	XP: $8	F16

Motor Inn

Location: Ohio Tpke, exit 91, on SR 53. 3701 SR 53 N 43420. **Fax:** 419/334-9551. **Facility:** 105 units. 103 one-bedroom standard units. 2 one-bedroom suites ($98-$175) with whirlpools. 2 stories, interior corridors. **Parking:** on-site. **Terms:** 3 day cancellation notice. **Amenities:** extended cable TV, hair dryers. **Pool(s):** heated outdoor. **Guest Services:** coin laundry. **Business Services:** meeting rooms, fax. **Cards:** AX, CB, DC, DS, JC, MC, VI. *(See color ad p 739)*

SOME UNITS

FEE

HOLIDAY INN-FREMONT   Phone: (419)334-2682

AAA SAVE

6/16-8/25	1P: $87-$129	2P: $87-$129
4/1-6/15 & 8/26-3/31	1P: $87-$105	2P: $87-$105

Motor Inn

Location: Ohio Tpke, exit 91, on SR 53. 3422 Port Clinton Rd 43420. **Fax:** 419/334-4086. **Facility:** 159 one-bedroom standard units, some with whirlpools. 2 stories, interior corridors. **Parking:** on-site. **Terms:** small pets only (in smoking units). **Amenities:** extended cable TV, video games, irons, hair dryers. **Dining:** restaurant, 6 am-2 & 5-10 pm, $8-$15, cocktails. **Pool(s):** heated outdoor. **Leisure Activities:** miniature golf, exercise room. **Guest Services:** coin laundry. **Business Services:** meeting rooms, fax. **Cards:** AX, CB, DC, DS, JC, MC, VI.

SOME UNITS

FEE   FEE FEE

GAHANNA —See Columbus p. 661.

GALION pop. 11,900

—— WHERE TO STAY ——

HOMETOWN INN   Phone: 419/468-9909

All Year	1P: $50-$100	2P: $60-$140	XP: $10	F18

Motel

Location: 1 mi w on SR 598, n of jct SR 309/61/19. 172 N Portland Way 44833. **Fax:** 419/462-5427. **Facility:** 31 one-bedroom standard units. 1-2 stories, interior/exterior corridors. **Parking:** on-site. **Terms:** 3 day cancellation notice, small pets only. **Amenities:** extended cable TV. **Cards:** AX, CB, DC, DS, JC, MC, VI.

SOME UNITS

—— WHERE TO DINE ——

JERRY'S AMERICAN CAFE   **Lunch:** $5-$8   **Dinner:** $8-$15   Phone: 419/468-9171

American

Location: 0.5 mi n of SR 61, on SR 598. 451 Portland Way 44833. **Hours:** 11 am-9 pm, Fri & Sat-10 pm. Closed: 1/1, 12/25. **Features:** casual dress; children's menu; carryout; cocktails. Patriotic decor splashes the comfortable, family-friendly restaurant with red, white and blue. Homemade specials include the tender and flavorful Lake Erie perch, excellent soups and scrumptious pies. Attentive servers always are wearing a smile. **Parking:** on-site. **Cards:** AX, MC, VI.

GALLIPOLIS pop. 4,800

—————— WHERE TO STAY ——————

SUPER 8 MOTEL-GALLIPOLIS
Phone: (740)446-8080
All Year 1P: $54-$74 2P: $59-$79 XP: $5 F12
Motel **Location:** SR 7, at jct US 35. 321 Upper River Rd 45631. Fax: 740/446-8080. **Facility:** 64 one-bedroom standard units, some with whirlpools. 2 stories, interior corridors. *Bath:* combo or shower only. **Parking:** on-site. **Terms:** 7 day cancellation notice-fee imposed. **Amenities:** extended cable TV. **Leisure Activities:** whirlpool.
Guest Services: coin laundry. **Cards:** AX, CB, DC, DS, MC, VI.

WILLIAM ANN MOTEL
Phone: (740)446-3373
All Year [ECP] 1P: $40-$45 2P: $50-$60 F16
Motel **Location:** 0.8 mi n on SR 7. 918 2nd Ave 45631. Fax: 740/446-1337. **Facility:** 50 one-bedroom standard units. 1-2 stories, exterior corridors. **Parking:** on-site. **Terms:** 3 day cancellation notice, small pets only. **Amenities:** extended cable TV. **Cards:** AX, DS, MC, VI. **Special Amenities:** free continental breakfast and free local telephone calls.

GAMBIER pop. 2,100

—————— WHERE TO STAY ——————

THE KENYON INN
Phone: (740)427-2202
All Year 1P: $110-$150 2P: $120-$160 XP: $10 F17
Country Inn **Location:** On campus of Kenyon College. 43022 W Wiggin St 43022 (PO Box 273). Fax: 740/427-2392. **Facility:** 32 one-bedroom standard units. 2 stories, interior corridors. **Parking:** on-site. **Terms:** package plans. **Amenities:** extended cable TV, irons, hair dryers. **Guest Services:** complimentary laundry. **Business Services:** meeting rooms. **Cards:** AX, CB, DS, MC, VI.

GENEVA pop. 6,600

—————— WHERE TO STAY ——————

HOWARD JOHNSON EXPRESS INN
Phone: (440)466-1168
5/24-9/30 [CP] 1P: $64-$74 2P: $74-$85 XP: $10 F17
4/1-5/23 & 10/1-3/31 [CP] 1P: $54-$60 2P: $60-$64 XP: $10 F17
Motel **Location:** I-90, exit 218, just n. SR 534 44041 (PO Box 30). Fax: 440/466-6544. **Facility:** 53 one-bedroom standard units. 2 stories, interior/exterior corridors. **Parking:** on-site. **Amenities:** extended cable TV. **Pool(s):** outdoor. **Business Services:** meeting rooms. **Cards:** AX, CB, DC, DS, MC, VI. **Special Amenities:** free continental breakfast and free newspaper.

GIRARD pop. 11,300

—————— WHERE TO DINE ——————

JIB JAB HOT DOG SHOPPE
Lunch: $4-$7 Dinner: $4-$7 Phone: 330/545-1129
American **Location:** I-80, exit 227, 0.4 mi w on US 422. 313 S State St 44420. **Hours:** 6:30 am-10 pm, Fri & Sat-11 pm, Sun 8 am-10 pm. Closed major holidays. **Features:** casual dress; carryout; a la carte. Specializing in hot dogs, burgers, and fresh cut french fries, this simple restaurant guards a chili recipe that has been handed down from generation to generation. **Parking:** on-site.

GLENDALE —*See Cincinnati p. 575.*

GRANDVIEW —*See Cincinnati p. 576.*

GRANVILLE —*See Columbus p. 661.*

GREEN pop. 3,600

—————— WHERE TO STAY ——————

SUPER 8 MOTEL
Phone: (330)899-9888
5/28-9/2 1P: $60-$70 2P: $66-$76 XP: $6 F17
4/1-5/27 1P: $55-$65 2P: $61-$71 XP: $6 F17
9/3-3/31 1P: $50-$60 2P: $56-$66 XP: $6 F17
Motel **Location:** I-77, exit 118, just w. 1605 Corporate Woods Pkwy 44685. Fax: 330/899-9888. **Facility:** 59 one-bedroom standard units, some with whirlpools. 3 stories. *Bath:* combo or shower only. **Parking:** on-site. **Terms:** pets ($6 extra charge). **Amenities:** extended cable TV, voice mail. *Some:* irons, hair dryers. **Pool(s):** heated indoor. **Leisure Activities:** whirlpool. **Business Services:** meeting rooms. **Cards:** AX, DC, DS, MC, VI. **Special Amenities:** free continental breakfast and free local telephone calls.

GREENVILLE pop. 12,900

------ WHERE TO STAY ------

COMFORT INN

[SAVE]

▼▼▼▼
Motel

All Year   1P: $63-$109   2P: $68-$109   XP: $5
Location: US 127, 0.6 mi w via Kruckeberg Rd. 1190 Russ Rd 45331. Fax: 937/316-5214. **Facility:** 57 one-bedroom standard units, some with whirlpools. 2 stories, interior corridors. *Bath:* combo or shower only. **Parking:** on-site. **Amenities:** extended cable TV, irons, hair dryers. **Pool(s):** heated indoor. **Leisure Activities:** whirlpool. **Guest Services:** coin laundry. **Business Services:** meeting rooms. **Cards:** AX, CB, DC, DS, JC, MC, VI.

Phone: (937)316-5252
F18

SOME UNITS

🆎 🛗 ♿ 🚭 ➰ 🛄 🎥 📠 🖨 / ✕ 🔌 🖼 ▭ /

GREENVILLE INN

[AAA] [SAVE]

▼▼▼▼
Motor Inn

All Year   1P: $60-$80
Location: Jct US 127 and 36, 0.3 mi w on SR 571. 851 E Martin 45331. Fax: 937/548-5851. **Facility:** 68 one-bedroom standard units. 2 stories, interior corridors. **Parking:** on-site. **Terms:** 3 day cancellation notice, [CP] meal plan available, pets ($75 deposit). **Amenities:** extended cable TV. *Some:* irons, hair dryers. **Dining:** restaurant, 6 am-9 pm, $7-$16, cocktails. **Guest Services:** valet laundry. **Business Services:** meeting rooms, fax. **Cards:** AX, DC, DS, MC, VI. **Special Amenities:** free continental breakfast and free local telephone calls.

Phone: (937)548-3613

SOME UNITS

🆎 🐾 🍽 🍸 🚭 🛄 🎥 📠 ▭ 🖨 / ✕ 🔌 🖼 /

------ WHERE TO DINE ------

CJ'S HIGHMARKS

▼▼ ◆◆
American

Lunch: $9-$18   **Dinner:** $9-$18   **Phone:** 937/548-1400
Location: US 27, 0.8 mi w via Kruckeburg and Ross rds, then just n. 1475 Wagner Ave 45331. **Hours:** 11 am-10 pm, Fri & Sat-11 pm. Closed major holidays. **Features:** casual dress; children's menu; carryout; cocktails & lounge. **Parking:** on-site. **Cards:** AX, DS, MC, VI.

✕

GROVE CITY —See Columbus p. 662.

HAMILTON pop. 61,400

------ WHERE TO STAY ------

THE HAMILTONIAN HOTEL

▼▼▼▼
Hotel

4/1-9/30   1P: $81   2P: $81
10/1-3/31   1P: $76   2P: $76
Location: Just off High St, on Front St. 1 Riverfront Plaza 45011. Fax: 513/896-9463. **Facility:** 120 one-bedroom standard units. 6 stories, interior corridors. **Parking:** on-site. **Terms:** package plans, pets ($50 deposit). **Amenities:** extended cable TV, video games, voice mail, irons, hair dryers. **Dining:** Alexander's Hearth, see separate listing. **Pool(s):** outdoor. **Guest Services:** valet laundry. **Business Services:** conference facilities. **Cards:** AX, CB, DC, DS, MC, VI. *(See color ad below)*

Phone: (513)896-6200

SOME UNITS

[ASK] 🐾 🍽 🍸 🚭 ➰ 🛄 🎥 📠 ▭ 🖨 / ✕ 🔌 🖼 /
FEE

------ WHERE TO DINE ------

ALEXANDER'S HEARTH

▼▼ ◆◆
American

Lunch: $6-$10   **Dinner:** $14-$20   **Phone:** 513/896-6200
Location: Just off High St, on Front St; in The Hamiltonian Hotel. 1 Riverfront Plaza 45011. **Hours:** 6:30 am-2 & 5-10 pm, Sat & Sun 7 am-2 & 5-9 pm. **Reservations:** accepted; Sat. **Features:** casual dress; Sunday brunch; children's menu; early bird specials; carryout; cocktails. Prime rib is a house specialty at the casually upscale restaurant, which delivers ample portions of steak, pasta and pork. Plate presentations are vibrant and appealing. The Friday prime rib and seafood buffet is a big draw. Save room for dessert. **Parking:** on-site. **Cards:** AX, CB, DC, DS, MC, VI. *(See color ad below)*

✕

HANOVERTON pop. 400

——— WHERE TO DINE ———

SPREAD EAGLE TAVERN Historical   **Lunch:** $6-$8   **Dinner:** $14-$26   **Phone:** 330/223-1583
▼▼▼▼ **Location:** Jct US 30 and SR 9, just ne. 10150 Historic Plymouth St 44423. **Hours:** 11:30 am-2 & 5-8 pm, Fri &
American Sat-10 pm. Closed major holidays. **Reservations:** suggested. **Features:** casual dress; children's menu;
carryout; cocktails & lounge. Impressive log fireplaces are among touches that lend an air of authenticity to
the restored three-story, Federal-style brick inn. The menu caters to palates of many persuasions, with
balanced offerings of traditional and not-so-traditional fare. **Parking:** on-site. **Cards:** DS, MC, VI.   ✕

HARRISON —See Cincinnati p. 576.

HEATH —See Columbus p. 663.

HEBRON —See Columbus p. 663.

HILLIARD —See Columbus p. 663.

HILLSBORO pop. 6,200

——— WHERE TO STAY ———

DAYS INN HILLSBORO   **Phone:** (937)393-0299
AAA SAVE 4/1-9/30 [ECP]   1P: $59-$99   2P: $69-$99   XP: $6   F16
10/1-3/31 [ECP]   1P: $54-$75   2P: $64-$75   XP: $6   F16
▼▼▼▼ **Location:** 1.4 mi n on US 62. 103 Harry Sauner Rd 45133. **Fax:** 937/393-0165. **Facility:** 42 one-bedroom stan-
Motel dard units, some with whirlpools. 2 stories, interior corridors. **Parking:** on-site. **Terms:** 7 day cancellation no-
tice. **Pool(s):** small outdoor. **Guest Services:** coin laundry. **Business Services:** meeting rooms, fax.
Cards: AX, DC, DS, MC, VI. **Special Amenities: free continental breakfast and free local telephone**
calls.

SOME UNITS

——— WHERE TO DINE ———

THE WOODEN SPOON RESTAURANT   **Lunch:** $5-$13   **Dinner:** $7-$16   **Phone:** 937/393-4956
▼ **Location:** 1.5 mi n on US 62. 1480 N High St 45133. **Hours:** 11 am-8:30 pm, Fri & Sat-9:30 pm, Sun-3 pm.
American Closed: 1/1, 11/28, 12/25; also Mon. **Features:** casual dress; carryout; salad bar; buffet. Along a major
artery of local traffic, the casual eatery lets diners choose from a variety of beef, chicken and fowl
selections, either from the menu or the daily buffet. The Early American dining room has some traditional
artifacts scattered throughout. **Parking:** on-site. **Cards:** MC, VI.   ✕

HOLLAND pop. 1,200 (See map p. 756; index p. 757)

——— WHERE TO STAY ———

COURTYARD BY MARRIOTT-TOLEDO/HOLLAND   **Phone:** (419)866-1001   ❶
AAA SAVE All Year [BP]   1P: $99-$129   2P: $99-$129
▼▼▼ **Location:** I-475, exit 8, 0.5 mi w on SR 2. 1435 E Mall Dr 43528. **Fax:** 419/866-9869. **Facility:** 149 one-bedroom
Motel standard units. 3 stories, interior corridors. **Bath:** combo or shower only. **Parking:** on-site. **Terms:** cancella-
tion fee imposed. **Amenities:** voice mail, irons, hair dryers. **Dining:** 6:30-10 am, Sat & Sun 7 am-noon.
Pool(s): heated indoor. **Leisure Activities:** whirlpool, exercise room. **Guest Services:** valet and coin
(See color ad card insert) laundry, area transportation. **Business Services:** meeting rooms. **Cards:** AX, CB, DC, DS, MC, VI.

SOME UNITS

CROSS COUNTRY INN   **Phone:** (419)866-6565   ❷
AAA SAVE All Year   1P: $40-$47   2P: $47-$54   XP: $2   F17
▼▼▼ **Location:** I-475, exit 8, just w on SR 2; behind the mall. 1201 E Mall Dr 43528. **Fax:** 419/866-6608. **Facility:** 128
Motel one-bedroom standard units. 2 stories, exterior corridors. **Bath:** combo or shower only. **Parking:** on-site.
Amenities: voice mail. **Pool(s):** heated indoor. **Cards:** AX, CB, DC, DS, JC, MC, VI. **Special Amenities:**
free local telephone calls and preferred room (subject to availability with advanced reservations).

SOME UNITS

EXTENDED STAY AMERICA   **Phone:** 419/861-1133   ❻
▼▼▼ Property failed to provide current rates
Extended Stay **Location:** I-475, exit 8, just e to Holland/Sylvania Rd, just n. 6155 Trust Dr 43528. **Fax:** 419/861-1144. **Facility:** 125
Motel one-bedroom standard units with efficiencies. 3 stories, interior corridors. **Bath:** combo or shower only.
Parking: on-site. **Amenities:** voice mail. **Guest Services:** coin laundry. **Cards:** AX, DC, DS, MC, VI.

SOME UNITS

(See map p. 756)

FAIRFIELD INN BY MARRIOTT-TOLEDO/HOLLAND
Phone: (419)867-1144 ④

(AAA) [SAVE]

◇◇ ◇◇
Motel

All Year [CP]   1P: $59-$89   2P: $59-$89
Location: I-475, exit 8, just w on SR 2; behind the mall. 1401 E Mall Dr 43528. **Fax:** 419/867-1144. **Facility:** 135 one-bedroom standard units. 3 stories, interior/exterior corridors. *Bath:* combo or shower only. **Parking:** on-site. **Amenities:** irons. **Pool(s):** heated outdoor. **Guest Services:** valet laundry, area transportation. **Cards:** AX, DC, DS, MC, VI. **Special Amenities:** free continental breakfast and free local telephone calls. *(See color ad card insert)*

SOME UNITS
⌂ ✈ ⑪ ◻ ⊇ ⊠ ⛶ [DATA PORT] 🖨 / ⊠ ▣ /
FEE

RED ROOF INN TOLEDO/HOLLAND
Phone: (419)866-5512 ③

(AAA) [SAVE]

◇◇ ◇◇
Motel

All Year   1P: $37-$59   2P: $44-$64   XP: $5   F18
Location: I-475, exit 8, just e on Holland-Sylvania Rd, just n to Trust Dr. 1214 Corporate Dr 43528. **Fax:** 419/866-5886. **Facility:** 108 one-bedroom standard units. 2 stories, exterior corridors. *Bath:* combo or shower only. **Parking:** on-site, winter plug-ins. **Amenities:** video games, voice mail. **Cards:** AX, CB, DC, DS, MC, VI. **Special Amenities:** free local telephone calls and free newspaper.

SOME UNITS
🐾 ◻ ⑪ [DATA PORT] 🖨 / ⊠ ▣ /
FEE

RESIDENCE INN BY MARRIOTT
Phone: (419)867-9555 ⑤

(AAA) [SAVE]

◇◇◇
Apartment

6/1-8/31   1P: $139-$159   2P: $139-$159
4/1-5/31 & 9/1-3/31   1P: $129-$159   2P: $129-$159
Location: I-475, exit 8, just e to Holland-Sylvania Rd, just n. 6101 Trust Dr 43528. **Fax:** 419/867-9475. **Facility:** 96 units. 72 one- & 24 two-bedroom standard units with kitchens. 2 stories, exterior corridors. *Bath:* combo or shower only. **Parking:** on-site. **Terms:** cancellation fee imposed, [ECP] meal plan available, package plans, pets ($50 fee, $10 extra charge). **Amenities:** extended cable TV, dual phone lines, voice mail, irons, hair dryers. **Pool(s):** heated outdoor. **Leisure Activities:** whirlpool, exercise room, sports court. **Guest Services:** coin laundry. **Business Services:** meeting rooms. **Cards:** AX, CB, DC, DS, JC, MC, VI. *(See color ad card insert)*

SOME UNITS
🐿 ✈ 🐾 ◻ ⊇ ⊠ ⛶ [DATA PORT] ▤ 🖴 ▣ 🖨 / ⊠ /

────── **WHERE TO DINE** ──────

EL MATADOR RESTAURANT   **Lunch:** $7-$9   **Dinner:** $9-$12   **Phone:** 419/866-8229 ②

◇
Mexican

Location: I-475, exit 8, 0.9 mi w on SR 2. 7011 Airport Hwy 43528. **Hours:** 11 am-11 pm. Closed major holidays. **Features:** casual dress; children's menu; carryout; cocktails & lounge; a la carte. This local chain serves all the traditional Mexican favorites. **Parking:** on-site. **Cards:** AX, DC, DS, MC, VI.

⊠

JOE'S CRAB SHACK   **Lunch:** $7-$10   **Dinner:** $10-$16   **Phone:** 419/866-8877 ①

◇◇◇
Seafood

Location: I-475, exit 8, 0.7 mi e on SR 2. 1435 Baronial Plaza Dr 43615. **Hours:** 11 am-10 pm, Fri & Sat-11 pm. Closed: 11/28, 12/25. **Features:** casual dress; children's menu; carryout; cocktails & lounge. The eclectic, high-energy dining room resembles an old fishing shanty, with lots of rustic memorabilia worked into a collage of fishing excursions. Steaks, American entrees and seafood, including the noteworthy fresh crab, make up the diverse menu. **Parking:** on-site. **Cards:** AX, CB, DC, DS, JC, MC, VI.

⊠

HUBER HEIGHTS pop. 38,700 (See map p. 672; index p. 674)

────── **WHERE TO STAY** ──────

COMFORT INN DAYTON/HUBER HEIGHTS
Phone: (937)237-7477 61

(AAA) [SAVE]

◇◇◇
Motel

4/1-8/31 [CP]   1P: $70-$75   2P: $75   XP: $10   F
9/1-3/31 [CP]   1P: $65   2P: $65   XP: $10   F
Location: I-70, exit 38, just s; at SR 201. 7907 Brandt Pk 45424. **Fax:** 937/237-5187. **Facility:** 53 one-bedroom standard units, some with whirlpools. 2 stories, interior corridors. *Bath:* combo or shower only. **Parking:** on-site. **Terms:** 7 day cancellation notice-fee imposed. **Amenities:** extended cable TV, irons, hair dryers. **Leisure Activities:** whirlpool, pool privileges, limited exercise equipment. **Guest Services:** coin laundry. **Cards:** AX, DC, DS, MC, VI.

SOME UNITS
🐿 ⑪ ⛷ ◻ ⊠ ⛶ [DATA PORT] 🖴 🖨 / ⊠ ▣ ▣ /
FEE

DAYS INN-HUBER HEIGHTS
Phone: (937)233-1836 63

(AAA) [SAVE]

◇◇ ◇◇
Motel

All Year [CP]   1P: $45-$65   2P: $55-$85   XP: $6   F17
Location: I-70, exit 36, just s. 7761 Old Country Ct 45424. **Fax:** 937/233-3079. **Facility:** 55 one-bedroom standard units, some with whirlpools. 2 stories, exterior corridors. *Bath:* combo or shower only. **Parking:** on-site. **Amenities:** extended cable TV, irons, hair dryers. **Pool(s):** outdoor. **Leisure Activities:** whirlpool. **Guest Services:** coin laundry. **Cards:** AX, DC, DS, MC, VI. **Special Amenities:** free continental breakfast and free newspaper.

SOME UNITS
⑪ ⛷ ◻ ⊇ ⛶ [DATA PORT] 🖨 / ⊠ ▣ ▣ /
FEE

HAMPTON INN
Phone: (937)233-4300 64

(AAA) [SAVE]

◇◇◇
Motel

All Year [CP]   1P: $89-$99   2P: $89-$99   XP: $10   F16
Location: I-70, exit 36, just s. 5588 Merily Way 45424. **Fax:** 937/233-4443. **Facility:** 72 one-bedroom standard units. 3 stories, interior corridors. *Bath:* combo or shower only. **Parking:** on-site. **Terms:** cancellation fee imposed. **Amenities:** extended cable TV, dual phone lines, voice mail, irons, hair dryers. **Pool(s):** heated indoor. **Leisure Activities:** sauna, whirlpool, exercise room. **Guest Services:** coin laundry. **Business Services:** meeting rooms, business center. **Cards:** AX, DC, DS, JC, MC, VI. **Special Amenities:** free continental breakfast and free local telephone calls.

SOME UNITS
🐿 ⑪ Ⓜ ⛷ ◻ ⊇ ⊠ ⛶ [DATA PORT] ▤ ▣ 🖨 / ⊠ /

(See map p. 672)

HOLIDAY INN EXPRESS & SUITES Phone: (937)235-2000 65
[AAA] [SAVE] 5/1-9/4 1P: $79 2P: $79
4/1-4/30 & 9/5-3/31 1P: $71 2P: $71
Motel **Location:** I-70, exit 36, just s on SR 202. 5612 Merily Way 45424. Fax: 937/235-2600. **Facility:** 65 one-bedroom standard units, some with whirlpools. 3 stories, interior corridors. *Bath:* combo or shower only. **Parking:** on-site. **Terms:** [CP] meal plan available. **Amenities:** extended cable TV, dual phone lines, voice mail, irons, hair dryers. **Pool(s):** heated indoor. **Leisure Activities:** whirlpool, exercise room. **Guest Services:** coin laundry. **Business Services:** meeting rooms. **Cards:** AX, DC, DS, JC, MC, VI. **Special Amenities: free continental breakfast and free local telephone calls.**

SOME UNITS

SUPER 8 MOTEL Phone: (937)237-1888 60
Motel All Year 1P: $48 2P: $51 XP: $3 F12
Location: I-70, exit 36. 8110 Old Troy Pike 45424. Fax: 937/237-2033. **Facility:** 63 one-bedroom standard units. 3 stories, interior corridors. *Bath:* combo or shower only. **Parking:** on-site. **Terms:** [ECP] meal plan available. **Amenities:** extended cable TV. **Pool(s):** heated indoor. **Leisure Activities:** whirlpool. **Guest Services:** coin laundry. **Cards:** AX, CB, DC, DS, MC, VI.

SOME UNITS

TRAVELODGE Phone: (937)236-9361 62
[AAA] [SAVE] 4/1-9/30 1P: $55 2P: $60 XP: $7 F16
10/1-3/31 1P: $55 2P: $55 XP: $7 F16
Motel **Location:** I-70, exit 38, just s, at SR 201. 7911 Brandt Pike 45424. Fax: 937/236-9361. **Facility:** 51 one-bedroom standard units. 2 stories, interior/exterior corridors. **Parking:** on-site. **Terms:** small pets only. **Amenities:** extended cable TV. **Pool(s):** outdoor. **Cards:** AX, CB, DC, DS, JC, MC, VI. **Special Amenities: free continental breakfast and free newspaper.**

SOME UNITS

———— WHERE TO DINE ————

THAI-WEST RESTAURANT **Lunch:** $9-$14 **Dinner:** $9-$14 Phone: 937/237-7767 45
Thai **Location:** I-70, exit 38, 1.6 mi s on SR 201, then just w. 6118 Chambersburg Rd 45424. **Hours:** 11 am-9 pm, Fri & Sat-10 pm. **Features:** casual dress; carryout; beer & wine only. The menu at this eatery includes a variety of Thai and Chinese dishes, as well as a handful of American entrees, served family style. Try the spicy red or green curry with your choice of meat. Situated in a shopping plaza, the restaurant has a simple decor. Smoke free premises. **Parking:** on-site. **Cards:** AX, DS, MC, VI.

HUDSON pop. 5,200

———— WHERE TO STAY ————

VIRGINIA MOTEL Phone: 330/650-0449
[AAA] [SAVE] 4/1-10/1 1P: $46-$51 2P: $60-$80 XP: $20
10/2-3/31 1P: $40-$45 2P: $50-$60 XP: $20
Motel **Location:** I-80, exit 180, 4.5 mi s. 5374 Akron-Cleveland Rd 44264. **Facility:** 13 one-bedroom standard units. 1 story, exterior corridors. *Bath:* combo or shower only. **Parking:** on-site. **Cards:** AX, DS, MC, VI.

———— WHERE TO DINE ————

THE INN AT TURNER'S MILL **Lunch:** $8-$13 **Dinner:** $19-$30 Phone: 330/656-2949
American **Location:** Just e of town square. 36 E Streetsboro St 44236. **Hours:** 11:30 am-2:30 & 5:30-9:30 pm, Fri & Sat-10 pm, Sun 4 pm-8 pm. Closed major holidays. **Reservations:** suggested. **Features:** dressy casual; carryout; cocktails & lounge; entertainment. The elegant, restored mill is a sophisticated setting for creative cuisine and relaxing jazz entertainment several nights a week. Both the food and service pamper diners, making the restaurant a favorite for special occasions. **Parking:** on-site. **Cards:** AX, DC, DS, MC, VI.

OLD WHEDON GRILLE **Lunch:** $6-$10 **Dinner:** $10-$20 Phone: 330/650-0013
American **Location:** Just n. 200 N Main St 44236. **Hours:** 11 am-midnight, Fri & Sat-2 am. Closed major holidays; also Sun. **Features:** casual dress; children's menu; carryout; cocktails. For a quick bite or a more traditional evening dining experience, this restaurant has a varied menu. They are located just a short drive from Six Flags and the Aurora Outlet Mall in the historic town of Hudson. The menu tends toward lighter fare and the seating is warm and cozy, especially in the cold winter. **Parking:** on-site. **Cards:** AX, MC, VI.

THE RED TOMATO **Lunch:** $5-$8 **Dinner:** $10-$20 Phone: 330/650-5050
Italian **Location:** West end of Hudson Shopping Plaza. 116 W Streetsboro Rd 44236. **Hours:** 11 am-2 & 4:30-10 pm, Fri-11 pm, Sat 4:30 pm-11 pm. Closed major holidays; also Sun. **Reservations:** suggested. **Features:** casual dress; children's menu; carryout; cocktails; a la carte. Try the linguine with meatballs and sausage; you'll be delighted not only with the taste but with the care paid to presentation. Most dishes are made from scratch and all employ fresh ingredients to enhance each meal. Limited seating is available. **Parking:** on-site. **Cards:** AX, DC, DS, MC, VI.

———— *The following restaurant has not been evaluated by AAA* ————
but is listed for your information only.

MARCELITA'S Phone: 330/650-2145
[fyi] Not evaluated. **Location:** 7774 Darrow Rd 44236. The relaxed atmosphere draws patrons to the restaurant for budget-friendly Mexican fare.

HURON pop. 7,000

——— WHERE TO STAY ———

COMFORT INN   **Phone:** (419)433-5359

[SAVE]

[icons]

Motel

6/22-9/1 [ECP]	1P: $69-$149	2P: $69-$149
4/1-6/21 [ECP]	1P: $39-$99	2P: $39-$99
9/2-10/26 [ECP]	1P: $39-$79	2P: $39-$79
10/27-3/31 [ECP]	1P: $39-$49	2P: $39-$49

Location: 2.8 mi w on US 6; SR 2, exit Rye Beach. 2119 W Cleveland Rd 44839. Fax: 419/433-5359. **Facility:** 43 one-bedroom standard units, some with whirlpools. 2 stories, interior corridors. **Parking:** on-site. **Amenities:** extended cable TV, hair dryers. *Some:* irons. **Pool(s):** heated outdoor. **Leisure Activities:** Fee: game room. **Guest Services:** coin laundry. **Business Services:** fax. **Cards:** AX, CB, DC, DS, JC, MC, VI. *(See color ad p 735 & p 739)*

SOME UNITS

[icons] / [icons] /

THE LODGE AT SAWMILL CREEK RESORT   **Phone:** 419/433-3800

(AAA) [SAVE]

[icons]

Resort

6/3-9/1	1P: $149-$189	2P: $149-$189	XP: $10	F18
9/2-10/28	1P: $117-$137	2P: $117-$137	XP: $10	F18
4/1-6/2	1P: $81-$127	2P: $81-$127	XP: $10	F18
10/29-3/31	1P: $85-$105	2P: $85-$105	XP: $10	F18

Location: 3 mi w on US 6; SR 2, exit Rye Beach. 400 Sawmill 44839. Fax: 419/433-7610. **Facility:** Closed 1/3-1/9. 240 one-bedroom standard units, some with whirlpools. 2 stories, interior corridors. *Bath:* combo or shower only. **Parking:** on-site. **Terms:** check-in 4 pm, 3 day cancellation notice-fee imposed, [BP] & [MAP] meal plans available, package plans, 15% service charge. **Amenities:** extended cable TV, voice mail, irons, hair dryers. *Some:* dual phone lines. **Dining:** restaurant, 7 am-10 pm, $15-$30, cocktails. **Pool(s):** heated indoor, heated indoor/outdoor. **Leisure Activities:** saunas, whirlpool, boating, marina, fishing, 3 tennis courts, nature program, exercise room. **Guest Services:** gift shop, massage (fee), valet laundry. **Business Services:** conference facilities, fax. **Cards:** AX, DS, MC, VI. **Special Amenities:** free newspaper and preferred room (subject to availability with advanced reservations). *(See color ad p 741)*

SOME UNITS

[icons] / [icons] /

PLANTATION MOTEL   **Phone:** 419/433-4790

(AAA) [SAVE]

[icons]

Motel

6/14-9/1	1P: $49-$69	2P: $69-$88	XP: $7	F10
5/3-6/13	1P: $35-$49	2P: $35-$59	XP: $7	F10
4/1-5/2 & 9/2-10/31	1P: $33	2P: $38	XP: $7	F10

Location: 3 mi e on US 6. 2815 E Cleveland Rd 44839. Fax: 419/433-3134. **Facility:** 26 one-bedroom standard units. 1 story, exterior corridors. *Bath:* combo or shower only. **Parking:** on-site. **Terms:** open 4/1-10/31, 3 day cancellation notice, pets ($7 extra charge). **Amenities:** extended cable TV. **Pool(s):** heated outdoor. **Cards:** MC, VI. **Special Amenities:** early check-in/late check-out and free local telephone calls. *(See ad p 743)*

SOME UNITS

[icons] / [icons] /

RIVER'S EDGE INN   **Phone:** (419)433-8000

(AAA) [SAVE]

[icons]

Motel

6/22-9/1 [ECP]	1P: $59-$149	2P: $59-$149
4/1-6/21 [ECP]	1P: $49-$99	2P: $49-$99
9/2-10/26 [ECP]	1P: $49-$79	2P: $49-$79
10/27-3/31 [ECP]	1P: $39-$49	2P: $39-$59

Location: Just 3 blks n on Williams St to South St, just e. 132 N Main St 44839. Fax: 419/433-8000. **Facility:** 65 one-bedroom standard units, some with whirlpools. 3 stories, interior corridors. *Bath:* combo or shower only. **Parking:** on-site. **Terms:** package plans - off season. **Amenities:** extended cable TV. *Some:* hair dryers. **Pool(s):** heated indoor. **Leisure Activities:** whirlpools, exercise room. **Guest Services:** coin laundry. **Business Services:** meeting rooms. **Cards:** AX, CB, DC, DC, MC, VI. **Special Amenities:** free continental breakfast and free local telephone calls. *(See color ad p 744)*

SOME UNITS

[icons] / [icons] /
FEE FEE

——— WHERE TO DINE ———

The following restaurants have not been evaluated by AAA but are listed for your information only.

JP'S DOWNUNDER   **Phone:** 419/433-2726

[fyi]   Not evaluated. **Location:** 356 N Main St 44839. Catchy names are bestowed on the restaurant's reasonably priced menu selections.

MARCONI'S   **Phone:** 419/433-4341

[fyi]   Not evaluated. **Location:** SR 6 & Berlin Rd 44839. The hometown favorite serves Italian, Sicilian and American dishes in a bistro-type setting.

INDEPENDENCE —See Cleveland p. 621.

JACKSON pop. 6,100

——— WHERE TO STAY ———

COMFORT INN   **Phone:** (740)286-7581

(AAA) [SAVE]

[icons]

Motel

All Year	1P: $70-$80	2P: $75-$85

Location: Jct SR 32, 0.5 mi n on SR 93. 605 E Main St 45640 (PO Box 667). Fax: 740/286-3657. **Facility:** 52 one-bedroom standard units, some with whirlpools. 2 stories, interior corridors. **Parking:** on-site. **Terms:** [CP] meal plan available. **Amenities:** extended cable TV, video tape library (fee), voice mail, irons, hair dryers. **Guest Services:** valet laundry. **Business Services:** meeting rooms. **Cards:** AX, CB, DC, DS, JC, MC, VI.

SOME UNITS

[icons] / [icons] /
FEE

KNIGHTS INN

Motel

MC, VI.

All Year · 1P: $40-$53 · 2P: $46-$59 · XP: $6 · F18
Location: 0.7 mi n on US 35 business route. 404 Chillicothe St 45640. Fax: 740/286-1714. **Facility:** 35 one-bedroom standard units. 1-2 stories, exterior corridors. *Bath:* combo or shower only. **Parking:** on-site. **Terms:** pets ($20 deposit). **Amenities:** extended cable TV. **Guest Services:** valet laundry. **Cards:** AX, DS,

Phone: (740)286-2135

SOME UNITS

——— WHERE TO DINE ———

LEWIS FAMILY RESTAURANT · **Lunch:** $6-$9 · **Dinner:** $7-$14 · **Phone:** 740/286-5413

American

Location: Jct SR 93 and US 32. 966 E Main St 45640. **Hours:** 7 am-9 pm, Sun 8 am-8 pm. Closed: 1/1, 11/28, 12/25. **Reservations:** suggested; weekends. **Features:** casual dress; carryout; salad bar. No need to wait for the holidays to enjoy a great turkey dinner. This restaurant specializes in fresh-from-the-farm turkey house specialties from the Lewis Family farm. The friendly staff also serves up steak, sandwiches and some seafood dishes. **Parking:** on-site. **Cards:** DS, MC, VI.

JEFFERSONVILLE pop. 1,300

——— WHERE TO STAY ———

AMERIHOST INN-JEFFERSONVILLE NORTH

[SAVE]

Motel

All Year [CP] · 1P: $78-$88 · 2P: $78-$88 · XP: $5 · F17
Location: I-71, exit 69 (SR 41). 10160 Carr Rd NW 43128. Fax: 740/426-6500. **Facility:** 61 one-bedroom standard units, some with whirlpools. 2 stories, interior corridors. *Bath:* combo or shower only. **Parking:** on-site. **Terms:** small pets only ($35 extra charge). **Amenities:** extended cable TV, voice mail, safes (fee), irons, hair dryers. **Pool(s):** heated indoor. **Leisure Activities:** sauna, whirlpool, exercise room. **Cards:** AX, CB, DC, DS, JC, MC, VI. **Special Amenities:** free continental breakfast and free newspaper.

Phone: (740)426-6400

SOME UNITS

FEE

AMERIHOST INN-JEFFERSONVILLE SOUTH

[SAVE]

Motel

All Year · 1P: $74 · 2P: $74 · XP: $6 · F18
Location: I-71, exit 65. 11431 Allen Rd NW 43128. Fax: 740/948-2110. **Facility:** 60 one-bedroom standard units, some with whirlpools. 2 stories, interior corridors. **Parking:** on-site. **Terms:** 14 day cancellation notice, package plans. **Amenities:** voice mail, safes (fee), irons, hair dryers. **Pool(s):** heated indoor. **Leisure Activities:** whirlpool, exercise bike, stair machine. **Business Services:** meeting rooms. **Cards:** AX, DC, DS, JC, MC, VI. **Special Amenities:** free continental breakfast and free newspaper.

Phone: (740)948-2104

SOME UNITS

FEE

HAMPTON INN

[SAVE]

Motel

All Year [ECP] · 1P: $74 · 2P: $74
Location: I-71, exit 65. 11484 Allen Rd NW 43128. Fax: 740/948-9498. **Facility:** 58 units. 57 one-bedroom standard units, some with whirlpools. 1 one-bedroom suite ($104-$124) with whirlpool. 3 stories, interior corridors. *Bath:* combo or shower only. **Parking:** on-site. **Terms:** 7 day cancellation notice. **Amenities:** extended cable TV, video tape library (fee), voice mail, irons, hair dryers. **Pool(s):** small heated indoor. **Leisure Activities:** whirlpool, exercise room. **Guest Services:** complimentary laundry. **Business Services:** meeting rooms. **Cards:** AX, CB, DC, DS, MC, VI.

Phone: (740)948-9499

SOME UNITS

KELLEYS ISLAND pop. 200

——— WHERE TO STAY ———

——— *The following lodging was either not evaluated or did not* ———
meet AAA rating requirements but is listed for your information only.

WATER'S EDGE RETREAT-LUXURY B & B

[fyi]

Not evaluated. **Location:** 827 E Lakeshore Dr 43438 (PO Box 839). Facilities, services, and decor characterize a mid-range property.

Phone: 419/746-2455

KENT pop. 28,800

——— WHERE TO STAY ———

ALDEN INN GROUP INC

Motel

6/1-9/14 [CP] · 1P: $50-$70 · 2P: $55-$75 · XP: $5 · F16
4/1-5/31 & 9/15-3/31 [CP] · 1P: $40-$60 · 2P: $45-$65 · XP: $5 · F16
Location: I-76, exit 33. (4386 SR 43, BRIMFIELD, 44240). Fax: 330/678-7695. **Facility:** 40 one-bedroom standard units, some with whirlpools. 3 stories, interior/exterior corridors. *Bath:* combo or shower only. **Parking:** on-site. **Terms:** cancellation fee imposed. **Amenities:** extended cable TV. **Guest Services:** coin laundry. **Business Services:** meeting rooms. **Cards:** AX, DS, MC, VI.

Phone: 330/678-9927

SOME UNITS

DAYS INN-AKRON KENT
Phone: (330)677-9400

[SAVE]

5/16-10/31 [CP]	1P: $76-$85	2P: $76-$85
11/1-3/31 [CP]	1P: $50-$65	2P: $50-$65
4/1-5/15 [CP]	1P: $50-$65	2P: $50-$65 XP: $5 F12

Motel
Location: I-76, exit 33. (4422 Edsen Rd, BRIMFIELD, 44240). Fax: 330/677-9456. **Facility:** 67 one-bedroom standard units, some with whirlpools. 2 stories, exterior corridors. *Bath:* combo or shower only. **Parking:** on-site. **Terms:** 7 day cancellation notice. **Amenities:** extended cable TV, safes (fee), hair dryers. *Some:* irons. **Pool(s):** heated outdoor. **Cards:** AX, DC, DS, MC, VI.

SOME UNITS
[icons] 🆂🅳 ... / 🗙 📠 💻 📺 💻 /

HAMPTON INN
Phone: (330)673-8555

[SAVE]

4/1-9/15 [ECP]	1P: $79	2P: $89
9/16-3/31 [ECP]	1P: $64	2P: $79

Motel
Location: I-76, exit 33. 4406 SR 43 44240. Fax: 330/673-4455. **Facility:** 80 one-bedroom standard units. 3 stories, interior corridors. *Bath:* combo or shower only. **Parking:** on-site. **Terms:** 14 day cancellation notice-fee imposed. **Amenities:** extended cable TV, high-speed Internet, voice mail, irons. *Some:* hair dryers. **Pool(s):** heated indoor. **Leisure Activities:** whirlpool, exercise room. **Guest Services:** valet and coin laundry. **Business Services:** meeting rooms. **Cards:** AX, CB, DC, DS, JC, MC, VI.

SOME UNITS
[icons] 🆂🅳 ... 📠 💻 💻 / 🗙 /
FEE

THE INN OF KENT
Phone: 330/673-3411

6/1-8/31	1P: $40-$80	2P: $40-$80
4/1-5/31	1P: $40-$75	2P: $45-$75
9/1-3/31	1P: $40-$75	2P: $40-$75 XP: $3

Motel
Location: Just e on SR 59. 303 E Main St 44240. Fax: 330/673-9878. **Facility:** 56 one-bedroom standard units, some with efficiencies. 2 stories, exterior corridors. *Bath:* combo or shower only. **Parking:** on-site. **Terms:** small pets only. **Amenities:** extended cable TV. **Pool(s):** heated indoor. **Guest Services:** coin laundry. **Cards:** AX, CB, DC, DS, MC, VI.

SOME UNITS
[icons] 🛏 🐾 📠 / 🗙 💻 💻 📠 /

RAMADA INN-AKRON/KENT
Phone: (330)678-0101

5/1-9/15	1P: $69-$99	2P: $79-$99 XP: $10 F17
4/1-4/30 & 9/16-3/31	1P: $59-$79	2P: $59-$89 XP: $10 F17

Motor Inn
Location: I-76, exit 33. 4363 SR 43 44240. Fax: 330/677-5001. **Facility:** 152 one-bedroom standard units. 2 stories, exterior corridors. **Parking:** on-site. **Terms:** check-in 4 pm, 3 day cancellation notice, package plans, pets ($50 deposit). **Amenities:** extended cable TV, irons, hair dryers. **Pool(s):** heated outdoor. **Leisure Activities:** whirlpool, exercise room. *Fee:* game room. **Guest Services:** gift shop, valet and coin laundry. **Business Services:** conference facilities. **Cards:** AX, CB, DC, DS, MC, VI.

SOME UNITS
[icons] 🅰🆂🅺 🆂🅳 🐾 🍴 📠 🐾 🗙 📺 💻 💻 / 🗙 /

SUPER 8 MOTEL
Phone: (330)678-8817

4/1-8/31	1P: $60-$80	2P: $70-$90 XP: $5 F18
9/1-12/31	1P: $45-$60	2P: $50-$60 XP: $5 F18
1/1-3/31	1P: $45-$60	2P: $50-$60 XP: $5 F18

Motel
Location: I-76, exit 33. 4380 Edson Rd 44240. Fax: 330/678-3138. **Facility:** 61 one-bedroom standard units. 3 stories, interior corridors. **Parking:** on-site. **Terms:** 7 day cancellation notice, pets ($5 extra charge). **Amenities:** extended cable TV, safes. **Cards:** AX, DC, DS, JC, MC, VI.

SOME UNITS
[icons] 🅰🆂🅺 🆂🅳 🐾 📠 📺 📠 / 🗙 💻 💻 /
FEE FEE

UNIVERSITY INN
Phone: 330/678-0123

[AAA] [SAVE]

6/1-8/31	1P: $49-$70	2P: $59-$89 XP: $5 F16
4/1-5/31 & 9/1-3/31	1P: $46-$62	2P: $50-$66 XP: $5 F16

Motel
Location: Just s on SR 43. 540 S Water St 44240. Fax: 330/678-7356. **Facility:** 60 one-bedroom standard units. 7 stories, exterior corridors. **Parking:** on-site. **Amenities:** extended cable TV, voice mail, hair dryers. **Dining:** coffee shop, 7 am-2 pm. **Pool(s):** heated outdoor. **Guest Services:** coin laundry. **Business Services:** meeting rooms. **Cards:** AX, DS, MC, VI. *(See color ad p 536)*

SOME UNITS
[icons] 🍴 🐾 📺 💻 💻 💻 💻 💻 / 🗙 /

─────── **WHERE TO DINE** ───────

PUFFERBELLY LTD   **Lunch:** $5-$8   **Dinner:** $8-$14   **Phone:** 330/673-1771

American
Location: Downtown; in historical district. 152 Franklin Ave 44240. **Hours:** 11 am-10 pm, Fri & Sat-11 pm, Sun 11 am-9 pm. Closed major holidays. **Reservations:** suggested; weekends. **Features:** casual dress; Sunday brunch; children's menu; carryout; cocktails & lounge. Antiques hang on the walls and candles sit on the tables in the quaint former train station, now a bustling, upbeat spot for family dining. The specialty chicken Pufferbelly consists of a pan-fried chicken breast served over fettuccine primavera. **Parking:** on-site. **Cards:** AX, DS, MC, VI.

[icon] 🗙

KENTON pop. 8,400

─────── **WHERE TO STAY** ───────

AMERIHOST INN-KENTON
Phone: (419)675-1400

[AAA] [SAVE]

All Year	1P: $69	2P: $95

Motel
Location: Jct US 68 and SR 67, just ne on SR 67 (E Columbus St). 902 E Columbus 43326. Fax: 419/675-1404. **Facility:** 60 one-bedroom standard units, some with whirlpools. 2 stories, interior corridors. *Bath:* combo or shower only. **Parking:** on-site. **Amenities:** extended cable TV, safes, irons, hair dryers. **Pool(s):** heated indoor. **Leisure Activities:** sauna, whirlpool, 18 hole golf course nearby, exercise room. **Guest Services:** valet laundry. **Business Services:** meeting rooms. **Cards:** AX, CB, DC, DS, JC, MC, VI. **Special Amenities:** free continental breakfast and free newspaper.

SOME UNITS
[icons] 🆂🅳 🍴 🆔 📠 🐾 🗙 📺 💻 💻 💻 / 🗙 💻 💻 /
FEE

KETTERING pop. 60,600   (See map p. 672; index p. 675)

———— WHERE TO DINE ————

L'AUBERGE
▼▲▲▲▼
French

Lunch: $11-$16   Dinner: $40-$50   Phone: 937/299-5536   [58]
Location: At jct of Stroop Rd and Far Hills Ave; just w of Town and Country Shopping Center. 4120 Far Hills Ave 45429. **Hours:** 11:30 am-2 & 5-10 pm, Fri & Sat-11 pm. Closed major holidays; also Sun. **Features:** casual dress; cocktails & lounge; a la carte. A recent visit found the pan-fried whitefish with crisp, colorful mixed vegetables a very good choice at L'Auberge. The seasonally changing menu offers a large variety of fish, lamb, game and veal dishes. Smoking is permitted only on the outdoor patio. **Parking:** on-site. **Cards:** AX, DC, MC, VI.   ⊗

MAMMA DISALVO'S ITALIAN RISTORANTE
▼▲▲▼ ▼▲▲▼
Italian

Lunch: $5-$12   Dinner: $7-$20   Phone: 937/299-5831   [56]
Location: I-675, exit 7, 0.5 mi w on Dorothy Ln to Stroop Rd, 3 mi w. 1375 E Stroop Rd 45429. **Hours:** 11 am-10 pm, Fri-11 pm, Sat 12:30 pm-11 pm, Sun 12:30 pm-10 pm. Closed major holidays; also Mon. **Features:** casual dress; Sunday brunch; carryout; cocktails & lounge; a la carte. Popular restaurant serving a wide variety of Italian food. Smoke free premises. **Parking:** on-site. **Cards:** AX, DS, MC, VI.   ⊗

PEASANT STOCK-A RESTAURANT
▼▲▲▼ ▼▲▲▼
American

Lunch: $7-$9   Dinner: $11-$18   Phone: 937/293-3900   [55]
Location: East end of Town and Country Shopping Center. 424 E Stroop Rd 45429. **Hours:** 11 am-10 pm, Fri & Sat-11 pm, Sun 10:30 am-2 pm. Closed major holidays. **Reservations:** suggested. **Features:** casual dress; Sunday brunch; children's menu; carryout; cocktails & lounge. Attractive dining rooms with country French appeal and a glass atrium complement your dining experience at Peasant Stock. House favorites range from fresh fish to chicken pot pie and the chef's monthly specials. Enclosed patio dining is available. **Parking:** on-site. **Cards:** AX, DC, DS, MC, VI.   ⊗

WELTONS RESTAURANT
▼▲▲▲▼
American

Dinner: $10-$17   Phone: 937/293-2233   [57]
Location: I-675, exit 7, 1 mi w; in Wilmington Heights Shopping Center. 4614 Wilmington Pike 45440. **Hours:** 5 pm-10 pm, Fri & Sat-11 pm. Closed: 1/1, 12/25; also Sun. **Features:** casual dress; carryout; cocktails & lounge. Specialties include pan-fried walleye and beef medallions sauteed in wine and topped with crabmeat, artichoke hearts and hollandaise. Beige and peach linens dress tables in the two dining rooms, which are decorated with paintings and light wood accents. **Parking:** on-site. **Cards:** AX, DS, MC, VI.   ⊗

———— *The following restaurants have not been evaluated by AAA* ————
but are listed for your information only.

AJANTA
[fyi]

Phone: 937/296-9201
Not evaluated. **Location:** 3063 Woodman Dr 45420. This popular restaurant serves up a wide variety of Indian cuisine.

CARMEL'S MEXICAN RESTAURANT AND LOUNGE
[fyi]

Phone: 937/294-1261
Not evaluated. **Location:** 1025 Shroyer Rd 45419. Mexican and American fare is offered at this restaurant.

KINGS MILLS —*See Cincinnati p. 576.*

LAKEWOOD —*See Cleveland p. 623.*

LANCASTER —*See Columbus p. 664.*

LEBANON —*See Cincinnati p. 576.*

LEXINGTON

———— WHERE TO DINE ————

———— *The following restaurants have not been evaluated by AAA* ————
but are listed for your information only.

BUCK'S BAR & GRILL
[fyi]

Phone: 419/884-2825
Not evaluated. **Location:** 192 E Main St 44813. Diners can enjoy seasonal sports events while sipping soup or munching on salads, pasta and subs.

PAUL REVERE'S FAMILY RESTAURANT
[fyi]

Phone: 419/884-1811
Not evaluated. **Location:** 157 SR 97 44813. Steak, chicken, pasta and seafood preparations line a menu that also includes many sandwiches.

LIBERTY

———— WHERE TO DINE ————

———— *The following restaurant has not been evaluated by AAA* ————
but is listed for your information only.

YOUNGSTOWN CRAB CO
[fyi]

Phone: 330/759-5480
Not evaluated. **Location:** 3917 Belmont Ave 44505. Anywhere from 6-16 market features, ranging from familiar to unusual, are printed daily.

LIMA pop. 45,500

─────── **WHERE TO STAY** ───────

COMFORT INN
⬥⬥⬥ [SAVE]
▽▽▽
Motor Inn

All Year   1P: $60-$75   2P: $65-$80   XP: $5   F18
Phone: (419)228-4251
Location: I-75, exit 127, just w on SR 81. 1210 Neubrecht Rd 45801. Fax: 419/224-4465. **Facility:** 121 one-bedroom standard units, some with whirlpools. 2 stories, interior corridors. **Parking:** on-site. **Terms:** [CP] meal plan available. **Amenities:** extended cable TV. *Some:* irons, hair dryers. **Dining:** restaurant, 11 am-10 pm, Fri & Sat-11 pm, $9-$12, cocktails. **Pool(s):** outdoor. **Guest Services:** valet and coin laundry. **Business Services:** meeting rooms, business center. **Cards:** AX, CB, DC, DS, MC, VI.

SOME UNITS

FAIRFIELD INN BY MARRIOTT
⬥⬥⬥ [SAVE]
▽▽▽▽
Motel

4/1-9/30 [CP]   1P: $70-$85   2P: $70-$85
10/1-3/31 [CP]   1P: $66-$79   2P: $66-$79
Phone: (419)224-8496
Location: West of downtown; at jct of SR 309 and Cable Rd. 2179 Elida Rd 45801. Fax: 419/224-8496. **Facility:** 64 one-bedroom standard units. 3 stories, interior corridors. *Bath:* shower only. **Parking:** on-site. **Amenities:** extended cable TV, irons. **Pool(s):** heated indoor. **Leisure Activities:** whirlpool. **Guest Services:** valet laundry. **Business Services:** meeting rooms. **Cards:** AX, DC, DS, MC, VI. **Special Amenities:** free continental breakfast and free local telephone calls. *(See color ad card insert)*

SOME UNITS
FEE

HAMPTON INN
[SAVE]
▽▽▽▽
Motel

All Year [ECP]   1P: $72-$85   2P: $79-$95
Phone: (419)225-8300
Location: I-75, exit 125A, at jct SR 117 and 309. 1933 Roschman Ave 45804. Fax: 419/225-8328. **Facility:** 98 one-bedroom standard units. 4 stories, interior corridors. *Bath:* combo or shower only. **Parking:** on-site. **Amenities:** extended cable TV, voice mail, irons, hair dryers. **Pool(s):** heated indoor. **Leisure Activities:** whirlpool, exercise room. **Guest Services:** valet laundry. **Business Services:** meeting rooms. **Cards:** AX, CB, DS, JC, MC, VI.

SOME UNITS
FEE

HOLIDAY INN LIMA
▽▽▽
Motor Inn

All Year   1P: $79-$104   2P: $79-$104
Phone: (419)222-0004
Location: I-75, exit 124A, at jct SR 117 and 309. 1920 Roschman Ave 45804. Fax: 419/222-2176. **Facility:** 150 one-bedroom standard units. 4 stories, interior corridors. *Bath:* combo or shower only. **Terms:** small pets only. **Amenities:** video games, irons, hair dryers. **Pool(s):** heated indoor. **Leisure Activities:** sauna, whirlpool, exercise room. **Guest Services:** gift shop, valet laundry. **Business Services:** conference facilities. **Cards:** AX, CB, DC, DS, JC, MC, VI.

SOME UNITS
FEE   FEE

KNIGHTS INN
⬥⬥⬥ [SAVE]
▽
Motel

All Year [ECP]   1P: $45-$50   2P: $50-$55   XP: $6   F18
Phone: (419)331-9215
Location: 4.5 mi w of jct I-75, on SR 309; w of Lima Mall. 2285 N Eastown Rd 45807. Fax: 419/331-9215. **Facility:** 63 one-bedroom standard units, some with whirlpools. 1 story, exterior corridors. **Parking:** on-site. **Terms:** 7 day cancellation notice, small pets only. **Amenities:** extended cable TV. **Pool(s):** outdoor. **Cards:** AX, DS, MC, VI. **Special Amenities:** free continental breakfast and free local telephone calls.

SOME UNITS

MOTEL 6 - 586
▽
Motel

5/23-9/21   1P: $39-$49   2P: $45-$55   XP: $3   F17
9/22-3/31   1P: $37-$47   2P: $43-$53   XP: $3   F17
4/1-5/22   1P: $35-$45   2P: $41-$51   XP: $3   F17
Phone: 419/228-0456
Location: I-75, exit 125, just e, at jct SR 117 and 309. 1800 Harding Hwy 45804. Fax: 419/228-4630. **Facility:** 95 one-bedroom standard units. 2 stories, exterior corridors. *Bath:* combo or shower only. **Parking:** on-site. **Terms:** small pets only. **Guest Services:** coin laundry. **Cards:** AX, CB, DC, DS, MC, VI.

SOME UNITS

WINGATE INN
▽▽▽
Motel

All Year   1P: $75-$85   2P: $75-$85
Phone: (419)228-7000
Location: Downtown; at the jct of W Market and Elizabeth sts. 175 W Market St 45801. Fax: 419/228-9752. **Facility:** 100 one-bedroom standard units, some with whirlpools. 6 stories, interior corridors. *Bath:* combo or shower only. **Parking:** on-site. **Amenities:** extended cable TV, video games, Web TV, high-speed Internet, dual phone lines, voice mail, safes, irons, hair dryers. **Leisure Activities:** whirlpool, exercise room. **Guest Services:** valet laundry. **Business Services:** meeting rooms, business center, administrative services, PC, fax. **Cards:** AX, CB, DC, DS, MC, VI.

SOME UNITS
FEE

─────── **WHERE TO DINE** ───────

BANDIDO'S RESTAURANTE MEXICANO
▽▽▽
Mexican

Lunch: $6-$8   **Dinner:** $7-$12   **Phone:** 419/331-0855
Location: Jct Cable Rd and SR 309 (Elida Rd), 0.3 mi w; opposite Lima Mall. 2613 Elida Rd 45801. **Hours:** 11 am-10 pm, Fri & Sat-11 pm. Closed: 11/28, 12/25. **Features:** casual dress; Sunday brunch; carryout; cocktails & lounge; a la carte. The lively energy of a Mexican cantina infuses the relaxed restaurant. Traditional favorites—such as chicken fajitas, enchiladas and Monterey chicken—pepper the menu. A wide selection of desserts includes apple chimichangas and fried ice cream. **Parking:** on-site. **Cards:** AX, DS, MC, VI.

BURGUNDY'S

▼▼ ▼▼

Italian

Lunch: $7-$10   **Dinner:** $9-$14   **Phone:** 419/224-5080

Location: Jct SR 309 and Cable Rd, just s; near Lima Mall. 1365 N Cable Rd 45805. **Hours:** 11 am-10:30 pm, Fri & Sat-11:30 pm, Sun-8 pm. Closed major holidays. **Features:** casual dress; children's menu; carryout; cocktails & lounge. American and Italian entrees mingle on a diverse menu that lists linguine with clam sauce, barbecue ribs and steak. Modern tavern decor adds to the friendly mood of the brightly illuminated dining room. Service are attentive and good with following up. Located on the west side of Lima near major mall and numerous retail shops. **Parking:** on-site. **Cards:** MC, VI.

MARK PI'S CHINA GATE

▼▼ ▼▼

Chinese

Lunch: $6-$8   **Dinner:** $8-$16   **Phone:** 419/224-4645

Location: I-75, exit 127, 2.3 mi w on SR 81. 702 W North St 45801. **Hours:** 11:30 am-2:30 & 4:30-9:30 pm, Fri & Sat-10 pm. Closed major holidays. **Reservations:** suggested. **Features:** casual dress; carryout; cocktails & lounge; a la carte, buffet. Szechwan and Mandarin specialties, such as spicy chicken with vegetables and glazed bananas, make up the restaurant's traditional menu. Tables topped with flowers and candles sit in a relaxed dining room decorated with attractive paintings. **Parking:** on-site. **Cards:** AX, MC, VI.

OLD BARN OUT BACK RESTAURANT

▼▼ ▼▼

American

Lunch: $6-$8   **Dinner:** $8-$12   **Phone:** 419/991-3075

Location: Jct Cable Rd and Elm St, 0.3 mi w. 3175 W Elm St 45805. **Hours:** 11 am-8 pm, Fri & Sat-9 pm, Sun 10:30 am-6 pm. Closed major holidays; also Mon. **Features:** casual dress; children's menu; salad bar; beer & wine only; buffet. Farm memorabilia and lots of wood set a rustic tone in the barnlike dining room. home-style favorites include barbecue ribs and fried chicken. The in-house bakery—which serves up fresh rolls, cinnamon buns and mouthwatering desserts—is a big hit. Smoke free premises. **Parking:** on-site. **Cards:** DS, MC, VI.

TUDOR'S DINING & TAVERN

▼▼ ▼▼

American

Lunch: $6-$8   **Dinner:** $8-$17   **Phone:** 419/331-2220

Location: Just w of jct Cable Rd and SR 309. 2383 Elida Rd 45806. **Hours:** 11 am-10:30 pm, Fri & Sat-11:30 pm, Sun-9 pm. Closed major holidays. **Features:** casual dress; Sunday brunch; children's menu; early bird specials; carryout; salad bar; cocktails & lounge. Fresh-cut steak, homemade pasta and barbecue chops are samplings of the variety on the cozy and quiet restaurant's menu. The casually upscale dining room is decorated in Tudor style, with attractive artwork and sophisticated furnishings. Large hot food bar area. Located on western side of Lima, near major mall. **Parking:** on-site. **Cards:** AX, DC, DS, MC, VI.

The following restaurants have not been evaluated by AAA but are listed for your information only.

BEEF & BOURBON AT FIRESIDE

[fyi]

Phone: 419/999-1331

Not evaluated. Location: 3801 Shawnee Rd 45804. Specialties at this restaurant include freshly cut steaks and chops.

CASA LU AL

[fyi]

Phone: 419/229-0774

Not evaluated. Location: 2323 N West St Rd 45804. On the menu are traditional Italian specialties and sizzling steaks.

LISBON pop. 4,400

--- **WHERE TO STAY** ---

DAYS INN LISBON

AAA [SAVE]

▼▼ ▼▼

Motel

All Year [ECP]   **1P:** $72   **2P:** $72   **XP:** $10   F17

Location: SR 11, exit SR 154, just w. 40952 SR 154 44432. Fax: 330/420-0113. **Facility:** 71 one-bedroom standard units, some with whirlpools. 2 stories, interior corridors. *Bath:* combo or shower only. **Parking:** on-site. **Amenities:** irons, hair dryers. **Leisure Activities:** exercise room. **Guest Services:** valet laundry. **Business Services:** meeting rooms. **Cards:** AX, DC, DS, MC, VI. **Special Amenities:** free continental breakfast and free local telephone calls.

SOME UNITS

[icons] FEE

LOGAN pop. 6,700

--- **WHERE TO STAY** ---

AMERIHOST INN-LOGAN

AAA [SAVE]

▼▼ ▼▼

Motel

All Year [CP]   **1P:** $55-$170   **2P:** $60-$175   **XP:** $6   F18

Location: Jct US 33 and SR 664, just n. 12819 SR 664 43138. Fax: 740/385-9288. **Facility:** 60 one-bedroom standard units, some with whirlpools. 2 stories, interior corridors. *Bath:* combo or shower only. **Parking:** on-site. **Amenities:** extended cable TV, safes (fee), irons, hair dryers. **Pool(s):** heated indoor. **Leisure Activities:** whirlpool, limited exercise equipment. **Business Services:** meeting rooms. **Cards:** AX, CB, DC, DS, JC, MC, VI. **Special Amenities:** free continental breakfast and free newspaper.

SOME UNITS

[icons] FEE

THE INN AT CEDAR FALLS

▼▼ ▼▼ ▼▼

Country Inn

Phone: (740)385-7489

4/1-11/30 & 3/16-3/31 [BP]   **2P:** $95-$110   **XP:** $25

12/1-3/15 [BP]   **2P:** $85-$99   **XP:** $25

Location: 9.5 mi s on SR 664, 1 mi s. 21190 SR 374 43138. Fax: 740/385-0820. **Facility:** Nestled in the Hocking Hills near Cedar Falls, this inn has a log lodge and cottages offering a wood stove, open kitchen and other rustic elements. 15 units. 12 one-bedroom standard units. 3 one-bedroom vacation rentals ($120-$245) with whirlpools. 2 stories, interior corridors. *Bath:* combo or shower only. **Parking:** on-site. **Terms:** 2 night minimum stay - weekends, 30 day cancellation notice-fee imposed, [AP] meal plan available, package plans. **Amenities:** *Some:* hair dryers. **Leisure Activities:** recreation program, hiking trails. **Guest Services:** gift shop. **Business Services:** meeting rooms. **Cards:** MC, VI.

SOME UNITS

[icons]

SHAWNEE INN
(AAA) (SAVE)
▼▼▼
Motel
All Year   1P: $45-$65   2P: $49-$70   Phone: (740)385-5674
                                                                      XP: $5   F13
Location: SR 664, just s of US 33. 30916 Lake Logan Rd 43138. **Fax:** 740/385-5675. **Facility:** 22 one-bedroom standard units. 2 stories, exterior corridors. **Parking:** on-site. **Terms:** small pets only ($5 extra charge). **Amenities:** extended cable TV. **Cards:** AX, DS, MC, VI. **Special Amenities:** early check-in/late check-out and free local telephone calls.

SOME UNITS
[symbols] /✕/

──────── **WHERE TO DINE** ────────

THE OLDE DUTCH RESTAURANT   **Lunch:** $5-$10   **Dinner:** $7-$12   **Phone:** 740/385-1000
▼▼▼
Regional American
Location: Jct US 33 and SR 664, just n. 12791 SR 664 S 43138. **Hours:** 11 am-9 pm, Sat from 8 am, Sun-8 pm; to 8 pm, Sun-7 pm 11/1-5/1. **Closed:** 1/1, 12/25; also at 5 pm 11/23 & at 3 pm 12/24. **Reservations:** accepted. **Features:** casual dress; Sunday brunch; children's menu; carryout; buffet. The family-friendly restaurant delivers simple and hearty Pennsylvania Dutch-style food, such as ham, meatloaf, Swiss steak and roast turkey and chicken. If freshly baked pies don't tempt the sweet tooth, there's a good chance the ice cream shop will. A petting zoo with white deer is on the property. Smoke free premises. **Parking:** on-site. **Cards:** AX, DS, MC, VI.

✕

LORAIN pop. 71,200

──────── **WHERE TO STAY** ────────

CLARION INN/SPITZER PLAZA HOTEL & MARINA   **Phone:** (440)246-5767
(AAA) (SAVE)
▼▼▼
Historic Motor Inn
4/1-5/31 & 9/1-3/31 [CP]   1P: $85-$121   2P: $95-$131   XP: $10   F18
6/1-8/31 [CP]   1P: $90-$120   2P: $100-$130   XP: $10   F18
Location: Corner of Broadway Ave and SR 6. 301 Broadway Ave 44052. **Fax:** 440/246-5393. **Facility:** 69 one-bedroom standard units, some with whirlpools. 5 stories, interior corridors. **Parking:** on-site. **Amenities:** video games, safes (fee), irons, hair dryers. **Dining:** restaurant, 7 am-2 & 5-10 pm, $10-$20. **Pool(s):** heated indoor. **Leisure Activities:** sauna, whirlpool, exercise room. **Guest Services:** valet laundry. **Business Services:** conference facilities, fax. **Cards:** AX, CB, DC, DS, JC, MC, VI. **Special Amenities:** free continental breakfast and free local telephone calls.

SOME UNITS
[symbols] /✕ ▯/
FEE   FEE

LOUDONVILLE pop. 2,900

──────── **WHERE TO STAY** ────────

LITTLE BROWN INN   **Phone:** 419/994-5525
▼▼▼
Motel
4/1-10/31   1P: $41-$51   2P: $51-$66   XP: $5   F13
11/1-3/31   1P: $41-$46   2P: $51-$66   XP: $5   F13
Location: 1 mi s on SR 3. 940 S Market St 44842. **Fax:** 419/994-5527. **Facility:** 20 one-bedroom standard units. 1 story, interior corridors. **Parking:** on-site. **Terms:** small pets only ($5 extra charge). **Amenities:** extended cable TV. **Cards:** AX, DS, MC, VI.

SOME UNITS
[symbols] /✕ [symbol]/

LOVELAND —See Cincinnati p. 577.

MACEDONIA pop. 7,500   (See map p. 600; index p. 603)

──────── **WHERE TO STAY** ────────

BAYMONT INN & SUITES CLEVELAND-MACEDONIA   **Phone:** (330)468-5400   [40]
(AAA) (SAVE)
▼▼▼▼
Motel
All Year   1P: $99-$119   2P: $99-$119
Location: I-271, exit 18, just s; I-80/90 (Ohio Tpke), exit 180, just n. 268 E Highland Rd 44056. **Fax:** 330/468-5500. **Facility:** 86 one-bedroom standard units. 4 stories, interior corridors. **Bath:** combo or shower only. **Parking:** on-site. **Terms:** small pets only. **Amenities:** video games, voice mail, irons, hair dryers. **Pool(s):** heated indoor. **Leisure Activities:** whirlpool. **Guest Services:** coin laundry. **Cards:** AX, CB, DC, DS, MC, VI. **Special Amenities:** free continental breakfast and free newspaper. *(See color ad opposite title page)*

SOME UNITS
[symbols] /✕ [symbol]/
FEE

CLEVELAND/AKRON TRAVELODGE   **Phone:** (330)467-1516   [38]
(AAA) (SAVE)
▼▼
Motel
5/24-9/3 [BP]   1P: $65-$75   2P: $75-$100   XP: $6   F17
4/1-5/23 & 9/4-3/31 [BP]   1P: $50-$60   2P: $50-$60   XP: $6   F17
Location: I-271, exit 18, just s; I-80/90 (Ohio Tpke), exit 180, 3 mi n. 275 Highland Rd 44056. **Fax:** 330/467-5089. **Facility:** 70 one-bedroom standard units. 2 stories, exterior corridors. **Parking:** on-site. **Terms:** 30 day cancellation notice. **Amenities:** extended cable TV. **Pool(s):** outdoor. **Guest Services:** valet laundry. **Business Services:** meeting rooms. **Cards:** AX, CB, DC, DS, JC, MC, VI. **Special Amenities:** free continental breakfast and free local telephone calls. *(See color ad p 613)*

SOME UNITS
[symbols] /✕ VCR [symbol]/

(See map p. 600)

COUNTRY INN & SUITES BY CARLSON Phone: (330)908-1700 39

	6/16-9/8	2P: $129	XP: $10 F17
	5/25-6/15	2P: $99	XP: $10 F17
Motel	4/1-5/24 & 9/9-3/31	2P: $79	XP: $10 F17

Location: I-271, exit 18, just s; I-80/90 (Ohio Tpke), exit 180, 3 mi n. 7820 Capital Blvd 44056. Fax: 330/908-1702. **Facility:** 54 one-bedroom standard units, some with efficiencies (no utensils) and/or whirlpools. 3 stories, interior corridors. **Parking:** on-site. **Amenities:** high-speed Internet (fee), dual phone lines, voice mail, irons, hair dryers. **Pool(s):** heated indoor. **Leisure Activities:** whirlpool, exercise room. **Guest Services:** valet and coin laundry. **Business Services:** meeting rooms. **Cards:** AX, DC, DS, MC, VI. *(See color ad p 646)*

SOME UNITS
ASK SD 🏊 🎥 DATA PORT 💻 🖨 / ✕ 🛏 🖥 / FEE

KNIGHTS INN-CLEVELAND/MACEDONIA Phone: (330)467-1981 41

	5/22-9/15	1P: $57-$79	2P: $57-$79
	4/1-5/21	1P: $45-$55	2P: $45-$55
Motel	9/16-3/31		2P: $45-$55

Location: I-271, exit 18, just s; I-80/90 (Ohio Tpke), exit 180, 3 mi n. 240 E Highland Rd 44056. Fax: 330/467-1981. **Facility:** 86 one-bedroom standard units. 1 story, exterior corridors. **Parking:** on-site. **Terms:** check-in 4 pm. **Amenities:** extended cable TV. **Pool(s):** outdoor. **Guest Services:** valet laundry. **Business Services:** meeting rooms. **Cards:** AX, CB, DC, DS, JC, MC, VI.

SOME UNITS
ASK SD 🐾 🍽 🏊 🎥 / ✕ VCR 🛏 🖥 💻 / FEE

MADEIRA —*See Cincinnati p. 577.*

MANCHESTER pop. 2,200

———— **WHERE TO DINE** ————

MOYER'S WINERY & RESTAURANT **Lunch:** $6-$11 **Dinner:** $9-$19 Phone: 937/549-2957
American **Location:** 3 mi w. 3859 US 52 45144. **Hours:** 11:30 am-9 pm, Fri & Sat-10 pm. Closed: 1/1, 11/28, 12/25; also Sun. **Reservations:** suggested; weekends. **Features:** casual dress; children's menu; carryout; wine only. The intimate dining room affords scenic views of the Ohio River Valley. A limited menu of such foods as steak and pasta is fittingly complemented by wines produced from the owner's vineyards. When the weather is nice, porch seating is popular. **Parking:** on-site. **Cards:** DS, MC, VI.

MANSFIELD pop. 50,600

———— **WHERE TO STAY** ————

AMERIHOST INN-MANSFIELD Phone: (419)756-6670
AAA SAVE

	All Year	1P: $45-$85	2P: $50-$105 XP: $5 F18

Motel **Location:** I-71, exit 169, jct SR 13 and Hanley Rd. 180 E Hanley Rd 44903. Fax: 419/756-9041. **Facility:** 60 one-bedroom standard units, some with whirlpools. 2 stories, interior corridors. *Bath:* combo or shower only. **Parking:** on-site. **Terms:** 14 day cancellation notice, [CP] meal plan available. **Amenities:** safes (fee), irons, hair dryers. **Pool(s):** heated indoor. **Leisure Activities:** sauna, whirlpool, exercise equipment available by pool. **Guest Services:** valet laundry. **Business Services:** meeting rooms. **Cards:** AX, CB, DC, DS, JC, MC, VI. **Special Amenities:** free continental breakfast and free local telephone calls. *(See color ad below)*

SOME UNITS
SD ♿ 🚫 🏊 ✕ 🎥 DATA PORT 💻 🖨 / ✕ 🛏 🖥 /

BAYMONT INN & SUITES-MANSFIELD Phone: (419)774-0005
AAA SAVE

	All Year	1P: $69-$79	2P: $69-$79

Motel **Location:** I-71, exit 169. 120 Stander Ave 44903. Fax: 419/774-9066. **Facility:** 87 one-bedroom standard units. 2 stories, interior corridors. *Bath:* combo or shower only. **Parking:** on-site. **Terms:** package plans. **Amenities:** extended cable TV, video games, voice mail, irons, hair dryers. **Pool(s):** heated indoor. **Leisure Activities:** whirlpool. **Guest Services:** valet and coin laundry. **Cards:** AX, CB, DC, DS, MC, VI. **Special Amenities:** free continental breakfast and free newspaper. *(See color ad opposite title page)*

SOME UNITS
SD 🐾 🍽 ♿ 🚫 🏊 🎥 DATA PORT 💻 🖨 / ✕ 🛏 🖥 / FEE

COMFORT INN
AAA **SAVE**
▽▽▽▽
Motel

Phone: (419)529-1000

All Year [ECP]   1P: $60   2P: $130
Location: Jct US 30 and Trimble Rd. 500 N Trimble Rd 44906. Fax: 419/529-2953. **Facility:** 114 one-bedroom standard units, some with efficiencies (no utensils) and/or whirlpools. 2 stories, interior corridors. **Parking:** on-site. **Terms:** 30 day cancellation notice. **Amenities:** extended cable TV, irons. *Some:* hair dryers. **Pool(s):** heated indoor. **Leisure Activities:** sauna, whirlpool. **Guest Services:** coin laundry. **Business Services:** meeting rooms. **Cards:** AX, DC, DS, MC, VI. **Special Amenities:** free continental breakfast and free local telephone calls.

SOME UNITS

ECONO LODGE
AAA **SAVE**
▽▽▽
Motel

Phone: (419)589-3333

5/16-8/31 [CP]	1P: $46-$55	2P: $48-$60	XP: $6	F16
4/1-5/15 [CP]	1P: $42-$50	2P: $44-$58	XP: $6	F16
9/1-10/31 [CP]	1P: $44-$50	2P: $46-$54	XP: $6	F16
11/1-3/31 [CP]	1P: $42-$46	2P: $44-$48	XP: $6	F16

Location: I-71, exit 176, just e. 1017 Koogle Rd 44903. Fax: 419/589-3333. **Facility:** 51 one-bedroom standard units. 2 stories, interior corridors. **Parking:** on-site. **Terms:** pets ($6 extra charge). **Amenities:** extended cable TV. **Pool(s):** outdoor. **Business Services:** meeting rooms. **Cards:** AX, CB, DC, DS, JC, MC, VI. **Special Amenities:** free continental breakfast and free local telephone calls.

SOME UNITS

FAIRFIELD INN
AAA **SAVE**
▽▽▽▽
Motel

Phone: (419)747-2200

All Year [CP]   1P: $61-$63   2P: $67-$69   XP: $6   F17
Location: Jct US 30 and Lexington-Springmill Rd, south side. 1065 N Lexington-Springmill Rd 44906. Fax: 419/747-2200. **Facility:** 62 one-bedroom standard units. 3 stories, interior corridors. *Bath:* combo or shower only. **Parking:** on-site. **Amenities:** extended cable TV, irons. **Pool(s):** heated indoor. **Guest Services:** valet laundry. **Cards:** AX, CB, DC, DS, MC, VI. **Special Amenities:** free continental breakfast and free local telephone calls. *(See color ad card insert)*

SOME UNITS

HAMPTON INN
SAVE
▽▽▽▽
Motel

Phone: (419)747-5353

10/1-3/31 [CP]	1P: $65-$159	2P: $79-$159
4/1-9/30 [CP]	1P: $67-$159	2P: $77-$159

Location: Jct US 30 and Lexington-Springmill Rd, south side. 1051 N Lexington-Springmill Rd 44906. Fax: 419/747-5368. **Facility:** 62 one-bedroom standard units. 3 stories, interior corridors. *Bath:* combo or shower only. **Parking:** on-site. **Terms:** 7 day cancellation notice. **Amenities:** extended cable TV, voice mail, irons. *Some:* hair dryers. **Pool(s):** heated indoor. **Leisure Activities:** whirlpool. **Guest Services:** valet laundry. **Cards:** AX, DC, DS, MC, VI.

SOME UNITS
FEE

HOLIDAY INN HOTEL & SUITES
▽▽▽▽
Motor Inn

Phone: 419/525-6000

Property failed to provide current rates
Location: Just w of downtown. 116 W Park Ave 44902. Fax: 419/525-0197. **Facility:** 139 units. 120 one-bedroom standard units. 19 one-bedroom suites, some with efficiencies (no utensils), kitchens and/or whirlpools. 6 stories, interior corridors. *Bath:* combo or shower only. **Parking:** on-site. **Terms:** package plans. **Amenities:** video games, dual phone lines, voice mail, irons, hair dryers. **Pool(s):** heated indoor. **Leisure Activities:** whirlpool, exercise room. **Guest Services:** valet and coin laundry. **Business Services:** conference facilities. **Cards:** AX, CB, DC, DS, JC, MC, VI.

SOME UNITS
FEE

KNIGHTS INN
AAA **SAVE**
▽
Motel

Phone: (419)529-2100

All Year [CP]   1P: $49-$100   2P: $49-$100
Location: Jct US 30 and Trimble Rd. 555 N Trimble Rd 44906. Fax: 419/529-6679. **Facility:** 88 one-bedroom standard units. 1 story, exterior corridors. **Parking:** on-site. **Amenities:** extended cable TV. **Guest Services:** valet laundry. **Business Services:** meeting rooms. **Cards:** AX, DC, DS, MC, VI. **Special Amenities:** free continental breakfast and free local telephone calls.

SOME UNITS

SUPER 8 MOTEL

Motel

All Year [CP]   1P: $45-$55   2P: $55-$65   XP: $6   F13

Phone: (419)756-8875

Location: I-71, exit 169; 2425 Interstate Cir 44903. Fax: 419/756-8875. **Facility:** 69 one-bedroom standard units. 3 stories, interior corridors. **Parking:** on-site. **Terms:** 30 day cancellation notice, package plans, pets ($50 deposit). **Amenities:** extended cable TV. **Cards:** AX, CB, DC, DS, JC, MC, VI.

SOME UNITS

FEE

——— WHERE TO DINE ———

EL CAMPESINO

Mexican

Lunch: $4-$7   Dinner: $5-$10   Phone: 419-529-5330

Location: Just e of Lexington-Springmill Rd. 1971 W 4th St 44902. **Hours:** 11 am-10 pm, Fri-10:30 pm, Sat noon-10:30 pm, Sun noon-9 pm. Closed major holidays. **Features:** casual dress; carryout; cocktails. Just minutes from the mall, the popular family restaurant prepares an extensive variety of traditional Mexican dishes, all served piping hot. The staff is friendly and attentive. **Parking:** on-site. **Cards:** AX, DS, MC, VI.

MAMA'S TOUCH OF ITALY

Italian

Lunch: $5-$8   Dinner: $7-$16   Phone: 419-526-5099

Location: Just w of downtown. 275 Park Ave W 44902. **Hours:** 11 am-2:30 & 5-8 pm, Fri & Sat-10 pm. Closed major holidays; also Sun. **Reservations:** required; on weekends. **Features:** casual dress; carryout; cocktails. Family owned and operated, the popular spot has an ordinary exterior, but its crowded interior is anything but. Delicious selections and owner specials are made from scratch, and the daily lunch bar is an excellent value. Attentive, personable servers make everyone feel welcomed. **Parking:** on-site. **Cards:** AX, DC, DS, MC, VI.

PAISLEY PARK

American

Lunch: $6-$10   Dinner: $6-$10   Phone: 419-756-3357

Location: 1 mi s on SR 42. 827 Lexington Ave 44902. **Hours:** 11 am-8 pm. Closed major holidays; also Sun. **Features:** casual dress; carryout. Hidden away in a small plaza, the delicatessen provides quick and efficient carry out, as well as a small dining room. The owner prepares several sandwich recipes not found elsewhere with premium ingredients. Smoke free premises. **Parking:** on-site. **Cards:** AX, DC, DS, MC, VI.

THE SKYWAY EAST

American

Dinner: $9-$20   Phone: 419-589-9929

Location: 3 mi e on SR 30, exit Reed Rd. 2461 Emma Ln 44903. **Hours:** 5 pm-9 pm, Fri & Sat-10:30 pm. Closed major holidays; also Sun. **Reservations:** required; weekends. **Features:** dressy casual; children's menu; carryout; cocktails. Mellow mood lighting contributes to the classic supper club atmosphere at this refined restaurant. An extensive wine list complements a menu with more than 20 appetizers and 80 entrees of fresh seafood, choice and prime steak, veal, lamb chops and pasta. **Parking:** on-site. **Cards:** AX, DC, DS, MC, VI.

STEVE'S DAKOTA GRILL

Steak House

Lunch: $5-$10   Dinner: $8-$16   Phone: 419-529-9064

Location: 6 mi w. 3101 Park Ave W 44906. **Hours:** 11:30 am-10 pm, Fri & Sat-11 pm, Sun noon-9 pm. **Features:** casual dress; carryout; cocktails. This restaurant has a bustling, yet casual atmosphere with a rustic decor. The portions are generous with USDA prime steak and chops aged and hand cut by the chef. Some seafood, chicken and pasta also available. The staff is energetic and attentive. **Parking:** on-site. **Cards:** AX, DC, DS, MC, VI.

SWEENEY'S TOO

American

Dinner: $10-$20   Phone: 419-756-2858

Location: 1 mi s on SR 42. 777 Lexington Ave 44907. **Hours:** 5 pm-9:30 pm, Fri & Sat-10 pm. Closed major holidays; also Sun. **Reservations:** suggested. **Features:** casual dress; children's menu; early bird specials; carryout; cocktails. Fresh ingredients and creativity go into innovative preparations of such foods as barbecue baby back ribs and calamari, both of which come with two sauces. The experienced wait staff is knowledgeable and attentive. Low lighting enhances the relaxed mood. **Parking:** on-site. **Cards:** DS, MC, VI.

The following restaurant has not been evaluated by AAA
but is listed for your information only.

R & B SOUTHERN STYLE BBQ   **Phone:** 419/529-9888
[fyi]   Not evaluated. **Location:** 1044 Park Ave W 44902. The barbecue joint offers drive-through, carry-out or patio dining
             in summer, with quick and efficient service.

MARBLEHEAD pop. 700

--------------------- **WHERE TO STAY** ---------------------

MARBLEHEAD INN   **Phone:** (419)798-8184
AAA [SAVE]   6/1-9/30   1P: $99-$149
             4/1-5/31 & 10/1-3/31   1P: $49-$69
◆◆ ◆   **Location:** 1 mi e of downtown, on SR 163. 614 E Main St 43440. Fax: 419/798-0414. **Facility:** 69 one-bedroom
Motel   standard units, some with whirlpools. 3 stories, interior corridors. *Bath:* combo or shower only. **Parking:** on-
             site. **Terms:** 3 day cancellation notice, [CP] meal plan available, package plans - seasonal. **Amenities:** ex-
             tended cable TV, hair dryers. **Leisure Activities:** fishing. **Business Services:** meeting rooms, fax.
Cards: AX, CB, DC, DS, JC, MC, VI. **Special Amenities: early check-in/late check-out and free continental breakfast.**

SOME UNITS
[S/D] [📷] [DATA PORT] [🖨] / [✕] [VCR] [🔒] [🍴] [📺] /

--------------------- **WHERE TO DINE** ---------------------

---
The following restaurant has not been evaluated by AAA
but is listed for your information only.

THE CROWS NEST   **Phone:** 419/798-8080
[fyi]   Not evaluated. **Location:** 2 mi n of SR 163 on SR 269. E Harbor Marina 43440. A popular local spot with a lively
             atmosphere and outside patio dining in the summer.

MARIETTA pop. 15,000

--------------------- **WHERE TO STAY** ---------------------

BEST WESTERN MARIETTA   **Phone:** (740)374-7211
AAA [SAVE]   All Year [CP]   1P: $59-$65   2P: $65-$74   XP: $5   F17
◆◆◆◆   **Location:** Center of town, 1.8 mi n on SR 60; I-77, exit 6, 3.5 mi sw. 279 Muskingum Dr 45750. Fax: 740/374-7211.
Motel   **Facility:** 47 one-bedroom standard units. 2 stories, exterior corridors. **Parking:** on-site. **Terms:** package
             plans. **Amenities:** extended cable TV. *Some:* hair dryers. **Leisure Activities:** boat dock, fishing. **Guest Serv-
             ices:** valet laundry. **Cards:** AX, CB, DC, DS, MC, VI. **Special Amenities: free continental breakfast and
             free local telephone calls.**

SOME UNITS
[S/D] [📶] [📷] [DATA PORT] [🔒] [🍴] / [✕] [📺] /

ECONO LODGE   **Phone:** (740)374-8481
AAA [SAVE]   6/1-9/15   1P: $50-$65   2P: $55-$75   XP: $5   F17
◆◆◆   9/16-12/1   1P: $45-$65   2P: $50-$75   XP: $5   F17
             4/1-5/31   1P: $42-$65   2P: $45-$70   XP: $5   F17
Motel   12/2-3/31   1P: $42-$50   2P: $45-$54   XP: $5   F17
             Location: I-77, exit 1. 702 Pike St 45750. Fax: 740/374-8481. **Facility:** 48 one-bedroom standard units. 2 sto-
             ries, exterior corridors. **Parking:** on-site. **Terms:** cancellation fee imposed, pets ($5 extra charge).
Amenities: extended cable TV, hair dryers. **Pool(s):** outdoor. **Cards:** AX, CB, DC, DS, MC, VI.

SOME UNITS
[S/D] [🛏] [🍴] [🏊] [📷] [🖨] / [✕] [📺] /

HOLIDAY INN   **Phone:** (740)374-9660
◆◆◆   All Year   1P: $65-$95   2P: $65-$95
             Location: I-77, exit 1. 701 Pike St 45750. Fax: 740/373-1762. **Facility:** 109 one-bedroom standard units. 2 sto-
Motor Inn   ries, interior corridors. **Parking:** on-site. **Terms:** package plans. **Amenities:** extended cable TV, voice mail,
             irons, hair dryers. **Pool(s):** outdoor, wading. **Leisure Activities:** exercise room. **Guest Services:** valet
laundry. **Business Services:** meeting rooms, PC, fax. **Cards:** AX, CB, DC, DS, JC, MC, VI.

SOME UNITS
[ASK] [S/D] [🍴] [🚭] [🏊] [📷] [DATA PORT] [📺] [🖨] / [✕] [VCR] [🔒] [🍴] /
                                              FEE   FEE

KNIGHTS INN   **Phone:** (740)373-7373
AAA [SAVE]   6/1-11/30 [CP]   1P: $49-$67   2P: $55-$73   XP: $6   F18
◆◆◆   12/1-3/31 [CP]   1P: $45-$63   2P: $51-$69   XP: $6   F18
             4/1-5/31 [CP]   1P: $44-$62   2P: $50-$68   XP: $6   F18
Motel   **Location:** I-77, exit 1. 506 Pike St 45750. Fax: 740/374-9466. **Facility:** 97 one-bedroom standard units, some
             with efficiencies and/or whirlpools. 1 story, exterior corridors. **Parking:** on-site. **Terms:** check-in 4 pm.
             Amenities: extended cable TV, high-speed Internet. *Some:* hair dryers. **Pool(s):** outdoor. **Guest Services:**
valet laundry. **Business Services:** meeting rooms. **Cards:** AX, CB, DC, DS, MC, VI. **Special Amenities: free continental
breakfast and free local telephone calls.**

SOME UNITS
[S/D] [🐕] [🍴] [🏊] [📷] [DATA PORT] [🖨] / [✕] [VCR] [🔒] [🍴] [📺] /
                                                              FEE

SUPER 8 MOTEL-MARIETTA   **Phone:** (740)374-8888
◆◆◆   5/17-9/30   1P: $49   2P: $54   XP: $5   F17
◆◆   4/1-5/16 & 10/1-3/31 1P: $43   2P: $48   XP: $5   F17
Motel   **Location:** I-77, exit 1, just w. 46 Acme St 45750. Fax: 740/374-8476. **Facility:** 62 one-bedroom standard units. 3
             stories, interior corridors. **Parking:** on-site. **Amenities:** extended cable TV, safes. **Cards:** AX, DC, DS,
MC, VI.

SOME UNITS
[ASK] [S/D] [🐕] [🍴] [🚭] [📷] [🖨] / [✕] [🔒] [🍴] /
                                   FEE

──────── The following lodging was either not evaluated or did not ────────
meet AAA rating requirements but is listed for your information only.

HAMPTON INN MARIETTA Phone: 740/373-5353
(fyi) All Year [ECP] 1P: $76-$109 2P: $86-$119 XP: $10 F18
Motel Too new to rate. **Location:** I-77, exit 1, 0.5 mi w. 508 Pike St 45750. Fax: 740/373-3803. **Amenities:** radios, coffeemakers, microwaves, refrigerators, pool. **Cards:** AX, DC, DS, MC, VI.

──────── **WHERE TO DINE** ────────

THE GUN ROOM Historical **Lunch:** $7-$10 **Dinner:** $11-$28 Phone: 740/373-5522
▼▼▼ **Location:** Town center; in Lafayette Hotel. 101 Front St 45750. **Hours:** 6:30 am-2 & 5-10 pm, Sun 7:30 am-9
American pm. Closed: 12/25. **Reservations:** suggested. **Features:** casual dress; Sunday brunch; children's menu;
cocktails & lounge; buffet. Vintage pictures and an 1800s gun room create the riverboat theme in the open,
airy dining room. Prime rib, beef tips and such seafood specialties as shrimp, scallops and king crab legs
are listed on a menu that also includes in-house desserts. **Parking:** on-site. **Cards:** AX, DC, DS, MC, VI. ✉

──────── The following restaurants have not been evaluated by AAA ────────
but are listed for your information only.

BRIDGEWATER 130 Phone: 740/374-6344
(fyi) Not evaluated. **Location:** 130 Front St 45750. The restaurant counts European-style baked goods among its choices.

MARIETTA BREWING COMPANY Phone: 740/373-8373
(fyi) Not evaluated. **Location:** 167 Front St 45750. Features include hand-cut steaks, pizza, hamburgers and a variety of
microbrews.

OLIVER'S FINE FOODS & SPIRITS Phone: 740/374-8278
(fyi) Not evaluated. **Location:** 203 Second St 45750. Gourmet hamburgers, steak, seafood and barbecue are among
offerings here.

THIRD STREET DELI Phone: 740/374-0003
(fyi) Not evaluated. **Location:** 343 Third St 45750. Gourmet sandwiches, soups, salads and desserts make up the bulk of
the menu.

MARION pop. 34,100

──────── **WHERE TO STAY** ────────

FAIRFIELD INN BY MARRIOTT Phone: (740)389-6636
(AAA) (SAVE) All Year [CP] 1P: $69-$99 2P: $69-$99 XP: $5 F17
▼▼▼▼ **Location:** Jct SR 95 and US 23. 227 James Way 43302. Fax: 740/389-6636. **Facility:** 57 one-bedroom standard
Motel units. 3 stories, interior corridors. **Parking:** on-site. **Terms:** 5 day cancellation notice. **Amenities:** extended
cable TV, irons. **Pool(s):** heated indoor. **Leisure Activities:** whirlpool. **Guest Services:** valet laundry.
Cards: AX, DC, DS, MC, VI. **Special Amenities:** free continental breakfast and free local telephone
calls. *(See color ad card insert)*
SOME UNITS
[icons] FEE

HOLIDAY INN EXPRESS & SUITES Phone: (740)389-4300
▼▼▼ All Year [ECP] 1P: $85 2P: $85 XP: $10 F20
Motel **Location:** Jct SR 95 and US 23. 1842 Marion-Mt Gilead Rd 43302. Fax: 740/386-5152. **Facility:** 81 one-bedroom
standard units, some with whirlpools. 3 stories, interior corridors. *Bath:* combo or shower only. **Parking:** on-
site. **Amenities:** extended cable TV, voice mail, irons, hair dryers. **Pool(s):** heated indoor. **Leisure Activities:** whirlpool, exercise room. **Business Services:** meeting rooms. **Cards:** AX, DC, DS, MC, VI.
SOME UNITS
[icons] FEE

MARION COMFORT INN Phone: (740)389-5552
(SAVE) All Year [CP] 1P: $59-$89 2P: $59-$89 XP: $5 F17
▼▼▼ **Location:** Jct SR 95 and US 23. 256 James Way 43302. Fax: 740/389-5552. **Facility:** 56 one-bedroom standard
Motel units. 2 stories, interior corridors. *Bath:* combo or shower only. **Parking:** on-site. **Terms:** 5 day cancellation
notice, small pets only ($10 extra charge). **Amenities:** extended cable TV. *Some:* irons, hair dryers. **Pool(s):**
heated indoor. **Leisure Activities:** whirlpool. **Guest Services:** valet laundry. **Cards:** AX, DC, DS, MC, VI.
SOME UNITS
[icons] FEE

MARION COUNTRY INN & SUITES Phone: (740)386-5451
▼▼▼ All Year [CP] 1P: $80 2P: $80
Motel **Location:** Jct SR 95 and US 23, just e. 2091 Marion-Mt Gilead Rd 43302. Fax: 740/386-5451. **Facility:** 63 one-
bedroom standard units. 3 stories, interior corridors. *Bath:* combo or shower only. **Parking:** on-site.
Terms: 10 day cancellation notice. **Amenities:** extended cable TV, irons, hair dryers. **Pool(s):** heated indoor.
Leisure Activities: whirlpool. **Cards:** AX, DC, DS, MC, VI. *(See color ad p 646)*
SOME UNITS
[icons] FEE

SUPER 8 MOTEL-MARION
Phone: (740)389-1998

▼▼▼ ▼▼▼
Motel

All Year   1P: $59-$64   2P: $64-$69   XP: $5   F12
Location: Jct SR 95 and US 23, just e. 2117 Marion-Mt Gilead Rd 43302. Fax: 740/389-1998. **Facility:** 63 one-bedroom standard units, some with whirlpools. 3 stories, interior corridors. *Bath:* combo or shower only. **Parking:** on-site. **Terms:** 7 day cancellation notice. **Amenities:** extended cable TV. **Pool(s):** heated indoor. **Leisure Activities:** whirlpool. **Guest Services:** valet and coin laundry. **Business Services:** meeting rooms. **Cards:** AX, DC, DS, MC, VI.

SOME UNITS

（ASK）(S▣) (T↑➞) (⟨⟩) (⊘) (⊇) (🖥) (DATA PORT) (🖨) / (✕) (VCR) (🔌) (☐) (💻) /
               FEE

――――― WHERE TO DINE ―――――

STEVE'S DAKOTA GRILL
Dinner: $10-$21   **Phone:** 740/725-9033

▼▼ ▼▼
Steak & Seafood

Location: Jct SR 95 and US 23, just w. 1950 Marion-Mt Gilead Rd 43302. **Hours:** 4 pm-10 pm, Fri & Sat-11 pm, Sun 11 am-9 pm. Closed: 12/25. **Features:** casual dress; children's menu; carryout; cocktails & lounge. Hearty cuts of choice steaks and fresh seafood are offered at the casual grill-style restaurant. **Parking:** on-site. **Cards:** AX, DS, MC, VI.

(✕)

――――― *The following restaurants have not been evaluated by AAA but are listed for your information only.* ―――――

GATEWAY SMORGASBORD
Phone: 740/389-4712

[fyi]   Not evaluated. **Location:** 1348 Mt Vernon Ave 43302. The spacious dining room includes a large buffet of home-cooked foods.

HOUSE OF HUNAN
Phone: 740/387-0032

[fyi]   Not evaluated. **Location:** 1583 Marion Waldo Rd 43302. Near Southland Mall, this restaurant serves cuisine from all the major provinces in China.

MARYSVILLE —See Columbus p. 665.

MASON —See Cincinnati p. 577.

MASSILLON pop. 31,000

――――― WHERE TO STAY ―――――

HAMPTON INN-CANTON/MASSILLON
Phone: (330)834-1144

SAVE
▼▼▼ ▼▼
Motel

All Year [ECP]   1P: $69-$79   2P: $79-$89
Location: Downtown. 44 First St SW 44647. Fax: 330/834-2960. **Facility:** 73 one-bedroom standard units. 5 stories, interior corridors. **Parking:** on-site. **Amenities:** extended cable TV, dual phone lines, voice mail, irons, hair dryers. **Leisure Activities:** exercise room. **Guest Services:** valet laundry. **Business Services:** meeting rooms. **Cards:** AX, DC, DS, MC, VI.

SOME UNITS

(🛏) (T↑➞) (🐾) (DATA PORT) (💻) (🖨) / (✕) /

MAUMEE pop. 15,600   (See map p. 756; index p. 757)

――――― WHERE TO STAY ―――――

COMFORT INN & SUITES
Phone: (419)897-5555 **17**

(AAA) SAVE
▼▼▼ ▼▼
Motel

All Year [ECP]   1P: $59-$74   2P: $64-$79
Location: I-80/90 (Ohio Tpke), exit 59, just s on US 20. 1702 Tollgate Dr 43537. Fax: 419/897-0055. **Facility:** 75 one-bedroom standard units, some with whirlpools. 3 stories, interior corridors. *Bath:* combo or shower only. **Parking:** on-site. **Amenities:** extended cable TV, voice mail, irons, hair dryers. **Pool(s):** heated indoor. **Leisure Activities:** whirlpool, exercise room. **Guest Services:** coin laundry. **Business Services:** meeting rooms. **Cards:** AX, DC, DS, MC, VI. **Special Amenities:** free continental breakfast and free newspaper.

(See color ad p 760)

SOME UNITS

(S▣) (T↑➞) (⟨M) (⟨⟩) (⊘) (⊇) (🖥) (DATA PORT) (🖨) / (✕) (🔌) (☐) (💻) /

COMFORT INN TOLEDO WEST/MAUMEE
Phone: (419)893-2800 **10**

(AAA) SAVE
▼▼▼ ▼▼
Motel

All Year [ECP]   1P: $49-$64   2P: $54-$69
Location: I-80/90 (Ohio Tpke), exit 59, just s on US 20. 1426 S Reynolds Rd 43537. Fax: 419/893-4517. **Facility:** 80 one-bedroom standard units. 2 stories, interior corridors. **Parking:** on-site. **Amenities:** irons, hair dryers. **Leisure Activities:** whirlpool. **Cards:** AX, CB, DC, DS, MC, VI. **Special Amenities:** free continental breakfast and free room upgrade (subject to availability with advanced reservations).

(See color ad p 760)

SOME UNITS

(S▣) (T↑➞) (🖥) (DATA PORT) (🖨) / (✕) (🔌) (☐) (💻) /

COUNTRY INN & SUITES BY CARLSON
Phone: (419)893-8576 **16**

▼▼▼ ▼▼
Motel

All Year [CP]   1P: $75-$85   2P: $75-$85   XP: $6   F17
Location: I-475, exit 6, just e. 541 W Dussel Dr 43537. Fax: 419/893-8576. **Facility:** 64 one-bedroom standard units. 1-3 stories, interior corridors. *Bath:* combo or shower only. **Parking:** on-site. **Terms:** 5 day cancellation notice, small pets only. **Amenities:** extended cable TV, voice mail, irons, hair dryers. **Pool(s):** heated indoor. **Leisure Activities:** whirlpool. **Guest Services:** valet laundry. **Business Services:** meeting rooms. **Cards:** AX, DC, DS, MC, VI. *(See color ad p 646)*

SOME UNITS

(ASK) (S▣) (🛏) (T↑➞) (⟨⟩) (⊘) (⊇) (🖥) (DATA PORT) (💻) (🖨) / (✕) (🔌) (☐) /
               FEE

(See map p. 756)

COURTYARD BY MARRIOTT-TOLDEO/MAUMEE   Phone: (419)897-2255 **18**

CAD SAVE

▽▽▽▽

Motel

All Year   1P: $104   2P: $104
Location: I-475, exit 6, 0.8 mi e. 415 W Dussel Dr 43537. Fax: 419/897-7680. **Facility:** 90 one-bedroom standard units, some with whirlpools. 3 stories, interior corridors. *Bath:* combo or shower only. **Parking:** on-site. **Amenities:** dual phone lines, voice mail, irons, hair dryers. **Dining:** coffee shop, 6:30-10 am, Sat & Sun 7 am-noon. **Leisure Activities:** whirlpool, exercise room. **Guest Services:** valet and coin laundry. **Business Services:** meeting rooms. **Cards:** AX, CB, DC, DS, MC, VI. *(See color ad card insert)*

SOME UNITS

🆘 🍴 📺 ᵫM 🚫 📡 📹 DATA PORT 💻 🖨 / ✕ 🛗 📠 /
　　　　　　FEE

CROSS COUNTRY INN TOLEDO/MAUMEE   Phone: (419)891-0880 **8**
                                                                              F17
▽▽▽

Motel

All Year   1P: $36-$43   2P: $43-$50   XP: $2
Location: I-80/90 (Ohio Tpke), exit 59, just s. 1704 Tollgate Dr 43537. Fax: 419/891-1017. **Facility:** 120 one-bedroom standard units. 2 stories, exterior corridors. *Bath:* combo or shower only. **Parking:** on-site. **Amenities:** video games, voice mail. **Pool(s):** heated outdoor. **Cards:** AX, CB, DC, DS, MC, VI.

SOME UNITS

ASK 🆘 🍴 🚫 📡 🏊 🎥 🖨 / ✕ /
　　　　　　　　　　　　FEE

DAYS INN TOLEDO ARROWHEAD   Phone: (419)893-9960 **15**

CAD SAVE

▽▽▽▽

Motel

6/1-9/3   1P: $50-$70   2P: $55-$80   XP: $6   F17
4/1-5/31   1P: $45-$50   2P: $50-$55   XP: $6   F17
9/4-3/31   1P: $45-$50   2P: $45-$55   XP: $6   F17
Location: I-80/90 (Ohio Tpke), exit 59, just s. 150 Dussel Dr 43537. Fax: 419/893-9559. **Facility:** 120 one-bedroom standard units, some with whirlpools. 2 stories, exterior corridors. **Parking:** on-site. **Amenities:** hair dryers. **Pool(s):** outdoor. **Business Services:** meeting rooms. **Cards:** AX, DS, MC, VI.
Special Amenities: free continental breakfast.

SOME UNITS

🆘 🐕 🍴 📡 🏊 🎥 🖨 / ✕ 🛗 📠 /

FAIRFIELD INN-TOLEDO/MAUMEE   Phone: (419)897-0865 **13**

CAD SAVE

▽▽▽▽

Motel

6/2-8/31 [CP]   1P: $75-$83   2P: $81-$85
4/1-6/1 & 9/1-3/31 [CP] 1P: $71-$79   2P: $75-$84
Location: I-475, exit 6, just e. 521 W Dussel Dr 43537. Fax: 419/897-0865. **Facility:** 64 one-bedroom standard units. 3 stories, interior corridors. *Bath:* combo or shower only. **Parking:** on-site. **Amenities:** extended cable TV, irons. **Pool(s):** heated indoor. **Leisure Activities:** whirlpool. **Guest Services:** valet laundry. **Cards:** AX, DC, DS, MC, VI. **Special Amenities:** free continental breakfast and free local telephone calls.

(See color ad card insert)

SOME UNITS

🆘 🍴 🚫 📡 🏊 🎥 DATA PORT 🖨 / ✕ 🛗 💻 /
　　　　　　　　　　FEE

HAMPTON INN TOLEDO SOUTH/MAUMEE   Phone: (419)893-1004 **11**

SAVE

▽▽▽▽

Motel

All Year [ECP]   1P: $77-$83   2P: $85-$95
Location: I-80/90 (Ohio Tpke), exit 59, just s on US 20. 1409 Reynolds Rd 43537. Fax: 419/893-4613. **Facility:** 128 one-bedroom standard units. 4 stories, interior corridors. **Parking:** on-site. **Amenities:** video games, dual phone lines, voice mail, irons, hair dryers. **Pool(s):** heated outdoor, heated indoor. **Leisure Activities:** whirlpool, exercise room. **Guest Services:** valet laundry. **Business Services:** meeting rooms. **Cards:** AX, CB, DC, DS, JC, MC, VI.

SOME UNITS

🆘 🔀 🍴 📡 🏊 🎥 DATA PORT 💻 🖨 / ✕ 🛗 📠 /
　　　　　　　　　FEE

KNIGHTS INN-TOLEDO WEST   Phone: (419)865-1380 **19**
                                                                              F17
▽▽

Motel

All Year   1P: $44-$150   2P: $44-$150   XP: $5
Location: I-475, exit 8, just e. 1520 S Holland-Sylvania Rd 43537. Fax: 419/865-0344. **Facility:** 162 one-bedroom standard units, some with whirlpools. 1 story, exterior corridors. **Parking:** on-site. **Terms:** 14 day cancellation notice, [ECP] meal plan available. **Amenities:** extended cable TV. **Pool(s):** small outdoor. **Guest Services:** coin laundry. **Business Services:** meeting rooms. **Cards:** AX, DC, DS, MC, VI.

SOME UNITS

ASK 🆘 🐕 🍴 🏊 🎥 / ✕ VCR 🛗 📠 /

RED ROOF INN-MAUMEE   Phone: (419)893-0292 **14**

CAD SAVE

▽▽▽▽

Motel

5/26-11/2   1P: $41-$63   2P: $47-$69   XP: $6   F18
11/3-3/31   1P: $39-$59   2P: $43-$65   XP: $6   F18
4/1-5/25   1P: $37-$57   2P: $43-$63   XP: $6   F18
Location: I-80/90 (Ohio Tpke), exit 59, just s. 1570 S Reynolds Rd 43537. Fax: 419/893-8767. **Facility:** 110 one-bedroom standard units. 2 stories, interior/exterior corridors. *Bath:* combo or shower only. **Parking:** on-site. **Terms:** small pets only. **Amenities:** video games, voice mail. **Cards:** AX, CB, DC, DS, MC, VI.
Special Amenities: free local telephone calls and free newspaper.

SOME UNITS

🐕 🍴 🚫 📡 🎥 DATA PORT 🖨 / ✕ 🛗 📠 /
　　　　　　　　　　FEE　　　　　　FEE FEE

SUPER 8 TOLEDO-MAUMEE   Phone: (419)897-3800 **7**

▽▽▽

Motel

5/25-9/1 [CP]   1P: $50-$80   2P: $55-$85   XP: $5   F16
4/1-5/24 & 9/2-3/31 [CP] 1P: $40-$60   2P: $45-$65   XP: $5   F16
Location: I-475, exit 6, just e. 1390 Arrowhead Rd 43537. Fax: 419/893-3860. **Facility:** 68 one-bedroom standard units. 2 stories, interior corridors. *Bath:* combo or shower only. **Parking:** on-site. **Amenities:** extended cable TV. **Guest Services:** coin laundry. **Business Services:** meeting rooms. **Cards:** AX, DC, DS, MC, VI.

SOME UNITS

ASK 🆘 🍴 🚫 📡 🎥 DATA PORT 💻 🖨 / ✕ 🛗 📠 /

(See map p. 756)

TOLEDO/MAUMEE HOMEWOOD SUITES BY HILTON　　　　　　**Phone:** (419)897-0980　🔢

SAVE	6/1-10/31 [ECP]	1P: $119
	4/1-5/31 & 2/1-3/31 [ECP]	1P: $109
▽▽▽	11/1-1/31 [ECP]	1P: $99

Apartment **Location:** I-475, exit 6, just e. 1410 Arrowhead Rd 43537. Fax: 419/897-1661. **Facility:** 78 one-bedroom standard units. 3 stories, interior corridors. **Parking:** on-site. **Terms:** [MAP] meal plan available. **Amenities:** extended cable TV, video games, dual phone lines, voice mail, irons, hair dryers. **Pool(s):** heated indoor. **Leisure Activities:** whirlpool, exercise room, sports court. **Guest Services:** valet and coin laundry. **Business Services:** meeting rooms, business center, PC. **Cards:** AX, DC, DS, MC, VI.

SOME UNITS

[icons] FEE　　/ X /

──────── **WHERE TO DINE** ────────

──────── *The following restaurants have not been evaluated by AAA* ────────
but are listed for your information only.

HOPS BAR & BREWERY　　　　　　**Phone:** 419/897-4677
[fyi]　Not evaluated. **Location:** 461 W Drussel 43537. Conveniently accessible from the bypass, the restaurant has a lively atmosphere and friendly wait staff.

MAUMEE CHOP HOUSE　　　　　　**Phone:** 419/897-6811
[fyi]　Not evaluated. **Location:** 1430 Holland Rd 43537. Generous portions of prime cuts, tempting appetizers and friendly servers are restaurant hallmarks.

RALPHIE'S FAMILY SPORTS EATERY　　　　　　**Phone:** 419/893-1212
[fyi]　Not evaluated. **Location:** 1320 Reynolds Rd 43537. Colorfully named sandwiches and wings with six sauces are favorites at the lively restaurant.

MAYFIELD —See Cleveland p. 624.

MAYFIELD HEIGHTS —See Cleveland p. 624.

MEDINA —See Cleveland p. 624.

MENTOR pop. 47,400

──────── **WHERE TO STAY** ────────

BEST WESTERN LAWNFIELD INN & SUITES　　　　　　**Phone:** (440)205-7378

AAA SAVE	All Year [CP]	1P: $79-$99	2P: $79-$99	XP: $20　F17

▽▽▽
Motel **Location:** I-90, exit 193, 2 mi n on SR 306, then 2 mi e. 8434 Mentor Ave 44060. Fax: 440/205-8436. **Facility:** 50 units. 23 one-bedroom standard units. 27 one-bedroom suites with efficiencies (no utensils). Interior corridors. *Bath:* combo or shower only. **Terms:** 7 day cancellation notice. **Amenities:** high-speed Internet, voice mail, irons, hair dryers. **Pool(s):** heated outdoor. **Leisure Activities:** exercise room. **Guest Services:** valet laundry. **Business Services:** meeting rooms, business center. **Cards:** AX, DC, DS, MC, VI. **Special Amenities:** free continental breakfast and free local telephone calls.

SOME UNITS

[icons]　/ X 📞 🖨 /

COMFORT INN　　　　　　**Phone:** (440)951-7333

AAA SAVE	5/24-8/2	1P: $79-$125	2P: $79-$125	XP: $10　F18
	8/3-3/31	1P: $59-$89	2P: $59-$89	
▽▽▽	4/1-5/23	1P: $59-$79	2P: $59-$89	XP: $10　F18

Motel **Location:** Just s of SR 2 on SR 306. 7701 Reynolds Rd 44060. Fax: 440/951-0961. **Facility:** 127 one-bedroom standard units, some with whirlpools. 4 stories, interior corridors. **Parking:** on-site. **Terms:** 7 day cancellation notice. **Amenities:** voice mail. **Pool(s):** heated indoor. **Leisure Activities:** exercise room. **Guest Services:** valet and coin laundry. **Business Services:** meeting rooms. **Cards:** AX, CB, DS, MC, VI. **Special Amenities:** free continental breakfast and free newspaper.

SOME UNITS

[icons]　/ X 📞 🖨 /

HOLIDAY INN EXPRESS HOTEL & SUITES AT LAMALFA CENTRE　　　　　　**Phone:** (440)357-0384

AAA SAVE	5/1-10/31	1P: $94	XP: $10　F18
▽▽▽	4/1-4/30 & 11/1-3/31	1P: $82	XP: $10　F18

Motel **Location:** Jct SR 2 and Heisley Rd, just w of jct SR 44. 5785 Heisley Rd 44060. Fax: 440/357-0560. **Facility:** 76 one-bedroom standard units, some with whirlpools. 3 stories, interior corridors. *Bath:* combo or shower only. **Parking:** on-site. **Amenities:** voice mail, irons, hair dryers. **Pool(s):** indoor. **Leisure Activities:** exercise room. **Guest Services:** complimentary evening beverages: Mon-Fri, valet laundry. **Business Services:** conference facilities. **Cards:** AX, CB, DC, DS, MC, VI.

SOME UNITS

[icons]　/ X 📞 🖨 /

──────── **WHERE TO DINE** ────────

MOLINARI'S　　**Lunch:** $8-$12　　**Dinner:** $15-$24　　**Phone:** 440/974-2750
▽▽ ▽▽　**Location:** US 20, 1.5 mi e of CR 615; in plaza. 8900 Mentor Ave 44060. **Hours:** 11:30 am-2 & 5:30-10 pm, Fri & Sat-11 pm, Mon-2 pm. Closed major holidays; also Sun. **Reservations:** required. **Features:** casual dress; American children's menu; carryout; cocktails; a la carte. Decidedly creative and attractive presentations make the European dining experience at Molinari's memorable. The eatery's special flair for Northern Italian and California cuisine is evident in an excellent stuffed pork loin wrapped in proscuitto. Great background music that is soothing and relaxing. A large variety of wine to choose from. **Parking:** on-site. **Cards:** AX, DC, DS, MC, VI.

X

MIAMISBURG pop. 17,800 (See map p. 672; index p. 674)

———— WHERE TO STAY ————

BEST WESTERN CONTINENTAL INN

Phone: (937)866-5500   36

Motel

DS, MC, VI.

All Year [CP]   1P: $60-$68   2P: $65-$73   XP: $5   F18
Location: I-75, exit 44, 0.5 mi w on SR 725. 155 Monarch Ln 45342. Fax: 937/866-8270. **Facility:** 60 one-bedroom standard units. 2 stories, interior corridors. **Parking:** on-site. **Amenities:** extended cable TV, voice mail, irons, hair dryers. **Guest Services:** valet laundry. **Business Services:** meeting rooms. **Cards:** AX, CB, DC,

SOME UNITS

COMFORT SUITES

Phone: (937)436-4529   40

SAVE

Motel

All Year [ECP]   1P: $85   2P: $85
Location: I-75, exit 44, just e on SR 725. (42 Prestige Plaza Dr, DAYTON, 45342). Fax: 937/436-4965. **Facility:** 57 one-bedroom standard units. 3 stories, interior corridors. *Bath:* combo or shower only. **Parking:** on-site. **Terms:** 14 day cancellation notice. **Amenities:** extended cable TV, dual phone lines, voice mail, irons, hair dryers. **Pool(s):** heated indoor. **Leisure Activities:** exercise room. **Guest Services:** valet and coin laundry. **Cards:** AX, DC, DS, MC, VI.

SOME UNITS

COURTYARD BY MARRIOTT

Phone: (937)433-3131   30

AAA SAVE

Motel

All Year   1P: $120-$130   2P: $120-$130
Location: I-75, exit 44, just e on SR 725; in Prestige Plaza Complex. 100 Prestige Pl 45342. Fax: 937/433-0285. **Facility:** 146 units. 134 one-bedroom standard units. 12 one-bedroom suites ($150). 3 stories, interior corridors. *Bath:* combo or shower only. **Parking:** on-site. **Terms:** cancellation fee imposed. **Amenities:** voice mail, irons, hair dryers. **Dining:** coffee shop, 6:30-10 am, Sat & Sun 7-11 am. **Pool(s):** heated indoor. **Leisure Activities:** whirlpool, exercise room. **Guest Services:** coin laundry. **Business Services:** meeting rooms. **Cards:** AX, CB, DC, DS, JC, MC, VI. *(See color ad card insert)*

SOME UNITS

DOUBLETREE GUEST SUITES-DAYTON MALL

Phone: (937)436-2400   35

SAVE

Suite Hotel

All Year   1P: $179-$194   2P: $179-$194   XP: $15   F18
Location: I-75, exit 44, just se on SR 725; in Prestige Plaza complex. 300 Prestige Pl 45342. Fax: 937/436-2886. **Facility:** 138 one-bedroom standard units. 3 stories, interior corridors. **Parking:** on-site. **Terms:** package plans. **Amenities:** voice mail, irons, hair dryers. **Pool(s):** heated indoor. **Leisure Activities:** whirlpool, exercise room. *Fee:* game room. **Guest Services:** coin laundry. **Business Services:** meeting rooms.

SOME UNITS

ENGLISH MANOR BED & BREAKFAST

Phone: (937)866-2288   33

Bed & Breakfast

All Year [BP]   1P: $79-$125   2P: $79-$125   XP: $10   F12
Location: I-75, exit 44, 3 mi w on SR 725, just s on 7th St, then just w. 505 E Linden Ave 45342. **Facility:** Smoke free premises. 4 one-bedroom standard units. 3 stories, interior corridors. *Bath:* some shared or private. **Parking:** street. **Terms:** 6 day cancellation notice-fee imposed. **Cards:** AX, DC, MC, VI.

HOLIDAY INN-DAYTON MALL

Phone: (937)434-8030   38

Motor Inn

All Year   1P: $98-$107   2P: $98-$107
Location: I-75, exit 44, just e on SR 725. 31 Prestige Plaza Dr 45342. Fax: 937/434-6452. **Facility:** 195 one-bedroom standard units. 3 stories, interior corridors. **Parking:** on-site. **Terms:** package plans. **Amenities:** voice mail, irons, hair dryers. **Pool(s):** outdoor, heated indoor, wading. **Leisure Activities:** sauna, whirlpool, putting green, exercise room. *Fee:* game room. **Guest Services:** coin laundry. **Business Services:** conference facilities. **Cards:** AX, CB, DC, DS, JC, MC, VI. *(See color ad p 677)*

SOME UNITS

HOMEWOOD SUITES HOTEL-DAYTON MALL

Phone: (937)432-0000   34

SAVE

Apartment

All Year [ECP]   1P: $129-$149   2P: $129-$149   XP: $10   F17
Location: I-75, exit 44, just e on SR 725; in Prestige Plaza Complex. 3100 Contemporary Ln 45342. Fax: 937/435-9411. **Facility:** 96 one-bedroom standard units with efficiencies. 5 stories, interior corridors. *Bath:* combo or shower only. **Parking:** on-site. **Terms:** [MAP] meal plan available, pets ($50 fee, $5 extra charge). **Amenities:** extended cable TV, video games, voice mail, irons, hair dryers. **Pool(s):** heated indoor. **Leisure Activities:** exercise room. **Guest Services:** coin laundry. **Business Services:** meeting rooms, business center, PC, fax. **Cards:** AX, DC, DS, MC, VI.

SOME UNITS

RED ROOF INN-SOUTH

Phone: (937)866-0705   39

AAA SAVE

Motel

5/5-8/24	1P: $47-$61	2P: $52-$66	XP: $5 F18
8/25-3/31	1P: $41-$56	2P: $46-$61	XP: $5 F18
4/1-5/4	1P: $39-$54	2P: $44-$59	XP: $5 F18

Location: I-75, exit 44, just w on SR 725. 222 Byers Rd 45342. Fax: 937/866-0700. **Facility:** 107 one-bedroom standard units. 2 stories, exterior corridors. *Bath:* combo or shower only. **Parking:** on-site, winter plug-ins. **Terms:** small pets only. **Amenities:** video games, voice mail. **Cards:** AX, CB, DC, DS, MC, VI.
Special Amenities: free local telephone calls and free newspaper.

SOME UNITS

(See map p. 672)

RESIDENCE INN BY MARRIOTT-DAYTON SOUTH

AAA (SAVE)

▽▽▽▽

Apartment

All Year [BP]   1P: $124   2P: $140   **Phone:** (937)434-7881   32

Location: I-75, exit 44, just e on SR 725. 155 Prestige Pl 45342. Fax: 937/434-9308. **Facility:** 96 units. 72 one- and 24 two-bedroom standard units with kitchens. 2 stories, exterior corridors. *Bath:* combo or shower only. **Parking:** on-site. **Terms:** pets ($150 deposit, $6 extra charge). **Amenities:** voice mail, irons, hair dryers. *Some:* dual phone lines. **Pool(s):** heated outdoor. **Leisure Activities:** whirlpool, sports court. **Guest Services:** coin laundry. **Cards:** AX, CB, DC, DS, JC, MC, VI. *(See color ad card insert)*

SOME UNITS

[icons] / [X] [VCR] /
FEE

SIGNATURE INN DAYTON SOUTH

▽▽▽▽

Motel

All Year [CP]   1P: $68-$78   2P: $68-$78   **Phone:** (937)865-0077   37

Location: I-75, exit 44, just w on SR 725. 250 Byers Rd 45342. Fax: 937/865-0077. **Facility:** 125 one-bedroom standard units, some with whirlpools. 3 stories, interior corridors. **Parking:** on-site. **Amenities:** extended cable TV, voice mail, irons, hair dryers. **Guest Services:** valet laundry. **Business Services:** meeting rooms, business center, PC. **Cards:** AX, DC, DS, MC, VI.

SOME UNITS

(ASK) [icons] / [X]

─────── **WHERE TO DINE** ───────

BULLWINKLES TOP HAT BISTRO

▽▽

American

Lunch: $9-$23   **Dinner:** $9-$23   **Phone:** 937/859-7677   19

Location: Just n of downtown. 19 N Main St 45342. **Hours:** 11 am-10:30 pm, Fri-11:30 pm, Sat noon-11:30 pm. Closed major holidays; also Sun. **Features:** casual dress; children's menu; carryout; cocktails & lounge. Diners at the downtown bistro can grill their own steak, seafood or ribs. **Parking:** on-site. **Cards:** AX, DC, DS, MC, VI.

[X]

PEERLESS MILL INN   Historical

AAA

▽▽▽

American

Dinner: $11-$18   **Phone:** 937/866-5968   21

Location: I-75, exit 44, 2.8 mi w on SR 725. 319 S 2nd St 45342. **Hours:** 5 pm-9 pm, Fri & Sat-10 pm, Sun 10 am-7 pm. Closed: 1/1, 7/4, 12/25; also Mon. **Reservations:** suggested; weekends. **Features:** casual dress; Sunday brunch; children's menu; cocktails & lounge. The former lumber mill is a quaint, comfortable spot to enjoy flavorful offerings, such as roast duck, chicken cordon bleu or prime rib. Desserts are made on the premises. A good selection of wine is offered. The weekend brunch draws a hungry, happy crowd. **Parking:** on-site. **Cards:** AX, CB, DC, MC, VI.

[X]

STEVE KAO'S CHINESE CUISINE

▽▽▽

Chinese

Lunch: $7-$8   **Dinner:** $10-$16   **Phone:** 937/435-5261   20

Location: Just s of Dayton Mall on SR 741. 8270 Springboro Pike SR 741 45342. **Hours:** 11:30 am-10 pm, Fri & Sat-11 pm, Sun noon-10 pm. Closed: 11/28. **Features:** casual dress; carryout; cocktails & lounge. In addition to traditional Szechuan, Hunan, Shanghai and Cantonese seafood cuisine, the moderately upscale restaurant delivers a few delightful surprises, such as shark fin soup and jellyfish. The well-maintained dining room is clean and comfortable. Attentive, well groomed staff. Located near Dayton Mall and I-75. **Parking:** on-site. **Cards:** AX, DC, DS, MC, VI.

[X]

─────── *The following restaurant has not been evaluated by AAA but is listed for your information only.* ───────

ALEX'S RESTAURANT

(fyi)

Phone: 937/866-2266

Not evaluated. **Location:** 125 Monarch Ln 45342. The menu includes Continental and American specialties.

MIDDLEBURG HEIGHTS —See Cleveland p. 625.

MIDDLETOWN —See Cincinnati p. 581.

MILAN pop. 1,500

─────── **WHERE TO STAY** ───────

COMFORT INN MILAN SANDUSKY

AAA (SAVE)

▽▽▽

Motel

7/20-9/1 [ECP]	1P: $60-$180	2P: $60-$180		
6/29-7/19 [ECP]	1P: $60-$140	2P: $60-$140		
4/1-6/28 & 9/2-3/31 [ECP]	1P: $42-$120	2P: $46-$120	XP: $4	F17

Phone: (419)499-4681

Location: I-80/90 (Ohio Tpke), exit 118, 2 mi n. 11020 US 250 Milan Rd 44846. Fax: 419/499-3159. **Facility:** 100 one-bedroom standard units, some with whirlpools. 2 stories, interior/exterior corridors. **Parking:** on-site. **Terms:** check-in 4 pm, 3 day cancellation notice. **Amenities:** safes (fee). *Some:* irons, hair dryers. **Pool(s):** heated indoor. **Leisure Activities:** sauna, whirlpool. *Fee:* game room. **Guest Services:** coin laundry. **Cards:** AX, DC, DS, MC, VI. **Special Amenities:** free continental breakfast and free local telephone calls. *(See color ad p 738)*

SOME UNITS

[icons] / [X] [DATA PORT] [icon] /

DAYS INN TURNPIKE

(SAVE)

▽▽▽

Motel

6/14-9/1 [CP]	1P: $69-$144	2P: $69-$144	XP: $8	F17
4/1-6/13 [CP]	1P: $40-$99	2P: $44-$99	XP: $8	F17
9/2-10/26 [CP]	1P: $40-$69	2P: $44-$69	XP: $8	F17
10/27-3/31 [CP]	1P: $40-$59	2P: $44-$59	XP: $8	F17

Phone: (419)499-4961

Location: I-80/90 (Ohio Tpke), exit 118, 1.5 mi n. 11410 US 250 44846. Fax: 419/499-4961. **Facility:** 66 one-bedroom standard units, some with kitchens and/or whirlpools. 2 stories, interior corridors. **Parking:** on-site. **Terms:** 3 day cancellation notice. **Amenities:** hair dryers. *Some:* irons. **Pool(s):** heated indoor. **Leisure Activities:** whirlpool, exercise room. **Guest Services:** coin laundry. **Business Services:** meeting rooms. **Cards:** AX, CB, DC, DS, MC, VI. *(See color ad p 742)*

SOME UNITS

[icons] / [X] [icons] /

HAMPTON INN

Phone: (419)499-4911

AAA [SAVE]

WWWW

Motel

6/15-9/3 [ECP]	1P: $98-$198	2P: $98-$198
5/12-6/14 [ECP]	1P: $88-$150	2P: $88-$150
4/1-5/11 [ECP]	1P: $68-$140	2P: $78-$140
9/4-3/31 [ECP]	1P: $58-$120	2P: $68-$120

Location: I-80/90 (Ohio Tpke), exit 118, just n. 11600 SR 250 44846. Fax: 419/499-4708. **Facility:** 50 one-bedroom standard units, some with whirlpools. 2 stories, interior corridors. **Parking:** on-site. **Terms:** cancellation fee imposed. **Amenities:** dual phone lines, voice mail, irons. **Pool(s):** indoor. **Leisure Activities:** whirlpool. **Guest Services:** valet laundry. **Cards:** AX, CB, DC, MC, VI. **Special Amenities:** free continental breakfast and free local telephone calls. *(See color ad p 741)*

SOME UNITS

[symbols]

MOTEL 6 - 4016

Phone: 419/499-8001

WWW

Motel

6/14-9/1	1P: $64-$139	2P: $64-$139	XP: $8	F17
4/1-6/13	1P: $36-$89	2P: $36-$89	XP: $8	F17
9/2-10/26	1P: $36-$59	2P: $36-$59	XP: $8	F17
10/27-3/31	1P: $36-$54	2P: $36-$54	XP: $8	F17

Location: I-80/90 (Ohio Tpke), exit 118 1.5 mi n. 11406 US 250 N 44846. Fax: 419/499-8029. **Facility:** 63 one-bedroom standard units. 3 stories, interior corridors. *Bath:* combo or shower only. **Parking:** on-site. **Terms:** 3 day cancellation notice, small pets only. **Pool(s):** heated outdoor. **Guest Services:** coin laundry. **Cards:** AX, CB, DC, DS, MC, VI. *(See color ad p 742)*

SOME UNITS

[symbols]

RAMADA LIMITED

Phone: 419/499-4347

WWWW

Motel

6/22-9/1 [ECP]	1P: $59-$149	2P: $59-$149	XP: $5	F17
4/1-6/21 [ECP]	1P: $39-$98	2P: $39-$109	XP: $5	F17
9/2-10/26 [ECP]	1P: $39-$69	2P: $39-$69	XP: $5	F17
10/27-3/31 [ECP]	1P: $39-$45	2P: $45-$49	XP: $5	F17

Location: I-80/90 (Ohio Tpke), exit 118, 0.5 mi n. 11303 Rt 250/Milan Rd 44846. Fax: 419/499-4347. **Facility:** 56 one-bedroom standard units, some with whirlpools. 2 stories, interior corridors. *Bath:* combo or shower only. **Parking:** on-site. **Terms:** 3 day cancellation notice. **Amenities:** voice mail, hair dryers. **Pool(s):** heated indoor. **Guest Services:** coin laundry. **Business Services:** meeting rooms. **Cards:** AX, CB, DC, DS, MC, VI. *(See color ad p 735 & p 739)*

SOME UNITS

[symbols] FEE

SUPER 8 MOTEL

Phone: 419/499-4671

WWW

Motel

6/22-9/1 [CP]	1P: $58-$138	2P: $58-$138	XP: $5	F17
4/1-6/21 [CP]	1P: $38-$98	2P: $38-$108	XP: $5	F17
9/2-10/26 [CP]	1P: $38-$58	2P: $38-$58	XP: $5	F17
10/27-3/31 [CP]	1P: $33-$36	2P: $36-$43	XP: $5	F17

Location: I-80/90 (Ohio Tpke), exit 118, 0.5 mi n. on SR 250. 11313 Milan Rd 44846 (2027 Cleveland Rd, SANDUSKY, 44870). Fax: 419/499-4671. **Facility:** 69 one-bedroom standard units, some with whirlpools. 2 stories, interior corridors. **Parking:** on-site. **Terms:** 3 day cancellation notice. **Amenities:** hair dryers. **Pool(s):** outdoor. **Guest Services:** coin laundry. **Business Services:** meeting rooms. **Cards:** AX, CB, DC, DS, MC, VI. *(See color ad p 735 & p 739)*

SOME UNITS

[symbols] FEE FEE FEE

WHERE TO DINE

HOMESTEAD INN RESTAURANT Historical

AAA

WWW

American

Lunch: $6-$10   **Dinner:** $12-$20   Phone: 419/499-4271

Location: I-80/90 (Ohio Tpke), exit 118, just s. 12018 US 250 44846. **Hours:** 11 am-9 pm. Closed major holidays. **Features:** casual dress; children's menu; carryout; cocktails & lounge; a la carte. Built by a local strawberry farmer, the 1883 mansion was converted into a restaurant in the late 1950s. The decor is decidedly Victorian, with authentic antiques and intricately carved ceilings. The Rathskeller Room is open for those desiring a more intimate atmosphere. Steak, Lake Erie perch and walleye, along with freshly baked bread and pastries, tempt the palate. **Parking:** on-site. **Cards:** AX, DC, DS, MC, VI.

[symbol]

MILFORD —*See Cincinnati p. 582.*

MILLBURY pop. 1,100

WHERE TO DINE

SALLOCK'S COOKHOUSE

WWW

American

Lunch: $6-$10   **Dinner:** $8-$19   Phone: 419/838-7223

Location: I-280, exit 2, just w on SR 795/Moline-Martin Rd. 27960 Cummings Rd 43447. **Hours:** 11 am-10 pm, Sat from 4 pm. Closed major holidays; also Sun. **Reservations:** accepted. **Features:** casual dress; children's menu; carryout; cocktails. Compact dining room decorated with antique photographs and license plates from the 50 states and beyond. Primarily serve American-style steak and seafood along with a variety Middle Eastern appetizers and entrees. For the hearty appetite try the Lebanese combo that features kibi, tabouli, tahini, and fetayer. Save room for the baklava. **Parking:** on-site. **Cards:** AX, DS, MC, VI.

[symbols]

MILLERSBURG pop. 3,100

WHERE TO STAY

COMFORT INN MILLERSBURG

Phone: (330)674-7400

AAA [SAVE]

WWW

Motel

4/1-10/31 [ECP]	1P: $69-$129	2P: $69-$129	XP: $6	F18
11/1-3/31 [ECP]	1P: $50-$129	2P: $50-$129	XP: $6	F18

Location: SR 39, 0.5 mi s on S Clay. 1102 Glen Dr 44654. Fax: 330/674-7910. **Facility:** 59 units. 58 one-bedroom standard units, some with whirlpools. 1 one-bedroom suite ($109-$139). 3 stories, interior corridors. *Bath:* combo or shower only. **Parking:** on-site. **Amenities:** extended cable TV, dual phone lines, voice mail, irons, hair dryers. **Pool(s):** heated indoor. **Leisure Activities:** whirlpool, exercise room. **Guest Services:** coin laundry. **Business Services:** meeting rooms, fax. **Cards:** AX, CB, DC, DS, JC, MC, VI. **Special Amenities:** free continental breakfast and free local telephone calls.

SOME UNITS

[symbols]

FIELDS OF HOME GUEST HOUSE BED & BREAKFAST

♦♦♦ ♦♦♦

Bed & Breakfast

Phone: 330/674-7152

	6/1-10/31 [ECP]	1P: $65-$130	2P: $65-$130	XP: $15
	4/1-5/31 & 3/1-3/31 [ECP]	1P: $60-$125	2P: $60-$125	XP: $15
	11/1-2/28 [ECP]	1P: $55-$125	2P: $55-$125	XP: $15

Location: 4 mi e on SR 39, 3.5 mi n. 7278 CR 201 44654. Fax: 330/674-4638. **Facility:** Smoke free premises. 6 one-bedroom standard units, some with whirlpools. 2 stories, interior corridors. *Bath:* combo or shower only. **Parking:** on-site. **Terms:** 10 day cancellation notice-fee imposed. **Amenities:** video tape library, CD players, irons. *Some:* hair dryers. **Cards:** DS, MC, VI.

SOME UNITS

⊠ 🅦 🖨 / 🆅🅲🆁 🔌 📠 💻 /

PORT WASHINGTON INN

♦♦♦ ♦♦♦

Bed & Breakfast

Phone: (330)674-7704

	8/1-11/30 [BP]	1P: $79-$99	2P: $79-$99	XP: $15
	5/1-7/31 & 12/1-3/31 [BP]	1P: $69-$99	2P: $69-$99	XP: $15
	4/1-4/30 [BP]	1P: $59-$99	2P: $59-$99	XP: $15

Location: 3 blks e, 1.3 mi s on Port Washington Rd. 4667 TR 312 44654. Fax: 330/674-7704. **Facility:** Near Amish country, this attractive Tudor-style home is set high atop a hill on a 45-acre estate with picturesque views of the countryside. Smoke free premises. 8 units. 4 one-bedroom standard units. 1 one-bedroom suite ($89-$149) with whirlpool. 3 one-bedroom vacation rentals ($119-$179) with whirlpools. 2 stories, exterior corridors. *Bath:* combo or shower only. **Parking:** on-site. **Terms:** age restrictions may apply, 7 day cancellation notice, package plans. **Amenities:** extended cable TV. *Some:* hair dryers. **Leisure Activities:** whirlpool. **Cards:** AX, DS, MC, VI.

SOME UNITS

⊠ 📹 🖨 / 🆅🅲🆁 🔌 📠 💻 /

──────── **WHERE TO DINE** ────────

THE WEST FORK RESTAURANT

♦♦♦ ♦♦♦

American

Lunch: $6-$11   **Dinner:** $6-$30   **Phone:** 330/674-2469

Location: 0.5 mi s on S Clay from SR 39. 170 Parkview 44654. **Hours:** 11 am-8:30 pm, Fri & Sat-9:30 pm. Closed major holidays; also Mon. **Reservations:** suggested; weekends. **Features:** casual dress; children's menu; carryout; beer & wine only. In the rolling hills of an Amish community, this family-owned and operated restaurant provides a taste of the American West. The atmosphere is relaxing in the spacious lodge-like dining rooms. Service is welcoming and responsive. Smoke free premises. **Parking:** on-site. **Cards:** MC, VI.   ⊠

MONROE pop. 4,500

──────── **WHERE TO STAY** ────────

DAYS INN CINCINNATI-MONROE

🅰🅰🅰 SAVE
♦♦♦ ♦♦♦

Motel

Phone: (513)539-2660

| | 7/1-9/3 [CP] | 1P: $60-$175 | 2P: $60-$175 | XP: $10 | F17 |
| | 4/1-6/30 & 9/4-3/31 [CP] | 1P: $50-$120 | 2P: $50-$120 | XP: $10 | F17 |

Location: I-75, exit 29, just e. 120 Senate Dr 45050. Fax: 513/539-2992. **Facility:** 68 one-bedroom standard units, some with whirlpools. 3 stories, interior corridors. *Bath:* combo or shower only. **Parking:** on-site. **Terms:** 14 day cancellation notice. **Amenities:** extended cable TV, voice mail, safes (fee), hair dryers. *Some:* irons. **Pool(s):** small heated indoor. **Guest Services:** coin laundry. **Business Services:** meeting rooms, fax (fee). **Cards:** AX, CB, DC, DS, JC, MC, VI. **Special Amenities:** free continental breakfast and free local telephone calls. *(See color ad p 578)*

SOME UNITS

🆂🄳 📶 🏊 🛗 📹 DATA PORT 🖨 / ⊠ 🔌 📠 💻 /

HAMPTON INN CINCINNATI/MONROE

SAVE
♦♦♦ ♦♦♦

Motel

Phone: 513/539-4400

	4/1-9/30 [ECP]	1P: $69-$89	2P: $75-$95
	10/1-11/30 & 2/1-3/31 [ECP]	1P: $69-$79	2P: $75-$85
	12/1-1/31 [ECP]	1P: $65-$69	2P: $69-$75

Location: I-75, exit 29, just w. 40 New Garver Rd 45050. Fax: 513/539-4664. **Facility:** 50 one-bedroom standard units. 2 stories, interior corridors. **Parking:** on-site. **Amenities:** extended cable TV, video games, high-speed Internet, dual phone lines, voice mail, irons, hair dryers. **Guest Services:** valet laundry. **Business Services:** fax (fee). **Cards:** AX, CB, DC, DS, MC, VI.

SOME UNITS

🆂🄳 🍴 🦻 📹 DATA PORT 💻 🖨 / ⊠ /
FEE

──────── **WHERE TO DINE** ────────

BRANDYWINE INN Historical

♦♦♦ ♦♦♦

American

Dinner: $14-$19   **Phone:** 513/539-8911

Location: I-75, exit 29, 1 mi w on SR 63, 0.3 mi s. 204 S Main St 45050. **Hours:** 6 pm-11 pm. Closed: 12/24, 12/25. **Reservations:** suggested. **Features:** dressy casual; cocktails; a la carte. This family-run, converted hotel/tavern stagecoach stop offers a distinctive dining experience with a menu that changes weekly and includes special tasting dinners, holiday meals and sophisticated, eclectic preparations. Credit cards are not accepted. Smoke free premises. **Parking:** on-site.   ⊠

MONTGOMERY —See Cincinnati p. 582.

MONTPELIER pop. 4,300

──────── **WHERE TO STAY** ────────

RAMADA INN

♦♦♦ ♦♦♦

Motor Inn

Phone: (419)485-5555

| | All Year | 1P: $99-$129 | 2P: $99-$129 |

Location: I-80/90 (Ohio Tpke), exit 13, just s. 13508 SR 15 43543. Fax: 419/485-4621. **Facility:** 159 one-bedroom standard units, some with whirlpools. 3 stories, interior corridors. **Parking:** on-site. **Terms:** check-in 4 pm, 3 day cancellation notice, small pets only. **Amenities:** voice mail, irons, hair dryers. **Pool(s):** heated indoor. **Leisure Activities:** sauna, whirlpool, exercise room. *Fee:* game room. **Guest Services:** valet and coin laundry. **Business Services:** meeting rooms. **Cards:** AX, CB, DC, DS, JC, MC, VI.

SOME UNITS

ASK 🆂🄳 🐾 🍴 🦻 🏊 ⊠ 📹 DATA PORT 💻 🖨 / ⊠ /
FEE

MORAINE pop. 6,000 (See map p. 672; index p. 674)

——— WHERE TO STAY ———

HOLIDAY INN HOTEL & SUITES
Phone: 937/294-1471 **27**
All Year 1P: $79 XP: $10 F12
▼▼▼▼ Motor Inn **Location:** I-75, exit 50A. 2455 Dryden Rd 45439. Fax: 937/294-4282. **Facility:** 178 units. 155 one-bedroom standard units. 23 one-bedroom suites ($99-$129). 2 stories, interior corridors. *Bath:* combo or shower only. **Parking:** on-site. **Terms:** 3 day cancellation notice-fee imposed, package plans, small pets only ($10 extra charge). **Amenities:** dual phone lines, voice mail, irons, hair dryers. **Pool(s):** heated indoor. **Leisure Activities:** whirlpool, exercise room. **Guest Services:** valet laundry. **Business Services:** meeting rooms. **Cards:** AX, CB, DC, DS, JC, MC, VI.

SOME UNITS
(ASK) 🛏 🍴 🐕 🐾 🚊 🎥 📠 💻 🖨 / ✕ 🛢 🖨 /
FEE

SUPER 8 MOTEL-MORAINE
Phone: (937)298-0380 **28**
All Year 1P: $49-$99 XP: $5 F
▼▼▼ Motel **Location:** I-75, exit 50A. 2450 Dryden Rd 45439. Fax: 937/298-0380. **Facility:** 70 one-bedroom standard units. 2 stories, exterior corridors. **Parking:** on-site. **Terms:** 10 day cancellation notice, small pets only ($10 deposit). **Amenities:** extended cable TV. **Pool(s):** outdoor. **Cards:** AX, DS, MC, VI.

SOME UNITS
(ASK) (S/D) 🛏 🍴+ 🚊 🎥 / ✕ /

MORELAND HILLS —See Cleveland p. 627.

MOUNT GILEAD pop. 2,800

——— WHERE TO STAY ———

BEST WESTERN EXECUTIVE INN
Phone: (419)768-2378
(AAA) (SAVE) 5/26-8/31 1P: $68-$74 2P: $75-$80 XP: $7 F11
9/1-9/30 1P: $66-$70 2P: $72-$75 XP: $7 F11
▼▼▼ 4/1-5/25 1P: $56-$60 2P: $62-$70 XP: $7 F11
Motel 10/1-3/31 1P: $55-$60 2P: $60-$70 XP: $5 F11
Location: I-71, exit 151, 1 mi e on SR 95. 3991 CR 172 43338. Fax: 419/768-2718. **Facility:** 33 one-bedroom standard units, some with whirlpools. 2 stories, interior corridors. **Parking:** on-site. **Terms:** [CP] meal plan available. **Amenities:** irons, hair dryers. **Pool(s):** heated outdoor. **Leisure Activities:** pool table. *Fee:* game room. **Cards:** AX, CB, DC, DS, MC, VI. **Special Amenities:** free continental breakfast.

SOME UNITS
(S/D) 🍴+ 🚊 🎥 📠 💻 🖨 / ✕ 🛢 🖨 /

KNIGHTS INN
Phone: (419)946-6010
(AAA) (SAVE) 6/1-9/6 1P: $50-$60 2P: $60-$65 XP: $5 F13
4/1-5/31 1P: $45-$50 2P: $55-$60 XP: $5 F13
▼▼▼ 9/7-10/1 1P: $45-$55 2P: $53-$60 XP: $5 F13
Motel 10/2-3/31 1P: $40-$45 2P: $50-$55 XP: $5 F13
Location: I-71, exit 151, 0.3 mi w. 5898 SR 95 43338. Fax: 419/946-6020. **Facility:** 44 one-bedroom standard units. 1 story, exterior corridors. **Parking:** on-site. **Terms:** pets ($15 deposit). **Guest Services:** coin laundry. **Business Services:** meeting rooms. **Cards:** AX, CB, DC, DS, MC, VI.

SOME UNITS
(S/D) 🛏 🎥 📠 / ✕ 🛢 🖨 🖨 /

MOUNT ORAB —See Cincinnati p. 583.

MOUNT STERLING —See Columbus p. 665.

MOUNT VERNON pop. 14,600

——— WHERE TO STAY ———

HOLIDAY INN EXPRESS
Phone: (740)392-1900
All Year [CP] 1P: $71-$80 2P: $71-$80 XP: $6 F19
▼▼▼ Motel **Location:** 3 mi e on US 36. 11555 Upper Gilchrist Rd 43050. Fax: 740/392-1925. **Facility:** 70 one-bedroom standard units, some with whirlpools. 3 stories, interior corridors. *Bath:* combo or shower only. **Parking:** on-site. **Terms:** 14 day cancellation notice, pets (in smoking units). **Amenities:** extended cable TV, voice mail, irons, hair dryers. **Pool(s):** heated indoor. **Leisure Activities:** whirlpool. **Guest Services:** valet and coin laundry. **Business Services:** meeting rooms. **Cards:** AX, CB, DC, DS, JC, MC, VI.

SOME UNITS
(ASK) (S/D) 🛏 🛏 (&M) 🐾 🚊 🎥 📠 💻 🖨 / ✕ (VCR) 🛢 🖨 /
FEE FEE

SUPER 8 MOTEL-MT VERNON
Phone: (740)397-8885
All Year 1P: $52-$62 2P: $57-$67 XP: $5 F12
▼▼▼ Motel **Location:** 1.8 mi e on US 36. 1000 Coshocton Rd 43050. Fax: 740/397-8885. **Facility:** 48 one-bedroom standard units, some with whirlpools. 2 stories, interior corridors. *Bath:* combo or shower only. **Parking:** on-site. **Terms:** 7 day cancellation notice. **Amenities:** extended cable TV, safes. **Pool(s):** heated indoor. **Leisure Activities:** whirlpool. **Guest Services:** coin laundry. **Business Services:** meeting rooms. **Cards:** AX, CB, DC, DS, MC, VI.

SOME UNITS
(ASK) (S/D) (&M) 🐕 🚊 🎥 📠 🖨 / ✕ 🛢 🖨 💻 /
FEE FEE

—— WHERE TO DINE ——

THE ALCOVE
◈◈ ◈◈
American

Lunch: $6-$10   **Dinner:** $10-$19   Phone: 740/392-3076
Location: Center. 116 S Main St 43050. **Hours:** 11 am-9 pm, Fri & Sat-9:30 pm. Closed major holidays; also Sun. **Reservations:** suggested. **Features:** casual dress; children's menu; carryout; cocktails & lounge. The long-established restaurant, which dates back to the early 20th-century, is a gathering place for locals to enjoy light tea-room fare, such as sandwiches, salads, pasta and desserts. Heartier appetites appreciate the specialty prime rib. **Parking:** street. **Cards:** AX, DC, DS, MC, VI.

MOUNT VICTORY

—— WHERE TO DINE ——

—— *The following restaurant has not been evaluated by AAA* ——
but is listed for your information only.

PLAZA INN
[fyi]

Phone: 937/354-2851
Not evaluated. **Location:** 491 Main St 43340. Established circa 1959, the family restaurant specializes in a variety of buffets.

NAPOLEON pop. 8,900

—— WHERE TO STAY ——

HOLIDAY INN EXPRESS HOTEL & SUITES
AAA [SAVE]
◈◈◈
Motel

Phone: 419/592-5599
All Year   1P: $77   2P: $77   XP: $7   F18
Location: Jct US 6 and 24, just n on SR 108. 590 Bonaparte Dr 43545. Fax: 419/592-5595. **Facility:** 56 one-bedroom standard units, some with whirlpools. 2 stories, interior corridors. *Bath:* combo or shower only. **Parking:** on-site. **Terms:** 3 day cancellation notice. **Amenities:** extended cable TV, irons, hair dryers. **Pool(s):** small heated indoor. **Leisure Activities:** whirlpool, exercise room. **Guest Services:** valet and coin laundry. **Business Services:** meeting rooms. **Cards:** AX, CB, DC, DS, JC, MC, VI. **Special Amenities:** free continental breakfast and free local telephone calls.

SOME UNITS
[S/D] [&M] [&] [⌖] [➳] [▦] [DATA PORT] [🖨] / [✕] [🛏] [🖼] /

NEWARK —See Columbus p. 665.

NEW CARLISLE pop. 6,000

—— WHERE TO DINE ——

MEL-O-DEE RESTAURANT
AAA
◈
American

Lunch: $6-$12   **Dinner:** $7-$12   Phone: 937/849-1378
Location: I-70, exit 41, 1.5 mi n on SR 235. 2350 Dayton Lakeview Rd 45344. **Hours:** 6 am-10 pm, Fri & Sat-11 pm. Closed: 12/25. **Features:** casual dress; children's menu; carryout. The colorful work of local artists hangs on the walls of the comfortable, family-oriented restaurant. The menu centers on home-style food, such as broasted chicken served with coleslaw and freshly baked bread. Service is attentive and friendly. **Parking:** on-site. **Cards:** MC, VI.

[✕]

NEW CONCORD pop. 2,100

—— WHERE TO STAY ——

FRIENDSHIP HOUSE BED & BREAKFAST
◈◈ ◈◈
Historic Bed
& Breakfast

Phone: 740/826-7397
All Year   1P: $75-$85   2P: $75-$85   XP: $15
Location: I-70, exit 169, 0.9 mi n on SR 83, just e. 62 W Main St 43762. **Facility:** Smoke free premises. 4 one-bedroom standard units. 2 stories, interior corridors. *Bath:* combo or shower only. **Parking:** on-site. **Terms:** 7 day cancellation notice. **Amenities:** extended cable TV. **Leisure Activities:** bicycles. **Business Services:** meeting rooms. **Cards:** MC, VI.

SOME UNITS
[✕] [🐾] / [VCR] [🛏] [🖼] [🖥] /

NEW PARIS pop. 1,800

—— WHERE TO STAY ——

FAIRFIELD INN BY MARRIOTT
AAA [SAVE]
◈◈◈
Motel

Phone: (937)437-8009
5/1-8/31 [ECP]   1P: $60-$65   2P: $60-$65
9/1-3/31 [ECP]   1P: $50-$62   2P: $50-$62
4/1-4/30 [ECP]   1P: $57-$60   2P: $57-$60
Location: I-70, exit 156B. 9797 Rt 40 W 45347. Fax: 937/437-8306. **Facility:** 57 one-bedroom standard units. 3 stories, interior corridors. *Bath:* combo or shower only. **Parking:** on-site. **Amenities:** irons. **Pool(s):** heated indoor. **Leisure Activities:** whirlpool. **Guest Services:** coin laundry. **Cards:** AX, CB, DC, DS, MC, VI. **Special Amenities:** free continental breakfast and free local telephone calls. *(See color ad card insert)*

SOME UNITS
[S/D] [🛗] [&M] [&] [⌖] [➳] [🕂] [▦] [DATA PORT] [🖨] / [✕] [🖼]

NEW PHILADELPHIA pop. 15,700

——— **WHERE TO STAY** ———

DAYS INN-NEW PHILADELPHIA   Phone: (330)339-6644

AAA SAVE   4/1-10/31   1P: $63   2P: $69   XP: $6   F17
             11/1-3/31   1P: $48   2P: $53   XP: $6   F17

Motel   **Location:** I-77, exit 81, just e. 1281 W High St 44663. Fax: 330/339-3774. **Facility:** 104 one-bedroom standard
             units, some with whirlpools. 2 stories, interior corridors. **Parking:** on-site. **Terms:** [ECP] meal plan available,
             pets ($10 deposit). **Amenities:** safes (fee), hair dryers. **Pool(s):** heated indoor. **Leisure Activities:** whirlpool.
             Guest Services: valet laundry. **Business Services:** meeting rooms. **Cards:** AX, CB, DC, DS, JC, MC, VI.
Special Amenities: free continental breakfast and free newspaper.   SOME UNITS

HAMPTON INN   Phone: (330)339-7000

SAVE   6/15-10/31 [ECP]   1P: $85-$99   2P: $85-$99
             4/1-6/14 & 11/1-3/31 [ECP] 1P: $69-$89   2P: $69-$89

Motel   **Location:** I-77, exit 81, just e. 1299 W High St 44663. Fax: 330/339-6609. **Facility:** 60 one-bedroom standard
             units, some with whirlpools. 3 stories. *Bath:* combo or shower only. **Parking:** on-site. **Terms:** 7 day cancel-
             lation notice, pets ($50 deposit). **Amenities:** extended cable TV, dual phone lines, voice mail, irons, hair
             dryers. **Pool(s):** heated indoor. **Leisure Activities:** whirlpool, exercise room. **Guest Services:** valet and coin
laundry. **Business Services:** meeting rooms, business center. **Cards:** AX, DC, DS, MC, VI.
                                                                                         SOME UNITS

HOLIDAY INN-NEW PHILADELPHIA/ DOVER   Phone: (330)339-7731

             6/16-11/1 [ECP]   1P: $79-$99   2P: $79-$99
             4/1-6/15 & 11/2-3/31 [ECP] 1P: $69-$79   2P: $69-$79

Motor Inn   **Location:** I-77, exit 81, 0.4 mi e. 131 Bluebell Dr SW 44663. Fax: 330/339-1565. **Facility:** 108 one-bedroom stan-
             dard units, some with whirlpools. 2 stories, interior corridors. *Bath:* combo or shower only. **Parking:** on-site.
Terms: package plans, pets ($15 fee). **Amenities:** extended cable TV, irons, hair dryers. **Pool(s):** outdoor, heated indoor.
Leisure Activities: whirlpool, exercise room. **Guest Services:** valet laundry. **Business Services:** conference facilities.
Cards: AX, DC, DS, MC, VI.
                                                                                         SOME UNITS
                                                                            FEE

MOTEL 6 - 254   Phone: 330/339-6446

             6/13-8/31   1P: $41-$55   2P: $47-$61   XP: $3   F17
             9/1-10/30   1P: $37-$47   2P: $43-$53   XP: $3   F17
             10/31-3/31   1P: $35-$45   2P: $41-$51   XP: $3   F17
Motel   4/1-6/12   1P: $29-$39   2P: $35-$45   XP: $3   F17

Location: I-77, exit 81, 0.4 mi e. 181 Bluebell Dr SW 44663. Fax: 330/339-7436. **Facility:** 83 one-bedroom standard units. 2 stories,
exterior corridors. *Bath:* shower only. **Parking:** on-site. **Terms:** small pets only. **Amenities:** extended cable TV. **Pool(s):** outdoor.
Guest Services: coin laundry. **Cards:** AX, CB, DC, DS, MC, VI.
                                                                                         SOME UNITS

SCHOENBRUNN INN BY CHRISTOPHER   Phone: (330)339-4334

AAA SAVE   All Year   1P: $69-$130   2P: $69-$130   XP: $5   F18

             Location: I-77, exit 81, 0.6 mi e. 1186 W High Ave 44663. Fax: 330/339-5749. **Facility:** 60 one-bedroom standard
             units, some with whirlpools. 2 stories, interior corridors. *Bath:* combo or shower only. **Parking:** on-site.
Motel   **Terms:** 30 day cancellation notice-fee imposed, package plans, pets ($16 fee). **Amenities:** extended cable
             TV, voice mail, irons, hair dryers. **Pool(s):** heated indoor. **Leisure Activities:** sauna, whirlpool, exercise
             room. **Guest Services:** coin laundry. **Business Services:** meeting rooms. **Cards:** AX, DC, DS, MC, VI.
Special Amenities: free continental breakfast and free local telephone calls.   SOME UNITS
                                                                            FEE

SUPER 8 MOTEL   Phone: (330)339-6500

             6/1-11/1   2P: $60-$70
             4/1-5/31   2P: $50-$60
Motel   11/2-3/31   2P: $56

             Location: I-77, exit 81, 0.4 mi e. 131 1/2 Blue-Bell Dr 44663. Fax: 330/339-6500. **Facility:** 42 one-bedroom stan-
dard units. 2 stories, interior corridors. **Parking:** on-site. **Amenities:** extended cable TV. **Cards:** AX, CB, DC, DS, MC, VI.
                                                                                         SOME UNITS
                                                                            FEE

——— **WHERE TO DINE** ———

DANTE'S PIZZA & PASTA HOUSE   **Lunch:** $5-$8   **Dinner:** $8-$12   **Phone:** 330/339-4444

             Location: Just w. 261 W High Ave 44663. **Hours:** 11 am-10 pm, Fri-11 pm, Sat 4 pm-11 pm. Closed major
             holidays; also Sun. **Features:** casual dress; carryout; beer & wine only. This restored Victorian home
Italian   downtown has seating in various elegantly decorated rooms yet retains a casual atmosphere. Many
             homemade dishes, such as the delicious Italian sausage braid, line a menu with all the classic Italian
favorites. Dressings, sauces and pasta all are made on the premises. Porcini sauce, prepared from a family recipe, is
available with most selections. Service is efficient, yet paced to make dining a relaxing, enjoyable experience. Smoke free
premises. **Parking:** on-site. **Cards:** AX, DC, DS, MC, VI.

RANDALLS

♢
American

Lunch: $6-$10   **Dinner:** $9-$14   **Phone:** 330/339-7667
Location: I-77, exit 81, 0.5 mi e on SR 39 to first light, then 1 mi se. 1013 Front Ave SW 44663. **Hours:** 7 am-8 pm, Fri & Sat-8:30 pm, Sun 11 am-3 pm. Closed: 5/27, 9/2, 12/24, 12/25. **Reservations:** suggested. **Features:** casual dress; Sunday brunch; children's menu; salad bar. Homemade soup and hand-rolled cinnamon buns are a tradition at the cozy, family-friendly restaurant. Menu favorites include Swiss steak, ham loaf and prime rib, as well as such desserts as hot fudge cake and mouthwatering Amish-style pies. **Parking:** on-site. **Cards:** MC, VI.

The following restaurants have not been evaluated by AAA but are listed for your information only.

COURT HOUSE CAFE

[fyi]

Phone: 330/343-7896
Not evaluated. **Location:** 110 S Broadway 44663. Daily specials are popular with devoted local clientele at this downtown favorite restaurant.

HOG HEAVEN

[fyi]

Phone: 330/308-0509
Not evaluated. **Location:** 152 Front St SW 44663. A popular place for good-sized portions of barbecue, this spot is a favorite for take-out food.

LAM'S ORIENTAL CUISINE

[fyi]

Phone: 330/343-9141
Not evaluated. **Location:** 347 Tuscarawas Ave NW 44663. Although the menu centers on large, reasonably priced selections of Chinese food, it also includes Americanized choices.

UNCLE PRIMO'S

[fyi]

Phone: 330/364-2349
Not evaluated. **Location:** Off Fourth St; behind Honda store. 435 Minnich Ave 44663. The chefs prepare everything, including coastal South specialties, from scratch.

NEWTON FALLS pop. 4,900

──── WHERE TO STAY ────

RODEWAY INN

ⓐⓐⓐ [SAVE]
♢
Motel

Phone: (330)872-0988
All Year   1P: $35-$89   2P: $35-$89   XP: $5   F17
Location: I-80, exit 209, just w. 4248 SR 5 44444. Fax: 330/872-1207. **Facility:** 35 one-bedroom standard units. 1 story, exterior corridors. **Parking:** on-site. **Terms:** cancellation fee imposed, pets ($5 extra charge). **Cards:** AX, DC, DS, MC, VI. **Special Amenities:** free continental breakfast and free local telephone calls.

SOME UNITS
[S/D] [🐕] [✆] [DATA PORT] [🖨] / [✕] [🔒] /
FEE

NILES pop. 21,100

──── WHERE TO STAY ────

DAY'S INN

ⓐⓐⓐ [SAVE]
♢ ♢
Motel

Phone: (330)544-1301
All Year   1P: $55-$65   2P: $60-$70   XP: $10   F18
Location: I-80, exit 227, 4 mi w on US 422. 1300 Youngstown-Warren Rd 44446. Fax: 330/544-0259. **Facility:** 74 one-bedroom standard units. 2 stories, interior/exterior corridors. **Parking:** on-site. **Amenities:** extended cable TV, hair dryers. **Pool(s):** outdoor. **Cards:** AX, DC, DS, MC, VI. **Special Amenities:** free continental breakfast and free newspaper.

SOME UNITS
[S/D] [📶] [🏊] [✆] [🔒] [🖨] / [✕] /

──── WHERE TO DINE ────

ALBERINI'S

ⓐⓐⓐ
♢ ♢ ♢
Nouvelle Italian

Lunch: $8-$12   **Dinner:** $13-$29   **Phone:** 330/652-5895
Location: I-80, exit 227, 4 mi n, then 4.5 mi e on US 422. 1201 Youngstown Rd 44446. **Hours:** 11:30 am-11 pm, Fri & Sat-1 am. Closed major holidays; also Sun. **Reservations:** suggested. **Features:** dressy casual; carryout; cocktails & lounge. Enjoy fine dining in a sociable and unpretentious atmosphere where menu selections include certified Angus beef, fresh seafood and classic Italian cuisine. Veal takes center stage on the list of house specialties along with tiramisu for dessert. **Parking:** on-site. **Cards:** AX, DC, DS, MC, VI.

PJ SNAPPERS

♢ ♢
Seafood
DS, MC, VI.

Lunch: $6-$9   **Dinner:** $10-$20   **Phone:** 330/505-9997
Location: I-80, exit 227, 5 mi nw on US 422. 5125 Youngstown-Warren Rd 44446. **Hours:** 11:30 am-10 pm, Fri & Sat-11 pm, Sun noon-9 pm. Closed major holidays. **Features:** casual dress; children's menu; early bird specials; carryout; cocktails. This popular spot has an extensive menu with daily specials and homemade soups. Lobster Scampi and Red Snapper Francoise are two local favorites. **Parking:** on-site. **Cards:** AX, DS, MC, VI.

The following restaurants have not been evaluated by AAA but are listed for your information only.

EL RODEO

[fyi]

Phone: 330/505-1093
Not evaluated. **Location:** 5400 Youngstown-Warren Rd 44446. Wallet-friendly Mexican dishes are served piping hot and in generous portions.

THE GREAT AMERICAN STEAK-OUT

[fyi]

Phone: 330/652-2254
Not evaluated. **Location:** 5115 Youngstown-Warren Rd 44446. Top-quality beef prepared over a wood-fired grill is at the heart of the menu.

OLD MAIN ALE CHOWDER HOUSE   Phone: 330/652-2300
(fyi)   Not evaluated. **Location:** 40 S Main St 44446. Old World charm exudes from the quaint pub, just a short walk from the McKinley Birthplace Memorial.

NORTH CANTON pop. 14,700—See also CANTON.

──────── WHERE TO STAY ────────

BEST WESTERN NORTH CANTON   Phone: (330)497-8799
▽▽▽   6/1-8/31 [ECP]   1P: $63-$94   2P: $68-$99   XP: $5   F18
      4/1-5/31 & 9/1-10/31 [ECP]   1P: $59-$84   2P: $64-$89   XP: $5   F18
Motel 11/1-3/31 [ECP]   1P: $49-$74   2P: $54-$79   XP: $5   F18
      Location: I-77, exit 111, just w. 6889 Sunset Strip Ave 44720. Fax: 330/497-8707. **Facility:** 54 one-bedroom standard units, some with whirlpools. 2 stories, interior corridors. *Bath:* combo or shower only. **Parking:** on-site. **Terms:** cancellation fee imposed, package plans. **Amenities:** extended cable TV, irons, hair dryers. **Pool(s):** heated indoor. **Leisure Activities:** whirlpool, exercise room. **Guest Services:** coin laundry. **Business Services:** meeting rooms. **Cards:** AX, CB, DC, DS, MC, VI.
                                                             SOME UNITS
      (ASK) (S/D) (🖥) (🏊) (▨) (DATA PORT) (📶) (📺) (🛏) (📠) / (✕) /
                              FEE

HOLIDAY INN CANTON   Phone: (330)494-2770
(AAA) (SAVE)   6/1-9/30   1P: $79-$125   2P: $79-$125   XP: $8   F19
             4/1-5/31 & 10/1-3/31   1P: $65-$95   2P: $65-$95   XP: $8   F19
▽▽▽▽ **Location:** I-77, exit 109, 0.5 mi e. 4520 Everhard Rd NW 44718. Fax: 330/494-6473. **Facility:** 194 one-bedroom standard units. 2-3 stories, interior corridors. *Bath:* combo or shower only. **Parking:** on-site. **Terms:** package plans, small pets only. **Amenities:** extended cable TV, video games, dual phone lines, voice mail, irons, hair
Motor Inn   dryers. **Dining:** restaurant, 6:30 am-2 & 5-10 pm, Sat & Sun from 7 am, $7-$14; cocktails, entertainment.
Pool(s): heated outdoor. **Leisure Activities:** exercise room. *Fee:* game room. **Guest Services:** valet laundry, area transportation-within 2 mi. **Business Services:** conference facilities. **Cards:** AX, CB, DC, DS, JC, MC, VI.
                                                             SOME UNITS
      (S/D) (✈) (🏇) (🍴) (🍸) (▨) (🏊) (▨) (DATA PORT) (📺) (📠) / (✕) (🛏) /
                              FEE

MICROTEL INN & SUITES   Phone: (330)966-7551
▽▽ ▽▽▽ All Year [CP]   1P: $59-$109   2P: $69-$139   XP: $10   F18
       Location: I-77, exit 111, just w. 7046 Sunset Strip Ave 44720. Fax: 330/966-9581. **Facility:** 62 one-bedroom standard units. 3 stories, interior corridors. *Bath:* combo or shower only. **Amenities:** extended cable TV, voice mail, irons, hair dryers. **Pool(s):** heated indoor. **Leisure Activi-
Motel   ties:** whirlpool, exercise room. **Guest Services:** coin laundry. **Cards:** AX, DC, DS, MC, VI.
                                                             SOME UNITS
      (ASK) (S/D) (▨) (🏊) (▨) (DATA PORT) (📠) / (✕) (🛏) (📺) (📶) /
                              FEE

SUPER 8 MOTEL CANTON NORTH   Phone: (330)492-5030
▽▽▽▽ 6/1-12/31 [ECP]   1P: $50-$60   2P: $65   XP: $5   F12
      4/1-5/31 & 1/1-3/31 [ECP]   1P: $45-$55   2P: $60   XP: $5   F12
Motel **Location:** I-77, exit 109 southbound, 0.3 mi e on Everhard Rd, 0.3 mi s on Whipple Ave; exit 109A northbound, 0.3 mi s on Whipple. 3950 Convenience Cir NW 44718. Fax: 330/492-5030. **Facility:** 101 one-bedroom standard units, some with whirlpools. 1 story, exterior corridors. **Parking:** on-site. **Terms:** check-in 4 pm, small pets only ($5 extra charge). **Amenities:** *Some:* hair dryers. **Pool(s):** outdoor. **Cards:** AX, DC, DS, MC, VI.
                                                             SOME UNITS
      (ASK) (S/D) (🐕) (🏊) (▨) (DATA PORT) (📠) / (✕) (🛏) (📶) (📺) /

──────── WHERE TO DINE ────────

356TH FIGHTER GROUP   Lunch: $5-$9   Dinner: $10-$19   Phone: 330/494-3500
(AAA)   **Location:** Behind Akron-Canton Airport. 4919 Mt. Pleasant Rd 44720. **Hours:** 11 am-10 pm, Fri & Sat-11 pm, Sun
▽▽▽   10:30 am-2:30 & 4-10 pm. Closed: 12/25. **Reservations:** suggested. **Features:** casual dress; Sunday brunch; children's menu; early bird specials; carryout; cocktails & lounge; entertainment. The charming French farmhouse is the kind of place Snoopy would go to have a root beer and curse the Red Baron.
American Memorabilia from both world wars decorates the walls; big-band music plays in the background. Seafood, steaks and pasta make up the menu. **Parking:** on-site. **Cards:** AX, DC, DS, MC, VI.
                                                                            (✕)

PANCHO'S SOUTHWESTERN GRILL   Lunch: $5-$8   Dinner: $8-$14   Phone: 330/497-0744
▽▽ ▽▽ **Location:** I-77, exit 109, 0.3 mi w on Everhard, 1.5 mi n. 6081 Dressler Rd 44720. **Hours:** 11 am-10 pm, Fri &
       Sat-11 pm. Closed major holidays. **Features:** casual dress; children's menu; carryout; cocktails & lounge.
Southwestern The menu centers on traditional dishes, such as burritos and enchiladas, with a few creative surprises to keep things interesting. Prices are reasonable and servings are plentiful. The dining room is bright and colorful, with Southwestern decorations. **Parking:** on-site. **Cards:** AX, DC, DS, MC, VI.
                                                                            (✕)

──────── *The following restaurants have not been evaluated by AAA* ────────
but are listed for your information only.

CITE GRILLE   Phone: 330/494-6758
(fyi)   Not evaluated. **Location:** I-77 exit 109, just e on Everhard Rd, 0.6 mi n. 6041 Whipple Ave 44720. Specialties on the casually elegant restaurant's menu of wood-fired rotisserie and grill dishes reflect a European flair.

RED ROBIN RESTAURANT   Phone: 330/305-1080
(fyi)   Not evaluated. **Location:** 6522 Sunset Strip Ave NW 44720. The conveniently located restaurant presents a menu of reliable choices, all served by the friendly staff.

NORTH HAMPTON pop. 400

——— WHERE TO STAY ———

MISS MOLLIE D'S VICTORIAN TEA ROOM/BED & BREAKFAST   **Phone:** 937/964-8228

▼▼▼ Property failed to provide current rates

Bed & Breakfast **Location:** 6 mi w of city of Springfield; 3 mi e of jct SR 235 and 41. 59 E Clark St 45349 (PO Box 114). Fax: 937/964-8118. **Facility:** Designated smoking area. 4 one-bedroom standard units. 2 stories, interior corridors. *Bath:* some shared or private. **Parking:** on-site. **Guest Services:** complimentary laundry.

NORTH KINGSVILLE

——— WHERE TO DINE ———

——— *The following restaurant has not been evaluated by AAA* ———
but is listed for your information only.

COVERED BRIDGE PIZZA PARLOR   **Phone:** 440/224-2252

[fyi] Not evaluated. **Location:** 6541 S Main St. A friendly wait staff serves menu selections here.

NORTH LIMA pop. 900

——— WHERE TO STAY ———

RODEWAY INN   **Phone:** (330)549-3988

6/1-9/6	1P: $50	2P: $65	XP: $5	F16
4/1-5/31 & 9/7-3/31	1P: $40	2P: $50	XP: $5	F16

Motel **Location:** I-76, exit 232, 0.3 mi s on SR 7. 10650 Market St 44452. Fax: 330/549-1976. **Facility:** 41 one-bedroom standard units. 1 story, exterior corridors. **Parking:** on-site. **Terms:** small pets only ($5 extra charge). **Amenities:** extended cable TV. **Cards:** AX, CB, DC, DS, MC, VI.

SOME UNITS

SUPER 8 MOTEL   **Phone:** (330)549-2187

5/26-9/5 [CP]	1P: $49-$85	2P: $49-$85	XP: $5	F12
4/1-5/25 [CP]	1P: $40-$65	2P: $40-$65	XP: $5	F12
9/6-11/30 [CP]	1P: $40-$55	2P: $40-$55	XP: $5	F12
12/1-3/31 [CP]	1P: $32-$50	2P: $32-$50	XP: $5	F12

Motel **Location:** I-76 (Ohio Tpke), exit 232, 0.7 mi n. 10076 Market St 44452. Fax: 330/549-0275. **Facility:** 87 one-bedroom standard units, some with whirlpools. 2 stories, exterior corridors. **Parking:** on-site. **Terms:** 7 day cancellation notice, pets ($5 extra charge). **Amenities:** extended cable TV. *Some:* hair dryers. **Pool(s):** outdoor. **Cards:** AX, DC, DS, MC, VI.

SOME UNITS

NORTH OLMSTED —*See Cleveland p. 627.*

NORTH RIDGEVILLE pop. 21,600 (See map p. 600; index p. 605)

——— WHERE TO STAY ———

SUPER 8 MOTEL   **Phone:** (440)327-0500   **109**

7/4-9/1 [ECP]	1P: $56-$79	2P: $66-$89	XP: $8	F12
5/24-7/3 [ECP]	1P: $49-$74	2P: $54-$84	XP: $8	F12
4/1-5/23 [ECP]	1P: $37-$52	2P: $48-$58	XP: $8	F12
9/2-3/31 [ECP]	1P: $39-$46	2P: $48-$56	XP: $8	F12

Motel **Location:** I-80, exit 152, 0.5 mi w on SR 10. 32801 Lorain Rd 44039. Fax: 440/327-0500. **Facility:** 55 one-bedroom standard units, some with whirlpools. 2 stories, interior corridors. **Parking:** on-site. **Guest Services:** coin laundry. **Cards:** AX, CB, DC, DS, MC, VI. *(See color ad p 739)*

SOME UNITS

TRAVELODGE NORTH RIDGEVILLE   **Phone:** (440)327-6311   **108**

All Year [CP]	1P: $41-$66	2P: $41-$66	XP: $5
			F12

Motel **Location:** I-80, exit 152, 0.6 mi w on SR 10. 32751 Lorain Rd 44039. Fax: 440/327-8412. **Facility:** 87 one-bedroom standard units. 2 stories, exterior corridors. *Bath:* shower only. **Parking:** on-site. **Terms:** 5 day cancellation notice. **Cards:** AX, DC, DS, MC, VI.

SOME UNITS

NORTHWOOD pop. 5,500 (See map p. 756; index p. 758)

——— WHERE TO STAY ———

MICROTEL INN & SUITES   **Phone:** (419)662-1200   **35**

All Year	1P: $49-$69	2P: $59-$79	XP: $5 F16

Motel **Location:** I-75, exit 198, just e on Wales Rd, then just s on Oregon Rd. 2600 Lauren Ln 43619. Fax: 419/662-1208. **Facility:** 82 one-bedroom standard units. 3 stories, interior corridors. *Bath:* combo or shower only. **Parking:** on-site. **Terms:** 10 day cancellation notice. **Amenities:** extended cable TV, voice mail. **Pool(s):** heated indoor. **Leisure Activities:** whirlpool, exercise room. **Guest Services:** valet and coin laundry. **Business Services:** meeting rooms, fax (fee). **Cards:** AX, DC, DS, MC, VI.

SOME UNITS

(See map p. 756)

─── WHERE TO DINE ───

SALLOCK'S STEAKHOUSE **Lunch:** $4-$6 **Dinner:** $7-$15 **Phone:** 419/693-1758 ⑮
▽▽▽ ▽▽▽ **Location:** I-280, exit 6 (Woodville/Curtice Rd), 0.5 mi w. 2900 Woodville Rd 43619. **Hours:** 11 am-9 pm, Fri-10 pm,
Steak House Sat noon-10 pm, Sun from noon. Closed major holidays; also Memorial weekend. **Features:** casual dress;
children's menu; carryout; cocktails; a la carte. Sallock's Steakhouse serves everything from T-bones and
ribeyes to Lebanese family recipes of ghanouj and fatayer. Enjoy their continental menu with drink specials
at the bar. **Parking:** on-site. **Cards:** AX, DS, MC, VI. ✕

NORTON

─── WHERE TO DINE ───

─── *The following restaurants have not been evaluated by AAA* ───
but are listed for your information only.

OLDE LOYAL OAK TAVERN **Phone:** 330/825-8280
fyi Not evaluated. **Location:** 3044 Wadsworth Rd. The tavern offers many wine selections from its large cellar.

TOMASOS ITALIAN VILLA **Phone:** 330/745-6063
fyi Not evaluated. **Location:** 3271 Barber Rd 44281. Traditional favorites are prepared alongside daily specials and
homemade soups.

NORWALK pop. 14,700

─── WHERE TO STAY ───

AMERIHOST INN AND SUITES-NORWALK **Phone:** (419)663-1922
AAA SAVE 7/1-9/30 [ECP] 1P: $63-$83 2P: $67-$87 XP: $5 F18
▽▽▽▽ 4/1-6/30 [ECP] 1P: $44-$80 2P: $59-$84 XP: $5 F18
  10/1-12/31 [ECP] 1P: $37-$71 2P: $42-$76 XP: $5 F18
Hotel 1/1-3/31 [ECP] 1P: $34-$45 2P: $37-$49 XP: $5 F18
Location: 4 mi n on SR 250; 5 mi s of I-80/90 (Ohio Tpke). 415 Milan Ave 44857. Fax: 419/663-1853. **Facility:** 64
one-bedroom standard units, some with whirlpools. 3 stories, interior corridors. **Parking:** on-site. **Terms:** cancellation fee imposed. **Amenities:** extended cable TV, voice mail, safes (fee); irons, hair dryers. **Pool(s):** heated indoor. **Leisure Activities:** exercise room. **Business Services:** meeting rooms. **Cards:** AX, CB, DC, DS, JC, MC, VI. **Special Amenities:** free continental breakfast and free local telephone calls. *(See color ad p 736)*
SOME UNITS

BEST WESTERN **Phone:** (419)663-3501
AAA SAVE 5/24-8/31 [ECP] 1P: $79-$129 2P: $84-$134 XP: $5 F18
▽▽▽▽ 9/1-10/31 [ECP] 1P: $59-$99 2P: $64-$104 XP: $85 F18
  4/1-5/23 [ECP] 1P: $49-$59 2P: $54-$64 XP: $5 F18
Motel 11/1-3/31 [ECP] 1P: $39-$49 2P: $44-$54 XP: $5 F18
Location: 3.5 mi n on SR 250; 5.5 mi s of I-80/90 (Ohio Tpke). 351 Milan Ave 44857. Fax: 419/663-3601. **Facility:** 61
one-bedroom standard units, some with whirlpools. 2 stories, interior corridors. *Bath:* combo or shower only.
Parking: on-site. **Terms:** cancellation fee imposed. **Amenities:** extended cable TV. *Some:* irons, hair dryers. **Pool(s):** heated
indoor. **Leisure Activities:** sauna, whirlpool, exercise room. **Business Services:** meeting rooms. **Cards:** AX, CB, DC, DS, JC,
MC, VI. **Special Amenities:** free continental breakfast and free local telephone calls. *(See color ad p 736)*
SOME UNITS

ECONO LODGE **Phone:** 419/668-5656
SAVE 6/22-9/1 [ECP] 1P: $48-$118 2P: $48-$118 XP: $5 F17
  4/1-6/21 [ECP] 1P: $32-$78 2P: $36-$78 XP: $5 F17
▽▽ 9/2-10/26 [ECP] 1P: $32-$68 2P: $32-$68 XP: $5 F17
Motel 10/27-3/31 [ECP] 1P: $32-$38 2P: $36-$42 XP: $5 F17
Location: 3 mi n on SR 250; 6 mi s of I-80/90 (Ohio Tpke), on SR 250. 342 Milan Ave 44857 (2027 Cleveland Rd,
SANDUSKY, 44870). Fax: 419/668-5656. **Facility:** 45 one-bedroom standard units. 1 story, exterior corridors.
Bath: combo or shower only. **Parking:** on-site. **Terms:** 3 day cancellation notice, pets ($25 deposit). **Amenities:** extended cable
TV. **Pool(s):** heated outdoor. **Leisure Activities:** Fee: game room. **Guest Services:** coin laundry. **Business Services:** meeting
rooms, fax. **Cards:** AX, CB, DC, DS, MC, VI. *(See color ad p 735 & p 739)*
SOME UNITS

GEORGIAN MANOR INN **Phone:** (419)663-8132
AAA SAVE 5/16-9/16 [BP] 1P: $125-$225 2P: $125-$225
▽▽▽▽ ▽▽▽▽ 4/1-5/15 & 9/17-3/31 [BP] 1P: $95-$165 2P: $95-$165
Historic Bed **Location:** Just w of town. 123 W Main St 44857. Fax: 419/668-3542. **Facility:** Elegant public areas and well-
& Breakfast maintained, manicured grounds create a refined ambience at this inn. Smoke free premises. 4 one-bedroom
standard units. 2 stories, interior corridors. **Parking:** on-site. **Terms:** age restrictions may apply, 7 day cancellation notice. **Amenities:** extended cable TV, hair dryers. **Guest Services:** valet laundry. **Business Services:** fax. **Cards:** AX, DC, MC, VI. **Special Amenities:** free continental breakfast and free local telephone
calls.
SOME UNITS

——— **WHERE TO DINE** ———

BERRY'S RESTAURANT   **Lunch:** $4-$7   **Dinner:** $6-$13   **Phone:** 419/668-2394
AAA   **Location:** Downtown. 15 W Main St 44857. **Hours:** 6 am-9 pm. Closed major holidays. **Features:** casual
          dress; children's menu; carryout. The landmark restaurant, build in the mid-1800s, delivers a familiar and
          varied menu of such options as prime rib, chicken marsala, Swiss steak, seafood salad, roast chicken and
American   turkey. A tin ceiling and antiques decorate the warm dining rooms. **Parking:** street. **Cards:** AX, DS, MC, VI.

⊗

NORWOOD —See Cincinnati p. 583.

OAKWOOD (MONTGOMERY COUNTY)

——— **WHERE TO DINE** ———

——— *The following restaurant has not been evaluated by AAA* ———
but is listed for your information only.

THE OAKWOOD CLUB   **Phone:** 937/293-6973
[fyi]   Not evaluated. **Location:** 2414 Far Hills Ave 45419. Creative American entrees are served at this restaurant.

OBERLIN pop. 8,200

——— **WHERE TO STAY** ———

OBERLIN INN   **Phone:** (440)775-1111
          All Year   1P: $115-$195   2P: $135-$215   XP: $10   F17
          Location: Center; on SR 58; at College and Main sts. 7 N Main St 44074. Fax: 440/775-0676. **Facility:** 72 units. 70
Motor Inn one-bedroom standard units. 2 one-bedroom suites. 2-3 stories, interior/exterior corridors. **Parking:** on-site.
          Terms: check-in 4 pm, package plans, small pets only. **Amenities:** extended cable TV. **Guest Services:** coin
laundry. **Business Services:** meeting rooms. **Cards:** AX, DC, DS, MC, VI.

SOME UNITS
🐕 🍴 📺 🏊 📶 [DATA PORT] 💻 🖨 / ⊗ 📞 FEE

OREGON pop. 18,300   (See map p. 756; index p. 758)

——— **WHERE TO STAY** ———

COMFORT INN EAST   **Phone:** (419)691-8911   [38]
AAA [SAVE]   4/1-9/15   1P: $64   2P: $74   XP: $5   F18
             9/16-3/31   1P: $59   2P: $69   XP: $5   F18
          Location: I-280, exit 7, just n on access road, then 0.5 mi e on SR 2 (Navarre Ave). 2930 Navarre Ave 43616.
Motel   Fax: 419/691-2107. **Facility:** 79 one-bedroom standard units, some with efficiencies and/or whirlpools. 2 sto-
          ries, interior corridors. **Parking:** on-site. **Amenities:** extended cable TV, video tape library (fee), voice mail,
          hair dryers. *Some:* irons. **Pool(s):** heated outdoor. **Guest Services:** valet laundry. **Business Services:**
meeting rooms. **Cards:** AX, CB, DC, DS, JC, MC, VI. **Special Amenities:** free continental breakfast and free room upgrade
(subject to availability with advanced reservations). *(See color ad p 759)*

SOME UNITS
[S] 🐕 🍴 📶 🏊 [VCR] 📶 [DATA PORT] 📞 💻 🖨 / ⊗ /

SLEEP INN & SUITES   **Phone:** (419)697-7800   [37]
AAA [SAVE]   4/1-9/15   1P: $69   2P: $79   XP: $5   F18
             9/16-3/31   1P: $64   2P: $74   XP: $5   F18
          Location: I-280, exit 6. 1761 Meijer Cir 43616. Fax: 419/697-7810. **Facility:** 89 one-bedroom standard units,
Motel   some with whirlpools. 3 stories, interior corridors. *Bath:* combo or shower only. **Parking:** on-site. **Terms:** pets
          ($20 fee). **Amenities:** extended cable TV, irons, hair dryers. **Pool(s):** small heated indoor. **Leisure Activi-
          ties:** sauna, steamroom, tanning booth, exercise room. **Guest Services:** coin laundry. **Business Services:**
meeting rooms. **Cards:** AX, CB, DC, DS, MC, VI. **Special Amenities:** free continental breakfast and free local telephone
calls. *(See color ad p 759)*

SOME UNITS
[S] 🐕 🛁 🏊 ⊗ 📶 [DATA PORT] 🖨 / ⊗ 📞 💻 /

ORRVILLE pop. 7,700

——— **WHERE TO STAY** ———

ROYAL STAR INN   **Phone:** 330/683-7827
          5/1-10/31 [ECP]   1P: $64-$69   2P: $69-$74   XP: $5   F16
          11/1-3/31 [ECP]   1P: $55-$64   2P: $55-$68   XP: $5   F16
          4/1-4/30 [ECP]   1P: $55-$62   2P: $55-$68   XP: $5   F16
Motel   **Location:** Jct US 30 and SR 57. 11980 Lincoln Way E 44667. Fax: 330/683-8224. **Facility:** 48 one-bedroom standard units, some with whirlpools. 2 stories, interior corridors. *Bath:* combo or shower only. **Parking:** on-site. **Amenities:** extended
cable TV, voice mail. **Guest Services:** valet laundry. **Business Services:** meeting rooms. **Cards:** AX, DS, MC, VI.

SOME UNITS
[ASK] [DATA PORT] / ⊗ 📞 💻 /

OTTAWA pop. 4,000

------ WHERE TO DINE ------

RED PIG INN

Barbecue

Lunch: $6-$13   **Dinner:** $10-$18   **Phone:** 419/523-6458
Location: 0.7 mi n on SR 65; northeast of downtown. 1470 N Perry 45875. **Hours:** 10 am-11 pm, Fri & Sat-midnight, Sun-10 pm. **Closed:** 12/25. **Reservations:** accepted. **Features:** casual dress; Sunday brunch; children's menu; carryout; cocktails & lounge; buffet. Award-winning barbecue is served in a family friendly atmosphere. Choose from slow roasted slabs of ribs, fire grilled chicken or seafood selections ranging from baked salmon to sweet and sour shrimp. **Parking:** on-site. **Cards:** MC, VI.

OXFORD pop. 18,900

------ WHERE TO STAY ------

AMERIHOST INN AND SUITES-OXFORD

Hotel

Phone: (513)523-2722
All Year [ECP]   1P: $65-$165   2P: $65-$165   XP: $6   F18
Location: 1 mi nw on SR 27. 5190 College Corner Pike 45056. Fax: 513/523-4103. **Facility:** 61 one-bedroom standard units, some with whirlpools. 3 stories, interior corridors. *Bath:* combo or shower only. **Parking:** on-site. **Terms:** 7 day cancellation notice. **Amenities:** voice mail, safes (fee), irons, hair dryers. **Pool(s):** heated indoor. **Leisure Activities:** whirlpool, exercise room. **Business Services:** meeting rooms, fax (fee). **Cards:** AX, CB, DC, DS, JC, MC, VI. **Special Amenities:** free continental breakfast and free newspaper.

SOME UNITS

BEST WESTERN SYCAMORE INN

Motel

Phone: (513)523-0000
5/1-8/31 [ECP]   1P: $79   2P: $89   XP: $5   F12
4/1-4/30 & 9/1-3/31 [ECP]   1P: $69   2P: $79   XP: $5   F12
Location: 0.5 mi n on SR 732. 6 E Sycamore St 45056. Fax: 513/523-2093. **Facility:** 61 one-bedroom standard units, some with whirlpools. 2 stories, interior corridors. **Parking:** on-site. **Amenities:** extended cable TV, irons, hair dryers. **Pool(s):** heated indoor. **Leisure Activities:** whirlpool, limited exercise equipment. **Business Services:** meeting rooms, fax (fee). **Cards:** AX, CB, DC, DS, JC, MC, VI. **Special Amenities:** free continental breakfast and free local telephone calls.

SOME UNITS

HAMPTON INN OXFORD

Motel

Phone: 513/524-0114
All Year   1P: $75-$95   2P: $85-$105
Location: 0.7 mi nw on US 27. 5056 College Corner Pike 45056. Fax: 513/524-1147. **Facility:** 66 one-bedroom standard units, some with whirlpools. 3 stories, interior corridors. *Bath:* combo or shower only. **Parking:** on-site. **Terms:** check-in 4 pm, cancellation fee imposed. **Amenities:** extended cable TV, voice mail, irons. **Pool(s):** small heated indoor. **Leisure Activities:** whirlpool, exercise room. **Guest Services:** valet laundry. **Business Services:** meeting rooms, fax (fee). **Cards:** AX, CB, DC, DS, JC, MC, VI.

SOME UNITS

------ WHERE TO DINE ------

DIPAOLO'S RESTAURANT

American

Lunch: $6-$8   **Dinner:** $12-$24   **Phone:** 513/523-1541
Location: Town center; corner of Beech and High sts. 12 S Beech St 45056. **Hours:** 11:30 am-2 & 5:30-9:30 pm, Fri & Sat-10:30 pm, Sun 11 am-2 & 5:30-9:30 pm. **Closed** major holidays. **Reservations:** suggested. **Features:** casual dress; Sunday brunch; carryout; cocktails. This is a little piece of Italy in the midst of the business community and nearby college campus. Small intimate dining area with sunlight streaming through overhead skylights illuminating glass clothed tabletops and captains chairs. Choice seafood appetizers. Many entrees not your typical Italian fare with alternatives of crayfish, salmon, rock shrimp, and your typical lasagna. Don't leave without viewing the mouth watering dessert tray with homemade tiramisu. **Parking:** on-site (fee). **Cards:** AX, DS, MC, VI.

PEDRO'S STEAKHOUSE

Mexican

Lunch: $4-$7   **Dinner:** $6-$20   **Phone:** 513/523-7529
Location: In town square. 40 E Park Pl 45056. **Hours:** 11 am-11 pm, Fri & Sat-midnight. **Closed:** 11/28, 12/25. **Reservations:** accepted. **Features:** casual dress; children's menu; carryout; cocktails & lounge. The relaxed atmosphere of the college town carries over into this cozy restaurant. The menu shows lots of variety, with certified Angus beef dishes, steaks and plenty of Tex-Mex fare. Dinners come with chips and salsa in two varieties: mild and spicy. **Parking:** on-site. **Cards:** AX, MC, VI.

PAINESVILLE pop. 15,700

------ WHERE TO STAY ------

RENAISSANCE QUAIL HOLLOW RESORT

Resort

Phone: (440)497-1100
All Year   1P: $89-$169   2P: $99-$179   XP: $10   F12
Location: I-90, exit 200, 0.3 mi s on SR 44, then just e on Auburn Rd. 11080 Concord-Hambden Rd 44077-9557. Fax: 440/497-1111. **Facility:** This modern lodge-style resort offers swimming, golf and tennis, as well as large conference facilities. 176 units. 175 one-bedroom standard units, some with whirlpools. 1 one-bedroom suite ($250-$375). 4 stories, interior corridors. **Parking:** on-site. **Terms:** check-in 4 pm, cancellation fee imposed, package plans. **Amenities:** extended cable TV, video games, high-speed Internet, voice mail, irons, hair dryers. *Some:* dual phone lines. **Dining:** dining room, 6:30 am-10 pm, Fri & Sat-11 pm, $15-$25, cocktails. **Pool(s):** heated outdoor, heated indoor, wading. **Leisure Activities:** sauna, whirlpool, 2 tennis courts, exercise room, horseshoes. *Fee:* golf-36 holes. **Guest Services:** gift shop, massage (fee), valet laundry. **Business Services:** conference facilities, business center. **Cards:** AX, CB, DC, DS, JC, MC, VI. *(See color ad card insert)*

SOME UNITS

——— WHERE TO DINE ———

REDHAWK GRILLE
American

Lunch: $5-$8   **Dinner:** $9-$16   **Phone:** 440/354-4040
Location: I-90, exit 200, just n on SR 44. 7481 Auburn Rd 44077. **Hours:** 11:30 am-10 pm, Fri & Sat-11 pm, Sun 4 pm-9 pm. Closed major holidays. **Features:** casual dress; children's menu; carryout; cocktails & lounge. Lots of memorabilia decorates the contemporary-styled dining room. The lively, bustling restaurant delivers mostly traditional fare, such as prime rib and fresh seafood, with a few more inventive choices. Service is efficient and friendly. **Parking:** on-site. **Cards:** AX, DC, DS, MC, VI.

RIDER'S INN   Historical
American

Lunch: $5-$10   **Dinner:** $12-$22   **Phone:** 440/354-8200
Location: On US 20, w of Lake Erie College; in Rider's Inn B&B. 792 Mentor Ave 44077. **Hours:** 11:30 am-9 pm, Fri & Sat-10 pm, Sun 10 am-8 pm. Closed: 5/27, 9/2, 12/25. **Reservations:** suggested. **Features:** casual dress; Sunday brunch; children's menu; carryout; cocktails. The restored 1812 stagecoach stop features white clapboard, large windows and many antique furnishings. The specialty prime rib is seasoned using an original recipe from the 1800s. Freshly baked desserts and breads are an irresistible temptation. **Parking:** on-site. **Cards:** AX, DS, MC, VI.

PARMA —*See Cleveland p. 628.*

PERRYSBURG   pop. 12,600   (See map p. 756; index p. 758)

——— WHERE TO STAY ———

BAYMONT INN & SUITES TOLEDO-PERRYSBURG
Motel

Phone: (419)872-0000   **51**
All Year   1P: $64-$74   2P: $64-$74
Location: I-75, exit 193, just w. 1154 Professional Dr 43551. Fax: 419/872-8650. **Facility:** 99 one-bedroom standard units. 3 stories, interior corridors. *Bath:* combo or shower only. **Parking:** on-site. **Terms:** small pets only. **Amenities:** video games, voice mail, irons, hair dryers. **Guest Services:** complimentary laundry. **Business Services:** meeting rooms. **Cards:** AX, CB, DC, DS, MC, VI. **Special Amenities:** free continental breakfast and free newspaper. *(See color ad opposite title page)*

SOME UNITS

DAYS INN OF TOLEDO-PERRYSBURG
Motel

Phone: (419)874-8771   **50**
All Year [CP]   1P: $65-$80   2P: $75-$90
Location: I-75, exit 193, just e on US 20 and 23. 10667 Fremont Pike 43551. Fax: 419/874-7926. **Facility:** 124 one-bedroom standard units. 2 stories, exterior corridors. **Parking:** on-site. **Terms:** pets ($3 extra charge). **Amenities:** safes (fee), hair dryers. *Some:* irons. **Pool(s):** outdoor. **Guest Services:** coin laundry. **Business Services:** meeting rooms. **Cards:** AX, CB, DC, DS, MC, VI.

SOME UNITS

HOLIDAY INN EXPRESS
Motel

Phone: (419)874-3101   **45**
5/25-9/2 [ECP]   1P: $92   2P: $92   XP: $7   F19
4/1-5/24 & 9/3-3/31 [ECP]   1P: $89   2P: $89   XP: $7   F19
Location: I-75, exit 193, just e on US 20 and 23. 10621 Fremont Pike 43551. Fax: 419/874-0287. **Facility:** 136 one-bedroom standard units. 2 stories, interior corridors. **Parking:** on-site. **Terms:** 3 day cancellation notice. **Amenities:** extended cable TV, video games, dual phone lines, voice mail, irons, hair dryers. **Pool(s):** heated indoor. **Leisure Activities:** sauna, whirlpool, exercise room. **Guest Services:** valet laundry. **Business Services:** conference facilities, fax. **Cards:** AX, CB, DC, DS, JC, MC, VI.

SOME UNITS

(See map p. 756)

HOLIDAY INN-FRENCH QUARTER   Phone: (419)874-3111   47

(AAA) (SAVE)   4/1-12/29 & 1/1-3/31   1P: $120-$180   2P: $120-$180   XP: $10   F18

▽▽▽▽   **Location:** I-75, exit 193, just e on US 20 and 23. 10630 Fremont Pike 43551 (PO Box 268). Fax: 419/874-0198.

Hotel   **Facility:** 299 units. 298 one-bedroom standard units. 1 two-bedroom suite ($230-$350) with efficiency (no utensils). 2-4 stories, interior/exterior corridors. *Bath:* combo or shower only. **Parking:** on-site. **Terms:** open 4/1-12/29 & 1/1-3/31, check-in 4 pm, cancellation fee imposed. **Amenities:** extended cable TV, video games, dual phone lines, voice mail, irons, hair dryers. **Dining:** dining room, restaurant, 6 am-10 pm, Sat-11 pm; Sunday brunch, $10-$17, cocktails, entertainment. **Pool(s):** heated outdoor, heated indoor. **Leisure Activities:** sauna, whirlpool, putting green, exercise room. *Fee:* game room, pool table, table tennis. **Guest Services:** gift shop, complimentary laundry. **Business Services:** conference facilities, business center, PC, fax. **Cards:** AX, CB, DC, DS, MC, VI.

SOME UNITS

⬛ ✈ 🍴 🍽 ⛨ ◻ 🛇 🏊 ✕ 📠 ⬛ 🖨 / ✕ ⬛ 🖼 /
                   FEE   DATA PORT   FEE

HOWARD JOHNSON INN TOLEDO SOUTH   Phone: (419)837-5245   46

(AAA) (SAVE)   5/24-8/31   1P: $36-$49   2P: $40-$55   XP: $3   F18

▽▽▽▽   4/1-5/23 & 9/1-3/31   1P: $34-$38   2P: $39-$45   XP: $3   F18

Motor Inn   **Location:** I-80/90 (Ohio Tpke), exit 71 to I-280, exit 1B. I-280 & Hanley Rd 43551. Fax: 419/837-5245. **Facility:** 142 one-bedroom standard units. 1-2 stories, interior/exterior corridors. **Parking:** on-site. **Terms:** [AP] meal plan available. **Amenities:** hair dryers. **Dining:** restaurant, 7 am-10 pm, Fri & Sat-11 pm, $8-$12, cocktails. **Pool(s):** heated indoor. **Business Services:** meeting rooms, fax. **Cards:** AX, CB, DC, DS, MC, VI.

(See color ad p 726)

SOME UNITS

⬛ 🐕 🍴 🍽 ◻ 🏊 ✕ 📠 ⬛ 🖨 / ✕ ⬛ 🖼 /

RAMADA LIMITED   Phone: (419)837-9500   53

(AAA) (SAVE)   5/1-10/31   1P: $54   2P: $59   XP: $5   F17

▽▽▽▽   4/1-4/30 & 11/1-3/31   1P: $50   2P: $54   XP: $5   F17

Motel   **Location:** I-80/90 (Ohio Tpke), exit 71 to I-280, exit 1B. 3484 Hanley Rd 43551. Fax: 419/837-0043. **Facility:** 83 one-bedroom standard units. 2 stories, exterior corridors. **Parking:** on-site. **Amenities:** extended cable TV, voice mail, irons, hair dryers. **Leisure Activities:** exercise room. **Business Services:** meeting rooms. **Cards:** AX, CB, DC, DS, MC, VI. **Special Amenities:** free continental breakfast and free local telephone calls.

SOME UNITS

⬛ 🍴 🦵 📠 ⬛ 🖨 / ✕ /
              DATA PORT

RED CARPET INN   Phone: (419)872-2902   52

(AAA) (SAVE)   All Year   1P: $35-$45   2P: $45-$55   XP: $5   F10

▽▽   **Location:** I-475, exit 2, just s. 26054 N Dixie Hwy 43551. Fax: 419/872-0133. **Facility:** 37 one-bedroom standard units. 1 story, exterior corridors. **Parking:** on-site. **Terms:** pets ($5 extra charge). **Cards:** AX, DS, MC, VI.

Motel   **Special Amenities:** early check-in/late check-out and free local telephone calls.

SOME UNITS

⬛ 🐕 🍴 🦵 / ✕ VCR ⬛ 🖼 /
               FEE   FEE

─────── **WHERE TO DINE** ───────

CASA BARRON RESTAURANTE   **Lunch:** $5-$6   **Dinner:** $5-$14   **Phone:** 419/874-5361   19

▽▽   **Location:** 209 Louisiana Ave. **Hours:** Closed major holidays; also Sun. **Features:** casual dress; children's menu; carryout; salad bar; cocktails; a la carte. Diners who come here expect traditional fare and interesting specials. **Parking:** on-site. **Cards:** AX, MC, VI.

Continental   ✕

CROY'S SUPPER CLUB   **Dinner:** $14-$21   **Phone:** 419/874-2117   20

▽▽   **Location:** I-75, exit 193, just e on US 20 and 23. 27096 Oakmead Dr 43551. **Hours:** 5 pm-10:30 pm, Fri & Sat-11 pm. Closed major holidays; also Sun. **Reservations:** suggested. **Features:** casual dress; children's menu; carryout; cocktails & lounge. Earth tones, background music and subtle lighting lend romantic warmth to the elegantly casual dining room. Thoughtful preparations of steak, fresh fish, and hand-pounded veal show the work of a dedicated chef. The wait staff is casual and friendly. **Parking:** on-site. **Cards:** AX, DC, DS, MC, VI.

American

FRICKER'S   **Lunch:** $6-$9   **Dinner:** $9-$15   **Phone:** 419/874-3605   21

▽   **Location:** I-75, exit 193, just e on US 20 and 23. 27390 Helen Dr 43551. **Hours:** 11 am-2:30 am. **Features:** casual dress; carryout; cocktails & lounge. Televisions broadcasting sporting events are spread out throughout the boisterous restaurant, which is decorated with sports memorabilia. The food—such as chicken wings, sandwiches and ribs—is familiar and filling. Service is casual and attentive. **Parking:** on-site. **Cards:** AX, DS, MC, VI.

American

─────── *The following restaurants have not been evaluated by AAA* ───────
but are listed for your information only.

CACTUS JACK'S CANTINA   **Phone:** 419/872-1230

[fyi]   Not evaluated. **Location:** 26611 N Dixie Hwy 43551. Traditional Mexican dishes and daily specials, all priced reasonably, are served in large portions.

FORTUNE HOUSE   **Phone:** 419/874-7077

[fyi]   Not evaluated. **Location:** 580 Craig Dr 43551. Chinese, Cantonese, Szechwan and American food can be eaten in the restaurant or carried out.

PETTISVILLE pop. 500

------ WHERE TO DINE ------

DAS ESSEN HAUS   **Lunch:** $7   **Dinner:** $8   **Phone:** 419/445-8456

◆◆◆

▽▽▽▽

American

Location: Jct SR 2/CR 19; 0.7 mi n of town center. SR 2 at CR 19 43553. **Hours:** 6 am-8 pm, Sun 11 am-2 pm. Closed major holidays. **Reservations:** accepted. **Features:** casual dress; children's menu; carryout; salad bar; buffet. Light streams in through the many windows around the country-decorated dining room to give it a cheerful feel. Amish-style cooking is the menu's focus, with such offerings as chicken, prime rib, seafood and turkey. The homemade bread pudding is delicious. Smoke free premises. **Parking:** on-site. **Cards:** MC, VI.

⊠

PICKERINGTON —See Columbus p. 666.

PIQUA pop. 20,600

------ WHERE TO STAY ------

COMFORT INN-PIQUA   **Phone:** (937)778-8100

SAVE

▽▽▽▽

Motel

4/1-8/24 [ECP]	1P: $73-$83	2P: $80-$90	XP: $6	F18
8/25-12/31 [ECP]	1P: $69-$79	2P: $78-$90	XP: $6	F18
1/1-3/31 [ECP]	1P: $67-$77	2P: $74-$84	XP: $6	F18

Location: I-75, exit 82; in the Miami Valley Centre Mall. 987 E Ash St 45356. **Fax:** 937/778-9573. **Facility:** 122 one-bedroom standard units, some with whirlpools. 5 stories, interior corridors. **Parking:** on-site. **Terms:** package plans, pets ($25 deposit). **Amenities:** extended cable TV, voice mail. *Some:* irons, hair dryers. **Pool(s):** heated indoor. **Leisure Activities:** whirlpool, exercise room. **Guest Services:** valet laundry. **Business Services:** meeting rooms. **Cards:** AX, CB, DC, DS, JC, MC, VI.

SOME UNITS

 🛏 🍴+ 📷 🐎 📹 [DATA PORT] 🖨 / ⊠ 🍴 🖵 🖵 /

RAMADA LIMITED   **Phone:** 937/615-0140

▽▽▽▽

Motel

All Year   1P: $64   2P: $70   XP: $6   F17

Location: I-75, exit 82, just w. 950 E Ash St 45356. **Fax:** 937/615-0142. **Facility:** 70 one-bedroom standard units, some with whirlpools. 3 stories, interior corridors. *Bath:* combo or shower only. **Parking:** on-site. **Terms:** 24 day cancellation notice-fee imposed, [CP] meal plan available, pets ($50 deposit). **Amenities:** extended cable TV, voice mail, irons, hair dryers. **Pool(s):** heated indoor. **Leisure Activities:** whirlpool. **Guest Services:** coin laundry. **Business Services:** meeting rooms. **Cards:** AX, DC, DS, MC, VI.

SOME UNITS

[ASK] 🛏 🍴+ ♿ 🐎 🐾+ 📹 [DATA PORT] 🖵 🖨 / ⊠ 🍴 🖵 /
                                            FEE

------ WHERE TO DINE ------

THE SPRINGS   **Dinner:** $10-$25   **Phone:** 937/773-7373

▽▽▽▽

American

Location: I-75, exit 78, 1.5 mi n. 5795 N CR 25A 45356. **Hours:** 4 pm-9 pm, Fri & Sat-10 pm. Closed: 12/24, Sun & Mon. **Features:** casual dress; children's menu; carryout; cocktails & lounge; a la carte. On the banks of the Miami River, the restaurant affords beautiful views of the great outdoors from every table. Steaks and fresh seafood are at the heart of a menu that also lists chops, chicken and pasta. The service staff is warm and friendly. **Parking:** on-site. **Cards:** AX, MC, VI.

⊠

PLAIN CITY —See Columbus p. 666.

POLAND pop. 3,000

------ WHERE TO STAY ------

FAIRFIELD INN   **Phone:** (330)726-5979

◆◆◆ **SAVE**

▽▽▽▽

Motel

5/1-9/5 [CP]	1P: $73-$79	2P: $73-$79	XP: $5	F17
4/1-4/30 & 9/6-3/31 [CP]	1P: $63-$69	2P: $63-$69	XP: $5	F17

Location: I-680, exit 11, just w. 7397 Tiffany S 44514. **Fax:** 330/726-5979. **Facility:** 64 one-bedroom standard units. 3 stories, interior corridors. **Parking:** on-site. **Terms:** 5 day cancellation notice. **Amenities:** extended cable TV, irons. **Pool(s):** heated indoor. **Leisure Activities:** whirlpool. **Guest Services:** valet laundry. **Cards:** AX, CB, DC, DS, MC, VI. **Special Amenities:** free continental breakfast and free local telephone calls. *(See color ad card insert)*

SOME UNITS

🛏 ♿ 🐎 📹 [DATA PORT] 🖨 / ⊠ 🍴 🖵 🖵 /
                            FEE

HAMPTON INN   **Phone:** (330)758-5191

SAVE

▽▽▽▽

Motel

4/1-11/2 [CP]	1P: $74-$84	2P: $80-$90	
11/3-3/31 [CP]	1P: $72-$79	2P: $79-$89	

Location: I-680, exit 11, just w. 7395 Tiffany S 44507. **Fax:** 330/758-9343. **Facility:** 64 one-bedroom standard units. 3 stories, interior corridors. *Bath:* combo or shower only. **Parking:** on-site. **Terms:** 14 day cancellation notice. **Amenities:** extended cable TV, voice mail, irons. **Pool(s):** heated indoor. **Leisure Activities:** whirlpool. **Guest Services:** valet laundry. **Cards:** AX, CB, DC, DS, JC, MC, VI.

SOME UNITS

 ♿ 📷 🐎 📹 [DATA PORT] 🖵 🖨 / ⊠ 🍴 🖵 /
                                    FEE

RED ROOF INN
(AAA) (SAVE)
◇◇◇◇
Motel
free newspaper.

6/16-9/15	1P: $49-$66	2P: $55-$72	XP: $6 F18
4/1-6/15 & 9/16-3/31	1P: $39-$49	2P: $45-$55	XP: $6 F18

Phone: (330)758-1999

Location: I-680, exit 11, just w. 1051 Tiffany S 44514. Fax: 330/758-8004. **Facility:** 117 units. 113 one-bedroom standard units. 4 one-bedroom suites with efficiencies (no utensils). 4 stories, interior corridors. *Bath:* combo or shower only. **Parking:** on-site. **Amenities:** extended cable TV, video games, voice mail. **Guest Services:** valet and coin laundry. **Cards:** AX, CB, DC, DS, MC, VI. **Special Amenities:** free local telephone calls and free newspaper.

SOME UNITS
🛏️ 🍽️ 📶 📷 📺 DATA PORT 🖨️ / ✕ 📱 🖥️ 💻 /
FEE

RESIDENCE INN
(AAA) (SAVE)
◇◇◇◇
Suite Motel

All Year [ECP]   1P: $109-$159   2P: $109-$159

Phone: 330/726-1747

Location: I-680, exit 11, just w. 7396 Tiffany S 44514. Fax: 330/726-1747. **Facility:** 78 units. 66 one- and 12 two-bedroom suites with kitchens. 3 stories, interior corridors. *Bath:* combo or shower only. **Parking:** on-site. **Terms:** pets ($200-$250 fee). **Amenities:** extended cable TV, voice mail, irons, hair dryers. **Pool(s):** heated indoor. **Leisure Activities:** whirlpool, exercise room, sports court. **Guest Services:** coin laundry. **Business Services:** meeting rooms. **Cards:** AX, CB, DC, DS, MC, VI. *(See color ad card insert)*

SOME UNITS
🛏️ 🍽️ 📶 📷 🏊 ✕ 📺 DATA PORT 📱 🖥️ 💻 🖨️ / ✕ /
FEE

─────── **WHERE TO DINE** ───────

SPRINGFIELD GRILLE   Lunch: $5-$9   Dinner: $8-$16   Phone: 330/726-0895
◇◇◇◇
Steak House

Location: I-680, exit 11, just w. 7413 Tiffany S 44507. **Hours:** 11:30 am-10:30 pm, Fri & Sat-11 pm. Closed: 11/28, 12/25. **Features:** casual dress; children's menu; cocktails. Natural wood grilling takes place in the steakhouse's open kitchen. Beef is not the only menu choice; also offered are fresh seafood, pasta, giant salads, a huge assortment of appetizers, homemade desserts and a variety of daily specials. **Parking:** on-site. **Cards:** AX, DC, DS, MC, VI.

✕

PORT CLINTON pop. 7,100

─────── **WHERE TO STAY** ───────

BEST BUDGET INN & SUITES
(AAA) (SAVE)
◇◇◇
Motel

6/14-9/2 [CP]	1P: $49-$139	2P: $49-$139	XP: $10 F18
4/1-6/13 [CP]	1P: $29-$109	2P: $39-$109	XP: $10 F18
9/3-10/31 [CP]	1P: $29-$79	2P: $39-$79	XP: $10 F18
11/1-3/31 [CP]	1P: $29	2P: $39	XP: $10 F18

Phone: 419/734-5633

Location: 1.4 mi e on SR 163, w of jct SR 2. 1735 E Perry St 43452. Fax: 419/734-5633. **Facility:** 61 one-bedroom standard units, some with efficiencies (no utensils) and/or whirlpools. 2 stories, interior/exterior corridors. **Parking:** on-site. **Terms:** cancellation fee imposed. **Amenities:** extended cable TV. *Some:* hair dryers. **Pool(s):** outdoor. **Guest Services:** coin laundry. **Cards:** AX, CB, DC, DS, MC, VI. **Special Amenities:** free continental breakfast and free local telephone calls. *(See color ad p 739 & below)*

SOME UNITS
S/D 🍽️ 🏊 📺 🖨️ / ✕ 📱 🖥️ /
FEE

BEST WESTERN PORT CLINTON

Phone: (419)734-2274

5/25-9/2	1P: $68-$128	2P: $78-$138	XP: $8	F16
4/1-5/24 & 9/3-10/31	1P: $48-$98	2P: $58-$108	XP: $8	F16
11/1-3/31	1P: $38-$58	2P: $58-$58	XP: $8	F16

Motel **Location:** 1.7 mi e on SR 163, w of jct SR 2. 1734 E Perry St 43452. Fax: 419/734-3845. **Facility:** 41 one-bedroom standard units, some with whirlpools. 2 stories, interior corridors. **Parking:** on-site. **Terms:** check-in 4 pm, 3 day cancellation notice. **Amenities:** extended cable TV. **Pool(s):** outdoor. **Guest Services:** coin laundry. **Business Services:** fax. **Cards:** AX, DC, DS, MC, VI. *(See color ad p 739 & p 729)*

SOME UNITS

COMFORT INN, WATERFRONT

Phone: (419)732-2929

6/14-9/2	1P: $69-$159	2P: $69-$159	XP: $10	F18
4/1-6/13	1P: $39-$129	2P: $49-$129	XP: $10	F18
9/3-10/31	1P: $39-$89	2P: $49-$89	XP: $10	F18
11/1-3/31	1P: $39	2P: $49	XP: $10	F18

Motel **Location:** 1.5 mi e on SR 163, w of jct SR 2. 1723 E Perry St 43452. Fax: 419/732-2929. **Facility:** 54 one-bedroom standard units, some with efficiencies (no utensils) and/or whirlpools. 2 stories, interior corridors. **Parking:** on-site. **Terms:** [ECP] meal plan available. **Amenities:** extended cable TV. *Some:* irons, hair dryers. **Pool(s):** heated outdoor. **Leisure Activities:** fishing. **Guest Services:** valet laundry. **Cards:** AX, CB, DC, DS, JC, MC, VI. *(See color ad p 739 & p 729)*

SOME UNITS
FEE

COUNTRY HEARTH INN

Phone: (419)732-2111

4/1-9/10 [CP]	1P: $57-$109	2P: $57-$109	XP: $6	F17
9/11-12/31 [CP]	1P: $50-$79	2P: $50-$79	XP: $6	F17
1/1-3/31 [CP]	1P: $53-$63	2P: $53-$63	XP: $6	F17

Motel **Location:** 1.2 mi e on SR 163, w of jct SR 2. 1815 E Perry St 43452. Fax: 419/732-0206. **Facility:** 66 one-bedroom standard units. 2 stories, interior/exterior corridors. **Parking:** on-site. **Terms:** small pets only. **Amenities:** extended cable TV, safes. **Pool(s):** outdoor. **Guest Services:** coin laundry. **Business Services:** meeting rooms. **Cards:** AX, CB, DC, DS, MC, VI.

SOME UNITS

DAYS INN PORT CLINTON

Phone: (419)734-4945

5/24-9/1 [CP]	1P: $88-$175	2P: $88-$175	XP: $8	F12
9/2-9/28 [CP]	1P: $38-$128	2P: $38-$128	XP: $8	F12
4/5-5/23 [CP]	1P: $38-$108	2P: $38-$108	XP: $8	F12

Motel **Location:** SR 2, exit SR 163, 0.3 mi e to Gill Rd, then 0.3 mi s. 2149 E Gill Rd 43452. Fax: 419/734-0495. **Facility:** 38 one-bedroom standard units. 1 story, exterior corridors. **Parking:** on-site. **Terms:** open 4/5-9/28, 3 day cancellation notice. **Amenities:** extended cable TV, hair dryers. **Pool(s):** outdoor. **Guest Services:** coin laundry. **Cards:** AX, CB, DC, DS, MC, VI.

SOME UNITS

FAIRFIELD INN BY MARRIOTT

Phone: (419)732-2434

6/14-9/2 [ECP]	1P: $59-$149	2P: $59-$149	XP: $10	F18
4/1-6/13 [ECP]	1P: $43-$119	2P: $49-$119	XP: $10	F18
9/3-10/31 [ECP]	1P: $43-$79	2P: $49-$79	XP: $10	F18
11/1-3/31 [ECP]	1P: $43	2P: $49	XP: $10	F18

Motel **Location:** SR 2, exit SR 53 N, just n. 3760 E State Rd 43452. Fax: 419/732-2434. **Facility:** 64 one-bedroom standard units, some with whirlpools. 2 stories, interior corridors. *Bath:* combo or shower only. **Parking:** on-site. **Amenities:** extended cable TV, irons. **Pool(s):** heated indoor. **Leisure Activities:** sauna, exercise room. **Guest Services:** coin laundry. **Business Services:** meeting rooms. **Cards:** AX, CB, DC, DS, JC, MC, VI. **Special Amenities:** free continental breakfast and free local telephone calls. *(See color ad p 739, p 729 & card insert)*

SOME UNITS

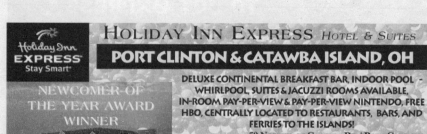

HOLIDAY INN EXPRESS HOTEL & SUITES Phone: (419)732-7322

(AAA) (SAVE)

Motel

7/2-10/31 [ECP]	1P: $60-$310	2P: $90-$310
5/2-7/1 [ECP]	1P: $60-$190	2P: $60-$190
4/1-5/1 & 11/1-3/31 [ECP]	1P: $60	2P: $60

Location: SR 2, exit SR 53 N, 2 mi n. 50 NE Catawba Rd 43452. Fax: 419/732-1919. **Facility:** 102 one-bedroom standard units, some with whirlpools. 3 stories, interior corridors. *Bath:* combo or shower only. **Parking:** on-site. **Amenities:** video games, dual phone lines, voice mail, irons, hair dryers. **Pool(s):** heated indoor. **Leisure Activities:** whirlpool. **Guest Services:** valet and coin laundry. **Business Services:** meeting rooms, business center, fax. **Cards:** AX, DC, DS, MC, VI. *(See color ad p 730)*

SOME UNITS

🅂🄳 🄶🄼 📺 ⛱ 🎥 DATA PORT ▯ 🖨 / ✖ 🍴 🖥 /
FEE

SLEEP INN Phone: (419)732-7707

(SAVE)

Motel

6/14-9/2 [ECP]	1P: $59-$149	2P: $59-$149	XP: $10	F18
4/1-6/13 [ECP]	1P: $39-$119	2P: $49-$119	XP: $10	F18
9/3-10/31 [ECP]	1P: $39-$89	2P: $49-$89	XP: $10	F18
11/1-3/31 [ECP]	1P: $39	2P: $49	XP: $10	F18

Location: SR 2, exit SR 53 N, just n. 947 SR 53 N 43452. Fax: 419/732-7707. **Facility:** 71 one-bedroom standard units, some with whirlpools. 3 stories, interior corridors. *Bath:* shower only. **Parking:** on-site. **Amenities:** *Some:* irons, hair dryers. **Pool(s):** heated indoor. **Guest Services:** valet and coin laundry. **Business Services:** meeting rooms. **Cards:** AX, DC, DS, MC, VI. *(See color ad p 739 & p 729)*

SOME UNITS

🅂🄳 🄶🄼 📺 🎥 ⛱ 🎥 DATA PORT 🖨 / ✖ 🍴 🖥 🖥 /

SUPER 8 Phone: (419)734-4446

Motel

5/25-9/2	1P: $68-$128	2P: $78-$138	XP: $8	F16
4/1-5/24 & 9/3-10/31	1P: $48-$98	2P: $58-$108	XP: $8	F16
11/1-3/31	1P: $38-$58	2P: $38-$58	XP: $8	F16

Location: 1.7 mi e on SR 163, w of jct SR 2. 1704 E Perry St 43452. Fax: 419/732-3370. **Facility:** 38 one-bedroom standard units, some with whirlpools. 2 stories, interior corridors. **Parking:** on-site. **Terms:** 3 day cancellation notice. **Cards:** AX, DC, DS, MC, VI. *(See color ad p 739 & p 729)*

SOME UNITS

(ASK) 🅂🄳 🍴 DATA PORT 🖨 / ✖ 🖥 /

——— WHERE TO DINE ———

CISCO & CHARLIE'S RESTAURANT & CANTINA Lunch: $5-$8 Dinner: $7-$15 Phone: 419/732-3126

Mexican

Location: 1 mi e on SR 163, w of jct SR 2. 1632 E Perry St 43452. **Hours:** 11 am-midnight, Fri & Sat-2 am. Closed: 11/28, 12/25. **Features:** casual dress; children's menu; carryout; cocktails & lounge; entertainment. Enjoy tasty Mexican food at this popular restaurant and cantina. They serve all your favorites and the prompt, cheerful service will ensure a great dining experience. **Parking:** on-site. **Cards:** AX, DS, MC, VI.

✖

GARDEN AT THE LIGHTHOUSE RESTAURANT Lunch: $4-$8 Dinner: $10-$20 Phone: 419/732-2151

(AAA)

American

Location: Just e. 226 E Perry St 43452. **Hours:** 11:30 am-2 & 4:30-10 pm; to 9:30 pm, Fri-10 pm 11/1-5/31. Closed major holidays. **Features:** casual dress; children's menu; early bird specials; carryout; cocktails. A former lighthouse keeper's house offers relaxed dining in airy and lush surroundings. House specials include fishmarket salad and certified black Angus beef entrees. Hours vary depending on the season. Outside dining is available in summer. **Parking:** on-site. **Cards:** AX, DC, DS, MC, VI.

✖

MON AMI RESTAURANT Lunch: $6-$10 Dinner: $12-$25 Phone: 419/797-4445

American

Location: SR 2, exit SR 53 N, 1.3 mi n. 3845 E Wine Cellar Rd 43452. **Hours:** 11:30 am-9 pm, Fri & Sat-10 pm. Closed: 1/1, 12/25; also Mon & Tues 10/1-4/30. **Reservations:** suggested. **Features:** casual dress; Sunday brunch; children's menu; carryout; cocktails. Old World tradition prevails on the grounds of this busy 1872 historic winery where fresh Lake Erie perch, walleye and a variety of steak are served in a congenial atmosphere. **Parking:** on-site. **Cards:** AX, DS, MC, VI.

✖

——— *The following restaurants have not been evaluated by AAA* ——— *but are listed for your information only.*

NATE'S Phone: 419/732-3033

(fyi)

Not evaluated. **Location:** 4046 E Harbor Rd 43452. Wholesome, budget-friendly American food can be sampled in the family restaurant.

PHIL'S INN RESTAURANT Phone: 419/734-9023

(fyi)

Not evaluated. **Location:** 1708 E Perry 43452. Well known landmark restaurant in business for over 50 years.

PORT JEFFERSON pop. 400

——— WHERE TO DINE ———

HUSSEY'S RESTAURANT Dinner: $8-$17 Phone: 937/492-8952

American

Location: I-75, exit 92, 7 mi e on SR 47, then just s. 8760 S Broad St 45360. **Hours:** 4 pm-9 pm, Fri & Sat-10 pm, Sun 3:30 pm-8:30 pm. Closed major holidays; also Mon. **Features:** casual dress; children's menu; carryout; cocktails & lounge. Operating since the early 1930s, the casual restaurant next to the Miami River has long been a favorite of the locals. Attractive wildlife pictures hang on the walls. The varied menu includes well-prepared selections of chicken, seafood and prime rib. **Parking:** on-site. **Cards:** AX, MC, VI.

✖

PORTSMOUTH pop. 22,700

-------- WHERE TO STAY --------

HOLIDAY INN EXPRESS
Phone: (740)353-3232

4/1-10/31	1P: $75-$89	2P: $75-$89	XP: $7	F16
11/1-3/31	1P: $73-$79	2P: $72-$79	XP: $7	F16

Motel
Location: 4 mi n of downtown. 5100 Old Scioto Tr 45662. Fax: 740/355-0415. **Facility:** 60 one-bedroom standard units, some with whirlpools. 2 stories, interior corridors. *Bath:* combo or shower only. **Parking:** on-site. **Terms:** 10 day cancellation notice. **Amenities:** extended cable TV, high-speed Internet, dual phone lines, voice mail, irons, hair dryers. **Pool(s):** heated indoor. **Guest Services:** valet and coin laundry. **Business Services:** meeting rooms. **Cards:** AX, DC, DS, JC, MC, VI.

SOME UNITS

PORTSMOUTH SUPER 8
Phone: (740)353-8880

All Year	1P: $52-$62	2P: $57-$67	XP: $5	F12

Motel
Location: 5 mi n. 4266 US Rt 23 N 45662. Fax: 740/553-8880. **Facility:** 51 one-bedroom standard units, some with whirlpools. 3 stories, interior corridors. *Bath:* combo or shower only. **Parking:** on-site. **Terms:** 7 day cancellation notice. **Amenities:** extended cable TV. **Pool(s):** heated indoor. **Leisure Activities:** whirlpool. **Business Services:** meeting rooms, fax (fee). **Cards:** AX, CB, DC, DS, MC, VI.

SOME UNITS
FEE

QUAKER CITY

-------- WHERE TO STAY --------

-------- *The following lodging was either not evaluated or did not* --------
meet AAA rating requirements but is listed for your information only.

WHISKEY RUN LODGE
Phone: 740-679-2422
[fyi]   Not evaluated. **Location:** I-70, exit 193, 11.5 mi s on SR 513, then 1.5 mi w. 55988 SR 147 43773. Facilities, services, and decor characterize a mid-range property.

REYNOLDSBURG —See Columbus p. 666.

RICHFIELD pop. 3,100   (See map p. 600; index p. 604)

-------- WHERE TO STAY --------

HOLIDAY INN-RICHFIELD
Phone: (330)659-6151   **45**

6/14-9/13	1P: $84	2P: $84	
5/1-6/13	1P: $72	2P: $72	
4/1-4/30 & 9/14-3/31	1P: $65	2P: $65	

Motor Inn
Location: I-80/90 (Ohio Tpke), exit 173, just s. 4742 Brecksville Rd 44286 (Rt 21). Fax: 330/659-3819. **Facility:** 217 units. 215 one-bedroom standard units. 2 one-bedroom suites. 2 stories, interior corridors. **Parking:** on-site. **Terms:** check-in 4 pm, 3 day cancellation notice-fee imposed. **Amenities:** extended cable TV, video games, voice mail, irons, hair dryers. **Dining:** dining room, 6:30 am-2 & 5-10 pm, $10-$19, cocktails. **Pool(s):** outdoor, heated indoor, wading. **Leisure Activities:** whirlpool, miniature golf, exercise room. *Fee:* game room. **Guest Services:** valet and coin laundry. **Business Services:** conference facilities. **Cards:** AX, CB, DC, DS, JC, MC, VI. **Special Amenities:** free newspaper.

SOME UNITS
FEE

SUPER 8 MOTEL
Phone: (330)659-6888   **44**

5/26-9/4 [CP]	1P: $60-$75	2P: $66-$82	XP: $7	F16
4/1-5/25 & 9/5-3/31 [CP]	1P: $50-$60	2P: $56-$67	XP: $7	F16

Motel
Location: I-80/90 (Ohio Tpke), exit 173, just s. 4845 Brecksville Rd 44286. Fax: 330/659-6888. **Facility:** 51 one-bedroom standard units. 3 stories, interior corridors. *Bath:* combo or shower only. **Parking:** on-site. **Amenities:** extended cable TV. **Pool(s):** heated indoor. **Leisure Activities:** whirlpool. **Cards:** AX, DC, DS, MC, VI.

SOME UNITS

RIO GRANDE pop. 1,000

-------- WHERE TO STAY --------

COLLEGE HILL MOTEL
Phone: 740/245-5326

All Year	1P: $34	2P: $43	XP: $3

Motel
Location: US 35, exit Rio Grande. 10987 State Rt 588 45674 (PO Box 172). **Facility:** 12 one-bedroom standard units. 1 story, exterior corridors. **Parking:** on-site. **Terms:** cancellation fee imposed. **Cards:** AX, DS, MC, VI.

SOME UNITS

ROCKBRIDGE pop. 500

——— WHERE TO STAY ———

GLENLAUREL-A SCOTTISH COUNTRY INN
All Year [BP]   2P: $119-$289   **Phone:** (740)385-4070

VVVVV   **Location:** Jct US 33 and SR 180, 4.8 mi w on SR 180, 0.5 mi s on Mt Olive Rd, follow signs. 14940 Mt Olive Rd 43149.   XP: $20
Country Inn   Fax: 740/385-9669. **Facility:** A bagpiper plays during meals at this Scottish-themed inn, which offers plush rooms and cottages in a wooded area of Hocking Hills. Smoke free premises. 20 units. 10 one-bedroom suites ($179-$229), some with whirlpools. 10 one-bedroom vacation rentals ($199-$299). 1-2 stories, interior/exterior corridors. *Bath:* combo or shower only. **Parking:** on-site. **Terms:** 2 night minimum stay - weekends, age restrictions may apply, 14 day cancellation notice-fee imposed, package plans. **Amenities:** CD players, voice mail, irons, hair dryers. *Some:* DVD players. **Leisure Activities:** hiking trails. **Guest Services:** gift shop, massage (fee). **Business Services:** meeting rooms, fax. **Cards:** AX, DC, DS, MC, VI.

SOME UNITS

ROCKY RIVER —*See Cleveland p. 628.*

ROSSFORD pop. 5,900   (See map p. 756; index p. 758)

——— WHERE TO STAY ———

COURTYARD BY MARRIOTT-PERRYSBURG/ROSSFORD   **Phone:** (419)872-5636   **42**
AAA SAVE   All Year [BP]   1P: $89   2P: $89
VVVV   **Location:** I-80/90 (Ohio Tpke), exit 4A; I-475 S to SR 795, 0.3 mi e. 9789 Clark Dr 43460. Fax: 419/872-5638.
Motel   **Facility:** 121 one-bedroom standard units, some with whirlpools. 3 stories, interior corridors. *Bath:* combo or shower only. **Parking:** on-site. **Amenities:** voice mail, irons, hair dryers. **Dining:** restaurant, 6:30-10 am, Sat & Sun 7 am-noon, $7-$9. **Pool(s):** heated indoor. **Leisure Activities:** whirlpool, exercise room. **Guest Services:** complimentary laundry. **Business Services:** meeting rooms. **Cards:** AX, DC, DS, MC, VI.
(See color ad card insert)

SOME UNITS
FEE

RUSSIA pop. 400

——— WHERE TO DINE ———

SHEP'S GOLDEN LANTERN   **Dinner:** $9-$20   **Phone:** 937/526-3553
VVVV   **Location:** Jct SR 48 and 47, 3 mi w on SR 47, 0.5 mi s. 2111 Miller Rd 45363. **Hours:** 4 pm-9 pm, Fri & Sat-9:30
American   pm, Sun 3:30 pm-8:30 pm. Closed major holidays; also Mon. **Features:** casual dress; cocktails & lounge; a la carte. A good selection of wines complements offerings of prime rib and fresh seafood. Oak wood, brass, framed prints and hanging plants are among touches that add to the dining room's laid-back ambience. Fresh flowers bloom in the front garden. **Parking:** on-site. **Cards:** AX, DC, DS, MC, VI.

ST. CLAIRSVILLE pop. 5,200

——— WHERE TO STAY ———

DAYS INN WHEELING WEST   **Phone:** (740)695-0100
SAVE   5/17-12/16 [ECP]   1P: $54-$64   2P: $59-$69   XP: $5   F17
VVVV   4/1-5/16 & 12/17-3/31 [ECP]   1P: $49-$59   2P: $54-$64   XP: $5   F17
Motor Inn **Location:** I-70, exit 220. 52601 Holiday Dr 43950. Fax: 740/695-4135. **Facility:** 137 one-bedroom standard units, some with whirlpools. 2 stories, exterior corridors. **Parking:** on-site. **Terms:** 14 day cancellation notice. **Amenities:** extended cable TV, hair dryers. **Pool(s):** outdoor. **Guest Services:** coin laundry. **Business Services:** meeting rooms. **Cards:** AX, DC, DS, MC, VI.

SOME UNITS
FEE FEE

HAMPTON INN-ST CLAIRSVILLE   **Phone:** (740)695-3961
SAVE   6/2-3/31 [ECP]   1P: $79-$89   2P: $84-$94
VVVV   4/1-6/1 [ECP]   1P: $76-$86   2P: $81-$91
Motel   **Location:** I-70, exit 218, 0.3 mi nw on US 40. 51130 E National Rd 43950-9118. Fax: 740/695-0739. **Facility:** 116 one-bedroom standard units. 2 stories, interior corridors. **Parking:** on-site. **Amenities:** extended cable TV, voice mail, irons, hair dryers. **Dining:** Undo's West, see separate listing. **Pool(s):** heated outdoor. **Leisure Activities:** exercise room. **Guest Services:** coin laundry. **Business Services:** meeting rooms. **Cards:** AX, CB, DC, DS, MC, VI.

SOME UNITS
FEE

HOLIDAY INN EXPRESS HOTEL & SUITES   **Phone:** (740)699-0010
VVVV   All Year [ECP]   1P: $71-$83   2P: $71-$83
Motel   **Location:** I-70, exit 218, 0.5 mi ne on US 40. 51654 National Rd 43950. Fax: 740/699-0662. **Facility:** 66 units. 65 one-bedroom standard units, some with whirlpools. 1 one-bedroom suite ($81-$87). 3 stories, interior corridors. *Bath:* combo or shower only. **Parking:** on-site. **Amenities:** extended cable TV. *Some:* irons, hair dryers. **Pool(s):** heated indoor. **Leisure Activities:** sauna, whirlpool, exercise room. **Guest Services:** coin laundry. **Cards:** AX, CB, DC, DS, JC, MC, VI.

SOME UNITS
FEE

KNIGHTS INN-ST. CLAIRSVILLE/WHEELING
AAA [SAVE]
◆◆ ◆◆
Motel

6/2-9/5	1P: $45-$64	2P: $51-$66	XP: $6	F18
4/1-6/1 & 9/6-3/31	1P: $39-$62	2P: $45-$66	XP: $6	F18

Location: I-70, exit 218, 0.5 mi ne on US 40. 51260 National Rd 43950. Fax: 740/695-3014. **Facility:** 104 one-bedroom standard units, some with kitchens and/or whirlpools. 1 story, exterior corridors. **Amenities:** extended cable TV. *Some:* hair dryers. **Pool(s):** outdoor. **Leisure Activities:** picnic area. **Guest Services:** coin laundry. **Cards:** AX, CB, DC, DS, MC, VI. **Special Amenities:** free continental breakfast and free local telephone calls.
Phone: (740)695-5038

SOME UNITS

RED ROOF INN
AAA [SAVE]
◆◆ ◆◆
Motel

5/20-8/25	1P: $41-$69	2P: $46-$74	XP: $5	F18
4/1-5/19	1P: $37-$49	2P: $42-$56	XP: $5	F18
8/26-3/31	1P: $39-$49	2P: $44-$54	XP: $5	F18

Location: I-70, exit 218. 68301 Red Roof Ln 43950. Fax: 740/695-6956. **Facility:** 108 one-bedroom standard units. 2 stories, exterior corridors. **Parking:** on-site. **Terms:** small pets only. **Amenities:** extended cable TV, video games, voice mail. **Cards:** AX, CB, DC, DS, MC, VI. **Special Amenities:** free local telephone calls and free newspaper.
Phone: (740)695-4057

SOME UNITS

——— WHERE TO DINE ———

BUFFALO WILD WINGS GRILL & BAR
◆
American

Lunch: $7-$15   **Dinner:** $7-$15   Phone: 740/695-2800
Location: I-70, exit 218, just n; in shopping plaza opposite Walmart. 50633 Valley Frontage Rd 43950. **Hours:** 11 am-1 am, Fri & Sat-2 am, Sun 11 am-midnight. Closed: 12/25. **Features:** casual dress; carryout; cocktails & lounge; a la carte, a la carte. Near Ohio Valley Mall, the sports bar entertains diners with wide-screen television and interactive trivia games. The fast-food menu centers on burgers, hot wings, Thai/Caribbean dishes and Tex-Mex entrees. **Parking:** on-site. **Cards:** AX, DS, MC, VI.

MEHLMAN'S CAFETERIA
◆
American

Phone: 740/695-1000
Location: I-70, exit 118 (Mall-Banfield Rd), 1 mi e; on US 40. 51800 National Rd 43950. **Hours:** 10:30 am-8 pm. Closed major holidays; also Mon. **Features:** casual dress; children's menu; carryout. The simple cafeteria is always busy, as diners choose from a good variety of familiar foods, such as broiled whitefish, baked ham, prime rib and roast beef. Pies, bread and rolls are baked fresh daily. Prices are great and portion sizes plentiful. **Parking:** on-site.

UNDO'S WEST
◆◆ ◆◆
Italian

Lunch: $7-$15   **Dinner:** $10-$22   Phone: 740/695-8888
Location: I-70, exit 218, 0.3 mi nw on US 40; in Hampton Inn-St Clairsville. 51130 National Rd 43950. **Hours:** 11:30 am-10 pm, Fri & Sat-10:30 pm, Sun-9 pm. Closed: 1/1, 12/25. **Features:** casual dress; Sunday brunch; children's menu; carryout; cocktails & lounge. Established in 1953, the family-owned restaurant doles out generous portions of original Italian dishes, including crunchy calzones, mozzarella pizza and a wide variety of pasta family dinners. **Parking:** on-site. **Cards:** AX, DC, DS, MC, VI.

ST. MARYS pop. 8,400

——— WHERE TO STAY ———

AMERIHOST INN-ST. MARYS
AAA [SAVE]
◆◆ ◆◆ ◆◆
Motel

5/29-9/15	1P: $78-$105	2P: $78-$105	XP: $6	F18
12/31-3/31	1P: $78-$95	2P: $78-$95	XP: $6	F18
9/16-12/30	1P: $75-$92	2P: $75-$92	XP: $6	F18
4/1-5/28	1P: $72-$90	2P: $72-$90	XP: $6	F18

Location: Jct US 33 and SR 29, just s. 1410 Commerce Dr 45885. Fax: 419/394-5710. **Facility:** 61 one-bedroom standard units, some with whirlpools. 2 stories, interior corridors. **Bath:** combo or shower only. **Parking:** on-site, winter plug-ins. **Terms:** 3 day cancellation notice, [ECP] meal plan available. **Amenities:** extended cable TV, safes (fee), irons, hair dryers. **Pool(s):** heated indoor. **Leisure Activities:** whirlpool, exercise room. **Business Services:** meeting rooms. **Cards:** AX, CB, DC, DS, JC, MC, VI. **Special Amenities:** free continental breakfast and free newspaper.
Phone: (419)394-2710

SOME UNITS

SANDUSKY pop. 29,800

——— WHERE TO STAY ———

BEST BUDGET INN
AAA [SAVE]
◆◆ ◆◆
Motel

6/22-9/1 [CP]	1P: $58-$98	2P: $58-$118	XP: $5	F17
4/1-6/21 [CP]	1P: $32-$88	2P: $38-$98	XP: $5	F17
9/2-10/26 [CP]	1P: $32-$48	2P: $38-$58	XP: $5	F17
10/27-3/31 [CP]	1P: $28-$32	2P: $32-$38	XP: $5	F17

Location: US 6, just e of Cedar Point Cswy. 2027 Cleveland Rd 44870. Fax: 419/627-9905. **Facility:** 47 one-bedroom standard units, some with whirlpools. 2 stories, interior/exterior corridors. **Parking:** on-site. **Terms:** 3 day cancellation notice. **Amenities:** extended cable TV, hair dryers. **Pool(s):** heated outdoor. **Leisure Activities:** Fee: game room. **Guest Services:** coin laundry. **Cards:** AX, CB, DC, DS, JC, MC, VI. **Special Amenities:** free continental breakfast and free local telephone calls. (See color ad p 735 & p 739)
Phone: 419/626-3610

SOME UNITS

BEST BUDGET INN

Phone: 419/625-7252

AAA [SAVE]
◇◇ ◇◇
Motel

6/22-9/1 [CP]	1P: $59-$149	2P: $59-$149
4/1-6/21 [CP]	1P: $39-$89	2P: $39-$89
9/2-10/26 [CP]	1P: $39-$79	2P: $39-$79
10/27-3/31 [CP]	1P: $34-$40	2P: $34-$40

Location: Jct SR 2 and US 250. 5918 Milan Rd 44870. Fax: 419/625-7252. **Facility:** 55 units. 53 one- and 2 two-bedroom standard units. 2 stories, interior/exterior corridors. **Parking:** on-site. **Amenities:** extended cable TV. **Pool(s):** outdoor. **Guest Services:** coin laundry. **Cards:** AX, CB, DC, DS, JC, MC, VI. **Special Amenities: free continental breakfast and free local telephone calls.** *(See color ad p 735 & p 739)*

SOME UNITS

[icons]

BEST WESTERN CEDAR POINT AREA

Phone: (419)625-9234

AAA [SAVE]
◇◇◇ ◇◇
Motor Inn

5/4-9/5	1P: $89-$199	2P: $99-$199
9/6-3/31	1P: $59-$159	2P: $69-$169
4/1-5/3	1P: $59-$89	2P: $69-$89

Location: 1.8 mi e on US 6; 0.3 mi w of Cedar Point Cswy. 1530 Cleveland Rd (US 6) 44870. Fax: 419/625-9971. **Facility:** 106 one-bedroom standard units, some with whirlpools. 2 stories, interior/exterior corridors. **Parking:** on-site. **Terms:** 3 day cancellation notice. **Amenities:** extended cable TV, hair dryers. *Some:* irons. **Dining:** dining room, 7 am-8 pm, $10-$18. **Pool(s):** heated outdoor. **Guest Services:** coin laundry. **Business Services:** meeting rooms. **Cards:** AX, CB, DC, DS, MC, VI. **Special Amenities: free local telephone calls and free room upgrade (subject to availability with advanced reservations).**

SOME UNITS

[icons]

BREAKER'S EXPRESS

Phone: 419/627-2109

◇◇◇
Motel

7/1-8/31	1P: $89-$179	2P: $89-$179	XP: $10
6/1-6/30	1P: $59-$179	2P: $59-$179	XP: $10
9/1-10/26	1P: $69-$159	2P: $69-$159	XP: $10
5/17-5/31	1P: $59-$109	2P: $59-$109	XP: $10

Location: 2 mi e on US 6, just n. 1201 Cedar Point Dr 44870. Fax: 419/609-3801. **Facility:** 350 one-bedroom standard units. 3 stories, interior corridors. *Bath:* combo or shower only. **Parking:** on-site. **Terms:** open 5/17-10/26, check-in 4 pm, 3 day cancellation notice-fee imposed, package plans. **Amenities:** extended cable TV, voice mail. **Pool(s):** heated outdoor. **Leisure Activities:** whirlpool. *Fee:* game room. **Guest Services:** coin laundry. **Cards:** DS, MC, VI.

SOME UNITS

[icons]

Travel Back to Yesterday

Let AAA help you visit a bygone era of romance and elegance with the *AAA Guide to North American Bed & Breakfasts and Country Inns*. This fascinating guide includes diamond ratings of more than 2,600 lodgings, with more than 1,500 illustrations and 100 full-color photos focusing on these tranquil accommodations. The guide also features maps illustrating scenic byways and listings of historical sites.

Bring a little of the past into the present. **Available at participating AAA club offices or web sites (aaa.com) or by calling 1-877-AAA-BOOK.**

CLARION INN SANDUSKY

SAVE

Motor Inn

Phone: (419)625-6280

| | 6/28-8/31 | 1P: $80-$130 | 2P: $80-$130 |
| | 4/1-6/27 & 9/1-3/31 | 1P: $55-$90 | 2P: $55-$90 |

Location: 1.5 mi n of SR 2, on US 250; in Sandusky Mall. 1119 Sandusky Mall Blvd 44870. Fax: 419/625-9080. **Facility:** 143 one-bedroom standard units. 2 stories, interior corridors. **Parking:** on-site. **Terms:** package plans - off season, small pets only. **Amenities:** irons, hair dryers. **Pool(s):** heated indoor. **Leisure Activities:** sauna, whirlpool, exercise room. *Fee:* game room. **Guest Services:** valet laundry. **Business Services:** conference facilities. **Cards:** AX, CB, DC, DS, MC, VI. *(See color ad below)*

SOME UNITS

COMFORT INN MAINGATE

AAA SAVE

Motel

Phone: (419)625-4700

	7/6-8/24 [ECP]	1P: $70-$210	2P: $70-$210
	5/25-7/5 [ECP]	1P: $60-$160	2P: $60-$160
	5/3-5/24 & 8/25-10/27 [ECP]	1P: $60-$110	2P: $60-$110

Location: 1.5 mi e on US 6. 1711 Cleveland Rd 44870. Fax: 419/625-4438. **Facility:** 63 one-bedroom standard units. 2 stories, exterior corridors. **Parking:** on-site. **Terms:** open 5/3-10/27, check-in 4 pm, 3 day cancellation notice. **Amenities:** extended cable TV. *Some:* irons, hair dryers. **Pool(s):** outdoor. **Cards:** AX, DC, DS, MC, VI. **Special Amenities:** free continental breakfast and free local telephone calls. *(See color ad p 738)*

SOME UNITS

COMFORT INN SANDUSKY

AAA SAVE

Motel

Phone: (419)621-0200

	7/14-8/24 [ECP]	1P: $70-$200	2P: $70-$200		
	6/16-7/13 [ECP]	1P: $60-$160	2P: $60-$160		
	4/1-6/15 & 8/25-3/31 [ECP]	1P: $39-$120	2P: $43-$120	XP: $4	F17

Location: Jct SR 2 and US 250. 5909 Milan Rd 44870. Fax: 419/621-0060. **Facility:** 209 one-bedroom standard units, some with whirlpools. 2 stories, interior corridors. *Bath:* combo or shower only. **Parking:** on-site. **Terms:** check-in 4 pm, 3 day cancellation notice. **Amenities:** extended cable TV, video games, voice mail. *Some:* irons, hair dryers. **Dining:** Baci Nite Club, see separate listing, nightclub. **Pool(s):** heated indoor. **Leisure Activities:** sauna, whirlpool. **Guest Services:** coin laundry. **Business Services:** meeting rooms. **Cards:** AX, DC, DS, MC, VI. **Special Amenities:** free continental breakfast and free local telephone calls. *(See color ad p 738)*

SOME UNITS

CORNADO MOTEL

Motel

Phone: 419/625-2954

	6/30-9/2	1P: $68-$117	2P: $68-$117	XP: $5	F12
	5/3-6/29	1P: $35-$65	2P: $40-$70	XP: $5	F12
	4/1-5/2 & 9/3-3/31	1P: $30-$60	2P: $35-$65	XP: $5	F12

Location: 1 mi e of SR 2. 4319 Venice Rd 44870. Fax: 419/625-8173. **Facility:** 22 one-bedroom standard units. 1 story, exterior corridors. *Bath:* combo or shower only. **Parking:** on-site. **Terms:** cancellation fee imposed, pets ($5 extra charge). **Amenities:** extended cable TV. **Pool(s):** outdoor. **Cards:** DS, MC, VI.

SOME UNITS

DAYS INN CENTRAL

SAVE

Motel

	Phone: (419)627-8884		
6/14-9/1 [CP]	1P: $79-$149	2P: $79-$149	XP: $8 F17
4/1-6/13 [CP]	1P: $34-$99	2P: $34-$99	XP: $8 F17
9/2-10/26 [CP]	1P: $34-$79	2P: $34-$79	XP: $8 F17
10/27-3/31 [CP]	1P: $34-$59	2P: $34-$55	XP: $8 F17

Location: US 250, 1.3 mi n of SR 2. 4315 Milan Rd 44870. **Fax:** 419/626-1316. **Facility:** 95 one-bedroom standard units, some with whirlpools. 2 stories, interior corridors. **Parking:** on-site. **Terms:** 3 day cancellation notice. **Amenities:** safes (fee), hair dryers. **Pool(s):** heated outdoor. **Guest Services:** coin laundry. **Cards:** AX, CB, DC, DS, MC, VI. *(See color ad p 742)*

SOME UNITS

ECONO LODGE

AAA SAVE

Motel

	Phone: (419)627-8000		
5/2-9/5	1P: $149	2P: $149	XP: $5 F18
9/6-10/31	1P: $99	2P: $99	XP: $5 F18
4/1-5/1 & 11/1-3/31	1P: $45	2P: $45	XP: $5 F18

Location: US 6, just w of Cedar Point Cswy. 1904 Cleveland Rd 44870. **Fax:** 419/627-8944. **Facility:** 118 one-bedroom standard units. 2 stories, exterior corridors. **Parking:** on-site. **Amenities:** extended cable TV. **Pool(s):** heated outdoor. **Cards:** AX, DC, DS, MC, VI. **Special Amenities:** free local telephone calls.

SOME UNITS

ECONO LODGE SOUTH

SAVE

Motel

	Phone: (419)626-8720		
6/14-9/1	1P: $69-$149	2P: $69-$149	XP: $8 F17
4/1-6/13	1P: $34-$99	2P: $34-$99	XP: $8 F17
9/2-10/26	1P: $34-$79	2P: $34-$79	XP: $8 F17
10/27-3/31	1P: $34-$59	2P: $34-$59	XP: $8 F17

Location: US 250, 2 mi n of SR 2. 3309 Milan Rd 44870. **Fax:** 419/626-4118. **Facility:** 32 one-bedroom standard units, some with whirlpools. 1 story, interior/exterior corridors. **Parking:** on-site. **Terms:** 3 day cancellation notice. **Amenities:** extended cable TV. **Pool(s):** outdoor. **Cards:** AX, CB, DC, DS, MC, VI. *(See color ad p 742)*

SOME UNITS

FAIRFIELD INN BY MARRIOTT

Phone: (419)621-9500

AAA SAVE
◊◊◊
Motel

6/22-9/1 [ECP]	1P: $79-$159	2P: $79-$159
4/1-6/21 [ECP]	1P: $43-$109	2P: $49-$109
9/2-10/26 [ECP]	1P: $43-$84	2P: $49-$84
10/27-3/31 [ECP]	1P: $43-$59	2P: $49-$59

Location: US 250, 0.5 mi s of SR 2. 6220 Milan Rd 44870. Fax: 419/621-9500. **Facility:** 63 one-bedroom standard units, some with whirlpools. 2 stories, interior corridors. **Parking:** on-site. **Amenities:** extended cable TV, voice mail, irons. **Pool(s):** heated indoor. **Guest Services:** coin laundry. **Business Services:** meeting rooms. **Cards:** AX, DC, DS, MC, VI. **Special Amenities:** free continental breakfast and free local telephone calls.
(See color ad p 735, p 739 & card insert)

SOME UNITS

S/D ⊞↑+ 🐕 🏊 🎥 DATA PORT 🖨 / ⊠
FEE

GREAT BEAR LODGE

Phone: (419)609-6000

AAA SAVE
◊◊◊
Resort

All Year   1P: $249-$339

Location: SR 2, 1 mi n on US 250. 4600 Milan Rd 44870. Fax: 419/609-6001. **Facility:** This is a family resort with a log lodge exterior look, six different rustic decor room styles and an indoor-outdoor waterpark for all to enjoy. 271 units. 249 one- and 22 two-bedroom standard units, some with whirlpools. 4 stories, interior corridors. *Bath:* combo or shower only. **Parking:** on-site. **Terms:** check-in 4 pm, 3 day cancellation notice-fee imposed, package plans. **Amenities:** video games, voice mail, hair dryers. **Dining:** dining room, restaurant, 7 am-9 pm, $8-$20. **Pool(s):** outdoor, 3 indoor, 2 small heated indoor, wading. **Leisure Activities:** whirlpools, waterslide, recreation program in summer, playground, exercise room. **Guest Services:** gift shop, coin laundry. **Business Services:** meeting rooms. **Cards:** AX, DC, DS, MC, VI. *(See color ad below)*

SOME UNITS

🍴 🍸 🏊 ⊠ 🎥 DATA PORT 🖬 🖭 🖳 🖨 / ⊠ /
FEE

GREENTREE INN

Phone: 419/626-6761

◊◊
Motel

6/14-9/1	1P: $64-$159	2P: $64-$159	XP: $10	F17
4/1-6/13	1P: $36-$89	2P: $36-$89	XP: $10	F17
9/2-10/26	1P: $36-$59	2P: $36-$59	XP: $10	F17
10/27-3/31	1P: $36-$54	2P: $36-$54	XP: $10	F17

Location: 2 mi e on US 6; at jct Cedar Point Cswy. 1935 E Cleveland Rd 44870. Fax: 419/621-8556. **Facility:** 91 one-bedroom standard units, some with whirlpools. 2 stories, interior/exterior corridors. **Parking:** on-site. **Terms:** 3 day cancellation notice-fee imposed, package plans. **Amenities:** extended cable TV, voice mail. **Pool(s):** indoor. **Leisure Activities:** whirlpool, exercise room. **Guest Services:** coin laundry. **Business Services:** conference facilities. **Cards:** AX, CB, DC, DS, JC, MC, VI. *(See color ad p 742)*

SOME UNITS

ASK S/D 🏊 🎥 DATA PORT 🖨 / ⊠ 🖬 🖳 /

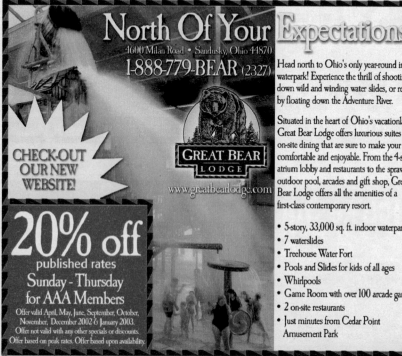

HOLIDAY INN EXPRESS   Phone: (419)624-0028

Motel

7/1-9/1	1P: $129-$169
5/16-6/30	1P: $119-$139
4/1-5/15 & 9/2-3/31	1P: $59-$109

Location: Jct SR 2 and US 250. 5513 1/2 Milan Rd 44870. Fax: 419/624-0988. **Facility:** 40 one-bedroom standard units. 2 stories, interior corridors. **Parking:** on-site. **Terms:** check-in 4 pm, 3 day cancellation notice-fee imposed. **Amenities:** extended cable TV, irons, hair dryers. **Guest Services:** valet laundry. **Business Services:** meeting rooms. **Cards:** AX, CB, DC, DS, JC, MC, VI.

SOME UNITS

HOLIDAY INN-SANDUSKY/CEDAR POINT AREA   Phone: (419)626-6671

Motor Inn

7/1-9/1	1P: $119-$169
5/16-6/30	1P: $79-$139
4/1-5/15 & 9/2-3/31	1P: $59-$109

Location: US 250, at jct SR 2. 5513 Milan Rd 44870. Fax: 419/626-9780. **Facility:** 175 one-bedroom standard units, some with whirlpools. 2 stories, interior/exterior corridors. **Parking:** on-site. **Terms:** check-in 4 pm, 3 day cancellation notice-fee imposed, package plans. **Amenities:** extended cable TV, irons, hair dryers. *Some:* video games. **Pool(s):** heated indoor. **Leisure Activities:** whirlpools, miniature golf, exercise room. *Fee:* game room. **Guest Services:** valet and coin laundry. **Business Services:** meeting rooms. **Cards:** AX, CB, DC, DS, JC, MC, VI.

SOME UNITS

HOWARD JOHNSON EXPRESS INN   Phone: (419)626-3742

(AAA) [SAVE]

Motel

5/1-10/31	1P: $40-$150	2P: $40-$150	F12
		XP: $10	

Location: Corner of Parkland Dr and Milan Rd (US 250). 2809 Milan Rd 44870 (29277 Hampshire Pl, WESTLAKE, 44145). Fax: 440/835-4242. **Facility:** 24 one-bedroom standard units. 2 stories, exterior corridors. *Bath:* combo or shower only. **Parking:** on-site. **Terms:** open 5/1-10/31, 3 day cancellation notice, [CP] meal plan available. **Amenities:** extended cable TV. **Pool(s):** outdoor. **Cards:** AX, DS, MC, VI. **Special Amenities:** free continental breakfast and free newspaper.

SOME UNITS

HOWARD JOHNSON EXPRESS INN NORTH   Phone: (419)625-1333

Motel

6/14-9/1	1P: $69-$149	2P: $69-$149	XP: $10	F17
4/1-6/13	1P: $34-$99	2P: $34-$99	XP: $10	F17
9/2-10/26	1P: $34-$79	2P: $34-$79	XP: $10	F17
10/27-3/31	1P: $34-$59	2P: $34-$59	XP: $10	F17

Location: 2 mi e on US 6; opposite Cedar Point Cswy. 1932 Cleveland Rd 44870. Fax: 419/626-4118. **Facility:** 68 one-bedroom standard units, some with whirlpools. 2 stories, exterior corridors. **Parking:** on-site. **Terms:** 3 day cancellation notice. **Amenities:** extended cable TV. **Pool(s):** heated outdoor. **Guest Services:** coin laundry. **Business Services:** meeting rooms. **Cards:** AX, CB, DC, DS, MC, VI. *(See color ad p 742)*

SOME UNITS

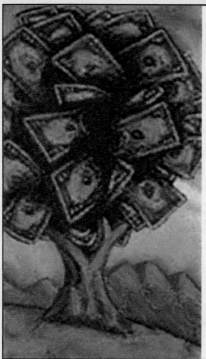

QUALITY INN & SUITES
Phone: (419)626-6766

AAA SAVE

Motel

6/14-9/4 [ECP]	1P: $88-$178	2P: $88-$178	XP: $6	F17
5/10-6/13 [ECP]	1P: $58-$130	2P: $58-$130	XP: $6	F17
9/5-3/31 [ECP]	1P: $43-$88	2P: $48-$98	XP: $6	F17
4/1-5/9 [ECP]	1P: $43	2P: $58	XP: $6	F17

Location: On US 250, 2 mi n of SR 2. 3304 Milan Rd 44870. Fax: 419/626-8882. **Facility:** 62 units. 52 one-bedroom standard units, some with whirlpools. 10 one-bedroom suites ($88-$275), some with efficiencies and/or whirlpools. 2 stories, interior/exterior corridors. **Parking:** on-site. **Terms:** cancellation fee imposed. **Amenities:** extended cable TV, hair dryers. **Pool(s):** heated outdoor, wading. **Cards:** AX, CB, DC, JC, MC, VI. *(See color ad below)*

SOME UNITS
FEE

RADISSON HARBOUR INN
Phone: (419)627-2500

AAA SAVE

Hotel

6/7-9/1	1P: $129-$240	2P: $129-$240
9/2-10/31	1P: $92-$159	2P: $92-$159
11/1-3/31	1P: $92-$145	2P: $92-$145
4/1-6/6	1P: $92-$135	2P: $92-$135

Location: US 6, just e of Cedar Point Cswy. 2001 Cleveland Rd 44870. Fax: 419/627-0745. **Facility:** 237 one-bedroom standard units, some with whirlpools. 4 stories, interior corridors. **Parking:** on-site. **Terms:** check-in 4 pm, 3 day cancellation notice-fee imposed, package plans. **Amenities:** video games, voice mail, irons, hair dryers. **Dining:** restaurant, 6:30 am-11 pm, $10-$18. **Pool(s):** heated indoor. **Leisure Activities:** whirlpool, boat dock, exercise room. **Guest Services:** gift shop, coin laundry. **Business Services:** conference facilities. **Cards:** AX, CB, DC, DS, JC, MC, VI.

SOME UNITS
FEE

RAMADA INN SANDUSKY
Phone: (419)626-9890

AAA SAVE

Motor Inn

7/28-9/1 [AP]	1P: $60-$180	2P: $60-$180		
6/23-7/27 [AP]	1P: $60-$150	2P: $60-$150		
4/1-6/22 [AP]	1P: $39-$120	2P: $44-$120	XP: $4	F17
9/2-3/31 [AP]	1P: $39-$100	2P: $44-$100	XP: $4	F17

Location: SR 250 at jct SR 2. 5608 Milan Rd, SR 250 44870. Fax: 419/626-0996. **Facility:** 100 one-bedroom standard units. 2 stories, interior corridors. **Parking:** on-site. **Terms:** 3 day cancellation notice. **Amenities:** extended cable TV, voice mail. **Dining:** dining room, 7 am-10 & noon-10 pm, Fri & Sat-11:30 pm, Sun 7 am-10 & noon-9 pm, $12-$18, cocktails. **Pool(s):** heated outdoor. **Cards:** AX, DC, DS, MC, VI. **Special Amenities:** free local telephone calls.
(See color ad p 738)

SOME UNITS

RED ROOF INN
Phone: 419/609-9000

AAA SAVE

◆◆◆

Motel

6/15-9/3 [ECP]	1P: $78-$178	2P: $78-$178
5/12-6/14 [ECP]	1P: $58-$118	2P: $58-$118
4/1-5/11 & 9/4-3/31 [ECP]	1P: $42	2P: $46

Location: SR 250, 0.5 mi s of SR 2. 6100 Milan Rd 44870. Fax: 419/609-8999. **Facility:** 50 one-bedroom standard units, some with whirlpools. 3 stories, interior corridors. **Parking:** on-site. **Terms:** cancellation fee imposed. **Amenities:** extended cable TV, voice mail. **Pool(s):** heated indoor. **Leisure Activities:** whirlpool, exercise room. **Guest Services:** coin laundry. **Cards:** AX, DC, DS, MC, VI. *(See color ad below)*

SOME UNITS

SEACREST MOTEL
Phone: 419/625-2522

◆◆◆

Motel

6/21-8/17	1P: $50-$80	2P: $60-$90
5/9-6/20 & 8/18-9/30	1P: $36-$50	2P: $44-$70

Location: 2.5 mi n on US 250 from jct SR 2, 0.5 mi w on Perkins Ave, then s. 2529 Columbus Ave 44870. **Facility:** 25 one-bedroom standard units. 1 story, exterior corridors. **Parking:** on-site. **Terms:** open 5/9-9/30, 3 day cancellation notice. **Amenities:** extended cable TV. **Pool(s):** heated indoor. **Cards:** AX, DS, MC, VI.

SLEEP INN
Phone: (419)625-6989

SAVE

◆◆◆

Motel

6/14-9/1 [CP]	1P: $69-$159	2P: $69-$159	XP: $10	F17
4/1-6/13 [CP]	1P: $49-$119	2P: $49-$119	XP: $10	F17
9/2-10/26 [CP]	1P: $49-$99	2P: $49-$99	XP: $10	F17
10/27-3/31 [CP]	1P: $39-$69	2P: $39-$69	XP: $10	F17

Location: Jct US 250 and SR 2. 5509 Milan Rd 44870. Fax: 419/625-1641. **Facility:** 68 one-bedroom standard units, some with whirlpools. 3 stories, interior corridors. **Bath:** combo or shower only. **Parking:** on-site. **Terms:** 3 day cancellation notice. **Amenities:** extended cable TV. *Some:* irons, hair dryers. **Pool(s):** heated indoor. **Leisure Activities:** whirlpool, exercise room. **Guest Services:** coin laundry. **Business Services:** meeting rooms, business center. **Cards:** AX, CB, DC, DS, MC, VI. *(See color ad p 742)*

SOME UNITS

Riverside Elegance

Our charming riverfront hotel is located in the heart of historic Huron, Ohio, just minutes from Cedar Point and all the area's exciting attractions. And, our low room rates make the River's Edge a family favorite!

SPECIAL AAA RATES:
Sun. - Thurs., $48-$68   July & Aug., $68-$98
double occupancy   double occupancy
(Fri. & Sat. not included, based on availability)

River's Edge INN
A Distinctively Different Hotel
132 Main Street • Huron, Ohio
800-947-3400 • 419-433-8000
www.cedarpointriversedge.com

Free Continental Breakfast
Large In-Door Pool
Jacuzzi

red roof inn

ALL NEW

"No French-milled soap.
No mints on the pillow.
No turn-down service.
No big bill either."

Rt. 250 & 2, Sandusky, Ohio 4 miles from Cedar Point

419-609-9000

www.redroof.com

For reservations call
1-800-THE-ROOF

red roof inns

SOUTH SHORE INN

				Phone: (419)626-4436	
▼▼▼	6/30-9/15	1P: $88-$148	2P: $88-$168	XP: $10	F
	4/1-6/29	1P: $68-$128	2P: $78-$128	XP: $10	F
Motel	9/16-3/31	1P: $48-$78	2P: $58-$88	XP: $10	F

Location: US 6, just e of Cedar Point Cswy. 2047 Cleveland Rd 44870. Fax: 419/626-0526. **Facility:** 100 one-bedroom standard units, some with efficiencies (no utensils) and/or whirlpools. 2 stories, interior/exterior corridors. **Parking:** on-site. **Amenities:** extended cable TV, voice mail, hair dryers. **Dining:** Graham's, see separate listing. **Pool(s):** heated outdoor. **Guest Services:** coin laundry. **Business Services:** meeting rooms. **Cards:** AX, CB, DC, DS, MC, VI. *(See color ad below)*

SOME UNITS

(A$K) (S☐) (†↑) (☒) (☞) (☜) (DATA PORT) (🖨) / (✕) (🖬) (🖴) (🖵) /

SUPER 8 MOTEL NORTH

				Phone: (419)625-7070
▼▼	6/22-9/1 [ECP]	1P: $69-$149	2P: $69-$149	
	4/1-6/21 [ECP]	1P: $39-$99	2P: $39-$99	
Motel	9/2-10/26 [ECP]	1P: $39-$79	2P: $39-$79	
	10/27-3/31 [ECP]	1P: $39-$49	2P: $39-$49	

Location: US 250, 0.3 mi n of SR 2. 5410 Milan Rd 44870. Fax: 419/625-7070. **Facility:** 68 one-bedroom standard units, some with whirlpools. 2 stories, exterior corridors. **Parking:** on-site. **Amenities:** extended cable TV. *Some:* irons, hair dryers. **Pool(s):** outdoor. **Guest Services:** coin laundry. **Cards:** AX, DC, DS, MC, VI. *(See color ad p 735 & p 739)*

SOME UNITS

(A$K) (S☐) (†↑) (☜) (☞) (DATA PORT) (🖨) / (✕) /

TRAVELODGE SANDUSKY

				Phone: (419)627-8971
(AAA) (SAVE)	6/29-8/24 [CP]	1P: $60-$160	2P: $60-$160	
▼▼	5/3-6/28 & 8/25-10/27 [CP]	1P: $50-$110	2P: $50-$110	
Motel				

Location: Jct SR 2 and US 250. 5906 Milan Rd 44870. Fax: 419/627-8114. **Facility:** 93 one-bedroom standard units, some with whirlpools. 2 stories, interior/exterior corridors. **Parking:** on-site. **Terms:** open 5/3-10/27, 3 day cancellation notice. **Amenities:** extended cable TV. *Some:* video games. **Pool(s):** outdoor. **Guest Services:** coin laundry. **Cards:** AX, DC, DS, MC, VI. **Special Amenities:** free continental breakfast and free local telephone calls. *(See color ad p 738)*

SOME UNITS

(S☐) (☜) (☞) (🖨) / (✕) (VCR) (🖬) (🖴) /

——— WHERE TO DINE ———

BACI NITE CLUB

▽▽▽▽

Northern
Italian

Dinner: $14-$25 **Phone: 419/624-9900**

Location: Jct SR 2 and US 250; in Comfort Inn Sandusky. 5909 Milan Rd 44870. **Hours:** 6 pm-2 am. Closed: Sun & Mon. **Reservations:** suggested. **Features:** dressy casual; carryout; cocktails. For a different experience, treat your special someone to an evening at Baci's, which means "KISSES" in Italian. You could begin your evening with a romantic dinner in one of the private alcoves and choose from a menu of certified black angus beef, fresh seafood and pasta all cooked in the style of Northern Italy. After 10 pm, enjoy dancing and a light show along with the fog bank. **Parking:** on-site. **Cards:** AX, DC, DS, MC, VI.

CEDAR VILLA

▽▽▽ ▽▽▽

Italian

MC, VI.

Dinner: $10-$18 **Phone: 419/625-8487**

Location: US 6, just w of Cedar Point Cswy. 1918 Cleveland Rd 44870. **Hours:** 4 pm-9 pm. Closed major holidays; also Sun, Mon & 9/17-10/8. **Features:** casual dress; children's menu; carryout; cocktails. At the entrance to Cedar Point, the cozy restaurant presents a menu of good, homemade Italian dishes, along with fresh perch and pickerel from Lake Erie. Smoke free premises. **Parking:** on-site. **Cards:** AX, DC, DS,

CHET & MATT'S

▽▽◆ ◆▽▽

American

Lunch: $4-$8 **Dinner: $6-$12** **Phone: 419/626-6000**

Location: 2 mi n of SR 2 on US 250, just e. 1013 E Strub Rd 44870. **Hours:** 11 am-10 pm, Fri-Sun to 1 am. Closed: 1/1, 11/28, 12/25. **Reservations:** suggested; Fri & Sat. **Features:** casual dress; carryout; salad bar; cocktails. This family oriented sports theme restaurant has a casual & comfortable atmosphere. They feature a wide variety of appetizers & the area's largest pizza as well as many specialty pizzas. Pictures of guests adorn the walls too. Smoke free premises. **Parking:** on-site. **Cards:** AX, DC, DS, MC, VI.

DIANNA'S DELI & RESTAURANT

▽▽ ▽▽

American

Lunch: $5-$9 **Dinner: $8-$14** **Phone: 419/625-9100**

Location: On US 250, 2.5 mi n of SR 2. 3002 Milan Rd 44870. **Hours:** 24 hours. **Features:** casual dress; children's menu; carryout. Among menu offerings are homemade soups and daily specials. **Parking:** on-site. **Cards:** AX, DC, DS, MC, VI.

GRAHAM'S

▽▽ ▽▽

American

Lunch: $7-$12 **Dinner: $7-$18** **Phone: 419/627-0011**

Location: US 6, just e of Cedar Point Cswy; in South Shore Inn. 2047 Cleveland Rd 44870. **Hours:** Open 5/1-10/15; 7 am-11:30 & 5-11 pm, Fri & Sat-midnight. **Features:** casual dress; children's menu; carryout; cocktails. The Lake Erie perch is a favorite at this restaurant, a popular spot for relaxed family dining. Preparations are tried and true, prices are reasonable, and portion sizes are hearty. Friendly, attentive servers seem to enjoy their jobs. **Parking:** on-site. **Cards:** AX, DS, MC, VI.

——— *The following restaurants have not been evaluated by AAA* ———
but are listed for your information only.

BARANEER'S CAFE

〔fyi〕

Not evaluated. **Location:** 116 Columbus Ave 44870. The downtown neighborhood cafe specializes in homemade cooking with reasonable prices.

BRENNAN'S STEAKHOUSE

〔fyi〕

Phone: 419/621-4134

Phone: 419/626-9733

Not evaluated. **Location:** 2916 Milan Rd 44870. Amply sized prime cuts stand out on the steakhouse's menu, as do the varied appetizers.

BUZZ'S EATING EXPERIENCE

〔fyi〕

Phone: 419/625-1551

Not evaluated. **Location:** 6201 Milan Rd 44870. Convenient to the turnpike and minutes from Cedar Point, the restaurant presents a varied menu and daily specials.

DEMORE'S FISH DEN

〔fyi〕

Phone: 419/626-8861

Not evaluated. **Location:** 302 W Perkins Ave 44870. Diners can relax on the seasonal patio while sampling preparations of fresh perch and pickerel.

THE LUNCH BOX

〔fyi〕

Phone: 419/626-3825

Not evaluated. **Location:** 154 Columbus Ave 44870. The restaurant prepares homemade soup, pie and daily specials.

SEAMAN pop. 100

——— WHERE TO STAY ———

RODEWAY INN

〔SAVE〕

▽▽ ◆

Motel

Phone: 937/386-2511

All Year [CP]   1P: $50-$65   2P: $55-$70   XP: $5   F18

Location: Jct SR 32 and 247. 55 Stern Dr 45679 (PO Box 277). Fax: 937/386-2100. **Facility:** 34 one-bedroom standard units, some with whirlpools. 2 stories, interior corridors. **Parking:** on-site. **Terms:** package plans. **Business Services:** meeting rooms. **Cards:** AX, DC, DS, JC, MC, VI.

SOME UNITS

FEE   FEE

SEVILLE pop. 1,800

——— WHERE TO STAY ———

SUPER 8 MOTEL-SEVILLE
▼▼▼ *Motel*
All Year [CP]   1P: $61-$69   2P: $61-$69   XP: $8   F18
Phone: (330)769-8880
Location: Jct SR 224 and Lake Rd. 6116 Speedway Dr 44273. Fax: 330/769-8880. **Facility:** 52 one-bedroom standard units. 2 stories, interior corridors. *Bath:* combo or shower only. **Parking:** on-site. **Terms:** pets ($50 deposit). **Amenities:** extended cable TV. **Guest Services:** coin laundry. **Cards:** AX, DC, DS, MC, VI.

SOME UNITS
(ASK) (S/D) 🛏 🐕 (🐾) 🎥 (DATA PORT) 🖨 / ✕ 🚪 🖥 /

SHAKER HEIGHTS —*See Cleveland p. 628.*

SHARONVILLE —*See Cincinnati p. 584.*

SHREVE pop. 1,600

——— WHERE TO DINE ———

DES DUTCH ESSENHAUS
▼▼▼ *American*
Lunch: $5-$10   **Dinner:** $6-$12   **Phone:** 330/567-2212
Location: 176 N Market St 44676. **Hours:** 7 am-8 pm, Fri & Sat-9 pm. Closed: 1/1, 12/25; also Sun. **Reservations:** suggested; weekends. **Features:** casual dress; children's menu; carryout; salad bar. The casual family restaurant servers dinners in the Amish tradition: chicken, ham, roast beef, turkey seafood and such delightful desserts as date pudding, apple dumplings, cinnamon rolls and freshly baked pies. Wood accents enhance the dining areas. **Parking:** street. **Cards:** DS, MC, VI.

✕

SIDNEY pop. 18,700

——— WHERE TO STAY ———

COMFORT INN
(AAA) (SAVE)
▼▼▼ *Motel*
4/1-9/1 [ECP]   1P: $61-$90   2P: $66-$95   XP: $5   F18
9/2-3/31 [ECP]   1P: $56-$80   2P: $61-$85
Phone: (937)498-9749
Location: I-75, exit 92, on SR 47. 1959 W Michigan Ave 45365. Fax: 937/497-8150. **Facility:** 71 one-bedroom standard units, some with whirlpools. 2 stories, interior corridors. **Parking:** on-site. **Terms:** pets ($25 deposit). **Amenities:** extended cable TV. *Some:* irons, hair dryers. **Pool(s):** heated outdoor. **Leisure Activities:** whirlpool, exercise room. **Guest Services:** valet laundry. **Business Services:** meeting rooms. **Cards:** AX, DC, DS, MC, VI. **Special Amenities:** free continental breakfast and free local telephone calls.

SOME UNITS
(S/D) 🛏 🍽 🏊 🎥 (DATA PORT) 🖥 / ✕ 🚪 (VCR) 🖥 🖨 /
FEE

DAYS INN
(AAA) (SAVE)
▼▼▼ *Motor Inn*
4/1-9/15 [ECP]   1P: $45-$75   2P: $45-$75   XP: $5   F11
9/16-3/31 [ECP]   1P: $43   2P: $43   XP: $5
Phone: (937)492-1104
Location: I-75, exit 92, at SR 47. 420 Folkerth Ave 45365. Fax: 932/492-1104. **Facility:** 119 one-bedroom standard units, some with whirlpools. 2 stories, exterior corridors. **Parking:** on-site. **Terms:** 3 day cancellation notice, pets ($5 extra charge). **Amenities:** extended cable TV, hair dryers. **Dining:** 2 restaurants, 4 pm-10 pm; closed Sun, $8-$17, cocktails. **Pool(s):** outdoor. **Leisure Activities:** playground. **Guest Services:** coin laundry. **Cards:** AX, DC, DS, JC, MC, VI. **Special Amenities:** free continental breakfast and free newspaper.

SOME UNITS
(S/D) 🛏 🍽 🏊 🎥 🖨 / ✕ 🚪 🖥 /

ECONO LODGE
(SAVE)
▼▼ *Motor Inn*
4/1-10/31   1P: $40   2P: $50   XP: $5   F16
11/1-3/31   1P: $36   2P: $46   XP: $5   F16
Phone: (937)492-9164
Location: I-75, exit 92, on SR 47. 2009 W Michigan St 45365. Fax: 937/492-9164. **Facility:** 98 one-bedroom standard units. 2 stories, interior/exterior corridors. **Parking:** on-site. **Amenities:** extended cable TV. **Pool(s):** outdoor. **Guest Services:** coin laundry. **Business Services:** meeting rooms. **Cards:** AX, DC, DS, JC, MC, VI.

SOME UNITS
(S/D) 🍽 🏊 / ✕ 🚪 🖥 /

GREATSTONE CASTLE
▼▼▼ *Historic Bed & Breakfast*
All Year   1P: $95-$145   2P: $95-$145   XP: $20
Phone: (937)498-4728
Location: I-75, exit 92, 1.2 mi e on SR 47, 3 blks n on West Ave. 429 N Ohio Ave 45365. Fax: 937/498-9950. **Facility:** Overlooking downtown, this 1895 stone-and-wood B&B has cathedral-like public areas featuring stained-glass windows and a grand staircase. Smoke free premises. 5 one-bedroom standard units. 2 stories, interior corridors. *Bath:* some shared or private. **Parking:** on-site. **Terms:** 7 day cancellation notice-fee imposed, no pets allowed (dog on premises). **Amenities:** extended cable TV. **Leisure Activities:** whirlpools, bicycles. **Guest Services:** massage (fee). **Cards:** AX, MC, VI.

SOME UNITS
✕ 🖨 / (VCR) /

HAMPTON INN
(AAA) (SAVE)
▼▼▼ *Motel*
All Year [ECP]   1P: $65   2P: $74
Phone: (937)498-8888
Location: I-75, exit 90, just w. 1600 Hampton Ct 45365. Fax: 937/498-8898. **Facility:** 68 one-bedroom standard units, some with whirlpools. 3 stories, interior corridors. *Bath:* combo or shower only. **Parking:** on-site. **Amenities:** extended cable TV, dual phone lines, voice mail, irons, hair dryers. **Pool(s):** heated indoor. **Leisure Activities:** exercise room. **Guest Services:** coin laundry. **Business Services:** meeting rooms, business center, PC. **Cards:** AX, DC, DS, JC, MC, VI.

SOME UNITS
(S/D) 🏊 🎥 (DATA PORT) 🖥 🖨 / ✕ 🚪 🖥 /

HOLIDAY INN

AAA SAVE

▼▼▼ ▼▼▼

Motor Inn

Phone: (937)492-1131

All Year   1P: $62   2P: $62   XP: $5   F19
Location: I-75, exit 92, just w. 400 Folkerth Ave 45365. Fax: 937/498-4655. **Facility:** 135 one-bedroom standard units. 2 stories, interior corridors. **Parking:** on-site. **Terms:** package plans, small pets only. **Amenities:** extended cable TV, voice mail, irons, hair dryers. **Dining:** dining room, 6:30 am-9 pm, Fri-10 pm, Sat 7 am-10 pm, Sun 7 am-8 pm, $7-$16, cocktails. **Pool(s):** outdoor. **Leisure Activities:** sauna, exercise room. **Guest Services:** coin laundry. **Business Services:** meeting rooms. **Cards:** AX, CB, DC, DS, JC, MC, VI.
Special Amenities: free local telephone calls and free newspaper.

SOME UNITS

[icons]

------ **WHERE TO DINE** ------

CJ'S HIGHMARKS

▼▼▼ ▼▼▼

American

Lunch: $7-$8   **Dinner:** $9-$18   **Phone:** 937/498-0072
Location: I-75, exit 92, 1 mi w on SR 47. 2599 W Michigan Ave 45365. **Hours:** 11 am-10 pm, Fri & Sat-11 pm. Closed: 11/28, 12/25. **Features:** casual dress; children's menu; carryout; cocktails & lounge. The upbeat family restaurant reflects the mood and stylings of a schoolhouse with a locker room-themed bar and lots of books and pencils. The menu, which resembles a folder, lists steak, seafood and specialty salads.
Parking: on-site. **Cards:** AX, DS, MC, VI.

[icon]

THE FAIRINGTON

▼▼▼ ▼▼▼

American

Lunch: $8-$10   **Dinner:** $15-$21   **Phone:** 937/492-6186
Location: Jct I-75 and Fair Rd, exit 90, just e. 1103 Fairington Dr 45365. **Hours:** 4:30 pm-9 pm, Fri & Sat-10 pm. Closed: 1/1, 7/4, 12/25; also Sun. **Features:** casual dress; children's menu; early bird specials; carryout; cocktails & lounge; buffet. An attractive wooded setting envelops the cozy restaurant, which overlooks a ravine. Candles and plants perk up the tavernlike dining room. The strength here is the food: flavorful preparations of steak, seafood and chicken, plus homemade dessert. **Parking:** on-site. **Cards:** AX, DS, MC, VI.

MICHAEL ANTHONY'S PASTA & GRILL

▼▼▼ ▼▼▼

Italian

Dinner: $9-$17   **Phone:** 937/497-9732
Location: I-75, exit 92, at SR 47. 420 Folkerth Ave 45365. **Hours:** 4 pm-9 pm, Fri & Sat-10 pm. Closed major holidays; also Sun. **Features:** casual dress; carryout; beer & wine only. Off the lobby of the Days Inn, the small restaurant offers a menu of Old World cuisine and classic American favorites. Smoke free premises. **Parking:** on-site. **Cards:** MC, VI.

[icon]

SMITHVILLE pop. 1,400

------ **WHERE TO DINE** ------

THE BARN RESTAURANT

▼▼▼ ▼▼▼

American

Lunch: $5-$8   **Dinner:** $7-$14   **Phone:** 330/669-2555
Location: 2 mi s on SR 585. 877 W Main St 44677. **Hours:** 10:30 am-8 pm, Fri & Sat-9 pm. Closed major holidays. **Features:** casual dress; children's menu; salad bar. Farming tools decorate the mid-1900s tri-level barn, which affords a wonderful view of the lake. Among menu offerings are barbecue chicken and pork ribs. The extensive salad bar is stocked with nicely displayed items. Smoke free premises. **Parking:** on-site. **Cards:** DS, MC, VI.

[icon]

SOLON —See Cleveland p. 629.

SPRINGBORO —See Cincinnati p. 587.

SPRINGDALE —See Cincinnati p. 587.

SPRINGFIELD pop. 70,500

------ **WHERE TO STAY** ------

COUNTRY INN & SUITES BY CARLSON

▼▼▼ ▼▼▼

Motel

Phone: (937)322-2200

All Year [ECP]   1P: $69-$105   2P: $69-$105
Location: Jct US 68 and SR 41. 1751 W 1st St 45504. Fax: 937/322-2200. **Facility:** 63 one-bedroom standard units. 3 stories, interior corridors. **Bath:** combo or shower only. **Parking:** on-site. **Amenities:** extended cable TV, voice mail, irons, hair dryers. **Pool(s):** heated indoor. **Leisure Activities:** whirlpool. **Guest Services:** valet and coin laundry. **Cards:** AX, DC, DS, MC, VI. **(See color ad p 646)**

SOME UNITS

[icons]

FAIRFIELD INN

AAA SAVE

▼▼▼ ▼▼▼

Motel

Phone: (937)323-9554

All Year [CP]   1P: $65-$85   2P: $65-$85   XP: $5   F17
Location: Jct US 68 and SR 41. 1870 W 1st St 45504. Fax: 937/323-9554. **Facility:** 63 one-bedroom standard units. 3 stories, interior corridors. **Bath:** combo or shower only. **Parking:** on-site. **Terms:** 5 day cancellation notice. **Amenities:** extended cable TV, irons. *Some:* dual phone lines. **Leisure Activities:** whirlpool. **Guest Services:** valet laundry. **Cards:** AX, DC, DS, MC, VI. **Special Amenities: free continental breakfast and free local telephone calls.** *(See color ad card insert)*

SOME UNITS

[icons] FEE

HAMPTON INN SPRINGFIELD

[SAVE]
▼▼▼
Motel

Phone: 937/325-8480

All Year [ECP]   1P: $79   2P: $84
Location: I-70, exit 54, just n. 101 W Leffel Ln 45506. Fax: 937/325-8634. **Facility:** 100 one-bedroom standard units. 4 stories, interior corridors. *Bath:* combo or shower only. **Parking:** on-site. **Amenities:** extended cable TV, video games, dual phone lines, voice mail, irons, hair dryers. **Pool(s):** heated indoor. **Leisure Activities:** whirlpool, exercise room. **Guest Services:** valet laundry. **Business Services:** meeting rooms. **Cards:** AX, DC, DS, MC, VI.

SOME UNITS

KNIGHTS INN

(AAA) [SAVE]
▼
Motel

Phone: (937) 325-8721

5/1-10/31   1P: $45-$52   2P: $50-$58   XP: $6   F18
4/1-4/30 & 11/1-3/31   1P: $36-$40   2P: $40-$45   XP: $6   F18
Location: I-70, exit 47, just e of US 68 on US 40. 2207 W Main St 45504. Fax: 937/322-0908. **Facility:** 39 one-bedroom standard units. 1 story, exterior corridors. **Parking:** on-site. **Terms:** small pets only ($10 extra charge). **Amenities:** extended cable TV. **Pool(s):** outdoor. **Cards:** AX, DC, DS, MC, VI. **Special Amenities: free continental breakfast.**

SOME UNITS

RAMADA LIMITED

(AAA) [SAVE]
▼▼ ▼▼
Motel

Phone: 937/328-0123

All Year [ECP]   1P: $70   2P: $75   XP: $6   F17
Location: I-70, exit 54, just n. 319 E Leffel Ln 45505. Fax: 937/322-4434. **Facility:** 46 one-bedroom standard units, some with whirlpools. 2 stories, interior corridors. **Parking:** on-site. **Terms:** pets ($10 extra charge). **Amenities:** extended cable TV, voice mail, safes (fee), irons, hair dryers. **Pool(s):** heated indoor. **Leisure Activities:** whirlpool, step machine. **Guest Services:** valet laundry. **Business Services:** meeting rooms. **Cards:** AX, DC, DS, JC, MC, VI.

SOME UNITS

RED ROOF INN

(AAA) [SAVE]
▼▼ ▼▼
Motel

Phone: (937) 325-5356

All Year [CP]   1P: $54-$99   2P: $59-$99   XP: $5   F17
Location: I-75, exit 54, just n, then w. 155 W Leffel Ln 45505. Fax: 937/322-9409. **Facility:** 58 units. 55 one-bedroom standard units, some with whirlpools. 3 one-bedroom suites ($79-$125). 3 stories, interior corridors. *Bath:* combo or shower only. **Parking:** on-site. **Terms:** 14 day cancellation notice-fee imposed, pets ($10 extra charge, designated units). **Amenities:** extended cable TV. **Pool(s):** heated indoor. **Cards:** AX, DS, MC, VI.

SOME UNITS

THE SPRINGFIELD INN

(AAA) [SAVE]
▼▼ ▼▼
Hotel

Phone: (937) 322-3600

All Year [CP]   1P: $69-$99   2P: $69-$99   XP: $10   F18
Location: I-70, exit 54, 2 mi n on SR 72, follow Limestone. 100 S Fountain Ave 45502. Fax: 937/322-0462. **Facility:** 124 one-bedroom standard units. 6 stories, interior corridors. **Parking:** on-site. **Terms:** package plans. **Amenities:** video games, voice mail, irons. *Some:* hair dryers. **Dining:** Ashley's Restaurant, see separate listing. **Guest Services:** valet laundry. **Business Services:** conference facilities. **Cards:** AX, CB, DC, DS, MC, VI. *(See color ad below)*

SOME UNITS

--- **WHERE TO DINE** ---

ASHLEY'S RESTAURANT

▼▼ ▼
American

Lunch: $8-$11   **Dinner:** $12-$20   Phone: 937/322-3600
Location: I-70, exit 54, 2 mi n on SR 72, follow Limestone; in Springfield Inn. 100 S Fountain Ave 45502. **Hours:** 6 am-2 & 5-9 pm, Fri & Sat-10 pm, Sun 11 am-2 & 5-9 pm. Closed: 12/25 7 am-2 pm. **Reservations:** suggested. **Features:** casual dress; Sunday brunch; children's menu; early bird specials; carryout; salad bar; cocktails & lounge. Creative seafood, prime rib and steak are menu mainstays along with several house specialties such as pot roast simmered in maple syrup and natural juices. The setting is Victorian with plenty of wood, windows, artwork and greenery to enhance your meal. Other entrees include far east pork chop accented with sweet sour sauce and fresh Norwegian salmon. **Parking:** on-site. **Cards:** AX, DC, DS, MC, VI. *(See color ad below)*

STEUBENVILLE pop. 22,100

------ WHERE TO STAY ------

HOLIDAY INN
AAA SAVE
▽▽▽
Motor Inn

Phone: (740)282-0901
All Year   1P: $80   2P: $80
Location: Jct US 22 and SR 7, 1 mi sw. 1401 University Blvd 43952. Fax: 740/282-9540. **Facility:** 120 one-bedroom standard units. 2-3 stories, interior/exterior corridors. *Bath:* some combo or shower only. **Parking:** on-site. **Terms:** 3 day cancellation notice. **Amenities:** extended cable TV, video games, voice mail, irons, hair dryers. **Dining:** dining room, 6:30 am-midnight, Fri-1 am, Sat 7 am-1 am, Sun 7 am-10 pm, $7-$13, cocktails. **Pool(s):** heated outdoor. **Leisure Activities:** exercise room. **Guest Services:** coin laundry. **Business Services:** meeting rooms. **Cards:** AX, CB, DC, DS, MC, VI. **Special Amenities: free local telephone calls and free newspaper.**

SUPER 8 MOTEL
▽▽▽
Motel

Phone: (740)282-4565
All Year   1P: $54-$64   2P: $54-$64   XP: $5   F12
Location: Jct US 22 and SR 7, 1 mi sw. 1505 University Blvd 43952. Fax: 740/282-4565. **Facility:** 63 one-bedroom standard units. 2 stories, interior corridors. *Bath:* combo or shower only. **Parking:** on-site. **Terms:** 7 day cancellation notice. **Amenities:** extended cable TV. *Some:* irons, hair dryers. **Business Services:** meeting rooms. **Cards:** AX, DC, DS, MC, VI.

------ WHERE TO DINE ------

NAPLES STEAK & SPAGETTI HOUSE
▽
Italian

Lunch: $5-$9   **Dinner: $7-$14**   **Phone: 740/283-3405**
Location: Downtown; jct of Fourth and North sts, just e. 329 North St 43952. **Hours:** 10:30 am-8 pm, Thurs & Fri-9 pm, Sat 11;30 am-9 pm, Sun 11:30 am-8 pm. Closed major holidays; also 7/1-7/7. **Features:** casual dress; children's menu; carryout; beer & wine only. Family-owned since 1923, the restaurant offers large portions and reasonable prices. **Parking:** on-site. **Cards:** DS, MC, VI.

THE VILLE RESTAURANT
▽
American

Lunch: $6-$17   **Dinner: $6-$17**   **Phone: 740/264-9887**
Location: Jct US 22 and John Scott Hwy, 2 mi sw to Fort Steubenville Mall; adjacent to Sears Department Store. Fort Steubenville Mall 43952. **Hours:** 11 am-10 pm, Fri & Sat-midnight, Sun noon-9 pm. Closed major holidays. **Features:** casual dress; children's menu; carryout; cocktails & lounge. More than 100 menu items are freshly prepared daily at the family-owned restaurant. **Parking:** on-site. **Cards:** AX, DS, MC, VI.

The following restaurants have not been evaluated by AAA but are listed for your information only.

FROEHLICH'S RIVERBOAT ROOM RESTAURANT
fyi

Phone: 740/283-9901
Not evaluated. **Location:** 909 Buckeye St 43952. The restaurant serves home-style dishes in a fine dining atmosphere.

HUNAN CHINESE RESTAURANT
fyi

Phone: 740/282-8952
Not evaluated. **Location:** 106 N 4th St 43952. The menu includes a variety of Cantonese, Mandarin, Hunan and spicy Szechwan dishes.

JAGGIN' AROUND RESTAURANT & PUB
fyi

Phone: 740/282-1010
Not evaluated. **Location:** 501 Washington St 43952. The restaurant is decorated in the 1930s art deco style.

STOW pop. 27,700

------ WHERE TO STAY ------

ECONOMY INN
AAA SAVE
▽▽▽
Motel

Phone: 330/929-8200
5/16-9/14 [CP]   1P: $65-$95   2P: $70-$95   XP: $11   F12
4/1-5/15 [CP]   1P: $55-$85   2P: $60-$85   XP: $9   F12
9/15-3/31 [CP]   1P: $55-$85   2P: $60-$85   XP: $11   F12
Location: SR 8, exit Graham Rd, just w. (1070 Graham Rd Circle, CUYAHOGA FALLS, 44223). Fax: 330/929-9299. **Facility:** 30 one-bedroom standard units, some with whirlpools. 1 story, exterior corridors. **Parking:** on-site. **Amenities:** extended cable TV, hair dryers. **Cards:** AX, DC, DS, MC, VI. **Special Amenities: free continental breakfast and preferred room (subject to availability with advanced reservations).**

STOW INN
AAA SAVE
▽
Motel

Phone: (330)688-3508
5/16-9/15   1P: $66-$91   2P: $66-$91   XP: $10   F18
4/1-5/15 & 9/16-3/31   1P: $51-$76   2P: $51-$76   XP: $8   F18
Location: 2 mi n on SR 91. 4601 Darrow Rd 44224. Fax: 330/688-3111. **Facility:** 32 one-bedroom standard units. 2 stories, interior corridors. **Parking:** on-site. **Amenities:** extended cable TV, hair dryers. **Cards:** DS, MC, VI. **Special Amenities: free local telephone calls.**

------ WHERE TO DINE ------

EL CAMPESINO
▽▽
Mexican

Lunch: $5-$8   **Dinner: $6-$12**   **Phone: 330/686-5561**
Location: 2 mi e of SR 43. 4360 Kent Rd 44224. **Hours:** 11 am-10 pm, Fri-10:30 pm, Sat noon-10 pm, Sun noon-9 pm. Closed major holidays. **Features:** casual dress; carryout; cocktails. The menu blends both traditional and more unusual dishes, all of which are served in huge portions. **Parking:** on-site. **Cards:** AX, DC, DS, MC, VI.

The following restaurants have not been evaluated by AAA but are listed for your information only.

HORIZON'S CLASSIC AMERICAN DINING   **Phone:** 330/686-3418
[fyi] Not evaluated. **Location:** 4410 Kent Rd 44224. The focus of the menu is on traditional selections, particularly homemade items.

MIKE'S BBQ & GRILL   **Phone:** 330/929-9995
[fyi] Not evaluated. **Location:** SR 8, exit Steels Corner. Bridgewater Plaza 44224. Although this place isn't fancy, it's popular for its large portions, food and friendly service.

STRASBURG pop. 2,000

——— WHERE TO STAY ———

RAMADA LIMITED DOVER/STRASBURG   **Phone:** (330)878-1400
(AAA) [SAVE] 5/1-10/31 [ECP]   1P: $70-$105   2P: $75-$110   XP: $5   F18
▼▼▼▼ 4/1-4/30 & 11/1-3/31 [ECP] 1P: $55-$90   2P: $60-$95   XP: $5   F18
Motel **Location:** I-77, exit 87, 0.4 mi n on US 250 and SR 21. 509 S Wooster Ave 44680. Fax: 330/878-1500. **Facility:** 58 one-bedroom standard units, some with whirlpools. 3 stories, interior corridors. *Bath:* combo or shower only.
Parking: on-site. **Terms:** package plans. **Amenities:** extended cable TV, voice mail. **Pool(s):** heated indoor. **Leisure Activities:** whirlpool, exercise room. **Guest Services:** coin laundry. **Business Services:** meeting rooms. **Cards:** AX, CB, DC, DS, JC, MC, VI. **Special Amenities:** free continental breakfast and free local telephone calls.

SOME UNITS
[S] [&M] [&] [🏊] [🌊] [🍴] [DATA PORT] [🖥] [🖨] / [✕] [🔒] [🖥] /

STREETSBORO pop. 9,900

——— WHERE TO STAY ———

BEST WESTERN INN & SUITES   **Phone:** (330)422-6446
(AAA) [SAVE] 5/25-9/4 [ECP]   1P: $125-$150   2P: $135-$160   XP: $10   F17
▼▼▼▼ 9/5-3/31 [ECP]   1P: $70-$80   2P: $75-$85   XP: $5   F17
Motel 4/1-5/24 [ECP]   1P: $65-$75   2P: $70-$80   XP: $5   F17
Location: I-80, exit 187, 1 mi s. 9172 Market Square Dr 44241. Fax: 330/422-0492. **Facility:** 66 one-bedroom standard units, some with whirlpools. 3 stories, interior corridors. *Bath:* combo or shower only. **Parking:** on-site.
Terms: 7 day cancellation notice. **Amenities:** voice mail, hair dryers. **Pool(s):** heated indoor. **Leisure Activities:** sauna, whirlpool, exercise room. *Fee:* game room. **Guest Services:** coin laundry. **Business Services:** meeting rooms. **Cards:** AX, DC, DS, MC, VI. **Special Amenities:** free continental breakfast and free local telephone calls.

SOME UNITS
[S] [🍴] [&] [🌊] [✕] [🌊] [DATA PORT] [🖨] / [✕] [🔒] [🖥] /

COMFORT INN   **Phone:** (330)626-5511
[SAVE] 5/1-9/10   1P: $60-$130   2P: $60-$130   XP: $7   F18
▼▼▼ 9/11-3/31   1P: $60-$90   2P: $60-$130   XP: $7   F18
Motel 4/1-4/30   1P: $60-$90   2P: $60-$90   XP: $7   F18
Location: I-80, exit 187, 0.5 mi s. 9789 SR 14 44241. Fax: 330/626-5724. **Facility:** 79 one-bedroom standard units, some with whirlpools. 2 stories, interior corridors. **Parking:** on-site. **Terms:** 14 day cancellation notice.
Amenities: extended cable TV, hair dryers. *Some:* irons. **Business Services:** meeting rooms. **Cards:** AX, CB, DC, DS, MC, VI.

SOME UNITS
[S] [🌊] [DATA PORT] [🖨] / [✕] [🔒] [🖥] [🖥] /

FAIRFIELD INN   **Phone:** (330)422-1166
(AAA) [SAVE] All Year   1P: $79-$179   2P: $79-$179   XP: $10   F18
▼▼▼ **Location:** I-80, exit 187, 0.8 mi s. 9783 SR 14 44241. Fax: 330/422-1140. **Facility:** 83 one-bedroom standard units, some with whirlpools. 3 stories, interior corridors. *Bath:* combo or shower only. **Parking:** on-site.
Motel **Amenities:** extended cable TV, dual phone lines, voice mail, irons. **Pool(s):** heated indoor. **Leisure Activities:** whirlpool, exercise room. **Guest Services:** coin laundry. **Business Services:** meeting rooms. **Cards:** AX, DC, DS, MC, VI. **Special Amenities:** free continental breakfast and free local telephone calls. *(See ad p 612 & color ad card insert & ad p 752)*

SOME UNITS
[S] [&M] [&] [🏊] [🌊] [✕] [DATA PORT] [🖨] / [✕] [🔒] [🖥] [🖥] /

HAMPTON INN & SUITES
AAA [SAVE]
▼▼▼▼▼
Motel

Phone: (330)422-0500

6/14-8/24 [ECP]	1P: $125-$145	2P: $125-$145
4/1-6/13 [ECP]	1P: $85-$125	2P: $85-$125
1/1-3/31 [ECP]	1P: $90-$110	2P: $90-$110
8/25-12/31 [ECP]	1P: $85-$105	2P: $85-$105

Location: I-80, exit 187, 0.8 mi s. 800 Mondial Pkwy 44241. Fax: 330/422-0600. **Facility:** 90 one-bedroom standard units, some with efficiencies and/or whirlpools. 3 stories, interior corridors. *Bath:* combo or shower only. **Parking:** on-site. **Amenities:** extended cable TV, dual phone lines, voice mail, irons. *Some:* hair dryers. **Pool(s):** heated indoor. **Leisure Activities:** whirlpool, exercise room. **Guest Services:** coin laundry. **Business Services:** meeting rooms. **Cards:** AX, CB, DC, DS, MC, VI. **Special Amenities:** free continental breakfast and free local telephone calls. *(See color ad p 613)*

SOME UNITS

HOLIDAY INN EXPRESS HOTEL AND SUITES
▼▼▼▼▼
Motel

Phone: (330)422-1888

5/24-9/2	1P: $109-$129	2P: $109-$129	XP: $10
4/1-5/23 & 9/3-3/31	1P: $49-$69	2P: $49-$69	XP: $10

Location: I-80, exit 187, 0.5 mi e. 9459 SR 14 44241. Fax: 330/422-0566. **Facility:** 72 one-bedroom standard units, some with whirlpools. 3 stories, interior corridors. *Bath:* combo or shower only. **Terms:** check-in 4 pm. **Amenities:** video games, dual phone lines, voice mail, irons, hair dryers. **Pool(s):** heated indoor. **Leisure Activities:** sauna, whirlpool, exercise room. **Guest Services:** coin laundry. **Cards:** AX, CB, DC, DS, MC, VI.

SOME UNITS

MICROTEL INN & SUITES OF STREETSBORO
▼▼▼▼ ▼▼▼▼
Motel

Phone: 330/422-1234

5/15-9/15	1P: $50-$149	2P: $50-$149	XP: $5	F16
4/1-5/14 & 9/16-3/31	1P: $30-$60	2P: $30-$60	XP: $5	F16

Location: I-80, exit 187, 1.2 mi s. 9371 SR 14 44241. Fax: 330/422-1232. **Facility:** 100 one-bedroom standard units. 3 stories, interior corridors. *Bath:* combo or shower only. **Parking:** on-site. **Terms:** cancellation fee imposed. **Amenities:** video games, voice mail. *Some:* irons, hair dryers. **Pool(s):** heated indoor. **Leisure Activities:** exercise room. **Guest Services:** coin laundry. **Business Services:** meeting rooms. **Cards:** AX, DC, DS, MC, VI.

SOME UNITS

SUPER 8 MOTEL
AAA [SAVE]
▼▼▼▼▼
Motel

Phone: (330)626-2888

6/1-9/6	1P: $75-$99	2P: $95-$125	XP: $6	F17
4/1-5/31 & 9/7-3/31	1P: $52-$59	2P: $55-$65	XP: $6	F17

Location: I-80, exit 187, 1 mi s. 9420 SR 14 44241. Fax: 330/626-2888. **Facility:** 57 one-bedroom standard units, some with whirlpools. 2 stories, interior corridors. **Parking:** on-site. **Amenities:** extended cable TV. **Pool(s):** outdoor. **Guest Services:** coin laundry. **Business Services:** meeting rooms. **Cards:** AX, CB, DC, DS, MC, VI. **Special Amenities:** free continental breakfast and free local telephone calls.

SOME UNITS

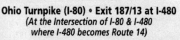

WINGATE INN

AAA [SAVE]
▽▽▽▽▽
Motel

6/2-9/1 [CP]	1P: $119-$139	2P: $119-$139	XP: $10 F18
4/1-6/1 & 9/2-3/31 [CP]	1P: $79-$89	2P: $79-$89	XP: $10 F18

Phone: (330)422-9900

Location: I-80, exit 187, 0.8 mi s. 9705 SR 14 44241. Fax: 330/422-0822. **Facility:** 85 one-bedroom standard units, some with whirlpools. 3 stories, interior corridors. *Bath:* combo or shower only. **Parking:** on-site. **Amenities:** extended cable TV, video games, high-speed Internet, dual phone lines, voice mail, safes, irons, hair dryers. **Pool(s):** heated indoor. **Leisure Activities:** whirlpool, exercise room. *Fee:* game room. **Guest Services:** valet and coin laundry. **Business Services:** meeting rooms, business center. **Cards:** AX, DC, DS, MC, VI. **Special Amenities: free continental breakfast and free newspaper.** *(See color ad p 752)*   SOME UNITS

[icons] FEE

The following lodging was either not evaluated or did not meet AAA rating requirements but is listed for your information only.

TOWNPLACE SUITES BY MARRIOTT

[fyi]
Hotel

6/2-9/3	1P: $99-$289
4/1-6/1 & 9/4-3/31	1P: $69-$139

Phone: 330/422-1855

Too new to rate. **Location:** 795 Mondial Pkwy 44241. Fax: 330/422-1450.
(See color ad card insert & ad p 752)

——— WHERE TO DINE ———

BRINKER'S SPORTS GRILL
▽▽
American

Lunch: $5-$8   **Dinner:** $6-$12   **Phone:** 330/626-2171

Location: Jct SR 43 and 14. 9230 SR 14 44241. **Hours:** 8:30 am-11 pm, Fri & Sat-midnight. Closed major holidays. **Features:** casual dress; Sunday brunch; children's menu; carryout; cocktails & lounge. The barbecue pork basket is just one homemade special to enjoy at this friendly neighborhood sports bar. Relax while watching the latest sports events. **Parking:** on-site. **Cards:** AX, DC, DS, MC, VI.   [X]

FINAL SCORE
▽▽ ▽▽▽
American

Lunch: $5-$9   **Dinner:** $6-$15   **Phone:** 330/626-9499

Location: 0.6 mi e of SR 43. 9062 SR 14 44241. **Hours:** 11 am-11 pm. **Features:** casual dress; children's menu; carryout; cocktails. Diners can cheer on their favorite team on one of 30 TVs mounted throughout this popular sports bar, which is just a short drive from Six Flags. Ample space can accommodate large crowds and the lively clientele who visit in the evenings. Sandwiches and dinner entrees can be washed down with 31 different beers. Service is fast and efficient. **Parking:** on-site. **Cards:** DS, MC, VI.   [X]

STRONGSVILLE —*See Cleveland p. 629.*

SUGARCREEK pop. 2,100

——— WHERE TO STAY ———

DUTCH HOST INN
▽▽▽▽
Motel

5/23-11/2 [ECP]	1P: $55-$80	2P: $60-$85	XP: $5 F12
4/1-5/22 [ECP]	1P: $45-$60	2P: $50-$65	XP: $5 F12
11/3-3/31 [ECP]	1P: $35-$50	2P: $40-$55	XP: $5 F12

Phone: 330/852-2468

Location: 1.5 mi e. State Rt 39 E, 1021 Dover Rd 44681. **Facility:** 32 units. 28 one-bedroom standard units. 4 one-bedroom suites with whirlpools. 1 story, exterior corridors. **Parking:** on-site. **Amenities:** extended cable TV, hair dryers. *Some:* irons. **Business Services:** meeting rooms. **Cards:** DS, MC, VI.   SOME UNITS

[icons]

——— WHERE TO DINE ———

BEACHY'S COUNTRY CHALET
▽▽▽ ▽▽
American

Lunch: $5-$8   **Dinner:** $8-$14   **Phone:** 330/852-4644

Location: Just e on E Main St. 115 Andreas Dr 44681. **Hours:** 11 am-10 pm. Closed: 11/28, 12/25; also Sun. **Features:** casual dress; children's menu; carryout. Family favorites, such as chicken, roast beef and turkey, mix with homemade soup, salad, dessert and bread on the Amish-style menu. Quilts, plants and flowers decorate the dining room, which features many windows. The patio is a nice place to relax. Smoke free premises. **Parking:** on-site. **Cards:** MC, VI.   [X]

DUTCH VALLEY RESTAURANT
▽▽▽ ▽▽▽
American

Lunch: $5-$8   **Dinner:** $7-$11   **Phone:** 330/852-4627

Location: 1 mi e on SR 39. **Hours:** 7 am-8 pm. Closed major holidays; also Sun. **Features:** casual dress; children's menu; carryout; salad bar. Good food, a convenient location and reasonable prices make this family-oriented eatery shine. Generous portions of fresh turkey, homemade mashed potatoes and green beans consistently earn a thumbs up from diners. Service is both attentive and prompt. Smoke free premises. **Parking:** on-site. **Cards:** DS, MC, VI.   [X]

SUNBURY —See Columbus p. 668.

SYLVANIA pop. 17,300 (See map p. 756; index p. 758)

——— WHERE TO DINE ———

CIAO! RISTORANTE
Dinner: $13-$23   **Phone:** 419/882-2334   **23**
Italian
Location: US 223/23, exit W Alexis/Monroe rds and SR 51/184, just w. 6064 Monroe St 43560. **Hours:** 5 pm-10 pm, Fri-11 pm, Sat 4 pm-11 pm, Sun 4 pm-9 pm. **Closed:** 1/1, 11/28, 12/25. **Reservations:** suggested. **Features:** dressy casual; children's menu; carryout; cocktails & lounge. An extraordinarily popular restaurant providing a gastronomic culinary delight of Italian cuisine served in a rustic setting. Sumptuous entrees like angel hair pasta tossed with house smoked salmon or the ravioli with ground veal, sage and cream reflect a few of the many pasta dishes. Lamb chops, veal, grilled fish and seafood are also deftly prepared. Be self-indulgent and top your meal off with the cannoli, tiramisu or one of the assorted flavors of gelatos and sorbets. Sparkly service. **Parking:** on-site. **Cards:** AX, DS, MC, VI.

FRICKER'S
Lunch: $6-$8   **Dinner:** $7-$13   **Phone:** 419/885-2141   **24**
American
Location: US 23, exit Sylvania, just w. 6339 Monroe St 43560. **Hours:** 11 am-2:30 am. Closed major holidays. **Features:** casual dress; carryout; cocktails & lounge. Televisions broadcasting sporting events are spread out throughout the boisterous restaurant, which is decorated with sports memorabilia. The food, such as chicken wings, sandwiches and ribs, is familiar and filling. Service is casual and attentive. **Parking:** on-site. **Cards:** AX, DS, MC, VI.

TIFFIN pop. 18,600

——— WHERE TO STAY ———

HAMPTON INN
Phone: 419/443-5300
SAVE
Motel
All Year [CP]   1P: $70-$95   2P: $75-$100
Location: 3 mi sw just off US 224. 2492 S SR 231 44883. Fax: 419/443-0140. **Facility:** 65 one-bedroom standard units, some with whirlpools. 3 stories, interior corridors. *Bath:* combo or shower only. **Parking:** on-site. **Terms:** 3 day cancellation notice, [ECP] meal plan available, pets ($50 fee, $200 deposit). **Amenities:** extended cable TV, voice mail, irons, hair dryers. **Pool(s):** heated indoor. **Leisure Activities:** whirlpool, exercise room. **Guest Services:** valet and coin laundry. **Business Services:** meeting rooms. **Cards:** AX, CB, DC, DS, JC, MC, VI.

SOME UNITS

HOLIDAY INN EXPRESS
Phone: (419)443-5100
AAA **SAVE**
Motel
All Year   1P: $70   2P: $75   XP: $5   F18
Location: Just w of mall. 78 Shaffer Park Dr 44883. Fax: 419/443-5200. **Facility:** 60 one-bedroom standard units, some with whirlpools. 3 stories, interior corridors. *Bath:* combo or shower only. **Parking:** on-site. **Amenities:** extended cable TV, voice mail, irons, hair dryers. **Pool(s):** heated indoor. **Leisure Activities:** exercise room. **Guest Services:** valet and coin laundry. **Business Services:** meeting rooms. **Cards:** AX, CB, DC, DS, JC, MC, VI. **Special Amenities:** free continental breakfast and free local telephone calls.

SOME UNITS

QUALITY INN
Phone: (419)447-6313
SAVE
Motor Inn
All Year [ECP]   1P: $75   2P: $81   XP: $6   F18
Location: 2 mi sw, at jct US 224 and SR 53. 1927 S SR 53 44883. Fax: 419/447-7024. **Facility:** 72 one-bedroom standard units, some with whirlpools. 2 stories, interior/exterior corridors. **Parking:** on-site. **Amenities:** extended cable TV. *Some:* irons, hair dryers. **Pool(s):** outdoor. **Guest Services:** coin laundry. **Business Services:** meeting rooms. **Cards:** AX, DC, DS, MC, VI.

SOME UNITS

——— WHERE TO DINE ———

PIONEER MILL OF TIFFIN Historical   **Lunch:** $6-$11   **Dinner:** $14-$20   **Phone:** 419/448-0100
American
Location: 3 blks n of Town Square on Washington, 0.6 mi e. 255 Riverside Dr 44883. **Hours:** 11 am-9 pm, Fri & Sat-10 pm, Sun 10 am-9 pm. Closed major holidays; also 12/24. **Reservations:** suggested; weekends. **Features:** casual dress; Sunday brunch; children's menu; early bird specials; carryout; cocktails & lounge. Built in 1822 by the founder of Tiffin, the historic mill is on the banks of the scenic, winding Sandusky River. Mill artifacts dominate the original brick and concrete walls. Tinkers Dam lounge is on the lower level. The menu features prime rib, as well as steaks, seafood and chicken. **Parking:** on-site. **Cards:** AX, DC, DS, MC, VI.

─── *The following restaurants have not been evaluated by AAA* ───
but are listed for your information only.

OLD OAKEN BUCKET   **Phone:** 419/639-2497
[fyi]   Not evaluated. **Location:** 5509 N SR 101 44883. The restaurant caters to the lunch and dinner crowds with its varied menu and daily specials.

ROSES SOUP & SUCH   **Phone:** 419/447-7562
[fyi]   Not evaluated. **Location:** 122 Miami St 44883. Diners seeking a lighter meal can choose from a variety of salads and soups.

TIPP CITY pop. 6,000

─────── **WHERE TO STAY** ───────

HOLIDAY INN EXPRESS   **Phone:** (937)667-1574

◆◆◆ SAVE	4/8-5/26 [CP]	1P: $86-$145	XP: $10	F18
▼▼▼	5/27-8/18 [CP]	1P: $74-$145	XP: $10	F18
	4/1-4/7 [CP]	1P: $69-$139	XP: $10	F18
Motel	8/19-3/31 [CP]	1P: $69-$74	XP: $10	F18

Location: I-75, exit 68, just w. 19 Weller Dr 45371. **Fax:** 937/667-0298. **Facility:** 56 one-bedroom standard units, some with whirlpools. 3 stories, interior corridors. *Bath:* combo or shower only. **Parking:** on-site. **Terms:** cancellation fee imposed. **Amenities:** extended cable TV, voice mail, irons, hair dryers. **Pool(s):** heated indoor. **Leisure Activities:** whirlpool. *Fee:* game room. **Guest Services:** coin laundry. **Business Services:** meeting rooms. **Cards:** AX, DC, DS, MC, VI. **Special Amenities:** free continental breakfast and free local telephone calls.

SOME UNITS

[🅢🅓] 🍴 📶 📺 🏊 📹 DATAPORT 📞 🖨 / ✖ 🔒 🧺 /

─────── **WHERE TO DINE** ───────

TIPP O' THE TOWN FAMILY RESTAURANT   **Lunch:** $5-$12   **Dinner:** $5-$12   **Phone:** 937/667-1168
▼▼   **Location:** I-75, exit 68, just w. 1150 W Main St 45371. **Hours:** 5:30 am-9 pm, Fri & Sat-10 pm, Sun-3 pm.
American   Closed major holidays. **Features:** casual dress; children's menu; carryout. The family-style restaurant offers a reliable menu of pasta, steak and chicken preparations. Breakfast is served anytime. **Parking:** on-site. **Cards:** DS, MC, VI.

✖

Look for a SAVE Place to Stay!

When selecting a AAA Approved lodging, look for properties that participate in our SAVE programs. These properties understand the value of AAA business and many offer discounts to AAA members.

• A red (SAVE) icon in their TourBook® guide listing indicates an **Official Appointment** property that offers a minimum 10% discount off published TourBook standard room rates or the lowest public standard room rate, at the time of booking, for the dates of stay.

• A black (SAVE) icon indicates a chain hotel that participates in the **Show Your Card & Save®** program. These properties offer a satisfaction guarantee and AAA's best rates for your dates of stay. Please refer to page 22 in the TourBook Navigator section for complete details and a list of participating hotel chains or call AAA/CAA's exclusive toll-free reservation number **866-AAA-SAVE** to make a reservation.

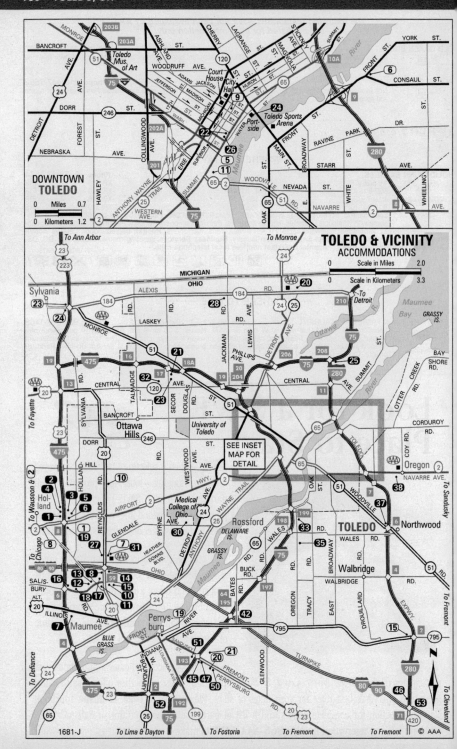

DOWNTOWN TOLEDO

Miles 0 — 0.7

Kilometers 0 — 1.2

TOLEDO & VICINITY ACCOMMODATIONS

Scale in Miles 0 — 2.0

Scale in Kilometers 0 — 3.3

1681-J

© AAA

Toledo and Vicinity

This index helps you "spot" where approved accommodations and restaurants are located on the corresponding detailed maps. Lodging rate ranges are for comparison only and show the property's high season; rates are per night, unless only weekly (W) or monthly (M) rates are available. Restaurant rate range is for dinner, unless only lunch (L) is served. Turn to the listing page for more detailed rate information and consult display ads for special promotions.

Spotter/Map Page Number	OA	HOLLAND - Lodgings	Diamond Rating	Rate Range High Season	Listing Page
1 / p. 756	AAA	Courtyard by Marriott-Toledo/Holland - see color ad card insert	◆◆◆	$99-$129 SAVE	695
2 / p. 756	AAA	Cross Country Inn	◆◆	$40-$54 SAVE	695
3 / p. 756	AAA	Red Roof Inn Toledo/Holland	◆◆	$37-$64 SAVE	696
4 / p. 756	AAA	Fairfield Inn by Marriott-Toledo/Holland - see color ad card insert	◆◆	$59-$89 SAVE	696
5 / p. 756	AAA	Residence Inn by Marriott - see color ad card insert	◆◆◆	$139-$159 SAVE	696
6 / p. 756		Extended Stay America	◆◆	Failed to provide	695
		HOLLAND - Restaurants			
① / p. 756		Joe's Crab Shack	◆◆	$10-$16	696
② / p. 756		El Matador Restaurant	◆	$9-$12	696
		MAUMEE - Lodgings			
7 / p. 756		Super 8 Toledo-Maumee	◆◆	$50-$85	711
8 / p. 756		Cross Country Inn Toledo/Maumee	◆◆	$36-$50	711
10 / p. 756	AAA	Comfort Inn Toledo West/Maumee - see color ad p 760	◆◆◆	$49-$69 SAVE	710
11 / p. 756		Hampton Inn Toledo South/Maumee	◆◆◆	$77-$95	711
12 / p. 756		Toledo/Maumee Homewood Suites by Hilton	◆◆◆	$119	712
13 / p. 756	AAA	Fairfield Inn-Toledo/Maumee - see color ad card insert	◆◆◆	$75-$85 SAVE	711
14 / p. 756	AAA	Red Roof Inn-Maumee	◆◆	$41-$69 SAVE	711
15 / p. 756	AAA	Days Inn Toledo Arrowhead	◆◆	$50-$80 SAVE	711
16 / p. 756		Country Inn & Suites By Carlson - see color ad p 646	◆◆◆	$75-$85	710
17 / p. 756	AAA	Comfort Inn & Suites - see color ad p 760	◆◆◆	$59-$79 SAVE	710
18 / p. 756	AAA	Courtyard by Marriott-Toldeo/Maumee - see color ad card insert	◆◆◆	$104 SAVE	711
19 / p. 756		Knights Inn-Toledo West	◆	$44-$150	711
		TOLEDO - Lodgings			
20 / p. 756	AAA	Comfort Inn-North	◆◆	$49-$89 SAVE	759
21 / p. 756	AAA	Comfort Inn Westgate	◆◆	$59-$99 SAVE	760
22 / p. 756	AAA	Radisson Hotel Toledo	◆◆◆	$135 SAVE	761
23 / p. 756	AAA	Clarion Hotel Westgate	◆◆◆	$79-$129 SAVE	759
24 / p. 756	AAA	Wyndham Toledo	◆◆◆	$99-$139 SAVE	762
25 / p. 756	AAA	Classic Inn	◆	$45-$125 SAVE	759
26 / p. 756	AAA	Ramada Inn & Suites - see color ad p 761	◆◆	$99-$139 SAVE	761
27 / p. 756		Holiday Inn Toledo West	◆◆◆	$99-$110	761
28 / p. 756	AAA	Crown Inn	◆	$57-$69 SAVE	760

Spotter/Map Page Number	OA	TOLEDO - Lodgings (continued)	Diamond Rating	Rate Range High Season	Listing Page
30 / p. 756	AAA	Hilton Toledo - see color ad p 760	◆◆◆	$99-$149 SAVE	761
31 / p. 756	AAA	Quality Hotel - see color ad p 759	◆◆	$70-$100 SAVE	761
32 / p. 756	AAA	Red Roof Inn Secor	◆◆	$44-$68 SAVE	762
33 / p. 756		Days Inn-Toledo	◆◆	$54-$60	760
		TOLEDO - Restaurants			
5 / p. 756		Spaghetti Warehouse	◆◆	$9-$15	762
6 / p. 756		Tony Packo's Cafe	◆◆	$8-$12	762
7 / p. 756		Dominic's	◆	$9-$15	762
8 / p. 756		El Matador Restaurant	◆	$9-$12	762
9 / p. 756		Georgio's Cafe International	◆◆◆	$18-$28	762
10 / p. 756		The Mango Tree	◆◆	$10-$18	762
11 / p. 756		Maumee Bay Brewing Company	◆◆	$11-$18	762
		NORTHWOOD - Lodgings			
35 / p. 756		Microtel Inn & Suites	◆◆	$49-$79	722
		NORTHWOOD - Restaurant			
15 / p. 756		Sallock's Steakhouse	◆◆	$7-$15	723
		OREGON - Lodgings			
37 / p. 756	AAA	Sleep Inn & Suites - see color ad p 759	◆◆◆	$69-$79 SAVE	724
38 / p. 756	AAA	Comfort Inn East - see color ad p 759	◆◆◆	$64-$74 SAVE	724
		ROSSFORD - Lodgings			
42 / p. 756	AAA	Courtyard by Marriott-Perrysburg/Rossford - see color ad card insert	◆◆◆	$89 SAVE	733
		PERRYSBURG - Lodgings			
45 / p. 756		Holiday Inn Express	◆◆◆	$92	726
46 / p. 756	AAA	Howard Johnson Inn Toledo South - see color ad p 726	◆◆	$36-$55 SAVE	727
47 / p. 756	AAA	Holiday Inn-French Quarter	◆◆◆	$120-$180 SAVE	727
50 / p. 756		Days Inn of Toledo-Perrysburg	◆	$65-$90	726
51 / p. 756	AAA	Baymont Inn & Suites Toledo-Perrysburg - see color ad opposite title page	◆◆◆	$64-$74 SAVE	726
52 / p. 756	AAA	Red Carpet Inn	◆	$35-$55 SAVE	727
53 / p. 756	AAA	Ramada Limited	◆◆	$54-$59 SAVE	727
		PERRYSBURG - Restaurants			
19 / p. 756		Casa Barron Restaurante	◆◆	$5-$14	727
20 / p. 756		Croy's Supper Club	◆◆	$14-$21	727
21 / p. 756		Fricker's	◆	$9-$15	727
		SYLVANIA - Restaurants			
23 / p. 756		Ciao! Ristorante	◆◆◆	$13-$23	754
24 / p. 756		Fricker's	◆	$7-$13	754

TOLEDO pop. 332,900   (See map p. 756; index p. 757)

———— WHERE TO STAY ————

CLARION HOTEL WESTGATE   Phone: (419)535-7070   23
(AAA) [SAVE]   All Year   1P: $79-$129   2P: $79-$129
▼▼▼▼   **Location:** I-475, exit 17, just s. 3536 Secor Rd 43606. Fax: 419/536-4836. **Facility:** 305 units. 303 one-bedroom
Hotel   standard units, some with whirlpools. 2 one-bedroom suites ($169-$395) with whirlpools. 3 stories, interior
corridors. **Parking:** on-site. **Amenities:** extended cable TV, voice mail, irons, hair dryers. **Dining:** restaurant,
6:30 am-2 & 5-9 pm, Sat 7:30 am-10 pm, Sun 8 am-2 pm, $11-$23, cocktails. **Pool(s):** heated indoor.
Leisure Activities: whirlpool, jogging, exercise room. **Guest Services:** valet laundry, airport transportation-
Toledo Express Airport, area transportation-within 5 mi, train depot, bus station. **Business Services:** conference facilities.
Cards: AX, CB, DC, DS, JC, MC, VI. **Special Amenities:** free local telephone calls and free newspaper.

SOME UNITS

[icons] FEE

CLASSIC INN   Phone: (419)729-1945   25
(AAA) [SAVE]   All Year   1P: $45-$125   2P: $45-$125
▼   **Location:** I-280, exit 12, just e; I-75, exit 208 (Manhattan Blvd) southbound; exit 207 northbound. 1821 E Manhattan Blvd
Motel   43608. Fax: 419/729-2920. **Facility:** 80 one-bedroom standard units. 2 stories, interior corridors. **Parking:**
on-site. **Terms:** [CP] meal plan available. **Pool(s):** outdoor. **Guest Services:** coin laundry. **Business Serv-
ices:** fax (fee). **Cards:** AX, DC, DS, MC, VI. **Special Amenities:** free continental breakfast.

SOME UNITS

[icons]

COMFORT INN-NORTH   Phone: (419)476-0170   20
(AAA) [SAVE]   All Year [ECP]   1P: $49-$69   2P: $59-$89   XP: $5   F18
▼▼ ▼▼   **Location:** I-75, exit 210, 2 mi w on SR 184; just e of jct US 24 and SR 184. 445 E Alexis Rd 43612. Fax: 419/476-6111.
Motel   **Facility:** 81 one-bedroom standard units, some with whirlpools. 2 stories, interior corridors. **Parking:** on-site.
Terms: small pets only ($10 fee). **Amenities:** extended cable TV, hair dryers. *Some:* irons. **Guest Services:**
valet and coin laundry. **Cards:** AX, DC, DS, MC, VI. **Special Amenities:** free continental breakfast and
free local telephone calls.

SOME UNITS

[icons]

(See map p. 756)

COMFORT INN WESTGATE
AAA SAVE

Motel

All Year [ECP]   1P: $59-$99   2P: $59-$99   **Phone:** (419)531-2666 **21**
Location: I-475, exit 17, just s. 3560 Secor Rd 43606. Fax: 419/531-4757. **Facility:** 70 one-bedroom standard units. 2 stories, interior corridors. **Parking:** on-site. **Amenities:** extended cable TV. *Some:* irons, hair dryers. **Leisure Activities:** jogging, indoor recreational facilities nearby. **Guest Services:** valet laundry. **Cards:** AX, CB, DC, DS, JC, MC, VI. **Special Amenities:** free continental breakfast and free local telephone calls.

SOME UNITS

CROWN INN
AAA SAVE

Motel

All Year [CP]   1P: $57-$64   2P: $62-$69   **Phone:** (419)473-1485 **28**
                                                    XP: $6   F15
Location: 2 mi w of jct US 24 and SR 184. 1727 W Alexis Rd 43613. Fax: 419/473-0364. **Facility:** 40 one-bedroom standard units, some with efficiencies and/or whirlpools. 1 story, exterior corridors. **Parking:** on-site. **Terms:** check-in 4 pm, small pets only ($5 fee, $40 deposit). **Amenities:** extended cable TV, video tape library (fee). **Cards:** AX, CB, DC, DS, MC, VI. **Special Amenities:** free continental breakfast and preferred room (subject to availability with advanced reservations).

SOME UNITS

FEE

DAYS INN-TOLEDO
SAVE

Motor Inn

4/1-8/1 [CP]   1P: $54-$60   2P: $54-$60   **Phone:** (419)666-5120 **33**
8/2-12/1 [CP]   1P: $50-$54   2P: $50-$54
12/2-3/31 [CP]   1P: $50   2P: $50
Location: I-75, exit 199 northbound; exit 199A southbound. 1800 Miami St 43605. Fax: 419/666-4298. **Facility:** 141 one-bedroom standard units. 3 stories, interior corridors. **Parking:** on-site. **Amenities:** extended cable TV, hair dryers. **Pool(s):** indoor. **Leisure Activities:** volleyball. **Guest Services:** coin laundry. **Business Services:** meeting rooms. **Cards:** AX, CB, DC, DS, MC, VI.

SOME UNITS

(See map p. 756)

HILTON TOLEDO

AAA SAVE
▼▼▼▼
Hotel

Phone: (419)381-6800   30
F17

All Year   1P: $99-$149   2P: $99-$149   XP: $10
Location: I-475, exit 8 (SR 2/Airport Hwy), 3.3 mi e, 0.8 mi s on Byrne Rd, then 0.5 mi e; on the campus of the Medical College of Ohio. 3100 Glendale Ave 43614. Fax: 419/381-0478. **Facility:** 213 units. 211 one-bedroom standard units. 2 one-bedroom suites. 6 stories, interior corridors. **Parking:** on-site. **Terms:** cancellation fee imposed, package plans. **Amenities:** dual phone lines, voice mail, irons, hair dryers. **Dining:** restaurant, 6:30 am-2 & 5-9 pm, Fri & Sat from 7 am, Sun 7 am-2 pm, $8-$20, cocktails. **Pool(s):** heated indoor. **Leisure Activities:** sauna, whirlpool, 3 lighted tennis courts, access to college recreational facilities. **Guest Services:** gift shop, valet laundry, area transportation. **Business Services:** conference facilities, business center, PC, fax. **Cards:** AX, CB, DC, DS, MC, VI. **Special Amenities:** early check-in/late check-out and free newspaper. *(See color ad p 760)*

SOME UNITS
[icons] FEE ... FEE FEE

HOLIDAY INN TOLEDO WEST

▼▼▼▼
Motor Inn

Phone: 419/865-1361   27

All Year [AP]   1P: $99-$110
Location: I-80/90 (Ohio Tpke), exit 59, just n on US 20. 2340 S Reynolds Rd 43614. Fax: 419/865-6177. **Facility:** 218 units. 210 one-bedroom standard units. 8 one-bedroom suites ($105-$129). 11 stories, interior corridors. *Bath:* combo or shower only. **Parking:** on-site. **Terms:** 30 day cancellation notice-fee imposed, package plans. **Amenities:** voice mail, irons, hair dryers. **Pool(s):** heated indoor. **Leisure Activities:** exercise room. **Guest Services:** gift shop, valet and coin laundry. **Business Services:** meeting rooms. **Cards:** AX, CB, DC, DS, MC, VI.

SOME UNITS
ASK [icons] FEE ... FEE

QUALITY HOTEL

AAA SAVE
▼▼▼
Motel

Phone: (419)381-8765   31
F18

All Year   1P: $70-$100   2P: $70-$100   XP: $7
Location: I-80/90 (Ohio Tpke), exit 59, just n on US 20. 2429 S Reynolds Rd 43614. Fax: 419/381-0129. **Facility:** 260 units. 249 one-bedroom standard units. 11 one-bedroom suites ($100-$125). 2-7 stories, interior corridors. **Parking:** on-site. **Amenities:** *Some:* irons, hair dryers. **Dining:** coffee shop, 4 pm-11 pm, $11-$22, cocktails. **Pool(s):** heated indoor. **Leisure Activities:** sauna, whirlpool, steamroom, playground, exercise room. *Fee:* game room. **Guest Services:** coin laundry. **Business Services:** conference facilities, fax. **Cards:** AX, CB, DC, DS, MC, VI. *(See color ad p 759)*

SOME UNITS
[icons]

RADISSON HOTEL TOLEDO

AAA SAVE
▼▼▼▼
Hotel

Phone: (419)241-3000   22
F18

All Year   1P: $135   2P: $135   XP: $10
Location: Downtown; between Jefferson and Monroe sts. 101 N Summit St 43604. Fax: 419/321-2099. **Facility:** 399 units. 388 one-bedroom standard units. 11 one-bedroom suites. 15 stories, interior corridors. **Parking:** *Fee:* on-site and valet. **Terms:** cancellation fee imposed, package plans, small pets only ($25 fee). **Amenities:** voice mail, irons, hair dryers. **Dining:** restaurant, 6:30 am-11 pm, $10-$17, cocktails. **Leisure Activities:** sauna. **Guest Services:** gift shop, valet laundry, area transportation-within 3 mi. **Business Services:** conference facilities. **Cards:** AX, CB, DC, DS, MC, VI. **Special Amenities:** free newspaper and preferred room (subject to availability with advanced reservations).

SOME UNITS
[icons] FEE

RAMADA INN & SUITES

AAA SAVE
▼▼ ▼
Motor Inn

Phone: (419)242-8885   26

6/1-8/31	1P: $99-$139	2P: $99-$139	XP: $10 F18
4/1-5/31 & 9/1-9/30	1P: $89-$129	2P: $89-$129	XP: $10 F18
10/1-3/31	1P: $79-$119	2P: $79-$119	XP: $10 F18

Location: Downtown; between Jefferson and Monroe sts. 141 N Summit St 43604. Fax: 419/242-1337. **Facility:** 211 units. 171 one-bedroom standard units, some with whirlpools. 40 one-bedroom suites, some with whirlpools. 19 stories, interior corridors. **Parking:** on-site (fee). **Terms:** 14 day cancellation notice, package plans, small pets only ($25 fee). **Amenities:** dual phone lines, voice mail, irons, hair dryers. **Dining:** restaurant, 5 am-2 pm, cocktails. **Pool(s):** heated indoor. **Leisure Activities:** exercise room. **Guest Services:** valet and coin laundry. **Business Services:** conference facilities, fax. **Cards:** AX, CB, DC, DS, JC, MC, VI. **Special Amenities:** early check-in/late check-out and free room upgrade (subject to availability with advanced reservations). *(See color ad below)*

SOME UNITS
[icons] FEE

(See map p. 756)

RED ROOF INN SECOR　　　　　　　　　　　　　　　　Phone: (419)536-0118　　32
AAA SAVE　All Year　　　　　　1P: $44-$63　　2P: $49-$68　　XP: $5　　F13
Location: I-475, exit 17, 0.5 mi s on Secor Rd, then just e. 3530 Executive Pkwy 43606. Fax: 419/536-1348.
Facility: 117 one-bedroom standard units. 3 stories, exterior corridors. *Bath:* combo or shower only. Parking: on-site. Terms: small pets only. Amenities: video games, voice mail. Business Services: meeting rooms.
Motel　Cards: AX, CB, DC, DS, MC, VI. Special Amenities: free local telephone calls and free newspaper.

SOME UNITS

WYNDHAM TOLEDO　　　　　　　　　　　　　　　　Phone: (419)241-1411　　24
AAA SAVE　All Year　　　　　　1P: $99-$139　　2P: $99-$139　　XP: $10　　F18
Location: Downtown; on river and adjacent to Promenade Park. 2 Seagate/Summit St 43604. Fax: 419/241-8161.
Facility: 241 units. 235 one-bedroom standard units. 6 one-bedroom suites. 13 stories, interior corridors.
Hotel　Parking: *Fee:* on-site and valet. Terms: cancellation fee imposed, package plans. Amenities: video games, high-speed Internet (fee), dual phone lines, voice mail, irons, hair dryers. *Some:* CD players. Dining: restaurant, 6:30 am-2 & 5-10 pm, $14-$27, cocktails. Pool(s): small heated indoor. Leisure Activities: sauna, whirlpool, exercise room. *Fee:* game room. Guest Services: valet laundry, area transportation-within 2 mi. Business Services: conference facilities, business center, PC, fax (fee). Cards: AX, CB, DC, DS, JC, MC, VI.

SOME UNITS

———— WHERE TO DINE ————

DOMINIC'S　　　　　　Lunch: $7-$9　　　　Dinner: $9-$15　　　Phone: 419/381-8822　　7
Location: I-80/90 (Ohio Tpke), exit 59, just n. 2121 S Reynolds Rd 43614. Hours: 4 pm-midnight, Sun noon-10 pm. Closed: 11/28, 12/25. Features: casual dress; children's menu; carryout; cocktails & lounge; buffet.
Italian　Subtle illumination from Tiffany-style lamps is a nice touch in the cozy dining room, which has the aura of a tavern. Traditional favorites, such as manicotti, calamari and lasagna, are fresh, tasty and served piping hot. Servers are friendly and prompt. Parking: on-site. Cards: AX, DC, DS, MC, VI.

EL MATADOR RESTAURANT　　　　Lunch: $7-$9　　　Dinner: $9-$12　　Phone: 419/476-2043　　8
Location: I-75, exit 210, 2.4 mi w on SR 184. 35 E Alexis Rd 43612. Hours: 11 am-10 pm, Fri & Sat-11 pm, Sun-9 pm. Closed major holidays. Features: casual dress; children's menu; carryout; cocktails & lounge; a
Mexican　la carte. This local chain restaurant serves all your Mexican favorites. A wide variety of menu items include nachos, tacos, chimichangas and grilled items. Parking: on-site. Cards: AX, DC, DS, MC, VI.

GEORGIO'S CAFE INTERNATIONAL　　　　Dinner: $18-$28　　　　Phone: 419/242-2424　　9
Location: Downtown; between Jackson and Adams sts. 426 N Superior St 43604. Hours: 5:30 pm-10 pm. Closed major holidays. Reservations: accepted. Features: dressy casual; cocktails & lounge. This local
American　award-winning restaurant suggests starting your meal with a Mediterranean influenced appetizer such as marinated octopus, stuffed grape leaves or escargot. The entrees include steaks, chops and chicken along with several featured fish of the day. The service is casual yet elegant in style. Parking: street. Cards: AX, MC, VI.

THE MANGO TREE　　　　　Lunch: $5-$10　　　Dinner: $10-$18　　Phone: 419/536-2883　　10
Location: I-80/90 (Ohio Tpke), exit 59, 2.5 mi n on SR 20. 217 S Reynolds Rd 43615. Hours: 11:30 am-10 pm, Fri-11 pm, Sat from 5 pm. Closed major holidays. Reservations: suggested; weekends. Features: casual
American　dress; children's menu; early bird specials; carryout; cocktails. The casual restaurant features steaks and seafood and has some of the area's most reasonable prices. Center-cut New York strip and macadamia nut-crusted snapper are two house specialties. Parking: on-site. Cards: AX, DC, DS, MC, VI.

MAUMEE BAY BREWING COMPANY Historical　　Lunch: $7-$9　　Dinner: $11-$18　　Phone: 419/241-1253　　11
Location: Just n of SR 2/65/51; between Clayton, Morris and Ottawa; in the Oliver House. 27 Broadway 43602. Hours: 11 am-10 pm, Fri-11 pm, Sat 3 pm-1 pm, Sun 3 pm-9 pm. Closed major holidays.
American　Reservations: accepted. Features: casual dress; children's menu; carryout; cocktails. Located in the historic Oliver House, originally a premier hotel opened in 1859, this micro-brewery restaurant offers an eclectic menu. The cheddar beer soup is a favorite. The well prepared entrees offer variety ranging from steak & mushroom pie, Polynesian salmon, Caribbean jerk chicken, inspiring pastas and wood-burning oven baked gourmet pizzas. The diverse handcrafted brews meld well as complements to the meal. Parking: on-site. Cards: AX, CB, DC, DS, MC, VI.

SPAGHETTI WAREHOUSE　　　　Lunch: $5-$10　　　Dinner: $9-$15　　Phone: 419/255-5038　　5
Location: Downtown; between S Summit and Huron sts, just s of Washington St. 42 S Superior St 43602. Hours: 11 am-10 pm, Fri & Sat-11 pm. Closed: 11/28, 12/25. Features: casual dress; children's menu; carryout;
Italian　cocktails & lounge. This national Italian-style restaurant chain creates a festive family atmosphere. All entrees include bottomless tossed salad or soup. Enjoy the plentiful portions of one of the classic dishes including ravioli, lasagna, baked penne or the richly flavored cannelloni Florentine. Splurge on one of the many desserts such as tiramisu, espresso mousse cake or carrot cake. Parking: on-site. Cards: AX, CB, DC, DS, MC, VI.

TONY PACKO'S CAFE　　　　Lunch: $6-$10　　　Dinner: $8-$12　　Phone: 419/691-6054　　6
Location: I-280, exit 9, 0.5 mi ne, corner of Front and Consaul sts. 1902 Front St 43605. Hours: 11 am-10 pm, Fri & Sat-11 pm, Sun noon-9 pm. Closed major holidays. Features: casual dress; children's menu; carryout;
Hungarian　cocktails. Fun and quirky decor, from the celebrity autographed ensconced hot dog buns to the brightly colored Tiffany-style chandeliers. Family owned and operated since 1935, this eatery achieved worldwide notoriety from recurrent mention in the hit TV show "MASH." The effervescent servers bring heaping plates of Hungarian fare such as cabbage rolls, sausages and chili dogs. Parking: on-site. Cards: AX, DC, DS, MC, VI.

**The following restaurants have not been evaluated by AAA
but are listed for your information only.**

BYBLOS   **Phone:** 419/382-1600
[fyi]   Not evaluated. **Location:** 1050 S Reynolds Rd 43614. Daily lunch specials and Lebanese and Italian dishes are what
           diners at this casual restaurant can expect.

COUSINO'S CAFE CHEZ VIN   **Phone:** 419/697-0017
[fyi]   Not evaluated. **Location:** 2022 Woodville Rd 43616. The bistro offers a menu of European choices.

DOLLY & JOE'S RESTAURANT   **Phone:** 419/385-2441
[fyi]   Not evaluated. **Location:** 1045 S Reynolds Rd 43614. Preparations of steak, seafood, chicken and chops factor
           heavily on the restaurant's menu.

FIFI'S RESTAURANT   **Phone:** 419/866-6777
[fyi]   Not evaluated. **Location:** 1423 Bernath Pkwy 43615. Continental selections make up the restaurant's menu.

HJ'S PRIME CUT   **Phone:** 419/476-1616
[fyi]   Not evaluated. **Location:** 206 N Towne Sq 43612. Menu offerings center on fresh steak and seafood.

MANCY'S RESTAURANT   **Phone:** 419/476-4154
[fyi]   Not evaluated. **Location:** 953 Phillips Ave 43612. Steak and seafood are served at this local landmark.

ROCKWELL'S   **Phone:** 419/241-1253
[fyi]   Not evaluated. **Location:** Just n of SR 65/2/51, between Clayton, Morris and Ottawa sts; in the Oliver House. 27
           Broadway St 43602.

RUSTY'S JAZZ CAFE   **Phone:** 419/381-9194
[fyi]   Not evaluated. **Location:** 2202 Tedrow "Jazz Ave" 43614. Home-style selections are served at this establishment.

VENTURA'S   **Phone:** 419/841-7523
[fyi]   Not evaluated. **Location:** 7742 W Bancroft 43617. On the restaurant's menu are traditional Mexican entrees.

TROY pop. 19,500

--- WHERE TO STAY ---

ALLEN VILLA BED & BREAKFAST   **Phone:** 937/335-1181
           All Year [BP]   1P: $65-$70   2P: $75-$80   XP: $10
Historic Bed **Location:** I-75, exit 73, 1 mi e on SR 55, then just n. 434 S Market St 45373. Fax: 937/335-4961. **Facility:** Antiques
& Breakfast   decorate the guest rooms of this 1874 B&B. Closed 12/24-12/26. Smoke free premises. 5 one-bedroom stan-
           dard units. 2 stories, interior corridors. *Bath:* combo or shower only. **Parking:** on-site. **Terms:** check-in 4 pm,
           5 day cancellation notice. **Amenities:** extended cable TV, hair dryers. **Cards:** AX, DS, MC, VI.
                                                                            SOME UNITS
                                         [VCR] [🖨] / [✕] [Ⓚ] [🛏] [🍴] /

FAIRFIELD INN & SUITES   **Phone:** (937)332-1446
(AAA) [SAVE]   4/1-9/2   1P: $59-$72   2P: $59-$72
           9/3-3/31   1P: $56-$65   2P: $56-$65
Motel   **Location:** I-75, exit 74, just w on SR 41. 83 Troy Town Dr 45373. Fax: 937/332-1447. **Facility:** 80 one-bedroom
           standard units, some with whirlpools. 3 stories, interior corridors. *Bath:* combo or shower only. **Parking:** on-
           site. **Amenities:** extended cable TV, voice mail, irons, hair dryers. **Pool(s):** heated indoor. **Leisure Activi-
           ties:** whirlpool, recreational facilities privileges. **Guest Services:** coin laundry. **Business Services:** meeting
rooms. **Cards:** AX, DC, DS, MC, VI. **Special Amenities:** free continental breakfast and free local telephone calls.
(See color ad card insert)
                                                                            SOME UNITS
                  [S🄳] [🍴+] [🔥M] [Ⓚ] [🌀] [🏊] [🏋] [DATA PORT] [🖨] / [✕] [🛏] [🍴] [💻] /

HAMPTON INN   **Phone:** (937)339-7801
[SAVE]   All Year   1P: $65-$85   2P: $65-$85
           Location: I-75, exit 74, on SR 41. 45 Troy Town Dr 45373. Fax: 937/335-7979. **Facility:** 60 one-bedroom standard
Motel   units, some with whirlpools. 3 stories, interior corridors. *Bath:* combo or shower only. **Parking:** on-site.
           Amenities: extended cable TV, high-speed Internet, voice mail, irons, hair dryers. **Pool(s):** heated indoor.
           Leisure Activities: exercise room. **Guest Services:** valet laundry. **Cards:** AX, CB, DC, DS, MC, VI.
                                                                            SOME UNITS
                     [🍴+] [Ⓚ] [🏊] [🏋] [DATA PORT] [🛏] [🍴] [💻] [🖨] / [✕] /
                                            FEE

HOLIDAY INN EXPRESS HOTEL & SUITES   **Phone:** (937)332-1700
(AAA) [SAVE]   All Year [ECP]   1P: $74-$79   2P: $74-$79
           Location: I-75, exit 74, just w on SR 41. 60 Troy Town Dr 45373. Fax: 937/332-1800. **Facility:** 65 one-bedroom
Motel   standard units. 3 stories, interior corridors. *Bath:* combo or shower only. **Parking:** on-site. **Terms:** small pets
           only. **Amenities:** extended cable TV, irons, hair dryers. *Some:* dual phone lines. **Pool(s):** heated indoor.
           Leisure Activities: whirlpool, exercise room. **Guest Services:** coin laundry. **Business Services:** meeting
           rooms. **Cards:** AX, CB, DC, DS, JC, MC, VI. **Special Amenities:** free continental breakfast and free local
telephone calls.
                                                                            SOME UNITS
                  [S🄳] [🐾] [🍴+] [Ⓚ] [🌀] [🏊] [🏋] [DATA PORT] [💻] [🖨] / [✕] [VCR] [🛏] [🍴] /

KNIGHTS INN TROY　　　　　　　　　　　　　　　　　　　　**Phone: (937)339-1515**

◆◆◆　All Year　　　　　　　　　　　1P: $46-$50
Motel　**Location:** I-75, exit 74, just w on SR 41. 30 Troy Town Dr 45373. Fax: 937/339-7031. **Facility:** 83 one-bedroom standard units. 1 story, exterior corridors. **Parking:** on-site. **Terms:** 7 day cancellation notice, small pets only. **Amenities:** extended cable TV, irons, hair dryers. **Leisure Activities:** basketball, volleyball. **Guest Services:** coin laundry. **Cards:** AX, DC, DS, MC, VI.

SOME UNITS
(ASK) (S/D) (🛏) (🍴) (❄) (🗄) (📠) (💻) / (X) /

RESIDENCE INN BY MARRIOTT　　　　　　　　　　　　　　**Phone: (937)440-9303**

(AAA) (SAVE)　4/1-9/2　　　　　　　1P: $89-$116　　　　　2P: $89-$116
◆◆◆ ◆◆◆　9/3-3/31　　　　　　1P: $84-$107　　　　　2P: $84-$107
Apartment　**Location:** I-75, exit 74, just w on SR 41. 87 Troy Town Dr 45373. Fax: 937/440-9403. **Facility:** 96 units. 80 one-bedroom standard units. 16 two-bedroom suites. 4 stories, interior corridors. **Bath:** combo or shower only. **Parking:** on-site. **Terms:** pets ($250 extra charge). **Amenities:** extended cable TV, video games, voice mail, irons, hair dryers. **Pool(s):** heated outdoor. **Leisure Activities:** whirlpool, exercise room, sports court. **Guest Services:** coin laundry. **Business Services:** meeting rooms. **Cards:** AX, CB, DC, DS, JC, MC, VI. *(See color ad card insert)*

SOME UNITS
(S/D) (🛏) (🍴) (📶) (📷) (🏊) (X) (❄) (DATA PORT) (🗄) (📠) (💻) (🖨) / (X) /
　　　　　　　　　　　FEE

─────── **WHERE TO DINE** ───────

CJ'S HIGHMARKS　　**Lunch: $7-$8**　　　**Dinner: $9-$18**　　　**Phone: 937/335-6569**

◆◆◆ ◆◆◆　**Location:** I-75, exit 74A. 1750 W Main St 45373. **Hours:** 11 am-10:30 pm, Fri & Sat-11:30 pm, Sun-10 pm. Closed: 11/28, 12/25. **Features:** casual dress; children's menu; carryout; cocktails & lounge. The upbeat American family restaurant reflects the mood and stylings of a schoolhouse, with hanging plastic crayons, a locker room-themed bar and lots of books and pencils. The menu, which resembles a folder, lists steak, seafood and specialty salads. **Parking:** on-site. **Cards:** AX, DS, MC, VI.

(X)

LA PIAZZA PASTA & GRILL　　**Lunch: $7-$9**　　　**Dinner: $10-$16**　　　**Phone: 937/339-5553**

◆◆◆ ◆◆◆　**Location:** Downtown; in public square. 2 N Market St 45373. **Hours:** 11 am-2 & 4:30-10 pm, Fri & Sat-11 pm, Italian　Sun 4 pm-9 pm. Closed major holidays. **Features:** casual dress; children's menu; carryout; cocktails & lounge; a la carte. In business since 1930, the warm, intimate restaurant has long been a favorite for such fare as pizza, antipasto and grilled dishes. The signature salad dressing is light and flavorful, and the in-house tiramisu and cannoli are well worth saving room for. **Parking:** on-site. **Cards:** AX, MC, VI.

(X)

LIZZIE'S RESTAURANT　　**Lunch: $5-$7**　　　**Dinner: $7-$12**　　　**Phone: 937/339-0706**

◆◆◆　**Location:** Just n of Town Square. 14 N Market St 45373. **Hours:** 11 am-9 pm, Sat-4 pm. Closed major holidays; also Sun. **Features:** casual dress; children's menu; carryout; cocktails. Home-style preparations of steak American and shrimp mingle with an assortment of charbroiled burgers, potatoes and omelets on the varied menu. Country decor, with lots of pictures and antiques, gives the dining room a comfortable, friendly ambience. **Parking:** on-site.

TAGGART'S ON THE SQUARE　　**Lunch: $7-$8**　　　**Dinner: $8-$16**　　　**Phone: 937/339-8911**

◆◆◆ ◆◆◆　**Location:** I-75, exit 74 northbound; exit 74A southbound, 2 mi e on SR 41; in Public Square. 5 S Market St 45373. **Hours:** 11 am-10 pm, Fri & Sat-11 pm. Closed major holidays; also Sun. **Reservations:** suggested. American **Features:** casual dress; children's menu; carryout; cocktails & lounge. Specializing in seafood, steaks, chicken and pasta, the warm restaurant caters to tourists. From the dining room-which is decorated with lots of oak, greenery and flowers-diners look out on the fountain in the square. The in-house desserts are delicious. **Parking:** on-site. **Cards:** AX, DC, DS, MC, VI.

(X)

TWINSBURG pop. 9,600　(See map p. 600; index p. 603)

─────── **WHERE TO STAY** ───────

HILTON GARDEN INN CLEVELAND/TWINSBURG　　　**Phone: (330)405-4488**　　(35)

(SAVE)　All Year　　　　　　　1P: $79-$169　　　2P: $79-$169　　　XP: $10　　F16
◆◆◆ ◆◆◆　**Location:** I-480, exit 36, just e on SR 82. 8971 Wilcox Dr 44087. Fax: 330/405-4499. **Facility:** 142 one-bedroom Motel　standard units, some with whirlpools. 5 stories, interior corridors. **Bath:** combo or shower only. **Parking:** on-site. **Terms:** check-in 4 pm. **Amenities:** video games, high-speed Internet (fee), dual phone lines, voice mail, irons, hair dryers. **Pool(s):** heated indoor. **Leisure Activities:** whirlpool, exercise room. **Guest Services:** valet and coin laundry. **Business Services:** conference facilities, business center, PC, fax. **Cards:** AX, CB, DC, DS, MC, VI. *(See ad p 751)*

SOME UNITS
(🍴) (🍷) (👤M) (📶) (📷) (🏊) (❄) (DATA PORT) (🗄) (📠) (💻) (🖨) / (X) (VCR) /
　　　　　　　　　　　FEE　　　　　　　　　　　　　　　　　FEE

TWINSBURG SUPER 8 MOTEL　　　　　　　　　**Phone: (330)425-2889**　　(36)

◆◆◆ ◆◆◆　6/16-9/1　　　1P: $80　　　　2P: $80-$85　　　XP: $5　　F18
◆◆　4/1-5/23　　　1P: $50-$73　　2P: $50-$79　　　XP: $5　　F18
Motel　5/24-6/15　　　1P: $65　　　　2P: $70-$75　　　XP: $5　　F18
　9/2-3/31　　　1P: $50　　　　2P: $50-$55　　　XP: $5　　F18
Location: I-480, exit 36, just w on SR 82. 8848 Twins Hills Dr 44087. Fax: 330/963-6658. **Facility:** 59 one-bedroom standard units. 2 stories, interior corridors. **Parking:** on-site. **Terms:** small pets only ($5.29 extra charge). **Amenities:** extended cable TV, safes. **Cards:** AX, DC, DS, JC, MC, VI.

SOME UNITS
(ASK) (S/D) (🛏) (🍴) (❄) (DATA PORT) (🖨) / (X) (🖨) (🖨)
　　　　　　　　FEE　　　　　　　　　　　　　FEE　FEE

(See map p. 600)

——— WHERE TO DINE ———

MAC LAREN'S **Lunch:** $7-$12 **Dinner:** $12-$25 **Phone:** 330/425-7979 (53)
▼▼▼
American **Location:** 4 mi s on SR 91. 8054 Darrow Rd 44087. **Hours:** 11 am-2 & 5-9 pm, Sat-10 pm. Closed: Sun & Mon. **Reservations:** required; weekends. **Features:** dressy casual; carryout; cocktails. The cuisine is very creative and imaginative here with seasonal changes. Their potato and bacon encrusted walleye served over sweet corn chowder is a local favorite and the French onion soup is always popular. They are located just a short drive from Six Flags and the Aurora Outlet Mall. Expect cozy seating. The staff is friendly, welcoming and always attentive to individual dinner requests. Smoke free premises. **Parking:** on-site. **Cards:** AX, DC, MC, VI. ✗

——— *The following restaurant has not been evaluated by AAA*
but is listed for your information only. ———

AMAZON TRAIL **Phone:** 330/425-7373
(fyi) Not evaluated. **Location:** 8870 Darrow Rd 44087. Fried bananas and fresh fish and seafood are favorites at the restaurant, which transports guests to the Amazon rain forest.

UHRICHSVILLE pop. 5,600

——— WHERE TO STAY ———

BEST WESTERN COUNTRY INN **Phone:** (740)922-0774
AAA (SAVE) 6/1-10/31 [ECP] 1P: $60-$70 2P: $66-$76 XP: $6 F18
▼▼▼▼ 4/1-5/31 & 11/1-3/31 [ECP] 1P: $50-$60 2P: $56-$66 XP: $6 F18
Motel **Location:** US 250, exit McCauley Dr. 111 McCauley Dr 44683. Fax: 740/922-2270. **Facility:** 48 one-bedroom standard units, some with whirlpools. 2 stories, exterior corridors. **Parking:** on-site. **Amenities:** extended cable TV, irons, hair dryers. **Business Services:** meeting rooms. **Cards:** AX, CB, DC, DS, MC, VI. **Special Amenities:** free continental breakfast and free local telephone calls.

SOME UNITS

[icons] 🅂🄳 🛎️ 🚫 📷 📠 🖥️ 🖨️ / ✗ 🔒 /

UNIONTOWN pop. 3,100

——— WHERE TO DINE ———

BELGRADE GARDENS SOUTH **Lunch:** $5-$10 **Dinner:** $7-$12 **Phone:** 330/896-3396
▼▼ ▼ **Location:** I-77, exit 118, 0.3 mi e. 3476 Massillon Rd 44685. **Hours:** 11 am-9 pm, Fri & Sat-9:30 pm. Closed: 11/28, 12/25. **Features:** casual dress; children's menu; carryout; beer & wine only. Original recipes dating
American back to 1933 result in tasty family-favorite foods, such as hot turkey, as well as a few more adventurous offerings, such as chicken paprikash. The converted farmhouse is comfortable and relaxed, with plenty of rustic decor. **Parking:** on-site. ✗

MENCHES BROS **Lunch:** $5-$8 **Dinner:** $7-$12 **Phone:** 330/896-2288
▼ **Location:** I-77, exit 118, just w. 3700 Massillon Rd 44685. **Hours:** 7 am-9 pm. Closed major holidays.
Features: casual dress; children's menu; carryout; beer & wine only. Original creators of the hamburger
American and ice cream cone, this restaurant still uses the original recipes and high quality ingredients today. Specialty sandwiches and homemade soups available daily. Smoke free premises. **Parking:** on-site.
Cards: AX, DS, MC, VI. ✗

UNIONVILLE pop. 500

——— WHERE TO DINE ———

THE OLD TAVERN Historical **Lunch:** $7-$12 **Dinner:** $12-$20 **Phone:** 440/428-2091
AAA **Location:** Jct SR 84 and County Line Rd. 7935 Middle Ridge Rd 44088. **Hours:** 11:30 am-8 pm, Sun 9 am-7 pm.
▼▼ ▼ Closed: 12/25; also Mon. **Reservations:** suggested. **Features:** Sunday brunch; children's menu; carryout;
cocktails. Originally a 1798 log cabin, the tavern was later converted to the cozy, informal dining spot it is
American today. The signature corn fritters, which were introduced in 1926, are served with maple syrup. Antiques sit throughout the charming restaurant. **Parking:** on-site. **Cards:** DC, DS, MC, VI. ✗

UPPER ARLINGTON —*See Columbus p. 668.*

UPPER SANDUSKY pop. 5,900

——— WHERE TO STAY ———

AMERIHOST INN-UPPER SANDUSKY **Phone:** (419)294-3919
AAA (SAVE) All Year 1P: $69-$189 2P: $74-$189 XP: $6 F16
▼▼ ▼ **Location:** Jct US 30 and 23. 1726 E Wyandot Ave 43351. Fax: 419/294-5684. **Facility:** 60 one-bedroom standard
Motel units; some with whirlpools. 2 stories, interior corridors. *Bath:* combo or shower only. **Parking:** on-site.
Terms: 14 day cancellation notice, pets ($25 fee). **Amenities:** extended cable TV, safes (fee), irons, hair dryers. **Pool(s):** heated indoor. **Leisure Activities:** sauna, whirlpool, exercise room. **Guest Services:** valet laundry. **Business Services:** meeting rooms. **Cards:** AX, CB, DC, DS, JC, MC, VI. **Special Amenities:** free continental breakfast and free newspaper.

SOME UNITS

[icons] 🅂🄳 🍴 🛎️ 🅼 ♿ 🚫 🏊 ✗ 🐕 📠 🖥️ 🖨️ / ✗ 🔒 📺 /
FEE

COMFORT INN

Motel

All Year	1P: $56	2P: $60	XP: $5	F18

Phone: (419)294-3891

Location: Jct US 30 and 23. 105 Comfort Dr 43351. **Fax:** 419/294-2540. **Facility:** 85 units. 81 one-bedroom standard units, some with whirlpools. 4 one-bedroom suites ($84-$89) with whirlpools. 2 stories, interior corridors. *Bath:* combo or shower only. **Parking:** on-site. **Terms:** [ECP] meal plan available. **Amenities:** extended cable TV, hair dryers. *Some:* irons. **Guest Services:** valet and coin laundry. **Business Services:** meeting rooms. **Cards:** AX, CB, DC, DS, JC, MC, VI.

─────── **WHERE TO DINE** ───────

THE STEER BARN

Steak & Seafood

Dinner: $10-$20 — Phone: 419/294-3860

Location: Jct US 30 and 23, 0.5 mi w. 1144 E Wyandot Ave 43351. **Hours:** 4 pm-9:30 pm. Closed major holidays; also Sun & Mon. **Features:** casual dress; cocktails & lounge. The 1897 restored barn setting, decorated with rustic pieces and farm implements, is a quaint and memorable place in which to savor tempting choice steaks and entrees of fresh seafood. A large relish Susan offers an interesting array of choices. **Parking:** on-site. **Cards:** AX, DS, MC, VI.

WOODY'S RESTAURANT

American

Lunch: $8-$12 — Dinner: $10-$19 — Phone: 419/294-1655

Location: US 23, exit 199 N, just w on SR 199 (N Warpool). 1351 Warpole St 43351. **Hours:** 11 am-2 & 4-9:30 pm. Closed major holidays; also Sun, Mon & Sat for lunch. **Reservations:** suggested. **Features:** casual dress; cocktails & lounge. Lace, woodwork and an antique sideboard are among Victorian appointments that give the cozy dining room a sophisticated aura. Prime rib, steak, seafood, pasta, veal and chicken make up the menu. The bread and desserts are made on the premises. **Parking:** on-site. **Cards:** AX, DS, MC, VI.

─────── *The following restaurants have not been evaluated by AAA* ───────
but are listed for your information only.

CORNER INN

[fyi]

Phone: 419/294-5201

Not evaluated. **Location:** 143 N Sandusky Ave 43351. Home-style meals and desserts are this restaurant's main offerings.

GREAT DRAGON

[fyi]

Phone: 419/294-2989

Not evaluated. **Location:** 1187 E Wyandot Ave 43351. Dishes reflect what is prepared in all regions of China.

KRONEYS

[fyi]

Phone: 419/294-9109

Not evaluated. **Location:** 136 S Main St 43351. Families are welcomed to try the restaurant's home-style dishes.

MJ MUGSY'S

[fyi]

Phone: 419/294-5355

Not evaluated. **Location:** 123 W Wyandot Ave 43351. The local hangout offers traditional American dishes.

THE POUR HOUSE

[fyi]

Phone: 419/294-9125

Not evaluated. **Location:** 130 N Sandusky Ave 43351. On the menu are popular American entrees and desserts.

URBANA pop. 11,400

─────── **WHERE TO STAY** ───────

LOGAN LODGE MOTEL

Motel

4/1-9/30	1P: $56	2P: $60	XP: $7	F5
10/1-3/31	1P: $50	2P: $56	XP: $7	F5

Phone: (937)652-2188

Location: 1.3 mi s on US 68. 2551 S US Hwy 68 43078. **Fax:** 937/652-2178. **Facility:** 30 one-bedroom standard units, some with whirlpools. 1-2 stories, exterior corridors. **Parking:** on-site. **Terms:** 7 day cancellation notice-fee imposed, [CP] & [ECP] meal plans available, pets ($15 fee). **Amenities:** extended cable TV, irons, hair dryers. **Pool(s):** heated outdoor. **Business Services:** meeting rooms. **Cards:** AX, DC, DS, MC, VI.

VANDALIA pop. 13,900 (See map p. 672; index p. 674)

─────── **WHERE TO STAY** ───────

CROSS COUNTRY INN

Motel

All Year	1P: $40-$47	2P: $47-$54	XP: $2	F17

Phone: (937)898-7636 56

Location: Jct US 40 and I-75, exit 63. 550 E National Rd 45377. **Fax:** 937/898-0630. **Facility:** 94 one-bedroom standard units. 3 stories, exterior corridors. *Bath:* combo or shower only. **Parking:** on-site. **Amenities:** video games, voice mail. **Pool(s):** heated outdoor. **Business Services:** meeting rooms. **Cards:** AX, CB, DC, DS, MC, VI. **Special Amenities:** free local telephone calls and preferred room (subject to availability with advanced reservations).

TRAVELODGE DAYTON AIRPORT

Motel

All Year	1P: $55-$90	2P: $55-$90	XP: $4	F12

Phone: (937)898-8321 57

Location: Across from Dayton International Airport; off National Rd. 75 Corporate Center Dr 45377-1155. **Fax:** 937/898-6334. **Facility:** 100 one-bedroom standard units, some with kitchens. 1 story, interior corridors. **Parking:** on-site. **Terms:** 10 day cancellation notice-fee imposed, package plans, small pets only ($10 extra charge). **Amenities:** extended cable TV, hair dryers. **Pool(s):** outdoor. **Leisure Activities:** exercise room. **Guest Services:** coin laundry, area transportation. **Business Services:** meeting rooms. **Cards:** AX, CB, DC, DS, JC, MC, VI. **Special Amenities:** free continental breakfast and free newspaper. (See ad p 678)

(See map p. 672)

──────── WHERE TO DINE ────────

FRICKER'S   **Lunch:** $7-$14   **Dinner:** $7-$14   **Phone:** 937/454-9464   43

▼▼▼

American

Location: I-75, exit 63, just e. 22 Foley Dr 45377. **Hours:** 11 am-1 am. Closed: 1/1, 12/25. **Features:** casual dress; carryout; cocktails & lounge. Lively sports fans gather to watch broadcast events and dine on fast-food fare, such as sandwiches, chicken wings and french fries. **Parking:** on-site. **Cards:** AX, DS, MC, VI.

ORIGINAL RIB HOUSE   **Dinner:** $8-$17   **Phone:** 937/898-4601   42

(AAA)

▼▼▼

American

Location: I-75, exit 63, just w. 275 E National Rd 45377. **Hours:** 4 pm-10 pm, Fri & Sat-11:30 pm, Sun 11:30 am-10 pm. Closed major holidays. **Features:** casual dress; children's menu; carryout; cocktails. As the relaxed restaurant's name suggests, ribs are a specialty. However, you'll also find broasted chicken and fish, steak and other well-prepared dishes on the menu. The sour cream apple pie is a sweet delight. Service is prompt and friendly. **Parking:** on-site. **Cards:** AX, DC, MC, VI.   ✗

VAN WERT pop. 10,900

──────── WHERE TO STAY ────────

HOLIDAY INN EXPRESS   **Phone:** (419)232-6040

▼▼▼   4/1-10/31   1P: $89-$99   2P: $89-$99   XP: $7   F18
          11/1-3/31   1P: $79-$99   2P: $79-$99   XP: $7   F18
Motel   **Location:** US 127, s of jct US 30 and 224. 840 N Washington St 45891. Fax: 419/232-6210. **Facility:** 57 one-bedroom standard units, some with efficiencies and/or whirlpools. 2 stories, interior corridors. *Bath:* combo or shower only. **Parking:** on-site. **Amenities:** extended cable TV, voice mail, irons, hair dryers. **Pool(s):** heated indoor. **Leisure Activities:** whirlpool, exercise room. **Guest Services:** valet and coin laundry. **Business Services:** meeting rooms. **Cards:** AX, DC, DS, JC, MC, VI.

SOME UNITS

(ASK) S/D 🍴 📶 ♿ 🎧 🏊 🎦 DATA/PORT 🖨 / ✗ 📁 🍽 💻 /

VERMILION pop. 11,100

──────── WHERE TO STAY ────────

HOLIDAY INN EXPRESS   **Phone:** (440)967-8770

▼▼▼   6/14-8/31 [ECP]   1P: $99-$139   2P: $99-$139   XP: $10   F18
          5/10-6/13 [ECP]   1P: $79-$129   2P: $79-$129   XP: $10   F18
Motel   4/1-5/9 & 9/1-3/31 [ECP] 1P: $45-$58   2P: $69-$99   XP: $10   F18
Location: Jct SR 60 and 2. 2417 SR 60 44089. Fax: 440/967-8772. **Facility:** 66 one-bedroom standard units, some with whirlpools. 2 stories, interior corridors. *Bath:* combo or shower only. **Parking:** on-site. **Terms:** small pets only. **Amenities:** voice mail, irons, hair dryers. *Some:* video games. **Pool(s):** heated indoor. **Leisure Activities:** whirlpool, exercise room. **Guest Services:** coin laundry. **Business Services:** meeting rooms, fax. **Cards:** AX, DC, DS, JC, MC, VI.

SOME UNITS

(ASK) S/D 🐾 📶 🎧 🏊 🎦 DATA/PORT 💻 🖨 / ✗ (VCR) 📁 🍽 /

MOTEL PLAZA   **Phone:** 440/967-3191

(AAA) [SAVE]   5/1-9/30   1P: $52-$75   2P: $62-$89
▼   4/1-4/30 & 10/1-3/31   1P: $45-$58   2P: $58-$78
Motel   **Location:** 2 mi e of SR 60; on US 6. 4645 Liberty Ave 44089. **Facility:** 14 one-bedroom standard units. 1 story, exterior corridors. *Bath:* shower only. **Parking:** on-site. **Terms:** small pets only ($20 deposit). **Amenities:** extended cable TV. **Cards:** AX, DS, MC, VI. **Special Amenities:** free local telephone calls and preferred room (subject to availability with advanced reservations).

SOME UNITS

S/D 🐾 📁 🍽 💻 🖨 / ✗ /

──────── WHERE TO DINE ────────

CHEZ FRANCOIS   **Dinner:** $10-$75   **Phone:** 440/967-0630

▼▼▼

French

Location: 555 Main St 44089. **Hours:** 5 pm-9 pm, Fri & Sat-10 pm, Sun 4 pm-9 pm. **Reservations:** suggested. **Features:** semi-formal attire; cocktails; a la carte. Overlooking the Vermilion River, the restaurant is known for a romantic atmosphere. Smoke free premises. **Parking:** on-site. **Cards:** MC, VI.

✗ 🍸

──────── *The following restaurant has not been evaluated by AAA* ────────
but is listed for your information only.

OLD PRAGUE RESTAURANT   **Phone:** 440/967-7182

[fyi]   Not evaluated. **Location:** 5586 Liberty Ave. Authentic central European dishes are served at this Czech eatery.

VERSAILLES pop. 2,400

──────── WHERE TO STAY ────────

THE INN AT VERSAILLES   **Phone:** 937/526-3020

▼▼▼   All Year [CP]   1P: $40-$116   XP: $10
Motor Inn **Location:** Downtown; at corner of Main and Center sts. 21 W Main St 45380. Fax: 937/526-3131. **Facility:** 20 one-bedroom standard units. 2 stories, interior corridors. **Parking:** on-site. **Terms:** package plans. **Amenities:** extended cable TV. **Dining:** restaurant, see separate listing. **Business Services:** meeting rooms. **Cards:** AX, CB, DC, DS, JC, MC, VI.

SOME UNITS

(ASK) S/D 🍴 📶 🎦 🖨 / ✗ 📁 🍽 💻 /

——— **WHERE TO DINE** ———

THE INN AT VERSAILLES RESTAURANT   **Lunch:** $5-$9   **Dinner:** $5-$17   **Phone:** 937/526-3020
▼▼▼▼ ▼▼▼▼   **Location:** Downtown; at corner of Main and Center sts; in The Inn at Versailles. 21 W Main St 45380. **Hours:** 11 am-9 pm, Fri-10 pm, Sat 4 pm-10 pm, Sun 11 am-3 & 4-8 pm. Closed major holidays. **Features:** casual
American   dress; Sunday brunch; children's menu; carryout; cocktails & lounge. Murals, imported furnishings and stone and marble fireplaces give the cozy restaurant the feel of a French country inn. A selection of domestic, European, North and South American wines complements the authentic, freshly prepared cuisine. **Parking:** on-site.
Cards: AX, DC, DS, MC, VI.
✕

WADSWORTH pop. 15,700

——— **WHERE TO STAY** ———

HOLIDAY INN EXPRESS HOTEL & SUITES   **Phone:** 330/334-7666
▼▼▼▼   4/1-8/31 [ECP]   1P: $69-$84   2P: $69-$84   XP: $10   F18
9/1-10/31 [ECP]   1P: $64-$79   2P: $64-$79   XP: $10   F18
Motel   11/1-3/31 [ECP]   1P: $59-$74   2P: $59-$74   XP: $10   F18
Location: I-76, exit 9, just n. 231 Park Center Dr 44281. **Fax:** 330/334-0214. **Facility:** 74 one-bedroom standard units, some with efficiencies (no utensils) and/or whirlpools. 3 stories, interior corridors. *Bath:* combo or shower only. **Parking:** on-site. **Amenities:** extended cable TV, dual phone lines, voice mail, irons, hair dryers. **Pool(s):** small heated indoor. **Leisure Activities:** sauna, whirlpool, exercise room. **Guest Services:** valet and coin laundry. **Business Services:** meeting rooms, business center, fax. **Cards:** AX, CB, DC, DS, MC, VI.
SOME UNITS
(ASK) (S/D) ✈ (†|+) ☞ ✕ (DATA PORT) ▭ 🖨 / ✕ 📻 (🖥) /

RAMADA LIMITED-AKRON/WADSWORTH   **Phone:** (330)336-7692
▼▼▼▼   6/1-8/31 [ECP]   1P: $69   2P: $69
4/1-5/31 & 9/1-10/31 [ECP]   1P: $62   2P: $62
Motel   11/1-3/31 [ECP]   1P: $59   2P: $59
Location: I-76, exit 9, just n. 5 Park Center Blvd 44281. **Fax:** 330/336-5984. **Facility:** 110 one-bedroom standard units, some with whirlpools. 5 stories, interior corridors. **Parking:** on-site. **Terms:** 3 day cancellation notice. **Amenities:** extended cable TV, dual phone lines, voice mail, irons, hair dryers. **Leisure Activities:** exercise room. **Guest Services:** valet laundry. **Business Services:** meeting rooms. **Cards:** AX, CB, DC, DS, JC, MC, VI.
SOME UNITS
(ASK) (S/D) (†|+) ☞ 📺 🖨 / ✕ 📻 (🖥) /

WALNUT CREEK pop. 700

——— **WHERE TO STAY** ———

CARLISLE VILLAGE INN   **Phone:** 330/893-3636
(AAA) (SAVE)   4/1-12/24 & 12/26-3/31 [CP]   1P: $98-$185   2P: $98-$185   XP: $8   F12
▼▼▼▼ ▼▼▼▼   **Location:** In town. 4949 SR 515 44687 (PO Box 177). **Fax:** 330/893-2056. **Facility:** Spacious rooms with Amish-style decor and views of the valley from private balconies make this inn interesting. Smoke free premises. 52
Motel   units. 48 one-bedroom standard units. 2 one- and 2 two-bedroom suites, some with whirlpools. 3 stories, interior corridors. *Bath:* combo or shower only. **Parking:** on-site. **Terms:** open 4/1-12/24 & 12/26-3/31, cancellation fee imposed, package plans - 11/1-4/30. **Amenities:** extended cable TV, video tape library (fee), voice mail, irons, hair dryers. **Business Services:** meeting rooms. **Cards:** AX, DS, MC, VI.
SOME UNITS
(†|+) (👟) (🖊) ✕ 📻 🖥 🖨 / (VCR) (🖥) /

THE INN AT WALNUT CREEK   **Phone:** 330/893-3599
▼▼ ▼▼   7/1-10/26   2P: $65-$100   XP: $7   F16
5/19-6/30   2P: $55-$100   XP: $7   F16
Motel   4/1-5/18   2P: $55-$75   XP: $7   F16
10/27-3/31   2P: $40-$65   XP: $7   F16
Location: In center of town. 4869 Olde Pump St 44687. **Facility:** Smoke free premises. 21 one-bedroom standard units. 2 stories, exterior corridors. **Parking:** on-site. **Terms:** 3 day cancellation notice-fee imposed. **Amenities:** extended cable TV. **Business Services:** meeting rooms. **Cards:** AX, DS, MC, VI.
SOME UNITS
(†|+) ✕ 🖨 / (DATA PORT) 📻 🖥 🖥 /

OAKRIDGE INN   **Phone:** (330)893-3811
▼▼▼   5/1-10/31 [CP]   1P: $69-$165   2P: $69-$165   XP: $8   F12
4/1-4/30 & 11/1-3/31 [CP]   1P: $59-$165   2P: $59-$165   XP: $8   F12
Motel   **Location:** Jct SR 39 and US 403. 4845 Milo Dr 44687 (PO Box 114). **Fax:** 330/893-3811. **Facility:** Smoke free premises. 8 units. 5 one-bedroom standard units, some with whirlpools. 1 one-bedroom suite with whirlpools. 1 story, interior corridors. *Bath:* combo or shower only. **Parking:** on-site. **Terms:** 3 day cancellation notice. **Amenities:** extended cable TV. *Some:* CD players. **Cards:** DS, MC, VI.
SOME UNITS
✕ 📻 🖥 🖨 / (VCR) 🖥 /

——— **WHERE TO DINE** ———

DER DUTCHMAN RESTAURANT   **Lunch:** $5-$8   **Dinner:** $8-$15   **Phone:** 330/893-2981
(AAA)   **Location:** SR 515; in Walnut Creek. 44687. **Hours:** 7 am-8 pm. Closed: 1/1, 11/28, 12/25; also Sun.
▼▼ ▼▼   **Features:** casual dress; children's menu; carryout; salad bar. Pan-fried chicken and roast beef baked in natural juices are among the Amish-style specialties of the charming, family-oriented restaurant. Freshly
American   baked bread is tasty. The dining room affords views of the Genza Bottom, a beautiful farming valley. Smoke free premises. **Parking:** on-site. **Cards:** DS, MC, VI.
✕

WAPAKONETA pop. 9,200

──────── WHERE TO STAY ────────

BEST WESTERN WAPAKONETA

(AAA) [SAVE]
▼▼▼▼
Motel

Phone: (419)738-8181

All Year [ECP]   1P: $59-$85   2P: $59-$85   XP: $5   F18
Location: On I-75 business loop at jct I-75, exit 111. 1510 Saturn 45895. Fax: 419/738-6478. **Facility:** 94 one-bedroom standard units. 4 stories, interior corridors. **Parking:** on-site. **Terms:** 10 day cancellation notice, package plans, pets ($10 extra charge). **Amenities:** extended cable TV. **Leisure Activities:** exercise room. **Guest Services:** coin laundry. **Business Services:** conference facilities. **Cards:** AX, CB, DC, DS, MC, VI. **Special Amenities:** free continental breakfast and free local telephone calls.

SOME UNITS

HOLIDAY INN EXPRESS

▼▼▼
Motel

Phone: (419)738-2050

All Year   1P: $69-$84   2P: $69-$84   XP: $5   F18
Location: I-75, exit 111, just w. 1008 Lunar Dr 45895. Fax: 419/738-2050. **Facility:** 55 one-bedroom standard units, some with whirlpools. 2 stories, interior corridors. *Bath:* combo or shower only. **Parking:** on-site. **Terms:** 7 day cancellation notice. **Amenities:** extended cable TV, dual phone lines, voice mail, safes, irons, hair dryers. **Pool(s):** heated indoor. **Leisure Activities:** whirlpool. **Guest Services:** valet laundry. **Cards:** AX, CB, DC, DS, MC, VI.

SOME UNITS

SUPER 8 MOTEL-WAPAKONETA

▼▼▼
Motel

Phone: 419/738-8810

All Year [CP]   1P: $46   2P: $49   XP: $4   F16
Location: I-75 business loop at jct I-75, exit 111. 1011 Lunar Dr 45895. Fax: 419/738-8810. **Facility:** 38 one-bedroom standard units, some with whirlpools. 2 stories, interior/exterior corridors. **Parking:** on-site. **Terms:** age restrictions may apply, pets ($10-$20 deposit). **Amenities:** extended cable TV, hair dryers. **Cards:** AX, CB, DC, DS, MC, VI.

SOME UNITS

WARREN pop. 50,800

──────── WHERE TO STAY ────────

AVALON INN

▼▼ ▼▼
Motor Inn

Phone: (330)856-1900

All Year   1P: $78-$85   2P: $85-$95   XP: $10   F
Location: 7 mi e on SR 82, 1.3 mi ne on Howland Wilson Rd, 0.5 mi e of SR 46. 9519 E Market St 44484. Fax: 330/856-2248. **Facility:** 144 one-bedroom standard units. 3 stories, interior corridors. *Bath:* combo or shower only. **Parking:** on-site. **Terms:** 3 day cancellation notice, package plans. **Amenities:** extended cable TV, voice mail, hair dryers. *Some:* irons. **Pool(s):** heated indoor. **Leisure Activities:** saunas, whirlpool. *Fee:* golf-36 holes, racquetball court. **Guest Services:** valet laundry. **Business Services:** conference facilities. **Cards:** AX, DC, DS, MC, VI.

SOME UNITS

FEE

BEST WESTERN DOWNTOWN MOTOR INN

(AAA) [SAVE]
▼▼▼▼
Motel

(See color ad below)

Phone: (330)392-2515

10/1-3/31 [ECP]   1P: $55-$75   2P: $60-$80   XP: $5   F18
4/1-9/30 [ECP]   1P: $50-$70   2P: $55-$75   XP: $5   F18
Location: 0.3 mi n of Courthouse Square. 777 Mahoning Ave 44483. Fax: 330/392-7099. **Facility:** 73 one-bedroom standard units. 2 stories, exterior corridors. **Parking:** on-site. **Terms:** 7 day cancellation notice. **Amenities:** extended cable TV. *Some:* hair dryers. **Guest Services:** valet laundry. **Cards:** AX, CB, DC, JC, MC, VI. **Special Amenities:** free continental breakfast and free local telephone calls.

SOME UNITS

FAIRFIELD INN   Phone: (330)544-5774

(AAA) (SAVE)   4/1-12/31 [CP]   1P: $72-$76   2P: $72-$76
▼▼▼▼▼   1/1-3/31 [CP]   1P: $67-$72   2P: $67-$72
             Location: Jct US 422 and SR 46, 1 mi n on SR 46. 1860 Niles-Cortland Rd 44484. Fax: 330/544-5774. **Facility:** 64
Motel   one-bedroom standard units. 3 stories, interior corridors. *Bath:* combo or shower only. **Parking:** on-site.
             Amenities: extended cable TV, irons. **Pool(s):** heated indoor. **Leisure Activities:** whirlpool. **Business Serv-**
ices: meeting rooms. **Cards:** AX, CB, DC, DS, JC, MC, VI. **Special Amenities: free continental breakfast**
and free local telephone calls. *(See color ad card insert)*

SOME UNITS

[icons] FEE

HOLIDAY INN EXPRESS HOTEL & SUITES   Phone: (330)544-8807
▼▼▼   All Year   1P: $139-$189   2P: $139-$189
             Location: Jct US 422 and SR 46, 1 mi n on SR 46. 135 Highland Terrace 44484. Fax: 330/544-8956. **Facility:** 78
Motel   units. 74 one-bedroom standard units, some with efficiencies (no utensils) and/or whirlpools. 4 one-bedroom
             suites ($149-$189) with efficiencies (no utensils) and whirlpools. 3 stories, interior corridors. *Bath:* combo or
shower only. **Parking:** on-site. **Amenities:** extended cable TV, video games, dual phone lines, voice mail, irons, hair dryers.
Some: safes. **Pool(s):** heated indoor. **Leisure Activities:** whirlpool, exercise room. **Guest Services:** valet laundry. **Business**
Services: meeting rooms, business center. **Cards:** AX, DC, DS, JC, MC, VI.

SOME UNITS

[icons] FEE

─────── **WHERE TO DINE** ───────

ABRUZZI'S CAFE 422   **Lunch:** $6-$9   **Dinner:** $9-$25   Phone: 330/369-2422
▼▼▼   **Location:** 3.5 mi se on US 422. 4422 Youngstown Rd 44484. **Hours:** 11 am-10 pm, Sun-9 pm; closing hours
             may vary. Closed: 12/25. **Features:** casual dress; children's menu; carryout; cocktails & lounge. Fresh
Italian   pasta and locally grown ingredients add to the flavor of such dishes as eggplant parmigiana and lasagna.
             The well-established restaurant has been in operation since the late 1930s. Attractive decorations give the
place a casual European feel. **Parking:** on-site. **Cards:** AX, DC, DS, MC, VI.

[icon]

HOT DOG SHOPPE   **Lunch:** $4-$7   **Dinner:** $4-$7   Phone: 330/395-7057
▼▼   **Location:** 0.8 mi w of Courthouse Square. 740 W Market St 44481. **Hours:** 10 am-10 pm. Closed major holidays.
             Features: casual dress; carryout; a la carte. Specializing in hot dogs, burgers and freshly cut fries, the
American   simple restaurant guards a chili recipe that has been handed down from generation to generation.
             Parking: on-site.

[icon]

─────── *The following restaurants have not been evaluated by AAA* ───────
but are listed for your information only.

BUENA VISTA CAFE   Phone: 330/372-4493
[fyi]   Not evaluated. **Location:** 1305 Buena Vista NE. Representative dishes here include Uncle Nick's Greek fried chicken
             and homemade soup.

CEASAR'S ITALIAN RESTAURANT   Phone: 330/898-1555
[fyi]   Not evaluated. **Location:** 2801 W Market St 44446. On the diverse menu are homemade pizzas, pasta and chicken
             dishes, sandwiches and wings.

ENZO'S   Phone: 330/372-3314
[fyi]   Not evaluated. **Location:** 2918 Elm Rd NE 44446. The restaurant blends a casual, comfortable atmosphere with
             traditional cuisine and good prices.

JIMMY CHIEFFO'S   Phone: 330/369-6507
[fyi]   Not evaluated. **Location:** 3860 Youngstown-Warren Rd. The restaurant is known for its varied menu and attentive
             service.

LEO'S RISTORANTE   Phone: 330/856-5291
[fyi]   Not evaluated. **Location:** 7042 E Market St 44446. Traditional offerings of classic Italian cuisine are prepared
             alongside creative daily specials, homemade soups and desserts.

MARY M'S RESTAURANT   Phone: 330/898-3846
[fyi]   Not evaluated. **Location:** 2940 Parkman Rd NW 44485. Homemade food with friendly service.

THE MOCHA HOUSE   Phone: 330/392-3020
[fyi]   Not evaluated. **Location:** 467 High St NE 44446. Signature items on a menu of homemade soups, New York-style
             cakes and pastries are wedding soup, California cheesecake and chicken walnut croissant.

SALVATORE'S ITALIAN GRILL   Phone: 330/609-7777
[fyi]   Not evaluated. **Location:** 8720 E Market St. Homemade pasta is used to prepare traditional Italian dishes.

WASHINGTON COURT HOUSE pop. 12,600

─────── **WHERE TO STAY** ───────

COUNTRY HEARTH INN WASHINGTON COURT HOUSE   Phone: (740)333-4478
▼▼ ▼▼   All Year   1P: $65-$110   2P: $65-$110
             Location: 1.5 mi n on US 62 and SR 3. 1810 Victorian St 43160. Fax: 740/333-4478. **Facility:** 40 one-bedroom
Motel   standard units, some with whirlpools. 2 stories, interior corridors. *Bath:* combo or shower only. **Parking:** on-
             site. **Amenities:** safes (fee), hair dryers. **Business Services:** fax (fee). **Cards:** AX, CB, DC, DS, MC, VI.

SOME UNITS

[icons]

KNIGHTS INN

(AAA) (SAVE)

◇◇◇
Motel

4/1-10/31 [CP]	1P: $45-$53	2P: $51-$59	XP: $6	F18
11/1-3/31 [CP]	1P: $40-$48	2P: $46-$54	XP: $6	F18

Phone: (740)335-9133

Location: 1.5 mi n on US 62 and SR 3. 1809 Columbus Ave 43160. Fax: 740/333-7938. **Facility:** 55 one-bedroom standard units, some with whirlpools. 1 story, exterior corridors. **Parking:** on-site. **Terms:** pets ($6 extra charge). **Amenities:** extended cable TV. **Business Services:** meeting rooms, fax (fee). **Cards:** AX, DC, DS, MC, VI. **Special Amenities:** free continental breakfast and free local telephone calls.

SOME UNITS

[icons]

WATERVILLE pop. 4,500

——— WHERE TO DINE ———

SMEDLAP'S SMITHY

◇◇ ◇◇
American

Lunch: $6-$9   **Dinner:** $10-$19   **Phone:** 419/878-0261

Location: Just s of US 24, on Farnsworth Rd (SR 64). 205 Farnsworth Rd 43566. **Hours:** 11:30 am-9:30 pm, Fri & Sat-10:30 pm. Closed major holidays; also Sun. **Reservations:** suggested; weekends. **Features:** casual dress; children's menu; early bird specials; carryout; cocktails & lounge; a la carte. In a 19th-century blacksmith shop, the restaurant is rustically decorated with horseshoes, antique coffee grinders and hay bale hooks. Prime ribs, king crab legs, salads and sandwiches make up the familiar menu. The atmosphere is warm and friendly. **Parking:** on-site. **Cards:** AX, DS, MC, VI.

[icon]

WAUSEON pop. 6,300

——— WHERE TO STAY ———

BEST WESTERN DEL MAR

(AAA) (SAVE)

◇◇◇
Motel

6/1-8/31	1P: $71-$160		XP: $10	F18
4/1-5/31 & 9/1-10/31	1P: $65-$115		XP: $10	F18
11/1-3/31	1P: $64-$109		XP: $10	F18

Phone: (419)335-1565

Location: I-80/90 (Ohio Tpke), exit 34, just s. 8319 SR 108 43567. Fax: 419/335-1828. **Facility:** 48 units. 46 one-bedroom standard units. 2 one-bedroom suites ($79-$109) with whirlpools. 1 story, exterior corridors. **Parking:** on-site. **Terms:** 3 day cancellation notice, pets ($17 extra charge). **Amenities:** extended cable TV, video tape library, irons, hair dryers. **Pool(s):** heated outdoor. **Leisure Activities:** playground. **Business Services:** meeting rooms. **Cards:** AX, CB, DC, DS, MC, VI. **Special Amenities:** free continental breakfast and free newspaper.

SOME UNITS

[icons]

——— WHERE TO DINE ———

SMITH'S RESTAURANT

(AAA)

◇◇
American

Lunch: $6-$8   **Dinner:** $9-$17   **Phone:** 419/335-4896

Location: I-80/90 (Ohio Tpke), exit 34, 0.3 mi s. SR 108 43567. **Hours:** 7 am-9 pm; 6:30 am-10 pm 6/1-9/15. Closed major holidays. **Features:** casual dress; children's menu; carryout; cocktails. Family-owned and operated since the early 1970s, this simple restaurant specializes in comfort food. The decor creates a homey environment. **Parking:** on-site. **Cards:** AX, DS, MC, VI.

[icon]

WAVERLY pop. 4,800

——— WHERE TO DINE ———

LAKE WHITE CLUB

◇◇ ◇◇
American

Dinner: $8-$16   **Phone:** 740/947-5000

Location: 2.5 mi sw on SR 552, via SR 104. 1166 SR 552 45690. **Hours:** 4 pm-9 pm, Sun noon-6:30 pm. Closed: 1/1, 11/28, 12/24, 12/25; also Mon. **Reservations:** suggested. **Features:** casual dress; children's menu; carryout; beer & wine only. Fried chicken is a specialty at the lakeside restaurant, once a private club for Ohio politicians. The quirky decor features family pictures in the foyer, and part of the building featuring timbers from an old log cabin. Service is prompt and attentive. **Parking:** on-site. **Cards:** MC, VI.

[icon]

WAYNESVILLE —See Cincinnati p. 588.

WEST CARROLLTON

——— WHERE TO DINE ———

——— *The following restaurants have not been evaluated by AAA*
but are listed for your information only. ———

EL MESON / MACARENA

(fyi)

Phone: 937/859-8229

Not evaluated. **Location:** 903 E Dixie Dr 45449. Spanish and Latin entrees line the restaurant's menu.

RED ROCK STEAKHOUSE & SALOON

(fyi)

Phone: 937/847-2400

Not evaluated. **Location:** 630 E Dixie Dr 45449. This eatery offers a variety of steaks, ribs and chicken dishes.

WEST CHESTER pop. 700   (See map p. 558; index p. 561)

———— WHERE TO STAY ————

CINCINNATI MARRIOTT NORTH   Phone: (513)874-7335   `105`

(AAA) (SAVE)   8/24-3/31   1P: $134-$152   2P: $134-$152
▽▽▽▽▽   4/1-8/23   1P: $131-$149   2P: $131-$149
          Location: I-75, exit 19. 6189 Muhlhauser Rd 45069. Fax: 513/874-7336. **Facility:** 295 units. 291 one-bedroom
Hotel   standard units. 4 one-bedroom suites ($259-$279), some with whirlpools. 8 stories, interior corridors. *Bath:*
          combo or shower only. **Parking:** on-site. **Terms:** package plans. **Amenities:** dual phone lines, voice mail,
irons, hair dryers. **Dining:** dining room, 6 am-11 pm, $10-$22. **Pool(s):** heated indoor. **Leisure Activi-**
ties: exercise room. **Guest Services:** gift shop, valet and coin laundry. **Business Services:** conference facilities, business
center, administrative services, PC, fax (fee). **Cards:** AX, CB, DC, DS, JC, MC, VI. *(See color ad card insert)*

SOME UNITS

🆂🅳 🍴 🍸 🔧Ⓜ 🛗 🚗 🏊 🎬 📠 💻 🖨 / ✕ 🔌
                                    FEE

WESTERVILLE —*See Columbus p. 668.*

WESTLAKE —*See Cleveland p. 630.*

WESTMINSTER

———— WHERE TO DINE ————

———— *The following restaurant has not been evaluated by AAA* ————
but is listed for your information only.

THE CANARY   Phone: 419/648-6400
(fyi)   Not evaluated. **Location:** 6590 Bellefontainerd 45850. Home-cooked meals are prepared at the rural, off-the-road
          restaurant.

WEST UNION pop. 3,100

———— WHERE TO STAY ————

THE MURPHIN RIDGE INN   Phone: 937/544-2263
▽▽▽   4/1-1/1 & 1/19-3/31   1P: $90-$130   2P: $90-$130   D12
          Location: 5.5 mi n on US 41, 2 mi w on Wheat Ridge Rd, 1 mi n. 750 Murphin Ridge Rd 45693. Fax: 937/544-8151.
Country Inn **Facility:** An art gallery occupies the second floor of this 1810 guest house; in a pastoral setting, it offers spa-
          cious, modern rooms. Smoke free premises. 13 units. 10 one-bedroom standard units. 3 one-bedroom va-
cation rentals ($135-$190). 2 stories, interior corridors. **Parking:** on-site. **Terms:** open 4/1-1/1 & 1/19-3/31, 2 night minimum stay
- weekends, cancellation fee imposed, [BP] meal plan available, package plans. **Pool(s):** heated outdoor. **Leisure Activi-**
ties: tennis court, hiking trails. **Guest Services:** gift shop. **Business Services:** meeting rooms. **Cards:** MC, VI.

SOME UNITS

🍴 🏊 ✕ 🅆 📠 🖨 / 🔌 💻 /

WHEELERSBURG pop. 5,100

———— WHERE TO STAY ————

COMFORT INN   Phone: (740)574-1046
(AAA) (SAVE)   All Year [ECP]   1P: $59-$98   XP: $5   F18
▽▽▽▽   **Location:** US 52, exit Wheelersburg. 8226 Ohio River Rd 45694. Fax: 740/574-5786. **Facility:** 52 one-bedroom
          standard units, some with whirlpools. 2 stories, interior corridors. *Bath:* combo or shower only. **Parking:** on-
Motel   site. **Amenities:** extended cable TV. *Some:* irons, hair dryers. **Pool(s):** small heated indoor. **Guest Services:**
          coin laundry. **Business Services:** meeting rooms, fax (fee). **Cards:** AX, CB, DC, DS, JC, MC, VI.
Special Amenities: free continental breakfast and free local telephone calls.

SOME UNITS

🆂🅳 🍴 🔧 🏊 🎬 📠 💻 / ✕ 💻 /

DAYS INN PORTSMOUTH-WHEELERSBURG   Phone: (740)574-8431
(AAA) (SAVE)   All Year [BP]   1P: $55-$65   2P: $60-$70   XP: $5   F17
▽▽ ▽   **Location:** US 52, exit Wheelersburg. 8340 Ohio River Rd 45694. Fax: 740/574-6398. **Facility:** 62 one-bedroom
          standard units. 2 stories, exterior corridors. **Parking:** on-site. **Amenities:** extended cable TV, hair dryers.
Motel   **Pool(s):** outdoor. **Business Services:** fax (fee). **Cards:** AX, CB, DC, DS, JC, MC, VI. **Special Amenities:**
          free continental breakfast and free newspaper.

SOME UNITS

🆂🅳 🍴 🏊 🎬 📠 🖨 / ✕ 🔌 💻 /

———— WHERE TO DINE ————

FRED'S RESTAURANT   Lunch: $5-$8   Dinner: $7-$10   Phone: 740/574-2507
(AAA)   **Location:** US 52, exit Wheelersburg. 8228 Ohio River Rd 45694. **Hours:** 11 am-11 pm, Fri & Sat-1 am. Closed
▽▽ ▽   major holidays. **Reservations:** accepted. **Features:** casual dress; children's menu; carryout; a la carte.
          Fred's is a casual, family-oriented restaurant with pizza, sandwiches, steak and pasta making an excellent
American menu showing for those not quite sure what they're in the mood for. The relaxed, informal atmosphere
          complements the Victorian-style setting. **Parking:** on-site. **Cards:** MC, VI.

WICKLIFFE pop. 14,600 (See map p. 600; index p. 602)

──────── WHERE TO STAY ────────

FOUR POINTS BY SHERATON CLEVELAND EAST Phone: (440)585-2750 **17**

5/3-9/3	1P: $99-$129	2P: $109-$139	XP: $10 F18
4/1-5/2 & 9/4-3/31	1P: $89-$119	2P: $99-$129	XP: $10 F18

Motor Inn **Location:** I-90, exit 186, just n. 28500 Euclid Ave 44092. Fax: 440/585-2775. **Facility:** 196 one-bedroom standard units, some with whirlpools. 4 stories, interior corridors. **Parking:** on-site. **Terms:** package plans. **Amenities:** video games, voice mail, irons, hair dryers. *Some:* CD players. **Pool(s):** heated indoor. **Leisure Activities:** sauna, whirlpool, miniature golf, exercise room, volleyball. **Guest Services:** complimentary laundry. **Business Services:** conference facilities, business center, fax. **Cards:** AX, CB, DC, DS, JC, MC, VI.

SOME UNITS
(ASK) (SD) (✈) (YI) (Y) (🖊) (🏊) (✕) (📹) (DATA PORT) (🖥) (🖨) / (✕) (📱) (📷) /
FEE   FEE FEE

HAMPTON INN-CLEVELAND/WICKLIFFE Phone: (440)944-4030 **16**

(SAVE)

6/1-8/31 [ECP]	1P: $89-$99	2P: $89-$99
9/1-3/31 [ECP]	1P: $79-$89	2P: $79-$89
4/1-5/31 [ECP]	1P: $75-$79	2P: $75-$79

Motel **Location:** I-90, exit 186, just n on US 20. 28611 Euclid Ave 44092. Fax: 440/944-6681. **Facility:** 124 one-bedroom standard units, some with whirlpools. 2-3 stories, interior corridors. **Parking:** on-site. **Amenities:** extended cable TV, video games, voice mail, irons, hair dryers. **Pool(s):** heated indoor. **Leisure Activities:** exercise room. **Guest Services:** complimentary laundry. **Business Services:** meeting rooms. **Cards:** AX, CB, DC, DS, JC, MC, VI.

SOME UNITS
(SD) (YI) (🖊) (🏊) (📹) (DATA PORT) (🖥) (🖨) / (✕) (📱) (📷) /
FEE   FEE FEE

HOLIDAY INN NORTH EAST Phone: (440)585-0600 **18**

(AAA) (SAVE)

4/1-9/30	1P: $105-$125	2P: $105-$135	XP: $10 F18
10/1-3/31	1P: $95-$115	2P: $120	XP: $10 F18

Motor Inn **Location:** I-90, exit 187, just s. 28600 Ridgehills Dr 44092. Fax: 440/585-1911. **Facility:** 215 one-bedroom standard units. 3-5 stories, interior corridors. *Bath:* combo or shower only. **Parking:** on-site. **Terms:** 3 day cancellation notice. **Amenities:** irons, hair dryers. **Dining:** restaurant, 6 am-2 & 5-11 pm, Sat & Sun from 7 am, $8-$17, cocktails. **Pool(s):** heated indoor. **Leisure Activities:** sauna, whirlpool, exercise room. **Guest Services:** massage (fee), valet laundry. **Business Services:** meeting rooms. **Cards:** AX, CB, DC, DS, MC, VI. **Special Amenities:** free newspaper.

SOME UNITS
(SD) (YI) (Y) (🖊) (🏊) (✕) (📹) (DATA PORT) (🖥) (🖨) / (✕) (📱) (📷) /
FEE

──────── WHERE TO DINE ────────

─── *The following restaurant has not been evaluated by AAA* ───
but is listed for your information only.

CLUB ALLEGRO Phone: 440/944-4119

(fyi) Not evaluated. **Location:** I-90, exit 186, just n. 28611 Euclid Ave 44092. A fun place with comedy club nights, yearly rib burn off & clambake and a summer boat cruise.

WILLARD pop. 6,200

──────── WHERE TO STAY ────────

COUNTRY HEARTH INN Phone: (419)935-8817

(AAA) (SAVE)

All Year [ECP]	1P: $57	2P: $57 XP: $10 F18

Motel **Location:** US 224 and SR 90. 1201 S Conwell Ave 44890. Fax: 419/935-1445. **Facility:** 116 one-bedroom standard units. 2 stories, interior corridors. *Bath:* combo or shower only. **Parking:** on-site. **Amenities:** extended cable TV, dual phone lines, voice mail, irons, hair dryers. **Dining:** deli, 6 am-8 pm, $6-$8. **Leisure Activities:** exercise room. **Guest Services:** valet laundry. **Cards:** AX, CB, DC, DS, MC, VI. **Special Amenities:** free continental breakfast and free newspaper.

SOME UNITS
(SD) (YI) (🖊) (🖊) (📹) (DATA PORT) (🖥) (🖨) / (✕) (📱) (📷) /

WILLOUGHBY pop. 20,500 (See map p. 600; index p. 602)

──────── WHERE TO STAY ────────

COURTYARD BY MARRIOTT Phone: (440)530-1100 **13**

(AAA) (SAVE)

All Year	1P: $79-$119

Motel **Location:** I-90, exit 189, just n on SR 91, then just e. 35103 Maple Grove Rd 44094. Fax: 440/530-1111. **Facility:** 90 one-bedroom standard units, some with whirlpools. 3 stories, interior corridors. *Bath:* shower or tub only. **Parking:** on-site. **Amenities:** extended cable TV, voice mail, irons, hair dryers. **Dining:** restaurant, 6:30-10 am, Sat & Sun 7-11 am. **Pool(s):** heated indoor. **Leisure Activities:** whirlpool, exercise room. **Guest Services:** valet laundry. **Business Services:** meeting rooms. **Cards:** AX, CB, DC, DS, JC, MC, VI.

(See color ad card insert)

SOME UNITS
(SD) (YI) (🏊) (📹) (DATA PORT) (🖥) (🖨) / (✕) (📱) (📷) /
FEE

DAYS INN-WILLOUGHBY Phone: (440)946-0500 **11**

(SAVE)

All Year	2P: $58

Motel **Location:** I-90, exit 193, just s. 4145 SR 306 44094. Fax: 440/946-5258. **Facility:** 113 one-bedroom standard units, some with whirlpools. 2 stories, interior corridors. *Bath:* combo or shower only. **Parking:** on-site. **Terms:** cancellation fee imposed, [CP] meal plan available, package plans. **Amenities:** extended cable TV, safes (fee), hair dryers. *Some:* irons. **Pool(s):** outdoor. **Guest Services:** coin laundry. **Business Services:** meeting rooms. **Cards:** AX, CB, DC, DS, JC, MC.

SOME UNITS

(SD) (YI) (🖊) (🏊) (📹) (DATA PORT) (🖨) / (✕) (📱) (📷) (🖥) /

(See map p. 600)

FAIRFIELD INN BY MARRIOTT-WILLOUGHBY   Phone: (440)975-9922   🔢12

🔺🔺🔺 SAVE   6/1-8/31 [ECP]   1P: $65-$89
🔻🔻🔻🔻   4/1-5/31 [ECP]   1P: $59-$69
              9/1-3/31 [ECP]   1P: $55-$69
Motel   **Location:** I-90, exit 189, just n, then just e. 35110 Maplegrove Rd 44094. **Fax:** 440/942-9928. **Facility:** 134 one-bedroom standard units. 3 stories, interior/exterior corridors. **Parking:** on-site. **Amenities:** voice mail, irons. **Pool(s):** heated outdoor. **Guest Services:** valet laundry. **Cards:** AX, DC, DS, MC, VI. **Special Amenities:** free continental breakfast and free local telephone calls. *(See color ad card insert)*

SOME UNITS

🅂🄳 🏨 🎿 📹 📠 / ✖ /
FEE

RAMADA INN CLEVELAND EAST   Phone: (440)944-4300   🔢14

🔺🔺🔺 SAVE   All Year [ECP]   1P: $50   2P: $60   XP: $10   F12
🔻🔻🔻   **Location:** I-90, exit 189, at jct SR 91. 6051 SOM Center Rd 44094. **Fax:** 440/944-7302. **Facility:** 148 one-bedroom standard units, some with whirlpools. 2 stories, interior corridors. *Bath:* combo or shower only. **Parking:** on-site. **Terms:** 12 day cancellation notice-fee imposed, package plans, pets ($35 fee). **Amenities:** extended
Hotel   cable TV, irons, hair dryers. *Some:* voice mail. **Pool(s):** wading. **Leisure Activities:** sauna, 2 lighted tennis courts, exercise room. **Guest Services:** coin laundry. **Business Services:** meeting rooms. **Cards:** AX, CB, DC, DS, JC, MC, VI. **Special Amenities:** early check-in/late check-out and free continental breakfast. *(See color ad p 615)*

SOME UNITS

🅂🄳 🐕 🏨 🎿 ✖ 📹 📠 💾 📠 / ✖ 🔌 🔲
FEE   FEE FEE

RED ROOF INN-EAST   Phone: (440)946-9872   🔢10

🔺🔺🔺 SAVE   6/28-9/2   1P: $56-$66   2P: $62-$72   XP: $6   F18
🔻🔻🔻   5/24-6/27   1P: $49-$66   2P: $55-$72   XP: $6   F18
              4/1-5/23 & 9/3-3/31   1P: $43-$63   2P: $49-$69   XP: $6   F18
Motel   **Location:** I-90, exit 193, just s. 4166 SR 306 44094. **Fax:** 440/946-3624. **Facility:** 108 one-bedroom standard units. 2 stories, exterior corridors. *Bath:* combo or shower only. **Parking:** on-site. **Terms:** small pets only. **Amenities:** extended cable TV, video games, voice mail. **Cards:** AX, CB, DC, DS, MC, VI.
Special Amenities: free local telephone calls and free newspaper.

SOME UNITS

🐕 🏨 🎿 🔌 📹 📠 📠 / ✖ /
FEE

──────── WHERE TO DINE ────────

GAVI'S ITALIAN CUISINE   **Lunch:** $7-$12   **Dinner:** $10-$20   Phone: 440/942-8008   🔢24
🔻🔻🔻   **Location:** 2 mi e of SR 91 off Euclid Ave. 38257 Glenn Ave 44094. **Hours:** 11:30 am-2 & 4:30-10 pm, Fri-11 pm, Sat noon-2 & 4:30-11 pm. Closed major holidays; also Sun & Mon. **Reservations:** suggested.
Italian   **Features:** dressy casual; carryout; cocktails. The century-old building sits atop the ravine of the Chagrin River. Homemade sausage and gnocchi are menu favorites. Cavatelli is prepared with a mildly spicy tomato-based sauce with peppers and ground mortadella. Servers show excellent follow up. **Parking:** on-site. **Cards:** AX, DC, DS, MC, VI.

✖

──────── *The following restaurant has not been evaluated by AAA but is listed for your information only.* ────────

DINO'S   Phone: 440/269-8000
[fyi]   Not evaluated. **Location:** I-90, exit 193, just s. 4145 SR 306 44094. Convenient access, reasonable prices, huge portions and friendly service are found at this popular spot.

WILMINGTON —*See Cincinnati p. 588.*

WILMOT pop. 300

──────── WHERE TO STAY ────────

THE INN AT AMISH DOOR   Phone: 330/359-7996
🔻🔻🔻   All Year [ECP]   1P: $59-$199   2P: $59-$199   XP: $10   F18
              Location: Jct SR 250, 0.5 mi w on US 62. 1210 Winesburg St 44689. **Fax:** 330/359-0102. **Facility:** The inn's spacious guest rooms and a lounge on its second-story deck allow views of the landscaped grounds and surrounding Amish countryside. Smoke free premises. 50 units. 47 one-bedroom standard units, some with
Country Inn whirlpools. 3 one-bedroom suites with whirlpools. 3 stories, interior corridors. **Parking:** on-site. **Terms:** package plans. **Amenities:** dual phone lines, voice mail, hair dryers. **Dining:** The Amish Door Restaurant & Village, see separate listing. **Pool(s):** heated indoor. **Leisure Activities:** whirlpool, exercise room. **Guest Services:** coin laundry. **Business Services:** meeting rooms. **Cards:** AX, CB, DC, DS, MC, VI.

SOME UNITS

🏨 🎿 ✖ 📹 📠 📠 / 🔌 🔲 🔲
FEE

──────── WHERE TO DINE ────────

ALPINE ALPA RESTAURANT   **Lunch:** $6-$7   **Dinner:** $7-$10   Phone: 330/359-5454
🔺🔺🔺   **Location:** 2.5 mi sw. 1504 US 62 44689. **Hours:** 11 am-8 pm. Closed major holidays. **Features:** children's menu; carryout; salad bar; a la carte. The dining room is all quaint ambience, with two animated dioramas of the Alps and a tumbling waterfall that cascades through copper kettles into a pond on the dining room floor. The menu includes Swiss and Amish cooking, including a tasty Swiss steak. Smoke free premises.
American   **Parking:** on-site. **Cards:** AX, DS, MC, VI.

✖

THE AMISH DOOR RESTAURANT & VILLAGE   **Lunch:** $5-$8   **Dinner:** $8-$10   **Phone:** 330/359-5464

(AAA)

♦♦ ♦♦

American

Location: Jct SR 250, 0.5 mi w on US 62; next to The Inn at Amish Door. 1210 Winesburg St US 62 44689. **Hours:** 7 am-8 pm. Closed major holidays; also Sun. **Features:** casual dress; children's menu; carryout; salad bar. Built to resemble a large Amish home, the casually sophisticated restaurant has a country atmosphere, with hand-crafted furniture, greenery and art. Broasted chicken, slow-roasted roast beef and a wide assortment of homemade pies are popular menu offerings. Smoke free premises. **Parking:** on-site. **Cards:** DS, MC, VI.

☒

WINCHESTER pop. 1,000

------ WHERE TO STAY ------

BUDGET HOST INN   **Phone:** (937)695-0381

(AAA) [SAVE]

♦♦ ♦♦

Motel

All Year	1P: $49-$69	2P: $55-$75	XP: $12

Location: Jct US 32 and SR 136. 18760 SR 136 45697. **Fax:** 937/695-1215. **Facility:** 19 one-bedroom standard units. 2 stories, exterior corridors. **Parking:** on-site. **Terms:** 30 day cancellation notice-fee imposed. **Amenities:** hair dryers. *Some:* irons. **Cards:** AX, DS, MC, VI. **Special Amenities: early check-in/late check-out and free local telephone calls.** *(See color ad p 529)*

SOME UNITS

[icons]

WINESBURG pop. 300

------ WHERE TO STAY ------

THE GRAPEVINE HOUSE BED & BREAKFAST   **Phone:** (330)359-7922

♦♦ ♦♦

Bed & Breakfast

4/1-12/31 [BP]	1P: $70	2P: $70	XP: $10
1/1-3/31 [BP]	1P: $55	2P: $55	XP: $10

Location: Center of town. 2140 Main St 44690 (PO Box 223). **Fax:** 330/893-4187. **Facility:** 6 units. 5 one-bedroom standard units. 1 one-bedroom suite. 2 stories, interior/exterior corridors. *Bath:* shower only. **Parking:** on-site. **Terms:** cancellation fee imposed. **Amenities:** extended cable TV. **Cards:** DS, MC, VI.

SOME UNITS

[icons]

WOOSTER pop. 22,200

------ WHERE TO STAY ------

AMERIHOST INN-WOOSTER EAST   **Phone:** (330)262-5008

(AAA) [SAVE]

♦♦ ♦♦ ♦♦

Motel

All Year [ECP]	1P: $69-$85	2P: $80-$90	XP: $6 F17

Location: 2.5 mi e on US 30. 2055 Lincolnway E 44691. **Fax:** 330/262-5084. **Facility:** 58 one-bedroom standard units, some with whirlpools. 2 stories, exterior corridors. *Bath:* combo or shower only. **Parking:** on-site. **Terms:** 7 day cancellation notice. **Amenities:** extended cable TV, voice mail, safes (fee), irons, hair dryers. **Pool(s):** heated indoor. **Leisure Activities:** sauna, exercise room. **Guest Services:** valet laundry. **Business Services:** meeting rooms. **Cards:** AX, CB, DC, DS, JC, MC, VI. **Special Amenities: free continental breakfast and free newspaper.**

SOME UNITS

[icons]   FEE

AMERIHOST INN-WOOSTER NORTH   **Phone:** (330)345-1500

(AAA) [SAVE]

♦♦ ♦♦ ♦♦

Motel

All Year	1P: $69-$80	2P: $85-$90	XP: $6 F17

Location: Jct SR 3 and Milltown Rd. 789 E Milltown Rd 44691. **Fax:** 330/345-2411. **Facility:** 60 units. 58 one-bedroom standard units. 2 one-bedroom suites ($140-$160) with whirlpools. 2 stories, interior corridors. *Bath:* combo or shower only. **Parking:** on-site. **Terms:** 7 day cancellation notice, [ECP] meal plan available. **Amenities:** extended cable TV, voice mail, safes (fee), irons, hair dryers. **Pool(s):** heated indoor. **Leisure Activities:** whirlpool, exercise room. **Guest Services:** valet laundry. **Business Services:** meeting rooms, fax. **Cards:** AX, CB, DC, DS, JC, MC, VI. **Special Amenities: free continental breakfast and free newspaper.**

SOME UNITS

[icons]   FEE

BEST WESTERN WOOSTER PLAZA   **Phone:** (330)264-7750

(AAA) [SAVE]

♦♦ ♦♦

Motor Inn

5/1-12/31	1P: $65-$85	2P: $65-$85	XP: $10 F17
4/1-4/30	1P: $55-$65	2P: $60-$70	XP: $10 F17
1/1-3/31	1P: $55-$70	2P: $55-$70	XP: $10 F17

Location: Just e of square. 243 E Liberty 44691. **Fax:** 330/262-5840. **Facility:** 100 one-bedroom standard units. 2 stories, interior corridors. *Bath:* combo or shower only. **Parking:** on-site. **Terms:** check-in 4 pm, package plans. **Amenities:** extended cable TV, video tape library (fee), hair dryers. **Dining:** dining room, 11 am-10 pm; closed Sun, $8-$18, cocktails. **Pool(s):** outdoor. **Leisure Activities:** exercise room. **Guest Services:** valet laundry. **Business Services:** meeting rooms. **Cards:** AX, CB, DC, DS, JC, MC, VI. **Special Amenities: free continental breakfast and free local telephone calls.**

SOME UNITS

[icons]   FEE

ECONO LODGE   **Phone:** (330)264-8883

(AAA) [SAVE]

♦♦ ♦♦ ♦♦

Motel

4/1-11/2	1P: $54-$74	2P: $59-$79	XP: $5 F17
11/3-3/31	1P: $48-$58	2P: $54-$64	XP: $5 F17

Location: 3 mi e on US 30. 2137 E Lincoln Way 44691. **Fax:** 330/263-0792. **Facility:** 98 one-bedroom standard units. 2 stories, exterior corridors. **Parking:** on-site. **Terms:** pets on-site ($5 extra charge). **Amenities:** extended cable TV, hair dryers. **Pool(s):** heated indoor. **Leisure Activities:** whirlpool, exercise room. **Guest Services:** coin laundry. **Business Services:** meeting rooms. **Cards:** AX, DC, DS, JC, MC, VI. **Special Amenities: free continental breakfast and free local telephone calls.**

SOME UNITS

[icons]

HAMPTON INN

SAVE

Motel

Phone: (330)345-4424

5/1-10/15 [ECP]	1P: $79-$89	2P: $79
4/16-4/30 & 10/16-3/31 [ECP]	1P: $69-$79	2P: $79

Location: US 30, 4 mi n on SR 83 (Burbank Rd). 4253 Burbank Rd 44691. Fax: 330/345-4724. **Facility:** 63 one-bedroom standard units. 3 stories, interior corridors. **Parking:** on-site. **Terms:** 7 day cancellation notice. **Amenities:** extended cable TV, voice mail, irons, hair dryers. **Pool(s):** heated indoor. **Leisure Activities:** exercise room. **Guest Services:** valet laundry. **Business Services:** fax. **Cards:** AX, DC, DS, MC, VI.

SOME UNITS

(icons) FEE

——— WHERE TO DINE ———

THE AMISH DOOR RESTAURANT OF WOOSTER   **Lunch:** $5-$8   **Dinner:** $7-$14   **Phone:** 330/263-0547

American

Location: 4 mi e on US 30. 6655 Lincolnway E 44691. **Hours:** 6 am-8 pm, Fri & Sat-9 pm. Closed major holidays; also Sun. **Features:** casual dress; children's menu; carryout; salad bar. The basic, family-oriented restaurant puts Amish kitchen cooking at the heart of its menu. Smoke free premises. **Parking:** on-site. **Cards:** DS, MC, VI.

(icon)

CW BURGERSTEINS   **Dinner:** $5-$14   **Phone:** 330/264-6263

American

Location: Just w. 359 W Liberty St 44691. **Hours:** 3 pm-midnight, Sat from 11 am. Closed major holidays; also Sun. **Features:** casual dress; children's menu; carryout; cocktails; a la carte. Sports fans can settle in at the rowdy, upbeat restaurant to watch the big game on any of a number of televisions or look around at all kinds of memorabilia. The menu offers up standard sports bar fare: appetizers, sandwiches and the ubiquitous burger. **Parking:** on-site. **Cards:** AX, DC, DS, MC, VI.

(icon)

EL-CANELO   **Lunch:** $4-$10   **Dinner:** $5-$10   **Phone:** 330/345-7005

Mexican

Location: 1.4 mi ne from jct US 83. 4782 Cleveland Rd 44691. **Hours:** 11 am-9 pm. Closed major holidays. **Features:** casual dress; children's menu; carryout; a la carte. Mild Mexican dishes are served in the festive spot, decorated with colorful pinatas and bright serapes. **Parking:** on-site. **Cards:** AX, DS, MC, VI.

(icon)

OLDE JAOL   **Dinner:** $8-$14   **Phone:** 330/262-3333

West American

Location: Just ne of town square. 215 N Walnut St 44691. **Hours:** 4:30 pm-10 pm, Fri-11 pm, Sat 5 pm-11 pm. Closed major holidays; also Sun. **Reservations:** suggested. **Features:** children's menu; carryout; cocktails. Once the county jail, the 19th-century building has intimate basement dining rooms that feature brick archways and iron grillwork. **Parking:** on-site. **Cards:** AX, DC, DS, MC, VI.

TJ'S RESTAURANT   **Lunch:** $5-$18   **Dinner:** $7-$18   **Phone:** 330/264-6263

American

Location: Downtown; just w. 359 W Liberty St 44691. **Hours:** 11 am-9:30 pm, Sat from 4:30 pm. Closed major holidays; also Sun. **Reservations:** suggested. **Features:** casual dress; children's menu; early bird specials; carryout; cocktails & lounge. Wood, marble and antiques lend an air of subtle sophistication to the comfortable restaurant, which has five dining rooms, including the warm, cozy bistro room. Well-seasoned prime rib mingles with lots of pasta and fresh fish on the varied menu. **Parking:** on-site. **Cards:** AX, DC, DS, MC, VI.

(icon)

WORTHINGTON —*See Columbus p. 669.*

XENIA pop. 24,700

——— WHERE TO STAY ———

BEST WESTERN REGENCY INN

Motel

Phone: (937)372-9954

All Year	1P: $43-$46	2P: $45-$48	XP: $6 F16

Location: 1 mi w. 600 Little Main St 45385. Fax: 937/372-9955. **Facility:** 19 one-bedroom standard units. 2 stories, exterior corridors. **Parking:** on-site. **Terms:** small pets only. **Amenities:** extended cable TV. **Cards:** AX, DC, DS, MC, VI.

SOME UNITS

(icons)

HOLIDAY INN-XENIA

SAVE

Motor Inn

Phone: (937)372-9921

4/1-11/1	1P: $81-$89	2P: $81-$89	XP: $10 F18
11/2-3/31	1P: $69-$79	2P: $69	XP: $10 F18

Location: 0.5 mi w on W Main St. 300 Xenia Towne Sq 45385. Fax: 937/372-9921. **Facility:** 88 one-bedroom standard units, some with whirlpools. 4 stories, interior corridors. **Parking:** on-site. **Amenities:** extended cable TV, voice mail, irons, hair dryers. **Dining:** restaurant, 6 am-10 & 4-9 pm, Fri 4 pm-10 pm, Sat 7 am-11 & 4-10 pm, Sun 7-11 am, $10-$17, cocktails. **Pool(s):** outdoor. **Leisure Activities:** exercise room. **Guest Services:** valet laundry. **Business Services:** meeting rooms. **Cards:** AX, DC, DS, MC, VI.

SOME UNITS

(icons) FEE

——— WHERE TO DINE ———

——— *The following restaurants have not been evaluated by AAA but are listed for your information only.* ———

COASTER'S GRILL   **Phone:** 937/372-4400

[fyi]   Not evaluated. **Location:** 44 Xenia Towne Sq. The small, downtown restaurant serves simple, American cuisine.

HUNAN GARDENS   **Phone:** 937/372-8898

[fyi]   Not evaluated. **Location:** 131 N Allison Ave 45385. Pork, chicken, beef and seafood are prepared in varied Chinese styles.

YOUNGSTOWN pop. 95,700

─── **WHERE TO STAY** ───

AUSTINTOWN SUPER 8 MOTEL

Motel

Phone: 330/793-7788

Property failed to provide current rates

Location: I-80, exit 223, just s on SR 46. 5280 76 Dr 44515. Fax: 330/793-9011. **Facility:** 62 one-bedroom standard units. 2 stories, interior corridors. **Parking:** on-site. **Amenities:** extended cable TV, safes (fee). **Guest Services:** coin laundry. **Cards:** AX, DC, DS, MC, VI.

SOME UNITS
FEE

BELMONT INN & SUITES

Motor Inn

Phone: (330)759-7850

4/1-9/15	1P: $79-$99	2P: $84-$104
9/16-3/31	1P: $59-$79	2P: $64-$84

Location: I-80, exit 229, just n. 4255 Belmont Ave 44505. Fax: 330/759-8147. **Facility:** 120 one-bedroom standard units, some with whirlpools. 2 stories, interior corridors. **Parking:** on-site. **Terms:** 14 day cancellation notice. **Amenities:** extended cable TV, voice mail. **Leisure Activities:** limited exercise equipment, basketball, horseshoes, volleyball. **Guest Services:** valet laundry. **Business Services:** conference facilities. **Cards:** AX, DC, DS, MC, VI.

SOME UNITS
FEE   FEE

COMFORT INN YOUNGSTOWN NORTH

SAVE
Motor Inn

Phone: (330)759-3180

All Year   1P: $45-$99   2P: $55-$99   XP: $10   F18

Location: I-80, exit 229, just s. 4055 Belmont Ave 44505. Fax: 330/759-7713. **Facility:** 144 one-bedroom standard units, some with whirlpools. 6 stories, interior corridors. **Parking:** on-site. **Terms:** 7 day cancellation notice. **Amenities:** extended cable TV, voice mail. *Some:* irons, hair dryers. **Dining:** Cancun Mexican Restaurant and Cantina, see separate listing. **Leisure Activities:** therapy pool. **Guest Services:** valet laundry. **Business Services:** meeting rooms. **Cards:** AX, CB, DC, DS, JC, MC, VI.

SOME UNITS

ECONO LODGE

(AAA) SAVE

Motel

Phone: (330)759-9820

All Year   1P: $39-$52   2P: $49-$75   XP: $7   F16

Location: I-80, exit 229, just s. 1615 E Liberty St 44420. Fax: 330/759-0469. **Facility:** 56 one-bedroom standard units. 2 stories, interior corridors. **Parking:** on-site. **Amenities:** extended cable TV. **Cards:** AX, DC, DS, MC, VI. **Special Amenities:** early check-in/late check-out and free room upgrade (subject to availability with advanced reservations).

SOME UNITS

HOLIDAY INN-AIRPORT METROPLEX
Phone: (330)759-0606

AAA SAVE ▽▽▽▽ Motor Inn

All Year 1P: $110-$140 2P: $110-$140
Location: I-80, exit 229, just n. 1620 Motor Inn Dr 44420. Fax: 330/759-7632. **Facility:** 153 one-bedroom standard units, some with whirlpools. 4 stories, interior corridors. **Parking:** on-site. **Terms:** [AP] meal plan available. **Amenities:** extended cable TV, video games, voice mail, irons, hair dryers. **Dining:** dining room, 6:30 am-2 & 5:30-10 pm, $9-$17, cocktails. **Pool(s):** outdoor. **Leisure Activities:** exercise room. **Guest Services:** valet laundry. **Business Services:** conference facilities. **Cards:** AX, CB, DC, DS, JC, MC, VI. **Special Amenities:** free newspaper.

SOME UNITS

(S D) ✈ 🍴 📺 ⊙ ≈ 🎥 DATA PORT 🛏 🖨 / ⊠ VCR 🔒 /
FEE FEE

─────── **WHERE TO DINE** ───────

CANCUN MEXICAN RESTAURANT AND CANTINA
Lunch: $5-$7 **Dinner:** $8-$10 **Phone:** 330/759-3301

▽▽ Mexican

Location: I-80, exit 229, just s; in Comfort Inn Youngstown North. 4055 Belmont Ave 44505. **Hours:** 11 am-10 pm, Fri & Sat-11 pm. **Features:** casual dress; children's menu; carryout; cocktails & lounge. Mexican cuisine is hard to come by in this area of Ohio, but the restaurant does a good job serving up freshly prepared traditional dishes. Everything from burritos, tacos and enchiladas to quesadillas, nachos and chalupas are on the varied menu. **Parking:** on-site. **Cards:** AX, DC, DS, MC, VI.

⊠

ZANESVILLE pop. 26,800

─────── **WHERE TO STAY** ───────

AMERIHOST INN-ZANESVILLE
Phone: (740)454-9332

AAA SAVE ▽▽▽▽ Motel

All Year [ECP] 1P: $79-$145 2P: $84-$155 XP: $5 F17
Location: I-70, exit 155. 230 Scenic Crest Dr 43701. Fax: 740/454-9342. **Facility:** 60 one-bedroom standard units, some with whirlpools. 2 stories, interior corridors. **Bath:** combo or shower only. **Parking:** on-site. **Amenities:** voice mail, safes, irons, hair dryers. **Pool(s):** heated indoor. **Leisure Activities:** whirlpool, exercise room. **Guest Services:** valet laundry. **Business Services:** meeting rooms. **Cards:** AX, CB, DC, DS, JC, MC, VI. **Special Amenities:** free continental breakfast and free newspaper.

SOME UNITS

(S D) 🍴 (⊙) 🐾 ≈ 🎥 DATA PORT 🛏 🖨 / ⊠ 🔒 📺 /
FEE

BEST WESTERN TOWN HOUSE
Phone: (740)452-4511

AAA SAVE ▽▽▽▽ Motor Inn

4/1-10/31 1P: $69-$89 2P: $74-$94 XP: $5 F18
11/1-3/31 1P: $49-$65 2P: $54-$70 XP: $5 F18
Location: I-70, exit 155 on SR 60, follow signs. 135 N 7th St 43701. Fax: 740/452-4511. **Facility:** 58 one-bedroom standard units. 2 stories, exterior corridors. **Parking:** on-site. **Terms:** pets ($10 extra charge, in smoking units). **Amenities:** extended cable TV, safes, irons, hair dryers. **Dining:** dining room, 6 am-2 & 5-9:30 pm, Fri & Sat 5 pm-10 pm, Sun 7 am-2 pm, $7-$15, cocktails. **Leisure Activities:** recreational facilities nearby. **Guest Services:** valet laundry. **Cards:** AX, CB, DC, DS, JC, MC, VI. **Special Amenities:** free continental breakfast and free local telephone calls. *(See color ad below)*

SOME UNITS

(S D) 🐾 🍴 ⊙ 🎥 DATA PORT 🛏 🖨 / ⊠ VCR 🔒 📺 /
FEE

COMFORT INN

Phone: (740)454-4144

4/1-10/31	1P: $69-$149	2P: $74-$159	XP: $5	F18
11/1-3/31	1P: $59-$139	2P: $64-$144	XP: $5	F18

Motel

Location: I-70, exit 155 westbound; exit 7th St eastbound, e on Elberon to light, just n on Underwood. 500 Monroe St 43701. Fax: 740/454-4144. **Facility:** 93 units. 87 one-bedroom standard units, some with whirlpools. 6 one-bedroom suites ($109-$169). 2 stories, interior corridors. *Bath:* combo or shower only. **Parking:** on-site. **Terms:** pets ($10 extra charge, in smoking units). **Amenities:** extended cable TV, safes, hair dryers. *Some:* irons. **Pool(s):** heated indoor. **Leisure Activities:** sauna, whirlpool, exercise room. **Guest Services:** valet and coin laundry. **Business Services:** meeting rooms. **Cards:** AX, CB, DC, DS, JC, MC, VI. **Special Amenities:** free continental breakfast and free local telephone calls. *(See color ad p 778)*

SOME UNITS

FAIRFIELD INN BY MARRIOTT

Phone: (740)453-8770

6/1-10/31 [CP]	1P: $77-$95	2P: $77-$95
4/1-5/31 [CP]	1P: $72-$88	2P: $72-$88
11/1-3/31 [CP]	1P: $62-$80	2P: $62-$80

Motel

Location: I-70, exit 155 westbound; exit 7th St eastbound, 0.5 mi n. 725 Zane St 43701. Fax: 740/453-8770. **Facility:** 63 one-bedroom standard units. 3 stories, interior corridors. **Parking:** on-site. **Terms:** 7 day cancellation notice. **Amenities:** extended cable TV, irons. **Pool(s):** heated indoor. **Leisure Activities:** whirlpool. **Guest Services:** valet laundry. **Cards:** AX, DC, DS, MC, VI. **Special Amenities:** free continental breakfast and free local telephone calls. *(See color ad card insert)*

SOME UNITS

HAMPTON INN

Phone: (740)453-6511

7/5-11/1 [CP]	1P: $90-$100	2P: $100-$105
4/1-7/4 [CP]	1P: $79-$93	2P: $83-$98
11/2-3/31 [CP]	1P: $64-$75	2P: $69-$79

Motel

Location: I-70, exit 155 westbound; exit 7th St eastbound, 0.5 mi n. 1009 Spring St 43701. Fax: 740/450-2899. **Facility:** 64 one-bedroom standard units. 3 stories, interior corridors. *Bath:* combo or shower only. **Parking:** on-site. **Amenities:** extended cable TV, voice mail, irons. **Pool(s):** heated indoor. **Leisure Activities:** whirlpool. **Guest Services:** valet laundry. **Cards:** AX, DC, DS, JC, MC, VI.

SOME UNITS

May I Take Your Order Please?

*W*hen you look through a AAA TourBook® guide in search of a place to dine while traveling, look for restaurants that advertise. These establishments are committed to increasing their AAA patronage, and are willing to go the extra mile to capture your attention ... and your appetite!

HOLIDAY INN CONFERENCE CENTER

Phone: 740/453-0771

Motor Inn

All Year　　　　1P: $74-$129　　　2P: $74-$129

Location: I-70, exit 160 on US 22 and 40. 4645 E Pike 43701. Fax: 740/453-0771. **Facility:** 130 units. 126 one-bedroom standard units, some with whirlpools. 4 one-bedroom suites ($99-$129). 2 stories, interior corridors. *Bath:* combo or shower only. **Parking:** on-site. **Terms:** check-in 4 pm, package plans, small pets only. **Amenities:** extended cable TV, voice mail, irons, hair dryers. **Dining:** Reflections, see separate listing. **Pool(s):** indoor, heated indoor. **Leisure Activities:** sauna, whirlpool, exercise room. **Guest Services:** coin laundry. **Business Services:** conference facilities, fax. **Cards:** AX, CB, DC, DS, MC, VI.

SOME UNITS

RED ROOF INN

Phone: (740)453-6300

Motel

11/1-3/31	1P: $44-$90	2P: $49-$95	XP: $5	F18
4/1-10/31	1P: $60-$74	2P: $65-$79	XP: $5	F18

Location: I-70, exit 160, just s. 4929 E Pike 43701. Fax: 740/453-3693. **Facility:** 78 one-bedroom standard units. 3 stories, interior corridors. *Bath:* combo or shower only. **Parking:** on-site. **Amenities:** extended cable TV, safes. **Pool(s):** heated indoor. **Leisure Activities:** whirlpool. **Guest Services:** coin laundry. **Business Services:** meeting rooms. **Cards:** AX, DC, DS, MC, VI. *(See color ad p 778)*

SOME UNITS

SUPER 8 MOTEL-ZANESVILLE

Phone: (740)455-3124

Motel

5/26-9/8 [CP]	1P: $60-$80	2P: $70-$90		
9/9-3/31 [CP]	1P: $50-$70	2P: $60-$90		
4/1-5/25 [CP]	1P: $50-$70	2P: $60-$90	XP: $5	F12

Location: I-70, exit 152, just n on SR 40 (National Rd). 2440 National Rd 43701. Fax: 740/455-3124. **Facility:** 62 one-bedroom standard units. 3 stories (no elevator), interior corridors. **Parking:** on-site. **Terms:** 7 day cancellation notice, pets (in carrier). **Amenities:** extended cable TV, safes. **Business Services:** meeting rooms. **Cards:** AX, DC, DS, MC, VI.

SOME UNITS

FEE

TRAVELODGE

Phone: (740)453-0611

Motel

4/1-6/30	1P: $65-$70	2P: $70-$75	XP: $5	F13
7/1-9/30	1P: $55-$60	2P: $60-$65	XP: $5	F13
10/1-12/31	1P: $45-$50	2P: $50-$55	XP: $5	F13
1/1-3/31	1P: $40-$45	2P: $45-$50	XP: $5	F13

Location: I-70, exit 155, on US 22 and SR 60, at jct 6th and Market sts. 58 N 6th St 43701. Fax: 740/453-9065. **Facility:** 54 one-bedroom standard units. 3 stories, interior/exterior corridors. *Bath:* combo or shower only. **Parking:** on-site, winter plug-ins. **Terms:** 10 day cancellation notice, [CP] meal plan available. **Amenities:** extended cable TV, hair dryers. *Some:* video games. **Guest Services:** coin laundry. **Cards:** AX, CB, DC, DS, MC, VI.

SOME UNITS

———— WHERE TO DINE ————

ADORNETTO'S ITALIAN FOODS

Dinner: $6-$9　　　**Phone:** 740/453-0789

Italian

Location: Jct SR 146 and Maple Ave, 0.8 mi n. 2224 Maple Ave 43701. **Hours:** 4 pm-10 pm, Sun from 11:30 am. Closed major holidays. **Features:** casual dress; children's menu; carryout. On popular retail strip, family style pizzeria serving wide variety of Italian specialties. The pizzas are really tempting. The dining room is quite spacious. A great place to bring the entire family. **Parking:** on-site. **Cards:** AX, MC, VI.

BRYAN PLACE RESTAURANT

Lunch: $8-$10　　　**Dinner:** $12-$20　　　**Phone:** 740/450-4004

American

Location: Downtown; between Main and Market sts. 49 N Sixth St 43701. **Hours:** 11 am-2:30 & 5-9 pm, Fri-10 pm, Sat 5 pm-10 pm, Sun 10:30 am-1:30 pm. Closed major holidays. **Reservations:** suggested; weekends. **Features:** casual dress; Sunday brunch; children's menu; carryout; cocktails & lounge. Built in the early 1920s, the facility once housed a YWCA. A Victorian presence is evident in the period furnishings. The Friday seafood dinner buffet and Sunday brunch draw good crowds. Prime rib, pasta primavera and fish and chips are popular entrees. **Parking:** on-site. **Cards:** AX, DS, MC, VI.

THE DINING CAR RESTAURANT

Lunch: $5-$7　　　**Phone:** 740/453-4007

American

Location: Downtown; at corner of Market and 3rd sts; in historic freight station. 231 Market St 43701. **Hours:** 10:30 am-2 pm, Sat from 11 am. Closed major holidays; also Sat 10/1-5/31. **Features:** casual dress; carryout. The small, rustic restaurant outfitted with a simple home decor, is the former ticket office of a 1917 railroad depot. The menu centers on generous portions of lighter fare: soup, salad and sandwiches. Casually dressed servers are friendly and attentive. Smoke free premises. **Parking:** on-site.

JUANITA'S RESTAURANT-NORTH

Lunch: $6-$8　　　**Dinner:** $8-$13　　　**Phone:** 740/454-2073

American

Location: Jct SR 60 (Maple Ave) and 146, just n of downtown. 1735 Maple Ave 43701. **Hours:** 7 am-8 pm, Sat & Sun-9 pm. Closed major holidays. **Features:** casual dress; carryout; salad bar. Thick baked steaks, marinated pork chops, mashed potatoes made from scratch and homemade desserts are among the home-cooked offerings of the family-oriented restaurant. Wallpaper and curtains add to the homey feel of the relaxed dining room. **Parking:** on-site. **Cards:** DS, MC, VI.

MARIA ADORNETTO'S RESTAURANT

Lunch: $6-$9　　　**Dinner:** $9-$20　　　**Phone:** 740/453-0643

Italian

Location: Downtown; just e of jct Market and Underwood sts. 953 Market St 43701. **Hours:** 11 am-2 & 4-11 pm. Closed major holidays; also Sun. **Reservations:** suggested; weekends. **Features:** dressy casual; children's menu; early bird specials; carryout; cocktails & lounge. Filet mignon and porterhouse steak, as well as plenty of seafood, make up the menu at the intimate restaurant. Tile, wall hangings and paintings are among the decorations that give the dining room an Italian feel. Entertainers perform on weekends. **Parking:** on-site. **Cards:** AX, DS, MC, VI.

OLD MARKET HOUSE INN

American

Dinner: $9-$19   **Phone:** 740/454-2555

Location: I-70, exit 154 eastbound, just s to Market St; exit 155 westbound, 0.3 mi s to Market St, just w. 424 Market St 43701. **Hours:** 5 pm-10:30 pm, Fri & Sat-11 pm. Closed major holidays; also Sun. **Reservations:** suggested; except Sat. **Features:** dressy casual; carryout; cocktails & lounge. A handful of seafood entrees complement selections of American and Italian food. Patterned after an English pub, the dining room has an appealing Old World atmosphere. Panamanican shrimp, served with a signature sauce, is a house specialty. **Parking:** on-site. **Cards:** AX, DC, DS, MC, VI.

REFLECTIONS

American

Lunch: $6-$8   **Dinner:** $10-$18   **Phone:** 740/453-0771

Location: I-70, exit 160, exit 160 on US 22 and 40; in Holiday Inn Conference Center. 4645 E Pike 43701. **Hours:** 6 am-2 & 5-9 pm, Fri-10 pm. Closed: 12/25. **Features:** casual dress; Sunday brunch; carryout; salad bar; cocktails & lounge; buffet. Mirrors, brass, glass and lots of oak wood add to the class and dignity of the casually upscale dining room. Steaks—such as the filet, New York strip and sirloin—and seafood, including shrimp cooked in a variety of ways, are the focus of the menu. **Parking:** on-site. **Cards:** AX, CB, DC, DS, MC, VI.

ZAK'S RESTAURANT

American

Lunch: $7-$11   **Dinner:** $9-$20   **Phone:** 740/453-2227

Location: Downtown; between Main and Market sts. 32 N 3rd St 43701. **Hours:** 11:30 am-10 pm, Fri-11 pm, Sat 5 pm-11 pm, Sun 5 pm-9 pm. Closed major holidays. **Reservations:** suggested; weekends. **Features:** casual dress; children's menu; carryout; cocktails & lounge. The eclectic menu dabbles in American, Mexican and Cajun cuisines, with such offerings as blackened and Cajun chicken, seafood specials, steak and the teriyaki combo, which unites steak and chicken on a bed of rice pilaf. The dining room is colorful and festive. **Parking:** on-site. **Cards:** AX, DC, DS, MC, VI.

——— *The following restaurants have not been evaluated by AAA* ———
but are listed for your information only.

EL MAGUEY MEXICAN RESTAURANT   **Phone:** 740/453-0971

[fyi]   Not evaluated. **Location:** 3523 Maple Ave 43701. The restaurant's menu features authentic Mexican cuisine.

GREAT NEW CHINA BUFFET   **Phone:** 740/450-8121

[fyi]   Not evaluated. **Location:** 3517 Maple Ave 43701. The buffet includes a wide variety of traditional favorites.

MARK PI'S CHINA GATE   **Phone:** 740/453-6655

[fyi]   Not evaluated. **Location:** 2502 Maple Ave 43701. Gourmet Chinese food includes spicy Szechwan and milder dishes.

OLDE FALLS INN   **Phone:** 740/452-2300

[fyi]   Not evaluated. **Location:** 3452 Newark Rd 43701. The pub-style restaurant serves everything from cheeseburgers to steak.

STEAK AND STEIN   **Phone:** 740/452-2576

[fyi]   Not evaluated. **Location:** 3190 Maple Ave 43701. Since 1951, the restaurant has served choice steaks and lobster tails.

ZOAR pop. 200

——— **WHERE TO DINE** ———

THE ZOAR TAVERN & INN

American

Lunch: $5-$8   **Dinner:** $10-$18   **Phone:** 330/874-2170

Location: In center of town. 162 Main St 44697. **Hours:** 11 am-10 pm, Fri & Sat-11 pm. Closed major holidays. **Reservations:** suggested. **Features:** casual dress; children's menu; carryout; cocktails. Originally the home of the village doctor, the relaxed tavern is a comfortable place to unwind and enjoy fresh seafood, steak, sandwiches and salad. Antique decorations cover the walls. Such desserts as bread pudding are tempting and tasty. **Parking:** on-site. **Cards:** AX, DS, MC, VI.

Look for the
Sign of Approval

W hen you're on the road, look for lodgings that display the AAA Approved sign. It's your sign that the property works hard to win AAA member business. In fact, these properties offer AAA members great room rates*.

When you see the AAA Approved sign, you know you've arrived.

See TourBook Navigator, page 16, for complete details.

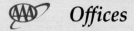 *Offices*

Cities with main offices are listed in **BOLD TYPE** and toll-free member service numbers in *ITALIC TYPE.*
All are closed Saturdays, Sundays and holidays unless otherwise indicated.

The type of service provided is designated below the name of the city where the office is located:

✚ Auto travel services, including books/maps, marked maps and on-demand Triptik maps
● Auto travel services, including books/maps, marked maps, but no on-demand Triptik maps
■ Provides books/maps only. No marked maps or on-demand Triptik maps available
▲ Travel agency services

NATIONAL OFFICE: 1000 AAA DRIVE, HEATHROW, FLORIDA 32746-5063, (407) 444-7000

ILLINOIS

ALTON—AAA MISSOURI, 217 E CENTER DR, 62002. MON-FRI 9-5, SAT 9-1. (618) 462-1091, *(800) 922-6813.*✚

ARLINGTON HEIGHTS—AAA-CHICAGO MOTOR CLUB, 1840 S ARLINGTON HEIGHTS, 60005. MON-FRI 9-5, SAT 9-1. (847) 364-0109.●▲

AURORA—**AAA-CHICAGO MOTOR CLUB,** 975 MERIDIAN LAKE DR, 60504. MON-FRI 8:30-5. (630) 328-7000.●▲

BEDFORD PARK—AAA-CHICAGO MOTOR CLUB, 6524 S LAVERGNE, 60638. SUMMER HOURS VARY MON-FRI 8-4:30. (708) 496-0614.✚▲

BLOOMINGTON—AAA-CHICAGO MOTOR CLUB, 2101 EASTLAND DR SUITE C, 61704. MON-FRI 9-5, SAT 9-12:30. (309) 663-6511.●▲

CARBONDALE—AAA MISSOURI, 1260 E MAIN, 62901. MON-FRI 9-5, SAT 9-1. (618) 457-8448, *(800) 554-8820.*✚

CHAMPAIGN—AAA-CHICAGO MOTOR CLUB, 1610 S NEIL ST, 61820. MON-FRI 9-5, SAT 9-1. (217) 398-3620.●▲

CHICAGO—AAA-CHICAGO MOTOR CLUB, 100 W RANDOLPH STE 213, 60601. MON-FRI 8:30-5. (312) 372-1818.●▲

CRYSTAL LAKE—AAA-CHICAGO MOTOR CLUB, 6234 NORTHWEST HWY, 60014. MON-FRI 9-5, SAT 9-1. (815) 455-7760.●▲

JOLIET—AAA-CHICAGO MOTOR CLUB, 50 BARNEY DR, 60435. MON-FRI 9-5, SAT 9-1. (815) 744-6940.●▲

LIBERTYVILLE—AAA-CHICAGO MOTOR CLUB, 1354 S MILWAUKEE AVE, 60048. MON-FRI 9-5, SAT 9-1. (847) 367-3363.●▲

MOLINE—AAA-CHICAGO MOTOR CLUB, 4500 16TH ST #605, 61265. MON-FRI 10-9, SAT 12-5. (309) 764-5914.●▲

MOLINE—AAA MINNESOTA/IOWA, QUAD CITY AIRPORT, 61265. MON-FRI 8-5:30. (309) 764-7970.▲

NAPERVILLE—AAA-CHICAGO MOTOR CLUB, 670 S RT 59, 60540. MON-FRI 9-6, MON & THU 9-7, SAT 9-6, SUN 12-5. (630) 357-6200.●▲

ORLAND HILLS—AAA-CHICAGO MOTOR CLUB, 9253 W 159TH ST, 60477. MON-FRI 9-5, SAT 9-1. (708) 873-0003.●▲

PEORIA—AAA-CHICAGO MOTOR CLUB, 7800 N SOMMER ST, 61615. MON-FRI 9-5, SAT 9-12. (309) 692-4728.●

ROCKFORD—AAA-CHICAGO MOTOR CLUB, 3910 N MILFORD STE 1200, 61114. MON-FRI 9-6, SAT 9-12. (815) 636-9050.●▲

SCHAUMBURG—AAA-CHICAGO MOTOR CLUB, 5 WOODFIELD MALL #E115, 60173. MON-FRI 10-9, SAT 10-7, SUN 11-6. (847) 517-8912.●▲

SKOKIE—AAA-CHICAGO MOTOR CLUB, 9245 SKOKIE BLVD, 60077. MON-FRI 9-5, SAT 9-1. (847) 679-8700.●▲

VILLA PARK—AAA-CHICAGO MOTOR CLUB, 130 W ROOSEVELT RD, 60181. MON-FRI 9-5, SAT 9-1. (630) 834-5923.●▲

INDIANA

ANDERSON—AAA HOOSIER MOTOR CLUB, 1803 N SCATTERFIELD #11, 46012. MON-FRI 8:30-5:30, SAT 9-1. (765) 649-2236.✚▲

AURORA—AAA CINCINNATI, 920 GREEN BLVD, 47001. MON-FRI 9-5, SAT 9-3. (812) 926-0212, *(800) 684-3062.*●▲

AVON—AAA HOOSIER MOTOR CLUB, 8100 E US HWY 36 #F, 46123. MON-FRI 8:30-5:45, SAT 9-1. (317) 272-5134.✚▲

BLOOMINGTON—AAA HOOSIER MOTOR CLUB, 2310 N WALNUT ST, 47404-2005. MON-FRI 8:30-5:30, SAT 9-1. (812) 336-1700.✚▲

CARMEL—AAA HOOSIER MOTOR CLUB, 1130 AAA WAY, 46032. MON-FRI 8:30-5:30, SAT 9-1. (317) 846-7399.✚▲

CLARKSVILLE—AAA HOOSIER MOTOR CLUB, 999 EASTERN BLVD, 47129. MON-FRI 8:30-5:30, SAT 9-1. (812) 282-7776.✚▲

COLUMBUS—AAA HOOSIER MOTOR CLUB, 811 LINDSEY, 47201. MON-FRI 8:30-5:30, SAT 9-1. (812) 372-7877.✚▲

CRAWFORDSVILLE—AAA HOOSIER MOTOR CLUB, 200 E MARKET ST, 47933. MON-FRI 8:30-5:30, SAT 9-1. (765) 362-3433.✚▲

EVANSVILLE—AAA MISSOURI, 7820 EAGLE CREST BLVD, 47715. MON-FRI 9-5:30. (812) 477-9966.✚▲

FORT WAYNE—AAA-CHICAGO MOTOR CLUB, 607 NORTHCREST SHPPNG CTR, 46805. MON-FRI 9-5, SAT 9-1. (219) 484-1541.●▲

INDIANAPOLIS—**AAA HOOSIER MOTOR CLUB,** 3750 GUION RD, 46222. MON-FRI 8-5. (317) 923-1500.▲

INDIANAPOLIS—AAA HOOSIER MOTOR CLUB, 3073 N HIGH SCHOOL RD, 46224. MON-FRI 8:30-5:30, SAT 9-1. (317) 297-4266.✚▲

INDIANAPOLIS—AAA HOOSIER MOTOR CLUB, 1309 E STOP 11 RD, 46227. MON-FRI 8:30-5:30, SAT 9-1. (317) 882-1521.✚▲

INDIANAPOLIS—AAA HOOSIER MOTOR CLUB, 8120 E 21ST ST, 46219. MON-FRI 8:30-5:30, SAT 9-1. (317) 899-4714.✚▲

INDIANAPOLIS—AAA HOOSIER MOTOR CLUB, 5180 ALLISONVILLE RD, 46205. MON-FRI 8:30-5:30, SAT 9-1. (317) 257-8101.✚▲

INDIANAPOLIS—AAA HOOSIER MOTOR CLUB, 8751 WESLEYAN RD, 46268. MON-FRI 8:30-5:30, SAT 9-1. (317) 875-4222.✚▲

INDIANAPOLIS—AAA HOOSIER MOTOR CLUB, 2727 E 86TH ST #132, 46240. MON-FRI 8:30-5:30, SAT 9-1. (317) 251-5854.✚▲

JASPER—AAA MISSOURI, 3555 N NEWTON ST, 47546. MON-FRI 9-5:30. (812) 634-1213, *(800) 880-7770.*✚

KOKOMO—AAA HOOSIER MOTOR CLUB, 3551 S LAFOUNTAIN ST, 46902. MON-FRI 8:30-5:30, SAT 9-1. (765) 453-7243.✚▲

LAFAYETTE—AAA HOOSIER MOTOR CLUB, 331 N 4TH ST, 47901. MON-FRI 8:30-5:30, SAT 9-1. (765) 423-1694.✚▲

MERRILLVILLE—AAA-CHICAGO MOTOR CLUB, 312 W 80TH PL, 46410. MON-FRI 9-5, MON 9-6, SAT 9-12. (219) 769-4818.●▲

MISHAWAKA—AAA-CHICAGO MOTOR CLUB, 5922 GRAPE RD, 46545. MON-FRI 9-5, SAT 9-12. (219) 277-5790.●▲

MUNCIE—AAA HOOSIER MOTOR CLUB, 4351 W. CLARA LANE, 47304. MON-FRI 8:30-5:30, SAT 9-1. (765) 289-7161.✚▲

NEW CASTLE—AAA HOOSIER MOTOR CLUB, 120 S MEMORIAL DR #F, 47362. MON-FRI 8:30-5:30, SAT 9-1. (765) 521-2135.✚▲

NOBLESVILLE—AAA HOOSIER MOTOR CLUB, 1950 E CONNER ST #C, 46060. MON-FRI 8:30-5:30, SAT 9-1. (317) 773-8235.✚▲

RICHMOND—AAA HOOSIER MOTOR CLUB, 3639 E MAIN ST, 47374. MON-FRI 8:30-5:30, SAT 9-1. (765) 966-3565.✚▲

TERRE HAUTE—AAA HOOSIER MOTOR CLUB, 1400 S THIRD ST, 47802. MON-FRI 8:30-5:30, SAT 9-1. (812) 232-2338.✚▲

OHIO

AKRON—**AAA AKRON AUTO CLUB,** 111 W CENTER ST, 44308. MON-FRI 8:40-5, SAT 8:40-12. (330) 762-0631.✚▲

AKRON—AAA AKRON AUTO CLUB, 506 CANTON RD, 44312. MON-FRI 8:40-5, SAT 8:40-12. (330) 798-0166.✚▲

ALLIANCE—**AAA ALLIANCE AUTO CLUB,** 2322 S UNION AVE, 44601. MON-FRI 9-5, SAT 9-12. (330) 823-9820.✚▲

ASHLAND—AAA ASHLAND COUNTY, 502 CLAREMONT AVE, 44805. MON-FRI 8-5, MON 8-6:30, SAT 8-12. (419) 289-8133.✦▲

ASHTABULA—AAA OHIO MOTORISTS ASSOCIATION, 2900 N RIDGE E (RT 20), 44004. MON-FRI 8:30-6, SUMMER HOURS SAT 8:30-1:30 SAT 9:30-1:30. (440) 997-5586.✦▲

ATHENS—AAA WEST PENN/W VIRGINIA/SO CENT OH, 130 E STATE ST, 45701. MON-FRI 9-5, SAT 9:30-12. (740) 593-6677.✦▲

BARBERTON—AAA OHIO AUTO CLUB, 139 E TUSCARAWAS AVE, 44203. MON-FRI 9-5, SAT 9-12. (330) 753-7779.✦▲

BEAVERCREEK—AAA MIAMI VALLEY, 2372 LAKEVIEW DR SUITE 1A, 45431. MON-FRI 9-5:30, OPENED 2ND & 4TH SATURDAY EVERY MONTH. SAT 9-12. (937) 427-5884, *(800) 624-2321.*✦▲

BELLEFONTAINE—AAA OHIO AUTO CLUB, 1790 S MAIN ST, 43311. MON-FRI 9-5. (937) 599-5154.✦▲

BOARDMAN—AAA OHIO MOTORISTS ASSOCIATION, 1275 BOARDMAN-CANFIELD RD, 44512. MON-FRI 8:30-6, SUMMER HOURS SAT 8:30-1:30 SAT 9:30-1:30. (330) 726-9083.✦▲

BOWLING GREEN—AAA NORTHWEST OHIO, 414 E WOOSTER ST, 43402. MON-FRI 8:45-5:30, SAT 9:30-12:30. (419) 352-5276, *(800) 328-4123.*✦▲

BRIDGEPORT—AAA OHIO AUTO CLUB, 318 HOWARD ST, 43912. MON-FRI 9-5, MON 9-6, SAT 9:30-12. (740) 635-2050.✦▲

BRYAN—AAA NORTHWEST OHIO, 1236 S MAIN ST, 43506. MON-FRI 8:45-5:30, SAT 9:30-12:30. (419) 636-5671, *(800) 342-3639.*✦▲

BUCYRUS—AAA OHIO AUTO CLUB, 314 S SANDUSKY AVE, 44820. MON-FRI 9-5, SAT 9-12. (419) 562-9969.✦▲

CAMBRIDGE—AAA OHIO AUTO CLUB, 902 WHEELING AVE, 43725. MON-FRI 9-5. (740) 432-7343.✦▲

CANAL FULTON—AAA MASSILLON AUTOMOBILE CLUB, 2382 LOCUST ST SE, 44614. MON-FRI 9-5, SAT 9-12. (330) 854-6616.✦▲

CANTON—AAA OHIO AUTO CLUB, 2722 FULTON DR NW, 44718. MON-FRI 9-5, MON & THU 9-6, SAT 9-12. (330) 455-6761.✦▲

CELINA—AAA OHIO AUTO CLUB, 105 N WALNUT ST, 45822. MON-FRI 9-5. (419) 586-2460.✦▲

CHESTERLAND—AAA OHIO MOTORISTS ASSOCIATION, 12628 CHILLICOTHE RD, 44026. CLOSED MONDAY EXCEPT IN THE SUMMER MON-FRI 8:30-6. SUMMER HOURS SAT 8:30-1:30 SAT 9:30-4. (440) 729-1938.✦▲

CHILLICOTHE—AAA WEST PENN/W VIRGINIA/SO CENT OH, 141 W MAIN ST, 45601. MON-FRI 9-5, SAT 9:30-12. (740) 702-3838.✦▲

CINCINNATI—AAA CINCINNATI, 15 W CENTRAL PKY, 45202. MON-FRI 8:30-6. (513) 762-3100, *(800) 543-2345.*✦▲

CINCINNATI—AAA CINCINNATI, 8176 MONTGOMERY RD, 45236. MON-FRI 9-6, SAT 9-3. (513) 984-3553, *(800) 543-2345.*✦▲

CINCINNATI—AAA CINCINNATI, 11711 PRINCETON PIKE #221, 45246. MON-FRI 9-6, SAT 9-3. (513) 671-1886, *(800) 543-2345.*✦▲

CINCINNATI—AAA CINCINNATI, 6558 GLENWAY AVE, 45211. MON-FRI 9-6, SAT 9-3. (513) 598-2500, *(800) 543-2345.*✦▲

CINCINNATI—AAA CINCINNATI, 8124 BEECHMONT AVE, 45255. MON-FRI 9-6, SAT 9-3. (513) 388-4222, *(800) 543-2345.*▲

CINCINNATI—AAA CINCINNATI, 9687 COLERAIN AVE, 45251. MON-FRI 9-6, SAT 9-3. (513) 385-0909, *(800) 543-2345.*✦▲

CINCINNATI—AAA CINCINNATI, 2712 ERIE AVE, 45208. MON-FRI 9-6, SAT 9-3. (513) 321-1222, *(800) 543-2345.*✦▲

CINCINNATI—AAA CINCINNATI, 4750 FIELDS ERTEL RD, 45249. MON-FRI 9-6, SAT 9-3. (513) 683-5200, *(800) 543-2345.*✦▲

CIRCLEVILLE—AAA OHIO AUTO CLUB, 23513 US RT 23 S, 43113. MON-FRI 9-5. (740) 477-2506.✦▲

CLEVELAND—AAA OHIO MOTORISTS ASSOCIATION, 6000 S MARGINAL RD, 44103. MON-FRI 8:30-6, SAT 9:30-1:30. (216) 416-1912.✦▲

COLUMBIANA—AAA COLUMBIANA COUNTY, 118 S MAIN ST, 44408. MON-FRI 9-5, SAT 9-12. (330) 482-3836.✦▲

COLUMBUS—AAA OHIO AUTO CLUB, 142 E TOWN ST, 43215. MON-FRI 9-5. (614) 228-2811.✦▲

COLUMBUS—AAA OHIO AUTO CLUB, 6023 E MAIN ST, 43213. MON-FRI 9-5, SAT 9-2. (614) 866-4420.✦▲

COLUMBUS—AAA OHIO AUTO CLUB, 2625 NORTHLAND PLZ DR, 43231. MON-FRI 9-5, SAT 9-2. (614) 899-1222.✦▲

COLUMBUS—AAA OHIO AUTO CLUB, 4701 REED RD, 43220. MON-FRI 9-5, SAT 9-2. (614) 457-2614.✦▲

CONNEAUT—AAA OHIO MOTORISTS ASSOCIATION, 191 MAIN ST, 44030. SUMMER HOURS SATURDAY 8:30-12:30 MON-FRI 8:30-5:30. (440) 593-6261.✦▲

COSHOCTON—AAA OHIO AUTO CLUB, 234 CHESTNUT ST, 43812. MON-FRI 9-5. (740) 622-2910.✦▲

CRESTLINE—AAA OHIO AUTO CLUB, 222 N SELTZER ST, 44827. MON-FRI 9-5. (419) 683-3053.✦▲

CUYAHOGA FALLS—AAA AKRON AUTO CLUB, 1945 23RD ST, 44223. MON-FRI 8:40-5, SAT 8:40-12. (330) 923-4826.✦▲

DAYTON—AAA MIAMI VALLEY, 825 S LUDLOW ST, 45402. MON-FRI 8:30-5. (937) 224-2801, *(800) 624-2321.*✦▲

DAYTON—AAA MIAMI VALLEY, 767 LYONS RD #100A, 45459. MON-FRI 9-5:30, OPENED 2ND & 4TH SATURDAY EVERY MONTH. SAT 9-12. (937) 435-7447, *(800) 624-2321.*✦▲

DAYTON—AAA MIAMI VALLEY, 6580 N MAIN ST, 45415. MON-FRI 9-5:30, OPENED 1ST, 3RD & 5TH SATURDAY EVERY MONTH. SAT 9-12. (937) 278-9195, *(800) 624-2321.*✦▲

DEFIANCE—AAA NORTHWEST OHIO, 1007 N CLINTON ST #2, 43512. MON-FRI 8:45-5:30, SAT 9:30-12:30. (419) 782-3876, *(800) 462-0045.*✦▲

DELAWARE—AAA OHIO AUTO CLUB, 1153 COLUMBUS PIKE, 43015. MON-FRI 9-5, SAT 9-12. (740) 363-1928.✦▲

EAST LIVERPOOL—AAA COLUMBIANA COUNTY, 516 BROADWAY, 43920. MON-FRI 9-5, SAT 9-12. (330) 385-2020.✦▲

EATON—AAA MIAMI VALLEY, 221 N AUKERMAN, 45320. MON-FRI 8:30-5:30. (937) 456-5678, *(800) 624-2321.*✦▲

ELYRIA—AAA OHIO MOTORISTS ASSOCIATION, 1839 MIDWAY MALL, 44035. MON-FRI 8:30-5, MON & THU 8:30-7, SAT 8:30-2. (440) 324-2090.▲

FAIRBORN—AAA MIAMI VALLEY, 2620 COLONEL GLENN HWY, 45324. MON-FRI 8:30-5:30. (937) 429-9903.▲

FAIRLAWN—AAA AKRON AUTO CLUB, 2709 W MARKET ST, 44333. MON-FRI 8:40-5, SAT 8:40-12. (330) 867-0694.✦▲

FINDLAY—FINDLAY AUTOMOBILE CLUB, 1550 TIFFIN RD, 45840. MON-FRI 9-5, MON 9-6, SAT 9-12. (419) 422-4961.✦▲

FOSTORIA—AAA OHIO AUTO CLUB, 520 PLAZA DR, 44830. MON-FRI 9-5. (419) 435-3125.✦▲

FREMONT—AAA OHIO AUTO CLUB, 1134 W STATE ST, 43420. MON-FRI 9-5. (419) 332-2602.✦▲

GALION—AAA OHIO AUTO CLUB, 222 PORTLAND WAY N, 44833. MON-FRI 9-5. (419) 468-3571.✦▲

GALLIPOLIS—AAA WEST PENN/W VIRGINIA/SO CENT OH, 360 SECOND AVE, 45631. MON-FRI 9-5, SAT 9:30-12. (740) 446-0699.✦▲

GREENVILLE—AAA MIAMI VALLEY, 302 S BROADWAY, 45331. MON-FRI 9-5. (937) 548-2230, *(800) 624-2321.*✦▲

HAMILTON—AAA OHIO AUTO CLUB, 744 NW WASHINGTON BLVD, 45013-1278. MON-FRI 9-5, MON 9-7, SAT 9-12. (513) 863-3200.✦▲

HILLIARD—AAA OHIO AUTO CLUB, 4601 LEAP CT, 43026. MON-FRI 9-5, SAT 9-2. (614) 771-5777.✦▲

HILLSBORO—AAA WEST PENN/W VIRGINIA/SO CENT OH, 125 W MAIN ST, 45133. MON-FRI 9-5, SAT 9:30-12. (937) 393-3489.✦▲

HUDSON—AAA AKRON AUTO CLUB, 178 W STREETSBORO RD, 44236. MON-FRI 8:40-5, SAT 8:40-12. (330) 650-6727.✦▲

INDEPENDENCE—AAA OHIO MOTORISTS ASSOCIATION, 5700 BRECKSVILLE RD, 44131-1514. MON-FRI 8:30-6, SUMMER HOURS SAT 8:30-1:30 SAT 9:30-1:30. (216) 606-6100, *(800) 711-5370.*✦▲

IRONTON—AAA WEST PENN/W VIRGINIA/SO CENT OH, 624 S FOURTH ST, 45638. MON-FRI 9-5, SAT 9:30-12. (740) 532-3242.✦▲

JACKSON—AAA WEST PENN/W VIRGINIA/SO CENT OH, 126 E GAY ST, 45640. MON-FRI 9-5, SAT 9:30-12. (740) 286-5077.✦▲

KENTON—AAA OHIO AUTO CLUB, 220 E FRANKLIN ST, 43326. MON-FRI 9-5. (419) 673-4249.✦▲

KETTERING—AAA MIAMI VALLEY, 1218 E STROOP RD, 45429. MON-FRI 9-5:30, OPENED 1ST, 3RD & 5TH SATURDAY EVERY MONTH. SAT 9-12. (937) 294-1695, *(800) 624-2321.*✦▲

LANCASTER—AAA OHIO AUTO CLUB, 714 N MEMORIAL DR, 43130. MON-FRI 9-5, SAT 9-12. (740) 653-0912.✦▲

LEBANON—AAA CINCINNATI, 102 E MULBERRY ST, 45036. MON-FRI 9-5. (513) 932-3300, *(800) 543-2345*.✛▲

LIMA—AAA OHIO AUTO CLUB, 2115 ALLENTOWN RD, 45805. MON-FRI 9-5, TUE & THU 9-6, SAT 9-12. (419) 228-1022.✛▲

LOGAN—AAA WEST PENN/W VIRGINIA/SO CENT OH, 82 W MAIN ST, 43138. MON-FRI 9-5, SAT 9:30-12. (740) 385-8595.✛▲

LYNDHURST—AAA OHIO MOTORISTS ASSOCIATION, 5356 MAYFIELD RD-TOWER PZ, 44124. CLOSED MONDAY EXCEPT IN THE SUMMER MON-FRI 8:30-6. SUMMER HOURS SAT 8:30-4 SAT 9:30-4. (440) 473-0700.✛▲

MANSFIELD—AAA OHIO AUTO CLUB, 2114 PARK AVE W, 44906. MON-FRI 9-5, TUE & THU 9-6, SAT 9-12. (419) 529-8500.✛▲

MARIETTA—AAA WEST PENN/W VIRGINIA/SO CENT OH, 148 B GROSS ST, 45750. MON-FRI 9-5, SAT 9:30-12. (740) 374-6821.✛▲

MARION—AAA OHIO AUTO CLUB, 1316 MT VERNON AVE, 43302. MON-FRI 9-5. (740) 389-3517.✛▲

MASSILLON—**AAA MASSILLON AUTOMOBILE CLUB,** 1972 WALES RD NE, 44646. MON-FRI 9-5, SAT 9-12. (330) 833-1084.✛▲

MASSILLON—AAA MASSILLON AUTOMOBILE CLUB, ONE FIRST NATIONAL PLZ, 44646. MON-FRI 9-5, SAT 9-12. (330) 837-3545.▲

MAUMEE—AAA NORTHWEST OHIO, 475 W DUSSEL DR, 43537. MON-FRI 8:45-5:30, SAT 9:30-12:30. (419) 897-4455.■▲

MEDINA—AAA OHIO AUTO CLUB, 150 NORTHLAND DR, 44256. MON-FRI 9-5, TUE & THU 9-6, SAT 9-12. (330) 725-5669.✛▲

MENTOR—AAA OHIO MOTORISTS ASSOCIATION, 6980 HEISLEY RD, 44060. MON-FRI 8:30-6, SUMMER HOURS SAT 8:30-1:30 SAT 9:30-1:30. (440) 974-0990.✛▲

MIAMISBURG—AAA MIAMI VALLEY, 8160 SPRINGBORO PIKE, 45342. MON-FRI 8-7, SAT 8-3. (973) 434-9718.▲

MIDDLETOWN—AAA OHIO AUTO CLUB, 120 S BREIEL BLVD, 45044. MON-FRI 9-5. (513) 424-5361.✛▲

MOUNT VERNON—AAA OHIO AUTO CLUB, 1 PUBLIC SQ, 43050. MON-FRI 9-5. (740) 397-2091.✛▲

NEW LEXINGTON—AAA OHIO AUTO CLUB, 119 N MAIN ST, 43764. MON-FRI 9-5, SAT 9-12. (740) 342-5166.✛▲

NEW PHILADELPHIA—**AAA TUSCARAWAS COUNTY,** 1112 FOURTH ST NW, 44663. MON-FRI 8:45-5, MON 8:45-7, SAT 8:45-12. (330) 343-4481.✛▲

NEWARK—AAA OHIO AUTO CLUB, 130 W MAIN ST, 43055. MON-FRI 9-5. (740) 345-4017.✛▲

NILES—AAA OHIO MOTORISTS ASSOCIATION, 937 YOUNGSTOWN-WARREN RD, 44446. MON-FRI 8:30-6, SUMMER HOURS SAT 8:30-1:30 SAT 9:30-1:30. (330) 652-6466.✛▲

NORWALK—AAA OHIO MOTORISTS ASSOCIATION, 275 BENEDICT AVE, 44857. SUMMER HOURS MON-FRI 8:30-6 MON-FRI 8:30-5:30. SUMMER HOURS SAT 8:30-1:30. (419) 668-1622.✛▲

OBERLIN—AAA OHIO MOTORISTS ASSOCIATION, 49 S MAIN ST, 44074. MON-FRI 8:30-6, SUMMER HOURS SAT 8:30-1:30 SAT 9:30-1:30. (440) 774-6971.✛▲

OREGON—AAA NORTHWEST OHIO, 3237 NAVARRE AVE, 43616. MON-FRI 8:45-5:30, SAT 9:30-12:30. (419) 691-2439.✛▲

ORRVILLE—AAA OHIO AUTO CLUB, 328 W HIGH ST, 44667. MON-FRI 9-5. (330) 684-2060.✛▲

OXFORD—AAA OHIO AUTO CLUB, PARK PL W, 45056. MON-FRI 9-5. (513) 523-6374.✛▲

PARMA—AAA OHIO MOTORISTS ASSOCIATION, 7917 DAY DR, 44129. CLOSED MONDAY EXCEPT IN THE SUMMER MON-FRI 8:30-6. SUMMER HOURS SAT 8:30-4 SAT 9:30-4. (440) 886-6161.✛▲

PERRYSBURG—AAA NORTHWEST OHIO, 26611 N DIXIE HWY #103, 43551. MON-FRI 8:45-5:30, SAT 9:30-12:30. (419) 872-5000.✛▲

PICKERINGTON—AAA OHIO AUTO CLUB, 1262 HILL RD N, 43147. MON-FRI 9-5, SAT 9-12. (614) 864-2224.✛▲

PIQUA—AAA CINCINNATI, 115 E HIGH ST, 45356. MON-FRI 9-5, SAT 9-12. (937) 773-3753.✛▲

PORT CLINTON—AAA NORTHWEST OHIO, 123-A MAPLE ST, 43452. MON-FRI 8:45-5:30, SAT 9:30-12:30. (419) 732-2161, *(800) 432-2161*.✛▲

PORTSMOUTH—AAA WEST PENN/W VIRGINIA/SO CENT OH, 710 WALLER ST, 45662. MON-FRI 9-5, SAT 9:30-12. (740) 354-5614.✛▲

RAVENNA—AAA OHIO MOTORISTS ASSOCIATION, 2641 STATE RT 59, 44266. SUMMER HOURS MON-FRI 8:30-6 MON-FRI 8:30-5:30. SUMMER HOURS SAT 8:30-1:30. (330) 296-3406.✛▲

ROCKY RIVER—AAA OHIO MOTORISTS ASSOCIATION, 3356 LINDEN RD WSTGATE ML, 44116. CLOSED MONDAY EXCEPT IN THE SUMMER MON-FRI 8:30-6. SUMMER HOURS SAT 8:30-4 SAT 9:30-4. (440) 333-5878.✛▲

ST. CLAIRSVILLE—AAA OHIO AUTO CLUB, 107 S MARIETTA ST, 43950. MON-FRI 10-5, THU 9-6, SAT 9:30-12. (740) 695-4030.✛▲

SALEM—AAA COLUMBIANA COUNTY, 600 E SECOND ST, 44460. MON-FRI 9-5, SAT 9-12. (330) 332-0371.●▲

SANDUSKY—AAA OHIO AUTO CLUB, 1437 SYCAMORE LINE, 44870. MON-FRI 9-5. (419) 625-5831.✛▲

SIDNEY—**AAA SHELBY COUNTY,** 920 WAPAKONETA AVE, 45365. MON-FRI 9-5, SAT 9-12. (937) 492-3167, *(800) 274-3129*.✛▲

SOLON—AAA OHIO MOTORISTS ASSOCIATION, 34050 SOLON RD, 44139. MON-FRI 8:30-6, SUMMER HOURS SAT 8:30-1:30 SAT 9:30-1:30. (440) 248-9000.✛▲

SPRINGFIELD—AAA MIAMI VALLEY, 755 BECHTLE AVE, 45504. MON-FRI 8:30-5. (937) 323-8661, *(800) 624-2321*.✛▲

STEUBENVILLE—AAA WEST PENN/W VIRGINIA/SO CENT OH, 2716 SUNSET BLVD, 43952. MON-FRI 9-5, SAT 9:30-12. (740) 264-7717.✛▲

SYLVANIA—AAA NORTHWEST OHIO, 5700 MONROE ST, 43560. MON-FRI 8:45-5:30, SAT 9:30-12:30. (419) 885-3555.✛▲

TIFFIN—AAA OHIO AUTO CLUB, 191 E MARKET ST, 44883. MON-FRI 9-5, TUE & THU 9-6, SAT 9-12. (419) 447-0551.✛▲

TOLEDO—**AAA NORTHWEST OHIO,** 7150 W CENTRAL AVE, 43617. MON-FRI 8:45-5:30, SAT 9:30-12:30. (419) 843-1200, *(800) 428-0060*.✛▲

TOLEDO—AAA NORTHWEST OHIO, 5106 HEATHERDOWNS BLVD, 43614. MON-FRI 8:45-5:30, SAT 9:30-12:30. (419) 381-1151.✛▲

TOLEDO—AAA NORTHWEST OHIO, 216 NEW TOWNE SQ DR, 43612. MON-FRI 8:45-5:30, SAT 9:30-12:30. (419) 478-2341.✛▲

TROY—AAA CINCINNATI, 1041 S DORSET RD, 45373. MON-FRI 9-5, MON 9-7, SAT 9-12. (937) 339-0112.✛▲

UNIONTOWN—AAA AKRON AUTO CLUB, 1840 TOWN PARK BLVD, 44685. MON-FRI 8:40-5, SAT 8:40-12. (330) 896-7390.✛▲

UPPER SANDUSKY—AAA OHIO AUTO CLUB, 235 N SANDUSKY AVE, 43351. MON-FRI 9-5. (419) 294-2315.✛▲

URBANA—AAA MIAMI VALLEY, 18 MONUMENT SQ, 43078. MON-FRI 9-5. (937) 653-7164, *(800) 624-2321*.✛▲

WADSWORTH—AAA OHIO AUTO CLUB, 133 W BOYER ST, 44281. MON-FRI 9-5. (330) 336-4900.✛▲

WASHINGTON COURT HOUSE—AAA WEST PENN/W VIRGINIA/SO CENT OH, 334 E COURT ST, 43160. MON-FRI 9-5, SAT 9:30-12. (740) 335-3950.✛▲

WAVERLY—AAA WEST PENN/W VIRGINIA/SO CENT OH, 217 W EMMITT AVE, 45690. MON-FRI 9-5, SAT 9:30-12. (740) 947-7775.✛▲

WILLARD—AAA OHIO MOTORISTS ASSOCIATION, 106 BLOSSOM CENTRE BLVD, 44890. MON-FRI 8:30-5:30, SUMMER HOURS SAT 8:30-1:30. (419) 935-0950.✛▲

WOOSTER—AAA OHIO AUTO CLUB, 2889 CLEVELAND RD, 44691. MON-FRI 9-5, TUE & THU 9-6, SAT 9-12. (330) 345-5550.✛▲

WORTHINGTON—**AAA OHIO AUTO CLUB,** 90 E WILSON BRIDGE RD, 43085. MON-FRI 9-5. (614) 431-7901.✛▲

ZANESVILLE—AAA OHIO AUTO CLUB, 1120 MAPLE AVE, 43701. MON-FRI 9-5, TUE & THU 9-6, SAT 9-12. (740) 454-1234.✛▲

The Symbols of Quality

*D*iamond ratings provide you an easy way to elect quality lodgings and restaurants with the amenities and degree of sophistication you desire. Each property receiving a Diamond rating is thoroughly inspected and rated using consistent, objective criteria.

One Diamond–This means an establishment meets our members' basic requirements. Lodgings are good but modest and designed for the budget-minded. Restaurants are clean, casual, and family-oriented.

Two Diamond–These establishments meet all of the One-Diamond requirements with enhanced furnishings for lodgings and broader menu selections for restaurants.

Three Diamond–They offer guests a degree of sophistication. Lodgings feature more luxury and amenities, while restaurants provide extensive menus and a skilled service staff.

Four Diamond–This rating is given to those establishments that create a truly memorable experience for guests. Lodgings feature a high level of service amid luxurious surroundings. Restaurants are geared toward an adult dining experience with a highly skilled staff and elegant atmosphere.

Five Diamond–AAA's highest award is given to those rare luxury establishments that are world-renowned. The service, quality, and sophistication are exceptional, creating an unforgettable experience.

Trust AAA to provide you objective and accurate ratings of thousands of lodgings and restaurants throughout North America. Know before you go what to expect when you get there.

Travel With Someone You Trust®

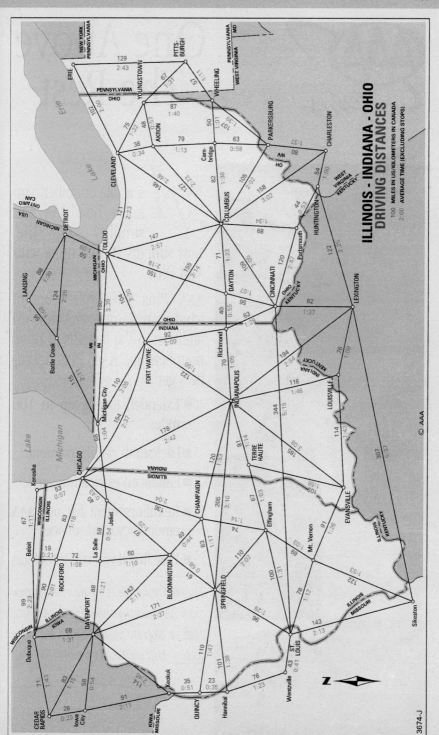

ILLINOIS - INDIANA - OHIO
DRIVING DISTANCES

100 MILES IN US/KILOMETERS IN CANADA
2:00 AVERAGE TIME (EXCLUDING STOPS)

© AAA

3674-J

Points of Interest Index

Index Legend

NB.	national battlefield	NR.	national river
NBP.	national battlefield park	NS.	national seashore
NC.	national cemetery	NWR.	national wildlife refuge
NF.	national forest	PHP.	provincial historic(al) park
NHM.	national historic(al) monument	PHS.	provincial historic(al) site
NHP.	national historic(al) park	PP.	provincial park
NHS.	national historic(al) site	SF.	state forest
NL.	national lakeshore	SHM.	state historic(al) monument
NME.	national memorial	SHP.	state historic(al) park
NMO.	national monument	SHS.	state historic(al) site
NMP.	national military park	SME.	state memorial
NP.	national park	SP.	state park
NRA.	national recreation area	SRA.	state recreation area

⬆ GEM: Points of Interest Offering a *Great Experience for Members*

EXHIBITS & COLLECTIONS-INDIAN

EXHIBITS & COLLECTIONS-MUSIC

EXHIBITS & COLLECTIONS-RELIGIOUS ITEMS

EXHIBITS & COLLECTIONS-REVOLUTIONARY WAR HISTORY

EXHIBITS & COLLECTIONS-SCIENCE

MUSIC HALLS & OPERA HOUSES

NATIONALITIES & ETHNIC AREAS

NATURAL PHENOMENA

NATURE CENTERS

SCHOOLS-INSTITUTES

SELF-GUIDING TOURS

SHIPS & BOATS

SHOPS, FIRMS & STORES

WALKING TOURS

WATERFALLS

WATER PARKS

WILDERNESS AREAS

WILDLIFE SANCTUARIES

SAVE *Attraction Admission Discount Index*

Bed & Breakfast Lodgings Index

Some bed and breakfasts listed below might have historical significance. Those properties are also referenced in the Historical index. The indication that continental [CP] or full breakfast [BP] is included in the room rate reflects whether a property is a Bed-and-Breakfast facility.

Country Inns Index

Some of the following country inns can also be considered as bed-and-breakfast operations. The indication that continental [CP] or full breakfast [BP] is included in the room rate reflects whether a property is a Bed-and-Breakfast facility.

Historical Lodgings & Restaurants Index

Some of the following historical lodgings can also be considered as bed-and-breakfast operations. The indication that continental [CP] or full breakfast [BP] is included in the room rate reflects whether a property is a Bed-and-Breakfast facility.

Resorts Index

Many establishments are located in resort areas; however, the following places have extensive on-premises recreational facilities:

Rules of the Road Can Change at State Borders

*S*peed limits are usually posted at state lines, but adherence to less known traffic regulations also is important for safe and enjoyable travel between states.

To assist the traveling motorists, AAA published the *Digest of Motor Laws* – a comprehensive description of the laws that govern motor vehicle registration and operation in the United States and Canada.

Examples of laws that differ include:

- In 33 state jurisdictions, police can only cite motorists for not wearing seat belts if they are stopped for another infraction. In the remaining 18 jurisdictions, police can stop motorists solely for failure to wear a seat belt.
- Drivers with a Learner's Permit are allowed to drive in their own states, subject to their state restrictions. 13 other states impose no additional restrictions while traveling in their respective states. 31 states impose additional restrictions and the remaining 7 jurisdictions prohibit vehicle operation by holders of an out-of-state learner's permit.
- While use of cellular telephones is permitted in all states, there may be local ordinances. Florida and Massachusetts have restrictions.

To obtain a copy of the *Digest of Motor Laws*, contact your local AAA club or AAA's National Office at the Traffic Safety Department, 1000 AAA Drive, Heathrow, FL 32746-5063. This glove-compartment-size book retails for $10.95.

Comprehensive City Index

Here is an alphabetical list of all cities appearing in this TourBook® guide. Cities are presented by state/province. Page numbers under the POI column indicate where points of interest text begins. Page numbers under the L&R column indicate where lodging and restaurant listings begin.

ILLINOIS	POI	L&R		POI	L&R
ALGONQUIN	N/A	324	DOWNTOWN CHICAGO	N/A	295
ALSIP	N/A	324	DU QUOIN	N/A	383
ALTON	44	269	EAST CAPE GIRARDEAU	N/A	384
ANTIOCH	N/A	324	EAST DUBUQUE	N/A	384
ARCOLA	44	270	EAST DUNDEE	76	N/A
ARLINGTON HEIGHTS	N/A	325	EAST PEORIA	88	384
ARTHUR	N/A	270	EAST ST. LOUIS	88	N/A
AURORA	75	327	EDWARDSVILLE	88	N/A
BANNOCKBURN	N/A	328	EFFINGHAM	N/A	384
BATAVIA	75	N/A	ELGIN	77	335
BEARDSTOWN	N/A	270	ELK GROVE VILLAGE	N/A	337
BEDFORD PARK	N/A	328	ELLIS GROVE	88	N/A
BELLEVILLE	44	270	ELMHURST	77	338
BEMENT	45	N/A	ELSAH	88	386
BISHOP HILL	45	N/A	EVANSTON	77	339
BLOOMINGDALE	N/A	329	FAIRFIELD	N/A	387
BLOOMINGTON	45	271	FAIRVIEW HEIGHTS	N/A	387
BLUE ISLAND	N/A	329	FORSYTH	N/A	388
BOLINGBROOK	N/A	330	FRANKLIN PARK	N/A	340
BOURBONNAIS	45	273	FREEPORT	88	388
BRIDGEVIEW	N/A	330	GALENA	89	389
BROOKFIELD	75	N/A	GALESBURG	89	390
BUFFALO GROVE	N/A	330	GENESEO	N/A	391
BURR RIDGE	N/A	331	GENEVA	N/A	340
CAHOKIA	46	N/A	GILMAN	N/A	391
CAIRO	46	N/A	GLEN CARBON	N/A	392
CALUMET CITY	N/A	331	GLEN ELLYN	N/A	341
CALUMET PARK	N/A	331	GLENCOE	78	N/A
CARBON CLIFF	N/A	273	GLENVIEW	78	341
CARBONDALE	46	274	GRAFTON	90	392
CARLINVILLE	46	275	GRAND DETOUR	90	N/A
CARLYLE	N/A	275	GRAYSLAKE	N/A	342
CARMI	47	N/A	GRAYVILLE	N/A	392
CAROL STREAM	N/A	331	GREENVILLE	N/A	392
CARTHAGE	47	N/A	GURNEE	78	342
CASEY	N/A	275	HARVARD	N/A	343
CASEYVILLE	N/A	276	HARVEY	N/A	344
CENTRALIA	N/A	276	HAVANA	91	N/A
CHAMPAIGN	47	276	HIGHLAND	N/A	393
CHARLESTON	47	277	HIGHLAND PARK	N/A	344
CHESTER	N/A	277	HILLSBORO	N/A	393
CHICAGO	48	278	HILLSIDE	N/A	344
CHICAGO NORTH	N/A	315	HINSDALE	N/A	344
CHICAGO SOUTH	N/A	322	HOFFMAN ESTATES	N/A	345
CHILLICOTHE	N/A	379	ITASCA	N/A	346
CLINTON	85	N/A	JACKSONVILLE	91	393
COAL VALLEY	85	N/A	JERSEYVILLE	N/A	394
COLLINSVILLE	85	379	JOLIET	78	346
COLUMBIA	N/A	380	KAMPSVILLE	91	N/A
COUNTRYSIDE	N/A	331	KANKAKEE	91	394
CRAINVILLE	N/A	380	KEWANEE	91	394
CRYSTAL LAKE	N/A	332	KICKAPOO	91	394
DANVILLE	85	380	LA SALLE	91	394
DECATUR	85	381	LAKE FOREST	N/A	349
DEERFIELD	N/A	332	LAKE ZURICH	N/A	349
DEKALB	87	383	LANSING	N/A	349
DES PLAINES	76	334	LAWRENCEVILLE	92	N/A
DIXON	87	383	LERNA	92	N/A
DOWNERS GROVE	N/A	335	LEWISTOWN	92	N/A

COMPREHENSIVE CITY INDEX (CONT'D)

COMPREHENSIVE CITY INDEX (CONT'D)

COMPREHENSIVE CITY INDEX (CONT'D)

COMPREHENSIVE CITY INDEX (CONT'D)

COMPREHENSIVE CITY INDEX (CONT'D)

LOOK FOR THE RED

Next time you pore over a AAA TourBook® guide in search of a lodging establishment, take note of the vibrant red AAA logo, SAVE icon, and Diamond rating just under a select group of property names! These Official Appointment properties place a high value on the business they receive from dedicated AAA travelers and offer members great room rates*.

See TourBook Navigator section, page 16, for complete details.

Photo Credit Index

One Perfect Gift

Give the gift of security, service, and savings—buy someone you care about a AAA gift membership. AAA memberships provide your loved ones more than emergency road service.

AAA members also have access to travel services, insurance, financial services, exclusive Show Your Card & Save® discounts, bail bond services, and more.

Give them more than a gift. Give them AAA. And let them discover how AAA can simplify their lives. Call or stop by your nearest AAA office today. And make AAA the one for you.

Now AAA is just a click away.
Welcome to aaa.com

When you visit aaa.com, you'll have a world of products, services, and more — at your fingertips. Membership services. Travel. Financial services. Insurance. Show Your Card & Save® discounts. And so much more. Log on to aaa.com today. And discover the many ways AAA can help you. www.aaa.com

AAA. Every Day.